The soul of Barone Pizzini
It embodies
the living nature of its vineyards

This wine is the crowning achievement of a long process
of pionering renewal, that led Barone Pizzini to become
the first organic grower and winemaker in Franciacorta.

BARONE PIZZINI
FRANCIACORTA 1870

 CAMPAGNA FINANZIATA AI SENSI DEL REGOLAMENTO CE N. 1308/13
CAMPAIGN FINANCED ACCORDING TO (EC) REGULATION NO. 1308/13

THE LOBSTER HAS PINCHED SOME IMPORTANT MEDALS.

Vermentino di Sardegna Aragosta.
Gold medal at Berliner Wein Trophy 2015,
Silver medal at Decanter 2015 and
Bronze medal at Wine Challenge 2015.

www.santamarialapalma.it

CANTINA SANTA MARIA LA PALMA

Alghero

—TENUTA DI—
LILLIANO

To the heart of the wine

umanironchi.com

Gambero Rosso
2017

Italian
Wines

VINI D'ITALIA 2017
GAMBERO ROSSO®

Gambero Rosso S.p.A.
via Ottavio Gasparri, 13/17 - 00152 Roma
tel. 06/551121 - fax 06/55112260
www.gamberorosso.it
email: gambero@gamberorosso.it

Senior Editors
Gianni Fabrizio
Eleonora Guerini
Marco Sabellico

Special Contributors
Antonio Boco
Paolo De Cristofaro
Lorenzo Ruggeri
Paolo Zaccaria

Regionali Coordinators
Nino Aiello
Giuseppe Carrus
Nicola Frasson
Massimo Lanza
Giorgio Melandri
Gianni Ottogalli
Nereo Pederzolli
Pierpaolo Rastelli

Contributors
Stefania Annese
Francesco Beghi
Sergio Bonanno
Michele Bressan
Pasquale Buffa
Dionisio Castello
Giacomo Mojoli
Franco Pallini
William Pregentelli
Leonardo Romanelli
Maurizio Rossi
Giulia Sampognaro
Herbert Taschler
Cinzia Tosetti

Other Contributors
Filippo Apollinari
Enrico Battistella
Claudia Cherchi
Lucio Chiesa
Francesca Ciancio
Mario De Benedittis
Mario Demattè
Pierluigi Fais
Maurizio Fava
Mario Josto D'Ascanio
Maurizio Marci
Leonardo Marco
Enrico Massidda
Enrico Melis
Michele Muraro
Nicola Piccinini
Michele Pico Palermo
Massimo Ponzanelli
Flavia Previtera
Walter Pugliese
Carlo Ravanello
Riccardo Rossetti
Simona Silvestri
Paolo Trimani
Vincenzo Verrastro
Liliana Zanellato
Danilo Zannella

Editorial Secretary
Giulia Sciortino

Coordination and Layout
Marina Proietti

Managing Editor Books
Laura Mantovano

Graphics
Chiara Buosi

Commercial Director
Francesco Dammicco

Production
Angelica Sorbara

**Editorial product distribution
and sales manager**
Eugenia Durando

Translation Coordinator
Angela Arnone

Translators and Revisors
Angela Arnone
Anthony Green
Dave Henderson
Sarah Ponting
Simon Tanner
Ailsa Wood

Publisher
Gr Usa Corp c/o Csc Services of Nevada Inc
2215-B RENAISSANCE DR
Las Vegas , NV 89119
email: gamberousa@aol.com

Distribution
USA and Canada
by Antique Collector's Club, Eastworks, 116
Pleasant St #18, Easthampton, MA 010207, USA;
UK and Australia by Antique Collector's Club Ltd
Sandy Lane, Old Martlesham, Woodbridge,
Suffolk IP12 4SD - United Kingdom

The final edit of Italian Wines was completed on
2 September 2016

ISBN 9781890142186

Printed in Italy for Gambero Rosso Holding S.p.A.
in November 2016 by
OMNIMEDIA S.r.l.
Piazza della Ferriera, 1
00015 Monterotondo Scalo (Roma)

SUMMARY

REGIONS

INDEXES

THE GUIDE

Despite our best efforts, it's not easy to write our introduction to the 30th edition of Italian Wines without giving ourselves a big pat on the back. But those who've been on board from the start can't fail to feel enormous satisfaction for having reached this milestone. Three decades is a long time and the world in general, not only the world of wine, has changed completely. For instance, in the summer of 1987, as the first pages of the first edition were taking shape (on a typewriter!), the Berlin wall, although crumbling, was still standing. And winemaking Italy was strenuously seeking to dig itself out of one of the blackest holes of its recent history. Getting the guide off the press was a great act of faith, a commitment to the thousand winemakers who, even then, were trying to express Italy's huge winemaking potential with enthusiasm and creativity. Above all, this was a service for a new generation of aficionados and gourmets – including ourselves – who were looking for guidance and suggestions in a production landscape in determined and tempestuous evolution. It was the Renaissance of Italian wine, as that moment in time was dubbed, a time of unbelievable excitement and news, when the foundations were laid for the international success of our wine industry. The success of the guide, then and now, is based on a number of factors we can try to sum up briefly. For a start, it is a group effort, where tastings are always undertaken by panels of at least three people, and where bottles are blind tasted, in other words the taster can't be swayed by the label. The 30-plus local panels, with over 70 experienced tasters, sample the most interesting wines, which are then reviewed by a commission including the guide's editors and the head tasters of the various regions. At this stage, the Tre Bicchieri (an expression acknowledged worldwide to mean "excellent wine") winners are selected from among 1,600 or so wines. This year we placed 429 wines on the top step of the podium, which are quite a few more than the 32 we chose for the first edition, but then we only had 1,500 wines to taste, whereas now we get through no less than 45,000 wines a year. And the wineries assessed have risen from 500 to 2,400. The first decade of the guide was dedicated to strengthening the organization and editorial framework, and right from the early years we commissioned translations of the guide into English and German, more recently adding Chinese and Japanese, to confirm the international mission of Gambero Rosso. Which has spent the last decade working to consolidate its international image, and now organizes more than 40 events around the world every year, where the star of the show is Italian wine. Over the years we turned a clever but small-scale publication for the Italian market into a handbook for international wine lovers, but it is also a formidable tool for international wine professionals, to the point that our Uno, Due and Tre Bicchieri scores are now applied like those of any international financial rating agency. A great success which wouldn't have been possible without the 1,000-plus tasters over the years. So our warmest thanks go to all of them and to all the institutions, associations and agencies that have worked with us, supporting us towards this amazing milestone.

Here we are, then, drawing the conclusions of our tastings for this historic 30th edition. The 429 Tre Bicchieri awards comprised 80 for Tuscany, 75 for Piedmont, 38 for Veneto, 27 for Alto Adige, 26 for Friuli, 23 for Lombardy, 22 for Campania, 21 for Sicily, 20 for Marche, 14 for Emilia Romagna, 12 for Abruzzo, Sardinia and Puglia, 10 for Umbria and Trentino, 7 for Lazio, 6 for Valle d'Aosta and Liguria, 4 for Basilicata, 3 for Calabria, 1 for Molise.

Every year we also decide who has given the best performance overall in our opinion and given them our Special Awards: Red of the Year is a great Gioia del Colle Primitivo, Chiaromonte's 2013 Muro Sant'Angelo Contrada Barbatto; White of the Year is Tenuta di Tavignano's truly refined, elegant 2015 Verdicchio dei Castelli di Jesi Classico Superiore Misco; Sparkler of the Year went to Ruggeri & C. for 2015, and 20th vintage of the iconic 2015 Valdobbiadene Giustino B., definitely one of the best sparkling wines made from glera we've ever tasted; Sweet Wine of the Year went to Friuli, to Tal Lùc Cuvée Speciale from Lis Neris, a great meditation wine blended from two vintages, 2006 and 2008. Then we have Winery of the Year, Bellavista the big Franciacorta outfit and a leader in the Terra Moretti group, vaunting a long list of top subsidiaries in Franciacorta and in Tuscany. Best Value for Money was the excellent 2015 Pecorino from Abruzzo's Tiberio. Grower of the Year is Aimone Vio, a talented Liguria vigneron of overwhelming passion. Up-and-Coming Winery is the Chianti-based Istine, a wonderful cellar with an assured future. The Sustainable Viticulture Award, a subject close to our hearts, goes to Roccafiore, in Umbria, which not only produces an excellent Grechetto di Todi but since its inception has been committed to sustainability. Readers will also find 88 Tre Bicchieri Verdi, wines produced by organic or certified biodynamic cellars. Last but not least, we include 88 award-winning wines available off the shelf for under 15 euros a bottle. We would like to thank Bolzano EOS, Cagliari and Perugia chambers of commerce, the Oltrepò Pavese Quality Wine District association, the coordinators of Strade del Vino e dell'Olio, the Arezzo Strada dei Vini wine trail, the Istituto Marchigiano di Tutela Vini di Jesi (IMT), and VINEA of Offida, ERSA Friuli Venezia Giulia, the Istituto Agronomico Mediterraneo of Valenzano, the Ente Vini Bresciani, Carcare (Savona) municipal council, Comitato Grandi Cru della Costa Toscana, Assovini Sicilia, the E. del Giudice Centro per l'Innovazione della Filiera Vitivinicola in Marsala. Also, the protection consortiums of Gavi, Barolo, Barbaresco, Alba, Langhe and Roero, Vini Colli Tortonesi, Nebbiolo dell'Alto Piemonte, Caluso, Carema and Canavese, Oltrepò Pavese, Vini di Valtellina, Franciacorta, Valcalepio and Vini Mantovani, Lugana, Valtenesi, Conegliano Valdobbiadene, Soave, Consorzio Vini Trentini, Bolgheri, as well as those of Bolgheri, Brunello di Montalcino, Chianti Classico, San Gimignano, Montepulciano, Chianti Rufina, Morellino di Scansano, Montecucco, Carmignano, Orvieto, Montefalco, and finally the Consorzio di Tutela Vini DOC Sicilia. Our thanks also to the regional wine cellars of Cassino Po in Lombardy, Roero and Nizza Monferrato, Canelli and Astesana; Cantina Comunale I Söri in Diano d'Alba, Bottega del Vino in Dogliani, University of Bologna – Degree Course in Viticulture and Oenology, Terre Naldi in Tebano, the Carpe Diem restaurant in Montaione, the Calidario in Venturina, Agriturismo Giuncola & Granaiolo of Rispescia, Città del Gusto in Rome and I Naples, the regional wine cellar of Basilicata in Venosa, Caneva in Mogliano Veneto, the Bouchon restaurant in Messina, and Acqua San Martino of Codrongianos.

And last but not least, we would like to thank our entire team for the heartfelt passion in putting together IW, from the local tastings to drafting the profiles and editing the volume, and to all those who have worked with us over the years, with special thanks to Nereo Pederzolli, who has been at our side with steadfast commitment from the very start.

Gianni Fabrizio, Eleonora Guerini, Marco Sabellico

TASTING WITH GAMBERO ROSSO

I received an invitation to join the tasting commission of Gambero Rosso while running the Tre Bicchieri event in Moscow in November of last year. You may imagine my reaction. By that time we'd arranged lots of Gambero Rosso events together and I had a great deal of experience in giving master classes during Gambero Rosso events in Russia. But I'd never had a chance to sit with Gambero Rosso experts at the tasting panel. We did share the same tables during some Anteprima events, but that is another story. While taking part in any presentation you can stand the weight of responsibility, but when you start thinking of those tens of thousands reading the Guide, their faith makes you concentrate more.

Initially I thought I would join the regional commission and as a result deepen my knowledge in some specific wine area, but unexpectedly, I spent several days judging the finals. The preselection was done meticulously, so the majority of the wines were very close to being named as Tre Bicchieri in terms of their points. I'd like to underline that point: their ratings were very close, but sometimes they didn't receive enough to be the best, as the final score for any wine was determined by average points from a group of experts. I don't have exact statistics, but reportedly only around 30% of the wines we tasted each day finally received a Tre Bicchieri rating. Don't you think that the judgment was extremely strict? Oh, yes, but that approach really increases the value of every Tre Bicchieri award. Undoubtedly, it means that the best wines listed in the Guide automatically become a benchmark of quality and could be considered as the gold standard by any producer.

The biggest challenge was to compare my marks with those of the rest of the panel, not because I underrate my personal opinion, but because it was surely a way to learn the philosophy of the Gambero Rosso experts. We openly discussed and exchanged opinions in order to understand each other's point of view. Those debates were really helpful in seeing the hidden beauty of wines that could occasionally be missed and in being twice as attentive while tasting wines that I initially detested for some reason.

So the Gambero Rosso experts let me take a more precise look at their verdicts, consequently broadening my horizons and giving me a better understanding of some peculiar styles of Italian wines.

My personal experience in judging for the most prestigious and well-known wine guide in Europe has increased my understanding of why the Gambero Rosso rating is considered synonymous with unbiased expertise and why it has earned the trust of all wine connoisseurs and lovers. This volume undoubtedly deserves to be a primary reference source while forming opinions about the best Italian wines.

Dmitry Fedotov
Wine Expert, Member of the Supervision Board
of the Union of Winegrowers and Winemakers of Russia

TRE BICCHIERI 2017

VALLE D'AOSTA

Valle d'Aosta Chambave Muscat Flétri '14	La Vrille	31
Valle d'Aosta Chardonnay Élevé en Fût de Chêne '15	Maison Anselmet	26
Valle d'Aosta Cornalin '15	Rosset Terroir	31
Valle d'Aosta Petite Arvine '15	Elio Ottin	30
Valle d'Aosta Pinot Gris '15	Lo Triolet	29
Valle d'Aosta Syrah Côteau La Tour '14	Les Crêtes	27

PIEDMONT

Barbaresco Albesani S. Stefano Ris. '11	Castello di Neive	78
Barbaresco Angelo '13	Albino Rocca	148
Barbaresco Asili '13	Ceretto	81
Barbaresco Asili Ris. '11	Ca' del Baio	62
Barbaresco Asili Ris. '11	Bruno Giacosa	103
Barbaresco Costa Russi '13	Gaja	100
Barbaresco Currà '12	Sottimano	164
Barbaresco Gallina '12	Piero Busso	61
Barbaresco Pajé '11	Roagna	148
Barbaresco Rabajà '12	Bruno Rocca	149
Barbaresco Rombone '12	Fiorenzo Nada	127
Barbera d'Asti Pomorosso '13	Coppo	89
Barbera d'Asti Sup. Nizza '13	Tenuta Olim Bauda	131
Barbera d'Asti Sup. Nizza La Court '13	Michele Chiarlo	82
Barbera d'Asti Sup. V. La Mandorla Edizione La Grisa '14	Luigi Spertino	165
Barbera del M.to Sup. Bricco Battista '13	Giulio Accornero e Figli	36
Barbera del M.to Sup. Pico Gonzaga '13	Castello di Uviglie	79
Barolo '12	Cascina Fontana	72
Barolo '12	Bartolo Mascarello	119
Barolo Bric dël Fiasc '12	Paolo Scavino	159
Barolo Bricco Boschis '12	Cavallotto	
	Tenuta Bricco Boschis	81
Barolo Bricco delle Viole '12	G. D. Vajra	170
Barolo Bricco Fiasco '12	Azelia	44
Barolo Bricco Pernice '11	Elvio Cogno	85
Barolo Brunate '12	Mario Marengo	117
Barolo Bussia 90 Dì Ris. '10	Giacomo Fenocchio	96
Barolo Bussia V. Mondoca Ris. '10	Poderi e Cantine Oddero	130
Barolo Cannubi '12	G. B. Burlotto	60
Barolo Cannubi '12	Marchesi di Barolo	116
Barolo Cerretta '12	Giovanni Rosso	152
Barolo Cerretta V. Bricco '10	Elio Altare - Cascina Nuova	39
Barolo del Comune di Barolo Essenze '12	Vite Colte	176
Barolo Francia '12	Giacomo Conterno	87
Barolo Giachini '12	Giovanni Corino	90
Barolo Ginestra Casa Maté '12	Elio Grasso	106
Barolo Ginestra Ris. '08	Paolo Conterno	88
Barolo Lazzarito Ris. '10	Ettore Germano	102
Barolo Liste '11	Giacomo Borgogno & Figli	52
Barolo Monprivato '11	Giuseppe Mascarello e Figlio	120
Barolo Monvigliero '12	F.lli Alessandria	37
Barolo Ornato '12	Pio Cesare	137
Barolo Paiagallo Casa E. di Mirafiore '12	Fontanafredda	99
Barolo Ravera '12	Vietti	172
Barolo Resa 56 '12	Brandini	54
Barolo Rocche dell'Annunziata '12	Mauro Veglio	170
Barolo Rocche di Castiglione '12	Brovia	60

Pinot Nero Bertone '13	Conte Vistarino	230
Valtellina Sforzato Albareda '13	Mamete Prevostini	238
Valtellina Sfursat 5 Stelle '13	Nino Negri	243
Valtellina Sup. Grumello Buon Consiglio Ris. '07	Ar.Pe.Pe.	216
Valtellina Sup. Sassella Ris. '12	Aldo Rainoldi	248
Valtellina Sup. Valgella Cà Moréi '13	Sandro Fay	233

TRENTINO

Fojaneghe Rosso '12	Bossi Fedrigotti	274
San Leonardo '11	Tenuta San Leonardo	285
Teroldego Rotaliano Pini '12	Roberto Zeni	286
Trento Brut Altemasi Graal Ris. '09	Cavit	274
Trento Brut Domini '10	Abate Nero	272
Trento Brut Giulio Ferrari Riserva del Fondatore '05	Ferrari	277
Trento Brut Ris. '10	Letrari	279
Trento Dosaggio Zero Ris. '11	Maso Martis	279
Trento Extra Brut Tridentum '09	Cesarini Sforza	275
Trento Rotari Flavio Ris. '08	Mezzacorona	280

ALTO ADIGE

A. A. Cabernet Puntay Ris. '12	Erste+Neue	298
A. A. Chardonnay Löwengang '13	Tenute Alois Lageder	317
A. A. Gewürztraminer Auratus Crescendo '15	Tenuta Ritterhof	312
A. A. Gewürztraminer Brenntal Ris. '14	Cantina Kurtatsch	306
A. A. Gewürztraminer Nussbaumer '14	Cantina Tramin	319
A. A. Gewürztraminer Vom Lehm '15	Castelfeder	295
A. A. Lago di Caldaro Scelto Sup. Bischofsleiten '15	Castel Sallegg	205
A. A. Lagrein Ris. '13	Erbhof Unterganzner - Josephus Mayr	297
A. A. Lagrein Taber Ris. '14	Cantina Bolzano	293
A. A. Pinot Bianco Praesulis '15	Gumphof - Markus Prackwieser	301
A. A. Pinot Bianco Sirmian '15	Cantina Nals Margreid	310
A. A. Pinot Grigio St. Valentin '14	Cantina Produttori San Michele Appiano	314
A. A. Pinot Nero Bachgart '13	Maso Hemberg	
	Klaus Lentsch	308
A. A. Pinot Nero Trattmann Mazon Ris. '13	Cantina Girlan	299
A. A. Santa Maddalena Cl. Rondell '15	Glögglhof - Franz Gojer	300
A. A. Sauvignon Lafóa '14	Cantina Produttori Colterenzio	296
A. A. Sauvignon Mervin '14	Cantina Meran Burggräfler	309
A. A. Terlano Nova Domus Ris. '13	Cantina Terlano	318
A. A. Terlano Pinot Bianco Eichhorn '15	Manincor	307
A. A. Val Venosta Riesling '14	Falkenstein Franz Pratzner	298
A. A. Val Venosta Riesling Unterortl '15	Tenuta Unterortl - Castel Juval	319
A. A. Valle Isarco Grüner Veltliner '15	Kuenhof - Peter Pliger	305
A. A. Valle Isarco Pinot Grigio '15	Köfererhof	
	Günther Kerschbaumer	304
A. A. Valle Isarco Sylvaner '14	Garlider - Christian Kerschbaumer	299
A. A. Valle Isarco Sylvaner '15	Taschlerhof - Peter Wachtler	317
A. A. Valle Isarco Sylvaner Aristos '15	Cantina Produttori Valle Isarco	320
A. A. Valle Isarco Sylvaner Praepositus '15	Abbazia di Novacella	292

VENETO

Amarone della Valpolicella Cl. Calcarole '11	Guerrieri Rizzardi	362
Amarone della Valpolicella Campo dei Gigli '12	Tenuta Sant'Antonio	387
Amarone della Valpolicella Cl. '12	Allegrini	330
Amarone della Valpolicella Cl. '08	Cav. G. B. Bertani	333

Amarone della Valpolicella Cl. '12	David Sterza	392
Amarone della Valpolicella Cl. '08	Villa Spinosa	402
Amarone della Valpolicella Cl. Casa dei Bepi '11	Viviani	403
Amarone della Valpolicella Cl. La Fabriseria Ris. '11	F.lli Tedeschi	394
Amarone della Valpolicella Cl. Monte Ca' Bianca '11	Lorenzo Begali	333
Amarone della Valpolicella Cl. Punta di Villa '11	Roberto Mazzi	368
Amarone della Valpolicella Cl. Sergio Zenato Ris. '10	Zenato	405
Amarone della Valpolicella Cl. Vaio Armaron Serègo Alighieri '11	Masi	367
Amarone della Valpolicella Cl. Vign. Monte Sant'Urbano '12	Viticoltori Speri	391
Amarone della Valpolicella Punta Tolotti '12	Ca' Rugate	342
Bardolino Cl. V. Morlongo '14	Vigneti Villabella	403
Cartizze Brut V. La Rivetta	Villa Sandi	402
Colli Euganei Cabernet Borgo delle Casette Ris. '12	Il Filò delle Vigne	358
Cristina V. T. '13	Roeno	383
Custoza Sup. Amedeo '14	Cavalchina	348
Custoza Sup. Ca' del Magro '14	Monte del Frà	370
Lugana Molceo Ris. '14	Ottella	378
Madre '14	Italo Cescon	350
Montello e Colli Asolani Il Rosso dell'Abazia '13	Serafini & Vidotto	390
Soave Cl. Campo Vulcano '15	I Campi	343
Soave Cl. La Rocca '14	Leonildo Pieropan	379
Soave Cl. Le Bine de Costiola '14	Tamellini	394
Soave Cl. Monte Carbonare '14	Suavia	392
Soave Cl. Staforte '14	Graziano Prà	380
Soave Sup. Il Casale '15	Agostino Vicentini	399
Soave Sup. Vign. Runcata '14	Dal Cero - Tenuta di Corte Giacobbe	355
Valdobbiadene Brut Particella 68 '15	Sorelle Bronca	339
Valdobbiadene Brut Rive di Col San Martino Cuvée del Fondatore Graziano Merotto '15	Merotto	369
Valdobbiadene Extra Dry Giustino B. '15	Ruggeri & C.	384
Valdobbiadene Rive di San Pietro di Barbozza Brut Nature Grande Cuvée del Fondatore Motus Vitae '13	Bortolomiol	337
Valpolicella Cl. Sup. Camporenzo '13	Monte dall'Ora	369
Valpolicella Sup. '12	Marco Mosconi	374
Valpolicella Sup. '13	Roccolo Grassi	382
Valpolicella Sup. Mithas '12	Corte Sant'Alda	354

FRIULI VENEZIA GIULIA

Carso Malvasia Dileo '15	Castelvecchio	427
Chardonnay '15	di Lenardo	432
Collio Bianco Broy '15	Eugenio Collavini	428
Collio Bianco Solarco '15	Livon	444
Collio Friulano '15	Fiegl	437
Collio Friulano '15	Doro Princic	454
Collio Friulano '15	Russiz Superiore	463
Collio Friulano '15	Schiopetto	465
Collio Malvasia '15	Ronco dei Tassi	461
Collio Ribolla Gialla di Oslavia Ris. '12	Primosic	453
Collio Sauvignon '15	Tiare - Roberto Snidarcig	471
Desiderium I Ferretti '13	Tenuta Luisa	444
FCO Bianco Illivio '14	Livio Felluga	436
FCO Bianco LaLinda '14	La Tunella	473
FCO Friulano '15	Tenuta di Angoris	416
FCO Friulano No Name '15	Le Vigne di Zamò	478

FCO Pinot Bianco Myò '15	Zorzettig	483
FCO Pinot Grigio '15	Torre Rosazza	472
FCO Sauvignon Liende '15	La Viarte	475
FCO Sauvignon Zuc di Volpe '15	Volpe Pasini	481
Friuli Grave Pinot Bianco '15	Le Monde	443
Malvasia '13	Skerk	468
Pinot Grigio '15	Jermann	440
Ribolla Gialla '08	Gravner	439
Ribolla Gialla '12	Damijan Podversic	452
Tal Lùc Cuvée Speciale	Lis Neris	443

EMILIA ROMAGNA

Colli di Parma Rosso MDV '14	Monte delle Vigne	508
Colli di Rimini Cabernet Sauvignon Montepirolo '12	San Patrignano	518
Lambrusco di Modena Brut Rosé M. Cl. '12	Cantina della Volta	497
Lambrusco di Sorbara del Fondatore '15	Cleto Chiarli Tenute Agricole	500
Lambrusco di Sorbara Secco Rito '15	Zucchi	525
Lambrusco di Sorbara V. del Cristo '15	Cavicchioli	498
Reggiano Lambrusco Concerto '15	Ermete Medici & Figli	508
Romagna Albana Passito Regina di Cuori Ris. '12	Gallegati	506
Romagna Albana Secco I Croppi '15	Celli	499
Romagna Sangiovese Modigliana I Probi di Papiano Ris. '13	Villa Papiano	524
Romagna Sangiovese Modigliana Sup. V. 1922 Ris. '13	Torre San Martino	521
Romagna Sangiovese Sup. Godenza '14	Noelia Ricci	515
Romagna Sangiovese Sup. Limbecca '14	Paolo Francesconi	505
Romagna Sangiovese Sup. V. del Generale Ris. '13	Fattoria Nicolucci	510

TUSCANY

Baron'Ugo '12	Monteraponi	613
Bolgheri Camarcanda '13	Ca' Marcanda	550
Bolgheri Rosso Sup. '13	Podere Sapaio	649
Bolgheri Rosso Sup. Grattamacco '13	Grattamacco	598
Bolgheri Rosso Sup. Millepassi '13	Donna Olimpia 1898	586
Bolgheri Sassicaia '13	Tenuta San Guido	645
Bolgheri Rosso Sup. Le Gonnare '13	Fabio Motta	617
Bolgheri Sup. Ornellaia '13	Ornellaia	620
Bolgheri Sup. Podere Ritorti '13	I Luoghi	606
Bolgheri Sup. Sondraia '13	Poggio al Tesoro	629
Brunello di Montalcino '11	Le Chiuse	572
Brunello di Montalcino '11	Poggio di Sotto	631
Brunello di Montalcino AdAlberto Ris. '10	Caprili	554
Brunello di Montalcino Giodo '11	Giodo	596
Brunello di Montalcino Madonna delle Grazie '11	Il Marroneto	608
Brunello di Montalcino Nello Ris. '10	Baricci	541
Brunello di Montalcino Ris. '10	Biondi Santi - Tenuta Il Greppo	545
Brunello di Montalcino Ris. '10	Canalicchio di Sopra	552
Brunello di Montalcino Ris. '10	Capanna	553
Brunello di Montalcino Ris. '10	Tenuta di Sesta	655
Brunello di Montalcino Trentennale '11	Talenti	654
Brunello di Montalcino V. Schiena d'Asino '10	Mastrojanni	609
Brunello di Montalcino V. V. '11	Le Ragnaie	637
Carmignano Le Farnete Ris. '13	Le Farnete/Cantagallo	588
Carmignano Ris. '13	Piaggia	623
Castello del Terriccio '11	Castello del Terriccio	561
Cepparello '13	Isole e Olena	600

Chianti Cl. '14	Borgo Salcetino	545
Chianti Cl. '13	San Felice	643
Chianti Cl. '13	Val delle Corti	663
Chianti Cl. Bugialla Ris. '13	Poggerino	628
Chianti Cl. Cigliano '13	Cigliano	573
Chianti Cl. Gran Sel. '13	Castello d'Albola	561
Chianti Cl. Gran Sel. Colledilà '13	Barone Ricasoli	541
Chianti Cl. Gran Sel. Riserva di Fizzano '13	Rocca delle Macìe	639
Chianti Cl. Gran Sel. San Lorenzo '13	Castello di Ama	562
Chianti Cl. Lamole di Lamole Et. Bianca '13	Lamole di Lamole	601
Chianti Cl. LeVigne Ris. '13	Istine	600
Chianti Cl. Ris. '13	Brancaia	547
Chianti Cl. Ris. '13	Castello di Radda	566
Chianti Cl. Ris. '13	Castello di Volpaia	567
Chianti Cl. Ris. '13	Tenuta di Lilliano	604
Chianti Cl. Ris. '13	Fattoria Nittardi	618
Chianti Cl. Villa Cerna Ris. '13	Famiglia Cecchi	570
Chianti Colli Fiorentini Badia a Corte Ris. '13	Torre a Cona	660
Chianti Rufina Nipozzano V. V. Ris. '13	Marchesi de' Frescobaldi	594
Colline Lucchesi Tenuta di Valgiano '13	Tenuta di Valgiano	664
Cortona Syrah Il Bosco '12	Tenimenti Luigi d'Alessandro	655
Do ut des '13	Fattoria Carpineta Fontalpino	555
Duemani '13	Duemani	586
I Sodi di S. Niccolò '12	Castellare di Castellina	560
Le Pergole Torte '13	Montevertine	615
Maremma Toscana Baffo Nero '14	Rocca di Frassinello	640
Maremma Toscana Ciliegiolo V. Vallerana Alta '14	Antonio Camillo	551
Maremma Toscana Sangiovese Carandelle '15	Podere San Cristoforo	643
Montecucco Rosso Ris. '13	Colle Massari	577
Montecucco Sangiovese Ad Agio Ris. '12	Basile	542
Morellino di Scansano Madrechiesa Ris. '13	Terenzi	657
Morellino di Scansano Ris. '13	Roccapesta	641
Nobile di Montepulciano '13	Maria Caterina Dei	584
Nobile di Montepulciano I Quadri '13	Bindella	544
Nobile di Montepulciano Il Nocio '12	Poderi Boscarelli	546
Nobile di Montepulciano Ris. '12	Tenuta di Gracciano della Seta	597
Nobile di Montepulciano Ris. '12	Tenute del Cerro	656
Orma '13	Orma	619
Paleo '13	Le Macchiole	607
Petra Rosso '13	Petra	622
Petresco '12	Le Cinciole	574
Pinot Nero '13	Podere della Civettaja	575
Rosso di Montalcino '14	Uccelliera	662
Saffredi '13	Fattoria Le Pupille	636
Sangioveto '10	Castello di Monsanto	565
Siepi '13	Castello di Fonterutoli	564
Terre di Pisa Nambrot '13	Tenuta di Ghizzano	595
Tignanello '13	Marchesi Antinori	534
Valdarno di Sopra Galatrona '13	Fattoria Petrolo	623
Valdarno di Sopra V. dell'Impero '13	Tenuta Sette Ponti	653
Vernaccia di S. Gimignano Albereta Ris. '13	Il Colombaio di Santa Chiara	579
Vernaccia di S. Gimignano Carato '12	Montenidoli	612
Vin Santo di Carmignano Ris. '09	Tenuta di Capezzana	553

MARCHE

Castelli di Jesi Verdicchio Cl. Crisio Ris. '13	CasalFarneto	700

Castelli di Jesi Verdicchio Cl. Lauro Ris. '13	Poderi Mattioli	713
Castelli di Jesi Verdicchio Cl. Salmariano Ris. '13	Marotti Campi	713
Castelli di Jesi Verdicchio Cl. San Paolo Ris. '13	Pievalta	718
Castelli di Jesi Verdicchio Cl. San Sisto Ris. '14	Fazi Battaglia	707
Castelli di Jesi Verdicchio Cl. Utopia Ris. '13	Montecappone	716
Castelli di Jesi Verdicchio Cl. Villa Bucci Ris. '14	Bucci	698
Conero Campo San Giorgio Ris. '11	Umani Ronchi	726
Kupra '13	Oasi degli Angeli	717
Offida Pecorino Artemisia '15	Tenuta Spinelli	724
Offida Pecorino Guido Cocci Grifoni '13	Tenuta Cocci Grifoni	702
Offida Pecorino Rêve '14	Velenosi	727
Offida Rosso Vignagiulia '13	Emanuele Dianetti	707
Verdicchio dei Castelli di Jesi Cl. Sup. Il Priore '14	Sparapani - Frati Bianchi	724
Verdicchio dei Castelli di Jesi Cl. Sup. Misco '15	Tenuta di Tavignano	725
Verdicchio dei Castelli di Jesi Cl. Sup. Sabbionare '15	Sabbionare	720
Verdicchio di Matelica Collestefano '15	Collestefano	703
Verdicchio di Matelica Mirum Ris. '14	La Monacesca	715
Verdicchio di Matelica Vign. B. '15	Belisario	696
Verdicchio di Matelica Vign. Fogliano '13	Bisci	697

UMBRIA

Brecciaro '14	Leonardo Bussoletti	739
Cervaro della Sala '14	Castello della Sala	741
Montefalco Sagrantino '12	F.lli Pardi	749
Montefalco Sagrantino Campo alla Cerqua '12	Giampaolo Tabarrini	753
Montefalco Sagrantino Collepiano '12	Arnaldo Caprai	739
Orvieto Cl. Sup. Campo del Guardiano '14	Palazzone	748
Orvieto Cl. Sup. Il Bianco '15	Decugnano dei Barbi	743
Orvieto Cl. Sup. Luigi e Giovanna '13	Barberani	737
Todi Grechetto Sup. Fiorfiore '14	Roccafiore	751
Turgiano Rosso Rubesco V. Monticchio Ris. '11	Lungarotti	746

LAZIO

Antium Bellone '15	Casale del Giglio	763
Cesanese del Piglio Sup. Hernicus '14	Antonello Coletti Conti	765
Fiorano Rosso '11	Tenuta di Fiorano	771
Frascati Sup. Epos Ris. '15	Poggio Le Volpi	769
Habemus '14	San Giovenale	770
Montiano '14	Falesco	766
Poggio della Costa '15	Sergio Mottura	767

ABRUZZO

Cerasuolo d'Abruzzo Villa Gemma '15	Masciarelli	787
Montepulciano d'Abruzzo '12	Valentini	794
Montepulciano d'Abruzzo '14	Villa Medoro	795
Montepulciano d'Abruzzo Amorino '12	Castorani	780
Montepulciano d'Abruzzo Chronicon '13	Ciccio Zaccagnini	795
Montepulciano d'Abruzzo Colline Teramane Zanna Ris. '11	Dino Illuminati	786
Montepulciano d'Abruzzo Luì '13	Tenuta Terraviva	791
Montepulciano d'Abruzzo Mo Ris. '12	Cantina Tollo	792
Pecorino '15	Tiberio	791
Pecorino Frontone '13	Luigi Cataldi Madonna	780
Trebbiano d'Abruzzo Bianchi Grilli per la Testa '14	Torre dei Beati	792
Trebbiano d'Abruzzo V. del Convento di Capestrano '14	Valle Reale	794

MOLISE

Molise Tintilia '13	Di Majo Norante 801

CAMPANIA

Caiatì '14	Alois 804
Campi Flegrei Piedirosso '15	Agnanum 804
Costa d'Amalfi Furore Bianco '15	Marisa Cuomo 810
Costa d'Amalfi Ravello Bianco V. Grotta Piana '15	Ettore Sammarco 824
Falanghina del Sannio Biancuzita '14	Torre a Oriente 829
Falanghina del Sannio Janare '15	La Guardiense 816
Falanghina del Sannio Svelato '15	Terre Stregate 828
Falanghina del Sannio Taburno '15	Fontanavecchia 814
Fiano di Avellino '15	Colli di Lapio 809
Fiano di Avellino '14	Ciro Picariello 821
Fiano di Avellino '14	Rocca del Principe 823
Fiano di Avellino '15	Tenuta Sarno 1860 826
Fiano di Avellino Pietramara '15	I Favati 813
Fiano di Avellino V. della Congregazione '15	Villa Diamante 831
Greco di Tufo '15	Pietracupa 822
Greco di Tufo V. Cicogna '15	Benito Ferrara 813
Montevetrano '14	Montevetrano 819
Paestum '15	San Giovanni 825
Sabbie di Sopra il Bosco '14	Nanni Copè 820
Taurasi Coste '11	Contrade di Taurasi 810
Trentenare '15	San Salvatore 825
Zagreo '15	I Cacciagalli 806

BASILICATA

Aglianico del Vulture Gricos '14	Grifalco della Lucania 844
Aglianico del Vulture Il Repertorio '14	Cantine del Notaio 842
Aglianico del Vulture Re Manfredi '13	Re Manfredi - Cantina Terre degli Svevi 846
Aglianico del Vulture Titolo '14	Elena Fucci 844

PUGLIA

Castel del Monte Nero di Troia Ottagono Ris. '14	Torrevento 864
Gioia del Colle Primitivo 17 '13	Polvanera 861
Gioia del Colle Primitivo Muro Sant'Angelo	
Contrada Barbatto '13	Chiaromonte 854
Gioia del Colle Primitivo Ris. '13	Cantine Tre Pini 864
Gioia del Colle Primitivo Senatore '10	Coppi 855
Negroamaro '14	Carvinea 853
Oltremé Susumaniello '15	Tenute Rubino 862
Primitivo di Manduria '15	Felline 856
Primitivo di Manduria Passo del Cardinale '14	Cantine Paolo Leo 858
Primitivo di Manduria Raccontami '14	Vespa - Vignaioli per Passione 866
Salice Salentino Rosso 50° Vendemmia '14	Leone de Castris 858
Salice Salentino Rosso Selvarossa Ris. '13	Cantine Due Palme 855

CALABRIA

Gravello '14	Librandi 878
Grisara '15	Roberto Ceraudo 876
Masino '14	iGreco 877

SICILY

Alcamo Beleda '15	Rallo 903
Cerasuolo di Vittoria Cl. Dorilli '14	Planeta 902

Cerasuolo di Vittoria Giambattista Valli Paris '12
Eloro Pachino Saro '13
Etna Bianco Alta Mora '14
Etna Rosso Prephylloxera La V. di Don Peppino '14
Etna Rosso San Lorenzo '14
Etna Rosso V. Barbagalli '13
Etna Rosso Zottorinoto Ris. '12
Faro '14
Faro Palari '12
Favinia La Muciara '14
Lorlando '15
Nero d'Avola Sosta Tre Santi '10
Passito di Pantelleria Ben Ryé '14
Saia '14
Shymer '13
Sicilia Carricante Tascante Buonora '15
Sicilia Mandrarossa Cartagho '14
SP 68 Rosso '15
Tripudium Rosso Duca di Castelmonte '13

Feudi del Pisciotto	894
Feudo Rudinì	904
Cusumano	891
Tenuta delle Terre Nere	907
Girolamo Russo	905
Pietradolce	901
Cottanera	891
Le Casematte	890
Palari	900
Firriato	896
Assuli	887
Cantine Nicosia	899
Donnafugata	892
Feudo Maccari	895
Baglio di Pianetto	888
Tasca d'Almerita	906
Cantine Settesoli	906
Occhipinti	900
Carlo Pellegrino	901

SARDINIA
Alghero Torbato Terre Bianche Cuvée 161 '15
Barrile '13
Cannonau di Sardegna Cl. D53 '13
Cannonau di Sardegna Cl. Dule '13
Cannonau di Sardegna Senes Ris. '12
Capichera '14
Carignano del Sulcis 6Mura '11
Carignano del Sulcis Buio Buio Ris. '13
Falconaro '11
Latinia '10
Vermentino di Gallura Sup. Sciala '15
Vermentino di Sardegna Stellato '15

Tenute Sella & Mosca	933
Attilio Contini	922
Cantina Dorgali	924
Giuseppe Gabbas	924
Argiolas	920
Capichera	920
Cantina Giba	925
Mesa	928
Cantine di Dolianova	923
Cantina di Santadi	932
Vigne Surrau	935
Pala	930

RETROSPECTIVE TRE BICCHIERI

Every ten years we give our Retrospective Tre Bicchieri award to wines which left us in doubt at time of tasting, or which simply slipped through the net, but over the years have been tasted again on many occasions and shown not only their worth, but also their undoubted longevity.

PIEDMONT

Barbaresco Rabajà '08	Giuseppe Cortese	92
Barbaresco Sorì Rio Sordo '06	Ca' Rome'	63
Barolo Cannubi '06	E. Pira & Figli Chiara Boschis	138
Barolo La Villa '10	F.lli Seghesio	161
Barolo Monvigliero Ris. '08	Castello di Verduno	80
Barolo Villero '10	Brovia	60

TRENTINO

Trentino Vino Santo '98	Pisoni	282

VENETO

Colli Euganoi Rosso Gemola '04	Vignalta	400

FRIULI VENEZIA GIULIA

Collio Bianco V.V. '08	Roncùs	462
Collio Bianco Jelka '11	Roberto Picéch	450
Collio Sauvignon '14	Tiare - Roberto Snidarcig	471

TUSCANY

Brunello di Montalcino Ris. '06	Tenuta Le Potazzine	635
Chianti Cl. Ris. '10	Fattoria Nittardi	618

MARCHE

Offida Pecorino Iosonogaia non sono Lucrezia '10	Le Caniette	699
Verdicchio di Matelica Collestefano '10	Collestefano	703

CAMPANIA

Taurasi '10	Pietracupa	822

PUGLIA

Primitivo di Manduria Archidamo '09	Felline	856

SICILY

Cerasuolo di Vittoria V. Para Para '02	Poggio di Bortolone	902

THE BEST

RED OF THE YEAR
GIOIA DEL COLLE PRIMITIVO MURO SANT'ANGELO CONTRADA BARBATTO '13 - CHIAROMONTE

WHITE OF THE YEAR
VERDICCHIO DEI CASTELLI DI JESI CL. SUP. MISCO '15 - TENUTA DI TAVIGNANO

SPARKLER OF THE YEAR
VALDOBBIADENE EXTRA DRY GIUSTINO B. '15 - RUGGERI

SWEET OF THE YEAR
TAL LÙC CUVÉE SPECIALE - LIS NERIS

WINERY OF THE YEAR
BELLAVISTA

BEST VALUE FOR MONEY
PECORINO '15 - TIBERIO

GROWER OF THE YEAR
AIMONE VIO (BIOVIO)

UP-AND-COMING WINERY
ISTINE

AWARD FOR SUSTAINABLE VITICULTURE
ROCCAFIORE

TRE BICCHIERI VERDI

The Tre Bicchieri Verdi award is applicable to wines produced with grapes from official organic and biodynamic certified plots (which are printed in red). This year we have 88 such wines, now accounting for just over 20% of our total awards. An important result, testifying how Italy's top wineries are now fully committed to the environmental process. There are more complex aspects, however, given that many wineries apply similar criteria but do not request certification. Moreover sustainability protocols are increasingly common among growers and these wineries are identified with the wording "Sustainable Winery" in their profiles.

Wine	Winery	Region
A. A. Chardonnay Löwengang '13	Tenute Alois Lageder	**Alto Adige**
A. A. Terlano Pinot Bianco Eichhorn '15	Manincor	**Alto Adige**
A. A. Valle Isarco Sylvaner '14	Garlider	
	Christian Kerschbaumer	**Alto Adige**
Aglianico del Vulture Gricos '14	Grifalco della Lucania	**Basilicata**
Aglianico del Vulture Il Repertorio '14	Cantine del Notaio	**Basilicata**
Alagmo Beleda '15	Rallo	**Sicily**
Amarone della Valpolicella Cl.		
Vign. Monte Sant'Urbano '12	Viticoltori Speri	**Veneto**
Barbaresco Asili '13	Cerello	**Piedmont**
Barolo Bricco Boschis '12	Cavallotto	
	Tenuta Bricco Boschis	**Piedmont**
Barolo Bricco Pernice '11	Elvio Cogno	**Piedmont**
Barolo Bussia V. Mondoca Ris. '10	Poderi e Cantine Oddero	**Piedmont**
Barolo del Comune di Barolo Essenze '12	Vite Colte	**Piedmont**
Barolo Resa 56 '12	Brandini	**Piedmont**
Barolo Rocche di Castiglione '12	Brovia	**Piedmont**
Barolo Sorì Ginestra '12	Conterno Fantino	**Piedmont**
Baron'Ugo '12	Monteraponi	**Tuscany**
Barrile '13	Attilio Contini	**Sardinia**
Bolgheri Rosso Sup. Grattamacco '13	Grattamacco	**Tuscany**
Bolgheri Sup. Podere Ritorti '13	I Luoghi	**Tuscany**
Brecciaro '14	Leonardo Bussoletti	**Umbria**
Brunello di Montalcino '11	Le Chiuse	**Tuscany**
Brunello di Montalcino '11	Poggio di Sotto	**Tuscany**
Brunello di Montalcino V. V. '11	Le Ragnaie	**Tuscany**
Castelli di Jesi Verdicchio Cl. Lauro Ris. '13	Poderi Mattioli	**Marche**
Castelli di Jesi Verdicchio Cl. San Paolo Ris. '13	Pievalta	**Marche**
Castelli di Jesi Verdicchio Cl. Villa Bucci Ris. '14	Bucci	**Marche**
Chianti Cl. '13	Val delle Corti	**Tuscany**
Chianti Cl. Bugialla Ris. '13	Poggerino	**Tuscany**
Chianti Cl. Ris. '13	Castello di Volpaia	**Tuscany**
Colli di Rimini Cabernet Sauvignon		
Montepirolo '12	San Patrignano	**Emilia Romagna**
Colline Lucchesi Tenuta di Valgiano '13	Tenuta di Valgiano	**Tuscany**
Conero Campo San Giorgio Ris. '11	Umani Ronchi	**Marche**
Cortona Syrah Il Bosco '12	Tenimenti	
	Luigi d'Alessandro	**Tuscany**
Do ut des '13	Fattoria Carpineta	
	Fontalpino	**Tuscany**
Duemani '13	Duemani	**Tuscany**
Etna Rosso Prephylloxera		
La V. di Don Peppino '14	Tenuta delle Terre Nere	**Sicily**
Etna Rosso San Lorenzo '14	Girolamo Russo	**Sicily**
Faro '14	Le Casematte	**Sicily**

Favinia La Muciara '14	Firriato	Sicily
Franciacorta Nature 61 '09	Guido Berlucchi & C.	Lombardy
Franciacorta Non Dosato		
Bagnadore Ris. '09	Barone Pizzini	Lombardy
Gioia del Colle Primitivo 17 '13	Polvanera	Puglia
Gioia del Colle Primitivo		
Muro Sant'Angelo Contrada Barbatto '13	Chiaromonte	Puglia
Gioia del Colle Primitivo Ris. '13	Cantine Tre Pini	Puglia
Grignolino del M.to Casalese '15	Vicara	Piedmont
Grisara '15	Roberto Ceraudo	Calabria
Habemus '14	San Giovenale	Lazio
Madre '14	Italo Cescon	Veneto
Malvasia '13	Skerk	Friuli Venezia Giulia
Maremma Toscana Ciliegiolo		
V. Vallerana Alta '14	Antonio Camillo	Tuscany
Maremma Toscana Sangiovese		
Carandelle '15	Podere San Cristoforo	Tuscany
Molise Tintilia '13	Di Majo Norante	Molise
Montecucco Rosso Ris. '13	Colle Massari	Tuscany
Montecucco Sangiovese Ad Agio Ris. '12	Basile	Tuscany
Montepulciano d'Abruzzo Amorino '12	Castorani	Abruzzo
Montepulciano d'Abruzzo Luì '13	Tenuta Terraviva	Abruzzo
Negroamaro '14	Carvinea	Puglia
Nero d'Avola Sosta Tre Santi '10	Cantine Nicosia	Sicily
Orvieto Cl. Sup. Luigi e Giovanna '13	Barberani	Umbria
Petresco '12	Le Cinciole	Tuscany
Pinot Nero '13	Podere della Civettaja	Tuscany
Poggio della Costa '15	Sergio Mottura	Lazio
Primitivo di Manduria '15	Felline	Puglia
Primitivo di Manduria		
Passo del Cardinale '14	Cantine Paolo Leo	Puglia
Ribolla Gialla '12	Damijan Podversic	Friuli Venezia Giulia
Riviera Ligure di Ponente Pigato		
Bon in da Bon '15	BioVio	Liguria
Roero Mompissano Ris. '13	Cascina Ca' Rossa	Piedmont
Romagna Sangiovese Sup. Limbecca '13	Paolo Francesconi	Emilia Romagna
Salice Salentino Rosso Selvarossa Ris. '13	Cantine Due Palme	Puglia
Soave Cl. La Rocca '14	Leonildo Pieropan	Veneto
Soave Cl. Staforte '14	Graziano Prà	Veneto
SP 68 Rosso '15	Occhipinti	Sicily
Taurasi Coste '11	Contrade di Taurasi	Campania
Teroldego Rotaliano Pini '12	Roberto Zeni	Trentino
Terre di Pisa Nambrot '13	Tenuta di Ghizzano	Toscana
Torgiano Rosso Rubesco		
V. Monticchio Ris. '11	Lungarotti	Umbria
Trebbiano d'Abruzzo		
Bianchi Grilli per la Testa '14	Torre dei Beati	Abruzzo
Trebbiano d'Abruzzo		
V. del Convento di Capestrano '14	Valle Reale	Abruzzo
Trentenare '15	San Salvatore	Campania
Trento Dosaggio Zero Ris. '11	Maso Martis	Trentino
Valpolicella Cl. Sup. Camporenzo '13	Monte dall'Ora	Veneto
Valpolicella Sup. Mithas '12	Corte Sant'Alda	Veneto
Verdicchio di Matelica Collestefano '15	Collestefano	Marche
Verdicchio di Matelica Vign. Fogliano '13	Bisci	Marche
Vernaccia di S. Gimignano Albereta Ris. '13	Il Colombaio di Santa Chiara	Tuscany
Vernaccia di S. Gimignano Carato '12	Montenidoli	Tuscany
Vin Santo di Carmignano Ris. '09	Tenuta di Capezzana	Tuscany
Zagreo '15	I Cacciagalli	Campania

TABLE OF VINTAGES
FROM 1990 TO 2015

The ratings below are shown as wine-bottle icons; the number in each cell indicates the count of bottle icons shown.

	BARBARESCO BAROLO	AMARONE	CHIANTI CLASSICO	BRUNELLO DI MONTALCINO	BOLGHERI	TAURASI	MONTEPULCIANO D'ABRUZZO
1990	5	5	4	5	5	5	4
1995	4	5	4	5	3	3	4
1996	4	3	2	2	2	2	4
1997	4	4	4	4	4	4	4
1999	5	4	4	4	4	4	2
2000	4	4	4	4	3	1	3
2001	5	4	4	5	4	4	4
2004	5	4	4	4	3	3	4
2005	4	3	3	2	3	3	3
2006	3	3	3	3	3	3	3
2007	5	5	5	5	5	5	4
2008	4	4	3	3	4	4	2
2009	4	3	2	2	4	3	1
2010	5	4	5	5	4	2	1
2011	4	3	3	3	4	2	4
2012	4	2	3	3	3		4
2013	4		3		5		4
2014			1				2

	ALTO ADIGE BIANCO	LUGANA SOAVE	FRIULI BIANCO	VERDICCHIO DEI CASTELLI DI JESI	FIANO DI AVELLINO	GRECO DI TUFO
2005	4	5	3	3	3	2
2006	3	4	5	5	4	5
2007	3	4	3	2	3	3
2008	3	4	3	4	3	3
2009	3	4	3	3	3	4
2010	4	4	2	3	4	4
2011	3	3	2	1	3	3
2012	4	3	4	4	4	4
2013	4	4	4	4	5	4
2014	3	3	3	3	3	3
2015	4	5	4	4	4	3

STARS

★★★★★
54
Gaja (Piedmonte)

★★★★
41
Ca' del Bosco (Lombardy)

★★★
38
La Spinetta (Piedmont)
35
Elio Altare - Cascina Nuova (Piedmont)
32
Allegrini (Veneto)
Castello di Fonterutoli (Tuscany)
Valentini (Abruzzo)

★★
28
Bellavista (Lombardy)
Giacomo Conterno (Piedmont)
Felsina (Tuscany)
Jermann (Friuli Venezia Giulia)
Masciarelli (Abruzzo)
Tenuta San Guido (Tuscany)
Cantina Produttori San Michele Appiano
(Alto Adige)
27
Castello della Sala (Umbria)
Ferrari (Trentino)
Planeta (Sicily)
26
Tasca d'Almerita (Sicily)
25
Marchesi Antinori (Tuscany)
Castello di Ama (Tuscany)
Poliziano (Tuscany)
Cantina Tramin (Alto Adige)
Vie di Romans (Friuli Venezia Giulia)
24
Livio Felluga (Friuli Venezia Giulia)
Feudi di San Gregorio (Campania)
Bruno Giacosa (Piedmont)
Gravner (Friuli Venezia Giulia)
Ornellaia (Tuscany)
Leonildo Pieropan (Veneto)
23
Argiolas (Sardinia)
Paolo Scavino (Piemonte)
22
Cantina Bolzano (Alto Adige)
Arnaldo Caprai (Umbria)
Domenico Clerico (Piedmont)
Fontodi (Tuscany)
Nino Negri (Lombardy)
Schiopetto (Friuli Venezia Giulia)
Villa Russiz (Friuli Venezia Giulia)
21
Barone Ricasoli (Tuscany)
Michele Chiarlo (Piedmont)
Falesco (Lazio)
Isole e Olena (Tuscany)

Tenute Sella & Mosca (Sardinia)
Cantina Terlano (Alto Adige)
20
Ca' Viola (Piedmont)
Cascina La Barbatella (Piedmont)
Castello del Terriccio (Tuscany)
Cantina Produttori Colterenzio (Alto Adige)
Dorigo (Friuli Venezia Giulia)
Montevetrano (Campania)
Tenuta San Leonardo (Trentino)
Vietti (Piedmont)
Elena Walch (Alto Adige)

★
19
Cantina di Caldaro (Alto Adige)
Les Crêtes (Valle d'Aosta)
Cusumano (Sicily)
Elio Grasso (Piemonte)
Serafini & Vidotto (Veneto)
Venica & Venica (Friuli Venezia Giulia)
Volpe Pasini (Friuli Venezia Giulia)
18
Abbazia di Novacella (Alto Adige)
Ca' Rugate (Veneto)
Castellare di Castellina (Tuscany)
Castello Banfi (Tuscany)
Conterno Fantino (Piedmont)
Matteo Correggia (Piedmont)
Gioacchino Garofoli (Marche)
Lis Neris (Friuli Venezia Giulia)
Le Macchiole (Tuscany)
Mastroberardino (Campania)
Montevertine (Tuscany)
Ruffino (Tuscany)
Luciano Sandrone (Piedmont)
Franco Toros (Friuli Venezia Giulia)
Le Vigne di Zamò (Friuli Venezia Giulia)
17
Brancaia (Tuscany)
Casanova di Neri (Tuscany)
Luigi Cataldi Madonna (Abruzzo)
Donnafugata (Sicily)
Massolino (Piedmont)
Palari (Sicily)
Querciabella (Tuscany)
Cantina di Santadi (Sardinia)
Sottimano (Piedmont)
Fattoria Zerbina (Emilia Romagna)
16
Antoniolo (Piedmont)
Aldo Conterno (Piedmont)
Romano Dal Forno (Veneto)
Firriato (Sicily)
Kuenhof - Peter Pliger (Alto Adige)
Livon (Friuli Venezia Giulia)
Masi (Veneto)
Miani (Friuli Venezia Giulia)
Monsupello (Lombardy)
Cantina Convento Muri-Gries (Alto Adige)
Fiorenzo Nada (Piedmont)
Fattoria Petrolo (Tuscany)
Giuseppe Quintarelli (Veneto)
Albino Rocca (Piedmont)

Bruno Rocca (Piedmont)
Ronco dei Tassi (Friuli Venezia Giulia)
San Patrignano (Emilia Romagna)
Umani Ronchi (Marche)
15
Roberto Anselmi (Veneto)
Lorenzo Begali (Veneto)
Bucci (Marche)
Coppo (Piedmont)
Doro Princic (Friuli Venezia Giulia)
Velenosi (Marche)
Roberto Voerzio (Piedmont)
14
Avignonesi (Tuscany)
Cav. G. B. Bertani (Veneto)
Biondi Santi - Tenuta Il Greppo (Tuscany)
Bricco Rocche - Bricco Asili (Piedmont)
Cavit (Trentino)
Tenuta di Ghizzano (Tuscany)
Librandi (Calabria)
Malvirà (Piedmont)
Franco M. Martinetti (Piedmont)
Bartolo Mascarello (Piedmont)
La Monacesca (Marche)
Oasi degli Angeli (Marche)
Produttori del Barbaresco (Piedmont)
Ronco del Gelso (Friuli Venezia Giulia)
Tenuta Sant'Antonio (Veneto)
Viticoltori Speri (Veneto)
Suavia (Veneto)
Uberti (Lombardy)
Tenuta Unterortl - Castel Juval (Alto Adige)
Vignalta (Veneto)
Viviani (Veneto)
13
Abbona (Piedmont)
Piero Busso (Piedmont)
Cavalleri (Lombardy)
Di Majo Norante (Molise)
Le Due Terre (Friuli Venezia Giulia)
Poderi Luigi Einaudi (Piedmont)
Falkenstein Franz Pratzner (Alto Adige)
Foradori (Trentino)
Grattamacco (Tuscany)
Dino Illuminati (Abruzzo)
Edi Keber (Friuli Venezia Giulia)
Lungarotti (Umbria)
Maculan (Veneto)
Pecchenino (Piedmont)
Pietracupa (Campania)
Graziano Prà (Veneto)
Rocca di Frassinello (Tuscany)
San Felice (Tuscany)
Tormaresca (Puglia)
Tua Rita (Tuscany)
12
F.lli Alessandria (Piedmont)
Azelia (Piedmont)
Poderi Boscarelli (Tuscany)
Braida (Piedmont)
Castello dei Rampolla (Tuscany)
Tenute Cisa Asinari dei Marchesi di Grésy
(Piedmont)
Elvio Cogno (Piedmont)
Tenuta Col d'Orcia (Tuscany)
Còlpetrone (Umbria)
Ferghettina (Lombardy)

Tenute Ambrogio e Giovanni Folonari (Tuscany)
Marchesi de' Frescobaldi (Tuscany)
Galardi (Campania)
Gini (Veneto)
Leone de Castris (Puglia)
Marchesi di Barolo (Piedmont)
Sergio Mottura (Lazio)
Piaggia (Tuscany)
Fattoria Le Pupille (Tuscany)
Dario Raccaro (Friuli Venezia Giulia)
Aldo Rainoldi (Lombardy)
Rocche dei Manzoni (Piedmont)
Russiz Superiore (Friuli Venezia Giulia)
Tenuta di Valgiano (Tuscany)
Valle Reale (Abruzzo)
Villa Medoro (Abruzzo)
Villa Sparina (Piedmont)
11
Abate Nero (Trentino)
Giulio Accornero e Figli (Piedmont)
Gianfranco Alessandria (Piedmont)
Benanti (Sicily)
Borgo San Daniele (Friuli Venezia Giulia)
Ca' del Baio (Piedmont)
Cavalchina (Veneto)
La Cerbaiola (Tuscany)
Eugenio Collavini (Friuli Venezia Giulia)
Dorigati (Trentino)
Elena Fucci (Basilicata)
Ettore Germano (Piedmont)
Köfererhof - Günther Kerschbaumer
(Alto Adige)
Cantina Kurtatsch (Alto Adige)
Mamete Prevostini (Lombardy)
La Massa (Tuscany)
Monchiero Carbone (Piedmont)
Cantina Nals Margreid (Alto Adige)
Prunotto (Piedmont)
G. D. Vajra (Piedmont)
Vigneti Massa (Piedmont)
Zenato (Veneto)
10
Maison Anselmet (Valle d'Aosta)
Brigaldara (Veneto)
Brovia (Piedmont)
Cascina Ca' Rossa (Piedmont)
Castello d'Albola (Tuscany)
Castello di Volpaia (Tuscany)
Cavallotto Tenuta Bricco Boschis (Piedmont)
F.lli Cigliuti (Piedmont)
Corte Sant'Alda (Veneto)
Cantine Due Palme (Puglia)
Cantina Girlan (Alto Adige)
Franz Haas (Alto Adige)
Hilberg - Pasquero (Piedmont)
Tenuta J. Hofstätter (Alto Adige)
Monte Rossa (Lombardy)
Poderi e Cantine Oddero (Piedmont)
Pio Cesare (Piedmont)
Poggio Antico (Tuscany)
Tenimenti Luigi d'Alessandro (Tuscany)
Tenuta delle Terre Nere (Sicily)
Tenute Alois Lageder (Alto Adige)
Torraccia del Piantavigna (Piedmont)
Torrevento (Puglia)
Villa Matilde (Campania)
Conti Zecca (Puglia)

HOW TO USE THE GUIDE

WINERY INFORMATION
ANNUAL PRODUCTION
HECTARES UNDER VINE
VITICULTURE METHOD

SYMBOLS
○ WHITE WINE
⊙ ROSÈ
● RED WINE

RATINGS
MODERATELY GOOD TO GOOD WINES IN THEIR RESPECTIVE CATEGORIES
VERY GOOD TO EXCELLENT WINES IN THEIR RESPECTIVE CATEGORIES
VERY GOOD TO EXCELLENT WINES THAT WENT FORWARD TO THE FINAL TASTINGS
EXCELLENT WINES IN THEIR RESPECTIVE CATEGORIES

WINES RATED IN PREVIOUS EDITIONS OF THE GUIDE ARE INDICATED BY WHITE GLASSES (♀, ♀♀, ♀♀♀), PROVIDED THEY ARE STILL DRINKING AT THE LEVEL FOR WHICH THE ORIGINAL AWARD WAS MADE.

STAR ★
INDICATES WINERIES THAT HAVE WON TEN TRE BICCHIERI AWARDS FOR EACH STAR

PRICE RANGES
1 up to 5 euro
3 from € 10.01 to € 15.00
5 from € 20.01 to € 30.00
7 from € 40.01 to € 50.00

2 from € 5.01 to € 10.00
4 from € 15.01 to € 20.00
6 from € 30.01 to € 40.00
8 more than € 50.01

PRICES INDICATED REFER TO AVERAGE PRICES IN WINE STORES

ASTERISK *
INDICATES ESPECIALLY GOOD VALUE WINES

ABBREVIATIONS

A. A.	Alto Adige	P.R.	Peduncolo Rosso (red bunchstem)
C.	Colli		
Cl.	Classico	P.	Prosecco
C.S.	Cantina Sociale (co-operative winery)	Rif. Agr.	Riforma Agraria (agrarian reform)
CEV	Colli Etruschi Viterbesi	Ris.	Riserva
Cons.	Consorzio	Sel.	Selezione
Coop.Agr.	Cooperativa Agricola (farming co-operative)	Sup.	Superiore
		TdF	Terre di Franciacorta
C. B.	Colli Bolognesi	V.	Vigna (vineyard)
C. P.	Colli Piacentini	Vign.	Vigneto (vineyard)
Et.	Etichetta (label)	V. T.	Vendemmia Tardiva (late harvest)
FCO	Friuli Colli Orientali		
M.	Metodo (method)	V. V.	Vecchia Vigna/Vecchie Vigne (old vine /old vines)
M.to	Monferrato		
OP	Oltrepò Pavese		

VALLE D'AOSTA

For the Valle d'Aosta, 2015 was perhaps the peak moment of a major climate change. For years, Aosta Valley winemakers have faced the challenge of getting their grapes to ripen completely. Global warming is now forcing them to deal with a different set of issues, for which they are not prepared. The 2015 growing year began with a very sultry spring, followed by a hot July, then a week of rain in August. A weather pattern of this kind restricted important areas, and vines in the first stage of ripening. Districts like Morgex and La Salle, whose production was heavily penalized, harvested many grapes overripe, leading to production of more alcoholic and less balanced wines than usual. All this has impacted typical mountain wine characteristics significantly, especially whites, their minerality and their acidity. On the other hand, it was a very satisfactory year for late-ripening grape varieties like syrah and fumin, and for those producers who very savvy enough to take the climate challenge in their stride. At the end of our tastings, six wines had scored top marks, and four of them were from the 2015 vintage. We are referring to Anselmet's Chardonnay Elevé en Fût de Chêne; Ottin's Petite Arvine; Lo Triolet's Pinot Gris; and the stunning Cornalin from Rosset Terroir, confirming its expertise as a producer. The other two award winners were 2014 vintages: Costantino Charrère's Syrah Côteau de la Tour di Les Crêtes, a name that needs no introduction; and another enchanting version of La Vrille's Chambave Muscat Flétri. We have six bijou masterpieces, all from a single growing area, from small vineyards (few regional cellars have more than five hectares under vine, except the cooperatives) and a genuine passion for wine and for these mountains. Rare wines, with few equals in Italy or in the world, and well worth seeking out for those who do not have the good fortune and delight of buying them in the beautiful Valle d'Aosta.

★Maison Anselmet

FRAZ. LA CRÊTE, 194
11018 VILLENEUVE [AO]
TEL. +39 3484127121
www.maisonanselmet.vievini.it

CELLAR SALES
PRE-BOOKED VISITS
ANNUAL PRODUCTION 75,000 bottles
HECTARES UNDER VINE 8.00

Winery owner Giorgio Anselmet breathed new life into his father Renato's estate. A rare combination of tradition and innovation that only someone who cares deeply for the terroir, with a love for family traditions and local products could achieve. The new cellar is the tangible proof of a vision that focuses on the future without forsaking the past. The brand offers a modern interpretation of traditional varieties, also sold on the international market. Maison Anselmet's great communication skills and innovative production have made it one of Valle d'Aosta's top outfits. This year, Anselmet was back on Tre Bicchieri form with a Chardonnay Elevé en Fût de Chêne of great elegance, showing a nose of hedgerow, apple and hazelnut, and an outstanding fresh palate. The excellent Semel Pater displays good structure, with spicy hints. We also liked Le Prisonnier, a blend with hints of red berry fruit with a sophisticated tannic weave.

Château Feuillet

LOC. CHÂTEAU FEUILLET, 12
11010 SAINT PIERRE
TEL. +39 3287673880
www.chateaufeuillet.vievini.it

CELLAR SALES
ACCOMMODATION AND RESTAURANT SERVICE
ANNUAL PRODUCTION 30,000 bottles
HECTARES UNDER VINE 5.00

We have used many adjectives to describe Maurizio Fiorano, the enterprising owner of Château Feuillet. We are no longer surprised by the flavour and quality of his wines. If anything we expect better wines and new arrivals every year so no disappointments on that front, with a new monovarietal petit rouge rosé, a perfect table companion for local charcuterie. Château Feuillet is located in one of the region's top growing areas, in Saint Pierre, north of Aosta, on south-facing hillsides, where both red and white varieties give a good account of themselves. The Petite Arvine reached the final, with its nose of apricots and almond, and its impressively full and balanced backbone. With their hints of ripe red berries and pleasing edge of greenness, the full-flavoured, firmly structured Torrette labels are true to type. We should also mention the Fumin, which though needing further ageing, displays attractively balsamic notes. The Chardonnay is tangy, layered and pleasant.

○ Valle d'Aosta Chardonnay Élevé en Fût de Chêne '15	♥♥♥ 5
● Le Prisonnier MMXIII	♥♥ 8
● Valle d'Aosta Cornalin Broblan '14	♥♥ 5
● Valle d'Aosta Pinot Noir Semel Pater '14	♥♥ 6
● Valle d'Aosta Fumin Élevé en Fût de Chêne '14	♥♥ 6
○ Valle d'Aosta Petite Arvine '15	♥♥ 3
○ Valle d'Aosta Pinot Gris '15	♥♥ 5
● Valle d'Aosta Syrah Henri '14	♥♥ 6
○ Valle d'Aosta Chardonnay Élevé en Fût de Chêne '11	♡♡♡ 5
○ Valle d'Aosta Chardonnay Élevé en Fût de Chêne '10	♡♡♡ 5
○ Valle d'Aosta Chardonnay Élevé en Fût de Chêne '09	♡♡♡ 5
● Valle d'Aosta Pinot Noir Semel Pater '13	♡♡♡ 8

○ Valle d'Aosta Petite Arvine '15	♥♥ 3*
○ Valle d'Aosta Chardonnay '15	♥♥ 3
● Valle d'Aosta Fumin '15	♥♥ 4
⊙ Valle d'Aosta Rosé '15	♥♥ 4
● Valle d'Aosta Torrette '15	♥♥ 3
● Valle d'Aosta Torrette Sup. '14	♥♥ 3
○ Valle d'Aosta Petite Arvine '12	♡♡♡ 3*
○ Valle d'Aosta Petite Arvine '11	♡♡♡ 3*
○ Valle d'Aosta Petite Arvine '10	♡♡♡ 3*
○ Valle d'Aosta Chardonnay '14	♡♡ 3
● Valle d'Aosta Fumin '14	♡♡ 4
○ Valle d'Aosta Petite Arvine '14	♡♡ 3*
○ Valle d'Aosta Petite Arvine '13	♡♡ 3*
● Valle d'Aosta Syrah '14	♡♡ 3
● Valle d'Aosta Torrette Sup. '13	♡♡ 3*
● Valle d'Aosta Torrette Sup. '12	♡♡ 3*

★Les Crêtes

LOC. VILLETOS, 50
11010 AYMAVILLES [AO]
TEL. +39 0165902274
www.lescretes.it

CELLAR SALES
PRE-BOOKED VISITS
ANNUAL PRODUCTION 180,000 bottles
HECTARES UNDER VINE 20.00
SUSTAINABLE WINERY

Les Crêtes definitely calls for a trip.
Costantino Charrères' new cellar, sited next
door to the old building, has both reception
and tasting rooms, and is without doubt
one of the most beautiful in Italy. This
wood, glass and stone construction building
is a "wine refuge", with stylized forms and
natural materials, fitting perfectly into its
mountain surroundings. But there is more
to Les Crêtes, with an old windmill and
charming vineyards, especially Côteau de
la Tour, all worth a visit, especially in the
company of Costantino. This year's Tre
Bicchieri goes to a red, the Syrah, with its
intensely brilliant ruby hues. Notes of red
berry fruit on the nose make way for spicy
tobacco hints and a nicely balanced, very
stylish mouth. Petite Arvine's Devin Ros cru
has hints of ripe fruit aromas and a
well-balanced palate. The Cuvée Bois has a
good structure and bodes well for the
future. The refreshing, fruit-forward
Chardonnay 2015 is worthy of mention.
Also pleasingly drinkable is the Pinot Nero.

● Valle d'Aosta Syrah Côteau La Tour '14	♀♀♀	4*
○ Valle d'Aosta Chardonnay Cuvée Bois '14	♀♀	6
○ Valle d'Aosta Petite Arvine Fleur V. Devin Ros '15	♀♀	5
○ Valle d'Aosta Chardonnay '15	♀♀	3
● Valle d'Aosta Pinot Noir '15	♀♀	3
○ Valle d'Aosta Chardonnay Cuvée Bois '13	♀♀♀	6
○ Valle d'Aosta Chardonnay Cuvée Bois '10	♀♀♀	6
○ Valle d'Aosta Chardonnay Cuvée Bois '09	♀♀♀	6
○ Valle d'Aosta Chardonnay Cuvée Bois '08	♀♀♀	6
○ Valle d'Aosta Chardonnay Cuvée Bois '07	♀♀♀	6
○ Valle d'Aosta Chardonnay Cuvée Bois '06	♀♀♀	6
○ Valle d'Aosta Chardonnay Cuvée Frissonnière Les Crêtes Cuvée Bois '05	♀♀♀	6
○ Valle d'Aosta Petite Arvine '13	♀♀♀	3*

La Crotta di Vegneron

P.ZZA RONCAS, 2
11023 CHAMBAVE [AO]
TEL. +39 016646670
www.lacrotta.it

CELLAR SALES
PRE-BOOKED VISITS
RESTAURANT SERVICE
ANNUAL PRODUCTION 300,000 bottles
HECTARES UNDER VINE 39.00

Crotta di Vegneron is on the main square,
in the village of Chambave. Staff from the
charming estate shop illustrate winery
production, while the restaurant next door
serves all Crotta wines, of course. This
cooperative has over 120 members, for
wines in various categories, while for a
Valle d'Aosta winery, quantities are
impressive. La Crotta's flagship is definitely
the Moscato Passito di Chambave, one of
Italy's best sweet wines. The Prieuré is
once again wonderful, with a concentrated
nose hinting at currants, ripe fruit and
honey, segued by a balanced, fresh, long
mouth. We enjoyed the Fumin, which was
very true to type, with its impenetrable
hues, delightful hints of black berry fruit
with blackcurrant to the fore; its green
nuance makes it magical, though it is still
rather austere in the mouth. The Syrah is a
welcome newcomer, with typical hints of
black pepper, and flowery nuances redolent
of violets; it has a balanced, elegant mouth.

○ Valle d'Aosta Chambave Moscato Passito Prieuré '14	♀♀	5
● Valle d'Aosta Fumin Esprit Follet '14	♀♀	5
● Valle d'Aosta Syrah Crème '14	♀♀	5
○ Valle d'Aosta Chambave Muscat '15	♀♀	3
○ Valle d'Aosta Nus Malvoisie '15	♀♀	3
○ Valle d'Aosta Chambave Moscato Passito Prieuré '13	♀♀♀	5
○ Valle d'Aosta Chambave Moscato Passito Prieuré '12	♀♀♀	5
○ Valle d'Aosta Chambave Moscato Passito Prieuré '11	♀♀♀	5
○ Valle d'Aosta Chambave Moscato Passito Prieuré '08	♀♀♀	5
● Valle d'Aosta Fumin Esprit Follet '09	♀♀♀	3

VALLE D'AOSTA

Di Barrò

LOC. CHÂTEAU FEUILLET, 8
11010 SAINT PIERRE
TEL. +39 0165903671
www.dibarro.vievini.it

CELLAR SALES
PRE-BOOKED VISITS
ANNUAL PRODUCTION 20,000 bottles
HECTARES UNDER VINE 2.50

Di Barrò is a small winery in Saint Pierre, a village with a beautiful medieval castle, on the road from Aosta up towards Mont Blanc. We are in the heart of the Torrette designation, where the main grape is petit rouge, which gives results unrivalled in any other part of the region. Its growing area covers 11 municipalities, and its acclaimed producers include Andrea Barmaz and Elvira Rini, who grow international varieties alongside their local grapes for their limited and meticulous range. This year, the Di Barrò winery took the brave step of not presenting any new vintages. They make wines of great structure, that need long ageing, so we have agreed to wait before tasting them. In the meantime, however, if you are passing through Valle d'Aosta, please pay them a visit and they will gladly give you a foretaste of their production.

○ Valle d'Aosta Chardonnay '12	♥♥♥	3*
● Valle d'Aosta Torrette Sup. V. de Torrette '06	♥♥♥	6
○ Valle d'Aosta Chardonnay '14	♥♥	3
● Valle d'Aosta Fumin '11	♥♥	4
● Valle d'Aosta Syrah V. de Conze '10	♥♥	3
● Valle d'Aosta Torrette Sup. Clos de Château Feuillet '12	♥♥	3
● Valle d'Aosta Torrette Sup. Clos de Château Feuillet '11	♥♥	3*
● Valle d'Aosta Torrette Sup. Clos de Château Feuillet '10	♥♥	3
● Valle d'Aosta Torrette Sup. Ostro '09	♥♥	5

Caves Cooperatives de Donnas

VIA ROMA, 97
11020 DONNAS [AO]
TEL. +39 0125807096
www.donnasvini.it

CELLAR SALES
PRE-BOOKED VISITS
ANNUAL PRODUCTION 150,000 bottles
HECTARES UNDER VINE 26.00

On terraces overlooking the town, on the left bank of the Dora Baltea, the ancient pergolas supported by stone pillars and a wooden structure help the local nebbiolo, known as picotendro, to ripen and repay the heroic efforts of the cooperative growers. After becoming a designation in 1971, and then a sub-designation of the regional DOC, Donnas is a flagship of this region's wines. One of the largest cooperatives in the Lower Aosta Valley, it has a monorail that reaches the most inaccessible, steep vineyards. Les Caves de Donnas is also a restaurant and is always open to visitors. Our favourite this year was the Donnas Vieilles Vignes, with its intense hues verging on ruby, its elegant nose of spices, leaf tobacco and liquorice, and a well-balanced mouth with good structure. Equally good is the Donnas 2013, slightly vegetal on the nose, with a long intense palate. The Napoléon is also intense, with a delicate hint of fruit and new oak. It has a savoury, tannin-heavy mouth and a long characterful finish.

● Valle d'Aosta Donnas '13	♥♥	4
● Valle d'Aosta Donnas Sup. V. V. '12	♥♥	5
● Valle d'Aosta Donnas Napoléon '13	♥♥	5
● Valle d'Aosta Donnas '11	♥♥	2*
● Valle d'Aosta Donnas Napoléon '11	♥♥	3
● Valle d'Aosta Donnas Napoléon '10	♥♥	3
● Valle d'Aosta Donnas Napoléon '07	♥♥	3
● Valle d'Aosta Donnas Sup. V. V. '07	♥♥	4
● Valle d'Aosta Donnas V. V. '09	♥♥	4

Lo Triolet

LOC. JUNOD, 7
11010 INTROD [AO]
TEL. +39 016595437
www.lotriolet.vievini.it

CELLAR SALES
PRE-BOOKED VISITS
ANNUAL PRODUCTION 42,000 bottles
HECTARES UNDER VINE 5.00

In the village of Introd, whose claim to fame was as a holiday destination for recent popes, Marco Martin's Lo Triolet, interprets pinot grigio and other varietals with the hand of a master. Like many others in Valle d'Aosta, the winery has a visitors' centre for tastings but is also a lovely place for holidays, set halfway up the slopes of Gran Paradiso. After years of replanting and expansion, Marco now has a decent area under vine, by regional standards, with great vineyards on sandy soils at an altitude of 600–900 metres. We gave the Pinot Gris 2015 a Tre Bicchieri for its nose of subtle, complex nuances of pear, paving the way for a mouth-caressing minerality, and a persistent, intense palate. Rosso Heritage is a pleasing, deep ruby red, with a fruit-driven, spicy nose, and a long, powerful palate. Ever pleasant is the barrique version of the Pinot Grigio, while the Fumin and Muscat Petit Grain are remarkable.

○ Valle d'Aosta Pinot Gris '15	♔♔♔	5
○ Valle d'Aosta Pinot Gris Élevé en Barriques '14	♔♔	6
● Valle d'Aosta Rosso Heritage '14	♔♔	6
● Valle d'Aosta Fumin '14	♔♔	5
○ Vallée d'Aoste Muscat Petit Grain '15	♔♔	4
○ Valle d'Aosta Pinot Gris '14	♔♔♔	3*
○ Valle d'Aosta Pinot Gris '13	♔♔♔	3*
○ Valle d'Aosta Pinot Gris '12	♔♔♔	3*
○ Valle d'Aosta Pinot Gris '09	♔♔♔	3
○ Valle d'Aosta Pinot Gris '08	♔♔♔	3*
○ Valle d'Aosta Pinot Gris '05	♔♔♔	3*
○ Valle d'Aosta Pinot Gris Élevé en Barriques '10	♔♔♔	5
● Valle d'Aosta Fumin '13	♔♔	5
○ Valle d'Aosta Pinot Gris Élevé en Barriques '13	♔♔	5

Cave du Mont Blanc de Morgex et La Salle

FRAZ. LA RUINE
CHEMIN DES ÎLES, 31
11017 MORGEX [AO]
TEL. +39 0165800331
www.caveduvinblanc.com

CELLAR SALES
PRE-BOOKED VISITS
ANNUAL PRODUCTION 140,000 bottles
HECTARES UNDER VINE 19.00

Leaving the motorway at Morgex and heading up the main road to nearby Courmayeur, the striking building on the right, constructed with the region's traditional materials of stone and wood, is the Cave du Vin Blanc de Morgex et de La Salle. In a mountain village at such altitudes it is hard to imagine that grape and wine can influence culture, traditions and local economy to such an extent. The pergolas on which the native, still ungrafted, priè blanc ripens are so low that some have to be tended lying down. The Blanc de Morgex 2015 is very good, with intense nose notes of Alpine herbs and sun-dried hay for a delicate wine of great balance. We enjoyed the Vini Estremi version, its bigger structure compared to the basic wine slightly hindering the bouquet. There are plenty of Metodo Classico versions of this wine, with a typical bouquet of Alpine herbs. This year we recommend the Cuvée du Prince Brut Nature, which reflects the typicity of the vine and has a noteworthy structure.

○ Valle d'Aosta Blanc de Morgex et de La Salle '15	♔♔	2*
○ Valle d'Aosta Blanc de Morgex et de La Salle Brut Nature Cuvée du Prince M. Cl. '09	♔♔	2*
○ Valle d'Aosta Blanc de Morgex et de La Salle Cuvée Gerbollier '12	♔♔	5
○ Valle d'Aosta Blanc de Morgex et de La Salle Vini Estremi '15	♔♔	3
○ Valle d'Aosta Blanc de Morgex et de La Salle Chaudelune '13	♔	2
○ Valle d'Aosta Blanc de Morgex et de La Salle '14	♔♔	2*
○ Valle d'Aosta Blanc de Morgex et de La Salle La Piagne '14	♔♔	5
○ Valle d'Aosta Blanc de Morgex et de La Salle Chaudelune '12	♔♔	2*

VALLE D'AOSTA

Elio Ottin

FRAZ. POROSSAN NEYVES, 209
11100 AOSTA
TEL. +39 3474071331
www.ottinvini.it

CELLAR SALES
PRE-BOOKED VISITS
ANNUAL PRODUCTION 30,000 bottles
HECTARES UNDER VINE 4.50
SUSTAINABLE WINERY

Elio Ottin, an iconic figure on the Valle d'Aosta wine scene, has his cellar on the hills around Aosta, within the city limits, on the road that goes to Roisan and then up to Great Saint Bernard. He produces his wines in keeping with local customs and traditions, innovating with sensitivity and intelligence, and his wines are from native varieties with the occasional international cultivar. Elio worked for years as an agricultural advisory officer for the regional council, and only in 2007 did he decide to make wine from his own grapes, which he had been growing for the local cooperative. A well-deserved Tre Bicchieri for the Petite Arvine, with its fruit-driven hints reminiscent of apricots, with citrusy nuances; on the palate elegance and finesse win out over power. A symphony of delicate balance, the Pinot Nero is very good. We would say the Fumin is a giant, with its impenetrable hues, spectacular nose, and fullness. The Torrette Supérieur is layered, balanced and well-orchestrated.

Ermes Pavese

S.DA PINETA, 26
11017 MORGEX [AO]
TEL. +39 0165800053
www.pavese.vievini.it

CELLAR SALES
PRE-BOOKED VISITS
ANNUAL PRODUCTION 35,000 bottles
HECTARES UNDER VINE 5.00

In northern Valle d'Aosta, among the high-altitude vineyards on the slopes of Mont Blanc, Blanc de Morgex is a gem of local culture, and Ermes Pavese is one of this traditional wine's most loyal makers. Ermes has reinterpreted priè blanc, the famous local grape, creating versions with a modern, alluring style. Here, at the upper limits for grape-growing, we stand in awe of the great work of winemakers like him, who struggle every year to keep these challenging vineyards going, with grapes that make wines of undisputed charm. In the finals again, the entry-level Blanc de Morgex is a refreshing, well-orchestrated wine, with pleasant hints of Alpine herbs on the nose are cloaked in a delicate minerality, leading into a light, flavoursome structure. Le Sette Scalinate is bright straw-yellow with greenish nuances; the intense yet refined nose of herbs and white-fleshed fruit progresses to a vibrant palate, slightly lacking in fullness but quite long and very dynamic. The Pas Dosé is a well-behaved, fragrant sparkler.

○ Valle d'Aosta Petite Arvine '15	♔♔♔ 5
● Valle d'Aosta Fumin '14	♔♔ 5
● Valle d'Aosta Pinot Noir '14	♔♔ 4
● Valle d'Aosta Torrette Sup. '14	♔♔ 5
○ Valle d'Aosta Petite Arvine Nuances '14	♔♔ 5
● Valle d'Aosta Fumin '12	♔♔♔ 3*
○ Valle d'Aosta Petite Arvine '14	♔♔♔ 4*
○ Valle d'Aosta Petite Arvine '12	♔♔♔ 3*
○ Valle d'Aosta Petite Arvine '11	♔♔♔ 3*
○ Valle d'Aosta Petite Arvine '10	♔♔♔ 3*
● Valle d'Aosta Fumin '13	♔♔ 4
● Valle d'Aosta Fumin '11	♔♔ 3*
● Valle d'Aosta Fumin '10	♔♔ 3*
○ Valle d'Aosta Petite Arvine '13	♔♔ 3*
● Valle d'Aosta Torrette Sup. '13	♔♔ 4
● Valle d'Aosta Torrette Sup. '11	♔♔ 4

○ Valle d'Aosta Vin Blanc de Morgex et La Salle '15	♔♔ 4
○ Valle d'Aosta Vin Blanc de Morgex et La Salle Le Sette Scalinate '14	♔♔ 5
○ Valle d'Aosta Vin Blanc de Morgex et La Salle Pavese XVIII Pas Dosé '13	♔♔ 5
○ Valle d'Aosta Vin Blanc de Morgex et La Salle Nathan '14	♔ 5
○ Valle d'Aosta Vin Blanc de Morgex et La Salle '14	♔♔ 2*
○ Valle d'Aosta Vin Blanc de Morgex et La Salle '13	♔♔ 2*
○ Valle d'Aosta Vin Blanc de Morgex et La Salle Nathan '12	♔♔ 2*

Rosset Terroir

LOC. TORRENT DE MAILLOD, 4
11020 QUART [AO]
TEL. +39 0165774111
www.rosseterroir.it

CELLAR SALES
PRE-BOOKED VISITS
ANNUAL PRODUCTION 20,000 bottles
HECTARES UNDER VINE 3.00

Founded in 2001, the Rosset winery is without doubt one of the most modern and innovative in the Valle d'Aosta. Focused market research, communication skills and eco sustainability soon paved the way to quality wines. Native and international varieties coexist in harmony, tended by young winemaker Matteo Moretto. Owner Nicola Rosset's experience in the international liqueur world opened the door for Rosset Terroir wines in the global market, making his winery one of the region's success stories. Rosset decided to present both vintages together. Though dissimilar, they have quality in common. Worthy of a Tre Bicchieri the fruit-driven, spicy 2015 Cornalin, from a native varietal, with notes of walnut and hazelnut on the nose, a full body, and a delicately balanced mouth. Both the 2014 and the 2015 Syrahs reach lofty heights, while the Chardonnay is still evolving.

● Valle d'Aosta Cornalin '15	♟♟♟ 4*
● Valle d'Aosta Syrah '15	♟♟ 4
● Valle d'Aosta Syrah '14	♟♟ 4
○ Valle d'Aosta Chardonnay '14	♟♟ 4
● Valle d'Aosta Cornalin '14	♟♟ 4
● Valle d'Aosta Syrah '13	♟♟♟ 4*
○ Valle d'Aosta Chardonnay '13	♀♀ 4
○ Valle d'Aosta Chardonnay '12	♀♀ 4
○ Valle d'Aosta Chardonnay '07	♀♀ 4
● Valle d'Aosta Cornalin '13	♀♀ 4
● Valle d'Aosta Syrah '12	♀♀ 4
● Valle d'Aosta Syrah '07	♀♀ 4
● Valle d'Aosta Syrah '06	♀♀ 4

La Vrille

LOC. GRANGEON, 1
11020 VERRAYES [AO]
TEL. +39 0166543018
www.lavrille-agriturisme.com

CELLAR SALES
PRE-BOOKED VISITS
ACCOMMODATION AND RESTAURANT SERVICE
ANNUAL PRODUCTION 16,000 bottles
HECTARES UNDER VINE 2.40
SUSTAINABLE WINERY

Hervé and Luciana Deguillaume's enchanting La Vrille is surrounded by an idyllic landscape, a natural amphitheatre formed by mountain peaks, all around the small cellar, its vineyards, and the farmhouse rooms and restaurant serving home-grown products, with wine at the top of the list. The Deguillaumes are pioneers of organic production and offer a small, carefully crafted range of labels based on traditional varieties, with Fumin and Cornalin alongside various versions of Moscato di Chambave. A Tre Bicchieri goes to the refined, layered Muscat Flétri, with a nose of over-ripe fruit caressed by caramel; the palate is balanced and well-behaved, with admirable length. The enthusiastic Fumin is true to type, inky, fruit-driven and spicy, with a nose of leaf tobacco and elegant overtones of greenness, a balanced mouth needing more time in the cellar. The Pinot Nero and the Cornalin are also very good.

○ Valle d'Aosta Chambave Muscat Flétri '14	♟♟♟ 7
● Valle d'Aosta Fumin '12	♟♟ 5
● Valle d'Aosta Cornalin '14	♟♟ 4
● Valle d'Aosta Pinot Noir '13	♟♟ 4
○ Valle d'Aosta Chambave Muscat '12	♀♀♀ 4*
○ Valle d'Aosta Chambave Muscat Flétri '11	♀♀♀ 6
○ Valle d'Aosta Chambave Muscat Flétri '10	♀♀♀ 5
○ Valle d'Aosta Chambave Muscat Flétri '07	♀♀♀ 4*
○ Valle d'Aosta Chambave Muscat '13	♀♀ 4
○ Valle d'Aosta Chambave Muscat Flétri '13	♀♀ 7

La Crotta de Tanteun e Marietta

VIA VEVEY, 23
11100 AOSTA
TEL. +39 3341822471
www.lacrottadetanteunemarietta.it

CELLAR SALES
PRE-BOOKED VISITS
ANNUAL PRODUCTION 10,000 bottles
HECTARES UNDER VINE 2.50

○ Valle d'Aosta Muscat Petit Grain '15	♟♟	5
● Valle d'Aosta Rouge Farouche '14	♟♟	5
○ Valle d'Aosta Pinot Gris Biselle '14	♟	5

Feudo di San Maurizio

FRAZ. MAILLOD, 44
11010 SARRE [AO]
TEL. +39 3383186831
www.vinievino.com

CELLAR SALES
PRE-BOOKED VISITS
ANNUAL PRODUCTION 40,000 bottles
HECTARES UNDER VINE 7.00

● Pierrots '14	♟♟	5
● Saro Djablo	♟♟	3
○ Valle d'Aosta Chardonnay '14	♟♟	3
● Valle d'Aosta Fumin '14	♟♟	4

F.lli Grosjean

VILLAGGIO OLLIGNAN, 1
11020 QUART [AO]
TEL. +39 0165775791
www.grosjean.vievini.it

CELLAR SALES
PRE-BOOKED VISITS
ANNUAL PRODUCTION 90,000 bottles
HECTARES UNDER VINE 10.00
VITICULTURE METHOD Certified Organic

● Valle d'Aosta Fumin V. Rovettaz '12	♟♟	6
○ Valle d'Aosta Petite Arvine V. Rovettaz '15	♟♟	5
● Valle d'Aosta Pinot Noir '15	♟♟	5

Institut Agricole Régional

LOC. RÉGION LA ROCHÈRE, 1A

11100 AOSTA
TEL. +39 0165215811
www.iaraosta.it

CELLAR SALES
PRE-BOOKED VISITS
ANNUAL PRODUCTION 50,000 bottles
HECTARES UNDER VINE 7.30

● Valle d'Aosta Vuillermin '14	♟♟	5
○ Valle d'Aosta Petite Arvine '15	♟	4
● Valle d'Aosta Pinot Noir Sang des Salasses '14	♟	5

La Source

LOC. BUSSAN DESSOUS, 1
11010 SAINT PIERRE
TEL. +39 0165904038
www.lasource.it

CELLAR SALES
PRE-BOOKED VISITS
ANNUAL PRODUCTION 40,000 bottles
HECTARES UNDER VINE 7.00

● Valle d'Aosta Torrette Sup. '13	♟♟	3
● Valle d'Aosta Cornalin '14	♟	3

Maison Albert Vevey

FRAZ. VILLAIR
S.DA DEL VILLAIR, 67
11017 MORGEX [AO]
TEL. +39 0165808930
www.vievini.it

CELLAR SALES
PRE-BOOKED VISITS
ANNUAL PRODUCTION 7,000 bottles
HECTARES UNDER VINE 1.50

○ Valle d'Aosta Blanc de Morgex et de La Salle '15	♟♟	4

A GUIDE TO THE LEADING 1100 COMPANIES PRODUCING FOODSTUFFS IN ITALY

An indispensable tool for foodies
but even more so for industry insiders
promoting the best of Made-in-Italy worldwide

COLLESI

BIRRA
ARTIGIANALE
COLLESI
Ego
BIONDA
IMPERALE

Birra Collesi... Sensazion*Ale*

www.collesi.com

PIEDMONT

No one dreams of doubting the cultural and qualitative superiority of the nebbiolo grape, which contributed to a whopping 58 Tre Bicchieri awards out of the 75 taken home by Piedmont in Italian Wines 2017. Nevertheless, it might be a good idea to try and imagine a turnaround. In a land that is slowly but very surely being overrun by nebbiolo, news is being made by varieties like barbera or moscato, long considered hoi polloi, or others already enjoying some international notoriety but strangers to most consumers, like dolcetto, cortese, erbaluce. Or even those like ruché or grignolino that never made it to the Tre Bicchieri podium, except in what can be considered prehistoric times for Italian wine, for example Scarpa's Rouchet Bricco Rosa 1990, a winner in the 1992 edition of the guide. In our way, we want to keep the faith with ideas that conjure up two words, quite unrelated to one another: secularism and biodiversity, which can live together peacefully and contribute to leading these lesser-known varieties to the top of the podium. Not that we give prizes to a grape type without assessing its real quality. We aim to quash the snobbery tof which they are victims and offer an opportunity for other exceptional wines to be appreciated. With the help of the fantastic 2015 vintage, a Grignolino garnered a first Tre Bicchieri and this is news because it also coincides with the first such award for Vicara, a winery that goes back a long way. A return to a top ranking for a Ruché, this time from Montalbera. The 2017 edition suggests that in the Alessandria growing area things have been turned upside down, as it loses the Tre Bicchieri for Timorasso and for Tortonese, struggling with the dismal 2014 vintage, while Gavi took three awards in one fell swoop, cashing in on the successful 2015 harvest, which also gave a helping hand to Moscato D'Asti, recovering its polish after showing slightly tarnished for climatic reasons. Noteworthy among the winners there is also a stunning performance from the Canelli subzone. Special praise goes to the six wineries making their Tre Bicchieri debut, and apart from those already mentioned we should remember Alto Piemonte's La Prevosturat, San Bartolomeo in the Gavi district, Palladino and Vite Colte in Langa.

460 Casina Bric

LOC. CASCINA BRICCO
FRAZ. VERGNE
VIA SORELLO, 1A
12060 BAROLO [CN]
TEL. +39 335283468
www.casinabric-barolo.it

CELLAR SALES
PRE-BOOKED VISITS
ANNUAL PRODUCTION 45,000 bottles
HECTARES UNDER VINE 10.00

Gianluca Viberti's motto is "Research and Patience", indicating his passion for studying the soil and work in the cellar, which continues to benefit from his experience year after year. Cascina Bric in Barolo is situated at an altitude of 460 metres and the vineyard in the hamlet of Serradenari in La Morra is even higher, ensuring a fresh, racy Barolo. The style of the wines is classic, lean and particularly elegant and focused, achieved by long maceration and the use of medium-sized oak. Just one Barolo was made from the 2012 harvest, blending all the grapes from the estate's six crus in the highest parts of La Morra and Barolo. The result is an extremely pleasant, vibrant wine with attractive notes of flowers and dried herbs, followed by hints of tobacco and liquorice, and a well-orchestrated palate with remarkable tannins and great acidity. While awaiting the next release of Nebbiolo d'Alba Metodo Classico, Nebbiolo Charmat Lungo Prêt-à-Porter is already very interesting.

● Barolo '12	♜♜ 6
⊙ Nebbiolo d'Alba Brut Rosè	
Prêt-à-Porter Collezione N°8	♜♜ 4
● Ansj	♜ 4
● Ansj '11	♕♕ 4
● Barolo '11	♕♕ 6
● Barolo '10	♕♕ 6
● Barolo Bricco delle Viole '11	♕♕ 7
● Barolo Bricco delle Viole '10	♕♕ 7

★Abbona

B.GO SAN LUIGI, 40
12063 DOGLIANI [CN]
TEL. +39 0173721317
www.abbona.com

CELLAR SALES
PRE-BOOKED VISITS
ANNUAL PRODUCTION 350,000 bottles
HECTARES UNDER VINE 50.00

Ever since his 1970s debut in the wine world, Marziano Abbona has refused to content himself with the international success of his Dolcetto Papà Celso, applying the same determination to Barolo with the purchase of prestigious crus in Novello and Monforte d'Alba. Neither has he neglected the Barbaresco, Nebbiolo d'Alba, and Langhe Nebbiolo, wines from the most representative grapes of the area, nor arneis, the typical white cultivar of neighbouring Roero. His sole concession to international varieties is viognier, used alone in the successful Langhe Bianco Cinerino. The 2015 vintage was a fabulous one for dolcetto and the Papà Celso is more concentrated and potent than ever, without foregoing its proverbial elegance and delicious drinkability. Its charming nose of blackberries and almonds helped it clinch our top accolade. Barolo Cerviano 2011 is splendidly balanced. The austere and undoubtedly ageworthy Barolo 2012 has plenty of fruit, while the pleasant Ravera of the same vintage is lighter.

● Dogliani Papà Celso '15	♜♜♜ 4*
● Barolo Cerviano '11	♜♜ 8
● Barolo Pressenda '12	♜♜ 7
● Barolo Ravera '12	♜♜ 7
● Dogliani San Luigi '15	♜♜ 3
○ Langhe Bianco Cinerino '15	♜♜ 4
● Nebbiolo d'Alba Bricco Barone '14	♜♜ 4
● Barbera d'Alba Rinaldi '15	♜ 4
● Barolo Cerviano '10	♕♕♕ 7
● Barolo Terlo Ravera '08	♕♕♕ 6
● Barolo Terlo Ravera '06	♕♕♕ 6
● Dogliani Papà Celso '13	♕♕♕ 4*
● Dogliani Papà Celso '11	♕♕♕ 3*
● Dogliani Papà Celso '09	♕♕♕ 3
● Dogliani Papà Celso '07	♕♕♕ 3
● Dogliani Papà Celso '06	♕♕♕ 3

Anna Maria Abbona

FRAZ. MONCUCCO, 21
12060 FARIGLIANO [CN]
TEL. +39 0173797228
www.annamariaabbona.it

Orlando Abrigo

VIA CAPPELLETTO, 5
12050 TREISO [CN]
TEL. +39 0173630533
www.orlandoabrigo.it

CELLAR SALES
PRE-BOOKED VISITS
ANNUAL PRODUCTION 75,000 bottles
HECTARES UNDER VINE 14.00

CELLAR SALES
PRE-BOOKED VISITS
ACCOMMODATION AND RESTAURANT SERVICE
ANNUAL PRODUCTION 80,000 bottles
HECTARES UNDER VINE 20.00
SUSTAINABLE WINERY

Anna Maria Abbona and Franco Schellino's estate is approaching its 20th anniversary and is an increasingly solid and determined feature of the rich Dogliani wine scene. Dolcetto obviously remains its focus, with three versions of Dogliani displaying varying degrees of complexity and firmness. However, over the years it has also confidently branched into the world of whites, with Langhe Riesling and Nascetta, and Barolo, now at its fourth vintage. The expansion of the range has been accompanied by a constant rise in quality. The quality of the Barolo has improved, with the 2012 vintage showing great length and fine harmony, with citrussy hints on the classic nose. The succulent Dogliani Superiore Maioli 2014 is certainly one of the finest Dolcettos of the vintage, with notes of dark fruit and liquorice, while the young Barbera d'Alba 2015 is uncomplicated but extremely drinkable.

Giovanni Abrigo is still relatively young, despite his long experience, and steadily continues to build his winery. Today he can boast top-notch vineyards that unfortunately do not always receive the attention they deserve due to their position in the wildest, southernmost reaches of the Barbaresco production zone. The house style favours fruity reds with plenty of flesh to counter the natural hardness derived from the soils of this subzone. The many innovative wines made from international grape varieties confirm Giovanni's love of experimentation. The trio of Barbarescos is characterized by an alluring, close-focused nose, testifying to the cellarmaster's skill and the soundness of the grapes. Montersino 2013 towers above the rest with delicious fruity flesh and a charming nose of dark berries and herbs. However, the entire range is very good, with the Livraie, a fresh, juicy Merlot, particularly worthy of note.

● Barolo '12	🏆🏆 6
● Dogliani Sup. Maioli '14	🏆🏆 3*
● Barbera d'Alba '15	🏆🏆 2*
● Dogliani Sorì dij But '15	🏆🏆 2*
● Dogliani Sup. San Bernardo '13	🏆🏆 4
● Langhe Nebbiolo '13	🏆🏆 3
⊙ Rosà '15	🏆🏆 3
● Langhe Dolcetto '15	🏆 2
○ Langhe Riesling L'Alman '14	🏆 3
● Langhe Rosso Cadò '12	🏆 5
● Dogliani Sup. San Bernardo '12	🏆🏆🏆 4*
● Dogliani Sup. San Bernardo '11	🏆🏆🏆 4*
● Barolo '11	🏆🏆 6
● Barolo '10	🏆🏆 6
● Barolo '09	🏆🏆 6
● Dogliani Sup. Maioli '10	🏆🏆 3*

● Barbaresco Montersino '13	🏆🏆 7
● Barbaresco Rongalio Ris. '11	🏆🏆 8
● Barbaresco Meruzzano '13	🏆🏆 5
● Barbera d'Alba Roreto '14	🏆🏆 3
● Langhe Rosso Livraie '13	🏆🏆 4
○ Langhe Très Plus '14	🏆🏆 3
● Langhe Nebbiolo Settevie '14	🏆 3
○ Moscato d'Asti '15	🏆 2
○ Sauvignon D'Amblè '15	🏆 3
● Barbaresco Meruzzano '12	🏆🏆 5
● Barbaresco Meruzzano '11	🏆🏆 5
● Barbaresco Montersino '12	🏆🏆 7
● Barbera d'Alba Mervisano '10	🏆🏆 3*
● Barbera d'Alba Roreto '13	🏆🏆 3
● Langhe Nebbiolo Settevie '13	🏆🏆 3
● Nebbiolo d'Alba Valmaggiore '12	🏆🏆 5

★Giulio Accornero e Figli

Cascina Ca' Cima, 1
15049 Vignale Monferrato [AL]
Tel. +39 0142933317
www.accornerovini.it

CELLAR SALES
PRE-BOOKED VISITS
ACCOMMODATION
ANNUAL PRODUCTION 100,000 bottles
HECTARES UNDER VINE 22.00
SUSTAINABLE WINERY

Ermanno's winemaking choices have always proven themselves to be very sound. His latest creation, Grignolino Vigne Vecchie, has become a driving force for much of the designation and is perfectly able to compete with world-famous Piedmont wines. The final step is the application for recognition of the Riserva type by the newly founded Consortium, in order to apply a common production protocol able to ensure uniformity. In the meantime, production figures are rising as the wine becomes increasingly popular with connoisseurs. Ermanno has lived up to our expectations, presenting an astounding list with three champions vying for our top accolade. The winner was a masterful version of Bricco del Bosco Vigne Vecchie 2011, which is concentrated and complex with an endless finish. Bricco Battista 2013 is also superb, with an incredibly complex nose and a majestic palate.

● Barbera del M.to Sup. Bricco Battista '13	♟♟♟ 5
● Barbera del M.to Sup. C ima Riserva della Casa '11	♟♟ 8
● Grignolino del M.to Casalese Bricco del Bosco V. V. '11	♟♟ 6
● Barbera del M.to Giulin '14	♟♟ 3
● Cabernet Sauvignon Centenario '11	♟♟ 5
● Casorzo Brigantino '15	♟♟ 2*
○ Fonsina '15	♟♟ 2*
● Grignolino del M.to Casalese Bricco del Bosco '15	♟♟ 2*
● M.to Girotondo '13	♟♟ 4
● Piemonte Barbera Campomoro '14	♟ 2
● Barbera del M.to Sup. Bricco Battista '12	♟♟♟ 5
● Barbera del M.to Sup. Bricco Battista '11	♟♟♟ 5

Marco e Vittorio Adriano

Fraz. San Rocco Seno d'Elvio, 13a
12051 Alba [CN]
Tel. +39 0173362294
www.adrianovini.it

CELLAR SALES
PRE-BOOKED VISITS
ANNUAL PRODUCTION 160,000 bottles
HECTARES UNDER VINE 27.00
SUSTAINABLE WINERY

Marco and Vittorio Adriano's handsome winery is in the little hamlet of San Rocco Seno d'Elvio, in the municipality of Alba. It is a story with a happy ending, considering the many sacrifices and stumbling blocks faced by the family during their early years as winemakers. Today their range is renowned for its consistent quality, distinctive style, and excellent value for money. This is particularly true for the Barbarescos, aged in 3,500–5,000-litre Slavonian oak barrels, from the Bricco and Frati vineyards for the Sanadaive, and the Basarin cru in Neive, also used for the Riserva since 2004. This year the Basarin Riserva 2011 put up the best performance, with sweet fruit and subtle confit notes mingling with hints of spice and roots, more evident on the austere, enfolding palate. The 2013 Sanadaive and Basarin are both still rather closed but the Sauvignon Basarico 2015 is exceptionally nice.

● Barbaresco Basarin Ris. '11	♟♟ 6
○ Ardì	♟♟ 2*
● Barbaresco Basarin '13	♟♟ 5
● Barbaresco Sanadaive '13	♟♟ 4
● Barbera d'Alba '15	♟♟ 2*
● Barbera d'Alba Sup. '13	♟♟ 2*
● Dolcetto'd'Alba '15	♟♟ 2*
○ Langhe Sauvignon Basarico '15	♟♟ 3
● Langhe Freisa '15	♟ 2
● Langhe Nebbiolo '14	♟ 3
○ Moscato d'Asti '15	♟ 3
● Barbaresco Basarin '12	♟♟ 4
● Barbaresco Sanadaive '12	♟♟ 4
● Langhe Nebbiolo '13	♟♟ 3

Claudio Alario

VIA SANTA CROCE, 23
12055 DIANO D'ALBA [CN]
TEL. +39 0173231808
www.alarioclaudio.it

CELLAR SALES
PRE-BOOKED VISITS
ANNUAL PRODUCTION 46,000 bottles
HECTARES UNDER VINE 10.00

Claudio Alario is a born vigneron who soon also proved himself a skilled cellarmaster, making consistently fruit-rich wines that are always clean, tasty, and very pleasant due to the well-calibrated use of oak. After several years of producing one of the finest versions of Dolcetto di Diano d'Alba, he moved onto Barolo, purchasing vineyards in the Riva Rocca cru in Verduno and the Sorano cru in Serralunga d'Alba. And he has done so maintaining friendly prices, making a name for himself both at home and abroad. Sorì Costa Fiore 2015 is powerful and assertive, destined to mellow over the coming months in bottle. Sorì Pradurent 2014 is slightly more evolved and vegetal, while Sorì Montagrillo 2015 is still decidedly youthful. The refined Barolo Riva Rocca 2012 has an intensely spicy nose and a palate focusing more on elegance than power.

● Barolo Riva Rocca '12	♔♔ 5
● Dolcetto di Diano d'Alba Costa Fiore '15	♔♔ 2*
● Barolo Sorano '12	♔♔ 6
● Dolcetto di Diano d'Alba Sorì Montagrillo '15	♔♔ 2*
● Dolcetto di Diano d'Alba Sup. Sorì Pradurent '14	♔ 3
● Barolo Sorano '05	♔♔♔ 7
● Barolo Riva Rocca '11	♔♔ 5
● Barolo Riva Rocca '10	♔♔ 6
● Barolo Sorano '09	♔♔ 6
● Dolcetto di Diano d'Alba Sorì Costa Fiore '14	♔♔ 2*
● Dolcetto di Diano d'Alba Sorì Costa Fiore '13	♔♔ 2*

★F.lli Alessandria

VIA B. VALFRÉ, 59
12060 VERDUNO [CN]
TEL. +39 0172470113
www.fratellialessandria.it

CELLAR SALES
PRE-BOOKED VISITS
ANNUAL PRODUCTION 80,000 bottles
HECTARES UNDER VINE 14.00

Pelaverga and nebbiolo are the perfect pair to explore the huge potential of the Verduno area and the wines crafted by the Alessandria brothers. Indeed, the know-how of Alessandro and Gian Battista, aided by his son Vittore, has long been yielding excellent results. The most representative wines are undoubtedly the Barolo crus: Monvigliero and San Lorenzo in Verduno, and Gramolere in Monforte d'Alba, which are veritable classics of the designation, simultaneously austere and airy. They are aged in tonneaux and 2,000 and 3,000-litre French oak barrels, but cellar choices increasingly play second fiddle to stylistic consistency. As usual, we were spoiled for choice with the commanding array of Barolos. Monvigliero 2012 took a Tre Bicchieri for its delicately refined palate and elegant aromas of fruit and spice. San Lorenzo 2012 has a nose of tar and dried herbs, and nice power without a hint of dryness on the palate. Gramolère 2012 is very classic, with notes of wild strawberries, tobacco, and liquorice.

● Barolo Monvigliero '12	♔♔♔ 6
● Barolo Gramolere '12	♔♔ 6
● Barolo San Lorenzo di Verduno '12	♔♔ 6
● Barolo '12	♔♔ 5
○ Langhe Favorita '15	♔♔ 2*
● Verduno Pelaverga Speziale '15	♔♔ 3
● Barolo Gramolere '11	♔♔♔ 6
● Barolo Gramolere '10	♔♔♔ 6
● Barolo Gramolere '05	♔♔♔ 6
● Barolo Monvigliero '09	♔♔♔ 6
● Barolo Monvigliero '06	♔♔♔ 6
● Barolo Monvigliero '00	♔♔♔ 6
● Barolo S. Lorenzo '08	♔♔♔ 6
● Barolo S. Lorenzo '04	♔♔♔ 6
● Barolo S. Lorenzo '01	♔♔♔ 6

★Gianfranco Alessandria

LOC. MANZONI, 13
12065 MONFORTE D'ALBA [CN]
TEL. +39 017378576
www.gianfrancoalessandria.com

CELLAR SALES
PRE-BOOKED VISITS
ANNUAL PRODUCTION 50,000 bottles
HECTARES UNDER VINE 7.00

Despite the large-scale return to tradition and large barrels by many Langhe estates, Gianfranco confidently continues in his modern style, using barriques and ruthless thinning in the conviction that they are the key to achieving consistently elegant, refined wines. Indeed, his entire range, particularly the two flagships, Barolo San Giovanni and Barbera d'Alba Vittoria, is regularly decidedly fruity and pervaded by spicy aromas, and always pleasantly toasty and smoky. Barolo San Giovanni 2012 reached our finals with elegant top notes of tobacco and liquorice on the nose, followed by leather and fresh, close-focused red berries, and a big, buttery palate with elegant tannins providing velvety backbone. The delectable Barbera d'Alba Vittoria 2013 is a sophisticated blend of ripe red fruit, the Barbera 2014 is fresh and simple, and the elegant Dolcetto d'Alba 2015 is full of juicy flesh.

Marchesi Alfieri

P.ZZA ALFIERI, 28
14010 SAN MARTINO ALFIERI [AT]
TEL. +39 0141976015
www.marchesialfieri.it

CELLAR SALES
PRE-BOOKED VISITS
ACCOMMODATION
ANNUAL PRODUCTION 100,000 bottles
HECTARES UNDER VINE 20.00

Marchesi Alfieri, owned by the San Martino di San Germano sisters, has been one of the leading producers in the province of Asti for over 30 years. Barbera, which accounts for over 75% of the area under vine, with plants up to 80 years old, grignolino, pinot nero and nebbiolo go to form a small range of top-quality reds, which are complex yet elegant, with firm structure and plenty of fruit. Barbera d'Asti Superiore Alfiera reconfirms its role as the estate's flagship wine with the 2013 vintage. Red berries and rain-soaked earth are followed by still evident notes of oak on the nose, while the firmly structured palate has good grip and staying power. Piemonte Pinot Nero San Germano 2012 has a typical nose of dark berries and a fresh, juicy palate with good pulp and fine-grained tannins. Both the nicely acidic Piemonte Grignolino Sansoero 2015 and the supple, approachable Barbera d'Asti La Tota 2014 are well made.

● Barbera d'Alba Vittoria '13	♛♛ 5
● Barolo S. Giovanni '12	♛♛ 7
● Barolo '12	♛♛ 6
● Dolcetto d'Alba '15	♛♛ 3
● Barbera d'Alba '15	♛ 3
● Barbera d'Alba Vittoria '11	♛♛♛ 5
● Barolo S. Giovanni '04	♛♛♛ 7
● Barolo S. Giovanni '01	♛♛♛ 7
● Barolo S. Giovanni '00	♛♛♛ 7
● Barolo S. Giovanni '99	♛♛♛ 8
● Barolo S. Giovanni '98	♛♛♛ 7
● Barolo S. Giovanni '97	♛♛♛ 7
● Barbera d'Alba Vittoria '12	♛♛ 5
● Barolo S. Giovanni '11	♛♛ 7
● Barolo S. Giovanni '10	♛♛ 7

● Barbera d'Asti Sup. Alfiera '13	♛♛ 5
● Barbera d'Asti La Tota '14	♛♛ 3
● Piemonte Grignolino Sansoero '15	♛♛ 2*
● Piemonte Pinot Nero San Germano '12	♛♛ 5
● M.to Rosso Sostegno '14	♛ 2
● Terre Alfieri Nebbiolo Costa Quaglia '12	♛ 4
● Barbera d'Asti Sup. Alfiera '07	♛♛♛ 5
● Barbera d'Asti Sup. Alfiera '05	♛♛♛ 5
● Barbera d'Asti Sup. Alfiera '01	♛♛♛ 5
● Barbera d'Asti La Tota '13	♛♛ 3*
● Barbera d'Asti Sup. Alfiera '12	♛♛ 5
● M.to Rosso Sostegno '13	♛♛ 2*
● Piemonte Grignolino Sansoero '14	♛♛ 2*

Giovanni Almondo

VIA SAN ROCCO, 26
12046 MONTÀ [CN]
TEL. +39 0173975256
www.giovannialmondo.com

PRE-BOOKED VISITS
ANNUAL PRODUCTION 110,000 bottles
HECTARES UNDER VINE 16.00
SUSTAINABLE WINERY

The Almondo family have lived in Roero for centuries. Today their winery, founded in 1978, is run by Domenico Almondo. All the estate's vineyards are in the municipality of Montà d'Alba, at altitudes between 280 and 360 metres, and include veritable crus, like Bricco delle Ciliegie for arneis and Bric Valdiana for nebbiolo. Production focuses chiefly on arneis, to which 12 of the 16 hectares under vine are planted. Roero Giovanni Almondo Riserva confirms itself one of the finest Roeros in recent years also in the 2013 version. It has a vibrant nose of red berries and tobacco, raspberries and spice, accompanied by a juicy, full-flavoured palate with impressive depth. The fresh Roero Arneis Bricco delle Ciliegie 2015 is also very well made, with jasmine and sweet citrus notes, and yellow-fleshed fruit on the long, pleasant finish. The rest of the range is well made.

● Roero Giovanni Almondo Ris. '13	♛♛♛	5
○ Roero Arneis Bricco delle Ciliegie '15	♛♛	3*
○ Langhe Riesling Sassi e Sabbia '15	♛	4
● Roero '14	♛	3
● Roero Bric Valdiana '11	♛♛♛	5
● Roero Bric Valdiana '07	♛♛♛	5
● Roero Bric Valdiana '03	♛♛♛	5
● Roero Giovanni Almondo Ris. '11	♛♛♛	5
● Roero Giovanni Almondo Ris. '09	♛♛♛	5
● Barbera d'Alba Valbianchèra '13	♛♛	3*
○ Roero Arneis Bricco delle Ciliegie '13	♛♛	3
● Roero Bric Valdiana '13	♛♛	5
● Roero Giovanni Almondo Ris. '12	♛♛	5

★★★Elio Altare
Cascina Nuova

FRAZ. ANNUNZIATA, 51
12064 LA MORRA [CN]
TEL. +39 017350835
www.elioaltare.com

CELLAR SALES
PRE-BOOKED VISITS
ANNUAL PRODUCTION 70,000 bottles
HECTARES UNDER VINE 11.00

The international success of the documentary film Barolo Boys has further credited the pioneering and visionary role played by Elio Altare in Langhe. His experiments with short maceration and small oak casks influenced an entire generation of vignerons when the scenario was very different from today. The time finally seems ripe for a detached analysis of the eternal debate between innovation and tradition in the nebbiolo world. Now as then, the focus is on vineyard work, in the Annunziata cru in La Morra, and more recently Bricco Cerretta in Serralunga, and Cannubi in Barolo, which have to all intents and purposes emerged as "new classics" of the designation. Barolo Cerretta Vigna Bricco 2010 is a delicately modern wine characterized by a splendidly well-orchestrated nose of alluring sweet spice and red berry fruit on a fresh background with typical Serralunga hints of pennyroyal, and an impressively structured palate with an endless finish. The harmonious Barolo Arborina 2012 is intensely spicy with fresh red berries.

● Barolo Cerretta V. Bricco '10	♛♛♛	8
● Barolo Arborina '12	♛♛	8
● Barbera d'Alba '15	♛♛	4
● Barolo '12	♛♛	8
● Langhe Giàrborina '14	♛♛	8
● Langhe La Villa '14	♛♛	8
● Langhe Larigi '14	♛♛	8
● Langhe Nebbiolo '15	♛♛	4
● Dolcetto d'Alba '15	♛	3
● Barolo Arborina '09	♛♛♛	8
● Barolo Cerretta V. Bricco '06	♛♛♛	8
● Barolo Cerretta V. Bricco '05	♛♛♛	8
● Langhe Arborina '08	♛♛♛	8
● Langhe Larigi '13	♛♛♛	8
● Langhe Larigi '12	♛♛♛	8
● Langhe Larigi '07	♛♛♛	7

Amalia Cascina in Langa

LOC. SANT'ANNA, 85
12065 CUNEO
TEL. +39 0173789013
www.cascinaamalia.it

CELLAR SALES
PRE-BOOKED VISITS
ACCOMMODATION
ANNUAL PRODUCTION 60,000 bottles
HECTARES UNDER VINE 14.00
SUSTAINABLE WINERY

Following its debut in our Guide last year, this year the estate has earned our full profile. The Boffa family pay great attention to detail and quality, as demonstrated by their lovely B&B in Sant'Anna di Monforte d'Alba and particularly by the art collection displayed in the cellar, which boasts works by Lodola and Schifano. However, the winery has also made giant technical progress in a very short space of time, with Barberas and Barolos that eloquently convey the great power conferred by this southern corner of the Barolo DOCG zone. Contrary to all expectations, Amalia's 2011 Barolos offer fresh fruity sensations while preserving the complexity of nebbiolo. Le Coste, with dense, close-woven tannins, is less approachable than the well-orchestrated and already highly drinkable Barolo 2011. The two exceptionally pleasant Barberas are stylistic opposites, with the 2015 offering an explosion of fruit, and the Superiore 2013 an attractive aristocratic character.

● Barolo '11	♥♥ 6
● Barolo Le Coste di Monforte '11	♥♥ 6
● Barbera d'Alba '15	♥♥ 4
● Barbera d'Alba Sup. '13	♥♥ 4
○ Langhe Rossese Bianco '14	♥♥ 4
● Barbera d'Alba '13	♀♀ 4
● Barolo Le Coste di Monforte '10	♀♀ 5

Antichi Vigneti di Cantalupo

VIA MICHELANGELO BUONARROTI, 5
28074 GHEMME [NO]
TEL. +39 0163840041
www.cantalupo.net

CELLAR SALES
PRE-BOOKED VISITS
ANNUAL PRODUCTION 200,000 bottles
HECTARES UNDER VINE 35.00

The Arluno family's winegrowing adventure commenced in the early 1800s and the Antichi Vigneti di Cantalupo brand was founded in 1977 by Carlo. Today the estate is run by his son Alberto, who tends its 35 hectares of vineyards, mainly planted to nebbiolo spanna and other typical varieties of the Colline Novaresi zone. The diverse range is centred on four versions of Ghemme: a basic one and three vineyard selections, interpreted according to the vintage using a combination of large and small oak. They are compact, austere reds that generally benefit from patient waiting to mellow any toasty and phenolic excesses. The style is perfectly embodied by Ghemme Collis Breclemae 2006, with tertiary notes of tobacco, petrol, and truffles on the nose, and a firm, hefty palate with still lively tannins. Carolus Bianco offers a fine blend of fullness and citrus nuances, while Primigenia 2013 has nicely controlled warmth.

○ Carolus	♥♥ 2*
● Colline Novaresi Primigenia '13	♥♥ 2*
● Ghemme Collis Breclemae '06	♥♥ 6
⊙ Colline Novaresi Nebbiolo Il Mimo '15	♥ 2
● Colline Novaresi Vespolina Villa Horta '13	♥ 2
● Ghemme '05	♀♀♀ 4
● Ghemme Collis Breclemae '00	♀♀♀ 6
● Colline Novaresi Agamium '09	♀♀ 3
● Colline Novaresi Vespolina Villa Horta '12	♀♀ 2*
● Ghemme Cantalupo Anno Primo '09	♀♀ 5
● Ghemme Cantalupo Anno Primo '08	♀♀ 5
● Ghemme Collis Breclemae '07	♀♀ 6
● Ghemme Collis Carellae '09	♀♀ 6
● Ghemme Collis Carellae '08	♀♀ 6
● Ghemme Signore di Bayard '08	♀♀ 6
● Ghemme Signore di Bayard '06	♀♀ 6

Antico Borgo dei Cavalli

VIA DANTE, 54
28010 CAVALLIRIO [NO]
TEL. +39 016380115
www.vinibarbaglia.it

CELLAR SALES
PRE-BOOKED VISITS
ANNUAL PRODUCTION 25,000 bottles
HECTARES UNDER VINE 3.00

Named after the scenic hamlet of Cavallirio, the Barbaglia family's small estate was founded after the war by Mario, who was succeeded by his son Sergio and his granddaughter Silvia. It covers just over three hectares in the little Boca designation in the province of Novara, whose revival has been boosted by the convincing versions of the wine made by Antico Borgo dei Cavalli over the last decade, in a sunny full-flavoured style. However, the Boca is not the only wine worthy of attention in the wide range, despite the small production figures. The Curticella line of sparklers is well worth trying, as are the monovarietals from nebbiolo, uva rara, croatina, vespolina, and erbaluce. The reliability of the entire range was confirmed by our latest tastings, commencing with Lucino Bianco 2015, with original sulphurous hints and a fat but balanced palate. The Boca 2012 also stands out, combining fresh fruit and tertiary notes of rust and herbs with a nicely layered palate.

● Boca '12	▼▼	5
○ Colline Novaresi Bianco Lucino '15	▼▼	3
○ Curticella Brut M. Cl.	▼▼	5
○ Curticella Dosaggio Zero M. Cl.	▼▼	5
● Colline Novaresi Nebbiolo Il Silente '12	▼	3
● Boca '11	♀♀	5
● Boca '10	♀♀	5
● Boca '09	♀♀	5
○ Colline Novaresi Bianco Biancaluce '14	♀♀	3
○ Colline Novaresi Bianco Lucino '13	♀♀	3
● Colline Novaresi Nebbiolo Il Silente '11	♀♀	3
● Colline Novaresi Nebbiolo Il Silente '09	♀♀	3
○ Curticella Caballi Regis Brut M. Cl.	♀♀	5
○ Curticella Caballi Regis Brut M. Cl.	♀♀	5

★Antoniolo

C.SO VALSESIA, 277
13045 GATTINARA [VC]
TEL. +39 0163833612
antoniolovini@bmm.it

CELLAR SALES
PRE-BOOKED VISITS
ANNUAL PRODUCTION 60,000 bottles
HECTARES UNDER VINE 12.00

Much of the credit for the revival of Gattinara reds, and northern Piedmont wines in general, is due to the determination of Rosanna Antoniolo and her children Alberto and Lorella. Indeed, it was no mean feat to maintain an even keel before such starkly pure and dynamic Nebbiolos had become popular. They are wines inextricably associated with the terroirs of vineyards like San Francesco, San Grato, Castelle, and Borelle, and minimal intervention in the cellar, based on long ageing. The estate's consistency has been rewarded with universal admiration and respect, which grows with each new release. The wines from the 2012 vintage are superb, with even the basic Gattinara displaying magnificent finesse and length, and the San Francesco offering a dark nose associated with a denser, more austere palate. The Osso San Grato is in many ways a combination of the two, showing big and complex with an endless finish.

● Gattinara Osso San Grato '12	▼▼▼	8
● Gattinara '12	▼▼	5
● Gattinara S. Francesco '12	▼▼	8
● Gattinara Le Castelle '12	▼▼	7
● Gattinara Osso S. Grato '11	♀♀♀	8
● Gattinara Osso S. Grato '10	♀♀♀	8
● Gattinara Osso S. Grato '09	♀♀♀	8
● Gattinara S. Francesco '08	♀♀♀	7
● Gattinara S. Francesco '07	♀♀♀	5
● Gattinara Vign. Osso S. Grato '06	♀♀♀	6
● Gattinara Vign. Osso S. Grato '05	♀♀♀	6
● Gattinara Vign. Osso S. Grato '04	♀♀♀	6
● Gattinara Vign. S. Francesco '06	♀♀♀	5
● Gattinara Vign. S. Francesco '05	♀♀♀	6
● Gattinara Vign. S. Francesco '03	♀♀♀	6

Odilio Antoniotti

V.LO ANTONIOTTI, 5
13868 SOSTEGNO [BI]
TEL. +39 0163860309
antoniottiodilio@libero.it

CELLAR SALES
PRE-BOOKED VISITS
ANNUAL PRODUCTION 10,500 bottles
HECTARES UNDER VINE 4.50

In the context of the widespread and welcome revival of northern Piedmont Nebbiolo, Bramaterra and Antoniotti, one of its leading producers, deserve special attention. True to local tradition, the blend of about 70% nebbiolo grapes also features variable amounts of croatina and vespolina, which give freshness and aromatic drive to the impressive underlying structure. The DOC zone is tiny, like the estate, but the results are splendid. At the time of our tastings only one wine was ready, the very elegant, youthful Bramaterra 2012, with a nose of raspberry jam and cherries and a palate with good pulp but still rather assertive tannins. The grapes come from a 40-year-old vineyard and the wine is aged in medium-sized used barrels for over 30 months.

Arbiola

LOC. ARBIOLA
REG. SALINE, 67
14050 SAN MARZANO OLIVETO [AT]
TEL. +39 0141856194
www.arbiola.it

CELLAR SALES
PRE-BOOKED VISITS
ACCOMMODATION AND RESTAURANT SERVICE
ANNUAL PRODUCTION 250,000 bottles
HECTARES UNDER VINE 30.00
VITICULTURE METHOD Certified Organic

The Terzano family's old estate overlooks the Nizza valley, on the border between Monferrato and Langhe, where the 17th-century cellar is flanked by a modern production facility. All the vineyards lie in the municipality of San Marzano Oliveto, on mainly marly soils. The focus is on barbera, which accounts for over 60% of the area under vine, with plants over 60 years old. It yields exuberant, fruit-rich modern wines with impressive aromatic focus. The wines we tasted are as well made as ever, but this year they seemed a little less stunning than in the past. Moscato d'Asti 2015 has a lovely nose of tropical fruit and lime, moss and sage, followed by a balanced palate with firm structure and a fairly juicy, long finish. Barbera d'Asti Superiore Nizza Romilda 2013 vaunts notes of coffee and ripe red berries, impressive stuffing, and particularly prominent acidity.

● Bramaterra '12	♥♥♥ 4
● Bramaterra '10	♥♥♥ 3*
● Bramaterra '11	♥♥ 3*
● Bramaterra '09	♥♥ 3*
● Bramaterra '08	♥♥ 3*
● Bramaterra '07	♥♥ 3*

● Barbera d'Asti Sup. Nizza Romilda '13	♥♥ 5
○ Moscato d'Asti '15	♥♥ 2*
● Barbera d'Asti Carlotta '14	♥ 3
● Barbera d'Asti Sup. Nizza Romilda XIV '09	♥♥♥ 5
● Barbera d'Asti Carlotta '13	♥♥ 3
● Barbera d'Asti Carlotta '12	♥♥ 2*
● Barbera d'Asti Carlotta '11	♥♥ 2*
● Barbera d'Asti Carlotta '09	♥♥ 2*
● Barbera d'Asti Sup. Nizza Romilda XV '10	♥♥ 5
● Barbera d'Asti Sup. Nizza Romilda XVI '11	♥♥ 5
● Barbera d'Asti Sup. Nizza Romilda XVII '12	♥♥ 4
○ Moscato d'Asti Ferlingot '10	♥♥ 2*
○ Nysus Brut M. Cl. '10	♥♥ 5

L'Armangia

FRAZ. SAN GIOVANNI, 122
14053 CANELLI [AT]
TEL. +39 0141824947
www.armangia.it

CELLAR SALES
PRE-BOOKED VISITS
ANNUAL PRODUCTION 95,000 bottles
HECTARES UNDER VINE 11.00
SUSTAINABLE WINERY

Although the Giovine family have lived in Canelli since the 17th century and fermented their own grapes since 1850, the first L'Armangia wines were not produced until 1993. Today the estate has vineyards in several municipalities, from Canelli, where mainly white grapes are grown, to Moasca, San Marzano Oliveto and Castel Boglione, which are home to the red varieties. The wines are modern in style, but very terroir true and well typed. Both versions of Barbera d'Asti Superiore Nizza presented this year were excellent. Titon 2013 has an elegant, concentrated nose of dark berries and sweet spice with still prominent oak, and a full, well-structured palate with great personality and length, while Vignali 2011 offers notes of coffee, cocoa powder, plum, and black damsons on the nose and a nicely acidic palate with fine structure and a long, juicy finish. The rest of the range is good, particularly the delicious, refreshing LorenzoMariaSole Extra Brut.

Paolo Avezza

REG. MONFORTE, 62
14053 CANELLI [AT]
TEL. +39 0141822296
www.paoloavezza.com

CELLAR SALES
PRE-BOOKED VISITS
ANNUAL PRODUCTION 25,000 bottles
HECTARES UNDER VINE 7.00

It has been 60 years since Natale Avezza decided to buy a handsome farmhouse surrounded by vineyards on the Canelli hills, and 15 since his grandson turned it into the family winery. Four of the estate's seven hectares of vineyards are in Nizza Monferrato and three in Canelli. Together, they yield five elegant wines: two Barberas, a Moscato, and two Metodo Classicos, all with remarkable aromatic focus. Barbera d'Asti Superiore Nizza Sotto La Muda 2013 proves itself among the best of the designation again. On the nose it offers very elegant, complex top notes of dark berry fruit and tobacco, while the palate is fresh, firm, and lingering, notwithstanding its still rather prominent oak. The approachable, easy-drinking Barbera d'Asti 2015 has beautifully fruity notes of fresh cherries, while Moscato d'Asti Canelli La Commenda 2015 is delicate with nice balance.

● Barbera d'Asti Sup. Nizza Titon '13	♟♟ 3*
● Barbera d'Asti Sup. Nizza Vignali '11	♟♟ 5
○ Lorenzomariasole Extra Brut M. Cl.	♟♟ 4
○ M.to Bianco Enneenne '14	♟♟ 2*
○ Moscato d'Asti Canelli '15	♟♟ 2*
○ Piemonte Chardonnay Pratorotondo '14	♟♟ 2*
○ Mesicaseu	♟ 3
● Piemonte Albarosso Macchiaferro '12	♟ 3
○ Piemonte Chardonnay Robi & Robi '14	♟ 4
● Barbera d'Asti Sopra Berruti '14	♟♟ 2*
● Barbera d'Asti Sup. Nizza Titon '12	♟♟ 3*
● Barbera d'Asti Sup. Nizza Titon '11	♟♟ 3*
○ Moscato d'Asti Canelli '14	♟♟ 2*

● Barbera d'Asti Sup. Nizza Sotto la Muda '13	♟♟ 4
● Barbera d'Asti '15	♟♟ 2*
○ Moscato d'Asti Canelli La Commenda '15	♟♟ 2*
○ Alta Langa Brut '12	♟ 4
● Barbera d'Asti Sup. Nizza Sotto la Muda '10	♟♟♟ 4*
● Barbera d'Asti Sup. Nizza Sotto la Muda '07	♟♟♟ 3*
● Barbera d'Asti '14	♟♟ 2*
● Barbera d'Asti '13	♟♟ 2*
● Barbera d'Asti '12	♟♟ 2*
● Barbera d'Asti Sup. Nizza Sotto la Muda '12	♟♟ 4
● Barbera d'Asti Sup. Nizza Sotto la Muda '11	♟♟ 4

★Azelia

Fraz. Garbelletto
via Alba-Barolo, 53
12060 Castiglione Falletto [CN]
Tel. +39 017362859
www.azelia.it

CELLAR SALES
PRE-BOOKED VISITS
ANNUAL PRODUCTION 80,000 bottles
HECTARES UNDER VINE 16.00
SUSTAINABLE WINERY

When Langhe wine was described in terms of outdated dichotomies, the estate founded almost a century ago by Lorenzo Scavino was regularly cited among the so-called modernists. Now that the deck has been reshuffled, it is worth focusing mainly on the winegrowing propensity of prestigious crus like Bricco Fiasco, Margheria, San Rocco, and Bricco Voghera, which also yields a Riserva in the finest vintages. Produced with the aid of roto-fermenters and aged in both barriques and large barrels, the impressive range is crafted by Luigi and his wife Lorella, along with their son Lorenzo, who represents the fifth generation to work in the Castiglione Falletto winery. Azelia's Barolos performed superbly, as usual. The juicy, dynamic Barolo Fiasco 2012 offers exceptionally classic notes of raspberries and tobacco, the Margheria 2012 is similar, but a tad more austere, and the San Rocco 2012 offers good balance and dynamism to compensate for slightly less backbone.

● Barolo Bricco Fiasco '12	♟♟♟ 8
● Barolo Margheria '12	♟♟ 8
● Barolo S. Rocco '12	♟♟ 8
● Barolo '12	♟♟ 6
● Barolo Bricco Fiasco '09	♛♛♛ 8
● Barolo Bricco Fiasco '01	♛♛♛ 7
● Barolo Bricco Fiasco '96	♛♛♛ 7
● Barolo Bricco Fiasco '95	♛♛♛ 7
● Barolo Bricco Fiasco '93	♛♛♛ 6
● Barolo Margheria '06	♛♛♛ 7
● Barolo S. Rocco '11	♛♛♛ 8
● Barolo S. Rocco '08	♛♛♛ 8
● Barolo S. Rocco '99	♛♛♛ 7
● Barolo Voghera Brea Ris. '01	♛♛♛ 8

Banfi Piemonte

via Vittorio Veneto, 76
15019 Strevi [AL]
Tel. +39 0144362600
www.castellobanfi.com

PRE-BOOKED VISITS
ANNUAL PRODUCTION 2,000,000 bottles
HECTARES UNDER VINE 76.00

In addition to dessert wines from moscato and brachetto, the estate also produces the terroir-oriented Dolcetto d'Acqui and Albarossa. However, its core business is sparkling winemaking, as revealed by a range of Metodo Classicos from pinot nero and chardonnay, flanked by the Charmat-method Tener from sauvignon and chardonnay. The latter is also produced in an Extra Dry version, dedicated to lovers of very soft sparklers. At our tastings it was the Alta Langa sparklers that really shone, with a fine, persistent bead, fruity aromas, and notes of crusty bread. They were followed by the Piemonte Albarosso with fine nose-palate symmetry. The many 2015 wines included Gavi Principessa Gavia, characterized by a fruity nose with a mineral backdrop and a fresh, full-bodied palate. L'Ardì is a Dolcetto d'Acqui with good varietal characteristics, while the Moscato d'Asti has a concentrated nose of peaches and sage, and a fresh, vibrant palate.

○ Alta Langa Cuvée Aurora '10	♟♟ 4
⊙ Alta Langa Cuvée Aurora Rosé '13	♟♟ 4
● Dolcetto d'Acqui L'Ardì '15	♟♟ 2*
○ Gavi Principessa Gavia '15	♟♟ 3
○ Moscato d'Asti Sciandor '15	♟♟ 2*
● Piemonte La Lus '13	♟♟ 4
● Brachetto d'Acqui Rosa Regale '15	♟ 3
○ Brut M. Cl.	♟ 5
○ Alta Langa Cuvée Aurora '09	♛♛ 5
⊙ Alta Langa Cuvée Aurora Rosé '12	♛♛ 6
● Dolcetto d'Acqui L'Ardì '14	♛♛ 3
○ Gavi Principessa Gavia '13	♛♛ 3
● Piemonte Albarossa La Lus '12	♛♛ 5
● Piemonte Albarossa La Lus '11	♛♛ 5

Osvaldo Barberis

B.TA VALDIBÀ, 42
12063 DOGLIANI [CN]
TEL. +39 017370054
www.osvaldobarberis.com

CELLAR SALES
PRE-BOOKED VISITS
ANNUAL PRODUCTION 20,000 bottles
HECTARES UNDER VINE 8.00
VITICULTURE METHOD Certified Organic

Langhe has almost become a single-crop area, with vineyards frequently replacing meadows and woodland. However, Osvaldo Barberis's estate continues the mixed farming tradition, continuing to maintain a small herd of around 20 bullocks. Its wines are the most spontaneous expression of the terroir, made from dolcetto, barbera, and nebbiolo grapes for the reds, and from a tiny plot of nascetta for the whites. The entire range is sound, with the steel-aged Dogliani Puncin and Nebbiolo d'Alba Muntajà, from a vineyard in Monforte, regularly standing out. We liked the exceptionally youthful nose of the Valdibà 2015, followed by a very generous, alluring palate with hints of almonds on the finish. Dogliani Avrì 2015 is stiffer and more down to earth, while Pinot Nero Ciabot Maifrin 2015 vaunts a particularly deep hue, a nose of red fruit, and an uncomplicated, tannic palate. Nascetta Anì is simple and supple.

Batasiolo

FRAZ. ANNUNZIATA, 87
12064 LA MORRA [CN]
TEL. +39 017350130
www.batasiolo.com

CELLAR SALES
PRE-BOOKED VISITS
ANNUAL PRODUCTION 2,500,000 bottles
HECTARES UNDER VINE 107.00

An extremely well-put-together range, derived from over 100 hectares of estate-owned vineyards, which focuses on the main traditional Langhe wines, plus a few experiments with international grape varieties, sparklers, and passitos. This is just a partial summary of the what the Dogliani family have achieved since purchasing the legendary Kiola winery. The large estate includes top-notch Barolo vineyards, such as Cerequio and Brunate in La Morra; Boscareto (also home to the resort of the same name) and Briccolina in Serralunga; Bricco di Vergne in Barolo; and Bussia Bofani in Monforte, which yield a basic wine and five vineyard selections. It's hard to choose from the magnificent line-up of 2012 Barolos. Ethereal touches mingle with hints of fruit on the Boscareto's very powerful palate. The Briccolina is even more classic and elegant, particularly in its extractive texture, whereas the Brunate is enlivened by its irrepressible, full-flavoured acid structure.

● Dogliani Valdibà '15	♟♟ 2*
● Langhe Pinot Nero Ciabot Maifrin '15	♟♟ 3
● Dogliani Avrì '15	♟ 3
○ Langhe Nascetta Anì '15	♟ 3
● Barbera d'Alba Castella '12	♟♟ 3*
● Barbera d'Alba Cesca '13	♟♟ 3
● Dogliani Sup. Puncin '13	♟♟ 3*
● Dogliani Sup. Puncin '12	♟♟ 3
● Dogliani Sup. Puncin '11	♟♟ 3*
● Dogliani Valdibà '14	♟♟ 2*
● Dogliani Valdibà '13	♟♟ 2*
● Dogliani Valdibà '12	♟♟ 2*
● Nebbiolo d'Alba Muntajà '13	♟♟ 3
● Nebbiolo d'Alba Muntajà '12	♟♟ 3
● Piemonte Barbera Brichat '13	♟♟ 2*

● Barolo Boscareto '12	♟♟ 7
● Barolo Briccolina '12	♟♟ 8
● Barbaresco '13	♟♟ 6
● Barbera d'Alba Sovrana '13	♟♟ 4
● Barolo Brunate '12	♟♟ 7
● Barolo Bussia Vign. Bofani '12	♟♟ 7
● Barolo Cerequio '12	♟♟ 7
● Barolo Ris. '07	♟♟ 6
○ Gavi del Comune di Gavi Granée '15	♟♟ 3
○ Langhe Chardonnay Vign. Morino '14	♟♟ 5
● Barolo '12	♟ 6
● Barolo Ris. '10	♟ 6
● Barolo Boscareto '05	♟♟♟ 7

Fabrizio Battaglino

LOC. BORGONUOVO
VIA MONTALDO ROERO, 44
12040 VEZZA D'ALBA [CN]
TEL. +39 0173658156
www.battaglino.com

CELLAR SALES
PRE-BOOKED VISITS
ANNUAL PRODUCTION 25,000 bottles
HECTARES UNDER VINE 5.00

Fabrizio Battaglino was founded in 1996 to continue the work of Riccardo, who already bottled his own wines in the 1960s, commended by Luigi Veronelli in 1973. It produces classic Roero wines from arneis, barbera, and nebbiolo. The arneis and nebbiolo vineyards lie on the Colla hill in Vezza d'Alba, on mainly sandy soils, while the barbera is grown on the Montebello hill in Guarene. The resulting wines are remarkably true to type. Fabrizio Battaglino presented a good list of wines, even though it lacked a top note. Roero Sergentin 2013 has a concentrated, delicate nose of mixed berries and liquorice, with vegetal hints, and a confident, full-flavoured palate with nice flesh and structure. The Sergentin Riserva 2012 is more ambitious, but the notes of aromatic herbs and dark berries are joined by rather prominent oak, echoed on the otherwise caressing, velvety palate. Nebbiolo d'Alba 2014 is fresh and pleasant.

Bava

S.DA MONFERRATO, 2
14023 COCCONATO [AT]
TEL. +39 0141907083
www.bava.com

CELLAR SALES
PRE-BOOKED VISITS
ACCOMMODATION
ANNUAL PRODUCTION 490,000 bottles
HECTARES UNDER VINE 55.00

Over a hundred harvests and four generations have passed since the Bava family founded their winery in Cocconato in 1911. Today the estate has vineyards in both Monferrato, planted mainly to barbera and white varietals, and Langhe, where the grapes for Barolo and Dolcetto d'Alba are grown. For almost four decades, the family have also owned the Giulio Cocchi brand, a leading producer of sparkling wines and aperitifs. Once again this year the Cocconato estate presented a series of reliable, quality wines. The fresh, creamy Alta Langa Brut Bianc 'd Bianc Giulio Cocchi 2010 made it into our finals, and the dynamic, racy Pas Dosé 2009 is also very sound. Barolo Scarrone 2011 has a sunny, open nose of ripe red fruit and a full-flavoured, fruity palate. We also liked the versions of Barbera d'Asti, like the elegant Nizza Piano Alto 2012 with good fruit, and the pleasant, approachable Libera 2014.

● Nebbiolo d'Alba '14	♛♛ 3
● Roero Sergentin '13	♛♛ 4
● Roero Sergentin Ris. '12	♛♛ 5
● Barbera d'Alba Munbèl '14	♛ 3
○ Roero Arneis '15	♛ 2
● Nebbiolo d'Alba V. Colla '07	♛♛♛ 3*
● Barbera d'Alba Munbèl '13	♛♛ 3
● Barbera d'Alba Munbèl '12	♛♛ 3*
● Nebbiolo d'Alba '13	♛♛ 3
● Nebbiolo d'Alba '12	♛♛ 3
● Nebbiolo d'Alba Colla '13	♛♛ 4
● Nebbiolo d'Alba Colla '12	♛♛ 4
● Roero Sergentin '12	♛♛ 4

○ Alta Langa Brut Bianc 'd Bianc Giulio Cocchi '10	♛♛ 6
○ Alta Langa Brut Toto Corde Giulio Cocchi '11	♛♛ 5
○ Alta Langa Pas Dosé Giulio Cocchi '09	♛♛ 6
● Barbera d'Asti Libera '14	♛♛ 3
● Barbera d'Asti Sup. Nizza PianoAlto '12	♛♛ 4
● Barolo Scarrone '11	♛♛ 7
○ Langhe Chardonnay Thou Bianc '15	♛ 3
● Malvasia di Castelnuovo Don Bosco Rosetta '15	♛ 3
○ Alta Langa Brut Bianc 'd Bianc Giulio Cocchi '09	♛♛ 6
○ Alta Langa Brut Toto Corde Giulio Cocchi '10	♛♛ 5
○ Alta Langa Pas Dosé Giulio Cocchi '08	♛♛ 6
● Barbera d'Asti Libera '13	♛♛ 3
● Barbera d'Asti Sup. Nizza Piano Alto '11	♛♛ 4

Bel Colle

FRAZ. CASTAGNI, 56
12060 VERDUNO [CN]
TEL. +39 0172470196
www.belcolle.eu

CELLAR SALES
PRE-BOOKED VISITS
ANNUAL PRODUCTION 180,000 bottles
HECTARES UNDER VINE 14.00

In August 2015, the venerable winery founded by brothers Franco and Carlo Pontiglione, with Giuseppe Priola, officially became part of the Bosio Family Estates of Santo Stefano Belbo. The passage from one dynasty of vignerons to another was part of an ongoing operation to upgrade the vineyards in Verduno and La Morra, which have subsequently been joined by estates in Roero, Barbaresco, and the province of Asti. The focus remains on pelaverga and nebbiolo, which achieved popularity under the previous management for their traditional but certainly not old-fashioned style, achieved using modular solutions for maceration and ageing. The well-made Barolo Monvigliero has a nose of fresh herbs and liquorice, and a confident, almost austere, classy palate with remarkable length and definition. The Simposio of the same vintage is less fleshy, while the agreeable Barbaresco 2012 is characterized by liquorice aromas and elegant tannins, and the spicy Pelaverga di Verduno is extremely alluring.

● Barbaresco '12	♟♟ 5
● Barolo Monvigliero '12	♟♟ 6
● Barbera d'Alba Sup. Le Masche '14	♟♟ 3
● Barolo Simposio '12	♟♟ 5
● Nebbiolo d'Alba La Reala '13	♟♟ 3
○ Roero Arneis '15	♟♟ 6
● Verduno Pelaverga '15	♟♟ 3
● Dolcetto d'Alba '15	♟ 2
○ Langhe Chardonnay '15	♟ 3
● Barbaresco Roncaglie Ris. '08	♟♟♟ 5
● Barolo Monvigliero '09	♟♟♟ 5
● Barolo Monvigliero '07	♟♟♟ 5
● Barolo Monvigliero '06	♟♟♟ 5
● Barbaresco Roncaglie '11	♟♟ 5
● Barbaresco Roncaglie '09	♟♟ 5
● Barolo Monvigliero '11	♟♟ 5

Bera

VIA CASTELLERO, 12
12050 NEVIGLIE [CN]
TEL. +39 0173630500
www.bera.it

CELLAR SALES
PRE-BOOKED VISITS
RESTAURANT SERVICE
ANNUAL PRODUCTION 140,000 bottles
HECTARES UNDER VINE 26.00

Valter Bera has been running the longstanding family winery with skill and passion since the early 1980s, accompanying it to the dizziest heights of moscato production, with both the semi-sparkling and Asti Spumante versions. The vineyards have an average age of around 40 years old and are mostly situated close to the winery on clayey-tufa hillsides, at altitudes between 320 and 380 metres. Bera also produces a range of dry still wines, from Barbaresco to several versions of Barbera. Moscato d'Asti Su Reimond 2015 has a concentrated, elegant nose of melon, medicinal herbs, citrus, and peaches, and a very fresh, balanced palate with a caressing long finish. The fresh, floral Asti 2015 is well made, as are the Barbaresco 2012, with fine grip and staying power; the deeper, more complex Barbaresco Rabajà Riserva, long and supple with notes of liquorice and truffles; and the two versions of Barbera d'Alba: the approachable, easy-drinking 2015 and the dense, spicy Superiore La Lena 2013.

○ Moscato d'Asti Su Reimond '15	♟♟ 3*
○ Asti '15	♟♟ 3
● Barbaresco '12	♟♟ 5
● Barbaresco Rabajà Ris. '11	♟♟ 5
● Barbera d'Alba '15	♟♟ 2*
● Barbera d'Alba Sup. La Lena '13	♟♟ 3
○ Langhe Arneis '15	♟♟ 2*
● Barbera d'Asti Sup. '14	♟ 2
● Piemonte Brachetto '15	♟ 2
● Barbaresco '11	♟♟ 5
● Barbera d'Alba Sup. La Lena '12	♟♟ 3
● Barbera d'Asti Sup. '12	♟♟ 2*
○ Moscato d'Asti '14	♟♟ 2*
○ Moscato d'Asti Su Reimond '14	♟♟ 3*

Cinzia Bergaglio

VIA GAVI, 29
15060 TASSAROLO [AL]
TEL. +39 0143342203
www.vinicinziabergaglio.it

CELLAR SALES
PRE-BOOKED VISITS
ANNUAL PRODUCTION 30,000 bottles
HECTARES UNDER VINE 9.00

Cinzia Bergaglio's tiny production, completely concentrated on the cortese from the estate's ten hectares of vineyards, is shaped by significant differences in soil, climate and style. La Fornace hails from the Tassarolo vineyards, characterized by iron-rich tufaceous soils, and is fermented using the classic off-the-skins method. Grifone delle Roveri, on the other hand, is made from grapes from the Gavi plots, which lie on clay and limestone marl soils, and undergoes brief maceration before fermentation and ageing in stainless steel. The differences are nonetheless brilliantly expressed in the consistent, true-to-type wines, focusing on freshness and drinkability. These are precious qualities for the sweltering 2015 vintage, as testified by the terrific Gavi La Fornace, with white-fleshed fruit and pennyroyal on a mineral backdrop, which is softer than usual, but with good tangy length. Grifone delle Roveri is similar but with greater texture and glycerine richness.

Nicola Bergaglio

FRAZ. ROVERETO
LOC. PEDAGGERI, 59
15066 GAVI [AL]
TEL. +39 0143682195
nicolabergaglio@alice.it

CELLAR SALES
PRE-BOOKED VISITS
ANNUAL PRODUCTION 140,000 bottles
HECTARES UNDER VINE 17.00
SUSTAINABLE WINERY

Gianluigi Bergaglio and his son Diego have long been considered benchmark figures by lovers of cellarable Cortese di Gavi, capable with ageing of developing mineral and tertiary notes worthy of the most renowned European whites. The merit for this is due chiefly to Minaia, a blend of the finest grapes grown on the Rovereto hill, which is patiently aged in steel and usually only reaches its best many years after release. However, the entire range is a safe bet due to its direct, linear style, without any tropical flourishes. We're celebrating the umpteenth spectacular pair of Gavis by Nicola Bergaglio. The 2015 has rich, fruity top notes of white peaches and damsons, with lively floral and mineral sensations on a full, edgy palate, while the Minaia of the same vintage has greater body and length, with hints of bracken and flint.

○ Gavi del Comune di Gavi Grifone delle Roveri '15	♟♟ 2*
○ Gavi La Fornace '15	♟♟ 2*
○ Gavi del Comune di Gavi Grifone delle Roveri '14	♟♟ 2*
○ Gavi del Comune di Gavi Grifone delle Roveri '13	♟♟ 2*
○ Gavi del Comune di Gavi Grifone delle Roveri '12	♟♟ 2*
○ Gavi del Comune di Gavi Grifone delle Roveri '11	♟♟ 2*
○ Gavi La Fornace '14	♟♟ 2*
○ Gavi La Fornace '13	♟♟ 2*
○ Gavi La Fornace '12	♟♟ 2*
○ Gavi La Fornace '10	♟♟ 2*

○ Gavi del Comune di Gavi Minaia '15	♟♟♟ 4*
○ Gavi del Comune di Gavi '15	♟♟ 2*
○ Gavi del Comune di Gavi Minaia '14	♟♟♟ 4*
○ Gavi del Comune di Gavi Minaia '11	♟♟♟ 4*
○ Gavi del Comune di Gavi Minaia '10	♟♟♟ 4
○ Gavi del Comune di Gavi Minaia '09	♟♟♟ 4
○ Gavi del Comune di Gavi '13	♟♟ 2*
○ Gavi del Comune di Gavi '07	♟♟ 2*
○ Gavi del Comune di Gavi Et. Bianca '14	♟♟ 3*
○ Gavi del Comune di Gavi Minaia '13	♟♟ 4
○ Gavi del Comune di Gavi Minaia '12	♟♟ 3*
○ Gavi del Comune di Gavi Minaia '08	♟♟ 3*
○ Gavi del Comune di Gavi Minaia '07	♟♟ 2*
○ Gavi del Comune di Gavi Minaia '06	♟♟ 2*
○ Gavi del Comune di Gavi Minaia '05	♟♟ 2*
○ Gavi del Comune di Gavi Minaia '04	♟♟ 2*

Bersano

P.ZZA DANTE, 21
14049 NIZZA MONFERRATO [AT]
TEL. +39 0141720211
www.bersano.it

CELLAR SALES
PRE-BOOKED VISITS
ANNUAL PRODUCTION 1,500,000 bottles
HECTARES UNDER VINE 230.00

Present in Nizza Monferrato since the beginning of the last century, and owned by the Massimelli and Soave families for the past 30 years, Bersano is undoubtedly one of the leading lights in the Asti area. The imposing winery comprises several estates in both Monferrato and Langhe, and produces well-made, terroir-true wines able to reconcile quantity and quality. Barbera d'Asti Superiore Nizza Generala 2013 remains the estate's top wine, with a very classic nose of cherries and rain-soaked earth, followed by nicely balanced spice. The concentrated, juicy palate is slightly tannic, with good acid grip and an extremely long, full-flavoured finish. Arturosé Brut Rosé is elegant and remarkably complex, while Barbera d'Asti Superiore Cremosina 2014 is fresh and balanced for its vintage, and Barolo Badarina 2010 has fine body and well-amalgamated tannins.

● Barbera d'Asti Sup. Nizza Generala '13	▼▼ 5
☉ Arturosè Brut Rosé M. Cl.	▼▼ 4
● Barbaresco Mantico '13	▼▼ 6
● Barbera d'Asti Sup. Cremosina '14	▼▼ 3
● Barolo Badarina '10	▼▼ 7
○ Arturo Bersano Brut M. Cl. '13	▼ 4
○ Moscato d'Asti Monteolivo '15	▼ 3
● Ruché di Castagnole Monferrato S. Pietro '15	▼ 3
● Barbera d'Asti Sup. Generala '97	♉♉♉ 5
○ Arturo Bersano Brut M. Cl. '11	♉♉ 4
● Barbera d'Asti Sup. Cremosina '12	♉♉ 3*
● Barbera d'Asti Sup. Nizza Generala '12	♉♉ 5
● Barolo Ris. '08	♉♉ 7

Guido Berta

LOC. SALINE, 53
14050 SAN MARZANO OLIVETO [AT]
TEL. +39 0141856193
www.guidoberta.com

CELLAR SALES
PRE-BOOKED VISITS
ANNUAL PRODUCTION 3,000 bottles
HECTARES UNDER VINE 12.00

It is 20 years since Guido Berta decided to found his winery in one of the finest barbera-growing areas. Most of the vineyards are in San Marzano Oliveto, on clayey limestone soils, but the estate also has plots in Calamandrana and Agliano Terme. Barbera accounts for the lion's share, with six hectares of vines planted between 1960 and 1988, followed by moscato and chardonnay. The wines are well typed and terroir true, with good aromatic focus. Barbera d'Asti Superiore Nizza Canto di Luna 2013 is among the best of the designation again, with a complex nose of cherries, tobacco, and spice, and a dense, caressing palate with good acidity. The fresh, approachable Barbera d'Asti Le Rondini 2015 is also well made, with plenty of fruit and a long, vibrant finish, as are Barbera d'Asti Superiore 2014, remarkably full for its vintage, and the spicy Monferrato Rosso 2011, from nebbiolo with a small amount of barbera, which has a lovely tannic weave.

● Barbera d'Asti Sup. Nizza Canto di Luna '13	▼▼ 5
● Barbera d'Asti Le Rondini '15	▼▼ 3
● Barbera d'Asti Sup. '14	▼▼ 3
● Monferrato Rosso '11	▼▼ 5
○ Moscato d'Asti '15	▼ 3
○ Piemonte Chardonnay '15	▼ 3
● Barbera d'Asti Sup. '13	♉♉ 3
● Barbera d'Asti Sup. '12	♉♉ 4
● Barbera d'Asti Sup. Nizza Canto di Luna '12	♉♉ 5
● Barbera d'Asti Sup. Nizza Canto di Luna '11	♉♉ 5
○ Moscato d'Asti '14	♉♉ 3
○ Moscato d'Asti '13	♉♉ 3
○ Moscato d'Asti '12	♉♉ 3

Enzo Boglietti

VIA FONTANE, 18A
12064 LA MORRA [CN]
TEL. +39 017350330
www.enzoboglietti.com

CELLAR SALES
PRE-BOOKED VISITS
ACCOMMODATION
ANNUAL PRODUCTION 100,000 bottles
HECTARES UNDER VINE 22.50
VITICULTURE METHOD Certified Organic
SUSTAINABLE WINERY

The charming, youthful Enzo Boglietti has
recently celebrated 25 vintages, having
started bottling his wines in 1991. Five years
later he was joined by his brother Gianni,
who has since focused particularly on work
in the vineyards. Their range consists
exclusively of red wines, headed by Barolo
selections largely from excellent crus in La
Morra, including Brunate and Case Nere, but
also an Arione from Serralunga d'Alba. The
style is always modern, with prominent oak
and ripe fruit, although a variety of
different-sized barrels is used, along with
concrete tanks. The charming, modern
Barbera d'Alba Roscaleto 2013 is fresher
than usual, showing caressing, spicy and
lively with good balance. Barolo Boiolo 2012
put up an excellent performance, showing a
beautifully well-orchestrated palate with
tannins that provide more backbone than
astringency. The Fossati 2012 has top
notes of dried roses and liquorice and a
deliciously fresh, balanced palate, while the
Brunate 2012 offers rich ripe red fruit and
oak, and the Case Nere 2012 is spicy with
medium body.

● Barbera d'Alba Roscaleto '13	♥♥ 5
● Barolo Boiolo '12	♥♥ 6
● Barolo Brunate '12	♥♥ 8
● Barolo Fossati '12	♥♥ 8
● Barbera d'Alba '15	♥♥ 3
● Barolo Arione '12	♥♥ 8
● Barolo Case Nere '12	♥♥ 8
● Barolo Ris. '08	♥♥ 8
○ Dolcetto d'Alba '15	♥♥ 2*
● Barolo Arione '06	♥♥♥ 8
● Barolo Arione '05	♥♥♥ 8
● Barolo Brunate '01	♥♥♥ 8
● Barolo Brunate '97	♥♥♥ 8
● Barolo Case Nere '04	♥♥♥ 8
● Barolo Case Nere '99	♥♥♥ 8
● Barolo V. Arione '07	♥♥♥ 8

Bondi - Cascina Banaia

S.DA CAPPELLETTE, 73
15076 OVADA [AL]
TEL. +39 0131299186
www.bondivini.it

CELLAR SALES
PRE-BOOKED VISITS
ANNUAL PRODUCTION 20,000 bottles
HECTARES UNDER VINE 5.00

The Bondi family's business focuses on
food and wine, and is split between the
winery in Ovada and the Locanda dell'Olmo
restaurant in Bosco Marengo. Both
enterprises focus on local traditions and
products, but also display the influences of
this borderland area, between Piedmont
and Liguria. The wines are all red, mainly
Barbera and Dolcetto di Ovada, offered
both as monovarietals and blended in the
Monferrato Rosso Le Guie. The range is
topped by Ovada D'Uien, which offers a
concentrated nose of red berries and
quinine accompanied by a palate with good
pulp and acidity and a somewhat husky
finish. Banaiotta has a fine nose of red fruit,
spice, and cocoa powder and a
well-orchestrated palate with a rather short
finish. Ansensò 2012 is still slightly hidden
by oak, although notes of ripe fruit still
shine through on the long, pervasive finish.

● Banaiotta	♥♥ 4
● Ovada D'Uien '13	♥♥ 3
● M.to Rosso Ansensò '12	♥ 4
● Barbera del M.to Banaiotta '10	♥♥ 2*
● Barbera del M.to Ruvrin '10	♥♥ 4
● Dolcetto di Ovada Nani '11	♥♥ 2*
● M.to Rosso Ansensò '11	♥♥ 4
● Ovada D'Uien '11	♥♥ 4

Gilberto Boniperti

via Vittorio Emanuele, 43/45
28010 Barengo [NO]
Tel. +39 0321997123
www.bonipertivignaioli.com

CELLAR SALES
ANNUAL PRODUCTION 12,000 bottles
HECTARES UNDER VINE 3.50

The estate owned by oenology graduate and committed interpreter of traditional northern Piedmontese grape varieties Gilberto Boniperti is about to celebrate ten years of bottling its own wines. The star of the show is a Fara, a tiny but very interesting designation, from mainly nebbiolo with a small amount of spicy vespolina. The Bartön is aged in different-sized barrels, while the fresher and readier drinking Colline Novaresi and Vespolina are aged exclusively in stainless steel. Fara Bartön 2013 focuses on delicacy and drinkability. It is not particularly complex but clean, lively, and racy, with hints of gentian on the nose. The pleasant, well-orchestrated Nebbiolo Carlin 2014 is refreshingly original with a spicy vegetal nose and an elegant, balanced palate.

● Fara Bartön '13	ΨΨ 4
● Colline Novaresi Nebbiolo Carlin '14	ΨΨ 4
⊙ Colline Novaresi Nebbiolo Rosadisera '15	Ψ 3
● Colline Novaresi Vespolina Favolalunga '14	Ψ 2
● Colline Novaresi Barbera Barblin '10	ΥΥ 4
● Colline Novaresi Nebbiolo Bartön '10	ΥΥ 4
● Colline Novaresi Nebbiolo Bartön '08	ΥΥ 4
● Colline Novaresi Nebbiolo Carlin '13	ΥΥ 4
● Colline Novaresi Nebbiolo Carlin '12	ΥΥ 4
● Colline Novaresi Nebbiolo Carlin '11	ΥΥ 4
● Colline Novaresi Nebbiolo Carlin '10	ΥΥ 4
● Colline Novaresi Vespolina Favolalunga '12	ΥΥ 3
● Fara Bartön '12	ΥΥ 4

Borgo Maragliano

via San Sebastiano, 2
14051 Loazzolo [AT]
Tel. +39 014487132
www.borgomaragliano.com

CELLAR SALES
PRE-BOOKED VISITS
ANNUAL PRODUCTION 315,000 bottles
HECTARES UNDER VINE 29.00
SUSTAINABLE WINERY

The Galliano family have been tending their vines in Loazzolo for over 50 years. Today the winery is run by Carlo and Silvia. The estate's vineyards are planted chiefly to moscato, which accounts for over 50% of the area under vine, and are situated between 360 and 750 metres above sea level, in a wooded area influenced by the Marin, a sea breeze that promotes the ripening and aromatic richness of the grapes. Its Metodo Classico sparkling wine, from pinot nero and chardonnay is also worthy of note. The estate's tradition of sparkling wine production continues to be its forte. Francesco Galliano Blanc de Blancs Brut 2013 has a remarkably complex nose of toast, damsons, and apples, and an elegant, firmly structured palate with great length, while Giuseppe Galliano Brut 2011 has riper notes and a powerful, creamy palate that is also fresh and nicely tangy. Loazzolo Vendemmia Tardiva 2012 displays remarkable balance and finesse.

○ Francesco Galliano Blanc de Blancs Brut M. Cl. '13	ΨΨ 4
○ Giuseppe Galliano Brut M. Cl. '11	ΨΨ 4
○ Dogma Blanc de Noirs M. Cl. '12	ΨΨ 5
○ El Calié '15	ΨΨ 2*
⊙ Giovanni Galliano Brut Rosè M. Cl. '12	ΨΨ 4
○ Loazzolo V. T. '12	ΨΨ 5
○ M.to Bianco PerFede '15	Ψ 3
○ Piemonte Chardonnay Crevoglio '15	Ψ 2
○ Giuseppe Galliano Ris. Brut M. Cl. '01	ΥΥΥ 4*
○ Francesco Galliano Blanc de Blancs Brut M. Cl. '12	ΥΥ 4
⊙ Giovanni Galliano Brut Rosé M. Cl. '11	ΥΥ 4
○ Giuseppe Galliano Brut M. Cl. Ris. '09	ΥΥ 5
○ Loazzolo V. T. '10	ΥΥ 5

Giacomo Borgogno & Figli

via Gioberti, 16
12060 Barolo [CN]
Tel. +39 017356108
www.borgogno.com

CELLAR SALES
PRE-BOOKED VISITS
ANNUAL PRODUCTION 110,000 bottles
HECTARES UNDER VINE 16.00
SUSTAINABLE WINERY

There is no point in even trying to condense Borgogno's time-honoured history into just a few lines. Taken over by the Farinetti family in 2008, it has become the symbol of Mr Eataly's adventures in the world of wine, with an extensive range featuring experimental provocations like No Name, Le Teorie, I Colori del Barolo, and Resistenza alongside the classics. This dual nature is also reflected in the style, which is traditional but far removed from the usual clichés. The grapes come from the estate's approximately 15 hectares of vineyards, over half of which planted to nebbiolo, concentrated in crus such as Cannubi, Cannubi San Lorenzo, Fossati, Liste and San Pietro delle Viole. Borgogno's latest arrival is the Cesare, made from a blend of nebbiolo-based wines of different vintages, which are shown on the label. It has thus renounced the use of the Barolo designation, creating a whirlwind of aromas and flavours that associate the freshness of recent vintages with the ethereal complexity of old ones. The unforgettable Liste 2011 is characterized by complex notes and great structure.

● Barolo Liste '11	♟♟♟ 8
● Barolo Cannubi '11	♟♟ 8
● Barolo Ris. '09	♟♟ 8
● Cesare 04 96 98 82	♟♟ 7
● Barolo '12	♟♟ 7
● Barolo Fossati '11	♟♟ 8
● Langhe Nebbiolo No Name '12	♟♟ 5
○ Langhe Riesling Era Ora '14	♟ 5
● Barolo Cl. '98	♟♟♟ 7
● Barolo Liste '10	♟♟♟ 8
● Barolo Liste '08	♟♟♟ 8
● Barolo Liste '07	♟♟♟ 7
● Barolo Liste '05	♟♟♟ 7
● Barolo V. Liste '06	♟♟♟ 7
● Barolo '11	♟♟ 7
● Barolo Cannubi '10	♟♟ 8

Francesco Boschis

fraz. San Martino di Pianezzo, 57
12063 Dogliani [CN]
Tel. +39 017370574
www.boschisfrancesco.it

CELLAR SALES
PRE-BOOKED VISITS
ANNUAL PRODUCTION 40,000 bottles
HECTARES UNDER VINE 11.00

The estate shuns herbicides and chemical fertilizers in the vineyard and favours a modern classic approach in the cellar, with the use of steel and controlled temperatures to ensure clean, wholesome wines. Dolcetto is king here, yielding four wines derived from different crus, alongside small amounts of Barbera (d'Alba and Langhe), Freisa, and Grignolino. There is also a tiny production of Sauvignon Blanc, sadly fewer than 2,000 bottles, which regularly stands out for its close-focused exotic aromatic sensations. Dogliani Vigne in Pianezzo 2015 has particularly rich structure, with still slightly assertive tannins and an alluring nose of bitter almonds, juniper, and black cherries. Vigna dei Prey 2014 is particularly good, bearing in mind its difficult vintage, with a more vegetal nose but a very satisfying palate, while Sauvignon Vigna dei Garisin 2015 has delicate notes of grapefruit and herbs and an agreeably bitterish finish.

● Dogliani V. in Pianezzo '15	♟♟ 2*
● Barbera d'Alba Sup. V. Le Masserie '13	♟♟ 3
● Dogliani Sorì San Martino '14	♟♟ 3
● Dogliani V. dei Prey '14	♟♟ 2*
○ Langhe Sauvignon V. dei Garisin '15	♟♟ 3
● Dogliani Sup. V. del Ciliegio '12	♟ 3
● Dogliani Sorì S. Martino '09	♟♟ 2*
● Dogliani Sorì S. Martino '08	♟♟ 2*
● Dogliani Sup. Sorì San Martino '12	♟♟ 3*
● Dogliani Sup. V. dei Prey '11	♟♟ 3*
● Dogliani V. dei Prey '10	♟♟ 2*
● Dogliani V. dei Prey '09	♟♟ 2*
● Dogliani V. dei Prey '08	♟♟ 2*
● Langhe Rosso nei Sorì '09	♟♟ 4
○ Langhe Sauvignon V. dei Garisin '12	♟♟ 3*

Luigi Boveri

LOC. MONTALE CELLI
VIA XX SETTEMBRE, 6
15050 COSTA VESCOVATO [AL]
TEL. +39 0131838165
www.boveriluigi.com

CELLAR SALES
PRE-BOOKED VISITS
ANNUAL PRODUCTION 80,000 bottles
HECTARES UNDER VINE 15.00

A pragmatic, enthusiastic vigneron, Luigi has made the most of Costa Vescovato's vineyards with his versions of Timorasso: the Filari, which ages an extra year in bottle to fully express its power and elegance, and the Derthona, which is generally readier but no less elegant. Another gem is the almost 100-year-old vineyard that yields the Vignalunga and Poggio delle Amarene, both potent and concentrated Barberas, the former aged in oak. Filari di Timorasso, a regular in our finals, topped the list presented this year. The 2013 has plenty of character and personality, while the Derthona 2014 is slightly leaner and reflects the unfortunate weather of its vintage. Vignalunga is concentrated and complex, slightly held back on the nose and palate by the effects of ageing in oak. The current Barbera Boccanera and Cortese Terre del Prete are both very interesting.

Gianfranco Bovio

FRAZ. ANNUNZIATA
B.TA CIOTTO, 63
12064 LA MORRA [CN]
TEL. +39 017350667
www.boviogianfranco.com

CELLAR SALES
PRE-BOOKED VISITS
ANNUAL PRODUCTION 75,000 bottles
HECTARES UNDER VINE 10.00

Gianfranco Bovio passed away at the beginning of 2016 after a life successfully spent entertaining the throngs of tourists who dined at his restaurants and tasted his estate's wines. It is now up to his daughter Alessandra and her husband Marco to run the important and complex business, aided in the winery by a talented oenologist and agronomist. The vineyards are in La Morra and include the prestigious Arborina and Gattera crus. On the nose Barolo Gattera has delicate fruit that immediately gives way to complex sensations of autumn leaves and medicinal herbs, with fine hints of rhubarb and dried roses, while the palate is smooth with medium structure. The Arborina 2012 is tannic and focuses slightly more on dark notes of quinine and juniper, and the 2012 Barolo, from a blend of different crus, is among the best of its vintage.

○ Colli Tortonesi Timorasso Derthona Filari di Timorasso '13	⧉⧉ 5
● Colli Tortonesi Barbera Boccanera '15	⧉⧉ 2*
● Colli Tortonesi Barbera Vignalunga '13	⧉⧉ 5
○ Colli Tortonesi Cortese Terre del Prete '15	⧉⧉ 2*
○ Colli Tortonesi Timorasso Derthona '14	⧉⧉ 4
● Colli Tortonesi Croatina Sensazioni '13	⧉ 4
○ Colli Tortonesi Timorasso Filari di Timorasso '12	⧉⧉⧉ 5
○ Colli Tortonesi Timorasso Filari di Timorasso '07	⧉⧉⧉ 3
● Colli Tortonesi Barbera Poggio delle Amarene '12	⧉⧉ 4
● Colli Tortonesi Barbera Vignalunga '12	⧉⧉ 5
○ Colli Tortonesi Timorasso Derthona '13	⧉⧉ 4

● Barolo '12	⧉⧉ 6
● Barolo Gattera '12	⧉⧉ 6
● Barbera d'Alba Sup. Regiaveja '13	⧉⧉ 4
● Barolo Arborina '12	⧉⧉ 6
● Dolcetto d'Alba Dabbene '15	⧉⧉ 2*
● Barbera d'Alba Il Ciotto '15	⧉ 2
○ Langhe Bianco Alessandro '15	⧉ 3
● Langhe Nebbiolo '14	⧉ 3
● Barolo Bricco Parussi Ris. '01	⧉⧉⧉ 6
● Barolo Gattera '11	⧉⧉⧉ 6
● Barolo Rocchettevino '06	⧉⧉⧉ 5*
● Barolo '11	⧉⧉ 6
● Barolo Arborina '11	⧉⧉ 6
● Barolo Arborina '10	⧉⧉ 6
● Barolo Rocchettevino '10	⧉⧉ 5
● Langhe Nebbiolo '13	⧉⧉ 3

★Braida

LOC. CIAPPELLETTE
S.DA PROVINCIALE 27, 9
14030 ROCCHETTA TANARO [AT]
TEL. +39 0141644113
www.braida.it

CELLAR SALES
PRE-BOOKED VISITS
ACCOMMODATION
ANNUAL PRODUCTION 650,000 bottles
HECTARES UNDER VINE 65.00
SUSTAINABLE WINERY

Braida is one of the renowned Piedmont estates and an undisputed model for the production of high-quality Barbera. Indeed, Raffaella and Giuseppe Bologna have continued the success of the family winery, confirming its role as a benchmark for the entire area that their father Giacomo established in the 1980s. The estate's vineyards are in Rocchetta Tanaro, which is home to its barbera crus, Costiglione d'Asti, Castelnuovo Calcea, Mango, and Trezzo Tinella. Barbera d'Asti Montebruna is back in the limelight with the 2014 vintage. It vaunts a concentrated, harmonious nose, with a nice balance of ripe cherries and fine spicy oak, and a fresh, delicate palate showing impressive acidity. Barbera d'Asti Bricco dell'Uccellone 2014 is as fine as ever, with a nose of fresh herbs, liquorice, charred oak, and black cherries, and a juicy palate with a long, gutsy finish. The rest of the list is well made.

Brandini

FRAZ. BRANDINI, 16
12064 LA MORRA [CN]
TEL. +39 017350266
www.agricolabrandini.it

CELLAR SALES
PRE-BOOKED VISITS
ACCOMMODATION AND RESTAURANT SERVICE
ANNUAL PRODUCTION 80,000 bottles
HECTARES UNDER VINE 15.00
VITICULTURE METHOD Certified Organic
SUSTAINABLE WINERY

In the scenic winery perched above La Morra you can already see the barrels in which the new Nebbiolo selections are ageing, due for release in the coming years. In the meantime, each year Barolo Resa 56 confirms itself a genuine thoroughbred, vinified in an intentionally classic style, always with velvety tannins, from painstakingly selected organic grapes. The Langhe Nebbiolo is also among the finest of its kind. The poolside views from the estate's elegant guest farm, complete with restaurant, are simply stunning. Barolo Resa 56 2012 has fine raspberry top notes on the nose, followed by cinnamon and cloves, with tobacco and liquorice adding complexity, and a powerful, full-flavoured palate with remarkable overall elegance. We rewarded its balance and finesse with a Tre Bicchieri. Nebbiolo Filari Corti 2014 is fruity and highly drinkable, while Alta Langa Rosé 2011 is beautifully fresh.

● Barbera d'Asti Bricco dell'Uccellone '14	♥♥ 7
● Barbera d'Asti Montebruna '14	♥♥ 3*
● Barbera d'Asti Bricco della Bigotta '14	♥♥ 7
● Grignolino d'Asti Limonte '15	♥♥ 3
● M.to Rosso Il Bacialè '14	♥♥ 3
○ Moscato d'Asti V. Senza Nome '15	♥♥ 3
○ Langhe Bianco Il Fiore '15	♥ 3
○ Langhe Riesling Re di Fiori '15	♥ 3
● Barbera d'Asti Bricco dell'Uccellone '12	♥♥♥ 7
● Barbera d'Asti Bricco dell'Uccellone '09	♥♥♥ 6
● Barbera d'Asti Bricco della Bigotta '07	♥♥♥ 6
● Barbera d'Asti Bricco della Bigotta '06	♥♥♥ 6
● Barbera d'Asti Montebruna '11	♥♥♥ 3*

● Barolo Resa 56 '12	♥♥♥ 8
● Barolo '12	♥♥ 7
☉ Alta Langa Brut Rosé '11	♥♥ 6
● Dolcetto d'Alba Filari Lunghi '15	♥♥ 3
● Langhe Nebbiolo Filari Corti '14	♥♥ 5
● Barbera d'Alba Sup. Rocche del Santo '14	♥ 5
○ Langhe Bianco Le Coccinelle '15	♥ 5
● Barolo Resa 56 '11	♥♥♥ 7
● Barolo Resa 56 '10	♥♥♥ 7
● Barbera d'Alba Sup. Rocche del Santo '13	♥♥ 3
● Barolo '11	♥♥ 5
● Barolo '10	♥♥ 5
● Dolcetto d'Alba Filari Lunghi '14	♥♥ 3
○ Langhe Bianco Le Coccinelle '14	♥♥ 4
● Langhe Nebbiolo Filari Corti '13	♥♥ 3

Brangero

VIA PROVINCIALE, 26
12055 DIANO D'ALBA [CN]
TEL. +39 017369423
www.brangero.com

PRE-BOOKED VISITS
ANNUAL PRODUCTION 50,000 bottles
HECTARES UNDER VINE 9.00

Marco Brangero has been running the
handsome winery on top of the hill
overlooking Diano d'Alba since 1999. The
vineyards are planted with the typical local
grape varieties: dolcetto, barbera, nebbiolo,
and arneis, with a few rows of international
cultivars. They surround the cellar, with the
exception of the estate's gem, the
Monvigliero vineyard in Verduno. The house
style favours moderate extraction, resulting
in wines that appeared more elegant and
defined in this year's tastings. Marco
Brangero also runs La Ginestraia, a fine
Ligurian estate in the province of Imperia.
The sophisticated, complex Barolo
Monvigliero 2012 has a nose of freshly
ground black pepper and roses on a
background of tobacco and liquorice, and a
palate with delicate, multilayered
development, silky tannins and a long, juicy
finish. Langhe Chardonnay Centofile 2015
is well made.

● Barolo Monvigliero '12	♟♟6
● Barbera d'Alba La Soprana '13	♟♟3
● Dolcetto di Diano d'Alba Sörì Rabino Soprano '15	♟♟2*
● Nebbiolo d'Alba Quattro Cloni '14	♟♟4
○ Langhe Chardonnay Centofile '15	♟3
● Barbera d'Alba La Soprana '12	♥♥3
● Barbera d'Alba La Soprana '11	♥♥3
● Barolo Monvigliero '11	♥♥6
● Barolo Monvigliero '10	♥♥6
○ Langhe Arneis Centofile '13	♥♥3
○ Langhe Chardonnay Centofile '13	♥♥3
● Langhe Rosso Tremarzo '11	♥♥4
● Nebbiolo d'Alba Bricco Bertone '12	♥♥4

Brema

VIA POZZOMAGNA, 9
14045 INCISA SCAPACCINO [AT]
TEL. +39 014174019
www.vinibrema.com

CELLAR SALES
PRE-BOOKED VISITS
ANNUAL PRODUCTION 150,000 bottles
HECTARES UNDER VINE 25.00
SUSTAINABLE WINERY

The Brema family have been making wine
in Incisa Scapaccino for five generations.
Their vineyards are scattered across
various municipalities in the province of
Asti, from Nizza Monferrato to Fontanile
d'Asti, San Marzano Oliveto, Incisa
Scapaccino, and Sessame d'Asti. The
emphasis is of course on barbera, from
which the top wines are made,
commencing with the Nizza Dedicato a
Luigi Veronelli, flanked by dolcetto,
grignolino, brachetto, moscato, and
cabernet sauvignon, forming a remarkably
well-typed range. Barbera d'Asti Superiore
Nizza A Luigi Veronelli 2013 has a
concentrated nose of red berries, tobacco
and spice, accompanied by a palate with
big structure and a long, juicy finish. We
also very much liked Monferrato Rosso
Umberto 2013, a Cabernet Sauvignon
with fruity and vegetal notes and plenty of
pulp and character; Barbera d'Asti
Superiore Volpettona 2013, offering
aromatic herbs and good fruit; and Barbera
d'Asti Ai Cruss 2014, which is leaner than
other vintages but very pleasant.

● Barbera d'Asti Sup. Nizza A Luigi Veronelli '13	♟♟6
● Barbera d'Asti Ai Cruss '14	♟♟2*
● Barbera d'Asti Sup. Volpettona '13	♟♟5
● M.to Rosso Umberto '13	♟♟4
● Barbera d'Asti Sup. Nizza A Luigi Veronelli '12	♥♥♥6
● Barbera d'Asti Sup. Nizza A Luigi Veronelli '06	♥♥♥6
● Barbera d'Asti Ai Cruss '13	♥♥2*
● Barbera d'Asti Ai Cruss '12	♥♥2*
● Barbera d'Asti Sup. Nizza A Luigi Veronelli '11	♥♥6
● Barbera d'Asti Sup. Volpettona '11	♥♥5
● Barbera del M.to Frizzante Castagnei '14	♥♥2*
● Barbera del M.to Frizzante Castagnei '13	♥♥2*
○ Moscato d'Asti Mariasole '12	♥♥2*

Giacomo Brezza & Figli

VIA LOMONDO, 4
12060 BAROLO [CN]
TEL. +39 0173560921
www.brezza.it

CELLAR SALES
PRE-BOOKED VISITS
ACCOMMODATION AND RESTAURANT SERVICE
ANNUAL PRODUCTION 100,000 bottles
HECTARES UNDER VINE 17.50
VITICULTURE METHOD Certified Organic
SUSTAINABLE WINERY

Time always seems to stand still when we visit the Brezza family and sit in their cellar-restaurant to listen to Oreste's many and varied tales and anecdotes. A few years ago this veritable repository of Langhe history handed over the running of the business to his son Enzo, who has further boosted its renown and that of its exemplary classic Nebbiolos. They hail from grand crus in the municipality of Barolo such as Cannubi, Castellero, and Sarmassa, whose grapes from the highest part are used to make Bricco in the finest vintages. The wines undergo long maceration and ageing for several years in medium and large barrels. Although we didn't award the winery our top accolade, Enzo Brezza's Barolos are nonetheless extremely well crafted The powerful, juicy Cannubi 2012 shows an austere, classic style and is destined to improve further in bottle, while the slightly more tannic Sarmassa 2012 has great personality, with prominent notes of strawberries, aniseed, and tobacco.

Gallino Domenico Bric Castelvej

MADONNA LORETO, 70
12043 CANALE [CN]
TEL. +39 017398108
www.briccastelvej.com

CELLAR SALES
PRE-BOOKED VISITS
ANNUAL PRODUCTION 100,000 bottles
HECTARES UNDER VINE 12.40

Bric Castelvej was founded by Domenico Gallino in 1956 and is now run by his son-in-law Mario Repellino with his son Cristiano. Its vineyards in Canale lie on mainly sandy soils, with some silt and clay, and are planted chiefly to the classic Roero grape varieties, from nebbiolo and arneis to barbera and favorita. Bric Castelvej was first featured in our Guide just last year, and has now earned a full profile with a particularly convincing series of wines. Roero Panera Alta Riserva 2013 has a nose of tobacco and Mediterranean scrubland against a charming fruity backdrop, and a balanced, full-bodied palate with nice length and fine-grained tannins. Roero Arneis Vigna Bricco Novara 2015 is also among the best of the designation, offering a floral nose with spicy hints and a fresh, tangy palate with a long, dynamic finish. The "basic" versions are also well made: the Roero 2013 with dark fruit and good thrust, and the pleasant, fruit-forward Roero Arneis 2015.

● Barolo Cannubi '12	♟♟ 6
● Barolo Sarmassa '12	♟♟ 7
● Barolo Castellero '12	♟♟ 6
● Barolo Bricco Sarmassa '08	♟♟♟ 7
● Barolo Bricco Sarmassa '07	♟♟♟ 7
● Barolo Cannubi '01	♟♟♟ 6
● Barolo Sarmassa '11	♟♟♟ 6
● Barolo Sarmassa '05	♟♟♟ 6
● Barolo Sarmassa '04	♟♟♟ 6
● Barolo Sarmassa '03	♟♟♟ 6
● Barolo Cannubi '11	♟♟ 6
● Barolo Castellero '11	♟♟ 6
● Barolo Sarmassa '10	♟♟ 6

○ Roero Arneis V. Bricco Novara '15	♟♟ 3*
● Roero Panera Alta Ris. '13	♟♟ 6
● Roero '13	♟♟ 4
○ Roero Arneis '15	♟♟ 2*
● Barbera d'Alba '15	♟ 2
● Barbera d'Alba Sup. V. Mompissano '14	♟ 2
○ Langhe Favorita '15	♟ 2
● Roero '12	♟♟ 4
● Roero Panera Alta Ris. '12	♟♟ 6

Bric Cenciurio

VIA ROMA, 24
12060 BAROLO [CN]
TEL. +39 017356317
www.briccenciurio.com

CELLAR SALES
PRE-BOOKED VISITS
ANNUAL PRODUCTION 45,000 bottles
HECTARES UNDER VINE 15.00

In the early 1990s Franco Pittatore and his brother-in-law Carlo Sacchetto pooled their efforts and vineyards to found Bric Cenciurio. Today the estate is run by Fiorella Sacchetto with her sons Alessandro and Alberto and her brother Carlo. The family's vineyards are divided between Langhe and Roero. The sandy soils of the Cenciurio di Castellinaldo hill yield exotic whites from arneis; the plots in Magliano Alfieri are home to the old barbera vines used for the powerful Barbera d'Alba Naunda; and the vineyards in the Coste di Rose and Monrobiolo di Bussia crus between Barolo and Monforte d'Alba are the source of the elegant Bric Cenciurio Barolos. Although it wasn't a very powerful vintage, the estate's Barolos generally display good body and tannins that still have a few rough edges. Riserva di Coste di Rose 2010 is already very drinkable, thanks to its complex aromas and alluring softness, and Coste di Rose 2012 has an exceptionally classic nose.

● Barbera d'Alba Sup. Naunda '13	♥♥ 4
● Barolo '12	♥♥ 5
● Barolo Coste di Rose '12	♥♥ 6
● Barolo Coste di Rose Ris. '10	♥♥ 7
● Barolo Monrobiolo di Bussia '12	♥♥ 5
● Langhe Nebbiolo '14	♥♥ 4
○ Roero Arneis Sito dei Fossili '14	♥♥ 3
● Barbera d'Alba '14	♥ 2
○ Langhe Riesling '14	♥ 3
● Barolo '11	♀♀ 5
● Barolo Monrobiolo di Bussia '11	♀♀ 5
○ Langhe Riesling '13	♀♀ 3
○ Roero Arneis Sito dei Fossili '13	♀♀ 3

Bricco del Cucù

LOC. BRICCO, 10
12060 BASTIA MONDOVÌ [CN]
TEL. +39 017460153
www.briccocucu.com

CELLAR SALES
PRE-BOOKED VISITS
ANNUAL PRODUCTION 50,000 bottles
HECTARES UNDER VINE 10.00

The estate run by Dario Sciolla eloquently expresses the characteristics of the Dogliani production zone, a corner of Piedmont that has not yet been fully explored. In the Bastìa area, the high altitude and fierce temperature fluctuations ensure firm acid backbone and good ageing potential. Dolcetto is the star of the well-assorted range of highly drinkable, fresh, vibrant wines. Be sure not to miss the prized hazelnuts that the estate also produces. The Dogliani 2015 is captivating, showing a deep, inky purplish ruby, with notes of jam, quinine, and liquorice on the nose, and a young, full-flavoured palate that is nonetheless caressing and very long, with excellent ageing prospects. We also liked Langhe Rosso Diavolisanti 2013, with a harmonious, concentrated nose of dark berries, tar, and roasted coffee beans, and a full-bodied palate with close-woven tannins and a long, fresh finish. Langhe Rosso Superboum 2013 has a nice balance of fresh sweet fruit and toasty notes.

● Dogliani '15	♥♥ 2*
○ Langhe Bianco Livor '15	♥♥ 2*
● Langhe Dolcetto '15	♥♥ 2*
● Langhe Rosso Diavolisanti '13	♥♥ 2*
● Langhe Rosso Superboum '13	♥♥ 2*
● Dogliani Sup. Bricco S. Bernardo '09	♥♥♥ 2*
● Dogliani '13	♀♀ 2*
● Dogliani Sup. Bricco S. Bernardo '12	♀♀ 2*
● Dogliani Sup. Bricco S. Bernardo '11	♀♀ 2*
● Langhe Dolcetto '13	♀♀ 2*
● Langhe Rosso Diavolisanti '12	♀♀ 2*
● Langhe Rosso Diavolisanti '11	♀♀ 2*
● Langhe Rosso Superboum '12	♀♀ 2*

Bricco Maiolica

FRAZ. RICCA
VIA BOLANGINO, 7
12055 DIANO D'ALBA [CN]
TEL. +39 0173612049
www.briccomaiolica.it

CELLAR SALES
PRE-BOOKED VISITS
ACCOMMODATION
ANNUAL PRODUCTION 110,000 bottles
HECTARES UNDER VINE 24.00
SUSTAINABLE WINERY

Beppe Accomo's sound cellar now offers a
range of 12 wines. The latest is a Barolo,
Contadin, whose first release is the 2012
vintage. It hails from a tiny vineyard in the
corner of Diano d'Alba that lies within the
Barolo production zone, and goes to join a
range based on the classic grape varieties
of the area, but also featuring selections of
Chardonnay, Sauvignon, Pinot Nero, and
Merlot. The winery is certainly worth a visit,
if possible combined with a stay at its
well-tended guest farm. The splendid Cumot
has won another Tre Bicchieri, this time with
the 2013 vintage. A veritable prototype of
the great Nebbiolo d'Alba, it is a perfect
harmony of delicate tannins, abundant fruity
flesh, and refreshing acidity. The complex
Barbera d'Alba Vigna Vigia 2013 proffers
plums, cherries, and cocoa powder on an
elegant oaky background, Chardonnay
Pensiero Infinito 2012 is modern and
elegantly caressing, and Barolo
Contadin 2012 has moderate structure.

● Nebbiolo d'Alba Sup. Cumot '13	▼▼▼	5
● Barbera d'Alba Sup. V. Vigia '13	▼▼	5
○ Langhe Bianco Pensiero Infinito '12	▼▼	6
● Barolo Contadin '12	▼▼	8
● Langhe Merlot Filius '13	▼▼	5
○ Langhe Sauvignon Castella '15	▼▼	3
● Barbera d'Alba '14	▼	3
● Dolcetto di Diano d'Alba '15	▼	3
○ Langhe Chardonnay Rolando '15	▼	3
● Langhe Pinot Nero Perlei '13	▼	5
● Diano d'Alba Sup. Sörì Bricco Maiolica '07	♛♛♛	3*
● Nebbiolo d'Alba Cumot '10	♛♛♛	4*
● Nebbiolo d'Alba Cumot '09	♛♛♛	4*
● Barbera d'Alba Sup. V. Vigia '12	♛♛	5
● Nebbiolo d'Alba Sup. Cumot '12	♛♛	5

Bricco Mondalino

REG. MONDALINO, 5
15049 VIGNALE MONFERRATO [AL]
TEL. +39 0142933204
www.gaudiovini.it

CELLAR SALES
PRE-BOOKED VISITS
ANNUAL PRODUCTION 80,000 bottles
HECTARES UNDER VINE 14.00

The estate boasts a particularly picturesque
setting in Mondalino, a hamlet of Vignale
Monferrato. It produces traditional
Monferrato wines, with excellent Barberas,
aged in oak or stainless steel, and a basic
and a bunch-selected Grignolino. The
semi-sparkling Freisas and Barberas should
not be underestimated, for when paired with
the right food, these easy-drinking wines
offer an interesting alternative to the
traditional accompaniment of young still
reds. Monte della Sala 2013 towers above
the other wines presented. It is a
concentrated Grignolino, with notes of spice
and tobacco on the nose, which continue on
the concentrated, caressing palate with a
very long finish. It's followed by a fine
version of Malvasia di Casorzo, deliciously
interpreted by Mauro Gaudio with
well-balanced residual sugar and acidity.
Barbera del Monferrato Superiore 2014 is
complex, with crisp fruit and a firm palate.

● Grignolino del M.to Casalese Monte della Sala '13	▼▼	4
● Barbera del M.to Sup. '14	▼▼	2*
● Malvasia di Casorzo Dolce Stil Novo '15	▼▼	2*
● Barbera d'Asti Il Bergantino '13	▼	3
● Grignolino del M.to Casalese '15	▼	3
● Barbera d'Asti Il Bergantino '12	♛♛	4
● Barbera d'Asti Il Bergantino '10	♛♛	3
● Barbera d'Asti Zerolegno '13	♛♛	4
● Barbera del M.to Gaudium Magnum '11	♛♛	6
● Grignolino del M.to Casalese '12	♛♛	2*
● Grignolino del M.to Casalese Bricco Mondalino '13	♛♛	2*
● Grignolino del M.to Casalese Bricco Mondalino '03	♛♛	2
● Malvasia di Casorzo Dolce Stil Novo '13	♛♛	2*
● Malvasia di Casorzo Dolce Stil Novo '12	♛♛	2*

Francesco Brigatti

VIA OLMI, 31
28019 SUNO [NO]
TEL. +39 032285037
www.vinibrigatti.it

CELLAR SALES
PRE-BOOKED VISITS
ANNUAL PRODUCTION 25,000 bottles
HECTARES UNDER VINE 6.50

MötZiflon, Mötfrei, and Campazzi are the three main hills around Suno that are home to the seven hectares of vineyards tended by Francesco Brigatti, an increasingly esteemed name of the Novara production zone. The small plots have very different aspects and soils, ranging from clay and sand to silt and iron deposits. They are reflected in individually tailored cellar processes for the top nebbiolo-based reds, with the MötZiflon and Ghemme Oltre il Bosco aged in 3,000-litre Slavonian oak casks and the Mötfrei in Allier tonneaux. The range is completed by wines from barbera, uva rara, vespolina, and erbaluce. The estate's versatility is evident in Vespolina Maria 2015 and Nebbiolo MötZiflon 2013, both firm, racy reds with excellent ageing prospects. Ghemme Oltre il Bosco 2011 has greater concentration and harmony, with notes of dried herbs and liquorice , red fruit and gentian, elegant tannins, and a long, savoury finish.

Broglia - Tenuta La Meirana

LOC. LOMELLINA, 22
15066 GAVI [AL]
TEL. +39 0143642998
www.broglia.it

CELLAR SALES
PRE-BOOKED VISITS
ACCOMMODATION
ANNUAL PRODUCTION 480,000 bottles
HECTARES UNDER VINE 65.00

Meirana is one of the most important Gavi estates, covering an area of almost 100 hectares, including more than 60 under vine. Founded by Bruno Broglia focusing entirely on cortese, today it is run by his sons Gian Piero and Paolo Broglia, but the white varietal remains the star of the range. Rigorously stainless steel fermented and characterized by a lean, racy style, the still versions are Il Doge, La Meirana, and the Bruno Broglia selection, which is aged for longer on the fine lees and is distinguished by riper, more opulent fruit. Then there are the two Roverello Spumante sparklers, and the red Le Pernici, from dolcetto and barbera. The Gavi di Gavi selections feature two very different vintages. The Bruno Broglia reveals the leanness of the 2014 harvest, offering a charming bouquet of fresh herbs and gunpowder, while the generous, sunny 2015 gives the La Meirana fruity ripeness and zesty vigour.

● Ghemme Oltre il Bosco '11	▼▼ 4
● Colline Novaresi Nebbiolo Mötziflon '13	▼▼ 3
● Colline Novaresi Vespolina Maria '15	▼▼ 3
● Colline Novaresi Barbera Campazzi '15	▼ 3
● Colline Novaresi Uva Rara Selvalunga '15	▼ 2
● Colline Novaresi Barbera Campazzi '13	♀♀ 3
○ Colline Novaresi Bianco Mottobello '14	♀♀ 2*
● Colline Novaresi Nebbiolo Mötfrei '12	♀♀ 3
● Colline Novaresi Nebbiolo Mötfrei '11	♀♀ 3*
● Colline Novaresi Nebbiolo MötZiflon '12	♀♀ 3*
● Colline Novaresi Nebbiolo MötZiflon '11	♀♀ 3
● Colline Novaresi Uva Rara Selvalunga '13	♀♀ 2*
● Colline Novaresi Vespolina Maria '14	♀♀ 2*
● Colline Novaresi Vespolina Maria '13	♀♀ 2*
● Ghemme Oltre il Bosco '10	♀♀ 4

○ Gavi del Comune di Gavi La Meirana '15	▼▼ 3*
○ Gavi del Comune di Gavi Bruno Broglia '14	▼▼ 5
● Barbera d'Asti Sup. '13	▼ 3
○ Gavi del Comune di Gavi Roverello Brut '14	▼ 3
○ Gavi del Comune di Gavi Bruno Broglia '12	♀♀♀ 5
○ Gavi del Comune di Gavi Bruno Broglia '08	♀♀♀ 5
○ Gavi del Comune di Gavi Bruno Broglia '07	♀♀♀ 5
○ Gavi del Comune di Gavi Bruno Broglia '13	♀♀ 5
○ Gavi del Comune di Gavi Bruno Broglia '11	♀♀ 5
○ Gavi Il Doge '13	♀♀ 2*
○ Gavi Il Doge '12	♀♀ 2*

★Brovia

VIA ALBA-BAROLO, 145
12060 CASTIGLIONE FALLETTO [CN]
TEL. +39 017362852
www.brovia.net

CELLAR SALES
PRE-BOOKED VISITS
ANNUAL PRODUCTION 60,000 bottles
HECTARES UNDER VINE 17.00
VITICULTURE METHOD Certified Organic

The name Brovia is first and foremost
about style, for it has long conjured up a
very precise idea of what a great Barolo
can and should be: almost rarefied
elegance and grace, meticulously mirroring
the terroir of superior vineyards like
Rocche, Villero, and Garblèt Sué in
Castiglione Falletto, or Cà Mia in
Serralunga. Traditionally made with
spontaneous fermentation in concrete vats
for 15-20 days and ageing in large barrels
for about three years, they are wines that
reflect the sensibility of those who craft
them today, sisters Cristina and Elena,
aided by Alejandro Sanchez Solana.
Brovia's Barolos put up a stunning
performance once again. For long cellaring
we recommend Brea Vigna Ca' Mia 2012,
initially closed and clenched but with
excellent stuffing. The full magnificence of
Rocche di Castiglione 2012 is already
evident, a veritable paradigm of the great
nebbiolo grape, with its symphony of
raspberries, aniseed, and tobacco. The
classic Villero has an enchanting nose.

● Barolo Rocche di Castiglione '12	♥♥♥ 8
● Barolo Brea V. Ca' Mia '12	♥♥ 8
● Barolo Villero '12	♥♥ 8
● Barolo Garblèt Sué '12	♥♥ 8
● Barolo Brea V. Ca' Mia '10	♀♀♀ 8
● Barolo Ca' Mia '09	♀♀♀ 8
● Barolo Ca' Mia '00	♀♀♀ 8
● Barolo Ca' Mia '96	♀♀♀ 8
● Barolo Monprivato '90	♀♀♀ 8
● Barolo Rocche dei Brovia '06	♀♀♀ 7
● Barolo Villero '11	♀♀♀ 8
● Barolo Villero '10	♀♀♀ 8
● Barolo Villero '08	♀♀♀ 7
● Barolo Villero '06	♀♀♀ 7

G. B. Burlotto

VIA VITTORIO EMANUELE, 28
12060 VERDUNO [CN]
TEL. +39 0172470122
www.burlotto.com

CELLAR SALES
PRE-BOOKED VISITS
ACCOMMODATION
ANNUAL PRODUCTION 60,000 bottles
HECTARES UNDER VINE 15.00

The top Langhe wineries can be recognized
by their natural transition from generation
to generation. G. B. Burlotto, founded in the
mid-19th century by "Il Commendatore"
Giovan Battista, is a good example. Today it
is run by the skilled oenologist Fabio
Alessandria, with his parents Giuseppe and
Maria. The estate vaunts around 15
hectares of vineyards, half of which planted
to nebbiolo: Monvigliero, Neirane, Breri, and
Rocche dell'Olmo in Verduno, and Cannubi
in Barolo. The rest is divided between
barbera, dolcetto, pelaverga, sauvignon,
and freisa, used to make an undisputedly
traditional range of wines. The Barolos are
aged in 3,500–5,000-litre oak barrels. A
Tre Bicchieri went to the harmonious,
sophisticated Cannubi 2012 that perfectly
embodies the classic style, with bright hints
of raspberries, roots, and medicinal herbs
echoed on a firm but nicely balanced
palate. The charming Monvigliero 2012 has
spicier aromas and restrained tannins,
while the Acclivi is slightly edgier.

● Barolo Cannubi '12	♥♥♥ 7
● Barolo Monvigliero '12	♥♥ 7
● Barolo Acclivi '12	♥♥ 6
○ Langhe Sauvignon Viridis '15	♥♥ 3
● Verduno Pelaverga '15	♥♥ 3
○ Langhe Sauvignon Dives '14	♥ 3
● Barolo Acclivi '11	♀♀♀ 6
● Barolo Acclivi '07	♀♀♀ 6
● Barolo Monvigliero '10	♀♀♀ 7
● Barbera d'Alba Aves '13	♀♀ 4
● Barolo '11	♀♀ 6
● Barolo Cannubi '11	♀♀ 7
● Barolo Vign. Monvigliero '11	♀♀ 7
○ Langhe Sauvignon Dives '13	♀♀ 3
● Verduno Pelaverga '14	♀♀ 3

★Piero Busso

VIA ALBESANI, 8
12052 NEIVE [CN]
TEL. +39 017367156
www.bussopiero.com

CELLAR SALES
PRE-BOOKED VISITS
ANNUAL PRODUCTION 45,000 bottles
HECTARES UNDER VINE 11.50
SUSTAINABLE WINERY

Albesani Borgese, Gallina, Santo Stefanetto, and Mondino from Balluro are the four Barbaresco crus that regularly play the lead role in Piero Busso's sound range. Aided by his wife Lucia and children Emanuela and Pierguido, he tends around a dozen hectares in Neive and Treiso, planted almost entirely to the typical Langhe grape varieties. Technical intransigence in the cellar is shunned in favour of flexible choices based on of the type of vintage and the characteristics of the individual vineyards. The resulting Nebbiolo wines are always in step with the times and highly regarded by many enthusiasts. Barbaresco Gallina 2012 epitomizes the classic style, earning a Tre Bicchieri with top notes of quinine and dried flowers on raspberries and wonderfully delicate, complex fruit, and a rich, juicy palate displaying progressive, fine-grained tannins and a very long finish. Vigna Borghese 2012 is particularly firm, with an exceptionally satisfying palate, while Albesani Viti Vecchie 2010 is simply splendid, although sadly only a few bottles were produced.

● Barbaresco Gallina '12	🏆🏆🏆 8
● Barbaresco Albesani V. Borgese '12	🏆🏆 7
● Barbaresco Albesani Viti Vecchie '10	🏆🏆 8
● Barbaresco Mondino '13	🏆🏆 5
● Barbaresco S. Stunet '13	🏆🏆 7
● Barbera d'Alba S. Stefanetto '13	🏆🏆 5
● Barbera d'Alba Majano '14	🏆 3
○ Langhe Bianco '14	🏆 3
● Langhe Nebbiolo '14	🏆 4
● Barbaresco Borgese '09	🏆🏆🏆 6
● Barbaresco Gallina '11	🏆🏆🏆 8
● Barbaresco Gallina '09	🏆🏆🏆 8
● Barbaresco S. Stunet '11	🏆🏆🏆 7

Ca' Bianca

REG. SPAGNA, 58
15010 ALICE BEL COLLE [AL]
TEL. +39 0144745420
www.cantinacabianca.it

CELLAR SALES
PRE-BOOKED VISITS
ANNUAL PRODUCTION 500,000 bottles
HECTARES UNDER VINE 24.00

Gruppo Italiano Vini's Piedmont estate has the characteristics and means to vinify the grapes from its vineyards in the best possible manner. Its well-organized, high-tech cellar produces several DOC and DOCG wines that form an extensive range. It features the white Arneis and Gavi, the red Dolcetto d'Acqui, Nebbiolo, and Barolo, and the sweet Moscato d'Asti, Asti Spumante, and Brachetto d'Acqui. Cà Bianca presented a small list featuring only a few of the wines in its range. The group was headed by Barbera d'Asti Superiore Chersì, with a beautiful nose and a fairly long finish. Fruity notes dominate the nose of the Arneis, followed by a fresh, tangy palate with a very long finish. The Dolcetto d'Acqui has a well-typed, varietal nose, while Barbera Antè 2014 betrays the unfortunate weather conditions of its vintage.

● Barbera d'Asti Sup. Chersì '13	🏆🏆 5
● Dolcetto d'Acqui '15	🏆🏆 3
○ Roero Arneis '15	🏆🏆 3
● Barbera d'Asti Sup. Antè '14	🏆 3
● Barbera d'Asti Sup. Antè '13	🏆🏆 3
● Barbera d'Asti Sup. Antè '12	🏆🏆 3
● Barbera d'Asti Sup. Antè '11	🏆🏆 3
● Barbera d'Asti Sup. Chersì '12	🏆🏆 3
● Barbera d'Asti Sup. Chersì '11	🏆🏆 5
● Barbera d'Asti Teis '14	🏆🏆 2*
● Barbera d'Asti Teis '13	🏆🏆 2*
● Dolcetto d'Acqui '14	🏆🏆 3
● Dolcetto d'Acqui '12	🏆🏆 3

Ca' d'Gal

FRAZ. VALDIVILLA
S.DA VECCHIA DI VALDIVILLA, 1
12058 SANTO STEFANO BELBO [CN]
TEL. +39 0141847103
www.cadgal.it

CELLAR SALES
PRE-BOOKED VISITS
ACCOMMODATION AND RESTAURANT SERVICE
ANNUAL PRODUCTION 95,000 bottles
HECTARES UNDER VINE 12.00

Alessandro Boido is undoubtedly one of the
leading names in Moscato production, in
terms of both the estate's history and his
ability to follow unusual paths, such as
releasing a Moscato d'Asti after five years
of bottle ageing. The majority of the estate's
vineyards lie on the hillsides of Santo
Stefano Belbo, on light, white sandy soils,
with vines over 60 years old, and also
include chardonnay, sauvignon, pinot nero,
and freisa. Canelli Sant'Ilario 2015 has an
elegant, concentrated nose of medicinal
herbs, mint, and lime, and an
extraordinarily full, complex palate that is
nonetheless delicate and very fresh. We
also very much liked the more
approachable but complex Lumine 2015,
full of personality, and Alessandro's
signature Vigna Vecchia 2010,with notes of
citrus, petrol, and aromatic herbs.

○ Moscato d'Asti Canelli Sant'Ilario '15	♛♛♛	3*
○ Moscato d'Asti Lumine '15	♛♛	3*
○ Moscato d'Asti V. Vecchia '10	♛♛	7
○ Asti	♛♛	3
● Barbera d'Asti '13	♛	3
○ Langhe Bianco '15	♛	3
○ Moscato d'Asti V. V. '11	♛♛♛	3*
○ Moscato d'Asti Sant'Ilario '14	♛♛	3*
○ Moscato d'Asti V. V. '12	♛♛	4
○ Moscato d'Asti V. V. '07	♛♛	3*
○ Moscato d'Asti V. Vecchia '13	♛♛	4
○ Moscato d'Asti V. Vecchia '09	♛♛	7
○ Moscato d'Asti V. Vecchia '08	♛♛	3*

★Ca' del Baio

VIA FERRERE SOTTANO, 33
12050 TREISO [CN]
TEL. +39 0173638219
www.cadelbaio.com

CELLAR SALES
PRE-BOOKED VISITS
ANNUAL PRODUCTION 130,000 bottles
HECTARES UNDER VINE 25.00

Giulio Grasso, who won our Grower of the
Year award in 2016, runs this family
winery with his wife Luciana and the
precious aid of their three young
daughters. Their sights are firmly set on
the future and production is slowly
increasing. Indeed, since 2011 the
excellent classic Barbaresco selections of
Marcarini, Vallegrande, Asili, and Pora have
been joined by the superb Riserva Asili,
while the array of white wines has been
expanded with a very fine Riesling, offering
outstanding quality across the entire
range. The sophisticated, complex
Barbaresco Pora 2012 boasts a layered
nose of tobacco, liquorice, and fresh red
berries, and a full-flavoured palate. The
Asili Riserva 2011 easily stole our top
accolade with its exceptionally broad,
complex nose and powerful yet exquisitely
delicate palate. Vallegrande 2013 is
excellent, while the elegant, potent
Asili 2013 is a worthy interpretation of a
great vineyard, bursting with notes of
raspberries and herbs in the sun.

● Barbaresco Asili Ris. '11	♛♛♛	8
● Barbaresco Asili '13	♛♛	6
● Barbaresco Pora '12	♛♛	6
● Barbaresco Vallegrande '13	♛♛	5
● Barbaresco Marcarini '13	♛♛	5
○ Langhe Riesling '14	♛♛	3
○ Moscato d'Asti 101 '15	♛♛	2*
○ Langhe Chardonnay Sermine '15	♛	3
● Barbaresco Asili '12	♛♛♛	6
● Barbaresco Asili '10	♛♛♛	6
● Barbaresco Asili '09	♛♛♛	5
● Barbaresco Asili '06	♛♛♛	5
● Barbaresco Pora '10	♛♛♛	6
● Barbaresco Pora '06	♛♛♛	6
● Barbaresco Pora '04	♛♛♛	6
● Barbaresco Valgrande '08	♛♛♛	5

Ca' Nova

via San Isidoro, 1
28010 Bogogno [NO]
Tel. +39 0322863406
www.cascinacanova.it

CELLAR SALES
PRE-BOOKED VISITS
ACCOMMODATION
ANNUAL PRODUCTION 35,000 bottles
HECTARES UNDER VINE 10.00

Two decades have already passed since
Giada Codecasa started envisaging her
ambitious plans for a winery with guest
accommodation in San Isidoro di Bogogno.
This enchantingly beautiful place is home
to most of her vineyards, along with the
Golf Club, the Relais Ca' Nova, and a
photovoltaic greenhouse for the production
of organic vegetables and green energy.
Nearby is the San Quirico vineyard, a
legendary nebbiolo cru that supplies the
fruit for the flagship wine and the Ghemme.
The range also features the two Metodo
Classicos of the Jad'Or line, the Rosé from
nebbiolo, and the Brut from erbaluce, which
is also used for the still dry white Rugiada.
Once again this year it was the nebbiolo
selections that convinced us most. Colline
Novaresi Melchiòr e San Quirico and
Ghemme Riserva 2009 share the same
ripe, foresty sensations, notes of rust and
roots, warm structure, and close-woven
tannins, while the Bocciolo 2015 is suppler
and leaner.

● Colline Novaresi Nebbiolo Melchiòr '09	♥♥ 3*
● Ghemme Ris. '09	♥♥ 5
● Colline Novaresi Nebbiolo Bocciòlo '15	♥♥ 2*
● Colline Novaresi Nebbiolo V. San Quirico '09	♥♥ 4
○ Colline Novaresi Bianco Rugiada '15	♥ 2
⊙ Colline Novaresi Nebbiolo Aurora '15	♥ 2
○ Jad'or Brut M. Cl.	♥ 4
○ Colline Novaresi Bianco Rugiada '14	♥♥ 2*
⊙ Colline Novaresi Nebbiolo Aurora '14	♥♥ 2*
● Colline Novaresi Nebbiolo V. San Quirico '07	♥♥ 4
○ Extra Brut M. Cl. Jad'Or	♥♥ 3
● Ghemme '09	♥♥ 5
● Ghemme '08	♥♥ 4
● Ghemme '07	♥♥ 4

Ca' Rome'

s.da Rabajà, 86
12050 Barbaresco [CN]
Tel. +39 0173635126
www.carome.com

CELLAR SALES
PRE-BOOKED VISITS
ANNUAL PRODUCTION 30,000 bottles
HECTARES UNDER VINE 5.00

The winery run by Romano Marengo with
the precious aid of his children Paola and
Giuseppe shuns the limelight, preferring to
keep a low profile, at least in Italy. Indeed,
its excellent wines are more commonly
found in restaurants in New York than in
Langhe or Italian cities, and feature more
frequently in British than in Italian wine
guides. They hail from great vineyards in
Barbaresco and Serralunga d'Alba and are
exclusively reds from nebbiolo and barbera,
which are big and powerful but never
aggressive, traditional and elegant, complex
and ageworthy. Barolo Rapet 2012 has a
deep, layered nose with fresh, fruity top
notes of raspberries, followed by tobacco
and liquorice, and then gentian, and a big,
full-flavoured palate with a long, caressing
finish. Barbaresco Maria di Brun 2011
continues to lives up to its well-deserved
fame, offering dried flowers and ripe red
berry fruit.

● Barbaresco Sorì Rio Sordo '13	♥♥ 6
● Barolo Rapet '12	♥♥ 7
● Barbaresco Chiaramanti '13	♥♥ 7
● Barbaresco Sorì Rio Sordo '06	♥♥♥ 6
● Barolo Rapet '11	♥♥♥ 7
● Barolo Rapet '08	♥♥♥ 7
● Barolo V. Cerretta '09	♥♥♥ 7
● Barbaresco Chiaramanti '12	♥♥ 7
● Barbaresco Maria di Brun '11	♥♥ 8
● Barbaresco Maria di Brun '10	♥♥ 7
● Barbaresco Rio Sordo '12	♥♥ 7
● Barolo Cerretta '11	♥♥ 7
● Barolo Cerretta '10	♥♥ 7
● Barolo Rapet '10	♥♥ 7
● Barolo Rapet Ris. '09	♥♥ 8

★★Ca' Viola

Borgata San Luigi, 11
12063 Dogliani [CN]
Tel. +39 017370547
www.caviola.com

CELLAR SALES
PRE-BOOKED VISITS
ACCOMMODATION AND RESTAURANT SERVICE
ANNUAL PRODUCTION 60,000 bottles
HECTARES UNDER VINE 12.00

Beppe Caviola pretends he hasn't noticed
he's been working for over 25 years and
continues his activity as both a renowned
consultant oenologist to top wineries all
over Italy and as a producer in his own
right, on his handsome Dogliani estate. His
first successes were the Dolcetto and
Barbera d'Alba, both from vineyards in
Rodello d'Alba, then it was the turn of the
Barolo, produced since 2006 and
constantly improving, partly due to the
increasing maturity of the vines of the
Sottocastello di Novello cru. Aged in the
cellar for over four years before release,
Barolo Sottocastello di Novello 2011 (9,000
bottles) earned a Tre Bicchieri for its
sophisticated nose of fresh red fruit and
balsamic notes, and perfectly balanced,
juicy palate that is already highly drinkable.
The 5,500 bottles of aromatic, citrus-tinged
Langhe Riesling, from a vineyard at an
altitude above 600 metres in the
municipality of Cissone, are an interesting
new addition to the range. We were also
impressed by Barbera Bric di Luv 2014.

● Barolo Sottocastello di Novello '11	▼▼▼	8
● Barbera d'Alba Bric di Luv '14	▼▼	5
○ Langhe Riesling '14	▼▼	5
● Barbera d'Alba Brichet '14	▼▼	4
● Dolcetto d'Alba Barturot '14	▼▼	4
● Dolcetto d'Alba Vilot '15	▼▼	3
● Langhe Nebbiolo '14	▼▼	5
● Barbera d'Alba Bric du Luv '12	♀♀♀	5
● Barbera d'Alba Bric du Luv '10	♀♀♀	5
● Barbera d'Alba Bric du Luv '07	♀♀♀	5
● Barolo Sottocastello '06	♀♀♀	7
● Barolo Sottocastello di Novello '10	♀♀♀	7
● Barolo Sottocastello di Novello '08	♀♀♀	7
● Dolcetto d'Alba Barturot '07	♀♀♀	3
● Dolcetto d'Alba Barturot '05	♀♀♀	3
● Langhe Nebbiolo '08	♀♀♀	5
● Langhe Rosso Bric du Luv '05	♀♀♀	5

Ca.Vi.Mon. - Cantina Iuli

Fraz. Montaldo
via Centrale, 27
15020 Cerrina Monferrato [AL]
Tel. +39 0142946657
www.iuli.it

CELLAR SALES
PRE-BOOKED VISITS
ACCOMMODATION
ANNUAL PRODUCTION 50,000 bottles
HECTARES UNDER VINE 8.50
VITICULTURE METHOD Certified Organic

Ca.Vi.Mon., namely Cantina Viticoltori del
Monferrato, founded in 1998, has now
come of age. These 18 vintages have made
it what it is today: one of the leading
wineries in Monferrato Casalese, an area
that is on the rise in terms of quality, but
above all one that is shaking off the notion
that it is capable of producing only basic
wines for everyday drinking. One of the
men behind this new philosophy is Fabrizio
Iuli, a practical and enlightened vigneron,
who has pursued his own idea of quality
without compromise. Despite lacking
several of the estate's top wines this year,
the list presented did extremely well, with a
special version of Barbera Rossore. Its
deep, almost inky, ruby hue is accompanied
by a fruity nose with notes of incense and
spice, and an impressively long, full-bodied
palate. The Nino, from pinot nero, has
vegetal hints on the nose and palate and
good overall balance.

● Rossore	▼▼	5
● Nino	▼	5
● Barbera del M.to Sup. Barabba '10	♀♀♀	6
● Barbera del M.to Sup. Barabba '04	♀♀♀	5
● Barbera del M.to Sup. Barabba '07	♀♀	5
● Barbera del M.to Sup. Barabba '06	♀♀	5
● Barbera del M.to Sup. Barabba '03	♀♀	5
● Barbera del M.to Sup. Barabba Magnum '04	♀♀	5
● Barbera del M.to Sup. Rossore '12	♀♀	5
● Barbera del M.to Sup. Rossore '10	♀♀	3*
● Barbera del M.to Sup. Rossore '09	♀♀	3*
● Barbera del M.to Sup. Rossore '07	♀♀	3*
● M.to Rosso Malidea '11	♀♀	5
● M.to Rosso Malidea '07	♀♀	5
● M.to Rosso Nino '10	♀♀	5

Cantina del Glicine

Via Giulio Cesare, 1
12052 Neive [CN]
Tel. +39 017367215
www.cantinadelglicine.it

CELLAR SALES
PRE-BOOKED VISITS
ANNUAL PRODUCTION 37,000 bottles
HECTARES UNDER VINE 6.00

Cantina del Glicine is a small family-run
estate owned by Adriana Marzi and Roberto
Bruno, whose magnificent 17th-century
cellars make it very popular with frequent
visitors to Langhe. Its vineyards cover an
area of around five hectares and are
planted mainly with traditional grape
varieties. The nebbiolo for Barbaresco is
fermented separately for the Currà,
Marcorino, and Vigne Sparse crus, while
the barbera goes to make the La
Sconsolata and La Dormiosa selections.
Together they form a range characterized
by precise, terroir-true wines that are also
extremely good value and accessible.
Unfortunately the close-knit team formed
by Adriana Marzi and Roberto Bruno didn't
repeat last year's impressive feat. The
wines, particularly the Barbaresco crus,
nonetheless put up a thoroughly decent
performance. This year there is no doubt
about it: the estate's crowning glory is the
Currà 2013, which displays fabulous
balance and finesse. The Marcorino 2013
appears less complete and still a little
coarse.

● Barbaresco Currà '13	¶¶	5
● Barbaresco Marcorino '13	¶¶	5
● Barbaresco Vigne Sparse '13	¶¶	5
● Barbera d'Alba Sup. La Dormiosa '14	¶¶	3
● Dolcetto d'Alba Olmiolo '15	¶¶	2*
● Nebbiolo d'Alba Calcabrume '14	¶¶	3
● Barbera d'Alba La Sconsolata '14	¶	3
○ Roero Arneis Il Mandolo '15	¶	3
● Barbaresco Currà '10	¶¶¶	4*
● Barbaresco Marcorino '12	¶¶¶	5
● Barbaresco Currà '12	¶¶	5
● Barbaresco Vigne Sparse '12	¶¶	5
● Barbera d'Alba La Sconsolata '13	¶¶	2*
● Barbera d'Alba Sup. La Dormiosa '13	¶¶	3

Cantina del Nebbiolo

Via Torino, 17
12050 Vezza d'Alba [CN]
Tel. +39 017365040
www.cantinadelnebbiolo.com

CELLAR SALES
PRE-BOOKED VISITS
ANNUAL PRODUCTION 300,000 bottles
HECTARES UNDER VINE 300.00
VITICULTURE METHOD Certified Organic

This longstanding cooperative winery,
founded as Cantina Sociale Parrocchiale di
Vezza d'Alba in 1901 and re-established
with its current name in 1959, is one of only
a handful of its kind in Roero. Today it has
175 grower-members with vineyards in 18
municipalities in Roero and Langhe. It
produces wines not only from nebbiolo, but
also from many other native grape varieties.
The wines are technically well made and
fully express the characteristics of the
terroir. The list presented this year seemed
a little lacklustre in respect to the past.
Nebbiolo d'Alba Vigna Valmaggiore 2014
has a concentrated floral nose with notes of
fresh red fruit and tobacco, and a beautifully
deep, complex palate. Barolo del Comune di
Serralunga d'Alba 2012 is somewhat
marked by oak on the nose, with notes of
sweet spice and hibiscus tea, while the juicy
palate is fruitier, with notes of raspberries
and currants. The other wines are
well-typed.

● Barolo del Comune di Serralunga d'Alba '12	¶¶	6
● Nebbiolo d'Alba V. Valmaggiore '14	¶¶	3
● Barbera d'Alba '14	¶	2
● Barolo '12	¶	5
○ Langhe Favorita '15	¶	2
○ Roero Arneis '15	¶	2
○ Roero Arneis Arenarium '15	¶	2
● Barbaresco '11	¶¶	4
● Barolo '10	¶¶	5
● Barolo Cannubi Boschis '11	¶¶	7
● Barolo del Comune di Serralunga d'Alba '11	¶¶	6
○ Langhe Nascetta Riveverse '14	¶¶	2*
● Nebbiolo d'Alba Valmaggiore '11	¶¶	2*

Cantina del Pino

S.DA OVELLO, 31
12050 BARBARESCO [CN]
TEL. +39 0173635147
www.cantinadelpino.com

ANNUAL PRODUCTION 38,000 bottles
HECTARES UNDER VINE 7.00

Renato Vacca is the great-grandson of
Domizio Cavazza, the legendary head of the
Royal Oenological School of Alba for over 20
years between the late 19th and early 20th
centuries. He has embraced this cultural and
productive legacy with admirable authority at
Cantina del Pino, following a long period as
technical director at Produttori del Barbaresco.
Everything revolves around the estate's
magnificent vineyards in important crus like
Ovello and Albesani. They yield Nebbiolos that
are theoretically modern in style, due to
ageing in small oak casks. However, these are
thoroughly classic Barbarescos, carefree yet
austere, which are consistently among the
finest of the DOCG. The release of Renato
Vacca's Barbarescos is always delayed by a
year as they require time to smooth out their
sharp edges. This year we tasted the 2012
vintage. The Ovello came within a hair's
breadth of a Tre Bicchieri with its nose of
aniseed and liquorice and its overall harmony
on the palate. The rugged Albesani, from a
vineyard in Neive, is destined for those who
know how to wait, and the basic Barbaresco
is also stunningly good.

● Barbaresco Albesani '12	♟♟ 6
● Barbaresco Ovello '12	♟♟ 6
● Barbaresco '12	♟♟ 5
● Dolcetto d'Alba '15	♟♟ 3
● Langhe Nebbiolo '15	♟♟ 4
● Barbera d'Alba '14	♟ 4
● Barbaresco '04	♟♟♟ 5*
● Barbaresco '03	♟♟♟ 4*
● Barbaresco Albesani '05	♟♟♟ 6
● Barbaresco Ovello '07	♟♟♟ 6
● Barbaresco Ovello '99	♟♟♟ 5
● Barbaresco '10	♟♟ 5
● Barbaresco '09	♟♟ 5
● Barbaresco Albesani '10	♟♟ 6
● Barbaresco Ovello '10	♟♟ 6
● Barbaresco Ovello '09	♟♟ 6
● Barbera d'Alba '10	♟♟ 4

La Caplana

VIA CIRCONVALLAZIONE, 4
15060 BOSIO [AL]
TEL. +39 0143684182
www.lacaplana.com

CELLAR SALES
PRE-BOOKED VISITS
ANNUAL PRODUCTION 120,000 bottles
HECTARES UNDER VINE 5.00

Loosely inspired by Amedeo Modigliani's
portraits of women, La Caplana's labels
recount the Guido family's several decades of
winemaking history in Bosio. Their small
estate has always had a dual focus, offering
Cortese di Gavi whites and Dolcetto d'Alba
reds, true to the tradition of an area that is a
border zone between the province of
Alessandria and the foothills of the Ligurian
Apennines, with their steep slopes and
clay-rich white soils Together with the
Barberas from the province of Asti, the
sparklers, and the Chardonnay, they form a
well-put-together range that is solid and
vigorous. La Caplana's top wines all
performed very well. Gavi di Gavi 2015
focuses more on character than details, while
Barbera d'Asti Rubis 2012 has a sedate,
concentrated nose of incense and plums,
slightly masked by oaky notes. Dolcetto di
Ovada Narcys 2013 appears the deepest and
most ageworthy, with notes of blackberries,
tobacco, and cocoa powder.

● Dolcetto di Ovada Narcys '13	♟♟ 3*
○ Gavi Villa Vecchia '15	♟♟ 2*
● Barbera d'Asti Rubis '12	♟♟ 3
● Dolcetto di Ovada '15	♟♟ 2*
○ Gavi del Comune di Gavi '15	♟♟ 2*
● Barbera d'Asti '14	♟ 2
○ Gavi '15	♟ 2
○ Piemonte Chardonnay '15	♟ 2
● Barbera d'Asti '13	♟♟ 2
● Barbera d'Asti Rubis '11	♟♟ 3
● Dolcetto di Ovada Narcys '12	♟♟ 3*
○ Gavi '14	♟♟ 2*
○ Gavi del Comune di Gavi '14	♟♟ 2*
○ Gavi del Comune di Gavi '13	♟♟ 2*
○ Gavi Villa Vecchia '14	♟♟ 2*
○ Gavi Villavecchia '13	♟♟ 2*

Tenuta Carretta

LOC. CARRETTA, 2
12040 PIOBESI D'ALBA [CN]
TEL. +39 0173619119
www.tenutacarretta.it

CELLAR SALES
PRE-BOOKED VISITS
ACCOMMODATION AND RESTAURANT SERVICE
ANNUAL PRODUCTION 480,000 bottles
HECTARES UNDER VINE 70.00

Tenuta Carretta is situated in an area characterized by a chalk outcrop, known and cited for its vineyards since the 12th century. The winery was purchased and entirely renovated by the Miroglio family in 1985, and boasts several estates – the vineyards close to the cellar for the classic Roero wines, several plots in the Barolo and Barbaresco designations, and the Malgrà estate in the Asti area – that allow it to offer a wide and diversified range. Barbera d'Asti Superiore Fornace di Cerreto 2013 has fresh red fruit with hints of toast on the nose and good stuffing underpinned by acidity on the palate, while Barbera d'Asti Superiore Gaiana 2013 is suppler, with notes of aromatic herbs. Barolo Cannubi 2011 is also well made, offering a concentrated nose of quinine and tobacco and a rather austere palate, as are the pleasant, harmonious Barbaresco Cascina Bordino 2012, with nicely amalgamated tannins, and the fresh, aromatic Roero Arneis Cayega 2015.

La Casaccia

VIA D. BARBANO, 10
15034 CELLA MONTE [AL]
TEL. +39 0142489986
www.lacasaccia.biz

CELLAR SALES
PRE-BOOKED VISITS
ANNUAL PRODUCTION 25,000 bottles
HECTARES UNDER VINE 6.70
VITICULTURE METHOD Certified Organic

The Ravas are making the most of their small Monferrato estate. Now that their winegrowing operation has reached the pinnacle of excellence, they are also welcoming tourists visiting Cella Monte, a magnificent snapshot of a corner of Piedmont, recognized by UNESCO as a unique collection of winegrowing landscapes, history and culture. La Casaccia contributes with organic wines from native grape varieties, to pair with local cheeses and charcuterie products, possibly while listening to a jazz quartet. The lovely Barbera Calichè 2013 made it into our finals with an almost impenetrable ruby hue and a nose with top notes of ripe fruit and sweet spice, echoed on a rich, firmly structured palate supported by good acidity. Bricco dei Boschi is a Barbera with tertiary aromas of dark berries and quinine, which exalt its personality and overall balance. Freisa Monfiorenza and the Brut from chardonnay and pinot nero grapes are also worthy of note.

● Barbaresco Cascina Bordino '12	♟♟ 6
● Barbera d'Asti Sup. Fornace di Cerreto '13	♟♟ 2*
● Barbera d'Asti Sup. Gaiana '13	♟♟ 3
● Barolo Cannubi '11	♟♟ 8
○ Roero Arneis Cayega '15	♟♟ 3
● Barbera d'Asti Briga della Mora '15	♟ 5
● Barbera d'Asti Sup. Nizza Mora dei Sassi '13	♟ 5
● Barolo Vign. in Cannubi '00	♟♟♟ 7
● Barbaresco Garassino '12	♟♟ 5
● Barbera d'Alba Sup. Bric Quercia '13	♟♟ 3
● Barbera d'Asti Sup. Fornace di Cerreto '12	♟♟ 2*
● Barolo Cascina Ferrero '11	♟♟ 6
○ Roero Arneis Cayega '14	♟♟ 3

● Barbera del M.to Calichè '13	♟♟ 3*
● Barbera del M.to Bricco dei Boschi '13	♟♟ 3
● M.to Freisa Monfiorenza '14	♟♟ 3
○ La Casaccia Brut M.Cl. '12	♟ 4
● Barbera d'Asti Sup. Calichè '06	♟♟ 3*
● Barbera del M.to Sup. Bricco del Bosco '07	♟♟ 2*
● Grignolino del M.to Casalese Poggeto '14	♟♟ 2*
● Grignolino del M.to Casalese Poggeto '10	♟♟ 2
● Grignolino del M.to Casalese Poggeto '08	♟♟ 2*
● Grignolino del M.to Casalese Poggeto '07	♟♟ 3*
○ La Casaccia Brut M.Cl. '10	♟♟ 4
● M.to Freisa Monfiorenza '13	♟♟ 3

Casalone

VIA MARCONI, 100
15040 LU [AL]
TEL. +39 0131741280
www.casalone.it

CELLAR SALES
PRE-BOOKED VISITS
ANNUAL PRODUCTION 50,000 bottles
HECTARES UNDER VINE 10.00

Lu Monferrato is a village with a population of just over 1,000, at the centre of the triangle formed by Alessandria, Asti, and Casale Monferrato. Its history encompasses the Celts and the Romans, and later the Gonzagas and the House of Savoy. In this ancient corner of Piedmont, Paolo Casalone continues in the footsteps of his ancestors, tending his vineyards to make veritable gems of country winemaking. Today his range features a dozen labels, from the classic Monferrato varieties and from internationals like merlot and pinot nero. His still white, a Metodo Classico sparkler, and a passito from the aromatic malvasia greca cultivar are particularly noteworthy. The wines presented for our tastings included the fantastic Grignolino La Caplëtta 2015, with a concentrated nose of black pepper and tobacco and a balanced, harmonious palate with a long, tannic finish. Barbera d'Asti Rubermillo is very well made, as are Monemvasia Brut and Monemvasia Bianco Affinato in Barrique, both from malvasia greca.

● Piemonte Grignolino La Caplëtta '15		🏆🏆 3*
● Barbera d'Asti Rubermillo '13		🏆🏆 3
○ Monemvasia Affinato Barrique		🏆🏆 4
○ Monemvasia Brut M. Cl.		🏆🏆 4
● Barbera del M.to Bricco Santa Maria '14		🏆 2
● Barbera del M.to Sup. Bricco Morlantino '12		🏆 2
○ Monemvasia		🏆 2
● Barbera d'Asti Rubermillo '11		🏆🏆 3*
● Barbera d'Asti Rubermillo '05		🏆🏆 2*
● Barbera del M.to Bricco Morlantino Sup. '06		🏆🏆 2*
● Barbera del M.to Sup. Bricco Morlantino '07		🏆🏆 2*
● M.to Rosso Rus '08		🏆🏆 3
● M.to Rosso Rus '07		🏆🏆 3*

Cascina Barisél

REG. SAN GIOVANNI, 30
14053 CANELLI [AT]
TEL. +39 0141824848
www.barisel.it

CELLAR SALES
PRE-BOOKED VISITS
ANNUAL PRODUCTION 35,000 bottles
HECTARES UNDER VINE 4.50

The Penna family have owned Cascina Barisel for more than half a century, and have been making and bottling their own wines for over 30 years. Their vineyard lies on the limestone soil surrounding the farm and is planted mainly to barbera and moscato, the classic grape varieties of the area. The average age of the vines is 40–60 years old, although some of the barbera plants are over 70. They produce the estate's finest wines, which show great trueness to both type and terroir. Barbera d'Asti Superiore La Cappelletta is always among the best of its kind. The 2013 vintage has an exuberant nose of plums with hints of balsam and tobacco, and a lovely big, well-orchestrated palate that is long with excellent fruit. The alluring, approachable Barbera d'Asti 2015 is also well made, focusing on vibrant acidity and fresh red fruit, as is Barbera d'Asti Superiore Listoria 2014, with good flesh and length.

● Barbera d'Asti Sup. La Cappelletta '13		🏆🏆 4
● Barbera d'Asti '15		🏆🏆 2*
● Barbera d'Asti Sup. Listoria '14		🏆🏆 2*
○ M.to Bianco Foravia '15		🏆 2
○ Moscato d'Asti Canelli Barisel '15		🏆 2
● Barbera d'Asti '14		🏆🏆 2*
● Barbera d'Asti '12		🏆🏆 2*
● Barbera d'Asti Sup. La Cappelletta '12		🏆🏆 4
● Barbera d'Asti Sup. Listoria '13		🏆🏆 2*
● Barbera d'Asti Sup. Listoria '12		🏆🏆 2*
● Barbera d'Asti Sup. Listoria '11		🏆🏆 2*
○ Moscato d'Asti Canelli '14		🏆🏆 2*
○ Moscato d'Asti Canelli '13		🏆🏆 2*

Cascina Bongiovanni

LOC. UCCELLACCIO
VIA ALBA BAROLO, 3
12060 CASTIGLIONE FALLETTO [CN]
TEL. +39 0173262184
www.cascinabongiovanni.com

CELLAR SALES
PRE-BOOKED VISITS
ACCOMMODATION
ANNUAL PRODUCTION 35,000 bottles
HECTARES UNDER VINE 7.20
SUSTAINABLE WINERY

Davide Mozzone is the custodian of a
deep-rooted viticultural tradition that
commenced with his grandfather Giovanni.
His small estate is in Castiglione Falletto, in
the heart of Langhe. In addition to prized
plots in the municipality, it also boasts two
vineyards in Serralunga d'Alba, another two
in Monforte d'Alba, and a dolcetto vineyard
in Diano d'Alba. The wide range of wines is
nicely diversified with a quietly extractive
style. Diano d'Alba 2015 is deliciously
juicy and true to its vintage, combining
fragrant fruit with flavour and remarkable
length, and the Dolcetto d'Alba of the same
vintage is also very good. The Barolo 2012
has an intense, layered nose of lively fruit
with fine background notes of tobacco,
and a progressive palate with creamy
tannins and acidity nicely balanced by the
juicy sweetness of the alcohol. Barolo
Pernanno 2012 is still slightly held back by
new oak.

★Cascina Ca' Rossa

LOC. CASCINA CA' ROSSA, 56
12043 CANALE [CN]
TEL. +39 017398348
www.cascinacarossa.com

CELLAR SALES
PRE-BOOKED VISITS
ANNUAL PRODUCTION 90,000 bottles
HECTARES UNDER VINE 16.00
VITICULTURE METHOD Certified Organic

The Ferro family offer some of the most
authentic and fascinating wines in all
Roero. Their estate comprises vineyards in
crus such as Audinaggio and Mompissano
for nebbiolo, and Mulassa for barbera,
which are among the finest in the area and
yield the flagship wines, from the Roeros to
the Barbera d'Alba. They are traditional in
style and fully express the typical elegance
and grace of the local sandy soils. Angelo
decided not to produce the vineyard
selections in 2014, so there is no Roero
Audinaggio or Barbera d'Alba Mulassa.
However, Roero Mompissano 2013 makes
up for it, winning a Tre Bicchieri. Its floral
nose has notes of aniseed and ripe red fruit
and is followed by a delicate yet complex,
spicy palate that is full and flavoursome,
with elegant tannins and a long finish.
Both the fresh Roero Arneis Merica 2015
and the pleasant, approachable Langhe
Nebbiolo 2015 are well made.

● Barolo Pernanno '12	▼▼ 7
● Dolcetto di Diano d'Alba '15	▼▼ 3*
● Barolo '12	▼▼ 6
● Dolcetto d'Alba '15	▼▼ 3
○ Langhe Arneis '15	▼ 3
● Barolo Pernanno '01	▼▼▼ 6
● Barbera d'Alba '13	▼▼ 3
● Barolo '11	▼▼ 5
● Barolo '10	▼▼ 5
● Barolo Pernanno '11	▼▼ 6
● Barolo Pernanno '10	▼▼ 6
● Dolcetto di Diano d'Alba '14	▼▼ 2*
● Langhe Rosso Faletto '13	▼▼ 4

● Roero Mompissano Ris. '13	▼▼▼ 5
● Langhe Nebbiolo '15	▼▼ 3
○ Roero Arneis Merica '15	▼▼ 3
● Barbera d'Alba Mulassa '04	▼▼▼ 4*
● Roero Audinaggio '07	▼▼▼ 5
● Roero Audinaggio '06	▼▼▼ 5
● Roero Mompissano Ris. '12	▼▼▼ 5
● Roero Mompissano Ris. '10	▼▼▼ 5
● Roero Mompissano Ris. '07	▼▼▼ 6
● Barbera d'Alba '14	▼▼ 3
● Barbera d'Alba Mulassa '11	▼▼ 5
● Langhe Nebbiolo '12	▼▼ 3
○ Roero Arneis Merica '14	▼▼ 3

Cascina Chicco

VIA VALENTINO, 14
12043 CANALE [CN]
TEL. +39 0173979411
www.cascinachicco.com

CELLAR SALES
PRE-BOOKED VISITS
ANNUAL PRODUCTION 410,000 bottles
HECTARES UNDER VINE 46.00
SUSTAINABLE WINERY

Founded in the 1950s with the purchase of a hectare of vineyards in Canale, over the years the Faccenda family's estate has become one of Roero's leading wineries. It now owns six vineyards, in crus in several municipalities, like Mompissano in Canale, Valmaggiore in Vezza d'Alba, and Ginestra in Monforte d'Alba, yielding a total of 14 wines ranging from Roero classics, first and foremost Roero and Roero Arneis, to Barolos. Barolo Ginestra Riserva 2009 is extremely well made, with notes of dried flowers and medicinal herbs, a long, supple palate, and silky tannins. The top wines also include two veritable Roero crus: Roero Valmaggiore Riserva 2013, displaying a fruity nose with notes of tobacco and spice and a juicy, firmly structured palate with slightly overly prominent tannins, and Nebbiolo d'Alba Mompissano 2014, with clear overtones of raspberries on a full, dense palate.

● Barolo Ginestra Ris. '09	♥♥ 7
● Nebbiolo d'Alba Monpissano '14	♥♥ 3*
● Roero Valmaggiore Ris. '13	♥♥ 4
● Barbera d'Alba Bric Loira '14	♥♥ 4
● Barbera d'Alba Granera Alta '15	♥♥ 2*
● Barolo Rocche di Castelletto '12	♥♥ 5
⊙ Cuvée Zero Rosé	♥♥ 4
○ Arcass V.T.	♥ 4
○ Cuvée Zero Extra Brut M. Cl.	♥ 4
○ Roero Arneis Anterisio '15	♥ 2
● Roero Montespinato '14	♥ 3
○ Arcàss Passito '04	♥♥♥ 4
● Roero Valmaggiore Ris. '12	♥♥♥ 4*

Cascina Corte

FRAZ. SAN LUIGI
B.TA VALDIBERTI, 33
12063 DOGLIANI [CN]
TEL. +39 0173743539
www.cascinacorte.it

CELLAR SALES
PRE-BOOKED VISITS
ACCOMMODATION
ANNUAL PRODUCTION 30,000 bottles
HECTARES UNDER VINE 5.00
VITICULTURE METHOD Certified Organic
SUSTAINABLE WINERY

Sandro Barosi, widely known as Sandrino, accurately reflects his Dogliani winery: straightforward and without artifice in both substance and appearance, and sincere to the core. He quietly tends his vineyards with organic methods, accepting and sharing the associated risks with his partner Amalia Battaglia. As the everyday wine of rural Langhe, Dolcetto was the natural choice for him. His Dogliani Superiore Pirochetta is from 60-year-old vines. The concept of a welcoming home is also evident in the charming B&B housed in an 18th-century farmhouse renovated with natural materials. Sandro's entire range is back on top form, with the help of the excellent 2015 vintage, particularly for dolcetto grapes, despite the absence of the Pirochetta that wasn't produced in 2014. Of course, our favourite was the Dogliani 2015 with its exuberant nose of dark berries and wonderfully firm yet velvety palate. However, the Nebbiolo is also one of the estate's finest wines, vaunting a delicate nose and a full-flavoured palate.

● Dogliani '15	♥♥ 3*
● Barbetto	♥♥ 2*
● Langhe Nebbiolo '14	♥♥ 4
● Langhe Barbera '14	♥ 3
● Dogliani Vecchie V. Pirochetta '08	♥♥♥ 3*
● Dogliani '14	♥♥ 3
● Dogliani '13	♥♥ 3
● Dogliani Pirochetta V. V. '10	♥♥ 3
● Dogliani Sup. Pirochetta V. V. '13	♥♥ 3
● Dogliani Sup. Pirochetta V. V. '12	♥♥ 3*
● Dogliani Sup. Pirochetta V. V. '11	♥♥ 3*
● Langhe Barbera '11	♥♥ 3
● Langhe Nebbiolo '13	♥♥ 4
● Langhe Nebbiolo '11	♥♥ 3

Cascina del Monastero

FRAZ. ANNUNZIATA
CASCINA LUCIANI, 112A
12064 LA MORRA [CN]
TEL. +39 0173509245
www.cascinadelmonastero.it

CELLAR SALES
PRE-BOOKED VISITS
ACCOMMODATION
ANNUAL PRODUCTION 40,000 bottles
HECTARES UNDER VINE 12.00
VITICULTURE METHOD Certified Organic
SUSTAINABLE WINERY

Giuseppe Grasso and his family have created a sound estate, which is also worth a visit for its beautiful premises and welcoming guest farm. Overall, the style of the wines is traditional, but not without those special touches that ensure elegance and finesse. The estate focuses almost exclusively on the local red grape varieties – nebbiolo, barbera, and dolcetto – plus a tiny amount of merlot and cabernet sauvignon that are used to make the two blends. The Barolos hail from both the Annunziata hamlet of La Morra and a huge, highly prized vineyard in Monforte d'Alba. Barolo Bricco Rocca Riund Riserva 2010 has a beautifully balanced nose of oak, red fruit, and tobacco, and a full-bodied palate with close-woven tannins and a fresh, long, juicy finish. Barolo Bricco Luciani 2012 vaunts penetrating notes of ripe mixed berries and hints of cocoa powder on the nose, followed by a full-bodied palate with good alcohol. The delicate, complex, balanced Nebbiolo 2012 is worthy of note.

Cascina Fonda

VIA SPESSA, 29
12052 MANGO [CN]
TEL. +39 0173677877
www.cascinafonda.com

CELLAR SALES
PRE-BOOKED VISITS
ACCOMMODATION
ANNUAL PRODUCTION 110,000 bottles
HECTARES UNDER VINE 12.00

Today the estate run by brothers Marco and Massimo Barbero is a renowned Moscato producer. Cascina Fonda owns several vineyards in Mango, where the winery is located, and in Neive, all planted primarily to moscato, with smaller amounts of traditional grape varieties like dolcetto, nebbiolo, and arneis. The majority are situated at an altitude of around 450 metres, and are home to vines between 35 and 60 years old. This year we particularly liked Moscato Spumante Tardivo 2014, with close-focused aromatic top notes on the nose, followed by blood oranges, ripe peaches, and candied peel, and a delicate, complex palate that is sweet and full but perfectly balanced by acidity. Both Asti Spumante Bel Piasì 2015, with a fresh nose of lime and mint, and a complex, sweet palate that is slightly cloying on the finish, and the pleasant, easy-drinking Dolcetto d'Alba Brusalino 2014 are well made.

● Barolo Bricco Rocca Riund Ris. '10	▼▼ 6
● Barbera d'Alba Sup. Parroco '13	▼▼ 3
● Barolo Bricco Luciani '12	▼▼ 6
● Barolo Perno '12	▼▼ 5
● Langhe Nebbiolo Monastero '12	▼▼ 3
○ Dolcetto d'Alba Sup. '13	▼ 2
● Barbera d'Alba Leprià '10	▽▽ 2*
● Barbera d'Alba Sup. Perno '12	▽▽ 3
● Barolo Bricco Luciani '11	▽▽ 6
● Barolo Bricco Luciani '10	▽▽ 6
● Barolo Bricco Luciani '09	▽▽ 5
● Barolo Bricco Rocca Riund Ris. '09	▽▽ 6
● Barolo Perno '11	▽▽ 5
● Barolo Perno '10	▽▽ 5
● Barolo Perno '09	▽▽ 5
● Barolo Riund Ris. '08	▽▽ 7

○ Moscato Spumante Tardivo '14	▼▼ 3*
○ Asti Spumante Bel Piasì '15	▼▼ 2*
● Dolcetto d'Alba Brusalino '14	▼▼ 2*
○ Moscato d'Asti Bel Piano '15	▼ 2
○ Umberto Extra Dry	▼ 4
○ Asti Spumante Bel Piasì '13	▽▽ 2*
○ Asti Spumante Bel Piasì '12	▽▽ 2*
● Barbaresco Bertola '12	▽▽ 5
● Barbaresco Bertola '10	▽▽ 5
○ Moscato d'Asti Bel Piano '14	▽▽ 2*
○ Moscato d'Asti Bel Piano '13	▽▽ 2*
○ Moscato Spumante Tardivo '12	▽▽ 3*
○ Moscato Spumante Tardivo '11	▽▽ 3

Cascina Fontana

LOC. PERNO
V.LO DELLA CHIESA, 2
12065 MONFORTE D'ALBA [CN]
TEL. +39 0173789005
www.cascinafontana.com

CELLAR SALES
PRE-BOOKED VISITS
ANNUAL PRODUCTION 25,000 bottles
HECTARES UNDER VINE 5.00
SUSTAINABLE WINERY

Mario Fontana, at 50, is a calm, optimistic man proud of having founded his own estate just over 20 years ago. His concept of wine is closely associated with naturalness and drinkability, leading him to shun intrusive oak, using concrete when necessary, and overly concentrated, muscular structure, in favour of meticulous attention to the grapes and the individual vintages. Since the 2012 vintage he has offered a single Barolo, made from the grapes of the vineyards in the municipalities of the Castiglione Falletto and La Morra, while a selection from the highly prized Villero cru is to be released soon. Pleasant notes of dried herbs mingle with hints of liquorice and raspberries in the remarkably complex, elegant Barolo 2012, whose classic palate vaunts glossy tannins and an impressively full, caressing finish, earning it our top accolade. The Barbera 2014 is lean, fresh, and close focused, while the Nebbiolo of the same vintage is complex and austere.

● Barolo '12	♥♥♥	6
● Barbera d'Alba '14	♥♥	3
● Langhe Nebbiolo '14	♥♥	4
● Dolcetto d'Alba '15	♥	2
● Barolo '10	♀♀♀	7
● Barbera d'Alba '13	♀♀	3
● Barbera d'Alba '12	♀♀	5
● Barbera d'Alba '11	♀♀	5
● Barbera d'Alba '09	♀♀	3
● Barolo '11	♀♀	6
● Barolo '09	♀♀	7
● Barolo '08	♀♀	7
● Dolcetto d'Alba '11	♀♀	3
● Langhe Nebbiolo '13	♀♀	4
● Langhe Nebbiolo '10	♀♀	4
● Langhe Nebbiolo '09	♀♀	3

Cascina Gilli

VIA NEVISSANO, 36
14022 CASTELNUOVO DON BOSCO [AT]
TEL. +39 0119876984
www.cascinagilli.it

CELLAR SALES
PRE-BOOKED VISITS
ACCOMMODATION
ANNUAL PRODUCTION 130,000 bottles
HECTARES UNDER VINE 17.00

Very few wineries offer a high-quality production from native grape varieties as traditional and uncommon as freisa and malvasia di Castelnuovo. Gianni Vergnano's Cascina Gilli offers several versions of Freisa, from semi-sparkling and still to vintage and wine for laying down, and malvasia di Castelnuovo, both still and sparkling, constituting a benchmark for the types and an authentic interpretation of the terroir. The estate also makes wines from barbera and bonarda. This year it was Barbera d'Asti Le More 2015 that stood out, with earthy notes and hints of dark fruit on the nose. The palate is dense and opulent, but not heavy, with fine-grained tannins and good acidity. Both Freisa d'Asti Il Forno 2014, with black pepper and tobacco on the nose, lifted by sensations of red fruit, and a long, austere palate with a bitterish finish, and the denser, fruit-forward Arvelé 2013 are excellent. The sweet Dlicà, from malvasia di Schierano grapes is well made.

● Barbera d'Asti Le More '15	♥♥	2*
● Dlicà	♥♥	3
● Freisa d'Asti Arvelé '13	♥♥	3
● Freisa d'Asti Il Forno '14	♥♥	2*
○ Piemonte Chardonnay Rafé '15	♥♥	2*
● Freisa d'Asti Frizzante Luna di Maggio '15	♥	2
● Piemonte Bonarda Sernù '14	♥	2
● Barbera d'Asti Le More '13	♀♀	2*
● Barbera d'Asti Le More '12	♀♀	2*
● Freisa d'Asti Arvelé	♀♀	3
● Malvasia di Castelnuovo Don Bosco '14	♀♀	2*
● Piemonte Bonarda Sernù '11	♀♀	2*

Cascina Giovinale

s.da San Nicolao, 102
14049 Nizza Monferrato [AT]
Tel. +39 0141793005
www.cascinagiovinale.it

CELLAR SALES
PRE-BOOKED VISITS
ANNUAL PRODUCTION 25,000 bottles
HECTARES UNDER VINE 7.00
SUSTAINABLE WINERY

Cascina Giovinale was founded in the early 1980s, the fruit of Bruno Ciocca and Anna Maria Solaini's passion for making quality wines with a strong sense of place. The vineyards, all on the San Nicolao hill, just outside Nizza Monferrato, lie on sandy limestone soil with a small amount of permeable clay. They are home to barbera, moscato, dolcetto, cortese, and cabernet sauvignon, with most of the vines planted between 1960 and 1970. The small estate presented only the two versions of Barbera d'Asti Superiore, both spectacular. Nizza Anssèma 2013 has a rich, concentrated nose of quinine, liquorice and black berries, and a full-flavoured palate with impressive structure and density that is nonetheless gutsy and nicely underpinned by acidity, resulting in a long, juicy finish. The 2012 vaunts a classic nose of plums and ripe cherries, accompanied by spicy notes on the succulent fresh palate that is balanced and very drinkable.

★★Cascina La Barbatella

s.da Annunziata, 55
14049 Nizza Monferrato [AT]
Tel. +39 0141701434
www.labarbatella.com

CELLAR SALES
PRE-BOOKED VISITS
ANNUAL PRODUCTION 25,000 bottles
HECTARES UNDER VINE 4.00

Consisting of a single plot of a few hectares around the farm in the hills above Nizza Monferrato, this long-standing estate is enthusiastically and competently run by the Perego family. The focus is on barbera, with vines over 70 years old, flanked by cabernet sauvignon, pinot nero, and less than half a hectare of the cortese and sauvignon white varieties. The flagship wines are modern, meticulously crafted interpretations of Barbera, both as a monovarietal and blended with international grape varieties. Barbera d'Asti Superiore Nizza La Vigna dell'Angelo 2013 has aromas of black cherries and rain-soaked earth with hints of quinine and liquorice, and a complex, juicy palate with great flesh and acidity, full flavour, and a very long finish. Monferrato Rosso Sonvico 2011, an equal blend of barbera and cabernet sauvignon, is also splendid, its fruity nose of currants and plums still showing traces of oak, and its dense, juicy palate vaunting splendid grip on a long, lingering finish.

- Barbera d'Asti Sup. '12 — ♙♙ 2*
- Barbera d'Asti Sup. Nizza Anssèma '13 — ♙♙ 3*
- Barbera d'Asti Sup. '11 — ♙♙ 2*
- Barbera d'Asti Sup. '10 — ♙♙ 2*
- Barbera d'Asti Sup. '09 — ♙♙ 2*
- Barbera d'Asti Sup. '07 — ♙♙ 2*
- Barbera d'Asti Sup. Nizza Anssèma '12 — ♙♙ 4
- Barbera d'Asti Sup. Nizza Anssèma '11 — ♙♙ 3
- Barbera d'Asti Sup. Nizza Anssèma '10 — ♙♙ 3*
- Barbera d'Asti Sup. Nizza Anssèma '09 — ♙♙ 3*
- Barbera d'Asti Sup. Nizza Anssèma '08 — ♙♙ 4
- Barbera d'Asti Sup. Nizza Anssèma '07 — ♙♙ 4
- Barbera d'Asti Sup. Nizza Anssèma '06 — ♙♙ 4*

- Barbera d'Asti Sup. Nizza V. dell'Angelo '13 — ♙♙ 5
- M.to Rosso Sonvico '11 — ♙♙ 6
- Barbera d'Asti La Barbatella '14 — ♙♙ 3
- M.to Rosso Ruanera '13 — ♙♙ 2*
- La Badessa Brut M. Cl. '12 — ♙ 4
- Barbera d'Asti Sup. Nizza V. dell'Angelo '11 — ♙♙♙ 5
- Barbera d'Asti Sup. Nizza V. dell'Angelo '07 — ♙♙♙ 5
- Barbera d'Asti Sup. Nizza V. dell'Angelo '01 — ♙♙♙ 5
- M.to Rosso Sonvico '09 — ♙♙♙ 6
- M.to Rosso Sonvico '06 — ♙♙♙ 5
- M.to Rosso Sonvico '04 — ♙♙♙ 5
- M.to Rosso Sonvico '03 — ♙♙♙ 5
- M.to Rosso Sonvico '10 — ♙♙ 6

Cascina Montagnola

S.DA MONTAGNOLA, 1
15058 VIGUZZOLO [AL]
TEL. +39 3480742701
www.cascinamontagnola.com

CELLAR SALES
PRE-BOOKED VISITS
ANNUAL PRODUCTION 30,000 bottles
HECTARES UNDER VINE 10.00

Over the years this estate has carved out a space for itself on the Tortona winegrowing scene. Production is monitored by oenologist Giovanni Bailo and is modern in style, but with carefully calibrated ageing in oak to avoid masking the characteristics deriving from the grape variety and the terroir. The range features around a dozen wines, mainly from the natives timorasso, cortese, barbera, and croatina, and the international chardonnay, sauvignon blanc, and merlot varieties. The range is nicely balanced, with the Morasso 2014 not yet fully expressed but displaying fine character and acidity, and the Margherita, from international grape varieties, boasting youth, power, and length, with still evident oak and lively tannins on the finish. The whites include the very well-made Cortese Dunin, with a nose of fresh herbs and mineral notes, followed by Sauvignon Blanc Alcesti and Chardonnay Risveglio.

Cascina Morassino

S.DA BERNINO, 10
12050 BARBARESCO [CN]
TEL. +39 0173635149
morassino@gmail.com

CELLAR SALES
PRE-BOOKED VISITS
ANNUAL PRODUCTION 20,000 bottles
HECTARES UNDER VINE 4.50
SUSTAINABLE WINERY

Cascina Morassino is a classic example of a family-run Langhe winery with a first-rate estate consisting of four hectares of well-tended vineyards and a couple of fabulous yet still little-known crus. It makes just two wines, dedicating artisanal care to the entire production process. Roberto Bianco, aided by his father Mauro, is a firm upholder of the traditional style, using carefully calibrated oak to craft precise, austere wines at very honest prices. Barbaresco Morassino 2013 possesses the magic of a great wine. Its concentrated, layered nose of fresh raspberries has close-focused notes of violets and liquorice, while the firmly-structured palate offers progressive, close-woven tannins, lively acidity, and a majestic long finish. Barbaresco Ovello 2013 has sensations of medicinal herbs and tobacco, on a background of fruit, accompanied by an austere palate with dry tannins and an underlying energy that promises very well for the coming years in bottle.

○ Colli Tortonesi Cortese Dunin '15	♥♥ 2*
○ Colli Tortonesi Timorasso Morasso '14	♥♥ 4
● Margherita	♥♥ 3
○ Alcesti '15	♥ 3
○ Risveglio '15	♥ 4
● Colli Tortonesi Barbera Amaranto '11	♀♀ 2*
● Colli Tortonesi Barbera Rodeo '10	♀♀ 5
● Colli Tortonesi Barbera Rodeo '09	♀♀ 5
○ Colli Tortonesi Cortese Dunin '12	♀♀ 2*
○ Colli Tortonesi Timorasso Derthona '10	♀♀ 3*
○ Colli Tortonesi Timorasso Morasso '13	♀♀ 4
○ Colli Tortonesi Timorasso Morasso '12	♀♀ 4
○ Colli Tortonesi Timorasso Morasso '11	♀♀ 4

● Barbaresco Morassino '13	♥♥ 5
● Barbaresco Ovello '13	♥♥ 6
● Barbaresco Morassino '09	♀♀♀ 5
● Barbaresco Morassino '12	♀♀ 5
● Barbaresco Morassino '11	♀♀ 5
● Barbaresco Morassino '10	♀♀ 5
● Barbaresco Morassino '08	♀♀ 5
● Barbaresco Ovello '12	♀♀ 6
● Barbaresco Ovello '11	♀♀ 6
● Barbera d'Alba Vignot '09	♀♀ 4
● Langhe Nebbiolo '09	♀♀ 3
● Langhe Rosso '09	♀♀ 4
● Langhe Rosso '08	♀♀ 4

Cascina Pellerino

LOC. SANT'ANNA, 93
12040 MONTEU ROERO [CN]
TEL. +39 0173978171
www.cascinapellerino.com

CELLAR SALES
PRE-BOOKED VISITS
ANNUAL PRODUCTION 50,000 bottles
HECTARES UNDER VINE 7.00
SUSTAINABLE WINERY

Cascina Pellerino, founded by the Bono family in 1980, has vineyards in several Roero municipalities, from Canale and Monteu Roero to Santo Stefano Roero and Vezza d'Alba. They are planted with the classic local grape varieties: arneis, nebbiolo, and barbera. In addition to the typical Roero wines, the range also includes a Metodo Classico from chardonnay, pinot nero, and arneis. The estate's wines are modern in style, offering good fruit and pleasant drinkability. It's a low-key year for Cristian Bono's estate in the absence of the flagship wines. Indeed, Barbera d'Alba Gran Madre 2014 was not produced due to the poor vintage and Roero Vigna del Padre Riserva 2013 was not bottled until the end of the summer, and so not in time for our tastings. In the meantime, our favourites were the Roero Vicot 2014, which is medium structured but juicy, with fine fruity flesh, nice balance, and elegant tannins, and the pleasant, fruity Barbera d'Alba Eleonora 2015.

● Barbera d'Alba Eleonora '15	♟♟ 3
● Roero Vicot '14	♟♟ 4
○ Langhe Favorita Caterina '15	♟ 3
○ Roero Arneis Atipico '15	♟ 3
○ Roero Arneis Boneur '15	♟ 3
● Barbera d'Alba Gran Madre '13	♟♟ 4
● Barbera d'Alba Gran Madre '12	♟♟ 4
● Barbera d'Alba Sup. Gran Madre '11	♟♟ 5
○ Roero Arneis Boneur '14	♟♟ 3
○ Roero Arneis Boneur '13	♟♟ 3
● Roero V. del Padre Ris. '12	♟♟ 5
● Roero V. del Padre Ris. '10	♟♟ 5
● Roero Vicot '13	♟♟ 4
● Roero Vigna del Padre Ris. '11	♟♟ 5

Cascina Salicetti

VIA CASCINA SALICETTI, 2
15050 MONTEGIOCO [AL]
TEL. +39 0131875192
www.cascinasalicetti.it

CELLAR SALES
PRE-BOOKED VISITS
ANNUAL PRODUCTION 25,000 bottles
HECTARES UNDER VINE 16.00

The Franzosi family's estate in Montegioco has been making wine for generations and is run today by oenologist Anselmo. This dynamic young man monitors the entire production chain in his hilltop realm consisting of winery surrounded by steeply sloping vineyards. His wines are full and powerful, expressing their terroir and the personality of their creator. They are almost exclusively from native grape varieties, with the exception of cabernet sauvignon, used alone in the intriguing Colli Tortonesi Rosso Il Seguito. Timorasso Ombra di Luna 2013 stole the show this year, with a nose and palate that nod to natural wines, before converging on a long, vibrant finish. Barbera Morganti 2013 has intense notes of red berries on the nose, followed by rather evident oak, and a long, concentrated palate ending in a slightly alcoholic finish. Colli Tortonesi Cortese Montarlino 2015 is worthy of note.

● Colli Tortonesi Barbera Morganti '13	♟♟ 4
○ Colli Tortonesi Timorasso Ombra di Luna '13	♟♟ 4
○ Colli Tortonesi Cortese Montarlino '15	♟ 4
● Colli Tortonesi Barbera Morganti '12	♟♟ 4
○ Colli Tortonesi Cortese Montarlino '14	♟♟ 4
○ Colli Tortonesi Cortese Montarlino '12	♟♟ 2*
● Colli Tortonesi Croatina Risulò '12	♟♟ 4
● Colli Tortonesi Dolcetto Di Marzi '12	♟♟ 2*
● Colli Tortonesi Rosso Il Seguito '12	♟♟ 2*
○ Colli Tortonesi Timorasso Ombra di Luna '12	♟♟ 4
○ Colli Tortonesi Timorasso Ombra di Luna '11	♟♟ 3*
○ Colli Tortonesi Timorasso Ombra di Luna '10	♟♟ 3
○ Colli Tortonesi Timorasso Principio '10	♟♟ 3

Cascina Val del Prete

S.DA SANTUARIO, 2
12040 PRIOCCA [CN]
TEL. +39 0173616534
www.valdelprete.com

CELLAR SALES
PRE-BOOKED VISITS
ANNUAL PRODUCTION 55,000 bottles
HECTARES UNDER VINE 11.00
VITICULTURE METHOD Certified Organic

Cascina Val del Prete is surrounded by a splendid amphitheatre of vineyards, considered by many a veritable cru. The estate was founded in 1977 by Bartolomeo and Carolina Roagna and has been managed since 1995 by their son Mario, who converted it to biodynamic principles in 2005. It grows the typical traditional Roero grape varieties: arneis, barbera, and nebbiolo, which it uses to craft an equally typical range of terroir-true wines. The Roero wines didn't perform as magnificently as in the past. They were headed by Roero Arneis Luèt 2015, with an alluring nose of aromatic herbs and tropical fruit and a firm, full palate with a pleasantly bitterish finish, and two versions of Barbera d'Alba. The Serra de' Gatti 2015 has a spicy nose of dark berries, good thrust, and length, while the Superiore Carolina 2014 is more marked by oak but full bodied and gutsy.

● Barbera d'Alba Serra de' Gatti '15	♟♟	3
● Barbera d'Alba Sup. Carolina '14	♟♟	5
○ Roero Arneis Luèt '15	♟♟	2*
● Roero Ris. '13	♟	5
● Roero V. di Lino '13	♟	5
● Nebbiolo d'Alba V. di Lino '00	♟♟♟	5
● Roero '04	♟♟♟	6
● Roero '03	♟♟♟	6
● Roero '01	♟♟♟	6
● Roero '00	♟♟♟	6
● Roero Bricco Medica '12	♟♟	3
● Roero Vigna di Lino '12	♟♟	4
● Roero Ris. '11	♟♟	5

Francesca Castaldi

VIA NOVEMBRE, 6
28072 BRIONA [NO]
TEL. +39 0321826045
www.cantinacastaldi.it

CELLAR SALES
PRE-BOOKED VISITS
ANNUAL PRODUCTION 10,000 bottles
HECTARES UNDER VINE 6.30

Francesca Castaldi and her brother Giuseppe could be defined the guardians of Fara, in light of their work in promoting the tiny Novara designation. Their small estate lies on the morainic hills of Briona, at the southern tip of the area, between Pianazze, Val Ceresole, and Belvedere. It covers an area of around six hectares, replanted to nebbiolo, vespolina, uva rara, and erbaluce in 1997 and tended with organic methods. The traditional grape varieties are expressed in a commanding range that is highly recommended to those seeking bright, food-friendly wines focusing more on progression than weight. The 2015 vintage shows the multifaceted personality of the range, from the fat, spicy Bianco Lucia with notes of grape skin, to the austere, dynamic fragrance of Rosato Rosa Alba, and the rustic exuberance of Vespolina Nina. Frara 2012 is more sophisticated, offering tobacco and quinine, and almost no discernible fruit on the lean palate, which is still settling.

● Fara '12	♟♟	5
○ Colline Novaresi Bianco Lucia '15	♟♟	3
⊙ Colline Novaresi Rosato Rosa Alba '15	♟♟	3
● Colline Novaresi Vespolina Nina '15	♟♟	3
● Colline Novaresi Barbera Martina '13	♟	3
● Colline Novaresi Nebbiolo Bigin '13	♟	3
● Colline Novaresi Nebbiolo Bigin '12	♟♟	3
● Colline Novaresi Nebbiolo Bigin '12	♟♟	3
● Colline Novaresi Vespolina Nina '13	♟♟	3
● Colline Novaresi Vespolina Nina '12	♟♟	3
● Crepuscolo	♟♟	4
● Fara '11	♟♟	5
● Fara '10	♟♟	5
● Fara '09	♟♟	5

Castellari Bergaglio

FRAZ. ROVERETO, 136R
15066 GAVI [AL]
TEL. +39 0143644000
www.castellaribergaglio.it

CELLAR SALES
PRE-BOOKED VISITS
ANNUAL PRODUCTION 90,000 bottles
HECTARES UNDER VINE 11.00

The latest generations at the helm of this long-standing Gavi winery are represented by Mario Bergaglio, active mainly in the vineyard, and his son Marco, who runs the cellar and commercial operations. Together they produce a range entirely dedicated to cortese, from approximately ten hectares of vineyards. It is used for seven different wines: the basic Salluvii; Fornaci and Rolona, which showcase the differences in soil and aspect of the vineyards in Tassarolo and Gavi; Rovereto, which is cold macerated; and Pilin, from the oldest vineyard, which is late-harvested and then aged in oak. There are also the Metodo Classico Ardé and the passito Gavium. The very diverse personalities of Castellari Bergaglio's Gavis were once again revealed in this year's tastings. Rovereto Vignavecchia 2013 is characterized by sweet, spicy sensations, while Rolona 2015 has a long, racy profile, and the stunning Fornaci 2015 is illuminated by the typical salty power of Tassarolo.

○ Gavi del Comune di Tassarolo Fornaci '15	♟♟ 2*
○ Gavi del Comune di Gavi Rovereto Vignavecchia '13	♟♟ 3
○ Gavi del Comune di Gavi Pilin '13	♟ 5
○ Gavi del Comune di Gavi Rolona '15	♟ 3
○ Gavi del Comune di Gavi Rolona '13	♟♟ 3*
○ Gavi del Comune di Gavi Rolona '12	♟♟ 3
○ Gavi del Comune di Gavi Rovereto Vignavecchia '12	♟♟ 3*
○ Gavi del Comune di Tassarolo Fornaci '14	♟♟ 2*
○ Gavi Fornaci '13	♟♟ 2*
○ Gavi Pilin '12	♟♟ 5
○ Gavi Salluvii '14	♟♟ 2*
○ Gavi Salluvii '13	♟♟ 2*
○ Gavi Salluvii '12	♟♟ 2*

Castello di Gabiano

VIA SAN DEFENDENTE, 2
15020 GABIANO [AL]
TEL. +39 0142945004
www.castellodigabiano.com

CELLAR SALES
PRE-BOOKED VISITS
ACCOMMODATION AND RESTAURANT SERVICE
ANNUAL PRODUCTION 120,000 bottles
HECTARES UNDER VINE 21.00

Today the splendid home of the Marchesi Cattaneo Adorno Giustiniani is also a popular tourist attraction, not only for its historical and scenic charm, but also for its gourmet food and wine. The fascinating experience is further enhanced by the elegant suites and apartments in the village next to the castle and by the restaurant housed in the old vinegar house. The estate's products also play a leading role, with a range of about ten labels featuring reds from barbera, freisa, grignolino, and pinot nero, and whites from chardonnay and sauvignon blanc. The standard-bearer of the DOC zone, Gabiano Riserva has a full, well-orchestrated nose and a powerful palate with a very long finish. It is closely followed by the elegant, spicy Grignolino Il Ruvo. Adornes 2011 has a nose of tobacco and quinine on a still fruity background, accompanied by a fresh, potent palate with a lingering finish. Gavius, Rubino di Cantavena, and La Braja are all well made.

● Gabiano A Matilde Giustiniani Ris. '10	♟♟ 6
● Barbera d'Asti La Braja '14	♟♟ 2*
● Barbera d'Asti Sup. Adornes '11	♟♟ 6
● Grignolino del M.to Casalese Il Ruvo '15	♟♟ 2*
● M.to Rosso Gavius '14	♟♟ 3
● Rubino di Cantavenna '14	♟♟ 3
○ M.to Bianco Corte '15	♟ 3
● Piemonte Chardonnay Castello '14	♟ 6
● Barbera d'Asti Sup. Adornes '10	♟♟ 5
● Barbera d'Asti Sup. Adornes '07	♟♟ 5*
● Gabiano Matilde Giustiniani Ris. '08	♟♟ 6
● Grignolino del M.to Casalese Il Ruvo '13	♟♟ 2*
○ M.to Bianco Corte '14	♟♟ 3
○ M.to Chiaretto Castelvere '14	♟♟ 2*
● M.to Rosso Gavius '12	♟♟ 3*
○ Piemonte Chardonnay Castello '13	♟♟ 5

Castello di Neive

c.so Romano Scagliola, 205
12052 Neive [CN]
Tél. +39 017367171
www.castellodineive.it

PRE-BOOKED VISITS
ANNUAL PRODUCTION 170,000 bottles
HECTARES UNDER VINE 26.00
SUSTAINABLE WINERY

A large, modern cellar for the production of wines from nebbiolo was added a few years ago, but the headquarters of the Stupino family are still housed in the historic castle after which the winery is named, and which houses the stunning barrel cellar. It receives the grapes from approximately 30 hectares of vineyards, all in Neive. Basarin, Cortini, Gallina, Marcorino, and Valtorta, are among the prized plots interpreted in a range completed by wines from barbera, dolcetto, pinot nero, grignolino, and riesling. The jewel in the crown is constituted by the Barbarescos from the Santo Stefano cru, also available as Riservas in the best vintages. The range features many fine wines, but the estate's flagship remains the Albesani Santo Stefano Riserva, which is magnificent even in a complicated vintage like 2011. Offering notes of blueberries, tobacco, and tar, it shows excellent progression, huge character, and velvety tannins on the complex, powerful palate.

Castello di Razzano

fraz. Casarello
via San Carlo, 2
15021 Alfiano Natta [AL]
Tel. +39 0141922124
www.castellodirazzano.it

CELLAR SALES
PRE-BOOKED VISITS
ACCOMMODATION
ANNUAL PRODUCTION 200,000 bottles
HECTARES UNDER VINE 30.00

The hamlet of Casarello lies on the main road between Alfiano Natta and Cardona, where the winery stands at the junction with Via San Carlo. It is the focus of all the estate's vinification, bottling and cellaring operations. The flagship wines are aged in oak barrels in the castle's cellars. Barbera d'Asti accounts for the lion's share of the production, with five versions, four of which Superiore. Grignolino, ruché, moscato d'Asti, merlot, pinot nero, sauvignon blanc, and chardonnay are the other varietals used. A single Barbera Superiore was presented this year, as the others are still ageing and will be tasted in the forthcoming editions of our Guide. Valentino Caligaris is simply splendid in every respect, from its impenetrable ruby hue and nose of plums, coffee, and chocolate, to its extraordinarily concentrated palate with fabulous tannic weave.

● Barbaresco Albesani S. Stefano Ris. '11	▼▼▼ 8
● Barbaresco Albesani S. Stefano '13	▼▼ 6
● Barbaresco Gallina '13	▼▼ 6
● Barbera d'Alba Sup. '13	▼▼ 5
● Dolcetto d'Alba V. Basarin '15	▼▼ 4
○ Langhe Arneis Montebertotto '15	▼▼ 3
● Langhe Pinot Nero I Cortini '15	▼ 5
● Piemonte Albarossa '13	▼▼ 5
○ Piemonte Pinot Nero Brut M. Cl. '12	▼▼ 5
● Barbera d'Alba V. S. Stefano '14	▼ 4
● Barbaresco Albesani S. Stefano '12	▽▽▽ 6
● Barbaresco S. Stefano Ris. '01	▽▽▽ 7
● Barbaresco S. Stefano Ris. '99	▽▽▽ 7
● Barbaresco '12	▽▽ 5

● Barbera d'Asti Sup. Valentino Caligaris '11	▼▼ 5
● Barbera d'Asti La Leona '15	▼▼ 2*
○ Costa al Sole '15	▼▼ 2*
● Grignolino del M.to Casalese Pianaccio '15	▼ 2
● Barbera d'Asti Sup. Campasso '07	▽▽ 2*
● Barbera d'Asti Sup. Campasso '06	▽▽ 2*
● Barbera d'Asti Sup. Del Beneficio '09	▽▽ 4
● Barbera d'Asti Sup. Eugenea '11	▽▽ 4
● Barbera d'Asti Sup. Eugenea '09	▽▽ 4
● Barbera d'Asti Sup. Eugenea '06	▽▽ 3*
● Barbera d'Asti Sup. Eugenea '05	▽▽ 3*
● Barbera d'Asti Sup. V. Valentino Caligaris '05	▽▽ 5
● Barbera d'Asti Sup. V. Valentino Caligaris '04	▽▽ 5

Castello di Tassarolo

CASCINA ALBORINA, 1
15060 TASSAROLO [AL]
TEL. +39 0143342248
www.castelloditassarolo.it

CELLAR SALES
PRE-BOOKED VISITS
ANNUAL PRODUCTION 130,000 bottles
HECTARES UNDER VINE 20.00
VITICULTURE METHOD Certified Organic
SUSTAINABLE WINERY

The Marchesi Spinola have owned Castello di Tassarolo for over seven centuries. Their 20 hectares of vineyards have been tended with organic methods for several years now. This decision was taken with great conviction by Bonifacio and his sister Massimiliana, aided by Vincenzo Muni and Henry Finzi-Constantine, during the restyling process that has also involved the production of experimental wines without added sulphites, like Monferrato Rosso, from barbera and cabernet sauvignon, and Barbera Titouan. However, the mainstay of the range has always been the cortese whites: Spinola, Il Castello, Titouan, Alborina, and most recently the Sparkling. Castello di Tassarolo's well-assorted range performed well. Spinola del Comune di Tassarolo stands out among the 2015 Gavis for its classic style, flesh, and backbone, with notes of moss and flint punctuating the nose. Alborina 2014 is at a far more controversial stage, showing tightly clenched but vigorous and linear.

Castello di Uviglie

VIA CASTELLO DI UVIGLIE, 73
15030 ROSIGNANO MONFERRATO [AL]
TEL. +39 0142488132
www.castellodiuviglie.com

CELLAR SALES
PRE-BOOKED VISITS
ANNUAL PRODUCTION 90,000 bottles
HECTARES UNDER VINE 25.00

Simone Lupano took over the winery in the 1980s and has worked hard and competently to transform it into the fine estate it is today, characterized by the high quality of its wines, even the basic range, and its important historical setting in Castello di Uviglie. He also takes the credit for some of the brave choices made over the years, focusing on boosting the quality of production and investing in unusual wines for Monferrato Casalese, such as the 1491 Barbera in albarossa, as well as the Metodo Classico sparkler and the passito from international grape varieties. The mighty range commences with the all-round fantastic Pico Gonzaga, whose nose of tobacco, spice, and liquorice heralds a complexity that is transformed into elegance and harmony on the palate. San Bastiano Terre Bianche surprised us with a stunningly elegant, well-typed nose, followed by a rich, powerful palate, with an elegant, lingering finish.

○ Gavi del Comune di Tassarolo Spinola '15	🏆🏆 2*
○ Gavi del Comune di Tassarolo Alborina '14	🏆 3
○ Gavi del Comune di Tassarolo Spinola No Solfiti '15	🏆 2
○ Gavi Il Castello '15	🏆 3
● Piemonte Barbera Titouan '14	🏆 3
○ Gavi del Comune di Tassarolo Alborina '13	🏆🏆 3
○ Gavi del Comune di Tassarolo Alborina '13	🏆🏆 3*
○ Gavi del Comune di Tassarolo Il Castello '14	🏆🏆 2*
○ Gavi del Comune di Tassarolo Il Castello '13	🏆🏆 2*
○ Gavi del Comune di Tassarolo Il Castello '12	🏆🏆 2*
○ Gavi del Comune di Tassarolo Spinola '13	🏆🏆 2*
○ Gavi del Comune di Tassarolo Spinola '12	🏆🏆 2*
○ Gavi del Comune di Tassarolo Titouan '13	🏆🏆 3

● Barbera del M.to Sup. Pico Gonzaga '13	🏆🏆🏆 5
● Grignolino del M.to Casalese San Bastiano Terre Bianche '12	🏆🏆 5
● Barbera del M.to Bricco del Conte '15	🏆🏆 2*
● Barbera del M.to Sup. Le Cave '14	🏆🏆 3
● Grignolino del M.to Casalese San Bastiano '15	🏆🏆 2*
○ Le Cave Extra Brut M. Cl. '12	🏆🏆 5
○ M.to Bianco San Martino '15	🏆🏆 2*
● M.to Rosso 1491 '13	🏆🏆 5
● Barbera del M.to Sup. Le Cave '13	🏆🏆🏆 3*
● Barbera del M.to Sup. Le Cave '09	🏆🏆🏆 3*
● Barbera del M.to Sup. Le Cave '07	🏆🏆🏆 3*
● Barbera del M.to Sup. Pico Gonzaga '07	🏆🏆🏆 4*
● Barbera del M.to Sup. Pico Gonzaga '12	🏆🏆 5
● Grignolino del M.to Casalese San Bastiano Terre Bianche '11	🏆🏆 5

Castello di Verduno

VIA UMBERTO I, 9
12060 VERDUNO [CN]
TEL. +39 0172470284
www.castellodiverduno.com

CELLAR SALES
PRE-BOOKED VISITS
ACCOMMODATION AND RESTAURANT SERVICE
ANNUAL PRODUCTION 68,000 bottles
HECTARES UNDER VINE 10.00
SUSTAINABLE WINERY

The evocative power of Castello di Verduno
is immediately evident, even to least
attentive eye. It derives not only from its
long history and production, but above all
from the sensation of harmony and peace
that pervades the enterprise headed by
Gabriella Burlotto and her husband Franco
Bianco. The whole range is very sound, but
the wines from pelaverga and nebbiolo
emanate the distinctive genius loci,
expressed in the versatile and spontaneous
style of the finest interpretations. This is
particularly true of the Barolo crus from
Massara and Monvigliero in Verduno and
the Barbarescos from Faset and Rabajà, all
aged in large barrels. This year the contest
between Castello di Verduno's top Nebbiolos
was fiercer than ever. Barolo Massara 2012
has a very convincing powerful, silky palate,
while the Monvigliero Riserva 2010 focuses
more on the contrasts between its graceful
nose and dry finish. Barbaresco Rabajà
Riserva 2011 offers balsamic vigour and a
balanced palate.

● Barbaresco Rabajà '13	♙♙ 6
● Barbaresco Rabajà Ris. '11	♙♙ 7
● Barolo Monvigliero Ris. '10	♙♙ 7
● Barbaresco '13	♙♙ 5
● Barbera d'Alba Bricco del Cuculo '14	♙♙ 4
● Barolo Massara '12	♙♙ 6
● Verduno Basadone '15	♙♙ 3
● Barbera d'Alba '15	♙ 3
● Langhe Nebbiolo '15	♙ 3
● Barbaresco Rabajà '04	♙♙♙ 6
● Barolo Massara '08	♙♙♙ 6
● Barolo Massara '01	♙♙♙ 6
● Barolo Monvigliero Ris. '08	♙♙♙ 7
● Barolo Monvigliero Ris. '04	♙♙♙ 7
● Barbaresco Rabajà '11	♙♙ 6
● Verduno Pelaverga Basadone '14	♙♙ 3

La Caudrina

S.DA BROSIA, 21
12053 CASTIGLIONE TINELLA [CN]
TEL. +39 0141855126
www.caudrina.it

CELLAR SALES
PRE-BOOKED VISITS
ANNUAL PRODUCTION 200,000 bottles
HECTARES UNDER VINE 24.00

The average age of the Dogliotti family's
vineyards at La Caudrina is over 40 years
old. Production focuses mainly on Moscato,
from grapes grown on mainly chalky
limestone soils in the municipality of
Castiglione Tinella, while the vineyards in
Nizza Monferrato are planted to barbera,
nebbiolo, and dolcetto, and those in Ottiglio
Monferrato to chardonnay. The wines are
distinguished by great aromatic focus.
Moscatos account for the lion's share.
Moscato d'Asti La Caudrina 2015 has fresh,
elegant nose of sage and peaches, with
tropical fruit and peppermint, followed by a
full-bodied palate with good residual sugar
balanced by vibrant acidity. Moscato d'Asti
La Galeisa 2015 has a beautifully long, full
nose of ripe and candied fruit with top notes
of sage and a soft, caressing palate.

○ Asti La Selvatica	♙♙ 3
○ Moscato d'Asti La Caudrina '15	♙♙ 3
○ Moscato d'Asti La Galeisa '15	♙♙ 3
● Barbera d'Asti La Solista '14	♙ 2
○ Lunatica Brut	♙ 4
○ Asti La Selvatica '12	♙♙ 3
● Barbera d'Asti La Solista '12	♙♙ 2*
● Barbera d'Asti La Solista '11	♙♙ 2*
● Barbera d'Asti Sup. Monte Venere '10	♙♙ 3
○ Moscato d'Asti '13	♙♙ 3*
○ Moscato d'Asti La Caudrina '11	♙♙ 3
○ Moscato d'Asti La Galeisa '12	♙♙ 3
○ Piemonte Moscato Passito Redento '11	♙♙ 4

★Cavallotto
Tenuta Bricco Boschis

LOC. BRICCO BOSCHIS
VIA ALBA-MONFORTE
12060 CASTIGLIONE FALLETTO [CN]
TEL. +39 017362814
www.cavallotto.com

CELLAR SALES
PRE-BOOKED VISITS
ANNUAL PRODUCTION 110,000 bottles
HECTARES UNDER VINE 25.00
VITICULTURE METHOD Certified Organic

Siblings Alfio, Giuseppe, and Laura Cavallotto have managed the difficult task of holding together a brand over ten years old with a very fresh, young, up-to-date image. They represent the latest generation at work at Tenuta Bricco Boschis in Castiglione Falletto, a single plot covering around 25 hectares tended with organic methods. The finest slopes are obviously home to nebbiolo for the Barolos: San Giuseppe and Vignolo, also released as a Riserva in the best vintages, fermented in roto-macerator tanks and aged in large barrels. Barbera, dolcetto, freisa, grignolino, pinot nero and chardonnay complete the range. The range of Barolos is impressive, topped by the Tre-Bicchieri-winning Bricco Boschis 2012, which is an excellent demonstration of the vintage's potential. It is out-and-out classic in style, vaunting a nose of raspberries and wild strawberries, with hints of tar and liquorice, and an austere but beautifully fleshy palate. Don't miss the 2013 vintage of Barbera Vigna del Cuculo 2013, which is one of the best ever.

● Barolo Bricco Boschis '12	♟♟♟ 8
● Barbera d'Alba Sup. V. del Cuculo '13	♟♟ 5
● Barolo Bricco Boschis V. San Giuseppe Ris. '10	♟♟ 8
● Barolo Vignolo Ris. '10	♟♟ 8
● Langhe Nebbiolo '14	♟♟ 5
● Dolcetto d'Alba V. Scot '15	♟ 3
● Barolo Bricco Boschis '05	♟♟♟ 6
● Barolo Bricco Boschis '04	♟♟♟ 7
● Barolo Bricco Boschis V. S. Giuseppe Ris. '05	♟♟♟ 8
● Barolo Vignolo Ris. '06	♟♟♟ 8
● Barolo Vignolo Ris. '04	♟♟♟ 8
● Barolo Bricco Boschis V. S. Giuseppe Ris. '09	♟♟ 8
● Barolo Vignolo Ris. '09	♟♟ 8

Ceretto

LOC. SAN CASSIANO, 34
12051 ALBA [CN]
TEL. +39 0173282582
www.ceretto.com

CELLAR SALES
PRE-BOOKED VISITS
ACCOMMODATION
ANNUAL PRODUCTION 900,000 bottles
HECTARES UNDER VINE 105.00
VITICULTURE METHOD Certified Organic
SUSTAINABLE WINERY

The conversion of the entire Ceretto estate to biodynamic methods represents one of the biggest new developments in recent years for the Piedmont wine world. It concerns not only the highly prized plots in the Barolo and Barbaresco production zones, commencing with Bricco Rocche and Bricco Asili, but also the Asti estates dedicated mainly to moscato, and the Roero properties famous for Arneis Blangé and other more innovative wines. This complete makeover is reflected in the style of an increasingly contemporary range, in which the technical details of fermentation and ageing definitely take a back seat. Further confirmation comes from the fantastic pair of 2013 Barbarescos. The Asili perfectly embodies the finesse, complexity and energy universally associated with this grand cru, while the Bernadot offers a lively nose of fresh fruit and medicinal herbs, and spirited, racy progression to compensate for less stuffing. The 2012 Barolos are sound although less vivacious.

● Barbaresco Asili '13	♟♟♟ 8
● Barbaresco Bernardot '13	♟♟ 8
● Barbera d'Alba Piana '15	♟♟ 4
● Barolo '12	♟♟ 6
● Barolo Bricco Rocche '12	♟♟ 8
● Barolo Brunate '12	♟♟ 8
● Langhe Rosso Monsordo '14	♟♟ 4
● Nebbiolo d'Alba Bernardina '15	♟♟ 5
● Dolcetto d'Alba Rossana '15	♟ 3
○ Langhe Bianco Monsordo '15	♟ 5
● Barbaresco Asij '97	♟♟♟ 5
● Barolo Bricco Rocche '11	♟♟♟ 8
● Barolo Bricco Rocche '09	♟♟♟ 8
● Barolo Bricco Rocche '00	♟♟♟ 8
● Barolo Prapò '06	♟♟♟ 8
● Barolo Prapò '05	♟♟♟ 8

★★Michele Chiarlo

S.DA NIZZA-CANELLI, 99
14042 CALAMANDRANA [AT]
TEL. +39 0141769030
www.chiarlo.it

CELLAR SALES
PRE-BOOKED VISITS
ACCOMMODATION
ANNUAL PRODUCTION 1,100,000 bottles
HECTARES UNDER VINE 120.00
SUSTAINABLE WINERY

The Chiarlo family have managed to create a successful and very solid estate that has been among the best known and esteemed in the province of Asti for over 50 years. Its vineyards in Monferrato, Langhe, and the Gavi zone, allow the winery to offer the most important Piedmont designations. It stands out for its ability to offer such a wide range, from different areas, with very high quality and consistency. This year the full, juicy Barbera d'Asti Superiore Nizza La Court 2013 took a Tre Bicchieri, brimming with fruit and with nice supporting acidity on a long, flavoursome palate. Barolo Cerequio 2012 is also excellent, with notes of quinine, tobacco, and liquorice underpinned by deep, sound fruit, as are Barolo Cannubi 2012, offering raspberries and aromatic herbs and progressive, close-woven tannins, and Barbera d'Asti Superiore Nizza Vignaveja 2011,which has great character and depth.

● Barbera d'Asti Sup. Nizza La Court '13	♟♟♟	5
● Barbera d'Asti Sup. Nizza VignaVeja '11	♟♟	5
● Barolo Cannubi '12	♟♟	7
● Barolo Cerequio '12	♟♟	7
● Barbaresco Reyna '13	♟♟	5
● Barbera d'Asti Sup. Nizza Cipressi '14	♟♟	3
● Barolo Tortoniano '12	♟♟	5
○ Gavi del Comune di Gavi Rovereto '15	♟	3
○ Moscato d'Asti Nivole '15	♟	2
● Piemonte Albarossa MonTald '13	♟	3
● Barbera d'Asti Sup. Nizza La Court '12	♟♟♟	5
● Barolo Cerequio '10	♟♟♟	7
● Barolo Cerequio '09	♟♟♟	7

Chionetti

B.TA VALDIBERTI, 44
12063 DOGLIANI [CN]
TEL. +39 017371179
www.chionettiquinto.com

CELLAR SALES
PRE-BOOKED VISITS
ANNUAL PRODUCTION 83,000 bottles
HECTARES UNDER VINE 15.00
VITICULTURE METHOD Certified Organic

The estate owned by Quinto Chionetti, universally recognized as one of the leading winemakers not just in Dogliani but in Langhe, confidently continues to expand its range focusing on dolcetto grapes, used to make the famous Briccolero and San Luigi. However, there have been some new developments under the management of his grandson Nicola, commencing with La Costa, a small selection of Dolcetto di Dogliani aged for a year in large barrels. Next will be a Barolo, thanks to the recent purchase of a vineyard on the prized Pianpolvere site in Monforte d'Alba. The heavyweight Dogliani Briccolero is concentrated and tannic, characterized by a nose of juniper and dark berries, and destined to improve further in bottle. The San Luigi of the same vintage is currently more balanced and elegant, with fine acidity that makes it delightfully drinkable. Langhe Nebbiolo La Chiusa 2014 has a nose of raspberries and pennyroyal, followed by a taut, clenched palate.

● Dogliani Briccolero '15	♟♟	3*
● Dogliani San Luigi '15	♟♟	3*
● Langhe Nebbiolo La Chiusa '14	♟♟	4
● Dolcetto di Dogliani Briccolero '07	♟♟♟	3*
● Dolcetto di Dogliani Briccolero '04	♟♟♟	3*
● Dogliani Briccolero '14	♟♟	3
● Dogliani Briccolero '13	♟♟	3
● Dogliani Briccolero '12	♟♟	3*
● Dogliani Briccolero '11	♟♟	3*
● Dogliani La Costa '13	♟♟	4
● Dogliani S. Luigi '12	♟♟	3
● Dogliani S. Luigi '11	♟♟	3*
● Dogliani San Luigi '13	♟♟	3
● Dolcetto di Dogliani Briccolero '09	♟♟	3*
● Langhe Nebbiolo '13	♟♟	3
● Langhe Nebbiolo La Chiusa '13	♟♟	4

Cieck

CASCINA CASTAGNOLA, 2
10090 SAN GIORGIO CANAVESE [TO]
TEL. +39 0124330522
www.cieck.it

CELLAR SALES
PRE-BOOKED VISITS
ANNUAL PRODUCTION 80,000 bottles
HECTARES UNDER VINE 13.00

Named after the eponymous farm in the
hamlet of San Grato di Aglié, Cieck is one
of the legendary names of the Canavese
district, with over 30 vintages behind it.
Headed today by Remo Falconieri and
Domenico Caretto, it is renowned above all
for its wines from erbaluce, produced in all
possible versions, from the sparkling
Calliope and San Giorgio to the Alladium
passito, plus the better-known still dry
wines. The basic Erbaluce di Caluso and
the Misobolo are fermented in steel, while
the T selection is aged in oak, and then in
bottle for six months before its release.
Nebbiolo, freisa and barbera are the other
grape varieties used. The estate confirms
its talent for sparkling wines with very
sound results across the board. Calliope
Brut 2013 has classic yeasty, bready notes
on the nose, and a dense, firmly structured
palate enlivened by carefully calibrated
acidity. Among the still whites, the Misobolo
is as sound as ever. The Nebbiolo is also
good, with the 2014 vintage offering
elegant aromas of raspberries and gentian.

○ Erbaluce di Caluso Brut Calliope M. Cl. '13	▼▼ 4
● Canavese Nebbiolo '14	▼▼ 3
⊙ Cieck Rosé Brut M.Cl.	▼▼ 3
○ Erbaluce di Caluso Brut San Giorgio '13	▼▼ 4
○ Erbaluce di Caluso Misobolo '15	▼▼ 3
○ Erbaluce di Caluso '15	▼ 2
○ Erbaluce di Caluso Passito Alladium '06	♈♈ 5
○ Erbaluce di Caluso Calliope Brut '10	♈♈ 4
○ Erbaluce di Caluso Misobolo '14	♈♈ 2*
○ Erbaluce di Caluso Misobolo '13	♈♈ 2*
○ Erbaluce di Caluso Passito Alladium '08	♈♈ 5
○ Erbaluce di Caluso T '13	♈♈ 3*
○ Erbaluce di Caluso T '12	♈♈ 3

★F.lli Cigliuti

VIA SERRABOELLA, 17
12052 NEIVE [CN]
TEL. +39 0173677185
www.cigliuti.it

CELLAR SALES
PRE-BOOKED VISITS
ANNUAL PRODUCTION 30,000 bottles
HECTARES UNDER VINE 7.50

Following a few mixed years, the fine
estate founded by the Cigliuti family over
half a century ago seems to have returned
to the glories of the turn of the millennium.
Today the founding brothers Leone and
Romualdo have been succeeded by
Renato, aided by his wife Dina and their
daughters Claudia and Silvia. They tend
approximately seven hectares of vineyards
in Neive, which form the basis for a small
but highly distinctive range of traditional
Langhe wines. Sometimes rather
unapproachable in their youth, the top
wines of Barbaresco, Dolcetto and Barbera
are from the Serraboella vineyard, and the
Bricco di Neive cru for Barbaresco Via Erte
and Langhe Nebbiolo. Barbaresco
Serraboella 2012 has an extraordinarily
delicate, well-defined nose, with sweet
tobacco and rhubarb mingling with fresh
raspberries, and a rather austere,
satisfying long palate. The Vie Erte of the
same vintage is equally good, with a
slightly more mature nose and an
unusually powerful, harmonious palate.

● Barbaresco Serraboella '12	▼▼ 8
● Barbaresco Vie Erte '12	▼▼ 6
● Barbera d'Alba Campass '13	▼▼ 5
● Barbaresco Serraboella '10	♈♈♈ 7
● Barbaresco Serraboella '09	♈♈♈ 7
● Barbaresco Serraboella '01	♈♈♈ 6
● Barbaresco Serraboella '00	♈♈♈ 6
● Barbaresco V. Erte '04	♈♈♈ 6
● Barbaresco Vie Erte '11	♈♈ 5
● Barbaresco Vie Erte '10	♈♈ 5
● Barbaresco Vie Erte '09	♈♈ 5
● Barbera d'Alba Campass '12	♈♈ 4
● Barbera d'Alba Campass '10	♈♈ 4

★Tenute Cisa Asinari dei Marchesi di Grésy

S.DA DELLA STAZIONE, 21
12050 BARBARESCO [CN]
TEL. +39 0173635222
www.marchesidigresy.com

CELLAR SALES
PRE-BOOKED VISITS
ANNUAL PRODUCTION 200,000 bottles
HECTARES UNDER VINE 35.00
SUSTAINABLE WINERY

The headquarters of Tenute Cisa Asinari, headed by Alberto de Grésy, have been situated on the slopes of the splendid Martinenga hill in Barbaresco for over 40 years, where the 12-hectare single plot yields the winery's most important and renowned nebbiolo reds: Camp Gros and Gauin. While they undergo relatively short maceration and ageing mainly in small oak casks, their finesse and cellarability set them apart from modern-style stereotypes. The winery also owns the La Serra and Monte Colombo estates in Cassine, in Monferrato, planted chiefly to moscato, barbera, and merlot, and Monte Aribaldo in Treiso, where dolcetto, chardonnay, and sauvignon are grown. Barbaresco Martinenga Gajun 2012 vaunts an exceptionally refined nose, with hints of cocoa powder and golden-leaf tobacco against a lovely background of dried roses, and a wonderfully balanced palate with elegant, mouthfilling tannins. The denser, more austere Riserva Camp Gros 2011 is destined to improve with bottle ageing. Villa Martis 2013, from nebbiolo and barbera, is enchantingly elegant.

● Barbaresco Camp Gros Martinenga Ris. '11	♥♥ 8
● Barbaresco Martinenga Gaiun '12	♥♥ 8
● Langhe Rosso Villa Martis '13	♥♥ 3*
● Barbaresco Martinenga '13	♥♥ 7
● Dolcetto d'Alba Monte Aribaldo '15	♥♥ 3
○ Langhe Bianco Villa Giulia '15	♥♥ 3
○ Langhe Chardonnay '15	♥♥ 3
● Langhe Nebbiolo Martinenga '15	♥♥ 4
○ Langhe Sauvignon '15	♥♥ 3
○ Moscato d'Asti '15	♥♥ 3
● Barbaresco Camp Gros '06	♥♥♥ 8
● Barbaresco Camp Gros Martinenga '09	♥♥♥ 8
● Barbaresco Camp Gros Martinenga '08	♥♥♥ 8

★★Domenico Clerico

LOC. MANZONI, 67
12065 MONFORTE D'ALBA [CN]
TEL. +39 017378171
www.domenicoclerico.com

PRE-BOOKED VISITS
ANNUAL PRODUCTION 110,000 bottles
HECTARES UNDER VINE 21.00

Domenico Clerico's hands tell the tale of his decades of work better than any technical description. This great vigneron, in the truest sense of the word, is universally loved for his contagious good humour, which he combines with a rare sense of hospitality. Not to mention his ability to channel the qualities of veritable grand crus like Ginestra and Mosconi in Monforte, in the Ciabot Mentin Ginestra, Pajana, and Percristina Barolo vineyard selections, and Briccotto and Aeroplanservaj in Serralunga. Long interpreted in a modern style, with ageing in small oak casks, a progressive restyling is evident in the latest vintages. In our tastings the highest scorers were the 2011 Barolos Pajana and Ciabot Mentin. The first is particularly youthful and fruity, with a strikingly potent palate, while the second has a more open nose of ripe red berries and a palate with commendable lively acidity. The Percristina, emerging from the cellar after ten years of ageing, has not lost its modern personality of spice and oak.

● Barolo Ciabot Mentin '11	♥♥ 8
● Barolo Pajana '11	♥♥ 8
● Barolo Percristina '06	♥♥ 8
● Barolo '12	♥♥ 6
● Barolo Aeroplanservaj '11	♥♥ 7
● Barolo Ciabot Mentin '08	♥♥♥ 8
● Barolo Ciabot Mentin Ginestra '05	♥♥♥ 8
● Barolo Ciabot Mentin Ginestra '04	♥♥♥ 8
● Barolo Ciabot Mentin Ginestra '01	♥♥♥ 7
● Barolo Percristina '01	♥♥♥ 8
● Barolo '11	♥♥ 6
● Barolo Pajana '10	♥♥ 8
● Barolo Percristina '07	♥♥ 8

★Elvio Cogno

VIA RAVERA, 2
12060 NOVELLO [CN]
TEL. +39 0173744006
www.elviocogno.com

CELLAR SALES
PRE-BOOKED VISITS
ACCOMMODATION
ANNUAL PRODUCTION 90,000 bottles
HECTARES UNDER VINE 15.00
VITICULTURE METHOD Certified Organic
SUSTAINABLE WINERY

Valter Fissore and his wife Nadia Cogno, daughter of Elvio after whom the handsome Novello winery is named, produce four Barolos in the best vintages: Vigna Elena, Ravera, Bricco Pernice, and Cascina Nuova. They are very different interpretations of nebbiolo, due to soil and climate differences in the vineyard, combined with different fermentation and ageing processes in the cellar. Yet a common style is still evident, characterized by a rich, close-knit tannic weave, which we also find in Barbaresco Bordini and the other wines from barbera, dolcetto, and nascetta. This consistency is well illustrated by the delicious, layered Barbera d'Alba Pre-Phylloxera 2014. Barolo Vigna Elena Riserva 2010 is more intense and nuanced, full of medicinal herbs and caressing tannins. The squaring of the circle becomes manifest with the Tre-Bicchieri-winning Bricco Pernice 2011, still austere but exceptionally fleshy and long. The Ravera 2012 is only slightly more delicate.

● Barolo Bricco Pernice '11	♈♈♈ 8
● Barolo Ravera '12	♈♈ 8
● Barolo V. Elena Ris. '10	♈♈ 8
● Barbera d'Alba Pre-Philloxera '14	♈♈ 6
● Barolo Cascina Nuova '12	♈♈ 6
○ Langhe Nascetta del Comune di Novello Anas-Cëtta '15	♈♈ 4
● Langhe Nebbiolo Montegrilli '15	♈♈ 4
● Barbaresco Bordini '13	♈ 5
● Barbera d'Alba Bricco dei Merli '14	♈ 4
○ Dolcetto d'Alba Mandorlo '15	♈ 3
● Barolo Bricco Pernice '09	♈♈♈ 8
● Barolo Bricco Pernice '08	♈♈♈ 8
● Barolo Ravera '11	♈♈♈ 7
● Barolo Ravera '07	♈♈♈ 7
● Barolo V. Elena Ris. '06	♈♈♈ 8

Poderi Colla

FRAZ. SAN ROCCO SENO D'ELVIO, 82
12051 ALBA [CN]
TEL. +39 0173290148
www.podericolla.it

CELLAR SALES
PRE-BOOKED VISITS
ANNUAL PRODUCTION 150,000 bottles
HECTARES UNDER VINE 26.00

Not everyone knows that the Colla family vaunt over 300 years of winemaking history. And that before they became world famous for their great Barolos and Barbarescos, they helped promote types that have been largely forgotten, such as rosatello, vino negro, moscatello, vermouth, and Asti spumantes. Then came the glorious years of the brothers Beppe and Tino, among the first in Langhe to ferment the grapes of the various crus separately during the post-war period. Today they are flanked by their children Federica and Pietro and tend 25 hectares in Cascina Drago near the cellar, Roncaglie in Barbaresco, and Dardi Le Rose in Bussia in Monforte, which they use to make very classic wines. Barbaresco Roncaglie 2013 has an alluring nose of myrtle, juniper, and white pepper, and fine acid-tannic balance. Barolo Bussia Dardi Le Rose 2012 is unexpectedly more placid and drinkable, brimming with floral and citrus hints, and showing sensual, silky development on the palate.

● Barbaresco Roncaglie '13	♈♈ 6
● Barolo Bussia Dardi Le Rose '12	♈♈ 6
● Barolo Bussia Dardi Le Rose '09	♈♈♈ 6
● Barolo Bussia Dardi Le Rose '99	♈♈♈ 6
● Barbaresco Roncaglie '12	♈♈ 6
● Barbaresco Roncaglie '11	♈♈ 6
● Barbera d'Alba Costa Bruna '13	♈♈ 3
● Barbera d'Alba Costa Bruna '12	♈♈ 3
● Barolo Bussia Dardi Le Rose '11	♈♈ 6
● Langhe Bricco del Drago '10	♈♈ 4
● Langhe Pinot Nero Campo Romano '12	♈♈ 4
○ Langhe Riesling '13	♈♈ 3
● Nebbiolo d'Alba '13	♈♈ 3
● Nebbiolo d'Alba '12	♈♈ 3

Colle Manora

S.DA BOZZOLA, 5
15044 QUARGNENTO [AL]
TEL. +39 0131219252
www.collemanora.it

CELLAR SALES
PRE-BOOKED VISITS
ACCOMMODATION
ANNUAL PRODUCTION 90,000 bottles
HECTARES UNDER VINE 20.00

Giorgio Schön has entrusted the
management of the estate to oenologist
Valter Piccinino, flanked by consultant Piero
Ballario since 2013. This year we can start
to see the results of this recent partnership
in the wines from the 2014 vintage, which
was rather an unfortunate one in terms of
weather conditions. The eight labels are
from traditional Piedmont and international
grape varieties: chardonnay, sauvignon
blanc, and viognier for the whites; pinot
nero, cabernet sauvignon, merlot, barbera,
and albarossa for the reds. Despite its
vintage, Mila 2014 has a complex nose of
sweet spice, apricots, and peaches,
followed by a concentrated, well-
orchestrated palate. Barbera Manora 2014
displays excellent nose-palate symmetry.
Ray, from albarossa, and Mimosa, from
sauvignon blanc, are also pleasant and
easy drinking.

● Barbera d'Asti Sup. Manora '14	♀♀ 3
○ M.to Bianco Mila '14	♀♀ 4
○ M.to Bianco Mimosa '15	♀♀ 2*
● Piemonte Albarossa Ray '14	♀♀ 3
● Barbera del M.to Pais '15	♀ 2
● M.to Rosso Barchetta '13	♀ 4
● Piemonte Pinot Nero Paloalto '13	♀ 4
● Barbera d'Asti Sup. Manora '13	♀♀ 3
● Barbera d'Asti Sup. Manora '07	♀♀ 3
● Barbera del M.to Manora '04	♀♀ 3
● Barbera del M.to Manora '00	♀♀ 3
○ M.to Bianco Mila '13	♀♀ 4
○ M.to Bianco Mimosa '14	♀♀ 2*
○ M.to Rosso Palo Alto '05	♀♀ 5
● M.to Rosso Ray '07	♀♀ 3
● Piemonte Albarossa Ray '13	♀♀ 3

La Colombera

S.DA COMUNALE PER VHO, 7
15057 TORTONA [AL]
TEL. +39 0131867795
www.lacolomberavini.it

CELLAR SALES
PRE-BOOKED VISITS
ANNUAL PRODUCTION 70,000 bottles
HECTARES UNDER VINE 24.00
SUSTAINABLE WINERY

Today the Semino family are one of the
pillars of the community of producers
responsible for the new direction of
viticulture in the Colli Tortonesi DOC zone.
The high quality of the estate's production
has enabled it to win our highest accolade
for both its wines from the area's most
important native grape varieties, Timorasso
and Barbera.. The feat has only one
precedent in the Tortona area and will thus
shake the convictions of those who
maintained that it was incapable of
producing great reds. La Colombera
presented an extensive list, headed by the
two 2014 Timorassos: Il Montino and
Derthona. Despite the difficult vintage, they
have managed to preserve their complexity
and character. The more approachable,
ready-drinking Derthona already shows
fairly complex minerality. Elisa is a
Barbera vaunting a complex, concentrated
nose and a balanced, harmonious palate,
with somewhat drying tannins on the
finish. Croatina La Romba 2015 is
surprisingly good.

○ Colli Tortonesi Timorasso Derthona '14	♀♀ 3*
○ Colli Tortonesi Timorasso Il Montino '14	♀♀ 5
● Colli Tortonesi Barbera Elisa '13	♀♀ 4
● Colli Tortonesi Croatina La Romba '15	♀♀ 3
● Colli Tortonesi Rosso Vegia Rampana '15	♀♀ 2*
○ Colli Tortonesi Cortese Bricco Bartolomeo '15	♀ 2
● Colli Tortonesi Croatina Arché '13	♀ 4
● Colli Tortonesi Rosso Suciaja '14	♀ 4
● Colli Tortonesi Barbera Elisa '11	♀♀♀ 3*
○ Colli Tortonesi Timorasso Il Montino '13	♀♀♀ 5
○ Colli Tortonesi Timorasso Il Montino '09	♀♀♀ 5
○ Colli Tortonesi Timorasso Il Montino '06	♀♀♀ 4
○ Colli Tortonesi Cortese Bricco Bartolomeo '14	♀♀ 2*
○ Colli Tortonesi Timorasso Derthona '13	♀♀ 3*

Diego Conterno

via Montà, 27
12065 Monforte d'Alba [CN]
Tel. +39 0173789265
www.diegoconterno.it

CELLAR SALES
PRE-BOOKED VISITS
ANNUAL PRODUCTION 40,000 bottles
HECTARES UNDER VINE 7.50

In 2000 Diego Conterno decided to found his own winery after working with his cousins Claudio Conterno and Guido Conterno for 20 years. Aided by his son Stefano, he soon made a name for himself as one of the most interesting "new" producers in Langhe, crafting a reliable range from around seven hectares of barbera, dolcetto, nascetta, and of course nebbiolo. His austere, ageworthy Barolos are made from grapes from the Le Coste and Ginestra crus in Monforte, processed in the cellar with a wide array of fermenting and ageing techniques, featuring concrete, stainless steel, tonneaux, and larger barrels. Barolo Ginestra 2012 is an excellent example of the modern style, full of fruit and subtle tertiary notes of cocoa powder, aniseed, and mint, beautifully underpinned by a firm, powerful palate without any overly toasty or oaky sensations. We very much liked the white Nascetta 2015, from a native grape variety, aged exclusively in steel, which is steadily conquering the market.

● Barolo Ginestra '12	♟♟ 7	
○ Langhe Nascetta '15	♟♟ 3	
● Barbera d'Alba Ferrione '14	♟ 3	
● Barolo Le Coste '09	♟♟♟ 6	
● Barbera d'Alba Ferrione '12	♟♟ 3	
● Barolo '10	♟♟ 6	
● Barolo '09	♟♟ 6	
● Barolo '07	♟♟ 6	
● Barolo Ginestra '11	♟♟ 6	
● Barolo Ginestra '10	♟♟ 6	
● Barolo Le Coste '08	♟♟ 6	
● Barolo Le Coste '07	♟♟ 6	
● Barolo Le Coste di Monforte '10	♟♟ 6	
● Nebbiolo d'Alba Baluma '12	♟♟ 3	
● Nebbiolo d'Alba Baluma '10	♟♟ 3	

★★Giacomo Conterno

loc. Ornati, 2
12065 Monforte d'Alba [CN]
Tel. +39 017378221
www.conterno.it

PRE-BOOKED VISITS
ANNUAL PRODUCTION 60,000 bottles
HECTARES UNDER VINE 23.00

Although it may seem surprising, it is only in recent years that the winery founded in the early 1900s by Giacomo Conterno, has joined the ranks of the superstars of the international wine world, with prices to match. Much of the merit for this is due to Roberto, representing the latest generation of the family, and his determination, sartorial sensitivity, meticulous attention to detail, historical awareness, and foresight, evident in the recent acquisition of vineyards like Cerretta and Arione in Serralunga. They join the Francia monopoly cru that yields the eponymous Barolo and Barbera, as well as the legendary Monfortino Riserva in the finest vintages. When the flagship wine of such a prestigious estate is missing, we all feel somewhat orphaned, but we evidently hadn't bargained for Roberto Conterno's great skill, for he made us forget all about the Monfortino with the excellent Barolo Francia 2012. Its naturally harmonious power contrasts with the Ceretta, which shows complex aromas of raspberries and tobacco, with a touch of alcohol.

● Barolo Francia '12	♟♟♟ 8	
● Barolo Cerretta '13	♟♟ 8	
● Barbera d'Alba V. Cerretta '14	♟♟ 5	
● Barbera d'Alba V. Francia '14	♟♟ 5	
● Barolo Cascina Francia '06	♟♟♟ 8	
● Barolo Cascina Francia '05	♟♟♟ 8	
● Barolo Francia '10	♟♟♟ 8	
● Barolo Monfortino Ris. '08	♟♟♟ 8	
● Barolo Monfortino Ris. '06	♟♟♟ 8	
● Barolo Monfortino Ris. '05	♟♟♟ 8	
● Barolo Monfortino Ris. '04	♟♟♟ 8	
● Barolo Monfortino Ris. '02	♟♟♟ 8	
● Barolo Monfortino Ris. '01	♟♟♟ 8	

Paolo Conterno

LOC. GINESTRA, 34
12065 MONFORTE D'ALBA [CN]
TEL. +39 017378415
www.paoloconterno.com

CELLAR SALES
PRE-BOOKED VISITS
ACCOMMODATION AND RESTAURANT SERVICE
ANNUAL PRODUCTION 72,000 bottles
HECTARES UNDER VINE 37.00
SUSTAINABLE WINERY

Set in the Ginestra cru in Monforte d'Alba, the estate founded 130 years ago by Paolo Conterno is now run by Giorgio and Marisa. It covers an area of around 13 hectares planted almost exclusively to nebbiolo, dolcetto, and barbera, at altitudes of 300–350 metres, on a particularly steep hillside with gradients over 40%. The flagship wines are undoubtedly both the vintage and the Riserva Barolo Ginestra, and the Riva del Bric, which have long been among the best of the designation due to their solid, juicy character, partly derived from ageing in 3,500-litre French oak barrels. The collection of excellent releases of Paolo Conterno's Barolo Ginestra has grown yet further with the 2012 vintage, which opens up immediately with a sophisticated nose of strawberries and oranges, bouquet garni, and iodine, before changing pace on the almost salty palate. Riserva di Ginestra 2008 took a Tre Bicchieri for its complex nose and powerful palate.

● Barolo Ginestra Ris. '08	♆♆♆	8
● Barolo Ginestra '12	♆♆	8
● Barbera d'Asti Bricco '15	♆♆	3
● Barolo Riva del Bric '12	♆♆	6
○ Langhe Arneis A Val '15	♆	4
● Barolo Ginestra '10	♆♆♆	8
● Barolo Ginestra '06	♆♆♆	8
● Barolo Ginestra '05	♆♆♆	8
● Barolo Ginestra Ris. '06	♆♆♆	8
● Barolo Ginestra Ris. '05	♆♆♆	8
● Barolo Ginestra Ris. '01	♆♆♆	8
● Barbera d'Alba Ginestra '13	♆♆	3
● Barolo Ginestra '11	♆♆	8
● Barolo Riva del Bric '11	♆♆	6
● Langhe Nebbiolo Bric Ginestra '11	♆♆	5

★Conterno Fantino

VIA GINESTRA, 1
12065 MONFORTE D'ALBA [CN]
TEL. +39 017378204
www.conternofantino.it

PRE-BOOKED VISITS
ANNUAL PRODUCTION 150,000 bottles
HECTARES UNDER VINE 27.00
VITICULTURE METHOD Certified Organic
SUSTAINABLE WINERY

Claudio Conterno and Guido Fantino's partnership is undoubtedly one of the longest and finest in Langhe. Together they have shaped some of the most celebrated modern-style Barolos, particularly since the early 1990s, without ever losing sight of the agricultural heart of their project, associated with top-level crus like Sorì Ginestra, Vigna del Gris, and Mosconi. Increasing attention has also been dedicated to energy-saving techniques and the use of renewable sources in the recently renovated and extended cellar. It has ushered in a new style, characterized by greater suppleness, authentic flavour, and confident development. Barolo Sorì Ginestra 2012 testifies to its excellence. Notes of currants, cinnamon, and roasted coffee beans on the nose announce a Nebbiolo in a fairly modern style, but development on the palate is far more classic, showing focused and fleshy, with crisp, vibrant acidity, and enfolding tannins.

● Barolo Sorì Ginestra '12	♆♆♆	8
● Barolo Mosconi '12	♆♆	8
● Barolo V. del Gris '12	♆♆	8
● Dolcetto d'Alba Bricco Bastia '15	♆♆	2*
○ Langhe Chardonnay Bastia '14	♆♆	5
○ Langhe Chardonnay Prinsipi '15	♆♆	2*
● Langhe Nebbiolo Ginestrino '14	♆♆	4
● Barolo Sorì Ginestra '10	♆♆♆	8
● Barolo Sorì Ginestra '07	♆♆♆	8
● Barolo Sorì Ginestra '00	♆♆♆	7
● Barolo Sorì Ginestra '99	♆♆♆	8
● Barolo Sorì Ginestra '98	♆♆♆	8
● Barolo V. del Gris '09	♆♆♆	8
● Barolo V. del Gris '04	♆♆♆	8
● Barolo V. del Gris '01	♆♆♆	8

Vigne Marina Coppi

VIA SANT'ANDREA, 5
15051 CASTELLANIA [AL]
TEL. +39 0131837089
www.vignemarinacoppi.com

CELLAR SALES
PRE-BOOKED VISITS
ANNUAL PRODUCTION 25,000 bottles
HECTARES UNDER VINE 4.50

Francesco Bellocchio and his wife Anna
have shared their winegrowing adventure
from the very first vintage. It represented a
change of lifestyle for them, a return to the
family roots, with an ethical and moral
approach that respects the area's traditions
and history. The estate grows only local
native grape varieties: timorasso, favorita,
barbera, and nebbiolo. They yield six wines,
which will become seven next year, when
we will taste the first vintage of the younger
sibling of the Fausto, which topped the list
this year with a beautiful 2014 version. It is
beautifully vibrant, with mineral notes
adding complexity to the fruity nose, and a
pervasive, lingering finish on the full-bodied
palate. The concentrated, fleshy
Sant'Andrea is particularly fresh and
intriguing, while I Grop 2012 is rather
austere, with still prominent tannins.
Nebbiolo Lindin 2013 is moderately
complex and the alluring Marine 2014 is
very drinkable.

★Coppo

VIA ALBA, 68
14053 CANELLI [AT]
TEL. +39 0141823146
www.coppo.it

CELLAR SALES
PRE-BOOKED VISITS
ANNUAL PRODUCTION 400,000 bottles
HECTARES UNDER VINE 52.00

Coppo's origins can be traced back to
1892 and its history goes hand in hand
with that of the family that made it a
benchmark winery for the area. Indeed, its
historic cellars, dating from the 18th
century and reaching 40 metres beneath
the Canelli hill, were recently declared a
UNESCO World Heritage Site. The estate's
wide range focuses chiefly on Barbera,
Metodo Classico sparklers, and
Chardonnay, and includes wines for laying
down. Barbera d'Asti Pomorosso has won
another Tre Bicchieri. The 2013 vintage has
a nose of ripe but fresh fruit with perfectly
calibrated oak ensuring fullness and
harmony, and a dense, rounded palate
superbly balanced by great acidity and
richness of flavour. Barbera d'Asti Camp du
Rouss 2014 is excellent, showing spicy,
fresh, and juicy, with notes of blackberries
and plums, as is the sophisticated, creamy
Riserva Coppo Brut 2008, offering yeasty
notes, white fruit, and spice.

● Colli Tortonesi Barbera Sant'Andrea '15	♔♔ 3*
○ Colli Tortonesi Timorasso Fausto '14	♔♔ 6
● Colli Tortonesi Barbera Sup. I Grop '12	♔♔ 5
○ Colli Tortonesi Favorita Marine '14	♔♔ 5
● Colli Tortonesi Rosso Lindin '13	♔♔ 5
○ Colli Tortonesi Timorasso Fausto '12	♕♕♕ 6
○ Colli Tortonesi Timorasso Fausto '11	♕♕♕ 6
○ Colli Tortonesi Timorasso Fausto '10	♕♕♕ 6
○ Colli Tortonesi Timorasso Fausto '09	♕♕♕ 6
● Colli Tortonesi Barbera Sant'Andrea '12	♕♕ 3*
● Colli Tortonesi Barbera Sup. I Grop '11	♕♕ 5
● Colli Tortonesi Barbera Sup. I Grop '10	♕♕ 5
○ Colli Tortonesi Timorasso Fausto '13	♕♕ 6

● Barbera d'Asti Pomorosso '13	♔♔♔ 7
● Barbera d'Asti Camp du Rouss '14	♔♔ 3*
○ Riserva Coppo Brut M. Cl. '08	♔♔ 5
● Barbera d'Asti L'Avvocata '15	♔♔ 2*
● Barbera d'Asti Sup. Nizza Riserva della Famiglia Ris. '07	♔♔ 3
● Barolo '10	♔♔ 8
○ Clelia Coppo Brut Rosé M. Cl. '11	♔♔ 5
○ Luigi Coppo Brut M. Cl.	♔♔ 4
○ Piemonte Chardonnay Costebianche '14	♔♔ 3
○ Piemonte Chardonnay Monteriolo '14	♔♔ 6
○ Moscato d'Asti Moncalvina '15	♔ 3
● Barbera d'Asti Pomorosso '12	♕♕♕ 7
● Barbera d'Asti Pomorosso '11	♕♕♕ 7

Giovanni Corino

FRAZ. ANNUNZIATA, 25B
12064 LA MORRA [CN]
TEL. +39 0173509452
www.corino.it

CELLAR SALES
PRE-BOOKED VISITS
ANNUAL PRODUCTION 45,000 bottles
HECTARES UNDER VINE 8.00

The transition from tenant farmer to entrepreneur was certainly not an easy one in post-war Langhe. However, the untiring Giovanni Corino managed it, with the invaluable support of his sons Renato and Giuliano, who decided to found their own separate wineries in 2005. This success story is set against the magnificent backdrop of the Annunziata hill and hamlet of La Morra, planted with around eight hectares of nebbiolo, barbera, and dolcetto, Both the basic Barolo and the Giachini, Arborina, and Vecchie Vigne crus are aged mainly in small oak casks and often require a little extra time for their toasted notes to be tamed and release their juicy, flavoursome driving power. The Giachini has sweet spicy nuances mingling with more classic notes of raspberries and roots, echoed on a palate with a captivating combination of freshness and plushness. A little more oakiness is evident in the Arborina, enhanced by delicate tannins. The other wines crafted by the capable Giuliano Corino hadn't been bottled at the time of our tastings.

Barolo Giachini '12	ᵀᵀᵀ 7
Barolo Arborina '12	ᵀᵀ 7
Barolo '12	ᵀᵀ 6
Barbera d'Alba V. Pozzo '97	♀♀♀ 5
Barbera d'Alba V. Pozzo '96	♀♀♀ 5
Barolo Giachini '11	♀♀♀ 7
Barolo Rocche '01	♀♀♀ 7
Barolo Rocche '90	♀♀♀ 7
Barolo V. Giachini '89	♀♀♀ 7
Barolo V. V. '99	♀♀♀ 8
Barolo V. V. '98	♀♀♀ 8

Renato Corino

FRAZ. ANNUNZIATA
B.TA POZZO, 49A
12064 LA MORRA [CN]
TEL. +39 0173500349
www.renatocorino.it

CELLAR SALES
PRE-BOOKED VISITS
ANNUAL PRODUCTION 50,000 bottles
HECTARES UNDER VINE 7.00

The estate boasts a splendid scenic position, a practical modern cellar, and the undisputed skill of Renato Corino, now increasingly enthusiastically flanked in both the vineyard and the cellar by his son Stefano. In the space of just 11 years, it has become a veritable beacon for the Barolo DOCG, also due to its fine vineyards in La Morra's Rocche dell'Annunziata and Arborina crus. In the finest vintages an alluring, firmly structured Riserva is also made from the grapes of vines over 50 years old. The estate focuses exclusively on red wines, all impeccably made. The spicy, complex, concentrated Barolo Rocche dell'Annunziata 2012 is an exceptionally elegant Nebbiolo. Its extraordinarily clean, well-orchestrated palate vaunts a very long, mouthfilling, tannic finish with fine acidity. Barolo Arborina 2012 is very fruity with notes of spicy oak and a balanced palate with pleasantly sweet tannins.

Barolo Arborina '12	ᵀᵀ 7
Barolo Rocche dell'Annunziata '12	ᵀᵀ 8
Barolo '12	ᵀᵀ 5
Barolo Rocche dell'Annunziata '11	♀♀♀ 8
Barolo Rocche dell'Annunziata '10	♀♀♀ 7
Barolo Rocche dell'Annunziata '09	♀♀♀ 7
Barolo Vign. Rocche '04	♀♀♀ 8
Barolo Vign. Rocche '03	♀♀♀ 8
Barbera d'Alba V. Pozzo '10	♀♀ 5
Barolo '06	♀♀ 5
Barolo Arborina '11	♀♀ 7
Barolo Arborina '09	♀♀ 7
Barolo Arborina '08	♀♀ 7
Barolo Arborina '07	♀♀ 7
Barolo V. V. Ris. '05	♀♀ 8

Cornarea

VIA VALENTINO, 150
12043 CANALE [CN]
TEL. +39 017365636
www.cornarea.com

CELLAR SALES
PRE-BOOKED VISITS
ACCOMMODATION
ANNUAL PRODUCTION 90,000 bottles
HECTARES UNDER VINE 14.00

Founded by the Bovone family in 1981, the Cornarea estate consists of a single plot of vineyards around the winery on the on the magnesium-rich clayey limestone soil of the eponymous hill. Planted by the family between 1975 and 1978, it is home to two of the most important local grape varieties: arneis, accounting for two-thirds of the area under vine, and nebbiolo. The winery's Roero Arneis has been a veritable benchmark for the designation for years. Tarasco 2012, a passito from arneis, is truly alluring, offering classic notes of honey and nuts, with hints of cocoa powder, coffee, and dried figs. Its very complex, concentrated palate shows remarkable clarity and is long and fresh with finely balanced sweetness and acidity. The pleasant, gutsy Roero Arneis 2015 is also excellent, with sensations of apricots and peaches, and hints of spice and Mediterranean scrubland, while the Roero 2013 is full and fruity.

○ Roero Arneis '15	♛♛ 3*
○ Tarasco Passito '12	♛♛ 5
● Roero '13	♛♛ 4
● Nebbiolo d'Alba '11	♛♛ 3
● Nebbiolo d'Alba '10	♛♛ 3
● Roero '12	♛♛ 4
● Roero '11	♛♛ 4
○ Roero Arneis '14	♛♛ 3*
○ Roero Arneis '13	♛♛ 3
○ Tarasco Passito '11	♛♛ 5
○ Tarasco Passito '10	♛♛ 5
○ Tarasco Passito '09	♛♛ 5
○ Tarasco Passito '08	♛♛ 5

★Matteo Correggia

LOC. GARBINETTO
VIA SANTO STEFANO ROERO, 124
12043 CANALE [CN]
TEL. +39 0173978009
www.matteocorreggia.com

CELLAR SALES
PRE-BOOKED VISITS
ANNUAL PRODUCTION 150,000 bottles
HECTARES UNDER VINE 20.00

Ornella Costa Correggia and her son Giovanni successfully continue the work commenced by Matteo in 1985. The estate's vineyards are mainly on mineral-rich sandy soils, with a low clay and silt content. The southern-facing plots, between Santo Stefano Roero and Canale, yield the nebbiolo and barbera used for Roero La Val dei Preti and Barbera d'Alba Marun, while the cooler areas are planted to arneis and brachetto, while the Roero Riserva Ròche d'Ampsèj is from a steep vineyard overlooking the Roero Rocks. Ròche d'Ampsèj 2012 has a beautifully complex nose of red berries and tobacco, oak and spice, and a rich, flavoursome palate showing well-behaved tannins and a long, supple finish. In the absence of Barbera d'Alba Marun 2014 and Roero Val dei Preti 2014, which the estate has decided to leave to age in the cellar for another year, we were very convinced by the dense, fruity Roero 2014 and the pleasant, juicy Barbera d'Alba 2014.

● Roero Ròche d'Ampsèj Ris. '12	♛♛ 6
● Barbera d'Alba '14	♛♛ 3
● Langhe Rosso Le Marne Grigie '13	♛♛ 6
● Roero '14	♛♛ 3
● Anthos '15	♛ 3
○ Roero Arneis '15	♛ 3
● Barbera d'Alba Marun '04	♛♛♛ 5
● Roero Ròche d'Ampsèj '04	♛♛♛ 6
● Roero Ròche d'Ampsèj Ris. '07	♛♛♛ 6
● Roero Ròche d'Ampsèj Ris. '06	♛♛♛ 6
● Barbera d'Alba '13	♛♛ 3
● Barbera d'Alba Marun '13	♛♛ 5
○ Langhe Sauvignon Matteo Correggia '13	♛♛ 5
● Roero '13	♛♛ 3

Giuseppe Cortese

S.DA RABAJÀ, 80
12050 BARBARESCO [CN]
TEL. +39 0173635131
www.cortesegiuseppe.it

CELLAR SALES
PRE-BOOKED VISITS
ACCOMMODATION
ANNUAL PRODUCTION 50,000 bottles
HECTARES UNDER VINE 8.00

Giuseppe Cortese is one of the first names
that comes to mind when drawing up a list
of top Barbaresco producers. Aided by his
wife Rossella and son Piercarlo, he has
further boosted the excellent work of the
cellar and vineyard, accurately reflected in
the entire range, from nebbiolo, dolcetto,
and barbera. The flagship is the impressive
Rabajà, in both vintage and Riserva
versions, aged in oak barrels of various
sizes and origins. It never ceases to
astonish with its magnificent combination
of delicious fruit and tannic backbone,
which associates eloquent immediacy with
eminent cellarability, a far cry from the
exclusively "masculine" stereotypes of the
cru. The 2013 vintage fully lived up to our
expectations, appearing almost ethereal,
focusing on citrus fruit, wild berries,
liquorice, and mint, with a light, lean,
minimalist palate in its quest for elegance
and finesse rather than power and
structure. Langhe Nebbiolo 2014 stands
out among the wines of its cool vintage.

Clemente Cossetti

VIA GUARDIE, 1
14043 CASTELNUOVO BELBO [AT]
TEL. +39 0141799803
www.cossetti.it

CELLAR SALES
PRE-BOOKED VISITS
ACCOMMODATION AND RESTAURANT SERVICE
ANNUAL PRODUCTION 500,000 bottles
HECTARES UNDER VINE 28.00

Cossetti is celebrating its 125th
anniversary. Founded by Giovanni Cossetti
in 1891, it is now run by the fourth
generation of the family. The estate's
vineyards are in Castelnuovo Belbo, near
Nizza, on medium-textured clay soil rich in
iron and magnesium. However, it also
vinifies purchased grapes, allowing it to
offer a wide range of wines featuring some
of the top Piedmont designations. Piemonte
Albarossa Amartè 2014 tops the list. Its
nose of blackberries and sweet spice is
followed by a full, velvety palate, with
particularly fine tannins for a grape like
albarossa, and a long, fresh finish. Moscato
d'Asti La Vita 2015 is also well made, with
nicely balanced sweetness and acidity and
aromatic notes of citrus, peaches, and
sage, as are the perfectly aromatic, floral
Ruché di Castagnole Monferrato 2015 and
the pleasant, fruity Barbera d'Asti Superiore
Nizza 2013.

● Barbaresco Rabajà '13		♟♟ 5
● Langhe Nebbiolo '14		♟♟ 3*
● Barbera d'Alba '15		♟♟ 3
● Dolcetto d'Alba '15		♟♟ 2*
○ Langhe Chardonnay Scapulin '15		♟ 3
● Barbaresco Rabajà '11		♟♟♟ 5
● Barbaresco Rabajà '10		♟♟♟ 5
● Barbaresco Rabajà '08		♟♟♟ 5
● Barbaresco Rabajà Ris. '96		♟♟♟ 8
● Barbaresco Rabajà '12		♟♟ 5
● Barbaresco Rabajà Ris. '08		♟♟ 8
● Barbera d'Alba '14		♟♟ 3
● Barbera d'Alba Morassina '13		♟♟ 3
● Barbera d'Alba Morassina '12		♟♟ 3
● Langhe Nebbiolo '13		♟♟ 3
● Langhe Nebbiolo '12		♟♟ 3

● Barbera d'Asti Sup. Nizza '13		♟♟ 4
○ Moscato d'Asti La Vita '15		♟♟ 2*
● Piemonte Albarossa Amartè '14		♟♟ 3
● Ruché di Castagnole Monferrato '15		♟♟ 3
● Barbera d'Asti La Vigna Vecchia '14		♟ 2
● Barbera d'Asti Venti di Marzo '15		♟ 3
● Barbera d'Asti La Vigna Vecchia '13		♟♟ 2*
● Barbera d'Asti La Vigna Vecchia '12		♟♟ 2*
● Barbera d'Asti Sup. Nizza '11		♟♟ 4
● Barbera d'Asti Venti di Marzo '14		♟♟ 3
● Barbera d'Asti Venti di Marzo '13		♟♟ 3
○ Grignolino d'Asti '14		♟♟ 2*
● Ruché di Castagnole Monferrato '13		♟♟ 3

Stefanino Costa

B.TA BENNA, 5
12046 MONTÀ [CN]
TEL. +39 0173976336
ninocostawine@gmail.com

CELLAR SALES
PRE-BOOKED VISITS
ANNUAL PRODUCTION 50,000 bottles
HECTARES UNDER VINE 9.50

In recent years Nino Costa has achieved good consistency in his production, whose traditional style is accompanied by clear aromatic focus. The estate's vineyards, situated on mainly sandy soils at altitudes of 350–400 metres above sea level in the municipalities of Canale, Montà, and Santo Stefano Roero, include veritable crus, such as Bric del Medic, and are home to 40-year-old vines. They're planted with the typical Roero grape varieties: arneis, barbera, brachetto, and nebbiolo. Roero Gepin 2012 earns a Tre Bicchieri for its concentrated floral nose, followed by hints of aniseed, red berries, and sweet tobacco, and remarkably complex palate that is fresh, compact, and flavoursome, with elegant tannins and a long, supple finish. The lip-smacking Roero Arneis Sarun 2015 is excellent, showing fleshy with good acid backbone, while Barbera d'Alba Superiore Genna 2013 is fruity and firmly structured.

Deltetto

C.SO ALBA, 43
12043 CANALE [CN]
TEL. +39 0173979383
www.deltetto.com

CELLAR SALES
PRE-BOOKED VISITS
ANNUAL PRODUCTION 170,000 bottles
HECTARES UNDER VINE 21.00
VITICULTURE METHOD Certified Organic
SUSTAINABLE WINERY

Antonio Deltetto has headed the family winery since 1977 and over the years has made it one of the most important in Roero. He has done so by flanking its traditional production based on local grape varieties, such as arneis, nebbiolo, and barbera, with sparkling wines from chardonnay and pinot nero, and also nebbiolo, as well as fine wines with other Piedmont designations, including Barolo and Gavi. Deltetto Extra Brut Metodo Classico 2010, from 60% pinot nero and 40% chardonnay, is extremely convincing, with complex toasty, yeasty notes on a nose of apples and pears, and a long, fresh palate. Roero Braja Riserva 2013 is also excellent, showing fruit rich and still tannic, but gutsy with good thrust. The rest of the range is good, including the pleasant, fresh Roero 2013, the soft, fruity Barbera d'Alba Superiore Bramé 2014, and the elegant, floral Brut Rosé.

● Roero Gepin '12	♥♥♥ 4*
○ Roero Arneis Sarun '15	♥♥ 3*
● Barbera d'Alba Sup. Genna '13	♥♥ 2*
● Roero Gepin '11	♀♀♀ 4*
● Roero Gepin '10	♀♀♀ 4*
● Barbera d'Alba Cichin '12	♀♀ 2*
○ Langhe Bianco Ricordi '13	♀♀ 3
○ Roero Arneis Sarun '13	♀♀ 3*
● Roero Bric del Medic '09	♀♀ 3*
● Roero Bric del Medic '07	♀♀ 3*
● Roero Medic '12	♀♀ 3
● Roero Medic '10	♀♀ 3*
● Roero V. V. '09	♀♀ 4
● Roero V. V. '08	♀♀ 4

○ Deltetto Extra Brut M. Cl. '10	♥♥ 5
● Roero Braja Ris. '13	♥♥ 4
● Barbera d'Alba Sup. Bramé '14	♥♥ 3
● Barolo Bussia '11	♥♥ 6
⊙ Deltetto Rosé Brut M. Cl.	♥♥ 5
● Roero '13	♥♥ 3
○ Deltetto Brut M. Cl. '11	♥ 4
○ Langhe Favorita '15	♥ 2
○ Roero Arneis Daivej '15	♥ 2
○ Roero Arneis San Michele '15	♥ 3
● Roero Braja Ris. '09	♀♀♀ 4*
● Roero Braja Ris. '08	♀♀♀ 4
● Roero Braja Ris. '07	♀♀♀ 4

Gianni Doglia

VIA ANNUNZIATA, 56
14054 CASTAGNOLE DELLE LANZE [AT]
TEL. +39 0141878359
www.giannidoglia.it

CELLAR SALES
PRE-BOOKED VISITS
ANNUAL PRODUCTION 80,000 bottles
HECTARES UNDER VINE 8.00

Gianni Doglia's production philosophy tends to interpret the personality of the individual grape varieties and the different possibilities they offer to the full. He thus presented two different versions of both Moscato d'Asti and Barbera d'Asti: the first uncomplicated and approachable, typical of these grapes, and two more complex selections like Casa di Bianco from moscato, aged in steel, and Genio from barbera, aged in oak, are the result of low yields and long ageing. The entire range is excellent. When the mouthfilling aromatic sensations of moscato grapes merge with the elegance of dozens of nuances of herbs, tropical fruit, and spices, and the usual softness of sugar makes way for a thousand delicate flavours, then we're talking of a truly great Moscato d'Asti: Tre Bicchieri for Casa Bianca 2015. The estate also shows great skill with Barbera d'Asti in the sophisticated, layered, fruity Genio 2014 and the approachable, fresh, close-focused Boscodonne 2015.

Dosio

REG. SERRADENARI, 6
12064 LA MORRA [CN]
TEL. +39 017350677
www.dosiovigneti.com

CELLAR SALES
PRE-BOOKED VISITS
ACCOMMODATION
ANNUAL PRODUCTION 65,000 bottles
HECTARES UNDER VINE 11.00

The takeover of the estate by the Lanci family a couple of years ago has revived work at this long-standing Langhe winery. Its vineyards are in the highest part of La Morra and include some of the highest crus of the entire production zone, peaking at altitudes around 500 metres. The experienced Marco Dotta, one of the region's most talented oenologists, acts as consultant. Barolo Serradenari 2012 is simply spectacular, slowly opening with notes of cloves and red berries on the nose. The powerful palate has dark, earthy notes and fresh acidity that perfectly balances its close-woven tannins and ensures good length. The 2012 Barolo has an approachable nose of crisp red berry fruit and a full, enfolding palate with a long, fresh finish with slightly drying oak notes. Roero Arneis 2015 is very enjoyable.

○ Moscato d'Asti Casa di Bianca '15	▼▼▼	3*
● Barbera d'Asti Sup. Genio '14	▼▼	4
● Barbera d'Asti Boscodonne '15	▼▼	2*
● Grignolino d'Asti '15	▼▼	2*
● M.to Rosso ! '13	▼▼	5
○ Moscato d'Asti '15	▼▼	2*
● Barbera d'Asti Sup. Genio '12	▽▽▽	4*
● Barbera d'Asti Boscodonne '14	▽▽	2*
● Barbera d'Asti Boscodonne '12	▽▽	2*
● Barbera d'Asti Sup. '10	▽▽	3*
● Barbera d'Asti Sup. '09	▽▽	3
● Barbera d'Asti Sup. '07	▽▽	3
● Barbera d'Asti Sup. Genio '11	▽▽	4
● M.to Rosso ! '12	▽▽	5
○ Moscato d'Asti Casa di Bianca '14	▽▽	3*
○ Moscato d'Asti Casa di Bianca '13	▽▽	3*
○ Moscato d'Asti Casa di Bianca '12	▽▽	3*

● Barolo Serradenari '12	▼▼	6
● Barolo '12	▼▼	5
● Dolcetto d'Alba '15	▼▼	2*
● Langhe Eventi '12	▼▼	4
● Langhe Nebbiolo Barilà '13	▼▼	5
○ Roero Arneis '15	▼▼	2*
● Barbera d'Alba Sup. '14	▼	3
● Nebbiolo d'Alba '13	▼	3
● Barbera d'Alba '13	▽▽	2*
● Barolo '10	▽▽	5
● Barolo Fossati '11	▽▽	5
● Barolo Fossati Ris. '08	▽▽	8
● Langhe Nebbiolo Barilà '12	▽▽	3*

★Poderi Luigi Einaudi

LOC. CASCINA TECC
B.TA GOMBE, 31/32
12063 DOGLIANI [CN]
TEL. +39 017370191
www.poderieinaudi.com

CELLAR SALES
PRE-BOOKED VISITS
ACCOMMODATION
ANNUAL PRODUCTION 250,000 bottles
HECTARES UNDER VINE 52.00

Matteo Sardagna has taken up the legacy of the estate founded by Italy's first President, Luigi Einaudi, in 1897 that has been a benchmark for the Piedmont wine world for decades. Its prime vineyards, commencing with Cannubi and Terlo for Barolo and Vigna Tecc for Dolcetto di Dogliani, ensure top-quality grapes, which are processed in the cellar by an exceptionally skilled staff. We recommend trying Langhe Rosso Luigi Einaudi, which is international in style, but full of personality. The elegant, welcoming Relais dei Poderi is in a splendid scenic position near the winery. Barolo Cannubi 2012 has a nose of raspberries and violets, followed by liquorice and sweet tobacco, and a firmly structured palate with fabulous balance, while the Terlo Vigna Costa Grimaldi 2012 is dry and surefooted, and the Terlo 2012 is still slightly marked by oak. The release of the new Dogliani Tecc has been postponed, and we are also awaiting the Barolo to be made from the grapes of the four hectares purchased in the Bussia cru of Monforte d'Alba in July 2016.

● Barolo Cannubi '12	♟♟ 8
● Langhe Rosso Luigi Einaudi '11	♟♟ 6
● Barolo Terlo '12	♟♟ 6
● Barolo Terlo V. Costa Grimaldi '12	♟♟ 7
● Dogliani '15	♟♟ 3
● Piemonte Barbera '13	♟♟ 3
● Langhe Nebbiolo '14	♟ 3
● Barolo Cannubi '11	♟♟♟ 8
● Barolo Cannubi '10	♟♟♟ 8
● Barolo Costa Grimaldi '05	♟♟♟ 8
● Barolo Costa Grimaldi '01	♟♟♟ 7
● Barolo nei Cannubi '00	♟♟♟ 8
● Barolo nei Cannubi '99	♟♟♟ 7
● Dogliani Sup. V. Tecc '10	♟♟♟ 3*
● Dogliani V. Tecc '06	♟♟♟ 4
● Langhe Rosso Luigi Einaudi '04	♟♟♟ 5

Tenuta Il Falchetto

FRAZ. CIOMBI
VIA VALLE TINELLA, 16
12058 SANTO STEFANO BELBO [CN]
TEL. +39 0141840344
www.ilfalchetto.com

CELLAR SALES
PRE-BOOKED VISITS
ANNUAL PRODUCTION 280,000 bottles
HECTARES UNDER VINE 47.00

The Forno family have lived in Santo Stefano Belbo since the mid-17th century and founded their estate in 1940, which is now headed by brothers Giorgio, Fabrizio, and Adriano. Its vineyards are divided between three estates in Santo Stefano Belbo and Castiglione Tinella and another three in Agliano Terme and Calosso. The lion's share of the plantings is accounted for by moscato and barbera, the traditional local grape varieties, which yield very concentrated, elegant, fruit-rich wines. Moscato d'Asti Ciombo 2015 had no trouble winning a Tre Bicchieri for its multifaceted nose of peaches, lime, sage, and citrus, and mighty palate with vibrant acidity underpinning its rich sweetness. The fresher, more linear Moscato d'Asti Tenuta del Fant 2015 is almost as good, with vegetal notes of pine needles and medicinal herbs, accompanied by aromas of apples and pears. The rest of the list is well made.

○ Moscato d'Asti Ciombo '15	♟♟♟ 2*
○ Moscato d'Asti Tenuta del Fant '15	♟♟ 2*
● M.to Rosso La Mora '13	♟♟ 3
○ Piemonte Chardonnay '15	♟♟ 2*
○ Piemonte Moscato Passito '12	♟♟ 4
● Barbera d'Asti Pian Scorrone '15	♟ 3
● Piemonte Pinot Nero Solo '13	♟ 3
○ Moscato d'Asti Tenuta del Fant '11	♟♟♟ 2*
○ Moscato d'Asti Tenuta del Fant '09	♟♟♟ 2*
● Barbera d'Alba Sup. La Rossa '11	♟♟ 3
● Barbera d'Asti Pian Scorrone '12	♟♟ 3
○ Moscato d'Asti Tenuta del Fant '14	♟♟ 2*
● Piemonte Pinot Nero Solo '12	♟♟ 3

Benito Favaro

S.DA CHIUSURE, 1BIS
10010 PIVERONE [TO]
TEL. +39 012572606
www.cantinafavaro.it

CELLAR SALES
PRE-BOOKED VISITS
ANNUAL PRODUCTION 20,000 bottles
HECTARES UNDER VINE 3.50

Long barely known outside its production zone, Erbaluce is gradually garnering attention and enthusiasm. Much of the credit for this is undoubtedly due to the efforts of Benito and Camillo Favaro, and the brilliant sequence of remarkable wines produced over the last decade. Teutonic complexity is combined with Caluso delicacy in the Le Chiusure whites, which faithfully echo the characteristics of the three hectares of vineyards clinging to the slopes of La Serra in Piverone. The basic version is aged in steel, while the 13 Mesi is fermented and partially aged in oak. The red wines, from syrah, freisa, nebbiolo, and barbera, are also very good. Erbaluce Le Chiusure 2015 is simply splendid, with a clean, close-focused nose of damsons and almonds, and a lively, enfolding palate displaying delightful, harmonious, almost salty acidity. The 13 Mesi 2014, delicately part-aged in oak, is a little more closed on the palate.

○ Erbaluce di Caluso Le Chiusure '15	♥♥	2*
○ Erbaluce di Caluso 13 Mesi '14	♥♥	3
☉ Rosacherosanonsei '15	♥♥	3
○ Sole d'Inverno '13	♥♥	5
○ Erbaluce di Caluso Le Chiusure '13	♥♥♥	2*
○ Erbaluce di Caluso Le Chiusure '12	♥♥♥	2*
○ Erbaluce di Caluso Le Chiusure '11	♥♥♥	2*
○ Erbaluce di Caluso Le Chiusure '10	♥♥♥	2*
○ Erbaluce di Caluso 13 Mesi '13	♀♀	3
○ Erbaluce di Caluso 13 Mesi '12	♀♀	3
○ Erbaluce di Caluso Le Chiusure '14	♀♀	2*
● Rossomeraviglia '13	♀♀	5
● Rossomeraviglia '12	♀♀	5

Giacomo Fenocchio

LOC. BUSSIA, 72
12065 MONFORTE D'ALBA [CN]
TEL. +39 017378675
www.giacomofenocchio.com

CELLAR SALES
PRE-BOOKED VISITS
ANNUAL PRODUCTION 90,000 bottles
HECTARES UNDER VINE 15.00
SUSTAINABLE WINERY

The story of the Fenoccio brothers' wines is in many ways emblematic of the contemporary Langhe wine scene. After having proceeded practically unnoticed for many years, the old estate found itself in the limelight not least for the excellent value of its range based on nebbiolo, dolcetto, barbera, and freisa. Indeed, its vineyards have big names like Cannubi in Barolo, Villero in Castiglione Falletto, and Bussia in Monforte, and the style of its wines has always been traditional but certainly not outmoded. The product of long maceration and patient ageing in Slavonian oak, they are Barolos that are both ageworthy and enjoyable when young. Fenocchio's Barolos have triumphed again, with a stellar Riserva Bussia 90 Dì exemplifying the full complexity of the nebbiolo grape with its nose of tobacco, liquorice, soot, and black cherries. Its majestic palate has juicy, close-woven tannins that impart an attractive chewiness. The Villero stands out among the excellent 2012 vintages.

● Barolo Bussia 90 Dì Ris. '10	♥♥♥	8
● Barolo Bussia '12	♥♥	6
● Barolo Villero '12	♥♥	6
● Barolo Cannubi '12	♥♥	6
☉ Barolo Castellero '12	♥♥	6
● Barolo Bussia '11	♀♀♀	6
● Barolo Bussia '09	♀♀♀	6
● Barolo Bussia '10	♀♀	6
● Barolo Bussia Ris. '09	♀♀	7
● Barolo Cannubi '11	♀♀	6
● Barolo Cannubi '10	♀♀	6
● Barolo Castellero '11	♀♀	6
● Barolo Villero '11	♀♀	6
● Barolo Villero '10	♀♀	6

Ferrando

via Torino, 599
10015 Ivrea [TO]
Tel. +39 0125633550
www.ferrandovini.it

CELLAR SALES
PRE-BOOKED VISITS
ANNUAL PRODUCTION 50,000 bottles
HECTARES UNDER VINE 5.00

The Ferrando family's wines embody a faith, extending far beyond production and sensory matters. Much of the credit for the survival of Carema, its spectacular terraced vineyards carved out of the rock, and mountain Nebbiolo, goes to the Ivrea estate now headed by Roberto. This decidedly uneconomical style of viticulture, is rewarded by many monumentally characterful and ageworthy versions of Etichetta Bianca and Etichetta Nera, which acts rather like a riserva in the best vintages. However, the estate's Erbaluce di Caluso is also noteworthy, with La Torrazza and Cariola still versions, two sweet wines, and a sparkler. While the release of the Riserva has been delayed, Ferrando won us over with the superb Carema 2012, which romped home with a Tre Bicchieri. The nose shows the typical aromas of nebbiolo grapes, from liquorice to dried flowers, with an attractive, unusual touch of iodine, while the imposing, balanced palate has confident, full stuffing supported by fine acidity and tannins. Erbaluce di Caluso Cariola is less fresh and lively than usual.

● Carema Et. Bianca '12	🍷🍷🍷 5
○ Caluso Passito '09	🍷🍷 5
○ La Torrazza Brut Cuvée Luigi Ferrando M. Cl.	🍷🍷 4
○ Erbaluce di Caluso Cariola '15	🍷 3
● Carema Et. Nera '11	ŸŸŸ 7
● Carema Et. Nera '09	ŸŸŸ 6
● Carema Et. Nera '08	ŸŸŸ 6
● Carema Et. Nera '07	ŸŸŸ 6
● Carema Et. Nera '06	ŸŸŸ 6
● Carema Et. Nera '05	ŸŸŸ 6
● Carema Et. Nera '01	ŸŸŸ 5

Roberto Ferraris

fraz. Dogliano, 33
14041 Agliano Terme [AT]
Tel. +39 0141954234
www.robertoferraris.com

CELLAR SALES
PRE-BOOKED VISITS
ANNUAL PRODUCTION 50,000 bottles
HECTARES UNDER VINE 10.50

Founded in the heart of the historic Barbera d'Asti zone by Stefano Ferraris in 1923, the family estate is now run by his grandson Roberto. Barbera accounts for 8.5 of the total 10.5 hectares of vineyards and the rest is a mixture of nebbiolo and grignolino, with vines on Vitis rupestris rootstocks planted between 1923 and 1930. The soils are mainly white limestone, with 65% silt and a little clay. The resulting wines are traditional in style and impressively terroir true. We particularly liked Barbera d'Asti Superiore La Cricca 2013, with a rich nose of fresh, ripe dark fruit and notes of spice, tobacco, and coffee, and a full palate with a fine tannic weave. The other versions of Barbera d'Asti are also well made, from the spicy, earthy Superiore Bisavolo 2013, offering notes of plums and black cherries, full flavour, and nice balance, to the Suôrì '15, with medium structure and an alluring fresh, long finish, and the approachable, supple Nobbio 2014.

● Barbera d'Asti Sup. La Cricca '13	🍷🍷 3*
● Barbera d'Asti Nobbio '14	🍷🍷 2*
● Barbera d'Asti Suôrì '15	🍷🍷 2*
● Barbera d'Asti Sup. Bisavolo '13	🍷🍷 3
● Barbera d'Asti Suôrì '14	🍷 2
● M.to Rosso Grixa '13	🍷 3
● Barbera d'Asti '13	ŸŸ 2*
● Barbera d'Asti '12	ŸŸ 2*
● Barbera d'Asti Nobbio '12	ŸŸ 2*
● Barbera d'Asti Sup. Bisavolo '12	ŸŸ 3
● M.to Rosso Grixa '12	ŸŸ 3
● M.to Rosso Grixa '11	ŸŸ 3
● M.to Rosso Grixa '11	ŸŸ 3

PIEDMONT

Carlo Ferro

FRAZ. SALERE, 41
14041 AGLIANO TERME [AT]
TEL. +39 0141954000
www.ferrovini.com

CELLAR SALES
PRE-BOOKED VISITS
ANNUAL PRODUCTION 15,000 bottles
HECTARES UNDER VINE 12.00

This family estate has been present in the Barbera d'Asti production zone for over a century, although it only started bottling its wines just over 20 years ago. Barbera, of course, accounts for the lion's share of the plantings, flanked by dolcetto, grignolino, nebbiolo, and cabernet sauvignon, used to make exclusively red wines. The wines are traditional in style, with a special eye to everyday drinkability. The small estate's range is always sound and reliable, particularly its Barbera d'Alba. The Notturno 2015 offers a nose of blood oranges, tobacco, morello cherries, and liquorice, accompanied by a traditional palate that has plenty of character but is possibly slightly too mature for a current Barbera; the Roche 2013 has remarkable structure and is fairly alcoholic, with plenty of flesh but still prominent oak; while the Giulia 2014 is simpler and lighter, partly due to its vintage, but fresh and pleasant.

● Barbera d'Asti Giulia '14	♟♟ 2*
● Barbera d'Asti Sup. Notturno '15	♟♟ 2*
● Barbera d'Asti Sup. Roche '13	♟♟ 3
● Barbera d'Asti '15	♟ 2
● Langhe Nebbiolo Tre Lune '14	♟ 2
● M.to Rosso Paolo '12	♟ 3
● Barbera d'Asti '14	♟♟ 2*
● Barbera d'Asti '13	♟♟ 1*
● Barbera d'Asti Giulia '13	♟♟ 2*
● Barbera d'Asti Giulia '11	♟♟ 2*
● Barbera d'Asti Sup. Notturno '12	♟♟ 2*
● Barbera d'Asti Sup. Roche '11	♟♟ 3
● Barbera d'Asti Superiore Notturno '10	♟♟ 2*

Fontanabianca

VIA BORDINI, 15
12057 NEIVE [CN]
TEL. +39 017367195
www.fontanabianca.it

CELLAR SALES
PRE-BOOKED VISITS
ANNUAL PRODUCTION 60,000 bottles
HECTARES UNDER VINE 14.00

Fontanabianca is a benchmark for the Neive hills. The turning point came in 1969, when the winery was founded and started bottling its own production after a long tradition as growers. Aldo Pola was one of the leading figures in the new phase of Barolo, with a modern style that has now given way to a more classic interpretation, with moderate extraction and more sparing use of new oak. This successful restyling has resulted in more drinkable wines that have lost nothing in terms of aromatic complexity. Quality is medium to high across the range, topped by Barbaresco Serraboella 2013, which offers a fresh nose of raspberries and liquorice, and a delicate, layered palate with lean, confident structure and a long, clean finish. Barbaresco Bordini 2013 has sweet tobacco and spice on the nose, and a juicy, austere palate with a precise, uncomplicated finish.

● Barbaresco Bordini '13	♟♟ 6
● Barbaresco '13	♟♟ 5
● Barbaresco Serraboella '13	♟♟ 5
● Barbera d'Alba Sup. '14	♟♟ 3
● Langhe Nebbiolo '14	♟ 3
● Barbaresco Serraboella '06	♟♟♟ 6
● Barbaresco Sorì Burdin '05	♟♟♟ 6
● Barbaresco Sorì Burdin '04	♟♟♟ 6
● Barbaresco '12	♟♟ 5
● Barbaresco Bordini '12	♟♟ 6
● Barbaresco Serraboella '12	♟♟ 5
● Barbera d'Alba Sup. '13	♟♟ 3
● Langhe Nebbiolo '13	♟♟ 3

Fontanafredda

VIA ALBA, 15
12050 SERRALUNGA D'ALBA [CN]
TEL. +39 0173626111
www.fontanafredda.it

CELLAR SALES
PRE-BOOKED VISITS
ACCOMMODATION AND RESTAURANT SERVICE
ANNUAL PRODUCTION 7,500,000 bottles
HECTARES UNDER VINE 100.00
SUSTAINABLE WINERY

The key to Fontanafredda's international prestige can be sought in its seemingly contradictory combination of ancient origins and modern business vision. It is a veritable colossus of Piedmont wine, with a production in excess of 7 million bottles and around 100 hectares of vineyards, largely converted to natural methods, bolstered by the partnership with Luca Baffigo, Oscar Farinetti, and Eataly. It's practically impossible to list all the different lines of the range, which includes selections and crus made with an "artisanal" approach, like the Casa E. di Mirafiore Barolos, commencing with the Paiagallo and Lazzarito. The stylistic austerity of Barolo Paiagallo 2012 stood out in our tastings, with its fresh fruit, medium body, caressing tannins, and captivating palate earning it a well-deserved Tre Bicchieri. Barolo Vigna La Rosa of the same vintage is concentrated and full, with irresistible close-focused notes of medicinal herbs and pink peppercorns. The Lazzarito 2010 has a darker, more austere nose.

● Barolo Paiagallo Casa E. di Mirafiore '12	♟♟♟	7
● Barolo Fontanafredda V. La Rosa '12	♟♟	7
● Barolo Lazzarito Casa E. di Mirafiore '10	♟♟	6
● Barbaresco Coste Rubin '13	♟♟	6
● Barolo Casa E. di Mirafiore '12	♟♟	8
● Barolo Casa E. di Mirafiore Ris. '07	♟♟	6
● Barolo del Comune di Serralunga d'Alba '12	♟♟	6
● Barolo Ris. '10	♟♟	8
● Langhe Nebbiolo Ebbio '14	♟♟	3
○ Moscato d'Asti Moncucco '15	♟♟	3
○ Roero Arneis Pradalupo '15	♟♟	3
● Barolo '12	♟	6
● Dolcetto d'Alba Casa E. di Mirafiore '15	♟	3
○ Gavi del Comune di Gavi '15	♟	3
○ Moscato d'Asti Le Fronde '15	♟	3
● Barolo Fontanafredda V. La Rosa '07	♟♟♟	7

Gabutti - Franco Boasso

B.TA GABUTTI, 3A
12050 SERRALUNGA D'ALBA [CN]
TEL. +39 0173613165
www.gabuttiboasso.com

CELLAR SALES
PRE-BOOKED VISITS
ACCOMMODATION
ANNUAL PRODUCTION 25,000 bottles
HECTARES UNDER VINE 7.00

The little estate founded by the Boasso family in the 1970s seems to be enjoying a second youth. Its close ties to the Serralunga area, where it has vineyards in the Gabutti, Meriame, and Margheria crus, are evident from its name alone. The grape varieties grown include barbera, dolcetto, moscato, and arneis, but it is of course nebbiolo that heads the fine range with the Barolos that can also be enjoyed at the delightful guest farm. Crafted with minimal intervention and aged mainly in large oak barrels, they are a benchmark for those seeking a restrained style and assertive flavours. Barolo Gabutti 2012 gave the umpteenth demonstration of its brilliance, with magnificent character and flavoursome full body, constantly enlivened by hints of violets, quinine, and Mediterranean scrubland. The Margheria 2012 is almost as good, with equally powerful, dynamic progression, but a slightly drying finish.

● Barolo Gabutti '12	♟♟	6
● Barbera d'Alba Sup. '13	♟♟	2*
● Barolo Margheria '12	♟♟	6
● Dolcetto d'Alba '15	♟	2
● Barolo Margheria '05	♟♟♟	5*
● Barbera d'Alba '12	♟♟	2*
● Barbera d'Alba '11	♟♟	2*
● Barolo del Comune di Serralunga d'Alba '11	♟♟	5
● Barolo del Comune di Serralunga d'Alba '10	♟♟	5
● Barolo Gabutti '11	♟♟	6
● Barolo Gabutti '10	♟♟	5
● Barolo Margheria '11	♟♟	6
● Barolo Margheria '10	♟♟	5
● Dolcetto d'Alba '13	♟♟	2*

Gaggino

S.DA SANT'EVASIO, 29
15076 OVADA [AL]
TEL. +39 0143822345
www.gaggino.it

★★★★★Gaja

VIA TORINO, 18
12050 BARBARESCO [CN]
TEL. +39 0173635158
info@gaja.com

CELLAR SALES
PRE-BOOKED VISITS
ANNUAL PRODUCTION 150,000 bottles
HECTARES UNDER VINE 20.00

ANNUAL PRODUCTION 350,000 bottles
HECTARES UNDER VINE 92.00

The estate founded by Leopoldo Gaggino in the 1920s has been handed down from father to son through the generations. Today it is run by the uncompromising Gabriele Gaggino, who is as forthright and honest as his wines. Characterized by their vibrancy and firm structure, some of them are immediately explosive while others are more poised and slower to express themselves, but always maintain their promise over the years. Despite the difficult vintage, Ovada Convivio offers a lovely young, concentrated nose that is echoed on a very well-orchestrated, vibrant palate. The excellent quality of the range continues with a rich, powerful version of Ovada Sant'Evasio. Barbera del Monferrato Lazzarina has lovely fruity top notes on the nose, echoed on the long, fresh palate. The sparkling Courteisa and Piemonte Bianco Pagliuzza are both worthy of note.

Today more than ever "venerable maestro", to use the Italian writer Alberto Arbasino's definition of the final stage in the career of successful Italians, Angelo Gaja, is undoubtedly the most famous producer abroad, not least for the great wines derived from his own unique interpretation of the magnificent legacy of his father Giovanni and his grandfather Angelo. Long flanked by his children Gaia, Rosanna, and Giovanni, and his wife Lucia, their Barbaresco cellar remains the nerve centre of the painstaking work focusing on a range topped by the Costa Russi, Conteisa, Sperss, Sorì San Lorenzo, and Sorì Tildin Langhe Nebbiolos. We tasted a sumptuous trio of Barbarescos. Costa Russi 2013 has the magic of a great wine, with a sophisticated, ethereal nose of freshly picked red berries, a sprinkling of spice, and a penetrating, long, layered, crystal-clear palate. Sorì Tildin 2013 is slightly weightier, also with astonishingly precisely extracted tannins. The Barbaresco 2013 is very good.

● Ovada Convivio '14	♼♼ 3*
● Barbera del M.to Lazzarina '14	♼♼ 3
○ Brut Courteisa	♼♼ 2*
● Ovada Sant'Evasio '12	♼♼ 4
○ Piemonte Bianco Pagliuzza '15	♼♼ 3
○ Cortese dell'Alto M.to '15	♼ 2
● Ovada Convivio '13	♼♼♼ 2*
● Barbera del M.to La Lazzarina '12	♼♼ 2*
● Barbera del M.to Sup. Il Ticco '11	♼♼ 3*
● Ovada S. Evasio '12	♼♼ 2*
● Ovada S. Evasio '10	♼♼ 2*

● Barbaresco Costa Russi '13	♼♼♼ 8
● Barbaresco '13	♼♼ 8
● Barbaresco Sorì Tildin '13	♼♼ 8
● Barbaresco '09	♼♼♼ 8
● Barbaresco '08	♼♼♼ 8
● Langhe Nebbiolo Costa Russi '10	♼♼♼ 8
● Langhe Nebbiolo Costa Russi '08	♼♼♼ 8
● Langhe Nebbiolo Costa Russi '07	♼♼♼ 8
● Langhe Nebbiolo Costa Russi '05	♼♼♼ 8
● Langhe Nebbiolo Costa Russi '04	♼♼♼ 8
● Langhe Nebbiolo Sorì S. Lorenzo '06	♼♼♼ 8
● Langhe Nebbiolo Sorì Tildin '11	♼♼♼ 8
● Langhe Nebbiolo Sorì Tildin '07	♼♼♼ 8
● Langhe Nebbiolo Sorì Tildin '06	♼♼♼ 8
● Langhe Nebbiolo Sperss '11	♼♼♼ 8
● Langhe Nebbiolo Sperss '04	♼♼♼ 8

Filippo Gallino

FRAZ. VALLE DEL POZZO, 63
12043 CANALE [CN]
TEL. +39 017398112
www.filippogallino.com

CELLAR SALES
PRE-BOOKED VISITS
ACCOMMODATION
ANNUAL PRODUCTION 100,000 bottles
HECTARES UNDER VINE 14.00
SUSTAINABLE WINERY

Founded in 1961, the estate has been successfully bottling its own wines for over 20 years now. Its vineyards, Briccola, Renesio, and Mompissano, lie on sandy clay soils in some of Roero's finest crus. They are planted with the classic local grapes: arneis, barbera, and nebbiolo. The resulting wines are simultaneously traditional and modern, attractive and fruit-rich. We particularly liked Barbera d'Alba Superiore 2012, with a close-focused nose of red fruit and star anise, and a complex, juicy palate that is still a little oaky, but vaunts good acidity and length, and Roero Arneis 2015, which offers notes of apricots and peaches with vegetal hints, fine stuffing, and good thrust and character on the finish. The Roero 2012 is fruity and firmly structured but has rather rugged tannins.

● Barbera d'Alba Sup. '12	♟♟ 4	
○ Roero Arneis '15	♟♟ 2*	
● Roero '12	♟♟ 4	
○ Seventy Brut M. Cl.	♟ 3	
● Barbera d'Alba Sup. '05	♟♟♟ 4*	
● Barbera d'Alba Sup. '04	♟♟♟ 4*	
● Roero '06	♟♟♟ 4*	
● Roero Sup. '03	♟♟♟ 3	
● Roero Sup. '01	♟♟♟ 5	
● Barbera d'Alba Sup. Bonora '10	♟♟ 4	
● Langhe Nebbiolo '13	♟♟ 2*	
○ Roero Arneis '14	♟♟ 2*	
○ Roero Arneis 4 Luglio '14	♟♟ 2*	
● Roero Sorano Ris. '11	♟♟ 3*	

Tenuta Garetto

S.DA ASTI MARE, 30
14041 AGLIANO TERME [AT]
TEL. +39 0141954068
www.garetto.it

CELLAR SALES
PRE-BOOKED VISITS
ANNUAL PRODUCTION 110,000 bottles
HECTARES UNDER VINE 18.00

Alessandro Garetto has been enthusiastically running the family estate for 20 years now. Its vineyards form a single plot on the hill that surrounds and overlooks the winery. Barbera accounts for 80% of the plantings on the silty clay soil with marl and limestone, while the remaining 20% is constituted by dolcetto, grignolino, and chardonnay. The resulting wines, particularly the Barberas, display exuberant fruit and are remarkably true to type. This year the three versions of Barbera d'Asti presented by Alessandro Garetto were simply splendid. Tra Neuit e Dì 2015 is a perfect current Barbera that is fruit forward, fresh and pleasant with remarkable length and good supporting acidity; Nizza Favà 2013 is deeper and firmer, with a complex nose and palate, offering spicy, earthy sensations and notes of ripe dark berries on a long, gutsy finish; and In Pectore 2014 is full, fresh, and assertive.

● Barbera d'Asti Sup. Nizza Favà '13	♟♟ 4	
● Barbera d'Asti Sup. In Pectore '14	♟♟ 5	
● Barbera d'Asti Tra Neuit e Dì '15	♟♟ 2*	
● Barbera d'Asti Sup. Nizza Favà '04	♟♟♟ 4	
● Barbera d'Asti Sup. In Pectore '13	♟♟ 5	
● Barbera d'Asti Sup. In Pectore '12	♟♟ 5	
● Barbera d'Asti Sup. Nizza Favà '12	♟♟ 4	
● Barbera d'Asti Sup. Nizza Favà '11	♟♟ 4	
● Barbera d'Asti Sup. Nizza Favà '10	♟♟ 4	
● Barbera d'Asti Sup. Nizza Favà '09	♟♟ 5	
● Barbera d'Asti Tra Neuit e Dì '14	♟♟ 2*	
● Barbera d'Asti Tra Neuit e Dì '13	♟♟ 2*	
● Barbera d'Asti Tra Neuit e Dì '12	♟♟ 2*	
○ M.to Bianco Il Biondo '13	♟♟ 3	

Generaj

B.TA TUCCI, 4
12046 MONTÀ [CN]
TEL. +39 0173976142
www.generaj.it

★Ettore Germano

LOC. CERRETTA, 1
12050 SERRALUNGA D'ALBA [CN]
TEL. +39 0173613528
www.germanoettore.com

CELLAR SALES
PRE-BOOKED VISITS
ANNUAL PRODUCTION 50,000 bottles
HECTARES UNDER VINE 12.00
SUSTAINABLE WINERY

CELLAR SALES
PRE-BOOKED VISITS
ACCOMMODATION
ANNUAL PRODUCTION 90,000 bottles
HECTARES UNDER VINE 16.00

The estate was founded by Giuseppe Viglione just after the war, and today it is passionately and successfully run by his grandson. It is planted with the typical Roero arneis, barbera, and nebbiolo grape varieties along with a small amount of bonarda and croatina. The estate's vineyards are in the southern part of Roero on different soils ranging from local typical sandy type to chalky and gravelly plots. Barbera d'Alba Superiore Ca' d' Pistola is among the best of its kind, with a nose of morello cherries and plums, followed by hints of cocoa powder against a backdrop of spice and roasted coffee beans, and a satisfyingly long, caressing palate. Roero Riserva Bric Aût 2012 is well made, focusing more on notes of Mediterranean scrubland and red berry fruit, but with rather austere tannins. Roero Bric Aût 2013 is pleasant and approachable, while Roero Arneis Quindicilune 2014 is less striking than past vintages.

The competitive Langhe region is full of estates that have risen to fame more on the strength of their top wines than on the general quality of their range. However, this is not the case of Sergio Germano, who is enjoying great success due to a comprehensive array of wines. Initially renowned mainly for his vigorous, multifaceted Barolos, from spectacular vineyards such as Prapò, Cerretta, and Lazzarito in Serralunga, he subsequently beguiled us with his white and sparkling wines from riesling, sauvignon, chardonnay, and pinot nero planted on the Aglié estate in Alta Langa. His success is deservedly consolidated with each new vintage. The range is once again spectacular, commencing with the fabulous Prapò and Ceretta 2012 Barolos, which complement each other very well. However, as usual, the Lazzarito Riserva is in a class of its own, with the monumental 2010 vintage vaunting aromatic contrasts, silky tannins, and exceptional length. Don't forget the very fine Riesling Hérzu.

● Barbera d'Alba Sup. Ca' d' Pistola '13	♟♟ 3*
● Roero Bric Aùt '13	♟♟ 4
● Roero Bric Aùt Ris. '12	♟♟ 5
○ Roero Arneis Bric Varomaldo '15	♟ 3
○ Roero Arneis Quindicilune '14	♟ 3
● Barbera d'Alba Sup. Ca' d' Pistola '12	♟♟ 3
○ Generaj Brut M. Cl. '11	♟♟ 5
○ Generaj Brut M. Cl. '10	♟♟ 5
○ Roero Arneis Quindicilune '13	♟♟ 3
○ Roero Arneis Quindicilune '12	♟♟ 3*
● Roero Bric Aût '12	♟♟ 4
● Roero Bric Aût '11	♟♟ 3

● Barolo Lazzarito Ris. '10	♟♟♟ 8
● Barolo Cerretta '12	♟♟ 7
● Barolo Prapò '12	♟♟ 7
○ Langhe Riesling Hérzu '14	♟♟ 4
○ Alta Langa Brut '12	♟♟ 5
● Barolo del Comune di Serralunga '12	♟♟ 6
○ Brut Rosé Rosanna M. Cl. '14	♟ 4
● Barolo Cerretta '05	♟♟♟ 8
● Barolo Cerretta '01	♟♟♟ 6
● Barolo Lazzarito Ris. '08	♟♟♟ 8
● Barolo Prapò '11	♟♟♟ 7
● Barolo Prapò '04	♟♟♟ 6
○ Langhe Bianco Hérzu '11	♟♟♟ 4*
○ Langhe Bianco Hérzu '10	♟♟♟ 4*
○ Langhe Bianco Hérzu '09	♟♟♟ 5
○ Langhe Bianco Hérzu '08	♟♟♟ 5

La Ghibellina

FRAZ. MONTEROTONDO, 61
15066 GAVI [AL]
TEL. +39 0143686257
www.laghibellina.it

CELLAR SALES
PRE-BOOKED VISITS
RESTAURANT SERVICE
ANNUAL PRODUCTION 60,000 bottles
HECTARES UNDER VINE 7.90

The estate founded in 2000 by Alberto and Maria Ghibellina vaunts an area of almost eight hectares under vine, planted mainly to cortese. It is located in Monterotondo, in the municipality of Gavi, long known for its concentrated, mineral whites with good ageing potential, like the estate's two Metodo Classicos: the Mainin, fermented in stainless steel; and the Altius aged partly in small oak casks. The reds are based on barbera, alone in Chiaretto Sandrino and Nero del Montone, and blended with merlot in the Pituj. Gavi di Gavi once again accounts for the lion's share, commencing with Altius 2014, boasting fine citrus-led aromatic persistence and zesty energy. Mainin 2015 is more concentrated and layered, with medicinal herbs, golden delicious apples, and river rocks on the nose, followed by a taut, luxuriant palate with a thirst-quenching balsamic finish.

○ Gavi del Comune di Gavi Altius '14	♈♈	5
○ Gavi del Comune di Gavi Mainin '15	♈♈	3*
○ Gavi del Comune di Gavi Brut Cuvée Marina M. Cl. '11	♈♈	7
○ Gavi del Comune di Gavi Cuvée Brut M. Cl. '13	♈	5
● M.to Rosso Pituj '14	♈	4
○ Gavi del Comune di Gavi Altius '13	♈♈	3*
○ Gavi del Comune di Gavi Altius '11	♈♈	3*
○ Gavi del Comune di Gavi Brut M. Cl. '11	♈♈	4
○ Gavi del Comune di Gavi Mainin '14	♈♈	3*
○ Gavi del Comune di Gavi Mainin '13	♈♈	3*
○ Gavi del Comune di Gavi Mainin '12	♈♈	3
● M.to Rosso Nero del Montone '10	♈♈	4
● M.to Rosso Pituj '13	♈♈	3
● M.to Rosso Pituj '12	♈♈	3

★★Bruno Giacosa

VIA XX SETTEMBRE, 52
12057 NEIVE [CN]
TEL. +39 017367027
www.brunogiacosa.it

ANNUAL PRODUCTION 300,000 bottles
HECTARES UNDER VINE 19.00
SUSTAINABLE WINERY

There are at least two reasons for Bruno Giacosa's legendary international standing. First of all, no other Italian producer has managed to raise the reputation of the figure of the négociant to such heights, for it should be remembered that many of his finest wines have been made from purchased grapes. But above all, he has produced stellar Barolos and Barbarescos with that unmistakable blend of delicious austerity, fruity sweetness, and unyielding structure. Aided by his daughter Bruna, he also established the Azienda Agricola Falletto label, under which the wines from the estate's own vineyards are marketed. Giacosa's style is exemplified by Barolo Falletto 2012 with undertones of camphor and liquorice, fresher fruity nuances initially concealed by tertiary notes, and an exceptionally full-flavoured, tannic palate that suggests a long, bright future. However, this year we could not fail to assign our highest accolade to the extraordinary Asili Riserva 2011, which associates the unique complexity of Nebbiolo with an incredibly deep palate.

● Barbaresco Asili Ris. '11	♈♈♈	8
● Barolo Falletto '12	♈♈	8
● Nebbiolo d'Alba V. Valmaggiore '14	♈♈	5
○ Roero Arneis '15	♈♈	4
● Barbaresco Asili '12	♈♈♈	8
● Barbaresco Asili '05	♈♈♈	8
● Barbaresco Asili Ris. '07	♈♈♈	8
● Barbaresco Asili Ris. '04	♈♈♈	8
● Barolo Falletto '07	♈♈♈	8
● Barolo Falletto '04	♈♈♈	8
● Barolo Le Rocche del Falletto '05	♈♈♈	8
● Barolo Le Rocche del Falletto '04	♈♈♈	8
● Barolo Le Rocche del Falletto Ris. '08	♈♈♈	8
● Barolo Le Rocche del Falletto Ris. '07	♈♈♈	8
● Barolo Le Rocche del Falletto Ris. '01	♈♈♈	8

Carlo Giacosa

S.DA OVELLO, 9
12050 BARBARESCO [CN]
TEL. +39 0173635116
www.carlogiacosa.it

CELLAR SALES
PRE-BOOKED VISITS
ANNUAL PRODUCTION 42,000 bottles
HECTARES UNDER VINE 5.50

Donato Giacosa founded his Barbaresco winery in 1968 with the purchase of some of the finest plots in the production zone. His work has been continued by his farsighted son Carlo, now flanked by his daughter Maria Grazia and Luca, the founder's great-grandson, in the cellar. In addition to Montefico, the estate also owns several legendary crus, such as Asili, Cole, Narin, and Ovello. Its consistent, reliable production, with sparing use of oak, is excellent value for money. Barbaresco Montefico 2013 towers above the other wines, showing a deep, bright ruby, with a concentrated nose of fresh flowers, liquorice, and sweet tobacco, and an elegant, complex palate offering fragrant wild berries, fine-grained, close-woven tannins, and a long, succulent finish. Barbera d'Alba Mucin 2015 vaunts exemplary cleanliness, concentration, and freshness on the palate, while Langhe Nebbiolo Maria Grazia 2014 has a subtle, ethereal nose of blossom and wild berries.

● Barbaresco Montefico '13	♟♟ 5
● Barbera d'Alba Mucin '15	♟♟ 3
● Langhe Nebbiolo Maria Grazia '14	♟♟ 3
○ Dolcetto d'Alba Cuchet '15	♟ 2
● Barbaresco Montefico '08	♟♟♟ 5*
● Barbaresco Luca Ris. '10	♟♟ 6
● Barbaresco Luca Ris. '09	♟♟ 6
● Barbaresco Montefico '12	♟♟ 5
● Barbaresco Montefico '11	♟♟ 5
● Barbaresco Narin '12	♟♟ 5
● Barbera d'Alba Lina '12	♟♟ 3
● Barbera d'Alba Mucin '14	♟♟ 3
● Langhe Nebbiolo Maria Grazia '13	♟♟ 3

F.lli Giacosa

VIA XX SETTEMBRE, 64
12057 NEIVE [CN]
TEL. +39 017367013
www.giacosa.it

CELLAR SALES
PRE-BOOKED VISITS
ANNUAL PRODUCTION 500,000 bottles
HECTARES UNDER VINE 50.00
SUSTAINABLE WINERY

Vaunting over a century of tradition, the estate owned by brothers Maurizio and Paolo Giacosa is as reliable as ever. Its production headquarters are in Neive, along with many prized plots for Barbaresco, while the Barolo hails from vineyards in Castiglione Falletto and Monforte d'Alba, the Dolcetto from Alba, and the Chardonnay from Trezzo Tinella. Consequently, the range of wines is wide and diversified, with solid quality throughout and fair prices. Barolo Scarrone Vigna Mandorlo 2011 displays a brilliant balance of rich fruit and darker notes of juniper berries and soot. It has a firmly structured palate with sweet, close-woven tannins and a very long finish. Barolo Bussia 2012 has an alluring, concentrated nose of red berries and subtle spicy hints, accompanied by a medium-structured palate with still slightly overbearing tannins and a long, well-sustained finish. Chardonnay Ca' Lunga 2015 is full, ripe, and racy.

● Barolo Scarrone V. Mandorlo '11	♟♟ 8
● Barbera d'Alba Maria Gioana '13	♟♟ 5
● Barolo Bussia '12	♟♟ 7
○ Langhe Chardonnay Ca' Lunga '15	♟♟ 5
● Nebbiolo d'Alba '14	♟ 5
● Barbaresco Basarin V. Gianmaté '12	♟♟ 6
● Barbaresco Basarin V. Gianmaté '11	♟♟ 6
● Barbera d'Alba Maria Gioana '12	♟♟ 5
● Barbera d'Alba Maria Gioana '11	♟♟ 4
● Barbera d'Alba Maria Gioana '10	♟♟ 4
● Barolo Bussia '11	♟♟ 6
● Barolo Scarrone V. Mandorlo '10	♟♟ 7
● Barolo V. Mandorlo '08	♟♟ 7
● Nebbiolo d'Alba '13	♟♟ 4

Giovanni Battista Gillardi

Cascina Corsaletto, 69
12060 Farigliano [CN]
Tel. +39 017376306
www.gillardi.it

CELLAR SALES
PRE-BOOKED VISITS
ANNUAL PRODUCTION 35,000 bottles
HECTARES UNDER VINE 7.00

The multi-talented Giacolino Gillardi has worked and played very hard with wine. Indeed, his Harys, from syrah, first released in 1993, rocked the Langhe tradition based on nebbiolo, dolcetto, and barbera. Although other experimental wines followed, produced in small amounts from merlot, cabernet sauvignon, and grenache, the estate's heart is still firmly embedded in the local tradition, with dolcetto remaining the principle grape used in the cellar. Following the purchase of a little cellar and vineyard in Barolo, the estate also started producing Barolo, commencing with the 2011 vintage. The 2015 vintage was a very difficult year for Giacolino Gillardi. One of his most important vineyards was struck by hail, halving the production of the Cursalet. After having flirted with French grape varieties for year, Giacolino has returned to dolcetto, his first love. In this extraordinary vintage, the Cursalet combines a carefree fruity nose with rare fullness for a Dolcetto. The Barolo 2012 is austere but nicely fleshy.

● Barolo '12	♟♟ 6
● Dogliani Cursalet '15	♟♟ 3*
● Dogliani Maestra '15	♟♟ 3
● Langhe Harys '14	♟♟ 7
● Langhe Ilmerlò '13	♟♟ 8
● Langhe Nebbiolo '14	♟♟ 4
● Langhe Fiore di Harys '14	♟ 4
● Barolo del Comune di Barolo '11	♟♟ 3*
● Dogliani Cursalet '14	♟♟ 3
● Dogliani Cursalet '13	♟♟ 3*
● Dogliani Cursalet '12	♟♟ 3*
● Dogliani Maestra '14	♟♟ 2*
● Langhe Harys '13	♟♟ 6
● Langhe Nebbiolo '13	♟♟ 6
● Langhe Rosso Harys '12	♟♟ 6
● Langhe Rosso Harys '11	♟♟ 6

La Gironda

s.da Bricco, 12
14049 Nizza Monferrato [AT]
Tel. +39 0141701013
www.lagironda.com

CELLAR SALES
PRE-BOOKED VISITS
ANNUAL PRODUCTION 60,000 bottles
HECTARES UNDER VINE 9.00
SUSTAINABLE WINERY

Founded by Agostino Galandrino in 2000, in recent years Gironda has become a leading player in the Asti wine world. Situated in Bricco Cremosino, a veritable barbera cru, where it vaunts a vineyard planted in 1963, the estate produces a small range, composed largely of Barberas. The wines are modern in style, with striking aromatic focus, and characterized by fresh fruit and attractive drinkability. Barbera d'Asti Superiore Nizza Le Nicchie 2013 has notes of quinine, with hints of ripe dark fruit and spice on the nose, and a full-bodied palate with prominent tannins. However, the whole range is well made. Barbera d'Asti La Lippa 2015 offers a nose of red berries with balsamic hints, and perfectly balanced structure, acidity, and alcohol; the leaner but exceptionally pleasant La Gena 2014 has notes of fresh red fruit; and the varietal Piemonte Sauvignon l'Aquilone 2015 is easy drinking.

● Barbera d'Asti La Gena '14	♟♟ 3
● Barbera d'Asti La Lippa '15	♟♟ 2*
● Barbera d'Asti Sup. Nizza Le Nicchie '13	♟♟ 5
○ Piemonte Sauvignon L'Aquilone '15	♟♟ 2*
● M.to Rosso Soul '13	♟ 5
○ Moscato d'Asti '15	♟ 2
● Barbera d'Asti Sup. Nizza Le Nicchie '11	♟♟♟ 5
● Barbera d'Asti La Gena '13	♟♟ 3
● Barbera d'Asti La Gena '12	♟♟ 3*
● Barbera d'Asti La Lippa '14	♟♟ 2*
● Barbera d'Asti Sup. Nizza Le Nicchie '12	♟♟ 5
● M.to Rosso Soul '12	♟♟ 5
○ Moscato d'Asti '13	♟♟ 2*

Tenuta La Giustiniana

FRAZ. ROVERETO, 5
15066 GAVI [AL]
TEL. +39 0143682132
www.lagiustiniana.it

CELLAR SALES
PRE-BOOKED VISITS
ANNUAL PRODUCTION 200,000 bottles
HECTARES UNDER VINE 39.00

Constantly cited as one of the first Gavi estates to have focused on single-vineyard selections, La Giustiniana is named after a splendid farm in the heart of the Rovereto hamlet. Covering an area of around 40 hectares, tended with organic methods and planted mainly to cortese, in recent years the Lombardini family's estate has received a further boost from its partnership with Enrico Tomalino. The flagship wines are represented by the various crus, all with different soils: grey marl for the Lugarara plots and iron-rich clay for Montessora, while Rovereto yields the Nostro Gavi, which undergoes long ageing on the lees in stainless-steel tanks. The contest between the 2015 Gavi crus ended in a tie: the Lugarara is tidy and supple, while the Montessora is more aromatic with almondy notes on the palate. Il Nostro Gavi 2012 is even better, enlivened with fresh notes of medicinal herbs and citrus on a beautifully salty wake.

○ Gavi del Comune di Gavi Il Nostro Gavi '12	♀♀ 4
○ Gavi del Comune di Gavi Lugarara '15	♀♀ 3
○ Gavi del Comune di Gavi Montessora '15	♀♀ 4
○ Gavi del Comune di Gavi Il Nostro Gavi '07	♀♀♀ 4
○ Gavi del Comune di Gavi Il Nostro Gavi '10	♀♀ 4
○ Gavi del Comune di Gavi Lugarara '14	♀♀ 3
○ Gavi del Comune di Gavi Lugarara '13	♀♀ 3*
○ Gavi del Comune di Gavi Lugarara '12	♀♀ 3*
○ Gavi del Comune di Gavi Lugarara '11	♀♀ 3
○ Gavi del Comune di Gavi Montessora '14	♀♀ 4
○ Gavi del Comune di Gavi Montessora '13	♀♀ 4
○ Gavi del Comune di Gavi Montessora '12	♀♀ 4

★Elio Grasso

LOC. GINESTRA, 40
12065 MONFORTE D'ALBA [CN]
TEL. +39 017378491
www.eliograsso.it

PRE-BOOKED VISITS
ANNUAL PRODUCTION 90,000 bottles
HECTARES UNDER VINE 18.00
SUSTAINABLE WINERY

One of the definitions of "classic" offered by the authoritative Treccani encyclopedia is "capable of serving as a model of a type and thus of establishing a tradition". It is a perfect description of the Barolos made by Elio Grasso with his wife Marina and their son Gianluca. Initially considered almost innovative in style, they soon became models of typicity on the dynamic Langhe wine scene. The technical specifications reveal ageing in 2,000-litre Slavonian oak barrels for the Casa Matè and Gavarini Vigna Chiniera, and in barriques for the Runcot Riserva, but these are just details in respect to the austere and nuanced nature of the three spectacular Monforte d'Alba crus. This year the customary contest between the Barolo 2012 crus was won by Ginestra Casa Maté. The Gavarini Chiniera is complex and layered, with a nice balance of close-woven tannins and luxuriant pulp, while the voluptuous Ginestra Casa Maté has a full nose of autumn leaves, liquorice, and juniper berries, followed by a delicious well-orchestrated palate with complex length.

● Barolo Ginestra Casa Maté '12	♀♀♀ 8
● Barbera d'Alba V. Martina '13	♀♀ 5
● Barolo Gavarini Chiniera '12	♀♀ 8
● Barolo Gavarini Chiniera '09	♀♀♀ 8
● Barolo Gavarini V. Chiniera '06	♀♀♀ 8
● Barolo Gavarini V. Chiniera '01	♀♀♀ 7
● Barolo Gavarini V. Chiniera '00	♀♀♀ 7
● Barolo Ginestra Casa Maté '07	♀♀♀ 8
● Barolo Ginestra V. Casa Maté '05	♀♀♀ 8
● Barolo Ginestra V. Casa Maté '04	♀♀♀ 8
● Barolo Ginestra V. Casa Maté '03	♀♀♀ 7
● Barolo Rüncot '01	♀♀♀ 8
● Barolo Rüncot '00	♀♀♀ 8

Silvio Grasso

FRAZ. ANNUNZIATA, 112
12064 LA MORRA [CN]
TEL. +39 017350322
www.silviograsso.com

CELLAR SALES
PRE-BOOKED VISITS
ANNUAL PRODUCTION 90,000 bottles
HECTARES UNDER VINE 14.00

Federico Grasso's estate has been bottling its own wines for 35 years, with consistently good results. The overall style is decidedly modern, with the two flagship Barolos, Bricco Luciani and Bricco Manzoni, aged in small new oak casks for two years. Barolo Turné, on the other hand follows the local tradition of blending the grapes of several vineyards, with very long maceration and ageing in a large used barrel. The other wines also performed exceptionally well, particularly Barbera d'Alba Fontanile. Barolo Bricco Luciani 2012 has elegant notes of new oak on a nose of red berries, and a full, complex palate with nicely balanced tannins and pulp. The traditional-style Turnè has charming top notes of mixed berries, followed by aniseed and mint, while the firm, tannic Barolo Annunziata Vigna Plicotti 2012 is characterized by hints of autumn leaves and dried herbs. Bricco Manzoni 2012 already has a very open nose, and the very drinkable Barolo 2012 is short on power, but displays great finesse.

● Barolo Bricco Luciani '12	♥♥ 7
● Barolo Turne' '12	♥♥ 7
● Barbera d'Alba Fontanile '13	♥♥ 5
● Barolo '12	♥♥ 5
● Barolo Annunziata V. Plicotti '12	♥♥ 7
● Barolo Bricco Manzoni '12	♥♥ 8
● Barolo Bricco Luciani '04	♥♥♥ 7
● Barolo Bricco Luciani '01	♥♥♥ 6
● Barolo Bricco Luciani '96	♥♥♥ 6
● Barolo Bricco Luciani '95	♥♥♥ 6
● Barolo Bricco Luciani '90	♥♥♥ 6
● Barolo Bricco Manzoni '10	♥♥♥ 7
● Barolo Bricco Luciani '11	♥♥ 7
● Barolo Bricco Luciani '10	♥♥ 7
● Barolo Bricco Luciani '09	♥♥ 7
● Barolo Bricco Manzoni '11	♥♥ 7

Bruna Grimaldi

VIA PAREA, 7
12060 GRINZANE CAVOUR [CN]
TEL. +39 0173262094
www.grimaldibruna.it

CELLAR SALES
PRE-BOOKED VISITS
ANNUAL PRODUCTION 70,000 bottles
HECTARES UNDER VINE 14.00

Most Barolo fans are unaware of Roddi, but a growing number of wineries are using its small but fine nebbiolo vineyards. Bruna Grimaldi does in her Barolo Bricco Ambrogio, always very drinkable and not too tannic. However, the estate's finest and best-known Barolo comes from the Badarina cru in Serralunga d'Alba, also the origin of a top Riserva, while the more delicate Barolo Camilla, from grapes grown in Grinzane Cavour, offers several excellent vintages. The range is completed by the clean, pleasant Nebbiolo, Dolcetto, and Barbera d'Alba, and a small production of Langhe Arneis, from Neive. Barolo Badarina 2012 has a concentrated, layered nose with fine tobacco and liquorice notes giving character and complexity to its ripe red fruit, with a well- structured palate of elegant tannins and rich flesh. Riserva Badarina 2012 is convincing, with sound fruit and a slightly rugged palate. The pleasant, delicately structured Barolo Bricco Ambrogio 2012 has top notes of raspberries and wild strawberries with spicy undertones of black pepper.

● Barolo Badarina '12	♥♥ 6
● Barolo Badarina Ris. '10	♥♥ 7
● Barbera d'Alba Sup. Scassa '13	♥♥ 3
● Barolo Bricco Ambrogio '12	♥♥ 5
● Barolo Camilla '12	♥♥ 5
● Dolcetto d'Alba '14	♥ 2
○ Langhe Arneis '15	♥ 2
● Nebbiolo d'Alba '13	♥ 3
● Barolo Badarina '11	♥♥ 6
● Barolo Badarina '10	♥♥ 6
● Barolo Badarina '09	♥♥ 6
● Barolo Badarina Ris. '09	♥♥ 6
● Barolo Badarina V. Regnola Ris. '06	♥♥ 6
● Barolo Bricco Ambrogio '10	♥♥ 5
● Barolo Bricco Ambrogio '09	♥♥ 5
● Barolo Bricco Ambrogio '08	♥♥ 5

Giacomo Grimaldi

VIA LUIGI EINAUDI, 8
12060 BAROLO [CN]
TEL. +39 0173560536
www.giacomogrimaldi.com

CELLAR SALES
PRE-BOOKED VISITS
ANNUAL PRODUCTION 50,000 bottles
HECTARES UNDER VINE 13.00

Today Ferruccio, yesterday Giacomo and
Ernesto: three generations of the Grimaldi
family continue to make their wine in
Barolo with great skill. The style is
traditional, producing austere young wines
that unbend after a few years, offering
great ageing potential. Barolo Le Coste
stands out for its great power, while the
Sotto Castello di Novello focuses more on
elegance. The vineyards around the
farmstead, belonging to the excellent Terlo
cru, supply the grapes for the basic Barolo.
This year the estate's best Barolo was the
Sotto Castello di Novello, which displays
aristocratic elegance. It fully expresses the
finesse of the cru in its classic nose of
roses, black pepper, and raspberries, and
the palate is equally good, characterized by
delicate tannins. Le Coste has a far darker
nose and a bigger, more rugged palate,
making it suitable for long ageing. The
Barolo 2012, from the Terlo and Ravera
vineyards, is rather austere.

● Barolo Sotto Castello di Novello '12	♟♟ 6
● Barbera d'Alba Pistin '15	♟♟ 3
● Barolo '12	♟♟ 6
● Barolo Le Coste '12	♟♟ 7
● Dolcetto d'Alba '15	♟ 2
○ Langhe Sauvignon '15	♟ 3
● Barolo Sotto Castello di Novello '05	♟♟♟ 6
● Barbera d'Alba Fornaci '12	♟♟ 4
● Barbera d'Alba Pistin '14	♟♟ 3
● Barolo '11	♟♟ 6
● Barolo Le Coste '11	♟♟ 7
● Barolo Le Coste '10	♟♟ 6
● Barolo Sotto Castello di Novello '11	♟♟ 6
● Barolo Sotto Castello di Novello '10	♟♟ 6
● Dolcetto d'Alba '14	♟♟ 2*

La Guardia

POD. LA GUARDIA, 74
15010 MORSASCO [AL]
TEL. +39 014473076
www.laguardiavilladelfini.it

CELLAR SALES
PRE-BOOKED VISITS
ANNUAL PRODUCTION 100,000 bottles
HECTARES UNDER VINE 35.00

The Priarone family commenced business
in the 1960s with seven hectares of
vineyards. Today they have around 35
hectares under vine and the winery is
housed in the splendid 17th-century Villa
Delfini in Morsasco, where the top wines
are aged in the old cellars, while the rest of
the property is used as a venue for
ceremonies and events. The wines are
made from both native barbera, dolcetto,
albarossa, brachetto, and cortese natives,
and international merlot, pinot nero,
cabernet sauvignon, and chardonnay. The
range opens with Ovada Riserva Il
Gamondino, vaunting a fruity nose with
undertones of spice and tobacco, and good
progression on the long palate. Monferrato
Rosso 805 has a vegetal nose and a firmly
structured palate with rather rugged
tannins on the finish. We also liked Doppio
Rosso, from dolcetto and barbera, and
Piemonte Chardonnay Villa Delfini.

● M.to Rosso 805 '11	♟♟ 3
● Ovada Il Gamondino Ris. '13	♟♟ 3
● Doppio Rosso '13	♟ 3
○ Piemonte Chardonnay Villa Delfini '15	♟ 3
● Barbera del M.to Ornovo '11	♟♟ 3
● Barbera del M.to Sup. La V. di Dante '08	♟♟ 4
● M.to Rosso Innominato '09	♟♟ 4
● M.to Rosso Leone '09	♟♟ 4
● M.to Rosso Leone '08	♟♟ 4
● M.to Rosso Sacro e Profano '09	♟♟ 4
● M.to Rosso Sacro e Profano '07	♟♟ 5
● Ovada Il Gamondino Ris. '11	♟♟ 3
● Ovada Vign. Bricco Riccardo '10	♟♟ 3

Clemente Guasti

C.SO IV NOVEMBRE, 80
14049 NIZZA MONFERRATO [AT]
TEL. +39 0141721350
www.guasti.it

CELLAR SALES
PRE-BOOKED VISITS
ANNUAL PRODUCTION 120,000 bottles
HECTARES UNDER VINE 27.00

Andrea and Alessandro run this
long-standing winery in the heart of Nizza
Monferrato, which is a benchmark for
Barbera d'Asti. Its vineyards are arranged
in four farmsteads: Boschetto Vecchio,
Fonda San Nicolao, Santa Teresa, and
Gessara–San Vitale, three in the Nizza area
and one near Mombaruzzo. The style of its
production is traditional, focusing mainly
on wines for laying down. Barbera d'Asti
Superiore Severa 2011 exemplifies the
house style, with notes of toast, followed
by mint, medicinal herbs, and bottled
cherries on the nose, and a complex, juicy
palate offering a nice balance of rich pulp
and fresh acidity. Barbera d'Asti Superiore
Boschetto Vecchio 2011 is spicy, with a
supple, evolved palate, while Moscato
d'Asti Santa Teresa 2015 has sweet, full
notes of orange peel and candied fruit,
and Barbera d'Asti Superiore Nizza
Barcarato 2011 is concentrated, dense,
and fruit rich.

● Barbera d'Asti Sup. Severa '11	▼▼ 3*
● Barbera d'Asti Sup. Boschetto Vecchio '11	▼▼ 4
● Barbera d'Asti Sup. Nizza Barcarato '11	▼▼ 5
○ Moscato d'Asti Santa Teresa '15	▼▼ 3
● Barbera d'Asti Desideria '13	▼ 3
● Barbera d'Asti Sup. Boschetto Vecchio '10	♡♡ 4
● Barbera d'Asti Sup. Boschetto Vecchio '09	♡♡ 4
● Barbera d'Asti Sup. Fonda San Nicolao '09	♡♡ 4
● Barbera d'Asti Sup. Nizza Barcarato '09	♡♡ 5
● Barbera d'Asti Sup. Severa '10	♡♡ 3
● Grignolino d'Asti '14	♡♡ 3
○ Moscato d'Asti Santa Teresa '13	♡♡ 3
○ Moscato d'Asti Santa Teresa '12	♡♡ 3

★Hilberg - Pasquero

VIA BRICCO GATTI, 16
12040 PRIOCCA [CN]
TEL. +39 0173616197
www.hilberg-pasquero.com

CELLAR SALES
PRE-BOOKED VISITS
ANNUAL PRODUCTION 24,000 bottles
HECTARES UNDER VINE 6.50
VITICULTURE METHOD Certified Organic

Michele Pasquero and Annette Hilberg
have created one of the best-known and
unique wineries in Roero, although none of
their wines bears the Roero designation. In
Bricco Gatti, on a hill overlooking Priocca,
the vineyards lie on white, silty and marly
soils, with a higher clay content than the
classic sandy Roero terrain, and are home
to red grape varieties only: barbera,
brachetto, and nebbiolo. This year our
favourite was the very drinkable Barbera
d'Alba 2015, flaunting a concentrated
nose of ripe cherries with earthy hints,
and a juicy but firmly structured palate.
Barbera d'Alba Superiore 2014 has notes
of cocoa powder, spice, and toast and
good stuffing, but rather fierce acidity
deriving from the difficult vintage. The
Vareij Rosso, a blend of 70% brachetto
and 30% barbera, is well made, showing
very aromatic with excellent grip.

● Barbera d'Alba '15	▼▼ 3*
● Barbera d'Alba Sup. '14	▼▼ 5
● Vareij Rosso	▼▼ 3
● Langhe Nebbiolo '14	▼ 4
● Barbera d'Alba Sup. '09	♡♡♡ 5
● Nebbiolo d'Alba '06	♡♡♡ 5
● Nebbiolo d'Alba '05	♡♡♡ 5
● Nebbiolo d'Alba '04	♡♡♡ 5
● Nebbiolo d'Alba '03	♡♡♡ 5
● Nebbiolo d'Alba '01	♡♡♡ 5
● Barbera d'Alba '14	♡♡ 3
● Langhe Nebbiolo '13	♡♡ 4
● Nebbiolo d'Alba '13	♡♡ 5

Icardi

LOC. SAN LAZZARO
S.DA COMUNALE BALBI, 30
12053 CASTIGLIONE TINELLA [CN]
TEL. +39 0141855159
www.icardivini.it

CELLAR SALES
PRE-BOOKED VISITS
ANNUAL PRODUCTION 360,000 bottles
HECTARES UNDER VINE 75.00
VITICULTURE METHOD Certified Biodynamic

Claudio and Mariagrazia Icardi run the
family winery founded in 1914 on the
border between Bassa Langa and
Monferrato. The vineyards next to the cellar
are flanked by others in Castiglione Tinella
and the finest winegrowing areas of
Monferrato and Langhe, offering a wide
range of wines, from Barolo and Barbaresco
to Barbera d'Asti and Moscato d'Asti. All of
them are focused, with plenty of fruit, and
highly drinkable from the moment of their
release, even in the case of the most
structured wines. The entire range
performed well, although there was no
absolute star. Barolo Parej 2012 made it
into our finals with its layered nose and
well-orchestrated palate, while the fruity
Barbaresco Montubert 2013 offers notes of
currants and a long finish. The white wines
are also well made, from the full, enfolding
Piemonte Bianco Pafoj 2015, from 60%
sauvignon and 40% chardonnay, which is
brimming with fruit, to Dadelio Bianco 2015,
a fresh aromatic blend of 70% cortese and
30% moscato.

● Barolo Parej '12	▼▼ 8
● Barbaresco Montubert '13	▼▼ 5
● Barbera d'Asti Sup. Nuj Suj '14	▼▼ 5
○ Dadelio Bianco '15	▼▼ 5
○ Moscato d'Asti La Rosa Selvatica '15	▼▼ 2*
○ Piemonte Bianco Pafoj '15	▼▼ 4
● Barbaresco Montubert '11	♀♀ 5
● Barbera d'Alba Surì di Mù '12	♀♀ 5
● Barbera d'Asti Nuj Suj '12	♀♀ 5
● Barolo Parej '11	♀♀ 8
● Langhe Rosso Dadelio Cascina San Lazzaro '11	♀♀ 5
● Langhe Rosso Pafoj '11	♀♀ 6
○ Piemonte Bianco Pafoj '14	♀♀ 4
○ Piemonte Bianco Pafoj '13	♀♀ 4

Ioppa

FRAZ. MAULETTA
VIA DELLE PALLOTTE, 10
28078 ROMAGNANO SESIA [NO]
TEL. +39 0163833079
www.viniioppa.it

CELLAR SALES
PRE-BOOKED VISITS
ANNUAL PRODUCTION 140,000 bottles
HECTARES UNDER VINE 20.50

The winery run by brothers Giampiero and
Giorgio Ioppa, with their sons Marco and
Andrea is certainly no newcomer to the
Novara production zone. Over the past few
years we have nonetheless noticed a
definite change in direction over the entire
range, hailing from about 20 hectares of
vineyards in Ghemme and Romagnano
Sesia. The focus is naturally reds from
nebbiolo although large areas are planted to
erbaluce, uva rara, and vespolina, the latter
used for the Stransì passito. The Ghemme
trio, formed by the basic version and the
Bricco Balsina and Santa Fé vineyard
selections, is modern and innovative, still
showing a little over-extracted and oaky in
its youth. The controversial 2011 vintage
has been brilliantly interpreted by the Ioppa
family. Their Santa Fé is strikingly fresh and
floral, with delicate texture, while the
Balsina has deeper aromas but leaner
development. The powerful Vespolina also
deserves a mention.

● Colline Novaresi Vespolina '11	▼▼ 3*
● Ghemme '11	▼▼ 4
● Ghemme Santa Fé '11	▼▼ 6
● Ghemme Bricco Balsina '11	▼▼ 6
● Colline Novaresi Nebbiolo '11	♀♀ 2*
● Colline Novaresi Nebbiolo '09	♀♀ 2*
⊙ Colline Novaresi Nebbiolo Rusin '13	♀♀ 2*
● Colline Novaresi Vespolina '07	♀♀ 3
● Ghemme '08	♀♀ 4
● Ghemme '07	♀♀ 4
● Ghemme Bricco Balsina '08	♀♀ 6
● Ghemme Bricco Balsina '07	♀♀ 4
● Ghemme Santa Fè '08	♀♀ 6
● Ghemme Santa Fè '07	♀♀ 6
● Stransì	♀♀ 5

Isolabella della Croce

REG. CAFFI, 3
14051 LOAZZOLO [AT]
TEL. +39 014487166
www.isolabelladellacroce.it

CELLAR SALES
PRE-BOOKED VISITS
ANNUAL PRODUCTION 90,000 bottles
HECTARES UNDER VINE 14.00

Borgo Isolabella and its vineyards are set among the woods in a south-facing natural amphitheatre over 500 metres above sea level in the little Loazzolo designation of Alta Langa, in the province of Asti, between the Belbo and Bormida valleys. Its range is composed of a dozen wines, from both native and international grape varieties. Pinot nero is the most important of the latter, in terms of both quantity and potential. The Nizza Augusta comes from the winery's estate in Calamandrana. The list of wines presented is as sound as ever, commencing with Barbera d'Asti Superiore Serena 2013, with a delicate, complex nose of fresh dark berries, tobacco, and rain-soaked earth, accompanied by a balanced palate with plenty of crisp fruit and lively acidity. Barbera d'Asti Superiore Nizza Augusta 2012 is still marked by oak but vaunts good structure and fullness. Moscato d'Asti Valdiserre 2015 is pleasant, while Piemonte Pinot Nero Bricco del Falco 2012 is rather austere.

● Barbera d'Asti Sup. Serena '13	♀♀ 4
● Barbera d'Asti Sup. Nizza Augusta '12	♀♀ 5
○ Moscato d'Asti Valdiserre '15	♀♀ 3
● Piemonte Pinot Nero Bricco del Falco '12	♀♀ 5
○ Loazzolo Solìo V. T. '07	♀ 5
○ Piemonte Chardonnay Solum '14	♀ 4
○ Piemonte Sauvignon Blanc '15	♀ 3
● Barbera d'Asti Sup. Nizza Augusta '11	♀♀ 4
● Barbera d'Asti Sup. Serena '12	♀♀ 4
● Barbera d'Asti Sup. Serena '11	♀♀ 4
○ Moscato d'Asti Valdiserre '14	♀♀ 3
○ Piemonte Sauvignon Blanc '14	♀♀ 3
○ Piemonte Sauvignon Blanc '13	♀♀ 3

Tenuta Langasco

FRAZ. MADONNA DI COMO, 10
12051 ALBA [CN]
TEL. +39 0173286972
www.tenutalangasco.it

CELLAR SALES
PRE-BOOKED VISITS
ANNUAL PRODUCTION 60,000 bottles
HECTARES UNDER VINE 22.00

Claudio Sacco's handsome winery stands in a magnificent position on the hill overlooking the towers of the town of Alba. The view is undeniably charming, despite the fact that much of the greenery has been replaced by buildings of various shapes and sizes over the past 40 years. Ever since its foundation in 1979, the winery has chosen to embrace the challenge of offering the entire array of local wines. They range from Langhe Arneis and Nebbiolo d'Alba to Moscato d'Asti and Dolcetto Madonna di Como, without forgetting Piemonte Brachetto and Langhe Favorita. Dolcetto Vigna Miclet 2015 made it into our finals, offering a classic nose of dark fruit and bitter almonds, and a complex, juicy palate with great personality. Barbera Sorì Coppa is also very good, with a nose of mixed berries enriched with toasty overtones and intriguing hints of quinine, followed by an impressively firm palate enlivened by balanced acidity.,

● Dolcetto d'Alba Madonna di Como V. Miclet '15	♀♀ 3*
● Barbera d'Alba Sortì '14	♀♀ 3
○ Gredo Brut M. Cl. '12	♀♀ 4
● Nebbiolo d'Alba Sorì Coppa '14	♀♀ 4
● Barbera d'Alba V. Madonna di Como '14	♀ 2
● Barbera d'Alba Madonna di Como '11	♀♀ 2*
● Barbera d'Alba Sortì '13	♀♀ 3
● Barbera d'Alba V. Madonna di Como '13	♀♀ 2*
● Barbera d'Alba V. Madonna di Como '12	♀♀ 2*
● Dolcetto d'Alba V. Madonna di Como '14	♀♀ 2*
● Dolcetto d'Alba V. Miclet '14	♀♀ 3
● Dolcetto d'Alba V. Miclet '13	♀♀ 3*
● Nebbiolo d'Alba Sorì Coppa '13	♀♀ 4
● Nebbiolo d'Alba Sorì Coppa '12	♀♀ 4
● Nebbiolo d'Alba Sorì Coppa '11	♀♀ 4

Ugo Lequio

VIA DEL MOLINO, 10
12057 NEIVE [CN]
TEL. +39 0173677224
www.ugolequio.it

CELLAR SALES
PRE-BOOKED VISITS
ANNUAL PRODUCTION 30,000 bottles
HECTARES UNDER VINE

We strongly recommend a detour to Molino di Neive to visit Ugo Lequio and enjoy his unique hospitality. Always calm and cordial, for over 30 years he has shown himself to be a reliable name in the Barbaresco zone, particularly with regard to the aristocratic Gallina vineyard selection, offered in basic and Riserva versions. Focusing on medium to long maceration and ageing mainly in 2,500-litre oak barrels, they are generally luxuriant and sunny, yet complex. The same style can be found across the rest of the range, from barbera and arneis. There is no doubt about the soundness of Barbaresco Gallina 2013, which instantly shakes off a few lingering hints of oak to reveal elegant, complex notes of golden-leaf tobacco and rhubarb. This dual personality is underscored on the palate by the still evident tannins of the oak associated with the classic austerity of Langhe Nebbiolo.

● Barbaresco Gallina '13	♟♟ 5
● Barbaresco Gallina '12	♟♟ 5
● Barbaresco Gallina '11	♟♟ 5
● Barbaresco Gallina '10	♟♟ 5
● Barbaresco Gallina '09	♟♟ 5
● Barbaresco Gallina '08	♟♟ 5
● Barbaresco Gallina '07	♟♟ 5
● Barbaresco Gallina Ris. '10	♟♟ 6
● Barbaresco Gallina Ris. '07	♟♟ 6
● Barbera d'Alba Sup. '11	♟♟ 4
● Barbera d'Alba Sup. Gallina '12	♟♟ 4
○ Langhe Arneis '13	♟♟ 3
○ Langhe Arneis '12	♟♟ 3

Podere Macellio

VIA ROMA, 18
10014 CALUSO [TO]
TEL. +39 0119833511
www.erbaluce-bianco.it

CELLAR SALES
PRE-BOOKED VISITS
ANNUAL PRODUCTION 25,000 bottles
HECTARES UNDER VINE 3.50

Podere Macellio, one of the finest estates in Caluso and home to the Bianco family's three and a half hectares of vineyards, can trace its winemaking origins back to the second half of the 18th century. In the 1960s Renato decided to bottle and sell his own wines and was later flanked and succeeded by his son Daniele. However, little has changed since then in the composition and style of the estate's beautifully traditional range. Made using simple vinification methods and long ageing, the wines are highly ageworthy Erbaluces, interpreted in excellent dry and passito versions, as well as Metodo Classico sparklers. The Erbaluce di Caluso 2015 gave an excellent performance, placing it among the best of its vintage. It has a particularly complex nose, with notes of medicinal herbs and pennyroyal, and a balanced, forthright palate showing good power and freshness, and a pleasant, lingering finish. Caluso Passito 2003 is magnificent, appearing complex yet balanced.

○ Erbaluce di Caluso '15	♟♟ 2*
○ Caluso Passito Ris. '03	♟♟ 5
○ Erbaluce di Caluso Extra Brut M. Cl.	♟♟ 3
○ Caluso Passito '09	♟♟ 5
○ Caluso Passito '08	♟♟ 5
○ Caluso Passito '07	♟♟ 5
○ Caluso Passito '06	♟♟ 5
○ Erbaluce di Caluso '13	♟♟ 2*
○ Erbaluce di Caluso '12	♟♟ 2*
○ Erbaluce di Caluso '11	♟♟ 2*
○ Erbaluce di Caluso '10	♟♟ 2*

Malabaila di Canale

VIA MADONNA DEI CAVALLI, 93
12043 CANALE [CN]
TEL. +39 017398381
www.malabaila.com

CELLAR SALES
PRE-BOOKED VISITS
ANNUAL PRODUCTION 100,000 bottles
HECTARES UNDER VINE 22.00
SUSTAINABLE WINERY

The first mention of wine production by the Malabaila family dates back to the 13th century. Today the 90-hectare Canale estate vaunts 22 hectares of vineyards on the well-drained, erosion-prone, loose, sandy marl soils typical of Roero, with gradients in excess of 50% and plants over 60 years old. The wines are terroir true, with particular emphasis on structure and rich fruit. Roero Castelletto Riserva 2012 is wonderfully firm and balanced, with rich red fruit, and fresh hints of aniseed on the long finish, while the lean, elegant Roero Bric Volta 2013 has a nose of wild berries with balsamic notes and a long, consistent, full-flavoured palate. This year we were more convinced by the Roero Arneis 2015 than the less brilliant Roero Arneis Pradvaj with notes of super-ripe fruit.

● Roero Bric Volta '13	♛♛ 3*
● Roero Castelletto Ris. '12	♛♛ 4
● Barbera d'Alba Giardino '15	♛♛ 2*
○ Roero Arneis '15	♛♛ 2*
○ Langhe Favorita Donna Costanza '15	♛ 2
○ Roero Arneis Pradvaj '15	♛ 3
● Barbera d'Alba Mezzavilla '11	♛♛ 3
● Nebbiolo d'Alba Bric Merli '13	♛♛ 3
○ Roero Arneis '14	♛♛ 2*
○ Roero Arneis Pradvaj '14	♛♛ 3*
● Roero Bric Volta '12	♛♛ 3*
● Roero Bric Volta '11	♛♛ 3
● Roero Castelletto Ris. '11	♛♛ 4
● Roero Castelletto Ris. '10	♛♛ 5

★Malvirà

LOC. CANOVA
VIA CASE SPARSE, 144
12043 CANALE [CN]
TEL. +39 0173978145
www.malvira.com

CELLAR SALES
PRE-BOOKED VISITS
ACCOMMODATION AND RESTAURANT SERVICE
ANNUAL PRODUCTION 300,000 bottles
HECTARES UNDER VINE 42.00

Brothers Massimo and Roberto Damonte have accompanied Malvirà to the heights of the Roero wine world The estate boasts vineyards in renowned Roero crus, from Mombeltramo and Renesio to Saglietto and San Michele, while the winery, hotel, and restaurant are set in the Trinità vineyard in Canale. The range consists of the typical local wines, based on arneis, barbera, and nebbiolo, plus a small amount of Barolo from a vineyard in the municipality of La Morra. Roero Mombeltrano Riserva has shown itself to be at the top again. The 2012 vintage has a vibrant nose of citrus, tobacco and red berries (strawberries and raspberries), and a firmly structured, balanced palate with great character and length. Roero Vigna Renesio Riserva 2012 is also excellent, showing leaner but supple and delicate, as is Barolo Boiolo 2012, with a complex nose of autumn leaves, porcini mushrooms, and tea leaves. The versions of Arneis aren't as brilliant as usual.

● Roero V. Mombeltramo Ris. '12	♛♛♛ 5
● Barolo Boiolo '12	♛♛ 7
● Roero V. Renesio Ris. '12	♛♛ 5
○ Roero Arneis V. Renesio '15	♛♛ 3
● Roero V. Trinità Ris. '12	♛♛ 5
○ Roero Arneis '15	♛ 2
○ Roero Arneis V. Saglietto '14	♛ 3
○ Roero Arneis V. Trinità '15	♛ 3
● Roero Mombeltramo Ris. '11	♛♛♛ 5
● Roero Mombeltramo Ris. '10	♛♛♛ 5
● Roero Mombeltramo Ris. '05	♛♛♛ 5
● Roero Renesio Ris. '05	♛♛♛ 5
● Roero Trinità Ris. '07	♛♛♛ 5

Giovanni Manzone

VIA CASTELLETTO, 9
12065 MONFORTE D'ALBA [CN]
TEL. +39 017378114
www.manzonegiovanni.com

CELLAR SALES
PRE-BOOKED VISITS
ANNUAL PRODUCTION 45,000 bottles
HECTARES UNDER VINE 7.50
SUSTAINABLE WINERY

The first time you climb up to the Castelletto hamlet of Monforte d'Alba you're likely to have trouble finding Giovanni and Mauro Manzone's winery. However, it's worth the effort because their wines are perfect examples of Langhe's proud country and artisanal traditions. The no-frills Barolos can be rather unapproachable when young, but show great ageing potential and have further improved in the last few years in terms of focused extract, thanks to illustrious crus like Gramolere, Bricat, and Castelletto. The picture is completed by a convincing range featuring the classic local wines, with the curious exception of Rossese Bianco. The trio of 2012 Barolos is as well assorted as ever. The Bricat has little in the way of fruity exuberance, favouring notes of woodland and a lean palate, while the Castelletto is currently more balanced and enjoyable than the Gramolere. The Gramolere Riserva 2009 is concentrated, with notes of mint and aniseed.

Paolo Manzone

LOC. MERIAME, 1
12050 SERRALUNGA D'ALBA [CN]
TEL. +39 0173613113
www.barolomeriame.com

CELLAR SALES
PRE-BOOKED VISITS
ACCOMMODATION
ANNUAL PRODUCTION 85,000 bottles
HECTARES UNDER VINE 10.00
SUSTAINABLE WINERY

The Meriame cru in Serralunga d'Alba is so small that its name wasn't specified on labels until recently. However, its soil and aspect are excellent, as demonstrated for over 30 years by the wines crafted by the experienced Paolo Manzone, obviously commencing with Barolo. The range closely reflects the terroir, hailing from vineyards planted to nebbiolo, barbera, and dolcetto, plus a few spilling over into Roero for the production of the fragrant Arneis. The adjoining guest farm lovingly run by Luisella offers a few handsome rooms for a relaxing break. Barolo Meriame is extremely classic, typical of the strong soils of Serralunga. On the nose it opens gradually with notes of tobacco and spice on a fine backdrop of raspberries and liquorice, and the palate is complex and full flavoured, with good pulp underpinning the rather stiff tannins. Barbera d'Alba Superiore Fiorenza 2014 has good personality, with notes of earth and red berries.

● Barolo Bricat '12	▼▼ 6
● Barolo Gramolere Ris. '09	▼▼ 8
● Barbera d'Alba Sup. La Marchesa '13	▼▼ 5
● Barolo Castelletto '12	▼▼ 6
● Barolo Gramolere '12	▼▼ 6
○ Langhe Rossese Bianco Rosserto '14	▼▼ 3
● Barolo Bricat '05	▼▼▼ 6
● Barolo Castelletto '09	▼▼▼ 5
● Barolo Gramolere Ris. '05	▼▼▼ 7
● Barolo Le Gramolere '04	▼▼▼ 6
● Barolo Le Gramolere Ris. '01	▼▼▼ 7
● Barolo Le Gramolere Ris. '00	▼▼▼ 7
● Barolo Le Gramolere Ris. '99	▼▼▼ 7

● Barolo Meriame '12	▼▼ 7
● Barbera d'Alba Sup. Fiorenza '14	▼▼ 3
● Barolo del Comune di Serralunga d'Alba '12	▼▼ 6
● Barolo Ris. '08	▼▼ 7
● Langhe Rosso Ardì '14	▼ 2
● Nebbiolo d'Alba Mirinè '14	▼ 3
● Barbera d'Alba Sup. Fiorenza '13	▼▼ 3
● Barolo del Comune di Serralunga d'Alba '12	▼▼ 6
● Barolo del Comune di Serralunga d'Alba '10	▼▼ 3*
● Barolo Meriame '11	▼▼ 7
● Barolo Meriame '10	▼▼ 7
● Barolo Meriame '09	▼▼ 7
● Langhe Rosso Luvì '12	▼▼ 3
● Nebbiolo d'Alba Miriné '13	▼▼ 3

Marcalberto

VIA PORTA SOTTANA, 9
12058 SANTO STEFANO BELBO [CN]
TEL. +39 0141844022
www.marcalberto.it

CELLAR SALES
PRE-BOOKED VISITS
ANNUAL PRODUCTION 30,000 bottles
HECTARES UNDER VINE 5.00

This little winery run by Marco and Alberto Cane, overseen by their father Piero, is entirely dedicated to the production of Metodo Classico sparklers, of which it offers four different versions: non-vintage, nature, rosé, and vintage. The estate's vineyards lie on the hillsides of Santo Stefano Belbo and Calosso and are planted to pinot nero and chardonnay. It is currently adding to its plots and renovating the cellar, with the addition of a stunning tasting room. This year Marcalberto Millesimo2mila11 Extra Brut 2011 rises above the rest of the range, showing a very fine, persistent bead, a fruity nose with hints of yeast, and a palate that focuses on fresh acidity and drinkability. Marcalberto Rosé combines a nose of red fruit with good stuffing, prominent acidity, and a long, vibrant finish, while Marcalberto Sansannée Brut is more vegetal and supple, perfect as an aperitif.

○ Marcalberto Extra Brut Millesimo2Mila11 M. Cl. '11	♟♟ 5
☉ Marcalberto Brut Rosé M. Cl.	♟♟ 4
○ Marcalberto Brut Sansannée M. Cl.	♟♟ 4
○ Marcalberto Brut Millesimo2Mila9 M. Cl. '09	♙♙ 5
○ Marcalberto Brut M. Cl. '08	♙♙ 5
○ Marcalberto Brut M. Cl. '07	♙♙ 5
○ Marcalberto Brut M. Cl. '06	♙♙ 5
○ Marcalberto Brut M. Cl. '05	♙♙ 5
○ Marcalberto Extra Brut Millesimo2Mila10 M. Cl. '10	♙♙ 5

Poderi Marcarini

P.ZZA MARTIRI, 2
12064 LA MORRA [CN]
TEL. +39 017350222
www.marcarini.it

CELLAR SALES
PRE-BOOKED VISITS
ACCOMMODATION
ANNUAL PRODUCTION 125,000 bottles
HECTARES UNDER VINE 20.00

In terms of style and geography, La Morra is regularly associated with rounder, more modern Barolos. Marcarini's Nebbiolos are the exception to the rule, for they have always conjured up a 19th-century atmosphere thanks to two vineyards that are among the finest assorted in the production zone. Brunate and La Serra are only a few metres apart as the crow flies, yet are virtual opposites in terms of expression, save for their luminous and almost Franciscan inspiration. Aged in 2,000 and 4,000-litre oak barrels, they are the jewels of the range crafted by Anna Bava Marcarini, aided by her daughter Luisa and son-in-law Manuel Marchetti. A comparison of the two 2012 Barolos reveals their different styles. The hot, albeit irregular, vintage is evident in the Brunate that already shows alluring tertiary notes of dried herbs, jam, and burnt firewood. La Serra, from a higher vineyard, appears fresher and more delicate and balanced but with softer structure.

● Barolo Brunate '12	♟♟ 7
● Barolo La Serra '12	♟♟ 7
● Barbera d'Alba Ciabot Camerano '13	♟♟ 3
○ Moscato d'Asti '15	♟♟ 2*
● Dolcetto d'Alba Boschi di Berri '14	♟ 3
● Dolcetto d'Alba Fontanazza '15	♟ 2
○ Roero Arneis '14	♟ 2
● Barolo Brunate '05	♙♙♙ 6
● Barolo Brunate '03	♙♙♙ 6
● Barolo Brunate '01	♙♙♙ 6
● Barolo Brunate '99	♙♙♙ 6
● Barolo Brunate '96	♙♙♙ 6
● Barolo Brunate Ris. '85	♙♙♙ 6
● Dolcetto d'Alba Boschi di Berri '96	♙♙♙ 4*

Marchese Luca Spinola

FRAZ. ROVERETO DI GAVI
LOC. CASCINA MASSIMILIANA, 97
15066 GAVI [AL]
TEL. +39 0143682514
www.marcheselucaspinola.it

CELLAR SALES
PRE-BOOKED VISITS
ANNUAL PRODUCTION 20,000 bottles
HECTARES UNDER VINE 15.00

Half of the 12 hectares of vineyards owned for generations by Marchesi Spinola are in Tassarolo and the other half in Rovereto di Gavi. The two old estates are planted entirely to cortese, which is used to make three wines clearly differentiated by technical style and terroir. Crafted from the grapes of both plots, Gavi di Gavi can be considered the basic wine and Tenuta Massimiliana, fermented for longer at lower temperatures, also in stainless steel, the flagship Lastly, there is the unique semi-sparkling Gavi del Comune di Tassarolo. This year the Gavi di Gavi made it into our tasting finals, with the Tenuta Massimiliana just a hair's breadth behind. The former is more approachable, proffering a nose of hedgerow and fresh herbs with hints of tobacco, and a firmly structured palate with a soft attack and a fine, long finish. Tenuta Massimiliana is fragrant with good structure.

○ Gavi del Comune di Gavi '15	▼▼	2*
○ Gavi del Comune di Gavi Tenuta Massimiliana '15	▼▼	3
○ Gavi del Comune di Gavi '12	▽▽	2*
○ Gavi del Comune di Gavi '11	▽▽	2*
○ Gavi del Comune di Gavi Et. Blu '14	▽▽	2*
○ Gavi del Comune di Gavi Tenuta Massimiliana '14	▽▽	3
○ Gavi del Comune di Gavi Tenuta Massimiliana '13	▽▽	3
○ Gavi del Comune di Gavi Tenuta Massimiliana '12	▽▽	3
○ Gavi del Comune di Tassarolo '13	▽▽	2*

★Marchesi di Barolo

VIA ALBA,12
12060 BAROLO [CN]
TEL. +39 0173564400
www.marchesibarolo.com

CELLAR SALES
PRE-BOOKED VISITS
RESTAURANT SERVICE
ANNUAL PRODUCTION 1,500,000 bottles
HECTARES UNDER VINE 194.00

The Abbona family are well accustomed to success. Years ago they took over Castello Falletti, the birthplace of Barolo and its legend since the time of Juliette Colbert, from the Agenzia della Tenuta Opera Pia. The added value of such a glorious legacy goes without saying, and it has been seamlessly incorporated into the demands of a contemporary plan by Anna and Ernesto, the latest generation at the helm of Marchesi di Barolo. It is clearly reflected in the composition and style of the comprehensive range of wines made from the Langhe, Roero, and Monferrato estates. The overall result is wonderful, particularly the 2012 crus. Our favourite was the sunny classic Cannubi, but the Sarmassa vaunts breezy progression, the Coste di Rose soft fullness, and the Barolo del Comune di Barolo carefree juiciness. Barbaresco Serragrilli 2013 is also noteworthy, showing fresh and lean.

● Barolo Cannubi '12	▼▼▼	8
● Barolo Coste di Rose '12	▼▼	7
● Barolo Sarrnassa '12	▼▼	8
● Barbaresco Serragrilli '13	▼▼	6
● Barbera d'Alba Peiragal '14	▼▼	5
● Barolo del Comune di Barolo '12	▼▼	8
● Dolcetto d'Alba Madonna del Dono '15	▼▼	3
○ Gavi del Comune di Gavi '15	▼▼	4
○ Langhe Bric Amel '15	▼▼	3
● Nebbiolo d'Alba Michet '14	▼▼	4
● Barbera d'Alba Ruvei '14	▼	3
○ Gavi '15	▼	3
○ Roero Arneis '15	▼	4
● Barolo Cannubi '11	▽▽▽	8
● Barolo Cannubi '10	▽▽▽	8
● Barolo Sarmassa '09	▽▽▽	8

Marchesi Incisa della Rocchetta

VIA ROMA, 66
14030 ROCCHETTA TANARO [AT]
TEL. +39 0141644647
www.marchesiincisawines.it

CELLAR SALES
PRE-BOOKED VISITS
ACCOMMODATION AND RESTAURANT SERVICE
ANNUAL PRODUCTION 80,000 bottles
HECTARES UNDER VINE 17.00

The entire Incisa della Rocchetta family work at the winery, which was renovated and modernized in 1990. Their estate's vineyards, lying partly in the Rocchetta Tanaro Nature Reserve, are on sandy clay soils and are planted chiefly to barbera, flanked by grignolino, pinot nero, and merlot. The wines from these vineyards are joined by others from various designations, such as Barolo, Roero Arneis, and Moscato d'Asti, all extremely well made and often alluring. Barbera d'Asti Valmorena 2014 is particularly well made, with a nose of black cherries and liquorice, velvety tannins, and a long, full-flavoured finish. Barbera d'Asti Superiore Sant'Emiliano 2014 is beautifully fresh, but needs more time for its oakiness to be tamed; Piemonte Pinot Nero Marchese Leopoldo 2014 is well made and fruit forward; and Grignolino d'Asti 2015 is spicy and easy drinking.

● Barbera d'Asti Valmorena '14	♈♈ 3*
● Barbera d'Asti Sup. Sant'Emiliano '14	♈♈ 5
● Grignolino d'Asti '15	♈♈ 3
● Piemonte Pinot Nero Marchese Leopoldo '14	♈♈ 5
● Piemonte Barbera Rollone '13	♈ 3
● Barbera d'Asti Sup. Sant'Emiliano '12	♈♈ 5
● Barbera d'Asti Sup. Sant'Emiliano '11	♈♈ 4
● Barbera d'Asti Valmorena '13	♈♈ 3
● Grignolino d'Asti '13	♈♈ 3
● Grignolino d'Asti '12	♈♈ 3
● M.to Rosso Colpo d'Ala '13	♈♈ 6
● M.to Rosso Rollone '12	♈♈ 3
● Piemonte Pinot Nero Marchese Leopoldo '13	♈♈ 4

Mario Marengo

LOC. SERRA DENARI, 2A
12064 LA MORRA [CN]
TEL. +39 017350115
marengo1964@libero.it

CELLAR SALES
PRE-BOOKED VISITS
ANNUAL PRODUCTION 35,000 bottles
HECTARES UNDER VINE 7.00

The first Barolos bottled by the Marengo family date from the late 19th century, which was a pioneering time for the "king of wines". Little has changed since then in the artisanal approach of the winery, with an estate of around seven hectares in La Morra, Castiglione Falletto, and Barolo, planted with typical Langhe grape varieties like dolcetto, barbera, and nebbiolo. While brief fermentation with the aid of vertical macerators, intense extraction, and ageing in barrique make them modern wines, the Barolos first and foremost echo the characteristics of prestigious vineyards like Brunate and Bricco delle Viole. Great vignerons tend to emerge in more uneven vintages, like the 2012 one. Bricco delle Viole combines fresh fruit and spicy vigour with phenolic power and focused extract, while the Brunate opens rather shyly on the nose, but expands magnificently on the plate with strawberries and pipe tobacco, earning a Tre Bicchieri for its beautifully blended tannins and length.

● Barolo Brunate '12	♈♈♈ 7
● Barolo Bricco delle Viole '12	♈♈ 6
● Barolo '12	♈♈ 5
● Dolcetto d'Alba '15	♈♈ 2*
● Barolo Brunate '11	♈♈♈ 7
● Barolo Brunate '09	♈♈♈ 6
● Barolo Brunate '07	♈♈♈ 6
● Barolo Brunate '06	♈♈♈ 6
● Barolo Brunate '05	♈♈♈ 6
● Barolo Brunate '04	♈♈♈ 6
● Barbera d'Alba Vign. Pugnane '13	♈♈ 3
● Barolo '11	♈♈ 5
● Barolo Bricco delle Viole '11	♈♈ 6
● Dolcetto d'Alba '14	♈♈ 2*
● Nebbiolo d'Alba Valmaggiore '13	♈♈ 3

Claudio Mariotto

S.DA PER SAREZZANO, 29
15057 TORTONA [AL]
TEL. +39 0131868500
www.claudiomariotto.it

CELLAR SALES
PRE-BOOKED VISITS
ANNUAL PRODUCTION 100,000 bottles
HECTARES UNDER VINE 32.00

Following his day in the vineyard, cellar, or workshop repairing his beloved farm vehicles, Claudio Mariotto turns into an attentive and curious producer, who often tastes old vintages of his wines to assess their development, and probably also to seek inspiration for his famously ageworthy red wines from barbera, dolcetto, croatina, and freisa, and whites from timorasso and cortese. The most difficult vintage in recent years has not shaken the solidity of Claudio's Timorasso, whose elegance and power is testified by the trio of wines that reached our finals. Once again the Derthona is the most ready, showing complex, and concentrated, followed by the Cavallina and the Pitasso, which are starting to develop minerality and the petrol notes that give Timorasso finesse and elegance. The Barbera and Croatina are both full and rich, focusing on tertiary aromas, the Poggio del Rosso 2013 offers bottled fruit, and the Montemirano 2014 has notes of tobacco and quinine.

Marsaglia

VIA MADAMA MUSSONE, 2
12050 CASTELLINALDO [CN]
TEL. +39 0173213048
www.cantinamarsaglia.it

CELLAR SALES
PRE-BOOKED VISITS
ANNUAL PRODUCTION 80,000 bottles
HECTARES UNDER VINE 15.00

Founded in 1900, the Marsaglia family's winery is one of the best known in Roero. The estate's vineyards are over 50 years old and are all in the municipality of Castellinaldo, but on different soils: sandier towards Canale, where its renowned Brich d'America cru is situated, and more compact towards Castagnito. They yield typical Roero wines, traditional in style and extremely reliable. Roero Brich d'America tops the range again and is among the best of the designation. The 2012 vintage has a vibrant nose of spice and red berries, accompanied by hints of liquorice, tobacco, and autumn leaves, while the full-flavoured palate shows great balance and length, with close-woven but never aggressive tannins. Barbera d'Alba San Cristoforo 2015 is well made, with classic earthy notes, exuberant fruit, and a pleasantly acidic finish.

○ Colli Tortonesi Timorasso Derthona '14	♼♼ 5
○ Colli Tortonesi Timorasso Derthona Cavallina '14	♼♼ 5
○ Colli Tortonesi Timorasso Derthona Pitasso '14	♼♼ 6
● Colli Tortonesi Croatina Montemirano '14	♼♼ 4
● Colli Tortonesi Freisa Braghè '15	♼♼ 3
● Colli Tortonesi Rosso Poggio del Rosso '13	♼♼ 5
○ Colli Tortonesi Bianco Pitasso '06	♼♼♼ 5
○ Colli Tortonesi Bianco Pitasso '05	♼♼♼ 4
○ Colli Tortonesi Bianco Pitasso '04	♼♼♼ 4
○ Colli Tortonesi Timorasso Pitasso '13	♼♼♼ 6
○ Colli Tortonesi Timorasso Pitasso '12	♼♼♼ 6
○ Colli Tortonesi Timorasso Pitasso '08	♼♼♼ 5
● Colli Tortonesi Croatina Montemirano '13	♼♼ 4
○ Colli Tortonesi Timorasso Cavallina '13	♼♼ 5

● Roero Brich d'America '12	♼♼ 4
● Barbera d'Alba S. Cristoforo '15	♼♼ 3
● Nebbiolo d'Alba '13	♼ 3
○ Roero Arneis Serramiana '15	♼ 3
○ Accordo Brut M. Cl.	♼♼ 4
● Barbera d'Alba Castellinaldo '11	♼♼ 4
● Barbera d'Alba S. Cristoforo '12	♼♼ 3
● Nebbiolo d'Alba '12	♼♼ 3
● Nebbiolo d'Alba San Pietro '11	♼♼ 3
○ Roero Arneis Serramiana '14	♼♼ 3
○ Roero Arneis Serramiana '13	♼♼ 3
● Roero Brich d'America '11	♼♼ 4
● Roero Brich d'America '10	♼♼ 4

★Franco M. Martinetti

c.so TURATI, 14
10128 TORINO
TEL. +39 0118395937
www.francomartinetti.it

PRE-BOOKED VISITS
ANNUAL PRODUCTION 140,000 bottles
HECTARES UNDER VINE 5.00

Franco Martinetti is a perfectionist, in terms of both wine and food, and their convivial pairing. Consequently, he has always used excellent growers for his wines, who have supplied him with their grapes and their experience. The result has been a succession of superlative whites like Colli Tortonesi Timorasso Martin and Gavi Minaia, and successful selections of Barbera d'Asti, such as the Montruc. However, Martinetti, who jokingly liked to call himself Franco Senza Terra, has recently decided to turn his hand to growing, leasing several fine vineyards for the purpose. The lovely fruity aromas of Barbera Montruc 2013 are underscored by good alcoholic thrust and the palate manages to remain austere and precise despite its remarkable fruit. Gavi Minaia 2015 is well made, vaunting an elegant, delicate nose and a particularly complex, caressing palate with good backbone, while the lovely sparkling Quarantatre 2005 has a honeyed nose and a fresh palate.

★Bartolo Mascarello

VIA ROMA, 15
12060 BAROLO [CN]
TEL. +39 017356125

CELLAR SALES
PRE-BOOKED VISITS
ANNUAL PRODUCTION 30,000 bottles
HECTARES UNDER VINE 5.00

Who knows what Langhe's most famous vigneron partisan would think to see his name acclaimed throughout the world like that of a rock star? His legacy is more than just oenological, consisting of values that are more important than ever today to protect and revive a specific concept of Barolo, with the benefit of hindsight. Maria Teresa, his daughter has drawn on this inspiration and further elevated it in an incredible series of great successes. Today the value of legendary plots like Cannubi, San Lorenzo, Rué, and Rocche has returned to the limelight to replace technical details such as length of maceration and barrel size. Maria Teresa's Barolos are made from the grapes of four different crus, ensuring a faithful interpretation of every single vintage. The fabulous 2012 strolled off with a Tre Bicchieri for its nose of wild berries and liquorice accompanied by a palate with exceptionally elegant tannins and a long finish.

● Barbera d'Asti Sup. Montruc '13	▼▼ 5	
○ Gavi Minaia '15	▼▼ 5	
○ Quarantatré Brut M. Cl. Ris. '05	▼▼ 6	
● Barbera d'Asti Bric dei Banditi '14	▼▼ 3	
● Barolo Marasco '12	▼▼ 8	
○ Colli Tortonesi Timorasso Martin '14	▼▼ 6	
○ Gavi del Comune di Gavi '15	▼▼ 3	
● M.to Rosso Sul Bric '13	▼▼ 6	
● Barbera d'Asti Sup. Montruc '06	♈♈♈ 5	
● Barbera d'Asti Sup. Montruc '01	♈♈♈ 5	
● Barolo Marasco '01	♈♈♈ 7	
● Barolo Marasco '00	♈♈♈ 7	
○ Colli Tortonesi Timorasso Martin '12	♈♈♈ 6	
● M.to Rosso Sul Bric '10	♈♈♈ 6	
● M.to Rosso Sul Bric '09	♈♈♈ 6	
● M.to Rosso Sul Bric '00	♈♈♈ 5	

● Barolo '12	▼▼▼ 8
● Barolo '11	♈♈♈ 8
● Barolo '10	♈♈♈ 8
● Barolo '09	♈♈♈ 8
● Barolo '07	♈♈♈ 8
● Barolo '06	♈♈♈ 8
● Barolo '05	♈♈♈ 8
● Barolo '01	♈♈♈ 8
● Barolo '99	♈♈♈ 8
● Barolo '98	♈♈♈ 8
● Barolo '89	♈♈♈ 8
● Barolo '85	♈♈♈ 8
● Barolo '84	♈♈♈ 8
● Barolo '83	♈♈♈ 8

Giuseppe Mascarello e Figlio

via Borgonuovo, 108
12060 Monchiero [CN]
Tel. +39 0173792126
www.mascarello1881.com

CELLAR SALES
PRE-BOOKED VISITS
ANNUAL PRODUCTION 60,000 bottles
HECTARES UNDER VINE 13.50

Although Langhe has long been a veritable land of opportunity in terms of average quality and pinnacles of excellence, the options for those seeking great old-style reds, in the truest sense, are very limited. This is why Mauro and Giuseppe Mascarello's winery is a place of constant pilgrimage: their chromatically transparent Nebbiolos, apparently light yet able to age for decades, are capable of conveying forgotten sensations. They hail from majestic vineyards in Castiglione Falletto like Villero, Santo Stefano di Perno, and Monprivato, which in great vintages also yields Cà d'Morissio, exclusively from the michet clone. We always expect the very best from such a prestigious estate, even when the weather conditions would caution against it. Mauro nonetheless managed to astonish us this year with a marvellous list of 2011 Barolos. The top prize goes to the legendary Monprivato, whose incredibly refined nose is followed by a majestic, never-ending palate. The Villero is characterized by fine balance and length.

● Barolo Monprivato '11	♛♛♛ 8
● Barolo Perno V. Santo Stefano '11	♛♛ 8
● Barolo Villero '11	♛♛ 8
● Barolo Monprivato '10	♕♕♕ 8
● Barolo Monprivato '09	♕♕♕ 8
● Barolo Monprivato '08	♕♕♕ 8
● Barolo Monprivato '01	♕♕♕ 8
● Barolo S. Stefano di Perno '98	♕♕♕ 8
● Barolo dai Vigneti di Proprietà '09	♕♕ 7
● Barolo Perno V. Santo Stefano '10	♕♕ 8
● Barolo S. Stefano di Perno '09	♕♕ 8
● Barolo Villero '10	♕♕ 8
● Barolo Villero '09	♕♕ 8

★Massolino

p.zza Cappellano, 8
12050 Serralunga d'Alba [CN]
Tel. +39 0173613138
www.massolino.it

CELLAR SALES
PRE-BOOKED VISITS
ANNUAL PRODUCTION 120,000 bottles
HECTARES UNDER VINE 24.00
SUSTAINABLE WINERY

If Nebbiolos from Serralunga d'Alba are consistently ranked among the most powerful, austere and ageworthy, much of the credit must go to the work of the Massolino family. In recent years their legendary vineyards like Parafada, Margheria, and Vigna Rionda on the western slope of Serralunga, have been joined by others in the Parussi cru in Castiglione Falletto. Today the winery is headed by brothers Franco and Roberto, who continue to refine the house style from vintage to vintage, adding ever more texture and focused extract. This is true not only of the top Barolos, but of the entire range, from barbera, dolcetto, chardonnay, and moscato. The trend is confirmed by the latest releases, commencing with the 2012 Barolos. The Parafada is initially shy, but opens up in the glass with an elegant nose of tobacco and medicinal herbs, followed by a dense, well-sustained palate, while the equally ageworthy Margheria has even better amalgamated rich tannins. However, the true champion remains the powerful Vigna Rionda from the splendid 2010 vintage.

● Barolo Vigna Rionda Ris. '10	♛♛♛ 8
● Barolo Margheria '12	♛♛ 8
● Barolo Parafada '12	♛♛ 8
● Barbera d'Alba '15	♛♛ 3
● Barolo '12	♛♛ 5
● Barolo Parussi '12	♛♛ 8
● Dolcetto d'Alba '15	♛♛ 2*
○ Langhe Chardonnay '14	♛♛ 3
● Langhe Nebbiolo '14	♛♛ 3
● Barolo Margheria '05	♕♕♕ 7
● Barolo Parafada '11	♕♕♕ 8
● Barolo Parafada '04	♕♕♕ 7
● Barolo V. Rionda Ris. '08	♕♕♕ 8
● Barolo V. Rionda Ris. '06	♕♕♕ 8
● Barolo Vigna Rionda Ris. '05	♕♕♕ 8
● Barolo Vigna Rionda Ris. '04	♕♕♕ 8

Tiziano Mazzoni

VIA ROMA, 73
28010 CAVAGLIO D'AGOGNA [NO]
TEL. +39 3488200635
www.vinimazzoni.it

CELLAR SALES
PRE-BOOKED VISITS
ANNUAL PRODUCTION 20,000 bottles
HECTARES UNDER VINE 4.50
SUSTAINABLE WINERY

Tiziano Mazzoni and his wife run this
classic family winery, aided by the patriarch
Nino and increasingly their young son
Gilles. It has always been a way of life for
them, underpinned by a strong urge to
return to nature and reap its fruits.
Nebbiolo is the most important grape
variety, yielding three wines: Ghemme dei
Mazzoni, Ghemme ai Livelli, and Colline
Novaresi Nebbiolo Monteregio. The key
concepts are small selections, great
respect for the environment, and
uncomplicated wines full of personality.
Vespolina Il Ricetto 2015 has an
exceptionally well-typed nose, with notes of
black pepper and spice on ripe red berries,
and a complex, juicy palate with a long
finish and slightly edgy tannins. The
straw-yellow Iris has greenish highlights
and a concentrated nose of fresh herbs and
white-fleshed fruit, accompanied by a
complex, firmly structured palate that's not
too lively but very pleasant. Nebbiolo del
Monteregio 2014 is easy drinking with
good tannins. Ghemme dei Mazzoni 2013
will be released shortly.

● Colline Novaresi Vespolina Il Ricetto '15	🍷🍷 3
○ Iris	🍷🍷 3
● Colline Novaresi Nebbiolo del Monteregio '14	🍷 3
● Ghemme dei Mazzoni '12	🍷🍷🍷 5
● Colline Novaresi Nebbiolo del Monteregio '13	🍷🍷 3
● Colline Novaresi Vespolina Al Ricetto '13	🍷🍷 2*
● Colline Novaresi Vespolina Il Ricetto '14	🍷🍷 3
● Ghemme ai Livelli '11	🍷🍷 6
● Ghemme ai Livelli '10	🍷🍷 6
● Ghemme ai Livelli '09	🍷🍷 6
● Ghemme dei Mazzoni '11	🍷🍷 5
● Ghemme dei Mazzoni '10	🍷🍷 5
● Ghemme dei Mazzoni '09	🍷🍷 5
○ Passito Le Masche	🍷🍷 4

La Mesma

FRAZ. MONTEROTONDO, 7
15066 GAVI [AL]
TEL. +39 0143342012
www.lamesma.it

CELLAR SALES
PRE-BOOKED VISITS
ACCOMMODATION
ANNUAL PRODUCTION 52,000 bottles
HECTARES UNDER VINE 25.00

The Rosina sisters' vineyards are divided
between Monterotondo, Novi Ligure, and
Tassarolo, where their cellar is located. Its
name, La Bella Alleanza, is inspired by a
treaty that was signed here during the
Napoleonic Wars. It is managed by Ivano
Rossi, who has extensive knowledge of
Gavi and the production zone, with the aid
of oenologist Massimo Azzolini. The range
consists of six wines: five from cortese and
one from barbera, merlot, and cabernet
sauvignon. The list commences with a
splendid version of Vigna della Rovere
Verde 2014, which is concentrated and
refined, with elegant mineral notes on a
nose of fresh herbs, followed by a very
refreshing palate with a very long,
full-flavoured finish. Etichetta Gialla offers
an elegant, fruity nose and a fleshy palate
with a flavoursome finish, while Etichetta
Nera is intriguing, with plenty of character.

○ Gavi del Comune di Gavi Et. Gialla '15	🍷🍷 2*
○ Gavi V. della Rovere Verde Ris. '14	🍷🍷 5
○ Gavi del Comune di Gavi Et. Nera '14	🍷🍷 3
○ Gavi Brut M. Cl. '09	🍷🍷 4
○ Gavi del Comune di Gavi Et. Gialla '14	🍷🍷 2*
○ Gavi V. della Rovere Verde Ris. '13	🍷🍷 3

Moccagatta

S.DA RABAJÀ, 46
12050 BARBARESCO [CN]
TEL. +39 0173635228
www.moccagatta.eu

CELLAR SALES
PRE-BOOKED VISITS
ANNUAL PRODUCTION 65,000 bottles
HECTARES UNDER VINE 12.00
SUSTAINABLE WINERY

Even before their success as winemakers, the Minuto brothers had earned well-deserved renown as growers among their vigneron colleagues in Barbaresco, who always speak of their work in the vineyard with great respect. However, their work in the cellar – thanks to Marc De Grazia and the winds of change of the 1980s – has also won them much attention, derived from the use of small new oak casks and complex, powerful wines. The cellar itself has been extended over the years, not to allow higher production but to ensure optimal fermentation and ageing. It is well worth a visit. The Minuto brothers' wines have remained the same as ever, with a well-extracted, modern style, very ripe dark fruit, and plenty of elegant oak. Barbaresco Bric Balin 2013 has striking notes of cocoa powder and a powerful, chewy palate displaying good flesh and rugged, austere tannins from the grapes and oak.

● Barbaresco Bric Balin '13	▼▼ 6
● Barbaresco Basarin '13	▼ 6
● Barbaresco Bric Balin '05	♈♈♈ 6
● Barbaresco Bric Balin '04	♈♈♈ 6
● Barbaresco Bric Balin '01	♈♈♈ 6
● Barbaresco Bric Balin '90	♈♈♈ 6
● Barbaresco Cole '97	♈♈♈ 6
● Barbaresco Basarin '11	♈♈ 6
● Barbaresco Basarin '10	♈♈ 6
● Barbaresco Bric Balin '12	♈♈ 6
● Barbaresco Bric Balin '11	♈♈ 6
● Barbaresco Bric Balin '10	♈♈ 6
● Barbaresco Cole '12	♈♈ 7
● Barbaresco Cole '11	♈♈ 6
● Barbaresco Cole '10	♈♈ 6

Mauro Molino

FRAZ. ANNUNZIATA GANCIA, 111A
12064 LA MORRA [CN]
TEL. +39 017350814
www.mauromolino.com

CELLAR SALES
PRE-BOOKED VISITS
ANNUAL PRODUCTION 95,000 bottles
HECTARES UNDER VINE 12.00
SUSTAINABLE WINERY

After having accrued extensive experienced at other wineries, in 1982 scrupulous oenologist Mauro Molino founded his own estate, which was an immediate success. The four Barolos are of course the jewels in its crown, but the range comprises all the classic Langhe types, along with a Chardonnay that represents the sole concession to international wines. After being joined by his determined children Martina and Matteo, the estate has expanded a little, with the addition of vineyards in Monforte d'Alba, planted to nebbiolo; Guarene for Barbera d'Alba; and, since 2015, Costigliole d'Asti for Barbera d'Asti Leradici. The sophisticated Barolo Conca 2012 has top notes of raspberries and a long, close-knit palate with remarkably firm structure, Bricco Luciani 2012 vaunts attractive sweet spice, good backbone and velvety smooth tannins, while the dry Barolo La Serra 2012 is still concealed by strong notes of toasty oak. Sadly the rest of the range had yet to be bottled at the time of our tastings.

● Barolo Conca '12	▼▼ 7
● Barolo Bricco Luciani '12	▼▼ 6
● Barolo La Serra '12	▼▼ 7
● Barbera d'Alba V. Gattere '00	♈♈♈ 5
● Barbera d'Alba V. Gattere '97	♈♈♈ 7
● Barbera d'Alba V. Gattere '96	♈♈♈ 7
● Barolo Gallinotto '11	♈♈♈ 6
● Barolo Gallinotto '03	♈♈♈ 6
● Barolo Gallinotto '01	♈♈♈ 6
● Barolo V. Conca '00	♈♈♈ 7
● Barolo V. Conca '97	♈♈♈ 7
● Barolo V. Conca '96	♈♈♈ 7

★Monchiero Carbone

VIA SANTO STEFANO ROERO, 2
12043 CANALE [CN]
TEL. +39 017395568
www.monchierocarbone.com

CELLAR SALES
PRE-BOOKED VISITS
ANNUAL PRODUCTION 180,000 bottles
HECTARES UNDER VINE 25.00
SUSTAINABLE WINERY

The Monchiero family have played a leading role in boosting the Roero wine scene with the high quality of their production and their commitment to promoting the local area and its wines. Their vineyards, which include some of the finest crus in the area, like Monbirone, Renesio, and Frailin, are situated mainly in Canale, on soils ranging from the typical sandy to more gravelly types suitable for the production of rich, structured wines, but also in Vezza d'Alba, Monteu Roero, and Priocca. The estate's wines have reached remarkable stylistic maturity. Roero Printi Riserva 2012 took our top award with its nose of spice and dark berries, and full, elegant palate that is simultaneously complex and delicate, long and flavoursome. The exceptionally fresh, juicy Roero Srü 2013 is also very good, as are the gutsy, fruit-forward Barbera d'Alba MonBirone and Roero Arneis Cecu d'La Biunda 2015, which is probably the best of its kind.

● Roero Printi Ris. '12	♟♟♟	5
● Barbera d'Alba MonBirone '13	♟♟	5
○ Roero Arneis Cecu d'La Biunda '15	♟♟	3*
● Roero Srü '13	♟♟	4
● Barbera d'Alba Pelisa '14	♟♟	2*
○ Roero Arneis Recit '15	♟♟	2*
● Barbera d'Alba MonBirone '10	♟♟♟	4*
● Roero Printi Ris. '11	♟♟♟	5
● Roero Printi Ris. '10	♟♟♟	5
● Roero Printi Ris. '09	♟♟♟	5
● Roero Printi Ris. '07	♟♟♟	5
● Roero Printi Ris. '06	♟♟♟	5
● Roero Srü '06	♟♟♟	3

Monfalletto
Cordero di Montezemolo

FRAZ. ANNUNZIATA, 67
12064 LA MORRA [CN]
TEL. +39 017350344
www.corderodimontezemolo.com

CELLAR SALES
PRE-BOOKED VISITS
ANNUAL PRODUCTION 240,000 bottles
HECTARES UNDER VINE 35.00

Cascina Monfalletto in La Morra belonged to the Fallettis for generations, until its purchase in 1920 by the Cordero di Montezemolo family, who turned it into one of Langhe's most striking estates. It is formed by a single plot of around 30 hectares of vineyards, divided into subplots planted to different varietals, with the lion's share reserved for nebbiolo and dolcetto, flanked by barbera, chardonnay, and arneis. The range comprises four Barolos: Monfalletto, Bricco Gattera, Gorette, and Enrico VI from the Villero cru in Castiglione Falletto, which share the same innovative but uncontrived style, the result of mainly short maceration and ageing in small French oak casks. Barolo Enrico VI once again towers over the rest, offering a good balance of fruit and oak and an elegant nose, while the palate displays tannins that remind us of its important pedigree. The Gattera is dominated by aromas of oriental spices and red berries, while the Monfalletto has a more traditional nose and leaner body.

● Barolo Enrico VI '12	♟♟	8
● Barbera d'Alba Sup. Funtanì '13	♟♟	5
● Barolo Gattera '12	♟♟	7
● Barolo Monfalletto '12	♟♟	6
○ Langhe Chardonnay Elioro '14	♟♟	5
● Barbera d'Alba '14	♟	3
● Dolcetto d'Alba '15	♟	3
● Barolo Enrico VI '04	♟♟♟	7
● Barolo Enrico VI '03	♟♟♟	7
● Barolo V. Bricco Gattera '99	♟♟♟	8
● Barolo V. Enrico VI '00	♟♟♟	7
● Barolo Bricco Gattera '11	♟♟	8
● Barolo Enrico VI '11	♟♟	8
● Barolo Enrico VI '10	♟♟	8

Montalbera

VIA MONTALBERA, 1
14030 CASTAGNOLE MONFERRATO [AT]
TEL. +39 0119433311
www.montalbera.it

CELLAR SALES
PRE-BOOKED VISITS
ANNUAL PRODUCTION 600,000 bottles
HECTARES UNDER VINE 175.00

About 30 years ago the Morando family started to buy up land to plant new vineyards. Today the winery is surrounded by a single plot of estate-owned vineyards arranged in an amphitheatre. They are planted mainly to ruché, flanked by barbera, grignolino, and viognier, on soils that range from clay to limestone. The estate also owns 15 hectares of moscato vineyards in Castiglione Tinella and several hectares of nebbiolo in La Morra, Barbaresco, and Neive. This year the estate presented a truly impressive array of Ruche di Castagnole Monferrato wines. La Tradizione 2015 is aromatic and fragrant, offering a fine varietal nose of roses and red fruit with charming peppery nuances, and a beautifully plush, juicy palate with a long characterful finish, earning it a Tre Bicchieri. Laccento 2015 is denser and more concentrated, but not quite as elegant, while the Vegan 2015 is varietal and gutsy. The fresh, full-flavoured Barbera d'Asti Superiore Nuda 2013 is also excellent.

Ruchè di Castagnole M.to La Tradizione '15	▼▼▼ 3*
Barbera d'Asti Sup. Nuda '13	▼▼ 7
Ruchè di Castagnole M.to Laccento '15	▼▼ 3*
Ruchè di Castagnole M.to Vegan '15	▼▼ 3*
Barolo Levoluzione '12	▼▼ 6
Grignolino d'Asti Grigné '15	▼▼ 2*
Ruchè di Castagnole M.to Limpronta '14	▼▼ 5
Barbera d'Asti Lequilibrio '14	▼ 3
Barbera d'Asti Solo Acciaio '15	▼ 2
Moscato d'Asti '15	▼ 2
Barbera d'Asti Sup. Nuda '12	♀♀ 7
Ruchè di Castagnole M.to La Tradizione '14	♀♀ 3*
Ruchè di Castagnole M.to Laccento '14	♀♀ 3*

Cecilia Monte

VIA SERRACAPELLI, 17
12052 NEIVE [CN]
TEL. +39 017367454
cecilia.monte@libero.it

CELLAR SALES
ANNUAL PRODUCTION 19,000 bottles
HECTARES UNDER VINE 3.50

At the turn of the millennium Cecilia Monte took over the management of the family winery, following the passion of her father Paolo, to whom she dedicated a Barbaresco from a small and particularly fine plot of the Serracapelli cru in the 2011 vintage. In almost 15 years of activity, the quality of the initially small, experimental production has reached remarkable heights. The well-made Barbaresco selection dedicated to Paolo made a fine debut, showing elegant and ethereal, with a nose of quinine and red berries and a long, powerful palate, still slightly stiff from the very close-woven tannins. Vigneto Serracapelli 2012 is already more concentrated and layered, with notes of medicinal herbs and tobacco mingling with liquorice and red berries. The Barbera d'Alba 2014 reflects its difficult vintage.

Barbaresco Serracapelli Dedicato a Paolo '11	▼▼ 6
Barbaresco Vign. Serracapelli '12	▼▼ 5
Barbera d'Alba '14	▼ 3
Barbaresco Ris. '06	♀♀ 5
Barbaresco Serracapelli '11	♀♀ 5
Barbaresco Serracapelli '05	♀♀ 5
Barbaresco Serracapelli '04	♀♀ 5
Barbaresco Serracapelli '03	♀♀ 5
Barbaresco Vign. Serracapelli '09	♀♀ 5
Barbaresco Vign. Serracapelli '07	♀♀ 5
Dolcetto d'Alba Montubert '05	♀♀ 3
Langhe Nebbiolo '12	♀♀ 3
Langhe Nebbiolo '10	♀♀ 3

Tenuta Montemagno

VIA CASCINA VALFOSSATO, 9
14030 MONTEMAGNO [AT]
TEL. +39 014163624
www.tenutamontemagno.it

CELLAR SALES
PRE-BOOKED VISITS
ACCOMMODATION AND RESTAURANT SERVICE
ANNUAL PRODUCTION 96,000 bottles
HECTARES UNDER VINE 15.00

In the space of a few years Tenuta Montemagno has shown impressive growth. All of its wines are not only sound, but tend towards excellence. The top of the range is aged in oak barrels of various sizes up to 2,500 litres, which enriches them without covering the typical aromas of the grape varieties. The wide range features aromatic red and white wines: Sauvignon Blanc and Ruché, but also Malvasia di Casorzo. The other wines are based on timorasso, grignolino, barbera, and syrah, the latter blended with barbera in the Violae. Barbera Superiore Mysterium topped the list. It is a very youthful version, commencing with its deep ruby hue, with a nose of plums and cherries and spicy undertones derived from the oak. On the palate it is full and juicy, with a fine tannic weave and a lingering finish. The other wines are very well made.

● Barbera d'Asti Sup. Mysterium '13	♟♟ 4
● Grignolino d'Asti Ruber '15	♟♟ 2*
○ M.to Bianco Musae '15	♟♟ 2*
○ M.to Bianco Solis Vis '14	♟♟ 2*
● Ruchè di Castagnole M.to '15	♟♟ 3
○ Tenuta Montemagno Brut 24 M. Cl.	♟♟ 5
● Barbera d'Asti Austerum '14	♟ 2
○ M.to Bianco Nymphae '15	♟ 2
● M.to Rosso Violae '14	♟ 2
● Malvasia di Casorzo d'Asti Dulcem '15	♟ 2
● Barbera d'Asti Sup. Mysterium '12	♟♟ 4
● Barbera d'Asti Sup. Mysterium '11	♟♟ 4
○ M.to Bianco Musae '13	♟♟ 2*
○ M.to Bianco Nymphae '14	♟♟ 2*
○ M.to Bianco Nymphae '12	♟♟ 2*
○ M.to Bianco Solis Vis '13	♟♟ 2*

Monti

FRAZ. CAMIE
LOC. SAN SEBASTIANO, 39
12065 MONFORTE D'ALBA [CN]
TEL. +39 017378391
www.paolomonti.com

CELLAR SALES
PRE-BOOKED VISITS
ANNUAL PRODUCTION 50,000 bottles
HECTARES UNDER VINE 16.00

In 1996 Pier Paolo Monti inaugurated his winery in the Bussia cru of Monforte. Little has changed since then, for he has lavished painstaking care on the production of sophisticated, full-bodied wines from the outset. Nebbiolo and barbera reign supreme in the vineyards, although they have been flanked by Bordeaux grape varieties, used chiefly in the Langhe Rosso and Langhe Merlot, along with riesling and chardonnay, which yield the white L'Aura. The wines are full of personality, beautifully varietal, and bear the faint traces of ageing in French oak, particularly in small casks. The powerful Barolo Bussia Riserva 2010 opens with pervasive notes of smoke, spice and toast, and continues with fine tannic grip on the palate. Barbera d'Alba 2013 is modern and elegant, with a nose brimming with dark fruit and sweet pulp on a refreshing palate with hints of oak. The elegant Barolo del Comune di Monforte d'Alba 2012 is still swathed in oak.

● Barbera d'Alba '13	♟♟ 5
● Barolo Bussia Ris. '10	♟♟ 8
● Barbera d'Alba Sup. '13	♟♟ 7
● Barolo del Comune di Monforte d'Alba '12	♟♟ 7
● Barbera d'Alba '12	♟♟ 5
● Barbera d'Alba '11	♟♟ 5
● Barbera d'Alba '09	♟♟ 5
● Barolo '09	♟♟ 7
● Barolo del Comune di Monforte d'Alba '11	♟♟ 7
● Barolo del Comune di Monforte d'Alba '10	♟♟ 7
● Langhe Dossi Rossi '11	♟♟ 5
● Nebbiolo d'Alba '12	♟♟ 4
● Nebbiolo d'Alba '11	♟♟ 4
● Nebbiolo d'Alba '10	♟♟ 4

Stefanino Morra

LOC. SAN PIETRO
VIA CASTAGNITO, 50
12050 CASTELLINALDO [CN]
TEL. +39 0173213489
www.morravini.it

CELLAR SALES
PRE-BOOKED VISITS
ANNUAL PRODUCTION 70,000 bottles
HECTARES UNDER VINE 11.00
SUSTAINABLE WINERY

The Morra family have been growing
grapes in Castellinaldo for three
generations and started bottling their own
wines in 1990. Their vineyards all lie on the
sandy limestone soils typical of Roero, in
Canale, Castellinaldo, and Vezza d'Alba.
They are planted with the classic local
grape varieties, from arneis and nebbiolo to
barbera and favorita, which are used to
make terroir-true wines with beautifully rich
fruit and full body. The list of wines
presented is excellent. Barbera d'Alba
Castellinaldo 2013 has a concentrated
nose of dark berries, rain-soaked earth,
liquorice, spice, and coffee, and a long,
velvety palate with impressive balance.
Barbera d'Alba Castlè 2012 is potent and
fruity, with lively acidity ensuring freshness
and length, while Roero Arneis 2015 is very
aromatic, with notes of yellow peaches, and
a refreshing, gutsy palate.

● Barbera d'Alba Castellinaldo '13	♥♥	4
● Barbera d'Alba Castlè '12	♥♥	5
○ Roero Arneis '15	♥♥	3*
● Barbera d'Alba '14	♥♥	3
● Roero '13	♥♥	4
● Roero Srai Ris. '12	♥♥	5
● Barbera d'Alba '13	♀♀	3*
● Barbera d'Alba '11	♀♀	3
● Barbera d'Alba Castellinaldo '12	♀♀	4
● Roero '12	♀♀	4
○ Roero Arneis '14	♀♀	3*
○ Roero Arneis '13	♀♀	3
● Roero Srai Ris. '11	♀♀	5

F.lli Mossio

FRAZ. CASCINA CARAMELLI
VIA MONTÀ, 12
12050 RODELLO [CN]
TEL. +39 0173617149
www.mossio.com

CELLAR SALES
PRE-BOOKED VISITS
ACCOMMODATION
ANNUAL PRODUCTION 50,000 bottles
HECTARES UNDER VINE 10.00
SUSTAINABLE WINERY

The Mossio family have always displayed
great skill and determination, which has
allowed them to make a name for
themselves on the international markets
with their Dolcetto d'Alba, a wine that has
suffered from the competition of
nebbiolo-based wines in Langhe. Our
favourites are always the complex Bricco
Caramelli and the fruitier Piano delli
Perdoni, but fans of more concentrated
Dolcetto will love the potent Superiore
Gamus, which is aged in large oak barrels,
and the Le Margherite passito. Dolcetto
d'Alba Bricco Caramelli successfully
interprets its rich vintage, with a pervasive
nose of red fruit and a particularly fresh,
powerful, enfolding palate. Piano delli
Perdoni of the same vintage is slightly more
tannic, offering a more austere nose of
dark berries with undertones of leather,
while the full-bodied Nebbiolo 2012 is a
little marked by ageing in oak.

● Dolcetto d'Alba Bricco Caramelli '15	♥♥	3*
● Barbera d'Alba '14	♥♥	4
● Dolcetto d'Alba Piano delli Perdoni '15	♥♥	2*
● Langhe Nebbiolo '12	♥♥	4
● Dolcetto d'Alba Bricco Caramelli '00	♀♀♀	3*
● Dolcetto d'Alba Bricco Caramelli '14	♀♀	3*
● Dolcetto d'Alba Bricco Caramelli '13	♀♀	3*
● Dolcetto d'Alba Bricco Caramelli '11	♀♀	3*
● Dolcetto d'Alba Bricco Caramelli '10	♀♀	3*
● Dolcetto d'Alba Bricco Caramelli '09	♀♀	3*
● Dolcetto d'Alba Piano delli Perdoni '12	♀♀	2*
● Dolcetto d'Alba Piano delli Perdoni '11	♀♀	2*
● Dolcetto d'Alba Sup. Gamus '13	♀♀	4
● Dolcetto d'Alba Sup. Gamvs '12	♀♀	4
● Langhe Nebbiolo '09	♀♀	4

★Fiorenzo Nada

VIA AUSARIO, 12c
12050 TREISO [CN]
TEL. +39 0173638254
www.nada.it

CELLAR SALES
PRE-BOOKED VISITS
ANNUAL PRODUCTION 45,000 bottles
HECTARES UNDER VINE 9.00
SUSTAINABLE WINERY

Originally a teacher, Bruno Nada has preserved his professional attention to detail and the message he wishes to convey, and remains a keen and engaging educator who never tires of keeping abreast of the latest developments. His steady goals, associated with his meticulous work in the vineyard, learnt from his father Fiorenzo, and in the cellar, are aimed at achieving the greatest possible elegance from his three beloved grape varieties: nebbiolo, barbera, and dolcetto. In addition to the multi-award-winning Barbaresco Rombone, we would also like to mention the Seifile, which remains a veritable beacon in the history of the Langhe Rosso DOC. We awarded a Tre Bicchieri to Barbaresco Rombone 2012, which has brilliant ageing prospects. Its concentrated, complex nose of raspberries with penetrating notes of liquorice and tar is followed by a fairly austere palate with very long, progressive tannic structure. The well-made Manzola 2012 is spicier and less fruity, while the dense, chocolatey Barbera d'Alba 2014 is among the best of its vintage.

● Barbaresco Rombone '12	▼▼▼ 7
● Barbaresco Manzola '12	▼▼ 6
● Barbera d'Alba '14	▼▼ 4
● Dolcetto d'Alba '15	▼▼ 2*
● Langhe Nebbiolo '14	▼▼ 3
● Langhe Rosso Seifile '12	▼▼ 7
● Barbaresco '01	♀♀♀ 6
● Barbaresco Manzola '08	♀♀♀ 6
● Barbaresco Manzola '06	♀♀♀ 6
● Barbaresco Rombone '10	♀♀♀ 7
● Barbaresco Rombone '09	♀♀♀ 7
● Barbaresco Rombone '07	♀♀♀ 7
● Barbaresco Rombone '06	♀♀♀ 7
● Barbaresco Rombone '05	♀♀♀ 7
● Barbaresco Rombone '04	♀♀♀ 7
● Langhe Rosso Seifile '01	♀♀♀ 6

Cantina dei Produttori Nebbiolo di Carema

VIA NAZIONALE, 32
10010 CAREMA [TO]
TEL. +39 0125811160
www.caremadoc.it

CELLAR SALES
PRE-BOOKED VISITS
RESTAURANT SERVICE
ANNUAL PRODUCTION 65,000 bottles
HECTARES UNDER VINE 17.00

Vaunting 17 hectares tended by around 80 members, this cooperative winery is the leading producer of the Carema designation. Numerically, with all that it entails for an area that is extreme in every respect, with its alpine climate, fragmented vineyards, and pergolas driven into the rock, but also stylistically, for it has not always been easy to offer and interpret the type of Nebbiolo that this terroir yields, apparently lean and almost fragile, yet capable of ageing for decades. The two main wines, aged in large barrels for 24–36 months, are the Carema Classico, which can be considered the basic version, and the Riserva. The 2013 vintage bestowed freshness and ensured good fruit on both the nose and palate, with Carema Etichetta Nera showing more confident and ready to drink and the Riserva 2012 slightly more closed and dense, lacking the raciness derived from acidity. This fine estate never disappoints, also due to its very reasonable prices.

● Carema Et. Nera '13	▼▼ 2*
● Carema Et. Bianca Ris. '12	▼▼ 3
● Carema Et. Bianca '07	♀♀♀ 3*
● Carema Et. Bianca Ris. '11	♀♀♀ 3*
● Carema Et. Bianca Ris. '09	♀♀♀ 3*
● Carema Et. Bianca Ris. '08	♀♀♀ 3*
● Carema Et. Bianca '06	♀♀ 3*
● Carema Et. Bianca '05	♀♀ 3
● Carema Et. Bianca Ris. '10	♀♀ 3*
● Carema Et. Nera '12	♀♀ 2*
● Carema Et. Nera '11	♀♀ 2*
● Carema Et. Nera '10	♀♀ 2*
● Carema Et. Nera '08	♀♀ 2*
● Carema Et. Nera '06	♀♀ 2*
● Carema Ris. '04	♀♀ 3*

Lorenzo Negro

FRAZ. SANT'ANNA, 55
12040 MONTEU ROERO [CN]
TEL. +39 017390645
www.negrolorenzo.com

CELLAR SALES
PRE-BOOKED VISITS
ANNUAL PRODUCTION 35,000 bottles
HECTARES UNDER VINE 8.00
SUSTAINABLE WINERY

In 2006 Lorenzo Negro decided to take a quantum leap and started bottling his own wine. The estate's vineyards, which surround the winery on the Serra Lupini hill, about 300 metres above sea level, are between 16 and 30 years old and lie on sandy soil with silt and clay. They are planted chiefly to arneis, nebbiolo, and barbera, plus a small amount of bonarda, dolcetto, and albarossa. Lorenzo Negro's wines are always well made, but this year they seemed slightly below par, particularly the Roero San Francesco Riserva 2012, which is lacking some of its usual character and complexity. The fruity Barbera d'Alba Superiore La Nanda 2012 has notes of Mediterranean scrubland and spice, and a long, velvety finish supported by good acidity. Roero Arneis Metodo Classico Brut 2010 is full and fresh, with pleasant notes of cake and ripe apricots and peaches.

● Barbera d'Alba Sup. La Nanda '12	♙♙	3
○ Roero Arneis Brut M. Cl. '10	♙♙	4
○ Roero Arneis '15	♙	2
● Roero San Francesco Ris. '12	♙	3
● Barbera d'Alba '13	♗♗	2*
● Barbera d'Alba '12	♗♗	2*
● Barbera d'Alba Sup. La Nanda '09	♗♗	3
● Barbera d'Alba Sup. La Nanda '07	♗♗	3
● Langhe Nebbiolo '12	♗♗	2*
○ Roero Arneis '12	♗♗	2*
○ Roero Arneis '11	♗♗	2*
● Roero San Francesco Ris. '10	♗♗	3
● Roero San Francesco Ris. '09	♗♗	3

Angelo Negro e Figli

FRAZ. SANT'ANNA, 1
12040 MONTEU ROERO [CN]
TEL. +39 017390252
www.negroangelo.it

CELLAR SALES
PRE-BOOKED VISITS
ANNUAL PRODUCTION 350,000 bottles
HECTARES UNDER VINE 60.00
SUSTAINABLE WINERY

The Negro family have lived in Roero since the 12th century. Today Giovanni and Marisa run one of the leading wineries in the production zone, aided by their children Angelo, Emanuela, Gabriele, and Giuseppe. Their vineyards, from which they craft the traditional local wines, are scattered across several municipalities, from Monteu Roero, where the winery is, and Canale to Magliano Alfieri and Santo Stefano Roero. They also own an estate in Neive, where Barbaresco and Dolcetto d'Alba are made. Roero Sudisfà Riserva 2013 won a well-deserved Tre Bicchieri with a nose of Mediterranean scrubland, liquorice, and red berries and hints of tobacco, and a fleshy, firmly structured palate with full flavour, velvety tannins, and a long finish nicely underpinned by acidity. Roero Prachiosso 2013 is also excellent, offering a floral nose with notes of spice and dark berries, as is the complex, flavoursome Roero Arneis Serra Lupini 2015, with pleasant notes of apples and pears.

● Roero Sudisfà Ris. '13	♙♙♙	6
○ Roero Arneis Serra Lupini '15	♙♙	3*
● Roero Prachiosso '13	♙♙	4
● Barbaresco Basarin '13	♙♙	5
○ Perdaudin Passito '11	♙♙	5
○ Roero Arneis Brut Giovanni Negro Dosage Zero '09	♙♙	5
○ Roero Arneis Perdaudin '15	♙♙	3
○ Roero Arneis Perdaudin '14	♙♙	3
● Roero San Giorgio Ris. '13	♙♙	5
● Roero Sudisfà Ris. '12	♗♗♗	6
● Roero Sudisfà Ris. '10	♗♗♗	6
● Roero Sudisfà Ris. '09	♗♗♗	5
● Roero Sudisfà Ris. '08	♗♗♗	5

Nervi

c.so Vercelli, 117
13045 Gattinara [VC]
Tel. +39 0163833228
www.gattinara-nervi.it

CELLAR SALES
PRE-BOOKED VISITS
ANNUAL PRODUCTION 120,000 bottles
HECTARES UNDER VINE 24.00

The oldest winery in Gattinara was founded by Luigi Nervi in 1906 and covers over 20 hectares planted to nebbiolo, located in veritable grand crus, such as Casacce, Garavoglie, and Valferana, not to mention the splendid amphitheatre formed by the Molsino vineyard. A few years ago the legendary estate was taken over by Erling Astrup and Christopher Moestue with two other Norwegian partners. They can be credited with a seamless transition in terms of both production and style, as demonstrated by the continued partnership with oenologist Enrico Fileppo. The top wines are as good as ever: vigorous, noble reds achieved using tailored cellar processes. The quality of the most recent wines is also improving, as exemplified by the fragrant Jefferson 1787 Metodo Classico Dosage Zéro Rosato, from nebbiolo, which is powerful with graceful effervescence. However, the star is again Gattinara Molsino, held back only by its still rugged tannins in the 2011 version.

● Gattinara Molsino '11	▼▼ 5
● Gattinara '12	▼▼ 4
● Gattinara Valferana '11	▼▼ 5
○ Erbaluce di Caluso Bianca '15	▼ 4
⊙ Jefferson 1787 Rosé Dosage Zéro M. Cl.	▼ 5
● Gattinara Podere dei Ginepri '01	♈♈♈ 5
● Gattinara Vign. Molsino '00	♈♈♈ 5
○ Erbaluce di Caluso Bianca '14	♈♈ 4
● Gattinara '10	♈♈ 4
● Gattinara '08	♈♈ 4
● Gattinara Molsino '09	♈♈ 5
● Gattinara Molsino '08	♈♈ 5
● Gattinara Valferana '09	♈♈ 5

Andrea Oberto

b.ta Simane, 11
12064 La Morra [CN]
Tel. +39 017350104
www.andreaoberto.com

CELLAR SALES
PRE-BOOKED VISITS
ANNUAL PRODUCTION 100,000 bottles
HECTARES UNDER VINE 16.00

For years La Morra vigneron Andrea Oberto's deep love of his land and vineyards inherited from his father led him to live a double life as a lorry driver and a farmer. After a hard week's work, he would find the time to tend his three hectares. Today, with the aid of his son Fabio, his estate boasts 16 hectares under vine in two of the finest Barolo crus: Brunate and Rocche dell'Annunziata. The same high quality characterizes his Barbera d'Alba Giada, first produced in 1988, which helped make the estate a familiar name in Italy and abroad. It is hard to decide which of the two Barolo crus is better. Rocche dell'Annunziata 2012 offers a concentrated toasty nose with alluring hints of cinnamon, close-woven tannins, and greater austerity than the previous vintage. The vibrant Brunate 2012 has hints of fruit and tobacco that alternate with floral notes on the nose. Its fine balance of tannins and firm structure ensures perfect smoothness.

● Barolo Brunate '12	▼▼ 6
● Barolo Rocche dell'Annunziata '12	▼▼ 7
● Barbera d'Alba Giada '13	▼▼ 5
● Barolo '12	▼▼ 6
● Barolo Albarella '12	▼▼ 7
● Barolo Vign. Albarella '01	♈♈♈ 7
● Barolo Vign. Brunate '05	♈♈♈ 8
● Barolo '11	♈♈ 6
● Barolo Albarella '11	♈♈ 7
● Barolo Brunate '11	♈♈ 6
● Barolo Rocche dell'Annunziata '11	♈♈ 7
● Dolcetto d'Alba '13	♈♈ 2*
● Langhe Rosso Fabio '09	♈♈ 7

Figli Luigi Oddero

LOC. BORGATA BETTOLOTTI
FRAZ. SANTA MARIA
TENUTA PARÀ, 95
12604 LA MORRA [CN]
TEL. +39 0173500386
www.figliluigioddero.it

CELLAR SALES
PRE-BOOKED VISITS
ANNUAL PRODUCTION 110,000 bottles
HECTARES UNDER VINE 35.00
SUSTAINABLE WINERY

Deservedly remembered as one of the great figures of the Langhe wine world, in 2006 Luigi Oddero founded his own winery after having run the eponymous Poderi e Cantine with his brother Giacomo for almost 50 years. Today the large estate is headed by his wife Lena and their children, who tend its prestigious vineyards, like the legendary Rive-Parà, Plaustra, and Bettolotti crus in La Morra; Rocche dei Rivera in Castiglione Falletto; and Vigna Rionda and Baudana in Serralunga d'Alba. Moscato from Cascina Fiori, in Trezzo Tinella, completes the fine range, composed of Barbera, Dolcetto, Freisa, and particularly the renowned and proudly traditional-style Nebbiolos. This stylistic concept is closely reflected in the latest wines from nebbiolo. Barbaresco Rombone 2013 has fine classic flesh countering its slightly rugged, granular development, while the excellent Barolo Rocche Rivera 2010 is more complex with strong personality, focusing on wild berries and spice.

● Barbaresco Rombone '13	♥♥ 5
● Barolo Rocche Rivera '10	♥♥ 6
● Barbera d'Alba '13	♥♥ 3
● Barolo '12	♥♥ 6
● Dolcetto d'Alba '15	♥♥ 2*
● Langhe Nebbiolo '12	♥♥ 3
● Barbaresco '11	♀♥ 5
● Barbaresco '10	♀♥ 5
● Barolo Rocche Rivera '09	♀♥ 8
● Barolo Rocche Rivera '08	♀♥ 8
● Barolo Specola '09	♀♥ 7
● Barolo V. Rionda '09	♀♥ 8
● Barolo V. Rionda '08	♀♥ 8
● Langhe Nebbiolo '11	♀♥ 3
● Langhe Nebbiolo '10	♀♥ 3

★Poderi e Cantine Oddero

FRAZ. SANTA MARIA
VIA TETTI, 28
12064 LA MORRA [CN]
TEL. +39 017350618
www.oddero.it

CELLAR SALES
PRE-BOOKED VISITS
ANNUAL PRODUCTION 150,000 bottles
HECTARES UNDER VINE 35.00
VITICULTURE METHOD Certified Organic

Mariacristina and Mariavittoria Oddero head one of the most important wineries in Langhe, with over 35 hectares under vine, almost half planted to nebbiolo destined for Barolo and Barbaresco. But it's not just about numbers, for the estate's assets include names like Villero and Rocche in Castiglione Falletto, Brunate in La Morra, Mondoca di Bussia Soprana in Monforte, Vigna Rionda in Serralunga, and Gallina in Barbaresco. These veritable grand crus are interpreted in an austere, penetrating style achieved by the skilled use of large oak barrels and smaller casks. Barbera, Dolcetto, and a few wines from international varietals complete the picture. A strong team of Barolos led a three-pronged attack. The Bussia Vigna Mondoca Riserva 2010 won us over with a charmingly complex nose and a long, dynamic palate, while the Rocche 2012 is still young and austere, and the Vignarionda 2006 is more complex and evolved.

● Barolo Bussia V. Mondoca Ris. '10	♥♥♥ 8
● Barbaresco Gallina '13	♥♥ 6
● Barolo Rocche di Castiglione '12	♥♥ 8
● Barolo Vignarionda Ris. '06	♥♥ 8
● Barbera d'Alba Sup. '13	♥♥ 4
● Barolo '12	♥♥ 6
● Barolo Brunate '12	♥♥ 8
● Barolo Villero '12	♥♥ 8
● Dolcetto d'Alba '15	♥♥ 3
○ Moscato d'Asti Cascina Fiori '15	♥♥ 3
○ Langhe Bianco Collaretto '14	♥ 3
● Langhe Nebbiolo '13	♥ 4
● Barbaresco Gallina '04	♀♀♥ 6
● Barolo Bussia V. Mondoca Ris. '08	♀♀♥ 8
● Barolo Mondoca di Bussia Soprana '04	♀♀♥ 7
● Barolo Rocche di Castiglione '09	♀♀♥ 7

Tenuta Olim Bauda

via Prata, 50
14045 Incisa Scapaccino [AT]
Tel. +39 0141702171
www.tenutaolimbauda.it

CELLAR SALES
PRE-BOOKED VISITS
ANNUAL PRODUCTION 183,000 bottles
HECTARES UNDER VINE 30.00

Over the past few years Diana, Dino, and Gianni Bertolino have accompanied the family winery, founded in 1961, to the highest pinnacles of Monferrato production, particularly in the case of Barbera, the area's most representative wine. Most of the estate's vineyards, planted to barbera and moscato, are in Nizza Monferrato. The same grapes are also grown in Isola d'Asti, Fontanile, and Castelnuovo Calcea, along with a small amount of grignolino. The winery's range also includes a Chardonnay and two Gavis. Barbera d'Asti Superiore Nizza 2013 won a Tre Bicchieri for its spicy nose of red fruit, accompanied by hints of quinine and autumn leaves, and its full-bodied, fleshy palate with fine balance and length. Barbera d'Asti Superiore Le Rocchette 2014 is also excellent, with a fruity, balsamic nose and a less compact but taut, elegant palate, as is the concentrated, complex Moscato Passito San Giovanni 2006, whose sweetness is nicely balanced by acidity.

● Barbera d'Asti Sup. Nizza '13	▼▼▼	5
● Barbera d'Asti Sup. Le Rocchette '14	▼▼	4
○ Piemonte Moscato Passito S. Giovanni '06	▼▼	5
● Barbera d'Asti La Villa '15	▼▼	3
○ Gavi del Comune di Gavi '15	▼▼	3
○ Moscato d'Asti Centive '15	▼▼	2*
● Grignolino d'Asti Isolavilla '15	▼	3
● Nebbiolo d'Alba San Pietro '13	▼	3
● Barbera d'Asti Sup. Nizza '12	▽▽▽	5
● Barbera d'Asti Sup. Nizza '11	▽▽▽	5
● Barbera d'Asti Sup. Nizza '08	▽▽▽	5
● Barbera d'Asti Sup. Nizza '07	▽▽▽	5
● Barbera d'Asti Sup. Nizza '06	▽▽▽	5

Orsolani

via Michele Chiesa, 12
10090 San Giorgio Canavese [TO]
Tel. +39 012432386
www.orsolani.it

CELLAR SALES
PRE-BOOKED VISITS
ANNUAL PRODUCTION 140,000 bottles
HECTARES UNDER VINE 19.00

Orsolani's wines have been a paean to the versatility of erbaluce for over half a century. The first experiments with sparkling wine production were carried out on the farmstead in San Giorgio Canavese after the war, when the potential of La Rustìa, a still dry type, was also recognized for a grape variety that had hitherto been used almost exclusively for passitos like Sulé, and the first vineyard selections were made. This dynamic approach has continued through the generations, with the transition from Gian Francesco to his son Gian Luigi, and is fuelled by magnificent vineyards that also extend over the morainic Mazzé and Caluso hills. We awarded a Tre Bicchieri to Erbaluce La Rustìa 2015, with a seductive, complex nose offering full, ripe notes of pears, damsons, and acacia honey, followed by refreshing herbs, and a long palate with great stuffing and attractive freshness. The 2009 vintage of Passito Sulé is as excellent as ever, combining elegant aromas of dried fruit and coffee.

○ Erbaluce di Caluso La Rustìa '15	▼▼▼	3*
○ Caluso Passito Sulé '09	▼▼	5
○ Caluso Brut Cuvée Tradizione M. Cl. '11	▼▼	5
○ Caluso Passito Sulé '04	▽▽▽	5
○ Caluso Passito Sulé '98	▽▽▽	5
○ Erbaluce di Caluso La Rustìa '13	▽▽▽	3*
○ Erbaluce di Caluso La Rustìa '12	▽▽▽	3*
○ Erbaluce di Caluso La Rustìa '11	▽▽▽	3*
○ Erbaluce di Caluso La Rustìa '10	▽▽▽	2*
○ Erbaluce di Caluso La Rustìa '09	▽▽▽	2*

Paitin

LOC. BRICCO
VIA SERRABOELLA, 20
12052 NEIVE [CN]
TEL. +39 017367343
www.paitin.it

CELLAR SALES
PRE-BOOKED VISITS
ACCOMMODATION
ANNUAL PRODUCTION 80,000 bottles
HECTARES UNDER VINE 17.00

The name Barbaresco, intended as a wine, was coined at the end of the 19th century, and the Pasquero Elia family started making wine in 1893. Their estate has gradually grown, and today Silvano and Giovanni vaunt a first-rate collection of vineyards, currently all under conversion to biodynamic methods. Following a period of prominent oak, typical of many wines of the 1990s, today the selections of Barbaresco Paitin are pure and true, always focusing on fruit. Riserva Vecchia Vigne is particularly impressive, from vines over 60 years old. The sound Barbaresco Serraboella 2013 has a close-focused nose of raspberries and a full-bodied palate with good body, slightly disrupted by young tannins. Dried roses, liquorice, and tar are slowly replacing red fruit in the Sorì Paitin 2013, which vaunts a complex palate and long finish. Barbaresco Sorì Paitin Vigne Vecchie Riserva 2011 has faintly salty top notes on the nose and a slightly alcoholic palate with full body.

Palladino

P.ZZA CAPPELANO, 9
12050 SERRALUNGA D'ALBA [CN]
TEL. +39 0173613108
www.palladinovini.com

CELLAR SALES
ACCOMMODATION
ANNUAL PRODUCTION 200,000 bottles
HECTARES UNDER VINE 11.00

This winery is a fairly large one by Langhe standards and supplements the fruit of its own vineyards with grapes purchased from selected growers. A few years ago Maurilio Palladino decided to give a qualitative boost to his Barolo selections, which now represent a valid benchmark for the extraordinary potential of Serralunga d'Alba. All the Barolos vaunt a classic, elegant style, with the Parafada and Riserva San Bernardo constituting pinnacles of excellence. The worthy product of a great vintage and a fine vineyard, Barolo Bernardo Riserva 2010 offers strawberries, raspberries, and blood oranges on the nose, followed by elegant hints of violets and liquorice, and a fabulously elegant, well-orchestrated palate that won the winery its first Tre Bicchieri. Barolo Parafada 2012 vaunts fine fresh fruit and a powerful, full-bodied palate with austere tannins, while the sound, firmly structured Ornato 2012 is slightly more compact and needs more time.

● Barbaresco Serraboella '13	♥♥ 5
● Barbaresco Sorì Paitin '13	♥♥ 6
● Barbaresco Sorì Paitin V. V. Ris. '11	♥♥ 8
○ Langhe Arneis Elisa '15	♥♥ 3
● Langhe Nebbiolo Starda '14	♥ 3
● Barbaresco Sorì Paitin '07	♥♥♥ 5
● Barbaresco Sorì Paitin '04	♥♥♥ 5
● Barbaresco Sorì Paitin '97	♥♥♥ 5
● Barbaresco Sorì Paitin '95	♥♥♥ 7
● Barbaresco Sorì Paitin V. V. '04	♥♥♥ 7
● Barbaresco Sorì Paitin V. V. '01	♥♥♥ 7
● Barbaresco Sorì Paitin V. V. '99	♥♥♥ 8
● Langhe Paitin '97	♥♥♥ 5
● Barbaresco Sorì Paitin '12	♥♥ 6
● Barbaresco Sorì Paitin '11	♥♥ 6
● Barbaresco Sorì Paitin '10	♥♥ 6

● Barolo San Bernardo Ris. '10	♥♥♥ 6
● Barolo Parafada '12	♥♥ 6
● Barbera d'Alba Sup. Bricco delle Olive '13	♥♥ 2*
● Barolo del Comune di Serralunga d'Alba '12	♥♥ 5
● Barolo Ornato '12	♥♥ 6
● Barbera d'Alba Sup. Bricco delle Olive '12	♥♥ 2*
● Barolo del Comune di Serralunga d'Alba '11	♥♥ 5
● Barolo Ornato '11	♥♥ 6
● Barolo Ornato '10	♥♥ 6
● Barolo Parafada '11	♥♥ 6
● Barolo Parafada '10	♥♥ 6

Armando Parusso

LOC. BUSSIA, 55
12065 MONFORTE D'ALBA [CN]
TEL. +39 017378257
www.parusso.com

CELLAR SALES
PRE-BOOKED VISITS
ANNUAL PRODUCTION 125,000 bottles
HECTARES UNDER VINE 23.00

The quest to achieve the fullest expression from the most natural grapes proceeds both in the vineyard, where biodynamic methods are increasingly prevalent, and in the cellar, commencing with a period of a few days during which the bunches are monitored before crushing. The resulting six Barolos are particularly complex and very ripe, more mouthfilling than delicate. However, the Parusso brothers are also skilled producers of white wines and their well-made Langhe Rovella, produced from sauvignon grapes since 1991, was joined by a very interesting Brut Metodo Classico from nebbiolo a couple of years ago. Sweet, spicy aromas of oak dominate the nose of Barolo Mariondino 2012, slightly masking the fruit and underscoring the tannins on the medium-structured palate. The Bussia 2012 is similar in style, perfect for lovers of thoroughly modern, spicy Barolos. The Barolo 2012 is more mature, showing soft and vegetal, still swathed in oak, while Parusso Brut 2012 is rich and mouthfilling.

● Barolo Bussia '12	▼▼	8
● Barolo '12	▼▼	6
● Barolo Le Coste di Monforte '12	▼▼	8
● Barolo Mariondino '12	▼▼	7
○ Parusso Brut M. Cl. '12	▼▼	6
● Barbera d'Alba Sup. '00	▼▼▼	5
● Barolo Bussia V. Munie '99	▼▼▼	8
● Barolo Bussia V. Munie '97	▼▼▼	8
● Barolo Bussia V. Munie '96	▼▼▼	8
● Barolo Le Coste Mosconi '03	▼▼▼	7
● Barolo V. V. in Mariondino Ris. '99	▼▼▼	8
● Langhe Rosso Bricco Rovella '96	▼▼▼	8
● Barolo Bussia Et. Oro Ris. '06	▽▽	8
● Barolo Le Coste Mosconi '09	▽▽	8
● Barolo Le Coste Mosconi '08	▽▽	8
● Barolo Mariondino '10	▽▽	7

Massimo Pastura
Cascina La Ghersa

VIA CHIARINA, 2
14050 MOASCA [AT]
TEL. +39 0141856012
www.laghersa.it

CELLAR SALES
PRE-BOOKED VISITS
ACCOMMODATION
ANNUAL PRODUCTION 150,000 bottles
HECTARES UNDER VINE 23.00

In recent years Massimo Pastura has transformed Cascina La Ghersa from a classic Monferrato winery, focusing almost exclusively on Barbera and Moscato, to a more complex operation in which the increasingly important and high-quality Barbera selections have been flanked by wines like Gavi and Colli Tortonesi Timorasso. The range is composed of 12 wines full of character, divided into the Vigneti Unici, I Classici, and Piagè product lines. Due to the poor vintage for Asti wines, this year it was the Tortona estate that gave the best performance, with the Colli Tortonesi Timorasso Timian Riserva 2013 offering a nose of dried herbs and tobacco with mint and rosemary, and a full palate nicely underpinned by acidity, ensuring a dynamic, long, fresh finish. The spicy Barbera d'Asti Superiore Le Cave 2013 is well made, vaunting a nose of plums and cocoa powder, and a dense palate with good extract and acidity.

○ Colli Tortonesi Timorasso Timian Ris. '13	▼▼	4
● Barbera d'Asti Sup. Le Cave '13	▼▼	3
● Barbera d'Asti Sup. Camparò '14	▼	2
● Barbera d'Asti Sup. Muascae '13	▼	6
● Barbera d'Asti Sup.Vignassa '13	▼	5
● Colli Tortonesi Croatina Smentià Ris. '13	▼	4
○ Colli Tortonesi Timorasso Sivoy '14	▼	4
○ Moscato d'Asti Giorgia '15	▼	2
● Barbera d'Asti Sup. Le Cave '12	▽▽	3
● Barbera d'Asti Sup. Muaschae '14	▽▽	6
● Barbera d'Asti Sup. Muaschae '11	▽▽	6
● Barbera d'Asti Sup.Vignassa '12	▽▽	5
○ Colli Tortonesi Timorasso Sivoy '12	▽▽	4

★Pecchenino

B.TA VALDIBERTI, 59
12063 DOGLIANI [CN]
TEL. +39 017370686
www.pecchenino.com

CELLAR SALES
PRE-BOOKED VISITS
ACCOMMODATION
ANNUAL PRODUCTION 130,000 bottles
HECTARES UNDER VINE 28.00
SUSTAINABLE WINERY

Orlando Pecchenino was elected Chairman of the Barolo, Barbaresco, Alba, Langhe, and Dogliani Consortium in May 2016. Knowing how wise and professional he is, we are sure he will make his own intelligent contribution to a winegrowing area with an annual production of over 60 million bottles and 11 different designations. New developments are also underfoot at his family winery, where a suitable cellar for Barolo is being built, while the splendid current headquarters will continue to produce the Dolcetto di Dogliani selections that have deservedly made it world famous. Barolo Le Coste di Monforte shows prominent oak, combined with a rich, full-flavoured palate with confident tannic entry, while the modern, well-defined Riserva 2008 from the same cru is softer. The new Barolo Bussia has hints of quinine and tobacco on the nose and focuses more on solidity than elegance, Dogliani Superiore Bricco Botti 2013 is complex and elegant, with a pleasant, unusually full-flavoured palate.

● Barolo Le Coste di Monforte '12	❧❧	7
● Barolo Le Coste di Monforte Ris. '08	❧❧	8
● Dogliani Sup. Bricco Botti '13	❧❧	4
● Barolo Bussia '12	❧❧	7
● Barolo San Giuseppe '12	❧❧	6
● Dogliani San Luigi '15	❧❧	3
○ Langhe Maestro '15	❧❧	3
● Langhe Nebbiolo Botti '14	❧❧	3
● Langhe Pinot Nero '13	❧	4
● Barolo Le Coste '05	❧❧❧	8
● Dogliani Bricco Botti '07	❧❧❧	4
● Dogliani Sirì d'Jermu '09	❧❧❧	3*
● Dogliani Sirì d'Jermu '06	❧❧❧	4
● Dogliani Sup. Bricco Botti '10	❧❧❧	4*
● Dolcetto di Dogliani Sirì d'Jermu '03	❧❧❧	3
● Dolcetto di Dogliani Sup. Bricco Botti '04	❧❧❧	4
● Langhe Pinot Nero '13	❧	4

Pelissero

VIA FERRERE, 10
12050 TREISO [CN]
TEL. +39 0173638430
www.pelissero.com

CELLAR SALES
PRE-BOOKED VISITS
ANNUAL PRODUCTION 250,000 bottles
HECTARES UNDER VINE 40.00

Giorgio represents the third generation of Pelissero vignerons and has had the farsightedness to preserve the family's old vineyards in the famous Barbaresco crus of Tre Stelle, Marcarini, and San Stefanetto. Covering an area of almost 40 hectares, planted chiefly to nebbiolo, barbera, and dolcetto, they yield a total of 250,000 bottles per year. Thanks to a modern vision of winegrowing applying new techniques, a progressive approach and a cutting-edge cellar, the estate is one of the most dynamic in the whole of Piedmont. The wines are contemporary in style, standing out for their power and extraction. The two Barbaresco vineyard selections interpret very different terroirs. The Vanotu, which borders three famous crus (Tre Stelle, Marcarini, and Basarin) is more civilized, while the Tulin, from a steep vineyard in the San Stefanetto cru between Treiso and Neviglie, is more explosive. Riesling Rigadin made a fine debut.

● Barbaresco Tulin '13	❧❧	7
● Barbaresco Vanotu '13	❧❧	8
● Barbaresco Nubiola '13	❧❧	5
● Dolcetto d'Alba Augenta '15	❧❧	3
● Dolcetto d'Alba Munfrina '15	❧❧	2*
○ Langhe Riesling Rigadin '15	❧❧	3
○ Langhe Favorita Le Nature '15	❧	2
● Langhe Nebbiolo '14	❧	3
● Barbaresco Vanotu '08	❧❧❧	8
● Barbaresco Vanotu '07	❧❧❧	8
● Barbaresco Vanotu '06	❧❧❧	8
● Barbaresco Vanotu '01	❧❧❧	7
● Barbaresco Vanotu '99	❧❧❧	7
● Barbaresco Vanotu '97	❧❧❧	6

Cantina Pertinace

LOC. PERTINACE, 2
12050 TREISO [CN]
TEL. +39 0173442238
www.pertinace.com

CELLAR SALES
PRE-BOOKED VISITS
ANNUAL PRODUCTION 500,000 bottles
HECTARES UNDER VINE 80.00

The strength of this cooperative lies in the work and determination of its members, who have created a new brand over the years, the symbol of terroir well suited for the production of great wines. The winery was founded in the Treiso hamlet of Pertinace between the end of 1972 and the beginning of 1973 by Mario Barbero and 13 other grower members. Today it is headed by chairman Bruno Fiori and manager oenologist Cesare Barbero, Mario's son who has inherited his determination and professionalism to guarantee all members high-quality production. Barbaresco Marcarini 2013 offers hints of cinnamon and tobacco on a classic nose of red berries, and a palate underpinned by creamy tannins and a very lively finish. The firmly structured Barbaresco Nervo 2013 appears slightly less complex, with plenty of pulp and assertive but not intrusive tannins.

● Barbaresco Marcarini '13	♟♟ 5	
● Barbaresco '13	♟♟ 5	
● Barbaresco Castellizzano '13	♟♟ 5	
● Barbaresco Nervo '13	♟♟ 5	
● Dolcetto d'Alba '15	♟♟ 2*	
● Langhe Arneis '15	♟♟ 3	
● Barbera d'Alba '14	♟ 2	
● Langhe Nebbiolo '15	♟ 3	
● Barbaresco Castellizzano '12	♟♟ 5	
● Barbaresco Marcarini '12	♟♟ 5	
● Barbera d'Alba '13	♟♟ 2*	
● Dolcetto d'Alba '14	♟♟ 2*	
● Langhe Nebbiolo '13	♟♟ 3	

Pescaja

VIA SAN MATTEO, 59
14010 CISTERNA D'ASTI [AT]
TEL. +39 0141979711
www.pescaja.com

PRE-BOOKED VISITS
ANNUAL PRODUCTION 200,000 bottles
HECTARES UNDER VINE 23.50

In 1990 Giuseppe Guido purchased his first vineyards and built the cellar in Cisterna d'Asti. Over the following years he bought the vineyards of the Pescaja Opera Pia estates in the Nizza zone, after which the winery is named, and planted four hectares in the Terre Alfieri area. Arneis, barbera, nebbiolo, and bonarda are the principle grape varieties grown. This year Pescaja has earned a full profile with a series of excellent wines. We liked Monferrato Solo Luna 2014, an Arneis offering a concentrated fruity nose of peaches and melons, with notes of sage and honey, accompanied by a beautifully orchestrated palate with fresh acidity. The taut, balanced Terre Alfieri Arneis 2015 is well made with fine notes of Mediterranean scrubland, as are Barbera d'Asti la Soliter 2015, displaying ripe dark fruit and remarkable structure for a current Barbera, and Nizza Solneri 2013, which is more marked by oak, but wonderfully rich with a very long finish.

● Barbera d'Asti Soliter '15	♟♟ 2*	
● Barbera d'Asti Sup. Nizza Solneri '13	♟♟ 4	
● Monferrato Rosso Solis '13	♟♟ 3	
○ Monferrato Solo Luna '14	♟♟ 5	
○ Terre Alfieri Arneis '15	♟♟ 2*	
⊙ Piemonte Rosato Fleury '15	♟ 2	
● Terre Alfieri Nebbiolo Tuké '14	♟ 3	
● Barbera d'Asti Soliter '14	♟♟ 2*	
● Barbera d'Asti Sup. Nizza Solneri '12	♟♟ 4	
● Monferrato Rosso Solis '11	♟♟ 3	
○ Terre Alfieri Arneis '14	♟♟ 2*	
○ Terre Alfieri Arneis '13	♟♟ 2*	
● Terre Alfieri Nebbiolo Tuké '13	♟♟ 3	

Le Piane

P.ZZA MATTEOTTI, 1
28010 BOCA [NO]
TEL. +39 3483354185
www.bocapiane.com

CELLAR SALES
PRE-BOOKED VISITS
ANNUAL PRODUCTION 45,000 bottles
HECTARES UNDER VINE 8.00
SUSTAINABLE WINERY

Christoph Künzli is rightly cited as one of
the "saviours" of Boca, a small DOC zone in
the province of Novara with ancient
traditions and a decidedly more uncertain
future, at least in the early 1990s. Indeed,
his decision to move to Le Piane after
having bought it from the elderly grower
Antonio Cerri, was one of the key moments
for the subsequent developments. These
include remarkable results from the
restored plots, some of which still use the
traditional "maggiorina" training system,
and the addition of new wines, such as the
Mimmo and the Plinius I, to the range
based on nebbiolo, croatina, and vespolina,
once again testifying to Christoph's
farsightedness. In the absence of the
Maggiorina and the Mimmo, only the
winery's two signature wines remained: the
Piane, from croatina vines between 70 and
100 years old, and the Boca. We preferred
the latter for its beautifully layered nose,
with notes of liquorice, rhubarb, blood, and
iodine) and complex, powerful palate with
tannins softened by exceptionally rich
flavour.

● Boca '11	♟♟♟	8
● Piane '12	♟♟	6
● Boca '10	♟♟♟	7
● Boca '08	♟♟♟	7
● Boca '06	♟♟♟	6
● Boca '05	♟♟♟	6
● Boca '04	♟♟♟	6
● Boca '03	♟♟♟	6
● Boca '07	♟♟	7
● Boca '01	♟♟	6
● Colline Novaresi Le Piane '09	♟♟	5
● Colline Novaresi Le Piane '07	♟♟	5
● Colline Novaresi Le Piane '06	♟♟	5
● Mimmo '11	♟♟	5
● Mimmo '10	♟♟	4
● Piane '11	♟♟	5

Le Pianelle

S.DA FORTE, 24
13862 BRUSNENGO [BI]
TEL. +39 3478772726
www.lepianelle.com

PRE-BOOKED VISITS
ANNUAL PRODUCTION 12,000 bottles
HECTARES UNDER VINE 3.00

Le Pianelle is a fabulous four-hectare
estate in northern Piedmont with a German
atmosphere, founded by the German Dieter
Heuskel and Peter Dipoli, from Alto Adige.
Although their initial idea dates from the
mid-1980s, it didn't become reality until
2002, immediately focusing on nebbiolo,
along with vespolina and croatina. Just two
wines are produced: the rosé Al Posto dei
Fiori, which is the fresh, fragrant version of
Langhe's most famous grape and was the
estate's first and only wine for several
years, and Bramaterra, a red with a great
personality. As is often the case for the
estate's wines, the only thing lacking is
quantity, with just two labels and a handful
of bottles, but quality is always very
present. Its Bramaterra is the least austere
of all Alto Piemonte Nebbiolos due to the
blend of grapes (croatina and vespolina)
that soften its indomitable spirit. The 2013
has a fruity nose and extracted flesh on the
palate, ensuring full flavour. Al Posto dei
Fiori is a fragrant, firmly structured rosé
capable of putting its Provençal
counterparts to shame.

● Bramaterra '13	♟♟	8
⊙ Coste della Sesia Rosato		
Al Posto dei Fiori '15	♟♟	3
● Bramaterra '12	♟♟	8
● Bramaterra '11	♟♟	8
⊙ Coste della Sesia Rosato		
Al Posto dei Fiori '14	♟♟	3
⊙ Coste della Sesia Rosato		
Al Posto dei Fiori '13	♟♟	3

Pico Maccario

VIA CORDARA, 87
14046 MOMBARUZZO [AT]
TEL. +39 0141774522
www.picomaccario.com

CELLAR SALES
PRE-BOOKED VISITS
ANNUAL PRODUCTION 650,000 bottles
HECTARES UNDER VINE 70.00

In 1997, brothers Pico and Vitaliano
Maccario decided to found a winery on an
estate comprised of 70 hectares of
vineyards in a single plot in Mombaruzzo, in
Alto Monferrato. About 60 hectares of
medium-textured soils are planted mainly
to the ubiquitous barbera, and the
remainder to merlot, cabernet sauvignon,
freisa, and favorita. The wines are modern
in style, focusing on rich body and fruit.
Despite its difficult vintage, Barbera d'Asti
Superiore Tre Roveri 2014 has a
concentrated nose of red berries with hints
of toast, and a balanced palate with an
attractive velvety finish that already appears
supple and ready to drink. The rest of the
range is also well made, from Barbera
d'Asti Superiore Epico 2014, which is
beautifully fresh notwithstanding the oak
notes that slightly conceal the fruit, to
Monferrato Bianco Vita 2015, a nicely
complex, varietal Sauvignon.

● Barbera d'Asti Sup. Tre Roveri '14	♀♀ 4
● Barbera d'Asti Lavignone '15	♀♀ 3
● Barbera d'Asti Sup. Epico '14	♀♀ 5
○ M.to Bianco Vita '15	♀♀ 4
● Barbera d'Asti Lavignone '14	♀♀ 3
● Barbera d'Asti Sup. Tre Roveri '13	♀♀ 4
● Barbera d'Asti Sup. Epico '12	♀ 5

★Pio Cesare

VIA CESARE BALBO, 6
12051 ALBA [CN]
TEL. +39 0173440386
www.piocesare.it

ANNUAL PRODUCTION 400,000 bottles
HECTARES UNDER VINE 70.00

This successful estate of almost 70
hectares is one of the oldest in Piedmont,
founded in the late 19th century and
headed today by Pio Boffa and Cesare
Benvenuto. Its first-class vineyards in
Bricco and Santo Stefanetto in the
Barbaresco production zone, and Ornato,
Colombaro, Gustava, Roncaglie, and Ravera
in the Barolo designation yield a wide and
eclectic range of nebbiolo reds with an
austerely modern flavour. However, it also
makes other wines from the traditional
local grape varieties of barbera, dolcetto,
grignolino, cortese, arneis, and moscato,
and a few based on chardonnay. As
expected, the top performers were the
Barolos, commencing with the entry-level
2012, which offers delicious hints of wild
strawberries, marjoram, and freshly
plucked roses, and a palate with good
power and backbone. The Ornato of the
same vintage adds a little extra depth of
flavour and tertiary complexity, earning a
well-deserved Tre Bicchieri. Both
Barbarescos are as excellent as ever.

● Barolo Ornato '12	♀♀♀ 8
● Barbaresco '12	♀♀ 8
● Barbaresco Il Bricco '12	♀♀ 8
● Barolo '12	♀♀ 8
● Barbera d'Alba Fides '14	♀♀ 5
○ Langhe Chardonnay Piodilei '14	♀♀ 6
● Langhe Rosso Il Nebbio '15	♀♀ 4
● Barolo Ornato '11	♀♀♀ 8
● Barolo Ornato '10	♀♀♀ 8
● Barolo Ornato '09	♀♀♀ 8
● Barolo Ornato '08	♀♀♀ 8
● Barolo Ornato '06	♀♀♀ 8
● Barolo Ornato '05	♀♀♀ 8

Luigi Pira

via XX Settembre, 9
12050 Serralunga d'Alba [CN]
Tel. +39 0173613106
pira.luigi@alice.it

CELLAR SALES
PRE-BOOKED VISITS
ANNUAL PRODUCTION 50,000 bottles
HECTARES UNDER VINE 12.00

The Pira family have been tending their Langhe vineyards on the Serralunga hillsides since the 1950s. The estate was founded by Luigi but only started bottling its own wines a couple of decades ago. Today Gianpaolo and Romolo are at the helm of an increasingly consistent and distinctive winery, whose style has become a little lighter over the past few years. The basic Barolo and the Margheria vineyard selection are aged for around two years in medium-sized oak barrels, while the Marenca and Vigna Rionda crus are aged in barriques and tonneaux for a year, followed by a further 12 months in 2,500-litre barrels. Technical details are increasingly insignificant in the face of the unwavering consistency of the top Barolos. The Marenca 2012 is well proportioned and ethereal, the opposite of the more rugged, introverted Margheria of the same vintage. But it was the Vignarionda that won us over with its power and complexity thanks to an alluring flavoursome backbone.

● Barolo Vignarionda '12	♥♥♥	8
● Barolo Marenca '12	♥♥	7
● Barolo del Comune di Serralunga '12	♥♥	5
● Barolo Margheria '12	♥♥	6
● Barolo Marenca '11	♥♥♥	7
● Barolo Marenca '09	♥♥♥	7
● Barolo Marenca '08	♥♥♥	7
● Barolo V. Marenca '01	♥♥♥	7
● Barolo V. Rionda '06	♥♥♥	8
● Barolo V. Rionda '04	♥♥♥	8
● Barolo V. Rionda '00	♥♥♥	8

E. Pira & Figli
Chiara Boschis

via Vittorio Veneto, 1
12060 Barolo [CN]
Tel. +39 017356247
www.pira-chiaraboschis.com

CELLAR SALES
PRE-BOOKED VISITS
ANNUAL PRODUCTION 35,000 bottles
HECTARES UNDER VINE 8.50
VITICULTURE METHOD Certified Organic

The daughter of vignerons, Chiara Boschis has always been a prominent member of the large group of Barolo producers who, commencing in the 1980s, chose the modern style to rejuvenate the great wine's image. The estate owns a few hectares planted to Barolo nebbiolo, with an excellent recently purchased vineyard in Monforte's Mosconi cru going to join the deservedly famous Cannubi and the more approachable Via Nuova. For further insight into Chiara's personality, we recommend the fine portrait penned by Mauro Fermariello in his book on Barolo. The complex Barolo Cannubi 2012, with a concentrated and ethereal nose underpinned by fresh, close-focused fruit and complex spicy hints, has a powerful, dense mouth. Close-woven tannins and alcohol ensure sweetness on a dense, powerful palate showing good acidity and a long finish. The Mosconi 2012 is complex and modern, while the plush Via Nuova of the same vintage is still slightly marked by oak.

● Barolo Cannubi '12	♥♥	8
● Barolo Mosconi '12	♥♥	8
● Barbera d'Alba Sup. '14	♥♥	4
● Barolo Via Nuova '12	♥♥	8
● Barolo '94	♥♥♥	7
● Barolo Cannubi '11	♥♥♥	8
● Barolo Cannubi '10	♥♥♥	8
● Barolo Cannubi '06	♥♥♥	8
● Barolo Cannubi '05	♥♥♥	8
● Barolo Cannubi '00	♥♥♥	8
● Barolo Cannubi '97	♥♥♥	8
● Barolo Cannubi '96	♥♥♥	8
● Barolo Ris. '90	♥♥♥	8
● Barolo Cannubi '09	♥♥	8
● Barolo Mosconi '11	♥♥	8
● Barolo Mosconi '10	♥♥	8
● Barolo Mosconi '09	♥♥	8

Marco Porello

c.so ALBA, 71
12043 CANALE [CN]
TEL. +39 0173979324
www.porellovini.it

CELLAR SALES
PRE-BOOKED VISITS
ANNUAL PRODUCTION 130,000 bottles
HECTARES UNDER VINE 15.00

During the 1930s Cesare Porello
transformed his small estate into a winery.
Today it is run by Marco, the third
generation of the family. The vineyards are
in Vezza d'Alba, on mainly sandy,
mineral-rich soils, planted to arneis,
favorita, brachetto, and nebbiolo, and
Canale, on medium-density clayey
limestone, planted to barbera, brachetto,
and nebbiolo. Roero Torretta 2013 has a
nose of dark fruit, Mediterranean
scrubland, and tobacco, with hints of
liquorice, and a firmly structured, elegant
palate with a long, supple, flavoursome
finish. The two versions of Barbera d'Alba
are very pleasant: the juicy, pulp-rich
Filatura 2014, with notes of ripe dark
berries and sweet spice, and the
fruit-forward Mommiano 2015 with
good supporting acidity. Roero Arneis
Camestrì 2015 has notes of tropical fruit
and fair depth and traction.

● Roero Torretta '13	♟♟ 3*
● Barbera d'Alba Filatura '14	♟♟ 3
● Barbera d'Alba Mommiano '15	♟♟ 2*
○ Roero Arneis Camestrì '15	♟♟ 3
○ Langhe Favorita '15	♟ 2
● Nebbiolo d'Alba '14	♟ 3
○ Roero Arneis '15	♟ 2
● Roero Torretta '06	♟♟♟ 3*
● Roero Torretta '04	♟♟♟ 3*
○ Langhe Favorita '14	♟♟ 2*
○ Roero Arneis '14	♟♟ 2*
○ Roero Arneis Camestrì '14	♟♟ 3
● Roero Torretta '11	♟♟ 3*

Guido Porro

VIA ALBA, 1
12050 SERRALUNGA D'ALBA [CN]
TEL. +39 0173613306
www.guidoporro.com

CELLAR SALES
PRE-BOOKED VISITS
ACCOMMODATION
ANNUAL PRODUCTION 35,000 bottles
HECTARES UNDER VINE 8.00

Guido Porro has had no need for fanfares
to establish his name as one of Langhe's
most respected vignerons. His attention is
concentrated exclusively on the family
estate that surrounds the cellar, on the
western slopes of Serralunga, between
Lazzairasco and Santa Caterina. Although
they are adjoining crus, they yield
profoundly different Barolos in terms of
aromatic expression and flavour: the first
very masculine and severe, the second
more lustrous and delicate. Both are
fermented in stainless steel and concrete,
before ageing in 2,500-litre Slavonian oak
barrels. We eagerly await the first Vigna
Rionda made from part of the plots that
belonged to Tommaso Canale. Barolo
Gianetto 2012 is very well made, standing
out for its classic notes of spice and roots,
and focusing more on proportions than
muscle. Lazzairasco 2012 is deeper and
more detailed, with a majestic palate
offering an array of flavours from red
berries to flowers, balsamic hints and
autumn leaves.

● Barolo V. Lazzairasco '12	♟♟♟ 5
● Barolo V. Santa Caterina '12	♟♟ 5
● Barbera d'Alba V. S. Caterina '15	♟♟ 3
● Barolo Gianetto '12	♟♟ 5
● Dolcetto d'Alba L'Pari '15	♟♟ 3
● Lange Nebbiolo Camilu '15	♟♟ 4
● Barolo V. Lazzairasco '11	♟♟♟ 5
● Barolo V. Lazzairasco '09	♟♟♟ 5
● Barolo V. Lazzairasco '07	♟♟♟ 5
● Barolo Santa Caterina '09	♟♟ 5
● Barolo V. Lazzairasco '10	♟♟ 5
● Barolo V. Lazzairasco '08	♟♟ 5
● Barolo V. Santa Caterina '10	♟♟ 5
● Barolo V. Santa Caterina '08	♟♟ 5*
● Lange Nebbiolo '09	♟♟ 3*

Post dal Vin
Terre del Barbera

FRAZ. POSSAVINA
VIA SALIE, 19
14030 ROCCHETTA TANARO [AT]
TEL. +39 0141644143
www.postdalvin.it

CELLAR SALES
PRE-BOOKED VISITS
ANNUAL PRODUCTION 80,000 bottles
HECTARES UNDER VINE 100.00

Post dal Vin–Terre del Barbera is a
cooperative winery that was founded in
1959. It now vaunts 100 members who
tend an area of 100 hectares under vine.
Almost all the vineyards are in the
municipalities of Rocchetta Tanaro,
Cortiglione, and Masio, with production
obviously focusing on Barbera, offered in
various types and versions, but also
includes several wines from other typical
Monferrato grape varieties, such as
grignolino, dolcetto, freisa, and moscato.
The various versions of Barbera d'Asti are
always reliable. Despite still showing some
oakiness, Castagnassa 2014 has good fruit
and stuffing, with notes of roots and
autumn leaves, while the pleasant
BriccoFiore 2014 is leaner, with vegetal
nuances and fresh but not aggressive
acidity. The semi-sparkling Barbera del
Monferrato La Matutona 2015 is
particularly well made and very drinkable,
with a slight earthiness on its fruity nose
and a pleasant, supple palate.

Giovanni Prandi

FRAZ. CASCINA COLOMBÈ
VIA FARINETTI, 5
12055 DIANO D'ALBA [CN]
TEL. +39 017369248
www.prandigiovanni.it

CELLAR SALES
PRE-BOOKED VISITS
ANNUAL PRODUCTION 20,000 bottles
HECTARES UNDER VINE 5.00
SUSTAINABLE WINERY

Dolcetto di Diano d'Alba is irresistibly fruity,
which makes it the ideal accompaniment to
many dishes, from pasta to white meats.
Alessandro Prandi is an excellent
interpreter of the wine, enhancing its
fruitiness by ageing exclusively in steel for
the entire range, topped by Sörì Cristina.
The estate is a small, family-run affair that
lavishes great attention on work in both the
vineyard and the cellar, making it a
veritable beacon of the production zone.
Connoisseurs of the delightful caressing
sensations of dolcetto grapes should not
miss these two 2015 selections. Both are
characterized by a nose of young red
berries and an elegant finish with hints of
bitter almonds, with the Sörì Colombè
showing slightly more plush and velvety.
The well-orchestrated Nebbiolo 2014 is
lean and delicate, while the close-focused
Barbera 2015 is fresh and easy drinking.

● Barbera d'Asti Sup. BriccoFiore '14	♙♙ 2*
● Barbera d'Asti Sup. Castagnassa '14	♙♙ 2*
● Barbera del M.to La Matutona '15	♙♙ 2*
● Barbera d'Asti Maricca '15	♙ 2
● Barbera d'Asti Castagnassa '13	♙♙ 2*
● Barbera d'Asti Maricca '14	♙♙ 2*
● Barbera d'Asti Maricca '12	♙♙ 2*
● Barbera d'Asti Sup. Bricco Fiore '13	♙♙ 2*
● Barbera d'Asti Sup. BriccoFiore '12	♙♙ 2*
● Barbera d'Asti Sup. Castagnassa '12	♙♙ 2*
● Barbera d'Asti Sup. Castagnassa '11	♙♙ 2*
● Grignolino d'Asti '13	♙♙ 1*
● Grignolino d'Asti '12	♙♙ 1*

● Dolcetto di Diano d'Alba Sörì Colombè '15	♙♙ 2*
● Dolcetto di Diano d'Alba Sörì Cristina '15	♙♙ 2*
● Barbera d'Alba '15	♙♙ 2*
● Nebbiolo d'Alba '14	♙♙ 3
○ Langhe Arneis '15	♙ 2
● Barbera d'Alba '14	♙♙ 2*
● Barbera d'Alba Santa Eurosia '12	♙♙ 2*
● Dolcetto di Diano d'Alba Sörì Colombè '14	♙♙ 2*
● Dolcetto di Diano d'Alba Sörì Cristina '14	♙♙ 2*
● Dolcetto di Diano d'Alba Sörì Cristina '13	♙♙ 2*
● Dolcetto di Diano d'Alba Sörì Cristina '12	♙♙ 2*
● Dolcetto di Diano Sörì Colombè '13	♙♙ 2*
● Dolcetto di Diano Sörì Colombè '12	♙♙ 2*
● Dolcetto di Diano Sörì Colombè '11	♙♙ 2*
● Nebbiolo d'Alba Colombè '12	♙♙ 3*
● Nebbiolo d'Alba Colombè '10	♙♙ 3

La Prevostura

Cascina Prevostura, 1
13853 Lessona [BI]
Tel. +39 0158853188
www.laprevostura.it

CELLAR SALES
PRE-BOOKED VISITS
RESTAURANT SERVICE
ANNUAL PRODUCTION 15,000 bottles
HECTARES UNDER VINE 4.00

The Bellini brothers' sandy vineyards are planted to red grape varieties alone, chiefly nebbiolo flanked by vespolina and croatina. Their flagship is the Lessona, from a vineyard 400 metres above sea level, which is aged in different-sized French oak barrels for two years. We also liked the more delicate Bramaterra, thanks to the fresh, spicy notes derived from grape varieties that complement the nebbiolo. The fragrant Coste della Sesia Rosato Corinna, also from nebbiolo with a lively swathe of acidity, also performed very well. The sophisticated, well-typed Bramaterra 2012 already shows great personality on the nose, an extraordinarily elegant tannic weave, and overall harmony on the palate. The Lessona 2012 is slightly more closed and youthful, earning a Tre Bicchieri for its lovely nose of dried herbs and liquorice and its firm, powerful palate, which make it a Nebbiolo with excellent ageing prospects. Rosso Muntacc 2012 is less fresh and fruity but won us over with its exceptionally pleasant, firm, enfolding palate. A memorable performance.

● Lessona '12	???	5
● Bramaterra '12	??	5
● Coste della Sesia Rosso Muntacc '12	??	3*
● Coste della Sesia Rosso Garsun '14	?	3
● Bramaterra '11	??	5
● Coste della Sesia Rosso Muntacc '11	??	3
● Coste della Sesia Rosso Muntacc '10	??	3
● Lessona '11	??	5
● Lessona '10	??	5
● Lessona '09	??	5

Prinsi

via Gaia, 5
12052 Neive [CN]
Tel. +39 017367192
www.prinsi.it

CELLAR SALES
PRE-BOOKED VISITS
ANNUAL PRODUCTION 60,000 bottles
HECTARES UNDER VINE 14.50

Daniele Lequio has gradually honed his winemaking skills and now competently runs a winery with 13 hectares of vineyards. They include some excellent crus planted to nebbiolo for Barbaresco: Gallina, Fausoni, and Gaia Principe. The charming cellar is well worth a visit and is home to different-sized French and Slavonian oak barrels. The vineyards are planted with the classic grape varieties of the area, with a few concessions to international white cultivars. The new Barbaresco selections performed splendidly. The Riserva Fausoni 2011 is complex , with a harmonious, layered nose of spicy fruit, and a beautifully firm, juicy palate without any oaky sweetness. Gaia Principe 2013 is only slightly less dense and firm, vaunting a close-woven, enfolding palate and no rough edges.

● Barbaresco Fausoni Ris. '11	??	5
● Barbaresco Gaia Principe '13	??	5
● Barbaresco Gallina '13	??	5
● Dolcetto d'Alba V. Basarin '15	?	3
○ Langhe Arneis li Nespolo '15	?	3
○ Langhe Chardonnay Tre Fichi '15	?	3
● Barbaresco Fausone Ris. '08	??	5
● Barbaresco Fausoni Ris. '10	??	5
● Barbaresco Gaia Principe '05	??	5
● Barbaresco Gallina '12	??	5
● Barbaresco Gallina '11	??	5
● Barbaresco Gallina '05	??	5
● Barbera d'Alba Sup. Il Bosco '11	??	3
● Barbera d'Alba Sup. Vign. Much '07	??	3

★Produttori del Barbaresco

VIA TORINO, 54
12050 BARBARESCO [CN]
TEL. +39 0173635139
www.produttoridelbarbaresco.com

CELLAR SALES
PRE-BOOKED VISITS
ACCOMMODATION
ANNUAL PRODUCTION 500,000 bottles
HECTARES UNDER VINE 105.00

Superfluous rhetoric aside, we cannot fail to stress once again the extraordinary progress made in less than 60 years by Cantina Produttori del Barbaresco. It represents a veritable pole of excellence in the world of cooperative wineries, not just in Piedmont and Italy, and is also one of the safest bets for connoisseurs seeking value for money. Its proudly traditional range focuses exclusively on the Nebbiolos from the grapes of 50 or so grower-members who cover a total area of around 100 hectares, with nine of the finest crus in Barbaresco offered in Riserva versions in the best vintages. The 2013 vintage of the entry-level Barbaresco once again exemplifies the winery's philosophy, appearing lean and enjoyable, without any unnecessary frills. This year the ever reliable range of Riservas was topped by the Rabajà, with a sophisticated classic nose and a powerful, fruity palate, together with the Muncagota and the Montefico.

● Barbaresco Montefico Rls. '11	♟♟	6
● Barbaresco Muncagota Ris. '11	♟♟	6
● Barbaresco Rabaja' Ris. '11	♟♟	6
● Barbaresco '13	♟♟	5
● Barbaresco Montestefano Ris. '11	♟♟	6
● Barbaresco Ovello Ris. '11	♟♟	6
● Barbaresco Paje' Ris. '11	♟♟	6
● Barbaresco Pora Ris. '11	♟♟	6
● Langhe Nebbiolo '14	♟	3
● Barbaresco Ovello Ris. '09	♟♟♟	6
● Barbaresco Vign. in Montestefano Ris. '05	♟♟♟	6
● Barbaresco Vign. in Ovello Ris. '08	♟♟♟	6
● Barbaresco Vign. in Pora Ris. '07	♟♟♟	6

Cantina Produttori del Gavi

VIA CAVALIERI DI VITTORIO VENETO, 45
15066 GAVI [AL]
TEL. +39 0143642786
www.cantinaproduttoridelgavi.it

CELLAR SALES
PRE-BOOKED VISITS
ANNUAL PRODUCTION 300,000 bottles
HECTARES UNDER VINE 220.00

One of Piedmont's leading cooperative wineries, Cantina Produttori del Gavi offers an impressive eight cortese wines in its consistently reliable range. Founded in the post-war period and renovated in the 1970s, when it acquired its current name, today it counts around 100 grower-members with over 200 hectares of vineyards, which allows it to achieve high production figures with a distinctive style. Apart from the Aureliana selection, all the whites are vinified and aged in steel without malolactic fermentation. The top wines regularly include Gavi di Gavi Etichetta Nera, G, and GG. The lavish 2015 vintage has partly disrupted this hierarchy, bringing Gavi di Gavi La Maddalena to the fore, with its Mediterranean sensations and alluring palate offering clear salty undertones. Gavi Primi Grappoli has even more classic hints of thyme, bracken, cedarwood, and flint.

○ Gavi del Comune di Gavi La Maddalena '15	♟♟	3*
○ Gavi Primi Grappoli '15	♟♟	2*
○ Gavi del Comune di Gavi Et. Nera '15	♟♟	2*
○ Gavi Il Forte '15	♟♟	2*
○ Gavi del Comune di Gavi Et. Nera '14	♟♟	2*
○ Gavi del Comune di Gavi Et. Nera '13	♟♟	2*
○ Gavi del Comune di Gavi Et. Nera '12	♟♟	2*
○ Gavi del Comune di Gavi GG '13	♟♟	3*
○ Gavi G '14	♟♟	3*
○ Gavi G '13	♟♟	2*
○ Gavi G '12	♟♟	3
○ Gavi GG '14	♟♟	3
○ Gavi Il Forte '14	♟♟	2*
○ Gavi La Maddalena '13	♟♟	2*
○ Gavi Primi Grappoli '14	♟♟	2*
○ Gavi Primi Grappoli '12	♟♟	2*

★Prunotto

c.so Barolo, 14
12051 Alba [CN]
Tel. +39 0173280017
www.prunotto.it

CELLAR SALES
PRE-BOOKED VISITS
ANNUAL PRODUCTION 850,000 bottles
HECTARES UNDER VINE 55.00

The Antinori family commenced their adventure in the world of Piedmont wine in the late 1980s, when they took over Prunotto from brothers Beppe and Tino Colla and Carlo Filiberti, who in turn had purchased the winery, previously used by the "Ai Vini delle Langhe" cooperative, from its founder Alfredo. This glorious history provided the launch pad for a solid, modern project, which has gradually been extended with vineyards in Bussia, Bric Turot, and Costamiole, and the renovation of the cellar, where the old 10,000-litre barrels have been replaced by barriques and medium-sized oak. The restyling of the Nebbiolos is well illustrated by Barbaresco Bric Turot 2012, with a diaphanous hue, a balsamic, vegetal nose, and a tight, edgy palate. Bussia Vigna Colonnello Riserva 2010 is a vigorous, traditional-style Barolo with hints of truffles and a caressing palate.

La Raia

s.da Monterotondo, 79
15067 Novi Ligure [AL]
Tel. +39 0143743685
www.la-raia.it

CELLAR SALES
PRE-BOOKED VISITS
ACCOMMODATION
ANNUAL PRODUCTION 150,000 bottles
HECTARES UNDER VINE 42.00
VITICULTURE METHOD Certified Biodynamic
SUSTAINABLE WINERY

Owned by the Tenimenti Rossi Cairo group, La Raia is a Demeter-certified biodynamic estate. It boasts an area of over 180 hectares of vineyards, arable crops, pasture, and woodland on the hillsides between Novi Ligure and Monterotondo. Oenologist Piero Ballario oversees the production of the five wines: three Gavis and two Barberas. We particularly liked the Gavi, whose quality is steadily rising and which is unusually ageworthy for a wine generally considered ready-drinking. This year's interesting list underscores the quality of the wines. Vigna della Madonnina offers a nose of damsons, with undertones of flowers and minerals, echoed on the long, fresh, full-flavoured palate. The basic Gavi is fantastic, its fruity nose showing hints of medicinal herbs and spices that mingle on the complex, velvety palate with a zesty finish. And the Pisé 2014 is equally good, with a fragrant nose of almonds and melted butter, and a full, potent palate.

● Barbaresco '13	♟♟ 5
● Barbaresco Bric Turot '12	♟♟ 6
● Barbera d'Alba Pian Romualdo '13	♟♟ 4
● Barolo Bussia V. Colonnello Ris. '10	♟♟ 8
● Nebbiolo d'Alba Occhetti '13	♟♟ 4
● Barbera d'Alba '15	♟ 3
● Barbera d'Asti Fiulòt '15	♟ 2
● Barolo '12	♟ 6
● M.to Bricco Colma '12	♟ 5
○ Moscato d'Asti '15	♟ 2
○ Roero Arneis '15	♟ 3
● Barbera d'Asti Costamiòle '99	♟♟♟ 4*
● Barolo Bussia '01	♟♟♟ 8
● Barolo Bussia '99	♟♟♟ 8
● Barolo Bussia '98	♟♟♟ 8
● Barolo Bussia '96	♟♟♟ 8

○ Gavi '15	♟♟ 3*
○ Gavi Pisé '14	♟♟ 4
○ Gavi V. della Madonnina Ris. '14	♟♟ 3*
● Piemonte Barbera Largé '11	♟ 5
○ Gavi '13	♟♟ 3
○ Gavi Pisé '12	♟♟ 4
○ Gavi Pisé '11	♟♟ 3*
○ Gavi Ris. '12	♟♟ 3*
○ Gavi V. della Madonnina Ris. '13	♟♟ 3*
● Piemonte Barbera '13	♟♟ 3
● Piemonte Barbera Largé '10	♟♟ 5

Renato Ratti

FRAZ. ANNUNZIATA, 7
12064 LA MORRA [CN]
TEL. +39 017350185
www.renatoratti.com

CELLAR SALES
PRE-BOOKED VISITS
ACCOMMODATION
ANNUAL PRODUCTION 300,000 bottles
HECTARES UNDER VINE 40.00

The fact that Barolo is one of the most
prestigious Italian designations today is
partly due to Renato Ratti. Between the
mid-1960s and late 1980s his untiring
research and exhaustive knowledge
underpinned his campaign for its
reclassification on the basis of two
fundamental points that seem obvious now,
but were not at the time: subzone and
vintage. His son Pietro has been confidently
following in his father's footsteps since
1988, making wines that appeal to the
tastes of Italian and international
consumers alike. Barolo Conca 2012 made
it into our finals with a very traditional,
complex, vibrant nose of ripe, fleshy fruit
with undertones of tar. The palate is still a
little stiff and held back by oak, but we're
sure it's just a youthful flaw. Rocche
dell'Annunziata 2012 is similar in style but
slightly more evolved.

● Barolo Conca '12	♟♟ 8
● Barbera d'Alba Battaglione '15	♟♟ 3
● Barolo Rocche dell'Annunziata '12	♟♟ 8
● Nebbiolo d'Alba Ochetti '14	♟♟ 4
● Dolcetto d'Alba Colombè '15	♟ 3
● Barolo Rocche '06	♟♟♟ 8
● Barolo Rocche Marcenasco '84	♟♟♟ 6
● Barolo Rocche Marcenasco '83	♟♟♟ 6
● Barolo Conca '11	♟♟ 8
● Barolo Marcenasco '11	♟♟ 6
● Barolo Rocche dell'Annunziata '11	♟♟ 8
● Dolcetto d'Alba Colombè '14	♟♟ 3
● Nebbiolo d'Alba Ochetti '13	♟♟ 4

Ressia

VIA CANOVA, 28
12052 NEIVE [CN]
TEL. +39 0173677305
www.ressia.com

CELLAR SALES
PRE-BOOKED VISITS
ANNUAL PRODUCTION 25,000 bottles
HECTARES UNDER VINE 5.50

The Ressia family have been making wine
for almost a century, but the turning point
in this long tradition came in 1997, when
Fabrizio commenced a veritable revolution.
Over the following couple of decades the
estate's Barbarescos joined the ranks of
the finest of the production zone, but it has
never neglected the other grape varieties
and the other zones in which its vineyards
lie. However, the heart of production
remains the carefully tended vineyard in the
Canova cru, which is south facing and fairly
high up, yielding grapes that produce
terroir-true wines with a strong personality.
They are exemplified by Barbaresco
Canova, whose concentrated swathe of
fruit perfectly balances its spicy nose, while
the initially full, powerful palate with
close-woven tannins becomes leaner on
the long, lively finish. Langhe Favorita
Miranda 2015 is extremely interesting,
showing complex, sumptuous, and full
flavoured, and the rest of the list is sound.

● Barbaresco Canova '13	♟♟ 5
○ Langhe Favorita La Miranda '15	♟♟ 2*
● Langhe Nebbiolo '13	♟ 3
● Barbaresco Canova '06	♟♟♟ 5*
● Barbaresco Canova '12	♟♟ 5
● Barbaresco Canova '11	♟♟ 5
● Barbaresco Canova '09	♟♟ 5
● Barbaresco Canova Ris. Oro '10	♟♟ 6
● Barbaresco Canova Ris. Oro '09	♟♟ 6
● Barbera d'Alba Sup. '12	♟♟ 5
○ Evien '13	♟♟ 2*
○ Evien	♟♟ 2*
● Langhe Nebbiolo Gepù '11	♟♟ 3

F.lli Revello

FRAZ. ANNUNZIATA, 103
12064 LA MORRA [CN]
TEL. +39 017350276
www.revellofratelli.it

CELLAR SALES
PRE-BOOKED VISITS
ACCOMMODATION
ANNUAL PRODUCTION 45,000 bottles
HECTARES UNDER VINE 8.00
SUSTAINABLE WINERY

After working together for over 20 years, brothers Carlo and Lorenzo Revello, along with their respective families, decided to part ways, with Lorenzo running the Fratelli Revello winery since late 2015 and Carlo striking out alone. The house style can be defined as modern, in the sense that roto-macerator tanks and small oak casks are used, but all the Barolos are exceptionally elegant and drinkable. We highly recommend a visit and a tasting in the splendid panoramic room next to the family's little guest farm. Barolo Gattera 2012 has a nose of sweet spice with delicate oaky undertones and a delicious palate despite still prominent tannins. The innovative Barolo Rocche dell'Annunziata 2012 has a full fruity nose and needs more time in bottle to reach its best, while sophisticated, elegant oak still dominates the palate of the Conca 2012, and the Giachini 2012 is a fine blend of modern and traditional.

● Barolo Gattera '12	♟♟ 6
● Barolo Rocche dell'Annunziata '12	♟♟ 8
● Barolo Conca '12	♟♟ 7
● Barolo Giachini '12	♟♟ 7
● Langhe Nebbiolo '14	♟♟ 3
● Barbera d'Alba Ciabot du Re '05	♟♟♟ 5
● Barbera d'Alba Ciabot du Re '00	♟♟♟ 5
● Barolo Rocche dell'Annunziata '01	♟♟♟ 8
● Barolo Rocche dell'Annunziata '00	♟♟♟ 8
● Barolo V. Conca '99	♟♟♟ 7
● Barolo '11	♟♟ 5
● Barolo Conca '11	♟♟ 7
● Barolo Gattera '11	♟♟ 6
● Barolo Giachini '11	♟♟ 7
● Barolo Rocche dell'Annunziata '11	♟♟ 8

Michele Reverdito

FRAZ. RIVALTA
B.TA GARASSINI, 74B
12064 LA MORRA [CN]
TEL. +39 017350336
www.reverdito.it

CELLAR SALES
PRE-BOOKED VISITS
ANNUAL PRODUCTION 70,000 bottles
HECTARES UNDER VINE 16.00

Silvano and Maria Reverdito made the decision to grow only native grape varieties, and their children Michele and Sabina are confidently following in their footsteps. The range focuses on Barolo but also features the excellent white Langhe Nascetta, and the pleasantly aromatic red Verduno Pelaverga. The nebbiolo vineyards include fine crus in La Morra, Serralunga, and Monforte, which yield the Riserva 10 Anni in the finest vintages. Ageing takes place in different-sized oak casks and barrels. Barolo Bricco Cogni 2012 has an elegant, harmonious nose with wonderful notes of tobacco and liquorice on a solid base of fruity pulp, and a very well-constructed palate with close-woven tannins and an impressive finish. Barolo Badarina 2012 is more austere and surefooted, with alluring notes of tobacco heralding fine development, while Barolo Riva Rocco 2012 has a moderately intense nose without much fruit, and a soft but well-orchestrated palate.

● Barolo Badarina '12	♟♟ 6
● Barolo Bricco Cogni '12	♟♟ 6
● Barolo Ascheri '12	♟♟ 5
● Barolo Riva Rocca '12	♟♟ 5
● Verduno Pelaverga '15	♟ 3
● Barolo Bricco Cogni '04	♟♟♟ 6
● Barolo 10 Anni Ris. '05	♟♟ 8
● Barolo Ascheri '11	♟♟ 5
● Barolo Badarina '11	♟♟ 5
● Barolo Badarina '10	♟♟ 5
● Barolo Bricco Cogni Ris. '09	♟♟ 6
● Barolo Castagni '10	♟♟ 5
● Barolo Riva Rocca '11	♟♟ 5
● Barolo Riva Rocca '10	♟♟ 5
● Langhe Nascetta '14	♟♟ 2*

Giuseppe Rinaldi

VIA MONFORTE, 5
12060 BAROLO [CN]
TEL. +39 017356156
carlotta.rinaldi@me.com

CELLAR SALES
PRE-BOOKED VISITS
ANNUAL PRODUCTION 35,000 bottles
HECTARES UNDER VINE 6.50

Beppe "Citrico" Rinaldi's marvellously anarchical Nebbiolos say more about this incredible man than a thousand words. He has definitively ascended the highest pinnacle of the international wine world, as testified by the mad rush for his bottles that ensues at the release of each new vintage. It is no coincidence that this consecration has coincided with the full-time commitment of his daughters Marta and Carlotta to the winery. The new energy and enthusiasm is clearly perceptible in the two new-look old Barolos, which have changed their names to Brunate and Tre Tine since the 2010 vintage, but not their combination of crus or minimal cellar techniques. Fans of Rinaldi's style will love the 2012 Barolos. The Tre Tine has a nose of dried flowers and bottled fruit, followed by a juicy palate with austere structure, while the Brunate has an even moodier nose and racier progressive tannins.

Francesco Rinaldi & Figli

VIA CROSIA, 30
12060 BAROLO [CN]
TEL. +39 0173440484
www.rinaldifrancesco.it

CELLAR SALES
PRE-BOOKED VISITS
ACCOMMODATION
ANNUAL PRODUCTION 70,000 bottles
HECTARES UNDER VINE 11.00

Paola and Piera Rinaldi head an estate over a century old, with huge vineyards and an extremely classic, terroir-true style. Their Barolo cellar is fabulously located in the Cannubi vineyard, affording stunning views of another of the estate's plots in the centre of the Brunate cru. After years of waiting, the long-standing Langhe winery with the familiar old-fashioned-style label has finally earned our full profile. Barolo Brunate 2012 has alluring classic notes of dried roses on the nose, enlivened by undertones of autumn leaves, and a firm, lively palate with nice proportions and a very pleasant finish. The flagship Barolo Cannubi 2012 vaunts an even fresher nose, offering layered notes of tobacco and liquorice and sound, young fruit, and a palate displaying the perfect harmony for which the cru is world famous.

● Barolo Brunate '12	♚♚7
● Barolo Tre Tine '12	♚♚7
● Barolo Brunate '11	♚♚♚7
● Barolo Brunate-Le Coste '07	♚♚♚7
● Barolo Brunate-Le Coste '06	♚♚♚7
● Barolo Brunate-Le Coste '01	♚♚♚6
● Barolo Brunate-Le Coste '00	♚♚♚6
● Barolo Cannubi S. Lorenzo-Ravera '04	♚♚♚6
● Barolo Brunate '10	♚♚7
● Barolo Brunate-Le Coste '09	♚♚7
● Barolo Cannubi S. Lorenzo-Ravera '09	♚♚7
● Barolo Tre Tine '11	♚♚7
● Barolo Tre Tine '10	♚♚7
● Langhe Nebbiolo '13	♚♚4

● Barolo Brunate '12	♚♚7
● Barolo Cannubi '12	♚♚7
● Barbaresco '13	♚♚5
● Dolcetto d'Alba Roussot '15	♚♚2*
● Barbera d'Alba '14	♚3
● Barbera d'Alba '13	♚♚3
● Barolo '10	♚♚6
● Barolo Brunate '11	♚♚6
● Barolo Brunate '10	♚♚7
● Barolo Cannubi '11	♚♚7
● Barolo Cannubi '10	♚♚7
● Barolo Cannubi '08	♚♚6
● Barolo Le Brunate '08	♚♚6

Massimo Rivetti

VIA RIVETTI, 22
12052 NEIVE [CN]
TEL. +39 017367505
www.rivettimassimo.it

CELLAR SALES
PRE-BOOKED VISITS
ANNUAL PRODUCTION 70,000 bottles
HECTARES UNDER VINE 25.00

This Neive winery has a strong masculine style honed by Massimo and his three young sons, all enthusiastically committed to their work. It attained organic certification this year, and makes its own compost using earthworms. The rest is ensured by excellent terroirs, such as the famous Serraboella cru, and delicate, attentive work in the cellar to ensure that the fruit is not overwhelmed by oak. The estate's wines can be tasted at the family's recently opened Porta San Rocco wine bar in Neive Alta, one of the most beautiful villages in Italy. Delays in bottling have led the Rivetti family to present just a few wines this year, and both the Barbaresco and Barbera Serraboella were missing. Despite the absence of the flagships, Barbaresco Froi and the 2013 Barbaresco both put up a spectacular performance. Characterized by bold fruit and a perfect palate, the former has few rivals.

● Barbaresco Froi '13	▼▼ 5
● Barbaresco '13	▼▼ 5
● Langhe Garasin '13	▼▼ 3
● Barbaresco Froi '12	♀♀ 5
● Barbaresco Froi '11	♀♀ 5
● Barbaresco Froi Ris. '09	♀♀ 6
● Barbaresco Serraboella '12	♀♀ 5
● Barbera d'Alba Sup. V. Serraboella '12	♀♀ 4
● Barbera d'Alba V. Serraboella '10	♀♀ 4

Rizzi

VIA RIZZI, 15
12050 TREISO [CN]
TEL. +39 0173638161
www.cantinarizzi.it

CELLAR SALES
PRE-BOOKED VISITS
ACCOMMODATION
ANNUAL PRODUCTION 70,000 bottles
HECTARES UNDER VINE 38.00
SUSTAINABLE WINERY

The reputation that the Dellapiana family have consolidated over the past decade in particular once again shows the power of word of mouth and the grapevine among the most attentive and curious wine lovers. However, it is not built on thin air, for the winery has more than 50 vintages under its belt and around 30 hectares of vineyards on the finest slopes around Treiso, commencing with the cru after which it is named. The heart of the very accessibly priced range is constituted by reds from dolcetto, barbera, and, of course, nebbiolo. The Rizzi, Pajorè, Nervo, and Boito Riserva Barbarescos are aged in medium to large Slavonian oak barrels. This time we tasted two very different vintages, excellently interpreted by the estate's crus. The classic 2013 is faithfully reflected in the delicate, racy, full-flavoured Pajorè, with notes of herbs and wild berries, while the warm, sunny 2011 gives the Boito Riserva fruity ripeness and glycerine-rich weight. The 2013 Barbera is complex and lively.

● Barbaresco Boito Ris. '11	▼▼ 7
● Barbaresco Pajorè '13	▼▼ 6
● Barbaresco Nervo '13	▼▼ 5
● Barbaresco Rizzi '13	▼▼ 5
● Barbera d'Alba '13	▼▼ 3
● Langhe Nebbiolo '14	▼▼ 3
● Barbaresco Boito Ris. '10	♀♀♀ 6
● Barbaresco Boito Ris. '09	♀♀ 6
● Barbaresco Nervo '11	♀♀ 5
● Barbaresco Nervo Fondetta '10	♀♀ 5
● Barbaresco Pajorè '11	♀♀ 6
● Barbaresco Pajorè '10	♀♀ 6
● Barbaresco Rizzi '12	♀♀ 5
● Barbaresco Rizzi '11	♀♀ 5
● Barbaresco Rizzi '10	♀♀ 5

Roagna

LOC. PAJÉ
S.DA PAGLIERI, 7
12050 BARBARESCO [CN]
TEL. +39 0173635109
www.roagna.com

CELLAR SALES
PRE-BOOKED VISITS
ANNUAL PRODUCTION 50,000 bottles
HECTARES UNDER VINE 15.00

Its fabulous vineyards meant it was only a matter of time before the Roagnas returned to the dizziest heights of the Langhe wine world. The distinctive characteristics of crus like Pajé, Montefico and Asili in Barbaresco; Pira in Castiglione Falletto; and Vigna Rionda in Serralunga, are respected by work in the vineyard aimed at maintaining the natural balance and soil vitality and minimal intervention in the cellar: spontaneous fermentation, long maceration, and patient ageing in large barrels. The magnificent 2011 vintage has made the estate's Barbarescos more spectacular than ever. The Pajé won a Tre Bicchieri for its wonderfully elegant, complex nose and delicately fresh, silky, harmonious palate. Montefico Vecchie Viti has stunningly powerful structure on the palate, with a delicate balsamic finish, and the innately elegant Crichët Pajé 2007 is incredibly fresh and youthful. The alluring Barolo 2011 Vecchie Viti is also remarkable, with notes of roses and raspberries.

● Barbaresco Pajé '11	♥♥♥ 8
● Barbaresco Crichët Pajé '07	♥♥ 8
● Barbaresco Montefico V. V. '11	♥♥ 8
● Barbaresco Pajè V. V. '11	♥♥ 8
● Barolo Pira V. V. '11	♥♥ 8
● Barbaresco Asili V. V. '11	♥♥ 8
● Barolo Pira '11	♥♥ 8
● Barbaresco Asili V. V. '07	♥♥♥ 8
● Barbaresco Crichët Pajé '06	♥♥♥ 8
● Barbaresco Crichët Pajé '05	♥♥♥ 8
● Barbaresco Crichët Pajé '04	♥♥♥ 8

★Albino Rocca

S.DA RONCHI, 18
12050 BARBARESCO [CN]
TEL. +39 0173635145
www.albinorocca.com

CELLAR SALES
PRE-BOOKED VISITS
ANNUAL PRODUCTION 100,000 bottles
HECTARES UNDER VINE 18.00
SUSTAINABLE WINERY

The concept of wine absorbing the character of its producers has become a cliché. However, each time we taste the Rocca family's wines we can't help thinking of the smiling charm that pervades their handsome Barbaresco cellar. First with the founder Albino and his son Angelo, and today in the faces of sisters Paola, Monica, and Daniela, who represent the fourth generation at work there, aided by Carlo Castellengo. The estate covers an area of around 20 hectares, planted to dolcetto, barbera, cabernet franc, cortese, chardonnay, and moscato, although the range is always topped by the reds from nebbiolo grown in the Montersino, Ovello, and Ronchi crus. The legend continues with yet another spectacular array of Barbarescos. The Ovello Vigna Loreto 2013 has a sweet nose of spice and Mediterranean scrubland, echoed on the supple palate, while the Angelo 2013 is more austere and restless, but classier and more ageworthy, thanks to its potent, full-flavoured palate and fine backbone. Cortese La Rocca is always one of Piedmont's finest whites.

● Barbaresco Angelo '13	♥♥♥ 5
● Barbaresco Ovello V. Loreto '13	♥♥ 6
● Barbaresco Ronchi Ris. '11	♥♥ 6
○ Piemonte Cortese La Rocca '15	♥♥ 4
● Barbaresco Montersino '13	♥♥ 6
● Barbaresco Ronchi '13	♥♥ 6
● Barbera d'Alba '15	♥♥ 2*
● Barbera d'Alba Gepin '14	♥♥ 5
● Dolcetto d'Alba '15	♥♥ 2*
● Nebbiolo d'Alba '14	♥♥ 3
● Barbaresco Ovello V. Loreto '11	♥♥♥ 6
● Barbaresco Ovello V. Loreto '09	♥♥♥ 6
● Barbaresco Ovello V. Loreto '07	♥♥♥ 6
● Barbaresco Ronchi '10	♥♥♥ 6
● Barbaresco Vign. Brich Ronchi Ris. '06	♥♥♥ 8
● Barbaresco Vign. Brich Ronchi Ris. '04	♥♥♥ 8

★Bruno Rocca

S.DA RABAJÀ, 60
12050 BARBARESCO [CN]
TEL. +39 0173635112
www.brunorocca.it

CELLAR SALES
PRE-BOOKED VISITS
ANNUAL PRODUCTION 70,000 bottles
HECTARES UNDER VINE 15.00

Truth, we know, is the daughter of time, and Bruno Rocca continues to harvest the fruits of his tireless work on the Rabajà estate, together with his children Francesco and Luisa. His Barbarescos are modern, at least according to the old dichotomy, and among the soundest and most reliable in terms of development. It is thus worth the patient wait to capture the nuances of the prestigious crus surrounding the winery or the Currà vineyard in Neive. Then there are the plots in Treiso and the Viglio Serra estate, from which the Barbera d'Asti hails, and where dolcetto, cabernet, and chardonnay are also grown. The result is a flawless range. Barbaresco Rabajà perfectly interprets the magnificent cru, with a nose of quinine, raspberries and spice, and a marvellous palate vaunting superbly balanced tannins and alcohol. The ready-drinking Coparossa 2013 is only slightly less firm, with a nose of sweet tobacco and aniseed.

● Barbaresco Rabajà '12	🍷🍷🍷 8
● Barbaresco Coparossa '13	🍷🍷 8
● Barbaresco '13	🍷🍷 6
● Barbera d'Alba '14	🍷🍷 5
● Barbera d'Asti '14	🍷🍷 4
● Dolcetto d'Alba Trifolè '15	🍷🍷 3
○ Langhe Chardonnay Cadet '14	🍷🍷 4
● Barbaresco Coparossa '04	🍸🍸🍸 8
● Barbaresco Maria Adelaide '07	🍸🍸🍸 8
● Barbaresco Maria Adelaide '04	🍸🍸🍸 8
● Barbaresco Maria Adelaide '01	🍸🍸🍸 8
● Barbaresco Rabajà '11	🍸🍸🍸 8
● Barbaresco Rabajà '10	🍸🍸🍸 8
● Barbaresco Rabajà '09	🍸🍸🍸 8
● Barbaresco Rabajà '01	🍸🍸🍸 8
● Barbaresco Rabajà '00	🍸🍸🍸 8

Rocche Costamagna

VIA VITTORIO EMANUELE, 8
12064 LA MORRA [CN]
TEL. +39 0173509225
www.rocchecostamagna.it

CELLAR SALES
PRE-BOOKED VISITS
ACCOMMODATION
ANNUAL PRODUCTION 95,000 bottles
HECTARES UNDER VINE 14.00

Rocca Costamagna was founded in 1841, making it one of Langhe's oldest wineries. Over the past few decades it has received a facelift, due to the work carried out by Claudia Ferraresi and her son Alessandro Lucarelli, who have built a new cellar in the Annunziata hamlet, complete with a shop and a guest farm. The wines have benefited too, with an increasingly precise identity and classic style. Barolo Bricco Francesco Riserva 2010 has a very traditional nose of fruit with hints of liquorice and violets, and a full-bodied palate vaunting caressing, glossy tannins, while Barolo Rocche dell'Annunziata 2012 is slightly marked by balsamic notes of oak. The 2012 Barolo has a pleasant, delicate nose of leather and orange peel, and a beautifully fresh palate with good tannins. The Barbera Rocche delle Rocche 2013 offers elegant fruit.

● Barbera d'Alba Sup. Rocche delle Rocche '13	🍷🍷 4
● Barolo Rocche dell'Annunziata Bricco Francesco Ris. '10	🍷🍷 6
● Barolo '12	🍷🍷 5
● Barolo Rocche dell'Annunziata '12	🍷🍷 6
○ Langhe Arneis '15	🍷 2
● Langhe Nebbiolo Roccardo '14	🍷 3
● Barolo Rocche dell'Annunziata '04	🍸🍸🍸 5
● Barbera d'Alba Sup. Rocche delle Rocche '11	🍸🍸 4
● Barolo Rocche dell'Annunziata '11	🍸🍸 6
● Barolo Rocche dell'Annunziata '10	🍸🍸 5
● Barolo Rocche dell'Annunziata '09	🍸🍸 5
● Barolo Rocche dell'Annunziata '07	🍸🍸 5
● Barolo Rocche dell'Annunziata Bricco Francesco Ris. '07	🍸🍸 6

★Rocche dei Manzoni

LOC. MANZONI SOPRANI, 3
12065 MONFORTE D'ALBA [CN]
TEL. +39 017378421
www.rocchedeimanzoni.it

CELLAR SALES
PRE-BOOKED VISITS
ANNUAL PRODUCTION 250,000 bottles
HECTARES UNDER VINE 40.00

Architecturally speaking, this winery is one of the most diverse and commanding, yet also bizarre and intriguing, in Langhe, as you can see from its website. Here, around 40 years ago, the talented and farsighted Valentino Migliorini commenced the ongoing task of creating a veritable Langhe chateau, now enthusiastically run by his son Rodolfo. The range is composed of innovative modern interpretations of the Langhe classics, first and foremost Barolo, along with two sound Metodo Classicos that continue the old Piedmontese tradition of sparkling wine production. Although we usually taste a series of the estate's Barolo crus, this year we had to content ourselves with just two. The Perno Vigna Cappella di Santo Stefano is in a class of its own, with a nose still slightly dominated by oaky notes, followed by a palate boasting extraordinary full body, pulp, and length, which will have no trouble balancing the oak. Of the other wines, we liked the buttery Angelica and the alluring Riserva Elena.

● Barolo Perno	
V. Cappella di S. Stefano '12	♟♟ 8
● Barolo '12	♟♟ 8
○ Langhe Chardonnay L'Angelica '13	♟♟ 8
● Langhe Rosso Bricco Manzoni '11	♟♟ 8
⊙ Valentino Brut Zero Rosé '11	♟♟ 8
○ Valentino Brut M. Cl. Riserva Elena '11	♟♟ 7
● Barbera d'Alba La Cresta '12	♟ 6
● Langhe Nebbiolo '14	♟ 6
● Barolo V. Cappella di S. Stefano '01	♟♟♟ 8
● Barolo V. d'la Roul '07	♟♟♟ 8
● Barolo Big 'd Big '10	♟♟ 8
● Barolo La Villa	
V. Madonna Assunta Ris. 10 anni '04	♟♟ 8
● Barolo Perno	
V. Cappella di S. Stefano '11	♟♟ 8
○ Valentino Brut M. Cl. Riserva Elena '10	♟♟ 5

Il Rocchin

LOC. VALLEMME, 39
15066 GAVI [AL]
TEL. +39 0143642228
www.ilrocchin.it

CELLAR SALES
PRE-BOOKED VISITS
ANNUAL PRODUCTION 50,000 bottles
HECTARES UNDER VINE 20.00

The winery and part of its vineyards lie between the hill that leads up to San Cristoforo from Gavi and the Lemme river, in an area bordering on the Ovada production zones. It is run by Angelo and Francesca Zerba, together with their father Bruno, who founded it in the early 1980s. Production focuses on Gavi, although a fair amount of Dolcetto and Barbera are also made. The Zerbo family are aided in the cellar by esteemed Piedmontese oenologist Mario Ronco. This year the estate earned our full profile, presenting a stunning 2015 vintage of Gavi di Gavi Il Bosco. Its concentrated nose, with peaches and damsons on a mineral background, is followed by a rich, powerful, complex palate with a very long, lip-smacking finish. The basic Gavi is slightly more ready drinking, due to its wonderful nose-palate symmetry and long, zesty finish, while the Dolcetto 2015 offers a concentrated, layered nose and a well-orchestrated palate.

○ Gavi del Comune di Gavi '15	♟♟ 2*
○ Gavi del Comune di Gavi Il Bosco '15	♟♟ 3*
● Dolcetto di Ovada '15	♟♟ 2*
○ Gavi del Comune di Gavi '14	♟♟ 2*
○ Gavi del Comune di Gavi '00	♟♟ 2*
○ Gavi del Comune di Gavi	
Vigna del Bosco '01	♟♟ 3

Roccolo di Mezzomerico

Cascina Roccolo Bellini, 4
28040 Mezzomerico [NO]
Tel. +39 0321920407
www.ilroccolovini.it

CELLAR SALES
PRE-BOOKED VISITS
ANNUAL PRODUCTION 30,000 bottles
HECTARES UNDER VINE 7.00

The Gelmini family's handsome estate is named after a building near the old fortress of Mezzomerico, a town in the province of Novara. Today Cascina Roccolo covers an area of around seven hectares, tended with environmentally friendly methods and planted to nebbiolo, uva rara, vespolina, erbaluce, and chardonnay. With the aid of Claudio Introini in the cellar, the grapes are used to make a range of over ten wines, some named after owner Pietro's daughters. Great attention is lavished on the passito and late-harvest wines, the fruit for which is sent to the beautiful drying pavilion, built especially for the purpose. This year it was the more unusual wines that stole the limelight. Nebbiolo Vendemmia Tardiva 2010 has spicy red fruit and smoky nuances, with good balance and fullness, and Siduri Francesca, a passito from erbaluce and chardonnay, is also harmonious and very drinkable.

● Colline Novaresi Nebbiolo Valentina V.T. '10	🍷🍷 5
○ Siduri Francesca	🍷🍷 5
● Colline Novaresi Nebbiolo Valentina '11	🍷 3
○ Colline Novaresi Bianco Francesca '13	🍷🍷 2*
● Colline Novaresi Nebbiolo Valentina '10	🍷🍷 3
● Colline Novaresi Nebbiolo Valentina '07	🍷🍷 3*
● Colline Novaresi Nebbiolo Valentina '06	🍷🍷 3*
● Colline Novaresi Nebbiolo Valentina V.T. '11	🍷🍷 5
● Colline Novaresi Nebbiolo Valentina V.T. Et. Oro '10	🍷🍷 4
● Colline Novaresi Nebbiolo Valentina V.T. Et. Oro '09	🍷🍷 4
● Gilgamesh Valentina	🍷🍷 5
○ Siduri Francesca Passito	🍷🍷 4
○ Siduri Francesca Vign. Il Ponticello	🍷🍷 4

Flavio Roddolo

Fraz. Bricco Appiani
loc. Sant'Anna, 5
12065 Monforte d'Alba [CN]
Tel. +39 017378535

CELLAR SALES
PRE-BOOKED VISITS
ANNUAL PRODUCTION 25,000 bottles
HECTARES UNDER VINE 6.00

Flavio Roddolo knows that patience and waiting are fundamental requirements for anyone aspiring to produce and drink great wines, particularly in Langhe. It is one of the reasons why he has expanded the cellar where he ages his bottles of Barolo (Ravera), Nebbiolo, Barbera, and Cabernet Sauvignon (Bricco Appiani) as long as he thinks necessary, without setting any dates. The different varietal interpretations always convey the character of this unique area of Monforte, also due to long ageing in mainly used small and medium oak casks. This year the list of wines was rather uneven. The splendid Nebbiolo d'Alba 2010 towered over all the others, opening with fine notes of violets and raspberries on the nose, followed by a rich, juicy palate with great tannic density and an exceptionally alluring fresh, long finish. The weighty Dolcetto d'Alba Superiore 2012 is more exuberant, while the husky Barolo Ravera 2010 is still very marked by tannins.

● Nebbiolo d'Alba '10	🍷🍷 4
● Barolo Ravera '10	🍷🍷 5
● Dolcetto d'Alba Sup. '12	🍷🍷 3
● Dolcetto d'Alba '13	🍷 2
● Barolo Ravera '08	🍷🍷🍷 5
● Barolo Ravera '07	🍷🍷🍷 5
● Barolo Ravera '04	🍷🍷🍷 5
● Barolo Ravera '01	🍷🍷🍷 5
● Barolo Ravera '97	🍷🍷🍷 5
● Bricco Appiani '99	🍷🍷🍷 5
● Dolcetto d'Alba '09	🍷🍷 2*
● Dolcetto d'Alba Sup. '11	🍷🍷 3*
● Dolcetto d'Alba Sup. '10	🍷🍷 3*
● Dolcetto d'Alba Sup. '09	🍷🍷 3*
● Nebbiolo d'Alba '08	🍷🍷 4
● Nebbiolo d'Alba '07	🍷🍷 4

Ronchi

S.DA RONCHI, 23
12050 BARBARESCO [CN]
TEL. +39 0173635156
www.aziendaagricolaronchi.it

CELLAR SALES
PRE-BOOKED VISITS
ANNUAL PRODUCTION 30,000 bottles
HECTARES UNDER VINE 7.00

Giancarlo Rocca remains a beacon for
lovers of high-quality wines at friendly
prices. His excellent vineyard planted to
nebbiolo produces two Barbarescos, the
finest being the Ronchi, thanks to careful
grape selection. All the vines are tended
using environmentally friendly methods and
small amounts of Barbera and Dolcetto
d'Alba are also produced, along with Freisa
and Chardonnay. A couple of years ago
Langhe Arneis was added to the range,
made from the grapes of a vineyard in
Guarene, in Roero. Partly because they
demand it and partly because his work in
the vineyards is so time-consuming,
Giancarlo Rocca started late bottling his
finest wines. Although the release of the
Barbaresco 2012 has been delayed again,
we were able to taste the Ronchi of the
same vintage, which is still very young and
influenced by oak, but already appears
highly ageworthy.

Giovanni Rosso

LOC. BAUDANA, 6
12050 SERRALUNGA D'ALBA [CN]
TEL. +39 0173613340
www.giovannirosso.com

CELLAR SALES
PRE-BOOKED VISITS
ANNUAL PRODUCTION 130,000 bottles
HECTARES UNDER VINE 18.00

In recent years Serralunga d'Alba has
witnessed a revival of estates that were
once prevalently growers but subsequently
started bottling their own wines, often with
excellent results. They include the operation
now run by Davide Rosso, which boasts an
outstanding range of elegant, powerful
wines. The four Barolos display the utmost
finesse and drinkability, with beautifully
amalgamated, well-tamed tannins, thanks
to the great crus and perfect work in the
cellar. The 2012 vintage has yielded a
fabulous array of Barolos. They are headed
by a particularly elegant, complex Cerretta,
with extraordinarily close-woven tannins
and full flesh, and a very fresh finish, which
walked off with our top accolade. The rare
Vigna Rionda Ester Canale Rosso selection
vaunts even more compact, powerful
structure. The exceptionally good Barolo del
Comune di Serralunga d'Alba is very fruity,
while the close-knit, mouthfilling Serra is
more austere.

● Barbaresco Ronchi '12	♥♥ 5
○ Langhe Arneis '15	♥♥ 2*
● Barbaresco Ronchi '04	♥♥♥ 6
● Barbaresco '11	♥♥ 5
● Barbaresco '10	♥♥ 5
● Barbaresco '09	♥♥ 5
● Barbaresco '07	♥♥ 5
● Barbaresco Et. Blu '08	♥♥ 5
● Barbaresco Ronchi '11	♥♥ 5
● Barbaresco Ronchi '07	♥♥ 5*
● Barbaresco Ronchi '06	♥♥ 5*
● Barbera d'Alba Terlé '11	♥♥ 3
● Dolcetto d'Alba '12	♥♥ 2*
○ Langhe Chardonnay '13	♥♥ 3
○ Langhe Chardonnay Ronchi '12	♥♥ 3*

● Barolo Cerretta '12	♥♥♥ 8
● Barolo del Comune di Serralunga d'Alba '12	♥♥ 5
● Barolo Serra '12	♥♥ 8
● Barolo Vigna Rionda Ester Canale Rosso '12	♥♥ 8
● Langhe Nebbiolo '14	♥♥ 5
● Barolo Cerretta '06	♥♥♥ 7
● Barolo La Serra '09	♥♥♥ 7
● Barolo La Serra '08	♥♥♥ 7
● Barolo Serra '10	♥♥♥ 7
● Barolo Vigna Rionda Ester Canale Rosso '11	♥♥♥ 8
● Barolo Cerretta '11	♥♥ 8
● Barolo Cerretta '10	♥♥ 7
● Barolo Cerretta '09	♥♥ 7

Poderi Rosso Giovanni

P.zza Roma, 36/37
14041 Agliano Terme [AT]
Tel. +39 0141954006
www.poderirossogiovanni.it

CELLAR SALES
PRE-BOOKED VISITS
ANNUAL PRODUCTION 45,000 bottles
HECTARES UNDER VINE 12.00

Founded in 1930, the estate now run by Lionello Rosso vaunts vineyards in the Agliano Terme area, one of the finest for Barbera production, near Cascina Perno and Cascina San Sebastiano. They are of course planted mainly to barbera, flanked by a small amount of cabernet sauvignon. The range has so far focused exclusively on red wines but plans for a sparkler are in the pipeline. This year the various versions of Barbera d'Asti were exceptionally good, earning the estate our full profile. Gioco dell'Oca 2013 has a nose of dark fruit, with notes of rain-soaked earth and leather, and a full, complex, compact palate with good supporting acidity on the juicy finish. The more delicate, balanced Carlinet 2013 is equally good, with notes of plums and cherries accompanied by hints of spice. Cascina Perno 2014 is fresh and supple, beautifully interpreting the difficult vintage, while San Bastian 2015 is fruit forward and very drinkable.

● Barbera d'Asti Sup. Carlinet '13	♀♀ 4
● Barbera d'Asti Sup. Gioco dell'Oca '13	♀♀ 6
● Barbera d'Asti San Bastian '15	♀♀ 2*
● Barbera d'Asti Sup. Cascina Perno '14	♀♀ 3
● M.to Infine '13	♀ 4
● Barbera d'Asti Podere San Bastian '14	♀♀ 2*
● Barbera d'Asti San Bastian '13	♀♀ 2*
● Barbera d'Asti San Bastian '11	♀♀ 2*
● Barbera d'Asti Sup. Cascina Perno '13	♀♀ 3
● Barbera d'Asti Sup. Cascina Perno '12	♀♀ 2*
● Barbera d'Asti Sup. Gioco dell'Oca '12	♀♀ 6
● Barbera d'Asti Sup. V. Carlinet '12	♀♀ 3
● M.to Infine '11	♀♀ 4

Rovellotti

Interno Castello, 22
28074 Ghemme [NO]
Tel. +39 0163841781
www.rovellotti.it

CELLAR SALES
ANNUAL PRODUCTION 50,000 bottles
HECTARES UNDER VINE 17.00

Antonello and Paolo Rovellotti's estate is one of the most surprising and stunning in the increasingly competitive upper Piedmont area. Their splendid winery is housed in the old Ricetto di Ghemme, an ideal home for a range of wines that defies narrow definitions of traditional and modern. Indeed, it juxtaposes traditional grape varieties like nebbiolo and vespolina with international types such as cabernet, merlot, and pinot nero, and classic interpretations with recently developed labels. The top reds are always Ghemme Chioso dei Pomi and Ghemme Salmino Riserva, which are bottled only after long ageing in oak. Once again the stars were the selections from nebbiolo. Colline Novaresi Valplazza 2012 has a nose of currants and cherries, quinine and liquorice, and the firm structure and pace of a great wine, held back only by its generous alcohol. Ghemme Chioso dei Pomi 2009 is more classic (white pepper, gentian, and rust) and harmonious, despite its stiff tannins.

● Ghemme Chioso dei Pomi '09	♀♀ 4
● Colline Novaresi Nebbiolo Valplazza '12	♀♀ 2*
⊙ Colline Novaresi Nebbiolo Rosato Valplazza '15	♀ 2
● Colline Novaresi Vespolina Ronco al Maso '15	♀ 2
○ Valdenrico Passito '12	♀ 6
● Ghemme Chioso dei Pomi '07	♀♀♀ 4*
○ Colline Novaresi Bianco Vitigno Innominabile Il Criccone '14	♀♀ 2*
● Ghemme Chioso dei Pomi '08	♀♀ 4
● Ghemme Costa del Salmino Ris. '07	♀♀ 5
○ Vitigno Innominabile Dosaggio Zero M. Cl.	♀♀ 2*

Podere Ruggeri Corsini

LOC. BUSSIA BOVI 18
12065 MONFORTE D'ALBA [CN]
TEL. +39 017378625
www.ruggericorsini.com

CELLAR SALES
PRE-BOOKED VISITS
ANNUAL PRODUCTION 75,000 bottles
HECTARES UNDER VINE 9.80
SUSTAINABLE WINERY

Loredana Addari and Nicola Argamante studied agronomy and oenology before founding their winery 20 years ago. Their extensive knowledge has allowed them to cultivate grape varieties that are unusual for Langhe, such as pinot nero and albarossa. However, the focus of production remains Barolo, offered in a modern, firmly structured version in the Bussia Corsini and in a classic style in the Bricco San Pietro. The powerful Barbera Armujan 2012 is vibrant, full of character, and destined to improve further. Barolo Bricco San Pietro 2012 offers a nose of red berries and a medium-structured palate with good harmony and stylistic precision but lacks personality, while the very classic Barolo Bussia Corsini 2012 has moderate, balanced structure and is slightly short on grip. The well-made Langhe Bianco 2015, from arneis, chardonnay, and sauvignon, is clean and buttery, and the Langhe Nebbiolo 2013 is young and fruity.

● Barbera d'Alba Sup. Armujan '12	▼▼ 3*
● Barolo Bricco San Pietro '12	▼▼ 5
● Barolo Bussia Corsini '12	▼▼ 5
○ Langhe Bianco '15	▼▼ 2*
● Langhe Nebbiolo '13	▼▼ 3
⊙ Langhe Rosato Rosin '15	▼ 2
● Barbera d'Alba '13	♀♀ 2*
● Barbera d'Alba Sup. Armujan '11	♀♀ 3
● Barbera d'Alba Sup. Armujan '09	♀♀ 3
● Barolo Bricco San Pietro '11	♀♀ 5
● Barolo Bricco San Pietro '10	♀♀ 5
● Barolo Bussia Corsini '11	♀♀ 5
● Barolo Bussia Corsini '10	♀♀ 5
● Barolo San Pietro '08	♀♀ 5
● Langhe Rosso Autenzio '11	♀♀ 4
● Langhe Rosso Autenzio '09	♀♀ 4

Josetta Saffirio

LOC. CASTELLETTO, 39
12065 MONFORTE D'ALBA [CN]
TEL. +39 0173787278
www.josettasaffirio.com

CELLAR SALES
PRE-BOOKED VISITS
ANNUAL PRODUCTION 30,000 bottles
HECTARES UNDER VINE 5.00
SUSTAINABLE WINERY

Young Sara Vezza, daughter of oenologist Roberto and agronomist Josetta Saffirio, is now fully autonomous and well versed in every aspect of the production process. The style of the wines focuses on finesse and elegance, offering a lovely variety of vibrant aromas, also in the three flagship Barolos. The fact that the estate also produces a small amount of extra-virgin olive oil from a grove set among its vineyards is proof of their excellent position. Barolo Persiera 2012, available in magnums only, is very harmonious and alluring, offering a nose of red fruit, tobacco, and liquorice, and a balanced, juicy palate with elegant tannins and good alcoholic sweetness. Barolo Millenovecento48 Riserva 2010 has a classic nose of black fruit and juniper berries, followed by a still very compact palate with rather low-key development and a stiff finish. Langhe Nebbiolo 2014 is particularly well made and the rare Rossese Bianco 2015 is complex and zesty.

● Barolo Persiera '12	▼▼ 8
● Barolo '12	▼▼ 5
● Barolo Millenovecento48 Ris. '10	▼▼ 7
● Langhe Nebbiolo '14	▼▼ 3
○ Langhe Rossese Bianco '15	▼▼ 3
● Barolo '89	♀♀♀ 6
● Barolo '88	♀♀♀ 6
● Barbera d'Alba '11	♀♀ 3*
● Barolo '11	♀♀ 5
● Barolo '10	♀♀ 5
● Barolo '09	♀♀ 5
● Barolo Francesco Millenovecento48 '07	♀♀ 7
● Barolo Millenovecento48 Ris. '08	♀♀ 7
● Barolo Persiera '10	♀♀ 7
● Barolo Persiera '09	♀♀ 7
● Barolo Persiera '08	♀♀ 7

San Bartolomeo

LOC. VALLEGGE
CASCINA SAN BARTOLOMEO, 26
15066 GAVI [AL]
TEL. +39 0143643180
www.sanbartolomeo-gavi.com

CELLAR SALES
PRE-BOOKED VISITS
ANNUAL PRODUCTION 50,000 bottles
HECTARES UNDER VINE 21.00
SUSTAINABLE WINERY

Named after the old monastery of San Bartolomeo, on the banks of the Lemme river just outside Gavi, the handsome winery run by Fulvio Bergaglio celebrates its centenary this year. The original ecclesiastical estate, which subsequently became a manor farm, was purchased by Fulvio's grandfather in 1916 and today vaunts 20 hectares of vineyards, planted solely to cortese. They yield a small range of classic wines, fermented and aged in stainless steel at controlled temperatures, featuring a basic Gavi and the Pelöia selection. As is normal for a ripe, textured vintage like 2015, the estate's whites seem to need more patience and attention in respect to the previous year. The Gavi Quinto offers aromas of white-fleshed fruit and balsamic vegetal notes on the balanced, flavoursome palate, while it is more reticent and clenched on the nose. The Pelöia, the estate's first fantastic Tre Bicchieri, can be cellared for several years.

○ Gavi del Comune di Gavi Pelöia '15	▼▼▼ 3*
○ Gavi Quinto '15	▼▼ 2*
○ Gavi '09	♈♈ 2*
○ Gavi del Comune di Gavi Pelöia '14	♈♈ 3*
○ Gavi del Comune di Gavi Pelöia '13	♈♈ 3*
○ Gavi del Comune di Gavi Pelöia '12	♈♈ 3
○ Gavi del Comune di Gavi Pelöia '11	♈♈ 3*
○ Gavi del Comune di Gavi Pelöia '09	♈♈ 3
○ Gavi Quinto '14	♈♈ 2*
○ Gavi Quinto '13	♈♈ 3*
○ Gavi Quinto '12	♈♈ 2*
○ Gavi Quinto '11	♈♈ 2*
○ Gavi Quinto '10	♈♈ 2*

Tenuta San Pietro

LOC. SAN PIETRO, 2
15060 TASSAROLO [AL]
TEL. +39 0143342422
www.tenutasanpietro.it

CELLAR SALES
PRE-BOOKED VISITS
ANNUAL PRODUCTION 250,000 bottles
HECTARES UNDER VINE 30.00
VITICULTURE METHOD Certified Organic
SUSTAINABLE WINERY

In the space of just a few years this certified-organic Tassarolo estate has established a virtuous cycle that has seen the quality of its wines rocket. Claudio Icardi oversees work in the vineyards and cellar, skilfully aided by expert cellarman Francesco Russo. The range consists of seven wines, four whites and three reds, from cortese, barbera, albarossa, cabernet sauvignon, and nibiö (dolcetto dal peduncolo rosso). Gavi del Comune di Tassarolo San Pietro is the flagship wine, showing concentrated, with an exceptionally elegant, long, vibrant nose of flowers and minerals. On the palate it is very fresh, with a lip-smacking lingering finish. Il Mandorlo focuses instead on delicate, elegant fruit, which converges on a rich, velvety palate with good balance and intensity. Nero San Pietro is worthy of note, vaunting a fine nose and a balanced palate.

○ Gavi del Comune di Tassarolo San Pietro '15	▼▼ 3*
○ Gavi del Comune di Tassarolo Il Mandorlo '15	▼▼ 5
● M.to Rosso Nero San Pietro '13	▼▼ 3
⊙ Brut Rosé	▼ 4
○ Brut San Pietro	▼ 4
● M.to Rosso Bellavita Nero '12	▼ 5
○ Gavi del Comune di Tassarolo Gorrina '12	♈♈ 6
○ Gavi del Comune di Tassarolo Il Mandorlo '14	♈♈ 5
○ Gavi del Comune di Tassarolo San Pietro '14	♈♈ 3

Tenuta San Sebastiano

Cascina San Sebastiano, 41
15040 Lu [AL]
Tel. +39 0131741353
www.dealessi.it

CELLAR SALES
PRE-BOOKED VISITS
ANNUAL PRODUCTION 70,000 bottles
HECTARES UNDER VINE 9.00

Every year Roberto De Alessi shows himself
to be an excellent interpreter of Barbera.
His entire range, including the basic wines,
is accorded the same painstaking attention
as the flagships. The skilled use of oak
barriques and tonneaux for ageing ensures
the wines remain true to their unique
terroir, while displaying the power that is
the estate's hallmark. The nine labels are
from traditional Monferrato and
international grape varieties. Grignolino
Monfiorato flew straight into our finals at its
first ever tasting. It put up an excellent
performance, offering a complex, layered
nose and a rich, powerful palate. The
balanced 2015 Grignolino is characterized
by a floral nose with classic notes of black
pepper, while the Barbera del Monferrato
has an approachable fruity nose and a
lovely back palate. The 2012 vintage was a
special one for Barbera Mepari, although it
is still a little closed due to its evolving oak
and tannins.

● Piemonte Grignolino Monfiorato '11	🍷🍷	4
● Barbera del M.to '14	🍷🍷	2*
● Piemonte Grignolino '15	🍷🍷	2*
● Barbera del M.to Sup. Mepari '12	🍷	4
○ M.to Bianco Sperilium '15	🍷	2
● Barbera del M.to '13	🏆🏆	2*
● Barbera del M.to Mepari '04	🏆🏆	3*
● Barbera del M.to Mepari '03	🏆🏆	3*
● Barbera del M.to Sup. Mepari '11	🏆🏆	4
● Barbera del M.to Sup. Mepari '08	🏆🏆	4
● Barbera del M.to Sup. Mepari '07	🏆🏆	4
● Barbera del M.to Sup. Mepari '06	🏆🏆	4
● Barbera del M.to Sup. Mepari '05	🏆🏆	3*
○ LV Quinquagesimaquinta Mansio Passito '13	🏆🏆	4
○ M.to Bianco '14	🏆🏆	2*
● M.to Rosso Sol-Do '05	🏆🏆	3*

★Luciano Sandrone

via Pugnane, 4
12060 Barolo [CN]
Tel. +39 0173560023
www.sandroneluciano.com

PRE-BOOKED VISITS
ANNUAL PRODUCTION 100,000 bottles
HECTARES UNDER VINE 27.00

For many reasons 1978 was a key year in
Langhe history, including Luciano
Sandrone's debut as a producer. It marked
the first vintage of his Barolo garage winery:
a few hundred bottles that were
immediately snapped up by collectors for
their original style, partly derived from
ageing in small oak casks. Like all
successful innovations, they subsequently
became established in the social imaginary
as classically contemporary Nebbiolos,
faithfully echoing the characteristics of
renowned vineyards like Cannubi Boschis,
Baudana, and Villero. Their fame has been
further boosted in recent years following the
full-time commitment of Luciano's daughter
Barbara and son Luca. The Sandrone family
have been offering a fabulous pair of
Barolos for 25 years. Cannubi Boschis 2012
is young and meaty, destined to acquire
better balance in bottle as the oak blends in.
Le Vigne 2012 is even denser and more
powerful, with notes of cherries, leather, and
green peppercorns, accompanied by good
rhythm and liveliness.

● Barolo Cannubi Boschis '12	🍷🍷	8
● Barolo Le Vigne '12	🍷🍷	8
● Nebbiolo d'Alba Valmaggiore '14	🍷🍷	5
● Barolo Cannubi Boschis '11	🏆🏆🏆	8
● Barolo Cannubi Boschis '10	🏆🏆🏆	8
● Barolo Cannubi Boschis '08	🏆🏆🏆	8
● Barolo Cannubi Boschis '07	🏆🏆🏆	8
● Barolo Cannubi Boschis '06	🏆🏆🏆	8
● Barolo Cannubi Boschis '05	🏆🏆🏆	8
● Barolo Cannubi Boschis '04	🏆🏆🏆	8
● Barolo Cannubi Boschis '03	🏆🏆🏆	8
● Barolo Cannubi Boschis '01	🏆🏆🏆	8
● Barolo Cannubi Boschis '00	🏆🏆🏆	8
● Barolo Le Vigne '99	🏆🏆🏆	8

Cantine Sant'Agata

reg. Mezzena, 19
14030 Scurzolengo [AT]
Tel. +39 0141203186
www.santagata.com

CELLAR SALES
PRE-BOOKED VISITS
RESTAURANT SERVICE
ANNUAL PRODUCTION 150,000 bottles
HECTARES UNDER VINE 12.00

The Cavallero family's estate, run by
brothers Claudio and Franco since 1992, is
celebrating its centenary. Cantine
Sant'Agata is a benchmark for wines from
ruché, of which it offers several versions,
alongside grignolino and barbera from the
Portacomaro vineyards, moscato from
Canelli, and Barolo from the La Fenice
estate between Barolo and Monforte,
produced in partnership with the Ghisolfi
family. The range is as reliable as ever, with
Barbera d'Asti Baby 2015 showing fresh
and balanced, with a nose of red fruit and
tobacco, and the Altea 2014 gutsy but
rather simple. Ruché di Castagnole
Monferrato 'Na Vota 2015 is aromatic, with
notes of quinine and rhubarb, while Il
Cavaliere 2015 has bigger, denser tannins.
The two Barolos are also well made, with
Bussia La Fenice 2010 appearing deeper
and more complex and La Fenice 2010
fresher and more approachable.

● Barbera d'Asti Baby '15	♼♼ 2*
● Barbera d'Asti Sup. Altea '14	♼♼ 3
● Barolo Bussia La Fenice '10	♼♼ 6
● Barolo La Fenice '10	♼♼ 6
● Ruché di Castagnole M.to 'Na Vota '15	♼♼ 3
● Ruché di Castagnole M.to Il Cavaliere '15	♼♼ 2*
● Ruché di Castagnole M.to Pro Nobis '13	♼ 3
● Barbera d'Asti Sup. Altea '12	♗♗ 3
● Barbera d'Asti Sup. Cavalé '12	♗♗ 4
● Barbera d'Asti Sup. Cavalé '11	♗♗ 4
● Barolo Bussia '09	♗♗ 7
● Ruché di Castagnole M.to Genesi '10	♗♗ 6
● Ruché di Castagnole M.to Il Cavaliere '14	♗♗ 2*

Paolo Saracco

via Circonvallazione, 6
12053 Castiglione Tinella [CN]
Tel. +39 0141855113
www.paolosaracco.it

CELLAR SALES
PRE-BOOKED VISITS
ANNUAL PRODUCTION 600,000 bottles
HECTARES UNDER VINE 46.00

The Saracco family started making
Moscato in the early 1900s. Managed by
Paolo since 1988, it has been firmly at the
top of the Moscato world for several years
now and vaunts 14 estates lying mainly on
sand, silt, and limestone soils at altitudes
between 300 and 460 metres. The small
range is competed by a Pinot Nero, a
Chardonnay, and a Riesling, made from
grapes grown in Castiglione Tinella and
Castagnole delle Lanze. Piemonte
Moscato d'Autunno is one of the most
famous Moscatos and the 2015 vintage is
one of the finest for the wine. It has a nose
of fresh apples and pears with
concentrated aromatic notes, and its usual
very full, sweet palate. The complex
Langhe Riesling 2014 is also very well
made, offering notes of Mediterranean
scrubland and fabulous structure, as are
Piemonte Pinot Nero 2013, with simpler
notes of wild berries, and the agreeable
Moscato d'Asti 2015.

○ Piemonte Moscato d'Autunno '15	♼♼ 3*
○ Langhe Riesling '14	♼♼ 3
○ Moscato d'Asti '15	♼♼ 3
● Piemonte Pinot Nero '13	♼♼ 5
○ Langhe Chardonnay Prasuè '15	♼ 3
○ Piemonte Moscato d'Autunno '09	♼♼♼ 3*
○ Moscato d'Asti '14	♗♗ 3
○ Moscato d'Asti '13	♗♗ 3
○ Piemonte Moscato d'Autunno '14	♗♗ 3*
○ Piemonte Moscato d'Autunno '13	♗♗ 3*
● Piemonte Pinot Nero '12	♗♗ 5
● Piemonte Pinot Nero '11	♗♗ 5
● Piemonte Pinot Nero '10	♗♗ 5
● Piemonte Pinot Nero '09	♗♗ 5

Roberto Sarotto

VIA RONCONUOVO, 13
12050 NEVIGLIE [CN]
TEL. +39 0173630228
www.robertosarotto.com

CELLAR SALES
PRE-BOOKED VISITS
ANNUAL PRODUCTION 700,000 bottles
HECTARES UNDER VINE 84.00

Roberto Sarotto is at the helm of this
extensive Piedmont estate vaunting
well-tended vineyards in the region's
best-known production zones, from Barolo
and Barbaresco to Gavi and Moscato d'Asti.
Two aspects are particularly worthy of note:
the concentrated, complex, juicy style of
the wines, and their very inviting prices.
Gavi del Comune di Gavi Bric Sassi Tenuta
Manenti 2015 reached our finals with
fragrant white fleshed-fruit, peaches,
melons, and mineral hints on the nose, and
a taut palate offering a long, flavoursome
finish. Barbaresco Currà Riserva 2008 is
very mature, vaunting complex spicy notes
of ginger and cinnamon mingling with
incense and ripe fruit on the nose, and a
big, alcohol-rich palate with a very long
finish. Barolo Audace 2012 has an
extracted style, with a nose of golden-leaf
tobacco and red berries, followed by a
delicate, creamy palate.

Scagliola

VIA SAN SIRO, 42
14052 CALOSSO [AT]
TEL. +39 0141853183
www.scagliolavini.com

CELLAR SALES
PRE-BOOKED VISITS
ANNUAL PRODUCTION 200,000 bottles
HECTARES UNDER VINE 37.00

A few years ago this leading Moscato
producer also started making a series of
first-rate Barberas. Now run by the fourth
generation of the Scagliola family, the
estate owns vineyards on medium-textured
clayey limestone soils in Calosso, planted
mainly to barbera, and on sandy marl in
Canelli, dedicated principally to moscato.
All the wines are elegant and terroir true.
Moscato d'Asti Volo di Farfalle 2015 has
benefited from the excellent vintage for
this type of wine, boasting particularly rich
notes of candied peel and custard, while
retaining a pleasant, fresh palate. The
Nizza designation made its debut with the
delicate Foravia 2014, offering a
dynamic palate refreshed by taut acidity,
while Barbera d'Asti Superiore SanSì
Antologia 2013 has a nose of sweet spice
and toast, plums, and cherries, and a
dense palate with impressive structure.

○ Gavi del Comune di Gavi Bric Sassi Tenuta Manenti '15	♟♟ 2*
● Barbaresco Currà Ris. '11	♟♟ 5
● Barbaresco Gaia Principe '13	♟♟ 6
● Barbera d'Alba Elena '13	♟♟ 5
● Barolo Audace '12	♟♟ 6
○ Gavi Aurora '15	♟♟ 2*
● Langhe Nebbiolo '13	♟ 3
● Barbaresco Currà Ris. '10	♟♟ 5
● Barbera d'Alba Elena La Luna '13	♟♟ 5
● Barolo Audace '11	♟♟ 6
○ Gavi Aurora '14	♟♟ 2*
○ Gavi del Comune di Gavi Bric Sassi Tenuta Manenti '14	♟♟ 2*
○ Piemonte Chardonnay Impuro '14	♟♟ 3

● Barbera d'Asti Sup. SanSì Antologia '13	♟♟ 8
○ Moscato d'Asti Volo di Farfalle '15	♟♟ 3*
● Nizza Foravia '14	♟♟ 5
● Barbera d'Asti Sup. SanSì '14	♟♟ 6
● M.to Rosso Azord '14	♟♟ 5
● M.to Dolcetto Busiord '15	♟ 3
○ Moscato d'Asti Primo Bacio '15	♟ 3
○ Piemonte Chardonnay Casot Dan Vian '15	♟ 3
● Barbera d'Asti Sup. SanSì Sel. '01	♟♟♟ 6
● Barbera d'Asti Sup. SanSì Sel. '00	♟♟♟ 6
● Barbera d'Asti Sup. SanSì Sel. '99	♟♟♟ 5
● Barbera d'Asti Sup. Nizza Foravia '13	♟♟ 5
● Barbera d'Asti Sup. SanSì '13	♟♟ 6

Giorgio Scarzello e Figli

VIA ALBA, 29
12060 BAROLO [CN]
TEL. +39 017356170
www.barolodibarolo.com

CELLAR SALES
PRE-BOOKED VISITS
ANNUAL PRODUCTION 25,000 bottles
HECTARES UNDER VINE 5.50

Federico Scarzello runs this small but important Langhe winery, which remains true to the long and prestigious local winemaking tradition. His estate, comprising just over five hectares of vineyards, produces straightforward, no-frills wines with great character and personality, which undergo long ageing before bottling and release. Their success on the international markets demonstrates that quality doesn't need to follow the latest trends. Vigna Merenda 2011 strolled into our finals. Its very traditional, concentrated nose offers notes of red berries, aniseed, dried herbs and tobacco. On the palate close-woven tannins are accompanied by well-calibrated, lively acidity, ensuring fresh, dynamic progression through to the long, caressing finish. Barolo del Comune di Barolo 2011 is also well made, showing ripe and very pleasant with delicate floral notes and good stuffing.

● Barolo Sarmassa V. Merenda '11	♥♥ 6
● Barolo del Comune di Barolo '11	♥♥ 5
● Barolo V. Merenda '99	♥♥♥ 5
● Barbera d'Alba Sup. '10	♥♥ 4
● Barbera d'Alba Sup. '08	♥♥ 4
● Barolo '07	♥♥ 5
● Barolo del Comune di Barolo '09	♥♥ 5
● Barolo del Comune di Barolo '08	♥♥ 5
● Barolo Sarmassa V. Merenda '09	♥♥ 6
● Barolo Sarmassa V. Merenda '08	♥♥ 6
● Langhe Nebbiolo '13	♥♥ 3
● Langhe Nebbiolo '12	♥♥ 3
● Langhe Nebbiolo '10	♥♥ 3

★★Paolo Scavino

FRAZ. GARBELLETTO
VIA ALBA-BAROLO, 157
12060 CASTIGLIONE FALLETTO [CN]
TEL. +39 017362850
www.paoloscavino.com

CELLAR SALES
PRE-BOOKED VISITS
ANNUAL PRODUCTION 130,000 bottles
HECTARES UNDER VINE 29.00

Enrico Scavino sits firmly atop the pinnacle of the Barolo winemaking world, thanks to his painstaking work in both the vineyard and his absolute gem of a cellar, which is well worth a visit. His most famous selections are Riserva Rocche dell'Annunziata and Bric dël Fiasc, but all the wines are beautifully elegant. Suzanne Hoffman's Labour of Love: Wine Family Women of Piemonte, published in June 2016 by Under Discovered, tells the story of the important female figures of the estate's past and present. We awarded a Tre Bicchieri to Barolo Bric dël Fiasc 2012, which already has complex notes of tobacco, medicinal herbs, liquorice, and tar on the nose, and an austere palate with very close-woven tannins supported by good flesh. The sophisticated Monvigliero 2012 has beautiful, close-focused top notes of fresh fruit and a very youthful palate with excellent backbone and fine flesh, while the fine Rocche dell'Annunziata Riserva 2010 is youthful, elegant, and well orchestrated.

● Barolo Bric dël Fiasc '12	♥♥♥ 8
● Barolo Bricco Ambrogio '12	♥♥ 8
● Barolo Monvigliero '12	♥♥ 8
● Barolo Rocche dell'Annunziata Ris. '10	♥♥ 8
● Barbera d'Alba '15	♥♥ 3
● Barolo Cannubi '12	♥♥ 8
● Barolo Carobric '12	♥♥ 8
● Barolo Enrico Scavino '12	♥♥ 7
● Langhe Nebbiolo '14	♥♥ 4
● Dolcetto d'Alba '15	♥ 3
○ Langhe Bianco Sorriso '15	♥ 3
● Barolo Bric dël Fiasc '11	♥♥♥ 8
● Barolo Bric dël Fiasc '09	♥♥♥ 8
● Barolo Bric dël Fiasc '06	♥♥♥ 8
● Barolo Monvigliero '08	♥♥♥ 8
● Barolo Rocche dell'Annunziata Ris. '08	♥♥♥ 8
● Barolo Rocche dell'Annunziata Ris. '05	♥♥♥ 8

Schiavenza

VIA MAZZINI, 4
12050 SERRALUNGA D'ALBA [CN]
TEL. +39 0173613115
www.schiavenza.com

CELLAR SALES
PRE-BOOKED VISITS
RESTAURANT SERVICE
ANNUAL PRODUCTION 43,000 bottles
HECTARES UNDER VINE 10.00
SUSTAINABLE WINERY

Schiavenza's austere, vigorous wines perfectly match the copybook descriptions of Serralunga Barolo. Due to long ageing in medium-sized barrels, they are not suited to those who aren't prepared to wait, but with time they reach a calmer, more resolved state. The ultra-traditional touch of Luciano Pira and his family intensifies the rugged personality of south-east-facing grand crus like Prapò, Bricco Cerretta, and Broglio, without forgetting the Perno vineyards in Monforte. A visit to the estate is also highly recommended for the local cuisine offered in the restaurant of the same name, to be enjoyed on the splendid terrace overlooking the vineyards. The 2012 vintage of the estate's Barolos is as enjoyable as ever. The Prapò is thick and austere, but less rugged than expected, while the Cerretta has a few rough edges and the Broglio is deliciously old fashioned, with a nose of dried fruit and tobacco, and an alluringly lean, flavoursome palate.

Mauro Sebaste

FRAZ. GALLO D'ALBA
VIA GARIBALDI, 222BIS
12051 ALBA [CN]
TEL. +39 0173262148
www.maurosebaste.it

CELLAR SALES
PRE-BOOKED VISITS
ANNUAL PRODUCTION 150,000 bottles
HECTARES UNDER VINE 30.00

Mauro Sebaste can proudly look back on his first 25 years of winemaking. His vineyards now cover an area of 30 hectares, the vines are mature and yield excellent grapes, and his wines are increasingly popular. The range focuses on three Barolos: the Riserva Ghé and the Prapò are from a single cru in Serralunga d'Alba, while the Trèsüri is made from the grapes of several vineyards, following the old local tradition. The cellar is very modern and practical, equipped with temperature-controlled stainless-steel tanks and French oak casks and barrels. Barolo Riserva Ghé 2010 is modern in style, with spicy notes of vanilla and cinnamon, and a firmly structured palate still dominated by the tannins of the oak. The Trèsüri 2012 is not particularly powerful but has good overall harmony on the nose and palate, while the Prapò 2012 is still rather rugged but has good ageing potential. The rest of the list is good.

● Barolo Broglio '12	♟♟ 6
● Barolo Prapò '12	♟♟ 6
● Barbera d'Alba '15	♟♟ 3
● Barolo Cerretta '12	♟♟ 6
● Barolo del Comune di Serralunga d'Alba '12	♟♟ 5
● Barolo Broglio '11	♟♟♟ 5
● Barolo Broglio '05	♟♟♟ 5
● Barolo Broglio '04	♟♟♟ 5
● Barolo Broglio Ris. '08	♟♟♟ 7
● Barolo Broglio Ris. '04	♟♟♟ 5
● Barolo Prapò '08	♟♟♟ 6
● Barolo Bricco Cerretta '11	♟♟ 6
● Barolo Prapò '11	♟♟ 6
● Barolo Prapò '10	♟♟ 6
● Barolo Prapò Ris. '08	♟♟ 7

● Barbera d'Asti Valvedani '15	♟♟ 5
● Barolo Ghé Ris. '10	♟♟ 8
● Barolo Prapò '12	♟♟ 8
● Barolo Trèsüri '12	♟♟ 6
● Nebbiolo d'Alba Parigi '14	♟♟ 5
● Barbera d'Alba Sup. Centobricchi '14	♟ 5
○ Langhe Bianco Centobricchi '15	♟ 3
○ Roero Arneis '15	♟ 3
● Barbera d'Alba Sup. Centobricchi '13	♟♟ 5
● Barbera d'Alba Sup. Centobricchi '12	♟♟ 4
● Barolo Ghé Ris. '09	♟♟ 8
● Barolo Ghé Ris. '08	♟♟ 8
● Barolo Prapò '11	♟♟ 7
● Nebbiolo d'Alba Parigi '11	♟♟ 4

F.lli Seghesio

Loc. Castelletto, 19
12065 Monforte d'Alba [CN]
Tel. +39 017378108
www.fratelliseghesio.it

CELLAR SALES
PRE-BOOKED VISITS
ANNUAL PRODUCTION 55,000 bottles
HECTARES UNDER VINE 10.00

A visit to this winery is not just an educational experience, but a moving one too, with breathtaking views over the Serralunga d'Alba hills and a family, headed by Riccardo, that humbly and skilfully dedicates itself to work in the vineyard and the cellar in a completely artisanal manner. The consistently delicious Barolo La Villa is flanked by Barbera d'Alba La Chiesa, among the best of the DOC zone. Three decades of virtuous winegrowing are summed up in consistently sound, fascinating wines. Barolo La Villa 2012 vaunts wonderful finesse, with very fresh, focused notes of raspberries and wild strawberries on the nose, followed by hints of golden-leaf tobacco and cinnamon, and magnificent undertones of violets, and an extraordinarily full bodied palate, with plenty of character and silky tannins. The entire range is sound, particularly the fruity, full-bodied Dolcetto 2015.

● Barolo La Villa '12	🍷🍷	7
● Barbera d'Alba '15	🍷🍷	3
● Barolo '12	🍷🍷	7
● Dolcetto d'Alba '15	🍷🍷	2*
● Langhe Nebbiolo '14	🍷	4
● Barbera d'Alba Vign. della Chiesa '00	🍷🍷🍷	4*
● Barbera d'Alba Vign. della Chiesa '97	🍷🍷🍷	4*
● Barolo La Villa '10	🍷🍷🍷	7
● Barolo Vign. La Villa '04	🍷🍷🍷	6
● Barolo Vign. La Villa '99	🍷🍷🍷	7
● Barbera d'Alba '13	🍷🍷	3
● Barbera d'Alba La Chiesa '12	🍷🍷	4
● Barbera d'Alba Vign. della Chiesa '10	🍷🍷	4
● Barolo '11	🍷🍷	7
● Barolo La Villa '11	🍷🍷	7
● Barolo La Villa '09	🍷🍷	7

Tenute Sella

via IV Novembre, 130
13060 Lessona [BI]
Tel. +39 01599455
www.tenutesella.it

CELLAR SALES
PRE-BOOKED VISITS
ANNUAL PRODUCTION 80,000 bottles
HECTARES UNDER VINE 22.00

The Sella family's range and cellars have always been an essential stop for anyone wishing to explore the many facets of nebbiolo from the Biella area, traditionally blended with vespolina and croatina. The wines express the personalities of the sandy soils of Lessona or the porphyry of Bramaterra, but share the same diligent work in the vineyard and cellar, with the top of the range undergoing long ageing in 2,500-litre Slavonian oak barrels and partly new barriques. This style has been preserved even after a series of changes in cellar management, closely reflecting the 20 hectares of vineyards distributed in prestigious crus like San Sebastiano allo Zoppo. The synergy of Bramaterra and Lessona is once again confirmed by the latest releases. The basic versions, from the 2011 and 2010 vintages, offer notes of sea air and woodland, alternating tannic power with edgy verve on the palate. Lessona Omaggio a Quintino Sella 2009 has a more layered nose and velvety palate.

● Lessona Omaggio a Quintino Sella '09	🍷🍷	7
● Bramaterra '11	🍷🍷	5
● Lessona '10	🍷🍷	5
⊙ Coste della Sesia Rosato Majoli '15	🍷	3
● Coste della Sesia Rosso Casteltorto '13	🍷	4
● Bramaterra I Porfidi '07	🍷🍷🍷	5
● Bramaterra I Porfidi '05	🍷🍷🍷	5
● Bramaterra I Porfidi '03	🍷🍷🍷	5
● Lessona Omaggio a Quintino Sella '06	🍷🍷🍷	7
● Lessona Omaggio a Quintino Sella '05	🍷🍷🍷	6
● Lessona S. Sebastiano allo Zoppo '04	🍷🍷🍷	5
● Lessona S. Sebastiano allo Zoppo '01	🍷🍷🍷	5
⊙ Coste della Sesia Rosato Majoli '13	🍷🍷	3
● Coste della Sesia Rosso Orbello '13	🍷🍷	3

Enrico Serafino

c.so Asti, 5
12043 Canale [CN]
Tel. +39 0173979485
www.enricoserafino.it

CELLAR SALES
PRE-BOOKED VISITS
ANNUAL PRODUCTION 500,000 bottles
HECTARES UNDER VINE 12.00

Enrico Serafino's new owners, the Krause family, have recently become famous for their buy-up campaign conducted in Langhe and the Asti area, with the purchase of Vietti, but it hasn't prevented them from keeping a close eye on production at the Roero winery. Its flagships remain the Roero classics and the Alta Langa sparklers. All the estate's vineyards are in Canale and are planted to nebbiolo, barbera, and arneis, while chardonnay and pinot nero are supplied by trusted growers. The Alta Langa wines are as excellent as ever. The Brut 2010 has a concentrated nose of white-fleshed fruit, citrus, and wholemeal, and a very taut, gutsy palate with fine fruity notes on the finish, while Brut Zero 2010 has hints of custard, saffron, and ginger on the nose and a fresh, elegant palate with good grip. We also particularly liked the balanced Barbera d'Alba Parduné 2013, with notes of tobacco and ripe cherries and lots of character.

○ Alta Langa Brut '10	♥♥ 4
○ Alta Langa Brut Zero '10	♥♥ 6
● Barbera d'Alba Parduné '13	♥♥ 4
⊙ Alta Langa Brut Rosè '13	♥♥ 5
● Barbera d'Alba Bacajé '15	♥♥ 3
● Nebbiolo d'Alba Diauleri '14	♥♥ 3
○ Roero Arneis Canteiò '15	♥♥ 3
● Roero Pasiunà '13	♥♥ 4
○ Alta Langa Brut Zero Cantina Maestra '09	♥♥♥ 6
○ Alta Langa Brut Zero Cantina Maestra '07	♥♥♥ 6
○ Alta Langa Brut Zero Cantina Maestra '06	♥♥♥ 6
○ Alta Langa Brut Zero Cantina Maestra Ris. '05	♥♥♥ 6
○ Alta Langa Brut Zero Sboccatura Tardiva Cantina Maestra '08	♥♥♥ 6

Sergio Grimaldi Ca' du Sindic

loc. San Grato, 15
12058 Santo Stefano Belbo [CN]
Tel. +39 0141840341
www.cadusindic.it

CELLAR SALES
PRE-BOOKED VISITS
ANNUAL PRODUCTION 100,000 bottles
HECTARES UNDER VINE 17.00
SUSTAINABLE WINERY

Ca' du Sindic's two Moscatos, Capsula Argento and Capsula Oro, have been benchmark wines for all moscato producers for several years now. The Grimaldi family's vineyards lie on the San Grato hill next to the winery, and on the San Maurizio, Bauda, and Moncuccuo hills in Santo Stefano Belbo, with vines up to 60 years old. Dolcetto, barbera, cortese, brachetto, favorita, pinot nero, and chardonnay are used for the rest of the range. Moscato d'Asti Capsula Oro 2015 is among the finest of its kind, vaunting a classic, concentrated nose of apples and pine needles, and nicely balanced flesh and acidity on a palate with a delicious, long finish. The varietal Moscato d'Asti Vigna Moncucco 2015 offers a nose of fresh aromatic herbs, and a full-flavoured, fruity palate with a dynamic, gutsy finish. We also liked the approachable Dolcetto d'Alba 2015 and the supple Ventuno Brut 2014.

○ Moscato d'Asti Ca' du Sindic '15	♥♥ 3*
○ Moscato d'Asti V. Moncucco '15	♥♥ 3*
● Dolcetto d'Alba '15	♥♥ 2*
○ Ventuno Brut '14	♥♥ 3
● Barbera d'Asti '12	♥♥ 2*
● Barbera d'Asti SanGrato '12	♥♥ 2*
○ Moscato d'Asti '14	♥♥ 2*
○ Moscato d'Asti '13	♥♥ 2*
○ Moscato d'Asti '12	♥♥ 2*
○ Moscato d'Asti Ca' du Sindic '14	♥♥ 3
○ Moscato d'Asti Ca' du Sindic '13	♥♥ 3
○ Moscato d'Asti Ca' du Sindic '12	♥♥ 3
○ Moscato d'Asti Ca' du Sindic '11	♥♥ 2*

Giovanni Silva

CASCINE ROGGE, 1B
10011 AGLIÈ [TO]
TEL. +39 3473075648
www.silvavini.com

CELLAR SALES
PRE-BOOKED VISITS
ANNUAL PRODUCTION 50,000 bottles
HECTARES UNDER VINE 12.00

The Silva family's vineyards lie on the morainic hilltops of Agliè around Cascina Rogge, bordering the grounds of the Castello Ducale. They cover an area of 12 hectares, tended by Giovanni with the aid of his grandson Stefano, the third generation to work at the winery in the space of 20 years. Their well-put-together range focuses chiefly on erbaluce, in all the different versions from the Dry Ice and Tre Ciochè still dry whites to the Passito Poetica, without forgetting the Charmat and Metodo Classico sparklers. However, small amounts of nebbiolo, barbera, freisa, and bonarda are also grown. Long ageing has given the interesting Erbaluce di Caluso Brut a dual personality, with a pervasive, mature nose of ripe white-fleshed fruit and honey, and astringent acidity on the palate. While the Dry Ice 2015 is not particularly firmly structured, it is pleasantly supple and alluring with hints of almonds on the finish.

○ Erbaluce di Caluso Brut M. Cl. '09	♟♟	5
○ Erbaluce di Caluso Dry Ice '15	♟♟	2*
○ Erbaluce di Caluso Tre Ciochè '15	♟♟	2*
○ Caluso Passito Poetica '03	♟♟	5
● Canavese Nebbiolo '08	♟♟	2*
○ Erbaluce di Caluso Dry Ice '14	♟♟	2*
○ Erbaluce di Caluso Dry Silva '12	♟♟	2*
○ Erbaluce di Caluso Passito Poetica '04	♟♟	5
○ Erbaluce di Caluso Tre Ciochè '14	♟♟	2*
○ Erbaluce di Caluso Tre Ciochè '13	♟♟	2*
○ Erbaluce di Caluso Tre Ciochè '12	♟♟	2*
○ Erbaluce di Caluso Tre Ciochè '06	♟♟	2*

La Smilla

VIA GARIBALDI, 7
15060 BOSIO [AL]
TEL. +39 0143684245
www.lasmilla.it

CELLAR SALES
ANNUAL PRODUCTION 100,000 bottles
HECTARES UNDER VINE 5.00

La Smilla's sensitivity towards cortese di Gavi has been evident for generations in the work of the Guido family on the hillsides of Bosio, the Piedmont municipality closest to the Ligurian Sea, less than ten kilometres away as the crow flies. The geography and climate say much, if not all, about the decidedly original nature of a range that combines spontaneity with expansiveness and is easily approachable yet ageworthy. The entire range is steel aged, with the exception of Gavi I Bergi and Barbera Calicanto, aged in small oak casks. This year it was the 2015 Gavis that put up the best performance. The basic Gavi has a very lively, powerful palate sustained by unusual herbal and smoky notes, while the Gavi del Comune di Gavi is similar in style but with more concentrated fruit and mineral thrust, and hints of damsons and apricots on the long finish. Gavi Metodo Classico Brut 2013 has a fine bead and zesty raciness.

○ Gavi '15	♟♟	2*
○ Gavi del Comune di Gavi '15	♟♟	2*
○ Gavi Brut M. Cl. '13	♟♟	3
● M.to Rosso Calicanto '12	♟♟	3
● Barbera del M.to '14	♟	2
● Dolcetto di Ovada '14	♟	2
○ Gavi I Bergi '14	♟	3
● Dolcetto di Ovada '13	♟♟	2*
● Dolcetto di Ovada '12	♟♟	2*
○ Gavi '14	♟♟	2*
○ Gavi '13	♟♟	2*
○ Gavi del Comune di Gavi '14	♟♟	2*
○ Gavi del Comune di Gavi '13	♟♟	2*
○ Gavi del Comune di Gavi '12	♟♟	2*
○ Gavi del Comune di Gavi I Bergi '11	♟♟	3
● M.to Rosso Calicanto '10	♟♟	3

Socré

S.DA TERZOLO, 7
12050 BARBARESCO [CN]
TEL. +39 3487121685
www.socre.it

CELLAR SALES
PRE-BOOKED VISITS
ANNUAL PRODUCTION 30,000 bottles
HECTARES UNDER VINE 5.50

A few years ago, following many more spent working in Turin, architect Marco Piacentino decided to take over the management of the family winery in his home town of Barbaresco. Quality has continued to improve steadily along with interest in his wines, as testified by his collection of important awards from international wine magazines and exports to many countries. The jewel in the crown is Barbaresco Roncaglie, released after long ageing in the cellar, but the entire range is very well made. Barbaresco Roncaglie 2012 has a delicately modern personality, with a touch of oak adding complexity to its fruit. The powerful, complex palate is remarkably balanced and has a very long, sophisticated finish. The 2013 Barbaresco has spicy fruit on the nose and, although a little lacking in weight, a nicely balanced, caressing palate.

● Barbaresco Roncaglie '12	♥♥♥ 6
● Barbaresco '13	♥♥♥ 5
● Cisterna d'Asti De Scapin '13	♥♥ 2*
● Langhe Nebbiolo '14	♥♥ 3
● Dolcetto d'Alba '15	♥ 2
● Barbaresco '12	♀♀ 5
● Barbaresco '11	♀♀ 5
● Barbaresco '10	♀♀ 5
● Barbaresco '08	♀♀ 5
● Barbaresco Roncaglie '11	♀♀ 6
● Barbaresco Roncaglie '10	♀♀ 7
● Barbaresco Roncaglie '09	♀♀ 7
● Barbera d'Alba Sup. '13	♀♀ 3
● Cisterna d'Asti De Scapin '12	♀♀ 2*

★Sottimano

LOC. COTTÀ, 21
12052 NEIVE [CN]
TEL. +39 0173635186
www.sottimano.it

CELLAR SALES
PRE-BOOKED VISITS
ANNUAL PRODUCTION 85,000 bottles
HECTARES UNDER VINE 18.00

The range of Barbarescos crafted by Rino and Anna Sottimano, aided by their children Andrea and Elena, is a sort of Neive "all-stars" team. Fausoni, Currà, Pajoré, Cottà: each cru is expressed in a style that can be defined as formally modern if we are forced to label it. Ageing takes place mainly in small oak casks (only part new), but work in the cellar is centred on high-quality fruit and extractive texture. A Barbaresco Riserva is produced in the finest vintages (from the grapes of the Cottà and Pajorè crus), and the range also includes Dolcetto Bric del Salto, Barbera Pairolero, and the dry Brachetto Maté. The range of Barbarescos stunned us once again. The Currà 2012 towers above the others with wonderfully balanced fruit and spice, and a finely austere palate that faithfully reflects the vintage, while the Pajoré has a seductive rich nose of red fruit, roots and herbs, and a juicy, velvety palate. The Cottà 2013 is fresher on the nose and more progressive on the palate.

● Barbaresco Currà '12	♥♥♥ 8
● Barbaresco Cottà '13	♥♥ 7
● Barbaresco Pajoré '13	♥♥ 7
● Barbaresco Fausoni '13	♥♥ 7
● Barbera d'Alba Pairolero '14	♥♥ 4
● Maté '15	♥♥ 3
● Barbaresco Cottà '05	♀♀♀ 7
● Barbaresco Currà '10	♀♀♀ 8
● Barbaresco Currà '08	♀♀♀ 7
● Barbaresco Currà '04	♀♀♀ 6
● Barbaresco Pajoré '10	♀♀♀ 7
● Barbaresco Pajoré '08	♀♀♀ 7
● Barbaresco Ris. '10	♀♀♀ 8
● Barbaresco Ris. '05	♀♀♀ 8
● Barbaresco Ris. '04	♀♀♀ 8

Luigi Spertino

VIA LEA, 505
14047 MOMBERCELLI [AT]
TEL. +39 0141959098
luigi.spertino@libero.it

CELLAR SALES
PRE-BOOKED VISITS
ANNUAL PRODUCTION 40,000 bottles
HECTARES UNDER VINE 9.00

The Spertino family have been tending their vineyards clinging to the steep hillsides for more than 35 years. They are home to barbera vines over 75 years old, which are flanked by grignolino, cortese, and pinot nero. Mauro's wines are highly original but also exceptionally authentic and terroir true, like Barbera La Mandorla, made from partially dried grapes, and Cortese Vilet, fermented on the skins. The 2014 vintage of Barbera d'Asti Superiore La Mandorla is labelled Edizione La Grisa, but confirms its uniqueness, winning a Tre Bicchieri. Notes of plums and cherries alternate with quinine and rain-soaked earth on the nose, followed by a fresh, dense, juicy palate with elegant tannins and wonderful flesh. Barbera d'Asti La Grisa 2014 is also excellent, with a nose of dark fruit, tobacco, and juniper berries, and a very full palate, nicely sustained by acidity and crisp fruit.

★★★La Spinetta

VIA ANNUNZIATA, 17
14054 CASTAGNOLE DELLE LANZE [AT]
TEL. +39 0141877396
www.la-spinetta.com

CELLAR SALES
PRE-BOOKED VISITS
ACCOMMODATION
ANNUAL PRODUCTION 500,000 bottles
HECTARES UNDER VINE 100.00
SUSTAINABLE WINERY

The style of Giorgio Rivetti's wines is associated mainly with super-ripe grapes and concentrated fruit, from which he crafts selections with a strong personality and a pervasive nose, always accompanied by rich tannins and impressive stuffing. In addition to the rightly famous Moscato d'Asti, the wide range focuses largely on Barolo (from the Campé vineyard in Grinzane Cavour) and Barbaresco, from crus in Neive and Treiso. However, the Bionzo Barbera d'Asti and the Gallina Barbera d'Alba are also excellent. The entire range performed very well, lacking only a touch of freshness to reach our top accolade. Barbaresco 2013 was the best of the fine line up, with a concentrated nose of peaches and oak, followed by a palate with great fruity flesh and supple tannins. The elegant Barbera d'Asti Bionzo is also among the best of its kind, as is the charming Moscato d'Asti Bricco Quaglia.

● Barbera d'Asti Sup. V. La Mandorla Edizione La Grisa '14	▼▼▼ 8
● Barbera d'Asti La Grisa '14	▼▼ 4
● Grignolino d'Asti '15	▼▼ 3*
● M.to Rosso '13	▼▼ 7
○ Piemonte Cortese Vilet '15	▼▼ 7
● Barbera d'Asti Sup. La Mandorla '13	♈♈♈ 8
● Barbera d'Asti Sup. La Mandorla '10	♈♈♈ 8
● Barbera d'Asti Sup. La Mandorla '09	♈♈♈ 8
● Barbera d'Asti Sup. La Mandorla '07	♈♈♈ 7
● Barbera d'Asti Sup. V. La Mandorla '12	♈♈♈ 8
● M.to Rosso La Mandorla '09	♈♈♈ 7
● M.to Rosso La Mandorla '07	♈♈♈ 5
● Barbera d'Asti '13	♈♈ 4

● Barbaresco Gallina '13	▼▼ 8
● Barbaresco Starderi '13	▼▼ 8
● Barbera d'Asti Sup. Bionzo '13	▼▼ 6
● Barolo Campè '12	▼▼ 8
○ Moscato d'Asti Bricco Quaglia '15	▼▼ 3*
● Barbaresco Valeirano '13	▼▼ 8
● Barbaresco Vign. Bordini '12	▼▼ 7
● Barolo Vign. Garretti '12	▼▼ 7
● Langhe Nebbiolo '13	▼▼ 5
● M.to Rosso Pin '13	▼▼ 6
○ Moscato d'Asti Biancospino '15	▼▼ 3
○ Piemonte Chardonnay Lidia '13	▼▼ 6
○ Piemonte Moscato Passito Oro '08	▼▼ 6
○ Langhe Bianco '13	▼ 6
● Barbaresco Gallina '11	♈♈♈ 8
● Barolo Campè '08	♈♈♈ 8

Sulin

v.le Pininfarina, 14
14035 Grazzano Badoglio [AT]
Tel. +39 0141925136
www.sulin.it

ANNUAL PRODUCTION 220,000 bottles
HECTARES UNDER VINE 19.50

In 2000 brothers Mauro and Fabio Fracchia decided to shake up the family business, founded in the 1920s, adopting new technologies and modern plantings in the vineyard, but without forgetting the history of the area. Two years of studies of various barbera clones in the family's old vineyards led to the clonal selection that has resulted in the Ornella vineyard and its splendid Barbera. The range consists of around a dozen wines, including the intriguing Chardonnay, fermented in large oak barrels, which is varietal and very ageworthy. Sulin didn't make it into the last edition of our Guide due to lack of space, but has hit the mark this year with an excellent list of wines. Ornella 2013 has a nose of dark berries with hints of black pepper and cocoa powder, echoed on a fresh, powerful palate with a very long finish. The complex, well-orchestrated Barbera 2014 is closely followed by the fruity, floral Chardonnay, and the classic, varietal Grignolino.

● Barbera del M.to Sup. Ornella '13	⦿⦿ 5
● Barbera del M.to '14	⦿⦿ 2*
● Grignolino del M.to Casalese '15	⦿⦿ 2*
○ Piemonte Chardonnay '15	⦿⦿ 2*

Sylla Sebaste

via San Pietro, 4
12060 Barolo [CN]
Tel. +39 017356266
www.syllasebaste.com

CELLAR SALES
PRE-BOOKED VISITS
RESTAURANT SERVICE
ANNUAL PRODUCTION 120,000 bottles
HECTARES UNDER VINE 7.00

Fabrizio Merlo, who has headed the winery for over two decades, is a Nebbiolo aficionado. This year he presented a new Barolo, Bricco delle Viole 2012, which is first and foremost a tribute to Langhe and Roero, listed as UNESCO World Heritage Sites just over a year ago. Opposite the cellar in the hamlet of Vergne, stands a handsome 14th-century church, the chapel of San Pietro delle Viole, and the magnificent vineyard from which the wine hails. Quality has steadily risen with the aid of consultant oenologist Luca Caramellino, with the Barolos always at the centre of attention. The new Barolo Bricco delle Viole 2012 made it into our finals with a complex, fruity nose of raspberries featuring evolved notes of tobacco and autumn leaves, and an enviably elegant palate displaying glossy, well-resolved tannins. Despite focusing on elegance, the Bussia 2012 offers a more layered nose, its fruit making way for hints of tar and liquorice.

● Barolo Bricco delle Viole '12	⦿⦿ 5
● Barolo '12	⦿⦿ 5
● Barolo Bussia '12	⦿⦿ 6
● Langhe Nebbiolo '13	⦿⦿ 3
○ Roero Arneis '15	⦿ 3
● Barolo Bussia '85	⦿⦿⦿ 6
● Barolo Bussia Ris. '84	⦿⦿⦿ 6
● Barbera d'Alba '13	⦿⦿ 3
● Barolo '11	⦿⦿ 6
● Barolo '10	⦿⦿ 6
● Barolo Bussia '11	⦿⦿ 6
● Barolo Bussia '10	⦿⦿ 6
● Nebbiolo d'Alba '12	⦿⦿ 3
● Nebbiolo d'Alba '11	⦿⦿ 3

Tacchino

VIA MARTIRI DELLA BENEDICTA, 26
15060 CASTELLETTO D'ORBA [AL]
TEL. +39 0143830115
www.luigitacchino.it

CELLAR SALES
PRE-BOOKED VISITS
ANNUAL PRODUCTION 12,000 bottles
HECTARES UNDER VINE 12.00

While Romina and her brother Alessio are certainly responsible for the leap in quality of the estate's production, their experience and love of the land is derived from a family history spanning three generations in the vineyards. They have achieved their goal by modernizing the production chain and starting to age their top wines in oak, associated with the necessary spirit of enterprise to make the estate an international name, a fundamental move at a time of severe recession for the domestic market. Hats off! Once again this year it was the Du Riva that touched our hearts with a nose of blackberries and currants on a spicy background and a powerful palate with an endless finish. The elegant, harmonious Barbera del Monferrato Albarola is characterized by great body and endless length. It is followed by a fine version of Monferrato Rosso Di Fatto and the 2014 versions of Barbera and Dolcetto, which vaunt excellent sensory characteristics despite their vintage.

● Dolcetto di Ovada Sup. Du Riva '13	♛♛♛ 4*
● Barbera del M.to Albarola '13	♛♛ 5
● Barbera del M.to '14	♛♛ 2*
● Dolcetto di Ovada '14	♛♛ 2*
○ Gavi del Comune di Gavi '15	♛♛ 3
● M.to Rosso Di Fatto '13	♛♛ 4
○ Cortese dell'Alto M.to Marsenca '15	♛ 2
● Dolcetto di Ovada Sup. Du Riva '12	♛♛♛ 5
● Dolcetto di Ovada Sup. Du Riva '11	♛♛♛ 5
● Dolcetto di Ovada Sup. Du Riva '10	♛♛♛ 4*
● Dolcetto di Ovada Sup. Du Riva '09	♛♛♛ 4*
● Dolcetto di Ovada Sup. Du Riva '08	♛♛♛ 4*
● Dolcetto di Ovada '13	♛♛ 2*
● Dolcetto di Ovada '12	♛♛ 2*
● M.to Rosso Di Fatto '12	♛♛ 4

Michele Taliano

C.SO A. MANZONI, 24
12046 MONTÀ [CN]
TEL. +39 0173975658
www.talianomichele.com

CELLAR SALES
PRE-BOOKED VISITS
ANNUAL PRODUCTION 60,000 bottles
HECTARES UNDER VINE 12.00

Founded in 1930 by Domenico Taliano, today the estate is run by the third generation of the family, brothers Ezio and Alberto. Initially all the vineyards were in the municipality of Montà, in the Bossola, Rolandi, and Benna areas, but plots and a farm in Montersino, in the Barbaresco zone, were subsequently purchased. The Roero vineyards are planted to native grape varieties like arneis, barbera, favorita, and nebbiolo, while in the Langhe there are nebbiolo, barbera, dolcetto, and moscato. Rochè Dra Bòssora Riserva 2012, the estate's Roero flagship, is simply brilliant, vaunting a spicy nose of fruit and tobacco, and a dense, tannic palate showing good balance and full flavour, with a long, juicy finish. The two Barbarescos presented are also well made: the Tera Mia Riserva 2009 with notes of dried flowers and tea leaves, still slightly marked by oak but with good fruit, and the fairly complex Ad Altiora Montersino 2012 that focuses more on fresh acidity.

● Roero Ròche dra Bòssora Ris. '12	♛♛ 3*
● Barbaresco Ad Altiora Montersino '12	♛♛ 5
● Barbaresco Tera Mia Ris. '09	♛♛ 5
● Barbera d'Alba A Bon Rendre '15	♛♛ 2*
● Barbera d'Alba Laboriosa Sup. '12	♛ 3
○ Roero Arneis Sernì '15	♛ 2
● Barbaresco Ad Altiora '11	♛♛ 5
● Barbaresco Ad Altiora '10	♛♛ 5
● Barbera d'Alba A Bon Rendre '13	♛♛ 2*
● Barbera d'Alba Laboriosa '11	♛♛ 3
● Nebbiolo d'Alba Blagheur '13	♛♛ 2*
○ Roero Arneis Sernì '13	♛♛ 2*
● Roero Ròche dra Bòssora Ris. '11	♛♛ 3*

Tenuta Tenaglia

S.DA SANTUARIO DI CREA, 5
15020 SERRALUNGA DI CREA [AL]
TEL. +39 0142940252
www.tenutatenaglia.it

CELLAR SALES
PRE-BOOKED VISITS
ACCOMMODATION
ANNUAL PRODUCTION 120,000 bottles
HECTARES UNDER VINE 30.00
SUSTAINABLE WINERY

Tenuta Tenaglia has a long history and is one of the touchstone wineries for Monferrato Casalese. Its wines modern in style, but carefully enhance the distinctive characteristics of the grape varieties. Barbera del Monferrato and Barbera d'Asti account for most of the wines produced, and are offered in versions differentiated by production volume and ageing. The chardonnay grapes are fermented alone or blended with timorasso, in the Monferrato Bianco, while the syrah is also fermented as a monovarietal. The fine list saw two great versions of Barbera d'Asti reach our finals. Emozioni and Giorgio Tenaglia have complex, concentrated tertiary notes on the nose, and an elegant, delicate palate with nice balance. The other wines presented, from the Syrah Paradiso to the current Grignolino and Barberas, underscore the overall quality of production.

Terre del Barolo

VIA ALBA-BAROLO, 8
12060 CASTIGLIONE FALLETTO [CN]
TEL. +39 0173262053
www.terredelbarolo.com

CELLAR SALES
PRE-BOOKED VISITS
ANNUAL PRODUCTION 3,800,000 bottles
HECTARES UNDER VINE 650.00
SUSTAINABLE WINERY

A vineyard area of 650 hectares is exceptionally large for Langhe, even for its most famous cooperative winery, based in Castiglione Falletto. The fact that it has been active for over 60 years testifies to its great attention to the terroir, and its wines are reliable and fairly priced, with a wide range of crus from which to choose. Its "Progetto Qualità", launched 15 years ago, drew on detailed knowledge of the different micro-zones of the 11 municipalities of the Barolo production zone. Today, the result of this investment can be seen in the many wines capable of satisfying different tastes and pockets. The estate's array of Barolos is simply flawless, commencing with the basic 2012, produced in accordance with the "Progetto Qualità", which offers good body and wonderful finesse. The single-vineyard selections are a few years older but preserve the same freshness. Of the two 2010 vintages, we prefer the classic, full elegance of the Ravera to the Monvigliero, while the 2009 Riservas have drier tannins.

● Barbera d'Asti Emozioni '10	♟♟ 5
● Barbera d'Asti Giorgio Tenaglia '10	♟♟ 3*
● Barbera d'Asti Bricco '15	♟♟ 2*
● Barbera del M.to Cappella III '15	♟♟ 2*
● Grignolino del M.to Casalese '15	♟♟ 2*
● M.to Rosso Paradiso '10	♟♟ 5
● Barbera del M.to Sup. 1930 Una Buona Annata '12	♟ 5
⊙ M.to Chiaretto Edenrose '15	♟ 2
○ Piemonte Chardonnay '15	♟ 2
● Barbera d'Asti Emozioni '99	♟♟♟ 4*
● Barbera del M.to Sup. 1930 Una Buona Annata '11	♟♟ 5
● Barbera del M.to Sup. 1930 Una Buona Annata '10	♟♟ 5
● Grignolino del M.to Casalese '13	♟♟ 2*

● Barolo Monvigliero '10	♟♟ 6
● Barolo Ravera '10	♟♟ 6
● Barolo '12	♟♟ 5
● Barolo Castello Ris. '09	♟♟ 6
● Barolo Rocche di Castiglione Ris. '09	♟♟ 7
● Barbera d'Alba Valdisera '12	♟♟ 2*
● Barolo Cannubi '09	♟♟ 7
● Barolo Cannubi '08	♟♟ 7
● Barolo Castello Ris. '08	♟♟ 6
● Barolo Castello Ris. '07	♟♟ 6
● Barolo Monvigliero '09	♟♟ 6
● Barolo Monvigliero '08	♟♟ 6
● Barolo Ravera '09	♟♟ 6
● Barolo Ravera '08	♟♟ 6

★Torraccia del Piantavigna

VIA ROMAGNANO, 20
28074 GHEMME [NO]
TEL. +39 0163840040
www.torracciadelpiantavigna.it

CELLAR SALES
PRE-BOOKED VISITS
ANNUAL PRODUCTION 150,000 bottles
HECTARES UNDER VINE 38.00
SUSTAINABLE WINERY

The name chosen by the Francoli brothers for their winery, universally acknowledged as one of the soundest and most ambitious in northern Piedmont, is not an invented moniker as many assume. Torraccia is the name of the Ghemme site where the first plot of nebbiolo was planted in the 1970s, while Piantavigna was the surname of the brothers' maternal grandfather who inspired the subsequent developments, with almost 40 hectares of vineyards purchased in at least six different zones of the provinces of Novara and Vercelli. The resulting range is wide and diversified, crafted with the aid of Beppe Caviola and focusing on big, austere reds, aged chiefly in large oak barrels and requiring medium to long cellaring. The 2011 vintage offers yet another perfectly typed Ghemme and Gattinara, with lively fruit, dense texture, and gutsy tannins, whose excellent performance is only the latest in a long series. Bianco ErbaVoglio 2015 is also very well made, showing linear but hefty.

● Ghemme '11	♟♟♟ 6
● Gattinara '11	♟♟ 6
○ Colline Novaresi Bianco ErbaVoglio '15	♟♟ 3
● Colline Novaresi Vespolina La Mostella '15	♟♟ 3
● Colline Novaresi Nebbiolo Ramale '13	♟ 4
⊙ Colline Novaresi Nebbiolo Rosato Barlàn '15	♟ 3
● Gattinara '09	♟♟♟ 5
● Gattinara '06	♟♟♟ 5
● Ghemme '10	♟♟♟ 5
● Ghemme '07	♟♟♟ 5
● Ghemme Ris. '07	♟♟♟ 5
● Ghemme Ris. '07	♟♟♟ 5
● Ghemme V. Pellizzane '10	♟♟♟ 6

Giancarlo Travaglini

VIA DELLE VIGNE, 36
13045 GATTINARA [VC]
TEL. +39 0163833588
www.travaglinigattinara.it

CELLAR SALES
PRE-BOOKED VISITS
ANNUAL PRODUCTION 250,000 bottles
HECTARES UNDER VINE 49.00
SUSTAINABLE WINERY

Owning almost 50 hectares of the total of just over 100 of the entire designation, this historic estate run by Cinzia Travaglini and her husband Massimo Collauto is a point of reference for Gattinara Nebbiolo. Its unmistakably lean, elegant character is due to the particular microclimate of the area, determined by the interplay of air currents flowing to and from the nearby Alps, and the porphyry-based soil. These characteristics are sensitively underscored in the basic version, the Tre Vigne selection, and the Riserva, aged in various sizes of oak barrels for different lengths of time. They are flanked by Nebbiolo Il Sogno, from super-ripe grapes. The role of basic wine seems rather unfitting for the classic, terroir-true Gattinara 2012, with clear-cut fruit, medicinal herbs and rhubarb, and a progressive palate. The 2011 Riserva is similar, but slightly more full blooded, with firm structure, good flesh, and rusty notes on a very promising long, flavoursome finish.

● Gattinara '12	♟♟ 6
● Gattinara Ris. '11	♟♟ 7
● Gattinara Tre Vigne '11	♟♟ 7
○ Nebolé Dosaggio Zero M. Cl. '11	♟♟ 8
● Coste della Sesia Nebbiolo '14	♟ 3
● Gattinara Ris. '04	♟♟♟ 5
● Gattinara Ris. '01	♟♟♟ 5
● Gattinara Tre Vigne '04	♟♟♟ 5
● Coste della Sesia Nebbiolo '13	♟♟ 3
● Gattinara '11	♟♟ 4
● Gattinara '10	♟♟ 4
● Gattinara Ris. '09	♟♟ 6
● Gattinara Tre Vigne '10	♟♟ 5

★ G. D. Vajra

LOC. VERGNE
VIA DELLE VIOLE, 25
12060 BAROLO [CN]
TEL. +39 017356257
www.gdvajra.it

CELLAR SALES
PRE-BOOKED VISITS
ANNUAL PRODUCTION 220,000 bottles
HECTARES UNDER VINE 50.00

According to many, Aldo and Milena Vajra's great achievement is their ability to reconcile two apparently opposite currents in their winery. Indeed, their well-established estate and standard-bearer of the finest Langhe tradition has expanded its viticultural horizons and successfully experimented with types that are less familiar in the area, like wines from riesling renano or pinot nero, but also freisa and sparklers. However, its natural focus remains its elegant, "feminine" Barolos from Bricco delle Viole and Vergne in Barolo, Ravera in Novello, and the vineyards taken over from Luigi Baudana in the Cerretta cru in Serralunga. Whether they're from Barolo or Serralunga d'Alba, the estate's Barolos are always impeccable, as shown by the Tre-Bicchieri-winning Bricco delle Viole, whose notes of raspberries and wild strawberries offer a beautifully classic interpretation of the DOCG. The multifaceted, layered Baudana has superb progression and flesh, while the Ravera is slightly less assertive.

● Barolo Bricco delle Viole '12	♙♙♙	8
● Barolo Baudana '12	♙♙	6
● Barolo Ravera '12	♙♙	7
● Barbera d'Alba Sup. '13	♙♙	5
● Barolo Albe '12	♙♙	6
○ Langhe Riesling '15	♙♙	5
○ Moscato d'Asti '15	♙♙	3
● Langhe Freisa Kyè '12	♙	5
● Barolo Baudana Luigi Baudana '09	♙♙♙	6
● Barolo Bricco delle Viole '10	♙♙♙	8
● Barolo Bricco delle Viole '05	♙♙♙	8
● Barolo Bricco delle Viole '01	♙♙♙	8
● Barolo Bricco delle Viole '00	♙♙♙	8
● Barolo Cerretta Luigi Baudana '08	♙♙♙	6

Mauro Veglio

FRAZ. ANNUNZIATA
CASCINA NUOVA, 50
12064 LA MORRA [CN]
TEL. +39 0173509212
www.mauroveglio.com

CELLAR SALES
PRE-BOOKED VISITS
ANNUAL PRODUCTION 80,000 bottles
HECTARES UNDER VINE 14.00
SUSTAINABLE WINERY

Mauro Veglio's estate consists of just under 15 hectares of vineyards on the hillsides of La Morra and Monforte d'Alba. Aided by his wife Daniela and his brother Elio, in the space of just a few years he has made a name for himself as one of the most authoritative interpreters of the modern style due to his discretion in the cellar that overshadows the technical details of short maceration times or ageing in small French oak casks. The range features five Barolos: the basic one and the Arborina, Roccche dell'Annunziata, Gattera, and Castelletto crus. However, the estate also has plots planted to barbera, including the Cascina Nuova cru, dolcetto, and cabernet sauvignon. The top Nebbiolos fared very well. Barolo Arborina 2012 combines fruity power with delicate extract, while the Castelletto of the same vintage is more introverted but equally precise and focused. Rocche dell'Annunziata 2012 earned a Tre Bicchieri for its austere sweetness enhanced by notes of cocoa powder and camphor, and its impressive stuffing, glossy tannins, and alluring freshness.

● Barolo Rocche dell'Annunziata '12	♙♙♙	8
● Barolo Arborina '12	♙♙	7
● Barolo Castelletto '12	♙♙	7
● Barbera d'Alba Cascina Nuova '14	♙♙	5
● Barolo '12	♙♙	5
● Barolo Gattera '12	♙♙	7
● Langhe Nebbiolo '14	♙♙	3
● Langhe Nebbiolo Angelo '15	♙♙	3
● Langhe Rosso L'Insieme '13	♙♙	6
● Barbera d'Alba '15	♙	3
● Barbera d'Alba Cascina Nuova '99	♙♙♙	5
● Barolo Arborina '10	♙♙♙	6
● Barolo V. Rocche '96	♙♙♙	8
● Barolo Vign. Arborina '01	♙♙♙	6
● Barolo Vign. Arborina '00	♙♙♙	6
● Barolo Vign. Gattera '05	♙♙♙	6

Giovanni Viberti

VIA DELLE VIOLE 30
12060 BAROLO [CN]
TEL. +39 017356192
www.viberti-barolo.com

CELLAR SALES
PRE-BOOKED VISITS
RESTAURANT SERVICE
ANNUAL PRODUCTION 80,000 bottles
HECTARES UNDER VINE 18.00

This estate has a long tradition, dating back almost a century, when it started making wine destined for consumption by the guests of the Locanda del Buon Padre, still a place of pilgrimage for foodies. Over the years output has risen and today Giovanni Viberti's name is well known on the other side of the Atlantic too. The vineyards, all famous and fully valorized by the estate, are mainly in the highest part of Barolo, with Bricco delle Viole reaching an altitude of 500 metres. The alluring Barolo Buon Padre 2012, from a blend of different crus, has top notes of violets and liquorice on the nose, embellished with vegetal hints of roots, and a particularly lively, juicy palate displaying almost crisp youthful freshness. Raspberries and liquorice are already evident on the nose of the classic Barolo Bricco delle Viole Riserva 2010, which is followed by an austere palate with very close-woven tannins and vibrant acidity.

Vicara

VIA MADONNA DELLE GRAZIE, 5
15030 ROSIGNANO MONFERRATO [AL]
TEL. +39 0142488054
www.vicara.it

CELLAR SALES
PRE-BOOKED VISITS
ANNUAL PRODUCTION 200,000 bottles
HECTARES UNDER VINE 40.00
VITICULTURE METHOD Certified Biodynamic

Domenico Ravizza is a dynamic, enterprising grower born and bred in Monferrato Casalese, which he now promotes with his wines and a production philosophy that follows the local winegrowing traditions. He uses mainly native Piedmont grape varieties, along with a few international cultivars. Personalized fermentation techniques are used in the cellar, yielding both ready-drinking and ageworthy wines. The former are produced with brief maceration at controlled temperatures, and the latter with long maceration and ageing in oak. This year Domenico has managed to scale a peak that had hitherto seemed impossible, winning a Tre Bicchieri with his Grignolino. This 2015 vintage has huge character, offering an inebriating nose of black pepper, quinine and tobacco followed by a stunning palate with dynamic tannins and a lingering finish. The other wines presented also performed very well, underscoring the high quality of the estate's production.

Wine	Rating
● Barolo Bricco delle Viole Ris. '10	▼▼ 7
● Barolo Buon Padre '12	▼▼ 6
● Barolo La Volta Ris. '10	▼▼ 8
● Barolo San Pietro Ris. '10	▼▼ 8
● Barbera d'Alba La Gemella '14	▼ 3
● Barbera d'Alba Sup. Bricco Airoli '11	♀♀ 4
● Barolo Buon Padre '11	♀♀ 6
● Barolo Buon Padre '10	♀♀ 6
● Barolo La Volta Ris. '07	♀♀ 8
● Barolo San Pietro Ris. '07	♀♀ 8
● Langhe Nebbiolo '13	♀♀ 3
● Langhe Nebbiolo '12	♀♀ 3

Wine	Rating
● Grignolino del M.to Casalese '15	▼▼▼ 3*
● Barbera del M.to Sup. Vadmò '12	▼▼ 4
● Barbera del M.to Sup. Cantico della Crosia '13	▼▼ 4
● Barbera del M.to Volpuva '15	▼▼ 3
● Grignolino del M.to Casalese L'Uccelletta '12	▼▼ 4
● M.to Rosso Rubello '11	▼▼ 4
○ M.to Airales '15	▼ 3
● Barbera del M.to Cascina Rocca 33 '13	♀♀ 3*
● Barbera del M.to La Rocca '10	♀♀ 3*
● Barbera del M.to Sup. Vadmò '11	♀♀ 4
● Barbera del M.to Sup. Vadmò '10	♀♀ 4
● Barbera del M.to Sup. Vadmò '06	♀♀ 3*
● Grignolino del M.to Casalese '12	♀♀ 3*

Giacomo Vico

VIA TORINO, 80/82
12043 CANALE [CN]
TEL. +39 0173970984
www.giacomovico.it

CELLAR SALES
PRE-BOOKED VISITS
ANNUAL PRODUCTION 92,300 bottles
HECTARES UNDER VINE 18.00

The Vico family have been part of the Roero
winegrowing world since the late 19th
century. Following the Second World War, the
business remained closed for many years
until production recommenced in the early
1990s. The estate's vineyards, which include
veritable crus, such as Valmaggiore, San
Michele, and Patarrone, lie on the typical
loose, sandy, limestone soil of the area and
are planted with the classic Roero grape
varieties, such as arneis, nebbiolo, barbera,
brachetto, and favorita. We very much liked
Roero Bricco Patarrone 2012, which is
among the best of the production zone, with
spicy notes of red fruit and impressive
backbone supported by vibrant acidity that
ensures a very long finish. Roero Riserva
Giacomo 2012 has a floral nose with hints of
aromatic herbs, and a juicy, full-flavoured
palate, while the 2012 Barolo focuses more
on notes of tobacco and dried flowers, and a
supple palate, which is already very open,
with velvety tannins and good acid grip.

● Roero Bricco Patarrone '12	♟♟	4
● Barolo '12	♟♟	5
● Roero Giacomo Ris. '12	♟♟	4
● Barbera d'Alba Sup. '13	♟	4
● Nebbiolo D'Alba Sup. V. Valmaggiore '12	♟	4
● Barbera d'Alba Sup. '12	♟♟	4
● Barolo '10	♟♟	5
● Barolo '09	♟♟	5
● Langhe Nebbiolo '12	♟♟	3
● Nebbiolo D'Alba Valmaggiore '11	♟♟	4
● Nebbiolo D'Alba Valmaggiore '10	♟♟	4
● Roero '11	♟♟	4
○ Roero Arneis '14	♟♟	3

★★Vietti

P.ZZA VITTORIO VENETO, 5
12060 CASTIGLIONE FALLETTO [CN]
TEL. +39 017362825
www.vietti.com

CELLAR SALES
PRE-BOOKED VISITS
ANNUAL PRODUCTION 250,000 bottles
HECTARES UNDER VINE 37.00

Recently purchased by the Krause group, the
estate, which is one of the most important
names in Italian wine, remains headed by
managing director Luca Currado and sales
director Mario Cordero. Its success can be
attributed to its great vineyards, a history of
excellence that keeps outdoing itself, and a
sound, reliable style across the range. It offers
six types of Barolo, all exquisitely crafted,
including the rare Riserva Villero that shines in
the best vintages. Barbera d'Asti La Crena
and Barbera d'Alba Vigna Scarrone are both
splendid. We awarded a Tre Bicchieri to Barolo
Ravera 2012 for its nose of close-focused,
young fruit and its palate with deliciously fresh
acidity and caressing tannins. The more
delicate Brunate 2012 offers notes of elegant
spice and liquorice and a beautifully balanced
palate, while Rocche di Castiglione 2012 has
a nose of sweet tobacco and spice followed
by a pervasive note of red berries, and a
velvety palate with medium body. Barolo
Lazzarito 2012 has a beautifully delicate nose
of red fruit and liquorice, and a wonderfully
caressing palate with spectacular character.

● Barolo Ravera '12	♟♟♟	8
● Barolo Brunate '12	♟♟	8
● Barolo Lazzarito '12	♟♟	8
● Barolo Rocche di Castiglione '12	♟♟	8
● Barbera d'Alba Tre Vigne '14	♟♟	3
● Barbera d'Asti Tre Vigne '14	♟♟	3
● Barolo Castiglione '12	♟♟	7
● Dolcetto d'Alba Tre Vigne '15	♟♟	3
● Langhe Nebbiolo Perbacco '13	♟♟	4
● Barbera d'Asti Sup. Nizza La Crena '09	♟♟♟	5
● Barolo Rocche '08	♟♟♟	8
● Barolo Rocche di Castiglione '11	♟♟♟	8
● Barolo Villero Ris. '07	♟♟♟	8
● Barolo Villero Ris. '06	♟♟♟	8
● Barolo Villero Ris. '04	♟♟♟	8

I Vignaioli di Santo Stefano

Loc. Marini, 26
12058 Santo Stefano Belbo [CN]
Tel. +39 0141840419
www.ivignaiolidisantostefano.it

CELLAR SALES
PRE-BOOKED VISITS
ANNUAL PRODUCTION 285,000 bottles
HECTARES UNDER VINE 35.00
SUSTAINABLE WINERY

Forty years have passed since the Ceretto, Santi, and Scavino families decided to found I Vignaioli di Santo Stefano, focusing exclusively on moscato. The vineyards are mainly in the municipality of Santo Stefano Belbo, including the prestigious rented San Maurizio estate, along with a few plots in Canelli and Calosso, all at altitudes between 320 and 450 metres. Production is limited to semi-sparking Moscato d'Asti and sparkling Asti Spumante. The 2015 Moscato d'Asti fully exploits its fine vintage, offering a nose of aromatic herbs, particularly thyme and sage, accompanied by typical notes of candied orange peel. On the palate it is fresh yet potent, with rather high residual sugar that is nonetheless nicely balanced by acidity. The refreshing Asti 2015 is almost as spectacular, with a close-focused nose of candied fruit and good thrust.

○ Moscato d'Asti '15	🍷🍷 3*
○ Asti '15	🍷🍷 3
○ Asti '14	🍷🍷 3
○ Asti '13	🍷🍷 3
○ Asti '12	🍷🍷 3
○ Asti '11	🍷🍷 3
○ Asti '10	🍷🍷 3
○ Moscato d'Asti '14	🍷🍷 5
○ Moscato d'Asti '13	🍷🍷 4
○ Moscato d'Asti '12	🍷🍷 4
○ Moscato d'Asti '11	🍷🍷 3
○ Moscato d'Asti '09	🍷🍷 4
○ Moscato d'Asti '08	🍷🍷 4

★Vigneti Massa

p.zza G. Capsoni, 10
15059 Monleale [AL]
Tel. +39 013180302
vignetimassa@libero.it

CELLAR SALES
PRE-BOOKED VISITS
ANNUAL PRODUCTION 120,000 bottles
HECTARES UNDER VINE 25.00
SUSTAINABLE WINERY

The Massa family have been vignerons for four generations, and before oenologist Walter took over the business, they sold their wine unbottled. Many other producers have followed the same path, partly dictated by the development of the consumer over the past 30 years. The only difference is that it possesses that rare creative spirit or stroke of genius that changes its horizons and, in the space of a few years catapults an area onto a global market that would otherwise be difficult to reach. This year the Timorassos presented for our tastings were from the 2014 vintage, which ensured fresher acidity but detracted a little from their complexity on the nose. However, the Montecitorio and Derthona still performed well, managing to express much of their potential. The 2012 Monleale is an intense wine, vaunting a powerful palate with an alcoholic finish, while the Grande Anarchia Costituzionale, from moscato, has a vibrant nose and a splendid, full, concentrated palate supported by exemplary acidity.

○ Derthona '14	🍷🍷 5
○ Montecitorio '14	🍷🍷 6
○ Anarchia Costituzionale '15	🍷🍷 3
● Monleale '12	🍷🍷 6
● Pietra del Gallo '15	🍷 2
● Sentieri '15	🍷 4
○ Colli Tortonesi Bianco Costa del Vento '05	🍷🍷🍷 7
○ Colli Tortonesi Bianco Sterpi '04	🍷🍷🍷 6
○ Colli Tortonesi Timorasso Derthona '06	🍷🍷🍷 5
○ Colli Tortonesi Timorasso Sterpi '08	🍷🍷🍷 7
○ Colli Tortonesi Timorasso Sterpi '07	🍷🍷🍷 7
○ Costa del Vento '12	🍷🍷🍷 6
○ Derthona '09	🍷🍷🍷 5
○ Montecitorio '11	🍷🍷🍷 6
○ Montecitorio '10	🍷🍷🍷 6
○ Sterpi '13	🍷🍷🍷 6

Vigneti Valle Roncati

VIA NAZIONALE, 10A
28072 BRIONA [NO]
TEL. +39 3355732548
www.vignetivalleroncati.it

CELLAR SALES
PRE-BOOKED VISITS
ANNUAL PRODUCTION 40,000 bottles
HECTARES UNDER VINE 10.00

Cecilia Bianchi is confidently approaching fine, consistent quality in her winemaking, as the awards from prestigious international trade magazines and our tastings are starting to show. Her handsome hillside vineyards are planted chiefly to nebbiolo, used to craft the area's most classic designations of Fara, Ghemme, and Sizzano, along with several red and white versions of Colline Novaresi. Il Pepin, an intriguing, satisfying passito from nebbiolo, is also worth tasting. The splendid Ghemme Leblanque 2011 has good personality, with notes of rain-soaked earth and quinine on the nose, followed by a particularly fresh, juicy, balanced palate. Sizzano San Bartolomeo 2012 has a layered nose with notes of gentian and rhubarb, and a powerful, velvety plate with a faintly bitterish finish. The delicate, spicy Bianco Particella 40 2015 has beautifully balanced alcohol and acidity, deserving a special mention.

● Ghemme Leblanque '11	♥♥ 5
● Sizzano San Bartolomeo '12	♥♥ 4
○ Colline Novaresi Bianco Particella 40 '15	♥♥ 2*
⊙ Colline Novaresi Nebbiolo Rosato Poderi di Sopra '15	♥ 3
● Colline Novaresi Vespolina '15	♥ 2
● Colline Novaresi Barbera V. di Mezzo '13	♥♥ 2*
● Colline Novaresi Nebbiolo V. di Sotto '09	♥♥ 2*
● Colline Novaresi Uva Rara '13	♥♥ 2*
● Colline Novaresi Vespolina '13	♥♥ 2*
● Colline Novaresi Vespolina '12	♥♥ 2*
● Fara Ciada '10	♥♥ 3*
● Fara V. di Sopra '10	♥♥ 3
● Sizzano San Bartolomeo '11	♥♥ 3*

Villa Giada

REG. CEIROLE, 10
14053 CANELLI [AT]
TEL. +39 0141831100
www.villagiada.wine

CELLAR SALES
PRE-BOOKED VISITS
ACCOMMODATION AND RESTAURANT SERVICE
ANNUAL PRODUCTION 180,000 bottles
HECTARES UNDER VINE 25.00

The Faccio family own three estates: the headquarters with the cellar and seven acres of moscato vineyards in Canelli, Cascina del Parroco in Calosso, and Dani in Agliano Terme, planted mainly to barbera. Nebbiolo, dolcetto, merlot, chardonnay, sauvignon, cortese, and gamba di pernice complete the array of grape varieties grown. The wines presented are well made and reliable, commencing with the versions of Moscato d'Asti. The Surì 2015 has a nose of candied peel and cakes, and a sweet, balanced palate, while the beautifully drinkable Canelli 2015 is fresh, with notes of sage and hints of white peaches. The spicy Gamba di Pernice is one of the few monovarietal wines from the grape and has good structure with plush tannins. Barbera d'Asti Surì 2015 is pleasant and fruit forward, while Barbera d'Asti Superiore Nizza Dedicato 2013 is more complex but less gutsy.

● Barbera d'Asti Sup. Nizza Dedicato a... '13	♥♥ 5
● Barbera d'Asti Surì '15	♥♥ 2*
● Gamba di Pernice	♥♥ 2*
○ Moscato d'Asti Canelli '15	♥♥ 2*
○ Moscato d'Asti Surì '15	♥♥ 2*
● Barbera d'Asti Ajan '15	♥ 2
● Barbera d'Asti Sup. La Quercia '14	♥ 3
● Barbera d'Asti Sup. La Quercia '13	♥♥ 3
● Barbera d'Asti Sup. Nizza Bricco Dani '13	♥♥ 4
● Barbera d'Asti Sup. Nizza Bricco Dani '11	♥♥ 4
● Barbera d'Asti Sup. Nizza Dedicato a... '10	♥♥ 5
○ Moscato d'Asti '13	♥♥ 2*
○ Moscato d'Asti Surì '14	♥♥ 2*

★Villa Sparina

FRAZ. MONTEROTONDO, 56
15066 GAVI [AL]
TEL. +39 0143633835
www.villasparina.it

PRE-BOOKED VISITS
ACCOMMODATION AND RESTAURANT SERVICE
ANNUAL PRODUCTION 550,000 bottles
HECTARES UNDER VINE 65.00

Villa Sparina frequently graces the society
pages of the press as the venue for events
frequented by members of the jet set from
the world of art. The credit for this goes to
siblings Stefano, Massimo, and Tiziana
Moccagatta, who have transformed the
splendid estate in Monterotondo di Gavi
into a welcoming resort complete with
hotel, restaurant and spa. However, they
continue to lavish equal attention on their
wine production, derived from over 60
hectares of vineyards planted mainly to
cortese, along with dolcetto and barbera
from the Cassinelle and Rivalta Bormida
estates. The result is an eclectic range,
which also features sparklers and white
wines designed for long ageing. This role is
fulfilled by Gavi di Gavi Monterotondo,
which won a Tre Bicchieri with a full,
layered nose with top notes of ginger and
medicinal herbs, and a stunning, very fresh
palate that promises to age well. The
supple Blanc de Blancs Brut 2012 is one of
the finest Metodo Classicos produced in
the province of Alessandria.

○ Gavi del Comune di Gavi Monterotondo '14	♟♟♟ 6
● Barbera del M.to Sup. Rivalta '13	♟♟ 6
○ Gavi del Comune di Gavi Et. Gialla '15	♟♟ 3
○ Villa Sparina Blanc de Blancs Brut '12	♟♟ 3
○ Gavi del Comune di Gavi Monterotondo '12	♟♟♟ 6
○ Gavi del Comune di Gavi Monterotondo '11	♟♟♟ 6
○ Gavi del Comune di Gavi Monterotondo '10	♟♟♟ 6
○ Gavi del Comune di Gavi Monterotondo '09	♟♟♟ 6
○ Gavi del Comune di Gavi Monterotondo '08	♟♟♟ 6

Cantina Sociale di Vinchio Vaglio Serra

FRAZ. REG. SAN PANCRAZIO, 1
S.DA PROV.LE 40 KM. 3,75
14040 VINCHIO [AT]
TEL. +39 0141950903
www.vinchio.com

CELLAR SALES
PRE-BOOKED VISITS
ANNUAL PRODUCTION 1,640,000 bottles
HECTARES UNDER VINE 420.00

Vinchio Vaglio Serra was founded as a
cooperative winery in 1959 by a group of
19 producers. It currently has 185
grower-members, with around 420 hectares
of vineyards, including several over 60 years
old, chiefly in Vinchio and Vaglio Serra, but
also in Incisa Scapaccino, Cortiglione, Nizza
Monferrato, Castelnuovo Belbo, Castelnuovo
Calcea, and Mombercelli. The wines are
technically well made and remarkably true
to type. The list of wines presented is as
valid as ever. Barbera d'Asti Superiore
Nizza Laudana 2013 has very well-typed
notes of red berries and rain-soaked earth,
with an elegant palate nicely underpinned
by acidity ensuring a long finish and
alluring drinkability. Barbera d'Asti Sorì dei
Mori 2015 also focuses on crisp red berries
but is more approachable, Grignolino d'Asti
Le Nocche 2015 is juicy and spicy, and
Moscato d'Asti Valamasca 2015 is fresh
and well typed.

● Barbera d'Asti Sorì dei Mori '15	♟♟ 2*
● Barbera d'Asti Sup. Nizza Laudana '13	♟♟ 3
● Grignolino d'Asti Le Nocche '15	♟♟ 2*
○ Moscato d'Asti Valamasca '15	♟♟ 2*
● Barbera d'Asti V. Vecchie '14	♟ 3
● Ruché di Castagnole Monferrato Rebus '15	♟ 2
● Barbera d'Asti Sup. Sei Vigne Insynthesis '01	♟♟♟ 6
● Barbera d'Asti Sup. I Tre Vescovi '13	♟♟ 2*
● Barbera d'Asti Sup. I Tre Vescovi '12	♟♟ 2*
● Barbera d'Asti Sup. Nizza Laudana '12	♟♟ 3*
● Barbera d'Asti Sup. Nizza Laudana '11	♟♟ 3
● Barbera d'Asti Sup. Vigne Vecchie '09	♟♟ 4
● Barbera d'Asti Vigne Vecchie 50 '13	♟♟ 3

Virna

VIA ALBA, 24
12060 BAROLO [CN]
TEL. +39 017356120
www.virnabarolo.it

CELLAR SALES
PRE-BOOKED VISITS
ANNUAL PRODUCTION 60,000 bottles
HECTARES UNDER VINE 12.00

The use of grapes from legendary crus in
the Barolo production zone and the
experience of Virna Borgogno, aided in the
cellar by her sister Ivana, have long
enabled this young estate to offer an
interesting range that is increasingly
convincing in terms of both quality and
price. Their Barolos, from crus such as
Sarmassa, Preda, and Cannubi Boschis, are
flanked by Dolcetto d'Alba, Barbera d'Alba,
Nebbiolo d'Alba and Langhe Nebbiolo, plus
several blends. The list of Barolos
performed very well, commencing with the
Cannubi Boschis 2012, with hints of cocoa
powder and liquorice on the nose, followed
by a very complex, juicy palate. The Barolo
Riserva 2010 is long and powerful, with
hints of incense and autumn leaves, and
close-woven but still unresolved tannins.
The pleasant, easy-drinking BaRosé 2015
is a very sound rosé.

Vite Colte

VIA BERGESIA, 6
12060 BAROLO [CN]
TEL. +39 0173564611
www.vitecolte.it

CELLAR SALES
PRE-BOOKED VISITS
ANNUAL PRODUCTION 1,200,000 bottles
HECTARES UNDER VINE 300.00
VITICULTURE METHOD Certified Organic
SUSTAINABLE WINERY

Terradavino, the huge cooperative winery
with its production headquarters in Langhe
and Monferrato, has chosen to use the
name Vite Colte for its top selections,
destined exclusively for the hotel and
restaurant trade. The fruit of much hard
work in the vineyard and cellar, they include
the famous Barbera d'Asti La Luna e I Falo,
also in the new Nizza version, and the
Barolo Essenze, without forgetting Moscato
Passito La Bella Estate. Barolo del Comune
di Barolo Essenze 2012 has fine top notes
of fresh herbs and tobacco on a
background of raspberries, liquorice and
spice, and a remarkably full palate with
stunning close-woven tannins that earned
it a Tre Bicchieri. The estate has always
lavished great attention on the rich,
balanced Moscato Passito, whose 2012
vintage is undoubtedly the best ever.
Despite its difficult vintage, the 2014 Nizza
offers pervasive fruity aromas and an
exceptionally full palate.

● Barolo Cannubi Boschis '12	▼▼ 6
● Barolo '12	▼▼ 5
● Barolo del Comune di Barolo '12	▼▼ 6
● Barolo Ris. '10	▼▼ 5
☉ BaRosé '15	▼▼ 3
○ Langhe Arneis Solouno '15	▼▼ 2*
● Langhe Rosso Le Sorelle '13	▼ 3
● Barolo '11	♈ 5
● Barolo Cannubi Boschis '11	♈ 6
● Barolo del Comune di Barolo '11	♈ 6
● Barolo Preda Sarmassa Limited Edition 10 Anni '06	♈ 8
● Barolo Sarmassa '11	♈ 6
● Langhe Nebbiolo '13	♈ 3

● Barolo del Comune di Barolo Essenze '12	▼▼▼ 6
● Nizza La Luna e I Falò '14	▼▼ 4
○ Piemonte Moscato Passito La Bella Estate '12	▼▼ 5
● Barbaresco La Casa in Collina '13	▼▼ 5
● Barbera d'Asti Sup. La Luna e I Falò '14	▼▼ 4
● Barolo del Comune di Serralunga d'Alba Essenze '11	▼▼ 7
● Barolo Essenze Ris. '07	▼▼ 8
● Barolo Paesi Tuoi '12	▼▼ 6
● Barbera d'Asti Sup. La Luna e I Falò '13	♈ 4
● Barbera d'Asti Sup. La Luna e I Falò '12	♈ 3
● Barbera d'Asti Sup. Nizza La Luna e I Falò '13	♈ 5
● Barolo del Comune di Barolo Essenze '11	♈ 6

F.lli Abrigo

LOC. BERFI
VIA MOGLIA GERLOTTO, 2
12055 DIANO D'ALBA [CN]
TEL. +39 017369104
www.abrigofratelli.com

CELLAR SALES
PRE-BOOKED VISITS
ANNUAL PRODUCTION 100,000 bottles
HECTARES UNDER VINE 27.00

● Diano d'Alba Sorì dei Berfi '15	♟♟ 3*
○ Alta Langa Brut Sivà '13	♟♟ 4
● Nebbiolo d'Alba Tardiss '14	♟♟ 3
● Barbera d'Alba Piasusa '15	♟ 2

Annamaria Alemanni

FRAZ. CHERLI INFERIORE, 64
15070 TAGLIOLO MONFERRATO [AL]
TEL. +39 0143896229
doppiaa@libero.it

CELLAR SALES
ACCOMMODATION
ANNUAL PRODUCTION 6,000 bottles
HECTARES UNDER VINE 4.00
SUSTAINABLE WINERY

● Dolcetto di Ovada Anvud '14	♟♟ 2*
● Dolcetto di Ovada Sup. Ansè '13	♟♟ 3
○ M.to Bianco Tre Lune '08	♟♟ 2*

Alice Bel Colle

REG. STAZIONE, 9
15010 ALICE BEL COLLE [AL]
TEL. +39 014474413
www.cantinaalicebc.it

CELLAR SALES
PRE-BOOKED VISITS
ANNUAL PRODUCTION 80,000 bottles
HECTARES UNDER VINE 370.00

● Barbera d'Asti Al Casò '15	♟♟ 2*
● Barbera d'Asti Filari Sociali '15	♟♟ 2*
● Barbera d'Asti Sup. Alix '13	♟♟ 3
○ Asti Classic M. Cl.	♟ 4

Antica Cascina Conti di Roero

LOC. VAL RUBIAGNO, 2
12040 VEZZA D'ALBA [CN]
TEL. +39 017365459
www.oliveropietro.it

CELLAR SALES
PRE-BOOKED VISITS
ANNUAL PRODUCTION 100,000 bottles
HECTARES UNDER VINE 13.50
SUSTAINABLE WINERY

○ Brut Rosé Maria Teresa M. Cl.	♟♟ 4
● Nebbiolo d'Alba '14	♟♟ 2*
○ Roero Arneis '15	♟ 2
● Roero V. Sant'Anna '13	♟ 3

L'Astemia Pentita

VIA CROSIA, 40
12060 BAROLO [CN]
TEL. +39 0173560501
www.astemiapentita.it

● Barolo Cannubi '12	♟♟ 8
● Barolo Terlo '12	♟♟ 8
● Dinamico	♟ 5

La Ballerina

FRAZ. TANA, 8
14048 MONTEGROSSO D'ASTI [AT]
TEL. +39 0141 956118
www.laballerina.it

● Barbera d'Asti Amoris '15	♟♟ 3
● Barbera d'Asti La Notte '10	♟♟ 3
● Grignolino d'Asti Alè '14	♟ 3
● M.to Rosso Infinitum '11	♟ 3

Cantina Sociale Barbera dei Sei Castelli

via Opessina, 41
14040 Castelnuovo Calcea [AT]
Tel. +39 0141957137
www.barberaseicastelli.it

CELLAR SALES
PRE-BOOKED VISITS
ANNUAL PRODUCTION 80,000 bottles
HECTARES UNDER VINE 620.00

● Barbera d'Asti 50 Anni di Barbera '14	🍷🍷 2*
● Barbera d'Asti Sup. Le Vignole '13	🍷🍷 3
● Barbera d'Asti Sup. Nizza '13	🍷🍷 4
● Barbera d'Asti '15	🍷 2

Battaglio

loc. Borbore
via Salerio, 15
12040 Vezza d'Alba [CN]
Tel. +39 017365423
www.battaglio.com

CELLAR SALES
PRE-BOOKED VISITS
ANNUAL PRODUCTION 35,000 bottles
HECTARES UNDER VINE 5.00

● Barbaresco '13	🍷🍷 6
● Barbaresco Serragrilli '13	🍷 6

Bea - Merenda con Corvi

s.da Santa Caterina, 8
10064 Pinerolo [TO]
Tel. +39 3356824880
www.merendaconcorvi.it

CELLAR SALES
PRE-BOOKED VISITS
ACCOMMODATION
ANNUAL PRODUCTION 4,500 bottles
HECTARES UNDER VINE 1.00

● Merlot '13	🍷🍷 5
● Pinerolese Barbera '13	🍷🍷 4
● Pinerolese Barbera Foravia '15	🍷🍷 3
● Bel Ami '13	🍷 7

Antonio Bellicoso

fraz. Molisso, 5a
14048 Montegrosso d'Asti [AT]
Tel. +39 0141953233
antonio.bellicoso@alice.it

CELLAR SALES
PRE-BOOKED VISITS
ANNUAL PRODUCTION 10,000 bottles
HECTARES UNDER VINE 4.00
SUSTAINABLE WINERY

● Barbera d'Asti Amormio '15	🍷🍷 2*
● Barbera d'Asti Merum '14	🍷🍷 4
● Freisa d'Asti '15	🍷 2

Marco Bonfante

s.da Vaglio Serra, 72
14049 Nizza Monferrato [AT]
Tel. +39 0141725012
www.marcobonfante.com

CELLAR SALES
PRE-BOOKED VISITS
ANNUAL PRODUCTION 270,000 bottles
HECTARES UNDER VINE 20.00

● Barbera d'Asti Sup. Stella Rossa '14	🍷🍷 2*
● Barolo Bussia '11	🍷🍷 6
● Piemonte Rosso Albarone '13	🍷🍷 5
● Langhe Nebbiolo Imma '13	🍷 4

F.lli Borgogno

via Crosia 12
12060 Barolo [CN]
Tel. +39 017356107
www.borgognoseriobattista.it

CELLAR SALES
PRE-BOOKED VISITS
ANNUAL PRODUCTION 60,000 bottles
HECTARES UNDER VINE 5.00

● Barolo Cannubi '11	🍷🍷 7
● Nebbiolo d'Alba '13	🍷🍷 3
● Barbera d'Alba Sup. '12	🍷 4

Boroli

Fraz. Madonna di Como, 34
12051 Alba [CN]
Tel. +39 0173365477
www.boroli.it

CELLAR SALES
PRE-BOOKED VISITS
ACCOMMODATION AND RESTAURANT SERVICE
ANNUAL PRODUCTION 200,000 bottles
HECTARES UNDER VINE 32.00
SUSTAINABLE WINERY

● Barolo Cerequio '12	♟♟	7
● Barolo '12	♟♟	6
● Barolo Villero '12	♟♟	7

Agostino Bosco

via Fontane, 24
12064 La Morra [CN]
Tel. +39 0173509466
www.barolobosco.com

CELLAR SALES
PRE-BOOKED VISITS
ANNUAL PRODUCTION 28,000 bottles
HECTARES UNDER VINE 5.50
SUSTAINABLE WINERY

● Barbera d'Alba Sup. Volupta '14	♟♟	3
● Barolo La Serra '12	♟♟	6
● Dolcetto d'Alba Vantrin '15	♟♟	2*
● Langhe Nebbiolo Rurem '14	♟	3

Giacomo Boveri

via Costa Vescovato, 15
15050 Costa Vescovato [AL]
Tel. +39 0131838223
www.vignetiboveri.it

ANNUAL PRODUCTION 25,000 bottles
HECTARES UNDER VINE 10.00

● Colli Tortonesi Barbera Sup. Bricco della Ginestra '13	♟♟	3
○ Colli Tortonesi Cortese Campo del Bosco '15	♟♟	2*

Renato Buganza

loc. Cascina Garbinotto, 4
12040 Piobesi d'Alba [CN]
Tel. +39 0173619370
www.renatobuganza.it

CELLAR SALES
PRE-BOOKED VISITS
ANNUAL PRODUCTION 35,000 bottles
HECTARES UNDER VINE 11.00
SUSTAINABLE WINERY

● Barbera d'Alba Sup. Gerbole '12	♟♟	2*
● Nebbiolo d'Alba Gerbole '11	♟	2
○ Roero Arneis dla Trifula '15	♟	2

Bussia Soprana

loc. Bussia, 88a
12065 Monforte d'Alba [CN]
Tel. +39 039305182
www.bussiasoprana.it

CELLAR SALES
PRE-BOOKED VISITS
ANNUAL PRODUCTION 60,000 bottles
HECTARES UNDER VINE 16.00

● Barbera d'Alba Mosconi '13	♟♟	4
● Barbera d'Alba Vin del Ross '07	♟♟	5
● Barolo Bussia V. Gabutti '11	♟♟	8

Oreste Buzio

V. Piave, 13
15049 Vignale Monferrato [AL]
Tel. +39 0142933197
www.orestebuzio.altervista.org

CELLAR SALES
PRE-BOOKED VISITS
ANNUAL PRODUCTION 25,000 bottles
HECTARES UNDER VINE 6.00
VITICULTURE METHOD Certified Organic

● Grignolino del M.to Casalese '15	♟♟	3*
● Grignolino del M.to Casalese '14	♟♟	3
● Barbera del M.to Sup. Riccardo II '11	♟	4

Marco Canato
FRAZ. FONS SALERA
LOC. CA' BALDEA, 18/2
15049 VIGNALE MONFERRATO [AL]
TEL. +39 0142933653
www.canatovini.it

CELLAR SALES
PRE-BOOKED VISITS
ANNUAL PRODUCTION 30,000 bottles
HECTARES UNDER VINE 11.00

● Barbera del M.to Gambaloita '15	❷❷	3
● Grignolino del M.to Casalese Celio '15	❷❷	3
○ Piemonte Chardonnay Piasì '15	❷	3

Pierangelo Careglio
LOC. APRATO, 15
12040 BALDISSERO D'ALBA [CN]
TEL. +39 017240436
www.cantinacareglio.com

CELLAR SALES
PRE-BOOKED VISITS
ANNUAL PRODUCTION 30,000 bottles
HECTARES UNDER VINE 8.00

● Roero '13	❷❷	2*
● Barbera d'Alba '14	❷	2
○ Langhe Favorita '15	❷	2
○ Roero Arneis '15	❷	2

Carussin
REG. MARIANO, 27
14050 SAN MARZANO OLIVETO [AT]
TEL. +39 0141831358
www.carussin.it

CELLAR SALES
PRE-BOOKED VISITS
RESTAURANT SERVICE
ANNUAL PRODUCTION 80,000 bottles
HECTARES UNDER VINE 15.00
VITICULTURE METHOD Certified Organic

● Barbera d'Asti Asinoi '15	❷❷	2*
● Barbera d'Asti Lia Vi '15	❷❷	3
○ Moscato d'Asti Filari Corti '15	❷❷	3
● Ciuchinoi	❷	3

Casavecchia
VIA ROMA, 2
12055 DIANO D'ALBA [CN]
TEL. +39 017369321
www.cantinacasavecchia.com

CELLAR SALES
PRE-BOOKED VISITS
ANNUAL PRODUCTION 40,000 bottles
HECTARES UNDER VINE 8.00

● Barbera d'Alba San Quirico '13	❷❷	2*
● Barolo del Comune di Castiglione Falletto '10	❷❷	5
● Nebbiolo d'Alba Piadvenza '12	❷❷	3

Cascina Castlet
S.DA CASTELLETTO, 6
14055 COSTIGLIOLE D'ASTI [AT]
TEL. +39 0141966651
www.cascinacastlet.com

CELLAR SALES
PRE-BOOKED VISITS
ANNUAL PRODUCTION 250,000 bottles
HECTARES UNDER VINE 30.00
SUSTAINABLE WINERY

● Barbera d'Asti '15	❷❷	2*
● Barbera d'Asti Sup. Litina '12	❷❷	4
● Barbera d'Asti Sup. Passum '12	❷❷	5
○ Moscato d'Asti '15	❷	2

Cascina Flino
VIA ABELLONI, 7
12055 DIANO D'ALBA [CN]
TEL. +39 017369231
cascinaflino@gmail.com

CELLAR SALES
PRE-BOOKED VISITS
ACCOMMODATION AND RESTAURANT SERVICE
ANNUAL PRODUCTION 10,000 bottles
HECTARES UNDER VINE 4.00

● Barolo San Lorenzo di Verduno '12	❷❷	5
● Diano di Diano d'Alba Sorì Cascina Flino '15	❷❷	2*
● Nebbiolo d'Alba Sup. '14	❷❷	3

Cascina Galarin Giuseppe Carosso

VIA CAROSSI, 12
14054 CASTAGNOLE DELLE LANZE [AT]
TEL. +39 0141878586
www.galarin.it

CELLAR SALES
ANNUAL PRODUCTION 20,000 bottles
HECTARES UNDER VINE 5.00
VITICULTURE METHOD Certified Organic

● Barbera d'Asti Le Querce '14	♥♥ 2*
○ Moscato d'Asti Prá Dône '15	♥♥ 2*
● Barbera d'Asti Superiore Tinella '13	♥ 5
● M.to Bricco Rorisso '12	♥ 4

Cascina La Maddalena

FRAZ. SAN GIACOMO
LOC. PIANI DEL PADRONE, 257
15078 ROCCA GRIMALDA [AL]
TEL. +39 0143876074
www.cascina-maddalena.com

CELLAR SALES
PRE-BOOKED VISITS
ACCOMMODATION
ANNUAL PRODUCTION 25,000 bottles
HECTARES UNDER VINE 4.00

● Bricco della Maddalena	♥ 5
● Pian del Merlo	♥ 2

Renzo Castella

VIA ALBA, 15
12055 DIANO D'ALBA [CN]
TEL. +39 017369203
renzocastella@virgilio.it

CELLAR SALES
PRE-BOOKED VISITS
ANNUAL PRODUCTION 20,000 bottles
HECTARES UNDER VINE 8.00

● Dolcetto di Diano d'Alba Sorì della Rivolia '15	♥♥ 2*
● Dolcetto di Diano d'Alba '15	♥♥ 2*
● Langhe Nebbiolo Madonnina '14	♥ 2

Castello del Poggio

LOC. POGGIO, 9
14100 PORTACOMARO [AT]
TEL. +39 0141202543
www.poggio.it

CELLAR SALES
PRE-BOOKED VISITS
ANNUAL PRODUCTION 800,000 bottles
HECTARES UNDER VINE 158.00

● Barbera d'Asti '14	♥♥ 2*
● Grignolino d'Asti '15	♥♥ 2*
○ Moscato d'Asti '15	♥♥ 2*
○ Asti	♥ 3

Cavalier Bartolomeo

VIA ALBA BAROLO, 55
12060 CASTIGLIONE FALLETTO [CN]
TEL. +39 017362866
www.cavalierbartolomeo.com

ANNUAL PRODUCTION 15,000 bottles
HECTARES UNDER VINE 3.50

● Barolo San Lorenzo '12	♥♥ 5
● Barolo Altenasso '12	♥♥ 5

Cerutti

VIA CANELLI, 205
14050 CASSINASCO [AT]
TEL. +39 0141851286
www.cascinacerutti.it

CELLAR SALES
PRE-BOOKED VISITS
ANNUAL PRODUCTION 20,000 bottles
HECTARES UNDER VINE 6.00
SUSTAINABLE WINERY

● Barbera d'Asti '15	♥♥ 2*
○ Moscato d'Asti Canelli Surì Sandrinet '15	♥♥ 2*
○ Piemonte Chardonnay Riva Granda '14	♥♥ 3
○ Enrico Cerutti Brut M. Cl.	♥ 3

Franco e Pierguido Ceste

c.so Alfieri, 1
12040 Govone [CN]
Tel. +39 017358635
www.cestevini.com

CELLAR SALES
PRE-BOOKED VISITS
ANNUAL PRODUCTION 180,000 bottles
HECTARES UNDER VINE 20.00

● Barolo '12	♟♟6
● Langhe Rosso Tubleu '13	♟♟3
● Barbaresco '13	♟3

Erede di Armando Chiappone

s.da San Michele, 51
14049 Nizza Monferrato [AT]
Tel. +39 0141721424
www.erededichiappone.com

CELLAR SALES
PRE-BOOKED VISITS
RESTAURANT SERVICE
ANNUAL PRODUCTION 35,000 bottles
HECTARES UNDER VINE 10.00

● Barbera d'Asti Sup. Nizza Ru '11	♟♟4
● Barbera d'Asti Brentura '13	♟♟2*

Il Chiosso

v.le Guglielmo Marconi 45-47a
13045 Gattinara [VC]
Tel. +39 0163826739
www.ilchiosso.it

CELLAR SALES
PRE-BOOKED VISITS
ANNUAL PRODUCTION 80,000 bottles
HECTARES UNDER VINE 12.00

● Gattinara '11	♟♟3
● Gattinara Galizja '11	♟♟5
● Ghemme '10	♟♟3
● Fara '12	♟3

Paride Chiovini

via Giuseppe Garibaldi, 20
28070 Sizzano [NO]
Tel. +39 3394304954
www.paridechiovini.it

CELLAR SALES
PRE-BOOKED VISITS
ANNUAL PRODUCTION 10,000 bottles
HECTARES UNDER VINE 3.00

● Ghemme '12	♟♟4
● Sizzano '11	♟♟4
● Colline Novaresi Uva Rara '15	♟3
● Colline Novaresi Vespolina Afrodite '15	♟2

Ciabot Berton

fraz. Santa Maria, 1
12064 La Morra [CN]
Tel. +39 017350217
www.ciabotberton.it

CELLAR SALES
PRE-BOOKED VISITS
ANNUAL PRODUCTION 55,000 bottles
HECTARES UNDER VINE 12.00

● Barolo del Comune di La Morra '12	♟♟5
● Barolo Rocchettevino '11	♟♟6
● Barolo Rocchettevino Ris. '10	♟♟8
● Barolo Roggeri '11	♟6

Cantina Clavesana

fraz. Madonna della Neve, 19
12060 Clavesana [CN]
Tel. +39 0173790451
www.inclavesana.it

CELLAR SALES
PRE-BOOKED VISITS
ANNUAL PRODUCTION 3,400,000 bottles
HECTARES UNDER VINE 520.00
SUSTAINABLE WINERY

● Barbera d'Alba Sup. Era '13	♟♟3
● Dogliani '15	♟♟2*
● Dogliani Sup. 110 '13	♟♟3
● Langhe Pinot Nero '14	♟♟3

Aldo Clerico

Loc. Manzoni, 69
12065 Monforte d'Alba [CN]
Tel. +39 017378509
www.aldoclerico.it

CELLAR SALES
PRE-BOOKED VISITS
ANNUAL PRODUCTION 30,000 bottles
HECTARES UNDER VINE 7.00

● Barolo '12	♟♟ 6
● Dolcetto d'Alba '15	♟♟ 2*
● Langhe Nebbiolo '14	♟♟ 3
● Barbera d'Alba '15	♟ 3

Col dei Venti

via La Serra, 38
14049 Vaglio Serra [AT]
Tel. +39 0141793071
www.coldeiventi.com

PRE-BOOKED VISITS
ANNUAL PRODUCTION 30,000 bottles
HECTARES UNDER VINE 10.00

● Barbaresco Túfoblu '13	♟♟ 6
● Barbera d'Asti '15	♟♟ 2*
● Barbera d'Asti Sup. '11	♟♟ 3
● Barolo Debútto '12	♟♟ 6

Collina Serragrilli

via Serragrilli, 30
12052 Neive [CN]
Tel. +39 0173677010
www.serragrilli.it

CELLAR SALES
PRE-BOOKED VISITS
ANNUAL PRODUCTION 100,000 bottles
HECTARES UNDER VINE 15.00

● Barbaresco Serragrilli '13	♟♟ 5
● Barbaresco Starderi '13	♟♟ 7
○ Langhe Grillobianco '15	♟ 2
● Langhe Grillorosso '13	♟ 3

Colombera & Garella

via Cascina Cottignano, 2
13866 Masserano [BI]
Tel. +39 01596967
colomberaegarella@gmail.com

CELLAR SALES
PRE-BOOKED VISITS
ANNUAL PRODUCTION 30,000 bottles
HECTARES UNDER VINE 9.00

● Bramaterra Cascina Cottignano '12	♟♟ 4
● Lessona Pizzaguerra '12	♟♟ 4
● Costa della Sesia Rosato	
Cascina Cottignano '13	♟ 4

Colombo - Cascina Pastori

reg. Cafra, 172b
14051 Bubbio [AT]
Tel. +39 0144852807
www.colombovino.it

CELLAR SALES
PRE-BOOKED VISITS
ANNUAL PRODUCTION 40,000 bottles
HECTARES UNDER VINE 10.00
SUSTAINABLE WINERY

○ Piemonte Chardonnay Spumante	
Blanc de Blancs Andrè M. Cl. '12	♟♟ 5
● Piemonte Pinot Nero Apertura '13	♟♟ 3
⊙ Alta Langa Brut Rosé Silvì Ris. '11	♟ 5

Contratto

via G. B. Giuliani, 56
14053 Canelli [AT]
Tel. +39 0141823349
www.contratto.it

CELLAR SALES
PRE-BOOKED VISITS
ANNUAL PRODUCTION 140,000 bottles
HECTARES UNDER VINE 21.00

○ For England Pas Dosé Blanc de Noirs '11	♟♟ 6
○ For England Pas Dosé Rosé M. Cl. '11	♟♟ 6
○ Millesimato Extra Brut M. Cl. '11	♟ 5

Cuvage

Stradale Alessandria, 90
15011 Acqui Terme [AL]
Tel. +39 0144371600
www.cuvage.com

ANNUAL PRODUCTION 80,000 bottles
HECTARES UNDER VINE 200.00

○ Brut Blanc de Blancs M. Cl.	♥♥ 3
⊙ Brut Rosé M. Cl.	♥ 3
○ Pas Dosé Cuvage de Cuvage M. Cl.	♥ 3

Dacapo

s.da Asti Mare, 4
14041 Agliano Terme [AT]
Tel. +39 0141964921
www.dacapo.it

CELLAR SALES
PRE-BOOKED VISITS
ANNUAL PRODUCTION 50,000 bottles
HECTARES UNDER VINE 8.50
VITICULTURE METHOD Certified Organic

● Barbera d'Asti Sup. Valrionda '13	♥♥ 3
● Ruchè di Castagnole M.to Majoli '15	♥♥ 2
● Barbera d'Asti Sanbastiàn '14	♥ 2
● Piemonte Pinot Nero Cantacucco '13	♥ 5

Giovanni Daglio

via Montale Celli, 10
15050 Costa Vescovato [AL]
Tel. +39 0131838262
www.vignetidaglio.com

CELLAR SALES
ANNUAL PRODUCTION 15,000 bottles
HECTARES UNDER VINE 10.00

○ Colli Tortonesi Timorasso Derthona Cantico '14	♥♥ 4
● Colli Tortonesi Barbera Pias '14	♥♥ 2*

F.lli Facchino

loc. Val del Prato, 210
15078 Rocca Grimalda [AL]
Tel. +39 014385401
www.vinifacchino.it

CELLAR SALES
PRE-BOOKED VISITS
ANNUAL PRODUCTION 60,000 bottles
HECTARES UNDER VINE 17.00

● Dolcetto di Ovada Poggiobello '14	♥♥ 2*
● M.to Rosso Note d'Autunno '11	♥♥ 3
● Barbera del M.to Terre del Re '13	♥ 2

Fabio Fidanza

via Rodotiglia, 55
14052 Calosso [AT]
Tel. +39 0141826921
a.a.fidanza@gmail.com

CELLAR SALES
PRE-BOOKED VISITS
ANNUAL PRODUCTION 20,000 bottles
HECTARES UNDER VINE 10.00

● M.to Rosso Que Duàn '14	♥♥ 3
○ Moscato d'Asti '15	♥♥ 2*
● Barbera d'Asti '14	♥ 2
● Barbera d'Asti Sup. Sterlino '14	♥ 4

Forteto della Luja

reg. Candelette, 4
14051 Loazzolo [AT]
Tel. +39 014487197
www.fortetodellaluja.it

CELLAR SALES
PRE-BOOKED VISITS
ANNUAL PRODUCTION 50,000 bottles
HECTARES UNDER VINE 11.00
VITICULTURE METHOD Certified Organic

○ Loazzolo V. T. Piasa Rischei '12	♥♥ 6
● Piemonte Brachetto Passito Pian dei Sogni '13	♥♥ 5
● Barbera d'Asti Mon Ross '15	♥ 2

La Fusina

B.GO SANTA LUCIA, 33
12063 DOGLIANI [CN]
TEL. +39 017370488
www.lafusina.com

CELLAR SALES
PRE-BOOKED VISITS
ANNUAL PRODUCTION 80,000 bottles
HECTARES UNDER VINE 20.00
SUSTAINABLE WINERY

● Barbera d'Alba '15	♟♟ 3
● Barolo '12	♟♟ 5
● Dogliani Sup. Cavagnè '14	♟♟ 3
○ Langhe Chardonnay '15	♟ 2

Garesio

LOC. SORDO, 1
12050 SERRALUNGA D'ALBA [CN]
TEL. +39 3667076775
www.garesiovini.it

ANNUAL PRODUCTION 11,000 bottles
HECTARES UNDER VINE 5.80

● Barbera d'Asti Superiore Nizza '13	♟♟ 4

Cantine Garrone

VIA SCAPACCIANO, 36
28845 DOMODOSSOLA [VB]
TEL. +39 0324242990
www.cantinegarrone.it

CELLAR SALES
PRE-BOOKED VISITS
ANNUAL PRODUCTION 50,000 bottles
HECTARES UNDER VINE 10.00

● Valli Ossane Rosso Cà d'Maté '13	♟♟ 3
● Valli Ossolane Nebbiolo Sup. Prünent '13	♟♟ 4
● Valli Ossolane Rosso Tarlàp '14	♟ 2

La Giribaldina

FRAZ. SAN VITO, 39
14042 CALAMANDRANA [AT]
TEL. +39 0141718043
www.giribaldina.com

CELLAR SALES
PRE-BOOKED VISITS
ACCOMMODATION
ANNUAL PRODUCTION 70,000 bottles
HECTARES UNDER VINE 11.00

● Barbera d'Asti Sup. Vign. della Val Sarmassa '14	♟♟ 3
● Barbera d'Asti Sup. Nizza Cala delle Mandrie '13	♟ 4

Tenuta L'Illuminata

LOC. SANT'ANNA, 30
12064 LA MORRA [CN]
TEL. +39 0302279601
www.lilluminata.it

CELLAR SALES
PRE-BOOKED VISITS
ACCOMMODATION
ANNUAL PRODUCTION 47,000 bottles
HECTARES UNDER VINE 11.00
SUSTAINABLE WINERY

● Barbera d'Alba Colbertina '13	♟♟ 3
● Barolo Tebavio '12	♟♟ 6
● Dolcetto d'Alba Savincato '15	♟♟ 3

Lagobava

CA' BERGANTINO, 5
15049 VIGNALE MONFERRATO [AL]
TEL. +39 3476900656
www.lagobava.it

CELLAR SALES
PRE-BOOKED VISITS
ANNUAL PRODUCTION 12,000 bottles
HECTARES UNDER VINE 5.00
VITICULTURE METHOD Certified Organic

● L'Ago '10	♟♟ 5
● M.to Rosso '09	♟♟ 6
● Piemonte Barbera '14	♟♟ 3
● M.to Rosso L'Amo '13	♟ 4

Maccagno

VIA BONORA, 29
12043 CANALE [CN]
TEL. +39 0173979438
www.cantinamaccagno.it

CELLAR SALES
PRE-BOOKED VISITS
ANNUAL PRODUCTION 50,000 bottles
HECTARES UNDER VINE 10.00

● Barbera d'Alba Sup. Arcalè '13	▼▼	3
○ Maccagno Brut M. Cl.	▼▼	3
○ Roero Arneis Excellence by Nikki '14	▼▼	3
● Roero S. Michele '12	▼▼	3

Tenuta La Marchesa

VIA GAVI, 87
15067 NOVI LIGURE [AL]
TEL. +39 0143743362
www.tenutalamarchesa.it

CELLAR SALES
PRE-BOOKED VISITS
ACCOMMODATION AND RESTAURANT SERVICE
ANNUAL PRODUCTION 250,000 bottles
HECTARES UNDER VINE 56.45

○ Gavi Etichetta Bianca '15	▼▼	2*
○ Gavi Etichetta Oro '15	▼▼	3

Marenco

P.ZZA VITTORIO EMANUELE II, 10
15019 STREVI [AL]
TEL. +39 0144363133
www.marencovini.com

CELLAR SALES
PRE-BOOKED VISITS
ACCOMMODATION
ANNUAL PRODUCTION 250,000 bottles
HECTARES UNDER VINE 80.00
SUSTAINABLE WINERY

● Brachetto d'Acqui Pineto '15	▼▼	3
○ Moscato d'Asti Scrapona '15	▼▼	3
○ Strevi Passri' di Scrapona '09	▼▼	6
● Dolcetto d'Acqui Marchesa '15	▼	3

Le Marie

VIA SAN DEFENDENTE, 6
12032 BARGE [CN]
TEL. +39 0175345159
www.lemarievini.eu

CELLAR SALES
PRE-BOOKED VISITS
RESTAURANT SERVICE
ANNUAL PRODUCTION 24,000 bottles
HECTARES UNDER VINE 8.00

○ Blanc de Lissart	▼▼	2*
⊙ Le Marie Pas Dosé Rosato M. Cl.	▼▼	3
● Pinerolese Barbera Colombe '13	▼▼	3
● Pinerolese Rosso Debárges '13	▼▼	3

La Masera

S.DA SAN PIETRO, 32
10010 PIVERONE [TO]
TEL. +39 0113164161
www.lamasera.it

CELLAR SALES
PRE-BOOKED VISITS
ANNUAL PRODUCTION 18,000 bottles
HECTARES UNDER VINE 5.00
SUSTAINABLE WINERY

○ Erbaluce di Caluso Anima '15	▼▼	2*
○ Erbaluce di Caluso Brut Masile M. Cl.	▼▼	4
○ Erbaluce di Caluso Macaria '14	▼▼	3
● Canavese Barbera Monte Gerbido '14	▼	2

Tenuta La Meridiana

FRAZ. TANA BASSA
VIA TANA BASSA, 5
14048 MONTEGROSSO D'ASTI [AT]
TEL. +39 0141956172
www.tenutalameridiana.com

CELLAR SALES
PRE-BOOKED VISITS
ANNUAL PRODUCTION 80,000 bottles
HECTARES UNDER VINE 10.00
VITICULTURE METHOD Certified Organic
SUSTAINABLE WINERY

● Barbera d'Asti Sup. Bricco Sereno '13	▼▼	4
● Barbera d'Asti Sup. Tra La Terra e Il Cielo '12	▼▼	4
○ Joaçaba Brut M. Cl.	▼▼	5

F.lli Monchiero

VIA ALBA-MONFORTE, 49
12060 CASTIGLIONE FALLETTO [CN]
TEL. +39 017362820
www.monchierovini.it

CELLAR SALES
PRE-BOOKED VISITS
ANNUAL PRODUCTION 40,000 bottles
HECTARES UNDER VINE 12.00

● Barolo Montanello Ris. '10	▼▼ 5
● Barolo Rocche di Castiglione Falletto '12	▼▼ 5
○ Langhe Arneis '15	▼ 2

Franco Mondo

REG. MARIANO, 33
14050 SAN MARZANO OLIVETO [AT]
TEL. +39 0141834096
www.francomondo.net

CELLAR SALES
PRE-BOOKED VISITS
ANNUAL PRODUCTION 75,000 bottles
HECTARES UNDER VINE 13.00

● Barbera d'Asti '15	▼▼ 2*
● Barbera d'Asti Sup. Il Salice '13	▼▼ 3
● Barbera d'Asti Sup. Nizza Le Rose '11	▼ 5
● M.to Rosso Di.Vino '13	▼ 3

Mongioia

FRAZ. VALDIVILLA, 40
12058 SANTO STEFANO BELBO [CN]
TEL. +39 0141847301
www.mongioia.com

ANNUAL PRODUCTION 40,000 bottles
HECTARES UNDER VINE 10.00

○ Meramentae Brut '14	▼▼ 5
○ Moscato d'Asti Belb '15	▼▼ 3
○ Moscato d'Asti Crivella '11	▼▼ 6
○ Moscato d'Asti La Moscata '15	▼ 3

La Montagnetta

FRAZ. BRICCO CAPPELLO, 4
14018 ROATTO [AT]
TEL. +39 0141938343
www.lamontagnetta.com

HECTARES UNDER VINE 10.00

● Barbera d'Asti Sup. Piovà '13	▼▼ 4
● Freisa d'Asti Bugianen '15	▼▼ 2*
● Piemonte Bonarda Frizzante Insopita '15	▼▼ 2*
● Barbera d'Asti Pi-Cit '15	▼ 2

Morgassi Superiore

CASE SPARSE SERMORIA, 7
15066 GAVI [AL]
TEL. +39 0143642007
www.morgassisuperiore.it

CELLAR SALES
PRE-BOOKED VISITS
ANNUAL PRODUCTION 130,000 bottles
HECTARES UNDER VINE 20.00

○ Gavi del Comune di Gavi Tuffo '15	▼▼ 3
○ M.to Bianco Timorgasso '13	▼▼ 4
○ Gavi del Comune di Gavi Volo '14	▼ 4

Diego Morra

VIA CASCINA MOSCA, 37
12060 VERDUNO [CN]
TEL. +39 3284623209
www.verdunopelaverga.it

CELLAR SALES
PRE-BOOKED VISITS
ANNUAL PRODUCTION 15,000 bottles
HECTARES UNDER VINE 30.00

● Barolo '11	▼▼ 6
○ Chardonnay '15	▼▼ 3
● Verduno Pelaverga '15	▼ 4

Ada Nada

LOC. ROMBONE
VIA AUSARIO, 12
12050 TREISO [CN]
TEL. +39 0173638127
www.adanada.it

CELLAR SALES
PRE-BOOKED VISITS
ACCOMMODATION AND RESTAURANT SERVICE
ANNUAL PRODUCTION 45,000 bottles
HECTARES UNDER VINE 9.00

● Barbera d'Alba Pierin '15	♆♆	3
○ Langhe Sauvignon Neta '15	♆	2

Giuseppe Negro

VIA GALLINA, 22
12052 NEIVE [CN]
TEL. +39 0173677468
www.negrogiuseppe.com

CELLAR SALES
PRE-BOOKED VISITS
ANNUAL PRODUCTION 55,000 bottles
HECTARES UNDER VINE 9.00

● Barbaresco Gallina '13	♆♆	6
● Barbaresco PianCavallo '13	♆♆	6
⊙ Langhe Rosato Monsù '15	♆♆	3

Cantina Sociale di Nizza

S.DA ALESSANDRIA, 57
14049 NIZZA MONFERRATO [AT]
TEL. +39 0141721348
www.nizza.it

CELLAR SALES
PRE-BOOKED VISITS
ANNUAL PRODUCTION 200,000 bottles
HECTARES UNDER VINE 560.00
VITICULTURE METHOD Certified Organic
SUSTAINABLE WINERY

● Barbera d'Asti Le Pole '15	♆♆	2*
● Barbera d'Asti Sup. Magister '14	♆♆	2*
● Barbera d'Asti Sup. Nizza Ceppi Vecchi '14	♆♆	4
● Piemonte Barbera Progetto in Origine '15	♆♆	2*

Silvano Nizza

FRAZ. BALLA LORA 29A
12040 SANTO STEFANO ROERO [CN]
TEL. +39 017390516
www.nizzasilvano.com

CELLAR SALES
PRE-BOOKED VISITS
ANNUAL PRODUCTION 65,000 bottles
HECTARES UNDER VINE 8.00

● Barbera d'Alba Sup. '14	♆♆	4
● Roero '13	♆♆	5
○ Roero Arneis '15	♆	3

Pace

FRAZ. MADONNA DI LORETO
CASCINA PACE, 52
12043 CANALE [CN]
TEL. +39 0173979544
dinonegropace@gmail.com

CELLAR SALES
PRE-BOOKED VISITS
ANNUAL PRODUCTION 60,000 bottles
HECTARES UNDER VINE 22.00

● Roero '13	♆♆	3
● Roero Ris. '12	♆♆	5
● Barbera d'Alba '14	♆	2
○ Roero Arneis '15	♆	2

Agostino Pavia e Figli

FRAZ. BOLOGNA, 33
14041 AGLIANO TERME [AT]
TEL. +39 0141954125
www.agostinopavia.it

CELLAR SALES
PRE-BOOKED VISITS
ACCOMMODATION
ANNUAL PRODUCTION 75,000 bottles
HECTARES UNDER VINE 9.00

● Barbera d'Asti Sup. Moliss '13	♆♆	3
● Barbera d'Asti Casareggio '15	♆	2
● Grignolino d'Asti '15	♆	2

Magda Pedrini

VIA PRATOLUNGO, 163
15066 GAVI [AL]
TEL. +39 0143667923
www.magdapedrini.it

CELLAR SALES
PRE-BOOKED VISITS
ANNUAL PRODUCTION 90,000 bottles
HECTARES UNDER VINE 10.50
SUSTAINABLE WINERY

○ Gavi del Comune di Gavi Domino '14	♥♥	4
○ Gavi del Comune di Gavi E' '15	♥♥	3
○ Gavi del Comune di Gavi La Piacentina '15	♥♥	3

Pelassa

B.GO TUCCI, 43
12046 MONTÀ [CN]
TEL. +39 0173971312
www.pelassa.com

CELLAR SALES
ANNUAL PRODUCTION 80,000 bottles
HECTARES UNDER VINE 14.00

● Barolo '12	♥♥	6
● Barolo Bussia '11	♥♥	6
● Roero Antaniolo Ris. '12	♥♥	4
● Barbera d'Alba Sup. San Pancrazio '14	♥	3

Pasquale Pelissero

CASCINA CROSA, 2
12052 NEIVE [CN]
TEL. +39 017367376
www.pasqualepelissero.com

CELLAR SALES
PRE-BOOKED VISITS
ANNUAL PRODUCTION 35,000 bottles
HECTARES UNDER VINE 8.00

● Barbaresco Cascina Crosa '13	♥♥	4
● Barbaresco San Giuliano Bricco '13	♥♥	5

Elio Perrone

S.DA SAN MARTINO, 3BIS
12053 CASTIGLIONE TINELLA [CN]
TEL. +39 0141855803
www.elioperrone.it

CELLAR SALES
PRE-BOOKED VISITS
ANNUAL PRODUCTION 200,000 bottles
HECTARES UNDER VINE 14.00
SUSTAINABLE WINERY

● Barbera d'Asti Sup. Mongovone '14	♥♥	5
● Barbera d'Asti Tasmorcan '15	♥	2
○ Moscato d'Asti Sourgal '15	♥	2

Guido Platinetti

VIA ROMA, 60
28074 GHEMME [NO]
TEL. +39 3389945783
platinettivini.com

CELLAR SALES
PRE-BOOKED VISITS
ANNUAL PRODUCTION 15,000 bottles
HECTARES UNDER VINE 5.50

● Colline Novaresi Nebbiolo '14	♥♥	3
● Colline Novaresi Vespolina '15	♥	2
● Ghemme V. Ronco Maso '11	♥	4

Poderi ai Valloni

VIA DELLA TRAVERSAGNA, 1
28010 BOCA [NO]
TEL. +39 032287332
www.podereaivalloni.it

CELLAR SALES
PRE-BOOKED VISITS
ANNUAL PRODUCTION 5,000 bottles
HECTARES UNDER VINE 3.00
SUSTAINABLE WINERY

● Boca V. Cristiana '10	♥♥	6
● Colline Novaresi Nebbiolo Gratus '14	♥	3

Paolo Giuseppe Poggio

VIA ROMA, 67
15050 BRIGNANO FRASCATA [AL]
TEL. +39 0131784929
www.cantinapoggio.com

CELLAR SALES
PRE-BOOKED VISITS
ANNUAL PRODUCTION 18,000 bottles
HECTARES UNDER VINE 3.50

○ Colli Tortonesi Timorasso Derthona Ronchetto '14	♟♟ 2*
○ Campogallo '15	♟ 1*
● Colli Tortonesi Barbera Campo La Bà '14	♟ 2

Pomodolce

VIA IV NOVEMBRE, 7
15050 MONTEMARZINO [AL]
TEL. +39 0131878135
www.pomodolce.it

CELLAR SALES
PRE-BOOKED VISITS
RESTAURANT SERVICE
ANNUAL PRODUCTION 14,000 bottles
HECTARES UNDER VINE 4.00
VITICULTURE METHOD Certified Organic

● Colli Tortonesi Monleale Marsen '13	♟♟ 4
○ Colli Tortonesi Timorasso Diletto '14	♟ 3

Punset

VIA ZOCCO, 2
12052 NEIVE [CN]
TEL. +39 017367072
www.punset.com

CELLAR SALES
PRE-BOOKED VISITS
ACCOMMODATION
ANNUAL PRODUCTION 100,000 bottles
HECTARES UNDER VINE 17.00
VITICULTURE METHOD Certified Organic

● Barbaresco Basarin Ris. '11	♟♟ 5
● Barbaresco San Cristoforo Campo Quadro '09	♟♟ 6

Gianmatteo Raineri

LOC. PANEROLE, 24
12060 NOVELLO [CN]
TEL. +39 3396009289
www.rainerivini.com

CELLAR SALES
PRE-BOOKED VISITS
ANNUAL PRODUCTION 20,000 bottles
HECTARES UNDER VINE 3.30
SUSTAINABLE WINERY

● Barbera d'Alba Sagrin '14	♟♟ 3
● Barolo Monserra '12	♟♟ 8
● Langhe Nebbiolo Snart '14	♟♟ 4
● Dogliani Cornole '15	♟ 3

Réva

LOC. SAN SEBASTIANO, 68
12065 MONFORTE D'ALBA [CN]
TEL. +39 0173789269
www.revamonforte.it

CELLAR SALES
PRE-BOOKED VISITS
ACCOMMODATION AND RESTAURANT SERVICE
ANNUAL PRODUCTION 35,000 bottles
HECTARES UNDER VINE 8.00
SUSTAINABLE WINERY

● Barolo '12	♟♟ 5
● Barolo Ravera '12	♟♟ 7
○ Langhe Sauvignon '15	♟ 3

Carlo Daniele Ricci

VIA MONTALE CELLI, 9
15050 COSTA VESCOVATO [AL]
TEL. +39 0131838115
www.aziendaagricolaricci.com

CELLAR SALES
PRE-BOOKED VISITS
ACCOMMODATION AND RESTAURANT SERVICE
ANNUAL PRODUCTION 40,000 bottles
HECTARES UNDER VINE 8.00

● Castellania	♟♟ 3
○ Il Giallo di Costa	♟♟ 4

Pietro Rinaldi

FRAZ. MADONNA DI COMO
12051 ALBA [CN]
TEL. +39 0173360090
www.pietrorinaldi.com

CELLAR SALES
PRE-BOOKED VISITS
ACCOMMODATION
ANNUAL PRODUCTION 70,000 bottles
HECTARES UNDER VINE 10.00

● Barbaresco San Cristoforo '13	🍷🍷 5
● Barolo Monvigliero '12	🍷🍷 6
● Langhe Nebbiolo Argante '13	🍷🍷 4
○ Langhe Arneis Hortensia '15	🍷 2

Silvia Rivella

LOC. MONTESTEFANO, 17
12050 BARBARESCO [CN]
TEL. +39 0173635040
www.agriturismorivella.it

CELLAR SALES
ACCOMMODATION AND RESTAURANT SERVICE
ANNUAL PRODUCTION 7,000 bottles
HECTARES UNDER VINE 1.50

● Barbaresco '13	🍷🍷 6
● Barbaresco Montestefano '13	🍷🍷 7

Rivetto

LOC. LIRANO, 2
12050 SINIO [CN]
TEL. +39 0173613380
www.rivetto.it

CELLAR SALES
PRE-BOOKED VISITS
ACCOMMODATION
ANNUAL PRODUCTION 100,000 bottles
HECTARES UNDER VINE 20.00

● Barolo Leon Ris. '10	🍷🍷 8
● Barbera d'Alba Zio Nando '13	🍷 5

Rossi Contini

S.DA SAN LORENZO, 20
15076 OVADA [AL]
TEL. +39 0143822530
www.rossicontini.com

CELLAR SALES
PRE-BOOKED VISITS
ANNUAL PRODUCTION 17,000 bottles
HECTARES UNDER VINE 4.50
SUSTAINABLE WINERY

● Barbera del M.to Sup. Cras Tibi '13	🍷🍷 3
○ Cortese dell'Alto M.to Cortesia '15	🍷 2
● Ovada Viign. Ninan '14	🍷 4

Sant'Anna dei Bricchetti

S.DA DEI BRICCHETTI, 11
14055 COSTIGLIOLE D'ASTI [AT]
TEL. +39 3484420363
www.santanna-dei-bricchetti.it

HECTARES UNDER VINE 5.00

● Barbera d'Asti Ricordi '14	🍷🍷 3
● Barbera d'Asti Sup. Bricchetti '13	🍷🍷 4
○ Moscato d'Asti '15	🍷 3

Tenuta Santa Caterina

VIA GUGLIELMO MARCONI, 17
14035 GRAZZANO BADOGLIO [AT]
TEL. +39 0141925108
www.tenuta-santa-caterina.it

ANNUAL PRODUCTION 50,000 bottles
HECTARES UNDER VINE 23.00

● Barbera d'Asti Sup. Setecàpita '12	🍷🍷 3
● Barbera d'Asti Sup. V. Lina '13	🍷🍷 3
● Freisa d'Asti Sorì di Giul '12	🍷🍷 3
● Grignolino d'Asti Arlandino '14	🍷 2

Giacomo Scagliola

REG. SANTA LIBERA, 20
14053 CANELLI [AT]
TEL. +39 0141831146
www.scagliola-canelli.it

CELLAR SALES
ANNUAL PRODUCTION 80,000 bottles
HECTARES UNDER VINE 15.00

● Barbera d'Asti Sup. Bric dei Mandorli '13	♀♀	3*
○ Moscato d'Asti Canelli Sifasol '15	♀♀	2*
● Barbera d'Asti '14	♀	2
● Barbera d'Asti Sup. La Faia '14	♀	2

Simone Scaletta

LOC. MANZONI, 61
12065 MONFORTE D'ALBA [CN]
TEL. +39 3484912733
www.simonescaletta.it

CELLAR SALES
PRE-BOOKED VISITS
ACCOMMODATION
ANNUAL PRODUCTION 20,000 bottles
HECTARES UNDER VINE 4.75

● Barolo Bricco San Pietro Chirlet '12	♀♀	6
● Dolcetto d'Alba Viglioni '15	♀	2
● Langhe Nebbiolo Autin 'd Madama '14	♀	3

Segni di Langa

LOC. RAVINALI, 25
12060 RODDI [CN]
TEL. +39 3803945151
www.segnidilanga.it

CELLAR SALES
PRE-BOOKED VISITS
ACCOMMODATION
ANNUAL PRODUCTION 6,000 bottles
HECTARES UNDER VINE 0.90
SUSTAINABLE WINERY

● Barbera d'Alba Greta '15	♀♀	4
● Langhe Pinot Nero '15	♀♀	4

Aurelio Settimo

FRAZ. ANNUNZIATA, 30
12064 LA MORRA [CN]
TEL. +39 017350803
www.aureliosettimo.com

CELLAR SALES
PRE-BOOKED VISITS
ANNUAL PRODUCTION 40,000 bottles
HECTARES UNDER VINE 6.64

● Barolo Rocche dell'Annunziata '12	♀♀	6
● Barolo '12	♀	5

Poderi Sinaglio

FRAZ. RICCA
VIA SINAGLIO, 5
12055 DIANO D'ALBA [CN]
TEL. +39 0173612209
www.poderisinaglio.it

CELLAR SALES
PRE-BOOKED VISITS
ACCOMMODATION
ANNUAL PRODUCTION 35,000 bottles
HECTARES UNDER VINE 13.00

● Dolcetto di Diano d'Alba Sorì Bric Maiolica '15	♀♀	2*
● Nebbiolo d'Alba Giachet '14	♀♀	3
● Barbera d'Alba Erta '14	♀	3

Sobrero Francesco

VIA PUGNANE, 5
12060 CASTIGLIONE FALLETTO [CN]
TEL. +39 017362864
www.sobrerofrancesco.it

CELLAR SALES
PRE-BOOKED VISITS
ACCOMMODATION
ANNUAL PRODUCTION 90,000 bottles
HECTARES UNDER VINE 16.00

● Barolo Ciabot Tanasio '12	♀♀	6
● Barolo Pernanno Ris. '10	♀♀	7
● Barbera d'Alba La Pichetera '13	♀	3

La Spinosa Alta

c.ne Cascina Spinosa Alta, 8
15038 Ottiglio [AL]
Tel. +39 0142921372
www.laspinosaalta.it

CELLAR SALES
PRE-BOOKED VISITS
ACCOMMODATION
ANNUAL PRODUCTION 12,000 bottles
HECTARES UNDER VINE 3.00

● Barbera del M.to Sup. La Punta '11	♟♟ 3
○ Solstizio	♟♟ 3
● Grignolino del M.to Casalese '14	♟ 2

Tenuta Cucco

loc. Cucco
via Mazzini, 10
12050 Serralunga d'Alba [CN]
Tel. +39 0173613003
www.tenutacucco.it

CELLAR SALES
PRE-BOOKED VISITS
ANNUAL PRODUCTION 70,000 bottles
HECTARES UNDER VINE 12.50

● Barolo Cerrati V. Cucco Ris. '10	♟♟ 8
● Barolo Cerrati '12	♟♟ 7
● Barolo del Comune di Serralunga d'Alba '12	♟♟ 6

La Toledana

loc. Sermoira, 5
15066 Gavi [AL]
Tel. +39 0141837287
www.latoledana.it

CELLAR SALES
PRE-BOOKED VISITS
ANNUAL PRODUCTION 145,000 bottles
HECTARES UNDER VINE 28.00

● Barolo Ravera Lo Zoccolaio '11	♟♟ 7
○ Gavi del Comune di Gavi La Toledana '15	♟♟ 5

La Torretta

s.da prov.le per Cavaglio, 10
28074 Ghemme [NO]
Tel. +39 0163840764
www.latorrettavinighemme.it

CELLAR SALES
PRE-BOOKED VISITS
ANNUAL PRODUCTION 15,000 bottles
HECTARES UNDER VINE 5.00

● Ghemme Il Motto '09	♟♟ 6
● Colline Novaresi Rosso Il Tordo '10	♟ 3

Tre Secoli

via Stazione, 15
14046 Mombaruzzo [AT]
Tel. +39 014177019
www.tresecoli.com

CELLAR SALES
PRE-BOOKED VISITS
ANNUAL PRODUCTION 400,000 bottles
HECTARES UNDER VINE 1200.00
VITICULTURE METHOD Certified Organic

● Barbera d'Asti San Pietro '15	♟♟ 2*
● Barbera d'Asti Sup. Nizza '13	♟♟ 4
● Barbera d'Asti Sup. Sorangela '13	♟♟ 3
● Piemonte Rosso Decoro '13	♟ 5

Trediberri

b.ta Torriglione, 4
12064 La Morra [CN]
Tel. +39 3391605470
www.trediberri.com

CELLAR SALES
PRE-BOOKED VISITS
ANNUAL PRODUCTION 35,000 bottles
HECTARES UNDER VINE 8.00
VITICULTURE METHOD Certified Organic

● Barolo '12	♟♟ 5
● Barolo Rocche dell'Annunziata '12	♟♟ 7
● Langhe Nebbiolo '15	♟♟ 2*
● Barbera d'Alba '15	♟ 3

F.lli Trinchero

VIA GORRA, 49
14048 MONTEGROSSO D'ASTI [AT]
TEL. +39 0141956167
www.fllitrincherovino.com

CELLAR SALES
PRE-BOOKED VISITS
ANNUAL PRODUCTION 50,000 bottles
HECTARES UNDER VINE 12.00

● Barbera d'Asti La Trincherina '15	♥♥ 2*
● Barbera d'Asti Sup. Rico '12	♥ 3

Poderi Vaiot

BORGATA LAIONE, 43
12046 MONTÀ [CN]
TEL. +39 0173976283
www.poderivaiot.it

ANNUAL PRODUCTION 25,000 bottles
HECTARES UNDER VINE 4.00

● Nebbiolo d'Alba '14	♥♥ 3
○ Roero Arneis '15	♥♥ 2*
● Barbera d'Alba Lupestre '14	♥ 2

Valfaccenda

FRAZ. MADONNA LORETO
LOC. VAL FACCENDA, 43
12043 CANALE [CN]
TEL. +39 3397303837
www.valfaccenda.it

CELLAR SALES
PRE-BOOKED VISITS
ANNUAL PRODUCTION 16,000 bottles
HECTARES UNDER VINE 3.00
SUSTAINABLE WINERY

● Roero '14	♥♥ 4
● Vindabeive '15	♥♥ 3
○ Roero Arneis '15	♥ 3

La Vecchia Posta

VIA MONTEBELLO, 2
15050 AVOLASCA [AL]
TEL. +39 0131876254
www.lavecchiaposta-avolasca.com

CELLAR SALES
PRE-BOOKED VISITS
ACCOMMODATION AND RESTAURANT SERVICE
ANNUAL PRODUCTION 10,000 bottles
HECTARES UNDER VINE 2.70
VITICULTURE METHOD Certified Organic

● Rosso Ciliegio	♥♥ 3
○ Colli Tortonesi Timorasso	
Il Selvaggio '14	♥ 3

Alessandro Veglio

FRAZ. ANNUNZIATA, 53
12064 LA MORRA [CN]
TEL. +39 3385699102
www.risveglioinlanga.it

ANNUAL PRODUCTION 10,000 bottles
HECTARES UNDER VINE 3.00

● Barolo Gattera '12	♥♥ 7
● Barolo '12	♥ 5

Alberto Voerzio

FRAZ. ANNUNZIATA, 103A
12064 LA MORRA [CN]
TEL. +39 3333927654
www.albertovoerzio.com

CELLAR SALES
PRE-BOOKED VISITS
ANNUAL PRODUCTION 12,000 bottles
HECTARES UNDER VINE 5.00

● Barolo '12	♥♥ 6
● Barolo La Serra '12	♥♥ 6

LIGURIA

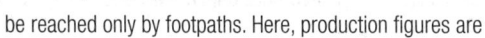

Winemaking Liguria is one of the most fascinating districts of the Italian viticultural scene. It is a region of small wineries, vineyards overlooking the sea, eked from the mountainside, held up by low, drystone walls, terraces that can be reached only by footpaths. Here, production figures are low: 0.4–0.5 percent of all Italian production. Fortunately, there is more to it than simple numbers. In recent years, Liguria's wines have begun to earn themselves a significant place on the wine lists of leading restaurants and in the hearts of aficionados. They are the offspring of wind and sea, of the native grapes that have always characterized this winegrowing. They are wines with extraordinary charm, both the reds and the whites, archetype of a razor-sharp, complex, minerally Mediterranean style, whose distinctive features are full flavour and iodine aromas. This year we gave awards to six wines, almost all from the warm, complicated 2015 vintage, with little rainfall, which endowed structure and alcohol (and we also tend to think ageing potential) to the whites. The only red in there is Terre Bianche's seductive, elegant Dolceacqua Bricco Arcagna 2014. For the rest, as we were saying, there are some great whites: from the east, three Colli di Luni Vermentinos by Lunae Bosoni, Lambruschi and La Baia del Sole, the latter a debutant Tre Bicchieri; from the west, two excellent Pigatos, La Ginestraia's Le Marige, another Tre Bicchieri first-timer, and a tempting Bon in da Bon from the family-run BioVio of Albenga, who is also our Grower of the Year. Overall a fine snapshot of a region that has made preservation of its winemaking heritage and growing areas its main objective. From pigato to vermentino, rossese, ormeasco, bosco, albarola, bianchetta genovese, and lumassina, the list is long, but Ligurian winemakers are very determined. We will be hearing more and more from them in coming years. Small businesses gradually get bigger, new ones open, and the region's wineries also offer farmhouse accommodation and cooking, and sell superb local products alongside wine. A model that is giving new life to this economy, just like other districts where vines are difficult to grow but are part of a landscape of outstanding beauty like Valle d'Aosta, Mount Etna, or the Amalfi Coast.

Massimo Alessandri

VIA COSTA PARROCCHIA, 42
18020 RANZO [IM]
TEL. +39 018253458
www.massimoalessandri.it

CELLAR SALES
PRE-BOOKED VISITS
RESTAURANT SERVICE
ANNUAL PRODUCTION 35,000 bottles
HECTARES UNDER VINE 7.00

Massimo Alessandri continues to invest in his vineyards. The new granaccia plantings in 2015 were part of the plan to produce black grapes which started up a few years ago. In addition, there is a new rossese vineyard of about 4,000m, planted three years ago at Ranzo, at about 400 metres altitude, and new rows of roussanne and viognier will be planted in the coming years to increase the estate's overall production, which focuses on white wines at the moment. Like the Pigato 2015, displaying vivid pale straw-yellow hues and very appealing sunny aromas with vibrant minerally sensations. Also intriguing, the Viorus 2014 has intense acacia and elder flowers on the nose, developing into chamomile, and a well-coordinated flavour culminating in a lingering finish. The Granaccia 2014 also impressed us, with forward hints of wild berries and velvety tannins balancing the flavour.

● Ligustico '13	♥♥ 6
● Riviera Ligure di Ponente Granaccia '14	♥♥ 4
○ Riviera Ligure di Ponente Pigato Costa de Vigne '15	♥♥ 3
● Riviera Ligure di Ponente Rossese '15	♥♥ 2*
○ Viorus Costa de Vigne '14	♥♥ 5
○ Riviera Ligure di Ponente Vermentino Costa de Vigne '15	♥ 3
● Riviera Ligure di Ponente Granaccia '13	♥♥ 4
○ Riviera Ligure di Ponente Pigato Costa de Vigne '14	♥♥ 3
○ Riviera Ligure di Ponente Pigato Costa de Vigne '13	♥♥ 3*
○ Riviera Ligure di Ponente Pigato Vigne Vegie '14	♥♥ 4
○ Viorus '13	♥♥ 5

Laura Aschero

P.ZZA VITTORIO EMANUELE, 7
18027 PONTEDASSIO [IM]
TEL. +39 0183710307
www.lauraaschero.it

CELLAR SALES
PRE-BOOKED VISITS
ANNUAL PRODUCTION 60,000 bottles
HECTARES UNDER VINE 50.00

At last the renovations to the Aschero cellar are complete, and the large vaulted ceilings with exposed brickwork are visible to the increasing numbers of customers and wine tourists. The location is easy to find, below the central square of the small town of Pontedassio, in a 15th-century building. Host Bianca, a marketing graduate who looks after all aspects of the estate, is the daughter of Carla and Marco Rizzo, and grand-daughter of Laura Aschero. As well as the cellar, 2015 saw completion of the long, challenging refurbishment of the drystone walls in the vineyards. With fresh greenish hues glimpsed in the bright, intense colour, Pigato 2015 reveals sunny aromas, and apple and pear fruit developing into hazelnuts. The classic palate is well-balanced, tangy, stylish and harmonious. The Vermentino 2015 is slightly below par, characterful but still lacking balance, with fruity and minerally aromas, and an appealing finish.

○ Riviera Ligure di Ponente Pigato '15	♥♥ 3*
○ Riviera Ligure di Ponente Vermentino '15	♥♥ 3
● Riviera Ligure di Ponente Rossese '15	♥ 3
○ Riviera Ligure di Ponente Vermentino '10	♥♥♥ 3*
○ Riviera Ligure di Ponente Pigato '14	♥♥ 3
○ Riviera Ligure di Ponente Pigato '13	♥♥ 3*
○ Riviera Ligure di Ponente Vermentino '14	♥♥ 3
○ Riviera Ligure di Ponente Vermentino '12	♥♥ 3*

La Baia del Sole - Federici

FRAZ. LUNI ANTICA
VIA FORLINO, 3
19034 ORTONOVO [SP]
TEL. +39 0187661821
www.cantinefederici.com

CELLAR SALES
PRE-BOOKED VISITS
ANNUAL PRODUCTION 150,000 bottles
HECTARES UNDER VINE 25.00

The Federici family's beautiful estate, inaugurated in June 2015, is of a modern design, structurally efficient and technologically advanced but with an eye to the environment and open to wine tourism. Few Ligurian estates can compete. Brothers Andrea and Luca have taken up the reins, the former managing the vineyards and sales; the latter engaged in the winemaking. The company looks to the future with new investments and very high quality. And the results have come: the Sarticola 2015 is a complex, intense wine with hints of rosemary and sage, summer flowers and ripe fruit, sea salt and medicinal herbs. The palate is mouthfilling and structured with bags of personality and assertive character. The Oro d'Isée 2015 is a great wine with natural balance, warm, tangy and minerally, with a satisfying vibrant finish. The characterful Solaris 2015 will be more polished with time.

○ Colli di Luni Vermentino Sarticola '15	♟♟♟ 4*
○ Colli di Luni Vermentino Oro d'Isée '15	♟♟ 4
● Colli di Luni Eutichiano '15	♟♟ 3
○ Colli di Luni Vermentino Gladius '15	♟♟ 2*
○ Colli di Luni Vermentino Solaris '15	♟♟ 3
○ Colli di Luni Gladius '14	♟♟ 2*
● Colli di Luni Terre d'Oriente Ris. '09	♟♟ 5
○ Colli di Luni Vermentino Oro d'Isée '13	♟♟ 3
○ Colli di Luni Vermentino Oro d'Isée '12	♟♟ 4
○ Colli di Luni Vermentino Sarticola '14	♟♟ 4
○ Colli di Luni Vermentino Sarticola '12	♟♟ 5
○ Colli di Luni Vermentino Solaris '14	♟♟ 3*
○ Colli di Luni Vermentino Solaris '13	♟♟ 2*

Maria Donata Bianchi

VIA MEREA, 101
18013 DIANO ARENTINO [IM]
TEL. +39 0183498233
www.aziendaagricolabianchi.it

CELLAR SALES
PRE-BOOKED VISITS
ACCOMMODATION
ANNUAL PRODUCTION 30,000 bottles
HECTARES UNDER VINE 4.00

This stunning estate, owned by Maria Donata and her husband, Emanuele Trevia, is situated in the municipal area of Diano Arentino, halfway to Diano Castello. It has grown and expanded over the years with accommodation and tourism facilities, and a new production cellar. This is where Emanuele works, producing attractive wines with prestigious character. An example is the Antico Sfizio, which undergoes lengthy maceration and spontaneous fermentation, without temperature control. This original product follows the principles of traditional winemaking, and it shows in the glass. The 2015 is an intense colour with golden hues, hints of dried flowers alongside distant nuances of lemon jelly, and beautifully balanced richness and extract on the palate. The young, bright Pigato 2015 displays generous sunny and almondy aromas. Heady alcohol sensations dominate the graceful structure, resolving tidily in a refined finish. The Vermentino 2015 is tangy and minerally with vibrant, mature aromas.

○ Riviera Ligure di Ponente Antico Sfizio '15	♟♟ 4
○ Riviera Ligure di Ponente Pigato '15	♟♟ 3
○ Riviera Ligure di Ponente Vermentino '15	♟♟ 3
○ Riviera Ligure di Ponente Pigato '12	♟♟♟ 3*
○ Riviera Ligure di Ponente Vermentino '09	♟♟♟ 3
○ Riviera Ligure di Ponente Vermentino '07	♟♟♟ 3*
○ Riviera Ligure di Ponente Pigato '14	♟♟ 3*
○ Riviera Ligure di Ponente Pigato '13	♟♟ 3*
○ Riviera Ligure di Ponente Pigato '11	♟♟ 4
○ Riviera Ligure di Ponente Vermentino '14	♟♟ 3
○ Riviera Ligure di Ponente Vermentino '13	♟♟ 3
○ Riviera Ligure di Ponente Vermentino '11	♟♟ 4
○ Riviera Ligure di Ponente Vermentino '10	♟♟ 3

BioVio

FRAZ. BASTIA
VIA CROCIATA, 24
17031 ALBENGA [SV]
TEL. +39 018220776
www.biovio.it

CELLAR SALES
PRE-BOOKED VISITS
ANNUAL PRODUCTION 40,000 bottles
HECTARES UNDER VINE 6.00
VITICULTURE METHOD Certified Organic

Winner of our 2017 Grower of the Year award for Aimone Vio's dedication to his vines over the years. The winery he started with wife Chiara is now run by daughters Caterina, Carolina and Camilla, future of this estate. Each has chosen one aspect of the overall task: the first winemaking, the second reception facilities, and sales for the youngest. The estate is expanding, having started with aromatic herbs, then moving on to wine and oil, it is now offering tourist accommodation with beautiful apartments. The investments are ongoing, with two new vineyards planted to granaccia and rossese in the Vallette area, inland from Albenga. The whites dominate the field, with a really superlative Pigato Bon in da Bon 2015: intense straw-yellow colour with bright hues, aromas of elderflower, medicinal herbs and almonds, and a complex, stylish palate with well-measured fresh, tangy and aromatic components. Not far behind is the Pigato Ma René 2015, with lovely hints of rosemary and thyme and fruity aromas.

○ Riviera Ligure di Ponente Pigato Bon in da Bon '15	♟♟♟ 2*
○ Riviera Ligure di Ponente Pigato Ma René '15	♟♟ 2*
○ Riviera Ligure di Ponente Vermentino Aimone '15	♟♟ 2*
● Granaccia Gigò '15	♟ 3
● Riviera Ligure di Ponente Rossese U Bastiò '15	♟ 2
○ Riviera Ligure di Ponente Vermentino Aimone '11	♟♟♟ 2*
○ Riviera Ligure di Ponente Pigato Albenganese Bon in da Bon '14	♟♟ 2*
○ Riviera Ligure di Ponente Pigato Albenganese Ma René '14	♟♟ 2*
○ Riviera Ligure di Ponente Vermentino Albenganese Aimone '14	♟♟ 2*

Samuele Heydi Bonanini

VIA SAN ANTONIO, 72
19017 RIOMAGGIORE [SP]
TEL. +39 0187920959
www.possa.it

CELLAR SALES
PRE-BOOKED VISITS
ANNUAL PRODUCTION 7,000 bottles
HECTARES UNDER VINE 1.50

The view from the Riomaggiore terraces is undoubtedly one of the most magical natural landscapes in Cinque Terre. Credit goes to a handful of winegrowers who devote themselves to protecting the geomorphological balance with their vineyards. One of these is Samuele Heydi Bonanini, an intrepid farmer who continues to work hard despite the difficulties of this fragile, arduous land, producing characterful wines with a strong identity that offer a perfect reading of the zone of origin. The grapes grown on the estate include albarola, vermentino, bosco, rossese bianco, canaiolo, and other native black grape varieties. Er Jancu 2015 has a wild, engaging personality, whose vintage year is omitted from the label. This is a Cinque Terre white grown at high altitude, and based mainly on albarola grapes, macerated on the skins for several weeks. The Cinque Terre 2015 is less complex and more down-to-earth. The Sciacchetrà 2014 is less flavoursome than usual but pleasantly botrytized.

○ Er Jancu '15	♟♟ 4
● U Neigru	♟♟ 5
○ Cinque Terre '15	♟♟ 5
○ Cinque Terre Sciacchetrà '14	♟♟ 8
○ Cinque Terre '13	♟♟♟ 5
○ Cinque Terre '12	♟♟♟ 5
○ Cinque Terre '14	♟♟ 5
○ Cinque Terre Sciacchetrà '12	♟♟ 8
○ Cinque Terre Sciacchetrà '11	♟♟ 8
○ Cinque Terre Sciacchetrà '10	♟♟ 8
○ Cinque Terre Sciacchetrà Ris. '10	♟♟ 8
○ Cinque Terre Sciacchetrà Ris. '09	♟♟ 8
● Passito '10	♟♟ 8
● Passito La Rinascita '11	♟♟ 8

Cantine Bregante

VIA UNITÀ D'ITALIA, 47
16039 SESTRI LEVANTE [GE]
TEL. +39 018541388
www.cantinebregante.it

CELLAR SALES
PRE-BOOKED VISITS
ANNUAL PRODUCTION 100,000 bottles
HECTARES UNDER VINE 1.00

Simona Bregante's husband, Sergio Sanguineti, runs this winery in the centre of Sestri Levante. The vineyards are situated in the hills, mainly at Sant'Anna, planted to vermentino, and San Bernardo, on the slopes above the Baia delle Favole, growing bianchetta genovese. Sergio loves working with this grape, transforming it into a Metodo Classico he describes as an artisan sparkling wine, made without clarification and keeping the must on the skins for a short time. The original 700 bottles per year have become 2,500, all pas dosé. The sweet, captivating Moscato 2015 has fine, concentrated mousse, sunny and varietal hints, and well-balanced acidity and sweetness enhancing the alluring palate. The Bianchetta Genovese 2015 shows intense straw-yellow colour with aromas of summer flowers and tobacco, and a fresh, minerally flavour, as yet lacking perfect balance.

○ Golfo del Tigullio Portofino Bianco '15	♥♥ 2*
○ Golfo del Tigullio Portofino Moscato '15	♥♥ 2*
○ Golfo del Tigullio Brut M. Cl. Baia delle Favole	♥ 5
○ Golfo del Tigullio Portofino Bianchetta Genovese '15	♥ 3
● Golfo del Tigullio Portofino Ca' du Diau '15	♥ 3
○ Golfo del Tigullio Portofino Vermentino '15	♥ 2
● Golfo del Tigullio Ca' du Diau '14	♥♥ 3
○ Portofino Bianchetta Genovese Segesta Tigullorium '13	♥♥ 2*
● Portofino Ca' du Diau '13	♥♥ 2*
○ Portofino Moscato '14	♥♥ 3
○ Portofino Moscato '13	♥♥ 3
○ Portofino Passito Sole della Costa '12	♥♥ 5

Bruna

FRAZ. BORGO
VIA UMBERTO I, 81
18020 RANZO [IM]
TEL. +39 0183318082
www.brunapigato.it

CELLAR SALES
PRE-BOOKED VISITS
ANNUAL PRODUCTION 40,000 bottles
HECTARES UNDER VINE 8.00

Marred by a heavy hailstorm in the Pigato U Baccan vineyard, 2014 is best forgotten, but 2015 made up for it. Francesca and her husband Roberto began the harvest on 31 August, in the lower vineyard at Pogli, between Ortovero and Ranzo, on the white soil that produces Pigato Majé. This is also where the estate has expanded, thanks to the recent purchase of a small strip of land planted in 2015, bringing the estate's total to eight hectares. The Pigato Majé 2015 is a bright, intense straw-yellow, with appealing sage and thyme aromas developing into ripe fruit, and clear minerally sensations, acidic structure and positive character on the palate. Intense fresh herb, apple and pear, and almond hints for the Pigato Le Russeghine 2015, the palate softened by minerally hints on a warm, well-structured body. The Rosso Bansìgu 2015 is also interesting: Parma violets and lovely blueberry and blackberry fruit notes, closing on tobacco, and a fresh, well-balanced palate.

○ Riviera Ligure di Ponente Pigato Le Russeghine '15	♥♥ 3*
○ Riviera Ligure di Ponente Pigato Majé '15	♥♥ 3*
● Bansìgu '15	♥♥ 3
● Pulin '14	♥ 4
● Riviera Ligure di Ponente Rossese '15	♥ 3
○ Riviera Ligure di Ponente Pigato U Baccan '13	♥♥♥ 5
○ Riviera Ligure di Ponente Pigato U Baccan '12	♥♥♥ 5
○ Riviera Ligure di Ponente Pigato U Baccan '11	♥♥♥ 5
○ Riviera Ligure di Ponente Pigato U Baccan '07	♥♥♥ 5
○ Riviera Ligure di Ponente Pigato U Baccan '06	♥♥♥ 4

LIGURIA

Cantine Calleri

LOC. SALEA
REG. FRATTI, 2
17031 ALBENGA [SV]
TEL. +39 018220085
www.cantinecalleri.com

ANNUAL PRODUCTION 55,000 bottles
HECTARES UNDER VINE 6.00

The winery is in the small village of Salea di Albenga. Established in 1968 by Aldo Calleri, it has continued to expand thanks to significant work in vineyard and cellar by meticulous, esteemed vigneron Marcello. The estate grows native grape varieties like pigato, bottled in the Albenga subzone; vermentino and rossese in the Albenga plain; ormeasco in the Arroscia valley. From this year there will also be a small quantity of dolceacqua. The Pigato Saleasco 2015 is youthful and stylish, with sunny aromas of sage and rosemary, and a polished, velvety, very harmonious palate. Not far behind is the Pigato di Albenga 2015 with intense hints of medicinal herbs and iodine on a generously tangy, fresh and well-structured palate. The appealing, harmonious Ormeasco 2015 shows bright, lively colour with red berries and bitter almonds on the nose and a heady, moderately structured palate. Attractive spicy aromas, generous red berries and a light hint of medicinal herbs characterize the Dolceacqua 2015, along with good structure and a long, heady finish.

○ Riviera Ligure di Ponente Pigato di Albenga Saleasco '15	♥♥ 3*
● Dolceacqua '15	♥♥ 3
● Ormeasco di Pornassio '15	♥♥ 2*
○ Riviera Ligure di Ponente Pigato di Albenga '15	♥♥ 3
○ Riviera Ligure di Ponente Vermentino I Müzazzi '15	♥♥ 3
○ Riviera Ligure di Ponente Pigato Albenga '12	♀♀ 3
○ Riviera Ligure di Ponente Pigato di Albenga '14	♀♀ 3*
○ Riviera Ligure di Ponente Vermentino I Müzazzi '14	♀♀ 3
○ Riviera Ligure di Ponente Vermentino I Müzazzi '12	♀♀ 3

Cheo

VIA BRIGATE PARTIGIANE, 1
19018 VERNAZZA [SP]
TEL. +39 0187821189
bartolocheo@gmail.com

CELLAR SALES
PRE-BOOKED VISITS
ANNUAL PRODUCTION 13,000 bottles
HECTARES UNDER VINE 2.00
SUSTAINABLE WINERY

Endless investments for Lise Bertram and Bartolomeo Lercari: after the flooding, renovations to the drystone walls, and purchases of new plots, they bought a ruined building in 2015. Landscaping regulations permitting, this will host the barrique cellar and tasting room. Increasing numbers of tourists visit the estate, and thanks to the quality of the wines and the beautiful surroundings the 13,000 bottles produced are soon gone. Of the wines we tasted, the Cinqueterre Sciacchetrà 2013 was excellent, with beautiful, intense amber tones, hints of tobacco and dried fruit, and a complex, stylish flavour with a lingering, very harmonious finish. The Perciò and Cheo, both 2015, also impressed: the former for its confident sunny aromas of sage and rosemary, developing into fruit, and the latter for the fresh, fragrant vegetal hints and spring flowers, with a velvety palate.

○ Cinque Terre Sciacchetrà '13	♥♥ 8
○ Cinque Terre Cheo '15	♥♥ 3
○ Cinque Terre Perciò '15	♥♥ 4
● Cheo Rosso '14	♥ 4
○ Cinque Terre Cheo '14	♀♀ 3
○ Cinque Terre Cheo '13	♀♀ 3*
○ Cinque Terre Cheo '11	♀♀ 3*
○ Cinque Terre Perciò '14	♀♀ 4
○ Cinque Terre Perciò '13	♀♀ 4
○ Cinque Terre Perciò '12	♀♀ 4
○ Cinque Terre Perciò '11	♀♀ 4
○ Cinque Terre Sciacchetrà '12	♀♀ 8
○ Cinque Terre Sciacchetrà '11	♀♀ 8

Cantina Cinque Terre

FRAZ. MANAROLA
LOC. GROPPO
19010 RIOMAGGIORE [SP]
TEL. +39 0187920435
www.cantinacinqueterre.com

PRE-BOOKED VISITS
ANNUAL PRODUCTION 200,000 bottles
HECTARES UNDER VINE 45.00

In order to understand the difficulties of winegrowing in Cinque Terre, an area bordered by the towns of Riomaggiore, Manarola, Corniglia, Vernazza, and Monterosso, we need to reveal some of the problems faced by this cooperative last year. To recover an old vineyard of about two hectares in a single plot (something of a rarity for this area) at about 400 metres altitude, owned by a new member, it was necessary to use a helicopter. It took about 40 flights to transport the large shafts indispensable for supporting the rows, due to the steeply sloping terrain. Sadly, we just enjoy the lovely wine, without knowing the difficulties in producing it. Pleasing qualities are what the Cinque Terre Sciacchetrà 2013 is all about: intense amber tones, appetizing aromas of dried herbs opening out into sweet dates and chestnut flower honey, and a velvety, harmonious palate rendered sublime by correctly dosed acidity. The Pergole Sparse 2015 is complex with a pleasantly lingering aftertaste.

○ Cinque Terre Sciacchetrà '13	🍷🍷 6
○ Cinque Terre Costa da' Posa '15	🍷🍷 3
○ Cinque Terre Pergole Sparse '15	🍷🍷 4
○ Cinque Terre '15	🍷 2
○ Cinque Terre Costa de Campu '15	🍷 3
○ Cinque Terre Vigne Alte '15	🍷 2
○ Cinque Terre '13	♀♀ 2*
○ Cinque Terre Costa da Posa '14	♀♀ 3
○ Cinque Terre Costa da' Posa '13	♀♀ 3
○ Cinque Terre Costa de Sèra '14	♀♀ 3
○ Cinque Terre Costa de Sèra '12	♀♀ 3
○ Cinque Terre Pergole Sparse '13	♀♀ 4
○ Cinque Terre Sciacchetrà '12	♀♀ 6
○ Cinque Terre Sciacchetrà '11	♀♀ 6

Fontanacota

FRAZ. PONTI
VIA PROVINCIALE, 137
18100 PORNASSIO [IM]
TEL. +39 3339807442
www.fontanacota.it

CELLAR SALES
PRE-BOOKED VISITS
ANNUAL PRODUCTION 40,000 bottles
HECTARES UNDER VINE 6.00

No significant changes in this winery for 2015, apart from extension of the vineyards, which will be appreciated only in the future. Marina and her brother Fabio Berta work in the ormeasco vineyard, about 1.3 hectares in Ponti a Pornasso. More space is reserved for white vermentino and pigato, and black rossese, about 3.5 hectares overall, lower down in Val Prino near Dolcedo, in the province of Imperia. The harvest was brought forward to late August for the white wines and ended in late September in the Pornassio vineyards. The grapes were healthy and very little treatment was applied overall. We enjoyed the 2015 Vermentino with bright, intense colour and hints of sage, rosemary and aromatic herbs. The palate is elegant, above all, with fresh, harmonious body. Just behind it is the Pigato 2015, with less evident structure, and fresh minerally aromas developing into an almondy aftertaste.

○ Riviera Ligure di Ponente Vermentino '15	🍷🍷 3*
● Pornassio '15	🍷🍷 3
○ Riviera Ligure di Ponente Pigato '15	🍷🍷 3
⊙ Pornassio Sciac-Trà '15	🍷 3
● Pornassio Sup. '14	🍷 3
○ Riviera Ligure di Ponente Pigato '11	♀♀♀ 3*
● Ormeasco di Pornassio Sup. '11	♀♀ 3
● Ormeasco di Pornassio Sup. '10	♀♀ 3
● Pornassio Sup. '12	♀♀ 3
○ Riviera Ligure di Ponente Pigato '14	♀♀ 3*
○ Riviera Ligure di Ponente Pigato '13	♀♀ 3*
○ Riviera Ligure di Ponente Pigato '12	♀♀ 3
○ Riviera Ligure di Ponente Pigato '10	♀♀ 2*
○ Riviera Ligure di Ponente Pigato '09	♀♀ 2*
○ Riviera Ligure di Ponente Vermentino '14	♀♀ 3
○ Riviera Ligure di Ponente Vermentino '12	♀♀ 3*

LIGURIA

Giacomelli

VIA PALVOTRISIA, 134
19030 CASTELNUOVO MAGRA [SP]
TEL. +39 0187674155
www.azagricolagiacomelli.it

CELLAR SALES
PRE-BOOKED VISITS
ANNUAL PRODUCTION 50,000 bottles
HECTARES UNDER VINE 12.00
SUSTAINABLE WINERY

New input on the estate in 2015, with replanting of a historic vineyard that will increase vermentino production. This is an enclosed plot of about 4,000 square metres, originally the garden of the Bishops of Luni, above the walls of Castelnuovo Magra. A new vineyard of 1.5 hectares is already productive, and as of this year has increased annual yield of Vermentino Pianacce to 35,000 bottles. Roberto Patacchi prefers to select his own grapes rather than use a vineyard selection, with meticulous methods in the rows, natural growing techniques that help preserve the environment, and harvesting the healthiest bunches. The Pianacce 2015 impressed us from the beginning with fresh, bright colour and complex flavour: generous hints of broom and elderflowers developing into apple and pear fruit, and a full-bodied, tangy and harmonious palate. The Boboli 2015 is still very young but already revealing impetuous structure, though it will show more polished behaviour after the summer.

○ Colli di Luni Vermentino Pianacce '15	🍷🍷 2*
○ Colli di Luni Vermentino Boboli '15	🍷🍷 4
○ Paduletti '15	🍷 2
● Colli di Luni Rosso Canal di Bocco '11	🍷🍷 4
○ Colli di Luni Vermentino Boboli '13	🍷🍷 4
○ Colli di Luni Vermentino Boboli '11	🍷🍷 4
○ Colli di Luni Vermentino Boboli '08	🍷🍷 4
○ Colli di Luni Vermentino Boboli '05	🍷🍷 4
○ Colli di Luni Vermentino Pianacce '14	🍷🍷 2*
○ Colli di Luni Vermentino Pianacce '12	🍷🍷 2*

La Ginestraia

VIA STERIA
18100 CERVO [IM]
TEL. +39 3272683692
www.laginestraia.com

ANNUAL PRODUCTION 50,000 bottles
HECTARES UNDER VINE 7.00

Marco Brangero's love for his vineyards and wines is almost unparalleled. Listening to him, we understand the extreme passion that drove him to invest in the Brangero family estate in Piedmont as well as in Liguria. The new cellar in San Bartolomeo al Mare, still under construction, is an eco-sustainable structure based on wood and stone. Across the Apennines the microclimate is completely different and the proximity to the sea fosters stylish minerally and salty features in the wines. This is true of Le Marige 2015, obtained from a vineyard in the Arnasco area at just 15 metres altitude, on red, stony soil ideal for the pigato grape. Fresh herbs and sage, and a full velvety body with hints of gunflint and almonds. A truly aristocratic wine. Ripe, sunny aromas developing into apple and pear fruit appear in the 2015 Pigato, with a generous palate supported by a rich, attractive salty sensation. The Vermentino 2015 is stylish with a less complex structure.

○ Riviera Ligure di Ponente Pigato Le Marige '15	🍷🍷🍷 3*
○ Riviera Ligure di Ponente Pigato '15	🍷🍷 3*
○ Riviera Ligure di Ponente Vermentino '15	🍷🍷 3
○ Riviera Ligure di Ponente Pigato Biancodamare '11	🍷🍷 3
○ Riviera Ligure di Ponente Pigato Via Maestra '14	🍷🍷 3*
○ Riviera Ligure di Ponente Pigato Via Maestra '12	🍷🍷 3
○ Riviera Ligure di Ponente Pigato Via Maestra '11	🍷🍷 3
● Riviera Ligure di Ponente Rossese '14	🍷🍷 3
○ Riviera Ligure di Ponente Vermentino '14	🍷🍷 3

Ka' Manciné

FRAZ. SAN MARTINO
VIA MACIURINA, 7
18036 SOLDANO [IM]
TEL. +39 339 3965477
www.kamancine.it

CELLAR SALES
PRE-BOOKED VISITS
ANNUAL PRODUCTION 20,000 bottles
HECTARES UNDER VINE 3.00

The estate is based in Soldano, a little village extending over the steep banks of the River Verbone, where vines have always grown and brought wealth to the town. Maurizio knows his land well, and skillfully cares for the vineyards, pouring heart and soul into the wines. This year, two small plots have been added to the Beragna vineyard, over 100 years old, bringing it up to around one hectare. The grapes are processed, at least in part, with local traditional methods, namely with the addition of 10–15% whole bunches, not destemmed during vinification. And the wines are really exciting: the Dolceacqua Beragna 2015 is a bright ruby red with vibrant aromas of dried herbs, damsons and black pepper on the nose, while the palate is rendered velvety by the polished tannins and long, pleasing flavour. The Galeae Angè Riserva 2014 is equally good, with bright, lively colour, releasing naturally elegant fruity aromas supported by a warm, silky palate that seems to go on, pleasantly, forever.

● Dolceacqua Beragna '15	♥♥	3*
● Dolceacqua Galeae Angè Ris. '14	♥♥	3*
● Dolceacqua Galeae '15	♥♥	3
⊙ Sciakk '15	♥	3
○ Tabaka '15	♥	3
● Dolceacqua Galeae '13	♥♥♥	3*
● Dolceacqua Beragna '14	♥♥	3*
● Dolceacqua Beragna '13	♥♥	3
● Dolceacqua Galeae '14	♥♥	3
● Dolceacqua Galeae Angè Ris. '13	♥♥	3*
● Dolceacqua Galeae Angè Ris. '12	♥♥	3*
● Rossese di Dolceacqua Beragna '12	♥♥	3
● Rossese di Dolceacqua Beragna '11	♥♥	3*
● Rossese di Dolceacqua Galeae '12	♥♥	3*

Ottaviano Lambruschi

VIA OLMARELLO, 28
19030 CASTELNUOVO MAGRA [SP]
TEL. +39 0187674261
www.ottavianolambruschi.com

CELLAR SALES
PRE-BOOKED VISITS
ANNUAL PRODUCTION 36,000 bottles
HECTARES UNDER VINE 10.00

Thinking of eastern Liguria in winemaking terms, one of the first names that comes to mind is Ottaviano Lambruschi. Head of the family, far-sighted pursuer of quality, he still oversees the work but leaves the running of the vineyard increasingly to his son Fabio, and the office and marketing department to his young grand-daughter Ylenia. No news for 2015, just the confirmation of steady, untarnished quality. Electing a best wine is tough since there is very little to choose between them. First up is the fresh-tasting Vermentino 2015, opening on lovely grassy, minerally tones with a complex, harmonious palate: full-bodied and stylish, rounded and boisterous, polished and refined. And what about the Maggiore 2015? Regal, sophisticated, with hints of fruit and medicinal herbs and a complex, well-rounded palate, captivating and distracting the mind in its pursuit of the most sublime appeal. Not far behind, the pleasing Costa Marina 2015 displays a multitude of ripe, sunny flavours.

○ Colli di Luni Vermentino Il Maggiore '15	♥♥♥	5
○ Colli di Luni Vermentino '15	♥♥	3*
○ Colli di Luni Vermentino Costa Marina '15	♥♥	4
● Colli di Luni Rosso Maniero '15	♥	2
○ Colli di Luni Vermentino Costa Marina '11	♥♥♥	4*
○ Colli di Luni Vermentino Costa Marina '09	♥♥♥	3
○ Colli di Luni Vermentino Il Maggiore '14	♥♥♥	5
○ Colli di Luni Vermentino Il Maggiore '13	♥♥♥	5
○ Colli di Luni Vermentino Il Maggiore '12	♥♥♥	4*
○ Colli di Luni Vermentino Sarticola '08	♥♥♥	3*
○ Colli di Luni Vermentino '14	♥♥	3*
○ Colli di Luni Vermentino Costa Marina '14	♥♥	4
○ Colli di Luni Vermentino Costa Marina '13	♥♥	4
○ Colli di Luni Vermentino Costa Marina '12	♥♥	4

Cantine Lunae Bosoni

FRAZ. ISOLA DI ORTONOVO
VIA BOZZI, 63
19034 ORTONOVO [SP]
TEL. +39 0187669222
www.cantinelunae.com

CELLAR SALES
PRE-BOOKED VISITS
ACCOMMODATION
ANNUAL PRODUCTION 450,000 bottles
HECTARES UNDER VINE 65.00

The Bosoni family is united by life and
work: Paolo, the perceptive head of the
family, is in charge of the vineyards and
cellar; his son Diego also oversees relations
with foreign clients, and his daughter
Debora manages events and sales in the
beautiful visitor centre; lastly, his wife
Antonella takes care of the accounting.
Thanks to this family, Cantina Lunae is
growing, with the purchase in 2015 of two
new plots in the Ortonovo area at around
250 metres altitude: about two hectares of
albarola at Camporegio, and three hectares
of vermentino on the famous Sarticola hill.
Once again the wines maintain a high
standard of quality: lovely straw-yellow
colour with greenish hues for the Etichetta
Nera 2015, with generous aromas ranging
from vegetal hints to tropical fruit like
mango and pineapple, and a velvety, firm
palate, well-balanced with a very lingering
aftertaste. The Cavagino 2015 is just as
good, still a bit young but plenty of rich, ripe
fruit and vegetal sensations. The intensely
warm palate is pleasantly lingering.

Maccario Dringenberg

VIA TORRE, 3
18036 SAN BIAGIO DELLA CIMA [IM]
TEL. +39 0184289947
maccariodringenberg@yahoo.it

CELLAR SALES
PRE-BOOKED VISITS
ANNUAL PRODUCTION 23,000 bottles
HECTARES UNDER VINE 4.00

San Biagio della Cima is a small town
nestled in the upper Vallecrosia, near
Bordighera immediately inland from
Imperia. This is where Giovanna Maccario
and her husband Goetz Dringenberg have
built their winemaking realm on consistent
work and high quality. The small cellar in
the old village is anything but functional,
requiring hands-on commitment and
attention when working there. For years
now this has been the birthplace of great
red wines like the Dolceacqua 2015:
intense colour and a floral nose, with hints
of ripe fruit, evolving towards tree bark and
black pepper. A graceful body and a long
finish. For the Dolceacqua Superiore
Luvaira 2014 the vintage changes but not
the quality, which is as high as ever. Ripe,
sunny aromas are enriched with hints of
the Orient, spices, liquorice and tobacco,
while the palate reveals the austerity and
elegance of a great structure. The
Dolceacqua Posaù 2014 is also very
inspiring.

○ Colli di Luni Vermentino Et. Nera '15	♈♈♈ 4*
○ Colli di Luni vermentino Albarola '15	♈♈ 4
○ Colli di Luni Vermentino Cavagino '15	♈♈ 5
○ Colli di Luni Bianco Fior di Luna '15	♈♈ 3
○ Colli di Luni Vermentino Et. Grigia '15	♈♈ 3
○ Colli di Luni Vermentino Numero Chiuso '11	♈♈ 6
● Colli di Luni Niccolò V '12	♈ 4
● Colli di Luni Niccolò V Ris. '09	♈ 5
○ Colli di Luni Vermentino Et. Nera '14	♈♈♈ 4*
○ Colli di Luni Vermentino Et. Nera '13	♈♈♈ 4*
○ Colli di Luni Vermentino Et. Nera '12	♈♈♈ 4*
○ Colli di Luni Vermentino Et. Nera '11	♈♈♈ 4*
○ Colli di Luni Vermentino Et. Nera '10	♈♈♈ 4
○ Colli di Luni Vermentino Et. Nera '09	♈♈♈ 4

● Rossese di Dolceacqua '15	♈♈ 3*
● Rossese di Dolceacqua Sup. Luvaira '14	♈♈ 4
● Rossese di Dolceacqua Sup. Posaù '14	♈♈ 3*
● Rossese di Dolceacqua Sup. Brae '15	♈♈ 3
● Rossese di Dolceacqua Sup. Posaù Biamonti '14	♈♈ 5
○ L'Amiral '15	♈ 3
● Dolceacqua Sup. Vign. Posaù '13	♈♈♈ 3*
● Rossese di Dolceacqua Sup. Vign. Luvaira '07	♈♈♈ 4*
● Rossese di Dolceacqua Sup. Vign. Posaù '10	♈♈♈ 3*
● Rossese di Dolceacqua Sup. Vign. Posaù '08	♈♈♈ 3
● Dolceacqua Brae '14	♈♈ 3
● Dolceacqua San Biagio della Cima '14	♈♈ 3

Maixei

Loc. Porto
18035 Dolceacqua [IM]
Tel. +39 0184205015
www.maixei.it

CELLAR SALES
PRE-BOOKED VISITS
ANNUAL PRODUCTION 45,000 bottles

As of this year, Maixei is producing a new wine, Mistral, a monovarietal syrah made from grapes contributed by a member who no longer makes wine. The estimable Fabio Corradi, winemaker and director, decided to ferment the grapes separately and in stainless steel, with a spell in second- and third-use barriques to boost its character. Still running the winery are chairman Giancarlo Cassini, and vice-chairman and agronomist Pasquale Restuccio. The wines have lost none of their identity and quality. The most impressive wine is the Dolceacqua Superiore 2014: lively, youthful colour, intense and multifaceted body, aromas of arbutus and myrtle fruits blending with lovely hints of tobacco and black pepper. The palate opens on a stylish, polished structure where the tannic and minerally textures meander to a long, tangy finish. The Mistral 2015 is vibrant, not too boisterous, harmonious and pleasantly lingering.

● Dolceacqua Sup. '14	♟♟ 4	
● Dolceacqua '15	♟♟ 3	
● Mistral '15	♟♟ 4	
● Dolceacqua Sup. Barbadirame '14	♟ 4	
● Dolceacqua '14	♟♟ 3*	
● Dolceacqua '12	♟♟ 3	
● Dolceacqua Rossese Sup. '10	♟♟ 4	
○ Dolceacqua Rossese Sup. '09	♟♟ 4	
○ Dolceacqua Rossese Sup. '08	♟♟ 4	
● Dolceacqua Sup. '13	♟♟ 4	
● Dolceacqua Sup. '12	♟♟ 4	
● Dolceacqua Sup. Barbadirame '12	♟♟ 4	

Il Monticello

Via Groppolo, 7
19038 Sarzana [SP]
Tel. +39 0187621432
www.ilmonticello.it

CELLAR SALES
PRE-BOOKED VISITS
ACCOMMODATION
ANNUAL PRODUCTION 68,000 bottles
HECTARES UNDER VINE 10.00

The Neri brothers continue to farm their vineyards with natural methods, prudent use of treatments, restricted to copper and lime. The cellarwork is customized, with the Poggio Paterno a vineyard selection obtained from the grapes of a single vineyard, making just over 2,000 bottles, while Groppolo is bottled following selection of grapes which have undergone three different vinification procedures: cold, carbonic, and conventional maceration. From 2015 the Poggio Paterno impressed us most: intense, brilliant straw-yellow colour and pleasing floral aromas, with ripe, sunny sensations on a minerally background. The palate is more stylish than complex, polished and harmonious, with a finish that is extremely pleasing rather than incisive. The Groppolo 2015 reveals intense colour and promising character: a buttery, rich palate balanced by well-measured acidity. It will develop further with time.

○ Colli di Luni Vermentino Poggio Paterno '15	♟♟ 3*	
● Colli di Luni Rosso Rupestro '15	♟♟ 2*	
○ Colli di Luni Vermentino Groppolo '15	♟♟ 3	
● Colli di Luni Rosso Poggio dei Magni Ris. '12	♟ 3	
● Colli di Luni Rosso Serasuolo '15	♟ 2	
● Colli di Luni Rosso Poggio dei Magni Ris. '11	♟♟ 3	
● Colli di Luni Rosso Rupestro '12	♟♟ 2*	
○ Colli di Luni Vermentino '12	♟♟ 3*	
○ Colli di Luni Vermentino Groppolo '14	♟♟ 3*	
○ Colli di Luni Vermentino Poggio Paterno '10	♟♟ 3*	
○ Passito dei Neri '12	♟♟ 4	
○ Poggio Paterno Il Bocciato '11	♟♟ 3*	

Conte Picedi Benettini

VIA MAZZINI, 57
19038 SARZANA [SP]
TEL. +39 0187625147
www.picedibenettini.it

CELLAR SALES
PRE-BOOKED VISITS
ACCOMMODATION
ANNUAL PRODUCTION 30,000 bottles
HECTARES UNDER VINE 7.00

Stubbornness and passion for vines have always been strong characteristics of engineer Papirio, aka Nino, esteemed grower and connoisseur, standard-bearer of a generation of diehards who changed the face of Italian wine production. He is assisted by the shy but increasingly consistent presence of his son Eugenio who is gradually bringing new energy to the estate, starting with accommodation: a farmhouse near the family home overlooks the vineyards and will be available for visitors when renovations are complete. The Vermentino 2015 was particularly interesting, with bright, intense colour, hints of medicinal herbs and rosemary, and polished character, nicely elegant with a pleasant aftertaste. Il Chioso 2015 is also young, vibrant, fresh and brilliant, with lovely melon and pineapple fruit and hints of dried herbs. Also worth a mention, the Passito del Chioso 2014 displays a nose of flowers and dried fruit, with a generous palate and powerful finish.

○ Colli di Luni Vermentino '15	♥♥ 2*
○ Colli di Luni Vermentino Il Chioso '15	♥♥ 3*
● Colli di Luni Rosso Villa Il Chioso '15	♥♥ 3
○ Colli di Luni Vermentino Stemma '15	♥♥ 3
○ Passito del Chioso '14	♥♥ 5
⊙ Ciliegiolo '15	♥ 2
○ Colli di Luni Vermentino Il Chioso '14	♥♥♥ 2*
○ Colli di Luni Vermentino '13	♀♀ 2*
○ Colli di Luni Vermentino '12	♀♀ 2*
○ Colli di Luni Vermentino Il Chioso '13	♀♀ 2*
○ Colli di Luni Vermentino Stemma '14	♀♀ 3
○ Colli di Luni Vermentino Stemma '13	♀♀ 3
○ Colli di Luni Vermentino Stemma '12	♀♀ 3
○ Colli di Luni Vermentino Stemma '11	♀♀ 3*

La Pietra del Focolare

LOC. ORTONOVO
FRAZ. ISOLA DI ORTONOVO
VIA ISOLA, 76
19034 ORTONOVO [SP]
TEL. +39 0187662129
www.lapietradelfocolare.it

CELLAR SALES
PRE-BOOKED VISITS
ANNUAL PRODUCTION 30,000 bottles
HECTARES UNDER VINE 6.00
SUSTAINABLE WINERY

Ortonovo is the easternmost town in Liguria, and the Tuscan border is just a few metres from the winery managed by Laura Angelini and Stefano Salvetti. The vineyards are divided into 13 small plots, for a total of almost seven hectares in the municipal areas of Ortonovo and Castelnuovo Magra, in the province of La Spezia. The meticulous work in the vineyards and cellar also respects the environment: for example, the latest vintage of reds were fermented without the addition of sulphites, while some labels have a natural shellac seal bearing the winery trademark instead of the usual foil capsule. The excellent Villa Linda 2015 displays very bright, brilliant colour and vibrant ripe apricot and plum aromas, while maintaining a fresh, minerally nuance. The warm, complex body finishes long and enjoyable. Pleasing ripe, sunny aromas and spring flowers for the Solarancio 2015, with a subtle, lingering palate.

○ Colli di Luni Vermentino Sup. Villa Linda '15	♥♥ 4
○ Colli di Luni Vermentino Augusto '15	♥♥ 3
○ Colli di Luni Vermentino Solarancio '15	♥♥ 4
● Colli di Luni Rosso La Merla dal Becco '12	♀♀ 5
○ Colli di Luni Vermentino L'Aura di Sarticola '14	♀♀ 6
○ Colli di Luni Vermentino Solarancio '11	♀♀ 5
○ Colli di Luni Vermentino Solarancio '10	♀♀ 4
○ Colli di Luni Vermentino Sup. Augusto '13	♀♀ 3*
○ Colli di Luni Vermentino Villa Linda '14	♀♀ 3*
○ Colli di Luni Vermentino Villa Linda '11	♀♀ 3*
○ Solarancio '13	♀♀ 3

Poggio dei Gorleri

FRAZ. DIANO GORLERI
VIA SAN LEONARDO
18013 DIANO MARINA [IM]
TEL. +39 0183495207
www.poggiodeigorleri.com

CELLAR SALES
PRE-BOOKED VISITS
ACCOMMODATION
ANNUAL PRODUCTION 80,000 bottles
HECTARES UNDER VINE 10.50

The Merano family's lovely, welcoming property is situated on the uplands of Diano Gorleri, a natural watershed dividing the two gulfs of Diano Marina to the east and Imperia to the west. The estate has been able to diversify its product range following purchases in the provinces of Imperia and Savona. The now-productive Arnasco vineyard is planted on terra rossa, ideal for the pigato grape, and the harvests are used to increase the production of Cycnus. Another great Cycnus from 2015: brilliant straw-yellow colour with cool, green hues, sunny aromas of rosemary, sage and peaches, truly stylish with a silky, well-structured palate. The Albium 2014 is flavoursome, vibrant and pleasantly warm, with medicinal herb aromas developing into chamomile and complex hints of bitter almonds and tobacco. Lovely black and red berries for the interesting Pornassio Peinetti 2015, a richly extracted, harmonious wine.

○ Riviera Ligure di Ponente Pigato Albium '14	♀♀ 5
○ Riviera Ligure di Ponente Pigato Cycnus '15	♀♀ 3*
● Ormeasco di Pornassio Peinetti '15	♀♀ 3
● Riviera Ligure di Ponente Granaccia Shalok '14	♀♀ 5
○ Riviera Ligure di Ponente Vermentino V. Sorì '15	♀♀ 3
○ Riviera Ligure di Ponente Vermentino '15	♀ 3
○ Riviera Ligure di Ponente Pigato Albium '13	♀♀♀ 5
○ Riviera Ligure di Ponente Pigato Cycnus '13	♀♀♀ 3*
○ Riviera Ligure di Ponente Pigato Cycnus '12	♀♀♀ 3*

Roberto Rondelli

FRAZ. BRUNETTI, 1
18033 CAMPOROSSO [IM]
TEL. +39 3280348055
rondellivini@gmail.com

CELLAR SALES
PRE-BOOKED VISITS
ACCOMMODATION AND RESTAURANT SERVICE
ANNUAL PRODUCTION 22,000 bottles
HECTARES UNDER VINE 3.50

This estate is not easy to reach, in the extreme west of Italian territory near the border between Liguria and France: harsh, almost wild terrain above the sea, with plenty of Mediterranean scrubland and woods. The small winery is beautifully situated on the green hillside, where a heavy silence reigns by night, and is suited to the estate's limited proportions. The vineyards are not close by but the courtyard offers a stunning view of the jewel in the crown, a new plot just beginning production, with enviable south-south-west aspecting. The wines respond with increasingly distinctive quality, above all, the stylish, impressive Dolceacqua 2015: aromas ranging from refined hints of violets to tree bark and spicy black pepper, and a powerful, characterful palate supported by elegant flavour and a lingering aftertaste. Powerful oaky sensations endow the Dolceacqua Migliarina 2013, also extremely interesting, with impressive character. The Pigato Vigna Ciotti 2015 is subtle and stylish.

● Dolceacqua '15	♀♀ 3*
● Dolceacqua Migliarina '13	♀♀ 3
○ Riviera Ligure di Ponente Pigato V. Ciotti '15	♀♀ 3
○ Pepin '15	♀ 3
○ Riviera Ligure di Ponente Vermentino '15	♀ 3
● Dolceacqua Migliarina '12	♀♀ 3
○ Riviera Ligure di Ponente Pigato V. Ciotti '14	♀♀ 3*
○ Riviera Ligure di Ponente Vermentino '14	♀♀ 3

Terenzuola

VIA VERCALDA, 14
54035 FOSDINOVO [MS]
TEL. +39 0187670387
www.terenzuola.it

ANNUAL PRODUCTION 137,000 bottles
HECTARES UNDER VINE 21.00

Ivan Giuliani runs the estate, while his partner Marco Nicolini is only concerned with the financial side. The farm extends over almost 22 hectares: a couple in the Cinque Terre and the rest in the Lunigiana area which straddles the border between Liguria and Tuscany. The estate is not open to the public, nor to direct and online sales, and the products are not to be found in large-scale retail. The potential 180,000 bottles produced in 2015 are distributed in restaurants and wine shops in Italy and abroad, thanks to a network of 50 agents and 20 importers. The wines tasted were very good indeed: the Vermentino Vigne Basse 2015 shows bright, lively hues and hints of Mediterranean scrubland, developing into ripe apple and pear fruit. The assertively fresh palate adds character without disturbing the harmonious feel. The La Merla della Miniera 2013, from canaiolo, massaretta and vermentino nero, offers pleasing hints of dried herbs and liquorice, and a multilayered, complex palate with marked personality.

○ Colli di Luni Vermentino V. Basse '15	♟♟ 3*
● Merla della Miniera '13	♟♟ 4
○ Colli di Luni Vermentino Sup. Fosso di Corsano '15	♟♟ 3
○ Colli di Luni Vermentino Sup. Fosso di Corsano '11	♟♟♟ 3*
○ Cinque Terre '13	♟♟ 4
○ Cinqueterre Sciacchetrà '09	♟♟ 7
○ Cinqueterre Sciacchetrà Ris. '10	♟♟ 4
○ Colli di Luni Vermentino Sup. Fosso di Corsano '14	♟♟ 3
○ Colli di Luni Vermentino Sup. Fosso di Corsano '13	♟♟ 3*
○ Colli di Luni Vermentino Sup. Fosso di Corsano '12	♟♟ 3*
● Merla della Miniera '12	♟♟ 4

Terre Bianche

LOC. ARCAGNA
18035 DOLCEACQUA [IM]
TEL. +39 018431426
www.terrebianche.com

CELLAR SALES
PRE-BOOKED VISITS
ACCOMMODATION
ANNUAL PRODUCTION 55,000 bottles
HECTARES UNDER VINE 8.50
SUSTAINABLE WINERY

An important agreement with a local estate no longer in production allowed owners Filippo Rondelli and Franco Laconi to increase the harvest of rossese di Dolceacqua and vermentino grapes. This made it possible to select and process grapes from the Terre Bianche vineyard, a significant single plot which lends its name to the winery itself. So a new wine has joined the range: Terrabianca. And the 2014 is one of the wines that most impressed us: hints of violets and ripe fruit, forest floor and tobacco, and a stylish complex palate with weighty, nicely balanced tannic texture. The Dolceacqua 2015 is on a par: brilliant, dense ruby red colour, and appealing, generous aromas of red berries with salty and sunny nuances, closing on black pepper and tree bark. The Bricco Arcagna as always breaks the bank. The 2014 is velvety, balanced, unfolding into elegant, well-coordinated spicy aromas. Tre Bicchieri.

● Dolceacqua Bricco Arcagna '14	♟♟♟ 5
● Dolceacqua Terrabianca '14	♟♟ 5
● Rossese di Dolceacqua '15	♟♟ 3*
○ Riviera Ligure di Ponente Pigato '15	♟♟ 3
○ Riviera Ligure di Ponente Vermentino '15	♟♟ 3
○ Riviera Ligure di Ponente Pigato Arcana '15	♟ 4
● Dolceacqua Bricco Arcagna '12	♟♟♟ 5
● Rossese di Dolceacqua '12	♟♟♟ 3*
● Rossese di Dolceacqua Bricco Arcagna '09	♟♟♟ 4
● Rossese di Dolceacqua Bricco Arcagna '08	♟♟♟ 5
● Dolceacqua '14	♟♟ 3*
● Dolceacqua '13	♟♟ 3*
● Dolceacqua Bricco Arcagna '13	♟♟ 5

Il Torchio

VIA DELLE COLLINE, 24
19033 CASTELNUOVO MAGRA [SP]
TEL. +39 3318585633
gildamusetti@gmail.com

CELLAR SALES
PRE-BOOKED VISITS
ACCOMMODATION AND RESTAURANT SERVICE
ANNUAL PRODUCTION 60,000 bottles
HECTARES UNDER VINE 12.00

Il Torchio has two branches. The winemaking, managed by uncle Claudio in the vineyards, Edoardo in the cellar, and his sister Gilda in sales; and the farmhouse restaurant, which brings the family together to run the spacious restaurant for counteless diners every week. A new wine, from vermentino grapes, joined the ranks in 2015: Stralunato, and thereby hangs a tale. After harvesting, with selection of the ripest grapes, the must ferments on the skins for three days, followed by long maceration on the fine lees for about three months, finally undergoing racking when the moon wanes, hence the name. For now, only 1,500 bottles are produced, all numbered. The wine wields its muscles on the palate, with mature sensations from the vinification process and the distant, fresh hints of Mediterranean aromas. Ethery ripe fruit aromas for the pleasantly tangy but restrained Vermentino 2015, while the Bianco 2015, rich in alcohol, needs to mature.

○ Colli di Luni Vermentino '15	♥♥ 3
○ Stralunato '15	♥♥ 3
○ Colli di Luni Vermentino Il Bianco '15	♥ 3
● Colli di Luni Rosso Il Torchio '13	♀♀ 4
○ Colli di Luni Vermentino '14	♀♀ 3*
○ Colli di Luni Vermentino Il Bianco '14	♀♀ 3
○ Colli di Luni Vermentino Il Bianco '13	♀♀ 3
○ Colli di Luni Vermentino Il Torchio '13	♀♀ 3*

Vis Amoris

LOC. CARAMAGNA
S.DA MOLINO JAVÈ, 23
18100 IMPERIA
TEL. +39 3483959569
www.visamoris.it

CELLAR SALES
PRE-BOOKED VISITS
ANNUAL PRODUCTION 24,000 bottles
HECTARES UNDER VINE 3.50
SUSTAINABLE WINERY

Roberto Tozzi and Rossana Zappa work only estate-owned vineyards and produce only four wines, all from pigato grapes, each quite different from the other. Vis Domé, fermented entirely in stainless steel, derives from clayey soil at altitudes of 70–80 metres; Verum is fermented on the skins for three–four days and then moved to steel vats; Sogno, harvested on a higher strip of rocky land is fermented partly in steel and partly in barriques, and released two years after the harvest, like Regis, which is fermented and aged in barriques. With plenty of personality, and peach and apricot aromas developing into medicinal herbs and almonds, the Verum 2015 is vibrant and complex with lingering alcohol sensations. The Sogno 2014 shows lovely bright, intense hues, while pleasing hints of oak appear hand-in-hand with the fresh flavour on the palate. The Regis 2014 is complex, appealing and nicely structured.

○ Riviera Ligure di Ponente Pigato Sogno '14	♥♥ 4
○ Riviera Ligure di Ponente Pigato Verum '15	♥♥ 3
○ Riviera Ligure di Ponente Pigato Vis Domè '15	♥ 3
○ Riviera Ligure di Ponente Regis '14	♥ 5
○ Vis Amoris Brut M. Cl.	♥ 5
○ Riviera Ligure di Ponente Pigato Domè '13	♀♀ 3*
○ Riviera Ligure di Ponente Pigato Sogno '13	♀♀ 4
○ Riviera Ligure di Ponente Pigato Sogno '12	♀♀ 4
○ Riviera Ligure di Ponente Pigato Vis Domè '14	♀♀ 3*
○ Verum '14	♀♀ 5

Carlo Alessandri

VIA UMBERTO I, 15
18020 RANZO [IM]
TEL. +39 0183318114
az.alessandricarlo@libero.it

CELLAR SALES
PRE-BOOKED VISITS
ANNUAL PRODUCTION 19,100 bottles
HECTARES UNDER VINE 2.13

● Ormeasco di Pornassio '15	♟♟ 3
○ Riviera Ligure di Ponente Vermentino '15	♟♟ 2*
○ Riviera Ligure di Ponente Pigato '15	♟ 3

Giovanni Ardissone

FRAZ. GAZZELLI
VIA DANTE ALIGHIERI, 2
18027 IMPERIA
TEL. +39 018352527

ANNUAL PRODUCTION 5,000 bottles
HECTARES UNDER VINE 0.60

○ Passito di Vermentino Gianni '12	♟♟ 3
○ Ramato Cippa Passito '15	♟ 3
○ Riviera Ligure di Ponente Vermentino Cian di Previ '15	♟ 3

Bisson

C.SO GIANELLI, 28
16043 CHIAVARI [GE]
TEL. +39 0185314462
www.bissonvini.it

CELLAR SALES
PRE-BOOKED VISITS
ANNUAL PRODUCTION 80,000 bottles
HECTARES UNDER VINE 12.00

○ Portofino Cimixià L'Antico '15	♟♟ 3*
○ Portofino Vermentino Intrigoso '15	♟♟ 3
○ Portofino Bianchetta Genovese U Pastine '15	♟ 2

Enoteca Andrea Bruzzone

VIA BOLZANETO, 96R
16162 GENOVA
TEL. +39 0107455157
www.andreabruzzonevini.it

CELLAR SALES
PRE-BOOKED VISITS

○ Val Polcevera Bianchetta Genovese Bunassa '15	♟♟ 2*
○ Val Polcèvera Coronata La Superba '15	♟♟ 2*
○ Val Polcevera Vermentino Armentin '15	♟ 2

Calvini

VIA SOLARO, 76/78A
18038 SANREMO [IM]
TEL. +39 0184660242
www.luigicalvini.com

CELLAR SALES
PRE-BOOKED VISITS
ANNUAL PRODUCTION 50,000 bottles
HECTARES UNDER VINE 3.50

○ Riviera Ligure di Ponente Vermentino '15	♟♟ 3
○ Prise de Mousse Brut '15	♟ 3

Altare Bonanni Campogrande

VIA DI LOCA, 189
19017 RIOMAGGIORE [SP]
TEL. +39 017350835
www.cinqueterre-campogrande.com

PRE-BOOKED VISITS
ANNUAL PRODUCTION 6,000 bottles
HECTARES UNDER VINE 2.00

○ Telemaco '15	♟♟ 7
○ Cinque Terre '15	♟♟ 7

Azienda Agricola Menconi Cantine Bondonor

VIA ISOLA ALTA, 53
19034 ORTONOVO [SP]
TEL. +39 3488713641
www.cantinebondonor.com

ANNUAL PRODUCTION 15,000 bottles
HECTARES UNDER VINE 3.00

○ Colli di Luni Vermentino Aegidius Vintage '15	♟♟ 3
○ Colli di Luni Vermentino Lunaris '15	♟♟ 3
⊙ RosaLuna '15	♟ 3

I Cerri

VIA GARIBOTTI
19012 CARRO [SP]
TEL. +39 3485102780
www.icerrivaldivara.it

ANNUAL PRODUCTION 8,000 bottles
HECTARES UNDER VINE 1.00

○ Campo Grande '15	♟♟ 3
● Fonte Dietro il Sole '15	♟♟ 3
○ Cian dei Seri '15	♟ 3

Azienda Agricola Durin

LOC. ORTOVERO
VIA ROMA, 202
17037 ORTOVERO [SV]
TEL. +39 0182547007
www.durin.it

CELLAR SALES
PRE-BOOKED VISITS
ACCOMMODATION AND RESTAURANT SERVICE
ANNUAL PRODUCTION 130,000 bottles
HECTARES UNDER VINE 16.50
SUSTAINABLE WINERY

○ Riviera Ligure di Ponente Pigato Braie '15	♟♟ 3*
○ Riviera Ligure di Ponente Pigato I S-cianchi '15	♟♟ 3

Gajaudo Cantina del Rossese

LOC. BUNDA
VIA ROMA, 33
18035 IMPERIA
TEL. +39 0184206958
www.cantinagajaudo.com

CELLAR SALES
PRE-BOOKED VISITS
ANNUAL PRODUCTION 150,000 bottles
HECTARES UNDER VINE 12.00

● Dolceacqua '15	♟♟ 3*
● Dolceacqua Arcagna '15	♟♟ 3
● Dolceacqua Luvaira '14	♟♟ 3
○ Riviera Ligure di Ponente Pigato '15	♟♟ 3

Nicola Guglierame

VIA CASTELLO, 4
18024 PORNASSIO [IM]
TEL. +39 3475696718
www.ormeasco-guglierame.it

ANNUAL PRODUCTION 18,000 bottles
HECTARES UNDER VINE 2.50

● Pornassio Sup. '13	♟♟ 3
● Pornassio '14	♟ 3
● Pornassio Sciac-Tra '14	♟ 3

Tenuta La Ghiaia

VIA FALCINELLO, 127
19038 SARZANA [SP]
TEL. +39 0187627307
www.tenutalaghiaia.it

CELLAR SALES
PRE-BOOKED VISITS
ACCOMMODATION
ANNUAL PRODUCTION 45,000 bottles
HECTARES UNDER VINE 5.50

○ Colli di Luni Vermentino Atys '14	♟♟ 3
● Colli di Luni Rosso 11 Nodi '14	♟ 3

Podere Lavandaro

via Castiglione
54035 Fosdinovo [MS]
Tel. +39 018768202
www.poderelavandaro.it

CELLAR SALES
PRE-BOOKED VISITS
ANNUAL PRODUCTION 22,000 bottles
HECTARES UNDER VINE 4.00

- ○ Colli di Luni Vermentino '15 — 🍷🍷 3*
- ○ Maséro '14 — 🍷 3
- ⊙ Merlarosa '15 — 🍷 3

Cantine Levante

via Villa Ragone, 21
16039 Sestri Levante [GE]
Tel. +39 0185 42466
cantinelevante@gmail.com

ANNUAL PRODUCTION 30,000 bottles

- ○ Portofino Bianchetta Genovese '15 — 🍷🍷 2*
- ● Portofino Ciliegiolo '15 — 🍷 2
- ● Portofino Cimixa '15 — 🍷 2
- ○ Portofino Vermentino '15 — 🍷 2

Podere Grecale

loc. Bussana
via Ciousse
18038 Sanremo [IM]
Tel. +39 01841956107
www.poderegrecale.it

CELLAR SALES
PRE-BOOKED VISITS
ANNUAL PRODUCTION 18,000 bottles
HECTARES UNDER VINE 3.00

- ○ Riviera Ligure di Ponente Pigato '15 — 🍷🍷 3*
- ○ Riviera Ligure di Ponente Vermentino '15 — 🍷 3
- ○ Riviera Ligure di Ponente Vermentino Maèn '14 — 🍷 3

Rossana Ruffini

via Tirolo, 58
19020 Bolano [SP]
Tel. +39 0187939988
g.brandani@libero.it

ANNUAL PRODUCTION 10,000 bottles
HECTARES UNDER VINE 3.00

- ○ Colli di Luni Vermentino Portolano '15 — 🍷🍷 2*
- ● Colli di Luni Rosso Logaiolo '14 — 🍷 2

Valdiscalve

loc. Reggimonti
s.da prov.le 42
19011 Bonassola [SP]
Tel. +39 0187818178
www.vermenting.com

CELLAR SALES
ANNUAL PRODUCTION 5,000 bottles
HECTARES UNDER VINE 1.00

- ○ Colline di Levanto Bianco Terre del Salice '15 — 🍷🍷 3
- ○ Colline di Levanto Bianco Costa di Macinara '15 — 🍷 2

La Vecchia Cantina

fraz. Salea
via Corta, 3
17031 Albenga [SV]
Tel. +39 3393733641
www.lavecchiacantinacalleri.it

CELLAR SALES
PRE-BOOKED VISITS
ANNUAL PRODUCTION 15,000 bottles
HECTARES UNDER VINE 4.00

- ○ Riviera Ligure di Ponente Albenganese Pigato '15 — 🍷🍷 3*
- ○ Riviera Ligure di Ponente Albenganese Vermentino '15 — 🍷🍷 3

LOMBARDY

A bumper year for Lombardy, for the average standard of tastings and for the number of awards received: 23 in all. With these results, the region confirms its role as a driving force in the Italian winemaking industry, with wines that are already extremely popular in Italy, and we are confident that exports will also benefit after a year of international media exposure, thanks to the success of ExpoMilano 2015. A stellar performance came in from Franciacorta, garnering an astonishing ten Tre Bicchieri. Over half a century has passed since it was established and there is no doubt that this district is in full command of its winemaking prowess, with its cuvées now starting to enjoy recognition around the world. A glance at the list of award-winning wines reveals that nine out of ten are Extra Brut or Pas Dosé, with the Franciacorta producers setting aside the cream of their production for these versions. The results are magical, since chardonnay and pinot nero grapes from the designation's best vineyards hardly need top-ups and bottling liquor to achieve excellence. The only Brut is Villa's seductive Rosé Boké 2012. Outstanding among the cellars on the podium was Bellavista, part of the Terra Moretti group, and Winery of the Year for this 30th edition of IW. Not so far away, Oltrepò is speeding along the quality route and won seven awards. A first-ever Tre Bicchieri was awarded to a Bonarda, the Campo del Monte 2015 by the Agnes brothers, whose elegant, fragrant wine is the perfect expression of this complex growing area. The rest of the mosaic is made up of excellent sparkling wines, whites and cruasés, whether they are DOCs or not matters little, and always from pinot nero, a grape has long been at home in this extraordinary hill habitat's calcareous soils. The proof of the pudding is in this year's success for red wines, with a Tre Bicchieri to Conte Vistarino's 2013 Bertone. Another great grape, another great terroir: nebbiolo or chiavennasca, and the Valtellina. Prizes went to five super reds, led by Negri's classic Sforzato 5 Stelle. Our review of award winners closes with a white, the amazing Lugana Molin from Ca' Maiol, making its fourth appearance on the podium, underscoring the importance of this designation shared with Veneto. And while these are the stars, remember that from the Valcalepio to Mantua, the Valcamonica to Botticino, oenological Lombardy is well on its way and always has more to offer.

Marchese Adorno

VIA GARLASSOLO, 30
27050 RETORBIDO [PV]
TEL. +39 0383374404
www.marcheseadorno-wines.it

CELLAR SALES
PRE-BOOKED VISITS
ANNUAL PRODUCTION 250,000 bottles
HECTARES UNDER VINE 85.00

After many changes, the winery owned by
Marchese Marcello Cattaneo Adorno has
found the course to follow in order to make
the most of its great resources and
potential. The substantial investments have
included the construction of a splendid
cellar and the renovation of the entire
estate. Under the technical management of
skilled oenologist Francesco Cervetti,
riesling, barbera, and pinot nero have been
identified as the main grape varieties on
which to focus in the quest for top-quality
wines. The range is already excellent,
scoring very high marks. Barbera Vigna del
Re 2014 is still young, with crisp fruit and
spice. The alluring fresh Bonarda 2015 is
also very good. Merlot Cliviano 2014 is the
Marchese's favourite wine, showing close
focused with good backbone and vibrant
aromas of currants and hay. The stylish
Pinot Nero Brugherio 2014 is exceptionally
well made, with a nose of medicinal herbs.

● OP Barbera V. del Re '14	▼▼	4
● OP Bonarda Vivace Costa del Sole '15	▼▼	2*
● Cliviano '14	▼▼	3
● OP Pinot Nero Brugherio '14	▼▼	2*
○ OP Pinot Grigio Dama d'Oro '15	▼	3
● OP Pinot Nero Rile Nero '14	▼	5
● Cliviano '13	♀♀	3
● OP Barbera V. del Re '12	♀♀	4
● OP Barbera V. del Re '11	♀♀	4
● OP Bonarda Costa del Sole '13	♀♀	2*
● OP Pinot Nero Rile Nero '13	♀♀	5
● OP Pinot Nero Rile Nero '11	♀♀	5
● OP Pinot Nero Rile Nero Riserva Privata '10	♀♀	5
○ OP Riesling Sup. Arcolaio '13	♀♀	3*
○ OP Riesling Sup. Arcolaio '12	♀♀	3*

F.lli Agnes

VIA CAMPO DEL MONTE, 1
27040 ROVESCALA [PV]
TEL. +39 038575206
www.fratelliagnes.it

CELLAR SALES
PRE-BOOKED VISITS
ANNUAL PRODUCTION 120,000 bottles
HECTARES UNDER VINE 21.00

Rovescala, in the eastern area of Oltrepò
Pavese, near the border with Emilia, is the
undisputed realm of Bonarda. Over the
years the determined brothers Sergio and
Cristiano Agnes have shown what they're
capable of with croatina, or rather pignola,
a subvariety with small, close-packed
bunches. The range of wines features all
the possible versions of the varietal – still
and semi-sparkling, dry and slightly sweet,
young and aged – with enviably consistent
quality. Campo Monte 2015 won a
memorable Tre Bicchieri for the area,
thanks also to the particularly good vintage:
a veritable delight of fragrant fruit, with
perfectly calibrated residual sugar. Cresta
del Ghiffi 2015 is almost as good, sweeter
but just as juicy, while Possessione del
Console 2015 is earthier and more austere.

● OP Bonarda Vivace Campo del Monte '15	▼▼▼	2*
● OP Bonarda Millennium '13	▼▼	4
● OP Bonarda Vivace Cresta del Ghiffi '15	▼▼	2*
● Possessione del Console '15	▼▼	3
● Loghetto '15	▼	3
● Loghetto '14	♀♀	3
● Loghetto '13	♀♀	3
● OP Bonarda Campo del Monte '13	♀♀	2*
● OP Bonarda Cresta del Ghiffi '13	♀♀	2*
● OP Bonarda Millennium '11	♀♀	4
● OP Bonarda Millennium '10	♀♀	4
● OP Possessione del Console '13	♀♀	3
● Poculum '12	♀♀	4

Anteo

LOC. CHIESA
27040 ROCCA DE' GIORGI [PV]
TEL. +39 038599073
www.anteovini.it

CELLAR SALES
PRE-BOOKED VISITS
ANNUAL PRODUCTION 200,000 bottles
HECTARES UNDER VINE 27.00

When it comes to Metodo Classico sparklers, this is one of the finest Oltrepò wineries. Founded late in life by Trento Cribellati, father of Ettore Piero and Antonella, its vaulted cellars housing stacks of bottles resting "sur lattes" and on riddling racks where they await disgorgement after turning by hand, offer a unique sight. The estate lies at the head of the Valle Versa and Valle Scuropasso, 380 metres above sea level, in the finest zone for the production of Oltrepò pinot nero sparklers. This year we particularly liked the close-focused, mineral Nature Ecru 2010, with a nose of berry fruit and pennyroyal, accompanied by good effervescence and stuffing. Riserva del Poeta 2008 is golden with firm structure, rich texture, and a distinctive evolved style. The coppery Cruasé is the most evolved of the two rosés, while the deeper-coloured Sabrage has a nose of herbs. The Bonarda and the vintage Moscato La Volpe e l'Uva are very varietal and well made.

○ La Volpe e l'Uva '15	▼▼ 3
● OP Bonarda Vivace Staffolo '15	▼▼ 2*
○ OP Pinot Nero Brut Riserva del Poeta '08	▼▼ 6
○ OP Pinot Nero Nature Écru '10	▼▼ 5
⊙ Brut Sabrage Rosé	▼ 4
⊙ OP Cruasé	▼ 4
○ OP Riesling Quadro di Mezzo '15	▼ 2
○ OP Pinot Nero Brut Cl. Nature Écru '03	♔♔♔ 4
○ OP Pinot Nero Brut Riserva del Poeta '07	♔♔ 6
○ OP Pinot Nero Nature Écru '09	♔♔ 5
○ OP Spumante Brut Tradition '09	♔♔ 4

Antica Fratta

VIA FONTANA, 11
25040 MONTICELLI BRUSATI [BS]
TEL. +39 030652068
www.anticafratta.it

CELLAR SALES
PRE-BOOKED VISITS
ANNUAL PRODUCTION 300,000 bottles
HECTARES UNDER VINE 4.00

The Ziliani family, who own Guido Berlucchi, also have another Franciacorta winery. Antica Fratta is housed in a handsome 18th-century palazzo that was restored in the late 1970s. It has always been known locally as the "Cantinon", due to its splendid vaulted cellars, laid out in the shape of a cross. Indeed, the palazzo was once the home of a rich wine merchant and is now the venue for events and receptions. The winery operates independently from Guido Berlucchi, using grapes from its small own estate and from trusted suppliers. Although Antica Fratta's production figures are much lower than its parent company's, in terms of quality it is every bit as good as the area's most prestigious wineries. This is demonstrated by the deep, fresh Riserva Quintessence 2007, which stood out in our finals for its complex balance, creaminess, and elegant close-focused oaky and tertiary nuances on a long finish.

○ Franciacorta Extra Brut Quintessence Ris. '07	▼▼ 7
○ Franciacorta Nature Essence '11	▼▼ 5
○ Franciacorta Rosé Essence '11	▼▼ 5
○ Franciacorta Satèn Essence '11	▼▼ 5
○ Franciacorta Brut Essence '08	♔♔ 5
○ Franciacorta Essence Nature '09	♔♔ 5
○ Franciacorta Extra Brut Quintessence Ris. '07	♔♔ 7
○ Franciacorta Extra Brut Quintessence Ris. '06	♔♔ 7
○ Franciacorta Rosé Essence '10	♔♔ 5
⊙ Franciacorta Rosé Essence '09	♔♔ 5
○ Franciacorta Satèn Essence '10	♔♔ 5
○ Franciacorta Satèn Essence '09	♔♔ 5

LOMBARDY

Antica Tesa

Loc. Mattina
via Merano, 28
25080 Botticino [BS]
Tel. +39 0302691500

CELLAR SALES
PRE-BOOKED VISITS
ANNUAL PRODUCTION 40,000 bottles
HECTARES UNDER VINE 10.00

Botticino is famous for its prized marbles, but the red wines made from its handsome south-facing vineyards, caressed by the winds and planted to sangiovese, barbera, marzemino, and schiava gentile, are distinctive and characterful. Pierangelo Noventa and has family lovingly tend their perfectly aspected organic plots, which enjoy splendid views at an altitude of 450 metres above sea level. They yield a series of excellent wines that accurately recount the terroir. Antica Tesa is the benchmark winery for this small DOC zone in the province of Brescia. This year we tasted an excellent Vigna del Gobbio 50 2012, aged for over 50 months, partly from dried grapes. Its attractive garnet hue is accompanied by a nose of ripe red berries, spices, and cocoa powder, and a palate with good structure and elegant balance. Pià de la Tesa 2012 is glorious, although it still has a few rough edges, while Colle degli Ulivi 2014 is simpler and suppler.

● Botticino V. del Gobbio 50 '12	▼▼ 5
● Botticino Pià de la Tesa '12	▼▼ 3
● Botticino Colle degli Ulivi '14	▼ 2
● Botticino Colle degli Ulivi	♀♀ 2*
● Botticino Pià de la Tesa '11	♀♀ 3
● Botticino Pià de la Tesa '10	♀♀ 3
● Botticino Pià de la Tesa '09	♀♀ 3
● Botticino Pià de la Tesa '07	♀♀ 3*
● Botticino Pià de la Tesa '06	♀♀ 3
● Botticino V. degli Ulivi '07	♀♀ 2*
● Botticino V. del Gobbio '11	♀♀ 5
● Botticino V. del Gobbio '10	♀♀ 5
● Botticino V. del Gobbio '09	♀♀ 5
● Botticino V. del Gobbio '08	♀♀ 5
● Botticino V. del Gobbio '06	♀♀ 5
● Botticino V. del Gobbio '05	♀♀ 5

Ar.Pe.Pe.

via del Buon Consiglio, 4
23100 Sondrio
Tel. +39 0342214120
www.arpepe.com

CELLAR SALES
PRE-BOOKED VISITS
ANNUAL PRODUCTION 80,000 bottles
HECTARES UNDER VINE 13.00

Patience has always been a virtue at Ar.Pe. Pe. The Pellizzatti Perego family's winery was one of the first to believe in the ageing potential of the Valtellina wines, sometimes releasing them more than ten years after harvest. They are the result of hard work in the vineyard, long maceration on the skins, large barrels only, and long bottle ageing. The range consists of increasingly well-defined, terroir-true mountain Nebbiolos that are complex and nuanced. In the 2014 vintage all the grapes were used for the Rosso di Valtellina, and we have to wait a further 12 months to taste Sassella Rocce Rosse Riserva 2007. Grumello Buon Consiglio 2007 is extraordinarily elegant, with original notes of rust, hints of raspberries, and unique complexity. On the palate it shows astonishing harmony and finesse, with a long, aristocratic finish. Vigna Regina 2007 is very complex and nuanced, offering a nose of tobacco, liquorice, and red berries with elegant rhubarb notes, and an alluring firm palate with an exceptionally long, full finish.

● Valtellina Sup. Grumello Buon Consiglio Ris. '07	▼▼▼ 6
● Valtellina Sup. Sassella Stella Retica Ris. '11	▼▼ 5
● Valtellina Sup. Sassella V. Regina Ris. '07	▼▼ 8
● Rosso di Valtellina '14	▼▼ 4
● Valtellina Sup. Grumello Rocca de Piro Ris. '11	▼▼ 5
● Valtellina Sup. Inferno Fiamme Antiche Ris. '11	▼▼ 5
● Valtellina Sup. Sassella Rocce Rosse Ris. '05	♀♀♀ 7
● Valtellina Sup. Sassella Stella Retica Ris. '10	♀♀♀ 5

Ballabio

via San Biagio, 32
27045 Casteggio [PV]
Tel. +39 0383805728
www.ballabio.net

CELLAR SALES
PRE-BOOKED VISITS
ANNUAL PRODUCTION 100,000 bottles
HECTARES UNDER VINE 60.00

This legendary winery was founded by Angelo Ballabio in 1905 and represented a milestone in the winemaking history of Oltrepò Pavese for years. Today, of course, everything has changed, including its handsome headquarters, in the Casteggio foothills. Above all, its huge, very modern cellar is now equipped for the production of sparkling wines, with presses fed by gravity conveyors. Filippo Nevelli is flanked by expert oenologist Carlo Casavechia in his quest for absolute quality. The elegant, crisp Brut Farfalla effortlessly won our Tre Bicchieri for the second year running: close-focused and lean, with the typical red-berry nose of pinot nero accompanied by intriguing notes of aromatic herbs, a fine bead and a long, flavoursome finish. The Rosé is also very good, with its usual pale hue and clean, sound aromas of strawberries and raspberries. Pinot Grigio Clastidium 2015 is harmonious and varietal, while the vintage Bonarda is fragrant and flavoursome.

○ Brut Farfalla	♟♟♟	4*
⊙ Brut Rosé Farfalla	♟♟	4
● OP Bonarda V. delle Cento Pertiche '15	♟♟	3
○ OP Pinot Grigio Clastidium '15	♟♟	2*
● Narbusto '13	♟	3
○ Brut Farfalla	♟♟♟♟	4*
● OP Bonarda V. delle Cento Pertiche '13	♟♟	3
● OP Bonarda V. delle Cento Pertiche '11	♟♟	2*
● OP Bonarda V. delle Cento Pertiche '10	♟♟	2*
● OP Bonarda Vivace V. delle Cento Pertiche '09	♟♟	2*
⊙ OP Pinot Nero Brut Cruasé '07	♟♟	4
⊙ OP Pinot Nero Brut Cruasé	♟♟	4

Barone Pizzini

via San Carlo, 14
25050 Provaglio d'Iseo [BS]
Tel. +39 0309848311
www.baronepizzini.it

CELLAR SALES
PRE-BOOKED VISITS
ACCOMMODATION
ANNUAL PRODUCTION 330,000 bottles
HECTARES UNDER VINE 47.00
VITICULTURE METHOD Certified Organic
SUSTAINABLE WINERY

Barone Pizzini has won the great challenge. Years of excellent production by the winery headed by Silvano Brescianini have demonstrated that environmentally friendly viticulture (organic and biodynamic) and sustainable, low-impact production facilities can yield top-level wines that fully express the unique characteristics of the terroir. And not just in Franciacorta either, but also at the winery's Marche estate, Pivalta, and at Ghiaccioforte in Maremma. Top honours went to one of the finest expressions of Franciacorta Riserva: Non Dosato Bagnadore 2009, a Chardonnay and Pinot Nero cuvée from vines over 20 years old in the Roccolo vineyard, which lies on the hillside, near a wood. After ageing for more than 70 months on the lees, it opens complex and elegant, with juicy fruit supported by a fresh swathe of acidity that ensures lively, dynamic progression through to the long finish of vanilla and cedarwood. Dosaggio Zero Naturae 2012 is also excellent.

○ Franciacorta Non Dosato Bagnadore Ris. '09	♟♟♟	6
○ Franciacorta Brut Naturae Edizione '12	♟♟	5
○ Franciacorta Brut Animante	♟♟	5
⊙ Franciacorta Brut Rosé Edizione '12	♟♟	5
○ Franciacorta Satèn Edizione '12	♟♟	5
○ Curtefranca Bianco '15	♟	3
● Curtefranca Rosso '14	♟	3
○ Franciacorta Brut	♟	5
○ Franciacorta Brut Naturae '11	♟♟♟	5
○ Franciacorta Brut Nature '10	♟♟♟	5
○ Franciacorta Brut Nature '09	♟♟♟	5
○ Franciacorta Brut Nature '08	♟♟♟	5
○ Curtefranca Polzina Bianco '12	♟♟	3
○ Franciacorta Brut Bagnadore Ris. '06	♟♟	5
⊙ Franciacorta Brut Rosé '09	♟♟	5
● San Carlo Sebino '09	♟♟	5

★★Bellavista

VIA BELLAVISTA, 5
25030 ERBUSCO [BS]
TEL. +39 0307762000
www.bellavistawine.it

CELLAR SALES
PRE-BOOKED VISITS
ANNUAL PRODUCTION 1,400,000 bottles
HECTARES UNDER VINE 190.00
SUSTAINABLE WINERY

Forty years from its foundation, Bellavista is one of the most prestigious names in the Italian wine world, successfully representing the Franciacorta DOCG throughout the world. Vittorio Moretti's estate, which sees the increasing involvement of his daughter Francesca alongside talented oenologist Mattia Vezzola, heads a group that also includes Contaldi Castaldi, and Petra and La Badiola in Tuscany. Forty years of accolades and extraordinary Franciacorta cuvées capable of defying time have earned Bellavista our Winery of the Year award. The delicately balanced Pas Operé 2009 deservedly took our top accolade. It is a little masterpiece of complexity and freshness, brimming with fruit and fresh citrusy nuances, deep and delightfully drinkable, epitomizing the Bellavista style. Brut Teatro alla Scala 2010 is juicy and zesty, with good backbone and a very fine bead. We awarded a Retrospective Tre Bicchieri to Meraviglioso, the extraordinary cuvée from Franciacorta Riservas spanning 30 years.

○ Franciacorta Pas Operé '09	♖♖♖	7
○ Franciacorta Brut Alma Cuvée	♖♖	5
○ Franciacorta Brut Teatro alla Scala '10	♖♖	7
○ Curtefranca Convento SS. Annunciata '13	♖♖	6
○ Curtefranca Uccellanda '13	♖♖	6
⊙ Franciacorta Brut Rosé '11	♖♖	7
○ Franciacorta Satèn '11	♖♖	7
○ Franciacorta Extra Brut Vittorio Moretti Ris. '08	♔♔♔	8
○ Franciacorta Extra Brut Vittorio Moretti Ris. '06	♔♔♔	8
○ Franciacorta Gran Cuvée Pas Operé '06	♔♔♔	8
○ Franciacorta Gran Cuvée Pas Operé '05	♔♔♔	7
○ Franciacorta Gran Cuvée Pas Operé '04	♔♔♔	7
○ Riserva Vittorio Moretti Meraviglioso	♔♔♔	8

Guido Berlucchi & C.

LOC. BORGONATO
P.ZZA DURANTI, 4
25040 CORTE FRANCA [BS]
TEL. +39 030984381
www.berlucchi.it

CELLAR SALES
PRE-BOOKED VISITS
ACCOMMODATION
ANNUAL PRODUCTION 4,400,000 bottles
HECTARES UNDER VINE 550.00
VITICULTURE METHOD Certified Organic
SUSTAINABLE WINERY

The estate that spawned the whole Franciacorta phenomenon just over 50 years ago is in excellent health. Franco Ziliani, its founder and chairman, is able to count on an extraordinary team formed by his children: oenologist Arturo, marketing manager Cristina, and Paolo, responsible for the business side. Several years ago the family went back to using only Franciacorta grapes for their cuvées, and together have earned the winery the status of leading Italian sparkling wine producer, with an annual output of over four million bottles and constantly growing exports. While the Extrême Riserva 2008 is still ageing on the lees, the estate shows its extraordinary potential with another cuvée, the Nature 2009 of the 61 range, named after Berlucchi's year of foundation. It is a complex, elegant wine that manages to combine depth and finesse with extraordinary drinkability, earning itself a well-deserved Tre Bicchieri. The same range also features an excellent Satèn and Rosé, while the Brut 2011 and Brut 61 are sound. Well done indeed!

○ Franciacorta Nature 61 '09	♖♖♖	5
○ Franciacorta Brut 61	♖♖	5
○ Franciacorta Brut Cellarius '11	♖♖	5
⊙ Franciacorta Rosé 61	♖♖	5
○ Franciacorta Satèn 61	♖♖	5
○ Franciacorta Brut Cellarius '08	♔♔♔	5
○ Franciacorta Brut Cellarius '07	♔♔♔	5
○ Franciacorta Brut Extrême Palazzo Lana '05	♔♔♔	6
○ Franciacorta Brut Extrême Palazzo Lana Ris. '06	♔♔♔	6
○ Franciacorta Extra Brut Extreme Palazzo Lana Ris. '07	♔♔♔	7
○ Franciacorta Satèn Palazzo Lana '06	♔♔♔	6

Cantina Bersi Serlini

LOC. CERETO
VIA CERETO, 7
25050 PROVAGLIO D'ISEO [BS]
TEL. +39 0309823338
www.bersiserlini.it

CELLAR SALES
PRE-BOOKED VISITS
ACCOMMODATION AND RESTAURANT SERVICE
ANNUAL PRODUCTION 200,000 bottles
HECTARES UNDER VINE 30.00
VITICULTURE METHOD Certified Organic

Located in the Torbiere di Iseo area, this
30-hectare estate that uses only its grapes,
is run by two women: Maddalena Bersi
Serlini and her sister Chiara. In 1886, their
family purchased the handsome estate in
Provaglio, on the shores of Lake Iseo,
which was once the grange of the nearby
Benedictine monastery of San Pietro in
Lamosa. Following extensive renovation
and extension work, today it is a charming
blend of old and new. As always, the range
of wines presented was excellent, topped
by the fresh, lively Extra Brut 2012, with a
soft, elegant nose of ripe fruit, cedarwood,
and floral nuances, a very fine bead, and a
spirited, racy, zesty palate. The Satèn is
excellent, showing complex and rounded,
while the 2012 vintage of Cuvée n. 4 is
spicy with good backbone. The complex,
well-orchestrated Brut Rosé is among the
best of its kind.

F.lli Bettini

LOC. SAN GIACOMO
VIA NAZIONALE, 4A
23036 TEGLIO [SO]
TEL. +39 0342786068
bettvini@tin.it

CELLAR SALES
PRE-BOOKED VISITS
ANNUAL PRODUCTION 200,000 bottles
HECTARES UNDER VINE 15.00

The winery in the Teglio hamlet of San
Giacomo has 130 years of experience and
is one of the best-known Valtellina
producers. It is situated in the heart of
Valgella, the largest of the three subzones
of the Valtellina Superiore designation, with
137 hectares of vineyards clinging to the
mountainsides. The estate comprises 15
hectares, scattered over the main Valtellina
subzones. The wide range is nicely
diversified, offering a concentrated,
expressive style with pronounced fruit, and
the use of new oak barrels for the flagship
wines. Sforzato Vigneti di Spina has been
steadily improving, as shown by the 2011
vintage with a complex nose of leather,
tobacco, and bottled cherries, and powerful
palate kept in check by close-knit tannins
and ending in a very long finish. The
elegant Valgella Vigna La Cornella 2011
has a delicate fruity, floral nose with a
swathe of medicinal herbs, and a
well-orchestrated palate with good acidity
and an original long finish.

○ Franciacorta Extra Brut '12	♟♟ 6
○ Franciacorta Brut Anniversario	♟♟ 6
○ Franciacorta Brut Anteprima	♟♟ 5
○ Franciacorta Brut Cuvée n. 4 '12	♟♟ 5
⊙ Franciacorta Brut Rosé	♟♟ 4
○ Franciacorta Brut Satèn	♟♟ 5
○ Franciacorta Non Dosato Mia Ris. '05	♟♟ 6
○ Franciacorta Demi Sec Nuvola	♟ 4
○ Franciacorta Brut '11	♟♟ 5
○ Franciacorta Brut Cuvée n. 4 '10	♟♟ 5
○ Franciacorta Brut Cuvée n. 4 '07	♟♟ 5
⊙ Franciacorta Brut Rosé Rosa Rosae	♟♟ 5
○ Franciacorta Extra Brut '08	♟♟ 6
○ Franciacorta Satèn '10	♟♟ 5

● Sforzato di Valtellina Vign. di Spina '11	♟♟ 7
● Valtellina Sup. Sant'Andrea '11	♟♟ 5
● Valtellina Sup. Sassella Reale '11	♟♟ 5
● Valtellina Sup. Valgella V. La Cornella '11	♟♟ 5
● Sforzato di Valtellina Vign. di Spina '10	♟♟ 6
● Valtellina Sfursat '11	♟♟ 5
● Valtellina Sfursat '10	♟♟ 5
● Valtellina Sup. Inferno Prodigio '10	♟♟ 4
● Valtellina Sup. Inferno Prodigio '09	♟♟ 3
● Valtellina Sup. Inferno Prodigio '08	♟♟ 3
● Valtellina Sup. Sant'Andrea '10	♟♟ 4
● Valtellina Sup. Sassella Reale '10	♟♟ 4
● Valtellina Sup. Sassella Reale '09	♟♟ 3
● Valtellina Sup. Valgella V. La Cornella '10	♟♟ 4
● Valtellina Sup. Valgella V. La Cornella '09	♟♟ 3

Bisi

LOC. CASCINA SAN MICHELE
FRAZ. VILLA MARONE, 70
27040 SAN DAMIANO AL COLLE [PV]
TEL. +39 038575037
www.aziendagricolabisi.it

CELLAR SALES
PRE-BOOKED VISITS
ANNUAL PRODUCTION 90,000 bottles
HECTARES UNDER VINE 30.00

Claudio Bisi is an emblematic case of what can happen in a land like Oltrepò Pavese. He shuns the limelight, preferring to let his wines to do the talking, which they undeniably do. Indeed, they have a strong personality, able to express the terroir of the various vineyards that Claudio tends with painstaking care. Although they are the product of different soils, microclimates, and grape varieties, they share the same commendable quality and emotional charge. This winery deserves more recognition and we gave our highest accolade to Bonarda Vivace La Peccatrice 2015, which was among the very best of a particularly fine vintage: concentrated but not overwhelming, fragrant, and dry with exceptionally fine tannins. The monovarietal Riesling LaGrà 2015 combines juiciness with finesse and a floral, citrusy nose with notes of aromatic herbs, Pinot Nero Calonga 2013 vaunts nice spicy notes, and Villa Marone Passito, from malvasia, is as good as ever. Barbera Roncolongo 2012 has impressive texture, which needs more time to be tamed.

● OP Bonarda Vivace La Peccatrice '15	♟♟	2*
● Barbera Senz'Aiuto '14	♟♟	3
○ Bianco Passito Villa Marone '12	♟♟	4
● OP Barbera Roncolongo '12	♟♟	3
● OP Pinot Nero Calonga '13	♟♟	3
○ OP Riesling LaGrà '15	♟♟	2*
● OP Barbera Pezzabianca '13	♟	4
● Calonga '12	♟♟	5
○ LaGrà '14	♟♟	3
○ LaGrà '13	♟♟	3*
● OP Bonarda Vivace La Peccatrice '14	♟♟	2*
● Pramattone '13	♟♟	3
● Roncolongo '11	♟♟	4
● Ultrapadum '13	♟♟	3

Castello Bonomi

VIA SAN PIETRO, 46
25030 COCCAGLIO [BS]
TEL. +39 0307721015
www.castellobonomi.it

CELLAR SALES
PRE-BOOKED VISITS
ANNUAL PRODUCTION 100,000 bottles
HECTARES UNDER VINE 20.00

The Paladin family have always been active in the wine sector in Veneto, and also own a Tuscan operation, Fattoria di Vescine, in Chianti Classico. A few years ago the Paladin brothers purchased this fine estate on the southern border of Franciacorta, and commenced its excellent production. Castello Bonomi vaunts an impressive 20 hectares of largely terraced vineyards at the foot of Monte Orfano, on the oldest soils of the area. Its cuvées are generally extraordinarily ageworthy. Franciacorta Dosage Zero 2009 worthily represented the estate in our finals. It is a cuvée of 50% Chardonnay and 50% Pinot Nero, which undergoes long ageing on the lees before disgorgement. The bright straw yellow hue is accompanied by a complex, evolved nose with top notes of apples and pears followed by delicate hints of vanilla and crusty bread. On the palate it is fruity with notes of aromatic herbs and a full, elegant finish.

○ Franciacorta Dosage Zero '09	♟♟	8
● Curtefranca Rosso Cordelio '11	♟♟	7
○ Franciacorta Brut Cru Perdü	♟♟	6
○ Franciacorta Extra Brut Cuvée Lucrezia Et. Nera '06	♟♟	8
⊙ Franciacorta Rosé	♟♟	7
○ Franciacorta Satèn	♟♟	7
○ Franciacorta Gran Cuvée	♟	6
○ Franciacorta Brut Cru Perdu '04	♟♟♟	7
○ Franciacorta Extra Brut Lucrezia Et. Nera '04	♟♟♟	8
⊙ Franciacorta Brut Rosé	♟♟	7
○ Franciacorta Dosage Zero '07	♟♟	8
○ Franciacorta Extra Brut Lucrezia '04	♟♟	8

La Boscaiola

VIA RICCAFANA, 19
25033 COLOGNE [BS]
TEL. +39 0307156386
www.laboscaiola.com

CELLAR SALES
PRE-BOOKED VISITS
ANNUAL PRODUCTION 50,000 bottles
HECTARES UNDER VINE 7.00

La Boscaiola was founded by the extraordinary Nelson Cenci, who was a writer, physician, and soldier. Born in Rimini, Nelson moved to Cologne in the 1960s to be near his beloved Alpini regiment, with which he fortunately returned safe and sound from the terrible expedition to the Russian front where the Tridentina division was deployed. Over the years he created a handsome estate specializing in Franciacortas, now passionately run by his daughters Giuliana and Maria Grazia, with seven hectares of fine vineyards on the slopes of Monte Orfano. The selection of wines presented this year was excellent. Brut La Capinera is taut and refreshing, with fruity, balsamic nuances, while the fresh Brut Sessanta 2007 boasts elegant floral aromas followed by attractive oaky nuances. The subtle, elegant Rosé La Capinera offers edgy, racy notes of red berries, and Extra Brut Nelson Cenci has a beautifully creamy, fruity personality underpinned by a lively swathe of acidity.

○ Franciacorta Brut La Capinera	♟♟ 4
○ Franciacorta Brut Sessanta '07	♟♟ 6
○ Franciacorta Extra Brut Nelson Cenci	♟♟ 6
○ Franciacorta Pas Dosé Zero	♟♟ 4
⊙ Franciacorta Rosé La Capinera	♟♟ 4
○ Franciacorta Satèn La Via della Seta	♟ 5
○ Franciacorta Brut '04	♟♟ 4

Tenuta Il Bosco

LOC. IL BOSCO
27049 ZENEVREDO [PV]
TEL. +39 0385245326
www.ilbosco.com

CELLAR SALES
PRE-BOOKED VISITS
ANNUAL PRODUCTION 1,000,000 bottles
HECTARES UNDER VINE 152.00

Almost 30 years ago the Zonin family purchased this handsome Oltrepò estate that belonged to the Monastery of Santa Maria Teodote in the Middle Ages. Since then the area under vine has increased from 30 to over 150 hectares, planted mainly with the most widespread locally grown varieties, such as barbera, croatina and pinot nero. The latter is not only fermented as a red wine, but is also the star of the estate's sparkling production that is now yielding excellent results under the capable guidance of manager Piernicola Olmo, following a few initial commercial uncertainties. Cruasé Oltrenero has taken another Tre Bicchieri two years after the first. A lively sparkler with a bright coppery hue, it has a concentrated nose of berries and pennyroyal, good stuffing, a fine bead, backbone, and minerality. The plush, aromatic Pinot Nero Brut Oltrenero also has creamy effervescence and fullness. Bonarda 2015 is exuberant and fruity, while the two Philéo sparklers are very fragrant.

⊙ OP Cruasé Oltrenero	♟♟♟ 5
● OP Bonarda Vivace '15	♟♟ 2*
○ OP Pinot Nero Brut Martinotti Philéo	♟♟ 3
○ OP Pinot Nero Brut Oltrenero	♟♟ 5
⊙ Philèo Extra Dry Rosé Martinotti	♟♟ 2
○ Brera '15	♟ 2
○ OP Malvasia Vivace '15	♟ 2
● OP Pinot Nero Poggio Pelato '13	♟ 3
○ OP Pinot Nero Brut Nature Oltrenero '10	♟♟ 6
● OP Pinot Nero Poggio Pelato '11	♟♟ 3

Bosio

FRAZ. TIMOLINE
VIA M. GATTI, 4
25040 CORTE FRANCA [BS]
TEL. +39 0309826224
www.bosiofranciacorta.it

CELLAR SALES
PRE-BOOKED VISITS
ANNUAL PRODUCTION 100,000 bottles
HECTARES UNDER VINE 30.00

Bosio was founded around 15 years ago by oenologist and agronomist Cesare Bosio and his economics graduate sister Laura, who pooled their expertise to extend the family vineyards to 30 hectares and built a modern new cellar in Corte Franca. The level of their Franciacortas and wines is excellent, due to the fine vineyards tended with Cesare's skill and the utmost respect for the environment. This year Bosio finally won its first Tre Bicchieri with Riserva Girolamo Bosio 2009, dedicated to the estate's founder, a cuvee from 70% pinot nero and 30% chardonnay, which ages on the lees for over five years. It vaunts creamy effervescence and a sophisticated nose of ripe fruit and summer flowers, with hints of vanilla and white chocolate. The palate is deep and well orchestrated, with a long, refreshing finish of aromatic herbs and white-fleshed fruit. Both the Nature 2011 and the Rosé 2012 are excellent.

Alessio Brandolini

FRAZ. BOFFALORA, 68
27040 SAN DAMIANO AL COLLE [PV]
TEL. +39 038575232
www.alessiobrandolini.com

ANNUAL PRODUCTION 50,000 bottles
HECTARES UNDER VINE 9.00

Alessio Brandolini is another young Oltrepò producer who gives us high hopes for the area's future. Immediately after completing his oenology degree, he lost his father Costante, along with his precious experience in vineyard management. However, Alessio did not give up and continued his quest to reveal the full potential of his vineyards, particularly suited for the production of red wines but also for pinot noir, which he was unable to resist turning into a sparkler, with very encouraging results. Bardughino 2015 is a still Malvasia with an intriguing nose of super-ripe tropical fruit. Beneficio 2012, a classic Rosso Oltrepò blend, is very juicy and requires bottle ageing to smooth out its tannins. Bonarda Vivace 2015 is well made, dry and balsamic, while the still version, Il Soffio 2015, is beefy and alcoholic. The two Metodo Classicos are pleasant: the delicate Luogo D'Agosto 2011 and the bigger Rosé Note d'Agosto 2011.

○ Franciacorta Pas Dosé Girolamo Bosio Ris. '09	♥♥♥ 5
○ Franciacorta Nature '11	♥♥ 5
⊙ Franciacorta Brut Rosé '12	♥♥ 5
○ Franciacorta Satèn	♥♥ 5
○ Franciacorta Brut	♥ 5
○ Franciacorta Brut '08	♀♀ 5
⊙ Franciacorta Brut Rosé '11	♀♀ 5
⊙ Franciacorta Brut Rosé '09	♀♀ 5
○ Franciacorta Extra Brut Boschedòr '10	♀♀ 5
○ Franciacorta Extra Brut Boschedòr '09	♀♀ 5
○ Franciacorta Extra Brut Boschedòr '09	♀♀ 5
○ Franciacorta Nature '10	♀♀ 5
○ Franciacorta Nature '09	♀♀ 5
○ Franciacorta Pas Dosé Girolamo Bosio Ris. '07	♀♀ 5

○ Il Bardughino '15	♥♥ 2*
● Il Beneficio '12	♥♥ 2*
● OP Bonarda Vivace Il Cassino '15	♥♥ 2*
○ Brut M. Cl. Luogo d'Agosto '11	♥ 3
⊙ Brut M. Cl. Rosé Note d'Agosto '11	♥ 3
● OP Bonarda Il Soffio '15	♥ 2
○ Brut M. Cl. Luogo d'Agosto '10	♀♀ 3
○ Il Bardughino '14	♀♀ 2*
○ Il Bardughino '13	♀♀ 2*
● Il Beneficio '11	♀♀ 2*
● OP Bonarda Vivace Il Cassino '14	♀♀ 2*
● OP Bonarda Vivace Il Cassino '13	♀♀ 2*

La Brugherata

FRAZ. ROSCIATE
VIA G. MEDOLAGO, 47
24020 SCANZOROSCIATE [BG]
TEL. +39 035655202
www.labrugherata.it

CELLAR SALES
PRE-BOOKED VISITS
ANNUAL PRODUCTION 40,000 bottles
HECTARES UNDER VINE 7.00

Always among the top producers in the Bergamo area, the estate owned by the Bendinelli family has the rare characteristic of offering a limited range of wines with a clearly identifiable style and quality year after year. Oenologist Beppe Bassi is an extremely reliable benchmark and the results are clear to see: clean, close-focused wines that always retain their personality, vintage after vintage. Moscato di Scanzo Doge 2013 is still young but full of promise. It has a nose of hay and aromatic herbs with typical notes of prunes and India rubber. The palate is mellow and voluptuous, with well-defined character and a nice finish. The big, solidly built Doglio Riserva 2012 is an evolved red with good, sound fruit offering notes of blackberries and blueberries. Rosso di Alberico 2015 is a pleasant, fragrant Merlot, while the white Vescovado del Feudo 2015 has an attractive tropical vein.

Cà Maiol

VIA COLLI STORICI, 119
25015 DESENZANO DEL GARDA [BS]
TEL. +39 0309910006
www.camaiol.it

CELLAR SALES
PRE-BOOKED VISITS
ANNUAL PRODUCTION 1,500,000 bottles
HECTARES UNDER VINE 160.00
SUSTAINABLE WINERY

Fabio and Patrizia Contato lovingly run the handsome family estate covering an area of over 150 hectares in the Lugana production zone. Years of work have brought the winery, once known as Provenza, to the height of excellence. The renovation of the vineyards and cellar, studies on oak and ageing of wines, the almost complete conversion to organic methods in the vineyards, and great attention to sustainability and renewable energy sources are just some of the ingredients of its success. Lugana Molin 2015 confirms itself one of the finest wines of the denomination once again, earning a Tre Bicchieri. It's a veritable model of refreshing fruit, expressive fullness, and mineral depth, which make it intriguingly drinkable when young, but also capable of long bottle ageing. The Fabio Contato 2014 selection, matured in new wood, is also very well made.

● Moscato di Scanzo Doge '13	♟♟ 7
● Rosso di Alberico '15	♟♟ 2*
● Valcalepio Rosso Doglio Ris. '12	♟♟ 4
○ Vescovado del Feudo '15	♟ 2
● Moscato di Scanzo Doge '12	♟♟ 7
● Moscato di Scanzo Doge '11	♟♟ 7
● Moscato di Scanzo Doge '10	♟♟ 7
● Moscato di Scanzo Doge '09	♟♟ 7
● Moscato Rosso Vermiglio di Roxia '13	♟♟ 3
● Priore '12	♟♟ 5
● Priore '09	♟♟ 3
● Valcalepio Rosso Vescovado '11	♟♟ 2*
○ Vescovado del Feudo '14	♟♟ 2*

○ Lugana Molin '15	♟♟♟ 3*
○ Lugana Sup. Sel. Fabio Contato '14	♟♟ 5
○ Lugana Brut M. Cl. 60 Mesi	♟♟ 4
○ Lugana Molin Bio '15	♟♟ 5
○ Lugana Prestige '15	♟♟ 3
○ Lugana Sup. Sel. Fabio Contato '12	♟♟ 5
○ Valtènesi Chiaretto '15	♟♟ 3
● Garda Cl. Groppello Joel '15	♟ 3
○ Lugana Molin '14	♟♟♟ 3*
○ Lugana Molin '13	♟♟♟ 3*
○ Lugana Molin '12	♟♟♟ 3*
○ Lugana Sel. Fabio Contato '07	♟♟♟ 5
○ Lugana Sup. Sel. Fabio Contato '11	♟♟♟ 5
○ Lugana Sup. Sel. Fabio Contato '10	♟♟♟ 5
○ Lugana Sup. Sel. Fabio Contato '09	♟♟♟ 5
○ Lugana Sup. Sel. Fabio Contato '06	♟♟♟ 5

★★★★ Ca' del Bosco

VIA ALBANO ZANELLA, 13
25030 ERBUSCO [BS]
TEL. +39 0307766111
www.cadelbosco.com

CELLAR SALES
PRE-BOOKED VISITS
ANNUAL PRODUCTION 1,470,000 bottles
HECTARES UNDER VINE 193.00
SUSTAINABLE WINERY

The estate headed by Maurizio Zanella is one of the very finest in Italy, and the array of awards it has managed to win in the 30-year history of our Guide is impressive. It represents the very pinnacle of Italian wine and ranks among the top producers in the world. We urge you to visit the estate's extremely modern headquarters: a welcoming cellar surrounded by woods and vineyards, equipped with the most sophisticated technologies and adorned with works of art. The product range, commencing with the Franciacortas, is very comprehensive and every single wine is excellent. We awarded Tre Bicchieri to the enthralling 2011 vintage of Dosage Zéro Vintage Collection, one of Cà del Bosco's great classics. It has a bright, greenish-yellow hue, an extraordinarily fine bead, and a nose with elegant, complex top notes of citrus fruit and flowers, followed by vanilla and white chocolate. It is unhesitatingly dry on the palate, with rare depth and linearity, and fresh, creamy fruit on the exceptionally long finish.

○ Franciacorta Dosage Zéro Vintage Collection '11	♟♟♟ 8
○ Curtefranca Chardonnay '12	♟♟ 8
○ Franciacorta Dosage Zéro Noir Vintage Collection '07	♟♟ 8
○ Franciacorta Satèn Vintage Collection '11	♟♟ 8
● Carmenero '09	♟♟ 8
○ Curtefranca Bianco '15	♟♟ 5
● Curtefranca Rosso '13	♟♟ 5
○ Franciacorta Brut Cuvée Prestige	♟♟ 5
○ Franciacorta Brut Vintage Collection '11	♟♟ 8
● Il Merlot '09	♟♟ 8
● Maurizio Zanella '11	♟♟ 8
● Pinéro '12	♟♟ 8
⊙ Franciacorta Rosé Cuvée Prestige	♟ 6
○ Franciacorta Dosage Zéro Noir Vintage Collection Ris. '06	♟♟♟ 8

Ca' del Gè

FRAZ. CA' DEL GÈ, 3
27040 MONTALTO PAVESE [PV]
TEL. +39 0383870179
www.cadelge.it

CELLAR SALES
PRE-BOOKED VISITS
ANNUAL PRODUCTION 180,000 bottles
HECTARES UNDER VINE 40.00

Enzo Padroggi, who founded the estate in 1985 and passed away before his time a few years ago, has left the family business in excellent hands. His capable children Carlo, Stefania, and Sara continue to run it with great care and dedication. The 40 hectares under vine, tended using low-impact methods, are split between Montalto Pavese, where the winery and the family home are and whose chalky limestone soils are ideal for riesling and pinot nero, and Cigognola, for the traditional reds. Riesling Renano Il Marinoni, Enzo Padroggi's pride and joy, is back in a "young" version. The 2015 vintage vaunts fragrant summer flowers and pennyroyal. The Metodo Classico, from pinot nero, is also very good: sound and firmly structured, but easy drinking. Riesling Italico Brinà 2015 is soft and caressing; Filagn Long 2015 is more floral. The rest of the range is as pleasant as ever.

○ Il Marinoni '15	♟♟ 2*
○ OP Pinot Nero Brut M. Cl. '11	♟♟ 3
○ OP Riesling Brinà '15	♟♟ 2*
● OP Bonarda Vivace Bricco del Prete '15	♟ 2
○ OP Moscato Frizzante '15	♟ 2
○ OP Riesling Filagn Long '15	♟ 2
● OP Bonarda Vivace '13	♟♟ 2*
● OP Bonarda Vivace '12	♟♟ 2*
● OP Buttafuoco Fajro '10	♟♟ 4
○ OP Moscato Frizzante '13	♟♟ 2*
○ OP Pinot Nero Brut '09	♟♟ 3
○ OP Pinot Nero Brut M. Cl. '10	♟♟ 3*
○ OP Riesling Brinà '14	♟♟ 2*

Ca' di Frara

via Casa Ferrari, 1
27040 Mornico Losana [PV]
Tel. +39 0383892299
www.cadifrara.com

CELLAR SALES
PRE-BOOKED VISITS
ANNUAL PRODUCTION 400,000 bottles
HECTARES UNDER VINE 46.00

Almost 20 years have passed since the young Luca Bellani took the helm of the family estate, inheriting the experience of his father Tullio, supported by his mother Daniela, and aided by his brother Matteo. We remember the huge leap in quality that, soon led Ca' di Frara to become one of the best-known Oltrepò wineries, even outside the region. Then came the ambitious Oltre il Classico project, dedicated to sparkling wines. Today the estate is a benchmark and we confidently await the final step that will take it to the pinnacles of excellence. The two Metodo Classicos presented were outstanding: the zesty, fruity, flavoursome Nature, with the coppery Cuvée Rosé, with a fine evolved nose of citrus fruit and red berries. The two 2015 vintages of Bonarda are also good: the still La Casetta and the semi-sparkling Monpezzato, both characterized by sound fruit and attractive drinkability. The Riesling 2015 is forthright and concentrated, with hints of citrus and aromatic herbs.

○ Brut Oltre il Classico Nature	♟♟	4
○ Brut Oltre il Classico Cuvée Rosé	♟♟	5
● OP Bonarda La Casetta '15	♟♟	3
● OP Bonarda Vivace Monpezzato '15	♟♟	2*
○ OP Riesling '15	♟♟	4
○ OP Pinot Grigio Selezione dei Vent'Anni '15	♟	4
● OP Pinot Nero '15	♟	3
● OP Pinot Nero '12	♟♟	3
○ OP Pinot Nero Brut Oltre il Classico Nature Ris. '04	♟♟	5
⊙ OP Pinot Nero Brut Oltre il Classico Rosé Ris. '08	♟♟	5
○ OP Riesling Oliva '12	♟♟	3

Ca' Lojera

loc. Rovizza
via 1866, 19
25019 Sirmione [BS]
Tel. +39 0457551901
www.calojera.com

CELLAR SALES
PRE-BOOKED VISITS
RESTAURANT SERVICE
ANNUAL PRODUCTION 120,000 bottles
HECTARES UNDER VINE 20.00

Franco and Ambra Tiraboschi have created one of the most interesting wineries in the Lugana production zone. Their Ca' Lojera, or house of wolves, has 20 hectares of vineyards. The flat land plots on the typical white soils close to the lake yield Lugana, while red grape varieties are grown on the hills. The modern cellar is part of a complex that also features a handsome guest farm and a restaurant. The Tiraboschi family presented three excellent versions of Lugana, confirming that Ca' Lojera is one of the most consistent producers in expressing this terroir. Our favourite was the Riserva del Lupo 2014, from super-ripe grapes, which has a deep, complex, nicely varietal nose, brimming with fruity and floral notes. The full, deep palate is fresh and edgy, with a long mineral finish. The Superiore 2014 is eminently drinkable, with fruity flesh and good body, while the 2015 offers approachable tropical fruit.

○ Lugana '15	♟♟	3
○ Lugana Riserva del Lupo '14	♟♟	5
○ Lugana Sup. '14	♟♟	3
⊙ Rosato Monte della Guardia '15	♟	2
○ Lugana '14	♟♟	3
○ Lugana del Lupo '10	♟♟	4
○ Lugana Riserva del Lupo '13	♟♟	5
○ Lugana Riserva del Lupo '12	♟♟	5
○ Lugana Riserva del Lupo '11	♟♟	4
○ Lugana Sup. '13	♟♟	3
○ Lugana Sup. '12	♟♟	3
○ Lugana Sup. '11	♟♟	3
○ Lugana Sup. '10	♟♟	3

Ca' Tessitori

VIA MATTEOTTI, 15
27043 BRONI [PV]
TEL. +39 038551495
www.catessitori.it

CELLAR SALES
PRE-BOOKED VISITS
ANNUAL PRODUCTION 120,000 bottles
HECTARES UNDER VINE 40.00

Step by step, with little ado, the family estate, run by Luigi Giorgi with the aid of his sons Giovanni and Francesco, has carved out a respectable niche for itself on the diversified Oltrepò wine scene. Located in the centre of Broni, the structure of the winery is in the old style. The cellar and its concrete vats serve as the foundations for the family home, while the vineyards are in Montecalvo Versiggia and Finigeto. The wines are full of character, with little or no use of wood, in favour of concrete, and great attention to tradition. The results, in terms of qualitative growth, are clear to see. Brut M.V., which narrowly missed our highest accolade last year, confirms itself a thoroughbred sparkler with the 2011 vintage, also focusing on an evolved style. The new Brut LB9 is very different, with an acid green label hinting at its fresher, more mineral and approachable style, despite ageing an extra year on the lees. Both the 2015 vintages of Bonarda are exemplary: the bottle-fermented Avita and especially the traditional Vivace, which reached our finals.

● OP Bonarda Vivace '15	♥♥ 3*
● OP Bonarda Avita '15	♥♥ 3
○ OP Pinot Nero Brut M. V. '11	♥♥ 4
● OP Rosso Borghesa '15	♥♥ 2*
○ Agòlo '15	♥ 2
○ OP Pinot Nero Brut LB9 '10	♥ 4
○ Agòlo '14	♀♥ 2*
● Gnese '11	♀♥ 3
● OP Bonarda Avita '14	♀♥ 2*
● OP Bonarda Vivace '13	♀♥ 2*
○ OP Pinot Nero Brut '11	♀♥ 4
○ OP Pinot Nero Brut M. V. '10	♀♥ 4

Calatroni

LOC. CASA GRANDE, 7
27040 MONTECALVO VERSIGGIA [PV]
TEL. +39 038599013
www.calatronivini.it

CELLAR SALES
PRE-BOOKED VISITS
RESTAURANT SERVICE
ANNUAL PRODUCTION 80,000 bottles
HECTARES UNDER VINE 15.00
SUSTAINABLE WINERY

In just a few years, the winery founded by Luigi Calatroni in 1964 with the purchase of the land at the end of a tenant-farming contract and now run by the fourth generation of the family, brothers Cristian and Stefano, has forged ahead: short profile, long profile, Tre Bicchieri. The credit goes to the skill of these boys born in the 1980s with the grapes that give the best results on the predominantly white soils of Montecalvo Versiggia, namely riesling and pinot nero. Now the winery just needs to continue with the same commitment and dedication and we are certain the results will keep coming. Last year the Brut 64 walked away with a Tre Bicchieri and the 2012 vintage is almost as good, also characterized by alluring creamy effervescence and a close-focused nose. However, this time it was outscored by the vibrant, gutsy Bonarda Vigiö 2015, which is taut and balanced. The two Rieslings also did very well: the 2013 more evolved and mineral, and Campo del Dottore 2015 fresher with a nose of basil and wild fennel.

○ Pinot Nero Brut 64 '12	♥♥ 5
● OP Bonarda Vivace Vigiö '15	♥♥ 2*
○ OP Riesling '13	♥♥ 2*
○ OP Riesling Campo del Dottore '15	♥♥ 2*
● OP Sangue di Giuda '15	♥♥ 3
○ Pinot Nero Brut 64 '11	♥♥♥ 5
● OP Bonarda Vivace Unico '13	♀♥ 2*
⊙ OP Cruasé '10	♀♥ 3
● OP Pinot Nero '13	♀♥ 2*
○ OP Riesling '14	♀♥ 2*
○ OP Riesling '09	♀♥ 2*
○ OP Riesling '07	♀♥ 2*

Camossi

VIA METELLI, 5
25030 ERBUSCO [BS]
TEL. +39 0307268022
www.camossi.it

CELLAR SALES
PRE-BOOKED VISITS
ANNUAL PRODUCTION 60,000 bottles
HECTARES UNDER VINE 30.00

Dario and Claudio Camossi represent the third generation of this fine Franciacorta estate founded by their grandfather Pietro. Wine production commenced in the early 1990s, and the first bottles of Franciacorta dei Camossi were released in 1996. Today the 30 hectares of vineyards in Erbusco, Paratico, and Provaglio d'Iseo supply excellent grapes for its high-quality range, made with the technical expertise of oenologist Nico Danesi and Giovanni Arcari. The boys' parents and grandfather, Pietro, also help at the winery. The selection of wines presented this year was excellent. We loved the density of Extra Brut 2009, which is fresh and tangy, with a nose of fruit and sap, and a lingering, juicy palate. The Satèn is characterized by a nose of aromatic herbs, echoed on the edgy, well-orchestrated palate. Extra Brut Riserva 2008 is delicately evolved, while the 2011 vintage focuses on fresh fruit and citrusy notes.

○ Franciacorta Extra Brut '11	♟♟ 6
○ Franciacorta Extra Brut '09	♟♟ 6
○ Franciacorta Extra Brut '08	♟♟ 6
○ Franciacorta Extra Brut Ris. '08	♟♟ 6
⊙ Franciacorta Extra Brut Rosé	♟♟ 6
○ Franciacorta Satèn	♟♟ 5
○ Franciacorta Brut	♟ 5
○ Franciacorta Extra Brut '08	♟♟ 6
○ Franciacorta Extra Brut '07	♟♟ 5
○ Franciacorta Extra Brut '07	♟♟ 5
○ Franciacorta Extra Brut Pietro Camossi Ris. '07	♟♟ 8

Cantrina

VIA COLOMBERA, 7
25081 BEDIZZOLE [BS]
TEL. +39 0306871052
www.cantrina.it

CELLAR SALES
ANNUAL PRODUCTION 35,000 bottles
HECTARES UNDER VINE 7.90

Cristina Inganni and Diego Lavo are partners in both the private and the professional sphere. They have been running Cantrina together since 1999 and have flanked international grape varieties with natives like groppello and rebo, well suited to the morainic hills of the Valtenesi. The small estate covers an area of less than eight hectares, planted with 33,000 vines with an average density of 5,500 per hectare. Nepomuceno was our favourite wine again this year. A blend of merlot, rebo and marzemino, it is released following long ageing in the cellar, in barrel and then in bottle. It has a nose of jammy fruit, with vegetal hints, forest floor, and spice, and good entry on the progressive, racy palate. Zerdì is a monovarietal Rebo, aged for around 10 months in small used oak casks, and offering evolved fruit, smooth tannins, and a spicy finish.

● Nepomuceno '11	♟♟ 5
● Zerdì '13	♟♟ 3
○ Rinè '14	♟ 3
⊙ Rosanoire '15	♟ 2
● Valtènesi '15	♟ 3
● Garda Cl. Groppello '12	♟♟ 2*
● Garda Cl. Groppello Libero Esercizio di Stile '11	♟♟ 2*
● Nepomuceno '09	♟♟ 5
○ Rinè '12	♟♟ 3
⊙ Rosanoire '14	♟♟ 2*
⊙ Rosanoire '13	♟♟ 2*
⊙ Rosanoire '11	♟♟ 2*
● Valtenesi '13	♟♟ 3
● Zerdì '09	♟♟ 3

CastelFaglia - Monogram

FRAZ. CALINO
LOC. BOSCHI, 3
25046 CAZZAGO SAN MARTINO [BS]
TEL. +39 0307751042
www.cavicchioli.it

CELLAR SALES
PRE-BOOKED VISITS
ANNUAL PRODUCTION 350,000 bottles
HECTARES UNDER VINE 22.00

Sandro Cavicchioli crafts elegant Metodo Classico cuvées in Franciacorta for CastelFaglia, the handsome estate in Cazzago San Martino that his family purchased a few years ago. It goes to join Bellei, in Emilia, also specializing in sparklers as well as Lambrusco, which has always been part of the genetic makeup of this Modena family. The estate offers two lines of Franciacorta cuvées, CastelFaglia and Monogram, from its 22 hectares of partially terraced vineyards bellow the old Faglia Castle. The top scorer in our tastings was Cuvée Monogram Dosaggio Zero 2012. It is an elegant, fruity Franciacorta, with clean, close-focused citrus and appley notes on the nose and the palate, accompanied by creamy effervescence derived from long bottle fermentation, which opens fresh and concentrated, well balanced, zesty and mineral, with nice length. The Satèn 2011 of the same range vaunts delicate notes of forest floor and vanilla, while the elegant Monogram Brut 2009 is characterized by medicinal herbs and chamomile.

○ Franciacorta Dosage Zero Cuvée Monogram '12	🍷🍷	5
○ Franciacorta Brut Cuvée Monogram '09	🍷🍷	5
⊙ Franciacorta Rosé Cuvée Monogram	🍷🍷	5
○ Franciacorta Satèn Cuvée Monogram '11	🍷🍷	5
○ Franciacorta Satèn Cuvée Monogram	🍷🍷	5
○ Franciacorta Brut Blanc de Blancs Monogram	🍷	5
○ Franciacorta Brut Monogram '07	YY	5
○ Franciacorta Brut Monogram '07	YY	5
○ Franciacorta Brut Monogram '02	YY	7
○ Franciacorta Dosage Zéro '09	YY	5
○ Franciacorta Dosage Zero Monogram '11	YY	5
○ Franciacorta Satèn Monogram '07	YY	5

Castello di Cigognola

P.ZZA CASTELLO, 1
27040 CIGOGNOLA [PV]
TEL. +39 0385284828
www.castellodicigognola.com

CELLAR SALES
PRE-BOOKED VISITS
ANNUAL PRODUCTION 75,000 bottles
HECTARES UNDER VINE 30.00

Castello di Cigognola is in a spectacular location, overlooking the Lombard Plain and the entrance to the Valle Scuropasso. Of ancient origins, it dates back to 1212 and the end of feudalism, later a Renaissance court, and became a winegrowing centre in the early 19th century. Today it is owned by Gianmarco and Letizia Moratti, who have renovated and transformed it into an operation producing fine wines with the aid of Riccardo Cotarella and Oltrepò oenologist Emilio Defilippi, as well as a research centre partnering Milan University to revive ancient local grape varieties. For the third year in a row, Brut Metodo Classico 'More garnered a Tre Bicchieri. The 2012 is even more elegant, close focused, vigorous, and zesty, with a nose of citrus and pennyroyal, and a long, well-sustained finish. The Rosé 2013 is subtler, commencing with its pale hue, and focuses chiefly on finesse and elegance. Barbera Dodicidodici 2014 is full, solid and chewy, with aromas of morello cherries. Barbera La Maga 2013 is more elegant and spicy, and still shows ample room for improvement.

○ OP Brut 'More '12	🍷🍷🍷	4*
⊙ Brut 'More Rosé '13	🍷🍷	4
● OP Barbera Dodicidodici '14	🍷🍷	3
● OP Barbera La Maga '13	🍷🍷	4
○ Bianca '15	🍷	3
○ Brut 'More '11	YYY	4*
○ Brut 'More '10	YYY	4*
● OP Barbera Castello di Cigognola '07	YYY	6
● OP Barbera Castello di Cigognola '06	YYY	6
● OP Barbera Dodicidodici '11	YYY	3*
● OP Barbera Poggio Della Maga '05	YYY	7
○ OP Pinot Nero Brut 'More '08	YYY	4*
○ La Bianca '14	YY	3
● OP Barbera Dodicidodici '13	YY	3
● OP Barbera Dodicidodici '12	YY	3
● OP Barbera La Maga '12	YY	4
● OP Barbera La Maga '11	YY	4

★Cavalleri

VIA PROVINCIALE, 96
25030 ERBUSCO [BS]
TEL. +39 0307760217
www.cavalleri.it

CELLAR SALES
PRE-BOOKED VISITS
ANNUAL PRODUCTION 250,000 bottles
HECTARES UNDER VINE 45.00
VITICULTURE METHOD Certified Organic

The Cavalleri were mentioned as landowners in Franciacorta in a deed as early as 1450, although it was not until 1968 that Gian Paolo and his son Giovanni started producing wine and Franciacortas. Today the estate is run by Giovanni's daughters Maria and Giulia, and grandchildren Francesco and Diletta, flanked by a competent staff. It vaunts an impressive 45 hectares of fine vineyards on the best-aspected sites in Erbusco. Pas Dosé is one of the specialities of this Franciacorta estate. Oenologist Paolo Turra offers us a very good 2011 from chardonnay, whose fresh, elegant personality is evident from its straw-yellow hue with greenish highlights, its fine bead, and its creamy effervescence. The nose has elegant top notes of white-fleshed fruit with hints of blossom and citron peel, while the palate is caressing and zesty with good balance and length. The quality of the rest of the range is also high.

○ Franciacorta Pas Dosé '11	♟♟ 6
○ Curtefranca Bianco '14	♟♟ 3
⊙ Franciacorta Blanc de Blancs	♟♟ 5
⊙ Franciacorta Brut Rosé '11	♟♟ 6
⊙ Franciacorta Brut Satèn	♟♟ 5
○ Franciacorta Brut Collezione '05	♟♟♟ 6
○ Franciacorta Brut Collezione Esclusiva Giovanni Cavalleri '05	♟♟♟ 8
○ Franciacorta Brut Collezione Esclusiva Giovanni Cavalleri '04	♟♟♟ 7
○ Franciacorta Brut Collezione Esclusiva Giovanni Cavalleri '01	♟♟♟ 7
○ Franciacorta Collezione Grandi Cru '08	♟♟♟ 6
○ Franciacorta Pas Dosé '07	♟♟♟ 5
○ Franciacorta Pas Dosé R. D. '06	♟♟♟ 6

Battista Cola

VIA INDIPENDENZA, 3
25030 ADRO [BS]
TEL. +39 0307356195
www.colabattista.it

CELLAR SALES
PRE-BOOKED VISITS
ANNUAL PRODUCTION 70,000 bottles
HECTARES UNDER VINE 10.00
SUSTAINABLE WINERY

Stefano Cola enthusiastically and competently continues the work commenced by his father Battista, the heir to an old family tradition, who started to make wine and Franciacortas from his little vineyard on Monte Alto, in Adro, in 1985. The vineyards now cover an area of 10 hectares, and annual production is around 70,000 bottles, but the wines and Franciacortas still have the authentic character of grower production, where work in the vineyard and cellar is prevalently manual and artisanal, and as sustainable as ever. Stefano Cola's wines are impeccable and once again this year the range is excellent, commencing with the basic, non-vintage Brut, which is fresh with a citrussy nose. The Brut 2011 is soft, deep, and juicy; Rosé Athena 2012 has good backbone and notes of red berries; the Non Dosato 2011 is complex, juicy, and well orchestrated; and the Satèn 2012 has alluring soft notes of ripe white-fleshed fruit and vanilla.

○ Franciacorta Brut '11	♟♟ 5
○ Franciacorta Brut	♟♟ 4
○ Franciacorta Extra Brut	♟♟ 4
○ Franciacorta Non Dosato '11	♟♟ 5
⊙ Franciacorta Rosé Athena '12	♟♟ 5
○ Franciacorta Satèn '11	♟♟ 5
○ Franciacorta Brut '10	♟♟ 5
○ Franciacorta Brut RD '06	♟♟ 5
○ Franciacorta Brut Ris. '07	♟♟ 5
○ Franciacorta Non Dosato '09	♟♟ 5
○ Franciacorta Satèn '10	♟♟ 5
○ Franciacorta Satèn '09	♟♟ 5
○ Franciacorta Satèn '07	♟♟ 5

Contadi Castaldi

LOC. FORNACE BIASCA
VIA COLZANO, 32
25030 ADRO [BS]
TEL. +39 0307450126
www.contadicastaldi.it

CELLAR SALES
PRE-BOOKED VISITS
ANNUAL PRODUCTION 1,000,000 bottles
HECTARES UNDER VINE 150.00
SUSTAINABLE WINERY

Although Contadi Castaldi in Adro
operates independently and has its own
large estate, it belongs to the Terra Moretti
group, headed by Bellavista. The cellar is
housed in Adro's ancient brick kilns and
uses grapes both from the estate-owned
and leased vineyards and from selected
growers. It is enthusiastically headed by
talented oenologist Gian Luca Uccelli, who
honed his craft during years spent at the
parent company. This year we awarded Tre
Bicchieri to the excellent Zero 2012. An
equal blend of Pinot Nero and Chardonnay
(part of the base wine is aged in oak), it is
aged on the lees for 40 months before
disgorgement, and then for a further six
before release. It has a dynamic, gutsy
nose of white-fleshed fruit and wild
berries, with hints of citrus peel and
aromatic herbs, accompanied by a firm,
fresh palate with good balance and depth,
and impressive aromatic length. The
Satèn is excellent and the other wines are
very sound.

○ Franciacorta Zero '12	♀♀♀	5
○ Franciacorta Satèn Soul '09	♀♀	6
○ Franciacorta Brut	♀♀	4
⊙ Franciacorta Rosé	♀♀	5
⊙ Franciacorta Rosé Soul '10	♀♀	5
○ Franciacorta Satèn '11	♀♀	5
○ Franciacorta Satèn Soul '06	♀♀♀	6
○ Franciacorta Satèn Soul '05	♀♀♀	6
○ Franciacorta Zero '09	♀♀♀	5
○ Franciacorta Satèn Soul '07	♀♀	6
○ Franciacorta Zero '11	♀♀	5
○ Franciacorta Zero '10	♀♀	5
○ Franciacorta Zero Pinònero Ris. '09	♀♀	6

Conte Vistarino

FRAZ. SCORZOLETTA, 82/84
27040 PIETRA DE' GIORGI [PV]
TEL. +39 038585117
www.contevistarino.it

CELLAR SALES
PRE-BOOKED VISITS
ANNUAL PRODUCTION 400,000 bottles
HECTARES UNDER VINE 200.00

One of the landmark moments in this
estate's long history occurred in 1865,
when Conte Giorgi Vimercati of Vistarino
and Conte Gancia pinpointed the upper part
of Valle Scuropasso as the ideal terroir for
planting pinot nero clones for the
production of bases for sparklers. Piedmont
wineries exploited this veritable goldmine
for decades. With the arrival of the young
Ottavia a few years ago, the estate of over
800 hectares, which is practically the entire
municipality of Rocca de' Giorgi, with 200
under vine, decided to aim for excellence,
as demonstrated by the three different crus
of Pinot Nero 2013 presented this year. The
legendary Pernice, which shows well
orchestrated, deep, elegant and balsamic,
has been joined by the warmer, Tavernetto,
with a nose of red berries, and the Bertone,
which has won a Tre Bicchieri at its debut
for its class, elegance, pervasive balsamic
notes, and caressing harmony. Our
favourite Metodo Classico was the Cruasé,
with its alluring complex texture.

● Pinot Nero Bertone '13	♀♀♀	5
● Pinot Nero Pernice '13	♀♀	5
● OP Bonarda L'Alcova '15	♀♀	2*
⊙ OP Cruasé Saignée della Rocca	♀♀	5
○ OP Pinot Nero Brut Conte Vistarino 1865 '09	♀♀	4
● Pinot Nero Tavernetto '13	♀♀	3
○ Brut Cépage '13	♀	4
○ Pinot Grigio Merlino '15	♀	3
○ OP Pinot Nero Brut Conte Vistarino 1865 '08	♀♀♀	4*
● OP Pinot Nero Pernice '06	♀♀♀	4*
○ OP Pinot Nero Brut 1865 '09	♀♀	5
● OP Pinot Nero Pernice '12	♀♀	5
● OP Pinot Nero Pernice '11	♀♀	5

La Costa

FRAZ. COSTA
VIA GALBUSERA NERA, 2
23888 PEREGO [LC]
TEL. +39 0395312218
www.la-costa.it

CELLAR SALES
PRE-BOOKED VISITS
ACCOMMODATION AND RESTAURANT SERVICE
ANNUAL PRODUCTION 40,000 bottles
HECTARES UNDER VINE 12.00
VITICULTURE METHOD Certified Organic

The Crippa family winery is one of the finest in Lombardy, with well-tended vineyards in the Montevecchia and Val Curone Regional Park in Brianza, in the province of Lecco. The 12-hectare estate, tended with organic methods, forms a steep natural amphitheatre, surrounded by woods. Riesling renano, pinot nero, merlot, and syrah are grown on the mineral-rich limestone soils, and significant temperature fluctuations ensure vibrant supporting acidity. The elegant, well-calibrated wines are fresh, subtle, and beautifully nuanced. Solesta 2014 is an exemplary Riesling, exceptionally well made, with white-fleshed fruit and very stylish citrus notes. The palate is rich, taut, and mouthfilling, with a long finish. Quattordici 2014, from merlot, syrah, pinot nero, and cabernet, is intriguing and nuanced, with a fruity, spicy nose and a well-orchestrated palate with good flesh.

Costaripa

VIA COSTA, 1A
25080 MONIGA DEL GARDA [BS]
TEL. +39 0365502010
www.costaripa.it

CELLAR SALES
PRE-BOOKED VISITS
ANNUAL PRODUCTION 400,000 bottles
HECTARES UNDER VINE 40.00

Mattia Vezzola is one of the stars of the Italian wine scene, thanks to his brilliant cuvées crafted in one of Franciacorta's legendary cellars. However, his family's heart has lain in the Valtenesi for generations. Today he splits his time between the two estates, aided by the fourth generation: his children Nicole, responsible for marketing, and Gherardo, oenology student. Their mission is to take the wines of the Valtenesi to the heights of the Italian wine world. We recommend by the tribute Chiaretto named after Senator Molmenti, who was already making great rosés on this shore of the lake in the 1800s. The 2012 has been released after years of ageing in large barrels and bottle, and has an intriguing, complex nose of alluring oak and invigorating red berries, followed by a firm, deep palate with attractive drinkability. The other wines are excellent, particularly the Rosamara and the sparklers.

○ Solesta '14	♟♟ 4
● Vino del Quattordici '14	♟♟ 3
● San Giobbe '13	♟♟ 4
● San Giobbe '12	♟♟ 4
● San Giobbe '11	♟♟ 4
● Serìz '11	♟♟ 3
○ Solesta '13	♟♟ 4
○ Solesta '12	♟♟ 3*
○ Solesta '11	♟♟ 3*
○ Solesta '10	♟♟ 3*

⊙ Valtènesi Chiaretto Molmenti '12	♟♟ 2*
○ Lugana Pievecroce '15	♟♟ 2*
○ Mattia Vezzola Brut '11	♟♟ 5
⊙ Mattia Vezzola Rosé '11	♟♟ 5
⊙ Mattia Vezzola Rosé	♟♟ 5
⊙ Valtènesi Chiaretto Rosamara '15	♟♟ 2*
● Valtènesi Rosso Campostarne '13	♟ 3
○ Costaripa Brut '08	♟♟ 5
⊙ Garda Cl. Chiaretto Molmenti '11	♟♟ 4
○ Lugana Pievecroce '14	♟♟ 2*
○ Mattia Vezzola Brut '10	♟♟ 5
⊙ Mattia Vezzola Rosé '10	♟♟ 5
● Valtènesi Le Castelline '12	♟♟ 3
● Valtènesi Maim '11	♟♟ 3

Derbusco Cives

VIA PROVINCIALE, 83
25030 ERBUSCO [BS]
TEL. +39 0307731164
www.derbuscocives.com

CELLAR SALES
PRE-BOOKED VISITS
RESTAURANT SERVICE
ANNUAL PRODUCTION 90,000 bottles
HECTARES UNDER VINE 12.00

Erbusco's wineries and exceptional terroir have earned it the fame of capital of Franciacorta. In 2004, a group of five friends, headed by Giuseppe Vezzoli, decided to underscore its unique status by founding a new winery that they named for the Citizens of Erbusco. It boasts 12 hectares of vineyards, in Erbusco, of course, and uses somewhat unconventional methods in the cellar, such as bottle fermentation with Franciacorta must and late disgorgement. The jewel in the estate's crown is the Doppio Erre Di, standing delayed disgorgement and recently disgorged, a Brut from chardonnay that undergoes long ageing on the lees and is disgorged immediately before delivery to the client. We tasted a beautifully full and brimming with fresh citrusy notes on both the nose and palate, where it opens out elegant, deep and fruity. We also liked the very sound Brut 2010, from chardonnay, which combines the freshness of lime and citron with elegant and more evolved notes of vanilla and attractive oak.

○ Franciacorta Brut Doppio Erre Di	🍷🍷 5
○ Franciacorta Brut '10	🍷🍷 6
○ Franciacorta Brut Blanc de Noir Crisalis '10	🍷 6
○ Franciacorta Brut '09	🍷🍷 6
○ Franciacorta Brut '08	🍷🍷 6
○ Franciacorta Brut '07	🍷🍷 6
○ Franciacorta Brut Doppio Erre Di '05	🍷🍷 5
○ Franciacorta Extra Brut '10	🍷🍷 8
○ Franciacorta Extra Brut '09	🍷🍷 7
○ Franciacorta Extra Brut '08	🍷🍷 7
○ Franciacorta Extra Brut '07	🍷🍷 6
⊙ Franciacorta Extra Brut Rosé '09	🍷🍷 6

Dirupi

LOC. MADONNA DI CAMPAGNA
VIA GRUMELLO, 1
23020 MONTAGNA IN VALTELLINA [SO]
TEL. +39 3472909779
www.dirupi.com

CELLAR SALES
PRE-BOOKED VISITS
ANNUAL PRODUCTION 15,000 bottles
HECTARES UNDER VINE 4.50

Davide Fasolino and Pierpaolo di Franco are two of the most interesting new faces on the Lombardy wine scene of the past few years. Their cellar is in Montagna, in the Valtellina and receives the grapes from incredibly steep old terraced vineyards, hence the winery's name, which means cliffs. The combination of manual work, creative spirit, enthusiasm, and energy has allowed their wines to make a name for themselves and gather quite a following. They show a lustrous pale red with a stylish, approachable nose, linear progression, and rare drinkability. Dirupi 2014 is magnificent, a veritable must in its class. Complex notes of rust and hints of rhubarb mingle nicely with undertones of raspberries on the nose, echoed on the surprisingly fresh palate, with a very stylish long finish. The Riserva 2013 is also excellent, with a complex, multifaceted nose of wild berries, medicinal herbs, and liquorice. On the palate it is firm, fleshy, and juicy with a long finish.

● Valtellina Sup. Dirupi '14	🍷🍷 4
● Valtellina Sup. Dirupi Ris. '13	🍷🍷 6
● Sforzato di Valtellina Vino Sbagliato '14	🍷🍷 6
● Rosso di Valtelina Olè '15	🍷 3
● Valtellina Sup. Dirupi Ris. '12	🍷🍷🍷 6
● Valtellina Sup. Dirupi Ris. '11	🍷🍷🍷 6
● Valtellina Sup. Dirupi Ris. '09	🍷🍷🍷 6
● Rosso di Valtelina Olè '14	🍷🍷 3
● Sforzato di Valtellina Vino Sbagliato '12	🍷🍷 6
● Valtellina Sup. Dirupi '13	🍷🍷 4
● Valtellina Sup. Dirupi '12	🍷🍷 4
● Valtellina Sup. Dirupi '11	🍷🍷 4
● Valtellina Sup. Dirupi Ris. '10	🍷🍷 6

F.lli Berlucchi

fraz. Borgonato
via Broletto, 2
25040 Corte Franca [BS]
Tel. +39 030984451
www.fratelliberlucchi.it

CELLAR SALES
PRE-BOOKED VISITS
ANNUAL PRODUCTION 400,000 bottles
HECTARES UNDER VINE 70.00

The Berlucchis are a long-standing Franciacorta family, who vaunt 70 hectares of fine vineyards. At the centre of the large estate, lovingly run on behalf of the siblings by Pia Donata and her daughter Tilli Rizzo, is the family's 16th-century villa, Casa delle Colonne, in Borgonato, which also houses the cellars. The range consists of two lines: Casa delle Colonne and Freccianera. The basic Brut 25 is the only non-vintage wine. Freccianera Rosa 2012 is a cuvée of 60% Pinot Nero (half fermented off the skins and half with rosé fermentation) and 40% Chardonnay, aged for over 45 months on the lees. It's an alluring pale pink with a very fine bead, an intriguing nose of wild berries, vanilla, and medicinal herbs, and an assertive, deep, zesty, fresh palate, which earned it a place in our finals. The wide range also includes the excellent Freccianera Satèn and Nature, both from the 2012 vintage.

⊙ Franciacorta Freccianera Rosa '12	🍷🍷 5
○ Franciacorta Nature Freccianera '12	🍷🍷 5
○ Franciacorta Brut Casa delle Colonne Ris. '09	🍷🍷 7
○ Franciacorta Brut Freccianera '11	🍷🍷 5
○ Franciacorta Casa delle Colonne Zero Ris. '09	🍷🍷 8
○ Franciacorta Satèn Freccianera '12	🍷🍷 5
○ Franciacorta Brut 25	🍷 4
○ Franciacorta Brut Freccianera '10	🍸🍸 6
○ Franciacorta Casa delle Colonne Brut Ris. '08	🍸🍸 7
○ Franciacorta Casa delle Colonne Zero Ris. '08	🍸🍸 8
⊙ Franciacorta Freccianera Rosa '11	🍸🍸 6
○ Franciacorta Satèn Freccianera '11	🍸🍸 7

Sandro Fay

loc. San Giacomo di Teglio
via Pila Caselli, 1
23030 Teglio [SO]
Tel. +39 0342786071
elefay@tin.it

CELLAR SALES
PRE-BOOKED VISITS
ANNUAL PRODUCTION 38,000 bottles
HECTARES UNDER VINE 13.00

Fay is practically synonymous with Valgella, one of the Valtellina's most evocative subzones, which is named after the many brooks, or valgel in the local dialect, that run through it. Founded by Sandro Fay in 1973, today it is brilliantly managed by his son Marco, increasingly committed to sustainable production. In-depth agronomical studies have led the estate to move production to higher altitudes, to enhance the unique characteristics of mountain viticulture, making the most of the individual vineyards, aspects, and height differences. The fine Valgella Cà Moréi 2013 is the fruit of skill and know-how, steadily becoming younger and fresher in style, with inspiring interactions between oak and red berries, complemented by ferrous notes. On the palate it shows extraordinarily dense fruit, tannic progression, and a long, flavoursome finish. Valgella Carterìa Riserva 2013 proffers a nose of tobacco, liquorice, raspberries and rust. The austere palate has close-knit tannins sustained by good fruity flesh, and a long finish full of promise.

● Valtellina Sup. Valgella Cà Moréi '13	🍷🍷🍷 5
● Valtellina Sup. Valgella Carterìa Ris. '13	🍷🍷 5
● La Faya '13	🍷🍷 5
● Valtellina Sup. Sassella Il Glicine '13	🍷🍷 4
● Valtellina Sforzato Ronco del Picchio '10	🍸🍸🍸 6
● Valtellina Sforzato Ronco del Picchio '09	🍸🍸🍸 6
● Valtellina Sforzato Ronco del Picchio '02	🍸🍸🍸 6
● Valtellina Sforzato Ronco del Picchio '11	🍸🍸 6
● Valtellina Sup. Valgella Cà Moréi '12	🍸🍸 5

★Ferghettina

VIA SALINE, 11
25030 ADRO [BS]
TEL. +39 0307451212
www.ferghettina.it

CELLAR SALES
PRE-BOOKED VISITS
ANNUAL PRODUCTION 400,000 bottles
HECTARES UNDER VINE 160.00
SUSTAINABLE WINERY

In the space of 20 years, Roberto Gatti and his family have created one of the finest Franciacorta wineries. Flanked by his wife Adreina, and with the precious help of his children Laura and Matteo, now oenologists, he has gone from a few hectares of leased vineyards to an estate of over 160 hectares, with stunning premises featuring a 6,000-square-metre cellar, and impressive production in terms of quantity and particularly quality. The 2009 vintage has earned Ferghettina another Tre Bicchieri, this time for Pas Dosé 33 Riserva, an extraordinarily elegant Blanc de Blancs aged on the lees for over 80 months. It shows a bright straw yellow, with a very fine, persistent bead, and a remarkably complex, elegant nose underscored by the fresh notes of citron and vanilla embellishing its close-focused fruit. On the palate it is caressing in spite of the dosage, almost velvety on the attack, before opening up full and fruity with citrus notes, followed by sophisticated hints of white chocolate and mint on the long finish.

○ Franciacorta Pas Dosé 33 Ris. '09	♥♥♥	6
○ Franciacorta Brut Milledì '12	♥♥	5
○ Franciacorta Extra Brut '10	♥♥	6
○ Curtefranca Bianco '15	♥♥	2*
○ Franciacorta Brut	♥♥	4
⊙ Franciacorta Brut Rosé Eronero '11	♥♥	6
○ Franciacorta Rosé Milledì '12	♥♥	5
○ Franciacorta Satèn '12	♥♥	5
● Curtefranca Rosso '14	♥	2
○ Franciacorta Extra Brut '09	♥♥♥	5
○ Franciacorta Extra Brut '06	♥♥♥	5
○ Franciacorta Pas Dosé 33 Ris. '07	♥♥♥	6
○ Franciacorta Pas Dosé 33 Ris. '06	♥♥♥	6

Fiamberti

VIA CHIESA, 17
27044 CANNETO PAVESE [PV]
TEL. +39 038588019
www.fiambertivini.it

CELLAR SALES
PRE-BOOKED VISITS
ANNUAL PRODUCTION 140,000 bottles
HECTARES UNDER VINE 18.00

The Fiamberti family's winery owns some of the finest vineyards in Canneto Pavese, the municipality that is home to many of the area's best red wines. Ambrogio concentrates on traditional wines and his son Giulio, who is also the chairman of the Buttafuoco Storico club, focuses in particular on Metodo Classico and Buttafuoco Storico. True to tradition, the estate produces red, white, still, semi-sparkling, and sparkling wine, whose the average quality continues to improve by leaps and bounds with each vintage. We now await the final sprint, which we know it's capable of achieving. The Brut is shedding its past heaviness, becoming more delicate and elegant, with attractive notes of berries and aromatic herbs, while the Cruasé has very prominent fruit. Buttafuoco Storico 2011 is admirable, showing dark, brooding, and earthy with notes of liquorice, tobacco, and coffee. Both the vintage Bonarda and Sangue di Giuda are good, forthright, fragrant wines, while the Pinot Nero 2013 is well made, clean and varietal.

● OP Bonarda Vivace La Briccona '15	♥♥	2*
● OP Buttafuoco Storico		
V. Sacca del Prete '11	♥♥	4
○ OP Pinot Nero Brut Fiamberti	♥♥	4
● OP Pinot Nero Nero '13	♥♥	2*
● OP Sangue di Giuda Lella '15	♥♥	2*
● OP Buttafuoco Cacciatore '12	♥	3
⊙ OP Cruasé Fiamberti	♥	4
● OP Buttafuoco Storico		
V. Sacca del Prete '09	♥♥	4
○ OP Riesling Italico		
V. Croce Monteveneroso '13	♥♥	2*
● OP Sangue di Giuda Lella '14	♥♥	2*
● OP Sangue di Giuda		
V. Costa Paradiso '13	♥♥	2*

Le Fracce

FRAZ. MAIRANO
VIA CASTEL DEL LUPO, 5
27045 CASTEGGIO [PV]
TEL. +39 038382526
www.lefracce.com

CELLAR SALES
PRE-BOOKED VISITS
ANNUAL PRODUCTION 180,000 bottles
HECTARES UNDER VINE 40.00

This is one of the finest wineries in all Oltrepò, lying on the Mairano hills, above Casteggio, where winemaking has been practised since time immemorial. It has belonged to the Fondazine Bussolera Branca for years and deserves a visit for both its wines and its splendid Italian gardens and collection of carriages and vintage cars. The soil of the vineyards is mixed, part chalky limestone, which yields sparklers and elegant white wines, in the style of oenologist Roberto Gerbino, and part clayey, planted with the typical local red grape varieties. However, we were expecting very different results from an estate like this. This year's tastings left us rather perplexed, especially in comparison to those of recent years. Bohemi 2010 has good flesh and backbone, but is still a little closed and needs more time. Bonarda La Rubiosa 2015 has nice fruit, while the vintage Riesling and Pinot Grigio are varietal and very drinkable, but lack the depth of previous vintages.

● OP Bonarda Vivace La Rubiosa '15	▼▼ 3
● OP Rosso Bohemi '10	▼▼ 6
● Garboso '14	▼ 3
○ OP Pinot Grigio Levriere '15	▼ 3
● OP Pinot Nero '12	▼ 5
○ OP Pinot Nero Extra Brut Martinotti Cuvée Bussolera '13	▼ 3
○ OP Riesling Landò '15	▼ 3
● OP Bonarda Vivace La Rubiosa '14	♀♀ 3
● OP Bonarda Vivace La Rubiosa '13	♀♀ 3
○ OP Riesling Landò '14	♀♀ 3
○ OP Riesling Landò '13	♀♀ 3
● OP Rosso Bohemi '08	♀♀ 6

Frecciarossa

VIA VIGORELLI, 141
27045 CASTEGGIO [PV]
TEL. +39 0383804465
www.frecciarossa.com

CELLAR SALES
PRE-BOOKED VISITS
ANNUAL PRODUCTION 120,000 bottles
HECTARES UNDER VINE 34.00

Among the loveliest Oltrepò estates, with the 19th-century Villa Odero overlooking the winery and vineyards, each year Frecciarossa continues to take another step along the difficult path to excellence. It vaunts a long history, being one of the first Italian wineries to export its production to the US, and a promising present, with Valeria Radici, Margherita Odero's daughter playing an increasingly active role in overseeing the team formed by agronomist Pierluigi Donna, oenologist Gianluca Scaglione, and sales manager (but also oenologist) Cristiano Garella, whose constant focus is the improvement of the range. Pinot Nero Giorgio Odero 2013 came within a hair's breadth of our highest accolade, perhaps because it's still a little immature. It nonetheless has enough body and elegance for us to predict a radiant future. The new Pinot Nero Carillo 2014 was a pleasant surprise, showing lively and dynamic, with a nose of blossom and berries. Riesling Gli Orti 2014 is edgy, with a nose of aromatic herbs.

● OP Pinot Nero Carillo '14	▼▼ 3*
● OP Pinot Nero Giorgio Odero '13	▼▼ 5
○ Frecciarossa Brut M. Cl. '10	▼▼ 6
○ I Moschettieri Brut M. Cl. '12	▼▼ 6
○ OP Riesling Gli Orti '14	▼▼ 2*
○ OP Bianco Margherita '15	▼ 4
○ OP Pinot Nero in bianco Sillery '15	▼ 2
● OP Pinot Nero Giorgio Odero '12	♀♀♀ 5
● OP Pinot Nero Giorgio Odero '11	♀♀♀ 5
● OP Pinot Nero Giorgio Odero '10	♀♀♀ 5
● OP Pinot Nero Giorgio Odero '08	♀♀♀ 5
● OP Pinot Nero Giorgio Odero '07	♀♀♀ 5
● OP Pinot Nero Giorgio Odero '05	♀♀♀ 5
● OP Pinot Nero Giorgio Odero '09	♀♀ 5
○ OP Riesling Gli Orti '13	♀♀ 2*
○ OP Riesling Renano Gli Orti '12	♀♀ 2*

Enrico Gatti

VIA METELLI, 9
25030 ERBUSCO [BS]
TEL. +39 0307267999
www.enricogatti.it

CELLAR SALES
PRE-BOOKED VISITS
ANNUAL PRODUCTION 120,000 bottles
HECTARES UNDER VINE 17.00

Lorenzo and Paola Gatti enthusiastically and lovingly run the estate founded over 40 years ago by their father Enrico, with the precious aid of Paola's husband Enzo Balzarini. The close-knit family team have accompanied the winery to the pinnacles of excellence. They use only the grapes from their own handsome vineyards, 17 hectares all in Erbusco, which give all their cuvees particularly firm structure, fullness, and opulent fruit, accompanied by remarkable acid backbone. Of the three wines tasted this year, we once again preferred the Nature, which won a place in our finals. In our opinion, it is the cuvée that best represents Gatti, offering rich fruity flesh combined with wonderful linearity derived from a remarkable swathe of acidity that gives this otherwise very rich wine its fantastic leaness and attractive drinkability. The Satèn 2012 is tangy and mineral, while the Brut is delightfully drinkable.

○ Franciacorta Nature	♟♟ 5
○ Franciacorta Brut	♟♟ 4
○ Franciacorta Satèn '12	♟♟ 5
○ Franciacorta Brut '05	♟♟♟ 6
○ Franciacorta Nature '07	♟♟♟ 5
○ Franciacorta Satèn '05	♟♟♟ 5
○ Franciacorta Satèn '03	♟♟♟ 5
○ Franciacorta Satèn '02	♟♟♟ 4
○ Franciacorta Satèn '01	♟♟♟ 4
○ Franciacorta Satèn '00	♟♟♟ 5
○ Franciacorta Brut Millesimo '09	♟♟ 6
○ Franciacorta Satèn '11	♟♟ 5
○ Franciacorta Satèn '09	♟♟ 5

I Gessi

FRAZ. FOSSA, 8
27050 OLIVA GESSI [PV]
TEL. +39 0383896606
www.cantineigessi.it

CELLAR SALES
PRE-BOOKED VISITS
ACCOMMODATION
ANNUAL PRODUCTION 160,000 bottles
HECTARES UNDER VINE 41.00

Fabbio Defilippi's handsome estate uses organic methods and comprises a guest farm. It boasts 41 hectares under vine, mainly on chalky limestone soils, as hinted at by its name and that of the Oltrepò municipality in which it is situated. The cellar is run by Fabbio's brother Emilio, an experienced oenologist, whose skill is evident in the sparklers in particular, as it was when he worked at Cantina di Casteggio. This year we were particularly struck by the elegant, racy Maria Cristina Pas Dosé 2010, a full, creamy Metodo Classico with plenty of character, with notes of toasted bread, resin, and aromatic herbs. The Rosé is well made, also with herbal notes alongside well-calibrated fruit, while the other Brut, Maria Cristina, has fragrant yellow-fleshed fruit and a slightly sweet finish. Pinot Grigio Crocetta 2015 is supple and varietal, and the Bonarda has a nose of dark berries and good stuffing.

○ OP Pinot Nero Pas Dosé Maria Cristina '10	♟♟ 5
● OP Bonarda I Gessi '15	♟♟ 2*
○ OP Pinot Grigio Crocetta '15	♟♟ 2*
◉ OP Pinot Nero Rosé Maria Cristina	♟♟ 3
● OP Barbera I Gessi '14	♟ 2
○ OP Pinot Nero Brut M. Cl. Maria Cristina	♟ 3
○ OP Riesling I Gessi '15	♟ 1*
● OP Barbera '13	♟♟ 2*
○ OP Pinot Nero Brut M. Cl. Maria Cristina '10	♟♟ 3
○ OP Riesling '13	♟♟ 1*
○ OP Riesling '12	♟♟ 1*
○ OP Riesling I Gessi '11	♟♟ 1*

F.lli Giorgi

FRAZ. CAMPONOCE, 39A
27044 CANNETO PAVESE [PV]
TEL. +39 0385262151
www.giorgi-wines.it

CELLAR SALES
PRE-BOOKED VISITS
ANNUAL PRODUCTION 1,600,000 bottles
HECTARES UNDER VINE 30.00

Although the Giorgi family's estate is one of the largest private wineries in Oltrepò, it has always preferred to focus chiefly on bottling. In recent years, Antonio's son Fabiano, aided by his sister Eleonora and his wife Ileana, has increasingly favoured high-quality wines, as the results of our tastings reveal. This is particularly true of Metodo Classico, whose annual production was in the range of a few thousand a few years ago, but reached over 100,000 for the last vintage. It was the 1870 that stood out again, the 2012 vintage as concentrated, creamy, and elegant as ever, earning it eight consecutive Tre Bicchieri. However, we also noted the progress of other wines like the Gianfranco Giorgi 2013, with a very fine bead, a nose of aromatic herbs, and wonderful length, and the fresh, well-paced Fusion, full of personality. Buttafuoco Storico 2012 is exceptionally deep, while Riesling Il Bandito 2015 is full and racy.

○ OP Pinot Nero Brut 1870 '12	♛♛♛ 5
○ Brut Fusion	♛♛ 4
● OP Bonarda Gallina '15	♛♛ 2*
● OP Bonarda Vivace La Brughera '15	♛♛ 2*
● OP Buttafuoco Storico V. Casa del Corno '12	♛♛ 3
○ OP Pinot Nero Brut Gianfranco Giorgi '13	♛♛ 5
○ OP Pinot Nero Brut Rosé 1870 '13	♛♛ 5
● OP Pinot Nero Monteroso '14	♛♛ 3
○ OP Riesling Il Bandito '15	♛♛ 4
○ Brut Top Zero	♛ 4
○ OP Pinot Nero Brut 1870 '11	♛♛♛ 5
○ OP Pinot Nero Brut 1870 '10	♛♛♛ 5
○ OP Pinot Nero Brut 1870 '09	♛♛♛ 5

Isimbarda

FRAZ. CASTELLO
CASCINA ISIMBARDA
27046 SANTA GIULETTA [PV]
TEL. +39 0383899256
www.isimbarda.com

CELLAR SALES
PRE-BOOKED VISITS
ANNUAL PRODUCTION 130,000 bottles
HECTARES UNDER VINE 40.00

Isimbarda lies in one of the most fascinating areas of Oltrepò, in the innermost part of the municipality of Santa Giulietta, towards Pietra de' Giorgi. In the 17th century it was the feud of the Marchesi Isimbardi and a century later it was already producing fine wine. Here Luigi Meroni has been tending his 40 hectares of vineyards for the past 35 years, aided by Veneto oenologist Daniele Zangelmi for many of these. The mixed soils of marly limestone and clay yield terroir-true wines, commencing with Riesling Renano, and more recently sparklers. Riesling Vigna Martina 2015 is still very young and struggles a little to express itself before revealing its usual elegance and a youthful nose of chamomile and aromatic herbs, promising very well for the future. Bonarda Vigna delle More 2015 is very fruity, fragrant, and flavoursome, while the pleasant sparklers focus more on drinkability than complexity.

● OP Bonarda Vivace V. delle More '15	♛♛ 2*
○ OP Riesling V. Martina '15	♛♛ 3
○ Brut Martinotti Riserva degli Isimbardi	♛ 3
⊙ OP Cruasé	♛ 4
○ OP Pinot Nero Brut Blanc de Noir	♛ 4
● OP Bonarda Vivace V. delle More '13	♛♛ 2*
● OP Pinot Nero V. del Cardinale '11	♛♛ 4
○ OP Riesling Renano V. Martina '14	♛♛ 2*
○ OP Riesling Renano V. Martina '13	♛♛ 2*
○ OP Riesling Renano V. Martina '12	♛♛ 2*
● OP Rosso Monplò '13	♛♛ 3
● OP Rosso Monplò '10	♛♛ 3

Lantieri de Paratico

LOC. COLZANO
VIA VIDETTI
25031 CAPRIOLO [BS]
TEL. +39 030736151
www.lantierideparatico.it

CELLAR SALES
PRE-BOOKED VISITS
ACCOMMODATION AND RESTAURANT SERVICE
ANNUAL PRODUCTION 140,000 bottles
HECTARES UNDER VINE 18.00
VITICULTURE METHOD Certified Organic

The Lantieri de Paratico family's presence in Franciacorta is documented since 930. In 1500 they settled in Capriolo, and their wine was already known and esteemed in Italy and at the European courts. Today Fabio Lantieri keeps the tradition alive and has created a well-equipped modern cellar in the old family home, where he makes his excellent cuvées from the grapes of his 18 hectares of handsome organic vineyards. Franciacorta Brut Arcadia 2012 reached our finals. A cuvée of 70% Chardonnay and 30% Pinot Nero from the estate's finest vineyards, it is aged for 42 months on the lees before disgorgement. It focuses on elegance and soft fruity notes, accompanied by good acid backbone and firm structure. The fresh, edgy non-vintage Extra Brut is among the finest of its kind, and the Satèn is excellent.

○ Franciacorta Brut Arcadia '12	♟♟	5
○ Franciacorta Brut	♟♟	4
○ Franciacorta Extra Brut	♟♟	4
○ Franciacorta Extra Brut Origines Ris. '10	♟♟	7
○ Franciacorta Satèn	♟♟	5
○ Franciacorta Brut Rosé	♟	5
○ Curtefranca Bianco '12	♟♟	2*
○ Franciacorta Brut Arcadia '11	♟♟	5
○ Franciacorta Brut Arcadia '10	♟♟	5
○ Franciacorta Brut Arcadia '09	♟♟	5
○ Franciacorta Extra Brut Origines Ris. '09	♟♟	7
○ Franciacorta Extra Brut Origines Ris. '08	♟♟	7

★Mamete Prevostini

VIA DON PRIMO LUCCHINETTI, 63
23020 MESE [SO]
TEL. +39 034341522
www.mameteprevostini.com

CELLAR SALES
PRE-BOOKED VISITS
RESTAURANT SERVICE
ANNUAL PRODUCTION 180,000 bottles
HECTARES UNDER VINE 20.00
SUSTAINABLE WINERY

Mamete Prevostini has always been a key figure of the Lombard winegrowing world. He is chairman of the Consorzio Vini di Valtellina and also of Ascovilo, the regional body for the promotion of Lombard wines abroad. However, he doesn't neglect his winery, which is constantly among the best in the Valtellina, due to its very sound range. His new cellar in the Valchiavenna is a model of environmental sustainability, which produces complex, nuanced, fruit-rich wines. Sforzato is a great wine, as shown by the confident and very elegant Albareda 2013, which is complex, with delicate tobacco notes that mingle nicely with hints of fresh fruit. The palate is suprisingly full and balanced, with a long, flavoursome finish. Sassella San Lorenzo is complex without being complicated, showing nuanced with notes of chocolate, jam, tobacco, and red berries, yet racy, with a very long, personal finish.

● Valtellina Sforzato Albareda '13	♟♟♟	6
● Valtellina Sforzato Corte di Cama '13	♟♟	6
● Valtellina Sup. Sassella San Lorenzo '13	♟♟	6
● Valtellina Sup. Ris. '12	♟♟	5
● Valtellina Sup. Sassella '14	♟♟	4
● Valtellina Sup. Sassella Sommarovina '14	♟♟	5
● Valtellina Sforzato Albareda '09	♟♟♟	6
● Valtellina Sforzato Albareda '08	♟♟♟	6
● Valtellina Sforzato Albareda '06	♟♟♟	6
● Valtellina Sforzato Albareda '05	♟♟♟	6
● Valtellina Sup. Ris. '09	♟♟♟	5
● Valtellina Sup. Sassella San Lorenzo '10	♟♟♟	5
● Valtellina Sup. Sassella Sommarovina '13	♟♟♟	5

Le Marchesine

VIA VALLOSA, 31
25050 PASSIRANO [BS]
TEL. +39 030657005
www.lemarchesine.it

CELLAR SALES
PRE-BOOKED VISITS
ANNUAL PRODUCTION 450,000 bottles
HECTARES UNDER VINE 47.00

Giovanni Biatta only founded Le Marchesine in the mid-1980s, but it is already one of the most prestigious wineries in the production zone, thanks to his son Loris and his children Alice and Andrea, who enthusiastically and competently continue his work. Today the estate boasts 47 hectares of fine vineyards, and an annual production of almost half a million bottles. French oenologist Jean-Pierre Valade, with international experience in the classic method, acts as consultant. This year it was the Franciacorta Satèn 2012 that represented the estate in our finals. It is from a single vineyard in Paderno and is fermented and aged in small casks prior to bottle fermentation for three years. Its bright straw yellow hue is accompanied by a concentrated nose of apples and pears, vanilla, and aromatic herbs, and a plush, taut, full-flavoured palate.

○ Franciacorta Satèn '12	♛♛	5
○ Franciacorta Brut	♛♛	4
○ Franciacorta Brut Blanc de Noir '12	♛♛	6
⊙ Franciacorta Brut Rosé '11	♛♛	5
○ Franciacorta Brut Secolo Novo '09	♛♛	7
○ Franciacorta Extra Brut	♛	5
○ Franciacorta Brut '04	♛♛♛	5
○ Franciacorta Brut Blanc de Noir '09	♛♛♛	5
○ Franciacorta Brut Secolo Novo '05	♛♛♛	7
○ Franciacorta Brut Blanc de Noir '11	♛♛	6
○ Franciacorta Brut Blanc de Noir '10	♛♛	5
○ Franciacorta Brut Nature Secolo Novo Giovanni Biatta '07	♛♛	5
○ Franciacorta Dosage Zero Secolo Novo Ris. '07	♛♛	7

Tenuta Mazzolino

VIA MAZZOLINO, 34
27050 CORVINO SAN QUIRICO [PV]
TEL. +39 0383876122
www.tenuta-mazzolino.com

CELLAR SALES
PRE-BOOKED VISITS
ANNUAL PRODUCTION 130,000 bottles
HECTARES UNDER VINE 22.00

Mazzolino is a real 19th-century hamlet, owned by the Braggiotti family since 1980, and one of those wineries everyone wants to visit on tours of Oltrepò Pavese. It was Giacomo Bologna who persuaded Enrico Braggiotti to ferment pinot nero on the skins, at the time with Giancarlo Scaglione, two legendary figures of the Piedmontese wine world. Then Kyriakos Kynigopoulos arrived from France, and pinot nero and chardonnay were confirmed as the main grape varieties. Sparkling wine production was added a few years ago. The award-winning Noir almost took our highest accolade, with the well-calibrated 2013 vintage vaunting elegant fruit and spice but, like others of its kind, requiring more time to reach its best. Blanco 2014, a barrique-aged Chardonnay, is as good as ever, with notes of honey, ripe tropical fruit, and vanilla, while Mazzolino 2015, a still Bonarda, is vinous with sound red berry fruit. The elegant Metodo Classico Blanc de Blancs, from chardonnay grapes, is particularly intriguing, showing salty and mineral with alluring hints of medicinal herbs.

● OP Pinot Nero Noir '13	♛♛	5
○ Brut Mazzolino Blanc de Blancs	♛♛	4
● OP Bonarda Mazzolino '15	♛♛	2*
○ OP Chardonnay Blanc '14	♛♛	3
○ Moscato '15	♛	2
⊙ OP Cruasé Mazzolino	♛	4
● Val di Prà '15	♛	3
● OP Pinot Nero Noir '12	♛♛♛	5
● OP Pinot Nero Noir '10	♛♛♛	5
● OP Pinot Nero Noir '09	♛♛♛	5
● OP Pinot Nero Noir '08	♛♛♛	5
● OP Pinot Nero Noir '07	♛♛♛	5
● OP Pinot Nero Noir '06	♛♛♛	5
○ OP Chardonnay Blanc '13	♛♛	3
● OP Pinot Nero Noir '11	♛♛	5

★Monsupello

VIA SAN LAZZARO, 5
27050 TORRICELLA VERZATE [PV]
TEL. +39 0383896043
www.monsupello.it

CELLAR SALES
PRE-BOOKED VISITS
ANNUAL PRODUCTION 260,000 bottles
HECTARES UNDER VINE 50.00

The estate owned by Pierangelo and Laura, the heirs of the late, lamented Carlo Boatti, one of the first to believe in the quality of Oltrepò wines, remains a benchmark for local winemaking. The cellar is skilfully run by oenologist Marco Bertelegni, whose strength is sparklers, as proven by his many awards won over the years. However, the family-run estate is also capable of producing impeccable still and semi-sparkling red and white wines. It's practically impossible not to award at least one Tre Bicchieri to the estate's sparklers, for even the non-vintage Brut scores very highly. This year the honour went to the 2011, which displays extraordinary finesse and matière, accompanied by a very complex nose and a focused, endless finish. The repeat award-winning Nature is just as good, showing rich, vibrant, and vigorous. Cuvée Ca' del Tava is weightier, but displays the same elegance and backbone.

Francesco Montagna

VIA CAIROLI, 67
27043 BRONI [PV]
TEL. +39 038551028
www.cantinemontagna.it

CELLAR SALES
PRE-BOOKED VISITS
RESTAURANT SERVICE
ANNUAL PRODUCTION 800,000 bottles
HECTARES UNDER VINE 18.00

This old winery, founded in 1895, has belonged to the Bertè and Cordini families for over 40 years, who have kept its original name. As in many similar cases in the area, it has evolved over time, and Natale Bertè has transformed it from a former largely commercial operation into an estate capable of producing high-quality wines at reasonable prices. The arrival of his son Matteo has given it new lifeblood, paying special attention to Metodo Classico sparklers. This year we particularly liked the Cuvée Tradizione 2012, with a lovely citrusy nose, creamy effervescence, firm structure, and a long finish. The taut Cruasé, with concentrated berries and orange peel, and the less exuberant Cuvée della Casa, dominated by red fruit, are also good. Bonarda 2015 is fragrant and juicy, and Buttafuoco 2013 is chewy, with a nose of blackberries, plums, and aromatic herbs.

○ Brut '11	▼▼▼ 5
○ Brut Nature	▼▼ 4
● Barbera I Gelsi '13	▼▼ 3
○ Brut	▼▼ 5
○ Brut Cuvée Ca' del Tava	▼▼ 6
○ Brut Rosé	▼▼ 4
● Cabernet Sauvignon Aplomb '09	▼▼ 5
○ Chardonnay '15	▼▼ 2*
● OP Bonarda Vivace Vaiolet '15	▼ 2
○ Brut '08	♀♀♀ 5
○ OP Brut Classese '06	♀♀♀ 5
○ OP Brut Classese '04	♀♀♀ 5
○ Brut '11	♀♀ 5

● OP Bonarda Sabion '15	▼▼ 2*
● OP Buttafuoco Bertè & Cordini '13	▼▼ 2*
⊙ OP Cruasé Bertè & Cordini	▼▼ 5
○ OP Pinot Nero Brut Cuvée Tradizione '12	▼▼ 4
○ OP Pinot Nero Brut M. Cl. Cuvée della Casa	▼▼ 5
○ OP Pinot Nero Brut M. Cl. Cuvée Nero d'Oro	▼ 4
● OP Rosso Valmaga '12	▼ 2
● OP Sangue di Giuda Bertè & Cordini '15	▼ 2
⊙ OP Cruasé Bertè & Cordini	♀♀ 5
○ OP Pinot Nero Brut Cuvée Tradizione '10	♀♀ 4
● OP Sangue di Giuda Bertè & Cordini '14	♀♀ 2*

★Monte Rossa

FRAZ. BORNATO
VIA MONTE ROSSA, 1
25040 CAZZAGO SAN MARTINO [BS]
TEL. +39 030725066
www.monterossa.com

CELLAR SALES
PRE-BOOKED VISITS
ANNUAL PRODUCTION 500,000 bottles
HECTARES UNDER VINE 70.00

Monte Rossa is one of Franciacorta's most typical long-standing wineries. It was founded by Paolo Rabotti and his wife Paola in 1972 and soon achieved iconic status. Today it is Emanuele Rabotti, in partnership with Oscar Farinetti, who runs the family estate with passion, painstaking care, and creativity, producing around 500,000 bottles of excellent wine each year from its 70 hectares of differently aspected vineyards. Cabochon 2011 reached our finals. It is a cuvée of 70% Chardonnay and 30% Pinot Nero, fermented and aged in small casks, prior to bottle ageing for around four years. It has a straw yellow hue with golden highlights, and vaunts a very fine, continuous bead and an elegant nose of ripe fruit, aromatic herbs, and chamomile, with elegant notes of oak and toast. On the palate it is deep, juicy, and complex. Satèn Sansevé and Rosé Flamingo are also excellent.

Tenuta Montenisa

FRAZ. CALINO
VIA PAOLO VI, 62
25046 CAZZAGO SAN MARTINO [BS]
TEL. +39 0307750838
www.montenisa.it

PRE-BOOKED VISITS
ANNUAL PRODUCTION 300,000 bottles
HECTARES UNDER VINE 60.00

In 1999 the Florentine Antinori family made a business agreement with the Maggi family for the management of this handsome Calino estate. Montenisa has been lovingly run by the Antinori sisters Albiera, Alessia, and Allegra, who have renovated the estate that today boasts 60 hectares of vineyards around the old buildings that now house the well-equipped modern cellars. The complex is dominated by the palazzo of the Conti Maggi, a fine 16th-century structure between two large colonnaded courtyards. This year's tastings confirm that this Lombard winery with a Tuscan soul has reached stylistic maturity. The complex, elegant Riserva Contessa Maggi 2007 is invigorating and lively, and made it into our finals. It is flanked by a series of good wines, particularly the sophisticated juicy Brut Blanc de Blancs and the floral, fruity Satèn Donna Cora 2011, vaunting a beautifully clean style.

○ Franciacorta Brut Cabochon '11	♛♛ 7
⊙ Franciacorta Brut Rosé Flamingo	♛♛ 6
⊙ Franciacorta Non Dosato Coupé	♛♛ 5
⊙ Franciacorta Satèn Sansevé	♛♛ 5
⊙ Franciacorta Brut Prima Cuvée	♛ 4
○ Franciacorta Brut Cabochon '05	♛♛♛ 6
○ Franciacorta Brut Cabochon '04	♛♛♛ 6
○ Franciacorta Brut Cabochon '03	♛♛♛ 6
○ Franciacorta Brut Cabochon '01	♛♛♛ 6
○ Franciacorta Brut Cabochon '09	♛♛ 7
○ Franciacorta Brut Cabochon '08	♛♛ 7
○ Franciacorta Extra Brut Salvadek '09	♛♛ 6
○ Franciacorta Extra Brut Salvadek '07	♛♛ 6

○ Franciacorta Brut Contessa Maggi Ris. '07	♛♛ 7
○ Franciacorta Brut Blanc de Blancs	♛♛ 5
○ Franciacorta Brut Satèn Donna Cora '11	♛♛ 6
○ Franciacorta Brut Conte Aimo '09	♛ 8
○ Franciacorta Brut Cuvée Royale	♛ 5
⊙ Franciacorta Brut Rosé	♛ 5
○ Franciacorta Brut Conte Aimo '07	♛♛ 8
○ Franciacorta Brut Contessa Camilla Maggi '02	♛♛ 7
○ Franciacorta Brut Contessa Maggi '06	♛♛ 7
○ Franciacorta Satèn '09	♛♛ 6
○ Franciacorta Satèn '06	♛♛ 6
○ Franciacorta Satèn '04	♛♛ 6
○ Franciacorta Satèn '04	♛♛ 6
○ Franciacorta Satèn '03	♛♛ 6

Monterucco

Valle Cima, 38
27040 Cigognola [PV]
Tel. +39 038585151
www.monterucco.it

CELLAR SALES
PRE-BOOKED VISITS
ANNUAL PRODUCTION 100,000 bottles
HECTARES UNDER VINE 20.00

This is the first full profile for the winery founded by Luigi Valenti and now run by his sons Silvano, in the vineyard, and Roberto, in the cellar. We've been keeping an eye on the slow but constant and significant improvement of the wines of this small estate in the Valle Scuropasso, with 20 hectares of vineyards scattered between Cigognola, Castana, and Canneto Pavese. Its traditional Oltrepò wines are almost unbeatable value for money. The star is often the Metodo Classico, which is no surprise as pinot nero for sparklers has been grown here for over 50 years. The 2011 vintage is particularly intense and complex, yet elegant, with a close-focused nose of wild berries, nice weight, and a coherent finish. Buttafuoco Sanluigi is good too, with notes of blackberries, blueberries, aromatic herbs, and violets, fine-grained tannins and attractive evolved fruit. Bonarda 2015 is exceptionally fragrant, juicy, and fruity, as is Sangue di Giuda 2015, offering just the right degree of sweetness.

○ Malvasia Valentina '15	♀♀ 2*
● OP Bonarda V. Il Modello '15	♀♀ 2*
● OP Buttafuoco Sanluigi '13	♀♀ 3
○ OP Pinot Nero Brut '11	♀♀ 3
● OP Sangue di Giuda '15	♀♀ 2*
○ Malvasia Valentina '14	♀♀ 2*
● OP Bonarda '13	♀♀ 2*
● OP Buttafuoco Sanluigi '10	♀♀ 3
○ OP Pinot Nero Brut '09	♀♀ 3

Monzio Compagnoni

via Nigoline, 98
25030 Adro [BS]
Tel. +39 0307457803
www.monziocompagnoni.com

CELLAR SALES
PRE-BOOKED VISITS
ANNUAL PRODUCTION 170,000 bottles
HECTARES UNDER VINE 17.00

In 1995, Marcello Monzio Compagnoni from the Valcalepio founded a handsome winery in Franciacorta, which now boasts a well-equipped modern cellar and extensive vineyards. The level of his Franciacorta production has always been high, and the cuvées made in the cellar in Adro are flanked by the wines from his estate in Scanzorosciate, in the province of Bergamo. Marcello has returned to our full profile and our finals with an excellent Satèn 2012, which perfectly embodies this style with vanilla notes on a delicate fruity nose, and a plush, rounded, supple palate characterized by fruit, ending in a long, fresh citrusy finish. The Brut of the same vintage is deeper and more complex, with a rich floral nose and a nicely rounded palate. Riserva Barone Monti della Corte 2008 is also very good, showing more austere and linear.

○ Franciacorta Satèn '12	♀♀ 5
○ Franciacorta Brut '12	♀♀ 5
○ Franciacorta Pas Dosé Barone Monti della Corte Ris. '08	♀♀ 6
● Moscato di Scanzo Don Quijote '09	♀♀ 6
● Valcalepio Rosso di Luna '10	♀♀ 5
○ Curtefranca Ronco della Seta '15	♀ 3
○ Franciacorta Extra Brut '04	♀♀♀ 5
○ Franciacorta Extra Brut '03	♀♀♀ 5
○ Franciacorta Brut '10	♀♀ 4
○ Franciacorta Brut '09	♀♀ 4
○ Franciacorta Extra Brut '09	♀♀ 5
○ Franciacorta Satèn '10	♀♀ 5
○ Franciacorta Satèn '09	♀♀ 5
● Moscato di Scanzo Don Quijote '08	♀♀ 5

Il Mosnel

LOC. CAMIGNONE
VIA BARBOGLIO, 14
25040 PASSIRANO [BS]
TEL. +39 030653117
www.ilmosnel.com

CELLAR SALES
PRE-BOOKED VISITS
RESTAURANT SERVICE
ANNUAL PRODUCTION 250,000 bottles
HECTARES UNDER VINE 40.00

Emanuela Barboglio converted the family estate to viticulture back in the 1960s, marking the start of wine and Franciacorta production of wines at Mosnel. Today the estate is lovingly and competently run by her children Giulio and Lucia Barzanò, who have perfectly restored the winery's headquarters, the 16th-century hamlet of Camignone di Passirano, set among its impressive 40 hectares of vineyards in a single plot. The range obviously focuses on Franciacortas, although it also features some still wines. Two of them our finals: Extra Brut EBB 2011, dedicated to the estate's founder, and Satèn 2012. The former is complex and well orchestrated, with top notes of fruit giving way to elegant blossom, cakes and vanilla; while the latter is soft and creamy, brimming with fruit but also displaying an enviable swathe of acidity that ensures grip and backbone.

○ Franciacorta Extra Brut EBB '11	♟♟	5
○ Franciacorta Satèn '12	♟♟	5
○ Franciacorta Brut	♟♟	4
⊙ Franciacorta Brut Rosé	♟♟	5
○ Franciacorta Pas Dosé	♟♟	4
○ Franciacorta Pas Dosé Parosé '10	♟♟	5
○ Franciacorta Extra Brut EBB '09	♟♟♟	5
○ Franciacorta Pas Dosé QdE Ris. '04	♟♟♟	6
○ Franciacorta Satèn '05	♟♟♟	5
○ Curtefranca Bianco Campolarga '14	♟♟	2*
○ Franciacorta Extra Brut EBB '10	♟♟	5
○ Franciacorta Satèn '11	♟♟	5
○ Franciacorta Satèn '10	♟♟	5

★★Nino Negri

VIA GHIBELLINI
23030 CHIURO [SO]
TEL. +39 0342485211
www.ninonegri.it

CELLAR SALES
PRE-BOOKED VISITS
RESTAURANT SERVICE
ANNUAL PRODUCTION 800,000 bottles
HECTARES UNDER VINE 36.00
SUSTAINABLE WINERY

Nino Negri is an important name in the history of the Valtellina, which it has brought to the attention of the rest of Italy and the world. Founded in 1897, and now owned by Gruppo Italiano Vini, it is one of the best-equipped wineries, focusing on research and experimentation to make the most of its unique estate with meticulously tended vineyards in the subzones of Valtellina Superiore: Sassella, Grumello, Inferno, and Valgella, where the Fracia vineyard is situated. The wines combine sense of place with sheer drinkability, in a quietly modern style. The flagship is Sfursat 5 Stelle, which won our Red Wine of the Year award with the 2001 vintage. The 2013 vintage sums up its dynamic history, offering a balsamic nose of incense, tobacco, and bottled cherries, with alluring spicy, gingery hints, and a sumptuous palate with big tannins and a promising endless finish. Inferno 2013 is beautifully harmonious and complex, with a nose of dark wild berries, spice, and medicinal herbs, and a juicy palate with progressive, close-woven tannins, and a long, aristocratic finish.

● Valtellina Sfursat 5 Stelle '13	♟♟♟	8
● Valtellina Sfursat Carlo Negri '13	♟♟	6
● Valtellina Sup. Inferno Carlo Negri '13	♟♟	5
○ Ca' Brione '15	♟♟	5
● Valtellina Sup. Grumello V. Sassorosso '13	♟♟	4
● Valtellina Sup. Mazer '13	♟♟	4
● Valtellina Sup. Sassella Le Tense '13	♟♟	4
● Valtellina Sfursat '05	♟♟♟	8
● Valtellina Sfursat 5 Stelle '11	♟♟♟	8
● Valtellina Sfursat 5 Stelle '10	♟♟♟	7
● Valtellina Sfursat 5 Stelle '09	♟♟♟	7
● Valtellina Sfursat 5 Stelle '07	♟♟♟	7
● Valtellina Sfursat 5 Stelle '06	♟♟♟	7
● Valtellina Sfursat Carlo Negri '11	♟♟♟	8
● Valtellina Sup. Vign. Fracia '08	♟♟♟	6

LOMBARDY

Pasini - San Giovanni

FRAZ. RAFFA
VIA VIDELLE, 2
25080 PUEGNAGO SUL GARDA [BS]
TEL. +39 0365651419
www.pasinisangiovanni.it

CELLAR SALES
PRE-BOOKED VISITS
RESTAURANT SERVICE
ANNUAL PRODUCTION 300,000 bottles
HECTARES UNDER VINE 36.00
SUSTAINABLE WINERY

The Pasini cousins form a close-knit team.
The third generation of a family of
vignerons, they founded this ambitious
estate designed to have minimal
environmental impact. Indeed the 36
hectares of vineyards in the Valtenesi and
Lugana are tended using organic methods
and the modern cellars use renewable
energy sources. This care and respect for
the terroir have resulted in a diverse range
of wines, with very interesting highlights
and still much potential for improvement.
This year we loved the elegant pale pink Il
Chiaretto 2015, vaunting well-calibrated
fruit and minerality, and a beautiful style.
Brut Centopercento is an original Blanc de
Noir from groppello. This year's version
offers notes of honey, hints of red berries,
and good backbone. The other wines are all
good, commencing with Ceppo 326 2008,
another Metodo Classico with long ageing
on the lees, from groppello grapes with a
small amount of chardonnay, and the
beautifully taut Lugana Bio 2015.

Perla del Garda

VIA FENIL VECCHIO, 9
25017 LONATO [BS]
TEL. +39 0309103109
www.perladelgarda.it

CELLAR SALES
PRE-BOOKED VISITS
ANNUAL PRODUCTION 120,000 bottles
HECTARES UNDER VINE 30.00
VITICULTURE METHOD Certified Organic

Giovanna Prandini, who has also been
president of Strada del Vino e Sapori del
Garda since 2006, has flanked dairy
farming on the family estate with wine
production. Today Perla del Garda vaunts
30 hectares of fine vineyards yielding
top-notch wines that are also exported. The
well-equipped modern winery is particularly
committed to attaining certification as a
sustainable low-impact operation. It
produces all the types of Lugana wines,
and this year presented a sound
Vendemmia Tardiva 2013, brimming with
tropical fruit, delicately sweet and balanced.
Lugana Perla 2015 is perfectly fruity and
tangy, while the Superiore Madonna della
Scoperta 2013, is more complex and
layered, with a fine mineral finish. Drajibo, a
Passito from turbiana, riesling and incrocio
Manzoni is extremely good, with notes of
candied peel and apricot jam.

○ Brut M. Cl. Centopercento	▼▼ 4
○ Brut M. Cl. Ceppo 326 '08	▼▼ 5
○ Lugana Il Lugana Bio '15	▼▼ 2*
⊙ Valtènesi Il Chiaretto '15	▼▼ 2*
○ Garda Cl. Bianco Il Renano '12	▼ 2
○ Lugana Brut	▼ 2
○ Lugana Il Lugana '15	▼ 2
● Valtènesi Picedo '13	▼ 2
⊙ Garda Cl. Chiaretto Il Chiaretto '09	♀♀ 2*
● Garda Cl. Groppello Vign. Arzane Ris. '09	♀♀ 5
● Garda Cl. Groppello Vign. Arzane Ris. '08	♀♀ 3*
● Garda Cl. Groppello Vign. Arzane Ris. '07	♀♀ 3*

○ Drajibo Passito	▼▼ 4
○ Lugana Perla '15	▼▼ 3
○ Lugana Sup. Madonna della Scoperta '13	▼▼ 4
○ Lugana V. T. '13	▼▼ 4
○ Drajibo Passito '09	♀♀ 5
● Leonatus '09	♀♀ 4
○ Lugana Madreperla '11	♀♀ 4
○ Lugana Perla '13	♀♀ 3
○ Lugana Perla '11	♀♀ 3
○ Lugana Sup. Madreperla '10	♀♀ 5
○ Lugana V. T. '11	♀♀ 4

Andrea Picchioni

FRAZ. CAMPONOCE, 8
27044 CANNETO PAVESE [PV]
TEL. +39 0385262139
www.picchioniandrea.it

CELLAR SALES
PRE-BOOKED VISITS
ACCOMMODATION
ANNUAL PRODUCTION 70,000 bottles
HECTARES UNDER VINE 10.00
VITICULTURE METHOD Certified Organic
SUSTAINABLE WINERY

Andrea Picchioni has been attracting the attention of the public and critics alike for many years with the wines made in his little cellar in Canneto Pavese, with the invaluable aid of his mother Rosa, father Antonio, and wife Silvia. They are proudly terroir-true, hailing mainly from the steep crests of Val Solinga, where Andrea grows the croatina, barbera, and ughetta used to make both young, early-drinking wines, in the traditional still and semi-sparkling versions, and big, characterful reds, which reach their best several years after bottling. This year Buttafuoco Bricco Riva Bianca 2012 reached our finals, offering a nose of dark wild berries that slowly unfolds to reveal cocoa powder and liquorice with a balsamic vein, and a firm, austere palate with lively, fine-grained tannins. It should age very well. Rosso d'Asia 2012 is readier to drink, fragrant and hefty, with a lovely almondy finish. The racy, harmonious Bonarda Vivace 2015 is among the best of the zone, with a concentrated nose of blueberries.

● OP Buttafuoco Bricco Riva Bianca '12	▼▼ 4
● OP Bonarda Vivace '15	▼▼ 2*
● Rosso d'Asia '12	▼▼ 4
● OP Buttafuoco Cerasa '15	▼ 2
● OP Sangue di Giuda Fior del Vento '15	▼ 2
● OP Buttafuoco Bricco Riva Bianca '11	♀♀ 4
● OP Buttafuoco Bricco Riva Bianca '10	♀♀ 4
● OP Buttafuoco Cerasa '14	♀♀ 2*
○ OP Profilo Brut Nature M. Cl. '00	♀♀ 5
● Pinot Nero Arfena '12	♀♀ 4
● Rosso d'Asia '11	♀♀ 4

Piccolo Bacco dei Quaroni

FRAZ. COSTAMONTEFEDELE
27040 MONTÙ BECCARIA [PV]
TEL. +39 038560521
www.piccolobaccodeiquaroni.it

CELLAR SALES
PRE-BOOKED VISITS
RESTAURANT SERVICE
ANNUAL PRODUCTION 35,000 bottles
HECTARES UNDER VINE 10.00
VITICULTURE METHOD Certified Organic

Piccolo Bacco is a small winery, but some of its wines have the potential for greatness. Situated in eastern Oltrepò, near the border with Emilia, the estate has four crus in the three municipalities of Montù Beccaria, Castana, and Bosnasco, with very different characteristics. They are tended with natural methods, without the use of pesticides, by agronomists Mario Cavalli and his wife Laura Brazzoli, who purchased it in 2001 and are now aided by their children, Giulia and oenologist Tommaso. Riesling Vigneto del Pozzo 2013 earned a place in our finals for its fine development that has revealed mineral notes while still retaining overtones of flowers and aromatic herbs. It is deep and elegant with impressive length. Bonarda Mons Acutus 2015 is also very good, juicy and highly drinkable with beautiful red fruit, a pervasive nose, and a stylish lean palate.

○ OP Riesling Vign. del Pozzo '13	▼▼ 3*
● OP Bonarda Mons Acutus '15	▼▼ 2*
● Il Moree '14	▼ 2
● OP Buttafuoco Ca' Padroni '12	▼ 3
● OP Barbera Gustavo '07	♀♀ 2
● OP Bonarda Mons Acutus '11	♀♀ 2*
● OP Bonarda Vivace Mons Acutus '07	♀♀ 2*
● OP Buttafuoco Vign. Ca' Padroni '04	♀♀ 3
☉ OP Cruasé PBQ '10	♀♀ 3
☉ OP Cruasé PBQ '09	♀♀ 3

Plozza Vini

VIA CAPPUCCINI, 26
23037 TIRANO [SO]
TEL. +39 0342701297
www.plozza.com

CELLAR SALES
PRE-BOOKED VISITS
ANNUAL PRODUCTION 350,000 bottles
HECTARES UNDER VINE 25.00

Andrea Zanolare is the owner and
oenologist of this legendary Valtellina
winery, founded by Pietro Plozza in 1919. It
has two cellars, one in Tirano, in the
province of Sondrio, and another in Brusio,
in the Swiss canton of Grisons. The
vineyards are planted entirely to nebbiolo
and lie between 400 and 700 metres
above sea level in Valtellina's main
subzones. The range comprises
easy-drinking wines and far more
structured, extracted selections, with long
ageing in small oak casks. Numero 1 2013
is complex and modern, offering a
concentrated nose of sweet oak, jammy
fruit and hints of cocoa powder, and a
warm, succulent palate with good structure
and a very long, elegant finish. The original
Sassella 2012 is characterized by red
berries, dried herbs, and tobacco, and a
full-bodied palate with prominent fruit,
close-woven tannins, and a long finish.

● Numero 1 '13	🍷🍷 7
● Sforzato di Valtellina Blackedition '12	🍷🍷 5
● Valtellina Sup. Inferno Rededition '12	🍷🍷 4
● Valtellina Sup. Sassella Rededition '12	🍷🍷 3
● Valtellina Numero Uno '01	🍷🍷🍷 7
● Sforzato di Valtellina Black Edition '11	🍷🍷 6
● Valtellina Numero 1 '12	🍷🍷 7
● Valtellina Numero Uno '11	🍷🍷 7
● Valtellina Numero Uno '10	🍷🍷 7
● Valtellina Sforzato Vin da Ca' '10	🍷🍷 5
● Valtellina Sforzato Vin da Ca' '09	🍷🍷 5
● Valtellina Sup. Inferno Red Edition '11	🍷🍷 5
● Valtellina Sup. Inferno Ris. '10	🍷🍷 3
● Valtellina Sup. Sassella La Scala Ris. '10	🍷🍷 3*
● Valtellina Sup. Sassella Red Edition '11	🍷🍷 5

Pratello

VIA PRATELLO, 26
25080 PADENGHE SUL GARDA [BS]
TEL. +39 0309907005
www.pratello.com

CELLAR SALES
ACCOMMODATION AND RESTAURANT SERVICE
ANNUAL PRODUCTION 600,000 bottles
HECTARES UNDER VINE 70.00
VITICULTURE METHOD Certified Organic

The dynamic Vincenzo Bertola's estate is
one of the finest in the entire Lake Garda
zone. The winery is housed in a large villa
with striking architecture near Padenghe
Castle, with fabulous views over the lake
and its valley; the cellar boasts cutting-
edge equipment; and the 70 hectares of
vineyards and olive groves are tended with
organic methods. Constant research into
the ageing potential of white wines has
frequently yielded surprises. This year Lieti
Conversari 2015, a fresh, zesty Incrocio
Manzoni, with a nose of white peaches and
aromatic herbs, performed very well.
Torrazzo 2015, from groppello, is also
good, with sound fruit and clear potential
for future development. Nero per Sempre is
a fragrant Marzemino, also with good fruit
and peppery notes. Our favourite of the two
2015 Luganas, was the Catulliano, with a
nose of flowers and tropical fruit and a firm
palate, while the Rivale focuses more on
super-ripeness.

○ Lieti Conversari '15	🍷🍷 4
○ Lugana Catulliano '15	🍷🍷 4
● Valtènesi Torrazzo '15	🍷🍷 3
○ Lugana Il Rivale '15	🍷 5
○ Riesling '15	🍷 3
⊙ Valtènesi Chiaretto Sant'Emiliano '15	🍷 3
○ Lugana Catulliano '14	🍷🍷 3
○ Lugana Il Rivale '14	🍷🍷 5
○ Lugana Il Rivale '12	🍷🍷 5
● Nero per Sempre '12	🍷🍷 5
● Rebo '08	🍷🍷 4
○ Riesling '14	🍷🍷 3
● Valtènesi Torrazzo '13	🍷🍷 3

Quadra

VIA SANT'EUSEBIO, 1
25033 COLOGNE [BS]
TEL. +39 0307157314
www.quadrafranciacorta.it

CELLAR SALES
PRE-BOOKED VISITS
RESTAURANT SERVICE
ANNUAL PRODUCTION 140,000 bottles
HECTARES UNDER VINE 32.00

In 2003 Ugo Ghezzi, an entrepreneur in the renewable energy sector, along with his children Cristina and Marco, decided to buy a small winery and the surrounding vineyards, whose management he subsequently entrusted to Mario Falcetti, an oenologist with a long career as a researcher. Today the estate boasts 32 hectares of vineyards. Alongside chardonnay, Ghezzi and Falcetti are working on valorizing pinot bianco, for which three highly complementary sites have been identified, and pinot nero, for which several plots on the morainic hillsides have been destined. This year it was Qsatèn 2011 that most impressed us. A Chardonnay cuvée with 30% Pinot Bianco, a small part of the base wine is aged in small casks and, after four years on the lees, displays an attractive bright greenish straw hue. The nose has top notes of white-fleshed fruit and citron peel, with hints of blossom, mountain herbs, and vanilla, and is accompanied by a delightful soft, spirited palate.

○ Franciacorta Brut QBlack	▼▼ 4
○ Franciacorta Dosaggio Zero EretiQ '11	▼▼ 6
○ Franciacorta Dosaggio Zero QZero '10	▼▼ 5
○ Franciacorta Extra Brut Cuvée 55 '10	▼▼ 5
○ Franciacorta QSatèn '11	▼▼ 5
○ Franciacorta Brut Green Vegan	▼ 5
○ Franciacorta QRosé	▼ 5
○ Franciacorta Brut Q39 '08	♀♀ 5
○ Franciacorta Dosaggio Zero EretiQ '10	♀♀ 6
○ Franciacorta Dosaggio Zero EretiQ '10	♀♀ 6
○ Franciacorta Extra Brut QZero '09	♀♀ 5
○ Franciacorta QSatèn '10	♀♀ 5
○ Franciacorta QSatèn '09	♀♀ 5
○ Franciacorta Quvée 46 '09	♀♀ 5

Francesco Quaquarini

LOC. MONTEVENEROSO
VIA CASA ZAMBIANCHI, 26
27044 CANNETO PAVESE [PV]
TEL. +39 038560152
www.quaquarinifrancesco.it

CELLAR SALES
PRE-BOOKED VISITS
ANNUAL PRODUCTION 650,000 bottles
HECTARES UNDER VINE 60.00
VITICULTURE METHOD Certified Organic

Despite its rather large dimensions for an extremely fragmented area like Oltrepò Pavese, the solid family estate belonging Francesco Quaquarini and his children Umberto and Maria Teresa, always manages to maintain very high average quality and excellent value for money, with stand-out wines in certain vintages. Its range is wide, as you'd expect in a growing zone whose production regulations provide for dozens of different types, with special attention to semi-sparkling wines. Pinot Nero Blau 2013 is well made and very drinkable, focusing on wild berries, with hints of citrus and a racy finish. The fruity Bonarda Vivace 2015 is good, with perceptible residual sugar, and the Sangue di Giuda of the same vintage is also nice, showing concentrated with a nose of plums and blackcurrants. The rest of the list is as reliable as ever.

● OP Bonarda Vivace '15	▼▼ 2*
● OP Pinot Nero Blau '13	▼▼ 3
● OP Sangue di Giuda '15	▼▼ 2*
● OP Barbera Poggio Anna '13	▼ 3
● OP Buttafuoco Storico V. Pregana '10	▼ 6
○ OP Cruasé Bio '11	▼ 5
○ OP Pinot Nero Brut Classese '09	▼ 4
● OP Barbera Poggio Anna '12	♀♀ 2*
● OP Barbera Poggio Anna '11	♀♀ 3
● OP Buttafuoco Storico V. Pregana '09	♀♀ 5
● OP Pinot Nero Blau '10	♀♀ 3
● OP Sangue di Giuda V. Acqua Calda '13	♀♀ 3

Cantina Sociale Cooperativa di Quistello

VIA ROMA, 46
46026 QUISTELLO [MN]
TEL. +39 0376618118
www.cantinasocialequistello.it

CELLAR SALES
PRE-BOOKED VISITS
ANNUAL PRODUCTION 1,000,000 bottles
HECTARES UNDER VINE 330.00

Lambrusco Mantovano is often wrongly considered the poor cousin of the Lambruscos from Emilia-Romagna. However, this south-eastern corner of Lombardy across the Po, along the River Secchia, is home to some very good producers and some extremely interesting wines. Their standard-bearer is the cooperative Cantina di Quistello, founded in 1928, which counts 300 members and 5 million kilograms of grapes crushed each year. In addition to Lambrusco, it also makes other typical local wines. The first of these is Gran Rosso Del Vicariato Di Quistello 2015, a bottle-fermented Lambrusco from ruberti and ancellotta, with an inky ruby hue, a fragrant nose of red berries and pennyroyal, and nice length. The 80 Vendemmie Rosso 2015, also bottle fermented at controlled temperature, is big and complex, with a prominent note of currants, while Rossissimo 2015, a blend of many different varieties, is brimming with fruit and alluring lively tannins.

★Aldo Rainoldi

FRAZ. CASACCE
VIA STELVIO, 128
23030 CHIURO [SO]
TEL. +39 0342482225
www.rainoldi.com

CELLAR SALES
PRE-BOOKED VISITS
ANNUAL PRODUCTION 180,000 bottles
HECTARES UNDER VINE 9.60

The Chiuro winery run by Aldo Rainoldi is rock solid and a benchmark for Valtellina wine. Aldo has steered the estate founded by his Uncle Peppino in a new direction, brilliantly upgrading it with the purchase of targeted plots – bringing the area under vine up to around ten hectares – and keenly promoting its image abroad. The wines have a strong sense of place, also thanks to the selections, and are the result of long, patient bottle ageing. Sassella Riserva 2012 is magnificent, combining tradition and future. Tobacco notes mingle with ripe fruit on the concentrated, elegant nose, while the rounded palate is characterized by fresh, crisp acidity, well-defined tannins, and a very long finish. Grumello Riserva 2010 is full of character, with a nose of raspberries nicely blended with classic hints of tobacco, quinine, and liquorice. The big palate has progressive, close-woven tannins, and a long, very personal finish.

● 80 Vendemmie Rosso '15	♟♟ 2*
● Gran Rosso del Vicariato di Quistello '15	♟♟ 2*
● Lambrusco Mantovano Rossissimo '15	♟♟ 2*
☉ 80 Vendemmie Rosato '15	♟ 2
● 80 Vendemmie '13	♟♟ 2*
● Gran Rosso del Vicariato di Quistello '13	♟♟ 2*
● Gran Rosso del Vicariato di Quistello '12	♟♟ 1*
● Lambrusco Mantovano Rossissimo '12	♟♟ 2*

● Valtellina Sup. Sassella Ris. '12	♟♟♟ 5
● Valtellina Sup. Crespino '12	♟♟ 5
● Valtellina Sup. Grumello Ris. '10	♟♟ 6
● Valtellina Sup. Grumello '12	♟♟ 3
● Valtellina Sup. Sassella '11	♟♟ 5
● Valtellina Sfursat '08	♟♟♟ 5
● Valtellina Sfursat Fruttaio Ca' Rizzieri '11	♟♟♟ 6
● Valtellina Sfursat Fruttaio Ca' Rizzieri '10	♟♟♟ 6
● Valtellina Sfursat Fruttaio Ca' Rizzieri '09	♟♟♟ 6
● Valtellina Sfursat Fruttaio Ca' Rizzieri '06	♟♟♟ 6
● Valtellina Sfursat Fruttaio Ca' Rizzieri '02	♟♟♟ 6
● Valtellina Sup. Sassella Ris. '06	♟♟♟ 5

Ricci Curbastro

VIA ADRO, 37
25031 CAPRIOLO [BS]
TEL. +39 030736094
www.riccicurbastro.it

CELLAR SALES
PRE-BOOKED VISITS
ACCOMMODATION
ANNUAL PRODUCTION 200,000 bottles
HECTARES UNDER VINE 27.00
SUSTAINABLE WINERY

Ricci Curbastro, founded in 1967, is one of Franciacorta's oldest estates. Today it is headed by agronomist and oenologist Riccardo, who also chairs the European Federation of Origin Wines and its Italian counterpart the FederDoc. He has been committed to environmental sustainability for years and is chairman of Equalitas, the company that drew up the relevant regulations for the Italian wine sector. The estate vaunts 27 hectares of vineyards on the finest sites in the production zone, and successfully exports its cuvées all over the world. We gave a well-deserved Tre Bicchieri to the Extra Brut 2012, which goes to join the winery's trophy collection. A cuvée of equal parts of Chardonnay and Pinot Nero, it vaunts a bright straw yellow hue with coppery highlights and a delicate, complex nose with top notes of fruit and elegant hints of barley sugar and vanilla. The full-flavoured palate is deep, firm, and dry, with excellent balance and freshness, making it highly drinkable. Satèn 2012 also performed well, showing vibrant and close focused.

○ Franciacorta Extra Brut '12	♟♟♟ 5
○ Curtefranca Bianco V. Bosco Alto '11	♟♟ 3
○ Franciacorta Extra Brut Museum Release '07	♟♟ 5
⊙ Franciacorta Rosé	♟♟ 5
○ Franciacorta Satèn '12	♟♟ 5
● Curtefranca Rosso '13	♟ 2
○ Franciacorta Brut	♟ 4
○ Franciacorta Demi Sec	♟ 4
○ Pinot Bianco '15	♟ 2
○ Franciacorta Dosaggio Zero Gualberto '06	♟♟♟ 6
○ Franciacorta Extra Brut '07	♟♟♟ 5
○ Franciacorta Extra Brut '11	♟♟ 5
○ Franciacorta Extra Brut '10	♟♟ 5
○ Franciacorta Extra Brut '09	♟♟ 5

Ronco Calino

FRAZ. TORBIATO
VIA FENICE, 45
25030 ADRO [BS]
TEL. +39 0307451073
www.roncocalino.it

CELLAR SALES
PRE-BOOKED VISITS
ANNUAL PRODUCTION 70,000 bottles
HECTARES UNDER VINE 10.00
VITICULTURE METHOD Certified Organic
SUSTAINABLE WINERY

In 1996 Paolo Radici decided to purchase the estate in Torbiato di Adro, which once belonged to the famous pianist Arturo Benedetti Michelangeli. It is lovingly run by Paolo's wife, Lara Imberti and specializes in Franciacortas. Vaunting a modern cellar and ten hectares of vineyards in a spectacular morainic amphitheatre, the boutique winery draws on the expertise of consultant oenologist Leonardo Valenti and agronomist Pierluigi Donna to produce a small but carefully crafted range of Franciacortas and local wines. It has a special talent for Satèn and once again this year we were struck by the wine's plush opulence, supported by a fresh swathe of acidity, which makes it alluringly drinkable, characterized by rich fruit and elegant vanillaed creaminess. The full, zesty, linear Nature 2010 is equally good, with attractive notes of oak and torrefaction on the complex finish. Pinot Nero L'Arturo 2012 is varietal, brimming with ripe red and black fruit.

● Curtefranca Rosso Ponènt '12	♟♟ 4
○ Franciacorta Brut	♟♟ 4
○ Franciacorta Brut Nature '10	♟♟ 5
○ Franciacorta Satèn	♟♟ 5
● Pinot Nero L'Arturo '12	♟♟ 5
○ Curtefranca Bianco Lèant '15	♟ 3
⊙ Franciacorta Rosé	♟ 5
○ Curtefranca Bianco Lèant '14	♟♟ 3
● Curtefranca Rosso Ponènt '11	♟♟ 4
● Curtefranca Rosso Ponènt '10	♟♟ 4
○ Franciacorta Extra Brut Centoventi '04	♟♟ 8
○ Franciacorta Nature '09	♟♟ 5
● Pinot Nero L'Arturo '11	♟♟ 5

San Cristoforo

FRAZ. VILLA D'ERBUSCO
VIA VILLANUOVA, 2
25030 ERBUSCO [BS]
TEL. +39 0307760482
www.sancristoforo.eu

CELLAR SALES
PRE-BOOKED VISITS
ANNUAL PRODUCTION 80,000 bottles
HECTARES UNDER VINE 10.00
SUSTAINABLE WINERY

In 1997 Bruno Dotti and his wife Claudia took over this little Franciacorta winery, already renowned for the high quality of its wines. In almost 20 years of work the keen couple have expanded the estate to ten hectares and renovated the cellar, installing the very latest equipment. Their production remains small scale, but the quality of their cuvées and wines continues to rise. Flanked by their daughter Celeste, they embody the philosophy of the grower-producer. The Dottis don't make Satèn, but favour undosed Franciacortas. Their Pas Dosé 2011 is one of the most interesting, combining finesse and firm structure, along with good sound fruit and a delicious citrussy finish. The refreshing Brut of the same vintage is excellent and earned a place in our finals with its rich fruit and creamy effervescence; the non-vintage Brut is dry, invigorating, taut and easy drinking; and the nicely complex undosed Celeste 2008 boasts an appealing clean style.

○ Franciacorta Brut '11	▼▼	6
○ Franciacorta Brut	▼▼	5
○ Franciacorta Dosaggio Zero '11	▼▼	6
○ Franciacorta Dosaggio Zero Celeste '08	▼▼	8
⊙ Franciacorta Rosé	▼	5
○ Franciacorta Brut '09	♈6	
○ Franciacorta Brut '08	♈6	
○ Franciacorta Brut '07	♈4	
○ Franciacorta Brut '06	♈4	
○ Franciacorta Pas Dosé '10	♈6	
○ Franciacorta Pas Dosé '09	♈6	
○ Franciacorta Pas Dosé '08	♈6	
○ Franciacorta Pas Dosé '07	♈5	
○ Franciacorta Pas Dosé '06	♈5	

Cantine Selva Capuzza

FRAZ. SAN MARTINO DELLA BATTAGLIA
LOC. SELVA CAPUZZA
25010 DESENZANO DEL GARDA [BS]
TEL. +39 0309910381
www.selvacapuzza.it

CELLAR SALES
PRE-BOOKED VISITS
ACCOMMODATION AND RESTAURANT SERVICE
ANNUAL PRODUCTION 300,000 bottles
HECTARES UNDER VINE 25.00

Selva Capuzza is a handsome 50-hectare estate, of which 25 under vine, that oenologist Vincenzo Formentini bought years ago and renamed the winery Colli a Lago. It lies in the morainic amphitheatre that marks the southern end of the lake and is home to the Lugana, San Martino della Battaglia, and Garda DOC zones. The winery uses only traditional grape varieties and is now run by Luca Formentini. Selva Capuzza also boasts an excellent restaurant and guest accommodation. The range of wines presented for the various designations is wide and very good. Our favourite Lugana was Riserva Menassasso 2012, a firmly structured, complex white with a variegated nose offering top notes of fruit, followed by mineral sensations and hints of saffron, and a deep, dense palate. San Vigilio 2015 is full flavoured and well orchestrated, and we also liked San Martino Campo al Soglio 2015 and the excellent Chiaretto San Donino 2015.

⊙ Garda Cl. Chiaretto San Donino '15	▼▼	2*
● Garda Cl. Groppello San Biagio '15	▼▼	4
○ Lugana Menasasso Ris. '12	▼▼	3
○ Lugana San Vigilio '15	▼▼	2*
○ Lugana Selva '15	▼▼	2*
○ San Martino della Battaglia Campo del Soglio '15	▼▼	3
⊙ Garda Brut Rosé Hirundo	▼	3
○ Lugana Dosaggio Zero Hirundo M. Cl.	▼	3
⊙ Garda Cl. Chiaretto San Donino '14	♈	2*
● Garda Cl. Groppello San Biagio '14	♈	3
○ Lugana San Vigilio '14	♈	2*
○ Lugana Selva '14	♈	2*

Lo Sparviere

VIA COSTA, 2
25040 MONTICELLI BRUSATI [BS]
TEL. +39 030652382
www.losparviere.com

CELLAR SALES
PRE-BOOKED VISITS
ANNUAL PRODUCTION 120,000 bottles
HECTARES UNDER VINE 30.00

Ugo Gussalli Beretta heads one of the world's oldest industrial dynasties, documented from 1526, and shares a great passion for wine and the countryside with his wife Monique. Over the years it has led them to found the Agricole Gussalli Beretta group, which also includes Castello di Radda in Chianti Classico, Orlandi Contucci Ponno in Abruzzo, and Cascina Pressenda in Castelletto di Monforte d'Alba. The Franciacorta estate covers an area of 150 hectares, including 30 under vine. Its beautiful winery is housed in a perfectly restored 16th-century villa with outbuildings. The Extra Brut 2009 is a Chardonnay cuvée that hails from a vineyard in Monticelli Brusati planted with vines over 20 years old. Part of the base wine is fermented and aged in small casks prior to bottle fermentation for at least five years. It is full and flavoursome, offering plenty of stuffing and firm, confident body with elegant hints of citrus, white-fleshed fruit, and vanilla, and lingering honeyed aromas.

○ Franciacorta Extra Brut '09	▼▼▼ 5
○ Franciacorta Brut '11	▼▼ 5
○ Franciacorta Satèn	▼▼ 6
○ Franciacorta Rosé Monique	▼ 5
○ Franciacorta Dosaggio Zero Ris. '08	♀♀♀ 6
○ Franciacorta Extra Brut '08	♀♀♀ 5
○ Franciacorta Extra Brut '07	♀♀♀ 5
○ Franciacorta Brut '09	♀♀ 5
○ Franciacorta Brut	♀♀ 5
○ Franciacorta Dosaggio Zero Ris. '07	♀♀ 6
○ Franciacorta Dosaggio Zero Ris. '06	♀♀ 8
○ Franciacorta Extra Brut	♀♀ 5

Pietro Torti

FRAZ. CASTELROTTO, 9
27047 MONTECALVO VERSIGGIA [PV]
TEL. +39 038599763
www.pietrotorti.it

CELLAR SALES
PRE-BOOKED VISITS
ACCOMMODATION
ANNUAL PRODUCTION 40,000 bottles
HECTARES UNDER VINE 18.00
VITICULTURE METHOD Certified Organic

This year marks a return to our full profile for Sandro Torti, son of Pietro after whom the winery is named. The friendly, tenacious Montecalvo vigneron is now aided by his young daughter Chiara, whom we hope will continue the history of the small but important Valle Versa estate. Its range reflects the classic Oltrepò tradition and has yielded excellent results this year. Campo Rivera 2012 stands out, for the particularly good vintage has yielded a remarkably deep, concentrated Barbera, with clean notes of black cherries, wild berries, and spice, supported by fine acidity and culminating in a long finish. Metodo Classico 2012 is also good, with a close-focused, fragrant nose, good backbone, and a fine bead, while the succulent Bonarda 2015 is among the best of its kind, with sound, crisp dark berries, perceptible residual sugar in the house style, and an almondy finish. We also liked the vinous, fruity Uva Rara 2015, with its distinctive peppery note.

● OP Barbera Campo Rivera '12	▼▼ 4
● OP Bonarda Vivace '15	▼▼ 2*
○ OP Pinot Nero Brut M. Cl. Torti '12	▼▼ 3
● Uva Rara '15	▼▼ 3
● Castelrotto '12	▼ 5
○ Fagù '15	▼ 3
● OP Bonarda Verzello '15	▼ 3
● OP Barbera Campo Rivera '10	♀♀ 3
● OP Bonarda '13	♀♀ 2*
● OP Bonarda Vivace '12	♀♀ 2*
⊙ OP Cruasé '11	♀♀ 3
⊙ OP Cruasé '10	♀♀ 2*
○ OP Pinot Nero Brut M. Cl. Torti '10	♀♀ 3

Travaglino

LOC. TRAVAGLINO, 6A
27040 CALVIGNANO [PV]
TEL. +39 0383872222
www.travaglino.it

CELLAR SALES
PRE-BOOKED VISITS
ACCOMMODATION AND RESTAURANT SERVICE
ANNUAL PRODUCTION 220,000 bottles
HECTARES UNDER VINE 80.00

Travaglino is a long-standing Oltrepò estate. Owned by the Comi family for almost 150 years, in the 1960s Vincenzo was among the first to realize the importance of cru, planting different grape varieties according to the characteristics of the soil. Today his granddaughter Cristina Cerri has taken over the management of the estate, drawing on the experience and skill of eminent oenologist Carlo Casavecchia, and the first signs of revival are already clear to see. The Brut Gran Cuvée reached our finals with its fresh cleanliness, attractive linearity, and creamy effervescence. We also liked the elegant sparkling Cruasé Monteceresino, with sound, complex notes of wild berries and hints of coffee, while the very nice Riserva Vincenzo Comi 2008 is still slightly held back by oak. Pinot Grigio Ramato 2015 is interesting, showing full, with a nose of pomegranates and nice backbone. Campo della Fojada, from Riesling, and Pernero 2015, from pinot nero, are also pleasant, varietal young wines with good fruit.

○ OP Brut Gran Cuvée	♈♈	4
○ Brut Cuvée 59 '13	♈♈	4
○ OP Pinot Grigio Ramato '15	♈♈	4
⊙ OP Pinot Nero Brut Cruasé Monteceresimo	♈♈	4
● OP Pinot Nero Pernero '15	♈♈	2*
○ OP Riesling Campo della Fojada '15	♈	3
● OP Pinot Nero Vincenzo Comi Ris. '08	♈	5
○ OP Riesling Campo della Fojada Ris. '13	♈	3
○ OP Brut Classese '09	♈♈	5
○ OP Brut Cuvée 59 '10	♈♈	5
⊙ OP Pinot Nero Brut Cruasé Monteceresimo '11	♈♈	4
○ OP Pinot Nero Brut Cuvée 59 '12	♈♈	3
○ OP Riesling Campo della Fojada '14	♈♈	3

★Uberti

LOC. SALEM
VIA E. FERMI, 2
25030 ERBUSCO [BS]
TEL. +39 0307267476
www.ubertivini.it

PRE-BOOKED VISITS
ANNUAL PRODUCTION 180,000 bottles
HECTARES UNDER VINE 25.00
VITICULTURE METHOD Certified Organic

The Uberti family's long history in the Brescia wine sector dates back to 1793. In 1980 Agostino and Eleonora founded the modern winery that immediately started garnering an incredible array of awards for the quality of its production that includes such famous names as Magnificentia and Comarì del Salem. Its secret probably lies in its first-rate vineyards, covering an area of 25 hectares in Erbusco, but also in the passion that the whole family lavishes on the estate. The couple are now flanked by their daughters, oenologist Silvia and Francesca, responsible for the administrative side of the business. The estate uses organic methods. Satèn Magnificentia 2012 did very well in our tastings, showing exceptionally expressive, balanced and full flavoured. It is a very consistent wine, which maintains its typical soft, full character year after year, along with a beautiful edgy finish with hints of aromatic herbs. Sublimis Riserva 2006 is complex and evolved, while the Extra Brut was our favourite of the fresher blends composing the Francesco I range.

○ Franciacorta Satèn Magnificentia '12	♈♈	6
○ Franciacorta Extra Brut Francesco I	♈♈	5
○ Franciacorta Non Dosato Sublimis Ris. '06	♈♈	7
○ Franciacorta Brut Francesco I	♈	5
⊙ Franciacorta Rosé Francesco I	♈	5
○ Franciacorta Brut Comarì del Salem '00	♈♈♈	6
○ Franciacorta Extra Brut Comarì del Salem '03	♈♈♈	6
○ Franciacorta Extra Brut Comarì del Salem '02	♈♈♈	6
○ Franciacorta Extra Brut Comarì del Salem '01	♈♈♈	6

Vanzini

FRAZ. BARBALEONE, 7
27040 SAN DAMIANO AL COLLE [PV]
TEL. +39 038575019
www.vanzini-wine.com

CELLAR SALES
PRE-BOOKED VISITS
ANNUAL PRODUCTION 600,000 bottles
HECTARES UNDER VINE 27.00

Oltrepò offers a huge and varied panorama. Some producers focus on reds for laying down, some on Metodo Classicos, and others on semi-sparkling wines from the classic local grape varieties. Siblings Antonio, Michela, and Pierpaolo Vanzini are an excellent example of the latter. Their Bonarda is always among the best in terms of fragrance, fruit and balance. The same is true of the sweet Sangue di Giuda and Moscato, both made in a semi-sparkling with standard cork and sparkling with mushroom cork. The white and rosé Extra Dry Metodo Martinotti, exclusively from estate-grown pinot nero, are also very good. Indeed, the white Martinotti Extra Dry reached our finals this year thanks to its elegance, fine bead, balance, floral nose, and depth. The Rosé also performed as well as ever, with fragrant, gutsy red berries. Aedo, which has a high percentage of white grapes, has notes of citrus and white-fleshed fruit, while the Bonarda and Sangue di Giuda 2015 are complex and exuberant, brimming with red berries. The Moscato Spumante is varietal and well made.

○ Pinot Nero Extra Dry Martinotti	♟♟	3
○ Moscato Spumante	♟♟	3
● OP Bonarda Vivace '15	♟♟	2*
● OP Sangue di Giuda '15	♟♟	3
○ Pinot Nero Extra Dry Martinotti Aedo	♟♟	3
⊙ Pinot Nero Extra Dry Martinotti Rosé	♟♟	3
● Barbera '15	♟	3
○ Pinot Grigio '15	♟	4
○ Riesling '15	♟	2
○ Moscato Spumante '14	♟♟	3
● OP Bonarda V. Guardia '13	♟♟	3
● OP Bonarda Vivace '14	♟♟	2*
● OP Sangue di Giuda '14	♟♟	3

Bruno Verdi

VIA VERGOMBERRA, 5
27044 CANNETO PAVESE [PV]
TEL. +39 038588023
www.brunoverdi.it

CELLAR SALES
PRE-BOOKED VISITS
ANNUAL PRODUCTION 90,000 bottles
HECTARES UNDER VINE 12.00

We have often extolled Paolo Verdi's skill. It's not easy to find yourself running a winery alone at the age of 20, following his father's premature death. Paolo has gone further, skilfully and doggedly transforming what was just one of many wineries 30 years ago into one of the finest estates in all Oltrepò today. It produces first-rate terroir-true reds, as attested by their frequent appearances in our finals, and surprisingly ageworthy Metodo Classico sparklers and whites. Vergomberra Nature 2011 is on top form this year: a taut, linear Metodo Classico with a nose of citrus fruit, particularly lime, and aromatic herbs, which is deep and concentrated. The unmistakable Cavariola 2012 is terrific, a powerful red, with sound fruit, balsamic notes of pennyroyal and cocoa powder, and a racy finish. Barbera Campo del Marrone 2013 is very muscular, with a nose of dark berries, while the vintage Bonarda and Sangue di Giuda offer attractive sound fruit.

○ OP Pinot Nero Nature Vergomberra '11	♟♟	4
● OP Rosso Cavariola Ris. '12	♟♟	5
● OP Barbera Campo del Marrone '13	♟♟	3
● OP Bonarda Vivace Possessione di Vergombera '15	♟♟	2*
● OP Sangue di Giuda Paradiso '15	♟♟	2*
● OP Buttafuoco '15	♟	2
○ OP Moscato '15	♟	2
○ OP Pinot Grigio '15	♟	2
● OP Rosso Cavariola Ris. '10	♟♟♟	5
● OP Rosso Cavariola Ris. '07	♟♟♟	4
● OP Barbera Campo del Marrone '12	♟♟	3*
⊙ OP Cruasé Vergomberra '10	♟♟	4
○ OP Pinot Nero Extra Brut Vergomberra '10	♟♟	4

Giuseppe Vezzoli

VIA COSTA SOPRA, 22
25030 ERBUSCO [BS]
TEL. +39 0307267579
www.vezzolivini.it

CELLAR SALES
PRE-BOOKED VISITS
ANNUAL PRODUCTION 190,000 bottles
HECTARES UNDER VINE 63.00

While his family have been vignerons for generations, Giuseppe Vezzoli founded his modern winery in 1994. Today the estate has an impressive annual production of 190,000 bottles, made from the grapes of over 60 hectares of vineyards, mainly in Erbusco, both estate-owned and leased. Giuseppe's children Jessica and Dario are now actively involved in the family business and have founded Sullali, an innovative little estate of their own. Once again this year the estate presented an excellent selection of wines. We were enchanted by the perfectly soft, creamy Satèn, with alluring notes of fresh fruit and nice pressure. The Dosaggio Zero has a floral nose and beautifully invigorating liveliness, while Nefertiti Dizeta 2010 is a complex, fragrant undosed Franciacorta that flaunts good structure and juicy white-fleshed fruit.

○ Franciacorta Brut '12	♥♥	5
○ Franciacorta Brut	♥♥	4
○ Franciacorta Brut Satèn	♥♥	5
○ Franciacorta Dosaggio Zero	♥♥	6
○ Franciacorta Extra Brut Nefertiti Dizeta '10	♥♥	6
○ Franciacorta Extra Brut Vendemmia Zero	♥	6
○ Franciacorta Brut '11	♀♀	5
○ Franciacorta Brut '10	♀♀	5
○ Franciacorta Brut '07	♀♀	5
○ Franciacorta Brut Nefertiti '05	♀♀	6
○ Franciacorta Extra Brut Nefertiti Dizeta '09	♀♀	6
○ Franciacorta Extra Brut Nefertiti Dizeta '07	♀♀	6

Villa Crespia

VIA VALLI, 31
25030 ADRO [BS]
TEL. +39 0307451051
www.arcipelagomuratori.it

CELLAR SALES
PRE-BOOKED VISITS
ANNUAL PRODUCTION 350,000 bottles
HECTARES UNDER VINE 60.00
SUSTAINABLE WINERY

The Muratori family have solid roots in agriculture and over the years have put together a group of first-rate estates known as Arcipelago Muratori. In addition to Villa Crespia in Franciacorta, it includes Rubbia al Colle in Maremma, Oppida Aminea in Sannio, and Giardini Arimei on Ischia. Villa Crespia is one of the most important estates in Franciacorta, with 60 hectares of vineyards ensuring a large production, achieved using sustainable methods. The technical management of the group is entrusted to oenologist Francesco Iacono, who crafts a series of cuvées expressing the estate's different terroirs. NumeroZero Dosaggio Zero represented the winery in our finals. It is made from chardonnay grapes grown on deep morainic soils, mainly in Erbusco, and is strikingly fresh and invigorating. The alluring citrusy nose is accompanied by a full palate, sustained by a marked acidic vein and creamy effervescence, and is echoed on the long fruity, floral finish.

○ Franciacorta Dosaggio Zero Numerozero	♥♥	5
○ Franciacorta Brut Novalia	♥♥	4
○ Franciacorta Brut Satèn Cesonato	♥♥	5
⊙ Franciacorta Extra Brut Rosé Brolese	♥♥	5
○ Franciacorta Brut Millè '08	♥	5
○ Franciacorta Brut Simbiotico	♥	5
○ Franciacorta Dosaggio Zero Cisiolo	♥	5
○ Franciacorta Dosaggio Zero Francesco Iacono Ris. '08	♥	7
○ Franciacorta Dosaggio Zero Francesco Iacono Ris. '04	♀♀♀	7
○ Franciacorta Brut Millè '07	♀♀	5
○ Franciacorta Dosaggio Zero Francesco Iacono Ris. '07	♀♀	7
○ Franciacorta Dosaggio Zero Francesco Iacono Ris. '05	♀♀	7

Villa Franciacorta

VIA VILLA, 12
25040 MONTICELLI BRUSATI [BS]
TEL. +39 030652329
www.villafranciacorta.it

PRE-BOOKED VISITS
ACCOMMODATION AND RESTAURANT SERVICE
ANNUAL PRODUCTION 300,000 bottles
HECTARES UNDER VINE 40.00

In the 1960s Alessandro Bianchi purchased the 16th-century hamlet of Villa, in Monticelli Brusati, and patiently converted it into a luxurious country hotel, complete with restaurant, restoring the old buildings and replanting the terraced vineyards on the adjoining slopes of Monte della Madonna della Rosa. Today the estate is run by Alessandra Bianchi and her husband Paolo Piziol. It covers an area of 100 hectares, of which 40 under vine, and vaunts a completely underground modern cellar that houses a million bottles awaiting riddling. We already liked Rosé di Villa very much last year, but this year it confidently walked off with our top accolade. Boké 2012 is a beautiful pale pink, with a concentrated, lingering nose of red berries featuring top notes of wild strawberries and redcurrants, and a taut, full-flavoured palate that confidently unfolds to reveal fresh, delicate fruit. Mon Satèn 2012 is equally good, brimming with white-fleshed fruit and floral notes. A vintage to remember.

⊙ Franciacorta Brut Rosé Boké '12	♥♥♥	5
○ Franciacorta Mon Satèn '12	♥♥	5
○ Franciacorta Brut Cuvette '08	♥♥	5
○ Franciacorta Brut Emozione '12	♥♥	5
⊙ Franciacorta Demi Sec Rosé Briolette	♥♥	5
○ Franciacorta Pas Dosé Diamant '10	♥♥	5
○ Curtefranca Pian della Villa '15	♥	3
● Curtefranca Rosso Gradoni '12	♥	5
○ Franciacorta Extra Brut Extra Blu '10	♥	5
● Sella Collezione '12	♥	3
○ Franciacorta Brut Emozione '09	♥♥♥	5
○ Franciacorta Extra Brut '98	♥♥♥	4*

Chiara Ziliani

VIA FRANCIACORTA, 7
25050 PROVAGLIO D'ISEO [BS]
TEL. +39 030981661
www.cantinachiaraziliani.it

PRE-BOOKED VISITS
ANNUAL PRODUCTION 300,000 bottles
HECTARES UNDER VINE 21.00

The talented Chiara Ziliani enthusiastically runs her 21-hectare estate on a morainic hill in Provaglio d'Iseo. She owns 17 of these hectares the top-quality grapes used to make a wide range of Franciacortas and local wines. The densely planted wines, with over 7,000 per hectare, are tended using methods with low environmental impact. The ideal location of the south and south-east-facing vineyards, 250 metres above sea level, and the care lavished on work in the cellar yield first-rate wines. Our pick of the many wines presented this year includes the excellent zesty, juicy Pas Dosé 2011 with a floral nose, the creamy Satèn 2011, and the fruity Brut with hints of vanilla, all from the Ziliani C range. Satèn Gran Cuvée Maddalena Cavalleri 2009 is creamy and well orchestrated, with attractive notes of oak, torrefaction, and croissant, while Satèn Conte di Provaglio is more delicate, refreshing, and approachable.

○ Franciacorta Brut Duca d'Iseo	♥♥	5
○ Franciacorta Brut Ziliani C '11	♥♥	4
○ Franciacorta Non Dosato Ziliani C '11	♥♥	5
⊙ Franciacorta Rosé Conte di Provaglio	♥♥	3
○ Franciacorta Satèn Conte di Provaglio	♥♥	3
○ Franciacorta Satèn Duca d'Iseo	♥♥	3
○ Franciacorta Satèn Gran Cuvée Maria Maddalena Cavalieri '09	♥♥	5
○ Franciacorta Satèn Ziliani C '11	♥♥	4
○ Franciacorta Satèn Ziliani C	♥♥	3
○ Franciacorta Brut Conte di Provaglio	♥	3
⊙ Franciacorta Brut Rosé Ziliani C	♥	4
○ Franciacorta Extra Brut Ziliani C '10	♥♥	4
○ Franciacorta Pas Dosé Ziliani C '09	♥♥	4
○ Franciacorta Satèn Ziliani C '10	♥♥	4

1701

P.ZZA MARCONI, 6
25046 CAZZAGO SAN MARTINO [BS]
TEL. +39 0307750875
www.1701franciacorta.it

CELLAR SALES
PRE-BOOKED VISITS
ANNUAL PRODUCTION 60,000 bottles
HECTARES UNDER VINE 10.00
VITICULTURE METHOD Certified Organic

○ Franciacorta Dosaggio Zero '11	♟♟	8
○ Franciacorta Satèn	♟♟	6
○ Franciacorta Brut	♟	6
⊙ Franciacorta Brut Rosé	♟	6

Elisabetta Abrami

S.DA VICINALE DELLE FOSCHE
25050 PROVAGLIO D'ISEO [BS]
TEL. +39 0306857185
www.vinielisabettaabrami.it

CELLAR SALES
ACCOMMODATION
ANNUAL PRODUCTION 60,000 bottles
HECTARES UNDER VINE 15.00
VITICULTURE METHOD Certified Organic

⊙ Franciacorta Brut Rosé	♟♟	5
○ Franciacorta Pas Dosé	♟♟	6
○ Franciacorta Brut	♟	5

Al Rocol

VIA PROVINCIALE, 79
25050 OME [BS]
TEL. +39 0306852542
www.alrocol.com

CELLAR SALES
PRE-BOOKED VISITS
ACCOMMODATION AND RESTAURANT SERVICE
ANNUAL PRODUCTION 60,000 bottles
HECTARES UNDER VINE 13.00

○ Franciacorta Brut Ca' del Luf	♟♟	5
○ Franciacorta Dosaggio Zero Castellini '12	♟♟	6
○ Franciacorta Satèn Martignac '12	♟♟	5

Annibale Alziati

LOC. SCAZZOLINO, 55
27040 ROVESCALA [PV]
TEL. +39 038575261
www.gaggiarone.it

CELLAR SALES
PRE-BOOKED VISITS
ANNUAL PRODUCTION 100,000 bottles
HECTARES UNDER VINE 19.00
VITICULTURE METHOD Certified Organic
SUSTAINABLE WINERY

● OP Barbera San Francesco '14	♟	4
● OP Bonarda Gaggiarone V. V. '12	♟	4

Tenuta Ambrosini

VIA DELLA PACE, 58
25046 CAZZAGO SAN MARTINO [BS]
TEL. +39 0307254850
www.tenutambrosini.it

ANNUAL PRODUCTION 55,000 bottles
HECTARES UNDER VINE 8.00

○ Franciacorta Brut '11	♟♟	5
○ Franciacorta Satèn '12	♟♟	5

Avanzi

VIA TREVISAGO, 19
25080 MANERBA DEL GARDA [BS]
TEL. +39 0365551013
www.avanzi.net

CELLAR SALES
PRE-BOOKED VISITS
ANNUAL PRODUCTION 600,000 bottles
HECTARES UNDER VINE 60.00

● Garda Cl. Groppello '14	♟♟	3
○ Lugana Borghetta Ris. '13	♟♟	3
○ Lugana Sirmione '15	♟♟	2*
● Rebo '13	♟♟	3

Barbacarlo - Lino Maga

s.da Bronese, 3
27043 Broni [PV]
Tel. +39 038551212
barbacarlodimaga@libero.it

CELLAR SALES
PRE-BOOKED VISITS
ANNUAL PRODUCTION 20,000 bottles
HECTARES UNDER VINE 12.00

● Barbacarlo '14	🍷🍷 5

Barboglio De Gaioncelli

fraz. Colombaro
via Nazario Sauro
25040 Corte Franca [BS]
Tel. +39 0309826831
www.barbogliodegaioncelli.it

CELLAR SALES
PRE-BOOKED VISITS
RESTAURANT SERVICE
ANNUAL PRODUCTION 90,000 bottles
HECTARES UNDER VINE 60.00

○ Franciacorta Pas Dosé Claro '08	🍷🍷 5
○ Franciacorta Satèn	🍷🍷 4
○ Franciacorta Extra Dry	🍷 4

La Basia

loc. La Basia
via Predefitte, 31
25080 Puegnago sul Garda [BS]
Tel. +39 0365555958
www.labasia.it

CELLAR SALES
PRE-BOOKED VISITS
ACCOMMODATION
ANNUAL PRODUCTION 28,000 bottles
HECTARES UNDER VINE 4.50
VITICULTURE METHOD Certified Organic

● Garda Marzemino '13	🍷🍷 3
● Valtènesi La Botte Piena '14	🍷 3

Cantina Sociale Bergamasca

via Bergamo, 10
24060 San Paolo d'Argon [BG]
Tel. +39 035951098
www.cantinabergamasca.it

CELLAR SALES
PRE-BOOKED VISITS
ANNUAL PRODUCTION 650,000 bottles
HECTARES UNDER VINE 90.00

○ Terre del Colleoni Brut Colleoni '12	🍷🍷 4
○ Terre del Colleoni Incrocio Manzoni '15	🍷🍷 2*
⊙ Terre del Colleoni Schiava '15	🍷🍷 2*

Bertagna

loc. Bande
s.da Madonna della Porta, 14
46040 Cavriana [MN]
Tel. +39 037682211
www.cantinabertagna.it

CELLAR SALES
PRE-BOOKED VISITS
ANNUAL PRODUCTION 120,000 bottles
HECTARES UNDER VINE 13.00

○ Lugana '15	🍷🍷 2*
● Montevolpe Rosso '12	🍷🍷 3
● Garda Cabernet '15	🍷 1*

Cantine Bertelegni

fraz. Gaminara
27052 Rocca Susella [PV]
www.oltrepovini.it

ANNUAL PRODUCTION 20,000 bottles
HECTARES UNDER VINE 5.00

● OP Bonarda Vergonia '15	🍷🍷 4
○ Brut M. Cl. Alexander Magnus	🍷 8

Podere Bignolino

LOC. BIGNOLINO
S.DA PROV.LE 44
27040 BRONI [PV]
TEL. +39 0383870160
www.poderebignolino.it

ANNUAL PRODUCTION 80,000 bottles
HECTARES UNDER VINE 40.00

● OP Barbera Costa Bercé '14	♟♟ 3
● OP Rosso Tre Colli Ris. '13	♟♟ 3
○ Riesling '15	♟♟ 2*

Bonaldi - Cascina del Bosco

LOC. PETOSINO
VIA GASPAROTTO, 96
24010 SORISOLE [BG]
TEL. +39 035571701
www.cascinadelbosco.it

CELLAR SALES
PRE-BOOKED VISITS
ANNUAL PRODUCTION 25,000 bottles
HECTARES UNDER VINE 4.00

○ Valcalepio Bianco '15	♟♟ 3
● Controcanto '13	♟ 4
● Valcalepio Rosso '14	♟ 4

Bonfadini

VIA L. DI BERNARDO, 85
25049 ISEO [BS]
TEL. +39 0309826721
www.bonfadini.it

CELLAR SALES
PRE-BOOKED VISITS
ANNUAL PRODUCTION 80,000 bottles
HECTARES UNDER VINE 10.00

○ Franciacorta Nature Veritas	♟♟ 5
⊙ Franciacorta Rosé Opera	♟♟ 5
○ Franciacorta Satèn Carpe Diem	♟♟ 5
○ Franciacorta Brut Nobilium	♟ 5

Borgo La Gallinaccia

VIA IV NOVEMBRE, 15
25050 RODENGO SAIANO [BS]
TEL. +39 030611314
www.borgolagallinaccia.it

CELLAR SALES
PRE-BOOKED VISITS
ANNUAL PRODUCTION 16,000 bottles
HECTARES UNDER VINE 3.40

● Colmo dei Colmi '11	♟♟ 4
○ Franciacorta Brut	♟♟ 4
○ Franciacorta Pas Dosé	♟♟ 5
○ Franciacorta Satèn	♟♟ 4

Ca' del Santo

LOC. CAMPOLUNGO, 4
27040 MONTALTO PAVESE [PV]
TEL. +39 0383870545
www.cadelsanto.it

CELLAR SALES
PRE-BOOKED VISITS
ANNUAL PRODUCTION 25,000 bottles
HECTARES UNDER VINE 6.00

● Il Nero '13	♟♟ 3
● OP Bonarda RossoPassione '15	♟♟ 2*

Patrizia Cadore

LOC. CAMPAGNA BIANCA
25010 POZZOLENGO [BS]
TEL. +39 0309918138
www.vinicadore.eu

ANNUAL PRODUCTION 25,000 bottles
HECTARES UNDER VINE 8.50

○ Lugana '15	♟♟ 3
○ Lugana Ris. '13	♟♟ 5
○ San Martino della Battaglia '15	♟ 3

Il Calepino

VIA SURRIPE, 1
24060 CASTELLI CALEPIO [BG]
TEL. +39 035847178
www.ilcalepino.it

CELLAR SALES
PRE-BOOKED VISITS
ANNUAL PRODUCTION 230,000 bottles
HECTARES UNDER VINE 15.00

○ Terre del Colleoni Brut	♟♟ 4
○ Valcalepio Bianco '15	♟ 2

Davide Calvi

FRAZ. PALAZZINA, 24
27040 CASTANA [PV]
TEL. +39 038582136
www.vinicalvi.it

CELLAR SALES
PRE-BOOKED VISITS
ANNUAL PRODUCTION 45,000 bottles
HECTARES UNDER VINE 8.00

○ Kantaros '14	♟ 3
● OP Buttafuoco V. Montarzolo '11	♟ 4

Le Cantorìe

FRAZ. CASAGLIO
VIA CASTELLO DI CASAGLIO, 24/25
25064 GUSSAGO [BS]
TEL. +39 0302523723
www.lecantorie.it

ANNUAL PRODUCTION 75,000 bottles
HECTARES UNDER VINE 12.00

○ Franciacorta Pas Dosé Armonia Ris. '09	♟♟ 6
⊙ Franciacorta Rosé Rosi delle Margherite	♟♟ 7
○ Franciacorta Satèn Armonia '12	♟♟ 5

Cascina Clarabella

VIA ENRICO MATTEI
25040 CORTE FRANCA [BS]
TEL. +39 0309821041
www.cascinaclarabella.it

CELLAR SALES
PRE-BOOKED VISITS
ANNUAL PRODUCTION 70,000 bottles
HECTARES UNDER VINE 11.00
VITICULTURE METHOD Certified Organic

○ Franciacorta Pas Dosé 180 '09	♟♟ 6
○ Franciacorta Pas Dosé E'ssenza	♟♟ 5
⊙ Franciacorta Brut Rosé Annalisa Faifer '11	♟ 5

Castello di Gussago La Santissima

VIA MANICA, 9
25064 GUSSAGO [BS]
TEL. +39 0302525267
www.castellodigussago.it

CELLAR SALES
PRE-BOOKED VISITS
ANNUAL PRODUCTION 120,000 bottles
HECTARES UNDER VINE 15.00

○ Franciacorta Brut	♟♟ 5
⊙ Franciacorta Extra Brut Rosé '11	♟♟ 5
○ Franciacorta Satèn '12	♟♟ 5

Castello di Luzzano

LOC. LUZZANO, 5
27040 ROVESCALA [PV]
TEL. +39 0523863277
www.castelloluzzano.it

CELLAR SALES
PRE-BOOKED VISITS
ACCOMMODATION AND RESTAURANT SERVICE
ANNUAL PRODUCTION 120,000 bottles
HECTARES UNDER VINE 76.00

● OP Bonarda Vivace Sommossa '15	♟♟ 2*
● OP Pinot Nero Umore Nero '15	♟ 2

Castello di Stefanago

LOC. CASTELLO DI STEFANAGO
27040 BORGO PRIOLO [PV]
TEL. +39 0383875227
www.baruffaldivini.it

CELLAR SALES
PRE-BOOKED VISITS
HECTARES UNDER VINE 20.00
VITICULTURE METHOD Certified Organic

○ Brut Ancestrale	♀4
○ Riesling San Rocco '12	♀3

Cantine Cavallotti

VIA EUROPA, 9A
20080 BUBBIANO [MI]
TEL. +39 0290848829
www.cantinecavallotti.it

CELLAR SALES
PRE-BOOKED VISITS
ANNUAL PRODUCTION 120,000 bottles
HECTARES UNDER VINE 14.00

● OP Bonarda Passo Gaio '15	♀♀4
☉ OP Cruasé Nero Puro '11	♀♀4

Le Chiusure

FRAZ. PORTESE
VIA BOSCHETTE, 2
25010 SAN FELICE DEL BENACO [BS]
TEL. +39 0365626243
www.lechiusure.net

CELLAR SALES
PRE-BOOKED VISITS
ACCOMMODATION
ANNUAL PRODUCTION 22,000 bottles
HECTARES UNDER VINE 4.00

☉ Valtènesi Chiaretto '15	♀♀3
● Campei '12	♀3
● Valtenesi Malborghetto '13	♀5

Citari

FRAZ. SAN MARTINO DELLA BATTAGLIA
LOC. CITARI, 2
25015 DESENZANO DEL GARDA [BS]
TEL. +39 0309910310
www.citari.it

CELLAR SALES
PRE-BOOKED VISITS
ANNUAL PRODUCTION 150,000 bottles
HECTARES UNDER VINE 22.00
SUSTAINABLE WINERY

○ Lugana Conchiglia '15	♀♀4
○ Lugana Torre '15	♀♀2*
○ Garda Cl. Chiaretto '15	♀3
○ Lugana Sorgente '15	♀3

AgriBioRelais Colletto

VIA COLLETTO, 6
24060 ADRARA SAN MARTINO [BG]
TEL. +39 035934253
www.collettoagribiorelais.it

ANNUAL PRODUCTION 25,000 bottles
HECTARES UNDER VINE 3.00

○ Brut Blanc de Blanc Fiore '09	♀♀5
☉ Brut Rosé '11	♀♀5
○ Brut Blanc de Blanc '09	♀5

Conti Ducco

LOC. CAMIGNONE
VIA DEGLI EROI, 70
25040 PASSIRANO [BS]
TEL. +39 0306850566
www.contiducco.it

PRE-BOOKED VISITS
ANNUAL PRODUCTION 400,000 bottles
HECTARES UNDER VINE 92.00

☉ Franciacorta Brut Rosé '11	♀♀5

Corte Anna

via Vigneto, 10
25019 Sirmione [BS]
Tel. +39 030919033
corte.anna@alice.it

ANNUAL PRODUCTION 40,000 bottles
HECTARES UNDER VINE 10.00

○ Lugana Antico Vign. Ris. '12	🍷🍷 4
○ Lugana '15	🍷 4

Corte Aura

via Colzano, 13
25030 Adro [BS]
Tel. +39 030 7357281
www.corteaura.it

CELLAR SALES
PRE-BOOKED VISITS
ANNUAL PRODUCTION 170,000 bottles
HECTARES UNDER VINE 5.00

○ Franciacorta Pas Dosé	🍷🍷 5
○ Franciacorta Satèn '10	🍷🍷 6
○ Franciacorta Satèn	🍷🍷 4
⊙ Franciacorta Brut Rosé	🍷 5

Tenuta La Costa

fraz. Costa, 68
27040 Castana [PV]
Tel. +39 0385241527
tenutalacosta@libero.it

CELLAR SALES
PRE-BOOKED VISITS
ANNUAL PRODUCTION 50,000 bottles
HECTARES UNDER VINE 12.00

● OP Buttafuoco V. Costa '13	🍷🍷 3
○ OP Pinot Nero Brut M. Cl. '09	🍷🍷 4
○ OP Riesling V. del Mattino '15	🍷 3

La Costaiola

fraz. Costaiola
via Costaiola, 25
27054 Montebello della Battaglia [PV]
Tel. +39 038383169
www.lacostaiola.it

CELLAR SALES
ACCOMMODATION
ANNUAL PRODUCTION 80,000 bottles
HECTARES UNDER VINE 13.00

● Pinot Nero Bricca '15	🍷🍷 3
● OP Bonarda Giada '15	🍷 2
○ Rossetti & Scrivani M. Cl. Brut	🍷 3
⊙ Rossetti & Scrivani M. Cl. Brut Rosé	🍷 3

De Toma

via Battisti, 7
24020 Scanzorosciate [BG]
Tel. +39 035657329

CELLAR SALES
PRE-BOOKED VISITS
ANNUAL PRODUCTION 5,000 bottles
HECTARES UNDER VINE 2.50

● Moscato di Scanzo '13	🍷🍷 7

Delai

via Moro, 1
25080 Puegnago sul Garda [BS]
Tel. +39 0365555527

ANNUAL PRODUCTION 80,000 bottles
HECTARES UNDER VINE 8.00

● Garda Bresciano Groppello Mogrì '14	🍷🍷 2*
⊙ Brut Rosé	🍷 3
⊙ Garda Bresciano Chiaretto Notterosa '15	🍷 3

Diana

VIA ROMA 63
27040 CASTANA [PV]
TEL. +39 0385249618
www.dianawine.it

CELLAR SALES
PRE-BOOKED VISITS
ANNUAL PRODUCTION 35,000 bottles
HECTARES UNDER VINE 9.00

● OP Barbera Sentiero della Guerra '13	♀♀ 3
● OP Buttafuoco Pozzo della Tromba '09	♀ 3

Due Pini

LOC. PICEDO
VIA NOVAGLIO, 16
25080 POLPENAZZE DEL GARDA [BS]
TEL. +39 0365675123

ANNUAL PRODUCTION 35,000 bottles
HECTARES UNDER VINE 6.00

● Garda Cl. Groppello '14	♀♀ 3
● Garda Cl. Rosso Sup. '12	♀♀ 4
⊙ Garda Bresciano Chiaretto '15	♀ 2

Luca Faccinelli

VIA CESURE, 19
23030 CHIURO [SO]
TEL. +39 3470807011
www.lucafaccinelli.it

CELLAR SALES
PRE-BOOKED VISITS
ANNUAL PRODUCTION 11,500 bottles
HECTARES UNDER VINE 2.00
SUSTAINABLE WINERY

● Valtellina Sup. Ortensio Lando '13	♀♀ 5
● Rosso di Valtellina Matteo Bandello '14	♀ 3

Feliciana

LOC. FELICIANA
25010 POZZOLENGO [BS]
TEL. +39 030918228
www.feliciana.it

ANNUAL PRODUCTION 120,000 bottles
HECTARES UNDER VINE 18.00

○ Lugana Felugan '15	♀♀ 3
○ Lugana Sercè Ris. '13	♀ 4

Il Feudo Nico

VIA SAN ROCCO, 63
27040 MORNICO LOSANA [PV]
TEL. +39 0383892452

ANNUAL PRODUCTION 40,000 bottles
HECTARES UNDER VINE 16.00

● Edoardo '13	♀♀ 4
○ Maria Antonietta M. Cl. Cuvée dei 100 Mesi '06	♀♀ 4
● Bonarda V. Castello '15	♀ 5

Finigeto

LOC. CELLA, 27
27040 MONTALTO PAVESE [PV]
TEL. +39 328 7095347
www.finigeto.com

CELLAR SALES
PRE-BOOKED VISITS
ACCOMMODATION
ANNUAL PRODUCTION 70,000 bottles
HECTARES UNDER VINE 33.00

○ Moscato '15	♀♀ 3
● OP Bonarda La Grintosa '15	♀♀ 2*
● OP Pinot Nero Il Nirò '14	♀♀ 3
○ OP Riesling Lo Spavaldo '15	♀ 2

La Fiòca

FRAZ. NIGOLINE
VIA VILLA, 13B
25040 CORTE FRANCA [BS]
TEL. +39 0309826313
www.lafioca.com

CELLAR SALES
PRE-BOOKED VISITS
ACCOMMODATION AND RESTAURANT SERVICE
ANNUAL PRODUCTION 35,000 bottles
HECTARES UNDER VINE 4.00

○ Franciacorta Dosaggio Zero '10	♟♟ 5
○ Franciacorta Extra Brut Ris. '09	♟♟ 6
○ Franciacorta Satèn	♟♟ 5

La Fiorita

VIA MAGLIO, 14
25020 OME [BS]
TEL. +39 030652279
www.lafiorita.bs.it

CELLAR SALES
PRE-BOOKED VISITS
ANNUAL PRODUCTION 60,000 bottles
HECTARES UNDER VINE 7.00

○ Franciacorta Brut Rosé	♟♟ 4
○ Franciacorta Dosaggio Zero	♟♟ 4
○ Franciacorta Extra Brut Eurosia Ris. '06	♟♟ 4
○ Franciacorta Satèn	♟♟ 4

Franca Contea

VIA VALLI, 130
25030 ADRO [BS]
TEL. +39 0307451217
www.francacontea.it

CELLAR SALES
PRE-BOOKED VISITS
ANNUAL PRODUCTION 70,000 bottles
HECTARES UNDER VINE 12.00

○ Franciacorta Brut '11	♟♟ 5
○ Franciacorta Dosaggio Zero Mia Dusàt	♟♟ 4
○ Franciacorta Satèn '11	♟ 5

Giubertoni

FRAZ. SAN NICOLÒ PO
VIA PAPA GIOVANNI XXIII
46031 BAGNOLO SAN VITO [MN]
TEL. +39 0376252762
www.cantinegiubertoni.it

ANNUAL PRODUCTION 100,000 bottles
HECTARES UNDER VINE 20.00

● Il Bel Angelin '15	♟♟ 2*
● Il Vecchio Ponte '15	♟♟ 2*

La Pergola - Civielle

VIA PERGOLA, 21
25080 MONIGA DEL GARDA [BS]
TEL. +39 0365502002
www.cantinelapergola.it

CELLAR SALES
PRE-BOOKED VISITS
ANNUAL PRODUCTION 500,000 bottles
HECTARES UNDER VINE 72.00
VITICULTURE METHOD Certified Organic

● Garda Cl. Groppello Elianto '15	♟♟ 2*
○ Lugana Biocòra '15	♟♟ 2*
○ Lugana Biocòra Bio '15	♟ 2
⊘ Valtènesi Chiaretto Selene '15	♟ 2

Lazzari

VIA MELLA, 49
25020 CAPRIANO DEL COLLE [BS]
TEL. +39 0309747387
www.lazzarivini.it

CELLAR SALES
PRE-BOOKED VISITS
ANNUAL PRODUCTION 35,000 bottles
HECTARES UNDER VINE 8.00
VITICULTURE METHOD Certified Organic
SUSTAINABLE WINERY

○ Capriano del Colle Bastian Contrario '13	♟♟ 5
● Capriano del Colle Marzemino Berzamì '15	♟ 2

Cantine Lebovitz

loc. Governolo
v.le Rimembranze, 4
46037 Roncoferraro [MN]
Tel. +39 0376668115
www.cantinelebovitz.it

CELLAR SALES
PRE-BOOKED VISITS
ANNUAL PRODUCTION 50,000 bottles

● Lambrusco Mantovano Rosso dei Concari '15	▼▼ 2*
● Scagarun '15	▼▼ 1*
● Sedamat '15	▼ 1*

Lovera

via Lovera, 14a
25030 Erbusco [BS]
Tel. +39 0307760491
www.cantinalovera.it

CELLAR SALES
PRE-BOOKED VISITS
ANNUAL PRODUCTION 150,000 bottles
HECTARES UNDER VINE 24.00

○ Franciacorta Brut '09	▼▼ 5
○ Franciacorta Brut La Gemma	▼▼ 4
○ Franciacorta Dosaggio Zero '08	▼▼ 5
○ Franciacorta Satèn	▼▼ 5

Lurani Cernuschi

via Convento, 3
24031 Almenno San Salvatore [BG]
Tel. +39 035642576
www.luranicernuschi.it

CELLAR SALES
PRE-BOOKED VISITS
RESTAURANT SERVICE
ANNUAL PRODUCTION 80,000 bottles
HECTARES UNDER VINE 13.00

● Lemine '15	▼▼ 2*
○ Opis '15	▼▼ 2*
● Valcalepio Rosso Tornago '13	▼ 4

Majolini

loc. Valle
via A. Manzoni, 3
25050 Ome [BS]
Tel. +39 0306527378
www.majolini.it

CELLAR SALES
PRE-BOOKED VISITS
ANNUAL PRODUCTION 150,000 bottles
HECTARES UNDER VINE 24.00
VITICULTURE METHOD Certified Organic
SUSTAINABLE WINERY

○ Franciacorta Satèn '11	▼▼ 5
○ Franciacorta Pas Dosé Aligi Sassu '08	▼▼ 5
○ Franciacorta Rosé Altera	▼ 5

Malavasi

loc. Casina Sacco, 1
fraz. San Giacomo
25010 Pozzolengo [BS]
Tel. +39 0309918759
www.malavasivini.it

ANNUAL PRODUCTION 100,000 bottles
HECTARES UNDER VINE 10.00

○ Bianco del Lago '15	▼▼ 3
● Nero del Lago '13	▼ 3

Manuelina

fraz. Ruinello di sotto, 3a
27047 Santa Maria della Versa [PV]
Tel. +39 0385278247
www.manuelina.com

CELLAR SALES
PRE-BOOKED VISITS
ANNUAL PRODUCTION 230,000 bottles
HECTARES UNDER VINE 22.00

○ Brut M. Cl. 137	▼▼ 3
⊙ OP Cruasé 145	▼▼ 3
○ Extra Dry Martinotti	▼ 3

Marangona

LOC. MARANGONA 1
25010 POZZOLENGO [BS]
TEL. +39 030919379
www.marangona.com

CELLAR SALES
PRE-BOOKED VISITS
ANNUAL PRODUCTION 30,000 bottles
HECTARES UNDER VINE 27.00

○ Lugana '15	♟♟ 2*
○ Lugana Bio '15	♟ 3
○ Lugana Il Rintocco Ris. '15	♟ 4

Marsadri

LOC. RAFFA DI PUEGNAGO
VIA NAZIONALE, 26
25080 PUEGNAGO SUL GARDA [BS]
TEL. +39 0365651005
www.cantinamarsadri.it

PRE-BOOKED VISITS
ANNUAL PRODUCTION 200,000 bottles
HECTARES UNDER VINE 15.00
SUSTAINABLE WINERY

⊙ Garda Bresciano Chiaretto '15	♟♟ 2*
● Garda Cl. Rosso Del Pioppo Sup. '14	♟♟ 4
● Garda Cl. Groppello Brolo '15	♟ 3
○ Lugana Brolo '15	♟ 3

Alberto Marsetti

VIA SCARPATETTI, 15
23100 SONDRIO
TEL. +39 0342216329
www.marsetti.it

ANNUAL PRODUCTION 20,000 bottles
HECTARES UNDER VINE 5.00

● Valtellina Sup. Grumello '12	♟♟ 5
● Valtellina Sup. Le Prudenze '13	♟♟ 5
● Sforzato di Valtellina '11	♟ 6

Martilde

FRAZ. CROCE, 4A
27040 ROVESCALA [PV]
TEL. +39 0385756280
www.martilde.it

CELLAR SALES
PRE-BOOKED VISITS
ANNUAL PRODUCTION 30,000 bottles
HECTARES UNDER VINE 15.00

○ Malvasia Piume '15	♟♟ 2*
○ Malvasia Dedica '15	♟ 3
● OP Bonarda '13	♟ 2

Marzaghe Franciacorta

VIA CONSOLARE, 19
25030 ERBUSCO [BS]
TEL. +39 0307267245
www.marzaghefranciacorta.it

CELLAR SALES
PRE-BOOKED VISITS
ACCOMMODATION
ANNUAL PRODUCTION 40,000 bottles
HECTARES UNDER VINE 7.00
SUSTAINABLE WINERY

○ Franciacorta Brut '11	♟♟ 6
○ Franciacorta Dosaggio Zero Superno '11	♟♟ 6
⊙ Franciacorta Brut Rosé	♟ 4
○ Franciacorta Satèn	♟ 4

Walter Menegola

VIA E. VANONI, 13C
CASTIONE ANDEVENNO [SO]
TEL. +39 349 6945516
www.cantinamenegola.it

ANNUAL PRODUCTION 25,000 bottles
HECTARES UNDER VINE 2.50

● Valtellina Sup. Orante '11	♟♟ 4
● Valtellina Sup. Sassella Rupestre '10	♟♟ 5
● Valtellina Sforzato '11	♟ 6
● Valtellina Sup. Sassella Ris. '10	♟ 5

Cantine di Mezzaluna

LOC. CASA TACCONI, 13
27040 MONTALTO PAVESE [PV]
TEL. +39 0383870282
www.cantinedimezzaluna.it

ANNUAL PRODUCTION 40,000 bottles
HECTARES UNDER VINE 13.00

● OP Pinot Nero '09	♈♈ 3

Mirabella

VIA CANTARANE, 2
25050 RODENGO SAIANO [BS]
TEL. +39 030611197
www.mirabellafranciacorta.it

CELLAR SALES
PRE-BOOKED VISITS
ANNUAL PRODUCTION 450,000 bottles
HECTARES UNDER VINE 50.00

○ Franciacorta Brut Cuvée Demetra	♈♈ 4
○ Franciacorta Brut Satèn	♈♈ 5
○ Franciacorta Extra Brut '09	♈♈ 5

Monte Cicogna

VIA DELLE VIGNE, 6
25080 MONIGA DEL GARDA [BS]
TEL. +39 0365503200
www.montecicogna.it

CELLAR SALES
PRE-BOOKED VISITS
ANNUAL PRODUCTION 150,000 bottles
HECTARES UNDER VINE 30.00

○ Garda Cl. Il Torrione '15	♈♈ 2*
○ Lugana Imperiale '15	♈♈ 2*
○ Lugana S.Caterina '15	♈ 2

Montelio

VIA D. MAZZA, 1
27050 CODEVILLA [PV]
TEL. +39 0383373090
montelio.gio@alice.it

CELLAR SALES
PRE-BOOKED VISITS
ACCOMMODATION AND RESTAURANT SERVICE
ANNUAL PRODUCTION 130,000 bottles
HECTARES UNDER VINE 27.00

○ Müller Thurgau '15	♈♈ 2*
● OP Pinot Nero Costarsa '12	♈♈ 4

La Montina

VIA BAIANA, 17
25040 MONTICELLI BRUSATI [BS]
TEL. +39 030653278
www.lamontina.it

CELLAR SALES
PRE-BOOKED VISITS
RESTAURANT SERVICE
ANNUAL PRODUCTION 450,000 bottles
HECTARES UNDER VINE 70.00

○ Franciacorta Brut	♈♈ 4
○ Franciacorta Brut Satèn	♈♈ 4
⊙ Franciacorta Extra Brut Rosé	♈♈ 5

Alfio Mozzi

VIA CA' BIANCA,19
23012 CASTIONE ANDEVENNO [SO]
TEL. +39 3393707018
www.alfiomozzi.com

CELLAR SALES
PRE-BOOKED VISITS
ANNUAL PRODUCTION 15,000 bottles
HECTARES UNDER VINE 3.50

● Valtellina Sup. Sassella Grisone Ris. '13	♈♈ 6
● Sforzato di Valtellina '13	♈ 7

Nettare dei Santi

via Capra, 17
20078 San Colombano al Lambro [MI]
Tel. +39 0371200523
www.nettaredeisanti.it

CELLAR SALES
PRE-BOOKED VISITS
ANNUAL PRODUCTION 600,000 bottles
HECTARES UNDER VINE 40.00

● Franco Riccardi '11	🍷🍷 4
○ San Colombano Bianco del Santo '15	🍷🍷 3
● San Colombano V. Roverone Ris. '13	🍷 3

Panigada - Banino

via della Vittoria, 13
20078 San Colombano al Lambro [MI]
Tel. +39 037189103
www.banino.it

CELLAR SALES
PRE-BOOKED VISITS
ANNUAL PRODUCTION 30,000 bottles
HECTARES UNDER VINE 5.00

● San Colombano Banino V. La Merla Ris. '10	🍷🍷 4
○ Aureum '13	🍷 4

Angelo Pecis

via San Pietro delle Passere, 12
24060 San Paolo d'Argon [BG]
Tel. +39 035959104
www.pecis.it

CELLAR SALES
PRE-BOOKED VISITS
ANNUAL PRODUCTION 25,000 bottles
HECTARES UNDER VINE 5.00

○ Brut M. Cl. Maximus '11	🍷🍷 4
● Valcalepio Moscato Passito Argo '12	🍷🍷 4
○ Valcalepio Bianco San Pietro delle Passere '15	🍷 2

Pian del Maggio

via Iseo,108
25030 Erbusco [BS]
Tel. +39 3467163590
www.piandelmaggio.it

PRE-BOOKED VISITS
ANNUAL PRODUCTION 25,000 bottles
HECTARES UNDER VINE 2.86

○ Franciacorta Brut Proscenio	🍷🍷 4
○ Franciacorta Satèn Capriccio	🍷🍷 5
⊙ Franciacorta Rosé...e Anna Sorrise	🍷 5

Plozza Ome

via Lizzana, 13
25050 Ome [BS]
Tel. +39 0306527775
www.plozzaome.it

CELLAR SALES
PRE-BOOKED VISITS
ANNUAL PRODUCTION 37,000 bottles
HECTARES UNDER VINE 7.00

○ Franciacorta Satèn	🍷🍷 5
○ Franciacorta Brut	🍷 5
⊙ Franciacorta Rosé	🍷 5

Prime Alture

via Madonna, 109
27045 Casteggio [PV]
Tel. +39 038383214
www.primealture.it

CELLAR SALES
PRE-BOOKED VISITS
ACCOMMODATION AND RESTAURANT SERVICE
ANNUAL PRODUCTION 40,000 bottles
HECTARES UNDER VINE 8.00

○ Brut M. Cl. Io per te	🍷🍷 5
○ Il Bianco '15	🍷 3
● OP Pinot Nero Centopercento '14	🍷 5

Le Quattro Terre

FRAZ. BORGONATO
VIA RISORGIMENTO, 11
25040 CORTE FRANCA [BS]
TEL. +39 030984312
www.quattroterre.it

CELLAR SALES
PRE-BOOKED VISITS
ACCOMMODATION AND RESTAURANT SERVICE
ANNUAL PRODUCTION 45,000 bottles
HECTARES UNDER VINE 7.00

○ Franciacorta Brut		♔♔ 5
⊙ Franciacorta Brut Rosé '11		♔♔ 5
○ Franciacorta Extra Brut		♔♔ 5

Rebollini

LOC. SBERCIA
27040 BORGORATTO MORMOROLO [PV]
TEL. +39 0383872295
www.rebollini.it

ANNUAL PRODUCTION 100,000 bottles
HECTARES UNDER VINE 36.00
SUSTAINABLE WINERY

● OP Bonarda '15		♔♔ 4
○ OP Pinot Nero Brut M. Cl. '11		♔♔ 4
○ OP Riesling '14		♔♔ 4

Riccafana - Fratus

VIA F.LLI FACCHETTI, 91
25033 COLOGNE [BS]
TEL. +39 0307156797
www.riccafana.com

CELLAR SALES
ANNUAL PRODUCTION 100,000 bottles
HECTARES UNDER VINE 12.00
VITICULTURE METHOD Certified Organic

○ Franciacorta Satèn '11		♔♔ 5
○ Franciacorta Zero Zero		♔ 6

Riva di Franciacorta

LOC. FANTECOLO
VIA CARLO ALBERTO, 19
25050 PROVAGLIO D'ISEO [BS]
TEL. +39 0309823701
www.rivadifranciacorta.it

CELLAR SALES
PRE-BOOKED VISITS
ANNUAL PRODUCTION 280,000 bottles
HECTARES UNDER VINE 32.00
SUSTAINABLE WINERY

○ Franciacorta Pas Dosé Rivalto 75		♔♔ 5
○ Franciacorta Satèn		♔♔ 5
○ Franciacorta Brut		♔ 5

Romantica

VIA VALLOSA, 29
25050 PASSIRANO [BS]
TEL. +39 030657362
www.romanticafranciacorta.com

CELLAR SALES
PRE-BOOKED VISITS
ACCOMMODATION AND RESTAURANT SERVICE
ANNUAL PRODUCTION 60,000 bottles
HECTARES UNDER VINE 10.00

○ Franciacorta Brut '12		♔♔ 4
○ Franciacorta Satèn		♔♔ 5
○ Franciacorta Brut		♔ 5

La Rovere

VIA G.B. MARCHESI, 18
24060 TORRE DE' ROVERI [BG]
TEL. +39 0354528972

ANNUAL PRODUCTION 25,000 bottles
HECTARES UNDER VINE 5.00

○ Valcalepio Bianco Concordia '15		♔♔ 2*
○ Valcalepio Moscato Passito '11		♔♔ 5
● Valcalepio Rosso Senesco '13		♔♔ 4

Santus

VIA BADIA, 68
25060 CELLATICA [BS]
TEL. +39 0308367074
www.santus.it

PRE-BOOKED VISITS
ANNUAL PRODUCTION 50,000 bottles
HECTARES UNDER VINE 9.00

○ Franciacorta Dosaggio Zero '12	♟♟ 5
⊙ Franciacorta Extra Brut Rosé	♟♟ 4
○ Franciacorta Satèn	♟♟ 4

Benedetto Tognazzi

FRAZ. CAIONVICO
VIA SANT'ORSOLA, 161
25135 BRESCIA
TEL. +39 0302692695
www.tognazzivini.it

CELLAR SALES
PRE-BOOKED VISITS
ANNUAL PRODUCTION 65,000 bottles
HECTARES UNDER VINE 12.00
SUSTAINABLE WINERY

● Botticino Cobio '13	♟♟ 4
○ Lugana Cascina Ardea '15	♟♟ 2*

Torrevilla

VIA EMILIA, 4
27050 TORRAZZA COSTE [PV]
TEL. +39 038377003
www.torrevilla.it

CELLAR SALES
PRE-BOOKED VISITS
ANNUAL PRODUCTION 3,000,000 bottles
HECTARES UNDER VINE 650.00

⊙ OP Cruasé La Genisia '12	♟♟ 4
● OP Bonarda La Genisia '15	♟ 2

F.lli Turina

VIA PERGOLA, 68
25080 MONIGA DEL GARDA [BS]
TEL. +39 0365502103
www.turinavini.it

CELLAR SALES
PRE-BOOKED VISITS
ANNUAL PRODUCTION 300,000 bottles
HECTARES UNDER VINE 20.00

○ Lugana V. Fenil Boi '15	♟♟ 2*
● Marzemino '14	♟♟ 2*
○ Lugana '15	♟ 2
⊙ Valtènesi Chiaretto '15	♟ 2

La Valle

VIA SANT'ANTONIO, 4
25050 RODENGO SAIANO [BS]
TEL. +39 0307722045
www.vinilavalle.it

CELLAR SALES
PRE-BOOKED VISITS
ANNUAL PRODUCTION 50,000 bottles
HECTARES UNDER VINE 6.00
SUSTAINABLE WINERY

○ Franciacorta Extra Brut Naturalis '10	♟♟ 5
⊙ Franciacorta Brut Rosé '12	♟♟ 5
○ Franciacorta Satèn '11	♟♟ 5

Vercesi del Castellazzo

VIA AURELIANO, 36
27040 MONTÙ BECCARIA [PV]
TEL. +39 0385262098
www.vercesidelcastellazzo.it

CELLAR SALES
PRE-BOOKED VISITS
ANNUAL PRODUCTION 80,000 bottles
HECTARES UNDER VINE 13.00

● OP Pinot Nero Luogo dei Monti '12	♟♟ 3*
● OP Bonarda Luogo della Milla '15	♟ 2
● Vespolino '15	♟ 2

Vigna Dorata

FRAZ. CALINO
VIA SALA, 80
25046 CAZZAGO SAN MARTINO [BS]
TEL. +39 0307254275
www.vignadorata.it

CELLAR SALES
PRE-BOOKED VISITS
ANNUAL PRODUCTION 70,000 bottles
HECTARES UNDER VINE 6.00

○ Franciacorta Extra Brut	♥♥ 5
⊙ Franciacorta Rosé	♥♥ 5
○ Franciacorta Satèn '09	♥♥ 6
○ Franciacorta Satèn	♥♥ 5

Tenuta Vinea Scerscé

VIA STELVIO, 18
23037 TIRANO [SO]
TEL. +39 3461542970
www.tenutascersce.it

CELLAR SALES
PRE-BOOKED VISITS
ANNUAL PRODUCTION 22,000 bottles
HECTARES UNDER VINE 3.50

● Valtellina Sforzato Infinito '10	♥♥ 7
● Valtellina Sup. Essenza '12	♥♥ 5
● Rosso di Valtellina '13	♥ 4

Visconti

FRAZ. SAN MARTINO DELLA BATTAGLIA
VIA SELVA CAPUZZA, 1
25010 DESENZANO DEL GARDA [BS]
TEL. +39 0309910381
www.viscontiwines.it

CELLAR SALES
PRE-BOOKED VISITS
ANNUAL PRODUCTION 250,000 bottles
HECTARES UNDER VINE 20.00

○ Lugana Collo Lungo '15	♥♥ 2*
○ Lugana Franco Visconti '15	♥♥ 3
⊙ Garda Cl. Chiaretto '15	♥ 3
○ Lugana Antica Casa '15	♥ 3

Vigne Olcru

VIA BUCA, 26
27047 SANTA MARIA DELLA VERSA [PV]
TEL. +39 0385799958
vigneolcru.com

PRE-BOOKED VISITS
ANNUAL PRODUCTION 100,000 bottles
HECTARES UNDER VINE 29.00

● OP Bonarda Buccia Rossa '15	♥♥ 4
○ Infinito	♥ 3

Cantine Virgili

VIA M. DONATI, 2
46100 MANTOVA
TEL. +39 0376322560
www.cantinevirgili.com

CELLAR SALES
PRE-BOOKED VISITS
ANNUAL PRODUCTION 300,000 bottles
HECTARES UNDER VINE 10.00

● Inciostar '15	♥♥ 2*
● Lambrusco Mantovano Rays '15	♥♥ 2*
● Pjafoc '15	♥♥ 2*

Zamichele

VIA ROVEGLIA PALAZZINA, 2
25010 POZZOLENGO [BS]
TEL. +39 030918631
cantinazamichele@alice.it

CELLAR SALES
PRE-BOOKED VISITS
ANNUAL PRODUCTION 45,000 bottles
HECTARES UNDER VINE 8.00

○ Lugana Gardè '14	♥♥ 2*
○ Lugana '15	♥ 2

TRENTINO

The Trentino growing area is one of the Italian
regions richest in opportunity. The great TrentoDoc
classic method sparkling wines, fine reds from
native grapes such as teroldego from Campi
Rotaliani, the preference for Bordeaux blends,
and the international varieties planted here over a century
ago, Italy's biggest chardonnay vineyards, and a series of leading whites from
high-altitude vineyards . . . not to mention many native grape varieties, both
red and white, and small productions of stunning sweet wines like Trentino Vino
Santo. This, in a nutshell, is the potential vaunted by the region. Each year, when
we summarize the work of the wine industry in the province of Trento, however,
we see that the results still do not do justice to this potential. The TrentoDoc
designation flies the Trentino flag, with seven excellent cuvées that are definitely
some of the best in Italy. Alongside Ferrari, Mezzacorona, Abate Nero, Cavit,
Letrari, and Cesarini Sforza, which are not new to success, we have the debut of
the Stelzer husband and wife team's Maso Martis with a dumbfounding Dosage
Zero 2011. The San Leonardo 2011 is at its usual high level, while Zeni encores
with an excellent Teroldego Rotaliano. Wines beyond reproach. Then we have
the 2012 Fojaneghe Rosso from Fedrigotti Bossi, taking its first award. But there
could be many more if only this wine country, also home to large cooperatives,
small, even micro cellars (some traditionalists and others young organic and
biodynamic devotees), could find the key and develop synergies with institutional
partners to make more impact on Italian and international markets, setting aside
local squabbles about a market hallmarked by large numbers, vineyard cultivation
choices, designation protocols (not least that involving Pinot Grigio Venezie with its
high yields and involving Trentino, Veneto and Friuli for business in the US market).
The 1996 edition of IW pondered: "In Trentino there are plenty of economic and
viticultural resources for us all to work together and grow the province to raise it
to the role deserves. A real shame . . .". Twenty years later, our considerations are
almost the same.

★Abate Nero

FRAZ. GARDOLO
S.DA TRENTINA, 45
38121 TRENTO
TEL. +39 0461246566
www.abatenero.it

CELLAR SALES
PRE-BOOKED VISITS
ANNUAL PRODUCTION 65,000 bottles
HECTARES UNDER VINE 65.00

Abate Nero's mission is to bring Trento closer to Pinot Nero, and to do so by raising the profile of much of this now long-established estate's range of sparklers, on which they focus exclusively. Founder members Luciano Lunelli and Eugenio de Castel Terlago have stubbornly and meticulously stuck to their tasks, helped by their respective children, Roberta and Andrea. Seven wine types, quality production, careful selection of the grapes on the vines tended with passion by expert growers from the local cooperative wineries. Once again, the Domini, from 100% chardonnay, deservedly wins a Tre Bicchieri. Its excellent structure displays golden highlights and rhythmic fizz, mellow wisdom, and a harmonious, lingering drinkability. Truly delightful. The spectacular Rosé slips down smoothly, with lively tropical fruit in the glass.

○ Trento Brut Domini '10	♈♈♈	5
○ Trento Brut	♈♈	4
⊙ Trento Domini Rosé '12	♈♈	5
○ Trento Extra Brut	♈♈	4
○ Trento Extra Dry	♈	4
○ Trento Brut Cuvée dell'Abate Ris. '04	♈♈♈	6
○ Trento Brut Cuvée dell'Abate Ris. '03	♈♈♈	5
○ Trento Brut Domini '07	♈♈♈	5
○ Trento Brut Domini '05	♈♈♈	5
○ Trento Brut Domini Nero '10	♈♈♈	5
○ Trento Brut Domini Nero '08	♈♈♈	5
○ Trento Domìni Nero '09	♈♈♈	5

Nicola Balter

VIA VALLUNGA II, 24
38068 ROVERETO [TN]
TEL. +39 0464430101
www.balter.it

CELLAR SALES
PRE-BOOKED VISITS
ANNUAL PRODUCTION 80,000 bottles
HECTARES UNDER VINE 10.00

The winery itself is tucked out of sight beneath the imposing walls of a castelliere, a fortified borough, testimony to the area's 19th-century rural nobility, now enjoying a new lease of life under Nicola Balter. Two members of the next generation, Giacomo and Clementina, are increasingly taking over responsibility within the firm, and Clementina in particular is also involved in the higher echelons of the Consorzio Vignaioli del Trentino. All production comes from vineyards surrounding the family-run winery, on a plateau planted to vine above Rovereto, amid woodlands and Dolomite rock. Nicola initially wished to create Bordeaux-style reds, but in recent vintages he has rightly shifted focus to sparklers, with excellent results. The Trento Riserva is still resting on the lees. We will console ourselves with a very pleasant Rosé. Almost as good were the still wines, especially the reds. The Barbanico 2013 is a supple, generous bordeaux with a dash of lagrein that shows plenty of flesh and elegance.

○ Trento Brut Rosé	♈♈	5
● Barbanico '13	♈♈	5
○ Trento Brut	♈♈	4
● Lagrein Merlot '15	♈	2
○ Sauvignon '15	♈	3
○ Trento Balter Ris. '06	♈♈♈	5
○ Trento Balter Ris. '05	♈♈♈	5
○ Trento Balter Ris. '04	♈♈♈	5
○ Trento Balter Ris. '01	♈♈♈	5
○ Trento Dosaggio Zero Ris. '10	♈♈♈	7
○ Trento Pas Dosé Balter Ris. '09	♈♈♈	5
○ Sauvignon '14	♈♈	3
○ Sauvignon '13	♈♈	3

Bellaveder

LOC. MASO BELVEDERE
38010 FAEDO [TN]
TEL. +39 0461650171
www.bellaveder.it

CELLAR SALES
PRE-BOOKED VISITS
ANNUAL PRODUCTION 70,000 bottles
HECTARES UNDER VINE 12.00
SUSTAINABLE WINERY

The Faedo alluvial fan, above San Michele all'Adige, has some of the most photographed vineyards in Trentino. Especially the ones surrounding this winery, as the name Bellaveder testifies, built by Tranquillo Lucchetta with the true dedication of a vigneron. His efficient approach is also reflected in the targeted harvests from his hillside plots in the Valle di Cavedine, between Lake Garda and the Brenta Dolomites. Two very distinct areas, Faedo and Cavedine, proudly blended into a range of wines with a crystal-clear identity, from a classico sparkler to an ever-finer Pinot Nero. Organic methods, vineyards tended like gardens and winemaking by Luca Gasperinatti, whose skills far outweigh his tender years. Despite its prickly rhythm, and touch of aromatic alpine herbs in harmony with citrusy aromas, the grippy Trento Brut Nature Riserva 2011 was pipped to the post for our top accolade. Pinot Nero has recently become one of the top sparkler varietals, and the 2013 again performed well.

○ Trento Brut Nature Ris. '11	♈♈	5
○ Sauvignon Faedi '15	♈♈	3
○ Trentino Müller Thurgau San Lorenz '15	♈♈	3
● Trentino Pinot Nero Faedi '13	♈♈	5
● Trentino Lagrein Dunkel Mansum Ris. '10	♈♈	4
● Trentino Lagrein Mansum '12	♈♈	4
● Trentino Lagrein Mansum '11	♈♈	4
○ Trentino Müller Thurgau San Lorenz '14	♈♈	3
● Trentino Pinot Nero '11	♈♈	5
● Trentino Pinot Nero Faedi Ris. '12	♈♈	5
○ Trentino Traminer '13	♈♈	3
○ Trento Brut Nature Ris. '10	♈♈	5

Borgo dei Posseri

LOC. POZZO BASSO, 1
38061 ALA [TN]
TEL. +39 0464671899
www.borgodeiposseri.com

CELLAR SALES
PRE-BOOKED VISITS
ANNUAL PRODUCTION 60,000 bottles
HECTARES UNDER VINE 21.00
VITICULTURE METHOD Certified Organic
SUSTAINABLE WINERY

The challenge began a few years ago, and results have been very promising. Now they are looking to relaunch a rather exciting wine-based project, seeking to breathe new life into a rural hamlet perched up on the Ala mountains, just below the Piccole Dolomiti. Dozens of hectares under vine, with plenty of woodland left to its own devices, scattered rural settlements created by back-breaking toil. Respect for the original habitat enhances their still evolving, yet very impressive, production. All credit is due to Martin Mainenti and his family, with invaluable help from Maria Marangoni. Wines that stand out. From every point of view. The high-altitude vineyards are the making of the Trento Tananai 2012, with its greenish hues and lively crystalline flavours, a relaxing, flavoursome wine. The supple, racy Merlot Rocol 2014 is also very good, displaying deep highlights and good density, with an enjoyable forthright finish.

● Merlot Rocol '14	♈♈	3
○ Müller Thurgau Quaron '15	♈♈	3
○ Traminer Arliz '15	♈♈	3
○ Trento Brut Tananai '12	♈♈	5
● Merlot Rocol '13	♈♈	3
○ Müller Thurgau Quaron '14	♈♈	3
○ Müller Thurgau Quaron '13	♈♈	3
● Pinot Nero Paradis '13	♈♈	3
○ Sauvignon Furiel '13	♈♈	3
○ Traminer Arliz '13	♈♈	3
○ Trento Brut Tananai '11	♈♈	5
○ Trento Brut Tananai '10	♈♈	5

Bossi Fedrigotti

VIA UNIONE, 43
38068 ROVERETO [TN]
TEL. +39 0456832511
www.masi.it

CELLAR SALES
PRE-BOOKED VISITS
ANNUAL PRODUCTION 160,000 bottles
HECTARES UNDER VINE 40.00
SUSTAINABLE WINERY

The Bossi Fedrigotti family grows its vines on the hillsides surrounding the winery, just a stone's throw from the ancient river port of Rovereto, where the Adige has laid down fertile soils, patiently sculpting the alluvial landscape of the Vallagarina. Though they have been harvesting their grapes traditionally for generations, they also welcome challenges, thus maintaining the family's reputation as well as its love of innovation. They recently joined forces with the Masi Agricola group. The subzone's first-ever Bordeaux blend, Fojaneghe, dates back to 1961, and is now back to its best. A splash of teroldego adds a local Dolomitic touch to an otherwise international style, featuring an attractively agile red berry fruit profile balanced by round tannins. By contrast, Vign'Asmara is a skilfully-blended chardonnay and traminer cuvée. The 2014 is tasty with intense hues, ready for the challenges posed by bottle ageing.

● Fojaneghe Rosso '12	♟♟♟ 5
○ Vign'Asmara '14	♟♟ 4
○ Valdadige Pinot Grigio Pian del Griso '15	♟ 3
● Fojaneghe Rosso '11	♟♟ 5
● Fojaneghe Rosso '10	♟♟ 5
● Fojaneghe Rosso '09	♟♟ 5
● Fojaneghe Rosso '08	♟♟ 5
● Mas'est '13	♟♟ 3
● Mas'est '12	♟♟ 3
● Trentino Marzemino '10	♟♟ 3
○ Trentino Traminer '11	♟♟ 4
○ Trento Brut Conte Federico '11	♟♟ 5
○ Vign'Asmara '13	♟♟ 4

★Cavit

VIA DEL PONTE, 31
38040 TRENTO
TEL. +39 0461381711
www.cavit.it

CELLAR SALES
PRE-BOOKED VISITS
ANNUAL PRODUCTION 70,000,000 bottles
HECTARES UNDER VINE 5500.00

Combining power and finesse, global footprint and respect for montane varietal stamping, some wines are for immediate mass consumption while others are to be sipped at leisure, rare exponents of rustic values. Cavit is all this. And maybe even more. It combines the global with the local, the international market with the protection of vineyard selections reserved for consumers seeking exclusivity. With over 5000 grower-members at the cooperatives that produce for the Cavit brand, business continues to expand with great acumen, offering a range of wines that demonstrate that big can also mean great. Not to mention delicious. Austere in its golden sheen, with an equally regal aromatic range and a decidedly satisfying smoothness to its flavours, the Altremasi Graal Riserva 2009 is once again one of the finest Trentos. But we very much enjoyed all the wines presented, including the classics from the forthright Bottega Vinai range, ideal for everyday use.

○ Trento Brut Altemasi Graal Ris. '09	♟♟♟ 6
○ Trentino Chardonnay Maso Toresella '14	♟♟ 4
○ Trentino Müller Thurgau Zeveri '15	♟♟ 3
● Trentino Pinot Nero Bottega Vinai '14	♟♟ 3
● Trentino Sup. Quattro Vicariati '12	♟♟ 4
○ Trento Brut Altemasi '11	♟♟ 4
● Teroldego Rotaliano Maso Cervara '07	♟♟♟ 4
○ Trento Altemasi Graal Brut Ris. '03	♟♟♟ 6
○ Trento Altemasi Graal Brut Ris. '02	♟♟♟ 6
○ Trento Brut Altemasi Graal Ris. '08	♟♟♟ 6
○ Trento Brut Altemasi Graal Ris. '06	♟♟♟ 6
○ Trento Brut Altemasi Graal Ris. '05	♟♟♟ 7
○ Trento Brut Altemasi Graal Ris. '04	♟♟♟ 7

Cesarini Sforza

FRAZ. RAVINA
VIA STELLA, 9
38123 TRENTO
TEL. +39 0461382200
www.cesarinisforza.com

CELLAR SALES
PRE-BOOKED VISITS
ANNUAL PRODUCTION 1,300,000 bottles
HECTARES UNDER VINE 800.00

The look and feel is completely new, featuring bright colours and uniquely-fashioned bottles, for a feel-good factor that reflects the alluring wines that await within. This long-established Trento-based sparkler winery, part of the La Vis group, continues to achieve market and critical success, even during the parent company's recent, albeit short-lived, trials and tribulations. Selecting only hill-grown grapes, from Val di Cembra, Valsugana and the higher slopes of Mount Baldo towards Garda, they make a dozen or so Metodo Classicos, as well as others made in pressurized vats. Sparkling wines of excellent workmanship, with some truly compelling gems, such as Aquila Reale. This long-established winery's sparklers have taken a turn for the better, with an original Tridentum Extra Brut 2009 earning itself a Tre Bicchieri. This monovarietal chardonnay reflects the grape's generosity in a pot pourri of exotic fruit and golden delicious apple, for a well-rounded fizz.

○ Trento Extra Brut Tridentum '09	♟♟♟ 4*
○ Cuvée Brut	♟♟ 4
○ Trento Brut Tridentum '12	♟♟ 4
○ Trento Dosaggio Zero Tridentum '12	♟♟ 5
⊙ Trento Tridentum Rosé '10	♟♟ 4
○ Trento Aquila Reale Ris. '05	♟♟♟ 7
○ Trento Aquila Reale Ris. '02	♟♟♟ 7
⊙ Trento Brut Rosé Tridentum '09	♟♟ 4
⊙ Trento Brut Rosé Tridentum '08	♟♟ 4
○ Trento Brut Tridentum '11	♟♟ 4
○ Trento Dosaggio Zero Tridentum '11	♟♟ 5
○ Trento Extra Brut Tridentum Ris. '08	♟♟ 5
○ Trento Tridentum Aquila Reale Ris. '07	♟♟ 6

De Vescovi Ulzbach

P.ZZA GARIBALDI, 12
38016 MEZZOCORONA [TN]
TEL. +39 0461605648
www.devescoviulzbach.it

CELLAR SALES
PRE-BOOKED VISITS
ANNUAL PRODUCTION 20,000 bottles
HECTARES UNDER VINE 3.50

What a pleasure to see how a single glass of Teroldego can express the wisdom handed down from generations of winemakers combined with the drinkability of a modern wine, perfectly in tune with today's lifestyles. Credit goes to this young, knowledgeable vigneron, Giulio De Vescovi, and to his Ulzbach dynasty, whose roots in Trentino winemaking go back some four centuries. Teroldego is the overriding passion, though down on the valley floor they also tend a variety of small plots with white varieties for future vinifications. Meanwhile, two versions of a Metodo Classico are also being tested, some vines being planted at 500 metres and others at nearly 1,000 on slopes above the winery. The Teroldego 2014 remains an illustrious thoroughbred. The Empeiria 2015, a blend of pinot bianco, sauvignon and incrocio Manzoni has an almost crunchy palate, while the rosé Teroldego 2015 with its berry aromas is most enjoyable.

● Teroldego Rotaliano '14	♟♟ 3*
○ Empeiria '15	♟♟ 5
○ Sauvignon '15	♟♟ 4
⊙ Teroldego Rotaliano Kretzer '14	♟ 3
● Teroldego Rotaliano Vigilius '12	♟♟♟ 5
● Teroldego Rotaliano '13	♟♟ 3
● Teroldego Rotaliano '12	♟♟ 3*
● Teroldego Rotaliano '11	♟♟ 3
● Teroldego Rotaliano '10	♟♟ 3
● Teroldego Rotaliano '07	♟♟ 3
● Teroldego Rotaliano Vigilius '13	♟♟ 5
● Teroldego Rotaliano Vigilius '11	♟♟ 5
● Teroldego Rotaliano Vigilius '09	♟♟ 5

★Dorigati

VIA DANTE, 5
38016 MEZZOCORONA [TN]
TEL. +39 0461605313
www.dorigati.it

CELLAR SALES
PRE-BOOKED VISITS
ANNUAL PRODUCTION 100,000 bottles
HECTARES UNDER VINE 10.00
SUSTAINABLE WINERY

Five generations of vignerons have now passed on their knowledge of the vineyard. They are well-qualified to do so, agronomic study and oenological research being part of the DNA in the Dorigati family, which has gradually built up an excellent all-round winery. Especially since the enthusiastic, highly-trained young cousins Michele and Paolo came on board, they have been proudly brandishing the winery foundation year of 1858, underlining all the experience his parents, grandparents and great-grandparents had built up. Making both Teroldego and Trento, honouring the past and setting out challenges for the future. Even though the Methius failed to land this year's top honours, its prestige remains intact. This blend of chardonnay and pinot nero shows strong personality and flavour, a vaguely resinous timbre, careful vinification and prodigious evolution in the bottle, making it unmistakably masculine, satisfying, as few other Trentos can. The fruity Diedri 2013 is harmonious, with suave tannins.

○ Trento Brut Methius '10	♥♥ 6
● Teroldego Rotaliano '14	♥♥ 3
● Teroldego Rotaliano Sup. Diedri '13	♥♥ 5
○ Trentino Chardonnay Majerla '14	♥♥ 3
● Trentino Lagrein '14	♥♥ 3
◉ Trentino Lagrein Kretzer '15	♥ 3
○ Trento Brut Methius Ris. '09	♥♥♥ 6
○ Trento Brut Methius Ris. '08	♥♥♥ 6
○ Trento Brut Methius Ris. '06	♥♥♥ 6
○ Trento Brut Methius Ris. '05	♥♥♥ 6
○ Trento Brut Methius Ris. '04	♥♥♥ 6
○ Trento Brut Methius Ris. '03	♥♥♥ 6
○ Trento Brut Methius Ris. '02	♥♥♥ 6

Endrizzi

LOC. MASETTO, 2
38010 SAN MICHELE ALL'ADIGE [TN]
TEL. +39 0461650129
www.endrizzi.it

CELLAR SALES
PRE-BOOKED VISITS
ANNUAL PRODUCTION 600,000 bottles
HECTARES UNDER VINE 55.00
SUSTAINABLE WINERY

Its 19th-century premises maintain an old-time charm, in contrast with the surprisingly high-tech winemaking equipment found inside. They tend the surrounding vines organically using experimental techniques, working hand in hand with international research centres. Endrizzi's Endrici may sound more like a Trentino dialect tongue-twister, but they are transforming their splendid property into a veritable hub of winemaking, spearheaded by the ambitious younger generation, diversifying their harvests, underscoring that innate passion for wines that are capable of winning over even the most select of marketplaces. The estate's excellent flagship wines, the Teroldego Rotaliano Tradizione 2014, tempered only by the difficult vintage, and the Superiore 2013 both impress. The spicy, citrussy Traminer 2015 stands out, as do two equally convincing reds, the Masetto Due 2014, from teroldego and cabernet, and the Masetto Nero 2015, a Bordeaux blend with teroldego and lagrein.

● Masetto Due '14	♥♥ 5
● Masetto Nero '13	♥♥ 3
● Teroldego Rotaliano Sup. '13	♥♥ 3
● Teroldego Rotaliano Tradizione '14	♥♥ 2*
○ Trentino Traminer Aromatico '15	♥♥ 2*
○ Trento Brut Pian di Castello '11	♥♥ 4
◉ Trento Brut Rosé Pian di Castello '09	♥♥ 4
● Gran Masetto '11	♥♥ 7
○ Masetto Bianco '13	♥♥ 3
○ Masetto Bianco '12	♥♥ 3
● Masetto Nero '12	♥♥ 3
● Masetto Nero '11	♥♥ 3
● Teroldego Rotaliano '13	♥♥ 2*
● Teroldego Rotaliano '11	♥♥ 3

★★Ferrari

VIA PONTE DI RAVINA, 15
38123 TRENTO
TEL. +39 0461972311
www.ferraritrento.it

CELLAR SALES
PRE-BOOKED VISITS
RESTAURANT SERVICE
ANNUAL PRODUCTION 4,450,000 bottles
HECTARES UNDER VINE 120.00
SUSTAINABLE WINERY

Their greatest claim to fame surely came at Expo 2015, where Ferrari was used for the official toasts, leading millions to savour one of Italy's most prestigious wines. At the same time, alongside its top range, the Lunelli family launched a series of commercial initiatives, first and foremost for its Proseccos, as well as for its fine Umbrian and Tuscan wines. A strictly Trento sparkle, combining respect for tradition with ecologically sound vineyard management, and genetic research for the vines of tomorrow. Investing heavily in the family jewels. The Maso Montalto 2013, a decidedly elegant and vibrant Pinot Nero with complex hints, surprisingly powerful in the mouth, looks to have a good future. The Trentos again live up to their fine reputation. The Giulio Ferrari 2005 defies the passage of time, with a mosaic of complexity, perhaps even more intriguing than previous vintages. Special mention for the Perlés, with the outstanding Nero 2009 and the compellingly lively Rosé 2010.

○ Trento Brut Giulio Ferrari Riserva del Fondatore '05	♆♆♆ 8
● Trentino Pinot Nero Maso Montalto '13	♆♆ 5
○ Trento Brut Perlé Nero '09	♆♆ 6
○ Trento Brut Perlé '10	♆♆ 6
○ Trento Brut Perlé Rosé '10	♆♆ 7
○ Trento Extra Brut Lunelli Ris. '08	♆♆ 7
○ Trento Brut Giulio Ferrari Riserva del Fondatore '04	♆♆♆ 8
○ Trento Brut Giulio Ferrari Riserva del Fondatore '01	♆♆♆ 8
○ Trento Extra Brut Lunelli Ris. '07	♆♆♆ 7
○ Trento Extra Brut Perlé Nero '07	♆♆♆ 8
○ Trento Extra Brut Perlé Nero '06	♆♆♆ 8
○ Trento Extra Brut Perlé Nero '05	♆♆♆ 8
○ Trento Extra Brut Perlé Nero '04	♆♆♆ 8

Fondazione Mach

VIA EDMONDO MACH, 1
38010 SAN MICHELE ALL'ADIGE [TN]
TEL. +39 0461615252
www.ismaa.it

CELLAR SALES
PRE-BOOKED VISITS
ANNUAL PRODUCTION 250,000 bottles
HECTARES UNDER VINE 60.00
VITICULTURE METHOD Certified Organic

The future of wine grapes will be played out here, in the Fondazione Mach's space-age laboratories, as the facilities at the San Michele all'Adige wine school are starting to be known. Founded by Edmund Mach, a leading light on the late 19th-century winemaking scene, perhaps the first person to grasp the importance of science for viticulture. It was here that the DNA of the grapevine and of many other plant species was unravelled, and scores of young people are learning to make environmentally-friendly wines. According to its founding mission, the vast range of wines made at the foundation serves to help hundreds of future oenologists to learn their trade. Their wines either confirmed previous year's results or showed progress. The Riesling Monastero 2015 is truly tantalizing and juicy, and looks set to improve even more with time. The other wines are equally impressive, including a distinctive Marzemino 2015, with a lightweight profile but rich fruit-forward notes. The crunchy Nosiola 2015 is flowery and fresh-tasting.

● Cabernet Franc Monastero '13	♆♆ 3
○ Manzoni Bianco Castel San Michele '15	♆♆ 4
● Trentino Marzemino '15	♆♆ 3
○ Trentino Nosiola '15	♆♆ 3
○ Trentino Riesling Monastero '15	♆♆ 5
○ Trento Mach Riserva del Fondatore '09	♆♆♆ 5
○ Trento Mach Riserva del Fondatore '07	♆♆♆ 5
○ Trento Mach Riserva del Fondatore '04	♆♆♆ 5
○ Trentino Pinot Bianco '14	♆♆ 2*
○ Trentino Pinot Bianco Monastero '13	♆♆ 3*
● Trentino Pinot Nero Monastero '10	♆♆ 6
○ Trento Mach Riserva del Fondatore '10	♆♆ 5
○ Trento Mach Riserva del Fondatore '08	♆♆ 5

Grigoletti

VIA GARIBALDI, 12
38060 NOMI [TN]
TEL. +39 0464834215
www.grigoletti.com

CELLAR SALES
PRE-BOOKED VISITS
ANNUAL PRODUCTION 60,000 bottles
HECTARES UNDER VINE 6.00

In the Nomi area, the Grigoletti family name means but one thing. A down-to-earth wine selection whose character is as genuine, forthright and uncompromising as its growers. The whole family is involved in running this independent winery, headed by Carmelo Grigoletti, ensuring that his father and winery founder, another Carmelo, can enjoy a well-earned rest. They tend vineyards scattered across the hills and alluvial soils on the right bank of the Adige, between Trento and Rovereto. No concessions to exclusivity, just the vinification of local varieties, for equally sincere wines. The Gonzalier 2015 shows good weight, backed up by a solid fruitiness, a balanced acidity and a tidy, lingering finish. The estate's flagship wine, the sinuously elegant Merlot Antica Vigna 2013, is flavoursome with great lustre and a lingering variegated finish. The purple-tinged Marzemino 2015, a must in its class, thoroughly deserves a mention,

● Gonzalier '15	♥♥ 5
● Trentino Marzemino '15	♥♥ 2*
● Trentino Merlot Antica Vigna '13	♥♥ 4
○ Retiko '14	♥ 3
○ San Martin Passito	♥ 4
○ Trentino Chardonnay '15	♥ 2
● Gonzalier '12	♥♥ 5
● Gonzalier '11	♥♥ 5
○ Retiko '13	♥♥ 3
○ Trentino Chardonnay L'Opera '14	♥♥ 3
○ Trentino Chardonnay L'Opera '13	♥♥ 3
● Trentino Marzemino '13	♥♥ 2*
● Trentino Merlot Antica Vigna '12	♥♥ 4

La-Vis/Valle di Cembra

VIA CARMINE, 7
38015 LAVIS [TN]
TEL. +39 0461440111
www.la-vis.com

CELLAR SALES
PRE-BOOKED VISITS
ACCOMMODATION AND RESTAURANT SERVICE
ANNUAL PRODUCTION 1,000,000 bottles
HECTARES UNDER VINE 850.00
SUSTAINABLE WINERY

La-Vis finds itself in the midst of a revolution. This renowned cooperative has completely renovated its management team, enabling it to overcome the financial hardships caused by previous administrations. Calm reigns once more and the 1,000-plus members are determined to consolidate each step in the production process, starting from the quality of the grapes from high-altitude vineyards, on mountain terraces planted only to highland varieties. A wide range of very affordable wines distributed in an intensive, exclusive network. Genuine Trentino wines. Praise for the almost unrivalled Trento Oro Rosso 60 Mesi 2012 from the Valle di Cembra, one of the finest Dolomite wines. The Traminer Maso Clinga 2015 is spicy, with flinty tones, and a lip-smacking, almost opulent, mouth. Powerful and complex with fruit-fuelled notes, the juicy Cabernet Sauvignon Riserva Ritratti 2012 shows a captivating finish. The organic Gewürztraminer Ai Padri and Teroldego Pergole Alte are both improving.

● Trentino Cabernet Sauvignon Ritratti '12	♥♥ 3*
○ Trentino Traminer Maso Clinga '15	♥♥ 4
○ Trento Brut Oro Rosso 60 Mesi	♥♥ 5
● Teroldego Pergole Alte Bio '15	♥♥ 2*
○ Trentino Gewürztraminer Ai Padri Bio '15	♥♥ 3
○ Trentino Müller Thurgau V. delle Forche '15	♥♥ 3
○ Ritratto Bianco '07	♥♥♥ 4
● Ritratto Rosso '03	♥♥♥ 4
○ Trentino Müller Thurgau V. delle Forche '14	♥♥♥ 3*
○ Trentino Müller Thurgau V. delle Forche '13	♥♥♥ 3*
○ Trentino Müller Thurgau V. delle Forche '12	♥♥♥ 3*
● Maso Franch L'Altro Manzoni '10	♥♥ 3*
○ Trentino Chardonnay Simboli '14	♥♥ 2*

Letrari

via Monte Baldo, 13/15
38068 Rovereto [TN]
Tel. +39 0464480200
www.letrari.it

CELLAR SALES
PRE-BOOKED VISITS
ANNUAL PRODUCTION 160,000 bottles
HECTARES UNDER VINE 23.00

Nello Letrari is unanimously regarded as the true patriarch of Trentino wines. This wise old octogenarian's trademark is his love of dialogue, investigating the whys and wherefores of oenology, dreaming up innovative strategies based on his almost 70 years of winemaking. He has passed on much of his knowledge to his daughter Lucia, from hviticulture to his unrivalled passion and determination, especially for Metodo Classico. This explains in part why the Letrari family is now producing a smaller range, concentrating specifically on their Trento sparklers. Fizz of great character, with a graceful vivaciousness. There are four particularly authoritative Trentos, with the as ever delicious Riserva 2010 once again taking home a Tre Bicchieri. With its crystalline golden brilliance and variegated aromatic expression, its exotic fragrances give way to white chocolate, candied citrus peel and a balanced vanilla finish. The forthright Millesimato 2013 is simple and laid-back.

○ Trento Brut Ris. '10	🏆🏆🏆 5
○ Trento Brut '13	🏆🏆 5
● Cabernet Franc '11	🏆🏆 4
● Trentino Marzemino '15	🏆🏆 3
○ Trento Brut Riserva del Fondatore 976 '06	🏆🏆 8
○ Trento Brut Letrari Ris. '09	🏆🏆🏆 5
○ Trento Brut Letrari Ris. '08	🏆🏆🏆 5
○ Trento Brut Letrari Ris. '07	🏆🏆🏆 5
○ Trento Brut Letrari Ris. '05	🏆🏆🏆 5
○ Trento Brut Ris. '06	🏆🏆🏆 5
○ Trento Brut Riserva del Fondatore 976 '05	🏆🏆🏆 8
○ Trento Letrari Quore Ris. '09	🏆🏆 5
○ Trento Letrari Riserva del Fondatore '04	🏆🏆 8

Maso Martis

loc. Martignano
via dell'Albera, 52
38121 Trento
Tel. +39 0461821057
www.masomartis.it

CELLAR SALES
PRE-BOOKED VISITS
ANNUAL PRODUCTION 65,000 bottles
HECTARES UNDER VINE 12.00
VITICULTURE METHOD Certified Organic

The winery name recalls Mars, the god of war, once venerated here on the slopes above today's city of Trento. The hillside vineyards on Mount Calisio produce the grapes for the Stelzer family to transform. In organically-tended rows, protected by characterful dry-stone walls, the vines are set against a mountain backdrop in decidedly rural surroundings. After 30 years of hospitality, and countless wine-related events, Roberta and Antonio Stelzer decided to focus mainly on Metodo Classico, with an unmistakable range of Trentos. and has been deserving of a Tre Bicchieri for some time. Indeed, the winery has been on the up for years, tirelessly promoting the designation. A peerless performance from two jewels in the crown, the stunning Riserva Madame Martis, with production limited to under a thousand bottles, and the splendid Dosaggio Zero 2011, dominated by pinot nero, making it compelling, gutsy and nonetheless gentle.

○ Trento Dosaggio Zero Ris. '11	🏆🏆🏆 5
○ Trento Madame Martis '06	🏆🏆 6
○ Trento Brut Bio	🏆🏆 4
○ Trento Brut Ris. '08	🏆🏆 5
○ Trento Rosé Ris. '11	🏆🏆 5
○ Trento Brut Ris. '07	🏆🏆 5
⊙ Trento Brut Rosé '11	🏆🏆 5
○ Trento Dosaggio Zero '10	🏆🏆 5
○ Trento Dosaggio Zero '09	🏆🏆 5
○ Trento Dosaggio Zero Ris. '10	🏆🏆 5
○ Trento Madame Martis Ris. '05	🏆🏆 6
○ Trento Madame Martis Ris. '04	🏆🏆 6
○ Trento Ris. '08	🏆🏆 5

Maso Poli

LOC. MASI DI PRESSANO, 33
38015 LAVIS [TN]
TEL. +39 0461871519
www.masopoli.com

CELLAR SALES
PRE-BOOKED VISITS
ACCOMMODATION
ANNUAL PRODUCTION 80,000 bottles
HECTARES UNDER VINE 13.00

With all the charm of high-altitude vines, on a terrace high above the Adige plain, the estate affords spectacular views across to the Brenta Dolomites and Paganella. This estate has been producing wines as far back as the 18th century, though the Togn family has only recently taken over. This dynasty of cellarmasters from Roverè della Luna also go by the name of Gaierhof, a name associated with pure excellence. On the slopes above Lavis, their success is based on a combination of territory, viticulture, winemaking and an undying passion for work in the rows. The decidedly matriarchal management team of Romina Togn and her sisters Martina and Valentina has come up with a traditional yet complete Trentino range, now including a classical Trento Riserva 2010, which immediately caught our attention, with its golden hue, compact yet clearly-defined aromas dominated by apple, and a juicy, angular palate. Top of the line is the Marmoram, from teroldego and lagrein, with its compact garnet highlights and rounded layers of redcurrant preserve.

○ Trentino Nosiola '15	▼▼	3
● Trentino Sorni Rosso Marmoram '12	▼▼	3
● Trentino Sup. Pinot Nero '13	▼▼	3
○ Trentino Traminer '15	▼▼	3
○ Trento Brut Ris. '10	▼▼	5
○ Trentino Pinot Grigio '15	▼	3
● Trentino Pinot Nero '12	▽▽	3
● Trentino Pinot Nero Sup. '08	▽▽	3
○ Trentino Riesling '13	▽▽	3
● Trentino Sorni Rosso Marmoram '11	▽▽	3
● Trentino Sorni Rosso Marmoram '10	▽▽	3
● Trentino Sup. Pinot Nero '11	▽▽	3
○ Trentino Traminer '13	▽▽	3

Mezzacorona

VIA DEL TEROLDEGO, 1E
38016 MEZZOCORONA [TN]
TEL. +39 0461616399
www.mezzacorona.it

CELLAR SALES
PRE-BOOKED VISITS
ACCOMMODATION
ANNUAL PRODUCTION 48,000,000 bottles
HECTARES UNDER VINE 2800.00
SUSTAINABLE WINERY

Mezzacorona is a colossus among wine producers, with clear-headed strategies for Trentino cooperative wines. They have turned the business around in a matter of a few years, with two modern facilities in Sicily at Feudo Arancio in the south-west near Agrigento, and Villa Albius in the south-east near Ragusa. Theirs is a vast wine market, which now includes a role in the Chinese e-commerce portal Alibaba. It has not severed all its ties with Trentino, though, as its Teroldego Rotaliano and Trentodoc attest. The winery has an extensive range of priorities, producing technically flawless wines that provide excellent value for money. Flavio 2008 is a thoroughbred Trento, with an austere attitude, generous bubbly disposition, piquant and juicy, taking its place as one of the greats of its class. A fine Tre Bicchieri for Rotari and Mezzacorona alongside various sparklers and a range of territory-dedicated wines.

○ Trento Rotari Flavio Ris. '08	▼▼▼	5
● Nerofino '13	▼▼	4
● Teroldego Rotaliano '15	▼▼	4
● Teroldego Rotaliano Castel Firmian Ris. '13	▼▼	2*
○ Trentino Pinot Grigio Castel Firmian Ris. '14	▼▼	4
● Teroldego Rotaliano Nos Ris. '04	▽▽▽	5
○ Trento Rotari Flavio Ris. '07	▽▽▽	5
○ Trento Rotari Flavio Ris. '06	▽▽▽	5
● Teroldego Rotaliano Castel Firmian Ris. '12	▽▽	2*
● Teroldego Rotaliano Nos '09	▽▽	5
○ Trentino Pinot Grigio Castel Firmian '13	▽▽	3
● Trentino Pinot Nero Castel Firmian '12	▽▽	3
○ Trento Extra Brut AlpeRegis '09	▽▽	5

Casata Monfort

VIA CARLO SETTE, 21
38015 LAVIS [TN]
TEL. +39 0461246353
www.cantinemonfort.it

CELLAR SALES
PRE-BOOKED VISITS
ANNUAL PRODUCTION 170,000 bottles
HECTARES UNDER VINE 40.00
SUSTAINABLE WINERY

Young Federico Simoni has very much taken over the reins at this family winery, following the traditions of his parents and focusing on making Casata Monfort wines even more appealing. He has proved to have a great knack, diversifying the selections to fit the various commercial strategies and marketplaces. His vast range of wines includes the fascinating Maso Cantanghel selection, named after an Austro-Hungarian fort which once protected the Valsugana side of Trento city and is now surrounded by vineyards. Here, Federico and his staff focus on pinot nero as well as on less common varieties, in a bid to preserve Trentino's winemaking traditions. The best performer of the year is without doubt the Pinot Nero 2012. Fragrant and traditional, from organic grapes, it has a well-balanced fruit profile of currants, a unique resin stamp, and a pleasant integrity of flavour. Also very good was the Traminer 2015, with its vibrant spiciness and juicy palate.

● Trentino Pinot Nero V. Cantanghel '12	▼▼ 5
○ Sotsas '13	▼▼ 3
☉ Trentino Pinot Grigio Rosé '15	▼▼ 3
○ Trentino Traminer Aromatico '15	▼▼ 3
○ Trento Brut Monfort	▼▼ 4
☉ Trento Monfort Rosé	▼ 4
○ Blanc de Sers '13	♀♀ 3
● Pinot Nero '13	♀♀ 3
● San Lorenzo '14	♀♀ 2*
○ Trentino Gewürztraminer '14	♀♀ 3
○ Trentino Traminer Aromatico V. Caselle '12	♀♀ 3
○ Trento Brut Ris. '09	♀♀ 5
○ Trento Brut Ris. '08	♀♀ 5

Moser

FRAZ. GARDOLO DI MEZZO
VIA CASTEL DI GARDOLO, 5
38121 TRENTO
TEL. +39 0461990786
www.cantinemoser.com

CELLAR SALES
PRE-BOOKED VISITS
ACCOMMODATION
ANNUAL PRODUCTION 120,000 bottles
HECTARES UNDER VINE 17.00

The Moser name is hitting the cycling headlines once again with young Moreno, while his uncle and former world champion Francesco has long since swapped his saddle for a seat in a tractor, cultivating the attractive estate around Gardolo di Mezzo, on the hillside north of Trento. Francesco's children Carlo and Francesca run the winery there. In more ways than one, this is a spectacular estate, which even has its own cycling mini-museum, blending spokes and oak casks, wine glasses and cycling trophies. And what better way to toast those victories than the estate's fine wines, including its classic Trento! In the final sprint, the Moser sparkler pedigree shone through, with a complex, slightly youthful yet truly gratifying Rosé dominated by red berry fruit. The Teroldego 2013, from hillside grapes grown close to Trento, is holding its own. Other team members in the winery's peloton include the Müller Thurgau and the Moscato Giallo, both 2015 vintages.

● Teroldego '13	▼▼ 3
○ Trento Brut 51,151	▼▼ 5
☉ Trento Rosé '12	▼▼ 5
○ Gewürztraminer '14	▼ 3
○ Moscato Giallo '15	▼ 3
○ Müller Thurgau '15	▼ 3
○ 51,151 '10	♀♀ 5
● Lagrein Dea Mater '09	♀♀ 3
● Lagrein Deamater '05	♀♀ 3
○ Moscato Giallo '14	♀♀ 3
○ Riesling '12	♀♀ 3
○ Riesling '10	♀♀ 2*
○ Trento 51,151 '09	♀♀ 5

Opera Vitivinicola in Valdicembra

Fraz. Verla
via 3 Novembre, 8
38030 Giovo [TN]
Tel. +39 0461684302
www.operavaldicembra.it

CELLAR SALES
PRE-BOOKED VISITS
ANNUAL PRODUCTION 60,000 bottles
HECTARES UNDER VINE 15.00

This small winery soon proved to be a winner, initially competing with the area's top names and then topping the Trento podium, with a few decidedly breathtaking versions of Metodo Classico. This was a source of great pride for the vignerons, underlining the value of these characterful wines from the Valle di Cembra, a mountain area which has finally earned recognition as a heroic winemaking subzone. This all-spumante operation has a modern structure of stainless steel, glass and porphyry, which despite being a very hard rock is rather gentle on the vines, giving the wines character, and protecting the vineyards with its dry-stone walls. The Riserva 2009 is magnificent, golden with porphyry highlights, reflecting the minerality of the Valle di Cembra, where the grapes for this classical Trento ripen. Textured and savoury, with spicy notes, its true character is set to come to the fore in years to come. Alpine fragrance and firm structure distinguish the monovarietal pinot nero, Opera Blanc 2010.

○ Trento Nature Opera '10	♥♥ 5
○ Trento Nature Opera Ris. '09	♥♥ 5
○ Trento Brut Opera '11	♥♥ 5
○ Trento Opera Blanc '10	♥♥ 5
○ Trento Brut Dosaggio Zero Opera Ris. '08	♥♥♥ 7
○ Trento Brut Opera '09	♀♥ 5
⊙ Trento Brut Rosé Noir '09	♀♥ 5
○ Trento Nature '08	♀♥ 4
○ Trento Nature Opera '09	♀♥ 5

Pisoni

loc. Sarche
fraz. Pergolese di Lasino
via San Siro, 7a
0461 Madruzzo
Tel. +39 0461564106
www.pisoni.net

CELLAR SALES
PRE-BOOKED VISITS
ANNUAL PRODUCTION 23,500 bottles
HECTARES UNDER VINE 16.00

A winemaking family for nearly two centuries, after agricultural college in San Michele all'Adige, they put their studies to use on the land, specialising in viticulture, cultivating the soil, vinifying the grapes, and distilling the pomace into traditional grappa. This close-knit family has a broad range of oenological skills. Marco and Stefano tend the vines with biodynamic methods, while their siblings and cousins run the cellar, the distillery and the special sparkler facility. Although the winery makes a complete range of wines, their pride and joy is the rare Vino Santo Trentino, a Pisoni family icon. The Trento Riserva 80 Mesi 2008 is truly stunning: layered, mature, with great aromatic weight and prickle, this is a full-flavoured, sound wine. The light-bodied Nature 2012 may be lively yet it has great poise, a good nose, and a forthright mouth with balanced acidity.

○ Trento Extra Brut 80 Mesi Ris. '08	♥♥ 5
○ Nosiola '15	♥♥ 2*
○ Trentino Vino Santo '02	♥♥ 6
○ Trento Brut Nature '12	♥♥ 4
⊙ Trento Rosé '12	♥♥ 5
● Reboro '12	♥ 4
○ Trentino Vino Santo '98	♀♀♀ 6
● Sarica Rosso '11	♀♥ 4
○ Trentino Vino Santo '01	♀♥ 6
○ Trentino Vino Santo '00	♀♥ 6
○ Trento Brut Nature '11	♀♥ 4
○ Trento Extra Brut '10	♀♥ 5
○ Trento Extra Brut 80 Mesi Ris. '07	♀♥ 5
○ Trento Extra Brut Ris. '08	♀♥ 5

Pojer & Sandri

LOC. MOLINI, 4
38010 FAEDO [TN]
TEL. +39 0461650342
www.pojeresandri.it

CELLAR SALES
PRE-BOOKED VISITS
ACCOMMODATION
ANNUAL PRODUCTION 200,000 bottles
HECTARES UNDER VINE 32.00
VITICULTURE METHOD Certified Organic

A tireless yet histrionic duo, who seek to capture the essence of grapes brought to them by growers, so as to transform them into equally remarkable wines. After over 40 vintages, with the help of the next generation and the entry into production of the new high-altitude vineyards in the nearby Cembra valley, this Faedo winery's prestige remains intact. This is due in no small part to its innovations, aiming to create new wines using grapes from nterspecific, naturally disease-resistant vines, and experimentation with grappas and special vinegars. The Pojer & Sandri sparklers are in their own league: whether resting on the lees or, like the Cuvée Rosé, a blend of the 2011 and 2012 vintages, the philosophy remains the same, with experimentation in both cellar and vineyard. Capturing the feel in just a few words is no mean feat. All the products have an intense, enfolding character, and the quality is well expressed by the grid.

● Pinot Nero Rodel Pianezzi '13	♟♟ 5	
☉ Spumante Rosé Cuvée 11-12	♟♟ 5	
○ Bianco Faye '12	♟♟ 5	
○ Chardonnay '15	♟♟ 3	
● Merlino	♟♟ 5	
○ Müller Thurgau Palai '15	♟♟ 3	
○ Traminer '15	♟♟ 4	
○ Bianco Faye '08	♟♟♟ 5	
○ Bianco Faye '01	♟♟♟ 5	
● Pinot Nero Rodel Pianezzi '09	♟♟♟ 5	
● Rosso Faye '05	♟♟♟ 5	
● Rosso Faye '00	♟♟♟ 5	
○ Palai '14	♟♟ 3*	
● Rosso Faye '11	♟♟ 6	

Pravis

LOC. LE BIOLCHE, 1
0461 MADRUZZO
TEL. +39 0461564305
www.pravis.it

CELLAR SALES
PRE-BOOKED VISITS
ANNUAL PRODUCTION 200,000 bottles
HECTARES UNDER VINE 32.00

The area is full of attractions: Castel Madruzzo, vineyards that cadence the landscape against a backdrop of the Brenta Dolomites and the myriad of lakes leading down to Garda. A pleasant area, caressed by the golden breeze which blows up from Garda, ensuring the perfect diurnal temperature range for the maturation of the grapes. Pravis' trio of owners have never sought to flaunt their winemaking prowess. They cultivate small fields, with tidy rows of negligible environmental impact. The next generation is following in their footsteps, with Alessio Chistè among the vines, Erika and Giulia Pedrini in the cellar, making remarkably simple wines of great significance. The matchless Fratagranda 2012, one of Trentino's best reds, plays on spicy aromas, with a resolute palate and a lush finish. After laying down it should evolve well. The other house red, Syrae 2013, is elegant, almost austere, with notes of spices and sandalwood. The best of the whites is the Cros del Mont 2015.

● Fratagranda '12	♟♟ 4	
● Syrae '13	♟♟ 4	
○ Kerner '15	♟♟ 2*	
○ Müller Thurgau St. Thomà '15	♟♟ 2*	
○ Sauvignon Teramara '15	♟♟ 3	
○ Traminer Cros del Mont '15	♟♟ 4	
● Fratagranda '10	♟♟♟ 4*	
● Fratagranda '07	♟♟♟ 4	
○ Vino Santo Arèle '06	♟♟♟ 6	
○ l'Ora '12	♟♟ 4	
● Madruzzo '12	♟♟ 3	
○ Stravino di Stravino '12	♟♟ 4	
○ Stravino di Stravino '11	♟♟ 4	
● Syrae '12	♟♟ 4	

Revì

VIA FLORIDA, 10
38060 ALDENO [TN]
TEL. +39 0461843155
www.revispumanti.com

CELLAR SALES
PRE-BOOKED VISITS
ANNUAL PRODUCTION 20,000 bottles
HECTARES UNDER VINE 1.70
VITICULTURE METHOD Certified Organic

Revì's fab four, or how a tiny family-run winery manages to come up with a winning range of Trentos. Years of constant oenological dedication from Paolo Malfer who founded the winery back in 1982, are paying dividends under the next generation, especially young Giacomo, an inspired sparkler master with a degree in marketing. The name Revì indicates the area where the grapes were destined to be made into the king's wine. The caressingly silky Dosaggio Zero 2012, from chardonnay, with its honeyed tones and a particularly lingering prickle, shows all the crunchiness of apples and freshly baked bread, well balanced by an elegant richness of flavour, while the greenish Brut 2011 has a racy, typically Trentino fragrance. The Cavaliere Nero 2009, from pinot nero, looks set to improve with time. No less impressive is the highly drinkable, approachable Rosé.

Cantina Rotaliana

VIA TRENTO, 65B
38017 MEZZOLOMBARDO [TN]
TEL. +39 0461601010
www.cantinarotaliana.it

CELLAR SALES
PRE-BOOKED VISITS
ANNUAL PRODUCTION 1,000,000 bottles
HECTARES UNDER VINE 330.00
SUSTAINABLE WINERY

The town of Mezzolombardo lies in an area of high vine density, almost exclusively planted to teroldego, a native cultivar which gives its name to a fine wine. Teroldego was first mentioned in the mid-1300s, and for the last century or so has characterized the lush countryside around Campo Rotaliano, where the Noce and Adige rivers meet. This successful cooperative, Rotaliana through and through, is inextricably linked with the subzone's geology, climate and traditions. Its flagship wine is Teroldego, in several versions, alongside various white grape selections and, last but not least, a Trento with attitude. The Redor 08 remains a classy wine, from chardonnay and pinot nero. The flagship grape for this subzone and winery remains teroldego, which has produced the fine Clesurae, Riserva and Etichetta Rossa. The Clesurae is well-structured, its oak needing just to offset the tannins. The Riserva 2013 is harmonious, while the Etichetta Rossa 2015 is easy-going and engaging.

○ Trento Brut '11	♈♈ 4
○ Trento Dosaggio Zero '12	♈♈ 5
○ Trento Extra Brut Cavaliere Nero '09	♈♈ 5
☉ Trento Rosé '12	♈♈ 5
○ Trento Brut Revì '09	♀♀ 4
○ Trento Brut Revì Mill. '10	♀♀ 4
○ Trento Brut Revì '11	♀♀ 4
○ Trento Dosaggio Zero Revì '10	♀♀ 5
○ Trento Dosaggio Zero Revì '09	♀♀ 5
○ Trento Extra Brut Bio Revì Paladino '09	♀♀ 7
○ Trento Extra Brut Paladino '10	♀♀ 7
○ Trento Revì Brut Mill. '08	♀♀ 4
☉ Trento Rosé Revì '11	♀♀ 5
☉ Trento Rosé Revì '09	♀♀ 5

● Teroldego Rotaliano Clesurae '13	♈♈ 6
● Teroldego Rotaliano Et. Rossa '15	♈♈ 3
● Teroldego Rotaliano Sup. Ris. '13	♈♈ 4
○ Trento Brut Redor Ris. '08	♈♈ 5
○ Trentino Pinot Bianco '15	♀ 2
○ Trentino Pinot Grigio '15	♀ 2
● Teroldego Rotaliano Clesurae '06	♀♀♀ 5
● Teroldego Rotaliano Clesurae '02	♀♀♀ 5
● Teroldego Rotaliano Ris. '04	♀♀♀ 3
● Teroldego Rotaliano Clesurae '12	♀♀ 6
● Teroldego Rotaliano Clesurae '11	♀♀ 6
● Teroldego Rotaliano Et. Rossa '14	♀♀ 2*
● Teroldego Rotaliano Ris. '11	♀♀ 4
○ Trento Brut Redor Ris. '07	♀♀ 5

★★Tenuta San Leonardo

FRAZ. BORGHETTO ALL'ADIGE
LOC. SAN LEONARDO
38060 AVIO [TN]
TEL. +39 0464689004
www.sanleonardo.it

CELLAR SALES
PRE-BOOKED VISITS
ANNUAL PRODUCTION 250,000 bottles
HECTARES UNDER VINE 34.00
SUSTAINABLE WINERY

Authoritative in all of its wines and a style so unmistakable as to make them unique. These are the wines of the Guerrieri Gonzaga, a noble dynasty who tirelessly tend the vines on their Borghetto d'Avio estate, on the Veneto border, in an effort to preserve the character of the local landscape. Vast woodland plots bedecked with new vineyards, exclusively planted to black grapes, grown organically throughout. The wines have something magical about them, reflecting the beauty and charm of their birthplace. Thus it is that Marchese Carlo and his son Anselmo reinforce their undisputed place as creators of fine wine, in Trentino and elsewhere. Harmony, complexity and texture. The magical caressing of a fine wine. For San Leonardo, 2011 was a marvellous vintage. The autumnal sensuality of the spicy fragrances is reminiscent of cigar leaf and woodland bark. The tannins are velvet-smooth, offset by perfect acidity. A decidedly polished wine, with no ifs or buts.

● San Leonardo '11	▼▼▼ 8
● Villa Gresti '11	▼▼ 5
● Terre di San Leonardo '13	▼▼ 3
○ Vette di San Leonardo '15	▼▼ 3
● Carmenère '07	♀♀♀ 8
● San Leonardo '10	♀♀♀ 7
● San Leonardo '08	♀♀♀ 7
● San Leonardo '07	♀♀♀ 7
● San Leonardo '06	♀♀♀ 7
● San Leonardo '05	♀♀♀ 7
● San Leonardo '04	♀♀♀ 7
● San Leonardo '03	♀♀♀ 7
● San Leonardo '01	♀♀♀ 7
● Villa Gresti '03	♀♀♀ 6

Toblino

FRAZ. SARCHE
VIA LONGA, 1
0461 MADRUZZO
TEL. +39 0461564168
www.toblino.it

CELLAR SALES
PRE-BOOKED VISITS
RESTAURANT SERVICE
ANNUAL PRODUCTION 400,000 bottles
HECTARES UNDER VINE 700.00
VITICULTURE METHOD Certified Organic

It was perhaps the first cooperative winery to involve all 600 of its members in a fully organic viticulture project, founding the Valle dei Laghi Bio District, in partnership with the new municipality of Madruzzo and a number of local agri-food associations, in vineyards going from the valley floor towards Lake Garda up to the slopes of Mount Bondone, with rows at altitudes of almost 800 metres. Toblino, like the lake of the same name, enjoys a fine microclimate, which enables the clusters to be left on the vine until super-ripe, as well as giving excellent yields for Trentino sparklers. The range is complete, including Trentos and some wines from the new organic Valle dei Laghi district. The best of the Trentos is the Antares 2011, with its impeccably lively prickle and cosseting expressive depth. Traminer Aromatico and Chardonnay show a rustic charm combined with an pleasingly unusual aromatic profile featuring rose petals and alpine fruits.

○ Trentino Chardonnay Bio '15	▼▼ 2*
○ Trentino Traminer Aromatico Bio '15	▼▼ 2*
○ Trento Brut Antares '11	▼▼ 3
○ Manzoni Bianco Bio '15	▼ 2
○ Trentino Müller Thurgau '15	▼ 2
○ Trentino Nosiola '15	▼ 2
○ L'Ora '11	♀♀ 3
○ Largiller '07	♀♀ 3
○ Manzoni Bianco '13	♀♀ 2*
○ Moscato Giallo Bio '14	♀♀ 2*
○ Trentino Chardonnay '13	♀♀ 2*
○ Trentino Müller Thurgau '13	♀♀ 2*
○ Trentino Nosiola '13	♀♀ 2*
○ Trento Brut Antares '10	♀♀ 3

Vallarom

FRAZ. MASI, 21
38063 AVIO [TN]
TEL. +39 0464684297
www.vallarom.it

CELLAR SALES
PRE-BOOKED VISITS
ACCOMMODATION AND RESTAURANT SERVICE
ANNUAL PRODUCTION 45,000 bottles
HECTARES UNDER VINE 7.00
VITICULTURE METHOD Certified Organic
SUSTAINABLE WINERY

Avio has been a winegrowing area since time immemorial. Mentioned by monks in eighth-century documents, with its impervious rocky crags on the banks of the Adige, in lower Vallagarina, transformed into the Campi Sarni vineyards by centuries of back-breaking toil, Avio produces fascinatingly original wines. Barbara Mottini and Filippo Scienza's family has set out to restore the area to its former glory. With great patience and following the rules to the letter, they have completely transformed all of their plots to organic, using green building techniques to turn their farmhouse-cellar into a splendid agriturismo. A blend of cabernet, merlot and syrah, the distinctive Fuflus 2012 has a caressing, well-rounded charm. As tradition requires, the brisk, alcohol-rich, unusually deep Marzemino 2015 is a delicate wine. The Cabernet Sauvignon 2013 impressed, with an intensity and balance befitting a bordeaux.

● Cabernet Sauvignon Bio '13	♟♟ 3
○ Enantio '15	♟♟ 3
● Fuflus '12	♟♟ 4
● Trentino Marzemino Bio '15	♟♟ 3
○ Vo'	♟♟ 4
⊙ Vo' Rosé	♟ 4
● Campi Sarni Rosso '10	♟♟ 4
● Trentino Marzemino '14	♟♟ 3
● Trentino Marzemino '13	♟♟ 3
○ Vadum Caesaris '01	♟♟ 2
● Vallagarina Campi Sarni '11	♟♟ 4
● Vallagarina Pinot Nero '13	♟♟ 4
○ Vo' Dosaggio Zero '12	♟♟ 4
○ Vo' Dosaggio Zero '10	♟♟ 4

Roberto Zeni

FRAZ. GRUMO
VIA STRETTA, 2
38010 SAN MICHELE ALL'ADIGE [TN]
TEL. +39 0461650456
www.zeni.tn.it

CELLAR SALES
PRE-BOOKED VISITS
ANNUAL PRODUCTION 150,000 bottles
HECTARES UNDER VINE 14.00
VITICULTURE METHOD Certified Organic

Inspired by their insatiable curiosity, over nearly 50 years of viticulture, brothers Andrea and Roberto Zeni's oenological insights encouraged young Rudy to set up his own micro cellar at Maso Nero in the Lavis hills, the viticultural heart of this charming family-owned winery. Their main vineyards are on the banks of the Adige, close to the cellar, at Grumo. Growers and makers of sparkling wines, they have boosted the prestige of their many wines, all cultivated using organic methods in vineyards scattered across the valley floor and on steep hillsides, the exclusive domain of aromatic grapes and classic Trento varietals. Their Teroldego, the Pini 2012, has few rivals in terms of power, and has reclaimed its place as one of the leading wines in its class. Unusually intense with its dark yet brilliant hues, and its liquorice and wild berry nose, this textured wine shows ripe fruit and a leisurely finish. Almost as good is another Teroldego, the versatile, agile Ternet 2013.

● Teroldego Rotaliano Pini '12	♟♟♟ 6
● Teroldego Ternet Schwarzhof '13	♟♟ 5
○ Traminer Schwarzhof '15	♟♟ 4
○ Trentino Nosiola Palustella '15	♟♟ 2*
○ Trento Brut Nero Maso Ris. '10	♟♟ 5
○ Trento Dosaggio Zero Maso Nero '11	♟♟ 5
● Ternet Schwarzhof '10	♟♟♟ 5
● Teroldego Rotaliano Pini '09	♟♟♟ 6
○ Müller Thurgau Lecroci '14	♟♟ 2*
● Rossara Legiare '14	♟♟ 2*
● Teroldego Rotaliano Lealbere '13	♟♟ 3
● Teroldego Rotaliano Pini '10	♟♟ 6
● Teroldego Ternet Schwarzhof '12	♟♟ 5
○ Trento Brut Nero Maso Ris. '09	♟♟ 5

Cantina Aldeno

VIA ROMA, 76
38060 ALDENO [TN]
TEL. +39 0461842511
www.cantinaaldeno.com

CELLAR SALES
PRE-BOOKED VISITS
ANNUAL PRODUCTION 240,000 bottles
HECTARES UNDER VINE 340.00

● Teroldego '15	♟♟ 2*
● Trentino San Zeno Ris. '11	♟♟ 4
○ Trentino Traminer '15	♟♟ 2*
○ Trento Extra Brut Altinum '10	♟♟ 5

Barone de Cles

VIA G. MAZZINI, 18
38017 MEZZOLOMBARDO [TN]
TEL. +39 0461601081
www.baronedecles.it

CELLAR SALES
PRE-BOOKED VISITS
ANNUAL PRODUCTION 80,000 bottles
HECTARES UNDER VINE 39.00

● Teroldego Rotaliano Cardinale '12	♟♟ 5
● Teroldego Rotaliano Maso Scari '13	♟♟ 3
● Teroldego Rotaliano Primo '14	♟ 3

Bolognani

VIA STAZIONE, 19
38015 LAVIS [TN]
TEL. +39 0461246354
www.bolognani.com

CELLAR SALES
PRE-BOOKED VISITS
ANNUAL PRODUCTION 70,000 bottles
HECTARES UNDER VINE 4.40

● Teroldego Armilo '14	♟♟ 3
○ Trentino Gewürztraminer Sanròc '14	♟♟ 3
○ Moscato Giallo '15	♟ 2
○ Sauvignon '15	♟ 3

Cantina Sociale di Trento

VIA DEI VITICOLTORI, 2/4
38123 VOLANO [TN]
TEL. +39 0461920186
www.cantinasocialetrento.it

CELLAR SALES
PRE-BOOKED VISITS
ANNUAL PRODUCTION 250,000 bottles
HECTARES UNDER VINE 50.00
SUSTAINABLE WINERY

● Trentino Heredia '13	♟♟ 3
● Trentino Merlot V. Novaline '13	♟♟ 4
○ Trento Brut Zell	♟♟ 5
○ Santacolomba Solaris '15	♟ 3

Cantina d'Isera

VIA AL PONTE, 1
38060 ISERA [TN]
TEL. +39 0464433795
www.cantinaisera.it

CELLAR SALES
PRE-BOOKED VISITS
ANNUAL PRODUCTION 500,000 bottles
HECTARES UNDER VINE 246.00
VITICULTURE METHOD Certified Organic

○ Sauvignon '15	♟♟ 3
● Trentino Marzemino Sup. Et. Verde '13	♟♟ 3
○ Trento Extra Brut	♟♟ 4
◉ Schiava Costa Felisa '15	♟ 4

Marco Donati

VIA CESARE BATTISTI, 41
38016 MEZZOCORONA [TN]
TEL. +39 0461604141
www.cantinadonatimarco.it

CELLAR SALES
PRE-BOOKED VISITS
ANNUAL PRODUCTION 100,000 bottles
HECTARES UNDER VINE 20.00
SUSTAINABLE WINERY

● Teroldego Rotaliano Sangue di Drago '13	♟♟ 5
● Teroldego Rotaliano Bagolari '14	♟ 4
● Trentino Marzemino Orme '15	♟ 3
○ Trentino Nosiola Sole Alto '15	♟ 3

Gaierhof

VIA IV NOVEMBRE, 51
38030 ROVERÉ DELLA LUNA [TN]
TEL. +39 0461658514
www.gaierhof.com

CELLAR SALES
PRE-BOOKED VISITS
ANNUAL PRODUCTION 500,000 bottles
HECTARES UNDER VINE 130.00

● Teroldego Rotaliano '14	♟♟ 2*
● Teroldego Rotaliano Sup. '13	♟♟ 3
○ Trento Brut Siris	♟♟ 4
○ Trentino Pinot Grigio '15	♟ 2

Bruno Grigolli

VIA SAN BERNARDINO,10
38065 MORI [TN]
TEL. +39 0464917368
www.grigollibruno.it

CELLAR SALES
ANNUAL PRODUCTION 13,000 bottles
HECTARES UNDER VINE 5.00

● Trentino Cabernet Germano '09	♟♟ 4
● Trentino Merlot Noal '10	♟♟ 6
⊙ Vallagarina Dumalis '13	♟ 5

Tenuta Maso Corno

LOC. VALBONA
38061 ALA [TN]
TEL. +39 0464421130
www.tenutamasocorno.it

PRE-BOOKED VISITS
ANNUAL PRODUCTION 10,000 bottles
HECTARES UNDER VINE 5.00

○ Trentino Chardonnay Villanova '13	♟♟ 6
● Trentino Pinot Nero Santa Maria '11	♟♟ 6
○ Trentino Sauvignon Declivi '13	♟ 4

Maso Grener

LOC. MASI DI PRESSANO
38015 LAVIS [TN]
TEL. +39 0461871514
www.masogrener.it

CELLAR SALES
PRE-BOOKED VISITS
ANNUAL PRODUCTION 18,000 bottles
HECTARES UNDER VINE 3.00

○ FP Chardonnay&Sauvignon '15	♟♟ 3
● Trentino Pinot Nero V. Bindesi '14	♟♟ 5
○ Trentino Sauvignon '15	♟ 4

Giuliano Micheletti

VIA E. CONCI, 74
38123 TRENTO
TEL. +39 3493306929
gm.limina@gmail.com

ANNUAL PRODUCTION 3,000 bottles
HECTARES UNDER VINE 3.00

● Merlot Limen '12	♟♟ 4
○ Riesling Limen '15	♟♟ 4

Mori - Colli Zugna

VIA DEL GARDA, 35
38065 MORI [TN]
TEL. +39 0464918154
www.cantinamoricollizugna.it

CELLAR SALES
PRE-BOOKED VISITS
ANNUAL PRODUCTION 220,000 bottles
HECTARES UNDER VINE 600.00

● Trentino Sup. Marzemino Terra di San Mauro '14	♟♟ 3
○ Trentino Traminer Pendici del Baldo '15	♟♟ 2*
○ Trento Brut Morus Ris. '12	♟♟ 5

Pedrotti Spumanti

VIA ROMA, 2A
38060 NOMI [TN]
TEL. +39 0464835111
www.predottispumanti.it

CELLAR SALES
ANNUAL PRODUCTION 30,000 bottles
HECTARES UNDER VINE 3.00
SUSTAINABLE WINERY

○ Trento Pas Dosé Ris. 111 '09	♟♟	6
⊙ Trento Brut Rosé Pedrotti '12	♟♟	5
○ Trento Dosaggio Zero Bouquet	♟♟	4
○ Trento Brut Bouquet	♟	4

Pelz

LOC. CAVADE, 3
38034 CEMBRA [TN]
TEL. +39 0461683051
www.cantinapelz.com

CELLAR SALES
PRE-BOOKED VISITS
ANNUAL PRODUCTION 28,000 bottles
HECTARES UNDER VINE 10.20

○ Müller Thurgau '15	♟♟	4
○ Riesling Dieci Vendemmie	♟♟	4
○ Trentino Riesling '13	♟♟	4
○ Trento Pas Dosé 3.Tre '12	♟	5

Riva del Garda

LOC. SAN NAZZARO, 4
38066 RIVA DEL GARDA [TN]
TEL. +39 0464552133
www.agririva.it

CELLAR SALES
PRE-BOOKED VISITS
ANNUAL PRODUCTION 250,000 bottles
HECTARES UNDER VINE 280.00

● Maso Lizzone '14	♟♟	3
● Teroldego Rivaldego '15	♟♟	2*
○ Trento Brut BrezzaRiva	♟♟	3
● Trentino Pinot Nero Maso Elesi '14	♟	4

Cantina Sociale Roverè della Luna

VIA IV NOVEMBRE, 9
38030 ROVERÈ DELLA LUNA [TN]
TEL. +39 0461658530
www.csrovere1919.it

CELLAR SALES
ANNUAL PRODUCTION 100,000 bottles
HECTARES UNDER VINE 420.00

○ Trento Brut Vervè '12	♟♟	4
● Trentino Lagrein '13	♟	2
○ Trentino Pinot Grigio '15	♟	2
○ Trentino Traminer V. Winchel '13	♟	4

Arcangelo Sandri

VIA VANEGGE, 4A
38010 FAEDO [TN]
TEL. +39 0461650935
www.arcangelosandri.it

CELLAR SALES
PRE-BOOKED VISITS
ANNUAL PRODUCTION 22,000 bottles
HECTARES UNDER VINE 3.00

● Trentino Lagrein Capòr '12	♟♟	3
○ Trentino Müller Thurgau Cosler '15	♟♟	2*
○ Trentino Traminer Razer '15	♟	2

Armando Simoncelli

VIA NAVICELLO, 7
38068 ROVERETO [TN]
TEL. +39 0464432373
www.simoncelli.it

CELLAR SALES
PRE-BOOKED VISITS
ANNUAL PRODUCTION 90,000 bottles
HECTARES UNDER VINE 10.50

● Trentino Marzemino '15	♟♟	4
○ Trentino Pinot Bianco '15	♟♟	4
● Trentino Cabernet Franc '13	♟	4

Enrico Spagnolli

VIA G. B. ROSINA, 4A
38060 ISERA [TN]
TEL. +39 0464409054
www.vinispagnolli.it

CELLAR SALES
PRE-BOOKED VISITS
ANNUAL PRODUCTION 85,000 bottles
HECTARES UNDER VINE 18.00

● Tebro '09	♟♟ 3
● Trentino Marzemino '14	♟♟ 2*
○ Trentino Moscato Giallo '15	♟♟ 2*
○ Vallagarina Riesling '15	♟ 2

Marco Tonini

LOC. FOLASO
VIA ROSMINI, 8
38060 ISERA [TN]
TEL. +39 3404991043

CELLAR SALES
PRE-BOOKED VISITS
ANNUAL PRODUCTION 8,000 bottles
HECTARES UNDER VINE 4.00

● Trentino Marzemino '14	♟♟ 4
○ Trento Brut '13	♟♟ 5

Villa Corniole

FRAZ. VERLA
VIA AL GREC', 23
38030 GIOVO [TN]
TEL. +39 0461695067
www.villacorniole.com

CELLAR SALES
PRE-BOOKED VISITS
ANNUAL PRODUCTION 60,000 bottles
HECTARES UNDER VINE 4.00
SUSTAINABLE WINERY

● Teroldego Rotaliano 7 Pergole '11	♟♟ 5
○ Trentino Müller Thurgau Petramontis '15	♟♟ 3
○ Trento Brut Salisa '12	♟♟ 5
○ Trento Dosaggio Zero Salisa '12	♟♟ 5

Vivallis

VIA PER BRANCOLINO, 4
38068 NOGAREDO [TN]
TEL. +39 0464834113
www.vivallis.it

CELLAR SALES
PRE-BOOKED VISITS
ANNUAL PRODUCTION 1,000,000 bottles
HECTARES UNDER VINE 730.00
VITICULTURE METHOD Certified Organic

○ Trentino Moscato Giallo Castel Beseno '15	♟♟ 4
● Trentino Sup. Marzemino '14	♟♟ 4
○ Trento Valentini di Weinfeld	♟♟ 5
● Vallagarina Suseya '13	♟ 3

Luigi Zanini

VIA DE GASPERI, 42
38017 MEZZOLOMBARDO [TN]
TEL. +39 0461601496
www.zaniniluigi.com

CELLAR SALES
PRE-BOOKED VISITS
ANNUAL PRODUCTION 90,000 bottles
HECTARES UNDER VINE 5.00

● Teroldego Rotaliano '15	♟♟ 2*
● Teroldego Rotaliano Le Cervare '14	♟♟ 3
○ Trentino Chardonnay '15	♟ 2
● Trentino Lagrein '15	♟ 3

Zanotelli

V.LE 4 NOVEMBRE, 52
38034 CEMBRA [TN]
TEL. +39 0461683131
www.zanotelliwines.com

CELLAR SALES
PRE-BOOKED VISITS
ANNUAL PRODUCTION 40,000 bottles
HECTARES UNDER VINE 11.00

○ Kerner Le Strope '15	♟♟ 4
○ Trentino Müller Thurgau '15	♟♟ 4
○ Trentino Riesling Le Strope '13	♟♟ 4
○ Trento Brut Forneri '12	♟♟ 5

ALTO ADIGE

There is a general notion that winemaking Alto Adige, as a district, offers a high standard of quality wines across the board. The numbers say that this notion is fairly accurate. Increasingly, however, the careful reader will grasp the nuances that each subzone is able to offer in the quest for the perfect balance of vines, winegrowing areas, and the winemaker's touch. Wineries, however, are very different from one another, with large cooperatives coexisting with smaller-scale vignerons, and with venerable Tyrol wine families, owners with extensive vineyard estates and equally extensive network of contributing growers. More and more cellars are specializing in wines that are a more precise expression of their terroir, as can be seen in true quality wine country like the Valle Isarco, a narrow valley that closes in to the north and enhances the fragrance and depth of Sylvaner, Riesling and Veltliner. Fleshy, refined Pinot Neros come from the eastern slope of Oltradige, and here Mazzon represents the true Italian Grand Cru for this grape variety. Then for the texture and class that distinguish Pinot Bianco we look to the areas of Appiano and Terlano. The region has a strong tradition for whites and all the wineries listed in IW make stunning versions, often with a Tre Bicchieri next to the name, or at least shining examples of the class that the growing area affords its wines. Of the 27 Alto Adige wines on the podium, no less than 20 are white, with Gewürztraminer and Sylvaner to the fore. These are varietals that show their full potential in well-defined areas along the hilly strip that stretches from Magrè to Caldaro for the former, and the Isarco Valley for the latter. A map of award-winning wines here will embrace the entire district, playing with altitude, aspecting and soils, allowing makers to emphasize features that on the surface may seem to be in contrast: the power of Lagreins from the Bolzano plain; the finesse of Val Venosta mountain Rieslings; the flavoursome, intriguing lightness of Lago di Caldaros and Santa Maddalenas; the depth of Terlaners. Last but not least, we should keep an eye out for the increasing number of stellar wines made in minute quantities: Cantina di Terlano's Terlaner I Grande Cuvée, Colterenzio's LR, and San Michele Appiano's Appius have opened a path now imitated by the labels of many wineries who have decided to challenge the big boys worldwide.

★Abbazia di Novacella

FRAZ. NOVACELLA
VIA DELL'ABBAZIA, 1
39040 VARNA/VAHRN [BZ]
TEL. +39 0472836189
www.abbazianovacella.it

CELLAR SALES
PRE-BOOKED VISITS
RESTAURANT SERVICE
ANNUAL PRODUCTION 650,000 bottles
HECTARES UNDER VINE 20.00

Valle Isarco is one of the emerging areas of
Alto Adige, with vineyards lying almost
exclusively high in the hills and climactic
conditions that exalt aroma and grip in its
wines. In the centre of the valley we find
Abbazia di Novacella, part of the complex of
the Abbazia dei Canonici Agostiniani, an
operation with around 20 hectares
distributed above all in the valley but also in
more southern areas of the province, such
as the Piana di Bolzano and Oltradige. The
winery's best labels nevertheless hark from
the northern zone, starting with an excellent
Sylvaner Praepositus, which exploited the
benefits of the 2015 growing year to the
full. Focused floral and citrus aromas on
the nose pave the way for great austerity
and length in the mouth, which gains in
elegance with ageing. The leaner
Riesling 2014 from the same line shows
an attractively clean finish.

Tenuta Baron Di Pauli

VIA CANTINE, 12
39052 CALDARO/KALTERN [BZ]
TEL. +39 0471963696
www.barondipauli.com

CELLAR SALES
PRE-BOOKED VISITS
ANNUAL PRODUCTION 46,000 bottles
HECTARES UNDER VINE 15.00

Baron di Pauli is located in the territory of
Oltradige, the area around Lake Caldaro,
whose aspects and altitudes allow grapes
to ripen gradually and consistently. Their
two vineyards, covering a total of a dozen
hectares, are at Arzenhof near Caldaro, and
Höfl unterm Stein at Söll. In the cellar,
production processes ensure the utmost
respect for the quality of the grapes, and
the wines are released only after judicious
ageing. The warmth of the area overlooking
the lake allowed the grapes of cabernet
and merlot to ripen to perfection, giving
Arzio a fruit-driven nose, developed on a
rich, almost dense palate, sustained by
focused, silky tannins. Enosi, a blend of
riesling, sauvignon and pinot bianco, boasts
rich flavour and harmony on a palate of
impressive length. The Lagrein Carano is
firm, crisp and beautifully taut.

○ A. A. Valle Isarco Sylvaner Praepositus '15	♛♛♛ 4*
○ A. A. Valle Isarco Grüner Veltliner Praepositus '14	♛♛ 3*
○ A. A. Valle Isarco Riesling Praepositus '14	♛♛ 4
● A. A. Pinot Nero Praepositus Ris. '12	♛♛ 4
○ A. A. Valle Isarco Gewürztraminer Praepositus '15	♛♛ 4
○ A. A. Valle Isarco Grüner Veltliner '15	♛♛ 3
○ A. A. Valle Isarco Kerner '15	♛♛ 3
○ A. A. Valle Isarco Kerner Praepositus '15	♛♛ 4
○ A. A. Valle Isarco Müller Thurgau '15	♛♛ 3
○ A. A. Valle Isarco Pinot Grigio '15	♛♛ 3
○ A. A. Valle Isarco Sylvaner '15	♛♛ 3
○ A. A. Valle Isarco Riesling Praepositus '13	♛♛♛ 4*
○ A. A. Valle Isarco Sylvaner Praepositus '12	♛♛♛ 4*
○ A. A. Valle Isarco Sylvaner Praepositus '11	♛♛♛ 4*
○ A. A. Valle Isarco Veltliner Praepositus '12	♛♛♛ 3

● A. A. Lagrein Carano Ris. '13	♛♛ 5
● A. A. Merlot - Cabernet Arzio '12	♛♛ 6
○ A. A. Sauvignon Kinesis '15	♛♛ 3
○ Enosi '14	♛♛ 3
○ A. A. Gewürztraminer Elix '15	♛ 6
○ A. A. Gewürztraminer Exilissi '12	♛ 6
● A. A. Lago di Caldaro Cl. Sup. Kalkofen '15	♛ 3
○ A. A. Riesling Dynamis '15	♛ 3
● A. A. Arzio Merlot Cabernet '11	♕♕ 6
● A. A. Carano Lagrein Ris. '12	♕♕ 5
○ A. A. Gewürztraminer Exilissi '11	♕♕ 6
○ A. A. Gewürztraminer Exilissi '09	♕♕ 6
● A. A. Lago di Caldaro Cl. Sup. Kalkofen '13	♕♕ 3*
● A. A. Lago di Caldaro Cl. Sup. Kalkofen '10	♕♕ 3
○ Enosi '13	♕♕ 3

Baron Widmann

ENDERGASSE, 3
39040 CORTACCIA/KURTATSCH [BZ]
TEL. +39 0471880092
www.baron-widmann.it

CELLAR SALES
PRE-BOOKED VISITS
ANNUAL PRODUCTION 35,000 bottles
HECTARES UNDER VINE 15.00

The Widmann family's winery is one of the area's historic operations, with vineyards covering 15 hectares in Bassa Atesina. The operation is based near Cortaccia, and on its low hillside plots, near the farm at Auhof, we find schiava and Bordeaux red grape varieties. For the white varieties we instead need to climb to 600 metres to the Sulzhof estate at Penon, where the cooler climate allows grapes to ripen without sacrificing aroma. We saw a fine performance from the Gewürztraminer, which despite the complicated 2014 growing year, showed a wonderfully intense nose, with classic aromas of tropical fruit and flowers swathed in attractive mineral notes, over a generous palate with zesty acidity. The pleasurable Weiss, a blend of chardonnay, petit manseng and pinot bianco, shows a well-rounded palate.

○ A. A. Gewürztraminer '14	♟♟	3
○ Weiss '15	♟♟	3
● A. A. Schiava '15	♟	3
● A. A. Cabernet Feld '91	♟♟♟	4*
● A. A. Cabernet-Merlot Auhof '97	♟♟♟	4*
● A. A. Merlot '93	♟♟♟	4*
○ Weiss '11	♟♟♟	5
○ A. A. Gewürztraminer '13	♟♟	3
○ A. A. Gewürztraminer '12	♟♟	3
○ A. A. Sauvignon '12	♟♟	3
● A. A. Schiava '14	♟♟	3
● A. A. Schiava '12	♟♟	3
○ Weiss '14	♟♟	3
○ Weiss '13	♟♟	3*
○ Weiss '12	♟♟	5

★★Cantina Bolzano

P.ZZA GRIES, 2
39100 BOLZANO/BOZEN
TEL. +39 0471270909
www.cantinabolzano.com

CELLAR SALES
PRE-BOOKED VISITS
ANNUAL PRODUCTION 3,000,000 bottles
HECTARES UNDER VINE 350.00
SUSTAINABLE WINERY

Over the years, we have seen some of the cooperative wineries in Alto Adige merge. A case in point can be found in the heart of Bolzano, with the wineries of Gries and Santa Maddalena, which came together around 15 years ago under the supervision of Stephan Filippi. Today, the operation boasts over 300 hectares under vine in all the main production zones. The winery style pursues fullness and varietal expression. Once again, the winery's champion was the Lagrein Taber, a wine that took advantage of the cooler growing year to benefit in terms of tautness and length, losing some of the exuberant tannins of previous versions and gaining in elegance and style. We were bowled over by the Gewürztraminer Kleinstein, which, from a winery renowned for its reds, gave a spectacular performance, with an intense nose of citrus and tropical fruit over a rich, full-flavoured palate.

● A. A. Lagrein Taber Ris. '14	♟♟♟	6
○ A. A. Gewürztraminer Kleinstein '15	♟♟	5
● A. A. Santa Maddalena Cl. Huck am Bach '15	♟♟	2*
● A. A. Cabernet Mumelter Ris. '14	♟♟	6
○ A. A. Chardonnay Ris. '13	♟♟	5
○ A. A. Lagrein - Merlot Mauritius '14	♟♟	5
● A. A. Lagrein Prestige Line Ris. '14	♟♟	4
○ A. A. Moscato Giallo Passito Vinalia '14	♟♟	3
○ A. A. Pinot Bianco Dellago '15	♟♟	4
● A. A. Pinot Nero Ris. '14	♟♟	5
○ A. A. Sauvignon Mock '15	♟♟	4
● A. A. Lagrein Taber Ris. '13	♟♟♟	6
● A. A. Lagrein Taber Ris. '12	♟♟♟	6
● A. A. Lagrein Taber Ris. '11	♟♟♟	6
● A. A. Lagrein Taber Ris. '10	♟♟♟	6

ALTO ADIGE

Josef Brigl

LOC. SAN MICHELE APPIANO
VIA MADONNA DEL RIPOSO, 3
39057 APPIANO/EPPAN [BZ]
TEL. +39 0471662419
www.brigl.com

CELLAR SALES
PRE-BOOKED VISITS
ANNUAL PRODUCTION 1,000,000 bottles
HECTARES UNDER VINE 50.00
SUSTAINABLE WINERY

There are many types of wineries in Alto
Adige, from cooperatives to small growers
and centuries-old operations with
impressive production figures. The latter
category includes Brigl, since time
immemorial an interpreter of the wines of
this region. For its raw materials, the estate
relies on 50 hectares of excellently-
aspected vineyards, supplemented by
grapes from a network of local growers. We
saw an excellent performance from the
Gewürztraminer Windegg, a white from
grapes at the Caldaro vineyard, which lies
at an elevation of 400 metres on clay and
limestone soil. The excellent 2015 growing
year resulted in an intense nose of citrus,
liquorice and spice, and a rich palate
underpinned by full flavour. We also liked
the varietal Riesling and Sauvignon, which
showed harmony and impressive focus on
the palate.

★Cantina di Caldaro

VIA CANTINE, 12
39052 CALDARO/KALTERN [BZ]
TEL. +39 0471963149
www.kellereikaltern.com

CELLAR SALES
PRE-BOOKED VISITS
ANNUAL PRODUCTION 2,000,000 bottles
HECTARES UNDER VINE 300.00

The longstanding cooperative in Caldaro
has for some time been one of the largest in
the territory, and is a superb interpreter of
Oltradige's wines, particularly those of Lake
Caldaro, the winery's heart and soul. It is
here that we find most of its 300-plus
hectares of vineyards farmed by 400
grower-members, giving wines with an
impressive sense of place year after year.
The winery's performance this year was just
short of perfect, with a range of wines
focusing once again on Schiava, as seen in
an excellent version of the Lago di Caldaro
Pfarrhof, with its fresh, elegant nose of
forest fruits interlaced with spice and floral
hints, over a firm, harmonious palate. The
Cabernet version is as always one of the
district's best, and shows a layered nose
and a combination of power and suppleness
on the palate. The Passito Serenade is an
example of harmony and finesse.

○ A. A. Gewürztraminer Windegg '15	♟♟ 3*
● A. A. Lagrein Briglhof Ris. '13	♟♟ 5
● A. A. Merlot Windegg Ris. '13	♟♟ 3
○ A. A. Pinot Bianco Haselhof '15	♟♟ 3
○ A. A. Riesling '15	♟♟ 3
○ A. A. Sauvignon '15	♟♟ 3
● A. A. Pinot Nero Briglhof Ris. '13	♟ 5
○ A. A. Pinot Grigio Windegg '11	♟♟♟ 3*
● A. A. Lagrein Briglhof '11	♟♟ 5
● A. A. Lagrein Kaltenburg '11	♟♟ 5
● A. A. Merlot Windegg '12	♟♟ 3
○ A. A. Pinot Bianco Haselhof '14	♟♟ 2*
● A. A. Pinot Nero Briglhof '12	♟♟ 5
● A. A. Schiava Grigia Kaltenburg '14	♟♟ 3

● A. A. Cabernet Sauvignon Pfarrhof Ris. '15	♟♟ 6
● A. A. Lago di Caldaro Scelto Cl. Sup. Pfarrhof '15	♟♟ 3*
○ A. A. Moscato Giallo Passito Serenade '13	♟♟ 6
● A. A. Cabernet Sauvignon Campaner Ris. '13	♟♟ 4
● A. A. Lagrein Solos '14	♟♟ 6
○ A. A. Pinot Bianco Hofstatt '15	♟♟ 2*
○ A. A. Pinot Grigio Söll '15	♟♟ 3
○ A. A. Sauvignon Castel Giovanelli '14	♟♟ 5
○ A. A. Sauvignon Premstaler '15	♟♟ 3
○ A. A. Kerner Carned '15	♟ 3
○ A. A. Pinot Bianco Vial '15	♟ 3
● A. A. Pinot Nero Saltner '14	♟ 4
● A. A. Lago di Caldaro Scelto Cl. Sup. Pfarrhof '13	♟♟♟ 3*

Castel Sallegg

V.LO DI SOTTO, 15
39052 CALDARO/KALTERN [BZ]
TEL. +39 0471963132
www.castelsallegg.it

CELLAR SALES
PRE-BOOKED VISITS
ANNUAL PRODUCTION 120,000 bottles
HECTARES UNDER VINE 30.00

From Piazzetta Rottemburg in the heart of the small town of Caldaro, visitors can admire a walled vineyard climbing up towards the castle. On either side of the short path running through it to the courtyard of the castle owned by the aristocratic Kuenburg family, they can enjoy a panoramic view of all the varieties grown in Alto Adige. The most important vineyards, at Preyhof, Leisenhof and Seehofare, lie around Lake Caldaro, and are planted to the region's main varieties. The historic Bischofsleiten vineyard gave us a fragrant, spicy Lago di Caldaro. While lacking great structure and power, it was deservedly awarded top honours thanks to its grip and elegant drinkability. We also loved the Cabernet Riserva 2013, which exploits the sun-kissed slopes where the grapes grow to forge a nose of rich red berry fruit and fines herbes over a firm, harmonious palate.

● A. A. Lago di Caldaro Scelto Sup. Bischofsleiten '15	♈♈♈	2*
● A. A. Cabernet Sauvignon Ris. '13	♈♈	3*
○ A. A. Bianco Cuvée Ars Lyrica '14	♈♈	3
○ A. A. Gewürztraminer '15	♈♈	3
○ A. A. Pinot Bianco '15	♈♈	3
○ A. A. Pinot Bianco Pratum '14	♈♈	3
● A. A. Pinot Nero '14	♈♈	3
● A. A. Merlot Nussleiten '12	♈	6
○ A. A. Pinot Grigio '15	♈	3
○ A. A. Sauvignon '15	♈	3
● A. A. Cabernet Sauvignon Ris. '11	♀♀	3
● A. A. Lago di Caldaro Scelto Bischofsleiten '14	♀♀	2*
☉ A. A. Moscato Rosa Passito '12	♀♀	6
○ A. A. Terlano Pinot Bianco Pratum '13	♀♀	3*

Castelfeder

VIA PORTICI, 11
39040 EGNA/NEUMARKT [BZ]
TEL. +39 0471820420
www.castelfeder.it

CELLAR SALES
PRE-BOOKED VISITS
ANNUAL PRODUCTION 400,000 bottles
HECTARES UNDER VINE 20.00

The reputation of Bassa Atesina is somewhat mixed, due to unexciting wines, often from vineyards on the valley floor, alternating with undisputed peaks of excellence, originating from some of the highest vineyards in the district. The Giovannet family is one of the best interpreters of the area, and relies on a vineyard covering around 20 hectares, supplemented by the grapes provided by a large network of local growers. The vineyards lie at elevations ranging from 200 to 700 metres, for wines of impressive quality and quantity. The Giovannet family presented an outstanding range of wines, with Pinot Bianco Tecum that makes the finals. This white, released only in magnums, presents great complexity on the nose. On the palate, we appreciated its firmness, and its dry, elegant, leisurely finish. The good 2015 growing year meanwhile endowed the Gewürztraminer Vom Lehm with exuberance and full flavour, for a well-earned Tre Bicchieri.

○ A. A. Gewürztraminer Vom Lehm '15	♈♈♈	3*
○ A. A. Pinot Bianco Tecum '14	♈♈	3*
● A. A. Cabernet Burgum Novum Ris. '13	♈♈	4
○ A. A. Pinot Bianco Vom Stein '15	♈♈	2*
○ A. A. Pinot Grigio '15	♈♈	2*
● A. A. Pinot Nero Burgum Novum Ris. '13	♈♈	5
● A. A. Pinot Nero Glener '14	♈♈	3
● A. A. Schiava Breitbacher '15	♈♈	2*
● A. A. Santa Maddalena Schallerhof '15	♈	2
○ Sauvignon Raif '15	♈	3
○ A. A. Pinot Bianco Tecum '10	♀♀♀	3*
○ A. A. Chardonnay Burgum Novum Ris. '12	♀♀	4
○ A. A. Pinot Bianco Tecum '13	♀♀	3*
● A. A. Pinot Nero Burgum Novum Ris. '12	♀♀	5
○ Sauvignon Raif '14	♀♀	3

★★Cantina Produttori Colterenzio

Loc. Cornaiano/Girlan
s.da del Vino, 8
39057 Appiano/Eppan [BZ]
Tel. +39 0471664246
www.colterenzio.it

CELLAR SALES
PRE-BOOKED VISITS
ANNUAL PRODUCTION 1,600,000 bottles
HECTARES UNDER VINE 300.00
SUSTAINABLE WINERY

Cantina di Colterenzio has been one of the driving forces behind the renaissance of the district, bringing out the great potential of the area in its wines. Today, the cooperative relies on the work of 300 members, with vineyards located above all in the zones of Oltradige and Bassa Atesina. Here, the rows lie on deeply varying soils which, together with a significant range of altitudes, allow each variety to achieve optimum ripeness. Cantina di Colterenzio has always been appreciated for its interpretations of varieties such as sauvignon and cabernet, and this year was no exception. The Sauvignon Lafóa is a paradigm of aromatic elegance, and earned a Tre Bicchieri with its aromas of white-fleshed fruit swathed in mineral notes, over a full, tangy palate of great length. Hot on its heels was the Cabernet Sauvignon version, with its rich, potent palate underpinned by attractive tannins.

Hartmann Donà

via Raffein, 8
39010 Cermes/Tscherms [BZ]
Tel. +39 3292610628
hartmann.dona@rolmail.net

ANNUAL PRODUCTION 35,000 bottles
HECTARES UNDER VINE 4.65

Hartmann Donà runs a handful of hectares in the hills above Merano and Cornaiano, dedicated to Tyrol's classic varieties, above all schiava and pinot nero, but there are also white berries. The experience gained in over 20 years of business means that Hartmann not only vaunts knowledge of the growing area and its potential, but has also developed a very personal vision of wine, which never lack elegance, tautness, and cellarability. The winery's Riservas were left to mature in the cellar, so our attention focused on the new Pinot Nero, with its delicate nose of wild berries and aromatic herbs, leading into a taut, linear, extremely pleasurable palate. Among the fresher wines, we appreciated the focused nose of the drinkable Chardonnay, with aromas of apple and white damson over a dry palate. We were intrigued by the lip-smacking Gewürztraminer, which showed dry and taut while remaining true to the variety's aromatic nature.

○ A. A. Sauvignon Lafóa '14	▼▼▼ 5
● A. A. Cabernet Sauvignon Lafóa '13	▼▼ 7
○ A. A. Chardonnay Formigar '14	▼▼ 5
○ A. A. Chardonnay Altkirch '15	▼▼ 2*
○ A. A. Gewürztraminer Perelise '15	▼▼ 5
● A. A. Merlot-Cabernet Sauvignon Cornelius '13	▼▼ 5
○ A. A. Pinot Bianco Weisshaus '14	▼▼ 3
○ A. A. Pinot Grigio Puiten '14	▼▼ 3
○ A. A. Sauvignon Prail '15	▼▼ 3
● A. A. Pinot Nero St. Daniel Ris. '13	▼ 4
● A. A. Schiava Menzen '15	▼ 2
● A. A. Cabernet Sauvignon Lafóa '12	▽▽▽ 7
● A. A. Cabernet Sauvignon Lafóa '11	▽▽▽ 7
● A. A. Cabernet Sauvignon Lafóa '10	▽▽▽ 7
● A. A. Cabernet Sauvignon Lafóa '09	▽▽▽ 7

○ A. A. Chardonnay '15	▼▼ 3
○ A. A. Gewürztraminer '15	▼▼ 3
● A. A. Pinot Nero '14	▼▼ 3
○ A. A. Sauvignon '15	▼▼ 3
○ A. A. Pinot Bianco '15	▼ 3
○ A. A. Gewürztraminer '13	▽▽ 3
● A. A. Lagrein '13	▽▽ 3
● A.A. Pinot Nero Donà Noir '11	▽▽ 3*
● A.A. Pinot Nero Donà Noir '10	▽▽ 3
○ A.A. Sauvignon '14	▽▽ 3
○ Donà Blanc '11	▽▽ 3
○ Donà Blanc '10	▽▽ 3
● Donà Rouge '10	▽▽ 3
● Donà Rouge '09	▽▽ 3

Tenuta Ebner
Florian Unterthiner

FRAZ. CAMPODAZZO, 18
39054 RENON/RITTEN [BZ]
TEL. +39 0471353386
www.weingutebner.it

CELLAR SALES
PRE-BOOKED VISITS
RESTAURANT SERVICE
ANNUAL PRODUCTION 20,000 bottles
HECTARES UNDER VINE 4.50

The Renon plateau lies to the north of the city of Bolzano, bordered by Val Sarentino to the west and the Valle Isarco to the east. It is here that the Unterthiner siblings, Florian and Brigitte, have developed Tenuta Ebner and are taking their parents' heritage into the future. They have a handful of hectares under vine in various areas, with the warmest and sunniest south-facing plots planted to red grape varieties, while the whites hark from the cooler, south-east-facing vineyards. The winery's labels improve with every passing year, and two of them made this year's finals. The first was the Sauvignon, which made the most of a superb growing year to unfurl a nose of great finesse and complexity, resulting in a rich palate brimming with flavour. The other finalist was a classic from the Valle Isarco, a Grüner Veltliner showing intense aromas of white-fleshed fruit and blossom, swathed in subtle smoky nuances. On the palate it is dry, powerful and long.

○ A. A. Sauvignon '15	♟♟ 3*
○ A. A. Valle Isarco Grüner Veltliner '15	♟♟ 3*
○ A. A. Pinot Bianco '15	♟♟ 3
● A. A. Pinot Nero '14	♟♟ 3
○ A. A. Valle Isarco Gewürztraminer '15	♟♟ 4
● A. A. Schiava '15	♟ 2
● A. A. Schiava '14	♟♟ 2*
○ A.A. Pinot Bianco '14	♟♟ 3
○ A.A. Pinot Bianco '12	♟♟ 3
○ A.A. Sauvignon '14	♟♟ 3
○ A.A. Sauvignon '13	♟♟ 3
○ A.A. Valle Isarco Gewürztraminer '14	♟♟ 4
○ A.A. Valle Isarco Veltliner '14	♟♟ 3
● Zweigelt '13	♟♟ 3

Erbhof Unterganzner
Josephus Mayr

FRAZ. CARDANO
VIA CAMPIGLIO, 15
39053 BOLZANO/BOZEN
TEL. +39 0471365582
www.tirolensisarsvini.it

CELLAR SALES
PRE-BOOKED VISITS
ANNUAL PRODUCTION 65,000 bottles
HECTARES UNDER VINE 9.00

Josephus and Barbara Mayr have extended the activity of the family winery over the years, adding the property of the Pignater farm to take their vineyard holdings to almost ten hectares. Every type of wine they produce aims to bring out the best of variety and vineyard, while not eschewing more original and characterful interpretations. In the higher vineyards we find white grapes, in the lower ones lagrein, schiava and Bordeaux varieties, in plots shared, unusually, with olive trees. Josephus has a clear vocation for reds, and presented an impeccable range of wines. At one end of the stylistic spectrum we find the Lamarein, from sun-dried grapes of lagrein, which proves its worth as a thoroughbred red of power and grip. At the other we have the Santa Maddalena, which won us over with its finesse and full flavour. In the middle, there is an extraordinary version of the Cabernet Kampill, showing firm, dry and harmonious, and a Lagrein Riserva that stands out for its aromatic balance and well-rounded yet supple palate. Tre Bicchieri.

● A. A. Lagrein Ris. '13	♟♟♟ 5
● A. A. Cabernet Kampill Ris. '13	♟♟ 5
● Lamarein '13	♟♟ 6
⊙ A. A. Lagrein Kretzer Rosato V. T. '15	♟♟ 3
● A. A. Santa Maddalena Cl. '14	♟♟ 3
○ A. A. Sauvignon Platt & Pignat '15	♟♟ 3
○ A. A. Chardonnay Platt&Pignat '15	♟ 3
○ A. A. Kerner '15	♟ 3
○ Marie Josephine Passito '14	♟ 5
● A. A. Lagrein Ris. '11	♟♟♟ 5
● A. A. Lagrein Scuro Ris. '05	♟♟♟ 4
● A. A. Lagrein Scuro Ris. '01	♟♟♟ 4
● A. A. Lagrein Scuro Ris. '00	♟♟♟ 4
● A. A. Lagrein Scuro Ris. '99	♟♟♟ 4
● Lamarein '05	♟♟♟ 6

Erste+Neue

VIA DELLE CANTINE, 5/10
39052 CALDARO/KALTERN [BZ]
TEL. +39 0471963122
www.erste-neue.it

CELLAR SALES
PRE-BOOKED VISITS
ANNUAL PRODUCTION 1,400,000 bottles
HECTARES UNDER VINE 250.00

This is the last time we will be dedicating a profile to the winery of Erste+Neue, as it has merged with the nearby Cantina di Caldaro to create the largest cooperative winery in the district. In dowry it brings a vineyard that covers 250 hectares, above all around the lake but also in the cooler, higher zones, tended by over 400 grower-members who proudly supply the winery with its grapes. They couldn't end in a better way, with a range of wines that fully convinced our tasting panels, starting with a sumptuous version of the Cabernet Puntay, a red that opens up slowly to show red berry fruit and spice, swathed in subtle, yet refreshing medicinal herbs. On the palate, we appreciated its potency and full flavour, and it romped off with top honours. Always one of the best Lago di Caldaro wines, Leuchtenburg, boasts wild berries and violet on the nose, over a racy, succulent palate.

★Falkenstein Franz Pratzner

VIA CASTELLO, 19
39025 NATURNO/NATURNS [BZ]
TEL. +39 0473666054
www.falkenstein.bz

CELLAR SALES
PRE-BOOKED VISITS
ANNUAL PRODUCTION 90,000 bottles
HECTARES UNDER VINE 12.00

Despite its relatively limited area under vine, Valle Venosta enjoys an excellent viticultural reputation, thanks to a number of small but important wineries. Franz Pratzner is one of the pioneering growers in the valley, and introduced wine lovers to the qualities of riesling from this warm area. His steep south-facing vineyards, combined with their altitude, allow the grapes to ripen to their full aromatic potential without losing freshness. Once again this year, the Pratzner's champion was the Riesling, with intense aromas of blossom and white-fleshed fruit, and deep yet still reticent mineral notes in the background. On the generous palate, it shows taut and gutsy, with an attractive, restless, rustic nature that endows tautness and character. Similar in style is the Pinot Bianco, with more abundant fruit on the nose but an equally rugged and grippy palate.

Wine	Rating
● A. A. Cabernet Puntay Ris. '12	♥♥♥ 5
● A. A. Lago di Caldaro Cl. Sup. Leuchtenburg '15	♥♥ 2*
● A. A. Lagrein Puntay Ris. '12	♥♥ 5
○ A. A. Chardonnay Salt '15	♥♥ 3
○ A. A. Gewürztraminer '15	♥♥ 3
● A. A. Lago di Caldaro Cl. Sup. Puntay '15	♥♥ 3
○ A. A. Pinot Bianco Prunar '15	♥♥ 3
○ A. A. Sauvignon Puntay '15	♥♥ 5
○ Anthos Bianco Passito '13	♥♥ 5
● A. A. Lago di Caldaro Cl. Sup. Leuchtenburg '14	♥♥♥ 2*
● A. A. Lago di Caldaro Cl. Sup. Leuchtenburg '12	♥♥♥ 2*
● A. A. Lago di Caldaro Cl. Sup. Puntay '10	♥♥♥ 3*
○ A. A. Sauvignon Puntay '06	♥♥♥ 4
○ Anthos Bianco Passito '10	♥♥♥ 5

Wine	Rating
○ A. A. Val Venosta Riesling '14	♥♥♥ 5
○ A. A. Val Venosta Pinot Bianco '14	♥♥ 4
● A. A. Val Venosta Pinot Nero '13	♥ 5
○ A. A. Val Venosta Sauvignon '14	♥ 4
○ A. A. Val Venosta Pinot Bianco '07	♥♥♥ 4
○ A. A. Val Venosta Riesling '12	♥♥♥ 5
○ A. A. Val Venosta Riesling '11	♥♥♥ 5
○ A. A. Val Venosta Riesling '10	♥♥♥ 5
○ A. A. Val Venosta Riesling '09	♥♥♥ 5
○ A. A. Val Venosta Riesling '08	♥♥♥ 5
○ A. A. Val Venosta Riesling '07	♥♥♥ 5
○ A. A. Val Venosta Riesling '06	♥♥♥ 5
○ A. A. Val Venosta Riesling '05	♥♥♥ 5
○ A. A. Val Venosta Riesling '00	♥♥♥ 3
○ A. A. Valle Venosta Riesling '13	♥♥♥ 5

Garlider
Christian Kerschbaumer

VIA UNTRUM, 20
39040 VELTURNO/FELDTHURNS [BZ]
TEL. +39 0472847296
www.garlider.it

CELLAR SALES
PRE-BOOKED VISITS
ANNUAL PRODUCTION 26,000 bottles
HECTARES UNDER VINE 4.20
VITICULTURE METHOD Certified Organic

Christian Kerschbaumer and his wife Veronika are at the helm of the beautiful Garlider winery in the Valle Isarco. In the space of a dozen or so years they have adopted organic farming methods for their vineyards, lying at elevations of between 550 and 800 metres. Except for a small production of pinot nero, only white grape varieties are grown, divided between the classic varieties of the district and those typical of this valley, grüner veltliner and sylvaner. In the Grüner Veltliner, intense sulphurous aromas initially overpower the fruit, only to make way for a tempest of smoke, pear and tropical fruit, perfectly mirrored on the taut, leisurely palate. Even more reticent on the nose is the Sylvaner, which however shows rich flavour, good body and grip in the mouth. This is a wine that it is difficult to forget.

★Cantina Girlan

LOC. CORNAIANO/GIRLAN
VIA SAN MARTINO, 24
39057 APPIANO/EPPAN [BZ]
TEL. +39 0471662403
www.girlan.it

CELLAR SALES
PRE-BOOKED VISITS
ANNUAL PRODUCTION 1,500,000 bottles
HECTARES UNDER VINE 220.00

In a territory that seems to have focused most of its aspirations on the aromatic qualities of Alto Adige varieties, Cantina Girlan has also continued to invest in more traditional varieties, such as schiava, pinot nero and pinot bianco. Gerhard Kofler works in close contact with the manager Oscar Lorandi and with all the members to bring out the excellent potential of this corner of Italy, in wines that exalt the symbiosis between the varieties and fine vineyards where they grow. It was in fact the best vineyards that gave the most interesting results, and among these Mazon once again proved its vocation for pinot nero. Il Trattmann is the usual thoroughbred, with a nose of forest fruits and medicinal herbs over a firm, yet enfolding body and an intriguing tannic weave that sustains the wine on its way to a succulent finish. The Pinot Bianco Plattenriegl was solid and elegant, while we loved the deep, taut Schiava Gschleier.

○ A. A. Valle Isarco Sylvaner '14	♟♟♟	3*
○ A. A. Valle Isarco Grüner Veltliner '14	♟♟	4
○ A. A. Valle Isarco Sylvaner '13	♟♟♟	3*
○ A. A. Valle Isarco Sylvaner '09	♟♟♟	3*
○ A. A. Valle Isarco Veltliner '08	♟♟♟	3*
○ A. A. Valle Isarco Veltliner '07	♟♟♟	3
○ A. A. Valle Isarco Veltliner '05	♟♟♟	3*
● A. A. Pinot Nero '12	♟♟	4
○ A. A. Valle Isarco Grüner Veltliner '12	♟♟	4
○ A. A. Valle Isarco Müller Thurgau '13	♟♟	3
○ A. A. Valle Isarco Sylvaner '12	♟♟	3*
○ A. A. Valle Isarco Sylvaner '11	♟♟	3
○ A. A. Valle Isarco Veltliner '13	♟♟	4
○ A. A. Valle Isarco Veltliner '11	♟♟	3*
○ Pinot Grigio '13	♟♟	4

● A. A. Pinot Nero Trattmann Mazon Ris. '13	♟♟♟	5
○ A. A. Pinot Bianco Plattenriegl '15	♟♟	3*
● A. A. Schiava Gschleier Alte Reben '14	♟♟	3*
○ 448 slm '15	♟♟	2*
○ A. A. Bianco Cuvée Flora Ris. '13	♟♟	5
○ A. A. Chardonnay Flora '14	♟♟	5
○ A. A. Gewürztraminer Flora '15	♟♟	6
○ A. A. Gewürztraminer Sandbichler H. Lun '15	♟♟	4
○ A. A. Pinot Bianco H. Lun '15	♟♟	3
○ A. A. Pinot Bianco Sandbichler H. Lun '15	♟♟	3
○ A. A. Pinot Grigio H. Lun '15	♟♟	2*
○ A. A. Sauvignon H. Lun '15	♟♟	3
○ A. A. Sauvignon Indra '15	♟♟	3
● A. A. Schiava Faß N° 9 '15	♟♟	2*
● A. A. Pinot Nero Trattmann Mazon Ris. '12	♟♟♟	5
● A. A. Pinot Nero Trattmann Mazon Ris. '11	♟♟♟	5

Glögglhof - Franz Gojer

FRAZ. SANTA MADDALENA
VIA RIVELLONE, 1
39100 BOLZANO/BOZEN
TEL. +39 0471978775
www.gojer.it

CELLAR SALES
PRE-BOOKED VISITS
ACCOMMODATION
ANNUAL PRODUCTION 55,000 bottles
HECTARES UNDER VINE 7.40

The Gojer family winery is based at Santa Maddalena, completely immersed in the vineyards but close to the centre of Bolzano. On the Glögglhof Franz estate, Maria Luise and Florian transform the grapes that arrive from the vineyards into products closely linked to tradition but with an international outlook. The vineyards are distributed in four zones: around the winery the grapes for the Santa Maddalena wines, on the plain of Gries; and at Rencio and in the area of Ora for the Lagreins. Lastly, from the higher vineyards of Cornedo all'Adige, come the grapes for the whites. The heart of the operation however remains faithfully bound to schiava, and there was never any doubt that the Santa Maddalena Rondell would seduce our tasting panels. An intense nose of berry fruits and spice paves the way for full flavour on the palate, resulting in a long, satisfyingly drinkable wine. We were also won over by the Lagrein Riserva, a potent red in which hefty stuffing is reined in by impressive grip.

● A. A. Santa Maddalena Cl. Rondell '15	♟♟♟	3*
○ A. A. Kerner Karneid '15	♟♟	3
● A. A. Lagrein Ris. '13	♟♟	4
○ A. A. Pinot Bianco Karneid '15	♟♟	3
● A. A. Santa Maddalena Cl. '15	♟♟	2*
○ A. A. Sauvignon Karneid '15	♟♟	3
● A. A. Vernatsch Alte Reben '15	♟♟	2*
○ A. A. Kerner Karneid '13	♟♟	3
● A. A. Lagrein Ris. '12	♟♟	4
○ A. A. Pinot Bianco Karneid '14	♟♟	3
● A. A. Santa Maddalena Cl. '14	♟♟	2*
● A. A. Santa Maddalena Cl. '13	♟♟	2*
● A. A. Santa Maddalena Cl. Rondell '14	♟♟	3*
● A. A. Vernatsch Alte Reben '14	♟♟	2*
● A. A. Vernatsch Alte Reben '13	♟♟	2*

Griesbauerhof
Georg Mumelter

VIA RENCIO, 66
39100 BOLZANO/BOZEN
TEL. +39 0471973090
www.griesbauerhof.it

CELLAR SALES
PRE-BOOKED VISITS
ANNUAL PRODUCTION 30,000 bottles
HECTARES UNDER VINE 3.80

The Mumelter family took over the Griesbauerhof farm around 150 years ago, and ever since have been dedicated to viticulture here. Today, Georg and his wife Margareth tend their few hectares under vine for labels which unusually for these parts do not envisage the use of aromatic varieties. Particular attention is given to the wines of Bolzano, and thus Santa Maddalena and Lagrein, while the vineyard at Appiano provides the raw materials for the production of whites. We saw a fine performance from the Lagrein, with intense notes of fruit and spice over a rich, potent palate, resulting in a wine of serious substance. The estate's sun-kissed vineyards also allow the Bordeaux varieties to reach perfect ripeness, as was evident in our tastings of the Cabernet Sauvignon Riserva, a reticent wine that unfolds slowly to reveal a firm body underpinned by solid tannins.

● A. A. Cabernet Sauvignon Ris. '13	♟♟	3
● A. A. Lagrein Ris. '13	♟♟	5
● A. A. Merlot Spitz '14	♟♟	3
● A. A. Lagrein '15	♟	3
⊙ A. A. Lagrein Kretzer '15	♟	3
○ A. A. Pinot Grigio '15	♟	3
● A. A. Santa Maddalena Cl. '15	♟	2
● A. A. Lagrein Ris. '09	♟♟♟	5
● A. A. Cabernet Sauvignon Ris. '12	♟♟	3
● A. A. Lagrein '13	♟♟	3*
● A. A. Lagrein Ris. '12	♟♟	5
○ A. A. Pinot Bianco '14	♟♟	3
● A. A. Santa Maddalena Cl. '14	♟♟	2*
● Schiava Isarcus '13	♟♟	3

Gummerhof - Malojer
VIA WEGGESTEIN, 36
39100 BOLZANO/BOZEN
TEL. +39 0471972885
www.malojer.it

CELLAR SALES
PRE-BOOKED VISITS
ANNUAL PRODUCTION 100,000 bottles
HECTARES UNDER VINE 18.00

The Malojer family's winery is located on the outskirts of Bolzano, almost at the mouth of Val Sarentino. The vineyards, covering just under 20 hectares, are spread all around the city and on the slopes of the Renon plateau. Here we find the classic Alto Adige varieties, above all lagrein and schiava, but also aromatic cultivars and international ones, such as merlot and cabernet, in a range of high-quality, reliable labels. Malojer produces a wide range of labels, and among these the most impressive this year was the Lagrein Gummerhof zu Gries, a red which was one of the most convincing of its type, despite the difficult growing year. A generous nose of black berry fruit and spice paves the way for a potent palate, whose weight is kept in check by full flavour and grip. The Cabernet Riserva shows an edgier nose, which needs time to express itself to the full. On the palate it displays polished tannins and admirable balance.

Gumphof Markus Prackwieser
LOC. NOVALE DI PRESULE, 8
39050 FIÈ ALLO SCILIAR/VÖLS AM SCHLERN [BZ]
TEL. +39 0471601190
www.gumphof.it

CELLAR SALES
PRE-BOOKED VISITS
ANNUAL PRODUCTION 45,000 bottles
HECTARES UNDER VINE 5.00

Markus Prackwieser is one of the leading interpreters of the unmistakable character to be found in the best wines of the Valle Isarco, with its unique climatic and geological conditions. Here, the warmth of the Bolzano basin joins forces with currents of cool air from the valley, while the soils benefit from disaggregated volcanic porphyry mixed with alluvial debris. The operation's few hectares of vineyards are farmed with expertise and respect for the environment, resulting in solid, reliable wines. The Pinot Bianco Praesulis 2015 is the usual thoroughbred, with aromas of fresh-cut flowers and white-fleshed fruit against a subtle citrus backdrop. On the palate, its charm lies in its finesse and grip rather than in its power, making it one of the most convincing of its type in the region. We also loved the Sauvignon version, another wine which plays on gracefulness and elegant harmony rather than pursuing potency for its own sake.

● A. A. Lagrein Gummerhof zu Gries '14	♛♛ 3*
○ A. A. Bianco Cuvée Bautzanum '15	♛♛ 4
● A. A. Cabernet Lagrein Bautzanum Cuvée Ris. '13	♛♛ 4
● A. A. Cabernet Ris. '13	♛♛ 4
○ A. A. Gewürztraminer Kui '15	♛♛ 3
● A. A. Lagrein Ris. '13	♛♛ 4
○ A. A. Müller Thurgau Kreiter '15	♛♛ 2*
● A. A. Pinot Nero Gstrein '13	♛♛ 3
● A. A. Pinot Nero Ris. '13	♛♛ 4
○ A. A. Pinot Bianco Kreiter '15	♛ 3
● A. A. Santa Maddalena Cl. Loamer '15	♛ 2
○ A. A. Sauvignon Gur zur Sand '15	♛ 3
● A. A. Lagrein Gries '09	♛♛♛ 2*
● A. A. Cabernet Ris. '12	♛♛ 4
● A. A. Lagrein Ris. '12	♛♛ 4

○ A. A. Pinot Bianco Praesulis '15	♛♛♛ 3*
○ A. A. Sauvignon Praesulis '15	♛♛ 4
○ A. A. Gewürztraminer Praesulis '15	♛♛ 4
● A. A. Pinot Nero Praesulis '14	♛♛ 5
○ A. A. Pinot Bianco Mediaevum '15	♛ 2
● A. A. Schiava Mediaevum '15	♛ 3
○ A. A. Pinot Bianco Praesulis '14	♛♛♛ 3*
○ A. A. Pinot Bianco Praesulis '06	♛♛♛ 3*
○ A. A. Sauvignon Praesulis '13	♛♛♛ 4*
○ A. A. Sauvignon Praesulis '09	♛♛♛ 3
○ A. A. Sauvignon Praesulis '07	♛♛♛ 3*
○ A. A. Sauvignon Praesulis '04	♛♛♛ 3*

ALTO ADIGE

★Franz Haas

VIA VILLA, 6
39040 MONTAGNA/MONTAN [BZ]
TEL. +39 0471812280
www.franz-haas.it

CELLAR SALES
PRE-BOOKED VISITS
ANNUAL PRODUCTION 350,000 bottles
HECTARES UNDER VINE 55.00
SUSTAINABLE WINERY

The winery of Franz Haas is located at
Montagna, a stone's throw from the area
that today is considered the cradle of Italian
pinot nero, Mazzon. The vineyards, now
covering over 50 hectares of the winery's
own land, rented plots and those of other
growers, are spread all over the region,
especially on high hillside sites. Aware of
the increasingly warm local climate, Franz
has invested in highland vineyards, with the
latest vineyard of pinot nero planted at an
altitude of 1,150 metres. The winery offers
a wide range of labels and interpretations,
while consistently focusing on elegance
and grip. Il Manna is a concentrated blend
of various cultivars, and exploits their
aromatic thrust in intense aromas of
flowers and citrus. With time, they become
less pungent and more harmonious,
exalting the full-flavoured, perfectly
balanced palate. We appreciated the more
intense, racy aromas of the Sauvignon, and
its generous, leisurely palate.

Wine	Rating
○ A. A. Sauvignon '14	♥♥ 5
○ Manna '14	♥♥ 5
○ A. A. Gewürztraminer '15	♥♥ 4
● A. A. Pinot Nero '14	♥♥ 5
○ A. A. Moscato Giallo '15	♥ 5
○ A. A. Pinot Bianco Lepus '15	♥ 3
● A. A. Moscato Rosa '12	♥♥♥ 5
● A. A. Moscato Rosa '11	♥♥♥ 5
● A. A. Moscato Rosa Schweizer '00	♥♥♥ 4
● A. A. Pinot Nero Schweizer '02	♥♥♥ 5
● A. A. Pinot Nero Schweizer '01	♥♥♥ 5
○ A. A. Sauvignon '13	♥♥♥ 5
○ Manna '07	♥♥♥ 4
○ Manna '05	♥♥♥ 4
○ Manna '04	♥♥♥ 4

Haderburg

FRAZ. BUCHOLZ
LOC. POCHI, 30
39040 SALORNO/SALURN [BZ]
TEL. +39 0471889097
www.haderburg.it

CELLAR SALES
PRE-BOOKED VISITS
ANNUAL PRODUCTION 100,000 bottles
HECTARES UNDER VINE 12.00
VITICULTURE METHOD Certified Biodynamic

Alois Ochsenreiter's operation has two
distinct souls, one expressed in sparkling
wine and the other rooted in the traditions
of Alto Adige. The former has led the winery
to produce not only some of the district's
best sparkling wine, but has seen it
become one of the forerunners of a
movement that has attracted many local
wineries. Its traditional side is more classic
in nature, and aims to bring the best out of
individual varieties. These two souls are
brought together by man, the custodian of
nature, as seen in the decision to use
biodynamic methods to exalt the fruits of
the land. We were impressed with the Pas
Dosé, a sparkler from chardonnay topped
up with pinot nero, which delights with a
captivating nose of white-fleshed fruit and
biscuits, over subtle mineral notes. The
taut, sumptuous palate shows great length
and power. The best of the still wines was
the Merlot Cabernet Erah.

Wine	Rating
○ A. A. Spumante Pas Dosé	♥♥ 4
● A. A. Merlot-Cabernet Sauvignon Erah Hausmannhof '12	♥♥ 5
● A. A. Pinot Nero Hausmannhof Ris. '13	♥♥ 6
○ A. A. Spumante Brut	♥♥ 5
○ A. A. Spumante Hausmannhof Brut Ris. '06	♥♥ 5
○ A. A. Sauvignon Hausmannhof '15	♥ 4
⊙ A. A. Spumante Brut Rosé	♥ 5
○ A. A. Valle Isarco Sylvaner Obermairlhof '05	♥♥♥ 3*
● A. A. Pinot Nero Hausmannhof '13	♥♥ 5
● A. A. Pinot Nero Hausmannhof Ris. '12	♥♥ 6
○ A. A. Sauvignon Hausmannhof '14	♥♥ 4
○ A. A. Spumante Pas Dosé '11	♥♥ 5

Kettmeir

VIA DELLE CANTINE, 4
39052 CALDARO/KALTERN [BZ]
TEL. +39 0471963135
www.kettmeir.com

CELLAR SALES
PRE-BOOKED VISITS
ANNUAL PRODUCTION 330,000 bottles
HECTARES UNDER VINE 36.00

It is 30 years since the historical winery in Caldaro became part of Santa Margherita, and a lot of water has flowed under the bridge. Today, Kettmeier can rely on three plots: one by the lake for the red grape varieties, with those for the spumante base wines planted in the higher-lying vineyards at Pochi di Salorno; one at the Reiner farm for chardonnay and pinot; and lastly at the Ebnicher estate in the Soprabolzano area on the Renon plateau for müller. In the cellar, with a panoramic view over Caldaro, Joseph Romen produces a solid, extremely reliable range. There are no weak points in Kettmeier's range this year, which includes an outstanding version of their Pinot Bianco Athesis, with its focused aromas of white-fleshed fruit swathed in blossom, over a zesty, beautifully harmonious palate. We also loved the Sauvignon, which made the best of the excellent growing year to offer a complex, intense nose and generous palate.

Tenuta Klosterhof
Oskar Andergassen

LOC. CLAVENZ, 40
39052 CALDARO/KALTERN [BZ]
TEL. +39 0471961046
www.garni-klosterhof.com

CELLAR SALES
PRE-BOOKED VISITS
ACCOMMODATION AND RESTAURANT SERVICE
ANNUAL PRODUCTION 20,000 bottles
HECTARES UNDER VINE 3.50

Oskar Andergassen, with the help of his son Hannes, runs the small family winery in Caldaro, covering a few hectares divided between the shores of the lake and the slopes leading to Pianizza di Sopra. In addition to running the winery, his commitments also include a hotel and the production of spirits. Wine production is however increasingly important, and the results are more convincing with every passing year. The superb Pinot Nero Panigl harks from a vineyard to the south of Caldaro, and offers forthright ripe red fruit over a full-bodied, generous, mouthfilling palate. We find a completely different style in the Pinot Bianco Trifall, from vineyards higher in the hills, with a more closed, pungent nose, but riper and more harmonious in the mouth, where elegant progression leads to a long finish.

○ A. A. Müller Thurgau Athesis '15	♥♥ 4
○ A. A. Pinot Bianco Athesis '14	♥♥ 3*
○ A. A. Sauvignon '15	♥♥ 3*
○ A. A. Chardonnay Maso Reiner '14	♥♥ 3
○ A. A. Gewürztraminer '15	♥♥ 3
● A. A. Moscato Rosa Athesis '12	♥♥ 5
○ A. A. Pinot Bianco '15	♥♥ 3
● A. A. Pinot Nero Maso Reiner '13	♥♥ 4
○ A. A. Spumante Brut Athesis '13	♥♥ 4
⊙ A. A. Spumante Rosé Brut Athesis	♥♥ 4
⊙ A. A. Lagrein Rosato '15	♥ 2
○ A. A. Chardonnay '14	♀♀ 3
○ A. A. Chardonnay Maso Reiner '13	♀♀ 3*
○ A. A. Müller Thurgau Athesis '14	♀♀ 4
● A. A. Pinot Nero Maso Reiner '12	♀♀ 4
○ A. A. Spumante Brut	♀♀ 3

○ A. A. Pinot Bianco Trifall '15	♥♥ 3
● A. A. Pinot Nero Panigl '13	♥♥ 5
● A. A. Pinot Nero Ris. '13	♥♥ 4
○ A. A. Pinot Bianco V. T. '14	♥♥ 4
● A. A. Lago di Caldaro Cl. Sup. Plantaditsch '15	♥ 2
● A. A. Lago di Caldaro Cl. Sup. Plantaditsch R. '15	♥ 3
○ Birnbaum '15	♥ 3
● A. A. Merlot Ris. '12	♀♀ 4
○ A. A. Moscato Giallo Birnbaum '14	♀♀ 3
○ A. A. Pinot Bianco Trifall '14	♀♀ 3
● A. A. Pinot Nero Panigl '12	♀♀ 5
⊙ A. A. Pinot Nero Rosé Summer '14	♀♀ 4
● A. A. Lago di Caldaro Cl. Sup. Plantaditsch '14	♀♀ 2*
○ A. A. Pinot Bianco Trifall '13	♀♀ 3*

ALTO ADIGE

★Köfererhof
Günther Kerschbaumer

FRAZ. NOVACELLA
VIA PUSTERIA, 3
39040 VARNA/VAHRN [BZ]
TEL. +39 3474778009
www.koefererhof.it

CELLAR SALES
PRE-BOOKED VISITS
RESTAURANT SERVICE
ANNUAL PRODUCTION 80,000 bottles
HECTARES UNDER VINE 10.00

Leaving behind the Bolzano basin and entering Valle Isarco, the landscape becomes more rugged, as the soft rolling hills gradually make way for the mountain ridges of the Dolomites. Here, at Varna, we find the winery of Günther Kerschbaumer, with a mere five hectares of his own vineyards plus a similar amount rented, at altitudes of almost 1,000 metres. Working exclusively with white grape varieties, he produces extremely interesting wines which combine approachability with depth and finesse. In this area, sylvaner reigns supreme, and Kerschbaumer pay it homage, exalting its smokiness and pear aromas on the nose and its dynamism and great length in the mouth. Even more convincing is the Pinot Grigio, which took top honours thanks to a subtle nose of fruit and blossom, paving the way for a potent palate with elegant progression and length.

Tenuta Kornell

FRAZ. SETTEQUERCE
VIA BOLZANO, 23
39018 TERLANO/TERLAN [BZ]
TEL. +39 0471917507
www.kornell.it

CELLAR SALES
PRE-BOOKED VISITS
ANNUAL PRODUCTION 100,000 bottles
HECTARES UNDER VINE 15.00

Going upriver along the Adige, near the provincial capital, the valley bends westwards and opens out into a lush plain on which vineyards and apple orchards vie for space. On the lands near the hill it is the vineyards which have pride of place, enjoying an ideal climate in which warm currents from the south meet those coming down from the Alps. Here, at Settequerce, we find Florian Brigl's winery and some of his vineyards, while other plots are at Appiano Monte and Gries. Merlot has found perfect conditions in this zone for ripening gradually and uniformly, as shown by the tasting of the Riserva Staves 2013. Its concentrated nose of ripe red berry fruit and spice is perfectly echoed on the long, full-flavoured palate, with intriguing smoky notes and aromatic herbs. We were also convinced by the Sauvignon, which combines intense aromas and a sumptuous palate.

○ A. A. Valle Isarco Pinot Grigio '15	♟♟♟ 3*
○ A. A. Valle Isarco Riesling '14	♟♟ 5
○ A. A. Valle Isarco Sylvaner '15	♟♟ 3*
○ A. A. Valle Isarco Grüner Veltliner '14	♟♟ 4
○ A. A. Valle Isarco Kerner '15	♟♟ 3
○ A. A. Valle Isarco Müller Thurgau '15	♟♟ 3
○ A. A. Valle Isarco Sylvaner R '14	♟♟ 5
○ A. A. Valle Isarco Pinot Grigio '13	♟♟♟ 3*
○ A. A. Valle Isarco Pinot Grigio '12	♟♟♟ 3*
○ A. A. Valle Isarco Pinot Grigio '11	♟♟♟ 3*
○ A. A. Valle Isarco Pinot Grigio '09	♟♟♟ 3*
○ A. A. Valle Isarco Riesling '10	♟♟♟ 4
○ A. A. Valle Isarco Sylvaner R '13	♟♟♟ 5
○ A. A. Valle Isarco Sylvaner R '09	♟♟♟ 4
○ A. A. Valle Isarco Sylvaner R '08	♟♟♟ 4

● A. A. Merlot Staves Ris. '13	♟♟ 5
○ A. A. Gewürztraminer Damian '15	♟♟ 3
● A. A. Lagrein Greif '15	♟♟ 3
● A. A. Lagrein Staves Ris. '13	♟♟ 5
● A. A. Sauvignon Oberberg '15	♟♟ 3
○ Eich '15	♟ 4
● Zeder '14	♟ 3
● A. A. Lagrein Staves Ris. '12	♟♟♟ 5
● A. A. Cabernet Sauvignon Staves Ris. '12	♟♟ 5
● A. A. Lagrein Greif '14	♟♟ 3
● A. A. Lagrein Greif '12	♟♟ 3
● A. A. Merlot Staves Ris. '11	♟♟ 3
○ A. A. Pinot Bianco Eich '13	♟♟ 3
○ A. A. Sauvignon Oberberg '14	♟♟ 3
● Zeder '13	♟♟ 3

Tenuta Kränzelhof
Graf Franz Pfeil

VIA PALADE, 1
39010 CERMES/TSCHERMS [BZ]
TEL. +39 0473564549
www.labyrinth.bz

CELLAR SALES
PRE-BOOKED VISITS
ANNUAL PRODUCTION 35,000 bottles
HECTARES UNDER VINE 6.00

Conte Franz Pfeil's Tenuta Kränzel estate is in Cermes, on the right bank of the Adige, with a splendid 650-year-old Gothic style house surrounded by a park and vineyards. These cover around six hectares, at elevations ranging from 300 to 600 metres, where each of the varieties grown finds its ideal habitat. Production alternates between international and traditional varieties, for limited amounts of top quality wines. We saw a fine performance from the Corona Segreto 2015, whose composition is a closely-guarded secret. On the nose, however, there is clearly evidence of gewürztraminer, providing intense aromas, while the dynamic palate boasts fleshy roundness. The Sagittarius 2012, a blend of cabernet sauvignon and lagrein, offers a fruity nose swathed in toasty notes and coffee grounds, followed by firmness and power in the mouth.

★Kuenhof - Peter Pliger

LOC. LA MARA, 110
39042 BRESSANONE/BRIXEN [BZ]
TEL. +39 0472850546
pliger.kuenhof@rolmail.net

CELLAR SALES
PRE-BOOKED VISITS
ANNUAL PRODUCTION 38,000 bottles
HECTARES UNDER VINE 6.00
SUSTAINABLE WINERY

Among the most appreciated wineries in the Valle Isarco is that of Peter Pliger and his wife Brigitte. Situated at Mara, just outside Bressanone, it comprises a vineyard covering only six hectares, which Peter tends with utmost care for the environment, to obtain wines with a marked sense of place. In the cellar, production is limited to four labels, all dedicated to the traditional white wines of this valley. Pliger's wines are a perfect way to get to know what Valle Isarco can produce. Elegant, deeply mineral aromas translate into richness on the palate combined with the full flavour and acidic freshness typical of wines from this valley. The deep, smoky Sylvaner displays a dynamic, racy palate, while the Riesling is tauter and leaner. The Veltliner, meanwhile, shows a strong character and a robust, restless, rustic nature.

○ Corona Segreto '15	♟♟ 4
● Pinot Nero '13	♟♟ 6
● Sagittarius '12	♟♟ 5
◉ Blanc de Noir '15	♟ 3
○ Helios Ris. '13	♟ 3
○ Pinot Bianco '15	♟ 4
● A. A. Meranese '13	♟♟ 3
● A. A. Meranese Baslan '12	♟♟ 3*
○ Corona '14	♟♟ 4
○ Dorado Passito '12	♟♟ 5
● Merlot '13	♟♟ 3
○ Pinot Bianco Helios '13	♟♟ 4
● Pinot Nero '12	♟♟ 6
● Pinot Nero '11	♟♟ 6
○ Sauvignon Blanc '14	♟♟ 3

○ A. A. Valle Isarco Grüner Veltliner '15	♟♟♟ 3*
○ A. A. Valle Isarco Riesling Kaiton '15	♟♟ 3*
○ A. A. Valle Isarco Sylvaner '15	♟♟ 3*
○ A. A. Valle Isarco Gewürztraminer '15	♟♟ 3
○ A. A. Valle Isarco Riesling Kaiton '12	♟♟♟ 4*
○ A. A. Valle Isarco Riesling Kaiton '11	♟♟♟ 4*
○ A. A. Valle Isarco Riesling Kaiton '10	♟♟♟ 4
○ A. A. Valle Isarco Riesling Kaiton '07	♟♟♟ 3*
○ A. A. Valle Isarco Riesling Kaiton '05	♟♟♟ 3*
○ A. A. Valle Isarco Sylvaner '14	♟♟♟ 3*
○ A. A. Valle Isarco Sylvaner '13	♟♟♟ 3*
○ A. A. Valle Isarco Sylvaner '08	♟♟♟ 3
○ A. A. Valle Isarco Sylvaner '06	♟♟♟ 3*
○ A. A. Valle Isarco Veltliner '09	♟♟♟ 3*

★Cantina Kurtatsch

S.DA DEL VINO, 23
39040 CORTACCIA/KURTATSCH [BZ]
TEL. +39 0471880115
www.cantina-cortaccia.it

CELLAR SALES
PRE-BOOKED VISITS
ANNUAL PRODUCTION 1,100,000 bottles
HECTARES UNDER VINE 190.00

Arriving from the south, one of the first towns you come across is the medieval Cortaccia, overlooking the Piana Atesina and lying on the first mountain spurs that separate Alto Adige from Trentino. Here, Cantina Cortaccia has developed an operation set up over a century ago, and today can count on just under 200 members, who tend vineyards at elevations of up to 900 metres and over. Their surefooted wines have a strong sense of place, and are based on red grape varieties from the warmer vineyards and whites from the cooler, higher plots. We are well aware that Cantina di Cortaccia enjoys some of the best aspects for gewürztraminer, but the 2014 version of the Brenntal is even more convincing than usual. The cool growing year did not prevent the wine from expressing a complex, elegant nose, rounded off by a lighter palate than in other vintages, but of great length and flavour. The Merlot Brenntal shows intense fruit and spice on the nose, and harmony in the mouth.

Laimburg

LOC. LAIMBURG, 6
39040 VADENA/PFATTEN [BZ]
TEL. +39 0471969700
www.laimburg.bz.it

CELLAR SALES
PRE-BOOKED VISITS
ANNUAL PRODUCTION 95,000 bottles
HECTARES UNDER VINE 15.00
SUSTAINABLE WINERY

The winery of the Centro di Sperimentazione Agraria e Forestale farms over 40 hectares of vineyards planted in the main viticultural areas of the district, from Termeno to the area around Merano, and lastly at Bressanone. A range of altitudes, training systems, soils and aspects are used to study the behaviour of various cultivars, which are then vinified and proposed in a wide range of varietal wines, as well as the more ambitious Maniero line of selections. Col de Réy is a blend of lagrein, petit verdot and tannat coming partly from the Gries vineyards and partly from those at Ölleiten near Caldaro, which after long ageing offers rich ripe fruit and spice, over a full, potent palate, reined in by the close-knit tannins typical of these grapes. The Lagrein Riserva Barbagòl, solely from grapes on the Gries plain, also boasts a rich, potent style.

○ A. A. Gewürztraminer Brenntal Ris. '14	♟♟♟ 5
● A. A. Cabernet Kirchhügel Ris. '13	♟♟ 4
● A. A. Merlot Brenntal Ris. '13	♟♟ 6
○ A. A. Müller Thurgau Graun '15	♟♟ 3*
● A. A. Lagrein Freienfeld Ris. '13	♟♟ 5
● A. A. Merlot-Cabernet Soma '13	♟♟ 5
● A. A. Pinot Nero Glen Ris. '13	♟♟ 5
○ Aruna Extreme Vintage '14	♟♟ 6
○ A. A. Chardonnay Pichl '15	♟ 4
○ A. A. Pinot Grigio Penóner '15	♟ 4
● A. A. Schiava Grigia Sonntaler '15	♟ 3
○ A. A. Gewürztraminer Brenntal '02	♟♟♟ 5
○ A. A. Gewürztraminer Brenntal '00	♟♟♟ 5
○ A. A. Gewürztraminer Brenntal Ris. '12	♟♟♟ 5
● A. A. Lagrein Scuro Fohrhof '00	♟♟♟ 5

● A. A. Cabernet Sauvignon Sass Roà Ris. '13	♟♟ 5
● A. A. Lagrein Barbagòl Ris. '13	♟♟ 5
○ A. A. Sauvignon Oyèll Ris. '14	♟♟ 4
○ A. A. Sauvignon Passito Saphir '14	♟♟ 6
● Col de Réy '11	♟♟ 6
○ A. A. Kerner Auròna '13	♟ 6
○ A. A. Pinot Bianco '15	♟ 2
● A. A. Pinot Nero Ris. '15	♟ 4
○ A. A. Riesling '15	♟ 4
● A. A. Lagrein Scuro Barbagòl Ris. '00	♟♟♟ 5
○ A. A. Gewürztraminer Elyònd Ris. '13	♟♟ 4
● A. A. Lagrein Barbagòl Ris. '12	♟♟ 5
● A. A. Pinot Nero Ris. '13	♟♟ 4
○ A. A. Sauvignon Oyèll '14	♟♟ 4

Loacker Schwarhof

LOC. SANCT JUSTINA, 3
39100 BOLZANO/BOZEN
TEL. +39 0471365125
www.loacker.bio

CELLAR SALES
PRE-BOOKED VISITS
ANNUAL PRODUCTION 60,000 bottles
HECTARES UNDER VINE 7.00
VITICULTURE METHOD Certified Organic
SUSTAINABLE WINERY

The winery of the Loacker family is to be found at Santa Justina, at the mouth of the Valle Isarco. Here, Hayo and Franz Josef farm the land using organic methods and adopt homeopathic techniques in their pursuit of the perfect combination of nature and human work. The vineyards are distributed over three plots, with one near the cellar and smaller vineyards at Kohlerhof and Kalter Keller, and offer wines of great character. We saw an impressive range this year from the Loacker family, with the Lagrein Gran Lareyn Riserva at the top of our list of favourites. A well-typed nose of black berry fruit and spice paves the way for a spectacular palate, offering serious concentration and power without sacrificing suppleness and continuity, resulting in an intriguing wine. The Merlot Ywain shows a similar style, while playing on its greater freshness.

● A. A. Lagrein Gran Lareyn Ris. '13	♥♥ 4
● Merlot Ywain '13	♥♥ 4
● A. A. Cabernet Lagrein Kastlet '13	♥♥ 4
○ Chardonnay '14	♥♥ 4
● Lagrein Gran Lareyn '14	♥♥ 4
● A. A. Santa Maddalena Cl. '15	♥ 3
○ Gewürztraminer Atagis '15	♥ 5
○ Sauvignon Blanc Tasnim '15	♥ 4
● A. A. Merlot Ywain '04	♥♥♥ 4*
● A. A. Lagrein Gran Lareyn '13	♥♥ 4
● A. A. Lagrein Gran Lareyn '12	♥♥ 4
○ Gewürztraminer Atagis '14	♥♥ 5
● Kastlet '12	♥♥ 5
● Kastlet '11	♥♥ 5
● Merlot Ywain '12	♥♥ 4

Manincor

LOC. SAN GIUSEPPE AL LAGO, 4
39052 CALDARO/KALTERN [BZ]
TEL. +39 0471960230
www.manincor.com

CELLAR SALES
PRE-BOOKED VISITS
ANNUAL PRODUCTION 300,000 bottles
HECTARES UNDER VINE 50.00
VITICULTURE METHOD Certified Biodynamic
SUSTAINABLE WINERY

In recent decades, Manincor has increasingly become a benchmark for the wines of this district. Sophie and Michael Goëss-Enzemberg, with the precious help of Helmut Zozin, have converted to biodynamic farming methods and built a new cellar perfectly integrated into the farmland setting, designed to optimize the efficient use of energy. They have no fewer than 50 hectares of vineyards in five plots, at elevations of between 230 and 500 metres. Mason's vineyards have provided a splendid Pinot Nero, which opens slowly on the nose to aromatic herbs and acidulous wild berry fruit. It shows its sweeter side on a graceful palate with a lingering finish. Among the whites, the Sauvignon Tannenberg won us over with its nose of tropical fruit and spice, and its dense, harmonious palate. The Pinot Bianco Eichhorn, meanwhile, offers a more reticent, subdued nose over a firm, crisp palate.

○ A. A. Terlano Pinot Bianco Eichhorn '15	♥♥♥ 5
● A. A. Pinot Nero Mason di Mason '13	♥♥ 7
○ A. A. Terlano Sauvignon Tannenberg '14	♥♥ 5
○ A. A. Terlano Réserve della Contessa '15	♥♥ 3
○ Le Petit Passito '14	♥♥ 6
○ A. A. Moscato Giallo '15	♥ 3
● Castel Campan '13	♥ 8
○ A. A. Terlano Pinot Bianco Eichhorn '13	♥♥♥ 5
○ A. A. Terlano Pinot Bianco Eichhorn '12	♥♥♥ 5
○ A. A. Terlano Pinot Bianco Eichhorn '10	♥♥♥ 4
○ A. A. Terlano Pinot Bianco Eichhorn '09	♥♥♥ 4
○ A. A. Terlano Sauvignon '08	♥♥♥ 4
○ A. A. Terlano Sauvignon Tannenberg '13	♥♥♥ 5
○ A. A. Terlano Réserve della Contessa '14	♥♥ 3*

K. Martini & Sohn

LOC. CORNAIANO
VIA LAMM, 28
39057 APPIANO/EPPAN [BZ]
TEL. +39 0471663156
www.martini-sohn.it

CELLAR SALES
PRE-BOOKED VISITS
ANNUAL PRODUCTION 230,000 bottles
HECTARES UNDER VINE 30.00

Gabriel Martini and his son Lukas are at the
helm of the family winery, established
around 40 years ago by Gabriel himself and
his father Karl. While owning limited land
under vine, they have managed to become a
leading name in the region's viticulture,
thanks to a network of growers that exploit
the best aspected plots to provide Gabriel
and Lukas with raw materials of the highest
quality, which they transform into a range of
outstanding wines. The wide range of wines
presented this year shows great variety, with
straightforward, fragrant, varietal wines to
imposing vineyard selections. The Lagrein
Maturum shows a complex, layered nose,
with fruit slowly making way for gamey and
mineral aromas. In the mouth, it is beautifully
balanced, potent and generous. The
focused Pinot Bianco Palladium, meanwhile,
boasts refreshing aromas and a racy,
succulent palate.

Maso Hemberg
Klaus Lentsch

S.DA REINSPERG, 18A
39057 APPIANO/EPPAN [BZ]
TEL. +39 0471967263
www.klauslentsch.eu

CELLAR SALES
PRE-BOOKED VISITS
ANNUAL PRODUCTION 50,000 bottles
HECTARES UNDER VINE 6.00

Just under ten years ago, Klaus Lentsch
took over the running of the Hemberg estate
at Campodazzo, at the mouth of the Valle
Isarco, starting out with a handful of labels
dedicated to the traditional varieties of the
valley, but soon adding further plots and
extending his range. In the new winery,
perfectly blending into the vineyards above
San Paolo, he now produces well-typed,
quality wines, dedicating care and energy to
each phase of the production process. We
were impressed by many of this year's
wines, starting with the Pinot Nero Bachgart,
a red unfolding focused aromas of wild
berries against a backdrop of oak and spice,
leading to an understated yet highly elegant,
taut palate. The Riserva offers a similar
aromatic profile but with greater complexity
and fullness. From the Valle Isarco,
meanwhile, we loved the firm, satisfyingly
drinkable Grüner Veltliner Eichberg.

● A. A. Lagrein Maturum '13	♟♟ 5
○ A. A. Pinot Bianco Palladium '15	♟♟ 2*
○ A. A. Chardonnay Maturum '14	♟♟ 4
● A. A. Lago di Caldaro Cl. Felton '15	♟♟ 2*
● A. A. Pinot Nero Palladium '14	♟♟ 3
○ A. A. Sauvignon Palladium '15	♟♟ 3
○ A. A. Kerner Palladium '15	♟ 2
● A. A. Lagrein Gurzan Rueslhof '15	♟ 2
⊙ A. A. Lagrein Rosé Grieser '15	♟ 2
○ A. A. Müller Thurgau Palladium '15	♟ 3
● A. A. Santa Maddalena Cl. '15	♟ 2
● A. A. Schiava Palladium '15	♟ 2
○ A. A. Sauvignon Palladium '04	♟♟♟ 2*
○ A. A. Pinot Bianco Palladium '14	♟♟ 2*
○ A. A. Sauvignon Palladium '14	♟♟ 3

● A. A. Pinot Nero Bachgart '13	♟♟♟ 4*
○ A. A. Pinot Bianco Amperg '15	♟♟ 2*
● A. A. Pinot Nero Bachgart Ris. '12	♟♟ 3
○ A. A. Valle Isarco Grüner Veltliner Eichberg '14	♟♟ 3
○ A. A. Gewürztraminer Fuchslahn '15	♟ 2
○ A. A. Moscato Giallo Amperg '15	♟ 2
○ A. A. Sauvignon Amperg '15	♟ 2
○ A. A. Moscato Giallo '14	♟♟ 2*
● A. A. Pinot Nero Bachgart '12	♟♟ 2*

Cantina Meran Burggräfler

VIA CANTINA, 9
39020 MARLENGO/MARLING [BZ]
TEL. +39 0473447137
www.cantinamerano.it

CELLAR SALES
PRE-BOOKED VISITS
ANNUAL PRODUCTION 1,000,000 bottles
HECTARES UNDER VINE 250.00

The winery is the result of the merger of two longstanding cooperatives in the Burgraviato area and has remained firmly linked to its territory, with vineyards covering around 250 hectares divided between almost 400 members, with some of the smallest average individual holdings in the district. The vineyards lie around Merano and nearby towns, above all in Val Venosta, and form the basis for various lines of excellent products. One of these, Sonnenberg, is dedicated precisely to the wines of the valley. We saw a splendid performance from the Sauvignon Mervin, from vineyards lying at an elevation of around 500 metres. On the nose, intense tropical fruit makes way for delicate mineral notes and underlying complexity. The rounded, juicy palate boasts full flavour and a long finish, earning it a Tre Bicchieri. A textbook example of how a red can exploit tautness and freshness to the full is the Schiava Schickenburg, while the Pinot Bianco Sonnenberg is crisp and harmonious.

★Cantina Convento Muri-Gries

P.ZZA GRIES, 21
39100 BOLZANO/BOZEN
TEL. +39 0471282287
www.muri-gries.com

CELLAR SALES
ANNUAL PRODUCTION 700,000 bottles
HECTARES UNDER VINE 55.00
SUSTAINABLE WINERY

Cantina Convento Muri Gries boasts around a century of history, and for around 50 years has been bottling its own wine. For 30 of these, lagrein has been its most important variety. For many years, Walter Bernard has been in charge of viticulture, and tends over 50 hectares of vineyards, mainly lying to the northeast of Bolzano, in the unique Klosteranger area, and near Appiano, where white grapes and some of the pinot nero are grown. Back at the cellar, meanwhile, Christian Werth is in charge, and brings the best out of the individual varieties. The winery's top label was left to mature for another year in the cellars, so our attention focused on an excellent version of the Bianco Abtei Muri, a blend of pinot bianco and pinot grigio grapes from vineyards at Appiano Monte, which ages in large oak. Its aromas of fruit and fresh-cut flowers are encored delightfully on the firm palate.

○ A. A. Sauvignon Mervin '14	♟♟♟ 4*
● A. A. Schiava Schickenburg Graf von Meran '15	♟♟ 2*
○ A. A. Val Venosta Pinot Bianco Sonnenberg '15	♟♟ 3*
○ A. A. Chardonnay Goldegg '14	♟♟ 4
○ A. A. Gewürztraminer Graf von Meran '15	♟♟ 3
● A. A. Merlot Freiherr Ris. '13	♟♟ 5
○ A. A. Moscato Giallo Passito Sissi '14	♟♟ 6
○ A. A. Pinot Bianco Graf von Meran '15	♟♟ 3
○ A. A. Pinot Bianco Tyrol '14	♟♟ 4
● A. A. Pinot Nero Zeno Ris. '13	♟♟ 4
○ A. A. Riesling Graf von Meran '15	♟♟ 4
○ A. A. Sauvignon Graf von Meran '15	♟♟ 4
○ A. A. Pinot Bianco Tyrol '13	♟♟♟ 4*
○ A. A. Valle Venosta Pinot Bianco Sonnenberg '13	♟♟♟ 3*

○ A. A. Bianco Abtei Muri Ris. '14	♟♟ 3*
● A. A. Lagrein '15	♟♟ 3
⊙ A. A. Lagrein Rosato '15	♟♟ 2*
● A. A. Moscato Rosa Abtei Muri V. T. '14	♟♟ 5
○ A. A. Pinot Grigio '15	♟♟ 3
○ A. A. Terlano Pinot Bianco '15	♟♟ 3
● A. A. Pinot Nero '15	♟ 3
● A. A. Lagrein Abtei Muri Ris. '12	♟♟♟ 5
● A. A. Lagrein Abtei Muri Ris. '11	♟♟♟ 5
● A. A. Lagrein Abtei Muri Ris. '10	♟♟♟ 5
● A. A. Lagrein Abtei Muri Ris. '09	♟♟♟ 5
● A. A. Lagrein Abtei Ris. '07	♟♟♟ 5
● A. A. Lagrein Abtei Ris. '06	♟♟♟ 4
● A. A. Lagrein Abtei Ris. '05	♟♟♟ 4
● A. A. Lagrein Abtei Ris. '04	♟♟♟ 4

★Cantina Nals Margreid

via Heiligenberg, 2
39010 Nalles/Nals [BZ]
Tel. +39 0471678626
www.kellerei.it

CELLAR SALES
PRE-BOOKED VISITS
ANNUAL PRODUCTION 950,000 bottles
HECTARES UNDER VINE 160.00
SUSTAINABLE WINERY

Cantina Nals Margreid covers over 150 hectares distributed over the district. The best grapes are found above all near Nalles, with vineyards that rise from the valley floor to the 700 metres of Sirmian. Near Magrè, meanwhile, we find the Bordeaux and white varieties, which need warmer temperatures, while in the Bolzano basin space is laid over to lagrein and schiava. In the cellar, it is Harald Schraffl who has the task of bringing out the best from these raw materials, in a range of characterful, elegant wines while Gottfried Pollinger runs the winery. It was once again the Pinot Bianco Sirmian that charmed our tasting panel, thanks to a graceful nose of crisp white-fleshed fruit against a backdrop of blossom and vegetal nuances. The full, caressing palate shows all the warmth of the growing year. We also loved the Passito Baronesse, with its intense aromas of spice, liquorice and dried flowers, over a harmonious, graceful palate.

Ignaz Niedrist

loc. Cornaiano/Girlan
via Ronco, 5
39057 Appiano/Eppan [BZ]
Tel. +39 0471664494
www.ignazniedrist.com

CELLAR SALES
PRE-BOOKED VISITS
ANNUAL PRODUCTION 45,000 bottles
HECTARES UNDER VINE 10.00
SUSTAINABLE WINERY

The Niedrist family has been producing wine for over 170 years, but it was with the arrival of Ignaz and his wife Elisabeth that the winery changed gear. The plots have been extended to cover around ten hectares in three different zones. The vineyards at Cornaiano lie at an elevation of around 500 metres, while those at Appiano Monte are on higher land. The gravelly soil and warmth of the valley floor at Gries, meanwhile, is exploited for lagrein. We saw convincing wines across the board from Niedrist this year, starting with a superlative version of its Pinot Nero, opening to a nose of autumn leaves, berries, medicinal herbs and rain-soaked earth. This paves the way for a richly flavoured, taut palate of great finesse. More intense and approachable on the nose, the Sauvignon offers thrust and full flavour in the mouth. The rich, almost meaty Lagrein Berger Gei still needs to mature before it can achieve perfect balance.

○ A. A. Pinot Bianco Sirmian '15	♟♟♟ 5
○ A. A. Moscato Giallo Passito Baronesse Baron Salvadori '13	♟♟ 6
○ A. A. Sauvignon Mantele '15	♟♟♟ 5
○ A. A. Chardonnay Magrè '15	♟♟ 4
○ A. A. Gewürztraminer Lyra '15	♟♟ 4
● A. A. Lagrein Gries Ris. '13	♟♟♟ 5
○ A. A. Pinot Bianco Penon '15	♟♟ 3
○ A. A. Pinot Grigio Punggl '15	♟♟ 4
● A. A. Merlot-Cabernet Anticus Baron Salvadori Ris. '13	♟ 6
○ A. A. Sauvignon Gennen '15	♟ 3
● A. A. Schiava Galea '15	♟ 3
○ A. A. Pinot Bianco Sirmian '14	♟♟♟ 5
○ A. A. Pinot Bianco Sirmian '13	♟♟♟ 4*
○ A. A. Pinot Bianco Sirmian '12	♟♟♟ 4*
○ A. A. Pinot Bianco Sirmian '11	♟♟♟ 3*

● A. A. Lagrein Gries Berger Gei '13	♟♟ 5
● A. A. Pinot Nero '13	♟♟ 5
○ A. A. Terlano Sauvignon '15	♟♟ 4
○ A. A. Riesling Berg '15	♟♟ 4
○ A. A. Terlano Pinot Bianco Berg '15	♟♟ 4
○ Trias '15	♟♟ 4
○ A. A. Riesling Berg '11	♟♟♟ 4*
○ A. A. Terlano Pinot Bianco '12	♟♟♟ 3*
○ A. A. Terlano Sauvignon '10	♟♟♟ 3
○ A. A. Terlano Sauvignon '00	♟♟♟ 3*
○ Trias '14	♟♟♟ 4*
● A. A. Lagrein Berger Gei '12	♟♟ 4
● A. A. Pinot Nero Vom Kalk '12	♟♟ 6

Niklaserhof - Josef Sölva

LOC. SAN NICOLÒ
VIA DELLE FONTANE, 31A
39052 CALDARO/KALTERN [BZ]
TEL. +39 0471963434
www.niklaserhof.it

CELLAR SALES
PRE-BOOKED VISITS
ANNUAL PRODUCTION 50,000 bottles
HECTARES UNDER VINE 6.00

Josef Sölva and his son Dieter run the family winery in the high part of Caldaro, at the foot of the Mendola massif that dominates the Oltradige area. Although the image of this zone is indissolubly linked to schiava and Lake Caldaro, the winery has made a name for its focused whites, produced from its six hectares of vineyards. Josef tends the rows, while Dieter is in charge of the fine cellar, practically carved out of the rock. Sölva offers a wide range of labels, among which pride of place goes to the Pinot Bianco Klaser Riserva 2013. Released after long ageing, it flaunts a brilliant, lustrous hue, and shows a nose of fruit and white pepper, against a backdrop of subtle yet persistent florality. In the mouth, it shows full-bodied, taut and supple. The Sauvignon offers more intense aromas and a racy palate, and we also liked the fresher version of the Pinot Bianco.

○ A. A. Pinot Bianco Klaser Ris. '13	♟♟	3*
○ A. A. Bianco Mondevinum Ris. '13	♟♟	4
○ A. A. Kerner '15	♟♟	2*
● A. A. Lago di Caldaro Cl. Charta '15	♟♟	2*
● A. A. Lago di Caldaro Scelto Cl. '15	♟♟	2*
● A. A. Lagrein Mondevinum Ris. '13	♟♟	4
● A. A. Lagrein-Cabernet Klaser Ris. '13	♟♟	4
○ A. A. Pinot Bianco '15	♟♟	2*
○ A. A. Sauvignon '15	♟♟	3
● A. A. Lagrein '15	♟	2
● A. A. Lago di Caldaro Scelto Cl. '14	♟♟	2*
● A. A. Lagrein '13	♟♟	2*
● A. A. Lagrein Mondevinum Ris. '12	♟♟	4
○ A. A. Pinot Bianco '14	♟♟	2*
○ A. A. Pinot Bianco Klaser Ris. '12	♟♟	3

Pacherhof - Andreas Huber

FRAZ. NOVACELLA
V.LO PACHER, 1
39040 VARNA/VAHRN [BZ]
TEL. +39 0472835717
www.pacherhof.com

CELLAR SALES
PRE-BOOKED VISITS
ACCOMMODATION AND RESTAURANT SERVICE
ANNUAL PRODUCTION 90,000 bottles
HECTARES UNDER VINE 8.50

One of the iconic wineries in Valle Isarco is that of Andreas Huber, lying on the western slope of the valley just above Novacella. His vineyards cover eight hectares at elevations which allow white grape varieties to develop intense, elegant aromas. In the cellar, housed in splendid building with 900 years of history, Andreas's philosophy is based on a perfect combination of variety and territory, which results in wines full of character. The winery's oldest vineyards provide the grapes for a Sylvaner Alte Reben of great character, with a deep sulphurous nose in which fruit comes only slowly to the fore, followed by a firm, gutsy palate with a long, dry finish. The Riesling meanwhile is more German in style, with an intense nose of blossom and white-fleshed fruit. This leads to attractive balance in the mouth, in which marked sweetness plays off against muscular, thrusting acidity.

○ A. A. Valle Isarco Riesling '15	♟♟	4
○ A. A. Valle Isarco Sylvaner Alte Reben '15	♟♟	5
○ A. A. Valle Isarco Grüner Veltliner '15	♟♟	4
○ A. A. Valle Isarco Müller Thurgau '15	♟♟	3
○ A. A. Valle Isarco Pinot Grigio '15	♟♟	4
○ A. A. Valle Isarco Sylvaner '15	♟♟	4
○ A. A. Valle Isarco Gewürztraminer '15	♟	5
○ A. A. Valle Isarco Kerner '15	♟	5
○ A. A. Valle Isarco Riesling '04	♟♟♟	3
○ A. A. Valle Isarco Sylvaner '13	♟♟♟	3*
○ A. A. Valle Isarco Sylvaner Alte Reben '05	♟♟♟	4
○ A. A. Valle Isarco Kerner '14	♟♟	3
○ A. A. Valle Isarco Pinot Grigio '14	♟♟	4
○ A. A. Valle Isarco Riesling '14	♟♟	4
○ A. A. Valle Isarco Sylvaner Alte Reben '14	♟♟	5

Pfannenstielhof
Johannes Pfeifer

VIA PFANNESTIEL, 9
39100 BOLZANO/BOZEN
TEL. +39 0471970884
www.pfannenstielhof.it

CELLAR SALES
PRE-BOOKED VISITS
ANNUAL PRODUCTION 43,000 bottles
HECTARES UNDER VINE 4.00

Only the railway separates the Pfeifer family's winery from the eastern outskirts of Bolzano, while its vineyards extend towards the hills of Santa Maddalena and Santa Justina. Johannes and his wife Margareth tend a few hectares mainly around the farmhouse, while a small plot dedicated to pinot nero is found at Pianizza in the Caldaro area. The remaining land is planted to schiava and lagrein, farmed with the utmost respect for the environment. Once again, Pfeifer's Santa Maddalena is one of the most convincing versions, and shows fresh yet deep, with a nose of berries, spice and fresh-cut flowers. It changes gear on the light, dynamic palate, where succulent, juicy fruit ensures great length and a dry, satisfying finish. We also loved the two completely different styles of the winery's brace of Lagreins: the rich, potent Riserva, and the approachable vom Boden with its crisp fruit.

Tenuta Ritterhof

S.DA DEL VINO, 1
39052 CALDARO/KALTERN [BZ]
TEL. +39 0471963298
www.ritterhof.it

CELLAR SALES
PRE-BOOKED VISITS
RESTAURANT SERVICE
ANNUAL PRODUCTION 300,000 bottles
HECTARES UNDER VINE 7.50

Driving along the SP14 on the way to Caldaro, as you enter the town you come across the historic Ritterhof winery, which in the 1990s was acquired by the Roner family. In just over a decade, Ludwig Kaneppele has given it a new lease of life, making it a benchmark for all lovers of Gewürztraminer. The winery's holdings cover less than ten hectares, but local growers working around 40 hectares provide further raw materials for its labels. Ludwig Kanepele clearly has a special touch when it comes to gewürztraminer, as our tastings of no fewer than three Ritterhof wines clearly showed. Our favourite, the Auratus Crescendo, took top honours, and exploited the full potential of the 2015 growing year, seducing us with rich aromas and a generous, leisurely palate. We also loved the Passito Sonus, a caressing, summery wine. The Lagrein Manu was rich, concentrated and potent.

● A. A. Santa Maddalena Cl. '15	♟♟ 3*
● A. A. Lagrein Ris. '13	♟♟ 5
● A. A. Lagrein vom Boden '15	♟♟ 3
⊙ Lagrein Rosé '15	♟♟ 2*
● A. A. Santa Maddalena Cl. '14	♟♟♟ 3*
● A. A. Santa Maddalena Cl. '09	♟♟♟ 2*
● A. A. Lagrein Ris. '12	♟♟ 5
● A. A. Lagrein Ris. '11	♟♟ 5
● A. A. Lagrein vom Boden '14	♟♟ 3
● A. A. Lagrein vom Boden '13	♟♟ 3
● A. A. Pinot Nero '12	♟♟ 4
● A. A. Pinot Nero '10	♟♟ 4
● A. A. Santa Maddalena Cl. '13	♟♟ 3*

○ A. A. Gewürztraminer Auratus Crescendo '15	♟♟♟ 4*
● A. A. Lagrein Manus Ris. '12	♟♟ 5
○ Gewürztraminer Passito Sonus '13	♟♟ 5
○ A. A. Gewürztraminer '15	♟♟ 3
● A. A. Lago di Caldaro Cl. Sup. Novis '15	♟♟ 3
○ A. A. Pinot Bianco '15	♟♟ 2*
○ A. A. Sauvignon '15	♟♟ 2*
○ A. A. Pinot Bianco Verus '15	♟ 3
● A. A. Pinot Nero Dignus '12	♟ 5
● A. A. Santa Maddalena Perlhof '15	♟ 2
○ A. A. Gewürztraminer Auratus Crescendo '14	♟♟♟ 5
○ A. A. Gewürztraminer Auratus Crescendo '13	♟♟♟ 4*
○ A. A. Gewürztraminer Auratus Crescendo '12	♟♟♟ 4*

Röckhof - Konrad Augschöll

VIA SAN VALENTINO, 22
39040 VILLANDRO/VILLANDERS [BZ]
TEL. +39 0472847130
roeck@rolmail.net

CELLAR SALES
PRE-BOOKED VISITS
RESTAURANT SERVICE
ANNUAL PRODUCTION 20,000 bottles
HECTARES UNDER VINE 3.50

Konrad Augschöll has turned his dream into reality, building a brand new, modern cellar perfectly set in the farmland around Villandro. The small plot lies on the western slopes of the Valle Isarco, perfectly aspected to the south east with views over the imposing monastery of Sabiona. The winery produces small but significant quantities of white wines, alongside the traditional zweigelt, while speck and other cured meats are stored in the cellar for visitors to Konrad's agriturismo. Konrad only presented three wines this year, but the Caruess cut a fine figure. This original blend of gewürztraminer, sylvaner and pinot grigio, aged almost exclusively in steel, displays a focused nose of blossom and citrus, followed by a full, complex palate with refreshing notes of medicinal herbs on the finish. The Grüner Veltliner and Müller Thurgau, meanwhile, are subtler and racier.

Tenuta Hans Rottensteiner

FRAZ. GRIES
VIA SARENTINO, 1A
39100 BOLZANO/BOZEN
TEL. +39 0471282015
www.rottensteiner-weine.com

CELLAR SALES
PRE-BOOKED VISITS
ANNUAL PRODUCTION 450,000 bottles
HECTARES UNDER VINE 95.00

Rottensteiner is an historic name in Alto Adige, a family-run business which has been operating for over 50 years in the area to the northwest of Trento. Right from the outset, the winery based its production on grapes from its own vineyards and those of around 60 growers, in three product lines: Classic for monovarietals; Cru for vineyard selections; and Select for the more ambitious labels. We were won over by the Sylvaner from vineyards in the Valle Isarco. The nose opens slowly, ushering in golden delicious apple followed first by subtle floral nuances and then powerful smoky notes. The palate plays on harmony rather than fullness, and offers full flavour and good length. The Pinot Bianco Carnol and Gewürztraminer Cancenai, meanwhile, are fine varietal expressions, and the Lagrein Select Riserva rich and well balanced.

○ Caruess Weiß '15	♙♙ 3*
○ A. A. Valle Isarco Grüner Veltliner Gail Fuass '15	♙♙ 3
○ A. A. Valle Isarco Müller Thurgau '15	♙♙ 3
○ A. A. Valle Isarco Riesling Viel Anders '08	♙♙♙ 3*
○ A. A. Valle Isarco Veltliner '11	♙♙♙ 3*
○ A. A. Valle Isarco Müller Thurgau '14	♙♙ 3
○ A. A. Valle Isarco Müller Thurgau '13	♙♙ 3
○ A. A. Valle Isarco Riesling Viel Anders '14	♙♙ 3*
○ A. A. Valle Isarco Riesling Viel Anders '13	♙♙ 3
○ A. A. Valle Isarco Veltliner Gail Fuass '14	♙♙ 3
○ A. A. Valle Isarco Veltliner Gail Fuass '13	♙♙ 3
○ A. A. Valle Isarco Veltliner Gail Fuass '12	♙♙ 3*
○ Caruess Weiß '14	♙♙ 3
○ Caruess Weiß '13	♙♙ 3

○ A. A. Gewürztraminer Cancenai '15	♙♙ 4
● A. A. Lagrein Grieser Select Ris. '13	♙♙ 5
○ A. A. Pinot Bianco Carnol '15	♙♙ 3
○ A. A. Valle Isarco Sylvaner '15	♙♙ 2*
● Prem '15	♙♙ 3
○ A. A. Chardonnay '15	♙ 2
⊙ A. A. Lagrein Rosato '15	♙ 2
○ A. A. Müller Thurgau '15	♙ 2
● A. A. Pinot Nero Select Ris. '13	♙ 5
● A. A. Santa Maddalena Cl. Premstallerhof '15	♙ 2
○ A. A. Sauvignon '15	♙ 3
● A. A. Schiava Kristplonerhof '15	♙ 2
● A. A. Lagrein Ris. '02	♙♙♙ 2*
● A. A. Pinot Grigio '14	♙♙ 2*
● A. A. Santa Maddalena Cl. Premstallerhof '14	♙♙ 2*

★★Cantina Produttori San Michele Appiano

VIA CIRCONVALLAZIONE, 17/19
39057 APPIANO/EPPAN [BZ]
TEL. +39 0471664466
www.stmichael.it

CELLAR SALES
PRE-BOOKED VISITS
ANNUAL PRODUCTION 2,200,000 bottles
HECTARES UNDER VINE 380.00

Cantina di San Michele Appiano is a benchmark for any wine lover, and has made a crucial contribution to the status of Alto Adige's wines over the last 20 years. At the helm, then as now, is Hans Terzer, a kellermeister of unquestionable technical skill, whose intuition and knowledge of the territory translate every year into a range of wines that combine superb quality and character. The Pinot Grigio Sanct Valentin, from vineyards at Appiano Monte lying at elevations of up to 600 metres, ages in oak for around a year. On the nose, intense fresh-cut flowers and pear come to the fore, against a backdrop of oak, providing complexity. On the rich, caressing palate, full flavour makes this a highly satisfying wine. The Sauvigon from the same line once more confirmed its thoroughbred status, and we were also impressed by the superb Chardonnay.

Cantina Produttori San Paolo

LOC. SAN PAOLO
VIA CASTEL GUARDIA, 21
39050 APPIANO/EPPAN [BZ]
TEL. +39 0471662183
www.kellereistpauls.com

CELLAR SALES
PRE-BOOKED VISITS
ANNUAL PRODUCTION 1,200,000 bottles
HECTARES UNDER VINE 175.00
SUSTAINABLE WINERY

Cantina di San Paolo is one of the district's oldest wineries, and has been in business for 100 years. With the passing of time, the number of members, now over 200, has grown. They tend plots above all in the Oltradige area, for a total of around 170 hectares. In the cellar, Wolfgang Tratter transforms the members' grapes into products divided into two lines: St. Paulus dedicated to more straightforward varietal wines; and Passion, which pursues the perfect union of territory and variety. It was this line which in fact gave the two most convincing wines, the Pinot Bianco Riserva and the Sauvignon. The former harks from old vines and ages for a year and a half in large oak. Its nose of pear swathed in delicate citrus and fines herbes paves the way for a satisfyingly weighty palate. The latter plays on intense aromas of tropical fruit and liquorice, perfectly echoed on the palate.

○ A. A. Pinot Grigio St. Valentin '14	♈♈♈ 5
○ A. A. Chardonnay Sanct Valentin '14	♈♈ 6
● A. A. Pinot Nero Sanct Valentin '13	♈♈ 5
○ A. A. Sauvignon Sanct Valentin '15	♈♈ 6
○ A. A. Gewürztraminer Passito Comtess' Sanct Valentin '13	♈♈ 7
○ A. A. Gewürztraminer Sanct Valentin '15	♈♈ 6
○ A. A. Pinot Bianco Sanct Valentin '15	♈♈ 6
○ A. A. Pinot Bianco Schulthauser '15	♈♈ 4
○ A. A. Sauvignon Lahn '15	♈♈ 5
○ A. A. Pinot Grigio Anger '15	♈ 4
○ A. A. Riesling Montiggl '15	♈ 5
○ A. A. Pinot Bianco St. Valentin '13	♈♈♈ 5
○ A. A. Pinot Bianco St. Valentin '11	♈♈♈ 5
○ A. A. Pinot Grigio Anger '11	♈♈♈ 3*
○ A. A. Sauvignon St. Valentin '13	♈♈♈ 5

○ A. A. Pinot Bianco Passion Ris. '14	♈♈ 5
○ A. A. Sauvignon Passion '15	♈♈ 5
○ A. A. Gewürztraminer Kössler '15	♈♈ 3
○ A. A. Gewürztraminer Passion '15	♈♈ 3
● A. A. Lagrein Passion Ris. '14	♈♈ 5
○ A. A. Pinot Grigio '15	♈ 3
● A. A. Pinot Nero Passion Ris. '14	♈♈ 5
○ A. A. Riesling '15	♈♈ 3
○ A. A. Sauvignon Kössler '15	♈♈ 2*
● A. A. Merlot Passion Ris. '13	♈ 7
○ A. A. Pinot Bianco Kössler '15	♈ 2
○ A. A. Pinot Bianco Plötzner '15	♈ 3
○ A. A. Pinot Grigio Kössler '15	♈ 2
○ A. A. Sauvignon Gfill '15	♈ 3
○ A. A. Pinot Bianco Passion '09	♈♈♈ 4
○ A. A. Pinot Bianco Passion Ris. '11	♈♈♈ 4*

Peter Sölva & Söhne

VIA DELL'ORO, 33
39052 CALDARO/KALTERN [BZ]
TEL. +39 0471964650
www.soelva.com

CELLAR SALES
PRE-BOOKED VISITS
ANNUAL PRODUCTION 75,000 bottles
HECTARES UNDER VINE 12.00

The vineyards of the Sölva family lie in the Bassa Atesina and Oltradige areas, where the higher temperatures result in wines of fullness and maturity. A dozen hectares of vineyards provide the raw materials for the winery's labels, divided into three lines with distinct styles. While the Vigneti wines are fragrant and approachable, Amistar and DeSilva offer a more complex and personal interpretation of the territory and its traditions. The most convincing results came precisely from these lines. First off was a Sauvignon DeSilva, which exalts the greener, more intense aromas of the variety, combined with a generous, supple palate. The Amistar Rosso, meanwhile, is a Bordeaux blend with the delightful addition of lagrein and small quantities of super-ripe grapes. Ripe, fleshy fruit on the nose leads into a potent, harmonious palate.

Stachlburg
Baron von Kripp

VIA MITTERHOFER, 2
39020 PARCINES/PARTSCHINS [BZ]
TEL. +39 0473968014
www.stachlburg.com

CELLAR SALES
PRE-BOOKED VISITS
ANNUAL PRODUCTION 30,000 bottles
HECTARES UNDER VINE 7.00
VITICULTURE METHOD Certified Organic

Val Venosta to the east of Merano offers a unique viticultural environment compared to the rest of Alto Adige, with vineyards rapidly climbing to high altitudes. The combination of low rainfall and high temperatures gives extremely attractive wines. It is here that we find Stachlburg, the winery of Barone Sigmund von Kripp, with seven hectares of organically farmed rows. Pinot Nero is not widely produced in these parts, but Kripp always offers convincing versions. On the nose, oak immediately comes to the fore, but soon makes way for wild berries and spice, revealing almost unexpected freshness. The palate unfolds with finesse and lightness, leading to a long, richly-flavoured finish. We also liked the Merlot, with up-front fruit and a generous palate. The rich, succulent Sauvignon, meanwhile, shows excellent continuity.

● Amistar Rosso '13	5
● A. A. Lago di Caldaro Cl. Sup. Peterleiten DeSilva '15	4
○ Amistar Bianco '14	6
● A. A. Lago di Caldaro Scelto Cl. Sup. Peterleiten DeSilva '15	2
○ A. A. Terlano Pinot Bianco DeSilva '15	3
○ A. A. Terlano Pinot Bianco DeSilva '10	3
○ A. A. Terlano Pinot Bianco DeSilva '09	3
● A. A. Lago di Caldaro Scelto Cl. Sup. Peterleiten '14	2*
○ A. A. Pinot Bianco DeSilva '14	4
○ A. A. Pinot Bianco DeSilva '13	4
○ Amistar Bianco '12	4
● Amistar Rosso '12	5

● A. A. Pinot Nero '13	3*
● A. A. Merlot '13	4
○ A. A. Terlano Sauvignon '15	4
○ A. A. Val Venosta Chardonnay '15	3
● A. A. Lagrein '15	3
⊙ A. A. Lagrein Kretzer '15	2
○ A. A. Pinot Grigio '15	2
○ A. A. Val Venosta Pinot Bianco '15	3
● Le Petit Passito '15	2
○ Praesepium Bianco '13	3
○ A. A. Valle Venosta Pinot Bianco '13	3*
○ A. A. Valle Venosta Pinot Bianco '10	3*
● A. A. Merlot '13	4
○ A. A. Terlano Sauvignon '14	4
○ A. A. Valle Venosta Chardonnay '14	3

Strasserhof
Hannes Baumgartner

FRAZ. NOVACELLA
LOC. UNTERRAIN, 8
39040 VARNA/VAHRN [BZ]
TEL. +39 0472830804
www.strasserhof.info

CELLAR SALES
PRE-BOOKED VISITS
ACCOMMODATION
ANNUAL PRODUCTION 45,000 bottles
HECTARES UNDER VINE 5.50

On the left side of Valle Isarco, the estate of
Hannes Baumgarner lies at an elevation of
700 metres, on a plateau overlooking the
Abbazia di Novacella, with south-east-
facing vineyards. The rows are planted
almost entirely to the typical varieties of the
valley, and benefit from mineral-rich soils
which bring out their aromas to the full. The
solid, elegant wines are aged almost
exclusively in steel. Hannes has a special
relationship with riesling, and this was
confirmed in our tastings of the 2015
vintage. A nose of white-fleshed fruit and
flowers gradually makes way for spicy
notes of white pepper, paving the way for
great concentration in the mouth,
counterpointed by tangy, cutting aciity. The
Grüner Veltliner offers a more
approachable, fragrant nose, mirrored on
the firm, grippy palate. The two Sylvaners
also performed admirably.

Stroblhof

LOC. SAN MICHELE
VIA PIGANÒ, 25
39057 APPIANO/EPPAN [BZ]
TEL. +39 0471662250
www.stroblhof.it

CELLAR SALES
PRE-BOOKED VISITS
ANNUAL PRODUCTION 40,000 bottles
HECTARES UNDER VINE 5.20

The fine Stroblhof estate, run by Rosmarie
Hanny and Andreas Nicolussi-Leck at
Appiano, covers just over five hectares on
the slopes of the mountains leading to the
Mendola massif. Here, at elevations of 500
metres, the vineyards are planted to the
region's typical varieties, with a preference
for pinot nero and pinot bianco, chardonnay
and sauvignon, and boast a style that
combines varietal expression with a sense
of place. The Pinot Nero Pigeno spends a
year in oak, and offers intense aromas of
wild berries and aromatic herbs over a
generous, creamy palate of great harmony
and length. The Pinot Bianco Strahler
shows initial reticence on the nose, but
finds full expression on the juicy, supple
palate, ending dry, tangy and beautifully
long. The drinkable Sauvignon Nico,
meanwhile, plays on its intense aromas and
racy palate.

○ A. A. Valle Isarco Grüner Veltliner '15	♟♟ 3*
○ A. A. Valle Isarco Riesling '15	♟♟ 4
○ A. A. Valle Isarco Kerner '15	♟♟ 3
○ A. A. Valle Isarco Sylvaner '15	♟♟ 3
○ A. A. Valle Isarco Sylvaner Anjo '15	♟♟ 4
○ A. A. Valle Isarco Gewürztraminer '15	♟ 4
○ A. A. Valle Isarco Müller Thurgau '15	♟ 3
○ A. A. Valle Isarco Riesling '12	♟♟♟ 3*
○ A. A. Valle Isarco Riesling '11	♟♟♟ 3*
○ A. A. Valle Isarco Veltliner '10	♟♟♟ 3*
○ A. A. Valle Isarco Veltliner '09	♟♟♟ 3*
○ A. A. Valle Isarco Kerner '14	♟♟ 3
○ A. A. Valle Isarco Müller Thurgau '14	♟♟ 3
○ A. A. Valle Isarco Riesling '14	♟♟ 4
○ A. A. Valle Isarco Sylvaner '14	♟♟ 3*

○ A. A. Pinot Bianco Strahler '15	♟♟ 3
● A. A. Pinot Nero Pigeno '13	♟♟ 5
○ A. A. Sauvignon Nico '15	♟♟ 4
○ A. A. Chardonnay Schwarzhaus '15	♟ 3
○ A. A. Pinot Bianco Strahler '09	♟♟♟ 3*
● A. A. Pinot Nero Ris. '05	♟♟♟ 5
○ A. A. Chardonnay Schwarzhaus '13	♟♟ 3
○ A. A. Chardonnay Schwarzhaus '12	♟♟ 3
○ A. A. Pinot Bianco Strahler '14	♟♟ 3
○ A. A. Pinot Bianco Strahler '13	♟♟ 3
○ A. A. Pinot Bianco Strahler '12	♟♟ 3
● A. A. Pinot Nero Pigeno '12	♟♟ 5
● A. A. Pinot Nero Ris. '11	♟♟ 6
◉ A. A. Pinot Nero Rosato Pinot Rosé '13	♟♟ 3
● Pinot Nero Ris. '12	♟♟ 6

Taschlerhof - Peter Wachtler

LOC. MARA, 107
39042 BRESSANONE/BRIXEN [BZ]
TEL. +39 0472851091
www.taschlerhof.com

CELLAR SALES
PRE-BOOKED VISITS
ANNUAL PRODUCTION 30,000 bottles
HECTARES UNDER VINE 4.20

Peter Watchler's winery lies on the steep slopes of the western side of Valle Isarco near Bressanone, where the grapes benefit from the early morning sun, and are constantly caressed by the breezes coming in from the Dolomites. He only grows white grape varieties, with particular attention to those which best represent the valley, namely riesling, kerner and sylvaner. Two of Taschler's wines made our finals, the Riesling and the Sylvaner. The former stands out thanks to its deep aromas, with white-fleshed fruit over citrus and fresh-cut flowers. The palate displays attractive balance, with residual sugar playing off against cutting acidity to provide impressive length. The latter is initially more closed on the smoky nose, before revealing focused fruit aromas, followed by intense flavour and grip in the mouth.

★Tenute Alois Lageder

LOC. TÒR LÖWENGANG
V.LO DEI CONTI, 9
39040 MAGRÈ/MARGREID [BZ]
TEL. +39 0471809500
www.aloislageder.eu

CELLAR SALES
PRE-BOOKED VISITS
RESTAURANT SERVICE
ANNUAL PRODUCTION 1,500,000 bottles
HECTARES UNDER VINE 160.00
VITICULTURE METHOD Certified Biodynamic
SUSTAINABLE WINERY

The Lageder family's estate is one of the largest in Alto Adige, and yet, despite its impressive production figures, one always has the impression of being on small farm. A pioneer of biodynamic methods in the zone, the winery tends 50 hectares of vineyards according to this philosophy, aware of the crucial role of man in the management and protection of the environment. This approach has also rubbed off on many of the growers that provide the winery with grapes. As always, the winery in Magrè presented a wide range, with excellence across the board. Once again, our favourites were the two wines from the Löwengang line, Cabernet and Chardonnay. The former, a 2012, reveals a graceful nose of aromatic herbs and red fruit against a backdrop of mineral notes and spice, supported by finesse and length in the mouth. The rich, potent, dry Chardonnay is zesty and harmonious, with a lingering finale. Tre Bicchieri.

○ A. A. Valle Isarco Sylvaner '15	♔♔♔	3*
○ A. A. Valle Isarco Riesling '15	♔♔	4
○ A. A. Valle Isarco Kerner '15	♔♔	4
○ A. A. Valle Isarco Sylvaner Lahner '14	♔♔	4
○ A. A. Valle Isarco Riesling '14	♔♔♔	4*
○ A. A. Valle Isarco Kerner '14	♔♔	4
○ A. A. Valle Isarco Kerner '13	♔♔	4
○ A. A. Valle Isarco Kerner '12	♔♔	3*
○ A. A. Valle Isarco Riesling '13	♔♔	4
○ A. A. Valle Isarco Sylvaner '14	♔♔	3*
○ A. A. Valle Isarco Sylvaner '13	♔♔	3*
○ A. A. Valle Isarco Sylvaner '12	♔♔	3
○ A. A. Valle Isarco Sylvaner Lahner '13	♔♔	4
○ A. A. Valle Isarco Sylvaner Lahner '12	♔♔	4
○ A. A. Valle Isarco Veltliner '14	♔♔	3*

○ A. A. Chardonnay Löwengang '13	♔♔♔	6
● A. A. Cabernet Löwengang '12	♔♔	7
○ A. A. Gewürztraminer Am Sand '14	♔♔	5
● A. A. Merlot '13	♔♔	3
● A. A. Pinot Nero Krafuss '12	♔♔	6
○ A. A. Sauvignon Lehen '14	♔♔	5
● Casòn '13	♔♔	6
○ Casòn Hirschprunn '13	♔♔	5
○ A. A. Riesling Rain '15	♔	4
○ Forra '14	♔	3
● A. A. Cabernet Löwengang '10	♔♔♔	7
● A. A. Cabernet Löwengang '07	♔♔♔	6
● A. A. Cabernet Sauvignon Cor Römigberg '11	♔♔♔	7
● A. A. Cabernet Sauvignon Cor Römigberg '08	♔♔♔	7

★★Cantina Terlano

VIA SILBERLEITEN, 7
39018 TERLANO/TERLAN [BZ]
TEL. +39 0471257135
www.cantina-terlano.com

CELLAR SALES
PRE-BOOKED VISITS
ANNUAL PRODUCTION 1,000,000 bottles
HECTARES UNDER VINE 165.00

Cantina di Terlano, established in the late 19th century, brings together 150 members, who farm small plots around the town. The vineyards are distributed above all over the south-west-facing slopes, on the slopes of Mount Zoccolo, whose red porphyry provides the wines with character and minerality. Today, under the technical guidance of the kellermeister Rudi Kofler, the winery mainly works with white grape varieties, for labels which in some cases undergo long cellar ageing. Nova Domus is a delicious blend di pinot bianco and chardonnay topped up with a splash of sauvignon which ages in oak of various sizes. The intense, elegant nose is dominated by white-fleshed fruit and blossom, against a backdrop of oak. In the mouth, it combines power and tautness, showing long and succulent. The Riserva Vorberg shows greater grip and depth, and yet again we loved the outstanding Pinot Bianco Rarità, a wine that ages with unbelievable confidence.

Tiefenbrunner

FRAZ. NICLARA
VIA CASTELLO, 4
39040 CORTACCIA/KURTATSCH [BZ]
TEL. +39 0471880122
www.tiefenbrunner.com

CELLAR SALES
PRE-BOOKED VISITS
RESTAURANT SERVICE
ANNUAL PRODUCTION 800,000 bottles
HECTARES UNDER VINE 25.00

The Bassa Atesina area includes a large number of valley floor vineyards, but at the same time also has the highest vineyards of the DOC zone, with plots at altitudes of up to 1,000 metres. The Tiefenbrunner family has been working the land here for centuries, and has 25 hectares of its own land, as well as relying on 40 hectares farmed by other local growers. The historic cellars in Niclara produce wines with marked varietal traits, as well as characterful, ageable selections. The estate's highest vineyards provide the grapes for its best-known wine, the Feldmarschall von Fenner, a Müller Thurgau whose generous nose offers tropical fruit swathed in spice and mineral notes. On the long, fruity palate, it combines power and tautness. We were also won over by the Riserva Linticlarus, a blend of merlot and cabernet that shows a nose of ripe fruit and a dynamic, generous palate.

○ A. A. Terlano Nova Domus Ris. '13	♥♥♥ 6
● A. A. Merlot Gant Andriano Ris. '13	♥♥ 4
○ A. A. Pinot Bianco Rarità '04	♥♥ 8
○ A. A. Terlano Pinot Bianco Vorberg Ris. '13	♥♥ 5
○ A. A. Terlano Sauvignon Quarz '14	♥♥ 6
○ A. A. Gewürztraminer Lunare '14	♥♥ 6
○ A. A. Gewürztraminer Movado Andriano '14	♥♥ 5
● A. A. Lagrein Andriano Tor di Lupo Ris. '13	♥♥ 4
● A. A. Lagrein Porphyr Ris. '13	♥♥ 6
○ A. A. Pinot Bianco '15	♥♥ 2*
○ A. A. Pinot Bianco Finado Andriano '15	♥♥ 2*
● A. A. Pinot Nero Anrar Ris. '13	♥♥ 5
● A. A. Pinot Nero Montigl Ris. '13	♥♥ 5
○ A. A. Terlaner Cl. '15	♥♥ 3
○ A. A. Terlano Sauvignon Winkl '15	♥♥ 3
○ A. A. Terlano Nova Domus Ris. '12	♡♡♡ 6

● A. A. Cabernet - Merlot Linticlarus Ris. '13	♥♥ 6
○ A. A. Müller Thurgau Feldmarschall von Fenner '14	♥♥ 4
○ A. A. Chardonnay Linticlarus Ris. '13	♥♥ 5
○ A. A. Chardonnay Turmhof '15	♥♥ 3
○ A. A. Gewürztraminer Castel Turmhof '15	♥♥ 5
○ A. A. Gewürztraminer Linticlarus V.T. '12	♥♥ 6
● A. A. Lagrein Linticlarus Ris. '13	♥♥ 5
○ A. A. Pinot Bianco Anna Turmhof '15	♥♥ 3
○ A. A. Pinot Grigio Turmhof '15	♥♥ 3
● A. A. Pinot Nero Linticlarus Ris. '13	♥♥ 6
○ A. A. Sauvignon Turmhof '15	♥♥ 4
○ A. A. Müller Thurgau Feldmarschall von Fenner zu Fennberg '13	♡♡♡ 5
○ A. A. Müller Thurgau Feldmarschall von Fenner zu Fennberg '12	♡♡♡ 5

★★Cantina Tramin

S.DA DEL VINO, 144
39040 TERMENO/TRAMIN [BZ]
TEL. +39 0471096633
www.cantinatramin.it

CELLAR SALES
PRE-BOOKED VISITS
ANNUAL PRODUCTION 1,500,000 bottles
HECTARES UNDER VINE 250.00

The 300 members of the the large Termeno cooperative farm around 250 hectares of vineyards, distributed almost entirely in Bassa Atesina, between the villages of Termeno, Ora, Egna and Montagna. Great attention is given to the rows and respect for the environment, which led to conversion to organic and also in part biodynamic methods. This philosophy is also promoted among its members. In the cellar, Willy Sturz exalts the qualities of raw materials from the best vineyards in a range of wines with great personality. Once again, Gewürztraminer ruled the roost at Cantina Tramin, and they presented a peerless range of wines dedicated to this variety. Best of the bunch was the Nussbaumer. Thanks to longer ageing, it has lost a touch of its exuberance to show its more relaxed, deeper nature, on a surefooted yet graceful palate. The Terminum, meanwhile, expressed more evidently the explosive aromas of the variety, and played on measure and harmony.

★Tenuta Unterortl Castel Juval

LOC. JUVAL, 1B
39020 CASTELBELLO CIARDES/KASTELBELL TSCHARS [BZ]
TEL. +39 0473667580
www.unterortl.it

CELLAR SALES
PRE-BOOKED VISITS
ANNUAL PRODUCTION 33,000 bottles
HECTARES UNDER VINE 4.00

At the mouth of Val Senales, looking towards the western slopes, a handful of vineyards can be seen clinging to steep terrain with perfect south-facing aspects, at elevations of up to 800 metres and over. These are the densely-planted rows of Martin and Gisela Aurich, dedicated almost exclusively to white grape varieties, mainly riesling but also pinot bianco and müller, with limited amounts of black grapes to complete the picture. The resulting wines show great finesse. Riesling is however the estate's most important variety, with no fewer than three labels dedicated to this lean white. Windbichel proved once again to be a thoroughbred, and despite the difficult 2014 growing year, offered intense appley aromas and blossom, against a backdrop of subtle but evident mineral notes. In the mouth, it proved firm and beautifully taut. We were impressed with the debut of Unterortl, which instead exploited the excellent 2015 growing year, resulting in aromatic finesse and a dynamic, grippy palate. Tre Bicchieri.

○ A. A. Gewürztraminer Nussbaumer '14	▼▼▼ 5
○ A. A. Gewürztraminer Passito Terminum V. T. '12	▼▼ 7
○ A. A. Pinot Bianco Moriz '15	▼▼ 2*
○ A. A. Pinot Grigio Unterebnerhof '14	▼▼ 4
○ A. A. Gewürztraminer Roen V. T. '14	▼▼ 5
○ A. A. Gewürztraminer Selida '15	▼▼ 3
● A. A. Lagrein Urban '14	▼▼ 5
● A. A. Pinot Nero Maglen Ris. '13	▼▼ 5
● A. A. Sauvignon Pepi '15	▼▼ 4
● A. A. Schiava Freisinger '15	▼▼ 3
○ A. A. Stoan '14	▼▼ 4
○ A. A. Chardonnay '15	▼ 2
○ A. A. Gewürztraminer Nussbaumer '13	▼▼▼ 5
○ A. A. Gewürztraminer Nussbaumer '12	▼▼▼ 5
○ A. A. Gewürztraminer Nussbaumer '11	▼▼▼ 5

○ A. A. Val Venosta Riesling Unterortl '15	▼▼▼ 4*
○ A. A. Val Venosta Riesling Windbichel '14	▼▼ 5
○ A. A. Val Venosta Müller Thurgau '15	▼▼ 3
○ A. A. Val Venosta Pinot Bianco '15	▼▼ 2*
○ A. A. Val Venosta Riesling Gletscherschliff '15	▼▼ 4
○ A. A. Val Venosta Pinot Nero '14	▼ 5
○ A. A. Val Venosta Pinot Bianco Castel Juval '12	▼▼▼ 3*
○ A. A. Val Venosta Riesling '10	▼▼▼ 4
○ A. A. Val Venosta Riesling '09	▼▼▼ 4
○ A. A. Val Venosta Riesling Castel Juval '11	▼▼▼ 4*
○ A. A. Valle Venosta Pinot Bianco Castel Juval '13	▼▼▼ 3*
○ A. A. Valle Venosta Riesling '14	▼▼▼ 4*

ALTO ADIGE

Cantina Produttori Valle Isarco

VIA COSTE, 50
39043 CHIUSA/KLAUSEN [BZ]
TEL. +39 0472847553
www.cantinavalleisarco.it

CELLAR SALES
PRE-BOOKED VISITS
ANNUAL PRODUCTION 750,000 bottles
HECTARES UNDER VINE 140.00

Cantina Produttori della Valle Isarco is the district's smallest cooperative, with over 130 growers working on average a hectare each. Almost impracticable vineyards cling to either side of the valley's slopes, giving wines mainly from white grape varieties, which in this corner of Alto Adige find ideal conditions to express their aromatic qualities to the full. The range is divided into a variety of lines, with the peerless Sabiona vineyard dedicated solely to sylvaner and kerner. The winery's champion this year was the Sylvaner Aristos, a white which slowly reveals its pear aromas, alongside smoky, almost salty notes. On the palate, its outstanding richness of flavour provides superb length, and earned it a Tre Bicchieri. The excellent 2015 growing year also benefited the Pinot Grigio from the same line, which presented complex fruit aromas with excellent follow-through on the palate.

Vivaldi - Arunda

VIA JOSEF-SCHWARZ, 18
39010 MELTINA/MÖLTEN [BZ]
TEL. +39 0471668033
www.arundavivaldi.it

CELLAR SALES
PRE-BOOKED VISITS
ANNUAL PRODUCTION 90,000 bottles
HECTARES UNDER VINE 12.00

Josef Reiterer's operation is located at Meltina near Terlano, but at an altitude of 1,200 metres. Here, Sepp and his wife Marianne have dedicated their energies to the production of Metodo Classico sparklers since the late 1970s, and are pioneers of spumante in the region. The base wines hark from a variety of zones and growers, and are selected to exalt the finesse that each grape achieves in its ideal growing area. Chardonnay is grown at Terlano, pinot nero at Salorno and, naturally, pinot bianco at Appiano. The Blanc de Blancs is a monovarietal Chardonnay which undergoes barrique ageing before bottle fermentation. It opens to a nose of ripe peachy fruit with just a hint of oak in the shadows, to be followed by a rich, zesty palate with good length and elegance. The Cuvée Marianna, meanwhile, is a blend of chardonnay topped up with pinot nero, boasting a complex nose and generous palate.

○ A. A. Valle Isarco Sylvaner Aristos '15	▼▼▼ 4*
○ A. A. Valle Isarco Pinot Grigio Aristos '15	▼▼ 4
○ A. A. Sauvignon Aristos '15	▼▼ 3
○ A. A. Valle Isarco Gewürztraminer Passito Nectaris '14	▼▼ 6
○ A. A. Valle Isarco Grüner Veltliner Aristos '15	▼▼ 4
○ A. A. Valle Isarco Kerner Aristos '15	▼▼ 4
○ A. A. Valle Isarco Kerner Sabiona '14	▼▼ 5
○ A. A. Valle Isarco Müller Thurgau Aristos '15	▼▼ 3
○ A. A. Valle Isarco Sylvaner Sabiona '14	▼▼ 5
○ A. A. Valle Isarco Gewürztraminer Aristos '15	▼ 4
○ A. A. Valle Isarco Kerner Aristos '05	♀♀♀ 3*
○ A. A. Valle Isarco Veltliner Aristos '03	♀♀♀ 3*
○ A. A. Valle Isarco Sylvaner Aristos '14	♀♀ 4

○ A. A. Spumante Blanc de Blancs Arunda Extra Brut	▼▼ 5
● A. A. Spumante Brut Rosé Arunda	▼▼ 5
○ A. A. Spumante Extra Brut Cuvée Marianna Arunda	▼▼ 5
○ A. A. Spumante Extra Brut Arunda	▼ 5
○ A. A. Spumante Extra Brut Arunda Ris. '10	▼ 5
○ A. A. Spumante Arunda Ris. '08	♀♀ 5
○ A. A. Spumante Arunda Ris. '07	♀♀ 5
○ A. A. Spumante Extra Brut Arunda Ris. '09	♀♀ 5
○ A. A. Spumante Extra Brut Ris. '08	♀♀ 5

★★Elena Walch

via A. Hofer, 1
39040 Termeno/Tramin [BZ]
Tel. +39 0471860172
www.elenawalch.com

CELLAR SALES
PRE-BOOKED VISITS
RESTAURANT SERVICE
ANNUAL PRODUCTION 500,000 bottles
HECTARES UNDER VINE 33.00

When entering the garden of Elena Walch's winery, it seems that nothing has changed, but underneath the lawn and courtyard the old cellar has been renovated and extended. After making huge investments in developing the vineyards, attention has shifted to the cellar, and since last year production methods have shown even greater respect for the grapes. The estate has impressive holdings, with the superb Kastelaz vineyard covering five hectares and a further 20 at Castel Ringberg. The winery presented an impeccable range of wines, with no fewer than three making our finals. The Gewürztraminer Vigna Kastelaz expresses all the exuberance of this variety, with concentrated aromas of citrus and tropical fruit, mirrored on the rich, full-flavoured, leisurely palate. The Lagrein Vigna Castel Ringberg shows an edgier nose, but beautifully combines power and suppleness in the mouth. The Beyond the Clouds offers a layered nose and a tangy, elegant palate.

○ A. A. Bianco Beyond the Clouds '14	🍷🍷 6
○ A. A. Gewürztraminer V. Kastelaz '15	🍷🍷 5
● A. A. Lagrein V. Castel Ringberg Ris. '12	🍷🍷 5
● A. A. Cabernet Sauvignon V. Castel Ringberg '13	🍷🍷 8
○ A. A. Chardonnay V. Castel Ringberg '13	🍷🍷 7
● A. A. Merlot V. Kastelaz Ris. '13	🍷🍷 6
○ A. A. Pinot Bianco Kristallberg '15	🍷🍷 4
○ A. A. Pinot Grigio V. Castel Ringberg '15	🍷🍷 4
● A. A. Pinot Nero Ludwig '13	🍷🍷 5
○ A. A. Sauvignon V. Castel Ringberg '15	🍷🍷 4
● Kermesse '12	🍷🍷 6
○ A. A. Gewürztraminer Kastelaz '13	🍷🍷🍷 5
○ A. A. Gewürztraminer Kastelaz '12	🍷🍷🍷 5
○ A. A. Gewürztraminer Kastelaz '11	🍷🍷🍷 5
● A. A. Lagrein Castel Ringberg Ris. '11	🍷🍷🍷 5

Tenuta Waldgries

loc. Santa Giustina, 2
39100 Bolzano/Bozen
Tel. +39 0471323603
www.waldgries.it

CELLAR SALES
PRE-BOOKED VISITS
ANNUAL PRODUCTION 65,000 bottles
HECTARES UNDER VINE 8.20

Christian Plattner's winery has a long history, as can be seen from his house, full of artefacts from a long viticultural heritage. The vineyards, covering just over ten hectares, lie in three different zones, each of which is planted to vines that best express their respective terroirs. Around the winery we find sun-kissed vineyards dedicated to schiava, at moderate elevations, while the plots at Appiano, used for the production of whites, are as high as 600 metres, Near Ora, meanwhile, lagrein benefits from alluvial, clayey soils. Plattner presented a wide range of convincing labels, and showed peerless ability in managing the impetuous exuberance of lagrein. Il Mirell harks from old vineyards, whose grapes are vinified with great care and attention in the cellar, for wines characterized by finesse and measured power. The Roblinus de Waldgries, meanwhile, comes from the Kirschleiten vineyard and reveals depth and concentration. Lastly, we loved the elegant Santa Maddalena Classico, a tangy, racy wine.

● A. A. Lagrein Mirell Ris. '13	🍷🍷 6
● A. A. Lagrein Roblinus de Waldgries Ris. '13	🍷🍷 8
● A. A. Santa Maddalena Cl. '15	🍷🍷 3*
● A. A. Lagrein Ris. '13	🍷🍷 5
● A. A. Moscato Rosa Passito '13	🍷🍷 5
○ A. A. Pinot Bianco Isos '15	🍷🍷 4
● A. A. Santa Maddalena Cl. Antheos '15	🍷🍷 5
○ A. A. Sauvignon Myra '15	🍷🍷 4
● A. A. Lagrein Mirell '09	🍷🍷🍷 6
● A. A. Lagrein Scuro Mirell '08	🍷🍷🍷 6
● A. A. Lagrein Scuro Mirell '07	🍷🍷🍷 6
● A. A. Lagrein Scuro Mirell '01	🍷🍷🍷 6
● A. A. Santa Maddalena Cl. Antheos '13	🍷🍷🍷 4*
● A. A. Santa Maddalena Cl. Antheos '12	🍷🍷🍷 4*
● A. A. Santa Maddalena Cl. Antheos '11	🍷🍷🍷 4*

Josef Weger

loc. Cornaiano
via Casa del Gesù, 17
39050 Appiano/Eppan [BZ]
Tel. +39 0471662416
www.wegerhof.it

CELLAR SALES
PRE-BOOKED VISITS
ACCOMMODATION AND RESTAURANT SERVICE
ANNUAL PRODUCTION 80,000 bottles
HECTARES UNDER VINE 8.00

This winery in Cornaiano has a complex history dating back to the early 1800s, and in the past also engaged in intense trade with towns to the north, leading to the opening of an office in Tyrol. Today, the operation is run by Johannes Weger, who farms eight hectares of vineyards giving reliable, quality wines. The Classica line offers labels focusing on varietal expression, while Maso delle Rose is dedicated to selections from the best-aspected sites. It was precisely this line that provided the most interesting wines, starting with the Merlot, which plays on the fruit and vegetal aromas typical of the variety, alternating warm, ripe notes with fresh, balsamic ones. The supple, stylish palate hinges on elegance and harmony. The Pinot Nero version, meanwhile, offers forest fruits on the nose swathed in smoke and spice, leading to a full palate with an attractive tannic weave.

● A. A. Merlot Maso delle Rose '13	🍷🍷 5
● A. A. Lagrein Stoa '14	🍷🍷 3
○ A. A. Pinot Bianco Maso delle Rose '15	🍷🍷 4
○ A. A. Pinot Grigio Ried '15	🍷🍷 3
● A. A. Pinot Nero Maso delle Rose '15	🍷🍷 5
○ A. A. Sauvignon Maso delle Rose '15	🍷🍷 4
○ A. A. Gewürztraminer Maso delle Rose '15	🍷 3
○ A. A. Müller Thurgau Pursgla '14	🍷🍷 3
○ A. A. Chardonnay Leite '14	🍷🍷 3
● A. A. Lagrein Stoa '13	🍷🍷 3
○ A. A. Pinot Bianco '13	🍷🍷 3
○ A. A. Pinot Bianco Lithos '14	🍷🍷 3
○ A. A. Pinot Bianco Maso delle Rose '13	🍷🍷 4
● A. A. Pinot Nero Johann '13	🍷🍷 3
○ A. A. Sauvignon Maso delle Rose '13	🍷🍷 4

Peter Zemmer

s.da del Vino, 24
39040 Cortina Sulla Strada del Vino/Kurtinig [BZ]
Tel. +39 0471817143
www.peterzemmer.com

CELLAR SALES
PRE-BOOKED VISITS
ANNUAL PRODUCTION 500,000 bottles
HECTARES UNDER VINE 65.00

The Zemmer family's winery, now run by Peter, is based in the southernmost part of the province, at Cortina sulla Strada del Vino, the only town in the zone located in the centre of the valley floor without plots on the surrounding mountain slopes. The vineyards, including those of growers who provide additional grapes, cover a large area, and Peter uses the raw materials to produce both wines with varietal character and selections aimed at showing off the vineyards of provenance to their best. We were convinced by the barrique-aged Chardonnay Selection R, from vineyards lying on the plains around Cortina, which reveals a floral nose against a subtle backdrop of oak, over a rich yet taut, supple palate. The Lagrein version, meanwhile, plays on rich fruit aromas and a powerful, warm body. We should also mention a fine performance from the highly pleasurable simpler labels, with their fresh aromas.

○ A. A. Chardonnay Selection R Ris. '14	🍷🍷 4
● A. A. Lagrein Selection R Ris. '14	🍷🍷 3*
○ A. A. Gewürztraminer Selection R '15	🍷🍷 4
○ A. A. Pinot Bianco Punggl '15	🍷🍷 3
○ A. A. Pinot Grigio Selection R Ris. '14	🍷🍷 3
○ A. A. Sauvignon Peter Zemmer '15	🍷🍷 3
○ Cortinie Bianco '15	🍷🍷 3
● Cortinie Rosso '14	🍷🍷 3
○ A. A. Chardonnay Peter Zemmer '15	🍷 3
○ A. A. Müller Thurgau Gfrill '15	🍷 3
○ A. A. Pinot Grigio Peter Zemmer '15	🍷 2
● A. A. Pinot Nero Rollhütt '15	🍷 4
○ A. A. Chardonnay Selection R '13	🍷🍷 4
● A. A. Lagrein Selection R '13	🍷🍷 3*
○ Cortinie Bianco '14	🍷🍷 3

Befehlhof

VIA VEZZANO, 14
39028 SILANDRO/SCHLANDERS [BZ]
TEL. +39 0473742197

CELLAR SALES
PRE-BOOKED VISITS
ANNUAL PRODUCTION 7,000 bottles
HECTARES UNDER VINE 1.20

○ A. A. Spumante Sällent Brut	♛♛	3
● Pinot Nero '13	♛♛	2*
○ Riesling '14	♛♛	3
○ Jera '15	♛	3

Bergmannhof

LOC. SAN PAOLO
RIVA DI SOTTO, 46
39050 APPIANO/EPPAN [BZ]
TEL. +39 0471637082
www.bergmannhof.it

CELLAR SALES
PRE-BOOKED VISITS
ANNUAL PRODUCTION 13,000 bottles
HECTARES UNDER VINE 2.20

● A. A. Lagrein Der Bergmann Ris. '13	♛♛	4
○ A. A. Chardonnay '15	♛	2
○ A. A. Chardonnay Der Bergmann Ris. '14	♛	4
● A. A. Merlot '15	♛	2

Bessererhof - Otmar Mair

LOC. NOVALE DI PRESULE, 10
39050 FIÈ ALLO SCILIAR/VÖLS AM SCHLERN [BZ]
TEL. +39 0471601011
www.bessererhof.it

CELLAR SALES
PRE-BOOKED VISITS
ANNUAL PRODUCTION 35,000 bottles
HECTARES UNDER VINE 1.50

○ A. A. Chardonnay Ris. '13	♛♛	3
○ A. A. Gewürztraminer '15	♛♛	4
○ A. A. Valle Isarco Kerner '15	♛♛	4
○ A. A. Pinot Bianco '15	♛	3

Brunnenhof
Kurt Rottensteiner

LOC. MAZZON
VIA DEGLI ALPINI, 5
39044 EGNA/NEUMARKT [BZ]
TEL. +39 0471820687
www.brunnenhof-mazzon.it

CELLAR SALES
PRE-BOOKED VISITS
ANNUAL PRODUCTION 35,000 bottles
HECTARES UNDER VINE 5.50
VITICULTURE METHOD Certified Organic

● A. A. Pinot Nero Ris. '13	♛♛	5
○ Eva '15	♛♛	4
○ A. A. Gewürztraminer '15	♛	4
● A. A. Lagrein V. V. '14	♛	3

Tenuta Donà

FRAZ. RIVA DI SOTTO
39057 APPIANO/EPPAN [BZ]
TEL. +39 0473221866
www.weingut-dona.com

CELLAR SALES
PRE-BOOKED VISITS
ACCOMMODATION
ANNUAL PRODUCTION 30,000 bottles
HECTARES UNDER VINE 6.00

● A. A. Lagrein '14	♛♛	4
○ A. A. Sauvignon '15	♛♛	3
○ A. A. Terlano Chardonnay '15	♛♛	3
● A. A. Schiava Cl. '15	♛	2

Himmelreichhof

LOC. CIARDEF
VIA CONVENTO, 15A
39020 CASTELBELLO CIARDES/KASTELBELL TSCHARS [BZ]
TEL. +39 0473624417
www.himmelreich-hof.info

ANNUAL PRODUCTION 20,000 bottles
HECTARES UNDER VINE 3.50

● A.A. Val Venosta Pinot Nero '14	♛♛	5
○ A.A. Val Venosta Riesling Geieregg '15	♛♛	4
○ A.A. Val Venosta Pinot Bianco '15	♛	4

Larcherhof - Spögler

VIA RENCIO, 82
39100 BOLZANO/BOZEN
TEL. +39 0471365034
larcherhof@yahoo.de

CELLAR SALES
PRE-BOOKED VISITS
ANNUAL PRODUCTION 30,000 bottles
HECTARES UNDER VINE 5.00

● A. A. Merlot '14	♟♟ 3
● A. A. Santa Maddalena Cl. '15	♟♟ 2*
● A. A. Lagrein '15	♟ 3
○ A. A. Pinot Grigio '15	♟ 3

Marinushof - Heinrich Pohl

LOC. MARAGNO
S.DA VECCHIA, 9B
39020 CASTELBELLO CIARDES/KASTELBELL TSCHARS [BZ]
TEL. +39 0473624717
www.marinushof.it

CELLAR SALES
PRE-BOOKED VISITS
ACCOMMODATION
ANNUAL PRODUCTION 8,000 bottles
HECTARES UNDER VINE 1.20

● A. A. Val Venosta Pinot Nero '14	♟♟ 5
○ A. A. Valle Venosta Riesling '15	♟♟ 4
○ A.A. Val Venosta Pinot Grigio '15	♟♟ 4
● Zweigelt '15	♟ 5

Lorenz Martini

LOC. CORNAIANO/GIRLAN
VIA PRANZOL, 2D
39057 APPIANO/EPPAN [BZ]
TEL. +39 0471664136
www.lorenz-martini.it

CELLAR SALES
PRE-BOOKED VISITS
ANNUAL PRODUCTION 15,000 bottles
HECTARES UNDER VINE 2.00

○ A. A. Spumante Brut Comitissa Gold Gran Riserva '06	♟♟ 5
○ A. A. Spumante Brut Comitissa Ris. '11	♟♟ 5

Messnerhof
Bernhard Pichler

LOC. SAN PIETRO, 7
39100 BOLZANO/BOZEN
TEL. +39 0471977162
www.messnerhof.net

CELLAR SALES
PRE-BOOKED VISITS
ANNUAL PRODUCTION 15,000 bottles
HECTARES UNDER VINE 2.90

○ A. A. Gewürztraminer '15	♟♟ 3
● A. A. Lagrein Ris. '13	♟♟ 4
● Belleus '13	♟♟ 4
○ A. A. Terlano Sauvignon '15	♟ 3

Pardellerhof Montin

VIA TERZO DI MEZZO, 15
39020 MARLENGO/MARLING [BZ]
TEL. +39 0473492575
www.pardellerhof.it

CELLAR SALES
PRE-BOOKED VISITS
ACCOMMODATION
ANNUAL PRODUCTION 10,000 bottles
HECTARES UNDER VINE 1.50

● A. A. Lagrein '14	♟♟ 4
○ A. A. Moscato Giallo Passito '13	♟♟ 5
○ A. A. Pinot Grigio '15	♟ 3

Tenuta Pfitscher

VIA DOLOMITI, 17
39040 MONTAGNA/MONTAN [BZ]
TEL. +39 04711681317
www.pfitscher.it

CELLAR SALES
PRE-BOOKED VISITS
ANNUAL PRODUCTION 60,000 bottles
HECTARES UNDER VINE 7.00

○ A. A. Gewürztraminer Stoass '15	♟♟ 4
● A. A. Merlot Kotznloater '14	♟♟ 4
○ A. A. Sauvignon Saxum '15	♟♟ 4
● A. A. Pinot Nero Matan Ris. '13	♟ 6

Thomas Pichler

VIA DELLE VIGNE, 4
39052 CALDARO/KALTERN [BZ]
TEL. +39 0471963094
www.thomas-pichler.it

CELLAR SALES
PRE-BOOKED VISITS
ANNUAL PRODUCTION 15,000 bottles
HECTARES UNDER VINE 1.50

● A. A. Lagrein Sond Ris. '14	🍷🍷 5
● Furioso '14	🍷🍷 8
○ A. A. Chardonnay Untermazzon '14	🍷 4
○ A. A. Pinot Bianco Im Feld '15	🍷 3

Schloss Englar

LOC. PIGENO, 42
39057 APPIANO/EPPAN [BZ]
TEL. +39 0471662628
www.weingut-englar.com

ANNUAL PRODUCTION 15,000 bottles
HECTARES UNDER VINE 7.00

○ A. A. Chardonnay '14	🍷🍷 4
○ A. A. Pinot Bianco '15	🍷🍷 3
○ A. A. Riesling '15	🍷🍷 4

Tenuta Seeperle

LOC. SAN GIUSEPPE AL LAGO, 28
39052 CALDARO/KALTERN [BZ]
TEL. +39 0471 960158
www.seeperle.it

ANNUAL PRODUCTION 15,000 bottles
HECTARES UNDER VINE 2.00

○ A. A. Gewürztraminer Scharf '15	🍷🍷 4
○ A. A. Pinot Bianco Seitensprung Ris. '14	🍷🍷 5
○ A. A. Sauvignon Echt Geil '15	🍷🍷 4

St. Quirinus - Robert Sinn

VIA PIANIZZA DI SOPRA, 4B
39052 CALDARO/KALTERN [BZ]
TEL. +39 329 8085003
www.st-quirinus.it

CELLAR SALES
PRE-BOOKED VISITS
ACCOMMODATION
ANNUAL PRODUCTION 12,000 bottles
HECTARES UNDER VINE 2.50
VITICULTURE METHOD Certified Organic

● A. A. Pinot Nero Ris. '13	🍷🍷 3
○ A. A. Sauvignon '15	🍷 3

Thurnhof - Andreas Berger

LOC. ASLAGO
VIA CASTEL FLAVON, 7
39100 BOLZANO/BOZEN
TEL. +39 0471288460
www.thurnhof.com

CELLAR SALES
PRE-BOOKED VISITS
ANNUAL PRODUCTION 25,000 bottles
HECTARES UNDER VINE 3.50

● A. A. Cabernet Sauvignon Weinegg Ris. '13	🍷🍷 5
● A. A. Lagrein Ris. '13	🍷🍷 4
○ Passaurum Passito '13	🍷🍷 4
○ A. A. Sauvignon 800 '15	🍷 3

Thomas Unterhofer

LOC. PIANIZZA DI SOPRA, 5
39052 CALDARO/KALTERN [BZ]
TEL. +39 0471669133
www.weingut-unterhofer.com

CELLAR SALES
PRE-BOOKED VISITS
ANNUAL PRODUCTION 12,000 bottles
HECTARES UNDER VINE 3.00

○ A. A. Sauvignon '15	🍷🍷 2*
● A. A. Schiava Campenn '15	🍷🍷 2*
○ Reitl Weiss '15	🍷🍷 3
○ A. A. Kerner '14	🍷 3

Untermoserhof Georg Ramoser

VIA SANTA MADDALENA, 36
39100 BOLZANO/BOZEN
TEL. +39 0471975481
untermoserhof@rolmail.net

CELLAR SALES
PRE-BOOKED VISITS
ACCOMMODATION
ANNUAL PRODUCTION 30,000 bottles
HECTARES UNDER VINE 3.70

● A. A. Lagrein Ris. '13	🍷🍷 5
● A. A. Merlot Ris. '13	🍷🍷 5

Von Blumen

VIA NAZIONALE, 9/1
39040 SALORNO/SALURN [BZ]
TEL. +39 0457230110
www.vonblumenwine.com

CELLAR SALES
PRE-BOOKED VISITS
ANNUAL PRODUCTION 380,000 bottles
HECTARES UNDER VINE 40.00

○ A. A. Pinot Bianco Flowers Selection '14	🍷🍷 3*
○ A. A. Gewürztraminer '15	🍷🍷 3
○ A. A. Pinot Bianco '15	🍷🍷 3
● A. A. Pinot Nero '14	🍷🍷 3

Waldner Tenuta Eichenstein

39020 MARLENGO/MARLING [BZ]
TEL. +39 0473 222020
www.eichenstein.it

ANNUAL PRODUCTION 15,000 bottles
HECTARES UNDER VINE 6.00
SUSTAINABLE WINERY

○ Riesling '15	🍷🍷 3
○ Sauvignon '15	🍷🍷 3
○ Gloria Dei '15	🍷 3

Wassererhof

LOC. NOVALE DI FIÈ, 21
39050 FIÈ ALLO SCILIAR/VÖLS AM SCHLERN [BZ]
TEL. +39 0471724114
www.wassererhof.com

CELLAR SALES
PRE-BOOKED VISITS
RESTAURANT SERVICE
ANNUAL PRODUCTION 35,000 bottles
HECTARES UNDER VINE 4.00

○ A. A. Pinot Bianco '15	🍷🍷 3
● A. A. Santa Maddalena Cl. Mumelterhof '15	🍷🍷 3
○ A. A. Sauvignon '15	🍷🍷 3

Weinberghof Christian Bellutti

IN DER AU, 4A
39040 TERMENO/TRAMIN [BZ]
TEL. +39 0471863224
www.weinberg-hof.com

ANNUAL PRODUCTION 20,000 bottles
HECTARES UNDER VINE 2.80

○ A. A. Gewürztraminer Plon '15	🍷🍷 3
○ A. A. Pinot Grigio Drau '15	🍷🍷 3
○ A. A. Lago di Caldaro Cl. Scelto Eichholz '15	🍷 3

Weingut Martin Abraham

VIA MADERNETO, 29
39057 APPIANO/EPPAN [BZ]
TEL. +39 047J664192
www.weingutabraham.it

ANNUAL PRODUCTION 16,000 bottles
HECTARES UNDER VINE 3.00

○ Pinot Bianco In der Lamm '14	🍷🍷 3
● Pinot Nero '13	🍷🍷 3
● Upupa Rot '13	🍷🍷 3
○ Pinot Bianco Abrahamart '13	🍷 3

VENETO

Veneto has put the thorny 2014 harvest firmly behind it and is back on top form. Production involves all the provinces in the region to some extent and each reveals varieties, traditions and types to satisfy even the most demanding enthusiasts, but there is also plenty of it. There are then two icons dominating the world wine stage: on one hand, the lightness and fragrance of Prosecco, the Italian sparkler now present around the globe; on the other, the muscle and cellarability of Amarone. The former relies on production that started out in the hills of Conegliano and Valdobbiadene but has now conquered much of the neighbouring provinces, and takes home our Sparkler of the Year award thanks to Ruggeri & C's 2015 Valdobbiadene Extra Dry Giustino B. The latter is a modern-style wine made thanks to age-old techniques, serving as a driver for the entire Verona district. Both wines come from the intense mosaic of zones and varietals, some light and fragrant, others deep and complex, clay soils interspersed with volcanic terrain, large and small wineries, and the ongoing changes that allow aficionados to get to know and appreciate the entire range offered by this region. Lots of news this year, reflecting developments that also involve lesser-known areas and producers perfecting their concept of better quality in wine, often paring down the impact of their business, mindful of their role in safeguarding the environment. In Bardolino we meet Villabella's Vigna Morlongo, and Soave vaunts the Dal Cero family as a new entry, with a Soave that shows how passion and capability get results even in difficult vintages. In a lively area like Valpolicella, Marco Mosconi at Illasi and the Sterza cousins at Casterna offer striking Valpolicella Superiore and Amarone. On the Treviso plain, the Cescon brothers have achieved surprising results with Manzoni bianco, a grape of great potential but not often used, proving that even a growing area wrongly considered minor can give great wines. For the rest, we have our usual crop of awards reaped by Valpolicella, with 18 Tre Bicchieris, followed by Soave, which took seven. In the wake of the benchmark wineries of these two DOC zones, awards were earned across all the major regional designations, from Custoza to Montello, the Valdobbiadene and Colli Euganei, not to mention Lugana and the Valdadige, where every year the Fugatti brothers produce one of Italy's best sweet wines.

A Mi Manera

FRAZ. LISON
VIA CADUTI PER LA PATRIA, 29
30026 PORTOGRUARO [VE]
TEL. +39 336592660
www.vinicolamimanera.com

CELLAR SALES
PRE-BOOKED VISITS
ANNUAL PRODUCTION 42,000 bottles
HECTARES UNDER VINE 7.00

Antonio Bigai, or Toni as he is known, is an eclectic winegrower who focused for years on his own property, a benchmark in the Lison area, then finally launched and directs this operation. His handful of hectares in the heart of the designation yields a cadre of personality-rich wines whose objective is to express their terroir. Whites predominate, with Chardonnay, Malvasia, and Tai, but the area's classic reds, Merlot and Cabernet, find their place in Toni's portfolio as well. The Malvasia, perhaps, best mirrors his approach, a tad clouded since he prefers it unfiltered. The nose is redolent of dried flowers, pear and white peach, and pungent scrub, while the full-volumed palate exhibits fine balance and snappy fruit, with a lengthy finish. Tai 2015 is similar, with a simpler nose perhaps, but equally solid and appealing in the mouth. Among the reds, we appreciated A Mi Manera, a Bordeaux blend with a touch of franconia and refosco, with its forthright countryish tone and juicy, incisive fruit.

● A Mi Manera Rosso	▼▼ 3
○ Malvasia '15	▼▼ 3
○ Tai '15	▼▼ 3
○ A Mi Manera Bianco	▼ 3
○ Chardonnay '15	▼ 3
● Pinot Nero '15	▼ 5
○ Lison-Pramaggiore Lison Cl. '09	♈♈ 2*
○ Malvasia d'Istria '12	♈♈ 2*
○ Tai '10	♈♈ 3

Stefano Accordini

FRAZ. CAVALO
LOC. CAMPAROL, 10
37022 FUMANE [VR]
TEL. +39 0457760138
www.accordinistefano.it

CELLAR SALES
PRE-BOOKED VISITS
ANNUAL PRODUCTION 120,000 bottles
HECTARES UNDER VINE 13.00

The Accordini family's wine cellar and vineyards occupied just a few hectares on the valley floor at Pedemonte. Today, their operation lies in the upper part of Valpolicella, seeming almost a balcony looking out over the designation. The vineyards have grown significantly, almost all in this area, where hours of sunlight and constant breezes preserve crisp aromatics and ensure sound fruit during the ripening process. The results are wines with a firmly-structured palate and good weight. Emerging from its lengthy maturation, Amarone Vigneto Il Fornetto 2010 unleashed a multi-faceted wealth of aromatics, with sweet, pulpy berry fruit leading a train of pungent spices and herbs, with the oak perfectly tucked in; the power and solidity on the palate is nicely checked by a dense suite of tannins. Amarone Acinatico 2012 is more exuberant and forward, with plenty of energy and succulence in the mouth.

● Amarone della Valpolicella Cl. Vign. Il Fornetto '10	▼▼ 8
● Amarone della Valpolicella Cl. Acinatico '12	▼▼ 7
● Recioto della Valpolicella Cl. Acinatico '13	▼▼ 5
● Valpolicella Cl. '15	▼▼ 2*
● Valpolicella Cl. Sup. Ripasso '14	▼▼ 3
● Recioto della Valpolicella Cl. Acinatico '04	♈♈♈ 6
● Recioto della Valpolicella Cl. Acinatico '00	♈♈♈ 8
● Amarone della Valpolicella Cl. Acinatico '11	♈♈ 7
● Recioto della Valpolicella Cl. Acinatico '12	♈♈ 5
● Valpolicella Cl. Sup. Ripasso Acinatico '13	♈♈ 3

Adami

FRAZ. COLBERTALDO
VIA ROVEDE, 27
31020 VIDOR [TV]
TEL. +39 0423982110
www.adamispumanti.it

CELLAR SALES
PRE-BOOKED VISITS
ANNUAL PRODUCTION 700,000 bottles
HECTARES UNDER VINE 12.00

Unlike most Prosecco producers, focused mainly on increasing production volume, Franco and Armando Adami prefer to remain faithful to their elected paradise, Valdobbiadene. In past years they have worked to acquire vineyard parcels contiguous to their Giardino property, but their attention is now on the Torri di Credazzo area, whose steep-sloped rows ensure taut, crackling fruit. Their winemaking is directed towards showcasing that crisp character in their wines, but never at the expense of a rich fruitiness. Col Credas 2015 testifies right from its name to its growing area, with crisp floral notes and even fresher vegetal tones balancing the fruit, and a compact, assertive palate drives through to an intriguing finish. In the opposite stylistic corner is Giardino 2015, whose intense ripe fruit and blossoms segue onto a silky palate and a pleasurable, dry conclusion.

○ Valdobbiadene Rive di Colbertaldo Dry Vign. Giardino '15	🍷🍷 3*
○ Valdobbiadene Rive di Farra di Soligo Brut Col Credas '15	🍷🍷 3*
○ Cartizze	🍷🍷 5
○ Valdobbiadene Brut Bosco di Gica	🍷🍷 3
○ Valdobbiadene Extra Dry Dei Casel	🍷🍷 3
○ Treviso Brut Garbel	🍷 2
○ Valdobbiadene Rive di Farra di Soligo Brut Col Credas '13	🍷🍷🍷 3*
○ Valdobbiadene Rive di Farra di Soligo Brut Col Credas '12	🍷🍷🍷 3*
○ Valdobbiadene Rive di Colbertaldo Dry Vign. Giardino '14	🍷🍷 3*

Ida Agnoletti

LOC. SELVA DEL MONTELLO
VIA SACCARDO, 55
31040 VOLPAGO DEL MONTELLO [TV]
TEL. +39 0423621555
www.agnoletti.it

CELLAR SALES
PRE-BOOKED VISITS
ANNUAL PRODUCTION 50,000 bottles
HECTARES UNDER VINE 7.00

Winegrower Ida Agnoletti combines driving curiosity with a firm bond to her growing area and its traditions. A little under ten hectares of vines flourish on the Montello hill's southern slope, yielding superb fruit, which she skilfully interprets, sometimes on the Bordeaux model, or with highly personal expressions dedicated to Manzoni bianco or glera. The resulting numbers may be limited, but the wines are intriguing and all of high quality. Agnoletti's tasting line-up this year lacks its more sought-after wines, which need a tad more ageing. The Merlot, in spite the difficult 2014 growing season, offers sweet, ripe fruit that gradually yields to hints of spice and herbs, and impressive grip on the palate makes for an utterly delicious red for every occasion. The Cabernet Sauvignon is somewhat closed on the nose, but it shows a taut palate and good length.

● Montello e Colli Asolani Merlot '14	🍷🍷 2*
○ Asolo Prosecco Il Tranquillo '15	🍷 2
○ Asolo Prosecco Selva n. 55	🍷 2
○ Manzoni 6.0.13 '14	🍷 2
● Montello e Colli Asolani Cabernet Sauvignon '14	🍷 2
○ PSL Always Frizzante	🍷 2
○ Manzoni Bianco Follia '13	🍷🍷 2*
○ Manzoni Bianco Follia '12	🍷🍷 2*
● Montello e Colli Asolani Merlot '13	🍷🍷 2*
● Montello e Colli Asolani Merlot La Ida '13	🍷🍷 2*
● Seneca '12	🍷🍷 3
● Vita Life is Red '13	🍷🍷 3
● Vita Life is Red '11	🍷🍷 3

★★★Allegrini

VIA GIARE, 5
37022 FUMANE [VR]
TEL. +39 0456832019
www.allegrini.it

CELLAR SALES
PRE-BOOKED VISITS
ACCOMMODATION AND RESTAURANT SERVICE
ANNUAL PRODUCTION 1,000,000 bottles
HECTARES UNDER VINE 120.00
SUSTAINABLE WINERY

Marilisa, Silvia, and Franco Allegrini's
operation certainly needs no introduction,
being one of the benchmarks not only in
Valpolicella but for wine-lovers worldwide.
In spite of some detours outside their
region, their spiritual centre is still
Valpolicella. They have constantly upgraded
the vineyards and manage them with deep
attention to the environment. More than
100 hectares of vineyard on hillslopes and
in the high hills yield grapes for a line of
wines uncompromisingly founded on deep
respect for the genuineness of their fruit.
Once again, Amarone is the undisputed
leader of the Allegrini team, this time the
2012. It pays tribute to tradition with its
standout qualities, namely intensely
fragrant, ripe fruit and spice, enriched by
hints of fines herbes that announce an
energy-laden palate of great elegance, with
a lovely partnership of power and crispness
that concludes in a lengthy, juicy finish.
Recioto Giovanni Allegrini 2013 is as usual
enchanting and finely balanced, while La
Poja 2012 unleashes a performance of rare
precision and refinement.

● Amarone della Valpolicella Cl. '12	♟♟♟	8
● La Poja '12	♟♟	8
● Recioto della Valpolicella Giovanni Allegrini '13	♟♟	7
● La Grola '13	♟♟	5
● Palazzo della Torre '13	♟♟	4
○ Soave '15	♟	3
● Valpolicella Cl. '15	♟♟	3
● Amarone della Valpolicella Cl. '11	♟♟♟	8
● Amarone della Valpolicella Cl. '10	♟♟♟	8
● Amarone della Valpolicella Cl. '09	♟♟♟	8
● Amarone della Valpolicella Cl. '08	♟♟♟	8
● Amarone della Valpolicella Cl. '07	♟♟♟	8
● Amarone della Valpolicella Cl. '06	♟♟♟	8
● Amarone della Valpolicella Cl. '05	♟♟♟	7
● Amarone della Valpolicella Cl. '04	♟♟♟	7

Andreola

VIA CAVRE,19
31010 FARRA DI SOLIGO [TV]
TEL. +39 0438989379
www.andreola.eu

CELLAR SALES
PRE-BOOKED VISITS
ANNUAL PRODUCTION 900,000 bottles
HECTARES UNDER VINE 70.00
SUSTAINABLE WINERY

The series of Stefano Pola's projects seems
endless, in his efforts to modernize his
family winery and to bring its Prosecco-
based production speedily up to the levels
it has now achieved. His new cellar in Via
Cavre boasts a multitude of new wines, all
characterized by rich aromas and
easy-quaffing approachability. In addition to
his considerable vineyard park, he buys in
fruit from many independent growers. One
of the best-aspected sites on Col San
Martino yields Brut 26° Primo, sporting ripe
apple and pear on the nose followed
closely by crisp, intense notes of citrus and
blossoms; it segues onto a palate notable
for its full fruit, creamy texture, and taut
grip. Dry 6° Senso boasts even more fruit,
and a rounded, soft palate that makes for a
deliciously appealing sparkler.

○ Valdobbiadene Brut Vign. Dirupo	♟♟	3
○ Valdobbiadene Dry 6° Senso	♟♟	3
○ Valdobbiadene Rive di Col San Martino Brut 26° Primo	♟♟	3
○ Valdobbiadene Dry '15	♟	2
○ Valdobbiadene Extra Dry Dirupo	♟	2
○ Valdobbiadene Prosecco Frizzante Casilir '15	♟	4
○ Valdobbiadene Prosecco Tranquillo Romit '15	♟	2
○ Valdobbiadene Rive Di Refrontolo Brut Col Del Forno	♟	3
○ Valdobbiadene Rive di Soligo Mas de Fer '15	♟	3
○ Cartizze '14	♟♟	5
○ Cartizze '13	♟♟	4

Antolini

via Prognol, 22
37020 Marano di Valpolicella [VR]
Tel. +39 0457755351
www.antolinivini.it

CELLAR SALES
PRE-BOOKED VISITS
ACCOMMODATION
ANNUAL PRODUCTION 60,000 bottles
HECTARES UNDER VINE 9.00
SUSTAINABLE WINERY

In just a few years, Pier Paolo and Stefano Antolini have succeeded in forging a superb reputation for their family winery, not so much as to quantity as to giving more importance to the role of a winegrower who respects the environment and protector of a worthy and delicately-balanced growing area. In like manner, winemaking seeks to develop local traditions, straying as little as possible from Valpolicella. The style that fully merits the term classic, but always concentrating on expression of fruit. The Amarones are sourced from growing areas with diverse characteristics and represent an unusual stylistic statement for this Verona-area classic wine. Ca' Coato 2012, from the Negrar valley, exuding warmth right from the nose, is soft and mouthfilling. Moròpio 2012, hailing from the Marano valley, offers impressively fragrant fruit and flowers, then power and equilibrium in the mouth. Ripasso 2014 compels attention with its combination of warmth, fruit of its raising process, and its taut crispness on the palate.

● Amarone della Valpolicella Cl. Moròpio '12	▼▼ 8
● Valpolicella Cl. Sup. Ripasso '14	▼▼ 5
● Amarone della Valpolicella Cl. Ca' Coato '12	▼▼ 8
● Corvina '13	▼▼ 4
● Recioto della Valpolicella Cl. '13	▼▼ 6
● Valpolicella Cl. '14	▼ 3
● Amarone della Valpolicella Cl. Ca' Coato '11	♀♀ 6
● Amarone della Valpolicella Cl. Moròpio '11	♀♀ 6
● Recioto della Valpolicella Cl. '11	♀♀ 5
● Theobroma '11	♀♀ 4
● Valpolicella Cl. Sup. Ripasso '13	♀♀ 4

Albino Armani

via Ceradello, 401
37020 Dolcè [VR]
Tel. +39 0457290033
www.albinoarmani.com

CELLAR SALES
PRE-BOOKED VISITS
ANNUAL PRODUCTION 900,000 bottles
HECTARES UNDER VINE 220.00
SUSTAINABLE WINERY

Dolcè is a large operation that in past decades has significantly enlarged its vineyard holdings, first in Vallagarina in Trentino, then quickly eastwards in Grave del Friuli and the province of Treviso, and southwards in Valpolicella. In each of these vineyards, production is centred on grape varieties and wine types classic to their respective growing areas. This year's most splendid results, however, arrive from the historic Verona-area operation. A superbly-expressive Foja Tonda 2012, made from casetta, releases refined aromas of wild fruit and black pepper, appealingly lifted by a crisp vein of medicinal herbs; the palate, compact, sinewy, and bright, is near endless. The impressive Pinot Grigio Colle Ara features pear and fresh blossoms, then builds to a full-volumed, harmonious performance in the mouth.

● Amarone della Valpolicella Cuslanus '10	▼▼ 6
● Valdadige Foja Tonda Casetta Terra dei Forti '12	▼▼ 3
○ Valdadige Terra dei Forti Pinot Grigio Colle Ara '15	▼▼ 2*
○ Sauvignon Campo Napoleone '15	▼ 2
● Valpolicella Cl. Sup. Ripasso '13	▼ 3
● Amarone della Valpolicella '08	♀♀ 5
● Amarone della Valpolicella Cl. Cuslanus '09	♀♀ 6
○ Trentino Chardonnay Capitel '14	♀♀ 2*
○ Trento Brut '10	♀♀ 4
○ Valdadige Pinot Grigio Corvara '14	♀♀ 2*
○ Valdadige Terra dei Forti Pinot Grigio Colle Ara '14	♀♀ 2*

Balestri Valda

VIA MONTI, 44
37038 SOAVE [VR]
TEL. +39 0457675393
www.vinibalestrivalda.com

CELLAR SALES
PRE-BOOKED VISITS
ANNUAL PRODUCTION 65,000 bottles
HECTARES UNDER VINE 13.00
SUSTAINABLE WINERY

The history of the Rizzotto family winery
may not be particularly long, but founder
Guido has spent his entire life in oenology.
As the years went by, he succeeded in
establishing his own wine operation,
shared with his wife Milena and children
Laura and Luca, the latter now at the helm,
but with Guido still on hand, always ready
to help. This attractive cellar lies in the hills
that seem to offer protection to the town of
Soave, and collectively represent the heart
of Soave Classico. We tasted Soave
Sengialta 2014, grown in black basaltic
soils, after it had aged a year in large
ovals. Apple, pear, and flowers waft up
first, backgrounded by an intriguing hint
of tropical fruit. Medium-bodied, it displays
a savouriness that conveys richness
without losing any elegance or taut
crispness. Lunalonga is dry and
one-dimensional, seemingly the result of
the difficult 2014 season.

○ Soave Cl. Vign. Sengialta '14	♟♟ 2*
○ Soave Cl. '15	♟ 2
○ Soave Cl. Lunalonga '14	♟ 3
○ Soave Cl. '12	♟♟ 2*
○ Soave Cl. '11	♟♟ 2*
○ Soave Cl. Lunalonga '12	♟♟ 3*
○ Soave Cl. Lunalonga '11	♟♟ 3
○ Soave Cl. Sengialta '11	♟♟ 2*
○ Soave Cl. Sengialta '10	♟♟ 2*
○ Soave Cl. Vign. Sengialta '13	♟♟ 2*
○ Soave Cl. Vign. Sengialta '12	♟♟ 2*

Barollo

VIA RIO SERVA, 4B
35123 PREGANZIOL [TV]
TEL. +39 0422633014
www.barollo.com

CELLAR SALES
PRE-BOOKED VISITS
ANNUAL PRODUCTION 57,000 bottles
HECTARES UNDER VINE 45.00

Young businessmen Marco and Nicola
Barollo were able to transform their
passion for wine into a flourishing
enterprise that has become a fine
expression of local winemaking traditions.
With more than 50 hectares of vineyard
south of Treviso testifying to a connection
with viticulture that the area risked losing.
Barollo's extensive and well-balanced
portfolio privileges full varietal fidelity, with
rich wines that remain eminently
approachable. This year, too, Frank! was
out in front of the team, a Cabernet Franc
that always eschews power in favour of
elegance and finesse on the palate. The
challenging 2014 season is obvious on a
somewhat troubled nose, its fruit veined
with wild herbs and spice, but the mouth
impresses with its crisp tension and fine
overall balance.

● Frank! '14	♟♟ 4
○ Manzoni Bianco '15	♟♟ 3
○ Piave Chardonnay '14	♟♟ 4
○ Sauvignon '15	♟♟ 3
○ Piave Chardonnay Frater '15	♟ 2
● Piave Merlot Frater '15	♟ 2
○ Pinot Bianco '15	♟ 3
○ Prosecco di Treviso Extra Dry '15	♟ 2
○ Alfredo Barollo Brut M. Cl. Ris. '10	♟♟ 4
● Frank! '13	♟♟ 4
● Frank! '12	♟♟ 4
○ Piave Chardonnay '13	♟♟ 4
○ Pinot Bianco '14	♟♟ 3
○ Sauvignon '13	♟♟ 3

★Lorenzo Begali

VIA CENGIA, 10
37020 SAN PIETRO IN CARIANO [VR]
TEL. +39 0457725148
www.begaliwine.it

CELLAR SALES
PRE-BOOKED VISITS
ANNUAL PRODUCTION 90,000 bottles
HECTARES UNDER VINE 12.00

With infinite care, Lorenzo Begali enlarged his estate vineyards, first those around the cellar in Cengia, followed by others across the contours of the Castelrotto hill, and finally on Masua, in a superb site in the Negrar valley. These dozen or so hectares are dedicated almost exclusively to local wine classics, all made in a very rigorous style that eschews the roundedness that has taken hold in this designation. This is precisely the style that characterizes Amarone Monte Ca' Bianca 2011, with gradually emerging aromas of cherry and dried plum, followed by medicinal herbs, and lastly spice. This fragrant complex nose carries over onto a solidly-built, rugged palate supported by tightly-woven tannins that heighten the crisp acidity so classic to these grapes and the growing area in general; it finishes long. Amarone Classico 2012 is brighter and more straightforward, equally complex on the nose, but crisp and less complicated in the mouth.

● Amarone della Valpolicella Cl. Monte Ca' Bianca '11	♔♔♔ 8
● Amarone della Valpolicella Cl. '12	♔♔ 6
● Tigiolo '12	♔♔ 5
● Valpolicella Cl. Sup. Ripasso La Cengia '14	♔♔ 3
● Valpolicella Cl. '15	♔ 2
● Amarone della Valpolicella Cl. Vign. Monte Ca' Bianca '09	♕♕♕ 8
● Amarone della Valpolicella Cl. Vign. Monte Ca' Bianca '08	♕♕♕ 8
● Amarone della Valpolicella Cl. Vign. Monte Ca' Bianca '07	♕♕♕ 8
● Amarone della Valpolicella Cl. Vign. Monte Ca' Bianca '06	♕♕♕ 8
● Amarone della Valpolicella Cl. Vign. Monte Ca' Bianca '05	♕♕♕ 8

★Cav. G. B. Bertani

VIA ASIAGO, 1
37023 GREZZANA [VR]
TEL. +39 0458658444
www.bertani.net

CELLAR SALES
PRE-BOOKED VISITS
ANNUAL PRODUCTION 2,100,000 bottles
HECTARES UNDER VINE 200.00
SUSTAINABLE WINERY

The strong suite of a winery such as Angelini lies in its ability to renew its human and technical resources without impinging on a style saluted worldwide for its classic expression and faithful interpretation of local tradition. Bertani demonstrates impressive expertise in managing its 200 hectares, most in Valpolicella, and every year offers wines of delicacy and fine balance. Amarone Classico 2008 unleashes a beautifully-honed performance, composed of ultra-ripe red berry fruit shot through with aromatic herbs and black pepper, with just a hint, still reticent, of earthy mineral. The palate showcases an elegance and delicacy that only a lengthy maturation can supply, which privilege even more effectively savouriness over silkiness and elegance over power, right through to a lengthy, succulent finish. The crisper, more youthful version from the Valpantena is likewise impressive, with its crisp aromatics complex and zesty drinkability.

● Amarone della Valpolicella Cl. '08	♔♔♔ 8
● Amarone della Valpolicella Valpantena '13	♔♔ 6
● Secco Bertani Vintage Edition '13	♔♔ 4
○ Soave Giovan Battista Bertani '14	♔♔ 3
○ Soave Sereole '15	♔ 3
● Valpolicella '15	♔ 3
● Amarone della Valpolicella Cl. '07	♕♕♕ 8
● Amarone della Valpolicella Cl. '06	♕♕♕ 8
● Amarone della Valpolicella Cl. '05	♕♕♕ 8
● Amarone della Valpolicella Cl. '04	♕♕♕ 8
● Amarone della Valpolicella Cl. '03	♕♕♕ 8
● Amarone della Valpolicella Cl. '01	♕♕♕ 8
● Amarone della Valpolicella Cl. '00	♕♕♕ 8
● Amarone della Valpolicella Cl. '99	♕♕♕ 8
● Valpolicella Cl. Sup. Vign. Ognisanti '06	♕♕♕ 4*

BiancaVigna

LOC. OGLIANO
VIA MONTE NERO, 8
31015 CONEGLIANO [TV]
TEL. +39 0438788403
www.biancavigna.it

CELLAR SALES
PRE-BOOKED VISITS
ACCOMMODATION
ANNUAL PRODUCTION 600,000 bottles
HECTARES UNDER VINE 30.20
SUSTAINABLE WINERY

The new cellar in Ogliano is finally up and running, set perfectly in the delicate fabric of the hills embracing Conegliano and the hamlets studding the countryside in the direction of Valdobbiadene. Here Elena and Enrico Moschetta direct their family winery, dedicated almost totally to Treviso-area sparklers and relying on some 30 hectares of vineyards as well as grapes contributed by local growers. Elena is the public image of this winery and Enrico is more reclusive, but his expertise shines in the cellar. Striving for concentration and vibrancy, and limiting as much as possible the softness that Prosecco often displays, is the house approach, which is brilliantly on display in Rive di Soligo. A Brut with a truly minimal amount of sugar, it impresses with cleanly-delineated aromas and appreciable weight in the mouth. Equally likeable are the Brut and Extra Dry versions, both with plenty of unexpected savouriness.

○ Conegliano Valdobbiadene Brut Rive di Soligo '15	♟♟ 3*
○ Conegliano Valdobbiadene Brut '15	♟♟ 3
○ Conegliano Valdobbiadene Extra Dry '15	♟♟ 3
○ Prosecco Brut	♟♟ 2*
○ Prosecco Extra Dry	♟♟ 2*
○ Prosecco Frizzante	♟ 2
⊙ Spumante Rosé Cuvée 1931	♟ 2
○ Conegliano Valdobbiadene Brut '14	♟♟ 3
○ Conegliano Valdobbiadene Brut '13	♟♟ 3
○ Conegliano Valdobbiadene Brut Rive di Soligo '14	♟♟ 3
○ Conegliano Valdobbiadene Extra Dry '14	♟♟ 3

Bisol

FRAZ. SANTO STEFANO
VIA FOLLO, 33
31049 VALDOBBIADENE [TV]
TEL. +39 0423900138
www.bisol.it

CELLAR SALES
PRE-BOOKED VISITS
ANNUAL PRODUCTION 1,800,000 bottles
HECTARES UNDER VINE 126.00

In an area as unremittingly dynamic as Prosecco, the Bisol family's operation manages a successful combination of two seemingly contradictory directions. They are intimately bound to the traditions of the growing areas around Valdobbiadene, and at the same time display an openness to the Prosecco world that does not disdain flatland vineyards. Theirs are among the area's most extensive holdings, and their wines among the most reliable and quality-oriented. From the best vineyards come the best wines, as proved by our tasting of Brut Garnei, a Valdobbiadene 2014 with extremely low sugar. On the nose, a longer maturation has brought to the fore clean-edged apple, pear, and blossoms, which continue onto a firm palate showing enviable balance and fruit. Cartizze 2015, on the other hand, encapsulates all the radiant extroversion of the growing area and of glera, in kaleidoscopic tropical fruit and candied almonds that lead into a succulent, enfolding palate.

○ Valdobbiadene Brut Private Garnei '14	♟♟ 3*
○ Brut M. Cl. '04	♟♟ 4
○ Cartizze '15	♟♟ 5
○ Cartizze Brut Private '13	♟♟ 5
○ Valdobbiadene Extra Dry Vign. del Fol '15	♟♟ 4
○ Prosecco Brut Belstar	♟ 3
○ Valdobbiadene Brut Jeio	♟ 2
○ Valdobbiadene Brut NoSo2	♟ 2
○ Cartizze '14	♟♟ 5
○ Cuvée del Fondatore Eliseo Bisol Brut M. Cl '04	♟♟ 5
○ Valdobbiadene Brut Garnei '13	♟♟ 3
○ Valdobbiadene Extra Dry Molera '14	♟♟ 3
○ Valdobbiadene Extra Dry Vign. del Fol '14	♟♟ 4

Bolla

Fraz. Pedemonte
via A. Bolla, 3
37029 San Pietro in Cariano [VR]
Tel. +39 0456836555
www.bolla.it

CELLAR SALES
PRE-BOOKED VISITS
ANNUAL PRODUCTION 11,000,000 bottles
HECTARES UNDER VINE 188.00

In the past, Bolla may have been synonymous worldwide with Italian wine, but today it is one of the venerable cellars focusing on a determined revival. Its 200 or so hectares throughout the Verona designations, plus grapes brought in by numerous growers, supply the raw materials for quite prestigious wines. Cristian Scrinzi's skilled hand has restored lustre to a line that increasingly reflects the classic qualities in one of Italy's most prized growing regions. The Valpolicella reds here have often given splendid results, but the barrel-aged Soave Tufaie 2015 is certainly at their level. The oak impressively liberates clean, bright fruit, while the palate is firmly-knit, rich, and vibrant. The house champion, though, remains Ripasso Le Poiane 2014, fragrant with super-ripe fruit and spices, and with tangy, rich fruit that expands the palate and achieves elegance.

● Valpolicella Cl. Sup. Ripasso Le Poiane '14	🍷🍷 4
○ Soave Cl. Sup. Tufaie '15	🍷🍷 3
● Amarone della Valpolicella Cl. Le Origini '09	🍷🍷 7
● Amarone della Valpolicella Cl. Le Origini Ris. '10	🍷🍷 6
● Amarone della Valpolicella Cl. Rhetico '10	🍷🍷 6
● Creso '12	🍷🍷 4
● Creso '11	🍷🍷 4
○ Custoza La Real Casa '14	🍷🍷 2*
○ Soave Cl. Sup. Tufaie '13	🍷🍷 3
● Valpolicella Cl. Sup. Colforte '13	🍷🍷 3
● Valpolicella Cl. Sup. Ripasso '12	🍷🍷 2*
● Valpolicella Cl. Sup. Ripasso Le Poiane '13	🍷🍷 4
● Valpolicella Cl. Sup. Ripasso Le Poiane '12	🍷🍷 4

Borgo Stajnbech

via Belfiore, 109
30020 Pramaggiore [VE]
Tel. +39 0421799929
www.borgostajnbech.com

CELLAR SALES
PRE-BOOKED VISITS
ANNUAL PRODUCTION 90,000 bottles
HECTARES UNDER VINE 15.00

The Valent family is among the most dynamic in the Lison-Pramaggiore district. Facing the Adriatic basin, this designation enjoys the mitigating effects of the nearby sea on its temperatures, while the high clay content in the soils is ideal for tai and refosco grapes, the star varieties here. Their 15 hectares of grapes produce mainly monovarietals, taut yet wonderfully quaffable wines. 150, a Lison Classico 2014, turned in a fine performance, ably conveying the variety's delicate, floral soul, heightened by notes of gooseberry and almond. In the mouth, full volume finds in a vein of vibrant acidity a fine complement, and the wine concludes dry and lengthy. Rosso Stajnbech 2013, a dry, finely balanced blend of refosco and cabernet sauvignon, did well too; straightforward aromas of crisp fruit contrast nicely with admirable depth and finesse on the palate.

○ Bianco Stajnbech '13	🍷🍷 3
○ Lison Cl. 150 '14	🍷🍷 3
● Refosco P. R. '14	🍷🍷 2*
● Rosso Stajnbech '13	🍷🍷 3
○ Sauvignon Bosco della Donna '15	🍷🍷 3
● Merlot Ywain '14	🍷 2
○ Pinot Grigio '15	🍷 2
● Pinot Nero '14	🍷 2
● Lison – Pramaggiore Refosco P.R. '12	🍷🍷 2*
○ Lison-Pramaggiore Cl. 150 '13	🍷🍷 3
● Lison-Pramaggiore Merlot '12	🍷🍷 2*
● Lison-Pramaggiore Refosco P.R. '13	🍷🍷 2*
● Malbech '12	🍷🍷 2*
● Stajnbech Rosso '11	🍷🍷 3

Borgoluce

LOC. MUSILE, 2
31058 SUSEGANA [TV]
TEL. +39 0438435287
www.borgoluce.it

CELLAR SALES
PRE-BOOKED VISITS
ACCOMMODATION AND RESTAURANT SERVICE
ANNUAL PRODUCTION 250,000 bottles
HECTARES UNDER VINE 70.00

This young Susegana-area operation boasts roots that go quite deep, since it represents a collaboration between the Collalto and Giustinian families, long-established producers here. They also rear stock and process products, but their viticultural efforts are impressive, mainly focused on Prosecco, which is styled to highlight fruit and a fine proportion of all the components on the palate. Only great grapes can go to make a great Brut, since the low dosage allows the delicate character of the variety to shine through, which is precisely the case with the appealing Borgoluce, a Brut with a delicate yet self-confident profile, and very savoury in the mouth. Still better is the wine grown in Collalto's finest vineyards, powerful yet well-balanced, beautifully showcasing the bright ripeness of fruit from the 2015 season.

Borin Vini & Vigne

FRAZ. MONTICELLI
VIA DEI COLLI, 5
35043 MONSELICE [PD]
TEL. +39 042974384
www.viniborin.it

CELLAR SALES
PRE-BOOKED VISITS
ANNUAL PRODUCTION 105,000 bottles
HECTARES UNDER VINE 28.00

The Borin family has been crafting wines in the Colli Euganei for more than 50 years now, from 30 hectares of vines subdivided into various parcels. The efforts of Gianni and Teresa are increasingly flanked by those of their sons Francesco and Paolo, the first overseeing production and the second keeping a watchful eye on market trends and directions to take. Their extensive, and reliable portfolio focuses mostly on monovarietals. After its lengthy stay in the cellar, Cabernet Sauvignon Mons Silicis already boasts a deep, multi-layered aromatic complex, with an initial fruit that gradually cedes to pencil lead and wild herbs, with a strictly secondary role for tones of oak. In the mouth, fine balance and savoury fruit outperform power, and it finishes quite long. Impressive too is the energy-laden Manzoni Bianco Corte Borin 2015.

○ Valdobbiadene Brut	♥♥ 3
○ Valdobbiadene Rive di Collalto Brut '15	♥♥ 2*
○ Valdobbiadene Extra Dry	♥ 3
○ Valdobbiadene Prosecco Frizzante Gaiante	♥ 3
○ Prosecco di Valdobbiadene Extra Dry '09	♀♀ 3
○ Prosecco di Valdobbiadene Extra Dry '08	♀♀ 2*
○ Valdobbiadene Rive di Collalto Brut '14	♀♀ 2*
○ Valdobbiadene Rive di Collalto Brut '13	♀♀ 2*
○ Valdobbiadene Rive di Collalto Extra Dry '14	♀♀ 2*
○ Valdobbiadene Rive di Collalto Extra Dry '13	♀♀ 2*
○ Valdobbiadene Rive di Collalto Extra Dry '12	♀♀ 2*
○ Valdobbiadene Rive di Collalto Extra Dry '11	♀♀ 2*

● Colli Euganei Cabernet Sauvignon Mons Silicis Ris. '12	♥♥ 4
○ Colli Euganei Fior d'Arancio '15	♥♥ 2*
○ Colli Euganei Fior d'Arancio Fiore di Gaia '15	♥♥ 2*
○ Colli Euganei Manzoni Bianco Corte Borin '15	♥♥ 3
● Colli Euganei Merlot Rocca Chiara Ris. '12	♥♥ 4
○ Sauvignon Blanc '15	♥♥ 4
● Colli Euganei Cabernet Sauvignon V. Costa '14	♥ 3
○ Colli Euganei Chardonnay V. Bianca '14	♥ 3
○ Colli Euganei Pinot Bianco Monte Archino '15	♥ 2
○ Colli Euganei Serprino '15	♥ 2
● Syrah Coldivalle '13	♥ 3

Bortolomiol

VIA GARIBALDI, 142
31049 VALDOBBIADENE [TV]
TEL. +39 04239749
www.bortolomiol.com

CELLAR SALES
PRE-BOOKED VISITS
RESTAURANT SERVICE
ANNUAL PRODUCTION 1,800,000 bottles
HECTARES UNDER VINE 5.00
SUSTAINABLE WINERY

Bortolomiol played a historic role in the rise of Prosecco. Founded in the last century by Giuliano, it has grown in harmony with its stunning setting and delicately-balanced agricultural fabric, of which it is a dedicated guardian. Giuliano's daughters have the helm today; their estate vineyards are few, but long-trusted local growers bring in the grapes that drive a production now almost at two million bottles a year. Painstaking attention to their Brut sparklers has its quality apogee in Prior, which lays out crisp apple and pear on the nose, followed by a thrusting palate that does just fine with no help needed from sugars. It finishes savoury and long. Motus Vitae, dedicated to the founder, undergoes a lengthy maturation before release; its complex aromatics feature Golden Delicious apple embracing dried flowers, seguing into a beautifully proportioned, delicate palate.

Carlo Boscaini

VIA SENGIA, 15
37015 SANT'AMBROGIO DI VALPOLICELLA [VR]
TEL. +39 0457731412
www.boscainicarlo.it

CELLAR SALES
PRE-BOOKED VISITS
ACCOMMODATION
ANNUAL PRODUCTION 60,000 bottles
HECTARES UNDER VINE 14.00

The Boscaini cellar, in Sant'Ambrogio di Valpolicella, comprises 14 hectares of vineyards distributed over the hills that surround the winery in Via Sengia, at an elevation of some 200 metres. The brothers produce about 60,000 bottles per year, dedicated exclusively on Valpolicella classics, and they strive to marry tradition to richness of flavour, and elegance to striking personality. The Zane vineyard yields Ripasso 2013, which enthused our tasting panels. Super-ripe berry fruit interweaves with pungent herbs on the nose, plus a note of rosemary, then glossy tannins and a zesty acidity duet together on a medium-full palate. Amarone San Giorgio 2012 impresses as well, with concentrated, ripe fruit, then a full-bodied, smooth-textured palate enlivened by a crisply acidic grip.

○ Valdobbiadene Rive di San Pietro di Barbozza Brut Nature Grande Cuvée del Fondatore Motus Vitae '13	♛♛♛ 4*
○ Valdobbiadene Brut Prior '15	♛♛ 3*
○ Cartizze	♛♛ 5
○ Valdobbiadene Brut Ius Naturae '15	♛♛ 3
○ Valdobbiadene Dry Maior '15	♛♛ 3
○ Valdobbiadene Extra Dry Senior '15	♛♛ 3
⊙ Filanda Rosé Brut '15	♛ 3
○ Riserva del Governatore Extra Brut '14	♛ 3
○ Valdobbiadene Demi Sec Suavis	♛ 3
○ Valdobbiadene Extra Dry Banda Rossa	♛ 3
○ Valdobbiadene Brut Prior '14	♛♛♛ 3*
○ Valdobbiadene Extra Dry Banda Rossa '14	♛♛ 3

● Amarone della Valpolicella Cl. San Giorgio '12	♛♛ 6
● Recioto della Valpolicella Cl. La Sengia '14	♛♛ 4
● Valpolicella Cl. Sup. La Preosa '14	♛♛ 3
● Valpolicella Cl. Sup. Ripasso Zane '13	♛♛ 4
● Valpolicella Cl. Ca' Bussin '15	♛ 2
● Amarone della Valpolicella Cl. San Giorgio '11	♛♛ 5
● Amarone della Valpolicella Cl. San Giorgio '10	♛♛ 5
● Amarone della Valpolicella Cl. San Giorgio '09	♛♛ 5
● Valpolicella Cl. Ca' Bussin '12	♛♛ 2*
● Valpolicella Cl. Sup. La Preosa '12	♛♛ 3
● Valpolicella Cl. Sup. La Preosa '11	♛♛ 3
● Valpolicella Cl. Sup. Ripasso Zane '11	♛♛ 4
● Valpolicella Cl. Sup. Ripasso Zane '09	♛♛ 3

Bosco del Merlo

Via Postumia, 12
30020 Annone Veneto [VE]
Tel. +39 0422768167
www.boscodelmerlo.it

CELLAR SALES
PRE-BOOKED VISITS
ANNUAL PRODUCTION 240,000 bottles
HECTARES UNDER VINE 84.00
SUSTAINABLE WINERY

Founded by Valentino in the mid-1900s, the Paladin cellar boasts a history in the Lison-Pramaggiore area that goes back more than 50 years. Nearly 100 hectares of estate vineyards yield grapes for the brothers' most ambitious wines; Bosco del Merlo is the family's standard-bearer. The house style privileges varietal clarity combined with an approachability that is refined and never flamboyant. Vineargenti, a blend of merlot and refosco dal peduncolo rosso, impresses with deep aromas of slowly-developing red berry fruit, which then yields to spice and floral essences. It is compact and full in the mouth, without losing a jot of its suppleness and delicacy. The merlot Campo Camino Riserva 2013 is no less impressive, but in this case with a clean expression of crisp, succulent fruit on the nose, then pulpy fruit on a delicious, easy-drinking palate.

- Lison-Pramaggiore Rosso
  Vineargenti Ris. '13 ▼▼ 6
- Lison-Pramaggiore Merlot
  Campo Camino Ris. '13 ▼▼ 4
- Lison-Pramaggiore Refosco P. R.
  Roggio dei Roveri Ris. '13 ▼▼ 5
- ○ Lison-Pramaggiore Sauvignon
  Turranio '15 ▼▼ 4
- Malbech Gli Aceri Paladin '13 ▼▼ 6
- ○ Venezia Pinot Grigio Tudajo '15 ▼▼ 3
- ○ Prosecco Brut ▼ 4
- ○ Prosecco Extra Dry ▼ 5
- ○ Venezia Chardonnay Nicopeja '15 ▼ 3
- Lison-Pramaggiore Merlot
  Campo Camino '11 ♀♀ 4
- Lison-Pramaggiore Refosco P.R.
  Roggio dei Roveri '12 ♀♀ 5

★Brigaldara

Fraz. San Floriano
Via Brigaldara, 20
37029 San Pietro in Cariano [VR]
Tel. +39 0457701055
www.brigaldara.it

CELLAR SALES
PRE-BOOKED VISITS
ANNUAL PRODUCTION 300,000 bottles
HECTARES UNDER VINE 50.00

The Cesaris have been making wine for almost 40 years in Valpolicella; in the last few decades they have enlarged their vineyards little by little, arriving at today's total of some 50 hectares, both within the classic zone as well as to the east. The winery itself is inserted in a traditional farmhouse next to the villa, perfectly integrated into the original architecture; its two levels allow fermentation operations to be separated from the subsequent ageing of the wines. A line-up of three Amarones might seem a bit much, but a tasting revealed the reasons for this trio: diverse vineyards, interpretations, and maturation periods, which heighten the differences between them. Riserva 2009 is all about depth and fruit ripeness; Case Vecie 2011, from the eastern vineyards, focuses on power and dynamics; while Classico 2012 shows sunny and lighter-bodied. Worth noting too, is Valpolicella Superiore Case Vecie 2014, which, at its first release, is full-volumed and of fine character.

- Amarone della Valpolicella
  Case Vecie '11 ▼▼ 6
- Amarone della Valpolicella Ris. '09 ▼▼ 8
- Valpolicella Sup. Case Vecie '14 ▼▼ 3*
- Amarone della Valpolicella Cl. '12 ▼▼ 6
- ○ Soave '15 ▼▼ 3
- Valpolicella '15 ▼ 3
- Valpolicella Cl. Sup. Ripasso
  Il Vegro '14 ▼ 4
- Amarone della Valpolicella
  Case Vecie '07 ♀♀♀ 7
- Amarone della Valpolicella Cl. '10 ♀♀♀ 7
- Amarone della Valpolicella Cl. '06 ♀♀♀ 6
- Amarone della Valpolicella Cl. '05 ♀♀♀ 6
- Amarone della Valpolicella Ris. '07 ♀♀♀ 8

Sorelle Bronca

FRAZ. COLBERTALDO
VIA MARTIRI, 20
31020 VIDOR [TV]
TEL. +39 0423987201
www.sorellebronca.com

CELLAR SALES
PRE-BOOKED VISITS
ACCOMMODATION
ANNUAL PRODUCTION 350,000 bottles
HECTARES UNDER VINE 24.00

The smooth-functioning quartet of Ersiliana and Antonella, assisted by daughter Elisa and husband Piero, directs Colbertaldo. They currently boast some 20 hectares of organically-farmed vines across the designation, ranging from steep-sloped vineyards such as those in Colbertaldo and Rolle, to the more gently-sloping terrain in Farrò. Some very impressive still wines complementing their classic Proseccos. Piero crafted masterful interpretations of the 2015 growing year, offering an array of astonishing sparklers, led once again by Particella 68, whose bright-edged, fruit-rich must yielded a Prosecco Brut that is dry, firmly-structured, yet refined. Ser Beleis a Bordeaux blend boasts an appealing, bright personality built on succulent red berry fruit. Finally, the most straightforward of the wines here, Sole Cielo Terra, deserves mention for its thoroughgoing pleasure.

○ Valdobbiadene Brut Particella 68 '15	▼▼▼ 4*
● Colli di Conegliano Rosso Ser Bele '13	▼▼ 5
○ Colli di Conegliano Bianco Delico '15	▼▼ 3
○ Valdobbiadene Brut	▼▼ 3
○ Valdobbiadene Extra Dry	▼▼ 3
○ Valdobbiadene Prosecco Frizzante Difetto Perfetto	▼ 3
● Colli di Conegliano Rosso Ser Bele '09	♀♀♀ 5
● Colli di Conegliano Rosso Ser Bele '05	♀♀♀ 5
○ Valdobbiadene Brut Particella 68 '13	♀♀♀ 4*
○ Colli di Conegliano Bianco Delico '12	♀♀ 3
● Colli di Conegliano Rosso Ser Bele '12	♀♀ 5
● Colli di Conegliano Rosso Ser Bele '11	♀♀ 5
○ Valdobbiadene Brut Particella 68 '14	♀♀ 4
○ Valdobbiadene Brut Particella 68 '12	♀♀ 4

Luigi Brunelli

VIA CARIANO, 10
37029 SAN PIETRO IN CARIANO [VR]
TEL. +39 0457701118
www.brunelliwine.com

CELLAR SALES
PRE-BOOKED VISITS
ACCOMMODATION
ANNUAL PRODUCTION 120,000 bottles
HECTARES UNDER VINE 14.00

Seen from the motorway, Brunelli's cellar appears perfectly integrated into the Valpolicella landscape, just behind the hill of San Pietro Incariano. Luigi, his wife Luciana, and son Alberto manage a dozen or so hectares, planted mainly to classic Valpolicella varieties, along with a few white grapes. The more straightforward wines are fruit-forward and approachable, while decisive power is the house style for the Amarones. Although they may not have reached the highest note this year, the overall line-up achieved impressive quality. Campo Inferi 2011 has shown, over the years, power and concentration; this vintage exhibits a difference in performance, with a touch more vibrancy and delicacy, adding up to great approachability and appeal. Valpolicella Praesel 2013, a complex, refined Superiore, performed well, too.

● Amarone della Valpolicella Cl. Campo Inferi Ris. '11	▼▼ 8
● Amarone della Valpolicella Cl. '12	▼▼ 8
● Amarone della Valpolicella Cl. Campo del Titari Ris. '11	▼▼ 8
● Recioto della Valpolicella Cl. '14	▼▼ 5
● Valpolicella Cl. Sup. Campo Praesel '13	▼▼ 3
● Valpolicella Cl. Sup. Ripasso Pa' Riondo '14	▼▼ 4
● Valpolicella Cl. '15	▼ 2
● Amarone della Valpolicella Cl. Campo del Titari '97	♀♀♀ 8
● Amarone della Valpolicella Cl. Campo del Titari '96	♀♀♀ 8
● Amarone della Valpolicella Cl. '11	♀♀ 8

Buglioni

FRAZ. CORRUBBIO
VIA CAMPAGNOLE, 55
37029 SAN PIETRO IN CARIANO [VR]
TEL. +39 0456760681
www.buglioni.it

CELLAR SALES
PRE-BOOKED VISITS
ACCOMMODATION
ANNUAL PRODUCTION 170,000 bottles
HECTARES UNDER VINE 48.00

Over the last few years, Mariano Buglioni has given this family operation a change in direction, not so much in the management of the many estate vineyards as in the winemaking. Oenologist Diego Bertoni oversees the entire ship, beginning with selection of the finest lots of grapes, since vineyard production greatly exceeds cellar needs. The new objective is a less soft and more elegant wine profile than in the past, and the results are increasingly impressive. The first release of Amarone Il Lussurioso 2011 is a standout. This Riserva unleashes rich, complex aromas that foreground ripe fruit gradually yielding to wild herbs and spice, while a close-knit palate shows surprising vibrancy, giving it suppleness and finesse. No less deserving is the Ripasso Il Bugiardo 2013, whose tannic structure supports considerable power.

● Amarone della Valpolicella Cl. Il Lussurioso Ris. '11	♟♟ 7
● Valpolicella Cl. Sup. L'Imperfetto '13	♟♟ 5
● Valpolicella Cl. Sup. Ripasso Il Bugiardo '13	♟♟ 5
● Amarone della Valpolicella Cl. L'Amarone '10	♟ 6
● Amarone della Valpolicella Cl. L'Amarone '04	♟ 6
● Valpolicella Cl. Sup. Il Ruffiano '13	♟ 3
● Valpolicella Cl. Sup. Ripasso Il Bugiardo '12	♟ 4

Ca' La Bionda

FRAZ. VALGATARA
VIA BIONDA, 4
37020 MARANO DI VALPOLICELLA [VR]
TEL. +39 0456801198
www.calabionda.it

CELLAR SALES
PRE-BOOKED VISITS
ANNUAL PRODUCTION 150,000 bottles
HECTARES UNDER VINE 29.00
VITICULTURE METHOD Certified Organic

Lying at the mid-point of the Marano valley, the Castellani operation is one of the designation's most impressive. Ably assisted by father Petro, the brothers tend some 30 hectares of hillslope vineyards, using organic methods, with the bare minimum of human intervention. Winemaking here relies not only on raising, but on continuous striving for a style that can best highlight the fragrant delicacy of the local grape varieties. For years now, Valpolicella Superiore Campo Casal Vegri has been a designation star, and this year too it stands out for its cleanly-delineated aromas of floral-veined fruit and fines herbes. Then it shifts into a higher gear in the mouth, displaying a bright tension complemented by spacious volume. Amarone Ravazzol 2012, on the other hand, offers warmer fruit on the nose then a lengthy progression and superb character that are the perfect foil to its rich complexity.

● Amarone della Valpolicella Cl. Vign. di Ravazzol '12	♟♟ 8
● Valpolicella Cl. Sup. Campo Casal Vegri '14	♟♟ 5
● Amarone della Valpolicella Cl. '12	♟♟ 6
● Recioto della Valpolicella Cl. Vign. Le Tordare '12	♟♟ 6
● Valpolicella Cl. '15	♟♟ 2*
● Valpolicella Cl. Sup. Ripasso Malavoglia '13	♟♟ 4
● Amarone della Valpolicella Cl. Vign. di Ravazzol '11	♟♟♟ 8
● Amarone della Valpolicella Cl. Vign. di Ravazzol '07	♟♟♟ 6
● Valpolicella Cl. Sup. Campo Casal Vegri '11	♟♟♟ 5

Ca' Lustra

LOC. FAEDO
VIA SAN PIETRO, 50
35030 CINTO EUGANEO [PD]
TEL. +39 042994128
www.calustra.it

CELLAR SALES
PRE-BOOKED VISITS
ANNUAL PRODUCTION 170,000 bottles
HECTARES UNDER VINE 25.50
VITICULTURE METHOD Certified Organic
SUSTAINABLE WINERY

The Euganean Hills, a small complex of volcanic origin at the middle of the Po Valley, enjoy both heat and constant breezes. This is one of the most intriguing growing areas in the region, perhaps of anywhere in Italy. The designation is part of the Parco Regionale, and Franco Zanovello is one of its leading figures. With son Marco increasingly at his side, he directs a winery that is a dynamic, careful guardian of its local environment. The warmth in this growing area enables cabernet sauvignon to consistently ripen, so that the wines show deep fruit and concentration, precisely what we find in spades in the long-matured Girapoggio, which puts on display fragrant pencil lead and spice, then a tannin perfectly woven into its texture. The result is a red of stunning balance and beauty. Moscato Secco 'A Cengia 2014, with its savoury, taut palate, is in a class of its own.

Ca' Orologio

VIA CA' OROLOGIO, 7A
35030 BAONE [PD]
TEL. +39 042950099
www.caorologio.com

CELLAR SALES
PRE-BOOKED VISITS
ACCOMMODATION
ANNUAL PRODUCTION 24,000 bottles
HECTARES UNDER VINE 12.00
VITICULTURE METHOD Certified Organic

Mariagioia Rosellini's cellar is located in the barchessa wing of the 16th-century Ca' Orologio villa. This tenacious producer has transformed her passion for the world of agriculture into one of the Euganean Hills' most impressive wineries. It is underpinned by a dozen or so hectares of organically-farmed vineyard, and low yields per vine translate into a portfolio of wines that is limited but of superb quality. Calaóne, a Bordeaux blend largely of merlot and the winery's most popular wine, releases clean notes of ripe red berry fruit lifted by a subtle hint of wild herbs, followed by a full-volumed succulence in the mouth, which lingers into a dry, glossy finish. In fine years, such as this 2013, Relógio is made with carmenère enriched with a tot of cabernet franc, giving it a rich, pulpy character.

● Colli Euganei Cabernet Girapoggio '09	▼▼ 3*
○ Colli Euganei Fior d'Arancio Spumante '15	▼▼ 3
● Marzemino Belvedere '13	▼▼ 2*
○ Moscato Secco 'A Cengia '14	▼▼ 3
● Nero Musqué '14	▼▼ 4
○ Colli Euganei Manzoni Bianco Pedevenda '14	▼ 3
○ Colli Euganei Serprino '15	▼ 2
● Marzemino Passito '12	▼ 2
● Colli Euganei Cabernet Girapoggio '05	▼▼▼ 3
○ Colli Euganei Fior d'Arancio Passito '07	▼▼▼ 4
● Colli Euganei Merlot Sassonero Villa Alessi '05	▼▼▼ 3
● Colli Euganei Cabernet '12	▼▼ 2*

● Colli Euganei Rosso Calaóne '13	▼▼ 4
● Relógio '13	▼▼ 5
○ Salaróla '15	▼▼ 3
● Colli Euganei Rosso Duemilaquattordici '14	▼ 4
● Colli Euganei Rosso Calaóne '05	▼▼▼ 3*
● Relógio '09	▼▼▼ 4*
● Relógio '07	▼▼▼ 4
● Relógio '06	▼▼▼ 4
● Relógio '04	▼▼▼ 4*
● Colli Euganei Rosso Calaóne '12	▼▼ 4
● Colli Euganei Rosso Calaóne '11	▼▼ 4
● Relógio '11	▼▼ 5
○ Salaróla '14	▼▼ 3
○ Salaróla '13	▼▼ 3

★Ca' Rugate

VIA PERGOLA, 36
37030 MONTECCHIA DI CROSARA [VR]
TEL. +39 0456176328
www.carugate.it

CELLAR SALES
PRE-BOOKED VISITS
ACCOMMODATION
ANNUAL PRODUCTION 600,000 bottles
HECTARES UNDER VINE 72.00
SUSTAINABLE WINERY

Michele Tessari is one of the most dynamic winegrowers in the crowded world of local viticulture, able to rely on hillslope vineyards in both the Soave and Valpolicella designations. His quality growth has been fuelled by newly-acquired vineyards, bringing his total to 40 in the Soave district, 30 or so in Valpolicella, and even a couple in Durello. His wines are a happy marriage of great character and unquestioned quality. Once again, the lineup here is one of the best we tasted, with high marks in particular for Amarone Punta Tolotti 2012 and Soave Monte Alto 2014. Year afer year, the former becomes ever more focused and refined on the nose, while it succeeds in tamping down Amarone's typical exuberance with great style. The Soave makes light of the difficult 2014, showcasing fine aromatic complexity and a truly magisterial palate, a masterpiece of winemaking art.

Giuseppe Campagnola

FRAZ. VALGATARA
VIA AGNELLA, 9
37020 MARANO DI VALPOLICELLA [VR]
TEL. +39 0457703900
www.campagnola.com

CELLAR SALES
PRE-BOOKED VISITS
ANNUAL PRODUCTION 5,000,000 bottles
HECTARES UNDER VINE 155.00

As head of the family winery, Giuseppe Campagnola faces the difficult challenge of wearing two hats, one of local grape grower and the other of the businessman who must, of course, keep the enterprise on a profitable track. He tends more than 100 hectares, but the lion's share of the grapes are bought in from dense network of local growers. The house style highlights the richness of the fruit without compromising tautness on the palate. A superb performance by Vallata di Marano 2013, which although it expresses the super-ripe warmth typical of its wine type, manages to bring to the fore its own resources of vibrancy and suppleness to deliver a crisp, utterly delicious approachability. Quite different is the Riserva Caterina Zardini 2011, showing deep and multi-layered on the nose, a rich palate nicely sculpted by tannins and acidity, and a majestic, stately progression.

● Amarone della Valpolicella Punta Tolotti '12	▼▼▼ 7
○ Lessini Durello Pas Dosé M. Cl. Amedeo '11	▼▼ 5
○ Recioto di Soave La Perlara '13	▼▼ 5
○ Soave Cl. Monte Alto '14	▼▼ 3*
○ Soave Cl. Monte Fiorentine '15	▼▼ 3*
● Valpolicella Sup. Campo Lavei '14	▼▼ 4
● Recioto della Valpolicella L'Eremita '12	▼▼ 5
○ Soave Cl. San Michele '15	▼▼ 2*
● Valpolicella Rio Albo '15	▼▼ 2*
○ Soave Cl. Monte Alto '13	▼▼▼ 3*
○ Soave Cl. Monte Alto '11	▼▼▼ 3*
○ Soave Cl. Monte Alto '10	▼▼▼ 3*
○ Soave Cl. Monte Alto '09	▼▼▼ 3*
○ Soave Cl. Monte Fiorentine '13	▼▼▼ 3*
○ Studio '10	▼▼▼ 4*

● Amarone della Valpolicella Cl. Caterina Zardini Ris. '11	▼▼ 6
● Amarone della Valpolicella Cl. Vign. Vallata di Marano '13	▼▼ 5
● Recioto della Valpolicella Cl. Casotto del Merlo '13	▼▼ 5
● Valpolicella Cl. Sup. Caterina Zardini '14	▼▼ 3
● Valpolicella Cl. Sup. Ripasso '14	▼▼ 3
⊘ Bardolino Cl. Chiaretto Roccolo del Lago '15	▼ 2
● Bardolino Cl. Roccolo del Lago '15	▼ 2
○ Pinot Grigio Arnaces '15	▼ 2
○ Prosecco Brut Arnaces	▼ 3
● Soave Cl. Monte Foscarino Le Bine '15	▼ 2
● Valpolicella Cl. Le Bine '15	▼ 2
● Valpolicella Cl. Sup. Caterina Zardini '05	▼▼▼ 3*

I Campi

LOC. ALLODOLA
FRAZ. CELLORE D'ILLASI
VIA DELLE PEZZOLE, 3
37032 ILLASI [VR]
TEL. +39 0456175915
www.icampi.it

CELLAR SALES
PRE-BOOKED VISITS
ANNUAL PRODUCTION 80,000 bottles
HECTARES UNDER VINE 12.00

Flavio Prà, with a long expertise acquired at various Verona-area wineries, launched a cellar modest in volume but high in quality, making wines from both Soave and Valpolicella. The hillslope vineyards, some at higher altitudes, are planted exclusively to traditional varieties. Prà takes different style paths for reds and white. The latter are fragrant and taut; the former privilege richness and varietal fruit, always striving for the perfect equilibrium between these two expressions. The outstanding 2015 harvest produced an absolutely stellar Soave Campo Vulcano, intensely fragrant with apple, pear, and blossoms, veined with a subtle herbaceousness that gives it crisp thrust. Supple energy in the mouth, the gift of a fine acidity and even brighter fruit, results in a palate of great finesse. The Ripasso Campo Ciotoli 2014, is also admirable, with stunning fruit, on generous display on a succulent, spacious palate.

○ Soave Cl. Campo Vulcano '15	♈♈♈ 3*
● Valpolicella Sup. Ripasso Campo Ciotoli '14	♈♈ 3*
● Amarone della Valpolicella Campi Lunghi '13	♈♈ 6
○ Soave Campo Base '15	♈♈ 2*
● Valpolicella Campo Base '14	♈ 3
○ Soave Cl. Campo Vulcano '13	♈♈♈ 3*
○ Soave Cl. Campo Vulcano '12	♈♈♈ 3*
○ Soave Cl. Campo Vulcano '11	♈♈♈ 5
○ Soave Cl. Campo Vulcano '10	♈♈♈ 3*
○ Soave Cl. Campo Vulcano '09	♈♈♈ 3*
○ Soave Cl. Campo Vulcano '08	♈♈♈ 3*
● Valpolicella Sup. Ripasso Campo Ciotoli '13	♈♈♈ 3*
○ Soave Cl. Campo Vulcano '14	♈♈ 3*

Canevel Spumanti

LOC. SACCOL
VIA ROCCAT E FERRARI, 17
31049 VALDOBBIADENE [TV]
TEL. +39 0423975940
www.canevel.it

PRE-BOOKED VISITS
ANNUAL PRODUCTION 700,000 bottles
HECTARES UNDER VINE 12.00

Canevel, one of the fabled Prosecco producers, owed its start in the late 1970s to Mario Caramel and Roberto De Lucchi. Today, by Mario's place had been taken by his wife Tatiana and son Carlo, working with Roberto to achieve their dream of producing an exceptional Prosecco that will showcase all the potential of the glera varietal. The grapes from a dozen or so hectares of organically-farmed vineyards are supplemented by those bought in many other area growers. There's not one weak point in Canevel's lineup this year. An excellent version of Valdobbiadene Brut is out in front, with the warm growing year conferring on it absolutely classic apple and pear; in the mouth, crisp acidity and varietally-faithful, rich fruit are a magisterial complement to its spacious breadth. The Extra Dry version is likewise delicious, displaying even more fruit on the nose, followed by a succulent, very satisfying palate.

○ Cartizze '15	♈♈ 5
○ Valdobbiadene Brut '15	♈♈ 4
○ Valdobbiadene Dosaggio Zero Vign. del Faè '15	♈♈ 4
○ Valdobbiadene Extra Dry '15	♈♈ 4
○ Valdobbiadene Extra Dry Il Millesimato '15	♈♈ 5
○ Cartizze '14	♈♈ 5
○ Valdobbiadene Brut '14	♈♈ 4
○ Valdobbiadene Dosaggio Zero Vign. del Faè '14	♈♈ 4
○ Valdobbiadene Dosaggio Zero Vign. del Faè '13	♈♈ 4
○ Valdobbiadene Extra Dry Il Millesimato '14	♈♈ 5
○ Valdobbiadene Extra Dry Mill. '13	♈♈ 5

Cantina del Castello

CORTE PITTORA, 5
37038 SOAVE [VR]
TEL. +39 0457680093
www.cantinacastello.it

CELLAR SALES
PRE-BOOKED VISITS
ANNUAL PRODUCTION 130,000 bottles
HECTARES UNDER VINE 13.00

Over the last 20 years, Arturo has neither striven for inordinate growth nor assembled vineyards across the designation to pump up production frantically. Instead, he has lavished attention on his splendid estate vineyards, streamlining or grubbing up and replanting them, always with the aim of improving fruit quality. His winemaking, though, consistently seeks a style whose hallmarks are delicacy and fragrance. Ably assisted by the 2016 growing year, the wines exhibit intense aromatics, as a whiff of Soave Pressoni will rapidly confirm, encountering fragrant white plum and flowers; a savoury, ultra-delicious palate quickly follows. The long-cellared Carniga offers more complexity: a nose of multi-layered impressions, then dense richness and admirable length in the mouth, demonstrating once again the cellarability of Soave white wines.

La Cappuccina

FRAZ. COSTALUNGA
VIA SAN BRIZIO, 125
37032 MONTEFORTE D'ALPONE [VR]
TEL. +39 0456175036
www.lacappuccina.it

CELLAR SALES
PRE-BOOKED VISITS
RESTAURANT SERVICE
ANNUAL PRODUCTION 300,000 bottles
HECTARES UNDER VINE 42.00
VITICULTURE METHOD Certified Organic

Sisto, Pietro, and Elena Tessari manage this family operation in Costalunga, on the eastern slope of the Soave designation. They have farmed their 40 hectares of vertically-trellised vineyards organically for over 30 years, with the result that La Cappuccina is one of the region's long-standing gems. Their winemaking focuses largely on Soave, bringing out its fragrance and easy drinkability, but the portfolio contains a few reds too, all of high quality. San Brizio hasn't performed so impressively for some years now, and that despite the difficult 2014 harvest. Fruit of the vineyard between the 16th-century villa and the new cellar, and aged about a year in wood,, it offers up rich, fragrant apple, pear, and flowers, with hints of oak perfectly tucked-in. The palate unfurls fine volume and vibrancy, along a lengthy progression marked by zesty fruit. Recioto Arzimo 2013 is a delicious passito, exuding tropical fruit and citrus.

○ Soave Cl. Carniga '13	♀♀ 3*
○ Soave Cl. Pressoni '15	♀♀ 3*
○ Soave Cl. Castello '15	♀♀ 2*
○ Recioto di Soave Cl. Cortepittora '13	♀ 5
○ Soave Cl. Sup. Monte Pressoni '01	♀♀♀ 3
○ Recioto di Soave Cl. Ardens '08	♀♀ 5
○ Soave Cl. Carniga '11	♀♀ 3*
○ Soave Cl. Carniga '10	♀♀ 3
○ Soave Cl. Carniga '08	♀♀ 3
○ Soave Cl. Castello '12	♀♀ 2*
○ Soave Cl. Castello '09	♀♀ 2
○ Soave Cl. Pressoni '14	♀♀ 3
○ Soave Cl. Pressoni '13	♀♀ 3

○ Soave San Brizio '14	♀♀ 3*
○ Basaltik Sauvignon '15	♀♀ 2*
● Campo Buri '11	♀♀ 4
○ Recioto di Soave Arzimo '13	♀♀ 5
○ Soave '15	♀♀ 2*
○ Soave Cl. Monte Stelle '14	♀♀ 3
○ Villa Buri Brut M. Cl. '10	♀♀ 4
● Madégo '15	♀ 2
○ Soave Fontégo '15	♀ 2
● Campo Buri '10	♀♀ 4
○ Recioto di Soave Arzimo '12	♀♀ 5
○ Recioto di Soave Arzimo '11	♀♀ 4
○ Soave '14	♀♀ 2*
○ Soave Fontégo '14	♀♀ 2*
○ Soave Fontégo '13	♀♀ 2*
○ Soave Monte Stelle '13	♀♀ 3

Le Carline

VIA CARLINE, 24
30020 PRAMAGGIORE [VE]
TEL. +39 0421799741
www.lecarline.com

CELLAR SALES
PRE-BOOKED VISITS
ANNUAL PRODUCTION 400,000 bottles
HECTARES UNDER VINE 18.00
VITICULTURE METHOD Certified Organic

The Piccinin family launched their cellar in the 1980s, pointing out that they were a rara avis, dedicating themselves to organic farming even in those early years. Today, Daniele and wife Diana rely increasingly on their children. They work some 20 hectares in the heart of a 400-hectare organic island that is truly difficult to find elsewhere in Italy. Production now exceeds 400,000 bottles a year, constituting three lines, or better, three projects: vegan-certified, no added sulphites, and, of course, organic. Dogale, a passito scented with dates and walnuts, is a sensitively-crafted Verduzzo. The palate is beautifully balanced between sweet and savoury, silkiness and vibrancy, right into a lengthy finish that is clean and dry. Metodo Classico Diana in impressive too, a Brut largely of chardonnay, slender yet luscious.

Carpenè Malvolti

VIA ANTONIO CARPENÈ, 1
31015 CONEGLIANO [TV]
TEL. +39 0438364611
www.carpene-malvolti.com

PRE-BOOKED VISITS
ANNUAL PRODUCTION 5,300,000 bottles
HECTARES UNDER VINE 26.00

If Prosecco has become the phenomenon that the world acknowledges today, some credit certainly goes to the producers who started down that road so many years ago, and that naturally includes Carpenè Malvolti as an important player. Their estate vineyards are few, but the advantage they enjoy is a broad network of local growers who have been bringing them fruit for generations and at very high quality levels. The production focuses almost exclusively on Prosecco. The Extra Dry version gets high plaudits for its magisterial expression of a great year. It is uncompromisingly fruit-forward, with floral notes consigned to a complementary role, while the lusciousness in the mouth is the fruit of a delicate equilibrium between sweetness and acidity, a partnership sealed with the saline thrust classic to the glera grape. The Brut version is not far behind, with a similar nosegay of fragrant fruit, but nervier and more sharp-edged on the palate.

○ Diana Brut M. Cl. '15	♟♟ 4
○ Dogale Passito	♟♟ 3
● Lison-Pramaggiore Cabernet '15	♟ 2
○ Spumante Brut	♟ 2
○ Venezia Pinot Grigio '15	♟ 2
● Carline Rosso '12	♟♟ 3
● Carline Rosso '11	♟♟ 3
● Carline Rosso '10	♟♟ 3
● Carline Rosso '07	♟♟ 4
● Carline Rosso '07	♟♟ 4
○ Lison Cl. '12	♟♟ 2*
○ Lison-Pramaggiore Lison '09	♟♟ 2*
○ Lison-Pramaggiore Pinot Grigio '09	♟♟ 2*
○ Lison-Pramaggiore Pinot Grigio '08	♟♟ 2*
● Lison-Pramaggiore Refosco P.R. senza solfiti aggiunti '13	♟♟ 2*

○ Conegliano Valdobbiadene Extra Dry 1868	♟♟ 3
○ Cartizze	♟ 5
○ Conegliano Valdobbiadene Brut 1868	♟ 3
○ Conegliano Valdobbiadene Dry 1868 '14	♟ 5

Casa Cecchin

VIA AGUGLIANA, 11
36075 MONTEBELLO VICENTINO [VI]
TEL. +39 0444649610
www.casacecchin.it

CELLAR SALES
PRE-BOOKED VISITS
ANNUAL PRODUCTION 30,000 bottles
HECTARES UNDER VINE 7.00

In the early 1970s, Renato Cecchin started the winery we know so well today, concentrating right from the beginning on the area's two historic varieties, durella and garganega. Even today, the vineyards number barely seven hectares, in the area of Agugliana, where the cellar is also located, planted in soils with a strong volcanic element, at 250 metres of elevation. The production remains just white wines, both still and sparking, the latter solely Metodo Classico. Full marks for the resounding Nostrum 2012, a durello that spends some three years sur lie. Its clean-contoured aromas conjure up apple, pear, and blossoms, with a hesitant nuance of mineral that should emerge more fully with age. The grape's typical acidity takes on a saline edge in the mouth, giving the palate a taut tanginess, but ample breadth as well. A good performance from the garganega San Nicolò 2015 too, with an energy-laden palate that just keeps developing.

○ Gambellara San Nicolò '15	🍷🍷 2*
○ Lessini Durello Extra Brut Nostrum M. Cl. '12	🍷🍷 4
○ Lessini Durello Pietralava '14	🍷🍷 2*
○ Lessini Durello Il Durello '15	🍷 2
○ Lessini Durello Extra Brut Nostrum M. Cl '10	🍷🍷 4
○ Lessini Durello Il Durello '14	🍷🍷 2*
○ Lessini Durello Il Durello '13	🍷🍷 2*
○ Lessini Durello Non Dosato M. Cl. Ris. '09	🍷🍷 5
○ Lessini Durello Pietralava '12	🍷🍷 2*
○ Lessini Durello San Nicolò '14	🍷🍷 2*

Casa Roma

VIA ORMELLE, 19
31020 SAN POLO DI PIAVE [TV]
TEL. +39 0422855339
www.casaroma.com

CELLAR SALES
PRE-BOOKED VISITS
ANNUAL PRODUCTION 200,000 bottles
HECTARES UNDER VINE 15.00

The Piave growing area teems with producers known for production of crisp white wines, but who have now largely converted to the Prosecco phenomenon. But in San Polo di Piave, Gigi Peruzzetto has managed to maintain a challenging equilibrium, turning out straightforward, quaffable whites, but retaining a strong attachment to the area's iconic raboso. Two lines, then, at two different speeds: straightforward and crisp one; depth and finesse for the other. This growing area is notable for the now-scarce presence of the marzemina bianca, once quite widespread on the Piave plain and today very hard to find. Gigi fashions it into a white fragrant with peach, apricot, and brined olives, slender-bodied yet with fine grip and tasty fruit. His Pro Fondo Rosso is exuberant, tasty, and exceptionally pleasurable, from raboso re-fermented in the bottle; it boasts intense fragrances and a self-confident, juicy palate.

○ Mazemina Bianca '15	🍷🍷 2*
● Pro Fondo Rosso Frizzante	🍷🍷 2*
○ San Dordi '15	🍷🍷 3
● Piave Carmenère '15	🍷 2
○ Piave Manzoni Bianco '15	🍷 2
● Raboso Sestier '15	🍷 2
● Venezia Cabernet Sauvignon '15	🍷 2
○ Venezia Chardonnay '15	🍷 2
● Venezia Merlot '15	🍷 2
○ Venezia Pinot Grigio '15	🍷 2
⊙ Nesio Brut M. Cl. '10	🍷🍷 5
● Piave Malanotte '09	🍷🍷 6
● Piave Raboso '10	🍷🍷 4
● Piave Raboso '09	🍷🍷 4
● Raboso Passito Callarghe '09	🍷🍷 5

Case Paolin

VIA MADONNA MERCEDE, 53
31040 VOLPAGO DEL MONTELLO [TV]
TEL. +39 0423871433
www.casepaolin.it

CELLAR SALES
PRE-BOOKED VISITS
ANNUAL PRODUCTION 75,000 bottles
HECTARES UNDER VINE 12.00
VITICULTURE METHOD Certified Organic
SUSTAINABLE WINERY

The family winery of the Pozzobon brothers is in Volpago del Montello, on the slopes of the Montello hill, which is enclosed by the Po Valley to the south and the River Piave to the north. Their dozen or so hectares of vineyard, on both hillslopes and plain, are planted to classic Bordeaux black grapes, at home here for over a century, as well as to the more interesting glera and incrocio Manzoni bianco. San Carlo is the iconic wine here, a cabernet sauvignon-dominant Bordeaux blend grown in the vineyards in Volpago del Montello. A deep ruby introduces super-ripe fruit and spices, while the impressively compact palate is well supported by densely-woven tannins. Likewise convincing is Costa degli Angeli 2014, a citrusy Manzoni bianco that offers up plenty of juicy, succulent fruit.

Michele Castellani

FRAZ. VALGATARA
VIA GRANDA, 1
37020 MARANO DI VALPOLICELLA [VR]
TEL. +39 0457701253
www.castellanimichele.it

CELLAR SALES
PRE-BOOKED VISITS
ANNUAL PRODUCTION 300,000 bottles
HECTARES UNDER VINE 50.00

Sergio Castellani's winery is in Valgatara, right at the mouth of the Marano Valley, is one of the most impressive in that area, thanks some 300,000 bottles per year that come from a full 50 hectares of vineyards. That many vines allows Sergio to use just the best lots, which he interprets in a style that unfailingly expresses both concentration and power. Amarone Cinquestelle 2012 vaunts super-ripe red berry fruit on the nose, enriched by spices and India ink, which tend to push the oak into the background. Sergio's hand is obvious on the palate, having crafted a rich, dense wine with a stately progression driven by a superb acidity and close-packed tannins. Recioto Monte Fasenara 2013 is its mirror opposite, exhibiting explosive fruit and an exuberant, joyous palate.

○ Asolo Brut	♟♟ 2*
○ Manzoni Bianco Costa degli Angeli '14	♟♟ 3
● Montello e Colli Asolani Rosso San Carlo '12	♟♟ 4
○ Prosecco di Treviso Extra Dry	♟♟ 2*
● Rosso del Milio '13	♟♟ 3
○ Asolo Frizzante Col Fondo	♟ 3
● Cabernet '15	♟ 2
○ Soér Passito	♟ 4
○ Manzoni Bianco Costa degli Angeli '13	♟♟ 3
● Montello e Colli Asolani Rosso del Milio '11	♟♟ 3
● Montello e Colli Asolani Sup. San Carlo '11	♟♟ 4
● Rosso del Milio '12	♟♟ 3

● Amarone della Valpolicella Cl. Cinquestelle Collezione Ca' del Pipa '12	♟♟ 7
● Recioto della Valpolicella Cl. Monte Fasenara I Castei '13	♟♟ 5
● Amarone della Valpolicella Cl. Campo Casalin I Castei '12	♟♟ 6
● Valpolicella Cl. Campo del Biotto I Castei '15	♟ 2
● Valpolicella Cl. Sup. Ripasso Costamaran I Castei '14	♟ 3
● Valpolicella Cl. Sup. Ripasso Costamaran I Castei '13	♟♟ 3

★Cavalchina

LOC. CAVALCHINA
FRAZ. CUSTOZA
VIA SOMMACAMPAGNA, 7
37066 SOMMACAMPAGNA [VR]
TEL. +39 045516002
www.cavalchina.com

CELLAR SALES
PRE-BOOKED VISITS
ANNUAL PRODUCTION 445,000 bottles
HECTARES UNDER VINE 50.00

Franco and Luciano Piona have given new drive to their family winery, starting with the venerable Bardolino and Custoza designations. They extended westwards and to the River Mincio for varietally-based wines, and eastwards and into Valpolicella for wines based on tradition. Wine styles mirror these directions, with richness and fruit definition in the west, fragrance and elegance in Custoza, and power and breadth in Valpolicella, for a large, reliable production overall. Not only is Custoza Amedeo once again team champion in the Piona stable, but it also enjoys star status on the national white-wine stage. One savours rich, elegant fragrances of pear, apple, and blossoms, against a captivating tot of citrus, with matching richness in the mouth and no loss of vibrancy or savoury fruit. Then the Custoza SP 2013 shows a racier, razor-sharp profile with keen acidity showcasing freshness. Among the reds, we appreciated the marriage of depth and finesse in Bardolino Santa Lucia 2014, as well as the full-volumed warmth of Amarone Torre d'Orti 2012.

○ Custoza Sup. Amedeo '14	♟♟♟ 3*
● Amarone della Valpolicella Torre d'Orti '12	♟♟ 6
● Bardolino '15	♟♟ 2*
⊙ Bardolino Chiaretto '15	♟♟ 2*
● Bardolino Sup. S. Lucia '14	♟♟ 3
● Garda Cabernet Sauvignon Falcone La Prendina '13	♟♟ 4
○ Garda Riesling Paroni La Prendina '15	♟♟ 2*
⊙ La Rosa Passito '15	♟♟ 3
○ Sauvignon Valbruna La Prendina '14	♟♟ 2*
● Garda Merlot Faial Prendina '13	♟ 5
○ Garda Pinot Bianco Prendina '15	♟ 3
○ Pinot Grigio Prendina '15	♟ 2
● Valpolicella Sup. Morari Torre d'Orti '13	♟ 4
● Valpolicella Sup. Ripasso Torre d'Orti '13	♟ 3

Cavazza

C.DA SELVA, 22
36054 MONTEBELLO VICENTINO [VI]
TEL. +39 0444649166
www.cavazzawine.com

CELLAR SALES
PRE-BOOKED VISITS
ACCOMMODATION
ANNUAL PRODUCTION 860,000 bottles
HECTARES UNDER VINE 150.00
SUSTAINABLE WINERY

The Cavazza family has been active for many years in the Gambellara growing district and the nearby Berici Hills. Production is now approaching a million bottles a year from vineyards that cover 150 hectares. The house style tends in two directions: on one hand the lightness and the fragrance of Gambellara, dedicated mostly to the renowned white; on the other, the richness and brightness of the Berici Hills, with a strongpoint in the Bordeaux varieties. The Colli Berici are the zone that brought us the most impressive wines this year, starting with a warm, ripe version of Merlot Cicogna. Smooth, well-ripened red berry fruit and spices greet the nose, assisted by a notes of coffee bean and cocoa powder that further sweeten the aromatic impact. Dense but glossy tannins drive a powerful, compact palate through to more warmth on the finish. Among the whites, high marks go to Bocara, a dynamic, juicy gambellara.

● Colli Berici Merlot Cicogna '13	♟♟ 5
○ Gambellara Cl. La Bocara '15	♟♟ 2*
○ Chardonnay Corì '15	♟ 3
● Colli Berici Cabernet Cicogna '12	♟♟ 4
● Colli Berici Cabernet Cicogna '11	♟♟ 4
● Colli Berici Merlot Cicogna '12	♟♟ 4
● Colli Berici Merlot Cicogna '11	♟♟ 4
● Colli Berici Tai Rosso Corallo '13	♟♟ 3
○ Gambellara Cl. Creari '12	♟♟ 3
○ Gambellara Cl. Creari '10	♟♟ 3
○ Gambellara Cl. La Bocara '12	♟♟ 2*
○ Recioto di Gambellara Cl. Capitel S. Libera '10	♟♟ 4

Giorgio Cecchetto

Fraz. Tezze di Piave
Via Piave, 67
31028 Vazzola [TV]
Tel. +39 043828598
www.rabosopiave.com

CELLAR SALES
PRE-BOOKED VISITS
ANNUAL PRODUCTION 200,000 bottles
HECTARES UNDER VINE 73.00
SUSTAINABLE WINERY

The Prosecco craze began in the Conegliano and Vadobbiadene hills, then took root and spread throughout the province of Treviso like wildfire. Giorgio Cecchetto and his wife Cristina, though not disdaining such fragrant sparklers, preferred to preserve their bond with raboso, which they produce in all the established types, from the partially-raisined Malanotte to the crisp, nervier Metodo Classico. Fruit of the 2012 harvest, Piave Raboso is the favourite wine this year. Wild berry and spice infuse the nose, lifted by pungent wild herbs, which continue unabated onto a palate that combines compactness with the acidic bite classic to this grape. Manzoni Bianco is a pleasure as well, an eloquent expression of the 2017 harvest, marrying fullness and suppleness to achieve a delightfully succulent white.

○ Manzoni Bianco '15	♥♥ 2*
● Piave Raboso '12	♥♥ 3
● Cabernet Sauvignon '15	♥ 2
● Carmenere '15	♥ 2
● Merlot Sante Rosso '13	♥ 3
● Malanotte Gelsaia '11	♀♀ 5
● Merlot Sante Rosso '11	♀♀ 3
● Merlot Sante Rosso '10	♀♀ 3
● Piave Raboso '11	♀♀ 3
● Raboso Passito RP	♀♀ 4
⊙ Rosa Bruna Cuvée 21 Brut M.Cl. '11	♀♀ 3
⊙ Rosa Bruna Cuvée 21 Brut M.Cl. '10	♀♀ 3
● Sante Rosso '12	♀♀ 3

Gerardo Cesari

Loc. Sorsei, 3
37010 Cavaion Veronese [VR]
Tel. +39 0456260928
www.cesariverona.it

CELLAR SALES
PRE-BOOKED VISITS
ANNUAL PRODUCTION 1,600,000 bottles
HECTARES UNDER VINE 109.00
SUSTAINABLE WINERY

From its 100 or so hectares of vineyards, Cesari produces over a million and a half bottle per year, but these numbers fail to convey its real passion for the wines of Valpolicella and of neighbouring designations, and the attention and expertise lavished on their production and lengthy maturation in the cellars in Cavaion and San Pietro. Their wide range of Amarones are subdivided by grape source and take time to reach the market. Amarone Bosan 2000, which we tasted for the first time, is one of the wines included in a portfolio of the winery's great vintages, just put on the market. At 16 years, it shows unexpected vibrancy, with fruit, spice, and aromatic herbs all on generous display, and the palate has achieved enviable harmony. Bosco, ten years younger, exhibits the same breed and tautness, with a palate that ably combines power and fine balance.

● Amarone della Valpolicella Bosan '00	♥♥ 7
● Amarone della Valpolicella Cl. '12	♥♥ 6
● Amarone della Valpolicella Cl. Il Bosco '10	♥♥ 7
○ Lugana Cento Filari '15	♥ 3
● Valpolicella Sup. Ripasso Mara '14	♥ 3
● Amarone della Valpolicella Bosan '06	♀♀ 8
● Amarone della Valpolicella Bosan '05	♀♀ 8
● Amarone della Valpolicella Cl. Il Bosco '09	♀♀ 7
● Amarone della Valpolicella Cl. Il Bosco '08	♀♀ 7
○ Lugana Cento Filari '14	♀♀ 3
○ Lugana Cento Filari '13	♀♀ 3
● Valpolicella Sup. Ripasso Bosan '11	♀♀ 5

Italo Cescon

FRAZ. RONCADELLE
P.ZZA DEI CADUTI, 3
31024 ORMELLE [TV]
TEL. +39 0422851033
www.cesconitalo.it

CELLAR SALES
PRE-BOOKED VISITS
ANNUAL PRODUCTION 800,000 bottles
HECTARES UNDER VINE 115.00
VITICULTURE METHOD Certified Organic
SUSTAINABLE WINERY

Gloria, Graziella, and Domenico Cescon radically renewed their family winery without losing touch with their roots. They have over 100 hectares of vineyard today, which they supplement with fruit bought in from a host of other local growers. The latter goes mainly to making their more straightforward wines, while the estate vineyards are the foundation for the more ambitious offerings, wines that are aromatic and with superb personalities. We have been expecting for years now the placing of the capstone in the Cescon enterprise, and here it is, in the appearance of a Manzoni Bianco that has no peer. Madre 2014 embodies superb aromatic expression, with understated use of wood that heightens the effect of citrus and tropical fruit, while the near-endless progression in the mouth is emphatic yet majestic. The cabernet-merlot Chieto 2013 is consistently improving as well, hallmarked by elegance and overall harmony of proportions.

○ Madre '14	▼▼▼	4*
● Chieto '13	▼▼	4
○ Manzoni Bianco Svejo '15	▼▼	3
○ Sauvignon Mejo '15	▼▼	3
● Amaranto 72 '12	♈♈	5
● Amaranto 72 '11	♈♈	5
● Chieto '12	♈♈	4
● Chieto '11	♈♈	3
● Chieto '10	♈♈	3
○ Manzoni Bianco Non Filtrato '13	♈♈	5
○ Manzoni Bianco Non Filtrato '12	♈♈	3
○ Manzoni Bianco Non Filtrato '11	♈♈	3
○ Manzoni Bianco Svejo '14	♈♈	3
○ Manzoni Bianco Svejo '11	♈♈	2*

Coffele

VIA ROMA, 5
37038 SOAVE [VR]
TEL. +39 0457680007
www.coffele.it

CELLAR SALES
PRE-BOOKED VISITS
ANNUAL PRODUCTION 120,000 bottles
HECTARES UNDER VINE 25.00
VITICULTURE METHOD Certified Organic

The Coffele family cellar lies in Castelcerino, at one of Soave's highest elevations, where some two dozen hectares are planted almost solely to garganega, with a few rows of trebbiano di Soave. The elevation ensures crisp, refined wines. They have recently added a small property in Cazzano di Tramigna dedicated to producing Valpolicella's classic reds. The excellent 2015 harvest gifted Soave Ca' Visco with particularly rich fruit, where tropical impressions meld into citrus and white peach. In the mouth, a zesty acidity enlivens its compact character, providing length and suppleness. As expected, one of the finest Reciotos is Le Sponde 2014, showcasing hazelnut and dried apricot, followed by a palate of seductive, harmonious sweetness.

○ Recioto di Soave Cl. Le Sponde '14	▼▼	5
○ Soave Cl. Ca' Visco '15	▼▼	3*
○ Soave Cl. Alzari '14	▼▼	3
○ Soave Cl. Castel Cerino '15	▼▼	3
○ Recioto di Soave Cl. Le Sponde '09	♈♈♈	5
○ Soave Cl. Ca' Visco '14	♈♈♈	3*
○ Soave Cl. Ca' Visco '05	♈♈♈	3*
○ Soave Cl. Ca' Visco '04	♈♈♈	2
○ Soave Cl. Ca' Visco '03	♈♈♈	2
○ Recioto di Soave Cl. Le Sponde '13	♈♈	5
○ Soave Cl. Alzari '13	♈♈	3
○ Soave Cl. Alzari '12	♈♈	3
○ Soave Cl. Ca' Visco '13	♈♈	3*

Col Vetoraz

fraz. Santo Stefano
s.da delle Tresiese, 1
31040 Valdobbiadene [TV]
Tel. +39 0423975291
www.colvetoraz.it

CELLAR SALES
PRE-BOOKED VISITS
ANNUAL PRODUCTION 800,000 bottles
HECTARES UNDER VINE 12.00

Steep and magical, the Vetoraz hill that gives the winery its name, soars over the Cartizze vines, a stone's throw from the centre of Valdobbiadene. The hilltop cellar is owned by partners Loris Dall'Acqua, Francesco Miotto, and Paolo De Bortoli, and is one of the most prestigious operations in the area. The secret lies in the expertise of its staff and the quality of its vineyards, part of which belong to the winery and part to the local growers who supply it. Plus the fact that only the finest lots of those grapes end up in the bottle. Grapes from the best sites, warm and sun-kissed, go to produce Brut Zero, a Prosecco that foregoes the boost of a sugar dosage in favour of quality based solely on perfectly-ripe grapes, which has the challenge of ensuring aromatic expressiveness and smooth suppleness in the mouth. That challenge is decisively met with the 2015 vintage. Its fragrances range through apple, pear, and blossoms, as well as a pungent hint of herbaceousness, then it shows pleasantly dry and emphatic in the mouth, concluding with a long-lingering, refined finale.

○ Valdobbiadene Brut Zero '15	🍷🍷 3*
○ Cartizze	🍷🍷 4
○ Valdobbiadene Brut	🍷🍷 3
○ Valdobbiadene Dry Mill. '15	🍷🍷 3
○ Valdobbiadene Extra Dry	🍷🍷 3
○ Valdobbiadene Tranquillo Tresiese '15	🍷 3
○ Cartizze '14	🍷🍷 4
○ Valdobbiadene Brut Zero '14	🍷🍷 3
○ Valdobbiadene Dry '13	🍷🍷 3
○ Valdobbiadene Dry '12	🍷🍷 3*
○ Valdobbiadene Dry Mill. '14	🍷🍷 3
○ Valdobbiadene Dry Mill. '11	🍷🍷 3

Vignaioli Contrà Soarda

s.da Soarda, 26
36061 Bassano del Grappa [VI]
Tel. +39 0424505562
www.contrasoarda.it

CELLAR SALES
PRE-BOOKED VISITS
RESTAURANT SERVICE
ANNUAL PRODUCTION 80,000 bottles
HECTARES UNDER VINE 20.00
VITICULTURE METHOD Certified Organic
SUSTAINABLE WINERY

The Gottardi family cellar is literally immersed in the hills, just a stone's throw from the Po Valley as well as from the nearby Valsugana, which sends the cool air currents that caress the grapes and ensure significant day-night temperature ranges during the summer. They grow some 20 hectares of both international and native grapes, farmed as sustainably as possible, for their extensive wine production, which ranges from the crisp and youthful to those aged at length in the cellar. Fragrant dried apricots, hazelnuts, and caramelled almonds characterize Torcolato Sarson 2013, freshened by a lovely hint of medicinal herbs. With no over-sweetness in the mouth, the acidity and savoury fruit keep all the components in beautiful proportion in the mouth. The merlot Terre di Lava 2011 impresses, too, its sweet, ripe fruit a tasty foil to the palate's vibrant richness, all the way to a dry, lengthy conclusion.

● Breganze Rosso Terre di Lava Ris. '11	🍷🍷 4
○ Breganze Torcolato Sarson '13	🍷🍷 5
● Pinot Nero Vigna Corejo '13	🍷🍷 7
● 121 b.C. Carmenere '13	🍷 5
○ 121 b.C. Vespaiolo '14	🍷 5
● Breganze Rosso Serafino Musso '07	🍷 4
○ Breganze Vespaiolo Soarda '15	🍷 3
○ Breganze Vespaiolo Vignasilan '13	🍷 4
● Marzemino Nero Gaggion '13	🍷 3
● Oliva Musso '11	🍷 4
● Breganze Pinot Nero Vignacorejo '12	🍷🍷 7
○ Breganze Torcolato Sarson Ris. '12	🍷🍷 5
● Musso Serafino '10	🍷🍷 3

Corte Adami

VIA CIRCONVALLAZIONE ALDO MORO, 32
37038 SOAVE [VR]
TEL. +39 0457680423
www.corteadami.it

CELLAR SALES
PRE-BOOKED VISITS
ANNUAL PRODUCTION 100,000 bottles
HECTARES UNDER VINE 38.00
SUSTAINABLE WINERY

Although the Adami family's winery was established just a few years back, its roots go quite deep in the Soave soil, first as grape growers and then some dozen years as bottlers. Their considerable vineyard area, almost 40 hectares, is even today used only partly for their own wines; the remainder goes to the cooperative. The wines are more than satisfactory, both from Soave and the nearby Valpolicella, including a superb Soave Vigna della Corte 2014. Ripe apricot, melon, and flowers meld together on the nose, seguing into a palate defined by a vibrant charge of acidity. Decennale 2013, on the other hand, from a more favourable season and given a lengthier ageing, focuses on complexity and overall harmony in the mouth. Among the reds, we liked Valpolicella Superiore 2013, fragrant with cherry and wild herbs, with its full body nicely counter-pointed by a taut vibrancy.

● Amarone della Valpolicella '12	♥♥	6
○ Soave Il Decennale '13	♥♥	6
○ Soave V. della Corte '14	♥♥	3
● Valpolicella Sup. '13	♥♥	3
○ Recioto di Soave '13	♥	4
○ Soave '15	♥	2
○ Soave Cl. Cimalta '15	♥	2
● Valpolicella Sup. Ripasso '13	♥	3
● Amarone della Valpolicella '11	♀♀	6
○ Soave Il Decennale '13	♀♀	2*
○ Soave V. della Corte '13	♀♀	3
○ Soave V. della Corte '12	♀♀	3
○ Soave V. della Corte '11	♀♀	3
○ Soave Vigna della Corte '09	♀♀	*

Corte Gardoni

LOC. GARDONI, 5
37067 VALEGGIO SUL MINCIO [VR]
TEL. +39 0457950382
www.cortegardoni.it

CELLAR SALES
PRE-BOOKED VISITS
ANNUAL PRODUCTION 200,000 bottles
HECTARES UNDER VINE 25.00

The southern area of Lake Garda, with its enfolding hills of morainic origin, presents a number of places for growing fine fruit for Bardolino, with grapes that are crisp yet compact and firm, qualities they transmit to the red wine here. The Piccoli family, among the area's most respected winegrowers, produces a good bit of Custoza as well, delicate and refined but with a fine tautness in the mouth. Mael 2015 is the house standard-bearer, a Custoza that explores the great potential of this category for yielding crisp, aromatic wines that are nevertheless rich and full on the palate. A sapient blend of the main grapes of the designation, Mael lays out intense notes of citrus and blossoms, then expands in the mouth with superb character and thrust towards a lengthy, sharp-edged finish. Fenili 2011 is a mostly garganega passito impressive for its near-miraculous equilibrium between sweetness, acidity, and savouriness.

○ Custoza Mael '15	♥♥	3*
☉ Bardolino Chiaretto '15	♥♥	2*
● Bardolino Le Fontane '15	♥♥	2*
● Becco Rosso '14	♥♥	3
○ Custoza '15	♥♥	2*
○ Fenili Passito '11	♥♥	5
● Rosso di Corte '13	♥♥	4
● Bardolino Le Fontane '14	♀♀	2*
● Bardolino Sup. Pradicà '13	♀♀	3*
● Bardolino Sup. Pradicà '12	♀♀	3*
● Bardolino Sup. Pradicà '11	♀♀	3*
● Becco Rosso '13	♀♀	3
○ Custoza '13	♀♀	2*
○ Custoza Mael '14	♀♀	3*
○ Fenili Passito '09	♀♀	5
● Rosso di Corte '11	♀♀	4

Corte Mainente

V.LE DELLA VITTORIA, 45
37038 SOAVE [VR]
TEL. +39 0457680303
www.cantinamainente.com

CELLAR SALES
PRE-BOOKED VISITS
ANNUAL PRODUCTION 7,700 bottles
HECTARES UNDER VINE 12.00
SUSTAINABLE WINERY

The Soave designation is teeming with winegrowers and every few hundred metres we find a new property, large and smaller wineries; growers who sell their crop to the cooperatives or to other bottlers. The Mainente family have been here a very long time, but in the last ten years they have changed direction, now concentrating on the garganega variety. They rely on a dozen or so hectares of vineyards divided between the Soave and Classico designations. Their iconic wine is Tovo al Pigno, a harmonious Soave that is pure pleasure. Netrroir is even more impressive, after a lengthy stay in the cellar. The nose reveals ripe apricot, melon, and yellow peach, plus a delicate whiff of minerally flint, and the full-volumed palate is well served by a tasty thrust of acidity that fuels its lengthy progression.

○ Recioto di Soave Luna Nova '14	🍷🍷 3
○ Soave Cl. Tovo al Pigno '15	🍷🍷 2*
○ Soave Netrroir '14	🍷🍷 2*
○ Soave Cengelle '15	🍷 2

Corte Moschina

VIA MOSCHINA, 1
37030 RONCÀ [VR]
TEL. +39 0457460788
www.cortemoschina.it

CELLAR SALES
PRE-BOOKED VISITS
ANNUAL PRODUCTION 75,000 bottles
HECTARES UNDER VINE 28.00
SUSTAINABLE WINERY

Corte Moschina is one of eastern Soave's most respected producers, ever since Patrizia Niero, with husband Silvano and sons Alessandro e Giacomo, changed the direction of this family operation. Their numerous estate vineyards yield a line that is still limited in quantity but of outstanding quality. Their whites explore the length and breadth of garganega, while the sparklers benefit from the taut crispness of durella. The all-garganega Soave Evaos 2015, matured in steel, expresses the designation's most vibrant and authentic potential. Only the finest vineyards, with their roots deep in the predominantly basaltic soils of Roncà, contribute to this Soave, and the winemaking is focused above all on preserving varietal fidelity. The result is a wine that eschews smoothness in favour of an energy-laden, super-savoury palate. I Tarai 2014 is richer and sunnier, offspring of a late harvest and partial maturation in oak.

○ Soave Evaos '15	🍷🍷 3*
○ Lessini Durello Brut M. Cl. Ris. '09	🍷🍷 5
○ Raìse '13	🍷🍷 5
○ Soave I Tarai '14	🍷🍷 3
○ Soave Roncathe '15	🍷🍷 2*
● Durello Frizzante Sui lieviti Puro Caso	🍷 5
○ Lessini Durello Brut M. Cl. '11	🍷 2
○ Lessini Durello Extra Brut M. Cl. '10	🍷🍷 4
○ Raise '12	🍷🍷 5
○ Recioto di Soave Incanto '11	🍷🍷 4
○ Recioto di Soave Incanto '10	🍷🍷 4
○ Soave Evaos '14	🍷🍷 2*
○ Soave Evaos '13	🍷🍷 2*
○ Soave I Tarai '13	🍷🍷 3
○ Soave I Tarai '12	🍷🍷 3*
○ Soave Roncathe '14	🍷🍷 2*

Corte Rugolin

FRAZ. VALGATARA
VIA RUGOLIN, 1
37020 MARANO DI VALPOLICELLA [VR]
TEL. +39 0457702153
www.corterugolin.it

CELLAR SALES
PRE-BOOKED VISITS
ANNUAL PRODUCTION 80,000 bottles
HECTARES UNDER VINE 12.00
SUSTAINABLE WINERY

Corte Rugolin has completely restyled its labels, but the real change lies inside the bottles. Over the years, Elena and Federico have worked out their own approach to interpreting Valpolicella and its wines, namely through soundness of fruit and good grip on the palate. Their 12 hectares of grapes yield fewer than 100,000 bottles, all focusing on traditional local reds, the sole and sporadic exception being a white passito. Amarone Crosara de le Strie 2011 plays the role of frontrunner here, richly redolent of wild berry fruit and spice, with an intriguing but fleeting whiff of powdered coffee. On the palate, taut verve and significant depth duet fruitfully together, into a long-lingering finale. San Giorgio 2014 displays a determination to be a new interpretation of Valpolicella Superiore, no longer based on mere power but on aromatic depth and an energetic thrust on the palate.

● Amarone della Valpolicella Cl. Crosara de le Strie '11	♥♥ 7
● Valpolicella Cl. Sup. San Giorgio '14	♥♥ 5
● Valpolicella Cl. Sup. Ripasso '13	♥♥ 5
● Valpolicella Cl. '15	♥ 3
● Amarone della Valpolicella Cl. Crosara de le Strie '10	♀♀ 6
● Amarone della Valpolicella Cl. Monte Danieli '10	♀♀ 7
● Recioto della Valpolicella Cl. '13	♀♀ 5
● Valpolicella Cl. '14	♀♀ 2*
● Valpolicella Cl. Sup. Ripasso '12	♀♀ 4
● Valpolicella Cl. Sup. Ripasso '11	♀♀ 4
● Valpolicella Cl. Sup. San Giorgio '13	♀♀ 5

★Corte Sant'Alda

LOC. FIOI
VIA CAPOVILLA, 28
37030 MEZZANE DI SOTTO [VR]
TEL. +39 0458880006
www.cortesantalda.it

CELLAR SALES
PRE-BOOKED VISITS
ACCOMMODATION
ANNUAL PRODUCTION 90,000 bottles
HECTARES UNDER VINE 19.00
VITICULTURE METHOD Certified Biodynamic

Marinella Camerani was one of the first to flee the world of the chemical-dominated farming and establish a rapport with wine expressed in terms of respect for the environment, local traditions, and the time required for its production. Today, assisted by her family and a fine group of young staff, she tends some 20 hectares, which yield wines limited in number but of distinguished quality, rich but not overly-concentrated, ripe but not opulent, with palates that always display good crisp grip. Valpolicella Mithas 2012 is simply stunning, a Superiore that veers decisively away from the Amarone model and shows instead an aromatic depth composed of fines herbes, smooth fruit, spice, and a hint of minerality which should grow apace. In the mouth, an uncompromising, yet elegant, compactness replaces the expected softness. Amarone 2010, also produced only in the best seasons, interweaves super-ripe fruit with black peppercorns and macerated flower petals, then impresses in the mouth with exquisite balance and fine length.

● Valpolicella Sup. Mithas '12	♥♥♥ 8
● Amarone della Valpolicella Mithas '10	♥♥ 8
⊙ Agathe '15	♥♥ 4
● Recioto della Valpolicella '13	♥♥ 6
○ Soave '15	♥♥ 3
● Valpolicella Ca' Fiui '15	♥♥ 3
● Valpolicella Sup. Ripasso Campi Magri '13	♥♥ 4
● Valpolicella Adalia '15	♥ 3
● Amarone della Valpolicella '10	♀♀♀ 8
● Amarone della Valpolicella '06	♀♀♀ 7
● Amarone della Valpolicella '00	♀♀♀ 7
● Amarone della Valpolicella '98	♀♀♀ 7
● Amarone della Valpolicella '90	♀♀♀ 7
● Amarone della Valpolicella Mithas '95	♀♀♀ 7
● Valpolicella Sup. '03	♀♀♀ 3*
● Valpolicella Sup. Mithas '04	♀♀♀ 6

Dal Cero
Tenuta di Corte Giacobbe

VIA MOSCHINA, 11
37030 RONCÀ [VR]
TEL. +39 0457460110
www.vinidalcero.com

CELLAR SALES
PRE-BOOKED VISITS
ANNUAL PRODUCTION 300,000 bottles
HECTARES UNDER VINE 40.00

The Dal Cero family has been successful in the difficult task of reconciling a peasant soul, always respectful of Nature's cadence, of traditions, and of classic wine types, with business demands, quick decision making, and an eye always on the market. In the space of a few years, they have increased their vineyards significantly, and have now networked to foster the production of Valpolicella reds, in addition to their Soaves and sparklers. Runcata, a Soave partly aged in ovals, stands out for its delectable fruit, which at this point is backgrounded perhaps a tad too much by oak. But things change on the palate, which expands with style and self-confidence, bolstered by a vibrant, tasty acidity that provides length and suppleness. Likewise impressive is Cuvée Augusto, a chardonnay and durella sparkler of great balance and élan.

○ Soave Sup. Vign. Runcata '14	♟♟♟ 2*	
● Amarone della Valpolicella '11	♟♟ 7	
○ Brut M. Cl.	♟♟ 3	
○ Dosaggio Zero M. Cl. Cuvée Augusto	♟♟ 5	
○ Soave '15	♟♟ 2*	
● Valpolicella Sup. Ripasso '14	♟♟ 5	
○ Pinot Grigio '15	♟ 2	
○ Pinot Grigio Ramato '15	♟ 2	
○ Dosaggio Zero M. Cl. Cuvée Augusto '10	♕♕ 5	
○ Dosaggio Zero M. Cl. Cuvée Augusto '09	♕♕ 2*	
○ Soave '14	♕♕ 2*	
○ Soave Corte Giacobbe '11	♕♕ 2*	
○ Soave Runcata '10	♕♕ 2*	
○ Soave Sup. Runcata '12	♕♕ 2*	
○ Soave Sup. Runcata '11	♕♕ 2*	
○ Soave Sup. Vign. Runcata '13	♕♕ 2*	

Dal Maso

C.DA SELVA, 62
36054 MONTEBELLO VICENTINO [VI]
TEL. +39 0444649104
www.dalmasovini.com

CELLAR SALES
PRE-BOOKED VISITS
ACCOMMODATION AND RESTAURANT SERVICE
ANNUAL PRODUCTION 450,000 bottles
HECTARES UNDER VINE 30.00
SUSTAINABLE WINERY

A respected leader in the Gambellara area, the Dal Maso family has extended its activities into the nearby Colli Berici, but continues its dedication to the traditional white grape here. Nicola directs this operation, with sisters Anna and Silvia, and oversees the 30 or so hectares of vineyards in both designations. Overall production is under a half million bottles, and style focuses on crispness and aromatics for the Gambellara wines, and bright, full-bodied Bericis. Montemitorio is a Tai Rosso that eschews the production area's usual extreme delicacy without veering into excessive concentration. What we find is a superb red showcasing intense scents of wild berry and spice on the nose and abundant crunchy, savoury fruit in the mouth, the gift too of its maturation in concrete and steel. Vin Santo di Gambellara 2004 is a different matter altogether: deeply concentrated and profoundly aromatic, with pure opulence in the mouth.

● Colli Berici Tai Rosso Montemitorio '14	♟♟ 2*	
○ Gambellara Cl. Vin Santo '04	♟♟ 8	
● Colli Berici Rosso Terra dei Rovi '13	♟♟ 5	
○ Gambellara Cl. Ca' Fischele '15	♟♟ 2*	
○ Gambellara Riva del Molino '15	♟♟ 3	
○ Recioto di Gambellara Riva dei Perari '13	♟♟ 5	
● Colli Berici Tai Rosso '15	♟ 2	
○ Lessini Durello Brut	♟ 2	
● Montebelvedere '14	♟ 3	
○ Gambellara Cl. Riva del Molino '07	♕♕♕ 2*	
● Colli Berici Tai Rosso Colpizzarda '13	♕♕ 4	
● Colli Berici Tai Rosso Colpizzarda '12	♕♕ 2*	
● Montebelvedere '13	♕♕ 3	
● Terra dei Rovi Rosso '13	♕♕ 5	

De Stefani

VIA CADORNA, 92
30020 FOSSALTA DI PIAVE [VE]
TEL. +39 042167502
www.de-stefani.it

CELLAR SALES
PRE-BOOKED VISITS
ANNUAL PRODUCTION 300,000 bottles
HECTARES UNDER VINE 50.00
SUSTAINABLE WINERY

Alessandro De Stefani, still enjoying the valiant assistance of father Tiziano, pursues his reorganization of the family winery year after year. An attractive new cellar graces the square on Via Cadorna, and the vineyards are benefiting from a gradual elimination of chemical treatments, while the property in Refrontolo will be the focus of vineyard renewals centred on the marzemino grape. The house style strives for richness of fruit and a taut crispness on the palate. Olmera, an impressive, and unusual, blend of sauvignon blanc and tai, has lost a bit of its smooth richness of years past, in favour of more authentic aromatic expression and a palate that is dry and seductively vibrant. The result is a wine that is ripe and stylish on those nose, and a rich palate with no need of residual sugar. Stefen 1624, exuding superb fruit, is ripe and power-filled in the mouth, ultra-appealing at every stage in its presentation. Good marks, finally, for Pinot Grigio 2015, straightforward but by no means banal.

- Cabernet Sauvignon '14   ▼▼ 3
- Colli di Conegliano Rosso
  Stefen 1624 '11   ▼▼ 8
- Kreda Refosco '13   ▼▼ 5
○ Olmera '15   ▼▼ 5
- Piave Raboso Vign. Terre Nobili '11   ▼▼ 4
○ Valdobbiadene Brut Mill. '15   ▼▼ 2*
○ Valdobbiadene Brut Nature '15   ▼▼ 2*
○ Venezia Pinot Grigio '15   ▼▼ 3
○ Piave Chardonnay Vitalys '15   ▼ 2
○ Prosecco di Treviso Zero Mill. '15   ▼ 4
○ Venis '15   ▼ 3
- Kreda Refosco '12   ♈ 5
- Plavis '13   ♈ 4
- Soler '13   ♈ 4
- Stefen 1624 '09   ♈ 8

Conte Emo Capodilista La Montecchia

VIA MONTECCHIA, 16
35030 SELVAZZANO DENTRO [PD]
TEL. +39 049637294
www.lamontecchia.it

CELLAR SALES
PRE-BOOKED VISITS
ACCOMMODATION
ANNUAL PRODUCTION 144,000 bottles
HECTARES UNDER VINE 30.00
SUSTAINABLE WINERY

The Euganean Hills, an isolated volcanic complex soaring upwards abruptly on the Po River plain, combine an almost Mediterranean climate with mineral-rich soils. Giordano Emo Capodilista runs the family wine estate here, both in the northern section, where white grapes and merlot flourish, as well as in the extreme south, the uncontested domain of cabernet sauvignon. Two wines stood out from the rest this year, Ireneo 2013 and Cuore di Donna Daria. The former, a cabernet sauvignon from the vineyards on Monte Castello, features rich, ripe fruit and spices, nicely lifted by pungent wild herbs and graphite, followed by a powerful, uncompromising palate that seems to go on forever. The second, on the other hand, is an unusual blend of ten years of Fior d'Arancio Passito, with a complex, multi-layered nose of mixed nuts and fruit alternating with candied citrus, while the palate is a tasty interplay between opulent richness and savoury fruit.

- Colli Euganei Cabernet Sauvignon
  Ireneo '13   ▼▼ 4
○ Cuore di Donna Daria   ▼▼ 8
- Colli Euganei Merlot '14   ▼▼ 5
- Godimondo Cabernet Franc '15   ▼▼ 2*
- Progetto Recupero Carmere '13   ▼▼ 3
- Ca' Emo '14   ▼ 2
○ Colli Euganei Fior d'Arancio Spumante   ▼ 2
○ Colli Euganei Pinot Bianco '15   ▼ 2
○ Piùchebello '15   ▼ 2
- Colli Euganei Cabernet Sauvignon
  Ireneo '12   ♈♈ 4*
○ Colli Euganei Fior d'Arancio Passito
  Donna Daria '06   ♈♈ 5

Farina

LOC. PEDEMONTE
VIA BOLLA, 11
37029 SAN PIETRO IN CARIANO [VR]
TEL. +39 0457701349
www.farinawines.com

CELLAR SALES
PRE-BOOKED VISITS
ANNUAL PRODUCTION 800,000 bottles
HECTARES UNDER VINE 45.00

Although history here goes back more than a century, the advent of Claudio, Elena, and Fabio was what gave this Pedemonte-based producer the image we recognize today. They cultivate some ten hectares of estate vineyards, but they purchase fruit from many other local growers, with whom they work closely during the growing season. The focus is on Valpolicella reds, but they also make a few Verona classics. The Montecorna 2014 Ripasso unfurls good aromatic depth with sweet, super-ripe fruit gearing down to pepper and thyme notes. Excellent follow-through as the wine expands with graceful confidence. A thumbs-up also for 2013 Amarone Classico, which belies its fast release with appreciable nose harmony and a palate with this wine's typical richness.

● Amarone della Valpolicella Cl. '13	▼▼ 5
● Valpolicella Cl. Sup. '14	▼▼ 2*
● Valpolicella Cl. Sup. Ripasso Montecorna '14	▼▼ 3
● Valpolicella Cl. '15	▼ 2
● Valpolicella Cl. Sup. Ripasso '14	▼ 2
● Amarone della Valpolicella Cl. '12	♀♀ 5
● Amarone della Valpolicella Cl. Montefante Ris. '10	♀♀ 8
● Amarone della Valpolicella Cl. Montefante Ris. '09	♀♀ 8
● Valpolicella Cl. Sup. Ripasso Montecorna '13	♀♀ 3
● Valpolicella Cl. Sup. Ripasso Montecorna '12	♀♀ 3
● Valpolicella Cl. Sup. Ripasso Remo Farina '13	♀♀ 2*

Fattori

FRAZ. TERROSSA
VIA OLMO, 6
37030 RONCÀ [VR]
TEL. +39 0457460041
www.fattoriwines.com

CELLAR SALES
PRE-BOOKED VISITS
ANNUAL PRODUCTION 280,000 bottles
HECTARES UNDER VINE 72.00
SUSTAINABLE WINERY

The wines from Roncà-based Fattori have always garnered high respect, but it is now winning increasing attention for its Soave, thanks to its extensive hillslope vineyard in that designation and to winemaking expertise that brings out the best from that fruit. In addition to their fine whites, their Valpolicella reds, produced in the new, efficient cellar atop the Col de la Bastia hill, are now attracting attention. High marks for Soave Danieli 2015, made in part from super-ripe fruit that gives the nose its intense scents of apricot, melon, yellow peach, and tropical fruit; the palate, however, builds and expands without any loss of grip and taut crispness. Recioto Motto Piane 2014 is fine as well, showing penetrating fragrances of dried fruit and nuts plus candied citrus, which also infuse the palate, where its superb sweetness is deliciously complemented by a notable acidity and, in particular, by ultra-crisp fruit. Very impressive, finally, is the Metodo Classico grown in the Monti Lessini zone.

● Amarone della Valpolicella '11	▼▼ 8
○ Lessini Durello Non Dosato M.Cl. '10	▼▼ 6
○ Recioto di Soave Motto Piane '14	▼▼ 5
○ Roncha '15	▼▼ 3
○ Soave Danieli '15	▼▼ 2*
○ Lessini Durello Brut M. Cl. '10	▼ 6
○ Lessini Durello Brut M. Cl. Roncà	▼ 4
○ Lessini Durello Brut Roncà di Roncà	▼ 3
○ Soave Cl. Runcaris '15	▼ 2
● Valpolicella Col de la Bastia '15	▼ 3
● Valpolicella Ripasso Col de la Bastia '14	▼ 5
○ Soave Cl. Danieli '14	♀♀ 2*
○ Soave Cl. Runcaris '14	♀♀ 2*
○ Soave Motto Piane '13	♀♀ 3

Filippi

LOC. CASTELCERINO
VIA LIBERTÀ, 55
37038 SOAVE [VR]
TEL. +39 0457675005
www.cantinafilippi.it

CELLAR SALES
PRE-BOOKED VISITS
ANNUAL PRODUCTION 60,000 bottles
HECTARES UNDER VINE 20.00
VITICULTURE METHOD Certified Organic

The Castelcerino district is one of Soave's finest growing zones, even though some of the vineyards fall outside the classic borders. Filippo Filippi has 20 hectares of organic hillslope vineyards there, many planted years ago, which he tends with passion. His winemaking style affords infinite care to the fruit and reduces interventions to a bare minimum. The result is that his wines show outstanding character. Monteseroni is a garganega grown in the designation's highest vineyards, in soils where basalt cedes quickly to limestone. The nose immediately intrigues, with pungent Mediterranean scrub and white plum; likewise impressive is the incisive sapidity and acidic grip on the palate. Of the two vintages of Soave Castelcerino, the 2015 is crisp and vibrant, while the 2014, after a lengthy maturation, hints at sea-salt and dried blossoms, followed by a solid, attractively countryish palate.

Il Filò delle Vigne

VIA TERRALBA, 14
35030 BAONE [PD]
TEL. +39 042956243
www.ilfilodellevigne.it

CELLAR SALES
PRE-BOOKED VISITS
ANNUAL PRODUCTION 50,000 bottles
HECTARES UNDER VINE 20.00

Filò della Vigne has shown a clear and steady course with both vineyards and winemaking, which over the years have yielded splendid results. The latest development is that the winery has been sold and Carlo Giordani is now at the helm. The estate vineyards cover some 20 hectares in the designation south of Padua, in sites with some of the area's finest exposures, and the resulting wines have always exhibited solid, compact palates. Borgo delle Casette 2012 seems a tad reluctant to reveal its charms, but then comes explosive fruit, framed by pencil lead and sweet spices, which continue onto the palate, an experience of magisterial power and amplitude effectively bolstered by a densely-woven, stylish suite of tannins. Merlot Casa del Merlo 2012, on the other hand, is more open-handed and extroverted, offering wild red berry fruit backgrounded by hints of forest floor, which animate a juicy palate that finishes long.

○ Monteseroni '14	♥♥ 2*
○ Soave Colli Scaligeri Castelcerino '15	♥♥ 3
○ Soave Colli Scaligeri Castelcerino 18 mesi sui lieviti '14	♥♥ 4
○ Castelcerino '14	♥ 2
○ Soave Colli Scaligeri V. della Brà '14	♥ 2
○ Soave Colli Scaligeri V. della Brà 18 mesi sui lieviti '13	♥ 3
○ Soave Castelcerino '13	♀♀ 2*
○ Soave Colli Scaligeri Monteseroni '13	♀♀ 2*
○ Soave Colli Scaligeri Monteseroni '06	♀♀ 2

● Colli Euganei Cabernet Borgo delle Casette Ris. '12	♥♥♥ 5
● Colli Euganei Merlot Casa del Merlo '12	♥♥ 4
● Colli Euganei Cabernet V. Cecilia di Baone Ris. '13	♥♥ 4
○ Il Calto delle Fate '11	♥♥ 4
○ Terralba di Baone '14	♥♥ 3
● Colli Euganei Cabernet Borgo delle Casette Ris. '10	♀♀♀ 5
● Colli Euganei Cabernet Borgo delle Casette Ris. '06	♀♀♀ 5
● Colli Euganei Cabernet Borgo delle Casette Ris. '11	♀♀ 5
● Colli Euganei Cabernet Borgo delle Casette Ris. '09	♀♀ 5
● Io di Baone '11	♀♀ 3*

Silvano Follador

LOC. FOLLO
FRAZ. SANTO STEFANO
VIA CALLONGA, 11
31040 VALDOBBIADENE [TV]
TEL. +39 0423900295
www.silvanofollador.it

CELLAR SALES
PRE-BOOKED VISITS
ANNUAL PRODUCTION 20,000 bottles
HECTARES UNDER VINE 3.50

The unusual path chosen by Alberta and Silvano Follador is no secret, but certain decisions clearly demonstrate their determination to promote the innate value of their growing area despite huge business interests hovering there. First, the decision to produce only dry wines with extremely low residual sugar, and then to go with Metodo Classico, and finally, instead of the distinctive Cartizze pedigree, to focus attention on a wine that embodies all the qualities that this historic area represents. Not to mention an approach ever more respectful of the environment. Here we are treated to a Prosecco of immense aromatic depth, in which any hint of fermentation is almost erased by ultra-fragrant apple, pear, and flowers, backgrounded by a fairly timid minerality. It opens wide in the mouth, with style and self-confidence, its pleasure heightened by a pulpy savouriness that expands its contours and drives a lengthy progression.

○ Valdobbiadene Brut Nature '15	♈♈	4
○ Cartizze Brut '08	♈♈♈	4
○ Cartizze Brut Nature '13	♈♈	4
○ Cartizze Brut Nature '11	♈♈	4
○ Cartizze Nature '12	♈♈	4
○ Valdobbiadene Brut Nature '14	♈♈	4
○ Valdobbiadene Brut Nature '13	♈♈	4
○ Valdobbiadene Brut Nature '12	♈♈	3*
○ Valdobbiadene Brut Nature '11	♈♈	3*
○ Valdobbiadene Sup. Brut Dosaggio Zero M. Cl. '12	♈♈	3

Le Fraghe

LOC. COLOMBARA, 3
37010 CAVAION VERONESE [VR]
TEL. +39 0457236832
www.fraghe.it

CELLAR SALES
PRE-BOOKED VISITS
ACCOMMODATION
ANNUAL PRODUCTION 120,000 bottles
HECTARES UNDER VINE 28.00
VITICULTURE METHOD Certified Organic

Matilde Poggi, who cultivates 30 or so hectares on the border between Verona and Trento, has always had a love for Bardolino, the Garda red that she interprets by striving for a balance of elegance, delicacy, and character. In the same perspective, her adoption of organic practices is more proof of her desire not to betray the growing area and its traditions. Hence her portfolio's focus almost solely on Bardolino, in various styles, plus a limited number of whites. The excellent 2015 harvest gifted a Bardolino that is still closed in, but ripe, pulpy wild berry fruit gradually emerges, then slowly yields to black pepper and sweet violets. The immensity of the palate is surprising, gift again of the hot season, but this expansiveness seems to have a relaxed elegance, emblematic of a Bardolino that treasures a vibrant suppleness. Ròdon 2015 is excellent, and the Chiaretto brine-edged, with crunchy, tasty fruit.

● Bardolino '15	♈♈	2*
⊙ Bardolino Chiaretto Ròdon '15	♈♈	2*
○ Garganega Camporengo '15	♈♈	2*
● Bardolino Cl. Brol Grande '12	♈♈♈	3*
● Bardolino Cl. Brol Grande '11	♈♈♈	3*
● Bardolino '14	♈♈	2*
● Bardolino '13	♈♈	2*
● Bardolino '12	♈♈	2*
⊙ Bardolino Chiaretto Ròdon '14	♈♈	2*
⊙ Bardolino Chiaretto Ròdon '13	♈♈	2*
● Bardolino Cl. Brol Grande '13	♈♈	3*
○ Garganega Camporengo '14	♈♈	2*
○ Garganega Camporengo '13	♈♈	2*
○ Garganega Camporengo '12	♈♈	2*
○ Garganega Camporengo '11	♈♈	2*
● Quaiare '12	♈♈	4
● Quaiare '11	♈♈	4

Marchesi Fumanelli

FRAZ. SAN FLORIANO
VIA SQUARANO, 1
37029 SAN PIETRO IN CARIANO [VR]
TEL. +39 0457704875
www.squarano.com

CELLAR SALES
PRE-BOOKED VISITS
RESTAURANT SERVICE
ANNUAL PRODUCTION 50,000 bottles
HECTARES UNDER VINE 23.00

Marchesi Fumanelli is sited in a privileged position, in the heart of Valpolicella Classica, on a slight rise dominated by the estate villa, surrounded by vineyards. Together with some more distant parcels, the estate comprises over 20 hectares, more than enough for the winery's limited production of bottles. Thus, only the finest lots are selected, which go mainly to vinification of the designation's venerable labels. We were impressed with Amarone Octavius 2010, a Riserva still somewhat closed in, its fruit opening slowly, until it suddenly explodes, accompanied by macerated flower petals and spices. On the palate, it is rich, full-volumed, and succulent, but not excessively so, auguring a radiant, complex future. No less satisfying is Valpolicella Squarano 2014, offering evolved, multi-layered fragrances and an impressively charged palate, a fine embodiment of the wine type. Amarone Classico 2011 privileges full-throated, exuberant fruit.

★Gini

VIA MATTEOTTI, 42
37032 MONTEFORTE D'ALPONE [VR]
TEL. +39 0457611908
www.ginivini.com

CELLAR SALES
PRE-BOOKED VISITS
ANNUAL PRODUCTION 200,000 bottles
HECTARES UNDER VINE 58.00
VITICULTURE METHOD Certified Organic

The Soave zone enjoys in Claudio and Sandro Gini ambassadors par excellence. For decades now, in their gorgeous cellar in Via Matteotti, they have been zealous interpreters of Soave, successful in demonstrating the cellarability of these wines. The true treasure of this winery, however, is the 50-hectares vineyard estate, predominantly of heirloom vines in the classic zone, with a few in Campiano. Salverenza 2013 gives a performance that should be treasured, redolent of well-ripened apple, pear, spices, and dried flower petals, hinting subtly of oak in the background. Its year and more spent in the cellar completed an enviable harmony of all components, giving us a solidly-built palate of superb length. Impressive, too, is Recioto Col Foscarin 2011, a passito infused with candied citrus and spice, then smooth and savoury in the mouth. Finally, kudos to the superbly-crafted Soave Classico 2015.

● Amarone della Valpolicella Cl. Octavius Ris. '10	▼▼	8
● Amarone della Valpolicella Cl. '11	▼▼	5
● Valpolicella Cl. Sup. Squarano '14	▼▼	3
● Amarone della Valpolicella Cl. '07	♀♀	5
● Amarone della Valpolicella Cl. '06	♀♀	5
● Amarone della Valpolicella Cl. Pralongo '03	♀♀	
● Valpolicella Cl. '08	♀♀	2*
● Valpolicella Cl. Sup. '11	♀♀	3
● Valpolicella Cl. Sup. '09	♀♀	3
● Valpolicella Cl. Sup. Squarano '10	♀♀	3
● Valpolicella Cl. Sup. Squarano '06	♀♀	3

○ Soave Cl. Contrada Salvarenza V. V. '13	▼▼	5
○ Recioto di Soave Cl. Col Foscarin '11	▼▼	4
○ Soave Cl. '15	▼▼	3
○ Soave Cl. Contrada Salvarenza V. V. '09	♀♀♀	5
○ Soave Cl. Contrada Salvarenza V. V. '08	♀♀♀	5
○ Soave Cl. Contrada Salvarenza V. V. '07	♀♀♀	5
○ Soave Cl. La Froscà '11	♀♀♀	4*
○ Soave Cl. La Froscà '06	♀♀♀	4*
○ Soave Cl. La Froscà '05	♀♀♀	4*
○ Soave Cl. Sup. Contrada Salvarenza V. V. '00	♀♀♀	5

Giusti Wine

VIA DEL VOLANTE, 4
31040 NERVESA DELLA BATTAGLIA [TV]
TEL. +39 0422720198
www.giustiwine.com

CELLAR SALES
PRE-BOOKED VISITS
ACCOMMODATION
ANNUAL PRODUCTION 200,000 bottles
HECTARES UNDER VINE 75.00
SUSTAINABLE WINERY

The Giusti family, headed by Ermenegildo, has written a new chapter in the Montello area, where it has become a major player in just a few years. The many hectares of vineyards extend in two directions, with those on the plains set aside for the more uncomplicated wines, while the hillslope grapes, planted in outstanding soils, are dedicated predominantly to Prosecco, but also to some Bordeaux-style wines. Giusti Wine's offerings are becoming increasingly impressive, this time with an Umberto I that almost made it into the final round. The nose abounds in sweet, ripe fruit that finds its appropriate counterpart in a compact, enfolding palate supported by densely-woven tannins. The Valpolicella Classica zone gives us Amarone 2012 with great aromatic depth, its fragrant cherry enriched by spices and medicinal herbs, followed by power and fine length in the mouth. Certainly deserving of mention is the well-crafted Asolo Brut.

● Amarone della Valpolicella Cl. '12	♟♟	8
● Antonio '14	♟♟	5
○ Asolo Brut	♟♟	2
○ Chardonnay Dei Carni '15	♟♟	3
● Umberto I '11	♟♟	8
● Valpolicella Ripasso Sup. '13	♟♟	5
○ Cuvée Extra Brut	♟	5
● Montello e Colli Asolani		
Recantina Augusto '14	♟	5
○ Pinot Grigio Longheri '15	♟	3
● Amarone della Valpolicella Cl. '11	♟♟	8
○ Pinot Grigio Longheri '14	♟♟	2*
● Umberto I '09	♟♟	8
● Umberto I '08	♟♟	2*

Gregoletto

FRAZ. PREMAOR
VIA SAN MARTINO, 83
31050 MIANE [TV]
TEL. +39 0438970463
www.gregoletto.com

CELLAR SALES
PRE-BOOKED VISITS
ANNUAL PRODUCTION 200,000 bottles
HECTARES UNDER VINE 18.00

Luigi Gregoletto's operation has managed to cope with the Prosecco craze without straining its winemaking habits and remaining focused on its historic wines. The 20 or so hectares of vineyards are completely embraced by the hills between Valdobbiadene and Conegliano, and are planted in part to glera and in part to Bordeaux varieties, classic Veneto white grapes, but also to some local natives pretty much neglected by everyone else but very much alive in Via San Martino. The outstanding 2015 harvest allowed Luigi to produce one of the finest versions ever of his Prosecco Tranquillo, which eschews fermentation aromas and sweet dosages and reveals instead, bit by bit, its subtle aromatic complex of blossoms, apple, and pear, and, in the mouth, its sculpted, utterly enchanting charms. Colli di Conegliano Rosso 2011, on the other hand, is mouth-filling, without recourse to either power or silky texture as its overall harmony is quite sufficient.

● Colli di Conegliano Rosso '11	♟♟	5
○ Conegliano Valdobbiadene		
Prosecco Tranquillo '15	♟♟	2*
● Cabernet '14	♟♟	3
● Merlot '14	♟♟	3
○ P. di Treviso Frizzante sui Lieviti '15	♟♟	4
○ Conegliano Valdobbiadene Extra Dry	♟	3
● Cabernet '12	♟♟	3
○ Chardonnay Zhopai '14	♟♟	3
○ Chardonnay Zhopai '13	♟♟	3
○ Conegliano Valdobbiadene		
Prosecco Tranquillo '14	♟♟	2*
○ Manzoni Bianco '14	♟♟	3
● Merlot '13	♟♟	3

Guerrieri Rizzardi

S.DA CAMPAZZI, 2
37011 BARDOLINO [VR]
TEL. +39 0457210028
www.guerrieri-rizzardi.it

CELLAR SALES
PRE-BOOKED VISITS
ANNUAL PRODUCTION 700,000 bottles
HECTARES UNDER VINE 100.00
SUSTAINABLE WINERY

Giuseppe and Agostino Rizzardi have pumped new energy into this venerable family operation, active in all the main Verona district designations. Some 100 hectares of estate vineyards provide the grapes for the new Bardolino facility, which turns out wines hallmarked by elegance and taut, crisp palates. The old cellar has been refurbished and repurposed for group and hospitality events themed to fine wine and food. Kudos to three reds from maison Rizzardi, starting with the superb Amarone Calcarole 2011, with a rich array of fragrances that include dried fruit, fines herbes, spice, and macerated flower petals that lead directly onto a palate where full volume and a vibrant crispness co-exist with stylish finesse. Bardolino Tacchetto 2015, one of the most impressive in the designation, boasts fragrant wild berry fruit and black pepper, with savoury fruit and a knife-sharp acidity that make for a delicious quaffer. Finally, Pojega 2014 is a Ripasso whose hallmarks are elegance and utter balance on the palate.

● Amarone della Valpolicella Cl. Calcarole '11	▼▼▼ 8
● Bardolino Cl. Tacchetto '15	▼▼ 2*
● Valpolicella Cl. Sup. Ripasso Pojega '14	▼▼ 3*
⊙ Bardolino Chiaretto Cl. '15	▼▼ 2*
● Bardolino Cl. '15	▼▼ 2*
● Clos Roareti '12	▼▼ 5
○ Soave Cl. Ferra '14	▼▼ 3
○ Soave Cl. '15	▼ 2
○ Soave Cl. Costeggiola '15	▼ 2
● Valpolicella Cl. '15	▼ 2
● Amarone della Valpolicella Cl. Calcarole '09	▼▼▼ 8
● Amarone della Valpolicella Cl. Villa Rizzardi '08	▼▼▼ 7
● Valpolicella Cl. Sup. Ripasso Pojega '13	▼▼▼ 3*

Inama

LOC. BIACCHE, 50
37047 SAN BONIFACIO [VR]
TEL. +39 0456104343
www.inamaaziendaagricola.it

CELLAR SALES
PRE-BOOKED VISITS
ANNUAL PRODUCTION 450,000 bottles
HECTARES UNDER VINE 62.00
VITICULTURE METHOD Certified Organic

The Inama family is increasingly dividing its attention between the Soave and the nearby Colli Berici designations. Their growing and winemaking activity in the former has long been impressive, of course, but continuous evolution is the key in the latter. The facility at Lonigo, immersed in the splendid pristine landscape, has been handsomely refurbished, sending out an impressive image and message. The house style maintains an equilibrium between richness of fruit and good grip on the palate. And it is precisely the Colli Berici that provide the most impressive wine, Bradisismo. Imama's historic red, a blend of cabernet sauvignon and carménère, exudes rich, fragrant fruit, particularly dried plum, haloed by pungent spice and wild herbs. Its extraordinarily full flavours in the mouth, along with its striking acidity and tannins, give it both delicacy and a vibrant energy. The Soave Foscarino 2014 is nicely crisp, which a multi-faceted bouquet and a long, juicy development.

● Bradisismo '12	▼▼ 5
○ Soave Cl. Vign. di Foscarino '14	▼▼ 4
● Carmenere Più '13	▼▼ 3
○ Soave Cl. Vin Soave '15	▼▼ 3
● Bradisismo '08	▼▼▼ 5
● Colli Berici Carmenère Oratorio di San Lorenzo Ris. '09	▼▼▼ 6
○ Soave Cl. Vign. di Foscarino '08	▼▼▼ 4
○ Soave Cl. Vign. Du Lot '05	▼▼▼ 2*
○ Soave Cl. Vign. Du Lot '01	▼▼▼ 4
● Bradisismo '11	▼▼ 5
● Colli Berici Carmenère Oratorio di San Lorenzo Ris. '11	▼▼ 6
○ Soave Cl. Vign. di Foscarino '13	▼▼ 4

La Giuva

VIA TREZZOLANO, 20c
37141 VERONA
TEL. +39 3421117089
www.lagiuva.com

CELLAR SALES
PRE-BOOKED VISITS
ANNUAL PRODUCTION 20,000 bottles
HECTARES UNDER VINE 9.50
VITICULTURE METHOD Certified Organic

Giulia and Valentina, whose acronym forms the name of their winery, are Alberto Malesani's young daughters. Together, the three launched this impressive operation in the upper Val Squarano, in eastern Valpolicella, an area still little known but with great viticultural promise. The family purchased vineyards and built a modern cellar, which is perfectly integrated into its surrounding landscape. Only four wines are produced, all of them clean and authentic, squarely within local traditions. We liked how Rientro 2013 performed, a Valpolicella Superiore made from partially dried grapes, which gives it alternating impressions of ripe red berry and crisp herbs and spices, while a zesty vein of acidity courses through rich fruit in the mouth. Likewise impressive was Valpo, a standard Valpolicella that is very tasty and crisp.

● Amarone della Valpolicella '12	▼▼ 7
● Valpolicella Il Valpo '15	▼▼ 3
● Valpolicella Sup. Il Rientro '13	▼▼ 5
● Recioto della Valpolicella '14	▼ 6
● Recioto della Valpolicella '13	♀♀ 3
● Recioto della Valpolicella '12	♀♀ 3
● Valpolicella '13	♀♀ 2*
● Valpolicella Sup. Il Rientro '12	♀♀ 3
● Valpolicella Sup. Il Rientro '11	♀♀ 3

Le Colture

LOC. SANTO STEFANO
VIA FOLLO, 5
31049 VALDOBBIADENE [TV]
TEL. +39 0423900192
www.lecolture.it

CELLAR SALES
PRE-BOOKED VISITS
ACCOMMODATION
ANNUAL PRODUCTION 750,000 bottles
HECTARES UNDER VINE 43.00

The Ruggeri operation is one that can boast a significant area of estate vineyards, over 30 hectares in various parcels in the Conegliano and Valdobbiadene designation, plus another estate near Nervesa della Battaglia in the neighbouring Montello zone. The brothers focus almost solely on Prosecco, with great respect for expressive fruit and savouriness on the palate. This was a memorable season for the Ruggeri brothers, with enviable quality right across the lineup. At the top of our list is Brut Fagher, with a seductive bouquet of clean-contoured lime blossom and pear. A low sugar dosage allows it to expand beautifully in the mouth, delicate and full-flavoured, through to a dry, very lengthy conclusion. Pianer and Cartizze turned in fine performances as well, two Proseccos that exhibit more obvious fruit and a softer mouthfeel.

○ Cartizze	▼▼ 3
○ Valdobbiadene Brut Fagher	▼▼ 3
○ Valdobbiadene Dry Cruner	▼▼ 3
○ Valdobbiadene Extra Dry Pianer	▼▼ 3
⊙ Brut Rosé	▼ 2
○ Valdobbiadene Sup. Rive di Santo Stefano Brut Gerardo '14	♀♀ 3
○ Valdobbiadene Sup. Rive di Santo Stefano Brut Gerardo '13	♀♀ 3

Conte Loredan Gasparini

FRAZ. VENEGAZZÙ
VIA MARTIGNAGO, 23
31040 VOLPAGO DEL MONTELLO [TV]
TEL. +39 0423870024
www.loredangasparini.it

CELLAR SALES
ACCOMMODATION
ANNUAL PRODUCTION 400,000 bottles
HECTARES UNDER VINE 62.00

This Venegazzù-based cellar, now run with skill and precision by Lorenzo Palla, has always been an important part of the history of Veneto red wines. The vineyards lie on the southern slopes of the Montello hill, divided largely into two sections, one around the cellar, planted to red grapes, and one in Giavera, which focuses on glera. The Bordeaux grapes produce a portfolio of wines whose cornerstones are richness of fruit and crisp palates. Capo di Stato 2011 unleashes a performance for the record books. Following a lengthy maturation, the fruit and spice are definitely out in full view, with the oak pushed well back in second place. In the mouth, it offers incisive vigour without seeming heavy, thanks to a bolstering acidity and tannins. Its younger brother, Venegazzù della Casa 2011, shows well too, with a similar character but slimmer palate.

★Maculan

VIA CASTELLETTO, 3
36042 BREGANZE [VI]
TEL. +39 0445873733
www.maculan.net

CELLAR SALES
PRE-BOOKED VISITS
ANNUAL PRODUCTION 650,000 bottles
HECTARES UNDER VINE 50.00

If Veneto wines enjoy world-wide respect today, credit goes to the region's quality pioneers, and Fausto Maculan was certainly a leader in that group. Today, daughters Angela and Maria Vittoria run the Breganze-based cellar, and they exhibit the same tenacity in proposing Veneto wines that can stand alongside the world's finest. Their portfolio vaunts feisty reds and elegant, refined dessert wines. Acininobili is made from Botrytis-infected vespaiola grapes, and only in the best growing years. The current version is exceptionally elegant, bursting with fragrant tropical fruit and blossoms, backgrounded by notes of candied citrus that shade into black liquorice and pungent scrub. In the mouth, the sweetness is well-calibrated, never cloying, expanding with finesse and verve. The fruit in Palazzotto 2013 is rich and crunchy, developing into a succulent, superbly-crafted palate.

● Montello e Colli Asolani Venegazzù Sup. Capo di Stato '11	♟♟ 6
● Falconera Merlot '12	♟♟ 3
● Montello e Colli Asolani Venegazzù della Casa '11	♟♟ 4
● Malbec '15	♟ 3
○ Asolo Extra Brut V. Monti '13	♕♕ 3
○ Asolo Extra Brut V. Monti '12	♕♕ 3
○ Asolo Extra Dry Cuvée Indigene '13	♕♕ 3
○ Asolo Extra Dry Cuvée Indigene '12	♕♕ 3
● Falconera Merlot '11	♕♕ 3
● Montello e Colli Asolani Cabernet Sauvignon '13	♕♕ 3
● Montello e Colli Asolani Cabernet Sauvignon '12	♕♕ 2*
● Montello e Colli Asolani Venegazzù Sup. Capo di Stato '09	♕♕ 5

○ Acininobili '11	♟♟ 8
● Breganze Cabernet Sauvignon Palazzotto '13	♟♟ 4
● Breganze Pinot Nero '13	♟♟ 3
● Brentino '14	♟♟ 3
● Crosara '13	♟♟ 8
● Fratta '13	♟♟ 8
● Speaia '13	♟♟ 3
○ Tre Volti Brut M. Cl.	♟♟ 5
○ Bidibi '15	♟ 2
○ Breganze Vespaiolo '15	♟ 2
● Cabernet '14	♟ 2
○ Chardonnay Ferrata '15	♟ 4
○ Costadolio '15	♟ 2
○ Dindarello '15	♟ 4
○ Pino & Toi '15	♟ 2

Manara

FRAZ. SAN FLORIANO
VIA DON CESARE BIASI, 53
37029 SAN PIETRO IN CARIANO [VR]
TEL. +39 0457701086
www.manaravini.it

CELLAR SALES
PRE-BOOKED VISITS
ANNUAL PRODUCTION 130,000 bottles
HECTARES UNDER VINE 11.00
SUSTAINABLE WINERY

This San Floriano-based cellar, which was enlarged a few years ago, adjoins the residence, almost underscoring the fact it is a family operation. Lorenzo, Fabio and Giovanni now run the winery founded by their father, faithful to the area's traditional wines, which they interpret with great rigour, avoiding over-concentration and commercial shortcuts. Their resource is a bit more than ten hectares of vineyard, which meets all their requirements. Ripasso Le Morete is a faithful expression of local traditions, which is quite obvious in its ripe, warm scents of dried fruit, macerated flower petals, and spices, as well as in the alcoholic warmth that softens the palate and heightens its flavours. Of the two Amarones produced, our choice fell on the more ambitious, Postera 2010. Although the nose is still somewhat closed, it already exhibits generous richness in the mouth and tannins that seem almost austere.

● Amarone della Valpolicella Cl. Postera '10		♟♟ 6
● Recioto della Valpolicella Cl. El Rocolo '12		♟♟ 5
● Valpolicella Cl. Sup. Ripasso Le Morete '13		♟♟ 3
● Valpolicella Cl. Sup. Vecio Belo '14		♟♟ 2*
● Amarone della Valpolicella Cl. Corte Manara '11		♟ 5
● Valpolicella Cl. '15		♟ 2
● Amarone della Valpolicella Cl. '00		♟♟♟ 5
● Amarone della Valpolicella Cl. Corte Manara '10		♟♟ 5
● Amarone della Valpolicella Cl. Postera '09		♟♟ 6
● Recioto della Valpolicella Cl. El Rocolo '11		♟♟ 5
● Valpolicella Cl. Sup. Le Morete Ripasso '12		♟♟ 3

Marcato

VIA PRANDI, 10
37030 RONCÀ [VR]
TEL. +39 0457460070
www.marcatovini.it

CELLAR SALES
PRE-BOOKED VISITS
ANNUAL PRODUCTION 450,000 bottles
HECTARES UNDER VINE 55.00

In just a few short years, Marcato has changed course in no uncertain terms, decreasing its portfolio and ensuring that each wine is correctly positioned, in terms of quality and price. Kudos go to Gianni Tessari, who handled the ownership change with finesse, without compromising the wines, and at the same time also enhanced their stylistic expression. Today, Soave and Durello sparklers constitute a solid base here in Roncà, with a style that is both pleasurable and up-to-date. Full marks this year too for Soave Pigno, brimming with crisp fruit and fragrant blossoms, its oak still noticeable enough to cloak delicate hints of citrus. Its lively acidity, gift of the 2014 harvest, gives the wine its vivaciousness and unexpected length. The Metodo Classicos continue to improve. A.R., which receives a lengthy ageing, stands out for its aromatic complexity and for the vibrant acidic charge that bolsters its rich fruit.

○ Soave Cl. Pigno Gianni Tessari '14		♟♟ 3*
● Colli Berici Cabernet Pian Alto Gianni Tessari '12		♟♟ 5
○ Lessini Durello Extra Brut A. R. M. Cl. '06		♟♟ 6
○ Lessini Durello Extra Brut 60mesi M. Cl. '08		♟♟ 5
○ Soave Cl. Monte Tenda Gianni Tessari '15		♟♟ 3
○ Chardonnay Gianni Tessari '15		♟ 2
● Due Gianni Tessari '13		♟ 2
○ Lessini Durello Brut 36mesi M. Cl.		♟ 3
○ Soave Cl. Pigno Gianni Tessari '13		♟♟♟ 3*
○ Lessini Durello Brut 60 Mesi '08		♟♟ 5
○ Lessini Durello Brut 60 Mesi '07		♟♟ 5
○ Soave Cl. Monte Tenda Gianni Tessari '14		♟♟ 3
○ Soave Cl. Pigno Gianni Tessari '12		♟♟ 3*

Marion

FRAZ. MARCELLISE
VIA BORGO MARCELLISE, 2
37036 SAN MARTINO BUON ALBERGO [VR]
TEL. +39 0458740021
www.marionvini.it

PRE-BOOKED VISITS
ANNUAL PRODUCTION 40,000 bottles
HECTARES UNDER VINE 14.00

Located in eastern Valpolicella, bordering on the classic zone, Stefano and Nicoletta Campedelli's operation is highly respected by aficionados of these wines. A little over ten hectares of vineyards yield solid, well-balanced wines, whose house standouts are Valpolicella Superiore and Amarone. They are complemented by two reds of the same style, from teroldego and cabernet sauvignon. It is difficult to decide which is better, the Valpolicella Superiore or the Amarone. The first offers up ideally-ripe fruit, with crisp, juicy cherry and red berry fruit, while an intriguing whiff of black pepper in the background lifts the entire bouquet. The palate is admirably compact, the finish endless. The second, on the other hand, exhibits super-ripe fruit, and more up-front spice and fines herbes. This wine wins kudos for its seductive, lively fruit, and for the way it effectively manages its considerable alcohol.

● Amarone della Valpolicella '11	♥♥ 7
● Valpolicella Sup. '12	♥♥ 4
● Cabernet Sauvignon '12	♥♥ 4
● Calto '10	♥♥ 4
● Valpolicella Borgomarcellise '14	♥♥ 3
● Amarone della Valpolicella '10	♀♀♀ 7
● Amarone della Valpolicella '06	♀♀♀ 7
● Amarone della Valpolicella '03	♀♀♀ 7
● Amarone della Valpolicella '01	♀♀♀ 7
● Valpolicella Sup. '10	♀♀♀ 4*
● Valpolicella Sup. '09	♀♀♀ 4*
● Valpolicella Sup. '06	♀♀♀ 4
● Valpolicella Sup. '05	♀♀♀ 4
● Amarone della Valpolicella '09	♀♀ 7
● Amarone della Valpolicella '08	♀♀ 7
● Calto '09	♀♀ 4
● Valpolicella Sup. '11	♀♀ 4

Masari

LOC. MAGLIO DI SOPRA
VIA BEVILACQUA, 2A
36078 VALDAGNO [VI]
TEL. +39 0445410780
www.masari.it

CELLAR SALES
PRE-BOOKED VISITS
ANNUAL PRODUCTION 30,000 bottles
HECTARES UNDER VINE 4.00

In just a few years, Massimo Dal Lago and Arianna Tessari have managed to transform their modest cellar in Valdagno into one of the region's most impressive outfits. Operating in a more or less pristine area has allowed them to expand their vineyards only in the most promising terrains, and to maintain a healthy balance between vineyards, meadows and woods, obvious in their new property in Cornedo, where only a part will be dedicated to viticulture. In the best growing years, Massimo takes some of the merlot from Masari and makes a monovarietal, which then undergoes a very lengthy maturation. We see it today, after eight years. Monte Pulgo 2009 is visually vibrant, with still-young aromas that alternate between red berry fruit and spice. Its elegance and length are stunning, its finish silk-smooth and refined. Masari 2013 is nervier, with more thrust, with broad, deep aromatics and gorgeous overall proportion in the mouth.

● Masari '13	♥♥ 5
● Monte Pulgo '09	♥♥ 8
○ AgnoBianco '14	♥♥ 2*
○ Leon Durello Dosaggio Zero M. Cl.	♥♥ 4
● Vicenza Rosso San Martino '14	♥♥ 3
○ AgnoBianco '13	♀♀ 2*
○ AgnoBianco '12	♀♀ 2*
○ Antico Pasquale Passito Bianco '07	♀♀ 8
○ Antico Pasquale Passito Bianco '06	♀♀ 8
○ Doro Passito Bianco '11	♀♀ 5
○ Leon Durello Dosaggio Zero M. Cl.	♀♀ 4
● Masari '12	♀♀ 5
● Masari '11	♀♀ 5
● Vicenza Rosso San Martino '12	♀♀ 3
● Vicenza Rosso San Martino '11	♀♀ 3*
● Vicenza Rosso San Martino '10	♀♀ 3*

★Masi

FRAZ. GARGAGNAGO
VIA MONTELEONE, 26
37015 SANT'AMBROGIO DI VALPOLICELLA [VR]
TEL. +39 0456832511
www.masi.it

CELLAR SALES
PRE-BOOKED VISITS
ACCOMMODATION
ANNUAL PRODUCTION 4,300,000 bottles
HECTARES UNDER VINE 670.00
SUSTAINABLE WINERY

In Valpolicella, the Boscaini family's large-scale winery is also one of historical prominence. Over the decades, Sandro Boscaini has transformed it into a cellar with a strong bond to its local growing area, and that in the broadest sense. The significant extent of production is the fruit of a relationship with a large number of local growers, whose grapes supplement those from the estate vineyards. We were presented with a full three Amarones this year, and this version of Vaio Armaron is truly memorable. The nose pours out intense impressions of dried red berry, chocolate, and cherry jam, which enrich the palate as well, where lively flavours and expressiveness are the dominant components. The tannins effectively shape its dry finish. The more complex and multi-layered Mazzano 2009 receives a lengthier maturation; its broad, expansive palate is supported by pleasingly rustic tannins.

Masottina

LOC. CASTELLO ROGANZUOLO
VIA BRADOLINI, 54
31020 SAN FIOR [TV]
TEL. +39 0438400775
www.masottina.it

CELLAR SALES
PRE-BOOKED VISITS
ANNUAL PRODUCTION 1,000,000 bottles
HECTARES UNDER VINE 230.00
SUSTAINABLE WINERY

The Dal Bianco's cellar dates back to just after WWII, but it was the advent of Adriano, Valerio and Renzo that brought about the quantum leap. Today, the latest generation of Filippo, Federico, and Edoardo, has brought new energy into maintaining the family standards. The hectares of vineyards have grown to quite a bit more than 100, part owned, part leased, largely in the Conegliano Valdobbiadene hills, with some on the plain near Treviso, which yield a few of the still wines. The finest vineyards in Ogliano, the historic designation's easternmost hill, provide the grapes for this Extra Dry, giving it tremendously intense fruit, quite typical for the area, and a palate showing an irresistible fusion between the mousse and its snappy fruit. Of the still wines, we liked the Merlot from the Gorgo al Monticano vineyards for its red berry and spices, shot through with crisp, pungent balsam. It is taut and elegant in the mouth, and utterly delicious right now.

● Amarone della Valpolicella Cl. Vaio Armaron Serègo Alighieri '11	♟♟♟ 8
● Amarone della Valpolicella Cl. Mazzano '09	♟♟ 8
● Amarone della Valpolicella Cl. Costasera Ris. '11	♟♟ 8
● Osar '09	♟♟ 7
● Recioto della Valpolicella Cl. Casal dei Ronchi Serego Alighieri '12	♟ 7
● Amarone della Valpolicella Cl. Campolongo di Torbe '09	♟♟♟ 8
● Amarone della Valpolicella Cl. Campolongo di Torbe '07	♟♟♟ 8
● Amarone della Valpolicella Cl. Costasera Ris. '09	♟♟♟ 8
● Amarone della Valpolicella Cl. Mazzano '06	♟♟♟ 8

○ Conegliano Valdobbiadene Extra Dry	♟♟ 6
○ Conegliano Valdobbiadene Rive di Ogliano Extra Dry '15	♟♟ 7
● Piave Merlot Ai Palazzi Ris. '10	♟♟ 6
○ Colli di Conegliano Bianco Rizzardo '13	♟ 8
● Colli di Conegliano Rosso Vign. Montesco '09	♟ 8
○ Conegliano Valdobbiadene Rive di Ogliano Brut Contrada Granda '15	♟ 7
○ Conegliano Valdobbiadene Rive di Ogliano Brut Contrada Granda '13	♟♟ 7
○ Conegliano Valdobbiadene Rive di Ogliano Extra Dry '14	♟♟ 7
○ Conegliano Valdobbiadene Rive di Ogliano Extra Dry '12	♟♟ 5
● Piave Cabernet Sauvignon Vign. ai Palazzi Ris. '09	♟♟ 4

Roberto Mazzi

Loc. San Peretto
via Crosetta, 8
37024 Negrar [VR]
Tel. +39 0457502072
www.robertomazzi.it

CELLAR SALES
PRE-BOOKED VISITS
ACCOMMODATION AND RESTAURANT SERVICE
ANNUAL PRODUCTION 45,000 bottles
HECTARES UNDER VINE 8.00

Despite Valpolicella's rampant success over the last decades, Antonio and Stefano Mazzi have preferred to keep their vineyards and cellar to a manageable scale, believing deeply in the concept of a family business in which all the operations are personally performed or at least supervised. The wines, all classic to the area, come from fewer than ten hectares of grapes sited in some of the Negrar valley's finest locations, such as Villa and Calcarole. We always expect the world from Amarone and Poiega, but we always impressed too by how often the brothers interpret Sanperetto, a Valpolicella Superiore, perfectly, conveying all the refined depth that these heirloom grapes can give. Black pepper, wild berry, and fines herbes meld together in a taut, tasty wine of succulent approachability. Poiega offers greater depth and ripeness, qualities that fairly explode in Punta di Villa, a complex, multi-nuanced Amarone that avoids exploiting power for power's sake, calibrating it for fine structure as tradition requires.

● Amarone della Valpolicella Cl. Punta di Villa '11	▼▼▼ 7
● Valpolicella Cl. Sup. Sanperetto '14	▼▼ 3*
● Valpolicella Cl. Sup. Vign. Poiega '13	▼▼ 4
● Amarone della Valpolicella Cl. Vign. Castel '12	▼▼ 7
● Valpolicella Cl. '15	▼▼ 2*
● Valpolicella Cl. Sup. Sanperetto '11	♀♀♀ 3*
● Amarone della Valpolicella Cl. Punta di Villa '10	♀♀ 7
● Amarone della Valpolicella Cl. Punta di Villa '09	♀♀ 7
● Amarone della Valpolicella Cl. Vign. Castel '10	♀♀ 7
● Valpolicella Cl. '14	♀♀ 2*
● Valpolicella Cl. Sup. Sanperetto '13	♀♀ 3
● Valpolicella Cl. Sup. Vign. Poiega '12	♀♀ 4

Menegotti

Loc. Acquaroli, 7
37069 Villafranca di Verona [VR]
Tel. +39 0457902611
www.menegotticantina.com

CELLAR SALES
PRE-BOOKED VISITS
ACCOMMODATION
ANNUAL PRODUCTION 250,000 bottles
HECTARES UNDER VINE 30.00
SUSTAINABLE WINERY

The Menegotti family's Villafranca cellar, in the Custoza countryside, boasts lengthy expertise in sparkling wine production, developed over decades for the delight of wine lovers. Launched in the aftermath of WWII, it expanded from the 1980s and now has some 30 hectares of vineyards, which yield wines that are a reliable reflection of the styles of Lake Garda. Antonio and Andrea produce an exemplary Custoza Elianto, redolent of apricot, melon, yellow peach, and blossoms, with a subtle vein of minerality that awaits full expression. It is faithful on the palate to the fragrance and delicacy classic to the designation, but also boasts satisfying volume. Of the sparklers, we liked Brut 2012, a chardonnay and corvina blend, fermented off the sins, which brings savoury fruit and a vibrant acidity, all of which add up to a lip-smacking wine of enviable balance. The Extra Dry version is also well-made.

○ Brut M. Cl. '12	▼▼ 4
○ Custoza '15	▼▼ 2*
○ Custoza Sup. Elianto '14	▼▼ 3
○ Extra Dry M. Cl.	▼▼ 3
● Bardolino '15	▼ 2
⊙ Bardolino Chiaretto '15	▼ 2
○ Biancospino	▼ 2
○ Biancospino Rosé	▼ 2
● Geodoro '12	▼ 5
● Le Bugne '14	▼ 2
○ Lugana '15	▼ 2
● Mezzacosta '13	▼ 3
○ Bianco di Custoza Sup. Elianto '12	♀♀ 2*
○ Brut M. Cl. '09	♀♀ 3
○ Custoza Sup. Elianto '13	♀♀ 2*
● Mezzacosta '12	♀♀ 2*

Merotto

LOC. COL SAN MARTINO
VIA SCANDOLERA, 21
31010 FARRA DI SOLIGO [TV]
TEL. +39 0438989000
www.merotto.it

CELLAR SALES
PRE-BOOKED VISITS
ANNUAL PRODUCTION 550,000 bottles
HECTARES UNDER VINE 21.00

Graziano Merotto founded this winery in the early 1970s, and it has been transforming itself ever since, with Prosecco always the focus of production. It is now a highly-respected local producer, relying on more than 20 hectares of vineyards and on strong relationships with trusted growers. Alongside their historic labels are the increasingly impressive wines from the most favourable sites, the Graziano Merotto and the new Castel. Maison Merotto debuted its new Prosecco, which, in counter-tendency to the very dry styles in vogue, returns to the classic Extra Dry style. Castel is sculpted with rare precision, intensely fragrant with wisteria blossoms and pear, then full flavours in the mouth are seductively heightened by its effervescence. Graziano Merotto, on the other hand, is more crisp and citrusy; it amazes for a palate that is so emphatically creamy and yet perfectly dry.

Monte dall'Ora

LOC. CASTELROTTO
VIA MONTE DALL'ORA, 5
37029 SAN PIETRO IN CARIANO [VR]
TEL. +39 0457704462
www.montedallora.com

CELLAR SALES
PRE-BOOKED VISITS
ANNUAL PRODUCTION 35,000 bottles
HECTARES UNDER VINE 6.00
VITICULTURE METHOD Certified Organic

Carlo and Alessandra Venturini manage their modest operation in Castelrotto with a firm commitment to making outstanding wines without damaging the environment. Their beliefs are deeply rooted and also look to the future, with respect not only for the world around them but for the traditions and heritage they will hand down to their children. Just six hectares of vines are enough for their Valpolicella classics, expressively rich and eminently drinkable. Camporenzo is a Valpolicella made from late-harvested grapes sourced from a vineyard not dedicated to Amarone. The nose is notable for the luminous ripeness of its fruit, lifted by dried blossoms and crisp medicinal herbs. It is full in the mouth, where rich flavours and a lively acidity nicely substitute for less power. Ripasso Saustò 2012 offers warmer, more enfolding aromatics, and skilfully manages a pulpy fullness in the mouth, with an admirable combination of delicacy and roundedness.

○ Valdobbiadene Brut Rive di Col San Martino Cuvée del Fondatore Graziano Merotto '15	♛♛♛ 4*
○ Valdobbiadene Extra Dry Castèl '15	♛♛ 3*
○ Le Fare Extra Brut	♛♛ 2*
○ Valdobbiadene Brut Bareta	♛♛ 3
○ Valdobbiadene Dry Rive di Col San Martino La Primavera di Barbara '15	♛♛ 3
○ Valdobbiadene Extra Dry Colbelo	♛♛ 3
○ Cartizze	♛ 5
⊙ Grani Rosa di Nero Brut	♛ 3
○ Prosecco di Treviso Dry Colmolina Mill. '15	♛ 3
○ Valdobbiadene Brut Rive di Col San Martino Cuvée del Fondatore Graziano Merotto '14	♚♚♚ 4*

● Valpolicella Cl. Sup. Camporenzo '13	♛♛♛ 4*
● Valpolicella Cl. Sup. Ripasso Saustò '12	♛♛ 5
● Amarone della Valpolicella Cl. Stropa '08	♛♛ 8
● Valpolicella Cl. Saseti '15	♛♛ 2*
● Valpolicella Cl. Sup. Camporenzo '11	♚♚♚ 4*
● Valpolicella Cl. Sup. Camporenzo '10	♚♚♚ 4*
● Valpolicella Cl. Sup. Ripasso Saustò '07	♚♚♚ 5
● Amarone della Valpolicella Cl. '09	♚♚ 6
● Amarone della Valpolicella Cl. Stropa '07	♚♚ 8
● Recioto della Valpolicella Cl. Sant' Ulderico '09	♚♚ 6
● Valpolicella Cl. Sup. Camporenzo '12	♚♚ 4
● Valpolicella Cl. Sup. Ripasso Saustò '11	♚♚ 5

Monte del Frà

S.DA PER CUSTOZA, 35
37066 SOMMACAMPAGNA [VR]
TEL. +39 045510490
www.montedelfra.it

CELLAR SALES
PRE-BOOKED VISITS
ANNUAL PRODUCTION 1,000,000 bottles
HECTARES UNDER VINE 197.00

With their large operation in Custoza, Marica and Massimo Bonomo have led the significant turnaround that has characterized that area in the last few years. Marica oversees marketing, while Massimo directs production; the result has been a leap both in quality and volume. Eligio and Claudio add expertise and talent, and Silvia, Dino, and a well-integrated team contribute to a line of wines that is winning increasing respect. Ca' del Magro is one of the most impressive white wines not only of the region but of the entire country. Over the past decade, it has become the Holy Grail for those who prize aromatic complexity and a palate that is rich, savoury, and lively, all at the same time. Among the Valpolicella offerings, thanks to this winery's ever-deepening commitment, we appreciated Scarnocchio, an Amarone marked not by power but by finesse, lean austerity, and a taut crispness.

Monte Faustino

VIA BURE ALTO
37029 SAN PIETRO IN CARIANO [VR]
TEL. +39 0457701651
www.fornaser.com

CELLAR SALES
PRE-BOOKED VISITS
ANNUAL PRODUCTION 70,000 bottles
HECTARES UNDER VINE 6.00

The success of Valpolicella in the international wine market over recent years has imposed great changes on many producers, who have not always known how to cope with such pressing demands. The Fornaser family, however, has improved wine quality and vineyard management practices, constantly expanding but without sending production through the roof. Their handful of hectares is sufficient to make their traditionally-styled wines, refined and never too forceful. Fruit of the hot 2011 season, Amarone Classico lays out super-ripe red berry fruit, with macerated flowers and spices providing an unexpected addition. In the mouth, considerable volume and alcohol are nicely checked by the acidity, and it finishes long and dry. Ripasso La Traversagna 2012, on the other hand, is more straightforward, with crisp, crunchy fruit, prominent oak, and a good vein of tangy acidity.

○ Custoza Sup. Ca' del Magro '14	♥♥♥ 3*
● Amarone della Valpolicella Cl. Scarnocchio Lena di Mezzo '11	♥♥ 7
● Amarone della Valpolicella Cl. Lena di Mezzo '12	♥♥ 6
● Bardolino '15	♥♥ 2*
⊙ Bardolino Chiaretto '15	♥♥ 2*
○ Custoza '15	♥♥ 2*
● Valpolicella Cl. Sup. Lena di Mezzo '14	♥♥ 3
● Valpolicella Cl. Sup. Ripasso Lena di Mezzo '14	♥♥ 3
● Valpolicella Cl. Lena di Mezzo '15	♥ 3
○ Custoza Sup. Ca' del Magro '13	♥♥♥ 3*
○ Custoza Sup. Ca' del Magro '12	♥♥♥ 2*
○ Custoza Sup. Ca' del Magro '11	♥♥♥ 2*
○ Custoza Sup. Ca' del Magro '10	♥♥♥ 2*
○ Custoza Sup. Ca' del Magro '09	♥♥♥ 2*

● Amarone della Valpolicella Cl. '11	♥♥ 7
● Recioto della Valpolicella Cl. '12	♥♥ 5
● Valpolicella Cl. '15	♥♥ 2*
● Valpolicella Cl. Sup. Ripasso La Traversagna '12	♥♥ 4
● Amarone della Valpolicella Cl. Maestro Fornaser Ris. '09	♥ 8
● Flò '11	♥ 3
● Amarone della Valpolicella Cl. '10	♥♥ 7
● Amarone della Valpolicella Cl. '09	♥♥ 7
● Amarone della Valpolicella Cl. Maestro Fornaser Ris. '08	♥♥ 8
● Amarone della Valpolicella Cl. Maestro Fornaser Ris. '07	♥♥ 8
● Pelara '11	♥♥ 3*
● Valpolicella Cl. Sup. La Traversagna '11	♥♥ 4

Monte Tondo

LOC. MONTE TONDO
VIA SAN LORENZO, 89
37038 SOAVE [VR]
TEL. +39 0457680347
www.montetondo.it

CELLAR SALES
PRE-BOOKED VISITS
ACCOMMODATION
ANNUAL PRODUCTION 200,000 bottles
HECTARES UNDER VINE 32.00

The Magnabosco family has long been active in Soave, and over the last decade their reliable local wines have been joined by a series of others from nearby Valpolicella. Their vineyards, distributed over numerous parcels, now amount to more than 30 hectares, and supply all their production. Founder Gino Magnabosco still has the reins solidly in hand, ably assisted by the entire family. Foscarin Slavinus, a Soave made from late-picked grapes grown on the steepest hillslopes on Mount Foscarino, ferments in large oak ovals and matures in steel. The result is intense scents of yellow peach, apricot, melon, and dried flowers, with a crisp hint of gunflint, while a tasty acidity effectively enlivens the full body. Casette Foscarin 2014 impresses too, showcasing smooth, sweet fruit and a warm, appealing palate.

Monte Zovo

LOC. ZOVO, 23A
37013 CAPRINO VERONESE [VR]
TEL. +39 0457281301
www.montezovo.com

CELLAR SALES
PRE-BOOKED VISITS
ACCOMMODATION AND RESTAURANT SERVICE
ANNUAL PRODUCTION 1,000,000 bottles
HECTARES UNDER VINE 100.00

The Cottini family officially founded their winery in 2000, although their roots in viticulture go back nearly a century. They were first growers, then sold wine in bulk; 2000 finally saw the beginning of their Monte Zovo project, which today boasts an impressive expanse of vineyards. Heart and soul of the operation is Diego, now increasingly assisted by sons Mattia, who handles marketing, and Michele, who takes after his father and spends his time in the vineyards and, above all, on the winemaking. The luminous ruby Amarone 2012 releases rich, well-ripened cherry, black pepper, and macerated flower petals. It opens to immediate concentration, dense and succulent, impressing with its combination of self-confidence and lean austerity. High marks for Ripasso 2014 too, offering still-youthful aromatics and a palate that privileges agility over power.

○ Soave Cl. Sup. Foscarin Slavinus '14	♔♔ 4
● Amarone della Valpolicella '12	♔♔ 6
○ Soave Cl. '15	♔♔ 2*
○ Soave Cl. Casette Foscarin '14	♔♔ 3
○ Soave Spumante Brut '15	♔ 2
● Valpolicella Sup. San Pietro '14	♔ 2
○ Soave Cl. Monte Tondo '06	♔♔♔ 2*
○ Soave Cl. '14	♔♔ 2*
○ Soave Cl. Casette Foscarin '14	♔♔ 3
○ Soave Cl. Casette Foscarin '13	♔♔ 3*
○ Soave Cl. Monte Tondo '13	♔♔ 2*
○ Soave Cl. Sup. Foscarin Slavinus '14	♔♔ 4
○ Soave Cl. Sup. Foscarin Slavinus '13	♔♔ 4
○ Soave Cl. Sup. Foscarin Slavinus '12	♔♔ 4

● Amarone della Valpolicella '12	♔♔ 6
○ Sauvignon '15	♔♔ 4
● Valpolicella Sup. Ripasso '14	♔♔ 4
● Ca' Linverno '12	♔ 4
○ Ca' Linverno Bianco '15	♔ 4
○ Lugana Le Civaie '15	♔ 3
● Amarone della Valpolicella '11	♔♔ 6
● Amarone della Valpolicella '07	♔♔ 7
● Amarone della Valpolicella '06	♔♔ 6
● Amarone della Valpolicella Ris. '09	♔♔ 8
● Amarone della Valpolicella Ris. '08	♔♔ 8
● Recioto della Valpolicella '10	♔♔ 5
● Valpolicella Sup. Ripasso '12	♔♔ 4
● Valpolicella Sup. Ripasso '11	♔♔ 4
● Valpolicella Sup. Ripasso '08	♔♔ 3

VENETO

Cantina Sociale di Monteforte d'Alpone

VIA XX SETTEMBRE, 24
37032 MONTEFORTE D'ALPONE [VR]
TEL. +39 0457610110
www.cantinadimonteforte.it

CELLAR SALES
PRE-BOOKED VISITS
ANNUAL PRODUCTION 2,000,000 bottles
HECTARES UNDER VINE

The Soave designation is typically split into many small properties, with thousands of growers owning just a hectare or two of vines. Over 600 of them are members of the Cantina Sociale di Monteforte, whose Gaetano Tobin knows how to coax quality wines out of grapes brought in by growers. Apart from the designation whites, of course, they also make some Valpolicella labels. Once again, Soave Castellaro 2014 is one of the stars of its designation, made from optimally-ripe garganega that ages about a year in oak. On the nose, rich fruit enfolds dried flowers and spice, while the palate demonstrates how a rich, power-filled wine can at the same time show suppleness and a vibrant crispness. Kudos to Soave Clivus 2015 as well, with crisp aromas and a dynamic palate.

Montegrande

VIA TORRE, 2
35030 ROVOLON [PD]
TEL. +39 0495226276
www.vinimontegrande.it

CELLAR SALES
PRE-BOOKED VISITS
ANNUAL PRODUCTION 250,000 bottles
HECTARES UNDER VINE 30.00

The Euganean Hills, one of the Veneto's finest growing areas, are a complex system of volcanic hills that boast mineral-rich soils and an uncommonly dry, sunny climate. Over the last ten years, the Cristofanon family has adjusted its production and its 30 or so hectares of vineyard today yield a very consistent line of wines with fine varietal expression. The most ambitious wines, Sereo and Vigna delle Roche, were not presented this year, but the fine 2015 season enabled Colli Euganei Rosso to strut a gorgeous array of fragrances, with zesty aromatic herbs and black pepper lifting well-ripened red berry fruit. In the mouth, the wine eschews depth and power in favour of a relaxed suppleness. Fior d'Arancio Passito 2013 is bright, ripe, and enfolding.

○ Soave Cl. Sup. Vign. di Castellaro '14	♟♟ 2*
○ Soave Cl. Clivus '15	♟♟ 1*
● Valpolicella Ripasso '14	♟♟ 2*
○ Lessini Durello Brut M. Cl.	♟ 3
○ Recioto di Soave Cl. Sigillo '13	♟ 3
○ Soave Cl. Il Vicario '15	♟ 2
● Amarone della Valpolicella Re Teodorico '11	♟♟ 5
○ Soave Cl. Clivus '14	♟♟ 1*
○ Soave Cl. Clivus '13	♟♟ 1*
○ Soave Cl. Il Vicario '13	♟♟ 2*
○ Soave Cl. Sup. Vign. di Castellaro '13	♟♟ 2*
○ Soave Cl. Sup. Vign. di Castellaro '12	♟♟ 2*
○ Soave Cl. Sup. Vign. di Castellaro '10	♟♟ 2*
● Valpolicella Ripasso '13	♟♟ 2*
● Valpolicella Ripasso '11	♟♟ 2*

○ Colli Euganei Fior d'Arancio Passito '13	♟♟ 3
● Colli Euganei Rosso '15	♟♟ 2*
○ Castearo '15	♟ 2
○ Colli Euganei Bianco Erto '15	♟ 2
● Colli Euganei Cabernet '15	♟ 2
○ Colli Euganei Fior d'Arancio Spumante '15	♟ 2
● Colli Euganei Merlot '15	♟ 2
○ Colli Euganei Pinot Bianco '15	♟ 2
○ Colli Euganei Seprino Extra Dry	♟ 2
● Colli Euganei Cabernet Sereo '12	♟♟ 3
● Colli Euganei Cabernet Sereo '11	♟♟ 3
○ Colli Euganei Fior d'Arancio Passito '12	♟♟ 3
○ Colli Euganei Fior d'Arancio Passito '11	♟♟ 3

Monteversa

VIA MONTE VERSA, 1024
35030 VÒ [PD]
TEL. +39 0499941092
www.monteversa.it

CELLAR SALES
PRE-BOOKED VISITS
ANNUAL PRODUCTION 23,000 bottles
HECTARES UNDER VINE 17.00
VITICULTURE METHOD Certified Organic

Monteversa has only been around a short time, but the hill on which it is built and its long-established vineyards are among the designation's most envied. Its slopes of red- and white-flaked soils face south, west, and north, so that the Voltazza family can ensure each variety receives the precise conditions it requires. The elevation is only 100 metres or so, but the rich soils allow the grapes to ripen with character and consistency. A champion performance from Bordeaux- blend Rosso Animaversa 2013. The nose is a tad reluctant at first, but it soon pours out fruit that is surrounded by forest floor, violets, and medicinal herbs. The palate shifts down a gear, expanding elegantly, then smooth, glossy tannins and a savoury acidity energize a full, pulpy mouthfeel. The explosive Versacinto 2015 is a generous red with ultra-expressive fruit and a straightforward, lip-smacking palate.

● Colli Euganei Rosso Animaversa '13	♈♈ 4
● Colli Euganei Rosso Versacinto '15	♈♈ 3
○ Versavò '15	♈♈ 2*
○ Colli Euganei Manzoni Bianco Animaversa '14	♈ 3
○ Primaversa Frizzante '15	♈ 3
○ Saver Frizzante '14	♈ 3
○ Colli Euganei Bianco Animaversa '12	♔♔ 3
○ Colli Euganei Bianco Versavò '13	♔♔ 2*
○ Colli Euganei Bianco Versavò '11	♔♔ 2*
● Colli Euganei Cabernet Animaversa '12	♔♔ 4
● Colli Euganei Rosso Animaversa '11	♔♔ 4
● Colli Euganei Rosso Animaversa '10	♔♔ 4
● Colli Euganei Rosso Versacinto '13	♔♔ 3
● Colli Euganei Rosso Versacinto '12	♔♔ 2*
● Colli Euganei Rosso Versacinto '11	♔♔ 2*
○ Versavò '14	♔♔ 2*

Le Morette - Valerio Zenato

FRAZ. SAN BENEDETTO DI LUGANA
V.LE INDIPENDENZA, 19D
37019 PESCHIERA DEL GARDA [VR]
TEL. +39 0457552724
www.lemorette.it

CELLAR SALES
PRE-BOOKED VISITS
ANNUAL PRODUCTION 350,000 bottles
HECTARES UNDER VINE 32.00
SUSTAINABLE WINERY

This family-run operation lies in the heart of the Lugana zone, very close to the tiny Frassino lake, whose clayey banks typify the conditions in which this variety gives impressive results. Some of the property supports a long-established and highly respected nursery business, but most of the vineyards are dedicated to grapes that Paolo and Fabio Zenato transform into a portfolio of solid, reliable wines reflecting this zone and its traditions. Zenato's Lugana Riserva, made solely of turbiana, is their finest expression of that wine category. The vineyards, grafted onto vines more than a century old, are in clay-rick soil; the wine spontaneously ferments, then matures two years, in both steel and glass, with only a small part on barrels. It shows off profound, multi-layered aromas, with camomile and gunflint coursing through ripe yellow peach, melon, and apricot, followed by an energy-infused, juicy palate.

○ Accordo Passito Bianco '12	♈♈ 4
● Bardolino Cl. '15	♈♈ 2*
○ Lugana Mandolara '15	♈♈ 3
○ Lugana Ris. '12	♈♈ 5
● Perseo '12	♈♈ 5
⊙ Bardolino Chiaretto Cl. '15	♈ 2
● Serai '14	♈ 2
○ Lugana Benedictus '14	♔♔ 3
○ Lugana Benedictus '11	♔♔ 3
○ Lugana Benedictus '07	♔♔ 3
○ Lugana Mandolara '14	♔♔ 2*
○ Lugana Mandolara '13	♔♔ 2*
○ Lugana Ris. '11	♔♔ 3
○ Lugana Vigna La Mandolara '08	♔♔ 2*

Marco Mosconi

VIA PARADISO, 5
37031 ILLASI [VR]
TEL. +39 0456529109
www.marcomosconi.it

CELLAR SALES
PRE-BOOKED VISITS
ANNUAL PRODUCTION 25,000 bottles
HECTARES UNDER VINE 10.00

Marco Mosconi happened into viticulture almost by chance. His family owned a fairly large vineyard, but had never paid much attention to farming, so when Marco showed interest in tending the vines, it was regarded as a bit odd. Leap forward ten years or so, and today it is one of the area's most prestigious operations, faithfully interpreting the designation's wines in a personal style that combines richness, power and grip. Two outstanding wines made the finals: a fragrant Valpolicella Superiore and a solid Amarone, both 2012. The first presents self-confident, clean-edged scents of wild berries and pungent herbs, then a full-volumed palate and a stimulating acidity driving the lengthy progression. The second shies away from the common approach of a soft, sweetish wine in favour of a more serious interpretation, with super-ripe fruit and spice that are at their best on a powerful yet dry palate and a magisterial progression.

● Valpolicella Sup. '12	▼▼▼	5
● Amarone della Valpolicella '12	▼▼	8
○ Soave Corte Paradiso '15	▼▼	2*
● Valpolicella Montecurto '15	▼▼	3
● Amarone della Valpolicella '11	♀♀	8
● Amarone della Valpolicella '09	♀♀	8
● Amarone della Valpolicella '08	♀♀	8
● Recioto della Valpolicella '11	♀♀	6
● Recioto della Valpolicella '07	♀♀	6
○ Recioto di Soave '13	♀♀	5
○ Soave Corte Paradiso '14	♀♀	2*
○ Soave Rosetta '13	♀♀	3
○ Soave Sup. Corte Paradiso '13	♀♀	2*
● Turan Cabernet Sauvignon '11	♀♀	3
● Valpolicella Montecurto '14	♀♀	3
● Valpolicella Sup. '11	♀♀	5
● Valpolicella Sup. '10	♀♀	5

Mosole

LOC. CORBOLONE
VIA ANNONE VENETO, 60
30029 SANTO STINO DI LIVENZA [VE]
TEL. +39 0421310404
www.mosole.com

CELLAR SALES
PRE-BOOKED VISITS
ANNUAL PRODUCTION 230,000 bottles
HECTARES UNDER VINE 30.00

In an area that is definitely true wine country but has all too often been linked to the idea of predictable, easy-drinking wine, Lucio Mosole's winery is the exception. In Corbolone, Lucio runs a vineyard of 30 hectares, planted mainly to Bordeaux varieties, where ripe, solid fruit was the mission pursued in the work of the last decade. In the cellar, the partnership with Gianni Menotti has elevated production to appreciable standards of quality. Merlot Ad Nonam 2013, one of the region's most impressive reds, has changed stylistic gears with respect to recent versions, surrendering a bit of opulence in favour of more refinement in terms of fruit and florality. The palate is well-built, admirably supported by silk-smooth tannins, with an acidity that moderates the heft and fuels a lengthy development. Passito 2014, on the other hand, is a glorious explosion of impressions of citrus, spice, and ripe apricot, well braced on the palate by vibrant flavours.

○ Ad Nonam Passito '14	▼▼	4
● Lison-Pramaggiore Merlot Ad Nonam '13	▼▼	5
○ Hora Prima '14	▼▼	4
○ Lison Eleo '15	▼▼	3
● Lison Pramaggiore Cabernet Hora Sexta '13	▼▼	4
○ Venezia Pinot Grigio '15	▼▼	2*
● Lison-Pramaggiore Cabernet Franc '15	▼	2
● Lison-Pramaggiore Merlot '15	▼	2
● Lison-Pramaggiore Refosco P. R. '15	▼	2
○ Sauvignon '15	▼	2
○ Tai '15	▼	2
○ Venezia Chardonnay '15	▼	2
○ Ad Nonam Passito '13	♀♀	4
● Lison-Pramaggiore Cabernet Hora Sexta '12	♀♀	3*

Il Mottolo

LOC. LE CONTARINE
VIA COMEZZARA, 13
35030 BAONE [PD]
TEL. +39 3479456155
www.ilmottolo.it

CELLAR SALES
PRE-BOOKED VISITS
ANNUAL PRODUCTION 27,000 bottles
HECTARES UNDER VINE 7.00

Sergio Fortin had been a grape grower for a decade or so, first just as a passion, then, as good results became ever more evident, with increasing commitment. Today, Mottolo is a lovely operation in the southern Euganean Hills, vaunting well-managed vineyards that yield perfect, ripe fruit. Winemaking here strives for harmony and elegance, a hallmark that even the most basic wines exhibit. Comezzara 2014 Merlot offered its usual fine performance, with straightforward, rich fruit and a palate both dense and succulent. The standard-bearer, though, is still Serro, a predominantly merlot Bordeaux blend, its nose profound and multi-layered, and with velvety tannins and a savoury acidity supporting a palate that is firmly-structured, dry, and superbly elegant. The richer and more concentrated Carmenere Vignànima 2013 features black pepper and spice that heighten its pulpy fruit.

Musella

LOC. FERRAZZE
VIA FERRAZZETTE, 2
37036 SAN MARTINO BUON ALBERGO [VR]
TEL. +39 045973385
www.musella.it

CELLAR SALES
PRE-BOOKED VISITS
ACCOMMODATION
ANNUAL PRODUCTION 260,000 bottles
HECTARES UNDER VINE 50.00
VITICULTURE METHOD Certified Biodynamic

Musella, a kind of pocket-size paradise just a stone's throw from Verona, is a venerable, wall-encircled wine estate that over the past ten years or so, has reached its winemaking apogee, under the guidance of the Pasqua family. The vineyards, winding for many hectares through a pristine landscape of woods and streams, are under biodynamic management, with diverse elevations and exposures. They yield wines that are limited in quantity but of inestimable character and quality. Musella may not have garnered the top award this year, but there are certainly no weaknesses in their line-up. Valpolicella Superiore, contrary to what the challenging 2014 led us to expect, is profoundly aromatic, with wild berry fruit and flowers, then a magisterial palate offers an interesting vein of rusticity. Of the three Amarones we tasted, our preference went to the 2011, which opens to fragrant spice and macerated flowers, followed only later by fragrant fruit. The palate impresses with full volume and vibrant tannins.

● Colli Euganei Rosso Serro '13	♙♙	4
● Vingnànima '13	♙♙	3*
● Comezzara Merlot '14	♙♙	2*
○ Le Contarine '15	♙♙	2*
● V. Marè Cabernet '14	♙	2
● Colli Euganei Rosso Serro '11	♙♙♙	3*
● Colli Euganei Rosso Serro '10	♙♙♙	3*
● Colli Euganei Rosso Serro '09	♙♙♙	3*
● Colli Euganei Cabernet V. Marè '13	♙♙	2*
● Colli Euganei Cabernet V. Marè '12	♙♙	2*
○ Colli Euganei Fior d'Arancio Passito V. del Pozzo '10	♙♙	3*
● Colli Euganei Merlot Comezzara '13	♙♙	2*
● Colli Euganei Rosso Serro '12	♙♙	3*
● Vingnànima '12	♙♙	3*
● Vingnànima '11	♙♙	3*
● Vingnànima '10	♙♙	3*

● Amarone della Valpolicella '11	♙♙	6
● Valpolicella Sup. '14	♙♙	3*
● Amarone della Valpolicella Ris. '10	♙♙	6
● Amarone della Valpolicella Senza Titolo '08	♙♙	8
○ Drago Bianco '15	♙♙	3
● Recioto della Valpolicella '12	♙♙	5
⊙ Drago Rosé '15	♙	3
● Amarone della Valpolicella Ris. '07	♙♙♙	6
● Valpolicella Sup. '13	♙♙♙	3*
● Valpolicella Sup. '12	♙♙♙	2*
● Amarone della Valpolicella '10	♙♙	6
● Amarone della Valpolicella '09	♙♙	6
● Amarone della Valpolicella Ris. '09	♙♙	6
● Valpolicella Sup. Ripasso '12	♙♙	4
● Valpolicella Sup. Ripasso '11	♙♙	4

Daniele Nardello

VIA IV NOVEMBRE, 56
37032 MONTEFORTE D'ALPONE [VR]
TEL. +39 0457612116
www.nardellovini.it

CELLAR SALES
PRE-BOOKED VISITS
ANNUAL PRODUCTION 50,000 bottles
HECTARES UNDER VINE 16.00

Step by step, Federica and Daniele Nardello
have built up their family winery, sited
along the southern slope of the hills
demarcating the classic Soave district. They
grow mostly garganega on their 15 or so
hectares of vineyard, along with small
amounts of chardonnay and trebbiano.
Since the yield is more than they need,
their wines are made only from the finest
lots of fruit. Ripe yellow peach, melon, and
apricot lead off in Soave Monte Zoppega,
nicely lifted by camomile flowers and dried
hay, followed by a full-volumed, delicious
palate, well supported by a savoury acidity.
The significant amount of trebbiano di
Soave in Vigna Turbian heightens the
category's traditional fragrance and
sculpted shape, providing even more length
and thrust.

○ Soave Cl. Monte Zoppega '14	♥♥ 3*
○ Recioto di Soave Suavissimus '11	♥♥ 4
○ Soave Cl. Meridies '15	♥♥ 2*
○ Soave Cl. V. Turbian '15	♥♥ 2*
○ Aetas Brut	♥ 2
○ Blanc De Fè '15	♥ 2
○ Blanc De Fè '14	♀♀ 2*
○ Soave Cl. Meridies '14	♀♀ 2*
○ Soave Cl. Meridies '13	♀♀ 2*
○ Soave Cl. Meridies '12	♀♀ 2*
○ Soave Cl. Monte Zoppega '13	♀♀ 3*
○ Soave Cl. Monte Zoppega '12	♀♀ 3
○ Soave Cl. V. Turbian '14	♀♀ 2*
○ Soave Cl. V. Turbian '13	♀♀ 2*
○ Soave Cl. V. Turbian '12	♀♀ 2*

Angelo Nicolis e Figli

VIA VILLA GIRARDI, 29
37029 SAN PIETRO IN CARIANO [VR]
TEL. +39 0457701261
www.vininicolis.com

CELLAR SALES
PRE-BOOKED VISITS
ANNUAL PRODUCTION 220,000 bottles
HECTARES UNDER VINE 42.00

The brothers Nicolis took good advantage
of the success that Valpolicella has
enjoyed to acquire a collection of quality
vineyards and upgrade their winemaking
cellar for production levels significant both
in volume and quality. Today, Beppe and
Giancarlo manage over 40 hectares of
vineyards spread over the various zones of
the designation, planted solely to the
traditional local varieties, from which they
produce solidly-styled wines. An Amarone
made only during the best harvests,
Ambrosan is sourced from the vineyard of
the same name in San Pietro in Cariano
and receives significant ageing, part in
botti and part in tonneaux. Ripe and warm
on the nose, its fruit is well grounded by
spices and baker's chocolate. It builds a
massive palate, but one kept beautifully in
check by the tannins and acidity. Equally
fine is Amarone Classico 2010, crisp and
ready right now.

● Amarone della Valpolicella Cl. Ambrosan '08	♥♥ 7
● Amarone della Valpolicella Cl. '10	♥♥ 6
● Recioto della Valpolicella Cl. '11	♥♥ 5
● Valpolicella Cl. Sup. Ripasso Seccal '13	♥♥ 3
● Valpolicella Cl. '15	♥ 2
● Amarone della Valpolicella Cl. Ambrosan '06	♀♀♀ 7
● Amarone della Valpolicella Cl. Ambrosan '98	♀♀♀ 7
● Amarone della Valpolicella Cl. Ambrosan '93	♀♀♀ 6
● Amarone della Valpolicella Cl. '09	♀♀ 6
● Amarone della Valpolicella Cl. Ambrosan '07	♀♀ 7
● Valpolicella Cl. Sup. Ripasso Seccal '12	♀♀ 3
● Valpolicella Cl. Sup. Ripasso Seccal '08	♀♀ 3

Nino Franco

VIA GARIBALDI, 147
31049 VALDOBBIADENE [TV]
TEL. +39 0423972051
www.ninofranco.it

CELLAR SALES
PRE-BOOKED VISITS
ACCOMMODATION AND RESTAURANT SERVICE
ANNUAL PRODUCTION 1,000,000 bottles
HECTARES UNDER VINE 3.50

The success that has impacted Valpolicella has led to some long-time operations preferring to come down out of the hills and set up commercial-scale production on the plains. Conversely, Primo Franco has remained loyal to his growing area, to the point of purchasing a vineyard right in the heart of Valdobbiadene, a small clos that imprints a distinctive character on the Via Garibaldi wines. Primo produces a million bottles a year of wines whose rich character welcomes ageing. Grave di Stecca receives its usual high marks, an eloquent example of how the Charmat method too is capable of producing champion sparklers. Of 100% glera grown almost in town, it receives a lengthy maturation, resulting in a complex nose where somewhat straightforward fruit interacts with dried flower petals and Mediterranean scrub. In the mouth, it shows dry, savoury, and classy. Riva di San Floriano is a more uncomplicated, fragrant Valdobbiadene Brut with a very well-crafted palate.

○ Brut Grave di Stecca '12	♟♟ 5
○ Valdobbiadene Brut V. della Riva di S. Floriano '15	♟♟ 3*
○ Cartizze '15	♟♟ 5
○ Valdobbiadene Brut	♟♟ 3
○ Valdobbiadene Dry Primo Franco '15	♟♟ 3
⊙ Faive Rosé Brut	♟ 3
○ Brut Grave di Stecca '11	♟♟♟ 5
○ Brut Grave di Stecca '09	♟♟♟ 5
○ Valdobbiadene Brut Grave di Stecca '08	♟♟♟ 5
○ Valdobbiadene Brut V. della Riva di S. Floriano '11	♟♟♟ 3*
○ Valdobbiadene Brut V. della Riva di S. Floriano '14	♟♟ 3*
○ Valdobbiadene Brut V. della Riva di S. Floriano '13	♟♟ 3
○ Valdobbiadene Dry Primo Franco '14	♟♟ 3*

Novaia

VIA NOVAIA, 1
37020 MARANO DI VALPOLICELLA [VR]
TEL. +39 0457755129
www.novaia.it

CELLAR SALES
PRE-BOOKED VISITS
ANNUAL PRODUCTION 45,000 bottles
HECTARES UNDER VINE 7.00
VITICULTURE METHOD Certified Organic
SUSTAINABLE WINERY

Traveling up the Marano Valley, the quasi-industrial area on its floor quickly gives way to vineyards on both the western and eastern hillslopes, an endless succession of pergolas, a handful of vertically-trellised vines, and clumps of woods. Giampaolo and Marcello Vaona farm their family's vineyards organically. The estate is just under ten hectares and the grapes produced are used only to make classic designation wines. If over recent years we have always drawn attention to the high quality of the more traditional wines, this year it was Amarone Le Balze 2011 that most impressed us, with plenty of super-ripe fruit and medicinal herbs on the nose, then power in the mouth, but carefully calibrated by enough acidity. Ripasso 2013 is another style altogether, exhibiting a complex nose of cherry infused with dry flowers and black liquorice and a full-flavoured palate that just goes on and on.

● Amarone della Valpolicella Cl. Le Balze '11	♟♟ 8
● Recioto della Valpolicella Cl. Le Novaje '14	♟♟ 4
● Valpolicella Cl. Sup. Ripasso '13	♟♟ 3
● Valpolicella Cl. '15	♟ 2
● Valpolicella Cl. Sup. I Cantoni '13	♟ 4
● Amarone della Valpolicella Cl. Corte Vaona '11	♟♟ 5
● Recioto della Valpolicella Cl. Le Novaje '13	♟♟ 4
● Recioto della Valpolicella Cl. Le Novaje '12	♟♟ 4
● Valpolicella Cl. '13	♟♟ 2*
● Valpolicella Cl. Sup. I Cantoni '12	♟♟ 4
● Valpolicella Cl. Sup. Ripasso '12	♟♟ 3

Ottella

FRAZ. SAN BENEDETTO DI LUGANA
LOC. OTTELLA
37019 PESCHIERA DEL GARDA [VR]
TEL. +39 0457551950
www.ottella.it

CELLAR SALES
PRE-BOOKED VISITS
ANNUAL PRODUCTION 350,000 bottles
HECTARES UNDER VINE 40.00

Ottella stands somewhat apart from Lake Garda, lying on the much less known and infinitely smaller Lake Frassino. This, however, is the cradle of Lugana, and the clay soils imprint their strength on local wines. Francesco and Michele Montresor's whites embody precisely that character, and with great refinement. They also produce a pair of reds, from the vineyards in Ponti sul Mincio, planted solely to red varieties. Lugana Molceo is a Riserva whose attractiveness is normally based less on power and more on aromatic depth, savouriness on the palate, and overall elegance. That is certainly true with the present vintage, with a heftier charge of acidy, child of the cool 2014 season, that makes the wine particularly crisp and electric. Le Creete, on the other hand, is more sun-kissed and riper, an ultra-delicious white boasting a lively, supple progression.

Pasqua - Cecilia Beretta

LOC. SAN FELICE EXTRA
VIA BELVEDERE, 135
37131 VERONA
TEL. +39 0458432111
www.pasqua.it

CELLAR SALES
PRE-BOOKED VISITS
ANNUAL PRODUCTION 13,000,000 bottles
HECTARES UNDER VINE 300.00

The Pasqua family has been involved in wine for over 90 years, and their bond with Valpolicella and its traditions has never waned. Many things have changed over the decades, and the renowned brand is now flanked by Cecilia Beretta, the family farm that experiments with and directs the entire production chain. Grapes from more than 100 hectares of estate vineyards are supplemented by those from a large cadre of local growers. Amarone Famiglia Pasqua 2012 stands out for the sheer depth of its fragrances, featuring super-ripe fruit shot through with pungent spice and macerated petals, and for the overall elegance of its palate, where tannins team with its acidity to give lift to a truly majestic palate. On the other hand, Amarone Terre di Cariano Riserva 2011, with its multi-layered bouquet, fairly crackles with energy on a near-austere palate. That cool 2014 harvest kept the progression of Ripasso Famiglia Pasqua crisp and charged.

○ Lugana Molceo Ris. '14	♟♟♟ 4*
● Campo Sireso '13	♟♟ 4
○ Lugana '15	♟♟ 2*
○ Lugana Le Creete '15	♟♟ 3
⊙ Roses Roses '15	♟♟ 2*
● Valpolicella Ripasso Ripa della Volta '13	♟♟ 4
○ Vignenuove '15	♟♟ 2*
● Amarone della Valpolicella Ripa della Volta '13	♟ 6
● Gemei Rosso '15	♟ 2
○ Lugana Molceo Ris. '13	♟♟♟ 4*
○ Lugana Molceo Ris. '12	♟♟♟ 4*
○ Lugana Sup. Molceo '11	♟♟♟ 4*
○ Lugana Sup. Molceo '10	♟♟♟ 4*
○ Lugana Sup. Molceo '09	♟♟♟ 4
○ Lugana Sup. Molceo '08	♟♟♟ 4
○ Lugana Sup. Molceo '07	♟♟♟ 4

● Amarone della Valpolicella Cl. Terre di Cariano Cecilia Beretta Ris. '11	♟♟ 8
● Amarone della Valpolicella Famiglia Pasqua '12	♟♟ 6
● Amarone della Valpolicella Cl. Villa Borghetti Pasqua '13	♟♟ 6
● Valpolicella Sup. Ripasso Famiglia Pasqua '14	♟♟ 4
○ Passimento Bianco '15	♟ 3
● Passimento Rosso '13	♟ 3
● Amarone della Valpolicella Cl. Terre di Cariano '04	♟♟♟ 8
● Amarone della Valpolicella Cl. Terre di Cariano Cecilia Beretta Ris. '10	♟♟ 8
● Amarone della Valpolicella Famiglia Pasqua '06	♟♟ 6

★★Leonildo Pieropan

VIA CAMUZZONI, 3
37038 SOAVE [VR]
TEL. +39 0456190171
www.pieropan.it

Albino Piona

FRAZ. CUSTOZA
VIA BELLAVISTA, 48
37060 SOMMACAMPAGNA [VR]
TEL. +39 045516055
www.albinopiona.it

CELLAR SALES
PRE-BOOKED VISITS
ANNUAL PRODUCTION 380,000 bottles
HECTARES UNDER VINE 62.00
VITICULTURE METHOD Certified Organic

CELLAR SALES
PRE-BOOKED VISITS
ANNUAL PRODUCTION 350,000 bottles
HECTARES UNDER VINE 77.00

Andrea and Dario Pieropan are playing an increasingly prominent role in this family operation, involved in the vineyards, in the cellar, and in all the marketing. What remains unaltered is their close bond with Soave, and, over the last ten years or more, with Valpolicella, where they embody the commitment and sensitivity inherited from parents Nino and Teresita. The vineyards are among the designation's largest, their production fairly limited but of absolutely superb quality. An aficionado wishing to make the acquaintance of Soave must taste Calvarino and La Rocca, two wines that embody the essence of the designation. Florality and crispness predominate in the first, combining with a taut, lengthy progression to comprise a wine of great attractiveness, while the second stands out for its aromatic complexity, the result of the interweaving of oak and fruit, spice and mineral, followed by a seductive, energy-charged palate that never tires the taster.

The Piona family occupies a prominent place on the Lake Garda winemaking stage. Albino gave the winery a great reputation for simple, straightforward quaffers, but the children are taking up the challenge of plumbing the true quality of the hillslopes south of the lake. Over 70 hectares of vines produce far more than is needed, so only the finest lots of grapes go to producing the family's wines, predominantly Bardolino and Custoza. To underscore Custoza's ageing potential, we tasted two long-matured exemplars. One, Campo del Selese 2013, is a partly oak-aged Superiore that lays out saffron and dried flowers, heightened by whiffs of gunflint. In the mouth, it is ripe and warm, with ultra-full flavours. Custoza SP 2013, however, shows a sharper, edgier profile, with keener acidity showcasing its fresh taste.

○ Soave Cl. La Rocca '14	▼▼▼ 5
○ Soave Cl. Calvarino '14	▼▼ 4
○ Soave Cl. '15	▼▼ 3
● Valpolicella Sup. Ruberpan V. Garzon '13	▼▼ 4
○ Soave Cl. Calvarino '13	♀♀♀ 4*
○ Soave Cl. Calvarino '09	♀♀♀ 4*
○ Soave Cl. Calvarino '08	♀♀♀ 4
○ Soave Cl. Calvarino '07	♀♀♀ 4
○ Soave Cl. Calvarino '06	♀♀♀ 4
○ Soave Cl. Calvarino '05	♀♀♀ 3
○ Soave Cl. Calvarino '04	♀♀♀ 3
○ Soave Cl. Calvarino '03	♀♀♀ 3
○ Soave Cl. Calvarino '02	♀♀♀ 3
○ Soave Cl. La Rocca '12	♀♀♀ 5
○ Soave Cl. La Rocca '11	♀♀♀ 5
○ Soave Cl. La Rocca '10	♀♀♀ 5
○ Soave Cl. La Rocca '02	♀♀♀ 5

○ Custoza SP '13	▼▼ 2*
○ Custoza Sup. Campo del Selese '13	▼▼ 2*
● Bardolino '15	▼▼ 2*
⊙ Bardolino Chiaretto '15	▼▼ 2*
○ Custoza '15	▼▼ 2*
○ Gran Cuvée Pas Dosé M. Cl.	▼▼ 4
⊙ Estro di Piona Rosé Brut	▼ 4
○ Verde Piona Frizzante	▼ 2
● Bardolino '14	♀♀ 2*
● Bardolino '13	♀♀ 2*
● Bardolino SP '12	♀♀ 2*
● Campo Massimo Corvina Veronese '12	♀♀ 2*
● Campo Massimo Corvina Veronese '11	♀♀ 2*
○ Custoza '14	♀♀ 2*
○ Custoza '13	♀♀ 2*

Piovene Porto Godi

FRAZ. TOARA
VIA VILLA, 14
36020 VILLAGA [VI]
TEL. +39 0444885142
www.piovene.com

CELLAR SALES
PRE-BOOKED VISITS
ANNUAL PRODUCTION 100,000 bottles
HECTARES UNDER VINE 36.00

The Colli Berici district shows tremendous quality potential, but the Piovene family, in Porto Godi, is one of the few really striving for quality, which they derive from more than 30 hectares of vineyard in the southern part of the designation. Tai rosso is the local cultivar of election, but the Bordeaux varieties are found there, too, and the more traditional garganega. The house style is crisp, fresh whites and fruit-expressive reds. Cabernet from the Pozzare vineyards is once again one of the area's most impressive reds, thanks to a profusion of fragrant fruit that slowly yields to pungent spice and herbs. In the mouth, radiantly-ripe fruit and chewy tannins fuse together to create a tight, compact palate. In Tai Rosso Thovara 2013, on the other hand, the aromas are more complex and riper, while its very full palate is impressively stylish.

● Colli Berici Cabernet Vign. Pozzare '13	🍷🍷 4
● Colli Berici Tai Rosso Thovara '13	🍷🍷 5
● Colli Berici Merlot Fra i Broli '13	🍷🍷 4
○ Colli Berici Pinot Bianco Polveriera '15	🍷🍷 4
● Colli Berici Tai Rosso Vign. Riveselle '15	🍷🍷 2*
○ Thovara Passito '13	🍷🍷 5
○ Colli Berici Sauvignon Vign. Fostine '15	🍷 2
● Colli Berici Cabernet Vign. Pozzare '12	🍸🍸🍸 4*
● Colli Berici Cabernet Vign. Pozzare '07	🍸🍸🍸 3
● Colli Berici Merlot Fra i Broli '12	🍸🍸 4
● Colli Berici Merlot Fra i Broli '11	🍸🍸 4
● Colli Berici Tai Rosso Thovara '12	🍸🍸 5
● Colli Berici Tai Rosso Thovara '11	🍸🍸 5

★Graziano Prà

VIA DELLA FONTANA, 31
37032 MONTEFORTE D'ALPONE [VR]
TEL. +39 0457612125
www.vinipra.it

CELLAR SALES
PRE-BOOKED VISITS
ACCOMMODATION
ANNUAL PRODUCTION 300,000 bottles
HECTARES UNDER VINE 35.00
VITICULTURE METHOD Certified Organic
SUSTAINABLE WINERY

Over the last ten years, Graziano Prà has extended his operation into nearby Valpolicella, but kept his now-consolidated white-wine style. His various Soave vineyards are distributed throughout the classic area, but in Valpolicella his only vineyard is in the upper Mezzane valley, planted in rocky, schist soils. The vines, organically farmed from the start, yield fragrant, refined wines. A wine produced only the better seasons, Collе Sant'Antonio receives lengthy ageing. It releases fragrant citrus, dried flowers, and gunflint, which are well complemented by a palate whose ageing ensures a wine of overall length and great appeal. Amarone 2010 hits the bullseye too, with a solidly-built, taut palate, while Soave Staforte 2014 shows its usual fine breed, multi-layered aromatics, with a long, beguiling finale. Tre Bicchieri.

○ Soave Cl. Staforte '14	🍷🍷🍷 4*
● Amarone della Valpolicella '10	🍷🍷 6
○ Soave Cl. Colle S. Antonio '12	🍷🍷 4
○ Soave Cl. Monte Grande '15	🍷🍷 4
○ Soave Otto '15	🍷🍷 2*
● Valpolicella Sup. Ripasso Morandina '14	🍷🍷 4
● Valpolicella Morandina '15	🍷 2
○ Soave Cl. Monte Grande '11	🍸🍸🍸 4*
○ Soave Cl. Monte Grande '08	🍸🍸🍸 4
○ Soave Cl. Monte Grande '06	🍸🍸🍸 4
○ Soave Cl. Monte Grande '05	🍸🍸🍸 3
○ Soave Cl. Monte Grande '04	🍸🍸🍸 3
○ Soave Cl. Monte Grande '03	🍸🍸🍸 2*
○ Soave Cl. Staforte '13	🍸🍸🍸 4*
○ Soave Cl. Staforte '11	🍸🍸🍸 4*
○ Soave Cl. Staforte '08	🍸🍸🍸 4
○ Soave Cl. Staforte '06	🍸🍸🍸 4*

★Giuseppe Quintarelli

VIA CERÈ, 1
37024 NEGRAR [VR]
TEL. +39 0457500016
giuseppe.quintarelli@tin.it

CELLAR SALES
PRE-BOOKED VISITS
ANNUAL PRODUCTION 60,000 bottles
HECTARES UNDER VINE 10.00

The extensive Valpolicella wine scene has no other cellar as powerfully evocative as that of the Quintarelli family, whose history runs deep here and who vaunt a tribe of fans across the globe. If the truth be told, theirs is a small operation, with very modest overall production from some ten hectares of vineyards in various locations in the classic zone. The wines are have evolved over time and are superbly representative of local traditions. We had to wait almost ten years to taste Amarone 2007, which is an exemplar of the qualities that this wine type can offer after lengthy ageing. Cherry preserves sensuously enfold pungent spices and roast espresso bean, while it expands, delicately but irresistibly, in the mouth. Recioto 2004, which needs a bit more time, shows dried fig and caramelled hazelnut, heightened by a well-calibrated sweetness in the mouth.

● Amarone della Valpolicella Cl. '07	♈♈ 8
● Recioto della Valpolicella Cl. '04	♈♈ 8
● Amarone della Valpolicella Cl. '06	♈♈♈ 8
● Amarone della Valpolicella Cl. '03	♈♈♈ 8
● Amarone della Valpolicella Cl. '98	♈♈♈ 8
● Amarone della Valpolicella Cl. '97	♈♈♈ 8
● Amarone della Valpolicella Cl. Sup. Monte Cà Paletta '00	♈♈♈ 8
● Amarone della Valpolicella Cl. Sup. Monte Cà Paletta '93	♈♈♈ 8
● Recioto della Valpolicella Cl. '01	♈♈♈ 8
● Recioto della Valpolicella Cl. '95	♈♈♈ 5
● Recioto della Valpolicella Cl. Monte Ca' Paletta '97	♈♈♈ 8
● Rosso del Bepi '96	♈♈♈ 8
● Valpolicella Cl. Sup. '99	♈♈♈ 7

Le Ragose

FRAZ. ARBIZZANO
VIA LE RAGOSE, 1
37024 NEGRAR [VR]
TEL. +39 0457513241
www.leragose.com

CELLAR SALES
PRE-BOOKED VISITS
ANNUAL PRODUCTION 120,000 bottles
HECTARES UNDER VINE 18.00

The Galli cellar was the first to bring world attention to the high hills of Valpolicella. When most vineyards lay on the valley floors and adjacent hillslopes, the Galli brothers were already making superb wines from vineyards at almost 400 metres in altitude. Many others have followed them, pushing rows even higher, but the Galli style of elegant, taut wines remains quite unmistakeable. Those high-elevation vineyards are the ones that yield Amarone Caloetto 2007. Appearing an intense ruby, it releases sweet, fleshy cherry nicely lifted by macerated flowers and pungent herbs, presaging a complexity that is immediately revealed on the palate, where the wine gracefully achieves full volume yet calibrates it effectively with a taut acidity. The intriguing Rhagos 2007 is a long-aged, velvet-smooth red that offers striking richness on the palate.

● Amarone della Valpolicella Cl. Caloetto '07	♈♈ 7
● Recioto della Valpolicella Cl. '13	♈♈ 5
● Rhagos Ammandorlato '07	♈♈ 8
● Valpolicella Cl. '15	♈♈ 2*
● Valpolicella Cl. Sup. Ripasso Le Sassine '12	♈ 3
● Amarone della Valpolicella Cl. Caloetto '06	♈♈♈ 7
● Amarone della Valpolicella Cl. Marta Galli '05	♈♈♈ 8
● Amarone della Valpolicella Cl. Marta Galli '07	♈♈ 7

F.lli Recchia

Loc. Jago
via Ca' Bertoldi, 30
37024 Negrar [VR]
Tel. +39 0457500584
www.recchiavini.it

CELLAR SALES
PRE-BOOKED VISITS
ANNUAL PRODUCTION 250,000 bottles
HECTARES UNDER VINE 100.00

Although its viticultural history in Valpolicella is a lengthy, the Recchia family has been producing wine under its own label for only a few years now. The winery quickly emerged as a major player, however, and the vineyards are extensive, particularly in the Negrar hill area, supplying a rapidly growing production. The wines are divided into two lines, Masua di Jago for the traditional offerings and a range for the more vineyard-expressive wines. Amarone Ca' Bertoldi 2010 unfolds with very ripe, sweet fruit, beautifully lifted by delicate balsam and spice. It progresses gradually, with a crisp acidity that keeps it advancing. Valpolicella Superiore Masua di Jago 2014 is a tad simpler on the nose but no less impressive, just as the mouth exemplifies drinkability and fidelity to the wine type rather than power and alcoholic warmth.

Roccolo Grassi

via San Giovanni di Dio, 19
37030 Mezzane di Sotto [VR]
Tel. +39 0458880089
www.roccolograssi.it

PRE-BOOKED VISITS
ANNUAL PRODUCTION 49,000 bottles
HECTARES UNDER VINE 14.00
SUSTAINABLE WINERY

If eastern Valpolicella has been recognized and appreciated for some 20 years now, that is thanks to producers such as Marco and Francesca Sartori. Retaining their legacy of simplicity and approachability, they revamped their cellar, disregarding fashion, trends and market demands, embodying instead a solid, weighty vision Valpolicella. Their vineyards, well-tended and managed with respect for the environment, produce a limited production of ultra-appealing wines. Painstaking attention is paid as well to the only white here, one of the designation's most impressive, not least since it exhibits no winemaking tricks, no over-the-top aromatics, and no sweetness. This pure thoroughbred is barrel aged with good weight. The house champion, though, remains Valpolicella Superiore 2013. It is still a bit closed on the nose but it shifts gears in the mouth, expanding very wide, with good control of the mouthfeel, on to a near-endless, admirable finish.

● Amarone della Valpolicella Cl. Ca' Bertoldi '10	▼▼ 5
● Recioto della Valpolicella Cl. Masua di Jago '14	▼▼ 4
● Valpolicella Cl. Sup. Masua di Jago '14	▼▼ 2*
● Korvilot '13	▼ 5
● Valpolicella Cl. Sup. Masua di Jago '15	▼ 2
● Valpolicella Cl. Sup. Ripasso Le Muraie '14	▼ 3
● Valpolicella Cl. Sup. Ripasso Masua di Jago '14	▼ 2
● Valpolicella Cl. Sup. Ripasso Le Muraie '13	♈♈ 3
● Valpolicella Cl. Sup. Ripasso Masua di Jago '13	♈♈ 2*

● Valpolicella Sup. '13	▼▼▼ 5
○ Soave Sup. La Broia '14	▼▼ 3*
● Amarone della Valpolicella Roccolo Grassi '07	♈♈♈ 8
● Amarone della Valpolicella Roccolo Grassi '00	♈♈♈ 7
● Amarone della Valpolicella Roccolo Grassi '99	♈♈♈ 7
● Valpolicella Sup. '11	♈♈♈ 5
● Valpolicella Sup. Roccolo Grassi '09	♈♈♈ 5
● Valpolicella Sup. Roccolo Grassi '07	♈♈♈ 5
● Valpolicella Sup. Roccolo Grassi '04	♈♈♈ 5
● Amarone della Valpolicella '11	♈♈ 8
● Amarone della Valpolicella '09	♈♈ 8
● Recioto della Valpolicella Roccolo Grassi '09	♈♈ 5
● Valpolicella Sup. '12	♈♈ 5

Roeno

via Mama, 5
37020 Brentino Belluno [VR]
Tel. +39 0457230110
www.cantinaroeno.com

CELLAR SALES
PRE-BOOKED VISITS
ACCOMMODATION AND RESTAURANT SERVICE
ANNUAL PRODUCTION 340,000 bottles
HECTARES UNDER VINE 60.00
SUSTAINABLE WINERY

The Valdadige, both border and corridor between north and south, over recent decades has experienced the installation of a viticulture that is intensive but of disappointing quality. The Fugatti brothers have broken this pattern, with extensive vineyards and wines that they are determined will reflect the best the growing area can produce. They cultivate both Trento and Verona varieties, plus the prized enantio grape, which yields the area's archetypal red. We know we should be used to it by now, but this wine, Cristina, leaves us speechless every year. This perfect fusion between pinot grigio, chardonnay, gewürztraminer, and sauvignon blanc pours out a cornucopia of fragrances, with citrus leading into spice, camomile into tropical fruit, and it then lays out an utterly scrumptious palate, at once sweet and savoury. Of rare finesse and depth, Riesling Collezione di Famiglia 2011 is a Mitteleuropean style of wine that will enthuse fans of this grape.

○ Cristina V. T. '13	♔♔♔	5
○ Riesling Renano Collezione di Famiglia '11	♔♔	6
○ Praecipuus Riesling Renano '14	♔♔	4
● Roeno '12	♔♔	4
○ Valdadige Pinot Grigio Tera Alta '15	♔♔	2*
● Valdadige Terra dei Forti Enantio '12	♔♔	4
● Valdadige Terra dei Forti Enantio Ris. '10	♔♔	8
● La Rua Marzemino '15	♔	2
○ Cristina V. T. '12	♕♕♕	5
○ Cristina V. T. '11	♕♕♕	5
○ Cristina V. T. '08	♕♕♕	5
○ Cristina V. T. '10	♕♕	5
○ Riesling Renano Collezione di Famiglia '14	♕♕	5

Rubinelli Vajol

fraz. San Floriano
via Paladon, 31
37029 San Pietro in Cariano [VR]
Tel. +39 0456839277
www.rubinellivajol.it

CELLAR SALES
PRE-BOOKED VISITS
ACCOMMODATION
ANNUAL PRODUCTION 50,000 bottles
HECTARES UNDER VINE 10.00

No one should be misled by the apparent youthfulness of this outfit, since Rubinelli family roots sick deep into Valpolicella soil, and the quality they embody stems not so much from history as from the location of their vineyards and their sensitive winemaking. The cellar and vineyards lie in the centre of a natural, south-facing bowl at 150–200 metres. Their wines are quite respectful of local traditions, offering impressively delicate versions of each wine type. Since Amarone missed the rollcall, needing a tad more time in the cellar, we focused on the excellent Valpolicella Superiore 2012. A lovely ruby, the nose parades cherry and wild berry fruit, followed by crisper impressions of black pepper and thyme. In the mouth it builds its usual bright acidity, which sustains quite a lengthy development. Recioto 2012 vaunts a much more forceful nose, then a magisterial harmony between sweetness and savouriness.

● Recioto della Valpolicella Cl. '12	♔♔	6
● Valpolicella Cl. Sup. '12	♔♔	4
● Valpolicella Cl. '15	♔	2
● Valpolicella Cl. Sup. Ripasso '13	♔	5
● Amarone della Valpolicella Cl. '11	♕♕	7
● Amarone della Valpolicella Cl. '10	♕♕	6
● Amarone della Valpolicella Cl. '07	♕♕	6
● Recioto della Valpolicella Cl. '11	♕♕	6
● Valpolicella Cl. '13	♕♕	2*
● Valpolicella Cl. Sup. '11	♕♕	4
● Valpolicella Cl. Sup. '10	♕♕	4
● Valpolicella Cl. Sup. Ripasso '12	♕♕	5
● Valpolicella Cl. Sup. Ripasso '11	♕♕	4

Ruggeri & C.

Loc. Valdobbiadene
Fraz. Zecchei
Via Prà Fontana, 4
31049 Valdobbiadene [TV]
Tel. +39 04239092
www.ruggeri.it

CELLAR SALES
PRE-BOOKED VISITS
ANNUAL PRODUCTION 1,000,000 bottles
HECTARES UNDER VINE 17.00
SUSTAINABLE WINERY

Over the decades, Paolo Bisol has rationalized the family operation in such a way that each of the individual lots of grapes arriving in the cellar is not only processed in the most appropriate fashion but is dedicated immediately to the most suitable wine type. These are the offspring of close relationships with a wealth of local growers, particularly Valdobbiadene, although Conegliano contributes its share as well. The line is reliable, with more than one real gem. Giustino B., created almost as a dare 21 years ago, is now a sine qua non for appreciating the Prosecco genre, and in fact it won the Sparkling Wine of the Year award. The superb growing season gifted it with intense floral-infused fruit, the hallmark of this wine, which gives it delicacy and crispness, while in the mouth it is the usual elegant, full-flavoured sparkler. Vecchie Viti, on the other hand, comes across as closed and rebarbative on the nose, but dry and solidly-built in the mouth. Finally, we note the consistency and reliability of the entire line of wines.

○ Valdobbiadene Extra Dry Giustino B. '15	🍷🍷🍷	4*
○ Valdobbiadene Brut V. V. '15	🍷🍷	5
○ Cartizze	🍷🍷	5
○ L'Extra Brut '15	🍷🍷	3
○ Valdobbiadene Brut Quartese	🍷🍷	3
○ Valdobbiadene Dry S. Stefano	🍷🍷	3
○ Valdobbiadene Extra Dry Altevigne	🍷🍷	4
○ Valdobbiadene Extra Dry Giall'Oro	🍷🍷	3
○ Valdobbiadene Brut V. V. '14	🍷🍷🍷	4*
○ Valdobbiadene Brut Vecchie Viti '13	🍷🍷🍷	4*
○ Valdobbiadene Extra Dry Giustino B. '12	🍷🍷🍷	3*
○ Valdobbiadene Extra Dry Giustino B. '11	🍷🍷🍷	3*
○ Valdobbiadene Extra Dry Giustino B. '10	🍷🍷🍷	3
○ Valdobbiadene Extra Dry Giustino B. '09	🍷🍷🍷	3
○ Valdobbiadene Extra Dry Giustino B. '14	🍷🍷	4
○ Valdobbiadene Extra Dry Giustino B. '13	🍷🍷	4

Le Salette

Via Pio Brugnoli, 11c
37022 Fumane [VR]
Tel. +39 0457701027
www.lesalette.it

CELLAR SALES
PRE-BOOKED VISITS
ANNUAL PRODUCTION 130,000 bottles
HECTARES UNDER VINE 20.00

When Valpolicella and its wine first made news, in the early 1980s, Le Salette was already a prized brand, thanks to Franco Scamperle, who slowly transformed the family cellar into an operation that was not very large but excelled at producing fine expressions of the traditional wine types. Today, their 20 or so hectares of vines are divided into numerous parcels, the foundation of a portfolio predominantly dedicated to the traditional categories. Amarone Pergole Vece is the iconic wine here, reinterpreting the tradition through the fragrance and clarity of its fruit, with macerated flowers and spice nicely framing ripe cherry. Its richness in the mouth is truly amazing, with a taut acidity and suppleness constantly in crescendo. The Amarone La Marega 2012 impressed us, styled for easy approachability and immediate enjoyment.

● Amarone della Valpolicella Cl. Pergole Vece '12	🍷🍷	8
● Amarone della Valpolicella Cl. La Marega '12	🍷🍷	6
● Recioto della Valpolicella Cl. Pergole Vece '13	🍷🍷	6
● Valpolicella Cl. Sup. Ripasso I Progni '14	🍷🍷	3
● Ca' Carnocchio '13	🍷	4
● Valpolicella Cl. '15	🍷	2
● Amarone della Valpolicella Cl. Pergole Vece '05	🍷🍷🍷	8
● Amarone della Valpolicella Cl. Pergole Vece '11	🍷🍷	8
● Amarone della Valpolicella Cl. Pergole Vece '10	🍷🍷	8
● Recioto della Valpolicella Cl. Pergole Vece '12	🍷🍷	6

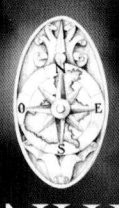

DOMÌNI VENETI

CANTINA
VALPOLICELLA
NEGRAR
ALLE ORIGINI DELL'AMARONE

Negrar - Verona - Italy
www.cantinanegrar.it

The 2016 vintage
will see a new look
for Val dei Molini.

Località Staffalo 1
37066 Custoza (Verona) - Italia
www.cantinadicustoza.it
info@cantinadicustoza.it
—
IMPORTED BY:
EUROWINES LTD LONDON

AN ENCHANTING TERROIR, A SINGLE VINEYARD, HARVESTED ENTIRELY BY-HAN
THE NEW, SECRET, SIDE OF PROSECCO.

Tenute SalvaTerra

Loc. Cengia
via Cengia, 8
37029 San Pietro in Cariano [VR]
Tel. +39 0456859025
www.tenutesalvaterra.it

CELLAR SALES
PRE-BOOKED VISITS
ANNUAL PRODUCTION 80,000 bottles
HECTARES UNDER VINE 16.00

The Furia brothers, among Valpolicella's largest growers, joined forces with a group of investors and founded SalvaTerra, which now grows grapes throughout the designation. The cellar and offices are located in the gorgeous Villa Giona, in Cengia, surrounded by a walled vineyard. Vineyards in Prun, Mezzane, Montorio, and Cazzano di Tramigna contribute to their Valpolicella reds. And it is the Prun property that yields the wine that impressed us the most, Amarone Riserva 2007, marked by deep, multi-layered super-ripe fruit shot through with wild herbs and a vein of mineral. We find none of the exaggerated forcefulness in the mouth that impedes pleasurable drinking, rather we enjoy fine proportion and a taut crispness. High marks to Amarone 2009 as well, which lays out sweet, gorgeous fruit on both nose and palate.

● Amarone della Valpolicella Cl. '09	♥♥ 8
● Amarone della Valpolicella Cl. Cave di Prun Ris. '07	♥♥ 8
● Valpolicella Cl. Sup. Ripasso '13	♥♥ 5
● Lazzarone '11	♥ 5
○ Pinot Grigio '15	♥ 5
○ Prosecco Extra Dry	♥ 4
● Valpolicella Cl. '14	♥ 3
● Amarone della Valpolicella Cl. '08	♀♀ 8
● Amarone della Valpolicella Cl. Cave di Prun Ris. '04	♀♀ 8
● Valpolicella Cl. Sup. Ripasso '12	♀♀ 5

Marco Sambin

Loc. Valnogaredo
via Fattorelle, 20a
35030 Cinto Euganeo [PD]
Tel. +39 3456812050
www.vinimarcus.com

CELLAR SALES
PRE-BOOKED VISITS
RESTAURANT SERVICE
ANNUAL PRODUCTION 10,000 bottles
HECTARES UNDER VINE 3.00
VITICULTURE METHOD Certified Organic
SUSTAINABLE WINERY

A professor specializing in agriculture, Marco Sambin established this small operation on the western slope of the Regional Park of the Euganean Hills. Its handful of vineyards, planted in clayey, white schist soils, with lengthy sunlight, are farmed organically, with a hint of biodynamics here and there. Yields are kept low, ensuring high-quality ripeness. Production too is limited, divided between Marcus and Alter, the most iconic offerings, and a series of experimental wines. 2013 Marcus once again shows off rich fragrances of sweet, ripe fruit, backgrounded by a subtle spice. The warmth characteristic of the vineyards where it grows emerges immediately in the mouth, with a palate that is silky, full, and seductive, supported by densely-woven tannins. Alter 2014, on the other hand, reflects its cooler season, with a crisper nose and more lively palate, gaining an overall delicacy and vibrancy.

● Alter '14	♥♥ 4
● Francisca XI Passito	♥♥ 5
● Marcus '13	♥♥ 5
○ Martha Frizzante '14	♥♥ 4
● Le Femminelle '15	♥ 3
○ Martha.due '15	♥ 3
● Alter '13	♀♀ 4
● Marcus '12	♀♀ 5
● Marcus '11	♀♀ 5
● Marcus '10	♀♀ 5
● Marcus '09	♀♀ 4
● Marcus '08	♀♀ 4
○ Martha.due '14	♀♀ 3
● Micael '11	♀♀ 5

San Rustico

FRAZ. VALGATARA DI VALPOLICELLA
VIA POZZO, 2
37020 MARANO DI VALPOLICELLA [VR]
TEL. +39 0457703348
www.sanrustico.it

CELLAR SALES
PRE-BOOKED VISITS
ANNUAL PRODUCTION 250,000 bottles
HECTARES UNDER VINE 22.00

Leaving behind the village of San Floriano and ascending Valpolicella's Marano valley, the semi-industrial areas gradually relinquish considerable space to viticulture, which is the real economic engine of this area; the road then begins to climb and penetrate the heart of the hills. And here lies the Campagnola cellar. These farmer-turned-entrepreneur brothers cultivate more than 20 hectares of vineyard, whose fruit goes to a line of wines withn a clearly traditional imprint. Gaso, the most striking estate vineyard, yielded the immensely-aromatic Amarone 2010, with macerated-flower oil and black pepper the foil to super-ripe fruit, followed by power on the palate that is well-checked by a dense-packed clutch of tannins. The nervy Ripasso 2012 comes from the same vineyard, while Amarone 2011 puts ripe red berry fruit on full display, which continues onto a juicy and pleasurably rustic palate.

La Sansonina

LOC. SANSONINA
37019 PESCHIERA DEL GARDA [VR]
TEL. +39 0457551905
www.sansonina.it

CELLAR SALES
ANNUAL PRODUCTION 21,000 bottles
HECTARES UNDER VINE 12.00

Carla Prospero launched Sansonina some 20 years ago, just as Lake Garda began to attract attention for rich, mouthwatering white wines. Contrary to what her colleagues were doing, however, Carla decided to risk everything on merlot, a variety that gives excellent results from the clay soils so prevalent around the lake. Today, the hectares have grown to well over ten, and the number of labels has increased too, with an initial Lugana now followed by the Cabernet Evaluna. This striking blend of cabernet sauvignon and franc, with smooth, ripe fruit alternating with delicate yet penetrating notes of pungent herbs. In the mouth, a suite of glossy tannins easily manage its full volume. Lugana Vigna del Moraro Verde, which ferments spontaneously, embodies the countryish side of this wine category, with its usual reliability and verve.

● Amarone della Valpolicella Cl. Gaso '10	▼▼ 8
● Amarone della Valpolicella Cl. '11	▼▼ 6
● Valpolicella Cl. Sup. '14	▼▼ 2*
● Valpolicella Cl. Sup. Ripasso Gaso '12	▼▼ 4
● Valpolicella Cl. '15	▼ 2
● Amarone della Valpolicella Cl. '10	♀♀ 6
● Amarone della Valpolicella Cl. '09	♀♀ 6
● Amarone della Valpolicella Cl. Gaso '09	♀♀ 8
● Amarone della Valpolicella Cl. Gaso '08	♀♀ 7
● Amarone della Valpolicella Cl. Gaso '07	♀♀ 6
● Amarone della Valpolicella Cl. Gaso '06	♀♀ 6
● Recioto della Valpolicella Cl. Gaso '13	♀♀ 5
● Valpolicella Cl. Sup. '12	♀♀ 2*
● Valpolicella Cl. Sup. Ripasso Gaso '11	♀♀ 4
● Valpolicella Cl. Sup. Ripasso Gaso '10	♀♀ 3

● Garda Evaluna '14	▼▼ 4
○ Lugana V. del Morano Verde '14	▼▼ 3
○ Lugana Sansonina '13	♀♀ 3
○ Lugana Sansonina '12	♀♀ 3
○ Lugana Sansonina '11	♀♀ 3
○ Lugana Sansonina '10	♀♀ 6
○ Lugana Sansonina '09	♀♀ 3*
○ Lugana Sansonina '08	♀♀ 3
● Sansonina '13	♀♀ 6
● Sansonina '12	♀♀ 6
● Sansonina '10	♀♀ 6
● Sansonina '09	♀♀ 6
● Sansonina '07	♀♀ 6

Tenuta Sant'Anna

Fraz. Loncon
via Monsignor P. L. Zovatto, 71
30020 Annone Veneto [VE]
Tel. +39 0422864511
www.tenutasantanna.it

CELLAR SALES
PRE-BOOKED VISITS
ANNUAL PRODUCTION 2,800,000 bottles
HECTARES UNDER VINE 140.00
SUSTAINABLE WINERY

The Po River plain, from Venice eastward, constitutes a vast area dedicated to viticulture, and the heart of the Lison Pramaggiore designation. This tongue of clayey land borders the Adriatic. Coast and is home to the Genagricola group winery, which vaunts well over 100 hectares, whose fruit goes to produce wines that show superb varietal expression. The nearby hills that constitute the historic zone of Prosecco yield this fragrant Valdobbiadene Extra Dry, the glass offering clean-contoured apple and pear, then a beguiling palate with a magisterial balance between sweetness, acidity, and mousse. Cartizze is quite similar, but the fruit is more forward, one of the reasons being its sweeter dosage. Among the still wines produced on the plains, we liked the aromatics of Chardonnay 2015.

○ Cartizze	🍷🍷 5
○ Valdobbiadene Extra Dry	🍷🍷 3
○ Brut di Pinot	🍷 2
○ Chardonnay Frizzante	🍷 2
○ Cuvée Blanche Extra Dry	🍷 2
⊙ Cuvée Rosé Brut	🍷 2
○ Lison-Pramaggiore Chardonnay Goccia '15	🍷 2
○ Lison-Pramaggiore Cl. Goccia '15	🍷 2
○ Lison-Pramaggiore Savignon Goccia '15	🍷 2
○ Moscato Spumante Dolce	🍷 2
○ Prosecco Brut	🍷 3
○ Prosecco Brut Mill. '15	🍷 3
○ Prosecco Extra Dry	🍷 3
○ Prosecco Frizzante	🍷 2
○ Traminer Goccia '15	🍷 2
○ Venezia Pinot Grigio Goccia '15	🍷 2

★Tenuta Sant'Antonio

Loc. San Zeno
via Ceriani, 23
37030 Colognola ai Colli [VR]
Tel. +39 0457650383
www.tenutasantantonio.it

CELLAR SALES
PRE-BOOKED VISITS
ANNUAL PRODUCTION 700,000 bottles
HECTARES UNDER VINE 100.00

The cellar that Armando, Tiziano, Paolo, and Massimo Castagnedi founded some 20 years ago has become almost a cult for lovers of Valpolicella. Their handful of initial bottles have become a production encountered worldwide. They have considerable estate vineyards, mostly in Valpolicella, but in nearby Soave also. The very consistent wines have a solid structure. Campo dei Gigli is the house champion, an Amarone that even with the 2012 vintage stands out as one of the designation's most impressive. Dense to the eye and nose, it lays out a melange of sweet ripe berry fruit, spice, and thyme, then builds a palate of huge yet vibrant concentration that leads into a lengthy, dry finish. La Bandina 2012 is a Valpolicella that is compact and vigorous.

● Amarone della Valpolicella Campo dei Gigli '12	🍷🍷🍷 8
● Valpolicella Sup. La Bandina '12	🍷🍷 5
● Amarone della Valpolicella Sel. Antonio Castagnedi '13	🍷🍷 6
○ Soave Monte Ceriani '14	🍷🍷 3
○ Soave V. V. '14	🍷🍷 3
● Valpolicella Sup. Ripasso Monti Garbi '14	🍷🍷 3
● Amarone della Valpolicella Campo dei Gigli '11	🍷🍷🍷 8
● Amarone della Valpolicella Campo dei Gigli '10	🍷🍷🍷 8
● Amarone della Valpolicella Campo dei Gigli '08	🍷🍷🍷 8
● Amarone della Valpolicella Campo dei Gigli '07	🍷🍷🍷 8
● Amarone della Valpolicella Campo dei Gigli '06	🍷🍷🍷 8

Santa Margherita

VIA ITA MARZOTTO, 8
30025 FOSSALTA DI PORTOGRUARO [VE]
TEL. +39 0421246111
www.santamargherita.com

CELLAR SALES
PRE-BOOKED VISITS
ANNUAL PRODUCTION 13,500,000 bottles
HECTARES UNDER VINE 50.00

The large Marzotto family operation has taken a sharp change of direction in its wine portfolio over the last ten years. Every detail received careful attention: first the estate vineyards, today covering some 50 hectares, then the new cellar, and now the entire historical complex in Fossalta di Portogruaro. Their efforts have been significant on the sparkling wine stage as well, where they strive to coax the maximum expression from their Prosecco grapes. It is Valdobbiadene that brings the most impressive performances, such as Rive di Refrontolo 2015, with clean, fragrant notes of pear and wisteria, and an admirably compact palate. Luna dei Feldi 2015 is excellent too, an aromatic blend of Alto Adige vineyards, releasing citrus and black liquorice heightened by a crisp florality. In the mouth, one enjoys its complexity, vibrant flavours, and taut grip.

○ A. A. Bianco Luna dei Feldi '15	▼▼ 3
○ A. A. Pinot Grigio Impronta del Fondatore '15	▼▼ 2*
○ Cartizze	▼▼ 4
○ Valdobbiadene Extra Dry 52	▼▼ 2*
○ Valdobbiadene Rive di Refrontolo Brut 52 '15	▼▼ 3
● Lison-Pramaggiore Malbech Impronta del Fondatore '14	▼ 2
● Lison-Pramaggiore Refosco P.R. Impronta del Fondatore '14	▼ 2
○ Lison-Pramaggiore Verduzzo Passito Dulcedo '11	▼ 3
○ Valdadige Pinot Grigio '15	▼ 2
○ Valdobbiadene Brut	▼ 2
● Venezia Cabernet Franc Impronta del Fondatore '14	▼ 2

Santa Sofia

FRAZ. PEDEMONTE DI VALPOLICELLA
VIA CA' DEDÉ, 61
37029 SAN PIETRO IN CARIANO [VR]
TEL. +39 0457701074
www.santasofia.com

CELLAR SALES
PRE-BOOKED VISITS
ANNUAL PRODUCTION 550,000 bottles
HECTARES UNDER VINE 38.00

After years of winegrowing, Luciano Begnoni imposed a sharp turn on his family winery. The purchase of a large property in Valpantena finally gives Santa Sofia some dozen hectares, only partially planted and constituting the first step for finally having available large quantities of its own grapes. A renewed winemaking approach took hold some time ago, resulting in wines that are still in line with tradition but also crisp and impressive. Amarone 2011 is an example of this change, brimming with fragrant impressions of very ripe yet still crunchy red berry, then a firmly-built palate with no hint of sweetness. It concludes with a vibrant, clean finish. Valpolicella Classico showed extremely well, despite the challenging 2014 harvest; the fruit of a year of ageing is a superb nose and seductive palate.

● Amarone della Valpolicella Cl. '11	▼▼ 7
● Valpolicella Cl. '14	▼▼ 2*
● Valpolicella Sup. Ripasso '13	▼▼ 4
● Amarone della Valpolicella Cl. '09	♈♈ 7
● Amarone della Valpolicella Cl. '08	♈♈ 6
● Amarone della Valpolicella Cl. '07	♈♈ 6
● Amarone della Valpolicella Cl. '06	♈♈ 6
● Amarone della Valpolicella Cl. Gioé '07	♈♈ 7
○ Lugana '12	♈♈ 2*
● Valpolicella Cl. Sup. Montegradella '11	♈♈ 4
● Valpolicella Cl. Sup. Montegradella '08	♈♈ 4
● Valpolicella Sup. Ripasso '12	♈♈ 4
● Valpolicella Sup. Ripasso '10	♈♈ 4

Santi

VIA UNGHERIA, 33
37031 ILLASI [VR]
TEL. +39 0456269600
www.carlosanti.it

CELLAR SALES
PRE-BOOKED VISITS
ANNUAL PRODUCTION 1,400,000 bottles
HECTARES UNDER VINE 50.00

Santi, owned by Gruppo Italiano Vini, has seen some recent developments, chief among them the arrival at the helm of Cristian Ridolfi. The respected oenologist has a deep understanding of the local area and its traditions, so the winery clearly intend to recover its former well-deserved prominence. The cellar is based in Illasi, in eastern Valpolicella, but it works vineyards in both the classic zone and further afield, offering rigorous, classic wines. When Amarone Proemio, the house champion, was not presented, Solane 2014 commanded our attention. This Ripasso always regales us with cleanly-delineated fruit, whose effect is notably heightened by spice and a note of crisp herbaceousness. The palate eschews power and opulence in favour of suppleness and a taut crispness, resulting in superb drinkability. Amarone Classico 2011 features more up-front, smooth fruit, and a juicy richness in the mouth.

● Amarone della Valpolicella Cl. '11	♟♟	6
● Bardolino Cl. Ca' Bordenis '15	♟♟	2*
● Valpolicella Cl. Sup. Ripasso Solane '14	♟♟	4
○ Lugana Melibeo '15	♟	3
● Amarone della Valpolicella Proemio '05	♟♟♟	6
● Amarone della Valpolicella Proemio '03	♟♟♟	6
● Amarone della Valpolicella Proemio '00	♟♟♟	5
● Valpolicella Cl. Sup. Ripasso Solane '09	♟♟♟	3*
● Amarone della Valpolicella Cl. '10	♟♟	6
● Amarone della Valpolicella Cl. '09	♟♟	6
● Amarone della Valpolicella Cl. Proemio '10	♟♟	7
● Bardolino Cl. Ca' Bordenis '14	♟♟	2*
○ Lugana Melibeo '14	♟♟	2*
● Valpolicella Cl. Le Caleselle '13	♟♟	2*
● Valpolicella Cl. Sup. Ripasso Solane '13	♟♟	4
● Valpolicella Cl. Sup. Ripasso Solane '12	♟♟	4

Casa Vinicola Sartori

FRAZ. SANTA MARIA
VIA CASETTE, 4
37024 NEGRAR [VR]
TEL. +39 0456028011
www.sartorinet.com

PRE-BOOKED VISITS
ANNUAL PRODUCTION 15,600,000 bottles
HECTARES UNDER VINE 120.00

Valpolicella comprises producers of every stripe, from the small grower just beginning to bottle their own wine, to the large cooperatives, and, of course, to wineries who have their own vineyards but buy in grapes from trusted grape growers. Sartori, in Santa Maria di Negrar, is one of the latter, cultivating more than 100 hectares and producing several millions of bottles per year. The Sartori family's line-up was smaller this year, but it was led by a superb Amarone Corte Brà 2009. Macerated flower extract and pungent forest floor enliven super-ripe fruit on the nose, and a crisp vein of tasty acidity drives a notably spacious palate. Regolo 2013 is a Ripasso marked by crisp, youthful aromas and delicious drinkability. The estate in eastern Valpolicella produced a rich, complex Amarone I Saltari 2009.

● Amarone della Valpolicella Cl. Corte Brà '09	♟♟	7
● Amarone della Valpolicella I Saltari '09	♟♟	8
● Valpolicella Sup. Ripasso Regolo '13	♟♟	4
○ Lugana La Musina '15	♟	4
○ Marani '14	♟	3
● Recioto della Valpolicella Cl. Rerum '13	♟	6
○ Recioto di Soave Vernus '14	♟	4
○ Soave Cl. Sella '15	♟	2
● Amarone della Valpolicella Cl. Reius '10	♟♟	7
● Amarone della Valpolicella Cl. Reius '09	♟♟	7
● Valpolicella Cl. Sup. Montegradella '12	♟♟	3
● Valpolicella Cl. Sup. Vign. di Montegradella '11	♟♟	3
● Valpolicella Sup. I Saltari '11	♟♟	4
● Valpolicella Sup. Ripasso Regolo '12	♟♟	3

Secondo Marco

v.le Campolongo, 9
37022 Fumane [VR]
Tel. +39 0456800954
www.secondomarco.it

PRE-BOOKED VISITS
ANNUAL PRODUCTION 50,000 bottles
HECTARES UNDER VINE 15.00

Some ten or so years back, Marco Speri left his family's winery to found Secondo Marco, a fine operation in the heart of Valpolicella Classica. His 15 or so hectares of grapes drive a constantly-growing production and testify to his ability in interpreting this growing area and its traditions. His wines, all of high quality, showcase the taut palates and delicate character of the traditional grapes, even when he practices raisining. The Amarone is still resting in the cellar, but Ripasso 2013 unleashed a truly stellar performance. Its appearance, not excessively dense, presages a version faithful to tradition, confirmed by red fruit that, while central, does not predominate; rather, cherry gradually yields sway to spice and wild herbs. The palate is solidly-constructed, with a firm acidity giving it excellent support all the way to a lengthy conclusion.

● Valpolicella Cl. Sup. Ripasso '13	▼▼ 5
● Valpolicella Cl. '14	▼▼ 3
● Amarone della Valpolicella Cl. '10	♈7
● Amarone della Valpolicella Cl. '09	♈7
● Amarone della Valpolicella Cl. '08	♈7
● Amarone della Valpolicella Cl. '07	♈7
● Recioto della Valpolicella Cl. '12	♈6
● Recioto della Valpolicella Cl. '11	♈6
● Recioto della Valpolicella Cl. '10	♈6
● Recioto della Valpolicella Cl. '10	♈6
● Valpolicella Cl. '13	♈3
● Valpolicella Cl. '12	♈2*
● Valpolicella Cl. '11	♈3
● Valpolicella Cl. Sup. Ripasso '12	♈5
● Valpolicella Cl. Sup. Ripasso '11	♈4
● Valpolicella Cl. Sup. Ripasso '10	♈4
● Valpolicella Cl. Sup. Ripasso '09	♈4

★Serafini & Vidotto

via Luigi Carrer, 8
31040 Nervesa della Battaglia [TV]
Tel. +39 0422773281
www.serafinividotto.it

CELLAR SALES
PRE-BOOKED VISITS
ANNUAL PRODUCTION 250,000 bottles
HECTARES UNDER VINE 23.00
SUSTAINABLE WINERY

Montello is a hillock enclosed on the south by the Po River valley and by the River Piave to the north, which also separate it from the Treviso Pre-Alps. Francesco Serafini and Antonello Vidotto chose this area for one of Veneto's most influential wineries. Focusing on Bordeaux blends, the wines are both faithful and original expressions of the varieties. The iron oxide-rich soils allow the grapes to ripen well while maintaining a fine acidic grip, which translates into wines that are elegant, sharply-delineated, and never over-muscled. World-class as usual, Rosso dell'Abazia 2013 is a predominantly cabernet sauvignon Bordeaux blend that makes a superb show of the expertise and passion of Francesco and Antonello. The nose opens slowly, juicy, pulpy fruit the first to appear, then impressions of pungent forest floor, sweet violets, and thyme. It shows admirably judicious volume in the mouth, relying on vibrant flavours and a nervy acidity. Phigaia 2013 and Bianco 2015 are solid performers, the former crisp and energetic, the second beautifully balanced and enticing.

● Montello e Colli Asolani Il Rosso dell'Abazia '13	▼▼▼ 6
○ Il Bianco '15	▼▼ 3
○ Montello e Colli Asolani Manzoni Bianco '15	▼▼ 2*
● Montello e Colli Asolani Phigaia '13	▼▼ 4
● Montello e Colli Asolani Recantina '15	▼▼ 3
● Pinot Nero '13	▼▼ 6
● Pinot Nero Giovane '14	▼▼ 6
☉ Bollicine Rosé Brut	▼ 3
○ P. di Treviso Extra Dry Bollicine di Prosecco	▼ 2
● Montello e Colli Asolani Il Rosso dell'Abazia '12	♈5
● Montello e Colli Asolani Il Rosso dell'Abazia '11	♈6
● Montello e Colli Asolani Il Rosso dell'Abazia '10	♈5

★Viticoltori Speri

LOC. PEDEMONTE
VIA FONTANA, 14
37029 SAN PIETRO IN CARIANO [VR]
TEL. +39 0457701154
www.speri.com

I Stefanini

VIA CROSARA, 21
37032 MONTEFORTE D'ALPONE [VR]
TEL. +39 0456175249
www.istefanini.it

CELLAR SALES
PRE-BOOKED VISITS
ANNUAL PRODUCTION 350,000 bottles
HECTARES UNDER VINE 60.00
VITICULTURE METHOD Certified Organic
SUSTAINABLE WINERY

CELLAR SALES
PRE-BOOKED VISITS
ANNUAL PRODUCTION 100,000 bottles
HECTARES UNDER VINE 17.00

The Speri family, one of Valpolicella's long-time producers, has been distributing the designation's wines throughout the world for some time now, and at the same time has always contributed to preserving local traditions. They organically farm some 60 hectares, which include prestigious parcels such as the famed Monte Sant'Urbano, a hill dividing the Fumane and Marano valleys, which supplies gapes for the most ambitious wines. The Speri wines are always among the designation's most impressive, and Amarone Sant'Urbano 2012 is their standout this year. Pulpy, self-confident red berry fruit predominates on the nose, but essence of macerated flowers and black pepper manage to appear as well. A zesty acidity and vigorous tannins combine to ensure a judicious dimension to the palate. Valpolicella Superiore 2014is solid and taut, and Recioto La Roggia 2013 displays more intense fruit and is truly enthralling in the mouth.

After only 15 or so years in business, Francesco Tessari's wines are much sought-after by fans of rich, powerful Soaves. What makes all this possible are some 20 hectares of outstanding vineyards lying partly in the level areas of the designation and partly on the hillslopes overlooking the cellar. The vines, all garganega, are trained to the traditional Verona pergola system. The line privileges three labels, all Soaves, whose hallmarks are a ripe, full richness. Soave Monte de Toni 2015 was at the top of our scorecard, bursting with apricot, yellow peach, and melon, all ripe and succulent, further enriched by dried flower petals and a hint of earthy mineral. In the mouth, the volume is nicely checked by a tasty acidic grip that brought the wine almost up to our highest award. Superiore Monte di Fice 2015, on the other hand, matches more complex aromatics with a firmly-built palate of surpassing energy.

● Amarone della Valpolicella Cl. Vign. Monte Sant'Urbano '12	▼▼▼ 7
● Recioto della Valpolicella La Roggia '13	▼▼ 6
● Valpolicella Cl. Sup. Sant'Urbano '13	▼▼ 4
● Valpolicella Cl. '15	▼ 3
● Amarone della Valpolicella Cl. Vign. Monte Sant'Urbano '09	▽▽▽ 7
● Amarone della Valpolicella Cl. Vign. Monte Sant'Urbano '08	▽▽▽ 7
● Amarone della Valpolicella Cl. Vign. Monte Sant'Urbano '07	▽▽▽ 7
● Amarone della Valpolicella Cl. Vign. Monte Sant'Urbano '06	▽▽▽ 7
● Amarone della Valpolicella Cl. Vign. Monte Sant'Urbano '04	▽▽▽ 7
● Amarone della Valpolicella Cl. Vign. Sant'Urbano '11	▽▽▽ 7

○ Soave Cl. Monte de Toni '15	▼▼ 2*
○ Soave Cl. Sup. Monte di Fice '15	▼▼ 3
○ Soave Il Selese '15	▼ 1*
○ Soave Cl. Monte de Toni '12	▽▽▽ 2*
○ Soave Cl. Sup. Monte di Fice '07	▽▽▽ 2*
○ Soave Cl. Monte de Toni '14	▽▽ 2*
○ Soave Cl. Monte de Toni '13	▽▽ 2*
○ Soave Cl. Monte de Toni '11	▽▽ 2*
○ Soave Cl. Monte de Toni '08	▽▽ 2*
○ Soave Cl. Monte di Fice '14	▽▽ 3
○ Soave Cl. Monte di Fice '10	▽▽ 2*
○ Soave Cl. Sup. Monte di Fice '13	▽▽ 3*
○ Soave Cl. Sup. Monte di Fice '12	▽▽ 3*
○ Soave Il Selese '14	▽▽ 1*
○ Soave Il Selese '12	▽▽ 1*
○ Soave Il Selese '11	▽▽ 1*
○ Soave Il Selese '10	▽▽ 1*

David Sterza

VIA CASTERNA, 37
37022 FUMANE [VR]
TEL. +39 0457704201
www.davidsterza.it

CELLAR SALES
PRE-BOOKED VISITS
ANNUAL PRODUCTION 30,000 bottles
HECTARES UNDER VINE 4.50

David Sterza and Paolo Mascanzoni direct this modest family operation located in Casterna, a hamlet in Fumane enfolded by the Valpolicella hills. Their few hectares of hillslope vineyards are used for a line of wines classic to the area, and winemaking is also carried out along traditional lines, with some reinterpretation. The resultant wines privilege richness and structure, fruit of the raising process, but without sacrificing character and tautness. Amarone 2012 greets the eye with an intense, compact ruby, presaging equally intense wild berry and mint, essence of macerated flowers and spice, in an aromatic mosaic of ever-changing combinations. The dry palate impresses with its density and power, yet it remains eminently drinkable and delicious. Ripasso 2014 lays out somewhat the same aromatic array, but the palate is a bit lighter, of course. We note the fine performance as well of Valpolicella 2015.

● Amarone della Valpolicella Cl. '12	▼▼▼	6
● Recioto della Valpolicella Cl. '14	▼▼	5
● Valpolicella Cl. Sup. Ripasso '14	▼▼	3
● Valpolicella Cl. '15	▼	2
● Amarone della Valpolicella Cl. '11	♀♀	6
● Amarone della Valpolicella Cl. '10	♀♀	6
● Amarone della Valpolicella Cl. '09	♀♀	6
● Amarone della Valpolicella Cl. '08	♀♀	6
● Recioto della Valpolicella Cl. '13	♀♀	5
● Recioto della Valpolicella Cl. '12	♀♀	5
● Valpolicella Cl. '14	♀♀	2*
● Valpolicella Cl. '13	♀♀	2*
● Valpolicella Cl. '12	♀♀	2*
● Valpolicella Cl. Sup. Ripasso '13	♀♀	3*
● Valpolicella Cl. Sup. Ripasso '12	♀♀	3
● Valpolicella Cl. Sup. Ripasso '11	♀♀	3
● Valpolicella Cl. Sup. Ripasso '10	♀♀	3

★Suavia

FRAZ. FITTÀ DI SOAVE
VIA CENTRO, 14
37038 SOAVE [VR]
TEL. +39 0457675089
www.suavia.it

CELLAR SALES
PRE-BOOKED VISITS
ANNUAL PRODUCTION 100,000 bottles
HECTARES UNDER VINE 12.00

Over the last 20 years, Suavia, under the direction of Meri, Valentina, and Alessandra, has become a benchmark for lovers of Verona's white wine. Their winery, deep in the Soave DOC hills, grows only historical varieties, with respect for the environment, and vineyard management improvements aligned with local traditions. Their winemaking approach aims to showcase the grape's assertive but refined character. The cool-weather 2014 season means that Soave Monte Carbonare displays intense, vibrant aromatics, with a lovely florality emerging initially, seguing slowly into apple and pear, along with a delicate note of citrus. It expands in the mouth with considerable energy and a crisp, refreshing acidity, to close with a lengthy, richly-flavoured finale. The Trebbiano Massifitti 2013 is more complex on the nose, then dry and perfectly proportioned in the mouth.

○ Soave Cl. Monte Carbonare '14	▼▼▼	3*
○ Massifitti '13	▼▼	3*
○ Le Rive '12	▼▼	4
○ Soave Cl. '15	▼▼	2*
○ Opera Semplice Dosaggio Zero M. Cl.	▼	4
○ Soave Cl. Le Rive '02	♀♀♀	4
○ Soave Cl. Monte Carbonare '12	♀♀♀	3*
○ Soave Cl. Monte Carbonare '11	♀♀♀	3*
○ Soave Cl. Monte Carbonare '10	♀♀♀	3*
○ Soave Cl. Monte Carbonare '09	♀♀♀	3*
○ Soave Cl. Monte Carbonare '08	♀♀♀	3*
○ Soave Cl. Monte Carbonare '07	♀♀♀	3*
○ Soave Cl. Monte Carbonare '06	♀♀♀	3*
○ Soave Cl. Monte Carbonare '05	♀♀♀	3*
○ Soave Cl. Monte Carbonare '04	♀♀♀	3
○ Soave Cl. Monte Carbonare '02	♀♀♀	3
○ Soave Cl. Sup. Le Rive '00	♀♀♀	4

Sutto

LOC. CAMPO DI PIETRA
VIA ARZERI, 34/1
31040 SALGAREDA [TV]
TEL. +39 0422744063
www.sutto.it

CELLAR SALES
PRE-BOOKED VISITS
ACCOMMODATION AND RESTAURANT SERVICE
ANNUAL PRODUCTION 153,000 bottles
HECTARES UNDER VINE 75.00

Indefatigable businessmen Stefano and
Luigi Sutto ably combine their agricultural
endeavours with other business activities.
The family winery in Salgareda has grown
mightily over the last few years, allowing
the brothers to dedicate just their best fruit
to their own wine portfolio and to send the
considerable remainder to other bottlers.
They produce wines from the Venetian
plains, but place great emphasis on
Prosecco, particularly on those grown in
the historic hills of Valdobbiadene. This
year definitely continues recent years'
growth in quality, as demonstrated by the
excellent Campo Sella, the cellar's iconic
wine sourced from the family's finest
merlot vineyard. Sweet, ripe fruit is on
generous display, and a classy suite of
tannins complements the spacious palate
and supports it into a lengthy finale. Among
the whites, our favourite was the
cleanly-aromatic Chardonnay 2015. We
were pleased to note the soundness of the
more uncomplicated wines as well, all
fragrant and delicious.

● Campo Sella '13	♟♟ 5
● Cabernet '15	♟♟ 2*
○ Chardonnay '15	♟♟ 2*
● Dogma Rosso '14	♟♟ 4
● Merlot '15	♟♟ 2*
○ Ultimo Passito '14	♟♟ 4
○ Valdobbiadene Extra Dry Batiso	♟♟ 3
○ Bianco di Sutto '15	♟ 2
○ Pinot Grigio '15	♟ 2
○ Prosecco Brut Batiso	♟ 2
○ Prosecco Extra Dry Batiso	♟ 2
● Cabernet '14	♟♟ 2*
● Campo Sella '12	♟♟ 5
○ Chardonnay '14	♟♟ 2*
● Dogma Rosso '12	♟♟ 4
○ Pinot Grigio '14	♟♟ 2*

T.E.S.S.A.R.I.

LOC. BROGNOLIGO
VIA FONTANA NUOVA, 86
37032 MONTEFORTE D'ALPONE [VR]
TEL. +39 0456176041
www.cantinatessari.com

CELLAR SALES
PRE-BOOKED VISITS
ANNUAL PRODUCTION 40,000 bottles
HECTARES UNDER VINE 17.00

The Tessari family, bearing one of the most
common surnames in the world of
Monteforte d'Alpone wine, manage their
operation in Brognoligo, in the heart of the
classic zone. They have just under 20
hectares planted to garganega and wine
production is still modest, allowing
Cornelia, Antonio, and Germano to work
with just the finest quality and sell the rest
to other local wineries. The best vineyards
are in Costalta, where some rows extend
for almost 400 metres, hence the wine
called Soave Bine Longhe, a late-harvest
garganega that is given a lengthy
maturation in steel in the cellar in Via
Fontana Nuova. The 2013 season gifts us
with a superb, luminous version of this
white, offering up richly-scented apricot,
yellow peach, and dried flower petals, then
a vein of gunflint that slowly grows more
prominent. In the mouth, an energy-laden,
tasty acidity sculpts and complements rich
fruit. Grisela 2015 is crisper, fruitier, and
more straightforward, a gorgeous,
well-balanced white for enjoying right now.

○ Soave Cl. Bine Longhe '13	♟♟ 3*
○ Recioto di Soave Tre Colli '13	♟♟ 5
○ Soave Cl. Grisela '15	♟♟ 2*
○ Garganega Brut	♟ 3
○ Soave Cl. Grisela '14	♟♟ 2*
○ Soave Cl. Grisela '13	♟♟ 2*
○ Soave Cl. Grisela '12	♟♟ 2*
○ Soave Cl. Grisela '11	♟♟ 2*
○ Soave Cl. Grisela '08	♟♟ 2*
○ Soave Cl. Grisela '07	♟♟ 2*
○ Soave Cl. Le Bine Longhe '10	♟♟ 5*
○ Soave Cl. Le Bine Longhe di Costalta '12	♟♟ 3
○ Soave Cl. Le Bine Longhe di Costalta '11	♟♟ 3

Tamellini

FRAZ. COSTEGGIOLA
VIA TAMELLINI, 4
37038 SOAVE [VR]
TEL. +39 0457675328
piofrancesco.tamellini@tin.it

CELLAR SALES
PRE-BOOKED VISITS
ANNUAL PRODUCTION 250,000 bottles
HECTARES UNDER VINE 27.00

The winery operation belonging to the Tamellini brothers now has almost 30 hectares of vineyard, planted solely to garganega, undisputed queen of this area. Over the years, Gaetano and Pio Francesco have added the Guyot training system to the traditional local pergola, without harming the profile of their Soave wines in the least. They strive for a seamless marriage of freshness and delicacy to character and depth. Their cellar is in Costeggiola, the extreme west of the classic zone, works only with stainless steel tanks. Annual production of each wine here is quite limited, but each is an eloquent expression of its terroir and vineyards. Le Bine de Costiola is a magisterial Soave Classico, redolent of citrus, apple, and pear; despite its cold 2014 season, it is a full-volumed, succulent delight, one of the designation's most impressive representatives. Soave 2015, on the other hand, displays more straightforward, juicy fruit, but this, too, translates into an appealing, joyous wine.

○ Soave Cl. Le Bine de Costiola '14	▼▼▼ 3*
○ Soave '15	▼▼ 2*
○ Soave Cl. Le Bine '04	♀♀♀ 3*
○ Soave Cl. Le Bine de Costiola '13	♀♀♀ 3*
○ Soave Cl. Le Bine de Costiola '11	♀♀♀ 3*
○ Soave Cl. Le Bine de Costiola '06	♀♀♀ 3*
○ Soave Cl. Le Bine de Costiola '05	♀♀♀ 3*
○ Soave '14	♀♀ 2*
○ Soave '11	♀♀ 2*
○ Soave Cl. '13	♀♀ 2*
○ Soave Cl. '12	♀♀ 2*
○ Soave Cl. Le Bine de Costiola '12	♀♀ 3*
○ Soave Cl. Le Bine de Costiola '10	♀♀ 3*
○ Soave Cl. Le Bine de Costiola '09	♀♀ 3*
○ Soave Cl. Le Bine de Costiola '08	♀♀ 3*

F.lli Tedeschi

FRAZ. PEDEMONTE
VIA G. VERDI, 4
37029 SAN PIETRO IN CARIANO [VR]
TEL. +39 0457701487
www.tedeschiwines.com

CELLAR SALES
PRE-BOOKED VISITS
ANNUAL PRODUCTION 500,000 bottles
HECTARES UNDER VINE 46.00
SUSTAINABLE WINERY

Tedeschi's focus has shifted eastwards, and the splendid Maternigo property, between Tregnago and Mezzane, is receiving increasing attention. Here, two hectares of olives and a full 50 hectares of woods separate about 50 hectares of vineyard from the other properties, making it possible to manage the vines with total respect for the environment. The winemaking remains as focused as ever on the traditional wines, here expressed in a rich yet austere style. Produced only in the finest growing years, Amarone La Fabriseria is an exemplar of both richness and austerity, and this 2011 turns in a performance to remember. True, its aromas seem still untamed and need further tempering, but the palate reveals its true breed: power, richness, and self-confidence, not to mention a perfect duet between alcohol and tannin. Valpolicella Maternigo 2013 is excellent as well, superbly-knit on both nose and palate.

● Amarone della Valpolicella Cl. La Fabriseria Ris. '11	▼▼▼ 8
● Amarone della Valpolicella Cl. Capitel Monte Olmi Ris. '10	▼▼ 8
● Valpolicella Sup. Maternigo '13	▼▼ 4
● Amarone della Valpolicella Cl. '12	▼▼ 6
● Recioto della Valpolicella Cl. Capitel Fontana '11	▼▼ 6
● Valpolicella Cl. Lucchine '15	▼▼ 2*
● Valpolicella Cl. Sup. La Fabriseria '12	▼▼ 5
● Valpolicella Sup. Capitel Nicolò '14	▼▼ 3
● Valpolicella Sup. Ripasso Capitel San Rocco '14	▼▼ 4
● Amarone della Valpolicella Cl. Capitel Monte Olmi '07	♀♀♀ 8
● Amarone della Valpolicella Cl. Capitel Monte Olmi '95	♀♀♀ 8
● Valpolicella Sup. Maternigo '11	♀♀♀ 4*

Le Tende

VIA TENDE, 35
37017 LAZISE [VR]
TEL. +39 0457590748
www.letende.it

CELLAR SALES
PRE-BOOKED VISITS
ANNUAL PRODUCTION 100,000 bottles
HECTARES UNDER VINE 12.50
VITICULTURE METHOD Certified Organic

The process of renewal now taking place in Bardolino is particularly impressive in wineries such as that of the Fortuna and Lucillini families. Mauro Fortuna organically farms some ten hectares, planted mostly to Lake Garda's traditional varieties, with a few internationals as well. The wines here exhibit the typical savoury freshness that are the hallmarks of many of the area's whites and reds. Corvina 2015 performed superbly, a perfect expression both of Mauro's concept of wine and of the quality potential of this growing area. Aromatic wild berry fruit, underbrush, and black pepper abound, and in the mouth it expands with delicacy into a savoury, succulent delight. Custoza, on the other hand, is the child of the 2015 harvest, with ripe apple and pear that flow onto a generous palate of pronounced vibrancy. High marks go to Bardolino Superiore 2014 as well, for its spicy nose and fine all-round proportion in the mouth.

● Bardolino Cl. Sup. '14	♟♟ 3
● Cicisbeo '13	♟♟ 4
● Corvina '15	♟♟ 3
○ Custoza '15	♟♟ 2*
⊙ Bardolino Chiaretto Brut Voluttà	♟ 3
⊙ Bardolino Chiaretto Cl. '15	♟ 2
● Bardolino Cl. '15	♟ 2
● Lucillini '15	♟ 3
● Bardolino Cl. '14	♟♟ 2*
● Bardolino Cl. '13	♟♟ 2*
● Bardolino Cl. Sup. '12	♟♟ 2*
● Bardolino Cl. Sup. '11	♟♟ 2*
● Bardolino Cl. Sup. '10	♟♟ 2*
○ Bianco di Custoza Lucillini '12	♟♟ 2*
● Cicisbeo '12	♟♟ 3
○ Custoza '14	♟♟ 2*

Viticoltori Tommasi

LOC. PEDEMONTE
VIA RONCHETTO, 2
37020 SAN PIETRO IN CARIANO [VR]
TEL. +39 0457701266
www.tommasiwine.it

CELLAR SALES
PRE-BOOKED VISITS
ANNUAL PRODUCTION 1,000,000 bottles
HECTARES UNDER VINE 162.00

Before looking at Tommasi as a wine operation, it has to be considered as a family that has always been deeply rooted in Valpolicella and committed to its protection and promotion on many fronts. The family's viticultural activities are impressive, with over 160 hectares of vineyard extending from Valpolicella Classica to the shores of Lake Garda. Giancarlo, in charge of winemaking, turns out wines that respect traditions yet show a contemporary edge and great refinement. Emerging after seven long years of ageing, Amarone Ca' Florian Riserva meets all expectations, revealing itself as a wine of superb depth. It releases sweet, super-ripe red berry and cherry fruit, veined with impressions of spice and mineral, on the way to a palate that is at once dense-packed, forceful, and agile. Amarone 2012 was impressive as well, somewhat crisper on the nose, with plenty of succulent fruit on a palate of some elegance.

● Amarone della Valpolicella Cl. Ca' Florian Ris. '09	♟♟ 7
● Amarone della Valpolicella Cl. '12	♟♟ 7
● Valpolicella Cl. Sup. Rafael '14	♟♟ 4
● Valpolicella Cl. Sup. Ripasso '14	♟♟ 4
● Recioto della Valpolicella Cl. Fiorato '13	♟ 4
● Amarone della Valpolicella Cl. '10	♟♟ 7
● Amarone della Valpolicella Cl. Ca' Florian Ris. '08	♟♟ 7
○ Lugana Il Sestante '14	♟♟ 2*
○ Lugana Le Fornaci '14	♟♟ 2*
○ Lugana Vign. San Martino Il Sestante '13	♟♟ 2*
● Valpolicella Cl. Sup. Rafael '13	♟♟ 4
● Valpolicella Cl. Sup. Rafael '12	♟♟ 3
● Valpolicella Cl. Sup. Ripasso '13	♟♟ 4
● Valpolicella Cl. Sup. Ripasso '12	♟♟ 4

Trabucchi d'Illasi

LOC. MONTE TENDA
37031 ILLASI [VR]
TEL. +39 0457833233
www.trabucchidillasi.it

CELLAR SALES
PRE-BOOKED VISITS
ANNUAL PRODUCTION 120,000 bottles
HECTARES UNDER VINE 25.00
VITICULTURE METHOD Certified Organic

Giuseppe and Raffaella Trabucchi have brought the world's attention to eastern Valpolicella, fortunate to have extensive vineyards and a consistent production of wines that are exquisite ambassadors of local traditions. They began organic viticulture before many even heard of it, and have always believed in non-invasive practices, as well as in letting their wines mature in their own time, releasing them only when ready. At that point, their wines display a rich intensity on the palate. Amarone 2008, presented only after a lengthy ageing, offers multi-layered aromatics that are quite reluctant to reveal their charms. Red berry and cherry, sweet and pulpy, emerge initially, then seem to stand aside, giving room to more delicate, complex impressions, now of spice, now of wild herbs. In the mouth, full body and dynamic thrust perfectly complement each other, bolstered by a backbone of acidity and the glossiest of tannins.

Spumanti Valdo

VIA FORO BOARIO, 20
31049 VALDOBBIADENE [TV]
TEL. +39 04239090
www.valdo.com

CELLAR SALES
PRE-BOOKED VISITS
ANNUAL PRODUCTION 9,000,000 bottles
HECTARES UNDER VINE 155.00

This great sparkling wine house, one of the most influential in the Valdobbiadene zone, which traces its origins back almost a century, is still directed by the Bolla family, today represented by Pierluigi. Its wines, of admirable consistency, are very expressive of the hillslope growing areas of the designation, due largely to the grapes that are brought in from a dense network of trusted growers. La Cuvée 1926, an Extra Dry Prosecco, showcases the intense expressiveness of its fruit, with apple and pear alternating against a background of notably crisp florality. The mouth, on the other hand, displays a notable equilibrium of sweetness, acidity, and mousse, a harmony that creates a succulent, appealing delight. Cuvée del Fondatore is unusual in that the cuvée contains some barrel-aged base wine. Complex yet bright on the nose, full flavours in the mouth are superbly supported by its mousse.

● Amarone della Valpolicella Alberto Trabucchi Ris. '08	▼▼ 8
● Recioto della Valpolicella '07	▼▼ 7
● Valpolicella Sup. Terre di S. Colombano '09	▼▼ 3
● Valpolicella Un Anno '15	▼▼ 2*
● Valpolicella Sup. La Gardellina '13	▼ 4
● Amarone della Valpolicella '06	♀♀♀ 8
● Amarone della Valpolicella '04	♀♀♀ 8
● Recioto della Valpolicella Cereolo '05	♀♀♀ 8
● Valpolicella Sup. Terre di S. Colombano '03	♀♀♀ 4*
● Valpolicella Sup. La Gardellina '12	♀♀ 4
● Valpolicella Sup. Terre del Cereolo '08	♀♀ 5
● Valpolicella Sup. Terre di S. Colombano '08	♀♀ 3

○ Valdobbiadene Brut Cuvée del Fondatore '14	▼▼ 3
○ Valdobbiadene Extra Dry Cuvée 1926	▼▼ 2
○ Cartizze Cuvée Viviana	▼ 5
○ Numero 10 Brut M. Cl. '11	▼ 4
○ Valdo 90 Brut M. Cl. '11	▼ 3
○ Valdobbiadene Brut Cuvée di Boj	▼ 2
○ Numero 10 Brut M. Cl. '10	♀♀ 4
○ Valdobbiadene Cuvée del Fondatore '13	♀♀ 3

Cantina Valpantena Verona

LOC. QUINTO
VIA COLONIA ORFANI DI GUERRA, 5B
37142 VERONA
TEL. +39 045550032
www.cantinavalpantena.it

CELLAR SALES
PRE-BOOKED VISITS
ANNUAL PRODUCTION 8,000,000 bottles
HECTARES UNDER VINE 750.00

Valpantena is the only subzone permitted
in the Valpolicella designation, testifying to
the importance this valley has enjoyed
down through the ages. The cooperative,
under the guidance of Luca Degani,
controls through its members, more than
700 hectares, which supply the grapes
both for the traditional wines as well as for
lighter, more fragrant offerings. Recioto
Tesauro 2012 expresses fragrant red berry
and cherry, sweet, fleshy, and inviting, with
the clean-edged cherry impressively
framed by notes of black pepper and
macerated-flower oil. All of this we find
clearly operative on a dense-packed
palate characterized by an exuberant,
yet beautifully integrated sweetness,
along with an acidity that provides delicacy
and a crisp edge. We applaud Amarone
Torre del Falasco 2012, youthfully aromatic
and self-confidently delicious. Valpantena
yielded Ritocco 2014, s well-balanced
Valpolicella.

● Amarone della Valpolicella Torre del Falasco '12	🍷🍷 6
● Recioto della Valpolicella Tesauro '12	🍷🍷 5
● Valpolicella Valpantena Ritocco '14	🍷🍷 3
● Amarone della Valpolicella '13	🍷 5
○ Chardonnay Baroncino '15	🍷 2
● Corvina Torre del Falasco '15	🍷 1*
○ Garganega Torre del Falasco '15	🍷 1*
○ Lugana Torre del Falasco '15	🍷 2
● Valpolicella Sup. Ripasso Torre del Falasco '14	🍷 3
● Valpolicella Sup. Torre del Falasco '14	🍷 2
● Amarone della Valpolicella '12	🍷🍷 5
● Valpolicella Sup. Ripasso Torre del Falasco '13	🍷🍷 3
● Valpolicella Valpantena Ritocco '13	🍷🍷 3

Cantina Valpolicella Negrar

VIA CA' SALGARI, 2
37024 NEGRAR [VR]
TEL. +39 0456014300
www.cantinanegrar.it

CELLAR SALES
PRE-BOOKED VISITS
RESTAURANT SERVICE
ANNUAL PRODUCTION 7,000,000 bottles
HECTARES UNDER VINE 700.00

The Cantina di Negrar is a large-sale
cooperative boasting some 20 members,
whose vineyards are distributed throughout
Valpolicella. Production is about seven
million bottles per year. In recent years
Daniele Accordini and his colleagues have
focused attention on taking full advantage
of the best-aspected vineyards. With the
support of their more skilled, their best
wines have been made from these vines.
We were presented with quite an array of
Amarones, and Espressioni headed our
scorecard. In Villa 2009, from a vineyard in
the Negrar valley, cherry and red berry fruit
predominate, fleshy and forceful, seguing
onto a palate of notable concentration and
forcefulness. Kept disciplined by fine
tannins, it drives into a warm, vibrant finish.
Recioto Vigneti di Moron 2012 boats
explosive fruit and an enviable succulence
on the palate.

● Amarone della Valpolicella Cl. Villa Domini Veneti '09	🍷🍷 5
● Recioto della Valpolicella Cl. Vign. di Moron Domini Veneti '12	🍷🍷 4
● Amarone della Valpolicella Cl. Castelrotto Domini Veneti '10	🍷🍷 7
● Amarone della Valpolicella Cl. Mater Domini Veneti Ris. '10	🍷🍷 8
● Amarone della Valpolicella Cl. Mazzurega Domini Veneti '10	🍷🍷 5
● Amarone della Valpolicella Cl. Monte Domini Veneti '10	🍷🍷 6
● Amarone della Valpolicella Cl. S. Rocco Domini Veneti '10	🍷🍷 8
● Amarone della Valpolicella Cl. Vign. di Jago '10	🍷🍷 7
● Valpolicella Cl. Sup. Ripasso La Casetta Domini Veneti '13	🍷🍷 4

Odino Vaona

LOC. VALGATARA
VIA PAVERNO, 41
37020 MARANO DI VALPOLICELLA [VR]
TEL. +39 0457703710
www.vaona.it

CELLAR SALES
PRE-BOOKED VISITS
ANNUAL PRODUCTION 70,000 bottles
HECTARES UNDER VINE 10.00
SUSTAINABLE WINERY

The narrow valley of Marano, perhaps the least known in all Valpolicella, heads northwards and quickly reaches and exceeds 300 metres in elevation. Here, immersed in nature and far from large towns, Alberto Vaona manages ten hectares of family vineyards, trained to both pergola and Guyot, producing wines that show a fine balance between richness and drinkability. Amarone Pegrandi appears dense indeed, and offers super-ripe and essence of macerated flowers, which slowly yield the stage to black pepper and to a hint of mineral, which has yet to evolve. Far from astounding with power and concentration, the wine grows step by step, revealing a good acidic thrust and a lengthy, dry finish. Ripasso Pegrandi impresses with a complex nose and fine proportion on the palate.

● Amarone della Valpolicella Cl. Pegrandi '12	▼▼6
● Valpolicella Cl. '15	▼▼2*
● Valpolicella Sup. Ripasso Pegrandi '14	▼▼3
● Amarone della Valpolicella Cl. Pegrandi '09	▼▼▼5
● Amarone della Valpolicella Cl. Pegrandi '08	▼▼▼5
● Amarone della Valpolicella Cl. Paverno '12	▼▼5
● Amarone della Valpolicella Cl. Paverno '11	▼▼5
● Amarone della Valpolicella Cl. Pegrandi '11	▼▼5
● Amarone della Valpolicella Cl. Pegrandi '10	▼▼5

Massimino Venturini

FRAZ. SAN FLORIANO
VIA SEMONTE, 20
37029 SAN PIETRO IN CARIANO [VR]
TEL. +39 0457701331
www.viniventurini.com

CELLAR SALES
PRE-BOOKED VISITS
ANNUAL PRODUCTION 100,000 bottles
HECTARES UNDER VINE 12.00

Daniele, Mirco, and Giuseppina inherited from their father Massimino the passionate commitment with which they manage the family wine operation. And the fourth generation is now emerging alongside them, taking their first steps in the vineyards and in the marketplace. Respect for tradition, vineyard practices inspired by venerable pergola training have not changed, nor has the concept of leaving the wine to age at length before release, or the style, which still strives for a balance of concentration and complexity. The Venturinis missed only the top award this year; their entire line-up shows the highest quality, beautiful expressions of the classic wine categories. Amarone Campomasua 2010 displays scents of dried cherry that meld together with oil of macerated flowers and medicinal herbs, and on the palate, an imposing structure is perfectly in synch with a thrust of vibrant acidity. Amarone Classico 2011 expresses quite similar aromatics, but it displays a richer concentration in the mouth.

● Amarone della Valpolicella Cl. '11	▼▼5
● Amarone della Valpolicella Cl. Campomasua '10	▼▼6
● Massimino '10	▼▼4
● Recioto della Valpolicella Cl. Le Brugnine '12	▼▼5
● Valpolicella Cl. Sup. Ripasso Semonte Alto '12	▼▼3
● Valpolicella Cl. '15	▼2
● Amarone della Valpolicella Cl. Campomasua '07	▼▼▼6
● Amarone della Valpolicella Cl. Campomasua '05	▼▼▼6
● Recioto della Valpolicella Cl. Le Brugnine '97	▼▼▼5
● Valpolicella Cl. '13	▼▼2*
● Valpolicella Cl. Sup. '12	▼▼2*

Agostino Vicentini

FRAZ. SAN ZENO
VIA C. BATTISTI, 62C
37030 COLOGNOLA AI COLLI [VR]
TEL. +39 0457650539
www.vinivicentini.com

CELLAR SALES
PRE-BOOKED VISITS
ANNUAL PRODUCTION 100,000 bottles
HECTARES UNDER VINE 20.00

Over the last 20 years, Agostino Vicentini has gradually left fruticulture behind, except for cherries, and dedicated himself body and soul to winemaking, in which he is assisted by the precious efforts of his wife Teresa and now by their children Manuele and Francesca. Their activities are deeply rooted in Soave, with excellent results, but their Valpolicella is also holding its own, with wines that are always bright-edged and incisive. Valpolicella, in fact, is home to one of that designation's most interesting wines, Palazzo di Campiano 2012, a Superiore made only from non-dried grapes that conveys the finesse and depth of its heirloom vines. The house champion, however, remains Casale 2015, a Soave Superiore that compels attention with the density of its aromas, with a fusion of fruit and fresh vegetable that heightens the innate vibrancy of the garganega. A solid-packed palate and a driving progression crown this truly memorable wine.

Vigna Roda

LOC. CORTELÀ
VIA MONTE VERSA, 1569
35030 VO [PD]
TEL. +39 0499940228
www.vignaroda.com

CELLAR SALES
PRE-BOOKED VISITS
ANNUAL PRODUCTION 52,000 bottles
HECTARES UNDER VINE 17.00

In his cellar on the centre-west slope of the Parco Regionale dei Colli Euganei, Gianni Strazzacappa is emerging as a real force on the Padua wine scene. His vineyards, which have gradually reached a total of 20 hectares, are planted mostly to the Bordeaux varieties, with some to white grapes and glera. The house winemaking philosophy aims for wines that are crisp, refreshing, and with good acidic grip. The most ambitious wine here is Scarlatto 2013, a predominantly merlot Bordeaux blend that displays youthful aromas of still-crunchy red berry lifted by lovely scents of forest floor and violets. In the mouth, a taut acidity supports considerable richness. Petali d'Ambra 2011, on the other hand, boasts near-explosive fruit, with spice, candied citrus, and dried fig in contradistinction to the nature of the grape. Fill in the mouth, it presents a tasty contrast between seductive smoothness and crisp acidity.

○ Soave Sup. Il Casale '15	♔♔♔ 3*
● Valpolicella Sup. Palazzo di Campiano '12	♔♔ 5
○ Soave Vign. Terre Lunghe '15	♔♔ 2*
● Valpolicella Sup. Idea Bacco '12	♔♔ 5
● Valpolicella Sup. '13	♔ 3
○ Soave Sup. Il Casale '14	♟♟♟ 3*
○ Soave Sup. Il Casale '13	♟♟♟ 3*
○ Soave Sup. Il Casale '12	♟♟♟ 3*
○ Soave Sup. Il Casale '09	♟♟♟ 3*
○ Soave Sup. Il Casale '08	♟♟♟ 3*
○ Soave Sup. Il Casale '07	♟♟♟ 3*
○ Soave Vign. Terre Lunghe '14	♟♟ 2*
○ Soave Vign. Terre Lunghe '13	♟♟ 2*
○ Soave Vign. Terre Lunghe '11	♟♟ 2*
● Valpolicella Sup. '12	♟♟ 3
● Valpolicella Sup. Idea Bacco '11	♟♟ 5
● Valpolicella Vign. Boccascalucce '14	♟♟ 2*

● Colli Euganei Cabernet Espero '15	♔♔ 2*
○ Colli Euganei Fior d'Arancio Passito Petali d'Ambra '11	♔♔♔ 4
○ Colli Euganei Fior d'Arancio Spumante '15	♔♔ 2*
● Colli Euganei Rosso Scarlatto '13	♔♔ 3
○ Colli Euganei Bianco '15	♔ 2
● Colli Euganei Rosso Probus '15	♔ 2
● Colli Euganei Cabernet Espero '14	♟♟ 2*
● Colli Euganei Cabernet Espero '13	♟♟ 2*
● Colli Euganei Cabernet Espero '12	♟♟ 2*
○ Colli Euganei Fior d'Arancio Spumante '14	♟♟ 2*
● Colli Euganei Rosso '13	♟♟ 2*
● Colli Euganei Rosso '12	♟♟ 2*
● Colli Euganei Rosso Scarlatto '12	♟♟ 3*
● Colli Euganei Rosso Scarlatto '11	♟♟ 3

Vignale di Cecilia

LOC. FORNACI
VIA CROCI, 14
35030 BAONE [PD]
TEL. +39 042951420
www.vignaledicecilia.it

PRE-BOOKED VISITS
ANNUAL PRODUCTION 20,000 bottles
HECTARES UNDER VINE 8.00
VITICULTURE METHOD Certified Organic

Paolo Brunello turned a passion into his main business, taking over the reins of his small family cellar a decade ago. Today the vineyards, farmed organically, amount to almost ten hectares; they are largely planted to merlot and cabernet, which consistently produce concentrated, perfectly ripe fruit. His line of whites is an impressive one, in an area traditionally given to reds, exhibiting a style that is clearly personal and of great character. In light of the difficult 2014 harvest, Paolo decided not to produce his standard-bearer, Passacaglia, and dedicated its grapes to Covolo 2014. The result is a red offering emphatic fruit and fines herbes, with an intriguing hint of mushroom in the background. In the mouth, Paolo has sculpted a firmly structured yet supple palate. Poldo, a somewhat restless and pleasantly countryish white, did very well; the palate rises to a final refreshing note of grapefruit.

● Colli Euganei Rosso Covolo '14	♟♟	3
○ Poldo	♟♟	3
○ Cocài '13	♟	3
○ Val di Spin Frizzante	♟	2
○ Benavides '11	♟♟	2*
○ Cocài '12	♟♟	3
○ Cocài '11	♟♟	3
○ Cocài '10	♟♟	3
● Colli Euganei Rosso Covolo '13	♟♟	3
● Colli Euganei Rosso Covolo '10	♟♟	3
● Colli Euganei Rosso Passacaglia '12	♟♟	4
● Colli Euganei Rosso Passacaglia '11	♟♟	4
● Colli Euganei Rosso Passacaglia '09	♟♟	4
● Colli Euganei Rosso Passacaglia '08	♟♟	4
● El Moro '08	♟♟	3*

★Vignalta

VIA SCALETTE, 23
35032 ARQUÀ PETRARCA [PD]
TEL. +39 0429777305
www.vignalta.it

CELLAR SALES
PRE-BOOKED VISITS
ANNUAL PRODUCTION 220,000 bottles
HECTARES UNDER VINE 35.00

Lucio Gomiero, the first to express full confidence in the winegrowing qualities of the Euganean Hills, founded his cellar Vignalta with the clear objective right from the start of making ambitious wines. Almost 40 years later, he has about 40 hectares of vineyard, and he is in the process of enlarging his cellar at Arquà, to provide more room for winemaking and for ageing. Bordeaux-style reds are closest to his heart, but some whites are standouts as well. The line is reliable across the board, with a battery led by Gemola and Alpianae. Gemola is the usual merlot-dominated Bordeaux blend expressing all the warmth of 2011: fruity, sweet and fleshy on the nose, the mouth unleashes a fullness nicely controlled by the acidity and the dense suite of tannins. Alpianae is a Fior d'arancio Passito 2013 that explores the more Mediterranean, caressing soul of the hills, showing citrusy and spicy on the nose, with delicately balanced mouth of sweetness and acidity.

○ Colli Euganei Fior d'Arancio Passito Alpianae '13	♟♟	5
● Colli Euganei Rosso Gemola '11	♟♟	6
○ Colli Euganei Manzoni Bianco Agno Casto '15	♟♟	3
○ Colli Euganei Moscato Secco Sirio '15	♟♟	3
○ Colli Euganei Pinot Bianco '15	♟♟	3
● Colli Euganei Rosso Ris. '11	♟♟	3
● Marrano '09	♟♟	5
● Pinot Nero '14	♟♟	5
○ Colli Euganei Fior d'Arancio Passito Alpianae '12	♟♟♟	5
● Colli Euganei Rosso Gemola '09	♟♟♟	5
● Colli Euganei Rosso Gemola '08	♟♟♟	5
● Colli Euganei Rosso Gemola '07	♟♟♟	5
● Colli Euganei Rosso Gemola '04	♟♟♟	5

Le Vigne di San Pietro

VIA SAN PIETRO, 23
37066 SOMMACAMPAGNA [VR]
TEL. +39 045510016
www.levignedisanpietro.it

CELLAR SALES
PRE-BOOKED VISITS
ANNUAL PRODUCTION 70,000 bottles
HECTARES UNDER VINE 10.00

As an architect with a bent for viticulture, Carlo Nerozzi has always striven to express his vision of nature through his wines. The cellar lies atop the San Pietro hill, a few kilometres from Lake Garda, and the ten or so hectares of vineyard are planted to the classic Garda varieties, as well as to cabernet sauvignon and merlot, the latter with but few vine-rows but of impressive quality. All the wines are marked by a certain refinement, with taut, crisp, elegant palates. There were three wines in our finals, emblematic of the high quality of the Garda designations. Custoza Sanpietro 2013 shows emphatic pear, apple, and minerally flint, expanding decisively in the mouth for a long, lingering finale. Always one of the most impressive, Bardolino 2015 offers wild red berry and black pepper, also infusing the palate, which is both rich and delicate. The Chiaretto CorDeRosa 2015 turned in a fine performance, with a lovely fusion of fragrance, gracefulness, and personality.

● Bardolino '15	♥♥	2*
⊙ Bardolino Chiaretto CorDeRosa '15	♥♥	2*
○ Custoza Sup. Sanpietro '13	♥♥	3*
● Bardolino Sup. '13	♥♥	3
○ Custoza '15	♥♥	2*
● Refolà '11	♥♥	6
● Bardolino '14	♥♥♥	2*
● Bardolino '11	♥♥♥	2*
● Refolà Cabernet Sauvignon '04	♥♥♥	6
○ Sud '95	♥♥♥	6
● Bardolino '15	♥♥	2*
● Bardolino '13	♥♥	2*
● Bardolino '12	♥♥	2*
○ Custoza '14	♥♥	2*
○ Custoza '13	♥♥	2*

Vigneto Due Santi

V.LE ASIAGO, 174
36061 BASSANO DEL GRAPPA [VI]
TEL. +39 0424502074
www.vignetoduesanti.it

CELLAR SALES
PRE-BOOKED VISITS
ANNUAL PRODUCTION 100,000 bottles
HECTARES UNDER VINE 18.00
SUSTAINABLE WINERY

Stefano and Adriano Zonta manage this family cellar in Bassano. They have gradually added to the vineyards, which now amount to 20 hectares, with the vines lie in the first rows of hills, caressed by cooling breezes out of the nearby Valsugana. Wine production has not changed, though, thanks to rigorous selection of the grapes as well of wines in barrels. Reds predominate, clean-edged, succulent and rich. The oldest and best-aspected vineyards grow the grapes for Cabernet Due Santi 2013, where ripe red berry, blueberry, and dried plum are shot through with pronounced mint and thyme, giving the nose its crisp fragrance. The compact palate is supported by a suite of ultra-polished, stylish tannins. Among the whites, we liked Rivana 2015, a blend of mostly tai, for its juicy palate.

● Breganze Cabernet Due Santi '13	♥♥	4
○ Breganze Bianco Rivana '15	♥♥	2*
● Breganze Merlot '13	♥♥	2*
○ Campo di Fiori '15	♥♥	2*
○ Breganze Sauvignon '15	♥	3
○ Breganze Torcolato '12	♥	5
○ Prosecco Extra Dry	♥	2
● Breganze Cabernet Vign. Due Santi '12	♥♥♥	4*
● Breganze Cabernet Vign. Due Santi '08	♥♥♥	4*
● Breganze Cabernet Vign. Due Santi '07	♥♥♥	4
● Breganze Cabernet Vign. Due Santi '05	♥♥♥	4
● Breganze Cabernet Vign. Due Santi '04	♥♥♥	4
● Breganze Cabernet Vign. Due Santi '03	♥♥♥	4*
● Breganze Cabernet Vign. Due Santi '00	♥♥♥	4
● Breganze Cabernet Vign. Due Santi '11	♥♥	4
● Breganze Rosso Cavallare '12	♥♥	4

Villa Sandi

VIA ERIZZO, 112
31035 CROCETTA DEL MONTELLO [TV]
TEL. +39 0423665033
www.villasandi.it

CELLAR SALES
PRE-BOOKED VISITS
ACCOMMODATION AND RESTAURANT SERVICE
ANNUAL PRODUCTION 5,000,000 bottles
HECTARES UNDER VINE 530.00
SUSTAINABLE WINERY

The Moretti Polegato winery is one of the leading operations in the Valdobbiadene area. The vineyards are quite extensive, some of the estate, others belonging to grape growers who supply their grapes to the winery. Star of the show is Prosecco, but they produce still wines, too, grown in vineyards on the Montello relief, both reds and whites that exhibit singular varietal expressiveness. Villa Sandi is certainly a benchmark for the Grand Cru of Valdobbiadene, Cartizze, for all of the aficionados of Treviso-area sparklers. This Brut summons up clean-edged notes of juicy pear and apple, perfectly complemented by a suite of delicate floral essences. Dry and full-flavoured, as well as tautly crisp, it embodies the delicacy classic to Prosecco. Serenissima Brut earns high marks too, with its self-confident, joyous expressiveness.

Villa Spinosa

LOC. JAGO
VIA JAGO DALL'ORA, 16
37024 NEGRAR [VR]
TEL. +39 0457500093
www.villaspinosa.it

CELLAR SALES
PRE-BOOKED VISITS
ACCOMMODATION
ANNUAL PRODUCTION 45,000 bottles
HECTARES UNDER VINE 20.00
SUSTAINABLE WINERY

Enrico Cascella has slowly transformed the family winery, with the result that alongside the 18th-century residence there is now a new cellar, beautifully integrated into its environment and the surrounding architecture, while a store and tasting room are now housed in the historic buildings next to the villa. All of the vineyards, some 20 hectares, have gradually been replanted and these are the true treasure of this operation. Amarone 2008, presented only after lengthy maturation, proffers a nose of significant compactness and depth, with extract of macerated fruit infused with crisp herbs and pungent black pepper. It then relaxes and expands in the mouth, building succulent, spacious flavours without ever becoming heavy. Valpolicella Figari 2012 is a Superiore that privileges aromatic fragrance and delicacy on the palate, an exemplar of the refined side of the designation.

○ Cartizze Brut V. La Rivetta	▼▼▼ 6
● Còrpore '13	▼▼ 5
○ Opere Trevigiane M. Cl. Ris. '13	▼▼ 5
○ Serenissima Opere Trevigiane Brut	▼▼ 5
○ Valdobbiadene Dry Cuvée Oris	▼▼ 3
○ Valdobbiadene Extra Dry	▼▼ 3
○ Marinali Manzoni Bianco '15	▼ 3
● Marinali Raboso '12	▼ 3
○ Prosecco di Treviso Il Fresco Brut	▼ 2
○ Cartizze Brut V. La Rivetta '11	♟♟♟ 4*
○ Cartizze Brut V. La Rivetta '10	♟♟♟ 4
○ Cartizze Brut V. La Rivetta '09	♟♟♟ 4
● Còrpore '12	♟♟ 5

● Amarone della Valpolicella Cl. '08	▼▼▼ 7
● Recioto della Valpolicella Cl. Francesca Finato Spinosa '11	▼▼ 5
● Valpolicella Cl. '14	▼▼ 2*
● Valpolicella Cl. Sup. Figari '12	▼▼ 3
● Valpolicella Cl. Sup. Ripasso Jago '11	♟♟♟ 3*
● Amarone della Valpolicella Cl. Anteprima '08	♟♟ 6
● Recioto della Valpolicella Cl. Francesca Finato Spinosa '08	♟♟ 5
● Valpolicella Cl. '13	♟♟ 2*
● Valpolicella Cl. '12	♟♟ 2*
● Valpolicella Cl. Sup. Figari '11	♟♟ 3
● Valpolicella Cl. Sup. Ripasso Jago '10	♟♟ 3

Vigneti Villabella

FRAZ. CALMASINO DI BARDOLINO
LOC. CANOVA, 2
37011 BARDOLINO [VR]
TEL. +39 0457236448
www.vignetivillabella.com

CELLAR SALES
PRE-BOOKED VISITS
ACCOMMODATION
ANNUAL PRODUCTION 500,000 bottles
HECTARES UNDER VINE 220.00

Over the years, the winery of the Cristoforetti and Delibori families has carved itself a major role among Lake Garda producers. With over 200 hectares of vineyard across the DOC area and the priceless estate surrounding Villa Cordevigo, the oasis of vineyards is managed with deep respect for the environment, the grapes used for the cellar's most prestigious wines. The style here has always been subtle and refined, and today's wines have also gained depth and finesse. Bardolino Vigna Morlongo 2014 is simply stunning in its ability to showcase the finest qualities of this Garda wine type. It appears the classic pale red, and its aromas, elegant yet pronounced, are dominated by a marriage of wild berry and black pepper, with a noble whiff of fines herbes hovering in the background. In the mouth, a savoury vein of acidity sculpts a palate that remains focused and utterly delicious. Chiaretto 2015 boasts emphatic, floral-based aromatics, and it is dry, supple, and appealing in the mouth.

★Viviani

VIA MAZZANO, 8
37020 NEGRAR [VR]
TEL. +39 0457500286
www.cantinaviviani.com

CELLAR SALES
PRE-BOOKED VISITS
ANNUAL PRODUCTION 80,000 bottles
HECTARES UNDER VINE 10.00
SUSTAINABLE WINERY

Claudio Viviani has taken the Valpolicella designation's incredible success in his stride, bringing a burnished reputation to his operation. No marble floors and no swimming pools in the garden, though, since the cellar has studiously preserved its agricultural character, concentrating all efforts on the excellent wines, which accurately express their terroir and its traditions. Only DOC wines are produced, with clean-contoured aromatics and great elegance on the palate. Of the first-class wines presented by Claudio, Amarone Casa dei Bepi 2011 stands out for its loyalty to the history of Valpolicella combined with contemporary appeal. The nose pays homage to the traditional super-ripe fruit and spice, but in the mouth this wine seems be exploring a new path, with grip, suppleness, and a taut crispness, for a memorable result. Likewise excellent is the compact Valpolicella Campo Morar 2013, intensely appealing for its full-flavoured balance on the palate.

● Bardolino Cl. V. Morlongo '14	♟♟♟ 2*
☉ Bardolino Chiaretto Cl. '15	♟♟ 2*
☉ Bardolino Chiaretto Cl. Villa Cordevigo '15	♟♟ 2*
○ Lugana Ca' del Lago '15	♟♟ 3
● Montemazzano '12	♟♟ 3
● Valpolicella Cl. Sup. Ripasso '14	♟♟ 3
☉ Bardolino Chiaretto Brut	♟ 2
○ Custoza '15	♟ 2
● Oseleta '08	♟ 5
● Valpolicella Cl. I Roccoli '15	♟ 2
● Amarone della Valpolicella Cl. Fracastoro Ris. '08	♕♕ 6
● Bardolino Cl. V. Morlongo '13	♕♕ 2*
● Bardolino Cl. V. Morlongo Anniversario '13	♕♕ 2*
● Valpolicella Cl. Sup. Ripasso '13	♕♕ 3

● Amarone della Valpolicella Cl. Casa dei Bepi '11	♟♟♟ 8
● Valpolicella Cl. Sup. Campo Morar '13	♟♟ 5
● Valpolicella Cl. '15	♟♟ 2*
● Amarone della Valpolicella Cl. Casa dei Bepi '10	♕♕♕ 8
● Amarone della Valpolicella Cl. Casa dei Bepi '09	♕♕♕ 8
● Amarone della Valpolicella Cl. Casa dei Bepi '05	♕♕♕ 8
● Amarone della Valpolicella Cl. Casa dei Bepi '04	♕♕♕ 8
● Amarone della Valpolicella Cl. Casa dei Bepi '01	♕♕♕ 8
● Amarone della Valpolicella Cl. Casa dei Bepi '00	♕♕♕ 8
● Valpolicella Cl. Sup. Campo Morar '09	♕♕♕ 5
● Valpolicella Cl. Sup. Campo Morar '05	♕♕♕ 5

Pietro Zanoni

FRAZ. QUINZANO
VIA ARE ZOVO, 16D
37125 VERONA
TEL. +39 0458343977
www.pietrozanoni.it

CELLAR SALES
PRE-BOOKED VISITS
ANNUAL PRODUCTION 20,000 bottles
HECTARES UNDER VINE 6.50

Pietro Zanoni's winery is not in a prominent position, almost at the very border of Valpolicella and almost overlooking Verona. His handful of hectares are planted solely to the classic varieties of the designation, in a style that marries tradition and richness of fruit, resulting in solid, multifaceted wines, few in number but of outstanding quality. It was difficult to select the best Zanoni wine because all of them won our panel's appreciation for their quality and how well they represented their various wine types. The Amarone Zovo 2011 is redolent of dark berry fruit and spice, and it continues in the mouth rich, warm, and forceful. Valpolicella Superiore 2014, on the other hand, boasts fruit that is more crunchy and straightforward, while the palate is concentrated, but dry and quite long, which makes for a grand, delicious wine.

● Amarone della Valpolicella Zovo '11	♟♟ 7
● Recioto della Valpolicella '11	♟♟ 5
● Valpolicella Sup. '14	♟♟ 2*
● Valpolicella Sup. Ripasso '13	♟♟ 4
● Amarone della Valpolicella Zovo '10	♟♟ 6
● Amarone della Valpolicella Zovo '09	♟♟ 6
● Amarone della Valpolicella Zovo '07	♟♟ 6
● Amarone della Valpolicella Zovo '04	♟♟ 6
● Recioto della Valpolicella '09	♟♟ 4
● Valpolicella Sup. '13	♟♟ 2*
● Valpolicella Sup. '08	♟♟ 4
● Valpolicella Sup. Campo Denari '11	♟♟ 4
● Valpolicella Sup. Campo Denari '10	♟♟ 4

Pietro Zardini

VIA DON P. FANTONI, 3
37029 SAN PIETRO IN CARIANO [VR]
TEL. +39 0456800989
www.pietrozardini.it

CELLAR SALES
PRE-BOOKED VISITS
ANNUAL PRODUCTION 20,000 bottles
HECTARES UNDER VINE 7.00

Pietro Zardini's winemaking operation has met with rapid success, thanks to the expertise he gained in working with top wineries in Valpolicella, as well as to his sensitive understanding of the entire growing area. The work in the vineyards is consolidated in his efficient new facility in San Pietro in Cariano, producing a portfolio of well-delineated wines embodying the qualities and traditions of the designation. Amarone Leone Zardini missed the top award be just a hairsbreadth. This Riserva 2009, in a classic traditional style, captivates for the depth of its aromatics, where essence of macerated flowers allows through intriguing impressions of dried flowers, wild herbs, spice, and hints of mineral. Its considerable body has finally found its true proportion and grace. Amarone 2011 puts its cards on rich, juicy fruit that makes it a straightforward delight, while Ripasso Austero 2012 is even more crisp and fruit-rich.

● Amarone della Valpolicella Leone Zardini Ris. '09	♟♟ 6
● Amarone della Valpolicella '11	♟♟ 6
● Valpolicella Sup. Ripasso Austero '12	♟♟ 4
○ Lugana '15	♟ 2
● Rosignol	♟ 4
☉ Rosignol Rosato Brut	♟ 3
● Amarone della Valpolicella '10	♟♟ 6
● Amarone della Valpolicella '05	♟♟ 6
● Amarone della Valpolicella '04	♟♟ 6
● Amarone della Valpolicella Cl. '07	♟♟ 6
● Amarone della Valpolicella Cl. '03	♟♟ 6
● Amarone della Valpolicella Cl. Leone Zardini Ris. '08	♟♟ 6
● Valpolicella Sup. Ripasso Austero '11	♟♟ 4
● Valpolicella Sup. Ripasso Austero '07	♟♟ 4

★Zenato

FRAZ. SAN BENEDETTO DI LUGANA
VIA SAN BENEDETTO, 8
37019 PESCHIERA DEL GARDA [VR]
TEL. +39 0457550300
www.zenato.it

CELLAR SALES
PRE-BOOKED VISITS
ANNUAL PRODUCTION 2,000,000 bottles
HECTARES UNDER VINE 75.00

The winery founded by Sergio Zenato, today run by his children Nadia and Alberto, occupies a special position in the word of Valpolicella. The estate vineyards, once quite limited, today cover more than 70 hectares, distributed in Valpolicella and in Lugana, where Zenato first began its activities. The house style follows two philosophies: aromatics and harmony for the whites; power and concentrated fruit for the reds. Amarone Sergio Zenato, a Riserva 2010 dedicated to the cellar's founder, is the very incarnation of forceful character, emanating red berry and cherry that is sun-bright, sweet, and succulent, enriched by emphatic, smooth spice. In the mouth, it is warm, enfolding, and velvety, refreshed on the finish by a rising thrust of tannins. In the Lugana category, we were enthused by the Riserva 2013, releasing ripe apricot and yellow peach, with a lovely creaminess and savoury fruit on the palate.

● Amarone della Valpolicella Cl. Sergio Zenato Ris. '10	♥♥♥ 8
○ Lugana Sergio Zenato Ris. '13	♥♥ 5
● Amarone della Valpolicella Cl. '11	♥♥ 6
● Cresasso '10	♥♥ 5
○ Lugana Brut M. Cl.	♥♥ 4
○ Lugana Massoni Santa Cristina '13	♥♥ 3
● Amarone della Valpolicella Cl. '05	♥♥♥ 6
● Amarone della Valpolicella Cl. Sergio Zenato '05	♥♥♥ 6
● Amarone della Valpolicella Cl. Sergio Zenato '03	♥♥♥ 6
● Amarone della Valpolicella Cl. Sergio Zenato '00	♥♥♥
● Amarone della Valpolicella Cl. Sergio Zenato Ris. '09	♥♥♥ 8
○ Lugana Sergio Zenato '08	♥♥♥ 4

Zeni 1870

VIA COSTABELLA, 9
37011 BARDOLINO [VR]
TEL. +39 0457210022
www.zeni.it

CELLAR SALES
PRE-BOOKED VISITS
ANNUAL PRODUCTION 1,000,000 bottles
HECTARES UNDER VINE 25.00

The Zeni family winery is a benchmark for all wine lovers living on the Venetian shore of Lake Garda. Winemaking activities here date way back and took the quantum leap under the guidance of Nino and his children Fausto, Elena, and Federica, who are now in charge. The estate vineyards are comparatively few, but trusted growers around Lake Garda and in nearby Valpolicella supply fruit that yields wines consistent both in numbers and in quality. The most impressive wines hail from Valpolicella, starting with Amarone Barrique 2011, which releases liqueur cherries and spice, with a subtle vein of fresh vegetable that lifts the aromatic mosaic. Its considerable body is matched and supported by a firm clutch of tannins that bolster the richness of the fruit. Bardolino Chiaretto 2015 acquitted itself well, a rosé with graceful fragrances and a crisply-flavoured, tasty palate.

● Amarone della Valpolicella Cl. Barrique '11	♥♥ 7
● Amarone della Valpolicella Cl. '13	♥♥ 6
● Amarone della Valpolicella Cl. Vigne Alte '12	♥♥ 6
⊙ Bardolino Chiaretto Cl. Vigne Alte '15	♥♥ 2*
○ Lugana Marogne '15	♥♥ 3
● Valpolicella Sup. Vigne Alte '14	♥♥ 2*
⊙ Bardolino Chiaretto Brut	♥ 2
● Bardolino Cl. Sup. '14	♥ 3
● Bardolino Cl. Vigne Alte '15	♥ 2
● Costalago Rosso '14	♥ 3
○ Lugana Vigne Alte '15	♥ 2
⊙ Rosato Marogne '15	♥ 2
● Valpolicella Sup. Ripasso Marogne '14	♥ 3

Zonin 1821

VIA BORGOLECCO, 9
36053 GAMBELLARA [VI]
TEL. +39 0444640111
www.zonin.it

CELLAR SALES
PRE-BOOKED VISITS
ANNUAL PRODUCTION 38,000,000 bottles
HECTARES UNDER VINE 2000.00

This impressive Gambellara maison, in business for almost a century, boasts very extensive vineyards, which have even crossed the Atlantic and taken root in the state of Virginia. They remain focused, of course, on the Vicenza area, but they produce regional in-vogue Prosecco and Amarone as well. Production is significant, with a style based on a crisp palate and varietal expressiveness. Found in the hills around Gambellara, Giangio brings us the most interesting wine, Recioto di Gambellara 2011, with its ripe, beguiling fragrances on a backdrop of intriguing hints of Botrytis. In the mouth, the quite delicate sweetness is well balanced by a combination of savouriness and acidity. Among the reds, we liked Amarone 2013's ripe yet crisp expressiveness, a wine that refrains from stupefying with sweetness or concentration, developing an agile, energy-laden crispness.

● Amarone della Valpolicella '13	▼▼ 6
○ Recioto di Gambellara Il Giangio '11	▼▼ 5
● Berengario '11	▼ 4
○ Prosecco Brut	▼ 2
○ Recioto di Gambellara Spumante	▼ 3
● Valpolicella Sup. Ripasso '14	▼ 3
● Amarone della Valpolicella '12	♈ 5
● Amarone della Valpolicella '11	♈ 6
● Amarone della Valpolicella '10	♈ 6
● Amarone della Valpolicella '09	♈ 6
○ Gambellara Cl. Podere Il Giangio '13	♈ 2*
● Valpolicella Sup. Ripasso '13	♈ 3
● Valpolicella Sup. Ripasso '12	♈ 3
● Valpolicella Sup. Ripasso '11	♈ 3

Zymè

LOC. SAN FLORIANO
VIA CA' DEL PIPA, 1
37029 SAN PIETRO IN CARIANO [VR]
TEL. +39 0457701108
www.zyme.it

CELLAR SALES
PRE-BOOKED VISITS
ANNUAL PRODUCTION 80,000 bottles
HECTARES UNDER VINE 30.00
SUSTAINABLE WINERY

Celestino Gaspari took a step-by-step approach to launching his cellar, first working as a consultant, then making his wines at other cellars, and finally the construction of his own gorgeous facility in San Pietro in Cariano. There are 30 hectares of vineyard, sited in various areas of the province, yielding the Valpolicella classics, but there are numerous imaginative wines too, fruit of Gasperi's commitment to experimentation. Amarone La Mattonara Riserva 2004, which appears after a maturation of more than ten years, displays an unexpected yet intriguing crispness, with still-fleshy fruit given a further thrust by pungent herbs. In the mouth, its powerful expression drives along with determination and length, thanks to a vibrant thrust of acidity. After such richness and complexity, Valpolicella Reverie 2015 ushers in fragrance and grace, fruit of its historic vineyards.

● Amarone della Valpolicella Cl. La Mattonara Ris. '04	▼▼ 8
● 60 20 20 '11	▼▼ 5
○ Il Bianco From Black to White '15	▼▼ 3
● Kairos '11	▼▼ 7
● Valpolicella Cl. Sup. '12	▼▼ 5
● Valpolicella Reverie '15	▼▼ 2*
● Amarone della Valpolicella Cl. '06	♈♈ 8
● Amarone della Valpolicella Cl. La Mattonara Ris. '03	♈♈ 8
● Amarone della Valpolicella Cl. La Mattonara Ris. '01	♈♈ 8
● Amarone della Valpolicella Cl. '08	♈ 8
● Valpolicella Cl. Sup. '11	♈ 5
● Valpolicella Cl. Sup. '10	♈ 5

Ai Galli

VIA LOREDAN, 28
30020 PRAMAGGIORE [VE]
TEL. +39 0421799314
www.aigalli.it

ANNUAL PRODUCTION 300,000 bottles
HECTARES UNDER VINE 50.00

○ Lison Cl. '15		♇♇ 2*
○ Lison-Pramaggiore Verduzzo Passito '11		♇♇ 3
● Lison-Pramaggiore Cabernet Franc '14		♇ 2
● Lison-Pramaggiore Refosco P. R. '14		♇ 2

Le Battistelle

LOC. BROGNOLIGO
VIA SAMBUCO, 110
37030 MONTEFORTE D'ALPONE [VR]
TEL. +39 0456175621
www.lebattistelle.it

CELLAR SALES
PRE-BOOKED VISITS
ANNUAL PRODUCTION 22,000 bottles
HECTARES UNDER VINE 9.00
SUSTAINABLE WINERY

○ Soave Cl. Battistelle '14		♇♇ 3
○ Soave Cl. Roccolo del Durlo '14		♇♇ 3
○ Soave Cl. Montesei '15		♇ 2

Bellussi Spumanti

VIA ERIZZO, 215
31049 VALDOBBIADENE [TV]
TEL. +39 0423983411
www.bellussi.com

CELLAR SALES
PRE-BOOKED VISITS
ANNUAL PRODUCTION 1,300,000 bottles

○ Cartizze Dry Belcanto		♇♇ 4
○ Valdobbiadene Extra Dry Belcanto		♇♇ 3
○ Valdobbiadene Brut Belcanto		♇ 3
○ Valdobbiadene Dry		♇ 3

Astoria Vini

VIA CREVADA, 12
31020 REFRONTOLO [TV]
TEL. +39 04236699
www.astoria.it

CELLAR SALES
PRE-BOOKED VISITS
ANNUAL PRODUCTION 15,000,000 bottles
HECTARES UNDER VINE 40.00
SUSTAINABLE WINERY

○ Valdobbiadene Extra Dry '15		♇♇ 4
○ Cartizze Arzanà		♇ 5
○ Valdobbiadene Brut Rive di Refrontolo Casa di Vittorino		♇ 4

Beato Bartolomeo

VIA ROMA, 100
36042 BREGANZE [VI]
TEL. +39 0445873112
www.cantinabreganze.it

CELLAR SALES
ANNUAL PRODUCTION 2,500,000 bottles
HECTARES UNDER VINE 700.00

● Breganze Merlot Sup. Bosco Grande '13		♇♇ 3
● Breganze Cabernet Kilò Ris. '13		♇ 4
● Breganze Cabernet Sup. Bosco Grande '13		♇ 3
● Breganze Cabernet Sup. Savardo '14		♇ 2

Bonotto delle Tezze

FRAZ. TEZZE DI PIAVE
VIA DUCA D'AOSTA, 16
31028 VAZZOLA [TV]
TEL. +39 0438488323
www.bonottodelletezze.it

CELLAR SALES
PRE-BOOKED VISITS
ANNUAL PRODUCTION 150,000 bottles
HECTARES UNDER VINE 48.00

● Piave Malanotte '12		♇♇ 6
○ Manzoni Bianco Novalis '15		♇ 2
● Piave Raboso Potestà '12		♇ 3
○ Venezia Pinot Grigio Montesanto '15		♇ 2

F.lli Bortolin

FRAZ. SANTO STEFANO
VIA MENEGAZZI, 5
31049 VALDOBBIADENE [TV]
TEL. +39 0423900135
www.bortolin.com

CELLAR SALES
PRE-BOOKED VISITS
ANNUAL PRODUCTION 300,000 bottles
HECTARES UNDER VINE 20.00

○ Valdobbiadene Dry	♟♟	2*
○ Valdobbiadene Extra Dry	♟♟	2*
○ Cartizze	♟	4
○ Valdobbiadene Extra Dry Ru' Mill. '15	♟	3

Ca' Bianca

LOC. FONTANAFREDDA
VIA CINTO, 5
35030 CINTO EUGANEO [PD]
TEL. +39 042994288

CELLAR SALES
RESTAURANT SERVICE
ANNUAL PRODUCTION 80,000 bottles
HECTARES UNDER VINE 20.00

● Colli Euganei Cabernet Ritocchino 42 '13	♟♟	3
○ Colli Euganei Chardonnay Passo di Santa Lucia '15	♟	3
○ Colli Euganei Serprino '15	♟	3

Ca' Corner

VIA CA CORNER SUD, 55
30020 MEOLO [VE]
TEL. +39 042161191
www.vinicacorner.com

ANNUAL PRODUCTION 70,000 bottles
HECTARES UNDER VINE 14.00

○ Erika Passito '11	♟♟	3
○ Manzoni Bianco '15	♟♟	2*
● Petalo Rosso '10	♟	2
● Piave Merlot '14	♟	2

Ca' Ferri

VIA CA' FERRI, 43
35020 CASALSERUGO [PD]
TEL. +39 049655518
www.vinicaferri.com

CELLAR SALES
PRE-BOOKED VISITS
ANNUAL PRODUCTION 10,000 bottles
HECTARES UNDER VINE 8.00

● Corti Benedettine del Padovano Merlot Ser Ugo '15	♟♟	2*
● Corti Benedettine del Padovano Cabernet Ser Ugo '15	♟	2

Castello di Roncade

VIA ROMA, 141
31056 RONCADE [TV]
TEL. +39 0422708736
www.castellodironcade.com

CELLAR SALES
PRE-BOOKED VISITS
ANNUAL PRODUCTION 200,000 bottles
HECTARES UNDER VINE 45.00

● Piave Raboso dell'Arnasa '12	♟♟	2*
● Villa Giustinian '12	♟♟	3
● Piave Merlot dell'Armata '13	♟	2
○ Venezia Chardonnay dell'Arnasa '14	♟	2

Tenuta Chiccheri

LOC. CHICCHERI, 1
37039 TREGNAGO [VR]
TEL. +39 0458774333
www.tenutachiccheri.it

CELLAR SALES
PRE-BOOKED VISITS
ANNUAL PRODUCTION 50,000 bottles
HECTARES UNDER VINE 11.00
SUSTAINABLE WINERY

● Amarone della Valpolicella Cl. Campo delle Strie '11	♟♟	8
● Valpolicella Sup. '11	♟♟	5
○ Montprè Cuvée del Fondatore Brut '10	♟	4

Conte Collalto

VIA XXIV MAGGIO, 1
31058 SUSEGANA [TV]
TEL. +39 0438435811
www.cantine-collalto.it

CELLAR SALES
PRE-BOOKED VISITS
ANNUAL PRODUCTION 850,000 bottles
HECTARES UNDER VINE 150.00
SUSTAINABLE WINERY

○ Conegliano Valdobbiadene Extra Dry	♥♥	3
● Incrocio Manzoni 2.15 '12	♥	2
○ Manzoni Bianco '15	♥	2
○ Rosabianco '15	♥	2

Corte Figaretto

FRAZ. POIANO
VIA CLOCEGO, 48A
37142 VERONA
TEL. +39 0458700753
www.cortefigaretto.it

CELLAR SALES
PRE-BOOKED VISITS
ANNUAL PRODUCTION 49,500 bottles
HECTARES UNDER VINE 7.50

● Amarone della Valpolicella Graal '12	♥♥	6
● Amarone della Valpolicella Valpantena		
Brolo del Figaretto '12	♥	5
● Valpolicella Valpantena '15	♥	3

Paolo Cottini

LOC. CASTELROTTO DI SAN PIETRO IN CARIANO
VIA BELVEDERE, 29
37029 VERONA
TEL. +39 0456837293
www.paolocottini.it

CELLAR SALES
PRE-BOOKED VISITS
ANNUAL PRODUCTION 30,000 bottles
HECTARES UNDER VINE 3.50

● Amarone della Valpolicella Cl. '12	♥♥	3
● PaCo '13	♥♥	2*
● Valpolicella Cl. '15	♥	3
● Valpolicella Cl. Sup. Ripasso '12	♥	3

Cantina di Custoza

LOC. CUSTOZA
VIA STAFFALO, 1
37066 SOMMACAMPAGNA [VR]
TEL. +39 045516200
www.cantinadicustoza.it

CELLAR SALES
PRE-BOOKED VISITS
ANNUAL PRODUCTION 4,000,000 bottles
HECTARES UNDER VINE 1000.00
VITICULTURE METHOD Certified Organic

○ Custoza Sup. Le Noci Custodia '14	♥♥	2*
○ Custoza Val dei Molini '15	♥	2

Dal Din

VIA MONTEGRAPPA, 29
31020 VIDOR [TV]
TEL. +39 0423987295
www.daldin.it

CELLAR SALES
PRE-BOOKED VISITS
ANNUAL PRODUCTION 200,000 bottles
HECTARES UNDER VINE 4.00

○ Valdobbiadene Dry Vidoro '15	♥♥	2*
○ Valdobbiadene Brut	♥	2
○ Valdobbiadene Extra Dry	♥	2

Fasoli

FRAZ. SAN ZENO
VIA C. BATTISTI, 47
37030 COLOGNOLA AI COLLI [VR]
TEL. +39 0457650741
www.fasoligino.com

CELLAR SALES
PRE-BOOKED VISITS
ANNUAL PRODUCTION 400,000 bottles
HECTARES UNDER VINE 40.00
VITICULTURE METHOD Certified Organic

● Amarone della Valpolicella Alteo '10	♥♥	8
● Merlot Calle '13	♥	6
○ Pieve Vecchia '12	♥	4
○ Soave Borgoletto '15	♥	2

Fongaro

VIA MOTTO PIANE, 12
37030 RONCÀ [VR]
TEL. +39 0457460240
www.fongarospumanti.it

CELLAR SALES
PRE-BOOKED VISITS
ANNUAL PRODUCTION 68,000 bottles
HECTARES UNDER VINE 7.00
VITICULTURE METHOD Certified Organic

○ Lessini Durello Brut Ris. '09	♥♥ 4
○ Lessini Pas Dosé Ris. '08	♥ 5

Gamba Gnirega

VIA GNIREGA, 19
37020 MARANO DI VALPOLICELLA [VR]
TEL. +39 0456801714
www.vini-gamba.it

CELLAR SALES
PRE-BOOKED VISITS
ANNUAL PRODUCTION 60,000 bottles
HECTARES UNDER VINE 7.00

● Amarone della Valpolicella Cl. Campedel '12	♥♥ 8
● Amarone della Valpolicella Cl. Campedel Ris. '10	♥♥ 8

Gorgo

FRAZ. CUSTOZA
LOC. GORGO
37066 SOMMACAMPAGNA [VR]
TEL. +39 045516063
www.cantinagorgo.com

ANNUAL PRODUCTION 350,000 bottles
HECTARES UNDER VINE 50.00

○ Custoza Sup. Summa '15	♥♥ 2*
○ Custoza San Michelin '15	♥♥ 2*
● Bardolino '15	♥ 2
○ Custoza '15	♥ 2

Io Mazzucato

VIA SAN GAETANO, 21
36042 BREGANZE [VI]
TEL. +39 0445308348
www.iomazzucato.it

ANNUAL PRODUCTION 70,000 bottles
HECTARES UNDER VINE 25.00

● Breganze Cabernet '12	♥♥ 2*
○ Breganze Pinot Grigio '15	♥ 2
● Roccolo '12	♥ 2

Lenotti

VIA SANTA CRISTINA, 1
37011 BARDOLINO [VR]
TEL. +39 0457210484
www.lenotti.com

CELLAR SALES
PRE-BOOKED VISITS
ANNUAL PRODUCTION 1,400,000 bottles
HECTARES UNDER VINE 105.00

● Amarone della Valpolicella Cl. '11	♥♥ 6
● Amarone della Valpolicella Cl. Di Carlo '10	♥♥ 8
⊙ Bardolino Chiaretto Cl. '15	♥ 3
○ Lugana Decus '15	♥ 3

Le Mandolare

LOC. BROGNOLIGO
VIA SAMBUCO, 180
37032 MONTEFORTE D'ALPONE [VR]
TEL. +39 0456175083
www.cantinalemandolare.com

CELLAR SALES
PRE-BOOKED VISITS
ANNUAL PRODUCTION 65,000 bottles
HECTARES UNDER VINE 20.00

○ Soave Cl. Il Roccolo '15	♥♥ 2*
○ Soave Cl. Monte Sella '13	♥♥ 3
⊙ Recioto di Soave Le Schiavette '14	♥ 5
○ Soave Cl. Corte Menini '15	♥ 2

Firmino Miotti

VIA BROGLIATI CONTRO, 53
36042 BREGANZE [VI]
TEL. +39 0445873006
www.firminomiotti.it

CELLAR SALES
PRE-BOOKED VISITS
ANNUAL PRODUCTION 25,000 bottles
HECTARES UNDER VINE 5.00

● Breganze Rosso '13	🍷🍷 3
● Gruajo	🍷 3
○ Le Colombare '15	🍷 2
○ Pedevendo Frizzante	🍷 2

Ornella Molon Traverso

FRAZ. CAMPO DI PIETRA
VIA RISORGIMENTO, 40
31040 SALGAREDA [TV]
TEL. +39 0422804807
www.ornellamolon.it

CELLAR SALES
PRE-BOOKED VISITS
RESTAURANT SERVICE
ANNUAL PRODUCTION 500,000 bottles
HECTARES UNDER VINE 42.00
SUSTAINABLE WINERY

● Piave Merlot Rosso di Villa '11	🍷🍷 5
○ Traminer '15	🍷 3
○ Treviso Prosecco Brut	🍷 3
● Vite Rossa '12	🍷 4

Monte Santoccio

LOC. SANTOCCIO, 6
37022 FUMANE [VR]
TEL. +39 3496461223
www.montesantoccio.it

ANNUAL PRODUCTION 14,000 bottles
HECTARES UNDER VINE 3.00

● Valpolicella Cl. Sup. '14	🍷🍷 2*
● Valpolicella Cl. Sup. Ripasso '13	🍷🍷 4

Walter Nardin

LOC. RONCADELLE
VIA FONTANE, 5
31024 ORMELLE [TV]
TEL. +39 0422851622
www.vinwalternardin.it

PRE-BOOKED VISITS
ANNUAL PRODUCTION 350,000 bottles
HECTARES UNDER VINE 30.00

● Refosco P. R. La Zerbaia '13	🍷🍷 3
● Rosso della Ghiaia La Zerbaia '12	🍷🍷 4
● Piave Raboso La Zerbaia '11	🍷 3
● Venezia Cabernet Franc '15	🍷 2

Orto di Venezia

LOC. ISOLA DI SANT'ERASMO
VIA DELLE MOTTE, 1
30141 VENEZIA
TEL. +39 0415237410
www.ortodivenezia.com

ANNUAL PRODUCTION 15,000 bottles
HECTARES UNDER VINE 4.50

○ Orto '12	🍷🍷 5

Pegoraro

VIA CALBIN, 24
36024 MOSSANO [VI]
TEL. +39 0444886461
www.cantinapegoraro.it

ANNUAL PRODUCTION 30,000 bottles
HECTARES UNDER VINE 7.00

● Colli Berici Tai Rosso '15	🍷🍷 2*
○ Colli Berici Tai '15	🍷 2

Tenuta Polvaro

VIA POLVARO, 35
30020 ANNONE VENETO [VE]
TEL. +39 0421281023
www.tenutapolvaro.it

CELLAR SALES
PRE-BOOKED VISITS
ANNUAL PRODUCTION 300,000 bottles
HECTARES UNDER VINE 60.00

○ Polvaro Oro '14	🍷🍷 2*
○ Prosecco Extra Dry	🍷 2
● Venezia Cabernet Sauvignon '14	🍷 2
○ Venezia Pinot Grigio '15	🍷 2

Progettidivini

LOC. SOLIGO
VIA I SETTEMBRE, 20
31010 FARRA DI SOLIGO [TV]
TEL. +39 0438983151
www.progettidivini.it

CELLAR SALES
ANNUAL PRODUCTION 500,000 bottles
HECTARES UNDER VINE 15.00

○ Cartizze 8	🍷🍷 4
○ Valdobbiadene Extra Dry 3 '15	🍷🍷 3
○ Valdobbiadene Brut 2	🍷 3
○ Valdobbiadene Extra Dry 1	🍷 3

Punto Zero

GALLERIA EZZELLINO, 5
35139 PADOVA
TEL. +39 0457701108
www.puntozerowine.it

CELLAR SALES
PRE-BOOKED VISITS
ANNUAL PRODUCTION 15,000 bottles
HECTARES UNDER VINE 10.00
SUSTAINABLE WINERY

● Dimezzo '12	🍷🍷 5
● Punto '12	🍷🍷 8
○ Trasparenza '15	🍷 3
● Virgola '13	🍷 8

Quota 101

VIA MALTERRENO, 12
35038 TORREGLIA [PD]
TEL. +39 0425410922
www.quota101.com

ANNUAL PRODUCTION 35,000 bottles
HECTARES UNDER VINE 7.50

○ Colli Euganei Fior d'Arancio Passito Il Gelso '13	🍷🍷 5
○ Colli Euganei Fior d'Arancio Secco '15	🍷 3
○ Colli Euganei Fior d'Arancio Spumante	🍷 2

Ettore Righetti

VIA SAN MARTINO, 8
37024 NEGRAR [VR]
TEL. +39 0457500062

CELLAR SALES
ANNUAL PRODUCTION 45,000 bottles
HECTARES UNDER VINE 5.00

● Amarone della Valpolicella Cl. '12	🍷🍷 6
● Recioto della Valpolicella Cl. '13	🍷🍷 5
● Valpolicella Cl. '14	🍷 3
● Valpolicella Cl. Sup. '13	🍷 4

Ronca

VIA VAL DI SONA, 7
37066 SOMMACAMPAGNA [VR]
TEL. +39 0458961641
www.cantinaronca.it

CELLAR SALES
PRE-BOOKED VISITS
ANNUAL PRODUCTION 30,000 bottles
HECTARES UNDER VINE 20.00

● Bardolino '15	🍷🍷 2*
● Corvina '15	🍷🍷 2*
○ Custoza '15	🍷🍷 2*
○ Bardolino Chiaretto Brut	🍷 3

San Nazario

LOC. CORTELÀ
VIA MONTE VERSA, 1519
35030 Vò [PD]
TEL. +39 0499940194
www.vinisannazario.it

CELLAR SALES
PRE-BOOKED VISITS
ANNUAL PRODUCTION 50,000 bottles
HECTARES UNDER VINE 10.00
VITICULTURE METHOD Certified Organic

○ Colli Euganei Fior d'Arancio Passito Messalino '11	♥♥ 4
○ Colli Euganei Bianco Dulcamara '15	♥ 2
● Colli Euganei Rosso Brolo delle Femmine '12	♥ 2

Santa Eurosia

FRAZ. SAN PIETRO DI BARBOZZA
VIA DELLA CIMA, 8
31040 VALDOBBIADENE [TV]
TEL. +39 0423973236
www.santaeurosia.it

PRE-BOOKED VISITS
ANNUAL PRODUCTION 270,000 bottles

○ Valdobbiadene Brut	♥♥ 2*
○ Cartizze	♥ 4
○ Conegliano Valdobbiadene Dry Mill. '15	♥ 4
○ Conegliano Valdobbiadene Extra Dry	♥ 2

Spagnol - Col del Sas

VIA SCANDOLERA, 51
31020 VIDOR [TV]
TEL. +39 0423987177
www.coldelsas.it

CELLAR SALES
PRE-BOOKED VISITS
ANNUAL PRODUCTION 450,000 bottles
HECTARES UNDER VINE 32.00

○ Valdobbiadene Extra Dry Col del Sas '15	♥♥ 2*
○ Valdobbiadene Rive di Solighetto Brut Col del Sas '14	♥♥ 3
○ Valdobbiadene Brut Col del Sas '15	♥ 2

Tanoré

FRAZ. SAN PIETRO DI BARBOZZA
VIA MONT DI CARTIZZE, 3
31040 VALDOBBIADENE [TV]
TEL. +39 0423975770
www.tanore.it

CELLAR SALES
PRE-BOOKED VISITS
ANNUAL PRODUCTION 90,000 bottles
HECTARES UNDER VINE 10.00

○ Cartizze	♥♥ 4
○ Valdobbiadene Brut	♥♥ 3
○ Valdobbiadene Dry Il Tanorè '15	♥ 3
○ Valdobbiadene Extra Dry	♥ 2

Giovanna Tantini

FRAZ. OLIOSI
LOC. I MISCHI
37014 CASTELNUOVO DEL GARDA [VR]
TEL. +39 3488717577
www.giovannatantini.it

CELLAR SALES
PRE-BOOKED VISITS
ACCOMMODATION
ANNUAL PRODUCTION 30,000 bottles
HECTARES UNDER VINE 11.50

● Bardolino '14	♥♥ 2*
⊙ Bardolino Chiaretto '15	♥♥ 2*
○ Custoza '15	♥ 2
● Greta '10	♥ 5

Terre di Leone

LOC. PORTA
37020 MARANO DI VALPOLICELLA [VR]
TEL. +39 0456895040
www.terredileone.it

CELLAR SALES
PRE-BOOKED VISITS
ANNUAL PRODUCTION 36,000 bottles
HECTARES UNDER VINE 10.00

● Amarone della Valpolicella Cl. '09	♥♥ 8
● Amarone della Valpolicella Re Pazzo '12	♥♥ 8
● Valpolicella Cl. Re Pazzo '14	♥ 3
● Valpolicella Sup. Ripasso Re Pazzo '13	♥ 5

Terre di San Venanzio Fortunato

VIA CAPITELLO FERRARI, 1
31049 VALDOBBIADENE [TV]
TEL. +39 0423974083
www.terredisanvenanzio.it

ANNUAL PRODUCTION 250,000 bottles

○ Cartizze	♟♟ 4
○ Valdobbiadene Dry '15	♟♟ 3
○ Valdobbiadene Brut	♟ 2
○ Valdobbiadene Brut Demi Long '14	♟ 4

Tezza

FRAZ. POIANO DI VALPANTENA
VIA STRADELLA MAIOLI, 4
37142 VERONA
TEL. +39 045550267
www.tezzawines.it

CELLAR SALES
PRE-BOOKED VISITS
ANNUAL PRODUCTION 200,000 bottles
HECTARES UNDER VINE 27.00

● Amarone della Valpolicella Valpantena Brolo delle Giare Ris. '06	♟♟ 7
● Valpolicella Valpantena Sup. Ripasso Brolo delle Giare '11	♟♟ 4

Villa Canestrari

VIA DANTE BROGLIO, 2
37030 COLOGNOLA AI COLLI [VR]
TEL. +39 0457650074
www.villacanestrari.com

CELLAR SALES
PRE-BOOKED VISITS
ANNUAL PRODUCTION 160,000 bottles
HECTARES UNDER VINE 18.00

● Amarone della Valpolicella 1888 Ris. '09	♟♟ 8
● Valpolicella Sup. '13	♟♟ 5
○ Soave Sup. Ris. '13	♟ 3
● Valpolicella Sup. Ripasso I Lasi '14	♟ 3

Villa Medici

VIA CAMPAGNOL, 11
37066 SOMMACAMPAGNA [VR]
TEL. +39 045515147
www.cantinavillamedici.it

ANNUAL PRODUCTION 220,000 bottles
HECTARES UNDER VINE 32.00

⊙ Bardolino Chiaretto '15	♟♟ 2*
○ Custoza Passito La Valle del Re '09	♟♟ 4
○ Custoza Sup. '14	♟♟ 2*
○ Custoza '15	♟ 2

Villa Minelli

VIA POSTIOMA, 66
31020 VILLORBA [TV]
TEL. +39 0422912355
www.villaminelli.it

CELLAR SALES
PRE-BOOKED VISITS
ANNUAL PRODUCTION 40,000 bottles
HECTARES UNDER VINE 9.50

● Merlot '13	♟♟ 4
○ Villa Persico Passito '11	♟♟ 3
○ Malvasia '15	♟ 3
● Rosso Villa Minelli '14	♟ 3

Zardetto

VIA MARTIRI DELLE FOIBE, 18
31015 CONEGLIANO [TV]
TEL. +39 0438394969
www.zardettoprosecco.com

CELLAR SALES
ANNUAL PRODUCTION 2,000,000 bottles
HECTARES UNDER VINE 40.00
VITICULTURE METHOD Certified Organic

○ Conegliano Valdobbiadene Brut Rive di Ogliano Treventi '15	♟♟ 3
○ Conegliano Valdobbiadene Dry Fòndego	♟♟ 2*

FRIULI VENEZIA GIULIA

The weather for the 2015 season, despite some high temperature spikes, suggested the harvest would be a good one, with perfectly ripe, healthy grapes. Satisfaction was clear on the face of every producer and the end result was beyond their wildest expectations: it was a great harvest. Probably the general enthusiasm stemmed from the problems that had left their stamp on the previous vintage. With grapes like this it was almost impossible to go wrong, and our tastings confirmed it. Competition in the finals was very fierce indeed, and in the end we awarded an astounding 26 Tre Bicchieri accolades. Friulano was the star this year, the benchmark native vine, but our first thoughts go to the plains wines, particularly the 2015 Pinot Bianco by Le Monde, confirmed for the fourth year in a row, and Lenardo's Chardonnay 2015 new entry. We awarded our top accolade to six Friulanos, all the latest vintage, the four produced on Collio by Doro Princic, Fiegl, Russiz Superiore, and Schiopetto, and two on the Colli Orientali hills, by Angoris and Le Vigne di Zamò, the latter provocatively named No Name. Malvasia 2015 is again represented on Collio by Ronco dei Tassi, and on Carso by another new entry, Castelvecchio, with Malvasia Dileo. Then there is Skerk's splendid lightly macerated and unfiltered 2013 Malvasia, also from Carso. Tre Bicchieri to Tiare's 2015 Sauvignon on Collio, and to La Viarte's 2015 Sauvignon Liende and Volpe Pasini's Sauvignon Zuc di Volpe on the Colli Orientali. The 2015 Collio Bianco gathers laurels with Collavini's Broy and Livon's Solarco. On the Colli Orientali, a Tre Bicchieri also to Livio Felluga's 2014 Illivio, La Tunella's 2014 La Linda, Zorzettig's 2015 Pinot Bianco, and Torre Rosazza's 2015 Pinot Grigio. Yet another award for Jermann, truly flying the flag of modern Friuli winemaking, with a 2015 Pinot Grigio, and an encore for Desiderium 2013 from Eddi Luisa. Outstanding macerated whites include a 2008 Ribolla from Josko Gravner, the acknowledged initiator, followed by Damijan Podversic's 2012 Ribolla Gialla, and Primosic's 2012 Ribolla Gialla Oslavia Riserva. Last but not least, the spectacular Lis Neris Tal Luc, a cuvée of dried grapes from a special selection of berries harvested in 2006 and 2008, which was our Sweet Wine of the Year.

Tenuta di Angoris

LOC. ANGORIS, 7
34071 CORMÒNS [GO]
TEL. +39 048160923
www.angoris.it

CELLAR SALES
PRE-BOOKED VISITS
RESTAURANT SERVICE
ANNUAL PRODUCTION 650,000 bottles
HECTARES UNDER VINE 110.00
SUSTAINABLE WINERY

In 1648, the Austrian Emperor Ferdinand III gave the 630-hectare Angoris Estate to Locatello Locatelli in recognition of his prowess in battle during the 30 Years' War. After passing through different hands, it happened to be purchased by another Locatelli, Luciano this time, in 1968. Many of the 110 hectares of vineyards surround the main villa in Cormòns, in the Friuli Isonzo wine region, while others are dotted around the nearby hills. Currently run by Luciano's daughter Marta, the winery has become one of the best in the region thanks to the invaluable assistance of the winery's oenologist Alessandro Dal Zovo. From one success to the next. Last year we praised the winery for its first Tre Bicchieri and this year there are more. This time thanks to the Friulano 2015, with its fragrant nose and well-orchestrated palate. The Chardonnay Spìule 2014 just missed the podium, and proves it is a great wine.

○ FCO Friulano '15	🍷🍷🍷 3*
○ FCO Chardonnay Spìule '14	🍷🍷 4
○ 1648 Brut '12	🍷🍷 5
○ Collio Bianco '14	🍷🍷 3
● FCO Merlot Ravost '13	🍷🍷 4
● FCO Pignolo '10	🍷🍷 5
○ FCO Ribolla Gialla '15	🍷🍷 3
● FCO Schioppettino '14	🍷 3
○ FCO Chardonnay Spìule '13	🍷🍷🍷 4*
⊙ 1648 Brut Rosé '11	🍷🍷 6
○ Collio Bianco '13	🍷🍷 3
○ FCO Picolit '10	🍷🍷 6
● FCO Schioppettino '12	🍷🍷 3

Antonutti

FRAZ. COLLOREDO DI PRATO
VIA D'ANTONI, 21
33037 PASIAN DI PRATO [UD]
TEL. +39 0432662001
www.antonuttivini.it

CELLAR SALES
PRE-BOOKED VISITS
ANNUAL PRODUCTION 780,000 bottles
HECTARES UNDER VINE 51.00
SUSTAINABLE WINERY

Skilfully run for many years by businesswoman Adriana Antonutti, this great name on the regional winemaking scene represents Grave del Friuli's potential to produce straightforward, forthright and highly drinkable wines. Way back in 1921, her grandfather Ignazio was inspired by this terrain, which covers a vast, rugged plain, sparse and stony, perfect for growing vines. Adriana is now continuing the family tradition with the help of her husband Lino and their children Caterina and Nicola. The vineyards adjacent to the historic winery are in Colloredo di Prato, while other highly prized grapes come from Barbeano, in the municipality of Spilimbergo. The Brut Metodo Classico Ant 2011 confirms the flattering reviews of the last vintage. The whites from the last harvest were striking true-to-type, consistent quaffers; the 2014 reds are truly pleasurable, and good value for money.

○ Brut M. Cl. Ant '11	🍷🍷 5
● Friuli Grave Cabernet Sauvignon '14	🍷🍷 2*
● Friuli Grave Merlot '14	🍷🍷 2*
● Friuli Grave Refosco P. R. '14	🍷🍷 2*
○ Friuli Grave Friulano '15	🍷 2
○ Friuli Grave Pinot Grigio '15	🍷 2
○ Friuli Grave Pinot Grigio Ramato '15	🍷 2
● Friuli Grave Pinot Nero '15	🍷 2
○ Friuli Grave Sauvignon '15	🍷 2
○ Friuli Grave Traminer Aromatico '15	🍷 2
○ Brut M. Cl. Ant '10	🍷🍷 5
● Friuli Grave Cabernet Sauvignon '13	🍷🍷 2*
○ Friuli Grave Chardonnay '13	🍷🍷 2*
○ Friuli Grave Friulano '13	🍷🍷 2*
○ Friuli Grave Sauvignon '14	🍷🍷 2*
○ Friuli Grave Sauvignon '13	🍷🍷 2*
○ Lindul '13	🍷🍷 6

TORRE ROSAZZA

www.torrerosazza.com

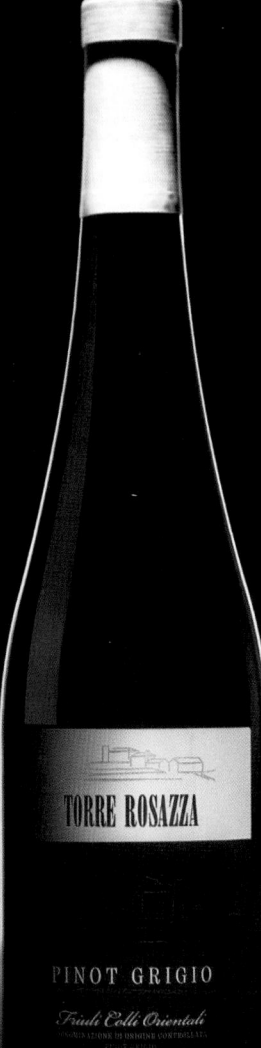

Wine Spectator

Pinot Grigio	TOP 100 2015
Pinot Grigio	90/100
Friulano	90/100
Sauvignon	90/100

Decanter

Pinot Grigio	92/100
Friulano	93/100
Ribolla Gialla	90/100

MUNDUS vini
THE GRAND INTERNATIONAL WINE AWARD

Pinot Grigio	Best of Show
Pinot Grigio	Gold Medal
Friulano	Silver Medal

GAMBERO ROSSO

Pinot Grigio	♈♈♈	2017
Pinot Bianco	♈♈♈	2016
Pinot Grigio	♈♈♈	2015
Pinot Grigio	♈♈	2014

WINE TRAVEL FOOD
GAMBERO ROSSO
30 YEARS OF SUCCESS
GAMBERO ROSSO
Gaia Gaja
BARBARESCO NATIVES
www.gamberorosso.it

KURTATSCH
KELLEREI · CANTINA

2017

tre bicchieri
Gambero Rosso

BRENNTAL

Gew... miner 2014
Riser...

SÜDTIROL
ALTO ADIGE
DOC

KURTATSCH
KELLEREI · CANTINA

Vineyard for Vineyard.
Wine for Wine.

www.kellerei-kurtatsch.it

Aquila del Torre

FRAZ. SAVORGNANO DEL TORRE
VIA ATTIMIS, 25
33040 POVOLETTO [UD]
TEL. +39 0432666428
www.aquiladeltorre.it

CELLAR SALES
PRE-BOOKED VISITS
ACCOMMODATION
ANNUAL PRODUCTION 50,000 bottles
HECTARES UNDER VINE 18.00
VITICULTURE METHOD Certified Organic

Aquila del Torre, founded early last century, draws its name from the little River Torre that runs past it and the fascinating layout of its vineyards that resembles the shape of an eagle's wing when seen from Udine. It was purchased in 1996 by the Ciani family and is now run by Michele, an experienced winemaker who skilfully undertakes the separate vinification of the fine grapes from 16 clearly differentiated plots. The vineyards extend over the steep northern hills of the Friuli Colli Orientali wine region, set amidst scenery of incomparable beauty, traversed by watercourses and set in luxuriant natural woodland. Reviews were generally excellent for the entire cadre but the Refosco SolSiRe 2012 performed especially well, with its brooding colour, delightful nose with hints of coffee and dark chocolate, plus a muscular, juicy mouth. The velvety, very fruity and delicately aromatic At Friulano 2015 is also worthy of mention.

● FCO SolSiRe '12	▼▼ 5
○ FCO At Friulano '15	▼▼ 3
● FCO At Refosco P. R. '13	▼▼ 3
○ FCO At Riesling '13	▼▼ 3
○ FCO At Sauvignon Blanc '15	▼▼ 3
○ COF At Friulano '13	♈♈ 3
○ COF At Picolit '12	♈♈ 6
● COF At Refosco P. R. '11	♈♈ 3
○ COF At Riesling '12	♈♈ 3
○ COF At Sauvignon Blanc '13	♈♈ 3
○ COF Friulano Ronc di Miez '12	♈♈ 5
○ COF Picolit '10	♈♈ 6
○ COF Sauvignon Vit dai Maz '12	♈♈ 5
○ FCO At Friulano '14	♈♈ 3
● FCO At Refosco P. R. '12	♈♈ 3
○ Oasi '12	♈♈ 6
○ Oasi '11	♈♈ 6

Bastianich

LOC. GAGLIANO
VIA DARNAZZACCO, 44/2
33043 CIVIDALE DEL FRIULI [UD]
TEL. +39 0432700943
www.bastianich.com

CELLAR SALES
PRE-BOOKED VISITS
ACCOMMODATION AND RESTAURANT SERVICE
ANNUAL PRODUCTION 270,000 bottles
HECTARES UNDER VINE 35.00

Joe Bastianich, co-owner of some famous restaurants in the US with mother Lidia, burst onto the regional scene in 1997 when he founded a winery, marking a return to his origins and a great challenge for a connoisseur of fine wines. After buying vineyards in Buttrio and Premariacco, he then purchased a winery in Gagliano, near Cividale del Friuli, which is the current company headquarters. He hired an experienced team and achieved great results immediately, distinguishing himself as an ambassador for regional excellence across Italy and overseas. This year's finalist was the Plus 2013, made with tocai friulano grapes from a single vineyard, over 60 years old. We were impressed by its opulence, both on the nose and on the palate, with clear candied peel notes, above all orange and tangerine, leaving lingering aromas.

○ Plus '13	▼▼ 6
● Calabrone '12	▼▼ 8
○ FCO Friulano '15	▼▼ 3
○ FCO Pinot Grigio '15	▼▼ 3
○ FCO Sauvignon '15	▼▼ 3
○ Vespa Bianco '14	▼▼ 5
● Vespa Rosso '13	▼▼ 5
○ FCO Ribolla Gialla '15	▼ 3
○ COF Tocai Friulano Plus '02	♈♈♈ 3*
○ Vespa Bianco '04	♈♈♈ 4
○ Vespa Bianco '03	♈♈♈ 4
○ Vespa Bianco '01	♈♈♈ 4
○ Vespa Bianco '00	♈♈♈ 3
○ Vespa Bianco '99	♈♈♈ 3*
○ Vespa Bianco '13	♈♈ 5
○ Vespa Bianco '12	♈♈ 5

Tenuta Beltrame

FRAZ. PRIVANO
LOC. ANTONINI, 4
33050 BAGNARIA ARSA [UD]
TEL. +39 0432923670
www.beltramewine.com

CELLAR SALES
PRE-BOOKED VISITS
ANNUAL PRODUCTION 80,000 bottles
HECTARES UNDER VINE 25.00

The ancient 40-hectare estate, including
25 hectares of vineyards, which once
belonged to the noble Antonini family, was
purchased by the Beltrame family in 1991
and entrusted to the then very young
Cristian. He set out enthusiastically to
reconvert and replant the vineyards,
focusing on native local varieties. The
historic cellars and main house dating back
to the 15th century were restored to their
former glory and now comprise a highly
attractive and functional complex. The vines
are now mature and exploit all the potential
of the predominantly clayey subsoil,
producing juicy and highly aromatic fruits.
The unanimous thumbs up for both red and
white wines proves that the entire range
has achieved and consolidated its quality.
The Merlot Riserva 2013 caught our
attention for the layered aromas and, above
all, for the boisterous tannins alternating
sweet notes with pleasurable bitter
nuances.

● Friuli Aquileia Cabernet Franc '14	♥♥ 3
● Friuli Aquileia Cabernet Sauvignon '14	♥♥ 3
○ Friuli Aquileia Chardonnay Pribus '13	♥♥ 3
● Friuli Aquileia Merlot Ris. '13	♥♥ 4
● Friuli Aquileia Refosco P.R. '14	♥♥ 3
○ Pinot Grigio '15	♥♥ 3
● Rebus '12	♥♥ 3
● Friuli Aquileia Cabernet Sauvignon Ris. '13	♥ 4
○ Friuli Aquileia Chardonnay '15	♥ 3
○ Friuli Aquileia Friulano '15	♥ 3
● Friuli Aquileia Merlot '14	♥ 3
○ Friuli Aquileia Sauvignon '15	♥ 3
● Pinot Nero '13	♥ 3
● Tazzelenghe '11	♥ 4
● Friuli Aquileia Cabernet Franc '13	♀♀ 2*
● Friuli Aquileia Refosco P. R. '13	♀♀ 2*

Borgo delle Oche

VIA BORGO ALPI, 5
33098 VALVASONE ARZENE [PN]
TEL. +39 0434840640
www.borgodelleoche.it

CELLAR SALES
PRE-BOOKED VISITS
ACCOMMODATION
ANNUAL PRODUCTION 35,000 bottles
HECTARES UNDER VINE 7.00
SUSTAINABLE WINERY

Borgo delle Orche is named after the
characteristic hamlet where it stands, in the
medieval town of Valvasone. It was founded
in 2004 by its current owner Luisa Menini,
who has a degree in food technology, and
her partner Nicola Pittini, agronomist and
oenologist. Luisa loves the great outdoors
and looks after the vines with an obsessive
passion and precision. Perfect grapes allow
Nicola to exploit the potential of the local
area to the full. They work together to
develop consistently high-quality wines,
demonstrating that fine results can even be
achieved even from grapes grown on the
plains by restricting the yields per hectare.
The Refosco dal Peduncolo Rosso 2013
deserved its place in the finals for its
refined nose profile and its sheer
drinkability, with a perfect and equally
persuasive consistency. Praise also for the
complex Lupi Terrae 2014, showing creamy
and fragrant on the nose, with a masterfully
balanced palate.

● Refosco P. R. '13	♥♥ 2*
○ Lupi Terrae '14	♥♥ 3
● Merlot '13	♥♥ 2*
● Rosso Svual '11	♥♥ 3
○ Terra & Cielo Brut '12	♥♥ 3
○ Traminer Aromatico '15	♥♥ 2*
○ Pinot Grigio '15	♥ 2
○ Sauvignon '15	♥ 2
○ Lupi Terrae '13	♀♀ 3
● Merlot '12	♀♀ 2*
● Merlot '11	♀♀ 2*
● Refosco P. R. '12	♀♀ 2*
● Rosso Svual '10	♀♀ 3
○ Terra & Cielo Brut '11	♀♀ 3
○ Traminer Aromatico '13	♀♀ 2*
○ Traminer Aromatico Alba '13	♀♀ 5

★Borgo San Daniele

VIA SAN DANIELE, 28
34071 CORMÒNS [GO]
TEL. +39 048160552
www.borgosandaniele.it

CELLAR SALES
PRE-BOOKED VISITS
ACCOMMODATION
ANNUAL PRODUCTION 57,000 bottles
HECTARES UNDER VINE 19.00
SUSTAINABLE WINERY

A few hectares of vineyards inherited from their grandfather Antonio in 1990 led the young siblings Mauro and Alessandra to change their lives, devoting themselves to these vines. A brave decision that immediately proved to be the right one. Mauro's innate ability took the company to the top of the regional wine scene. Its production of just a few select labels conveys all the potential of the local area. The blends bear the name Arbis, meaning herbs, commemorating the fact that wild herbs are allowed to grow in the vineyards to mitigate the vigour of the vines and the negative effects of monoculture. The Malvasia 2014, from a tragic year in terms of weather conditions, is a real work of art. Straight to the finals and just missing the number one spot by a whisker. The magical sauvignon, chardonnay, friulano, and pinot bianco Arbis Blanc 2014 blend is also marvellous.

Borgo Savaian

VIA SAVAIAN, 36
34071 CORMÒNS [GO]
TEL. +39 048160725
stefanobastiani@libero.it

CELLAR SALES
PRE-BOOKED VISITS
ANNUAL PRODUCTION 100,000 bottles
HECTARES UNDER VINE 18.00

The old tale of peasant families who have devoted themselves to winemaking and are enriched by new life blood, renewed energy and enthusiasm with each new generation is something that never changes. In 2001 Stefano and Rosanna Bastiani took over from their father Mario and started out on a new road, combining winemaking studies with first-hand experience in running the family firm. Stefano is demonstrating an ability to exploit the great potential offered by the Collio Goriziano, and also knows how to make the most of grapes from vineyards extending over the flat expanses of the Fruili Isonzo wine region. A sunkissed summer imprinted wild flowers and wheat notes on this Friulano 2015 del Collio, delighting the nose and echoing on the back palate. A delicious Collio Pinot Grigio 2015 is fruity and fragrant; the Friuli Isonzo Cabernet Franc 2014 continues to live up to its name.

○ Arbis Blanc '14	♀♀ 5
○ Friuli Isonzo Malvasia '14	♀♀ 4
● Arbis Ròs '11	♀♀ 5
○ Friuli Isonzo Pinot Grigio '14	♀♀ 4
○ Arbis Blanc '10	♀♀♀ 4*
○ Arbis Blanc '09	♀♀♀ 4
○ Arbis Blanc '05	♀♀♀ 4
○ Friuli Isonzo Friulano '08	♀♀♀ 4*
○ Friuli Isonzo Friulano '07	♀♀♀ 4*
○ Friuli Isonzo Pinot Grigio '04	♀♀♀ 4
○ Friuli Isonzo Tocai Friulano '03	♀♀♀ 3
● Gortmarin '03	♀♀♀ 5

○ Collio Friulano '15	♀♀ 3*
○ Collio Pinot Grigio '15	♀♀ 3
○ Collio Sauvignon '15	♀♀ 3
● Friuli Isonzo Cabernet Franc '14	♀♀ 3
● Collio Merlot '14	♀ 3
○ Collio Ribolla Gialla '15	♀ 3
○ Friuli Isonzo Malvasia '15	♀ 3
○ Collio Friulano '13	♀♀ 3
● Collio Merlot Tolrem '09	♀♀ 3
○ Collio Pinot Bianco '12	♀♀ 3
○ Collio Ribolla Gialla '14	♀♀ 3
○ Collio Ribolla Gialla '13	♀♀ 3
○ Collio Sauvignon '12	♀♀ 3
● Friuli Isonzo Cabernet Franc '13	♀♀ 3
● Friuli Isonzo Cabernet Franc '12	♀♀ 3*
○ Friuli Isonzo Malvasia '14	♀♀ 3
○ Friuli Isonzo Malvasia '12	♀♀ 3

Cav. Emiro Bortolusso

VIA OLTREGORGO, 10
33050 CARLINO [UD]
TEL. +39 043167596
www.bortolusso.it

CELLAR SALES
PRE-BOOKED VISITS
ACCOMMODATION
ANNUAL PRODUCTION 120,000 bottles
HECTARES UNDER VINE 40.00

The winery now run by Sergio and Clara Bortolusso is based in Carlino, in the Friuli Annia wine region, a beautiful strip of land. The vineyards extend over Friuli's vast flatlands, often surrounded by coppices and overlooking the nearby Adriatic Sea. The mild climate ensures that the grapes reach perfect levels of maturity, while the beneficial sea breezes help to establish the varietal aromas. This family-run firm has been producing a very respectable number of bottles for a number of years now. Consistent quality and good prices have also enabled it to keep expanding. The Pinot Grigio 2015, with nose notes of hay meadow flowers and Golden Delicious, is perfectly balanced and tasty in the mouth. The Friulano 2015 conjures up appley notes but still lacks maturity; the Chardonnay 2015 displays iodine notes and aromatic herbs on the nose, with a fresh, tangy mouth.

○ Chardonnay '15	♟♟ 2*
○ Friuli Annia Friulano '15	♟♟ 2*
○ Malvasia '15	♟♟ 2*
○ Pinot Grigio '15	♟♟ 2*
○ Sauvignon '15	♟♟ 2*
○ Traminer Aromatico '15	♟♟ 2*
○ Chardonnay '13	♟♟ 2*
○ Friulano '13	♟♟ 2*
○ Friuli Annia Friulano '14	♟♟ 2*
○ Friuli Annia Malvasia '12	♟♟ 2*
○ Malvasia '14	♟♟ 2*
○ Pinot Grigio '14	♟♟ 2*
○ Sauvignon '14	♟♟ 2*
○ Sauvignon '13	♟♟ 2*
○ Traminer Aromatico '14	♟♟ 2*
○ Traminer Aromatico '13	♟♟ 2*
○ Verduzzo Friulano '14	♟♟ 3

Branko

LOC. ZEGLA, 20
34071 CORMÒNS [GO]
TEL. +39 0481639826
www.brankowines.com

CELLAR SALES
PRE-BOOKED VISITS
ANNUAL PRODUCTION 45,000 bottles
HECTARES UNDER VINE 9.00

Igor Erzetic should be credited with having transformed a small family-run firm into a regional winemaking gem. In 1950 his father Branko formally founded the firm, but its roots are lost in time, as there has been an intimate link between the land and man in the historic Collio since time immemorial. The small size of the cellar and the limited number of labels allow Igor to devote all his efforts to looking after the vines and processing the grapes. His wines reflect his personality. These great ambassadors for the local area possess an exemplary cleanliness and propriety, respecting the varietal characteristics. This year the Pinot Grigio 2015 lives up to its name yet again, and deserved its place in our finals, accompanied by a surprising Sauvignon of the same vintage. The tempting nose shows elderflower and pear notes; the tasty mouth closes on whispers of tropical fruit.

○ Collio Pinot Grigio '15	♟♟ 4
○ Collio Sauvignon '15	♟♟ 4
○ Capo Branko '15	♟♟ 4
○ Collio Chardonnay '15	♟♟ 4
○ Collio Friulano '15	♟♟ 4
● Red Branko '13	♟♟ 4
○ Collio Pinot Grigio '14	♟♟♟ 4*
○ Collio Pinot Grigio '08	♟♟♟ 3*
○ Collio Pinot Grigio '07	♟♟♟ 3
○ Collio Pinot Grigio '06	♟♟♟ 3
○ Collio Pinot Grigio '05	♟♟♟ 3
○ Capo Branko '14	♟♟ 4
○ Collio Chardonnay '14	♟♟ 4
○ Collio Chardonnay '13	♟♟ 4
○ Collio Pinot Grigio '12	♟♟ 4
○ Collio Sauvignon '14	♟♟ 4
● Red Branko '12	♟♟ 4

Livio e Claudio Buiatti

VIA LIPPE, 25
33042 BUTTRIO [UD]
TEL. +39 0432674317
www.buiattivini.it

CELLAR SALES
PRE-BOOKED VISITS
ANNUAL PRODUCTION 35,000 bottles
HECTARES UNDER VINE 8.00

The Buiatti family boasts over a century of experience in growing grapes on the Buttrio hills, which are close to the sea and exposed to the hot rays of the sun. Claudio Buiatti, who now runs the company together with his wife Viviana, inherited the wonderful vineyards from his father and has successfully combined past experience with present needs. He has progressively modernized the firm, increasing the equipment and restricting production with drastic pruning. These essential measures have produced the desired effects, taking the entire range to a very high level of quality, with some truly excellent highlights, all at very good prices. The Friulano 2015 carries the imprint of the season's positive conditions and displays an intense nose of wild flowers, dried thyme and acacia honey, with a fragrant, flavoursome palate. The Momon Ros Riserva 2012 stands out for structure and personality, steeping the palate in memories of morello cherry and liquorice.

○ FCO Friulano '15	♟♟	3
○ FCO Malvasia '15	♟♟	3
● FCO Momon Ros Ris. '12	♟♟	4
○ FCO Sauvignon '15	♟♟	3
● FCO Cabernet Franc '14	♟	3
● FCO Refosco P. R. '14	♟	3
○ FCO Verduzzo Friulano Momon d'Aur '15	♟	3
● COF Cabernet Franc '12	♟♟	3
● COF Merlot '12	♟♟	3
● COF Momon Ros Ris. '10	♟♟	3
○ COF Pinot Grigio '13	♟♟	3
○ COF Sauvignon '13	♟♟	3
○ COF Verduzzo Friulano Momon d'Aur '12	♟♟	4
○ FCO Friulano '14	♟♟	3
○ FCO Malvasia '14	♟♟	3
● FCO Merlot '13	♟♟	3
○ FCO Pinot Grigio '14	♟♟	3

La Buse dal Lôf

VIA RONCHI, 90
33040 PREPOTTO [UD]
TEL. +39 0432701523
www.labusedallof.com

CELLAR SALES
PRE-BOOKED VISITS
ANNUAL PRODUCTION 100,000 bottles
HECTARES UNDER VINE 25.00

Many people are interested in the origins of the strange name of this Prepotto-based winery. As in other cases, it is all to do with the topographic name given to its location. Ancient maps often mention these zones with expressions deriving from the local language and La Buse dal Lôf means The Wolf's Den. It was back in 1972 that Giuseppe Pavan founded the firm, later employing his son Michele, who has managed to promote it thanks to his great passion and innate ability. The vineyards extend over 25 hectares, which is a fair size in this part of the Friuli Colli Orientali wine region. Year after year results continue to improve and the entire cadre has stabilized at an admirable level of quality, without peaks of excellence but with textbook constancy. This year's flagship is the 2015 Pinot Bianco In Bocca al Lupo 2015, whose name is a good omen in Italy.

● FCO Cabernet Franc '14	♟♟	3
○ FCO Chardonnay '15	♟♟	3
○ FCO Friulano '15	♟♟	3
○ FCO Pinot Bianco In Bocca al Lupo '15	♟♟	3
○ FCO Ribolla Gialla '15	♟♟	3
○ FCO Sauvignon '15	♟♟	3
● FCO Schioppettino di Prepotto '12	♟♟	4
○ FCO Pinot Grigio '15	♟	3
○ COF Pinot Bianco In Bocca al Lupo '13	♟♟	3
● COF Refosco P. R. '11	♟♟	3
● COF Schioppettino di Prepotto '11	♟♟	4
○ FCO Friulano '14	♟♟	3
○ FCO Sauvignon '14	♟♟	3

Valentino Butussi

VIA PRÀ DI CORTE, 1
33040 CORNO DI ROSAZZO [UD]
TEL. +39 0432759194
www.butussi.it

CELLAR SALES
PRE-BOOKED VISITS
ACCOMMODATION
ANNUAL PRODUCTION 120,000 bottles
HECTARES UNDER VINE 18.00
VITICULTURE METHOD Certified Organic
SUSTAINABLE WINERY

Tobia, Filippo, Mattia and Erika represent the next generation in the company management, but their father Angelo is emblematic, heading a truly cohesive and synchronized family group that shares the various tasks and is ready to switch roles when required. Credit should be given to their grandfather Valentino, who founded the company at the start of the last century and passed on the concept of upholding the values of the peasant culture. Team spirit is the added value that has enabled this brand to stand out on Friuli's crowded wine scene, enabling it to produce a large number of labels at fair, competitive prices. Not only the white wines of the vintage but also the reds, the sweet dessert wines, and the sparklers met with unanimous approval, confirming the quality offered by the entire range. The Merlot 2013 shows aromas of sweet spice and great drinkability. We noted the forthright Friuliano 2015 for its fragrance and tanginess.

● FCO Cabernet Sauvignon '13	♟♟	3
○ FCO Friulano '15	♟♟	2*
● FCO Merlot '13	♟♟	3
○ FCO Picolit '10	♟♟	6
● FCO Pignolo '11	♟♟	5
○ FCO Sauvignon '15	♟♟	2*
○ Ribolla Gialla Brut	♟♟	5
○ FCO Chardonnay '15	♟	2
○ FCO Pinot Grigio '15	♟	2
○ FCO Ribolla Gialla '15	♟	2
○ FCO Verduzzo Friulano '12	♟	2
○ COF Friulano '13	♟♟	2*
● FCO Cabernet Franc '13	♟♟	3
● FCO Cabernet Sauvignon '12	♟♟	3
○ FCO Chardonnay '14	♟♟	2*
● FCO Refosco P. R. '12	♟♟	3*
○ FCO Ribolla Gialla '14	♟♟	2*

Maurizio Buzzinelli

LOC. PRADIS, 20
34071 CORMÒNS [GO]
TEL. +39 048160902
www.buzzinelli.it

CELLAR SALES
PRE-BOOKED VISITS
ACCOMMODATION
ANNUAL PRODUCTION 120,000 bottles
HECTARES UNDER VINE 35.00

Natural beauty and the need to survive attracted Luigi back in 1937, leading him and his entire family to settle on the Pradis hills, near Cormòns. Gently rolling slopes form a sun-kissed amphitheatre, exposed to the breeze from the nearby Adriatic, taking him progressively away from mixed agriculture towards intensive grape growing. Maurizio represents the third generation of the family to grow these wonderful vines. He supervises the entire production chain in person, achieving great results both from the white grapes grown on the Collio and from the red grapes that exploit the characteristics of the Friuli Isonzo wine region. As is customary we only received the new vintage Collio whites, and the scores obtained confirm the quality was what we have come to expect. The 2015 Malvasia and 2015 Chardonnay have the edge but the others follow hot on their heels.

○ Collio Chardonnay '15	♟♟	3
○ Collio Friulano '15	♟♟	3
○ Collio Malvasia '15	♟♟	2*
○ Collio Ribolla Gialla '15	♟♟	3
○ Collio Sauvignon '15	♟♟	3
○ Collio Chardonnay '14	♟♟	3
○ Collio Chardonnay '12	♟♟	3
○ Collio Friulano '14	♟♟	3
○ Collio Friulano '13	♟♟	3
○ Collio Friulano '12	♟♟	3*
○ Collio Malvasia '13	♟♟	2*
○ Collio Pinot Grigio '13	♟♟	3*
○ Collio Pinot Grigio '12	♟♟	3
○ Collio Ribolla Gialla '14	♟♟	3
○ Collio Ribolla Gialla '13	♟♟	3
○ Collio Sauvignon '14	♟♟	3*
○ Collio Sauvignon '13	♟♟	2*

Ca' Bolani

VIA CA' BOLANI, 2
33052 CERVIGNANO DEL FRIULI [UD]
TEL. +39 043132670
www.cabolani.it

CELLAR SALES
PRE-BOOKED VISITS
ANNUAL PRODUCTION 2,700,000 bottles
HECTARES UNDER VINE 550.00

The Ca' Bolani estate belonged to the eponymous family, whose most famous member was Conte Domenico Bolani, Friuli's public prosecutor for the Venetian Republic in the first half of the 16th century, until it was acquired by the Veneto-based Zonin group in 1970. Covering 550 hectares, it is the largest vineyard not just in the region, but in the whole of northern Italy. The high number of bottles produced here, which is unusual on the regional winemaking scene, does not have a negative effect on quality which, together with competitive prices, is Ca' Bolani's strong point. The winery has an experienced team, managed with great ability by the oenologist Marco Rabino. Quality has settled at more than respectable levels. The Ca' Bolani brand is absolutely reliable and adds lustre to the entire Friuli Aquileia designation. Our favourite? The excellent Merlot Superiore 2014, a nose of ripe sour cherries and a gratifying palate.

● Friuli Aquileia Cabernet Franc Sup. '14	♟♟	3
● Friuli Aquileia Merlot Sup. '14	♟♟	3
○ Friuli Aquileia Pinot Bianco Opimio '14	♟♟	4
● Friuli Aquileia Refosco P. R. '14	♟♟	3
○ Friuli Aquileia Friulano Sup. '15	♟	3
○ Friuli Aquileia Pinot Bianco Sup. '15	♟	3
○ Friuli Aquileia Pinot Grigio Sup. '15	♟	3
○ Friuli Aquileia Sauvignon Sup. '15	♟	3
○ Friuli Aquileia Traminer Aromatico Sup. '15	♟	3
○ Prosecco Brut	♟	3
○ Friuli Aquileia Pinot Bianco '09	♟♟♟	2*
○ Friuli Aquileia Pinot Grigio Sup. '13	♟♟	3
● Friuli Aquileia Refosco P. R. Sup. '13	♟♟	3
○ Friuli Aquileia Sauvignon Aquilis '14	♟♟	2*
○ Friuli Aquileia Traminer Aromatico Sup. '14	♟♟	3

Ca' Tullio

VIA BELIGNA, 41
33051 AQUILEIA [UD]
TEL. +39 0431919700
www.catullio.it

CELLAR SALES
PRE-BOOKED VISITS
ANNUAL PRODUCTION 200,000 bottles
HECTARES UNDER VINE 100.00

Ca' Tullio is based in Aquileia, in a large turn-of-the-century building once used for drying tobacco, which was purchased by Paolo Calligaris in 1994. After skilful renovation work, it was transformed into a modern and functional winery, without damaging its wonderful architecture in any way. The winemaking process is entrusted to the winery oenologist Francesco Visintin. Most of the grapes are grown on the Manzano hills, in the Friuli Colli Orientali wine region, while other vineyards surround the winery itself, where traminer can still be cultivated ungrafted in the sandy ground of the Viola area. In the last edition, the Sdricca di Manzano line was well ahead of the Ca' Tullio but the roles are reversed this year, mainly thanks to the 2015 whites, showing lots of flower and citrus notes on the nose, with consistent, excellent drinkability.

● FCO Pignolo '12	♟♟	3
○ FCO Ribolla Gialla '15	♟♟	3
○ FCO Sauvignon '15	♟♟	3
● FCO Schioppettino '13	♟♟	3
○ Friuli Aquileia Pinot Grigio '15	♟♟	2*
○ Friuli Aquileia Traminer Viola '15	♟♟	2*
● FCO Cabernet Franc '15	♟	2
○ FCO Friulano Sdricca di Manzano '15	♟	3
● FCO Merlot '15	♟	3
○ Friuli Aquileia Chardonnay '15	♟	2
○ Prosecco Extra Dry '15	♟	2
● Cabernet Franc '13	♟♟	2*
○ FCO Ribolla Gialla Sdricca di Manzano '14	♟♟	3
○ FCO Sauvignon Sdricca di Manzano '14	♟♟	3
○ Friuli Aquileia Chardonnay '13	♟♟	2*
● Merlot '13	♟♟	2*

Cadibon

VIA CASALI GALLO, 1
33040 CORNO DI ROSAZZO [UD]
TEL. +39 0432759316
www.cadibon.com

CELLAR SALES
PRE-BOOKED VISITS
RESTAURANT SERVICE
ANNUAL PRODUCTION 55,000 bottles
HECTARES UNDER VINE 14.00
VITICULTURE METHOD Certified Organic

This flourishing winery in Corno di Rosazzo, founded in 1977 by Gianni Bon, is now run by Luca and Francesca who, as well as having introduced a breath of fresh air and new energy, have also started working towards organic and biodynamic production. The wines have benefitted from brave decision to opt for natural fermentation and, despite deriving from elaborating processing techniques, stand out for their freshness and drinkability. Luca looks after the vineyards in three different wine regions: Friuli Colli Orientali, Friuli Grave and Collio. Cadibon is also an invitation, an expression in the local dialect meaning "Here on the Bon estate". Quality has grown in leaps and bounds recently and tickled even the most demanding palates. The fragrance of the forthright Friulano Bontaj 2015 confirms its flagship role but consistent, taut and delicately balanced the Ronco del Nonno 2015 sauvignon, friulano, chardonnay, and verduzzo blend is not far behind.

Fernanda Cappello

S.DA DI SEQUALS, 15
33090 SEQUALS [PN]
TEL. +39 042793291
www.fernandacappello.it

CELLAR SALES
PRE-BOOKED VISITS
RESTAURANT SERVICE
ANNUAL PRODUCTION 100,000 bottles
HECTARES UNDER VINE 126.00
SUSTAINABLE WINERY

In 1988 Fernanda Cappello took over the winery acquired by her father in the late 1970s. Her entrepreneurial ability saw the launch of a modernization process that promoted the firm and made it a key name on the regional wine scene. A good 126 hectares of the 135-hectare estate are under vine, covering one of the biggest expanses in western Friuli. The land is dry, lean and rocky, ideal for growing grapes, and composed of Dolomitic limestone alluvial sediments from the Cellina and Meduna rivers. The invaluable winemaking advice of Fabio Coser has contributed to the leap in quality of the entire range of wines. The Cabernet Sauvignon 2014 concedes hints of golden-leaf tobacco, rhubarb and damson jam, segued by a well-balanced palate of softness and lively tannins. The Chardonnay Perla dei Sassi 2014, shows scents of hawthorn flanked by subtle fresh notes of peppermint encoring on the palate.

○ Collio Sauvignon '15	♟♟ 3
● FCO Cabernet Franc '15	♟♟ 3
○ FCO Friulano Bontaj '15	♟♟ 3
○ FCO Pinot Grigio '15	♟♟ 3
● FCO Refosco P. R. '14	♟♟ 3
○ FCO Ribolla Gialla '15	♟♟ 3
● FCO Schioppettino '14	♟♟ 3
○ Ronco del Nonno '15	♟♟ 3
○ Collio Chardonnay '15	♟ 3
○ Moscato '15	♟ 3
○ Collio Sauvignon '14	♟♟ 3
○ Collio Sauvignon '13	♟♟ 3
○ FCO Friulano Bontaj '14	♟♟ 3
● FCO Refosco P. R. '13	♟♟ 3
● FCO Schioppettino '13	♟♟ 3
○ Ronco del Nonno '14	♟♟ 3
○ Ronco del Nonno '13	♟♟ 3

● Friuli Grave Cabernet Sauvignon '14	♟♟ 2*
○ Friuli Grave Chardonnay Perla dei Sassi '14	♟♟ 3
○ Friuli Grave Chardonnay '15	♟ 2
○ Friuli Grave Friulano '15	♟ 2
○ Friuli Grave Pinot Grigio '15	♟ 2
○ Friuli Grave Sauvignon '15	♟ 2
○ Friuli Grave Traminer Aromatico '15	♟ 2
○ Prosecco Extra Dry	♟ 2
● Friuli Grave Cabernet Franc '13	♟♟ 2*
○ Friuli Grave Chardonnay '14	♟♟ 2*
○ Friuli Grave Friulano '14	♟♟ 2*
○ Friuli Grave Friulano '13	♟♟ 2*
○ Friuli Grave Pinot Grigio '13	♟♟ 2*
○ Friuli Grave Sauvignon '14	♟♟ 2*
○ Friuli Grave Sauvignon '13	♟♟ 2*
○ Friuli Grave Traminer Aromatico '12	♟♟ 2*

Carlo di Pradis

LOC. PRADIS, 22B
34071 CORMÒNS [GO]
TEL. +39 048162272
www.carlodipradis.it

CELLAR SALES
PRE-BOOKED VISITS
ANNUAL PRODUCTION 70,000 bottles
HECTARES UNDER VINE 15.00

For some time, brothers Boris and David Buzzinelli have been running the company inherited from their father Carlo. The firm has been handed down from one generation to the next, as is typical of small family-run wineries dotting the Pradis hills, a flourishing district of the Collio Goriziano wine region, which benefits from great exposure overlooking the plain, caressed by the breeze from the nearby Adriatic Sea. Around half of the vineyards surround the winery, while the rest are in the Friuli Isonzo wine region. Boris and David manage to get the very best from both areas, focusing on agreeableness and structure. Freshness and fragrance are the common denominators that characterize the entire range of wines, in particular the Friuliano 2015. The Pinot Grigio 2015 is another excellent offering, with hay meadow flowers and wheat aromas, while both the 2015 Sauvignons are especially citrusy and varietal.

○ Collio Friulano '15	♥♥	3
○ Collio Pinot Grigio '15	♥♥	3
○ Collio Sauvignon '15	♥♥	3
○ Friuli Isonzo Sauvignon '15	♥♥	2*
○ Collio Ribolla Gialla '15	♥	3
○ Friuli Isonzo Chardonnay '15	♥	3
○ Collio Friulano '14	♀♀	3*
○ Collio Friulano '13	♀♀	3
○ Collio Friulano '12	♀♀	3
○ Collio Pinot Grigio '13	♀♀	3
○ Collio Pinot Grigio '12	♀♀	3
○ Collio Sauvignon '14	♀♀	3
○ Collio Sauvignon '12	♀♀	3*
○ Friuli Isonzo Chardonnay '13	♀♀	3
○ Friuli Isonzo Chardonnay '12	♀♀	3
○ Friuli Isonzo Sauvignon '14	♀♀	2*
○ Friuli Isonzo Sauvignon '12	♀♀	2*

Il Carpino

LOC. SOVENZA, 14A
34070 SAN FLORIANO DEL COLLIO [GO]
TEL. +39 0481884097
www.ilcarpino.com

CELLAR SALES
PRE-BOOKED VISITS
ANNUAL PRODUCTION 70,000 bottles
HECTARES UNDER VINE 16.00

Despite coming from peasant stock, Anna and Franco Sosol both worked in different fields before deciding to join forces in 1987 and enter the world of agriculture. They founded Il Carpino brand and still run this wonderful winery that occupies a key position on the regional wine scene. The winery is based in San Floriano del Collio, in the Sovenza area, not far from the border with Slovenia. Traditions die hard here and there is a strong tendency to look to the past. Modern technology is reserved for the vinification of grapes from younger vineyards, while the best products are the result of slow maceration using historic techniques. An impressive three wines made our finals, all from white grapes harvested in 2012. The colours are vibrant, intense and marked for wines that beguile on the nose with intriguing notes of honey, almonds and tropical fruit, while the palate is a sequence of unusual but very elegant aromas and flavours.

○ Collio Ribolla Gialla V. Runc '12	♥♥	5
○ Exordium '12	♥♥	5
○ Malvasia '12	♥♥	5
○ Collio Ribolla Gialla '15	♥♥	4
○ Friuli Isonzo Bianco Runc '15	♥♥	3
○ Vis Uvae '12	♥♥	5
○ Collio Bianco V. Runc '10	♀♀♀	2*
○ Collio Malvasia V. Runc '11	♀♀♀	3*
○ Malvasia '11	♀♀♀	5
○ Collio Malvasia V. Runc '14	♀♀	3*
○ Collio Sauvignon V. Runc '13	♀♀	2*
○ Exordium '11	♀♀	5
○ Friuli Isonzo Bianco Runc '13	♀♀	3
○ Friuli Isonzo Friulano V. Runc '13	♀♀	3
○ Vis Uvae '11	♀♀	5

Castello di Buttrio

VIA DEL POZZO, 5
33042 BUTTRIO [UD]
TEL. +39 0432673015
www.castellodibuttrio.it

CELLAR SALES
PRE-BOOKED VISITS
ACCOMMODATION AND RESTAURANT SERVICE
ANNUAL PRODUCTION 60,000 bottles
HECTARES UNDER VINE 25.00

The Castello di Buttrio estate extends over the gently rolling hills of the Friuli Colli Orientali wine region. The first hills overlooking the sea dominate the extensive Friuli plain. The horizon fades into the distance and it is no coincidence that a castle once stood here. Alessandra Felluga has patiently restored the ancient structure to its former glory, converting it into an avant-garde winery while respecting the original architecture. Castello di Buttrio wines have captured the attention of the most refined palates thanks to their improved quality, which can be attributed to the expert hand of the oenologist Hartmann Donà. The Sauvignon Ettaro Riserva 2013 made an excellent debut, winning unanimous approval for its elegant, refined floral and fruit nose notes, enhanced by an undercurrent of medicinal herbs and bay leaf. The rich palate is flavoursome with intriguing aromatic nuances and minty hints.

Castello di Spessa

VIA SPESSA, 1
34070 CAPRIVA DEL FRIULI [GO]
TEL. +39 048160445
www.castellodispessa.it

CELLAR SALES
PRE-BOOKED VISITS
ACCOMMODATION AND RESTAURANT SERVICE
ANNUAL PRODUCTION 300,000 bottles
HECTARES UNDER VINE 83.00

The elegant 13th-century Castello di Spessa perches on a small hill and is surrounded by a magnificent Italian garden, in the heart of the Collio Goriziano wine region. Its eventful history goes back almost 1000 years, while its beauty exerts a subtle charm over even the most distracted visitor. In 1987, the current owner Loretto Pali created a winery here, converting back the neighbouring vineyards and restoring the castle at the same time. Excellent results were quick to arrive thanks to the advice of the best consultants. The winery's now-experienced team still works with expert oenologist Enrico Paternoster. This year there was further proof that the entire battery is utterly worthy, but the pleasurable Pinot Bianco 2015 was the latest vintage of a long series that is a cut above the rest for elegance and fragrance. Unsurprisingly it made the finals accompanied by an equally great Sauvignon Segrè 2015.

○ FCO Bianco Mon Blanc '14	♟♟ 3
○ FCO Friulano '15	♟♟ 4
● FCO Merlot '12	♟♟ 4
● FCO Rosso Mon Rouge '13	♟♟ 3
○ FCO Sauvignon Ettaro Ris. '13	♟♟ 6
● FCO Refosco P. R. '14	♟ 4
○ FCO Ribolla Gialla '15	♟ 4
○ COF Friulano '13	♟♟ 3
○ COF Bianco Mon Blanc '13	♟♟ 3
○ COF Sauvignon '13	♟♟ 3
○ FCO Friulano '14	♟♟ 3
● FCO Pignolo '10	♟♟ 5
○ FCO Sauvignon '14	♟♟ 3
○ FCO Torre Butria Ris. '11	♟♟ 5
○ FCO Verduzzo Friulano Mille e una Botte '12	♟♟ 5

○ Collio Pinot Bianco '15	♟♟ 3*
● Collio Sauvignon Segrè '15	♟♟ 5
○ Collio Friulano '15	♟♟ 3
● Collio Merlot V. Rosaris '13	♟♟ 5
○ Collio Pinot Grigio '15	♟♟ 3
● Collio Pinot Nero Casanova '12	♟♟ 5
○ Collio Sauvignon '15	♟♟ 3
● Friuli Isonzo Cabernet Franc '14	♟♟ 3
● Friuli Isonzo Cabernet Sauvignon '14	♟♟ 3
○ Ribolla Gialla Brut Pertè '15	♟♟ 4
○ Collio Pinot Bianco '14	♟♟♟ 3*
○ Collio Pinot Bianco '13	♟♟♟ 3*
○ Collio Pinot Bianco '11	♟♟♟ 3*
○ Collio Pinot Bianco '06	♟♟♟ 3*
○ Collio Sauvignon Segrè '03	♟♟♟ 5
○ Collio Tocai Friulano '05	♟♟♟ 3*

Castello Sant'Anna

LOC. SPESSA
VIA SANT'ANNA, 9
33043 CIVIDALE DEL FRIULI [UD]
TEL. +39 0432716289
centasantanna@libero.it

CELLAR SALES
PRE-BOOKED VISITS
ANNUAL PRODUCTION 25,000 bottles
HECTARES UNDER VINE 7.00
VITICULTURE METHOD Certified Organic

Andrea Giaiotti represents the third
generation of the same family to run
Castello Sant'Anna, in Spessa di Cividale,
a winery founded by 1966 by his
grandfather Giuseppe, who decided to
leave his industrial career behind and
return to his peasant origins. Once the
summer residence of noble families from
Cividale, the castle is surrounded by
vineyards. Andrea has worked tirelessly to
reorganize the old vines and construct a
new underground cellar that ensures
natural humidity and a constant
temperature. This winery is run on a
human scale, making it possible to carry
out the agricultural labour and the winery
operations. In previous editions our praise
was mainly for the reds while this year we
were more impressed by the white wines
of the last vintage. In particular, the
fragrant, tasty Pinot Grigio 2015 made a
well-deserved entry to the finals for its
appealing nose and sheer drinkability.

Castelvecchio

VIA CASTELNUOVO, 2
34078 SAGRADO [GO]
TEL. +39 048199742
www.castelvecchio.com

CELLAR SALES
PRE-BOOKED VISITS
ACCOMMODATION AND RESTAURANT SERVICE
ANNUAL PRODUCTION 180,000 bottles
HECTARES UNDER VINE 35.00
SUSTAINABLE WINERY

Castelvecchio, owned by the Terraneo
family, is in the northernmost part of the
karst plateau, in the province of Gorizia. Its
elevated position offers an all-round view of
the region, from the sea to the mountains.
The predominantly rocky ground is rich in
iron and limestone. The beautiful landscape
encompasses the noble and ancient origins
of these places, still evident today in the
Renaissance villa and the stunning gardens
planted with age-old cypresses and oaks.
The microclimate is ideal and the perfect
grapes that grow here are entrusted to the
expert oenologist Saverio Di Giacomo,
aided by the expert advice of Gianni
Menotti. In the last edition we said that
seeing a wine reach the finals is always
very satisfying, but this year the Malvasia
Dileo 2015 went further, taking the first Tre
Bicchieri for its maker. A sun-drenched,
fragrant wine with citrus and iodine notes,
and a creamy palate that is zippy, thrusting
and in no hurry to sign off.

○ FCO Pinot Grigio '15	♀♀ 3*
● FCO Cabernet Franc '13	♀♀ 4
○ FCO Friulano '15	♀♀ 3
● FCO Merlot '12	♀♀ 4
○ FCO Ribolla Gialla '15	♀♀ 3
○ FCO Sauvignon '15	♀♀ 3
○ COF Friulano '12	♀♀ 3
● COF Merlot '11	♀♀ 4
○ COF Pinot Grigio '12	♀♀ 3*
○ COF Pinot Grigio '11	♀♀ 3*
○ COF Ribolla Gialla '12	♀♀ 3*
● FCO Cabernet Franc '12	♀♀ 4
○ FCO Friulano '13	♀♀ 3
○ FCO Pinot Grigio '13	♀♀ 3
● FCO Refosco P. R. '11	♀♀ 4
○ FCO Sauvignon '13	♀♀ 3
● FCO Schioppettino '11	♀♀ 5

○ Carso Malvasia Dileo '15	♀♀♀ 4*
● Carso Cabernet Franc '13	♀♀ 3
● Carso Cabernet Sauvignon '13	♀♀ 3
● Carso Refosco P. R. '12	♀♀ 3
○ Carso Traminer Aromatico '15	♀♀ 3
○ Carso Vitovska '15	♀♀ 3
⊙ Terrano Brut Rosé	♀♀ 4
○ Carso Malvasia '15	♀ 3
○ Carso Pinot Grigio '15	♀ 3
○ Carso Sauvignon '15	♀ 3
● Carso Terrano '15	♀ 3
● Carso Cabernet Franc '12	♀♀ 3
● Carso Cabernet Sauvignon '12	♀♀ 3
○ Carso Malvasia '14	♀♀ 3
○ Carso Traminer Aromatico '14	♀♀ 3

★Eugenio Collavini

LOC. GRAMOGLIANO
VIA DELLA RIBOLLA GIALLA, 2
33040 CORNO DI ROSAZZO [UD]
TEL. +39 0432753222
www.collavini.it

CELLAR SALES
PRE-BOOKED VISITS
RESTAURANT SERVICE
ANNUAL PRODUCTION 1,200,000 bottles
HECTARES UNDER VINE 140.00
SUSTAINABLE WINERY

The business founded by Eugenio Collavini in 1896 is one of the region's historic wineries. Its headquarters are in Corno di Rosazzo, in a 16th-century fortified villa that once belonged to the noble Zucco di Cuccanea family. Today it is run by Manlio Collavini, who started a process of progressive improvements in the 1970s, expanding it without negatively affecting the quality of the wine. An expert agronomist employed by the winery supervises operations in its own vineyards and in those belonging to its suppliers. The brothers Luigi and Giovanni represent the next generation of the family, actively collaborating in the business for years. Yet another Tre Bicchieri for the Collio Bianco Broy 2015, almost a byword for the award, which is collects year after year with enviable regularity. In such a positive vintage it is especially fragrant with citrus notes of lime and citron, and irresistible aromatic layers.

○ Collio Bianco Broy '15	♔♔♔ 5
● FCO Pignolo '07	♔♔ 6
○ Collio Pinot Grigio '15	♔♔ 3
○ Collio Sauvignon Blanc Fumât '15	♔♔ 3
○ FCO Ribolla Gialla Turian '15	♔♔ 4
○ Collio Bianco Broy '14	♔♔♔ 5
○ Collio Bianco Broy '13	♔♔♔ 5
○ Collio Bianco Broy '11	♔♔♔ 4*
○ Collio Bianco Broy '10	♔♔♔ 4
○ Collio Bianco Broy '09	♔♔♔ 4*
○ Collio Bianco Broy '08	♔♔♔ 4*
○ Collio Bianco Broy '07	♔♔♔ 4
○ Collio Bianco Broy '06	♔♔♔ 4
○ Collio Bianco Broy '04	♔♔♔ 4*
○ Collio Bianco Broy '03	♔♔♔ 4

Colle Duga

LOC. ZEGLA, 10
34071 CORMÒNS [GO]
TEL. +39 048161177
www.colleduga.com

CELLAR SALES
PRE-BOOKED VISITS
ANNUAL PRODUCTION 50,000 bottles
HECTARES UNDER VINE 9.00

Damijan Princic named his company Colle Duga, taking the name from local names that name the hill on which his vineyards are situated as Duga. The Princic family have been cultivating vines and the art of winemaking on this hill for generations. Damijan took over the management of the winery in 1991. He is still assisted by his father Luciano in the vineyards, while the family is completed by his wife Monica and his young children Karin and Patrik, who also participate enthusiastically in the business. The wines have a strong personality and reflect the simple and honest peasant philosophy. At least two Colle Duga wines have made it to our finals for many years now, and this year both the Collio Bianco 2015 and the Friulano 2015 earned this acknowledgement. Both are very fruity, with tropical hints putting in an appearance, but above all they are balanced, full-flavoured and a joy for the palate.

○ Collio Bianco '15	♔♔ 4
○ Collio Friulano '15	♔♔ 3*
○ Collio Chardonnay '15	♔♔ 3
○ Collio Pinot Grigio '15	♔♔ 3
○ Collio Sauvignon '15	♔♔ 3
○ Collio Bianco '11	♔♔♔ 4*
○ Collio Bianco '08	♔♔♔ 3*
○ Collio Bianco '07	♔♔♔ 3
○ Collio Friulano '09	♔♔♔ 3*
○ Collio Tocai Friulano '06	♔♔♔ 3*
○ Collio Tocai Friulano '05	♔♔♔ 3*
○ Collio Bianco '14	♔♔ 4
○ Collio Chardonnay '15	♔♔ 3
○ Collio Chardonnay '14	♔♔ 3*
○ Collio Chardonnay '13	♔♔ 3*
○ Collio Friulano '14	♔♔ 3

Colmello di Grotta

Loc. Grotta
via Gorizia, 133
34072 Farra d'Isonzo [GO]
Tel. +39 0481888445
www.colmello.it

CELLAR SALES
PRE-BOOKED VISITS
ANNUAL PRODUCTION 75,000 bottles
HECTARES UNDER VINE 15.00

Francesca Bortolotto runs this great winery inherited from her mother Luciana Bennati, who set out to restore a run-down hamlet in 1965, transforming it into an efficient and well-equipped production site. The winery's vineyards are on the plain and the hill, which have very different climates. Thanks to the winemaking expertise of Fabio Coser, the wines reflect the local potential to the full. Wines produced in the Friuli Isonzo wine region are characterized by their linearity, rich aromas and great drinkability, while those from the Collio grapes display a markedly complex nose and powerful structure. The top performance from the growing season's wines, especially the Collio, was integrated by a good show from the Rondon Rosso 2013, a blend of merlot and cabernet sauvignon. The complex nose shows macerate sour cherries, violets, dark spice and cocoa powder; the palate is rich, mouthfilling and juicy.

○ Collio Bianco Sanfilip '15	♟♟ 3
○ Collio Chardonnay '15	♟♟ 3
○ Collio Friulano '15	♟♟ 3
○ Collio Pinot Grigio '15	♟♟ 3
○ Collio Sauvignon '15	♟♟ 3
○ Friuli Isonzo Chardonnay '15	♟♟ 3
● Rondon '13	♟♟ 5
○ Collio Ribolla Gialla '15	♟ 3
○ Friuli Isonzo Pinot Grigio '15	♟ 3
○ Friuli Isonzo Sauvignon '15	♟ 3
○ Collio Chardonnay '13	♟♟ 3*
○ Collio Pinot Grigio '14	♟♟ 3
○ Collio Pinot Grigio '13	♟♟ 3
● Friuli Isonzo Cabernet Franc '14	♟♟ 3
○ Friuli Isonzo Chardonnay '14	♟♟ 2*
● Friuli Isonzo Merlot '12	♟♟ 3
○ Friuli Isonzo Pinot Grigio '14	♟♟ 2*

Gianpaolo Colutta

via Orsaria, 32a
33044 Manzano [UD]
Tel. +39 0432510654
www.coluttagianpaolo.com

CELLAR SALES
PRE-BOOKED VISITS
ANNUAL PRODUCTION 150,000 bottles
HECTARES UNDER VINE 30.00

The noble Colutta family boasts documented agricultural experience going back more than 1000 years in the Manzano area. With 30 hectares of vineyard on the Buttrio, Manzano and Premariacco hills, Gianpaolo Colutta decided to found his own winery in 1999, running it in partnership with his daughter Elisabetta. His love of the land and respect for traditions led him to enhance the area, replanting some vineyards with clones of ancient native varieties that had almost disappeared. This brave decision, which went against the flow, soon produced the desired results, making the winery stand out on the crowded regional wine scene. This year's wines again garnered flattering scores, confirming the excellent quality established over time. The Friuliano 2015 stood out for its freshness and fragrance, while the very tasty Pinot Grigio 2015 echoed with elderflower and pomegranate on the nose.

○ FCO Chardonnay '15	♟♟ 3
○ FCO Friulano '15	♟♟ 3
○ FCO Pinot Grigio '15	♟♟ 3
● FCO Rosso Frassinolo '12	♟♟ 5
○ FCO Verduzzo Friulano '14	♟♟ 4
● FCO Schioppettino '15	♟ 5
○ COF Bianco Prarion '13	♟♟ 4
○ COF Bianco Prarion '12	♟♟ 4
○ COF Friulano '13	♟♟ 3
● COF Merlot '09	♟♟ 3
● COF Schioppettino '12	♟♟ 5
● COF Tazzelenghe '07	♟♟ 6
○ FCO Chardonnay '14	♟♟ 3
○ FCO Pinot Grigio '14	♟♟ 3
● FCO Refosco P. R. '11	♟♟ 3
○ FCO Verduzzo Friulano '14	♟♟ 4

Giorgio Colutta

VIA ORSARIA, 32
33044 MANZANO [UD]
TEL. +39 0432740315
www.colutta.it

CELLAR SALES
PRE-BOOKED VISITS
ACCOMMODATION
ANNUAL PRODUCTION 140,000 bottles
HECTARES UNDER VINE 21.00

Giorgio Colutta's vineyards are in the prestigious Parco della Vite e del Vino, in the far south of the natural amphitheatre formed by the gently rolling slopes of the Friuli Colli Orientali wine region, overlooking the Adriatic Sea and sheltered by the Julian Alps. Giorgio's winery, which is named Bandut after an ancient estate, is in Manzano, in an 18th-century stately villa. With a perfect combination of tradition and innovation, it has always offered exemplarily precise and linear wines. The traditional range has been enhanced by some intriguing sparkling whites, with some high-quality selections during the best years. A superb, slim-bodied, fragrant Friulano 2015 with notes of ripe fruit, including yellow-fleshed, enriched with hints of confectioner's cream and lime blossom honey. The Ribolla Gialla 2015 has citrus on the nose and has a fresh, symmetrical palate. The complex Pignolo 2010 is rich and solidly built, underpinned by some powerful tannin.

○ FCO Friulano '15	♈♈ 3
● FCO Pignolo '10	♈♈ 7
○ FCO Pinot Grigio '15	♈♈ 3
○ FCO Ribolla Gialla '15	♈♈ 4
○ FCO Sauvignon '15	♈♈ 3
● FCO Schioppettino '12	♈♈ 5
○ FCO Chardonnay '15	♈ 3
○ Prosecco Brut	♈ 2
○ COF Pinot Grigio '13	♉♉ 3
● COF Refosco P. R. '12	♉♉ 3
○ COF Sauvignon '13	♉♉ 3
● COF Schioppettino '11	♉♉ 5
○ FCO Friulano '14	♉♉ 3
○ FCO Pinot Grigio '14	♉♉ 3
● FCO Refosco P. R. '13	♉♉ 3
○ FCO Ribolla Gialla '14	♉♉ 4

Paolino Comelli

CASE COLLOREDO, 8
33040 FAEDIS [UD]
TEL. +39 0432711226
www.comelli.it

CELLAR SALES
PRE-BOOKED VISITS
ACCOMMODATION AND RESTAURANT SERVICE
ANNUAL PRODUCTION 60,000 bottles
HECTARES UNDER VINE 12.50
SUSTAINABLE WINERY

Pierluigi Comelli and his wife Daniela have finished restoring an old abandoned hamlet in the Colloredo di Soffumbergo hills, in the Friuli Colli Orientali wine region. Most of the credit should be given to Paolino, who demonstrated great forward thinking in the aftermath of the First World War, transforming it into a farm. Now those once decaying rural buildings provide attractive holiday accommodation, vaunting with every comfort and furnished in the typical local style. The winery staff, aided by Emilio Del Medico, ensure a consistent quality that makes the winery one of the best in the region. Many wines were borderline excellent but the top accolades go to the 2014 Malvasia, which made it to the final selections for and intriguing nose of lemon cream and sage, and especially for its drinkability and back palate. Also excellent the clean-tasting, typical Friuliano 2015.

○ FCO Malvasia '14	♈♈ 3*
○ FCO Friulano '15	♈♈ 3
○ FCO Pinot Grigio Amplius '15	♈♈ 3
○ Soffumbergo Bianco '13	♈♈ 4
● Soffumbergo Rosso '13	♈♈ 4
● FCO Pignolo '10	♈ 5
○ FCO Sauvignon '15	♈ 3
○ COF Sauvignon '13	♉♉ 3*
● Esprimo Red '13	♉♉ 2*
○ Esprimo White '13	♉♉ 2*
○ Esprimo White '12	♉♉ 2*
○ FCO Malvasia Locum Nostrum '13	♉♉ 2
○ FCO Picolit Eoos '12	♉♉ 6
○ FCO Pinot Grigio Amplius '14	♉♉ 3
○ Soffumbergo Bianco '12	♉♉ 4
● Soffumbergo Rosso '11	♉♉ 4

Dario Coos

VIA RAMANDOLO, 5
33045 NIMIS [UD]
TEL. +39 0432790320
www.dariocoos.it

CELLAR SALES
PRE-BOOKED VISITS
ANNUAL PRODUCTION 65,000 bottles
HECTARES UNDER VINE 10.00

Coos is synonymous with Ramandolo. The Coos family have made wine on the steep slopes of the northernmost Friuli Colli Orientali wine region since the early 19th century. In 1986, Dario founded the company that still bears his name, although it is now run by a small group of enthusiastic partners. The verduzzo giallo grown on the Ramandolo hills is a variety that produces small bunches of grapes with a thick, resilient skin, perfect for raisining. The firm now produces a wide range of wines, mainly made from local grapes, which act as ambassadors for the area. The winery is run by an efficient team, led by Andrea Pittana. This year quite a few wines were sent for tasting, both the classic sweet dessert wines produced on site, and the whites and the reds. The scores speak for themselves: all excellent, and the best of is the Friuliano 2015, with its refined scent of flowers and fruit with a touch of pennyroyal in the close.

○ FCO Friulano '15	♟♟ 3*
○ Chardonnay '15	♟♟ 4
○ FCO Picolit '13	♟♟ 6
○ Malvasia '15	♟♟ 3
○ Pinot Grigio '15	♟♟ 3
○ Ramandolo V.T. '14	♟♟ 4
● Refosco P.R. '13	♟♟ 4
○ Sauvignon '15	♟♟ 3
○ Ramandolo Il Longhino '13	♟ 4
○ Ribolla Gialla '15	♟ 3
● Schioppettino '14	♟ 4
○ FCO Picolit '12	♟♟ 6
○ Ramandolo V.T. '12	♟♟ 4
● Refosco P.R. '12	♟♟ 4
○ Sauvignon '14	♟♟ 3

Cantina Produttori Cormòns

VIA VINO DELLA PACE, 31
34071 CORMÒNS [GO]
TEL. +39 048162471
www.cormons.com

CELLAR SALES
PRE-BOOKED VISITS
ACCOMMODATION AND RESTAURANT SERVICE
ANNUAL PRODUCTION 2,250,000 bottles
HECTARES UNDER VINE 471.00
SUSTAINABLE WINERY

In 1968, a number of winemakers from Cormons, who were unable to act alone, decided to join forces and promote the local potential. They therefore founded the Cantina Produttori di Cormòns, which now has more than 200 partners dotted around the best wine regions. The suppliers have to follow a strict code of conduct and have been monitored for over 30 years by the expert agronomist Gianni Rover. The production manager is Rodolfo Rizzi, who has been appointed general director. He is responsible for safeguarding a brand that has always succeeded in combining quality with large volumes. We decided to reward the 1987 Vino della Pace, which was probably presented to prove how the whites around can hold their for even 30 years. The burnished hue is the prelude to memories of marsala, with raisins and bottled figs on the nose, but and incredibly fresh, fragrant palate is still going strong.

○ Vino della Pace '87	♟♟ 5
○ Collio Bianco Collio & Collio '15	♟♟ 3
○ Collio Friuliano '15	♟♟ 3
○ Friuli Isonzo Malvasia '15	♟♟ 2*
○ Collio Pinot Bianco '15	♟ 3
○ Collio Pinot Grigio '15	♟ 3
○ Friuli Isonzo Chardonnay '15	♟ 2
○ Collio Bianco Collio & Collio '14	♟♟ 3
○ Collio Friuliano '13	♟♟ 3
○ Collio Pinot Bianco '14	♟♟ 3
○ Collio Pinot Bianco '13	♟♟ 3
○ Collio Pinot Grigio '13	♟♟ 3
○ Collio Pinot Grigio '11	♟♟ 3
○ Friuli Isonzo Malvasia Istriana '12	♟♟ 3
○ Vino della Pace '09	♟♟ 5
○ Vino della Pace '08	♟♟ 5

Crastin

LOC. RUTTARS, 33
34070 DOLEGNA DEL COLLIO [GO]
TEL. +39 0481630310
www.vinicrastin.it

CELLAR SALES
PRE-BOOKED VISITS
ANNUAL PRODUCTION 35,000 bottles
HECTARES UNDER VINE 6.00

Sergio Collarig is the perfect example of a wine artisan. He looks after his vineyards himself, using traditional methods handed down by peasant families and combining them with the most advanced technological innovations. Realizing the potential of the 2.5 hectares of vineyards he inherited from his father Olivo in 1980, he set about adding to them. In 1990 he started bottling his own wine, serving it to guests at the farm restaurant he had opened in the meantime with his sister on the beautiful Ruttars hills, in the Collio Goriziano wine region. The winery currently covers 6 hectares, mostly used to grow white grapes. Just like last year, the Friulano 2015 scored top marks and made it to our finals, confirming the stellar quality obtained from this grape. Showing nose notes of citron, apple and sage, with shades of confectioner's cream, the taste is mouthfilling and pleasantly persistent.

○ Collio Friulano '15	🍷🍷 3*
● Collio Cabernet Franc '14	🍷🍷 3
● Collio Merlot '13	🍷🍷 4
○ Collio Pinot Grigio '15	🍷🍷 3
○ Collio Ribolla Gialla '15	🍷🍷 3
○ Collio Sauvignon '15	🍷🍷 3
● Collio Cabernet Franc '13	🍷🍷 3
○ Collio Friulano '14	🍷🍷 2*
○ Collio Friulano '13	🍷🍷 2*
● Collio Merlot '12	🍷🍷 2*
○ Collio Pinot Grigio '14	🍷🍷 3
○ Collio Pinot Grigio '13	🍷🍷 3
○ Collio Ribolla Gialla '14	🍷🍷 2*
○ Collio Ribolla Gialla '13	🍷🍷 2*
○ Collio Sauvignon '14	🍷🍷 3
○ Collio Sauvignon '13	🍷🍷 3

di Lenardo

FRAZ. ONTAGNANO
P.ZZA BATTISTI, 1
33050 GONARS [UD]
TEL. +39 0432928633
www.dilenardo.it

CELLAR SALES
PRE-BOOKED VISITS
ANNUAL PRODUCTION 750,000 bottles
HECTARES UNDER VINE 55.00
SUSTAINABLE WINERY

Despite not being able to reap the benefits of hillside winemaking, Massimo di Lenardo has managed to make his winery one of the best on the regional scene. His wines demonstrate how winemaking can be carried out on the plain in an intelligent and entrepreneurial fashion, combining large volumes with quality. The wines are often characterized by particularly inviting hints, distinguished by exemplary simplicity and linearity. The winery exports 80% of its production, acting as a real ambassador for the region around the world, particularly overseas. The winery's range embraces all types and offers a wide choice of products at very friendly prices. There was a great team performance and we would suggest keeping an eye out for the forceful, mineral-rich Chardonnay 2015.

○ Chardonnay '15	🍷🍷🍷 2*
● Cabernet '15	🍷🍷 2*
● Merlot '15	🍷🍷 2*
● Merlot Just Me '13	🍷🍷 4
○ Pinot Grigio '15	🍷🍷 2*
○ Pinot Grigio Ramato Gossip '15	🍷🍷 2*
○ Chardonnay Father's Eyes '15	🍷 3
○ Friulano Toh! '15	🍷 2
○ Pass the Cookies '15	🍷 3
○ Ribolla Gialla Comemivuoi '15	🍷 2
● Ronco Nolè Rosso '14	🍷 2
○ Sarà Brut	🍷 3
○ Sauvignon '15	🍷 2
○ Chardonnay '14	🍷🍷 2*
○ Friulano Toh! '14	🍷🍷 2*
○ Pinot Grigio '14	🍷🍷 2*

★★Dorigo

S.DA PROV.LE 79
33040 PREMARIACCO [UD]
TEL. +39 0432634161
www.dorigowines.com

CELLAR SALES
PRE-BOOKED VISITS
ANNUAL PRODUCTION 120,000 bottles
HECTARES UNDER VINE 20.00
SUSTAINABLE WINERY

Representing the new generation, Alessio
Dorigo reorganized the company a few
years ago, acquiring a new, modern and
well-equipped headquarters, which stands
out for its cutting-edge architecture on the
main road from Udine to Cividale del Friuli.
Enthusiastic, keen to learn and innovative,
Alessio pays homage to the Dorigo brand
created by his father Girolamo 50 years
ago. Half a century of experiments and
changes, which have written an important
page in the regional winemaking history.
The particular focus on sparkling wine
production using the metodo classico is key
to the winery's flagship products. This
could well be the first time a non-
macerated Ribolla Gialla made it to our
finals. All our respect goes to the first
winery to believe in the potential of this
variety. Rosso Dorigo made an excellent
debut, too, with mighty structure and
delightful juicy raisining notes.

○ FCO Ribolla Gialla '15	♟♟	3*
○ Blanc de Blancs Pas Dosé	♟♟	5
○ Blanc de Noir Dosage Zéro	♟♟	5
○ Dorigo Brut Cuvée	♟♟	4
● Dorigo Rosso	♟♟	4
○ FCO Chardonnay Ronc di Juri '14	♟♟	5
○ FCO Friulano '15	♟♟	3
● FCO Merlot '14	♟♟	3
○ FCO Picolit '14	♟♟	6
○ FCO Sauvignon '15	♟♟	3
● COF Pignolo di Buttrio '03	♟♟♟	8
● COF Pignolo di Buttrio '02	♟♟♟	8
● COF Rosso Montsclapade '06	♟♟♟	6
● COF Rosso Montsclapade '04	♟♟♟	6
● COF Rosso Montsclapade '01	♟♟♟	6

Draga

LOC. SCEDINA, 8
34070 SAN FLORIANO DEL COLLIO [GO]
TEL. +39 0481884182
www.draga.it

CELLAR SALES
PRE-BOOKED VISITS
ANNUAL PRODUCTION 40,000 bottles
HECTARES UNDER VINE 14.00
SUSTAINABLE WINERY

The Miklus family has been looking after its
vineyards in San Floriano del Collio with
great love and passion for three
generations. The winery is currently run by
Milan Miklus, assisted by his wife Anna and
children Denis and Mitja. In 1982 Milan
started renewing the vineyards, divided into
two plots, Draga and Breg, and ten years
later he started bottling his own wines. The
Draga label comprises very refined and
drinkable wines, while the Miklus label
features wines made in keeping with the
ancient local tradition, which involves long
periods of maceration on the skins, even
for the white whites, with intense aromatic
extracts deriving from ancestral techniques.
Miklus wines start to cast their spell right
from the intense, glistening hue, ushering
in intriguing hints on the nose. Above all the
Pinot Grigio Miklus 2011, with notes of
almond crunch, candied fruit, black tea,
and caramel. The palate is surprisingly
slim-bodied, consistent, tasty and rich in
aromatic notes.

○ Collio Pinot Grigio Miklus '11	♟♟	4
○ Collio Friulano '15	♟♟	3
○ Collio Malvasia Miklus '13	♟♟	4
○ Collio Ribolla Gialla Miklus Natural Art '09	♟♟	5
○ Collio Sauvignon '15	♟♟	3
○ Collio Malvasia Miklus '10	♟♟♟	7
○ Collio Friulano '14	♟♟	3
○ Collio Pinot Grigio '14	♟♟	3
● Collio Rosso Miklus Negro di Collina '12	♟♟	4
○ Collio Sauvignon '14	♟♟	3
○ Collio Sauvignon '13	♟♟	3
○ Miklus Pas Dosé M. Cl. '12	♟♟	5
○ Ribolla Gialla Miklus '09	♟♟	5

Drius

via Filanda, 100
34071 Cormòns [GO]
Tel. +39 048160998
www.drius.it

CELLAR SALES
PRE-BOOKED VISITS
ANNUAL PRODUCTION 50,000 bottles
HECTARES UNDER VINE 15.00
SUSTAINABLE WINERY

Over almost two centuries of history, the Drius family, involved in various fields of agriculture and cattle farming, set an example of cohesion and love of the land in Cormòns, spanning the Friuli Isonzo and Collio wine regions. Many years ago, Mauro Drius, supported by his wife Nadia, turned the business around, switching to winemaking. A proud peasant and wine artisan, Mauro is a punctilious winemaker able to exploit the local potential, expressed in enviably forthright, character-packed wines. He has already involved his very young son Denis in the business, placing him in charge of the winemaking process. This year's finalist was the Bianco Vignis di Siris 2013, a Friuli Isonzo DOC, a noteworthy blend of tocai friulano, sauvignon, and pinot bianco all from the same plot. The refined nose is complex and the palate is perfectly symmetrical, balanced, and softly charming.

○ Friuli Isonzo Bianco Vignis di Siris '13	🍷🍷	3*
○ Collio Friulano '15	🍷🍷	3
● Friuli Isonzo Cabernet Sauvignon '13	🍷🍷	4
○ Friuli Isonzo Malvasia '15	🍷🍷	3
● Friuli Isonzo Merlot '13	🍷🍷	4
○ Friuli Isonzo Pinot Bianco '15	🍷🍷	3
○ Friuli Isonzo Pinot Grigio '15	🍷🍷	3
○ Friuli Isonzo Friulano '15	🍷	3
○ Collio Tocai Friulano '05	ΥΥΥ	3*
○ Collio Tocai Friulano '02	ΥΥΥ	2*
○ Friuli Isonzo Bianco Vignis di Siris '02	ΥΥΥ	3*
○ Friuli Isonzo Friulano '07	ΥΥΥ	3
○ Friuli Isonzo Malvasia '08	ΥΥΥ	3*
○ Friuli Isonzo Pinot Bianco '09	ΥΥΥ	3*
○ Friuli Isonzo Pinot Bianco '00	ΥΥΥ	3*
○ Collio Friulano '14	ΥΥ	3*

★Le Due Terre

via Roma, 68b
33040 Prepotto [UD]
Tel. +39 0432713189
fortesilvana@libero.it

CELLAR SALES
PRE-BOOKED VISITS
ANNUAL PRODUCTION 18,000 bottles
HECTARES UNDER VINE 5.00

Flavio Basilicata and Silvana Forte own a tiny company that they have run with enviable synergy for over 30 years, producing organic wine. With just a few hectares of vineyard, the couple look after every production phase meticulously. For some years now, Le Due Terre wines have numbered among the best in the region and nationwide. The winery's grape blends, called Sacrisassi, are made solely from native varieties. Sacrisassi Rosso is a mix of schioppettino and refosco dal peduncolo rosso in equal parts, while friulano prevails in the Sacrisassi Bianco, with an abundant measure of ribolla gialla. The range is completed by the Merlot and Pinot Nero. It speaks volumes about Flavio's skilful handling of a tricky vintage like 2014 when three of his four wines got to the finals. Still, we were sad that Rosso Sacrisassi got left behind, after its amazing seven consecutive years as a Tre Bicchieri winner.

○ FCO Bianco Sacrisassi '14	🍷🍷	5
● FCO Merlot '14	🍷🍷	5
● FCO Rosso Sacrisassi '14	🍷🍷	5
● FCO Pinot Nero '14	🍷🍷	5
○ COF Bianco Sacrisassi '05	ΥΥΥ	5
● COF Merlot '03	ΥΥΥ	5
● COF Merlot '02	ΥΥΥ	5
● COF Merlot '00	ΥΥΥ	5
● COF Rosso Sacrisassi '12	ΥΥΥ	5
● COF Rosso Sacrisassi '11	ΥΥΥ	5
● COF Rosso Sacrisassi '10	ΥΥΥ	5
● COF Rosso Sacrisassi '09	ΥΥΥ	5
● COF Rosso Sacrisassi '08	ΥΥΥ	5
● COF Rosso Sacrisassi '07	ΥΥΥ	5
● FCO Rosso Sacrisassi '13	ΥΥΥ	5

Ermacora

FRAZ. IPPLIS
VIA SOLZAREDO, 9
33040 PREMARIACCO [UD]
TEL. +39 0432716250
www.ermacora.it

CELLAR SALES
PRE-BOOKED VISITS
ANNUAL PRODUCTION 180,000 bottles
HECTARES UNDER VINE 47.00
SUSTAINABLE WINERY

In the world of wine, Ermacora is synonymous with absolute quality. This guarantee has become established over the years, ever since the brothers Antonio and Giuseppe Ermacora began making wine on the Ipplis hills in 1922, creating the necessary conditions for fine wines. They started a family-run business that has been handed down over the years. The cutting-edge winery is now run by another two brothers, Dario and Luciano. "Doing little to achieve the best, with the subtle use of the most advanced technology." These words, based on a simple philosophy, sum up the desire to follow the pace set by nature, avoiding force and excess. The Friulano 2015 repeated last season's feat and is reconfirmed as the leader of a range of wines of excellent level. This Mediterranean wine shows dried flowers, light honey and thyme on the nose, and an excellent mouth balance. The juicy, persuasive Pinot Grigio 2015, with a fragrant lime and grapefruit finale, is also top notch.

○ FCO Friulano '15	🍷🍷 3*
○ FCO Picolit '13	🍷🍷 6
● FCO Pignolo '10	🍷🍷 5
○ FCO Pinot Bianco '15	🍷🍷 3
○ FCO Pinot Grigio '15	🍷🍷 3
○ FCO Ribolla Gialla '15	🍷🍷 3
○ FCO Sauvignon '15	🍷🍷 3
● FCO Merlot '14	🍷 3
● FCO Riul '12	🍷 4
● COF Pignolo '00	🍷🍷🍷 5
○ FCO Friulano '14	🍷🍷 3*
○ FCO Picolit '12	🍷🍷 6
○ FCO Pinot Bianco '14	🍷🍷 3
○ FCO Pinot Grigio '14	🍷🍷 3
○ FCO Ribolla Gialla '14	🍷🍷 3
○ FCO Sauvignon '14	🍷🍷 3
● FCO Schioppettino '13	🍷🍷 3

Fantinel

FRAZ. TAURIANO
VIA TESIS, 8
33097 SPILIMBERGO [PN]
TEL. +39 0427591511
www.fantinel.com

CELLAR SALES
PRE-BOOKED VISITS
RESTAURANT SERVICE
ANNUAL PRODUCTION 5,000,000 bottles
HECTARES UNDER VINE 300.00
SUSTAINABLE WINERY

The winery run by the Fantinel family offers a vast collection of wines able to meet market demands, satisfying the palate of all consumer types. Their products are distributed in more than 90 countries worldwide and are therefore ambassadors for regional specialities Their flagship products are the Collio wines from the Sant'Elena estate, which are full-bodied with a strong personality. But the big numbers derive from the freshness and drinkability of the wines from the plains, where sparkling wines also play a key role. The huge company headquarters in Tauriano di Spilimbergo, surrounded by vineyards, is a typical example of art, culture and functionality. Once again this year the friulano, pinot bianco and chardonnay blend Collio Bianco Frontiere Sant'Helena 2014 was much appreciated. Showing tropical notes of passion fruit and mango, followed by notes of rum baba, wheat and tea, it has a soft, juicy, mouthfilling palate that is fresh and fruity.

● Cabernet Sauvignon Sant'Helena '12	🍷🍷 3
○ Collio Bianco Frontiere Sant'Helena '14	🍷🍷 4
○ Collio Pinot Grigio Sant'Helena '15	🍷🍷 3
● Collio Rosso Venko Sant'Helena '10	🍷🍷 4
○ Collio Sauvignon Sant'Helena '15	🍷🍷 3
○ Brut Rosé One & Only '14	🍷 3
○ Prosecco Brut One & Only	🍷 3
○ Prosecco Brut The Indipendent '15	🍷 3
● Refosco P. R. Sant'Helena '11	🍷 3
○ Ribolla Gialla Brut	🍷 3
○ Ribolla Gialla Sant'Helena '15	🍷 3
○ Collio Pinot Grigio Sant'Helena '14	🍷🍷 3
● Collio Rosso Venko Sant'Helena '08	🍷🍷 3
○ Collio Sauvignon Sant'Helena '14	🍷🍷 3
● Refosco P. R. Sant'Helena '10	🍷🍷 3
○ Ribolla Gialla Sant'Helena '14	🍷🍷 3

★★Livio Felluga

FRAZ. BRAZZANO
VIA RISORGIMENTO, 1
34071 CORMÒNS [GO]
TEL. +39 048160203
www.liviofelluga.it

PRE-BOOKED VISITS
ANNUAL PRODUCTION 800,000 bottles
HECTARES UNDER VINE 160.00
SUSTAINABLE WINERY

Early in the second half of last century, Livio Felluga, the patriarch of regional winemaking, who is now over 100 years old, together with a small bunch of entrepreneurial winemakers, promoted an initiative unheard-of in Italy at the time: making great white wines. He founded the winery in Brazzano di Cormòns and had the foresight to purchase the first vineyards in Rosazzo. The historic label developed in 1956 and recognized worldwide today, features a map of the hills. The winery is now run by his four children and has expanded considerably, encompassing the Abbazia di Rosazzo, at the centre of Friuli's winemaking culture. With three wines in the final, the odds of garnering the top award were high. The Tre Bicchieri went to the Bianco Illivio 2014, repeating the success of just a few years ago. It is less opulent than its fellows but that, combined with simplicity and fragrance, may well be the secret of its success.

○ FCO Bianco Illivio '14	▼▼▼	5
● FCO Rosazzo Sossó '12	▼▼	7
○ Rosazzo Terre Alte '14	▼▼	7
○ FCO Chardonnay '15	▼▼	4
○ FCO Friulano '15	▼▼	4
○ FCO Picolit '11	▼▼	8
● FCO Refosco P. R. '12	▼▼	7
○ Rosazzo Abbazia di Rosazzo '13	▼▼	7
○ COF Bianco Illivio '10	♀♀♀	5
○ COF Rosazzo Bianco Terre Alte '09	♀♀♀	7
○ COF Rosazzo Bianco Terre Alte '08	♀♀♀	7
○ COF Rosazzo Bianco Terre Alte '07	♀♀♀	7
○ COF Rosazzo Bianco Terre Alte '06	♀♀♀	6
○ COF Rosazzo Bianco Terre Alte '04	♀♀♀	6
○ Rosazzo Terre Alte '12	♀♀♀	7
○ Rosazzo Terre Alte '11	♀♀♀	7

Marco Felluga

VIA GORIZIA, 121
34072 GRADISCA D'ISONZO [GO]
TEL. +39 048199164
www.marcofelluga.it

CELLAR SALES
PRE-BOOKED VISITS
RESTAURANT SERVICE
ANNUAL PRODUCTION 600,000 bottles
HECTARES UNDER VINE 100.00
SUSTAINABLE WINERY

Roberto Felluga runs the company founded in 1956 by his father Marco, who is now over 90 and considered a pioneer and great innovator. Despite the difficult times, he glimpsed the potential of Collio wines and made them world famous. Roberto, with just as much entrepreneurial skill and forward thinking, has launched a daring project over recent years to enhance the shelf-life of white wines, selecting a few reserves released onto the market several years after harvesting. These more mature wines educate the consumer in the appreciation of sensory characteristics resulting from long ageing in the bottle. For the fourth year in a row we find the Pinot Grigio Mongris Riserva 2013 in the final, a clear sign that its characteristics are widely appreciated and although it just missed the top accolade, it is one of the most interesting wines in the region for quality.

○ Collio Pinot Grigio Mongris Ris. '13	▼▼	5
○ Collio Chardonnay '15	▼▼	5
○ Collio Friulano '15	▼▼	3
○ Collio Sauvignon '15	▼▼	3
○ Collio Pinot Grigio '15	▼	5
○ Collio Ribolla Gialla '15	▼	3
○ Collio Bianco Molamatta '13	♀♀	5
○ Collio Friulano '14	♀♀	3
● Collio Merlot '12	♀♀	3
○ Collio Pinot Grigio '14	♀♀	5
○ Collio Pinot Grigio Mongris Ris. '12	♀♀	5
○ Collio Pinot Grigio Mongris Ris. '11	♀♀	6
○ Collio Ribolla Gialla '14	♀♀	3
○ Collio Sauvignon '13	♀♀	5

Fiegl

FRAZ. OSLAVIA
LOC. LENZUOLO BIANCO, 1
34170 GORIZIA
TEL. +39 0481547103
www.fieglvini.com

CELLAR SALES
PRE-BOOKED VISITS
ANNUAL PRODUCTION 150,000 bottles
HECTARES UNDER VINE 30.00
SUSTAINABLE WINERY

Lenzuolo Bianco, on Collio Goriziano, is home to a number of big names on the regional winemaking scene. It is a borderland, battered by wars, which has churned out generations of peasants proud of their land and their vineyards. The Fiegl family from nearby Austria has lived and worked here for over two centuries. It is currently owned by three brothers, Alessio, Giuseppe and Rinaldo, but the day-to-day running has been entrusted to the energetic new generation, formed by Martin, Robert and Matej. Their hard work, boosted by significant investments in the vineyards and winery, has produced a leap in quality. An outstanding performance for the full range of wines, of which three went through to our finals, with the Friuliano 2015 taking the Tre Bicchieri. An alluring nose of acacia flowers, Golden Delicious and fresh almonds, following through nicely in mouth and back palate.

Gigante

VIA ROCCA BERNARDA, 3
33040 CORNO DI ROSAZZO [UD]
TEL. +39 0432755835
www.adrianogigante.it

CELLAR SALES
PRE-BOOKED VISITS
ACCOMMODATION
ANNUAL PRODUCTION 100,000 bottles
HECTARES UNDER VINE 25.00

The Rocca Bernarda is home to numerous leading names on the regional wine scene. The winery owned by Adriano Gigante, on the slope overlooking Corno di Rosazzo, is an established business that honours the unique features of the Friuli Colli Orientali wine region. The Storico vineyard planted with tocai friulano is known for its potential, giving rise to the winery and still the pride and joy of this great firm. Now construction work has been completed on the new building, Adriano has plenty of space to process his grapes, using the latest technology and combining tradition with high quality. This year two wines again made the finals, both produced with native vines, one white and the other red, confirming the excellent quality of the entire range. The Friulano Vigneto Storico 2015 is an old acquaintance while the Refosco dal Peduncolo Rosso Riserva 2013 is a welcome addition.

○ Collio Friulano '15	🍷🍷🍷	3*
○ Collio Ribolla Gialla Oslavia '14	🍷🍷	5
● Collio Rosso Leopold Cuvée Rouge '09	🍷🍷	5
○ Collio Bianco Cuvée Blanc '14	🍷🍷	4
○ Collio Malvasia '15	🍷🍷	3
● Collio Merlot Leopold '10	🍷🍷	5
○ Collio Sauvignon '15	🍷🍷	3
⊙ Fiegl Rosé	🍷🍷	4
○ Collio Pinot Grigio '15	🍷	3
○ Collio Ribolla Gialla '15	🍷	3
○ Collio Pinot Grigio '04	🍷🍷🍷	2*
○ Collio Bianco Cuvée Blanc '13	🍷🍷	4
○ Collio Chardonnay '14	🍷🍷	3
○ Collio Friulano '14	🍷🍷	3
○ Collio Sauvignon '14	🍷🍷	3

○ FCO Friulano Vign. Storico '15	🍷🍷	4
● FCO Refosco P. R. Ris. '13	🍷🍷	3*
○ FCO Friulano '15	🍷🍷	3
○ FCO Pinot Grigio '15	🍷🍷	3
○ FCO Ribolla Gialla '15	🍷🍷	3
○ FCO Sauvignon '15	🍷🍷	3
○ FCO Verduzzo Friulano '11	🍷🍷	3
● FCO Cabernet Franc '14	🍷	3
⊙ Prima Nera Brut Rosé	🍷	3
○ Ribolla Gialla Brut	🍷	3
○ COF Tocai Friulano Vign. Storico '06	🍷🍷🍷	4
○ COF Tocai Friulano Vign. Storico '05	🍷🍷🍷	4
○ COF Tocai Friulano Vign. Storico '03	🍷🍷🍷	4
○ FCO Picolit '08	🍷🍷🍷	6

Gori

VIA G.B. GORI, 14
33045 NIMIS [UD]
TEL. +39 0432878475
www.goriagricola.it

PRE-BOOKED VISITS
ANNUAL PRODUCTION 45,000 bottles
HECTARES UNDER VINE 18.00

Gianpiero Gori's recently founded winery in Nimis, in the north of the Friuli Colli Orientali wine region, is already making a name for itself thanks to its wines and great architecture. Perched on top of a hill overlooking the town below, the main villa stands on top of the underground cellars. The northern side of the building recalls a stone and steel bastion, while the southern side enjoys a wonderful view over the valley. An ambitious promotion project has introduced pinot nero to the winery. The vineyards are managed by the expert agronomist Giovanni Bigot, while Natale Favretto supervises the winemaking process. The Refosco dal Peduncolo Rosso Redelbosco 2013 was at the top of our rankings for the second year in a row and went through to the finals. We voted its layered fruity, spicy nose, but also and especially its structure and balance.

● Refosco P. R. Redelbosco '13	♟♟3*
● FCO Merlot Toni Vasùt '14	♟♟3
○ FCO Sauvignon Busseben '14	♟♟3
● Rosso Meni Vasùt '13	♟♟3
○ FCO Chardonnay Giugiù '14	♟3
● Pinot Nero Nemas I '14	♟4
○ Chardonnay Giugiù '13	♟♟4
● Merlot Toni Vasùt '13	♟♟4
● Refosco P. R. Redelbosco '12	♟♟4
● Rosso Meni Vasùt '12	♟♟4

Gradis'ciutta

LOC. GIASBANA, 10
34070 SAN FLORIANO DEL COLLIO [GO]
TEL. +39 0481390237
www.gradisciutta.eu

CELLAR SALES
PRE-BOOKED VISITS
ANNUAL PRODUCTION 100,000 bottles
HECTARES UNDER VINE 20.00

The Princic family made wine in Kosana, in nearby Slovenia, from 1780 onwards. The decline of the House of Habsburg, the Great War and sharecropping brought their great-grandfather Filip to Giasbana, near San Floriano del Collio. Robert Princic, the current owner, was practically born in the vineyard, but the winery was founded when he joined the company in 1997, working alongside his father Isidoro. Some vineyards by the headquarters have been planted with vines for more than 80 years, a unique legacy safeguarded with diligence and professionalism. The other vineyards, in various locations and at different altitudes, offer terrain suitable for each variety. Almost every year we have at least a couple of wines from Robert Princic in the final. This year it was the turn of the Friulano 2015 and the Collio Bianco Bratinis 2014. Both showed outstanding fragrance, freshness and consistency, both on the nose and on the palate, a hair's breadth from the top award.

○ Collio Bianco Bratinis '14	♟♟3*
○ Collio Friulano '15	♟♟3*
○ Collio Bianco Ris. '09	♟♟3
○ Collio Chardonnay '15	♟♟3
○ Collio Malvasia '15	♟♟3
○ Collio Pinot Grigio '15	♟♟3
○ Collio Ribolla Gialla '15	♟♟3
○ Collio Sauvignon '15	♟♟3
○ Collio Bianco Bratinis '13	♟♟3*
○ Collio Bianco Bratinis '12	♟♟3*
○ Collio Chardonnay '14	♟♟3
○ Collio Malvasia '13	♟♟3
○ Collio Pinot Grigio '14	♟♟3
○ Collio Pinot Grigio '13	♟♟3
○ Collio Ribolla Gialla '14	♟♟3
○ Collio Sauvignon '14	♟♟3

★★ Gravner

FRAZ. OSLAVIA
LOC. LENZUOLO BIANCO, 9
34070 GORIZIA
TEL. +39 048130882
www.gravner.it

CELLAR SALES
PRE-BOOKED VISITS
ANNUAL PRODUCTION 30,000 bottles
HECTARES UNDER VINE 18.00

Josko Gravner is a great winemaker and a reticent man whose wines speak for him. He loves to recall the early days when he tried out all the latest technology, but his winery no longer contains steel vats or even barriques. All that can be seen are partially buried amphorae from the Caucasus, where red and white grapes are macerated for over six months. The wines are then aged in large wooden barrels for years: at least seven for Ribolla Gialla, more than ten for the reds. They are powerful, structured and rich in everything, even colour, especially in the case of the whites that acquire an amber hue, but they are also genuine, intriguing, exciting and very drinkable. Only two wines but what wines they are! It was no mean feat to choose between the two giants of regional wine our podium went to Pinot Grigio 2008, with its nose of crema catalana, almond crunch, thyme and eucalyptus, and a very dry but juicy, silky mouth.

○ Ribolla Gialla '08	▼▼▼	5
○ Bianco Breg '08	▼▼	7
○ Breg '00	♀♀♀	8
○ Breg Anfora '06	♀♀♀	7
○ Breg Anfora '03	♀♀♀	7
○ Breg Anfora '02	♀♀♀	7
○ Chardonnay '87	♀♀♀	7
○ Chardonnay '83	♀♀♀	7
○ Ribolla Anfora '05	♀♀♀	7
○ Ribolla Anfora '04	♀♀♀	7
○ Ribolla Anfora '02	♀♀♀	7
○ Ribolla Anfora '01	♀♀♀	7
○ Ribolla Gialla '07	♀♀♀	5
● Rosso Gravner '04	♀♀♀	7

Iole Grillo

VIA ALBANA, 60
33040 PREPOTTO [UD]
TEL. +39 0432713201
www.vinigrillo.it

CELLAR SALES
PRE-BOOKED VISITS
ACCOMMODATION
ANNUAL PRODUCTION 40,000 bottles
HECTARES UNDER VINE 9.00

Anna Muzzolini, a young and energetic wine entrepreneur, assisted by her husband Andrea, runs the winery founded by her father Sergio in the 1970s, which he dedicated to his wife Iole Grillo. It is based in Albana di Prepotto, in an old 18th-century house that has been skilfully renovated. The vineyards cover the beautiful Judrio river valley, battered systematically by relatively cool winds that keep the grapes dry and create the perfect microclimate for their complete maturation. Anna loves supervising the various phases of the production cycle personally, counting on the proven winemaking ability of Giuseppe Tosoratti. The Schioppettino di Prepotto 2013, a flagship not only for the winery but for the entire sector, garnered top ratings but the other wines, both vintage reds and whites, were close behind with more than flattering appraisals, confirming the excellent quality of the entire range.

○ FCO Friulano '15	▼▼	3
● FCO Merlot Ris. '12	▼▼	3
● FCO Refosco P. R. '12	▼▼	3
○ FCO Sauvignon '15	▼▼	3
● FCO Schioppettino di Prepotto '13	▼▼	3
○ FCO Ribolla Gialla '15	▼	3
○ COF Il Sauvignon '12	♀♀	4
● COF Merlot Ris. '09	♀♀	3
● COF Refosco P. R. '11	♀♀	3
● COF Rosso Guardafuoco '11	♀♀	3
○ COF Sauvignon '13	♀♀	3
○ COF Sauvignon '12	♀♀	3
● COF Schioppettino di Prepotto '11	♀♀	3
● FCO Merlot Ris. '11	♀♀	3
● Rosso Duedonne	♀♀	3

Jacùss

FRAZ. MONTINA
V.LE KENNEDY, 35A
33040 TORREANO [UD]
TEL. +39 0432715147
www.jacuss.it

CELLAR SALES
PRE-BOOKED VISITS
ANNUAL PRODUCTION 50,000 bottles
HECTARES UNDER VINE 11.00

In 1990, the brothers Sandro and Andrea Iacuzzi decided to transform their mixed farm into a specialist winery, calling it Jacùss, their surname in the local dialect. Like most small family-run concerns, they look after both the vineyards and the winemaking process. They are one of the few to still grow tazzelenghe, a native grape with an ancient peasant tradition, which is packed with flavour but characterized by sharp tannins. Their vineyards extend over the hills of the small district of Montina, in Torreano di Cividale, in the Friuli Colli Orientali wine region. Again this year the red wines reaped the benefits of some ageing and scored more points than the vintage whites. In particular, the Merlot 2012 is still very fruity but shows a nice, mouthfilling blend of spices and aromatic herbs.

★★Jermann

FRAZ. RUTTARS
LOC. TRUSSIO, 11
34072 DOLEGNA DEL COLLIO [GO]
TEL. +39 0481888080
www.jermann.it

CELLAR SALES
PRE-BOOKED VISITS
ANNUAL PRODUCTION 900,000 bottles
HECTARES UNDER VINE 160.00

In the 1970s the young Silvio Jermann took the helm of the company and soon made its wines some of the best in the world. The wonderful new winery in Ruttars, where technological innovation is skilfully combined with architectural tradition in a magical atmosphere, is surrounded by more than 20 hectares of vineyards and was designed especially for the vinification of Capo Martino, Vigna Truss, W… Dreams… … … and Vintage Tunina, the wine that has determined the success of the Jermann label more than any other. All the other wines are made in the historic headquarters in Villanova di Farra. The sheer quality of the complex and ever-intriguing Vintage Tunina 2014 will raise few eyebrows. The real news comes in the form of the splendid performance of the Pinot Grigio 2015, that even in the finals captured palates for its fragrance and the engaging sea-breeze tanginess. Tre Bicchieri!

● FCO Cabernet Sauvignon '12	♟♟ 3
○ FCO Friulano '15	♟♟ 3
● FCO Merlot '12	♟♟ 3
○ FCO Picolit '10	♟♟ 6
○ FCO Sauvignon '15	♟♟ 3
● FCO Schioppettino Fucs e Flamis '14	♟♟ 3
○ FCO Verduzzo Friulano '11	♟♟ 3
○ FCO Pinot Bianco '15	♟ 3
● FCO Tazzelenghe '11	♟ 3
○ COF Picolit '09	♟♟ 6
○ COF Verduzzo Friulano '09	♟♟ 3
● FCO Merlot '11	♟♟ 3
○ FCO Pinot Bianco '14	♟♟ 3
● FCO Refosco P. R. '12	♟♟ 3
● FCO Schioppettino Fucs e Flamis '13	♟♟ 3
● FCO Tazzelenghe '10	♟♟ 3

○ Pinot Grigio '15	♟♟♟ 4*
○ Capo Martino '14	♟♟ 7
○ Vintage Tunina '14	♟♟ 7
○ W… Dreams… … … '14	♟♟ 8
○ Chardonnay '15	♟♟ 4
● Pignolo Pignacolusse '09	♟♟ 5
○ Ribolla Gialla Vinnae '15	♟♟ 4
○ Sauvignon '15	♟♟ 4
○ Capo Martino '10	♟♟♟ 8
○ Vintage Tunina '13	♟♟♟ 6
○ Vintage Tunina '12	♟♟♟ 6
○ Vintage Tunina '11	♟♟♟ 6
○ Vintage Tunina '08	♟♟♟ 7
○ W… Dreams… … … '12	♟♟♟ 8
○ W… Dreams… … … '09	♟♟♟ 6

Kante

FRAZ. SAN PELAGIO
LOC. PREPOTTO, 1A
34011 DUINO AURISINA [TS]
TEL. +39 040200255
www.kante.it

ANNUAL PRODUCTION 45,000 bottles
HECTARES UNDER VINE 13.00

Edi Kante's name is associated with Trieste's karst plain, home to a heroic style of winemaking. The rocky ground requires a lot of hard work to create vineyards exposed to the sun, benefitted by the influx from the sea and ventilated by the bora. In the wonderful underground winery carved entirely out of the rock, a monument to winemaking, orderly rows of barrels and barriques follow the elliptical shape of the fascinating jagged walls, where the wines continue to breathe in the salty air from mysterious subterranean inlets that ensure a constant temperature and humidity in the karstic depths. With three wines in the finals there is little to add. The Malvasia and the Vitovska have always been Edi's masterpieces and gems in the Carso crown, but the real pearl is the 2008 Chardonnay La Bora di Kante, a wine whose aromatics are the echo of its terroir: iodine, rock and Mediterranean maquis.

○ Chardonnay La Bora di Kante '08	♥♥	4
○ Malvasia '13	♥♥	4
○ Vitovska '13	♥♥	4
○ Chardonnay '13	♥♥	4
○ Sauvignon '13	♥♥	5
○ Vitovska Sel. '07	♥♥	5
○ Carso Malvasia '07	♥♥♥	5
○ Carso Malvasia '06	♥♥♥	5
○ Carso Malvasia '05	♥♥♥	5
○ Carso Malvasia '98	♥♥♥	5
○ Carso Sauvignon '92	♥♥♥	5
○ Carso Sauvignon '91	♥♥♥	5
○ Chardonnay '94	♥♥♥	5
○ Chardonnay '90	♥♥♥	5
○ Malvasia '12	♥♥♥	4*
○ Vitovska '11	♥	4

★Edi Keber

LOC. ZEGLA, 17
34071 CORMÒNS [GO]
TEL. +39 048161184
www.edikeber.it

CELLAR SALES
PRE-BOOKED VISITS
ACCOMMODATION
ANNUAL PRODUCTION 50,000 bottles
HECTARES UNDER VINE 12.00

The Edi Keber label has been synonymous with Collio for some time. It produces a single wine, identified by the name of the wine region only. This wine is the result of extensive research and years of experimentation, focusing solely on its success, from grape preparation to vinification. It is simply a return to the origins, when Collio wine was understood to mean a white of superior quality, made from a blend of native regional varieties: tocai friulano, malvasia istriana and ribolla gialla. Edi Keber and his son Kristian made a great choice. Only one wine. Yet there are always new things to say about it, each year showing its different faces. So the Collio 2015 reveals a very complex, sophisticated nose, with well-integrated floral and gentian aromas, and an impeccable palate balance.

○ Collio '15	♥♥	3*
○ Collio Bianco '10	♥♥♥	3*
○ Collio Bianco '09	♥♥♥	3
○ Collio Bianco '08	♥♥♥	3*
○ Collio Bianco '04	♥♥♥	3*
○ Collio Bianco '02	♥♥♥	3
○ Collio Tocai Friulano '07	♥♥♥	3
○ Collio Tocai Friulano '06	♥♥♥	3
○ Collio Tocai Friulano '05	♥♥♥	3
○ Collio Tocai Friulano '03	♥♥♥	3*
○ Collio Tocai Friulano '01	♥♥♥	3
○ Collio Tocai Friulano '99	♥♥♥	3*
○ Collio Tocai Friulano '97	♥♥♥	3
○ Collio Tocai Friulano '95	♥♥♥	3*
○ Collio '14	♥♥	3*
○ Collio '13	♥♥	3*

Alessio Komjanc

LOC. GIASBANA, 35
34070 SAN FLORIANO DEL COLLIO [GO]
TEL. +39 0481391228
www.komjancalessio.com

CELLAR SALES
PRE-BOOKED VISITS
ANNUAL PRODUCTION 70,000 bottles
HECTARES UNDER VINE 24.00
SUSTAINABLE WINERY

The history of the Komjanc family in San Floriano del Collio is lost in the dawn of time. We know that Alessio's great grandparents made wine here in the early 19th century. The company headquarters on the side of the hill enjoy a spectacular panoramic view over the valley below, framed by the Prealps and the Eastern Alps. The first label featuring the Alessio Komjanc name dates to 1973, but the real turnaround came in 2000, when all four sons, Beniamin, Roberto, Patrik and Ivani, joined the firm definitively, dividing up the tasks between them and optimizing the entire production chain. We may have to thank a particularly satisfactory growing year, but all the wines, monovarietal as usual, garnered praise for the quality, especially when considering the price. Malvasia Istriana 2015, in particular, shows energy and character both on the nose and in the mouth, with vibrant touches of balsam.

○ Malvasia Istriana '15	♥♥ 3*
○ Collio Chardonnay '15	♥♥ 2*
○ Collio Friulano '15	♥♥ 2*
○ Collio Sauvignon '15	♥♥ 2*
○ Collio Pinot Grigio '15	♥ 2
○ Collio Ribolla Gialla '15	♥ 2
○ Collio Chardonnay '13	♥♥ 2*
○ Collio Friulano '14	♥♥ 2*
○ Collio Friulano '13	♥♥ 2*
○ Collio Sauvignon '13	♥♥ 2*
○ Malvasia Istriana '14	♥♥ 2*

Anita Vogric Kurtin

LOC. NOVALI, 9
34071 CORMÒNS [GO]
TEL. +39 048160685
www.winekurtin.it

CELLAR SALES
PRE-BOOKED VISITS
ANNUAL PRODUCTION 60,000 bottles
HECTARES UNDER VINE 10.00

The Kurtin family settled in Novali, near Cormòns, in 1906, and having realized the area's potential for winemaking, especially whites, they started growing vines in the natural amphitheatre that looks out from the Collio towards Slovenia. Albino Kurtin, from the third generation, formally founded the company and began bottling its wines as part of a process targeted at achieving a compromise between local traditions and market demands dictated by international tastes. His recent early death has placed all the responsibility for running the winery in the hands of his very young son Alessio, who has already proved himself to be up to the task. The wines we were able to taste this year are all well-made whites that mirror the characteristics of the vintage: marked fragrance and slim-bodied, refreshing drinkability. The Friulano 2015 is especially sunny, with delightful nose and mouth showing notes of dried thyme, almond and honey.

○ Collio Chardonnay '15	♥♥ 3
○ Collio Friulano '15	♥♥ 3
○ Opera Prima Bianco '15	♥♥ 3
○ Collio Sauvignon '15	♥ 3
○ Collio Chardonnay '13	♥♥ 3
○ Collio Friulano '12	♥♥ 3
○ Collio Friulano '11	♥♥ 3
○ Collio Malvasia '11	♥♥ 3
○ Collio Malvasia '10	♥♥ 3
○ Collio Ribolla Gialla '10	♥♥ 3
○ Collio Sauvignon '14	♥♥ 3
○ Collio Sauvignon '12	♥♥ 3
○ Collio Sauvignon '11	♥♥ 3
○ Opera Prima Bianco '14	♥♥ 3
○ Opera Prima Bianco '13	♥♥ 4
○ Opera Prima Bianco '12	♥♥ 3

Le Monde

LOC. LE MONDE
VIA GARIBALDI, 2
33080 PRATA DI PORDENONE [PN]
TEL. +39 0434622087
www.lemondewine.com

CELLAR SALES
PRE-BOOKED VISITS
ANNUAL PRODUCTION 250,000 bottles
HECTARES UNDER VINE 50.00
SUSTAINABLE WINERY

Alex Maccan, a young entrepreneur, took over this flourishing business on the Tagliamento in 2008, soon taking it to the top of the regional winemaking scene. The vineyards extend between the banks of the Livenza and Meduna rivers, in the Friuli Grave wine region, where the clayey and limestone terrain gives a unique characteristic to Le Monde, which is therefore considered a subzone with a great vocation for vine growing. The high quality of the products is the result of the rare decision in this area to pursue very low yields per hectare, counting on vines that are more than 30 years old on average. The Pinot Bianco took another Tre Bicchieri, this time for the 2015 growing years. The constancy of this winery is commendable and it always hits the mark with this wine. But it is surprising even the provision of full range, regardless of the type, with ratings that, compared to the price, are the absolute value.

★Lis Neris

VIA GAVINANA, 5
34070 SAN LORENZO ISONTINO [GO]
TEL. +39 048180105
www.lisneris.it

CELLAR SALES
PRE-BOOKED VISITS
ACCOMMODATION
ANNUAL PRODUCTION 400,000 bottles
HECTARES UNDER VINE 70.00
SUSTAINABLE WINERY

Alvaro Pecorari, who took over Lis Neris in 1981, managed to transform a smallholding into a winery. Slowly but surely it has grown to a very respectable size, now representing one of Italy's most important firms. The vineyards are on a deep gravel plateau between the Slovenian border and the right bank of the River Isonzo, forming four separate sites: Gris, Picol, Jurosa and Neris. Alvaro has managed to promote the unique features of each area, establishing a highly personal style and making the most of the strong temperature variations that assist the slow maturation of the grapes, making them more solid and better balanced. With four wines in the final, the Tre Bicchieri and the Sweet Wine of the Year went to the very sweet Tal Lùc Cuvée Speciale, produced from raisined verduzzo friulano grapes topped up with a small percentage of riesling. The belief is that sweet wines require the cuvées of several vintages for solutions with enhanced potential.

○ Friuli Grave Pinot Bianco '15	♟♟♟	2*
● Friuli Grave Cabernet Sauvignon '14	♟♟	2*
○ Friuli Grave Chardonnay '15	♟♟	2*
○ Friuli Grave Friulano '15	♟♟	2*
● Friuli Grave Merlot '14	♟♟	2*
○ Friuli Grave Pinot Grigio '15	♟♟	2*
● Friuli Grave Refosco P. R. '14	♟♟	2*
● Friuli Grave Refosco P. R. Inaco Ris. '11	♟♟	4
○ Pratum '13	♟♟	4
○ Friuli Grave Sauvignon '15	♟	2
○ Ribolla Gialla '15	♟	3
○ Ribolla Gialla Brut	♟	3
○ Friuli Grave Pinot Bianco '14	♟♟♟	2*
○ Friuli Grave Pinot Bianco '13	♟♟♟	2*
○ Friuli Grave Pinot Bianco '12	♟♟♟	2*
○ Friuli Grave Pinot Bianco '01	♟♟♟	2

○ Tal Lùc Cuvée Speciale	♟♟♟	8
○ Confini '13	♟♟	5
○ Friuli Isonzo Pinot Grigio Gris '14	♟♟	4
○ Lis '13	♟♟	5
○ Friuli Isonzo Chardonnay Jurosa '14	♟♟	4
○ Friuli Isonzo Sauvignon Picòl '14	♟♟	4
● Lis Neris '10	♟♟	6
○ Fiore di Campo '06	♟♟♟	3
○ Friuli Isonzo Pinot Grigio Gris '13	♟♟♟	4*
○ Friuli Isonzo Pinot Grigio Gris '12	♟♟♟	4*
○ Friuli Isonzo Pinot Grigio Gris '11	♟♟♟	4*
○ Friuli Isonzo Pinot Grigio Gris '10	♟♟♟	4*
○ Friuli Isonzo Pinot Grigio Gris '09	♟♟♟	4*
○ Lis '03	♟♟♟	5
○ Pinot Grigio Gris '08	♟♟♟	4*
○ Pinot Grigio Gris '04	♟♟♟	4*
○ Sauvignon Picòl '06	♟♟♟	3*

★Livon

FRAZ. DOLEGNANO
VIA MONTAREZZA, 33
33048 SAN GIOVANNI AL NATISONE [UD]
TEL. +39 0432757173
www.livon.it

CELLAR SALES
PRE-BOOKED VISITS
ACCOMMODATION
ANNUAL PRODUCTION 850,000 bottles
HECTARES UNDER VINE 180.00

With more than 50 years of activity under its belt, Livon, now run by Valneo and Toino, is a historic brand that has helped keep small regional businesses among the very best Italian and international names. The next generation is represented by their respective children, Matteo and Francesca, who have been employed by the company for some time. The famous winged woman who distinguishes the parent company has now been joined by: RoncAlto on Collio Goriziano, Villa Chiopris on the Friuli plain, Borgo Salcetino in Tuscany and Colsanto in Umbria. All the production sites rely on the proven expertise of the winery oenologist Rinaldo Stocco. Along with the usual Braide Alte 2014, there is also a debut finalist, the Collio Bianco Solarco, which won our Tre Bicchieri. A friulano and ribolla gialla blend of these two utterly representative native varieties, it is fragrant, with notes of lime and crisp fruit, with an energetic, lively mouth.

Tenuta Luisa

FRAZ. CORONA
VIA CAMPO SPORTIVO, 13
34070 MARIANO DEL FRIULI [GO]
TEL. +39 048169680
www.tenutaluisa.com

CELLAR SALES
PRE-BOOKED VISITS
ACCOMMODATION
ANNUAL PRODUCTION 350,000 bottles
HECTARES UNDER VINE 100.00
SUSTAINABLE WINERY

Eddi Luisa is an emblematic figure on the regional winemaking scene. Proud of his peasant roots, he loves to repeat that since the age of 13 he has been working from sun to sun, never looking at his watch. He farmed cattle for many years, before devoting himself almost exclusively to vineyards. Slowly but surely, he has managed to expand the business, equipping it with a wonderful winery surrounded by green vines. Supported by his wife Nella, he heads a close-knit family group, although he handed over the running of the business to his children some time ago: Michele handles vinification and Davide deals with the agricultural side of things. The two I Ferretti line wines earned a place in the finals and the Desiderium 2013 took a Tre Bicchieri. This skilful blend of chardonnay, friulano and sauvignon seduces the nose with forward notes of fruit and tropical fruit, and shows sublime aromatic palate nuances.

○ Collio Bianco Solarco '15	♔♔♔ 3*
○ Braide Alte '14	♔♔ 5
○ Collio Malvasia Soluna '15	♔♔ 3
● Collio Merlot Tiare Mate '13	♔♔ 5
○ Collio Pinot Grigio Braide Grande '15	♔♔ 3
○ Collio Ribolla Gialla Roncalto '15	♔♔ 3
○ Collio Sauvignon Valbuins '15	♔♔ 3
● FCO Pignolo Eldoro '12	♔♔ 5
● FCO Refosco P. R. Riul '13	♔♔ 3
● TiareBlù '13	♔♔ 5
○ Braide Alte '13	♔♔♔ 5
○ Braide Alte '11	♔♔♔ 5
○ Braide Alte '09	♔♔♔ 5
○ Braide Alte '07	♔♔♔ 5
○ Collio Braide Alte '08	♔♔♔ 3
○ Collio Friulano Manditocai '12	♔♔♔ 5
○ Collio Friulano Manditocai '10	♔♔♔ 5

○ Desiderium I Ferretti '13	♔♔♔ 4*
○ Friuli Isonzo Friulano I Ferretti '13	♔♔ 3*
● Friuli Isonzo Cabernet Franc '14	♔♔ 3
● Friuli Isonzo Merlot '14	♔♔ 3
● Friuli Isonzo Refosco P. R. I Ferretti '11	♔♔ 4
○ Friuli Isonzo Sauvignon '15	♔♔ 3
○ Ribolla Gialla '15	♔♔ 3
○ Friuli Isonzo Chardonnay '15	♔ 3
○ Traminer Aromatico '15	♔ 3
● Desiderium Sel. I Ferretti '09	♔♔♔ 4*
○ Chardonnay I Ferretti '07	♔♔ 4
● Friuli Isonzo Cabernet I Ferretti '07	♔♔ 4
● Friuli Isonzo Cabernet Sauvignon I Ferretti '11	♔♔ 4
○ Friuli Isonzo Friulano I Ferretti '12	♔♔ 3*
○ Friuli Isonzo Pinot Bianco '06	♔♔ 2*
● Friuli Isonzo Refosco P. R. '08	♔♔ 3*

Magnàs

LOC. BOATINA
VIA CORONA, 47
34071 CORMÒNS [GO]
TEL. +39 048160991
www.magnas.it

CELLAR SALES
PRE-BOOKED VISITS
ACCOMMODATION AND RESTAURANT SERVICE
ANNUAL PRODUCTION 25,000 bottles
HECTARES UNDER VINE 10.00

Magnàs is a small artisanal firm run by Andrea Visintin, but founded by his father Luciano who, in the early 1970s, decided to put his own stamp on a brand new business, making the most of the centuries-old experience of a family always linked with agriculture. Magnàs is the nickname given to this branch of the Visintin family for generations, conveying their loyalty, pride, dignity and spirt of sacrifice. With just a few hectares of vineyards, Andrea is able to look after every vine with great care. The winery only has a few labels and its production is limited, but the quality is high and the prices very reasonable. Our excellent opinion of all the wines is racked up a notch by the performance of the Pinot Grigio 2015. The nose regales us with inviting notes of dried flowers and fruity hints of pear and white peach, all subtly veiled with vanilla and acacia honey. The palate follows through, velvety and balanced.

Valerio Marinig

VIA BROLO, 41
33040 PREPOTTO [UD]
TEL. +39 0432713012
www.marinig.it

CELLAR SALES
PRE-BOOKED VISITS
ANNUAL PRODUCTION 25,000 bottles
HECTARES UNDER VINE 9.00

As often happens in traditional family-run firms in Friuli, which operate on a human scale, there is a factotum who runs it. This role is now entrusted to Valerio Marinig, who exploits the ancestral know-how handed down from one generation to the next. His father Sergio still plays an active role, especially in the countryside, with his wife Michela and mother Marisa completing the family group. The nine hectares of vineyard are situated on a hillside in the municipality of Prepotto, the homeland of the schioppettino grape, where the unique morphology and climate have created the necessary conditions for quality wine production. The Refosco dal Peduncolo Rosso 2014 which made last year's finals is again at the top of wine rankings. The growing year whites confirm their great fragrance and coherence, while the reds vaunt good structure, with tannins still a tad sharp but promising well for the future.

○ Pinot Grigio '15	▼▼	3*
○ Collio Bianco '15	▼▼	3
○ Friuli Isonzo Friulano '15	▼▼	3
○ Malvasia '15	▼▼	3
● Merlot '13	▼▼	3
○ Sauvignon '14	▼▼	3
○ Collio Bianco '13	♀♀	3*
○ Collio Bianco '12	♀♀	3
○ Friuli Isonzo Chardonnay '13	♀♀	3
○ Friuli Isonzo Friulano '14	♀♀	3
○ Friuli Isonzo Friulano '13	♀♀	3
○ Friuli Isonzo Sauvignon '13	♀♀	3
○ Friuli Isonzo Sauvignon '12	♀♀	3
○ Malvasia '14	♀♀	3
○ Malvasia '13	♀♀	3
○ Pinot Grigio '14	♀♀	3

● FCO Biel Cûr Rosso '13	▼▼	4
○ FCO Friulano '15	▼▼	2*
● FCO Refosco P. R. '14	▼▼	3
○ FCO Sauvignon '15	▼▼	3
● FCO Schioppettino di Prepotto '12	▼▼	4
○ FCO Pinot Bianco '15	▼	2
○ FCO Verduzzo Friulano '15	▼	3
● Biel Cûr Rosso '11	♀♀	4
○ COF Friulano '13	♀♀	2*
○ COF Picolit '12	♀♀	6
● COF Pignolo '09	♀♀	4
○ COF Pinot Bianco '13	♀♀	2*
○ COF Sauvignon '13	♀♀	3
● COF Schioppettino di Prepotto '10	♀♀	4
○ FCO Pinot Bianco '14	♀♀	2*
● FCO Schioppettino di Prepotto '11	♀♀	4

Masùt da Rive

VIA MANZONI, 82
34070 MARIANO DEL FRIULI [GO]
TEL. +39 048169200
www.masutdarive.com

CELLAR SALES
PRE-BOOKED VISITS
ANNUAL PRODUCTION 80,000 bottles
HECTARES UNDER VINE 22.00
SUSTAINABLE WINERY

Masùt da Rive is playing an important part in the relaunch of pinot nero in the region, a grape that many have stopped growing over recent years. Credit should be given to Silvano Gallo for having always believed in it and handed down this passion to his sons Fabrizio and Marco. Years of research and experimentation have revealed that particular vinification measures are needed to make the most of this grape, often using the stalks, and the results have been quick to come. The rapidly growing Masùt da Rive is offering increasingly interesting and convincing wines, with marked local features that highlight the potential of the Friuli Isonzo wine region. We missed the Pinot Nero Maurus that made the finals for two years in a row as it is only made in the best vintages. Meanwhile we were able to enjoy the refined nose, delicate spice and clean taste of the Cabernet Sauvignon 2014.

Davino Meroi

VIA STRETTA, 7B
33042 BUTTRIO [UD]
TEL. +39 0432673369
www.meroidavino.com

CELLAR SALES
PRE-BOOKED VISITS
RESTAURANT SERVICE
ANNUAL PRODUCTION 45,000 bottles
HECTARES UNDER VINE 19.00
SUSTAINABLE WINERY

Paolo Meroi is also well-known in the area as an established restaurateur, but his best role involves running the winery founded by his father Davino, from whom he inherited the experience garnered in vineyards forged by his grandfather Domenico, on the gentle slopes of Buttrio. Vines of over 30 years old, very low yields and meticulous selections are what is needed to achieve healthy, rich and concentrated grapes, giving the wines a personal style, resulting from the skilful vinification in wood. He can now also count on the support of his son Damiano, who handles the marketing, while Mirko Degan provides invaluable assistance in the vineyard and winery. We are now accustomed to seeing at least two wines in the final, and this year it fell to Verduzzo Friulano 2013 and Merlot Ros di Buri 2013. The former is very sweet, with candied citrus, macaroons and vanilla on the nose, while the Merlot is complex, tasty, chewy, mellow, and mouthfilling.

● Friuli Isonzo Cabernet Sauvignon '14	♟♟ 3
● Friuli Isonzo Pinot Nero '14	♟♟ 5
● Friuli Isonzo Rosso Semidis '13	♟♟ 5
○ Friuli Isonzo Sauvignon '15	♟♟ 3
○ Pinot Grigio '15	♟♟ 3
○ Friuli Isonzo Chardonnay '15	♟ 3
● Friuli Isonzo Merlot '14	♟ 4
○ Ribolla Gialla '15	♟ 3
○ Friuli Isonzo Tocai Friulano '04	♟♟♟ 3*
● Friuli Isonzo Cabernet Sauvignon '12	♟♟ 3
○ Friuli Isonzo Chardonnay Rive Alte '14	♟♟ 3
○ Friuli Isonzo Chardonnay Rive Alte '13	♟♟ 3
● Friuli Isonzo Pinot Nero '13	♟♟ 4
● Friuli Isonzo Refosco P. R. '12	♟♟ 3
○ Friuli Isonzo Sauvignon Rive Alte '14	♟♟ 3
○ Friuli Isonzo Sauvignon Rive Alte '13	♟♟ 3

● FCO Merlot Ros di Buri '13	♟♟ 5
○ FCO Verduzzo Friulano '13	♟♟ 5
○ FCO Chardonnay '14	♟♟ 5
○ FCO Sauvignon '14	♟♟ 4
○ COF Friulano '11	♟♟♟ 5
○ COF Friulano '10	♟♟♟ 5
○ COF Verduzzo Friulano '08	♟♟♟ 5
○ COF Chardonnay '12	♟♟ 5
○ COF Friulano '13	♟♟ 5
● COF Merlot Ros di Buri '12	♟♟ 5
● COF Merlot V. Dominin '11	♟♟ 8
○ COF Sauvignon '12	♟♟ 4
○ FCO Malvasia Zitelle Durì '13	♟♟ 6
● FCO Merlot V. Dominin '12	♟♟ 8
○ FCO Picolit '13	♟♟ 6
○ FCO Sauvignon '13	♟♟ 4
○ FCO Verduzzo Friulano '12	♟♟ 5

Muzic

Loc. Bivio, 4
34070 San Floriano del Collio [GO]
Tel. +39 0481884201
www.cantinamuzic.it

CELLAR SALES
PRE-BOOKED VISITS
ANNUAL PRODUCTION 90,000 bottles
HECTARES UNDER VINE 21.00
SUSTAINABLE WINERY

Elija and Fabijan Muzic are ready to pick up the baton from their father Giovanni, better known locally as Ivan, a wine artisan and lover of the great outdoors. In his turn, Ivan inherited the winery from his parents, who purchased the first five hectares of vineyard in 1963 after working as sharecroppers on the sunny slopes of San Floriano del Collio. Elija and Fabijan have diligently divided the tasks and have been working in perfect harmony for some time. Their mother Orieta still supervises their work, an added value for this family group that makes cohesion its trump card and now play a leading role on the regional wine scene. The peerless quality of the entire range is confirmed. Now a stalwart in our finals, we are in no way surprised by yet another feat from Friulano Vigna Valeris, this time from 2015. The Malvasia 2015 is a pleasant novelty, with its yellow peach and medlar nose, and a creamy, fragrant, flavoursome mouth.

Paraschos

Loc. Bucuie, 13a
34070 San Floriano del Collio [GO]
Tel. +39 0481884154
www.paraschos.it

CELLAR SALES
PRE-BOOKED VISITS
ANNUAL PRODUCTION 14,000 bottles
HECTARES UNDER VINE 6.00

The showy Greek Pi that distinguishes the labels of Evangelos Paraschos leaves no doubts as to his origins. Having settled in San Floriano del Collio in 1979, he immediately assimilated the local winemaking traditions, combining them with those from the Vipacco valley, in nearby Slovenia. Biodynamic cultivation is followed by vinification involving long periods of maceration with the skins, for red and white grapes alike, in open oak vats from Slavonia or terracotta amphorae, with no temperature controls, entrusting the process to indigenous yeasts. The wines are bottled after at least two years without being filtered, clarified or stabilized, with no added sulphur dioxide. Again this year, we were able to taste only a couple of wines and the accolades of previous editions still ring true. In particular, the Pinot Grigio Not 2013 was outstanding, for its sunny nature with dried wild flowers and candied fruit on the nose, while dry and tasty on the palate.

○ Collio Friulano V. Valeris '15	♥♥ 3*
○ Collio Malvasia '15	♥♥ 3*
○ Collio Bianco '15	♥♥ 3
○ Collio Chardonnay '15	♥♥ 3
● Collio Merlot '14	♥♥ 3
○ Collio Pinot Grigio '15	♥♥ 3
○ Collio Ribolla Gialla '15	♥♥ 3
○ Collio Sauvignon V. Pàjze '15	♥♥ 3
○ Collio Bianco '13	♀♀ 3
● Collio Cabernet Sauvignon '12	♀♀ 3
○ Collio Chardonnay '13	♀♀ 3
○ Collio Malvasia '13	♀♀ 3
○ Collio Pinot Grigio '13	♀♀ 3
○ Collio Ribolla Gialla '13	♀♀ 3
○ Collio Sauvignon V. Pàjze '14	♀♀ 3
○ Collio Sauvignon V. Pàjze '12	♀♀ 3

○ Pinot Grigio Not '13	♥♥ 5
○ Ponka '11	♥♥ 5
○ Amphoreus Bianco '09	♀♀ 5
○ Amphoreus Malvasia '10	♀♀ 6
○ Chardonnay '09	♀♀ 3
○ Chardonnay '08	♀♀ 3
○ Kaj '11	♀♀ 5
○ Kaj '09	♀♀ 5
○ Malvasia Amphoreus '11	♀♀ 6
● Merlot '10	♀♀ 3*
● Merlot '09	♀♀ 4
○ Pinot Grigio Not '11	♀♀ 5
○ Ponka '10	♀♀ 5
○ Ponka '09	♀♀ 5
● Ros di Lune '09	♀♀ 3
● Skala '07	♀♀ 5

Alessandro Pascolo

LOC. RUTTÀRS, 1
34070 DOLEGNA DEL COLLIO [GO]
TEL. +39 048161144
www.vinipascolo.com

CELLAR SALES
PRE-BOOKED VISITS
ANNUAL PRODUCTION 25,000 bottles
HECTARES UNDER VINE 7.00
SUSTAINABLE WINERY

A very recent winery founded in 2006 by
Alessandro Pascolo who, after studying
winemaking and agronomy, decided to
follow up and make the most of his
grandfather Angelo's great idea of investing
in the countryside in the 1970s, when he
bought a farmhouse surrounded by
vineyards on the sunny slopes of Ruttàrs
hill, a wonderful part of the Dolegna del
Collio wine region. Seven hectares of
vineyard enjoying ideal exposure, with some
old vines too, that Alessandro now manages
himself, interpreting the land with great skill,
demonstrating that vineyards are in his
blood and his heart is in the vineyards,
converting this love into emotions in his
wines. We were unanimous in our approval
of all the wines, for their sheer drinkability
and, above all, for being so true to the
varietal characteristics of each grape. In
particular, the Malvasia 2015 made it to our
finals, where it garnered praise for its
complex nose and lingering palate.

○ Collio Malvasia '15	🍷🍷 3*
○ Collio Bianco Agnul '14	🍷🍷 4
○ Collio Friulano '15	🍷🍷 3
● Collio Merlot Sel. '13	🍷🍷 5
○ Collio Sauvignon '15	🍷🍷 3
○ Collio Pinot Bianco '15	🍷 3
○ Collio Bianco Agnul '13	🍷🍷 4
○ Collio Malvasia '13	🍷🍷 3
● Collio Merlot Sel. '12	🍷🍷 5
● Pascal '11	🍷🍷 3
○ Riesling Briach '07	🍷🍷 4

Pierpaolo Pecorari

VIA TOMMASEO, 56
34070 SAN LORENZO ISONTINO [GO]
TEL. +39 0481808775
www.pierpaolopecorari.it

CELLAR SALES
PRE-BOOKED VISITS
ANNUAL PRODUCTION 150,000 bottles
HECTARES UNDER VINE 30.00

Vignerons by tradition, the Pecorari family
have written several pages of history in the
world of regional winemaking. In 1970,
when he was very young, Pierpaolo
Pecorari founded his own business and
started a process that soon made him one
of the most important winemakers in the
Friuli Isonzo wine region. His philosophy
has always been one of bottling the great
personality that only this location is able to
offer. Because of this, all his wines are
strictly monovarietal and make the most of
the growing area's features to present
marked minerality, showing very true to
type. The white wines matured in wood
show elegant notes of whipped cream,
candied citrus, and vanilla, with a soft,
fragrant mouth. The top scores went to the
2015 Malvasia for its complexity and
seductive nose, but above all for its fresh,
dynamic palate.

○ Malvasia '15	🍷🍷 3*
● Merlot '14	🍷🍷 3
○ Pinot Grigio Olivers '14	🍷🍷 5
● Refosco P. R. Tao '12	🍷🍷 5
○ Sauvignon Kolaus '14	🍷🍷 5
○ Friuli Isonzo Friulano '15	🍷 3
○ Chardonnay Soris '11	🍷🍷 5
○ Friuli Isonzo Friulano '11	🍷🍷 3*
● Merlot Baolar '11	🍷🍷 4
○ Pinot Grigio Olivers '12	🍷🍷 5
○ Pinot Grigio Olivers '11	🍷🍷 5
● Refosco P. R. '12	🍷🍷 3
○ Sauvignon Blanc '10	🍷🍷 3
○ Sauvignon Blanc Altis '11	🍷🍷 4
○ Sauvignon Kolaus '12	🍷🍷 5
○ Sauvignon Kolaus '11	🍷🍷 5*

Perusini

LOC. GRAMOGLIANO
VIA DEL TORRIONE, 13
33040 CORNO DI ROSAZZO [UD]
TEL. +39 0432759151
www.perusini.com

CELLAR SALES
PRE-BOOKED VISITS
ACCOMMODATION AND RESTAURANT SERVICE
ANNUAL PRODUCTION 90,000 bottles
HECTARES UNDER VINE 15.00
VITICULTURE METHOD Certified Organic
SUSTAINABLE WINERY

Teresa Perusini owns this winery in Friuli founded in the late 19th century by her grandfather Giacomo Perusini. A lover of art, the beautiful and the good, Teresa has enhanced the work of her forebears, proving herself to be a skilled winemaker, able to interpret the local area and convey her enthusiasm to the next generation represented by Carlo Tommaso and Michele, who have been involved for some time. The introduction of young energies has coincided with a substantial leap forward, affecting the entire production line. Both the white and red wines have stabilized at very high quality levels, with Picolit the winery's flagship product. Freshness, mineral notes and fragrance are to the fore in all the growing season's white wines, but the Pinot Grigio 2015 was a cut above, its exotic whispers showcasing the citrus notes of citron and tangerine zest. The reds show excellent, spruced up fruity and balsamic tones.

○ FCO Pinot Grigio '15	♟♟	3*
● FCO Cabernet Franc '13	♟♟	3
● FCO Merlot '13	♟♟	3
○ FCO Picolit '13	♟♟	8
● FCO Refosco P.R. '13	♟♟	3
● FCO Rosso del Postiglione '13	♟♟	3
○ FCO Sauvignon '15	♟♟	3
○ FCO Chardonnay '15	♟	3
○ FCO Ribolla Gialla '15	♟	3
● COF Merlot '12	♟♟	3
○ COF Picolit '12	♟♟	8
● COF Refosco P.R. '12	♟♟	3
● COF Rosso del Postiglione '12	♟♟	3
○ FCO Pinot Grigio '14	♟♟	3
○ FCO Ribolla Gialla '14	♟♟	3
○ FCO Sauvignon '14	♟♟	3

Petrucco

VIA MORPURGO, 12
33042 BUTTRIO [UD]
TEL. +39 0432674387
www.vinipetrucco.it

CELLAR SALES
PRE-BOOKED VISITS
ANNUAL PRODUCTION 80,000 bottles
HECTARES UNDER VINE 25.00

A business born out of a couple's love of their land: Lina and Paolo Petrucco. In 1981 they settled on the sunny slopes of Buttrio, on the edge of Friuli's beautiful natural amphitheatre formed by hills exposed to the sea breeze, founding a winery here. They entrusted themselves to the winemaking and agronomic experience of Flavio Cabas, who still runs the production chain today. He is responsible for looking after the historic vineyards planted before the Great War by Italo Balbo, husband of Contessa Emanuela Florio, used to grow the grapes for producing the Riserva Ronco del Balbo wines, the company's pride and joy. Petrucco has always produced monovarietal wines, but this year they will be making their market of Bianco Cabas Ronco del Balbo 2015, a blend of chardonnay, sauvignon, friulano and malvasia, which we fell for on the spot and showered with praise.

○ FCO Bianco Cabas Ronco del Balbo '15	♟♟	4
○ FCO Malvasia '15	♟♟	3
● FCO Merlot Ronco del Balbo '13	♟♟	4
● FCO Pignolo Ronco del Balbo '11	♟♟	5
○ FCO Pinot Bianco '15	♟♟	3
○ FCO Pinot Grigio '15	♟♟	3
● FCO Refosco P. R. Ronco del Balbo '13	♟♟	4
○ FCO Sauvignon '15	♟♟	3
○ FCO Friulano '15	♟	3
● COF Merlot Ronco del Balbo '12	♟♟	4
● COF Merlot Ronco del Balbo '11	♟♟	3*
● COF Refosco P. R. Ronco del Balbo '12	♟♟	4
○ FCO Chardonnay '14	♟♟	3
○ FCO Friulano '14	♟♟	3
○ FCO Pinot Bianco '14	♟♟	3*
○ FCO Pinot Grigio '14	♟♟	3

Petrussa

VIA ALBANA, 49
33040 PREPOTTO [UD]
TEL. +39 0432713192
www.petrussa.it

CELLAR SALES
PRE-BOOKED VISITS
ACCOMMODATION
ANNUAL PRODUCTION 40,000 bottles
HECTARES UNDER VINE 10.00

It was the siren song of a return to one's
origins that in 1986 convinced brothers
Gianni and Paolo Petrussa to take over from
their parents the reins of their family
operation. Their first goal was to fully
understand the particular characteristics of
their growing area, Albana di Prepotto, a
modest corner of earth considered to be the
cradle of ribolla gialla, a native grape that
yields Schioppettino. Their estate vineyards
are divided into small parcels throughout
the northern section of the Friuli Colli
Orientali denomination, near the Julian
Pre-Alps, in a valley protected from the
strong east winds and enjoying its own
unique climate. This was definitely an
impressive year for the entire line, all of
which show progress in quality. The whites
of the recent vintage display marked varietal
fidelity and delicious approachability, while
the reds boast the aromatic complexity
gained from slow maturation.

○ FCO Friulano '15	🍷🍷 3
● FCO Merlot Rosso Petrussa '13	🍷🍷 5
○ FCO Pinot Bianco '15	🍷🍷 3
○ FCO Ribolla Gialla '15	🍷🍷 3
○ FCO Sauvignon '15	🍷🍷 3
● FCO Schioppettino di Prepotto '13	🍷🍷 5
○ Pensiero '13	🍷🍷 5
○ FCO Chardonnay S. Elena '14	🍷 4
○ COF Cabernet '12	🍷🍷 3
○ COF Chardonnay S. Elena '13	🍷🍷 4
● COF Rosso Petrussa '12	🍷🍷 5
○ COF Sauvignon '13	🍷🍷 3
○ FCO Friulano '14	🍷🍷 3
○ FCO Pinot Bianco '14	🍷🍷 3
○ Pensiero '12	🍷🍷 5
○ Pensiero '11	🍷🍷 5

Roberto Picéch

LOC. PRADIS, 11
34071 CORMÒNS [GO]
TEL. +39 048160347
www.picech.com

CELLAR SALES
PRE-BOOKED VISITS
ACCOMMODATION
ANNUAL PRODUCTION 30,000 bottles
HECTARES UNDER VINE 7.00
SUSTAINABLE WINERY

Roberto Picéch runs a highly-respected
operation in the Collio, a benchmark for the
area. Rising atop a hill near Pradis, not far
from Cormòns, it is surrounded by superb
vineyards inherited from his father Egidio; a
local legend whose nickname was "il ribèl",
he is universally remembered for his strong
personality, his tenacity and determination,
but for his generosity as well and for his
readiness in dispensing help and advice.
The apple has not fallen far from the tree,
and Roberto has eschewed following trends
and market demands, producing wines that
reflect his own character--pure, authentic,
incisive, and at times a tad hard to read.
Collio Rosso 2014 shows the thrust classic
to cabernet franc, with its signature
herbaceous notes of willow bark and
liquorice root, while merlot and cabernet
sauvignon, which complete the blend,
convey delicious macerated cherry and
sweet tobacco, on both nose and finish.

● Collio Rosso '14	🍷🍷 3*
○ Collio Friulano '15	🍷🍷 3
○ Collio Malvasia '15	🍷🍷 3
○ Collio Pinot Bianco '15	🍷🍷 3
○ Collio Bianco Athena '05	🍷🍷🍷 7
○ Collio Bianco Jelka '11	🍷🍷🍷 4*
○ Collio Bianco Jelka '99	🍷🍷🍷 7
○ Collio Pinot Bianco '13	🍷🍷🍷 3*
○ Collio Bianco Athena Magnum '12	🍷🍷 7
○ Collio Bianco Athena Magnum '11	🍷🍷 7
○ Collio Bianco Jelka '13	🍷🍷 4
○ Collio Bianco Jelka '12	🍷🍷 4
○ Collio Malvasia '14	🍷🍷 3*
○ Collio Pinot Bianco '14	🍷🍷 3
● Collio Rosso '13	🍷🍷 3
● Collio Rosso '12	🍷🍷 3
● Collio Rosso Ruben Ris. '12	🍷🍷 6

Vigneti Pittaro

VIA UDINE, 67
33033 CODROIPO [UD]
TEL. +39 0432904726
www.vignetipittaro.com

CELLAR SALES
PRE-BOOKED VISITS
ACCOMMODATION
ANNUAL PRODUCTION 400,000 bottles
HECTARES UNDER VINE 90.00
SUSTAINABLE WINERY

Piero Pittaro comes from an ancient local family boasting 450 years of winegrowing activity. Most of the vineyards surround the impressive cellar in Codroipo, a nonpareil example of symbiosis between architecture and functionality, are set in the vast, rocky expanse of the Friuli Grave denomination, while others lie in the northernmost hills of Friuli Colli Orientali, near Ramandolo. These diverse terroirs yield equally diverse wines, in a generous line that answers the range of market demands, a cadre that includes a prestigious series of classic method sparklers that are the fruit of the lengthy expertise of managing director Stefano Trinco. Pittaro Brut Etichetta Oro 2009, which always seem to be one step ahead of the pack, stands out as usual among the regional sparklers for its aromas and full-flavours. It leads a team of wines of various types, all well-crafted and varietally eloquent, each an effective ambassador of its growing area.

○ Pittaro Brut Et. Oro '09	♟♟ 5
○ FCO Friulano Ronco Vieri '15	♟♟ 3
○ FCO Picolit Ronco Vieri '13	♟♟ 6
● Friuli Grave Cabernet '13	♟♟ 3
○ Friuli Grave Chardonnay Mousquè '15	♟♟ 3
● Friuli Grave Rosso Agresto '11	♟♟ 4
○ Pittaro Brut Et. Argento	♟♟ 4
⊙ Pittaro Brut Pink	♟♟ 5
○ Ramandolo Ronco Vieri '14	♟♟ 3
○ Ribolla Gialla Brut	♟♟ 3
○ Friuli Grave Sauvignon Blanc '15	♟ 3
○ Manzoni Bianco '15	♟ 3
● Friuli Grave Rosso Agresto '08	♙♙ 4
○ Pittaro Brut Et. Oro '08	♙♙ 5
○ Pittaro Brut Et. Oro '07	♙♙ 5

Denis Pizzulin

VIA BROLO, 43
33040 PREPOTTO [UD]
TEL. +39 0432713425
www.pizzulin.com

CELLAR SALES
PRE-BOOKED VISITS
ANNUAL PRODUCTION 30,000 bottles
HECTARES UNDER VINE 11.00

Just a handful of hectares and wines find their effective foil in overriding passion and inborn winemaking skills, the qualities that have enabled Denis Pizzulin to gain benchmark status in the area of Prepotto. This narrow, wind-protected valley bordering Slovenia and the Collio hums with the activities of small family operations inheriting expertise from generations of ancestors. This is the home of the ribolla nera, which produces Schioppettino, which is Pizzulin's iconic wine as well, although his entire line receives his careful attention. His Rarisolchi wines, both white and red, are barrel-aged blends. The year was very felicitous for the whites, all fragrant, straightforward, citrusy and delicious. But Merlot Scaglia Rossa Riserva 2013 steals the show, thanks to its firm structure and velvety palate, infused with crushed cherry, smooth spice, and black liquorice.

● FCO Merlot Scaglia Rossa Ris. '13	♟♟ 4
○ FCO Friulano '15	♟♟ 3
○ FCO Pignolo '11	♟♟ 6
○ FCO Pinot Grigio '15	♟♟ 3
○ FCO Sauvignon '15	♟♟ 3
● FCO Pinot Nero '13	♟ 4
● COF Merlot '13	♙♙ 3
● COF Merlot '12	♙♙ 3
○ COF Pinot Bianco '13	♙♙ 3
● COF Refosco P. R. '12	♙♙ 4
● COF Refosco P. R. Ris. '09	♙♙ 4
● COF Rosso Rarisolchi Ris. '09	♙♙ 4
○ COF Sauvignon '13	♙♙ 3
● COF Schioppettino di Prepotto '12	♙♙ 3
● COF Schioppettino di Prepotto '11	♙♙ 3
● COF Schioppettino di Prepotto '10	♙♙ 3

Renata Pizzulin

via Celso Macor, 1
34070 Moraro [GO]
Tel. +39 0432713027
www.renatapizzulin.it

CELLAR SALES
PRE-BOOKED VISITS
ANNUAL PRODUCTION 10,000 bottles
HECTARES UNDER VINE 3.00
SUSTAINABLE WINERY

This miniscule, freshly-minted cellar has grabbed attention for the fragrance and approachability of its wines. The youthful couple Alberto Peloan and Renata Pizzulin has shown impressive understanding, planting their vineyards in clayey, iron-rich soils on the right bank of the Isonzo, to varieties appropriate to the weather and soil conditions of each parcel. They have assigned to each toponyms taken from ancient tax maps, namely Teolis, Melaris, Paladis, Murellis, and Clagnis. Their debut is breath-taking, and now Alberto must live up to expectations. To ensure optimal expression, the wines are given lengthy bottle-ageing and released after a minimum of two years following the harvest. We tasted all the 2014s, and that challenging year did not, in fact, diminish the performances across the line.

○ Friuli Isonzo Bianco Teolis '14	🍷🍷 4
○ Friuli Isonzo Chardonnay Paladis '14	🍷🍷 4
● Refosco P. R. Murellis '13	🍷🍷 4
○ Friuli Isonzo Malvasia Melaris '14	🍷 3
○ Friuli Isonzo Bianco Teolis '13	🍷🍷 3
○ Friuli Isonzo Bianco Teolis '12	🍷🍷 3
○ Friuli Isonzo Chardonnay Paladis '13	🍷🍷 3
○ Friuli Isonzo Chardonnay Paladis '12	🍷🍷 3
○ Friuli Isonzo Malvasia Melaris '13	🍷🍷 3
○ Friuli Isonzo Malvasia Melaris '12	🍷🍷 3
● Friuli Isonzo Refosco P. R. Murellis '12	🍷🍷 3
● Murellis '12	🍷🍷 3

Damijan Podversic

via Brigata Pavia, 61
34170 Gorizia
Tel. +39 048178217
www.damijanpodversic.com

CELLAR SALES
PRE-BOOKED VISITS
ANNUAL PRODUCTION 24,000 bottles
HECTARES UNDER VINE 10.00
VITICULTURE METHOD Certified Organic
SUSTAINABLE WINERY

From Monte Calvario, one of the highest hills in the Collio area, one's gaze takes in the undulating contours of nearby reliefs, then descends to the immense plain below and to glimpses of the sea beyond. It is a breath-taking panorama that Damijan Podversic has the good fortune to enjoy every day, as he tends his vineyards with near-maniacal meticulousness. An authentic, proud farmer, relying on love for his earth and on age-old winemaking methods, he privileges lengthy macerations on the skins, even for his white wines, and eschews anything that might alter the natural process of transformation. A glance at the table below will confirm the quality of Damijan's wines, with a full four wines in the final round this year. Ribolla Gialla 2012 garnered the Tre Bicchieri, boasting ginger, beeswax, incense, raisin, and liqueur figs, and an almost-peppery palate that completes a tangy, savoury wine.

○ Ribolla Gialla '12	🍷🍷🍷 8
○ Kaplja '12	🍷🍷 6
○ Malvasia '12	🍷🍷 8
● Rosso Prelit '12	🍷🍷 6
○ Nekaj '12	🍷🍷 6
○ Kaplja '08	🍷🍷🍷 6
○ Malvasia '10	🍷🍷🍷 6
○ Malvasia '09	🍷🍷🍷 6
○ Kaplja '11	🍷🍷 6
○ Kaplja '10	🍷🍷 6
○ Kaplja '09	🍷🍷 6
○ Kaplja '07	🍷🍷 6
○ Nekaj '11	🍷🍷 6
○ Ribolla Giall '10	🍷🍷 6
○ Ribolla Gialla '11	🍷🍷 6
○ Ribolla Gialla '09	🍷🍷 6
○ Ribolla Gialla '07	🍷🍷 5

Isidoro Polencic

Loc. Plessiva, 12
34071 Cormòns [GO]
Tel. +39 048160655
www.polencic.com

CELLAR SALES
PRE-BOOKED VISITS
ACCOMMODATION
ANNUAL PRODUCTION 120,000 bottles
HECTARES UNDER VINE 28.00

Memories of the Polencic family's settlement in the Collio are lost in the mists of time. Stubborn, committed to agriculture, and, of course, to grapegrowing, their heir is Isidoro Polencic, splendidly skilled in both vineyard and cellar. He founded this winery in 1968, then directed it for many years, achieving an impressive dimension for a family-run cellar. The helm is now shared by his three children, Elisabetta, Michele, and Alex, who have shown unusual self-confidence, particularly given their youth. The standard-bearer here is Fisc, made from a vineyard that was re-planted with genetic material from an ultra-centenarian tocai friulano vineyard. The entire line we tasted gave a truly superb performance, all latest-vintage whites from the Collio, fitting ambassadors of a celebrated region. Each is admirably expressive of its source grape, and all display nonpareil aromatics.

Primosic

Fraz. Oslavia
Loc. Madonnina di Oslavia, 3
34070 Gorizia
Tel. +39 0481535153
www.primosic.com

CELLAR SALES
PRE-BOOKED VISITS
ANNUAL PRODUCTION 210,000 bottles
HECTARES UNDER VINE 30.00

Young brothers Marko and Boris Primosic manage this operation founded in 1956 by their father Silvestro in Oslavia, an area with quite a number of family-run cellars that have written the history of the Collio, and continue to do so. Winemaking practices here are handed down from previous generations, common on all sides of the borders, with lengthy macerations on the skins, even for the whites and particularly for Ribolla Gialla. Use is made of modern technology too, of course, which makes possible valuable additions to the line, offering the international market a broad array of local interpretations. The overall fine performance of the wines, given additional lustre by Bianco Klin 2011's competition in the final round, was crowned by Tre Bicchieri for Ribolla Gialla di Oslavia Riserva 2012, which repeats last year's triumph. Kudos to the Collio, Oslavia, and the Primosics.

○ Collio Chardonnay '15	♟♟ 3
○ Collio Friulano '15	♟♟ 3
○ Collio Pinot Bianco '15	♟♟ 3
○ Collio Pinot Grigio '15	♟♟ 3
○ Collio Ribolla Gialla '15	♟♟ 3
○ Collio Sauvignon '15	♟♟ 3
○ Collio Friulano Fisc '07	♟♟♟ 3*
○ Collio Pinot Bianco '07	♟♟♟ 3
○ Collio Pinot Grigio '98	♟♟♟ 3*
○ Collio Tocai Friulano '04	♟♟♟ 3*
○ Collio Chardonnay '14	♟♟ 3
○ Collio Friulano '14	♟♟ 3
○ Collio Friulano Fisc '13	♟♟ 4
○ Collio Pinot Bianco '13	♟♟ 3
○ Collio Pinot Grigio '14	♟♟ 3
○ Oblin Blanc '12	♟♟ 4

○ Collio Ribolla Gialla di Oslavia Ris. '12	♟♟♟ 5
○ Collio Bianco Klin '11	♟♟ 5
○ Collio Chardonnay Gmajne '13	♟♟ 5
● Collio Merlot Murno '12	♟♟ 4
○ Collio Pinot Grigio Murno '15	♟♟ 4
○ Collio Pinot Grigio Ris. '12	♟♟ 4
○ Collio Sauvignon '15	♟♟ 3
○ Collio Sauvignon Gmajne '15	♟♟ 5
○ Ribolla Gialla '15	♟ 3
○ Collio Chardonnay Gmajne '11	♟♟♟ 4*
○ Collio Ribolla Gialla di Oslavia Ris. '11	♟♟♟ 5
○ Collio Bianco Klin Ris. '10	♟♟ 5
○ Collio Friulano Belvedere '14	♟♟ 3
● Collio Merlot Murno '11	♟♟ 3
○ Collio Sauvignon Gmajne '14	♟♟ 4

★Doro Princic

LOC. PRADIS, 5
34071 CORMÒNS [GO]
TEL. +39 048160723
doroprincic@virgilio.it

CELLAR SALES
PRE-BOOKED VISITS
ANNUAL PRODUCTION 60,000 bottles
HECTARES UNDER VINE 10.00

The winery founded by Doro Princic in 1950 is an institution the entire Collio is proud of, a brand whose hallmark is absolute quality, all thanks to Alessandro, a classic, vineyard-savvy wine artisan, and an imposing figure both in physique and in character, with a knowing smile beneath his Austro-Hungarian-style moustache. He and his wife Mariagrazia make a truly warm couple. As a true believer in monovarietals, he is able to coax out the best qualities from each grape variety, with no manipulation or excess, and with full respect for nature's rhythms. Although Malvasia 2015 deservedly went to the final round, it failed to maintain its seven-year consecutive winner's record. Instead, Friulano 2015 pulled out all the stops and took home our Tre Bicchieri.

Puiatti - Bertani Domains

LOC. ZUCCOLE, 4
34076 ROMANS D'ISONZO [GO]
TEL. +39 0481909608
www.puiatti.com

CELLAR SALES
PRE-BOOKED VISITS
ANNUAL PRODUCTION 400,000 bottles
HECTARES UNDER VINE 50.00
SUSTAINABLE WINERY

When the subject arises of the qualitative leap taken in the 1960s by this region's winemaking, much credit must go to the great Vittorio Puiatti. He succeeded in given his wines an inimitable style, based on a deep respect for each variety, without being swayed by that era's overweening use of oak, responding to, and sometimes anticipating, changes in taste and demand. The new owner, the Tenimenti Angelini group, shares and, if possible, is improving that style, entrusting to winemaker Giuriato Andrea the task of marrying together the maestro's teachings and today's demands. The standard vintage whites are characterized by crispness and low alcohols, but Ribolla Gialla Archetipi 2014 simply outruns them. Its unusual vinification process features the addition of a certain amount of whole berries into the base wine.

○ Collio Friulano '15	♀♀♀	5
○ Collio Malvasia '15	♀♀	5
● Collio Merlot '12	♀♀	5
○ Collio Pinot Bianco '15	♀♀	5
○ Collio Pinot Grigio '15	♀♀	5
○ Collio Sauvignon '15	♀♀	5
○ Collio Ribolla Gialla '15	♀	5
○ Collio Malvasia '14	♀♀♀	5
○ Collio Malvasia '13	♀♀♀	5
○ Collio Malvasia '12	♀♀♀	5
○ Collio Malvasia '11	♀♀♀	5
○ Collio Malvasia '10	♀♀♀	4
○ Collio Malvasia '09	♀♀♀	4*
○ Collio Malvasia '08	♀♀♀	4
○ Collio Pinot Bianco '07	♀♀♀	3
○ Collio Pinot Bianco '05	♀♀♀	3
○ Collio Tocai Friulano '06	♀♀♀	3*

○ Friuli Isonzo Friulano Vuj '15	♀♀	3
○ Ribolla Gialla Archetipi '14	♀♀	5
○ Ribolla Gialla Extra Brut M. Cl.	♀♀	4
○ Sauvignon Fun '15	♀♀	3
○ Pinot Grigio Sal '15	♀	3
○ Traminer Aromatico Cur '15	♀	2
● Collio Pinot Nero Ruttars '08	♀♀	3
○ Friuli Isonzo Friulano Vuj '14	♀♀	3
○ Friuli Isonzo Ribolla Gialla Archetipi '12	♀♀	3
○ Friuli Isonzo Ribolla Gialla Lus '13	♀♀	4
○ Oltre il Metodo Extra Brut '06	♀♀	5
○ Ribolla Gialla Archetipi '13	♀♀	5
○ Ribolla Gialla Lus '14	♀♀	3

★Dario Raccaro

FRAZ. ROLAT
VIA SAN GIOVANNI, 87
34071 CORMÒNS [GO]
TEL. +39 048161425
az.agr.raccaro@alice.it

CELLAR SALES
PRE-BOOKED VISITS
ANNUAL PRODUCTION 30,000 bottles
HECTARES UNDER VINE 6.00

Dario Raccaro's operation is a classic example of how, with few vineyards and even fewer wines, it is possible to be an influential figure. The story of the Raccaros in the Collio goes back to 1928, when Giuseppe Raccaro abandoned the dry, inhospitable Natisone valley and settled in a venerable farmhouse beneath Monte Quarin, the hill that dominates Cormòns. He was quick to realize that the surrounding land was ideal for growing high-quality grapes, and in the 1980s he decided to devote all his energy to winegrowing. In addition to his own vineyards, he leased an old tocai friulano vineyard, the Vigna del Rolàt. This year only two wines were presented, and it was no surprise that both earned high marks. Friulano Rolat 2015 as usual was in the finals, and the winery's iconic wine proved that it stands in the top ranks of the region's finest expressions of the area's finest variety.

La Rajade

LOC. PETRUS, 2
34070 DOLEGNA DEL COLLIO [GO]
TEL. +39 0481639273
www.larajade.it

CELLAR SALES
PRE-BOOKED VISITS
ANNUAL PRODUCTION 50,000 bottles
HECTARES UNDER VINE 6.50

The recently-established Rajade, a combination of a farm property cum winecellar and already-producing vineyard, lies in northern Collio, in the Judrio river valley, along the Slovenia border. The vineyards slope down from the Petrus relief, following the contour of the hill, which affords outstanding exposure to the sun, a fact that inspired owner Sergio Campeotto to adopt the name Rajade, which in the local dialect means sunbeam. Diego Zanin, experienced man of all seasons here, directs both vineyard and winemaking operations. For the second year in a row, Cabernet Sauvignon Riserva 2013 is the line's standout, competing in our final round. Ripe Morello cherry, baker's chocolate, and clove grace the nose, while the palate is very appealing, with tannins that are lively but remarkably glossy.

○ Collio Friulano Rolat '15	❦❦ 4
○ Collio Malvasia '15	❦❦ 5
○ Collio Bianco '03	❦❦❦ 3
○ Collio Bianco '02	❦❦❦ 3
○ Collio Friulano V. del Rolat '09	❦❦❦ 4
○ Collio Friulano V. del Rolat '08	❦❦❦ 4
○ Collio Friulano V. del Rolat '07	❦❦❦ 4
○ Collio Malvasia '12	❦❦❦ 5
○ Collio Malvasia '11	❦❦❦ 4*
○ Collio Tocai Friulano '05	❦❦❦ 3
○ Collio Tocai Friulano '04	❦❦❦ 3
○ Collio Tocai Friulano '01	❦❦❦ 3*
○ Collio Tocai Friulano '00	❦❦❦ 3*
○ Collio Tocai Friulano V. del Rolat '06	❦❦❦ 4
○ Collio Friulano V. del Rolat '14	❦❦ 4
○ Collio Friulano V. del Rolat '13	❦❦ 4

● Collio Cabernet Sauvignon Ris. '13	❦❦ 4
○ Collio Friulano '15	❦❦ 3
● Collio Merlot Ris. '13	❦❦ 4
○ Collio Pinot Grigio '15	❦❦ 3
○ Collio Ribolla Gialla '15	❦❦ 3
○ Collio Sauvignon '15	❦❦ 3
○ Collio Caprizi Ris. '13	❦ 4
○ Collio Bianco '14	❦❦ 3
○ Collio Bianco '13	❦❦ 3
● Collio Cabernet Sauvignon Ris. '11	❦❦ 4
● Collio Merlot Ris. '12	❦❦ 4
○ Collio Pinot Grigio '14	❦❦ 3
○ Collio Pinot Grigio '13	❦❦ 3
○ Collio Ribolla Gialla '14	❦❦ 3
○ Collio Ribolla Gialla '13	❦❦ 3
○ Collio Sauvignon '14	❦❦ 3

Rocca Bernarda

FRAZ. IPPLIS
VIA ROCCA BERNARDA, 27
33040 PREMARIACCO [UD]
TEL. +39 0432716914
www.sagrivit.it

CELLAR SALES
PRE-BOOKED VISITS
ANNUAL PRODUCTION 100,000 bottles
HECTARES UNDER VINE 38.50

Rocca Bernarda, rising on the hill of the same name, is located in a venerable mansion boasting four striking cylindrical towers that dates back to the mid-16th century and was used over the centuries as the summer residence of noble Cividale families. Pages and pages of history have been written within these walls, and in the late 1800s it witnessed the rebirth of Conte Asquini's Picolit, brought here by then-owners Conti Perusini. In 1977, the latter turned the property over to the Knights of Malta, and since 2006 the wine operation has been directed by the Società Agricola Vitivinicola Italiana. The magnificent natural bowls of terraced vineyards that surround the complex complete a thoroughly striking landscape. Only a few wines were presented this year, and we missed in particular Picolit, which in recent years has been the winery standout. But Refosco dal Peduncolo Rosso 2014 and Sauvignon 2015 are superbly crafted, and fine representatives of the cellar's quality level.

● FCO Refosco P. R. '14	🍷🍷 3
○ FCO Sauvignon '15	🍷🍷 3
○ Novecento 1113-2013 '15	🍷 3
● COF Merlot Centis '99	🍷🍷🍷 7
○ COF Picolit '03	🍷🍷🍷 7
○ COF Picolit '98	🍷🍷🍷 7
○ COF Picolit '97	🍷🍷🍷 7
○ COF Chardonnay '13	🍷🍷 3
○ COF Friulano '13	🍷🍷 3
○ COF Friulano '12	🍷🍷 3
● COF Merlot Centis '09	🍷🍷 4
● COF Pignolo Novecento 1113-2013 '08	🍷🍷 5
○ COF Pinot Grigio '13	🍷🍷 3
● COF Refosco P. R. '13	🍷🍷 3
○ COF Sauvignon '13	🍷🍷 3
○ Novecento 1113-2013 '13	🍷🍷 3

Paolo Rodaro

LOC. SPESSA
VIA CORMONS, 60
33043 CIVIDALE DEL FRIULI [UD]
TEL. +39 0432716066
www.rodaropaolo.it

CELLAR SALES
PRE-BOOKED VISITS
ANNUAL PRODUCTION 200,000 bottles
HECTARES UNDER VINE 50.00
SUSTAINABLE WINERY

The Rodaros were already making wine in 1846, and now the sixth generation, in the person of Paolo Rodaro, who bears the same name as the founder, has put the operation on a firm base, following the path trod by his father Luigi and uncle Edo, who between the 1960s and '70s transformed a modest farm into one of the region's largest and most highly-respected producers. The Romain line, fruit of the purchase of the prestigious Conte Romano estate, offers a range of superbly-structured reds produced from loft-dried grapes, while the wines of the standard lines have been lightened. The classic method sparklers are now receiving significant attention. Friulano 2015 and Malvasia 2015 embody the lovely fragrances of the standard-vintage white wines here, and are eloquent of their respective grapes. No less outstanding are Metodo Classico Rosé Pas Dosé 2012 and, in particular, Rosso Romain di Romain '09, the latter powerful, fat, and seductive.

● FCO Rosso Romain di Romain '09	🍷🍷 6
○ FCO Friulano '15	🍷🍷 3
○ FCO Malvasia '15	🍷🍷 2*
● FCO Schioppettino Romain '11	🍷🍷 5
⊙ Rosé Pas Dosé M.Cl. '12	🍷🍷 5
○ FCO Pinot Grigio '15	🍷 3
○ FCO Ribolla Gialla '15	🍷 3
● COF Refosco P. R. Romain '03	🍷🍷🍷 6
⊙ Ronc '00	🍷🍷🍷 3
● COF Merlot Romain '09	🍷🍷 5
● COF Schioppettino Romain '08	🍷🍷 4

Ronc di Vico

FRAZ. BELLAZOIA
VIA CENTRALE, 5
33040 POVOLETTO [UD]
TEL. +39 3208822002
roncdivicobellazoia@libero.it

CELLAR SALES
PRE-BOOKED VISITS
ANNUAL PRODUCTION 12,000 bottles
HECTARES UNDER VINE 7.00

The very recently-established Ronc di Vico quickly garnered attention, thanks to Gianni del Fabbro's inspired moves after he inherited in 2004 a few hectares of old vineyards scattered in the northernmost area of the Friuli Colli Orientali denomination. It experiences significant day-night temperature differentials, conditions ideal for concentration of aromatics. Well-advised by a friend and expert grower, he began re-structuring the vineyards, assisted by his very young son Lodovico, who grew up amidst the vine-rows and today directs both vineyard and winemaking operations. They may have few vineyards and wines, but they are rich in passion, and quality is outstanding. A lovely Refosco dal Peduncolo Rosso 2013 stands out from its colleagues and gained entrance to the finals, thanks to its utter deliciousness. Its offers toasty oak, heightened by spice and balsam, and the tannins are wondrously smooth and rounded.

● FCO Refosco P. '13	▼▼ 6
○ FCO Il Friulano '15	▼▼ 4
○ FCO Sauvignon '15	▼▼ 4
● FCO Vicorosso '13	▼▼ 4
○ COF Il Friulano '09	♉♉♉ 4
○ COF Il Friulano '08	♉♉♉ 4*
○ COF Il Friulano '12	♉♉ 4
○ COF Picolit '11	♉♉ 7
● COF Refosco P. R. '11	♉♉ 6
○ COF Sauvignon '12	♉♉ 4
● COF Titut Ros '11	♉♉ 6
● COF Titut Ros '09	♉♉ 5
● COF Vicorosso '11	♉♉ 4
● COF Vicorosso '10	♉♉ 4
● FCO Titut Ros '12	♉♉ 6
● FCO Vicorosso '12	♉♉ 4

Ronc Soreli

LOC. NOVACUZZO, 46
33040 PREPOTTO [UD]
TEL. +39 0432713005
www.roncsoreli.com

CELLAR SALES
ANNUAL PRODUCTION 100,000 bottles
HECTARES UNDER VINE 42.00

In 2008, Flavio Schiratti took over this wine operation in the ancient Borgo di Novacuzzo, near Prepotto, and with his business experience leading to immediatel-set high goals, he launched a re-structuring of the product line, backed by the assistance of well-known agronomy and winemaking consultants. The fruits were soon apparent. The name Ronc Soreli, which in the local dialect refers to a hill kissed by the sun, underscores the constant exposure of the vineyards to the sun, favoured by the unusual contours of the hillslopes as they gently descend, alongside the Bosco Romagno natural park. Friulano Vigna delle Robinie 2015 has become a fixture in our final round, which simply proves this region's magisterial touch with its benchmark grape. Redolent of Golden Delicious apple, sun-dried hay, honey, and dried thyme, it offers in the mouth complementary smooth texture and crisp, full flavours.

○ FCO Friulano V. delle Robinie '15	▼▼ 3*
○ FCO Picolit '10	▼▼ 5
○ FCO Pinot Grigio Ramato '15	▼▼ 3
● FCO Schioppettino di Prepotto '10	▼▼ 5
○ FCO Sauvignon V. dei Peschi '15	▼ 3
○ COF Friulano V. delle Robinie '12	♉♉ 3
○ COF Pinot Grigio V. dei Melograni '12	♉♉ 3
● COF Ribolla Nera V. delle Marasche '11	♉♉ 3
● COF RossoRe '11	♉♉ 5
● COF Schioppettino di Prepotto Ris. '09	♉♉ 5
● COF Schioppettino V. delle Marasche '11	♉♉ 3
○ FCo Friulano V. delle Robinie '13	♉♉ 3*
○ FCO Pinot Grigio V. dei Melograni '13	♉♉ 3
○ FCO Ribolla Gialla V. dei Nespoli '13	♉♉ 3
○ FCO Sauvignon V. dei Peschi '13	♉♉ 3
○ Friulano Otto Lustri '11	♉♉ 5

La Roncaia

FRAZ. CERGNEU
VIA VERDI, 26
33045 NIMIS [UD]
TEL. +39 0432790280
www.laroncaia.it

CELLAR SALES
PRE-BOOKED VISITS
ANNUAL PRODUCTION 50,000 bottles
HECTARES UNDER VINE 22.00

The Fantinel group, involved in viticulture for three generations, acquired in 1998 an operation that had thirty years of activities in Cergneu, a small village near Nimis, in the extreme north of the Friuli Colli Orientali zone, famous for Ramandolo and Picolit, both of which were being made here from dense-planted vineyards of modern design. These two much-prized sweet wines increase the already-broad Fantinel line, whose number of properties is impressive both in the Collio and in the vast Grave zone, and they can thus offer the international market a full array of regional-character wines. We were able to taste only two wines, so we did not have a representative sample of the entire line, but the scores are eloquent enough. Bianco Eclisse 2014, in particular, which is largely sauvignon blanc with a tot of Picolit, once again missed the highest award by just a hairsbreadth.

Il Roncal

FRAZ. COLLE MONTEBELLO
VIA FORNALIS, 148
33043 CIVIDALE DEL FRIULI [UD]
TEL. +39 0432730138
www.ilroncal.it

CELLAR SALES
PRE-BOOKED VISITS
ACCOMMODATION AND RESTAURANT SERVICE
ANNUAL PRODUCTION 130,000 bottles
HECTARES UNDER VINE 20.00

Roncal is a woman-directed cellar, with Martina Moreale as both owner and hands-on manager of the entire operation. Her husband Roberto Zorzettig died prematurely in 2006, and with true grit and commitment, Moreale, in just a brief time, completed the construction of the new cellar, started by Zorzettig. Along with the estate villa, it now stands proudly on the Montebello hill, in the heart of the Friuli Colli Orientali zone, offering a stupendous view, right to the far horizon, of woods and meadows that complement the geometrical shapes of the vineyards carpeting the sinuous hillslope contours. Bianco Ploe di Stelis 2014, a blend of chardonnay, sauvignon, and white riesling in almost equal parts, received high marks. The nose presents rich, multi-layered fragrances, including tropical fruit, and appealing floral impressions, while the palate's rounded texture is complemented by a piercing acidity.

○ Bianco Eclisse '14	♟♟ 5
● FCO Refosco P.R. '12	♟♟ 5
○ Eclisse '12	♟♟♟ 4*
○ COF Bianco Eclisse '13	♟♟ 4
● COF Cabernet Sauvignon '09	♟♟ 3
○ COF Friulano '12	♟♟ 4
○ COF Friulano '11	♟♟ 4
● COF Merlot '11	♟♟ 4
● COF Merlot '10	♟♟ 4
● COF Merlot '09	♟♟ 3
○ COF Picolit '10	♟♟ 5
● COF Refosco P.R. '11	♟♟ 5
○ FCO Friulano '13	♟♟ 4
● FCO Merlot '12	♟♟ 4
○ FCO Picolit '11	♟♟ 5
○ Ramandolo '11	♟♟ 5

○ FCO Bianco Ploe di Stelis '14	♟♟ 4
● FCO Merlot '13	♟♟ 3
● FCO Pignolo '10	♟♟ 5
○ FCO Ribolla Gialla '15	♟♟ 3
○ FCO Friulano '15	♟ 3
○ COF Bianco Ploe di Stelis '12	♟♟ 4
● COF Cabernet Franc '10	♟♟ 5
● COF Pignolo '08	♟♟ 5
● COF Refosco P.R. '11	♟♟ 4
● COF Refosco P.R. '10	♟♟ 4
● COF Rosso Civon '09	♟♟ 4
● COF Schioppettino '10	♟♟ 4
○ FCO Bianco Ploe di Stelis '13	♟♟ 4
● FCO Pignolo '09	♟♟ 5
● FCO Ribolla Gialla '14	♟♟ 3
● FCO Schioppettino '12	♟♟ 4

Il Roncat - Giovanni Dri

LOC. RAMANDOLO
VIA PESCIA, 7
33045 NIMIS [UD]
TEL. +39 0432790260
www.drironcat.com

CELLAR SALES
PRE-BOOKED VISITS
ANNUAL PRODUCTION 40,000 bottles
HECTARES UNDER VINE 10.00

Worth discussion is whether Giovanni Dri is synonymous with Ramandolo or whether Ramandolo is synonymous with Giovanni Dri. In any case, the success of this wine and its growing area coincide with the period that saw Dri introducing it to the world. The grape is verduzzo giallo, a local native of low productivity in danger of extinction, and Dri succeeded in resurrecting and improving it, with the tenacity of one born among these local rocks on the steep slopes of Monte Bernardia, in the extreme north of the Friuli Colli Orientali zone. Using ancient materials, he constricted a spacious, efficient cellar, integrated perfectly into its surroundings, whose workings are entrusted to his already-expert daughter Stefania. This year too we tasted three different styles of Ramandolo, and high marks for all three confirm the superb quality of this sweet ambassador of the region. Equally outstanding were Picolit and the reds, all with appealing spice and pungent resin.

Ronchi di Manzano

VIA ORSARIA, 42
33044 MANZANO [UD]
TEL. +39 0432740718
www.ronchidimanzano.com

CELLAR SALES
PRE-BOOKED VISITS
ANNUAL PRODUCTION 200,000 bottles
HECTARES UNDER VINE 60.00

This gorgeous facility is an all-woman operation, with the trio of Roberta Borghese and her young daughters Lisa and Nicole. I Ronchi di Manzano vaunts a rich history, with the Conti Trento producing wine here that went to the nobles of the Austrian-Hungarian Empire. The Borghese family purchased it in 1984 and put the very young but business-savvy Roberta in charge, and she immediately won it wide respect. Sensitive to fine style, she imprinted her feminine sensitivity on every detail, which translates into wines of elegance and grace. Those looking for added value will find it in the enchanting vineyards in Rosazzo. All of the wines here are well-crafted and enviably straightforward, even though only the white Ellégri 2015 received high enough scores to go into the final tasting. It is a magical mix of friulano and chardonnay with a touch of sauvignon blanc that releases intriguing, subtle fragrances.

● FCO Merlot '12	▼▼ 3
● FCO Refosco P.R. '12	▼▼ 3
● FCO Schioppettino Monte dei Carpin '12	▼▼ 4
○ Picolit Il Roncat '12	▼▼ 7
○ Ramandolo Il Roncat '11	▼▼ 5
○ Ramandolo Uve Decembrine '11	▼▼ 5
● FCO Cabernet '12	▼ 3
○ FCO Sauvignon '15	▼ 4
○ Ramandolo '12	▼ 4
● COF Cabernet '11	♀♀ 3
● COF Merlot '11	♀♀ 3
○ COF Picolit '10	♀♀ 7
● COF Refosco P.R. '10	♀♀ 3
● COF Refosco P.R. '11	♀♀ 3
○ Picolit Il Roncat '11	♀♀ 7
○ Ramandolo Uve Decembrine '10	♀♀ 5

○ FCO Bianco Ellégri '15	▼▼ 3*
● FCO Cabernet Franc '13	▼▼ 3
● FCO Cabernet Sauvignon '13	▼▼ 3
○ FCO Chardonnay '15	▼▼ 3
○ FCO Friulano '15	▼▼ 3
● FCO Merlot '13	▼▼ 3
○ FCO Pinot Grigio '15	▼▼ 3
○ FCO Sauvignon '15	▼▼ 3
○ FCO Verduzzo Friulano '15	▼▼ 2*
○ FCO Pinot Grigio Ramato '15	▼ 3
○ FCO Ribolla Gialla di Rosazzo '15	▼ 3
○ COF Ellegri '13	♀♀♀ 3*
○ COF Friulano '10	♀♀♀ 3
○ COF Friulano '09	♀♀♀ 3*
○ COF Rosazzo Bianco Ellégri '11	♀♀♀ 3*
○ Rosazzo Bianco '13	♀♀♀ 3*
○ FCO Bianco Ellégri '14	♀♀ 3*

Ronchi San Giuseppe

VIA STRADA DI SPESSA, 8
33043 CIVIDALE DEL FRIULI [UD]
TEL. +39 0432716172
www.ronchisangiuseppe.com

CELLAR SALES
PRE-BOOKED VISITS
ANNUAL PRODUCTION 400,000 bottles
HECTARES UNDER VINE 70.00
SUSTAINABLE WINERY

The Zorzettig family, of Spessa in Cividale del Friuli, has produced over the years talented winegrowers, who, with their individual families, established their own wine operations. Franco, with his son Fulvio, has maintained the original operation, Ronchi San Giuseppe. To his considerable merit, he was considerably ahead of his time in dedicating attention to raising the quality of native grapes that were little-known or used just for local wines. Fulvio's energy and innovative thrust have given the winery an impressive trajectory that keeps its wines up with the times and in constant demand. This year too, high marks went to the entire line, which vaunts more than fine quality and quite reasonable prices. Both the standard-vintage whites and the reds, including the Verduzzo are frank, supple, and varietally expressive.

○ FCO Friulano '15		♟♟ 2*
● FCO Refosco P. R. '14		♟♟ 2*
○ FCO Ribolla Gialla '15		♟♟ 2*
○ FCO Sauvignon '15		♟♟ 2*
● FCO Schioppettino '14		♟ 2
○ FCO Verduzzo Friulano '14		♟ 2
○ COF Friulano '13		♟♟ 2*
○ COF Pinot Grigio '13		♟♟ 2*
○ COF Pinot Grigio '12		♟♟ 2*
○ COF Sauvignon '13		♟♟ 2*
● COF Schioppettino '12		♟♟ 2*
○ FCO Friulano '14		♟♟ 2*
○ FCO Pinot Grigio '14		♟♟ 2*
● FCO Refosco P. R. '13		♟♟ 2*
○ FCO Sauvignon '14		♟♟ 2*
● FCO Schioppettino '13		♟♟ 2*

Ronco Blanchis

VIA BLANCHIS, 70
34070 MOSSA [GO]
TEL. +39 048180519
www.roncoblanchis.it

PRE-BOOKED VISITS
ANNUAL PRODUCTION 60,000 bottles
HECTARES UNDER VINE 14.00
SUSTAINABLE WINERY

The Blanchis hill, one of the highest in the Gorizia area of the Collio, enjoys a superb exposure and its own climate, which has made it famous for very high-quality wines. Giancarlo Palla, with sons Alberto and Lorenzo, is its current owner. The name Blanchis suggests a predisposition of this hill for growing white wines, and that is exactly the case here. Only four are monovarietals, while the best grapes, from the oldest vineyards, go to make up a single wine, Collio, the most eloquent expression of the area. The Palls have availed themselves of the consulting assistance of Gianni Menotti, and the results are clear. Once again, we see superb performances and successful twins. Collio 2015, a 50-50 blend of friulano and chardonnay, and the most representative of its growing area, was as fine as the best previous vintages and competed in our finals. It was accompanied by another blend, Collio Blanc de Blanchis 2015.

○ Collio '15		♟♟ 5
○ Collio Blanc de Blanchis '15		♟♟ 3*
○ Collio Friulano '15		♟♟ 4
○ Collio Sauvignon '15		♟♟ 4
○ Collio Pinot Grigio '15		♟ 4
○ Collio '13		♟♟♟ 3*
○ Collio '12		♟♟♟ 3*
○ Collio Blanc de Blanchis '14		♟♟ 3
○ Collio Friulano '14		♟♟ 3*
○ Collio Friulano '13		♟♟ 3
○ Collio Friulano Blanchis '11		♟♟ 3
○ Collio Pinot Grigio '14		♟♟ 3
○ Collio Pinot Grigio '13		♟♟ 3
○ Collio Pinot Grigio '12		♟♟ 3
○ Collio Sauvignon '13		♟♟ 3
○ Collio Sauvignon '11		♟♟ 3

★Ronco dei Tassi

LOC. MONTONA, 19
34071 CORMÒNS [GO]
TEL. +39 048160155
www.roncodeitassi.it

CELLAR SALES
PRE-BOOKED VISITS
ANNUAL PRODUCTION 110,000 bottles
HECTARES UNDER VINE 18.00

Ronco dei Tassi, one of the most impressive producers in the region, was founded in 1989 by Fabio Coser, a fine oenologist with a deep understanding of the character and potential of the Collio. The winery went immediately into the ranks of the top producers in the Cormòns area, winning prestigious accolades and, more importantly, maintaining its leading position. Fabio's sons Matteo and Enrico have been playing important roles in the winery for some time now, and as with most family-run enterprises, they do a bit of everything. Ambition and market needs have spurred Fabio to establish another operation, Vigna del Lauro. In the last edition, we expressed a desire to taste Fosarin 2014, and our expectations were fully met. Impressions of citron, mint, and juniper grace the nose, and the palate is velvety and full-flavoured. But, once again, the Tre Bicchieri goes to the cellar jewel, Malvasia 2015.

○ Collio Malvasia '15	♔♔♔	3*
○ Collio Bianco Fosarin '14	♔♔	3*
○ Collio Friulano '15	♔♔	3
○ Collio Pinot Grigio '15	♔♔	3
● Collio Rosso Cjarandon Ris. '12	♔♔	5
○ Collio Sauvignon '15	♔♔	3
○ Collio Ribolla Gialla '15	♔	3
○ Collio Bianco Fosarin '10	♔♔♔	3
○ Collio Bianco Fosarin '09	♔♔♔	3*
○ Collio Bianco Fosarin '08	♔♔♔	3*
○ Collio Bianco Fosarin '07	♔♔♔	3
○ Collio Bianco Fosarin '06	♔♔♔	3
○ Collio Malvasia '14	♔♔♔	3*
○ Collio Malvasia '13	♔♔♔	3*
○ Collio Malvasia '12	♔♔♔	3*
○ Collio Malvasia '11	♔♔♔	3*
○ Collio Sauvignon '05	♔♔♔	3*

Ronco delle Betulle

LOC. ROSAZZO
VIA ABATE COLONNA, 24
33044 MANZANO [UD]
TEL. +39 0432740547
www.roncodellebetulle.it

CELLAR SALES
PRE-BOOKED VISITS
ANNUAL PRODUCTION 60,000 bottles
HECTARES UNDER VINE 12.00
SUSTAINABLE WINERY

The tenacious and entrepreneurial Ivana Adami created the Ronco delle Betulle brand, linking her name to the cellar that she has directed for a quarter century. It was her grandfather, Giovanbattista, who had the brilliant idea, long before others, of focusing attention on the hills of Rosazzo, which had always been recognized as a protection zone for local native grapes. With her long experience, skills, and classically-feminine meticulousness, Adami personally directs the vinifications, determined to preserve the traditional local styles of the wines. For some time now, her son Simone has assisted her across the process, and the third generation is now ready to take over the reins. In the earlier editions, we noted that our tastings revealed that the wines here "take turns" being the top scorer, underlining the painstaking attention given here to every wine. This year, the laurels go to Pignolo Rosazzo 2009, energy-laden and powerful on the palate.

● FCO Rosazzo Pignolo '09	♔♔	6
● FCO Cabernet Franc '13	♔♔	3
○ FCO Friulano '15	♔♔	3
● FCO Merlot '13	♔♔	3
○ FCO Ribolla Gialla '15	♔♔	3
● FCO Rosazzo Rosso Narciso '11	♔♔	5
○ FCO Sauvignon '15	♔♔	3
○ FCO Pinot Grigio '15	♔	3
● Franconia '12	♔	3
● FCO Bianco Vanessa '13	♔♔	3
● FCO Cabernet Franc '11	♔♔	3*
○ FCO Friulano '14	♔♔	3
● FCO Merlot '12	♔♔	3
● FCO Refosco P. R. '12	♔♔	3
● Franconia '11	♔♔	3
○ Rosazzo Bianco '12	♔♔	4

Ronco Severo

VIA RONCHI, 93
33040 PREPOTTO [UD]
TEL. +39 04337133440
www.roncosevero.it

CELLAR SALES
PRE-BOOKED VISITS
ANNUAL PRODUCTION 22,000 bottles
HECTARES UNDER VINE 8.00
VITICULTURE METHOD Certified Organic

Stefano Novello, who directs the operation
founded by his father Severo, personally
works his handful of hectares, with
impressive passion and attention to detail,
applying organic and biodynamic
principles. His winemaking too is conducted
along ancestral lines, using natural
fermentations with ambient yeasts. The
musts, even the whites, remain on the
skins for a few weeks, at times for months
even; consequently, he adds no chemicals
or preservatives. All of Stefano's wines
were greeted with unanimous enthusiasm;
we found them rich, succulent, and
eminently worthy of demanding palates.
The full-flavoured Ribolla Gialla 2014 is
laden with fragrant candied orange peel,
dried flowers, and propolis, while the
complex nose of Merlot Artiûl Riserva 2013
is fully matched by its smooth, creamy
palate, which nonetheless offers vibrant
tannins as well.

Roncùs

VIA MAZZINI, 26
34076 CAPRIVA DEL FRIULI [GO]
TEL. +39 0481809349
www.roncus.it

CELLAR SALES
PRE-BOOKED VISITS
ACCOMMODATION
ANNUAL PRODUCTION 40,000 bottles
HECTARES UNDER VINE 10.00

Marco Perco, a true artisanal, meticulous
winegrower and faithful observer of
nature's rhythms, imprints his wines with
his own personal stamp, unusual in this
area, giving the musts' lengthy stays on
ambient yeasts, à la Alsace winemaking.
This gives a greater aromatic
concentration and contributes to
cellarability, which in turn means that they
are aged longer and released at least a
year and a half following harvest. The
vineyards are divided into small parcels
spread over the "ronchi" of Capriva del
Friuli, most of them exceeding 50 years
old. Collio Bianco Vecchie Vigne 2012, an
all-native blend of malvasia istriana, tocai
friulano, and ribolla gialla, has always
gathered the laurels here. It offers dried
blossoms, passion fruit, dandelion honey,
and wild herbs, while the palate is creamy
and smooth, with a touch of sea-brine.

● FCO Merlot Artiûl Ris. '13	5
○ Ribolla Gialla '14	4
○ FCO Friulano Severo Bianco '08	4
● FCO Refosco P.R. '13	5
● FCO Schioppettino di Prepotto '13	4
○ Pinot Grigio '14	4
○ Severo Bianco '14	4
○ Severo Bianco '12	4*
○ COF Friulano Ris. '12	4
● COF Merlot Artiûl Ris. '11	5
○ COF Pinot Grigio '12	4
● FCO Merlot Artiûl Ris. '12	5
● FCO Schioppettino di Prepotto '12	4
○ Pinot Grigio '13	4
○ Ribolla Gialla '13	4
○ Severo Bianco '13	4

○ Collio Bianco V. V. '12	5
○ Collio Bianco '14	3
○ Collio Friulano '15	4
○ Pinot Bianco '14	4
○ Ribolla Gialla '15	3
○ Collio Bianco V. V. '08	5
○ Roncùs Bianco V. V. '01	5
○ Collio Bianco '12	3
○ Collio Bianco V. V. '10	5
○ Collio Friulano '13	4
○ Collio Friulano '12	4
● Merlot '12	3
○ Pinot Bianco '13	4
○ Ribolla Gialla '14	3
● Val di Miez '12	5
● Val di Miez '09	5

★Russiz Superiore

VIA RUSSIZ, 7
34070 CAPRIVA DEL FRIULI [GO]
TEL. +39 048180328
www.marcofelluga.it

CELLAR SALES
PRE-BOOKED VISITS
ACCOMMODATION
ANNUAL PRODUCTION 180,000 bottles
HECTARES UNDER VINE 50.00
SUSTAINABLE WINERY

Far-sighted, nonpareil innovator Marco Felluga realized the quality potential of the vineyards surrounding the 13th-century hamlet of Russiz Superiore, acquired property there, and settled among its storied walls. Roberto Felluga, wood of the same grain, has directed for many years now this estate of 50 hectares of vineyard spreading over the hillslopes of the Collio near Gorizia, in the commune of Capriva del Friuli, where the grapevine has found its terrestrial paradise. Felluga has given the operation a reliable continuity and achieved significant objectives. He has also launched a project to accustom consumers to the unique charms of age-worthy white wines. Friulano 2015 leads the team once more and again takes home the Tre Bicchieri. This year, Col Disôre 2013 joined it in the final round, an intriguing marriage of local white grapes that release citrus, yellow peach, and elderflower syrup, followed by a fragrant, rounded palate with generous, tangy flavours.

○ Collio Friulano '15	♛♛♛ 4*
○ Collio Bianco Col Disôre '13	♛♛ 5
● Collio Cabernet Franc '13	♛♛ 4
○ Collio Pinot Bianco '15	♛♛ 4
○ Collio Pinot Grigio '15	♛♛ 4
● Collio Rosso Ris. degli Orzoni '10	♛♛ 5
○ Collio Sauvignon '15	♛♛ 4
○ Collio Bianco Russiz Disôre '01	♛♛♛ 5
○ Collio Bianco Russiz Disôre '00	♛♛♛ 4
○ Collio Friulano '14	♛♛♛ 4*
○ Collio Pinot Bianco '07	♛♛♛ 4
○ Collio Pinot Grigio '11	♛♛♛ 4*
○ Collio Sauvignon '05	♛♛♛ 3
○ Collio Sauvignon '04	♛♛♛ 5
○ Collio Sauvignon '98	♛♛♛ 4*
○ Collio Tocai Friulano '99	♛♛♛ 3*

Sant'Elena

VIA GASPARINI, 1
34072 GRADISCA D'ISONZO [GO]
TEL. +39 048192388
www.sant-elena.com

CELLAR SALES
PRE-BOOKED VISITS
ANNUAL PRODUCTION 130,000 bottles
HECTARES UNDER VINE 30.00

Dominic Nocerino, successful importer of Italian wines to the American shores, relaunched this historic house, whose beginnings date back to 1893. Only in the mid-1960s, realizing the quality of the terroir, were the fields converted into vineyards, and in 1997 Nocerino purchased the property, determined to produce wines that would faithfully showcase the qualities of the Friuli Isonzo denomination. The surface soils here are a thin, reddish layer of alluvial origin, rich in iron, lying over clay and gravel, which imbues the grapes with a minerality that translates in the wines into fine structure and aromatic depth. In the last edition, we mentioned that only red wines were presented, while this year it was an all-white affair, including Mil Rosis 2013, largely chardonnay with a notable aromatic imprint from traminer and white riesling.

○ Friuli Isonzo Friulano Rive Alte '15	♛♛ 3
○ Friuli Isonzo Pinot Grigio Rive Alte '15	♛♛ 3
○ Friuli Isonzo Chardonnay Rive Alte '15	♛ 3
○ Friuli Isonzo Sauvignon Rive Alte '15	♛ 4
○ Friuli Isonzo Traminer Aromatico '15	♛ 4
○ Mil Rosis '13	♛ 5
● Cabernet Franc '11	♛♛ 3
● Friuli Isonzo Pignolo Quantum '11	♛♛ 7
○ Friuli Isonzo Pinot Grigio Rive Alte '13	♛♛ 3
○ Friuli Isonzo Sauvignon Blanc Rive Alte '13	♛♛ 4
● Merlot '11	♛♛ 4
● Merlot '10	♛♛ 4
● Merlot '09	♛♛ 3
● Merlot Ròs di Rôl '10	♛♛ 5
● Tato '10	♛♛ 5
● Tato '09	♛♛ 5

Marco Sara

FRAZ. SAVORGNANO DEL TORRE
VIA DEI MONTI, 3A
33040 POVOLETTO [UD]
TEL. +39 0432666066
www.marcosara.com

CELLAR SALES
PRE-BOOKED VISITS
ANNUAL PRODUCTION 20,000 bottles
HECTARES UNDER VINE 8.00
VITICULTURE METHOD Certified Organic

The still-young Marco Sara has for some years now been at the helm of this family operation, whose philosophy has always been natural viticulture. The vineyards extend over the hill zone of Povoletto, which has always been marked by a plethora of small producers, a fragmentation that has led to small vineyard parcels in many different locations, each with its own exposure and weather conditions. This allows each individual variety to express itself to the fullest. In Riu Falcon, where the vines are oldest, cool temperatures and clay soils are superb for white grapes, which can develop Botrytis, while the higher area of Roncus experiences significant day-night temperature differentials that are beneficial for aroma development. Picolit 2014, the standard-bearer of the entire hill zone of the province of Udine, was enthusiastically received and, just as last year, competed in our final round. Crunchy almond, barley sugar, dates, and honey make for an exciting bouquet, and it is seductively sweet in the mouth.

○ FCO Picolit '14	▼▼ 5
○ FCO Friulano '14	▼▼ 3
○ FCO Verduzzo '14	▼▼ 3
● FCO Cabernet Franc Frank '14	▼ 3
● COF Cabernet Franc Frank '13	♀♀ 3
○ COF Erba Alta '13	♀♀ 4
○ COF Picolit '13	♀♀ 5
● COF Refosco P. R. El Re '13	♀♀ 3
● COF Schioppettino '13	♀♀ 3
● COF Schioppettino '12	♀♀ 3*
○ FCO Friulano '13	♀♀ 2*

Sara & Sara

LOC. SAVORGNANO DEL TORRE
VIA DEI MONTI, 5
33040 POVOLETTO [UD]
TEL. +39 04323859042
www.saraesara.com

CELLAR SALES
PRE-BOOKED VISITS
ANNUAL PRODUCTION 25,000 bottles
HECTARES UNDER VINE 7.50

The tiny operation of Sara & Sara is a real jewel on the region's wine scene. Very young Alessandro Sara, assisted by brother Manuele, has already won full standing among local winegrowers who use ancestral practices to make modern wines of great character and pleasure. The cellar lies in Savorgnano del Torre, a village in the extreme west of the Friuli Colli Orientali zone, and the vineyards climb the steep hillslopes that are furrowed by streams and subjected to the cold northern winds. The resulting weather conditions favour formation of Botrytis on the clusters. This year too, Alessandro presented only sweet wines, which are the focus of this operation and of all the surrounding cellars. Both Verduzzo Friulano Crei 2013 and Picolit 2011 offer up a mixed drink of tropical fruit, caramelized figs, candied citron, and saffron, then pleasure the palate with an enfolding sweetness.

○ FCO Verduzzo Friulano Crei '13	▼▼ 5
○ FCO Picolit '11	▼▼ 6
○ COF Friulano '12	♀♀ 3
○ COF Friulano '10	♀♀ 3
○ COF Picolit '10	♀♀ 5
○ COF Picolit '09	♀♀ 5
○ COF Picolit '07	♀♀ 5
○ COF Picolit '06	♀♀ 5
● COF Refosco P. R. '10	♀♀ 3
● COF Rosso Il Rio Falcone '08	♀♀ 3
○ COF Verduzzo Friulano Crei '11	♀♀ 5
○ COF Verduzzo Friulano Crei '09	♀♀ 5
○ COF Verduzzo Friulano Crei '08	♀♀ 5
○ FCO Verduzzo Friulano Crei '12	♀♀ 5
● Il Rio Falcone	♀♀ 3
○ Sauvignon '12	♀♀ 2*

★★Schiopetto

VIA PALAZZO ARCIVESCOVILE, 1
34070 CAPRIVA DEL FRIULI [GO]
TEL. +39 048180332
www.schiopetto.it

CELLAR SALES
PRE-BOOKED VISITS
ANNUAL PRODUCTION 190,000 bottles
HECTARES UNDER VINE 30.00
SUSTAINABLE WINERY

1965-2015. Exactly 50 years ago, Mario Schiopetto bottle his first 100% Tocai Friulano. Today more than ever, Friulano (no longer Tocai) is the iconic wine of this ultra-awarded cellar in the Gorizia area of the Collio. Schiopetto's heritage has been solidly in the hands of the Rotolo family for three years now, more precisely in those of the young Francesco and Alessandro, who, with passion, humility, and youthful enthusiasm, and with a helping hand from di Lorenzo Landi, has ensured that Schiopetto enjoys even more lustre today. The 2015 vintage was a great one, as is the performance of Friulano 2015, which equalled those of the two previous editions and again conquered the Tre Bicchieri. It excites the nose with notes of fresh-mown hay, grapefruit and tropical fruit, then enthuses the palate with a skilfully-crafted fusion of silky texture and crisp acidity.

○ Collio Friulano '15	♀♀♀ 4*
○ Collio Pinot Bianco '15	♀♀ 4
○ Collio Sauvignon '15	♀♀ 4
○ Blanc des Rosis '15	♀♀ 4
○ Collio Malvasia '15	♀♀ 4
○ Collio Pinot Grigio '15	♀♀ 4
● Poderi dei Blumeri '13	♀♀ 5
● Rivarossa '13	♀♀ 4
○ Blanc des Rosis '07	♀♀♀ 4
○ Blanc des Rosis '06	♀♀♀ 4
○ Collio Friulano '14	♀♀♀ 4*
○ Collio Friulano '13	♀♀♀ 4*
○ Mario Schiopetto Bianco '08	♀♀♀ 5
○ Mario Schiopetto Bianco '07	♀♀♀ 5
○ Mario Schiopetto Bianco '03	♀♀♀ 5
○ Mario Schiopetto Bianco '02	♀♀♀ 5

La Sclusa

LOC. SPESSA
VIA STRADA DI SANT'ANNA, 7/2
33043 CIVIDALE DEL FRIULI [UD]
TEL. +39 0432716259
www.lasclusa.it

CELLAR SALES
PRE-BOOKED VISITS
ACCOMMODATION
ANNUAL PRODUCTION 160,000 bottles
HECTARES UNDER VINE 30.00

The trunk of the Zorzettig family bears the name of Giobatta, ancestor of a generation of winegrowers who since 1963 have been busy in Spessa, a village south of Cividale del Friuli which has always been synonymous with vines and wines. Each branch of the family eventually fashioned its own identity, and carved on one of those branches is the name of Gino, who guided his own operation for over 40 years and then passed it on to his sons Germano, Maurizio, and Luciano. The winemaking philosophy, shared by a compact, well-meshed family, reflects the traditions of farmers who work the earth to gain its finest fruits, following the rhythms of nature and avoiding any forcing or excess. Friulano 2015 won plaudits for its superb varietal expression on both nose and palate. Chardonnay 2015 offers fruit-rich impressions of white melon, nectarine, and yellow plum, while Ribolla Gialla 2015 stands out for its refreshing crispness, aromatics, and straightforward pleasure.

○ FCO Chardonnay '15	♀♀ 3
○ FCO Friulano '15	♀♀ 3
○ FCO Picolit '12	♀♀ 7
○ FCO Ribolla Gialla '15	♀♀ 3
○ FCO Sauvignon '15	♀♀ 3
○ FCO Pinot Grigio '15	♀ 3
○ COF Chardonnay '12	♀♀ 3
● COF Merlot '12	♀♀ 3
○ COF Picolit '10	♀♀ 6
○ COF Ribolla Gialla '13	♀♀ 3
○ COF Ribolla Gialla '12	♀♀ 3
○ FCO Chardonnay '14	♀♀ 3
○ FCO Friulano '14	♀♀ 3
○ FCO Picolit '11	♀♀ 6
○ FCO Pinot Grigio '14	♀♀ 2*
○ FCO Ribolla Gialla '14	♀♀ 3

Roberto Scubla

FRAZ. IPPLIS
VIA ROCCA BERNARDA, 22
33040 PREMARIACCO [UD]
TEL. +39 0432716258
www.scubla.com

CELLAR SALES
PRE-BOOKED VISITS
ANNUAL PRODUCTION 60,000 bottles
HECTARES UNDER VINE 12.00

A majestic, centuries-old mulberry rises in the courtyard in front of the cellar, seeming to guard the farm residence rising upon one of the first hills of Rocca Bernarda, where Roberto Scubla settled and built an operation that in short order became a pearl of local winemaking. The geologic structure of the nearby hills facilitates the entrance of the bora winds, which not only ensures a constant ventilation for the vineyards, but naturally dries the verduzzo grapes laid out in the open on trays under a roof. Gianni Menotti, more a friend of old than a consultant, assists in the cellar. In the final tasting, we welcomed back old friends, such as Verduzzo Friulano Cràtis 2013 and the white Pomèdes, wines whose high qualities we have always appreciated. And we met a newcomer as well, Friulano 2015, which takes full advantage of a felicitous vintage to express to the fullest extent possible the qualities of this native grape that is the pride of the region.

○ FCO Bianco Pomèdes '14	♟♟ 5
○ FCO Friulano '15	♟♟ 3*
○ FCO Verduzzo Friulano Cràtis '13	♟♟ 5
● FCO Cabernet Franc '14	♟♟ 3
● FCO Cabernet Sauvignon '14	♟♟ 3
● FCO Merlot '14	♟♟ 3
○ FCO Pinot Bianco '15	♟♟ 3
● FCO Rosso Scuro '13	♟♟ 4
○ FCO Sauvignon '15	♟♟ 3
○ RS Brut M. Cl.	♟♟ 7
○ COF Bianco Pomèdes '04	♟♟♟ 4
○ COF Bianco Pomèdes '99	♟♟♟ 4*
○ COF Verduzzo Friulano Cràtis '09	♟♟♟ 5
○ COF Verduzzo Friulano Cràtis '06	♟♟♟ 5
○ COF Verduzzo Friulano Cràtis '04	♟♟♟ 5
○ COF Verduzzo Friulano Graticcio '99	♟♟♟ 5

Renzo Sgubin

VIA FAET, 15/1
34071 CORMÒNS [GO]
TEL. +39 0481630297
www.renzosgubin.it

CELLAR SALES
PRE-BOOKED VISITS
ANNUAL PRODUCTION 28,000 bottles
HECTARES UNDER VINE 12.00
SUSTAINABLE WINERY

Renzo Sgubin, one of the region's most skilled wine artisans, is a proud farmer and grapegrower, connected to his land by a love inherited from his ancestors. His dozen hectares of vineyards lie in Pradis, near Cormòns, some of them on the hillslopes of the Collio near Gorizia, while others are in the Friuli Isonzo zone. He did his initial bottling in 2003, then in an amazingly short period of time, established his operation on an enviable level of quality. The modest size of his cellar makes it possible for him to personally perform all the steps in making his wines. 3,4,3. 2015, a blend of mostly friulano, chardonnay, and malvasia istriana, turned in a terrific performance, helped by a graceful aromatic touch that makes it even more intriguing on both nose and palate. Collio-grown Merlot 2013 is opulent, fruit-rich, full-bodied, and full of promise.

○ 3, 4, 3 '15	♟♟ 3
● Collio Merlot '13	♟♟ 3
○ Friuli Isonzo Chardonnay '15	♟♟ 3
○ Friuli Isonzo Malvasia '15	♟♟ 3
○ Friuli Isonzo Pinot Grigio '15	♟♟ 3
○ Plagnis '11	♟♟ 3
○ Friuli Isonzo Friulano '15	♟ 3
○ Friuli Isonzo Sauvignon '15	♟ 3
● Collio Merlot '12	♟♟ 3
● Collio Merlot '11	♟♟ 3
○ Friuli Isonzo Chardonnay '14	♟♟ 3
○ Friuli Isonzo Chardonnay '13	♟♟ 3
○ Friuli Isonzo Friulano '14	♟♟ 3
○ Friuli Isonzo Friulano '13	♟♟ 3
○ Friuli Isonzo Malvasia '14	♟♟ 3
● Plagnis '09	♟♟ 3

Simon di Brazzan

FRAZ. BRAZZANO
VIA SAN ROCCO, 17
34070 CORMÒNS [GO]
TEL. +39 048161182
www.simondibrazzan.com

CELLAR SALES
PRE-BOOKED VISITS
ANNUAL PRODUCTION 70,000 bottles
HECTARES UNDER VINE 13.00
VITICULTURE METHOD Certified Organic

Simon di Brazzan is a fine winery in Cormòns, owned by Enrico Veliscig who, at the venerable age of 98, still lends a hand in the rows to his grandson Daniele Drius, who has been at the helm for over 20 years. Daniele immediately abandoned the use of chemical treatments in the vineyard, introducing exclusively natural practices, and for some years now has been a convinced exponent of biodynamic viticulture. Infusions of horsetail and nettle are sprayed on the leaves, and the soil is treated with a mix of grasses sowed in alternate rows. In late May, after flowering, the grass is cut and turned into the soil. Naturally, the vinification processes are also traditional. The winery, extremely well known in the area, had never submitted its wines for tasting. Finally this year, Daniele decided to do so and the results were quite simply outstanding. We were won over by the whole range and some made our finals. A good start...

Sirch

VIA FORNALIS, 277/1
33043 CIVIDALE DEL FRIULI [UD]
TEL. +39 0432709835
www.sirchwine.com

CELLAR SALES
PRE-BOOKED VISITS
ANNUAL PRODUCTION 150,000 bottles
HECTARES UNDER VINE 25.00

We are all by now aware of the link between Sirch and Feudi di San Gregorio, the leading winery in Campania that boasts an international market of significant importance and deals with distribution of the entire line of wines produced in Friuli by Luca Sirch. This line of wines represents the complete range of regional types, and is the result of a simple philosophy that eschews excess and aims at exalting the unique characteristics of each variety. Luca has 25 hectares under vine, all on hillside sites, divided into small plots with a variety of subsoils and microclimates, which allows him to choose the best location for each individual variety. We were offered the opportunity to taste a number of wines and the grid below shows the consistent quality achieved. The Bianco Cladrecis 2014 carved out a place in our finals. It had been some time since this last happened, and the well-deserved recognition bodes well for the future.

○ Blanc di Simon '15	♈♈ 3*
○ Ri.nè Blanc '14	♈♈ 3*
○ Blanc di Simon Tradizion '10	♈♈ 5
● Cabernet Franc '14	♈♈ 3
○ Malvasia '15	♈♈ 3
● Merlot '13	♈♈ 4
○ Pinot Grigio '15	♈♈ 3
○ Pinot Grigio Tradizion '14	♈♈ 5
○ Sauvignon '15	♈♈ 3
○ Blanc di Simon '06	♈♈ 3
○ Blanc di Simon '04	♈♈ 2*
○ Friuli Isonzo Sauvignon '03	♈♈ 3*
○ Pinot Grigio '05	♈♈ 3*

○ FCO Bianco Cladrecis '14	♈♈ 3*
● FCO Cabernet '14	♈♈ 3
○ FCO Chardonnay '15	♈♈ 3
○ FCO Friulano '15	♈♈ 3
● FCO Merlot '14	♈♈ 3
○ FCO Pinot Grigio '15	♈♈ 3
○ FCO Ribolla Gialla '15	♈♈ 3
● FCO Rosso Cladrecis '13	♈♈ 3
○ FCO Sauvignon '15	♈♈ 3
● FCO Schioppettino '14	♈♈ 3
● FCO Refosco P.R. '14	♈ 3
○ COF Friulano '07	♈♈♈ 2*
○ FCO Bianco Cladrecis '13	♈♈ 3
○ FCO Chardonnay '14	♈♈ 3
○ FCO Ribolla Gialla '14	♈♈ 3
○ FCO Sauvignon '14	♈♈ 3

Skerk

FRAZ. SAN PELAGIO
LOC. PREPOTTO, 20
34011 DUINO AURISINA [TS]
TEL. +39 040200156
www.skerk.com

CELLAR SALES
PRE-BOOKED VISITS
RESTAURANT SERVICE
ANNUAL PRODUCTION 22,000 bottles
HECTARES UNDER VINE 7.00
VITICULTURE METHOD Certified Organic

Sandi Skerk is a real artisan of wine, and one of the best growers on the Karst plateau. His production is based on local traditions, that envisage maceration of the skins in the must for some weeks, followed by racking in the first days of the waning moon, without clarification and above all without filtration. These time-honoured techniques give character and personality to richly flavored wines with aromatic nuances of rare elegance. In the splendid winery cut out of the rock, a real masterpiece of human creativity, draughts from unreachable crevices ensure cool temperatures and constant humidity throughout the year. After four years, the splendid series of top honours for Ograde has come to an end, but it still made our finals, while its crown was taken by the Malvasia 2013, which earned a Tre Bicchieri. It opens to a delightful nose, with wafts of iodine and hints of candyfloss, to then envelop on the palate with salty notes of Mediterranean scrub.

Skerlj

VIA SALES, 44
34010 SGONICO [TS]
TEL. +39 040229253
www.agriturismoskerlj.com

CELLAR SALES
PRE-BOOKED VISITS
ACCOMMODATION AND RESTAURANT SERVICE
ANNUAL PRODUCTION 5,000 bottles
HECTARES UNDER VINE 2.00
VITICULTURE METHOD Certified Organic

The wineries located in the harsh rocky territory of Carso, with some rare exceptions, are tiny, but of great interest due to the originality and fragrance of the wines they produce. Matej and Kristina Skerlj only have two hectares of vineyards inherited from their grandparents, but precisely the small size of the holdings allow them to tend the vines with meticulous care and to vinify the grapes using time-honored local techniques. It is superfluous to say that almost all the work is done by hand. On Carso, tradition envisages the cultivation of solely native varieties, which over time have adapted to survive the summer droughts and the buffeting bora wind. Malvasia and vitovska are the most representative white grape varieties, and we have seen how for some years those by Matej regularly alternate in our finals. This year it was the turn of the Malvasia 2013, whose plushness offsets notes of iodine and salty Mediterranean scrub.

○ Malvasia '13	♥♥♥ 5
○ Ograde '13	♥♥ 5
○ Vitovska '13	♥♥ 5
● Terrano '13	♥ 5
○ Carso Malvasia '08	♀♀♀ 4
○ Ograde '12	♀♀♀ 5
○ Ograde '11	♀♀♀ 5
○ Ograde '10	♀♀♀ 4
○ Ograde '09	♀♀♀ 4*
○ Malvasia '12	♀♀ 5
○ Malvasia '11	♀♀ 5
● Terrano '12	♀♀ 5
● Terrano '11	♀♀ 5
● Terrano Ris. '06	♀♀ 5
● Terrano Sel. '11	♀♀ 5
○ Vitovska '12	♀♀ 5
○ Vitovska '11	♀♀ 5

○ Malvasia '13	♥♥ 5
○ Vitovska '13	♥♥ 5
● Terrano '13	♥ 5
○ Malvasia '12	♀♀ 5
○ Malvasia '11	♀♀ 5
○ Malvasia '10	♀♀ 5
○ Malvasia '07	♀♀ 4
○ Malvasia '06	♀♀ 4
● Terrano '12	♀♀ 5
● Terrano '07	♀♀ 4
○ Vitovska '12	♀♀ 5
○ Vitovska '11	♀♀ 5
○ Vitovska '10	♀♀ 5
○ Vitovska '08	♀♀ 4
○ Vitovska '07	♀♀ 4
○ Vitovska '06	♀♀ 4

Edi Skok

LOC. GIASBANA, 15
34070 SAN FLORIANO DEL COLLIO [GO]
TEL. +39 3408034045
www.skok.it

CELLAR SALES
PRE-BOOKED VISITS
ANNUAL PRODUCTION 38,000 bottles
HECTARES UNDER VINE 11.00

Edi and Orietta Skok have been running for some time this fine operation based in San Floriano del Collio, at Giasbana, in an area unanimously acknowledged to be ideal for viticulture, especially based on white grape varieties. It enjoys excellent aspects and a wide variety of microclimates, making it adaptable to each variety. While being anchored to local traditions, deeply rooted in the farming origins of his family, Edi has always been open to innovation, and for some time has stopped using long macerations to adopt more modern techniques, with the aim of obtaining more fragrant wines that maintain varietal traits. With enviable consistency, all the wines achieved high levels of quality. An elegant Friulano Zabura 2015 regales us with a nose of blossom and fragrant, also tropical fruit, and delights on the palate with soft, salty notes, to end with delicate aromatic notes of bitter almond and pennyroyal.

○ Collio Friulano Zabura '15	🍷🍷 3
● Collio Merlot Villa Jasbinae '11	🍷🍷 3
○ Collio Pinot Grigio '15	🍷🍷 3
○ Collio Sauvignon '15	🍷🍷 3
○ Collio Bianco Pe Ar '13	🍷🍷 3
○ Collio Bianco Pe Ar '12	🍷🍷 3
○ Collio Bianco Pe Ar '11	🍷🍷 3
○ Collio Chardonnay '14	🍷🍷 2*
○ Collio Chardonnay '13	🍷🍷 2*
○ Collio Chardonnay '12	🍷🍷 2*
○ Collio Friulano Zabura '14	🍷🍷 3
● Collio Merlot '13	🍷🍷 3
○ Collio Pinot Grigio '14	🍷🍷 3
○ Collio Pinot Grigio '13	🍷🍷 3
○ Collio Pinot Grigio '12	🍷🍷 3
○ Collio Sauvignon '13	🍷🍷 3

Leonardo Specogna

VIA ROCCA BERNARDA, 4
33040 CORNO DI ROSAZZO [UD]
TEL. +39 0432755840
www.specogna.it

CELLAR SALES
PRE-BOOKED VISITS
ANNUAL PRODUCTION 120,000 bottles
HECTARES UNDER VINE 18.00
VITICULTURE METHOD Certified Organic

The winery established by Leonardo Specogna over 50 years ago is continuously and constantly evolving. The entrepreneurial spirit and oenological skills of the young Michele and Cristian, who are now at the helm, have brought it into the top flight of the region's operations, and it is unanimously recognized as an ambassador for the territorial traits of the Friuli Colli Orientali DOC zone. Not only does the family winery now have new vineyards on Rocca Bernarda, but Michele and Cristian are working on a project that sees them as major players in the subzone of Ramandolo, where some years ago they established the Toblâr winery, a brave move crowned with success. The large number of wines presented allowed us to try almost all the winery's range, and the scores achieved bears witness to the high level of quality across the board. Moreover, no fewer than two wines made our finals. Identità 2013 is composed solely of native varieties: friulano, malvasia and ribolla gialla.

○ FCO Identità '13	🍷🍷 6
● FCO Oltre '11	🍷🍷 6
○ FCO Chardonnay '14	🍷🍷 3
○ FCO Friulano '15	🍷🍷 3
○ FCO Picolit '12	🍷🍷 6
● FCO Pignolo '11	🍷🍷 6
● FCO Refosco P. R. '14	🍷🍷 3
○ FCO Ribolla Gialla '15	🍷🍷 3
○ FCO Sauvignon '15	🍷🍷 3
○ Sauvignon Duality '13	🍷🍷 6
● FCO Merlot '14	🍷 4
○ FCO Pinot Grigio '15	🍷 3
● COF Merlot '13	🍷🍷 4
● COF Oltre '11	🍷🍷 6
● COF Pignolo '10	🍷🍷 6
● COF Refosco P. R. '13	🍷🍷 3

Tenuta Stella

LOC. SCRIÒ
VIA SDENCINA, 1
34070 DOLEGNA DEL COLLIO [GO]
TEL. +39 0499318135
www.tenutastellacollio.it

CELLAR SALES
PRE-BOOKED VISITS
ANNUAL PRODUCTION 32,000 bottles
HECTARES UNDER VINE 7.00
VITICULTURE METHOD Certified Organic
SUSTAINABLE WINERY

Despite being a new name on the regional viticultural scene, Tenuta Stella immediately made a name for itself thanks to the high quality of its wines, solely whites, produced exclusively from native varieties. It relies on around 12 hectares under vine in the highest part of Collio, in the district of Dolegna at Scriò, where the steep slopes ensure ideal aspects and exposure to sun, but mean that most of the work needs to be done by hand. The soils are composed of marl and sandstone of oceanic origin, known as "ponca", brought to the surface by the rising Adriatic seabed. All the wines obtained excellent scores, confirming the performances seen in previous editions. The classic still wines of Collio were joined by two excellent Metodo Classico sparklers. The Cuvée Tanni Brut perfectly combines fragrance, softness, flavour and ageing potential.

○ Collio Friulano Scriò '14	🍷🍷 3
○ Collio Malvasia '14	🍷🍷 4
○ Collio Ribolla Gialla '14	🍷🍷 4
○ Cuvée Tanni Brut	🍷🍷 5
○ Ribolla Gialla Brut	🍷🍷 4
○ Collio Bianco '12	🍷🍷 3
○ Collio Friulano Scriò '13	🍷🍷 3
○ Collio Friulano Scriò '12	🍷🍷 3*
○ Collio Malvasia '13	🍷🍷 4
○ Collio Malvasia '12	🍷🍷 4
○ Collio Ribolla Gialla '13	🍷🍷 4
○ Collio Ribolla Gialla '12	🍷🍷 4

Subida di Monte

LOC. SUBIDA
VIA SUBIDA, 6
34071 CORMÒNS [GO]
TEL. +39 048161011
www.subidadimonte.it

CELLAR SALES
PRE-BOOKED VISITS
ACCOMMODATION
ANNUAL PRODUCTION 45,000 bottles
HECTARES UNDER VINE 9.00

Subida di Monte is family-run winery managed by Cristian and Andrea Antonutti, established in 1972 by their father, Luigi Antonutti, one of the regional pioneers of quality viticulture, who managed to crown his dream of living as a grower full-time. This modern winery, with extensive room both for vinification and visitors, is situated in a strategic position in the Collio area near Gorizia, surrounded by vineyards and set in an unspoilt natural environment of woods and grassland. Cristian and Andrea have enthusiastically taken up the winery's philosophy, aimed at producing natural, genuine, fragrant wines which respect varietal traits. An outstanding Malvasia 2015 reveals an attractive mix of candied peel, white peach, annurca apple and bay leaves, over a richly-flavoured, lingering palate. The Cabernet Franc 2014 offers liqueur cherries and rain-soaked grass, with light toasty notes both on the nose and on the finish.

● Collio Cabernet Franc '14	🍷🍷 3
○ Collio Friulano '15	🍷🍷 3
○ Collio Malvasia '15	🍷🍷 3
○ Collio Sauvignon '15	🍷🍷 3
○ Collio Pinot Grigio '15	🍷 3
● Collio Cabernet Franc '12	🍷🍷 3
○ Collio Friulano '14	🍷🍷 3
○ Collio Friulano '13	🍷🍷 3
○ Collio Friulano '12	🍷🍷 3
○ Collio Malvasia '14	🍷🍷 3
● Collio Merlot '13	🍷🍷 3
● Collio Merlot '11	🍷🍷 3
○ Collio Pinot Grigio '13	🍷🍷 3
● Collio Rosso Poncaia '12	🍷🍷 4
○ Collio Sauvignon '14	🍷🍷 3
○ Collio Sauvignon '13	🍷🍷 3

Matijaz Terčič

LOC. BUCUIE, 4A
34070 SAN FLORIANO DEL COLLIO [GO]
TEL. +39 0481884920
www.tercic.com

CELLAR SALES
PRE-BOOKED VISITS
ANNUAL PRODUCTION 30,000 bottles
HECTARES UNDER VINE 9.50

The winery established and run by Matijaz Terčič is one of the most interesting and renowned in the wine scene of San Floriano del Collio. This zone is considered one of the most interesting of the foothills of eastern Friuli. On the steep slopes the rows trace geometric patterns interspersed with long rows of cherry trees, leading down to the beautiful valley below. Here, for many generations, the Terčič family has been dedicated to viticulture and transforming grapes into wine, but it is thanks to Matijaz that excellence has been achieved. He has an unmistakable personal style, based on forthright, approachable, drinkable wines. The superb Merlot Seme 2011 is in the company of a series of excellently made white wines, with pride of place going to the Vino degli Orti 2013, a blend of friulano and malvasia in equal measure, with a nose of orange blossom, peach, apricot and green tea, over a perfectly balanced creamy, sumptuous palate with aromatic nuances.

○ Vino degli Orti '13	♥♥ 3*
○ Collio Bianco Planta '12	♥♥ 4
● Collio Merlot Seme '11	♥♥ 5
○ Collio Pinot Grigio Dar '12	♥♥ 4
○ Collio Sauvignon '14	♥♥ 3
○ Friuli Isonzo Friulano '14	♥♥ 3
○ Collio Pinot Grigio '07	♥♥♥ 3*
○ Collio Bianco Planta '11	♀♀ 4
○ Collio Chardonnay '12	♀♀ 3*
○ Collio Chardonnay '11	♀♀ 3
● Collio Merlot '10	♀♀ 4
○ Collio Pinot Grigio '13	♀♀ 3
○ Collio Pinot Grigio '12	♀♀ 3*
○ Collio Sauvignon '13	♀♀ 3
○ Collio Sauvignon '12	♀♀ 3
○ Vino degli Orti '12	♀♀ 3

Tiare - Roberto Snidarcig

FRAZ. VENCÒ
LOC. SANT'ELENA, 3A
34070 DOLEGNA DEL COLLIO [GO]
TEL. +39 048162491
www.tiaredoc.com

CELLAR SALES
PRE-BOOKED VISITS
RESTAURANT SERVICE
ANNUAL PRODUCTION 90,000 bottles
HECTARES UNDER VINE 10.00
SUSTAINABLE WINERY

Roberto Snidarcig's love for the land he farms inspired the name he gave to his winery, since Tiare in the local dialect in fact means "land". Starting out small, beginning with a single hectare of vineyards on the slopes of Mount Quarin, the high hill that protects the town of Cormòns from the cold winds that blow down the Valle del Vipacco, he has managed to develop his operation both in terms of volume and quality, transforming it in a short time into one of the region's most renowned wineries. It is now based at Dolegna del Collio, in a spacious new, functional facility, where, with the precious help of his wife Saundra, he continues unperturbed in his plans for expansion. The thrilling fragrance and aromas revealed by the Sauvignon 2015 obtain top honours, taking home a Tre Bicchieri. For lovers of this variety, this is a benchmark wine, showing superb balance, elegance, and intriguing mineral notes. And a Retrospective Tre Bicchieri for the excellent 2014.

○ Collio Sauvignon '15	♥♥♥ 5
○ Collio Chardonnay '15	♥♥ 3
○ Collio Friulano '15	♥♥ 4
○ Collio Malvasia '15	♥♥ 3
○ Collio Ribolla Gialla '15	♥♥ 4
○ Il Tiare '15	♥♥ 3
● Schioppettino '14	♥♥ 3
○ Collio Pinot Grigio '15	♥ 4
○ Collio Sauvignon '14	♀♀♀ 5
○ Collio Sauvignon '13	♀♀♀ 3*
○ Collio Friulano '14	♀♀ 4
○ Collio Malvasia '14	♀♀ 3*
○ Collio Malvasia '13	♀♀ 3
○ Collio Pinot Grigio '13	♀♀ 3
● Collio Pinot Nero '14	♀♀ 2*
○ Collio Ribolla Gialla '14	♀♀ 4
○ Collio Ribolla Gialla '13	♀♀ 3*

★Franco Toros

LOC. NOVALI, 12
34071 CORMÒNS [GO]
TEL. +39 048161327
www.vinitoros.com

CELLAR SALES
PRE-BOOKED VISITS
ANNUAL PRODUCTION 60,000 bottles
HECTARES UNDER VINE 11.00

Franco Toros is a great grower, an artisan of wine, and a real artist. This modest man, who moves in silence among the rows and avoids publicity, comes from a family of expert growers who at the beginning of the last century settled at Novali, neat Cormòns. Already back then, the Collio district was home to a white wine with such a marked personality that it attracted connoisseurs from Austria and nearby Veneto. Franco exploits the traditional knowledge stratified over time in every family, which is handed down from generation to generation. His wines are universal benchmarks, an example to imitate, and a source of regional pride. The fact that this year Franco Toros failed to take top honours will probably make the news. The wines are in any case superb, the result of a good growing year, especially the fresh, soft Friulano 2015, and the aromatic, full-flavoured Pinot Bianco 2015, which deservedly made our finals.

○ Collio Friulano '15	♥♥ 4
○ Collio Pinot Bianco '15	♥♥ 4
○ Collio Chardonnay '15	♥♥ 4
○ Collio Pinot Grigio '15	♥♥ 4
○ Collio Sauvignon '15	♥♥ 4
○ Collio Friulano '12	♥♥♥ 4*
○ Collio Friulano '11	♥♥♥ 4*
○ Collio Friulano '10	♥♥♥ 4*
○ Collio Friulano '09	♥♥♥ 4*
○ Collio Friulano '08	♥♥♥ 4*
○ Collio Pinot Bianco '14	♥♥♥ 4*
○ Collio Pinot Bianco '13	♥♥♥ 4*
○ Collio Pinot Bianco '08	♥♥♥ 4*
○ Collio Pinot Bianco '07	♥♥♥ 4
○ Collio Pinot Bianco '05	♥♥♥ 4
○ Collio Tocai Friulano '06	♥♥♥ 4
○ Collio Tocai Friulano '04	♥♥♥ 4

Torre Rosazza

FRAZ. OLEIS
LOC. POGGIOBELLO, 12
33044 MANZANO [UD]
TEL. +39 0422864511
www.torrerosazza.com

CELLAR SALES
PRE-BOOKED VISITS
ANNUAL PRODUCTION 200,000 bottles
HECTARES UNDER VINE 90.00
SUSTAINABLE WINERY

Torre Rosazza is the pride of Le Tenute di Genagricola, a group of companies that boasts holdings in various regions of Italy, but which particularly in Friuli has expanded by creating the brands Poggiobello, Borgo Magredo and Tenuta Sant'Anna. The winery is run by Enrico Raddi, who acts as its general manager, and is based in the 18th-century Palazzo De Marchi, which stands out on the summit of a hill in the municipality of Manzano. It is surrounded by two splendid natural terraced amphitheatres, whose aspect and microclimate are a real jewel in this area of the Colli Orientali. They are home to native varieties such as pignolo and ribolla gialla, the pride of viticulture in Friuli. The winery's two Pinots alternate at the height of excellence, and this year it was the turn of the Pinot Grigio 2015, which reclaimed a Tre Bicchieri. It was joined in the finals by an outstanding, fruit-fuelled Friulano 2015 with attractive balsamic notes.

○ FCO Pinot Grigio '15	♥♥♥ 3*
○ FCO Friulano '15	♥♥ 3*
○ Blanc di Neri Brut	♥♥ 5
○ FCO Picolit '12	♥♥ 5
○ FCO Pinot Bianco '15	♥♥ 3
● FCO Refosco P. R. '14	♥♥ 3
○ FCO Ribolla Gialla '15	♥♥ 3
○ FCO Sauvignon '15	♥♥ 3
● FCO Pinot Nero Ronco del Palazzo '09	♥ 3
○ FCO Verduzzo Friulano '13	♥ 3
○ COF Pinot Grigio '13	♥♥♥ 3*
○ COF Pinot Grigio '12	♥♥♥ 3*
○ FCO Pinot Bianco '14	♥♥♥ 3*
● COF Cabernet Sauvignon '13	♥♥ 3
● COF Refosco P. R. '13	♥♥ 3
○ FCO Sauvignon '14	♥♥ 3

La Tunella

FRAZ. IPPLIS
VIA DEL COLLIO, 14
33040 PREMARIACCO [UD]
TEL. +39 0432716030
www.latunella.it

CELLAR SALES
PRE-BOOKED VISITS
ANNUAL PRODUCTION 390,000 bottles
HECTARES UNDER VINE 70.00
SUSTAINABLE WINERY

La Tunella is unanimously acknowledged on an international level as one of the most prestigious wineries in Friuli. This year they celebrate 30 years since Livio Zorzettig left the original company and settled in Ipplis, where he set up in business on his own. The operation is now run by the two brothers Massimo and Marco who together with their mother Gabriella have managed to exploit the experiences accumulated by three generations of growers. Vinification is in the hands of Luigino Zamparo, who works in the impressively designed spacious hi-tech winery. His is the task of transforming the grapes into quality wines that exalt the territory while preserving the typical traits of each individual variety. Once again, no fewer than two wines made our finals, and a Tre Bicchieri went to the LaLinda 2014, a splendid blend of native varieties: friulano, malvasia istriana and ribolla gialla. A nose of candied lemon peel, white peach, incense and sweet spice is followed by a velvety, focused palate with a touch of saltiness.

○ FCO Bianco LaLinda '14	♟♟♟ 4*
○ FCO BiancoSesto '14	♟♟ 4
○ FCO Friulano Col Livius '14	♟♟ 4
○ FCO Pinot Grigio '15	♟♟ 3
○ FCO Ribolla Gialla Col de Bliss '14	♟♟ 4
○ FCO Ribolla Gialla Rjgialla '15	♟♟ 3
● FCO Rosso L'Arcione '11	♟♟ 5
● FCO Sauvignon Col Matiss '14	♟♟ 4
● FCO Schioppettino '12	♟♟ 4
○ Noans '14	♟♟ 5
○ COF BiancoSesto '11	♟♟♟ 4*
○ COF BiancoSesto '07	♟♟♟ 3
○ COF BiancoSesto '06	♟♟♟ 3*
○ Noans '12	♟♟♟ 5
○ COF BiancoSesto '13	♀♟ 4
○ COF Friulano Col Livius '13	♀♟ 4
● COF Schioppettino '11	♀♟ 4

Valchiarò

FRAZ. TOGLIANO
VIA DEI LAGHI, 4C
33040 TORREANO [UD]
TEL. +39 0432715502
www.valchiaro.it

CELLAR SALES
PRE-BOOKED VISITS
ANNUAL PRODUCTION 45,000 bottles
HECTARES UNDER VINE 14.00
SUSTAINABLE WINERY

Valchiarò is a fine story of passion and friendship. It was 1990 when six small producers, engaged in various professions, decided to come together and pool their grapes, opening the winery at Torreano di Cividale. This example of cooperation started out 25 years ago but still today is a fine example of team spirit based on mutual esteem and understanding. Its history has seen important changes, including the building of a large, modern winery, which opened its doors in 2006, where vinification is entrusted to the highly experienced Gianni Menotti. The white wines benefited from the good growing year and perfectly express the varietal characteristics of each cultivar with excellent fragrance but above all with a wide variety of original notes and aromatic nuances. In particular, the Friulano Nexus 2015 combines softness with marked marine saltiness.

○ FCO Friulano '15	♟♟ 3
○ FCO Friulano Nexus '15	♟♟ 3
○ FCO Picolit '11	♟♟ 6
○ FCO Pinot Grigio '15	♟♟ 3
● FCO Refosco P. R. Ris. '12	♟♟ 3
○ FCO Sauvignon '15	♟♟ 3
○ FCO Verduzzo Friulano '12	♟♟ 4
● FCO Cabernet '12	♟ 3
● COF Cabernet '11	♀♟ 3
● COF Merlot Ris. '11	♀♟ 3
○ COF Picolit '10	♀♟ 6
○ COF Verduzzo Friulano '11	♀♟ 4
○ COF Verduzzo Friulano '10	♀♟ 4
○ FCO Friulano '14	♀♟ 3
○ FCO Pinot Grigio '14	♀♟ 3
○ FCO Sauvignon '14	♀♟ 3

Valpanera

VIA TRIESTE, 5A
33059 VILLA VICENTINA [UD]
TEL. +39 0431970395
www.valpanera.it

CELLAR SALES
PRE-BOOKED VISITS
ANNUAL PRODUCTION 450,000 bottles
HECTARES UNDER VINE 55.00

Valpanera is a consolidated operation and one of the most representative of the potential of the Friuli Aquileia DOC zone. Set up by Giampietro Dal Vecchio and now run together with his son Giovanni, it has taken on the mission of bringing the best out of refosco dal peduncolo rosso, the region's most representative native red grape variety. The brave decision to focus mainly on this variety was dictated by studies and research that showed the ideal growing conditions of the district with its clay soils and constant air circulation provided by the bora wind. Optimum ripening of the grapes is ensured by the warm breezes from the nearby Adriatic. The Riserva, which generally gives a fine performance, was not presented this year, but the other two versions nevertheless proved to be superb. The Refosco dal Peduncolo Rosso Superiore 2013 is richly spiced, with black pepper and cloves on the nose, leading into a richly-flavoured, caressing palate.

● Friuli Aquileia Refosco P. R. '14	♆♆	2*
● Friuli Aquileia Refosco P. R. Sup. '13	♆♆	3
● Friuli Aquileia Rosso Alma '11	♆♆	5
○ Friuli Aquileia Verduzzo Friulano '13	♆♆	4
○ Friuli Aquileia Sauvignon '15	♆	3
● Le Tre Uve '15	♆	2
● Friuli Aquileia Refosco P. R. '13	♀♀	2*
● Friuli Aquileia Refosco P. R. '12	♀♀	2*
● Friuli Aquileia Refosco P. R. Ris. '11	♀♀	5
● Friuli Aquileia Refosco P. R. Ris. '08	♀♀	5
● Friuli Aquileia Refosco P. R. Ris. '07	♀♀	5
● Friuli Aquileia Refosco P. R. Sup. '12	♀♀	3
● Friuli Aquileia Refosco P. R. Sup. '10	♀♀	3
● Friuli Aquileia Rosso Alma '08	♀♀	5
● Rosso di Valpanera '12	♀♀	2*
● Rosso di Valpanera '10	♀♀	2*

★Venica & Venica

LOC. CERÒ, 8
34070 DOLEGNA DEL COLLIO [GO]
TEL. +39 048161264
www.venica.it

CELLAR SALES
PRE-BOOKED VISITS
ACCOMMODATION
ANNUAL PRODUCTION 280,000 bottles
HECTARES UNDER VINE 39.00

Gianni and Giorgio are the Venicas who transformed a small farm into a huge model estate, modern, dynamic, well-organized, famous and much appreciated throughout the world. With the team spirit typical of farming families, undisputed artisanal skills and business acumen, they have made the operation an example of regional excellence. Ornella and Giampaolo are widely known because they deal with public relations, but the whole staff contributes to the success of the Venica & Venica brand, which is a guarantee of absolute quality, offering a wide range of products that bring out the best of the unique traits of Collio Goriziano. With three wines in the final, there remains a certain disappointment that none took top honours, although this is yet further confirmation of the potential of this winery, which presented a Sauvignon Ronco delle Mele 2015, a Friulano Ronco delle Cime 2015 and a Pinot Bianco Tàlis 2015 of the highest level, the pride of Collio and the whole region.

○ Collio Friulano Ronco delle Cime '15	♆♆	4
○ Collio Pinot Bianco Tàlis '15	♆♆	4
○ Collio Sauvignon Ronco delle Mele '15	♆♆	6
○ Collio Malvasia Pètris '15	♆♆	4
○ Collio Pinot Grigio Jesera '15	♆♆	4
● Collio Refosco P. R. Bottaz '12	♆♆	5
○ Collio Sauvignon Ronco del Cerò '15	♆♆	5
○ Collio Traminer Aromatico '15	♆♆	4
○ Collio Sauvignon Ronco delle Mele '13	♀♀	6
○ Collio Sauvignon Ronco delle Mele '12	♀♀	6
○ Collio Sauvignon Ronco delle Mele '11	♀♀	6
○ Collio Sauvignon Ronco delle Mele '10	♀♀	5
○ Collio Sauvignon Ronco delle Mele '09	♀♀	5
○ Collio Sauvignon Ronco delle Mele '08	♀♀	5
○ Collio Sauvignon Ronco delle Mele '07	♀♀	5
○ Collio Tocai Friulano Ronco delle Cime '06	♀♀	4

La Viarte

VIA Novacuzzo, 51
33040 Prepotto [UD]
Tel. +39 0432759458
www.laviarte.it

CELLAR SALES
PRE-BOOKED VISITS
ACCOMMODATION
ANNUAL PRODUCTION 100,000 bottles
HECTARES UNDER VINE 27.00
SUSTAINABLE WINERY

The winery's name of La Viarte, which in local direct means "spring", was chosen by the Ceschin family when they started out 40 years ago. Since then, they have become a major name in regional wine production. The current owner, Alberto Piovan, decided to further develop the unique traits of this territory, thanks to mature vineyards, and without compromising the winery style, set himself the goal of bringing out its unexpressed potential, with extremely low yields and excellent quality. Being a farsighted businessman, he decided to avail himself of the precious help of Gianni Menotti. Excellent performance across the range is the demonstration that the winery is on track, and satisfying results have not been long in coming. The well-typed Sauvignon Liende 2015 perhaps performed above expectations, and earned a Tre Bicchieri, with its fragrant nose and leisurely palate.

Vidussi

VIA Spessa, 18
34071 Capriva del Friuli [GO]
Tel. +39 048180072
www.vinimontresor.it

CELLAR SALES
PRE-BOOKED VISITS
ANNUAL PRODUCTION 500,000 bottles
HECTARES UNDER VINE 30.00

The family-owned Vidussi estate has been leased out to the Veronese group Montresor since the year 2000. It is based in Capriva del Friuli, in the heart of Collio, and the majority of the vineyards lie in that district, while other plots are located in the Friuli Isonzo and Friuli Colli Orientali DOC zones. The growing conditions of the territory mean that the majority of grapes grown are white varieties, and the choice falls above all on the use of native cultivars, with particular focus on a winery favorite, ribolla gialla. The wide range of wines covers all the sectors of the market, and displays excellent value for money. Year after year, we mention the excellent flavour displayed by this operation's wines, and their superb consistency. Forthright and coherent, they are without frills or superfluities, and while being highly drinkable, are at the same time well managed and extremely tasty.

○ FCO Sauvignon Liende '15	♟♟♟ 5
○ FCO Friulano Liende '15	♟♟ 5
○ Arteus '15	♟♟ 3
○ COF Sauvignon '15	♟♟ 3
○ FCO Friulano '15	♟♟ 3
● FCO Merlot '12	♟♟ 4
○ FCO Ribolla Gialla '15	♟♟ 3
☉ La Viarte Rosé Brut	♟♟ 4
● COF Merlot '11	♟♟ 4
○ COF Pinot Grigio '13	♟♟ 3
○ COF Sauvignon '13	♟♟ 3*
○ COF Sauvignon Liende '13	♟♟ 5
● COF Tazzelenghe '09	♟♟ 5
○ FCO Chardonnay '14	♟♟ 3
○ FCO Friulano '14	♟♟ 3
○ FCO Pinot Bianco '14	♟♟ 3

○ Collio Chardonnay '15	♟♟ 2*
○ Collio Friulano '15	♟♟ 3
○ Collio Malvasia '15	♟♟ 2*
○ Collio Pinot Grigio '15	♟♟ 2*
○ Collio Sauvignon '15	♟♟ 2*
○ Collio Traminer Aromatico '15	♟♟ 2*
○ Collio Ribolla Gialla '15	♟ 2
● Ribolla Nera o Schioppettino '15	♟ 3
○ Collio Chardonnay '14	♟♟ 3
○ Collio Friulano '14	♟♟ 3
○ Collio Malvasia '14	♟♟ 2*
○ Collio Pinot Bianco '14	♟♟ 3
○ Collio Pinot Grigio '14	♟♟ 2*
○ Collio Ribolla Gialla '14	♟♟ 2*
○ Collio Traminer Aromatico '14	♟♟ 2*
● Ribolla Nera o Schioppettino '14	♟♟ 3

★★Vie di Romans

Loc. Vie di Romans, 1
34070 Mariano del Friuli [GO]
Tel. +39 048169600
www.viediromans.it

CELLAR SALES
PRE-BOOKED VISITS
ANNUAL PRODUCTION 250,000 bottles
HECTARES UNDER VINE 55.00
SUSTAINABLE WINERY

Vie di Romans is a prestigious brand, a model company, and a real jewel on the region's viticultural scene. Gianfranco Gallo is the man behind this masterpiece, the result of exceptional qualities which result in a style based on precise viticultural strategies combined with meticulous vinification. The wines, above all the whites, display marked territorial expression and impressive structure. The vineyards all lie in the Friuli Isonzo DOC zone, a few kilometres from the Bay of Trieste, where the continental climate meets that of the Mediterranean. The soils are on the plains, but enjoy an ideal microclimate and subsoils rich in minerals. It may seem absurd to have four wines in the finals, as happens with enviable regularity, although hardly ever with the same labels, and not take home top honours. On the contrary; it confirms the excellent quality offered by the winery across the board, both with its wines aged in steel and those in oak.

○ Dut'un '13	♥♥ 6
○ Friuli Isonzo Bianco Flors di Uis '14	♥♥ 4
○ Friuli Isonzo Chardonnay Ciampagnis Vieris '14	♥♥ 4
○ Friuli Isonzo Sauvignon Piere '14	♥♥ 5
○ Friuli Isonzo Chardonnay Vie di Romans '14	♥♥ 5
○ Friuli Isonzo Friulano Dolée '14	♥♥ 5
○ Friuli Isonzo Malvasia Dis Cumieris '14	♥♥ 5
○ Friuli Isonzo Pinot Grigio Dessimis '14	♥♥ 6
○ Friuli Isonzo Sauvignon Vieris '14	♥♥ 5
○ Friuli Isonzo Bianco Flors di Uis '09	♥♥♥ 4*
○ Friuli Isonzo Chardonnay Ciampagnis Vieris '13	♥♥♥ 4*
○ Friuli Isonzo Friulano Dolée '12	♥♥♥ 5
○ Friuli Isonzo Friulano Dolée '11	♥♥♥ 4*
○ Friuli Isonzo Sauvignon Piere '10	♥♥♥ 4*

Vigna del Lauro

Loc. Montona, 19
34071 Cormòns [GO]
Tel. +39 0481629549
www.vignadellauro.it

CELLAR SALES
PRE-BOOKED VISITS
ANNUAL PRODUCTION 60,000 bottles
HECTARES UNDER VINE 10.00

Vigna del Lauro is a family winery run by Fabio Coser, previously owner of Ronco dei Tassi, his wife Daniela, and their sons Matteo and Enrico. It was set up in 1994 as the result of a joint project with a German importer of Italian wines, Eberhard Spangenberg, who needed to differentiate products to satisfy the needs of the German market. The winery philosophy is based on the concept that attention and the respect of raw materials during production are crucial to bringing out varietal character and a sense of place. The result is genuine, coherent wines which are approachable and drinkable, at extremely competitive prices. Once again this year, the wines of Collio have a little extra something, although those from the plain are also extremely interesting. The Merlot 2014 opens to a nose of cherries, and shows attractive spice, coming back to the fore on the palate. The Traminer Aromatico 2015 offers elderflower syrup, quince and white peach.

○ Collio Friulano '15	♥♥ 3
○ Collio Pinot Grigio '15	♥♥ 3
○ Collio Ribolla Gialla '15	♥♥ 3
○ Collio Sauvignon '15	♥♥ 3
● Friuli Isonzo Merlot '14	♥♥ 2*
○ Friuli Isonzo Traminer Aromatico '15	♥♥ 2*
○ Friuli Isonzo Friulano '15	♥ 2
○ Friuli Isonzo Sauvignon '15	♥ 2
○ Collio Sauvignon '99	♥♥♥ 2*
○ Collio Friulano '14	♀♀ 3
○ Collio Pinot Grigio '14	♀♀ 3
○ Collio Ribolla Gialla '14	♀♀ 3
○ Collio Sauvignon '14	♀♀ 3
○ Collio Sauvignon '13	♀♀ 3
● Friuli Isonzo Cabernet Franc '13	♀♀ 2*
● Friuli Isonzo Merlot '12	♀♀ 2*

Vigna Petrussa

VIA ALBANA, 47
33040 PREPOTTO [UD]
TEL. +39 0432713021
www.vignapetrussa.it

CELLAR SALES
PRE-BOOKED VISITS
ANNUAL PRODUCTION 30,000 bottles
HECTARES UNDER VINE 6.50

In 1995, Hilde Petrussa decided to move back to the family estate, which after flourishing in the early 20th century, had since fallen into neglect. She found she had to convert the vineyards, trying to give priority to native cultivars, training them with the Guyot system, increasing plants per hectare and cover-cropping the entire area under vine. Of course she devoted most attention to ribolla nera, the variety from which Schioppettino is made, which seems to have originated in this valley and where it has in any case always existed. Together with a large group of other local growers, she has for years been campaigning for official recognition of the Schioppettino di Prepotto subzone. Hilde generally proposes mature wines, already well aged, with evolved, tucked-in aromas, but this year the real news is a surprising Friulano 2015, which is universally appreciated thanks to its intensity, complexity and attractive nose, but above all for its grippy, enfolding palate.

○ FCO Friulano '15		♟♟ 3*
○ FCO Picolit '12		♟♟ 5
● FCO Schioppettino di Prepotto '12		♟♟ 4
○ Richenza '13		♟♟ 4
● FCO Refosco P. R. '13		♟ 4
● COF Cabernet Franc '12		♟♟ 3
● COF Cabernet Franc '10		♟♟ 3
○ COF Friulano '13		♟♟ 3
○ COF Friulano '12		♟♟ 3
○ COF Picolit '11		♟♟ 5
○ COF Sauvignon '12		♟♟ 3
● COF Schioppettino di Prepotto '11		♟♟ 4
● COF Schioppettino di Prepotto '10		♟♟ 4
○ FCO Sauvignon '14		♟♟ 3
○ Richenza '12		♟♟ 4
○ Richenza '11		♟♟ 4

Vigna Traverso

VIA RONCHI, 73
33040 PREPOTTO [UD]
TEL. +39 0422804807
www.vignatraverso.it

CELLAR SALES
PRE-BOOKED VISITS
RESTAURANT SERVICE
ANNUAL PRODUCTION 100,000 bottles
HECTARES UNDER VINE 22.00
SUSTAINABLE WINERY

The Vigna Traverso wiery, once called Ronco di Castagneto, has for almost 20 years been owned by the Molon Traverso family, the owners of the famous winery based in nearby Veneto. For some time now it has been run by Stefano Traverso who, despite still being young, has wide experience in the sector and deals both with vinification and the rows, focusing in particular on renovating old vineyards planted to native varieties. For some years, he has been working in the new cellar at Prepotto, equipped with the latest technology, but which has also reintroduced concrete tanks, a classic example of respect for tradition. We saw an excellent performance from the white vintages but greater development rewarded the Bianco Sottocastello 2013 and the Refosco dal Peduncolo Rosso 2012, which reached our finals. The former offers a nose of custard and pot pourri, the latter leaf tobacco and spice, while both vaunt a rich palate and balsamic finish.

○ FCO Bianco Sottocastello '13		♟♟ 4
● FCO Refosco P. R. '12		♟♟ 3*
○ FCO Friulano '15		♟♟ 3
○ FCO Ribolla Gialla '15		♟♟ 3
○ FCO Sauvignon '15		♟♟ 3
● FCO Troj '12		♟♟ 3
○ FCO Pinot Grigio '15		♟ 3
● FCO Schioppettino di Prepotto '12		♟ 4
○ COF Bianco Sottocastello '12		♟♟ 3
○ COF Bianco Sottocastello '11		♟♟ 4
● COF Merlot '11		♟♟ 3
● COF Rosso Troj '11		♟♟ 3
○ COF Sauvignon '13		♟♟ 3
● COF Schioppettino di Prepotto '11		♟♟ 4
○ FCO Friulano '14		♟♟ 3
○ FCO Sauvignon '14		♟♟ 3

Vigne del Malina

FRAZ. ORZANO
VIA PASINI VIANELLI, 9
33047 REMANZACCO [UD]
TEL. +39 0432649258
www.vignedelmalina.com

CELLAR SALES
PRE-BOOKED VISITS
ANNUAL PRODUCTION 45,000 bottles
HECTARES UNDER VINE 10.00

In the first half of the last century, many young entrepreneurs from Friuli, including Alberto Bacchetti, went to seek their fortune in Venezuela. Having achieved some success, and longing to come back to their homeland, in 1967 the Bacchetti family purchased an estate at Orzano set around a fine 19th century house, Villa Pasini Vianelli. In 2007 Roberto Bacchetti and Maria Luisa Trevisan decided to set up a winery with the declared intent of obtaining the utmost quality, releasing their wines on the market only when they had achieved the best possible sensory characteristics resulting from long ageing. We will have to wait for next year to taste wines from the 2013 harvest. In the meantime, the winery presented two whites obtained after maceration of the grapes, and thus from even earlier vintages. They were both superb, but in particular the Sauvignon Aur 2009, with a complex, deep nose and fragrant palate.

★Le Vigne di Zamò

LOC. ROSAZZO
VIA ABATE CORRADO, 4
33044 MANZANO [UD]
TEL. +39 0432759693
www.levignedizamo.com

CELLAR SALES
PRE-BOOKED VISITS
ANNUAL PRODUCTION 280,000 bottles
HECTARES UNDER VINE 67.00
SUSTAINABLE WINERY

The reputation of this prestigious brand is linked to the name of its legendary founder Tullio Zamò, a perfect example of what it takes to be an entrepreneur. He started out by establishing Vigne dal Leon on the hill of Rocca Bernarda, some years later set up Abbazia di Rosazzo, and in 1996 together with his sons Pierluigi and Silvano, established Le Vigne di Zamò. The operation has now become part of the Farinetti group, and this has led to significant consolidation of the winery, as well as increasing its visibility on international markets. The winery headquarters lie on the hillside near the famous abbey, while the modern production facility is entirely set into the hillside. The quality of the entire range has always been outstanding, but for some years top honours have eluded the winery. It was the Friulano No Name 2015 that changed this, putting the winery back among the region's best and earning aTre Bicchieri with its most representative native variety.

○ Sauvignon Aur '09	▼▼	5
○ Pinot Grigio Ram '09	▼▼	4
● Cabernet Franc '11	♀♀	3
● Cabernet Franc '09	♀♀	3
○ Chardonnay '12	♀♀	3
○ Friuli Grave Chardonnay '07	♀♀	4
● Friuli Grave Refosco P.R. '07	♀♀	4
○ Friuli Grave Sauvignon '09	♀♀	3
○ Friuli Grave Sauvignon '08	♀♀	2*
○ Pinot Grigio '12	♀♀	3
○ Pinot Grigio '11	♀♀	3
○ Pinot Grigio '10	♀♀	3
● Refosco P.R. '09	♀♀	4
○ Sauvignon '12	♀♀	3
○ Sauvignon '11	♀♀	3

○ FCO Friulano No Name '15	▼▼▼	5
○ FCO Bianco Ronco delle Acacie '13	▼▼	5
● FCO Merlot V. Cinquant'Anni '12	▼▼	6
○ FCO Ribolla Gialla '15	▼▼	3
○ FCO Sauvignon '15	▼▼	3
○ FCO Pinot Grigio '15	▼	3
○ COF Friulano V. Cinquant'Anni '09	♀♀♀	5
○ COF Friulano V. Cinquant'Anni '08	♀♀♀	5
● COF Merlot V. Cinquant'Anni '09	♀♀♀	5
● COF Merlot V. Cinquant'Anni '06	♀♀♀	5
● COF Merlot V. Cinquant'Anni '99	♀♀♀	5
○ COF Rosazzo Bianco Ronco delle Acacie '01	♀♀♀	4
● COF Rosazzo Pignolo '01	♀♀♀	6
○ COF Tocai Friulano V. Cinquant'Anni '06	♀♀♀	5

Villa de Puppi

VIA ROMA, 5
33040 MOIMACCO [UD]
TEL. +39 0432722461
www.depuppi.it

CELLAR SALES
PRE-BOOKED VISITS
ANNUAL PRODUCTION 70,000 bottles
HECTARES UNDER VINE 25.00
SUSTAINABLE WINERY

Caterina and Valfredo de Puppi, today at the helm of the winery, represent the latest generation of the aristocratic family which since time immemorial has been dedicated to farming the family estates around the splendid ancestral home. The merit for their reputation on the region's wine scene should be given to the farsightedness of Conte Luigi de Puppi, who sensed its potential and in the late 20th century reorganized the old vineyards before handing them over to his young children. The winery's success was later consolidated with the purchase of around ten hectares under vine on the hills of Rosazzo and with the takeover of the prestigious Rosa Bosco brand. The wines presented from the entry-level line do not hark from the last growing year, an evident sign that the winery decided to delay bottling to let the wines mature. Our finals were graced by the Sauvignon Blanc di Rosa Bosco 2013, which offers a nose of lemon cream and dried medicinal herbs over a rich, tasty palate.

○ Sauvignon Blanc di Rosa Bosco '13	♚♚ 5
○ Chardonnay '14	♚♚ 3
● Merlot Il Boscorosso di Rosa Bosco '11	♚♚ 6
○ Pinot Grigio '14	♚♚ 3
○ Ribolla Gialla di Rosa Bosco '14	♚♚ 4
○ Taj Blanc '14	♚♚ 3
○ Sauvignon '14	♚ 3
● Cabernet '12	♛♛ 2*
● Merlot Il Boscorosso di Rosa Bosco '10	♛♛ 4
● Refosco P. R. '12	♛♛ 3
● Refosco P.R. Cate '10	♛♛ 5
○ Ribolla Gialla di Rosa Bosco '13	♛♛ 4
○ Ribolla Gialla di Rosa Bosco '11	♛♛ 4
○ Sauvignon '13	♛♛ 2*
○ Sauvignon Blanc di Rosa Bosco '12	♛♛ 4
○ Taj Blanc '13	♛♛ 2*

★★Villa Russiz

VIA RUSSIZ, 4/6
34070 CAPRIVA DEL FRIULI [GO]
TEL. +39 048180047
www.villarussiz.it

CELLAR SALES
PRE-BOOKED VISITS
ANNUAL PRODUCTION 220,000 bottles
HECTARES UNDER VINE 45.00
SUSTAINABLE WINERY

Among the historic brands in the region, one that stands out is that of Villa Russiz, established in 1869 by the French count Teodoro de La Tour, who decided to move to Capriva del Collio with his Austrian wife Elvine Ritter. He was clearly a skilled grower, and realizing the ideal conditions for viticulture, imported rooted cuttings from his homeland and planted them on the hills of the area. The varieties soon adapted perfectly to the environment, and due to the quality of the wines they produced, spread throughout the territory. In addition to the winery, Villa Russiz is also home to a charitable institution for children in need. With two wines of this quality, we imagined that the finals would bring top honours. Despite the disappointment that this did not happen, it does not change the fact that the Malvasia 2015 and the Chardonnay Gräfin de La Tour 2012 are equally excellent, although diferent, showing elegance both on the nose and in the mouth.

○ Collio Chardonnay Gräfin de La Tour '12	♚♚ 7
○ Collio Malvasia '15	♚♚ 4
○ Collio Friulano '15	♚♚ 4
○ Collio Pinot Bianco '15	♚♚ 4
○ Collio Pinot Grigio '15	♚♚ 4
○ Collio Sauvignon de La Tour '15	♚♚ 6
● Collio Merlot '13	♚ 4
● Collio Merlot Gräf de La Tour '02	♛♛♛ 6
○ Collio Pinot Bianco '07	♛♛♛ 3
○ Collio Sauvignon de La Tour '08	♛♛♛ 5
○ Collio Sauvignon de La Tour '05	♛♛♛ 5
○ Collio Tocai Friulano '04	♛♛♛ 3

Tenuta Villanova

LOC. VILLANOVA
VIA CONTESSA BERETTA, 29
34072 FARRA D'ISONZO [GO]
TEL. +39 0481889311
www.tenutavillanova.com

CELLAR SALES
PRE-BOOKED VISITS
ANNUAL PRODUCTION 600,000 bottles
HECTARES UNDER VINE 105.00

Tenuta Villanova boasts over five centuries of history, and was established in 1499. Naturally, over time, it has had various owners, and in 1932 was purchased by the businessman Arnaldo Bennati, whose wife Giuseppina Grossi still runs the operation, helped by her grandson Alberto, who acts as the general manager. Of historical interest is the fact that in 1869, the owner at the time, Alberto Levi, hosted Louis Pasteur, who was in Friuli for his studies, and who discovered that Villanova's wines were in no way inferior to those of his French homeland. The winery boasts a young, united team of staff, supported by the experience of outstanding technicians. The excellent performance this year confirms the consistent quality of the whole range of wines, among which pride of place goes to the Friulano Ronco Cucco 2015, making our finals with its complex, graceful nose of fruit and balsam, and an attractively nuanced, aromatic, full-flavoured palate.

○ Collio Friulano Ronco Cucco '15	▼▼	4
○ Collio Pinot Grigio Ronco Cucco '15	▼▼	3
○ Collio Ribolla Gialla Ronco Cucco '15	▼▼	3
○ Collio Sauvignon Ronco Cucco '15	▼▼	4
● Fraja '10	▼▼	5
● Friuli Isonzo Refosco P. R. '13	▼▼	2*
○ Friuli Isonzo Chardonnay '15	▼	2
○ Friuli Isonzo Sauvignon '15	▼	2
○ Collio Picolit Ronco Cucco '10	♈♈	5
○ Collio Pinot Grigio Ronco Cucco '14	♈♈	3
○ Collio Pinot Grigio Ronco Cucco '13	♈♈	3
○ Collio Ribolla Gialla Ronco Cucco '14	♈♈	3
○ Friuli Isonzo Malvasia '13	♈♈	2*
○ Friuli Isonzo Pinot Grigio '13	♈♈	2*
● Friuli Isonzo Refosco P. R. '12	♈♈	2*
○ Friuli Isonzo Sauvignon '14	♈♈	2*

Andrea Visintini

VIA GRAMOGLIANO, 27
33040 CORNO DI ROSAZZO [UD]
TEL. +39 0432755813
www.vinivisintini.com

CELLAR SALES
PRE-BOOKED VISITS
ANNUAL PRODUCTION 110,000 bottles
HECTARES UNDER VINE 28.00
VITICULTURE METHOD Certified Organic
SUSTAINABLE WINERY

Oliviero Visintini, with his sisters Cinzia and Palmira, has been managing the family winery inherited from his father Andrea for some time. This is one of the most successful operations in the area of Corno di Rosazzo, the pride of the Friuli Colli Orientali DOC zone. The winery is built on the ruins of the historic Castello di Gramogliano, destroyed and then rebuilt various times over the centuries, and also boasts a perfectly preserved circular watchtower dating back to 1560. Oliviero's winemaking philosophy envisages extremely limited intervention in the rows, with the aim of maintaining the aromas of each individual variety intact. All the wines in the range stand out for their excellent value for money, especially considering their performance in our tastings. The vintage whites, all superb, were joined by the Pignolo 2009, offering a well-developed, complex nose and a powerful palate with lively, still untamed tannins.

○ FCO Friulano '15	▼▼	2*
● FCO Pignolo '09	▼▼	4
○ FCO Pinot Bianco '15	▼▼	2*
○ FCO Sauvignon '15	▼▼	2*
○ Malvasia '15	▼▼	2*
○ FCO Pinot Grigio '15	▼	2
○ FCO Ribolla Gialla '15	▼	2
○ COF Bianco '13	♈♈	2*
● COF Merlot '12	♈♈	2*
○ COF Pinot Bianco '13	♈♈	2*
○ COF Pinot Grigio '13	♈♈	2*
○ COF Ribolla Gialla '13	♈♈	2*
○ COF Sauvignon '13	♈♈	2*
○ FCO Bianco '14	♈♈	2*
○ FCO Sauvignon '14	♈♈	2*
○ Malvasia '14	♈♈	2*

Vitas 1907

LOC. STRASSOLDO
VIA SAN MARCO, 5
33052 CERVIGNANO DEL FRIULI [UD]
TEL. +39 043193083
www.vitas.it

CELLAR SALES
PRE-BOOKED VISITS
ACCOMMODATION
ANNUAL PRODUCTION 130,000 bottles
HECTARES UNDER VINE 15.00
SUSTAINABLE WINERY

A historic 18th-century house set in a centuries-old park, reached by a long avenue flanked by magnolia trees and vineyards, is home to Villa Vitas, a fine winery set on clay and sandy soils rich in mineral detritus, located within the Friuli Aquileia DOC zone. Roberto Vitas, who represents the fourth generation of passionate growers, took over at the helm in 1993, and with his youthful enthusiasm and energy reorganized the vineyard holdings, introducing high density training systems. The low production levels and beneficial effects of the nearby sea ensure perfect ripening of the grapes. We saw yet another fine performance from all the wines, both reds and whites, but were particularly impressed with the Marlet 2014, a blend of chardonnay, sauvignon and malvasia istriana, which seduces on the nose and palate with intriguing suggestions of candied peel, pineapple, mixed flower honey, vanilla and pennyroyal.

★Volpe Pasini

FRAZ. TOGLIANO
VIA CIVIDALE, 16
33040 TORREANO [UD]
TEL. +39 0432715151
www.volpepasini.it

CELLAR SALES
PRE-BOOKED VISITS
ACCOMMODATION
ANNUAL PRODUCTION 400,000 bottles
HECTARES UNDER VINE 52.00
SUSTAINABLE WINERY

A single day is not enough to properly visit this splendid operation in the Colli Orientali area of Friuli. Villa Volpe Pasini, with its centuries-old park including a small vineyard of ribolla gialla, is of breathtaking beauty, and is also home to the modern winery, in the hands of the expert oenologist John Turato. The vineyards are tended with a care usually dedicated to gardens, but the operation's greatest asset is without doubt its staff, who have always aimed at the highest quality, while increasingly focusing on environmental sustainability. Francesco and Alessandro Rotolo, together with Lorenzo Landi, have given us great wines from the magnificent 2015 growing year. These include the Sauvignon Zuc di Volpe 2015, which romps off with its seventh Tre Bicchieri in a row. Once again, it was not alone in the finals, and was in the company of the Pinot Bianco 2015 and the Pinot Grigio 2015 from the Zuc di Volpe line, and a surprising Friulano 2015 from the Volpe Pasini line.

● Friuli Aquileia Cabernet Franc '14	🏆🏆 2*
● Friuli Aquileia Refosco P. R. '14	🏆🏆 2*
○ Marlet '14	🏆🏆 3
● Vign. Romano '11	🏆🏆 3
○ Friuli Aquileia Friulano '15	🏆 2
○ Friuli Aquileia Sauvignon '15	🏆 2
○ Traminer Aromatico '15	🏆 2
● Friuli Aquileia Cabernet Franc '12	🏆🏆 2*
● Friuli Aquileia Refosco dal P. R. '12	🏆🏆 3
● Friuli Aquileia Refosco P. R. '13	🏆🏆 2*
○ Friuli Aquileia Sauvignon '14	🏆🏆 2*
○ Marlet '13	🏆🏆 3
○ Marlet '12	🏆🏆 4
○ Traminer Aromatico '14	🏆🏆 2*
● Vign. Romano '10	🏆🏆 3
● Vign. Romano '09	🏆🏆 3

○ FCO Sauvignon Zuc di Volpe '15	🏆🏆🏆 5
○ FCO Friulano Volpe Pasini '15	🏆🏆 3*
○ FCO Pinot Bianco Zuc di Volpe '15	🏆🏆 5
● FCO Cabernet Volpe Pasini '13	🏆🏆 3
● FCO Merlot Togliano Volpe Pasini '13	🏆🏆 3
○ FCO Pinot Grigio Grivò Volpe Pasini '15	🏆🏆 3
○ FCO Pinot Grigio Zuc di Volpe '15	🏆🏆 4
● FCO Refosco P. R. Zuc di Volpe '13	🏆🏆 5
○ FCO Ribolla Gialla Zuc di Volpe '15	🏆🏆 4
○ COF Pinot Bianco Zuc di Volpe '12	🏆🏆🏆 4*
○ COF Pinot Bianco Zuc di Volpe '10	🏆🏆🏆 4
○ COF Sauvignon Zuc di Volpe '13	🏆🏆🏆 4*
○ COF Sauvignon Zuc di Volpe '12	🏆🏆🏆 4*
○ COF Sauvignon Zuc di Volpe '11	🏆🏆🏆 4*
○ COF Sauvignon Zuc di Volpe '10	🏆🏆🏆 3*
○ FCO Sauvignon Zuc di Volpe '14	🏆🏆🏆 5

Francesco Vosca

FRAZ. BRAZZANO
VIA SOTTOMONTE, 19
34071 CORMÒNS [GO]
TEL. +39 048162135
www.voscavini.it

CELLAR SALES
PRE-BOOKED VISITS
ANNUAL PRODUCTION 50,000 bottles
HECTARES UNDER VINE 8.50

Francesco Vosca's winery is one of the classic family-run operations with proud farming origins that in the last decades of the 20th century progressively decided to abandon mixed farming and livestock rearing to dedicate themselves exclusively to winegrowing. This important step, not without its risks, was based on the awareness of the territory's potential, but also of how difficult it is to work such difficult terrain, unsuitable for mechanized farming. Francesco's wife Anita helps in the rows, while their son Gabriele deals with vinification. We saw excellent performance across the range, although the wines from Collio seem to have a little extra something, especially in terms of fragrance and structure. As always, the best of the bunch was the Malvasia 2015 with its trademark aromatic nose and marine saltiness in the mouth.

○ Collio Friulano '15	🍷🍷	3
○ Collio Malvasia '15	🍷🍷	3
○ Collio Ribolla Gialla '15	🍷🍷	3
○ Friuli Isonzo Chardonnay '15	🍷🍷	3
○ Friuli Isonzo Pinot Grigio '15	🍷🍷	3
○ Friuli Isonzo Sauvignon '15	🍷	3
○ Collio Friulano '14	🍷🍷	3
○ Collio Friulano '13	🍷🍷	3
○ Collio Malvasia '14	🍷🍷	3
○ Collio Malvasia '13	🍷🍷	3
● Collio Merlot '11	🍷🍷	4
○ Collio Ribolla Gialla '14	🍷🍷	3
○ Collio Ribolla Gialla '13	🍷🍷	3
○ Friuli Isonzo Pinot Grigio '14	🍷🍷	3
○ Friuli Isonzo Pinot Grigio '13	🍷🍷	3
○ Friuli Isonzo Sauvignon '14	🍷🍷	3

Zidarich

LOC. PREPOTTO, 23
34011 DUINO AURISINA [TS]
TEL. +39 040201223
www.zidarich.it

CELLAR SALES
PRE-BOOKED VISITS
ANNUAL PRODUCTION 28,000 bottles
HECTARES UNDER VINE 8.00

Beniamino Zidarich, with little land but an indomitable spirit and enviable determination, established his estate in 1988 in the Trieste section of the Karst plateau, at Prepotto in the municipality of Duino Aurisina. Set among the vines and typical Karst vegetation, this estate enjoys remarkable aspects over the Bay of Trieste. The continental climate on the plateau is characterized by the influence of the sea and the cold, often violent bora wind. Although this limits the choice of grape varieties, vitovska and terrano are always here. The cellar is a real monument to oenology, and in its niches carved from the rock, oak barrels maintain the wines at cool underground temperatures. Of the four wines presented, two deservedly made our finals. The Malvasia 2013 shows a nose of candied fruit, cumin, green tea and peaches in syrup, while the Prulke 2013, a blend of sauvignon, malvasia istriana and vitovska, shows a complex nose and the mineral notes of the local karst rock.

○ Malvasia '13	🍷🍷	5
○ Prulke '13	🍷🍷	5
● Terrano '13	🍷🍷	5
○ Vitovska '13	🍷🍷	5
○ Carso Malvasia '09	🍷🍷🍷	5
○ Carso Malvasia '06	🍷🍷🍷	5
○ Carso Vitovska V. Collezione '09	🍷🍷🍷	8
○ Prulke '10	🍷🍷🍷	5
○ Prulke '08	🍷🍷🍷	5
● Carso Terrano '11	🍷🍷	5
○ Prulke '12	🍷🍷	5
● Ruje '10	🍷🍷	7
● Ruje '07	🍷🍷	5
● Terrano '12	🍷🍷	5
○ Vitovska '11	🍷🍷	5
○ Vitovska Kamen '13	🍷🍷	7

Zorzettig

FRAZ. SPESSA
S.DA SANT'ANNA, 37
33043 CIVIDALE DEL FRIULI [UD]
TEL. +39 0432716156
www.zorzettigvini.it

CELLAR SALES
PRE-BOOKED VISITS
ACCOMMODATION AND RESTAURANT SERVICE
ANNUAL PRODUCTION 800,000 bottles
HECTARES UNDER VINE 110.00
SUSTAINABLE WINERY

Annalisa Zorzettig is an innovative, dynamic grower, full of ideas, and the classic example of a successful businesswoman. Her brother Alessandro, meanwhile, prefers to deal with attending the rows. Together, they run the winery established by their father, Cavalier Giuseppe Zorzettig, who in 1986 had the opportunity to purchase a historic farmstead, moved there with his family, and soon transformed it into a modern, functional winery. As the operation has continued to expand, they have never sacrificed value for money, and have also achieved excellence in the selections of the Myò line, entrusted to the expert hands of oenologist Fabio Coser. What we mentioned last year as a pleasant surprise has proved this year to be a splendid reality. The Pinot Bianco Myò 2015 once again took home a Tre Bicchieri and confirmed its place as the best of the range. It was joined in the finals by an excellent, beautifully-typed Friulano Myò 2015.

○ FCO Pinot Bianco Myò '15	���� 4*
○ FCO Friulano Myò '15	�� 4
○ FCO Malvasia Myò '15	�� 4
● FCO Pignolo Myò '12	�� 6
○ FCO Ribolla Gialla '15	�� 3
○ FCO Sauvignon Myò '15	�� 4
● FCO Schioppettino Myò '13	�� 5
○ Ribolla Giall Brut Optimum '15	�� 3
○ FCO Chardonnay '15	� 3
○ FCO Friulano '15	� 3
○ FCO Pinot Grigio '15	� 3
○ FCO Pinot Bianco Myò '14	��� 4*
○ COF Friulano Myò '13	�� 4
● COF Pignolo Myò '11	�� 6
● COF Refosco P.R. Myò '12	�� 4
● COF Schioppettino Myò '12	�� 5
○ FCO Friulano Myò '14	�� 4

Zuani

LOC. GIASBANA, 12
34070 SAN FLORIANO DEL COLLIO [GO]
TEL. +39 0481391432
www.zuanivini.it

CELLAR SALES
PRE-BOOKED VISITS
ACCOMMODATION
ANNUAL PRODUCTION 75,000 bottles
HECTARES UNDER VINE 15.00

Zuani is the expression of a philosophy accumulated over years of experience among the rows and in the cellar by Patrizia Felluga, supported by knowledge acquired thanks to her business skills. A daughter of growers, Patrizia has in turn managed to transmit to her children Antonio and Caterina a love for the land and viticulture. The result of an ambitious project, Zuani only releases a single wine, the Collio Bianco, produced with grapes from 15 hectares of vineyards purchased specifically for this purpose at Giasbana on the splendid slopes of San Floriano del Collio. A small proportion of the grapes is set aside for Zuani Riserva, which is aged in wood, while Zuani Vigne is produced in stainless steel. Usually, when a wine is good, it is of little importance what grapes it has been produced with, and this does not need to be specified on the label. For the curious, in this case, half the blend is made up of friulano and chardonnay, with other varieties completing the picture. The delightful Zuani Vigne 2015 is fragrant and lively, and shows good progression.

○ Collio Bianco Zuani Vigne '15	�� 4
○ Collio Bianco Zuani Ris. '13	�� 5
○ Collio Bianco Zuani Vigne '10	��� 3
○ Collio Bianco Zuani Vigne '07	��� 3
○ Collio Bianco Zuani '08	�� 5
○ Collio Bianco Zuani '07	�� 5
○ Collio Bianco Zuani Ris. '12	�� 5
○ Collio Bianco Zuani Ris. '11	�� 5
○ Collio Bianco Zuani Ris. '10	�� 5
○ Collio Bianco Zuani Ris. '09	�� 5
○ Collio Bianco Zuani Vigne '14	�� 4
○ Collio Bianco Zuani Vigne '13	�� 4
○ Collio Bianco Zuani Vigne '12	�� 3*
○ Collio Bianco Zuani Vigne '11	�� 3
○ Collio Bianco Zuani Vigne '09	�� 3
○ Collio Bianco Zuani Vigne '08	�� 3*

Anzelin

VIA PLESSIVA, 4
34071 CORMÒNS [GO]
TEL. +39 0481639821
www.anzelin.it

CELLAR SALES
PRE-BOOKED VISITS
ANNUAL PRODUCTION 24,000 bottles
HECTARES UNDER VINE 9.00

○ Collio Pinot Bianco '15	♟♟ 3*
○ Collio Pinot Grigio '15	♟♟ 3
○ Collio Sauvignon '15	♟♟ 3
○ Collio Friulano '15	♟ 3

Maurizio Arzenton

FRAZ. SPESSA
VIA CORMONS, 221
33043 CIVIDALE DEL FRIULI [UD]
TEL. +39 0432716139
www.arzentonvini.it

CELLAR SALES
PRE-BOOKED VISITS
ANNUAL PRODUCTION 30,000 bottles
HECTARES UNDER VINE 10.00

○ FCO Friulano '15	♟♟ 2*
○ FCO Pinot Grigio '15	♟♟ 2*
○ FCO Sauvignon '15	♟♟ 3
○ FCO Chardonnay '15	♟ 2

Attems

FRAZ. CAPRIVA DEL FRIULI
VIA AQUILEIA, 30
34070 GORIZIA
TEL. +39 0481806098
www.attems.it

CELLAR SALES
PRE-BOOKED VISITS
ANNUAL PRODUCTION 420,000 bottles
HECTARES UNDER VINE 44.00

○ Chardonnay '15	♟♟ 3
○ Collio Friulano '15	♟♟ 3
○ Collio Sauvignon Blanc Cicinis '14	♟♟ 5
○ Pinot Grigio '15	♟ 3

La Bellanotte

S.DA DELLA BELLANOTTE, 3
34072 FARRA D'ISONZO [GO]
TEL. +39 0481888020
www.labellanotte.it

CELLAR SALES
PRE-BOOKED VISITS
ANNUAL PRODUCTION 100,000 bottles
HECTARES UNDER VINE 12.00
SUSTAINABLE WINERY

○ Bianco Armonico '14	♟♟ 2*
○ Collio Pinot Grigio '15	♟♟ 3
○ Friuli Isonzo Bianco Luna de Ronchi '15	♟♟ 3
○ Vento dell'Est	♟♟ 8

Tenuta di Blasig

VIA ROMA, 63
34077 RONCHI DEI LEGIONARI [GO]
TEL. +39 0481475480
www.tenutadiblasig.it

CELLAR SALES
PRE-BOOKED VISITS
RESTAURANT SERVICE
ANNUAL PRODUCTION 120,000 bottles
HECTARES UNDER VINE 16.00

● Friuli Isonzo Merlot '13	♟♟ 3
○ Friuli Isonzo Pinot Grigio '15	♟♟ 3
● Friuli Isonzo Refosco P. R. '14	♟♟ 3
● Friuli Isonzo Refosco P. R. Affreschi '13	♟♟ 3

Blason

LOC. BRUMA
VIA ROMA, 32
34072 GRADISCA D'ISONZO [GO]
TEL. +39 048192414
www.blasonwines.com

CELLAR SALES
PRE-BOOKED VISITS
ANNUAL PRODUCTION 60,000 bottles
HECTARES UNDER VINE 18.00

● Cabernet Sauvignon '15	♟♟ 3
○ Friuli Isonzo Friulano '15	♟♟ 2*
○ Ribolla Gialla '15	♟♟ 2*

Blazic

LOC. ZEGLA, 16
34071 CORMÒNS [GO]
TEL. +39 048161720
www.blazic.it

CELLAR SALES
PRE-BOOKED VISITS
ANNUAL PRODUCTION 20,000 bottles
HECTARES UNDER VINE 6.50

○ Collio Friulano '15	♙♙ 3*
○ Collio Malvasia '15	♙♙ 3
○ Collio Pinot Grigio '15	♙ 3
○ Collio Ribolla Gialla '15	♙ 3

Tenuta Borgo Conventi

S.DA DELLA COLOMBARA, 13
24070 FARRA D'ISONZO [GO]
TEL. +39 0481888004
www.borgoconventi.it

CELLAR SALES
PRE-BOOKED VISITS
ANNUAL PRODUCTION 350,000 bottles
HECTARES UNDER VINE 40.00

○ Collio Friulano '15	♙♙ 3
○ Collio Ribolla Gialla '15	♙♙ 3
○ Collio Sauvignon '15	♙♙ 3
○ Friuli Isonzo Chardonnay '15	♙♙ 2*

Borgo Judrio - Cornium

VIA AQUILEIA, 79
33040 CORNO DI ROSAZZO [UD]
TEL. +39 0432755896
www.viniborgojudrio.it

CELLAR SALES
PRE-BOOKED VISITS
ANNUAL PRODUCTION 20,000 bottles
HECTARES UNDER VINE 12.00

○ FCO Friulano '15	♙♙ 2*
○ FCO Sauvignon '15	♙♙ 2*
● FCO Merlot '15	♙ 2
○ FCO Ribolla Gialla '15	♙ 2

Borgo Magredo

LOC. TAURIANO
VIA BASALDELLA, 5
33090 SPILIMBERGO [PN]
TEL. +39 0422864511
www.borgomagredo.it

CELLAR SALES
PRE-BOOKED VISITS
ANNUAL PRODUCTION 45,000 bottles
HECTARES UNDER VINE 105.00
SUSTAINABLE WINERY

● Friuli Grave Cabernet Sauvignon '15	♙ 2
○ Friuli Grave Pinot Grigio '15	♙ 2
● Friuli Grave Refosco P. R. '15	♙ 2
○ Friuli Grave Sauvignon '15	♙ 2

Ca' Ronesca

FRAZ. LONZANO
VIA CASALI ZORUTTI, 2
34070 DOLEGNA DEL COLLIO [GO]
TEL. +39 048160034
www.caronesca.it

CELLAR SALES
PRE-BOOKED VISITS
ANNUAL PRODUCTION 250,000 bottles
HECTARES UNDER VINE 55.00

○ Collio Bianco Marnà '12	♙♙ 4
○ Collio Friulano '15	♙♙ 3
○ Collio Pinot Grigio '15	♙♙ 3
○ Collio Sauvignon '15	♙ 3

Cantarutti

VIA RONCHI, 9
33048 SAN GIOVANNI AL NATISONE [UD]
TEL. +39 0432756317
www.cantaruttialfieri.it

CELLAR SALES
PRE-BOOKED VISITS
ACCOMMODATION AND RESTAURANT SERVICE
ANNUAL PRODUCTION 110,000 bottles
HECTARES UNDER VINE 54.00

○ FCO Bianco Canto '14	♙♙ 2*
○ FCO Pinot Grigio '15	♙♙ 2*
○ FCO Sauvignon '15	♙♙ 3
⊙ Prologo Brut Rosé '06	♙♙ 4

I Clivi

LOC. GRAMOGLIANO 20
33040 CORNO DI ROSAZZO [UD]
TEL. +39 3287269979
www.clivi.it

CELLAR SALES
PRE-BOOKED VISITS
ANNUAL PRODUCTION 50,000 bottles
HECTARES UNDER VINE 12.00
VITICULTURE METHOD Certified Organic

○ FCO Bianco Clivi Galea '14	🍷🍷 4
○ Collio Friulano Clivi Brazan '14	🍷🍷 4
○ Collio Malvasia 80 Anni '15	🍷🍷 4
○ FCO Friulano San Pietro '15	🍷🍷 3

Colli di Poianis

VIA POIANIS, 34A
33040 PREPOTTO [UD]
TEL. +39 0432713185
www.collidipoianis.it

CELLAR SALES
PRE-BOOKED VISITS
ACCOMMODATION
ANNUAL PRODUCTION 50,000 bottles
HECTARES UNDER VINE 11.00
SUSTAINABLE WINERY

○ FCO Friulano '15	🍷🍷 3
○ FCO Malvasia '15	🍷🍷 3
○ FCO Pinot Grigio '15	🍷🍷 3
● FCO Schioppettino di Prepotto '13	🍷🍷 5

Tenuta Conte Romano

VIA DELLE PRIMULE, 12
33044 MANZANO [UD]
TEL. +39 0432755339
info@tenutaconteromano.it

PRE-BOOKED VISITS
ANNUAL PRODUCTION 40,000 bottles
HECTARES UNDER VINE 10.00

○ FCO Friulano '15	🍷🍷 3
○ FCO Malvasia '15	🍷🍷 3
○ FCO Sauvignon '15	🍷🍷 2*

Viticoltori Friulani La Delizia

VIA UDINE, 24
33072 CASARSA DELLA DELIZIA [PN]
TEL. +39 0434869564
www.ladelizia.com

CELLAR SALES
PRE-BOOKED VISITS
ANNUAL PRODUCTION 16,000,000 bottles
HECTARES UNDER VINE 1,950.00

● Friuli Grave Merlot Sass Ter' '15	🍷🍷 2*
○ Friuli Grave Pinot Grigio Sass Ter' '15	🍷🍷 2*
○ Jadèr Cuvée Brut	🍷🍷 2*
○ Ribolla Gialla Brut	🍷🍷 2*

Le Due Torri

LOC. VICINALE DEL JUDRIO
VIA SAN MARTINO, 19
33040 CORNO DI ROSAZZO [UD]
TEL. +39 0432759150
www.le2torri.com

CELLAR SALES
PRE-BOOKED VISITS
ANNUAL PRODUCTION 36,000 bottles
HECTARES UNDER VINE 7.60

● Cabernet Sauvignon '13	🍷🍷 2*
○ Friuli Grave Friulano '15	🍷🍷 2*
○ Ribolla Gialla '15	🍷🍷 2*
○ Friuli Grave Sauvignon '15	🍷 2

Le Favole

LOC. TERRA ROSSA
VIA DIETRO CASTELLO, 7
33077 CANEVA [PN]
TEL. +39 0434735604
www.lefavole-wines.com

CELLAR SALES
PRE-BOOKED VISITS
ACCOMMODATION
ANNUAL PRODUCTION 70,000 bottles
HECTARES UNDER VINE 20.00

○ Friuli Annia Pinot Grigio '15	🍷🍷 2*
○ Friuli Annia Traminer Aromatico '15	🍷🍷 2*
○ Giallo di Roccia Brut	🍷🍷 4
○ Friuli Annia Friulano '15	🍷 2

Fedele Giacomo

LOC. GRAMOGLIANO, 5
33040 CORNO DI ROSAZZO [UD]
TEL. +39 3406078929
fedele.giacomo@alice.it

CELLAR SALES
PRE-BOOKED VISITS
HECTARES UNDER VINE 18.50

● FCO Cabernet Franc '14	♟♟ 2*
● FCO Refosco P.R. '13	♟♟ 2*
○ FCO Sauvignon '14	♟♟ 2*
○ Ribolla Gialla '14	♟ 2

I Feudi di Romans

FRAZ. PIERIS
VIA CÀ DEL BOSCO, 16
34075 SAN CANZIAN D'ISONZO [GO]
TEL. +39 048176445
www.ifeudidiromans.it

CELLAR SALES
ANNUAL PRODUCTION 500,000 bottles
HECTARES UNDER VINE 90.00

● Friuli Isonzo Cabernet Franc '14	♟♟ 3
○ Friuli Isonzo Friulano '15	♟♟ 3
● Friuli Isonzo Refosco P.R. '14	♟♟ 3
○ Malvasia Istriana '15	♟ 2

Foffani

FRAZ. CLAUIANO
P.ZZA GIULIA, 13
33050 TRIVIGNANO UDINESE [UD]
TEL. +39 0432999584
www.foffani.com

CELLAR SALES
PRE-BOOKED VISITS
ACCOMMODATION AND RESTAURANT SERVICE
ANNUAL PRODUCTION 80,000 bottles
HECTARES UNDER VINE 10.00
SUSTAINABLE WINERY

○ Friuli Aquileia Friulano TerVinum '15	♟♟ 3
● Friuli Aquileia Refosco P. R. TerVinum '12	♟♟ 3
○ Friuli Sauvignon '15	♟ 2
○ Merlot Bianco '15	♟ 3

Fossa Mala

VIA BASSI, 81
33080 FIUME VENETO [PN]
TEL. +39 0434957997
www.fossamala.it

CELLAR SALES
PRE-BOOKED VISITS
ACCOMMODATION AND RESTAURANT SERVICE
ANNUAL PRODUCTION 130,000 bottles
HECTARES UNDER VINE 37.00

○ Friuli Grave Friulano '15	♟♟ 2*
● Friuli Grave Merlot '13	♟♟ 2*
○ Friuli Grave Traminer Aromatico '15	♟♟ 2*
○ Friuli Grave Chardonnay '15	♟ 2

Albano Guerra

LOC. MONTINA
V.LE KENNEDY, 39A
33040 TORREANO [UD]
TEL. +39 0432715479
www.guerraalbano.it

CELLAR SALES
PRE-BOOKED VISITS
ANNUAL PRODUCTION 60,000 bottles
HECTARES UNDER VINE 10.00

○ FCO Friulano '15	♟♟ 2*
○ FCO Malvasia '15	♟♟ 2*
● FCO Merlot '11	♟♟ 2*
○ FCO Sauvignon '15	♟♟ 2*

Humar

LOC. VALERISCE, 20
34070 SAN FLORIANO DEL COLLIO [GO]
TEL. +39 0481884197
www.humar.it

CELLAR SALES
PRE-BOOKED VISITS
ANNUAL PRODUCTION 60,000 bottles
HECTARES UNDER VINE 12.00

○ Collio Friulano '15	♟♟ 3
○ Collio Pinot Grigio '15	♟♟ 3
○ Collio Ribolla Gialla '15	♟♟ 3
○ Collio Sauvignon '15	♟ 2

Isola Augusta

Casali Isola Augusta, 4
33056 Palazzolo dello Stella [UD]
Tel. +39 043158046
www.isolaugusta.com

CELLAR SALES
PRE-BOOKED VISITS
ACCOMMODATION AND RESTAURANT SERVICE
ANNUAL PRODUCTION 270,000 bottles
HECTARES UNDER VINE 65.00
SUSTAINABLE WINERY

○ Chardì Extra Brut	♟3
○ Friuli Latisana Chardonnay '15	♟2
○ Friuli Latisana Sauvignon '15	♟2
○ Prosecco Brut '15	♟3

Job

fraz. Coia
via Coia di Levante, 26
33017 Tarcento [UD]
Tel. +39 0432783226
job.agricoltura@gmail.com

CELLAR SALES
PRE-BOOKED VISITS
ACCOMMODATION
ANNUAL PRODUCTION 3,000 bottles
HECTARES UNDER VINE 1.00

● FCO Refosco P. R. '09	♟♟3
○ Ramandolo '09	♟♟3
○ Ramandolo '06	♟♟3

Rado Kocjancic

fraz. Dolina
via Dolina, 528
34018 San Dorligo della Valle [TS]
Tel. +39 3483063298
www.radokocjancic.eu

CELLAR SALES
PRE-BOOKED VISITS
ANNUAL PRODUCTION 15,000 bottles
HECTARES UNDER VINE 5.00

○ Carso Malvasia '15	♟♟2*
○ Vitovska '15	♟♟3

Modeano

via Casali Modeano, 1
33056 Palazzolo dello Stella [UD]
Tel. +39 043158244
www.modeano.it

CELLAR SALES
PRE-BOOKED VISITS
ANNUAL PRODUCTION 40,000 bottles
HECTARES UNDER VINE 31.00

● Friuli Latisana Cabernet Sauvignon '13	♟♟2*
● Friuli Latisana Refosco P. R. '13	♟♟2*
○ Friuli Latisana Chardonnay '15	♟2
○ Pinot Grigio '15	♟2

Mulino delle Tolle

fraz. Sevegliano
via Mulino delle Tolle, 15
33050 Bagnaria Arsa [UD]
Tel. +39 0432924723
www.mulinodelletolle.it

CELLAR SALES
PRE-BOOKED VISITS
ACCOMMODATION AND RESTAURANT SERVICE
ANNUAL PRODUCTION 100,000 bottles
HECTARES UNDER VINE 22.00

○ Friuli Aquileia Chardonnay '15	♟♟3
○ Friuli Aquileia Malvasia '15	♟♟3
● Friuli Aquileia Rosso Sabellius '13	♟♟3

Obiz

b.go Gortani, 2
33052 Cervignano del Friuli [UD]
Tel. +39 043131900
www.obiz.it

CELLAR SALES
ANNUAL PRODUCTION 100,000 bottles
HECTARES UNDER VINE 25.00

● Friuli Aquileia Cabernet Franc Cromazio '15	♟♟2*
● Friuli Aquileia Refosco P.R. Teodoro '14	♟♟2*
○ Friuli Aquileia Friulano Tampia '15	♟2

Parovel

LOC. CARESANA, 81
34018 SAN DORLIGO DELLA VALLE [TS]
TEL. +39 040227050
www.parovel.com

ANNUAL PRODUCTION 35,000 bottles
HECTARES UNDER VINE 11.00
SUSTAINABLE WINERY

○ Matos Nonet '12	♥♥ 6
○ Carso Malvasia Poje '14	♥♥ 5
○ Carso Vitovska Onavè '13	♥♥ 5
● Terrano Hodì '14	♥♥ 4

Norina Pez

VIA ZORUTTI, 4
34070 DOLEGNA DEL COLLIO [GO]
TEL. +39 0481639951
www.norinapez.it

CELLAR SALES
PRE-BOOKED VISITS
ANNUAL PRODUCTION 40,000 bottles
HECTARES UNDER VINE 7.00

○ Collio Friulano '15	♥♥ 2*
● Collio Merlot '13	♥♥ 2*
● Schioppettino '13	♥♥ 3
○ Collio Sauvignon '15	♥ 2

Pighin

FRAZ. RISANO
V.LE GRADO, 11/1
33050 PAVIA DI UDINE [UD]
TEL. +39 0432675444
www.pighin.com

CELLAR SALES
PRE-BOOKED VISITS
ANNUAL PRODUCTION 1,000,000 bottles
HECTARES UNDER VINE 180.00

○ Collio Malvasia '15	♥♥ 3
○ Collio Pinot Grigio '15	♥♥ 5
○ Friuli Grave Risano '15	♥♥ 4
○ Collio Friulano '15	♥ 5

Tenuta Pinni

VIA SANT'OSVALDO, 3
33098 SAN MARTINO AL TAGLIAMENTO [PN]
TEL. +39 0434899464
www.tenutapinni.com

CELLAR SALES
PRE-BOOKED VISITS
ANNUAL PRODUCTION 30,000 bottles
HECTARES UNDER VINE 23.55
SUSTAINABLE WINERY

○ Pinot Grigio '15	♥♥ 2*
○ Sauvignon '15	♥♥ 2*
○ Traminer Aromatico '15	♥♥ 2*
○ Friuli Grave Friulano '15	♥ 2

Pitars

VIA TONELLO, 10
33098 SAN MARTINO AL TAGLIAMENTO [PN]
TEL. +39 043488078
www.pitars.it

CELLAR SALES
PRE-BOOKED VISITS
ANNUAL PRODUCTION 250,000 bottles
HECTARES UNDER VINE 125.00
SUSTAINABLE WINERY

● Friuli Grave Cabernet Franc '14	♥♥ 2*
● Friuli Grave Merlot '14	♥♥ 2*
○ Friuli Grave Pinot Grigio '15	♥♥ 2*
○ Malvasia '15	♥♥ 2*

La Ponca

LOC. SCRIÒ, 3
34070 DOLEGNA DEL COLLIO [GO]
TEL. +39 048162396
www.laponca.it

CELLAR SALES
PRE-BOOKED VISITS
ANNUAL PRODUCTION 24,000 bottles
HECTARES UNDER VINE 10.00

○ Collio Friulano '15	♥♥ 3
○ Collio Malvasia '15	♥♥ 3
○ Collio Sauvignon '15	♥♥ 3
● Schioppettino '13	♥♥ 3

Flavio Pontoni

VIA PERUZZI, 8
33042 BUTTRIO [UD]
TEL. +39 0432674352
www.pontoni.it

CELLAR SALES
PRE-BOOKED VISITS
ACCOMMODATION
ANNUAL PRODUCTION 30,000 bottles
HECTARES UNDER VINE 4.50

○ FCO Chardonnay '15	♟♟ 2*
○ FCO Malvasia '15	♟♟ 2*
○ FCO Pinot Grigio '15	♟♟ 2*
● FCO Cabernet Franc '15	♟ 2

Pradio

FRAZ. FELETTIS
VIA UDINE, 17
33050 BICINICCO [UD]
TEL. +39 0432990123
www.pradio.it

CELLAR SALES
PRE-BOOKED VISITS
ANNUAL PRODUCTION 300,000 bottles
HECTARES UNDER VINE 33.00

○ Friuli Grave Friulano Gaiare '15	♟♟ 2*
○ Friuli Grave Pinot Grigio Priara '15	♟♟ 2*
● Friuli Grave Refosco P. R. Tuaro '14	♟♟ 2*
○ Friuli Grave Sauvignon Sobaja '15	♟♟ 2*

Reguta

VIA BASSI, 16
33050 POCENIA [UD]
TEL. +39 0432779157
www.giuseppeeluigivini.it

CELLAR SALES
PRE-BOOKED VISITS
ANNUAL PRODUCTION 2,000,000 bottles
HECTARES UNDER VINE 240.00

● Altropasso '14	♟♟ 3
● Collio Cabernet Sauvignon '15	♟♟ 3
○ Collio Friulano '15	♟♟ 3
○ Collio Chardonnay '15	♟ 3

Ronco dei Pini

VIA RONCHI, 93
33040 PREPOTTO [UD]
TEL. +39 0432713239
www.roncodeipini.it

CELLAR SALES
PRE-BOOKED VISITS
ANNUAL PRODUCTION 90,000 bottles
HECTARES UNDER VINE 15.00

○ Biglia '15	♟♟ 3
○ FCO Pinot Grigio '15	♟♟ 3
○ FCO Sauvignon '15	♟♟ 5
● FCO Schiopettino di Prepotto '12	♟♟ 5

Ronco Margherita

LOC. PINZANO AL TAGLIAMENTO
VIA XX SETTEMBRE, 106
33094 PINZANO AL TAGLIAMENTO [PN]
TEL. +39 0432950845
www.roncomargherita.it

CELLAR SALES
PRE-BOOKED VISITS
ANNUAL PRODUCTION 100,000 bottles
HECTARES UNDER VINE 40.00

○ FCO Chardonnay '15	♟♟ 3
○ FCO Friulano '15	♟♟ 3
○ FCO Picolit '13	♟♟ 5
○ FCO Ribolla Gialla '15	♟♟ 3

Ronco Scagnet

LOC. CIME DI DOLEGNA, 7
34070 DOLEGNA DEL COLLIO [GO]
TEL. +39 0481639870
www.roncoscagnet.it

CELLAR SALES
PRE-BOOKED VISITS
ANNUAL PRODUCTION 80,000 bottles
HECTARES UNDER VINE 10.00

○ Collio Pinot Grigio '15	♟♟ 2*
○ Collio Ribolla Gialla '15	♟♟ 2*
○ Collio Sauvignon '15	♟♟ 2*
○ Raggio di Sole '15	♟♟ 2*

Russolo

VIA SAN ROCCO, 58A
33080 SAN QUIRINO [PN]
TEL. +39 0434919577
www.russolo.it

CELLAR SALES
PRE-BOOKED VISITS
ANNUAL PRODUCTION 165,000 bottles
HECTARES UNDER VINE 16.00
SUSTAINABLE WINERY

● Borgo di Peuma '12	♥♥ 5
○ Doi Raps '15	♥♥ 3
● Refosco P. R. '13	♥♥ 3
○ Sauvignon Ronco Calaj '15	♥♥ 3

San Simone

LOC. RONDOVER
VIA PRATA, 30
33080 PORCIA [PN]
TEL. +39 0434578633
www.sansimone.it

CELLAR SALES
PRE-BOOKED VISITS
ANNUAL PRODUCTION 900,000 bottles
HECTARES UNDER VINE 85.00
SUSTAINABLE WINERY

● Friuli Grave Cabernet Sauvignon Nexus '11	♥♥ 3
○ Friuli Grave Friulano Case Sugan '15	♥♥ 2*
○ Friuli Grave Sauvignon '15	♥♥ 2*

Scarbolo

FRAZ. LAUZACCO
V.LE GRADO, 4
33050 PAVIA DI UDINE [UD]
TEL. +39 0432675612
www.scarbolo.com

CELLAR SALES
PRE-BOOKED VISITS
RESTAURANT SERVICE
ANNUAL PRODUCTION 160,000 bottles
HECTARES UNDER VINE 30.00

○ Bianco My Time '13	♥♥ 4
● Friuli Grave Merlot '14	♥♥ 3
○ Pinot Grigio Ramato XL '13	♥♥ 4
● Refosco dal P. R. '12	♥♥ 4

Scolaris

VIA BOSCHETTO, 4
34070 SAN LORENZO ISONTINO [GO]
TEL. +39 0481809920
www.scolaris.it

CELLAR SALES
PRE-BOOKED VISITS
ANNUAL PRODUCTION 600,000 bottles
HECTARES UNDER VINE 20.00
SUSTAINABLE WINERY

○ Collio Friulano '15	♥♥ 3
○ Collio Malvasia '14	♥♥ 3
○ Collio Sauvignon '15	♥ 3

F.lli Stanig

VIA ALBANA, 44
33040 PREPOTTO [UD]
TEL. +39 0432713234
www.stanig.it

CELLAR SALES
ACCOMMODATION AND RESTAURANT SERVICE
ANNUAL PRODUCTION 45,000 bottles
HECTARES UNDER VINE 9.00

● FCO Schioppettino di Prepotto '13	♥♥ 3*
○ FCO Friulano '15	♥♥ 3
● FCO Rosso del Gelso '11	♥ 4
○ FCO Sauvignon '15	♥ 3

Stocco

VIA CASALI STOCCO, 12
33050 BICINICCO [UD]
TEL. +39 0432934906
www.vinistocco.it

CELLAR SALES
PRE-BOOKED VISITS
RESTAURANT SERVICE
ANNUAL PRODUCTION 150,000 bottles
HECTARES UNDER VINE 44.20

● Cabernet Franc '14	♥♥ 2*
○ Pinot Grigio '15	♥♥ 2*
○ Pinot Grigio Ramato '15	♥♥ 2*
○ Ribolla Gialla '15	♥ 2

Tarlao

VIA SAN ZILI, 41
33051 AQUILEIA [UD]
TEL. +39 043191417
www.tarlao.eu

CELLAR SALES
PRE-BOOKED VISITS
ANNUAL PRODUCTION 18,000 bottles
HECTARES UNDER VINE 5.00

○ Friuli Aquileia Malvasia '15	🍷🍷 3
○ Friuli Aquileia Pinot Bianco Poc ma Bon '15	🍷🍷 3
● Friuli Aquileia Refosco P. R. Mosaic Ros '12	🍷🍷 3

Terre del Faet

V.LE ROMA, 82
34071 CORMÒNS [GO]
TEL. +39 3470103325
www.terredelfaet.it

PRE-BOOKED VISITS
ANNUAL PRODUCTION 1,000 bottles
HECTARES UNDER VINE 3.00

○ Collio Friulano '15	🍷🍷 3
○ Collio Friulano Sel. '14	🍷🍷 3

Terre di Ger

FRAZ. FRATTINA
S.DA DELLA MEDUNA, 17
33076 PRAVISDOMINI [PN]
TEL. +39 0434644452
www.terrediger.it

CELLAR SALES
PRE-BOOKED VISITS
ANNUAL PRODUCTION 100,000 bottles
HECTARES UNDER VINE 50.00

○ Limine '13	🍷🍷 3*
○ Brut M. Cl.	🍷🍷 4
○ Friuli Grave Chardonnay '15	🍷🍷 2*
○ Sauvignon Blanc '15	🍷 3

Vicentini Orgnani

LOC. VALERIANO
VIA SOTTOPLOVIA, 4A
33094 PINZANO AL TAGLIAMENTO [PN]
TEL. +39 0432950107
www.vicentiniorgnani.it

CELLAR SALES
PRE-BOOKED VISITS
ANNUAL PRODUCTION 50,000 bottles
HECTARES UNDER VINE 18.00
SUSTAINABLE WINERY

● Cabernet Sauvignon '12	🍷🍷 2*
● Merlot '12	🍷🍷 3
○ Pinot Grigio '14	🍷🍷 2*
● Cabernet Franc '12	🍷 2

Villa Parens

VIA DANTE, 69
34072 FARRA D'ISONZO [GO]
TEL. +39 0481888198
www.villaparens.com

CELLAR SALES
PRE-BOOKED VISITS
ANNUAL PRODUCTION 50,000 bottles
HECTARES UNDER VINE 6.00

● Blanc de Blancs Extra Brut	🍷🍷 5
⊙ Rosé de Noirs Dosage Zero '13	🍷🍷 5
● Pinot Nero '15	🍷 3
○ Ribolla Gialla '15	🍷 3

Zaglia

LOC. FRASSINUTTI
VIA CRESCENZIA, 10
33050 PRECENICCO [UD]
TEL. +39 0431510320
www.zaglia.com

CELLAR SALES
PRE-BOOKED VISITS
ANNUAL PRODUCTION 100,000 bottles
HECTARES UNDER VINE 15.00

● Friuli Latisana Cabernet Franc V. degli Amanti Ris. '10	🍷🍷 2*
○ Friuli Latisana Pinot Grigio '15	🍷🍷 2*
● Friuli Latisana Refosco P. R. '14	🍷🍷 2*

EMILIA ROMAGNA

For 2,200 years, Via Emilia has connected Rimini to Piacenza, across the amazing variety of regional growing areas, and in many ways all these terroirs are not completely understood. Starting from the north, the first is the Colli Piacentini, a complex system of valleys and districts that could deliver much in terms of quality and character. Sadly the road of territorial identity is still a dream and the area stays afloat thanks to correct wines lacking personality. Next, we reach the world of Lambrusco, a growing area in which enthusiasm and energy abound, especially in the de facto capital of Modena, represented by a hotbed of artisans, cooperatives and large private wineries in practice covering the whole supply chain. A reality in which each plays their role and contributes to raising the quality of the wines but, above all, developing a narrative that is increasingly clear and legible to the onlooker. The process is positive and is really widening the gap between those who choose to work towards quality wines with strong identity, and those who continue along the path of sweet, soft standards. From a quality perspective, Sorbara and Metodo Classico are the most centred. The Colli Bolognesi district has taken up the gauntlet of the new Pignoletto designation and, with teamwork, is finally defining the conditions that will give voice to a growing area of incredible potential for minerality and freshness. The last leg of the journey is Romagna, with its 150 km of valleys and diversity, a heritage nicely expressed in recent years by the subzones falling within the Sangiovese di Romagna designation. Romagna is in a transitional phase that is redrafting quality boundaries. The venerable wineries are struggling to interpret Sangiovese in a modern style as a fresh, territorial wine, and are stuck in the rut of over-rich, over-alcoholic riservas, dragged down by long ageing in small ovals. The Superiore, however, seems to be offering better freshness, quality and longevity. To close, we want to mention albana, the white grape with great potential and distinctive identity. Rather than exploiting its acidity, Romagna's growers are seeking to draw out its richness with super ripening and small top-ups of the raisined wine. A stylistic notion that is encountering some consensus in the district but hinders these wines from playing the role that will give them a reputation on markets outside the region and outside of Italy. The Tre Bicchieri for Celli's I Croppi 2015, one of the few makers looking for freshness and drinkability, is therefore an invitation to head down this path for albana.

Agrintesa

VIA G. GALILEI, 15
48018 FAENZA [RA]
TEL. +39 059952511
www.agrintesa.it

ANNUAL PRODUCTION 350,000 bottles
HECTARES UNDER VINE 44.00

The Agrintesa cooperative's project of producing quality wines hinges on a small group of members in the Modigliana area. The vinification facility, in Valle del Marzeno, near the town of Modigliana, is thus provided with extraordinary grapes from the highest land in Romagna. The manager, Elisa Muccinelli, has given free rein to the capable young oenologist Nicola Zoli, and the results are already surprising. Their new way of conceiving wine, paying great attention to territory, makes them one of the most interesting operations in Romagna. The Sangiovese 2015 has character and finesse, with a vertical, austere nose over a salty, taut palate, in the vibrant, elegant style of this growing area. The dry Superiore 2015 has impressive stuffing, with beautifully focused pomegranate fruit, for a composed, austere, full-flavoured, razor-sharp wine. The Albana 2015 relies on thrusting acidity to provide progression and length.

● Romagna Sangiovese Poderi delle Rose '15	▼▼ 2*
○ Albana di Romagna Secco Poderi delle Rose '15	▼▼ 2*
● Romagna Sangiovese Sup. Poderi delle Rose '15	▼▼ 2*
○ Albana di Romagna Secco I Calanchi Loveria '12	♀♀ 2*
○ Albana di Romagna Secco I Calanchi Spighea '14	♀♀ 2*
○ Albana di Romagna Secco Poderi delle Rose '15	♀♀ 2*
● Romagna Sangiovese Poderi delle Rose '15	♀♀ 2*
● Romagna Sangiovese Sup. Poderi delle Rose '15	♀♀ 2*

Ancarani

VIA SAN BIAGIO ANTICO, 14
48018 FAENZA [RA]
TEL. +39 0546642162
www.viniancarani.it

CELLAR SALES
PRE-BOOKED VISITS
RESTAURANT SERVICE
ANNUAL PRODUCTION 30,000 bottles
HECTARES UNDER VINE 14.00

Claudio Ancarani, now joined by his wife Rita Babini, has vineyards near Torre di Oriolo, a small zone which is making a name for itself as perfect wine country for albana and the rare native variety centesimino. The labels are classic and traditional, although the winery is gradually shedding excessive richness for lighter wines, and a fresher, more elegant style. The most important wine is as always the Albana Santa Lusa, which combines, power, acidity and the tannins typical of this white variety. The 2014's dense, complex nose has a touch of warmth, followed by a taut, vibrant palate, where acidity gives depth and mineral nuances. The Sangiovese Oriolo 2015 is supple, fresh and peppery, with well-expressed fruit. Uvappesa 2012 embodies the fresher aspects of the variety's aromatic traits, in a nose of roses, orange zest and geraniums, as well as good overall balance.

○ Romagna Albana Secco Santa Lusa '14	▼▼ 3
● Sangiovese di Romagna Oriolo '15	▼▼ 2*
● Sâvignon Rosso Centesimino '15	▼▼ 2*
○ Signore '15	▼▼ 2*
● Uvappesa Centesimino '12	▼▼ 4
○ Albana di Romagna Santa Lusa '11	♀♀ 3
○ Albana di Romagna Santa Lusa '10	♀♀ 3
○ Romagna Albana Secco Santa Lusa '13	♀♀ 3
● Sangiovese di Romagna Oriolo '12	♀♀ 2*
● Sangiovese di Romagna Oriolo '11	♀♀ 2
● Sangiovese di Romagna Sup. Biagio Antico '11	♀♀ 2*
● Sâvignon Rosso '10	♀♀ 3
● Sâvignon Rosso Centesimino '12	♀♀ 3
● Uvappesa '11	♀♀ 4
● Uvappesa '10	♀♀ 4
● Uvappesa '09	♀♀ 4

Balìa di Zola

VIA CASALE, 11
47015 MODIGLIANA [FC]
TEL. +39 0546940577
www.baliadizola.com

CELLAR SALES
PRE-BOOKED VISITS
ANNUAL PRODUCTION 30,000 bottles
HECTARES UNDER VINE 5.00

The lands of the Acerreta valley, in the Modigliana area, produce wines of unique elegance, typical of this subzone, but also with clenched, close-knit tannins which ensure cellarability and complexity. Veruska Eluci and her husband Claudio Fiore arrived in Romagna from Tuscany in 1999 and believed in this territory to the point that in 2003 they invested in a small winery of their own. The vineyards planted back then are now producing at full steam, and the range of labels, reliable across the board, bears witness to their quality. Balitore 2015, from sangiovese topped up with cabernet sauvignon, is a savoury, dynamic wine, with pomegranate fruit, as is typical of the Modigliana area. On the taut, complex palate, freshness and dynamic progression end to citrus notes. The focused, supple Redinoce 2013 combines cool fruit with elegant grassy and peppery notes over a full-bodied, clenched, richly-flavoured palate.

Le Barbaterre

LOC. BERGONZANO
VIA CAVOUR, 2A
42020 QUATTRO CASTELLA [RE]
TEL. +39 0522247573
www.barbaterre.it

CELLAR SALES
PRE-BOOKED VISITS
ACCOMMODATION AND RESTAURANT SERVICE
ANNUAL PRODUCTION 20,000 bottles
HECTARES UNDER VINE 8.00
VITICULTURE METHOD Certified Organic
SUSTAINABLE WINERY

This small yet important artisanal winery in Emilia symbolizes the wine renaissance of the hills around Modena and Reggio Emilia. The limited production is entirely dedicated to sparklers that undergo second fermentation in the bottle, often without disgorgement. Erika Tagliavini farms eight hectares of vineyards on loose soils of silt, clay and marl at an elevation of 350 metres near Val d'Enza, in the hills near Quattro Castella, in the heart of the territory that Matilda of Canossa defended with a series of castles at Pianello, Rossena, Canossa, Sarzano and Carpineti. The graceful Lambrusco 2015 shows earthy, citrus notes over a dry, dynamic palate. The Blanc de Noirs 2010, from pinot nero, is mineral and delicately spicy, fresh and vertical, with a savoury, floral finish. The vibrant, taut Sauvignon 2015 shows a classic repertoire of citrus and mineral notes.

● Romagna Sangiovese Sup. Balitore '15	♟♟ 2*
● Sangiovese di Romagna Sup. Redinoce Ris. '13	♟♟ 4
● Sangiovese di Romagna Redinoce Ris. '09	♟♟♟ 4*
● Sangiovese di Romagna Redinoce Ris. '08	♟♟♟ 4*
● Romagna Sangiovese Modigliana Redinoce Ris. '12	♟♟ 4
● Romagna Sangiovese Sup. Balitore '14	♟♟ 2*
● Sangiovese di Romagna Balitore '10	♟♟ 2*
● Sangiovese di Romagna Balitore '09	♟♟ 2
● Sangiovese di Romagna Balitore '08	♟♟ 2
● Sangiovese di Romagna Redinoce Ris. '11	♟♟ 4
● Sangiovese di Romagna Redinoce Ris. '10	♟♟ 4

○ Blanc de Noirs Brut M. Cl. '10	♟♟ 6
● Lambrusco Rifermentato in Bottiglia '15	♟♟ 3*
⊙ Besmein Capoleg Marzemino Frizzante Rosé Rifermantato in Bottiglia '15	♟♟ 2*
○ Sauvignon Frizzante Rifermentato in Bottiglia '15	♟♟ 3
⊙ Besmein Capoleg Marzemino Frizzante Rosé '12	♟♟ 2*
⊙ Besmein Capoleg Marzemino Frizzante Rosé '11	♟♟ 2*
○ CSC Pinot Nero Spumante L'Orlando Bianco '11	♟♟ 5
● Lambrusco dell'Emilia '13	♟♟ 2*
● Lambrusco dell'Emilia '12	♟♟ 2*
○ Sauvignon Brut M. Cl. '11	♟♟ 3
○ Sauvignon Frizzante '13	♟♟ 3

Francesco Bellei

FRAZ. CRISTO DI SORBARA
VIA NAZIONALE, 132
41030 BOMPORTO [MO]
TEL. +39 059902009
www.francescobellei.it

CELLAR SALES
PRE-BOOKED VISITS
ANNUAL PRODUCTION 70,000 bottles
HECTARES UNDER VINE 5.00

This operation near Modena, with a long tradition of Metodo Classico sparklers, has an ace up its sleeve in the form of the experienced, talented Sandro Cavicchioli, who has been in charge of vinification since 2003. Francesco Bellei's wines show greater focus with each passing year, and their crosses of sorbara and pignoletto, the native grapes of this area, vinified using time-honoured fermentation methods, result in elegant, complex original wines. Sandro Cavicchioli's project envisages the opening of a small winery near Cristo di Sorbara, aimed at attracting visitors and promoting the potential of this incredible territory. The Modena Rifermentazione Ancestrale 2015, a monovarietal Sorbara, is a whirlwind of aromas and surprises, passing from spiced notes of cloves and mace to delicate nuances of bitter orange zest and tangerine. In the mouth, it shows savoury, lean and taut, with impressive grip and finesse. The linear, full-flavoured Rosé 2012 is fresh, nuanced, citrusy and floral.

⊙ Cuvée Brut Rosé M.Cl. '12		♥♥ 5
● Lambrusco di Modena Rifermentazione Ancestrale '15		♥♥ 3*
○ Cuvée Brut M.Cl.		♥♥ 5
● Modena Pignoletto Rifermentazione Ancestrale '15		♥♥ 3
⊙ Cuvée Brut Rosé M.Cl. '11		♀♀ 5
● Lambrusco di Modena Rifermentazione Ancestrale '14		♀♀ 3*
● Lambrusco di Modena Rifermentazione Ancestrale '13		♀♀ 2*
● Lambrusco di Modena Rifermentazione Ancestrale '12		♀♀ 2*
● Modena Pignoletto Rifermentazione Ancestrale '14		♀♀ 3
● Modena Pignoletto Rifermentazione Ancestrale '13		♀♀ 2*

Braschi

VIA ROMA, 37
47025 MERCATO SARACENO [FC]
TEL. +39 054791061
www.cantinabraschi.com

CELLAR SALES
PRE-BOOKED VISITS
ANNUAL PRODUCTION 125,000 bottles
HECTARES UNDER VINE 34.50

Endless ideas, fresh energy and irrepressible enthusiasm are the basis for the renaissance of this historic estate in Romagna's Valle del Savio, established in 1949. The men behind it are Vincenzo Vernocchi, oenologist, and Davide Moky Castagnoli, sales manager, who have been here since 2011. The range of wine shows great focus, and combines basic labels with territorial selections of various cultivars. Their well-made, classic, traditional wines clearly express the various terroirs, from Bertinoro to Valle del Savio. Monte Sasso 2014 is a Sangiovese vinified in large oak, from grapes grown in selected vineyards in Valle del Savio. The elegant, nuanced nose offers aromas of mace and tangerine, leading into a taut, supple, dynamic palate with a long finish. Campo Mamante 2014 is an Albana with two souls, the thrusting, cutting soul expressing the growing year, and another, richer and more candied, which shows the variety's incredible capacity to produce grapes rich in sugars and polyphenols.

○ Albana di Romagna Secco Campo Mamante '14		♥♥ 3
● Sangiovese di Romagna San Vicinio Monte Sasso '14		♥♥ 3
● Sangiovese di Romagna San Vicinio Monte Sasso '12		♀♀♀ 3*
○ Albana di Romagna '12		♀♀ 2*
● Romagna Sangiovese Bertinoro Il Costone Ris. '12		♀♀ 4
● Romagna Sangiovese San Vicinio Monte Sasso '13		♀♀ 3*
● Sangiovese di Romagna Sup. Il Costone '12		♀♀ 3
● Sangiovese di Romagna Sup. Il Costone '11		♀♀ 3
● Sangiovese di Romagna Sup. Il Gelso '13		♀♀ 3

Cantina della Volta

VIA PER MODENA, 82
41030 BOMPORTO [MO]
TEL. +39 0597473312
www.cantinadellavolta.com

CELLAR SALES
PRE-BOOKED VISITS
ANNUAL PRODUCTION 120,000 bottles
HECTARES UNDER VINE 14.00

The confident, talented Christian Bellei is experiencing a period of impressive success, thanks to increasingly focused, elegant wines of high quality and reliability. In addition to sorbara, eight hectares of new vineyards have been planted to pinot nero in the high hills near Modena. Chardonnay, meanwhile, is found on the dark soils of Riccò di Serramazzoni, a small growing area that over the years has proved its worth and consistency in the production of base wines for Metodo Classico sparklers. The subtle, delicate Rosé 2012 is bursting with energy and dynamism. The full, highly nuanced nose paves the way for good progression on the consistent, tangy, citrusy palate, ending with blossom and white-fleshed fruit. The savoury, focused Rimosso 2015 is rustic in the most refined way possible, with delicate aromas of forest fruits and flowers. The lees are evident, but so is great elegance.

⊙ Lambrusco di Modena Brut Rosé M. Cl. '12	♉♉♉ 5
● Lambrusco di Sorbara Secco Rimosso '15	♉♉ 3*
● Lambrusco di Modena Brut M. Cl. Trentasei '12	♉♉ 4
● Lambrusco di Sorbara Rimosso '13	♉♉♉ 3*
● Lambrusco di Sorbara Rimosso '12	♉♉♉ 3*
○ Il Mattaglio Brut M. Cl '11	♉♉ 5
○ La Base Chardonnay Fermo '13	♉♉ 3
● Lambrusco di Modena Brut M. Cl. Trentasei '10	♉♉ 4
⊙ Lambrusco di Modena Brut Rosé M. Cl. '11	♉♉ 5
● Lambrusco di Sorbara Rimosso '10	♉♉ 3*
● Lambrusco di Sorbara Secco Rimosso '14	♉♉ 3*

Cantina Sociale di Carpi e Sorbara

VIA CAVATA
41012 CARPI [MO]
TEL. +39 059 643071
www.cantinadicarpiesorbara.it

HECTARES UNDER VINE 2,300.00

If the Modena viticultural scene is so well-developed in terms of hectares under vine and ability to interpret the terroir, it is because in the early 1900s, sector pioneer Gino Friedman promoted the cooperative winery concept, which preserved and safeguarded local winemaking culture. Today, these wineries control most of the region's viticulture to all intents and purposes, and are starting to bottle their own wine, with increasingly convincing results, both for quality and the possibility to choose from a wide range of raw materials. Now this operation, the merger of two wineries: Carpi and Sorbara, established in 1903 and 1923 respectively, vinifies grapes from 2,300 hectares of vineyards farmed by 1,600 members. The austere, savoury Omaggio a Gino Friedmann Fermentazione in Bottiglia 2015 is lean and citrusy, with tangerine zest to the fore. Omaggio a Gino Friedmann 2015 shows a nose of blossom, apples and pears, followed by a focused, mineral, incisive palate.

● Lambrusco di Sorbara Secco Omaggio a Gino Friedmann '15	♉♉ 3*
● Lambrusco di Sorbara Secco Omaggio a Gino Friedmann FB '15	♉♉ 3*
● Lambrusco di Sorbara Amabile Emma '15	♉♉ 2*
● Lambrusco di Sorbara Secco Villa Badia '15	♉ 2
● Lambrusco di Sorbara Secco Omaggio a Gino Friedmann '13	♉♉♉ 3*
● Lambrusco di Sorbara Secco Omaggio a Gino Friedmann FB '14	♉♉♉ 3*
● Lambrusco di Sorbara Amabile Emma '14	♉♉ 2*
● Lambrusco di Sorbara Secco Le Bolle '14	♉♉ 2*
● Lambrusco di Sorbara Secco Omaggio a Gino Friedmann '14	♉♉ 3*
● Lambrusco Salamino di S. Croce Secco Novecento03 '14	♉♉ 2*

Cavicchioli

VIA CANALETTO, 52
41030 SAN PROSPERO [MO]
TEL. +39 059812412
www.cavicchioli.it

CELLAR SALES
PRE-BOOKED VISITS
ANNUAL PRODUCTION 10,000,000 bottles
HECTARES UNDER VINE 90.00

The extension of the facility and significant investments in production equipment testify to this winery's view of the future, also thanks to a perfect opportunity for growth in the union between the brothers Sandro and Claudio Cavicchioli, and Gruppo Italiano Vini. The wines clearly express this confidence and sense of ambition. The selections of Sorbara are always some of the best in the DOC zone, and the classic labels of the most popular brands such as those in the Tre Medaglie line are always among the most reliable and convincing. The consistent Vigna del Cristo 2015 opens to a floral nose of rose tea, making way for elegant spice and citrus, with tangerine to the fore. The lean, grippy palate is reticent but potent. The complex yet delicate Rosé del Cristo 2012 is reminiscent of a country landscape overlooking the sea, with notes of herbs and hedgerow, ending with nuances of hazelnut and mace.

Caviro

VIA CONVERTITE, 12
48018 FAENZA [RA]
TEL. +39 0546629111
www.caviro.it

CELLAR SALES
ANNUAL PRODUCTION 25,000,000 bottles
HECTARES UNDER VINE 31.00

Caviro brings together 32 co-operatives from eight different regions, which overall vinify the grapes of 12,000 growers, managing a certified production chain that is unique in terms of depth and size. Alongside popular, reliable table wines such as Tavernello, produced by blending wines from all over Italy, there are products from Romagna, which remains the home of this colossus, and it is in these territorial roots that we find the most interesting expressions. Romio Albana 2015 is a wine of character and quality, opening to a well-typed nose of fresh, delicate fruit over a dry, vibrant palate. The Pignoletto Frizzante Romio 2015 opens to an interesting repertoire of herbs, with sage, absinthe and burnet, over a fresh, rounded palate. The full-flavoured, aromatic Trebbiano Terre Forti 2015 shows attractive acidity.

● Lambrusco di Sorbara V. del Cristo '15	♟♟♟ 2*
⊙ Lambrusco di Sorbara Brut Rosé del Cristo M. Cl. '12	♟♟ 4
⊙ Lambrusco di Modena Rosé Extra Dry 1928 '15	♟ 2*
● Lambrusco di Sorbara Tre Medaglie '15	♟♟ 2*
● Lambrusco di Sorbara V. del Cristo '14	♟♟♟ 2*
● Lambrusco di Sorbara V. del Cristo '13	♟♟♟ 2*
● Lambrusco di Sorbara V. del Cristo '12	♟♟♟ 2*
● Lambrusco di Sorbara V. del Cristo '11	♟♟♟ 2*
● Lambrusco di Modena 1928 '14	♟♟ 2*
● Lambrusco di Sorbara Secco Marchio Storico '13	♟♟ 2*
● Lambrusco di Sorbara Tre Medaglie '14	♟♟ 2*
● Lambrusco Grasparossa di Castelvetro Amabile Tre Medaglie '13	♟♟ 2*

○ Pignoletto Frizzante Romio '15	♟♟ 2*
○ Romagna Albana Secco Romio '15	♟♟ 2*
○ Romagna Trebbiano Terre Forti '15	♟♟ 1*
● Romagna Sangiovese Sup. Romio '14	♟ 3
○ Romagna Albana Secco Romio '14	♟♟ 2*
● Romagna Sangiovese Sup. Terragens Ris. '12	♟♟ 4
● Sangiovese di Romagna Brumale '13	♟♟ 2*
● Sangiovese di Romagna Brumale '12	♟♟ 2*
● Sangiovese di Romagna Terre Forti '13	♟♟ 2*
● Sangiovese di Romagna Terre Forti '12	♟♟ 2*

Celli

V.LE CARDUCCI, 5
47032 BERTINORO [FC]
TEL. +39 0543445183
www.celli-vini.com

CELLAR SALES
PRE-BOOKED VISITS
ANNUAL PRODUCTION 280,000 bottles
HECTARES UNDER VINE 30.00

The winery is celebrating 50 years of business and has become a symbol of continuity and history in a territory where still in the 1990s you could count local wineries on the fingers of one hand. The 30 hectares of vineyards, partly owned and partly rented, are all in the territory of Bertinoro on typical limestone soils rich in spungone rock. The Sirri and Casadei families proudly take forward the idea of approachable yet territorial wines with good ageing potential. Even the simpler labels are becoming more interesting year after year. I Croppi 2015 is a benchmark for style, a full-flavoured, dry wine that does not betray Albana's rustic tradition but rather exalts it and brings it into the modern world. Dry, taut and citrusy, it shows a rich palate of great suppleness, with salty, cutting acidity. The Sangiovese Le Grillaie 2015 has upfront fruit and a dynamic peppery note, over a slightly dry but supple, fresh palate.

Umberto Cesari

LOC. CASTEL SAN PIETRO TERME
VIA STANZANO, 1120
40024 CASTEL SAN PIETRO TERME [BO]
TEL. +39 0516947811
www.umbertocesari.it

CELLAR SALES
PRE-BOOKED VISITS
ANNUAL PRODUCTION 3,500,000 bottles
HECTARES UNDER VINE 350.00

In 2014, Umberto Cesari celebrated its 50th harvest. This long success story has seen the winery become the standard-bearer of Romagna on many foreign markets. At the helm there is now Gianmaria, who has inherited his father's entrepreneurial spirit and vision, and who looks to the future with ambitions to focus even more on quality. His wines pursue territorial character in response to increasingly discerning markets. The Liano 2013 shows a spicy nose and ripe, rich fruit, with focused aromas, leading into close-knit tannins on the palate, which is however supple and fresh. The austere, clenched, elegant Riserva 2013 is the winery's most classic, traditional wine, and ages for two years in large Slavonian oak.

○ Romagna Albana Secco I Croppi '15	♛♛♛ 2*
○ Romagna Albana Dolce Le Querce '15	♛♛ 2*
● Romagna Sangiovese Sup. Le Grillaie '15	♛♛ 2*
○ Romagna Pagadebit Campi di Fratta '15	♛ 2
○ Albana di Romagna Dolce Le Querce '12	♛♛ 2*
○ Albana di Romagna Passito Solara '11	♛♛ 4
○ Albana di Romagna Passito Solara '08	♛♛ 3
○ Albana di Romagna Secco I Croppi '13	♛♛ 2*
○ Albana di Romagna Secco I Croppi '12	♛♛ 2*
○ Albana di Romagna Secco I Croppi '10	♛♛ 2*
● Bron & Rusèval Sangiovese '11	♛♛ 3
○ Romagna Albana Dolce Le Querce '14	♛♛ 2*
○ Romagna Albana Secco I Croppi '14	♛♛ 2*
○ Romagna Pagadebit Campi di Fratta '14	♛♛ 2*
● Romagna Sangiovese Sup. Le Grillaie '14	♛♛ 2*
● Sangiovese di Romagna Sup. Le Grillaie '12	♛♛ 2*

● Liano Rosso '13	♛♛ 4
● Romagna Sangiovese Sup. Ris. '13	♛♛ 3
○ Liano Bianco '14	♛ 4
● Moma Rosso '14	♛ 2
● Yemula Rosso '13	♛ 4
● Liano '12	♛♛ 4
● Liano '09	♛♛ 5
● Romagna Sangiovese Sup. Ris. '12	♛♛ 3
● Sangiovese di Romagna Laurento Ris. '10	♛♛ 3
● Sangiovese di Romagna Laurento Ris. '09	♛♛ 3

Cleto Chiarli Tenute Agricole

VIA BELVEDERE, 8
41014 CASTELVETRO DI MODENA [MO]
TEL. +39 0593163311
www.chiarli.it

CELLAR SALES
PRE-BOOKED VISITS
ANNUAL PRODUCTION 900,000 bottles
HECTARES UNDER VINE 100.00

Without the intuition of Cleto Chiarli, the visionary restaurateur at Pomposa in the heart of Modena, the story of Lambrusco would not have been the same. In the mid-1800s, this extraordinary figure began to sell quality bottles of what until then had been a country wine, produced and consumed in homes without the entrepreneurial approach that has since made it one if Italy's most important wines. In harmony with the spirit of this past is Chiarli 1860. Anselmo and Mauro Chiarli established this winery that vinifies solely its own grapes, boosting quality and with it giving the territory new ambitions and a modern view of the market which in the meantime has changed completely. The extremely graceful Fondatore 2015 finds its energy in a subtle, salty body with notes of citrus and blossom. Sic et Simpliciter 2015, from a selection of old clones, is the archetype of what a Grasparossa should be: elegance sustained by acidity and tannins.

● Lambrusco di Sorbara del Fondatore '15	♈♈♈ 3*
● Lambrusco di Sorbara Vecchia Modena Premium '15	♈♈ 2*
● Lambrusco Grasparossa di Castelvetro Vign. Cialdini '15	♈♈ 2*
● Lambrusco Grasparossa di Castelvetro Vign. Cialdini Sic et Simpliciter '15	♈♈ 2*
⊙ Rosé Brut '15	♈♈ 2*
○ Modena Modén Blanc Brut '15	♈ 2
● Lambrusco di Sorbara del Fondatore '14	♈♈♈ 3*
● Lambrusco di Sorbara del Fondatore '12	♈♈♈ 3*
● Lambrusco di Sorbara del Fondatore '11	♈♈♈ 2*
● Lambrusco di Sorbara del Fondatore '09	♈♈♈ 2*
● Lambrusco di Sorbara Vecchia Modena Premium '13	♈♈♈ 2*
● Lambrusco di Sorbara Vecchia Modena Premium '10	♈♈♈ 2*

Condé

LOC. FIUMANA DI PREDAPPIO
VIA LUCCHINA, 27
47016 PREDAPPIO [FC]
TEL. +39 0543940860
www.conde.it

CELLAR SALES
PRE-BOOKED VISITS
ACCOMMODATION AND RESTAURANT SERVICE
ANNUAL PRODUCTION 150,000 bottles
HECTARES UNDER VINE 77.00
SUSTAINABLE WINERY

On one hand this winery can rely on the vision of Francesco Condello and his energy; on the other, on the determination and commitment of his daughter Chiara, who has taken over the agronomic and technical side of the operation. In only a few years, Chiara has revolutionized the winery philosophy, adopting farming methods which fully respect the land. In the cellar, with Tuscan oenologist Federico Staderini, she aims for an elegant, demanding style. This change in direction is supported by the new cellar, which opened in 2014. Predappio Riserva 2012, obtained from a selection of grapes grown in the highest vineyards, is a full, classic wine, with a palate that unfolds with great freshness. The Superiore 2012 is an austere, elegant Sangiovese, with a complex nose of reticent fruit, citrus and herbs. In the mouth it shows attractive freshness and overall grace.

● Romagna Sangiovese Predappio Ris. '12	♈♈ 6
● Romagna Sangiovese Sup. '12	♈♈ 3
● Massera Merlot '12	♈♈ 3
● Romagna Sangiovese Predappio '12	♈♈ 3
● Romagna Sangiovese Predappio Ris. '11	♈♈ 2*
● Sangiovese di Romagna '09	♈♈ 2
● Sangiovese di Romagna Capsula Nera '10	♈♈ 2*
● Sangiovese di Romagna Sup. '11	♈♈ 2*
● Sangiovese di Romagna Sup. '09	♈♈ 2*
● Sangiovese di Romagna Sup. Condè Capsula Blu Ris. '09	♈♈ 5
● Sangiovese di Romagna Sup. Condè Capsula Rossa '10	♈♈ 3
● Sangiovese di Romagna Sup. Ris. '10	♈♈ 2*
● Sangiovese di Romagna Sup. Ris. '08	♈♈ 2*

Leone Conti

loc. Santa Lucia
via Pozzo, 1
48018 Faenza [RA]
Tel. +39 0546642149
www.leoneconti.it

CELLAR SALES
PRE-BOOKED VISITS
ANNUAL PRODUCTION 80,000 bottles
HECTARES UNDER VINE 17.00

Leone Conti, today assisted by his nephew Francesco, was one of the first to believe in the potential of albana, and his wines have always borne witness to this. If it has now been rediscovered and appreciated, especially in dry versions, much of the merit goes to Leone and his Progetto 1, which epitomizes the rebirth of Albana. He has always shown a certain sensitivity towards minor native varieties, as seen by his current interest in centesimino and uva ruggine. Various important wines are missing from this edition of the Guide, but we had the benchmark Albana Progetto 1. The 2015 perfectly expresses the growing year, showing warm, hefty, and complex on the nose. On the palate, it finds energy and typical varietal traits, with a dry finish that evokes the traditional character of this extraordinary native white grape.

○ Romagna Albana Secco La mia Albana Progetto 1 '15	ΨΨ 3
● Romagna Sangiovese Sup. Never Walk Alone '15	Ψ 2
○ Romagna Trebbiano Duit '15	Ψ 2
○ Albana di Romagna Passito Nontiscordardime '07	ΥΥΥ 6
○ Albana di Romagna Secco Progetto 1 '13	ΥΥ 3
○ Albana di Romagna Secco Progetto 1 '12	ΥΥ 3
⊙ Impressioni di Settembre '14	ΥΥ 2*
○ Romagna Albana Secco La mia Albana Progetto 1 '14	ΥΥ 3
● Romagna Sangiovese Sup. Le Betulle '12	ΥΥ 3
● Sangiovese di Romagna Sup. Never Walk Alone '13	ΥΥ 2*
● Sangiovese di Romagna Sup. Never Walk Alone '12	ΥΥ 2*

Costa Archi

loc. Serra
via Rinfosco, 1690
48014 Castel Bolognese [RA]
Tel. +39 3384818346
costaarchi.wordpress.com

CELLAR SALES
PRE-BOOKED VISITS
ANNUAL PRODUCTION 15,000 bottles
HECTARES UNDER VINE 13.00

Gabriele Succi is an enthusiastic grower who in the space of a few years, thanks also to hard work and dedication, has taken this winery to the top of the DOC zone. His proud, rebellious nature has given the small subzone of Serra an excellent spokesman, who is taking a credible message of quality and style beyond the region's borders. The estate's 13 hectares are divided into two distinct plots in the hills near Castel Bolognese: at Beneficio, lying at an elevation of around 80 metres, and at Monte Brullo, lying at around 160 metres. The dry, savoury Sangiovese Monte Brullo Riserva 2012 shows mature, close-knit tannins and stuffing, with cutting acidity to provide perfect balance, and a citrus finish of impressive length. GS 2013 needs to breathe to shed some of its overpowering oak, but then opens up on the taut, richly nuanced, surprising palate. Assiolo 2014 displays austere fruit and a delicate yet characterful palate.

● GS Sangiovese '13	ΨΨ 5
● Romagna Sangiovese Serra Monte Brullo Ris. '12	ΨΨ 2*
● Romagna Sangiovese Sup. Assiolo '14	ΨΨ 2*
● Romagna Sangiovese Sup. Assiolo '13	ΥΥΥ 4*
● Colli di Faenza Prima Luce '09	ΥΥ 2*
● GS Sangiovese '12	ΥΥ 5
● GS Sangiovese '11	ΥΥ 3*
● Sangiovese di Romagna Sup. Assiolo '12	ΥΥ 2*
● Sangiovese di Romagna Sup. Assiolo '11	ΥΥ 2*
● Sangiovese di Romagna Sup. Assiolo '10	ΥΥ 2*
● Sangiovese di Romagna Sup. Monte Brullo Ris. '10	ΥΥ 2*
● Sangiovese di Romagna Sup. Monte Brullo Ris. '09	ΥΥ 2*

Denavolo

LOC. GATTAVERA
FRAZ. DENAVOLO
29020 TRAVO [PC]
TEL. +39 3356480766
denavolo@gmail.com

CELLAR SALES
ANNUAL PRODUCTION 15,000 bottles
HECTARES UNDER VINE 3.00
SUSTAINABLE WINERY

Giulio Armani and his son Jacopo produce white wines from a few hectares of vineyards planted on the lean, loose soils of the upper Val Trebbia. On one hand we see the tradition of the territory's historic white grapes, in the form of ortrugo, malvasia di Candia aromatica, trebbiano romagnolo, marsanne; on the other, vinification based on long macerations, of which Giulio is an undisputed master. The result is complex wines, multifaceted and nuanced on the nose, and fresh, dry and vibrant in the mouth. Surprisingly complex aromas of herbs, honey, dried fruit, iodine and minerals are followed by freshness and rhythm on the palate, making these wines highly drinkable. Denavolo did not present any wines for the 2017 edition; the Dinavolo 2014 was not produced due to the unfavourable growing year and the Dinavolino 2015 was left to mature further.

○ Catavela '14		♀♀ 2*
○ Catavela '13		♀♀ 2*
○ Catavela '12		♀♀ 2*
○ Catavela '11		♀♀ 2*
○ Dinavolino '14		♀♀ 5
○ Dinavolino '12		♀♀ 5
○ Dinavolino '10		♀♀ 2*
○ Dinavolino '09		♀♀ 2*
○ Dinavolo '10		♀♀ 4
○ Dinavolo '09		♀♀ 4
○ Dinavolo '08		♀♀ 4
○ Dinavolo '07		♀♀ 4
○ Dinavolo '06		♀♀ 5
○ Dinavolo '05		♀♀ 5

Donelli

VIA CARLO SIGONIO, 54
41100 MODENA
TEL. +39 0522908715
www.donellivini.it

CELLAR SALES
ANNUAL PRODUCTION 30,000,000 bottles
HECTARES UNDER VINE 120.00

Antonio Giacobazzi, today assisted by three of his four children, has deep knowledge of the territories of Lambrusco, and his experience allows him to select reliable grapes and wines. This translates into a high overall standard for the 30 million bottles that the winery exports all over the world. With grapes from the 120 hectares of his own vineyards, he instead produces the Sergio Scaglietti line, named after the famous Ferrari coachbuilder who designed the bottle. This dedication shows the family's relationship with Ferrari and the world of Formula 1. In 2015, the Giacobazzi family also reacquired their brand. The Reggiano Sergio Scaglietti 2015 is an elegant, beautifully fresh wine, with notes of blood orange in the mouth and a rounded, mineral finish. The aromatic, delicately balsamic Sorbara Sergio Scaglietti 2015 is consistent and full-flavoured.

● Lambrusco di Sorbara Brut Sergio Scaglietti '15		♀♀ 2*
● Reggiano Lambrusco Brut Sergio Scaglietti '15		♀♀ 2*
● Lambrusco di Sorbara Secco Sergio Scaglietti '14		♀♀ 2*
● Lambrusco di Sorbara Secco Sergio Scaglietti '13		♀♀ 2*
● Lambrusco di Sorbara Secco Sergio Scaglietti '12		♀♀ 2*
● Lambrusco Reggiano Secco Sergio Scaglietti '13		♀♀ 2*
● Lambrusco Reggiano Secco Sergio Scaglietti '12		♀♀ 2*
● Reggiano Lambrusco Secco Sergio Scaglietti '14		♀♀ 2*

Drei Donà Tenuta La Palazza

LOC. MASSA DI VECCHIAZZANO
VIA DEL TESORO, 23
47121 FORLÌ
TEL. +39 0543769371
www.dreidona.it

CELLAR SALES
PRE-BOOKED VISITS
ANNUAL PRODUCTION 130,000 bottles
HECTARES UNDER VINE 27.00
SUSTAINABLE WINERY

In the early 1980s, Claudio Drei Donà dedicated himself to a quality project in his family's Forlì estates, establishing what was de facto one of Romagna's first prestigious wineries, when the region was still linked to cheap unbottled wine. This made Drei Donà's work revolutionary and pioneering in many ways. The idea was to promote Romagna worldwide, and today the efforts of Enrico Drei Donà, now at the helm, target mainly the international market. It is no coincidence, then, that Drei Donà is a brand strong in Romagna but also well known abroad. For some years now this historic operation has been toying with a style that focuses on rich, oaky wines. The austere, citrusy Riserva Palazza 2013 offers spicy nuances over a dry yet fresh, dynamic palate. The Magnificat 2012 has fruit and flavour, close-knit, mature tannins and a character combining richness and tautness.

● Magnificat Cabernet Sauvignon '12	♥♥	5
● Notturno Sangiovese '14	♥♥	3
● Romagna Sangiovese Sup. Palazza Ris. '13	♥♥	5
● Romagna Sangiovese Sup. Pruno Ris. '13	♥♥	5
○ Il Tornese '15	♥	3
● Sangiovese di Romagna Sup. Pruno Ris. '08	♥♥♥	5
● Sangiovese di Romagna Sup. Pruno Ris. '07	♥♥♥	5
● Sangiovese di Romagna Sup. Pruno Ris. '06	♥♥♥	5
● Sangiovese di Romagna Sup. Pruno Ris. '01	♥♥♥	4*

Emilia Wine

VIA 11 SETTEMBRE 2001, 3
42019 SCANDIANO [RE]
TEL. +39 0522989107
www.emiliawine.eu

ANNUAL PRODUCTION 300,000 bottles
HECTARES UNDER VINE 1,900.00

Emilia Wine was created in 2014 from the merger of three Reggio cooperatives: Arceto, Correggio and Prato. Together, the members of this new operation vinify grapes from around 1,900 hectares under vine, for a total of 35 million litres of wine. This is a great community, but above all an extraordinary production chain comprising a mosaic of vineyards, for a detailed map of this land of Lambrusco. The forward-looking approach of chairman Davide Frascari and the technical expertise of oenologist Luca Tognoli are true resources for the growing area at the highest level. The supple, taut Niveo 2015, a salamino-heavy blend, shows a citrus nose over a palate where bitter orange encores, alongside a rustic note which endows character and complexity, with a dry, mineral finish. The lively, vibrant Rossospino 2015 is an everyday drinker, rustic in the best sense of the term, and ends to orange and mature tannins. The elegant, complex Rosaspino 2015 shows a nuanced nose and supple palate.

⊙ Colli di Scandiano e di Canossa Lambrusco Rosaspino Cantina di Arceto '15	♥♥	2*
● Colli di Scandiano e di Canossa Lambrusco Rossospino Cantina di Arceto '15	♥♥	2*
● Reggiano Lambrusco Secco Niveo Cantina di Arceto '15	♥♥	2*
● Colli di Scandiano e di Canossa Grasparossa Cardinale Pighini Cantina di Arceto '15	♥	1*
● Migliolungo Lambrusco '15	♥	2
● Colli di Scandiano e di Canossa Grasparossa Cardinale Pighini Cantina di Arceto '14	♥♥	1*
● Colli di Scandiano e di Canossa Lambrusco Rossospino Cantina di Arceto '14	♥♥	2*

Stefano Ferrucci

VIA CASOLANA, 3045/2
48014 CASTEL BOLOGNESE [RA]
TEL. +39 0546651068
www.stefanoferrucci.it

CELLAR SALES
PRE-BOOKED VISITS
ANNUAL PRODUCTION 95,000 bottles
HECTARES UNDER VINE 16.00

Ferrucci boasts a solid tradition, now in the hands of the young sisters Ilaria and Serena. The vineyards all lie in the subzone of Serra, and the Sangioveses bear the tangy hallmark of the clay and limestone soils of these hills, along with incisive tannins. The winery's top label is the Domus Caia, obtained from lightly dried grapes, which was created in the 1980s by Stefano Ferrucci, and is still one of Romagna's most prestigious and appreciated wines. Ilaria Ferrucci should be given merit for having interpreted this wine over the years with ever greater finesse, without however sacrificing the essential traits given by drying. Domus Caia 2013 displays the complexity provided by partial drying of the grapes, and sacrifices the fresher, more austere notes of sangiovese for a balsamic, variegated nose, with notes of dried fruits, Mediterranean scrub, spice and orange zest. On the taut, clenched palate it shows mature, never overly dry tannins.

Fiorini

VIA PUGLIE, 4
41056 SAVIGNANO SUL PANARO [MO]
TEL. +39 059733151
www.poderifiorini.com

CELLAR SALES
PRE-BOOKED VISITS
ANNUAL PRODUCTION 100,000 bottles
HECTARES UNDER VINE 9.00

Fiorini, established in 1919, is an historic Modena name in Lambrusco production, set up in the growing area for sorbara, of which it is still a masterful interpreter. The winery, managed by Alberto Fiorini and his sister Cristina, has various plots: the grasparossa vineyard at Riccò, at 450 metres; the Torre dei Nannicplot at Savignano sul Panaro; and the venerable sorbara estate between Secchia and Villanova, covering nine hectares of vineyards on loose sand and silt soils. Vignadelpadre 2015 is an original, salty Sorbara Rifermentato in Bottiglia with a delicately spiced nose and a taut, savoury palate, ending to notes of flint and grapefruit. Corte degli Attimi 2015 displays a dry, rustic soul and a finish of roses and tangerine. Terre al Sole 2015, a vineyard selection with second fermentation in the bottle followed by disgorgement, is taut and full-flavoured, with blood orange to the fore on the earthy, mineral palate. The closed, focused Becco Rosso 2015 is an elegant wine with notes of herbs and tangerine zest.

● Romagna Sangiovese Auriga '15	🍷🍷 2*
● Romagna Sangiovese Sup. Domus Caia Ris. '13	🍷🍷 5
● Romagna Sangiovese Sup. Centurione '15	🍷 2
○ Romagna Trebbiano Mattinale '15	🍷 1*
○ Albana di Romagna Passito Domus Aurea '12	🍷🍷 5
○ Romagna Albana Passito Domus Aurea '13	🍷🍷 5
● Romagna Sangiovese Sup. Centurione '14	🍷🍷 2*
● Romagna Sangiovese Sup. Domus Caia Ris. '12	🍷🍷 5
● Sangiovese di Romagna Auriga '11	🍷🍷 2*
● Sangiovese di Romagna Sup. Centurione '11	🍷🍷 2*
● Sangiovese di Romagna Sup. Domus Caia Ris. '11	🍷🍷 5

● Lambrusco di Sorbara Brut Corte degli Attimi '15	🍷🍷 2*
● Lambrusco di Sorbara Vignadelpadre Rifermentato in Bottiglia '15	🍷🍷 2*
● Lambrusco Grasparossa di Castelvetro Becco Rosso '15	🍷🍷 3
● Lambrusco Grasparossa di Castelvetro Terre al Sole '15	🍷🍷 2*
● Lambrusco di Sorbara Corte degli Attimi '14	🍷🍷 2*
● Lambrusco di Sorbara Corte degli Attimi '13	🍷🍷 2*
● Lambrusco di Sorbara Corte degli Attimi '12	🍷🍷 2*
● Lambrusco Grasparossa di Castelvetro Terre al Sole '14	🍷🍷 2*
● Lambrusco Grasparossa di Castelvetro Terre al Sole '13	🍷🍷 2*

Paolo Francesconi

LOC. SARNA
VIA TULIERO, 154
48018 FAENZA [RA]
TEL. +39 054643213
www.francesconipaolo.it

CELLAR SALES
PRE-BOOKED VISITS
RESTAURANT SERVICE
ANNUAL PRODUCTION 20,000 bottles
HECTARES UNDER VINE 8.00
VITICULTURE METHOD Certified Organic

Paolo Francesconi is an artisan to the core, and supervises every phase of his work, from managing the rows, which for years have been farmed using biodynamic methods, to vinification. He is a skilled interpreter of the red clay soils of the first band of hills near Faenza, which give sangiovese bright fruitiness and close-knit tannins. He also does interesting things with albana, which may be fermented off the skins or undergo long maceration on them. The Sangiovese Limbecca 2014 displays an impeccable style and a territorial, classic soul, with austere fruit and earthy notes which disperse as it breathes, and a full-flavoured palate sustained by attractive acidity. This is a reticent wine, that needs time to open up, but then offers complexity. Le ladi 2012 shows pomegranate fruit and a fresh, dry palate where a vibrant finish brings notes of tangerine zest. Vite in Fiore 2015 is full of energy, and shows a lingering, salty, dry palate.

Maria Galassi

LOC. PADERNO DI CESENA
VIA CASETTE, 688
47023 CESENA [FC]
TEL. +39 054721177
www.galassimaria.it

CELLAR SALES
PRE-BOOKED VISITS
ANNUAL PRODUCTION 18,000 bottles
HECTARES UNDER VINE 18.00
VITICULTURE METHOD Certified Organic

Maria Galassi's winery is located between the Savio Valley and Bertinoro, in a position that is, however, closer to the latter in terms of soil characteristics, with active lime and the presence of spungone, the typical marine tufa. From the winery's almost 20 hectares of vineyards, farmed using organic methods for over 20 years, the best batches of grapes are selected and then vinified in steel or large oak, in line with an elegant style which exalts minerality and gracefully expresses the abundant tannins of sangiovese from the Bertinoro area. The elegant, tangy Paternus 2014 shows graceful progression in the mouth, with full flavour and grip. On the nose, citrus and floral notes come to the fore, with blood orange encoring on the palate, but never overpowering. Smembar 2014 opens slowly to express light citrus fruit over a light, salty palate of great finesse. The rounded, close-knit NatoRe 2012 is slightly drying on the palate, but dynamic and fresh.

● Romagna Sangiovese Sup. Limbecca '14	♟♟♟ 3*
● Romagna Sangiovese Sup. Le ladi Ris. '12	♟♟ 5
○ Arcaica '15	♟♟ 3
● Vite in Fiore '15	♟♟ 3
○ Luna Nuova '15	♟ 2
● Sangiovese di Romagna Sup. Limbecca '11	♟♟♟ 3*
● Sangiovese di Romagna Sup. Limbecca '10	♟♟♟ 3*
○ Arcaica '14	♟♟ 3
○ Arcaica '13	♟♟ 3*
○ Arcaica '12	♟♟ 3
● Romagna Sangiovese Sup. Limbecca '13	♟♟ 3
● Sangiovese di Romagna Sup. Limbecca '12	♟♟ 3*

● Romagna Sangiovese Sup. Smembar '14	♟♟ 5
● Romagna Sangiovese Bertinoro natoRe Ris. '12	♟♟ 2*
● Romagna Sangiovese Sup. Paternus '14	♟♟ 2*
● Sangiovese di Romagna Sup. natoRe '10	♟♟♟ 2*
● Romagna Sangiovese Sup. natoRe '13	♟♟ 2*
● Romagna Sangiovese Sup. Paternus '13	♟♟ 2*
● Sangiovese di Romagna Sup. natoRe Ris. '11	♟♟ 2*
● Sangiovese di Romagna Sup. Paternus '11	♟♟ 2*
● Sangiovese di Romagna Sup. Paternus '10	♟♟ 2*
● Sangiovese di Romagna Sup. Smembar '13	♟♟ 5

Gallegati

via Lugo, 182
48018 Faenza [RA]
Tel. +39 0546621149
www.aziendaagricolagallegati.it

CELLAR SALES
PRE-BOOKED VISITS
ACCOMMODATION
ANNUAL PRODUCTION 15,000 bottles
HECTARES UNDER VINE 6.00

The brothers Cesare and Antonio Gallegati are artisanal producers of classic wines, eschewing fashion, in line with the decision taken some years ago to produce territorial wines, consistent with the growing year and the hefty, close-knit wines that come from the pure clay soils between Faenza and Brisighella. The brothers personally take meticulous care of the vineyards, and every year try to interpret the raw materials in the most direct, respectful way possible. The captivating Regina di Cuori 2012 plays polyphenols off against acidity. A nose of dried figs, apricots, horehound, absinthe, black tea and freshly ground coffee paves the way for candied peel and grapefruit in the mouth, for a wine that is rustic and yet aristocratic at the same time. Corallo Nero 2013 is a clenched, weighty Sangiovese from clay soils offering meaty, austere fruit over a palate where acidity provides dynamism, with notes of blood orange on the finish.

○ Romagna Albana Passito Regina di Cuori Ris. '12	🍷🍷🍷 4*
● Romagna Sangiovese Brisighella Corallo Nero Ris. '13	🍷🍷 4
○ Romagna Albana Secco Corallo Giallo '15	🍷🍷 4
● Romagna Sangiovese Brisighella Corallo Nero Ris. '12	🍷🍷 4
● Romagna Sangiovese Brisighella Corallo Rosso '14	🍷🍷 2*
○ Albana di Romagna Passito Regina di Cuori Ris. '10	🍷🍷🍷 4*
○ Albana di Romagna Passito Regina di Cuori Ris. '09	🍷🍷🍷 4*
● Sangiovese di Romagna Sup. Corallo Nero Ris. '06	🍷🍷🍷 3
● Sangiovese di Romagna Sup. Corallo Nero Ris. '10	🍷🍷 4

Gruppo Cevico

via Fiumazzo, 72
48022 Lugo [RA]
Tel. +39 0545284711
www.gruppocevico.com

CELLAR SALES
PRE-BOOKED VISITS
ANNUAL PRODUCTION 20,000,000 bottles
HECTARES UNDER VINE 6700.00

Love for the land and a commitment to promoting Romagna, expressed with dedication and determination by the president Ruenza Santandrea, make this large cooperative a crucial player in the process of Romagna's affirmation in the world of wine. The community of 4,500 growers is an incredible force that today allows Cevico to invest in projects of quality and to choose grapes from their 6,700 hectares under vine. They can now achieve territorial interpretations that were unthinkable in the past, resulting in popular wines with a real sense of identity. The main brands are Terre Cevico, Vigneti Galassi, Sancrispino, Ronco, Romandiola and Bernardi. Vigneti Galassi is an example of what it means to combine quantity and quality, offering good reliable, territorial wines at extremely accessible prices. The everyday Superiore 2015 is a chewy, fruit-driven wine, with freshness supporting progression on the palate.

○ Albana di Romagna Secco Romandiola '15	🍷🍷 3
○ Colli di Imola Pignoletto Frizzante Romandiola '15	🍷🍷 2*
● Romagna Sangiovese Sup. Vign. Galassi '15	🍷🍷 2*
● Bosco Eliceo Merlot Terre Cevico '14	🍷🍷 1*
● Romagna Sangiovese Sup. Romandiola Novilunio '14	🍷🍷 2*
● Romagna Sangiovese Sup. Terre Cevico '14	🍷🍷 2*
● Romagna Sangiovese Sup. Vign. Galassi '14	🍷🍷 2*
● Romagna Sangiovese Terre Cevico '14	🍷🍷 2*

Lusenti

LOC. CASA PICCIONI, 57
29010 ZIANO PIACENTINO [PC]
TEL. +39 0523868479
www.lusentivini.it

CELLAR SALES
PRE-BOOKED VISITS
ANNUAL PRODUCTION 100,000 bottles
HECTARES UNDER VINE 17.00
VITICULTURE METHOD Certified Organic

Ludovica Lusenti tends 17 hectares in the high part of Val Tidone, near the regional border. At around 300 metres above sea level, this area shows great potential for wines with freshness and elegance. For some years now, Ludovica has been moving closer to the world of natural wine, as seen in the two products made using the technique of bottle refermentation without disgorgement: the reliable, interesting Malvasia Frizzante Emiliana and Gutturnio Frizzante Tournesol. The complex, nuanced Emiliana 2015 shows an elegant nose of tangerine, herby notes of oregano, sage, absinthe and curry plant, and balsamic notes with a touch of bay leaves. In the mouth, it is mineral and dynamic, with a savoury, floral finish. The Piriolo 2011 is a wine of great complexity, with a nose of figs, apricots, candied lemon peel and oregano. Attractive acidity on the palate provides progression and leads to a finish with salty notes of black olives and capers.

○ C. P. Malvasia Frizzante Emiliana '15	♥♥	2*
○ C. P. Malvasia Passito Il Piriolo '11	♥♥	5
○ C. P. Ortrugo Ciano '14	♥♥	2*
⊙ Pinot Nero Rosé Nature M. Cl. '11	♥♥	3
● C. P. Gutturnio Frizzante '10	♀♀	2*
● C. P. Gutturnio Frizzante Tournesol '11	♀♀	2*
● C. P. Gutturnio Frizzante Tournesol '10	♀♀	2*
○ C. P. Malvasia Frizzante Emiliana '12	♀♀	2*
○ C. P. Malvasia Frizzante Emiliana '11	♀♀	2*
○ C. P. Malvasia Passito Il Piriolo '10	♀♀	5
⊙ C. P. Pinot Nero Rosé Frizzante Fiocco di Rose '13	♀♀	4
● Gutturnio Frizzante Tournesol '12	♀♀	2*

Giovanna Madonia

LOC. VILLA MADONIA
VIA DE' CAPPUCCINI, 130
47032 BERTINORO [FC]
TEL. +39 0543444361
www.giovannamadonia.it

CELLAR SALES
PRE-BOOKED VISITS
RESTAURANT SERVICE
ANNUAL PRODUCTION 60,000 bottles
HECTARES UNDER VINE 13.00

Since the 1990s, Giovanna Madonia has focused on providing precise interpretations of the character of the Monte May subzone, the cold part of Bertinoro, with its characteristic soils rich in active lime, where the grapes ripen more slowly, resulting in wines that need time to fully express themselves. They show rich stuffing, with close-knit, mature tannins, modulated by the attractive acidity of the sangiovese. These artisanal wines are always perfect expressions of their growing years. Ombroso 2012 shows character and a nose that needs to breathe to reveal earthy, gamey notes, followed by pomegranate fruit. The consistent, full-flavoured palate is dense but supple, and signs off with delicate citrus. Fermavento 2013 shows a touch of alcoholic warmth, but offers a supple, dynamic palate. Barlume 2013 offers austere, focused fruit over good balance in the mouth.

● Colli Romagna Centrale Barlume Ris. '13	♥♥	4
○ Romagna Albana Secco Neblina '15	♥♥	2*
● Romagna Sangiovese Bertinoro Ombroso Ris. '12	♥♥	5
● Romagna Sangiovese Sup. Fermavento '13	♥♥	3
○ Romagna Albana Secco Neblina '14	♀♀♀	2*
● Sangiovese di Romagna Sup. Ombroso Ris. '06	♀♀♀	5
● Sangiovese di Romagna Sup. Ombroso Ris. '01	♀♀♀	5
● Colli Romagna Centrale Barlume Ris. '11	♀♀	4
● Romagna Sangiovese Bertinoro Ombroso Ris. '11	♀♀	5
● Sangiovese di Romagna Sup. Fermavento '10	♀♀	3
● Tenentino '12	♀♀	2*

Ermete Medici & Figli

LOC. GAIDA
VIA NEWTON, 13A
42040 REGGIO EMILIA
TEL. +39 0522942135
www.medici.it

CELLAR SALES
PRE-BOOKED VISITS
ANNUAL PRODUCTION 800,000 bottles
HECTARES UNDER VINE 75.00
SUSTAINABLE WINERY

Alberto Medici has been travelling all over the world for 30 years, promoting an idea of Lambrusco linked to quality. He was a pioneer of a new concept of growing area and the incredible reputation of his wines is the result of what was originally groundbreaking work. With the arrival of the Cevico group, joint owners with the Medici family, the winery is now in an ideal position to further develop this philosophy and look to the future with optimism. Medici also produces an excellent Aceto Balsamico Tradizionale di Reggio Emilia and has an estate equipped for visitors, even including a small Lambrusco museum. The focused, creamy Concerto 2015 shows classic, expressive, elegant fruit and vibrancy on the palate, in a style that over the years has reduced sweetness to benefit in finesse. The deep, taut Unique 2013 shows a nuanced nose alternating tertiary aromas of hazelnut and absinthe with mineral and salty notes.

Monte delle Vigne

LOC. OZZANO TARO
VIA MONTICELLO, 13
43046 COLLECCHIO [PR]
TEL. +39 0521309704
www.montedellevigne.it

CELLAR SALES
PRE-BOOKED VISITS
ACCOMMODATION
ANNUAL PRODUCTION 350,000 bottles
HECTARES UNDER VINE 60.00

Andrea Ferrari and Paolo Pizzarotti have built their project around their 60 hectares of vineyards, farmed using solely organic methods, on hillside sites above Parma characterized by clay and limestone soils. The farming side of the operation is supervised by Federico Curtaz, while the grapes are vinified in the modern new winery according to the instructions of an external consultant, the oenologist Attilio Pagli. In recent years, the production of still wines has also been accompanied by sparklers, especially Lambrusco obtained from Maestri grapes. It is in the simpler labels most linked to territorial tradition that the winery gives of its best. A case in point is MDV, a red from barbera and bonarda, which evokes the tradition of the hills near Parma and Piacenza, where it is called Gutturnio. The elegant, vibrant 2014, vinified in steel, shows fruity and nuanced, with good progression on the palate provided by barbera's attractive acidity.

● Reggiano Lambrusco Concerto '15	♟♟♟ 2*
⊙ Brut Rosé M. Cl. Unique '13	♟♟ 3*
● C. P. Bonarda Castelli del Duca Ottavio '13	♟♟ 3
○ C. P. Malvasia Castelli del Duca Isabella '15	♟♟ 3
○ C. P. Sauvignon Castelli del Duca Vittoria '15	♟♟ 3
● Colli di Scandiano e di Canossa Grasparossa Bocciolo '15	♟♟ 2*
● Reggiano Lambrusco Assolo '15	♟ 2
● Reggiano Lambrusco I Quercioli '15	♟ 1*
● Reggiano Lambrusco Concerto '14	♟♟♟ 2*
● Reggiano Lambrusco Concerto '13	♟♟♟ 2*
● Reggiano Lambrusco Concerto '12	♟♟♟ 2*
● Reggiano Lambrusco Concerto '11	♟♟♟ 2*
● Reggiano Lambrusco Concerto '10	♟♟♟ 2*

● Colli di Parma Rosso MDV '14	♟♟♟ 2*
○ Colli di Parma Malvasia Frizzante '15	♟♟ 2*
● Colli di Parma Lambrusco I Calanchi '15	♟ 5
○ Colli di Parma Malvasia Poem '15	♟ 2
● Lambrusco Emilia '15	♟ 2
● Argille Malvasia '08	♟♟ 5
○ Callas Malvasia '12	♟♟ 2*
○ Callas Malvasia '11	♟♟ 4
○ Colli di Parma Malvasia Frizzante '14	♟♟ 2*
○ Colli di Parma Malvasia Poem '14	♟♟ 2*
● Colli di Parma Malvasia Poem '12	♟♟ 2*
● Colli di Parma Malvasia Poem '11	♟♟ 2*
○ Colli di Parma Sauvignon '13	♟♟ 2*
● Lambrusco Emilia '14	♟♟ 2*
○ Malvasia Frizzante Dolce '12	♟♟ 2*
⊙ Rubina Brut Rosé '13	♟♟ 4

Fattoria Monticino Rosso

VIA MONTECATONE, 7
40026 IMOLA [BO]
TEL. +39 054240577
www.fattoriadelmonticinorosso.it

CELLAR SALES
PRE-BOOKED VISITS
ANNUAL PRODUCTION 70,000 bottles
HECTARES UNDER VINE 18.00

The Zeoli family have an extraordinary bond with the land, and their dynamism bears witness to the faith they have in their growing area. Every year they invest and plan to raise production figures and increase the winery's reputation. They can always count on Giancarlo Soverchia, a great man, and an inspiring oenologust, who is the winery's driving force. Over the years, they have become a benchmark for the production of white wines and in particular Albana, of which they even produce small limited edition series, resulting from patient maturation and special techniques. The original Codronchio is obtained from botrytized albana grapes vinified to achieve a dry wine. The complex, nuanced 2014 shows savoury and dry, with herb notes of sage, oregano and absinthe on the finish. S 2015 is a simple, fruit-infused wine, slightly weighed down by its drying tannins, but full of flavour, with acidity providing thrust.

○ Romagna Albana Passito '11	♟♟ 4
○ Romagna Albana Secco Codronchio '14	♟♟ 3
● Romagna Sangiovese Sup. S '15	♟♟ 2*
○ Colli d'Imola Pignoletto P '15	♟ 2
○ Romagna Albana Secco A '15	♟ 2
● Romagna Sangiovese Sup. Le Morine '12	♟ 3
○ Albana di Romagna Secco Codronchio '08	♟♟♟ 3*
○ Albana di Romagna Secco A '13	♟♟ 2*
○ Albana di Romagna Secco Codronchio '12	♟♟ 3
○ Colli d'Imola Pignoletto P '14	♟♟ 2*
○ Romagna Albana Secco A '14	♟♟ 2*
○ Romagna Albana Secco Codronchio '13	♟♟ 3
● Romagna Sangiovese Sup. Le Morine '11	♟♟ 3
● Romagna Sangiovese Sup. S '14	♟♟ 2*

Fattoria Moretto

VIA TIBERIA, 13B
41014 CASTELVETRO DI MODENA [MO]
TEL. +39 059790183
www.fattoriamoretto.it

CELLAR SALES
PRE-BOOKED VISITS
ANNUAL PRODUCTION 65,000 bottles
HECTARES UNDER VINE 10.00
VITICULTURE METHOD Certified Organic
SUSTAINABLE WINERY

Fausto and Fabio Altariva are artisanal growers who tend their rows in the hills around Modena, in the heart of the growing area of lambrusco grasparossa. For years, they have safeguarded the genuine territorial identity of this variety, and have shown their ability to give a modern interpretation of this its more rustic nature. Their wines in fact display a tannic weave of character and personality, dry palates and austere, sober fruit. Their vineyards lie at elevations of 200 metres with south and south-west aspects on clayey soils, in an ideal microclimate for organic farming methods. They were the first to vinify grasparossa vineyard by vineyard, based on a concept of interpreting the various soils which is rare in the world of Lambrusco. The two Canova and Monovitigno crus are, as always, at the highest level. Monovitigno 2015 offers an original nose of roses and lavender, paving the way for a dense, citrusy palate and a mineral finish, where the fruit finally comes to the fore.

● Lambrusco Grasparossa di Castelvetro Secco Monovitigno '15	♟♟ 3*
● Lambrusco Grasparossa di Castelvetro Secco Canova '15	♟♟ 3
● Lambrusco Grasparossa di Castelvetro Secco Tasso '15	♟ 2
● Lambrusco Grasparossa di Castelvetro Secco Canova '14	♟♟ 3*
● Lambrusco Grasparossa di Castelvetro Secco Canova '13	♟♟ 3*
● Lambrusco Grasparossa di Castelvetro Secco Monovitigno '14	♟♟ 3
● Lambrusco Grasparossa di Castelvetro Secco Monovitigno '13	♟♟ 3
● Lambrusco Grasparossa di Castelvetro Secco Tasso '13	♟♟ 2*

Poderi Morini

LOC. ORIOLO DEI FICHI
VIA GESUITA
48018 FAENZA [RA]
TEL. +39 0546634257
www.poderimorini.com

ANNUAL PRODUCTION 100,000 bottles
HECTARES UNDER VINE 26.00
SUSTAINABLE WINERY

Alessandro Morini is an artisan from
Faenza who vinifies the grapes of his 26
hectares of vineyards at Oriolo dei Fichi, a
hillside area that boasts an extraordinary
tapestry of small producers. This group,
together with Alessandro, has done a great
deal of work on minor varieties from the
past, relaunching the old red aromatic
variety centesimino and other little-known
native cutivars. The zone is also extremely
interesting for albana, which here achieves
full flavour and good stuffing. The Albana
Sette Note 2015 opens to a herby nose of
sage, absinthe and burnet, leading into a
rich, expressive palate. Its fruity soul
emerges on the finish, with white damson
leading the way. The simple, classic
Sangiovese Morale 2015 is dry and
peppery. Savignone 2015 shows the typical
vegetal notes of Centesimino to the fore,
and expresses its aromatic nature with a
certain austerity. On the nose, rose,
petunia, white pepper and tangerine
alternate with a delicate hint of cloves.

○ Romagna Albana Secco Sette Note '15	🍷🍷 2*
● Romagna Sangiovese Sup. Morale '15	🍷🍷 3
● Savignone Centesimino '15	🍷🍷 2*
○ Morale DOC '15	🍷 2
● Sangiovese di Romagna Sup. Morale '14	🍷🍷 3
● Sangiovese di Romagna Sup. Morale '10	🍷🍷 3
● Sangiovese di Romagna Sup. Nonno Rico Ris. '10	🍷🍷 2*
● Sangiovese di Romagna Sup. Nonno Rico Ris. '09	🍷🍷 2*
● Sangiovese di Romagna Sup. Torre di Oriolo '11	🍷🍷 3
● Sangiovese di Romagna Sup. Torre di Oriolo '10	🍷🍷 3
● Savignone '11	🍷🍷 2*
● Savignone Centesimo '13	🍷🍷 2*
● Traicolli '10	🍷🍷 2*

Fattoria Nicolucci

LOC. PREDAPPIO ALTA
VIA UMBERTO PRIMO, 21
47016 PREDAPPIO [FC]
TEL. +39 0543922361
www.vini-nicolucci.it

CELLAR SALES
PRE-BOOKED VISITS
ANNUAL PRODUCTION 70,000 bottles
HECTARES UNDER VINE 10.00
SUSTAINABLE WINERY

Alessandro Nicolucci, heir to a family
tradition now in its fifth generation, is a
precious asset for the whole of Romagna,
and today is reaping the fruits of a stylistic
consistency that he has pursued with
determination over the years. His classic,
ageable Sangioveses, aged in concrete and
large oak, are perfect interpretions of a
unique terroir which alternates clays and
veins of sulphur. The Predappio Alta growing
area, not to be confused with Predappio,
boasts time-honoured bush vines and a
clone of eliptical berry grapes which is its
original trademark. The beautifully nuanced
Vigna del Generale 2013 is an elegant,
classic Sangiovese of infinite grace,
showing austere fruit. This earthy,
sulphurous, savoury wine is subtle, supple
and close-knit, and offers a seemingly
infinite palette of aromas, including pencil
lead, herbs and tangerine zest. The
expressive, taut Tre Rocche 2015 is dry,
full-flavoured and complex, and shows the
mineral notes typical of the Predappio Alta
growing area.

● Romagna Sangiovese Sup. V. del Generale Ris. '13	🍷🍷🍷 5
● Romagna Sangiovese Sup. Tre Rocche '15	🍷🍷 3*
● Romagna Sangiovese Sup. V. del Generale Ris. '12	🍷🍷🍷 5
● Sangiovese di Romagna Predappio di Predappio V. del Generale '11	🍷🍷🍷 5
● Sangiovese di Romagna Sup. V. del Generale Ris. '10	🍷🍷🍷 5
● Sangiovese di Romagna Sup. V. del Generale Ris. '08	🍷🍷🍷 5
● Sangiovese di Romagna V. del Generale Ris. '09	🍷🍷🍷 5
● Sangiovese di Romagna V. del Generale Ris. '05	🍷🍷🍷 4

Enio Ottaviani

LOC. SANT'ANDREA IN CASALE
VIA PIAN DI VAGLIA, 17
47832 SAN CLEMENTE [RN]
TEL. +39 0541952608
www.enioottaviani.it

CELLAR SALES
PRE-BOOKED VISITS
ANNUAL PRODUCTION 130,000 bottles
HECTARES UNDER VINE 12.00

The winery run by Davide and Massimo Lorenzi together with their cousins Marco and Milena represents the transformation of the commercial activity of their grandfather Enio Ottaviani, which is now also a farming operation. The 12 hectares of vineyards are found in the southern part of Romagna, on the hills behind Cattolica, at the feet of Valle del Conca. Massimo's love for this growing area and the meticulous work of Davide in the cellar have allowed the winery to make a serious leap forwards in terms of quality, to the benefit of the whole Rimini area. The family also has an extraordinary capacity to make visitors feel welcome, and embody the authentic character of Romagna and its spirit of hospitality. The relaxed, fruit-infused Caciara 2015 shows a taut, tangy palate, and is aged in the concrete tanks that Davide has recently restored. The spicy Merlot 2013 shows beautifully fresh currant and blackberry fruit, over a well-balanced palate whose appeal is provided by attractive, mature tannins.

○ Clemente Primo '15		♥♥ 2*
● Merlot '13		♥♥ 2*
● Romagna Sangiovese Caciara '15		♥♥ 3
● Romagna Sangiovese Sup. Sole Rosso Ris. '13		♥♥ 4
● Romagna Sangiovese Primalba '15		♥ 2
○ Clemente Primo '14		♥♥ 2*
● Romagna Sangiovese Primalba '14		♥♥ 2*
● Romagna Sangiovese Sup. Caciara '14		♥♥ 2*
● Romagna Sangiovese Sup. Primalba '13		♥♥ 2*
● Romagna Sangiovese Sup. Sole Rosso Ris. '11		♥♥ 3

Gianfranco Paltrinieri

FRAZ. SORBARA
VIA CRISTO, 49
41030 BOMPORTO [MO]
TEL. +39 059902047
www.cantinapaltrinieri.it

CELLAR SALES
PRE-BOOKED VISITS
ANNUAL PRODUCTION 90,000 bottles
HECTARES UNDER VINE 15.00

Paltrinieri is a byword for artisanal Lambrusco, the demonstration of how this wine is going beyond the idea of brand to become part of a more territorial concept, taken by Alberto as far as the extreme idea of cru. The loose soils of this strip of land between Secchia and Panaro are the great terroir of sorbara, and the 15 hectares of the estate's own vineyards are in the heart of its DOC zone. The wines of Paltrinieri, farmers in spirit but wonderful communicators, are focused, delicate and dynamic. The crown-cap version of Radice Lambrusco di Modena 2015 is lean, essential and pure, with the graceful soul of sorbara and an unbelievable reserve of power and energy. In the mouth, it shows the salty acidity typical of this variety, as well as incredible progression, unfolding a series of aromas from blossom to notes of the sea. This description also holds good for the cork-top version, obtained from the same base.

● Lambrusco di Sorbara Radice '15		♥♥ 2*
● Radice Tappo a Corona '15		♥♥ 2*
● Lambrusco di Sorbara Leclisse '15		♥♥ 2*
● Lambrusco di Sorbara Sant'Agata '15		♥♥ 2*
● Brut Grosso M. Cl. '13		♥♥ 2*
● Lambrusco di Sorbara Leclisse '10		♥♥♥ 3*
● Lambrusco di Modena Greto '13		♥♥ 2*
● Lambrusco di Modena M. Cl. Grosso '12		♥♥ 2*
● Lambrusco di Modena M. Cl. Grosso '11		♥♥ 2*
● Lambrusco di Sorbara La Piria '13		♥♥ 2*
● Lambrusco di Sorbara La Piria '12		♥♥ 2*
● Lambrusco di Sorbara Leclisse '14		♥♥ 2*
● Lambrusco di Sorbara Leclisse '13		♥♥ 2*
● Lambrusco di Sorbara Leclisse '12		♥♥ 2*
● Lambrusco di Sorbara Radice '14		♥♥ 2*

Fattoria Paradiso

LOC. CAPOCOLLE
VIA PALMEGGIANA, 285
47032 BERTINORO [FC]
TEL. +39 0543445044
www.fattoriaparadiso.com

CELLAR SALES
PRE-BOOKED VISITS
ANNUAL PRODUCTION 500,000 bottles
HECTARES UNDER VINE 100.00

The story of wine in Romagna was one of farming traditions until some important new wineries opened in the 1970s, changed its course. One of these was Fattoria Paradiso, the place where for the first time there were thoughts of a Riserva version of the Sangiovese di Romagna, and where Veronelli urged Mario Pezzi to start thinking, in what was a revolutionary way for this area, about the idea of vineyard selections. Graziella Pezzi has carried on this family tradition over time, and with the recent involvement of her son Jacopo, the winery has found a new lease of life, with reliable, interesting wines across the range. Vigna del Molino 2015 shows fruit, complexity and an elegant, fleshy palate leading to a full-flavoured finish adorned with delicate notes of orange zest. Vigna delle Lepri 2013 shows a fresh, taut palate with close-knit, mature tannins. The Barbarossa 2013, from aromatic native red grapes, is peppery and vegetal, fresh and dry. The Mito 2013 is a classic, rounded Bordeaux blend.

Tenuta Pertinello

S.DA ARPINETO PERTINELLO, 2
47010 GALEATA [FC]
TEL. +39 0543983156
www.tenutapertinello.it

CELLAR SALES
PRE-BOOKED VISITS
ANNUAL PRODUCTION 70,000 bottles
HECTARES UNDER VINE 14.00
VITICULTURE METHOD Certified Organic

The vineyards, planted on loose soils of marl and sandstone, are among the highest in Romagna and in some way mark a border between the Apennines, whose woods arrive as far as Tuscany, and the clayey hills bordering the Via Emilia. The winery of Moreno Mancini, which started life up here, has given a new lease of life to the tradition of Valle del Bidente, a heartland of quality viticulture with its bush vines and entirely manual production methods. Pertinello exploits the potential for elegance of this growing area with products of great finesse. Pertinello 2013 shows austere, spicy fruit over a palate that unfolds with the territorial traits typical of sangiovese grown on high ground: grip, finesse and elegant tannins. The expressive, relaxed Bosco 2015 offers full flavour and fruit, with light progression on the palate leading to citrus on the finish.

○ Albana V.T. '15	♟♟ 2*
● Barbarossa Il Dosso '13	♟♟ 4
● Mito '13	♟♟ 6
● Romagna Sangiovese Sup. V. Del Molino Maestri di Vigna '15	♟♟ 2*
● Romagna Sangiovese Sup. V. delle Lepri Ris. '13	♟♟ 3
○ Romagna Albana Secco '15	♟ 2
● Romagna Sangiovese Sup. Petit Paradiso '15	♟ 3
● Mito '10	♟♟ 6
● Sangiovese di Romagna Cuvée Rina Pezzi Ris. '11	♟♟ 3
● Sangiovese di Romagna Cuvée Rina Pezzi Ris. '10	♟♟ 3
● Sangiovese di Romagna Sup. V. delle Lepri Ris. '12	♟♟ 3

● Colli Romagna Centrale Sangiovese Pertinello '13	♟♟ 3*
● Colli Romagna Centrale Sangiovese Il Bosco '15	♟♟ 2*
● Colli Romagna Centrale Sangiovese Il Sasso Ris. '11	♟♟ 5
● Colli Romagna Centrale Sangiovese Pertinello '08	♟♟♟ 3
● Colli Romagna Centrale Sangiovese Il Bosco '14	♟♟ 2*
● Colli Romagna Centrale Sangiovese Il Sasso Ris. '10	♟♟ 5
● Colli Romagna Centrale Sangiovese Il Sasso Ris. '09	♟♟ 5
● Colli Romagna Centrale Sangiovese Pertinello '12	♟♟ 3
● Colli Romagna Centrale Sangiovese Pertinello '11	♟♟ 3

Poderi dal Nespoli

LOC. NESPOLI
VILLA ROSSI, 50
47012 CIVITELLA DI ROMAGNA [FC]
TEL. +39 0543989911
www.poderidalnespoli.com

CELLAR SALES
PRE-BOOKED VISITS
ANNUAL PRODUCTION 900,000 bottles
HECTARES UNDER VINE 30.00

Valle del Bidente is home to an operation that has made its knowledge of the growing area the basis for a project that combines the entrepreneurial spirit of the Martini family and the roots of the Ravaioli family in a special alchemy. Since 1929 Poderi dal Nespoli has been the symbol and pride of its district. Its ability to interpret the fruits of these hills at the foot of the Apennines as quality wines has been handed down over the generations. If people in this nook of Romagna identify with these wines, it is because they see shared values in them and the ability to represent them, both close to home and all over the world. The Nespoli 2013 shows fruit to the fore and exceptional focus, with a close knit, clenched palate and appealing, mature tannins. The Prugneto 2015 is a beautifully plush, creamy wine with an open, floral, fruity nose. Borgo dei Guidi 2013 vaunts an international style with spice, complexity and elegant progression in the mouth.

● Borgo dei Guidi '13		▼▼ 5
○ Romagna Albana Campodora '15		▼▼ 4
● Romagna Sangiovese Sup. Il Nespoli Ris. '13		▼▼ 4
● Romagna Sangiovese Sup. Il Prugneto '15		▼▼ 2*
● Sangiovese di Romagna Sup. Il Nespoli Ris. '07		♔♔♔ 4*
● Sangiovese di Romagna Sup. Il Nespoli Ris. '06		♔♔♔ 4*
● Borgo dei Guidi '12		♔♔ 5
● Sangiovese di Romagna Sup. Il Nespoli Ris. '11		♔♔ 4
● Sangiovese di Romagna Sup. Il Prugneto '14		♔♔ 2*
● Sangiovese di Romagna Sup. Il Prugneto '13		♔♔ 2*

Il Pratello

VIA MORANA, 14
47015 MODIGLIANA [FC]
TEL. +39 0546942038
www.ilpratello.net

CELLAR SALES
PRE-BOOKED VISITS
ANNUAL PRODUCTION 20,000 bottles
HECTARES UNDER VINE 5.50
VITICULTURE METHOD Certified Organic

Modigliana is a territory able to produce salty, vertical wines, ageable like no others in Romagna. The uniquely lean, loose soils with marl and sandstone, the altitude which favours slow maturation which normally occurs in October, and an unspoilt environment, mainly of woodland, make this area unique in the region. To these qualities, Emilio Placci adds talent and rare sensitivity, and the determination that allows him to produce without compromise. The result is wines which age well and with time regale extraordinary complexity. Badia 2011 is an ageable wine, a small masterpiece that only artisans with extraordinary sensitivity can produce. After breathing, its nose slowly reveals autumn leaves, topsoil and a hint of fruit and spice. The dense, austere palate offers full flavour that unexpectedly comes to the fore and leads to a tangy, incisive finish.

● Badia Raustignolo '11		▼▼ 5
● Morana '12		▼▼ 2*
● Colli di Faenza Sangiovese Mantignano V. V. Ris. '04		♔♔♔ 3*
● Mantignano V. V. '08		♔♔♔ 3*
● Badia Raustignolo '08		♔♔ 5
● Castagnara '11		♔♔ 4
● Colli di Faenza Rosso Calenzone '04		♔♔ 3
○ Le Campore '13		♔♔ 2*
○ Le Campore '10		♔♔ 2*
○ Le Campore '08		♔♔ 2*
○ Le Campore '06		♔♔ 2
● Mantignano V. V. '09		♔♔ 3
● Mantignano Vecchie Vigne '07		♔♔ 2*
● Sangiovese di Romagna Morana '10		♔♔ 2*
● Sangiovese di Romagna Morana '09		♔♔ 2*
● Sangiovese di Romagna Morana '08		♔♔ 2

EMILIA ROMAGNA

Quarticello

VIA MATILDE DI CANOSSA, 1A
42027 MONTECCHIO EMILIA [RE]
TEL. +39 0522866220
www.quarticello.it

ANNUAL PRODUCTION 25,000 bottles
HECTARES UNDER VINE 5.00

Roberto Maestri has been running this hillside winery on the Reggio side of the River Enza since 2001, obtaining increasingly high-quality results. He is one of the few artisans in the world of Lambrusco, a grower who personally tends his five hectares of vineyards and deals with the entire vinification process. He always adopts natural techniques in the cellar, with second fermentation in the bottle, as tradition demands. The result is reliable, focused, extremely classic, austere wines with a real sense of place. The Malvasia Despina 2015 opens up in the glass to reveal a complex nose ranging from mineral notes of flint, iodine and salt to balsamic aromas of sage and eucalyptus. In the mouth, acidity ensures good progression, leading to an attractive savoury finish. The Lambrusco Ferrando 2015 opens to earthy notes followed by orange zest, rose, and delicate spice. The taut, dry palate is elegant and dynamic. The Malvasia Passita Stradora 2015 shows a beautifully variegated nose of freshly ground coffee, dried figs, curry plant, absinthe and apricots.

○ Despina Rifermentato in Bottiglia '15	🍷🍷	2*
⊙ Ferrando Rifermentato in Bottiglia '15	🍷🍷	2*
○ Stradora '15	🍷🍷	3
○ Despina '14	🍷🍷	2*
○ Despina '13	🍷🍷	2*
○ Despina '12	🍷🍷	2*
⊙ Ferrando '14	🍷🍷	2*
⊙ Ferrando '13	🍷🍷	2*
⊙ Ferrando '11	🍷🍷	2*
⊙ Ferrando '11	🍷🍷	2*
○ Stradora '13	🍷🍷	3*

Quinto Passo

LOC. SOZZIGALLI DI SOLIERA
VIA CANALE, 267
410109 MODENA
TEL. +39 0593163311
www.quintopasso.it

CELLAR SALES
ANNUAL PRODUCTION 40,000 bottles
HECTARES UNDER VINE 12.00

The experience in Metodo Classico in the Modena area and the availability of an extraordinary variety like sorbara – acidity, sea salt, grace and elegance – is stimulating the best and most enlightened producers to invest in important projects. A case in point is the Chiarli family, which has dedicated a winery solely to Metodo Classico, and is renovating an old dairy at Sozzigalli for production. This radical decision underlines just how motivated and serious the family are in embarking on this new adventure. The focused, pure Rosé 2013, a monovarietal Sorbara, offers a delicate floral, citrus nose, leading to a potent palate with a crisp, focused finish and the full flavour typical of this variety. The Pas Dosé 2013, from chardonnay topped up with sorbara, is taut, graceful and nuanced, and offers an attractive finish of delicate herbs, including balsamic sage and absinthe.

⊙ Modena Rosé Brut M. Cl. '13	🍷🍷	4
⊙ Pas Dosé '13	🍷🍷	5
○ Cuvée Paradiso Brut '13	🍷	4
⊙ Modena Rosé Brut M. Cl. '12	🍷🍷	4

Noelia Ricci

FRAZ. FIUMANA
VIA PANDOLFA, 35
47016 PREDAPPIO [FC]
TEL. +39 0543940073
info@noeliaricci.it

PRE-BOOKED VISITS
ACCOMMODATION
ANNUAL PRODUCTION 200,000 bottles
HECTARES UNDER VINE 9.00
SUSTAINABLE WINERY

Marco Cirese has revolutionized the family's historic estate, Tenuta Pandolfa, with an extraordinary staff full of energy: Francesco Bordini supervising work in the rows and cellar, and Francesco Guazzugli Marini dealing with sales. The change has been so extreme and overwhelming that they decided on a new name that underlined how different this project was. This brand brings together grapes selected from the Pandolfa estate and the family's historic vineyards. Godenza 2014 is a subtle, complex wine of great finesse, with earthy, spicy notes and well-managed fruit on the nose, over a supple, fresh, consistent, focused palate with delicate citrus notes. The Sangiovese 2015, known to all as "the wasp" due to the large insect depicted on the label, is open and full-flavoured, with attractively simple aromas.

Cantine Riunite & Civ

VIA G. BRODOLINI, 24
42040 CAMPEGINE [RE]
TEL. +39 0522905711
www.riuniteciv.it

CELLAR SALES
ANNUAL PRODUCTION 130,000,000 bottles
HECTARES UNDER VINE 3500.00
SUSTAINABLE WINERY

This major cooperative brings together 2,600 growers and vinifies the grapes from 3,500 hectares under vine. These extraordinary figures together with the turnover achieved by Gruppo Italiano Vini make this operation Italy's leading producer. Its soul, however, despite its size, is rooted in country farming values and solidarity, as seen in the chairman Corrado Casoli. In recent years Lambrusco production has been increasingly convincing and Vanni Lusetti's wines are increasingly territorial and authentic. The 2015 range shows excellent quality across the board. The light, graceful Lambrusco FB 2015 is a subtle, vibrant wine with a nose of hedgerow, mace and damson followed by upfront citrus in the mouth. The Reggiano Albinea Canali 2015 displays a certain rustic quality, with austere fruit and close-knit tannins. The dense, meaty Foglie Rosse 2015 shows Parma violets on the nose over a supple, rounded palate. The floral, focused Pignoletto Righi 2015 has a herby finish.

● Romagna Sangiovese Sup. Godenza '14	♥♥♥ 3*
○ Bro '15	♥♥ 3
● Romagna Sangiovese Sup. Il Sangiovese '15	♥♥ 2*
● Romagna Sangiovese Sup. Il Sangiovese '14	♥♥♥ 2*
○ Bro '14	♥♥ 3
● Romagna Sangiovese Sup. '13	♥♥ 2*
● Romagna Sangiovese Sup. Godenza '13	♥♥ 2*

● Lambrusco Emilia FB Metodo Ancestrale Albinea Canali '15	♥♥ 2*
● Colli di Scandiano e di Canossa Lambrusco Grasparossa Frizzante Codarossa '15	♥♥ 2*
● L'Oscuro Gaetano Righi '15	♥♥ 2*
● Lambrusco di Modena Vecchio Ducato '15	♥♥ 2*
● Lambrusco di Sorbara Secco Gaetano Righi '15	♥♥ 2*
● Lambrusco Salamino di S. Croce Secco Gaetano Righi '15	♥♥ 2*
○ Pignoletto Spumante Gaetano Righi '15	♥♥ 2*
● Reggiano Lambrusco Albinea Canali '15	♥♥ 2*
● Reggiano Lambrusco Foglie Rosse Albinea Canali '15	♥♥ 2*
● Lambrusco Grasparossa di Castelvetro Secco Gaetano Righi '15	♥ 2

EMILIA ROMAGNA

Cantine Romagnoli

LOC. VILLÒ
VIA GENOVA, 20
29020 VIGOLZONE [PC]
TEL. +39 0523870904
www.cantineromagnoli.it

CELLAR SALES
PRE-BOOKED VISITS
ANNUAL PRODUCTION 300,000 bottles
HECTARES UNDER VINE 45.00
SUSTAINABLE WINERY

This historic Piacenza winery has been recently taken over by the Perini family. Production is in the hands of the oenologist Luciana Biondo, who has given it a new lease of life and faced the challenge with great commitment. Here, in one of the prime territories of the Piacenza area, Val Nure, regarded as the cradle of viticulture around Piacenza, the valley is brimming with established, well-known wineries. Cantine Romagnoli own 45 hectares under vine on ancient red clay soils, which owe their colour to the iron sediments they contain. The austere, fresh Colto Vitato del Cicotto 2015, a monovarietal Barbera, with a focused nose of rich fruit over a relaxed, limpid, citrus palate of impressive weight, with elegant encores of blood orange and tangerine, for a terroir-true wine. The rounded, full-flavoured Colto Vitato della Bellaria 2015 is taut and supple.

● Colto Vitato del Cicotto '15	♟♟ 2*
● Gutturnio Sup. Colto Vitato della Bellaria '15	♟♟ 2*
○ C. P. Ortrugo Frizzante Sasso Nero del Nure '15	♟ 2
● Caravaggio '14	♟ 5
● Gutturnio Frizzante Sasso Nero del Nure '15	♟ 3
● Caravaggio '12	♟♟ 5
● Colto Vitato del Cicotto '14	♟♟ 2*
○ Sasso Nero del Nure Bianco '14	♟♟ 2*
○ Sasso Nero del Nure Malvasia '14	♟♟ 2*

I Sabbioni

LOC. SABBIONI
VIA DEI SABBIONI, 22
47121 FORLÌ
TEL. +39 0543755711
www.isabbioni.it

CELLAR SALES
ANNUAL PRODUCTION 46,000 bottles
HECTARES UNDER VINE 7.00

The winery lies in the hills between Forlì and Faenza in the subzone of Oriolo. Here, the soils are characterized by an unusual lens of yellow molasse, at points emerging on the surface. This unique terroir moderates the vigour of some varieties and ensures flavourful wines. Here, in the 1980s, a find of great naturalistic value was uncovered, the cranium of a Mammuthus Meridionalis, today conserved in the Museo Civico di Scienze Naturali in Faenza. This extraordinary find bears witness to how geologically unique this place is. Bonadea 2015 is a perfect interpretation of this growing area, a fresh wine with forest fruits on the nose and full flavour on the vibrant palate. This is a highly approachable wine, subtle and full of energy, as well as stylistically perfect. The Sisto 2014, from vineyards planted on sand, shows an interesting palate with attractive acidity but is marred by slightly drying tannins.

● Romagna Sangiovese Rubrarosa Oriolo Sisto '14	♟♟ 2*
● Romagna Sangiovese Sup. Rubrarosa Bonadea '15	♟♟ 2*
● Romagna Sangiovese Sup. Rubrarosa Bonadea '14	♟♟ 2*
● Romagna Sangiovese Sup. Rubrarosa Elaide Ris. '13	♟♟ 4

San Biagio Vecchio

VIA SALITA DI ORIOLO, 13
48018 FAENZA [RA]
TEL. +39 3393523168
www.cantinasanbiagiovecchio.com

CELLAR SALES
PRE-BOOKED VISITS
ANNUAL PRODUCTION 8,000 bottles
HECTARES UNDER VINE 5.50

Andrea Balducci inherited the amazing experience of Antonio Baldassari, the parish priest of San Biagio, but above all a specialist in rustic, marvellous, sweet Albanas. Inspired by that experience, Andrea and his wife, Lucia Ziniti, have developed a dry wine that expresses the difficult but wonderful identity of this white vine variety and its acidity, power and tannins. Sabbiagialla owes its name to the sands of Pleistocene origin that characterize the soil on which the vines were planted 30 years ago following a long mass selection from old clones present in the area. The 2015, as usual the result of various growing years, opens to an attractive concentrated nose which fades quickly, but which will ensure complexity and longevity. The savoury, nuanced palate shows a herby finish. Bay leaf, curry plant, grapefruit, saffron and honey are among the many aromas this wine has to offer.

Vigne di San Lorenzo

VIA CAMPIUME, 6
48013 BRISIGHELLA [RA]
TEL. +39 3391137070
www.vignedisanlorenzo.it

CELLAR SALES
PRE-BOOKED VISITS
ACCOMMODATION AND RESTAURANT SERVICE
ANNUAL PRODUCTION 10,000 bottles
HECTARES UNDER VINE 3.00
VITICULTURE METHOD Certified Organic

In Valle del Lamone, a few kilometres to the north of Brisighella, on the road from Faenza to Florence, we find the town of Campiume, a place of extraordinary beauty that Filippo Manetti converted into a small winery and five rooms for guests. A grower and intellectual, he has for years been pursuing an artisanal style, and his wines are fine, ageable expressions of the growing year. Campiume 2012 is a complex, gamey, earthy Sangiovese, with a nose of extremely austere fruit over a savoury, vibrant palate which shows close-knit tannins and delicate pomegranate fruit. This austere wine will give of its best after ageing. The Oudeis 2011, a monovarietal Sangiovese aged in large oak, vaunts nuanced complexity, with a concentrated nose and great elegance on the palate. Rich aromas of autumn leaves, earthy minerality and gaminess come once again to the fore on the finish.

○ Sabbiagialla '15	♟♟ 2*
○ MammaMia! '15	♟ 2
○ Ambrosia Albana Passito '07	♟♟ 3
● Centesimino Passito '12	♟♟ 4
○ Quintessenza Albana Passito '12	♟♟ 3
○ Sabbiagialla '14	♟♟ 2*
○ Sabbiagialla '13	♟♟ 2*
○ Sabbiagialla '12	♟♟ 2*
○ Sabbiagialla '11	♟♟ 3
● Sangiovese di Romagna Sup. Barbatello '12	♟♟ 3
● Sangiovese di Romagna Sup. Serraglio '10	♟♟ 3
● Sangiovese di Romagna Sup. Serraglio '09	♟♟ 2*

● Campiume '12	♟♟♟ 4
● Oudeis '11	♟♟♟ 5
● Campiume '11	♟♟ 4
● Campiume '09	♟♟ 4
● Campiume '08	♟♟ 4
● San Lorenzo '11	♟♟ 4
● San Lorenzo '09	♟♟ 4
● San Lorenzo '08	♟♟ 4
● San Lorenzo '07	♟♟ 4
● Sangiovese Campaglione '11	♟♟ 2*
● Sangiovese di Romagna Sup. Campiume Ris. '07	♟♟ 4
● Sangiovese di Romagna Sup. Campiume Ris. '06	♟♟ 4

★San Patrignano

VIA SAN PATRIGNANO, 53
47853 CORIANO [RN]
TEL. +39 0541362111
www.spaziosanpa.com

PRE-BOOKED VISITS
RESTAURANT SERVICE
ANNUAL PRODUCTION 500,000 bottles
HECTARES UNDER VINE 110.00
VITICULTURE METHOD Certified Organic

The assets of 110 hectares of vineyards planted in the 1990s are today precious for the entire zone of Rimini, which sees in this winery a benchmark of absolute quality. Riccardo Cotarella and the local staff have risen to the challenge, pursuing a stylistic interpretation which increasingly expresses the territory. The operation is set in the hills near Rimini, where a climate mitigated by the closeness to the sea endows the wines with expressive fruit and appealing tannins, even in the case of sangiovese, which is generally edgy and stiff. In particular, the Bordeaux varieties find here an ideal climate, and comparing the area to Bolgheri is not an exaggeration. The Cabernet Sauvignon Montepirolo 2012 is a supple, taut wine of great finesse, unfolding spice and austere fruit. This fine example of a balance between richness and elegance shows how the area around Rimini has a particular vocation for Bordeaux varieties. The ripe Avi 2012 offers full flavour and close-knit tannins.

San Valentino

FRAZ. SAN MARTINO IN VENTI
VIA TOMASETTA, 13
47900 RIMINI
TEL. +39 0541752231
www.vinisanvalentino.com

CELLAR SALES
PRE-BOOKED VISITS
ACCOMMODATION
ANNUAL PRODUCTION 120,000 bottles
HECTARES UNDER VINE 20.00
VITICULTURE METHOD Certified Biodynamic

San Valentino is a time-honoured operation in the hills near Rimini, with vineyards overlooking the sea benefitting from temperature ranges softened by the Adriatic and regular summer air circulation. Over the years, Roberto Mascarin has not lacked the courage to take radical decisions and revolutionize farming techniques, converting to solely biodynamic methods with the help of the French agronomist Michel Barbaud. The aim is to produce wines which have artisanal character but formal precision. The complex, dry Vivian 2014, from sangiovese, Montepulciano and syrah, shows real character, with a variegated nose of forest floor, topsoil, fruit and herbs, swathed in delicate spice, over a rounded, elegant palate. Contesse Muschetti 2000 is to all effects a Vin Santo, and expresses the aromas typical of this type, with freshly ground coffee, dried fruits, figs, walnut skin, dates, curry plant and absinthe. The Luna Nuova 2014, a monovarietal Cabernet Franc, is vegetal and peppery.

● Colli di Rimini Cabernet Sauvignon Montepirolo '12	♟♟♟ 4*
○ Aulente Bianco '15	♟♟ 2*
● Romagna Sangiovese Sup. Ris. Avi '12	♟♟ 4
● Aulente Rosso '15	♟ 2
● Colli di Rimini Cabernet Montepirolo '06	♟♟♟ 5
● Colli di Rimini Cabernet Montepirolo '04	♟♟♟ 5
● Colli di Rimini Rosso Noi '04	♟♟♟ 4
● Romagna Sangiovese Sup. Avi Ris. '11	♟♟♟ 5
● Sangiovese di Romagna Sup. Avi Ris. '08	♟♟♟ 5
● Sangiovese di Romagna Sup. Avi Ris. '07	♟♟♟ 5
● Sangiovese di Romagna Sup. Avi Ris. '06	♟♟♟ 5
● Sangiovese di Romagna Sup. Avi Ris. '05	♟♟♟ 5
● Sangiovese di Romagna Sup. Ora '12	♟♟♟ 3*
● Sangiovese di Romagna Sup. Ora '11	♟♟♟ 3*

● Vivian '14	♟♟ 3*
○ Colli di Rimini Rebola Passito Contesse Muschietti 15 Anni '00	♟♟ 8
○ Colli di Rimini Rebola Scabi Bianco '15	♟♟ 2*
○ Due Bianco '15	♟♟ 3
● Luna Nuova '14	♟♟ 5
● Sangiovese di Romagna Sup. Scabi '14	♟ 2
● Sangiovese di Romagna Sup. Terra di Covignano Ris. '05	♟♟♟ 5
● Sangiovese di Romagna Sup. Terra di Covignano Ris. '03	♟♟♟ 4
● Sangiovese di Romagna Sup. Terra di Covignano Ris. '02	♟♟♟ 4
● Sangiovese di Romagna Sup. Terra di Covignano Ris. '01	♟♟♟ 4

Cantina Sociale Santa Croce

s.s. 468 DI CORREGGIO, 35
41012 CARPI [MO]
TEL. +39 059664007
www.cantinasantacroce.it

CELLAR SALES
PRE-BOOKED VISITS
ANNUAL PRODUCTION 400,000 bottles
HECTARES UNDER VINE 500.00

This historic operation, dating back to 1907, is located at Santa Croce, near Carpi, in the heart of the zone that gives its name to Lambrusco Salamino. Its 250 member-growers farm more than 500 hectares of vineyard, mostly in the plains south of Modena, although sme members are in the province of Reggio Emilia, just north of the loose-textured soils ideal for growing sorbara, at Limidi and Sozzigalli, on the left bank of the Secchia, which here acquires superb elegance. If you are looking to understand the essential identity of this variety, try the wines of Maurizio Boni, who has stepped in to replace the excellent Villiam Friggeri, taken from us before his time. The fruity, creamy Linea 2015 is a well-typed, territorial wine offering full flavour and freshness, with austere fruit and elegant tannins. Tradizione 2015 is full rounded and close-knit, with cherries and blackberries to the fore.

● Lambrusco Salamino di S. Croce Secco Linea '15	▼▼ 1*
● Lambrusco Salamino di S. Croce Tradizione '15	▼▼ 1*
● Lambrusco Salamino di S. Croce Amabile Linea '15	▼ 1*
☉ 100 Vendemmie Rosé Brut '14	♀♀ 2*
● Lambrusco Grasparossa di Castelvetro Secco '14	♀♀ 2*
● Lambrusco Salamino di S. Croce Enoteca '13	♀♀ 1*
● Lambrusco Salamino di S. Croce Tradizione '14	♀♀ 1*
● Lambrusco Salamino di S. Croce Tradizione '13	♀♀ 1*

Tenuta Santini

FRAZ. PASSANO
VIA CAMPO, 33
47853 CORIANO [RN]
TEL. +39 0541656527
www.tenutasantini.com

CELLAR SALES
PRE-BOOKED VISITS
ANNUAL PRODUCTION 40,000 bottles
HECTARES UNDER VINE 22.00

We are near Coriano, on the foothills rising behind Rimini and Riccione, between San Marino and Val Marecchia. These open rolling hills, with fairly uniform clay and limestone soils, enjoy temperature ranges influenced by the sea, which, especially in the summer, takes the edge off the heat and guarantees air circulation in the form of breezes. The result is fruity, approachable, somewhat graceful Sangioveses, with unaggressive tannins. More interesting are the wines from Bordeaux varieties, which here manage to give deep, complex, elegant wines with original character. It is no coincidence that this area is spoken of as the Adriatic's Bolgheri. Battarreo 2014, from cabernet sauvignon and merlot, is a graceful, focused wine, with elegant spice and rounded, austere fruit on the nose, followed by a richly-flavoured, taut, lingering palate. Beato Enrico 2015 offers a warm seductive nose and freshness in the mouth.

● Battarreo '14	▼▼ 3*
● Romagna Sangiovese Sup. Beato Enrico '15	▼▼ 2*
● Romagna Sangiovese Sup. Cornelianum Ris. '13	▼▼ 4
● Battarreo '09	♀♀ 3
● Sangiovese di Romagna Sup. Beato Enrico '11	♀♀ 2*
● Sangiovese di Romagna Sup. Cornelianum Ris. '12	♀♀ 4
● Sangiovese di Romagna Sup. Cornelianum Ris. '10	♀♀ 4
● Sangiovese di Romagna Sup. Cornelianum Ris. '09	♀♀ 4
● Sangiovese di Romagna Sup. Cornelianum Ris. '08	♀ 4

Cantina Sociale Settecani

VIA MODENA, 184
41014 CASTELVETRO DI MODENA [MO]
TEL. +39 059702505
www.cantinasettecani.it

CELLAR SALES
ANNUAL PRODUCTION 1,000,000 bottles
HECTARES UNDER VINE 530.00

Established in 1923, this small cooperative vinifies the grapes of 180 members for a total of around 300 hectares of vineyards. We are in the historic Borgo di Castelvetro, in the beautiful hills around Modena, and above all we are in the heart of the growing area of lambrusco grasparossa. Only a small part of the production is bottled and the wines proposed by the winery are classic and territorial, with a generally reliable, consistent range of good quality and matchless value for money. The classic, fruit-infused Grasparossa Secco 2015 is the quintessential everyday drinker, with a creamy, rounded palate and a citrusy, earthy finish. The complex Vini del Re 2015 shows a rustic soul, and shows mineral notes over a palate of blood orange, sea salt and herbs, swathed in refreshing savoury nuances. Divino 2015 shows austere and composed, with aromas of blackberry, currants and black tea.

La Stoppa

LOC. ANCARANO
29029 RIVERGARO [PC]
TEL. +39 0523958159
www.lastoppa.it

CELLAR SALES
PRE-BOOKED VISITS
RESTAURANT SERVICE
ANNUAL PRODUCTION 160,000 bottles
HECTARES UNDER VINE 32.00
VITICULTURE METHOD Certified Organic

Elena Pantaleoni is an important part of the story of this winery, which was already ground-breaking when it started out in the early 1900s with a lawyer from Genoa, before passing into the hands of the Pantaleoni family in 1973. The stylistic maturity and production figures make La Stoppa a symbol of Italian natural wine, an operation that has inspired dozens of growers through its revolutionary approach to viticulture and willingness to engage in discussion. On these wonderfully lean soils, Elena and Giulio Armani produce complex, pure, austere wines of incredible depth, with superb ageing potential. Trebbiolo Fermo 2014, from barbera and bonarda, needs to breathe to open up and express its focused fruit and earthy, mineral notes. On the taut, incisive palate, it offers full flavour and citrus. The complex Ageno 2010, a macerated white, shows a nose of dried fruits, curry plant, absinthe and eucalyptus, leading into a light, refreshing palate.

● Lambrusco Grasparossa di Castelvetro Secco '15	▼▼ 1*
● Lambrusco Grasparossa di Castelvetro Secco Divino '15	▼▼ 1*
● Lambrusco Grasparossa di Castelvetro Secco Vini del Re '15	▼▼ 1*
● Lambrusco Grasparossa di Castelvetro Amabile '14	♈ 1*
● Lambrusco Grasparossa di Castelvetro Amabile '13	♈ 1*
● Lambrusco Grasparossa di Castelvetro Secco '14	♈ 1*
● Lambrusco Grasparossa di Castelvetro Secco '13	♈ 1*
● Lambrusco Grasparossa di Castelvetro Secco '12	♈ 1*

● Trebbiolo Rosso Fermo '14	▼▼ 2*
○ Ageno '10	▼▼ 4
● Trebbiolo Rosso Frizzante '14	▼▼ 2*
● C. P. Cabernet Sauvignon Stoppa '96	♈♈♈ 5
○ C. P. Malvasia Passito V. del Volta '06	♈♈♈ 5
○ C. P. Malvasia Passito V. del Volta '04	♈♈♈ 5
○ C. P. Malvasia Passito V. del Volta '03	♈♈♈ 4
○ C. P. Malvasia Passito V. del Volta '97	♈♈♈ 4*
● Macchiona '06	♈♈♈ 4*
● Macchiona '05	♈♈♈ 4
○ Vigna del Volta '08	♈♈♈ 5
○ Ageno '11	♈ 4
● Barbera della Stoppa '10	♈ 4
● Barbera della Stoppa '09	♈ 4
● Macchiona '09	♈ 4
● Trebbiolo '13	♈ 2*

Tenuta Saiano

FRAZ. MONTEBELLO
VIA CASONE, 30
47824 TORRIANA [RN]
TEL. +39 3667862921
www.tenutasaiano.it

CELLAR SALES
PRE-BOOKED VISITS
ACCOMMODATION AND RESTAURANT SERVICE
ANNUAL PRODUCTION 15,000 bottles
HECTARES UNDER VINE 11.00
VITICULTURE METHOD Certified Organic

Established in 2003 by the businessman Manlio Maggioli, Saiano vinifies the grapes from ten hectares of its own vineyards planted on the chalky marl around Torriana, at an elevation of 400 metres in the hills near Rimini. The chalky soils endow the wines with a certain elegance and a salty palate, which is found across the range. The estate provides wines for a famous trattoria, La Sangiovesa di Santarcangelo di Romagna, also owned by the Maggioli family, and base wines for the artisanal production of excellent Vermouth. Saiano 2015, a blend of cabernet sauvignon, merlot and sangiovese, vaunts an overwhelming palate of great power and energy. This is a supple, spicy, fruit-infused wine, which elegantly combines the vegetal notes of cabernet and the fruitiness of merlot, with sangiovese providing grace and grip in the mouth. The fruity, floral Gianciotto 2015 plays on freshness to exalt its subtle, delicate soul.

● Romagna Sangiovese Sup. Gianciotto '15	🍷🍷 2*
● Saiano Rosso '15	🍷🍷 2*
● Romagna Sangiovese Sup. Gianciotto '14	🍷🍷 2*
● Romagna Sangiovese Sup. Gianciotto '13	🍷🍷 2*
● Saiano Rosso '14	🍷🍷 2*
● Saiano Rosso '13	🍷🍷 2*

Torre San Martino

VIA SAN MARTINO IN MONTE
47015 MODIGLIANA [FC]
TEL. +39 0689786312
www.torre1922.it

CELLAR SALES
PRE-BOOKED VISITS
ANNUAL PRODUCTION 38,000 bottles
HECTARES UNDER VINE 7.50

The vineyards of Torre San Martino lie at Modigliana, at an elevation of 350 metres on sandstone soils, which give finesse and longevity. In particular, we are a stone's throw from Valle dell'Acerreta, one of the three valleys which rise up from Modigliana towards the Apennines. Of the three, this is the one with the most clayey soils. Although expressing marked territorial identity, with salty palates, elegant tannins and cutting acidity, here the the wines show greater stuffing and grip, and fine-grained finesse. The winery also owns the oldest vineyard in Romagna, dating back to 1922, planted to bush vines patiently restored by Francesco Bordini, the winery's agronomist and oenologist. The Sangiovese Vigna 1922 2013 is mineral and balsamic, with pencil lead and elegant fresh green notes. On the palate, salty acidity provides progression and is underpinned by close-knit, compact tannins. Gemme 2015 expresses focused, austere fruit, with hints of pomegranate and delicate citrus nuances.

● Romagna Sangiovese Modigliana Sup. V. 1922 Ris. '13	🍷🍷🍷 6
● Romagna Sangiovese Modigliana Sup. Gemme '15	🍷🍷 3*
● Colli di Faenza V. Claudia Ris. '13	🍷🍷 3
○ V. della Signora '15	🍷🍷 5
● Romagna Sangiovese Sup. Gemme '14	🍷🍷🍷 3*
● Sangiovese di Romagna V. 1922 Ris. '11	🍷🍷🍷 6
○ Colli di Faenza Torre '12	🍷🍷 2*
● Colli di Faenza V. Claudia Ris. '12	🍷🍷 3
● Romagna Sangiovese Sup. V. 1922 Ris. '12	🍷🍷 6
● Sangiovese di Romagna V. 1922 '08	🍷🍷 6

Venturini Baldini

FRAZ. RONCOLO
VIA TURATI, 42
42020 QUATTRO CASTELLA [RE]
TEL. +39 0522249011
www.venturinibaldini.it

CELLAR SALES
PRE-BOOKED VISITS
RESTAURANT SERVICE
ANNUAL PRODUCTION 300,000 bottles
HECTARES UNDER VINE 35.00
VITICULTURE METHOD Certified Organic

Venturini Baldini was established in 1975, but its roots go back much further, being set around a villa built in 1670. Here, in the hills near Reggio Emilia, lie its 35 hectares under vine, organically tended for 20 years, surrounded by 150 hectares of woodland and meadow. This property has recently been bought up by a large Italian wine holding owned by the Iverna investment company. The winery is now run by Giuseppe Prestia, who has worked hard together with Lorenzo Tersi and Monica Franceschetti to bring this established brand into the group's portfolio, with a steadfast belief in the potential both of the area and of top-quality Lambrusco. Denny Bini, the winery's long-standing cellarman, has put his experience to the service of Carlo Ferrini, now on his second harvest, and the result is an extremely interesting range of wines. Manodori 2015 is an elegant wine of great finesse, showing fresh citrus and delicate fruit.

- ● Reggiano Lambrusco Secco
  Marchese Manodori '15 ⚑⚑ 3*
- ○ Colli di Scandiano e di Canossa
  Malvasia Frizzante Secco Graniers '15 ⚑⚑ 2*
- ⊙ Reggiano Lambrusco Rosato
  Spumante Secco Cadelvento '15 ⚑⚑ 3
- ● Reggiano Lambrusco Secco
  Spumante Rubino del Cerro '15 ⚑⚑ 3
- ● Reggiano Lambrusco Rosso
  Spumante Brut Quaranta '15 ⚑ 3
- ⊙ Reggiano Lambrusco Rosato Secco '14 ⚑⚑ 2*
- ● Reggiano Lambrusco Secco '14 ⚑⚑ 2*
- ● Rubino del Cerro Mater Spumante '14 ⚑⚑ 2*

Francesco Vezzelli

FRAZ. SAN MATTEO
VIA CANALETTO NORD, 878A
41122 MODENA
TEL. +39 059318695
aavezzelli@gmail.com

CELLAR SALES
PRE-BOOKED VISITS
ANNUAL PRODUCTION 120,000 bottles
HECTARES UNDER VINE 15.00

This operation near Modena has been producing wine since 1958, and now sees the third generation at work in the cellar. The production facility is in the small village of San Matteo, just outside Modena, while the vineyards are at Sozzigalli, in the floodplains between the lowest river levees and the main levee, the Secchia. These loose, lean soils are perfect for lambrusco sorbara because they exalt its floral traits and minerality. The Grasparossas are produced using grapes bought from other growers at Levizzano Rangone. The incisive, mineral Selezione 2015 needs to breathe before expressing delicate, austere fruit. On the palate, full flavour combines with a floral finish of roses, Parma violets and hawthorn, alongside gunflint. This vibrant, rustic wine shows elegant nuances, and shows taut, lean and pure.

- ● Lambrusco di Sorbara Il Selezione '15 ⚑⚑ 2*
- ● Lambrusco di Sorbara Secco
  Soldino '15 ⚑⚑ 2*
- ⊙ Lambrusco di Sorbara
  Spumante Brut MoRosa Rosé '15 ⚑⚑ 2*
- ● Lambrusco Grasparossa di Castelvetro
  Secco Rive dei Ciliegi '15 ⚑ 2
- ● Lambrusco di Sorbara Il Selezione '14 ⚑⚑ 2*
- ⊙ Lambrusco di Sorbara Rosé MoRosa '14 ⚑⚑ 2*
- ● Lambrusco Grasparossa di Castelvetro
  Rive dei Ciliegi '14 ⚑⚑ 2*

Villa di Corlo

LOC. BAGGIOVARA
S.DA CAVEZZO, 200
41126 MODENA
TEL. +39 059510736
www.villadicorlo.com

CELLAR SALES
PRE-BOOKED VISITS
ANNUAL PRODUCTION 85,000 bottles
HECTARES UNDER VINE 26.50

Maria Antonietta Munari perfectly represents the hardworking, optimistic spirit of Modena and its people, and their extraordinary, time-honoured love for the land. The winery lies around an old stately home just off the Via Emilia, on ideal soils for grasparossa, which is in fact the basis for the estate's best wines. The house also contains the vinegar room, one of Modena's oldest and finest, which produces an Aceto Balsamico Tradizionale of outstanding quality. The Corleto 2015 is a quality wine that vaunts a fruity, seductive style, far from the supple, highly drinkable versions of some years ago. This is the result of a conscious decision by the owners, but we feel that the high quality grapes produced by this small winery have greater potential. The Grasparossa 2015, convincing but with slightly overripe fruit on the nose, shows a fresh palate, but is sadly marred by drying tannins.

Villa Liverzano

FRAZ. RONTANA
VIA VALLONI, 47
48013 BRISIGHELLA [RA]
TEL. +39 054680461
www.liverzano.it

CELLAR SALES
PRE-BOOKED VISITS
ACCOMMODATION
ANNUAL PRODUCTION 15,000 bottles
HECTARES UNDER VINE 3.20
VITICULTURE METHOD Certified Organic

Marco Montanari tends his rows in a unique terroir, on original soils with abundant outcrops of Brisighella chalk, which provide potential for extreme finesse, consistently interpreted in expressive, fruit-driven wines which enjoy great success in his native Switzerland. His is a constant struggle against the harshness of the highest land in Brisighella, and demonstrates that wine is also a cultural product embodying the story of each producer. The wines bear the signature of the agronomist and wine maker Francesco Bordini. Don 2013, from cabernet franc and carmenere, is a wine with a clear identity and great character. The complex nose shows abundant fruit and spice, with notes of pomegranate and fresh nuances, leading into a close-knit, dense, dry palate with full flavour and depth. Rebello 2012, from sangiovese and merlot, offers silky tannins and crisp, focused fruit.

● Lambrusco Grasparossa di Castelvetro Corleto '15	♟♟ 2*
⊙ Lambrusco Grasparossa di Castelvetro Rosato Spumante Brut '15	♟ 2
● Lambrusco Grasparossa di Castelvetro Secco '15	♟ 2
○ Pignoletto Extra Dry '15	♟ 2
● Lambrusco di Sorbara Primevo '14	♟♟ 2*
● Lambrusco di Sorbara Primevo '13	♟♟ 2*
● Lambrusco Grasparossa di Castelvetro Amabile '13	♟♟ 2*
● Lambrusco Grasparossa di Castelvetro Corleto '13	♟♟ 2*

● Don '13	♟♟ 6
● Rebello '12	♟♟ 5
● Donna Merlot '11	♟♟ 7
● Don '11	♟♟ 6
● Don '10	♟♟ 6
● Don '09	♟♟ 6
● Don '08	♟♟ 6
● Donna '09	♟♟ 7
● Rebello '11	♟♟ 5
● Rebello '10	♟♟ 5
● Rebello '08	♟♟ 5
● Rebello '07	♟♟ 5
● Trecento '12	♟♟ 4
● Trecento '11	♟♟ 4
● Trecento '10	♟♟ 4

EMILIA ROMAGNA

Villa Papiano

VIA IBOLA, 24
47015 MODIGLIANA [FC]
TEL. +39 0546941790
www.villapapiano.it

CELLAR SALES
PRE-BOOKED VISITS
ANNUAL PRODUCTION 50,000 bottles
HECTARES UNDER VINE 10.00

Francesco Bordini is a seasoned professional, able to perfectly interpret the territorial traits of Modigliana, and in fact manages to bring out to the full the potential of these marl and sandstone soils in vertical, richly-flavoured wines, without sacrificing the complexity that Valle dell'Ibola, on the northern slopes of Mount Chioda, at an altitude of 500 metres, gives sangiovese grapes. The resulting wines are austere, showing rarified tannins and unbeatable longevity. The vineyards at Villa Papiano are some of the highest in the region, and vie for space with woodland and pastures, perfectly set in an unspoilt natural environment. I Probi 2013, a monovarietal Sangiovese aged in large oak, is a composed wine of great elegance, and shows deep, austere and clenched. On the nose, it shows layered and follows through with a consistent, savoury palate, with hard, rarefied tannins, which will help the wine age well. The richly-flavoured, fruity Le Papesse 2015 is crisp and forthright.

Villa Venti

LOC. VILLAVENTI DI RONCOFREDDO
VIA DOCCIA, 1442
47020 FORLÌ
TEL. +39 0541949532
www.villaventi.it

CELLAR SALES
PRE-BOOKED VISITS
ACCOMMODATION
ANNUAL PRODUCTION 27,500 bottles
HECTARES UNDER VINE 7.00
VITICULTURE METHOD Certified Organic

The vineyards of Villa Venti are now producing at full capacity, and are supported by the experience of Mauro Giardini and Davide Castellucci, who meticulously exploit to their advantage every small variation in the soil. This what makes Villa Venti a benchmark for the territory, releasing year after year increasingly artisanal, classic products, without any of the rhetoric so often associated with natural and organic wines. Go and pay these authentic growers a visit, and let them tell you about their work and territory. Primo Segno was the first Sangiovese to challenge the conventions of the Romagna wine world: a Superiore with the ambitions of a Riserva, based on the conviction that quality in this growing area can include fresh, austere, subtle wines without oak ageing. The elegant, supple, taut 2013 shows mature tannins alongside delicate hints of spice and attractive tangerine fruit.

● Romagna Sangiovese Modigliana I Probi di Papiano Ris. '13	¶¶¶ 3*
● Romagna Sangiovese Sup. Le Papesse di Papiano '15	¶¶ 2*
○ Terra! '15	¶¶ 3
○ Tregenda Albana Passita V. T. '13	¶¶ 3
● Romagna Sangiovese I Probi di Papiano Ris. '12	¶¶¶ 3*
● Sangiovese di Romagna I Probi di Papiano Ris. '11	¶¶¶ 3*
● Sangiovese di Romagna I Probi di Papiano Ris. '10	¶¶¶ 3*

● Sangiovese di Romagna Sup. Primo Segno '13	¶¶ 3*
○ Colli della Romagna Centrale Felis Leo '10	¶¶ 3
● Sangiovese di Romagna Longiano Primo Segno '11	¶¶¶ 3*
● Sangiovese di Romagna Sup. Primo Segno '09	¶¶¶ 3*
● Sangiovese di Romagna Sup. Primo Segno '08	¶¶¶ 3*
● Romagna Sangiovese Longiano Ris. '12	¶¶ 4
● Sangiovese di Romagna Longiano Ris '11	¶¶ 4

★Fattoria Zerbina

FRAZ. MARZENO
VIA VICCHIO, 11
48018 FAENZA [RA]
TEL. +39 054640022
www.zerbina.com

CELLAR SALES
PRE-BOOKED VISITS
ANNUAL PRODUCTION 220,000 bottles
HECTARES UNDER VINE 33.00

The extreme discipline in caring for the rows, mainly of mature bush vines, ensure that Cristina Geminiani and her partners can count on exceptional raw materials. The experience of 30 harvests does the rest, along with traditional techniques and respect for the typical traits endowed by the red clay of the small subzone of Marzeno. The overall reliability of their Sangioveses is extraordinary, but they also do magnificent work with albana, traditionally used for sweet wines but also now in an interesting dry version. Pietramora 2012 is in the classic Zerbina style: rich and weighty, potent and forthright. Attractive acidity provides dynamism on the palate, finishing to citrus notes of orange zest. This warm wine shows close-woven tannins and bears the mark of the red clay soils from which it harks. Torre di Ceparano 2012 is drying in the mouth, but remains supple thanks to its freshness. The Albana Ceparano 2015 offers a herby nose, with faint hints of peat and aniseed, over a citrusy, incisive palate.

○ Albana di Romagna Passito Arrocco '13	♥♥	5
○ Albana di Romagna Secco Ceparano '15	♥♥	2*
● Romagna Sangiovese Sup. Pietramora Ris. '12	♥♥	5
● Sangiovese di Romagna Sup. Torre di Ceparano Ris. '12	♥♥	3
○ Tergeno Albana Secco V. T. '14	♥♥	3
● Romagna Sangiovese Sup. Ceregio '15	♥	2
○ Romagna Trebbiano Ceregio Bianco '15	♥	2
○ Albana di Romagna Passito AR Ris. '06	♥♥♥	8
● Marzieno '08	♥♥♥	4*
● Sangiovese di Romagna Sup. Pietramora Ris. '08	♥♥♥	6

Zucchi

LOC. SAN LORENZO
VIA VIAZZA, 64
41030 SAN PROSPERO [MO]
TEL. +39 059908934
www.vinizucchi.it

CELLAR SALES
PRE-BOOKED VISITS
ANNUAL PRODUCTION 130,000 bottles
HECTARES UNDER VINE 10.00

The winery boasts a long tradition, and has been producing small but excellent quantities of Sorbara for over 60 years from its own vineyards. Bottling began with Bruno Zucchi before passing to the hands of his son Davide and the latter's wife Maura. With the arrival of his youngest daughter, Silvia, the experience of Davide, who is loved and respected in the area, combines with by her great energy and desire to look to the future with ambition and uncompromising quality. This has led to new ideas, although they are actually traditional, such as manual harvesting and vinification focusing as far as possible on dry wines. The crisp, lean Rito 2015 shows a delicate nose of flowers and herbs with a hint of fruit, over a dynamic palate in which acidity provides rhythm and tautness. On the finish, we find lemon and tangerine zest and Sorbara's trademark saltiness. The Metodo Classico 2013 is complex and deep.

● Lambrusco di Sorbara Secco Rito '15	♥♥♥	2*
● Lambrusco di Sorbara Dosaggio Zero M. Cl. '13	♥♥	2*
● Lambrusco di Sorbara Secco '15	♥♥	2*
● Lambrusco di Sorbara Secco Rifermentazione in Bottiglia '14	♥♥	2*
● Lambrusco di Sorbara Rito '14	♥♥♥	2*
● Lambrusco di Sorbara Secco '14	♥♥	2*
● Lambrusco di Sorbara Secco '13	♥♥	2*
● Lambrusco di Sorbara Secco Rito '13	♥♥	2*
● Modena Lambrusco Marascone '14	♥♥	2*

Ariola Vigne e Vini

LOC. CALICELLA DI PILASTRO
FRAZ. PILASTRO
S.DA DELLA BUCA, 5A
43010 LANGHIRANO [PR]
TEL. +39 0521637678
www.viniariola.it

CELLAR SALES
PRE-BOOKED VISITS
RESTAURANT SERVICE
ANNUAL PRODUCTION 800,000 bottles
HECTARES UNDER VINE 48.00

○ Forte Rigoni Nature Malvasia Brut '15	♥♥ 3
● Marcello Dry '15	♥♥ 3
● Marcello Nature Brut '15	♥♥ 3

Raffaella Alessandra Bissoni

LOC. CASTICCIANO
VIA COLECCHIO, 280
47032 BERTINORO [FC]
TEL. +39 0543460382
www.vinibissoni.com

CELLAR SALES
PRE-BOOKED VISITS
ANNUAL PRODUCTION 25,000 bottles
HECTARES UNDER VINE 5.00
SUSTAINABLE WINERY

○ Albana di Romagna Passito '11	♥♥ 5
● Sangiovese di Romagna Sup. Girapoggio '14	♥ 3

Ca' di Sopra

LOC. MARZENO
VIA FELIGARA, 15
48013 BRISIGHELLA [RA]
TEL. +39 3284927073
www.cadisopra.com

CELLAR SALES
PRE-BOOKED VISITS
ANNUAL PRODUCTION 24,000 bottles
HECTARES UNDER VINE 28.00
SUSTAINABLE WINERY

○ Romagna Albana Secco '15	♥♥ 3
● Romagna Sangiovese Sup. Crepe '15	♥♥ 2*

Calonga

LOC. CASTIGLIONE
VIA CASTEL LEONE, 8
47100 FORLÌ
TEL. +39 0543753044
www.calonga.it

CELLAR SALES
PRE-BOOKED VISITS
ANNUAL PRODUCTION 30,000 bottles
HECTARES UNDER VINE 8.00

● Ordelaffo '15	♥♥ 2*
● Romagna Sangiovese Sup. Michelangiolo Ris. '12	♥♥ 4

Tenuta Carbognano

VIA CARBOGNANO, 3
47855 GEMMANO [RN]
TEL. +39 0541984507
www.tenutacarbognano.it

CELLAR SALES
PRE-BOOKED VISITS
ACCOMMODATION
ANNUAL PRODUCTION 10,000 bottles
HECTARES UNDER VINE 3.00
VITICULTURE METHOD Certified Organic

● Ali '13	♥♥ 3

Carra di Casatico

LOC. CASATICO
S.DA LA NAVE, 10B
43013 LANGHIRANO [PR]
TEL. +39 0521863510
www.carradicasatico.com

CELLAR SALES
PRE-BOOKED VISITS
ANNUAL PRODUCTION 120,000 bottles
HECTARES UNDER VINE 25.00

○ Colli di Parma Malvasia Frizzante '15	♥♥ 2*
● Torcularia Lambrusco Emilia '15	♥ 2

Castelluccio

LOC. POGGIOLO DI SOTTO
VIA TRAMONTO, 15
47015 MODIGLIANA [FC]
TEL. +39 0546942486
www.ronchidicastelluccio.it

CELLAR SALES
PRE-BOOKED VISITS
ACCOMMODATION
ANNUAL PRODUCTION 100,000 bottles
HECTARES UNDER VINE 16.00

○ Ronco del Re '09	♀♀ 5
● Sangiovese di Romagna Le More '15	♀♀ 2*

La Collina

VIA PAGLIA, 19
48013 BRISIGHELLA [RA]
TEL. +39 054683110
www.lacollina-vinicola.com

CELLAR SALES
ANNUAL PRODUCTION 17,000 bottles
HECTARES UNDER VINE 4.00

● Cupola '13	♀♀ 4
● Sangiovita '13	♀♀ 3

Divinalux

VIA CADUTI DI CRIVELLARI, 50
48025 RIOLO TERME [RA]
TEL. +39 3314948859
www.divinaluxwinery.com

PRE-BOOKED VISITS
ANNUAL PRODUCTION 25,000 bottles
HECTARES UNDER VINE 7.00

○ Hilla Trebbiano '14	♀♀ 6
○ Romagna Albana Secco Dar '14	♀♀ 6

Cantina Sociale Formigine Pedemontana

VIA RADICI IN PIANO, 228
41043 FORMIGINE [MO]
TEL. +39 059558122
www.lambruscodoc.it

CELLAR SALES
PRE-BOOKED VISITS
ANNUAL PRODUCTION 960,000 bottles
HECTARES UNDER VINE 580.00
VITICULTURE METHOD Certified Organic

⊙ Modena Lambrusco For.Mo.Sa. Brut Rosé '15	♀♀ 2*
○ Pignoletto For.Mo.Sa. Brut '15	♀♀ 2*

Gavioli

VIA PROVINCIALE OVEST
41015 NONANTOLA [MO]
TEL. +39 059545462
www.gaviolivini.com

CELLAR SALES
PRE-BOOKED VISITS
ANNUAL PRODUCTION 250,000 bottles
HECTARES UNDER VINE 60.00

● Lambrusco di Sorbara Secco '15	♀♀ 2*
● Lambrusco Emilia M. Cl. Brut '12	♀♀ 4
● Modena Lambrusco Rifermentazione Ancestrale '14	♀ 3

Isola

FRAZ. MONGIORGIO
VIA G. BERNARDI, 3
40050 MONTE SAN PIETRO [BO]
TEL. +39 0516768428
isola1898@interfree.it

CELLAR SALES
PRE-BOOKED VISITS
ANNUAL PRODUCTION 60,000 bottles
HECTARES UNDER VINE 12.50

○ C. B. Pignoletto Cl. V. V. '13	♀♀ 3
○ C. B. Pignoletto Picrì Brut '15	♀♀ 2*

Lini 910

FRAZ. CANOLO
VIA VECCHIA CANOLO, 7
42015 CORREGGIO [RE]
TEL. +39 0522690162
www.lini910.it

CELLAR SALES
PRE-BOOKED VISITS
ANNUAL PRODUCTION 400,000 bottles
HECTARES UNDER VINE 25.00

● In Correggio Lambrusco Scuro '15   ♥♥ 2*

Alberto Lusignani

LOC. VIGOLENO
VIA CASE ORSI, 9
29010 VERNASCA [PC]
TEL. +39 0523895178
lusignani@agonet.it

CELLAR SALES
PRE-BOOKED VISITS
ANNUAL PRODUCTION 3,000 bottles
HECTARES UNDER VINE 10.00

○ C. P. Vin Santo di Vigoleno '06   ♥♥ 8
● Barbera Frizzante '15   ♥♥ 1*

Manaresi

LOC. BELLA VISTA
VIA BERTOLONI , 14
40069 ZOLA PREDOSA [BO]
TEL. +39 051751491
www.manaresi.net

CELLAR SALES
PRE-BOOKED VISITS
ANNUAL PRODUCTION 45,000 bottles
HECTARES UNDER VINE 11.00
SUSTAINABLE WINERY

○ C.B. Pignoletto Frizzante '15   ♥♥ 2*
○ C.B. Pignoletto Cl. '15   ♥ 2

Tenuta Masselina

LOC. SERRÀ
VIA POZZE, 1030
48014 CASTEL BOLOGNESE [RA]
TEL. +39 0545651004
www.masselina.it

CELLAR SALES
ANNUAL PRODUCTION 35,000 bottles
HECTARES UNDER VINE 16.00

○ Romagna Albana Secco '14   ♥♥ 2*
● Romagna Sangiovese Sup. 138 '15   ♥♥ 2*

Mattarelli

VIA MARCONI, 35
44049 VIGARANO MAINARDA [FE]
TEL. +39 053243123
www.mattarelli-vini.it

CELLAR SALES
PRE-BOOKED VISITS
ANNUAL PRODUCTION 300,000 bottles
HECTARES UNDER VINE 11.00

○ Bosco Eliceo Bianco Frizzante '15   ♥♥ 3
● Bosco Eliceo Fortana Frizzante '15   ♥♥ 3

Cantina Puianello e Coviolo

FRAZ. PUIANELLO
VIA C. MARX, 19A
42020 QUATTRO CASTELLA [RE]
TEL. +39 0522889120
www.cantinapuianello.it

CELLAR SALES
PRE-BOOKED VISITS
ANNUAL PRODUCTION 980,000 bottles
HECTARES UNDER VINE 240.00
VITICULTURE METHOD Certified Organic

⊙ Ancestrale Lambrusco Emilia
  Rosé Frizzante Secco '14   ♥♥ 2*
● Reggiano Lambrusco Barghi
  L'Incontro '15   ♥♥ 2*

Rocca Le Caminate

S.DA MELDOLA ROCCA DELLE CAMINATE, 15A
47014 MELDOLA [FC]
TEL. +39 0543493482
www.roccalecaminate.it

CELLAR SALES
PRE-BOOKED VISITS
ANNUAL PRODUCTION 20,000 bottles
HECTARES UNDER VINE 6.00
VITICULTURE METHOD Certified
OrganicCertified Biodynamic

● Romagna Sangiovese Predappio Sbargoleto '13	♥♥ 3
● Romagna Sangiovese Predappio Bramabene '13	♥ 2

Le Rocche Malatestiane

VIA EMILIA, 104
47900 RIMINI
TEL. +39 0541743079
www.lerocchemalatestiane.it

CELLAR SALES
PRE-BOOKED VISITS
ANNUAL PRODUCTION 800,000 bottles
HECTARES UNDER VINE 800.00

● Romagna Sangiovese Sup. Tre Miracoli '15	♥♥ 2*
● Romagna Sangiovese Sup. I Diavoli '15	♥♥ 2*
● Romagna Sangiovese Sup. Sigismondo '15	♥♥ 2*

Fondo San Giuseppe

VIA TURA
48013 BRISIGHELLA [RA]
TEL. +39 3284333271
www.fondosangiuseppe.it

PRE-BOOKED VISITS
ANNUAL PRODUCTION 20,000 bottles
HECTARES UNDER VINE 4.50
VITICULTURE METHOD Certified Organic

● Ca' Bianca Sangiovese '15	♥♥ 3
○ Fiorile Albana '15	♥♥ 3

Tenuta Santa Lucia

VIA GIARDINO, 1400
47025 MERCATO SARACENO [FC]
TEL. +39 054790441
www.santaluciavinery.it

CELLAR SALES
PRE-BOOKED VISITS
ACCOMMODATION
ANNUAL PRODUCTION 90,000 bottles
HECTARES UNDER VINE 16.00
VITICULTURE METHOD Certified Organic
SUSTAINABLE WINERY

○ Albana di Romagna Secco Alba Rara '15	♥♥ 2*
● Sangiovese di Romagna Sup. Taibo '15	♥ 2

Santodeno

VIA VILLA ROSSI, 50
47012 CIVITELLA DI ROMAGNA [FC]
TEL. +39 3356556747
fabio.ravaioli@santodeno.it

CELLAR SALES
PRE-BOOKED VISITS
ACCOMMODATION
ANNUAL PRODUCTION 400,000 bottles
HECTARES UNDER VINE 70.00

● Romagna Sangiovese Sup. '15	♥♥ 2*

Il Teatro

VIA MONTE TREBBIO, 17
47015 MODIGLIANA [FC]
TEL. +39 3351358688
ilteatrodivino@icloud.com

CELLAR SALES
PRE-BOOKED VISITS
ANNUAL PRODUCTION 5,000 bottles
HECTARES UNDER VINE 2.50

● Romagna Sangiovese Modigliana Violano '15	♥♥ 4
● Romagna Sangiovese Sup. Atto II '15	♥♥ 3

Terraquilia

VIA CALDANA
41052 GUIGLIA [MO]
TEL. +39 059931023
www.terraquilia.it

CELLAR SALES
PRE-BOOKED VISITS
ANNUAL PRODUCTION 40,000 bottles
HECTARES UNDER VINE 6.00
VITICULTURE METHOD Certified Organic

● Falcorubens '15	♥♥ 2*
○ Terrebianche '15	♥♥ 2*

Terre della Pieve

FRAZ. DIEGARO
VIA EMILIA PONENTE, 2412
47023 CESENA [FC]
TEL. +39 0547611535
www.terredellapieve.com

PRE-BOOKED VISITS
ANNUAL PRODUCTION 25,000 bottles
HECTARES UNDER VINE 5.00

● Sangiovese di Romagna Sup. Nobis Ris. '12	♥♥ 3

Azienda Agricola Trerè

LOC. MONTICORALLI
VIA CASALE, 19
48018 FAENZA [RA]
TEL. +39 054647034
www.trere.com

CELLAR SALES
PRE-BOOKED VISITS
ACCOMMODATION AND RESTAURANT SERVICE
ANNUAL PRODUCTION 150,000 bottles
HECTARES UNDER VINE 30.00

● Sangiovese di Romagna Sup. Sperone '15	♥♥ 2*
○ Albana di Romagna Arlùs '15	♥ 2

Vallona

LOC. FAGNANO
40050 CASTELLO DI SERRAVALLE [BO]
TEL. +39 0516703333
www.fattorievallona.it

CELLAR SALES
PRE-BOOKED VISITS
ANNUAL PRODUCTION 100,000 bottles
HECTARES UNDER VINE 31.00

○ C. B. Pignoletto Cl. Amestesso '11	♥♥ 4
○ Pignoletto Frizzante '15	♥ 2

Marta Valpiani

LOC. CASTROCARO TERME
VIA BAGNOLO, 156/158
47011 FORLÌ
TEL. +39 0543769598
www.vinimartavalpiani.it

CELLAR SALES
PRE-BOOKED VISITS
ANNUAL PRODUCTION 20,000 bottles
HECTARES UNDER VINE 8.00

○ Bianco '15	♥♥ 2*
● Romagna Sangiovese Sup. '14	♥♥ 2*

Podere Vecciano

VIA VECCIANO, 23
47852 CORIANO [RN]
TEL. +39 0541658388
www.poderevecciano.it

CELLAR SALES
PRE-BOOKED VISITS
ANNUAL PRODUCTION 100,000 bottles
HECTARES UNDER VINE 15.00
VITICULTURE METHOD Certified Organic
SUSTAINABLE WINERY

⊙ Ramante Rosé Brut '15	♥♥ 2*
● Romagna Sangiovese Sup. Vignalmonte '13	♥♥ 3

TUSCANY

In this year's guide, Tuscany continues to lead Tre Bicchieri rankings, with 80 cellars on the podium, but even more importantly, the region has the biggest number of wineries taking their first ever award, ten in all and well over ten percent of the regional total. It is no coincidence that for the second year in a row the Up-and-Coming Winery is Tuscan: Angela Fronti's admirable Istine from the Chianti Classico district. Not to mention that from the same area Cigliano also hit the bullseye as did Torre a Cona, in the Colli Fiorentini. To these we can add 16 Tre Bicchieri awards to other Chianti Classicos and eight to IGTs from the same zone. Not bad for an area that is oh-so-wrongly considered sluggish, hidebound by the local giants who seem unable to renew themselves. Hopefully the growers themselves will start to believe it and thus find a way to exploit the assets at their disposal, also from an economic perspective, given that designation grapes are selling far too cheaply. Montalcino garnered 14 awards, with one to Uccelliera's Rosso. The 2010 Riservas just pipped the 2011 Brunellos at the post by seven to six, and it is worth underscoring that the 2011 is a very good vintage so it seems a little unfair to see it overshadowed by a much-hyped 2010. There were also two Montalcino debut Tre Bicchieri awards, going to Tenuta di Sesta and to Oenologist Carlo Ferrini's small Giodo. The Bolgheris recover their glory in the 2013 vintage and waltz away with 11 awards for great balance, grip and structure, and perfectly ripe tannins, and we would be willing to bet they even cellar well. Things are moving here too, as our guide was happy to award a Tre Bicchieri to Fabio Motta and his Le Gonnare 2013. The Nobile di Montepulciano designation confirms last year's feeling that the wine is increasingly focused, especially the tannins, which tend to be tricky because of the nature of the terroir, and it also has a Tre Bicchieri new entry: Tenuta di Gracciano della Seta. Maremma's Morellino and Montecucco are certainly not resting on their laurels either, and hold on to the winning less-is-more approach in preference to muscle, because when the growing area and climate are generous, the vigneron must learn to use a light not a heavy hand. The Tre Bicchieri debutant winners here are Antonio Camillo and his 2014 Maremma Toscana Ciliegiolo Vigna Vallerana Alta, an elegant, refined reading of the delicate vine, as well as Podere della Civettaja's 2013 Pinot Nero, a stubborn rebel from the Tuscan Apennines showing elegance, finesse and delicacy.

Acquabona

LOC. ACQUABONA
57037 PORTOFERRAIO [LI]
TEL. +39 0565933013
www.acquabonaelba.it

CELLAR SALES
PRE-BOOKED VISITS
ANNUAL PRODUCTION 90,000 bottles
HECTARES UNDER VINE 18.00

Acquabona's earliest nucleus stood around a freshwater spring between Portoferraio and Porto Azzurro in the early 1700s. A few vines grew among the larger plantations of cereal crops and fodder for the livestock farm, and over time they took on a prevalent role in the farm's economy, until the winegrowing estate was established just under 60 years ago. In 1987 three agronomist friends decided to take over the farm with a view to relaunching Aleatico Passito dell'Elba and Ansonica, and creating a modern, functional winegrowing estate. The Aleatico Passito is almost a classic presence in the finals. The 2011 shows a slightly gamey nose with hints of ripe fruit. The palate is succulent and weighty, stylish and full-bodied, with a lovely, gutsy, truly lingering finish. Floral aromas for the Elba Ansonica 2015, with hints of almonds, and a firm but fresh and enjoyable palate. The Elba Bianco 2015 is tantalisingly uncomplicated with hints of lime on the nose and a mouthwatering, fresh and appetizing flavour.

● Elba Aleatico Passito '11	♥♥ 3*
○ Elba Ansonica '15	♥♥ 3
○ Elba Bianco '15	♥♥ 2*
● Voltraio '12	♥♥ 4
⊙ Elba Rosato '15	♥ 2
● Elba Rosso '14	♥ 2
● Elba Rosso Camillo Bianchi Ris. '15	♥ 4
○ Elba Vermentino '15	♥ 3
● Benvenuto '13	♀♀ 2*
● Benvenuto '11	♀♀ 2*
○ Elba Ansonica '13	♀♀ 3
○ Elba Bianco '13	♀♀ 2*
○ Elba Vermentino '14	♀♀ 3
● Voltraio '10	♀♀ 4

Agricoltori del Chianti Geografico

LOC. MULINACCIO, 10
53013 GAIOLE IN CHIANTI [SI]
TEL. +39 0577749489
www.chiantigeografico.it

CELLAR SALES
PRE-BOOKED VISITS
ACCOMMODATION
ANNUAL PRODUCTION 1,100,000 bottles
HECTARES UNDER VINE 270.00

The estate has a recent but very rich history. It began as a cooperative in 1961, thanks to 17 winegrowers who decided to join forces and strongly reiterate their sense of belonging to this historic terroir. Over the years the number of member growers has increased, joined more recently by longstanding local producers, the Piccini family, making a relaunch possible with good prospects of development. Chianti Classico is still the main product, in all its multifaceted versions. The Riserva Montegiachi 2012 displays characteristically clear-cut aromas, from ripe red berries to light spice, and a relaxed texture with nicely blended tannins, and a pleasing, broad finish. The enjoyable Contessa di Radda 2013 has classic aromas, well-measured structure with fresh acidity, and a clean finish. The Chianti Classico 2013 is delicious, tempting and succulent.

● Chianti Cl. '13	♥♥ 3
● Chianti Cl. Contessa di Radda '13	♥♥ 3
● Chianti Cl. Montegiachi Ris. '12	♥♥ 4
● Ferraiolo '13	♥♥ 5
● Pulleraia '13	♥ 3
○ Vernaccia di S. Gimignano '15	♥ 2
● Chianti Cl. Montegiachi Ris. '09	♀♀♀ 4*
● Chianti Cl. Montegiachi Ris. '07	♀♀♀ 4
● Chianti Cl. Montegiachi Ris. '05	♀♀♀ 4
● Brunello di Montalcino Castello Tricerchi '07	♀♀ 7
● Chianti Cl. Contessa di Radda '11	♀♀ 3
● Chianti Cl. Lucignano '12	♀♀ 3
● Chianti Cl. Molin Lungo '12	♀♀ 3
● Pulleraia '10	♀♀ 5

Altesino

LOC. ALTESINO, 54
53024 MONTALCINO [SI]
TEL. +39 0577806208
www.altesino.it

CELLAR SALES
PRE-BOOKED VISITS
ACCOMMODATION
ANNUAL PRODUCTION 250,000 bottles
HECTARES UNDER VINE 49.00

The history of the Altesino brand is closely linked to the Consonni family, who established it in the 1970s, and the famous Montosoli hill, a true grand cru on the northern slope of Montalcino. Elisabetta Gnudi Angelini took over the estate in 2002 and gradually transformed it into a property of over 40 hectares, buying other significant vineyards at Castelnuovo dell'Abate and Pianezzine. The estate's grape varieties include merlot, cabernet, chardonnay, vermentino, viognier, trebbiano and malvasia, but sangiovese naturally takes the lion's share, starting with the three Brunellos in a moderately modern style. The latest tastings reveal a good, solid range led by the 2011 Brunello: a hint of sweet oak, as well as citrus fruit, spices and balsamic herbs and a supple palate with good grip. The Montosoli selection of the same year seems darker and more austere in this phase, but might find a more harmonious balance in the bottles, like the 2010 Riserva.

● Brunello di Montalcino '11	♥♥	6
● Brunello di Montalcino Montosoli '11	♥♥	8
● Brunello di Montalcino Ris. '10	♥♥	8
● Toscana Rosso '14	♥♥	3
● Rosso di Montalcino '14	♥	3
● Brunello di Montalcino '10	♀♀	6
● Brunello di Montalcino '00	♀♀	6
● Brunello di Montalcino Montosoli '10	♀♀	8

Amiata

LOC. MONTEGIOVI
58033 CASTEL DEL PIANO [GR]
TEL. +39 3396902444
www.amiatavini.it

CELLAR SALES
PRE-BOOKED VISITS
ANNUAL PRODUCTION 12,000 bottles
HECTARES UNDER VINE 3.00

Back in the Guide, after a break of just a year, for the young estate owned by Simone Toninelli and Stefania Colombini. As the name indicates, it is situated on the slopes of huge Mount Amiata, an old extinct volcano that forms the backdrop for three hectares of vineyards mainly planted to sangiovese, the leading local grape variety. The Montecucco designation is right next to the Montalcino DOC zone, and has shown itself capable of excellent results: Amiata wines are the solid proof. Into the finals, a hair's breadth from the bullseye, the Cenere 2010 is an earthy sangiovese with a dark nose detailed with aromatic herbs, bay leaves and minerally sensations. The enthralling earthy notes reappear on the palate alongside ripe cherries and blackberries on a close-woven, fine-grained tannic structure. No less interesting, the Lavico 2011 displays generous aromas of ripe black berries and tight-knit tannins.

● Montecucco Sangiovese Cenere Ris. '10	♥♥	5
● Montecucco Sangiovese Lavico '11	♥♥	4
● Lapillo '09	♀♀	3
● Montecucco Sangiovese Cenere Ris. '09	♀♀	5
● Montecucco Sangiovese Cenere Ris. '08	♀♀	3
● Montecucco Sangiovese Cenere Ris. '07	♀♀	3
● Montecucco Sangiovese Lavico '10	♀♀	4
● Montecucco Sangiovese Lavico '09	♀♀	3*
● Montecucco Sangiovese Lavico '08	♀♀	3*

Ampeleia

FRAZ. ROCCATEDERIGHI
LOC. MELETA
58028 ROCCASTRADA [GR]
TEL. +39 0564567155
www.ampeleia.it

CELLAR SALES
PRE-BOOKED VISITS
ANNUAL PRODUCTION 135,000 bottles
HECTARES UNDER VINE 35.00
VITICULTURE METHOD Certified Organic
SUSTAINABLE WINERY

Fattoria di Meleta was one of the Tuscan wineries in the first edition of the Guide, 30 years ago. In 2002, three friends, all entrepreneurs, built their future winegrowing success on the remains of that estate. Thomas Widmann left and Elisabetta Foradori and Giacomo Pondini continued the Ampelaia project of 35 hectares of vineyards at three altitudes. One is the biodynamic Ampelaia di Sopra plot, consisting of 15 hectares at 450–600 metres, planted mainly to cabernet franc. There are just a few rows of sangiovese on the estate and the rest are non-natives that have adapted to the Mediterranean climate. A blend of alicante nero, carignano and alicante bouschet, the Kepos 2014 went through to the finals thanks to grassy aromas reminiscent of Mediterranean scrubland and a dark palate with close-knit tannins and an appealing spicy finish. The very enjoyable Carignano 2015 shows clear cherry aromas and a relaxed, well-sustained palate. The Alicante 2015 is fresh and lively with red berry fruit and well-balanced acidity.

● Kepos '14	♥♥	4
● Alicante '15	♥♥	5
● Carignano Campo Al Finocchio '15	♥♥	5
● Ampeleia '13	♥	5
● Cabernet Franc '15	♥	5
● Unlitro '15	♥	3
● Ampeleia '12	♀♀	5
● Ampeleia '11	♀♀	5
● Ampeleia '09	♀♀	5
● Kepos '13	♀♀	4
● Kepos '12	♀♀	4
● Kepos '11	♀♀	3*
● Kepos '10	♀♀	3*

★★Marchesi Antinori

P.ZZA DEGLI ANTINORI, 3
50123 FIRENZE
TEL. +39 05523595
www.antinori.it

CELLAR SALES
PRE-BOOKED VISITS
ACCOMMODATION AND RESTAURANT SERVICE
ANNUAL PRODUCTION 2,000,000 bottles
HECTARES UNDER VINE 2350.00

There is no doubt that Italian wine would not have achieved the prestige it enjoys today without Antinori. Their confident marketing, technical and productive strategies triggered the country's winemaking renaissance in the mid-Eighties and the estate, still family-run despite the industrial production quantities, played a fundamental role. The wines are technically flawless and their quality reliable, meeting the demands of various market sectors, from the beautifully styled entry level wines to the rarefied and exclusive top products. 2013 is a very high profile version of the Tignanello, delivering vibrant, multifaceted aromas and a deep, succulent palate in this king of Super Tuscans, made from sangiovese, cabernet sauvignon and cabernet franc. The Chianti Classico Marchese Antinori Riserva 2013 has light iron-like aromas and a soft, lively palate. The 2014 Chianti Classico Pèppoli is an utterly appealing wine.

● Tignanello '13	♥♥♥	8
● Chianti Cl. Marchese Antinori Ris. '13	♥♥	5
● Maremma Botrosecco Le Mortelle '14	♥♥	3*
● Chianti Cl. Pèppoli '14	♥♥	3
● Nobile di Montepulciano Santa Pia La Braccesca Ris. '12	♥♥	5
● Solaia '13	♥♥	8
● Cortona Syrah Achelo La Braccesca '14	♥	5
● Maremma Poggio alle Nane Le Mortelle '13	♥	6
○ Maremma Viva Le Mortelle '15	♥	4
● Solaia '07	♀♀♀	8
● Solaia '06	♀♀♀	8
● Tignanello '09	♀♀♀	8
● Tignanello '08	♀♀♀	8

Tenuta Argentiera

LOC. I PIANALI
FRAZ. DONORATICO
VIA AURELIA, 412A
57022 CASTAGNETO CARDUCCI [LI]
TEL. +39 0565773176
www.argentiera.eu

CELLAR SALES
PRE-BOOKED VISITS
ANNUAL PRODUCTION 450,000 bottles
HECTARES UNDER VINE 75.00

Tenuta Argentiera, managed by Corrado and Marcello Fratini, can boast over 70 hectares of vineyards in some of the DOC's leading subzones and produces some of the best wines in the area. The vineyards are planted on clayey and stony soil, ideal for achieving excellent results from the classic Bolgheri grape varieties: cabernet sauvignon and franc, merlot, syrah. Cellarwork completes the process to offer hugely complex and elegant red wines. A reliable landing place for fans of the type. The Bolgheri Rosso Superiore 2013 shows dark colour and beautifully concentrated fruit. The hints of toasted oak guide the wine into complex, richly extracted sensations and a clenched, slightly drying tannic texture. The Bolgheri Villa Donoratico 2013 is similar in style with some marked differences.

Artimino

FRAZ. ARTIMINO
V.LE PAPA GIOVANNI XXIII, 1
59015 CARMIGNANO [PO]
TEL. +39 0558751423
www.artimino.com

CELLAR SALES
PRE-BOOKED VISITS
ACCOMMODATION AND RESTAURANT SERVICE
ANNUAL PRODUCTION 420,000 bottles
HECTARES UNDER VINE 88.00

Overlooking the village of Artimino, the beautiful Medici villa Ferdinanda was the summer residence of the Grand Dukes of Tuscany from the late 16th century. Today Artimino is a large estate with over 700 hectares of land, operating in different sectors: hotel, country holiday homes, restaurant, receptions. But on the Carmignano hills, Artimino has 80 hectares of vineyards, producing local classics from Vin Ruspo and Vin Santo to extra virgin olive oil. In 1533 Caterina de' Medici introduced cabernet sauvignon grapes to this area, and today it is rightly considered a traditional grape. This year our tastings met with excellent results. The Vin Santo Occhio di Pernice 2009 breezed through to the finals with lovely amber mahogany colour, and generous aromas of raisins, candied citrus, walnuts, hazelnuts and vanilla. The weighty palate is subtly sweet with stylish, lingering nuances of dried figs and wild fennel. The excellent Carmignano 2013 confirms the recent new direction undertaken by Artimino.

● Bolgheri Rosso Sup. '13	♟♟ 8
● Bolgheri Villa Donoratico '13	♟♟ 5
● Bolgheri Sup. Lavinia Maria '12	♟ 8
○ Poggio ai Ginepri '15	♟ 3
● Bolgheri Sup. '11	♟♟♟ 8
● Bolgheri Sup. Argentiera '10	♟♟♟ 7
● Bolgheri Sup. Argentiera '06	♟♟♟ 7
● Bolgheri Sup. Argentiera '05	♟♟♟ 7
● Bolgheri Sup. Argentiera '04	♟♟♟ 7
● Bolgheri Rosso Poggio ai Ginepri '13	♟♟ 3
● Bolgheri Sup. '12	♟♟ 8
● Giorgio Bartholomaus '12	♟♟ 8
● Giorgio Bartholomaus '11	♟♟ 8
● Lavinia Maria '11	♟♟ 8

● Vin Santo di Carmignano Occhio di Pernice '09	♟♟ 5
● Carmignano '13	♟♟ 3
● Carmignano Ris. '12	♟♟ 4
○ Vin Santo di Carmignano '12	♟♟ 4
● Barco Reale '15	♟ 2
⊙ Barco Reale Vin Ruspo '15	♟ 2
● Carmignano V. Grumarello Ris. '11	♟ 4
● Carmignano '11	♟♟ 3
● Carmignano '10	♟♟ 3
● Carmignano V. Grumarello Ris. '10	♟♟ 4
● Carmignano V. Grumarello Ris. '09	♟♟ 4
● Carmignano Villa Artimino Ris. '09	♟♟ 2*
○ Vin Santo di Carmignano '10	♟♟ 4

Assolati

FRAZ. MONTENERO
POD. ASSOLATI, 47
58040 CASTEL DEL PIANO [GR]
TEL. +39 0564954146
www.assolati.it

CELLAR SALES
PRE-BOOKED VISITS
ACCOMMODATION
ANNUAL PRODUCTION 18,000 bottles
HECTARES UNDER VINE 5.00

Loriano Giannetti inherited over 100 hectares of land on the hillsides between Mount Amiata and the Maremma from his grandparents and parents, along with the determination and self-denial necessary to make the harsh, woody land suitable for growing vines and olive trees. Today, with five hectares of vineyards, his winegrowing activity has changed from simple subsistence farming to fine quality products. In the renovated former farmhouse, Loriano has set up a flourishing agritourism business focusing on cooking and local dishes as well as oil and wine. The range presented this year for our tastings was really impressive. The 2013 Riserva reached the finals thanks to austere aromas with strictly measured fruity, balsamic hints. The palate shows fine-grained tannin, although not fully blended, and significant supporting acidity livening up the flavour. The vibrant, fresh-tasting Montecucco Rosso 2014 displays lovely hints of Seville oranges and aromatic herbs.

● Montecucco Sangiovese Ris. '13	♟♟ 4
● Montecucco Rosso '14	♟♟ 2*
● Montecucco Sangiovese '13	♟♟ 3
○ Dionysos '15	♟ 2
● Montecucco Rosso '12	♟♟ 2*
● Montecucco Rosso '11	♟♟ 2*
● Montecucco Rosso '10	♟♟ 2*
● Montecucco Rosso '08	♟♟ 2*
● Montecucco Sangiovese '09	♟♟ 3
● Montecucco Sangiovese Ris. '12	♟♟ 3
● Montecucco Sangiovese Ris. '10	♟♟ 3
● Montecucco Sangiovese Ris. '09	♟♟ 4
● Montecucco Sangiovese Ris. '07	♟♟ 4

★Avignonesi

FRAZ. VALIANO DI MONTEPULCIANO
VIA LODOLA, 1
53045 MONTEPULCIANO [SI]
TEL. +39 0578724304
www.avignonesi.it

CELLAR SALES
PRE-BOOKED VISITS
RESTAURANT SERVICE
ANNUAL PRODUCTION 700,000 bottles
HECTARES UNDER VINE 180.00
VITICULTURE METHOD Certified Organic

The Valiano estate, which also uses the vineyards and winery of Tenuta Lodola Nuova, is the focus of an ambitious wine project created by Virginie Saverys, concentrating on the environment. Following the adoption of organic farming methods the estate is now close to obtaining biodynamic certification for all the vineyards. Avignonesi thus remains one of Montepulciano's most emblematic wineries, making harmonious wines with good personality, as well as Vin Santo, a great traditional Montepulciano product always honoured by this winery in memorable versions. The Nobile 2013 displays a generous array of aromas and firm, assertive flavour. The Vin Santo di Montepulciano 2001 is a majestic wine as ever, very fragrant, weighty and creamy. The well-focused Nobile Grandi Annate 2012 has a spicy nose and full, succulent flavour, with just slightly too much oak. The Vin Santo Montepulciano Occhio di Pernice 2001 is outstanding, as it should be.

● Nobile di Montepulciano '13	♟♟ 5
○ Vin Santo di Montepulciano '01	♟♟ 8
● Nobile di Montepulciano Grandi Annate '12	♟♟ 7
● 50 & 50 '11	♟ 8
● Rosso di Montepulciano '14	♟ 3
● Vin Santo di Montepulciano Occhio di Pernice '01	♟ 8
● Nobile di Montepulciano '12	♟♟♟ 4*
○ Vin Santo '98	♟♟♟ 8
○ Vin Santo '96	♟♟♟ 8
○ Vin Santo '95	♟♟♟ 8
○ Vin Santo '93	♟♟♟ 8
● Vin Santo Occhio di Pernice '97	♟♟♟ 8
● Vin Santo Occhio di Pernice '93	♟♟♟ 8
● Vin Santo Occhio di Pernice '90	♟♟♟ 8

Badia a Coltibuono

LOC. BADIA A COLTIBUONO
53013 GAIOLE IN CHIANTI [SI]
TEL. +39 0577746110
www.coltibuono.com

CELLAR SALES
PRE-BOOKED VISITS
ACCOMMODATION AND RESTAURANT SERVICE
ANNUAL PRODUCTION 240,000 bottles
HECTARES UNDER VINE 62.00
VITICULTURE METHOD Certified Organic
SUSTAINABLE WINERY

As a historic brandname in the Chianti Classico designation, Badia a Coltibuono is a good example of highly developed Italian winegrowing. Not only due to organic certification, held by this estate since 2000, but also the great sensitivity shown throughout the production process which favours stylistically polished, elegant, complex wines able to pass the test of time. Brother and sister team Roberto and Emanuela Stucchi run the estate, definitively focusing on consistent quality and excellence in recent years. Very attractive earthy, floral aromas displayed by the Chianti Classico Riserva 2012, with a mouthwatering, almost airy palate. The flavour is deep and persistent, appealing but certainly not without personality. The Chianti Classico RS 2014 is undoubtedly affected by the complicated year, with clean aromas and a slender but generously savoury palate.

● Chianti Cl. Ris. '12	▼▼	5
● Chianti Cetamura '15	▼▼	2*
● Chianti Cl. RS '14	▼▼	2*
● Chianti Cl. '14	▼	3
● Montebello '11	▼	7
● Chianti Cl. '13	♀♀♀	3*
● Chianti Cl. '12	♀♀♀	3*
● Chianti Cl. '06	♀♀♀	3*
● Chianti Cl. Cultus Boni '09	♀♀♀	4*
● Chianti Cl. Ris. '09	♀♀♀	5
● Chianti Cl. Ris. '07	♀♀♀	5
● Chianti Cl. Ris. '04	♀♀♀	5
● Chianti Cl. RS '13	♀♀	2*

Badia di Morrona

VIA DEL CHIANTI, 6
56030 TERRICCIOLA [PI]
TEL. +39 0587658505
www.badiadimorrona.it

CELLAR SALES
PRE-BOOKED VISITS
ACCOMMODATION AND RESTAURANT SERVICE
ANNUAL PRODUCTION 350,000 bottles
HECTARES UNDER VINE 110.00

Badia di Morrona, between Pisa and Volterra, is a prestigious place of considerable historic and artistic value. The estate's origins date back to the year 1000, and it is known to have been a Benedictine monastery. In the late 1930s it passed into the hands of the Gaslini Alberti family. 100 hectares of the huge 600-hectare property are under vine, and the modern-style wines produced are among the best-typed in the area. Sangiovese dominates the black grape varieties on the estate, alongside cabernet, merlot and syrah. The Taneto 2013 is a weighty and complex wine that will definitely need bottle ageing, though it is already expressive: mainly syrah-based, with forward toasty sensations softened by fruit, and a generous, flavoursome profile, solidly-built and deep. We found the same standard of quality in the N'Antia 2013. The 2015 I Sodi del Paretaio is a well-typed Chianti with appealing, drinkable flavour, mouthwatering hints of wild plums and fine spice, by no means cropped and nicely racy.

● Chianti I Sodi del Paretaio '15	▼▼	2*
○ Felciaio '15	▼▼	2*
● N'Antia '13	▼▼	5
● Taneto '13	▼▼	3
○ Vin Santo del Chianti '10	▼	4
○ Felciaio '14	♀♀	2*
● N'Antia '10	♀♀	5
● Taneto '12	♀♀	3
● Taneto '11	♀♀	3*
● VignAalta '10	♀♀	5
● VignAalta '09	♀♀	5
○ Vin Santo del Chianti '09	♀♀	4

Tenuta La Badiola

LOC. BADIOLA
58043 CASTIGLIONE DELLA PESCAIA [GR]
TEL. +39 0564944919
www.tenutalabadiola.it

CELLAR SALES
ACCOMMODATION AND RESTAURANT SERVICE
ANNUAL PRODUCTION 150,000 bottles
HECTARES UNDER VINE 30.00

Before joining the Terra Moretti group of estates (which includes Petra in Tuscany and Contadi Castaldi and Bellavista in Franciacorta), this was a summer residence used by the court of Leopold II of Lorraine, Grand Duke of Tuscany. Vittorio Moretti has made it a leading local winegrowing estate and added a luxury hotel, L'Andana. The 30 hectares of vineyards are planted to vermentino and viognier for the white and merlot, sangiovese and shiraz for the red. Alicante grapes are also grown for use in the rosé. All the wines share a common denominator, a sunny Mediterranean quality that offers an expression of their terroir of origin. Like the Acquagiusta Rosso 2014: aromas of ripe strawberries and cherries, scrubland and juniper, and a dynamic, well-paced palate thanks to the harmonious supporting acidity and spicy finish. The equally consistent Vermentino 2015 has spring flowers with whiffs of sea salt, echoed on the palate in the fragrant, taut flavour.

● Maremma Toscana Acquagiusta Rosso '14	♙♙ 3
○ Maremma Toscana Vermentino Acquagiusta '15	♙♙ 3
⊙ Maremma Toscana Rosato Acquagiusta '15	♙ 3
○ Acquadoro '11	♙♙ 4
● Acquagiusta Rosso '12	♙♙ 3*
● Acquagiusta Rosso '08	♙♙ 2*

Fattoria di Bagnolo

VIA IMPRUNETANA PER TAVARNUZZE, 36
50023 IMPRUNETA [FI]
TEL. +39 0552313403
www.bartolinibaldelli.it

CELLAR SALES
PRE-BOOKED VISITS
ANNUAL PRODUCTION 25,000 bottles
HECTARES UNDER VINE 10.00

Since the 15th century the hills overlooking Florence have been the home of this estate, owned by the Bartolini Baldelli family since about 1800. Marco runs it today along with the other properties: Castello di Montozzi at Pergine Valdarno, in the province of Arezzo, and Fattoria di Scaletta at San Miniato, in the province of Pisa. Here in the municipal area of Impruneta, the estate's ten hectares of vineyards are mainly planted to sangiovese, as well as other native varieties like colorino, canaiolo, malvasia, and trebbiano, and two international grapes, cabernet sauvignon and merlot. Alongside wine and oil, the other important activity is the expanding agritourism facility. Back to the finals again for the Riserva: the 2013 version presents a harmonious, multifaceted nose ranging from morello and black cherries to pipe tobacco and balsamic hints. A polished tannic structure, with echoes of fruit in the flavour and a background tanginess. The 2014 Chianti, more supple and coherent, is very pleasing.

● Chianti Colli Fiorentini Ris. '13	♙♙ 4
● Chianti Colli Fiorentini '14	♙♙ 2*
● Capro Rosso '13	♙ 5
● Capro Rosso '12	♙♙ 5
● Capro Rosso '11	♙♙ 5
● Capro Rosso '10	♙♙ 5
● Capro Rosso '09	♙♙ 5
● Chianti Colli Fiorentini '13	♙♙ 2*
● Chianti Colli Fiorentini Ris. '12	♙♙ 4
● Chianti Colli Fiorentini Ris. '11	♙♙ 4
● Chianti Colli Fiorentini Ris. '10	♙♙ 4
● Chianti Colli Fiorentini Ris. '08	♙♙ 3
○ Vin Santo del Chianti Ris. '04	♙♙ 5

I Balzini

Loc. Pastine, 19
50021 Barberino Val d'Elsa [FI]
Tel. +39 0558075503
www.ibalzini.it

CELLAR SALES
PRE-BOOKED VISITS
ANNUAL PRODUCTION 70,000 bottles
HECTARES UNDER VINE 12.00
SUSTAINABLE WINERY

In 1980, professional accountant Vincenzo d'Isanto found some suitable land for planting vineyards and producing wine, on the border between the provinces of Florence and Siena. In the subsequent years his wife Antonella also left her profession as a labour consultant, not only to work in the vineyard and cellar but overseeing the organization too, and today her daughter Diana is also involved in this side of the business. This family estate, named for the terraced land on which the vineyards are planted, extends around the old farmhouse, and includes olive groves. The White Label 2013, sangiovese and cabernet sauvignon, has blackberries and cherries on the nose, light hints of spice and grassy nuances. The palate is supple, with excellent mouthfeel, succulent and nicely sustained. The Black Label 2013, cabernet sauvignon and merlot, is richly extracted and warm with generous spicy aromas of cinnamon and juniper, hints of roasted coffee and a soft, mouthfilling flavour with perceptible tannins and a long finish.

● I Balzini Black Label '13	♟♟ 6
● I Balzini Red Label '14	♟♟ 3
● I Balzini White Label '13	♟♟ 5
● I Balzini Green Label '15	♟ 3
☉ I Balzini Pink Label '15	♟ 2
● I Balzini Black Label '12	♟♟ 6
● I Balzini Black Label '11	♟♟ 6
● I Balzini Black Label '10	♟♟ 6
● I Balzini Black Label '09	♟♟ 6
● I Balzini Green Label '12	♟♟ 2*
● I Balzini Green Label '11	♟♟ 2*
● I Balzini Red Label '11	♟♟ 3
● I Balzini White Label '12	♟♟ 5
● I Balzini White Label '11	♟♟ 5

Bandini - Villa Pomona

Loc. Pomona, 39
s.da Chiantigiana
53011 Castellina in Chianti [SI]
Tel. +39 0577740473
www.fattoriapomona.it

CELLAR SALES
PRE-BOOKED VISITS
ACCOMMODATION
ANNUAL PRODUCTION 16,000 bottles
HECTARES UNDER VINE 4.70
VITICULTURE METHOD Certified Organic

Villa Pomona is run by Monica Raspi and Enrico Selvi, who converted this small winery into a go-to place for all who love Chianti Classico made comme il faut. The vines are tended with organic methods on marly limestone with some alberese. No invasive cellar techniques for Villa Pomona, with the wines just left to express all the traits endowed by these soils. The results are truly enjoyable and original labels showing one of the most solid links with the growing area of all those currently seen in Chianti ranges. The Chianti Classico Riserva 2013 has a well-defined, very fresh nose with distinctive and elegant hints of red berries always in the foreground. The palate is well co-ordinated and characterful, perhaps just lacking a little complexity. The Chianti Classico 2014 is subtle and fluent, as we might expect from this problematic vintage year.

● Chianti Cl. Ris. '13	♟♟ 4
● Chianti Cl. '14	♟♟ 3
● Chianti Cl. '13	♟♟♟ 3*
● Chianti Cl. '12	♟♟♟ 3*
● Chianti Cl. '11	♟♟ 3
● Chianti Cl. '10	♟♟ 3
● Chianti Cl. '09	♟♟ 3
● Chianti Cl. Ris. '12	♟♟ 4
● Chianti Cl. Ris. '11	♟♟ 4
● Chianti Cl. Ris. '10	♟♟ 4
● Chianti Cl. Ris. '09	♟♟ 4
● Chianti Cl. Ris. '08	♟♟ 4
● Chianti Cl. Ris. '07	♟♟ 4

Baracchi

LOC. CEGLIOLO, 21
52044 CORTONA [AR]
TEL. +39 0575612679
www.baracchiwinery.com

CELLAR SALES
PRE-BOOKED VISITS
ACCOMMODATION AND RESTAURANT SERVICE
ANNUAL PRODUCTION 140,000 bottles
HECTARES UNDER VINE 32.00
SUSTAINABLE WINERY

Riccardo Baracchi carries forward one of his family's business activities, wine production, which began five generations ago in 1860. A brilliant character, full of initiative, Riccardo has created a very attractive resort alongside the winery, with hotel, restaurant and spa, surrounded by some of the vineyards. These are situated in four separate locations: San Martino, Gabbiano, la Pietraia and Montanare. Today he is helped by his son Benedetto on a very focused project: modern winegrowing practice with respect for the local area. Into the finals for the Cortona Syrah Riserva 2013, with a generous, complex nose in which spices appear alongside the red and black berry aromas, with light hints of animal skins and leather. A broad, appealing entry with a good, dynamic mid-palate and excellent development to the finish.

● Cortona Syrah Ris. '13	♥♥ 6
● Cortona Smeriglio Syrah '13	♥♥ 4
● Pinot Nero '13	♥♥ 6
⊙ Brut Sangiovese Rosé M. Cl. '14	♥ 5
○ Brut Trebbiano M. Cl. '13	♥ 5
● Ardito '12	♀♀ 6
● Ardito '11	♀♀ 6
○ Astore '13	♀♀ 3
● Cortona Merlot Smeriglio '13	♀♀ 4
● Cortona Sangiovese Smeriglio '13	♀♀ 4
● Cortona Smeriglio Sangiovese '12	♀♀ 4
● Cortona Syrah Smeriglio '13	♀♀ 4
● O'Lillo '14	♀♀ 2*
● Pinot Nero '12	♀♀ 6

Fattoria dei Barbi

LOC. PODERNOVI, 170
53024 MONTALCINO [SI]
TEL. +39 0577841111
www.fattoriadeibarbi.it

CELLAR SALES
PRE-BOOKED VISITS
ACCOMMODATION AND RESTAURANT SERVICE
ANNUAL PRODUCTION 600,000 bottles
HECTARES UNDER VINE 66.00

Podernovi, a historic location in the central-eastern zone of Montalcino, is home to Fattoria dei Barbi's winery and museum, and the greater portion of the estate's 70-odd hectares planted to sangiovese. This is a traditional winery in the most authentic sense, managed with the greatest passion by Stefano Cinelli Colombini, heir to a family dynasty active in the wine sector since the late 18th century. The most famous labels are the three Brunellos, which differ slightly from one another in the processes of vinification and ageing (mainly in small and medium-sized oak barrels) but share aristocratic and austere expressive features. A stylistic score that echoes throughout the range of wines tested in this round of tastings. The Brunello Riserva 2010 is outstanding, with a multitude of aromas including juniper, incense, and tree bark, a vigorous, flavoursome mid-palate and slightly stiff finish. The Brunello 2011 is pleasantly old-style, while the Vigna del Fiore 2011 is more vigorous and rich in extract.

● Brunello di Montalcino Ris. '10	♥♥ 7
● Brunello di Montalcino '11	♥♥ 5
● Brunello di Montalcino V. del Fiore '11	♥♥ 7
● Rosso di Montalcino '14	♥♥ 3
● Brunello di Montalcino '10	♀♀ 5
● Brunello di Montalcino '09	♀♀ 5
● Brunello di Montalcino '08	♀♀ 5
● Brunello di Montalcino '07	♀♀ 5
● Brunello di Montalcino Ris. '08	♀♀ 7
● Brunello di Montalcino Ris. '07	♀♀ 7
● Brunello di Montalcino V. del Fiore '10	♀♀ 7
● Brunello di Montalcino V. del Fiore '08	♀♀ 7
● Brunello di Montalcino V. del Fiore '07	♀♀ 7
● Brunello di Montalcino V. del Fiore '06	♀♀ 7
● Morellino di Scansano '11	♀♀ 3
● Rosso di Montalcino '12	♀♀ 3

Baricci

loc. COLOMBAIO DI MONTOSOLI, 13
53024 MONTALCINO [SI]
TEL. +39 0577848109
www.baricci.it

CELLAR SALES
PRE-BOOKED VISITS
ANNUAL PRODUCTION 30,000 bottles
HECTARES UNDER VINE 5.00

The year 1955 holds deep symbolic value for Montalcino's history, for many reasons, including the purchase of the Colombaio estate by Nello Baricci, a true pioneer of Brunello in a period in stark contrast with today's glory. He has enjoyed a well-deserved rest for some time now, but the wines named after him remain extremely faithful to the earthy, lustrous style typical of Montosoli sangioveses. Credit is due to his children Graziano and Graziella, his son-in-law Piero Buffi, and grandsons Federico and Francesco, all of whom work on the estate's five hectares and the cellar processes, which include long maceration and ageing in 20- and 40-hectolitre Slavonian oak barrels. The first Riserva di Brunello made at Baricci in 60 years of history is from the acclaimed 2010 vintage. Dedicated to founder Nello, this wine describes a modern yet retro inspiration with an interplay of damsons and dried flowers, freshly dug earth and coffee powder, faithfully echoed in the taut, biting palate.

● Brunello di Montalcino Nello Ris. '10	♟♟♟ 6
● Brunello di Montalcino '11	♟♟ 6
● Rosso di Montalcino '14	♟♟ 4
● Brunello di Montalcino '10	♟♟♟ 6
● Brunello di Montalcino '09	♟♟♟ 5
● Brunello di Montalcino '07	♟♟♟ 5
● Brunello di Montalcino '83	♟♟♟ 5
● Brunello di Montalcino '08	♟♟ 5
● Rosso di Montalcino '13	♟♟ 4
● Rosso di Montalcino '11	♟♟ 3*
● Rosso di Montalcino '10	♟♟ 3

★★Barone Ricasoli

loc. MADONNA A BROLIO
53013 GAIOLE IN CHIANTI [SI]
TEL. +39 05777301
www.ricasoli.it

CELLAR SALES
PRE-BOOKED VISITS
ACCOMMODATION
ANNUAL PRODUCTION 2,500,000 bottles
HECTARES UNDER VINE 235.00
SUSTAINABLE WINERY

The Barone Ricasoli brand is an anchor in the Chianti Classico designation. One of the oldest estates in the world, it has been producing wine since 1141. Today it is also among the largest estate-owned vineyards in the DOC zone, and over about 20 years Francesco Ricasoli has driven the winery forwards, transforming it into one of the most interesting in Italy. The modern style is now remarkably well-balanced and the flawlessly made wines are also characterful, elegant and terroir-true. The Chianti Classico Gran Selezione Colledilà 2013 displays the gait of a great wine. The clearly defined aromas reveal a blend of red fruits, spices and earthy nuances while the palate is complex, lively and deep. The Chianti Classico Rocca Guicciarda Riserva 2013 is also very good: succulent and lipsmacking, with a full-bodied, satisfying flavour.

● Chianti Cl. Gran Sel. Colledilà '13	♟♟♟ 8
● Chianti Cl. Rocca Guicciarda Ris. '13	♟♟ 5
● Casalferro '13	♟♟ 8
● Chianti Cl. Bettino '13	♟♟ 4
● Chianti Cl. Brolio Ris. '13	♟♟ 6
● Chianti Cl. Gran Sel. Castello di Brolio '13	♟♟ 8
● Chianti Cl. Brolio '14	♟ 3
● Casalferro '08	♟♟♟ 8
● Chianti Cl. Castello di Brolio '07	♟♟♟ 8
● Chianti Cl. Castello di Brolio '06	♟♟♟ 8
● Chianti Cl. Castello di Brolio '04	♟♟♟ 7
● Chianti Cl. Castello di Brolio '03	♟♟♟ 5
● Chianti Cl. Castello di Brolio '01	♟♟♟ 6
● Chianti Cl. Colledilà '10	♟♟♟ 7
● Chianti Cl. Gran Sel. Colledilà '11	♟♟♟ 8
● Chianti Cl. Rocca Guicciarda Ris. '12	♟♟♟ 5

Fattoria di Basciano

V.LE DUCA DELLA VITTORIA, 159
50068 RUFINA [FI]
TEL. +39 0558397034
www.renzomasibasciano.it

CELLAR SALES
PRE-BOOKED VISITS
ANNUAL PRODUCTION 200,000 bottles
HECTARES UNDER VINE 35.00

The Masi family has been at the helm of
this estate since 1925, established by
Renzo and managed today by his son Paolo
and wife Anna Rita. The vineyards grow on
gravelly soil at about 300 metres altitude,
on a hillside that serves as a division
between the Argomenna valley and the
banks of the Sieve. The 35 hectares under
vine are used for the Fattoria di Basciano
line, while the Renzo Masi brand indicates
wines made from grapes bought from
trusted growers. As well as wine and oil,
the farm is the heart of a flourishing holiday
accommodation business. A fluctuating
range presented for tasting this year, partly
due to the problematic 2014 vintage. Two
outstanding wines, however: the Chianti
Riserva 2013, with generous, pervasive
aromas of ripe damsons and vanilla pods,
and a soft, warm palate where the spicy
oak sensations are a little too forward; and
a lovely Vin Santo 2009, with vibrant
almonds and dried figs on the nose and a
balanced, harmonious palate.

● Chianti Ris. '13	♥♥ 2*
○ Vin Santo Chianti Rufina '09	♥♥ 3
● Chianti Rufina '14	♥ 2
● Chianti Rufina Ris. '13	♥ 3
● I Pini '14	♥ 4
● Il Corto '14	♥ 3
● Chianti Rufina '13	♀♀ 2*
● Chianti Rufina Ris. '12	♀♀ 3
● Erta e China '13	♀♀ 2*
● Erta e China '12	♀♀ 2*
● I Pini '13	♀♀ 4
○ Vin Santo Chianti Rufina '08	♀♀ 3
○ Vin Santo Chianti Rufina Ris. '07	♀♀ 3

Basile

POD. MONTE MARIO
58044 CINIGIANO [GR]
TEL. +39 0564993227
www.basilessa.it

CELLAR SALES
PRE-BOOKED VISITS
ANNUAL PRODUCTION 50,000 bottles
HECTARES UNDER VINE 8.00
VITICULTURE METHOD Certified Organic
SUSTAINABLE WINERY

From Naples to the Cinigiano hills in the
heart of the Montecucco DOC zone: this
was Glovanbattista Basile's journey, starting
in 1999 when he left the southern city to
start making wine in Tuscany. His path was
clear on the fields left untended for
decades: modern winegrowing techniques
based on organic principles, respecting the
local area. The eight hectares of vineyards
meandering across limestone marl, on
hillsides between 330 and 380 metres
altitude, are mainly south-west facing and
planted to sangiovese, merlot and ciliegiolo
as well as a few rows of vermentino,
viognier and petit manseng used in
production of the estate's only white wine,
Artéteca. The 2012 Riserva, more assertive
and captivating than other vintages, earns
Tre Bicchieri: spice, red berries and
balsamic hints introduce the fresh,
flavoursome palate with smooth tannins
and minerally sensations. A very dynamic
flavour with a crescendo finish. The 2013
Cartacanta also gave a good performance,
more coherent with lovely grip.

● Montecucco Sangiovese Ad Agio Ris. '12	♥♥♥ 5
● Montecucco Sangiovese Cartacanta '13	♥♥ 3
○ Artéteca '15	♥ 2
● Maremma Toscana Comandante '13	♥ 3
● Maremma Comandante '12	♀♀ 3
● Montecucco Ad Agio Ris. '08	♀♀ 3
● Montecucco Cartacanta '11	♀♀ 3
● Montecucco Cartacanta '08	♀♀ 2*
● Montecucco Sangiovese Ad Agio Ris. '11	♀♀ 5
● Montecucco Sangiovese Ad Agio Ris. '09	♀♀ 3
● Montecucco Sangiovese Cartacanta '12	♀♀ 3

Pietro Beconcini

FRAZ. LA SCALA
VIA MONTORZO, 13A
56028 SAN MINIATO [PI]
TEL. +39 0571464785
www.pietrobeconcini.com

CELLAR SALES
PRE-BOOKED VISITS
ANNUAL PRODUCTION 95,000 bottles
HECTARES UNDER VINE 12.00

A tempranillo vine has grown on this land, owned by the Marchesi Ridolfi, since the early 20th century. In the mid-1950s Leonardo's grandfather bought the farmland where he was sharecropping and it was handed down to Leonardo through his father Pietro, who had decided to become a full-time wine producer. Leonardo and Eva Bellagamba have taken farming of their vineyards in a new direction, focusing on the mixtures of grapes: as well as the Spanish tempranillo variety, there are sangiovese, canaiolo, malvasia bianca and nera, colorino. The IXE 2014, tempranillo with a small percentage of sangiovese, displays aromas of bay leaves and forest floor, with ripe blackberries and hints of liquorice. The palate opens firm and meaty, relaxing into an appealing finish, lingering and pleasantly satisfying. Also excellent, Vigna alle Nicchie 2012 is a monovarietal Tempranillo with toasty sensations, blackberry jam and grassy hints, and a tight-knit texture, nicely distributed tannins and a flavoursome, consistent finish.

● Chianti Ris. '13	♟♟ 2*
● IXE '14	♟♟ 3
● Vigna alle Nicchie '12	♟♟ 6
○ Vin Santo del Chianti Caratello '08	♟♟ 5
● Maurleo '14	♟ 2
● IXE '13	♟♟ 3
● Vigna alle Nicchie '11	♟♟ 6
● Vigna alle Nicchie '09	♟♟ 6

Podere Le Berne

LOC. CERVOGNANO
VIA POGGIO GOLO, 7
53040 MONTEPULCIANO [SI]
TEL. +39 0578767328
www.leberne.it

CELLAR SALES
ANNUAL PRODUCTION 25,000 bottles
HECTARES UNDER VINE 6.00

Andrea Natalini has not allowed himself to be overwhelmed by the flattering results obtained recently, and continues to work with the same commitment and passion among the rows of his vineyards in Cervognano, one of the most important crus in the Montepulciano area. His wines have achieved a very focused stylistic clarity: while they don't fear the passing of time, they are still very drinkable and well-typed with marked characteristic features. Delicate cherry aromas with hints of pipe tobacco and spice mark the Nobile Riserva 2012, harmonious overall with a generous, succulent palate. The Nobile 2013 has an edgier flavour, though racy and tangy. It performs best on the nose with fruity aromas combining floral hints and lovely freshness. The Rosso di Montepulciano 2015 is fragrant and delicious, a really appealing wine with a palate as relaxed as it is flavoursome.

● Nobile di Montepulciano Ris. '12	♟♟ 5
● Nobile di Montepulciano '13	♟♟ 3
● Rosso di Montepulciano '15	♟♟ 2*
● Nobile di Montepulciano '11	♟♟♟ 3*
● Nobile di Montepulciano '06	♟♟♟ 3
● L'Affronto '11	♟♟ 2*
● Nobile di Montepulciano '12	♟♟ 3*
● Nobile di Montepulciano '09	♟♟ 3
● Nobile di Montepulciano Ris. '11	♟♟ 5
● Nobile di Montepulciano Ris. '10	♟♟ 5
● Nobile di Montepulciano Ris. '09	♟♟ 5
● Nobile di Montepulciano Ris. '08	♟♟ 5
○ Vin Santo di Montepulciano Ada '07	♟♟ 5
○ Vin Santo di Montepulciano Ada '06	♟♟ 5

Tenuta di Bibbiano

VIA BIBBIANO, 76
53011 CASTELLINA IN CHIANTI [SI]
TEL. +39 0577743065
www.bibbiano.com

CELLAR SALES
PRE-BOOKED VISITS
ACCOMMODATION
ANNUAL PRODUCTION 100,000 bottles
HECTARES UNDER VINE 25.00
VITICULTURE METHOD Certified Organic
SUSTAINABLE WINERY

This Castellina in Chianti winery sold its first bottles in 1969, and its style has remained substantially the same, with some of the most consistent expressions of this designation. The vineyards are organically farmed and the cellar procedures are reduced to a minimum, focusing on the quality of the fruit. The resulting wines show good character and personality, and have provided reassuringly consistent proof of clear expression and a connection to the terroir. They are aged in both large and small oak. After a hesitant start, the Chianti Classico Montornello Riserva 2013 opens up on the nose with floral, earthy aromas. The palate shows complex structure developing smoothly with a lovely tangy note in the finish. Lingering reductive sensations dull the nose of the slim-bodied, uncomplicated Chianti Classico 2014. Its strongpoint is a well-paced, fresh flavour.

● Chianti Cl. '14	♟♟ 3
● Chianti Cl. Montornello Ris. '13	♟♟ 4
● Chianti Cl. '13	♟♟ 3*
● Chianti Cl. '11	♟♟ 3*
● Chianti Cl. '10	♟♟ 3
● Chianti Cl. '07	♟♟ 3*
● Chianti Cl. Montornello '11	♟♟ 3
● Chianti Cl. Montornello '09	♟♟ 3
● Chianti Cl. Montornello '08	♟♟ 3
● Chianti Cl. Montornello '06	♟♟ 2*
● Chianti Cl. Montornello Ris. '12	♟♟ 4
● Chianti Cl. V. del Capannino Gran Sel. '10	♟♟ 5
● Chianti Cl. V. del Capannino Ris. '10	♟♟ 5
● Chianti Cl. V. del Capannino Ris. '06	♟♟ 5

Bindella

FRAZ. ACQUAVIVA
VIA DELLE TRE BERTE, 10A
53045 MONTEPULCIANO [SI]
TEL. +39 0578767777
www.bindella.it

CELLAR SALES
PRE-BOOKED VISITS
ANNUAL PRODUCTION 160,000 bottles
HECTARES UNDER VINE 36.50

Vallocaia, named after the location, is considered to be one of the historic estates of Montepulciano, with over 30 harvests under its belt. Deep roots, therefore, but above all a terroir that is able to yield good results. The Swiss owners are familiar with and experienced in wine production and catering, and the efficient, close-knit staff are capable of increasing results and an impressive process, the most immediate proof of which are the wines themselves. The Nobile I Quadri 2013 is simply wonderful: uproarious personality, shrewd and moody on the palate, deep yet airy. Salty sensations and fruity sweetness, within a really polished texture: it walks away with Tre Bicchieri. An honourable mention for the Vin Santo Occhio di Pernice Sinfonia 2007, with a heart-rendingly classic profile.

● Nobile di Montepulciano I Quadri '13	♟♟♟ 5
● Vin Santo di Montepulciano Occhio di Pernice Dolce Sinfonia '07	♟♟ 7
● Nobile di Montepulciano '13	♟♟ 4
● Rosso di Montepulciano Fosso Lupaio '14	♟ 2
● Nobile di Montepulciano I Quadri '12	♟♟♟ 5
● Nobile di Montepulciano '12	♟♟ 4
● Nobile di Montepulciano '11	♟♟ 4
● Nobile di Montepulciano I Quadri '11	♟♟ 5
● Nobile di Montepulciano Vallocaia Ris. '10	♟♟ 5
○ Vin Santo di Montepulciano Dolce Sinfonia '11	♟♟ 5

★Biondi Santi
Tenuta Il Greppo

Loc. Villa Greppo, 183
53024 Montalcino [SI]
Tel. +39 0577848087
www.biondisanti.it

CELLAR SALES
PRE-BOOKED VISITS
ACCOMMODATION
ANNUAL PRODUCTION 80,000 bottles
HECTARES UNDER VINE 25.00

Rumours have been circulating in recent months about possible changes in the Biondi Santi company structure, which is and always will be an essential benchmark for fans of Brunello di Montalcino around the world. In many ways the epic journey of this great vin de garde began at the Greppo estate and the legendary, undamaged, late 19th-century bottles are still there to bear witness. This is why it is always worth patiently waiting for the estate's reds, especially the Riserva, to complete their long ageing period in large barrels and reveal that unmistakable spirited and racy character. Two masterful versions: the Brunello del Greppo 2011 and the Riserva 2010. We were pushed to decide which we like best, and really comes down to nuance. Because on paper these two vintages could not be more different, the former more approachable, and the 2010 rigorous, but in interpretation there is a very fine line. The flavoursome Riserva wins it, with velvety tannin and whippy acidity. Or perhaps not.

● Brunello di Montalcino Ris. '10	♟♟♟ 8
● Brunello di Montalcino '11	♟♟ 8
● Brunello di Montalcino '10	♟♟♟ 8
● Brunello di Montalcino '09	♟♟♟ 8
● Brunello di Montalcino '06	♟♟♟ 7
● Brunello di Montalcino '04	♟♟♟ 8
● Brunello di Montalcino '03	♟♟♟ 8
● Brunello di Montalcino '01	♟♟♟ 8
● Brunello di Montalcino Ris. '07	♟♟♟ 8
● Brunello di Montalcino Ris. '06	♟♟♟ 8
● Brunello di Montalcino Ris. '04	♟♟♟ 8
● Brunello di Montalcino Ris. '01	♟♟♟ 8

Borgo Salcetino

Loc. Lucarelli
53017 Radda in Chianti [SI]
Tel. +39 0577733541
www.livon.it

PRE-BOOKED VISITS
ANNUAL PRODUCTION 95,000 bottles
HECTARES UNDER VINE 15.00

Friuli winemaking family Livon has found a very interesting context in Borgo Salcetino, expressing all the potential of the designation to its fullest extent. The estate, situated in the excellent growing area of Radda in Chianti, was purchased in the mid-Nineties and is yielding significant results thanks to consistent choices and avoidance of pointless excess. The estate's style is faithful to the Chianti Classico principles, starting with ageing in large oak casks, and the wines show lively flavour and attractive features. Without beating about the bush, the Chianti Classico 2014 is one of the best in this vintage year, and it was a complex year, especially for this designation. However the version presented by Borgo Salcetino hits the bullseye. Airy, polished aromas of red berries, light spice and a hint of forest floor, while the palate is beautifully balanced with pleasantly spirited flavour.

● Chianti Cl. '14	♟♟♟ 3*
● Chianti Cl. '13	♟♟♟ 3*
● Chianti Cl. '11	♟♟♟ 3*
● Rossole '12	♟♟♟ 3*
● Chianti Cl. '10	♟♟ 3
● Chianti Cl. '09	♟♟ 3
● Chianti Cl. '08	♟♟ 3
● Chianti Cl. '07	♟♟ 3*
● Chianti Cl. Lucarello Ris. '12	♟♟ 4
● Chianti Cl. Lucarello Ris. '11	♟♟ 4
● Chianti Cl. Lucarello Ris. '10	♟♟ 4
● Chianti Cl. Lucarello Ris. '07	♟♟ 4
● Rossole '08	♟♟ 3

Il Borro

FRAZ. SAN GIUSTINO VALDARNO
LOC. IL BORRO, 1
52020 LORO CIUFFENNA [AR]
TEL. +39 055977053
www.ilborro.it

CELLAR SALES
PRE-BOOKED VISITS
ACCOMMODATION AND RESTAURANT SERVICE
ANNUAL PRODUCTION 160,000 bottles
HECTARES UNDER VINE 45.00

The first definite record of Borro dates back
to 1254 when the castle was purchased by
a Milanese nobleman, Marchese Borro
Borri, who had been made podestà of
Arezzo. Under leading political figure
Alessandro dal Borro the Borro estate
definitively took on the appearance we see
today. After visiting for many years, in 1993
Ferruccio Ferragamo decided to purchase
the whole estate and carried out extensive
renovations. The first vintage was produced
in 1999. Il Borro 2013 kept its date with
the finals: made from merlot and cabernet
sauvignon, with small additions of petit
verdot and syrah, it has a subtle, complex
nose, in which pepper and cinnamon soften
the cherry fruit base. An appealing entry on
the nicely weighty, velvety palate, pleasantly
fresh-tasting, with nice acidic backbone
and a flavoursome crescendo finish. A
lovely new entry is Bolle di Borro 2011, a
Metodo Classico made from sangiovese,
with a floral nose and lively palate.

● Il Borro '13	♥♥ 7
⊙ Brut Bolle di Borro '11	♥♥ 8
● Pian di Nova '13	♥♥ 3
● Polissena '12	♥ 5
● Il Borro '12	♀♀ 7
● Il Borro '09	♀♀ 4
● Il Borro '08	♀♀ 6
● Pian di Nova '09	♀♀ 3
● Polissena '11	♀♀ 5
● Vin Santo del Chianti Occhio di Pernice '09	♀♀ 7
○ Vin Santo del Chianti Occhio di Pernice '08	♀♀ 5
○ Vin Santo del Chianti Occhio di Pernice '07	♀♀ 5

★Poderi Boscarelli

LOC. CERVOGNANO
VIA DI MONTENERO, 28
53045 MONTEPULCIANO [SI]
TEL. +39 0578767277
www.poderiboscarelli.com

CELLAR SALES
PRE-BOOKED VISITS
ANNUAL PRODUCTION 100,000 bottles
HECTARES UNDER VINE 14.00

Boscarelli might well represent the pinnacle
benchmark of Sangiovese production in
Montepulciano. The estate owned by the
De Ferrari family since 1962 has never lost
sight of the centrality of this fundamental
area for Vino Nobile production, with
versions rich in personality and character.
The wines show distinctive, confident
continuity of style and quality thanks to
meticulous choices in the vineyards and
cellar, and turning a blind eye to passing
oenological trends. A flawless range of
wines from this Cervognano winery, but not
for the first time, with absolutely excellent
quality from the Nobile di Montepulciano Il
Nocio 2012. This is quite simply one of the
most consistent expressions of Sangiovese
in Tuscany, and is rarely less than excellent.
The Nobile di Montepulciano Sottocasa
Riserva 2011 is also intriguing, fragrant
and dynamic, and the Vin Santo di
Montepulciano Familiae 2004 is a sweet
surprise. The rest of the range is firmly
reliable.

● Nobile di Montepulciano Il Nocio '12	♥♥♥ 8
● Nobile di Montepulciano Sottocasa Ris. '11	♥♥ 6
○ Vin Santo di Montepulciano Familiae '04	♥♥ 7
● Cortona Merlot '12	♥♥ 4
● Nobile di Montepulciano '13	♥♥ 5
● De Ferrari '15	♥ 3
● Rosso di Montepulciano Prugnolo '15	♥ 3
● Nobile di Montepulciano Il Nocio '11	♀♀♀ 8
● Nobile di Montepulciano Nocio dei Boscarelli '10	♀♀♀ 8
● Nobile di Montepulciano Nocio dei Boscarelli '09	♀♀♀ 8
● Nobile di Montepulciano Nocio dei Boscarelli '08	♀♀♀ 8
● Nobile di Montepulciano Nocio dei Boscarelli '07	♀♀♀ 8

★Brancaia

Loc. Poppi, 42
53017 Radda in Chianti [SI]
Tel. +39 0577742007
www.brancaia.it

CELLAR SALES
PRE-BOOKED VISITS
ACCOMMODATION
ANNUAL PRODUCTION 700,000 bottles
HECTARES UNDER VINE 80.00
SUSTAINABLE WINERY

Brancaia continues to offer a consistent and above average standard of quality, in wines with a well-defined and coherent style. The wines have a modern feel, aged mostly in barriques, but are also harmonious and elegant, revealing fresh, dynamic features. This well-judged combination places both the Chianti wines and those produced in the Maremma vineyards among the benchmark products for this designation and Tuscany in general. The Chianti Classico Riserva 2013 is polished with airy, nicely accessible aromas and a dynamic, fragrant palate. Also good, the Chianti Classico 2014 is slender-bodied but not insubstantial. Its strongpoint is appealing flavour. Il Blu 2012, from sangiovese, cabernet sauvignon and merlot, has enthralling aromas while the palate displays lovely mouthfeel, slightly held back by the oak. The Ilatraia 2013, a Maremma blend of cabernet sauvignon, franc and petit verdot, is balsamic and well-paced, despite rather evident oakiness.

● Chianti Cl. Ris. '13	▼▼▼ 5
● Il Blu '12	▼▼ 7
● Chianti Cl. Brancaia '14	▼▼ 4
● Ilatraia '13	▼▼ 6
● Brancaia Il Blu '08	♈♈♈ 8
● Brancaia Il Blu '07	♈♈♈ 7
● Brancaia Il Blu '06	♈♈♈ 6
● Brancaia Il Blu '05	♈♈♈ 6
● Brancaia Il Blu '04	♈♈♈ 6
● Chianti Cl. Brancaia '13	♈♈♈ 4*
● Chianti Cl. Ris. '11	♈♈♈ 5
● Chianti Cl. Ris. '10	♈♈♈ 4*
● Chianti Cl. Ris. '09	♈♈♈ 7

Brancatelli

Loc. Riotorto
Casa Rossa, 2
57025 Piombino [LI]
Tel. +39 056520655
www.brancatelli.eu

CELLAR SALES
PRE-BOOKED VISITS
ACCOMMODATION AND RESTAURANT SERVICE
ANNUAL PRODUCTION 75,000 bottles
HECTARES UNDER VINE 15.00
VITICULTURE METHOD Certified Organic

Giuseppe Brancatelli left Sicily and his father's vineyard in the province of Messina as a young man and went to work in the Netherlands. Working in catering brought success and satisfaction and nurtured his passion for wine, but he missed the daily contact with the land and nature to be moulded and transformed. So he decided to look for a farm, and after some years he found one he liked in Val di Cornia, between the mountains and the sea. Since the 1990s he has reorganized the vineyards, planted new ones, tended the olive trees and begun production. A good performance from the Segreto 2012, a Cabernet Sauvignon, with grassy, green pepper aromas alongside wild berries and leather. The palate is fluent, appealing, succulent with a lively, flavoursome and lingering finish. We also enjoyed the Questo Dedicato A 2014, made from an equal blend of cabernet franc, cabernet sauvignon, petit verdot and syrah, with cherry jam on the nose and hints of cinnamon and cloves. A warm, mouthfilling flavour with a lingering, appetizing finish.

● Cabernet Sauvignon Segreto '12	▼▼ 7
● Questo Dedicato A '14	▼▼ 3
○ Ansonica Splendente '15	▼ 3
⊙ Loren '15	▼ 3
● Valle delle Stelle '14	▼ 3
○ Ansonica Splendente '14	♈♈ 3
● Cabernet Sauvignon Segreto '11	♈♈ 7
● Cabernet Sauvignon Segreto '10	♈♈ 7
● Giuseppe Brancatelli '12	♈♈ 4
● Giuseppe Brancatelli '11	♈♈ 4
● Valle del Sogno '12	♈♈ 4
● Valle delle Stelle '13	♈♈ 3
● Valle delle Stelle '12	♈♈ 3

Brunelli - Le Chiuse di Sotto

LOC. PODERNOVONE, 157
53024 MONTALCINO [SI]
TEL. +39 0577849337
www.giannibrunelli.it

CELLAR SALES
PRE-BOOKED VISITS
ACCOMMODATION AND RESTAURANT SERVICE
ANNUAL PRODUCTION 30,000 bottles
HECTARES UNDER VINE 6.50
SUSTAINABLE WINERY

With sheer determination, Maria Laura Vacca Brunelli continues the project begun by her late husband Gianni, a leading Montalcino winegrower. Just over six hectares under vine, in two terroirs of different soil and weather features: Le Chiuse di Sotto, in the north-east, above the Canalicchio, and the Podernovo farm, south-east of the village. The Brunellos from the combination of their expressive features have a contemporary profile, thanks to medium-long maceration and ageing in 20- and 30-hectolitre oak. These are meticulous reds with a bite, not sprinters, and worth the wait. It wouldn't have been easy to repeat last year's exploit, but this is still an excellent performance from Gianni Brunelli's Sangioveses. Floral and mineral essences outline the soft, light Brunello 2011, which is like the alter ego of the more expansive and mature 2010 Riserva, too held back in this phase by austerely grained tannins.

● Brunello di Montalcino '11	♥♥ 6
● Brunello di Montalcino Ris. '10	♥♥ 8
● Rosso di Montalcino '14	♥ 4
● Amor Costante '05	♥♥♥ 5
● Brunello di Montalcino '10	♥♥♥ 6
● Amor Costante '10	♥♥ 5
● Brunello di Montalcino '09	♥♥ 6
● Brunello di Montalcino '08	♥♥ 6
● Brunello di Montalcino '07	♥♥ 6
● Brunello di Montalcino '06	♥♥ 6
● Brunello di Montalcino Ris. '07	♥♥ 8
● Brunello di Montalcino Ris. '06	♥♥ 8
● Rosso di Montalcino '13	♥♥ 4
● Rosso di Montalcino '12	♥♥ 4

Bruni

FRAZ. FONTEBLANDA
LOC. LA MARTA, 6
58010 ORBETELLO [GR]
TEL. +39 0564885445
www.aziendabruni.it

CELLAR SALES
PRE-BOOKED VISITS
ANNUAL PRODUCTION 400,000 bottles
HECTARES UNDER VINE 36.00

The Bruni estate, run by brothers Marco and Moreno, boasts flawlessly made, beautifully drinkable wines in a confident style capable, in some particular cases, of highlighting considerable complexity and strongly original features. They are mainly aged in small oak, although large barrels have also reached this estate, underlining the pursuit of stylistic development that makes this Fonteblanda cellar one of the most dynamic in the Maremma wine scenario. The Maremma Grenache Oltreconfine 2014 shows the gait of a complex, elegant wine, veiled on the nose, with sound, sweet and pervasive aromas in which the berry fruit is reminiscent of Burgundy. The slender-bodied palate is well-paced and deep with a fresh, sustained flavour. The Morellino di Scansano Laire Riserva 2013, in a completely different style, is characterful and edgy with pleasing hardness and vibrant aromas.

● Maremma Toscana Grenache Oltreconfine '14	♥♥ 5
● Morellino di Scansano Laire Ris. '13	♥♥ 4
○ Maremma Toscana Vermentino Perlaia '15	♥♥ 3
○ Maremma Toscana Vermentino Brut Plinio Cuvée	♥ 3
○ Maremma Toscana Vermentino Plinio '15	♥ 3
● Morellino di Scansano Marteto '15	♥ 2
● Syrah Perlaia '15	♥ 3
● Grenache Oltreconfine '13	♥♥♥ 2*
○ Dolce Muffato Perlaia '13	♥♥ 5
● Morellino di Scansano Laire Ris. '12	♥♥ 4
● Morellino di Scansano Marteto '13	♥♥ 2*
● Morellino di Scansano Marteto '12	♥♥ 2*
● Syrah Perlaia '13	♥♥ 3

Bulichella

LOC. BULICHELLA, 131
57028 SUVERETO [LI]
TEL. +39 0565829892
www.bulichella.it

CELLAR SALES
PRE-BOOKED VISITS
ACCOMMODATION AND RESTAURANT SERVICE
ANNUAL PRODUCTION 60,000 bottles
HECTARES UNDER VINE 17.00
VITICULTURE METHOD Certified Organic

The estate was established in 1983 by four families from various parts of Italy who decided to live together and share their experiences, farming with full respect for the environment. Their immediate choice to farm organically was well ahead of its time. In 1999 one of the founding families, consisting of Hideyuki Miyakawa, his wife Marisa Bassano and their children, took over ownership and carried forward the original plan, with renovations to the cellar and extension of the vineyards. A new style for the estate's wines and an excellent performance from the Coldipetrerosse 2013: balsam and mint on the nose supported by hints of cinnamon and cloves on a fruity base, rounded off by wild berries. The palate opens creamy smooth and nicely weighty with appealing tannins and a lingering, succulent finish. Also interesting, the Hide 2013 is a monovarietal Syrah with gamy aromas of animal skins and leather, alongside spicy hints of pepper. The palate is chewy, succulent and well-sustained.

● Suvereto Cabernet Coldipietrerosse '13	¶¶ 5
● Suvereto Merlot Maria Shizuko '13	¶¶ 6
● Suvereto Sangiovese Tuscanio '13	¶¶ 5
● Syrah Hide '13	¶¶ 5
● Rubino '14	¶ 2
● Aleatico Sfiziale '13	♀♀ 4
● Aleatico Sfiziale '12	♀♀ 4
● Suvereto Cabernet Sauvignon Coldipietrerosse '12	♀♀ 5
● Suvereto Sangiovese Tuscanio '11	♀♀ 5
● Syrah Hide '12	♀♀ 5
● Val di Cornia Merlot Maria Shizuko '10	♀♀ 6
● Val di Cornia Suvereto Coldipietrerosse '12	♀♀ 5
● Val di Cornia Suvereto Merlot Maria Shizuko '12	♀♀ 5
● Val di Cornia Suvereto Tuscanio '12	♀♀ 5

Tenuta del Buonamico

LOC. CERCATOIA
VIA PROVINCIALE DI MONTECARLO, 43
55015 MONTECARLO [LU]
TEL. +39 058322038
www.buonamico.it

CELLAR SALES
PRE-BOOKED VISITS
ACCOMMODATION
ANNUAL PRODUCTION 250,000 bottles
HECTARES UNDER VINE 43.00

A historic estate currently undergoing extensive renewal, Tenuta di Buonamico is situated at Cercatoia, near Montecarlo. Established in the 1960s, it is run today by the Fontana family who have decided to launch it at an international level. In technical terms the wines are modern, free from traditional references both in stylistic terms and the types produced, as demonstrated by the predilection for fizz. The Montecarlo Bianco 2015 is a lovely expression of a modern white, made from a blend of six different grapes, fermented separately: trebbiano, pinot bianco, sauvignon, semillon, roussanne and chardonnay. The aromas are vibrantly fruity, lightly aromatic and very striking, while the palate is smooth, soft and fresh but not too acidulous. The 2013 Cercatoja has a really open nose with forward jammy sensations while the palate is rather tannic and restrained in the finish.

○ Montecarlo Bianco '15	¶¶ 2*
● Cercatoja '13	¶ 5
● Cercatoja Rosso '11	♀♀ 5
● Cercatoja Rosso '10	♀♀ 5
● Cercatoja Rosso '09	♀♀ 5
● Cercatoja Rosso '06	♀♀ 5
● Il Fortino '12	♀♀ 6
● Il Fortino Syrah '10	♀♀ 6
● Montecarlo Rosso '11	♀♀ 3
○ Vasario '12	♀♀ 4

Ca' Marcanda

LOC. SANTA TERESA, 272
57022 CASTAGNETO CARDUCCI [LI]
TEL. +39 0565763809
info@camarcanda.com

CELLAR SALES
PRE-BOOKED VISITS
ANNUAL PRODUCTION 450,000 bottles
HECTARES UNDER VINE 120.00

Angelo Gaja's estate on the Tuscan coast is making consistent, coherent progress. The landscape at Ca' Marcanda is scattered with olive trees, vineyards and a handsome cellar designed by architect Giovanni Bo, perfectly and harmoniously blended with the surrounding environment. The grapes grown here are the usual Bolgheri area varieties, above all merlot and cabernet sauvignon. The wines narrate the winery's style and language in different ways: focused, stylish, and in the best cases, sophisticated. Gaja wines, in other words. The Bolgheri Rosso Camarcanda 2013 is astonishing for its intensity, varied aromas and underlying finesse. The nose opens on black berry fruit, but soon aromatic herbs, very fine spice and a light, consistent whiff of balsam steal the scene. The palate is complex, racy and holds together well, with a very long, engaging finish.

● Bolgheri Camarcanda '13	♛♛♛	8
● Bogheri Magari '14	♛	8
● Promis '14	♛	1*
● Bolgheri Camarcanda '07	♛♛♛	8
● Bolgheri Camarcanda '01	♛♛♛	8
● Bolgheri Camarcanda '12	♛♛	8
● Bolgheri Camarcanda '11	♛♛	8
● Bolgheri Camarcanda '10	♛♛	8
● Bolgheri Camarcanda '09	♛♛	8
● Bolgheri Camarcanda '08	♛♛	8

Tenuta Le Calcinaie

LOC. SANTA LUCIA, 36
53037 SAN GIMIGNANO [SI]
TEL. +39 0577943007
www.tenutalecalcinaie.it

CELLAR SALES
PRE-BOOKED VISITS
ANNUAL PRODUCTION 60,000 bottles
HECTARES UNDER VINE 9.50
VITICULTURE METHOD Certified Organic

A passion for wine was always in Simone Santini's blood, so much so that he decided to attend the agricultural institute in Siena where he graduated as a wine technician. In 1986 he began his career as a winegrower, planting vineyards and starting to make wines in 1993. He soon converted the estate to organic methods, leading to certification of the vinification process too, in 2001. The subsequent addition of the new cellar, has enabled him to work even more consistently, with respect for the environment. Through to the finals for the Vernaccia Vigna ai Sassi Riserva 2013, thanks to complex and varied aromas: medicinal herbs combining with fruity hints of apples and apricots, a light citrus nuances. The fine-tuned, weighty palate shows well-organized structure with an appealing finish and aromatic herbs in the aftertaste. We also liked the Vernaccia 2015: fresh aromas of lemon and marjoram with hints of plums, and a well-balanced palate with good acidic backbone and an impressive finish.

○ Vernaccia di S. Gimignano V. ai Sassi Ris. '13	♛♛	3*
○ Vernaccia di S. Gimignano '15	♛♛	2*
● Chianti Colli Senesi Santa Maria Ris. '13	♛	4
● Chianti Colli Senesi '12	♛♛	2*
● Gabriele '07	♛♛	4
● Teodoro '07	♛♛	4
○ Vernaccia di S. Gimignano '13	♛♛	2*
○ Vernaccia di S. Gimignano '12	♛♛	2*
○ Vernaccia di S. Gimignano '10	♛♛	2*
○ Vernaccia di S. Gimignano Ris. '08	♛♛	2*
○ Vernaccia di S. Gimignano V. ai Sassi Ris. '10	♛♛	3*
○ Vernaccia di S. Gimignano V. ai Sassi Ris. '09	♛♛	3*

Camigliano

LOC. CAMIGLIANO
VIA D'INGRESSO, 2
53024 MONTALCINO [SI]
TEL. +39 0577844068
www.camigliano.it

Antonio Camillo

LOC. PIANETTI DI MONTEMERANO
FRAZ. MONTEMERANO
58014 MANCIANO [GR]
TEL. 3391525224
info@antoniocamillo.com

CELLAR SALES
PRE-BOOKED VISITS
ANNUAL PRODUCTION 350,000 bottles
HECTARES UNDER VINE 92.00
SUSTAINABLE WINERY

CELLAR SALES
PRE-BOOKED VISITS
ANNUAL PRODUCTION 50,000 bottles
HECTARES UNDER VINE 9.00
VITICULTURE METHOD Certified Organic

Ancient Camigliano, taken over by the Ghezzi family in 1957, is one of the last outposts of Montalcino, at the western border where it becomes Maremma. Gualtiero was passionate about restoring the hamlet to life, saving it from the sprawl of Mediterranean vegetation. Overlooked by the Colline Metallifere, his pleasant renovations have made it a centre of operations, today more than ever. The estate has just under 100 hectares, mainly planted to sangiovese, whose warm and powerful nature is easy to recognize in the two Brunellos aged in 25- and 60-hectolitre French oak. Consistency with the terroir and vintage year are mainly evident in the 2011 version: bottled cherries, yellow peaches, piquant spice, and a chewy, appealing palate that unfolds without losing poise. The Gualto Riserva 2010 is even more airy and approachable, after some aromatic hesitancy, and the palate is mouthfilling and well-paced. The Rosso 2014 and Gamal 2015 are a step below.

Antonio Camillo is almost without equal in terms of his winemaking and, especially, winegrowing experience in Maremma. In addition, he shows particular sensitivity and skill in reintroducing the positive qualities of an old variety like ciliegiolo into the area. His best wines are those obtained from this grape, and they stand out for their meticulous and easily recognizable style in which the variety abandons its huskiness in favour of more pleasing qualities as well as a rediscovered originality in some of their features. The Ciliegiolo Vallerana Alta obtains a well-deserved Tre Bicchieri. This is the most accomplished expression of the grape and its extremely drinkable qualities demonstrate the finesse and complexity of a great wine. The 2014 version is fresh, multilayered and elegant aromas leading into a deep palate with polished nuancing. Also worth a mention, the Morellino Cotozzino 2015 is developing well.

● Brunello di Montalcino '11	▼▼ 6
● Brunello di Montalcino Gualto Ris. '10	▼▼ 7
○ Gamal '15	▼ 2
● Rosso di Montalcino '14	▼ 2
● Brunello di Montalcino '10	♈ 6
● Brunello di Montalcino '09	♈ 6
● Brunello di Montalcino '08	♈ 6
● Brunello di Montalcino '08	♈ 6
● Brunello di Montalcino '06	♈ 6
● Brunello di Montalcino Gualto Ris. '09	♈ 7
● Brunello di Montalcino Gualto Ris. '07	♈ 7
● Brunello di Montalcino Gualto Ris. '06	♈ 7
● Brunello di Montalcino Gualto Ris. '05	♈ 7
○ Moscadello di Montalcino L'Aura '10	♈ 5
● Rosso di Montalcino '13	♈ 3

● Maremma Toscana Ciliegiolo V. Vallerana Alta '14	▼▼▼ 3*
● Maremma Toscana Ciliegiolo Principio '15	▼▼ 2*
● Morellino di Scansano Cotozzino '15	▼▼ 3
○ Vermentino '15	▼ 2
● Ciliegiolo Vallerana Alta '10	♈ 3*
● Maremma Toscana Ciliegiolo Principio '14	♈ 2*
● Maremma Toscana Ciliegiolo Principio '13	♈ 2*
● Maremma Toscana Ciliegiolo Principio '11	♈ 2*
● Maremma Toscana Ciliegiolo V. Vallerana Alta '13	♈ 3*
● Maremma Toscana Ciliegiolo V. Vallerana Alta '12	♈ 3*

Canalicchio - Franco Pacenti

LOC. CANALICCHIO DI SOPRA, 6
53024 MONTALCINO [SI]
TEL. +39 0577849277
www.canalicchiofrancopacenti.it

CELLAR SALES
PRE-BOOKED VISITS
RESTAURANT SERVICE
ANNUAL PRODUCTION 40,000 bottles
HECTARES UNDER VINE 10.00

The link with the famous placename in the north of Montalcino is stated in the brand name, chosen by Rosildo Pacenti in the 1960s for this farm. It was later converted into a bottling estate by his son Franco, who runs the 10-hectare farm with his wife Carla and children Lisa, Serena and Lorenzo. The vineyards are planted at about 300 metres altitude on medium-textured, mainly clayey soil, and exclusively with sangiovese, which undergoes mid-long maceration and ageing in largeish Slavonian oak. With their classic feel and contemporary texture, we recommend these wines particularly to those who don't mind some youthful rough edges and will give them due time at the table. The Franco Pacenti style is nicely captured in the 2011 Brunello: an autumnal nose with truffles and fresh soil, and clear fruit on the fresher palate. The double aspect of lightness and austerity is confirmed in the rugged but assertive and tangy flavour. The 2010 Riserva is more mature and curbed in texture.

● Brunello di Montalcino '11	♥♥ 5
● Brunello di Montalcino Ris. '10	♥♥ 7
● Rosso di Montalcino '14	♥ 3
● Brunello di Montalcino '04	♀♀♀ 5
● Brunello di Montalcino '10	♀♀ 5
● Brunello di Montalcino '09	♀♀ 5
● Brunello di Montalcino '08	♀♀ 5
● Brunello di Montalcino '07	♀♀ 5
● Brunello di Montalcino '06	♀♀ 5
● Brunello di Montalcino '05	♀♀ 5
● Brunello di Montalcino Ris. '07	♀♀ 7
● Brunello di Montalcino Ris. '04	♀♀ 7
● Rosso di Montalcino '13	♀♀ 3
● Rosso di Montalcino '10	♀♀ 3

Canalicchio di Sopra

LOC. CASACCIA, 73
53024 MONTALCINO [SI]
TEL. +39 0577848316
www.canalicchiodisopra.com

CELLAR SALES
PRE-BOOKED VISITS
ACCOMMODATION
ANNUAL PRODUCTION 55,000 bottles
HECTARES UNDER VINE 15.00

A long-time scaler of the Brunello hit parade heights, Canalicchio di Sopra is based primarily on the combination of two families historically linked to Montalcino winemaking. In 1962 the Pacenti branch began producing wine at the Canalicchi estate, in the north where the winery stands, to which they added the Montosoli plots planted by the Ripaccioli, in the 1980s. Separated by just a few hundred metres, they mould sangiovese grapes with almost identical character, skillfully combined according to the vintage in the estate's two Brunellos. Aged in 20-30-hectolitre oak, they are usually a blend of verve and close-knit texture, extremely reliable for ageing. Yet again Tre Bicchieri for the Brunellos presented by Canalicchio di Sopra: first the 2010 standard label, and then for the Riserva, in the exemplary style we know and love. Wild berries, damp earth, and tar on the nose, and a proud, compact gait that displays all its long ageing potential.

● Brunello di Montalcino Ris. '10	♥♥♥ 8
● Brunello di Montalcino '11	♥♥ 6
● Rosso di Montalcino '14	♥♥ 3
● Brunello di Montalcino '10	♀♀♀ 6
● Brunello di Montalcino '07	♀♀♀ 6
● Brunello di Montalcino '06	♀♀♀ 6
● Brunello di Montalcino '04	♀♀♀ 6
● Brunello di Montalciodi Montalcino Ris. '07	♀♀♀ 8
● Brunello di Montalcino Ris. '04	♀♀♀ 7
● Brunello di Montalcino Ris. '01	♀♀♀ 7
● Brunello di Montalcino '05	♀♀ 5
● Brunello di Montalcino Ris. '06	♀♀ 8
● Rosso di Montalcino '13	♀♀ 3
● Rosso di Montalcino '12	♀♀ 3
● Rosso di Montalcino '11	♀♀ 3
● Rosso di Montalcino '09	♀♀ 3

Capanna

LOC. CAPANNA, 333
53024 MONTALCINO [SI]
TEL. +39 0577848298
www.capannamontalcino.com

CELLAR SALES
PRE-BOOKED VISITS
ANNUAL PRODUCTION 70,000 bottles
HECTARES UNDER VINE 21.00

The Capanna estate purchased by the Cencioni family in 1957 extends over the northern sector of Montalcino, overlooking Montosoli from a splendid hilltop at about 300 metres altitude on limestone-marl soil. The 20-odd hectares of vineyards are almost exclusively planted to sangiovese, which forms the basis of Brunellos in a contemporary retro style, sometimes unruly while young but capable of very prestigious expression over time. The hands behind the wines are those of Patrizio, a meticulous vigneron and exponent who has always followed the classic procedures, including maturation in 10- and 30-hectolitre oak. Another Tre Bicchieri for Capanna thanks to the monumental Brunello Riserva 2010: wild strawberries, red currants, topsoil, and a salty base are followed by a lively, assertive pace, thanks mainly to the generous but never harsh tannins. An honourable mention for the 2011 Brunello and the 2014 Rosso, similar in expressive style, succulent and dynamic.

● Brunello di Montalcino Ris. '10	♔♔♔	8
● Brunello di Montalcino '11	♔♔	6
● Rosso di Montalcino '14	♔♔	3
● Brunello di Montalcino Ris. '06	♔♔♔	7
● Brunello di Montalcino Ris. '04	♔♔♔	7
● Brunello di Montalcino Ris. '90	♔♔♔	6
● Brunello di Montalcino '10	♔♔	6
● Brunello di Montalcino '09	♔♔	6
● Brunello di Montalcino '08	♔♔	6
● Brunello di Montalcino Ris. '07	♔♔	7
○ Moscadello di Montalcino '14	♔♔	3
○ Moscadello di Montalcino '13	♔♔	3
● Rosso del Cerro '10	♔♔	2*
● Rosso di Montalcino '13	♔♔	3
● Sant'Antimo Rosso '10	♔♔	4

Tenuta di Capezzana

LOC. SEANO
VIA CAPEZZANA, 100
59015 CARMIGNANO [PO]
TEL. +39 0558706005
www.capezzana.it

CELLAR SALES
PRE-BOOKED VISITS
ACCOMMODATION AND RESTAURANT SERVICE
ANNUAL PRODUCTION 450,000 bottles
HECTARES UNDER VINE 90.00
VITICULTURE METHOD Certified Organic

The estate owned by the Conti Contini Bonacossi estate has made fine quality wines for over 1,200 years. Today, with 90 hectares of lovely vineyards it is the top winery in Carmignano and still family-run, producing some of the best local wines as well as an outstanding extra virgin olive oil. Credit goes to these products for making this historic Tuscan designation famous around the world. The old cellar at Capezzana is worth visiting, as is the nearby Villa di Trefiano, both with reception facilities. Our Tre Bicchieri couldn't fail to reward an extraordinary Vin Santo Riserva, the 2009, captivating in expressive intensity, balance, depth and complexity. But the excellent Carmignano Villa di Capezzana 2013 also made the finals: balsamic, iron-like aromas, fruity and tangy, with very fine-grained tannins. The Riserva di Trefiano 2012 is elegant and well-structured and the Trebbiano 2015 is the best version in the region. The rest of the range shows a very high standard, as ever.

○ Vin Santo di Carmignano Ris. '09	♔♔♔	6
● Carmignano Villa di Capezzana '13	♔♔	5
● Carmignano Trefiano Ris. '12	♔♔	6
○ Chardonnay '15	♔♔	3
● Ghiaie della Furba '12	♔♔	6
○ Trebbiano '15	♔♔	4
● Barco Reale '14	♔	3
⊙ Barco Reale Vin Ruspo '15	♔	2
● Carmignano Villa di Capezzana '07	♔♔♔	4
● Carmignano Villa di Capezzana '05	♔♔♔	4
● Carmignano Villa di Capezzana '99	♔♔♔	5
● Ghiaie della Furba '01	♔♔♔	5
○ Vin Santo di Carmignano Ris. '08	♔♔♔	6
○ Vin Santo di Carmignano Ris. '07	♔♔♔	6
○ Vin Santo di Carmignano Ris. '05	♔♔♔	5

Cappella Sant'Andrea

LOC. CASALE, 26
53037 SAN GIMIGNANO [SI]
TEL. +39 0577940456
www.cappellasantandrea.it

CELLAR SALES
PRE-BOOKED VISITS
RESTAURANT SERVICE
ANNUAL PRODUCTION 45,000 bottles
HECTARES UNDER VINE 9.00
VITICULTURE METHOD Certified Organic
SUSTAINABLE WINERY

An estate created out of a love for the land and family tradition: this is the story of Cappella Sant'Andrea, and protagonists Flavia and Francesco who ended up in the wine sector almost by chance. The estate run by Flavia's grandfather was left unexpectedly with no-one in charge, hence their decision to dedicate their lives to winegrowing. Art enthusiast Francesco transferred his passion to vineyards and wines, but the most important choice was to farm the land organically from the beginning. The Vernaccia Prima Luce 2013 displays fresh aromas, rich in fruit: grapefruit, balsamic sensations and hints of wood resin, and a tangy, minerally, long and lingering flavour. The Vernaccia Casanuova 2014 has a pleasing, rather stylish nose with aromatic herbs, hints of butter and apples, and a nicely full-bodied, supple, generous palate with a tangy finish. The other wines are all appealing and very drinkable.

○ Vernaccia di S. Gimignano Casanuova '14	♥♥	3
○ Vernaccia di S. Gimignano Prima Luce '13	♥♥♥	5
● Serreto '12	♥	4
○ Vernaccia di S. Gimignano Rialto '15	♥	3
○ Vernaccia di S. Gimignano '11	♀♀	2*
○ Vernaccia di S. Gimignano '10	♀♀	2*
○ Vernaccia di S. Gimignano Rialto '13	♀♀	3
○ Vernaccia di S. Gimignano Rialto '12	♀♀	3
○ Vernaccia di S. Gimignano Rialto '09	♀♀	3

Caprili

FRAZ. TAVERNELLE
LOC. CAPRILI, 268
53024 MONTALCINO [SI]
TEL. +39 0577848566
www.caprili.it

CELLAR SALES
PRE-BOOKED VISITS
ACCOMMODATION
ANNUAL PRODUCTION 75,000 bottles
HECTARES UNDER VINE 21.00
SUSTAINABLE WINERY

With almost 40 harvests to its name, the Bartolommei family farm is by no means an up-and-coming estate in the crowded Montalcino DOC zone. But Caprili has only quite recently changed gear towards stylistic and territorial consistency. With Nordic precision and Mediterranean warmth, the estate's Brunellos faithfully reflect the characteristic features of a sunny, steep, breezy subzone with prevalently stony soil rich in sand and limestone. The 15-odd hectares are mainly planted to sangiovese, with separate harvests for the various plots and final blending following lengthy maturation in large oak barrels. To repeat ourselves: Caprili's Brunello Riserva is up there on Montalcino's dais for consistency and peaks. The 2010, dedicated AdAlberto, provides yet more proof of this. Irresistible from the first, clearly fruity impact, with resin and plasticine aromas and an even more delightful palate, eager and flavoursome.

● Brunello di Montalcino AdAlberto Ris. '10	♥♥♥	8
● Brunello di Montalcino '11	♥♥	6
● Rosso di Montalcino '14	♥♥	3
● Brunello di Montalcino '10	♀♀♀	6
● Brunello di Montalcino '06	♀♀♀	7
● Brunello di Montalcino Ris. '08	♀♀♀	7
● Brunello di Montalcino Ris. '06	♀♀♀	7
● Brunello di Montalcino Ris. '04	♀♀♀	5
● Brunello di Montalcino '09	♀♀	5
● Brunello di Montalcino '08	♀♀	5
● Brunello di Montalcino '07	♀♀	5
● Brunello di Montalcino '05	♀♀	5
● Rosso di Montalcino '13	♀♀	3

Fattoria Carpineta Fontalpino

FRAZ. MONTAPERTI
LOC. CARPINETA
53019 CASTELNUOVO BERARDENGA [SI]
TEL. +39 0577369219
www.carpinetafontalpino.it

CELLAR SALES
PRE-BOOKED VISITS
ACCOMMODATION
ANNUAL PRODUCTION 100,000 bottles
HECTARES UNDER VINE 23.00
VITICULTURE METHOD Certified Organic

This Monteaperti-based estate is firmly established among the best in the designation. The wines produced at Carpineta Fontalpino are generous, rich in personality and flawlessly made. The style is modern, with prevalent and well-measured use of small oak casks, nicely extracted colour and significant structure, but also good acidity and spirited tannins. A winning combination that yields consistently impressive wines. The Do ut des 2013 is very good, as always: a sturdy blend of cabernet sauvignon, sangiovese and merlot with clear-cut aromas of lush fruit, spices and hints of forest floor. The palate is generous and well-textured with a succulent flavour and lengthy finish. The salient features of the Chianti Classico Riserva 2013 are vibrant aromas and tangy flavour while the Chianti Classico 2014 stands out for its fresh, relaxed and drinkable palate.

● Do ut des '13	▼▼▼	5
● Chianti Cl. Fontalpino '14	▼▼	3
● Chianti Cl. Fontalpino Ris. '13	▼▼	5
● Montaperto '14	▼	3
● Do ut des '12	♀♀♀	5
● Do ut des '11	♀♀♀	5
● Do ut des '10	♀♀♀	5
● Do ut des '09	♀♀♀	5
● Do ut des '07	♀♀♀	5
● Dofana '10	♀♀♀	7
● Dofana '07	♀♀♀	8
● Chianti Cl. Fontalpino '13	♀♀	3
● Chianti Cl. Fontalpino '12	♀♀	3

Casa alle Vacche

FRAZ. PANCOLE
LOC. LUCIGNANO, 73A
53037 SAN GIMIGNANO [SI]
TEL. +39 0577955103
www.casaallevacche.it

CELLAR SALES
PRE-BOOKED VISITS
ACCOMMODATION AND RESTAURANT SERVICE
ANNUAL PRODUCTION 115,000 bottles
HECTARES UNDER VINE 28.00

The farm is immersed in the countryside a few kilometres from San Gimignano's famous towers. Its name is a specific reference to its original purpose many years ago: in the 1800s the estate's oldest building was a stable for the livestock used to pull carts and work in the fields. Since then the Ciappi family have been passionately devoted to working the land and producing wine and oil. They have used integrated farming techniques for some time, demonstrating special interest in the environment. The Vernaccia Riserva Crocus 2013 presents a fruity, vegetal nose with white peaches and slightly minty sensations. The palate is elegant, layered, complex and nicely buttery with a long, flavoursome finish. Also interesting, the Vernaccia I Macchioni 2015 shows more traditional aromas of apples and almonds, and a tidy, perfectly tangy palate with vigorous, interesting acidity. The other wines are well made, with typically clean aromas and nice structure.

○ Vernaccia di S. Gimignano Crocus Ris. '13	▼▼	3
○ Vernaccia di S. Gimignano I Macchioni '15	▼▼	2*
☉ Rosato '15	▼	2
● Sangiovese '15	▼	2
○ Vernaccia di S. Gimignano '15	▼	2
● Aglieno '12	♀♀	2*
○ Vernaccia di S. Gimignano '13	♀♀	2*
○ Vernaccia di S. Gimignano '11	♀♀	2*
○ Vernaccia di S. Gimignano Crocus Ris. '11	♀♀	2*
○ Vernaccia di S. Gimignano Crocus Ris. '10	♀♀	2*
○ Vernaccia di S. Gimignano I Macchioni '14	♀♀	2*
○ Vernaccia di S. Gimignano I Macchioni '11	♀♀	2*

Casa Emma

LOC. CORTINE
S.DA PROV.LE DI CASTELLINA IN CHIANTI, 3
50021 BARBERINO VAL D'ELSA [FI]
TEL. +39 0558072239
www.casaemma.com

CELLAR SALES
PRE-BOOKED VISITS
RESTAURANT SERVICE
ANNUAL PRODUCTION 90,000 bottles
HECTARES UNDER VINE 25.00

Casa Emma, owned by the Bucalossi family, has vineyards divided over the Castellina in Chianti and Barberino Val d'Elsa areas. These specific zones are clearly defined in the wines, and sometimes successfully mixed together. The style typically shows good ripe fruit and complex structure, in a concept of wine that is well-balanced and characterful. Ageing mainly takes place in small oak casks. The Chianti Classico Riserva 2013 has clear, sweet fruity aromas, especially cherries, nicely blended with the oak. The palate is weighty and mouthfilling with a well-paced flavour. The Chianti Classico Gran Selezione 2012 is more about finesse and a multifaceted, complex profile. The aromas are more stylish although toasty notes are clearly evident. The Chianti Classico 2014 is fresh-tasting and the Soloìo, a monovarietal Merlot, is impressive.

Fattoria Casabianca

FRAZ. CASCIANO DI MURLO
LOC. CASABIANCA
53016 MURLO [SI]
TEL. +39 0577811033
www.fattoriacasabianca.it

CELLAR SALES
PRE-BOOKED VISITS
ACCOMMODATION AND RESTAURANT SERVICE
ANNUAL PRODUCTION 230,000 bottles
HECTARES UNDER VINE 70.00
VITICULTURE METHOD Certified Organic
SUSTAINABLE WINERY

Fattoria Casabianca is situated in the southern part of the province of Siena, near Murlo. These southernmost hills of the Chianti Colli Senesi zone usually enjoy warmer weather than the rest of the area. 70 of the estate's 650 hectares are planted to vineyards, certified organic since 2015. The wines are aged in both barriques and large barrels, and the style is drinkable and elegant with a range designed above all to be enjoyed. Two Chianti Colli Senesi Riservas from 2013, both definitely well made. The first has clean aromas and a well-paced, nicely supple flavour. The other, Belsedere, made from grapes grown in the vineyard of the same name, is fragrant and gutsy with a long finish. The 15 Staiori 2013, a monovarietal Merlot, is also good: not at all ingratiating, with fresh, delicate aromas, refreshing herbal nuances and a tangy, vigorous palate.

● Chianti Cl. Gran Sel. '12	🍷🍷 5
● Chianti Cl. Ris. '13	🍷🍷 5
● Chianti Cl. '14	🍷🍷 3
● Soloìo '12	🍷🍷 6
● Chianti Cl. Ris. '95	🍷🍷🍷 4*
● Chianti Cl. Ris. '93	🍷🍷🍷 5
● Soloìo '94	🍷🍷🍷 4*
● Chianti Cl. '13	🍷🍷 3
● Chianti Cl. '10	🍷🍷 3
● Chianti Cl. Ris. '11	🍷🍷 5
● Chianti Cl. Ris. '08	🍷🍷 5
● Chianti Cl. Vignalparco '12	🍷🍷 3
● Chianti Cl. Vignalparco '11	🍷🍷 3

● 15 Staiori '13	🍷🍷 5
● Chianti Colli Senesi Belsedere Ris. '13	🍷🍷 5
● Chianti Colli Senesi Ris. '13	🍷🍷 3
● Chianti Colli Senesi '11	🍷🍷 2*
● Chianti Colli Senesi Ris. '07	🍷🍷 3*
● Loccareto '11	🍷🍷 4
● Loccareto '08	🍷🍷 3*

Tenuta Casadei

loc. San Rocco
57028 Suvereto [LI]
Tel. +39 0558300411
www.tenutacasadei.it

PRE-BOOKED VISITS
ANNUAL PRODUCTION 80,000 bottles
HECTARES UNDER VINE 17.00
VITICULTURE METHOD Certified Organic
SUSTAINABLE WINERY

Stefano Casadei has longstanding experience in the wine sector. He started out working on his father's estate, specializing in planting, equipment and consultancy for wine and olive oil production. Later he turned his hand personally, with his wife Anna Baj Macario and brother Andrea, to running three estates: Castello di Trebbio, another modern and dynamic estate on the Olianas hills in Sardinia, and Casa Dei at Suvereto, which was purchased in 1997 to start producing wines that reflect the typical aromas of the Tuscan coast. The appealing Filare 18, from 100% cabernet franc, reaches the finals thanks to varied aromas: grilled green peppers alongside ripe wild berries with fresh, enthralling grassy sensations. The palate is stylish, docile, nicely soft, with a flavoursome, relaxed finish. The Filare 41, from petit verdot, displays vibrant aromas of blackberries and blueberries, with Mediterranean scrubland and aromatic herbs, and an elegant, well-defined structure with a rounded, dynamic finish.

- Filare 18 '14 🍷🍷 6
- Filare 41 '14 🍷🍷 6
- Armonia '15 🍷 3
- Sogno Mediterraneo '14 🍷 4
- Armonia '10 ΥΥ 2*
- Armonia '08 ΥΥ 3
- Filare 18 '13 ΥΥ 6
- Filare 18 '09 ΥΥ 5
- Filare 22 '08 ΥΥ 5
- Filare 41 '13 ΥΥ 6
- Filare 41 '11 ΥΥ 5
- Filare 41 '07 ΥΥ 5
- Sogno Mediterraneo '13 ΥΥ 4
- Syrah Le Anfore '14 ΥΥ 5

Casale dello Sparviero Fattoria Campoperi

loc. Casale, 93
53011 Castellina in Chianti [SI]
Tel. +39 0577743228
www.casaledellosparviero.it

CELLAR SALES
PRE-BOOKED VISITS
ACCOMMODATION
ANNUAL PRODUCTION 127,000 bottles
HECTARES UNDER VINE 88.00

A 380-hectare estate of which 90 are under vine, Casale dello Sparviero is situated in the subzone of Castellina in Chianti, further down with a warmer microclimate, which produces assertive, generous wines. These features are consistently reflected in the wines from this estate. Barriques are mainly used for ageing the wines, as well as large casks, an impressive mixture that delivers well-balanced, technically flawless wines. The Chianti Classico 2013 is fresh and very supple with clearly defined fruity aromas. The same basic features appear in the Chianti Classico Riserva 2013, along with a more complex structure and spicy aromas with balsamic hints. The powerful, firm Chianti Classico Gran Selezione Vigna Paronza 2012 is generous, succulent and satisfying with complex aromas and nuanced shading.

- Chianti Cl. '13 🍷🍷 3
- Chianti Cl. Gran Sel. V. Paronza '12 🍷🍷 3
- Chianti Cl. Ris. '13 🍷🍷 3
- Chianti Cl. Gran Sel. Ada Andrighetti '12 🍷 3
- Chianti Sup. '14 🍷 3
- Chianti Cl. '08 ΥΥ 3

Fattoria Le Casalte

FRAZ. SANT'ALBINO
VIA DEL TERMINE, 2
53045 MONTEPULCIANO [SI]
TEL. +39 0578798246
www.lecasalte.com

CELLAR SALES
PRE-BOOKED VISITS
ANNUAL PRODUCTION 50,000 bottles
HECTARES UNDER VINE 13.00

Chiara Barioffi is a skilled, sensitive winegrower with clear-sighted vision. The estate was purchased by her father and she started to lend a hand in the vineyard and cellar at a very young age. The land is clayey especially in the Quercetonda cru. Today the vineyards are organically farmed and there is not much interference in the cellar. The wines, aged in medium-large and smaller barrels, are personal and elegant in style, never pursuing frills or excess. The Nobile Quercetonda 2013 is well focused: enthralling aromas with outstanding personality, opening on subtle floral hints and moving into red currants and wild strawberries, shot through with minerally, pebbly sensations. The palate continues to ride this aromatic wave, supple, unpredictable, nicely racy though a little grassy in the finish. A spicier, closer-knit texture for the Nobile 2013.

★Casanova di Neri

POD. FIESOLE
53024 MONTALCINO [SI]
TEL. +39 0577834455
www.casanovadineri.com

PRE-BOOKED VISITS
ACCOMMODATION
ANNUAL PRODUCTION 225,000 bottles
HECTARES UNDER VINE 63.00

The winery established in the 1970s and managed by Giacomo, Gianlorenzo and Giovanni Neri is now, more than ever, an international star in the Montalcino firmament. Credit is undoubtedly due to sangiovese-based wines in a strongly characteristic style: dense colour, firm structure and ripe fruit. Other factors include the vineyard management choices and the features of the estate's different plots, scattered between the north-eastern area of Torrenieri, Cava dell'Onice at Castelnuovo dell'Abate, and Sesta to the south. Alongside the standard Brunello in the best vintage years are the Tenuta Nuova and Cerretalto selections, matured in small, new oak barrels. This time the fruity, lively Brunello 2011 tickles our fancy: generous aromas of cherry jam, balsam, and charred oak, ahead of the open, accomplished flavour, just slightly edgy in the finish. The Tenuta Nuova of the same vintage, with darker aromas, is less accessible in this phase.

● Nobile di Montepulciano Quercetonda '13	♟♟ 5
● Nobile di Montepulciano '13	♟♟ 3
● Nobile di Montepulciano '08	♟♟ 3
● Nobile di Montepulciano Quercetonda '12	♟♟ 5
● Nobile di Montepulciano Quercetonda '07	♟♟ 5
● Nobile di Montepulciano Quercetonda '04	♟♟ 5
● Rosso di Montepulciano '13	♟♟ 2*
● Rosso di Montepulciano '10	♟♟ 2*
● Rosso Toscano '08	♟♟ 2*
○ Vin Santo di Montepulciano '03	♟♟ 7
○ Vin Santo di Montepulciano '00	♟♟ 7
○ Vin Santo di Montepulciano '99	♟♟ 7

● Brunello di Montalcino '11	♟♟ 6
● Brunello di Montalcino Tenuta Nuova '11	♟♟ 8
● Rosso di Montalcino '14	♟♟ 5
● Brunello di Montalcino '09	♟♟♟ 6
● Brunello di Montalcino '06	♟♟♟ 5
● Brunello di Montalcino Cerretalto '07	♟♟♟ 8
● Brunello di Montalcino Cerretalto '06	♟♟♟ 8
● Brunello di Montalcino Cerretalto '04	♟♟♟ 8
● Brunello di Montalcino Cerretalto '01	♟♟♟ 8
● Brunello di Montalcino Cerretalto '99	♟♟♟ 8
● Brunello di Montalcino Tenuta Nuova '06	♟♟♟ 8
● Brunello di Montalcino Tenuta Nuova '05	♟♟♟ 7
● Brunello di Montalcino Tenuta Nuova '01	♟♟♟ 6
● Brunello di Montalcino Tenuta Nuova '99	♟♟♟ 6
● Pietradonice '05	♟♟♟ 8
● Sant'Antimo Pietradonice '01	♟♟♟ 8

Castell'in Villa

LOC. CASTELL'IN VILLA
53019 CASTELNUOVO BERARDENGA [SI]
TEL. +39 0577359074
www.castellinvilla.com

CELLAR SALES
PRE-BOOKED VISITS
ANNUAL PRODUCTION 100,000 bottles
HECTARES UNDER VINE 54.00

Coralia Pignatelli wines are firmly positioned at the absolute peak of the most authentic and consistent Chianti Classico production. Vibrant but nuanced, stylish but also spirited, they offer an uncompromising interpretation of the noblest, most unyielding soul of the Castelnuovo Berardenga subzone. Very elegant, unusually complex and ageable, these products continue to trace the expressive path of Tuscan auteur wines, enhancing the huge potential of sangiovese with innate spontaneity. Quite simply, a safe bet in this DOC zone and the rest of Italy. The Chianti Classico 2012 is a little compressed, with hints of ripe fruit, strawberry jam, forest floor, mushrooms and gamy hints. The palate is mouthfilling, lightly alcoholic, with a drying finish. The 2010 Riserva also suffers from rather excessive tannin the finish, but can boast a whippy acidity. Mature sensations on the nose and palate for the Santacroce 2008.

● Chianti Cl. '12	▼▼ 5
● Chianti Cl. Ris. '10	▼▼ 6
⊙ La Gazzera '15	▼ 3
● Santacroce '08	▼ 6
● Chianti Cl. '11	♀♀♀ 5
● Chianti Cl. '09	♀♀♀ 5
● Chianti Cl. '08	♀♀♀ 5
● Chianti Cl. Poggio delle Rose Ris. '10	♀♀ 6

Castellani

FRAZ. SANTA LUCIA
VIA DEL POPOLO, 90E
56025 PONTEDERA [PI]
TEL. +39 0587292900
www.castelwine.com

CELLAR SALES
PRE-BOOKED VISITS
ANNUAL PRODUCTION 25,000,000 bottles
HECTARES UNDER VINE 150.00

The estate's history dates back over a century when founder Alfredo began bottling and selling his own wine in the late 19th century. His work ethic was passed on to his sons Duilio and Mario, who transformed the estate from a simple farm into a well-organized, efficient estate, also in economic and distribution terms. The vineyards are situated on various estates in the province of Pisa, with another property in Chianti Classico. The appealing Ciliegiolo 2014 from Tenuta Santa Lucia has vibrant aromas with hints of raspberries and cherries, pipe tobacco and leather, and a chewy, tangy palate with a long, succulent finish. The interesting Violetta 2012, from Tenuta di Ceppaiano, is based on sangiovese with cabernet sauvignon: vibrant fruity aromas, a consistent palate with good acidity and relaxed, flavoursome finish. The captivating Travalda 2011 is a classic Bordeaux blend: spicy sensations on a creamy, lively palate.

● Alle Viole Tenuta di Ceppaiano '13	▼▼ 3
● Ciliegiolo Tenuta di Santa Lucia '14	▼▼ 3
● Travalda Tenuta Santa Lucia '11	▼▼ 3
● Violetta Tenuta di Ceppaiano '12	▼▼ 3
● Casone Tenuta di Poggio al Casone '13	▼ 3
● La Cattura Tenuta di Poggio al Casone '13	▼ 3
○ Vermentino Tenuta Santa Lucia '15	▼ 3

★Castellare di Castellina

LOC. CASTELLARE
53011 CASTELLINA IN CHIANTI [SI]
TEL. +39 0577742903
www.castellare.it

CELLAR SALES
PRE-BOOKED VISITS
ACCOMMODATION
ANNUAL PRODUCTION 200,000 bottles
HECTARES UNDER VINE 28.00

Over time Castellare di Castellina has managed to build itself a leading role in the Chianti Classico DOC. The well-established results derive from the choice to make wines that meticulously reveal the deepest expression, linked to the terroir, immune to passing fanciful trends. The style of this Castellina in Chianti estate is firmly rooted in the pursuit of balance and elegance, also enhanced by careful use of oak for ageing, revealing wines with nice grip and plenty of character. I Sodi di S. Niccolò 2012 has stylish character, with lovely complex aromas and a sharp flavour: in other words, it is very good, as it often is. Not far behind, the Chianti Classico Il Poggiale Riserva 2013 has medicinal herbs and earthy aromas, with a weighty, nicely dynamic flavour. Also very good, the Chianti Classico Riserva 2013 is succulent, well paced and flavoursome.

● I Sodi di S. Niccolò '12	🍷🍷🍷 8
● Chianti Cl. Il Poggiale Ris. '13	🍷🍷 5
● Chianti Cl. Ris. '13	🍷🍷 4
● Chianti Cl. '14	🍷 3
● Chianti Cl. V. Il Poggiale Ris. '01	🍷🍷🍷 5
● I Sodi di S. Niccolò '11	🍷🍷🍷 8
● I Sodi di S. Niccolò '10	🍷🍷🍷 8
● I Sodi di S. Niccolò '09	🍷🍷🍷 8
● I Sodi di S. Niccolò '08	🍷🍷🍷 7
● I Sodi di S. Niccolò '07	🍷🍷🍷 7
● I Sodi di S. Niccolò '06	🍷🍷🍷 7
● I Sodi di S. Niccolò '05	🍷🍷🍷 7
● I Sodi di S. Niccolò '04	🍷🍷🍷 7
● I Sodi di S. Niccolò '03	🍷🍷🍷 7
● I Sodi di S. Niccolò '02	🍷🍷🍷 7
● I Sodi di San Niccolò '01	🍷🍷🍷 7

★Castello Banfi

LOC. SANT'ANGELO SCALO
CASTELLO DI POGGIO ALLE MURA
53024 MONTALCINO [SI]
TEL. +39 0577840111
www.castellobanfi.com

CELLAR SALES
PRE-BOOKED VISITS
ACCOMMODATION AND RESTAURANT SERVICE
ANNUAL PRODUCTION 10,000,000 bottles
HECTARES UNDER VINE 850.00
SUSTAINABLE WINERY

Despite its well-documented, centuries-old roots, Montalcino and its emblematic wine would probably never have achieved the fame they enjoy today without the efforts of the Mariani family, from the 1970s onwards. First they purchased Castello Banfi, a farm with over 800 hectares of vineyards, managed today by Enrico Viglierchio and Remo Grassi, then added Vigne Regali in Piedmont and the Banfi Toscana line. The result is a generous, well-assorted range, also in terms of grape varieties, spearheaded as ever by the classic sangiovese-based reds, well-rounded and fruity in style. A lovely choral performance just missing a top note, with some outstanding solos from the Brunellos. Like the excellent Poggio alle Mura 2011, well focused and supple, or the Poggio all'Oro Riserva 2010, more evolved and mature, but with impressively well-defined tannins. Not to mention the sunny Fontanelle Chardonnay 2015, unquestionably one of the best whites from Montalcino.

● Brunello di Montalcino Poggio alle Mura '11	🍷🍷 6
● Brunello di Montalcino '11	🍷🍷 6
● Brunello di Montalcino Poggio all'Oro Ris. '10	🍷🍷 8
● Brunello di Montalcino Poggio alle Mura Ris. '10	🍷🍷 8
○ Fontanelle Chardonnay '15	🍷🍷 4
● Rosso di Montalcino '14	🍷🍷 2*
● Excelsus '12	🍷 6
● Rosso di Montalcino Poggio alle Mura '14	🍷 4
● Brunello di Montalcino Poggio all'Oro Ris. '04	🍷🍷🍷 8
● Brunello di Montalcino Poggio all'Oro Ris. '85	🍷🍷🍷 8
● Sant'Antimo Mandrielle '04	🍷🍷🍷 3

★Castello d'Albola

Loc. Pian d'Albola, 31
53017 Radda in Chianti [SI]
Tel. +39 0577738019
www.albola.it

CELLAR SALES
PRE-BOOKED VISITS
ANNUAL PRODUCTION 800,000 bottles
HECTARES UNDER VINE 157.00

In Zonin's gigantic archipelago of wineries, Castello d'Albola is the most interesting productive estate, as we have underlined many times. Not only for the pedoclimatic context of the vineyards, in one of the best areas of the Radda in Chianti subzone, but also because the team working on the estate seem to have fully and coherently grasped the expressive potential of locally produced wines. Albola wines are technically flawless and highlight character and personality which places them in the exclusive elite of the best in the designation. The 2013 version of the Chianti Classico Gran Selezione is absolutely dazzling. The stylish aromas range from red berries to hints of forest floor and gunflint, while the palate is fragrant, succulent, and richly nuanced with a crescendo finish. The Chianti Classico 2013 is the paradigm of its type: full-bodied, fresh and flavoursome with tempting, appealing aromas.

★★Castello del Terriccio

Loc. Terriccio
via Bagnoli, 16
56040 Castellina Marittima [PI]
Tel. +39 050699709
www.terriccio.com

CELLAR SALES
PRE-BOOKED VISITS
ANNUAL PRODUCTION 150,000 bottles
HECTARES UNDER VINE 60.00

The castle has a 1000-year-old history in the heart of an extensive estate, over 1800 hectares between the sea and the inland foothills. Cereal crops were prevalent until current owner Gian Annibale Rossi di Medelana increased the vineyard acreage and continued to modernize the estate, which often happens when the bond between wine and culture is celebrated. Today, as well as vineyards, Castello di Terriccio grows organic spelt, wheat, fodder and olives. Castello di Terriccio 2011 is blend of mainly syrah and petit verdot with elegant, complex aromas combining iodine hints, medicinal herbs, blackcurrants and blackberries. The palate opens fresh and lively with a harmonious texture, slender tannins and a nice lingering finish. A breezy Tre Bicchieri. The Lupicaia 2012, cabernet sauvignon with petit verdot, displays vibrant forest floor aromas with minty nuances, and a succulent, harmonious palate.

● Chianti Cl. Gran Sel. '13	▼▼▼ 5
● Chianti Cl. '13	▼▼ 3*
● Acciaiolo '13	▼▼ 6
● Chianti Cl. Ris. '12	▼▼ 4
● Acciaiolo '06	♈♈♈ 6
● Acciaiolo '04	♈♈♈ 6
● Acciaiolo '01	♈♈♈ 6
● Chianti Cl. Il Solatio Gran Sel. '11	♈♈♈ 5
● Chianti Cl. Il Solatio Gran Sel. '10	♈♈♈ 5
● Chianti Cl. Le Ellere '08	♈♈♈ 3
● Chianti Cl. Ris. '09	♈♈♈ 4*
● Chianti Cl. Ris. '08	♈♈♈ 4*
● Chianti Cl. Le Ellere '12	♈♈ 3*

● Castello del Terriccio '11	▼▼▼ 8
● Lupicaia '12	▼▼ 8
● Tassinaia '12	▼▼ 6
● Castello del Terriccio '07	♈♈♈ 8
● Castello del Terriccio '04	♈♈♈ 8
● Castello del Terriccio '03	♈♈♈ 8
● Castello del Terriccio '01	♈♈♈ 8
● Lupicaia '11	♈♈♈ 8
● Lupicaia '10	♈♈♈ 8
● Lupicaia '07	♈♈♈ 8
● Lupicaia '06	♈♈♈ 8
● Lupicaia '05	♈♈♈ 8
● Lupicaia '04	♈♈♈ 8
● Lupicaia '01	♈♈♈ 8

Castello del Trebbio

Via Santa Brigida, 9
50065 Pontassieve [FI]
Tel. +39 0558304900
www.castellodeltrebbio.it

CELLAR SALES
PRE-BOOKED VISITS
ANNUAL PRODUCTION 300,000 bottles
HECTARES UNDER VINE 52.00
SUSTAINABLE WINERY

A nucleus dating back to 1184, a building once owned by the de' Pazzi family, historic cellars which can still be visited, renovated farmhouses scattered over the Colli Fiorentini: this is the heritage acquired by the Baj Macario family in 1968 as well as an estate of 380 hectares, 52 under vine. Alongside on-site holiday accommodation, wine tourism, and special crops like saffron, wine production is the fulcrum of the family business. Stefano Casadei, husband of owner Anna, manages another two estates belonging to Baj Macario: Tenute Casa Dei, in Val di Cornia, and Tenuta Olianas, in Sardinia. Through to the finals for the Lastricato 2012, a hair's breadth from our highest accolade. A fresh, floral nose slightly held back by spiciness from the oak, and a palate with lively tannins on a tangy background, and echoes of aromatic herbs and spice. The Chianti Superiore 2014 is also very appealing, supple and slender.

● Chianti Rufina Lastricato Ris. '12	♟♟	5
● Chianti Sup. '14	♟♟	2*
○ Brut M. Cl. '13	♟	3
○ Congiura '15	♟	4
● Chianti Rufina Lastricato Ris. '11	♟♟♟	4*
○ Bianco della Congiura '14	♟♟	3
● Cabernet Franc Casa Dei '12	♟♟	5
● De' Pazzi '11	♟♟	4
○ Pazzesco '11	♟♟	5
● Petit Verdot Casa Dei '12	♟♟	5
● Sangiovese '13	♟♟	5
○ Vin Santo del Chianti '07	♟♟	4
○ Viognier Casa Dei '13	♟♟	4

★★Castello di Ama

Loc. Ama
53013 Gaiole in Chianti [SI]
Tel. +39 0577746031
www.castellodiama.com

CELLAR SALES
PRE-BOOKED VISITS
ANNUAL PRODUCTION 300,000 bottles
HECTARES UNDER VINE 90.00

Castello di Ama is firmly established in a prominent position on the crowded Chianti wine production scene. Lorenza Sebasti and Marco Pallanti offer impeccably made wines that express unusual authenticity in a blend of energy and elegance. The meticulously tended vineyards are mainly situated at 500 metres altitude, and divided into four plots: Bellavista, Casuccia, Montebuoni and San Lorenzo. The wines are aged in small, previously used oak casks. The Chianti Classico San Lorenzo Gran Selezione 2013 shows the rhythm of a great wine: multifaceted, very fresh aromas, and generous, succulent flavour perked up by lively, consistent acidity. The single variety Merlot, L'Apparita 2013, is firm-structured and not without character. The 2014 Chianti Classico Ama is slender-bodied with approachable flavour and slightly hazy aromas. The Haiku 2013, from sangiovese cabernet franc and merlot, displays lush fruit aromas and slightly excessive oakiness in the flavour.

● Chianti Cl. Gran Sel. San Lorenzo '13	♟♟♟	6
● L'Apparita '13	♟♟	8
● Chianti Cl. Ama '14	♟	4
● Haiku '13	♟	6
● Chianti Cl. Ama '11	♟♟♟	4*
● Chianti Cl. Bellavista '01	♟♟♟	8
● Chianti Cl. Bellavista '99	♟♟♟	8
● Chianti Cl. Castello di Ama '05	♟♟♟	5
● Chianti Cl. Castello di Ama '03	♟♟♟	5
● Chianti Cl. Castello di Ama '01	♟♟♟	5
● Chianti Cl. Castello di Ama '00	♟♟♟	5
● Chianti Cl. La Casuccia '04	♟♟♟	8
● Chianti Cl. La Casuccia '01	♟♟♟	8
● L'Apparita '01	♟♟♟	8

Castello di Bolgheri

LOC. BOLGHERI
S.DA LAURETTA, 7
57020 CASTAGNETO CARDUCCI [LI]
TEL. +39 0565762110
www.castellodibolgheri.eu

CELLAR SALES
PRE-BOOKED VISITS
ACCOMMODATION
ANNUAL PRODUCTION 80,000 bottles
HECTARES UNDER VINE 50.00

This veteran estate with a long pedigree was part of the huge property owned by the Conti della Gherardesca. It is not all about history, however, since Castello di Bolgheri is a modern business with a high standard of quality. It belongs today to the Zileri al Verme family, who are tasked with protecting and promoting the considerable extent of vineyards: about 50 hectares on sandy and clayey land rich in stony material and limestone. They rise to the occasion beautifully, to judge by the excellent quality shown by the wines every year. The Bolgheri Rosso Superiore 2013 is very unusual. To be honest, it is difficult to pick out in a blind tasting, thanks to an unusual, strongly citrus aroma with marked hints of pink grapefruit and orange fruit gums. It is juicy and fruity, with a consistent, accomplished palate, and certainly very drinkable. Citrus and vegetal hints also appear in the Bolgheri Rosso Varvàra 2014.

Castello di Bossi

LOC. BOSSI IN CHIANTI
53019 CASTELNUOVO BERARDENGA [SI]
TEL. +39 0577359330
www.bacciwines.it

CELLAR SALES
PRE-BOOKED VISITS
ACCOMMODATION
ANNUAL PRODUCTION 700,000 bottles
HECTARES UNDER VINE 124.00

A mosaic of estates ranging from Chianti Classico to Maremma via Montalcino. A clearly defined, modern style offering firmly structured, powerful wines with strong support from the oak used for ageing, mainly barriques. These are the salient production features of the Bacci family, who started as winegrowers in 1980. Their range of well-made wines showed a steady standard of quality and in the past have scaled the heights of absolute excellence. The Corbaia 2012 feels like an old-style sangiovese and cabernet sauvignon blend, with vibrant aromas and oak-led but succulent flavour. The Chianti Classico Berardo Riserva 2012 displays fruity aromas and a powerful palate, slightly dry in the finish. The Mega Tenuta di Renieri 2012 is another sangiovese and cabernet sauvignon blend, very similar to its older brother. The Morellino di Scansano Tempo Terre di Talamo Riserva 2012 is more relaxed.

● Bolgheri Rosso Sup. '13	♟♟ 7
● Bolgheri Varvàra '14	♟ 4
● Bolgheri Sup. Castello di Bolgheri '12	♟♟♟ 6
● Bolgheri Sup. Castello di Bolgheri '10	♟♟♟ 6
● Bolgheri Sup. Castello di Bolgheri '09	♟♟♟ 6
● Bolgheri Sup. Castello di Bolgheri '07	♟♟♟ 6
● Bolgheri Rosso Varvàra '10	♟♟ 4
● Bolgheri Rosso Varvàra '09	♟♟ 4
● Bolgheri Rosso Varvàra '08	♟♟ 4
● Bolgheri Sup. Castello di Bolgheri '11	♟♟ 6
● Bolgheri Varvàra '13	♟♟ 4
● Bolgheri Varvàra '12	♟♟ 4

● Brunello di Montalcino Renieri '11	♟♟ 7
● Chianti Cl. Berardo Ris. '12	♟♟ 5
● Corbaia '12	♟♟ 8
● Mega Tenuta di Renieri '12	♟♟ 6
● Morellino di Scansano Tempo Terra di Talamo Ris. '12	♟♟ 5
● Brunello di Montalcino Renieri Ris. '10	♟ 7
● Chianti Cl. '13	♟ 4
● Chianti Cl. Tenuta di Renieri '13	♟ 5
● Grido Tenuta di Renieri '13	♟ 6
○ Vermentino Vento Terre di Talamo '15	♟ 5
○ Viogner Vento Teso Terre di Talamo '15	♟ 4
● Corbaia '03	♟♟♟ 6

★★★Castello di Fonterutoli

LOC. FONTERUTOLI
VIA OTTONE III DI SASSONIA, 5
53011 CASTELLINA IN CHIANTI [SI]
TEL. +39 057773571
www.mazzei.it

CELLAR SALES
PRE-BOOKED VISITS
ACCOMMODATION AND RESTAURANT SERVICE
ANNUAL PRODUCTION 800,000 bottles
HECTARES UNDER VINE 117.00
SUSTAINABLE WINERY

The Mazzei family are a piece of Chianti Classico history, and more besides. The style of Fonterutoli wines is clearly readable and synonymous with opulent, full extract and soft flavour, flawless technical precision and excellent grip, guaranteeing elegant, lively wines. They are the result of meticulous attention to ripeness of the fruit and ageing in small oak casks. This stylistic process is also repeated in Tenuta Belguardo, in Maremma. Siepi 2013, a sangiovese and merlot blend, is polished and stylish with complex, vibrant aromas and a firm, soft flavour. 30 years on from the last vintage produced, the Concerto is back in the 2013 version: a fragrant and succulent blend of sangiovese and cabernet sauvignon, this is a classic Fonterutoli wine made for the first time in 1981. The Philip 2013, a monovarietal Cabernet Sauvignon, is lively and mouthfilling with roasted coffee beans and red berries on the nose.

● Siepi '13	♥♥♥ 8
● Chianti Cl. Ser Lapo Ris. '13	♥♥ 5
● Concerto '13	♥♥ 8
● Philip '13	♥♥ 6
● Morellino di Scansano Bronzone Tenuta di Belguardo '13	♥♥ 4
● Poggio Badiola '14	♥♥ 3
● Serrata di Belguardo Tenuta di Belguardo '14	♥♥ 4
● Chianti Cl. Fonterutoli '14	♥ 5
● Mix36 '12	♥ 7
● Tenuta Belguardo '12	♥ 5
● Tirreno Tenuta di Belguardo '14	♥ 4
○ Vermentino Tenuta di Belguardo '15	♥ 4
● Mix36 '11	♥♥♥ 8
● Siepi '11	♥♥♥ 8

Castello di Gabbiano

FRAZ. MERCATALE VAL DI PESA
VIA GABBIANO, 22
50020 SAN CASCIANO IN VAL DI PESA [FI]
TEL. +39 055821053
www.castellogabbiano.it

CELLAR SALES
PRE-BOOKED VISITS
ACCOMMODATION AND RESTAURANT SERVICE
ANNUAL PRODUCTION 1,000,000 bottles
HECTARES UNDER VINE 145.00

Significant quantities both in bottles sold and acreage of vineyards make this a leading productive estate in the Chianti subzone of San Casciano Val di Pesa, south of Florence. The wines are modern in style and well-modulated, both in ripeness of the fruit and in the use of oak, mainly small casks. This is a well-made range of products, perhaps slightly lacking in personality but enjoyable and, in some cases, in harmony with the features of their terroir of origin. The Chianti Classico Bellezza Gran Selezione 2012 is well made with clear, mature aromas and a soft, succulent, nicely balanced flavour. The Chianti Classico Riserva 2013 is also accomplished, although the oak can take over at times. Very simple but enjoyable, the Chianti Classico 2014 has veiled aromas and a supple palate.

● Chianti Cl. Gran Sel. Bellezza '12	♥♥ 5
● Chianti Cl. Ris. '13	♥♥ 5
● Chianti Cl. '14	♥ 3
● Alleanza '08	♥♥ 5
● Alleanza '05	♥♥ 5
● Bellezza '06	♥♥ 5
● Bellezza '05	♥♥ 5
● Bellezza '04	♥♥ 5
● Chianti Cl. '11	♥♥ 3
● Chianti Cl. Gran Sel. Bellezza '11	♥♥ 5
● Chianti Cl. Ris. '12	♥♥ 5
● Chianti Cl. Ris. '09	♥♥ 5
● Chianti Cl. Ris. '07	♥♥ 5
● Chianti Cl. Ris. '06	♥♥ 4

Castello di Meleto

LOC. MELETO
53013 GAIOLE IN CHIANTI [SI]
TEL. +39 0577749217
www.castellomeleto.it

CELLAR SALES
PRE-BOOKED VISITS
ACCOMMODATION AND RESTAURANT SERVICE
ANNUAL PRODUCTION 600,000 bottles
HECTARES UNDER VINE 144.00
SUSTAINABLE WINERY

With over 140 hectares of vineyards Castello di Meleto, in the Gaiole in Chianti subzone, is a benchmark for the designation both in size and in suitability of the vineyard locations. The wines preserve the typical features of Chianti in terms of the choice of grapes, preferring sangiovese, and ageing in oak, where the large cask is coming back into vogue. The Chianti Classico Meleto 2013 is slender and succulent with a tasty, multilayered flavour and rounded, well-sustained aromas alternating spicy hints and red berry fruit. The Chianti Classico Vigna Casi Riserva 2013 reveals mature aromas with a generous, soft flavour.

● Chianti Cl. Meleto '13	♟♟ 3*
● Chianti Cl. V. Casi Ris. '13	♟♟ 5
● Chianti Cl. Pieve di Spaltenna Ris. '12	♟ 3
● Chianti Cl. Ris. '03	♟♟♟ 4
● Chianti Cl. V. Casi Ris. '11	♟♟♟ 5
● Borgaio '11	♟♟ 3
● Chianti Cl. '13	♟♟ 3
● Chianti Cl. '09	♟♟ 3
● Chianti Cl. Gran Sel. '10	♟♟ 6
● Chianti Cl. V. Casi Ris. '12	♟♟ 5
● Fiore '10	♟♟ 5
● Fiore '09	♟♟ 5
○ Vin Santo del Chianti Cl. '08	♟♟ 5

Castello di Monsanto

VIA MONSANTO, 8
50021 BARBERINO VAL D'ELSA [FI]
TEL. +39 0558059000
www.castellodimonsanto.it

CELLAR SALES
PRE-BOOKED VISITS
ANNUAL PRODUCTION 450,000 bottles
HECTARES UNDER VINE 72.00

Castello di Monsanto has recently celebrated half a century of business, and started making wine thanks to the foresight of Fabrizio Bianchi, assisted today on the estate by his daughter Laura. The typical winery style displays elegant aromas and fine-grained tannic texture. The wines have plenty of personality, although this is not always fully evident on their release, and are uncommonly ageworthy: longstanding benchmark products for those who love auteur wines. First created in 1974 as a Sangiovese selection, and among the first single variety wines successfully based on this grape, it is known today as Sangioveto and the 2010 version is really well typed. The aromas are elegant and clearly defined while the palate is well balanced and lipsmacking with complex, succulent flavour. The Chianti Classico 2014 is fresh, slender-bodied and very drinkable.

● Sangioveto '10	♟♟♟ 7
● Chianti Cl. '14	♟♟ 3*
● Chianti Cl. Il Poggio Ris. '11	♟♟ 7
● Chianti Cl. Ris. '13	♟♟ 5
● Chianti Cl. '11	♟♟♟ 3*
● Chianti Cl. Cinquantenario Ris. '08	♟♟♟ 6
● Chianti Cl. Il Poggio Ris. '10	♟♟♟ 8
● Chianti Cl. Il Poggio Ris. '06	♟♟♟ 6
● Chianti Cl. Ris. '11	♟♟♟ 5
● Chianti Cl. '13	♟♟ 3*
● Chianti Cl. Il Poggio Ris. '09	♟♟ 7
● Chianti Cl. Ris. '12	♟♟ 5
● Nemo '10	♟♟ 6

Castello di Potentino

LOC. POTENTINO, 6
58038 SEGGIANO [GR]
TEL. +39 0564950014
www.potentino.com

CELLAR SALES
PRE-BOOKED VISITS
ACCOMMODATION
ANNUAL PRODUCTION 20,000 bottles
HECTARES UNDER VINE 4.00

In the Middle Ages castles were built for
defence. But when English writer and
journalist Charlotte Horton renovated the
castle in Seggiano she threw it open to the
local community, as a place where art
comes together with the best local food
and wine products. And where her wine
mirrors the terroir. The four hectares of
vineyards planted to sangiovese, alicante
and pinot noir are situated a few kilometres
from the southern limit of the Brunello di
Montalcino zone. Here, in a sheltered valley
among the ridges of nearby Mt. Amiata, an
extinct volcano, Charlotte makes wines with
mineral, even features which never cede to
excessive texture. We especially liked the
Balaxus 2011, from grenache, fermented
and aged in 50-hectolitre French oak. The
vintage offers rounded body without
sacrificing flavour and liveliness. The
aromas are immediately enfolding, with rich
ripe cherries, spices and wood resin, and a
chewy palate as broad as it is deep. The
Sangiovese Sacromonte 2012 is good,
while the 2012 Pinot Nero Piropo is less
vibrant than other vintages.

● Balaxus '11	♟♟ 4
● Sacromonte '12	♟♟ 3
☉ Jaspidem '14	♟ 3
● Piropo '12	♟ 5
● Balaxus '08	♟♟ 3
● Piropo '11	♟♟ 4
● Piropo '10	♟♟ 4
● Sacromonte '11	♟♟ 3*
● Sacromonte '10	♟♟ 3*

Castello di Radda

LOC. IL BECCO
53017 RADDA IN CHIANTI [SI]
TEL. +39 0577738992
www.castellodiradda.it

CELLAR SALES
PRE-BOOKED VISITS
ANNUAL PRODUCTION 100,000 bottles
HECTARES UNDER VINE 33.00

Agricole Gussalli Beretta, owned by the
Beretta family, is working well at Castello di
Radda, with a coherent grasp of the
features of this area and no forcing of
procedures in the cellar. The grapes are
grown in vineyards of various ages and
aspects, and aged alternately in large oak
casks and barriques, creating a
well-judged, efficient mixture. The signature
wines are elegant and enjoyable, while
showing character and complexity. The
Chianti Classico Riserva 2013 has
multilayered, lively aromas that herald a
succulent, deep, nicely fresh flavour.
Equally interesting is the Chianti Classico
Gran Selezione 2012: slightly veiled aromas
in this phase but a full, generous and
pleasantly warm palate. The Chianti
Classico 2014 is well focused, especially
considering the critical year, with a supple,
slender body and nuanced, defined aromas.

● Chianti Cl. Ris. '13	♟♟♟ 5
● Chianti Cl. Gran Sel. '12	♟♟ 3*
● Chianti Cl. '14	♟♟ 3
● Chianti Cl. Ris. '12	♟♟♟ 5
● Chianti Cl. Ris. '11	♟♟♟ 6
● Chianti Cl. Ris. '07	♟♟♟ 5
● Chianti Cl. '08	♟♟ 3
● Chianti Cl. Castello di Radda '10	♟♟ 3
● Chianti Cl. Gran Sel. '11	♟♟ 3
● Chianti Cl. Gran Sel. '10	♟♟ 3
● Chianti Cl. Poggio Selvale '10	♟♟ 3
● Guss '11	♟♟ 6
● Guss '09	♟♟ 6

★Castello di Volpaia

LOC. VOLPAIA
P.ZZA DELLA CISTERNA, 1
53017 RADDA IN CHIANTI [SI]
TEL. +39 0577738066
www.volpaia.com

CELLAR SALES
PRE-BOOKED VISITS
ACCOMMODATION AND RESTAURANT SERVICE
ANNUAL PRODUCTION 200,000 bottles
HECTARES UNDER VINE 46.00
VITICULTURE METHOD Certified Organic
SUSTAINABLE WINERY

The estate owned by the Mascheroni Stianti family combines organically farmed vineyards with solid, unimpeachable winemaking technique. The resulting wines are usually elegant in a flawless modern style, starting with ageing in mainly small oak casks, which removes nothing of their personality and character. A now-consolidated overall harmony characterizes the Castello di Volpaia range with reassuring continuity, and the wines are among the benchmark products in the Radda in Chianti subzone. The Chianti Classico Riserva 2013 is wonderful: clearly defined, sunny aromas and a deep, succulent, nicely paced flavour. The Balifico 2012, a blend of sangiovese, cabernet sauvignon and merlot, has lush fruit on the nose and a sweet, lively palate. The Chianti Classico 2014 displays fresh aromas and a pleasantly edgy flavour, while the Chianti Classico Coltassala Riserva 2012 is still slightly hard.

Castello Romitorio

LOC. ROMITORIO, 279
53024 MONTALCINO [SI]
TEL. +39 0577847212
www.castelloromitorio.com

CELLAR SALES
PRE-BOOKED VISITS
ACCOMMODATION
ANNUAL PRODUCTION 150,000 bottles
HECTARES UNDER VINE 15.00

The "modernist" label is increasingly evident for the Castello Romitorio range, especially considering the releases of recent years. The Chia family makes Brunellos with mouthfilling fruit, ably blending texture and finesse, and guiding the temperament of western Montalcino into the glass. This is where the 15 or so hectares of vineyards are located, mostly planted to sangiovese. The plots purchased in the Chianti Colli Senesi and Morellino di Scansano areas complete the overview of a mature agricultural and oenological project, which lives up to the worldwide fame of the artist and founder, an outstanding exponent of the transavantgarde. Further confirmation comes from the range of Brunellos, led by a minimalist, dynamic 2011, even more surprising than the splendid 2010, and just lacking a little depth to repeat its success. The excellent Brunello Filo di Seta 2011 and Riserva 2010 are in a warmer, more richly extracted style.

● Chianti Cl. Ris. '13	♚♚♚ 5
● Balifico '12	♚♚ 7
● Chianti Cl. '14	♚♚ 3
● Chianti Cl. Coltassala Ris. '12	♚♚ 7
● Chianti Cl. Gran Sel. Il Puro '11	♚♚ 8
● Chianti Cl. '13	♚♚♚ 3*
● Chianti Cl. Coltassala Ris. '04	♚♚♚ 6
● Chianti Cl. Coltassala Ris. '01	♚♚♚ 6
● Chianti Cl. Il Puro Vign. Casanova Ris. '08	♚♚♚ 8
● Chianti Cl. Il Puro Vign. Casanova Ris. '06	♚♚♚ 8
● Chianti Cl. Ris. '10	♚♚♚ 5
● Chianti Cl. Ris. '08	♚♚♚ 5
● Chianti Cl. Ris. '07	♚♚♚ 5

● Brunello di Montalcino '11	♚♚ 8
● Brunello di Montalcino Filo di Seta '11	♚♚ 8
● Brunello di Montalcino Ris. '10	♚♚ 8
● Brunello di Montalcino '10	♚♚♚ 8
● Brunello di Montalcino '05	♚♚♚ 8
● Brunello di Montalcino Ris. '97	♚♚♚ 8
● Brunello di Montalcino '09	♚♚ 8
● Brunello di Montalcino '08	♚♚ 7
● Brunello di Montalcino Filo di Seta '10	♚♚ 8
● Brunello di Montalcino Ris. '07	♚♚ 8
● Morellino di Scansano '13	♚♚ 3
● Morellino di Scansano Ghiaccio Forte '11	♚♚ 5
● Rosso di Montalcino '12	♚♚ 5
● Rosso di Montalcino '11	♚♚ 4
● Rosso di Montalcino '10	♚♚ 4

Castello Sonnino

VIA VOLTERRANA NORD, 6A
50025 MONTESPERTOLI [FI]
TEL. +39 0571609198
www.castellosonnino.it

CELLAR SALES
PRE-BOOKED VISITS
ACCOMMODATION
ANNUAL PRODUCTION 250,000 bottles
HECTARES UNDER VINE 40.00

All that remains today of the oldest part of
Castello Sonnino is the 13th-century tower
overlooking the surrounding valley. Although
the castle has been owned by the De Renzis
Sonnino family since the early 19th century,
the turning point towards high quality farm
products only came in 1987. Credit goes to
Alessandro and Caterina who extensively
renovated the property and breathed new life
into the winegrowing aspect, bringing the
estate up among the leaders of the Chianti
Montespertoli DOC. Sangiovese and canaiolo
are the main native varieties grown, although
international grapes are to be found
alongside them, such as merlot, petit verdot,
syrah, cabernet sauvignon and malbec. The
Cantinino 2010, 100% sangiovese, has
fruity blackberry and cherry jam aromas and
a weighty palate with a lovely mouthwatering
finish. The Chianti Montespertoli Castello
di Sonnino 2013 is fragrant and tangy,
while the Vin Santo 2009 is appealing and
enthralling.

● Cantinino '10	▼▼ 4
● Chianti Montespertoli Castello di Sonnino '13	▼▼ 2*
○ Vin Santo del Chianti '09	▼▼ 5
● Chianti Montespertoli '15	▼ 2
● Leone Rosso '15	▼ 2
● Cantinino '09	♀♀ 4
● Cantinino '08	♀♀ 5
● Cantinino '07	♀♀ 4
● Cantinino '06	♀♀ 4
● Cantinino '05	♀♀ 4
● Chianti Montespertoli '13	♀♀ 2*

Castello Vicchiomaggio

LOC. LE BOLLE
VIA VICCHIOMAGGIO, 4
50022 GREVE IN CHIANTI [FI]
TEL. +39 055854079
www.vicchiomaggio.it

CELLAR SALES
PRE-BOOKED VISITS
ACCOMMODATION AND RESTAURANT SERVICE
ANNUAL PRODUCTION 300,000 bottles
HECTARES UNDER VINE 38.00
SUSTAINABLE WINERY

Castello di Vicchiomaggio wines have
earned themselves a leading role on the
Chianti Classico production scene. The
vineyards are planted in the Florentine area
of the designation at Greve in Chianti, and
the fine quality grapes are processed in the
cellar without unnecessary procedures. The
results show a reassuring continuity in
quality, with a range of reliable wines in a
modern but never excessive style. The
winery also produces the Tenuta
Vallemaggiore wines in Maremma.
Harmonious flavour and clear-cut aromas
are the salient features of the beautifully
made Chianti Classico Vigna La Prima Gran
Selezione 2012. The Ripa delle More 2013,
a blend of sangiovese, cabernet sauvignon
and merlot, has consistent, lipsmacking
flavour but the aromas are a little confused
at times. The Chianti Classico Agostino Petri
da Vicchiomaggio Riserva 2013 is firm and
austere while the Maremma Colle Alto 2013
from Villa Vallemaggiore is fresh and soft.

● Chianti Cl. V. La Prima Gran Sel. '12	▼▼ 7
● Chianti Cl. Agostino Petri da Vicchiomaggio Ris. '13	▼▼ 5
● Ripa delle More '13	▼▼ 5
● Chianti Cl. San Jacopo da Vicchiomaggio '14	▼ 3
● Governo Villa Vallemaggiore '15	▼ 3
● Maremma Poggio Re Villa Vallemaggiore '14	▼ 4
● Ripa delle Mandorle '14	▼ 2
○ Vermentino Villa Vallemaggiore '15	▼ 3
● Chianti Cl. Vigna La Prima Gran Sel. '10	♀♀♀ 7
● FSM '07	♀♀♀ 8
● FSM '04	♀♀♀ 5
● Chianti Cl. San Jacopo da Vicchiomaggio '13	♀♀ 3

Castelvecchio

LOC. SAN PANCRAZIO
VIA CERTALDESE, 30
50026 SAN CASCIANO IN VAL DI PESA [FI]
TEL. +39 0558248032
www.castelvecchio.it

CELLAR SALES
PRE-BOOKED VISITS
ACCOMMODATION
ANNUAL PRODUCTION 120,000 bottles
HECTARES UNDER VINE 22.00
VITICULTURE METHOD Certified Organic
SUSTAINABLE WINERY

Medieval notary documents clearly show that this farmstead belonged to the Cavalcanti family in around 1200. Today it is owned by the Rocchi family who took it over in the early 1960s. Renzo started building the winery and planting the first vineyards while in the mid-Nineties Carlo, with his children Filippo and Stefania, chose to follow the hard path towards quality winegrowing, with excellent results. The vineyards benefit from ideal locations: while sangiovese, cabernet sauvignon and petit verdot enjoy the sunshine on a south-east facing hillside, the cooler altitudes to the north-west are planted to canaiolo nero, merlot and malvasia. Evident vegetal aromas mark the presence of petit verdot in the Brecciolino 2013, joined by merlot and sangiovese in the blend: green peppers stand out over a spicy, fruity background, while the palate shows good grip and balance with more spice and hints of black berry fruit in the finish. The Riserva Vigna La Quercia of the same vintage is more austere and stylish.

● Chianti Colli Fiorentini	
V. La Quercia Ris. '13	♟♟ 4
● Il Brecciolino '13	♟♟ 5
● Orme in Rosso '13	♟ 3
● Solo Uno '13	♟ 6
● Il Brecciolino '11	♟♟♟ 5
● Chianti Colli Fiorentini	
Il Castelvecchio '13	♟♟ 2*
● Il Brecciolino '12	♟♟ 5
● Numero Otto '13	♟♟ 3
● Orme in Rosso '11	♟♟ 3
● Solo Uno '11	♟♟ 7
○ Vin Santo del Chianti	
Chiacchierata Notturna '04	♟♟ 6

Castiglion del Bosco

LOC. CASTIGLION DEL BOSCO
53024 MONTALCINO [SI]
TEL. +39 05771913750
www.castigliondelbosco.com

CELLAR SALES
PRE-BOOKED VISITS
ACCOMMODATION AND RESTAURANT SERVICE
ANNUAL PRODUCTION 250,000 bottles
HECTARES UNDER VINE 62.00
VITICULTURE METHOD Certified Organic

It is practically impossible to condense into a few lines all the splendour of the Castiglio del Bosco project, as Massimo Ferragamo conceived it after he bought the estate in 2003. The north-western part of Montalcino is a basically unspoilt oasis immersed in woodlands, and this is the location of the 60-odd hectares of sangiovese vineyards as well as the luxurious holiday village, with two restaurants, a spa, private golf club, and much more. The two main farms, Capanna and Gauggiole, bring to life a generous, varied range in continual stylistic evolution, led by the three Brunellos. The range shows consistent growth, supported by our latest tastings, starting with the Campo del Drago 2011: crisp, clear fruit, reordered and enhanced in the emerging earthy, smoky sensations. The Brunello of the same year is tighter, but similar in expressive style, with hints of raspberries and thyme. The Riserva 1100 2010, on the other hand, shows a more evolved and dry character.

● Brunello di Montalcino '11	♟♟ 6
● Brunello di Montalcino	
Campo del Drago '11	♟♟ 8
● Brunello di Montalcino Ris. 1100 '10	♟♟ 6
● Rosso di Montalcino '14	♟ 3
● Brunello di Montalcino '07	♟♟ 6
● Brunello di Montalcino	
Campo del Drago '10	♟♟ 8
● Brunello di Montalcino	
Campo del Drago '08	♟♟ 8
● Brunello di Montalcino	
Campo del Drago '07	♟♟ 8
● Brunello di Montalcino	
Campo del Drago '04	♟♟ 8
● Brunello di Montalcino Ris. 1100 '10	♟♟ 6
● Rosso di Montalcino '11	♟♟ 3

Famiglia Cecchi

LOC. CASINA DEI PONTI, 56
53011 CASTELLINA IN CHIANTI [SI]
TEL. +39 057754311
www.cecchi.net

PRE-BOOKED VISITS
ANNUAL PRODUCTION 8,000,000 bottles
HECTARES UNDER VINE 330.00
SUSTAINABLE WINERY

The Cecchi brandname has always
represented once of the leading estates in
the Chianti Classico designation, and not
only in terms of quantity. The recent
improvement in quality revealed by the
wines, especially the more rigorous
selections, has thrust the Castellina in
Chianti estate irreversibly forwards. Credit
goes to strict stylistic choices, above all
emphasis on increasingly marked identity.
The estate also owns Castello di Montauto at
San Gimignano and the Val delle Rose estate
in Maremma. A lovely interpretation from the
Chianti Classico Villa Cerna Riserva 2013,
both of the year and the terroir. Clearly
defined aromas alternating fruit and hints of
spice and forest floor. The multilayered
palate shows firm progression and a deep,
succulent palate. The Chianti Classico
Riserva di Famiglia 2013 is also very good,
but the oak sometimes takes over.

Centolani

LOC. FRIGGIALI
S.DA MAREMMANA
53024 MONTALCINO [SI]
TEL. +39 0577849454
www.tenutafriggialiepietranera.it

CELLAR SALES
PRE-BOOKED VISITS
ACCOMMODATION
ANNUAL PRODUCTION 260,000 bottles
HECTARES UNDER VINE 70.00

The Peluso Centolani family's wines are
moulded from several leading estate-owned
farms in areas of the jagged-shaped
Montalcino DOC zone showing different
altitudes and microclimates. The Friggiali
estate is situated in the western part of the
zone at 250 to 400 metres altitude in an
open, breezy area, on marly soil with very
little clay. Tenuta Pietranera is a short
distance from the Abbey of Sant'Antimo, to
the south, at much lower altitudes, on more
compact soil. These territorial variables are
supported by the vinification and ageing
processes for the leading Sangioveses,
which mainly use 30- and 50-hectolitre
Slavonian oak. As often happens, the battle
of the house Brunellos ends in a draw. The
Friggiali 2011 is currently a little held
back by marked oaky sensations, but the
fruit is impressively intact. The Pietranera
of the same vintage is more open and
mature with a mouthfilling mid-palate and
vigorous finish.

● Chianti Cl. Villa Cerna Ris. '13	♟♟♟ 5
● Chianti Cl. Primo Colle Villa Cerna '14	♟♟ 3
● Chianti Cl. Riserva di Famiglia '13	♟♟ 5
○ Maremma Vermentino Litorale Val delle Rose '15	♟♟ 3
● Morellino di Scansano Poggio al Leone Val delle Rose Ris. '13	♟♟ 4
● Chianti Castello Montauto '14	♟ 2
● Maremma Aurelio '13	♟ 4
● Morellino di Scansano Val delle Rose '15	♟ 3
○ Vernaccia di S. Gimignano Castello di Montauto '15	♟ 3
● Chianti Cl. Villa Cerna Ris. '12	♟♟♟ 5
● Chianti Cl. Villa Cerna Ris. '08	♟♟♟ 5
● Coevo '11	♟♟♟ 8
● Coevo '10	♟♟♟ 7

● Brunello di Montalcino Pietranera '11	♟♟ 5
● Brunello di Montalcino Tenuta Friggiali '11	♟♟ 6
● Brunello di Montalcino Pietranera Ris. '10	♟♟ 6
● Brunello di Montalcino Poggiotondo '11	♟ 6
● Rosso di Montalcino Pietranera '14	♟ 3
● Brunello di Montalcino Tenuta Friggiali '04	♟♟♟ 5
● Brunello di Montalcino Tenuta Friggiali Ris. '99	♟♟♟ 7
● Brunello di Montalcino Pietranera '10	♟♟ 5
● Brunello di Montalcino Pietranera '09	♟♟ 5
● Brunello di Montalcino Poggiotondo '10	♟♟ 5
● Brunello di Montalcino Poggiotondo '09	♟♟ 5
● Brunello di Montalcino Tenuta Friggiali '10	♟♟ 5

★La Cerbaiola

P.ZZA CAVOUR, 19
53024 MONTALCINO [SI]
TEL. +39 0577848499
www.aziendasalvioni.com

PRE-BOOKED VISITS
RESTAURANT SERVICE
ANNUAL PRODUCTION 15,000 bottles
HECTARES UNDER VINE 4.00

Giulio Salvioni, who recently celebrated 30 harvests, is universally acclaimed as a great veteran of Montalcino wine. Assisted by his wife Mirella and children David and Alessia, he tends four hectares of vineyards in the north-eastern zone, at Cerbaie Alte's 400-odd metres altitude. This is a true cru which has always been cared for in a traditional, but not academic, style with spontaneous fermentation and ageing in 20-hectolitre Slavonian oak. The textured, characterful Brunellos are sometimes a tad unapproachable when young, but capable of composure and expansion over time. The 2011 version seems to be no exception: blackberry jam, piquant spice, toasty hints, juicy fruit and expansive supporting acidity, although the flavour seems curbed and cumbersome. The Rosso 2014 is remarkably well made, generous and organized on hints of summer fruit and Mediterranean scrubland, with a firm, tasty flavour and just a little too much burred tannin in the finish.

Vincenzo Cesani

LOC. PANCOLE, 82D
53037 SAN GIMIGNANO [SI]
TEL. +39 0577955084
www.cesani.it

CELLAR SALES
PRE-BOOKED VISITS
ACCOMMODATION
ANNUAL PRODUCTION 100,000 bottles
HECTARES UNDER VINE 21.00
VITICULTURE METHOD Certified Organic

The Cesani family came here from the Marche region in the 1950s. Vincenzo began working to achieve a higher production standard, and 60 years on this dedication to work has translated into organic farming whose fruits are also used as ingredients for a line of cosmetics. The farm is still family-run with the same work ethic by Maria Luisa and Letizia, current Chair of the producers' association, and has also focused on rediscovering an ancient San Gimignano product: saffron. Through to the finals for the Vernaccia Sanice Riserva 2013, with hints of aromatic herbs, white peaches, and plums on the nose and a firm, very generous, invigorating palate with nicely recognizable and lingering tangy flavour. The Chianti Colli Senesi 2015 is pleasantly uncomplicated with clear aromas of cherries and damsons, alongside floral hints of violets. The palate is slim-bodied, harmonious and nicely drinkable thanks to well-balanced acidity. The rest of the wines are all well made.

● Brunello di Montalcino '11	♟♟ 8
● Rosso di Montalcino '14	♟♟ 8
● Brunello di Montalcino '09	♟♟♟ 8
● Brunello di Montalcino '06	♟♟♟ 8
● Brunello di Montalcino '04	♟♟♟ 8
● Brunello di Montalcino '00	♟♟♟ 8
● Brunello di Montalcino '99	♟♟♟ 8
● Brunello di Montalcino '97	♟♟♟ 8
● Brunello di Montalcino '90	♟♟♟ 8
● Brunello di Montalcino '89	♟♟♟ 8
● Brunello di Montalcino '88	♟♟♟ 8
● Brunello di Montalcino '87	♟♟♟ 8
● Brunello di Montalcino '85	♟♟♟ 8
● Brunello di Montalcino '10	♟♟ 8
● Brunello di Montalcino '08	♟♟ 8
● Brunello di Montalcino '07	♟♟ 8

○ Vernaccia di S. Gimignano Sanice Ris. '13	♟♟ 3*
● Chianti Colli Senesi '15	♟♟ 2*
● Luenzo '12	♟♟ 4
⊙ Serarosa '15	♟ 2
○ Vernaccia di S. Gimignano '15	♟ 2
● Luenzo '99	♟♟♟ 4
● Luenzo '97	♟♟♟ 4*
● Chianti Colli Senesi '13	♟♟ 2*
● Luenzo '11	♟♟ 4
● San Gimignano Rosso Cellori '09	♟♟ 4
● Serisè '12	♟♟ 3
○ Vernaccia di S. Gimignano '13	♟♟ 2*
○ Vernaccia di S. Gimignano '12	♟♟ 2*
○ Vernaccia di S. Gimignano Sanice '11	♟♟ 2*
○ Vernaccia di S. Gimignano Sanice Ris. '12	♟♟ 3*

Giovanni Chiappini

Loc. Felciaino
via Bolgherese, 189c
57020 Bolgheri [LI]
Tel. +39 0565765201
www.giovannichiappini.it

CELLAR SALES
PRE-BOOKED VISITS
ANNUAL PRODUCTION 70,000 bottles
HECTARES UNDER VINE 23.00
VITICULTURE METHOD Certified Organic
SUSTAINABLE WINERY

Although this is a small, family-run winery it has nonetheless achieved considerable international success. The story of the project's origin describes humble farmers from the Marche region who moved to Bolgheri in the 1950s and decided to start up a small farm, which gradually assumed an importance far beyond any expectations. The vineyards, organically farmed since 2010, are divided into separate plots. Often the grapes are fermented separately to create different wines, also from the different varieties grown. A good year for this estate's wines. The Bolgheri Rosso Superiore Guado de' Gemoli is very good: a fruity profile that is both sweet and fresh, nicely supported by leather and tobacco sensations. The palate is very well balanced and confident, with a velvety, lingering texture and grassy hints in the lovely finish.

● Bolgheri Sup. Guado de' Gemoli '13	▼▼ 8
● Lienà Cabernet Franc '13	▼▼ 8
○ Bolgheri Le Grottine '15	▼ 3
● Lienà Petit Verdot '13	▼ 8
● Bolgheri Felciaino '13	♙♙ 4
● Bolgheri Rosso Felciaino '12	♙♙ 3
● Bolgheri Rosso Ferrugini '11	♙♙ 3
● Bolgheri Sup. Gaudo de' Gemoli '09	♙♙ 6
● Lienà Cabernet Franc '12	♙♙ 8
● Lienà Cabernet Franc '11	♙♙ 7
● Lienà Cabernet Franc '08	♙♙ 7
● Lienà Cabernet Sauvignon '10	♙♙ 7
● Lienà Cabernet Sauvignon '08	♙♙ 7

Le Chiuse

Loc. Pullera, 228
53024 Montalcino [SI]
Tel. +39 055597052
www.lechiuse.com

CELLAR SALES
PRE-BOOKED VISITS
ACCOMMODATION
ANNUAL PRODUCTION 30,000 bottles
HECTARES UNDER VINE 8.00
VITICULTURE METHOD Certified Organic

Back in 1986 Simonetta Valiani and her husband Nicolò Magnelli started making their own Brunello from the Le Chiuse estate, inherited from Fiorella Biondi Santi and consisting of a single plot of eight hectares planted exclusively with sangiovese in the heart of northern Montalcino, overlooking the Montosoli hillside. Its glorious history finds continuity in meticulously tended vineyards, the adoption of organic farming principles back when no-one would have imagined applying them, and above all a classic expressive sensitivity in the best sense of the term. This last takes place through spontaneous fermentation, long maceration and ageing in 20-, 30- and 50-hectolitre oak barrels. The 2011 version joins the list of the best Brunellos made by Le Chiuse. Wild berries, topsoil, and clear-cut spice in an original, solid profile, very drinkable flavour with nuanced tannins, and a final spurt into the vigorous finish. The Rosso di Montalcino 2014 is also a success, delicious and streamlined.

● Brunello di Montalcino '11	▼▼▼ 7
● Rosso di Montalcino '14	▼▼ 4
● Brunello di Montalcino '10	♙♙♙ 7
● Brunello di Montalcino '07	♙♙♙ 7
● Brunello di Montalcino Ris. '07	♙♙♙ 8
● Brunello di Montalcino Ris. '09	♙♙ 8
● Brunello di Montalcino Ris. '06	♙♙ 8
● Rosso di Montalcino '13	♙♙ 4
● Rosso di Montalcino '12	♙♙ 4
● Rosso di Montalcino '11	♙♙ 4
● Rosso di Montalcino '10	♙♙ 3

Cigliano

VIA CIGLIANO, 17
50026 SAN CASCIANO IN VAL DI PESA [FI]
TEL. +39 055820033
www.villadelcigliano.it

CELLAR SALES
PRE-BOOKED VISITS
ANNUAL PRODUCTION 40,000 bottles
HECTARES UNDER VINE 25.00

This is probably one of the most interesting estates in Chianti Classico today. The wines reflect a clear and coherent pursuit of a connection with the production zone, San Casciano Val di Pesa in the area of the designation nearest to Florence, and the results proclaim its success. The wines are elegant and harmonious with classic style, also due to a traditional mix of ageing vessels, concrete vats and large oak casks. The Chianti Classico 2013 shows a very dynamic flavour: fresh, well paced and not without complexity, definitely among the best of its type, with clearly defined, very fragrant aromas. The Chianti Classico Riserva 2012 is austere and less focused, with hazy aromas, and a rounded flavour that still needs to relax. The Suganella 2012, from sangiovese, cabernet sauvignon and merlot, displays grassy sensations on both the nose and palate.

● Chianti Cl. Cigliano '13	♟♟♟ 3*
● Chianti Cl. Villa Cigliano Ris. '12	♟ 4
● Suganella '12	♟ 4
● Chianti Cl. '10	♟♟ 2*
● Chianti Cl. '07	♟♟ 2*
● Chianti Cl. Cigliano '12	♟♟ 3*
● Chianti Cl. '11	♟♟ 3
● Chianti Cl. Villa Cigliano Ris. '11	♟♟ 4
● Chianti Cl. Villa Cigliano Ris. '09	♟♟ 4
● Suganella '06	♟♟ 4

Fattoria di Cinciano

LOC. CINCIANO, 2
53036 POGGIBONSI [SI]
TEL. +39 0577936588
www.cinciano.it

ANNUAL PRODUCTION 70,000 bottles
HECTARES UNDER VINE 25.00

The estate owned by the Garré family since 1983 is situated between Poggibonsi and Barberino Val d'Elsa. The vineyards are farmed with great respect for the environment and no unnecessary forcing takes place in the cellar. Mainly large oak casks are used for ageing, in a particularly well-judged dosage. The resulting range of wines is very interesting, a masterful blend of drinkable flavour and elegance, reflecting the terroir nicely and with recognizable identity. The Chianti Classico Riserva 2013 displays elegant, layered aromas with marked berry fruit polished with spicy hints, leading into a well-focused and nicely paced palate, not without shading. The sturdier Chianti Classico Gran Selezione 2012 reveals rounded, mature aromas and a slightly less supple flavour. The Chianti Classico 2014 is very slender-bodied, uncomplicated and eminently drinkable.

● Chianti Cl. Ris. '13	♟♟ 3*
● Chianti Cl. Gran Sel. '12	♟♟ 5
● Chianti Cl. '14	♟ 3
● Chianti Cl. '12	♟♟ 3
● Chianti Cl. '11	♟♟ 3
● Chianti Cl. '06	♟♟ 3
● Chianti Cl. Gran Sel. '11	♟♟ 5
● Chianti Cl. Ris. '12	♟♟ 3*
● Chianti Cl. Ris. '11	♟♟ 3
● Chianti Cl. Ris. '10	♟♟ 3*
● Chianti Cl. Ris. '06	♟♟ 4
● Chianti Cl. Ris. '05	♟♟ 4
● Pietraforte '11	♟♟ 2*
● Pietraforte '07	♟♟ 4

Le Cinciole

VIA CASE SPARSE, 83
50020 PANZANO [FI]
TEL. +39 055852636
www.lecinciole.it

CELLAR SALES
PRE-BOOKED VISITS
ANNUAL PRODUCTION 45,000 bottles
HECTARES UNDER VINE 11.00
VITICULTURE METHOD Certified Organic
SUSTAINABLE WINERY

Luca and Valeria Orsini run this small but interesting productive estate in the Panzano subzone. The vineyards are organically farmed and wines are aged in both barriques and large casks. The consolidated winery style favours fresh, drinkable, harmonious flavour, as well as ageability, and the wines often show character and personality. The 2012 is one of the best versions of Petresco, a monovarietal Sangiovese: fresh aromas of red berries, hints of spice and freshly mown grass and a nuance of forest floor. The palate is well paced and complex with deep, particularly supple and mouthwatering flavour. The Chianti Classico A Luigi Riserva 2012 displays interesting aromas of fruit combined with hints of pebbles. The palate is dynamic and harmonious, but unfortunately a little hard in the finish. An outstandingly fresh and drinkable flavour marks the Chianti Classico 2013.

● Petresco '12	🍷🍷🍷 5
● Chianti Cl. '13	🍷🍷 3
● Chianti Cl. A Luigi Ris. '12	🍷🍷 3
● Cinciorosso '13	🍷🍷 3
● Camalaione '04	🍷🍷🍷 7
● Chianti Cl. '12	🍷🍷🍷 3*
● Chianti Cl. Petresco Ris. '01	🍷🍷🍷 5
● Chianti Cl. '11	🍷🍷 3
● Chianti Cl. '10	🍷🍷 3
● Chianti Cl. Petresco Ris. '08	🍷🍷 5
● Chianti Cl. Petresco Ris. '07	🍷🍷 5
● Cinciorosso '12	🍷🍷 3
● Petresco '10	🍷🍷 5
☉ Rosato '13	🍷🍷 2*

Citille di Sopra

FRAZ. TORRENIERI
LOC. CITILLE DI SOPRA, 46
53024 MONTALCINO [SI]
TEL. +39 0577832749
www.citille.com

CELLAR SALES
PRE-BOOKED VISITS
ANNUAL PRODUCTION 35,000 bottles
HECTARES UNDER VINE 6.00

The small town of Torrenieri in north-eastern Montalcino lends its name to the lovely estate established in the 1950s by Fulvio Innocenti and run today by his son Fabio. Just under six hectares of vineyards at around 300 metres altitude, on clayey soil rich in stony material, with silty ferrous components and veins of tufa rock. This unusual land formation is explored in the estate's three Brunellos (basic version, Poggio Ronconi cru and Riserva) with cellar procedures that vary according to the type of harvest. The technical particulars support the austere, meticulous pace of confidently full-bodied Sangioveses which demand a little patience. The latest tastings revealed a profile in many ways open-ended for the most ambitious wines, among which the unusually sunny and warm Poggio Ronconi 2011 deserves a mention. However, the Rosso 2014 seems particularly well made, with joyous fruity sensations enlivening a pleasing and dynamic flavour.

● Brunello di Montalcino V. Poggio Ronconi '11	🍷🍷 5
● Rosso di Montalcino '14	🍷🍷 3
● Brunello di Montalcino Ris. '10	🍷 7
● Brunello di Montalcino '06	🍷🍷🍷 5
● Brunello di Montalcino V. Poggio Ronconi '07	🍷🍷🍷 5
● Brunello di Montalcino '10	🍷🍷 5
● Brunello di Montalcino '08	🍷🍷 5
● Brunello di Montalcino V. Poggio Ronconi '10	🍷🍷 5
● Brunello di Montalcino V. Poggio Ronconi '09	🍷🍷 5
● Brunello di Montalcino V. Poggio Ronconi '08	🍷🍷 5
● Rosso di Montalcino '12	🍷🍷 3

Podere della Civettaja

VIA DI CASINA ROSSA, 5A
52100 AREZZO
TEL. 3397098418
www.civettaja.it

CELLAR SALES
PRE-BOOKED VISITS
ANNUAL PRODUCTION 7,000 bottles
HECTARES UNDER VINE 3.00
VITICULTURE METHOD Certified Organic

Vincenzo Tommasi, a capable, thoughtful grower and sensitive, inspired winemaker, has a small estate in Romena di Pratovecchio, deep in Casentino. These are the Apennine foothills that in recent years have proved to be a welcoming habitat for a capricious varietal like pinot nero. Specifically this is a closed and quite cool valley, with land under vine rising to 500 metres on clayey limestone. There is documented evidence that pinot nero was present here in ancient times, while the Civettaja project also develops thanks to Burgundian trips and insights. The pinot nero grapes are fermented without addition of cultured yeasts, in stainless steel and concrete vats, before ageing in used barriques. We loved the 2010 but the 2013 is even better: a delicious wine from start to finish, with alchemic balance of sweet fruit, tangy mineral sensations and lively acidity. Sharpish and lingering, destined for further maturation in the bottles.

● Pinot Nero '13	♥♥♥ 4*
● Pinot Nero '12	♀♀ 3
● Pinot Nero '11	♀♀ 3

★Tenuta Col d'Orcia

VIA GIUNCHETI
53020 MONTALCINO [SI]
TEL. +39 057780891
www.coldorcia.it

CELLAR SALES
PRE-BOOKED VISITS
ANNUAL PRODUCTION 800,000 bottles
HECTARES UNDER VINE 142.00
VITICULTURE METHOD Certified Organic
SUSTAINABLE WINERY

The centuries-old Col d'Orcia estate, taken over in 1973 by the Marone Cinzano family and managed today by Conte Francesco, overlooks the extreme fringes of southern Montalcino. More than 140 hectares of vineyards are wedged between Sant'Angelo in Colle and the Orcia river in a warm area, tempered by nearby Mt. Amiata and linked to generally loose soil structure, rich in stony and limestone material. The vineyards are not exclusively planted to sangiovese but the Brunellos head the range of wines, starting with the Poggio al Vento cru, aged for almost four years in 25- and 75-hectolitre Allier and Slavonian oak barrels. The leading wine was not made in 2009 but the range has its highpoints even in this reorganized formation. With its bright, invigorating aromas, the Brunello 2011 maintains its tidy flavour despite a lack of grip. The toasty imperfections are a little more marked in the Olmaia 2012, but it is nonetheless true to type as a warm, sunny Cabernet.

● Brunello di Montalcino '11	♥♥ 7
● Sant'Antimo Cabernet Olmaia '12	♥♥ 6
● Rosso di Montalcino '14	♥ 4
● Sant'Antimo Nearco '12	♥ 4
● Brunello di Montalcino Poggio al Vento Ris. '06	♀♀♀ 8
● Brunello di Montalcino Poggio al Vento Ris. '04	♀♀♀ 8
● Brunello di Montalcino Poggio al Vento Ris. '99	♀♀♀ 8
● Brunello di Montalcino Poggio al Vento Ris. '97	♀♀♀ 7
● Brunello di Montalcino Poggio al Vento Ris. '83	♀♀♀ 7
● Olmaia '01	♀♀♀ 7
● Olmaia '00	♀♀♀ 7

Col di Bacche

FRAZ. MONTIANO
S.DA DI CUPI
58010 MAGLIANO IN TOSCANA [GR]
TEL. +39 0564589538
www.coldibacche.com

CELLAR SALES
PRE-BOOKED VISITS
ANNUAL PRODUCTION 80,000 bottles
HECTARES UNDER VINE 13.50

Alberto Carnasciali runs a model farm that has confidently established itself in the Maremma winemaking sector too much ado. The estate has a relatively short history though, because the vineyards were planted in 1998 and the first wines reached the shelves in 2004. Today it has achieved a very stable, prominent and indeed almost authoritative position. The simple secret to this success is the hard and consistent work of a true oenological craftsman. The Morellino di Scansano Rovente Riserva 2013 is very good, with a lovely hint of blood-rich meat on the nose and very dynamic, gutsy, tangy flavour. The Cupi winery's Morellino di Scansano 2015 is probably the best of the vintage: lovely drinkable flavour with generous, vibrant aromas and considerable detailing. The Cupinero 2013, from merlot and cabernet sauvignon, is lively and well paced with nicely readable varietal features and a fresh flavour.

● Morellino di Scansano '15	▼▼ 3*
● Morellino di Scansano Rovente Ris. '13	▼▼ 5
● Cupinero '13	▼▼ 5
○ Vermentino '15	▼ 2
● Morellino di Scansano Rovente '05	▼▼▼ 4
● Cupinero '12	♀♀ 5
● Cupinero '11	♀♀ 5
● Maremma Toscana Cupinero '10	♀♀ 5
● Morellino di Scansano '11	♀♀ 3
● Morellino di Scansano Rovente Ris. '12	♀♀ 5
● Morellino di Scansano Rovente Ris. '11	♀♀ 5
● Morellino di Scansano Rovente Ris. '10	♀♀ 5

Fattoria Collazzi

LOC. TAVARNUZZE
VIA COLLERAMOLE, 101
50023 IMPRUNETA [FI]
TEL. +39 0552374902
www.collazzi.it

CELLAR SALES
PRE-BOOKED VISITS
ANNUAL PRODUCTION 80,000 bottles
HECTARES UNDER VINE 32.00

The Marchi family took over the estate in 1933: over 400 hectares at the gates of Florence with a beautiful villa at its heart, said to be designed by Michelangelo Buonarroti. A large part of the estate is covered with olive trees while wine has gradually assumed fundamental importance, especially from the 1990s onwards. Since then, the vineyards have been completely reorganized with greater focus on agronomical and oenological management, entrusted to the care of Lamberto Frescobaldi. Through to the finals for the Collazzi 2013, a blend of merlot, cabernet sauvignon and cabernet franc: appealing aromas of wild berries and spice with balsamic hints, a warm, harmonious and mouthfilling palate and a lingering flavoursome finish. The Ferro 2013 is an interesting monovarietal Petit Verdot with grilled peppers on the nose, vegetal hints, and a mouthfilling, dynamic palate with a relaxed, appealing finish.

● Collazzi '13	▼▼ 6
● Ferro '13	▼▼ 5
● Libertà '13	▼▼ 3
○ Otto Muri '15	▼▼ 3
● Chianti Cl. I Bastioni '11	♀♀ 3
● Collazzi '11	♀♀ 6
● Collazzi '10	♀♀ 6
● Collazzi '09	♀♀ 6
● Ferro '12	♀♀ 5
● Libertà '12	♀♀ 2*
● Libertà '11	♀♀ 2*
● Libertà '10	♀♀ 2*
○ Otto Muri '14	♀♀ 3
○ Otto Muri '12	♀♀ 3

Colle Massari

LOC. POGGI DEL SASSO
58044 CINIGIANO [GR]
TEL. +39 0564990496
www.collemassari.it

CELLAR SALES
PRE-BOOKED VISITS
ACCOMMODATION
ANNUAL PRODUCTION 500,000 bottles
HECTARES UNDER VINE 110.00
VITICULTURE METHOD Certified Organic
SUSTAINABLE WINERY

Claudio Tipa and his sister Maria Iris sparked the success of the Montecucco DOC zone. Claudio, a pharmaceutical entrepreneur, purchased the 1,200-hectare Castello di Colle Massari estate in 1998, including 60 hectares of olive groves, 400 of arable land and 110 under vine. This was just the starting point from which he expanded the property into some of Tuscany's most prestigious winegrowing areas, like Bolgheri and Montalcino. Here in Cinigiano, on the slopes of Mt. Amiata overlooking the Tyrrhenian coast, sangiovese is the uncontested king of the vineyards, the result of mass selections developed in partnership with the University of Pisa. The Montecucco Rosso Riserva 2013 walks away with Tre Bicchieri: an appealing nose with enthralling sweet spice enriching the clear cherry and red berry fruit, while the palate is taut and flavoursome with compact tannic texture. The well-balanced acidity leads the flavour towards a really pleasing finish.

● Montecucco Rosso Ris. '13	♀♀♀ 3*
● Montecucco Sangiovese Poggio Lombrone Ris. '12	♀♀ 6
● Montecucco Rigoleto '14	♀♀ 2*
● Montecucco Sangiovese Rigomoro Ris. '13	♀♀ 5
☉ Montecucco Gròttolo '15	♀ 2
○ Montecucco Irisse '15	♀ 3
○ Montecucco Melacce '15	♀ 3
● Montecucco Sangiovese Lombrone Ris. '11	♀♀♀ 6
● Montecucco Sangiovese Lombrone Ris. '10	♀♀♀ 6
● Montecucco Sangiovese Lombrone Ris. '09	♀♀♀ 6
● Montecucco Sangiovese Lombrone Ris. '08	♀♀♀ 6

Colle Santa Mustiola

VIA DELLE TORRI, 86A
53043 CHIUSI [SI]
TEL. +39 057820525
www.poggioaichiari.it

CELLAR SALES
PRE-BOOKED VISITS
ANNUAL PRODUCTION 18,000 bottles
HECTARES UNDER VINE 5.00
SUSTAINABLE WINERY

This is definitely one of the most interesting Tuscan wineries for fans of authentic Sangioveses. Colle Santa Mustiola is situated in the Chiusi area, near the border with Umbria, and is capable of producing brilliant, elegant wines with bags of ageing potential. Credit goes to sensitive, skilled winegrower Fabio Cenni, and an original terroir, once a sea-bed, with a high content of sand, pebbles and clay. Outstanding work with the sangiovese grape, from cloning to very high profile growing practices. The cellar, of Etruscan origin, is incredible. It is not easy to read the original Poggio ai Chiari, released after a lengthy ageing in the cellar. The sensations are clearly more mature than the average red wine we tasted, but the character of this wine is indisputable. The 2009 has earthy aromas with dried flowers and wild berries, tracing a very appealing, almost Burgundy-style profile closing on a nicely forward and lipsmacking tannic texture. The Vigna Flavia is always nicely focused.

● Poggio ai Chiari '09	♀♀ 6
● Vigna Flavia '12	♀♀ 5
● Poggio ai Chiari '06	♀♀♀ 6
● Poggio ai Chiari '08	♀♀ 6
● Poggio ai Chiari '05	♀♀ 6
● Poggio ai Chiari '04	♀♀ 6
● Poggio ai Chiari '03	♀♀ 6
● Poggio ai Chiari '02	♀♀ 6
● Poggio ai Chiari '01	♀♀ 6
● Vigna Flavia '11	♀♀ 5
● Vigna Flavia '10	♀♀ 5
● Vigna Flavia '09	♀♀ 5

Fattoria Colle Verde

FRAZ. MATRAIA
LOC. CASTELLO
55010 LUCCA
TEL. +39 0583402310
www.colleverde.it

CELLAR SALES
PRE-BOOKED VISITS
ANNUAL PRODUCTION 30,000 bottles
HECTARES UNDER VINE 7.00

A specific lifestyle choice led Piero Tartagni and Francesca Pardini to leave the city and move here to the country. They did not choose any old place, but the magnificent hills of Matraia, undoubtedly suitable but not wholly explored at that time. The vineyard plantation and consequent choices were clear and determined from the start. Today Fattoria Colle Verde is farmed according to biodynamic principles, producing original, flavoursome wines. The Nero della Spinosa 2013 is good, nicely extracted from syrah grapes, with hints of pomegranate on the nose and a spicy timbre that enhances the pleasing complexity. The palate is rich in extract. The Brania delle Ghiandaie isn't bad either: subtle and quite stylish if rather tannic from the mid-palate onwards.

Collelceto

LOC. CAMIGLIANO
POD. LA PISANA
53024 MONTALCINO [SI]
TEL. +39 0577816606
www.collelceto.it

CELLAR SALES
PRE-BOOKED VISITS
ANNUAL PRODUCTION 22,000 bottles
HECTARES UNDER VINE 6.00

A canyon overlooking the Ombrone river, in south-western Montalcino: this is the first impression of the Colle degli Elci estate (named after the holm oak trees), where the Palazzesi family have their vineyards and winery. The six or so hectares are almost exclusively planted to sangiovese, which expresses itself hereabouts with cheerful yet robust tones, due to the moderate Tyrrhenian winds, clay loam soil rich in stony material and altitudes rarely over 200 metres. The recognizable style is pursued in the Collelceto reds through technical choices adapted to the vintage year, and ageing in both barriques and medium-sized oak. Although it doesn't scale last year's heights, Brunello 2011 and Riserva Elia 2010 make a well matched pairing just the same. The former is delicious and multifaceted, but overly warm and fluffy on the palate. The Riserva is weightier and more austere, with dark streaks of extract holding back the finish.

● Colline Lucchesi Rosso Brania delle Ghiandaie '13	♼♼ 5
● Nero della Spinosa '13	♼♼ 5
○ Brania del Cancello '13	♼♼ 4
○ Colline Lucchesi Bianco Terre di Matraja '13	♼♼ 2*
● Colline Lucchesi Disinòpia '11	♼♼ 4
● Colline Lucchesi Rosso Brania delle Ghiandaie '12	♼♼ 5
● Colline Lucchesi Rosso Brania delle Ghiandaie '11	♼♼ 5
● Colline Lucchesi Rosso Terre di Matraja '12	♼♼ 2*
● Colline Lucchesi Rosso Terre di Matraja '11	♼♼ 2*
● Nero della Spinosa '11	♼♼ 5

● Brunello di Montalcino '11	♼♼ 5
● Brunello di Montalcino Elia Ris. '10	♼♼ 6
● Rosso di Montalcino '14	♼ 3
● Brunello di Montalcino '10	♼♼♼ 5
● Brunello di Montalcino '06	♼♼♼ 5
● Brunello di Montalcino '09	♼♼ 5
● Brunello di Montalcino '08	♼♼ 5
● Brunello di Montalcino '07	♼♼ 5
● Brunello di Montalcino '03	♼♼ 5
● Brunello di Montalcino '01	♼♼ 5
● Rosso di Montalcino '13	♼♼ 3
● Rosso di Montalcino '12	♼♼ 3
● Rosso di Montalcino '10	♼♼ 3*

Tenuta di Collosorbo

FRAZ. CASTELNUOVO DELL'ABATE
LOC. VILLA A SESTA, 25
53024 MONTALCINO [SI]
TEL. +39 0577835534
www.collosorbo.com

CELLAR SALES
PRE-BOOKED VISITS
ANNUAL PRODUCTION 100,000 bottles
HECTARES UNDER VINE 27.00

A welcome return to the main section of our Guide for Giovanna Ciacci's estate, which originated in 1995 from the divided inheritance of Tenuta di Sesta. Assisted by her daughters, oenologist Laura and agronomist Lucia, Giovanna cares for the 25-odd hectares of vineyards mainly located in southern Montalcino, bringing to life Brunellos with a contemporary feel, created without adhering to strict models for maceration and ageing. Each plot is fermented separately using 12-54 hectolitre French and Slavonian oak, although the multifaceted character of these reds, earthy yet graceful in the best versions, is more important than the technical minutiae. This is exactly the profile revealed by the 2010 Riserva. A few reductive imperfections are soon forgotten in the parade of herbs and roots: a woody trail is even more evident in the flavour, austere in texture but lush and iodine at the same time. When character is worth more than the individual elements.

● Brunello di Montalcino Ris. '10	♟♟ 8
● Brunello di Montalcino '11	♟♟ 6
● Brunello di Montalcino '10	♟♟ 6
● Brunello di Montalcino '07	♟♟ 6
● Brunello di Montalcino '06	♟♟ 6
● Brunello di Montalcino '05	♟♟ 6
● Brunello di Montalcino '03	♟♟ 6
● Brunello di Montalcino '01	♟♟ 5
● Brunello di Montalcino Ris. '07	♟♟ 8
● Brunello di Montalcino Ris. '04	♟♟ 8
● Rosso di Montalcino '08	♟♟ 4
● Sant'Antimo '09	♟♟ 3

Il Colombaio di Santa Chiara

LOC. RACCIANO
VIA SAN DONATO, 1
53037 SAN GIMIGNANO [SI]
TEL. +39 0577942004
www.colombaiosantachiara.it

CELLAR SALES
PRE-BOOKED VISITS
ACCOMMODATION
ANNUAL PRODUCTION 90,000 bottles
HECTARES UNDER VINE 12.00
VITICULTURE METHOD Certified Organic

As you leave San Gimignano towards Volterra, you will come across the land owned by the estate where Mario Logi's three sons, Alessio, Stefano and Giampiero, work according to the idea that wine is produced by the land. So no use of pesticides, and meticulous care in the vineyard, followed by painstaking grape selection during the harvest. The estate is enhanced by the presence of the 12th-century Romanesque church, the Pieve di San Donato. Through to the finals for the Vernaccia Albereta Riserva 2013, with varied, complex aromas of apples and peaches alongside fresh hints of basil and other aromatic herbs with subtle nuances of mixed spice. The pleasing entry shows mouthfilling flavour, free of excess, with appetizing acidity and a long, succulent finish. The Vernaccia Selvabianca 2015 is well made with vegetal hints and a light, well-balanced body into a lingering finish.

○ Vernaccia di S. Gimignano Albereta Ris. '13	♟♟♟ 3*
○ Vernaccia di San Gimignano Selvabianca '15	♟♟ 3
● Chianti Colli Senesi Campale '14	♟ 3
● Chianti Colli Senesi Il Priore '12	♟ 4
⊙ Cremisi Rosato '15	♟ 3
○ Vernaccia di S. Gimignano Campo della Pieve '14	♟ 4
○ Vernaccia di S. Gimignano Albereta Ris. '12	♟♟♟ 5
○ Vernaccia di S. Gimignano Albereta Ris. '11	♟♟♟ 4*
○ Vernaccia di S. Gimignano Campo della Pieve '11	♟♟♟ 3*

Conte Guicciardini

LOC. POPPIANO
VIA FEZZANA, 45/49
50025 MONTESPERTOLI [FI]
TEL. +39 05582315
www.conteguicciardini.it

CELLAR SALES
PRE-BOOKED VISITS
ANNUAL PRODUCTION 270,000 bottles
HECTARES UNDER VINE 130.00
SUSTAINABLE WINERY

Castello di Poppiano has overlooked the
Virginio valley since the Middle Ages.
Owned by the Guicciardini family, who have
always been active local farmers, the estate
is now run by Ferdinando Guicciardini with
the help of his nephew Bernardo. The
whole estate covers about 250 hectares of
farmland, 130 of which are planted to
vineyards. But the family also own Massi di
Mandorlaia, 56 hectares of vineyards in
Maremma, in the Morellino designation,
and have recently purchased another
estate, Belvedere Campoli, about ten
hectares in the Chianti Classico DOC zone.
A good performance from the 2013
Riserva, made from sangiovese with a
small addition of merlot and cabernet:
sweet spice and ripe red berries on the
nose, and a firm, compact palate. Another
good showing comes from the La Historia,
a vibrant, mouthfilling monovarietal Merlot.
The wines from the Scansano area are not
so impressive, as both Morellinos are
slightly curbed by the oak.

● Chianti Colli Fiorentini Ris. '13	♥♥ 4
● La Historia '13	♥♥ 5
● Chianti Colli Fiorentini Il Cortile '14	♥ 2
● Morellino di Scansano I Massi '14	♥ 3
● Morellino di Scansano Massi di Mandorlaia Ris. '13	♥ 4
● Toscoforte '14	♥ 4
● Tricorno '13	♥ 6
● Chianti Colli Fiorentini Il Cortile '13	♀♀ 2*
● Chianti Colli Fiorentini Ris. '11	♀♀ 4
● La Historia '12	♀♀ 5
● Syrah '13	♀♀ 3
● Toscoforte '13	♀♀ 3
● Tricorno '12	♀♀ 6

Contucci

VIA DEL TEATRO, 1
53045 MONTEPULCIANO [SI]
TEL. +39 0578757006
www.contucci.it

CELLAR SALES
PRE-BOOKED VISITS
ACCOMMODATION
ANNUAL PRODUCTION 100,000 bottles
HECTARES UNDER VINE 21.00

The Contucci family have been involved in
winegrowing since time immemorial. Their
cellars, situated in the old town centre, are
a pleasing haven for the large and very old
barrels that represent the estate's principal
ageing method. From a winery like this we
naturally expect very traditional wines that
shun trends, even at the cost of stylistic
flaws, which we have noted particularly in
the recent past, and which have slightly
undermined the estate's quality continuity.
It often happens that at least one wine from
this winery, overlooking Montepulciano's
Piazza Grande, makes an excellent
impression, with typical features and very
good complexity. This time it is the Nobile di
Montepulciano Riserva 2012. The aromas
are multilayered, with floral and iron-like
hints with light spice, and the palate is
succulent, vigorous and nicely paced. The
Nobile Pietra Rossa 2013 is a little more
rugged, but still fresh and flavoursome.

● Nobile di Montepulciano Ris. '12	♥♥ 5
● Nobile di Montepulciano Pietra Rossa '13	♥♥ 5
● Nobile di Montepulciano '13	♥ 3
● Nobile di Montepulciano Mulinvecchio '13	♥ 5
● Nobile di Montepulciano Mulinvecchio '12	♀♀ 5
● Nobile di Montepulciano Pietra Rossa '10	♀♀ 4
● Rosso di Montepulciano '14	♀♀ 2*

Il Conventino

FRAZ. GRACCIANO
VIA DELLA CIARLIANA, 25B
53040 MONTEPULCIANO [SI]
TEL. +39 0578715371
www.ilconventino.it

CELLAR SALES
PRE-BOOKED VISITS
ANNUAL PRODUCTION 55,000 bottles
HECTARES UNDER VINE 12.00
VITICULTURE METHOD Certified Organic

The wines produced by the Brini brothers' organic estate, purchased in 2003, are substantial: the standard-label Nobile stands out for its supple palate while the Nobile Riserva offers a fuller-bodied, more complex structure. The winery's focused and classic style leans towards austere, nuanced, elegant features, making it one of the most interesting in Montepulciano in the last decade. The wines are mostly aged in large oak barrels, and the estate grows exclusively local grapes: sangiovese, canaiolo and colorino. The Nobile di Montepulciano Riserva 2012 displays fragrant aromas nuanced with pipe tobacco, forest floor and violets. A stylish, characterful palate with edgy tannins, nice depth and a fresh, lipsmacking flavour. The Nobile di Montepulciano 2013 has more relaxed aromas of fresh cherries, flowers and raspberries. The Rosso di Montepulciano 2015 is enjoyable.

● Nobile di Montepulciano Ris. '12	♟♟ 5
● Nobile di Montepulciano '13	♟♟ 4
● Rosso di Montepulciano '15	♟ 2
● Nobile di Montepulciano '10	♟♟♟ 4*
● Nobile di Montepulciano '12	♟♟ 4
● Nobile di Montepulciano '11	♟♟ 4
● Nobile di Montepulciano '09	♟♟ 4
● Nobile di Montepulciano Ris. '11	♟♟ 5
● Nobile di Montepulciano Ris. '10	♟♟ 5
● Nobile di Montepulciano Ris. '09	♟♟ 5
● Nobile di Montepulciano Ris. '08	♟♟ 5
● Rosso di Montepulciano '12	♟♟ 2*

La Corsa

S.DA VICINALE DEL PRATACCIONE, 19
58015 ORBETELLO [GR]
TEL. +39 0564880007
www.lacorsawine.it

CELLAR SALES
PRE-BOOKED VISITS
ANNUAL PRODUCTION 25,000 bottles
HECTARES UNDER VINE 14.00

The ongoing winegrowing project at the Maremma estate owned by Marco Bassetti and his wife Stefania Craxi is developing nicely. It started in 2005 with the help of winemakers Vittorio Fiore and Barbara Tamburini, and now consists of 14 hectares of vineyards between Capalbio and Ansedonia, a particularly unspoilt area, wooded, with red soils rich in sand, clay and good skeleton texture. Alongside sangiovese grapes are unusual varieties for this area such as teroldego and petit verdot, the latter seeming to adapt well to the warm but temperate microclimate of this subzone, among the least rainy in the region. Barbadonna 2014, a vineyard designated petit verdot, stands out for its complex and multifaceted profile: subtle notes of freshly ground black pepper and cigar smoke, nicely articulated grassy sensations and beautifully nuanced tangy flavour. The Mandrione 2014 is a Sangiovese with floral aromas and a very weighty palate, with lingering smoky hints. The Aghiloro 2015 is well focused.

● Aghiloro '15	♟♟ 3
● Barbadonna '14	♟♟ 8
● Mandrione '14	♟♟ 7
⊙ Macchiatonda '15	♟ 3
● Petit Verdot '15	♟ 4
● Settefinestre '15	♟ 3

Villa Le Corti

LOC. LE CORTI
VIA SAN PIERO DI SOTTO, 1
50026 SAN CASCIANO IN VAL DI PESA [FI]
TEL. +39 055829301
www.principecorsini.com

CELLAR SALES
PRE-BOOKED VISITS
ACCOMMODATION
ANNUAL PRODUCTION 150,000 bottles
HECTARES UNDER VINE 50.00
VITICULTURE METHOD Certified Organic

Organically farmed vineyards, generally pared-down cellar procedures, and the use of concrete vats, large oak barrels and barriques for ageing: this is the recipe for producing wine on the estate run by Duccio Corsini. The style bears the imprint of Chianti tradition, executed with flawless craftsmanship, and the wines are all lively and very drinkable, while characterful and terroir-true. The Corsini family also produce wine in Tenuta Marsiliana, in Maremma. The Chianti Classico 2013 displays floral aromas and a taut, nicely layered palate, well paced and very drinkable. The Chianti Classico Cortevecchia Riserva 2013 is delicious: clean, vibrant aromas and a well-balanced flavour, just slightly rugged in the finish with a touch too much oak. The enjoyable Birillo 2013 from Maremma is a blend of cabernet sauvignon and merlot. The Marsiliana 2012, also made in Maremma is a more robust combination of cabernet sauvignon, merlot and petit verdot.

Fattoria Corzano e Paterno

LOC. CORZANO
FRAZ. SAN PANCRAZIO
VIA SAN VITO DI SOPRA
50020 SAN CASCIANO IN VAL DI PESA [FI]
TEL. +39 0558248179
www.corzanoepaterno.com

CELLAR SALES
PRE-BOOKED VISITS
ACCOMMODATION
ANNUAL PRODUCTION 85,000 bottles
HECTARES UNDER VINE 19.00
VITICULTURE METHOD Certified Organic

The 19 hectares of vineyards stand on pebbly hillsides at about 300 metres altitude just south of Florence. In 1969 Swiss architect Wendelin Gelpke purchased the estate and gradually involved his whole family in the business. Today Aljoscha Goldschmidt and Arianna Gelpke, nephew and daughter of the founder respectively, run the wine estate. The vineyards are planted to classic local grapes: alongside sangiovese are canaiolo, malvasia and trebbiano as well as international varieties like cabernet sauvignon, merlot and chardonnay. Through to the finals for the Chianti I Tre Borri Riserva 2013, with subtle, very clean aromas with hints of cherries and redcurrants, alongside aromatic herbs like bay and sage. The palate is supple and fluent with good acidity, nicely blended tannins and a subtly lingering flavour. The interesting Corzano 2013, from cabernet sauvignon, merlot and sangiovese, has balsamic, minerally aromas, a full-bodied structure, subtle, evident tannins and a fresh aftertaste.

● Chianti Cl. '13	▼▼ 3*
● Birillo Tenuta Marsiliana '13	▼▼ 3
● Chianti Cl. Cortevecchia Ris. '13	▼▼ 4
● Marsiliana '12	▼▼ 5
● Chianti Cl. '12	▼▼▼ 3*
● Chianti Cl. Cortevecchia Ris. '05	▼▼▼ 4
● Chianti Cl. Le Corti '10	▼▼▼ 3*
● Birillo Tenuta Marsiliana '11	▼▼ 5
● Chianti Cl. A-101 Ris. '07	▼▼ 3
● Chianti Cl. Cortevecchia Ris. '11	▼▼ 4
● Chianti Cl. Don Tommaso Gran Sel. '11	▼▼ 5
● Chianti Cl. Don Tommaso Gran Sel. '10	▼▼ 5
● Chianti Cl. Le Corti '11	▼▼ 3

● Chianti I Tre Borri Ris. '13	▼▼ 5
● Chianti Terre di Corzano '14	▼▼ 2*
● Il Corzano '13	▼▼ 5
● Chianti I Tre Borri Ris. '07	▼▼▼ 5
● Il Corzano '05	▼▼▼ 5
● Chianti I Tre Borri Ris. '12	▼▼ 5
● Chianti I Tre Borri Ris. '11	▼▼ 5
● Chianti I Tre Borri Ris. '09	▼▼ 5
○ Il Corzanello '14	▼▼ 2*
○ Il Corzano '11	▼▼ 5
○ Il Corzano '10	▼▼ 5
○ Il Corzano '09	▼▼ 5
○ Passito di Corzano '11	▼▼ 6
○ Passito di Corzano '02	▼▼ 6

Andrea Costanti

loc. Colle al Matrichese
53024 Montalcino [SI]
Tel. +39 0577848195
www.costanti.it

CELLAR SALES
PRE-BOOKED VISITS
ANNUAL PRODUCTION 60,000 bottles
HECTARES UNDER VINE 12.00

Andrea Costanti proudly lays claim to Colle al Matrichese's centuries of productive history. The estate counts around ten hectares located at 300-450 metres altitude on the eastern route linking the village of Montalcino to Torrenieri. This is poor soil, principally limestone marl in composition, which brings to life Brunellos hanging in the balance between austere tannin and citrus, salty elegance. The lengthy maceration is followed by mixed ageing in large Slavonian oak barrels and tonneaux, but further bottle ageing is highly recommended for the more powerful, austere vintages. These recommendations will probably be useful for the 2010 Riserva: it is currently in a dark, dry phase with clear jammy aromas but prolonged aeration allows it to settle into a more placid and harmonious profile. The Brunello 2011 is similar, clearer in its classic nuances of leather and spices, shrubs and roots, but slightly sandy in texture.

La Cura

loc. Cura Nuova, 12
58024 Massa Marittima [GR]
Tel. +39 0566918094
www.cantinalacura.it

CELLAR SALES
PRE-BOOKED VISITS
ANNUAL PRODUCTION 30,000 bottles
HECTARES UNDER VINE 15.00
SUSTAINABLE WINERY

Andrea Corsi bought this estate in 1968. At the time only vegetables and cereals were grown on the land, but his passion for wine led Andrea to plant the first two hectares of vineyards. Today, his son Enrico has brought the total up to 15 hectares, mainly planted to international grape varieties, and created a winery that fully respects environmental sustainability and produces the electricity required for its procedures using a photovoltaic system. A good version of the Merlot stands out in the range this year, a perfect reading of the 2013 vintage: typical aromas of ripe damsons and floral sensations, a soft, relaxed palate with docile, rounded tannins. The Trinus 2015 is a fresh, appealing blend of chardonnay, vermentino and malvasia with clear hints of peach and apricot fruit and summer flowers. The Cavaliere d'Italia 2015, from sangiovese, is also very pleasant, flavoursome, consistent and crisp.

● Brunello di Montalcino Ris. '10	♟♟ 8
● Brunello di Montalcino '11	♟♟ 6
● Brunello di Montalcino '06	♟♟♟ 6
● Brunello di Montalcino '88	♟♟♟ 6
● Brunello di Montalcino '10	♟♟ 6
● Brunello di Montalcino '09	♟♟ 6
● Brunello di Montalcino '08	♟♟ 6
● Brunello di Montalcino '07	♟♟ 6
● Brunello di Montalcino '99	♟♟ 6
● Brunello di Montalcino Calbello '00	♟♟ 6
● Brunello di Montalcino Ris. '07	♟♟ 8
● Brunello di Montalcino Ris. '06	♟♟ 8
● Brunello di Montalcino Ris. '01	♟♟ 8
● Rosso di Montalcino '11	♟♟ 4

● Maremma Toscana Merlot '13	♟♟ 5
● Predicatore '15	♟♟ 3
○ Trinus '15	♟♟ 2*
● Maremma Toscana Cavaliere d'Italia '15	♟ 2
● Monteregio di Massa Marittima Rosso Breccerosse '14	♟ 3
● Maremma Merlot La Cura '12	♟♟ 5
● Maremma Podere di Monte Muro Vedetta '11	♟♟ 3
● Monteregio di Massa Marittima Rosso Breccerosse '13	♟♟ 3
● Predicatore '13	♟♟ 3
○ Trinus '14	♟♟ 2*
● Vedetta '13	♟♟ 4

Casale Daviddi

VIA NOTTOLA, 9
53045 MONTEPULCIANO [SI]
TEL. +39 0578738257
www.casaledaviddi.it

ANNUAL PRODUCTION 100,000 bottles
HECTARES UNDER VINE 20.00

The Daviddi family boasts a long farming tradition that dawned in the early 17th century. The local area is Valiano, a true appendix to the DOC zone, on the border with Umbria and Lake Trasimeno. The land where the vineyards are planted shows medium levels of clay with plenty of stony material. As well as Valiano, the vineyards are situated at Gracciano, Abbadia and Acquaviva. The classic grape varieties are grown here, and the wines are linked to a clear concept of tradition. A well-deserved place in the Guide for this wonderful Vino Nobile di Montepulciano 2013. The tastings were suffused with pleasing aromas as subtle as they are focused, with hints of wild strawberries and forest floor. The palate is appealing, nicely elegant, lingering and fresh without losing the tangy background. Just one cloud in the sky: excessive tannic texture.

● Nobile di Montepulciano '13	♟♟ 4
● Nobile di Montepulciano Ris. '12	♟ 5
● Nobile di Montepulciano '12	♟♟ 4

Maria Caterina Dei

VIA DI MARTIENA, 35
53045 MONTEPULCIANO [SI]
TEL. +39 0578716878
www.cantinedei.com

CELLAR SALES
PRE-BOOKED VISITS
ACCOMMODATION
ANNUAL PRODUCTION 230,000 bottles
HECTARES UNDER VINE 55.00
SUSTAINABLE WINERY

Since 1991 Maria Caterina Dei has run the family estate which originates from the purchase of the Bossona vineyard in 1964 and the Martiena farmstead, now the estate's headquarters, in 1973. The first wines were bottled in 1985 and since then Dei products have gradually conquered a leading position in the Nobile di Montepulciano overview, thanks to a range of firm-structured but very drinkable wines, capable of harmonious expansion. Without beating around the bush, the Nobile di Montepulciano 2013 definitely moves like a great wine and is probably the best of its vintage year. Clear-cut, multifaceted aromas with fruity sensations alongside floral hints, coffee powder and spice. Fine-grained tannins on the palate with a complex, succulent flavour, pleasing and coherent. A really good wine. Good overall quality from the rest of the wines.

● Nobile di Montepulciano '13	♟♟♟ 4*
● Nobile di Montepulciano Bossona Ris. '11	♟ 6
● Nobile di Montepulciano '11	♟♟ 4
● Nobile di Montepulciano '10	♟♟ 4
● Nobile di Montepulciano '09	♟♟ 4
● Nobile di Montepulciano '08	♟♟ 4
● Nobile di Montepulciano Bossona Ris. '10	♟♟ 6
● Nobile di Montepulciano Bossona Ris. '09	♟♟ 6
● Nobile di Montepulciano Bossona Ris. '08	♟♟ 5
● Nobile di Montepulciano Bossona Ris. '07	♟♟ 5
● Rosso di Montepulciano '12	♟♟ 2*
● Rosso di Montepulciano '11	♟♟ 2*
○ Vin Santo di Montepulciano '07	♟♟ 5

Fabrizio Dionisio

FRAZ. OSSAIA
LOC. IL CASTAGNO
52044 CORTONA [AR]
TEL. +39 063223541
www.fabriziodionisio.it

PRE-BOOKED VISITS
ANNUAL PRODUCTION 35,000 bottles
HECTARES UNDER VINE 15.00
SUSTAINABLE WINERY

Driven by the desire, back in the Seventies, to find a beautiful location in the Tuscan countryside, Fabrizio's father Sergio Dionisio chose a farmhouse with seven hectares of vineyards and olive groves on the hills overlooking Cortona. 20 or so years later, the purchase of a new plot of land brought the estate to its current size and laid the foundations to begin a modern winegrowing business. Helped by his wife Alessandra in running the farm, Fabrizio decided to replant the old vineyards adding syrah, which offers good expression in this area. The Cortona Syrah Il Castagno 2013 reveals an excellent complex nose, with nicely concentrated aromas of currants and raspberries, cloves and vanilla, in a supple palate with nicely blended tannins and a pleasing finish. The excellent Castagnino 2015 displays very fresh, fruity aromas and a lively, refreshing, delicious flavour with a lingering, lipsmacking finish.

● Cortona Syrah Il Castagno '13	♟♟ 5
● Cortona Syrah Castagnino '15	♟♟ 3
⊙ Rosa del Castagno '15	♟ 3
● Cortona Syrah Il Castagno '12	♟♟♟ 5
● Cortona Syrah Il Castagno '11	♟♟♟ 5
● Cortona Syrah Il Castagno '10	♟♟♟ 5
● Cortona Syrah '07	♟♟ 4
● Cortona Syrah Castagnino '14	♟♟ 3
● Cortona Syrah Castagnino '09	♟♟ 3*
● Cortona Syrah Cuculaia '10	♟♟ 7
● Cortona Syrah Cuculaia '09	♟♟ 6
● Cortona Syrah Cuculaia '08	♟♟ 6
● Cortona Syrah Il Castagno '09	♟♟ 5
● Cortona Syrah Il Castagno '08	♟♟ 5

Donna Olga

LOC. FRIGGIALI
S.DA MAREMMANA
53024 MONTALCINO [SI]
TEL. +39 0577849454
www.tenutedonnaolga.it

CELLAR SALES
PRE-BOOKED VISITS
ACCOMMODATION
ANNUAL PRODUCTION 25,000 bottles
HECTARES UNDER VINE 11.00

Olga Peluso Centolani's Sangioveses come from two separate estates, situated on land between 270 and 400 metres altitude. The land overlooking the sea from the hill where the village is located is mainly volcanic in origin, while the plots near Castello della Velona, in the south-east, are mainly of a stony, limestone marl composition. The happy blend of microclimates and lands contributes to making soberly innovative Brunellos, half of which are matured in 30- and 50-hectolitre Slavonian oak and the rest in tonneaux. Expressive wines once again thrown into disorder by a Brunello Riserva 2010, classic from the very first impact of clear fruit, balsamic herbs and iodine. The palate progresses, flavoursome and penetrating, to the sweet, polished finish, just lacking a boost in roundness and depth to make it unforgettable.

● Brunello di Montalcino Ris. '10	♟♟ 6
● Brunello di Montalcino '11	♟♟ 7
● Brunello di Montalcino '09	♟♟♟ 7
● Brunello di Montalcino '06	♟♟♟ 7
● Brunello di Montalcino '01	♟♟♟ 6
● Brunello di Montalcino Collezione Arte '06	♟♟♟ 7
● Brunello di Montalcino Ris. '01	♟♟♟ 6
● Brunello di Montalcino '10	♟♟ 7
● Brunello di Montalcino '08	♟♟ 7
● Brunello di Montalcino '07	♟♟ 7
● Brunello di Montalcino Favorito '07	♟♟ 7
● Brunello di Montalcino Favorito Collezione Arte '09	♟♟ 7
● Brunello di Montalcino Ris. '07	♟♟ 6

Donna Olimpia 1898

FRAZ. BOLGHERI
LOC. MIGLIARINI, 142
57020 CASTAGNETO CARDUCCI [LI]
TEL. +39 0302279601
www.donnaolimpia1898.it

CELLAR SALES
ACCOMMODATION AND RESTAURANT SERVICE
ANNUAL PRODUCTION 250,000 bottles
HECTARES UNDER VINE 45.00
SUSTAINABLE WINERY

The estate named after Olimpia Alliata, Lady of Biserno, is run today by Guido Folonari, who belongs to one of the most famous and esteemed Tuscan winemaking families. The 45 hectares of vineyards are planted to traditional varieties for the Bolgheri area with a few less common elements: petit verdot for the reds, vermentino, viognier and petit manseng for the whites. The vineyard clonal project is the result of a partnership with Professor Scienza of the University of Milan. A great year for the scintillating Bolgheri Rosso Superiore Millepassi 2013: vibrant and engaging with ripe fruit, crushed herbs and spice on the nose alongside still-forward but elegant toasty hints. The palate is also wonderful, with well-measured alcohol, a mouthfilling entry and a carefree, focused flavour unfolding towards fine-grained, flavoursome tannins. The Bolgheri Rosso 2013 is not bad at all, less impressive in the finish but crisp and delicious.

● Bolgheri Rosso Sup. Millepassi '13	▼▼▼ 6
● Bolgheri Rosso '13	▼▼ 5
● Tageto '14	▼ 2
● Bolgheri Rosso Sup. Millepassi '11	♀♀♀ 8
● Bolgheri Rosso '12	♀♀ 5
● Bolgheri Rosso '10	♀♀ 5
● Bolgheri Rosso '09	♀♀ 5
● Bolgheri Rosso '08	♀♀ 4
● Bolgheri Rosso Sup. Millepassi '12	♀♀ 6
● Bolgheri Rosso Sup. Millepassi '09	♀♀ 8
● Bolgheri Rosso Sup. Millepassi '08	♀♀ 6
● Tageto '09	♀♀ 2

Duemani

LOC. ORTACAVOLI
56046 RIPARBELLA [PI]
TEL. +39 0583975048
www.duemani.eu

ANNUAL PRODUCTION 40,000 bottles
HECTARES UNDER VINE 10.00
VITICULTURE METHOD Certified Biodynamic
SUSTAINABLE WINERY

Luca D'Attoma has fulfilled the dream of many oenologists: a winegrowing estate of his own. Along with his wife Elena Celli, he chose to find a location in the province of Pisa to work with his favourite grape varieties, cabernet franc, syrah and merlot. In 2000 his search was rewarded on the hills of Riparbella, overlooking the sea: "an extreme, difficult, wild and magnetic place, an unspoilt and exciting landscape", is how Elena and Luca describe it. The story of Duemani began here, with replanting of the vineyards now farmed according to biodynamic principles. Tre Bicchieri for the Duemani 2013, a monovarietal Cabernet Franc: fresh balsamic aromas, Mediterranean scrubland, clean, clear-cut wild berries and a mouthfilling, flavoursome palate with beautifully blended tannins and a crescendo finish. The Suisassi 2013, a Syrah, is also enjoyable: medicinal herbs, cinchona, leather, and lively ripe wild berries on the nose. The palate is generous and multilayered with a clenched, lingering finish.

● Duemani '13	▼▼▼ 8
● Cifra '14	▼▼ 5
● Suisassi '13	▼▼ 8
● Altrovino '14	▼ 6
⊙ Si	▼ 5
● Duemani '12	♀♀♀ 8
● Duemani '09	♀♀♀ 8
● Suisassi '10	♀♀♀ 8
● Altrovino '13	♀♀ 5
● Altrovino '11	♀♀ 5
● Cifra '11	♀♀ 4
● Duemani '10	♀♀ 8
● Suisassi '12	♀♀ 8
● Suisassi '11	♀♀ 8
● Suisassi '09	♀♀ 8

Eucaliptus

VIA BOLGHERESE, 275A
57022 LIVORNO
TEL. +39 0565763511
www.agriturismoeucaliptus.com

PRE-BOOKED VISITS
ACCOMMODATION AND RESTAURANT SERVICE
ANNUAL PRODUCTION 20,000 bottles
HECTARES UNDER VINE 5.00

Pasqualino Di Vaira runs this lovely Bolgheri estate with a skilful and steady hand. It was set up in the 1960s to sell unbottled wine, but a great deal has changed since then: today Eucaliptus is a modern winegrowing estate, one of the most interesting in the region. The varieties grown here are merlot, cabernet sauvignon, petit verdot, syrah and sangiovese, not to mention white grapes like vermentino and chardonnay. The wines are on top form as usual, and the latest tastings brought a good response. The Bolgheri Superiore Ville Rustiche 2013 impressed us with enthralling, very clear, vibrant and multifaceted aromas, ranging from blackberries to ripe blueberries. The palate is nicely sweet, broader than it is deep, refreshed by lovely grassy and citrus sensations. The Bolgheri Rosso Clarice 2014 is astute, more succulent and linear but nevertheless mature. The Vermentino Le Pinete is less complex.

● Bolgheri Rosso Clarice '14	♟♟ 3
● Bolgheri Sup. Ville Rustiche '13	♟♟ 5
○ Bolgheri Le Pinete '15	♟ 3
● Bolgheri Rosso Clarice '13	♟♟ 3
● Bolgheri Rosso Clarice '12	♟♟ 3
● Bolgheri Rosso Clarice '11	♟♟ 3
● Bolgheri Sup. Ville Rustiche '12	♟♟ 5
● Bolgheri Sup. Ville Rustiche '11	♟♟ 5
● Bolgheri Sup. Ville Rustiche '10	♟♟ 5

I Fabbri

LOC. LAMOLE
VIA CASOLE, 52
50022 GREVE IN CHIANTI [FI]
TEL. 339412622
www.agricolaifabbri.it

CELLAR SALES
PRE-BOOKED VISITS
ANNUAL PRODUCTION 35,000 bottles
HECTARES UNDER VINE 11.00
VITICULTURE METHOD Certified Organic

In the early 2000s Susanna Grassi took back direct running of the family wine estate after renting it for a long period. Situated in the subzone of Lamole, the estate produces wines in a polished, forthright style. The grapes are grown organically, and in the cellar they are processed in stainless steel, concrete and tonneaux. I Fabbri wines show lovely personality, combining freshness and a very dynamic flavour. The Chianti Classico Terre di Lamole 2013 is definitely very good: floral, earthy, spicy aromas and a crisp, nicely lively palate, especially the tannins, with an edgy, lipsmacking finish. The delicious Chianti Classico Olinto 2014 has a fresh, relaxed flavour with clear, fragrant aromas. The Chianti Classico Riserva 2012 is more rugged, with nuanced aromas but a little too much oak, also holding back a palate that is less than fluent.

● Chianti Cl. Terra di Lamole '13	♟♟ 3*
● Chianti Cl. Olinto '14	♟♟ 4
● Chianti Cl. Ris. '12	♟ 4
● Chianti Cl. '13	♟♟ 4
● Chianti Cl. '12	♟♟ 4
● Chianti Cl. '10	♟♟ 4
● Chianti Cl. Gran Sel. '11	♟♟ 6
● Chianti Cl. Lamole '11	♟♟ 2*
● Chianti Cl. Olinto '12	♟♟ 4
● Chianti Cl. Olinto '10	♟♟ 4
● Chianti Cl. Olinto '08	♟♟ 4
● Chianti Cl. Ris. '11	♟♟ 4
● Chianti Cl. Ris. '10	♟♟ 4
● Chianti Cl. Terra di Lamole '10	♟♟ 2*

Tenuta Fanti

FRAZ. CASTELNUOVO DELL'ABATE
PODERE PALAZZO, 14
53020 MONTALCINO [SI]
TEL. +39 0577835795
www.tenutafanti.it

CELLAR SALES
PRE-BOOKED VISITS
ANNUAL PRODUCTION 200,000 bottles
HECTARES UNDER VINE 50.00

With over 300 hectares, 50 under vine, the Fanti family estates make up one of the largest farming properties in the south-east of Montalcino. Just a stone's throw from Castelnuovo dell'Abate, where the warm, airy climate and limestone marl soil work together to shape a Sangiovese with powerful character. Filippo, who established the farm in the 1970s now runs it jointly with his daughter Elisa. They have always been attentive to the expressive input in the Brunello universe, but at the same time able to offer a coherent style with mixed ageing methods, using both medium-sized barrels and barriques. Once again we must underline an excellent overall performance from Fanti wines, starting with the two 2011 Brunellos: the basic is already quite open and mature, more evolved fruit and forward tannin for the Vallocchio. The Vigna Le Macchiarelle Riserva 2010 reveals tertiary aromas as well as a better standard of extract.

Le Farnete/Cantagallo

VIA VALICARDA, 35
50050 CAPRAIA E LIMITE [FI]
TEL. +39 0571910078
www.tenutacantagallo.it

CELLAR SALES
PRE-BOOKED VISITS
ACCOMMODATION AND RESTAURANT SERVICE
ANNUAL PRODUCTION 180,000 bottles
HECTARES UNDER VINE 30.00
SUSTAINABLE WINERY

The Pierazzuoli family's lovely estate was established in the 1970s and is divided into two locations: Le Farnete, in the Carmignano designation, and Tenuta Cantagallo in nearby Chianti Montalbano, for a total of over 30 hectares of vineyards. Enrico Pierazzuoli and his family work with enthusiasm in the vineyards and cellar as well as running the adjacent agritourism facilities and restaurant. The Pierazzuoli haven't taken home Tre Bicchieri since 2001, for a splendid 1997 Riserva di Carmignano. But the Riserva 2013 earns the accolade again, thanks to really superior elegance and clean styling. This great red is not only weighty and richly extracted, it is above all complex, harmonious and elegant. However, the whole range is of an excellent standard.

● Brunello di Montalcino '11	♟♟ 6
● Brunello di Montalcino V. Le Macchiarelle Ris. '10	♟♟ 6
● Brunello di Montalcino Vallocchio '11	♟♟ 6
● Rosso di Montalcino '14	♟ 3
● Brunello di Montalcino '07	♟♟♟ 5
● Brunello di Montalcino '00	♟♟♟ 6
● Brunello di Montalcino '97	♟♟♟ 5
● Brunello di Montalcino Ris. '95	♟♟♟ 5
● Brunello di Montalcino '10	♟♟ 6
● Brunello di Montalcino '09	♟♟ 6
● Brunello di Montalcino V. Le Macchiarelle Ris. '09	♟♟ 6
● Brunello di Montalcino Vallocchio '10	♟♟ 6

● Carmignano Le Farnete Ris. '13	♟♟♟ 4*
● Gioveto Tenuta Cantagallo '13	♟♟ 4
● Carmignano Le Farnete '14	♟♟ 3
● Chianti Montalbano Tenuta Cantagallo Ris. '13	♟♟ 3
● Barco Reale Le Farnete '15	♟ 2
● Chianti Montalbano Tenuta Cantagallo '15	♟ 2
● Carmignano Le Farnete Ris. '97	♟♟♟ 6
● Carmignano Le Farnete '13	♟♟ 3
● Carmignano Le Farnete Ris. '12	♟♟ 4
● Carmignano Le Farnete Ris. '11	♟♟ 4
● Chianti Montalbano Ris. '12	♟♟ 3
● Gioveto '12	♟♟ 4

Fattoi

LOC. SANTA RESTITUTA
POD. CAPANNA, 101
53024 MONTALCINO [SI]
TEL. +39 0577848613
www.fattoi.it

CELLAR SALES
PRE-BOOKED VISITS
ANNUAL PRODUCTION 50,000 bottles
HECTARES UNDER VINE 9.00

With almost 40 harvests under its belt, this is by no means an up-and-coming estate, and nor should we be surprised by the quality of the wines originating from Pieve Santa Restituta, a true Montalcino grand cru. But in the last few years, above all, the winery established by Ofelio Fattoi has been described as one of the best choices for Brunello, thanks to its original and characteristic style, increasingly skilled in compensating some tannic and reductive huskiness with natural expressivity and mouthwatering flavour. These are respected Sangioveses made with artisan sensitivity, not to mention the ageing procedure, using large Slavonian oak barrels. An excellent overall performance from the Fattoi reds, just missing a high note. Mulberry blossom, raspberries and a hint of confit in an airy, breathable Brunello 2011, penalized by the vintage's dry texture. The Riserva 2010 is also held back by basic ruggedness, though its lively, spontaneous gait is satisfying.

● Brunello di Montalcino '11	▼▼ 5
● Brunello di Montalcino Ris. '10	▼▼ 7
● Rosso di Montalcino '14	▼▼ 3
● Brunello di Montalcino '09	♀♀ 5
● Brunello di Montalcino '07	♀♀ 6
● Brunello di Montalcino '06	♀♀ 6
● Brunello di Montalcino '04	♀♀ 5
● Brunello di Montalcino '03	♀♀ 5
● Brunello di Montalcino Ris. '08	♀♀ 7
● Brunello di Montalcino Ris. '07	♀♀ 7
● Brunello di Montalcino Ris. '06	♀♀ 4
● Brunello di Montalcino Ris. '03	♀♀ 5
● Rosso di Montalcino '13	♀♀ 3
● Rosso di Montalcino '12	♀♀ 3
● Rosso di Montalcino '10	♀♀ 3
● Rosso di Montalcino '05	♀♀ 3

★★Felsina

VIA DEL CHIANTI, 101
53019 CASTELNUOVO BERARDENGA [SI]
TEL. +39 0577355117
www.felsina.it

CELLAR SALES
PRE-BOOKED VISITS
ANNUAL PRODUCTION 480,000 bottles
HECTARES UNDER VINE 94.00
VITICULTURE METHOD Certified Organic
SUSTAINABLE WINERY

Progressive and consistent conversion to biodynamic farming methods in the vineyards, alongside a decisive change in the style of the wines, are the distinguishing features marking the evolution of Felsina, an estate which has made a considerable contribution to the success of Chianti Classico and the most authentic representation of the Castelnuovo Berardenga subzone. The wines have achieved a more contemporary level of expression, with brighter hues, stronger oaky aromas and weightier extract. The Sangiovese Maestro Raro 2013 is still a very enjoyable Supertuscan, with rounded, fragrant aromas of violets and cherries, supported by spice from the oak, and a lovely sweet, succulent, well-paced flavour. The Chianti Classico Riserva and Chianti Classico Rancia Riserva, both 2013, are heavily affected by the oak used for ageing, which also influences the aromas and flavour of the Fontalloro 2013, a monovarietal Sangiovese.

● Maestro Raro '13	▼▼ 6
● Chianti Cl. Berardenga Ris. '13	▼ 5
● Chianti Cl. Rancia Ris. '13	▼ 6
● Fontalloro '13	▼ 7
○ I Sistri '14	▼ 4
● Chianti Cl. Rancia Ris. '07	♀♀♀ 6
● Chianti Cl. Rancia Ris. '05	♀♀♀ 5
● Chianti Cl. Rancia Ris. '04	♀♀♀ 5
● Chianti Cl. Rancia Ris. '03	♀♀♀ 5
● Fontalloro '10	♀♀♀ 6
● Fontalloro '07	♀♀♀ 6
● Fontalloro '06	♀♀♀ 6
● Fontalloro '05	♀♀♀ 6
● Maestro Raro '08	♀♀♀ 6

Le Filigare

Loc. Le Filigare
via Sicelle, 35
50020 Barberino Val d'Elsa [FI]
Tel. +39 0558072796
www.lefiligare.it

CELLAR SALES
PRE-BOOKED VISITS
ANNUAL PRODUCTION 45,000 bottles
HECTARES UNDER VINE 10.00

Le Filigare consists of ten hectares of vineyards in the Florentine area of Chianti Classico, close to the province of Siena. The land is typically a mix of clay and dense skeleton texture, traditional elements in this area of Chianti, and the vineyards are planted at an altitude of around 300 metres. The cellar makes use of both large and small oak casks, producing wines of a generally harmonious style, avoiding pointless forcing in the winemaking procedures, or overly buffed-up wines. The Chianti Classico Lorenzo 2013 proves to be the revelation of the year, coming close to our highest accolade. Aromas of fruit and blood-rich meat are refined by hints of liquorice and forest floor, while the palate is supple and juicy, well paced and nuanced with a deep, tangy crescendo finish. The Chianti Classico 2014 is also worthy, slender-bodied with shaded aromas and a light, multifaceted flavour. The Podere Le Rocce 2013, from sangiovese and cabernet sauvignon, is firm-bodied and impressive.

● Chianti Cl. Lorenzo '13	♟♟ 4
● Chianti Cl. '14	♟♟ 4
● Podere Le Rocce '13	♟♟ 4
● Chianti Cl. Lorenzo '06	♟♟ 4
● Chianti Cl. Lorenzo '04	♟♟ 4
● Chianti Cl. Maria Vittoria Ris. '05	♟♟ 5
● Chianti Cl. Maria Vittoria Ris. '04	♟♟ 5
● Pietro '01	♟♟ 8
● Podere Le Rocce '01	♟♟ 6

★Tenute Ambrogio e Giovanni Folonari

Loc. Passo dei Pecorai
via di Nozzole, 12
50022 Greve in Chianti [FI]
Tel. +39 055859811
www.tenutefolonari.com

CELLAR SALES
PRE-BOOKED VISITS
ACCOMMODATION
ANNUAL PRODUCTION 1,400,000 bottles
HECTARES UNDER VINE 200.00

One of the leading winemaker families in Italy, with Tuscany as the undisputed homeland of their various properties, consisting of several estates in the region's best terroirs: Nozzole, at Greve in Chianti, in the Chianti Classico DOC zone, La Fuga at Montalcino, Torcalvano at Montepulciano, Campo al Mare at Bolgheri and Vigne a Porrona in Maremma. The wines are generally modern in style, do not turn their nose up at considerable use of oak for ageing, and aim for approachable, generous fruit. Among the wines tasted from the different estates, we were very impressed with those from La Fuga, the 2011 Brunello and the Riserva Le Due Sorelle 2010, both mouthfilling but with nicely defined acidity. The Chianti Classico 2013 is less focused, with excessively tannic extract, as is the Cabreo La Pietra 2014, where the oak is too forward. The Bolgheri wines are reliably good.

● Brunello di Montalcino Tenuta La Fuga '11	♟♟ 6
● Brunello di Montalcino Le Due Sorelle Tenuta La Fuga Ris. '10	♟♟ 7
● Cabreo Il Borgo '13	♟♟ 6
● Bolgheri Campo al Mare '14	♟ 3
● Bolgheri Sup. Baia al Vento Campo al Mare '12	♟ 6
○ Cabreo La Pietra '14	♟ 6
● Chianti Cl. '13	♟ 4
● Il Pareto '09	♟♟♟ 7
● Il Pareto '07	♟♟♟ 7
● Il Pareto '04	♟♟♟ 7
● Il Pareto '01	♟♟♟ 7

★★Fontodi

FRAZ. PANZANO IN CHIANTI
VIA SAN LEOLINO, 89
50020 GREVE IN CHIANTI [FI]
TEL. +39 055852005
www.fontodi.com

CELLAR SALES
PRE-BOOKED VISITS
ACCOMMODATION
ANNUAL PRODUCTION 300,000 bottles
HECTARES UNDER VINE 80.00
VITICULTURE METHOD Certified Organic

Fontodi is a reliable brand name and its wines display a clear and highly approachable style. These reds are sturdy, generous and extremely ageable, while showing well-balanced expression. The high quality grapes, organically farmed, respect the generous nature of the Panzano in Chianti subzone. The wines are mainly aged in barriques which sometimes tends to mask their natural energy, particularly in the early phase of development. The Chianti Classico 2013 is of an excellent standard: fragrant, well-defined fruity and floral aromas, and a lively, multifaceted, and very supple flavour. The Pinot Nero Case Via 2014 is also interesting, probably enhanced by the good year, with subtle, clean aromas and a consistent, fruity flavour, the finish just held back by slightly excessive oak.

Fornacelle

LOC. FORNACELLE, 232A
57022 CASTAGNETO CARDUCCI [LI]
TEL. +39 0565775575
www.fornacelle.it

CELLAR SALES
PRE-BOOKED VISITS
ANNUAL PRODUCTION 35,000 bottles
HECTARES UNDER VINE 15.00

The Billi Batistoni family farm their vineyards and make their wines personally. This is a small artisan business, skilled in authentic and very interesting processes. The name originates from the many kilns that once stood here, their remains still visible under the cellar. Although the family has run the farm for four generations, the turning point came in 1998 thanks to a thorough renewal of the vineyards and meticulous choices in the cellar. All the wines are worth consideration. The Bolgheri Superiore Guarda Boschi 2013 is excellent, with enthralling iodine, salty sensations from the vintage year. The palate is racy, not too concentrated, and tangy, with marked but not bitter tannins. The other 2013 Bolgheri Superiore, Foglio 38, appeared more evolved and equally well made.

● Chianti Cl. '13	♟♟ 4
● Pinot Nero Case Via '14	♟♟ 5
● Chianti Cl. Gran Sel. V. del Sorbo '13	♟ 6
● Chianti Cl. '10	♟♟♟ 4*
● Flaccianello della Pieve '12	♟♟♟ 8
● Flaccianello della Pieve '09	♟♟♟ 8
● Flaccianello della Pieve '08	♟♟♟ 8
● Flaccianello della Pieve '07	♟♟♟ 6
● Flaccianello della Pieve '05	♟♟♟ 6
● Flaccianello della Pieve '03	♟♟♟ 6
● Chianti Cl. V. del Sorbo Gran Sel. '11	♟♟ 6
● Flaccianello della Pieve '10	♟♟ 8

● Bolgheri Sup. Foglio 38 '13	♟♟ 6
● Bolgheri Sup. Guarda Boschi '13	♟♟ 6
○ Bolgheri Bianco Zizzolo '15	♟ 3
● Bolgheri Rosso Zizzolo '14	♟ 3
○ Bianco Fornacelle '10	♟♟ 2
● Bolgheri Rosso Zizzolo '13	♟♟ 3
● Bolgheri Rosso Zizzolo '12	♟♟ 3
● Bolgheri Rosso Zizzolo '09	♟♟ 6
● Bolgheri Sup. Guarda Boschi '12	♟♟ 6
● Bolgheri Sup. Guarda Boschi '11	♟♟ 6
● Bolgheri Sup. Guarda Boschi '08	♟♟ 6
○ Bolgheri Vermentino Zizzolo '14	♟♟ 3
● Foglio 38 '11	♟♟ 6

Podere Fortuna

VIA SAN GIUSTO A FORTUNA, 7
50038 SCARPERIA E SAN PIERO [FI]
TEL. +39 0558487214
www.poderefortuna.com

CELLAR SALES
PRE-BOOKED VISITS
ACCOMMODATION
ANNUAL PRODUCTION 25,000 bottles
HECTARES UNDER VINE 6.00

The location is Mugello, alongside the Cafaggiolo castle built by the Medici family and part of Lorenzo the Magnificent's possessions. A document dated 1465 shows that wine was already being produced there at the time. Fortuna was one of the 12 farms on the Castello di Cafaggiolo property. When Alessandro Brogi decided to start up the winegrowing business again in the late Nineties, having studied the land and climate, he decided to plant some chardonnay and above all pinot noir, which was certainly not commonly grown in Tuscany. The pinot nero selection, 1465, is good: fresh, well-typed aromas with wild berries alongside grassy hints, supported by light minty sensations. The palate makes a weighty entry, pleasant, broad and tempting, not too full-bodied, with a progressive, lingering finish. The Coldaia 2013 is more approachable and accessible, with a compact nose and soft palate, with a refreshing flavour and crescendo finish.

● 1465 MCDLXV '11	♟♟	8
● Coldaia '13	♟♟	5
● Fortuni '11	♟♟	6
● 1465 MCDLXV '10	♟♟♟	8
● 1465 MCDLXV '09	♟♟	8
● 1465 MCDLXV '07	♟♟	8
● Ardito del Mugello '10	♟♟	3
● Coldaia '11	♟♟	5
● Coldaia '09	♟♟	5
● Fortuni '12	♟♟	5
● Fortuni '10	♟♟	6
● Fortuni '09	♟♟	6
○ Greto alla Macchia '12	♟♟	5
○ Greto alla Macchia '10	♟♟	5

La Fralluca

LOC. BARBICONI, 153
57028 SUVERETO [LI]
TEL. +39 0565829076
www.lafralluca.com

CELLAR SALES
PRE-BOOKED VISITS
ANNUAL PRODUCTION 40,000 bottles
HECTARES UNDER VINE 10.00
SUSTAINABLE WINERY

Fralluca stands for Francesca and Luca: she is from Pisa and he is Milanese, both worked in the fashion sector. They met in Milan in the late Nineties and built a family with two children and a dream: to move to Tuscany and make wine. After three years of research they fell in love with a place on top of a hill at Suvereto, with an abandoned farmhouse and a splendid view of woodlands. This was the beginning of the farm's story and of theirs as winegrowers. They planted the vineyards about ten years ago and began to bring their project to life. The 2013 Cabernet Franc has tomato leaves, grilled green peppers and ripe blackberry and raspberry fruit on the nose, with hints of spice. The palate opens warm and mouthfilling, nicely weighty with well-balanced, fresh acidity and an appetizing finish. The enthralling Bauci 2014 is a Viognier with primarily vegetal and floral aromas, fruity hints of lemon and plums, and a subtle, balanced palate.

○ Bauci '14	♟♟	3
● Cabernet Franc '13	♟♟	5
○ Filemone '15	♟	3
● Fillide '13	♟	3
● Suvereto Ciparisso '13	♟	5
● Suvereto Sangiovese Ciparisso '12	♟♟	5
● Cabernet Franc '12	♟♟	5
● Cabernet Franc '11	♟♟	6
● Fillide '12	♟♟	3
● Syrah Pitis '12	♟♟	5
● Syrah Pitis '10	♟♟	3
○ Viognier '11	♟♟	2*
○ Viognier Bauci '13	♟♟	3
○ Viognier Bauci '12	♟♟	3

Frank & Serafico

FRAZ. ALBERESE
S.DA SPERGOLAIA
58100 GROSSETO
TEL. +39 0564418491
www.frankeserafico.com

CELLAR SALES
PRE-BOOKED VISITS
RESTAURANT SERVICE
ANNUAL PRODUCTION 90,000 bottles
HECTARES UNDER VINE 25.00

This estate has a recent history, established in 2010 when Fabrizio Testa and Pierpaolo Pratesi joined forces. The vineyards are scattered over the province of Grosseto: in the Alberese nature reserve, in Campagnatico, Magliano and Capalbio. The style of the estate's various wines favours approachable, drinkable qualities and probably needs a bit longer to develop more original features. The wines have a good basis and are well-made without wasting time on pointless forcing. Clean, well-structured aromas in the Montalzato 2013, a blend of cabernet sauvignon, merlot and sangiovese, with a flavoursome, nicely judged palate. The Maremma Sangiovese 2012 shows equally supple flavour and clean, subtle aromas. The Serafico 2013 is atypical but interesting: made from vermentino grapes dried on the vine, it reveals vibrant aromas and a lightly salty flavour. The Frank 2014 is well made but lacks a little personality. The rest of the wines are delicious.

● Maremma Toscana Sangiovese '12	♼♼ 4
● Montalzato '13	♼♼ 2*
○ Serafico '13	♼♼ 4
● Frank '14	♼ 3
● Maremma Toscana Rosso Redola '15	♼ 2
● Morellino di Scansano Mr '14	♼ 2
○ Vermentino VR '15	♼ 2
● Frank '09	♼♼ 6
● Morellino di Scansano Mr '13	♼♼ 2*
● Morellino di Scansano Mr '12	♼♼ 2*
● Sangiovese '11	♼♼ 4

Frascole

LOC. FRASCOLE, 27A
50062 DICOMANO [FI]
TEL. +39 0558386340
www.frascole.it

CELLAR SALES
PRE-BOOKED VISITS
ACCOMMODATION
ANNUAL PRODUCTION 65,000 bottles
HECTARES UNDER VINE 16.00
VITICULTURE METHOD Certified Organic

Dicomano is a small town between the valleys of Mugello and Valdisieve. Frascole's 16 hectares of vineyards cover the hillsides overlooking the village, farmed with the greatest respect for the area and environment, and certified organic. As well as vineyards, the estate includes arable land and olive groves. The Lippi and Santoni families who own the farm have succeeded over the years in creating a pleasant location through restoration and recovery of some of Medieval buildings. This year the winery sent us a Passito from 2002 for tasting. The grapes are the classic trebbiano and malvasia bianca used to make Vin Santo, producing here one of the most attractive sweet wines we tasted during the selections. Light hints of medical herbs blend with dried peach and apricot fruit, while the palate is weighty, creamy and not at all cloying. The Rufina 2014 is also well made, spicy, and nicely dynamic.

○ Passito '02	♼♼ 8
● Chianti Rufina '14	♼♼ 2*
● Chianti Rufina Ris. '13	♼ 3
○ Bianco InAlbis '13	♼♼ 2*
○ Bianco InAlbis Sulle Bucce '11	♼♼ 2*
● Chianti Rufina '13	♼♼ 2*
● Chianti Rufina '11	♼♼ 2*
● Chianti Rufina Ris. '12	♼♼ 3*
● Chianti Rufina Ris. '11	♼♼ 3
● Limine '10	♼♼ 2*
● Rosso Limine '09	♼♼ 2*
○ Vin Santo del Chianti Rufina '05	♼♼ 7

★Marchesi de' Frescobaldi

VIA SANTO SPIRITO, 11
50125 FIRENZE
TEL. +39 05527141
www.frescobaldi.it

CELLAR SALES
PRE-BOOKED VISITS
ANNUAL PRODUCTION 7,000,000 bottles
HECTARES UNDER VINE 923.00

One of the classic Italian winemaking names, a family whose roots reach back to the 14th century, and an estate that started with in Rufina and nearby Pomino, to extend its property across different areas of Tuscany, from Montalcino to Maremma, from Scansano to Colli Fiorentini, and outside the region in Friuli. For a few years now, Lamberto Frescobaldi has been the chairman of the group which has effected an extraordinary transformation in the vineyards and cellar, focusing mainly on the concept of ecosustainability. Another Tre Bicchieri for one of the estate's most representative wines, the Rufina Vecchie Viti Riserva 2013. A stylish nose with hints of wild berries and blood oranges, opening out with tidy, harmonious tannic texture enlivened by well-balanced acidity and a juicy tang. One of the Montalcino wines makes the finals: Luce 2013 presents cherry and blackberry aromas with spicy hints of black pepper and cinnamon. The palate is engaging and succulent, lingering and nicely weighty, with a long, flavoursome finish.

● Chianti Rufina Nipozzano V. V. Ris. '13 ▼▼▼ 5
● Luce '13 ▼▼ 8
● Chianti Rufina Nipozzano Ris. '13 ▼▼▼ 5
● Lucente '14 ▼▼ 4
● Morellino di Scansano Pietraregia dell'Ammiraglia Ris. '12 ▼▼ 5
● Tenuta di Castiglioni '13 ▼▼ 4
○ Pomino Bianco '15 ▼ 3
○ Pomino Bianco Benefizio Ris. '14 ▼ 5
○ Pomino Brut Leonia '12 ▼ 6
○ Pomino Vin Santo '08 ▼ 6
● Chianti Rufina Montesodi '01 ♚♚♚ 6
● Chianti Rufina Montesodi '99 ♚♚♚ 5
● Chianti Rufina V. V. Ris. '11 ♚♚♚ 6
● Mormoreto '05 ♚♚♚ 7
● Mormoreto '01 ♚♚♚ 7
● Mormoreto '97 ♚♚♚ 7

Fuligni

VIA SALONI, 33
53024 MONTALCINO [SI]
TEL. +39 0577848710
www.fuligni.it

CELLAR SALES
PRE-BOOKED VISITS
ANNUAL PRODUCTION 52,000 bottles
HECTARES UNDER VINE 12.00

At altitudes between 380 and 450 metres, Cottimelli is one of the highest estates in the Montalcino DOC. The Fuligni family have concentrated their efforts here in the north-eastern part of the zone for almost a century, led with great enthusiasm by Signora Maria Flora and her trusted staff. The ten or so hectares of vineyards are planted on soil rich in limestone marl and stones, forming the basis of firm, stylish Brunellos aged in 30-hectolitre oak casks after a spell in tonneaux. These reds are sometimes unruly and, to some extent, obscure in the early years, but worth the wait to enjoy their gentler, calmer side. The wines we tasted effectively fit this overall description. First of all, the 2011 Brunello generated contrasting impressions, with evolved aromas including dried fruit, forest floor, tanned leather, and somewhat held back in this phase by dry, austere tannins. This limitation is shared by the Rosso Ginestreto 2014, simpler and tighter but nicely drinkable.

● Brunello di Montalcino '11 ▼▼ 6
● Rosso di Montalcino Ginestreto '14 ▼ 4
● Brunello di Montalcino '10 ♚♚♚ 6
● Brunello di Montalcino Ris. '01 ♚♚♚ 8
● Brunello di Montalcino Ris. '97 ♚♚♚ 8
● Brunello di Montalcino '09 ♚♚ 6
● Brunello di Montalcino '08 ♚♚ 6
● Brunello di Montalcino '07 ♚♚ 6
● Brunello di Montalcino '06 ♚♚ 6
● Brunello di Montalcino Ris. '07 ♚♚ 8
● Brunello di Montalcino Ris. '06 ♚♚ 8
● Brunello di Montalcino Ris. '04 ♚♚ 8
● Rosso di Montalcino Ginestreto '13 ♚♚ 4
● Rosso di Montalcino Ginestreto '10 ♚♚ 3
● S. J. '12 ♚♚ 3

★Tenuta di Ghizzano

FRAZ. GHIZZANO
VIA DELLA CHIESA, 4
56037 PECCIOLI [PI]
TEL. +39 0587630096
www.tenutadighizzano.com

CELLAR SALES
PRE-BOOKED VISITS
ACCOMMODATION
ANNUAL PRODUCTION 80,000 bottles
HECTARES UNDER VINE 20.00
VITICULTURE METHOD Certified Organic

Ginevra Venerosi Pesciolini is one of the best-known and most competent women in the Italian wine sector, and the owner of this spectacular estate that is a balance between old traditions and a spirit of innovation. Over 350 hectares in a lush, attractive, natural location, with vineyards planted on sandy, loamy soil of marine origin, rich in fossils. The farming methods were originally organic and are now biodynamic. The wines are full-bodied, Mediterranean in style, and as modern as they are flavoursome. A simply extraordinary performance from memorable wines that come close to and win Tre Bicchieri. The Nambrot 2013 is excellent, polished and stylish with a cloud of spice, grassy nuances and balsamic hints, enclosing a Bordeaux structure with a fragrant, racy, infinitely deep flavour. A great wine, like the Veneroso of the same year: more compact but complex and certain to develop.

● Terre di Pisa Nambrot '13	♈♈♈	6
● Terre di Pisa Veneroso '13	♈♈	5
○ San Germano Passito '13	♈♈	5
○ Il Ghizzano Bianco '15	♈	3
● Il Guizzano Rosso '14	♈	3
● Nambrot '09	♈♈♈	6
● Nambrot '08	♈♈♈	6
● Nambrot '06	♈♈♈	6
● Nambrot '05	♈♈♈	6
● Nambrot '04	♈♈♈	6
● Nambrot '03	♈♈♈	6
● Terre di Pisa Nambrot '12	♈♈♈	6
● Veneroso '10	♈♈♈	5
● Veneroso '07	♈♈♈	5
● Veneroso '04	♈♈♈	5
● Terre di Pisa Veneroso '12	♈♈	5

Marchesi Ginori Lisci

FRAZ. PONTEGINORI
LOC. QUERCETO
56040 MONTECATINI VAL DI CECINA [PI]
TEL. +39 058837443
www.marchesiginorilisci.it

CELLAR SALES
ACCOMMODATION AND RESTAURANT SERVICE
ANNUAL PRODUCTION 35,000 bottles
HECTARES UNDER VINE 17.00
VITICULTURE METHOD Certified Organic

The property covers 2000 hectares in the inland area of Val di Cecina. At the heart of the estate is the Castello Ginori di Querceto, whose long history is entwined with that of the Marchesi Ginori Lisci family, famous for china manufacturing. In the late 20th century Lionardo Ginori and his nephew Luigi Malenchini started to transform the estate by planting new vineyards and finding space to build a more modern and functional cellar. Holiday apartments are available in the hamlet. The appealing Macchion del Lupo 2013, from cabernet sauvignon, has an enthralling, dark nose with aromatic herbs like sage and bay, balsamic and fruity sensations of damsons and blackberries. The palate is tangy, tempting, and fresh with a lingering finish. The Castello Ginori, a Merlot, is also good, with hints of raspberry and strawberry jam, spices like juniper and cloves, and a soft, succulent, weighty palate with a generous, creamy finish and beautifully lingering flavour. The other wines are all lovely.

● Montescudaio Cabernet Macchion del Lupo '13	♈♈	3
● Montescudaio Merlot Castello Ginori '12	♈♈	2*
⊙ Bacio '15	♈	2
● Montescudaio Rosso Campordigno '14	♈	2
○ Virgola '15	♈	2
● Montescudaio Cabernet Macchion del Lupo '11	♈♈	3*
● Montescudaio Cabernet Macchion del Lupo '09	♈♈	3
● Montescudaio Merlot '08	♈♈	2*
● Montescudaio Merlot Campordigno '12	♈♈	2*
● Montescudaio Merlot Castello Ginori '11	♈♈	2*
● Montescudaio Merlot Castello Ginori '09	♈♈	4
● Montescudaio Rosso Campordigno '10	♈♈	2*

Giodo

LOC. PIAZZINI
53011 MONTALCINO [SI]
carlo.ferrini27@gmail.com

ANNUAL PRODUCTION 8,000 bottles
HECTARES UNDER VINE 2.50
SUSTAINABLE WINERY

Carlo Ferrini is one of Italy's best-known and most sought-after oenologists, who set up his own project in the early 2000s, in Montalcino. Just over two hectares in the south, on the road from Castelnuovo dell'Abate to Sant'Angelo in Colle, to make a single Brunello, first released in the 2009 vintage and produced outside its own designation zone. Podere Giodo soon earned its slot among the DOC's best wineries, thanks to its recognizable signature style. In many ways, the reds are post-modern, expressing sartorial awareness of agricultural design and winemaking haute couture. And Carlo Ferrini's creation is an instant success, making a debut in the main section of the Guide and winning Tre Bicchieri with the Brunello Giodo 2011. Raspberry jelly, Mediterranean shrubs, pencil lead, and a mouthfilling, flavoursome palate that compensates a slight lack of sinew with tangy, dense acidity.

● Brunello di Montalcino Giodo '11	▼▼▼ 8
● Giodo '13	▼▼ 6

I Giusti & Zanza Vigneti

LOC. FAUGLIA
VIA DEI PUNTONI, 9
56043 FAUGLIA [PI]
TEL. +39 058544354
www.igiustiezanza.it

CELLAR SALES
PRE-BOOKED VISITS
ACCOMMODATION
ANNUAL PRODUCTION 100,000 bottles
HECTARES UNDER VINE 17.00
VITICULTURE METHOD Certified Organic

Fauglia, in the hills between Pisa and Livorno, is where Paolo Giusti brought his project to life. It all began in the 1990s, pursuing a specific idea regarding promotion of the area and an identity harmonizing with nature, and today the estate is biodynamically farmed. The vineyards are planted on sandy, loamy soil with plenty of gravelly content. The wines reflect their terroir with personality, character and a judiciously modern appearance. An indeterminate year for the 2014 wines, Belcore and Perbruno, both Syrahs. The slender structure, due to the difficult weather in 2014, is excessively supported by the oak which holds back length and sweetness in the back palate. The Dulcamara 2103, mostly cabernet, is more focused but still very oaky.

● Dulcamara '13	▼▼ 5
● Belcore '14	▼ 3
● Perbruno '14	▼ 4
● Belcore '13	♀♀ 3
● Belcore '12	♀♀ 3
● Dulcamara '12	♀♀ 5
● Dulcamara '11	♀♀ 5
● Dulcamara '10	♀♀ 5
● Dulcamara '09	♀♀ 5
● Dulcamara '08	♀♀ 5
○ Nemorino Bianco '12	♀♀ 2*
● Perbruno '13	♀♀ 4
● Perbruno '12	♀♀ 4
● Perbruno '10	♀♀ 4

Tenuta di Gracciano della Seta

FRAZ. GRACCIANO
VIA UMBRIA, 59
53045 MONTEPULCIANO [SI]
TEL. +39 0578708340
www.graccianodellaseta.com

CELLAR SALES
PRE-BOOKED VISITS
ANNUAL PRODUCTION 100,000 bottles
HECTARES UNDER VINE 18.00
SUSTAINABLE WINERY

A 315-hectare estate which includes olive groves, cereal crops, woods and, naturally, vineyards. This is the farm owned by Donatella Gondi and her brother Bernardo, with his sons Gerardo and Lapo, the heirs to this property belonging to the aristocratic family since the late 1500s. Once harvested, the grapes grown in the 19-hectare vineyard are fermented in the old vaulted cellars below the villa. The estate includes another farmstead, Volmiano, on the slopes of Mt. Morello. The Nobile di Montepulciano Riserva 2012 is really superlative, an exciting wine with minerally, earthy personality and high calibre and complexity. Relaxed and nuanced with beautiful aromas of raspberries and other wild berries, enfolded in subtle hints of leather and golden tobacco. A consistent, vibrant palate, succulent and racy yet firm with flavoursome tannic backbone. The Nobile 2013 is focused, spicy and piquant.

● Nobile di Montepulciano Ris. '12	▼▼▼ 5
● Nobile di Montepulciano '13	▼▼ 4
● Rosso di Montepulciano '14	▼ 3
● Nobile di Montepulciano '11	♈♈ 3
● Nobile di Montepulciano '06	♈♈ 5
● Nobile di Montepulciano Ris. '10	♈♈ 5
● Nobile di Montepulciano Ris. '06	♈♈ 5
● Nobile di Montepulciano Ris. '04	♈♈ 5

Bibi Graetz

VIA DI VINCIGLIATA, 19
50014 FIESOLE [FI]
TEL. +39 055597289
www.bibigraetz.com

PRE-BOOKED VISITS
ANNUAL PRODUCTION 500,000 bottles
HECTARES UNDER VINE 10.00

Bibi Graetz is an unusual, non-conformist character who turned to winegrowing after initially following, as a painter, in the artistic footsteps of his father, an internationally famed sculptor. He brought old vineyards back to life in the Fiesole area, little known for winegrowing, and revalued varieties that were almost sidelined, bringing them back into the limelight with an appearance suited to international tastes. Proof of this is his choice to make a wine like Ansonica del Giglio, selecting the grapes himself from the island and persuading the farmers not to abandon the vines. Monovarietal Sangiovese Testamatta 2013 goes through to the finals: clean, simple aromas of redcurrants and cherries, fresh sensations, and a stylish palate, not too powerful, with lovely acidity and a long, flavoursome, well-measured finish. The enthralling Colore 2011 is an equal blend of sangiovese, canaiolo and colorino with vibrant jammy aromas and evolved sensations, and a clenched, close-knit texture.

● Testamatta '13	▼▼ 8
● Colore '11	▼▼ 8
● Soffocone di Vincigliata '14	▼▼ 5
⊙ Bollamatta	▼ 3
○ Scopeto '15	▼ 3
○ Bugia '14	♈♈ 6
○ Bugia '13	♈♈ 6
○ Casamatta Bianco '11	♈♈ 2*
○ Gigliese '11	♈♈ 3
● Grilli del Testamatta '10	♈♈ 5
● It's a Game '10	♈♈ 2*
● Soffocone di Vincigliata '13	♈♈ 5
● Testamatta '12	♈♈ 8
● Testamatta '09	♈♈ 8

★Grattamacco

Loc. Lungagnano
57022 Castagneto Carducci [LI]
Tel. +39 0565765069
www.collemassari.it

CELLAR SALES
PRE-BOOKED VISITS
ANNUAL PRODUCTION 120,000 bottles
HECTARES UNDER VINE 16.00
VITICULTURE METHOD Certified Organic
SUSTAINABLE WINERY

Grattamacco is one of the best-known names in Bolgheri winemaking. The estate, established in the 1970s, is now run by the Tipa brothers who also own Colle Massari and Poggio di Sotto, and have recently bought some more land. The magnificent and painstakingly farmed vineyards stand on different types of soil, from sandy to limestone marl. The wines are capable of revealing confident character, finesse and elegance, and are among the best we tasted in this DOC . The marvellous Bolgheri Rosso Superiore Grattamacco 2013 is enhanced with even more class and finesse by the wonderful year. Enticing, ripe, fresh red berries and an array of spices on the nose, and an appealing, subtle palate with a strong structure. We particularly enjoyed this wine, more elegant than it is weighty and rich in extract. The L'Alberello 2013 is also excellent, and the Bolgheri Rosso 2014 is well typed but obviously easier.

● Bolgheri Rosso Sup. Grattamacco '13	♥♥♥	8
● Bolgheri Rosso '14	♥♥	4
● Bolgheri Sup. L'Alberello '13	♥♥	6
● Bolgheri Rosso Sup. Grattamacco '12	♀♀♀	8
● Bolgheri Rosso Sup. Grattamacco '10	♀♀♀	7
● Bolgheri Rosso Sup. Grattamacco '09	♀♀♀	7
● Bolgheri Rosso Sup. Grattamacco '07	♀♀♀	7
● Bolgheri Rosso Sup. Grattamacco '06	♀♀♀	7
● Bolgheri Rosso Sup. Grattamacco '05	♀♀♀	7
● Bolgheri Rosso Sup. Grattamacco '04	♀♀♀	7
● Bolgheri Rosso Sup. Grattamacco '03	♀♀♀	7
● Bolgheri Sup. L'Alberello '11	♀♀♀	6

Guado al Melo

Loc. Murrotto, 130a
57022 Castagneto Carducci [LI]
Tel. +39 0565763238
www.guadoalmelo.it

CELLAR SALES
PRE-BOOKED VISITS
ANNUAL PRODUCTION 150,000 bottles
HECTARES UNDER VINE 20.00
VITICULTURE METHOD Certified Organic
SUSTAINABLE WINERY

In the last edition of the Guide Michele Scienza's estate was elected best Up-and-Coming Winery, and is one of those in best shape in Bolgheri. The 17 hectares of vineyards are scattered with many different varieties, both Mediterranean and Caucasian, condensed in the Jassarte label, and reflect a desire to experiment. Meticulous cellar work produces wines that are as flawlessly made as they are terroir-true. The varieties include vermentino and sangiovese as well as the classic cabernet sauvignon and franc, and merlot. After tasting, we believe the Bolgheri Superiore Atis 2013 is still the winery's best wine. Compared to the previous version, which was enchanting, it has lost something of the fruit and intensity, throwing open the doors to more strongly marked grassy, balsamic aromas. The palate is very good, though, elegant and succulent. The Bolgheri Rosso Rute 2014 and Jassarte 2013 are good but rather simple.

● Bolgheri Rosso Sup. Atis '13	♥♥	6
● Bolgheri Rosso Rute '14	♥	4
● Jassarte '13	♥	5
● Bolgheri Rosso Sup. Atis '12	♀♀♀	6
● Bolgheri Rosso Rute '13	♀♀	5

Tenuta Guado al Tasso

LOC. BOLGHERI
S.DA BOLGHERESE KM 3,9
57020 CASTAGNETO CARDUCCI [LI]
TEL. +39 0565749735
www.guadoaltasso.it

CELLAR SALES
ANNUAL PRODUCTION 1,500,000 bottles
HECTARES UNDER VINE 300.00

Guado al Tasso is a lovely estate of 1000 hectares including vineyards, woodlands and Mediterranean scrubland, and wine production obviously plays a leading role in this marvellous natural landscape. The 300 or so hectares under vine include the zone's most representative grape varieties: merlot, cabernet sauvignon, petit verdot, sangiovese for the reds, and the all-important vermentino for the whites. The estate belongs to the historic Antinori constellation, among the top Italian wine producers. The Bolgheri Rosso Superiore Guado al Tasso 2013 offers very positive sensations: full, mature yet fresh aromas of red and black berries, enfolded by polished spicy and toasty notes, with a well-structured, meaty, quite lingering palate. The Bruciato 2014 simpler, but still among the best Bolgheri Rossos of its year tasted so far.

● Bolgheri Rosso Il Bruciato '14	▼▼ 5
● Bolgheri Rosso Sup. Guado al Tasso '13	▼▼ 8
○ Bolgheri Vermentino '15	▼ 3
● Bolgheri Rosso Sup. Guado al Tasso '01	♀♀♀ 8
⊙ Bolgheri Rosato Scalabrone '11	♀♀ 3
⊙ Bolgheri Rosato Scalabrone '10	♀♀ 3*
● Bolgheri Rosso Il Bruciato '13	♀♀ 5
● Bolgheri Rosso Il Bruciato '12	♀♀ 4
● Bolgheri Rosso Sup. Guado al Tasso '12	♀♀ 8
● Bolgheri Rosso Sup. Guado al Tasso '10	♀♀ 8
○ Bolgheri Vermentino '14	♀♀ 3
○ Bolgheri Vermentino '13	♀♀ 3
○ Bolgheri Vermentino '12	♀♀ 3
○ Bolgheri Vermentino '11	♀♀ 3

Tenute Guicciardini Strozzi

LOC. CUSONA, 5
53037 SAN GIMIGNANO [SI]
TEL. +39 0577950028
www.guicciardinistrozzi.it

CELLAR SALES
PRE-BOOKED VISITS
ANNUAL PRODUCTION 800,000 bottles
HECTARES UNDER VINE 115.00

530 hectares and over 1000 years of history: this is how we might describe the Cusona estate, through the memory of the Mona Lisa painted by Leonardo Da Vinci, counted among the family ancestors. The father of current owner Girolamo Strozzi first bottled Vernaccia in Bordeaux bottles in 1933. About 20 years ago the winegrowing activity expanded into Tuscan's Maremma area, between Bolgheri, Scansano and Montemassi, and to Pantelleria, producing 22 different types of wine. The Vernaccia Riserva 2013 made it to the finals thanks to its elegant profile, starting with the aromas: hints of aromatic herbs alongside nuances of citron. The palate makes a good impact, not too powerful but balanced with elegant structure and a light, simple finish. The Sòdole 2011, a Sangiovese, is enjoyable, with austere aromas in which tobacco and leather overcome the fruit. The palate is juicy and meaty with a simple, slightly drawn finish. The remaining Vernaccias are well made.

○ Vernaccia di S. Gimignano Ris. '13	▼▼ 3*
● Sòdole '11	▼▼ 5
○ Arabesque '15	▼ 2
● Chianti Colli Senesi Titolato Strozzi '15	▼ 2
○ Vernaccia di S. Gimignano Cusona 1933 '14	▼ 3
○ Vernaccia di S. Gimignano Titolato Strozzi '15	▼ 2
● Millanni '08	♀♀ 6
● Morellino di Scansano Titolato Strozzi '12	♀♀ 2*
○ Vernaccia di S. Gimignano Cusona 1933 '12	♀♀ 3
○ Vernaccia di S. Gimignano Ris. '12	♀♀ 3
○ Vernaccia di S. Gimignano Titolato Strozzi '12	♀♀ 2*

★★Isole e Olena

Loc. Isole, 1
50021 Barberino Val d'Elsa [FI]
Tel. +39 0558072763
www.isoleolena.it

CELLAR SALES
PRE-BOOKED VISITS
ANNUAL PRODUCTION 200,000 bottles
HECTARES UNDER VINE 56.00

Paolo De Marchi's estate is widely
acknowledged to be one of the best in
Chianti Classico and has shown no fall in
standards over its many years of textbook
stylistic continuity, based on fully ripe fruit
and judicious selection of oak for
maturation. Another distinctive feature of
Isole e Olena wines is the faithful
interpretation of the terroir, making them a
sound and consistent model for the whole
DOC zone. The Cepparello 2013 is an
impressive version, probably one of the
best. The aromas are very complex,
blending hints of blood-rich meat, flowers
and forest floor, polished by well-defined
nuances of fresh cherries. The palate is
weighty and broad, with a succulent, deep
flavour and a delightful salty hint in the
finish. The fragrant, and relaxed Chianti
Classico is well made and easily overcomes
the problems of the vintage.

Istine

via Roma, 11
53017 Radda in Chianti [SI]
Tel. +39 0577733684
www.istine.it

ANNUAL PRODUCTION 32,000 bottles
HECTARES UNDER VINE 34.00

Istine's ambitious project, earning it the
Up-and-Coming Winery award, consists of
three separate vineyards. Two are in the
Radda subzone and one in Gaiole in
Chianti, with distinct aspect, altitude and
soil composition, organic methods,
pared-down traditional cellar procedures
such as ageing in large oak barrels. In
addition, Angela Fronti, founder of the
estate, always offers particularly elegant,
invigorating wines with a well-focused,
highly readable profile. The Chianti Classico
LeVigne Riserva 2013 is really delicious,
and one of the best of its type. Not only
does it combine complexity and appeal in
the flavour, the aromas are accomplished,
fragrant and multilayered. The Chianti
Classico 2014 is also very good: with
subtle aromas and a slender-bodied,
vigorous palate. The Chianti Classico Vigna
Cavarchione 2014 is good, slightly veiled
on the nose but with a progressive,
flavoursome palate.

● Cepparello '13	▼▼▼ 8
● Cabernet Sauvignon Collezione De Marchi '12	▼▼ 8
● Chianti Cl. '14	▼▼ 5
● Cepparello '12	♈♈♈ 8
● Cepparello '09	♈♈♈ 8
● Cepparello '07	♈♈♈ 8
● Cepparello '06	♈♈♈ 8
● Cepparello '05	♈♈♈ 8
● Cepparello '03	♈♈♈ 7
● Cepparello '01	♈♈♈ 6
● Cepparello '00	♈♈♈ 6
● Cepparello '11	♈♈ 8
● Cepparello '08	♈♈ 8
● Chianti Cl. '13	♈♈ 5

● Chianti Cl. LeVigne Ris. '13	▼▼▼ 3*
● Chianti Cl. '14	▼▼ 3*
● Chianti Cl. V. Cavarchione '14	▼▼ 3
● Chianti Cl. V. Istine '14	▼▼ 3
● Chianti Cl. '13	♈♈ 3
● Chianti Cl. '11	♈♈ 3
● Chianti Cl. '10	♈♈ 3*
● Chianti Cl. Le Vigne Ris. '12	♈♈ 3*
● Chianti Cl. V. Casanova '13	♈♈ 3*
● Chianti Cl. V. Casanova '12	♈♈ 3
● Chianti Cl. V. Istine '13	♈♈ 3
● Chianti Cl. V. Istine '12	♈♈ 3

Maurizio Lambardi

LOC. CANALICCHIO DI SOTTO, 8
53024 MONTALCINO [SI]
TEL. +39 0577848476
www.lambardimontalcino.it

CELLAR SALES
PRE-BOOKED VISITS
ANNUAL PRODUCTION 17,000 bottles
HECTARES UNDER VINE 6.50

Canalicchio di Sotto, owned by the Lambardi family since 1965, is located in the north-eastern area of Montalcino. About six hectares of vineyards are mainly planted to sangiovese at altitudes of around 350 metres, on clayey tuffstone soil with plenty of stony material. Maurizio is at the helm today, carrying forward and even strengthening the stylistic imprint of lengthy maceration and ageing in 30- and 50-hectolitre Slavonian oak. The reds are traditional but not retro, and the best versions achieve a happy medium between supple structure and vigour, northern aromatic qualities and a much more southern tannic texture. An unquestionably effective identikit for the Brunello 2011: a truly classic nose with pipe tobacco, topsoil, dried flowers, apparently more open and approachable than the palate. The tannins still have plenty of bite but the sound fruit and close-knit, tangy texture are indicative of a good year.

● Brunello di Montalcino '11	🍷🍷 5
● Rosso di Montalcino '14	🍷 3
● Brunello di Montalcino '10	🍷🍷 5
● Brunello di Montalcino '09	🍷🍷 5
● Brunello di Montalcino '08	🍷🍷 5
● Brunello di Montalcino '07	🍷🍷 5
● Brunello di Montalcino '06	🍷🍷 5
● Brunello di Montalcino '05	🍷🍷 5

Lamole di Lamole

LOC. LAMOLE
50022 GREVE IN CHIANTI [FI]
TEL. +39 0559331411
www.lamole.com

CELLAR SALES
PRE-BOOKED VISITS
RESTAURANT SERVICE
ANNUAL PRODUCTION 242,000 bottles
HECTARES UNDER VINE 57.00
SUSTAINABLE WINERY

Villa Vistarenni at Gaiole in Chianti, Sassoregale in Maremma and Lamole di Lamole in Greve, the latter in a particularly well-suited area of the wonderful Chianti mosaic: these are the locations chosen by the Santa Margherita group for their Tuscan wine production. The Chianti Classico DOC wines present a very well-focused style, typically drinkable, harmonious and elegant. This is due to sustainable winegrowing practices and meticulous cellarwork, culminating in judicious use of large and small oak barrels. The Chianti Classico Etichetta Bianca 2013 is really delicious: fragrant, airy aromas and a lively, complex palate with a coherent and almost irresistible flavour. The Chianti Classico Etichetta Blu 2013 is also good: more modern in style, with more focus on sweetness than contrasts. The well-made Chianti Classico Riserva 2012 presents subtle aromas of spice and fruit with a deep, firm flavour.

● Chianti Cl. Lamole di Lamole Et. Bianca '13	🍷🍷🍷 3*
● Chianti Cl. Lamole di Lamole Et. Blu '13	🍷🍷 3
● Chianti Cl. Ris. '12	🍷🍷 3
● Maremma Merlot Sassoregale '14	🍷🍷 3
● Maremma Sangiovese Sassoregale '14	🍷🍷 3
● Chianti Cl. Gran Sel. Vign. di Campolungo '10	🍷🍷🍷 5
● Chianti Cl. Lamole di Lamole Et. Blu '12	🍷🍷🍷 3*
● Chianti Cl. Vign. di Campolungo Ris. '09	🍷🍷🍷 5
● Chianti Cl. Vign. di Campolungo Ris. '08	🍷🍷🍷 5
● Chianti Cl. Gran Sel. Vign. di Campolungo '11	🍷🍷 5
● Chianti Cl. Lamole di Lamole Et. Bianca '12	🍷🍷 3
● Chianti Cl. Lamole di Lamole Et. Blu '11	🍷🍷 3
● Chianti Cl. Lamole di Lamole Ris. '10	🍷🍷 4

La Lastra

FRAZ. SANTA LUCIA
VIA R. DE GRADA, 9
53037 SAN GIMIGNANO [SI]
TEL. +39 0577941781
www.lalastra.it

CELLAR SALES
PRE-BOOKED VISITS
ANNUAL PRODUCTION 58,000 bottles
HECTARES UNDER VINE 7.00
SUSTAINABLE WINERY

Environment before business, people before
brand, substance before appearance: these
are the principles of La Lastra's company
philosophy. The estate was established in
the mid-Nineties by Nadia Betti and her
husband Renato Spanu, after a decade of
studies and work as winegrowing
consultants. Nadia's brother Christian
immediately became involved in the project
along with friends Enrico Paternoster and
Valerio Zorzi, with the aim of producing fine
quality, eco-sustainable wines that express
the features of their terroir. Through to the
finals for the Vernaccia Riserva 2014:
stylish, elegant aromas, recognizable
aromatic herbs like thyme and mint,
followed by apples and floral hints, blended
well into a beautifully toned palate, with
clearly defined freshness, tempting juicy
fruit and a lengthy, well-sustained finish.
The Rovaio 2011 is an equal blend of
sangiovese, cabernet sauvignon, and
merlot which opens well on the nose,
slightly grassy but interesting, with a
slender, supple body, fine-grained tannins,
excellent length.

○ Vernaccia di S. Gimignano Ris. '14	♟♟ 3*
● Rovaio '11	♟♟ 4
○ Vernaccia di S. Gimignano '15	♟ 2
○ Vernaccia di S. Gimignano Ris. '09	♟♟♟ 3*
● Rovaio '09	♟♟ 4
○ Vernaccia di S. Gimignano '13	♟♟ 2*
○ Vernaccia di S. Gimignano '12	♟♟ 2*
○ Vernaccia di S. Gimignano '11	♟♟ 2*
○ Vernaccia di S. Gimignano '10	♟♟ 2*
○ Vernaccia di S. Gimignano Ris. '12	♟♟ 3*
○ Vernaccia di S. Gimignano Ris. '11	♟♟ 3*
○ Vernaccia di S. Gimignano Ris. '10	♟♟ 3*

Fattoria Lavacchio

VIA DI MONTEFIESOLE, 55
50065 PONTASSIEVE [FI]
TEL. +39 0558317472
www.fattorialavacchio.com

CELLAR SALES
PRE-BOOKED VISITS
ACCOMMODATION AND RESTAURANT SERVICE
ANNUAL PRODUCTION 120,000 bottles
HECTARES UNDER VINE 22.00
VITICULTURE METHOD Certified Organic
SUSTAINABLE WINERY

From the top of the Montefiesole hill, at
450 metres altitude, a typical Tuscan
landscape of olive groves and vineyards
unfolds. This is the home of Lavacchio, built
in the 1700s by the Peruzzi family and run
today by Faye Lottero. This was one of the
first local estates to strongly believe in the
importance and necessity of organic
farming. Today the 22-hectare vineyard, the
olive groves and the cereal crops, are
farmed with full respect for the
environment and terroir. Other satellite
businesses have grown up around the
farm, such as a restaurant, agritourism
centre, shop and typical, fully functional
windmill, renovated in 2011 to grind the
farm's own wheat. In the absence of the
Riserva Ludiè this year, the Cedro leads
the range: ripe red berries blended with
spice from the oak herald the succulent,
coherent palate. A good performance from
the Fontegalli 2011 too, from merlot and
syrah, with a soft palate, velvety tannins
and vanilla in the finish.

● Chianti Rufina Cedro '14	♟♟ 2*
● Fontegalli '11	♟♟ 4
● Chianti Puro '15	♟ 2
● Chianti Rufina Cedro Ris. '11	♟ 3
○ Oro del Cedro V. T. '14	♟ 5
● Chianti Rufina Cedro '12	♟♟ 2*
● Chianti Rufina Cedro Ris. '10	♟♟ 4
● Chianti Rufina Ludié Ris. '10	♟♟ 5
● Fontegalli '08	♟♟ 5
○ Oro del Cedro V. T. '12	♟♟ 5
○ Pachar '13	♟♟ 4
○ Pachar '12	♟♟ 4
○ Vin Santo del Chianti Rufina Ris. '09	♟♟ 5
○ Vin Santo del Chianti Rufina Ris. '08	♟♟ 5

La Lecciaia

LOC. VALLAFRICO
53024 MONTALCINO [SI]
TEL. +39 0583928366
www.lecciaia.it

PRE-BOOKED VISITS
ANNUAL PRODUCTION 200,000 bottles
HECTARES UNDER VINE 16.00

La Lecciaia, in eastern Montalcino, was taken over and extensively renovated in the early Eighties by Mauro Pacini. About 16 of the overall 70 hectares are under vine and sangiovese takes the lion's share, naturally able to reflect the unique pedoclimatic conditions of altitudes around 450 metres, sandy and clayey soil rich in stony material, and dry, breezy weather. The basic Brunello and the Vigna Manapetra cru, both produced in Riserva version in the most favourable years, are mainly aged in large oak barrels after 2-3 weeks temperature-controlled maceration. The range appears in its entirety with the four La Lecciaia Brunellos. The most impressive was the Vigna Manapetra Riserva 2010, with prestigious citrus and balsam shading, not fully supported by the almondy flavour. The Riserva of the same year is slightly more slender with a similar profile, including hints of mandarins.

● Brunello di Montalcino Ris. '10	❦❦ 6
● Brunello di Montalcino V. Manapetra Ris. '10	❦❦ 6
● Brunello di Montalcino '11	❦ 5
● Brunello di Montalcino V. Manapetra '11	❦ 6
● Brunello di Montalcino V. Manapetra '09	❦❦❦ 6
● Brunello di Montalcino '10	♈♈ 5
● Brunello di Montalcino Ris. '09	♈♈ 6
● Brunello di Montalcino Ris. '08	♈♈ 6
● Brunello di Montalcino V. Manapetra '10	♈♈ 6
● Brunello di Montalcino V. Manapetra '08	♈♈ 5
● Brunello di Montalcino V. Manapetra Ris. '08	♈♈ 6
● Rosso di Montalcino '11	♈♈ 3

Tenuta Lenzini

FRAZ. GRAGNANO
VIA DELLA CHIESA, 44
55012 CAPANNORI [LU]
TEL. +39 0583974037
www.tenutalenzini.it

CELLAR SALES
PRE-BOOKED VISITS
ACCOMMODATION
ANNUAL PRODUCTION 60,000 bottles
HECTARES UNDER VINE 14.00
VITICULTURE METHOD Certified Organic

Gragnano is a splendid area, particularly well-suited to cultivating olives and vines. Here in the hills around Lucca, Tenuta Lenzini farms 13 hectares of vineyards planted to merlot, cabernet sauvignon, syrah, and alicante bouschet. Apart from the grape varieties, the encouraging results are due to well thought-out winegrowing methods, and cellar practices that respect the fruit. The estate has ancient farming roots but the business as we know it today started in 2007. Light and dark shading is our overall impression this year due to the different vintages. The Vermignon, from vermentino and sauvignon grapes, presents vibrant, stylish aromas with quite juicy fruit. The Colline Lucchesi Rosso Casa e Chiesa 2014 is strongly marked by the vintage year, with light spice aromas and a tannic palate.

○ Vermignon '15	❦❦ 3
● Colline Lucchesi Rosso Casa e Chiesa '14	❦ 3
● Poggio de' Paoli '12	❦ 4
● Poggio de' Paoli '07	♈♈ 4
● Syrah '12	♈♈ 5
● Syrah '11	♈♈ 5
● Syrah '07	♈♈ 4
○ Vermignon '14	♈♈ 3

Cantine Leonardo da Vinci

VIA PROVINCIALE MERCATALE, 291
50059 VINCI [FI]
TEL. +39 0571902444
www.cantineleonardo.it

CELLAR SALES
PRE-BOOKED VISITS
ACCOMMODATION AND RESTAURANT SERVICE
ANNUAL PRODUCTION 4,500,000 bottles
HECTARES UNDER VINE 750.00

Numbers are a bit impersonal but sometimes they tell a better story than a thousand words. 1961: 30 members, 70 hectares. Today, about 200 members and over 750 hectares of vineyards. Credit goes to a group of winegrowers who have believed in their terroir and in fine quality wine, and refused to be held back. They bought the Cantina di Montalcino in 1990 and in little more than 50 years have achieved exponential growth in quality and organization, so much so that in 2002 the estate created a secondary branch for distribution, Delle Vigne. Another turning point came in 2012 when the estate joined the Caviro group. The Chianti Da Vinci Riserva 2013 made the final tastings: a subtle, stylish bouquet of wild berries, light spice aromas of cloves and cinnamon, and balsamic hints. The palate makes a good entry, warm and harmonious, with a lipsmacking, lingering, flavoursome finish. The enjoyable Leonardo 2014 displays vanilla and juniper, raspberries and strawberries on the nose, and a creamy, gentle, soft and generous flavour.

● Chianti Da Vinci Ris. '13	♟♟ 3*
○ Bianco dell'Empolese	
Vin Santo Da Vinci '09	♟♟ 5
● Brunello di Montalcino	
Cantina di Montalcino '11	♟♟ 5
● Leonardo '14	♟♟ 2*
● Chianti '15	♟ 2
● Rosso di Montalcino	
Cantina di Montalcino '14	♟ 3
● Chianti Da Vinci Ris. '12	♟♟ 3*
● Chianti Da Vinci Ris. '11	♟♟ 3*
● Chianti Da Vinci Ris. '10	♟♟ 3

Tenuta di Lilliano

LOC. LILLIANO, 8
53011 CASTELLINA IN CHIANTI [SI]
TEL. +39 0577743070
www.lilliano.com

CELLAR SALES
PRE-BOOKED VISITS
ACCOMMODATION
ANNUAL PRODUCTION 150,000 bottles
HECTARES UNDER VINE 35.00

The earliest inspiration for Tenuta di Lilliano, owned by the Ruspoli family for almost a century, came from figures like Enzo Morganti and Giulio Gambelli, who shaped the history of Chianti Classico. Today the products have absorbed more prominent contemporary elements, while still respecting Chianti tradition. The result is a range of wines in a meticulous style, with typically lush fruit and harmonious use of large and small oak, often revealing character and complexity over time. The Chianti Classico Riserva 2013 tends towards the austere: elegant and well made with all the traditional components of its type, starting with floral, earthy aromas and a dynamic, flavoursome palate. The Chianti Classico Gran Selezione 2012 is a bit more modern in style, with sweeter flavour and enthralling, vibrant aromas. The Chianti Classico 2014 is appealing although very simple.

● Chianti Cl. Ris. '13	♟♟♟ 5
● Chianti Cl. Gran Sel. '12	♟♟ 5
● Chianti Cl. '14	♟ 3
● Chianti Cl. '10	♟♟♟ 3*
● Chianti Cl. '09	♟♟♟ 3
● Chianti Cl. Gran Sel. '11	♟♟♟ 5
● Chianti Cl. Gran Sel. Ris. '10	♟♟♟ 6
● Chianti Cl. '13	♟♟ 3
● Chianti Cl. '11	♟♟ 3
● Chianti Cl. '08	♟♟ 4
● Chianti Cl. Ris '08	♟♟ 5
● Chianti Cl. Ris. '11	♟♟ 5
● Chianti Cl. Ris. '10	♟♟ 5
● Chianti Cl. Ris. '09	♟♟ 5

Lisini

FRAZ. SANT'ANGELO IN COLLE
POD. CASANOVA
53024 MONTALCINO [SI]
TEL. +39 0577844040
www.lisini.com

CELLAR SALES
PRE-BOOKED VISITS
ANNUAL PRODUCTION 90,000 bottles
HECTARES UNDER VINE 21.00

The Lisini family, active in Montalcino since the late 19th century, is among the few who can lay claim to a cellar of bottles dating back to the 1960s, making it a historic estate in the truest sense of the world. This legacy is still relevant today and is primarily based on about 20 hectares of vineyards, all planted to sangiovese, mostly in the Sesta area, with one significant exception: the Ugolaia cru, with its recognizable red and tuffstone soil. Holding the compact range together is a concept of flavoursome, austere Brunellos designed to last over time, aged in medium-sized Slavonian oak. The contest between the 2010 Lisini wines ends pretty much in a draw. The Brunello Riserva is all about minimalism, with classic aromas of truffles, dried flowers and leather. The Ugolaia presents darker fruit and richer texture, more curbed in this phase by vigorous tannins and generous alcohol.

● Brunello di Montalcino Ris. '10	♟♟ 7	
● Brunello di Montalcino Ugolaia '10	♟♟ 8	
● Brunello di Montalcino '11	♟ 6	
● San Biagio '14	♟ 2	
● Brunello di Montalcino '90	♟♟♟ 5	
● Brunello di Montalcino '88	♟♟♟ 5	
● Brunello di Montalcino Ugolaia '06	♟♟♟ 8	
● Brunello di Montalcino Ugolaia '04	♟♟♟ 8	
● Brunello di Montalcino Ugolaia '01	♟♟♟ 8	
● Brunello di Montalcino Ugolaia '00	♟♟♟ 7	
● Brunello di Montalcino Ugolaia '91	♟♟♟ 7	

Livernano

LOC. LIVERNANO, 67A
53017 RADDA IN CHIANTI [SI]
TEL. +39 0577738353
www.livernano.it

CELLAR SALES
PRE-BOOKED VISITS
ACCOMMODATION AND RESTAURANT SERVICE
ANNUAL PRODUCTION 100,000 bottles
HECTARES UNDER VINE 25.00

Livernano's distinctive trait is extreme vineyard management, starting with the almost exclusive use of the bush-training system and a planting density of 7,000 per hectare. Barriques take pride of place in the cellar, underlining the confidently modern approach, and the wines produced are full-bodied and rich in texture with the constant presence of well-handled fruit and toasting to keep the acidity at bay without coarseness. The estate also owns the Casalvento winery in the Radda in Chianti area. The Chianti Classico 2013 is very good, especially thanks to the consistent, well-paced and very tangy flavour, supported by clear-cut, nicely fragrant aromas. The Chianti Classico Casalvento 2013 is also good: nicely contrasting, lipsmacking flavour and aromas of spice and pencil lead which slightly overwhelm the hints of fruit. The Chianti Classico Riserva 2013 presents more austere aromas but the palate is firm with close-knit tannins, generous and succulent.

● Chianti Cl. '13	♟♟ 3*	
● Chianti Cl. Casalvento '13	♟♟ 5	
● Chianti Cl. Ris. '13	♟♟ 4	
● Chianti Cl. Ris. '04	♟♟♟ 4	
● Livernano '05	♟♟♟ 6	
● Livernano '03	♟♟♟ 6	
● Livernano '99	♟♟♟ 7	
● Chianti Cl. '12	♟♟ 3*	
● Chianti Cl. '10	♟♟ 3	
● Chianti Cl. Gran Selezione '11	♟♟ 7	
● Chianti Cl. Ris. '11	♟♟ 4	
● Chianti Cl. Ris. '10	♟♟ 4	
○ L'Anima '14	♟♟ 3	
● Purosangue '10	♟♟ 5	

Lunadoro

FRAZ. VALIANO
LOC. TERRAROSSA PAGLIERETO
53040 MONTEPULCIANO [SI]
TEL. 348 2215188
wwww.lunadoro.com

CELLAR SALES
PRE-BOOKED VISITS
ACCOMMODATION
ANNUAL PRODUCTION 60,000 bottles
HECTARES UNDER VINE 12.00
VITICULTURE METHOD Certified Organic
SUSTAINABLE WINERY

The estate recently purchased by Swiss company Schenk Italian Wineries is situated in the Valiano area. Established in 2002, it is one of the youngest productive estates in the Nobile di Montepulciano DOC zone. The wines display clearly focused style and excellent quality with very reassuring consistency. Credit is due to painstaking and meticulous work in both vineyard and cellar, where pointless forcing is avoided during the vinification process. Clear-cut, nicely complex aromas in the Nobile di Montepulciano Quercione Riserva 2012, blending with spice from the oak and lovely fresh, sound fruit. The palate is coherent, broad and supple, and not without depth. The Nobile Pagliareto 2013 is more fragrant and well paced, with a tangy flavour just lacking a bit of complexity. Perhaps one of the best, the Rosso di Montepulciano Prugnanello 2014 is absolutely appealing, with a sweet entry and delicious flavour.

I Luoghi

LOC. CAMPO AL CAPRIOLO, 201
57022 CASTAGNETO CARDUCCI [LI]
TEL. +39 0565777379
www.iluoghi.it

CELLAR SALES
ANNUAL PRODUCTION 15,000 bottles
HECTARES UNDER VINE 3.80
VITICULTURE METHOD Certified Organic

Stefano Granata and his wife Paola have set up a delightful little winery with its own vineyard, a definitely original addition to the Bolgheri area. The couple runs the estate lovingly and intimately, taking care of all the phases of vineyard management (on two separate plots), vinification, ageing and sales of wine. The house style is unmistakeably elegant and personal, never too rich or full-bodied. One of the most successful family-run artisan wineries in the area. A fantastic Podere Ritorti 2013 breezes away with Tre Bicchieri. This wine is far removed from packaged or standardized styles, with earthy, minerally aromas and lovely hints of leather and pipe tobacco. The texture is very elegant and flavoursome, never too groomed but extremely pleasing. The Campo al Fico 2013 is less clearly defined, with aromas slightly veiled by foxy sensations, but engaging nonetheless.

● Nobile di Montepulciano Quercione Ris. '12	♟♟♟ 4
● Nobile di Montepulciano Pagliareto '13	♟♟ 3
● Rosso di Montepulciano Prugnanello '14	♟♟ 2*
● Nobile di Montepulciano '11	♟♟ 4
● Nobile di Montepulciano '09	♟♟ 4
● Nobile di Montepulciano '08	♟♟ 3
● Nobile di Montepulciano Pagliareto '12	♟♟ 4
● Nobile di Montepulciano Quercione '11	♟♟ 4
● Nobile di Montepulciano Quercione '10	♟♟ 4
● Nobile di Montepulciano Quercione Ris. '09	♟♟ 5
● Rosso di Montepulciano Primo Senso '11	♟♟ 3

● Bolgheri Sup. Podere Ritorti '13	♟♟♟ 5
● Bolgheri Sup. Campo al Fico '13	♟♟ 7
● Bolgheri Sup. Campo al Fico '10	♟♟♟ 7
● Bolgheri Sup. Campo al Fico '09	♟♟♟ 7
● Bolgheri Sup. Campo al Fico '08	♟♟♟ 7
● Bolgheri Sup. Campo al Fico '07	♟♟ 7
● Bolgheri Sup. Campo al Fico '06	♟♟ 7
● Bolgheri Sup. Podere Ritorti '12	♟♟ 5
● Bolgheri Sup. Podere Ritorti '11	♟♟ 5
● Bolgheri Sup. Podere Ritorti '10	♟♟ 5
● Bolgheri Sup. Podere Ritorti '09	♟♟ 5
● Bolgheri Sup. Podere Ritorti '08	♟♟ 5
● Bolgheri Sup. Podere Ritorti '07	♟♟ 4

★Le Macchiole

LOC. BOLGHERI
VIA BOLGHERESE, 189A
57022 CASTAGNETO CARDUCCI [LI]
TEL. +39 0565766092
www.lemacchiole.it

PRE-BOOKED VISITS
ANNUAL PRODUCTION 157,000 bottles
HECTARES UNDER VINE 27.00

Le Macchiole tells one of the loveliest, most fascinating stories of Bolgheri wine. So it deserves to be a benchmark brand for Made in Italy wines, as one of the first to bring out the area's emerging potential. The foundation dates back to 1983, thanks to Eugenio Campolmi and Cinzia Merli, who were able to translate their passion into a business. Today Le Macchiole is a dynamic, estate, attentive to changes in the wine sector and looking to express these with skill and originality. As it always has. The best wine we tasted this year is the Paleo 2013: a very intense red led by the vintage year along a path of elegance and depth. Black berry fruit and forest floor on the nose, with stylish balsamic and grassy hints. A few toasty sensations still need to blend in, but bottle ageing should complete the picture. The Paleo Bianco 2014 also made a very good impression.

Le Macioche

S.DA PROV.LE 55 DI SANT'ANTIMO KM 4,850
53024 MONTALCINO [SI]
TEL. +39 0577849168
www.lemacioche.it

CELLAR SALES
PRE-BOOKED VISITS
ACCOMMODATION
ANNUAL PRODUCTION 18,000 bottles
HECTARES UNDER VINE 3.00

It will take a few years to assess any productive and stylistic changes at Le Macioche, the historic Montalcino estate recently taken over by friends (and now business partners) Riccardo Calieri, Stefano Brunetto and Massimo Bronzato. The headquarters is still the small estate with three hectares of vineyards extending over the south-west slopes of Sant'Antimo, on soil of marine origin rich in limestone and marl. Until now we have been used to airy, sometimes almost lean Brunellos, their character supported by pared-down cellar procedures: spontaneous fermentation in wooden vats and lengthy ageing in 40-hectolitre barrels. Just one wine in this round of tastings, the excellent 2011 Brunello. In true Le Macioche style, it displays penetrating hints of citrus, berries, and dried spices, and enters the palate with streamlined, youthful ease, perhaps too much so for the imposing tannic weight.

● Paleo Rosso '13	▼▼▼ 8
○ Bolgheri Bianco Paleo '14	▼▼ 6
● Messorio '13	▼▼ 8
● Scrio '13	▼▼ 8
● Messorio '07	♀♀♀ 8
● Messorio '06	♀♀♀ 8
● Paleo Rosso '12	♀♀♀ 8
● Paleo Rosso '11	♀♀♀ 8
● Paleo Rosso '10	♀♀♀ 8
● Paleo Rosso '09	♀♀♀ 8
● Paleo Rosso '03	♀♀♀ 8
● Paleo Rosso '01	♀♀♀ 8
● Scrio '08	♀♀♀ 8

● Brunello di Montalcino '11	▼▼ 7
● Brunello di Montalcino '10	♀♀ 7
● Brunello di Montalcino '09	♀♀ 7
● Brunello di Montalcino '08	♀♀ 7
● Brunello di Montalcino '07	♀♀ 7
● Brunello di Montalcino '06	♀♀ 6
● Brunello di Montalcino '04	♀♀ 6
● Brunello di Montalcino '00	♀♀ 5
● Brunello di Montalcino Ris. '06	♀♀ 8
● Brunello di Montalcino Ris. '01	♀♀ 6
● Rosso di Montalcino '13	♀♀ 4
● Rosso di Montalcino '11	♀♀ 4
● Rosso di Montalcino '10	♀♀ 4
● Rosso di Montalcino '09	♀♀ 4

La Mannella

LOC. LA MANNELLA, 322
53024 MONTALCINO [SI]
TEL. +39 0577848268
www.lamannella.it

PRE-BOOKED VISITS
ANNUAL PRODUCTION 35,000 bottles
HECTARES UNDER VINE 8.00

Marco Cortonesi is one of the most highly esteemed winegrowers in Montalcino, and not only for the excellent Brunellos he has produced since 1990 at La Mannella. The estate was created in the early 1970s and totals about eight hectares under vine in the north, above the winery, at 200-250 metres altitude on clayey soil, and in the south-east, at almost 400 metres, on stony limestone marl. The leading wines undergo lengthy temperature-controlled maceration in stainless steel and varying ageing periods in Slavonian oak, while a percentage of the I Poggiarelli cru matures in barriques. At the risk of repeating ourselves, once again the solid teamwork stands out more than one single peak. However the Brunello Riserva 2010 is a lot of fun, rich in aromas of colonial spice and roots with classic, solid flavour. The Brunello I Poggiarelli 2011 seems to lack a little energy and weight, but while the nose offers bottled fruit and talcum powder.

● Brunello di Montalcino Ris. '10	♥♥♥	6
● Brunello di Montalcino I Poggiarelli '11	♥♥	5
● Rosso di Montalcino '14	♥♥	3
● Brunello di Montalcino '11	♥	5
● Brunello di Montalcino '10	♀♀	5
● Brunello di Montalcino '09	♀♀	5
● Brunello di Montalcino '08	♀♀	5
● Brunello di Montalcino '07	♀♀	5
● Brunello di Montalcino Ris. '06	♀♀	6
● Brunello di Montalcino I Poggiarelli '10	♀♀	5
● Brunello di Montalcino I Poggiarelli '09	♀♀	5
● Brunello di Montalcino I Poggiarelli '08	♀♀	5
● Brunello di Montalcino I Poggiarelli '07	♀♀	5
● Rosso di Montalcino '13	♀♀	3

Il Marroneto

LOC. MADONNA DELLE GRAZIE, 307
53024 MONTALCINO [SI]
TEL. +39 0577849382
www.ilmarroneto.it

CELLAR SALES
PRE-BOOKED VISITS
ANNUAL PRODUCTION 30,000 bottles
HECTARES UNDER VINE 6.00
SUSTAINABLE WINERY

This old chestnut drying room overlooking the Montosoli hillside was converted into a winery by Giuseppe Mori in the 1970s, hence its name, Il Marroneto. Today, the farm managed by his son Alessandro has become one of the brightest stars in the Montalcino firmament, thanks above all to the worldwide fame of the Madonna delle Grazie cru. Credit is due to the unmistakeable style, with little interference, that was just waiting to be fully understood. Lengthy ageing in Slavonian oak barrels of various ages and sizes sets free the purest, northern soul of the Brunello, a gift of authentic delight for those who treasure it patiently. The winning run of great versions continues with the Madonna delle Grazie 2011: the hot year is clear in the aromas of dark fruit, but the hints of wood resin, incense and balsam suggest complexity and breadth. Not to mention the amazingly tangy tannic texture, as vigorous as it is defined, leaving us in no doubt as to its ageability.

● Brunello di Montalcino Madonna delle Grazie '11	♥♥♥	8
● Brunello di Montalcino '11	♥♥	7
● Brunello di Montalcino Madonna delle Grazie '10	♀♀♀	8
● Brunello di Montalcino Madonna delle Grazie '08	♀♀♀	8
● Brunello di Montalcino '10	♀♀	7
● Brunello di Montalcino '09	♀♀	7
● Brunello di Montalcino '08	♀♀	7
● Brunello di Montalcino Madonna delle Grazie '09	♀♀	8
● Rosso di Montalcino Ignaccio '13	♀♀	3
● Rosso di Montalcino Ignaccio '11	♀♀	3*

Cosimo Maria Masini

VIA POGGIO AL PINO, 16
56028 SAN MINIATO [PI]
TEL. +39 0571465032
www.cosimomariamasini.it

CELLAR SALES
PRE-BOOKED VISITS
ANNUAL PRODUCTION 35,000 bottles
HECTARES UNDER VINE 17.00

The Masini family purchased the estate in 2000. As business entrepreneurs from a different sector, they chose it for its ideal location, a single plot of 40 hectares, and because the organization set up by former owner Cosmo Ridolfi, founder of the agricultural science faculty in Pisa, was suited to winegrowing based on biodynamic methods. This choice was embraced and carried forward by passionate current owner, Cosimo Masini. We liked the Nicole 2015, a monovarietal Sangiovese with fresh, pleasing hints of wild berries and aromatic herbs, and a fluent, slender body with good acidity and a succulent finish. The Cosimo 2015 is based on sangiovese alongside rare varieties like sanforte and buonamico, hints of medicinal herbs and fresh fruit, and a racy, lively, sound palate.

● Cosimo '15	♟♟ 5
○ Daphné '15	♟♟ 4
● Nicole '15	♟♟ 3
○ Vin Santo del Chianti Fedardo '08	♟♟ 4
○ Annick '15	♟ 2
⊙ Matilde '15	♟ 2
● Sincero '15	♟ 2
● Nicole '12	♟♟ 3
● Sincero '13	♟♟ 2*
○ Vin Santo del Chianti Fedardo '06	♟♟ 4

Mastrojanni

FRAZ. CASTELNUOVO DELL'ABATE
POD. LORETO SAN PIO
53024 MONTALCINO [SI]
TEL. +39 0577835681
www.mastrojanni.com

CELLAR SALES
PRE-BOOKED VISITS
ACCOMMODATION
ANNUAL PRODUCTION 110,000 bottles
HECTARES UNDER VINE 33.00

Once again we must say: in a period of profound structural upheaval for the historic Montalcino estates, Mastrojanni has probably been most successful in harmonizing the transition from old to new property. Thanks are due to the Illy group, with Andrea Machetti, who have provided continuity for the agronomical and stylistic input concentrated on true grands crus from the south-east of Castelnuovo dell'Abate. These include Vigna Loreto, grown on tuffstone soil and aged in large barrels, and Vigna Schiena d'Asino, from sandy soils and matured in 16-hectolitre oak. Continuing on course, then, with an almost textbook classic rendering that overshadows the oenological details. Another memorable performance, starting with an airy, multilayered 2014 Rosso. Vigna Schiena d'Asino 2010 wins the Brunello contest this time: a symphony of delicious fruit and spices that enfold the palate from the first drop to the last. But the Vigna Loreto 2011 is a close second in breadth and flavour.

● Brunello di Montalcino V. Schiena d'Asino '10	♟♟♟ 8
● Brunello di Montalcino V. Loreto '11	♟♟ 7
● Rosso di Montalcino '14	♟♟ 3*
● Brunello di Montalcino '11	♟♟ 5
● Brunello di Montalcino '97	♟♟♟ 7
● Brunello di Montalcino '90	♟♟♟ 7
● Brunello di Montalcino Ris. '88	♟♟♟ 6
● Brunello di Montalcino Schiena d'Asino '08	♟♟♟ 8
● Brunello di Montalcino Schiena d'Asino '93	♟♟♟ 7
● Brunello di Montalcino Schiena d'Asino '90	♟♟♟ 7
● Brunello di Montalcino V. Loreto '10	♟♟♟ 7
● Brunello di Montalcino V. Loreto '09	♟♟♟ 7

Giorgio Meletti Cavallari

VIA CASONE UGOLINO,12
57022 CASTAGNETO CARDUCCI [LI]
TEL. +39 0565775620
www.giorgiomeletticavallari.it

CELLAR SALES
PRE-BOOKED VISITS
ACCOMMODATION
ANNUAL PRODUCTION 40,000 bottles
HECTARES UNDER VINE 10.00

The Meletti Cavallari are certainly no novices when it comes to Bolgheri wines but Giorgio, who represents the younger generation of the family, has established a new estate consisting of two distinct vineyards on soil rich in stony, skeletal material. Piastraia is situated on the Castagneto hill while Vallone is lower down. The style seems focused, producing mouthwatering, racy wines. The wines presented this year showed alternating highs and lows. The most focused is the Bolgheri Rosso Superiore Impronte 2013: lovely fruity aromas and a supple palate, with hints of wild berries and appealing spicy nuances. The Bolgheri Rosso 2014 is paler, showing the limitations of the year.

● Bolgheri Sup. Impronte '13	🏆🏆 5
● Bolgheri Rosso '14	🏆 3
○ Bolgheri Bianco Borgeri '14	🏆🏆 3
● Bolgheri Rosso Borgeri '13	🏆🏆 3
● Bolgheri Rosso Borgeri '12	🏆🏆 3
● Bolgheri Rosso Borgeri '06	🏆🏆 3
● Bolgheri Rosso Impronte '04	🏆🏆 5
● Bolgheri Sup. Impronte '12	🏆🏆 5
● Bolgheri Sup. Impronte '11	🏆🏆 5

Melini

LOC. GAGGIANO
53036 POGGIBONSI [SI]
TEL. +39 0577998511
www.cantinemelini.it

CELLAR SALES
PRE-BOOKED VISITS
ANNUAL PRODUCTION 3,100,000 bottles
HECTARES UNDER VINE 136.00

Melini and Macchiavelli are the Chianti estates owned by Gruppo Italiano Vini. The history of this Poggibonsi-located brand is the history of Chianti Classico itself: in 1860 Laborel Melini first used the straw flask, resistant to the pressure of the machine-inserted cork, which contributed towards the spread and success of Chianti around the world. Today, the GIV wines produced in the Chianti Classico DOC zone show unparalleled flawless craftsmanship alongside good personality, and sometimes achieve absolute excellence. The strongpoint of the Chianti Classico Terrarossa Gran Selezione 2012 is the aromas, with well-defined fruity and spicy hints, alongside light balsamic nuances. The palate is full-flavoured with a nicely lingering finish echoing toasty and fruity hints. The I Coltri 2015 is a juicy and really delicious blend of sangiovese, cabernet sauvignon and merlot.

● Chianti Cl. Gran Sel. Terrarossa '12	🏆🏆 5
● I Coltri '15	🏆🏆 2*
○ Vernaccia di S. Gimignano Le Grillaie '15	🏆🏆 3
● Chianti Cl. '15	🏆 4
● Chianti Cl. Granaio '14	🏆 4
● Chianti Governo all'uso Toscano '13	🏆 3
● Chianti San Lorenzo '15	🏆 3
● Il Principe Fattoria Machiavelli '14	🏆 5
● Chianti Cl. La Selvanella Ris. '06	🏆🏆🏆 5
● Chianti Cl. La Selvanella Ris. '03	🏆🏆🏆 4
● Chianti Cl. La Selvanella Ris. '01	🏆🏆🏆 4
● Chianti Cl. La Selvanella Ris. '00	🏆🏆🏆 4
● Chianti Cl. La Selvanella Ris. '12	🏆🏆 5

Mocali

LOC. MOCALI
53024 MONTALCINO [SI]
TEL. +39 0577849485
www.mocali.eu

CELLAR SALES
PRE-BOOKED VISITS
ANNUAL PRODUCTION 120,000 bottles
HECTARES UNDER VINE 9.00
VITICULTURE METHOD Certified Organic
SUSTAINABLE WINERY

Tiziano Ciacci has embraced the teachings
of grandfather Dino, often mentioned
among the founding members of the
Corsorzio Brunello di Montalcino in the
post-War period, with a decisive
contribution to the prestigious ten-hectare
Mocali estate, situated mostly on the south-
west route of the DOC zone. The
sangiovese vineyards are situated at
altitudes between 350 and 400 metres, on
compact soil with alberese and limestone
marl, and produce multifaceted reds,
simultaneously even and full-bodied. Their
nature is respected in the cellar, with
procedures adapted to the cru or vintage
(20- and 50-hectolitre oak for the leading
wines). We tasted four Brunellos for this
edition, all excellent, though we slightly
preferred the two 2010 Riservas: the basic
presents a very original woodland and
seafaring profile, and slightly rugged
texture, while the Vigna delle Raunate
shows stronger extract and darker aromas.

Mocine

LOC. MOCINE CHIUSURE
53041 ASCIANO [SI]
TEL. +39 0577707075
www.mocine.it

CELLAR SALES
PRE-BOOKED VISITS
ACCOMMODATION
ANNUAL PRODUCTION 18,000 bottles
HECTARES UNDER VINE 4.00
VITICULTURE METHOD Certified Organic

Mocine is situated in an area of Siena, the
Crete Senesi, which is very well-known for
tourism but less so for wine. This
cooperative could be the first winery to
break this rule. The 800-hectare estate,
which includes a game reserve, an
agritourism and an olive grove, currently
only devotes four hectares to vineyards.
The organically grown grapes are
exclusively traditional Tuscan varieties and
from the province of Siena: sangiovese,
colorino, foglia tonda, barsaglina and
vermentino. Nicely made wines with good,
frank character, aged in small oak casks.
S'indora 2013 is a monovarietal Foglia
Tonda, alternating floral and spicy aromas
and a dynamic, lipsmacking flavour. The
Santa Marta 2015, a blend of sangiovese,
colorino and barsaglina, is fresh and
relaxed on the palate. The interesting Otto
Rintocchi 2014 is a blend of sangiovese,
foglia tonda, colorino and barsaglina, with
just a little too much oakiness.

● Brunello di Montalcino '11	♥♥ 5
● Brunello di Montalcino Ris. '10	♥♥ 7
● Brunello di Montalcino V. delle Raunate '11	♥♥ 6
● Brunello di Montalcino V. delle Raunate Ris. '10	♥♥ 8
● Rosso di Montalcino '14	♥ 2
● Brunello di Montalcino V. delle Raunate '08	♥♥♥ 6
● Brunello di Montalcino '10	♥♥ 5
● Brunello di Montalcino '09	♥♥ 5
● Brunello di Montalcino Ris. '07	♥♥ 7
● Brunello di Montalcino V. delle Raunate '10	♥♥ 6
● Brunello di Montalcino V. delle Raunate '09	♥♥ 6

● Otto Rintocchi '14	♥♥ 4
● S'indora '13	♥♥ 8
● Santa Marta '15	♥♥ 3
○ Alba '15	♥ 3
● Mocine '14	♥ 3

Fattoria Montellori

VIA PISTOIESE, 1
50054 FUCECCHIO [FI]
TEL. +39 0571260641
www.fattoriamontellori.it

CELLAR SALES
PRE-BOOKED VISITS
ACCOMMODATION AND RESTAURANT SERVICE
ANNUAL PRODUCTION 250,000 bottles
HECTARES UNDER VINE 50.00
VITICULTURE METHOD Certified Organic
SUSTAINABLE WINERY

A family estate established in 1895, when leather salesman Giuseppe Nieri purchased the villa and land that make up the historic nucleus and committed himself to farming with passion and good results. In over 100 years the vineyards have been extended and the cellar fitted with more modern equipment, to bring to life remarkable wines in an area of Tuscany that is less appreciated than others with a greater tradition of wine production. In the mid-1980s the farm took on its current identity with Alessandro in charge. The Dicatum 2013, 100% sangiovese, made it to the finals: floral and spicy cardamom aromas, lovely style with a well-balanced palate and a succulent, mouthfilling finish. The Spumante Pas Dosé, from chardonnay grapes, confirms its quality with fresh, lightly citrusy aromas of lime, apples and white peaches, and crusty bread. Generous and nicely textured on the palate with good acidity and a powerful, lingering finish.

● Dicatum '13	♟♟ 5
○ Bianco dell'Empolese Vin Santo '10	♟♟ 5
○ Montellori Pas Dosé '12	♟♟ 5
● Chianti '14	♟ 2
○ Mandorlo '15	♟ 2
● Moro '13	♟ 3
☉ Rosato '15	♟ 5
○ Bianco dell'Empolese Vin Santo '09	♟♟ 5
○ Bianco dell'Empolese Vin Santo '07	♟♟ 5
○ Montellori Pas Dosé '11	♟♟ 5
● Moro '12	♟♟ 3
● Salamartano '12	♟♟ 6
● Salamartano '11	♟♟ 5

Montenidoli

LOC. MONTENIDOLI
53037 SAN GIMIGNANO [SI]
TEL. +39 0577941565
www.montenidoli.com

CELLAR SALES
ACCOMMODATION
ANNUAL PRODUCTION 100,000 bottles
HECTARES UNDER VINE 24.00
VITICULTURE METHOD Certified Organic

Elisabetta Fagiuoli moved to this part of Tuscany with Sergio Muratori, her life partner of 45 years. This decision was not only based on a love of the land and the fruits it can yield when treated with respect, but also on a commitment to facilitating the dialogue between older and younger generations in difficulty and talking about education. A production philosophy took shape in this climate: only native grapes, biodynamic farming, protection of the environment. This translates into a special spirit of hospitality towards the guests in the agritourism facility. Tre Bicchieri for the Vernaccia Carato 2012: nicely complex aromas with hints of mango and peaches alongside light, intriguing nuances of wood resin and a little spice. The palate is sumptuous, nicely blended, with harmonious acidity, fresh and vigorous, and a lingering, flavoursome finish. The Vernaccia Tradizionale 2014 presents tempting aromas, mainly of peaches and apricots, and a good, firm, flavoursome palate with a tangy, well-styled finish.

○ Vernaccia di S. Gimignano Carato '12	♟♟♟ 4*
○ Vernaccia di S. Gimignano Tradizionale '14	♟♟ 2*
○ Il Templare '12	♟♟ 4
● Chianti Colli Senesi Il Garrulo '14	♟ 2
● Sono Montenidoli '09	♟ 5
○ Vernaccia di S. Gimignano Fiore '14	♟ 3
○ Vernaccia di S. Gimignano Carato '11	♟♟♟ 4*
○ Vernaccia di S. Gimignano Carato '05	♟♟♟ 5
○ Vernaccia di S. Gimignano Carato '02	♟♟♟ 5
○ Vernaccia di S. Gimignano Fiore '09	♟♟♟ 3
○ Vernaccia di S. Gimignano Tradizionale '12	♟♟♟ 2*

Montepeloso

loc. Montepeloso, 82
57028 Suvereto [LI]
Tel. +39 0565828180
www.montepeloso.it

ANNUAL PRODUCTION 22,000 bottles
HECTARES UNDER VINE 7.00
SUSTAINABLE WINERY

This small estate was purchased in the late Nineties by Fabio Chiarelotto who, until then, had cultivated an interest in history and religions. His passion for wine led him to a search for areas that might inspire him to take the next step and become a producer. So he arrived in Suvereto and unearthed this farm, tasted its wines and was convinced of the area's huge potential. This was the start of his adventure, which took shape without a lot of fuss but at a steady, gradual pace, and is beginning to yield results. Back into the finals for the Nardo, a blend of sangiovese, Montepulciano and cabernet sauvignon. The 2013 offers a deep, generous bouquet of black berries and fresh, minty sensations, with a broad, succulent, soft palate and lingering finish with a spicy back palate. The appealing Eneo 2013, from sangiovese, colorino and merlot, presents aromas of leather and animal skins, ripe fruit and a good consistent flavour.

● Nardo '13	♟♟ 8
● Eneo '13	♟♟ 5
● Gabbro '13	♟♟ 8
● A Qu '14	♟ 5
● Gabbro '02	♟♟♟ 8
● Nardo '01	♟♟♟ 8
● Nardo '00	♟♟♟ 8
● A Quo '13	♟♟ 5
● Eneo '12	♟♟ 5
● Gabbro '12	♟♟ 8
● Gabbro '08	♟♟ 8
● Gabbro '06	♟♟ 8
● Nardo '12	♟♟ 8
● Nardo '08	♟♟ 8

Monteraponi

loc. Monteraponi
53017 Radda in Chianti [SI]
Tel. +39 0577738280
www.monteraponi.it

CELLAR SALES
PRE-BOOKED VISITS
ACCOMMODATION
ANNUAL PRODUCTION 50,000 bottles
HECTARES UNDER VINE 10.00
VITICULTURE METHOD Certified Organic

Since 2003 Michele Braganti has managed to build up one of the finest and most attractive wine estates in Chianti Classico, through organic winegrowing and traditional cellar methods, starting with the exclusive use of large oak. His wines display a clear and approachable style, with all the elegance and complexity that sangiovese is capable of endowing with generosity, especially in the best areas, alongside the most engaging international varieties. The Baron'Ugo may have left the designation to become an IGT, but nonetheless a great wine. The 2012 presents nuanced aromas of flowers and game, with a gutsy palate full of flavour and depth. Almost to the same standard, the Chianti Classico Il Campitello Riserva 2013 aromas are slightly marked by excessive oak, and persistent gamy hints, but also subtly floral with earthy sensations. The palate is very tangy, dynamic and consistent.

● Baron'Ugo '12	♟♟♟ 8
● Chianti Cl. Il Campitello Ris. '13	♟♟ 5
● Chianti Cl. '14	♟ 3
● Chianti Cl. Baron'Ugo Ris. '10	♟♟♟ 7
● Chianti Cl. Baron'Ugo Ris. '09	♟♟♟ 7
● Chianti Cl. Baron'Ugo Ris. '07	♟♟♟ 5
● Chianti Cl. '13	♟♟ 3
● Chianti Cl. '12	♟♟ 3
● Chianti Cl. '11	♟♟ 3
● Chianti Cl. Baron'Ugo Ris. '11	♟♟ 7
● Chianti Cl. Il Campitello Ris. '12	♟♟ 5
● Chianti Cl. Il Campitello Ris. '11	♟♟ 5
● Chianti Cl. Il Campitello Ris. '10	♟♟ 5
● Vin Santo del Chianti Cl. '05	♟♟ 6

Tenuta Monteti

S.DA DELLA SGRILLA, 6
58011 CAPALBIO [GR]
TEL. +39 0564896160
www.tenutamonteti.it

CELLAR SALES
PRE-BOOKED VISITS
ANNUAL PRODUCTION 120,000 bottles
HECTARES UNDER VINE 28.00
SUSTAINABLE WINERY

The Monteti hill, from which the estate takes its name, shelters the 28 hectares of vineyards from winds blowing from the sea, no more than 15 kilometres away. Here among the woods and Mediterranean vegetation of the Maremma, Paolo Baratta decided back in 1998 to plant black international grape varieties: cabernet sauvignon e franc, petit verdot, merlot and alicante bouchet. The estate is managed today by Eva Baratta and her husband Javier Pedrazzini, with the help of consultant winemaker Carlo Ferrini. The 28 separate vineyard plots are fermented separately and blended only after the first stage of maturation. A good performance from the Monteti 2012, a blend of petit verdot, cabernet franc and cabernet sauvignon: lovely medicinal herbs on the nose and a stylish, nicely consistent palate with lively tannins on a tangy background creating a lingering, mouthwatering flavour. The Caburnio 2012 is also good: the combination of cabernet sauvignon, alicante bouchet and merlot grapes create a more approachable wine, though still a little curbed by oak in this phase.

● Monteti '12	♟♟ 5
● Caburnio '12	♟♟ 3
⊙ TM Rosé '15	♟ 3
● Caburnio '11	♟♟ 3
● Caburnio '06	♟♟ 3
● Monteti '11	♟♟ 5
● Monteti '07	♟♟ 5
● Monteti '05	♟♟ 5
● Monteti '04	♟♟ 5

Monteverro

S.DA AURELIA CAPALBIO, 11
58011 CAPALBIO [GR]
TEL. +39 0564890721
www.monteverro.com

CELLAR SALES
ANNUAL PRODUCTION 120,000 bottles
HECTARES UNDER VINE 30.00

The vineyards are a few kilometres from Capalbio, but the language spoken on the estate is international. Not only because the vineyards contain few native grape varieties, but because the owners and staff come from various different European countries. Julia and Georg Weber are the German owners who found the perfect terroir for their concept of wine, and decided to stay in Maremma. Alongside Michel Rolland, they chose to make wines able to compete on an international level, bringing together a confidently modern style and the Mediterranean features of the area. These features are clearly present in the Monteverro 2013, a Bordeaux blend with aromas of black and morello cherries alongside aromatic herbs ahead of the concentrated, rounded but not too weighty palate. The Tinata 2013 is up to the same standard: syrah and grenache play the spice card on a flavoursome, nicely developed palate. The Terra di Monteverro 2013 is also really enjoyable.

○ Chardonnay '13	♟♟ 8
● Monteverro '13	♟♟ 8
● Terra di Monteverro '13	♟♟ 7
● Tinata '13	♟♟ 8
● Monteverro '12	♟♟ 8
● Monteverro '08	♟♟ 8
● Terra di Monteverro '12	♟♟ 7
● Terra di Monteverro '09	♟♟ 5
● Tinata '12	♟♟ 8
● Tinata '08	♟♟ 8

★Montevertine

LOC. MONTEVERTINE
53017 RADDA IN CHIANTI [SI]
TEL. +39 0577738009
www.montevertine.it

PRE-BOOKED VISITS
ANNUAL PRODUCTION 85,000 bottles
HECTARES UNDER VINE 15.00

The estate was bought by the Manetti family in 1967 and the first bottles were released in 1971, a period of history when Chianti Classico certainly did not have the same prestige it enjoys today. Since then the wines have become a sort of stylistic model for the whole area, standing out for what is probably one of the most polished versions of sangiovese in Tuscany and an unmistakeable, original and well-balanced style that places Montevertine at the absolute peak of Italian winemaking. The wines from a magical year like 2013 could not be anything but superlative. The Le Pergole Torte has a captivating nose with recognizable shading, plenty of freshness, and complexity that is still embedded for now, but perceptible. The palate dances between peaks of acidity and tannin, flowers and berry fruit. Sangiovese-style elegance. An indisputable Tre Bicchieri.

Cantina Vignaioli del Morellino di Scansano

LOC. SARAGIOLO
58054 SCANSANO [GR]
TEL. +39 0564507288
www.cantinadelmorellino.it

CELLAR SALES
PRE-BOOKED VISITS
ANNUAL PRODUCTION 2,000,000 bottles
HECTARES UNDER VINE 470.00

The Cantina Cooperativa del Morellino di Scansano was established in 1972 in response to the recession in the mining sector. Now managed by committed and passionate experts and Maremma farmers, it is on the way to becoming one of the most modern winemaking cooperatives, with improved, consistent quality, and flawlessly made wines that fully represent their type. Regular monitoring of the members' vineyards, and cellar processes that combine quality and quantity, guarantee good reliable products, although we are still waiting for that leap forward to absolute excellence. Lovely sensations from the Vignabenefizio 2015, a Morellino di Scansano with clean aromas and a generally succulent, delicious flavour. The two 2015 Roggianos are really well made, very pleasing and extremely drinkable.

● Le Pergole Torte '13	♟♟♟ 8
● Montevertine '13	♟ 6
● Pian del Ciampolo '14	♟ 4
● Le Pergole Torte '12	♟♟♟ 8
● Le Pergole Torte '11	♟♟♟ 8
● Le Pergole Torte '10	♟♟♟ 8
● Le Pergole Torte '09	♟♟♟ 8
● Le Pergole Torte '07	♟♟♟ 8
● Le Pergole Torte '04	♟♟♟ 8
● Le Pergole Torte '03	♟♟♟ 7
● Le Pergole Torte '01	♟♟♟ 8
● Montevertine '04	♟♟♟ 5
● Montevertine '01	♟♟♟ 5

● Morellino di Scansano Vignabenefizio '15	♟♟ 2*
● Morellino di Scansano Roggiano '15	♟♟ 2*
● Morellino di Scansano Roggiano Bio '15	♟♟ 2*
○ Vermentino V. Fiorini V.T. '15	♟♟ 2*
● Maremma Toscana Ciliegiolo Capoccia '15	♟ 2
● Morellino di Scansano Roggiano Ris. '13	♟ 3
● Morellino di Scansano Sicomoro Ris. '12	♟ 3
● Sangiovese Scantianum '15	♟ 1*
○ Vermentino Scantianum '15	♟ 2
● Morellino di Scansano Roggiano '14	♟♟ 2*
● Morellino di Scansano Roggiano Bio '13	♟♟ 2*
● Morellino di Scansano Roggiano Ris. '12	♟♟ 3
● Morellino di Scansano Vignabenefizio '13	♟♟ 2*

Morisfarms

loc. Cura Nuova
Fattoria Poggetti
58024 Massa Marittima [GR]
Tel. +39 0566919135
www.morisfarms.it

CELLAR SALES
PRE-BOOKED VISITS
ACCOMMODATION
ANNUAL PRODUCTION 300,000 bottles
HECTARES UNDER VINE 71.00

The estate's most ancient history informs us that about 200 years ago the Moris family left Spain to settle in Maremma. More recent history tells us, on the other hand, that in the late 1980s Adolfo Parentini effected an upswing in quality. Today his son Giulio works alongside him in running the estate's two farms, one at Poggio La Mozza, near Grosseto, with 33 hectares under vine, and the other at Poggetti, near Massa Marittima, with 37 hectares. In 1990 replanting began and today sangiovese is the principal variety used in production. In the absence of the Avvoltore, the Mandriolo leads the range: sangiovese with a small addition of international grapes, and an intriguing nose ranging from Mediterranean scrubland to ripe cherries, while docile tannins and a tangy flavour open out the palate nicely. The Morellino Riserva 2013 is warm and mouthfilling. The estate's white wines are appealing and delicious: Santa Chiara 2015, with hints of apple and pear fruit and breakfast cereal, and the floral, very drinkable Vermentino.

● Maremma Toscana Mandriolo '15	♥♥	1*
● Morellino di Scansano Ris. '13	♥♥	4
☉ Maremma Toscana Mandriolo Rosato '15	♥	2
○ Monteregio di Massa Marittima Bianco Santa Chiara '15	♥	2
● Morellino di Scansano '15	♥	2
○ Vermentino '15	♥	2
● Avvoltore '06	♥♥♥	5
● Avvoltore '04	♥♥♥	5
● Avvoltore '01	♥♥♥	5
● Avvoltore '00	♥♥♥	5
● Avvoltore '12	♥♥	6
● Avvoltore '11	♥♥	6
○ Vermentino '14	♥♥	2*

Mormoraia

loc. Sant'Andrea, 15
53037 San Gimignano [SI]
Tel. +39 0577940096
www.mormoraia.it

CELLAR SALES
PRE-BOOKED VISITS
ACCOMMODATION
ANNUAL PRODUCTION 230,000 bottles
HECTARES UNDER VINE 40.00

The estate has belonged to the Passoni family since 1980, enabling them to fulfil their dream of finding somewhere to live in Tuscany, their ideal location. Renovations began in 1990 on the old convent, whose name derives from the murmuring of the nuns as they prayed. Since then many things have changed: the adoption of organic farming methods for the vineyards and olive groves, another very interesting crop for the owners, and the opening of an agritourism with adjacent restaurant. The Vernaccia Riserva 2014 made the finals with balsamic hints on the nose alongside aromatic herbs, apple and peach fruit, and a firm, nicely weighty, harmonious palate with a flavoursome, lingering finish. We also liked the Vernaccia Ostrea 2015, which plays the citrus card with hints of tropical fruit and a lively, nicely racy palate with a succulent finish. The Chianti Colli Senesi 2014 is pleasantly uncomplicated: clean, impressive aromas and a slender, flavoursome, beautifully drinkable palate.

○ Vernaccia di S. Gimignano Ris. '14	♥♥	3*
● Chianti Colli Senesi '14	♥♥	2*
○ Vernaccia di S. Gimignano Ostrea '15	♥♥	3
○ Vernaccia di S. Gimignano '15	♥	2
● Chianti Colli Senesi '11	♥♥	2*
● Syrah '12	♥♥	3
● Syrah '11	♥♥	2*
○ Vernaccia di S. Gimignano '14	♥♥	2*
○ Vernaccia di S. Gimignano '13	♥♥	2*
○ Vernaccia di S. Gimignano '12	♥♥	2*
○ Vernaccia di S. Gimignano Ostrea '13	♥♥	3
○ Vernaccia di S. Gimignano Ostrea '12	♥♥	3*
○ Vernaccia di S. Gimignano Ris. '11	♥♥	3*

Fabio Motta

Vigna al Cavaliere, 61
57022 Castagneto Carducci [LI]
Tel. +39 0565773041
www.mottafabio.it

CELLAR SALES
PRE-BOOKED VISITS
ANNUAL PRODUCTION 23,000 bottles
HECTARES UNDER VINE 6.50

Less than ten years have passed since Fabio Motta, equipped with a degree in agriculture and cellar experience, decided the time had come for adventure, to go it alone. The black grape vineyards, situated at the foot of the Castagneto Carducci hill at Le Pievi, are over 20 years old and occupy about four hectares of land. The vermentino grapes come from Fornacelle. This small and fairly new winery is already managing to stand out and make some significant wines. Crystal-clear proof of the value of this project comes from the superlative Bolgheri Rosso Superiore Le Gonnare 2013. A good year and a wine that opens and lightens up after a clenched, slightly dark impact, into bright, relaxed fruit, focused and appealing. The palate is equally good, with lovely extract and sublime texture, closing on subtly spicy tones. The Bolgheri Rosso Pievi 2014 is simpler and grassier.

● Bolgheri Sup. Le Gonnare '13	♼♼♼	8
○ Bolgheri Bianco Nova '15	♼	4
● Bolgheri Rosso Pievi '14	♼	4

Tenute Silvio Nardi

loc. Casale del Bosco
53024 Montalcino [SI]
Tel. +39 0577808269
www.tenutenardi.com

CELLAR SALES
PRE-BOOKED VISITS
ANNUAL PRODUCTION 250,000 bottles
HECTARES UNDER VINE 80.00

With 50 hectares of registered Brunello vineyards, out of a total of 80, and at least 30 in different plots, the estates taken over by Silvio Nardi in the 1950s make up one of Montalcino's most significant farms. He was one of the first "foreigners" to invest in this Tuscan DOC zone in very different times from today's glory, and Emilia devotedly carries on the work today. The main farms are Casale del Bosco in the north-western zone and Manachiara, to the east. Sangiovese is the undisputed protagonist in the varied range, based on mixed maturation in large barrels and tonneaux for the leading wines. The pair of Brunellos provide positive confirmation: the standard version from 2011 focuses on mature aromas of pears, melon, raspberry jam and spicy, oaky sensations, more evident in the abrupt finish. Some acidic imperfections also appear in the Vigneto Poggio Doria Riserva 2010, but it's nicely typed with a close-knit, austere gait.

● Brunello di Montalcino '11	♼♼	6
● Brunello di Montalcino Vign. Poggio Doria Ris. '10	♼♼	8
● Rosso di Montalcino '14	♼	3
● Brunello di Montalcino Manachiara '99	♼♼♼	7
● Brunello di Montalcino Manachiara '97	♼♼♼	7
● Brunello di Montalcino '10	♼♼	5
● Brunello di Montalcino Manachiara '06	♼♼	8
● Brunello di Montalcino Manachiara '04	♼♼	8
● Brunello di Montalcino Vign. Manachiara '10	♼♼	8
● Brunello di Montalcino Vign. Poggio Doria '10	♼♼	8
● Rosso di Montalcino '07	♼♼	3

Tenute Niccolai - Palagetto

VIA MONTEOLIVETO, 46
53037 SAN GIMIGNANO [SI]
TEL. +39 0577943090
www.tenuteniccolai.it

CELLAR SALES
PRE-BOOKED VISITS
ACCOMMODATION
ANNUAL PRODUCTION 250,000 bottles
HECTARES UNDER VINE 44.00

This is the heart of the Niccolai family estates, rooted in San Gimignano. Sabrina carries forward the work of her father Luano, an industrialist with a passion for nature and the countryside, who in turn inherited this love for the land from his own father and father-in-law, both cellarmen. The Tenute Niccolai estate includes Podere Bellarina in Montalcino and Pian de' Cerri in the Montecucco area, but the most important work takes place at Palagetto, in the modern, functional cellar, where most of the wines from all the farms are produced. An excellent overall performance from this broad, varied range. The Vernaccia Vent'anni 2014 made the finals with a classic bouquet of almonds and floral pot-pourri, a firm, nicely layered palate with fresh sensations to balance the mouthfilling texture, and a long, full-bodied finish. The Vernaccia Riserva 2014 is good: hints of melon and apple fruit, a good mouthwatering structure, and a tangy finish.

Fattoria Nittardi

LOC. NITTARDI
53011 CASTELLINA IN CHIANTI [SI]
TEL. +39 0577740269
www.nittardi.com

CELLAR SALES
PRE-BOOKED VISITS
ANNUAL PRODUCTION 94,000 bottles
HECTARES UNDER VINE 29.00

The style of this Castellina in Chianti estate is modern and well-focused yet, at the same time, the wines are endowed with marked terroir characteristics and personality. Fattoria di Nittardi reds have an approachable, enjoyable flavour, vibrant aromas and invigorating development on the palate. They are matured in judiciously dosed small oak, which contributes to the very impressive results. Fattoria Nittardi also owns 37 hectares of vineyards in Maremma, where the wines are often among the best of their type. Nicely balanced fruit and oak in the Chianti Classico Riserva 2013, with clean, airy aromas and a pleasantly flavoursome palate. We are happy to gamble on this wine. The Nectar Dei 2014 is a powerful and richly extracted blend of cabernet sauvignon, merlot and petit verdot with vibrant aromas. The Chianti Classico Casanuova di Nittardi 2014 is flavoursome and well paced with clean, fragrant aromas.

○ Vernaccia di S. Gimignano Vent'anni '14	♈♈ 3*
○ Sauvignon '15	♈♈ 3
○ Vernaccia di S. Gimignano '15	♈♈ 2*
○ Vernaccia di S. Gimignano Ris. '14	♈♈ 3
○ Vernaccia di S. Gimignano V. Santa Chiara '14	♈♈ 2*
● Chianti Colli Senesi '14	♈ 2
○ l'Niccolò '15	♈ 3
○ l'Niccolò '14	♈♈ 3
● San Gimignano Sangiovese Merlot Uno di Quattro '10	♈♈ 6
○ Vernaccia di S. Gimignano Ris. '12	♈♈ 3
○ Vernaccia di S. Gimignano Ris. '10	♈♈ 3*
○ Vernaccia di S. Gimignano V. Santa Chiara '13	♈♈ 2*

● Chianti Cl. Ris. '13	♈♈♈ 6
● Chianti Cl. Casanuova di Nittardi '14	♈♈ 4
● Nectar Dei '14	♈♈ 7
● Chianti Cl. Belcanto '14	♈ 4
● Ad Astra '08	♈♈♈ 3
● Chianti Cl. Ris. '11	♈♈♈ 6
● Chianti Cl. Ris. '10	♈♈♈ 6
● Ad Astra '13	♈♈ 3
● Ad Astra '12	♈♈ 3
● Chianti Cl. Belcanto '13	♈♈ 4
● Chianti Cl. Casanuova di Nittardi '12	♈♈ 4
● Chianti Cl. Casanuova di Nittardi '11	♈♈ 4
● Chianti Cl. Ris. '12	♈♈ 6
● Nectar Dei '12	♈♈ 7
● Nectar Dei '10	♈♈ 7

Orma

VIA BOLGHERESE
57022 CASTAGNETO CARDUCCI [LI]
TEL. +39 0575477857
tenutasetteponti@tenutasetteponti.it

ANNUAL PRODUCTION 30,000 bottles
HECTARES UNDER VINE 5.50
SUSTAINABLE WINERY

Orma belongs to the estates of Antonio
Moretti, a successful entrepreneur who has
poured his passion into the wine sector.
The mother company is Tenuta Setteponti,
near Arezzo, but there is also the lovely
estate in Sicily, Feudo Maccari. The two
labels are Orma, which is not officially a
Bolgheri DOC wine but effectively one of
the best reds in the area, and a basic
Bolgheri. They are made from the grapes
grown on just five hectares of vineyards on
clayey, pebbly soil which endows them with
complexity and elegance. The 2013 wins
another Tre Bicchieri, from one of the best
recent years for the Bolgheri area. Vibrant
berry fruit, balsamic hints, Mediterranean
scrubland and a fragrant hint of bay leaves.
The palate combines the structure of
cabernet and merlot with the fine
craftsmanship that provides an excellent
interpretation of this generous, light-filled
area. Acidity is never absent from the
flavour and the tannin is masterfully
extracted, to say the least. Keep it up!

● Orma '13	▼▼▼ 8
● Orma '12	▼▼▼ 8
● Orma '11	▼▼▼ 8
● Orma '10	▼▼▼ 7
● Orma '09	▼▼▼ 6
● Orma '08	▼▼▼ 6
● Orma '07	▼▼▼ 5
● Orma '06	▼▼▼ 6
● Orma '05	▼▼ 6

Fattoria Ormanni

LOC. ORMANNI, 1
53036 POGGIBONSI [SI]
TEL. +39 0577937212
www.ormanni.it

CELLAR SALES
PRE-BOOKED VISITS
ACCOMMODATION
ANNUAL PRODUCTION 70,000 bottles
HECTARES UNDER VINE 68.00

A historic brandname in this designation,
Ormanni has been owned by the Brini
Batacchi family since 1818. The vineyards,
over 40 years old, are planted between the
provinces of Florence and Siena. The grapes
for the Chianti Classico wines come from
the Florence area. The Barberino Val d'Elsa
land is rich in skeletal material and situated
at a higher altitude (350 metres above sea
level). The cellar procedures tend to be
traditional, starting with the use of large oak
casks. The resulting wines are rigorous,
sometimes austere, but appealing and
characterful. As in the case of the Chianti
Classico Borro del Diavolo Riserva 2012,
with ripe cherry and earthy aromas and
succulent flavour, with pleasant hardness.
The Chianti Classico 2012 is also good
and spicy with a nice contrast of sweetness
and acidity. The Chianti Classico Gran
Selezione 2011 is more powerful but
perhaps a little less intriguing, while the
Julius 2012, from sangiovese, merlot and
syrah, is flavoursome.

● Chianti Cl. Borro del Diavolo Ris. '12	▼▼ 4
● Chianti Cl. '12	▼▼ 3
● Chianti Cl. Gran Sel. '11	▼▼ 3
● Julius '12	▼▼ 5
● Chianti Cl. '10	▽▽ 3*
● Chianti Cl. '08	▽▽ 3
● Chianti Cl. '04	▽▽ 2
● Chianti Cl. '03	▽▽ 3
● Chianti Cl. Borro del Diavolo Ris. '08	▽▽ 4
● Chianti Cl. Borro del Diavolo Ris. '06	▽▽ 3
● Chianti Cl. Borro del Diavolo Ris. '01	▽▽ 3
● Chianti Cl. Borro del Diavolo Ris. '00	▽▽ 5
● Julius '00	▽▽ 5

★★Ornellaia

FRAZ. BOLGHERI
LOC. ORNELLAIA, 191
57022 CASTAGNETO CARDUCCI [LI]
TEL. +39 056571811
www.ornellaia.it

PRE-BOOKED VISITS
ANNUAL PRODUCTION 930,000 bottles
HECTARES UNDER VINE 112.00

Ornellaia is one of the brightest stars in Italy's winemaking firmament, shining brightly around the world. Established in the 1980s, the winery has found incredible success with critics and even the most demanding enthusiasts. The estate consists of a single plot with the same name plus another vineyard at Bellaria. The wines are of a very high standard, and excel at an international level. Today this property is owned by the Frescobaldi, a prestigious Tuscan dynasty of great lineage. The Bolgheri Rosso Superiore Ornellaia repeats last year's performance with a second Tre Bicchieri. The 2013 harvest brings us a wine that is still somewhat compressed but holds many cards in its hand, indicating a definitely bright future. The profile in this phase is definitely dark, both in fruit and in the influence of the oak used for ageing. So, a compact wine, capable of combining rich texture and an unusual propensity for depth.

● Bolgheri Sup. Ornellaia '13	▼▼▼	8
● Masseto '13	▼▼	8
● Bolgheri Sup. Ornellaia '12	♀♀♀	8
● Bolgheri Sup. Ornellaia '10	♀♀♀	8
● Bolgheri Sup. Ornellaia '07	♀♀♀	8
● Bolgheri Sup. Ornellaia '05	♀♀♀	8
● Bolgheri Sup. Ornellaia '04	♀♀♀	8
● Bolgheri Sup. Ornellaia '02	♀♀♀	8
● Bolgheri Sup. Ornellaia '01	♀♀♀	8
● Masseto '11	♀♀♀	8
● Masseto '09	♀♀♀	8
● Masseto '06	♀♀♀	8
● Masseto '04	♀♀♀	8

Siro Pacenti

LOC. PELAGRILLI, 1
53024 MONTALCINO [SI]
TEL. +39 0577848662
www.siropacenti.it

CELLAR SALES
PRE-BOOKED VISITS
ANNUAL PRODUCTION 60,000 bottles
HECTARES UNDER VINE 22.00

The earliest bottled wines date back to 1988 at Siro Pacenti, established in 1971 as an offshoot of one of the most prestigious Montalcino wine dynasties. At the helm today is Giancarlo, one of the first distinguished exponents to experiment with barriques and tonneaux to age his Brunellos, which are far removed from the "modernist" stereotype. The hub of the estate are the Pelagrilli vineyards situated at 350 metres altitude on clayey, silty soil and used for the Brunello of the same name and for the PS Riserva. In addition, there are the southern vineyards at Piancornello, a warmer area with mainly pebbly soil, which contributes grapes for the Vecchie Vigne and the Rosso. Once again Giancarlo Pacenti succeeds in placing all his Brunellos in the finals. The PS Riserva 2010 offers its best in interwoven floral and earthy sensations, while the Pelagrilli 2011 suffers from rough extract, though it lacks neither texture nor energy. The Vecchie Vigne 2011 shows the most accomplished harmony and flavour.

● Brunello di Montalcino Pelagrilli '11	▼▼	6
● Brunello di Montalcino PS Ris. '10	▼▼	8
● Brunello di Montalcino V. V. '11	▼▼	8
● Brunello di Montalcino '97	♀♀♀	7
● Brunello di Montalcino '96	♀♀♀	7
● Brunello di Montalcino '95	♀♀♀	7
● Brunello di Montalcino '88	♀♀♀	7
● Brunello di Montalcino PS Ris. '07	♀♀♀	8
● Brunello di Montalcino V. V. '10	♀♀♀	8
● Brunello di Montalcino '09	♀♀	8
● Brunello di Montalcino '07	♀♀	8
● Brunello di Montalcino '06	♀♀	8
● Brunello di Montalcino Pelagrilli '10	♀♀	6
● Brunello di Montalcino PS '04	♀♀	8
● Brunello di Montalcino PS Ris. '06	♀♀	8
● Rosso di Montalcino PS '11	♀♀	5

Panizzi

<small>LOC. SANTA MARGHERITA, 34
53037 SAN GIMIGNANO [SI]
TEL. +39 0577941576
www.panizzi.it</small>

CELLAR SALES
PRE-BOOKED VISITS
ACCOMMODATION
ANNUAL PRODUCTION 210,000 bottles
HECTARES UNDER VINE 50.00

Lombard Giovanni Panizzi fell in love with Tuscany, and in the late Seventies he chose San Gimignano as the place to start his life as a winegrower. He set up a farm which contributed in just a few years to reviving Vernaccia. In 2005 Luano Niccolai took over ownership of the estate, but Giovanni continued to contribute his passion and experience until he passed away in 2010. Today Simone Niccolai runs the farm, leading a far-reaching process of reinforcement and expansion. An excellent performance in the finals from the Vernaccia Vigna Santa Margherita 2014 with subtle, fine aromas: intriguing vegetal hints of thyme and marjoram, lovely melon and peach fruit, and a well-structured and measured palate, balanced by a fresh, harmonious finish. The enthralling Passito 2013 displays a complex nose with dried figs, apricots and hints of hazelnuts. The palate is mouthfilling, opulent, generous and nicely weighty, sweet and beautifully sustained.

○ Vernaccia di San Gimignano V. Santa Margherita '14	3*
○ Passito '13	4
⊙ Ceraso Rosato '15	2
● Chianti Colli Senesi Vertunno Ris. '12	2
● San Gimignano Rosso Folgore '10	5
○ Vernaccia di S. Gimignano '15	2
○ Vernaccia di S. Gimignano Ris. '07	5
○ Vernaccia di S. Gimignano Ris. '05	5
○ Vernaccia di S. Gimignano Ris. '98	4*
○ Vernaccia di S. Gimignano '13	2*
○ Vernaccia di S. Gimignano Ris. '12	5
○ Vernaccia di S. Gimignano Ris. '11	5

Parmoleto

<small>LOC. MONTENERO D'ORCIA
POD. PARMOLETONE, 44
58040 CASTEL DEL PIANO [GR]
TEL. +39 0564954131
www.parmoleto.it</small>

CELLAR SALES
PRE-BOOKED VISITS
ACCOMMODATION AND RESTAURANT SERVICE
ANNUAL PRODUCTION 23,000 bottles
HECTARES UNDER VINE 6.00

The Sodi family, originally from Montalcino, has owned this portion of Val d'Orcia since the early 20th century. But Duilio Sodi only decided to convert six of his 72 hectares to vineyards in the 1990s. As well as producing olive oil, legumes, spelt and saffron, and a flourishing pig farm, Parmoleto has become one of the most solid and terroir-rooted wine estates in the Montecucco area. The old farmstead overlooking the gently rolling Tuscan hills is also an agritourism centre. Talking of territorial features and solidity, we encountered these same features in the great Montecucco Sangiovese Riserva, which reached our final tastings and was among the best wines in its designation. Fresh aromatic herbs and black berries introduce a sound, relaxed palate with balanced tannin and alcohol, refreshed with acidic backbone. The Sangiovese 2012 is also of a high standard, with aromas of Mediterranean scrubland and a graceful, coherent flavour.

● Montecucco Sangiovese Ris. '11	3*
● Montecucco Sangiovese '12	3
● Montecucco Rosso '13	2
○ Carabatto '10	2*
● Montecucco Sangiovese '11	3
● Montecucco Sangiovese Ris. '10	3
● Sormonno '08	4
● Sormonno '05	4

Tenuta La Parrina

FRAZ. ALBINIA
S.DA DELLA PARRINA
58010 ORBETELLO [GR]
TEL. +39 0564862636
www.parrina.it

CELLAR SALES
PRE-BOOKED VISITS
ACCOMMODATION AND RESTAURANT SERVICE
ANNUAL PRODUCTION 200,000 bottles
HECTARES UNDER VINE 60.00
VITICULTURE METHOD Certified Organic

The estate was established back in 1830, when Florentine banker Michele Giuntini decided to invest in a virgin farming area. Today Franca Spinola runs the estate, restored to its former glory in just a few decades. The 60 hectares of vineyards fall within a DOC zone that shares the name of the estate, Parrina (rarely the case in Italy), and covers the lower hillsides of Orbetello. But the estate does not only produce wine: alongside the vineyards are olives, vegetables, cereals, fruit, as well as sheep, goats and cows, in the name of protecting the local area and respecting its biodiversity. The Muraccio, from sangiovese with a small percentage of cabernet sauvignon and merlot, shows no ill effects from the problematic 2014, with a range of aromas based on ripe red berries blending into spicy, tertiary aromas. The Poggio della Fata 2015, from sauvignon and vermentino, is also succulent, dynamic and enjoyable.

● Parrina Rosso Muraccio '14		♀♀ 3*
○ Costa dell'Argentario Ansonica '15		♀♀ 3
○ Poggio della Fata '15		♀♀ 3
○ Parrina Bianco '15		♀ 2
● Parrina Merlot Radaia '14		♀ 6
● Parrina Sangiovese '15		♀ 2
● Parrina Sangiovese Ris. '13		♀ 5
○ Parrina Vermentino '15		♀ 3
○ Ansonica Costa dell'Argentario '14		♀♀ 3
○ Parrina Bianco '12		♀♀ 2*
● Parrina Radaia '13		♀♀ 6
● Parrina Rosso Muraccio '13		♀♀ 3
● Parrina Rosso Muraccio '11		♀♀ 3
● Parrina Sangiovese '10		♀♀ 4
● Parrina Sangiovese Ris. '12		♀♀ 5

Petra

LOC. SAN LORENZO ALTO, 131
57028 SUVERETO [LI]
TEL. +39 0565845308
www.petrawine.it

CELLAR SALES
PRE-BOOKED VISITS
ANNUAL PRODUCTION 350,000 bottles
HECTARES UNDER VINE 94.00
SUSTAINABLE WINERY

From Franciacorta to Val di Cornia: this was the ideal journey of Vittorio Moretti's passion for wine. After his success with Franciacorta di Bellavista and Contadi Castaldi, his entrepreneurial curiosity drove him to Tuscany, as far as Maremma, and the Badiola estate, though the decisive stage was the previous one at Petra. This is where the cellar created and designed by Mario Botta stands, both symbolic and functional. Francesca runs it all with the same intense passion of her father, committed to creating wines that describe a love for this unique area. An excellent overall performance from the Moretti estate. Tre Bicchieri to the Petra 2013, cabernet sauvignon and merlot, with forward hints of green peppers, blueberries and currants, followed by minty, grassy sensations. The palate is pliant, generous, enthralling, and relaxed in the appetizing finish. The very good Potenti 2013 has minerally, balsam aromas, and supple, succulent, pleasant and lingering flavour.

● Petra Rosso '13		♀♀♀ 8
● Potenti '13		♀♀ 6
● Alto '12		♀♀ 6
○ Belvento Vermentino '15		♀♀ 3
○ La Balena '13		♀♀ 6
● Quercegobbe '13		♀♀ 6
● Belvento Cabernet Sauvignon '14		♀ 3
● Belvento Sangiovese '14		♀ 3
⊙ Belvento Velarosa '15		♀ 3
○ Belvento Viognier '15		♀ 3
● Hebo '14		♀ 3
● Petra Rosso '12		♀♀♀ 8
● Petra Rosso '11		♀♀♀ 8
● Petra Rosso '04		♀♀♀ 7

★Fattoria Petrolo

FRAZ. MERCATALE VALDARNO
VIA PETROLO, 30
52021 BUCINE [AR]
TEL. +39 0559911322
www.petrolo.it

PRE-BOOKED VISITS
ACCOMMODATION
ANNUAL PRODUCTION 70,000 bottles
HECTARES UNDER VINE 27.00

Although there are traces of Etruscan settlements in the area, Petrolo has Roman origins: its name derives from the term petroliarum, denoting a country villa with a praetorium. The extensively wooded area has always cultivated vines and olive groves, and produced fine wines. This is documented by the notice issued in 1716 by Tuscan Grand Duke Cosimo III, who identified it as one of four prestigious winegrowing areas: Chianti, Carmignano, Pomino and Val d'Arno di Sopra, where Petrolo is situated. The estate has been run by the Bazzocchi-Sanjust family for four generations, since 1947 when it was purchased by the grandfather of current owner Luca Sanjust. Monovarietal Merlot Galatrona does not miss its regular appointment with Tre Bicchieri. The 2013 preserves the elegant fruity aromas with spicy hints of cloves, black pepper and vanilla. The palate opens creamy, warm and mouthfilling, nicely full-bodied, with a long, enjoyable finish.

● Valdarno di Sopra Galatrona '13	♥♥♥	8
● Valdarno di Sopra Boggina '14	♥♥	6
● Valdarno di Sopra Bogginanfora '14	♥♥	7
● Valdarno di Sopra Inarno '15	♥	2
● Valdarno di Sopra Torrione '14	♥	5
● Galatrona '12	♀♀♀	8
● Galatrona '11	♀♀♀	8
● Galatrona '10	♀♀♀	8
● Galatrona '09	♀♀♀	8
● Galatrona '08	♀♀♀	8
● Galatrona '07	♀♀♀	8
● Galatrona '06	♀♀♀	8
● Galatrona '05	♀♀♀	8
● Torrione '11	♀♀♀	5

★Piaggia

LOC. POGGETTO
VIA CEGOLI, 47
59016 POGGIO A CAIANO [PO]
TEL. +39 0558705401
www.piaggia.com

CELLAR SALES
PRE-BOOKED VISITS
ANNUAL PRODUCTION 75,000 bottles
HECTARES UNDER VINE 15.00

The continuing success of this lovely Carmignano estate is built on solid foundations. The Vannucci family is passionately devoted to this farm, established in the mid-1970s by Mauro Vannucci and his wife Rita. Their daughter Silvia has worked alongside them for a few years, supervising sales development, and was also Chair of the local producers' consortium. Today, Piaggia is a 25-hectare estate, 15 of which are meticulously tended vineyards, and the remainder olive groves. Alberto Antonini and Emiliano Falsini are the technical consultants. The umpteenth crowning success for the Riserva 2013: a great red, richly extracted and generous, aged in fine quality new oak casks and confidently straddling the border between international style and elegant terroir-bound features. A symphony of ripe red fruits supported by fresh acidity and velvety tannins accompany the flavour towards the very lingering spicy, balsamic finish. The equally good Cabernet Franc Poggio de' Colli 2014 offers generous blackberry and blueberry fruit, blending with hints of mint, chocolate and coffee.

● Carmignano Ris. '13	♥♥♥	6
● Poggio de' Colli '14	♥♥	7
● Carmignano Il Sasso '14	♥♥	5
● Carmignano Ris. '12	♀♀♀	6
● Carmignano Ris. '11	♀♀♀	6
● Carmignano Ris. '08	♀♀♀	5
● Carmignano Ris. '07	♀♀♀	5
● Carmignano Ris. '99	♀♀♀	5
● Carmignano Ris. '98	♀♀♀	5
● Carmignano Ris. '97	♀♀♀	5
● Carmignano Sasso '07	♀♀♀	4
● Il Sasso '01	♀♀♀	4
● Poggio de' Colli '11	♀♀♀	7
● Poggio de' Colli '10	♀♀♀	6

Piancornello

LOC. PIANCORNELLO
53024 MONTALCINO [SI]
TEL. +39 0577844105
piancornello@libero.it

CELLAR SALES
PRE-BOOKED VISITS
ANNUAL PRODUCTION 50,000 bottles
HECTARES UNDER VINE 10.00

Regularly named among the most recognizable and consistent choices in the southern area of Montalcino, Piancornello is owned by Silvana Pieri and Claudio Monaci. It is nourished by 10 hectares of vineyards, detached from the winery on an upland overlooking Mt. Amiata and the river Orcia. This unique terroir is inextricably linked to the Mediterranean microclimate and its stony, rocky soil, sloping and well-drained, the origin of mouthfilling, sunny sangiovese wines. Don't expect approachable, ready-to-drink Brunellos: on the contrary, the vigorous tannin component, reinforced by ageing in barriques and tonneaux, demands attention and patience. Myrtle, juniper, black pepper, balsamic herbs, candied citrus fruit: from the nose onwards, the Brunello 2011 embodies our expectations of an area and a generous year. It does lack that something extra in energy and depth, but this is fully compensated by the lipsmacking, sunny flavour. The Rosso 2014 seems to suffer more from the complicated year.

● Brunello di Montalcino '11	♛♛ 6
● Rosso di Montalcino '14	♛ 3
● Brunello di Montalcino '10	♛♛♛ 6
● Brunello di Montalcino '06	♛♛♛ 6
● Brunello di Montalcino '99	♛♛♛ 6
● Brunello di Montalcino '09	♛♛ 6
● Brunello di Montalcino '08	♛♛ 6
● Brunello di Montalcino '07	♛♛ 6
● Brunello di Montalcino '04	♛♛ 6
● Brunello di Montalcino '03	♛♛ 6
● Brunello di Montalcino Ris. '06	♛♛ 6
● Brunello di Montalcino Ris. '04	♛♛ 6
● Rosso di Montalcino '11	♛♛ 3
● Rosso di Montalcino '08	♛♛ 3*

Piandaccoli

VIA DI PIANDACCOLI, 7
50055 LASTRA A SIGNA [FI]
TEL. +39 0550750005
www.piandaccoli.it

CELLAR SALES
PRE-BOOKED VISITS
ACCOMMODATION
ANNUAL PRODUCTION 90,000 bottles
HECTARES UNDER VINE 20.00

Protection and promotion of native Tuscan grape varieties has been central to the Piandaccoli project for years, since owner Giampaolo Bruni decided to inject strength and originality into the wines produced on his family estate. The grapes he has saved from neglect and used in his wines are: barsaglina, a native Tuscan grape documented back in the late 19th century; colorino, which takes its name from the richly coloured skin; foglia tonda; mammolo; pugnitello, whose bunches are shaped like little fists; and the inevitable sangiovese. Through to the finals for the Pugnitello del Rinascimento 2013: fruity aromas of cherries and blackberries, enthralling hints of spice, a firm, edgy body, taut, with nicely embedded tannins, and a long, mouthwatering finish. The enjoyable Foglia Tonda del Rinascimento 2013 displays prevalent aromas of bell peppers and vegetal hints, damson fruit, and a firm, nicely defined structure with pleasantly lingering flavour.

● Pugnitello del Rinascimento '13	♛♛ 6
● Foglia Tonda del Rinascimento '13	♛♛ 6
● Maiorem '13	♛♛ 5
● Chianti Cosmus Ris. '13	♛ 2
● In Primis '13	♛ 3
⊙ Operandi '15	♛ 3
● Chianti Cosmus '11	♛♛ 2*
● Chianti Cosmus Ris. '12	♛♛ 2*
● Foglia Tonda del Rinascimento '12	♛♛ 6
● Maiorem '12	♛♛ 5
● Maiorem '11	♛♛ 5
● Maiorem '10	♛♛ 5

Pietrafitta

Loc. Cortennano, 54
53037 San Gimignano [SI]
Tel. +39 0577943200
www.pietrafitta.com

CELLAR SALES
PRE-BOOKED VISITS
ACCOMMODATION
ANNUAL PRODUCTION 230,000 bottles
HECTARES UNDER VINE 80.00

This estate, which began all-round renewal work a few years ago, has a long history. It dates back to 961 AD, when it was part of the Fosci estate, owned by Marchese Ugo Salico. Over the centuries it has changed hands many times but with the House of Savoy it received a considerable boost in wine and olive-growing, and the early 20th century saw the construction of the well-designed and still perfectly functional cellar. A good performance from the Vernaccia Il Borghetto 2015: concentrated, very fruity aromas and hints of medicinal herbs, and a nicely juicy palate with tempting acidity and a dynamic, flavoursome finish. The Vernaccia La Costa Riserva 2012 is appealing, with mainly minerally aromas alongside hints of dried flowers and clear-cut peach fruit. The broad palate opens with good texture, and the finish is appetizing. The enthralling Vin Santo 2007 offers the classic aromas of dates and almonds with a sumptuous, creamy palate and a lingering, enjoyable finish.

○ San Gimignano Vin Santo '07	♟♟ 5	
○ Vernaccia di S. Gimignano Il Borghetto '15	♟♟ 3	
○ Vernaccia di S. Gimignano La Costa Ris. '12	♟♟ 4	
● Chianti dei Colli Senesi '12	♟ 2	
○ Vernaccia di S. Gimignano La Costa Ris. '15	♟ 2	
● Chianti Colli Senesi '07	♟♟ 2*	
○ S. Gimignano Vin Santo '04	♟♟ 5	
○ Vernaccia di S. Gimignano La Costa Ris. '11	♟♟ 4	
○ Vernaccia di S. Gimignano La Costa Ris. '08	♟♟ 3	
○ Vernaccia di S. Gimignano V. La Costa Ris. '06	♟♟ 3	

Pietroso

Loc. Pietroso, 257
53024 Montalcino [SI]
Tel. +39 0577848573
www.pietroso.it

CELLAR SALES
PRE-BOOKED VISITS
ANNUAL PRODUCTION 30,000 bottles
HECTARES UNDER VINE 5.00

Three vineyard plots, all planted to sangiovese, contribute to the small and increasingly interesting range produced by Gianni Pignatti and his family. The Pietroso vineyard surrounds the winery, at almost 500 metres altitude, on poor soil with plenty of rocks and stones. To the south, at 400 metres altitude near the Abbey of Sant'Antimo, the Colombaiolo vineyards grow on clayey, tuffstone-based land, while the Fornello plot is situated at 350 metres in the northern part of Montalcino, on soil rich in limestone marl. The grapes from each plot are processed separately and follow a specific ageing process in 30-hectolitre oak, prior to final blending. Just the cherry was missing from a masterfully prepared cake with quality ingredients like the Brunello Riserva 2010. Classic tertiary aromas of black cherries, pipe tobacco and mostarda, its essential nature confirmed on a palate just held back by a dry finish. The Brunello 2011 also offers sweetness and austerity.

● Brunello di Montalcino Ris. '10	♟♟ 6	
● Brunello di Montalcino '11	♟♟ 6	
● Rosso di Montalcino '14	♟♟ 4	
● Brunello di Montalcino '09	♟♟♟ 6	
● Brunello di Montalcino '10	♟♟ 6	
● Brunello di Montalcino '08	♟♟ 6	
● Brunello di Montalcino '04	♟♟ 5	
● Rosso di Montalcino '13	♟♟ 4	
● Rosso di Montalcino '12	♟♟ 4	
● Rosso di Montalcino '11	♟♟ 3*	
● Rosso di Montalcino '07	♟♟ 3	

Pieve de' Pitti

LOC. PIEVE DE' PITTI, 7BIS
56030 TERRICCIOLA [PI]
TEL. +39 0587635724
www.pievedepitti.it

CELLAR SALES
PRE-BOOKED VISITS
ANNUAL PRODUCTION 60,000 bottles
HECTARES UNDER VINE 16.00

There are 198 hectares of woods, arable land and above all vineyards and olive groves, surrounding Terricciola, spreading out like rays over the hillside overlooked by the villa and the Castello di Pava. Meet Pieve de' Pitti, named for the Florentine Pitti family who owned the farm until the mid-17th century, and the parish church of San Giovanni, built on the ruins of an ancient Etruscan church, and still consecrated today. Sangiovese is the main variety here but space and care are also devoted to other, less common grapes in this area, such as vermentino, trebbiano and syrah. The lovely Syrah 2013 offers spicy aromas of black pepper and liquorice, and hints of leather on a base of cherries and blackberries. The palate is relaxed, nicely supported by alcohol, with a lingering, very clean finish. The Appunto 2012, from sangiovese and merlot is appealing: aromas of currants and blueberries, and nicely blended tannin and alcohol on a lively, fresh palate with a lovely appetizing finish.

● Appunto '12	▼▼ 2*
● Moro di Pava '11	▼▼ 4
● Syrah '13	▼▼ 2*
○ Aprilante '15	▼ 2
● Chianti Sup. Cerretello '12	▼ 2
○ Aprilante '14	♈♈ 2*
● Scopaiolo '11	♈♈ 3

Pieve Santo Stefano

LOC. SARDINI
55100 LUCCA
TEL. +39 0583394115
www.pievedisantostefano.com

CELLAR SALES
PRE-BOOKED VISITS
ACCOMMODATION
ANNUAL PRODUCTION 45,000 bottles
HECTARES UNDER VINE 10.60
SUSTAINABLE WINERY

The current owners of this ancient site on the hills above Lucca are husband-and-wife Francesca Bogazzi and Antoine Hiriz, who have perfectly grasped the potential of the vineyards' location, with clay loam soil rich in skeletal material. At this altitude, between 200 and 300 metres, the microclimate is typically rainier than in Lucca and temperature variation is emphatic, and these conditions are a very positive combination for producing slender-bodied, very fresh-tasting wines. These are the main stylistic features of the winery's products, which are generally well-balanced and elegant, also due to the shrewd use of large and small oak casks. Pinot-like aromas and a tangy, deep flavour and the main features of the Colline Lucchesi Ludovico Sardini 2013. The Villa Sardini 2015 is juicy and really delicious, while the Lippo 2014, from cabernet franc and merlot, is slender and nicely paced.

● Colline Lucchesi Ludovico Sardini '13	▼▼ 4
● Colline Lucchesi Villa Sardini '15	▼▼ 2*
● Lippo '14	▼▼ 4
● Colline Lucchesi Ludovico '08	♈♈ 2*
● Colline Lucchesi Ludovico Sardini '12	♈♈ 4
● Colline Lucchesi Ludovico Sardini '11	♈♈ 2*
● Colline Lucchesi Villa Sardini '13	♈♈ 2*
● Colline Lucchesi Villa Sardini '12	♈♈ 2*
● Lippo '11	♈♈ 3
● Lippo '10	♈♈ 3
● Ludovico Sardini '12	♈♈ 3

Podere 414

LOC. MAIANO LAVACCHIO, 10
58051 MAGLIANO IN TOSCANA [GR]
TEL. +39 0564507818
www.podere414.it

CELLAR SALES
PRE-BOOKED VISITS
ANNUAL PRODUCTION 150,000 bottles
HECTARES UNDER VINE 22.00
VITICULTURE METHOD Certified Organic

Simone Castelli gambled on the Maremma area from the beginning and built up his winemaking project in the heart of this area, starting in 1998. The name of the estate is actually the number assigned to it by the Ente Maremma in the 1960s during the process of splitting up large agricultural estates, which emphasizes the historical link with between this farm and fortunes of the local area. A link which is echoed in the style of the wines: pared-down, not without personality, resulting from the exclusive use of grape varieties historically grown in this zone. The strongpoint of the 2014 Morellino di Scansano is its flavour: supple, racy, very fresh and deep with a lovely salty tang in the finish. The aromas are clean, light and nicely defined with lush fruit, especially fresh cherries. The Rosato Flower Power 2015, from drawn-off sangiovese, offers a crisp, tasty flavour and fragrant, persistent aromas.

● Morellino di Scansano '14	▼▼ 3
⊙ Rosato Flower Power '15	▼▼ 2*
● Aleatico Passito '14	♀♀ 7
● Aleatico Passito '13	♀♀ 7
● Morellino di Scansano '13	♀♀ 3
● Morellino di Scansano '12	♀♀ 3

Poderi del Paradiso

LOC. STRADA, 21A
53037 SAN GIMIGNANO [SI]
TEL. +39 0577941500
www.poderidelparadiso.it

CELLAR SALES
PRE-BOOKED VISITS
ACCOMMODATION
ANNUAL PRODUCTION 130,000 bottles
HECTARES UNDER VINE 27.00

Historical evidence dates the arrival of a certain Puccio di Cetto in San Gimignano at around the year 1000. Documents dated just over two centuries later mention Podere Paradiso. The land and buildings were purchased by the Cetti family in 1973 and these represent the original nucleus around which the estate has more recently been built. The vineyards have been renovated, providing space for international varieties alongside more traditional grapes like vernaccia and sangiovese. The appealing Vernaccia Biscondola 2014 has lovely aromas of spices blending with fruity hints of peaches and apricots, rounded off with aromatic herbs. The palate is nicely fresh and full-bodied, with well-measured tangy flavour, and an enthralling finish. The Silicum 2013, a blend of sangiovese, merlot and syrah, is also good: fruity aromas of cherries and damsons, well-judged hints of balsam, black pepper and cinnamon, and a firm-bodied palate with nicely embedded tannins and a fresh, lingering finish.

● Silicum '13	▼▼ 3
○ Vernaccia di S. Gimignano Biscondola '14	▼▼ 3
● Chianti Colli Senesi '14	▼ 2
● San Gimignano Rosso Bottaccio '13	▼ 3
● A Filippo '02	♀♀♀ 4
● Saxa Calida '00	♀♀♀ 5
● Saxa Calida '99	♀♀♀ 4
● Chianti Colli Senesi Ris. '12	♀♀ 3
● San Gimignano Sangiovese Bottaccio '11	♀♀ 4
● San Gimignano Sangiovese Bottaccio '10	♀♀ 5
○ San Gimignano Vin Santo '07	♀♀ 5
○ Vernaccia di S. Gimignano '12	♀♀ 3
○ Vernaccia di S. Gimignano Biscondola '11	♀♀ 3

Podernuovo a Palazzone

LOC. LE VIGNE, 203
53040 SAN CASCIANO DEI BAGNI [SI]
TEL. +39 057856056
www.podernuovoapalazzone.com

ANNUAL PRODUCTION 130,000 bottles
HECTARES UNDER VINE 20.00
SUSTAINABLE WINERY

The Podernuovo estate and winemaking project belongs to Giovanni Bulgari, son of Paolo, jeweller and chairman of the well-known maison of the same name. The estate's 20 hectares of vineyards are planted to sangiovese, Montepulciano, cabernet sauvignon, franc and merlot, on clayey, limestone soil mixed with sandstone and fossils. This area of Tuscany is not usually linked to winegrowing today, although it once had a strong tradition. The wines are modern in style, made without pointless forcing procedures, and above all, with well-judged use of oak. The Therra 2013 is a fragrant and nicely drinkable blend of sangiovese, Montepulciano, cabernet sauvignon, cabernet franc and merlot. The more complex and stylish Argirio 2013, from cabernet sauvignon and franc, offers clear-cut aromas and a soft flavour, with some depth. The Sotirio 2011 is a monovarietal Sangiovese with rather evolved aromas and a tangy but oaky flavour.

● Argirio '13	♟♟ 6
● Therra '13	♟♟ 5
● Sotirio '11	♟ 7

Poggerino

LOC. POGGERINO, 6
53017 RADDA IN CHIANTI [SI]
TEL. +39 0577738958
www.poggerino.com

CELLAR SALES
PRE-BOOKED VISITS
ACCOMMODATION
ANNUAL PRODUCTION 60,000 bottles
HECTARES UNDER VINE 11.30
VITICULTURE METHOD Certified Organic

The wines of Fattoria Poggerino in the Radda in Chianti area, managed by Piero and Benedetta Lanza, are increasingly clear-cut and approachable, and very appealing. The style displays marked acidity alongside sharpish tannins in the early stage of development, for characterful and dynamic wines. Biodynamic vineyard practices have replaced organic, and large barrels are gradually being adopted in the cellar instead of barriques and tonneaux. The Chianti Classico Bugialla Riserva 2013 confirms its distinctive great wine character with clear-cut, complex aromas, in which fresh red fruit alternates with spicy and floral hints polished with earthy sensations. Mouthwatering, lingering flavour and close-knit tannins nicely supported by lively acidity, contrasting with the oak, sometimes a little forward due to the wine's youth. The fragrant Chianti Classico 2013 is firm and well paced.

● Chianti Cl. Bugialla Ris. '13	♟♟♟ 5
● Chianti Cl. '13	♟♟ 4
● Chianti Cl. Bugialla Ris. '12	♟♟♟ 5
● Chianti Cl. Bugialla Ris. '09	♟♟♟ 5
● Chianti Cl. Bugialla Ris. '08	♟♟♟ 5
● Primamateria '01	♟♟♟ 5
● Chianti Cl. '12	♟♟ 3*
● Chianti Cl. '08	♟♟ 3
● Chianti Cl. '06	♟♟ 3*
● Chianti Cl. Bugialla Ris. '10	♟♟ 5
● Primamateria '10	♟♟ 5
● Primamateria '07	♟♟ 5
● Primamateria '06	♟♟ 5

Poggio al Gello

LOC. GELLO
58045 CIVITELLA PAGANICO [GR]
TEL. +39 0564906025
www.poggioalgello.it

CELLAR SALES
PRE-BOOKED VISITS
ANNUAL PRODUCTION 20,000 bottles
HECTARES UNDER VINE 4.00
VITICULTURE METHOD Certified Organic
SUSTAINABLE WINERY

The estate was established in 1998 by Alda Chiarini and Giorgio Nelli. The guidelines of their concept were clear from the beginning: full respect for the environment, scrupulous care over every stage of production, minimal interference in the vineyard and cellar, allowing the land to express its true nature. The four hectares of certified organic vineyards are exclusively planted to native local grape varieties: alongside sangiovese are lesser known cultivars like pugnitello or foglia tonda, older varieties that have recently been rediscovered and yield good results in the bottles. The Rosso del Gello, a monovarietal Sangiovese, opens on dark tones of roots and topsoil, opening out into an array of fruity aromas, like blackberries and cherries. These fruity sensations return on the palate in a juicy, nicely relaxed flavour with compact tannins. The Fosso del Nibbio 2012 is also good, flavoursome and appealing.

● Montecucco Rosso Fosso del Nibbio '12	▼▼	3
● Montecucco Sangiovese Rosso del Gello '13	▼▼	3
● Agellus '14	▼	4
● Montecucco Sangiovese Rosso del Gello '11	♀♀	3*
● Montecucco Sangiovese Rosso del Gello Ris. '11	♀♀	4

Poggio al Tesoro

LOC. FELCIAINO
VIA BOLGHERESE, 189B
57022 BOLGHERI [LI]
TEL. +39 0565773051
www.poggioaltesoro.it

CELLAR SALES
PRE-BOOKED VISITS
ANNUAL PRODUCTION 330,000 bottles
HECTARES UNDER VINE 65.00

Thanks to increased quality and the quite original stylistic definition of recent years, Poggio al Tesoro is becoming one of the most interesting estates in the Bolgheri area. The vineyards are obviously very important: the typical grapes of this DOC zone are planted on different types of soil, sometimes quite compact, in other cases sandy or rich in stony material. The estate style, as we mentioned, is quite individual, focusing on aromatic nuances and consistent flavours. The farm is part of the Valpolicella-based Allegrini group, a famous name in Italian winemaking. A splendid 2013 version of the Bolgheri Rosso Superiore Sondraia: very complex and multi-shaded, ranging from fruity, grassy tones of currants and red peppers to pipe tobacco and dried mint leaves. The palate is firm and warm with luxuriant tannins. The Dedicato a Walter 2013 is excellent, if grassy and unpredictable, with hints of green peppers and a light foxy sensations.

● Bolgheri Sup. Sondraia '13	▼▼▼	5
● Bolgheri Sup. Dedicato a Walter '13	▼▼	7
○ Bolgheri Vermentino Solosole '15	▼▼	3
● Bolgheri Sup. Sondraia '11	♀♀♀	5
● Bolgheri Sup. Sondraia '10	♀♀♀	5
● Dedicato a Walter '12	♀♀♀	7
● Dedicato a Walter '09	♀♀♀	7
⊙ Bolgheri Rosato Cassiopea '13	♀♀	2*
● Bolgheri Sup. Sondraia '12	♀♀	5
○ Bolgheri Vermentino Solosole '13	♀♀	3
● Dedicato a Walter '11	♀♀	7
● Dedicato a Walter '10	♀♀	7
● Mediterra '13	♀♀	3
● Mediterra '12	♀♀	3

★Poggio Antico

LOC. POGGIO ANTICO
53024 MONTALCINO [SI]
TEL. +39 0577848044
www.poggioantico.com

CELLAR SALES
PRE-BOOKED VISITS
RESTAURANT SERVICE
ANNUAL PRODUCTION 120,000 bottles
HECTARES UNDER VINE 32.00

The name of Poggio Antico evokes unforgettable emotions for avid connoisseurs of Montalcino wines. The Riservas produced back in the Seventies and Eighties made the DOC's history, and its present is no less illustrious thanks to the passionate and scrupulous work of Paola Gloder and Alberto Montefiori. With surgical precision, their elegant, racy Brunellos reflect the features of a very unusual zone, among the highest and airiest in the south-western area and most greatly exposed to the influence of the Tyrrhenian coast. A very light hand in the cellar backs up the style with ageing in 37- and 55-hectolitre oak for the basic and Riserva wines, and tonneaux for the Altero selection. Once again, the Riserva is the diamond point of the range. Very varied aromas in the 2010 version: with hints of cherries, watermelon, pencil lead, and a clear touch of confit on the palate, contrasting with tannins which are too forward at the moment. The pair of 2011 Brunellos also show excellent promise.

● Brunello di Montalcino Ris. '10	♥♥	8
● Brunello di Montalcino '11	♥♥	7
● Brunello di Montalcino Altero '11	♥♥	8
● Madre '13	♥	6
● Rosso di Montalcino '14	♥	5
● Brunello di Montalcino '05	♥♥♥	7
● Brunello di Montalcino '88	♥♥♥	7
● Brunello di Montalcino Altero '09	♥♥♥	7
● Brunello di Montalcino Altero '07	♥♥♥	8
● Brunello di Montalcino Altero '06	♥♥♥	8
● Brunello di Montalcino Altero '04	♥♥♥	8
● Brunello di Montalcino Altero '99	♥♥♥	8
● Brunello di Montalcino Ris. '01	♥♥♥	7

Poggio Argentiera

LOC. ALBERESE
S.DA BANDITELLA, 2
58010 GROSSETO
TEL. 3484952767
www.poggioargentiera.com

CELLAR SALES
PRE-BOOKED VISITS
ANNUAL PRODUCTION 200,000 bottles
HECTARES UNDER VINE 22.00
VITICULTURE METHOD Certified Organic

Last year the estate established by Giampaolo Paglia was rented for a 20-year period to Tua Rita of Suvereto, but the general direction seems unchanged. This is one of the leading winemaking estates in the Maremma area, and its production standard remains at an excellent level. The wines reveal a style that is still a work in progress, but based on solid foundations, such as good quality fruit, consistent winemaking choices and the utmost attention to appealing features, as demanded by the types of product on offer. The Morellino di Scansano Capatosta 2013 presents nicely settled aromas, especially red berries, polished with spices, and a well paced, long and consistent palate. The Morellino di Scansano Bellamarsilia 2015 is more approachable, as juicy and soft on the palate as it is vibrant and fragrant on the nose. The crisp, peppery Maremmante 2015, and equal blend of syrah and alicante, is fresh and beautifully drinkable.

● Maremmante '15	♥♥	2*
● Morellino di Scansano Bellamarsilia '15	♥♥	3
● Morellino di Scansano Capatosta '13	♥♥	5
● Finisterre '07	♥♥♥	6
● Morellino di Scansano Capatosta '00	♥♥♥	5*
○ Guazza '13	♥♥	2*
● Morellino di Scansano Bellamarsilia '13	♥♥	3*
● Morellino di Scansano Bellamarsilia '12	♥♥	2*
● Morellino di Scansano Bellamarsilia '11	♥♥	2*
● Morellino di Scansano Capatosta '12	♥♥	5
● Morellino di Scansano Capatosta '11	♥♥	5
● Morellino di Scansano Capatosta '10	♥♥	5

Poggio Bonelli

VIA DELL'ARBIA, 2
53019 CASTELNUOVO BERARDENGA [SI]
TEL. +39 057756661
www.poggiobonelli.it

CELLAR SALES
PRE-BOOKED VISITS
ACCOMMODATION
ANNUAL PRODUCTION 125,000 bottles
HECTARES UNDER VINE 87.00

Poggio Bonelli and Villa Chigi Saracini are the MPS Tenimenti brands, owned by the Montepaschi di Siena banking group. The Sienese company took over full management in 2000 although Poggio Bonelli had existed since the 1950s as had Villa Chigi Saracini, owned by the Sienese family of that name. The winery style consists of well-structured, fruit-rich wines, faithful and well-balanced in expression, despite the often considerable use of mainly small oak. The well-made Poggiassai 2013 is a blend of sangiovese and cabernet sauvignon: fruity aromas polished with hints of spice and vanilla, and a soft, consisten palate with a long finish, just slightly drying. The Chianti Villa Chigi Saracini 2015 is succulent and drinkable, with cherry aromas and a lively, flavoursome palate. The Chianti Classico 2014 is slower to open out on the palate, slender-bodied with somewhat excessive support from the oak.

● Chianti Villa Chigi Saracini '15	♥♥	3
● Poggiassai '13	♥♥	6
● Chianti Cl. '14	♥	3
● Poggiassai '11	♥♥♥	6
● Poggiassai '10	♥♥♥	6
● Poggiassai '08	♥♥♥	5
● Poggiassai '07	♥♥♥	5
● Poggiassai '06	♥♥♥	5
● Tramonto d'Oca '10	♥♥♥	5
● Chianti Cl. '13	♥♥	3
● Chianti Villa Chigi Saracini '14	♥♥	3
● Chianti Villa Chigi Saracini '13	♥♥	3
● Chianti Villa Chigi Saracini '12	♥♥	3

Poggio di Sotto

FRAZ. CASTELNUOVO DELL'ABATE
LOC. POGGIO DI SOTTO
53024 MONTALCINO [SI]
TEL. +39 0577835502
www.collemassari.it

CELLAR SALES
PRE-BOOKED VISITS
ACCOMMODATION
ANNUAL PRODUCTION 35,000 bottles
HECTARES UNDER VINE 12.00
VITICULTURE METHOD Certified Organic
SUSTAINABLE WINERY

The stable of estates under the Tipa family umbrella is increasing and its Montalcino presence has doubled with the purchase of the La Velona properties. No offence to its "sister" wineries (Collemassari in Maremma and Grattamacco at Bolgheri), but the most exciting gamble was taking over Poggio di Sotto in 2011, the estate established by Piero Palmucci and acclaimed as one of the brightest stars in the Brunello firmament. The new direction highlights even more clearly the general desire for expressive continuity, focusing on the temperaments of the Castelnuovo dell'Abate plots and ageing in 30-hectolitre Slavonian oak. The best possible demonstration of this comes from the Brunello 2011, the first vintage to be completely produced by the new staff. Aromas of watermelon, roots, medicinal herbs reveal the Poggio di Sotto style, like the light, luxurious flavour with some contrasting features. The lustrous Rosso 2013 is slightly perfunctory but equally engaging.

● Brunello di Montalcino '11	♥♥♥	8
● Rosso di Montalcino '13	♥♥	8
● Brunello di Montalcino Ris. '10	♥♥	8
● Brunello di Montalcino '10	♥♥♥	8
● Brunello di Montalcino '07	♥♥♥	8
● Brunello di Montalcino '04	♥♥♥	8
● Brunello di Montalcino '99	♥♥♥	8
● Brunello di Montalcino Ris. '07	♥♥♥	8
● Brunello di Montalcino Ris. '99	♥♥♥	8
● Brunello di Montalcino Ris. '95	♥♥♥	8
● Rosso di Montalcino '07	♥♥♥	6

Poggio Rubino

LOC. LA SORGENTE, 62
S.DA PROVINCIALE CASTIGLION DEL BOSCO
53024 MONTALCINO [SI]
TEL. +39 05771698133
www.poggiorubino.it

CELLAR SALES
PRE-BOOKED VISITS
ACCOMMODATION AND RESTAURANT SERVICE
ANNUAL PRODUCTION 32,000 bottles
HECTARES UNDER VINE 7.00

The seven-hectare estate owned by
Edward Corsi and Alessandra Marzocchi is
planted entirely to sangiovese and farmed
according to biocompatible methods. The
plots are located in different areas of the
DOC zone, but the centre is Poggio Rubino
in the central-western sector of Montalcino.
This area is known for high altitudes,
almost 450 metres, and land rich in
limestone and stony material with some
silty components. These are ideal
pedoclimatic conditions for Brunellos which
are traditional but not retro in style,
undergoing long maceration of up to a
month and aged in 25- and 30-hectolitre
oak barrels. Never a false move from the
contained Poggio Rubino range. We were
most impressed with the hard, sharply
focused Brunello 2011, with vegetal and
balsamic hints and confident sinew. The
2010 Riserva is darker initially, with hints of
coffee and tree-bark, but brilliantly
redeemed by the firm, tangy structure.

● Brunello di Montalcino '11	▼▼ 6
● Brunello di Montalcino Ris. '10	▼▼ 7
● Rosso di Montalcino '14	▼ 3
● Brunello di Montalcino '10	♀♀ 6
● Brunello di Montalcino '09	♀♀ 6
● Brunello di Montalcino '08	♀♀ 6
● Brunello di Montalcino '07	♀♀ 6
● Brunello di Montalcino '06	♀♀ 6
● Brunello di Montalcino Ris. '07	♀♀ 7
● Brunello di Montalcino Ris. '06	♀♀ 6
● Rosso di Montalcino '12	♀♀ 3

Poggio Trevvalle

FRAZ. ARCILLE
S.DA PROV.LE 24 FRONZINA, KM 0,600
58042 CAMPAGNATICO [GR]
TEL. +39 0564998142
www.poggiotrevvalle.it

CELLAR SALES
PRE-BOOKED VISITS
ANNUAL PRODUCTION 80,000 bottles
HECTARES UNDER VINE 13.35
VITICULTURE METHOD Certified Organic
SUSTAINABLE WINERY

Poggio Trevvalle has origins outside the
Maremma but has become a good example
of the area's artisan winemaking style.
Brothers Umberto and Bernardo Valle,
originally from Naples and with
winegrowing experience in Puglia, settled
in southern Tuscany in 1999 and breathed
life into a wine estate with vineyards
between the Montecucco and Morellino
DOC zones, organically farmed from the
outset. This choice was carried forward
confidently alongside pared-down cellar
techniques to form the basis of agreeable,
characterful wines. Passera is one of the
best 2015 Morellinos, with sunny aromas
blending lush fruit and spicy, lightly earthy
hints. The palate is succulent, broad and
deep with lovely piquant sensations in the
finish. The Montecucco Rosso 2015 is very
good, youthful with a fresh, relaxed palate.
The Sangiovese Torello 2014, also
fresh-tasting and well-paced, suffers from
slightly excessive oak used for ageing.

● Morellino di Scansano Passera '15	▼▼ 2*
● Montecucco Rosso '15	▼▼ 3
● Morellino di Scansano '15	▼ 3
● Torello '14	▼ 2
● Morellino di Scansano '12	♀♀♀ 2*
● Morellino di Scansano '11	♀♀ 2*
● Morellino di Scansano Larcille Ris. '12	♀♀ 4
● Morellino di Scansano Pàssera '14	♀♀ 3
● Morellino di Scansano Pàssera '13	♀♀ 2*
● Morellino di Scansano Pàssera '12	♀♀ 2*
● Rafele '08	♀♀ 2

Tenuta Il Poggione

FRAZ. SANT'ANGELO IN COLLE
LOC. MONTEANO
53024 MONTALCINO [SI]
TEL. +39 0577844029
www.tenutailpoggione.it

CELLAR SALES
PRE-BOOKED VISITS
ACCOMMODATION
ANNUAL PRODUCTION 600,000 bottles
HECTARES UNDER VINE 127.00

Fabrizio Bindocci and the Franceschi family, who have owned Il Poggione for five generations, are linked by much more than a professional relationship. For many years Fabrizio has run one of Montalcino's largest estates, with over 120 hectares of vineyards in the southern area of Sant'Angelo in Colle. The sangiovese grapes used in the basic and Vigna Paganelli Riserva versions of Brunello have always been treated with traditional methods, such as maceration for about 20 days and ageing in 30- and 50-hectolitre French oak. Small quantities of merlot, vermentino and chardonnay complete the range of grapes grown. The 2010 is one of the best Vigna Paganelli Riservas of the last decade, with sound, juicy fruit enhanced by woody, spicy sensations, and a very slightly curt finish. The whole range is of an excellent standard, however, from the generous 2011 Brunello to the racy, inexpensive Rosso di Montalcino 2014.

● Brunello di Montalcino V. Paganelli Ris. '10	♟♟ 8
● Brunello di Montalcino '11	♟♟ 7
● Rosso di Montalcino '14	♟♟ 4
● Toscana Rosso '13	♟♟ 3
○ Bianco di Toscana Vermentino Chardonnay '15	♟ 3
● Brunello di Montalcino Ris. '97	♟♟♟ 7
● Brunello di Montalcino '10	♟♟ 7
● Brunello di Montalcino '09	♟♟ 6
● Brunello di Montalcino '08	♟♟ 6
● Brunello di Montalcino V. Paganelli Ris. '07	♟♟ 7
● Brunello di Montalcino V. Paganelli Ris. '06	♟♟ 7
● Rosso di Montalcino '13	♟♟ 4
● Rosso di Montalcino '12	♟♟ 3

Poggiotondo

LOC. CERRETO GUIDI
VIA TORRIBINA, 83
50050 CERRETO GUIDI [FI]
TEL. +39 0571559167
www.poggiotondowines.com

PRE-BOOKED VISITS
ACCOMMODATION
ANNUAL PRODUCTION 300,000 bottles
HECTARES UNDER VINE 20.00

We are in Cerreto Guidi, in the midst of the typical Tuscan landscape, halfway between Florence and Pisa. Winemaker Alberto Antonini, helped by his wife Alessandra, runs the estate owned by his family for generations, with organically and biodynamically farmed vineyards, obtaining wines that offer an authentic interpretation of the terroir. Minimal cellar procedures make sure the wines are as natural as possible. The Chianti Riserva Vigna del 1928 beautifully made, with a delightful floral bouquet of violets and cherry and blackberry fruit, light minty sensations and a well-structured, fresh, lively palate with tannins held in check by the alcohol and a consistent, relaxed finish. The Chianti Vigna delle Conchiglie 2013 displays more feral aromas with pleasing hints of forest floor, and a chewy, appetizing, full-bodied palate with a tangy, lingering finish.

● Chianti V. del 1928 Ris. '13	♟♟ 6
● Chianti V. delle Conchiglie '13	♟♟ 6
○ Vermentino '14	♟♟ 2*
● Chianti Ris. '13	♟ 5
● Chianti Sup. '14	♟ 2
● Chianti Sup. '10	♟♟ 2*
● Chianti V. delle Conchiglie '10	♟♟ 6

Poggioventoso

S.DA DI TERENZANA, 5
56046 RIPARBELLA [PI]
TEL. 3938973677
www.poggioventoso.wine

CELLAR SALES
PRE-BOOKED VISITS
ANNUAL PRODUCTION 25,000 bottles
HECTARES UNDER VINE 6.00

This relatively new estate, over ten years old, enjoys a magnificent location at Riparbella, near Pisa. The vineyards are situated in an ideal pedoclimatic context, and the name of the estate was not chosen by chance: the winds are a constant influence in both summer and winter. The technical management is good and solid. This winery was designed, created and carried forward with great passion by Maricla Affatato and family and the wines continue to grow in quality and style. Fruity, grassy aromas with hints of bell peppers, and a broad, succulent palate for the nicely warm and ageable Fuochi 2013, mainly merlot. The Poetico 2015, made from vermentino with an addition of malvasia and petit manseng, is graceful and fluent, with fairly vibrant fruit, juice and tanginess.

● Fuochi '13	♟♟ 6
○ Poetico '15	♟♟ 5
● Fuochi '12	♟♟ 6

★★Poliziano

FRAZ. MONTEPULCIANO STAZIONE
VIA FONTAGO, 1
53045 MONTEPULCIANO [SI]
TEL. +39 0578738171
www.carlettipoliziano.com

CELLAR SALES
PRE-BOOKED VISITS
ANNUAL PRODUCTION 650,000 bottles
HECTARES UNDER VINE 160.00

In the relatively short time of 30 years, Federico Carletti has managed to become and consistently remain a unanimously acknowledged benchmark of winemaking in Tuscany and beyond. Not only have his wines achieved an excellent level of quality, they maintain it every year. More recently, they have successfully changed their signature style, moving away from weighty structure and extract towards elegance and complexity. The strong suit of the Nobile di Montepulciano Asinone 2013 is the nose: polished, complex aromas ranging from lush fruit to iron-like sensations with light hints of toasted coffee. The palate is lively, with rounded, edgy tannins and a tangy, lingering finish. The Nobile di Montepulciano 2013 is deliciously drinkable, and the flavoursome, fragrant Morellino di Scansano Lhosa 2014 is certainly well-focused. A high standard throughout the range.

● Nobile di Montepulciano Asinone '13	♟♟ 7
● Cortona Merlot In Violas '13	♟♟ 4
● Mandrone di Lohsa '12	♟♟ 5
● Morellino di Scansano Lohsa '14	♟♟ 3
● Nobile di Montepulciano '13	♟♟ 5
● Rosso di Montepulciano '14	♟ 3
● Le Stanze '03	♟♟♟ 6
● Nobile di Montepulciano '09	♟♟♟ 4*
● Nobile di Montepulciano Asinone '12	♟♟♟ 7
● Nobile di Montepulciano Asinone '11	♟♟♟ 7
● Nobile di Montepulciano Asinone '07	♟♟♟ 6
● Nobile di Montepulciano Asinone '06	♟♟♟ 6
● Nobile di Montepulciano Asinone '05	♟♟♟ 6
● Nobile di Montepulciano Asinone '04	♟♟♟ 6
● Nobile di Montepulciano Asinone '03	♟♟♟ 6
● Nobile di Montepulciano Asinone '01	♟♟♟ 6

Tenuta Le Potazzine

LOC. LE PRATA, 262
53024 MONTALCINO [SI]
TEL. +39 0577846168
www.lepotazzine.it

CELLAR SALES
PRE-BOOKED VISITS
RESTAURANT SERVICE
ANNUAL PRODUCTION 50,000 bottles
HECTARES UNDER VINE 4.70

Le Potazzine are growing up: youngsters Viola and Sofia Gorelli are increasingly involved in the family estate, which bears their own childhood nickname, the Tuscan word for great tits, the birds shown on the label. They reflect the radiant, carefree style of the Sangiovese wines shaped by Giuseppe and Gigliola Giannetti with incredible consistency. The wines originate from two farms: Le Prata, three and a half hectares in the western Montalcino area at high altitudes close to 500 metres, with a sunny, breezy microclimate and iron-rich soil; and Torre, just over one hectare in the south, between Sesta and Sant'Angelo in Colle, producing more powerful, austere wines. The most recent releases are particularly effective in portraying the character of le Potazzine products, starting with the 2014 Rosso: open and jovial, with an aggressive, racy palate. The herby, citrus 2011 Brunello just lacks a bit more weight and length.

● Brunello di Montalcino '11	♟♟ 7
● Rosso di Montalcino '14	♟♟ 4
● Parus '14	♟ 3
● Brunello di Montalcino '10	♟♟♟ 7
● Brunello di Montalcino '08	♟♟♟ 7
● Brunello di Montalcino Ris. '06	♟♟♟ 8
● Brunello di Montalcino '09	♟♟ 7
● Brunello di Montalcino '07	♟♟ 6
● Brunello di Montalcino '04	♟♟ 7
● Brunello di Montalcino Ris. '04	♟♟ 7
● Rosso di Montalcino '13	♟♟ 4
● Rosso di Montalcino '12	♟♟ 4
● Rosso di Montalcino '10	♟♟ 4

Fabrizio Pratesi

LOC. SEANO
FRAZ. CARMIGNANO
VIA RIZZELLI, 10
59011 CARMIGNANO [PO]
TEL. +39 0558704108
www.pratesivini.it

CELLAR SALES
PRE-BOOKED VISITS
RESTAURANT SERVICE
ANNUAL PRODUCTION 60,000 bottles
HECTARES UNDER VINE 12.00

With the greatest passion Fabrizio Pratesi runs the family estate established by his ancestor Pietro back in 1875, as well as covering the institutional role of Chairman of the Carmignano wine producers' consortium. Following the various purchases and replanting at a high density of plants per hectare, there are now 12 hectares of vineyards and production is of a very high standard. The Pratesi style is based on rich extract and long ageing potential. The Riserva Il Circo Rosso 2013 made a good showing in our final tastings, with generous character and powerful structure. Dark ruby red colour, enthralling aromas of ripe black berry fruit blending into minty, balsamic sensations, and a clear hint of spice. The palate is generous, alcohol-rich, weighty but well balanced and lingering. The Carmione 2014 is succulent and richly extracted, with smooth tannins and lovely hints of red and black berries and Mediterranean scrubland. The Barco Reale is sound.

● Carmignano Il Circo Rosso Ris. '13	♟♟ 6
● Carmione '14	♟♟ 6
● Barco Reale '15	♟ 2
● Carmignano '13	♟♟ 4
● Carmignano '12	♟♟ 3
● Carmignano '08	♟♟ 4
● Carmignano Circo Rosso Ris. '11	♟♟ 5
● Carmignano Circo Rosso Ris. '10	♟♟ 4
● Carmignano Circo Rosso Ris. '08	♟♟ 5
● Carmignano Il Circo Rosso Ris. '12	♟♟ 6
● Carmione '10	♟♟ 4
● Carmione '08	♟♟ 5
● Carmione '07	♟♟ 5
● Merlot Barche di Bacchereto '12	♟♟ 3
● Merlot Barche di Barchereto '10	♟♟ 3

★Fattoria Le Pupille

S.DA PIAGGE DEL MAIANO
58100 GROSSETO
TEL. +39 0564409517
www.fattorialepupille.it

CELLAR SALES
PRE-BOOKED VISITS
ACCOMMODATION
ANNUAL PRODUCTION 450,000 bottles
HECTARES UNDER VINE 80.00

Elisabetta Geppetti is deservedly the protagonist of Maremma's winemaking history, especially in Morellino di Scansano. Le Pupille's first vintages date back to the early 1980s but the real upswing in production for the Istia d'Ombrone estate came with the release of Saffredi, 30 years ago now. Today this winery is a well-established leader, and one of the leading productive estates in Italy's whole winemaking overview. The Morellino di Scansano Riserva 2013 gave us good sensations, with nicely integrated, generally stylish aromas and a layered, progressive flavour with both length and breadth. The Saffredi 2013, a blend of cabernet sauvignon, merlot and petit verdot, displays vibrant, multifaceted aromas, though the oak used for ageing is not yet fully absorbed. The Pelofino 2015 is a fresh and relaxed blend of sangiovese, syrah, cabernet sauvignon and franc.

La Querce

VIA IMPRUNETANA PER TAVARNUZZE, 41
50023 IMPRUNETA [FI]
TEL. +39 0552011380
www.laquerce.com

CELLAR SALES
PRE-BOOKED VISITS
ACCOMMODATION
ANNUAL PRODUCTION 35,000 bottles
HECTARES UNDER VINE 8.00

In the early 1960s, Gino Marchi was inspired by his passion for wine to buy this estate on the hills surrounding Impruneta, a few kilometres south of Florence. Today his son Massimo runs the 42-hectare estate (with eight under vine), assisted by his children Donatella, Benedetta and Giulio who also manage the accommodation facilities in the historic villa. The vineyards are mostly south-facing and have been extensively replanted in recent years with traditional grape varieties like sangiovese and colorino, and also with merlot. And these three grapes provide the basis of the Sorrettole 2015, a Chianti with the winning card of supple drinkable flavour up its sleeve. The nose and palate both reveal fresh red fruit, with a succulent and extremely delicious flavour. The same applies to the Canaiolo Belrosso 2015, flavoursome and very drinkable. The La Torretta 2014 falls short of our expectations, a little below par.

● Saffredi '13	♥♥♥ 8
● Morellino di Scansano Ris. '13	♥♥ 6
● Morellino di Scansano '14	♥ 2
● Morellino di Scansano Poggio Valente Ris. '12	♥ 5
● Pelofino '15	♥ 2
● Morellino di Scansano Poggio Valente '04	♥♥♥ 5
● Saffredi '05	♥♥♥ 8
● Saffredi '04	♥♥♥ 8
● Saffredi '03	♥♥♥ 8
● Saffredi '02	♥♥♥ 7
● Saffredi '01	♥♥♥ 7
● Saffredi '00	♥♥♥ 7

● Belrosso '15	♥♥ 2*
● Chianti Sorrettole '15	♥♥ 2*
● Chianti Colli Fiorentini La Torretta '14	♥ 2
● La Querce '13	♥ 5
● La Querce '11	♥♥♥ 5
● Chianti Colli Fiorentini La Torretta '13	♥♥ 2*
● Chianti Colli Fiorentini La Torretta '12	♥♥ 2*
● La Querce '12	♥♥ 5
● La Querce '10	♥♥ 5
● La Querce '09	♥♥ 5
● La Querce '08	♥♥ 5
● M '09	♥♥ 6
● M '07	♥♥ 6

Querce Bettina

loc. La Casina di Mocali, 275
53024 Montalcino [SI]
Tel. +39 0577848588
www.quercebettina.it

CELLAR SALES
PRE-BOOKED VISITS
ANNUAL PRODUCTION 15,000 bottles
HECTARES UNDER VINE 2.50

It is worth recommending the wines of Querce Bettina if only for the wonderful natural environment from which they originate. Two and a half hectares were planted by the Morettis in the late Nineties in an unspoilt area, literally camouflaged by the woods in the extreme south-western areas of Montalcino. At altitudes of over 400 metres, the land is rich in clay and silty, limestone marl mixed with stones. This light-filled, airy zone is reflected in Brunellos interpreted in anything but two-dimensional terms, and aged in 25-hectolitre Austrian oak with a moderately southern imprint. Querce Bettina's Sangioveses are always interesting for their expressive originality, as further demonstrated by the crisp, succulent Brunello 2011: lemon and orange sweets on the nose with medicinal herbs, and a pleasing, delicious palate. Oddly, the aromas and flavours of the Rosso 2013 are more mature in comparison.

● Brunello di Montalcino '11	♟♟ 7
● Rosso di Montalcino '13	♟♟ 4
● Brunello di Montalcino '06	♟♟♟ 7
● Brunello di Montalcino '10	♟♟ 7
● Brunello di Montalcino '09	♟♟ 7
● Brunello di Montalcino '08	♟♟ 6
● Brunello di Montalcino '07	♟♟ 7
● Brunello di Montalcino '05	♟♟ 7
● Brunello di Montalcino Ris. '07	♟♟ 8
● Brunello di Montalcino Ris. '06	♟♟ 8

Le Ragnaie

loc. Le Ragnaie
53024 Montalcino [SI]
Tel. +39 0577848639
www.leragnaie.com

CELLAR SALES
PRE-BOOKED VISITS
ACCOMMODATION
ANNUAL PRODUCTION 80,000 bottles
HECTARES UNDER VINE 15.50
VITICULTURE METHOD Certified Organic

Riccardo Campinoti, one of the most highly esteemed exponents of Brunello, has a first class set of vineyards on the estate properly named Le Ragnaie, surrounding the winery at the Lume Spento pass, one of the highest points in Montalcino at 600 metres. Vigna Fornace, on the other hand, is situated at Loreto di Castelnuovo dell'Abate in the extreme south-east, with the Pietroso plots above the village. These are profoundly different terroirs whose expressive common thread is to be found in invigorating fruit and a graceful profile, explored through flexible cellar solutions according to the vintage year. This stylistic model appears again in the latest, brilliant releases, above all the Brunello Vecchie Vigne 2011: clear-cut, complex, with a hint of the Orient, the ever-changing aromatic tone fills every space of the flavour with vibrant, tangy energy. The Fornace of the same year is equally serene and relaxed on the palate, with a warmer, more austere texture.

● Brunello di Montalcino V. V. '11	♟♟♟ 8
● Brunello di Montalcino Fornace '11	♟♟ 8
● Brunello di Montalcino '11	♟♟ 7
● Rosso di Montalcino '13	♟♟ 5
● Chianti Colli Senesi '14	♟ 2
☉ Rosato '14	♟ 5
● Brunello di Montalcino Fornace '08	♟♟♟ 8
● Brunello di Montalcino V. V. '10	♟♟♟ 8
● Brunello di Montalcino V. V. '07	♟♟♟ 5
○ Bianco '11	♟♟ 4
● Brunello di Montalcino '10	♟♟ 6
● Brunello di Montalcino '09	♟♟ 6
● Brunello di Montalcino V. V. '09	♟♟ 8
● Chianti Colli Senesi '13	♟♟ 2*

Podere La Regola

Loc. San Martino
56046 Riparbella [PI]
Tel. +39 0586698145
www.laregola.com

CELLAR SALES
PRE-BOOKED VISITS
ANNUAL PRODUCTION 90,000 bottles
HECTARES UNDER VINE 20.00

In the early 20th century the Nuti family purchased a plot of land five kilometres from the sea, at La Regola, to produce olive oil and wine for family consumption. Just over 20 years ago Luca received his degree in agricultural science and decided to transform the little family farm into a properly structured wine estate, planting more vineyards and monitoring the production process to obtain increasingly natural and recognizable wines. A few years later his brother Flavio, a lawyer, joined him in running the farm, in marketing and sales. The Strido 2013, 100% merlot, reached the finals with a generous array of aromas: coffee and toasty hints, followed by forest fruits and hints of vanilla. The palate is mouthfilling, creamy, with tannins blended into the alcohol, fresh-tasting with an appetizing finish. The excellent Vallino 2013, a Cabernet Sauvignon, has a minty, balsamic nose with fresh fruity notes and a dynamic, succulent palate.

● Strido '13	♥♥	8
● La Regola '13	♥♥	6
○ Steccaia Bianco '15	♥♥	3
● Vallino '13	♥♥	5
● Beloro '13	♥	6
○ Lauro Bianco '12	♥	4
○ Le Prode '15	♥	3
● Ligustro '14	♥	3
● Montescudaio Rosso Le Prode '14	♥	2
○ Spumante Brut M. Cl.	♥	4
● La Regola '12	♥♥	6
○ Sondrete '05	♥♥	6
● Strido '11	♥♥	8
● Syrah '13	♥♥	3
● Vallino '11	♥♥	5

Podere Le Ripi

Loc. Le Ripi
53021 Montalcino [SI]
Tel. +39 0577835641
www.podereleripi.it

CELLAR SALES
PRE-BOOKED VISITS
ANNUAL PRODUCTION 25,000 bottles
HECTARES UNDER VINE 12.00
VITICULTURE METHOD Certified Biodynamic
SUSTAINABLE WINERY

Enthusiasts around the world heard the news of Francesco Illy's visionary project even before getting to know his wines. He arrived in Montalcino in the late 1990s to create a new winegrowing estate at Castelnuovo dell'Abate, consisting of 12 hectares of vineyards out of the estate's total 50, biodynamically farmed. The various plots include the now famous "bonsai vineyard", planted at over 60,000 vines per hectare and contributing to the small sangiovese production. Then there is the so-called "golden cellar", the HQ of a stylistic work in progress already noted for its delicious fruit and natural drinkability. Podere Le Ripi debuts straight into the main section thanks to an original range led by the Brunello Lupi e Sirene Riserva 2010. Simply delightful hints of catmint and orange zest, spreading out fluently into a consistent, refreshing flavour, slightly cropped in the finish by tannic bite.

● Brunello di Montalcino Lupi e Sirene Ris. '10	♥♥	6
● Rosso di Montalcino '11	♥♥	5

Rocca delle Macìe

LOC. LE MACÌE, 45
53011 CASTELLINA IN CHIANTI [SI]
TEL. +39 05777321
www.roccadellemacie.com

CELLAR SALES
PRE-BOOKED VISITS
ACCOMMODATION AND RESTAURANT SERVICE
ANNUAL PRODUCTION 3,700,000 bottles
HECTARES UNDER VINE 194.00
SUSTAINABLE WINERY

The estate owned by Sergio Zingarelli, once again elected chairman of the Chianti Classico producers' association, is a benchmark for this DOC. Starting with the less ambitious labels, Rocca delle Macìe wines stand out for their clean craftsmanship and approachable, enjoyable qualities. The style of the leading wines is obviously more complex, while avoiding commonplace or quantity-based choices like excessive use of oak or fruit, preferring harmony and elegance. The Maremma wines, Campomaccione and Casamaria, are also a safe bet for quality. Outstanding finesse and elegance in the Chianti Classico Riserva di Fizzano Gran Selezione 2013, with multifaceted aromas and a sweet entry with a taut, lipsmacking flavour. The Chianti Classico Sergio Zingarelli Gran Selezione 2012 is a little more affected by the oak, with clear-cut aromas and a beautifully detailed palate. The Chianti Classico Sergio Zingarelli 2014 and Riserva 2013 are both delicious.

Rocca di Castagnoli

LOC. CASTAGNOLI
53013 GAIOLE IN CHIANTI [SI]
TEL. +39 0577731004
www.roccadicastagnoli.com

CELLAR SALES
PRE-BOOKED VISITS
ACCOMMODATION AND RESTAURANT SERVICE
ANNUAL PRODUCTION 500,000 bottles
HECTARES UNDER VINE 132.00
SUSTAINABLE WINERY

A clear-cut, consistent style displaying the typical harmony and elegance of Chianti Classico: this is probably the most distinctive feature of Rocca di Castagnoli wines. The estate includes Tenuta di Capraia in the subzone of Castellina in Chianti, and Poggio Maestrino Spiaggiole in Maremma. These wines show consistent, reliable quality and character over time, and plenty of grip without pointless forcing. The Chianti Classico Poggio ai Frati Riserva 2013 is a well-made wine with nicely defined, complex aromas and a succulent, consistent flavour. The more approachable Chianti Classico Rocca di Castagnoli 2014 is extremely drinkable with a relaxed, lipsmacking flavour. The Chianti Classico Tenuta di Capraia Riserva 2013 displays warm aromas, a nicely layered palate and deep finish. The Buriano 2012 is a vibrant Cabernet Sauvignon.

● Chianti Cl. Gran Sel. Riserva di Fizzano '13	▼▼▼ 6
● Chianti Cl. Gran Sel. Sergio Zingarelli '12	▼▼ 8
● Chianti Cl. Famiglia Zingarelli '14	▼▼ 3
● Chianti Cl. Famiglia Zingarelli Ris. '13	▼▼ 4
● Morellino di Scansano Campomaccione '15	▼▼ 3
● Roccato '13	▼▼ 6
● Chianti Cl. Tenuta S. Alfonso '14	▼ 5
● Ser Gioveto '13	▼ 6
● Chianti Cl. Famiglia Zingarelli Ris. '09	▽▽▽ 3*
● Chianti Cl. Fizzano Ris. '10	▽▽▽ 5
● Chianti Cl. Gran Sel. Sergio Zingarelli '11	▽▽▽ 8
● Chianti Cl. Famiglia Zingarelli '13	▽▽ 3*
● Chianti Cl. Gran Sel. Riserva di Fizzano '12	▽▽ 6

● Chianti Cl. Poggio ai Frati Ris. '13	▼▼ 4
● Chianti Cl. Rocca di Castagnoli '14	▼▼ 3
● Chianti Cl. Tenuta di Capraia Ris. '13	▼▼ 5
● Le Pratola '12	▼▼ 6
● Buriano '12	▼ 6
● Chianti Cl. Tenuta di Capraia '14	▼ 4
● Morellino di Scansano Spiaggiole Poggio Maestrino '14	▼ 3
● Morellino di Scansano Spiaggiole Poggio Maestrino Ris. '13	▼ 3
● Chianti Cl. Capraia Ris. '07	▽▽▽ 4
● Chianti Cl. Poggio ai Frati Ris. '08	▽▽▽ 4
● Chianti Cl. Poggio ai Frati Ris. '06	▽▽▽ 4*
● Chianti Cl. Tenuta di Capraia Ris. '06	▽▽▽ 4*

★Rocca di Frassinello

LOC. GIUNCARICO
58023 GAVORRANO [GR]
TEL. +39 056688400
www.roccadifrassinello.it

CELLAR SALES
PRE-BOOKED VISITS
ACCOMMODATION
ANNUAL PRODUCTION 400,000 bottles
HECTARES UNDER VINE 80.00

The gamble was to succeed in making a great wine in an area that was still a winegrowing question mark in the early 2000s. Over the years the gamble has proved a winner and has brought this part of Maremma, wedged between the DOC zones of Bolgheri, to the north, and Morellino di Scansano to the south, into the spotlight on worldwide markets. Editor and owner Paolo Panerai was already producing wine in Chianti Classico, with Castellare di Castellina, and in Sicily with Feudi del Pisciotto. This estate currently numbers 80 hectares under vine planted to native and international grapes producing powerfully structured wines with good evident Mediterranean features. Like the Baffo Nero, 100% merlot, which manages to earn itself Tre Bicchieri despite the difficult year. The nose opens on ripe damsons, with well-dosed hints of juniper berries and aromatic herbs. The palate is warm and mouthfilling, richly extracted and luxurious.

Rocca di Montegrossi

FRAZ. MONTI IN CHIANTI
53010 GAIOLE IN CHIANTI [SI]
TEL. +39 0577747977
www.roccadimontegrossi.it

CELLAR SALES
PRE-BOOKED VISITS
ANNUAL PRODUCTION 80,000 bottles
HECTARES UNDER VINE 18.00
VITICULTURE METHOD Certified Organic

Marco Ricasoli Firidolfi runs his estate in the most consistent, authentic Chianti style, perfected back in the 1980s which, thanks to necessary technical adjustments, characterizes the products of this Monti in Chianti estate today. The wines pursue harmony and elegance, starting with the shrewd use of both barriques and large oak casks for ageing. Among the best in the designation, the excellent Vin Santo is a traditional wine "threatened with extinction". The 2007 is charming, with iodine, dried fruit and dates on the nose and a generous creamy palate with lively acidity. The Chianti Classico Vigneto San Marcellino Gran Selezione 2012 is nicely made with clear, warm aromas and a firm, succulent flavour, just slightly held back by excessive tannic hardness. The Geremia 2012, merlot and cabernet sauvignon, is richly textured and fruity.

● Maremma Toscana Baffo Nero '14	♟♟♟	8
● Maremma Toscana Le Sughere di Frassinello '14	♟♟	4
● Maremma Toscana Ornello '14	♟♟	3
● Maremma Toscana Rocca di Frassinello '14	♟♟	6
○ Maremma Toscana Vermentino '15	♟♟	3
● Maremma Toscana Poggio alla Guardia '14	♟	3
● Baffo Nero '12	♟♟♟	8
● Baffo Nero '11	♟♟♟	8
● Baffo Nero '10	♟♟♟	8
● Baffo Nero '09	♟♟♟	8
● Le Sughere di Frassinello '10	♟♟♟	4*
● Maremma Toscana Baffo Nero '13	♟♟♟	8
● Rocca di Frassinello '12	♟♟♟	6
● Rocca di Frassinello '11	♟♟♟	6

○ Vin Santo del Chianti Cl. '07	♟♟	5
● Chianti Cl. Gran Sel. Vign. S. Marcellino '12	♟♟	5
● Geremia '12	♟♟	6
● Chianti Cl. Vign. S. Marcellino '07	♟♟♟	6
● Chianti Cl. Vign. S. Marcellino Ris. '99	♟♟♟	4
● Chianti Cl. '13	♟♟	3
● Chianti Cl. '12	♟♟	3
● Chianti Cl. Vign. S. Marcellino '11	♟♟	5
● Chianti Cl. Vign. S. Marcellino '10	♟♟	5
● Chianti Cl. Vign. S. Marcellino '09	♟♟	5
● Chianti Cl. Vign. S. Marcellino '08	♟♟	3
○ Vin Santo del Chianti Cl. '06	♟♟	5
○ Vin Santo del Chianti Cl. '04	♟♟	5

Rocca di Montemassi

LOC. PIAN DEL BICHI
FRAZ. MONTEMASSI
S.DA PROV.LE 91
58036 ROCCASTRADA [GR]
TEL. +39 0564579700
www.roccadimontemassi.it

CELLAR SALES
PRE-BOOKED VISITS
ACCOMMODATION AND RESTAURANT SERVICE
ANNUAL PRODUCTION 200,000 bottles
HECTARES UNDER VINE 165.00
SUSTAINABLE WINERY

The winery is part of the Zonin group, whose Tuscan properties include Castello d'Albola in Chianti Classico and Abbazia Monte Oliveto near San Gimignano. The 460-hectare Maremma estate, 165 under vine, was purchased in 1999 and is situated between the Tyrrhenian coast and the Colline Metallifere. Renovations were carried out in full respect of the local area, including restoration of the old farmhouses and planting of vegetation to preserve the rural landscape's biodiversity and identity. The vineyards speak the local language, with a foreign accent. Their rows include non-native varieties which have fully acclimatized to the Mediterranean environment, such as cabernet sauvignon and franc, merlot, petit verdot and viognier, alongside the two main typical local varieties, sangiovese and vermentino. The Sassabruna 2014, sangiovese with a small addition of syrah and merlot, is excellent, just lacking that final extra surge to achieve the highest accolade. Ripe black berries, chocolate and vanilla pods lead into a richly opulent palate.

● Maremma Toscana Sassabruna '14	♥♥ 3*
● Maremma Toscana Sangiovese Le Focaie '15	♥♥ 3
○ Maremma Toscana Calasole '15	♥ 3
● Maremma Toscana Rocca di Montemassi '14	♥ 5
○ Maremma Toscana Viognier Astraio '15	♥ 4
● Maremma Toscana Rocca di Montemassi '13	♥♥♥ 5
● Rocca di Montemassi '10	♥♥♥ 5
● Rocca di Montemassi '09	♥♥♥ 5
● Maremma Rocca di Montemassi '12	♥♥ 5
● Monteregio di Massa Marittima Sassabruna '11	♥♥ 3
● Rocca di Montemassi '11	♥♥ 5
● Rocca di Montemassi '08	♥♥ 5

Roccapesta

LOC. MACERETO, 9
50854 SCANSANO [GR]
TEL. +39 0564599252
www.roccapesta.it

CELLAR SALES
PRE-BOOKED VISITS
ANNUAL PRODUCTION 100,000 bottles
HECTARES UNDER VINE 18.50

Roccapesta has risen very quickly. In 2003 Milanese manager Alberto Tanzini decided to change his life and devote his time to winegrowing. Today his estate is a well-established benchmark, thanks to his clear-sighted and determined choices. The use of older vineyards, like 40-year-old Calestaia, as well as long maceration, large oak barrels and generous bottle ageing produce polished, ageable wines with lovely personality, which was unimaginable in Scansano only a few years ago. Outstanding among a very good range of wines from Roccapesta, the Morellino di Scansano Riserva 2013 displays enchanting aromas blending earthy sensations and fragrant fruit with hints of pipe tobacco and flowers. The flavour is consistent, tangy and sometimes edgy, closing on cherry sensations. The Morellino di Scansano Ribeo 2014 is no less delicious, with a well-paced and slender palate, and light, elegant aromas.

● Morellino di Scansano Ris. '13	♥♥♥ 4*
● Morellino di Scansano Ribeo '14	♥♥ 3*
● Maremma Toscana Masca '14	♥♥ 2*
● Morellino di Scansano '14	♥♥ 3
● Pugnitello '13	♥♥ 6
● Morellino di Scansano Calestaia Ris. '11	♥♥♥ 5
● Morellino di Scansano Calestaia Ris. '10	♥♥♥ 5
● Morellino di Scansano Calestaia Ris. '09	♥♥♥ 5
● Masca '13	♥♥ 2*
● Masca '12	♥♥ 2*
● Morellino di Scansano '13	♥♥ 3*
● Morellino di Scansano Ribeo '13	♥♥ 3
● Morellino di Scansano Ris. '12	♥♥ 4
● Morellino di Scansano Ris. '11	♥♥ 4
● Pugnitello '12	♥♥ 5

Salcheto

FRAZ. SANT'ALBINO
VIA DI VILLA BIANCA, 15
53045 MONTEPULCIANO [SI]
TEL. +39 0578799031
www.salcheto.it

CELLAR SALES
PRE-BOOKED VISITS
ACCOMMODATION AND RESTAURANT SERVICE
ANNUAL PRODUCTION 300,000 bottles
HECTARES UNDER VINE 50.00
VITICULTURE METHOD Certified Organic
SUSTAINABLE WINERY

Despite ancient origins the estate only underwent a transformation with the arrival of Michele Manelli in 1997. He was responsible for turning Salcheto into one of the most innovative wineries in the world in terms of environmental sustainability. The whole structure is a model of ecological efficiency and technological innovation, and the vineyard is also managed with a careful eye on the environment. The oldest plots, Vigna del Salco and Vigna del Laghetto, produce competing versions of Nobile di Montepulciano Salco. The 2012 version of this great wine has a strongly Mediterranean, sunny character with aromas immediately focusing on ripe fruit, with some hints of cigar smoke, pencil lead and liquorice. The palate is consistent and well structured with open fruity sensations, hints of scrubland and lipsmacking tannins, if rather drying. The 2012 Riserva is a little evolved, while the Nobile 2013 has hints of roots and spices.

● Nobile di Montepulciano Salco '12	▼▼ 6
● Nobile di Montepulciano '13	▼▼ 4
● Nobile di Montepulciano Ris. '12	▼▼ 5
● Nobile di Montepulciano '10	▼▼▼ 4*
● Nobile di Montepulciano '97	▼▼▼ 3*
● Nobile di Montepulciano Salco '11	▼▼▼ 6
● Nobile di Montepulciano Salco '10	▼▼▼ 5
● Nobile di Montepulciano Salco Evoluzione '06	▼▼▼ 6
● Nobile di Montepulciano Salco Evoluzione '01	▼▼▼ 6
● Nobile di Montepulciano '11	▽▼ 4
● Nobile di Montepulciano Ris. '10	▽▼ 4
● Rosso di Montepulciano '14	▽▼ 2*

Leonardo Salustri

FRAZ. POGGI DEL SASSO
LOC. LA CAVA, 7
58044 CINIGIANO [GR]
TEL. +39 0564990529
www.salustri.it

CELLAR SALES
PRE-BOOKED VISITS
ACCOMMODATION
ANNUAL PRODUCTION 80,000 bottles
HECTARES UNDER VINE 25.00
VITICULTURE METHOD Certified Organic
SUSTAINABLE WINERY

In the late 19th century, Secondo Salustri began planting his vineyard at Poggi del Sasso, in the heart of Maremma, on the lowest foothills of Mount Amiata. Today that vineyard still exists in the meticulous clonal selection carried out by Leonardo Salustri, current owner of the estate. He started planting his own vineyards in the 1950s, and renewed them all in the Nineties in a partnership with the Faculty of Oenology of the University of Pisa. Such a perfectly acclimatized vineyard in perfect harmony with the terroir cannot help but produce deeply land-rooted wines with a strong identity. So much so, that two wines made it to the finals, the Sangiovese Santa Marta 2013 and the Grotte Rosse of the same year. The former displays enthralling aromas of blood oranges and currants, with a sound flavour, lovely grip, and echoes of Seville oranges in the finish alongside still-lively tannins, certain to develop further. The latter wine is slightly more opulent with ripe black fruit on the nose and a relaxed, mouthfilling palate.

● Montecucco Sangiovese Grotte Rosse '13	▼▼ 6
● Montecucco Sangiovese Santa Marta '13	▼▼ 4
● Montecucco Sangiovese Terre d'Alviero '13	▼▼ 8
● Montecucco Grotte Rosse '08	▼▼▼ 6
● Montecucco Grotte Rosse '07	▼▼▼ 5
● Montecucco Santa Marta '06	▼▼▼ 4
● Montecucco Grotte Rosse '11	▽▼ 6
● Montecucco Grotte Rosse '10	▽▼ 6
● Montecucco Grotte Rosse '06	▽▼ 5
● Montecucco Santa Marta '12	▽▼ 4
● Montecucco Santa Marta '10	▽▼ 4
● Montecucco Santa Marta '09	▽▼ 4
● Montecucco Santa Marta '08	▽▼ 4
● Montecucco Santa Marta '07	▽▼ 4

Podere San Cristoforo

LOC. BAGNO
VIA FORNI
58023 GAVORRANO [GR]
TEL. 3358212413
www.poderesancristoforo.it

CELLAR SALES
PRE-BOOKED VISITS
ACCOMMODATION
ANNUAL PRODUCTION 50,000 bottles
HECTARES UNDER VINE 16.00
VITICULTURE METHOD Certified Organic

Lorenzo Zonin, owner and winemaker of the estate, developed his winegrowing project according to biodynamic principles. Little technology, a great deal of manual work, respect for the environment and local area: these are the guidelines for running the cellar and, above all, the 15 hectares of vineyards on the 45-hectare estate along with two hectares of olive groves, and 20 planted to cereal crops and sunflowers. Sangiovese takes the lion's share of the vineyards, as well as petit verdot, syrah, vermentino and trebbiano, in a range of wines aiming at full expression of their terroir. The Carandelle 2015 is a really good Sangiovese with a subtle, ethereal nose with lovely floral hints and intriguing nuances of pink pepper. The palate is lively and dynamic with elegant acidity and smooth tannins. The clean, clear-cut Amaranti 2015 is fresh tasting with slightly piquant tannins, and fluent, coherent body. A good performance also from the Luminoso 2015, from trebbiano, malvasia and vermentino: tangy, salty, vibrant and mouthwatering.

● Maremma Toscana Sangiovese Carandelle '15	♈♈♈ 3*
○ Maremma Toscana Luminoso '15	♈♈ 3
● Maremma Toscana Sangiovese Amaranto '15	♈♈ 3
● Maremma Toscana Podere San Cristoforo '13	♈♈♈ 3*
● Maremma Toscana Sangiovese Amaranto '14	♈♈ 2*
● Podere San Cristoforo '12	♈♈ 5
● San Cristoforo '10	♈♈ 5
● San Cristoforo '09	♈♈ 4

★San Felice

LOC. SAN FELICE
53019 CASTELNUOVO BERARDENGA [SI]
TEL. +39 05773991
www.agricolasanfelice.it

CELLAR SALES
PRE-BOOKED VISITS
ACCOMMODATION AND RESTAURANT SERVICE
ANNUAL PRODUCTION 900,000 bottles
HECTARES UNDER VINE 140.00

San Felice has been a strong presence in the Chianti Classico DOC for 40 years now, and its wines are definitely influenced by the microclimate of the Castelnuovo Berardenga subzone, displaying extremely drinkable appeal and sturdy structure throughout the range. The estate belongs to the Allianz insurance group, along with the Campogiovanni farm at Montalcino and Periolla in Maremma, creating a productive mosaic across some of Tuscany's top growing areas. The Chianti Classico 2013 is very good, perhaps one of the best. A detailed nose with red berries, earthy hints and forest floor, and a fresh, flavoursome palate with nicely harmonious, progressive flavour. The Chianti Classico Il Grigio Gran Selezione 2013 displays well-organized aromas despite a few evolved nuances, while the flavour is succulent and rounded.

● Chianti Cl. '13	♈♈♈ 3*
● Brunello di Montalcino Il Quercione Campogiovanni Ris. '10	♈♈ 6
● Chianti Cl. Gran Sel. Il Grigio da San Felice '13	♈♈ 5
● Chianti Cl. Gran Sel. Poggio Rosso '11	♈ 6
● Rosso di Montalcino Campogiovanni '14	♈ 3
● Vigorello '12	♈ 6
● Chianti Cl. Gran Sel. Il Grigio da San Felice '11	♈♈♈ 5
● Chianti Cl. Gran Sel. Il Grigio da San Felice '10	♈♈♈ 5
● Pugnitello '07	♈♈♈ 6
● Pugnitello '06	♈♈♈ 6
● Vigorello '10	♈♈♈ 6
● Vigorello '08	♈♈♈ 6

San Ferdinando

LOC. CIGGIANO
VIA DEL GARGAIOLO, 33
52041 CIVITELLA IN VAL DI CHIANA [AR]
TEL. +39 0575440355
www.sanferdinando.eu

CELLAR SALES
PRE-BOOKED VISITS
ACCOMMODATION
ANNUAL PRODUCTION 30,000 bottles
HECTARES UNDER VINE 10.00

San Ferdinando is a lovely, original project, which has increased the prestige of the whole winegrowing context of Val di Chiana. It was started up in 1998 by the Grifoni family who not only planted the vineyards, but also built a modern cellar, inaugurated in 2009. Everything is based on promoting native Tuscan grape varieties, sangiovese and ciliegiolo above all, as well as pugnitello and vermentino among the white grapes. The training methods respect the natural environment, just as the vinification and ageing procedures protect the wines' natural expression. The Ciliegiolo 2015 is full, refreshing, and tangy with sweet fruity texture, enhanced by subtle, appealing hints of black pepper. The Pugnitello 2013 is similar in style: obviously more mature but no less delicious and drinkable. The Chianti Podere Gamba 2014 is also excellent, while the 2015 Vermentino is more open and less vibrant than usual.

San Giusto a Rentennano

LOC. SAN GIUSTO A RENTENNANO, 20
53013 GAIOLE IN CHIANTI [SI]
TEL. +39 0577747121
www.fattoriasangiusto.it

CELLAR SALES
PRE-BOOKED VISITS
ANNUAL PRODUCTION 80,000 bottles
HECTARES UNDER VINE 27.00
VITICULTURE METHOD Certified Organic
SUSTAINABLE WINERY

The Martini di Cigala family estate is firmly established in the category of the best in the DOC zone, and their basic Chianti Classico is rarely excluded from the best wines. However their legendary signature style, with bags of energy especially in the more prestigious wines, continues to suffer from excessive use of oak in the maturation phase. While the whole range still offers a faithful interpretation of the Monti subzone, this flaw is detrimental to fruit that could potentially display prime quality. The Chianti Classico Le Baròncole Riserva 2013 is a well-made wine overall, with alternating fruity and spicy aromas and a weighty, gutsy palate. The 2014 Chianti Classico is generally more focused and pleasing, despite the tricky year, while the Percarlo 2012, 100% sangiovese, is less confident, with markedly toasty aromas and a clean but rather strained flavour.

● Chianti Podere Gamba '14	♥♥ 2*
● Ciliegiolo '15	♥♥ 2*
● Pugnitello '13	♥♥ 3
○ Vermentino '15	♥ 3
● Ciliegiolo '12	♀♀ 2*
● Ciliegiolo '10	♀♀ 2*
● Sangiovese '10	♀♀ 3

● Chianti Cl. Le Baròncole Ris. '13	♥♥ 5
● Chianti Cl. '14	♥♥ 4
● Percarlo '12	♥ 8
● Chianti Cl. '10	♥♥♥ 4*
● Percarlo '07	♥♥♥ 7
● Percarlo '99	♥♥♥ 7
● Percarlo '97	♥♥♥ 6
● Percarlo '95	♥♥♥ 6
● Percarlo '88	♥♥♥ 6
● Chianti Cl. '09	♀♀ 3
● Chianti Cl. Le Baròncole Ris. '11	♀♀ 5
● Chianti Cl. Le Baròncole Ris. '10	♀♀ 5
● Chianti Cl. Le Baròncole Ris. '09	♀♀ 5
● Chianti Cl. Le Baròncole Ris. '07	♀♀ 5
● Chianti Cl. Le Baròncole Ris. '06	♀♀ 5
● Percarlo '05	♀♀ 7

★★Tenuta San Guido

FRAZ. BOLGHERI
LOC. LE CAPANNE, 27
57022 CASTAGNETO CARDUCCI [LI]
TEL. +39 0565762003
www.sassicaia.com

PRE-BOOKED VISITS
RESTAURANT SERVICE
ANNUAL PRODUCTION 780,000 bottles
HECTARES UNDER VINE 90.00

A large portion of credit for Bolgheri's amazing current international success goes to the Marchesi Incisa della Rocchetta. They were behind the Tenuta San Guido project, back when no-one imagined its potential, and launched one of the most significant Italian wines ever onto the market, Sassicaia. The vineyards are divided over several areas with different soil types and aspect, some near the sea and others on the hills. The grapes are cabernet sauvignon and franc, and the wines are aged in French oak barriques. Watch out: the 2013 Sassicaia is an insanely good wine. To find a version this impressive, we'd have to go back to 2009, though it was profoundly different, almost the opposite, we might say. And that's not all: in outlook this 2013 is undoubtedly better, and will find a place among the greatest years of all time. Clenched and vigorous, vibrant and appealing, as complex as it is lively and deep, and endlessly lingering. A masterpiece.

● Bolgheri Sassicaia '13	♛♛♛ 8
● Guidalberto '14	♛♛ 6
● Bolgheri Sassicaia '12	♛♛♛ 8
● Bolgheri Sassicaia '11	♛♛♛ 8
● Bolgheri Sassicaia '10	♛♛♛ 8
● Bolgheri Sassicaia '09	♛♛♛ 8
● Bolgheri Sassicaia '08	♛♛♛ 8
● Bolgheri Sassicaia '07	♛♛♛ 8
● Bolgheri Sassicaia '06	♛♛♛ 8
● Bolgheri Sassicaia '05	♛♛♛ 8
● Bolgheri Sassicaia '04	♛♛♛ 8
● Bolgheri Sassicaia '03	♛♛♛ 8
● Guidalberto '08	♛♛♛ 6
● Guidalberto '04	♛♛♛ 6

San Michele a Torri

VIA SAN MICHELE, 36
50020 SCANDICCI [FI]
TEL. +39 055769111
www.fattoriasanmichele.it

CELLAR SALES
PRE-BOOKED VISITS
ANNUAL PRODUCTION 200,000 bottles
HECTARES UNDER VINE 55.00
VITICULTURE METHOD Certified Organic

Transport entrepreneur Paolo Nocentini owns this estate which, in his capable hands, has become a virtuous example of intelligent traditional farming, promoting the most authentic face of Tuscany. With 55 hectares under vine, some in the Chianti Classico DOC zone, the estate is also the nerve centre for typical local products: olive oil of course, but also Cinta Senese cured meats, eggs, meat, vegetables, bread, legumes, honey, jams and flours made from old traditional grains. All these are used in the farm's restaurant in Florence. Both the versions of the Chianti Colli Fiorentini are very impressive. The Riserva San Giovanni Novantasette shows weighty texture and rounded tannins that soften the flavour. The 2014 is darting and lively, with a small amount of canaiolo, colorino and merlot in the blend: currants, raspberries and floral sensations on the nose, and an expressive, pleasing palate.

● Chianti Colli Fiorentini '14	♛♛ 2*
● Chianti Colli Fiorentini S. Giovanni Novantasette Ris. '13	♛♛ 4
● Chianti Cl. '11	♛♛ 3
● Chianti Colli Fiorentini '13	♛♛ 2*
● Chianti Colli Fiorentini '10	♛♛ 2*
● Chianti Colli Fiorentini '09	♛♛ 2*
● Chianti Colli Fiorentini S. Giovanni Novantasette Ris. '12	♛♛ 4
○ Chianti Colli Fiorentini Vin Santo '07	♛♛ 3
● Murtas '11	♛♛ 5
● Murtas '09	♛♛ 5
● Murtas '07	♛♛ 5
○ Vin Santo '08	♛♛ 6

San Polo

LOC. PODERNOVI, 161
53024 MONTALCINO [SI]
TEL. +39 0577835101
www.poggiosanpolo.com

CELLAR SALES
PRE-BOOKED VISITS
ANNUAL PRODUCTION 150,000 bottles
HECTARES UNDER VINE 17.00

The Allegrini family's Montalcino project
seems to have settled into a polished
productive and stylistic appearance.
Everything focuses on the 17-hectare
estate at Podernovi, a historic location in
the east, at 450 metres altitude on loamy
limestone soil. The Brunellos fermented in
concrete vats and matured in both
barriques and 30-hectolitre Slavonian and
Allier oak are a blend of clarity and vitality.
Completing the range alongside the Rosso
are the Mezzopane IGT, a sangiovese-
heavy blend, and the Rubio, a monovarietal
sangiovese aged in large oak barrels.
Undoubtedly the best performance ever for
San Polo, with the Brunello Riserva 2010
in the final. Black berries, colonial spice,
hints of cocoa powder, and a sweet,
rounded palate with a little harshness in
the finish due to the oaky sensations. The
Brunello 2011 is also beautifully made,
and already quite approachable with hints
of cherries and coffee.

● Brunello di Montalcino Ris. '10	▼▼ 7
● Brunello di Montalcino '11	▼▼ 6
● Rosso di Montalcino '14	▼ 3
● Brunello di Montalcino '10	♀♀ 6
● Brunello di Montalcino '09	♀♀ 6
● Brunello di Montalcino '08	♀♀ 6
● Brunello di Montalcino '07	♀♀ 6
● Brunello di Montalcino '06	♀♀ 6
● Brunello di Montalcino Ris. '06	♀♀ 7
● Brunello di Montalcino Ris. '04	♀♀ 7
● Rosso di Montalcino '13	♀♀ 3
● Rosso di Montalcino '12	♀♀ 3
● Rosso di Montalcino '11	♀♀ 3
● Rubio '10	♀♀ 2*
● Rubio '08	♀♀ 2

Tenuta San Vito

VIA SAN VITO, 59
50056 MONTELUPO FIORENTINO [FI]
TEL. +39 057151411
www.san-vito.com

CELLAR SALES
PRE-BOOKED VISITS
ACCOMMODATION AND RESTAURANT SERVICE
ANNUAL PRODUCTION 150,000 bottles
HECTARES UNDER VINE 35.00
VITICULTURE METHOD Certified Organic

The Drighi family bought this estate around
1960. Roberto planted the vineyards and
olive groves, and started the construction
of the cellar and oil mill. Tenuta San Vito
can boast that it was one of the first
Tuscan estates to seriously commit to
organic production methods, obtaining
certification in 1985 after the strenuous
efforts of Roberto's daughter Laura. Today,
on the Montelupo Fiorentino hills, a few
kilometres from Florence, the estate's
farmhouses house a flourishing
agritourism business, run by Roberto's
nephew Neri Gazulli, as well as the cellar.
We were particularly taken with the Chianti
San Vito 2015, a monovarietal Sangiovese,
fresh and firm with lovely red fruit aromas,
tempting and really enjoyable. The Poggio
Alto 2013 wasn't bad either: a blend of
colorino, canaiolo, ciliegiolo and merlot,
with black berries and spice on the nose
and an invigorating palate with a lovely
peppery finish.

● Chianti San Vito '15	▼▼ 2*
● Poggio Alto '13	▼▼ 4
● Chianti Colli Fiorentini Darno '13	▼ 2
○ Amantiglio '05	♀♀ 2
● Chianti dei Colli Fiorentini Darno '12	♀♀ 2*
● Chianti dei Colli Fiorentini Darno '06	♀♀ 2*
● Chianti dei Colli Fiorentini Darno '05	♀♀ 2*
● Colle dei Mandorli '11	♀♀ 6
● Colle dei Mandorli '10	♀♀ 6
● Colle dei Mandorli '07	♀♀ 5
● Colle dei Mandorli '06	♀♀ 5
● Colle dei Mandorli '05	♀♀ 5
● Madiere '06	♀♀ 3
● Madiere '05	♀♀ 3
○ Vin Santo del Chianti Malmatico '07	♀♀ 5

Sangervasio

LOC. SAN GERVASIO
VIA DEI CIPRESSI, 13
56036 PALAIA [PI]
TEL. +39 0587483360
www.sangervasio.com

CELLAR SALES
PRE-BOOKED VISITS
ACCOMMODATION AND RESTAURANT SERVICE
ANNUAL PRODUCTION 100,000 bottles
HECTARES UNDER VINE 22.00
VITICULTURE METHOD Certified Organic

A 16th-century hamlet surrounded by 400 hectares of land: this is the San Gervasio estate purchased in 1960 by the Tommasini family. Luca effected a profound change on the property in the mid-Nineties: he opted for organic methods in the vineyards, renovated the old cellars, regrafted old vines, purchased new hectares of land, and created avantgarde vineyards on them. The result is a noticeable increase in the quality of the wines. The Cabernet Sauvignon 2011 is deep and vibrant with balsamic sensations alongside hints of cloves and cinnamon, and a broad, well-measured palate, lively and fresh with a lingering, gentle finish. The impressive I Renai 2011, 100% merlot, shows a bouquet of wild red berries on the nose and a harmonious palate with well-blended tannins, lively and mouthwatering with a powerful finish. The Vin Santo Recinaio 2005 displays classic aromas of dates and dried figs with hints of toasted almonds, a creamy, mouthfilling palate and velvety finish.

● Cabernet Sauvignon '11	♀♀ 5	
○ Colli dell'Etruria Centrale Vin Santo Recinaio '05	♀♀ 5	
● I Renai '11	♀♀ 5	
● Chianti Sangervasio '15	♀ 2	
● Terre di Pisa Sangiovese a Sirio '11	♀ 4	
● I Renai '09	♀♀ 5	
● I Renai '03	♀♀ 5	
○ Sangervasio Bianco '05	♀♀ 2	
● Sangervasio Rosso '09	♀♀ 2*	
● Sangervasio Rosso '05	♀♀ 2	
● Terre di Pisa Sangervasio '11	♀♀ 4	

Podere Sanlorenzo

POD. SANLORENZO, 280
53024 MONTALCINO [SI]
TEL. 3396070930
www.poderesanlorenzo.net

CELLAR SALES
PRE-BOOKED VISITS
ANNUAL PRODUCTION 18,000 bottles
HECTARES UNDER VINE 4.50

Bramante Ferretti's birthday has become a real drinkable feast for the people of Montalcino. At over 100 years old he is there to advise and inspire his grandson Luciano Ciolfi who, in 2003, decided to convert Sanlorenzo into a bottling estate, with immediately interesting results. Sangiovese is the only variety growing on the farm's four hectares in the south-western area of Montalcino, at about 500 metres altitude, on soil with medium loam content and rich in limestone marl. This is the origin of austerely powerful, supple, full-bodied Brunellos, their nature nurtured by lengthy maceration and ageing in 30-hectare Slavonian oak. We always recommend patience with the Sanlorenzo reds, and the 2011 Bramante is no exception: the aromas are already quite nicely defined, with earthy, woody nuances while the palate is still a little overwhelmed by the extract, though it displays strength and grip. The exquisite Rosso 2014 is much more accomplished.

● Brunello di Montalcino Bramante '11	♀♀ 6	
● Rosso di Montalcino '14	♀♀ 3	
● Brunello di Montalcino Bramante '07	♀♀♀ 6	
● Brunello di Montalcino Bramante '07	♀♀♀ 8	
● Brunello di Montalcino Bramante '10	♀♀ 6	
● Brunello di Montalcino Bramante '09	♀♀ 6	
● Brunello di Montalcino Bramante '08	♀♀ 6	
● Brunello di Montalcino Bramante '04	♀♀ 6	
● Rosso di Montalcino '13	♀♀ 3	
● Rosso di Montalcino '11	♀♀ 3	
● Rosso di Montalcino '10	♀♀ 3	

Sant'Agnese

LOC. CAMPO ALLE FAVE, 1
57025 PIOMBINO [LI]
TEL. +39 0565277069
www.santagnesefarm.it

CELLAR SALES
PRE-BOOKED VISITS
ANNUAL PRODUCTION 25,000 bottles
HECTARES UNDER VINE 6.00
SUSTAINABLE WINERY

In 1994 the Gigli family made a longstanding dream come true when they bought a farm at auction, nestling in the hills overlooking the sea. Although faced with abandoned lands and buildings in need of renovations, their passion and enthusiasmkept the upper hand, and they made a successful start to their life as fine wine producers. Today the Gigli brothers manage a respectable winery, a small but well-organized family estate where grapes that have adapted to this ideal habitat grow alongside traditional Tuscan varieties. Fiori Blu 2010 is a Cabernet Sauvignon with evolved aromas of leather and pipe tobacco, followed by balsamic sensations and ripe fruit. The palate is powerful and generous with perceptible, blended tannins and a lively, succulent finish. The Rubido 2013, 100% merlot, is also interesting, with raspberry and cherry jam and tomato leaves on the nose, and a nicely weighty, warm and harmonious palate.

● I Fiori Blu '10	♟♟ 6
● Rubido '13	♟♟ 2*
☉ A Rose is a Rose '15	♟ 2
○ Kalendamaia '15	♟ 2
● I Fiori Blu '08	♟♟ 6
● Libatio '08	♟♟ 4
● Merlot I Fiori Blu '09	♟♟ 6
● Rubido '12	♟♟ 2*
● Rubido '11	♟♟ 2*
● Spirto '09	♟♟ 5
● Spirto '08	♟♟ 5
● Spirto '06	♟♟ 5
○ Val di Cornia Kalendamaia '11	♟♟ 2*
● Val di Cornia Rubido '09	♟♟ 2*
● Val di Cornia Rubido '08	♟♟ 2*

Santa Lucia

FRAZ. FONTEBLANDA
S.DA STAT.LE AURELIA, 264
58015 ORBETELLO [GR]
TEL. +39 0564885474
www.azsantalucia.com

CELLAR SALES
PRE-BOOKED VISITS
ACCOMMODATION
ANNUAL PRODUCTION 150,000 bottles
HECTARES UNDER VINE 35.00
SUSTAINABLE WINERY

Luciano Scotto's definitely family-run winery vaunts 35 hectares under vine and has potential production of about 80,000 bottles. In the past the cellar has alternated interesting products and respectable, but little more than correct performance. The house style is one of generous wines, decidedly Mediterranean and at times this strong tendency can lead to some uncertainty in grape ripening or use of wood. This year Luciano seems to have hit the right note, safeguarding his style but refining it and rendering it more solid. Clean, tempting, well-focused aromas and a really lovely flavour for the Morellino di Scansano A Luciano 2015, while the equally delicious Morellino di Scansano Torre del Moro 2014 is a refreshing glassful with a pleasing iodine sensation in the finish. The Morellino Tore del Moro Riserva 2013 is richly contrasted and complex with spicy, fruity aromas and a sturdy, impressive flavour.

● Betto '13	♟♟ 3
● Maremma Toscana Losco '15	♟♟ 2*
● Morellino di Scansano A Luciano '15	♟♟ 2*
● Morellino di Scansano Tore del Moro '14	♟♟ 2*
● Morellino di Scansano Torre del Moro Ris. '13	♟♟ 4
○ Maremma Toscana Ansonica '15	♟ 2
○ Maremma Toscana Vermentino Brigante '15	♟ 2
○ Maremma Vermentino Brigante '12	♟♟ 2*
● Morellino di Scansano A Luciano '14	♟♟ 2*
● Morellino di Scansano A Luciano '13	♟♟ 2*
● Morellino di Scansano Tore del Moro '12	♟♟ 2*
● Morellino di Scansano Tore del Moro '11	♟♟ 2*

Podere Sapaio

Loc. Lo Scopaio, 212
57022 Castagneto Carducci [LI]
Tel. +39 0565765187
www.sapaio.it

PRE-BOOKED VISITS
ANNUAL PRODUCTION 75,000 bottles
HECTARES UNDER VINE 25.00

Podere Sapaio is a lovely winegrowing project set up by Massimo Piccini in 1999. His family, originally from Veneto, invested in the Bolgheri terroir long before it made its name, convinced of its potential and capacity to produce something original. And so it was. Today, Sapaio wines are among the most recognizable and interesting in the DOC zone. The land is sandy with limestone, and the Bordeaux variety grapes produce powerful wines whose intensity is enhanced by ageing in oak. We were really impressed with the interpretation of the vintage shown by the Bolgheri Rosso Superiore 2013, following the same model as ever, but more harmonious and elegant, starting with spicy, toasty aromas. These are followed by ripe, dark fruit streaked through with refreshing vegetal and balsamic sensations. The palate is full-bodied and rich in extract but, as we said, capable of dynamic, racy development.

● Bolgheri Rosso Sup. '13	▼▼▼ 7	
● Bolgheri Volpolo '14	▼ 5	
● Bolgheri Rosso Sup. '12	♈♈♈ 7	
● Bolgheri Rosso Sup. '11	♈♈♈ 7	
● Bolgheri Sup. Sapaio '10	♈♈♈ 6	
● Bolgheri Sup. Sapaio '09	♈♈♈ 6	
● Bolgheri Sup. Sapaio '08	♈♈♈ 6	
● Bolgheri Sup. Sapaio '07	♈♈♈ 6	
● Bolgheri Sup. Sapaio '06	♈♈♈ 6	
● Bolgheri Sup. Sapaio '05	♈♈ 6	
● Bolgheri Volpolo '13	♈♈ 5	
● Bolgheri Volpolo '12	♈♈ 4	
● Bolgheri Volpolo '11	♈♈ 4	
● Bolgheri Volpolo '08	♈♈ 4	
● Bolgheri Volpolo '07	♈♈ 4	

Michele Satta

Loc. Vigna al Cavaliere, 61b
57022 Castagneto Carducci [LI]
Tel. +39 0565773041
www.michelesatta.com

CELLAR SALES
PRE-BOOKED VISITS
ANNUAL PRODUCTION 150,000 bottles
HECTARES UNDER VINE 20.00

Michele Satta is a well-known name in the Tuscan wine sector, and original exponent of the Bolgheri terroir. His passion for sangiovese motivates him to keep making space for this variety on his estate, alongside the most commonly grown Bordeaux grapes in this area. This aside, Satta's style is really impressive. He has plenty of experience, having established his winery in the 80s, as well as a sensitive mind and hands which he applies to winemaking. This is a charming estate, especially if you are looking for authentic wines and less usual methods. The Bolgheri Rosso Superiore I Castagni 2012 should be interpreted in this light: it is capable of balance and a certain finesse rather than excessive extract, almost slender at times, certainly linear, but always delicious, which lengthens and enhances the pleasing flavour. The Bolgheri Bianco Costa di Giulia 2015 has lovely white peach aromas and a fresh, juicy palate.

○ Bolgheri Bianco Costa di Giulia '15	▼▼ 4	
● Bolgheri Rosso Sup. I Castagni '12	▼▼ 8	
● Bolgheri Sup. Piastraia '13	▼ 6	
● Bolgheri Rosso Piastraia '02	♈♈♈ 6	
● Bolgheri Rosso Piastraia '01	♈♈♈ 6	
⊙ Bolgheri Rosato '13	♈♈ 2*	
● Bolgheri Rosso '13	♈♈ 3	
● Bolgheri Rosso '12	♈♈ 3	
● Bolgheri Rosso '11	♈♈ 3	
● Bolgheri Rosso Piastraia '12	♈♈ 5	
● Bolgheri Rosso Piastraia '11	♈♈ 5	
● Bolgheri Rosso Piastraia '10	♈♈ 5	
● Syrah '12	♈♈ 5	

Savignola Paolina

VIA PETRIOLO, 58
50022 GREVE IN CHIANTI [FI]
TEL. +39 0558546036
www.savignolapaolina.it

CELLAR SALES
PRE-BOOKED VISITS
ACCOMMODATION
ANNUAL PRODUCTION 35,000 bottles
HECTARES UNDER VINE 6.00

The farmstead, originally called Savignola, was purchased by the Fabbri family in the mid-1800s. In the period between the two World Wars, Paolina added her own name and started the winegrowing business which singled her out as one of the pioneers of the designation. Today her great-grand-daughter/niece Ludovica, who runs the estate, has created a clearly defined style for the wines, which undergo skilful technical procedures during vinification and are aged in small oak casks, preserving the character and nature of Chianti Classicos grown in a cool location. The Chianti Classico Riserva 2013 is a really well-focused wine, with precise, vibrant aromas alternating strawberries and flowers with spicy and earthy hints. The palate is more flavoursome than powerful, lipsmacking and coherent, up to the nicely tangy finish. The Chianti Classico 2014, subtle but not without substance, also offers lovely sensations: approachably fragrant with a supple flavour and simple, nicely defined aromas.

● Chianti Cl. '14	♥♥	3
● Chianti Cl. Ris. '13	♥♥	4
● Chianti Cl. '10	♀♀	3
● Chianti Cl. '09	♀♀	3
● Chianti Cl. Ris. '11	♀♀	4
● Chianti Cl. Ris. '08	♀♀	4
● Chianti Cl. Ris. '06	♀♀	4
● Chianti Cl. Ris. '05	♀♀	4
● Chianti Cl. Ris. '04	♀♀	4
● Chianti Cl. Ris. '03	♀♀	3
● Granaio '08	♀♀	4
● Granaio '07	♀♀	4
● Granaio '06	♀♀	4

La Selva

LOC. FONTE BLANDA
S.DA PROV.LE 81 OSA, 7
58010 ORBETELLO [GR]
TEL. +39 0564885669
www.laselva-bio.it

CELLAR SALES
PRE-BOOKED VISITS
ACCOMMODATION
ANNUAL PRODUCTION 200,000 bottles
HECTARES UNDER VINE 32.00
VITICULTURE METHOD Certified Organic

These are the pillars of Karl Egger's winegrowing estate: organic farming methods since the beginning in 1980, attention to local grape varieties, and even more care over sustainable cellar procedures. In addition, the prices are particularly fair, making this Orbetello estate one of the most strongly established in Maremma's overview, offering a consistently enjoyable range of labels, especially recently. Full of flavour, almost piquant, the Morellino di Scansano Colli dell'Uccellina Riserva 2013 has fresh, vibrant aromas and a gutsy, well-paced flavour. The rich, layered Morellino di Scansano 2015 is more approachable and open but equally delicious. The Maremma Ciliegiolo 2013 is subtle and edgy with elegant, well-defined fruit and a moreish flavour. The succulent, fragrant Nudo Sangiovese 2014 is made by Roland Krebser, La Selva's winemaker, with Stefano Bambagioni.

● Maremma Toscana Ciliegiolo '13	♥♥	3
● Morellino di Scansano '15	♥♥	2*
● Morellino di Scansano Colli dell'Uccellina Ris. '13	♥♥	3
● Nudo Sangiovese '14	♥♥	2*
● Maremma Toscana Privo '15	♥	2
○ Maremma Toscana Vermentino '15	♥	2
● Pugnitello '12	♥	5
○ Vermentino Nudo '15	♥	3
○ Bianco Toscano '14	♀♀	2*
● Maremma Toscana Ciliegiolo '12	♀♀	3
● Prima Causa '11	♀♀	5
● Pugnitello '11	♀♀	5

Fattoria Selvapiana

Loc. Selvapiana, 43
50068 Rufina [FI]
Tel. +39 0558369848
www.selvapiana.it

CELLAR SALES
PRE-BOOKED VISITS
ANNUAL PRODUCTION 220,000 bottles
HECTARES UNDER VINE 60.00

The farm's roots date back to the Middle Ages when it served as a defensive fortress for the city of Florence, along the Sieve river. Today the estate is run by brother and sister Silvia and Federico Giuntini Massetti, the last heirs of a tradition that has set Chianti Rufina apart from other subzones, as Cosimo Il de' Medici realized. The Selvapiana estate currently covers 250 hectares with 60 under vine, in the foothills of the Apennines where the weather stays cool even in summer. Since 1990 the vineyard and olive groves have been organically farmed. Into the finals once again for the Bucerchiale with a 2013 that opens on lovely black and red berries, and unfolds with dynamic energy, powerful and nicely textured. We also tasted a good version of the Chianti Rufina, the 2014: cherry fruit on the nose with light grassy hints and a tangy, fluent palate.

Sensi

via Cerbaia, 107
51035 Lamporecchio [PT]
Tel. +39 057382910
www.sensivini.com

CELLAR SALES
PRE-BOOKED VISITS
ANNUAL PRODUCTION 2,000,000 bottles
HECTARES UNDER VINE 80.00

In 1895, Pietro Sensi was already selling his wine in the district markets. His sons, Vittorio and Armido founded Fratelli Sensi and delivered wine door-to-door from their horse-drawn wagon. After the war, Vittorio's sons, Pietro and Giovanni grew the winery to national level. Today's owners, Massimo and Roberta, have turned it into an international venture. The family has two estates: Tenuta del Poggio and Fattoria di Calappiano. Through to the finals again for the Chianti Vinciano Riserva 2013, thanks to an array of clear fruit aromas, cherries above all, hints of forest floor and a nuance of pipe tobacco. The palate is supported by lovely acidity, a light body and fine-grained tannins, with a succulent, lingering finish. The enjoyable Testardo 2014, sangiovese and cabernet sauvignon, has good, spicy aromas with balsamic hints and a soft, broad and mouthfilling palate with a long, flavoursome finish.

● Chianti Rufina Bucerchiale Ris. '13	🍷🍷 5
● Chianti Rufina '14	🍷🍷 2*
● Pomino '12	🍷 2
○ Selvapiana '15	🍷 2
● Chianti Rufina '13	🍷🍷 2*
● Chianti Rufina '12	🍷🍷 2*
● Chianti Rufina '11	🍷🍷 2*
● Chianti Rufina Bucerchiale Ris. '12	🍷🍷 5
● Chianti Rufina Bucerchiale Ris. '11	🍷🍷 5
● Fornace '11	🍷🍷 5
● Fornace '09	🍷🍷 5
● Pomino Villa Petrognano '12	🍷🍷 2*
○ Vin Santo del Chianti Rufina '07	🍷🍷 2*

● Chianti Vinciano Fattoria di Calappiano Ris. '13	🍷🍷 6
● Bolgheri Sabbiato '14	🍷🍷 5
● Brunello di Montalcino Boscoselvo '11	🍷🍷 7
● Mantello '14	🍷🍷 4
● Morellino di Scansano Pretorio '15	🍷🍷 3
● Testardo '14	🍷🍷 4
● Chianti Campoluce '15	🍷 2
● Chianti Sup. Vagante '15	🍷 3
● Chianti Vinciano '15	🍷 4
● Ninfato '15	🍷 4
● Chianti Dalcampo Ris. '12	🍷🍷 3
● Chianti Vinciano Fattoria di Calappiano Ris. '12	🍷🍷 6
● Lungarno Fattoria di Calappiano '13	🍷🍷 7
● Mantello '13	🍷🍷 4

Serpaia

LOC. FONTEBLANDA
VIA GOLDONI, 15
58100 GROSSETO
TEL. +39 0461650129
www.serpaiamaremma.it

ANNUAL PRODUCTION 134,500 bottles
HECTARES UNDER VINE 30.00

Trento company Endrizzi landed here at Fonteblanda in the southern part of the Morellino di Scansano DOC zone, in 2000. The encounter between two very different winemaking traditions was successful in building a solid, very readable blend. No forcing goes into the sangiovese production process, thanks to meticulous growing techniques and moderate fermentation, and the result is beautifully enjoyable wines with good clean aromas. Ageing in both large oak and barriques enhances the wines with balance and finesse. The wines from this Monteblanda-based estate are solid and well made. The Morellino di Scansano 2014 displays clearly approachable aromas focused on fruit, polished with spicy and toasty hints. The palate is very fresh, well-paced and tangy. The Serpaiolo 2014 is an equally well-made blend of merlot, cabernet sauvignon and sangiovese, with well-defined, fresh aromas and generous, layered flavour.

● Morellino di Scansano '14	♥♥ 2*
● Serpaiolo '14	♥♥ 2*
● Morellino di Scansano '13	♀♀ 2*
● Morellino di Scansano '12	♀♀ 2*
● Morellino di Scansano Dono Ris. '11	♀♀ 3
● Morellino di Scansano Dono Ris. '08	♀♀ 3

Serraiola

FRAZ. FRASSINE
LOC. SERRAIOLA
58025 MONTEROTONDO MARITTIMO [GR]
TEL. +39 0566910026
www.serraiola.it

CELLAR SALES
PRE-BOOKED VISITS
ANNUAL PRODUCTION 40,000 bottles
HECTARES UNDER VINE 12.00

On the border between the provinces of Grosseto and Livorno, Serraiola is the furthest extremity of the Monteregio DOC zone. The Lenzi family bought the land in the late Sixties and immediately began planting the first vineyards. Today Fiorella is at the helm, and credit goes to her for turning the estate around, enabling the wines to achieve a reliable standard of quality and establishing the winery among the most interesting in the DOC. The 12-odd hectares under vine have gradually been replanted to more suitable clonal selections and the addition of a few international grape varieties: sangiovese and merlot for the reds and trebbiano, malvasia, vermentino, chardonnay and sauvignon for the whites. The Campo Montecristo 2014 is a monovarietal Merlot with hints of raspberries and ripe cherries blending with tertiary aromas. The cool year has endowed this wine with a more fluent, drinkable palate, but cost a little of its usual softness. The Sangiovese Lentisco 2014 is well-paced with consistent flavour.

● Campo Montecristo '14	♥♥ 5
● Lentisco '14	♥♥ 3
● Maremma Toscana Sassonero '15	♥ 2
○ Maremma Toscana Violina '15	♥ 3
○ Serrabacio '15	♥ 3
● Shiraz '14	♥ 3
● Campo Montecristo '13	♀♀ 5
● Campo Montecristo '09	♀♀ 5
● Campo Montecristo '08	♀♀ 5
● Campo Montecristo '07	♀♀ 5
● Monteregio di Massa Marittima Lentisco '11	♀♀ 3
● Monteregio Massa Marittima Lentisco '13	♀♀ 3
● Shiraz '13	♀♀ 3
● Shiraz '07	♀♀ 3
○ Vermentino '13	♀♀ 2*

Sesti - Castello di Argiano

FRAZ. SANT'ANGELO IN COLLE
LOC. CASTELLO DI ARGIANO
53024 MONTALCINO [SI]
TEL. +39 0577843921
www.sestiwine.com

CELLAR SALES
PRE-BOOKED VISITS
ANNUAL PRODUCTION 61,000 bottles
HECTARES UNDER VINE 9.00

Castello di Argiano, the estate established by Giuseppe Sesta and run today with his daughter Elisa, is situated in the heart of an ancient Etruscan settlement in the extreme south-west of Montalcino. The castle-hamlet watches over the vineyards, inspiring what is in many ways an ancestral task, linked to natural procedures and operating timetables dependent on the lunar cycle. Basically, it is not just about farming, but also history, geology, and astronomy, all of which affect the cellar decisions as much as technical reflections in producing serene Brunellos, as you might expect from an area with a strongly Tyrrhenian influence, and largely ecocenic soils. The well-made 2011 Brunello is textbook: aromas ranging from flowers to Mediterranean essences, soft and mouthfilling on the palate despite a slight loss in vigour. The Phenomena Riserva 2010 also appears well-prepared, with a blend of topsoil, strawberry jam and black olives on the nose and a drier, more expansive flavour.

● Brunello di Montalcino Phenomena Ris. '10	♟♟ 8
● Brunello di Montalcino '11	♟♟ 6
● Rosso di Montalcino '14	♟♟ 4
○ Sauvignon '15	♟♟ 3
● Grangiovese '14	♟ 2
☉ Rosato '15	♟ 2
● Brunello di Montalcino '06	♟♟♟ 6
● Brunello di Montalcino Phenomena Ris. '07	♟♟♟ 8
● Brunello di Montalcino Phenomena Ris. '01	♟♟♟ 8
● Brunello di Montalcino Ris. '04	♟♟♟ 8
● Brunello di Montalcino '10	♟♟ 6
● Rosso di Montalcino '13	♟♟ 4

Tenuta Sette Ponti

VIA SETTE PONTI, 71
52029 CASTIGLION FIBOCCHI [AR]
TEL. +39 0575477857
www.tenutasetteponti.it

CELLAR SALES
PRE-BOOKED VISITS
ACCOMMODATION
ANNUAL PRODUCTION 225,000 bottles
HECTARES UNDER VINE 55.00
SUSTAINABLE WINERY

The Moretti family purchased the estate in the 1950s from Margherita and Maria Cristina di Savoia. It was used as a country residence and conventional farm, with grapes included among the crops grown. When fashion entrepreneur Antonio Moretti joined the business, it was a turning point for the estate which owes its name to him, as a tribute to the Via dei Sette Ponti, connecting the banks of the River Arno between Florence and Arezzo. Two wines through to the finals: the Oreno, from merlot, cabernet sauvignon and petit verdot is a regular, and the 2013 greatly impressed us with its broad range of aromas, fine-grained, subtle tannins, firm, nicely blended texture and very lingering finish, as ever. But we couldn't help but award Tre Bicchieri to the Sangiovese Vigna dell'Impero 2013: elegant, vibrant, clean, outstandingly stylish, a true thoroughbred.

● Valdarno di Sopra V. dell'Impero '13	♟♟♟ 8
● Oreno '13	♟♟♟ 8
● Crognolo '14	♟♟ 5
○ Grisoglia '12	♟♟ 5
● Chianti V. di Pallino '15	♟ 2
● Chianti V. di Pallino Ris. '13	♟ 3
● Oreno '12	♟♟♟ 7
● Oreno '11	♟♟♟ 7
● Oreno '10	♟♟♟ 7
● Oreno '09	♟♟♟ 7
● Oreno '05	♟♟♟ 7
● Oreno '00	♟♟♟ 5

Talenti

FRAZ. SANT'ANGELO IN COLLE
LOC. PIAN DI CONTE
53020 MONTALCINO [SI]
TEL. +39 0577844064
www.talentimontalcino.it

CELLAR SALES
PRE-BOOKED VISITS
ANNUAL PRODUCTION 100,000 bottles
HECTARES UNDER VINE 21.00

Back in 1980 Pierluigi Talenti decided to move from Romagna to Montalcino and purchase the Pian di Conte property overlooking the Orcia river valley a stone's throw from the village of Sant'Angelo in Colle. About 20 hectares of vineyards, mainly planted to sangiovese, are divided over various plots at altitudes between 200 and 400 metres, with loamy, limestone, and sandy soil. At the helm is Riccardo, Piero's grandson, who shapes a small, distinguished range of wines according to different ageing processes (medium-sized oak and tonneaux for the Brunellos). Talenti is celebrating its thirtieth anniversary with the 2011 vintage, beautifully expressed in the Brunello Trentennale: clear-cut fruit, roots, medicinal herbs and a hushed complexity bounding across the palate with sweet and savoury hints, lengthened by mouthwatering and beautifully extracted tannins. Also excellent are the Pian di Conte Riserva 2010 and Rosso 2014.

● Brunello di Montalcino Trentennale '11	▼▼▼ 8
● Brunello di Montalcino Pian di Conte Ris. '10	▼▼ 7
● Rosso di Montalcino '14	▼▼ 3
● Brunello di Montalcino '04	♀♀♀ 8
● Brunello di Montalcino '88	♀♀♀ 8
● Brunello di Montalcino Ris. '99	♀♀♀ 6
● Brunello di Montalcino V. del Paretaio Ris. '01	♀♀♀ 6
● Brunello di Montalcino '10	♀♀ 6
● Brunello di Montalcino '09	♀♀ 6
● Brunello di Montalcino '08	♀♀ 6
● Brunello di Montalcino '06	♀♀ 6

Fattoria della Talosa

VIA TALOSA, 8
53045 MONTEPULCIANO [SI]
TEL. +39 0578758277
www.talosa.it

CELLAR SALES
PRE-BOOKED VISITS
ANNUAL PRODUCTION 100,000 bottles
HECTARES UNDER VINE 35.00

A visit to the historic Talosa cellar in the underground areas beneath two old buildings in the centre of Montepulciano offers a meaningful picture of the important role wine has always played in this area. The estate has been owned by Angelo Jacorossi since the early 1970s. The vineyards are planted in some of the DOC zone's best growing areas, at altitudes between 350 and 400 metres. The wines show generous personality and excellent ageing potential, confirmed by tasting some classic riservas. A nuanced performance from the wines tasted this year. The Nobile di Montepulciano 2013 is of a high standard in particular, with confident redcurrant and cherry aromas and a beautifully relaxed palate, classy and deep with a fresh, clenched and linear finish. The Rosso di Montepulciano 2015 is less impressive, quite acidulous and grassy.

● Nobile di Montepulciano '13	▼▼ 4
● Rosso di Montepulciano '15	▼ 2
● Nobile di Montepulciano '11	♀♀ 4
● Nobile di Montepulciano '10	♀♀ 3
● Nobile di Montepulciano '08	♀♀ 3
● Nobile di Montepulciano '07	♀♀ 3
● Nobile di Montepulciano '07	♀♀ 4
● Nobile di Montepulciano '06	♀♀ 3
● Nobile di Montepulciano Filai Lunghi '11	♀♀ 5
● Nobile di Montepulciano Filai Lunghi '07	♀♀ 5
● Nobile di Montepulciano Ris. '10	♀♀ 4
● Nobile di Montepulciano Ris. '07	♀♀ 4

★Tenimenti Luigi d'Alessandro

VIA MANZANO, 15
52042 CORTONA [AR]
TEL. +39 0575618667
www.tenimentidalessandro.it

CELLAR SALES
PRE-BOOKED VISITS
ACCOMMODATION AND RESTAURANT SERVICE
ANNUAL PRODUCTION 130,000 bottles
HECTARES UNDER VINE 37.00
VITICULTURE METHOD Certified Organic

Since the 18th century Tenimenti
d'Alessandro has been one of the leading
farms in the Val di Chiana. The estate is
run today by the Calabresi family, who
bring to fruition the innovative winegrowing
work started in the 1960s by the
d'Alessandro family who planted the first
syrah vineyards, now the most widespread
grape in the Cortona area. The vineyards
have been organically farmed since the
2013 harvest and in 2016 the estate
obtained organic certification. These wines
show impressively consistent quality. The
Migliara 2011 made the finals with tertiary,
complex aromas and a more structured,
generous palate with a lovely lingering,
flavourful finish. Bosco 2012 is more
straightforward and satisfying, focused on
wild berry aromas, with a relaxed,
appealing palate. All the range is sound,
including the whites, especially the
monovarietal Viognier, Fontarca.

● Cortona Syrah Il Bosco '12	♟♟♟ 6
● Cortona Syrah Migliara '11	♟♟ 8
○ Bianco del Borgo '15	♟♟ 3
● Cortona Syrah Borgo '14	♟♟ 3
● Cortona Syrah V. V. '12	♟♟ 5
○ Cortona Vin Santo '04	♟♟ 6
○ Fontarca '14	♟♟ 5
● Cortona Il Bosco '09	♟♟♟ 6
● Cortona Il Bosco '06	♟♟♟ 6
● Cortona Il Bosco '04	♟♟♟ 5
● Cortona Il Bosco '03	♟♟♟ 5
● Cortona Syrah Migliara '08	♟♟♟ 8
● Cortona Syrah Migliara '07	♟♟♟ 8

Tenuta di Sesta

FRAZ. CASTELNUOVO DELL'ABATE
LOC. SESTA
53024 MONTALCINO [SI]
TEL. +39 0577835612
www.tenutadisesta.it

CELLAR SALES
PRE-BOOKED VISITS
ANNUAL PRODUCTION 150,000 bottles
HECTARES UNDER VINE 30.00

The Tenuta di Sesta name proudly
announces its indissoluble association with
one of the best growing areas in southern
Montalcino. Situated practically halfway
between Sant'Angelo in Colle and
Castelnuovo dell'Abate, the estate
established by Tiziano Ciacci in the 1960s is
run today by Giovanni and Francesca. Its
vineyard plots are located at around 350
metres altitude, on generally lean soil, rich
in limestone with some tuffstone. This is an
ideal starting point for rangy, airy Brunellos,
their nature enhanced by pared-down
cellarwork, with long ageing in medium-
sized oak. An original style bravely explored
in the Riserva: the 2010 is in many ways
the squaring of the circle, with a light-footed
gait, with an almost springtime feel in the
hints of jasmine, mandarins, ginger and
wildflowers. Not as slender as it looks, as
shown by the progressive, penetrating
flavour with a long, balsamic aftertaste.

● Brunello di Montalcino Ris. '10	♟♟♟ 7
● Brunello di Montalcino '11	♟ 5
● Brunello di Montalcino '10	♟♟ 5
● Brunello di Montalcino '09	♟♟ 5
● Brunello di Montalcino '08	♟♟ 5
● Brunello di Montalcino '07	♟♟ 5
● Brunello di Montalcino '06	♟♟ 5
● Brunello di Montalcino '05	♟♟ 5
● Brunello di Montalcino Ris. '09	♟♟ 7
● Brunello di Montalcino Ris. '07	♟♟ 7
● Brunello di Montalcino Ris. '06	♟♟ 7
● Poggio d'Arna '11	♟♟ 2*
● Poggio d'Arna '10	♟♟ 2*
● Rosso di Montalcino '13	♟♟ 3
● Rosso di Montalcino '11	♟♟ 3
● Rosso di Montalcino '10	♟♟ 3*

Tenuta di Trinoro

VIA VAL D'ORCIA, 15
53047 SARTEANO [SI]
TEL. +39 05782671100578267110
www.tenutaditrinoro.it

PRE-BOOKED VISITS
ANNUAL PRODUCTION 70,000 bottles
HECTARES UNDER VINE 20.00

The first experimental bottles from this
winemaking estate date back to 1995,
when owner Andrea Franchetti immediately
succeeded in endowing his wines with a
characteristic, focused and readable style.
A great deal is owed to the Bordeaux
winemaking and growing approach but the
personality expressed by his wines is by no
means a secondary aspect, achieved
through harvesting as late as possible,
fermentation in concrete vats, considerable
extraction and the use of small oak casks.
The resulting products always reveal very
vibrant aromas and a dynamic, satisfying
flavour. There's no lack of oak in the Tenuta
Trinoto 2014, a blend of cabernet franc,
cabernet sauvignon, merlot and petit
verdot, but it is rich in texture and verve. Of
the three single variety Cabernet Francs,
presented for the first time, we liked the
Campo di Tenaglia 2014 best: lightly citrus,
earthy aromas and a deep flavour with a
spicy finish.

● Campo di Tenaglia '14	♟♟ 8
● Tenuta di Trinoro '14	♟♟ 8
● Campo di Camagi '14	♟♟ 8
● Campo di Magnacosta '14	♟♟ 8
● Palazzi '14	♟♟ 8
● Le Cupole '14	♟ 5
● Tenuta di Trinoro '08	♟♟♟ 8
● Tenuta di Trinoro '04	♟♟♟ 8
● Tenuta di Trinoro '03	♟♟♟ 8
● Magnacosta '13	♟♟ 8
● Palazzi '13	♟♟ 8
● Tenuta di Trinoro '13	♟♟ 8
● Tenuta di Trinoro '12	♟♟ 8

Tenute del Cerro

FRAZ. ACQUAVIVA
VIA GRAZIANELLA, 5
53045 MONTEPULCIANO [SI]
TEL. +39 0578767722
www.tenutedelcerro.it

CELLAR SALES
PRE-BOOKED VISITS
ACCOMMODATION AND RESTAURANT SERVICE
ANNUAL PRODUCTION 1,700,000 bottles
HECTARES UNDER VINE 233.00

Tenute del Cerro, owned by Unipol Group,
comprises leading Italian wine estates, for
almost 5,000 hectares of land. As well as
Montepulciano, (Fattoria del Cerro), the
farms are situated in the Brunello di
Montalcino (La Poderina) and Montefalco
Sagrantino areas (Còlpetrone), and at
Monterufoli, growing vermentino. Fattoria
del Cerro, with 94 hectares of vineyards, is
the jewel in the crown, as one of the
largest, most attractive and best-suited
estates in the Vino Nobile di Montepulciano
designation. The leader of the group of
wines tasted was the Vino Nobile di
Montepulciano Riserva 2012, a marvel of
texture and vibrant sensations.
Immediately impressive with fresh yet
mature aromas, swinging between floral,
fruity and spicy sensations, with an
approachable, chewy, vigorous palate and
very lingering flavour. Focused and vibrant:
what more could we ask?

● Nobile di Montepulciano Ris. '12	♟♟♟ 4*
● Nobile di Montepulciano '13	♟♟ 3
○ La Grazianella Brut	♟ 2
● Montefalco Rosso Còlpetrone '13	♟ 3
○ Vermentino '15	♟ 2
○ Vin Santo '12	♟ 5
● Nobile di Montepulciano '11	♟♟♟ 3*
● Nobile di Montepulciano '10	♟♟♟ 3*
● Nobile di Montepulciano '90	♟♟♟ 3*
● Nobile di Montepulciano Ris. '11	♟♟♟ 4*
● Nobile di Montepulciano Ris. '06	♟♟♟ 4
● Nobile di Montepulciano Vign. Antica Chiusina '00	♟♟♟ 6
● Nobile di Montepulciano Vign. Antica Chiusina '99	♟♟♟ 6
● Nobile di Montepulciano Vign. Antica Chiusina '98	♟♟♟ 6

Terenzi

LOC. MONTEDONICO
58054 SCANSANO [GR]
TEL. +39 0564599601
www.terenzi.eu

CELLAR SALES
PRE-BOOKED VISITS
ACCOMMODATION AND RESTAURANT SERVICE
ANNUAL PRODUCTION 350,000 bottles
HECTARES UNDER VINE 60.00

The Terenzi family released its first labels onto the market in 2007. A few years to settle, and then the wines took their rightful place among the benchmark products of Morellino. Uncompromising choices, always with an eye to local tradition, have honed a style characterized by balance and drinkability, with well-measured oak and moderate extraction. The leading products always express the personality and gait of great wines. The Morellino di Scansano Madrechiesa Riserva 2013 is again among the best of its type. Complex, multifaceted aromas of flowers, spices and balsamic, minty sensations. The palate is gutsy and elegant with a really succulent, deep flavour. Equally well made is the Morellino di Scansano Purosangue Riserva 2013, making its debut, with similar stylistic features to the Madrechiesa but more marked by oakiness.

Terre del Marchesato

FRAZ. BOLGHERI
LOC. SANT'UBERTO, 164
57022 CASTAGNETO CARDUCCI [LI]
TEL. +39 0565749752
www.terredelmarchesato.com

CELLAR SALES
PRE-BOOKED VISITS
ACCOMMODATION
ANNUAL PRODUCTION 80,000 bottles
HECTARES UNDER VINE 15.00

The community who moved from the Marche region to Bolgheri in the mid-20th century is quite numerous and includes Emilio Fuselli, who owns land that used to belong to the Marchesi Incisa della Rocchetta. After successive generations of the family the project is more animated than ever, showing a modern aspect and outstanding vocation for winegrowing. Once again the Marchesale 2013 is of a high standard, with clear-cut toasty, spicy sensations, generous wild berries and coffee beans. A definitely modern, richly extracted wine that requires some bottle ageing, but very well made and deep. Also excellent, the Nobilis 2013 is Sauternes-like, with hints of honey and white peaches on the nose, and a weighty but fluent and fresh palate. The Aldone 2013 is juicy and full-bodied.

● Morellino di Scansano Madrechiesa Ris. '13	♟♟♟ 5
● Morellino di Scansano Purosangue Ris. '13	♟♟ 4
● Maremma Toscana Bramaluce '14	♟♟ 3
● Morellino di Scansano '15	♟♟ 3
○ Petit Manseng Passito '13	♟♟ 5
○ Maremma Toscana Vermentino Balbino '15	♟ 2
● Morellino di Scansano Madrechiesa Ris. '12	♟♟♟ 5
● Morellino di Scansano Madrechiesa Ris. '11	♟♟♟ 5
● Morellino di Scansano Madrechiesa Ris. '10	♟♟♟ 5
● Morellino di Scansano Madrechiesa Ris. '09	♟♟♟ 5

● Marchesale '13	♟♟ 6
● Aldone '13	♟♟ 7
○ Nobilis '13	♟♟ 5
○ Papeo '15	♟♟ 4
○ Emilio Primo Bianco '15	♟ 3
● Tarabuso '13	♟ 5
● Bolgheri Rosso Emilio I '13	♟♟ 3
● Bolgheri Rosso Emilio I '12	♟♟ 3
○ Emilio I '13	♟♟ 5
● Inedito '13	♟♟ 2*
● Marchesale '12	♟♟ 7
○ Nobilis '11	♟♟ 5
○ Papeo '13	♟♟ 6
● Tarabuso '12	♟♟ 6
● Tarabuso '11	♟♟ 6

Terre Nere

Loc. Castelnuovo dell'Abate
53024 Montalcino [SI]
Tel. 3358107743
www.terreneremontalcino.it

CELLAR SALES
PRE-BOOKED VISITS
ACCOMMODATION
ANNUAL PRODUCTION 50,000 bottles
HECTARES UNDER VINE 10.00

Due to a lack of space we have been unable to talk about the Terre Nere wines in the main section of our Guide until now. This fairly young estate was set up by Pasquale Vallone and Piera Campigli who took over the three hectares, now about ten, in the 1990s. The area has typically dark soil, expressed in pedigree Sangioveses mainly aged in 30- and 50-hectolitre Slavonian oak. These delightfully old-style Brunellos, often achieving a natural expression on the first tasting, have been developed over recent years thanks also to the help of Pasquale and Piera's children Francesca and Federico, who now work on the estate full-time. Pomegranate, lemon zest, dried flowers, colonial spice: the 2010 Brunello Riserva shows original aromas to say the least, and the palate is similar, with a light-footed gait, flavourful and focused, just lacking an extra spurt to be truly great. Along the same lines is the delicious 2011 Brunello.

● Brunello di Montalcino Ris. '10	🏆🏆 6
● Brunello di Montalcino '11	🏆🏆 5
● Rosso di Montalcino '14	🏆 3
● Brunello di Montalcino '10	🏆🏆 5
● Brunello di Montalcino '09	🏆🏆 5

Teruzzi & Puthod

Loc. Casale, 19
53037 San Gimignano [SI]
Tel. +39 0577940143
www.teruzzieputhod.it

CELLAR SALES
PRE-BOOKED VISITS
ANNUAL PRODUCTION 1,000,000 bottles
HECTARES UNDER VINE 94.00

In the mid-Seventies Enrico Teruzzi and Carmen Puthod left Milan and moved to what they believed to be the most suitable area in Tuscany to consolidate their passion for winegrowing. So here they are in San Gimignano where their great innovative spirit and excellent choice of partners and strategies have earned them a recognizable space among the producers, thanks above all to the quality of their wines. In 2013 the estate was purchased by the Campari group which invested effort in new purchases and modernization of the vineyards. The Vernaccia Riserva 2011 makes the final tastings with elegant, complex aromas in which minerally sensations appear alongside fruity hints of apricots and lemons and vegetal aromatic herbs. The palate is beautifully juicy, flavoursome and mouthwatering with acid backbone, and a rounded, enthralling finish. The appealing, flavourful Vernaccia 2015 has stylish aromas of peach fruit and an elegant, subtle palate with good texture and pleasantly lingering flavour.

○ Vernaccia di S. Gimignano Ris. '11	🏆🏆 4
○ Carmen Puthod '14	🏆🏆 3
○ Vernaccia di S. Gimignano '15	🏆🏆 2*
● Peperino '13	🏆 2
○ Terre di Tufi '14	🏆 4
○ Vernaccia di S. Gimignano Sant'Elena '15	🏆 3
● Peperino '12	🏆🏆 2*
○ Vernaccia di S. Gimignano '14	🏆🏆 2*
○ Vernaccia di S. Gimignano '13	🏆🏆 2*
○ Vernaccia di S. Gimignano '12	🏆🏆 2*
○ Vernaccia di S. Gimignano '11	🏆🏆 2*
○ Vernaccia di S. Gimignano Ris. '10	🏆🏆 4

Tolaini

LOC. VALLENUOVA
S.DA PROV.LE 9 DI PIEVASCIATA, 28
53019 CASTELNUOVO BERARDENGA [SI]
TEL. +39 0577356972
www.tolaini.it

CELLAR SALES
PRE-BOOKED VISITS
ANNUAL PRODUCTION 300,000 bottles
HECTARES UNDER VINE 50.00
SUSTAINABLE WINERY

Meticulous care in the vineyards following the Bordeaux model, avoidance of pointless interference in the cellar and international consultants: these are the keys to making Pierluigi Tolaini's estate in the hills between Pianella and Vagliagli one of the most important to emerge in Chianti Classico in recent years. The wines show a harmonious style, modern but not lacking grip and supple development. Although mainly aged in small oak, this is never intrusive and rather enhances their elegance and finesse. The Al Passo 2012 is a blend of sangiovese and merlot, fragrant with soft but lively and tangy flavour. The firm-bodied Valdisanti 2012, from sangiovese, cabernet sauvignon and franc, shows ripe, lush fruit and a generous, mouthfilling flavour. The Picconero 2011, from merlot, cabernet sauvignon and petit verdot, is more marked by the oak used for ageing.

● Al Passo '12	▼▼ 4
● Valdisanti '12	▼▼ 5
● Picconero '11	▼ 8
● Picconero '10	▼▼▼ 8
● Picconero '09	▼▼▼ 8
● Valdisanti '08	▼▼▼ 8
● Al Passo '09	▼▼ 4
● Al Passo '07	▼▼ 4
● Chianti Cl. Gran Sel. '11	▼▼ 5
● Chianti Cl. Montebello Vign. n.7 Ris. '10	▼▼ 6
● Chianti Cl. Ris. '10	▼▼ 5
● Chianti Cl. Ris. '08	▼▼ 5
● Valdisanti '11	▼▼ 5
● Valdisanti '09	▼▼ 8

Fattoria La Torre

VIA PROV.LE DI MONTECARLO, 7
55015 MONTECARLO [LU]
TEL. +39 058322981
www.fattorialatorre.it

CELLAR SALES
PRE-BOOKED VISITS
ACCOMMODATION AND RESTAURANT SERVICE
ANNUAL PRODUCTION 43,500 bottles
HECTARES UNDER VINE 6.50

A small, very dynamic estate owned by the Cerri family, with only a few but meticulously farmed vineyards, as well as a resort and restaurant. Wine production is recorded here since 1887, in Montecarlo which was one of the first areas to use French grapes. The winery has chosen to preserve the building but equip it with modern facilities, like the cellar which was built from an existing building. The Esse 2013, 100% syrah, has clear wild berry aromas, spicy sensations and hints of leather and animal skins. The warm palate shows firm structure, with perceptible but well-blended tannins, and a finish that is fully satisfying if not especially lingering. The Altair 2015, a blend of vermentino and viognier, displays appealing floral and fruity hints with clear apple and white peach fruit. A smooth entry on the palate, edgy and succulent with a clean finish. The spicy, flavoursome, dynamic Stringaio 2015 is made from syrah with a small addition of cabernet sauvignon.

○ Altair '15	▼▼ 3
● Esse Syrah '13	▼▼ 5
● Stringaio '14	▼▼ 3
● Albireo '14	▼ 4
○ Montecarlo Vermentino '15	▼ 2
● Esse '07	▼▼ 7
● Esse '01	▼▼ 7
○ Montecarlo Bianco '11	▼▼ 2*
● Stringaio '07	▼▼ 3

Torre a Cona

LOC. SAN DONATO IN COLLINA
50067 RIGNANO SULL'ARNO [FI]
TEL. +39 055699000
www.torreacona.com

CELLAR SALES
PRE-BOOKED VISITS
ACCOMMODATION
ANNUAL PRODUCTION 75,000 bottles
HECTARES UNDER VINE 14.00

Built on the ruins of a former Medieval
settlement, Torre a Cona is one of
Tuscany's most beautiful and elegant
estates, developing over time to its current
appearance dating back to the 18th
century. The farm passed through the
hands of various families until the Conti
Rossi di Montelera bought it in 1937. The
younger generations have intensified the
wine and olive-growing activity as well as
the accommodation facilities. The vineyards
are planted to sangiovese, the
unchallenged leader in this area, as well as
merlot for a monovarietal wine. For the first
time this estate crosses the finish line with
Tre Bicchieri: the wine in question is the
Riserva Badia a Corte, which had come
close to the accolade several times.
Multifaceted, glowing aromas of wild black
berries, aromatic herbs and hints of
balsam. The palate is mouthwatering with
perfect balance between tannins and a
pleasantly tangy background.

● Chianti Colli Fiorentini Badia a Corte Ris. '13	▼▼▼ 4*
● Chianti Colli Fiorentini '14	▼▼ 2*
● Merlot '13	▼▼ 5
● Terre di Cino '13	▼▼ 3
● Chianti Colli Fiorentini '13	♀♀ 3
● Chianti Colli Fiorentini Badia a Corte Ris. '12	♀♀ 4
● Chianti Colli Fiorentini Badia a Corte Ris. '11	♀♀ 4
● Chianti Colli Fiorentini Badia a Corte Ris. '10	♀♀ 4
● Merlot '12	♀♀ 3*
● Merlot '11	♀♀ 3*
● Terre di Cino '12	♀♀ 3
● Terre di Cino '11	♀♀ 3

Le Torri

VIA SAN LORENZO A VIGLIANO, 31
50021 BARBERINO VAL D'ELSA [FI]
TEL. +39 0558076161
www.letorri.net

CELLAR SALES
PRE-BOOKED VISITS
ACCOMMODATION AND RESTAURANT SERVICE
ANNUAL PRODUCTION 170,000 bottles
HECTARES UNDER VINE 28.00
SUSTAINABLE WINERY

Tuscany has always had a strong attraction
for wine enthusiasts and this applied to a
group of friends who decided to buy this
strip of land bordering Chianti Classico to
the east, in the 1980s. The 28 hectares of
vineyards cover the hillsides at 300-350
metres altitude, planted to sangiovese, of
course, as well as colorino, canaiolo and
trebbiano, and international varieties like
cabernet sauvignon, merlot, syrah and
chardonnay. At the helm is Beatrice
Mozzi, daughter of one of the owners, to
whom credit is due for the wave of
innovations on the estate. We enjoyed the
very solid qualities of the Riserva Colli
Fiorentini 2103, with vibrant aromas of
fresh plums and cherries contrasting with
sweet spice and cinnamon opening the
way to an elegant, relaxed and lingering
flavour. The Chianti 2014 is also well made
with a fruity, floral nose and coherent,
harmonious palate. The Meridius 2014 is
easy and carefree.

● Chianti Colli Fiorentini Ris. '13	▼▼ 3
● Chianti Colli Fiorentini '14	▼ 2
● Meridius '14	▼ 2
● Chianti Colli Fiorentini '10	♀♀ 2*
● Chianti Colli Fiorentini Ris. '12	♀♀ 3*
● Chianti Colli Fiorentini Ris. '11	♀♀ 3
● Chianti Colli Fiorentini Ris. '10	♀♀ 3
● Magliano '12	♀♀ 5
● Magliano '10	♀♀ 5
● Magliano '09	♀♀ 5
● Magliano '08	♀♀ 5
● Meridius '13	♀♀ 2*
● San Lorenzo '12	♀♀ 5
● Vigliano '08	♀♀ 5
● Vigliano '04	♀♀ 5

Travignoli

VIA TRAVIGNOLI, 78
50060 PELAGO [FI]
TEL. +39 0558361098
www.travignoli.com

CELLAR SALES
PRE-BOOKED VISITS
ANNUAL PRODUCTION 250,000 bottles
HECTARES UNDER VINE 70.00

An Etruscan stele discovered in the estate's fields, depicting scenes of feasts and libations, demonstrates that even in ancient times this area was devoted to winegrowing. Travignoli has a long history, starting in the late 15th century and leading up to the present. Today Giovanni Busi runs the winery and is also chairman of the Chianti producers' association. The 70 hectares of vineyards wind across the hills of the Rufina subzone on marly soil at altitudes between 250 and 400 metres. Southern exposure guarantees perfectly ripe grapes while fresh breezes from the nearby Apennines cool the air perfectly, especially in summer. Another good performance from the Riserva Tegolaia 2013: the usual jammy aromas with grassy hints and ripe black berries echoed on the palate, blending into the tangy texture and nicely rounded tannin. The Vin Santo 2010 shows classic features, with walnuts and dates ushering in a biscuity palate balanced by light acidity.

● Chianti Rufina Tegolaia Ris. '13	▼▼ 3*
○ Vin Santo Chianti Rufina '10	▼▼ 4
● Calice del Conte '08	♀♀ 5
● Chianti Rufina '12	♀♀ 2*
● Chianti Rufina Ris. '05	♀♀ 3
● Chianti Rufina Tegolaia Ris. '12	♀♀ 3
● Chianti Rufina Tegolaia Ris. '11	♀♀ 3
● Chianti Rufina Tegolaia Ris. '10	♀♀ 3
● Chianti Rufina Tegolaia Ris. '09	♀♀ 3
● Chianti Rufina Tegolaia Ris. '08	♀♀ 3
● Chianti Rufina Tegolaia Ris. '07	♀♀ 3
● Tegolaia '06	♀♀ 4
○ Vin Santo Chianti Rufina '09	♀♀ 4
○ Vin Santo Chianti Rufina '01	♀♀ 4

★Tua Rita

LOC. NOTRI, 81
57028 SUVERETO [LI]
TEL. +39 0565829237
www.tuarita.it

PRE-BOOKED VISITS
ANNUAL PRODUCTION 250,000 bottles
HECTARES UNDER VINE 35.00
VITICULTURE METHOD Certified Organic

Just over 30 years ago Rita Tua and Virgilio Bisti decided to buy a country house in Val di Cornia with a little land around it, to have a lovely place for their retirement. Their enhancement of the location's vocation for winegrowing was still in the quite distant future, but they shared a passion for wine and have come a long way since then. The vineyards have been extended and now form the heart of the functioning farm's activity, organized by the couple's daughter Simona and son-in-law Stefano Frascolla. The Giusto di Notri 2013, from cabernet sauvignon, merlot and cabernet franc, displays a complex, layered nose with fresh sensations of mint and lemongrass, wild berries and the barest hint of spice. The palate is fresh and broad with well-blended tannins and a flavoursome, lingering finish. The Perlato del Bosco 2014, sangiovese and cabernet sauvignon, has a pared-down nose and a firm, racy palate.

● Giusto di Notri '13	▼▼ 8
● Perlato del Bosco Rosso '14	▼▼ 5
● Rosso dei Notri '15	▼▼ 4
● Redigaffi '08	♀♀♀ 8
● Redigaffi '07	♀♀♀ 8
● Redigaffi '06	♀♀♀ 8
● Redigaffi '04	♀♀♀ 8
● Redigaffi '03	♀♀♀ 8
● Redigaffi '02	♀♀♀ 8
● Redigaffi '01	♀♀♀ 8
● Giusto di Notri '11	♀♀ 8
● Giusto di Notri '10	♀♀ 8
● Giusto di Notri '10	♀♀ 8
● Rosso dei Notri '14	♀♀ 4
● Rosso dei Notri '12	♀♀ 3
● Syrah Per Sempre '12	♀♀ 8

Uccelliera

FRAZ. CASTELNUOVO DELL'ABATE
POD. UCCELLIERA, 45
53020 MONTALCINO [SI]
TEL. +39 0577835729
www.uccelliera-montalcino.it

CELLAR SALES
PRE-BOOKED VISITS
ANNUAL PRODUCTION 60,000 bottles
HECTARES UNDER VINE 6.00

Uccelliera Brunellos have always been a compulsory benchmark for anyone wishing to further their knowledge of the Montalcino terroir, especially its more southern character, linked to the area overlooking Castelnuovo dell'Abate on loamy-sandy soil at altitudes around 250 metres. The distinctive wines are shaped by the untiring Andrea Cortonesi, a layman in the best possible sense: there is no pre-defined recipe governing his cellar choices, just vinification to suit each plot and the particular features of each harvest, with barriques sometimes alongside the untoasted Slavonian oak. Our highest accolade for the Rosso 2014, which will be no surprise to those who know Uccelliera wines. A below-par year and very fine extract for the Sangiovese, hot-blooded and raring to go, with lovely clear fruit and beautifully textured flavour. An example of the typical strength of this area, combined with pace and control, which are somewhat lacking in the Brunello 2011.

● Rosso di Montalcino '14	▼▼▼	4*
● Brunello di Montalcino '11	▼▼	6
● Brunello di Montalcino '10	♀♀♀	6
● Brunello di Montalcino '08	♀♀♀	7
● Brunello di Montalcino Ris. '97	♀♀♀	8
● Brunello di Montalcino '09	♀♀	6
● Brunello di Montalcino '07	♀♀	7
● Brunello di Montalcino '06	♀♀	7
● Brunello di Montalcino Ris. '08	♀♀	8
● Brunello di Montalcino Ris. '07	♀♀	8
● Brunello di Montalcino Ris. '06	♀♀	8
● Brunello di Montalcino Ris. '04	♀♀	8
● Rapace '08	♀♀	5
● Rosso di Montalcino '11	♀♀	4
● Rosso di Montalcino '10	♀♀	4
● Rosso di Montalcino '09	♀♀	4

F.lli Vagnoni

LOC. PANCOLE, 82
53037 SAN GIMIGNANO [SI]
TEL. +39 0577955077
www.fratellivagnoni.com

CELLAR SALES
PRE-BOOKED VISITS
ACCOMMODATION
ANNUAL PRODUCTION 120,000 bottles
HECTARES UNDER VINE 17.00
VITICULTURE METHOD Certified Organic

For over 60 years now the Vagnoni brothers' winery has occupied a lovely portion of the Pancole hillside, where one of the two vineyards is located. The other is at San Biagio with the cellar, opened in 2007 alongside the old one. This includes a large tasting space, a drying room for the grapes (for Vinsanto production), a vinification and ageing area, and a barrique cellar entirely covered with tuffstone with electronic temperature and humidity control. Along with the vineyards the farm has olive groves, orchards, and arable land, all organically farmed. Through to the finals for the La Riserva I Mocali 2013, with complex and tempting aromas combining spicy hints of vanilla and cinnamon with tropical mango and pineapple fruit. The palate is complex from the entry, broad and weighty with lovely juicy fruit, and a long, well-judged and flavoursome finish. The Vernaccia 2015 is simple but nicely balanced, with fresh aromas, hints of lemon and aromatic herbs, and a slender, harmonious palate with an easy, relaxed finish.

○ Vernaccia di S. Gimignano I Mocali Ris. '13	▼▼	3*
○ Vernaccia di S. Gimignano '15	▼▼	2*
● Chianti Colli Senesi '14	▼	2
○ Vinbrusco '14	▼	1*
● Chianti Colli Senesi Capanneto Ris. '11	♀♀	3
● San Gimignano Vin Santo Occhio di Pernice '07	♀♀	5
● Sodi Lunghi '11	♀♀	3
○ Vernaccia di S. Gimignano '13	♀♀	2*
○ Vernaccia di S. Gimignano Fontabuccio '13	♀♀	2*
○ Vernaccia di S. Gimignano I Mocali Ris. '12	♀♀	3
○ Vernaccia di S. Gimignano I Mocali Ris. '11	♀♀	3*

Val delle Corti

loc. La Croce, 141
53017 Radda in Chianti [SI]
Tel. +39 0577738215
www.valdellecorti.it

CELLAR SALES
PRE-BOOKED VISITS
ACCOMMODATION
ANNUAL PRODUCTION 30,000 bottles
HECTARES UNDER VINE 6.00
VITICULTURE METHOD Certified Organic

Roberto Bianchi, who has managed the family farm since 1999, has succeeded in bringing it into the category of Radda's best wine estates while maintaining close links to traditional methods and care for the environment. The organically farmed vineyards are gradually being converted to biodynamic methods and the wines are aged primarily in large oak. Though not approachable, Val delle Corti wines offer uniquely profound flavour and authentic sense of place, qualities that can be hard to find in an extraordinary area like Chianti Classico. Roberto Bianchi's Chianti Classico 2013 is wonderful: a wine with clearly defined, very fresh aromas and an assertive, tangy palate making the flavour extremely appealing. The Chianti Classico Riserva 2013 is just as good, with clean, elegant aromas and a nicely complex palate with crisp, flavoursome tannins.

● Chianti Cl. '13	▼▼▼ 4*
● Chianti Cl. Ris. '13	▼▼ 5
● Chianti Cl. '12	♀♀♀ 4*
● Chianti Cl. '11	♀♀♀ 3*
● Chianti Cl. '10	♀♀♀ 3*
● Chianti Cl. '09	♀♀♀ 2*
● Chianti Cl. '06	♀♀ 2*
● Chianti Cl. '05	♀♀ 2*
● Chianti Cl. '04	♀♀ 2*
● Chianti Cl. Ris. '11	♀♀ 5
● Chianti Cl. Ris. '09	♀♀ 5
● Chianti Cl. Ris. '07	♀♀ 4
● Il Campino	♀♀ 2*

Tenuta Valdipiatta

via della Ciarliana, 25a
53040 Montepulciano [SI]
Tel. +39 0578757930
www.valdipiatta.it

CELLAR SALES
PRE-BOOKED VISITS
ACCOMMODATION
ANNUAL PRODUCTION 80,000 bottles
HECTARES UNDER VINE 23.00

Over the years, the wines from the estate run by Miriam Caporali have taken on a highly recognizable style, whose basic features are harmony and elegance. The result is a range of wines that are reliable in terms of continuous quality, nicely consistent, with good personality. For over 20 years they have been one of the best examples of the potential of sangiovese in the Montepulciano area. The Nobile Vigna d'Alfiero 2013 reveals fruity, dark-toned aromas, lovely texture and complexity, just slightly curbed by excessive oak which marks the finish with grassy sensations. The most distinctive features of the Nobile 2013 are balance and delicious flavour: fragrant and mouthwatering with edgy, flavourful tannin. The same stylistic tone is echoed to a slightly lesser extent in the Rosso di Montepulciano 2014, a fragrant, slender and supple wine with very drinkable flavour.

● Nobile di Montepulciano '13	▼▼ 4
● Nobile di Montepulciano V. d'Alfiero '13	▼▼ 6
● Rosso di Montepulciano '14	▼ 3
● Nobile di Montepulciano Ris. '90	♀♀♀ 5
● Nobile di Montepulciano V. d'Alfiero '99	♀♀♀ 5
● Nobile di Montepulciano '12	♀♀ 4
● Nobile di Montepulciano '11	♀♀ 4
● Nobile di Montepulciano '10	♀♀ 4
● Nobile di Montepulciano '09	♀♀ 4
● Nobile di Montepulciano '08	♀♀ 4
● Nobile di Montepulciano V. d'Alfiero '12	♀♀ 6
● Nobile di Montepulciano V. d'Alfiero '10	♀♀ 6
● Nobile di Montepulciano V. d'Alfiero '08	♀♀ 6
● Rosso di Montepulciano '10	♀♀ 3

★Tenuta di Valgiano

VIA DI VALGIANO, 7
55015 LUCCA
TEL. +39 0583402271
www.valgiano.it

CELLAR SALES
PRE-BOOKED VISITS
ANNUAL PRODUCTION 70,000 bottles
HECTARES UNDER VINE 20.00
VITICULTURE METHOD Certified Biodynamic

Valgiano is a world of its own. Moreno
Petrini and Laura di Collobiano designed
and created a fantastic project in all
possible ways, named after the magical
location. Biodynamic farming methods, of
which Saverio Petrilli is one of Italy's leading
experts, support and enhance the area's
suitability for agriculture and winegrowing.
The style of the wines is a direct
consequence of all this, as well as the
sensitivity of the exponents. This is a
well-balanced project and one of Italy's
brightest wine businesses. The 2013
version of the Tenuta di Valgiano is as
charming as it is unpredictable: paler than
usual, beautifully elegant, it should be
judged on its potential and certainly requires
bottle ageing. Zooming in, beautiful aromas
of fresh, ripe black berries, hints of
pomegranate and black pepper, and an
austere, succulent palate, clenched and still
hard but very engaging. A long finish carried
by flavour rather than texture.

● Colline Lucchesi Tenuta di Valgiano '13 ▼▼▼ 8
● Colline Lucchesi Palistorti
   di Valgiano '13 ▼▼ 5
● Colline Lucchesi Tenuta di Valgiano '12 ▼▼▼ 6
● Colline Lucchesi Tenuta di Valgiano '11 ▼▼▼ 6
● Colline Lucchesi Tenuta di Valgiano '10 ▼▼▼ 6
● Colline Lucchesi Tenuta di Valgiano '09 ▼▼▼ 6
● Colline Lucchesi Tenuta di Valgiano '08 ▼▼▼ 6
● Colline Lucchesi Tenuta di Valgiano '07 ▼▼▼ 6
● Colline Lucchesi Tenuta di Valgiano '06 ▼▼▼ 6
● Colline Lucchesi Tenuta di Valgiano '05 ▼▼▼ 6
● Colline Lucchesi Tenuta di Valgiano '04 ▼▼▼ 6
● Colline Lucchesi Tenuta di Valgiano '03 ▼▼▼ 6
● Colline Lucchesi Tenuta di Valgiano '01 ▼▼▼ 8

Varramista

LOC. VARRAMISTA
VIA RICAVO
56020 MONTOPOLI IN VAL D'ARNO [PI]
TEL. +39 057144711
www.varramista.it

CELLAR SALES
PRE-BOOKED VISITS
ACCOMMODATION
ANNUAL PRODUCTION 65,000 bottles
HECTARES UNDER VINE 14.20

The story began in the 1950s when the
Piaggio and Agnelli families chose this
place as their country residence. But it is
thanks to Giovanni Alberto Agnelli that the
winegrowing project took off, and the family
estate was gradually transformed into a
real farm. Several different varieties are
grown here, with a preference for
sangiovese, the classic Tuscan red wine
grape, and syrah, which finds ideal growing
conditions on this estate. An excellent
choice, at least as far as the well-made
Syrah 2011 is concerned: richly extracted
with firm acid backbone, and markedly
varietal aromas of pepper and freshly
picked black berries. The Frasca 2013,
from sangiovese, merlot and syrah, is also
excellent, with toasty and spicy aromas
from the oak and a clean, fluent palate with
consistent aromas and a lovely finish.

● Frasca '13 ▼▼ 4
● Syrah '11 ▼▼ 6
● Varramista '00 ▼▼▼ 6
● Chianti Monsonaccio '12 ▼▼ 2*
● Frasca '08 ▼▼ 3
● Frasca Rosso '11 ▼▼ 3
● Ottopioppi '08 ▼▼ 3
● Sterpato '12 ▼▼ 2*
● Sterpato '11 ▼▼ 2*
● Varramista '08 ▼▼ 6
● Varramista '07 ▼▼ 6

I Veroni

VIA TIFARITI, 5
50065 PONTASSIEVE [FI]
TEL. +39 0558368886
www.iveroni.it

CELLAR SALES
PRE-BOOKED VISITS
ACCOMMODATION
ANNUAL PRODUCTION 110,000 bottles
HECTARES UNDER VINE 20.00
VITICULTURE METHOD Certified Organic

In the early 12th century the Conti Guidi owned a landed estate that occupied part of Emilia Romagna and Tuscany, and built a series of watchtowers to monitor their land between the Arno and Sieve rivers. One of these has been incorporated into the various layers of the farm, managed today with a great deal of passion by Lorenzo Mariani. Around the 1990s the estate underwent extensive replanting, increasing the density per hectare. Of the 20 hectares under vine, 16 are planted to sangiovese, two with international varieties and the rest with white grapes for Vin Santo production. Some excellent results from the range presented for tasting, with one of the wines through to the finals. This is the Riserva 2013, offering sound aromas of black berry fruit, and a throbbing, dynamic palate, flavoursome and vibrant with sober streaks of acidity. The 2014 version is also very pleasing, fresh and fluent.

● Chianti Rufina Ris. '13	🍷🍷 5
● Chianti Rufina '14	🍷🍷 3
○ Vin Santo del Chianti Rufina '07	🍷🍷 5
● Chianti Rufina '13	ΥΥ 2*
● Chianti Rufina '12	ΥΥ 2*
● Chianti Rufina '11	ΥΥ 2*
● Chianti Rufina Ris. '12	ΥΥ 4
● Chianti Rufina Ris. '11	ΥΥ 4
● Chianti Rufina Ris. '10	ΥΥ 4
● Chianti Rufina Ris. '09	ΥΥ 4
● Chianti Rufina Ris. '08	ΥΥ 4
● Rosso di Toscana '13	ΥΥ 2*
○ Vin Santo del Chianti Rufina '06	ΥΥ 5
○ Vin Santo del Chianti Rufina '05	ΥΥ 5
○ Vin Santo del Chianti Rufina '04	ΥΥ 5

Vignamaggio

VIA DI PETRIOLO, 5
50022 GREVE IN CHIANTI [FI]
TEL. +39 055854661
www.vignamaggio.com

CELLAR SALES
PRE-BOOKED VISITS
ACCOMMODATION AND RESTAURANT SERVICE
ANNUAL PRODUCTION 350,000 bottles
HECTARES UNDER VINE 62.50
VITICULTURE METHOD Certified Organic

Situated in the subzone of Greve in Chianti, about 30 kilometres from Florence and Siena, Villa Vignamaggio has over 300 years of winegrowing history. The modern winery was built in 2010 and the wines are aged in the historic 15th-century building, which offers ideal conditions for maturing without technological interference. In 2014 the estate began conversion to organic farming methods, alongside work to recover old varieties like occhiorosso. The Chianti Classico Terre di Prenzano 2014 is definitely well made with subtle, flavourful tannic texture and well-defined, beautifully fresh aromas. The Cabernet Franc 2013 is also of a high standard, refreshed by spicy, pleasantly grassy aromas and with a firm, nicely paced flavour. A delicious impact from the Morino 2015, from a blend of sangiovese and merlot grown in the estate's youngest vineyards.

● Cabernet Franc '13	🍷🍷 8
● Chianti Cl. Terre di Prenzano '14	🍷🍷 3
● Il Morino '15	🍷 2
● Vignamaggio '06	ΥΥΥ 7
● Vignamaggio '05	ΥΥΥ 7
● Vignamaggio '04	ΥΥΥ 6
● Vignamaggio '01	ΥΥΥ 6
● Vignamaggio '00	ΥΥΥ 6
● Chianti Cl. Gherardino '13	ΥΥ 3
● Chianti Cl. Gran Sel. Castello di Monna Lisa '10	ΥΥ 5
● Chianti Cl. Terre di Prenzano '13	ΥΥ 3
● Chianti Cl. Terre di Prenzano '12	ΥΥ 3
● Chianti Cl. Terre di Prenzano '11	ΥΥ 3

Villa Calcinaia

FRAZ. GRETI
VIA CITILLE, 84
50022 GREVE IN CHIANTI [FI]
TEL. +39 055853715
www.villacalcinaia.it

CELLAR SALES
PRE-BOOKED VISITS
ACCOMMODATION
ANNUAL PRODUCTION 90,000 bottles
HECTARES UNDER VINE 27.00
VITICULTURE METHOD Certified Organic

The Villa Calcinaia estate has taken important steps forward on the path to quality in recent times. Sebastiano Capponi, at the helm, has added to his vineyards, now 27 hectares and organically farmed, but maintained the traditional varieties. In the cellar, the wines are aged both in barriques and, to a progressively greater extent, in large oak. The resulting wines are appealing, with good flavour, personality, a link to the terroir, and are often elegant and harmonious. Vibrant fruit aromas and earthy hints for the Chianti Classico Gran Selezione Vigna Bastignano 2013, with a well-paced and nuanced palate. The Chianti Classico Riserva 2013 has a pleasantly confident, almost edgy palate, and iron-like aromas with hints of forest floor. The strongpoint of the Chianti Classico Gran Selezione Vigna Contessa Luisa 2013 is a particularly well-balanced and flavoursome palate.

● Chianti Cl. Gran Sel. V. Bastignano '13	♥♥ 6
● Chianti Cl. Gran Sel. V. Contessa Luisa '13	♥♥ 6
● Chianti Cl. Villa Calcinaia Ris. '13	♥♥ 5
● Casarsa '13	♥ 5
● Chianti Cl. '13	♥ 3
● Chianti Cl. '10	♥♥ 3*
● Chianti Cl. '01	♥♥ 3
● Chianti Cl. Ris. '10	♥♥ 3
● Chianti Cl. Ris. '05	♥♥ 5
● Chianti Cl. Ris. '04	♥♥ 5
● Chianti Cl. Ris. '03	♥♥ 5
● Chianti Cl. V. Bastignano Ris. '09	♥♥ 4

Villa Sant'Anna

FRAZ. ABBADIA
VIA DELLA RESISTENZA, 143
53045 MONTEPULCIANO [SI]
TEL. +39 0578708017
www.villasantanna.it

CELLAR SALES
PRE-BOOKED VISITS
ANNUAL PRODUCTION 80,000 bottles
HECTARES UNDER VINE 18.00

A growing winery worthy of attention, according to our yearly tastings. The historic property belongs to the maternal side of Simona Ruggeri Fabroni's family, and today the estate is mainly run by women. The modern vineyards are planted to a high density per hectare and the cellar equipment, barrels and barriques have been renewed. The wines, which appear confident, well-focused in style, and definitely improving in quality, are aged in the historic underground cellars at natural temperatures. An excellent Nobile di Montepulciano 2013 earns a place in our final tastings. Multifaceted and complex, this wine changes its appearance in the glass, showing more dynamic energy. Forward fruity aromas alongside dark spicy hints and almost blood-like sensations. The palate is basically light, fresh, well textured and juicy.

● Nobile di Montepulciano '13	♥♥ 4
● Rosso di Montepulciano '13	♥♥ 2*
● Chianti Colli Senesi '13	♥ 2
● Nobile di Montepulciano '10	♥♥ 4
● Nobile di Montepulciano '07	♥♥ 4
● Nobile di Montepulciano '06	♥♥ 4
● Nobile di Montepulciano '02	♥♥ 3
● Nobile di Montepulciano '01	♥♥ 3
● Nobile di Montepulciano Poldo '05	♥♥ 5
● Nobile di Montepulciano Poldo '03	♥♥ 5
● Nobile di Montepulciano Poldo '01	♥♥ 5
○ Vin Santo '99	♥♥ 8
○ Vin Santo di Montepulciano '06	♥♥ 8
○ Vin Santo di Montepulciano '05	♥♥ 8
○ Vin Santo di Montepulciano '04	♥♥ 8

Tenuta Vitereta

VIA CASANUOVA, 108/1
52020 LATERINA [AR]
TEL. +39 057589058
www.tenutavitereta.com

CELLAR SALES
PRE-BOOKED VISITS
ACCOMMODATION
ANNUAL PRODUCTION 45,000 bottles
HECTARES UNDER VINE 45.00
VITICULTURE METHOD Certified Organic

In the early 1970s, agronomist and winemaker Marcello Bidini purchased the estate that would, over time, become the modern and efficient farm he runs today with the help of his daughters Francesca and Martina. Certified organic since 2009, the farm has various types of crops, and the whole project shows a great deal of respect for the land of the environment. As far as wine is concerned, interference in the various procedures is deliberately kept to a minimum. The two Vin Santos are the feathers in the estate's cap thanks to rich extract and astoundingly different styles: the Occhio di Pernice 2009 is richer and velvety, while the Supremo 2005 is stylish with clear-cut flavour. The Ripa della Mozza 2013 is a Sangiovese with distinctive fruity hints and a gentle, fluent palate with a pleasing vein of acidity, while the Donnaurora 2013 has aromas of grapeskins and a well-sustained, tangy, nicely lingering flavour.

○ Donnaurora '13	♟♟ 4
● Ripa della Mozza '13	♟♟ 3
● Vin Santo del Chianti Occhio di Pernice '09	♟♟ 8
● Vin Santo del Chianti Occhio di Pernice '08	♟♟ 8
○ Vin Santo del Chianti Supremo '05	♟♟ 8
● Chianti Casarossa Ris. '13	♟ 4
● Ripa della Mozza '11	♟♟ 3
● Ripa della Mozza '10	♟♟ 3
● Vin Santo del Chianti Occhio di Pernice '07	♟♟ 8
● Vin Santo del Chianti Occhio di Pernice '06	♟♟ 8

Fattoria Viticcio

VIA SAN CRESCI, 12A
50022 GREVE IN CHIANTI [FI]
TEL. +39 055854210
www.fattoriaviticcio.com

CELLAR SALES
PRE-BOOKED VISITS
ACCOMMODATION
ANNUAL PRODUCTION 250,000 bottles
HECTARES UNDER VINE 30.00
SUSTAINABLE WINERY

Viticcio's 30 hectares of vineyards are mainly located in the Chianti Classico DOC zone, as well as Maremma and Bolgheri. The estate's signature style tends towards richly textured wines with a marked presence of oak, though confident acidity sometimes guarantees a good dose of personality. The range shows a high standard of quality, including some wines that can stand alongside the best of their type. The Chianti Classico Riserva 2013 makes a lovely entry on the palate, broad and rounded, with clearly defined, powerful aromas and echoes of spice and toasted oak. The Chianti Classico 2014 reveals edgy but pleasant tannin, and shines with its supple flavour. The Chianti Classico Prunaio 2013 is still a work in progress: well made but lacks a change in pace in the finish, currently supported by oaky sensations alone.

● Chianti Cl. '14	♟♟ 3
● Chianti Cl. Ris. '13	♟♟ 4
● Chianti Cl. Gran Sel. Prunaio '13	♟ 6
○ Vermentino '15	♟ 3
● Chianti Cl. '12	♟♟ 3
● Chianti Cl. Gran Sel. Beatrice '11	♟♟ 5
● Chianti Cl. Ris. '12	♟♟ 4
● Chianti Cl. Ris. '11	♟♟ 4
● Monile '11	♟♟ 6
● Prunaio '11	♟♟ 6
● Prunaio '08	♟♟ 6

Abbadia Ardenga

FRAZ. TORRENIERI
VIA ROMANA, 139
53028 MONTALCINO [SI]
TEL. +39 0577834150
www.abbadiardengapoggio.it

CELLAR SALES
PRE-BOOKED VISITS
ANNUAL PRODUCTION 40,000 bottles
HECTARES UNDER VINE 10.00

● Brunello di Montalcino '11	♟ 5
● Brunello di Montalcino Ris. '09	♟ 6
● Brunello di Montalcino V. Piaggia '11	♟ 5

Acquacalda

LOC. ACQUA CALDA
57033 MARCIANA MARINA [LI]
TEL. +39 0565998111
www.tenutaacquacalda.com

CELLAR SALES
PRE-BOOKED VISITS
ANNUAL PRODUCTION 15,000 bottles
HECTARES UNDER VINE 2.00

○ Elba Ansonica '15	♟♟ 2*
○ Elba Bianco '15	♟♟ 2*
○ Elba Vermentino '15	♟ 2

Agrisole

LOC. LA SERRA
VIA SERRA, 64
56028 SAN MINIATO [PI]
TEL. +39 0571409825
www.agri-sole.it

CELLAR SALES
ANNUAL PRODUCTION 30,000 bottles
HECTARES UNDER VINE 7.00

● Mafefa '12	♟♟ 2*
● Colorino '14	♟ 6
● Sangiovese '14	♟ 5

Podere Albiano

LOC. PETROIO
POD. ALBIANO
53020 TREQUANDA [SI]
TEL. +39 0577665386
www.poderealbiano.it

CELLAR SALES
PRE-BOOKED VISITS
ANNUAL PRODUCTION 20,000 bottles
HECTARES UNDER VINE 4.00

● Albiano '11	♟♟ 5
● Orcia Tribolo Ris. '11	♟♟ 5
● Citto '11	♟ 2
● Orcia Ciriè '11	♟ 3

Fattoria Ambra

VIA LOMBARDA, 85
59015 CARMIGNANO [PO]
TEL. +39 3358282552
www.fattoriaambra.it

CELLAR SALES
PRE-BOOKED VISITS
ANNUAL PRODUCTION 80,000 bottles
HECTARES UNDER VINE 20.00
VITICULTURE METHOD Certified Organic

● Carmignano Montalbiolo Ris. '12	♟♟ 5
● Carmignano Santa Cristina in Pilli '13	♟♟ 3
○ Trebbiano '15	♟♟ 2*
○ Vin Santo di Carmignano '08	♟♟ 5

Stefano Amerighi

LOC. POGGIOBELLO DI FARNETA
FRAZ. FARNETA
VIA DI POGGIOBELLO
52044 CORTONA [AR]
TEL. +39 0575648340
www.stefanoamerighi.it

CELLAR SALES
PRE-BOOKED VISITS
ANNUAL PRODUCTION 28,000 bottles
HECTARES UNDER VINE 8.50
VITICULTURE METHOD Certified Biodynamic
SUSTAINABLE WINERY

● Cortona Syrah '13	♟♟ 5

Tenuta di Arceno - Arcanum

LOC. ARCENO
FRAZ. SAN GUSMÉ
53010 CASTELNUOVO BERARDENGA [SI]
TEL. +39 0577359346
www.tenutadiarceno.com

CELLAR SALES
PRE-BOOKED VISITS
ANNUAL PRODUCTION 250,000 bottles
HECTARES UNDER VINE 92.00

● Valadorna '11	♟♟ 7
● Arcanum '11	♟ 8
● Chianti Cl. '14	♟ 3
● Chianti Cl. Ris. '13	♟ 5

Argiano

FRAZ. SANT'ANGELO IN COLLE
53024 MONTALCINO [SI]
TEL. +39 0577844037
www.argiano.net

PRE-BOOKED VISITS
ACCOMMODATION
ANNUAL PRODUCTION 350,000 bottles
HECTARES UNDER VINE 55.00

● Brunello di Montalcino '11	♟ 7
● Brunello di Montalcino Ris. '10	♟ 8
● Rosso di Montalcino '14	♟ 4
● Solengo '13	♟ 8

Arizzi Wine

LOC. CASCIANO
VIA FONTAZZI, 6
53016 MURLO [SI]
TEL. +39 05771655845
www.arizziwine.it

CELLAR SALES
PRE-BOOKED VISITS
ANNUAL PRODUCTION 60,000 bottles
HECTARES UNDER VINE 12.00

○ Il Lato Social del Vivere '15	♟♟ 3
● Chianti Colli Senesi Il Lato Selvaggio del Vivere '15	♟ 3

Arrighi

LOC. PIAN DEL MONTE, 1
57036 PORTO AZZURRO [LI]
TEL. +39 3356641793
www.arrighivigneolivi.it

CELLAR SALES
PRE-BOOKED VISITS
ANNUAL PRODUCTION 30,000 bottles
HECTARES UNDER VINE 6.00

● Tresse '12	♟♟ 5
○ V.I.P. '15	♟♟ 4
● Elba Aleatico Passito Silosò '15	♟ 5
○ Elba Ansonica Mattanto '15	♟ 3

Fattoria di Bacchereto

LOC. BACCHERETO
VIA FONTEMORANA, 179
59015 CARMIGNANO [PO]
TEL. +39 0558717191
terreamano@gmail.com

CELLAR SALES
PRE-BOOKED VISITS
ACCOMMODATION
ANNUAL PRODUCTION 15,000 bottles
HECTARES UNDER VINE 8.00

● Carmignano '12	♟♟ 5
○ Sassocarlo '14	♟♟ 4

Le Badelle

FRAZ. ACQUAVIVA
POD. BADELLE
53045 MONTEPULCIANO [SI]
TEL. +39 0577679156
www.lebadelle.it

ANNUAL PRODUCTION 5,000 bottles
HECTARES UNDER VINE 6.00

● Nobile di Montepulciano '13	♟♟ 4
● Nobile di Montepulciano Rubeo '13	♟ 5

Alfonso Baldetti

LOC. PIETRAIA, 71A
52044 CORTONA [AR]
TEL. +39 057567077
www.baldetti.com

CELLAR SALES
PRE-BOOKED VISITS
ANNUAL PRODUCTION 100,000 bottles
HECTARES UNDER VINE 15.00
SUSTAINABLE WINERY

● Cortona Sangiovese Marius '12		♟♟ 4
● Cortona Syrah Crano '12		♟♟ 4
○ Chagré '14		♟ 2
⊙ Piet Rosé '15		♟ 3

Erik Banti

LOC. FOSSO DEI MOLINI
58054 SCANSANO [GR]
TEL. +39 0564508006
www.erikbanti.com

CELLAR SALES
PRE-BOOKED VISITS
ANNUAL PRODUCTION 350,000 bottles
HECTARES UNDER VINE 25.00
VITICULTURE METHOD Certified Organic

● Morellino di Scansano '15		♟♟ 2*
● Morellino di Scansano Ciabatta '13		♟♟ 4
○ Il Vermentino '15		♟ 2
● Morellino di Scansano Carato '13		♟ 3

Cantine Bellini

VIA PIAVE, 1
50068 RUFINA [FI]
TEL. +39 0558396025
www.bellinicantine.it

CELLAR SALES
ANNUAL PRODUCTION 900,000 bottles
HECTARES UNDER VINE 15.00

● Chianti Rufina Ris. '13		♟♟ 2*
● Chianti '15		♟ 1*
● Le Lodole '12		♟ 2

Podere Bellosguardo

LOC. SANTA MARIA POPPIENA
52015 PRATOVECCHIO STIA [AR]
bellosguardo.miraglia@virgilio.it

CELLAR SALES
ANNUAL PRODUCTION 1,400 bottles
HECTARES UNDER VINE 2.00

● Syrah '13		♟♟ 5
● Pied Franc '13		♟♟ 8
○ Il Passito		♟ 5
● Syrah '14		♟ 5

Le Bertille

VIA DELLE COLOMBELLE, 7
53045 MONTEPULCIANO [SI]
TEL. +39 0578758330
www.lebertille.com

CELLAR SALES
PRE-BOOKED VISITS
ACCOMMODATION
ANNUAL PRODUCTION 65,000 bottles
HECTARES UNDER VINE 14.00
SUSTAINABLE WINERY

● Nobile di Montepulciano '12		♟♟ 3
● Nobile di Montepulciano Ris. '11		♟ 5

Buccelletti Winery

VIA SANTA CRISTINA, 16
52043 CASTIGLION FIORENTINO [AR]
TEL. +39 0575650179
www.famigliabuccelletti.it

CELLAR SALES
PRE-BOOKED VISITS
ACCOMMODATION
ANNUAL PRODUCTION 10,000 bottles
HECTARES UNDER VINE 3.00
VITICULTURE METHOD Certified Organic

● Merigge '11		♟♟ 3
● Poventa '11		♟♟ 3
⊙ Albestre '15		♟ 2
○ Paggino '15		♟ 2

Caccia al Piano 1868

LOC. BOLGHERI
VIA BOLGHERESE, 279
57022 CASTAGNETO CARDUCCI [LI]
TEL. +39 0565763394
www.berlucchi.it

CELLAR SALES
PRE-BOOKED VISITS
ANNUAL PRODUCTION 127,000 bottles
HECTARES UNDER VINE 18.00
SUSTAINABLE WINERY

● Bolgheri Sup. Levia Gravia '13	♟♟ 7
● Bolgheri Ruit Hora '14	♟ 4

Cacciagrande

FRAZ. TIRLI
LOC. AMPIO
58040 CASTIGLIONE DELLA PESCAIA [GR]
TEL. +39 0564944168
www.cacciagrande.com

CELLAR SALES
PRE-BOOKED VISITS
ANNUAL PRODUCTION 100,000 bottles
HECTARES UNDER VINE 20.00
SUSTAINABLE WINERY

● Cortigliano '15	♟♟ 3
○ Maremma Toscana Vermentino '15	♟♟ 3
● Castiglione '14	♟ 4
● Maremma Toscana Rosso Cacciagrande '15	♟ 2

Caiarossa

LOC. SERRA ALL'OLIO, 59
56046 RIPARBELLA [PI]
TEL. +39 0586699016
www.caiarossa.com

CELLAR SALES
PRE-BOOKED VISITS
ANNUAL PRODUCTION 120,000 bottles
HECTARES UNDER VINE 32.00
VITICULTURE METHOD Certified Biodynamic

● Caiarossa '12	♟♟ 6
● Aria di Caiarossa '12	♟♟ 5
● Pergolaia '12	♟♟ 3
○ Oro di Caiarossa '09	♟ 6

Calafata

P.ZZALE ARRIGONI, 2
55100 LUCCA
TEL. +39 0583 430939
info@calafata.it

ANNUAL PRODUCTION 13,000 bottles
HECTARES UNDER VINE 10.00

○ Levato di Gronda '15	♟♟ 4
● Levato di Majulina '13	♟♟ 4

Campo alla Sughera

LOC. CACCIA AL PIANO, 280
57020 BOLGHERI [LI]
TEL. +39 0565766936
www.campoallasughera.com

CELLAR SALES
PRE-BOOKED VISITS
ANNUAL PRODUCTION 110,000 bottles
HECTARES UNDER VINE 16.50

● Bolgheri Rosso Adeo '14	♟♟ 4
● Bolgheri Sup. Arnione '13	♟♟ 6
○ Arioso '15	♟ 5
○ Bolgheri Achenio '15	♟ 5

Camporignano

FRAZ. MONTEGUIDI
53031 CASOLE D'ELSA [SI]
TEL. +39 0577963915
www.camporignano.com

CELLAR SALES
ANNUAL PRODUCTION 30,000 bottles
HECTARES UNDER VINE 10.00

● Cerronero '13	♟♟ 5
● Terre di Casole Mattaione '13	♟♟ 3
● Camporignano '15	♟ 2
⊙ Rosa Rosa '15	♟ 3

Candialle

via Chiantigiana, km 34,00
50020 Panzano [FI]
Tel. +39 055852201
www.candialle.com

CELLAR SALES
PRE-BOOKED VISITS
ANNUAL PRODUCTION 35,000 bottles
HECTARES UNDER VINE 11.30
SUSTAINABLE WINERY

● La Misse '14	▼▼ 3
● Mimas '14	▼▼ 4
● Ciclope '13	▼ 4

Podere Il Carnasciale

loc. Il Carnasciale
52020 Mercatale Valdarno [AR]
Tel. +39 0559911142
www.caberlot.eu

PRE-BOOKED VISITS
ANNUAL PRODUCTION 10,000 bottles
HECTARES UNDER VINE 4.50
SUSTAINABLE WINERY

● Caberlot '13	▼▼ 8

Carusvini

loc. Mercatale val di Pesa
via Perseto, 20
50026 San Casciano in Val di Pesa [FI]
Tel. +39 0558218296
www.carusvini.it

CELLAR SALES
ANNUAL PRODUCTION 30,000 bottles
HECTARES UNDER VINE 13.00
SUSTAINABLE WINERY

● Chianti Cl. Gaudio '12	▼▼ 5
● Tespero '12	▼▼ 4
● Chianti Cl. Baldero '12	▼ 3
● Robeo '12	▼ 4

Fattoria Casa di Terra

fraz. Bolgheri
loc. Le Ferruggini, 162a
57022 Castagneto Carducci [LI]
Tel. +39 0565749810
www.fattoriacasaditerra.com

CELLAR SALES
PRE-BOOKED VISITS
ACCOMMODATION
ANNUAL PRODUCTION 180,000 bottles
HECTARES UNDER VINE 44.50

● Bolgheri Rosso Mosaico '13	▼▼ 5
○ Bolgheri Vermentino '15	▼▼ 3
● Bolgheri Rosso Sup. Maronea '12	▼ 6
● Lenaia '15	▼ 2

Casa Lucii

loc. Santa Maria a Villacastelli
53037 San Gimignano [SI]
Tel. +39 0577950199
www.casalucii.it

ANNUAL PRODUCTION 120,000 bottles
HECTARES UNDER VINE 100.00

○ Vernaccia di S. Gimignano Mareterra Ris. '13	▼▼ 6
● Chianti Colli Senesi Senarum '13	▼ 5
○ Vernaccia di S. Gimignano '15	▼ 4

Casavyc

loc. Poggioferro
pod. Camporomano, 43
58054 Scansano [GR]
Tel. +39 3356880673
www.casavyc.it

CELLAR SALES
PRE-BOOKED VISITS
ANNUAL PRODUCTION 40,000 bottles
HECTARES UNDER VINE 14.00

○ Brut M. Cl. A Riveder Le Stelle	▼▼ 3
○ Piano Piano Poco Poco '15	▼▼ 6
○ Vedorosa '15	▼ 3

Castelfalfi

LOC. CASTELFALFI
50050 MONTAIONE [FI]
TEL. +39 0571891400
www.castelfalfi.it

ANNUAL PRODUCTION 50,000 bottles
HECTARES UNDER VINE 23.00

● Poggio alla Fame '13   🍷🍷 5
● Poggionero '13   🍷 3

Castello di Querceto

LOC. QUERCETO
VIA A. FRANÇOIS, 2
50022 GREVE IN CHIANTI [FI]
TEL. +39 05585921
www.castellodiquerceto.it

CELLAR SALES
PRE-BOOKED VISITS
ACCOMMODATION
ANNUAL PRODUCTION 600,000 bottles
HECTARES UNDER VINE 60.00

● Chianti Cl. Ris. '13   🍷🍷 4
● Chianti Cl. Gran Sel. Il Picchio '13   🍷 5

Castello Tricerchi

LOC. ALTESI
S.DA PROV.LE 45 DEL BRUNELLO KM 1,700
53024 MONTALCINO [SI]
TEL. +39 0577806081
www.castellotricerchi.com

CELLAR SALES
PRE-BOOKED VISITS
ANNUAL PRODUCTION 30,000 bottles
HECTARES UNDER VINE 13.00

● Brunello di Montalcino '11   🍷🍷 6
● Rosso di Montalcino '14   🍷 4

Castelsina

FRAZ. SINALUNGA
LOC. OSTERIA, 54A
53011 SINALUNGA [SI]
TEL. +39 0577663595
www.castelsina.it

CELLAR SALES
PRE-BOOKED VISITS
ANNUAL PRODUCTION 2,000,000 bottles
HECTARES UNDER VINE 400.00

● Chianti '15   🍷🍷 2*
● Chianti Ris. '11   🍷🍷 2*
● Orcia '15   🍷🍷 3

Castelvecchi

LOC. CASTELVECCHI
53017 RADDA IN CHIANTI [SI]
TEL. +39 0577735612
www.chianticastelvecchi.it

CELLAR SALES
PRE-BOOKED VISITS
ACCOMMODATION AND RESTAURANT SERVICE
ANNUAL PRODUCTION 70,000 bottles
HECTARES UNDER VINE 18.00
SUSTAINABLE WINERY

● Chianti Cl. Capotondo '14   🍷🍷 5
● Chianti Cl. Lodolaio Ris. '12   🍷 6

Castelvecchio

LOC. SEANO
VIA DELLE MANNELLE, 19
59011 CARMIGNANO [PO]
TEL. +39 0558705451
www.castelvecchio.net

CELLAR SALES
PRE-BOOKED VISITS
ANNUAL PRODUCTION 40,000 bottles
HECTARES UNDER VINE 10.00

● Carmignano '12   🍷🍷 3*

I Cavallini

LOC. CAVALLINI
58014 MANCIANO [GR]
TEL. +39 0564609008
www.icavallini.it

ANNUAL PRODUCTION 25,000 bottles
HECTARES UNDER VINE 9.50

- Alicante '14 ⟐⟐ 3
- Maremmma Merlot Pause '14 ⟐⟐ 5
- ○ Maremma Toscana Vermentino Diaccio '15 ⟐ 3
- Morellino di Scansano '15 ⟐ 3

Ceralti

VIA DEI CERALTI, 77
57022 CASTAGNETO CARDUCCI [LI]
TEL. +39 0565763989
www.ceralti.com

CELLAR SALES
PRE-BOOKED VISITS
ACCOMMODATION
ANNUAL PRODUCTION 50,000 bottles
HECTARES UNDER VINE 9.00
VITICULTURE METHOD Certified Organic

- Bolgheri Sup. Sonoro '13 ⟐⟐ 7
- ○ Bolgheri Vermentino '15 ⟐ 3
- ○ Lillarae '15 ⟐ 4

Il Cerchio

VIA VALMARINA, 24
58011 CAPALBIO [GR]
TEL. +39 0564898856
www.ilcerchiobio.it

CELLAR SALES
PRE-BOOKED VISITS
HECTARES UNDER VINE 5.00
VITICULTURE METHOD Certified Organic
SUSTAINABLE WINERY

- Maremma Toscana Alicante Tinto '13 ⟐⟐ 4
- ○ Ansonica Costa dell'Argentario '15 ⟐ 2
- ○ Ansonica Passito l'Altro '15 ⟐ 3
- Maremma Toscana Valmarina '14 ⟐ 3

La Cerreta

VIA CAMPAGNA SUD, 143
57020 SASSETTA [LI]
TEL. +39 0565794352
www.lacerreta.it

ANNUAL PRODUCTION 20,000 bottles
HECTARES UNDER VINE 8.00
VITICULTURE METHOD Certified Biodynamic

- Sangiovese '13 ⟐⟐ 3
- ○ Matis '13 ⟐ 3
- Rio de' Messi '11 ⟐ 3
- Solatio della Cerreta '13 ⟐ 3

La Ciarliana

FRAZ. GRACCIANO
VIA CIARLIANA, 31
53040 MONTEPULCIANO [SI]
TEL. +39 0578758423
www.laciarliana.it

CELLAR SALES
PRE-BOOKED VISITS
ANNUAL PRODUCTION 30,000 bottles
HECTARES UNDER VINE 12.00

- Nobile di Montepulciano '13 ⟐⟐ 4
- Rosso di Montepulciano '14 ⟐ 3

Donatella Cinelli Colombini

LOC. CASATO, 17
53024 MONTALCINO [SI]
TEL. +39 0577662108
www.cinellicolombini.it

CELLAR SALES
PRE-BOOKED VISITS
ACCOMMODATION AND RESTAURANT SERVICE
ANNUAL PRODUCTION 120,000 bottles
HECTARES UNDER VINE 34.00

- Brunello di Montalcino Ris. '10 ⟐⟐ 8
- Rosso di Montalcino '14 ⟐ 3

La Cipriana

LOC. CAMPASTRELLO, 176B
57022 CASTAGNETO CARDUCCI [LI]
TEL. +39 0565775568
www.lacipriana.com

CELLAR SALES
PRE-BOOKED VISITS
ACCOMMODATION AND RESTAURANT SERVICE
ANNUAL PRODUCTION 30,000 bottles
HECTARES UNDER VINE 8.00

● Bolgheri Rosso Sup. San Martino '13	♥♥ 6
● Bolgheri Rosso Scopaio '14	♥♥ 4
○ Bolgheri Vermentino Paguro '15	♥ 2

Colle di Bordocheo

LOC. SEGROMIGNO IN MONTE
VIA DI PIAGGIORI BASSO, 123
55012 CAPANNORI [LU]
TEL. +39 0583929821
www.colledibordocheo.com

CELLAR SALES
PRE-BOOKED VISITS
ACCOMMODATION
ANNUAL PRODUCTION 30,000 bottles
HECTARES UNDER VINE 10.00

○ Bianco dell'Oca '15	♥♥ 3
● Colline Lucchesi Rosso Picchio Rosso '13	♥♥ 3
○ Quinto Vendemmia Tardiva	♥ 5

Collemattoni

FRAZ. SANT'ANGELO IN COLLE
LOC. COLLEMATTONI, 100
53024 MONTALCINO [SI]
TEL. +39 0577844127
www.collemattoni.it

CELLAR SALES
PRE-BOOKED VISITS
ANNUAL PRODUCTION 60,000 bottles
HECTARES UNDER VINE 11.00
VITICULTURE METHOD Certified Organic
SUSTAINABLE WINERY

● Rosso di Montalcino '14	♥♥ 4
● Brunello di Montalcino V. Fontelontano Ris. '10	♥ 8

Le Colline di Sopra

VIA DELLE COLLINE, 17
56040 MONTESCUDAIO [PI]
TEL. +39 0586650377
www.collinedisopra.com

CELLAR SALES
PRE-BOOKED VISITS
ANNUAL PRODUCTION 27,000 bottles
HECTARES UNDER VINE 5.10
VITICULTURE METHOD Certified Organic
SUSTAINABLE WINERY

○ Tredici '15	♥♥ 3
● Eola '15	♥ 3
● Montescudaio Sangiovese Sopra '13	♥ 6

Colline San Biagio

LOC. BACCHERETO
VIA SAN BIAGIO 6/8
59015 CARMIGNANO [PO]
TEL. +39 0558717143
www.collinesanbiagio.it

CELLAR SALES
PRE-BOOKED VISITS
ACCOMMODATION
ANNUAL PRODUCTION 35,000 bottles
HECTARES UNDER VINE 7.00
SUSTAINABLE WINERY

● Carmignano Sancti Blasii '10	♥♥ 4
● Sangiovese Donna Mingarda '12	♥♥ 4
⊙ Balè Rosato '15	♥ 3

Colognole

LOC. COLOGNOLE
VIA DEL PALAGIO, 15
50065 PONTASSIEVE [FI]
TEL. +39 0558319870
www.colognole.it

CELLAR SALES
PRE-BOOKED VISITS
ACCOMMODATION AND RESTAURANT SERVICE
ANNUAL PRODUCTION 90,000 bottles
HECTARES UNDER VINE 27.00

● Chianti Sinopie '15	♥♥ 2*
● Chianti Rufina '13	♥ 3
○ Sinopie '15	♥ 2

Corte dei Venti

LOC. PIANCORNELLO, 35
53024 MONTALCINO [SI]
TEL. +39 3473653718
www.lacortedeiventi.it

CELLAR SALES
PRE-BOOKED VISITS
ANNUAL PRODUCTION 20,000 bottles
HECTARES UNDER VINE 5.00

● Brunello di Montalcino '11	♟♟ 8
● Brunello di Montalcino Donna Elena Ris. '10	♟♟ 8
● Sant'Antimo Poggio dei Lecci '14	♟♟ 3

Cupelli Spumanti

V.LE MARCONI, 203
56028 SAN MINIATO [PI]
TEL. +39 057143801
www.cupellivini.com

CELLAR SALES
PRE-BOOKED VISITS
RESTAURANT SERVICE
ANNUAL PRODUCTION 30,000 bottles
HECTARES UNDER VINE 8.00

○ L'Erede Limited Edition	♟♟ 4
○ L'Erede	♟ 4
⊙ L'Erede Rosé	♟ 5

Dal Cero
Tenuta Montecchiesi

LOC. MONTECCHIO DI CORTONA
CASE SPARSE, 403
52044 CORTONA [AR]
TEL. +39 0575618503
www.vinidalcero.com

CELLAR SALES
PRE-BOOKED VISITS
ANNUAL PRODUCTION 300,000 bottles
HECTARES UNDER VINE 65.00

● Cortona Syrah Klanis '12	♟♟ 5
● Sangiovese '14	♟♟ 2*
○ Vermentino Chardonnay Montecchiesi '15	♟ 2

Dalle Nostre Mani

VIA DEI CIPRESSI, 14
50124 FUCECCHIO [FI]
TEL. +39 3395734846
www.dallenostremani.com

CELLAR SALES
PRE-BOOKED VISITS
ACCOMMODATION AND RESTAURANT SERVICE
ANNUAL PRODUCTION 50,000 bottles
HECTARES UNDER VINE 19.00
VITICULTURE METHOD Certified Organic
SUSTAINABLE WINERY

● Foglia Punta Riserva di Botte '13	♟♟ 4
● Foglia Tonda Riserva di Botte '13	♟♟ 4
● Arialdo '14	♟ 2
● Foglia Punta '13	♟ 3

Diadema

VIA IMPRUNETANA PER TAVARNUZZE, 19
50023 IMPRUNETA [FI]
TEL. +39 0552311330
www.diadema-wine.com

CELLAR SALES
PRE-BOOKED VISITS
ACCOMMODATION
ANNUAL PRODUCTION 240,000 bottles
HECTARES UNDER VINE 15.00

● D'Amare Rosso '14	♟♟ 5
● Diadema '14	♟♟ 8
● D'Ado '14	♟ 2
○ D'Amare Bianco '15	♟ 3

Dianella

VIA DIANELLA, 48
50059 VINCI [FI]
TEL. +39 0571508166
www.dianella.wine

CELLAR SALES
PRE-BOOKED VISITS
ACCOMMODATION
ANNUAL PRODUCTION 70,000 bottles
HECTARES UNDER VINE 25.00
SUSTAINABLE WINERY

○ Dolci Ricordi V.T.	♟♟ 5
● Il Matto delle Giuncaie '13	♟♟ 2*
⊙ All'Aria Aperta '15	♟ 2
● Le Veglie di Neri '15	♟ 3

Dievole

Fraz. Vagliagli
via Dievole, 6
53010 Castelnuovo Berardenga [SI]
Tel. +39 0577322613
www.dievole.it

CELLAR SALES
PRE-BOOKED VISITS
ACCOMMODATION AND RESTAURANT SERVICE
ANNUAL PRODUCTION 350,000 bottles
HECTARES UNDER VINE 80.00

● Chianti Cl. Ris. '13	♥♥ 5
● Chianti Cl. '14	♥ 4

Donne Fittipaldi

loc. Bolgheri
via Bolgherese, 198
57022 Castagneto Carducci [LI]
Tel. +39 0565762175
www.donnefittipaldi.it

ANNUAL PRODUCTION 60,000 bottles
HECTARES UNDER VINE 9.50

● Bolgheri Rosso Sup. Superior '13	♥♥ 6

Podere Fedespina

loc. Bosco Arpiola, 1
54026 Mulazzo [MS]
Tel. +39 0187439610
www.poderefedespina.it

ANNUAL PRODUCTION 5,000 bottles
HECTARES UNDER VINE 1.00

● Ca' '12	♥♥ 5
● Spinorosso '13	♥♥ 4

Fattoria di Fiano

loc. Fiano
via Firenze, 11
50050 Certaldo [FI]
Tel. +39 0571669048
www.ugobing.it

CELLAR SALES
PRE-BOOKED VISITS
ANNUAL PRODUCTION 150,000 bottles
HECTARES UNDER VINE 22.00

● Chianti Colli Fiorentini Ris. '13	♥♥ 2*
● Chianti Colli Fiorentini '14	♥ 2

Ficomontanino

loc. Ficomontanino
53043 Chiusi [SI]
Tel. +39 065561283
www.agricolaficomontanino.it

CELLAR SALES
PRE-BOOKED VISITS
ANNUAL PRODUCTION 40,000 bottles
HECTARES UNDER VINE 9.00

● Chianti Colli Senesi Terre del Fico '15	♥♥ 2*
● Lucumone del Fico '12	♥ 5

Il Fitto

Fraz. Cignano
loc. Chianacce, 126
52042 Cortona [AR]
Tel. +39 0575648988
www.podereilfitto.com

CELLAR SALES
PRE-BOOKED VISITS
ACCOMMODATION
ANNUAL PRODUCTION 30,000 bottles
HECTARES UNDER VINE 8.00

● Cortona Sangiovese Il Fitto '14	♥♥ 2*
● Cortona Syrah Il Fitto '14	♥♥ 3

Poderi Fontemorsi

VIA DELLE COLLINE
56040 MONTESCUDAIO [PI]
TEL. +39 3356843438
www.fontemorsi.it

CELLAR SALES
ACCOMMODATION
ANNUAL PRODUCTION 50,000 bottles
HECTARES UNDER VINE 8.50
VITICULTURE METHOD Certified Organic

● Montescudaio Rosso Spazzavento '12	♟♟ 2*
● Volterrano '12	♟♟ 4
● Guadipiani '12	♟ 4
○ Tresassi '15	♟ 2

Le Fonti

FRAZ. PANZANO IN CHIANTI
LOC. LE FONTI
50022 GREVE IN CHIANTI [FI]
TEL. +39 055852194
www.fattorialefonti.it

CELLAR SALES
PRE-BOOKED VISITS
ANNUAL PRODUCTION 45,000 bottles
HECTARES UNDER VINE 8.81
VITICULTURE METHOD Certified Organic

● Chianti Cl. '13	♟♟ 3
● Chianti Cl. Ris. '12	♟ 4
● Fontissimo '12	♟ 5

La Fornace

POD. FORNACE, 154A
53024 MONTALCINO [SI]
TEL. +39 0577848465
www.agricola-lafornace.it

CELLAR SALES
PRE-BOOKED VISITS
ANNUAL PRODUCTION 15,000 bottles
HECTARES UNDER VINE 4.50

● Rosso di Montalcino '14	♟♟ 4

Fattoria di Fubbiano

LOC. SAN GENNARO
VIA DI TOFORI FUBBIANO
55010 CAPANNORI [LU]
TEL. +39 0583978011
www.fattoriadifubbiano.it

CELLAR SALES
PRE-BOOKED VISITS
ACCOMMODATION
ANNUAL PRODUCTION 100,000 bottles
HECTARES UNDER VINE 20.00

○ Colline Lucchesi Vermentino '15	♟♟ 2*
● Schiller '15	♟ 3

Gattavecchi

LOC. SANTA MARIA
VIA DI COLLAZZI, 74
53045 MONTEPULCIANO [SI]
TEL. +39 0578757110
www.gattavecchi.it

CELLAR SALES
PRE-BOOKED VISITS
RESTAURANT SERVICE
ANNUAL PRODUCTION 280,000 bottles
HECTARES UNDER VINE 40.00

● Nobile di Montepulciano '13	♟♟ 4
● Nobile di Montepulciano Riserva dei Padri Serviti '12	♟ 5

Gentili

VIA DEL TAMBURINO, 120
53040 CETONA [SI]
TEL. +39 0578244038
www.gentiliwine.com

CELLAR SALES
PRE-BOOKED VISITS
ANNUAL PRODUCTION 100,000 bottles
HECTARES UNDER VINE 15.00

● Le Favorite '13	♟♟ 5
● Matero '15	♟♟ 1*
○ Chardonnay '15	♟ 2
○ Costa del Sole '15	♟ 1*

La Gerla

LOC. CANALICCHIO
POD. COLOMBAIO, 5
53024 MONTALCINO [SI]
TEL. +39 0577848599
www.lagerla.it

CELLAR SALES
PRE-BOOKED VISITS
ANNUAL PRODUCTION 80,000 bottles
HECTARES UNDER VINE 11.50

● Rosso di Montalcino '14	♟♟ 3
● Brunello di Montalcino '11	♟ 6

Giomi Zannoni

VIA AURELIA NORD, 63
57029 CAMPIGLIA MARITTIMA [LI]
TEL. +39 0565846416
www.giomi-zannoni.com

CELLAR SALES
PRE-BOOKED VISITS
RESTAURANT SERVICE
ANNUAL PRODUCTION 18,000 bottles
HECTARES UNDER VINE 7.00

● Aldò 917 '15	♟♟ 5
● Val di Cornia Sangiovese Solemare '15	♟♟ 2*
○ Val di Cornia Bianco Corniola '15	♟ 3
○ Vermentino Ninà 910 '15	♟ 3

Marchesi Gondi
Tenuta Bossi

LOC. BOSSI
VIA DELLO STRACCHINO, 32
50065 PONTASSIEVE [FI]
TEL. +39 0558317830
www.tenutabossi.com

CELLAR SALES
PRE-BOOKED VISITS
ACCOMMODATION
ANNUAL PRODUCTION 50,000 bottles
HECTARES UNDER VINE 19.00

● Chianti Rufina Pian dei Sorbi Ris. '12	♟♟ 3
● Chianti Rufina San Giuliano '13	♟ 2

Greppone Mazzi
Tenimenti Ruffino

LOC. GREPPONE
53024 MONTALCINO [SI]
TEL. +39 0556499717
www.ruffino.it

PRE-BOOKED VISITS
ANNUAL PRODUCTION 45,000 bottles
HECTARES UNDER VINE 13.00

● Brunello di Montalcino '11	♟♟ 7

Fattoria di Grignano

VIA DI GRIGNANO, 22
50065 PONTASSIEVE [FI]
TEL. +39 0558398490
www.fattoriadigrignano.com

CELLAR SALES
PRE-BOOKED VISITS
ANNUAL PRODUCTION 200,000 bottles
HECTARES UNDER VINE 53.00
VITICULTURE METHOD Certified Organic
SUSTAINABLE WINERY

● Chianti Rufina '13	♟♟ 2*
● Salicaria '10	♟ 5

Fattoria Il Lago

FRAZ. CAMPAGNA, 23
50062 DICOMANO [FI]
TEL. +39 055838047
www.fattoriaillago.com

CELLAR SALES
PRE-BOOKED VISITS
ACCOMMODATION
ANNUAL PRODUCTION 50,000 bottles
HECTARES UNDER VINE 17.00
SUSTAINABLE WINERY

● Pinot Nero '12	♟♟ 5
● Chianti Rufina '13	♟ 2

Tenuta La Macchia

LOC. CASAGIUSTRI, 3
56040 MONTESCUDAIO [PI]
TEL. +39 3381258469
www.tenutalamacchia.com

ANNUAL PRODUCTION 15,000 bottles
HECTARES UNDER VINE 2.20

○ Aura '15	♟♟ 3
● Scutum '14	♟♟ 3
⊙ Materia '15	♟ 4

Leuta

VIA PIETRAIA, 21
52044 CORTONA [AR]
TEL. +39 3385033560
www.leuta.it

CELLAR SALES
PRE-BOOKED VISITS
ANNUAL PRODUCTION 25,000 bottles
HECTARES UNDER VINE 12.60

● Cortona Cabernet Franc 2,618 '13	♟♟ 5
● Cortona Sangiovese Solitario '12	♟♟ 6
● Cortona Merlot 1.618 '11	♟ 5
● Cortona Syrah 0,618 '13	♟ 5

Lornano

LOC. LORNANO, 11
53035 MONTERIGGIONI [SI]
TEL. +39 0577309059
www.lornano.it

CELLAR SALES
PRE-BOOKED VISITS
ACCOMMODATION
ANNUAL PRODUCTION 250,000 bottles
HECTARES UNDER VINE 45.00

● Chianti Cl. Gran Sel. '12	♟♟ 6
● Chianti Cl. Ris. '12	♟ 3

La Magia

LOC. LA MAGIA
53024 MONTALCINO [SI]
TEL. +39 0577835667
www.fattorialamagia.it

ANNUAL PRODUCTION 80,000 bottles
HECTARES UNDER VINE 15.00

● Brunello di Montalcino '11	♟♟ 6
● Brunello di Montalcino Ris. '10	♟♟ 8
● Rosso di Montalcino '14	♟ 3

Fattoria di Magliano

LOC. STERPETI, 10
58051 MAGLIANO IN TOSCANA [GR]
TEL. +39 0564593040
www.fattoriadimagliano.it

CELLAR SALES
PRE-BOOKED VISITS
ACCOMMODATION AND RESTAURANT SERVICE
ANNUAL PRODUCTION 300,000 bottles
HECTARES UNDER VINE 50.00
VITICULTURE METHOD Certified Organic

● Morellino di Scansano Heba '15	♟♟ 3
● Perenzo '13	♟ 6
● Poggio Bestiale '13	♟ 5

Malenchini

LOC. GRASSINA
VIA LILLIANO E MEOLI, 82
50015 BAGNO A RIPOLI [FI]
TEL. +39 055642602
www.malenchini.it

CELLAR SALES
PRE-BOOKED VISITS
ANNUAL PRODUCTION 120,000 bottles
HECTARES UNDER VINE 17.00

● Chianti Colli Fiorentini '14	♟♟ 2*
● Chianti Colli Fiorentini '15	♟ 2

Fattoria Mantellassi

LOC. BANDITACCIA, 26
58051 MAGLIANO IN TOSCANA [GR]
TEL. +39 0564592037
www.fattoriamantellassi.it

CELLAR SALES
PRE-BOOKED VISITS
ANNUAL PRODUCTION 900,000 bottles
HECTARES UNDER VINE 72.00

● Morellino di Scansano Mentore '15	♟♟ 2*
○ Maremma Toscana Scalandrino '15	♟ 2

Máté

LOC. SANTA RESTITUTA
53024 MONTALCINO [SI]
TEL. +39 0577847215
www.matewine.com

CELLAR SALES
PRE-BOOKED VISITS
ANNUAL PRODUCTION 28,000 bottles
HECTARES UNDER VINE 6.50

● Brunello di Montalcino '11	♟♟ 6
● Brunello di Montalcino Ris. '10	♟♟ 7
● Rosso di Montalcino '14	♟♟ 3

Le Miccine

LOC. LE MICCINE
S.DA STAT.LE TRAVERSA CHIANTIGIANA, 44
53013 GAIOLE IN CHIANTI [SI]
TEL. +39 0577749526
www.lemiccine.com

CELLAR SALES
PRE-BOOKED VISITS
ACCOMMODATION
ANNUAL PRODUCTION 30,000 bottles
HECTARES UNDER VINE 7.00
VITICULTURE METHOD Certified Organic

● Chianti Cl. Ris. '13	♟♟ 5
● Chianti Cl. '14	♟ 4

Mola

LOC. GELSARELLO, 2
57031 PORTO AZZURRO [LI]
TEL. +39 0565958151
www.tenutepavoletti.it

CELLAR SALES
PRE-BOOKED VISITS
ANNUAL PRODUCTION 47,000 bottles
HECTARES UNDER VINE 12.00

● Elba Aleatico Passito '12	♟♟ 4
○ Cuvée Brut A '14	♟ 3
○ Elba Ansonica '15	♟ 3
○ Elba Vermentino '15	♟ 2

Il Molinaccio

VIA ANTICA CHIUSINA, 12
53045 MONTEPULCIANO [SI]
TEL. +39 0578758660
www.ilmolinaccio.com

CELLAR SALES
ACCOMMODATION AND RESTAURANT SERVICE

● Nobile di Montepulciano '13	♟♟ 4
● Nobile di Montepulciano '12	♟♟ 4

Podere Monastero

LOC. MONASTERO
53011 CASTELLINA IN CHIANTI [SI]
TEL. +39 0577740436
www.poderemonastero.com

CELLAR SALES
PRE-BOOKED VISITS
ACCOMMODATION
ANNUAL PRODUCTION 7,000 bottles
HECTARES UNDER VINE 3.00

● La Pineta '14	♟♟ 6
● Campanaio '14	♟♟ 6

Montemercurio

VIA DI TOTONA, 25A
53045 MONTEPULCIANO [SI]
TEL. +39 0578716610
www.montemercurio.com

CELLAR SALES
PRE-BOOKED VISITS
ANNUAL PRODUCTION 40,000 bottles
HECTARES UNDER VINE 10.00
VITICULTURE METHOD Certified Organic

● Rosso di Montepulciano Petaso '12	♥♥	3

Montepepe

VIA SFORZA, 76
54038 MONTIGNOSO [MS]
TEL. +39 0585831042
www.montepepe.com

CELLAR SALES
PRE-BOOKED VISITS
ANNUAL PRODUCTION 20,000 bottles
HECTARES UNDER VINE 5.40

○ Montepepe Bianco '14	♥♥	4
○ Montepepe Bianco Vintage '11	♥	5

Fattoria Montereggi

VIA BOSCONI, 44
50014 FIESOLE [FI]
TEL. +39 055540005
www.fattoriamontereggi.it

CELLAR SALES
PRE-BOOKED VISITS
ANNUAL PRODUCTION 100,000 bottles
HECTARES UNDER VINE 15.00
SUSTAINABLE WINERY

● Chianti Ris. '10	♥♥	3*
● Chianti '14	♥♥	2*

Monterinaldi

LOC. LUCARELLI
53017 RADDA IN CHIANTI [SI]
TEL. +39 0577733533
www.monterinaldi.it

ANNUAL PRODUCTION 400,000 bottles
HECTARES UNDER VINE 65.00

● Chianti Cl. Campopazzo '13	♥♥	3
● Chianti Cl. Ris. '13	♥♥	4

Monterotondo

LOC. MONTEROTONDO, 12
53013 GAIOLE IN CHIANTI [SI]
TEL. +39 0577 749089
www.agriturismomonterotondo.net

PRE-BOOKED VISITS
ACCOMODATION
ANNUAL PRODUCTION 20,000 bottles
HECTARES UNDER VINE 4.00
VITICULTURE METHOD Certified Organic

● Chianti Cl. Vaggiolata '12	♥♥	3*
● Chianti Cl. Ris. '11	♥	4

Podere Morazzano

S.DA MORAZZANO 5
56040 MONTESCUDAIO [PI]
TEL. +39 0445529693
www.poderemorazzano.it

ANNUAL PRODUCTION 20,000 bottles
HECTARES UNDER VINE 5.00

● Eriva '11	♥♥	5
● Montescudaio Rerosso '11	♥♥	4
● Ribuio '12	♥	2

Giacomo Mori

FRAZ. PALAZZONE
P.ZZA SANDRO PERTINI, 8
53040 SAN CASCIANO DEI BAGNI [SI]
TEL. +39 0578227005
www.giacomomori.it

CELLAR SALES
PRE-BOOKED VISITS
ACCOMMODATION
ANNUAL PRODUCTION 40,000 bottles
HECTARES UNDER VINE 11.00
VITICULTURE METHOD Certified Organic

● Chianti Castelrotto Ris. '13	♟♟ 3
● Chianti '14	♟ 2

Mario Motta

LOC. BANDITELLA ALBERESE
58100 GROSSETO
TEL. +39 0564405105
www.mottavini.com

CELLAR SALES
PRE-BOOKED VISITS
ANNUAL PRODUCTION 40,000 bottles
HECTARES UNDER VINE 9.00

● Ciliegiolo '15	♟♟ 3
● Morellino di Scansano Ris. '13	♟♟ 5
● Morellino di Scansano '15	♟ 3

Nottola

FRAZ. GRACCIANO
LOC. BIVIO DI NOTTOLA, 9A
53045 MONTEPULCIANO [SI]
TEL. +39 0578707060
www.cantinanottola.it

CELLAR SALES
PRE-BOOKED VISITS
ACCOMMODATION AND RESTAURANT SERVICE
ANNUAL PRODUCTION 120,000 bottles
HECTARES UNDER VINE 20.00

● Nobile di Montepulciano '13	♟♟ 4
● Rosso di Montepulciano '14	♟ 2

Cantina Olivi Le Buche

VIA CASELFAVA, 25
53047 SARTEANO [SI]
TEL. +39 0578274066
www.lebuche.com

CELLAR SALES
PRE-BOOKED VISITS
ACCOMMODATION AND RESTAURANT SERVICE
ANNUAL PRODUCTION 100,000 bottles
HECTARES UNDER VINE 30.00
SUSTAINABLE WINERY

● I Puri Syrah '11	♟♟ 8
● Orcia Le Buche '12	♟♟ 5
● Chianti Sup. Olivi '13	♟ 3
● Orcia Coreno '15	♟ 3

Oliviera

S.DA PROV.LE 102 DI VAGLIAGLI, 36
53019 CASTELNUOVO BERARDENGA [SI]
TEL. +39 3498950188
www.oliviera.it

ANNUAL PRODUCTION 30,000 bottles
HECTARES UNDER VINE 9.00

● Chianti Cl. Ris. '12	♟♟ 4
● Chianti Cl. '14	♟ 3

Ottomani

VIA DI PANCOLE, 119
50027 GREVE IN CHIANTI [FI]
TEL. +39 3407105484
www.ottomanivino.com

ANNUAL PRODUCTION 25,000 bottles
HECTARES UNDER VINE 12.00

● Chianti Colli Fiorentini '14	♟♟ 2*
● Sangiovese '13	♟♟ 4
● Canaiolo '12	♟ 5

Fattoria Il Palagio

FRAZ. CASTEL SAN GIMIGNANO
LOC. IL PALAGIO
53030 COLLE DI VAL D'ELSA [SI]
TEL. +39 0577953004
www.ilpalagio.it

CELLAR SALES
PRE-BOOKED VISITS
ANNUAL PRODUCTION 800,000 bottles
HECTARES UNDER VINE 79.00

○ Chardonnay Chioppaia '15	♥♥ 3
○ Sauvignon Melaia '15	♥ 3
○ Vernaccia di San Gimignano Le Ginestrelle '15	♥ 3

Il Palagione

VIA PER CASTEL SAN GIMIGNANO, 36
53037 SAN GIMIGNANO [SI]
TEL. +39 0577953134
www.ilpalagione.com

CELLAR SALES
PRE-BOOKED VISITS
ACCOMMODATION
ANNUAL PRODUCTION 40,000 bottles
HECTARES UNDER VINE 16.00
VITICULTURE METHOD Certified Organic

○ Vernaccia di S. Gimignano Ori Ris. '14	♥♥ 3
● Chianti Colli Senesi Caelum '14	♥ 2
● Chianti Colli Senesi Drago Ris. '13	♥ 3
⊙ Sunrosé '15	♥ 2

La Palazzetta

FRAZ. CASTELNUOVO DELL'ABATE
VIA PODERE LA PALAZZETTA, 1P
53024 MONTALCINO [SI]
TEL. +39 0577835531
palazzettafanti@gmail.com

CELLAR SALES
PRE-BOOKED VISITS
ACCOMMODATION
ANNUAL PRODUCTION 70,000 bottles
HECTARES UNDER VINE 20.00

● Brunello di Montalcino '11	♥♥ 5

Palazzo

LOC. PALAZZO, 144
53024 MONTALCINO [SI]
TEL. +39 0577849226
www.aziendapalazzo.it

CELLAR SALES
PRE-BOOKED VISITS
ANNUAL PRODUCTION 21,000 bottles
HECTARES UNDER VINE 4.00
VITICULTURE METHOD Certified Biodynamic

● Brunello di Montalcino Ris. '10	♥♥ 7
● Brunello di Montalcino '11	♥ 6
● Rosso di Montalcino '14	♥ 3

Tenuta Il Palazzo

LOC. ANTRIA
52100 AREZZO
TEL. +39 0575 361338
www.tenutailpalazzo.it

CELLAR SALES
PRE-BOOKED VISITS
ANNUAL PRODUCTION 300,000 bottles
HECTARES UNDER VINE 40.00

● Syrah '12	♥♥ 3
○ Vin Santo del Chianti Ris. '07	♥♥ 4
● Chianti Il Palazzo '14	♥ 3
● Chianti Il Palazzo Ris. '11	♥ 3

Palazzo Vecchio

FRAZ. VALIANO
VIA TERRAROSSA, 5
53040 MONTEPULCIANO [SI]
TEL. +39 0578724170
www.vinonobile.it

CELLAR SALES
PRE-BOOKED VISITS
RESTAURANT SERVICE
ANNUAL PRODUCTION 40,000 bottles
HECTARES UNDER VINE 25.00

● Nobile di Montepulciano Maestro '13	♥♥ 4

Fattoria Pancole

LOC. PANCOLE
53037 SAN GIMIGNANO [SI]
TEL. +39 0577955078
www.fattoriadipancole.it

CELLAR SALES
PRE-BOOKED VISITS
ACCOMMODATION
ANNUAL PRODUCTION 120,000 bottles
HECTARES UNDER VINE 17.00
VITICULTURE METHOD Certified Organic
SUSTAINABLE WINERY

● Terraisassi '12	♟♟ 5
● Chianti dei Colli Senesi '15	♟ 2
● Dogato '12	♟ 4
○ Vernaccia di S. Gimignano '15	♟ 2

Fattoria di Petroio

FRAZ. QUERCEGROSSA
VIA DI MOCENNI, 7
53019 CASTELNUOVO BERARDENGA [SI]
TEL. +39 0577328045
www.fattoriapetroio.it

CELLAR SALES
PRE-BOOKED VISITS
RESTAURANT SERVICE
ANNUAL PRODUCTION 40,000 bottles
HECTARES UNDER VINE 15.00
VITICULTURE METHOD Certified Organic

● Poggio al Mandorlo '14	♟♟ 5

La Piana

VIA REGINA MARGHERITA, 4
57032 CAPRAIA ISOLA [LI]
TEL. +39 3920592988
www.lapianacapraia.it

PRE-BOOKED VISITS
ANNUAL PRODUCTION 8,000 bottles
HECTARES UNDER VINE 5.50
VITICULTURE METHOD Certified Organic

● Cristino '15	♟♟ 5
○ Palmazio '15	♟♟ 3
⊙ Asfoledo Rosé '15	♟ 3
⊙ Rosa della Piana '15	♟ 3

Perazzeta

LOC. MONTENERO D'ORCIA
VIA DELL'AIA, 14
58040 CASTEL DEL PIANO [GR]
TEL. +39 0564954158
www.perazzeta.it

CELLAR SALES
PRE-BOOKED VISITS
ANNUAL PRODUCTION 40,000 bottles
HECTARES UNDER VINE 7.50

● Montecucco Rosso Alfeno '14	♟♟ 2*
⊙ Sara Rosé '15	♟ 2

Pian delle Querci

VIA GIACOMO LEOPARDI, 10
53024 MONTALCINO [SI]
TEL. +39 0577834174
www.piandellequerci.it

CELLAR SALES
PRE-BOOKED VISITS
ANNUAL PRODUCTION 53,000 bottles
HECTARES UNDER VINE 8.50

● Brunello di Montalcino '11	♟♟ 5
● Brunello di Montalcino Ris. '10	♟♟ 5
● Rosso di Montalcino '14	♟ 3

Piandibugnano

LOC. PIAN DI BUGNANO
58038 SEGGIANO [GR]
TEL. +39 0564950773
www.piandibugnano.com

CELLAR SALES
PRE-BOOKED VISITS
ANNUAL PRODUCTION 27,800 bottles
HECTARES UNDER VINE 3.80

● Montecucco Sangiovese L'Erpico '13	♟♟ 5
● Nanerone Aleatico Passito '14	♟ 5

Pianirossi

LOC. PORRONA
POD. SANTA GENOVEFFA, 1
58044 CINIGIANO [GR]
TEL. +39 0564990573
www.pianirossi.it

CELLAR SALES
PRE-BOOKED VISITS
ACCOMMODATION AND RESTAURANT SERVICE
ANNUAL PRODUCTION 50,000 bottles
HECTARES UNDER VINE 14.00

- Montecucco Sidus '14   ♥♥ 2*
- Pianirossi '13   ♥ 6
- Solus '13   ♥ 3

Fattoria Piccaratico

LOC. SPICCHIO
VIA PICCARATICO, 9
50059 VINCI [FI]
TEL. +39 0571509143
www.fattoriapiccaratico.it

CELLAR SALES
PRE-BOOKED VISITS
ACCOMMODATION
ANNUAL PRODUCTION 28,000 bottles
HECTARES UNDER VINE 10.00

- ○ Bianco dell'Empolese Vin Santo
  Semiramis '07   ♥♥ 5
- Rosso del Rinserrato '13   ♥♥ 3
- Chianti Colle dei Fossili '15   ♥ 2

Agostina Pieri

FRAZ. SANT'ANGELO SCALO
LOC. PIANCORNELLO
53024 MONTALCINO [SI]
TEL. +39 0577844163
www.pieriagostina.it

ANNUAL PRODUCTION 45,000 bottles
HECTARES UNDER VINE 10.78

- Brunello di Montalcino '11   ♥♥ 6
- Rosso di Montalcino '14   ♥♥ 3

La Pierotta

LOC. LA PIEROTTA, 19
58020 SCARLINO [GR]
TEL. +39 056637218
www.@lapierotta.it

CELLAR SALES
PRE-BOOKED VISITS
ANNUAL PRODUCTION 50,000 bottles
HECTARES UNDER VINE 13.00

- Monteregio di Massa Marittima Rosso
  Selvaneta '14   ♥♥ 2*
- Monteregio di Massa Marittima
  Scarilius '13   ♥ 3

Pieve Santa Restituta

LOC. CHIESA DI SANTA RESTITUTA
53024 MONTALCINO [SI]
TEL. +39 0577848610
info@pievesantarestituta.com

ANNUAL PRODUCTION 75,000 bottles
HECTARES UNDER VINE 27.00

- Brunello di Montalcino Sugarille '11   ♥♥ 8
- Brunello di Montalcino Rennina '11   ♥ 8

Pinino

LOC. PININO, 327
53024 MONTALCINO [SI]
TEL. +39 0577849381
www.pinino.com

CELLAR SALES
PRE-BOOKED VISITS
ANNUAL PRODUCTION 90,000 bottles
HECTARES UNDER VINE 16.00

- Brunello di Montalcino '11   ♥♥ 7
- Brunello di Montalcino Pinone Ris. '10   ♥♥ 8
- Rosso di Montalcino Pinino '14   ♥ 3

Cantina Cooperativa di Pitigliano

VIA NICOLA CIACCI, 974
58017 PITIGLIANO [GR]
TEL. +39 0564616133
www.cantinadipitigliano.it

CELLAR SALES
PRE-BOOKED VISITS
ANNUAL PRODUCTION 3,000,000 bottles
HECTARES UNDER VINE 1000.00
VITICULTURE METHOD Certified Organic

● Maremma Toscana Ciliegiolo '15		♟♟ 3
● Sovana Sup. Vignamurata Sangiovese '15		♟♟ 2*
○ Bianco di Pitigliano Sup. Ildebrando '15		♟ 2

Podere dell'Anselmo

LOC. ANSELMO
VIA PANFI, 12
50025 MONTESPERTOLI [FI]
TEL. +39 0571671951
www.forconi.net

CELLAR SALES
PRE-BOOKED VISITS
ACCOMMODATION AND RESTAURANT SERVICE
ANNUAL PRODUCTION 40,000 bottles
HECTARES UNDER VINE 13.00

● Pax '12		♟♟ 6
● Terre di Bracciatica '14		♟♟ 2*
● Chianti Montespertoli '13		♟ 2
● Chianti Montespertoli Ingannamatti Ris. '12		♟ 3

Poggio al Tufo

LOC. POGGIO CAVALLUCCIO
58017 PITIGLIANO [GR]
TEL. +39 0457701266
www.tommasiwine.it

CELLAR SALES
ANNUAL PRODUCTION 165,000 bottles
HECTARES UNDER VINE 66.00

● Cabernet Sauvignon '14		♟♟ 2*
● Alicante '13		♟ 3
● Rompicollo '14		♟ 2

Poggio Nicchiaia

VIA SAN MARTINO, 7
56037 PECCIOLI [PI]
TEL. +39 0587697139
www.poggionicchiaia.it

ANNUAL PRODUCTION 80,000 bottles
HECTARES UNDER VINE 50.00

● Mania '13		♟♟ 3
● Chianti Filetto '14		♟ 2
○ Fiore del Borgo '15		♟ 2

Tenuta Poggio Rosso

FRAZ. POPULONIA
LOC. POGGIO ROSSO, 1
57025 PIOMBINO [LI]
TEL. +39 056529553
www.tenutapoggiorosso.it

CELLAR SALES
PRE-BOOKED VISITS
ANNUAL PRODUCTION 35,000 bottles
HECTARES UNDER VINE 6.00

● Velthune '13		♟♟ 6
○ Feronia '15		♟ 4
○ Losna '14		♟ 6
○ Phylika '15		♟ 3

Fattoria Pogni

LOC. MARCIALLA
VIA POGNI DI SOPRA, 159
50052 CERTALDO [FI]
TEL. +39 3331334379
www.fattoriapogni.it

CELLAR SALES
PRE-BOOKED VISITS
ACCOMMODATION
ANNUAL PRODUCTION 100,000 bottles
HECTARES UNDER VINE 12.00

● Nappolaio '12		♟♟ 3
● Terrasole '12		♟♟ 4
● Chianti Poggio ai Falchi Ris. '11		♟ 3
● Gorgogli '12		♟ 4

Pometti

LOC. LA SELVA, 16
53020 TREQUANDA [SI]
TEL. +39 057747833
www.pometti.it

CELLAR SALES
PRE-BOOKED VISITS
ACCOMMODATION AND RESTAURANT SERVICE
ANNUAL PRODUCTION 40,000 bottles
HECTARES UNDER VINE 11.00

● Tinotre '13	♥♥ 4
● Tarchun Us '12	♥ 3

Il Ponte

S.DA CARIGE ALTA, 15
58010 CAPALBIO [GR]
TEL. +39 068547928
www.agricolailponte.it

CELLAR SALES
PRE-BOOKED VISITS
ANNUAL PRODUCTION 25,000 bottles
HECTARES UNDER VINE 14.00

● Maremma Toscana Balto '12	♥♥ 4
● Capalbio Rosso T-Lex '14	♥ 4
○ Costa dell'Argentario Ansonica T-Lex '15	♥ 4

Provveditore

LOC. SALAIOLO, 174
58054 SCANSANO [GR]
TEL. +39 3487018670
www.provveditore.net

CELLAR SALES
PRE-BOOKED VISITS
RESTAURANT SERVICE
ANNUAL PRODUCTION 15,000 bottles
HECTARES UNDER VINE 30.00

● Morellino di Scansano '14	♥♥ 3
○ Maremma Toscana Sauvignon Il Bargaglino '15	♥ 3
● Morellino di Scansano Irio '15	♥ 2

La Rasina

LOC. RASINA, 132
53024 MONTALCINO [SI]
TEL. +39 0577848536
www.larasina.it

CELLAR SALES
PRE-BOOKED VISITS
ACCOMMODATION
ANNUAL PRODUCTION 60,000 bottles
HECTARES UNDER VINE 12.50

● Brunello di Montalcino '11	♥♥ 6
● Brunello di Montalcino Il Divasco Ris. '10	♥♥ 8

Riecine

LOC. RIECINE
53013 GAIOLE IN CHIANTI [SI]
TEL. +39 0577749098
www.riecine.com

CELLAR SALES
PRE-BOOKED VISITS
ANNUAL PRODUCTION 60,000 bottles
HECTARES UNDER VINE 11.00
VITICULTURE METHOD Certified Organic

● Riecine di Riecine '12	♥♥ 5
● La Gioia '12	♥ 6

Rigoli

LOC. CAFAGGIO
VIA DEGLI ULMI, 8
57021 CAMPIGLIA MARITTIMA [LI]
TEL. +39 0565843079
www.rigolivini.com

ANNUAL PRODUCTION 30,000 bottles
HECTARES UNDER VINE 5.00

● N'Etrusco '15	♥♥ 1*
○ Stradivino '15	♥♥ 1*
● Assiolo '11	♥ 1*

Tenute delle Ripalte

LOC. RIPALTE
57031 CAPOLIVERI [LI]
TEL. +39 056594211
www.tenutadelleripalte.it

CELLAR SALES
PRE-BOOKED VISITS
ACCOMMODATION AND RESTAURANT SERVICE
ANNUAL PRODUCTION 60,000 bottles
HECTARES UNDER VINE 15.00
SUSTAINABLE WINERY

● Elba Aleatico Passito Alea Ludendo '12	♥♥ 6
● Alicante '14	♥♥ 3
⊙ Rosato delle Ripalte '15	♥ 3
○ Vermentino '15	♥ 3

San Benedetto

LOC. SAN BENEDETTO, 4A
53037 SAN GIMIGNANO [SI]
TEL. +39 3386958705
www.agrisanbenedetto.com

CELLAR SALES
ANNUAL PRODUCTION 40,000 bottles
HECTARES UNDER VINE 25.00

○ Vernaccia di San Gimignano Ris. '13	♥♥ 2*
● Chianti '14	♥ 2
○ Vermentino '15	♥ 2
○ Vernaccia di San Gimignano '15	♥ 2

Fattoria Sardi

FRAZ. MONTE SAN QUIRICO
VIA DELLA MAULINA, 747
55100 LUCCA
TEL. +39 0583341230
www.fattoriasardi.com

CELLAR SALES
PRE-BOOKED VISITS
ACCOMMODATION
ANNUAL PRODUCTION 110,000 bottles
HECTARES UNDER VINE 14.00
VITICULTURE METHOD Certified Organic

● Colline Lucchesi Rosso Sebastiano '13	♥♥ 5
⊙ Fattoria Sardi Rosé '15	♥ 3

Sada

S.DA PROV.LE DEI 3 COMUNI
56040 CASALE MARITTIMO [PI]
TEL. +39 0586650180
www.agricolasada.com

CELLAR SALES
PRE-BOOKED VISITS
ANNUAL PRODUCTION 60,000 bottles
HECTARES UNDER VINE 11.50
VITICULTURE METHOD Certified Organic

● Bolgheri Sup. '13	♥♥ 6
● Integolo '13	♥♥ 6
○ Vermentino '15	♥ 3

Fattoria San Felo

LOC. PAGLIATELLI
58051 MAGLIANO IN TOSCANA [GR]
TEL. +39 05641836727
www.fattoriasanfelo.it

PRE-BOOKED VISITS
ANNUAL PRODUCTION 200,000 bottles
HECTARES UNDER VINE 30.00

○ Chardonnay '15	♥♥ 3
● Morellino di Scansano Lampo '13	♥♥ 3
○ Le Stoppie '15	♥ 2

Vasco Sassetti

LOC. CASTELNUOVO DELL'ABATE
VIA BASSOMONDO, 7
53024 MONTALCINO [SI]
TEL. +39 0577835619
lanzini.massimo@tiscali.it

CELLAR SALES
PRE-BOOKED VISITS
RESTAURANT SERVICE
ANNUAL PRODUCTION 100,000 bottles
HECTARES UNDER VINE 20.00

● Brunello di Montalcino '11	♥♥ 6
● Rosso di Montalcino '14	♥♥ 4
● Brunello di Montalcino Ris. '10	♥ 7

SassodiSole

FRAZ. TORRENIERI
LOC. SASSODISOLE, 85
53024 MONTALCINO [SI]
TEL. +39 0577834303
www.sassodisole.it

CELLAR SALES
PRE-BOOKED VISITS
ANNUAL PRODUCTION 30,000 bottles
HECTARES UNDER VINE 8.00
SUSTAINABLE WINERY

- ● Brunello di Montalcino '11 — 🍷🍷 5
- ● Brunello di Montalcino Ris. '10 — 🍷🍷 8

Il Sassolo

VIA CITERNA, 5
59015 CARMIGNANO [PO]
TEL. +39 0558706488
www.ilsassolo.it

ANNUAL PRODUCTION 9,000 bottles
HECTARES UNDER VINE 5.50

- ● Carmignano '13 — 🍷🍷 3
- ⊙ Barco Reale Vin Ruspo '15 — 🍷 2

Sassotondo

LOC. PIAN DI CONATI, 52
58010 SOVANA [GR]
TEL. +39 0564614218
www.sassotondo.it

CELLAR SALES
PRE-BOOKED VISITS
ANNUAL PRODUCTION 50,000 bottles
HECTARES UNDER VINE 12.00
VITICULTURE METHOD Certified Organic

- ● Maremma Toscana Ciliegiolo San Lorenzo '13 — 🍷🍷 6
- ● Sovana Rosso Sup. Ombra Blu '14 — 🍷 3
- ● Tufo Rosso '15 — 🍷 2

Sedime

POD. SEDIME, 63
53026 PIENZA [SI]
TEL. +39 0578748436
www.capitoni.eu

CELLAR SALES
PRE-BOOKED VISITS
ANNUAL PRODUCTION 12,000 bottles
HECTARES UNDER VINE 5.00

- ● Orcia Rosso Capitoni Ris. '12 — 🍷🍷 4
- ● Orcia Sangiovese Troccolone '15 — 🍷🍷 3

Fulvio Luigi Serni

LOC. LE LAME, 237
57022 CASTAGNETO CARDUCCI [LI]
TEL. +39 0565763585
www.sernifulvioluigi.it

CELLAR SALES
PRE-BOOKED VISITS
ANNUAL PRODUCTION 20,000 bottles
HECTARES UNDER VINE 3.50

- ● Bolgheri Rosso Tegoleto '14 — 🍷🍷 3
- ○ Bolgheri Bianco Le Lame '15 — 🍷 2
- ⊙ Bolgheri Rosato Arcanto '15 — 🍷 2
- ● Bolgheri Rosso Acciderba '13 — 🍷 4

Solaria - Cencioni Patrizia

POD. CAPANNA, 102
53024 MONTALCINO [SI]
TEL. +39 0577849426
www.solariacencioni.com

CELLAR SALES
PRE-BOOKED VISITS
ANNUAL PRODUCTION 35,500 bottles
HECTARES UNDER VINE 9.00

- ● Brunello di Montalcino 123 Ris. '10 — 🍷🍷 8
- ● Brunello di Montalcino '11 — 🍷 6
- ● Rosso di Montalcino '14 — 🍷 3

Borgo La Stella

Loc. Vagliagli
B.go La Stella, 60
53017 Radda in Chianti [SI]
Tel. +39 0577740699
www.borgolastella.com

ANNUAL PRODUCTION 21,000 bottles
HECTARES UNDER VINE 4.50

● Cronos '14	♟♟ 5
● Chianti Cl. '14	♟ 3

Tenuta di Sticciano

via di Sticciano, 207
50052 Certaldo [FI]
Tel. +39 0571669191
www.tenutadisticciano.it

CELLAR SALES
PRE-BOOKED VISITS
ACCOMMODATION
ANNUAL PRODUCTION 65,000 bottles
HECTARES UNDER VINE 25.00
VITICULTURE METHOD Certified Organic

● Chianti Villa di Sticciano Ris. '12	♟♟ 3
● Chianti Maggiano '14	♟ 2

Stomennano

Loc. Stomennano
53035 Monteriggioni [SI]
Tel. +39 0577304033
www.stomennano.it

PRE-BOOKED VISITS
ACCOMMODATION
ANNUAL PRODUCTION 50,000 bottles
HECTARES UNDER VINE 11.00
SUSTAINABLE WINERY

● Chianti Cl. '14	♟♟ 5

Suveraia

Loc. Campetroso, 26
58025 Monterotondo Marittimo [GR]
Tel. +39 3356211060
www.suveraia.it

CELLAR SALES
PRE-BOOKED VISITS
ANNUAL PRODUCTION 30,000 bottles
HECTARES UNDER VINE 6.00

● Monteregio di Massa Marittima Bacucco di Suveraia '12	♟♟ 5
● Monteregio di Massa Marittima Rosso di Campetroso '15	♟♟ 3

Tassi

.le P. Strozzi, 1/3
53024 Montalcino [SI]
Tel. +39 0577848025
www.tassimontalcino.com

ANNUAL PRODUCTION 20,000 bottles
HECTARES UNDER VINE 5.00

● Brunello di Montalcino '11	♟♟ 7
● Brunello di Montalcino Franci Ris. '10	♟♟ 8
● Brunello di Montalcino Franci '11	♟ 8

Tenuta degli Dei

via San Leolino, 56
50022 Greve in Chianti [FI]
Tel. +39 055852593
www.deglidei.it

PRE-BOOKED VISITS
ANNUAL PRODUCTION 65,000 bottles
HECTARES UNDER VINE 9.00

● Chianti Cl. '14	♟♟ 3
● Le Redini '14	♟ 4

Tenuta La Chiusa

Loc. Magazzini, 93
57037 Portoferraio [LI]
Tel. +39 0565933046
lachiusa@elbalink.it

CELLAR SALES
PRE-BOOKED VISITS
ACCOMMODATION
ANNUAL PRODUCTION 25,000 bottles
HECTARES UNDER VINE 7.50

● Elba Aleatico Passito '14	♥♥ 6
○ Elba Bianco '15	♥ 2
○ Elba Vermentino '15	♥ 2

Terre dell'Etruria Il Poderone

Loc. Poderone
58051 Magliano in Toscana [GR]
Tel. +39 0564593011
www.terretruria.it

CELLAR SALES
PRE-BOOKED VISITS
ANNUAL PRODUCTION 200,000 bottles
HECTARES UNDER VINE 90.00

● Briglia Ciliegiolo '14	♥♥ 2*
● Morellino di Scansano Giogo '15	♥ 2
○ Vermentino Marmato '15	♥ 2

Tenuta Tre Rose

Fraz. Valiano
via della Stella, 3
53040 Montepulciano [SI]
Tel. +39 0577804101
www.tenutatrerose.it

CELLAR SALES
PRE-BOOKED VISITS
ANNUAL PRODUCTION 650,000 bottles
HECTARES UNDER VINE 102.00

● Nobile di Montepulciano Simposio '11	♥♥ 6
● Rosso di Montepulciano Salterio '15	♥♥ 3

Tenuta di Trecciano

S.da prov.le 52 della Montagnola, 16
53018 Sovicille [SI]
Tel. +39 0577314357
www.trecciano.it

CELLAR SALES
PRE-BOOKED VISITS
ANNUAL PRODUCTION 80,000 bottles
HECTARES UNDER VINE 15.50

● Chianti Colli Senesi '15	♥♥ 2*
● I Campacci '14	♥♥ 4
● Suavis Locus Ille '14	♥ 4

Tringali - Casanuova

Loc. Casa al Piano, 68
57022 Castagneto Carducci [LI]
Tel. +39 0565774101
www.tringalipro.it

CELLAR SALES
PRE-BOOKED VISITS
ACCOMMODATION
ANNUAL PRODUCTION 35,000 bottles
HECTARES UNDER VINE 4.00

● Bolgheri Casa al Piano '14	♥♥ 3
● Bolgheri Sup. Renzo '13	♥ 6

Tuttisanti

Loc. Fiorentina
57025 Piombino [LI]
Tel. +39 056535226

CELLAR SALES
PRE-BOOKED VISITS
ANNUAL PRODUCTION 20,000 bottles
HECTARES UNDER VINE 4.60

● Val di Cornia Merlot '15	♥♥ 2*
○ Val di Cornia Vermentino '15	♥♥ 2*
○ Val di Cornia Bianco '15	♥ 2
⊙ Val di Cornia Rosato '15	♥ 2

Fattoria Uccelliera

VIA PONTITA, 26
56043 FAUGLIA [PI]
TEL. +39 050662747
www.uccelliera.com

CELLAR SALES
PRE-BOOKED VISITS
ACCOMMODATION
ANNUAL PRODUCTION 100,000 bottles
HECTARES UNDER VINE 17.00

● Ginepraia '15	♟♟ 2*
○ Ficaia '15	♟ 2
○ Lupinaio '15	♟ 3
● Poggio alla Pietra '14	♟ 4

Urlari

LOC. URLARI
56046 RIPARBELLA [PI]
TEL. +39 335215031
www.urlari.com

CELLAR SALES
PRE-BOOKED VISITS
ANNUAL PRODUCTION 30,000 bottles
HECTARES UNDER VINE 6.00

● Pervale '13	♟♟ 3
● L'Urlo '13	♟ 5
● Ritasso '13	♟ 5

Usiglian Del Vescovo

VIA USIGLIANO, 26
56036 PALAIA [PI]
TEL. +39 0587622138
www.usigliandelvescovo.it

CELLAR SALES
PRE-BOOKED VISITS
ANNUAL PRODUCTION 150,000 bottles
HECTARES UNDER VINE 28.00
SUSTAINABLE WINERY

● Il Barbiglione '13	♟♟ 5
○ Il Ginestraio '15	♟ 5
● Il Grullaio '15	♟ 3

Val di Suga

LOC. VAL DI CAVA
53024 MONTALCINO [SI]
TEL. +39 0577804101
www.valdisuga.it

CELLAR SALES
PRE-BOOKED VISITS
ANNUAL PRODUCTION 270,000 bottles
HECTARES UNDER VINE 55.00

● Brunello di Montalcino Poggio al Granchio '10	♟♟ 8
● Brunello di Montalcino V. Spuntali '10	♟ 8
● Brunello di Montalcino Val di Suga '11	♟ 6

Val di Toro

LOC. POGGIO LA MOZZA
S.DA DELLE CAMPORE, 18
58100 GROSSETO
TEL. +39 0564409600
www.valditoro.it

CELLAR SALES
PRE-BOOKED VISITS
ANNUAL PRODUCTION 70,000 bottles
HECTARES UNDER VINE 10.00

● Morellino di Scansano Reviresco '14	♟♟ 3
○ Maremma Toscana Auramaris '15	♟ 2

Valdonica

FRAZ. SASSOFORTINO
LOC. CASALONE DELL'EBREO
58036 ROCCASTRADA [GR]
TEL. +39 0564567251
www.valdonica.com

CELLAR SALES
PRE-BOOKED VISITS
ANNUAL PRODUCTION 35,000 bottles
HECTARES UNDER VINE 10.00
VITICULTURE METHOD Certified Organic

● Maremma Toscana Ciliegiolo '12	♟♟ 6
● Monteregio di Massa Marittima Sangiovese Ris. '12	♟♟ 4
● Monteregio Saragio '12	♟ 5

Valentini

LOC. VALPIANA
POD. FIORDALISO, 69
58024 MASSA MARITTIMA [GR]
TEL. +39 0566918058
www.agricolavalentini.it

CELLAR SALES
PRE-BOOKED VISITS
ACCOMMODATION
ANNUAL PRODUCTION 40,000 bottles
HECTARES UNDER VINE 5.50

● Monteregio di Massa Marittima '14	🍷🍷 2*

Vecchia Cantina di Montepulciano

VIA PROVINCIALE, 7
53045 MONTEPULCIANO [SI]
TEL. +39 0578716092
www.vecchiacantina.com

CELLAR SALES
PRE-BOOKED VISITS
ANNUAL PRODUCTION 5,000,000 bottles
HECTARES UNDER VINE 1000.00

○ Vin Santo di Montepulciano '10	🍷🍷 6
● Nobile di Montepulciano Briareo Ris. '11	🍷 5
● Rosso di Montepulciano '14	🍷 2

Ventolaio

LOC. VENTOLAIO, 51
53024 MONTALCINO [SI]
TEL. +39 0577835779

CELLAR SALES
PRE-BOOKED VISITS
ANNUAL PRODUCTION 70,000 bottles
HECTARES UNDER VINE 14.00

● Brunello di Montalcino Ris. '10	🍷🍷 8
● Brunello di Montalcino '11	🍷 6
● Rosso di Montalcino '13	🍷 3

Verbena

LOC. VERBENA, 100
53024 MONTALCINO [SI]
TEL. +39 0577846035
www.aziendaverbena.it

CELLAR SALES
PRE-BOOKED VISITS
ANNUAL PRODUCTION 50,000 bottles
HECTARES UNDER VINE 10.00

● Brunello di Montalcino '11	🍷🍷 5
● Brunello di Montalcino Ris. '10	🍷 7
● Rosso di Montalcino '14	🍷 3

Villa Corliano

LOC. BRUCIANESI
VIA DI CORLIANO, 4
50058 LASTRA A SIGNA [FI]
TEL. +39 0558734542
www.villacorliano.com

CELLAR SALES
PRE-BOOKED VISITS
ANNUAL PRODUCTION 35,000 bottles
HECTARES UNDER VINE 6.78

● Ghirigoro '12	🍷🍷 3
○ Vin Santo Dedicato '06	🍷🍷 5
○ Italobianco Trebbiano Viognier '15	🍷 2
● Italorosso Sangiovese Syrah '14	🍷 2

Tenuta Vitanza

FRAZ. TORRENIERI
POD. BELVEDERE, 145
52024 MONTALCINO [SI]
TEL. +39 0577832882
www.tenutavitanza.it

CELLAR SALES
PRE-BOOKED VISITS
ANNUAL PRODUCTION 200,000 bottles
HECTARES UNDER VINE 26.00

● Brunello di Montalcino '11	🍷 5
● Rosso di Montalcino '14	🍷 3

MARCHE

In this edition of IW, Marche is extending its list of excellent wines with several more whites. Of the 20 Tre Bicchieri awarded, a splendid 14 go to Verdicchio, arriving from the Jesi and the Matelica growing areas, while three are for Offida Pecorino. However eloquent numbers may be, they are not sufficient to explain the great vitality and raised quality bar we are observing in the aforementioned districts. The first effect is the ongoing turnover of award winners: each year, every winery has to prove it deserves praise and there is no resting on laurels. So we should raise our glasses to folks like Bucci, Casalfarneto, Tenuta Spinelli, Velenosi, Tenuta di Tavignano (whose 2015 Verdicchio dei Castelli di Jesi Classico Superiore Misco also took home our White of the Year Award), Sparapani-Frati Bianchi, Belisario and Collestefano, who have improved their 2016 performance and hold their own against seasoned colleagues. Back on the Tre Bicchieri podium, after a year or even more of absence, we see Pievalta, Poderi Mattioli, Marotti Campi, Montecappone, Bisci, and La Monacesca. And we have our new entries, regardless of size, from the high-profile artisan style of Sabbionare to Tenuta Cocci Grifoni, one of the best known names in the region, who has finally garnered the coveted award with a magnificent wine dedicated to Guido Cocci Grifoni, the man who rescued the pecorino varietal and was the first to spread the good word along the hills connecting Marche to Abruzzo. Struggling to keep pace, we have the regional reds. While the Conero designation was back in a top slot thanks to Umani Ronchi's prodigious Campo San Giorgio 2011, important winegrowing districts like Piceno and Macerata slipped back. The seasons of poor weather for Montepulciano, sangiovese, and black grapes in general, certainly did not help, but makers must not lower their guard in terms of phenolic maturity, appropriate use of wood, and excessive concentrations of fruit and extract. We found the Kupra 2013 to be a brilliantly modern gem, produced by an experienced vigneron like Marco Casolanetti, but equally amazing was the 2013 Offida Rosso Vignagiulia 2013 from the incredibly passionate newcomer, Emanuele Dianetti, which took us all by surprise. In any case, we should look beyond the Tre Bicchieri and keep an eye on the short profiles, which list many new names in this edition, and is a hotbed of talent, probably nurturing a star or two of the future. Prepare nose and palate, and start searching. We are certain consumers will not be disappointed.

Aurora

LOC. SANTA MARIA IN CARRO
C.DA CIAFONE, 98
63073 OFFIDA [AP]
TEL. +39 0736810007
www.viniaurora.it

CELLAR SALES
PRE-BOOKED VISITS
ACCOMMODATION
ANNUAL PRODUCTION 53,300 bottles
HECTARES UNDER VINE 9.50
VITICULTURE METHOD Certified Organic

Here at Aurora, winemaking is a form of religion and the members of this little cooperative are outright devotees, deeply attached to the impressive vineyards of Contrada Ciafone. They have banned all types of chemical product and external interference in the rows and in the cellars, with unwavering integrity, even in the face of market trends or demands. This resolute approach produces spontaneous, lively wines inspired by the Piceno district's age-old traditions. The Offida Rosso Barricadiero 2013 is the best example: full-bodied, approachable, bursting with energy that translates the occasional rugged feature into unparalleled character. The Pecorino Fiobbo 2014 has aniseed, aromatic herbs and apples on the nose, with a mouthwatering palate, of edgy acidity, and a deep finish. A lovely performance from the Rosso Piceno 2015 too, with genuine, traditional heady and fruity aromas, and a simple but not commonplace palate.

○ Offida Pecorino Fiobbo '14	🍷🍷 3*
● Offida Rosso Barricadiero '13	🍷🍷 4
● Rosso Piceno '15	🍷🍷 2*
● Rosso Piceno Sup. '13	🍷🍷 2*
⊙ Rosato '14	🍷 2
● Barricadiero '10	🍷🍷🍷 4*
● Barricadiero '09	🍷🍷🍷 4
● Barricadiero '06	🍷🍷🍷 4
● Barricadiero '04	🍷🍷🍷 3
● Barricadiero '03	🍷🍷🍷 3*
● Barricadiero '02	🍷🍷🍷 3
● Barricadiero '01	🍷🍷🍷 3*
● Offida Rosso Barricadiero '11	🍷🍷🍷 4*
○ Offida Pecorino Fiobbo '11	🍷🍷 2*
○ Offida Pecorino Fiobbo '10	🍷🍷 2*
○ Offida Pecorino Fiobbo '09	🍷🍷 2*

Belisario

VIA ARISTIDE MERLONI, 12
62024 MATELICA [MC]
TEL. +39 0737787247
www.belisario.it

CELLAR SALES
PRE-BOOKED VISITS
ANNUAL PRODUCTION 1,000,000 bottles
HECTARES UNDER VINE 300.00

In the wine industry, cooperatives are not always the success story they might be, but when they work, they can act as a flywheel for the entire district. This is true of Belisario, which has been a driving force in the Verdicchio di Matelica designation for 45 years, dissuading small-scale growers from uprooting vineyards, driving the DOC with a series of wines that highlight its versatility, and making quality available at the right price. The team of experts led by Roberto Potentini supervise members directly and make the wines in the large, well-appointed cellar. Vigneti B. 2015 has a sublime, invigorating palate with record-breaking length, and a seductive nose with hints of hawthorn, almonds and pebbles. A splendid standard-label Matelica. The Cambrugiano 2013 brings out oaky aromas among the summer fruits and broom flowers, with a mouthfilling, richly flavoursome palate. The other wines are all reliably good, especially the nicely-typed Del Cerro 2015.

○ Verdicchio di Matelica Vign. B. '15	🍷🍷🍷 3*
○ Verdicchio di Matelica Cambrugiano Ris. '13	🍷🍷 3
○ Verdicchio di Matelica Del Cerro '15	🍷🍷 2*
○ Verdicchio di Matelica L'Anfora '15	🍷🍷 2*
○ Verdicchio di Matelica Terre di Valbona '15	🍷🍷 2*
○ Verdicchio di Matelica Meridia '13	🍷 3
○ Verdicchio di Matelica Cambrugiano Ris. '12	🍷🍷🍷 3
○ Verdicchio di Matelica Cambrugiano Ris. '08	🍷🍷🍷 3
○ Verdicchio di Matelica Cambrugiano Ris. '06	🍷🍷🍷 3*
○ Verdicchio di Matelica Cambrugiano Ris. '02	🍷🍷🍷 3*
○ Verdicchio di Matelica Meridia '10	🍷🍷🍷 3*
○ Verdicchio di Matelica Meridia '07	🍷🍷🍷 3*

Bisci

Via Fogliano, 120
62024 Matelica [MC]
Tel. +39 0737787490
www.bisci.it

CELLAR SALES
PRE-BOOKED VISITS
ANNUAL PRODUCTION 120,000 bottles
HECTARES UNDER VINE 20.00
VITICULTURE METHOD Certified Organic

Today the winery is run by Mauro Bisci, respectively son and nephew of Giuseppe and Pierino, founders in 1980. As a staunch supporter of Verdicchio, Mauro opted to cut back on the quantities of black grapes, now restricted to just two hectares of sangiovese and merlot, and upped amounts of white varieties. The magnificent location of the vineyards on the Mount San Vicino hills guarantees a must rich in acidity and extract, which translates into wines of renowned ageability. The concrete vats from the old cellar remain, and are used to age the Matelica. Another Tre Bicchieri for the Vigneto Fogliano 2013, in a polished version opening on intimately typical Matelica aromas, with hints of aniseed, citrus fruit and almonds. The palate follows with an elegant and cohesive pace with minerally sensations providing magnetic charm in the finish. The Matelica 2015 displays generous floral aromas and a lingering, drinkable flavour.

○ Verdicchio di Matelica Vign. Fogliano '13	▼▼▼	3*
○ Verdicchio di Matelica '15	▼▼	3
○ Verdicchio di Matelica Vign. Fogliano '10	▽▽▽	3*
○ Verdicchio di Matelica Vign. Fogliano '08	▽▽▽	3*
○ Verdicchio di Matelica '14	▽▽	2*
○ Verdicchio di Matelica '13	▽▽	3
○ Verdicchio di Matelica '12	▽▽	2*
○ Verdicchio di Matelica '11	▽▽	3
○ Verdicchio di Matelica '10	▽▽	2*
○ Verdicchio di Matelica Senex '09	▽▽	4
○ Verdicchio di Matelica Vign. Fogliano '11	▽▽	3*
○ Verdicchio di Matelica Vign. Fogliano '07	▽▽	3*

Boccadigabbia

loc. Fontespina
c.da Castelletta, 56
62012 Civitanova Marche [MC]
Tel. +39 073370728
www.boccadigabbia.com

CELLAR SALES
PRE-BOOKED VISITS
ANNUAL PRODUCTION 100,000 bottles
HECTARES UNDER VINE 25.00

Elvio Alessandri has refocused his Boccadigabbia estate with renewed vigour, putting an end to the rocky period that followed his glory days at the end of the 20th century. For the 2014 harvest he followed his instinct and entrusted Tuscan winemaker Emiliano Falsini with the task of restoring personality and cohesion to a range composed chiefly of international varieties like cabernet, merlot and chardonnay, although Elvio has a place in his heart for the natives and his Villamagna estate vineyards in Macerata are planted to Montepulciano, sangiovese and ribona. A beautiful performance from the holdover Akronte 2012, a Cabernet Sauvignon: streaks of balsam, black berries and a hint of green peppers pinpoint the grape variety, with a powerful, explosive entry supported by very solid structure. Not far behind is the Pix 2012, a gracefully fruity Merlot with a silky texture. The Le Grane 2015 is unashamedly citrusy, while the Saltapicchio 2012 is weighty and warm on the palate.

● Akronte '12	▼▼	8
● Pix '12	▼▼	6
○ Colli Maceratesi Ribona Le Grane '15	▼▼	3
● Rosso Piceno '13	▼▼	3
● Saltapicchio '12	▼▼	4
○ La Castelletta '15	▼	3
● Akronte '98	▽▽▽	7
● Akronte '97	▽▽▽	7
● Akronte '95	▽▽▽	7
● Akronte '94	▽▽▽	7
● Akronte '93	▽▽▽	7
● Akronte Cabernet '92	▽▽▽	7
● Akronte '10	▽▽	8
● Akronte '08	▽▽	7
● Pix '10	▽▽	6
● Pix '09	▽▽	6

Borgo Paglianetto

Loc. Pagliano, 393
62024 Matelica [MC]
Tel. +39 073785465
www.borgopaglianetto.it

CELLAR SALES
PRE-BOOKED VISITS
ANNUAL PRODUCTION 60,000 bottles
HECTARES UNDER VINE 25.00
VITICULTURE METHOD Certified Organic

If the overall quality of Verdicchio di
Matelica is high, this is partly due to Borgo
Paglianetto. Over the years, winemaker
Aroldo Bellelli and his team have developed
well-typed wines, even at entry level, that
are true to this terroir of distinctive
features. The grapes come from the
single, well-aspected plot of vineyards in
Contrada Pagliano and are all fermented in
stainless steel. The ripeness of the grapes
and the subsequent cellaring processes
determine the character of the various
wines. This year we were particularly
impressed by the Petrara 2015, with
polished aromas of acacia flowers, pebbles
and limes, echoed on a well-crafted palate
with an open, salty finish. Not far behind it,
the Terravignata 2015 has a supple palate
suffused with appetizing, citrusy freshness.
The Jera 2012 has lovely floral tones and a
weighty, flavoursome palate in which the
soft contours of the components play a
leading role.

○ Verdicchio di Matelica Petrara '15	♈♈ 2*
○ Verdicchio di Matelica Jera Ris. '12	♈♈ 4
○ Verdicchio di Matelica Terravignata '15	♈♈ 2*
○ Verdicchio di Matelica Jera Ris. '10	♈♈♈ 4*
○ Verdicchio di Matelica Vertis '09	♈♈♈ 3*
○ Verdicchio di Matelica Aja Lunga '05	♈♈ 2*
○ Verdicchio di Matelica Jera Ris. '11	♈♈ 4
○ Verdicchio di Matelica Jera Ris. '09	♈♈ 4
○ Verdicchio di Matelica Petrara '09	♈♈ 2*
○ Verdicchio di Matelica Terravignata '11	♈♈ 2*
○ Verdicchio di Matelica Vertis '13	♈♈ 3*
○ Verdicchio di Matelica Vertis '12	♈♈ 3*
○ Verdicchio di Matelica Vertis '10	♈♈ 3*
○ Verdicchio di Matelica Vertis '08	♈♈ 3*

★Bucci

Fraz. Pongelli
via Cona, 30
60010 Ostra Vetere [AN]
Tel. +39 071964179
www.villabucci.com

CELLAR SALES
PRE-BOOKED VISITS
ANNUAL PRODUCTION 120,000 bottles
HECTARES UNDER VINE 31.00
VITICULTURE METHOD Certified Organic

If understatement is still a virtue in wine,
this is also thanks to that courteous
gentleman, Ampelio Bucci. His wines are
typically elegant and eminently ageworthy,
made from grapes grown in eight plots
scattered across the areas of Serra de'
Conti, Montecarotto and Barbara. The
vineyards are of varying ages, the oldest
verging on half a century. All the batches
are fermented separately and the best
continue to mature in large wood. The close
working relationship between Ampelio and
his longstanding consultant Giorgio Grai is
behind the blend for wines sold under the
Villa Bucci label. Not even the terrible 2014
could mar the character of the Villa Bucci.
Just the opposite: its legendary grace is
enhanced by well-focused hints of aniseed,
chard and chamomile and an airy, very
complex palate. Don't underestimate the
Classico: the 2014 is mature and weighty,
while the 2015 moves with carefree pace,
a multifaceted palate and wonderfully
extended finish.

○ Castelli di Jesi Verdicchio Cl. Villa Bucci Ris. '14	♈♈♈ 6
○ Verdicchio dei Castelli di Jesi Cl. Sup. '15	♈♈ 3*
○ Verdicchio dei Castelli di Jesi Cl. Sup. '14	♈♈ 3*
● Rosso Piceno Villa Bucci '13	♈♈ 5
○ Castelli di Jesi Verdicchio Cl. Villa Bucci Ris. '13	♈♈♈ 6
○ Castelli di Jesi Verdicchio Cl. Villa Bucci Ris. '12	♈♈♈ 6
○ Castelli di Jesi Verdicchio Cl. Villa Bucci Ris. '10	♈♈♈ 6
○ Verdicchio dei Castelli di Jesi Cl. Villa Bucci Ris. '09	♈♈♈ 6
○ Verdicchio dei Castelli di Jesi Cl. Villa Bucci Ris. '07	♈♈♈ 6
○ Verdicchio dei Castelli di Jesi Cl. Villa Bucci Ris. '06	♈♈♈ 6

_e Caniette

.DA CANALI, 23
63065 RIPATRANSONE [AP]
TEL. +39 07359200
www.lecaniette.it

CELLAR SALES
PRE-BOOKED VISITS
ANNUAL PRODUCTION 60,000 bottles
HECTARES UNDER VINE 16.00
VITICULTURE METHOD Certified Organic

Hard, methodical graft is the secret to the success of the Vagnoni brothers and their current position as a benchmark in Piceno winemaking. The journey to their expertise in managing the exuberant Montepulciano grape, the backbone of the estate's red wine production was long, and included some trial and error with pecorino, resulting in the unfiltered Veronica and a version matured in small wood. A polished modern style is applied overall, without severing ties with local tradition. Light mint and vibrant citrus sensations mark the 2014 Iosonogaia, with a racy, mouthwatering, harmonious palate. The Veronica 2015 is less challenging with very fresh flavour. A great performance from the Cinabro 2012, made from bordò grapes: the nose is a whirlwind of white chocolate, garrigue and oriental spices, echoed on the vibrant, polished palate with close-woven tannins. A slightly evolved, oaky nose for the Morellone 2011 with a silky tannic texture on the palate.

● Cinabro '12	♟♟ 8
○ Offida Pecorino Iosonogaia non sono Lucrezia '14	♟♟ 4
● Piceno Sup. Morellone '11	♟♟ 4
○ Offida Pecorino Veronica '15	♟♟ 3
● Piceno Nero di Vite '09	♟♟ 6
● Piceno Rosso Bello '14	♟♟ 2*
○ Lucrezia '15	♟ 2
○ Offida Pecorino Iosonogaia non sono Lucrezia '10	♟♟♟ 4*
● Piceno Morellone '10	♟♟♟ 4*
● Piceno Morellone '08	♟♟♟ 4*
● Cinabro '11	♟♟ 8
○ Offida Pecorino Iosonogaia non sono Lucrezia '13	♟♟ 4
○ Offida Pecorino Iosonogaia non sono Lucrezia '12	♟♟ 4

Carminucci

VIA SAN LEONARDO, 39
63013 GROTTAMMARE [AP]
TEL. +39 0735735869
www.carminucci.com

CELLAR SALES
ANNUAL PRODUCTION 200,000 bottles
HECTARES UNDER VINE 52.00
VITICULTURE METHOD Certified Organic

Carminucci is a big winery found at the entrance to the Valtesino, a few kilometres from the Adriatic. It processes grapes from the estate's many hectares of vineyards, the best of which are in the Offida area, organically farmed for some years. Piero Carminucci is the champion of an approachable, drinkable style, qualities enhanced by the pursuit of fruity appeal that is never affected or forced. The range is based on the typical Piceno cultivars, using stainless steel to increase the freshness of pecorino and passerina, and small and medium wood for the Montepulciano and sangiovese. For some years Belato has dominated our tastings with an intense and flavoursome performance. The 2015 shines thanks to harmonious acidity and softness on a palate with deep hints of citrus fruit. The same sensations, but less complex, appear in the Casta 2015. The Piceno Superiore Naumakos 2013 is reliable as ever with clear aromas of black cherries and sweet spices and a fresh, lively palate.

○ Offida Pecorino Belato '15	♟♟ 2*
○ Offida Passerina Casta '15	♟♟ 2*
● Rosso Piceno Sup. Naumakos '13	♟♟ 2*
○ Falerio Grotte sul Mare '15	♟ 1*
○ Falerio Naumakos '14	♟ 2
⊙ Rosato Grotte sul Mare '15	♟ 2
● Rosso Piceno Grotte sul Mare '15	♟ 1*
○ Falerio Naumachos '14	♟♟ 2*
○ Falerio Naumachos '13	♟♟ 2*
○ Offida Pecorino Belato '14	♟♟ 2*
○ Offida Pecorino Belato '13	♟♟ 2*
○ Offida Pecorino Belato '12	♟♟ 2*
● Paccaosso '09	♟♟ 7
● Rosso Piceno Sup. Naumachos '12	♟♟ 2*
● Rosso Piceno Sup. Naumachos '11	♟♟ 2*
● Rosso Piceno Sup. Naumachos '10	♟♟ 2*

CasalFarneto

VIA FARNETO, 12
60030 SERRA DE' CONTI [AN]
TEL. +39 0731889001
www.casalfarneto.it

CELLAR SALES
PRE-BOOKED VISITS
ANNUAL PRODUCTION 580,000 bottles
HECTARES UNDER VINE 32.00

After taking over CasalFarneto, the Togni family, and manager Danilo Solustri, set no deadlines or compulsory objectives to be achieved. The Serra De' Conti hills is perfect wine country where strictly defined parcels were mapped out to identify the features of each plot, carefully observing the verdicchio ripening curves. The harvesting period, whether early, exact or late, and modern vinification techniques shape the unambiguous character of the various labels, all with typical unobtrusive energy. The Crisio 2013 benefits from longer in the bottle: enticing hints of ginger and citrus, and smoky sensations are echoed on the beautifully balanced, layered palate with a deep finish. Grancasale 2014 reveals balsamic hints on the nose with a vigorous, well-crafted palate closing on hints of aromatic herbs, almonds and pine needles. The polished Passito Ikòn 2012 is velvety and supple with hints of tinned peaches and thyme.

○ Castelli di Jesi Verdicchio Cl. Crisio Ris. '13	♟♟♟ 3*
○ Verdicchio dei Castelli di Jesi Cl. Sup. Grancasale '14	♟♟ 3*
○ Cimaio '13	♟♟ 4
○ Verdicchio dei Castelli di Jesi Cl. Sup. Fontevecchia '15	♟♟ 2*
○ Verdicchio dei Castelli di Jesi Passito Ikòn '12	♟♟ 5
● Merago '12	♟ 3
○ Castelli di Jesi Verdicchio Cl. Crisio Ris. '12	♟♟♟ 3*
○ Castelli di Jesi Verdicchio Cl. Crisio Ris. '11	♟♟♟ 3*
○ Verdicchio dei Castelli di Jesi Cl. Crisio Ris. '10	♟♟♟ 3*
○ Verdicchio dei Castelli di Jesi Cl. Sup. Grancasale '13	♟♟♟ 3*

Maria Pia Castelli

C.DA SANT'ISIDORO, 22
63813 MONTE URANO [FM]
TEL. +39 0734841774
www.mariapiacastelli.it

CELLAR SALES
PRE-BOOKED VISITS
ANNUAL PRODUCTION 25,000 bottles
HECTARES UNDER VINE 8.00

The mid-Tenna valley area still has a large number of micro-vineyards growing mainly for personal consumption. In the early 2000s, Enrico Bartoletti and his wife Maria Pia Castelli decided to turn the family passion into a profession: they planted new vineyards, taking care to choose only local cultivars, and built a modern, well-appointed cellar, under the guidance of consultant Marco Casolanetti. Their precise purpose was to make only a few bottles but with superior and original characteristics. And indeed, their wines are complex, sometimes difficult, requiring patience in the glass. Erasmo Castelli 2012 is a dour Montepulciano with hints of iron filings and blood-rich meat and generous salty aromas of capers, while the palate is engagingly dynamic in character. Stella Flora 2014 is a blend of pecorino, passerina, trebbiano and malvasia aged in small oak: dried apricots, aromatic herbs and hazelnuts are echoed on a palate with plenty of mouthfeel and exuberant acidity.

● Erasmo Castelli '12	♟♟ 5
○ Stella Flora '14	♟♟ 5
● Erasmo Castelli '06	♟♟♟ 5
● Erasmo Castelli '11	♟♟ 5
● Erasmo Castelli '10	♟♟ 5
● Erasmo Castelli '09	♟♟ 5
● Erasmo Castelli '07	♟♟ 5
● Orano '11	♟♟ 4
● Orano '10	♟♟ 3
⊙ Sant'Isidoro '13	♟♟ 2*
○ Stella Flora '12	♟♟ 5
○ Stella Flora '11	♟♟ 5
○ Stella Flora '10	♟♟ 5
○ Stella Flora '09	♟♟ 5
○ Stella Flora '08	♟♟ 5
○ Stella Flora '07	♟♟ 5

Cherri d'Acquaviva

Via Roma, 40
63075 Acquaviva Picena [AP]
Tel. +39 0735764416
www.vinicherri.it

CELLAR SALES
PRE-BOOKED VISITS
ANNUAL PRODUCTION 160,000 bottles
HECTARES UNDER VINE 33.00

The Acquaviva Picena vineyards are found in the inland Piceno area, protected from the impact of the salty Adriatic breezes by the hill, crowned by the town's splendid castle. In this landscape Paolo Cherri's vineyards glean strength and lustre to pour into the wines, filtered through the dynamic Montepulciano and sangiovese black grapes, and pecorino, passerina and trebbiano for the whites. A modern, clean style is common to all the wines, which are fruity and not without elegant qualities. Confirmation comes from the Altissimo 2015, a Pecorino with citrus and wild herb aromas minutely blended and spread smoothly over the palate. The nicely-typed Offida Passerina Radiosa 2015 is fresh-tasting with skilful play between fruit and tangy flavour, while the Passerina 2015 is simpler but still a flavoursome and moreish basic wine. The Piceno Superiore 2014 stands out among the reds: supple, with well-measured structure and lovely cherries in the finish.

○ Offida Passerina Radiosa '15	♈♈ 3	
○ Offida Pecorino Altissimo '15	♈♈ 3	
○ Passerina '15	♈ 2*	
● Rosso Piceno Sup. '14	♈♈ 2*	
◑ Ancella '15	♈ 2	
○ Faelrio Pecorino '15	♈ 2	
● Offida Rosso Tumbulus '12	♈ 4	
○ Pecorino Brut	♈ 3	
● Rosso Piceno '15	♈ 2	
○ Offida Pecorino Altissimo '14	♈♈ 3	
○ Offida Pecorino Altissimo '13	♈♈ 3*	
● Rosso Piceno '14	♈♈ 2*	
● Rosso Piceno '13	♈♈ 2*	
● Rosso Piceno Sup. '13	♈♈ 2*	
● Rosso Piceno Sup. '12	♈♈ 2*	

Ciù Ciù

Loc. Santa Maria in Carro
C.da Ciafone, 106
63035 Offida [AP]
Tel. +39 0736810001
www.ciuciuvini.it

CELLAR SALES
PRE-BOOKED VISITS
ACCOMMODATION AND RESTAURANT SERVICE
ANNUAL PRODUCTION 800,000 bottles
HECTARES UNDER VINE 180.00
VITICULTURE METHOD Certified Organic

Brothers Walter and Massimiliano Bartolomei manage one of the most enterprising wineries in the Piceno area. In recent years, Ciù Ciù has purchased land in the excellent growing areas between Offida and Acquaviva Picena, taking care to give the black grapes a sunny location, while preferring cooler slopes for the white berries, applying organic methods across the board. The large, well-appointed cellar can handle the growing numbers of bottles, with typically meticulous processing, distinctive aromas and clearly defined fruit. Oppidum 2012, from Montepulciano, is their best calling-card: marked black cherry fruit softened by floral and spicy sensations, and a powerful palate enhancing mouthfilling fruit without requiring excessive extract. Esperanto 2010 is still very sound, with a mellow tannic texture. The Oris 2015 stands out among the whites with clear hints of Golden Delicious apples enriching the supple, pleasantly tangy flavour. Merlettaie 2015 has green olive and floral aromas on a close-knit palate.

● Oppidum '12	♈♈ 4	
○ Faelrio Oris '15	♈♈ 2*	
○ Offida Pecorino Merlettaie '15	♈♈ 2*	
● Offida Rosso Esperanto '10	♈♈ 5	
● Rosso Piceno Sup. Gotico '13	♈♈ 2*	
○ Altamarea Brut	♈ 2	
○ Evoé '15	♈ 2	
● Rosso Piceno Bacchus '15	♈ 2	
○ Faelrio Oris '13	♈♈ 2*	
○ Offida Pecorino Le Merlettaie '14	♈♈ 2*	
○ Offida Pecorino Le Merlettaie '13	♈♈ 2*	
○ Offida Pecorino Le Merlettaie '12	♈♈ 2*	
● Offida Rosso Esperanto '09	♈♈ 5	
● Oppidum '08	♈♈ 4	
● Rosso Piceno Sup. Gotico '12	♈♈ 2*	
● Rosso Piceno Sup. Gotico '11	♈♈ 2*	

Tenuta Cocci Grifoni

loc. San Savino
c.da Messieri, 12
63038 Ripatransone [AP]
Tel. +39 073590143
www.tenutacoccigrifoni.it

CELLAR SALES
PRE-BOOKED VISITS
ACCOMMODATION
ANNUAL PRODUCTION 380,000 bottles
HECTARES UNDER VINE 50.00
SUSTAINABLE WINERY

The Cocci Grifoni family, owners of vineyards between Ripatransone and Offida since 1933, defines themselves simply yet effectively as custodians of the land, but this does not stand in the way of progress. In recent years, sisters Marilena and Paola have renovated the cellar, bought new vineyards, and converted their childhood home into pleasant holiday accommodation. The wines have a classic feel, especially the reds, matured at length in Slavonian oak barrels. Pecorino has found a new lease of life here, saved from probable extinction by their father Guido. The first vintage of Guido Cocci Grifoni, a Pecorino obtained from a vineyard planted in 1987, takes home Tre Bicchieri. This modern, polished white displays all the potential of the grape: a very fresh nose with chard and aniseed, and a layered palate with contrasting saltiness and elegance. Il Grifone 2010 is a precious jewel: sound, minerally, with composed energy and a broad palate.

Col di Corte

via San Pietro, 19a
60036 Montecarotto [AN]
Tel. +39 073189435
www.coldicorte.it

CELLAR SALES
PRE-BOOKED VISITS
ANNUAL PRODUCTION 40,000 bottles
HECTARES UNDER VINE 11.50
VITICULTURE METHOD Certified Organic
SUSTAINABLE WINERY

The project started by Giacomo Rossi, Carl Giudice and Paolo Marcellini, partners at Col di Corte since 2011, is starting to take shape. Embracing organic principles and artisan work with determination, they shun shortcut so a considerable amount of time is needed for a style to emerge. In this sense, a few experiments are uner way for biodynamic vineyard methods, and use of spontaneous fermentation, so far tested only on the Vigneto di Tobia. White wine production is centred on verdicchio, flanke by typical local black grapes like Montepulciano. The very good Sant'Ansovino Riserva 2014, matured for 12 months in small wood, shows compelling citrus features and a relaxed, mouthfilling and very flavoursome palate. We also liked the Classico Superiore 2015, with hints of aniseed and almonds in a beautifully authentic palate. The Verdicchio Vigneto di Tobia 2015 was less impressive than the others, with acidulous and baked apple tones covering the aromas.

○ Offida Pecorino Guido Cocci Grifoni '13	🍷🍷🍷 4*
● Offida Rosso Il Grifone '10	🍷🍷 5
○ Falerio Pecorino Le Torri '15	🍷🍷 2*
● Rosso Piceno '15	🍷🍷 2*
○ Adamantea '15	🍷 2
○ Passerina Brut Gaudio Magno '15	🍷 3
○ Offida Pecorino Colle Vecchio '14	🍷🍷 3
○ Offida Pecorino Colle Vecchio '13	🍷🍷 3
○ Offida Pecorino Podere Colle Vecchio '12	🍷🍷 3
○ Offida Pecorino Podere Colle Vecchio '10	🍷🍷 3*
● Rosso Piceno Sup. Le Torri '11	🍷🍷 2*
● Rosso Piceno Sup. Le Torri '10	🍷🍷 3
● Rosso Piceno Sup. Le Torri '08	🍷🍷 3
● Rosso Piceno Sup. Tenute Messieri '10	🍷🍷 4
● Rosso Piceno Sup. V. Messieri '10	🍷🍷 4
● Rosso Piceno Sup. V. Messieri '07	🍷🍷 4

○ Castelli di Jesi Verdicchio Cl. Sant'Ansovino Ris. '14	🍷🍷 5
○ Verdicchio dei Castelli di Jesi Cl. Sup. '15	🍷🍷 3
○ Verdicchio dei Castelli di Jesi Cl. Vign. di Tobia '15	🍷 3
○ Castelli di Jesi Verdicchio Cl. Ris. '12	🍷🍷 3*
○ Verdicchio dei Castelli di Jesi Cl. '05	🍷🍷 1*
○ Verdicchio dei Castelli di Jesi Cl. Anno I '14	🍷🍷 2*
○ Verdicchio dei Castelli di Jesi Cl. Sup. Anno Zero '12	🍷🍷 3
○ Verdicchio dei Castelli di Jesi Cl. Vign. di Tobia '06	🍷🍷 2*
○ Verdicchio dei Castelli di Jesi Cl. Vign. di Tobia '04	🍷🍷 2*

Collestefano

LOC. COLLE STEFANO, 3
62022 CASTELRAIMONDO [MC]
TEL. +39 0737640439
www.collestefano.com

CELLAR SALES
PRE-BOOKED VISITS
ACCOMMODATION
ANNUAL PRODUCTION 110,000 bottles
HECTARES UNDER VINE 17.50
VITICULTURE METHOD Certified Organic

It may be a cliché, but Fabio Marchionni is firmly convinced that vineyards should be treated like gardens. A profound rapport with the land can be achieved only by following the cycles and traits of the plants, supporting their climatic whims, and avoiding pesticides and herbicides. Fabio does not destem clusters and he uses soft crushing, cultured yeasts, controlled temperatures, fermenting in stainless steel. The other ingredients are verdicchio grapes, sunlight, and the Rustano terroir. Fabio has learned to manage the hotter years too, his Achilles' heel. With several selections in the harvest he manages to preserve the typical acidity of the grapes without sacrificing firmer structure. The result is a 2015 Matelica with a delicious, captivating flavour, driven by the usual well-defined aromas of rain-washed pebbles and citrus fruit. Turning to the sparklers, the Extra Brut 2013, is increasingly focused and pleasing.

○ Verdicchio di Matelica Collestefano '15	♟♟♟	2*
○ Verdicchio di Matelica Extra Brut M. Cl. '13	♟♟	3*
○ Verdicchio di Matelica Collestefano '14	♟♟♟	2*
○ Verdicchio di Matelica Collestefano '13	♟♟♟	2*
○ Verdicchio di Matelica Collestefano '12	♟♟♟	2*
○ Verdicchio di Matelica Collestefano '10	♟♟♟	2*
○ Verdicchio di Matelica Collestefano '07	♟♟♟	2*
○ Verdicchio di Matelica Collestefano '06	♟♟♟	2*

Cantina dei Colli Ripani

C.DA TOSCIANO, 28
63065 RIPATRANSONE [AP]
TEL. +39 07359505
www.colliripani.it

CELLAR SALES
PRE-BOOKED VISITS
ANNUAL PRODUCTION 1,300,000 bottles
HECTARES UNDER VINE 700.00
VITICULTURE METHOD Certified Organic

Leading cooperative winery Colli Ripani has coordinated and managed the work of many small winegrowers between Ripatransone and Offida since 1969. The cellars play a strong social role, preventing destruction of vineyards and supplementing the farming income of many families. This affects the final consumer too, who can buy affordable modern wines made with traditional methods. The huge Contrada Tosciano facility is home to large wood and a few barriques for the patient maturing of several Rosso Picenos, while the whites are always aged in stainless steel. Very clear morello cherry fruit for the Castellano 2013 streaked through with spicy hints and light smoky sensations, and a nicely balanced palate with muted tannins. The Piceno Superior Settantase77e 2012 is similar but suppler and more fluent. Among the whites, the Rugaro Gold 2015 has lovely notes of lemon curd and a fruity palate, while the Falerio Pecorino Bio 2015 is soft and citrusy.

○ Falerio Pecorino Bio '15	♟♟	2*
○ Offida Pecorino Rugaro Gold '15	♟♟	2*
● Rosso Piceno Sup. Castellano '13	♟♟	2*
● Rosso Piceno Sup. Settantase77e '12	♟♟	2*
○ Falerio Pecorino 9 '15	♟	2
○ Offida Passerina Ninfa Ripana Gold '15	♟	2
● Rosso Piceno Bio '15	♟	2
● Rosso Piceno Rupe Nero Gold '15	♟	2
○ Falerio Brezzolino '13	♟♟	1*
○ Falerio Pecorino Rugaro '14	♟♟	2*
○ Falerio Pecorino Rugaro '13	♟♟	2*
● Khorakhanè '09	♟♟	5
○ Offida Passerina Passito Anima Mundi '08	♟♟	4
○ Offida Pecorino Rugaro Gold '14	♟♟	2*
○ Offida Pecorino Rugaro Gold '13	♟♟	2*

Colonnara

VIA MANDRIOLE, 6
60034 CUPRAMONTANA [AN]
TEL. +39 0731780273
www.colonnara.it

CELLAR SALES
PRE-BOOKED VISITS
ANNUAL PRODUCTION 1,000,000 bottles
HECTARES UNDER VINE 120.00

The fact that Cupramontana is known as the capital of Verdicchio is also thanks to Colonnara. Since 1959 this cooperative winery has collected the grape harvest of its many members and produced wines with deep roots in local winemaking heritage. Grapes from the higher, cooler slopes are used for sparkling wines: Colonnara's solid reputation for spumantes is based on these grapes, rich in acidity and extract. Anyone visiting the underground cellars will notice plenty of Verdicchio Metodo Classico awaiting dégorgement. The Ubaldo Rosi 2009 reconfirms its reputation as the best Metodo Classico in the region: a very subtle, almondy nose with balsamic and aniseed hints, followed by a firmly structured palate with peaks of prickle enhancing the creamy flavour. Those looking for something less challenging without losing complexity, should try the Luigi Ghislieri. The Cuprese 2015 is slightly closed on the nose with an edgy palate, but bound to develop over time.

○ Verdicchio dei Castelli di Jesi Brut M. Cl. Ubaldo Rosi Ris. '09	♟♟ 5
● Tornamagno '12	♟♟ 3
○ Verdicchio dei Castelli di Jesi Brut M. Cl. Luigi Ghislieri	♟♟ 4
○ Verdicchio dei Castelli di Jesi Cl. Lyricus '15	♟♟ 2*
○ Verdicchio dei Castelli di Jesi Cl. Sup. Cuprese '15	♟♟ 2*
○ Verdicchio dei Castelli di Jesi M. Cl. Brut Ubaldo Rosi Ris. '06	♟♟♟ 5
○ Verdicchio dei Castelli di Jesi Brut M. Cl. Ubaldo Rosi '07	♟♟ 5
○ Verdicchio dei Castelli di Jesi Brut M. Cl. Ubaldo Rosi Ris. '08	♟♟ 5
○ Verdicchio dei Castelli di Jesi Cl. Sup. Cuprese '12	♟♟ 2*

Il Conte Villa Prandone

C.DA COLLE NAVICCHIO, 28
63033 MONTEPRANDONE [AP]
TEL. +39 073562593
www.ilcontevini.it

CELLAR SALES
PRE-BOOKED VISITS
ANNUAL PRODUCTION 200,000 bottles
HECTARES UNDER VINE 50.00

Emmanuel De Angelis is the face of this estate, presenting his labels in wine stores around the world. He is supported by a well-coordinated family unit consisting of siblings, in-laws and parents, each with their own role to play in managing the many hectares planted with traditional Piceno grapes, as well as a few rows of international cultivars. Very ripe black and white grapes are used to make wines with a quite richly extracted style, the true offspring of a warm, sunny terroir like the Tronto valley. The most glowing example is the LuKont 2013, a monovarietal Montepulciano: mouthfilling, with close-knit texture and juicy ripe black cherries. Powerful structure and full body are also features of the fruity Zipolo 2013. The nicely-typed Donello 2015 is a floral Sangiovese, unpretentious but flavoursome Among the whites the soft and mouthfilling Navicchio 2015 stands out with herbs and citrus fruit on the nose.

● Donello '15	♟♟ 2*
○ Emmanuel Maria Extra Dry	♟♟ 3
● LuKont '13	♟♟ 6
○ Offida Pecorino Navicchio '15	♟♟ 3
● Zipolo '13	♟♟ 5
○ Falerio Aurato '15	♟ 2
○ L'Estro del Mastro '13	♟ 4
○ Offida Passerina Cavaceppo '15	♟ 2
● Rosso Piceno Conte Rosso '15	♟ 2
● Rosso Piceno Sup. Marinus '14	♟ 3
● Donello '14	♟♟ 2*
● LuKont '12	♟♟ 6
● LuKont '11	♟♟ 6
○ Offida Pecorino Navicchio '14	♟♟ 3
● Zipolo '12	♟♟ 5
● Zipolo '11	♟♟ 5

Conti di Buscareto

FRAZ. PIANELLO
VIA SAN GREGORIO, 66
60010 OSTRA [AN]
TEL. +39 0717988020
www.contidibuscareto.com

CELLAR SALES
PRE-BOOKED VISITS
ANNUAL PRODUCTION 250,000 bottles
HECTARES UNDER VINE 70.00

The estate owned by partners Enrico
Giacomelli and Claudio Gabellini includes
various plots. Verdicchio grapes are grown
in a single plot in the mountainous Ripalta
di Arcevia; the lacrima nera comes mainly
from the excellent Sant'Amico cru at Morro
d'Alba, and a small amount from the
vineyards surrounding the winery at
Pianello di Ostra; Montepulciano,
sangiovese and international varieties are
grown at Monte San Vito and Camerata
Picena. The cellar is large and well-
appointed with white wines fermented and
aged in stainless steel, and the reds in
wood. Ammazzaconte 2013 is an excellent
choice: alternating hints of almonds and
orange peel, while the palate opens fresh
and strongly citrus, with a lingering finish.
The Compagnia della Rosa 2013 is also
charming, with typical floral aromas
blending with spicy sensations, and a
flavoursome, tannic, characterful palate.
The Brut Rosé, from lacrima grapes, is
well-focused and pleasantly drinkable.

○ Verdicchio dei Castelli di Jesi		
Ammazzaconte '13	🍷🍷 3*	
⊙ Brut Rosé	🍷🍷 3	
● Lacrima di Morro d'Alba Sup.		
Compagnia della Rosa '13	🍷🍷 4	
○ Brut Bianco	🍷 3	
● Lacrima di Morro d'Alba '15	🍷 2	
● Rosso Piceno '15	🍷 2	
○ Verdicchio dei Castelli di Jesi '15	🍷 2	
● Bisaccione '09	🍷🍷 4	
○ Castelli di Jesi Verdicchio		
Ammazzaconte Ris. '10	🍷🍷 3	
● Lacrima di Morro d'Alba Passito '11	🍷🍷 3*	
● Lacrima di Morro d'Alba Passito '10	🍷🍷 3*	
● Lacrima di Morro d'Alba Sup.		
Compagnia della Rosa '08	🍷🍷 4	

Fattoria Coroncino

C.DA CORONCINO, 7
60039 STAFFOLO [AN]
TEL. +39 0731779494
www.coroncino.it

CELLAR SALES
PRE-BOOKED VISITS
ANNUAL PRODUCTION 45,000 bottles
HECTARES UNDER VINE 9.50

Lucio Canestrari is one of the most
respected names in Verdicchio winemaking,
thanks to his stubborn refusal to aim only
for quantities and sales. His motto appears
on each bottle: "ndo arivo metto n'segno",
meaning he does what he can, remaining
within the family and artisan scope where
he began. His famous style is based on very
lengthy maturation, yielding powerful,
alcohol-rich, very flavourful wines. The
Verdicchios are sometimes extreme but
definitely show unconventional charm and
consistent style. Not even a cool, rainy year
like 2014 can soften the powerful
Gaiospino, with extremely vibrant aromas of
peaches, apricots and almonds and a
sweet, weighty, very dynamic, glycerine
palate. The small oak casks used for ageing
are noticeable in the Stracacio 2014, with
toasty sensations blending with floral and
citrusy hints, and a mouthfilling palate with
plenty of tangy phases. The Coroncino 2014
is powerful, velvety and tropical.

○ Verdicchio dei Castelli di Jesi Cl. Sup.		
Gaiospino '14	🍷🍷 4	
○ Verdicchio dei Castelli di Jesi Cl. Sup.		
Stracacio '14	🍷🍷 5	
○ Verdicchio dei Castelli di Jesi Cl. Sup.		
Il Bacco '15	🍷 2	
○ Verdicchio dei Castelli di Jesi Cl. Sup.		
Il Coroncino '14	🍷 2	
○ Verdicchio dei Castelli di Jesi Cl. Sup.		
Gaiospino '03	🍷🍷🍷 4	
○ Verdicchio dei Castelli di Jesi Cl. Sup.		
Gaiospino '13	🍷🍷 4	
○ Verdicchio dei Castelli di Jesi Cl. Sup.		
Gaiospino Fumé '12	🍷🍷 5	
○ Verdicchio dei Castelli di Jesi Cl. Sup.		
Il Coroncino '13	🍷🍷 2*	

Tenuta De Angelis

VIA SAN FRANCESCO, 10
63030 CASTEL DI LAMA [AP]
TEL. +39 073687429
www.tenutadeangelis.it

CELLAR SALES
PRE-BOOKED VISITS
ANNUAL PRODUCTION 500,000 bottles
HECTARES UNDER VINE 50.00

It was 1958 and the economic boom was still to come when the De Angelis family started producing and selling wine. The real turning point came in the early 1990s, when they decided to introduce a range of bottled wines alongside their extensive unbottled products. Since then they have never strayed from the path of promoting local designations, offering excellent value for money, and a dependable style that showcases expressive fruit and robust acidity, especially in the reds from Montepulciano and sangiovese. The Rosso Picenos are, in fact, the protagonists of our tastings: the Superiore Oro 2012 combines dark, coffee aromas with a liquorice base, while the palate is complex with nicely blended flavour. The Superiore 2014 offers well-focused varietal hints of morello cherries and black olives, echoed in a full-bodied, chewy flavour. The Quiete 2015 is a sound, unfiltered Pecorino with a confidently fruity, flavoursome feel.

○ Offida Pecorino Quiete '15	♟♟ 2*
● Rosso Piceno '15	♟♟ 1*
● Rosso Piceno Sup. '14	♟♟ 2*
● Rosso Piceno Sup. Oro '12	♟♟ 3
○ Offida Passerina '15	♟ 2
○ Offida Pecorino '15	♟ 2
● Anghelos '12	♟ 3
● Anghelos '11	♟ 3
○ Offida Passerina '12	♟ 2*
○ Offida Pecorino '14	♟ 2*
○ Offida Pecorino '13	♟ 2*
○ Offida Pecorino '12	♟ 2*
● Rosso Piceno Sup. '13	♟ 2*
● Rosso Piceno Sup. '12	♟ 2*
● Rosso Piceno Sup. '11	♟ 2*
● Rosso Piceno Sup. '10	♟ 2*
● Rosso Piceno Sup. Oro '11	♟ 3

Fattoria Dezi

C.DA FONTEMAGGIO, 14
63839 SERVIGLIANO [FM]
TEL. +39 0734710090
fattoriadezi@hotmail.com

CELLAR SALES
PRE-BOOKED VISITS
ACCOMMODATION
ANNUAL PRODUCTION 45,000 bottles
HECTARES UNDER VINE 15.00

Fattoria Dezi was the first quality winery in the Tenna valley. Brothers Davide and Stefano improved on their parents' work and gave a boost to quality in the early 1990s. The vineyards in Contrada Fontemaggio enjoy a sunny, sloping location with full view of the Ete valley. Thanks to short pruning and a quite inland position at a good altitude, the site has little influence on the ripening of the grapes, which is usually quite pronounced. The reds made from Montepulciano and sangiovese are tannic while young, with generous alcohol content. Ageing in small and medium wood guarantees slow development in the bottle. The whites, aged in concrete, tend to show broad, flavoursome dimensions rather than depth. Solo 2014 is dark and minerally with cut flowers and oriental spices on the nose and a confidently paced palate with a liquorice finish. The Dezio 2014 has black cherry aromas and a fruity, tannic finish.

● Solo '14	♟♟ 6
● Dezio '14	♟♟ 3
○ Falerio Pecorino Servigliano P. '14	♟ 3
○ Solagne '14	♟ 3
● Regina del Bosco '06	♟♟♟ 6
● Regina del Bosco '05	♟♟♟ 6
● Regina del Bosco '03	♟♟♟ 6
● Solo Sangiovese '05	♟♟♟ 6
● Solo Sangiovese '01	♟♟♟ 5
● Solo Sangiovese '00	♟♟♟ 6
● Dezio '13	♟ 3
● Dezio '12	♟ 3
○ Falerio Pecorino P. '11	♟ 3
● Regina del Bosco '11	♟ 6
● Regina del Bosco '10	♟ 6
● Regina del Bosco '09	♟ 6
● Solo '12	♟ 6

Emanuele Dianetti

C.DA VALLEROSA, 25
63063 CARASSAI [AP]
TEL. +39 3383928439
www.dianettivini.it

CELLAR SALES
PRE-BOOKED VISITS
ANNUAL PRODUCTION 6,600 bottles
HECTARES UNDER VINE 2.00

Emanuele Dianetti's day job is in a bank, but winemaking is not simply a hobby for him. He dedicates passion and respect for his family's values to it and to pursue a business that requires considerable energy and long hours, he relies on the full support of his mother, Giulia, a crucial figure tending the few hectares of vineyards planted mainly with traditional Piceno grapes, and of Michele Quagliarini. A healthy artisan style stamps the whole production process, from hand-picking to the architectural details of the cellar with its stainless steel tanks for the whites and small, used wood for the reds. Emanuele prioritizes healthy fruit and acidic backbone, both of which are concentrated in the Offida Rosso Vignagiulia 2013. Finely focused tannic texture makes this a stylish, pleasantly succulent wine. Citrus fruit and seashells on the nose for the Offida Pecorino Vignagiulia 2015, with a palate streaked through with salty sensations.

● Offida Rosso Vignagiulia '13	♟♟♟	5
○ Offida Pecorino Vignagiulia '15	♟♟	3*
○ Offida Pecorino Vignagiulia '14	♟♟	3*
○ Offida Pecorino Vignagiulia '13	♟♟	3
● Offida Rosso Vignagiulia '12	♟♟	4
● Offida Rosso Vignagiulia '11	♟♟	4

Fazi Battaglia

VIA ROMA, 117
60031 CASTELPLANIO [AN]
TEL. +39 073181591
www.fazibattaglia.it

CELLAR SALES
PRE-BOOKED VISITS
ANNUAL PRODUCTION 450,000 bottles
HECTARES UNDER VINE 130.00

Bought out last year by Bertani Domains, this Castelplanio estate has undergone in-depth refurbishment across the board, all with a single aim: to promote Verdicchio and a historically significant brand-name. Many hectares of vineyards, some in enviably wine country, produce a range of completely distinct labels that express the versatile character of the Castelli di Jesi grape. Aged in barriques for one year, San Sisto 2014 is subtle and stylish with clear nuances of toasted almonds and star anise. The palate is linear and streamlined, just slightly held back in the finish. Massaccio 2014, matured in concrete on the fine lees for six months, reveals more weightier structure and nicely handled, flavoursome, full body. Arkezia 2013 is subtle with hints of ripe pears and well-balanced sweetness offering alluring and lingering aromas.

○ Castelli di Jesi Verdicchio Cl. San Sisto Ris. '14	♟♟♟	4*
○ Arkezia '13	♟♟	5
○ Verdicchio dei Castelli di Jesi Cl. Sup. Massaccio '14	♟♟	3
○ Verdicchio dei Castelli di Jesi Cl. Le Moie '15	♟	2
○ Verdicchio dei Castelli di Jesi Cl. Titulus '15	♟	2
○ Castelli di Jesi Verdicchio Cl. San Sisto Ris. '10	♟♟♟	4*
○ Verdicchio dei Castelli di Jesi Cl. San Sisto Ris. '09	♟♟♟	4*
○ Verdicchio dei Castelli di Jesi Cl. San Sisto Ris. '07	♟♟♟	4
○ Verdicchio dei Castelli di Jesi Cl. San Sisto Ris. '05	♟♟♟	4

Andrea Felici

VIA SANT'ISIDORO, 28
62021 APIRO [MC]
TEL. +39 0733611431
www.andreafelici.it

CELLAR SALES
PRE-BOOKED VISITS
ANNUAL PRODUCTION 53,000 bottles
HECTARES UNDER VINE 9.00
VITICULTURE METHOD Certified Organic

As soon as he returned to his home town of Apiro, young Leo Felici made up his mind to dedicate himself in a world as familiar as it was mysterious, that of winemaking. Now he is an expert vigneron with a specific project in mind and a clear vision, and has become one of the cornerstones of this designation. His taut, sharpish, salty wines are the purest expression of a terroir underpinned by its unmistakable Apennine origins. Stainless steel and concrete are used to age the Verdicchio, from the only variety planted in the new vineyards alongside the old Cantico della Figura plot. Leo has decided to let the Cantico Riserva 2013 mature for longer, so you won't find it the table below. We'll talk about it next year. A lovely version of the Andrea Felici makes up for it though: the 2015 displays aromas of almonds and acacia flowers with an irresistible citrusy flourish. The palate shows backbone, vigour and lengthy flavour.

○ Verdicchio dei Castelli di Jesi Cl. Sup. Andrea Felici '15	♥♥ 3*
○ Castelli di Jesi Verdicchio Cl. Il Cantico della Figura Ris. '12	♥♥♥ 4*
○ Castelli di Jesi Verdicchio Cl. Il Cantico della Figura Ris. '11	♥♥♥ 4*
○ Castelli di Jesi Verdicchio Cl. Il Cantico della Figura Ris. '10	♥♥♥ 4*
○ Verdicchio dei Castelli di Jesi Cl. Il Cantico della Figura Ris. '09	♥♥♥ 4*
○ Verdicchio dei Castelli di Jesi Cl. Sup. Andrea Felici '14	♥♥ 3*
○ Verdicchio dei Castelli di Jesi Cl. Sup. Andrea Felici '13	♥♥ 2*
○ Verdicchio dei Castelli di Jesi Cl. Sup. Andrea Felici '12	♥♥ 2*

Fiorano

C.DA FIORANO, 19
63067 COSSIGNANO [AP]
TEL. +39 073598446
www.agrifiorano.it

CELLAR SALES
PRE-BOOKED VISITS
ACCOMMODATION
ANNUAL PRODUCTION 30,000 bottles
HECTARES UNDER VINE 6.00
VITICULTURE METHOD Certified Organic

A glance from the terrace of the holiday farm, especially as the sun sets on a hot summer's day, suffices to enchant visitors admiring the amphitheatre of vineyards and olive groves. It's easy to grasp what the plants have always known, the special light that shines on Contrada Fiorano. Paolo Beretta and Paola Massi have invested in this area with courage and intuition, choosing organic methods, and setting up a perfectly efficient cellar. Their wines are expressive with chiselled aromas, correctly influenced by the vintage like every wine that promises to be the solely the fruit of the vine. Thus the Donna Orgilla from the very hot 2015 is less citrusy and salty than usual but nicely complex. The Giulia Erminia 2014, a Pecorino matured in small new oak barrels, has fresh butter, lemons and aromatic herbs on the nose with palate that is flavoursome, taut, creamy all at once. Black cherries and good balance are the features of the Terre di Giobbe 2013.

○ Giulia Erminia '14	♥♥ 2*
● Fiorano Sangiovese '15	♥♥ 2*
○ Offida Pecorino Donna Orgilla '15	♥♥ 3
● Rosso Piceno Sup. Terre di Giobbe '13	♥♥ 3
⊙ Rosato '15	♥ 2
○ Offida Pecorino Donna Orgilla '14	♥♥♥ 3*
● Fiorano '14	♥♥ 2*
○ Offida Pecorino Donna Orgilla '13	♥♥ 3*
○ Offida Pecorino Donna Orgilla '12	♥♥ 3
○ Offida Pecorino Donna Orgilla '11	♥♥ 3
● Rosso Piceno Sup. Terre di Giobbe '12	♥♥ 3
● Rosso Piceno Sup. Terre di Giobbe '11	♥♥ 3
● Rosso Piceno Sup. Terre di Giobbe '10	♥♥ 3
● Sangiovese '11	♥♥ 2*

Cantine Fontezoppa

C.DA SAN DOMENICO, 38
62012 CIVITANOVA MARCHE [MC]
TEL. +39 0733790504
www.cantinefontezoppa.it

CELLAR SALES
PRE-BOOKED VISITS
ACCOMMODATION AND RESTAURANT SERVICE
ANNUAL PRODUCTION 290,000 bottles
HECTARES UNDER VINE 38.00

Fontezoppa offers a very varied range, which is understandable since the grapes come from three very different production areas. A wide range of varieties were planted so as to verify the suitability of each. With the exception of Matelica, where verdicchio reigns supreme. After almost 20 years of work, it can be said that the best results have come from ribona and cabernet sauvignon grown at Civitanova, and from the vernaccia nera from Serrapetrona. Pinot nero is also grown here, in a climate with Apennine nuances, and yields wines with a special charm. The Morò 2013 has berry fruit aromas with hints of black pepper typical of vernaccia. The palate is firm-footed with a determined finish on earthy sensations. The Pinot Nero San Marone 2012 is subtle and stylish with smoky nuances on a mature, relaxed palate. Carapetto 2012 is a Cabernet Sauvignon with mint, cedarwood and blackberry aromas and a compact, slightly alcohol-rich palate.

● Serrapetrona Morò '13	♀♀	5
● Carapetto '12	♀♀	5
● San Marone '12	♀♀	5
⊙ M. Cl. Extra Brut Rosé	♀	5
○ Colli Maceratesi Ribona '12	♀	3
⊙ Frapiccì '15	♀	2
○ Verdicchio di Matelica Vardì '15	♀	3
● Carapetto '11	♀♀	5
● Dedicato a Piero '09	♀♀	5
● I Terreni di San Severino Cascià Passito '07	♀♀	4
● Serrapetrona Carpignano '09	♀♀	2*
● Serrapetrona Falcotto '12	♀♀	4
● Serrapetrona Falcotto '09	♀♀	4
● Serrapetrona Morò '09	♀♀	5

★Gioacchino Garofoli

VIA CARLO MARX, 123
60022 CASTELFIDARDO [AN]
TEL. +39 0717820162
www.garofolivini.it

CELLAR SALES
PRE-BOOKED VISITS
ANNUAL PRODUCTION 2,000,000 bottles
HECTARES UNDER VINE 42.00

Over a century of history along with a style consolidated over time, shaped by the same hand for four decades, make Garofoli a greatly respected Marche name. The renovated Castelfidardo cellar, spacious and hi-tech to make work easier, produces Verdicchios of unquestionable character, with a classic feel. Jewels in the crown of regional winemaking that in no way steal attention from the winery's long tradition in sparklers or its mighty, polished Montepulciano del Coneros, with their stunning cellar potential. The Podium 2014 is the best choice: citrus, acacia flowers, gunflint and a hint of saffron on the nose, and a graceful palate with emphasized detail but lacking the depth of the better versions. Sweet aromas betray the barrique ageing for the Serra Fiorese 2012, with a vigorous, flavoursome palate and soft finish. The dark and iron-like Agontano 2012 displays personality and austere charm.

○ Verdicchio dei Castelli di Jesi Cl. Sup. Podium '14	♀♀	4
● Camerlano '11	♀♀	4
○ Castelli di Jesi Verdicchio Cl. Serra Fiorese Ris. '12	♀♀	4
● Conero Grosso Agontano Ris. '12	♀♀	5
● Rosso Conero Piancarda '13	♀♀	3
● Rosso Piceno Colle Ambro '13	♀♀	2*
○ Verdicchio dei Castelli di Jesi Brut M. Cl. Ris. '09	♀♀	4
⊙ Kòmaros '15	♀	2
○ Verdicchio dei Castelli di Jesi Brut M. Cl. Delìs '12	♀	4
○ Verdicchio dei Castelli di Jesi Cl. Sup. Macrina '15	♀	2
○ Verdicchio dei Castelli di Jesi Cl. Sup. Podium '13	♀♀♀	4*

Marco Gatti

VIA LAGUA E SAN MARTINO, 2
60043 CERRETO D'ESI [AN]
TEL. +39 0732677012
www.gattiagri.it

CELLAR SALES
PRE-BOOKED VISITS
ANNUAL PRODUCTION 10,000 bottles
HECTARES UNDER VINE 7.00

Marco Gatti is a talented vigneron and nurseryman. He personally manages a few hectares, some rented and some owned, in the northernmost Cerreto d'Esi part of the Verdicchio di Matelica designation. Small plots are fermented separately to extract the best qualities of the terroir. The best wine country is the Quadrelle di Cerreto d'Esi cru, which provides the top selections. Only stainless steel is used for fermentation. The wines are naturally full-bodied and flavoursome, which points to meticulous selection of the ripest grapes. Even without the leading wine, Millo Riserva, not produced in 2014, the other wines all show classy features. We liked the Villa Marilla 2015 best, with hawthorn blossom, apples and pears on the nose and a vigorous, complex, extremely succulent palate. The Casale Venza 2015 shows good texture on a harmonious palate with typical fresh almond nuances. The baby of the family, Aristo 2015, is a jolly glassful with hints of citron peel.

○ Verdicchio di Matelica Aristo '15	♥♥ 2*
○ Verdicchio di Matelica Casale Venza '15	♥♥ 2*
○ Verdicchio di Matelica Villa Marilla '15	♥♥ 2*
○ Verdicchio di Matelica '14	♀♀ 2*
○ Verdicchio di Matelica '13	♀♀ 2*
○ Verdicchio di Matelica Millo Ris. '13	♀♀ 3*
○ Verdicchio di Matelica Millo Ris. '12	♀♀ 3
○ Verdicchio di Matelica Villa Marilla '14	♀♀ 2*
○ Verdicchio di Matelica Villa Marilla '13	♀♀ 2*

Luciano Landi

VIA GAVIGLIANO, 16
60030 BELVEDERE OSTRENSE [AN]
TEL. +39 073162353
www.aziendalandi.it

CELLAR SALES
PRE-BOOKED VISITS
ACCOMMODATION
ANNUAL PRODUCTION 80,000 bottles
HECTARES UNDER VINE 20.00

Belvedere Ostrense is one of six municipalities north of the Esino river that fall within the limited Lacrima DOC zone. Luciano Landi is one of its most reliable winemakers and has created a quite generous style using short pruning and fully ripe grapes grown on clay and limestone soils. Luciano is thus able to overcome the agronomical limitations of a capricious grape variety even in more difficult years. Alongside the inevitable verdicchio, he also grows smaller quantities of Montepulciano and international varieties in his vineyards. Black cherries and an enticing, lightly piquant sensation for the Lacrima Superiore Gavigliano 2014. The palate shows fresh, dynamic energy with hints of orange zest in a lovely finish. Flowers and candied red berries on the nose of the Lacrima 2015 are consolidated on the weighty palate. Don't underestimate the mouthwatering, flavoursome, mouthfilling Verdicchio Classico 2015. Nobilnero 2010 is a powerful, balsamic Montepulciano.

● Lacrima di Morro d'Alba Sup. Gavigliano '14	♥♥ 3
● Nobilnero '10	♥♥ 6
○ Verdicchio dei Castelli di Jesi Cl. '15	♥♥ 2*
● Kore '10	♥ 3
● Lacrima di Morro d'Alba '15	♥ 2
● Ragosto '13	♥ 2
● Goliardo '10	♀♀ 4
● Lacrima di Morro d'Alba '14	♀♀ 2*
● Lacrima di Morro d'Alba Sup. Gavigliano '13	♀♀ 3
● Lacrima di Morro d'Alba Sup. Gavigliano '11	♀♀ 3
● Ragosto '11	♀♀ 2*
● Ragosto '10	♀♀ 2*
⊙ Syla '13	♀♀ 2*

Conte Leopardi Dittajuti

VIA MARINA II, 24
60026 NUMANA [AN]
TEL. +39 0717390116
www.conteleopardi.it

CELLAR SALES
PRE-BOOKED VISITS
ANNUAL PRODUCTION 350,000 bottles
HECTARES UNDER VINE 49.00

Many of the estate's vineyards are inside the Parco Naturale del Conero, a limestone promontory overlooking the Adriatic. The unusual soil composition, proximity to a sea that acts as a thermal flywheel, and constant breezes make Conero the northernmost location where Montepulciano grapes are able to ripen consistently. Piervittorio Leopardi's modern touch in the cellar softens their husky nature and excessive alcohol, and he applies his skills in different ways across many labels. The two 2013 Conero Riservas are both aged at length in barriques. Pigmento displays morello cherries with light vegetal streaks and a lovely compact palate. Artemano is more complex with lovely dark fruit and a palate that displays strength and character. A good performance, unsurprisingly, from the Villa Marina 2014, with aromas of leather and morello cherries and a dry, flavoursome palate with minerally hints. Of the younger wines, Fructus 2015 offers a lovely fresh, supple palate with mouthwatering, fruity texture.

● Conero Artemano Ris. '13	¶¶	5
● Conero Pigmento Ris. '13	¶¶	5
● Lacrima di Morro d'Alba '14	¶¶	2*
● Rosso Conero Fructus '15	¶¶	2*
● Rosso Conero Villa Marina '14	¶¶	3
○ Bassamarea '15	¶	2
○ Calcare '15	¶	3
● Rose del Coppo '15	¶	2
● Rosso Conero Antichi Poderi del Conte '13	¶	2
● Rosso Conero Casirano '14	¶	4
○ Verdicchio dei Castelli di Jesi Cl. Castelverde '15	¶	2
● Conero Pigmento Ris. '12	¶¶	5
● Rosso Conero Casirano '13	¶¶	4
● Rosso Conero Villa Marina '13	¶¶	3

Roberto Lucarelli

LOC. RIPALTA
VIA PIANA, 20
61030 CARTOCETO [PU]
TEL. +39 0721893019
www.laripe.com

CELLAR SALES
PRE-BOOKED VISITS
ANNUAL PRODUCTION 200,000 bottles
HECTARES UNDER VINE 32.00

Roberto Lucarelli is one of the most talented of Pesaro's winegrowers. He has doggedly created a gem of an estate among his vineyards in the verdant Cartoceto area, where a landscape of olive trees steals the scene from the vineyards. His specialities are bianchello and sangiovese, alongside a far fromm shy presence of international grapes. The style is modern, judiciously safeguarding the fresh, drinkable traits and clean aromas, and overall pleasurable quality that is never commonplace or too simple. The Rocho, processed in both steel and tonneaux, is the most complex and elegant Bianchello of 2015, with aromas of apple and pear fruit and rain-washed pebbles followed by a harmonious, polished palate. Also well-typed, the Bianchello La Ripe 2015 is all summer fruit, with a supple, gutsy palate. Turning to the reds, we liked the Goccione 2012 best: spicy, perfectly mature aromas with a hints of cloves and rhubarb and a tangy, relaxed flavour with resolved tannic texture.

○ Bianchello del Metauro La Ripe '15	¶¶	2*
○ Bianchello del Metauro Sup. Rocho '15	¶¶	2*
○ Collemare '15	¶¶	2*
● Colli Pesaresi Sangiovese Goccione '12	¶¶	3
○ Verdicchio dei Castelli di Jesi Cl. Villa Piana '15	¶¶	2*
● Colli Pesaresi Sangiovese La Ripe '15	¶	2
⊙ Rosato '15	¶	2
○ Bianchello del Metauro La Ripe '12	¶¶	2*
○ Bianchello del Metauro Rocho '11	¶¶	2*
○ Bianchello del Metauro Sup. Rocho '12	¶¶	2*
○ Chardonnay '12	¶¶	2*
● Colli Pesaresi Sangiovese Goccione '11	¶¶	3
● Colli Pesaresi Sangiovese Insieme Ris. '11	¶¶	4
● Colli Pesaresi Sangiovese La Ripe '12	¶¶	2*

La Marca di San Michele

VIA TORRE, 13
60034 CUPRAMONTANA [AN]
TEL. +39 0731781183
www.lamarcadisanmichele.com

CELLAR SALES
PRE-BOOKED VISITS
ACCOMMODATION
ANNUAL PRODUCTION 25,000 bottles
HECTARES UNDER VINE 6.00
VITICULTURE METHOD Certified Organic

In 2007, Alessandro and Beatrice Bonci and Daniela Quaresima founded their estate. As firm supporters of an ethical approach to farming, they immediately embarkd on a path that strictly applied organic principles, which means plenty of work in the vineyards and a few essential winemaking procedures in the cellar. In this way the grapes that grow in the San Michele cru are free to offer a well-focused expression of the nature of this terroir and the value of the vintage. The wines are boisterous and without restriction, lively and with a really charming authentic feel. The Passolento 2014, aged for nine months in large oak followed by maturation in stainless steel and bottles, opens on vegetal hints of freshly mown hay and celery, moving into clear aromas of toasted almonds and a crescendo of complexity in the finish of a succulent palate. Aromas of flowers and bitter herbs for the Capovolto 2015, and a subtle, salty palate with a long, almondy finish, the indelible mark of the most typical Verdicchios.

○ Castelli di Jesi Verdicchio Cl. Passolento Ris. '14	▼▼ 4
○ Verdicchio dei Castelli di Jesi Cl. Sup. Capovolto '15	▼▼ 3
○ Verdicchio dei Castelli di Jesi Cl. Sup. Capovolto '13	♀♀♀ 3*
○ Verdicchio dei Castelli di Jesi Cl. Sup. Capovolto '10	♀♀♀ 3*
○ Capovolto '12	♀♀ 3
○ Verdicchio dei Castelli di Jesi Cl. Il Pigro Ris. '08	♀♀ 5
○ Verdicchio dei Castelli di Jesi Cl. Sup. Capovolto '14	♀♀ 3
○ Verdicchio dei Castelli di Jesi Cl.Sup. Capovolto '09	♀♀ 2*

Maurizio Marchetti

FRAZ. PINOCCHIO
VIA DI PONTELUNGO, 166
60131 ANCONA
TEL. +39 071897386
www.marchettiwines.it

CELLAR SALES
PRE-BOOKED VISITS
ANNUAL PRODUCTION 60,000 bottles
HECTARES UNDER VINE 20.00

A piece of Conero history exists here at Maurizio Marchetti's estate. His father Mario developed production and sales of wine in the 1960s, although the estate can boast a century of history. Maurizio has continued his father's quest for quality, helped along the way by Lorenzo Landi. Together they have renewed the vineyards on the sunny slopes of Candia, where the best spots are reserved for Montepulciano. The pair prefer short pruning with a focus on ripe, fruity grapes for a modernized range of products that has not altered traditional features. Villa Bonomi 2013, aged for 16 months in barriques, offers clear aromas of morello cherries, a hint of coffee powder and smoky sensations, and a smooth-textured entry with healthy fruit. Younger brother Castro di San Silvestro 2015 is also very fruity, but slightly lacking in suppleness. The Verdicchio 2015 is approachable and really flavoursome.

● Conero Villa Bonomi Cento Vendemmie Mario Marchetti Ris. '13	▼▼ 5
○ Verdicchio dei Castelli di Jesi Cl. '15	▼▼ 2*
● Rosso Conero Castro di San Silvestro '15	▼ 2
○ Verdicchio dei Castelli di Jesi Cl. Sup. Tenuta del Cavaliere '15	▼ 3
● Rosso Conero Villa Bonomi Ris. '02	♀♀♀ 4
● Conero Villa Bonomi Ris. '12	♀♀ 5
● Conero Villa Bonomi Ris. '11	♀♀ 5
● Conero Villa Bonomi Ris. '10	♀♀ 4
○ Verdicchio dei Castelli di Jesi Cl. Sup. Tenuta del Cavaliere '14	♀♀ 3
○ Verdicchio dei Castelli di Jesi Cl. Sup. Tenuta del Cavaliere '13	♀♀ 3

Marotti Campi

VIA SANT'AMICO, 14
60030 MORRO D'ALBA [AN]
TEL. +39 0731618027
www.marotticampi.it

CELLAR SALES
PRE-BOOKED VISITS
ACCOMMODATION
ANNUAL PRODUCTION 220,000 bottles
HECTARES UNDER VINE 68.00

A glance at the statistics for this winery appears to suggest little more than an artisan estate, but in actual fact, Marotti Campi is a true colossus in the small but important Lacrima designation. Over the years, Lorenzo's wines have proved very reliable. Credit goes to a planning strategy based on well-managed vineyards, meticulous winemaking, and well-judged variation within the range. Verdicchio takes a leading role in the generous array of wines on offer. And indeed the Salmariano 2013 brings Tre Bicchieri home to Morro d'Alba. A very vibrant nose with lemon curd and aromatic herbs is followed by a confident entry, unstoppable development and a long finish reverberating with aromatic sensations. Its red alter ego, Orgiolo 2014, is just as good: stylish spice, excellent grip, leaving a vivid trace of black cherries on the palate. The Donderè 2012 is peppery with a lovely dynamic palate.

○ Castelli di Jesi Verdicchio Cl. Salmariano Ris. '13	♟♟♟ 3*
● Lacrima di Morro d'Alba Sup. Orgiolo '14	♟♟ 3*
⊙ Brut Rosé	♟♟ 3
● Donderè '12	♟♟ 3
● Lacrima di Morro d'Alba Rùbico '15	♟♟ 2*
○ Verdicchio dei Castelli di Jesi Cl. Sup. Luzano '15	♟♟ 2*
● Xyris	♟♟ 2
○ Verdicchio dei Castelli di Jesi Cl. Albiano '15	♟ 1*
○ Verdicchio dei Castelli di Jesi Cl. Salmariano Ris. '08	♟♟♟ 3*
○ Verdicchio dei Castelli di Jesi Cl. Salmariano Ris. '07	♟♟♟ 2*

Poderi Mattioli

VIA FARNETO, 17A
60030 SERRA DE' CONTI [AN]
TEL. +39 0731878676
www.poderimattioli.it

CELLAR SALES
PRE-BOOKED VISITS
ANNUAL PRODUCTION 18,000 bottles
HECTARES UNDER VINE 6.50
VITICULTURE METHOD Certified Organic

The large photos showing scenes of country life in the 1960s might seem to clash with the architecture of the modern winery, but they effectively sum up the estate philosophy: a successful blend of inherited skills and state-of-the-art knowledge. Giordano Mattioli looks after the vineyards, comprising three crus with distinct features. His brother Giacomo is busy with fermentation and ageing of the wines. The grapes for Lauro, the family's Riserva, come from the Mogliette vineyard. The 2013 version has a well-defined profile moving towards a light blend of citrus and almonds with clear aniseed aromas identifying the terroir. The palate is vivid, subtle and dynamic, its stylish pace leaving a persistent salty sensation in the finish. Also well-made with nice, lively, tangy flavour, the Dosaggio Zero is a meticulous verdicchio-based Metodo Classico with 15% chardonnay.

○ Castelli di Jesi Verdicchio Cl. Lauro Ris. '13	♟♟♟ 3*
○ M. Cl. Dosaggio Zero '11	♟♟ 5
○ Verdicchio dei Castelli di Jesi Cl. Sup. Ylice '12	♟♟♟ 2*
○ Verdicchio dei Castelli di Jesi Cl. Sup. Lauro '10	♟♟ 3*
○ Verdicchio dei Castelli di Jesi Cl. Sup. Ylice '14	♟♟ 3
○ Verdicchio dei Castelli di Jesi Cl. Sup. Ylice '13	♟♟ 3
○ Verdicchio dei Castelli di Jesi Cl. Sup. Ylice '11	♟♟ 2*

Valter Mattoni

VIA PESCOLLA, 1
63030 CASTORANO [AP]
TEL. +39 073687329
www.valtermattoni.it

CELLAR SALES
PRE-BOOKED VISITS
ANNUAL PRODUCTION 6,000 bottles
HECTARES UNDER VINE 3.50

Despite the limited production quantities, Valter Mattoni's wines are widely distributed among enthusiasts. A few rows of trebbiano, Montepulciano and bordò provide perfectly terroir-rooted wines that respect tradition, obtained using natural methods and avoiding any kind of dogmatic procedures. Wines that roar in the glass, slow to express themselves but forthright and impetuous once they get going. Small wood reigns in the compact, recently-built cellar, used to age the reds and the Trebbien, which is the only white produced. A lovely performance from all the wines. The Rossobordò 2013, made from a grenache clone, is uniquely subtle, rich in nuances of black cherries, lavender and liquorice. Arshura 2014 is the opposite, with very vibrant aromas of morello cherries and soot, and a dark, minerally, chewy palate: an ode to the truest, most generous of Montepulciano. Apple aromas in the Trebbien 2014, with pleasantly husky, perky features.

● Arshura '14	♥♥ 5
● Rossobordò '13	♥♥ 8
○ Trebbien '14	♥♥ 3
● Arshura '11	♥♥♥ 3*
● Arshura '13	♥♥ 5
● Arshura '12	♥♥ 5
● Arshura '10	♥♥ 3*
● Arshura '09	♥♥ 3
● Arshura '08	♥♥ 3
● Rosso Bordò '10	♥♥ 8
● Rossobordò '12	♥♥ 8
● Rossobordò '11	♥♥ 8
○ Trebbien '13	♥♥ 3
○ Trebbien '12	♥♥ 2*

Federico Mencaroni

VIA OLMIGRANDI, 72
60013 CORINALDO [AN]
TEL. +39 0717975625
www.mencaroni.eu

PRE-BOOKED VISITS
ANNUAL PRODUCTION 30,000 bottles
HECTARES UNDER VINE 7.50

Corinaldo is the northernmost municipality in Castelli di Jesi, an area of gentle hills of moderate altitudes, intensely planted with vines set against the Adriatic sea. Federico Mencaroni, the fourth generation of a winemaking family, completed his studies and work experience in other parts of Italy, before deciding to continue the work of his uncle, Nevio. Clear ideas, young support staff, and plenty of courage explain the tens of thousands of champagne bottles piled up in the underground cellar today, for a project concentrating on verdicchio sparklers. Contatto 2011 spends 40 months on the yeasts a vibrant floral nose and a sparkling palate with a harmonious blend of acidity, tangy texture and sweetness from the liqueur d'expedition. Apollonia 2011, 50 months of lees contact, shows more vigour and grip but less harmony, revealing some vegetal hesitancy. Good news from the still wines: Isola 2013 is a dry, salty Verdicchio with lively backbone.

○ Verdicchio dei Castelli di Jesi M. Cl. Brut Contatto '11	♥♥ 4
○ Verdicchio dei Castelli di Jesi Isola '13	♥♥ 3
○ Verdicchio dei Castelli di Jesi M. Cl. Brut Nature Apollonia '11	♥♥ 5
○ Verdicchio dei Castelli di Jesi Isola '11	♥♥ 3
○ Verdicchio dei Castelli di Jesi Isola '10	♥♥ 2*
○ Verdicchio dei Castelli di Jesi M. Cl. Brut Apollonia '09	♥♥ 5
○ Verdicchio dei Castelli di Jesi M. Cl. Brut Contatto '10	♥♥ 4
○ Verdicchio dei Castelli di Jesi M. Cl. Brut Nature Apollonia '10	♥♥ 5

★La Monacesca

C.DA MONACESCA
62024 MATELICA [MC]
TEL. +39 0733672641
www.monacesca.it

CELLAR SALES
PRE-BOOKED VISITS
ANNUAL PRODUCTION 180,000 bottles
HECTARES UNDER VINE 30.00

Aldo Cifola manages the estate with a firm hand, and has brought it up to the top levels of Italian white wine production. His full-bodied, flavoursome Verdicchios, for which he never uses wood, have become a benchmark for the area, with a very recognizable style. As of this year a third Verdicchio di Matelica is on offer after many years' absence: a combination of the free-and-easy basic Matelica and the full, complex Mirum, the leading wine in the range. The cold vintage year has endowed the Mirum 2014 with unexpected suppleness, and hasn't done any harm to the complex mid-palate, driven by lovely minerally energy up to the extremely nuanced finish. The Terra di Mezzo 2012 has hints of botrytis and broom, supported by a mature, full-bodied, multilayered palate. The Verdicchio 2014 offers citrusy acidity and a mouthwatering flavour. Ecclesia 2015 is a surprisingly original Chardonnay, broad rather than deep, and very pleasing.

○ Verdicchio di Matelica Mirum Ris. '14	▼▼▼ 5
○ Ecclesia '15	▼▼ 3
○ Verdicchio di Matelica '14	▼▼ 3
○ Verdicchio di Matelica Terra di Mezzo '12	▼▼ 4
○ Verdicchio di Matelica Mirum Ris. '12	♀♀♀ 5
○ Verdicchio di Matelica Mirum Ris. '11	♀♀♀ 5
○ Verdicchio di Matelica Mirum Ris. '10	♀♀♀ 4*
○ Verdicchio di Matelica Mirum Ris. '09	♀♀♀ 4
○ Verdicchio di Matelica Mirum Ris. '08	♀♀♀ 4
○ Verdicchio di Matelica Mirum Ris. '07	♀♀♀ 4*
○ Verdicchio di Matelica Mirum Ris. '06	♀♀♀ 4
○ Verdicchio di Matelica Mirum Ris. '04	♀♀♀ 4
○ Verdicchio di Matelica Mirum Ris. '02	♀♀♀ 3

Monte Schiavo

FRAZ. MONTESCHIAVO
VIA VIVAIO
60030 MAIOLATI SPONTINI [AN]
TEL. +39 0731700385
www.monteschiavo.it

CELLAR SALES
PRE-BOOKED VISITS
ANNUAL PRODUCTION 950,000 bottles
HECTARES UNDER VINE 103.00
SUSTAINABLE WINERY

With a whopping 103 hectares available, the Pieralisi family's Monteschiavo estate is one of the Marche region's largest private wine producers. The land is split into many plots, including the outstanding Tassanare located between Arcevia and Rosora. Carlo Ferrini is in charge of the spacious cellar, and his work aims to offer a modern interpretation of the classic Jesi designations. Verdicchio takes the lion's share, of course, but the reds provide a valid snapshot of DOCs like Lacrima and Rosso Piceno. Le Giuncare 2013 displays a generous array of aromas ranging from ripe fruit like pineapples and peaches, to sweeter spice, toasted almonds and cocoa butter. The palate shows well-balanced structure and length, with a flavoursome, persistent finish. Pieralisi for Friends 2013 has black cherries, smoky hints and cloves on the nose and an original palate with considerable tannic texture.

○ Castelli di Jesi Verdicchio Cl. Le Giuncare Ris. '13	▼▼ 3*
● Esino Rosso Pieralisi for Friends '13	▼▼ 5
● Lacrima di Morro d'Alba Marzaiola '15	▼ 2
● Rosso Piceno Sassaiolo '13	▼ 2
○ Verdicchio dei Castelli di Jesi Cl. Coste del Molino '15	▼ 2
○ Verdicchio dei Castelli di Jesi Cl. Sup. Pallio di S. Floriano '15	▼ 3
○ Verdicchio dei Castelli di Jesi Cl. Sup. Pallio di S. Floriano '11	♀♀♀ 2*
○ Verdicchio dei Castelli di Jesi Cl. Sup. Pallio di S. Floriano '10	♀♀♀ 2*
○ Verdicchio dei Castelli di Jesi Cl. Sup. Pallio di S. Floriano '09	♀♀♀ 2*

Montecappone

VIA COLLE OLIVO, 2
60035 JESI [AN]
TEL. +39 0731205761
www.montecappone.com

CELLAR SALES
PRE-BOOKED VISITS
ANNUAL PRODUCTION 150,000 bottles
HECTARES UNDER VINE 70.00

Gianluca Mirizzi is very satisfied with his new six-hectare plot between Cupramontana and Monteroberto, in a cool location and aspect. He finds it ideal for his concept of wine, to preserve the acidic vigour and citrusy aromas in whites, and the healthy fruit in the Montepulciano-based reds. The spacious Jesi cellar is home to the pressurized vats for the two Charmat method wines based on verdicchio and sauvignon, the stainless steel and concrete vats for the whites which are all fermented with the aid of cold reduction, and barriques for the leading reds. Utopia 2103 makes the very best of an almost perfect year, displaying citrus tones gently invigorated by hints of wild herbs, and a stylish palate with persistent, tangy grip in the finish. Tre Bicchieri. The Federico II 2015 reveals lovely aromas of aniseed and flowers, followed by a very effective, energetic entry on the palate. Among the reds, the Rosso Piceno Utopia 2013 performs well, with clear and characteristic fruitiness.

○ Castelli di Jesi Verdicchio Cl. Utopia Ris. '13	♛♛♛ 4*
○ La Breccia '15	♛♛ 3
● Rosso Piceno Utopia '13	♛♛ 5
○ Verdicchio dei Castelli di Jesi Cl. '15	♛♛ 2*
○ Verdicchio dei Castelli di Jesi Cl. Sup. Federico II a.D. 1194 '15	♛♛ 3
⊙ Pergolesi a. D. 1710 '15	♛ 2
● Rosso Piceno '15	♛ 2
○ Sauvignon Extra Dry '15	♛ 3
○ Tabano '15	♛ 3
○ Verdicchio dei Castelli di Jesi Cl. Utopia Ris. '08	♛♛♛ 4
○ Verdicchio dei Castelli di Jesi Cl. Utopia Ris. '07	♛♛♛ 4*
○ Castelli di Jesi Verdicchio Cl. Utopia Ris. '12	♛♛ 4

Alessandro Moroder

VIA MONTACUTO, 121
60029 ANCONA
TEL. +39 071898232
www.moroder-vini.it

CELLAR SALES
PRE-BOOKED VISITS
ANNUAL PRODUCTION 130,000 bottles
HECTARES UNDER VINE 18.00
VITICULTURE METHOD Certified Organic
SUSTAINABLE WINERY

Alessandro Moroder, the founding father of Conero designations, has worked hard in recent years to convert all the vineyards to organic methods and to give his wines an even more terroir-true profile. He is joined in the vineyards and cellar by his son Marco, and recently also by talented winemaker Marco Gozzi. Together they offer a reliable, classic range of wines: reds matured at length in various sizes of wood, and uncomplicated, easy-drinking whites matured in stainless steel. Dorico still rules our selections, this time in the 2011 version: evolved aromas with hints of leather, liquorice and spices, and a mature, polished palate thanks to the resolved tannins. In a different style, the Conero Moroder Riserva 2012 has a very fruity feel, with a sturdy palate and plenty of prominent tannins. The Rosso Conero Aiòn 2014 is compromised by the difficult year, showing a few vegetal aromas, redeemed by the dry, fresh, dynamic palate.

● Conero Dorico Ris. '11	♛♛ 5
● Conero Moroder Ris. '12	♛♛ 5
● Rosso Conero Aiòn '14	♛♛ 2*
○ Candiano '15	♛ 2
○ Malvasia '15	♛ 2
⊙ Rosa di Moroder '15	♛ 2
● Rosso Conero '13	♛ 2
● Conero Dorico Ris. '05	♛♛♛ 5
● Conero Dorico Ris. '09	♛♛ 5
● Conero Dorico Ris. '08	♛♛ 5
● Conero Dorico Ris. '07	♛♛ 5
● Conero Moroder Ris. '11	♛♛ 5
● Rosso Conero Aiòn '13	♛♛ 2*
● Rosso Conero Moroder '12	♛♛ 2*
● Rosso Conero Moroder '08	♛♛ 2*

Muròla

C.DA VILLAMAGNA, 9
62010 URBISAGLIA [MC]
TEL. +39 0733506843
www.murola.it

CELLAR SALES
PRE-BOOKED VISITS
ANNUAL PRODUCTION 700,000 bottles
HECTARES UNDER VINE 60.00

Back in 2004, the Mosiewicz family decided to use part of their massive property in one of the most beautiful parts of the Macerata countryside to bring to life the Murola project. Today they have an avant-garde cellar and vineyards at altitudes between 250 and 300 metres, on clay-rich soil. The whites are matured in stainless steel while the leading reds undergo lengthy ageing and maturation in barriques. The use of ribona grapes to make a Metodo Classico aged for 36 months on the yeasts is very interesting indeed. The Teodoro 2013 stands firm as the best wine: morello cherries blended with spicy sensations, perfectly echoing the Montepulciano grapes, and a soft, mouthfilling palate with muted tannins. The Jurek Metodo Classico is an excellent glass of fizz: fruity, delicately salty, lipsmacking. The Sangiovese Agello 2014 is light and floral, with good flavour and aromatic nuances even though it is precociously mature.

Wine	Rating
● Teodoro '13	♟♟ 3*
● Agello '14	♟♟ 2*
○ Colli Maceratesi Ribona Agar '15	♟♟ 2*
○ Jurek M.Cl. Brut	♟♟ 4
⊙ Millerose '15	♟♟ 2*
○ Verdicchio di Matelica Vitige '15	♟♟ 3
○ Baccius '15	♟ 2
○ Gremone '15	♟ 2
⊙ Jole Brut '14	♟ 3
○ Varà Brut Passerina '15	♟ 2
● Teodoro '12	♟♟♟ 3*
● Camà '12	♟♟ 2*
● Camà '11	♟♟ 3*
● Camà '10	♟♟ 4
● Sangiovese '14	♟♟ 2*
● Teodoro '11	♟♟ 3

★Oasi degli Angeli

C.DA SANT'EGIDIO, 50
63012 CUPRA MARITTIMA [AP]
TEL. +39 0735778569
www.kurni.it

CELLAR SALES
PRE-BOOKED VISITS
ANNUAL PRODUCTION 5,000 bottles
HECTARES UNDER VINE 16.00

Two decades have passed since Marco Casolanetti and Eleonora Rossi picked their first Montepulciano grapes for the 1996 Permatilde, a sort of one-off Kurni prototype. The following year the project that would give this type cult status in Italian winemaking was officially up and running, attracting many fans as well as a few dissenters who complained of excessive liveliness and extract. But moving on, today Kurni enjoys global fame and is considered a classic of its style. Marco's research is ongoing and has led to a rediscovery of bordò, a clone of grenache replicated from a 100-year-old vine and used for another red, the Kupra. Kupra 2013 has a varied and very polished nose: myrtle, chard, berries, a hint of incense, white chocolate and charred oak. The palate makes a subtle entry before taking flight with impressive development. The Kurni 2014 reveals hints of damsons and morello cherries on the usual extract-rich, explosive palate.

Wine	Rating
● Kupra '13	♟♟♟ 8
● Kurni '14	♟♟ 8
● Kupra '12	♟♟♟ 8
● Kupra '10	♟♟♟ 8
● Kurni '10	♟♟♟ 8
● Kurni '09	♟♟♟ 8
● Kurni '08	♟♟♟ 8
● Kurni '07	♟♟♟ 8
● Kurni '04	♟♟♟ 8
● Kurni '03	♟♟♟ 8
● Kurni '02	♟♟♟ 8
● Kurni '01	♟♟♟ 8
● Kurni '00	♟♟♟ 8
● Kurni '98	♟♟♟ 8
● Kurni '97	♟♟♟ 8

Pantaleone

VIA COLONNATA ALTA, 118
63100 ASCOLI PICENO
TEL. +39 3478757476
www.pantaleonewine.com

PRE-BOOKED VISITS
ANNUAL PRODUCTION 60,000 bottles
HECTARES UNDER VINE 13.00
VITICULTURE METHOD Certified Organic

Woods, badlands, broom. The estate owned by sisters Francesca and Federica Pantaloni is just a few minutes from Ascoli Piceno, but it feels far removed from any urban settlement. The looming bulk of Mount Ascensione impacts the climate, leaving its mark on the unusually fresh-tasting wines made from native grape varieties. The link with traditional grapes like Montepulciano, pecorino and passerina can be seen in a project to revive and showcase the bordò grape, a local grenache clone. Onirocep 2015 releases its usual fresh aromas with hints of grapefruit zest, green apples and sage. The palate is gutsy and flavoursome thanks to vibrant acidity creating a racy, appealingly supple finish. Chicca 2015, from passerina, is generous, well-defined and delightfully citrus. The only red is the Ribalta 2102, from bordò grapes: appealing sunny, ripe aromas and a powerful structure resting on smooth, tangy tannins, with a lingering flavour.

○ Falerio Pecorino Onirocep '15	🍷🍷	2*
● Ribalta '12	🍷🍷	8
○ Chicca '15	🍷	2
● Atto I '10	🍷🍷	2*
● Atto I '09	🍷🍷	2*
● Boccascena '12	🍷🍷	3
○ Chicca '13	🍷🍷	2*
○ Falerio Pecorino Onirocep '14	🍷🍷	2*
○ Falerio Pecorino Onirocep '13	🍷🍷	2*
● La Ribalta '10	🍷🍷	8
○ Onirocep '11	🍷🍷	2*
○ Onirocep '10	🍷🍷	3
● Sipario '09	🍷🍷	2*
● Sipario '06	🍷🍷	2*

Pievalta

VIA MONTESCHIAVO, 18
60030 MAIOLATI SPONTINI [AN]
TEL. +39 0731705199
www.baronepizzini.it

CELLAR SALES
PRE-BOOKED VISITS
ANNUAL PRODUCTION 110,000 bottles
HECTARES UNDER VINE 26.50
VITICULTURE METHOD Certified Biodynamic

As of this year the back label of the winery's Verdicchio, and is the cornerstone of production at 90,000 bottles, shows the faces of Alessandro Fenino and Silvano Brescianini, respectively cellar manager and director of Barone Pizzini, Franciacorta-based owner of Pievalta. The message is identity, clarity, responsibility: important values that combine with the biodynamic spirit driving production, aiming for wines that offer an authentic reading of the spirit of this area and the most typical Castelli di Jesi grapes. The San Paolo Riserva 2013 is hard to forget: multi-toned aromas of citrus fruit, basil, flowers, sweet almonds, and a hint of aniseed, introduce an explosive palate on which acidity, structure and minerally sensations are perfectly blended in a very deep flavour bursting with tanginess. A masterpiece. The Dominè 2015 has sweet aromas of candied citrus fruit and a subtle lift endowing the delicately salty palate with vibrant energy.

○ Castelli di Jesi Verdicchio Cl. San Paolo Ris. '13	🍷🍷🍷	3*
○ Perlugo Zero M. Cl.	🍷🍷	3
○ Verdicchio dei Castelli di Jesi Cl. Sup. Dominè '15	🍷🍷	2*
○ Verdicchio dei Castelli di Jesi Cl. Sup. Pievalta '15	🍷🍷	2*
● Rosso Pievalta '14	🍷	2
○ Castelli di Jesi Verdicchio Cl. San Paolo Ris. '10	🍷🍷🍷	3*
○ Verdicchio dei Castelli di Jesi Cl. Sup. Pievalta '09	🍷🍷🍷	2*
○ Castelli di Jesi Verdicchio Cl. San Paolo Ris. '12	🍷🍷	3*
○ Verdicchio dei Castelli di Jesi Cl. San Paolo Ris. '09	🍷🍷	3*
○ Verdicchio dei Castelli di Jesi Passito Curina '11	🍷🍷	3*

Podere sul Lago

Loc. Borgiano
via Castello, 20
62020 Serrapetrona [MC]
Tel. +39 3333017380
www.poderesullago.it

CELLAR SALES
PRE-BOOKED VISITS
ANNUAL PRODUCTION 10,000 bottles
HECTARES UNDER VINE 4.00
SUSTAINABLE WINERY

Lake Caccamo offers picture-postcard views of the area's typical foothills, where the vineyards are bordered by woods and temperature changes are keenly felt. This is the realm of vernaccia nera. Instead of producing a sparkling wine with it, as local tradition demands, Sandrine Quadraroli makes two still Serrapetrona reds. His other favourite grape, merlot, is used for the pure Il Ruggero, and in equal parts with vernaccia for the Cercis. 2014 was handled well despite its issues: the Lacus, aged in barriques, has appealing black pepper aromas with hints of bay leaves and incense, while the palate is delicately salty with prominent backbone. Hints of cherries for the Il Torcular aged in stainless steel, over a vegetal undercurrent which leaves the tangy spice undisturbed. Il Ruggero is much fruitier, with smooth tannins and mouthfilling sensations. Zio Sergio, from dried vernaccia grapes, is very spicy with nicely measured residual sweetness.

● Il Ruggero '14	♟♟ 5
● Serrapetrona Lacus '14	♟♟ 5
● Serrapetrona Torcular '14	♟♟ 2*
● Zio Sergio '14	♟♟ 5
● Cercis '14	♟ 3
○ Cercis '13	♟♟ 3
● Il Ruggero '13	♟♟ 5
● Serrapetrona Torcular '13	♟♟ 2*

Il Pollenza

c.da Casone, 4
62029 Tolentino [MC]
Tel. +39 0733961989
www.ilpollenza.it

CELLAR SALES
PRE-BOOKED VISITS
ANNUAL PRODUCTION 300,000 bottles
HECTARES UNDER VINE 80.00
SUSTAINABLE WINERY

Having stepped down from running the oil company he established, Conte Brachetti Peretti now spends much of his time at his wine estate between Pollenza and Tolentino. The sumptuously restored villas, one of which is used as the cellar, the high professional standard of the technical team, and the atmosphere of order and beauty are inevitably reminiscent of a Bordeaux château. This is reflected in the use of the land too. Recently, ribona and Montepulciano have found a niche among the dominant international varieties. The Cosmino 2013, a Cabernet, shows green and balsamic aromas and red berries and spice which livens up the flavour. The magnificent Pius IX Mastai 2014 is a Sauvignon Passito with peaches, basil and chamomile creating subtle, mouthwatering, very lingering flavour.

● Cosmino '13	♟♟ 5
○ Pius IX Mastai '14	♟♟ 6
○ Colli Maceratesi Ribona Angera '15	♟♟ 3
○ Brianello '15	♟ 3
● Porpora '13	♟ 3
● Il Pollenza '12	♟♟♟ 8
● Il Pollenza '11	♟♟♟ 7
● Il Pollenza '10	♟♟♟ 7
● Il Pollenza '09	♟♟♟ 7
● Il Pollenza '07	♟♟♟ 7
● Cosmino '12	♟♟ 5
● Cosmino '11	♟♟ 5
● Cosmino '09	♟♟ 5
○ Pius IX '13	♟♟ 6
○ Pius IX '10	♟♟ 6

Alberto Quacquarini

VIA COLLI, 1
62020 SERRAPETRONA [MC]
TEL. +39 0733908180
www.quacquarini.it

CELLAR SALES
ANNUAL PRODUCTION 140,000 bottles
HECTARES UNDER VINE 25.00

Alberto Quacquarini is considered the father of Vernaccia di Serrapetrona, a special red sparkling wine obtained from vernaccia grapes and a complex method of second fermentation, partly activated by dried grape must. In 1958, he began to replicate the ancient rural practice of hanging the grapes in a drying room to obtain a must rich in sugars and aromas. Today, Mauro and Luca Quacquarini continue his work, strenuously defending tradition while attentive to modern winemaking practices. The spacious renovated cellar accommodates small wood and steel vats for the still reds, as well as the drying room and pressurized tanks. Serrapetrona 2014, the winery's youngest wine, offers a particularly vibrant expression of the grape's peppery aromas on a light, flavoursome and moreish palate. The Petronio, 100% dried vernaccia grapes, displays clear hints of raisins, black pepper and bottled black cherries. The two Vernaccias are well-made, and we especially liked the sweet version.

● Serrapetrona '14	♟♟	2*
● Colli della Serra '12	♟♟	2*
● Petronio '10	♟♟	5
● Vernaccia di Serrapetrona Dolce	♟♟	2
● Vernaccia di Serrapetrona Secco	♟♟	3
○ Verdicchio di Matelica '15	♟	2
● Petronio '02	♟♟	5
● Petronio '01	♟♟	5
● Serrapetrona '10	♟♟	2*
● Serrapetrona '08	♟♟	2

Sabbionare

VIA SABBIONARE, 10
60036 MONTECAROTTO [AN]
TEL. +39 0731889004
www.sabbionare.it

CELLAR SALES
PRE-BOOKED VISITS
ANNUAL PRODUCTION 35,000 bottles
HECTARES UNDER VINE 15.00

Contrada Sabbionare owes its name to the signifcant presence of sand in the soil. In the mid-1990s, Donatella Paoloni and her husband Sauro Paolucci decided to take their amateur wine business to the next level, and built a cellar near the vineyard. With the supervision of real Jesi grape experts, like agronomist Pierluigi Donna and winemaker Sergio Paolucci, they have increased production by managing other vineyards, almost all located at Montecarotto. Their Verdicchios are always well-defined, flavoursome and tangy. The vintage wines aged in stainless steel are good now but also ageable. The Sabbionare 2015 is up there with the best: a well-focused blend of varietal tones, like almonds and acacia flowers, and fresh citrusy aromas with a hint of white peaches. The palate is taut, well-sustained and delicately salty. A masterful Tre Bicchieri. The second wine, El Filetto 2015, is reliable as ever, supple, fragrant and nicely typed.

○ Verdicchio dei Castelli di Jesi Cl. Sup. Sabbionare '15	♟♟♟	2*
○ Verdicchio dei Castelli di Jesi Cl. El Filetto '15	♟♟	1*
○ Verdicchio dei Castelli di Jesi Cl. I Pratelli '11	♟♟	1*
○ Verdicchio dei Castelli di Jesi Cl. I Pratelli '10	♟♟	1*
○ Verdicchio dei Castelli di Jesi Cl. Sup. Sabbionare '13	♟♟	2*
○ Verdicchio dei Castelli di Jesi Cl. Sup. Sabbionare '12	♟♟	2*
○ Verdicchio dei Castelli di Jesi Cl. Sup. Sabbionare '10	♟♟	2*
○ Verdicchio dei Castelli di Jesi Cl. Sup. Sabbionare '09	♟♟	2*

Saladini Pilastri

VIA SALADINI, 5
63078 SPINETOLI [AP]
TEL. +39 0736899534
www.saladinipilastri.it

CELLAR SALES
PRE-BOOKED VISITS
ANNUAL PRODUCTION 1,000,000 bottles
HECTARES UNDER VINE 150.00
VITICULTURE METHOD Certified Organic
SUSTAINABLE WINERY

The winery was established back in 1986
but the Saladini Pilastri estate has a history
of several centuries. The family's vast
properties cover a wide area between the
municipalities of Spinetoli and
Monteprandone. For several years, the
estate has been organically farmed, thanks
also to its excellent aspect and the dry local
climate. The cellarwork supports the
generous features of Montepulciano and
the character of sangiovese, creating
considerably fruity wines with compact
structure that release their energy slowly.
The vinification methods are modern and
the wines are aged in woods of different
sizes, with smaller sizes used for the more
ambitious reds. The Montetinello 2014 has
red berry and charred oak aromas and a
lively, nicely textured palate. Vigna
Monteprandone 2014 has morello cherries
and damsons on the nose with a close-knit,
tannic palate, worth the wait. Among the
whites we liked the floral, nicely vigorous
Passerina 2015.

San Giovanni

C.DA CIAFONE, 41
63035 OFFIDA [AP]
TEL. +39 0736889032
www.vinisangiovanni.it

PRE-BOOKED VISITS
ANNUAL PRODUCTION 180,000 bottles
HECTARES UNDER VINE 35.00
VITICULTURE METHOD Certified Organic

San Giovanni, established by the Di
Lorenzo family in 1990, has undergone
extensive renovation in recent years with
profound changes to the property and
cellar, without involving the vineyards in
Contrada Ciafone, historically and
universally acknowledged as one of
Piceno's best growing districts. The whole
estate has been organically farmed for
several years and offers a range based on
traditional cultivars. The wines are openly
modern in style, especially the Gyo line.
Kiara's star is shining again in 2015: a
blend of herbs and citrus fruit create a
polished nose while the palate is taut,
captivating and lively. Among the best
wines tasted this year. The wines in the
Gyo line all stand out for fruity aromas and
very attractive flavour, on a supple but
nicely organized palate. Zeii 2012 is an
impressive red with black cherry and
coffee aromas and a fruity palate with
close-knit tannins.

● Rosso Piceno Sup. Montetinello '14	♥♥	3
● Rosso Piceno Sup. V. Monteprandone '14	♥♥	5
○ Falerio Palazzi '15	♥	3
○ Offida Passerina '15	♥	3
○ Offida Pecorino '15	♥	3
● Pregio del Conte '14	♥	5
● Rosso Piceno '15	♥	3
● Rosso Piceno Sup. V. Monteprandone '00	♥♥♥	3
○ Offida Pecorino '14	♀♀	3
○ Offida Pecorino '10	♀♀	2*
● Pregio del Conte Rosso '10	♀♀	4
● Rosso Piceno Sup. Montetinello '13	♀♀	3
● Rosso Piceno Sup. V. Monteprandone '13	♀♀	5
● Rosso Piceno Sup. V. Monteprandone '10	♀♀	4
● Rosso Piceno Sup. V. Montetinello '10	♀♀	2*
● Rosso Piceno V. Piediprato '11	♀♀	3

○ Offida Pecorino Kiara '15	♥♥	3*
○ Falerio Pecorino Gyo '15	♥♥	2*
● Offida Rosso Zeii '12	♥♥	3
○ Passerina Gyo '14	♥♥	2*
● Rosso Piceno Sup. Gyo '14	♥♥	2*
○ Marta '15	♥	2
○ Marta Passerina Brut	♥	3
○ Offida Pecorino Zagros '13	♥	4
○ Falerio Pecorino Gyo '14	♀♀	2*
○ Offida Pecorino Kiara '13	♀♀	3
○ Offida Pecorino Kiara '12	♀♀	3
○ Offida Pecorino Kiara '11	♀♀	3
○ Offida Pecorino Kiara '10	♀♀	2*
● Rosso Piceno Sup. Leo Guelfus '11	♀♀	3
● Rosso Piceno Sup. Leo Guelfus '07	♀♀	2*
○ Zagros '11	♀♀	3

MARCHE

Poderi San Lazzaro

FRAZ. BORGO MIRIAM
C.DA SAN LAZZARO, 88
63073 OFFIDA [AP]
TEL. +39 0736889189
www.poderisanlazzaro.it

CELLAR SALES
PRE-BOOKED VISITS
ANNUAL PRODUCTION 50,000 bottles
HECTARES UNDER VINE 7.50
VITICULTURE METHOD Certified Organic

The concept of artisan production and its blurred boundaries can easily be misappropriated when it comes to wine production. But when we talk about Paolo Capriotti's work, rest assured that we are using it in the most authentic sense. He supervises everything personally, with plenty of help from his family in the vineyards. In the cellar he swaps ideas with Marco Casolanetti to create wines with plenty of personality, a little rustic in youth but later revealing the generous Piceno weave. The reds are on top form. Podere 72 2013 reveals appealing aromas of strawberries, cherries and more complex charred oak, and lovely fruity texture on a palate with perceptible but not harsh tannins. The Bordò 2012 aged in tonneaux is naturally expressive with a plush, mouthfilling texture and confident, spicy development. The Polesio 2015 is a floral Sangiovese with refreshing flavour. The Pistillo 2015 is vegetal and flavoursome but also a little static.

● Bordò '12	♟♟	7
● Piceno Sup. Podere 72 '13	♟♟	2*
● Polesio '15	♟♟	2*
○ Offida Passerina Passina '15	♟	2
○ Offida Pecorino Pistillo '15	♟	2
● Offida Rosso Grifola '11	♟♟♟	4*
● Bordò '11	♟♟	7
● Grifola '10	♟♟	4
● Offida Rosso Grifola '12	♟♟	4
● Piceno Sup. Podere 72 '12	♟♟	2*
● Piceno Sup. Podere 72 '11	♟♟	2*
● Polesio '14	♟♟	2*
● Polesio '13	♟♟	2*
● Polesio '11	♟♟	2*
● Rosso Piceno Sup. Podere 72 '10	♟♟	2*
● Rosso Piceno Sup. Podere 72 '09	♟♟	2*

San Savino - Poderi Capecci

LOC. SAN SAVINO
VIA SANTA MARIA IN CARRO, 13
63065 RIPATRANSONE [AP]
TEL. +39 073590107
www.sansavino.com

CELLAR SALES
PRE-BOOKED VISITS
ANNUAL PRODUCTION 120,000 bottles
HECTARES UNDER VINE 22.00
VITICULTURE METHOD Certified Organic

Simone Capecci is a striking example of the vigneron who fuses the experience of generations of winemakers and the modern traits of someone who can take the best from tradition using it to offer a new interpretation in a contemporary style. The grapes from the vineyards at Acquaviva and the cool slopes of Santa Maria in Carro are processed with different methods in the cellar: the pecorino and passerina in a reductive environment using cold maceration and stainless steel vats; the superior reds rely on patient fermentation and small wood. Simone presented us with three excellent wines. Ciprea 2015 has aromas of herbs, aniseed, and white peaches in a delicately salty palate, invigorating and easy to drink. Fedus 2014, an unusual Sangiovese, is full-bodied with a vigorous, rounded palate and layered aromas with plenty of fruity sensations. Quinta Regio 2012 is styled on aromas of ripe morello cherries and sweet oak, with luxurious, concentrated, healthy fruit on the palate.

○ Offida Pecorino Ciprea '15	♟♟	3*
● Offida Rosso Quinta Regio '12	♟♟	5
● Fedus '14	♟♟	4
● Rosso Piceno Sup. Picus '14	♟♟	2*
○ Tufilla '15	♟	2
● Fedus Sangiovese '06	♟♟♟	4
○ Offida Pecorino Ciprea '10	♟♟♟	3*
○ Offida Pecorino Ciprea '09	♟♟♟	3*
○ Offida Pecorino Ciprea '08	♟♟♟	3*
● Quinta Regio '01	♟♟♟	5
● Quinta Regio '00	♟♟♟	5
○ Offida Pecorino Ciprea '14	♟♟	3*
● Quinta Regio '10	♟♟	5
● Quinta Regio '08	♟♟	5
● Rosso Piceno Sup. Picus '13	♟♟	2*

Santa Barbara

B.GO MAZZINI, 35
60010 BARBARA [AN]
TEL. +39 0719674249
www.vinisantabarbara.it

CELLAR SALES
PRE-BOOKED VISITS
ANNUAL PRODUCTION 650,000 bottles
HECTARES UNDER VINE 40.00

Stefano Antonucci, aka Mossi, is a larger-than-life character who often makes the headlines with his Santa Barbara estate. One of his main, but lesser known merits is that he has developed a tight-knit team that includes Pierluigi Lorenzetti and young Daniele and Roberto Rotatori, stalwarts of his technical production department. New ideas, an up-to-date style and close collaboration are the secret of the cellar's successful wines of appealing flavour and clean aromas. The best are unexpectedly ageworthy, especially the Verdicchios and Le Vaglie is one of the year's best with a bright, refreshing palate and a very tangy finish. Along the same lines but with a little less depth is the Pignocco 2015. The Superiore Stefano Antonucci 2014 has tropical fruit aromas, candied citrus and a smooth palate. The Mossone 2013 is a really well-typed Merlot with surprising texture, an array of aromas, sweet tannins and a lingering finish.

● Mossone '13	▼▼ 8
○ Verdicchio dei Castelli di Jesi Cl. Le Vaglie '15	▼▼ 3*
○ Animale Celeste '15	▼▼ 3
● Mossi Passito '14	▼▼ 5
● Pathos '14	▼▼ 6
○ Stefano Antonucci Brut M. Cl.	▼▼ 5
● Stefano Antonucci Rosso '14	▼▼ 4
○ Verdicchio dei Castelli di Jesi Back to Basic '14	▼▼ 5
○ Verdicchio dei Castelli di Jesi Cl. Pignocco '15	▼▼ 2*
○ Verdicchio dei Castelli di Jesi Cl. Sup. Stefano Antonucci '14	▼▼ 4
● Rosso Piceno Il Maschio da Monte '14	▼ 5
○ Verdicchio dei Castelli di Jesi Stefano Antonucci '15	▼ 2

Sartarelli

VIA COSTE DEL MOLINO, 24
60030 POGGIO SAN MARCELLO [AN]
TEL. +39 073189732
www.sartarelli.it

CELLAR SALES
PRE-BOOKED VISITS
ANNUAL PRODUCTION 280,000 bottles
HECTARES UNDER VINE 55.00

Even the most hardened verdicchio vignerons have a few rows of other varieties in their vineyard. But not Sartarelli. Total devotion to the Jesi grape has always reigned supreme. Patrizio Chiacchierini and Donatella Sartarelli own some of the loveliest vineyards on the left bank of the Esino, and use the grapes to make some distinctly classic wines. The spacious cellar overlooks a steep, scenic carpet of vines in one of the region's loveliest landscapes. Inside, only stainless steel vats for ageing all the wines. The Classico 2015 is what it says it is on the label: dried fruit and ripe apples on the nose and echoed on a palate whose greatest virtue is a generous flavour. The Balciana 2014 made from late-harvested grapes has yellow peaches, honey and thyme on the nose and a creamy, rather glycerine palate with a very vibrant, slightly sugary finish. The Tralivio 2014 is less focused than usual: blame the terrible year for its loss of complexity.

○ Verdicchio dei Castelli di Jesi Cl. '15	▼▼ 2*
○ Verdicchio dei Castelli di Jesi Cl. Sup. Balciana '14	▼▼ 5
○ Brut	▼ 3
○ Verdicchio dei Castelli di Jesi Cl. Sup. Tralivio '14	▼ 3
○ Verdicchio dei Castelli di Jesi Passito '14	▼ 5
○ Verdicchio dei Castelli di Jesi Cl. Sup. Balciana '09	▼▼▼ 5
○ Verdicchio dei Castelli di Jesi Cl. Sup. Balciana '04	▼▼▼ 5
○ Verdicchio dei Castelli di Jesi Cl. Sup. Contrada Balciana '98	▼▼▼ 5
○ Verdicchio dei Castelli di Jesi Cl. Sup. Contrada Balciana '97	▼▼▼ 5

Sparapani - Frati Bianchi

VIA BARCHIO, 12
60034 CUPRAMONTANA [AN]
TEL. +39 0731781216
www.fratibianchi.it

CELLAR SALES
PRE-BOOKED VISITS
RESTAURANT SERVICE
ANNUAL PRODUCTION 40,000 bottles
HECTARES UNDER VINE 14.00

Judging by the results, the move from the old, cramped building to the new, modern cellar has clearly allowed the Sparapani brothers to unleash their talent. Although young, they have been skilled artisans for many years, raised among the rows by their father Settimio. They have built up vast expertise and specialized in Verdicchio, and more than ever their wines express in full the concept of sturdy structure and tangy character guaranteed by the Cupramontana terroir. Only stainless steel is used in the cellar except for the Riserva Donna Cloe, aged for 16 months in medium-sized wood. The Priore 2014 easily overcomes the problems of the harvest and releases elegant floral and almond aromas, their appeal intensified by minerally and salty hints. The palate sweeps along to a crackling finish. Donna Cloe Riserva 2012 is complex and vigorous, while the Salerna 2015 is an excellent standard-label Verdicchio: citrus and delicately salty with a refreshing flavour.

○ Verdicchio dei Castelli di Jesi Cl. Sup. Il Priore '14	♥♥♥ 2*
○ Castelli di Jesi Verdicchio Cl. Donna Cloe Ris. '12	♥♥ 5
○ Verdicchio dei Castelli di Jesi Cl. Salerna '15	♥♥ 2*
○ Verdicchio dei Castelli di Jesi Cl. Sup. Il Priore '13	♀♀♀ 2*
○ Verdicchio dei Castelli di Jesi Cl. Sup. Il Priore '12	♀♀♀ 2*
○ Verdicchio dei Castelli di Jesi Cl. Sup. Il Priore '06	♀♀♀ 2*

Tenuta Spinelli

VIA LAGO, 2
63032 CASTIGNANO [AP]
TEL. +39 0736821489
www.tenutaspinelli.it

CELLAR SALES
PRE-BOOKED VISITS
ACCOMMODATION
ANNUAL PRODUCTION 30,000 bottles
HECTARES UNDER VINE 7.00

One of the most appealing aspects of winegrowing is the passion shown by those involved. Despite the effort required to run everything personally, Simone Spinelli is ever more enamoured of his work. This passion has led him to plant vineyards on higher ground, gleaning plots of useful land from the rocks of Mount Ascensione. The excellent results quickly brought new challenges: ongoing projects regarding pinot nero and perfecting his pecorino-based Metodo Classico. The cellar is small but is equipped to be very efficient. The umpteenth Tre Bicchieri for talented Simone arrives with Artemisia 2015, which sidesteps the pitfalls of the very hot year presenting multifaceted, crystal clear aromas. The palate makes an authoritative entry, curves with hints of summer fruit and leaps to the finish with vibrant structure. Eden 2015 is a monovarietal Passerina with a captivating nose and a palate that combines fresh, citrus qualities with sugary sensuality, and enjoyably lingering aromas.

○ Offida Pecorino Artemisia '15	♥♥♥ 2*
○ Eden '15	♥♥ 2*
○ Offida Pecorino Artemisia '14	♀♀♀ 2*
○ Offida Pecorino Artemisia '13	♀♀♀ 2*
○ Offida Pecorino Artemisia '12	♀♀♀ 2*
○ Eden '13	♀♀ 2*
○ Eden '11	♀♀ 2*
○ Méroe Pecorino M. Cl. '09	♀♀ 3
○ Offida Pecorino Artemisia '11	♀♀ 2*

Tenuta di Tavignano

loc. Tavignano
62011 Cingoli [MC]
Tel. +39 0733617303
www.tenutaditavignano.it

CELLAR SALES
PRE-BOOKED VISITS
ANNUAL PRODUCTION 100,000 bottles
HECTARES UNDER VINE 30.00
SUSTAINABLE WINERY

Ondine de la Feld is the niece of Stefano Aymerich, founder of this lovely estate on the ridge between the Musone and Esino valleys. She joined the winery a few years ago, bringing a breath of fresh air with graphic restyling, supporting the creation of new products like Pestifero, a sparkling wine of second bottle fermentation without dégorgement, and increasing visibility and presence on developed markets. Her job is made easier by the rising fame of the winery's Verdicchios, ideal examples of strength, character and tangy flavour achieved without interfering with the variety. Tre Bicchieri and the White of the Year award for Misco Superiore 2015: very stylish and extremely varietal aromas, deep and consistent, precede a flawless palate. The Misco Riserva 2014 is wonderful, with its aromas of chard, almonds and orange zest blending on a firmly structured palate with a harmonious, sensual finish. Vigna Verde 2015 has lemony aromas and a harmonious, pleasing and delicious mouth.

○ Verdicchio dei Castelli di Jesi Cl. Sup. Misco '15	♟♟♟ 3*
○ Castelli di Jesi Verdicchio Cl. Misco Ris. '14	♟♟ 4
● Rosso Piceno Cervidoni '14	♟♟ 2*
○ Verdicchio dei Castelli di Jesi Cl. Sup. Villa Torre '15	♟♟ 2*
○ Verdicchio dei Castelli di Jesi Cl. V. Verde '15	♟♟ 2*
⊙ Buonasera Signorina '15	♟ 3
○ Il Pestifero Pas Dosé '15	♟ 2
○ Passerina '15	♟ 2
○ Verdicchio dei Castelli di Jesi Cl. Sup. Misco '14	♟♟♟ 3*
○ Verdicchio dei Castelli di Jesi Cl. Sup. Misco '13	♟♟♟ 3*

Terre Cortesi Moncaro

via Pianole, 7a
63036 Montecarotto [AN]
Tel. +39 073189245
www.moncaro.com

CELLAR SALES
PRE-BOOKED VISITS
RESTAURANT SERVICE
ANNUAL PRODUCTION 7,500,000 bottles
HECTARES UNDER VINE 1200.00

Despite being a huge cooperative for a region dominated by small producers, Moncaro has never eschewed the desire to offer quality wines. The massive number of vineyards provides plenty of opportunity to select the best grapes, almost always from native local varieties, which are fermented separately in the three cellars at Castelli di Jesi, Conero, and Acquaviva Picena. The best harvests translate into wines offering a modern interpretation of a consolidated style based on vibrant fruity aromas and appealing drinkable flavour. A kidney punch from the Moncaro white winemaking spirit, placing two emblematic wines from their respective terroirs at the top of the table. Vigna Novali 2013 has an iridescent nose with balsamic sensations and hints of aniseed and almonds echoed on a beautifully mouthfilling, relaxed, smooth palate. Ofithe 2015 displays irresistibly fluid hints of herbs and lemon zest. The prestigious Fondiglie 2015 has delicious flavour.

○ Castelli di Jesi Verdicchio Cl. V. Novali Ris. '13	♟♟ 3*
○ Offida Pecorino Ofithe '15	♟♟ 3*
● Conero Vign. del Parco Ris. '11	♟♟ 4
● Piceno Sup. Roccaviva '13	♟♟ 2*
● Rosso Conero Le Silve '15	♟♟ 3
○ Verdicchio dei Castelli di Jesi Cl. Sup. Fondiglie '15	♟♟ 3
● Conero Cimerio Ris. '13	♟ 3
● Conero Montescuro Ris. '13	♟ 3
○ Verdicchio dei Castelli di Jesi Cl. Le Vele '15	♟ 3
○ Verdicchio dei Castelli di Jesi Cl. Sup. Verde Ca' Ruptae '15	♟ 3
○ Castelli di Jesi Verdicchio Cl. V. Novali Ris. '10	♟♟♟ 3*
● Rosso Piceno Sup. Roccaviva '12	♟♟♟ 2*

★Umani Ronchi

VIA ADRIATICA, 12
60027 OSIMO [AN]
TEL. +39 0717108019
www.umanironchi.com

CELLAR SALES
PRE-BOOKED VISITS
ANNUAL PRODUCTION 3,000,000 bottles
HECTARES UNDER VINE 230.00
VITICULTURE METHOD Certified Organic
SUSTAINABLE WINERY

The numbers may place it among the largest Marche wineries in terms of acreage and bottles produced, but Umani Ronchi is still a family business at heart. For several years Michele Bernetti has run the estate set up by his father Massimo and uncle Stefano, developing new projects that aim for quality. These include conversion to organic farming for most of the vineyards, found around Castelli di Jesi, Conero, and in Abruzzo. Casal di Serra is the estate's first certified organic wine. The Campo San Giorgio Riserva 2011 shows what is achievable in elegance and minerality for Montepulciano del Conero. A marvel of polished expressiveness. Its younger brother, Cùmaro 2012 is bright and fruity, with firm acidity interwoven with smooth tannins. Plenio 2013 is graceful and dynamic, with generous varietal features and palate powered by extraordinary energy. Maximo 2013 is a botrytized Sauvignon: alluring, plush, and very lingering.

● Conero Campo San Giorgio Ris. '11	🍷🍷🍷	7
● Conero Cùmaro Ris. '12	🍷🍷	4
○ Maximo '13	🍷🍷	4
○ Verdicchio dei Castelli di Jesi Cl. Sup. V.V. '14	🍷🍷	4
○ Castelli di Jesi Verdicchio Cl. Ris. Plenio '13	🍷🍷	4
○ La Hoz M. Cl. Brut Nature '10	🍷🍷	5
● Montepulciano d'Abruzzo Jorio '14	🍷🍷	3
● Pelago '12	🍷🍷	5
● Rosso Conero San Lorenzo '14	🍷🍷	3
● Rosso Conero Serrano '15	🍷🍷	2*
○ Vellodoro '15	🍷🍷	2*
○ Verdicchio dei Castelli di Jesi Cl. Sup. Casal di Serra '15	🍷🍷	3
○ Verdicchio dei Castelli di Jesi Cl. Villa Bianchi '15	🍷🍷	2*

Vallerosa Bonci

VIA TORRE, 15
60034 CUPRAMONTANA [AN]
TEL. +39 0731789129
www.vallerosa-bonci.com

CELLAR SALES
PRE-BOOKED VISITS
ANNUAL PRODUCTION 250,000 bottles
HECTARES UNDER VINE 26.00

Peppe Boni is a walking Verdicchio encyclopedia. He knows practically everything about it, having accumulated personal experience of countless harvests, hosted in his own vineyards the most complete clonal research ever undertaken (by the University of Milan), and experimented with all types of vinification. His various plots of land at different altitudes and aspects, but all in the Cupramontana area, provide grapes of varying character and ripeness, to create very distinct wines. The best choice is still San Michele, obtained from the south-facing cru of the same name. The cool 2014 season lightened up the alcohol and structure without affecting the usual tanginess and mouthwatering flavour. Manciano 2015 is also definitely sound, with clear-cut citrus aromas and a fluid palate with streaks of saltiness. The Brut is as reliable as ever, a beautifully framed Charmat with hints of almonds and crusty bread and approachable features.

○ Verdicchio dei Castelli di Jesi Cl. Manciano '15	🍷🍷	2*
○ Verdicchio dei Castelli di Jesi Cl. Sup. S. Michele '14	🍷🍷	3
○ Verdicchio dei Castelli di Jesi Brut	🍷	2
○ Verdicchio dei Castelli di Jesi Cl. Viatorre '15	🍷	2
○ Verdicchio dei Castelli di Jesi Cl. Pietrone Ris. '04	🍷🍷🍷	3
○ Verdicchio dei Castelli di Jesi Cl. Sup. S. Michele '10	🍷🍷🍷	3*
○ Verdicchio dei Castelli di Jesi Cl. Sup. S. Michele '06	🍷🍷🍷	3
○ Verdicchio dei Castelli di Jesi Cl. Sup. S. Michele '00	🍷🍷🍷	3*

★Velenosi

Loc. Monticelli
via dei Biancospini, 11
63100 Ascoli Piceno
Tel. +39 0736341218
www.velenosivini.com

CELLAR SALES
PRE-BOOKED VISITS
ANNUAL PRODUCTION 2,500,000 bottles
HECTARES UNDER VINE 192.00

All trains, even the smallest, need an engine. In the regional overview, few wineries have been able to place Marche-made wines in points-of-sale worldwide. Velenosi is one of those few, playing an important role and growing its presence on the global market every year. Piceno wines are the cornerstone of the wide range, but the best Marche designations are represented thanks to trusted growers or well-established partnerships. From sparklers to whites from local grapes and powerful reds, this enviably reliable winery has countless strong suits. Rêve 2014 has very vibrant aromas, with clearly defined hints of grapefruit zest perked up by a fresh array of aromatic herbs. The sinuous palate has a full, lingering flavour. Roggio del Filare 2013 displays fruity aromas with a subtle vegetal hint, more prominent on the soft palate, and juicy texture.

Roberto Venturi

via Case Nuove, 1a
60010 Castelleone di Suasa [AN]
Tel. +39 3381855566
www.viniventuri.it

CELLAR SALES
PRE-BOOKED VISITS
ANNUAL PRODUCTION 60,000 bottles
HECTARES UNDER VINE 8.00

Roberto Venturi was not intimidated by the worldwide recession and paid no heed to traditional Marche caution. Pursuing his aims, he has fulfilled his dream of building a new cellar, which has no manias of grandeur, fitting seamlessly into his artisan estate, although the architecture and rooms are modern. The roof terrace enjoys a splendid view, encompassing all the vineyards except the Montecarotto site. Vinification is chiefly in stainless steel. Qudì 2014 has wild herbs and almonds on the nose and robust structure, as well as firm, tangy texture. Younger brother San Martino 2015 is also very sound, with hints of aniseed and a lovely succulent palate. Desiderio 2015, a monovarietal Moscato, is an explosion of citrus and spicy aromas, marking the light and really flavoursome palate. Balsamino 2015, from aleatico, is a simple, no-frills wine with lively aromas.

○ Offida Pecorino Rêve '14	♆♆♆ 5
● Rosso Piceno Sup. Roggio del Filare '13	♆♆ 7
○ Falerio Pecorino Villa Angela '15	♆♆ 4
● Lacrima di Morro d'Alba Querciantica '15	♆♆ 4
○ Offida Pecorino Villa Angela '15	♆♆ 4
○ Passerina Brut	♆♆ 3
○ Passerina Villa Angela '15	♆♆ 4
● Rosso Piceno Sup. Brecciarolo '14	♆♆ 4
● Rosso Piceno Sup. Brecciarolo Gold '14	♆♆ 5
○ Verdicchio dei Castelli di Jesi Cl. Querciantica '15	♆♆ 4
○ Chardonnay Villa Angela '15	♆ 4
● Offida Rosso Ludi '13	♆ 7
● Rosso Piceno Sup. Roggio del Filare '12	♆♆♆ 7
● Rosso Piceno Sup. Roggio del Filare '11	♆♆♆ 7
● Rosso Piceno Sup. Roggio del Filare '10	♆♆♆ 5

○ Desiderio '15	♆♆ 2*
○ Verdicchio dei Castelli di Jesi Cl. Sup. Qudì '14	♆♆ 2*
○ Verdicchio dei Castelli di Jesi San Martino '15	♆♆ 2*
● Balsamino '15	♆ 2
○ Verdicchio dei Castelli di Jesi Cl. Sup. Qudì '13	♆♆♆ 2*
○ Desiderio '14	♆♆ 2*
○ Desiderio '13	♆♆ 2*
○ Verdicchio dei Castelli di Jesi Cl. Sup. Qudì '12	♆♆ 2*

Vicari

VIA POZZO BUONO, 3
60030 MORRO D'ALBA [AN]
TEL. +39 073163164
www.vicarivini.it

CELLAR SALES
PRE-BOOKED VISITS
ANNUAL PRODUCTION 110,000 bottles
HECTARES UNDER VINE 22.00

Nazzareno Vicari is a Lacrima legend and his work in this designation is now justly promoted by his children. They form a close-knit team: young Valentina is busy with trade events, presentations and the point-of-sale, while Vico has carved himself the role of untiring driving force in both vineyards and cellar. Their Lacrimas benefit from various stages of maturation and different production methods, including carbonic maceration or raisining, which produce vibrantly fruity wines with lively personality. Essenza 2015 reveals extraordinarily vibrant aromas with hints of sour cherries and cloves. The creamy texture of the palate makes it less approachable but charms the senses. The Insolito 2014 is a typical Morro d'Alba Verdicchio: powerful, efficient and confident in releasing its exuberant fruity energy. Amaranto is a viscous, sugary Passito: an admirable concentration of the most floral and fruity Lacrima character.

● Lacrima di Morro d'Alba Dasempre del Pozzo Buono '15	♔♔ 2*
● Lacrima di Morro d'Alba Essenza del Pozzo Buono '15	♔♔ 3
● Lacrima di Morro d'Alba Passito Amaranto del Pozzo Buono '12	♔♔ 4
○ Verdicchio dei Castelli di Jesi Cl. del Pozzo Buono '15	♔♔ 2*
○ Verdicchio dei Castelli di Jesi Cl. Sup. Insolito del Pozzo Buono '14	♔♔ 3
● Lacrima di Morro d'Alba Sup. del Pozzo Buono '14	♔ 3
● Lacrima di Morro d'Alba Dasempre del Pozzo Buono '13	♕♕ 2*
● Lacrima di Morro d'Alba Sup. del Pozzo Buono '13	♕♕ 3

Vignamato

VIA BATTINEBBIA, 4
60038 SAN PAOLO DI JESI [AN]
TEL. +39 0731779197
www.vignamato.com

CELLAR SALES
PRE-BOOKED VISITS
ANNUAL PRODUCTION 100,000 bottles
HECTARES UNDER VINE 27.00

Andrea Ceci grew up among the verdicchio vineyards, and it was no sacrifice for him to take over the estate developed by his father Maurizio and mother Serenella. His confident personality, still a tad wet behind the ears, is perfectly balanced by the experience and placid nature of popular winemaker Pierluigi Lorenzetti. Together they have worked to add texture, elegance and tangy flavour to the estate's style, typifided over the years by the sturdy, flavoursome Verdicchios. The generously fruity features of Versiano 2015 meet an edgy surge of acidity on the palate, creating tangy flavour and lengthening the pace and assertive finish. The Valle della Lame 2015, a very supple and fluid Verdicchio, has white peach aromas with subtle streaks of aniseed. Our praise goes to the Antares 2011, one of the best dried grape wines in the region: mouthfilling and rich in fruit with tinned peaches, toasted almonds and melon. The palate is creamy but fresh and perky.

○ Verdicchio dei Castelli di Jesi Cl. Sup. Versiano '15	♔♔ 3*
○ Verdicchio dei Castelli di Jesi Passito Antares '11	♔♔ 4
● Campalliano '13	♔♔ 3
○ Castelli di Jesi Verdicchio Cl. Ambrosia Ris. '12	♔♔ 3
○ Verdicchio dei Castelli di Jesi Cl. Sup. Eos '15	♔♔ 2*
○ Verdicchio dei Castelli di Jesi Cl. Valle delle Lame '15	♔♔ 2*
○ Versus '15	♔ 2
○ Verdicchio dei Castelli di Jesi Cl. Sup. Eos '14	♕♕ 2*
○ Verdicchio dei Castelli di Jesi Cl. Valle delle Lame '14	♕♕ 2*

Maria Letizia Allevi

via P. C. Orazi, 58
63081 Castorano [AP]
Tel. +39 073687646
www.vinimida.it

CELLAR SALES
PRE-BOOKED VISITS
ANNUAL PRODUCTION 8,000 bottles
HECTARES UNDER VINE 3.00
VITICULTURE METHOD Certified Organic

- ○ Offida Pecorino Mida '15 — 🍷🍷 3
- ● Offida Rosso Mida '13 — 🍷🍷 4

Ca' Liptra

via San Michele, 21
60034 Cupramontana [AN]
Tel. +39 3491321442
www.caliptra.it

CELLAR SALES
PRE-BOOKED VISITS
HECTARES UNDER VINE 2.30
VITICULTURE METHOD Certified Organic
SUSTAINABLE WINERY

- ○ Castelli di Jesi Verdicchio Cl. S. M. 21 Ris. '14 — 🍷🍷 4
- ○ Verdicchio dei Castelli di Jesi Cl. Sup. Kypra '15 — 🍷🍷 3

La Calcinara

fraz. Candia
via Calcinara, 102a
60131 Ancona
Tel. +39 3285552643
www.lacalcinara.it

CELLAR SALES
PRE-BOOKED VISITS
ANNUAL PRODUCTION 26,000 bottles
HECTARES UNDER VINE 13.00
SUSTAINABLE WINERY

- ● Conero Terra Calcinara Ris. '13 — 🍷🍷 3
- ⊙ Mun '15 — 🍷🍷 2*
- ● Rosso Conero Il Cacciatore di Sogni '14 — 🍷 2

Cantine di Castignano

c.da San Venanzo, 31
63072 Castignano [AP]
Tel. +39 0736822216
www.cantinedicastignano.com

CELLAR SALES
PRE-BOOKED VISITS
ANNUAL PRODUCTION 450,000 bottles
HECTARES UNDER VINE 527.00
VITICULTURE METHOD Certified Organic

- ○ Gramelot '14 — 🍷🍷 2*
- ● Templaria '14 — 🍷🍷 2*
- ○ Falerio Pecorino Destriero '15 — 🍷 1*

Cavalieri

via Raffaello, 1
62024 Matelica [MC]
Tel. +39 073784859
www.cantinacavalieri.it

PRE-BOOKED VISITS
ANNUAL PRODUCTION 15,000 bottles
HECTARES UNDER VINE 8.24

- ○ Verdicchio di Matelica Gegè '14 — 🍷🍷 3
- ● Sangiovese '13 — 🍷 3
- ○ Verdicchio di Matelica '15 — 🍷 2

Giacomo Centanni

c.da Aso, 159
63062 Montefiore dell'Aso [AP]
Tel. +39 0734938530
www.vinicentanni.it

CELLAR SALES
ACCOMMODATION
ANNUAL PRODUCTION 100,000 bottles
HECTARES UNDER VINE 30.00
VITICULTURE METHOD Certified Organic

- ● Monte Floris '14 — 🍷🍷 2*
- ○ Offida Pecorino '15 — 🍷🍷 2*
- ○ Offida Passerina '15 — 🍷 2

Cantina Cològnola
Tenuta Musone

LOC. COLOGNOLA, 22A BIS
62011 CINGOLI [MC]
TEL. +39 0733616438
www.tenutamusone.it

CELLAR SALES
PRE-BOOKED VISITS
ANNUAL PRODUCTION 150,000 bottles
HECTARES UNDER VINE 25.00

○ Verdicchio dei Castelli di Jesi Cl. Sup. Via Condotto '15	♟♟ 2*
○ Verdicchio dei Castelli di Jesi Cl. Sup. Ghiffa '14	♟ 3

Colpaola

LOC. COLPAOLA
FRAZ. BRACCANO
62024 MATELICA [MC]
TEL. +39 0737768300
www.cantinacolpaola.it

CELLAR SALES
ANNUAL PRODUCTION 18,000 bottles
HECTARES UNDER VINE 9.00
VITICULTURE METHOD Certified Organic

○ Verdicchio di Matelica '15	♟♟ 2*
○ Verdicchio di Matelica '14	♟♟ 2*

Conti degli Azzoni

VIA DON MINZONI, 26
62010 MONTEFANO [MC]
TEL. +39 0733850219
www.degliazzoni.it

CELLAR SALES
PRE-BOOKED VISITS
ACCOMMODATION AND RESTAURANT SERVICE
ANNUAL PRODUCTION 100,000 bottles
HECTARES UNDER VINE 130.00

● Passatempo '13	♟♟ 5
● Rosso Piceno '13	♟♟ 2*
○ Colli Maceratesi Ribona '15	♟ 2

Domodimonti

VIA MENOCCHIA, 195
63010 MONTEFIORE DELL'ASO [AP]
TEL. +39 0734930010
www.domodimonti.com

CELLAR SALES
PRE-BOOKED VISITS
ACCOMMODATION AND RESTAURANT SERVICE
ANNUAL PRODUCTION 200,000 bottles
HECTARES UNDER VINE 40.00

● Il Messia '12	♟♟ 5
○ Offida Pecorino LiCoste '15	♟♟ 3
● Passione e Visione '12	♟ 8

Filodivino

VIA SERRA, 46
60030 SAN MARCELLO [AN]
TEL. +39 0731026139
www.filodivino.it

CELLAR SALES
ACCOMMODATION AND RESTAURANT SERVICE
ANNUAL PRODUCTION 52,000 bottles
HECTARES UNDER VINE 15.50

○ Castelli di Jesi Verdicchio Cl. Dino Ris. '14	♟♟ 4
○ Verdicchio dei Castelli di Jesi Filotto '14	♟♟ 3
● Lacrima di Morro d'Alba Diana '14	♟ 3

Fiorini

VIA GIARDINO CAMPIOLI, 5
61040 BARCHI [PU]
TEL. +39 072197151
www.fioriniwines.it

CELLAR SALES
PRE-BOOKED VISITS
ACCOMMODATION
ANNUAL PRODUCTION 200,000 bottles
HECTARES UNDER VINE 45.00

○ Bianchello del Metauro Sup. Andy '14	♟♟ 2*
○ Bianchello del Metauro Sup. Tenuta Campioli '15	♟♟ 2*
● Colli Pesaresi Rosso Bartis '13	♟♟ 3

Luca Guerrieri

VIA SAN FILIPPO, 24
61030 PIAGGE [PU]
TEL. +39 0721890152
www.aziendaguerrieri.it

CELLAR SALES
PRE-BOOKED VISITS
ACCOMMODATION
ANNUAL PRODUCTION 250,000 bottles
HECTARES UNDER VINE 44.40

● Colli Pesaresi Sangiovese Galileo Ris. '13	🍷🍷	3
○ Guerriero Bianco '14	🍷🍷	2*
○ Lisippo '15	🍷🍷	2*

Esther Hauser

C.DA CORONCINO, 1A
60039 STAFFOLO [AN]
TEL. +39 0731770203
www.estherhauser.it

CELLAR SALES
PRE-BOOKED VISITS
ANNUAL PRODUCTION 6,000 bottles
HECTARES UNDER VINE 1.00

● Il Cupo '13	🍷🍷	5
● Il Ceppo '13	🍷	4

La Valle del Sole

VIA SAN LAZZARO, 46
63035 OFFIDA [AP]
TEL. +39 0736889658
valledelsoleoffida@gmail.com

PRE-BOOKED VISITS
HECTARES UNDER VINE 11.00
VITICULTURE METHOD Certified Organic

○ Offida Pecorino '15	🍷🍷	2*
● Rosso Piceno Sup. '14	🍷🍷	2*
○ Offida Passerina '15	🍷	2

Laila Libenzi

VIA SAN FILIPPO SUL CESANO, 27
61040 MONDAVIO [PU]
TEL. +39 0721979353
www.lailalibenzi.it

CELLAR SALES
PRE-BOOKED VISITS
ANNUAL PRODUCTION 130,000 bottles
HECTARES UNDER VINE 33.00

● Torrile '14	🍷🍷	2*
○ Verdicchio dei Castelli di Jesi Casalta '14	🍷🍷	2*
● Rosso Conero Zizzero '14	🍷	2

Stefano Mancinelli

VIA ROMA, 62
60030 MORRO D'ALBA [AN]
TEL. +39 073163021
www.mancinellivini.it

CELLAR SALES
PRE-BOOKED VISITS
ACCOMMODATION
ANNUAL PRODUCTION 150,000 bottles
HECTARES UNDER VINE 25.00

● Terre dei Goti '11	🍷🍷	5
● Lacrima di Morro d'Alba '14	🍷	2
● Lacrima di Morro d'Alba Sensazioni di Frutto '15	🍷	2

Mancini

FRAZ. MOIE
60030 MAIOLATI SPONTINI [AN]
TEL. +39 0731702975
www.manciniwines.it

CELLAR SALES
PRE-BOOKED VISITS
RESTAURANT SERVICE
ANNUAL PRODUCTION 140,000 bottles
HECTARES UNDER VINE 20.00

○ Verdicchio Castelli di Jesi Cl. S. Lucia '15	🍷🍷	2*
○ Verdicchio Castelli di Jesi Cl. Sup. Villa Talliano '15	🍷🍷	3

Filippo Maraviglia

LOC. PIANNÉ, 593
62024 MATELICA [MC]
TEL. +39 0737786340
www.vinimaraviglia.com

CELLAR SALES
PRE-BOOKED VISITS
ACCOMMODATION
ANNUAL PRODUCTION 30,000 bottles
HECTARES UNDER VINE 27.00

● Colli Maceratesi Rosso Onorio '15	♀♀ 2*
○ Verdicchio di Matelica Alarico '15	♀♀ 2*
○ Verdicchio di Matelica Grappoli d'Oro Ris. '13	♀ 3

Clara Marcelli

VIA FONTE VECCHIA, 8
63030 CASTORANO [AP]
TEL. +39 073687289
www.claramarcelli.it

PRE-BOOKED VISITS
ANNUAL PRODUCTION 40,000 bottles
HECTARES UNDER VINE 14.00
VITICULTURE METHOD Certified Organic

● Ruggine '11	♀♀ 8
● K'un '13	♀♀ 3
○ Offida Pecorino Irata '14	♀ 3

Maurizio Marconi

VIA MELANO, 25
60030 SAN MARCELLO [AN]
TEL. +39 0731267223
www.marconivini.it

CELLAR SALES
PRE-BOOKED VISITS
ANNUAL PRODUCTION 220,000 bottles
HECTARES UNDER VINE 50.50

○ Lilith '14	♀♀ 3
● Rosso Piceno '15	♀♀ 2*
○ Verdicchio dei Castelli di Jesi Cl. Sup. Istinto '15	♀♀ 2*

Enzo Mecella

VIA DANTE, 112
60044 FABRIANO [AN]
TEL. +39 073221680
www.enzomecella.com

CELLAR SALES
PRE-BOOKED VISITS
ANNUAL PRODUCTION 200,000 bottles
HECTARES UNDER VINE 12.00

● Braccano '12	♀♀ 4
○ Verdicchio di Matelica Pagliano '15	♀♀ 2*

Claudio Morelli

V.LE ROMAGNA, 47B
61032 FANO [PU]
TEL. +39 0721823352
www.claudiomorelli.it

CELLAR SALES
PRE-BOOKED VISITS
ANNUAL PRODUCTION 110,000 bottles
HECTARES UNDER VINE 40.00

○ Bianchello del Metauro Borgo Torre '15	♀♀ 2*
○ Bianchello del Metauro S. Cesareo '15	♀♀ 2*
○ Bianchello del Metauro La Vigna delle Terrazze '15	♀ 2

Cantina Offida

VIA DELLA REPUBBLICA , 70
63073 OFFIDA [AP]
TEL. +39 0736880104
www.cantinaoffida.com

CELLAR SALES
PRE-BOOKED VISITS
ANNUAL PRODUCTION 400,000 bottles
HECTARES UNDER VINE 300.00
VITICULTURE METHOD Certified Organic

○ Offida Passerina '15	♀♀ 2*
○ Offida Pecorino '15	♀♀ 2*
● Offida Rosso Serpente Aureo '10	♀ 4

La Pila

VIA MICHELANGELO, 2
63833 MONTEGIORGIO [FM]
TEL. +39 0734277801
www.vinilapila.it

ANNUAL PRODUCTION 12,000 bottles
HECTARES UNDER VINE 4.00

● Cinabrum '15	♥♥ 2*
● Furnace '13	♥♥ 3
○ Refolo '15	♥♥ 2*
○ Emmar '15	♥ 3

Rocca di Castiglioni

VIA CASTIGLIONI, 50
63072 CASTIGNANO [AP]
TEL. +39 0736821876
www.rocca-di-castiglioni.it

CELLAR SALES
PRE-BOOKED VISITS
ACCOMMODATION
ANNUAL PRODUCTION 25,000 bottles
HECTARES UNDER VINE 12.00

○ Offida Pecorino Valeo Si Vales '15	♥♥ 3*
● Rosso Piceno Console Castino '15	♥♥ 2*
○ Offida Passerina Alba Plena '15	♥ 2

San Filippo

LOC. BORGO MIRIAM
C.DA CIAFONE, 17A
63035 OFFIDA [AP]
TEL. +39 0736889828
www.vinisanfilippo.it

CELLAR SALES
PRE-BOOKED VISITS
ANNUAL PRODUCTION 20,000 bottles
HECTARES UNDER VINE 35.00
VITICULTURE METHOD Certified Organic

○ Offida Pecorino '15	♥♥ 2*
● Rosso Piceno Sup. Katharsis '14	♥♥ 2*
● Offida Rosso Lupo del Ciafone '13	♥ 3

Tenuta San Marcello

VIA MELANO, 30
60030 SAN MARCELLO [AN]
TEL. +39 0731831008
www.tenutasanmarcello.net

CELLAR SALES
ACCOMMODATION AND RESTAURANT SERVICE
ANNUAL PRODUCTION 4,000 bottles
HECTARES UNDER VINE 3.50

● Lacrima di Morro d'Alba Bastaro '15	♥♥ 2*
● Lacrima di Morro d'Alba Sup. Melano '15	♥♥ 3
○ Verdicchio dei Castelli di Jesi Cl. Buca della Marcona '15	♥ 2

San Michele a Ripa

C.DA SAN MICHELE, 24
63065 RIPATRANSONE [AP]
TEL. +39 3356833088
www.sanmichelearipa.it

CELLAR SALES
PRE-BOOKED VISITS
ANNUAL PRODUCTION 20,000 bottles
HECTARES UNDER VINE 5.00

○ Offida Pecorino Falchetti '15	♥♥ 3
● Periplo '14	♥♥ 3
○ Offida Passerina Brancuna '15	♥ 2

Fattoria Serra San Martino

VIA SAN MARTINO, 1
60030 SERRA DE' CONTI [AN]
TEL. +39 0731878025
www.serrasanmartino.com

CELLAR SALES
PRE-BOOKED VISITS
ANNUAL PRODUCTION 13,000 bottles
HECTARES UNDER VINE 3.00
VITICULTURE METHOD Certified Organic

● Lysipp '12	♥♥ 5
● Il Paonazzo '13	♥♥ 5
● Roccuccio '13	♥♥ 3
● Costa dei Zoppi '12	♥ 4

La Staffa

VIA CASTELLARETTA, 19
60039 STAFFOLO [AN]
TEL. +39 0731779810
www.vinilastaffa.it

CELLAR SALES
PRE-BOOKED VISITS
ANNUAL PRODUCTION 30,000 bottles
HECTARES UNDER VINE 8.00
VITICULTURE METHOD Certified Organic

○ Verdicchio dei Castelli di Jesi Cl. Sup. La Staffa '15	🍷🍷 3
○ Mai Sentito	🍷 2

Fattoria Le Terrazze

VIA MUSONE, 4
60026 NUMANA [AN]
TEL. +39 0717390352
www.fattorialeterrazze.it

CELLAR SALES
PRE-BOOKED VISITS
ANNUAL PRODUCTION 100,000 bottles
HECTARES UNDER VINE 20.00

⊙ Donna Giulia Brut Rosé M. Cl. '13	🍷🍷 4
● Conero Sassi Neri Ris. '12	🍷 5
● Rosso Conero '14	🍷 2

Fulvia Tombolini

C.DA CAVALLINE, 2
60039 STAFFOLO [AN]
TEL. +39 0731770330
www.fulviatombolini.it

ANNUAL PRODUCTION 160,000 bottles
HECTARES UNDER VINE 28.00

○ Castelli di Jesi Verdicchio Cl. Fulvia Tombolini Ris. '13	🍷🍷 3
○ Verdicchio dei Castelli di Jesi Cl. Sup. Fulvia Tombolini '15	🍷🍷 3

Tenuta dell'Ugolino

VIA COPPARONI, 32
60031 CASTELPLANIO [AN]
TEL. +39 07310731 812569
www.tenutaugolino.it

CELLAR SALES
PRE-BOOKED VISITS
ANNUAL PRODUCTION 50,000 bottles
HECTARES UNDER VINE 7.00
SUSTAINABLE WINERY

○ Verdicchio dei Castelli di Jesi Cl. Le Piaole '15	🍷🍷 2*
○ Verdicchio dei Castelli di Jesi Passito Dolce Cate '09	🍷🍷 5

Le Vigne di Clementina Fabi

C.DA FRANILE, 3
63069 MONTEDINOVE [AP]
TEL. +39 338 7463441
www.levignediclementinafabi.it

CELLAR SALES
PRE-BOOKED VISITS
ACCOMMODATION
ANNUAL PRODUCTION 55,000 bottles
HECTARES UNDER VINE 7.32
VITICULTURE METHOD Certified Organic

○ Offida Pecorino '15	🍷🍷 2*
● Dal Tino '13	🍷🍷 2*
○ Offida Passerina '15	🍷 2

Zaccagnini

VIA SALMAGINA, 9/10
60039 STAFFOLO [AN]
TEL. +39 0731779892
www.zaccagnini.it

CELLAR SALES
PRE-BOOKED VISITS
ACCOMMODATION AND RESTAURANT SERVICE
ANNUAL PRODUCTION 250,000 bottles
HECTARES UNDER VINE 35.00

○ Verdicchio dei Castelli di Jesi Cl. Sup. Terratufo '15	🍷🍷 3
○ Verdicchio dei Castelli di Jesi Cl. Sup. Viterosa '15	🍷🍷 3

UMBRIA

Winemaking Umbria vaunts important historical roots, that are specific and well documented, proving its significance. Despite being a small region it is easy to identify its various districts, sub-zones and growing areas, differing in terms of soil, climate and varieties cultivated. More recently, Umbria's wine success was for reds, in line with a national and international trend, but that is now changing rapidly and the region's whites are being given their rightful dues. Not surprisingly, Orvieto is the most renowned area, since time immemorial, nor is it a coincidence that in recent years it has shown encouraging signs and renewed vitality. The 2015 growing season was dry and sunny, enhancing the Mediterranean profile of the wines, raising average quality and fuelling the white-wine trend. A thorough reading of IW and its top wines will confirm this. The Tre Bicchieri awards do not stop at the excellent 2014 Cervaro della Sala, played out on sheer finesse, however, also singling out stellar versions of the 2014 Campo del Guardiano Palazzone and Decugnano dei Barbi's Orvieto Classico Superiore 2015 Il Bianco. Around the corner, Todi Grechetto is very lively, with plenty of wines worth mentioning, although the leader is the 2014 Superiore Fiorfiore from the brilliant Roccafiore winery, reaching unprecedented heights and taking away the Sustainable Viticulture Award for its efforts since its inception. If we factor in the many Trebbiano Spoletinos that came up trumps, the overview is complete. And the red wines? Lots of news here too, starting with the delicious Ciliegiolo di Narnis, a wine from a variety that local producers obstinately brought back to life. There is a long list of labels that should be mentioned but the best, in our opinion, is Leonardo Bussoletti's 2014 Brecciaro. For its finesse and elegance, we would add Lungarotti's legendary Torgiano Rosso Riserva Rubesco Vigna Monticchio, in the 2011 vintage, showing the same mouthwatering charm as ever. To close, a mention for the most structured reds, inevitably pointing to the generous and rightly celebrated Montefalco growing area, which has fewer winners than usual, due to a 2012 vintage whose wines seem to be more laboured, tannin-heavy and stiff than in other years. Despite this, three Sagrantinos were outstanding: Marco Caprai's surefooted yet brilliant Collepiano; Giampaolo Tabarrini's original and tasty Campo alla Cerqua cru; and a newcomer from a winemaker with a hallmark seductive, refined style, Pardi, finally making it to the top step of our podium.

Adanti

VIA BELVEDERE, 2
06031 BEVAGNA [PG]
TEL. +39 0742360295
www.cantineadanti.com

CELLAR SALES
PRE-BOOKED VISITS
ANNUAL PRODUCTION 160,000 bottles
HECTARES UNDER VINE 30.00
SUSTAINABLE WINERY

Austere tradition, classical rigour, and the power of time-honoured concepts that take root in the present are all Adanti hallmarks, evident in the wines crafted in the villa which houses the cellar, set among the vineyards. Only native yeasts are used during fermentation, extraction is moderate, and maturation in the wood is carefully gauged. The reds need time to develop, but are capable of thrilling after many years of bottle ageing. This is true of the wonderfully austere Montefalco Sagrantino 2010, which proffers a marvellous nose. The dry, firm palate is also in a class of its own, although held back by very hard tannins. The Passito 2008 is among the best of the DOCG zone.

● Montefalco Sagrantino '10	♟♟ 5
○ Montefalco Bianco '15	♟♟ 2*
● Montefalco Sagrantino Passito '08	♟♟ 6
○ Colli Martani Grechetto '15	♟ 2
● Montefalco Sagrantino Arquata '08	♟♟♟ 6
● Montefalco Sagrantino Arquata '06	♟♟♟ 5
● Montefalco Sagrantino Arquata '05	♟♟♟ 5
○ Colli Martani Grechetto '12	♟♟ 2*
○ Montefalco Bianco '14	♟♟ 2*
● Montefalco Rosso '11	♟♟ 2*
● Montefalco Rosso '10	♟♟ 2*
● Montefalco Rosso Ris. '10	♟♟ 4
● Montefalco Rosso Ris. '09	♟♟ 3*
● Montefalco Sagrantino '09	♟♟ 5
● Montefalco Sagrantino Arquata '07	♟♟ 5
● Montefalco Sagrantino Il Domenico '08	♟♟ 6
● Montefalco Sagrantino Il Domenico '07	♟♟ 6

Antonelli - San Marco

LOC. SAN MARCO, 60
06036 MONTEFALCO [PG]
TEL. +39 0742379158
www.antonellisanmarco.it

CELLAR SALES
PRE-BOOKED VISITS
ACCOMMODATION
ANNUAL PRODUCTION 350,000 bottles
HECTARES UNDER VINE 50.00
VITICULTURE METHOD Certified Organic
SUSTAINABLE WINERY

This legendary Montefalco estate is in the illustrious San Marco subzone, long renowned as prime farmland. It vaunts 170 hectares of land, in a single plot, of which 50 under vine. Organic methods in the vineyard and great sensitivity in the cellar, with moderate extraction and skilled use of large and medium-sized oak barrels, make Antonelli's wines personal and distinctive. Each bottle is faithful to a specific stylistic concept and terroir. The excellent Sagrantino 2011 reached our finals with a convincing, elegant nose offering fine notes of wild berries and spice, along with a few toasty notes still to be tamed. It is accompanied by a nicely balanced, racy palate with rather drying tannins on the finish. The average level of the other wines is generally very high.

● Montefalco Sagrantino '11	♟♟ 5
● Baiocco '15	♟♟ 2*
● Montefalco Rosso '13	♟ 3
● Montefalco Sagrantino Chiusa di Pannone '09	♟♟ 6
○ Spoleto Trebbiano Spoletino Trebium '15	♟♟ 3
○ Colli Martani Grechetto '15	♟ 2
● Montefalco Sagrantino '09	♟♟♟ 5
● Montefalco Sagrantino '08	♟♟♟ 5
● Montefalco Sagrantino Chiusa di Pannone '04	♟♟♟ 6
○ Spoleto Trebbiano Spoletino Trebium '14	♟♟♟ 3*
● Montefalco Rosso '12	♟♟ 3
● Montefalco Rosso '11	♟♟ 3
● Montefalco Sagrantino '10	♟♟ 5

Barberani

Loc. Cerreto
05023 Baschi [TR]
Tel. +39 0763341820
www.barberani.it

CELLAR SALES
PRE-BOOKED VISITS
ACCOMMODATION
ANNUAL PRODUCTION 350,000 bottles
HECTARES UNDER VINE 55.00
VITICULTURE METHOD Certified Organic
SUSTAINABLE WINERY

History and terroir encounter the liveliness
and verve of the new generations in
Barberani, a well-established yet dynamic
estate, which is tracing an exciting new
path that appears sound and clearly
defined. Origins and future, classic wines
and innovative projects blend seamlessly
thanks to the increasing attention lavished
on the vineyards, commencing with certified
organic methods, and an increasingly
confident hand in the cellar. The delightful
Orvieto Classico Superiore Luigi e Giovanna
once again came out top in our tastings.
The 2013 vintage is highly convincing,
vaunting sweet fruit balanced by racy citrus
and mineral notes, good density and
freshness, roundness and linearity. It is a
complete wine, with a few tertiary nuances.
Castagnolo 2015 is very good and the rest
of the range is above average.

○ Orvieto Cl. Sup. Luigi e Giovanna '13	♥♥♥	5
● Aleatico Passito '09	♥♥	6
○ Grechetto '15	♥♥	3
○ Moscato Passito Villa Monticelli '13	♥♥	6
○ Orvieto Cl. Sup. Castagnolo '15	♥♥	3
○ Orvieto Cl. Sup. Muffa Nobile Calcaia '13	♥	7
● Lago di Corbara Rosso Villa Monticelli '04	♥♥♥	4
○ Orvieto Cl. Sup. Luigi e Giovanna Villa Monticelli '11	♥♥♥	5
○ Orvieto Cl. Sup. Muffa Nobile Calcaia '10	♥♥♥	5
○ Orvieto Cl. Sup. Castagnolo '13	♥♥	3*
○ Orvieto Cl. Sup. Luigi e Giovanna Villa Monticelli '12	♥♥	5
○ Orvieto Cl. Sup. Muffa Nobile Calcaia '12	♥♥	5

Tenuta Bellafonte

Loc. Torre del Colle
via Colle Nottolo, 2
06031 Bevagna [PG]
Tel. +39 0742710019
www.tenutabellafonte.it

CELLAR SALES
PRE-BOOKED VISITS
ACCOMMODATION
ANNUAL PRODUCTION 15,000 bottles
HECTARES UNDER VINE 9.00
SUSTAINABLE WINERY

Tenuta Bellafonte's original, high-quality
wines set it apart from other recent
Umbrian operations. The credit for this goes
to its experienced manager Peter Heilbron,
who decided to invest in a magnificent
estate near Bevagna for his own winery. He
has done so with great skill and
confidence, commencing with an elegant,
pondered style that immediately stands out
from that of other local producers. The
terroir, non-invasive cellar techniques, and
careful ageing yield wines with great
personality and natural expressiveness. Of
course, this makes vintage the decisive
factor, so a few ups and downs are to be
expected, reflected in the very good
Sagrantino 2012. Juicy and fragrant on the
palate with attractive shifts in rhythm, but
slightly marred by a faint foxy sensation
that also affects the tannins, less elegant
than usual but still above average.
Trebbiano Spoletino Arnèto 2014 is
absolutely charming and better than ever.

○ Arnèto '14	♥♥	5
● Montefalco Sagrantino Collenottolo '12	♥♥	6
● Montefalco Sagrantino '09	♥♥♥	6
● Montefalco Sagrantino Collenottolo '11	♥♥♥	6
● Montefalco Sagrantino Collenottolo '10	♥♥♥	6
● Montefalco Sagrantino '08	♥♥	5

Bocale

LOC. MADONNA DELLA STELLA
VIA FRATTA ALZATURA
06036 MONTEFALCO [PG]
TEL. +39 0742399233
www.bocale.it

CELLAR SALES
PRE-BOOKED VISITS
ANNUAL PRODUCTION 25,000 bottles
HECTARES UNDER VINE 4.20

Despite its small dimensions, the estate's style is increasingly consistent and well defined, capable of offering an original interpretation of the typical Montefalco wines. After the initial hesitant vintages, the Valentini family's wines are starting to find a convincing style. The reds are perfectly extracted, with balanced oak, especially since the arrival of large barrels for ageing. Trebbiano Spoletino, the new white, also seems to have got off on the right foot. We can start with two splendid reds. The delightful Sagrantino 2013 is fresh yet concentrated, full-flavoured and fruit-rich. Its length is marred only by the finish, which is still a tad too tannic. Once this has been smoothed out, it could reach the dizziest heights of the designation. Montefalco Rosso 2014 is juicy and highly drinkable.

● Montefalco Sagrantino '13	▼▼	5
● Montefalco Rosso '14	▼▼	3
○ Trebbiano Spoletino '15	▼▼	3
● Montefalco Rosso '13	♀♀	3
● Montefalco Rosso '12	♀♀	2*
● Montefalco Rosso '09	♀♀	4
● Montefalco Rosso '08	♀♀	4
● Montefalco Sagrantino '12	♀♀	5
● Montefalco Sagrantino '11	♀♀	5
● Montefalco Sagrantino '10	♀♀	5
● Montefalco Sagrantino '09	♀♀	5
● Montefalco Sagrantino '07	♀♀	5
● Montefalco Sagrantino '06	♀♀	5
● Montefalco Sagrantino Passito '09	♀♀	5

Briziarelli

VIA COLLE ALLODOLE, 10
06031 BEVAGNA [PG]
TEL. +39 07587461
www.cantinebriziarelli.it

CELLAR SALES
PRE-BOOKED VISITS
ACCOMMODATION AND RESTAURANT SERVICE
ANNUAL PRODUCTION 70,000 bottles
HECTARES UNDER VINE 18.50

The winery is owned by a family of successful building materials entrepreneurs, who started with one of the agricultural estates they purchased in the past, splendidly located between Bevagna and Montefalco. Now that the cellar has been completed, it is true to say that the operation is a leader in the production zone, its wines following suit, becoming more interesting with each new vintage. Sagrantino Vitruvio confirms our good impressions of the previous vintage. The 2010 is complete and complex, with a style that avoids excessive extraction and toastiness. UnoNoveZeroSei 2011 is excellent, offering spicy texture and a caressing palate with slight hints of tar.

● Montefalco Rosso '12	▼▼	2*
● Montefalco Rosso Mattone '12	▼▼	4
● Montefalco Sagrantino Vitruvio '10	▼▼	6
● UnoNoveZeroSei '11	▼▼	5
● Montefalco Rosso '11	♀♀	2*
● Montefalco Rosso '10	♀♀	2*
● Montefalco Rosso Mattone '11	♀♀	3
● Montefalco Sagrantino Vitruvio '09	♀♀	4

Leonardo Bussoletti

LOC. MIRIANO
S.DA DELLE PRETARE, 62
05035 NARNI [TR]
TEL. +39 0744715687
www.leonardobussoletti.it

PRE-BOOKED VISITS
ANNUAL PRODUCTION 20,000 bottles
HECTARES UNDER VINE 7.00
VITICULTURE METHOD Certified Organic

Leonardo Bussoletti is one of the region's most brilliant and promising vignerons. A veteran of the wine world, he recently started his own business, immediately making headlines and intriguing press and connoisseurs alike with his wines. The cellar and vineyards are near Narni, vaunting a large number of venerable old vines, and local ciliegiolo is the favoured grape variety. Much care is lavished in the cellar and ageing in oak is increasingly successful. The average level of the wines, both red and white, is exceptionally high, and they are all terroir true. The elegant Brecciaro 2014 is the first Ciliegiolo di Narni to win our Tre Bicchieri. It is a delightful red, with a delicate, lively nose of cherries, raspberries, and black pepper. The elegant, full-flavoured palate is supple and luscious. Grechetto Colle Ozio 2014 is also splendid, with a nose of spring flowers and earthy notes on the palate.

● Brecciaro '14	▼▼▼ 3*
○ Colle Ozio Grechetto '14	▼▼ 3*
● 05035 Rosso '15	▼▼ 2*
○ Colle Murello '15	▼▼ 3
● Vigna Vecchia '13	▼▼ 7
○ 05035 Bianco '15	▼ 2
○ Colle Ozio Grechetto '12	▽▽▽ 3*
● 05035 Narni Rosso '14	▽▽ 2*
● Brecciaro '13	▽▽ 3*
● Brecciaro '12	▽▽ 3
● Brecciaro '11	▽▽ 3
● Brecciaro '10	▽▽ 3
● Ciliegiolo di Narni V. V. '11	▽▽ 7
● Ciliegiolo di Narni V. V. '10	▽▽ 7
● Ciliegiolo di Narni Vigna Vecchia '12	▽▽ 7
○ Colle Ozio '12	▽▽ 3

★★Arnaldo Caprai

LOC. TORRE
06036 MONTEFALCO [PG]
TEL. +39 0742378802
www.arnaldocaprai.it

CELLAR SALES
PRE-BOOKED VISITS
ANNUAL PRODUCTION 800,000 bottles
HECTARES UNDER VINE 136.00
SUSTAINABLE WINERY

Caprai has played a fundamental role in developing the Montefalco and Umbria wine industry in general, and not just in promoting Sagrantino. The estate was founded in the 1970s and achieved international acclaim in the early 1990s. Today the Caprai family's enterprise seems to have entered a new phase. The cornerstones remain the same, but renowned consultant oenologist Michel Rolland has been tasked with the stylistic and technical supervision of the wines. The new course has only just been set; time will show where it will lead. Sagrantino Collepiano 2012 is a great wine that was among the very finest tasted this year. A red in the distinctive house style, focusing on elegance and exceptional depth, it is brimming with flavour. The toasty notes are very refined and allow the aromas to develop through to attractive nuances of leather and cedarwood. We were also very struck by the Vigna del Lago of the same vintage, with its bewitching notes of pencil lead.

● Montefalco Sagrantino Collepiano '12	▼▼▼ 7
● Montefalco Sagrantino 25 Anni '12	▼▼ 8
○ Chardonnay '15	▼▼ 5
○ Colli Martani Grechetto Grecante '15	▼▼ 4
○ Montefalco Bianco '15	▼▼ 3
● Montefalco Rosso '14	▼▼ 4
● Montefalco Rosso V. Flaminia Maremmana '14	▼▼ 4
● Montefalco Sagrantino V. del Lago '12	▼▼ 8
● Montefalco Sagrantino 25 Anni '10	▽▽▽ 8
● Montefalco Sagrantino 25 Anni '09	▽▽▽ 8
● Montefalco Sagrantino 25 Anni '08	▽▽▽ 8
● Montefalco Sagrantino 25 Anni '07	▽▽▽ 8
● Montefalco Sagrantino 25 Anni '06	▽▽▽ 8
● Montefalco Sagrantino Collepiano '11	▽▽▽ 7
● Montefalco Sagrantino Collepiano '08	▽▽▽ 6

La Carraia

LOC. TORDIMONTE, 56
05018 ORVIETO [TR]
TEL. +39 0763304013
www.lacarraia.it

CELLAR SALES
PRE-BOOKED VISITS
ANNUAL PRODUCTION 580,000 bottles
HECTARES UNDER VINE 119.00

The consolidated Gialletti–Cotarella partnership continues to produce excellent wines with the vigneron's perseverance and the technical skill of a great winemaker: a winning combination that has shown its steadfastness over the years with rare and equally persistent continuity. La Carraia makes a wide range of wines and blends from different grape varieties, clean and austere, with good personality. The benchmark, not just among the whites, is Orvieto Classico Superiore Poggio Calvelli. The 2015 vintage is very good, although it needs further time in bottle to develop. It has an alluring nose of medicinal herbs and lavender, and dense, luscious peaches and apricots on the bright, deep palate. Tizzonero 2014 is fine, showing dark and toasty with good extraction and texture, and Sangiovese 2015 is juicy.

○ Orvieto Cl. Sup. Poggio Calvelli '15	♀♀	2*
● Sangiovese '15	♀♀	2*
● Tizzonero '14	♀♀	3
○ Le Basque '15	♀	3
○ Vermentino Porticina '15	♀	2
● Fobiano '03	♀♀♀	4
● Fobiano '99	♀♀♀	4*
● Fobiano '98	♀♀♀	4*
● Fobiano '12	♀♀	5
● Fobiano '11	♀♀	5
● Fobiano '10	♀♀	4
○ Orvieto Cl. Poggio Calvelli '10	♀♀	2*
○ Orvieto Cl. Sup. Poggio Calvelli '14	♀♀	2*
○ Orvieto Cl. Sup. Poggio Calvelli '13	♀♀	2*
● Tizzonero '12	♀♀	3

Tenuta Castelbuono

LOC. BEVAGNA
VOC. CASTELLACCIO, 9
06031 PERUGIA
TEL. +39 0742361670
www.tenutacastelbuono.it

ANNUAL PRODUCTION 123,000 bottles
HECTARES UNDER VINE 32.00

Named after its location, Castelbuono is a splendid estate belonging to the Tenute Lunelli group, which also owns Margon in Trentino and Podernovo in Tuscany. Located just outside Bevagna, the winery is a veritable work of art designed by the great Arnaldo Pomodoro, with vineyards in Bevagna and Montefalco. The technical project is still being drawn up, with plenty of new features that will definitely bring surprises in the near future. We will keep a watchful eye on progress. For now we'll enjoy the two very good Sagrantinos from the 2012 vintage. The dry version is delicate and nuanced, at least for this type of wine. It has a nose of wild cherries, flowers, and Mediterranean scrub, accompanied by a deep, linear palate just slightly held back by assertive tannins on the finish. The delicious Passito is very balanced, with notes of ripe damsons.

● Montefalco Sagrantino Carapace '12	♀♀	5
● Montefalco Sagrantino Passito '12	♀♀	5
● Montefalco Rosso '10	♀♀	3
● Montefalco Rosso '09	♀♀	3
● Montefalco Rosso '07	♀♀	3*
● Montefalco Rosso Lampante Ris. '10	♀♀	5
● Montefalco Rosso Ris. '09	♀♀	5
● Montefalco Rosso Ris. '08	♀♀	5
● Montefalco Rosso Ziggurat '11	♀♀	3
● Montefalco Sagrantino '10	♀♀	5
● Montefalco Sagrantino '08	♀♀	5
● Montefalco Sagrantino '07	♀♀	5
● Montefalco Sagrantino Carapace '09	♀♀	5

★★Castello della Sala

LOC. SALA
05016 FICULLE [TR]
TEL. +39 076386127
www.antinori.it

CELLAR SALES
PRE-BOOKED VISITS
ANNUAL PRODUCTION 760,000 bottles
HECTARES UNDER VINE 140.00

When Marchesi Antinori started looking for a terroir suitable for the production of great white wines to add to their well-established production of reds in Tuscany, they confidently chose Umbria, not far from Orvieto. The estate covers an area of 500 hectares, including 140 under vine, on fossil-rich clay soils at altitudes between 200 and 450 metres. Cervaro della Sala, from chardonnay with a small amount of grechetto, fermented and aged in barrique, is one of the most famous and acclaimed Italian white wines. The 2014 vintage is a masterful interpretation, characterized by elegance and grace. It still displays toasted notes from ageing in oak, but that is only to be expected at this stage. Underneath lies splendid fruit, along with hints of citrus and flint. The palate is stylish but full, with good extract.

Cantina Castello Monte Vibiano Vecchio

LOC. MONTE VIBIANO VECCHIO DI MERCATELLO
VOC. PALOMBARO, 22
06072 MARSCIANO [PG]
TEL. +39 0758783386
www.montevibiano.it

CELLAR SALES
PRE-BOOKED VISITS
ANNUAL PRODUCTION 300,000 bottles
HECTARES UNDER VINE 35.00
SUSTAINABLE WINERY

The Fasola Bologna family's estate, run by the visionary Lorenzo, is set in a breathtaking spot in the Perugia hills. The operation vaunts a solid winemaking background and an innovative sustainability policy. The cellar was built in 2002 and welcomes visitors, who are shown around the vineyards in electric off-road vehicles. In recent years the wines have reached very high standards in terms of quality, modern style, focus, and consistency. The flagship Colli Perugini Rosso L'Andrea is back, with the 2012 vintage. Its complex, concentrated nose is well orchestrated, with notes ranging from ripe dark berry fruit to spice. On the palate it is chewy and caressing, smooth until the austere, assertive tannins emerge. The white Maria Camilla 2015 is good and the Villa Monte Vibiano Rosso of the same vintage is surprising.

○ Cervaro della Sala '14	♈♈♈ 6
○ Bramito del Cervo '15	♈♈ 3
○ Conte della Vipera '15	♈♈ 5
○ Muffato della Sala '11	♈♈ 6
○ Orvieto Cl. Sup. San Giovanni della Sala '15	♈♈ 3
● Pinot Nero '14	♈ 6
○ Cervaro della Sala '13	♈♈♈ 6
○ Cervaro della Sala '12	♈♈♈ 6
○ Cervaro della Sala '11	♈♈♈ 6
○ Cervaro della Sala '10	♈♈♈ 6
○ Cervaro della Sala '09	♈♈♈ 6
○ Cervaro della Sala '08	♈♈♈ 6
○ Cervaro della Sala '07	♈♈♈ 6
○ Cervaro della Sala '06	♈♈♈ 6
○ Cervaro della Sala '05	♈♈♈ 6

● Colli Perugini Rosso L'Andrea '12	♈♈ 5
○ Maria Camilla '15	♈♈ 3
● Villa Monte Vibiano Rosso '15	♈♈ 1*
○ Villa Monte Vibiano Bianco '15	♈ 2
● Colli Perugini Rosso L'Andrea '08	♈♈♈ 5
● Colli Perugini Rosso L'Andrea '10	♈♈ 5
● Colli Perugini Rosso L'Andrea '09	♈♈ 5
● Colli Perugini Rosso Monvì '12	♈♈ 2*
● Colli Perugini Rosso Monvì '10	♈♈ 2*
● Colli Perugini Rosso Monvì '09	♈♈ 2*
○ Maria Camilla '14	♈♈ 3
○ Maria Camilla '13	♈♈ 3
○ Villa Monte Vibiano Bianco '14	♈♈ 2*

UMBRIA

Cantina Cenci

FRAZ. SAN BIAGIO DELLA VALLE
VOC. ANTICELLO, 1
06072 MARSCIANO [PG]
TEL. +39 3805198980
www.cantinacenci.it

CELLAR SALES
PRE-BOOKED VISITS
ANNUAL PRODUCTION 20,000 bottles
HECTARES UNDER VINE 5.00
SUSTAINABLE WINERY

Giovanni Cenci exudes pure energy: a man in perpetual motion, both physical and mental, who is very sure of his ideas and shuns all compromises. He is also very competent and is gradually building his viticultural experience, underpinned by a solid knowledge of farming and winemaking. His vineyards are set in a splendid natural landscape in San Biagio, between Perugia and Marsciano, which was once the site of the rural settlements of the Olivetan order. All the wines can be defined as typical of the growing area, powerful with good acidity, and an accurate reflection of their vintage. Sangiovese Piantata is excellent once again. The 2014 vintage is a delicate red, with a lustrous pale hue, which vaunts a floral nose with hints of spice. The elegant palate is long and juicy, with good acid-tannin balance. Grechetto Anticello 2015 is richer and more potent than the previous vintage, but equally balanced and drinkable. It is a very cellarable wine for teaming with hearty dishes.

Fattoria Colleallodole

VIA COLLEALLODOLE, 3
06031 BEVAGNA [PG]
TEL. +39 0742361897
www.fattoriacolleallodole.it

CELLAR SALES
PRE-BOOKED VISITS
ANNUAL PRODUCTION 70,000 bottles
HECTARES UNDER VINE 20.00

The Antano family played an important role in the history of Sagrantino and the typical local wines. Several of their wines were the reason the great Montefalco red at its finest was noted by the wine-drinking public, bewitching even Luigi Veronelli. Fattoria Colleallodole's wines are more delightful than ever today, vaunting a unique and genuinely artisanal style without any compromises. The new, bigger and more efficient cellar will certainly play a role in further development. The 2013 vintage of Colleallodole is a little contradictory. A very good, intriguing wine, with a nose of ripe blackberries, autumn leaves and hints of toast, but the luxuriant, silky palate is hampered by an imposing tannic weave and bitterish notes. The plush, ripe Montefalco Rosso Riserva 2013 is nicely complex.

○ Alago Stellato '15	♥♥ 2*
○ Anticello '15	♥♥ 2*
○ Giole '15	♥♥ 2*
● Piantata '14	♥♥ 4
● Ascheria '14	♥ 4
● Sanbiagio '14	♥ 3
○ Alago '12	♀♀ 3
○ Anticello '14	♀♀ 2*
○ Anticello '12	♀♀ 2*
○ Giole '14	♀♀ 2*
● Piantata '13	♀♀ 4
● Piantata '12	♀♀ 2*

● Montefalco Sagrantino Colleallodole '13	♥♥ 8
● Montefalco Rosso Ris. '13	♥♥ 5
● Montefalco Sagrantino '13	♥♥ 6
● Montefalco Rosso '14	♥ 3
● Montefalco Rosso Ris. '08	♀♀♀ 5
● Montefalco Sagrantino '12	♀♀♀ 6
● Montefalco Sagrantino Colleallodole '10	♀♀♀ 8
● Montefalco Sagrantino Colleallodole '09	♀♀♀ 8
● Montefalco Sagrantino Colleallodole '06	♀♀♀ 6
● Montefalco Sagrantino Colleallodole '05	♀♀♀ 6
● Montefalco Rosso Ris. '11	♀♀ 5
● Montefalco Sagrantino '10	♀♀ 5
● Montefalco Sagrantino '09	♀♀ 5
● Montefalco Sagrantino '08	♀♀ 8
● Montefalco Sagrantino Colleallodole '12	♀♀ 8
● Montefalco Sagrantino Colleallodole '11	♀♀ 8
● Montefalco Sagrantino Passito '07	♀♀ 8

Fattoria Colsanto

LOC. MONTARONE
06031 BEVAGNA [PG]
TEL. +39 0742360412
www.livon.it

CELLAR SALES
PRE-BOOKED VISITS
ACCOMMODATION
ANNUAL PRODUCTION 50,000 bottles
HECTARES UNDER VINE 15.00

The winery sits atop a little hill surrounded by vineyards at the end of a long avenue of cypress trees. This beautiful setting is the site of the Livon family's Umbrian estate, in the heart of the Sagrantino zone, near Bevagna, and produces typical local grapes and wines. Following an initial running-in period, Colsanto's wines are now perfect in terms of quality and style. The reds are aged solely in classic large barrels. Our top accolade went to the Sagrantino once again. The 2012 vintage of the great Montefalco red has an alluring, relaxed nose ranging from mixed berries to earthy, mineral notes. Concentrated and gutsy, with good stuffing, it is nevertheless highly drinkable, ending in a dry finish with rather stiff tannins. The lively, approachable Montefalco Rosso is similar in style, although obviously with different aromas and flavours, and has good backbone.

Decugnano dei Barbi

LOC. FOSSATELLO, 50
05018 ORVIETO [TR]
TEL. +39 0763308255
www.decugnano.it

CELLAR SALES
PRE-BOOKED VISITS
ANNUAL PRODUCTION 130,000 bottles
HECTARES UNDER VINE 32.00

The estate is certainly among the Umbrian wineries most worthy of a visit for the magnificent scenic location steeped in history. The vineyards are planted on soils of marine origin, containing seashells and fossils, ideal for growing white grape varieties. Also worth visiting for the Etruscan tufa grotto, where several of the wines, including the Metodo Classico, are still aged today. All in all, a fabulous operation, founded on the love, wisdom, and patience of the Barbi family. Orvieto Classico Superiore Il Bianco 2015 is one of Umbria's very finest wines. The vintage has given it ripeness, flavour, and fullness without detracting from its freshness. We'd go as far as saying that this little masterpiece is almost a northern wine with its vibrancy, linearity and sharpness, and its wonderful aromas of citrus and green apples.

● Montefalco Rosso '13	♟♟ 3
● Montefalco Sagrantino '12	♟♟ 5
● Montefalco Rosso '10	♟♟ 3
● Montefalco Rosso '09	♟♟ 3*
● Montefalco Sagrantino '11	♟♟ 5
● Montefalco Sagrantino '10	♟♟ 5
● Montefalco Sagrantino '09	♟♟ 5
● Montefalco Sagrantino '08	♟♟ 5
● Montefalco Sagrantino '07	♟♟ 5
● Montefalco Sagrantino '03	♟♟ 5
● Ruris Rosso '13	♟♟ 2*
● Ruris Rosso '12	♟♟ 2*

○ Orvieto Cl. Sup. Il Bianco '15	♟♟♟ 4*
○ Decugnano Dosaggio Zero '10	♟♟ 4
● Il Rosso '14	♟♟ 3
○ Orvieto Cl. Pourriture Noble '14	♟♟ 5
○ Orvieto Cl. Villa Barbi Bianco '15	♟♟ 3
● Villa Barbi Rosso '14	♟ 3
● "IL" Rosso '98	♟♟♟ 5
○ Orvieto Cl. Sup. "IL" '11	♟♟♟ 3*
○ Orvieto Cl. Sup. Il Bianco '12	♟♟♟ 3*
○ Orvieto Cl. Sup. Il Bianco '10	♟♟♟ 3
○ Orvieto Cl. Sup. Il Bianco '09	♟♟♟ 4
● Il Rosso '13	♟♟ 3
● Il Rosso '12	♟♟ 4
○ Orvieto Cl. Sup. Il Bianco '14	♟♟ 3*
○ Orvieto Cl. Sup. Il Bianco '13	♟♟ 3*
○ Orvieto Cl. Sup. Pourriture Noble '13	♟♟ 5
● Villa Barbi Rosso '13	♟♟ 2*

Di Filippo

voc. Conversino, 153
06033 Cannara [PG]
Tel. +39 0742731242
www.vinidifilippo.com

CELLAR SALES
PRE-BOOKED VISITS
ANNUAL PRODUCTION 227,000 bottles
HECTARES UNDER VINE 35.00
VITICULTURE METHOD Certified Organic
SUSTAINABLE WINERY

Di Filippo is an estate with a fair number of vintages under its belt, which lies in a borderland between two distinct winegrowing areas. Organic methods have long been used in all the vineyards, planted to different grape varieties, including the traditional local mainstays. The range is composed of many lines and labels, and average quality has risen greatly in recent years, accompanied by an excellent, terroir-true style. We particularly liked Colli Martani Grechetto 2015, which reiterates the estate's talent for interpreting the most widely grown Umbrian cultivar. It has a fresh citrussy nose with notes of fruit skins, and a long, firm palate that faithfully echoes the characteristics of the grape. Our favourite red was the Sagrantino 2012, which is concentrated yet fresh and fragrant, with notes of cherries and forest floor.

Duca della Corgna

via Roma, 236
06061 Castiglione del Lago [PG]
Tel. +39 0759652493
www.ducadellacorgna.it

CELLAR SALES
PRE-BOOKED VISITS
ANNUAL PRODUCTION 280,000 bottles
HECTARES UNDER VINE 55.00

The hills around Lake Trasimeno, practically on the border with Tuscany, have long been considered fine farming and winegrowing country. However, this heritage has not always been fully exploited in terms of winemaking, partly due to the widespread use of non-native grape varieties. Duca della Corgna, the quality star of a venerable local cooperative winery, can be credited with always having wagered on Trasimeno gamay, a grape variety resembling grenache, which could become a benchmark for producers in the area. The deep, stylish Corniolo 2013 is back at the top, with an elegant toasty note that gives complexity without detracting from its vigour. Baccio del Rosso 2015 is juicy and excellent value, and Trasimeno Gamay Divina Villa Etichetta Bianca 2015 is first rate. All the other wines are very decent.

○ Colli Martani Grechetto '15	🍷🍷 2*
○ Colli Martani Grechetto Sassi d'Arenaria '14	🍷🍷 3
● Colli Martani Sangiovese Properzio Ris. '13	🍷🍷 3
● Colli Martani Vernaccia di Cannara '15	🍷🍷 5
● Montefalco Sagrantino '12	🍷🍷 5
● Sangiovese '15	🍷 3
○ Colli Martani Grechetto Planiarche '14	🍷🍷 2*
● Colli Martani Sangiovese Properzio '11	🍷🍷 3
● Colli Martani Vernaccia di Cannara '14	🍷🍷 4
● Montefalco Rosso '13	🍷🍷 2*
● Montefalco Rosso Sallustio '12	🍷🍷 3
● Montefalco Sagrantino '11	🍷🍷 5
● Montefalco Sagrantino '10	🍷🍷 5
● Terre di S. Nicola Rosso '11	🍷🍷 3

● C. del Trasimeno Rosso Corniolo Ris. '13	🍷🍷 4
○ Ascanio '15	🍷🍷 2*
● C. del Trasimeno Baccio del Rosso '15	🍷🍷 2*
● C. del Trasimeno Gamay Divina Villa Et. Bianca '15	🍷🍷 2*
○ C. del Trasimeno Baccio del Bianco '15	🍷 2
○ C. del Trasimeno Grechetto Nuricante '15	🍷 2
○ C. del Trasimeno Baccio del Bianco '13	🍷🍷 2*
● C. del Trasimeno Baccio del Rosso '14	🍷🍷 2*
● C. del Trasimeno Baccio del Rosso '13	🍷🍷 2*
● C. del Trasimeno Gamay Divina Villa Et. Bianca '14	🍷🍷 2*
● C. del Trasimeno Gamay Divina Villa Et. Bianca '13	🍷🍷 2*
● C. del Trasimeno Gamay Divina Villa Ris. '12	🍷🍷 3

Podere Fontesecca

voc. Fontesecca, 30
06062 Città della Pieve [PG]
Tel. +39 3496180516
www.fontesecca.it

CELLAR SALES
PRE-BOOKED VISITS
ACCOMMODATION
ANNUAL PRODUCTION 10,000 bottles
HECTARES UNDER VINE 3.00
VITICULTURE METHOD Certified Organic

Paolo Bolla has created a little gem just a stone's throw from the centre of Città del Pieve, a splendid Umbrian town on the border with Tuscany and Lazio. Fontesecca is a small winery by any standards, with a few hectares of vineyards, planted to traditional local varieties of white grechetto, trebbiano, and malvasia, and black sangiovese, ciliegiolo, and canaiolo. Despite its small scale, it is renowned above all among lovers of authentic, gourmet wines, the fruit of clean farming and sensitive hands. These are not wines for everyone, requiring attention and patience, but after an initial hint of reduction, the reds and whites are thirst quenching and full of personality. Pino 2013 is more convincing than ever, one of the best examples of Umbrian Sangiovese, and Ciliegiolo 2014 and Elso 2015 are splendid.

Cantina La Spina

fraz. Spina
via Emilio Alessandrini, 1
06055 Marsciano [PG]
Tel. +39 0758738120
www.cantinalaspina.it

CELLAR SALES
PRE-BOOKED VISITS
ANNUAL PRODUCTION 16,000 bottles
HECTARES UNDER VINE 2.20
SUSTAINABLE WINERY

La Spina is a successful little Perugia winery that has garnered a great following. Moreno Peccia is an old-style figure with the dual soul of conscientious vigneron and thoughtful winemaker, who has styled his enterprise in his own image. The vineyards lie near a village among the hills between Perugia and Marsciano, home to grape varieties dictated more by tradition than by fashion or profit. The wines are pleasant, flavoursome, and never over-extracted, and the whites are meeting with increasing success. The flagship Rosso Spina 2014 is the wine that really stands out, showing concentrated and caressing, yet fragrant, lean, and drinkable. The revelation of the year is Merlato 2015, with a nose of mixed berries and a firm, luscious palate.

● Ciliegiolo '14	♥♥ 3*
● Pino Sangiovese '13	♥♥ 3*
○ Elso '15	♥♥ 2*
○ Bianco Fontesecca '09	♥♥ 3
⊙ Canaiolo '14	♥♥ 3
⊙ Canaiolo '13	♥♥ 3
⊙ Canaiolo '12	♥♥ 3
⊙ Canaiolo '10	♥♥ 3
● Ciliegiolo '13	♥♥ 3
● Ciliegiolo '12	♥♥ 3
● Ciliegiolo '11	♥♥ 3
● Ciliegiolo '10	♥♥ 3*
○ Elso '13	♥♥ 2*
○ Elso '12	♥♥ 2*
● Pino Sangiovese '09	♥♥ 3*
● Pino Sangiovese '08	♥♥ 4

○ Filare Maiore '15	♥♥ 2*
● Merlato '15	♥♥ 2*
● Rosso Spina '14	♥♥ 3
○ Eburneo '15	♥ 2
● Polimante della Spina '14	♥ 4
○ Eburneo '14	♥♥ 2*
○ Eburneo '13	♥♥ 2*
○ Filare Maiore '14	♥♥ 2*
● Polimante della Spina '11	♥♥ 3
● Polimante della Spina '10	♥♥ 3
● Rosso Spina '13	♥♥ 3
● Rosso Spina '12	♥♥ 3
● Rosso Spina '11	♥♥ 3
● Rosso Spina '10	♥♥ 3
● Rosso Spina '09	♥♥ 3
○ V. Maiore '13	♥♥ 2*
○ V. Maiore '12	♥♥ 2*

★Lungarotti

V.LE G. LUNGAROTTI, 2
06089 TORGIANO [PG]
TEL. +39 075988661
www.lungarotti.it

CELLAR SALES
PRE-BOOKED VISITS
ACCOMMODATION AND RESTAURANT SERVICE
ANNUAL PRODUCTION 2,400,000 bottles
HECTARES UNDER VINE 250.00
VITICULTURE METHOD Certified Organic
SUSTAINABLE WINERY

Hugh Johnson, the British wine expert, once
wrote that Lungarotti put Umbria on the
world wine map, and it remains the best
description of the estate's importance for
the region's industry. Following the winery's
beginnings, in the 1960s, and the
unstoppable growth of the subsequent
decades, the family faced a complete
renovation around the turn of the
millennium. Today we can say that it is now
back on its game again, commencing with
the style of its top wines. Commencing with
the last vintages of the first decade of the
millennium, Vigna Monticchio has developed
a modern style of interpreting the past. Part
of the wine is aged in large barrels again,
and from 2009 onwards only sangiovese
has been used, considered ready to star
alone. The 2011 vintage is marvellous,
richer than 2010 but unrivalled in quality.
Rubesco 2013 is a veritable delight!

La Madeleine

S.DA MONTINI, 38
05035 NARNI [TR]
TEL. +39 3453208914
www.cantinalamadeleine.it

PRE-BOOKED VISITS
ANNUAL PRODUCTION 40,000 bottles
HECTARES UNDER VINE 6.50

Linda and Massimo D'Alema chose to keep
the name of the old farm that they bought
in 2008, now owned by their children Giulia
and Francesco. Apart from that, everything
else at La Madeleine has changed since
then. The estate covers an area of 15
hectares, of which 6.5 are under vine,
embraced by the lovely hills around Narni
and Otricoli. The extensive work carried out
has transformed the estate into a modern
winegrowing operation, with vineyards
planted to various grape varieties, primarily
international. We very much liked the juicy
Sfide 2014, from cabernet franc, which is
concentrated and silky, with good texture. It
has a close-focused nose of dark berries,
with grassy hints and notes of toast. The
excellent Pinot Nero 2014 is stylish and
racy, very consistent and tasty.

● Torgiano Rosso Rubesco V. Monticchio Ris. '11	♟♟♟ 6
● Torgiano Rosso Rubesco '13	♟♟ 3*
● Montefalco Rosso '13	♟♟ 3
● Montefalco Sagrantino '11	♟♟ 5
○ Torgiano Bianco Torre di Giano '15	♟♟ 2*
○ Torgiano Bianco Torre di Giano V. il Pino Ris. '08	♟♟♟ 3*
● Torgiano Rosso Rubesco V. Monticchio Ris. '07	♟♟♟ 6
● Torgiano Rosso V. Monticchio Ris. '10	♟♟♟ 6
● Torgiano Rosso V. Monticchio Ris. '09	♟♟♟ 6
● Torgiano Rosso V. Monticchio Ris. '08	♟♟♟ 6
● Torgiano Rosso V. Monticchio Ris. '06	♟♟♟ 5
● Torgiano Rosso V. Monticchio Ris. '05	♟♟♟ 5*
● Torgiano Rosso V. Monticchio Ris. '04	♟♟♟ 5

● Sfide '14	♟♟ 3*
● Pinot Nero '14	♟♟ 6
● NarnOt '13	♟ 6
⊙ Nerosé	♟ 5
● NarnOt '11	♟♟ 6
● Sfide '13	♟♟ 3*

Madrevite

LOC. VAIANO
VIA CIMBANO, 36
06061 CASTIGLIONE DEL LAGO [PG]
TEL. +39 0759527220
www.madrevite.com

CELLAR SALES
PRE-BOOKED VISITS
RESTAURANT SERVICE
ANNUAL PRODUCTION 45,000 bottles
HECTARES UNDER VINE 10.00

This small winery is an original example of winegrowing in the Lake Trasimeno zone, which respects the local history and terroir. Madrevita was born in 2001 from of the restructuring of the Chiucchiurlotto family estate, and stands on the site of the old Podere Mastronuccio, indicated as a farm in a document dated 1651. Its single 20-hectare plot, including ten under vine, is home to both local and international grape varieties. The stylish, racy Reminore 2015 is a splendid example of Trebbiano Spoletino grown outside the classic zone: bright and concentrated, full of flavour and stuffing, with salty notes. Glanio 2014, from sangiovese, Trasimeno gamay, and merlot, is also very good. It has an alluring nose dominated by fresh, ripe wild berries, and an elegant toasty note, accompanied by a long, juicy palate.

○ Il Reminore '15	♟♟ 3*
● Capofoco '12	♟♟ 4
● Glanio '14	♟♟ 3
⊙ La Bisbetica Rosé '15	♟ 3
● Colli del Trasimeno Glanio '12	♟♟ 3
● Colli del Trasimeno Glanio '11	♟♟ 3
● Colli del Trasimeno Glanio '10	♟♟ 3*
○ Il Reminore '14	♟♟ 3
○ Il Reminore '13	♟♟ 3
○ La Bisbetica Rosé '13	♟♟ 3
○ Re Minore '12	♟♟ 2*
○ Re Minore '11	♟♟ 2*

Moretti Omero

LOC. SAN SABINO, 20
06030 GIANO DELL'UMBRIA [PG]
TEL. +39 074290426
www.morettiomero.it

CELLAR SALES
PRE-BOOKED VISITS
ACCOMMODATION AND RESTAURANT SERVICE
ANNUAL PRODUCTION 75,000 bottles
HECTARES UNDER VINE 13.00
VITICULTURE METHOD Certified Organic
SUSTAINABLE WINERY

Aided today by his whole family, Omero Moretti is an old-style artisan, farmer, olive and grape grower, completely focused on his work and direct contact with the land. His vineyards and cellar lie in a splendid area, near Giano dell'Umbria and the Martani Mountains. He is a firm believer in organic farming and obtained certification for his vineyards many years ago. The same philosophy extends to the wines, which are genuine and personal, rather than focused on technical perfection. The Sagrantino 2012 is an excellent interpretation of the vintage, offering an intriguing, earthy nose with hints of topsoil and roots on the ripe, fruity middle notes. The supple palate has good texture and grip, with well-typed flavours and precise tannins that are still a bit stiff. It will develop well in the bottle. Passito Argo 2012, also from sagrantino, is fantastic.

● Argo Passito '12	♟♟ 5
○ Montefalco Bianco '15	♟♟ 3
● Montefalco Sagrantino '12	♟♟ 5
○ Grechetto '15	♟ 2
○ Grechetto '14	♟♟ 2*
○ Grechetto '12	♟♟ 2*
○ Grechetto dell'Umbria '10	♟♟ 2
● Montefalco Rosso '10	♟♟ 3
● Montefalco Rosso '09	♟♟ 5
● Montefalco Sagrantino '11	♟♟ 5
● Montefalco Sagrantino '09	♟♟ 5
● Montefalco Sagrantino '08	♟♟ 5
○ Nessuno '14	♟♟ 2*
○ Nessuno '13	♟♟ 2*
○ Nessuno '12	♟♟ 2*

La Palazzola

LOC. VASCIGLIANO
05039 STRONCONE [TR]
TEL. +39 0744609091
www.lapalazzola.it

ANNUAL PRODUCTION 150,000 bottles
HECTARES UNDER VINE 28.00

Stefano Grilli is one of the most original producers in the Umbrian wine world. His cellar in Vascigliano, near Terni, frequently releases new creations that are a blend of experimentation, innovation, skill, and foresight. The range includes the pioneering Metodo Ancestrale sparklers, the extraordinary Vin Santos and sweet wines in general, and charming reds and whites. In an age in which standardization is rife, we can find consolation in La Palazzola's highly personal wines. Who, for instance, would have expected such a Verdello? A classy revival of a traditional variety, aged in terracotta jars, showing an earthy, salty nose of medicinal herbs, curry plant, and wild fennel, with a racy, full-flavoured palate. Riesling Brut Metodo Ancestrale is very good and individual, as usual.

Palazzone

LOC. ROCCA RIPESENA, 68
05019 ORVIETO [TR]
TEL. +39 0763344921
www.palazzone.com

CELLAR SALES
PRE-BOOKED VISITS
ACCOMMODATION AND RESTAURANT SERVICE
ANNUAL PRODUCTION 130,000 bottles
HECTARES UNDER VINE 24.00

Giovanni Dubini is an extraordinary vigneron whose innate sensitivity is associated with long experience. His estate is certainly a benchmark for Umbrian wine, particularly whites, as his own production proves year after year. The winery stands on a splendid hill, surrounded by vineyards, between Rocca Ripesena and Il Romitorio, near Orvieto. Work in the cellar respects the grapes and the terroir, in a contemporary traditional style. Palazzone's wines are wonderful and a source of pride for the entire area. All the wines presented were excellent, particularly the monumental Campo del Guardiano 2014, with a magnetic nose of quinces, Mediterranean herbs and berries, flowers and flint. The vibrant, three-dimensional palate is deep and full flavoured, with hints of summer flowers and fresh, green sensations, followed by flint, earth and medicinal herbs on the delicious finish.

○ Riesling Brut Metodo Ancestrale '12	♼♼ 3*
○ Verdello '14	♼♼ 3*
○ Amelia Vin Santo '12	♼♼ 4
● Amelia Vin Santo Occhio di Pernice '12	♼♼ 5
○ Gran Cuvée Brut '13	♼♼ 4
○ Brut '11	♼ 4
● Syrah '13	♼ 3
● Merlot '97	♼♼♼ 4*
○ Amelia Vin Santo '11	♼♼ 4
○ Riesling Brut Metodo Ancestrale '11	♼♼ 3
○ Riesling Brut Metodo Ancestrale '10	♼♼ 3*
● Rubino '09	♼♼ 5
● Syrah '11	♼♼ 3

○ Orvieto Cl. Sup. Campo del Guardiano '14	♼♼♼ 3*
● Armaleo '13	♼♼ 5
○ Orvieto Cl. Sup. Muffa Nobile '15	♼♼ 5
○ Orvieto Cl. Sup. Terre Vineate '15	♼♼ 2*
○ Viognier '15	♼ 3
● Armaleo '00	♼♼♼ 5
● Armaleo '98	♼♼♼ 5
● Armaleo '97	♼♼♼ 5
● Armaleo '95	♼♼♼ 5
○ Orvieto Cl. Sup. Campo del Guardiano '11	♼♼♼ 2*
○ Orvieto Cl. Sup. Campo del Guardiano '09	♼♼♼ 3
○ Orvieto Cl. Sup. Campo del Guardiano '07	♼♼♼ 3
○ Orvieto Cl. Sup. Terre Vineate '11	♼♼♼ 2*

F.lli Pardi

VIA G. PASCOLI, 7/9
06036 MONTEFALCO [PG]
TEL. +39 0742379023
www.cantinapardi.it

CELLAR SALES
PRE-BOOKED VISITS
ANNUAL PRODUCTION 56,000 bottles
HECTARES UNDER VINE 11.00

The Pardi family have an important
entrepreneurial past in Montefalco, in
which wine is both an age-old and a
contemporary element. The estate has
long been producing it, with excellent
results, but only in recent years has it
assumed its current form. Its vineyards lie
in several sub-zones of the designation,
with very different characteristics. The
wines vaunt an impeccable, highly
distinctive style, which is elegant and
drinkable with aromatic nuances. The
sublime Sagrantino 2012 came out on top
at our tastings of the vintage in
Montefalco. We were thoroughly convinced
by this delightful crisp wine, with an
alluring nose of cherries, blackberries and
red berry fruit, balanced extract, a long,
silky weave, and a citrussy finish.
Montefalco Rosso 2014 and Trebbiano
Spoletino 2015 are also excellent.

● Montefalco Sagrantino '12	♟♟♟ 5
○ Colli Martani Grechetto '15	♟♟ 2*
● Montefalco Rosso '14	♟♟ 2*
● Montefalco Sagrantino Sacrantino '11	♟♟ 6
○ Spoleto Trebbiano Spoletino '15	♟♟ 2*
○ Colli Martani Grechetto '13	♟♟ 2*
○ Colli Martani Grechetto '12	♟♟ 2*
● Montefalco Rosso '12	♟♟ 3
● Montefalco Rosso '11	♟♟ 2*
● Montefalco Sagrantino '11	♟♟ 5
● Montefalco Sagrantino '10	♟♟ 5
● Montefalco Sagrantino Sacrantino '10	♟♟ 6
● Montefalco Sagrantino Sacrantino '08	♟♟ 6
○ Spoleto Trebbiano Spoletino '14	♟♟ 2*
○ Spoleto Trebbiano Spoletino '13	♟♟ 2*

Cantina Peppucci

LOC. SANT'ANTIMO
FRAZ. PETRORO, 4
06059 TODI [PG]
TEL. +39 0758947439
www.cantinapeppucci.com

CELLAR SALES
PRE-BOOKED VISITS
ACCOMMODATION
ANNUAL PRODUCTION 70,000 bottles
HECTARES UNDER VINE 12.50

Cantina Peppucci is one of the region's
up-and-coming wineries. Its vineyards lie in
the municipality of Todi, on the border with
the Sagrantino production zone, and yield
increasingly convincing wines in terms of
style and quality. The whites are reaching
truly dizzy heights, with a personality that
was inconceivable until a few years ago,
while the reds are modern, nicely
calibrated, and well typed, capable of
ageing well in the bottle. Peppucci has
released a new version of Grechetto, which
has cut a very fine figure on its debut. The
oakiness derived from barrel ageing still
needs adjusting, but the rest promises very
well. It is firm and solid, with a balanced
nose and notes of vanilla and crusty bread
on the rich, full-flavoured palate. Our
favourite red was the superb Petroro 4.

○ Todi Grechetto Sup. I Rovi '14	♟♟ 3*
● Todi Rosso Petroro 4 '15	♟♟ 2*
● Altro Io '12	♟♟ 5
○ Todi Grechetto Montorsolo '15	♟♟ 2*
● Altro Io '11	♟♟ 5
● Altro Io '10	♟♟ 5
○ Colli Martani Grechetto di Todi Montorsolo '10	♟♟ 2
● Giovanni '10	♟♟ 4
● Giovanni '09	♟♟ 4
● Petroro 4 '11	♟♟ 2*
○ Todi Grechetto Montorsolo '14	♟♟ 2*
○ Todi Grechetto Montorsolo '13	♟♟ 2*
○ Todi Petroro 4 '12	♟♟ 2*
● Todi Rosso Petroro 4 '14	♟♟ 2*
● Todi Rosso Petroro 4 '13	♟♟ 2*

Perticaia

LOC. CASALE
06036 MONTEFALCO [PG]
TEL. +39 0742379014
www.perticaia.it

CELLAR SALES
PRE-BOOKED VISITS
ANNUAL PRODUCTION 120,000 bottles
HECTARES UNDER VINE 15.50
SUSTAINABLE WINERY

Perticaia has quickly become one of the most illustrious names in Umbrian wine, thanks to its first-rate terroir in Casale di Montefalco, and its excellent technical management. The estate has recently changed hands, from its founder Guido Guardigli to a Luxembourg family of entrepreneurs of Umbrian origin. As far as we know, the continuity of the project is not in question, and nothing will actually change, apart from the aim to achieve even higher quality and with Guardigli still at the helm during the transitional period. We will keep a close eye on new developments. Trebbiano Spoletino 2015 is very good, promising to age well in bottle. The fresh, delicate white, with notes of citron and lemon leaf and a slight hint of bay, is bound to improve. Montefalco Sagrantino 2012 is among the best, as usual, showing lush and racy, just slightly held back by still rather intrusive, stiff tannins. Umbria Rosso 2015 is delightful and worth buying in bulk.

● Montefalco Sagrantino '12	♟♟ 5
○ Spoleto Trebbiano Spoletino '15	♟♟ 2*
● Montefalco Rosso '13	♟ 3
● Umbria Rosso '15	♟ 2
● Montefalco Sagrantino '11	♟♟♟ 5
● Montefalco Sagrantino '10	♟♟♟ 5
● Montefalco Sagrantino '09	♟♟♟ 5
● Montefalco Sagrantino '07	♟♟♟ 5
● Montefalco Sagrantino '06	♟♟♟ 5
● Montefalco Sagrantino '05	♟♟♟ 5
● Montefalco Sagrantino '04	♟♟♟ 5
● Montefalco Rosso '11	♟♟ 3
● Montefalco Rosso Ris. '11	♟♟ 4
● Montefalco Rosso Ris. '09	♟♟ 4
● Montefalco Rosso Ris. '08	♟♟ 4
● Montefalco Sagrantino '08	♟♟ 5

Pucciarella

LOC. VILLA DI MAGIONE
VIA CASE SPARSE, 39
06063 MAGIONE [PG]
TEL. +39 0758409147
www.pucciarella.it

CELLAR SALES
PRE-BOOKED VISITS
ACCOMMODATION
ANNUAL PRODUCTION 250,000 bottles
HECTARES UNDER VINE 58.50
SUSTAINABLE WINERY

Everything at Pucciarella is on the grand scale, commencing with its sheer size, covering almost 300 hectares between Magione and Corciano, towards Lake Trasimeno. Flanked by fields of crops and olive groves, the vineyards lie at an average altitude of around 300 metres, on mainly loose gravelly, stony soils, and are largely registered in the local designation. The range is reliable, with several pinnacles of excellence and labels offering fantastic value for money. The red Empireo is very elegant, characterized by a fine nose of red berries, delicate sweet spice and a touch of rose water, and an equally good sound, balanced palate with nice extract. Colli del Trasimeno Vin Santo 2013 is also stunning, with almonds on the nose and a complex, full-flavoured palate. Agnolo 2015 is clean and refreshing.

● Empireo '13	♟♟ 3*
○ Arsiccio '15	♟♟ 3
● Colli del Trasimeno Sant'Anna di Pucciarella '13	♟♟ 3
○ Colli del Trasimeno Vin Santo '13	♟♟ 4
○ Agnolo '15	♟ 2
○ Arsiccio '13	♟♟ 3
○ Arsiccio '11	♟♟ 3
● C. del Trasimeno Rosso Berlingero '13	♟♟ 2*
● C. del Trasimeno Rosso Sant'Anna Ris. '10	♟♟ 2*
● C. del Trasimeno Rosso Sant'Anna Ris. '09	♟♟ 2*
○ C. del Trasimeno Vin Santo '10	♟♟ 3*
○ C. del Trasimeno Vin Santo '09	♟♟ 3
○ C. del Trasimeno Vin Santo '08	♟♟ 3

Raina

LOC. TURRI
VIA CASE SPARSE, 42
06036 MONTEFALCO [PG]
TEL. +39 0742621356
www.raina.it

CELLAR SALES
PRE-BOOKED VISITS
RESTAURANT SERVICE
ANNUAL PRODUCTION 60,000 bottles
HECTARES UNDER VINE 10.00
VITICULTURE METHOD Certified Organic
SUSTAINABLE WINERY

Francesco Mariani is a brilliant young
vigneron from Montefalco, who is making a
name for himself on the region's wine
scene. He's doing so via an increasingly
personal route and extremely original,
seductive wines. His vineyards are in Turri
di Montefalco and are tended with organic
methods tending increasingly to the
biodynamic. The wines are very digestible,
with an artisan flavour and personality,
and moderate extraction. The typical local
reds are very good, while the style of the
whites is still being defined. Trebbiano
Spoletino 2015 already seems to be on the
right track. It is an alluring, moody wine
with some fanciful nuances, which is
difficult to pigeonhole. The nose offers
notes of fruit peel and cereals, green tea,
and dried lemons, while the bright, vibrant
palate is fresh and flavoursome. Rosso
della Gobba 2014 is splendid.

Roccafiore

FRAZ. CHIOANO
VOC. COLLINA, 110A
06059 TODI [PG]
TEL. +39 0758942416
www.roccafiorewines.com

CELLAR SALES
PRE-BOOKED VISITS
ACCOMMODATION AND RESTAURANT SERVICE
ANNUAL PRODUCTION 120,000 bottles
HECTARES UNDER VINE 15.00
SUSTAINABLE WINERY

Roccafiore is a charming, well-organized
winery with a contemporary feel, fully
committed to sustainability to the point that
we gave it our Sustainable Viticulture Award.
Its beautiful setting, among the rolling hills
of Todi, is one of the most picturesque in
Umbria. Here the vineyards are tended with
non-invasive methods and planted mainly to
local grape varieties, and the cellar also
enjoys a light hand. The wines continue to
improve from year to year, in terms of both
overall quality and style. An example is the
fantastic Fiorfiore 2014, a naturally
fermented Grechetto aged in large oak
barrels. The vintage has resulted in a
dazzling, fragrant white, which confidently
juxtaposes soft and tangy sensations with
racy acidity. Prova d'Autore 2013 is also
excellent, while all the reds appear very
encouraging, with an ever-clearer style.

○ Spoleto Trebbiano Spoletino '15	♥♥♥ 3*
☉ La Peschiera di Pacino '15	♥♥ 2*
● Montefalco Rosso '13	♥♥ 3
● Rosso della Gobba '14	♥♥ 2*
○ Grechetto '15	♥ 2
● Montefalco Rosso '12	♀♀ 2*
● Montefalco Rosso '11	♀♀ 2*
● Montefalco Rosso '10	♀♀ 3
● Montefalco Sagrantino '08	♀♀ 5
● Montefalco Sagrantino Campo di Raina '10	♀♀ 4
● Montefalco Sagrantino Le Pretelle '10	♀♀ 5
● Rosso della Gobba '13	♀♀ 2*
● Rosso della Gobba '12	♀♀ 2*
○ Spoleto Trebbiano Spoletino '14	♀♀ 3
○ Trebbiano Spoletino '12	♀♀ 2*

○ Todi Grechetto Sup. Fiorfiore '14	♥♥♥ 3*
● Prova d'Autore '13	♥♥ 5
● Il Roccafiore '14	♥♥ 3
○ Todi Bianco Fiordaliso '15	♥♥ 2*
● Todi Rosso Melograno '14	♥♥ 2*
● Collina d'Oro Passito '15	♥ 5
○ Fiordaliso '12	♀♀ 2*
● Prova d'Autore '12	♀♀ 4
○ Todi Bianco Fiordaliso '13	♀♀ 2*
○ Todi Grechetto Sup. Fiorfiore '13	♀♀ 3*
○ Todi Grechetto Sup. Fiorfiore '12	♀♀ 3*
○ Todi Grechetto Sup. Fiorfiore '11	♀♀ 3*
● Todi Rosso Melograno '12	♀♀ 2*
● Todi Rosso Melograno '11	♀♀ 2*
● Todi Sangiovese Rosso '10	♀♀ 2*
● Todi Sangiovese Sup. Il Roccafiore '12	♀♀ 3
● Todi Sangiovese Sup. Il Roccafiore '11	♀♀ 3*

Romanelli

LOC. COLLE SAN CLEMENTE, 129A
06036 MONTEFALCO [PG]
TEL. +39 0742371245
www.romanelli.se

CELLAR SALES
PRE-BOOKED VISITS
ANNUAL PRODUCTION 40,000 bottles
HECTARES UNDER VINE 7.50

Romanelli has gradually ascended the
ladder of success to reach the very top of
the crowded Montefalco wine scene. We
consider its wines among the finest of the
production zone, the fruit of meticulous
work in the vineyard and accurate choices
in the cellar. It is not only the quality that is
impressive, but the style too with wines that
stand out for their elegance, carefully
calibrated extraction, balance, and aromatic
expressiveness. The vineyards lie on silty
clay soils at an altitude of 350 metres
above sea level. Although the winery
usually produces some of the most original
Sagrantinos, this year we detected a lack of
consistency among the bottles tasted.
Medeo 2011 is nonetheless splendid,
showing relaxed and elegant, earthy, almost
rusty and decadent at times, but with good,
strong backbone. The Sagrantino 2012 is
also excellent, although perhaps a little
more tannic and drying than usual.

Scacciadiavoli

LOC. CANTINONE, 31
06036 MONTEFALCO [PG]
TEL. +39 0742371210
www.scacciadiavoli.it

CELLAR SALES
PRE-BOOKED VISITS
ANNUAL PRODUCTION 200,000 bottles
HECTARES UNDER VINE 32.00
SUSTAINABLE WINERY

Scacciadiavoli has a long history, as
testified by its handsome cellar that is a
rare example of the area's industrial
archaeology and well worth a visit.
However, the Pambuffetti family, who own
it, has not rested on its laurels. In the early
2000s, both vineyards and fermentation
and ageing methods were overhauled
completely and today Scacciadiavoli wines
are modern, meticulously crafted,
consistent, and reliable, a benchmark for
the Montefalco production zone. Montefalco
Sagrantino 2011 has a ripe nose of plums
and vanilla pods. On the palate it is
powerful but racy, slightly held back by
prominent chewy tannins. We also liked the
sprightly Montefalco Rosso 2013, the
well-made Montefalco Bianco 2014, and
Sagrantino Passito 2010, which is almost
as good.

● Montefalco Sagrantino '12	♥♥ 5
● Montefalco Sagrantino Medeo '11	♥♥ 8
○ Colli Martani Grechetto '15	♥♥ 2*
● Montefalco Rosso '12	♥ 3
● Montefalco Sagrantino '11	♥♥♥ 5
● Montefalco Sagrantino '10	♥♥♥ 5
○ Colli Martani Grechetto '13	♥♥ 2*
○ Colli Martani Grechetto '12	♥♥ 2*
○ Colli Martani Grechetto '11	♥♥ 2*
○ Colli Martani Grechetto '08	♥♥ 2
● Montefalco Rosso '11	♥♥ 3
● Montefalco Rosso '10	♥♥ 2*
● Montefalco Rosso '09	♥♥ 2*
● Montefalco Rosso '08	♥♥ 3
● Montefalco Rosso '07	♥♥ 3
● Montefalco Rosso Ris. '09	♥♥ 3
● Montefalco Sagrantino Passito '08	♥♥ 5

● Montefalco Sagrantino '11	♥♥ 5
○ Montefalco Bianco '14	♥♥ 3
● Montefalco Rosso '13	♥♥ 3
● Montefalco Sagrantino Passito '10	♥ 5
● Montefalco Sagrantino '10	♥♥♥ 5
○ Montefalco Bianco '13	♥♥ 3
● Montefalco Rosso '12	♥♥ 3
● Montefalco Rosso '11	♥♥ 3
● Montefalco Rosso '10	♥♥ 3
● Montefalco Rosso '09	♥♥ 3*
● Montefalco Rosso '08	♥♥ 3
● Montefalco Sagrantino '09	♥♥ 5
● Montefalco Sagrantino '08	♥♥ 5
● Montefalco Sagrantino '07	♥♥ 5
● Montefalco Sagrantino Passito '07	♥♥ 5

Sportoletti

VIA LOMBARDIA, 1
06038 SPELLO [PG]
TEL. +39 0742651461
www.sportoletti.com

CELLAR SALES
PRE-BOOKED VISITS
ANNUAL PRODUCTION 230,000 bottles
HECTARES UNDER VINE 30.00

Now that the young generations of the Sportoletti family have become a permanent part of the business, the handsome estate's prospects for the future are rosy. After all, the estate has solid farming roots, but also an undeniable capacity for innovation, as it has recently shown. The well-aspected vineyards lie on the Spello hills and are planted with local and international grape varieties, which are often blended in the flagship wines. Both the reds and the whites are soundly modern in style, capable of simultaneously surprising and satisfying. An impressive two wines reached our finals, testifying to the excellence of the bottles presented for our tastings. In addition to the usual Villa Fidelia Rosso, with luxuriant notes of fruit and toast, Assisi Rosso 2015 is also exceptionally good. Considering the price, we recommend stocking up.

● Assisi Rosso '15	♟♟	2*
● Villa Fidelia Rosso '14	♟♟	4
○ Villa Fidelia Bianco '14	♟♟	3
○ Assisi Grechetto '15	♟	1*
● Villa Fidelia Rosso '98	♟♟♟	4*
○ Assisi Grechetto '13	♟♟	1*
● Assisi Rosso '14	♟♟	2*
● Assisi Rosso '13	♟♟	2*
○ Villa Fidelia Bianco '13	♟♟	3
○ Villa Fidelia Bianco '12	♟♟	3
○ Villa Fidelia Bianco '11	♟♟	3
● Villa Fidelia Rosso '13	♟♟	4
● Villa Fidelia Rosso '12	♟♟	4
● Villa Fidelia Rosso '11	♟♟	4
● Villa Fidelia Rosso '10	♟♟	4
● Villa Fidelia Rosso '08	♟♟	5
● Villa Fidelia Rosso '07	♟♟	5

Giampaolo Tabarrini

FRAZ. TURRITA
06036 MONTEFALCO [PG]
TEL. +39 0742379351
www.tabarrini.com

CELLAR SALES
PRE-BOOKED VISITS
ANNUAL PRODUCTION 70,000 bottles
HECTARES UNDER VINE 18.00
SUSTAINABLE WINERY

Gianpaolo Tabarrini is a real character, full of surprises and always on the go, constantly seeking anything able to improve or distinguish his business. He is a restless spirit, in the finest sense of the word, who has enabled his winery to develop year after year, making its name one of the most illustrious in the production zone. The vineyards are skilfully managed and both the red and white wines have a well-defined identity, with the flagship vineyard selections made separately. The difficult 2012 vintage has yielded Sagrantinos that struggle to unbend fully. Campo alla Cerqua nonetheless manages to hit the bull's-eye, particularly in terms of potential. It is a seductive red, with a nose of spice, resin and concentrated fruit, accompanied by a warm palate with very assertive tannins full of promise. Adarmando 2014 is fresher and more delicate than usual, and Piantagrero, from a local grape variety undergoing a revival, is well worth trying.

● Montefalco Sagrantino Campo alla Cerqua '12	♟♟♟	6
○ Adarmando '14	♟♟	4
● Montefalco Rosso Boccatone '13	♟♟	3
● Montefalco Sagrantino Colle alle Macchie '12	♟♟	6
● Montefalco Sagrantino Colle Grimaldesco '12	♟♟	5
● Piantagrero '13	♟♟	4
● Montefalco Sagrantino Campo alla Cerqua '11	♟♟♟	6
● Montefalco Sagrantino Campo alla Cerqua '10	♟♟♟	6
● Montefalco Sagrantino Campo alla Cerqua '08	♟♟♟	6
● Montefalco Sagrantino Colle alle Macchie '09	♟♟♟	6

Terre de la Custodia

LOC. PALOMBARA
06035 GUALDO CATTANEO [PG]
TEL. +39 0742929586
www.terredelacustodia.it

CELLAR SALES
PRE-BOOKED VISITS
ANNUAL PRODUCTION 1,000,000 bottles
HECTARES UNDER VINE 160.00
SUSTAINABLE WINERY

The Farchionis, who own Terre de la
Custodia brand, are a top Umbrian
entrepreneurial family. In addition to wine,
they also produce oil, flour, and craft beer,
all of which are extraordinarily successful.
The fermentation and ageing cellar is a
handsome building, receiving grapes from
vineyards in Gualdo Cattaneo and Todi,
where white varieties flourish. The wines
are flawless and modern, clean cut, and
very expressive. The delicious, juicy
Montefalco Riserva 2013 is lean with lovely
texture and a delicate nose of raspberries
and wild strawberries. Sagrantino 2011 is
almost as good, showing nuanced with
attractive fruity notes of cherries and
blackberries, despite a rather tannic finish.
The smooth, ripe Grechetto Plentis 2014 is
convincingly full with a concentrated nose.

Terre Margaritelli

FRAZ. CHIUSACCIA
LOC. MIRALDUOLO
06089 TORGIANO [PG]
TEL. +39 0757824668
www.terremargaritelli.com

CELLAR SALES
PRE-BOOKED VISITS
ANNUAL PRODUCTION 120,000 bottles
HECTARES UNDER VINE 52.00
VITICULTURE METHOD Certified Organic

Founded in the 1950s as a family farm,
the estate received an entrepreneurial
boost in the early 2000s. Today it vaunts
60 hectares of certified organic land,
including more than 50 under vine in a
single plot, all on the Miralduolo hill in
Torgiano, which has always been fine
winegrowing country. Several different
grape varieties are grown, including the
classic black sangiovese and canaiolo, and
the white grechetto and trebbiano. The
wines are modern and constantly
improving. Torgiano Rosso Riserva Freccia
degli Scacchi 2013 strode confidently into
our finals. This big, complex red shows
well-orchestrated fruit accompanied by a
rich array of oriental spices. The long, deep
palate has a fine weave and good acidity,
albeit with a certain warmth. Torgiano
Bianco Costellato 2015 is also good, with
sweet fruit and full flavour.

● Montefalco Rosso Ris. '13	▼▼ 5
○ Colli Martani Grechetto Plentis '14	▼▼ 3
● Montefalco Sagrantino '11	▼▼ 6
○ Sublimis Gladius Brut M. Cl. '10	▼▼ 4
● Montefalco Sagrantino Exubera '06	▼ 8
● Colli Martani Collezione '12	♀♀ 2*
○ Colli Martani Grechetto '14	♀♀ 2*
○ Colli Martani Grechetto '13	♀♀ 2*
○ Colli Martani Grechetto '11	♀♀ 2*
○ Colli Martani Grechetto Plentis '12	♀♀ 3
○ Colli Martani Grechetto Plentis '11	♀♀ 3
● Montefalco Rosso '12	♀♀ 4
● Montefalco Rosso '10	♀♀ 4
● Montefalco Sagrantino '10	♀♀ 6
● Montefalco Sagrantino '09	♀♀ 6
● Montefalco Sagrantino Passito Melanto '11	♀♀ 5

● Torgiano Rosso Freccia degli Scacchi Ris. '13	▼▼ 5
○ Greco di Renabianca '15	▼▼ 3
● Roccascossa '15	▼▼ 2*
○ Torgiano Bianco Costellato '15	▼▼ 2*
○ Pietramala '15	▼ 2
● Malot '11	♀♀ 3
● Roccascossa '11	♀♀ 2*
● Roccascossa '10	♀♀ 2*
○ Torgiano Bianco Costellato '14	♀♀ 2*
○ Torgiano Costellato '13	♀♀ 2*
● Torgiano Freccia degli Scacchi '10	♀♀ 5
● Torgiano Freccia degli Scacchi '09	♀♀ 5
● Torgiano Mirantico '08	♀♀ 2*
● Torgiano Mirantico '07	♀♀ 2*
● Torgiano Rosso Freccia degli Scacchi Ris. '10	♀♀ 5

Todini

FRAZ. ROSCETO
VIA COLLINA, 29
06059 TODI [PG]
TEL. +39 075887122
www.cantinafrancotodini.com

CELLAR SALES
PRE-BOOKED VISITS
ACCOMMODATION AND RESTAURANT SERVICE
ANNUAL PRODUCTION 300,000 bottles
HECTARES UNDER VINE 20.00

Todini is an important and complex
business operation with a well-established
winery set in a beautiful area. The estate
covers an area of 120 hectares, of which
20 under vine, and includes a handsome
cellar and a delightful hotel. It grows both
local and international grape varieties,
which yield well-made modern wines.
All the wines did very well, with some of
the flagships reaching peaks of excellence.
The top performers were Nero della
Cevara 2013 and Todi Sangiovese 2014.
The former appeared far more stylish and
fragrant than in the past, not in the least bit
overwhelmed by the notes of oak. On the
contrary, it is fresh and elegant, with hints
of Mediterranean scrubland and spice, and
a luscious, original palate. The latter is
colonial and earthy, brimming with flavour.

Tudernum

LOC. PIAN DI PORTO, 146
06059 TODI [PG]
TEL. +39 0758989403
www.tudernum.it

CELLAR SALES
PRE-BOOKED VISITS
ACCOMMODATION AND RESTAURANT SERVICE
ANNUAL PRODUCTION 2,000,000 bottles
HECTARES UNDER VINE 240.00

Tudernum is a cooperative winery that
stands out for its capable management and
spirit of innovation, which has allowed it to
make the quantum leap from relatively
minor producer to benchmark in the space
of a decade. Its wines are flawless, and
frequently excellent, well able to face the
competition and win points on the
international markets. They express local
grape varieties, first and foremost
sangiovese and sagrantino, very well
indeed, and are more than reasonably
priced. The excellent Rojano 2013
combines generous stuffing with rare
progression. A nose of leather and red
berries, with hints of tobacco, is followed by
a vibrant, compact palate, still young but
full of promise. The alluring, relaxed
Sagrantino 2011 offers notes of tobacco
and rain-soaked earth and a fine weave,
while Todi Rosso 2015 is a gem.

● Nero della Cervara '13	▾▾▾ 5
● Todi Sangiovese '14	▾▾▾ 4
○ Marte Bianco '15	▾▾▾ 2*
● Marte Rosso '15	▾▾▾ 2*
● Merlot '14	▾▾▾ 2*
○ Todi Grechetto '15	▾▾▾ 2*
○ Todi Grechetto Sup. Bianco del Cavaliere '14	▾▾ 3
○ Chardonnay '15	▾ 2
● Colli Martani Sangiovese Rubro '11	♑♑ 4
○ Grechetto di Todi Bianco del Cavaliere Sup. '11	♑ 3
○ Grechetto Riesling '12	♑♑ 2*
● Marte '14	♑♑ 2*
● Merlot '13	♑♑ 2*
● Relais Rosso '13	♑♑ 3
● Relais Rosso '12	♑♑ 2*

● Montefalco Sagrantino Fidenzio '11	▾▾ 4
● Todi Rosso Sup. Rojano '13	▾▾ 3*
○ Todi Grechetto '15	▾▾ 2*
● Todi Rosso '15	▾▾ 2*
○ Todi Bianco '15	▾ 2
● Montefalco Rosso '09	♑♑ 3
● Montefalco Sagrantino Fidenzio '10	♑♑ 4
● Montefalco Sagrantino Fidenzio '09	♑♑ 4
● Montefalco Sagrantino Fidenzio '08	♑♑ 5
○ Todi Grechetto '14	♑♑ 2*
○ Todi Grechetto '12	♑♑ 2*
○ Todi Grechetto Sup. Colle Nobile '13	♑♑ 2*
○ Todi Grechetto Sup. Colle Nobile '12	♑♑ 2*
● Todi Rosso '14	♑♑ 2*
● Todi Rosso Sup. Rojano '12	♑♑ 3
● Todi Rosso Sup. Rojano '11	♑♑ 3*
● Todi Sangiovese '12	♑♑ 2*

Tenuta Le Velette

FRAZ. CANALE DI ORVIETO
LOC. LE VELETTE, 23
05019 ORVIETO [TR]
TEL. +39 076329090
www.levelette.it

CELLAR SALES
PRE-BOOKED VISITS
ANNUAL PRODUCTION 320,000 bottles
HECTARES UNDER VINE 119.00

The Bottai family own one of the most beautiful Orvieto estates, on the volcanic side of the DOC zone, east of the cliff, where they built their winery long ago. The results have been excellent. Many grape varieties, both red and white, are grown in the vineyards, which cover an area of over 100 hectares. Work in the cellar is very efficient and ageing takes place in old caves. The distinctive wines are impeccably styled, blending terroir and modernity. Once again, our favourite was a white wine. Orvieto Classico Berganorio 2015 struck us with its traction and stuffing. Its stylish, complex nose is dominated by tempting fruit and wild herbs, while good acidity makes its flinty palate satisfyingly long and interesting. Calanco 2012 is the best of the reds, offering a menthol nose with hints of bay leaf and dark berry fruit, and a juicy although rather tannic palate.

○ Orvieto Cl. Berganorio '15	⏆⏆ 2*
● Calanco '12	⏆⏆ 4
○ Orvieto Cl. Sup. Lunato '15	⏆⏆ 2*
● Rosso Orvietano Rosso di Spicca '14	⏆ 2
● Calanco '03	⏆⏆⏆ 4
● Calanco '95	⏆⏆⏆ 4*
● Gaudio '03	⏆⏆⏆ 4
● Accordo '10	⏆⏆ 2*
● Calanco '08	⏆⏆ 4
● Gaudio '10	⏆⏆ 4
● Gaudio '08	⏆⏆ 4
○ Orvieto Cl. Berganorio '14	⏆⏆ 2*
○ Orvieto Cl. Berganorio '13	⏆⏆ 2*
○ Orvieto Cl. Sup. Lunato '14	⏆⏆ 2*
● Rosso Orvietano Rosso di Spicca '13	⏆⏆ 2*
○ Sole Uve '13	⏆⏆ 3

Villa Mongalli

VIA DELLA CIMA, 52
06031 BEVAGNA [PG]
TEL. +39 0742360703
www.villamongalli.com

CELLAR SALES
ACCOMMODATION
ANNUAL PRODUCTION 70,000 bottles
HECTARES UNDER VINE 15.00

The Menghini family are increasingly involved in their winegrowing operation. Their splendid vineyards are in some of the finest plots in Montefalco and their winery boasts efficient fermentation and ageing cellars. The no-frills style is terroir true, enhancing the characteristics of the grapes used, which are mainly traditional local varieties. Solely native yeasts are used for fermentation and most of the wines undergo long ageing before release. A slight foxy note, which we found quite pleasant, does nothing to mar the very well-made Sagrantino Pozzo del Curato 2012. The captivating, juicy palate progresses naturally with full flavour and hints of wild berries, culminating in a beautiful finish. Full and ripe, as its vintage dictates, Trebbiano Spoletino Calicanto 2015 remains as bright as ever.

● Montefalco Sagrantino Pozzo del Curato '12	⏆⏆ 7
● Montefalco Rosso Le Grazie '14	⏆⏆ 5
○ Trebbiano Spoletino Calicanto '15	⏆⏆ 5
● Montefalco Sagrantino Colcimino '08	⏆⏆⏆ 3*
● Montefalco Sagrantino Della Cima '10	⏆⏆⏆ 8
● Montefalco Sagrantino Della Cima '06	⏆⏆⏆ 6
● Montefalco Sagrantino Pozzo del Curato '09	⏆⏆⏆ 6
○ Calicanto Trebbiano Spoletino '13	⏆⏆ 5
● Montefalco Rosso Le Grazie '12	⏆⏆ 5
● Montefalco Rosso Le Grazie '11	⏆⏆ 5
● Montefalco Sagrantino Colcimino '12	⏆⏆ 8
● Montefalco Sagrantino Colcimino '11	⏆⏆ 8
● Montefalco Sagrantino Colcimino '10	⏆⏆ 3*
● Montefalco Sagrantino Della Cima '08	⏆⏆ 3*
○ Trebbiano Spoletino Calicanto '14	⏆⏆ 5

Argillae

loc. Pomarro, 45
05010 Allerona [TR]
Tel. +39 0763624604
www.argillae.eu

CELLAR SALES
PRE-BOOKED VISITS
ANNUAL PRODUCTION 65,000 bottles
HECTARES UNDER VINE 70.00

○ Orvieto '15	♟♟ 2*
● Sinuoso '15	♟♟ 2*
○ Grechetto '15	♟ 2
○ Orvieto Sup. Panata '15	♟ 2

Berioli

loc. Case Sparse, 21
06063 Magione [PG]
Tel. +39 3355498173
www.cantinaberioli.it

ANNUAL PRODUCTION 15,000 bottles
HECTARES UNDER VINE 12.00

○ Grechetto Vercanto '15	♟♟ 3
○ Toppo Bianco '15	♟♟ 3
● Colli del Trasimeno Spiridione '11	♟ 3

Bigi

loc. Ponte Giulio
05018 Orvieto [TR]
Tel. +39 0763315888
www.cantinebigi.it

PRE-BOOKED VISITS
ANNUAL PRODUCTION 4,000,000 bottles
HECTARES UNDER VINE 248.00

○ Orvieto Cl. Secco '15	♟♟ 2*
○ Orvieto Cl. Torricella '15	♟♟ 3
○ Grechetto Strozzavolpe '15	♟ 3
● Vipra Rossa '15	♟ 2

Carini

loc. Canneto
fraz. Colle Umberto
s.da del Tegolaro, 3
06133 Perugia
Tel. +39 0756059495
www.agrariacarini.it

CELLAR SALES
PRE-BOOKED VISITS
ANNUAL PRODUCTION 40,000 bottles
HECTARES UNDER VINE 10.00

○ C. del Trasimeno Rile '15	♟♟ 2*
○ Lumìa V. T.	♟♟ 4
● Òscano '15	♟♟ 2*
○ Poggio Canneto '14	♟♟ 3

Castello di Corbara

loc. Corbara, 7
05018 Orvieto [TR]
Tel. +39 0763304035
www.castellodicorbara.it

CELLAR SALES
PRE-BOOKED VISITS
ANNUAL PRODUCTION 200,000 bottles
HECTARES UNDER VINE 100.00

○ Orvieto Cl. Sup. '15	♟♟ 2*
○ Orzalume '15	♟♟ 3
● Sangiovese Merlot '15	♟♟ 2*
● Lago di Corbara '14	♟ 3

Castello di Magione

v.le Cavalieri di Malta, 31
06063 Magione [PG]
Tel. +39 0755057319
www.sagrivit.it

CELLAR SALES
PRE-BOOKED VISITS
ANNUAL PRODUCTION 200,000 bottles
HECTARES UNDER VINE 41.00

⊙ Belfiore '15	♟♟ 2*
○ C. del Trasimeno Grechetto Monterone '15	♟♟ 2*
○ Chardonnay '15	♟♟ 3
● Nerocavalieri '13	♟♟ 4

Chiorri

LOC. SANT'ENEA
VIA TODI, 100
06132 PERUGIA
TEL. +39 075607141
www.chiorri.it

CELLAR SALES
PRE-BOOKED VISITS
ACCOMMODATION AND RESTAURANT SERVICE
ANNUAL PRODUCTION 100,000 bottles
HECTARES UNDER VINE 25.00

○ Grechetto '15	🍷🍷 2*
● Sangiovese '15	🍷🍷 2*
⊙ Colli Perugini Rosato '15	🍷 2

Le Cimate

FRAZ. CASALE
LOC. CECAPECORE, 41
06036 MONTEFALCO [PG]
TEL. +39 0742290136
www.lecimate.it

CELLAR SALES
PRE-BOOKED VISITS
ACCOMMODATION AND RESTAURANT SERVICE
ANNUAL PRODUCTION 800,000 bottles
HECTARES UNDER VINE 20.00
SUSTAINABLE WINERY

● Montefalco Sagrantino '12	🍷🍷 5
○ Trebbiano Spoletino '15	🍷🍷 3

Cantina Colle Ciocco

VIA PIETRAUTA
06036 MONTEFALCO [PG]
TEL. +39 0742379859
www.colleciocco.it

CELLAR SALES
PRE-BOOKED VISITS
ANNUAL PRODUCTION 45,000 bottles
HECTARES UNDER VINE 15.00

● Montefalco Rosso '12	🍷🍷 3
● Montefalco Sagrantino '10	🍷🍷 5
○ Spoleto Trebbiano Spoletino Tempestivo '15	🍷🍷 3

Coste del Faena

VOC. CHERABÒ
06054 FRATTA TODINA [PG]
TEL. +39 0758745043
www.costedelfaena.com

CELLAR SALES
PRE-BOOKED VISITS
ANNUAL PRODUCTION 40,000 bottles
HECTARES UNDER VINE 14.00

● Merlot '15	🍷🍷 3
○ Todi Grechetto '15	🍷🍷 4

Custodi

LOC. CANALE
V.LE VENERE
05018 ORVIETO [TR]
TEL. +39 076329053
www.cantinacustodi.com

CELLAR SALES
PRE-BOOKED VISITS
ANNUAL PRODUCTION 65,000 bottles
HECTARES UNDER VINE 40.00

○ Orvieto Cl. Belloro '15	🍷🍷 2*
○ Orvieto Cl. Sup. Pertusa V. T. '15	🍷🍷 5
● Piancoleto '15	🍷 2

Fattoria Giro di Vento

LOC. SCHIFANOIA
S.DA COLLESPINO, 39
05035 NARNI [TR]
TEL. +39 3356136353
www.fattoriagirodivento.it

CELLAR SALES
PRE-BOOKED VISITS
ANNUAL PRODUCTION 30,000 bottles
HECTARES UNDER VINE 10.50
SUSTAINABLE WINERY

● Ciliegiolo di Narni Spiffero '15	🍷🍷 2*
○ Raggio '15	🍷 2

Roberto Lepri

S.DA SAN VETTURINO, 16
06126 PERUGIA
TEL. +39 3388156147
www.robertolepri.com

ANNUAL PRODUCTION 10,000 bottles
HECTARES UNDER VINE 3.50

● Gamay Perugino '14	♟♟ 2*
○ Gocce di Stelle '15	♟♟ 2*
● Fiore d'Alba '10	♟ 3
● Luce di Gemma '11	♟ 2

Morami

FRAZ. PANICAROLA
VOC. MORAMI
06060 CASTIGLIONE DEL LAGO [PG]
TEL. +39 0759589107
www.morami.it

CELLAR SALES
PRE-BOOKED VISITS
ACCOMMODATION
ANNUAL PRODUCTION 20,000 bottles
HECTARES UNDER VINE 11.00

○ Cardissa '14	♟♟ 5
○ Pratolungo '15	♟♟ 3

Cantine Neri

LOC. BARDANO, 28
05018 ORVIETO [TR]
TEL. +39 0763316196
www.neri-vini.it

ANNUAL PRODUCTION 65,000 bottles
HECTARES UNDER VINE 52.00

○ Orvieto Cl. Sup. Ca' Viti '15	♟♟ 2*
○ Bianco dei Neri Chardonnay '15	♟♟ 2*
○ Bianco dei Neri Grechetto '14	♟♟ 3
○ Poggio Forno '13	♟♟ 5

Cantina Ninni

FRAZ. TERRAIA
06049 SPOLETO [PG]
TEL. +39 3355450523
www.cantinaninnispoleto.com

CELLAR SALES
PRE-BOOKED VISITS
ANNUAL PRODUCTION 15,000 bottles
HECTARES UNDER VINE 3.00

● Diavolacciu '13	♟♟ 3
○ Spoleto Trebbiano Spoletino	
Poggio del Vescovo '15	♟♟ 2*
○ Misluli Bianco '15	♟ 2

Domenico Pennacchi

FRAZ. MARCELLANO
VIA SANT'ANGELO, 10
06035 GUALDO CATTANEO [PG]
TEL. +39 0742920069
pennacchidomenico@tiscalinet.it

CELLAR SALES
PRE-BOOKED VISITS
ANNUAL PRODUCTION 12,000 bottles
HECTARES UNDER VINE 6.00

● Colli di Fontivecchie Rosso '12	♟♟ 2*
● Montefalco Rosso Ris. '12	♟♟ 4
○ Colli di Fontivecchie Grechetto '15	♟ 2

La Plani Arche

VOC. CONVERSINO, 160A
06033 CANNARA [PG]
TEL. +39 3356389537
www.planiarche.it

ANNUAL PRODUCTION 15,000 bottles
HECTARES UNDER VINE 6.00
VITICULTURE METHOD Certified Organic
SUSTAINABLE WINERY

● Colli Martani Vernaccia di Cannara '15	♟♟ 5
● Montefalco Sagrantino Brown Label '11	♟♟ 4
○ Spoleto Trebbiano Spoletino '15	♟♟ 2*

Pomario

LOC. POMARIO
06066 PIEGARO [PG]
TEL. +39 064818418
www.pomario.it

CELLAR SALES
PRE-BOOKED VISITS
ANNUAL PRODUCTION 8,000 bottles
HECTARES UNDER VINE 6.00
VITICULTURE METHOD Certified Organic

○ Arale '15	🍷🍷 4
● Sariano '13	🍷🍷 3
⊙ Rondirose '15	🍷 3

Sandonna

LOC. SELVE
05024 GIOVE [TR]
TEL. +39 0744992274
www.cantinasandonna.it

CELLAR SALES
PRE-BOOKED VISITS
ANNUAL PRODUCTION 28,000 bottles
HECTARES UNDER VINE 5.50

● Ciliegiolo di Narni '15	🍷🍷 2*
● Jovio '13	🍷🍷 2*
● Selve di Giove '13	🍷 4

Cantina Santo Iolo

S.DA MONTINI, 36
05035 NARNI [TR]
TEL. +39 0744796754
www.santoiolo.it

CELLAR SALES
PRE-BOOKED VISITS
ANNUAL PRODUCTION 15,000 bottles
HECTARES UNDER VINE 3.50
SUSTAINABLE WINERY

○ Pratalia '15	🍷🍷 3
● Santoiolo '12	🍷🍷 4
● Rossoiolo '13	🍷 3

Sasso dei Lupi

VIA CARLO FAINA, 18
06055 MARSCIANO [PG]
TEL. +39 0758749523
www.sassodeilupi.it

ANNUAL PRODUCTION 400,000 bottles
HECTARES UNDER VINE 400.00

● L'Intruso '15	🍷🍷 1*
○ Luno '14	🍷 5
○ Montali '15	🍷 2

Tenuta di Titignano

LOC. CIVITELLA DEL LAGO
VOC. SALVIANO, 44
05020 BASCHI [TR]
TEL. +39 0744950459
info@titignano.it

CELLAR SALES
PRE-BOOKED VISITS
ANNUAL PRODUCTION 150,000 bottles
HECTARES UNDER VINE 70.00

○ Orvieto Cl. Sup. Salviano '15	🍷🍷 2*
● Lago di Corbara Rosso Solideo '13	🍷 2

Zanchi

VIA ORTANA, 122
05022 AMELIA [TR]
TEL. +39 0744970011
www.cantinezanchi.it

CELLAR SALES
PRE-BOOKED VISITS
ANNUAL PRODUCTION 80,000 bottles
HECTARES UNDER VINE 31.00
SUSTAINABLE WINERY

● Amelia Rosso Armané '13	🍷🍷 2*
● Amelia Rosso Sciurio Ris. '09	🍷🍷 4
○ Vignavecchia '12	🍷🍷 5
● Amelia Ciliegiolo Carmino '15	🍷 2

LAZIO

After a couple of years in which we had noted improvement and overall upswing in quality for regional production, this year we have to backtrack to less positive considerations. Certainly, this can be attributed to two less than positive vintages, which impacted many of the wines tasted, but it also reflects the general fragility of the sector. Far too few makers accept the idea that the only way Lazio wine will get itself back to competitive level is they aim for quality, even at the cost of a drastic reduction in yields, or deciding not to produce in some harvests. In short, 2014's heavy rains and hailstorms hit key areas for the region's wines, for instance the cesanese terroir, and was followed by the tropical heat of 2015, which initially seemed to be a godsend but ended up producing whites that are very often heavy, lacking freshness and the right acidity for length and drinkability, tripping up Lazio wineries. In any case, apart from the usual suspects, it seems to be a struggle to ensure reliable quality in general and specifically in production. This is a critical issue and has been highlighted above all in the Castelli Romani zone and for the Frascati DOC, but has also left its mark in other areas, like Viterbo and the province of Latina, where we are forced to admit that 2014 whites, which many of us deemed to be inferior to previous vintages, are actually more satisfactory that the 2015 counterparts. It is no coincidence that only three Lazio whites were awarded a Tre Bicchieri in a region where 70% of total production is white. On the subject of Tre Bicchieri, we can make two announcements: one absolute and one relative. One spotlights Emanuele Pangrazi's San Giovenale winery and its Habemus 2014, a wine that has literally invented a growing area and created a new entry on the Lazio wine list; the other is a welcome return for Alessandrojacopo Boncompagni Ludovisi, with his Fiorano Rosso, following in the footsteps of the white version. The 2011 vintage will trigger fond memories for those who consumed and loved the Fioranos made way back when by Alessandrojacopo's uncle, Alberico. As for the other award-winning wines, we have the classics, such as Sergio Mottura's Poggio della Costa, or Falesco's Montiano, then those working their way up to classic status like Poggio Le Volpi's Cesanese del Piglio Superiore Hernicus, not to mention the validation that Casale del Giglio's Antonio Santarelli was spot on when he saw the sandy soils of Anzio were just the ticket for making a pure Bellone like Antium.

Antiche Cantine Migliaccio

VIA PIZZICATO
04027 PONZA [LT]
TEL. +39 3392822252
lucianasabino@libero.it

CELLAR SALES
PRE-BOOKED VISITS
ANNUAL PRODUCTION 10,000 bottles
HECTARES UNDER VINE 2.50

Ancient traditions meet modern winemaking techniques. This mix enabled Emanuele Vittorio and his wife Luciana Sabino to found the Antiche Cantine Migliaccio winery in 2000, following in the footsteps of one of their ancestors, who first made wine at Punta Fieno on the island of Ponza back in 1734. The vineyards overlook the sea, on sandy-clayey soils, partly planted to ungrafted natives, including biancolella, forastera, guarnaccia, aglianico and piedirosso. Fieno di Ponza Bianco 2015 is a classic citrusy, gutsy blend obtained from 80% biancolella and forastera, a supple, focused wine which embodies all of the island's flavours. The Biancolella di Ponza 2015 has an appley nose, its full-flavoured minerally palate displaying good staying power. Lastly, the Fieno di Ponza Rosso 2014 is pleasant, redolent of black and red berries, with notes of bramble, a light backdrop of garden vegetables, and a sea-breeze hint of tannins.

○ Fieno di Ponza Bianco '15	▼▼	4
○ Biancolella di Ponza '15	▼▼	5
● Fieno di Ponza Rosso '14	▼	4
○ Biancolella di Ponza '14	♀♀	5
○ Biancolella di Ponza '13	♀♀	5
○ Biancolella di Ponza '12	♀♀	5
○ Fieno di Ponza Bianco '14	♀♀	4
● Fieno di Ponza Rosso '13	♀♀	4

Marco Carpineti

S.DA PROV.LE VELLETRI-ANZIO, 3
04010 CORI [LT]
TEL. +39 069679860
www.marcocarpineti.com

CELLAR SALES
PRE-BOOKED VISITS
ANNUAL PRODUCTION 300,000 bottles
HECTARES UNDER VINE 52.00
VITICULTURE METHOD Certified Organic

Marco Carpineti's natural leaning towards an organic regime is reflected in his recent decision to go back to using horses in his vineyards, on the pebble-rich tufa and limestone volcanic soils. He combines this with a judicious use of state-of-the-art equipment in the winery. The resulting range is good throughout, as shown by the Capolemole Bianco 2015, a finalist that is excellent value for money, with balanced, polished flavours. Compared to the previous vintage, the Moro 2014 is more firmly structured and undeveloped, but gradually becomes clearer with every tasting, which bodes well for the future. The Kius Brut 2013, with its well-consolidated stylish qualities, is now joined by the lively, mature though still rather uneven Kius Rosato 2012. In the absence of Dithyrambus, a noteworthy basic red is the usual drinkable Tufaliccio 2015, while the Capolemole Rosso 2013 is well-typed.

○ Capolemole Bianco '15	▼▼	2*
○ Moro '14	▼▼	3*
○ Kius Brut '13	▼▼	3
● Tufaliccio '15	▼▼	2*
● Capolemole Rosso '13	▼	3
⊙ Kius Extra Brut Rosato '12	▼	5
○ Capolemole Bianco '14	♀♀	2*
○ Capolemole Bianco '13	♀♀	2*
● Capolemole Rosso '12	♀♀	2*
● Dithyrambus '10	♀♀	5
○ Kius Brut '12	♀♀	3
○ Moro '13	♀♀	3*
○ Moro '12	♀♀	3*
⊙ Os Rosae '13	♀♀	2*
● Tufaliccio '13	♀♀	2*

Casale del Giglio

Loc. Le Ferriere
S.da Cisterna-Nettuno km 13
04100 Latina
Tel. +39 0692902530
www.casaledelgiglio.it

CELLAR SALES
PRE-BOOKED VISITS
ANNUAL PRODUCTION 1,276,600 bottles
HECTARES UNDER VINE 164.00
SUSTAINABLE WINERY

Based on biancolella grown on Ponza and processed in an ancient local cellar, and on heirloom bellone from Anzio, some ungrafted, Antonio Santarelli and Paolo Tiefenthaler's native varietals project looks set to hit interesting new heights. In the meantime, the results speak for themselves, with another Tre Bicchieri deservedly going to the Antium 2015, with its wealth of polished nuances at every sip, whereas the Faro della Guardia 2015 is more pedestrian. The Mater Matuta 2013 is back in the finals after a year out of production, with its excellent fruit-oak balance, while the Tempranijo 2014 is a first-time finalist, almost a Valpolicella-style Ripasso, where mature notes are offset by excellent tannic weave. The rest of the huge range remains of good quality, in particular the Albiola 2015, one of the region's top Rosatos, and the Petit Manseng 2015, the best we have tasted so far, with its long, full nose and mouth.

○ Antium Bellone '15	♛♛♛ 4*	
● Mater Matuta '13	♛♛ 7	
● Tempranijo '14	♛♛ 5	
○ Albiola Rosato '15	♛♛ 3	
○ Antinoo '14	♛♛ 5	
○ Biancolella Faro della Guardia '15	♛♛ 5	
● Madreselva '13	♛♛ 5	
○ Petit Manseng '15	♛♛ 4	
○ Chardonnay '15	♛ 3	
○ Satrico '15	♛ 3	
● Shiraz '14	♛ 4	
○ Viognier '15	♛ 3	
○ Antium Bellone '14	♛♛♛ 4*	
○ Biancolella Faro della Guardia '13	♛♛♛ 5	

Castel de Paolis

via Val de Paolis
00046 Grottaferrata [RM]
Tel. +39 069413648
www.casteldepaolis.com

CELLAR SALES
PRE-BOOKED VISITS
RESTAURANT SERVICE
ANNUAL PRODUCTION 80,000 bottles
HECTARES UNDER VINE 11.00

The winery was set up in the mid-1980s by Giulio Santarelli, a man of great experience in politics and agriculture. With his wife Adriana, he restored to ancient splendour the medieval fortress of Castel de Paolis, built on the ruins of a Roman villa. They also restored the surrounding vineyards, focusing both on reviving native varieties and on experimenting with international grape types under the watchful eye of University of Milan professor Attilio Scienza. The winery is in the process of converting to organic. Fabrizio Santarelli and oenologist Fabrizio Bono produce a fine series of wines from their 11 hectares under vine. We especially enjoyed the Donna Adriana 2015, a blend of viognier and malvasia del Lazio. It has backbone and attitude, a delicate bouquet of peach and summer flowers, and a complex, fresh-tasting and fragrant palate. The piquant, balanced Frascati 2015 has plenty of flavour and alcoholic warmth. The long, juicy Campo Vecchio Rosso 2014 has hints of black pepper and dark berry fruit.

● Campo Vecchio Rosso '14	♛♛ 3	
○ Donna Adriana '15	♛♛ 4	
○ Frascati Sup. '15	♛♛ 3	
○ Frascati Campo Vecchio '15	♛ 2	
● I Quattro Mori '12	♛ 5	
● Rosathea '15	♛ 4	
● Campo Vecchio Rosso '12	♛♛ 3	
○ Frascati Campo Vecchio '14	♛♛ 2*	
○ Frascati Sup. '12	♛♛ 3	
● I Quattro Mori '11	♛♛ 5	
○ Muffa Nobile '11	♛♛ 5	

Cincinnato

VIA CORI-CISTERNA, KM 2
04010 CORI [LT]
TEL. +39 069679380
www.cincinnato.it

CELLAR SALES
PRE-BOOKED VISITS
ACCOMMODATION AND RESTAURANT SERVICE
ANNUAL PRODUCTION 600,000 bottles
HECTARES UNDER VINE 400.00
SUSTAINABLE WINERY

As we know, vines have flourished on the hills of Cori since Ancient Roman times, remembered in this cooperative winery's name, but human labour is equally important. Mindful of this, Nazareno Milita and Carlo Morettini have been overseeing the state-of-the-art cellar and ensuring their growers apply strict vineyard management, all of which has led to the successes of the last 20 years. Production revolves around two great native varietals, nero buono and bellone, whose main versions, the rounded yet balanced Ercole Nero Buono 2013 and the emphatic, minerally, full-flavoured Pozzodorico Bellone 2014, both reached the finals. The natives are well represented by the Cori Rosso Raverosse 2013 and Cori Bianco Illirio 2015, while greco gialo, also known locally as moro, is used for Pantaleo 2015, with its pleasingly husky, almondy mouth. The other wines were also well-typed, though we certainly remember better vintages.

● Ercole Nero Buono '13	🍷🍷 3*
○ Pozzodorico Bellone '14	🍷🍷 2*
○ Cori Bianco Illirio '15	🍷🍷 2*
● Cori Rosso Raverosse '13	🍷🍷 2*
○ Pantaleo '15	🍷🍷 2*
● Arcatura '14	🍷 2
○ Castore '15	🍷 2
● Arcatura '13	🍾 2*
○ Castore '14	🍾 2*
○ Cori Bianco Illirio '13	🍾 2*
● Ercole Nero Buono '12	🍾 3
● Ercole Nero Buono '11	🍾 3
○ Pantaleo '14	🍾 2*
○ Pozzodorico Bellone '12	🍾 2*

Damiano Ciolli

VIA DEL CORSO
00035 OLEVANO ROMANO [RM]
TEL. +39 069563334
www.damianociolli.it

CELLAR SALES
PRE-BOOKED VISITS
ANNUAL PRODUCTION 25,000 bottles
HECTARES UNDER VINE 5.00
SUSTAINABLE WINERY

Damiano Ciolli's winery opened in 2001, but his family has been growing grapes here for four generations. His small production figures are entirely made up of cesanese for the Olevano Romano designation. His vineyards, from 15 to 35 years of age, lie at an altitude of around 450 metres on volcanic terra rossa soils; one hectare, planted by Damiano's grandfather in 1953, is dedicated to the Cirsium vineyard selection, growing only cesanese di Affile. This is a slightly below par edition for Ciolli wines. His Cesanese di Olevano Romano Cirsium Riserva 2012 shows black berry fruit and Mediterranean scrub on the nose, with hints of sweet oak, while the palate displays good mouthfeel, but somewhat rougher tannins. By contrast, the Cesanese di Olevano Romano Superiore Silene 2014 is lighter, almost insubstantial, as befits the 2014 vintage, but has fresh, full-flavoured, pleasing fruitiness.

● Cesanese di Olevano Romano Cirsium Ris. '12	🍷🍷 5
● Cesanese di Olevano Romano Sup. Silene '14	🍷🍷 3
● Cesanese di Olevano Cirsium '08	🍾 5
● Cesanese di Olevano Romano Cirsium '11	🍾 5
● Cesanese di Olevano Romano Sup. Cirsium '09	🍾 5
● Cesanese di Olevano Romano Sup. Cirsium Ris. '10	🍾 5
● Cesanese di Olevano Romano Sup. Silene '13	🍾 3
● Cesanese di Olevano Romano Sup. Silene '12	🍾 3
● Cesanese di Olevano Romano Sup. Silene '10	🍾 3
● Cesanese di Olevano Silene '11	🍾 2*

Antonello Coletti Conti

VIA VITTORIO EMANUELE, 116
03012 ANAGNI [FR]
TEL. +39 0775728610
www.coletticonti.it

CELLAR SALES
PRE-BOOKED VISITS
ANNUAL PRODUCTION 20,000 bottles
HECTARES UNDER VINE 20.00

Antonello Coletti Conti's tiny estate lies at the heart of the Cesanese del Piglio designation, and it comes as no surprise that this heirloom grape is the winery's mainstay. That said, with his curious and adventurous spirit, Antonello also explores other pathways, including bordeaux and incrocio Manzoni varieties, as well as recent plantings of traditional passerina. This year, for the first time, he is pleased enough with the results to present the complete range. Both Cesaneses reached the final, while we preferred their younger sibling, Hernicus 2014 for its breadth, complexity and surprising balance at such an early stage. The Romanico 2014 will also achieve that balance, though its rich fruitiness needs to open up to absorb some of the oakiness. The Cabernet Franc Cosmato 2014 sets a rather international tone, while of the two whites, the Incrocio Manzoni Arcadia 2015 displays an elegance that time can only enhance.

● Cesanese del Piglio Sup. Hernicus '14	♟♟♟	3*
● Cesanese del Piglio Sup. Romanico '14	♟♟	5
○ Arcadia '15	♟♟	3
● Cosmato '14	♟♟	5
○ Passerina del Frusinate Hernicus '15	♟	3
● Cesanese del Piglio Romanico '11	♟♟♟	5
● Cesanese del Piglio Romanico '07	♟♟♟	5
● Cesanese del Piglio Sup. Hernicus '12	♟♟♟	3*
● Cesanese del Piglio Hernicus '11	♟♟	3*
● Cesanese del Piglio Romanico '12	♟♟	5
● Cesanese del Piglio Romanico '10	♟♟	5
● Cesanese del Piglio Sup. Hernicus '13	♟♟	3
● Cesanese del Piglio Sup. Romanico '13	♟♟	5
● Cosmato '12	♟♟	5

Paolo e Noemia D'Amico

LOC. PALOMBARO
FRAZ. VAIANO
01024 CASTIGLIONE IN TEVERINA [VT]
TEL. +39 0761948034
www.paoloenoemiadamico.it

CELLAR SALES
PRE-BOOKED VISITS
RESTAURANT SERVICE
ANNUAL PRODUCTION 150,000 bottles
HECTARES UNDER VINE 30.00
SUSTAINABLE WINERY

Different life stories join forces here to write a chapter in winemaking. Paolo is the third generation of a ship-owning family and grew up surrounded by vines; while Noemia, of Portuguese origin, inherited her grandparents' love of wine. In the heart of Tuscia, they found fertile terrain for their shared passion. The winery's vineyards are found here among the badlands of the upper Tiber valley, planted mainly to international varietals. With an unusually subdued Calanchi Vaiano 2015, the labels which impressed us most this year are the Chardonnay Falesia 2014, with its nose of peach and apricot, hints of hedgerow, and good thrust on the palate, and the spicy and agreeable Notturno dei Calanchi 2013, a crisp, succulent Pinot Nero with classic notes of forest fruits. Also nicely crafted is the Orvieto Noe dei Calanchi 2015 with its notes of citrus and tropical fruit, while the fragrant blend from 70% sémillon and sauvignon, Terre di Ala 2015, dances across the palate.

○ Falesia '14	♟♟	5
● Notturno dei Calanchi '13	♟♟	5
○ Calanchi di Vaiano '15	♟	3
○ Orvieto Noe dei Calanchi '15	♟	2
○ Terre di Ala '15	♟	3
● Villa Tirrena '12	♟	3
● Atlante '12	♟♟	5
○ Calanchi di Vaiano '12	♟♟	3
○ Falesia '11	♟♟	4
● Notturno dei Calanchi '12	♟♟	5
● Notturno dei Calanchi '11	♟♟	5
○ Seiano Bianco '11	♟♟	2*
● Seiano Rosso '11	♟♟	2*
○ Terre di Ala '13	♟♟	3

LAZIO

★★Falesco

LOC. SAN PIETRO
05020 MONTECCHIO [TR]
TEL. +39 07449556
www.falesco.it

CELLAR SALES
PRE-BOOKED VISITS
ACCOMMODATION
ANNUAL PRODUCTION 4,100,000 bottles
HECTARES UNDER VINE 370.00

Falesco is a family winery, started in 1979 by Renzo and Riccardo Cotarella, and continuing today with the new generations, who still combine science with their passion for wine. The original vineyards are planted to both international and native varieties, and lie between Montefiascone and Lake Bolsena, in Lazio. Its Umbrian estate, on the hills south of Orvieto is home to merlot, cabernet, sangiovese, verdicchio, and vermentino, along with a few experimental cultivars. Montiano 2014, from merlot, is as good as ever, with a nose of dark berries, liquorice, and sweet oak, and a long, gutsy palate. The plush, juicy Trentanni 2014 is an equal blend of merlot and sangiovese, with notes of blackberries and spice, while Est! Est!! Est!!! di Montefiascone Poggio dei Gelsi 2015 offers nuances of sage and apples. However, the entire range is good, underscoring the estate's consistent performance.

● Montiano '14	♟♟♟	6
● Trentanni '14	♟♟	4
● Appunto '15	♟♟	1*
○ Est! Est!! Est!!! di Montefiascone Accenno '15	♟♟	2
○ Est! Est!! Est!!! di Montefiascone Poggio dei Gelsi '15	♟♟	2*
○ Falesco Brut M. Cl. '11	♟♟	4
○ Ferentano '14	♟♟	4
● Messidoro '15	♟♟	1*
○ Soente '15	♟♟	3
○ Tellus Oro '15	♟♟	2*
● Tellus Syrah '15	♟	3
● Vitiano Rosso '15	♟	2
○ Vitiano Vermentino '15	♟	3
● Montiano '13	♟♟♟	6
● Montiano '12	♟♟♟	6

Fontana Candida

VIA FONTANA CANDIDA, 11
00040 MONTE PORZIO CATONE [RM]
TEL. +39 069401881
www.fontanacandida.it

CELLAR SALES
PRE-BOOKED VISITS
RESTAURANT SERVICE
ANNUAL PRODUCTION 3,700,000 bottles
HECTARES UNDER VINE 97.00

One of Gruppo Italiano Vini's best-known brands, Fontana Candida, is also one of Castelli Romani's biggest producers. At the heart of the Frascati district, the winery processes around 50,000 quintals of grapes, from over 190 growers, produced on the area's volcanic soils rich in potassium, phosphorus, calcium, magnesium, iron, and trace elements. Making mainly whites, the winery's top labels are from local varieties. The whole Frascati range is well-typed, especially the Superiore Luna Mater Riserva 2015, displaying ripe tropical fruit and good structure, with background notes of oak and spices. The Superiore Terre dei Grifi 2015 has notes of aromatic herbs and citrus underpinned by acidity, while the Superiore Vigneto Santa Teresa 2015 captures white-fleshed fruit and lemon, with a vegetal hint. Sweet citrus fruit accompanied by hints of sage mark the Roma Malvasia Puntinata 2015.

○ Frascati Sup. Luna Mater Ris. '15	♟♟	3*
○ Frascati Sup. Terre dei Grifi '15	♟♟	2*
○ Frascati Sup. Vign. Santa Teresa '15	♟♟	2*
○ Roma Malvasia Puntinata '15	♟♟	3
○ Frascati Secco '15	♟	2
○ Sesto 21 Passito '12	♟	4
● Sesto 21 Syrah '13	♟	4
○ Frascati Secco '14	♟♟	2*
○ Frascati Sup. Luna Mater Ris. '14	♟♟	4
○ Frascati Sup. Terre dei Grifi '14	♟♟	2*
○ Frascati Sup. Vign. Santa Teresa '14	♟♟	2*
○ Frascati Sup. Vign. Santa Teresa '13	♟♟	2*
● Siroe '14	♟♟	3

★Sergio Mottura

LOC. POGGIO DELLA COSTA, 1
01020 CIVITELLA D'AGLIANO [VT]
TEL. +39 0761914533
www.motturasergio.it

CELLAR SALES
PRE-BOOKED VISITS
ACCOMMODATION AND RESTAURANT SERVICE
ANNUAL PRODUCTION 97,000 bottles
HECTARES UNDER VINE 37.00
VITICULTURE METHOD Certified Organic

Sergio Mottura must be the greatest craftsman of grechetto, a variety he has championed since the early 1960s. Varietal stamping, quality and environmental sustainability are the watchwords for this winery, which uses the porcupine on its labels as the symbol of its quality and authenticity. Sergio experiments widely with organic methods on his 37 hectares under vine, set among the clay gullies of Civitella d'Agliano and the Tiber valley, dominated by native vine varieties such as grechetto, drupeggio, verdello and procanico. Repeating last year's Tre Bicchieri success is the Grechetto Poggio della Costa 2015 with its nose profile of citrus, saffron and summer flowers, and full-flavoured palate supported by an elegant gutsy mouthfeel. The complex, generous Latour a Civitella 2014 is back to its best, with spicy citrusy sweet notes, while the richly-flavoured and spicy Orvieto Tragugnano 2015 remains exceptional. Lastly, the 2015 Civitella Rosato is well-orchestrated, delicate and pleasing.

Omina Romana

VIA FONTANA PARATA, 75
00049 VELLETRI [RM]
TEL. +39 0696430193
www.ominaromana.com

CELLAR SALES
PRE-BOOKED VISITS
ANNUAL PRODUCTION 130,000 bottles
HECTARES UNDER VINE 80.00

In 2004, German entrepreneur Anton F. Börner invested in an 80-hectare estate in Velletri, in the Colli Albani, to make quality wines with a rather international feel to them. The character of the territory, its volcanic hillside soils and constant sea breezes are, as the winery name suggests, good omens for top-quality production. Winemaker Claudio Gori and agronomist Paula Pacheco decided to focus mainly on reds, processing 12 different varietals, some local and others international. This year's top of the range is the long, close-knit Cabernet Franc Linea Ars Magna 2013, with its notes of black berry fruit, sweet oak and rain-soaked earth. Also impressive is the Hermes Diactoros 2013, a refreshing Bordeaux blend displaying good fruitiness, spice and well-managed tannins. The 2013 Merlot is well-typed, with sound, dense fruit, and notes of leaf tobacco and cocoa powder, while the Bellone Brut 2014 is pleasantly fresh.

○ Poggio della Costa '15	▲▲▲ 3*
○ Grechetto Latour a Civitella '14	▲▲ 5
○ Orvieto Tragugnano '15	▲▲ 3*
◉ Civitella Rosato '15	▲▲ 3
● Civitella Rosso '14	▲ 3
○ Orvieto Secco '15	▲ 3
○ Grechetto Latour a Civitella '11	▽▽▽ 4*
○ Grechetto Latour a Civitella '06	▽▽▽ 4*
○ Grechetto Poggio della Costa '14	▽▽▽ 3*
○ Grechetto Poggio della Costa '10	▽▽▽ 3*
○ Grechetto Poggio della Costa '09	▽▽▽ 3*
○ Grechetto Poggio della Costa '08	▽▽▽ 3*
○ Poggio della Costa '12	▽▽▽ 3*
○ Poggio della Costa '11	▽▽▽ 3*

● Cabernet Franc Linea Ars Magna '13	▲▲ 8
○ Bellone Brut '14	▲▲ 4
● Hermes Diactoros '13	▲▲ 4
● Merlot '13	▲▲ 7
● Cabernet Sauvignon '11	▽▽ 7
● Diana Nemorensis I '12	▽▽ 6
● Merlot '12	▽▽ 7

Principe Pallavicini

VIA ROMA, 121
00030 COLONNA [RM]
TEL. +39 069438816
www.vinipallavicini.com

CELLAR SALES
PRE-BOOKED VISITS
RESTAURANT SERVICE
ANNUAL PRODUCTION 600,000 bottles
HECTARES UNDER VINE 65.00

Principe Pallavicini is one of the pillars of
the region's wine-making. Soils once tended
by princes, cardinals and popes, are today
in the hands of Maria Camilla, committed to
maximizing the potential of the Frascati
designation. Most of her vineyards are
situated in Castelli Romani, where white
grapes thrive on the volcanic soils. The
winery is made up of the venerable cellar
and administrative offices in Colonna, and
the Cerveteri estate with its limestone,
pebble-rich soils, ideal for sangiovese,
merlot and syrah. The well-made Cesanese
Amarasco 2014 has a fruit-driven bouquet,
leading into a palate of crisp black berry
fruit and a tasty, drinkable finish. Also well
made, though we felt not quite up to last
year's levels, is the austere Frascati
Superiore Poggio Verde 2015, with plenty of
stuffing, backed up by good vegetal
nuances. Also interesting is the pleasingly
refreshing Roma Malvasia Puntinata 2015,
with its nose of sage and roses.

○ Frascati Sup. Poggio Verde '15	♥♥ 2*
● Amarasco '14	♥♥ 3
○ Roma Malvasia Puntinata '15	♥♥ 2*
● Soleggio '14	♥ 3
○ Stillato '14	♥ 3
● Syrah '14	♥ 2
○ Frascati Sup. Poggio Verde '13	♥♥♥ 2*
● Amarasco '11	♀♀ 3
● Casa Romana '12	♀♀ 5
○ Frascati '13	♀♀ 2*
○ Frascati Sup. Poggio Verde '14	♀♀ 2*
○ Frascati Sup. Poggio Verde '12	♀♀ 2*
○ Stillato '13	♀♀ 3*
○ Stillato '12	♀♀ 3

Tenuta La Pazzaglia

S.DA DI BAGNOREGIO, 4
01024 CASTIGLIONE IN TEVERINA [VT]
TEL. +39 0761947114
www.tenutalapazzaglia.it

CELLAR SALES
PRE-BOOKED VISITS
ACCOMMODATION
ANNUAL PRODUCTION 56,000 bottles
HECTARES UNDER VINE 12.00

The Verdecchia family celebrates 25 years
in the winemaking world. After starting up
Tenuta La Pazzaglia, in the Valle dei
Calanchi, in 1991, they began a journey
through tradition and innovation, trial and
error. Randolfo and Agnese's son
Pierfrancesco tends the vineyards, and his
sister Maria Teresa handles the vinification.
The winery processes both native grape
types, especially grechetto, as well as
international varieties. Another finalist is the
Grechetto Poggio Triale 2014, with a
bouquet of hedgerow and apricots, a palate
showing plenty of mouthfeel, elegance and
richness of flavour. We once again enjoyed
the Grechetto 109, the gutsy 2015 version
displaying hints of refreshing white-fleshed
fruit, jasmine and citrus. The deep, savoury
2015 Corno from grechetto, chardonnay
and pinot bianco, has notes of peach,
apricot and orange blossom. Finally, the
Orvieto Vignamia 2015, with its citrusy
notes, shows good fruit.

○ Poggio Triale '14	♥♥ 3*
○ Grechetto 109 '15	♥♥ 3
○ Il Corno '15	♥♥ 2*
○ Orvieto Vignamia '15	♥ 2
○ Grechetto 109 '14	♀♀ 3
○ Grechetto 109 '13	♀♀ 3*
○ Il Corno '14	♀♀ 2*
○ Il Corno '12	♀♀ 2*
○ Orvieto '12	♀♀ 2*
○ Orvieto '11	♀♀ 2*
○ Poggio Triale '12	♀♀ 3
⊙ Rosé Marie '14	♀♀ 2*

Pietra Pinta

VIA LE PASTINE KM 20,200
04010 CORI [LT]
TEL. +39 069678001
www.pietrapinta.com

CELLAR SALES
PRE-BOOKED VISITS
ACCOMMODATION AND RESTAURANT SERVICE
ANNUAL PRODUCTION 300,000 bottles
HECTARES UNDER VINE 33.00
VITICULTURE METHOD Certified Organic
SUSTAINABLE WINERY

The Ferretti family has long been a resourceful promoter of the Cori area's traits and beauty, producing fine olive oil and wines and, in the last decade, also running a welcoming holiday farm. We are delighted that Colle Amato, the wine which launched this winery on a nationwide level, is back to its usual excellence. The full-bodied yet balanced 2012 shows dark berry fruit and liquorice to the fore. It is backed up by two more contemporary whites, the result of a recent focus on international varietals, the Chardonnay 2015 with a charming and rather unusual richness of flavour, and Viognier 2015, with citrus alongside peach and apricot. The other wines have taken the same path, and we had a slight preference for the whites, due to the pleasant aromatic profile of both the Malvasia Puntinata 2015 and the Sauvignon 2015.

○ Chardonnay '15	▼▼ 2*	
● Colle Amato '12	▼▼ 4	
○ Viognier '15	▼▼ 2*	
○ Costa Vecchia Bianco '15	▼ 2	
● Costa Vecchia Rosso '15	▼ 2	
○ Malvasia Puntinata '15	▼ 2	
○ Sauvignon '15	▼ 2	
● Shiraz '14	▼ 2	
○ Chardonnay '13	♀♀ 2*	
● Colle Amato '10	♀♀ 4	
○ Costa Vecchia Bianco '14	♀♀ 2*	
● Costa Vecchia Rosso '13	♀♀ 2*	
○ Malvasia Puntinata '14	♀♀ 2*	
● Nero Buono '13	♀♀ 2*	
○ Sauvignon '14	♀♀ 2*	

Poggio Le Volpi

VIA COLLE PISANO, 27
00040 MONTE PORZIO CATONE [RM]
TEL. +39 069426980
www.poggiolevolpi.it

CELLAR SALES
PRE-BOOKED VISITS
RESTAURANT SERVICE
ANNUAL PRODUCTION 300,000 bottles
HECTARES UNDER VINE 70.00

During the 1990s, Felice Mergè was a young winemaker who decided to take over the family cellars, exploiting the traits of commitment, tradition, research, and experimentation that had made the business successful. The resulting wines are modern and distinctive, much of the credit going to the volcanic clay soils at an altitude of 400 metres, on the slopes of Mount Porzio Catone, where mainly native varieties are grown. Tre Bicchieri for the Frascati Superiore Epos Riserva 2015 with its sweet citrus nose with hints of garden vegetables, following through to an enveloping palate, with good matière and yet refreshing. True to type the Frascati Cannellino 2011, with a nose of medlar and spring flowers, a healthy balance of sweetness and acidity. The Nero Buono di Cori Baccarossa 2014 is pleasant, with fruit-driven hints despite the oakiness. Lastly, the outstanding Donnaluce 2015, from malvasia puntinata, greco and chardonnay, shows appley fruit and wood resin.

○ Frascati Sup. Epos Ris. '15	▼▼▼ 3*	
● Baccarossa '14	▼▼ 5	
○ Donnaluce '15	▼▼ 4	
○ Frascati Cannellino '11	▼▼ 4	
● Baccarossa '13	♀♀♀ 4*	
● Baccarossa '11	♀♀♀ 4*	
○ Frascati Sup. Epos '13	♀♀♀ 2*	
○ Frascati Sup. Epos '11	♀♀♀ 2*	
○ Frascati Sup. Epos '10	♀♀♀ 2*	
○ Frascati Sup. Epos '09	♀♀♀ 2*	
● Baccarossa '12	♀♀ 4	
○ Donnaluce '13	♀♀ 3	
○ Donnaluce '12	♀♀ 3	
○ Frascati Sup. Epos '14	♀♀ 2*	

San Giovenale

LOC. LA MACCHIA
01010 BLERA [VT]
TEL. +39 066877877
www.sangiovenale.it

CELLAR SALES
PRE-BOOKED VISITS
ACCOMMODATION AND RESTAURANT SERVICE
ANNUAL PRODUCTION 7,000 bottles
HECTARES UNDER VINE 10.00
VITICULTURE METHOD Certified Organic
SUSTAINABLE WINERY

An organic winery with a focus on land conservation, San Giovenale vaunts a fully sustainable cellar, with living roofs, ventilated walls and roofing, as well as geothermal temperature control. They have made similarly significant decisions in the vineyard, planting grenache, syrah, carignano and cabernet franc, blending the first three into Habemus Etichetta Bianca, while the Habemus Cabernet Etichetta Rossa is a monovarietal Franc. Since its launch four years ago, Habemus had earned itself a place among the region's finest reds, and the 2014 brings home a Tre Bicchieri. Its nose of spices, tapenade and ripe black berry fruit gives way to a typically close-woven palate escorted by elegant tannins, balanced by an unexpected freshness, for a wine of great complexity and personality. Meanwhile, the Habemus Cabernet 2013 Etichetta Rossa shows exemplary grip, body and drinkability.

Sant'Andrea

LOC. BORGO VODICE
VIA RENIBBIO, 1720
04019 TERRACINA [LT]
TEL. +39 0773755028
www.cantinasantandrea.it

CELLAR SALES
PRE-BOOKED VISITS
ANNUAL PRODUCTION 1,000,000 bottles
HECTARES UNDER VINE 85.00

Their attractive vineyards, some rented, are in the best wine country for the Circeo designations, especially Moscato di Terracina, which Andrea and Gabriele Pandolfo have brought to nationwide attention. A few years ago, they introduced Hum as a sister wine to Oppidum, which was slightly disappointing in 2015. It seems to have been a wise decision to age the wines longer, and the result, for Hum 2013, is a concentrated aromatic profile full of Mediterranean warmth. They are backed up by the deep, elegant Circeo Bianco Dune 2014, with its courageous wood-aged malvasia with trebbiano, and the Sogno 2011, from merlot and cesanese, which shows good nose-palate harmony. A special mention for the Riflessi range, which has good average quality levels at competitive prices. We especially liked the Circeo Bianco 2015, and we were taken too by the Circeo Rosato 2015, from merlot, and by the Extra Dry, a slightly off-dry sparkler from trebbiano and malvasia.

● Habemus '14	♟♟♟ 7
● Habemus Cabernet '13	♟♟ 8
● Habemus '13	♟♟ 7
● Habemus '12	♟♟ 7
● Habemus '11	♟♟ 7
● Habemus '10	♟♟ 4

○ Circeo Bianco Dune '14	♟♟ 2*
○ Circeo Bianco Riflessi '15	♟♟ 2*
○ Moscato di Terracina Hum '13	♟♟ 5
● Sogno '11	♟♟ 3
⊙ Circeo Rosato Riflessi '15	♟ 2
● Circeo Rosso Incontro al Circeo '12	♟ 2
○ Moscato di Terracina Amabile Templum '15	♟ 2
○ Moscato di Terracina Secco Oppidum '15	♟ 2
○ Riflessi Extra Dry	♟ 2
⊙ Circeo Rosato Riflessi '14	♟♟ 2*
● Circeo Rosso Riflessi '14	♟♟ 2*
○ Moscato di Terracina Passito Capitolium '13	♟♟ 4

Tenuta di Fiorano

VIA DI FIORANELLO, 19-31
00134 ROMA
TEL. +39 0679340093
www.tenutadifiorano.it

CELLAR SALES
PRE-BOOKED VISITS
RESTAURANT SERVICE
ANNUAL PRODUCTION 18,000 bottles
HECTARES UNDER VINE 6.00

Just a few miles outside Rome, time seems to have forgotten this corner of paradise, its charm undiminished, as is its fine winemaking tradition. Tenuta di Fiorano has a fascinating history, and is now run by Alessandrojacopo Boncompagni Ludovisi, since his uncle, Prince Alberico, handed over replanting rights to him in the late 1990s. The black grapes on his five hectares are unchanged, including cabernet sauvignon and merlot, whereas malvasia and semillon have been replaced by grechetto and viognier. The 2011 Fiorano Rosso is splendid, its nose of Mediterranean scrubland, cep mushrooms and black berry fruit giving way to a very firmly structured palate, which is both mouthfilling and elegant. The Fiorano Bianco 2014 has a highly complex bouquet and palate, with its flowery, saffrony notes of apple and spice. Also well-made are the Fioranello Rosso 2014, with its notes of black berry fruit and quinine, and the fresh-tasting, citrusy Fioranello Bianco 2015.

● Fiorano Rosso '11	♟♟♟ 7
○ Fiorano Bianco '14	♟♟ 5
○ Fioranello Bianco '15	♟♟ 3
● Fioranello Rosso '14	♟♟ 4
○ Fiorano Bianco '13	♟♟♟ 5
○ Fiorano Bianco '12	♟♟♟ 4*
○ Fiorano Bianco '10	♟♟♟ 5
○ Fioranello Bianco '14	♟♟ 3
● Fioranello Rosso '13	♟♟ 4
○ Fiorano Bianco '11	♟♟ 4
● Fiorano Rosso '10	♟♟ 7
● Fiorano Rosso '09	♟♟ 7
● Fiorano Rosso '07	♟♟ 4

Giovanni Terenzi

VIA FORESE, 13
03010 SERRONE [FR]
TEL. +39 0775594286
www.viniterenzi.com

CELLAR SALES
PRE-BOOKED VISITS
ANNUAL PRODUCTION 150,000 bottles
HECTARES UNDER VINE 12.00

Over the last 50 years, the Terenzi winery has focused on Cesanese, with top-quality vineyards both in the Piglio designation and in the nearby Olevano Romano DOC zone, on volcanic and limestone soils. So it comes as quite a surprise that the most successful wine is the Quercia Rossa 2012, from sangiovese, with a full-flavoured, coherent fruitiness, tertiary notes and well-balanced tannins. Of the Cesaneses, after the excellent 2011 and 2012 vintages, the Vajoscuro 2013 confirms its top spot. It is no coincidence that this is the cellar's most ambitious wine, aged long, with spicy nuances of quinine and rhubarb, and a fully-rounded mouth. Lacking in breadth and complexity, which perhaps makes them more drinkable, are the Velobra 2014 and the 2013 Colle Forma. Almondy notes for an unusual version of the Passerina Villa Santa 2015, though recent vintages have seemed more convincing and varietal.

● Cesanese del Piglio Sup. Vajoscuro Ris. '13	♟♟ 4
● Quercia Rossa '12	♟♟ 3
● Cesanese del Piglio Sup. Colle Forma '13	♟ 4
● Cesanese del Piglio Velobra '14	♟ 2
○ Passerina Villa Santa '15	♟ 2
● Cesanese del Piglio Sup. Colle Forma '11	♟♟ 4
● Cesanese del Piglio Sup. Vajoscuro Ris. '12	♟♟ 4
● Cesanese del Piglio Sup. Vajoscuro Ris. '11	♟♟ 4
● Cesanese del Piglio Vajoscuro '10	♟♟ 5
● Cesanese del Piglio Velobra '13	♟♟ 2*
● Cesanese del Piglio Velobra '12	♟♟ 2*
● Cesanese del Piglio Velobra '11	♟♟ 2*
● Cesanese di Olevano Romano Colle S. Quirico '13	♟♟ 2*

Trappolini

VIA DEL RIVELLINO, 65
01024 CASTIGLIONE IN TEVERINA [VT]
TEL. +39 0761948381
www.trappolini.com

CELLAR SALES
PRE-BOOKED VISITS
ANNUAL PRODUCTION 150,000 bottles
HECTARES UNDER VINE 30.00

Roberto and Paolo took over from their
father Mario who had started up his winery
selling bulk wine from his own vineyards on
the Lazio-Umbria border in the early 1960s.
They have since renewed and enhanced the
range. Production is based almost entirely
on natives, including aleatico, sangiovese,
violone, procanico, and grechetto, which
make the most of the typical mix of volcanic
clayey soils. Of note, too, the focus on black
grapes, which is unusual for this area.
Among the whites, the Grechetto 2015 put
in a good show, with yellow-fleshed fruit
and saffron on the nose, its palate
embellished with hints of almond, for a rich
and harmonious finish. We also liked the
pleasant if a touch rustic Est! Est!! Est!!! di
Montefiascone 2015, with its bouquet of
Golden Delicious apple and lemon. The
outstanding red is Paterno 2014, with tones
of violets and red berries, consistent and
fresh on the palate, with hints of black
pepper and spices. Notes of red pepper and
leaf tobacco make the Cabernet Franc 2014
flavoursome and varietal.

○ Grechetto '15	⚐⚐ 2*
● Cabernet Franc '14	⚐⚐ 3
○ Est! Est!! Est!!! di Montefiascone '15	⚐⚐ 2*
● Paterno '14	⚐⚐ 4
○ Brecceto '15	⚐ 3
● Canaiolo Nero '14	⚐ 2
● Cenereto '15	⚐ 2
● Idea '15	⚐ 4
○ Orvieto '15	⚐ 2
○ Sartei '15	⚐ 2
○ Grechetto '14	⚐⚐⚐ 2*
● Cabernet Franc '13	⚐⚐ 3
● Paterno '13	⚐⚐ 4
● Paterno '12	⚐⚐ 4

Valle Vermiglia

VIA A. GRAMSCI, 7
00197 ROMA
TEL. +39 3487221073
www.vallevermiglia.it

CELLAR SALES
ANNUAL PRODUCTION 30,000 bottles
HECTARES UNDER VINE 8.00
SUSTAINABLE WINERY

Mario Masini's project began back in 2000,
when he planted up native vine stock on
the slopes of Mount Tuscolo, aiming to
produce an elegant, territorial wine. The
plot stands 600 metres above sea level on
volcanic soils surrounding the cloistered
Benedictine abbey of Monte Corona (whose
strict rules forbid women from entering).
Strictly hand-picked malvasia di Candia
and malvasia del Lazio, trebbiano giallo,
trebbiano toscano, and bombino bianco are
the grapes used for the winery's only label.
Its high altitude, its vineyards set in
woodland, in perhaps the coolest part of
the designation, are usually regarded as
the winery's strengths, though in a difficult
year such as 2014 they were more of a
problem than anything else. Hence, while
the fruit-rich Frascati Superiore Eremo
Tuscolano is still an excellent wine, with
remarkable freshness and charm, it lacks
the 2013's depth.

○ Frascati Sup. Eremo Tuscolano '14	⚐⚐ 3*
○ Frascati Sup. Eremo Tuscolano '13	⚐⚐⚐ 3*
○ Frascati Sup. Eremo Tuscolano '12	⚐⚐ 3*

Casale Cento Corvi

VIA AURELIA KM 45,500
00052 CERVETERI [RM]
TEL. +39 069903902
www.casalecentocorvi.it

CELLAR SALES
PRE-BOOKED VISITS
ANNUAL PRODUCTION 300,000 bottles
HECTARES UNDER VINE 35.00

● Giacchè Rosso '12	▼▼ 6
● La Nostra Scelta '13	▼ 5

Casale della Ioria

LOC. LA GLORIA
S.DA PROV.LE 118 ANAGNI-PALIANO
03012 ANAGNI [FR]
TEL. +39 077556031
www.casaledellaioria.com

CELLAR SALES
PRE-BOOKED VISITS
ANNUAL PRODUCTION 65,000 bottles
HECTARES UNDER VINE 38.00
SUSTAINABLE WINERY

● Cesanese del Piglio Sup. Torre del Piano Ris. '13	▼▼ 4
○ Passerina Colle Bianco '15	▼ 2

Cominium

VIA RITINTO
03041 ALVITO [FR]
.TEL. +39 0776510683
www.cantinacominium.it

CELLAR SALES
ANNUAL PRODUCTION 70,000 bottles
HECTARES UNDER VINE 18.00

● Atina Cabernet Satur '13	▼▼ 3
○ Maturano '15	▼▼ 2*
● Atina Cabernet Ris. '13	▼ 5
● Colle Alto '15	▼ 2

Cordeschi

LOC. ACQUAPENDENTE
VIA CASSIA KM 137,400
00121 ACQUAPENDENTE [VT]
TEL. +39 3356953547
www.cantinacordeschi.it

CELLAR SALES
PRE-BOOKED VISITS
ANNUAL PRODUCTION 35,000 bottles
HECTARES UNDER VINE 8.50

● Ost '14	▼▼ 3
● Saìno '13	▼▼ 3
○ Palea '15	▼ 2
○ Siele '15	▼ 2

Corte dei Papi

LOC. COLLETONNO
03012 ANAGNI [FR]
TEL. +39 0775769271
www.cortedeipapi.it

CELLAR SALES
PRE-BOOKED VISITS
ANNUAL PRODUCTION 40,000 bottles
HECTARES UNDER VINE 25.00

● Cesanese del Piglio Colle Ticchio '15	▼▼ 2*
● Cesanese del Piglio San Magno '14	▼ 4
○ Colle Sape '15	▼ 2
○ Passerina '15	▼ 2

Agricola Emme

VIA MAGGIORE, 126
03010 PIGLIO [FR]
TEL. +39 0775769859
www.agricolaemme.com

ANNUAL PRODUCTION 25,000 bottles
HECTARES UNDER VINE 25.70

● Cesanese del Piglio Sup. Casal Cervino Ris. '12	▼▼ 4
○ Passerina Casal Cervino '15	▼▼ 2*
● Cesanese del Piglio Hyperius '15	▼ 2

Federici

VIA SANTA APOLLARIA VECCHIA, 30
00039 ZAGAROLO [RM]
TEL. +39 0695461022
www.vinifederici.com

CELLAR SALES
PRE-BOOKED VISITS
ANNUAL PRODUCTION 350,000 bottles
HECTARES UNDER VINE 3.00

● Cesanese del Piglio Sapiens '15	🍷🍷	4
● Cesanese del Piglio Sup. Nunc '13	🍷🍷	5
○ Le Coste '15	🍷	2
● Wwwine '15	🍷	3

La Ferriera

VIA FERRIERA, 723
03042 ATINA [FR]
TEL. +39 0776691226
www.laferriera.it

CELLAR SALES
PRE-BOOKED VISITS
ANNUAL PRODUCTION 50,000 bottles
HECTARES UNDER VINE 15.00

● Atina Cabernet Real Magona '12	🍷🍷	3
○ Real Magona Brut '12	🍷🍷	4
● Atina Cabernet Real Magona Ris. '12	🍷	5
● Ferrato '13	🍷	2

Formiconi

LOC. FARINELLA
00021 AFFILE [RM]
TEL. +39 3470934541
www.cantinaformiconi.it

ANNUAL PRODUCTION 7,500 bottles
HECTARES UNDER VINE 1.80

● Cesanese di Affile Capozzano Ris. '14	🍷🍷	4
● Cesanese di Affile Cisinianum '14	🍷🍷	3

Alberto Giacobbe

C.DA SAN GIOVENALE
03018 PALIANO [FR]
TEL. +39 0775579198
www.vinigiacobbe.it

PRE-BOOKED VISITS
ANNUAL PRODUCTION 25,000 bottles
HECTARES UNDER VINE 9.00

● Cesanese del Piglio Sup. Lepanto Ris. '13	🍷🍷	4
○ Passerina Duchessa '15	🍷	2
○ Passerina Maddalena '14	🍷	2

Donato Giangirolami

B.GO MONTELLO
FRAZ. LE FERRIERE
VIA DEL CAVALIERE, 1414
04100 LATINA
TEL. +39 3358394890
www.donatogiangirolami.it

CELLAR SALES
PRE-BOOKED VISITS
ANNUAL PRODUCTION 80,000 bottles
HECTARES UNDER VINE 38.00
VITICULTURE METHOD Certified Organic

○ Propizio '15	🍷🍷	2*
○ Apricor Passito '13	🍷🍷	4
○ Regius '15	🍷🍷	2*
● Pancarpo '13	🍷	3

Gotto d'Oro

LOC. FRATTOCCHIE
VIA DEL DIVINO AMORE, 115
00040 MARINO [RM]
TEL. +39 0693022211
www.gottodoro.it

CELLAR SALES
PRE-BOOKED VISITS
ANNUAL PRODUCTION 9,000,000 bottles
HECTARES UNDER VINE 1400.00

● Mitreo Mithra '14	🍷🍷	2*
● Mitreo Korex '14	🍷	2
○ Mitreo Sol '15	🍷	2
○ Mitreo Taurus '14	🍷	2

Podere Grecchi

S.DA SAMMARTINESE, 8
01100 VITERBO
TEL. +39 0761305671
www.poderegrecchi.com

CELLAR SALES
PRE-BOOKED VISITS
ANNUAL PRODUCTION 70,000 bottles
HECTARES UNDER VINE 10.50
SUSTAINABLE WINERY

● CEV Merlot Poggio Ferrone '15	♥♥ 2*
○ CEV Rossetto Il Fedele '15	♥♥ 2*
○ San Silvestro '15	♥ 2
○ Sauvignon '15	♥ 2

Antica Cantina Leonardi

VIA DEL PINO, 12
01027 MONTEFIASCONE [VT]
TEL. +39 0761826028
www.cantinaleonardi.it

CELLAR SALES
PRE-BOOKED VISITS
ACCOMMODATION
ANNUAL PRODUCTION 100,000 bottles
HECTARES UNDER VINE 37.00
VITICULTURE METHOD Certified Organic

● Don Carlo '13	♥♥ 2*
○ Luce di Lago '15	♥♥ 2*
○ Est! Est!! Est!!! di Montefiascone Poggio del Cardinale '15	♥ 2

Casale Marchese

VIA DI VERMICINO, 68
00044 FRASCATI [RM]
TEL. +39 069408932
www.casalemarchese.it

CELLAR SALES
PRE-BOOKED VISITS
ANNUAL PRODUCTION 150,000 bottles
HECTARES UNDER VINE 40.00

○ Clemens '14	♥♥ 3
○ Frascati Sup. '15	♥♥ 2*
○ Cannellino di Frascati '14	♥ 3

Antonella Pacchiarotti

VIA ROMA, 14
01024 GROTTE DI CASTRO [VT]
TEL. +39 0763796852
www.vinipacchiarotti.it

CELLAR SALES
PRE-BOOKED VISITS
ANNUAL PRODUCTION 10,000 bottles
HECTARES UNDER VINE 3.50
SUSTAINABLE WINERY

● Cavarosso '15	♥♥ 3
○ Matée '15	♥♥ 3
○ Ramatico '11	♥♥ 3

Tenuta Ronci di Nepi

VIA RONCI 2072
01036 NEPI [VT]
TEL. +39 0761555125
www.roncidinepi.it

CELLAR SALES
PRE-BOOKED VISITS
ANNUAL PRODUCTION 130,000 bottles
HECTARES UNDER VINE 18.00

○ Grechetto '15	♥♥ 2*
○ Manti '14	♥ 4
○ Oro di Nè '15	♥ 2
● Veste Porpora '14	♥ 2

Le Rose

VIA PONTE TRE ARMI, 25
00045 GENZANO DI ROMA [RM]
TEL. +39 0693709671
www.aziendaagricolalerose.com

CELLAR SALES
PRE-BOOKED VISITS
ANNUAL PRODUCTION 70,000 bottles
HECTARES UNDER VINE 10.00
VITICULTURE METHOD Certified Organic
SUSTAINABLE WINERY

○ La Faiola '15	♥♥ 5
○ Artemisia '15	♥ 4
○ Tre Armi '15	♥ 3

Tenuta Sant'Isidoro

LOC. PORTACCIA
01016 TARQUINIA [VT]
TEL. +39 0766869716
www.santisidoro.net

CELLAR SALES
PRE-BOOKED VISITS
ANNUAL PRODUCTION 65,000 bottles
HECTARES UNDER VINE 57.00

● Soremidio '12	🏆🏆 4
○ Forca di Palma '15	🏆 2
○ Soraluisa '15	🏆 3
● Terzolo '15	🏆 2

Stefanoni

LOC. ZEPPONAMI
VIA STEFANONI, 48
01027 MONTEFIASCONE [VT]
TEL. +39 0761825651
www.cantinastefanoni.it

CELLAR SALES
PRE-BOOKED VISITS
ANNUAL PRODUCTION 100,000 bottles
HECTARES UNDER VINE 10.00

○ Est! Est!! Est!!! di Montefiascone Cl. Foltone '15	🏆🏆 2*
○ Brut M. Cl. '13	🏆 3
● Fanum '13	🏆 3

Terra delle Ginestre

S.DA ST.LE 630 AUSONIA, 59
04020 SPIGNO SATURNIA [LT]
TEL. +39 3495617153
www.terradelleginestre.it

CELLAR SALES
PRE-BOOKED VISITS
ANNUAL PRODUCTION 15,000 bottles
HECTARES UNDER VINE 4.00

● Il Generale '14	🏆🏆 3
○ Lentisco '14	🏆🏆 3
○ Letizia '15	🏆 2

Villa Caviciana

LOC. TOJENA CAVICIANA
01025 GROTTE DI CASTRO [VT]
TEL. +39 0763798212
www.villacaviciana.com

CELLAR SALES
PRE-BOOKED VISITS
ANNUAL PRODUCTION 25,000 bottles
HECTARES UNDER VINE 16.00
VITICULTURE METHOD Certified Organic

○ Lorenzo Brut	🏆🏆 3
● Maddalena '11	🏆🏆 5
☉ Tadzio '15	🏆🏆 2*
● Faustina '13	🏆 6

Villa Gianna

B.GO SAN DONATO
S.DA MAREMMANA
04010 SABAUDIA [LT]
TEL. +39 0773250034
www.villagianna.it

CELLAR SALES
PRE-BOOKED VISITS
ACCOMMODATION
ANNUAL PRODUCTION 1,000,000 bottles
HECTARES UNDER VINE 65.00
VITICULTURE METHOD Certified Organic

○ Circeo Bianco Innato '15	🏆🏆 2*
○ Moscato di Terracina Secco '15	🏆🏆 2*
● Rudestro '14	🏆 2
○ Vigne del Borgo Sauvignon '15	🏆 2

Cantine Volpetti

VIA NETTUNENSE, 21
00040 ARICCIA [RM]
TEL. +39 069342000
www.cantinevolpetti.it

CELLAR SALES
PRE-BOOKED VISITS
ANNUAL PRODUCTION 450,000 bottles
HECTARES UNDER VINE 40.00

○ Malvasia del Lazio V.T.	🏆🏆 3
● Shiraz Le Piantate '14	🏆🏆 2*
● Cesanese Le Piantate '14	🏆 2
○ Frascati Sup. Le Piantate '14	🏆 2

ABRUZZO

The Abruzzo wine sector has never been so sound. At least judging by the average standard of production, which continues to rise, and is increasingly competitive as far as value for money is concerned. Not many places in Europe come to mind where you can drink so well spending so little. A perfect example is Tiberio's Pecorino 2015, winner of the Best Value for Money award. A double-edged sword nonetheless. The amazing affordability of entry-level ranges increases the risk of detracting interest from more ambitious projects. And Abruzzo wines competing in the premium segment with the world's most iconic labels from legendary terroirs are the exception rather than the rule. Add to this the significant percentage of bulk wine bottled outside the region and it becomes clear why Abruzzo is still struggling to gain proper recognition with professional consumers. Nonetheless, the scenario is definitely encouraging if the energy evident in every round of tastings is anything to go by. The range of dependable, typical wines is growing with each vintage, which makes our job more difficult when selecting wineries for a full profile in our guide. Many are left out only for reasons of space. The top rankings show a peaceful coexistence of venerable brands and emerging names, small businesses and large enterprises, not to mention the extensive network of efficient cooperatives meeting market challenges. Across the board there is also a growing number of green wineries, applying biocompatible protocols in the vineyard, and up-to-date cellar solutions inspired by ancient methods: spontaneous fermentations, less-is-more vinification, modular aging, using amphorae and cement alongside wood and steel. Consequently, the marked reduction in the number of Tre Bicchieri awarded may be misleading. The reason is to be sought in the challenges posed by the vintages presented in the most recent battery of tastings: the cold and damp of 2014 made life complicated for the more representative reds, while the conversely hot dry 2015 left whites and rosés struggling to achieve their tangy depth and their sinew. As always, Montepulciano is king of the heap for regional excellence, with its many terroir and style expressions, including the Cerasuolo versions. But we were also delighted by the more impressive interpretations of Pecorino and Trebbiano, showing that special fusion of Adriatic and Apennines that makes the Abruzzo landscape so unique.

Agriverde

LOC. CALDARI
VIA STORTINI, 32A
66026 ORTONA [CH]
TEL. +39 0859032101
www.agriverde.it

CELLAR SALES
PRE-BOOKED VISITS
RESTAURANT SERVICE
ANNUAL PRODUCTION 900,000 bottles
HECTARES UNDER VINE 65.00
VITICULTURE METHOD Certified Organic
SUSTAINABLE WINERY

The De Carlos have been vignerons for almost two centuries. The estate is now composed of plots found in Caldari, Ortona, Rogatti, Frisa and Crecchio, and the Colline Teatine zone. Agriverde was one of Italy's first wineries to focus on biocompatible protocols and has become an outright eco-friendly hub, the architecture of its cellar, boutique hotel and spa perfectly integrated with the landscape, and a full range of wines to meet the requests of contemporary awareness. The company's renown is owed chiefly to its reds from montepulciano, but Cerasuolo, Pecorino, Trebbiano, and various other wines are also playing in the big league these days. And there is plenty of choice in the winery's magnificent range. An especially bright star is the Montepulciano Solàrea 2012, with its mature aromas and hint of jammy fruit supported in a consistently broad, smoky palate. The Pecorino Eikos 2015 is hot on its heels, with musky and flowery hints.

● Montepulciano d'Abruzzo Solàrea '12	♥♥	4
○ Eikos Pecorino '15	♥♥	3
● Montepulciano d'Abruzzo Eikos '14	♥♥	3
● Montepulciano d'Abruzzo Natum Biovegan '15	♥♥	2*
○ Riseis Pecorino '15	♥♥	3
○ Trebbiano d'Abruzzo Piane di Maggio '15	♥♥	2*
○ Abruzzo Cococciola Riseis '15	♥	2
⊙ Cerasuolo d'Abruzzo Natum Biovegan '15	♥	2
⊙ Cerasuolo d'Abruzzo Solàrea '15	♥	3
● Montepulciano d'Abruzzo Piane di Maggio '15	♥	2
● Montepulciano d'Abruzzo Riseis '14	♥	3
○ Natum Pecorino Biovegan '15	♥	2
○ Riseis Passerina '15	♥	3
● Montepulciano d'Abruzzo Plateo '04	♥♥♥	6

Barone Cornacchia

C.DA TORRI, 20
64010 TORANO NUOVO [TE]
TEL. +39 0861887412
www.baronecornacchia.it

CELLAR SALES
PRE-BOOKED VISITS
ACCOMMODATION
ANNUAL PRODUCTION 300,000 bottles
HECTARES UNDER VINE 42.00
VITICULTURE METHOD Certified Organic

The noble roots that allowed the Cornacchia family to acquire an extensive agricultural fief date back to the 16th century. The estate was located near the fortress of Civitella, in the today's Colline Teramane zone, and about 40 hectares still survive, mostly concentrated in a single, spectacular plot influenced by the climate produced by the Adriatic Sea and Mount Gran Sasso. Filippo and Caterina are at the helm today, with all the might of organic certification behind the whole product range. In an area when Montepulciano selections are always to the fore, we are now also noting increasing solidity and stylistic consistency in whites from pecorino, trebbiano and passerina, not to mention the Cerasuolos. The latest tastings were further evidence of some great teamwork. The Controguerra Passerina Villa Torri 2015 is a stunner, with a hint of maceration in the profile, it follows through nice and airy thanks to a vigorous salty backbone. The 2013 Poggio Varano is again a mouthfilling, composed Montepulciano.

⊙ Cerasuolo d'Abruzzo Sup. '15	♥♥	2*
○ Controguerra Passerina Villa Torri '15	♥♥	2*
○ Controguerra Pecorino Villa Torri '15	♥♥	2*
● Montepulciano d'Abruzzo Colline Teramane Vizzarro '12	♥♥	5
● Montepulciano d'Abruzzo Poggio Varano Antico Feudo '13	♥♥	3
○ Trebbiano d'Abruzzo Sup. Bio '15	♥♥	2*
● Montepulciano d'Abruzzo Bio '14	♥	2
● Montepulciano d'Abruzzo '13	♀♀	2*
● Montepulciano d'Abruzzo Colline Teramane Vizzarro '11	♀♀	5
● Montepulciano d'Abruzzo Poggio Varano '12	♀♀	3
● Montepulciano d'Abruzzo V. Le Coste '12	♀♀	3*

Tenute Barone di Valforte

c.da Piomba, 11
64029 Silvi Marina [TE]
Tel. +39 0859353432
www.baronedivalforte.it

CELLAR SALES
PRE-BOOKED VISITS
ANNUAL PRODUCTION 280,000 bottles
HECTARES UNDER VINE 50.00

The Sorricchio family has owned the Valforte fief since the 1300s, tending about 50 hectares of vineyards in the Colline Teramane zone, scattered around the municipal areas of Atri, Mutignano, Casoli and Silvi Marina, the latter home to the cellar. The area offers a wide variety of soil types that produces pecorino, trebbiano, passerina, Montepulciano, and some international varieties, coming together in a compact but persuasive interpretation, and with only a passing nod to technical diktats. The young reds are, as usual, the strongpoint: supple and sprightly, yet retaining a good level of complexity. Indeed, the 2014 Montepulciano Colle Sale shows appealing, eloquent liquorice and caramel notes, underpinned by a far from languid flavour. If possible, the pattern is even more perfect in the 2015 Montepulciano, a lusciously simple wine yet with awesome deep hints of ink and pencil lead, and close-knit tannin grain.

● Montepulciano d'Abruzzo '15	♍♍ 2*
● Montepulciano d'Abruzzo Colle Sale '14	♍♍ 4
○ Pecorino '15	♍ 2
○ Trebbiano d'Abruzzo Villa Chiara '15	♍ 2
● Montepulciano d'Abruzzo '13	♍♍ 2*
⊙ Montepulciano d'Abruzzo Cerasuolo Valforte Rosé '14	♍♍ 2*
● Montepulciano d'Abruzzo Colline Teramane Colle Sale '13	♍♍ 3*
● Montepulciano d'Abruzzo Colline Teramane Colle Sale '10	♍♍ 3*
○ Passerina '14	♍♍ 2*
○ Pecorino '14	♍♍ 2*
○ Trebbiano d'Abruzzo Villa Chiara '14	♍♍ 2*

Nestore Bosco

c.da Casali, 147
65010 Nocciano [PE]
Tel. +39 085847345
www.nestorebosco.com

CELLAR SALES
PRE-BOOKED VISITS
ANNUAL PRODUCTION 600,000 bottles
HECTARES UNDER VINE 75.00

Cavaliere Bosco left his son Giovanni and grandchildren, Nestore (now working in production) and Stefania (in administration), a kind of spiritual legacy. More than a century of history, based on a significant heritage of vineyards, approximately 75 hectares in the Colli Pescaresi zone, including the Nocciano, estate surrounding the lovely underground cellar, and the more recently acquired Valle Subequana land, on Mount Majella. The result is a multifaceted range revolving around Abruzzo's main cultivars, embracing Montepulcianos, Trebbianos, Pecorinos, and Passerinas, where classic interpretations are flanked by some modern concepts. Cavalier Bosco's entire battery was admirable with the 2013 Montepulcianos heading the list: the classic R hints at an almost nebbiolo-like character with its continuity of herbs and berries; the Nestore Bosco shows more brooding, earthy aromas, but is also broader and more dynamic mid-palate.

● Montepulciano d'Abruzzo Nestore Bosco '13	♍♍ 4
● Montepulciano d'Abruzzo R '13	♍♍ 3*
⊙ Cerasuolo d'Abruzzo Donna Bosco Rosé '15	♍♍ 2*
⊙ Cerasuolo d'Abruzzo Sup. '15	♍♍ 3
● Montepulciano d'Abruzzo Donna Bosco '14	♍♍ 3
● Montepulciano d'Abruzzo Pan Ris. '12	♍♍ 4
● Montepulciano d'Abruzzo Don Bosco Ris. '12	♍ 4
○ Passerina '14	♍ 2
○ Pecorino '15	♍ 3
○ Pecorino Donna Bosco '15	♍ 2
○ Trebbiano d'Abruzzo Sup. '15	♍ 3
● Montepulciano d'Abruzzo '12	♍♍ 2*
● Montepulciano d'Abruzzo 110 Ris. '10	♍♍ 6

Castorani

LOC. C.DA ORATORIO
VIA CASTORANI, 5
65020 ALANNO [PE]
TEL. +39 3466355635
www.castorani.it

CELLAR SALES
PRE-BOOKED VISITS
ANNUAL PRODUCTION 1,000,000 bottles
HECTARES UNDER VINE 72.00
VITICULTURE METHOD Certified Organic

In the late 1700s, celebrated surgeon Raffaele Castorani was the founder of this venerable Alanno winery, between the Adriatic coast and Majella's Pescara slope. Now owned by retired Formula One racing driver Jarno Trulli and his partners, in just over 15 years they have turned it into a modern outfit combining high quality with large numbers of bottles, made from the grapes growing on over 70 hectares of certified organic land. It would be no mean feat to list all the labels of a full range of Abruzzo wines, comprising various lines for each price bracket and winemaking style, whose declared mission is intense fruitiness and pleasurable drinkability. The ratings shown below say all that needs to be said about Castorani's ace performance. The star is the 2012 Montepulciano Amorino with blood orange and bottle cherry charting a spirited yet Mediterranean weave, underscored by the warm, lush flavour. The 2014 Cadetto is hot on its heels for expression.

★Luigi Cataldi Madonna

LOC. PIANO
67025 OFENA [AQ]
TEL. +39 0862954252
www.cataldimadonna.com

CELLAR SALES
PRE-BOOKED VISITS
ANNUAL PRODUCTION 240,000 bottles
HECTARES UNDER VINE 31.00
SUSTAINABLE WINERY

The Ofena plateau, described as "the furnace of Abruzzo", is the setting for the Cataldi Madonna family's winemaking exploits up in L'Aquila. The heart of Gran Sasso National Park is an area unique in many ways for its soil and climate, and dizzying day-night temperature changes due to the proximity of Calderone, the only Apennine glacier. Thus we expect and we get powerful, textured but taut, spirited wines, often at their best after lengthy cellaring. And it is increasingly difficult to delineate a hierarchy for the Montepulciano, Cerasuolo and Pecorino selections, which are top notch in all the price ranges. The Pecorino Frontone 2013 is merely the tip of a splendid iceberg fronted by Cataldi Madonna's flawless range. Balsamic herbs, citrus fruits and iodine make a white with complex structure, grip and flavour, while a brilliant bitter orange finale points to a long life.

● Montepulciano d'Abruzzo Amorino '12	♥♥♥	3*
● Montepulciano d'Abruzzo Cadetto '14	♥♥	2*
○ Abruzzo Pecorino Sup. Amorino '15	♥♥	3
⊙ Cerasuolo d'Abruzzo Cadetto '15	♥♥	2*
● Montepulciano d'Abruzzo Coste delle Plaie '13	♥♥	3
● Montepulciano d'Abruzzo Le Paranze '14	♥♥	2*
● Montepulciano d'Abruzzo Podere Castorani Ris. '12	♥♥	5
○ Trebbiano d'Abruzzo Cadetto '15	♥♥	2*
○ Trebbiano d'Abruzzo Coste delle Plaie '15	♥♥	3
○ Trebbiano d'Abruzzo Majolica '15	♥♥	1*
○ Trebbiano d'Abruzzo Podere Castorani '13	♥♥	3
⊙ Cerasuolo d'Abruzzo Majolica '15	♥	1*
⊙ Cerasuolo d'Abruzzo Sup. Podere Castorani '15	♥	3
● Montepulciano d'Abruzzo Jarno '13	♥	2

○ Pecorino Frontone '13	♥♥♥	5
⊙ Cerasuolo d'Abruzzo Piè delle Vigne '14	♥♥	3*
⊙ Cataldino '15	♥♥	2*
⊙ Cerasuolo d'Abruzzo '15	♥♥	2*
○ Pecorino Giulia '15	♥♥	2*
○ Trebbiano d'Abruzzo '15	♥♥	2*
● Montepulciano d'Abruzzo Malandrino '14	♥	3
● Montepulciano d'Abruzzo Malandrino '13	♥♥♥	3*
● Montepulciano d'Abruzzo Malandrino '12	♥♥♥	3*
● Montepulciano d'Abruzzo Tonì '07	♥♥♥	5
○ Pecorino '11	♥♥♥	5
○ Pecorino '10	♥♥♥	5
○ Pecorino '09	♥♥♥	5
○ Pecorino '08	♥♥♥	5

Centorame

VIA DELLE FORNACI, 15
64030 ATRI [TE]
TEL. +39 0858709115
www.centorame.it

CELLAR SALES
PRE-BOOKED VISITS
ANNUAL PRODUCTION 100,000 bottles
HECTARES UNDER VINE 12.00
SUSTAINABLE WINERY

Lamberto Vannucci's Centorame was
officially founded in 1987, covering over
ten hectares in Casoli d'Atri, a scenic area
in the Teramo hills badlands, just a stone's
throw from the sea, about 180 metres in
altitude. The winery bottled its first labels in
2002, but it soon soared to the top of
Abruzzo production, thanks to a highly
versatile range based on Montepulciano,
trebbiano, pecorino, and passerina
varieties. The cellar offers the San Michele,
Scuderie Ducali and Castellum Vetus lines,
in a battery of wines know for bright but
laid-back eloquence that shuns textbook
winemaking techniques. It was precisely
the eclectic range that aroused our interest
in the most recent tastings. Above all, the
2015 Trebbiano San Michele, with a
distinctive aromatic profile that appears
even more sun-drenched in the tasty,
medicinal flavour. Equally enchanting is the
2014 Montepulciano San Michele with an
old-style approach of petrol, forest floor
and coffee bean notes.

Cirelli

LOC. TRECIMINIERE
VIA COLLE SAN GIOVANNI, 1
64032 ATRI [TE]
TEL. +39 0858700106
www.agricolacirelli.com

CELLAR SALES
PRE-BOOKED VISITS
ACCOMMODATION AND RESTAURANT SERVICE
ANNUAL PRODUCTION 26,000 bottles
HECTARES UNDER VINE 5.00
VITICULTURE METHOD Certified Organic

Wine is just one of many prestige products
offered by the Cirelli brand from its certified
organic farm, located on the Atri badlands
in the Teramo hills. Overlooking the Adriatic,
this small winery has just five hectares, but
it has progressed in leaps and bounds over
the last vintages, both for the average
quality of the wine and for personality in the
more aspirational labels. We find the
Amphora selections of Montepulciano,
Cerasuolo and Trebbiano to be very
interesting, a hint of anarchy and caprice
when young, but increasingly reliable for
medium-term aging. The Collina Biologica
is a thoroughly drinkable organic wine sold
in screw-cap bottles. The proof of further
development is instantly clear in the slew of
good wines and satisfaction for reaching
the final with the 2015 Cerasuolo Amphora.
Tangerine, wildflowers and medlar drive the
lively, racy pace of the best Mediterranean
rosés. Once the tannins settle, they will be
at their best.

○ Trebbiano d'Abruzzo San Michele '15	♟♟ 2*
○ Abruzzo Passerina San Michele '15	♟♟ 2*
⊙ Cerasuolo d'Abruzzo San Michele '15	♟♟ 2*
● Montepulciano d'Abruzzo San Michele '14	♟♟ 2*
● Montepulciano d'Abruzzo Scuderie Ducali '14	♟♟ 2*
● Montepulciano d'Abruzzo Colline Teramane Castellum Vetus '13	♟ 4
● Montepulciano d'Abruzzo Liberamente '15	♟ 2
○ Scuderie Ducali '15	♟ 2
○ Trebbiano d'Abruzzo Castellum Vetus '14	♟ 3
○ Tuapina Pecorino '15	♟ 2
● Montepulciano d'Abruzzo San Michele '11	♟♟ 2*
● Montepulciano d'Abruzzo San Michele '10	♟♟ 2*
● Montepulciano d'Abruzzo San Michele '09	♟♟ 2*

⊙ Cerasuolo d'Abruzzo Amphora '15	♟♟ 5
⊙ Cerasuolo d'Abruzzo La Collina Biologica '15	♟♟ 2*
● Montepulciano d'Abruzzo La Collina Biologica '15	♟♟ 2*
○ Trebbiano d'Abruzzo '15	♟♟ 2*
● Montepulciano d'Abruzzo Amphora '15	♟ 5
○ Trebbiano d'Abruzzo La Collina Biologica '15	♟ 2
● Montepulciano d'Abruzzo '14	♟♟ 2*
● Montepulciano d'Abruzzo Amphora '14	♟♟ 5
⊙ Montepulciano d'Abruzzo Cerasuolo '14	♟♟ 2*
⊙ Montepulciano d'Abruzzo Cerasuolo Amphora '14	♟♟ 5
○ Trebbiano d'Abruzzo Amphora '14	♟♟ 5
○ Trebbiano d'Abruzzo Amphora '13	♟♟ 5

Codice Citra

C.DA CUCULLO
66026 ORTONA [CH]
TEL. +39 0859031342
www.citra.it

CELLAR SALES
PRE-BOOKED VISITS
ANNUAL PRODUCTION 18,000,000 bottles
HECTARES UNDER VINE 6000.00

Codice Citra vaunts 43 vintages, 6,000
hectares tended by over 3,000 cooperative
members, an annual output of nearly 20
million bottles, and plays a major role on
the Abruzzo wine scene. It is a cooperative
to end all cooperatives, embracing nine
wineries in the province of Chieti, offering a
range dominated by traditional varieties,
above all Montepulciano, trebbiano,
passerina, and pecorino. Given the large
number of labels, there is no single stylistic
imprint, but the results are interesting both
for early-drinkers and for cellarable
selections to observe over time. The
Montepulcianos head up this top-notch
battery, each with its own vintage profile.
The 2014 Ferzo balances a supple palate
with the year's austere, phenolic profile.
The 2010 Caroso adds the complexity of
citrus and spice notes, and stern depth.
Damson and peach endow the Pecorino
Superiore Ferzo 2015 with sunny
Mediterranean nuances.

○ Abruzzo Pecorino Sup. Ferzo '15	♟♟ 2*
● Montepulciano d'Abruzzo Caroso '10	♟♟ 4
● Montepulciano d'Abruzzo Ferzo '14	♟♟ 3
○ Abruzzo Cococciola Sup. Ferzo '15	♟ 3
⊙ Cerasuolo d'Abruzzo Palio '15	♟ 2
● Montepulciano d'Abruzzo Laus Vitae Ris. '09	♟ 5
○ Pecorino Palio '15	♟ 2
○ Aer '14	♟♟ 3
○ La Volpe all'Uva Pecorino '12	♟♟ 3*
● Montepulciano d'Abruzzo Aulicus '12	♟♟ 3*
⊙ Montepulciano d'Abruzzo Cerasuolo Palio '14	♟♟ 2*
○ Pecorino Palio '14	♟♟ 2*
○ Trebbiano d'Abruzzo Palio '14	♟♟ 2*

Collefrisio

LOC. PIANE DI MAGGIO
66030 FRISA [CH]
TEL. +39 0859039074
www.collefrisio.it

CELLAR SALES
PRE-BOOKED VISITS
ANNUAL PRODUCTION 500,000 bottles
HECTARES UNDER VINE 50.00
VITICULTURE METHOD Certified Organic
SUSTAINABLE WINERY

The joint venture initiated by Amedeo De
Luca and Antonio Patricelli makes explicit
reference to the place of origin: the Chieti
hills in Frisa. A relatively young, organic
winery with about 50 hectares under vine,
of which two-thirds are its own, the estate
comprises three macro blocks that are
quite different in microclimate and altitude.
Montepulciano and trebbiano come
predominantly from Valle del Moro and
Tenuta Morracine; higher up, the Tenuta
Giuliano Teatino produces pecorino and
other white grape varieties. The solid,
compact range has a neoclassical feel and
tasty, appealing expressiveness. Which
describes Montepulciano 2014 to
perfection. One of Collefrisio's best
products, showing scrubland, wood resin,
and black olive, this red is Mediterranean to
the core, with its tasty, refreshing flavour. A
tad less open and polished, the 2012
Montepulciano Vignaquadra vaunts
phenolic backbone and warmth.

○ Falanghina Vignaquadra '15	♟♟ 2*
● Montepulciano d'Abruzzo '14	♟♟ 2*
● Montepulciano d'Abruzzo Vignaquadra '12	♟♟ 3
○ Trebbiano d'Abruzzo Filarè '15	♟♟ 2*
○ Collefrisio di Collefrisio Bianco '12	♟ 5
● Montepulciano d'Abruzzo Collefrisio di Collefrisio '09	♟ 5
● Montepulciano d'Abruzzo Morrecine '14	♟ 2
● Montepulciano d'Abruzzo '11	♟♟ 2*
⊙ Montepulciano d'Abruzzo Cerasuolo '14	♟♟ 2*
● Montepulciano d'Abruzzo Morrecine '13	♟♟ 2*
● Montepulciano d'Abruzzo Morrecine '12	♟♟ 2*
○ Passerina Vignaquadra '14	♟♟ 2*
○ Pecorino Vignaquadra '14	♟♟ 2*
○ Trebbiano d'Abruzzo Filarè '14	♟♟ 2*

Contesa

LOC. CAPARRONE
S.DA DELLE VIGNE, 28
65010 COLLECORVINO [PE]
TEL. +39 0858205078
www.contesa.it

CELLAR SALES
PRE-BOOKED VISITS
RESTAURANT SERVICE
ANNUAL PRODUCTION 260,000 bottles
HECTARES UNDER VINE 40.00
SUSTAINABLE WINERY

The successful winery opened in 2000 by
Rocco Pasetti is located on the Lombard
site of Collecorvino, in the province of
Pescara. Its name is inspired by the
infamous land dispute that involved
great-grandfather Antonio just after the
Unification of Italy. Most of the 40 hectares
under vine are found around the cellar, on a
hillside overlooking the Adriatic at 250
metres. These are ideal conditions for racy,
spirited wines, with plenty of scope for
enhancing natural expression and
drinkability. The winery uses the region's
traditional varieties of Montepulciano,
trebbiano, pecorino, and passerina,
marketing under the Contesa, Antica Persia
and Vigna Corvino labels. Both Contesa's
whites and reds are garnering success.
Typically floral and full-bodied, the 2015
Trebbiano S'ha fatte da Sole shares the
same frank, bracing taste of the
Montepulciano Vigna Corvino. The 2014
Montepulciano has a huskier, more closed
profile but its heart is in the right place.

● Montepulciano d'Abruzzo '14	🏆🏆 3
● Montepulciano d'Abruzzo V. Corvino '15	🏆🏆 2*
○ Trebbiano d'Abruzzo S'ha fatte da Sole '15	🏆🏆 3
○ Abruzzo Passerina V. Corvino '15	🏆 2
○ Abruzzo Pecorino '15	🏆 3
⊙ Cerasuolo d'Abruzzo '15	🏆 3
● Montepulciano d'Abruzzo Ris. '11	🏆 4
● Montepulciano d'Abruzzo Ris. '08	🏆🏆🏆 3*
● Montepulciano d'Abruzzo Ris. '10	🏆🏆 4
● Montepulciano d'Abruzzo Ris. '09	🏆🏆 4
○ Passerina Vigna Corvino '14	🏆🏆 2*
○ Pecorino '14	🏆🏆 3
○ Pecorino '13	🏆🏆 3
○ Trebbiano d'Abruzzo '13	🏆🏆 2*

De Angelis Corvi

C.DA PIGNOTTO
64010 CONTROGUERRA [TE]
TEL. +39 086189475
www.deangeliscorvi.it

CELLAR SALES
PRE-BOOKED VISITS
ANNUAL PRODUCTION 40,000 bottles
HECTARES UNDER VINE 8.00
VITICULTURE METHOD Certified Organic

The small wine and EVO business founded
in 2002 by Corrado De Angelis Corvi is
located in Controguerra, almost on the
border between the Colline Teramane zone
and the Val Vibrata. There are eight certified
organic hectares under vine, devoted
mainly to Montepulciano, with trebbiano,
malvasia and passerina sharing out the
rest. The range of wines shows a
traditional, but certainly not traditionalist
twist, and year after year reveals surprising
progress as far as reliable performance and
expressive balance are concerned, not only
for the entry-level labels like Fonte
Raviliano, but also the more prestigious
selections like Elévito. A trend confirmed by
the latest round of tastings, with an
outstanding 2015 Trebbiano Fonte
Raviliano. The aromatic profile is still
evolving but the palate leaves no doubts as
to its Adriatic nature with the exciting
contrast between the mature fruity flesh
and the exciting salty streak. Both
Montepulcianos are also commendable.

● Montepulciano d'Abruzzo Colline Teramane Elévito '11	🏆🏆 5
● Montepulciano d'Abruzzo Fonte Raviliano '13	🏆🏆 3
○ Trebbiano d'Abruzzo Fonte Raviliano '15	🏆🏆 2*
⊙ Cerasuolo d'Abruzzo Sup. '15	🏆 2
⊙ Montepulciano d'Abruzzo Cerasuolo Sup. '14	🏆🏆 2*
● Montepulciano d'Abruzzo Colline Teramane Elévito Ris. '10	🏆🏆 5
● Montepulciano d'Abruzzo Fonte Raviliano '12	🏆🏆 3
○ Trebbiano d'Abruzzo Sup. Fonte Raviliano '14	🏆🏆 2*
○ Trebbiano d'Abruzzo Sup. Fonte Raviliano '13	🏆🏆 2*

Nicoletta De Fermo

c.da Cordano
65014 Loreto Aprutino [PE]
Tel. +39 0858289136
www.defermo.it

CELLAR SALES
PRE-BOOKED VISITS
ANNUAL PRODUCTION 26,000 bottles
HECTARES UNDER VINE 17.00
VITICULTURE METHOD Certified Biodynamic
SUSTAINABLE WINERY

Loreto Aprutino continues to build its reputation as one of the Abruzzo wine capitals, and the credit can also be attributed to a number of up-and-coming artisanal wineries scaling the upper echelons after just a few harvests. One example is the cellar run by Nicoletta De Fermo with her husband Stefano Papetti Ceroni. Just over 15 hectares, only some of them used for its own production and mainly given over to pecorino, chardonnay and Montepulciano. These varieties take centre stage in a small range with strong stylistic traits forged by spontaneous fermentations and patient maturing in steel and concrete to achieve sizzling, food-friendly flavour. The Cerasuolo Superiore Le Cince just missed a Tre Bicchieri by a hair's breadth, and is nonetheless one of the region's best 2015 rosés. The "sponty" touch is rather more noticeable than usual, but the wait is rewarded by the lively fusion of medicinal herbs and orange peel, and above all its racy, thirst-quenching energy.

⊙ Cerasuolo d'Abruzzo Sup. Le Cince '15	▼▼ 4
○ Abruzzo Pecorino Sup. Don Carlino '15	▼▼ 4
○ Launegild Chardonnay '14	▼▼ 5
● Montepulciano d'Abruzzo Concrete '15	▼▼ 4
⊙ Montepulciano d'Abruzzo Cerasuolo Le Cince '14	▽▽▽ 4*
● Montepulciano d'Abruzzo Prologo '12	▽▽▽ 5
○ Don Carlino '13	▽▽ 4
○ Don Carlino Pecorino '14	▽▽ 4
○ Launegild '13	▽▽ 5
● Montepulciano d'Abruzzo Prologo '13	▽▽ 5
● Montepulciano d'Abruzzo Prologo '11	▽▽ 5
○ Piè Tancredi '11	▽▽ 4

Eredi Legonziano

c.da Nasuti, 169
66034 Lanciano [CH]
Tel. +39 087245210
www.eredilegonziano.it

CELLAR SALES
PRE-BOOKED VISITS
ANNUAL PRODUCTION 200,000 bottles
HECTARES UNDER VINE 500.00

Eredi Legonziano's advertising slogan is "100% Abruzzo" and no declaration could be more accurate. This cooperative winery is almost 50 years old and can be found on the slopes of Lanciano, a town in the lower Chieti area with production traditions lost in the mists of time. It is precisely the interaction between the Adriatic and Majella that emerges in the style profile of a range centred mainly around Montepulciano, Cerasuolo and Pecorino, the latter also available as very palatable sparklers. There are a few plots of passerina and cococciola, but the classics of the Anxanum line are really the most successful expression of a crisp, no-nonsense character. In this respect, the 2014 Montepulciano Anxanum is a paradigm: dried flowers, wild herbs, roots, and a close-knit tannin profile promising interesting prospects for the future. But the jewel in the Eredi Legonziano crown is still the Metodo Classico 36 Mesi: invigorating, creamy and totally unique.

○ Abruzzo Brut M. Cl. 36 Mesi	▼▼ 4
○ Anxanum Pecorino '15	▼▼ 2*
⊙ Cerasuolo d'Abruzzo Anxanum '15	▼▼ 2*
● Montepulciano d'Abruzzo Anxanum '14	▼▼ 2*
○ Abruzzo M. Cl. Carmine Festa '10	▼ 3
● Montepulciano d'Abruzzo Diocleziano '10	▽▽ 2*
○ Pecorino Anxanum '13	▽▽ 2*
○ Pecorino Methys '13	▽▽ 2*

Tenuta I Fauri

s.da Corta, 9
66100 Chieti
Tel. +39 0871332627
www.tenutaifauri.it

CELLAR SALES
PRE-BOOKED VISITS
ANNUAL PRODUCTION 150,000 bottles
HECTARES UNDER VINE 35.00

Domenico and Valentina Di Camillo run a winery that is one of the most successful on the very competitive Abruzzo winemaking scene, specifically the Colline Teatine zone. The 30-hectare estate seems almost to hang in the air between the Adriatic coast and Majella's slopes. Using the main regional cultivars, wines are produced to modular style concepts that define the various lines: Baldovino, Santa Cecilia, Pecorino, Montepulciano Ottobre Rosso, sparklers and semi-sparklers. Vinification is low-key, with spontaneous fermentations, aging in steel and concrete, with an eye to substance rather than form, for very food-flexible wines. A theme that emerges clearly in a nice, complete range whose best expression is in the Baldovino Montepulcianos. The 2015 quickly shrugs off any reductive reticence to unfold a sweet, juicy thrust, not lacking in contrast. Raring to go, the untamed Cerasuolo has the same profile.

⊙ Cerasuolo d'Abruzzo Baldovino '15	🍷🍷 2*
● Montepulciano d'Abruzzo Baldovino '15	🍷🍷 2*
○ Abruzzo Pecorino '15	🍷🍷 2*
● Montepulciano d'Abruzzo Ottobre Rosso '15	🍷🍷 2*
○ Trebbiano d'Abruzzo Baldovino '15	🍷🍷 2*
○ Passerina '15	🍷 2
○ Spumante Brut	🍷 2
○ Abruzzo Pecorino '14	🍷🍷🍷 2*
○ Abruzzo Pecorino '13	🍷🍷🍷 2*
● Montepulciano d'Abruzzo Baldovino '14	🍷🍷 2*
● Montepulciano d'Abruzzo Ottobre Rosso '14	🍷🍷 2*
○ Passerina '14	🍷🍷 2*
○ Trebbiano d'Abruzzo Baldovino '14	🍷🍷 2*

Feudo Antico

via Perruna, 35
66010 Tollo [CH]
Tel. +39 0871969128
www.feudoantico.it

CELLAR SALES
PRE-BOOKED VISITS
ANNUAL PRODUCTION 60,000 bottles
HECTARES UNDER VINE 20.00

Feudo Antico is one of the few wineries to have developed the potential of the new Tullum designation with conviction. This young cooperative was founded in 2008 and encompasses some 20 hectares, owned by its 50 members and scattered in winemaking country like Pedine, Colle Secco, San Pietro, Colle dei Campli, not to mention the Castel di Sangro high-altitude experiments with pecorino at Michelin-star chef Niko Romito's Casadonna vineyards. The latter is simply the cherry on a cake of extremely reliable entry-level Montepulcianos, Cerasuolos and Pecorinos, also available in organic versions, aged in steel and concrete to streamline the sensory profile. Feudo Antico's skill in white wines can be seen right from its extrovert, pleasing 2015 Tullum Pecorino Biologico, but even more so in the 2014 Pecorino Casadonna, irresistible from the word go with its citrus and riverbank notes, meticulously following through in the mouthfilling flavour.

○ Pecorino Casadonna '14	🍷🍷 7
○ Tullum Pecorino Biologico '15	🍷🍷 3
● Montepulciano d'Abruzzo '13	🍷 3
⊙ Rosato Bio '15	🍷 2
○ Tullum Pecorino '15	🍷 3
● Tullum Rosso Ris. '12	🍷 5
⊙ Rosato '14	🍷🍷 2*
⊙ Rosato Terre di Chieti '13	🍷🍷 2*
○ Tullum Bianco '13	🍷🍷 3
○ Tullum Bianco '11	🍷🍷 3
○ Tullum Brut	🍷🍷 5
○ Tullum Passerina '14	🍷🍷 3
○ Tullum Pecorino '14	🍷🍷 3*
○ Tullum Pecorino '12	🍷🍷 3*
● Tullum Rosso '11	🍷🍷 3

Gentile

VIA DEL GIARDINO, 7
67025 OFENA [AQ]
TEL. +39 0862956618
www.gentilevini.it

CELLAR SALES
PRE-BOOKED VISITS
ANNUAL PRODUCTION 90,000 bottles
HECTARES UNDER VINE 12.00

Although not yet 40, Riccardo Gentile is already a veteran of the Abruzzo winemaking craft. And thanks to him fans have discovered the wonders of Ofena, a village wedged between the Gran Sasso massif and the hot plateaux overlooking the sea. The unique heat regulation and uncompromising day-night temperature ranges leave an unmistakeable mark on a limited line produced from the winery's ten hectares. The key is the supple drinkability of the four Pié della Grotta labels of Montepulciano, Cerasuolo, Trebbiano, and Pecorino, while the Plot 417 selections and the Vecchie Vigne line offer extra mouthfeel and complexity. For the best Gentile labels we would call it a draw. The Pié della Grotta line offers a juicy, spicy 2014 Montepulciano, and a well-defined 2015 Pecorino true to the varietal stamp. But the 2015 Particella 417 is not far behind, with its hint of the wild, and refreshing, dynamic palate.

● Montepulciano d'Abruzzo Pié della Grotta '14	♈♈ 5
○ Particella 417 Pecorino '15	♈♈ 3
○ Pecorino Pié della Grotta '15	♈♈ 2*
⊙ Cerasuolo d'Abruzzo Pié della Grotta '15	♈ 3
● Montepulciano d'Abruzzo V. V. '12	♈ 4
○ Trebbiano d'Abruzzo Pié della Grotta '15	♈ 1*
⊙ Montepulciano d'Abruzzo Cerasuolo Pié della Grotta '14	♈♈ 3
⊙ Montepulciano d'Abruzzo Cerasuolo Pié della Grotta '13	♈♈ 3
● Montepulciano d'Abruzzo Pié della Grotta '13	♈♈ 2*
○ Pecorino Pié della Grotta '14	♈♈ 2*
○ Pecorino Pié della Grotta '13	♈♈ 2*
○ Trebbiano d'Abruzzo Pié della Grotta '14	♈♈ 1*
○ Trebbiano d'Abruzzo Pié della Grotta '13	♈♈ 1*

★Dino Illuminati

C.DA SAN BIAGIO, 18
64010 CONTROGUERRA [TE]
TEL. +39 0861808008
www.illuminativini.it

CELLAR SALES
PRE-BOOKED VISITS
ANNUAL PRODUCTION 1,150,000 bottles
HECTARES UNDER VINE 130.00

The late Cavaliere Dino Illuminati's commitment as the ambassador of Abruzzo wine worldwide is no secret. The winery was founded in the latter 1800s, a time when winegrowing in Teramo was very different, and which gradually developed an identity in no small measure thanks to the choices made by the Controguerra cellar. Today the company is managed full-time by offspring Lorenzo, Stefano and Anna, now vaunting over 100 hectares of land, with most vineyards at about 300 metres above sea level. Illuminati thus produces a complete selection of traditional types, and as always the mighty, austere Zanna and Pieluni Montepulciano Riservas are the top of the range. Illuminati sent us their usual astounding battery, with Montepulcianos again to the fore. The 2015 Riparosso unfolds blackberry, cocoa powder and embers, a step ahead of an entry-level wine. Its modern style is replicated and reinforced in the 2011 Zanna Riserva, with its aromas of pepper and coffee.

● Montepulciano d'Abruzzo Colline Teramane Zanna Ris. '11	♈♈♈ 5
● Montepulciano d'Abruzzo Riparosso '15	♈♈ 2*
○ Controguerra Bianco Costalupo '15	♈♈ 2*
○ Controguerra Bianco Pligia '15	♈♈ 2*
● Controguerra Rosso Lumen Ris. '11	♈♈ 5
⊙ Cerasuolo d'Abruzzo Campirosa '15	♈ 2
⊙ Cerasuolo d'Abruzzo Sitara '15	♈ 2
○ Controguerra Passerina '15	♈ 2
○ Controguerra Pecorino '15	♈ 2
● Montepulciano d'Abruzzo Ilico '14	♈ 2
● Montepulciano d'Abruzzo Spiano '15	♈ 2
● Montepulciano d'Abruzzo Colline Teramane Pieluni Ris. '10	♈♈♈ 6
● Montepulciano d'Abruzzo Colline Teramane Zanna Ris. '10	♈♈♈ 5

★★Masciarelli

VIA GAMBERALE, 1
66010 SAN MARTINO SULLA MARRUCINA [CH]
TEL. +39 087185241
www.masciarelli.it

CELLAR SALES
PRE-BOOKED VISITS
ACCOMMODATION
ANNUAL PRODUCTION 2,500,000 bottles
HECTARES UNDER VINE 300.00
SUSTAINABLE WINERY

Anyone who has observed developments on the Abruzzo winemaking scene in the last 30 years will acknowledge the importance of the work of Gianni Masciarelli. A man who put his heart and soul into his production, a man who was able to make his international dreams come true thanks to a simply spectacular vineyard estate, 300 hectares distributed around four provinces. The style of winemaking was openly modern, self-contained, and progressively developed by his heirs into the five Classica, Gianni Masciarelli, Marina Cvetic, Castello di Semivicoli, and Villa Gemma lines of native and non-native monovarietals, for a total of about 20 labels. A new approach that can be seen clearly, especially in the 2015 Cerasuolo Villa Gemma, definitely showing coastal hints of pine resin and Mediterranean maquis, certainly leaning more to savoury than to depth, suggesting it will evolve further in the bottle. Rich but quite brooding and dry, the Montepulciano Villa Gemma 2011.

⊙ Cerasuolo d'Abruzzo Villa Gemma '15	♥♥♥ 3*
● Montepulciano d'Abruzzo	
Villa Gemma '11	♥♥ 7
○ Abruzzo Pecorino	
Castello di Semivicoli '15	♥♥ 3
● Castello di Semivicoli Rosso '14	♥♥ 3
● Montepulciano d'Abruzzo	
Colline Teramane Iskra '11	♥♥ 5
● Montepulciano d'Abruzzo	
Gianni Masciarelli '14	♥♥ 2*
● Montepulciano d'Abruzzo	
Marina Cvetic San Martino '14	♥♥ 4
○ Trebbiano d'Abruzzo	
Gianni Masciarelli '15	♥♥ 2*
⊙ Cerasuolo d'Abruzzo	
Gianni Masciarelli '15	♥ 2
● Marina Cvetic Merlot '13	♥ 5
● Marina Cvetic Syrah '14	♥ 5

Camillo Montori

LOC. PIANE TRONTO, 80
64010 CONTROGUERRA [TE]
TEL. +39 0861809900
www.montorivini.it

CELLAR SALES
PRE-BOOKED VISITS
ACCOMMODATION AND RESTAURANT SERVICE
ANNUAL PRODUCTION 600,000 bottles
HECTARES UNDER VINE 50.00

In an era when technical contrasts are increasingly nuanced, the Montori family is emerging as one of the few truly traditional cellars. Founded in the latter 1800s, it now covers over 50 hectares in the Controguerra hills of the province of Teramo, planted mainly to Montepulciano and trebbiano, then similar amounts of pecorino, passerina, chardonnay, sauvignon, sangiovese, merlot, and cabernet. Nonetheless, the more traditional varieties are the guiding light of the top Casa Montori and Poderi di Fonte Cupa lines, part of an extensive battery always characterized by the unobtrusive style of expression, preferring follow-through to intensity. A style profile confirmed in full during these tastings, spotlighting first of all the 2015 Cerasuolo Fonte Cupa's subtle floral grace. The two Montepulcianos are close behind, however: the more approachable 2011 Casa Montori has greater verve; the 2008 Fonte Cupa Riserva shows a better weave without losing any of its liveliness.

⊙ Cerasuolo d'Abruzzo Fonte Cupa '15	♥♥ 2*
● Montepulciano d'Abruzzo	
Colline Teramane Casa Montori '11	♥♥ 2*
● Montepulciano d'Abruzzo	
Colline Teramane Fonte Cupa Ris. '08	♥♥ 5
○ Controguerra Passerina Fonte Cupa '15	♥ 2
○ Pecorino Fonte Cupa '15	♥ 3
○ Trebbiano d'Abruzzo Fonte Cupa '15	♥ 2
⊙ Montepulciano d'Abruzzo Cerasuolo	
Fonte Cupa '14	♀♀ 2*
● Montepulciano d'Abruzzo	
Colline Teramane Casa Montori '10	♀♀ 2*
● Montepulciano d'Abruzzo Fonte Cupa '11	♀♀ 2*
○ Pecorino Fonte Cupa '14	♀♀ 3

Fattoria Nicodemi

C.DA VENIGLIO
64024 NOTARESCO [TE]
TEL. +39 085895493
www.nicodemi.com

CELLAR SALES
PRE-BOOKED VISITS
ANNUAL PRODUCTION 250,000 bottles
HECTARES UNDER VINE 30.00

Elena and Alessandro Nicodemi are the second generation working in what is effectively a veteran outfit in the Teramo wine scene, founded by father Bruno in the 1970s. The winery vaunts an estate of about 30 hectares set around the cellar in Notaresco's Contrada Veniglio, practically a single plot in which Montepulciano and trebbiano share the best aspects. This is a Mediterranean terroir despite Gran Sasso at its back, and it forges wines that unfold in a crescendo of might and fruit-rich stuffing found in the Le Murate and Notàri lines, with Neromoro Riserva laying claim to aspirations of being a rich, austere, cellarable red. The Nicodemi siblings continue to fly the quality flag. The spice and balsamic notes of the Montepulciano Notàri 2014 make for a commendable multifaceted aromatic profile, verging on the oriental and held back only by a French nuance. Conversely, the Neromoro 2012 shows more mature on the nose, with a harmonious, mellow mouth.

- Montepulciano d'Abruzzo
  Colline Teramane Neromoro Ris. '12   ♈♈ 5
- Montepulciano d'Abruzzo
  Colline Teramane Notàri '14   ♈♈ 4
- ○ Trebbiano d'Abruzzo Le Murate '15   ♈♈ 2*
- ⊙ Cerasuolo d'Abruzzo Le Murate '15   ♈ 2
- Montepulciano d'Abruzzo
  Colline Teramane Le Murate '14   ♈ 3
- ○ Trebbiano d'Abruzzo Sup. Notàri '14   ♈ 3
- Montepulciano d'Abruzzo
  Colline Teramane Neromoro Ris. '09   ♈♈♈ 5
- Montepulciano d'Abruzzo
  Colline Teramane Neromoro Ris. '03   ♈♈♈ 5

Orlandi Contucci Ponno

LOC. PIANA DEGLI ULIVI, 1
64026 ROSETO DEGLI ABRUZZI [TE]
TEL. +39 0858944049
www.orlandicontucci.com

CELLAR SALES
PRE-BOOKED VISITS
ANNUAL PRODUCTION 180,000 bottles
HECTARES UNDER VINE 31.00

Can a business that is over 50 years old be up and coming? Yes, if we are in the dynamic Teramo district, which encourages established traditional wineries to review their ranges and style constantly. This is the path taken by Orlandi Contucci Ponno, especially after the 2007 takeover by the Gussalli Beretta family. The result is a multifaceted range of native and international varieties whose image continues to grow thanks to a happy-go-lucky and racy twist, both in entry-level labels and in the crus and Riservas selected from nearly 30 hectares in the Roseto area, a stone's throw from the sea. And there are at least two champions in this round of tastings. Black berry fruit, cocoa powder and charred wood for the 2012 Colline Teramane Riserva, a compact, vigorous Montepulciano not lacking extractive delicacy. On equal footing, we scored the 2015 Cerasuolo Vermiglio with brilliant citrus notes and a dynamic palate.

- ⊙ Cerasuolo d'Abruzzo Vermiglio '15   ♈♈ 2*
- Montepulciano d'Abruzzo
  Colline Teramane Ris. '12   ♈♈ 5
- Montepulciano d'Abruzzo
  Colline Teramane La Regia Specula '13   ♈♈ 3
- Montepulciano d'Abruzzo Rubiolo '15   ♈♈ 2*
- ○ Trebbiano d'Abruzzo Sup.
  Colle della Corte Gusalli Beretta '15   ♈♈ 2*
- Liburnio '12   ♈ 5
- ○ Sauvignon Ghiaiolo '15   ♈ 3
- Colle Funaro '11   ♈♈ 3
- Montepulciano d'Abruzzo
  Colline Teramane
  Podere La Regia Specula '12   ♈♈ 3
- Montepulciano d'Abruzzo
  Colline Teramane Ris. '11   ♈♈ 5

Pasetti

LOC. C.DA PRETARO
VIA SAN PAOLO, 21
66023 FRANCAVILLA AL MARE [CH]
TEL. +39 08561875
www.pasettivini.it

CELLAR SALES
PRE-BOOKED VISITS
ACCOMMODATION AND RESTAURANT SERVICE
ANNUAL PRODUCTION 600,000 bottles
HECTARES UNDER VINE 70.00

The Pasetti brand's production is more than ever characterized by the terrific fusion of sea and mountain milieus. Now in the capable hands of Mimmo and Laura, the venerable cellar is in Francavilla al Mare, on the Adriatic coast, but the bulk of the vineyards are to be found inland, in the provinces of Pescara, at Pescosansonesco at the foot of Mount Majella, and L'Aquila, at Capestrano, near Gran Sasso. The range comprises five lines, including one named for the famous Tenuta Testarossa estate, and reflects a dual interpretation showing juiciness and verve, based on innovative yet offbeat cellar protocols. Already well-respected, we hope Pasetti wines will make a further quantum leap. The spotlight is on two Pecorinos: a 2015 given full rein, compensating one or two aromatic quirks with its approachability; a 2014 Colle Civetta persuasive for its citrusy, salty pace, with an almost Teutonic consistency and backbone.

○ Abruzzo Pecorino '15	♀♀	2*
○ Abruzzo Pecorino Colle Civetta '14	♀♀	3
○ Abruzzo Passito Gesmino '14	♀	4
○ Passerina Testarossa '15	♀	2
⊙ Testarossa Rosato '15	♀	2
○ Abruzzo Pecorino '14	♀♀	2*
○ Abruzzo Pecorino Colle Civetta '13	♀♀	3
● Montepulciano d'Abruzzo '12	♀♀	2*
● Montepulciano d'Abruzzo Testarossa '11	♀♀	4
● Montepulciano d'Abruzzo Testarossa '10	♀♀	4
○ Passerina Testarossa '13	♀♀	2*
⊙ Testarossa Rosato '14	♀♀	2*
○ Trebbiano d'Abruzzo Zarachè '14	♀♀	2*
○ Trebbiano d'Abruzzo Zarachè '13	♀♀	2*

Emidio Pepe

VIA CHIESI, 10
64010 TORANO NUOVO [TE]
TEL. +39 0861856493
www.emidiopepe.com

CELLAR SALES
PRE-BOOKED VISITS
ACCOMMODATION AND RESTAURANT SERVICE
ANNUAL PRODUCTION 80,000 bottles
HECTARES UNDER VINE 15.00
VITICULTURE METHOD Certified Biodynamic
SUSTAINABLE WINERY

Emidio Pepe is universally elevated to semi-god status in the Abruzzo artisanal winemaking Valhalla. In the 1960s, the Torano Nuovo farming business established in 1899, was converted into a bottling facility. On the northern edge of the region, today's 15 hectares of organic and biodynamic vineyards are planted to typical Teramo varieties, mainly Montepulciano and trebbiano. Recently the helm has been taken over by his daughters Sofia and Daniela, but little or nothing has changed of the small and proudly traditional range, with its renowned spontaneous fermentation and long aging in concrete and bottle. The Pepe family's wines are always unmistakable. The Trebbiano 2014 shows strong hints of cider, honey and dried flowers, and wagers on gutsy tastiness. Bergamot, pine resin and chimney soot for an equally well-made Montepulciano 2013, slightly hindered by the alcohol grip in a bitterish, austere palate.

● Montepulciano d'Abruzzo '13	♀♀	6
○ Trebbiano d'Abruzzo '14	♀♀	5
⊙ Cerasuolo d'Abruzzo '15	♀♀	5
○ Pecorino '14	♀♀	6
● Montepulciano d'Abruzzo '98	♀♀♀	8
● Montepulciano d'Abruzzo '12	♀♀	6
● Montepulciano d'Abruzzo '11	♀♀	6
● Montepulciano d'Abruzzo '10	♀♀	6
● Montepulciano d'Abruzzo '09	♀♀	5
⊙ Montepulciano d'Abruzzo Cerasuolo '14	♀♀	5
⊙ Montepulciano d'Abruzzo Cerasuolo '13	♀♀	5
⊙ Montepulciano d'Abruzzo Cerasuolo '12	♀♀	5
○ Trebbiano d'Abruzzo '13	♀♀	5
○ Trebbiano d'Abruzzo '12	♀♀	5
○ Trebbiano d'Abruzzo '11	♀♀	5

La Quercia

C.DA COLLE CROCE
64020 MORRO D'ORO [TE]
TEL. +39 0858959110
www.vinilaquercia.it

CELLAR SALES
PRE-BOOKED VISITS
ANNUAL PRODUCTION 200,000 bottles
HECTARES UNDER VINE 21.00

La Quercia is the result of a friendship that led to the purchase of the winery in 2000 by four colleagues who had worked for the Teramo-based company. Elisabetta Di Berardino, Antonio Lamona, Luca Moretti, and Fabio Pedicone acquired the 20 hectares, some owned, some rented, concentrated mainly between the municipal districts of Morro d'Oro, Bisenti and Cermignano, and planted to a wide range of local varieties, and international chardonnay and pinot nero. Used for different lines, from Classici to Primamadre, Peladi and Santapupa, and the Mastrobono Riservas, aged in wood and cellared. A memorable performance for La Quercia's limited range. The Montepulciano Primamadre is spirited and lively following a blood-rich, tertiary start, combining charm and substance. Certainly on equal footing are the agile, smooth Montepulciano La Quercia 2013 and the delicate, fruity Montonico Santapupa 2015.

San Lorenzo Vini

C.DA PLAVIGNANO, 2
64035 CASTILENTI [TE]
TEL. +39 0861999325
www.sanlorenzovini.com

CELLAR SALES
PRE-BOOKED VISITS
ANNUAL PRODUCTION 800,000 bottles
HECTARES UNDER VINE 150.00

Founded in 1890, in many ways San Lorenzo is the most Bordeaux influenced of Abruzzo wineries, with about 150 hectares of vineyard concentrated near the Castilenti cellar, on the border between the provinces of Teramo and Pescara. It lies midway between the Adriatic Sea and Mount Gran Sasso, in wine country with a tradition for aspiring to quality and quantity. San Lorenzo's identity is openly declared in its rich range of both traditional styles and innovative labels, affordable early-drinkers alongside selections and Riservas (especially Montepulciano) that play out on more austere autumnal expressiveness, and applying different technical protocols. A superb presentation from San Lorenzo with its worthy Montepulciano Sirio 2014 in the front line. This red hints at a modern feel of bottled cherries, chocolate and ashes, showing feistier in the assertive, tasty palate with nicely textured tannins. The 2014 Bio and Antàres are also commendable.

● Montepulciano d'Abruzzo Primamadre '12	🏆🏆 2*
○ Abruzzo Montonico Sup. Santapupa '15	🏆🏆 2*
○ Abruzzo Passerina Sup. Santapupa '15	🏆🏆 2*
● Montepulciano d'Abruzzo La Quercia '13	🏆🏆 2*
● Montepulciano d'Abruzzo '11	🏆🏆 2*
◉ Montepulciano d'Abruzzo Cerasuolo Peladi '13	🏆🏆 1*
● Montepulciano d'Abruzzo Colline Teramane Mastrobono Ris. '07	🏆🏆 5
● Montepulciano d'Abruzzo Colline Teramane Primamadre '08	🏆🏆 3
● Montepulciano d'Abruzzo Colline Teramane Primamadre '07	🏆🏆 3
● Montepulciano d'Abruzzo Primamadre '10	🏆🏆 2*

● Montepulciano d'Abruzzo Sirio '14	🏆🏆 1*
○ Chardonnay Chioma di Berenice '15	🏆🏆 2*
● Montepulciano d'Abruzzo Bio Raccolto a Mano '14	🏆🏆 3
● Montepulciano d'Abruzzo Colline Teramane Antàres '14	🏆🏆 3
○ Abruzzo Pecorino Il Pecorino '15	🏆 2
◉ Cerasuolo d'Abruzzo Sirio '15	🏆 1*
○ La Passerina '15	🏆 2
● Montepulciano d'Abruzzo Casabianca '14	🏆 2
● Montepulciano d'Abruzzo Colline Teramane Escol Ris. '11	🏆 5
● Montepulciano d'Abruzzo Colline Teramane Oinos '12	🏆 4
◉ Rosato '15	🏆 2
○ Trebbiano d'Abruzzo Casabianca '15	🏆 2
○ Trebbiano d'Abruzzo Sirio '15	🏆 1*

Tenuta Terraviva

VIA DEL LAGO, 19
64081 TORTORETO [TE]
TEL. +39 0861786056
www.tenutaterraviva.it

CELLAR SALES
PRE-BOOKED VISITS
ANNUAL PRODUCTION 65,000 bottles
HECTARES UNDER VINE 18.00
VITICULTURE METHOD Certified Organic

Tenuta Terraviva is experiencing a sort of second youth with its most recent vintages. The changes were driven by some extensive rethinking of their agricultural philosophy, followed by conversion to organic protocols of about 20 hectares of estate in Teramo province's Tortoreto hills. Cellar methods were also changed to accommodate spontaneous fermentation and a recognizable style that manages to weave in a hint of jazz, focusing on drinking flexibility. There is little point in drafting a risk-laden default hierarchy of this winery's entry-level Montepulcianos, Cerasuolos, Trebbianos, and Pecorinos, and its more muscular selections. We confirm a fantastic performance, with at least three peaks of excellence. The 2015 Ekwo is an eager, impulsive Pecorino, showing a similar personality to the Cerasuolo of the same vintage. The textured, well-defined character of the Montepulciano Luì 2013 shows loam, blood orange, and green pepper notes.

● Montepulciano d'Abruzzo Luì '13	♟♟♟ 3*
○ Abruzzo Pecorino Ekwo '15	♟♟ 3*
○ Cerasuolo d'Abruzzo Giusi '15	♟♟ 2*
● Montepulciano d'Abruzzo Terraviva '13	♟♟ 2*
○ Trebbiano d'Abruzzo '15	♟♟ 2*
○ Trebbiano d'Abruzzo Mario's 42 '15	♟♟ 3
○ Trebbiano d'Abruzzo Terraviva '15	♟♟ 2*
○ Abruzzo Passerina '15	♟ 2
● Montepulciano d'Abruzzo Colline Teramane Polyphemos '10	♟ 6
● Solorosso '14	♟ 3
○ Abruzzo Pecorino Ekwo '14	♟♟ 3
● Montepulciano d'Abruzzo '13	♟♟ 2*
○ Trebbiano d'Abruzzo '14	♟♟ 2*
○ Trebbiano d'Abruzzo Mario's 41 '13	♟♟ 3

Tiberio

C.DA LA VOTA
65020 CUGNOLI [PE]
TEL. +39 0858576744
www.tiberio.it

CELLAR SALES
PRE-BOOKED VISITS
ANNUAL PRODUCTION 90,000 bottles
HECTARES UNDER VINE 30.00

Agricola Tiberio only took ten years or so to become a fully-fledged member of the Abruzzo winemaking club. It all started with Riccardo, who bought an old trebbiano vineyard in Cugnoli, on the Pescara hills, off towards Mount Majella, at about 350 metres. Throughout the Noughties, other plots, planted to Montepulciano, aglianico, pecorino, and moscato di Castiglione, were acquired for a total of about 30 hectares. Offspring Cristiana and Antonio are now at the helm and have developed a commendable battery of wines, with some noteworthy and very food-friendly labels, both racy, mineral-rich whites, and elegantly woven reds. Undoubtedly one of the best whites of the centre-south to come from the sun-kissed 2015 harvest, Tiberio's Pecorino enchants from the start: bright and multifaceted, it unfolds lemon peel and mint, freshly-baked bread and damp sand. A layered profile backed up by the full, well-paced palate, at such an affordable price tag that it took our Best Value For Money award.

○ Pecorino '15	♟♟♟ 3*
● Montepulciano d'Abruzzo '14	♟♟ 2*
○ Trebbiano d'Abruzzo '15	♟♟ 2*
⊙ Cerasuolo d'Abruzzo '15	♟ 2
● Montepulciano d'Abruzzo '13	♟♟♟ 2*
○ Pecorino '13	♟♟♟ 3*
○ Pecorino '12	♟♟♟ 3*
○ Pecorino '11	♟♟♟ 3*
○ Pecorino '10	♟♟♟ 3
⊙ Montepulciano d'Abruzzo Cerasuolo '14	♟♟ 2*
○ Pecorino '14	♟♟ 3*
○ Pecorino FS '14	♟♟ 3*
○ Trebbiano d'Abruzzo '14	♟♟ 2*
○ Trebbiano d'Abruzzo '13	♟♟ 2*

Cantina Tollo

Via Garibaldi, 68
66010 Tollo [CH]
Tel. +39 087196251
www.cantinatollo.it

CELLAR SALES
ANNUAL PRODUCTION 13,000,000 bottles
HECTARES UNDER VINE 3,200.00

Apart from being one of the most famous of Abruzzo's wineries, it is also a leading European cooperative with 822 members, over 3,000 hectares under vine, and 13 million bottles produced each year. A stately flagship that has achieved the miracle of navigating a modern business approach combined with a rational range of various complementary lines with distinct styles. Cantina Tollo, in short, assures consumers some very affordable Montepulciano, Cerasuolo, Trebbiano, Pecorino, Passerina, and Cococciola labels, but there are also more complex, layered interpretations for cellaring with confidence. The standard and reliability of the Cantina Tollo range are astounding, with a perfectly balanced pair of Montepulcianos heading the list. The 2015 Biologico is simply luscious but also shows complex hints of orange, roots and bitter herbs; the 2012 Mo Riserva expresses sea-salt tones in an austere, compact palate.

● Montepulciano d'Abruzzo Mo Ris. '12	♟♟♟ 2*
● Montepulciano d'Abruzzo Biologico '15	♟♟ 2*
● Montepulciano d'Abruzzo Cagiòlo Ris. '12	♟♟ 5
● Montepulciano d'Abruzzo Colle Secco Rubì '13	♟♟ 2*
● Montepulciano d'Abruzzo Heliko '15	♟♟ 3
○ Trebbiano d'Abruzzo Biovegano '15	♟♟ 2*
⊙ Cerasuolo d'Abruzzo Hedòs '15	♟ 3
○ Pecorino '15	♟ 3
○ Trebbiano d'Abruzzo Aldiano '15	♟ 2
● Montepulciano d'Abruzzo Cagiòlo Ris. '09	♟♟♟ 4*
● Montepulciano d'Abruzzo Mo Ris. '11	♟♟♟ 2*
○ Trebbiano d'Abruzzo C'Incanta '11	♟♟♟ 4*
○ Trebbiano d'Abruzzo C'Incanta '10	♟♟♟ 4*

Torre dei Beati

c.da Poggioragone, 56
65014 Loreto Aprutino [PE]
Tel. +39 0854916069
www.torredeibeati.it

CELLAR SALES
PRE-BOOKED VISITS
ANNUAL PRODUCTION 100,000 bottles
HECTARES UNDER VINE 20.00
VITICULTURE METHOD Certified Organic
SUSTAINABLE WINERY

In 1999 a precious 1400s fresco in the church of Santa Maria in Piano, in Loreto Aprutino, inspired the name for the Torre dei Beati project. Today Adriana Galasso and Fausto Albanese manage 20 hectares of owned and rented vineyards, perched on the Pescara hills at 250–300 metres of altitude, in an area influenced by the significant day-night temperature fluctuations brought by nearby Gran Sasso. From the start, the business has been organic, with region's typical montepulciano, trebbiano and pecorino varieties interpreted with artisanal sensitivity for a charming, kaleidoscopic range, reflected in the imaginative labels. Individual ratings apart, the Torre dei Beati range overall is confirmed as one of the most original and consistent in the region. The best results come from the Trebbiano Bianchi Grilli per la Testa 2014, with apricot, propolis and dried fruit, sustained by a glycerine-rich backbone, winding down slightly in the finale.

○ Trebbiano d'Abruzzo Bianchi Grilli per la Testa '14	♟♟♟ 4
○ Abruzzo Pecorino Giocheremo con i Fiori '15	♟♟ 3
○ Abruzzo Pecorino Bianchi Grilli per la Testa '14	♟♟ 4
⊙ Cerasuolo d'Abruzzo Rosa-ae '15	♟♟ 2*
● Montepulciano d'Abruzzo '07	♟♟♟ 2*
● Montepulciano d'Abruzzo Cocciapazza '11	♟♟♟ 4*
● Montepulciano d'Abruzzo Cocciapazza '10	♟♟♟ 4*
● Montepulciano d'Abruzzo Cocciapazza '09	♟♟♟ 4*
● Montepulciano d'Abruzzo Cocciapazza '08	♟♟♟ 4
● Montepulciano d'Abruzzo Cocciapazza '07	♟♟♟ 4

Tenuta Ulisse

VIA SAN POLO, 40
66014 CRECCHIO [CH]
TEL. +39 0871407733
www.tenutaulisse.it

CELLAR SALES
PRE-BOOKED VISITS
ANNUAL PRODUCTION 550,000 bottles
HECTARES UNDER VINE 75.00

Brothers Antonio and Luigi Ulisse decided to aim for the big time from the word go, when they started their project in 2006. The estate they took over in San Polo, at Crecchio in the Chieti hills, has now grown to 75 controlled hectares, most converted to organic production. The plots are found along a stretch connecting the Adriatic and to Mount Majella, ideal wine country for Montepulciano, Cerasuolo, Pecorino, Trebbiano, Passerina, and Cococciola, each with its own personality, emphasized in the various lines thanks to spontaneous fermentation at low temperature. Results are increasingly persuasive both for whites and reds, entry-level labels and more ambitious selections. A dual direction explored with confidence in the latest releases. On the one hand, a sappy 2015 Pecorino with terpene hints and an invigorating citrus trace on the palate; on the other, the Montepulciano Nativae of the same year, intense and nuanced, showing the stuff of an awe-inspiring wine.

○ Abruzzo Pecorino Nativae '15	♟♟ 4
● Montepulciano d'Abruzzo Nativae '15	♟♟ 4
○ Pecorino '15	♟♟ 3*
○ Cococciola '15	♟♟ 3
⊙ Cerasuolo d'Abruzzo '15	♟ 3
⊙ Merlot Rosé '15	♟ 3
● Montepulciano d'Abruzzo '15	♟ 4
● Montepulciano d'Abruzzo Amaranta '14	♟ 4
○ Passerina '15	♟ 3
○ Trebbiano d'Abruzzo '15	♟ 3
○ Trebbiano d'Abruzzo Nativae '15	♟ 4
○ Abruzzo Pecorino Nativae '13	♟♟♟ 4*
● Montepulciano d'Abruzzo Nativae '14	♟♟♟ 4*
● Montepulciano d'Abruzzo Nativae '12	♟♟♟ 4*

La Valentina

VIA TORRETTA, 52
65010 SPOLTORE [PE]
TEL. +39 0854478158
www.lavalentina.it

CELLAR SALES
PRE-BOOKED VISITS
ANNUAL PRODUCTION 350,000 bottles
HECTARES UNDER VINE 40.00
VITICULTURE METHOD Certified Organic
SUSTAINABLE WINERY

Originally opened in 1990, and acquired some years later by Sabatino, Roberto and Andrea Di Properzio, La Valentina is one of the best-known cellars of those at the forefront of today's Abruzzo wine scene. Always attentive to the dictates of biocompatible agriculture, the winery now covers about 40 hectares and at least five plots of vineyards in the Pescara hills: Spoltore and Cavaticchi near the coast; Scafa, San Valentino and Penne inland, and at significantly higher altitudes. The Classica line of fragrant, affable wines comprises Montepulcianos, Cerasuolos and Trebbianos, as does the Terroir line, with the noteworthy muscle and energy of the Spelt label. Tastings of the Trebbiano Superiore Spelt confirmed the 2015 vintage to be in line with the classic medlar, fresh hazelnut and sappy profile, true to its Mediterranean nature. Not far behind, the 2012 Montepulciano Spelt Riserva showed black cherry, chimney soot, and pencil lead, combining intense fruitiness with tangy momentum.

● Montepulciano d'Abruzzo Spelt Ris. '12	♟♟ 4
○ Trebbiano d'Abruzzo Sup. Spelt '15	♟♟ 3*
⊙ Cerasuolo d'Abruzzo Spelt '15	♟♟ 3
● Montepulciano d'Abruzzo '14	♟♟ 2*
● Montepulciano d'Abruzzo Bellovedere '12	♟♟ 6
● Montepulciano d'Abruzzo Binomio Ris. '12	♟♟ 5
○ Ahuà Fiano '15	♟ 3
⊙ Cerasuolo d'Abruzzo '15	♟ 2
○ Pecorino '15	♟ 2
● Montepulciano d'Abruzzo Bellovedere '05	♟♟♟ 6
● Montepulciano d'Abruzzo Spelt '08	♟♟♟ 3*
● Montepulciano d'Abruzzo Spelt '07	♟♟♟ 3
● Montepulciano d'Abruzzo Spelt '05	♟♟♟ 3
● Montepulciano d'Abruzzo Spelt Ris. '11	♟♟♟ 4*
● Montepulciano d'Abruzzo Spelt Ris. '10	♟♟♟ 3*

★★★Valentini

VIA DEL BAIO, 2
65014 LORETO APRUTINO [PE]
TEL. +39 0858291138

ANNUAL PRODUCTION 30,000 bottles
HECTARES UNDER VINE 60.00

Francesco Paolo Valentini is the latest in line of a charismatic family that has taken Abruzzo artisanal winemaking, and more, to its apex. The agricultural roots go back to the first half of the 1600s and continue to inspire work based not only on protocols but also, even more so, on a glocal philosophy of life that voices concerns about global warming and the Earth's life cycle. All of which explains why the Loreto Aprutino house-winery has become a place of pilgrimage for the many aficionados who love the timeless stamp of his Montepulciano, Cerasuolo and Trebbiano, entranced by a resolute rejection of any rigid approach. Valentini's long-awaited and legendary 2006 Montepulciano certainly lived up to expectations. The 2012 version is already memorable with its unmistakable earthy, blood-rich notes that quickly usher in a flavour monumental for the sheer might of the fruit, velvety tannins and refreshing thrust.

★Valle Reale

LOC. SAN CALISTO
65026 POPOLI [PE]
TEL. +39 0859871039
www.vallereale.it

CELLAR SALES
PRE-BOOKED VISITS
ANNUAL PRODUCTION 250,000 bottles
HECTARES UNDER VINE 49.00
VITICULTURE METHOD Certified Organic
SUSTAINABLE WINERY

A trip up to Valle Reale will make it clear at first glance how much the mountains and the Apennines impact farming economy here. In early 1998, the Pizzolo family began to make the most of these local traits for their production concept, adding the finishing touches in 2007 with new acquisitions, organic procedures, spontaneous fermentations, and vinification by plot. Today they have about 50 hectares under vine, on the border between the provinces of Pescara and L'Aquila, between Popoli at the mouth of the Val Peligna and Capestrano, overlooking the Ofena Plain, both natural amphitheatres that forge tasty, graceful Trebbiano, Cerasuolo and Montepulciano. This year the talent for white winemaking was to the fore, thanks to a fantastic range of Trebbianos. The 2014 duel played out between the deliciously summery Vigneto di Popoli and the more intense, deep Vigna del Convento di Capestrano, unfurling flowers and citrus fruits, mineral swathe and flavour.

● Montepulciano d'Abruzzo '12	♥♥♥ 8
● Montepulciano d'Abruzzo '06	♥♥♥ 8
● Montepulciano d'Abruzzo '02	♥♥♥ 8
● Montepulciano d'Abruzzo '01	♥♥♥ 8
⊙ Montepulciano d'Abruzzo Cerasuolo '09	♥♥♥ 6
⊙ Montepulciano d'Abruzzo Cerasuolo '08	♥♥♥ 6
⊙ Montepulciano d'Abruzzo Cerasuolo '06	♥♥♥ 6
○ Trebbiano d'Abruzzo '12	♥♥♥ 6
○ Trebbiano d'Abruzzo '11	♥♥♥ 6
○ Trebbiano d'Abruzzo '10	♥♥♥ 6
○ Trebbiano d'Abruzzo '09	♥♥♥ 6
○ Trebbiano d'Abruzzo '08	♥♥♥ 6
○ Trebbiano d'Abruzzo '07	♥♥♥ 6
○ Trebbiano d'Abruzzo '05	♥♥♥ 6
○ Trebbiano d'Abruzzo '04	♥♥♥ 6
○ Trebbiano d'Abruzzo '02	♥♥♥ 6

○ Trebbiano d'Abruzzo V. del Convento di Capestrano '14	♥♥♥ 5
○ Trebbiano d'Abruzzo Vign. di Popoli '14	♥♥ 5
○ Trebbiano d'Abruzzo '15	♥♥ 2*
⊙ Cerasuolo d'Abruzzo '15	♥ 2
● Montepulciano d'Abruzzo '15	♥ 2
● Montepulciano d'Abruzzo '06	♥♥♥ 3*
● Montepulciano d'Abruzzo San Calisto '08	♥♥♥ 5
● Montepulciano d'Abruzzo San Calisto '07	♥♥♥ 5
● Montepulciano d'Abruzzo San Calisto '06	♥♥♥ 5
● Montepulciano d'Abruzzo San Calisto '05	♥♥♥ 5
○ Trebbiano d'Abruzzo V. di Capestrano '13	♥♥♥ 5
○ Trebbiano d'Abruzzo V. di Capestrano '12	♥♥♥ 5
○ Trebbiano d'Abruzzo V. di Capestrano '11	♥♥♥ 5
○ Trebbiano d'Abruzzo V. di Capestrano '10	♥♥♥ 5
○ Trebbiano d'Abruzzo V. di Capestrano '08	♥♥♥ 4

★Villa Medoro

C.DA MEDORO
64030 ATRI [TE]
TEL. +39 0858708142
www.villamedoro.it

CELLAR SALES
PRE-BOOKED VISITS
ACCOMMODATION
ANNUAL PRODUCTION 300,000 bottles
HECTARES UNDER VINE 100.00

Named after the renowned Atri district of Medoro, on the Colline Teramane hills, the splendid Morricone family winery opened officially in 1997, after two decades of experimentation. It then spread its wings as an up-and-coming outfit in the stagnant Abruzzo district of the time, thanks to a solid range that grew to nearly 100 hectares with the acquisition of Tenuta Fontanelle and Fonte Corvo. Villa Medoro makes no secret of its modern approach, which it confirms in the cellar, developing a tasty, mouthfilling style, gradually honed in recent vintages, and which hallmarks both the monovarietal Villa Medoro line and the cellared Montepulciano selections. In this round of tastings we encountered a range that was impeccable on all fronts, starting with a plump, full-blooded 2014 Montepulciano showing original floral and sea-salt hints, and which may well relax an austere, demanding mouth. The Adrano 2013 is darker and sterner, but with aromatic persistence.

● Montepulciano d'Abruzzo '14	▼▼▼	2*
● Montepulciano d'Abruzzo Colline Teramane Adrano '13	▼▼	4
● Montepulciano d'Abruzzo Rosso del Duca '14	▼▼	3*
○ Pecorino '15	▼▼	2*
○ Trebbiano d'Abruzzo '15	▼▼	2*
⊙ Cerasuolo d'Abruzzo '15	▼	2
○ Montonico '15	▼	2
○ Passerina '15	▼	2
○ Trebbiano d'Abruzzo Chimera '15	▼	2
● Montepulciano d'Abruzzo Colline Teramane Adrano '12	♈♈♈	4*
● Montepulciano d'Abruzzo Colline Teramane Adrano '10	♈♈♈	4*
● Montepulciano d'Abruzzo Rosso del Duca '12	♈♈♈	3*

Ciccio Zaccagnini

C.DA POZZO
65020 BOLOGNANO [PE]
TEL. +39 0858880195
www.cantinazaccagnini.it

CELLAR SALES
PRE-BOOKED VISITS
ANNUAL PRODUCTION 1,500,000 bottles
HECTARES UNDER VINE 300.00

Abruzzo wine would never have travelled the world without Zaccagnini's decades of hard work on the markets. A family business but now vaunting about 300 hectares of land around Bolognano, on the Pescara hills, where Majella seems to tumble into the Adriatic, the winery now produces one of the region's most multifaceted and pocket-friendly ranges, with various styles of Pecorino, Trebbiano, Montepulciano, and Cerasuolo, not to mention the famous Tralcetto wines and the experimental sparklers, or those without added sulphites. The modern cellar also hosts prestigious art exhibitions, and has long been a rendezvous for wine lovers and other members of the public. A stunning selection of Montepulcianos, each with its own amazing quality. The San Clemente Riserva 2013 is a thoroughbred whose youth is holding it back but we are in no doubt that a few months will be sufficient to hone it. The fruity balsamic, well-structured, tannin-rich Chronicon 2013, however, is perfect. The Pecorino Cuvée dell'Abate is to die for.

● Montepulciano d'Abruzzo Chronicon '13	▼▼▼	3
○ Abruzzo Pecorino La Cuvée dell'Abate '15	▼▼	2*
● Montepulciano d'Abruzzo S. Clemente Ris. '13	▼▼	5
○ Abruzzo Pecorino Yamada '15	▼▼	3
⊙ Cerasuolo d'Abruzzo Myosotis '15	▼▼	3
○ Abruzzo Bianco San Clemente '14	▼	4
● Capsico Rosso '09	▼	4
○ Ispira Passerina '15	▼	3
● Montepulciano d'Abruzzo Cuvée dell'Abate '14	▼	2
● Montepulciano d'Abruzzo Il Vino dal Tralcetto '14	▼	2
● Montepulciano d'Abruzzo No So2 '15	▼	2
● Montepulciano d'Abruzzo S. Clemente Ris. '12	♈♈♈	5

Angelucci

C.DA VICENNE, 7
65020 CASTIGLIONE A CASAURIA [PE]
TEL. +39 0857998193
www.angeluccivini.it

CELLAR SALES
PRE-BOOKED VISITS
ANNUAL PRODUCTION 200,000 bottles
HECTARES UNDER VINE 30.00

○ Leonate Pecorino '15	♥ 3
○ Moscatello Passito '11	♥ 4
○ Travertine Moscatello '15	♥ 3
○ Trebbiano d'Abruzzo Leonate '15	♥ 2

Bove

VIA ROMA, 216
67051 AVEZZANO [AQ]
TEL. +39 086333133
info@cantinebove.it

CELLAR SALES
PRE-BOOKED VISITS
ANNUAL PRODUCTION 1,200,000 bottles
HECTARES UNDER VINE 60.00

● Montepulciano d'Abruzzo Indio '13	♥♥ 2*
● Montepulciano d'Abruzzo Poggio d'Albe '14	♥ 2
○ Trebbiano d'Abruzzo Poggio d'Albe '15	♥ 2

Cerulli Spinozzi

S.S. 150 DEL VOMANO KM 17,600
64020 CANZANO [TE]
TEL. +39 086157193
www.cerullispinozzi.it

CELLAR SALES
PRE-BOOKED VISITS
ACCOMMODATION
ANNUAL PRODUCTION 200,000 bottles
HECTARES UNDER VINE 53.00

○ Cortalto Pecorino '15	♥♥ 2*
○ Trebbiano d'Abruzzo '15	♥ 2

Col del Mondo

C.DA CAMPOTINO, 35C
65010 COLLECORVINO [PE]
TEL. +39 0858207831
www.coldelmondo.com

CELLAR SALES
PRE-BOOKED VISITS
ANNUAL PRODUCTION 80,000 bottles
HECTARES UNDER VINE 12.00

● Montepulciano d'Abruzzo Sunnae '15	♥♥ 2*
○ Abruzzo Bianco Sunnae '15	♥ 2
○ Kerrias Pecorino '15	♥ 2

Antonio Costantini

S.DA MIGLIORI, 20
65013 CITTÀ SANT'ANGELO [PE]
TEL. +39 0859699169
www.costantinivini.it

CELLAR SALES
PRE-BOOKED VISITS
ACCOMMODATION AND RESTAURANT SERVICE
ANNUAL PRODUCTION 450,000 bottles
HECTARES UNDER VINE 60.00

● Montepulciano d'Abruzzo Febe '15	♥♥ 2*
○ Abruzzo Pecorino '15	♥ 3
○ Trebbiano d'Abruzzo '15	♥ 2
○ Trebbiano d'Abruzzo Febe '15	♥ 2

Coste di Brenta

C.DA CAMICIE, 50
66034 LANCIANO [CH]
TEL. +39 0872895280
www.costedibrenta.it

CELLAR SALES
PRE-BOOKED VISITS
ANNUAL PRODUCTION 180,000 bottles
HECTARES UNDER VINE 15.00
VITICULTURE METHOD Certified Organic

○ Abruzzo Pecorino '15	♥♥ 2*
○ Abruzzo Pecorino Elisio '15	♥♥ 2*
● Montepulciano d'Abruzzo '14	♥ 2
○ Trebbiano d'Abruzzo Elisio '15	♥ 2

Faraone

s.s. 80, 290
64021 GIULIANOVA [TE]
TEL. +39 0858071804
www.faraonevini.it

CELLAR SALES
PRE-BOOKED VISITS
ANNUAL PRODUCTION 50,000 bottles
HECTARES UNDER VINE 9.00

⊙ Cerasuolo d'Abruzzo	
Le Vigne di Faraone '15	❦❦ 2*
○ Colle Pietro Passerina '15	❦ 2

Fontefico

VIA DIFENZA, 38
66054 VASTO [CH]
TEL. +39 3284113619
www.fontefico.it

CELLAR SALES
PRE-BOOKED VISITS
RESTAURANT SERVICE
ANNUAL PRODUCTION 30,000 bottles
HECTARES UNDER VINE 15.00
VITICULTURE METHOD Certified Organic
SUSTAINABLE WINERY

● Montepulciano d'Abruzzo Fontefico '13	❦❦ 3
⊙ Cerasuolo d'Abruzzo Sup. '15	❦ 3
● Montepulciano d'Abruzzo	
Colline Teramane Titinge Ris. '12	❦ 5

Cantina Frentana

VIA PERAZZA, 32
66020 ROCCA SAN GIOVANNI [CH]
TEL. +39 087260152
www.cantinafrentana.it

CELLAR SALES
PRE-BOOKED VISITS
ACCOMMODATION
ANNUAL PRODUCTION 800,000 bottles
HECTARES UNDER VINE 22.00

○ Abruzzo Pecorino Costa del Mulino '15	❦❦ 1*
● Montepulciano d'Abruzzo Panarda Ris. '13	❦ 2
● Montepulciano d'Abruzzo Torre Vinaria '14	❦ 2

Lepore

C.DA CIVITA, 29
64010 COLONNELLA [TE]
TEL. +39 086170860
www.vinilepore.it

CELLAR SALES
PRE-BOOKED VISITS
ANNUAL PRODUCTION 330,000 bottles
HECTARES UNDER VINE 43.00

● Montepulciano d'Abruzzo '14	❦❦ 2*
● Montepulciano d'Abruzzo	
Colline Teramane Re '12	❦❦ 3

Marchesi De' Cordano

C.DA CORDANO, 43
65014 LORETO APRUTINO [PE]
TEL. +39 0858289526
www.cordano.it

CELLAR SALES
PRE-BOOKED VISITS
ANNUAL PRODUCTION 180,000 bottles
HECTARES UNDER VINE 50.00
VITICULTURE METHOD Certified Organic
SUSTAINABLE WINERY

○ Brilla Cococciola '15	❦❦ 3
● Montepulciano d'Abruzzo Aida '13	❦❦ 2*
● Santagiusta '11	❦ 4
○ Trebbiano d'Abruzzo Aida '15	❦ 2

Cantine Mucci

C.DA VALLONE DI NANNI, 65
66020 TORINO DI SANGRO [CH]
TEL. +39 0873913366
www.cantinemucci.com

CELLAR SALES
PRE-BOOKED VISITS
ANNUAL PRODUCTION 250,000 bottles
HECTARES UNDER VINE 24.00

○ Pecorino Valentino '15	❦❦ 2*
⊙ Cerasuolo d'Abruzzo Valentino '15	❦ 2
● Montepulciano d'Abruzzo Valentino '15	❦ 2
○ Trebbiano d'Abruzzo '15	❦ 2

Tommaso Olivastri

C.DA QUERCIA DEL CORVO, 37
66038 SAN VITO CHIETINO [CH]
TEL. +39 087261543
www.vinioilvastri.com

CELLAR SALES
PRE-BOOKED VISITS
ANNUAL PRODUCTION 50,000 bottles
HECTARES UNDER VINE 15.00

● Montepulciano d'Abruzzo La Grondaia '12	♥♥ 2*
⊙ Cerasuolo d'Abruzzo Marcantonio '15	♥ 2
○ Coccociola L'Ariosa '15	♥ 2

Pietrantonj

VIA SAN SEBASTIANO, 38
67030 VITTORITO [AQ]
TEL. +39 0864727102
www.vinipietrantonj.it

CELLAR SALES
PRE-BOOKED VISITS
ANNUAL PRODUCTION 650,000 bottles
HECTARES UNDER VINE 60.00

⊙ Cerasuolo d'Abruzzo Arboreo '15	♥ 2
⊙ Cerasuolo d'Abruzzo Sup. Cerano '15	♥ 3

San Giacomo

C.DA NOVELLA, 51
66020 ROCCA SAN GIOVANNI [CH]
TEL. +39 0872620504
www.cantinasangiacomo.it

CELLAR SALES
PRE-BOOKED VISITS
ANNUAL PRODUCTION 20,000 bottles
HECTARES UNDER VINE 300.00
VITICULTURE METHOD Certified Organic

● Montepulciano d'Abruzzo '13	♥♥ 1*
● Montepulciano d'Abruzzo Casino Murri '14	♥♥ 2*
○ Pecorino '14	♥♥ 1*
○ Pecorino Casino Murri '15	♥♥ 2*

Strappelli

VIA TORRI, 16
64010 TORANO NUOVO [TE]
TEL. +39 0861887402
www.cantinastrappelli.it

CELLAR SALES
PRE-BOOKED VISITS
ANNUAL PRODUCTION 65,000 bottles
HECTARES UNDER VINE 10.00
VITICULTURE METHOD Certified Organic

⊙ Cerasuolo d'Abruzzo Sup. Colle Trà Sup. '15	♥♥ 2*
⊙ Trebbiano d'Abruzzo '15	♥♥ 2*
● Montepulciano d'Abruzzo '14	♥ 2

Valle Martello

C.DA VALLE MARTELLO, 10
66010 VILLAMAGNA [CH]
TEL. +39 0871300330
www.vallemartello.it

CELLAR SALES
PRE-BOOKED VISITS
ACCOMMODATION
ANNUAL PRODUCTION 120,000 bottles
HECTARES UNDER VINE 40.00
SUSTAINABLE WINERY

○ Cococciola Brado '15	♥♥ 3
● Montepulciano d'Abruzzo Prima Terra '10	♥♥ 4
○ Pecorino Brado '15	♥♥ 3
○ Cococciola Brut	♥ 3

Valori

VIA TORQUATO AL SALINELLO, 8
64027 SANT'OMERO [TE]
TEL. +39 087185241
www..vinivalori.it

PRE-BOOKED VISITS
ANNUAL PRODUCTION 150,000 bottles
HECTARES UNDER VINE 26.00
VITICULTURE METHOD Certified Organic
SUSTAINABLE WINERY

○ Abruzzo Pecorino '15	♥♥ 2*
● Montepulciano d'Abruzzo Colline Teramane V. Sant'Angelo '11	♥♥ 4
● Montepulciano d'Abruzzo '15	♥ 2

MOLISE

When we talk about heroic viticulture, we mean not only some challenging soil and weather conditions that characterize a number of the most fascinating mountain and coastal terroirs, we also mean the challenging lives of courageous, determined growers and makers who work in places that in many ways are uncharted on the world wine map. This is a compulsory starting point for our annual reconnaissance of Molise's best bottles and wineries. We received a scant selection and these cellars should be encouraged and supported, regardless of technical or rating details. There is no doubt that sooner or later the true added value of this outlying frontier, a crossroads of peoples and cultures, a natural bridge between southern Abruzzo and inland Frosinone, Sannio and Daunia, the Adriatic and the Apennines, will emerge in full. Not surprisingly, it is influenced by its mosaic of geology and altitudes, as well as by the vast array of traditional production methods and grape varieties, a mosaic difficult to assess overall. Sadly, this diversity of growing areas all too often results in confusion or, worse, is crushed by a largely outdated, antiquated, and ultimately naïve winemaking approach. Hurdles in marketing and positioning notwithstanding, the region's most ambitious winemakers could, and should, be more resourceful in showcasing the unique personality of their reds, from montepulciano, from aglianico and, above all, from tintilia. Not to mention the fragrant, fresh-tasting white wines from falanghina, greco, trebbiano, malvasia, with some international flavour from sauvignon and chardonnay. Further growth, in our opinion, can be achieved by taking the road now travelled by healthy wineries like Borgo di Colloredo, Claudio Cipressi, and Tenimenti Grieco, permanent flagbearers of our Molise selection. A total of three labels getting as far as the national finals is a result to be reckoned with, given the limited number of samples sent. Equally, the only Tre Bicchieri awarded is worth shouting from the rooftops, assigned to a 2013 Molise Tintilia from Di Majo Norante, a venerable Campomarino winery and undisputed leader of regional winemaking.

Borgo di Colloredo

LOC. NUOVA CLITERNIA
VIA COLLOREDO, 15
86042 CAMPOMARINO [CB]
TEL. +39 087557453
www.borgodicolloredo.com

CELLAR SALES
PRE-BOOKED VISITS
ACCOMMODATION AND RESTAURANT SERVICE
ANNUAL PRODUCTION 200,000 bottles
HECTARES UNDER VINE 70.00
SUSTAINABLE WINERY

Local tales describe an ancient farmhouse just outside Campomarino, on the Saccione River plain. This was Colloredo and gave its name to one of the top Molise wineries, launched in 1960 by Silvio Di Giulio. Now in the capable hands of brothers Enrico and Pasquale, there are about 70 hectares of vineyards that make up various estates. traditional varieties of Montepulciano, tintilia, aglianico, greco, trebbiano, malvasia, and falanghina, as well as others from further afield, like garganega, chardonnay and syrah, used in the Biferno Gironia, Nobili Vitigni and Classici lines. We recommend a trip out to savour them at the splendid Masseria San Martino in Pensilis, in the heart of the L'Aquila–Foggia Trattturo Magno. We consider this to be a good performance from Borgo di Colloredo, confirming its feel for theoretically more straightforward types like the delicate, juicy Gironia Rosato 2015, or pocket-friendly whites. The winery is equally skilled, however, with more muscular labels vaunting ripe fruitiness, like its Aglianico 2013.

● Aglianico '13		♟♟ 3
⊙ Biferno Rosato Gironia '15		♟♟ 2*
○ Biferno Bianco Gironia '15		♟ 3
○ Greco '15		♟ 2
○ Molise Falanghina '15		♟ 2
● Aglianico '10		♟♟♟ 3*
○ Biferno Bianco Gironia '14		♟♟ 3
○ Biferno Bianco Gironia '13		♟♟ 2*
○ Biferno Bianco Gironia '12		♟♟ 2*
● Biferno Rosso Gironia Ris. '08		♟♟ 4
● Molise Montepulciano '10		♟♟ 2*
● Molise Rosso '12		♟♟ 2*

Claudio Cipressi

C.DA MONTAGNA, 11B
86030 SAN FELICE DEL MOLISE [CB]
TEL. +39 3351244859
www.claudiocipressi.it

CELLAR SALES
PRE-BOOKED VISITS
ACCOMMODATION
ANNUAL PRODUCTION 40,000 bottles
HECTARES UNDER VINE 15.00
VITICULTURE METHOD Certified Organic
SUSTAINABLE WINERY

Clear ideas and a surfeit of passion are the production secrets of Claudio Cipressi, a winemaker in San Felice del Molise, the most rugged inland part of the province of Campobasso. The estate covers about 15 hectares and has been certified organic since the first harvest. Claudio grows mainly tintilia, the local star variety, which he uses for his small range, comprising a base wine, the 66 and Macchiarossa selections, the Collequinto rosé, and the Macchianera blend of largely Montepulciano. The picture is completed by his Falanghina Vananh and Trebbiano Le Scoste, which share the same graceful, low-key profile. Once again the group is successful with the tintilia-based labels. Choose between the 2013 Settevigne's lively tertiary aromas and the autumn symphony of roots and forest floor offered by the 2011 66, but without overlooking the 2012 Macchiarossa with a similar profile but with distinctive bitter herbs and blood-rich nuances. The 2015 whites are a notch behind.

● Molise Tintilia 66 '11		♟♟ 7
● Molise Tintilia Macchiarossa '12		♟♟ 4
● Molise Tintilia Settevigne '13		♟♟ 4
⊙ Molise Rosato Collequinto '15		♟ 3
● Molise Rosso Macchianera '11		♟ 5
○ Molise Trebbiano Le Scoste '15		♟ 4
○ Voira Falanghina '15		♟ 4
○ Falanghina '13		♟♟ 2*
○ Falanghina Voira '13		♟♟ 3
● Molise Rosso Mekan '11		♟♟ 3*
● Molise Rosso Rumen '09		♟♟ 2*
● Molise Tintilia Macchiarossa '11		♟♟ 4
● Molise Tintilia Macchiarossa '10		♟♟ 4
● Molise Tintilia Settevigne '14		♟♟ 4
○ Molise Trebbiano Le Scoste '13		♟♟ 3

★Di Majo Norante

FRAZ. NUOVA CLITERNIA
VIA COLLE SAVINO, 6
86042 CAMPOMARINO [CB]
TEL. +39 087557208
www.dimajonorante.com

CELLAR SALES
PRE-BOOKED VISITS
ANNUAL PRODUCTION 800,000 bottles
HECTARES UNDER VINE 125.00
VITICULTURE METHOD Certified Organic

Campomarino is at the heart of a unique territorial and cultural crossroads where southern Abruzzo meets Daunia and Sannio. A multifaceted identity that is reflected in the wines of Di Majo Norante, arguably the world's best-known Molise winery, now run by Alessio. He has about 135 hectares, cultivated with biocompatible protocols, planted to an extensive range of vines typical of the southern Apennines, and beyond: blacks, like Montepulciano, aglianico, tintilia, and sangiovese; trebbiano, malvasia, moscato, falanghina, and greco for the whites. The moderately modern range hangs together well, applying an expressive approach well represented by the finalists. Cherry compote, quinine and coffee notes for the 2013 Tintilia, underpinned chiefly by its tannin framework. The 2014 Aglianico Biorganic has a more faceted aromatic profile, and a vigorous and lively palate with energetic freshness in the long finish.

Tenimenti Grieco

C.DA DIFENSOLA
86045 PORTOCANNONE [CB]
TEL. +39 0875590032
www.tenimentigrieco.it

CELLAR SALES
PRE-BOOKED VISITS
ANNUAL PRODUCTION 700,000 bottles
HECTARES UNDER VINE 85.00

Tenimenti Grieco has literally forged ahead, proving it is among Molise's leading wineries after just a few vintages. The location is Portocannone, the most densely planted in the region, where the four partners have managed to put together almost 100 hectares and fierce battery of wines divided into six lines: Anima Osca, Maré, the Chapeau sparklers, Costali, Molisani, Passo alle Tremiti. The range comes from a wide variety including falanghina, sauvignon, chardonnay, pinot bianco, tintilia, Montepulciano, cabernet sauvignon, and syrah, with a cellar style that focuses on fruitiness, flavour and drinkability. This year's tastings suggest a further step forward for Tenimenti Grieco's aspirations. The average standard of wines is high and the Tintilia 200 Metri 2015 is a worthy flagship, plump and pleasant, without clichés, harmonizing the pushy dark fruit notes with smoky, spicy nuances.

● Molise Tintilia '13	♟♟♟ 3*
● Molise Aglianico Biorganic '14	♟♟ 3*
● Moli Rosso '15	♟♟ 2*
○ Molise Falanghina Biorganic '15	♟♟ 2*
● Sangiovese '15	♟♟ 2*
○ Moli Bianco '15	♟ 2
○ Molise Falanghina '15	♟ 2
○ Molise Greco '15	♟ 2
● Molise Aglianico Biorganic '11	♟♟♟ 2*
● Molise Aglianico Contado Ris. '10	♟♟♟ 3*
● Molise Aglianico Contado Ris. '09	♟♟♟ 3*
● Molise Aglianico Contado Ris. '07	♟♟♟ 2*
● Molise Don Luigi Ris. '08	♟♟♟ 5
● Molise Rosso Don Luigi Ris. '12	♟♟♟ 5
● Molise Rosso Don Luigi Ris. '11	♟♟♟ 5

● Molise Tintilia 200 Metri '15	♟♟ 2*
● Biferno Bosco delle Guardie '14	♟♟ 3
⊙ Molise Rosato Passo alle Tremiti '15	♟♟ 3
● Triassi '13	♟♟ 5
● Lenda '14	♟ 5
○ Molise Falanghina Passo alle Tremiti '15	♟ 3
● Molise Rosso Passo alle Tremiti '14	♟ 3
○ Passo alle Tremiti Sauvignon '15	♟ 3
● Cabernet Sauvignon '09	♟♟ 2
○ Falanghina '08	♟♟ 2
● Molise Monterosso '13	♟♟ 2*
⊙ Molise Rosato Passo alle Tremiti '14	♟♟ 2*
● Molise Rosso Podere di Sot '08	♟♟ 2*
● Molise Tintilia '14	♟♟ 2*
● Molise Tintilia Cupaia '13	♟♟ 3

Cantine Catabbo

C.DA PETRIERA
86046 SAN MARTINO IN PENSILIS [CB]
TEL. +39 0875604945
www.catabbo.it

CELLAR SALES
ANNUAL PRODUCTION 160,000 bottles
HECTARES UNDER VINE 54.00

● Molise Tintilia S '13	♥ 4
● Petriera Merlot '15	♥ 2
☉ Petriera Rosé '15	♥ 2
● Petriera Rosso '15	♥ 1*

Angelo D'Uva

C.DA MONTE ALTINO, 23A
86035 LARINO [CB]
TEL. +39 0874822320
www.cantineduva.com

CELLAR SALES
PRE-BOOKED VISITS
ACCOMMODATION AND RESTAURANT SERVICE
ANNUAL PRODUCTION 70,000 bottles
HECTARES UNDER VINE 20.00
SUSTAINABLE WINERY

○ Biferno Bianco Kantharos '15	♥ 2
○ Keres Falanghina '15	♥ 2
● Molise Rosso Ricupo '13	♥ 2

Cantine Salvatore

C.DA VIGNE
86049 URURI [CB]
TEL. +39 0874830656
www.cantinesalvatore.it

CELLAR SALES
PRE-BOOKED VISITS
ANNUAL PRODUCTION 80,000 bottles
HECTARES UNDER VINE 15.00
SUSTAINABLE WINERY

○ L'IndoVINO Falanghina '15	♥♥ 2*
● L'IndoVINO Rosso '14	♥♥ 2*
○ Molise Falanghina Nysias '15	♥ 3
● Molise Rosso Biberius '12	♥ 2

Terresacre

C.DA MONTEBELLO
86036 MONTENERO DI BISACCIA [CB]
TEL. +39 0875960191
www.terresacre.net

CELLAR SALES
PRE-BOOKED VISITS
ACCOMMODATION AND RESTAURANT SERVICE
ANNUAL PRODUCTION 100,000 bottles
HECTARES UNDER VINE 35.00

○ Molise Falanghina '15	♥ 3
● Molise Tintilia '13	♥ 5
○ Molise Trebbiano Orovite '15	♥ 2

CAMPANIA

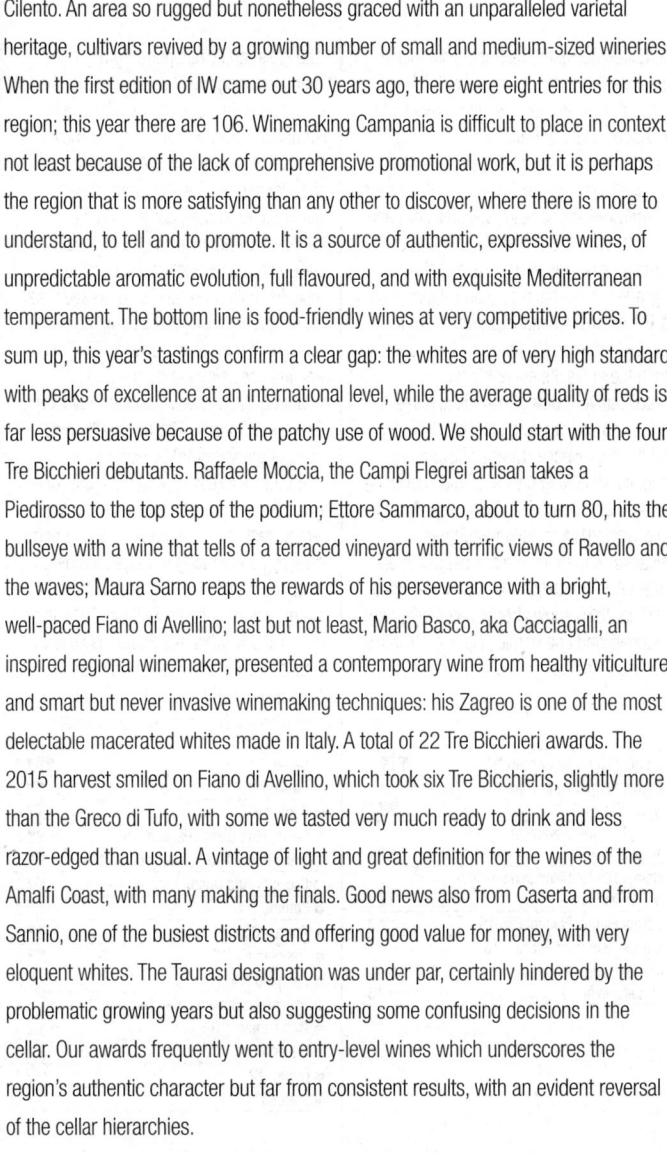

Beautiful and unpredictable are the two descriptors we choose for Campania wines. First of all, the region's vineyards are located on some of the most spectacular sites in Italy: the Amalfi coast, the islands, the slopes of extinct volcanoes, the Picentini mountains, natural parks overlooking the sea, like Cilento. An area so rugged but nonetheless graced with an unparalleled varietal heritage, cultivars revived by a growing number of small and medium-sized wineries. When the first edition of IW came out 30 years ago, there were eight entries for this region; this year there are 106. Winemaking Campania is difficult to place in context, not least because of the lack of comprehensive promotional work, but it is perhaps the region that is more satisfying than any other to discover, where there is more to understand, to tell and to promote. It is a source of authentic, expressive wines, of unpredictable aromatic evolution, full flavoured, and with exquisite Mediterranean temperament. The bottom line is food-friendly wines at very competitive prices. To sum up, this year's tastings confirm a clear gap: the whites are of very high standard, with peaks of excellence at an international level, while the average quality of reds is far less persuasive because of the patchy use of wood. We should start with the four Tre Bicchieri debutants. Raffaele Moccia, the Campi Flegrei artisan takes a Piedirosso to the top step of the podium; Ettore Sammarco, about to turn 80, hits the bullseye with a wine that tells of a terraced vineyard with terrific views of Ravello and the waves; Maura Sarno reaps the rewards of his perseverance with a bright, well-paced Fiano di Avellino; last but not least, Mario Basco, aka Cacciagalli, an inspired regional winemaker, presented a contemporary wine from healthy viticulture and smart but never invasive winemaking techniques: his Zagreo is one of the most delectable macerated whites made in Italy. A total of 22 Tre Bicchieri awards. The 2015 harvest smiled on Fiano di Avellino, which took six Tre Bicchieris, slightly more than the Greco di Tufo, with some we tasted very much ready to drink and less razor-edged than usual. A vintage of light and great definition for the wines of the Amalfi Coast, with many making the finals. Good news also from Caserta and from Sannio, one of the busiest districts and offering good value for money, with very eloquent whites. The Taurasi designation was under par, certainly hindered by the problematic growing years but also suggesting some confusing decisions in the cellar. Our awards frequently went to entry-level wines which underscores the region's authentic character but far from consistent results, with an evident reversal of the cellar hierarchies.

Agnanum

VIA VICINALE ABBANDONATA AGLI ASTRONI, 3
80125 NAPOLI
TEL. +39 3385315272
www.agnanum.it

CELLAR SALES
PRE-BOOKED VISITS
ANNUAL PRODUCTION 25,000 bottles
HECTARES UNDER VINE 7.50

Raffaele Moccia, the stubborn winemaker who runs this virtuous winery with its terraced vineyards on the steep slopes of the Astroni Natural Park, has over seven hectares under vine, half falanghina and half piedirosso. His exquisitely crafted wines faithfully reflect the black volcanic soils and sun-drenched Mediterranean climate of the Campi Flegrei. His yields are low, his vines ungrafted, while his production volumes are off the record. A historic achievement for the Piedirosso 2015, the first of its variety to reach the finals. Its enchantingly approachable profile of medicinal herbs and spring flowers, and nose of rosemary and thyme, reveal a dynamic flavour and deep, lip-smacking palate, with a chewy fruit and soft finish. The Piediroso Vigna delle Volpi 2014 is darker and more balsamic, with hints of black pepper and roots, while the delightful Falanghina Vigna del Pino 2015 shows bright notes of spring meadows and chamomile, signing off with a seemingly endless smoky finish.

● Campi Flegrei Piedirosso '15	♟♟♟ 4*
○ Campi Flegrei Falanghina V. del Pino '15	♟♟ 3*
● Campi Flegrei Piedirosso V. delle Volpi '14	♟♟ 4
○ Campi Flegrei Falanghina V. del Pino '14	♟♟ 3
○ Campi Flegrei Falanghina '15	♟ 3
● Campi Flegrei Piedirosso '13	♟♟ 3*
● Campi Flegrei Piedirosso V. delle Volpi '12	♟♟ 5

Alois

LOC. AUDELINO
VIA RAGAZZANO
81040 PONTELATONE [CE]
TEL. +39 0823876710
www.vinialois.it

CELLAR SALES
PRE-BOOKED VISITS
ANNUAL PRODUCTION 220,000 bottles
HECTARES UNDER VINE 30.00
SUSTAINABLE WINERY

The Alois family has gone from manufacturing precious silks in the shadow of the sumptuous Reggia di Caserta to embarking upon a viticultural journey. Brothers Massimo and Michele run one of the region's most interesting wineries, aiming to promote Caserta's native varieties, using a viticultural philosophy based on monovarietals. Production includes pallagrello bianco, to make Caiatì, an excellent vineyard selection, as well as pallagrello nero and casavecchia. Donna Paolina specializes in Irpinia wines, featuring the classic Avellino trio of Fiano, Greco and Taurasi. The unusually deep hues of the Caiatì 2014 usher in an authentic, expressive wine, and star of an exceptional range. Overtones of peach, lemon zest and wheat give way to a rich, creamy palate nicely underpinned by a long, menthol finish. The Trebulanum 2012 champs at the bit, the Settimo 2014 is taut and crunchy, while the Fiano di Avellino Donna Paolina 2015 shows elegant extractive weight and admirable acid backbone with a tasty, complex finish.

○ Caiatì '14	♟♟♟ 3*
○ Caulino '15	♟♟ 2*
● Cunto '13	♟♟ 4
○ Falanghina Donna Paolina '15	♟♟ 3
○ Fiano di Avellino Donna Paolina '15	♟♟ 3
○ Greco di Tufo Donna Paolina '15	♟♟ 3
● Settimo '14	♟♟ 2*
● Taurasi Donna Paolina '11	♟♟ 5
● Trebulanum '12	♟♟ 5
● Campole '14	♟ 3
○ Pallagrello Bianco Caiatì Morrone '13	♟♟♟ 2*
● Trebulanum '10	♟♟♟ 5
○ Caulino '14	♟♟ 2*
● Cunto '12	♟♟ 4
● Settimo '13	♟♟ 2*

Cantine Astroni

VIA SARTANIA, 48
80126 NAPOLI
TEL. +39 0815884182
www.cantineastroni.com

CELLAR SALES
PRE-BOOKED VISITS
RESTAURANT SERVICE
ANNUAL PRODUCTION 330,000 bottles
HECTARES UNDER VINE 25.00
VITICULTURE METHOD Certified Organic
SUSTAINABLE WINERY

The winery lies on the outer slopes of the Astroni crater, between Naples and Pozzuoli, part of the beautiful Campi Flegrei subzone, where piedirosso and falanghina have long held court. Astroni is one of the district's biggest wineries, owning 13 hectares under vine, plus another 12 tended by a network of long-serving grower- members. Gerardo Vernazzaro runs the winery, helped by his wife Emanuela Russo and his cousin Vincenzo. The range offers a series of elegant, true-to-type wines. The Piedirosso Colle Rotondella 2015 made the finals for a profile hinging on appealing, ripe red fruit, and we enjoyed a deep, balsamic palate against dark spices, and a fresh, invigorating citrus finish. The Falanghina Colle Imperatrice 2015 shows impressively deep flavours. A hint of maceration and a minerally nose distinguish the Falanghina Vigna Astroni 2014, with its pleasantly bitterish palate.

● Campi Flegrei Piedirosso Colle Rotondella '15	♟♟ 3*
○ Campi Flegrei Falanghina Colle Imperatrice '15	♟♟ 2*
○ Campi Flegrei Falanghina V. Astroni '14	♟♟ 3
○ Strione '11	♟ 4
○ Campi Flegrei Falanghina Colle Imperatrice '14	♟♟ 2*
○ Campi Flegrei Falanghina Colle Imperatrice '12	♟♟ 2*
○ Campi Flegrei Falanghina V. Astroni '13	♟♟ 3
● Campi Flegrei Piedirosso Colle Rotondella '12	♟♟ 2*
○ Strione '10	♟♟ 4

Bambinuto

VIA CERRO
83030 SANTA PAOLINA [AV]
TEL. +39 0825964634
www.cantinabambinuto.com

PRE-BOOKED VISITS
ANNUAL PRODUCTION 25,000 bottles
HECTARES UNDER VINE 6.00

Like many small wineries in Irpinia, Bambinuto grew out of a desire to vinify grapes that had for years simply been sold on to larger producers. Here in Santa Paolina, in the heartland of Greco di Tufo production, the vines grow on clayey limestone soils with plenty of calcium and potassium content. Assisted by oenologist Antonio Pesce, Marilena Aufiero vinifies two Grecos in steel, a basic wine and Picoli, from the eponymous vineyard, which uses riper grapes with extra structure. Marilena sees a wine make the finals for the first time. The complex, elegant Greco di Tufo 2014, with its chalky iodine fragrances and hint of aromatic herbs is an invigorating yet graceful wine, with a sea salt finish. The Picoli 2013, which we were tasting for the first time, was just as good, with a Riesling-like aromatic brightness. The Picoli 2015 was richer, dense and creamy with a nose of broom and apricot. Falanghina Insania 2015 was expressive.

○ Greco di Tufo '14	♟♟ 2*
○ Greco di Tufo Picoli '15	♟♟ 4
○ Greco di Tufo Picoli '13	♟♟ 4
○ Irpinia Falanghina Insania '15	♟♟ 2*
○ Greco di Tufo '13	♟♟ 2*
○ Greco di Tufo '12	♟♟ 3
○ Greco di Tufo Picoli '11	♟♟ 4
○ Greco di Tufo Picoli '10	♟♟ 4
● Taurasi '07	♟♟ 5

I Cacciagalli

LOC. CAIANELLO
FRAZ. AORIVOLA
VIA TEANO, 3
81059 TEANO [CE]
TEL. +39 0823875216
www.icacciagalli.it

CELLAR SALES
PRE-BOOKED VISITS
ACCOMMODATION
ANNUAL PRODUCTION 20,000 bottles
HECTARES UNDER VINE 9.00
VITICULTURE METHOD Certified Organic

Mario Basco and Diana Iaccannone's micro-winery is a rising star on the local wine scene. Here in Aorivola, north of Caserta, a few kilometres from the extinct volcano of Roccamonfina, the philosophy is biodynamic, using large barrels and terracotta amphorae with stainless steel lids in the cellar. The wines already showing commendable stylistic maturity, combining intensity, vitality, and natural expressiveness, are true quaffers and very contemporary. The new arrival is the Mille, from piedirosso with aglianico top-up, aged in concrete tanks, a tribute to the 1860 meeting in Teano between Garibaldi and Vittorio Emanuele II. The Zagreo 2015 is one of Italy's best macerated whites, with a nose of wheat, ripe peaches and black tea, aniseed, orange zest and a tangy, supple and fragrant palate, with full-flavoured, bitterish overtones, acquiring balance in a lively finale that is very moreish. Equally quaffable, the Mille 2015, all rhythm and grip, with darker notes of black olives and pencil lead, and a dynamic mouth, with no-nonsense tannins and appetizing acidity.

○ Zagreo '15	♟♟♟	4*
○ Zagreo '14	♟♟	4*
● Mille '15	♟♟	3
○ Aorivola '15	♟	3
○ Aorivola '13	♟♟	4
● Lucno '13	♟♟	4
● Masseria Cacciagalli '11	♟♟	4
● Phos '13	♟♟	4
● Sphaeranera '13	♟♟	4
○ Zagreo '13	♟♟	4

Antonio Caggiano

C.DA SALA
83030 TAURASI [AV]
TEL. +39 082774723
www.cantinecaggiano.it

CELLAR SALES
PRE-BOOKED VISITS
RESTAURANT SERVICE
ANNUAL PRODUCTION 155,000 bottles
HECTARES UNDER VINE 25.00

Photography, travel and wine are Antonio Caggiano's three passions. After searching far and wide for the perfect shot, he set up one of Campania's finest wineries, creating spectacular niches for his bottles, alongside traditional winemaking exhibits, making for a truly fine museum. Today, his son Giuseppe is increasingly to be found at the helm, with vineyards that enjoy some of the best aspects in the Taurasi production area. Vigna Macchia dei Goti was the first of its kind, one of the DOC's first vineyard-designated wines to be aged exclusively in barrels. The 2012 Vigna Macchia dei Goti has a ripe bouquet of black berry fruit and blood orange, lively backbone and balanced tannin, for a juicy, full-bodied wine with dark spices and a nicely soft, tasty finish. Mel, a blend of fiano and greco, remains one of Campania's best sweet wines, with its aromas of saffron and candied peel, and its dense yet stylish palate, with understated sugars. Béchar 2015 is succulent with a delicate, resinous smack.

● Taurasi V. Macchia dei Goti '12	♟♟	5
○ Fiano di Avellino Béchar '15	♟♟	3
○ Greco di Tufo Devon '15	♟♟	3
○ Mel	♟♟	5
● Irpinia Aglianico Taurì '14	♟	2
● Irpinia Campi Taurasini Salae Domini '14	♟	5
○ Fiano di Avellino Béchar '13	♟♟♟	3*
● Taurasi V. Macchia dei Goti '08	♟♟♟	5
● Taurasi V. Macchia dei Goti '04	♟♟♟	5
○ Fiano di Avellino Béchar '14	♟♟	3*
● Irpinia Aglianico Taurì '13	♟♟	2*
● Taurasi V. Macchia dei Goti '11	♟♟	5
● Taurasi V. Macchia dei Goti '10	♟♟	5

Cantina del Taburno

via Sala, 16
82030 Foglianise [BN]
Tel. +39 0824871338
www.cantinadeltaburno.it

CELLAR SALES
PRE-BOOKED VISITS
ANNUAL PRODUCTION 1,000,000 bottles
HECTARES UNDER VINE 600.00

Cantina del Taburno belongs to Benevento's Consorzio Agrario Provinciale, that has played such a major role in the growth of winemaking in the Sannio area since 1901. The cooperative brings together 300 members, working a total area under vine of 600 hectares on Mount Taburno, on mainly clayey slopes. They produce all the main Sannio designations, especially Falanghina, Piedirosso, Aglianico, Sciascinoso, Coda di Volpe, Greco and Fiano. Pleasant, approachable whites, juicy extractive reds, as well as passitos and Charmat-method sparklers. As we await the new vintages of Bue Apis and Delius, we were impressed by an approachable, pleasing Falanghina del Sannio Taburno. The 2015 offers fragrant notes of aniseed and almond, and a stable aromatic mouth profile, full-flavoured with a linear progression that flows across the palate. Cesco dell'Eremo 2015 also impressed, with its nose of green apple, a succulent palate and acidity well-integrated with the backbone.

○ Falanghina del Sannio Taburno '15	🍷🍷 2*
○ Cesco dell'Eremo '15	🍷🍷 2*
○ Coda di Volpe Amineo '15	🍷 2
○ Greco '15	🍷 2
● Sannio Aglianico Fidelis '13	🍷 2
● Aglianico del Taburno Bue Apis '04	YYY 8
● Aglianico del Taburno Delius '09	YYY 4*
● Bue Apis '00	YYY 6
○ Bue Apis '99	YYY 6
● Aglianico del Taburno Bue Apis '11	YY 8
○ Cesco dell'Eremo '13	YY 2*
○ Coda di Volpe Amineo '14	YY 2*
○ Fiano '14	YY 2*
○ Greco '14	YY 2*
● Sannio Aglianico Fidelis '11	YY 2*

Cautiero

c.da Arbusti
82030 Frasso Telesino [BN]
Tel. +39 3387640641
www.cautiero.it

CELLAR SALES
ACCOMMODATION
ANNUAL PRODUCTION 18,000 bottles
HECTARES UNDER VINE 4.00
VITICULTURE METHOD Certified Organic

Fulvio Cautiero and Imma Cropano's boutique is celebrating its 15th anniversary. In 2002, they both left their day jobs to concentrate on making wine on abandoned plots in the Parco Regionale del Taburno-Camposauro, near Benevento. The grapes come from their four organically-managed hectares of high-trained vines, on clay- and pebble-rich soils. Ruling the roost here is their Falanghina, consistently among the best of its type, a hallmark of the Cautiero house style based on cleanness, fragrance and tautness, which go to enhance a very pure progression. The Falanghina is again among the best of the designation, with its ripe, sunny progression and shades of chamomile and elderflower, and a rich, lively palate both flavoursome and savoury. Also good is the quaffable Erba Bianca 2015, reminiscent of macerated herbs and wheat, over a lean, racy, powerful palate and an inviting finish of green tea. The reds were less well-typed.

○ Erba Bianca '15	🍷🍷 2*
○ Falanghina del Sannio Fois '15	🍷🍷 2*
● Sannio Aglianico Fois '13	🍷🍷 2*
○ Sannio Greco Trois '15	🍷🍷 2*
● Piedirosso '15	🍷 2
● Sannio Aglianico Donna Candida '11	🍷 4
○ Falanghina del Sannio Fois '13	YYY 2*
○ Erba Bianca '14	YY 2*
○ Falanghina del Sannio Fois '14	YY 2*
● Piedirosso '13	YY 2*
● Sannio Aglianico Fois '12	YY 2*
○ Sannio Greco Trois '14	YY 2*
○ Sannio Greco Trois '13	YY 2*

Tenuta Cavalier Pepe

VIA SANTA VARA
83050 SANT'ANGELO ALL'ESCA [AV]
TEL. +39 082773766
www.tenutapepe.it

CELLAR SALES
PRE-BOOKED VISITS
ACCOMMODATION AND RESTAURANT SERVICE
ANNUAL PRODUCTION 300,000 bottles
HECTARES UNDER VINE 50.00
SUSTAINABLE WINERY

Italian President Oscar Luigi Scalfaro granted Angelo Pepe the honorific title of Cavaliere del Lavoro for his invaluable contribution to gastronomy in Belgium, where he ran six renowned restaurants. After working in the Netherlands and specializing in France, his daughter Milena took over her father's winemaking operations in Sant'Angelo all'Esca, expanding to what is now 50 hectares under vine. Production embraces all of Irpinia's designations, achieving constantly high levels throughout the range, with a few peaks that have repeatedly come close to excellence. On the nose, the Fiano di Avellino Refiano 2015 is sunny and focused, both fragrant and mature, with a stylish, slim-bodied palate over hints of aromatic herbs, and a clean, consistent finish. The sun-drenched Taurasi Opera Mia 2011, with its concentrated tertiary notes of myrtle and Mediterranean scrub, displays a warm, juicy, full-flavoured mouth, reinforced by a savoury finale that draws out an already rich, opulent wine.

○ Fiano di Avellino Refiano '15	♟♟ 3
○ Greco di Tufo Nestor '15	♟♟ 3
● Taurasi Opera Mia '11	♟♟ 5
○ Fiano di Avellino Brancato '14	♟ 4
● Irpinia Aglianico Terra del Varo '12	♟ 2
● Irpinia Rosso Sanserino '13	♟ 2
○ Fiano di Avellino Refiano '14	♟♟ 3
○ Fiano di Avellino Refiano '13	♟♟ 3
● Irpinia Aglianico Terra del Varo '11	♟♟ 2*
● Taurasi La Loggia del Cavaliere Ris. '09	♟♟ 6
● Taurasi La Loggia del Cavaliere Ris. '08	♟♟ 6
● Taurasi La Loggia del Cavaliere Ris. '07	♟♟ 6
● Taurasi Opera Mia '10	♟♟ 5
● Taurasi Opera Mia '09	♟♟ 5

Cenatiempo Vini d'Ischia

VIA BALDASSARRE COSSA, 84
80077 ISCHIA [NA]
TEL. +39 081981107
www.vinicenatiempo.it

CELLAR SALES
PRE-BOOKED VISITS
ANNUAL PRODUCTION 70,000 bottles
HECTARES UNDER VINE 4.00

After three impressive rounds of tastings, Cenatiempo has earnt itself a place in the finals with the rest of the full profiles. Founded right after the war, in 1945, by Francesco Cenatiempo, pioneer of modern winegrowing on Ischia, it is now run by his son Pasquale. They process only the grapes from their four hectares under vine, using only copper and sulphur, with year-round cover cropping. Production revolves around the island's main varieties, biancolella, forastera, piedirosso, and a few rows planted to guarnaccia. These wines seem to showcase a better combination of rich aromatics and more defined, supple structures each season, especially the whites. The exemplary Ischia Biancolella 2015, an invitingly fresh wine of character and substance with a citrusy stamp and a caressingly taut progression, shows graceful precision. Slightly riper, but very creamy and complex, the Ischia Forastera 2015 is one of the best we tasted.

○ Ischia Biancolella '15	♟♟ 3*
○ Ischia Biancolella Kalimera '14	♟♟ 4
○ Ischia Forastera '15	♟♟ 4
○ Ischia Bianco Lefkos '15	♟ 4
● Ischia Per' 'e Palummo '15	♟ 3
○ Ischia Biancolella Kalimera '13	♟♟ 4
● Ischia Per' 'e Palummo '14	♟♟ 3

Colli di Lapio

VIA ARIANIELLO, 47
83030 LAPIO [AV]
TEL. +39 0825982184
www.collidilapio.it

CELLAR SALES
PRE-BOOKED VISITS
ANNUAL PRODUCTION 6,000 bottles
HECTARES UNDER VINE 8.00

Lapio is the cradle of Fiano di Avellino. On clayey, marl-rich soils with plenty of limestone, at 400-600 metres above sea level, Fiano offers some of the most fascinating whites anywhere in Italy, supple and lean, full-flavoured and elegant with great aromatic precision. Wines with an unusually northern profile, a delicate smokiness and a piercing acidity that gives them good ageing potential. Known to all as La Signora del Fiano, Clelia Romano runs the winery, along with oenologist Angelo Pizzi and her children Carmela and Federico. The Fiano di Avellino once again goes home with a Tre Bicchieri. The 2015 is readier to drink than its predecessors, but equally complex and multifaceted. The nose expresses meadow flowers, sun-dried hay, and peach, while the entry is delicious, fragrant and taut, with a slightly richer finish displaying softer, riper overtones, underpinning its assertiveness and verve. The other two were less well-typed.

Michele Contrada

C.DA TAVERNA, 31
83040 CANDIDA [AV]
TEL. +39 0825988434
www.vinicontrada.it

CELLAR SALES
PRE-BOOKED VISITS
ANNUAL PRODUCTION 60,000 bottles
HECTARES UNDER VINE 10.00

Campania is dotted with a whole host of artisans and small wineries that enliven an already extremely dynamic wine scene, full of undiscovered surprises. Gerardo Contrada is another tenacious Irpinia winemaker. During the final heats of the tastings, his little winery scored very well both for its basic wines and for its vineyard selections of heirloom varieties. The Fiano di Avellino, in particular, captures the characteristics of the Candida area, with a mineral stamp and a unique aromatic richness. Greco di Tufo and Coda di Volpe complete the array of whites, all made solely in stainless steel. The Fiano di Avellino 2015's fruity framework is bright and well-focused, including peach and aromatic herbs, for an appealing harmonious palate, with a satisfying, well-coordinated drinkability. The well-typed Taurasi 2011 has a bouquet of black olives and capers, rustic and mature in its mouth profile. Tropical fruit and toasted almond notes dominate the Falanghina del Sannio 2015.

○ Fiano di Avellino '15		♛♛♛ 4*
○ Greco di Tufo Alexandros '15		♛ 3
● Irpinia Campi Taurasini Donna Chiara '14		♛ 3
○ Fiano di Avellino '14		♛♛♛ 4*
○ Fiano di Avellino '13		♛♛♛ 4*
○ Fiano di Avellino '10		♛♛♛ 4
○ Fiano di Avellino '09		♛♛♛ 4
○ Fiano di Avellino '08		♛♛♛ 4*
○ Fiano di Avellino '07		♛♛♛ 4
○ Fiano di Avellino '05		♛♛♛ 4
○ Fiano di Avellino '04		♛♛♛ 4
○ Greco di Tufo Alèxandros '14		♛♛ 3
○ Greco di Tufo Alèxandros '13		♛♛ 3
● Taurasi V. Andrea '11		♛♛ 5

○ Fiano di Avellino '15		♛♛ 3*
● Taurasi '11		♛♛ 5
○ Falanghina del Sannio '15		♛ 2
○ Fiano di Avellino Selvecorte '12		♛♛♛ 3*
○ Fiano di Avellino '12		♛♛ 3*
○ Fiano di Avellino Selvecorte '13		♛♛ 3*
○ Fiano di Avellino Selvecorte '11		♛♛ 3*
○ Greco di Tufo '12		♛♛ 3
○ Greco di Tufo Gaudioso '13		♛♛ 2*
○ Greco di Tufo Gaudioso '12		♛♛ 3
● Taurasi Hirpus '08		♛♛ 5

Contrade di Taurasi

VIA MUNICIPIO, 41
83030 TAURASI [AV]
TEL. +39 082774483
www.cantinelonardo.it

CELLAR SALES
PRE-BOOKED VISITS
ANNUAL PRODUCTION 18,000 bottles
HECTARES UNDER VINE 5.00
VITICULTURE METHOD Certified Organic

With technical support from Vincenzo
Mercurio, Alessandro Lonardo stands at the
helm of a virtuoso Irpinia winery, officially
launched in 1998. His figures reflect the size
of this artisanal operation, which works only
the grapes from his five hectares of land,
using solely ambient yeasts, on an organic
basis. The only white released was the
Grecomusc', true to the native rovello
varietal. There is also a Taurasi, a Taurasi
Riserva as well as Coste and Vigne d'Alto,
both Taurasi vineyard selections from vines
over 80 years old. The house style features
wines with very pure aromas, with
nicely-concentrated extractions and sinuous,
elegant profiles. The Taurasi Coste 2011 hits
the bullseye. Initial hints of leather, black
pepper and blood orange are the prelude to
a very minerally wine, with a complex acidity,
and a long finish with notes of golden-leaf
tobacco and roots. The Vigne d'Alto 2011 is
flinty, full-flavoured and austere, while the
Taurasi 2011 is taut and racy, with a slightly
drying, tannin-rich finish. The Grecomusc'
Burlesque makes a promising debut.

● Taurasi Coste '11	♔♔♔	8
● Taurasi '11	♔♔	6
○ Grecomusc' '14	♔♔	5
○ Grecomusc' Burlesque '14	♔♔	5
● Taurasi Vigne d'Alto '11	♔♔	8
○ Grecomusc' '12	♔♔♔	4*
○ Grecomusc' '10	♔♔♔	4*
● Taurasi '10	♔♔♔	6
● Taurasi '04	♔♔♔	6
● Taurasi Coste '08	♔♔♔	7
○ Grecomusc' '13	♔♔	4
● Irpinia Aglianico '12	♔♔	3
● Taurasi '08	♔♔	5
● Taurasi Coste '09	♔♔	7
● Taurasi Vigne d'Alto '09	♔♔	5
● Taurasi Vigne d'Alto '08	♔♔	7

Marisa Cuomo

VIA G. B. LAMA, 16/18
84010 FURORE [SA]
TEL. +39 089830348
www.marisacuomo.com

CELLAR SALES
PRE-BOOKED VISITS
RESTAURANT SERVICE
ANNUAL PRODUCTION 109,000 bottles
HECTARES UNDER VINE 18.00

According to an unwritten law, great wines
can be produced only in particularly stunning
landscapes. As if there were some sort of
exchange between the soul of the place and
its fruits. That law would seem to apply to
the wines which Marisa Cuomo, Andrea
Ferraioli and their children Raffaele and Dora
make. Furore, a UNESCO heritage site on the
Amalfi Coast, offers breathtaking views of
sea cliffs and terraces draped in heirloom
vines of such native varieties as fenile,
pepella, and tintore. This is where inimitable
whites with a sunny, sea-salt laden aromatic
complexity come from. Our favourite this
year was the Furore Bianco 2015, an
irresistible white of class and distinction. The
nose profile unmistakably recalls its origins,
with a bouquet of freshly-cut lemons.
Invitingly fresh, taut and bracing, with a
crescendo of menthol and fruit to finish. The
Fiorduva 2015 is generous and well-coordinated, the only flaw a marked aromatic
sweetness. Make sure a Costa d'Amalfi
Rosato 2015 is always to hand, preferably
chilled.

○ Costa d'Amalfi Furore Bianco '15	♔♔♔	4*
○ Costa d'Amalfi Furore Bianco Fiorduva '15	♔♔	7
○ Costa d'Amalfi Ravello Bianco '15	♔♔	3
⊙ Costa d'Amalfi Rosato '15	♔♔	4
● Costa d'Amalfi Furore Rosso '15	♔	3
● Costa d'Amalfi Ravello Rosso Ris. '13	♔	5
○ Costa d'Amalfi Fiorduva '08	♔♔♔	6
○ Costa d'Amalfi Fiorduva '07	♔♔♔	6
○ Costa d'Amalfi Fiorduva '06	♔♔♔	6
○ Costa d'Amalfi Fiorduva '05	♔♔♔	6
○ Costa d'Amalfi Furore Bianco '10	♔♔♔	4
○ Costa d'Amalfi Furore Bianco Fiorduva '14	♔♔♔	7
○ Costa d'Amalfi Furore Bianco Fiorduva '10	♔♔♔	6

D'Ambra Vini d'Ischia

FRAZ. PANZA
VIA MARIO D'AMBRA, 16
80077 FORIO [NA]
TEL. +39 081907210
www.dambravini.com

CELLAR SALES
PRE-BOOKED VISITS
ANNUAL PRODUCTION 450,000 bottles
HECTARES UNDER VINE 14.00

The first in Campania, and one of the first in Italy, the Ischia designation celebrates its 50th anniversary this year. The d'Ambra family represents the collective memory of the island's wine sector, which used to produce much higher volumes than it does today. Officially founded in 1888, Casa D'Ambra has vineyards on various sides of the island, including the famous Tenuta Frassitelli, where the slopes are so steep that a narrow-gauge railway is used for the harvest. The vineyards overlooking the sea, at the foot of the extinct volcano of Epomeo, give rise to the relaxed cadences of Biancolella, mainstay of a large, well-segmented range. Time will tell whether we have been over-zealous in our interpretation of the Biancolella Tenuta Frassitelli 2015, with its subtly aromatic, tasty nuances of mint and wood smoke, with a finish that is rather too one-dimensional to aspire to higher goals. Intriguingly grassy and balsamic notes distinguish the Rosso Dedicato a Mario d'Ambra 2013, while La Vigna dei Mille Anni 2013 shows earthy coffee cream aromas.

○ Ischia Biancolella '15	🍷🍷	3
○ Ischia Biancolella Tenutta Frassitelli '15	🍷🍷	4
● Ischia Per'e Palummo La Vigna dei Mille Anni '13	🍷🍷	5
● Ischia Rosso Dedicato a Mario D'Ambra '13	🍷🍷	4
○ Gocce D'Ambra	🍷	5
○ Ischia Bianco '15	🍷	2
○ Ischia Forastera '15	🍷	3
○ Ischia Biancolella Tenuta Frassitelli '12	🍷🍷🍷	3*
○ Ischia Biancolella Tenuta Frassitelli '14	🍷🍷	3*
○ Ischia Biancolella Tenuta Frassitelli '13	🍷🍷	3*
○ Ischia Forastera Euposia '14	🍷🍷	3
○ Ischia Forastera Euposia '13	🍷🍷	3
● Ischia Rosso Dedicato a Mario D'Ambra '11	🍷🍷	4

Di Meo

C.DA COCCOVONI, 1
83050 SALZA IRPINA [AV]
TEL. +39 0825981419
www.dimeo.it

CELLAR SALES
PRE-BOOKED VISITS
RESTAURANT SERVICE
ANNUAL PRODUCTION 450,000 bottles
HECTARES UNDER VINE 30.00
SUSTAINABLE WINERY

It is no easy task to navigate Generoso and Roberto di Meo's range, which surprises us each year with releases of vintages after long ageing in the bottle and plenty of new selections. Production includes the area's classic whites, such as Fiano di Avellino, Greco di Tufo, Falanghina and Aglianico. The estate's flagship vineyard is Montemarano, at over 600 metres above sea level. Its extremely powerful yet gripping Taurasi needs plenty of bottle ageing to smooth out the rough edges and find the right balance. A good overall performance from the Di Meo range sees a Fiano F 2015 which opens up slowly with aromas of Mediterranean scrub and orange peel, finishing with a crescendo of delicately smoky flavours. The Greco 2007 shows admirable longevity, still bright with a slightly musky progression of toasted almond and a well-supported, savoury finish. Though both were muscular and far-sighted, their two Taurasis differed in their aromatic profile.

○ Fiano di Avellino F '15	🍷🍷	3*
○ Greco di Tufo G '07	🍷🍷	3
● Taurasi Sel. Hamilton Ris. '08	🍷🍷	7
● Taurasi V. Olmo Ris. '10	🍷🍷	5
○ Coda di Volpe C '15	🍷	2
○ Falanghina '15	🍷	2
○ Greco di Tufo G '15	🍷	3
● Taurasi Ris. '06	🍷🍷🍷	5
○ Falanghina '14	🍷🍷	2*
○ Fiano di Avellino Alessandra '10	🍷🍷	3
○ Fiano di Avellino Colle dei Cerri '10	🍷🍷	4
○ Fiano di Avellino F '12	🍷🍷	3
○ Fiano di Avellino F Sel. Alessandra '11	🍷🍷	3
● Taurasi V. Olmo Ris. '08	🍷🍷	5

Di Prisco

C.DA ROTOLE, 27
83040 FONTANAROSA [AV]
TEL. +39 0825475738
www.cantinadiprisco.it

CELLAR SALES
PRE-BOOKED VISITS
ANNUAL PRODUCTION 100,000 bottles
HECTARES UNDER VINE 10.00

A typical Irpinia vigneron, Pasqualino Di Prisco is a tireless worker, very attached to his terroir. He is one of the few regional producers capable of producing whites and reds of equal calibre at a very reasonable price. His winery is in Fontanarosa, an area fabled for its abundant limestone and wild temperature swings. The whites are markedly saline, while the outstanding feature of his reds is their gracefully contoured character, with less mouthfeel and extraction than most. The Greco di Tufo Pietra Rosa 2013's initial impact on the nose shows notes of petrol, sage and white pepper, while the mouth is stony, musky, with smoky, lactic notes, showing impressively deep flavours, ushering in a long, assertive finish. The Greco di Tufo 2015, with its crystalline fragrance of citrus and broom, its attractively nuanced, rather brief yet cadenced palate and mellow finish, also grows in the glass.

○ Greco di Tufo '15	🍷🍷	3
○ Greco di Tufo Pietra Rosa '13	🍷🍷	3
● Irpinia Campi Taurasini '12	🍷	3
○ Greco di Tufo '11	YYY	2*
● Taurasi '06	YYY	5
● Taurasi '05	YYY	5*
○ Fiano di Avellino '12	YY	2*
○ Greco di Tufo '13	YY	3*
○ Greco di Tufo '12	YY	2*
○ Greco di Tufo Pietra Rosa '12	YY	3*
○ Greco di Tufo Pietra Rosa '11	YY	3*
○ Greco di Tufo Pietra Rosa '10	YY	3*
○ Irpinia Fiano Rotole '14	YY	3
● Taurasi '10	YY	5
● Taurasi '07	YY	5

Donnachiara

LOC. PIETRACUPA
VIA STAZIONE
83030 MONTEFALCIONE [AV]
TEL. +39 0825977135
www.donnachiara.com

CELLAR SALES
PRE-BOOKED VISITS
RESTAURANT SERVICE
ANNUAL PRODUCTION 200,000 bottles
HECTARES UNDER VINE 27.00

Donnachiara is a solid winery from Avellino's competitive wine district. In the 10 years since its foundation in 2005, it has managed to carve out a nice little niche for itself, thanks to Italia Petitto's hard work and determination. In addition to owning 24 hectares under vine, it rents another three, for an extensive range covering Irpinia's main designations, vinified in a quietly modern style. The whites are vinified in steel, with long periods on the lees, while the Taurasi are aged mainly in small oak casks. We really enjoyed the Greco di Tufo 2015, with its elegant aniseed and bay leaf notes, and its piquant, focused mouth leading to a soft creamy finish with bergamot hints. The Coda di Volpe is once again good, the juicy, caressing 2015 with its sage and bay leaf nose being fruit-driven with a racy palate. Sweet, well-balanced fruitiness distinguishes the Falanghina 2015, while the Taurasi di Umberto 2012 has a still rather oaky aromatic framework.

○ Falanghina '15	🍷🍷	2*
○ Greco di Tufo '15	🍷🍷	3
○ Irpinia Coda di Volpe '15	🍷🍷	3
● Aglianico '14	🍷	2
○ Fiano di Avellino '15	🍷	3
● Irpinia Aglianico '13	🍷	3
● Taurasi di Umberto '12	🍷	5
○ Falanghina '14	YY	2*
○ Falanghina del Beneventano '13	YY	2*
○ Fiano di Avellino '13	YY	3
○ Fiano di Avellino '12	YY	3
○ Greco di Tufo '14	YY	2*
○ Greco di Tufo '12	YY	3
● Irpinia Coda di Volpe '14	YY	2*

I Favati

P.ZZA DI DONATO
83020 CESINALI [AV]
TEL. +39 0825666898
www.cantineifavati.it

CELLAR SALES
PRE-BOOKED VISITS
ANNUAL PRODUCTION 80,000 bottles
HECTARES UNDER VINE 10.00

Rossanna Petrozziello and siblings Piersabino and Giancarlo Favati have come up with a range that is solid and well-managed. The jewel in the estate's crown, the Fiano di Avellino grapes come from the Pietramora vineyard near Atripalda, while Greco di Tufo comes from vines in Montefusco. Both are vinified in steel, and in the best years grapes from the same plots are used to make another two Etichette Bianche selections of the finest quality, as confirmed by the recent re-tasting of some old vintages. The reds, meanwhile, have greater mouthfeel and extraction. Their Fiano di Avellino Pietramara earns the winery top marks, living up to its classy reputation. Its nutty, smoky notes are particularly attractive, against a background of pencil lead, followed by a perky, perfectly mature white-fleshed fruit, for a lively, biting white, with an energetic, well-rounded, confident finale. The Taurasi Terzo Tratto Etichetta Bianca Riserva 2010 is muscular and extracted, juicy with more than a hint of good roasted coffee beans.

○ Fiano di Avellino Pietramara '15	♛♛♛ 3*
● Taurasi Terzo Tratto Et. Bianca Ris. '10	♛♛ 7
○ Greco di Tufo Terrantica '15	♛ 2
● Irpinia Campi Taurasini Cretarossa '12	♛ 3
● Taurasi Terzo Tratto '10	♛ 5
○ Fiano di Avellino Pietramara '13	♛♛♛ 3*
○ Fiano di Avellino Pietramara '12	♛♛♛ 3*
○ Fiano di Avellino Pietramara '14	♛♛ 3*
○ Fiano di Avellino Pietramara Et. Bianca '13	♛♛ 5
○ Greco di Tufo Terrantica '14	♛♛ 2*
● Taurasi Terzo Tratto '09	♛♛ 5
● Taurasi Terzo Tratto Et. Bianca '08	♛♛ 7

Benito Ferrara

FRAZ. SAN PAOLO, 14A
83010 TUFO [AV]
TEL. +39 0825998194
www.benitoferrara.it

CELLAR SALES
PRE-BOOKED VISITS
ANNUAL PRODUCTION 55,000 bottles
HECTARES UNDER VINE 13.00

Vigna Cicogna was one of Greco di Tufo's first vineyard selections, dating back to 1996. The true expression of a single two-hectare vineyard in the village of San Paolo di Tufo, 500 metres above sea level: south-facing on clay- and sulphur-rich soils. Bearing the signatures of Gabriella and Sergio Ferrara, this concentrate of flavour never loses rhythm and verve. They also make two aglianico-based reds, from the Quattro Confini vineyard, while this year a Fiano and a Greco sport new labels and names. The Vigna Cicogna 2015 leaves the well-trodden path of recent vintages, the higher temperatures making for a softer, riper fruitiness. The entry on the palate is almost sweet, offset by an elegant smokiness and a rich mouthfeel supported by plenty of salty energy, for a slightly sulphurous, lingering finale. The more slim-bodied Greco di Tufo Terre d'Uva 2015 displays a nose of aniseed, melon and spring meadows, supported by a lengthy acidity.

○ Greco di Tufo V. Cicogna '15	♛♛♛ 4*
○ Fiano d'Avellino Sequenzha '15	♛♛ 4
○ Greco di Tufo Terra d'Uva '15	♛♛ 4
● Taurasi V. Quattro Confini '12	♛ 6
○ Greco di Tufo V. Cicogna '14	♛♛♛ 4*
○ Greco di Tufo V. Cicogna '13	♛♛♛ 5
○ Greco di Tufo V. Cicogna '12	♛♛♛ 4*
○ Greco di Tufo V. Cicogna '10	♛♛♛ 4
○ Greco di Tufo V. Cicogna '09	♛♛♛ 4
○ Fiano di Avellino '13	♛♛ 4
○ Fiano di Avellino '12	♛♛ 4
○ Greco di Tufo '13	♛♛ 4
○ Greco di Tufo '12	♛♛ 3*
○ Greco di Tufo V. Cicogna '11	♛♛ 4
● Taurasi V. Quattro Confini '10	♛♛ 6

★★Feudi di San Gregorio

LOC. CERZA GROSSA
83050 SORBO SERPICO [AV]
TEL. +39 0825986683
www.feudi.it

CELLAR SALES
PRE-BOOKED VISITS
RESTAURANT SERVICE
ANNUAL PRODUCTION 3,500,000 bottles
HECTARES UNDER VINE 250.00
VITICULTURE METHOD Certified Organic

Feudi di San Gregorio, the Sorbo Serpico-based leading light in Campania's wine trade, this year celebrates its 30th anniversary. Under the leadership of chairman Antonio Capaldo, ably assisted by agronomist Pierpaolo Sirch, the estate has successfully tweaked its stylistic identity. It has become more terroir-true, increasingly geared towards bringing out the best in its vast wine heritage. The reds have become livelier with time with less extraction, while some of the white selections offer significant performances. The latest project is called Feudi Studi, a limited edition designed to further raise the bar. Fiano d'Avellino Pietracalda 2015 showcases extraordinary compactness, with a focused nose of peach and apricot and fine, complex, well-defined aromatics. The Greco di Tufo Cutizzi 2015 displays good stylistic consistency, based around white flowers and citrus. The new Dubl Esse Dosaggio Zero, from greco, is worthy of a separate mention, being the finest Campania sparkler for fragrance, thrust, beading and full, fresh finish.

○ Dubl Esse	♟♟ 5
○ Fiano di Avellino Pietracalda '15	♟♟ 4
○ Dubl + Brut '13	♟♟ 5
○ Greco di Tufo Cutizzi '15	♟♟ 4
● Irpinia Aglianico Serpico '12	♟♟ 7
○ Irpinia Fiano Passito Privilegio '14	♟♟ 6
● Taurasi '12	♟♟ 5
○ Dubl Brut	♟ 4
⊙ Dubl Brut Rosé	♟ 5
○ Falanghina del Sannio Serrociclo '15	♟ 3
● Taurasi Piano di Montevergine Ris. '11	♟ 6
○ Fiano di Avellino Pietracalda '09	♟♟♟ 3
○ Greco di Tufo Cutizzi '12	♟♟♟ 3*
○ Greco di Tufo Cutizzi '10	♟♟♟ 3
○ Greco di Tufo Cutizzi '07	♟♟♟ 3*
● Taurasi Piano di Montevergine Ris. '07	♟♟♟ 6

Fontanavecchia

VIA FONTANAVECCHIA, 7
82030 TORRECUSO [BN]
TEL. +39 0824876275
www.fontanavecchia.info

CELLAR SALES
PRE-BOOKED VISITS
ACCOMMODATION AND RESTAURANT SERVICE
ANNUAL PRODUCTION 160,000 bottles
HECTARES UNDER VINE 18.00

Fontanavecchia is one of the most solid and consistent estates on the Sannio wine scene, a benchmark for the whole Benevento area. As well as running the estate, Libero Rillo is also chairperson of the Sannio Wine Consortium. His contribution to the revival of the designation has been priceless, creating a constructive climate among winegrowers. The winery owns 14 hectares under vine at the foot of Mount Taburno, along with a few rented plots. The extensive range includes refreshing, dynamic whites and more firmly structured reds, aged mostly in small oak casks. The Falanghina del Sannio 2015 has an attractively nuanced progression, with a mature profile and sure-footed palate. It shows rich fruit and acidic verve, with a well-sustained, lengthy, fresh finish. The exemplary Sannio Rosso 2015, a vintage red vinified only in stainless steel, whose main quality is its succulent, ripe red fruitiness, offset by appetizing balsamic notes.

○ Falanghina del Sannio Taburno '15	♟♟♟ 2*
● Aglianico del Taburno '11	♟♟ 3
● Aglianico del Taburno V. Cataratte '09	♟♟ 5
● Sannio Rosso '15	♟♟ 2*
○ Sannio Fiano '15	♟ 2
○ Sannio Greco '15	♟ 2
● Sannio Piedirosso '15	♟ 2
○ Falanghina del Sannio Taburno '14	♟♟♟ 2*
○ Falanghina del Sannio Taburno '13	♟♟♟ 2*
○ Falanghina del Sannio Taburno '12	♟♟♟ 2*
● Aglianico del Taburno '09	♟♟ 3
● Aglianico del Taburno V. Cataratte Ris. '08	♟♟ 4
○ Sannio Fiano '13	♟♟ 2*
● Sannio Piedirosso '12	♟♟ 2*

Fonzone

LOC. SCORZAGALLINE
83052 PATERNOPOLI [AV]
TEL. +39 08271730100
www.fonzone.it

CELLAR SALES
PRE-BOOKED VISITS
ANNUAL PRODUCTION 57,000 bottles
HECTARES UNDER VINE 22.00
SUSTAINABLE WINERY

Surgeon Lorenzo Fonzone Caccese opened his winery in 2005, in Paternopoli, an area famous for its Taurasi. The grapes from his 20 hectares are processed in a state-of-the-art underground cellar, blending in perfectly with its surroundings. No herbicides are used in the rows, cover cropping is year-round, and grasses are sown to maintain soil biodiversity. Greco di Tufo, Fiano di Avellino and Falanghina are made solely in stainless steel vats, giving them exceptional fragrance and grip. The Taurasi Riserva Scorzagalline is aged in new oak, also briefly used for Irpinia Campi Taurasini and Fiano Sequoia. This year's tastings showcase Fonzone excellence. Fresh tasting yet multifaceted, the Greco di Tufo 2014 displays an inviting bouquet in its typical notes of almond, aniseed and spring meadows, while the palate is caressing and creamy, with a vibrant dynamism. We also liked the Fiano di Avellino 2014, whose supple profile is woven with notes of bay leaf and dried fruit, followed by a light but very tasty palate.

○ Greco di Tufo '14	♀♀ 3*
○ Fiano di Avellino '14	♀♀ 3
● Taurasi Scorzagalline Ris. '10	♀♀ 5
○ Greco di Tufo '13	♀♀♀ 3*
● Aglianico '12	♀♀ 3
○ Fiano di Avellino '13	♀♀ 3*
○ Fiano di Avellino '12	♀♀ 3
○ Greco di Tufo '12	♀♀ 2*
● Irpinia Campi Taurasini '10	♀♀ 3
○ Irpinia Fiano Sequoia '13	♀♀ 5

La Fortezza

LOC. TORA II, 20
82030 TORRECUSO [BN]
TEL. +39 0824886155
www.lafortezzasrl.it

CELLAR SALES
PRE-BOOKED VISITS
ANNUAL PRODUCTION 300,000 bottles
HECTARES UNDER VINE 50.00

This dynamic Torrecuso winery has a total of 50 hectares under vine near Benevento, 30 of which are estate-owned, in various districts of the Sannio, mainly on the eastern slopes of the Taburno Camposauro Regional Park. The ample range includes the Classica and Noi beviamo con la testa lines, mainly Aglianicos, Falanghinas, Grecos and Fianos. The well-equipped winery affords spectacular views, with a restaurant and comfortable rooms with imposing stone arches. The range is improving, with one wine, the approachable, no-frills Falanghina del Sannio Taburno 2015, reaching the finals. Its nose of citrus and freshly-cut grass is followed by a supple yet linear, persistent palate. A compact wine with lustrous aromas and good acidic verve, the Sannio Fiano 2015 features a delicate, smoky finish. One of the best of its type, the Falanghina Brut Maleventum uses a long Charmat method.

○ Falanghina del Sannio Taburno '15	♀♀ 2*
● Aglianico del Taburno '12	♀♀ 3
○ Falanghina Brut Maleventum	♀♀ 3
○ Sannio Fiano '15	♀♀ 2*
○ Sannio Greco '15	♀♀ 2*
○ Fiano Noi beviamo con la testa '15	♀ 2
● Sannio Aglianico Ris. '09	♀ 4
● Aglianico del Taburno Ris. '07	♀♀ 4
● Aglianico Noi Beviamo con la Testa '11	♀♀ 3
○ Beneventano Falanghina '14	♀♀ 2*
○ Falanghina del Sannio Taburno '14	♀♀ 2*
○ Falanghina del Sannio Taburno '13	♀♀ 2*
○ Sannio Fiano '13	♀♀ 2*

La Guardiense

c.da Santa Lucia, 104/106
82034 Guardia Sanframondi [BN]
Tel. +39 0824864034
www.laguardiense.it

CELLAR SALES
PRE-BOOKED VISITS
RESTAURANT SERVICE
ANNUAL PRODUCTION 3,700,000 bottles
HECTARES UNDER VINE 1900.00

La Guardiense is a modern cooperative with 1000 members tending almost 2000 hectares under vine throughout the Sannio area. The task of running such a huge winery is down to Domizio Pigna, who has successfully managed its growth, with production that in recent years very much seems to have struck the right balance. Its new-found stability is based on highly reliable standards, as is patently clear in the more ambitious selections. The broad, multi-layered range includes basic wines at highly competitive prices and occasional forays into the world of sparklers and sweet wines. The soft Falanghina del Sannio Janare 2015 displays notes of citrus and tropical fruit on a complex, juicy palate, leading to a consistent, expansive finish. We were impressed by the glowering, fruit-driven Sannio Guardia Sanframondi Janare Riserva 2013 with above-average tannin, a creamy, rich, dense mouth with a modern blend of spices, without sacrificing suppleness and verve.

○ Falanghina del Sannio Janare '15	♥♥♥ 2*
● Sannio Guardia Sanframondi Janare Ris. '13	♥♥ 2*
● Sannio Aglianico Janare '15	♥ 2
● Sannio Aglianico Lucchero Janare '14	♥ 3
○ Sannio Fiano Janare '15	♥ 2
○ Sannio Greco Janare '15	♥ 2
○ Falanghina del Sannio Janare '14	♥♥♥ 2*
○ Falanghina del Sannio Janare '13	♥♥♥ 2*
○ Falanghina del Sannio Calvese '13	♥♥ 2*
○ Sannio Fiano Colle di Tilio '13	♥♥ 3
○ Sannio Fiano Janare '14	♥♥ 2*
● Sannio Piedirosso Janare '12	♥♥ 2*

Lunarossa

via V. Fortunato P.I.P. Lotto 10
84095 Giffoni Valle Piana [SA]
Tel. +39 0898021016
www.viniepassione.it

CELLAR SALES
PRE-BOOKED VISITS
ANNUAL PRODUCTION 50,000 bottles
HECTARES UNDER VINE 4.50

Last year, we praised the progress of this young winery at the foot of the Picentini, a mountain range in the Campania Apennines overlooking the Gulf of Salerno. With agronomist Mario Mazzitelli at the helm, it is at the forefront of attempts to bring out the best in heirloom vines in a still rather forgotten production area, with a keen eye for environmental and social sustainability. Its summery, genuine wines display measured extractive weight, being mature yet refreshing and very drinkable. Wines which reflect the sea breezes as well as the wild temperature swings of the Apennines. This year's range is headed by the highly enjoyable Costacielo Rosso 2015, with its notes of crisp red berries and a balsamic, fragrant palate, leading into a taut, limpid finish. We also enjoyed the Camporeale Bianco, with its nose of wheat and hedgerow, drive in the mouth and succulent, yellow-fleshed fruit. The close-woven Camporeale Rosso 2015 shows smoky, organic tones, unfolding pleasantly across the palate.

○ Camporeale Falanghina '15	♥♥ 2*
● Camporeale Rosso '15	♥♥ 2*
● Costacielo Rosso '15	♥♥ 3
◉ Costacielo Rosato '15	♥ 3
○ Quartara '13	♥ 5
● Rossomarea '11	♥ 4
● Borgomastro '09	♥♥ 6
● Borgomastro '08	♥♥ 6
● Borgomastro '07	♥♥ 6
○ Camporeale '14	♥♥ 2*
○ Costacielo Bianco '13	♥♥ 3*
● Marea Rosso '09	♥♥ 3
● Rossomarea '08	♥♥ 4

Masseria Felicia

FRAZ. CARANO
LOC. SAN TERENZANO
81037 SESSA AURUNCA [CE]
TEL. +39 0823935095
www.masseriafelicia.it

CELLAR SALES
PRE-BOOKED VISITS
ANNUAL PRODUCTION 25,000 bottles
HECTARES UNDER VINE 5.00

Maria Felicia Brini and her father Alessandro run one of the most interesting wineries in the Massico volcanic district. Their winery stands on the north-western slopes of the Ager falernus, where Ancient Rome's finest wines were produced, as much Classical literature attests. The winery uses solely native varieties from its five hectares of vines, whose roots enjoy the area's loose, ash-rich volcanic soils. By the time they are bottled, the wines display a lively aromatic profile, making them exceptionally food-friendly. Notes of currants and myrtle in the Falerno del Massico Rosso Etichetta Bronzo Riserva 2012, embellished by pencil lead and bay leaf. This juicy, sun-drenched red gathers pace on the palate, despite its firm structure. The still-evolving volcanic edge released from the glass by the Falerno del Massico Bianco Anthologia 2015 combines well with a mouth full of flavours reminiscent of melon and summer flowers.

○ Falerno del Massico Anthologia '15	♀♀	3
● Falerno del Massico Rosso Et. Bronzo Ris. '12	♀♀	5
● Falerno del Massico Rosso Et. Bronzo '10	♀♀♀	5
○ Falerno del Massico Bianco Anthologia '13	♀♀	3
○ Falerno del Massico Bianco Anthologia '12	♀♀	3
● Falerno del Massico Rosso '12	♀♀	2*
● Falerno del Massico Rosso '11	♀♀	2*
● Falerno del Massico Rosso Ariapetrina '11	♀♀	3*
● Falerno del Massico Rosso Ariapetrina '10	♀♀	3
● Falerno del Massico Rosso Et. Bronzo '11	♀♀	2*
● Falerno del Massico Rosso Et. Bronzo '11	♀♀	5

★Mastroberardino

VIA MANFREDI, 75/81
83042 ATRIPALDA [AV]
TEL. +39 0825614111
www.mastroberardino.com

CELLAR SALES
PRE-BOOKED VISITS
ACCOMMODATION AND RESTAURANT SERVICE
ANNUAL PRODUCTION 2,000,000 bottles
HECTARES UNDER VINE 300.00
SUSTAINABLE WINERY

The story of the Mastroberardino family reflects the recent history of Campanian wine, Antonio and Walter being leading figures on the modern Irpinia wine scene. They currently have 300 hectares at their disposal, covering all of Irpinia's finest subzones. Under the watchful eye of Piero Mastroberardino, the winery works all year round to promote its native varieties around the world, with a highly diversified range and a collection of old vintages that is second to none. A restricted range with a high average quality. The Taurasi Radici 2012 offers good dark fleshy fruit, accompanied by classic notes of black olives and orange peel, while the palate is weighty but still held back by dominant toasty flavours, which end up drying it out. The Fiano di Avellino Radici 2015 has a well-coordinated taste profile, displaying notes of pollen and wheat and a lively, full mouth with well-defined finish. The rest of the range is solid

○ Fiano di Avellino Radici '15	♀♀	3*
● Taurasi Radici '12	♀♀	5
○ Greco di Tufo Novaserra '15	♀♀	3
● Taurasi Naturalis Historia '09	♀♀	6
● Taurasi Radici Ris. '09	♀♀	5
○ Fiano di Avellino '87	♀♀♀	2
○ Greco di Tufo Novaserra '07	♀♀♀	3*
○ Greco di Tufo Novaserra '06	♀♀♀	3*
● Taurasi Naturalis Historia '04	♀♀♀	6
● Taurasi Radici '08	♀♀♀	5
● Taurasi Radici '07	♀♀♀	5
● Taurasi Radici '06	♀♀♀	5
● Taurasi Radici '05	♀♀♀	5
● Taurasi Radici Ris. '04	♀♀♀	5
● Taurasi Radici Ris. '01	♀♀♀	5

Salvatore Molettieri

C.DA MUSANNI, 19B
83040 MONTEMARANO [AV]
TEL. +39 082763722
www.salvatoremolettieri.com

CELLAR SALES
PRE-BOOKED VISITS
ANNUAL PRODUCTION 65,000 bottles
HECTARES UNDER VINE 13.00

Winemaker Salvatore Molettieri has toiled indefatigably for 33 years, creating wines which accurately reflect the character of the soils in the Montemarano and Castelfranci area. Harvesting at his vineyards, at over 600 metres above sea level, surrounded by mountains, can even occur in late November once snow is forecast. Yields are almost laughable, but in the winery Salvatore combines large and small oaks to make muscular, full-bodied, rich yet austere wines with an assertively acidic, tannin-heavy energy. Rebellious wines that only time can tame in the bottle. The Vigna Cinque Querce 2010 reflects the winery's traditional style, all firm structure and energy, with particularly compact, elegant tannins, an energetic, full-flavoured and well-sustained grip leading to a long finish of mint and orange peel. The Taurasi Renonno 2011 is on the same lines, though slightly richer in fruit and less extracted. Our bottle of Taurasi Riserva Vigna Cinque Riserva 2009 was already showing quite evolved notes.

○ Greco di Tufo '14	🏆🏆 3
● Taurasi Renonno '11	🏆🏆 5
● Taurasi V. Cinque Querce '10	🏆🏆 6
○ Fiano di Avellino Apianum '14	🏆 3
● Irpinia Aglianico Cinque Querce '12	🏆 3
● Irpinia Aglianico O'Calice Rosso '13	🏆 3
● Irpinia Rosso Ischia Piana '12	🏆 3
● Taurasi V. Cinque Querce Ris. '09	🏆 7
● Taurasi Renonno '08	🏆🏆🏆 5
● Taurasi V. Cinque Querce '05	🏆🏆🏆 6
● Taurasi V. Cinque Querce '04	🏆🏆🏆 6
● Taurasi V. Cinque Querce '01	🏆🏆🏆 5
● Taurasi V. Cinque Querce Ris. '05	🏆🏆🏆 7
● Taurasi V. Cinque Querce Ris. '04	🏆🏆🏆 7
● Taurasi V. Cinque Querce Ris. '01	🏆🏆🏆 7

Montesole

LOC. SERRA DI MONTEFUSCO
VIA SERRA
83030 MONTEFUSCO [AV]
TEL. +39 0825963972
www.montesole.it

PRE-BOOKED VISITS
ANNUAL PRODUCTION 1,200,000 bottles
HECTARES UNDER VINE 120.00

This winery lies on the border between Irpinia and Sannio. The Montesole brand is named after the original denomination for the town of Montefusco, some 700 metres above sea level. Founded in 1995, it has no estate-owned vines, but has signed long-term agreements and buys in grapes carefully, processing them in a state-of-the-art cellar. Their range is broad, covering the main Irpinia and Sannio varieties, with several gems which are well-nigh excellent. Centre stage was taken by the Fiano di Avellino Vigna Acquaviva 2015, with its soft, concentrated fragrance of flowers, sage, basil, wisteria, and juicy yellow peach. A rangy, agile wine with a pervasive rush of flavour, with a musky progression, leading into a subtle yet elegant finish. Initially brooding and earthy with rooty hints, the Taurasi 2009 displays an energetic, gutsy palate of sound fruit, while the Taurasi Vigna Vinieri 2009 is nicely evolved.

○ Fiano di Avellino V. Acquaviva '15	🏆🏆 4
● Taurasi '09	🏆🏆 4
○ Falanghina del Sannio V. Zampino '15	🏆 3
○ Greco di Tufo V. Breccia '15	🏆 4
● Taurasi V. Vinieri '09	🏆 6
○ Falanghina del Sannio V. Zampino '14	🏆🏆 3*
○ Fiano di Avellino '14	🏆🏆 3
○ Fiano di Avellino '13	🏆🏆 3
○ Fiano di Avellino V. Acquaviva '14	🏆🏆 4
○ Fiano di Avellino V. Acquaviva '13	🏆🏆 4
○ Greco di Tufo V. Breccia '13	🏆🏆 4
○ Grilae Brut	🏆🏆 3
● Sairus '08	🏆🏆 3
● Taurasi V. Vinieri '08	🏆🏆 6

★★Montevetrano

LOC. NIDO
VIA MONTEVETRANO, 3
84099 SAN CIPRIANO PICENTINO [SA]
TEL. +39 089882285
www.montevetrano.it

CELLAR SALES
PRE-BOOKED VISITS
ACCOMMODATION
ANNUAL PRODUCTION 25,000 bottles
HECTARES UNDER VINE 5.00

Ambitious and far-sighted, Silvia Imparato combines her two passions for photography and for wine into one. Right from the start of her winemaking career, she began raising the bar, imagining a wine that would not only be representative of its growing area, but also compete with the world's finest wines in a frontierless market. And she has succeeded. Her Montevetrano, a blend of aglianico, cabernet and merlot, is one of the Italy's great reds, its first vintage coming in 1991. This year saw the launch of the estate's first white, Core Bianco, a blend of fiano and greco. A Tre Bicchieri for the Montevetrano 2014, with its good texture and substance, elegant nose of Mediterranean scrub and thyme, crisp red fruit and hints of aubergine; the palate is zesty, with a suffused, fresh-tasting structure and plenty of thrust and back palate; the long, well-defined finish is reminiscent of black tea. We very much enjoyed the Core 2014 for its approachable black berry fruit and refreshing balsamic vein.

● Montevetrano '14	▼▼▼ 7
● Core '14	▼▼ 3
● Montevetrano '12	♀♀♀ 7
● Montevetrano '11	♀♀♀ 7
● Montevetrano '10	♀♀♀ 7
● Montevetrano '09	♀♀♀ 7
● Montevetrano '08	♀♀♀ 7
● Montevetrano '07	♀♀♀ 7
● Montevetrano '06	♀♀♀ 7
● Montevetrano '05	♀♀♀ 7
● Montevetrano '04	♀♀♀ 7
● Montevetrano '03	♀♀♀ 7
● Montevetrano '02	♀♀♀ 7
● Montevetrano '01	♀♀♀ 7
● Montevetrano '00	♀♀♀ 6

Mustilli

VIA CAUDINA, 10
82019 SANT'AGATA DE' GOTI [BN]
TEL. +39 0823718142
www.mustilli.com

CELLAR SALES
PRE-BOOKED VISITS
ACCOMMODATION AND RESTAURANT SERVICE
ANNUAL PRODUCTION 150,000 bottles
HECTARES UNDER VINE 21.00

Credit to the Mustilli family for their re-discovery and promotion of falanghina. They were among the first to believe in the variety, bottling a monovarietal back in 1979, after carefully researching the biotypes that best responded to the clayey limestone soils of Sant'Agata de' Goti, the smallest of the Sannio subzones. Today the 21 hectares under vine are run by sisters Paola and Annachiara, for a solid, reliable range of wines. Don't miss the atmospheric old cellars dug out of the tufa below Palazzo Rainone, whose 18th-century bedrooms are available for overnight stays. The vibrant, sun-drenched Falanghina del Sannio Sant'Agata dei Goti 2015 features pear and cedarwood notes, a lively, well-sustained palate, and a slightly smoky finish. The Greco 2015 has a solid structure, with an attractively nuanced framework of aromatic richness and fresh acidity. Pale hues and increasingly intense fragrances are the hallmarks of the bold, snappy Piedirosso 2015, with its hints of sun-dried tomatoes and black pepper.

○ Falanghina del Sannio Sant'Agata dei Goti '15	▼▼ 3*
● Sannio Piedirosso '15	▼▼ 3
○ Sannio Sant'Agata dei Goti Greco '15	▼▼ 3
● Sannio Aglianico '14	▼ 3
● Sannio S'Agata dei Goti Aglianico Cesco di Nece '13	▼ 3
○ Falanghina del Sannio Sant'Agata dei Goti '14	♀♀ 2*
○ Falanghina del Sannio Sant'Agata dei Goti '13	♀♀ 2*
● Sannio Aglianico '12	♀♀ 4
● Sannio Piedirosso '13	♀♀ 2*
○ Sannio Sant'Agata dei Goti Greco '14	♀♀ 2*

Nanni Copè

VIA TUFO, 3
81041 VITULAZIO [CE]
TEL. +39 330879815
www.nannicope.it

CELLAR SALES
PRE-BOOKED VISITS
ANNUAL PRODUCTION 7,500 bottles
HECTARES UNDER VINE 3.50
SUSTAINABLE WINERY

Manager, wine writer, producer. This summary of Giovanni Ascione's career culminated in his 2007 purchase of two and a half hectares in Caserta's Caitine Hills, at Monticelli di Castel Campagnano. His only wine, Sabbie di Sopra il Bosco, a blend of pallagrello nero with small amounts of aglianico and casavecchia, began life in his garage. Better known to all as Nanni, Giovanni's first vintage, in 2008, proved he could get the best out of Caiazzo's sandstone soils. Its contemporary style, capable of bringing out the varietal's fragrance, full-flavoured energy and edgy acid, makes for a wine of great drinkability. Giovanni's sagacious ability to read the vintage year can be seen in his 2014 wines. Right from the off, the Sabbie di Sopra il Bosco 2014 is intense and dynamic, with smoky notes of pencil lead and black pepper. The mouth is enjoyably mature, very well nuanced, full-flavoured and expansive with a long finish that never wavers or becomes diluted. Perky and invigorating, full of verve, it is one of this vintage's most interesting reds.

● Sabbie di Sopra il Bosco '14	▼▼▼ 5
● Sabbie di Sopra il Bosco '12	♀♀♀ 5
● Sabbie di Sopra il Bosco '11	♀♀♀ 5
● Sabbie di Sopra il Bosco '10	♀♀♀ 5
● Sabbie di Sopra il Bosco '09	♀♀♀ 5
● Sabbie di Sopra il Bosco '13	♀♀ 5
● Sabbie di Sopra il Bosco '08	♀♀ 5

Perillo

C.DA VALLE, 19
83040 CASTELFRANCI [AV]
TEL. +39 082772252
cantinaperillo@libero.it

CELLAR SALES
PRE-BOOKED VISITS
ANNUAL PRODUCTION 20,000 bottles
HECTARES UNDER VINE 5.00

Michele Perillo is unlikely to be found out and about in Italy and the rest of the world promoting his wines, as his place is very much in his vineyards, around the Castelfranci winery and at Montemarano at elevations of almost 700 metres. The soil is rich in clay and silica, some plots dating back as far as the 1930s, while yields are minimal and the vinification wholly traditional. Every year, his Taurasis stand out from the crowd, one step ahead of the rest, with reds that are powerful but never heavy, with outstanding verve on the palate. That extra something that only a few of the world's great wines have. The Taurasi Riserva 2007 is certainly not lacking in attitude. An energetic, weighty wine, with a full-flavoured palate against a distinctively ashy background. A slightly more brooding profile than the same vintage last year, with inky tones and a slightly more evident spiciness. The mouth suggests thrust and progression, the vibrant palate being underpinned by biting tannins and a very lengthy finish.

● Taurasi Ris. '07	▼▼ 6
● Taurasi '07	♀♀♀ 6
● Taurasi '05	♀♀♀ 4
● Taurasi Ris. '06	♀♀♀ 6
○ Irpinia Coda di Volpe '12	♀♀ 3
● Taurasi '06	♀♀ 4
● Taurasi '04	♀♀ 4*
● Taurasi '03	♀♀ 5
● Taurasi Ris. '05	♀♀ 5
● Taurasi Ris. '04	♀♀ 5
● Taurasi Ris. '01	♀♀ 5

Ciro Picariello

VIA MARRONI, 18A
83010 SUMMONTE [AV]
TEL. +39 082533848
www.ciropicariello.it

CELLAR SALES
PRE-BOOKED VISITS
ANNUAL PRODUCTION 50,000 bottles
HECTARES UNDER VINE 15.00
SUSTAINABLE WINERY

In recent years, Fiano d'Avellino has emerged strongly as one of the top names in Italy, in terms of number of awards, average quality and ageing capacity. Credit for this is down to the new winemakers, Ciro Picariello and Rita Guerriero. From the vineyards, equally divided between Montefredane and Summonte, they have been able to produce wines of great charm, aromatically subtle but with a piercing acid edge, the result of partial malolactic fermentation. Grapes from one Summonte plot, the Fiano Ciro 906, with its refined smoky peatiness, was bottled separately after the 2012 harvest. With its outstanding balance and innate sense of proportion, the Fiano di Avellino 2014 is without doubt one of the best of its type. A wine that seems to develop on tiptoe, with clear-cut aromas and a racy yet lightweight structure, linear acid backbone and pervasive flavour, leading to a very fresh-tasting, lustrous finish.

○ Fiano di Avellino '14	▼▼▼ 4*
○ Brut Contadino	▼▼ 4
○ Fiano di Avellino Ciro 906 '13	▼▼ 4
○ Fiano di Avellino '10	♈♈♈ 3*
○ Fiano di Avellino '08	♈♈♈ 3*
○ Fiano di Avellino '13	♈♈ 4
○ Fiano di Avellino '11	♈♈ 3*
○ Fiano di Avellino '09	♈♈ 3
○ Fiano di Avellino '07	♈♈ 3*
○ Fiano di Avellino '06	♈♈ 3*
○ Fiano di Avellino '05	♈♈ 3*
○ Fiano di Avellino Ciro 906 '12	♈♈ 4

La Pietra di Tommasone

VIA PROV.LE FANGO, 98
80076 LACCO AMENO [NA]
TEL. +39 0813330330
www.tommasonevini.it

CELLAR SALES
PRE-BOOKED VISITS
ANNUAL PRODUCTION 100,000 bottles
HECTARES UNDER VINE 11.00

Once again, the full-length profiles included Ischian wines from Antonio Monti and daughter Lucia, the winery oenologist and estate manager. After his father Tommaso died in 1980, Antonio left the island to seek his fortune in Germany, where he met his future wife and opened an Italian restaurant. Ten years later, he headed back to Lacco Ameno to restore his father's old vineyard. He refurbished the cellar and planted up new plots of land that he now tends with his entire family. A contrasting range of perky whites and lacklustre reds, dominated by the two Biancolellas. The graceful, elegant La Vigna dei Preti 2015 shows a nose of broom and melon, with a whispery progression, as if on tiptoe, and a long, mineral salt finish. The Ischia Biancolella 2015 has a smoky profile reminiscent of oriental spices, while though lacking a pronounced supporting acidity, the Epomeo Bianco 2015 displays an appetizing iodine finale.

○ Epomeo Bianco '15	▼▼ 3
○ Ischia Biancolella '15	▼▼ 2*
○ Ischia Biancolella V. dei Preti '15	▼▼ 4
○ Pithecusa Bianco '15	▼▼ 3
● Pithecusa Rosso '13	▼ 3
⊙ Rosamonti '15	▼ 2
○ Epomeo Bianco '13	♈♈ 3
● Epomeo Rosso '11	♈♈ 3
○ Ischia Biancolella '14	♈♈ 2*
○ Ischia Biancolella '12	♈♈ 2*
● Ischia Per' 'e Palummo '13	♈♈ 3
● Pignanera '07	♈♈ 6
○ Terradei '13	♈♈ 3

★Pietracupa

C.DA VADIAPERTI, 17
83030 MONTEFREDANE [AV]
TEL. +39 0825607418
pietracupa@email.it

CELLAR SALES
PRE-BOOKED VISITS
ANNUAL PRODUCTION 50,000 bottles
HECTARES UNDER VINE 7.50

From the Montefredane hill come great wines and brilliant madmen like Sabino Loffredo, who revolutionized the winery founded in 1990 by his father Peppino, making it a sure bet for Irpinia's great whites, Fiano di Avellino and Greco di Tufo. His wines are bright, with a lingering acid profile, very dependent on the vagaries of the vintage. Wines that age with a special grace. The Taurasi he's been making since 2000, a red with great personality and a refined balsamic tone, is worthy of a separate mention. The crystalline aromas of grapefruit and crushed stone, full-flavoured body and a endless mint and citrus fruit finish, make the Greco di Tufo 2015 electrifying. As usual, the Fiano di Avellino 2015 lags a tad behind, weighed down by its aromatics but with a deep, layered palate. Given enough bottle ageing, it will no doubt give great pleasure. The juicy, ethery Taurasi 2011 is one of the most focused of its vintage.

○ Greco di Tufo '15	♛♛♛	3*
○ Fiano di Avellino '15	♛♛	3*
● Taurasi '11	♛♛	5
○ Cupo '10	♛♛♛	5
○ Cupo '08	♛♛♛	5
○ Cupo '05	♛♛♛	5
○ Cupo '03	♛♛♛	3*
○ Fiano di Avellino '13	♛♛♛	3*
○ Fiano di Avellino '12	♛♛♛	3*
○ Greco di Tufo '14	♛♛♛	3*
○ Greco di Tufo '10	♛♛♛	3*
○ Greco di Tufo '09	♛♛♛	3*
○ Greco di Tufo '08	♛♛♛	3*
○ Greco di Tufo '07	♛♛♛	3*
○ Greco di Tufo '06	♛♛♛	3*
● Taurasi '10	♛♛♛	5

Quintodecimo

VIA SAN LEONARDO, 27
83036 MIRABELLA ECLANO [AV]
TEL. +39 0825449321
www.quintodecimo.it

CELLAR SALES
PRE-BOOKED VISITS
ACCOMMODATION
ANNUAL PRODUCTION 60,000 bottles
HECTARES UNDER VINE 18.00
SUSTAINABLE WINERY

Known in the trade as the Campania wine professor, Luigi Moio makes instantly recognizable wines of good stylistic consistency. The estate was named after Quintum decimum, a Sannite town 15 miles from the ancient principality of Benevento. After teaching for years at the Agricultural Sciences Faculty, in 2001 Luigi started up the wine project with his wife Laura di Marzo. Today they own 18 hectares under vine, in some of the finest vineyards in their designations: theirs are wines of great structure, weight and flavour, designed to last and evolve over time. More stylish than in previous years, though just as layered and edgy, the Fiano di Avellino Exultet 2014 romped into the finals. With a nose of aniseed, melon and dried fruits, it is full and racy, with a resinous feel at the back. Yet again, the distinctive balsamic profile of the Taurasi Vigna Grande Cerzito 2011 recalls the aromatic intensity of Sichuan peppercorns, a smooth mouthfeel leading to a bitter chocolate finish.

○ Fiano di Avellino Exultet '14	♛♛	6
○ Greco di Tufo Giallo D'Arles '14	♛♛	6
○ Irpinia Falanghina Via Del Campo '14	♛♛	5
● Taurasi V. Grande Cerzito Ris. '11	♛♛	8
● Irpinia Aglianico Terra d'Eclano '13	♛	6
○ Fiano di Avellino Exultet '09	♛♛♛	6
○ Fiano di Avellino Exultet '13	♛♛	6
○ Fiano di Avellino Exultet '12	♛♛	6
○ Fiano di Avellino Exultet '11	♛♛	6
○ Greco di Tufo Giallo d'Arles '13	♛♛	6
○ Greco di Tufo Giallo d'Arles '12	♛♛	6
● Irpinia Aglianico Terra d'Eclano '11	♛♛	6
● Taurasi V. Grande Cerzito Ris. '09	♛♛	8
● Taurasi V. Quintodecimo Ris. '10	♛♛	8
● Taurasi V. Quintodecimo Ris. '07	♛♛	8

Fattoria La Rivolta

C.DA RIVOLTA
82030 TORRECUSO [BN]
TEL. +39 0824872921
www.fattorialarivolta.com

CELLAR SALES
PRE-BOOKED VISITS
ACCOMMODATION
ANNUAL PRODUCTION 180,000 bottles
HECTARES UNDER VINE 29.00
VITICULTURE METHOD Certified Organic

The greatest supporters of the Sannio area's winegrowing potential include Paolo Cotroneo, a pharmacist by trade, at the helm of one of the best-known and most consistent Sannio wineries. Over the years he has shored up a wide range based on the main Campania varieties, made into monovarietals and sold at very reasonable prices. It all started in the Rivolta district in 1997, at the heart of Torrecuso, close to Mount Taburno. The cellar churned out refreshing whites with good varietal aromas, while the reds are firmer and more extractive. With its nose of berry fruit, medicinal herbs and ash, the Aglianico del Taburno 2013 also made it to our finals. The mouth is austere with good acidic verve and a citrus finish. The delicate, juicy Sannio Fiano 2015 shows a lively finish of tangerine and aromatic herbs. Held back by toastiness and still mouth-drying tannins, the Terra di Rivolta Riserva 2013 could do with some fine-tuning. The very drinkable Aglianico Rosato, with a juicy, fruit-driven profile, is unusual in colour, almost red.

● Aglianico del Taburno '13	♟♟ 3*
○ Sannio Taburno Fiano '15	♟♟ 3
⊙ Aglianico del Taburno Rosato Le Mongolfiere a San Bruno '15	♟ 3
● Aglianico del Taburno Terra di Rivolta Ris. '13	♟ 5
○ Falanghina del Sannio Taburno '15	♟ 2
○ Sannio Taburno Greco '15	♟ 3
● Sannio Taburno Piedirosso '15	♟ 3
● Aglianico del Taburno '10	♟♟♟ 3*
● Aglianico del Taburno Terra di Rivolta Ris. '08	♟♟♟ 5
● Aglianico del Taburno Terra di Rivolta Ris. '12	♟♟ 5
○ Sannio Taburno Greco '14	♟♟ 3

Rocca del Principe

VIA ARIANIELLO, 9
83030 LAPIO [AV]
TEL. +39 08251728013
www.roccadelprincipe.it

CELLAR SALES
PRE-BOOKED VISITS
ANNUAL PRODUCTION 30,000 bottles
HECTARES UNDER VINE 6.50

Lapine is the heartland of Fiano di Avellino, with the greatest percentage of hectares under vine. Here, in 2004, after working as growers for several years, Ercole Zarella, his wife Aurelia Fabrizio and his brother Antonio decided to produce and bottle their own wines. The vines reflect Arianello hill, the highest part of the town, with its colder climate, late harvests, and pumice-rich volcanic soils. The Zarella estate's Fiano d'Avellino has a unique aromatic signature, both fresh-tasting and full of backbone, with a smoky nose, slow to open up but with an unstoppable follow-through. Despite opening up slowly with hints of aniseed, and a delicate profile of herbs, sage and yellow peach, the new Zarrella Fiano di Avellino 2014 yet again takes home a Tre Bicchieri. As it progresses, it takes possession of the glass, unfolding a smoky minerality with hints of lime and new-mown hay, with the merest touch of a tannic kick, making the palate pleasantly three-dimensional, closing on a long, piquant finish.

○ Fiano di Avellino '14	♟♟♟ 3*
○ Fiano di Avellino '13	♟♟♟ 3*
○ Fiano di Avellino '12	♟♟♟ 3*
○ Fiano di Avellino '10	♟♟♟ 3*
○ Fiano di Avellino '08	♟♟♟ 2*
○ Fiano di Avellino '07	♟♟♟ 2*
○ Fiano di Avellino '11	♟♟ 3*
○ Fiano di Avellino '09	♟♟ 3*
● Irpinia Aglianico '11	♟♟ 3*
● Taurasi Master Domini '07	♟♟ 5
● Taurasi Mater Domini '09	♟♟ 5
● Taurasi Mater Domini '08	♟♟ 5
● Taurasi Ris. '10	♟♟ 5

Ettore Sammarco

VIA CIVITA, 9
84010 RAVELLO [SA]
TEL. +39 089872774
www.ettoresammarco.it

CELLAR SALES
PRE-BOOKED VISITS
ANNUAL PRODUCTION 66,000 bottles
HECTARES UNDER VINE 13.00

For the first time, the beautiful Medieval town of Ravello, overlooking the sea at the heart of the Amalfi Coast, has garnered a Tre Bicchieri award. Credit to Ettore Sammarco, a true pioneer who founded the winery back in 1962 and even today, as he nears his 80th birthday, he tends its terraced vineyards, together with his children Bartolo, Maria Rosaria and Antonella. Accessible only on foot, at an altitude of 500 metres on the slopes of Mount Brusara, Vigna Grotta Piana made it to the finals. For a couple of months, this blend of ginestrella, falanghina and biancolella rests on the fine lees in a barrique. The 2015 is harmonious and refined, with a nose of almond, anise and dried herbs, followed by a lively, well-sustained and tasty palate with barely hinted toasty notes, and closing on a long chamomile and yellow citrus finale. That said, the range as a whole steals the limelight, after making the most of the excellent growing conditions for the 2015 vintage.

○ Costa d'Amalfi Ravello Bianco V. Grotta Piana '15	♛♛♛ 4*
○ Costa d'Amalfi Ravello Bianco Selva delle Monache '15	♛♛ 3
⊙ Costa d'Amalfi Ravello Rosato Selva delle Monache '15	♛♛ 3
● Costa d'Amalfi Ravello Rosso Selva delle Monache '15	♛♛ 3
● Costa d'Amalfi Ravello Rosso Selva delle Monache Ris. '12	♛♛ 5
⊙ Costa d'Amalfi Rosato Terre Saracene '15	♛♛ 3
● Costa d'Amalfi Terre Sarecene Rosso '14	♛ 3
● Costa d'Amalfi Ravello Rosso Selva delle Monache Ris. '10	♛♛ 4

Tenuta San Francesco

FRAZ. CORSANO
VIA SOFILCIANO, 18
84010 TRAMONTI [SA]
TEL. +39 089876748
www.vinitenutasanfrancesco.com

CELLAR SALES
PRE-BOOKED VISITS
ACCOMMODATION
ANNUAL PRODUCTION 40,000 bottles
HECTARES UNDER VINE 10.00

Tenuta San Francesco was set up by the Bove, D'Avino and Giordano families, bound first by friendship and then as business partners, becoming one of the Amalfi Coast's finest winegrowing areas, namely the Tramonti subzone. Still agriculturally pristine, this area has an exceptional grape heritage, as witnessed by its heirloom ungrafted vines and ancient terraces. An unmissable experience. The wines are full-flavoured, attractively nuanced and true to native varietals such as falanghina, biancolella, ginestra, tintore, piedirosso, and aglianico. Alluringly earthy, smoky notes encapsulate the E' Iss 2012, a red from tintore grafted onto ancient, pre-phylloxera rootstock. More caressing than taut, its nose of currants and sun-dried tomatoes is followed by a soft yet gripping mouth with great attitude and personality. The true-to-type Costa d'Amalfi Per Eva 2014 has a classic profile with delicate lactic, dried herb and peach notes leading into a palate that is fruity, supple and long.

○ Costa d'Amalfi Bianco Per Eva '14	♛♛ 4
○ Costa d'Amalfi Tramonti Bianco '15	♛♛ 2*
● Costa d'Amalfi Tramonti Rosso Quattrospine Ris. '12	♛♛ 5
● E' Iss '12	♛♛ 5
⊙ Costa d'Amalfi Tramonti Rosato '15	♛ 2
○ Costa d'Amalfi Bianco Per Eva '13	♛♛♛ 4*
○ Costa d'Amalfi Tramonti Bianco '14	♛♛ 2*
⊙ Costa d'Amalfi Tramonti Rosato '14	♛♛ 2*
● Costa d'Amalfi Tramonti Rosso '12	♛♛ 3
● Costa d'Amalfi Tramonti Rosso Quattrospine Ris. '11	♛♛ 5
● Costa d'Amalfi Tramonti Rosso Quattrospine Ris. '10	♛♛ 5
● E' Iss '11	♛♛ 5

San Giovanni

C.DA TRESINO
84048 CASTELLABATE [SA]
TEL. +39 0974965136
www.agricolasangiovanni.it

CELLAR SALES
PRE-BOOKED VISITS
ACCOMMODATION
ANNUAL PRODUCTION 20,000 bottles
HECTARES UNDER VINE 4.00

Punta Tresino is one of the beauty spots
along the coast south of Salerno, in the heart
of the Cilento National Park. Architect Mario
Corrado and his lawyer wife Ida left their
hometown of Salerno to settle in this corner
of paradise with their three children. They
chose life in harmony with the environment,
restoring a series of rural houses and the
estate cellar. They have four hectares under
vine, planted to fiano, aglianico and
piedirosso. The wines reveal a decidedly
exquisite Mediterranean and marine
temperament. Our tastings overturned the
winery's own hierarchy. The Paestum 2015
walked off with the Tre Bicchieri. This
exhilaratingly sun-drenched Fiano, with very
pure fruit, displays aromas of peach and
broom, a mouthfilling, tasty palate and a
never-ending salty finish. Not to be missed.
The multi-faceted Tresinus 2015 has a
smoky feel to it and a slightly resinous finish,
while the Ficonera 2014 from piedirosso is
lip-smackingly peppery.

○ Paestum '15	♗♗♗	2*
○ Fiano Tresinus '15	♗♗	3
● Ficonera '14	♗♗	5
● Maroccia '12	♗	5
○ Fiano Tresinus '12	♗♗♗	3*
● Castellabate '11	♗♗	3
○ Fiano Tresinus '14	♗♗	3
○ Fiano Tresinus '13	♗♗	3*
○ Fiano Tresinus '11	♗♗	3
● Ficonera '11	♗♗	5
● Maroccia '07	♗♗	5
○ Paestum Bianco '14	♗♗	2*

San Salvatore

VIA DIONISIO
84050 GIUNGANO [SA]
TEL. +39 08281990900
www.sansalvatore1988.it

CELLAR SALES
ACCOMMODATION AND RESTAURANT SERVICE
ANNUAL PRODUCTION 160,000 bottles
HECTARES UNDER VINE 23.00
VITICULTURE METHOD Certified Biodynamic
SUSTAINABLE WINERY

The San Salvatore estate combines a
traditional approach with a modern offering.
We are in the beautiful Cilento National
Park, in an area between Stio and the
Greek temples of Paestum and Giungano.
Giuseppe Pagano's biodynamically
cultivated estate produces wine, olive oil
and excellent buffalo mozzarella. The
photovoltaic system minimizes energy
consumption, with everything being
recycled, starting with their organic
fertilizers. Their 23 hectares of land
produce textbook wines with a strong local
identity. This round of tastings went very
well, with plenty of wines scoring top
marks. The best was the Trentenare 2015
Fiano with nice iodine-like notes, a nose of
almond and cedarwood, and a subtle yet
energetic finish of aromatic herbs. We
expect the Pian di Stio 2015, with its
fragrant green apple and citrus notes, to
improve with more bottle ageing. We also
liked the Palinuro, the Cecerale and the
summery Aglianico Omaggio a Gillo
Dorfles 2013.

○ Trentenare '15	♗♗♗	3*
○ Pian di Stio '15	♗♗	4
● Aglianico Omaggio a Gillo Dorfles '13	♗♗	6
○ Calpazio '15	♗♗	3
○ Cecerale Senza Solfiti Aggiunti '15	♗♗	3
○ Palinuro '15	♗♗	2*
● Vetere '15	♗♗	3
● Aglianico Corleto '14	♗	2
⊙ Joi Brut Rosé '13	♗	5
● Jungano '14	♗	3
○ Pian di Stio '14	♗♗♗	4*
○ Pian di Stio '13	♗♗♗	4*
○ Pian di Stio '12	♗♗♗	3*
● Aglianico Corleto '13	♗♗	2*
○ Calpazio '14	♗♗	3
○ Falanghina '14	♗♗	3

Sanpaolo
di Claudio Quarta Vignaiolo

C.DA SAN PAOLO
VIA AUFIERI, 25
83010 TORRIONI [AV]
TEL. +39 0832704398
www.claudioquarta.it

CELLAR SALES
PRE-BOOKED VISITS
ACCOMMODATION
ANNUAL PRODUCTION 115,000 bottles
HECTARES UNDER VINE 22.00

Claudio Quarta and his daughter
Alessandra have an all-consuming passion
for wine. After an interlude in America, they
came up with a well-structured plan to
bring out the best in Southern Italian
winegrowing, focusing on the three core
areas of research, sustainability and
biodiversity. They also own three wineries:
two in Puglia, Moros and Tenute Emèra;
one in Irpinia, Sanpaolo, based in Torrioni.
They produce some outstanding regional
natives, including falanghina from the
Pietrelcina vineyards near Benevento, greco
from suppliers in Montefusco and Tufo,
while their Aglianico and Taurasi wines are
the fruits of their Paternopoli site. Initially
held back by oak, the Taurasi Riserva 2010
reveals a wild berry juiciness, well backed
up by acidity and whiffs of black pepper
and orange zest. This year's hot vintage is
reflected in the Greco di Tufo Selezione
Claudio Quarta 2015, with its notes of
mixed flower honey and almond. Dense
flavour gives way to a broad caressing
palate. This year's Falanghina is again
attractively nuanced.

● Taurasi Ris. '10	🍷🍷	5
○ Falanghina '15	🍷🍷	2*
○ Fiano di Avellino '15	🍷🍷	2*
○ Greco di Tufo Claudio Quarta '15	🍷🍷	6
○ Greco di Tufo '15	🍷	2
● Irpinia Aglianico '14	🍷	2
○ Greco di Tufo Claudio Quarta '13	🍷🍷🍷	6
○ Greco di Tufo Claudio Quarta '12	🍷🍷🍷	6
○ Falanghina '13	🍸🍸	2*
○ Fiano di Avellino '13	🍸🍸	2*
○ Greco di Tufo '13	🍸🍸	2*
○ Greco di Tufo '12	🍸🍸	2*
● Taurasi Ris. '09	🍸🍸	5
● Taurasi Ris. '08	🍸🍸	5

Tenuta Sarno 1860

C.DA SERRONI, 4B
83100 AVELLINO
TEL. +39 082526161
www.tenutasarno1860.it

ANNUAL PRODUCTION 15,000 bottles
HECTARES UNDER VINE 6.00

Maura Sarno's commitment is a 24/7 deal.
Her Fiano di Avellino is a true mirror of
Candida, an Irpinia village at 600 metres in
altitude. Here the soils are mainly clay and
rich in limestone, with stunning day-night
temperature ranges. With Vincenzo
Mercurio to help out, Sarno produces wines
of eloquent, high-spirited aromatic profiles,
deeply nuanced and complex. The Fiano is
processed in steel at controlled
temperatures, maturing for at least six
months on the fine lees. This year heralds
the debut of the first sparkler, a lengthy
Charmat Method from the winery's single
vineyard plot dedicated entirely to fiano.
The 2015 growing season brought the first
Tre Bicchieri for the Fiano, which goes
straight to the heart with glowing notes of
broom, aniseed and chamomile. The
caressing, sinuous palate is tangy,
progressing in its own sweet time to a
broad, multifaceted finale closing with a
long hint of meadow herbs. Citrus notes to
the fore in the fresh-tasting, vibrant 2015
Sarno 1860 Pas Dosé.

○ Fiano di Avellino '15	🍷🍷🍷	4*
○ Sarno 1860 Pas Dosé '15	🍷🍷	4
○ Fiano di Avellino '14	🍸🍸	3*
○ Fiano di Avellino '13	🍸🍸	3*
○ Fiano di Avellino '12	🍸🍸	3*
○ Fiano di Avellino '11	🍸🍸	3
○ Fiano di Avellino '10	🍸🍸	3*

La Sibilla

FRAZ. BAIA
VIA OTTAVIANO AUGUSTO, 19
80070 BACOLI [NA]
TEL. +39 0818688778
www.sibillavini.com

CELLAR SALES
PRE-BOOKED VISITS
ANNUAL PRODUCTION 70,000 bottles
HECTARES UNDER VINE 9.50

La Sibilla wines are the mirror Campi Flegrei and its volcanic soil, with its texture of ash and lapilli, the mild climate, and the influence of the Gulf of Naples. Vincenzo di Meo has a wealth of valuable ungrafted vines, marked by a focused, juicy style, capable of making various types of wine with excellent levels of success. Production relies heavily on Falanghina and Piedirosso, especially the Falanghina Cruna deLago, aged in steel for over six months on the lees, and released over a year after harvest. Although now something of a cliché, the term minerally fits the style of the Falanghina Cruna deLago 2014, with its unique petrol and ripe apple notes, and full, lively, pervasive flavour, leading to a vibrant finish of dried fruits and citrus. The more predictable yet focused Falanghina 2015 is fresh and delicately smoky. The Piedirosso 2015 shows Mediterranean notes of sun-dried tomatoes and oregano.

○ Campi Flegrei Falanghina '15	🍷🍷 2*
○ Campi Flegrei Falanghina Cruna deLago '14	🍷🍷 4
● Campi Flegrei Piedirosso '15	🍷🍷 3
● Campi Flegrei V. Madre '13	🍷 4
○ Campi Flegrei Falanghina '13	YYY 2*
○ Campi Flegrei Falanghina '14	YY 3
○ Campi Flegrei Falanghina Cruna deLago '13	YY 4
○ Campi Flegrei Falanghina Cruna deLago '12	YY 4
● Campi Flegrei Piedirosso '14	YY 4
● Campi Flegrei Piedirosso '13	YY 3*
● Campi Flegrei Piedirosso V. Madre '12	YY 4

Luigi Tecce

C.DA TRINITÀ, 6
83052 PATERNOPOLI [AV]
TEL. +39 3492957565
ltecce@libero.it

PRE-BOOKED VISITS
ANNUAL PRODUCTION 10,000 bottles
HECTARES UNDER VINE 5.00

Unpredictability is a key factor in understanding Luigi Tecce's wines. Visiting him in his Paternopoli vineyards, where the clayey soils contain more limestone and sand, means clambering up to the hilltops. His wines are never clarified or filtered, sulphur dioxide levels rarely exceed 40 mg/L, while the vinification and ageing process varies according to harvest conditions. He may plump for amphorae, open chestnut vats, or tonneau with a lengthy stay on the fine lees. His painstaking work in the vineyard is clear to see, with very low yields and only two wines, a Taurasi and an Irpinia Campi Taurasini. The Taurasi Poliphemo 2012 impressed, with its nose of ripe berries, wild cherry and hints of chimney soot and orange zest, giving way to a fragrant, tangy palate with good thrust and a long warm finish. Showing concentrated and wild tones of leather and sun-dried tomatoes, the Satyricon 2013 has tenacious tannins and a characterful finish.

● Taurasi Poliphemo '12	🍷🍷 6
● Irpinia Campi Taurasini Satyricon '13	🍷🍷 4
● Taurasi Poliphemo '08	YYY 6
● Taurasi Poliphemo '07	YYY 6
● Irpinia Campi Taurasini Satyricon '12	YY 5
● Irpinia Campi Taurasini Satyricon '10	YY 5
● Irpinia Campi Taurasini Satyricon '09	YY 4
● Taurasi Poliphemo '11	YY 6
● Taurasi Poliphemo '10	YY 6
● Taurasi Poliphemo '09	YY 7
● Taurasi Poliphemo '06	YY 6
● Taurasi Poliphemo '05	YY 6

Terre del Principe

LOC. SQUILLE
S.DA 325 SS GIOVANNI E PAOLO, 30
81010 CASTEL CAMPAGNANO [CE]
TEL. +39 0823867126
www.terredelprincipe.com

CELLAR SALES
PRE-BOOKED VISITS
ANNUAL PRODUCTION 50,000 bottles
HECTARES UNDER VINE 11.00
VITICULTURE METHOD Certified Organic
SUSTAINABLE WINERY

The chief feature of the land between the Taburno and Matese mountain ranges is the presence of Caiazzo sandstones, dating back five to seven million years, from the late Miocene, enriching and characterizing the soil. Peppe Mancini and Manuela Piancastelli have devoted their lives to tending the hills around Squille, making the most of their 11 hectares of pallagrello bianco, pallagrello nero and casavecchia. Their wines show remarkable aromatic richness and big structure, with the use of both new and second-passage small wood, followed by lengthy bottle ageing. A Pallagrello Bianco with an excellent aromatic profile, Le Sèrole 2014, all citrus fruit and green tea, with a slightly sulphurous edge vaunting impressively stylish acidity well integrated with the backbone, got through to the final. The compact, brooding Ambruco 2013 shows concentrated and persistent, while the Centomoggia has a classic profile with black pepper and liquorice notes.

○ Le Sèrole '14	🍷🍷 5
● Ambruco '13	🍷🍷 5
● Centomoggia '13	🍷🍷 5
● Piancastelli '13	🍷🍷 6
● Ambruco '06	🍷🍷🍷 5
● Ambruco Pallagrello Nero '10	🍷🍷🍷 5
● Centomoggia '11	🍷🍷🍷 5
● Centomoggia '08	🍷🍷🍷 5
● Centomoggia '07	🍷🍷🍷 5
○ Le Sèrole Pallagrello Bianco '13	🍷🍷🍷 5
● Ambruco '12	🍷🍷 5
● Castello delle Femmine '13	🍷🍷 3
● Castello delle Femmine '12	🍷🍷 3
○ Le Sèrole '12	🍷🍷 5
○ Pallagrello Bianco Fontanavigna '14	🍷🍷 3
● Sasso di Riccardo '14	🍷🍷 5

Terre Stregate

LOC. SANTA LUCIA
VIA MUNICIPIO, 105
82034 GUARDIA SANFRAMONDI [BN]
TEL. +39 0824817857
www.terrestregate.it

CELLAR SALES
PRE-BOOKED VISITS
ANNUAL PRODUCTION 100,000 bottles
HECTARES UNDER VINE 22.00
SUSTAINABLE WINERY

Filomena and Carlo Iacobucci have given a real boost to their Sannio winery, which won the Best Value for Money award in last year's Guide. The workload is shared equally between vineyard and the recently-built cellat, and there is also an ongoing commitment to promoting this growing area which was ravaged last year by a massive flood. Last year's yields fell, but the area's altitude and extreme temperature swings made for healthy, perfectly ripe grapes. In turn, this gives a broad range dominated by Falanghina, with four different labels, each reflecting different profiles and nuances. A Tre Bicchieri goes to the Falanghina Sannio Svelato 2015, with its nose of honey and nuts soon giving way to fresher, more fragrant sensations. Its rich, dense mouth, reinforced by a balsamic hint leads to a long, flavoursome, mint and aniseed finish. With its wheat and espresso notes, the Falanghina Trama 2015 is truly captivating.

○ Falanghina del Sannio Svelato '15	🍷🍷🍷 2*
○ Falanghina Trama '15	🍷🍷 2*
● Sannio Aglianico Manent '14	🍷🍷 2*
○ Falanghina Caracara '14	🍷 6
○ Sannio Fiano Genius Loci '15	🍷 2
○ Sannio Greco Aurora '15	🍷 2
○ Falanghina del Sannio Svelato '14	🍷🍷🍷 2*
○ Falanghina del Sannio Svelato '13	🍷🍷🍷 2*
○ Falanghina del Sannio Svelato Sur Lies '13	🍷🍷 3*
● Sannio Aglianico Manent '13	🍷🍷 2*
○ Sannio Fiano Genius Loci '14	🍷🍷 2*
○ Sannio Fiano Genius Loci '13	🍷🍷 2*

Terredora Di Paolo

VIA SERRA
83030 MONTEFUSCO [AV]
TEL. +39 0825968215
www.terredora.com

CELLAR SALES
PRE-BOOKED VISITS
ACCOMMODATION
ANNUAL PRODUCTION 1,000,000 bottles
HECTARES UNDER VINE 200.00

Terredora Di Paolo is one of Irpinia's biggest wineries, with 200 hectares under vine, including some of the vineyards with the best-exposed slopes and a long history of winemaking. The winery was founded in 1994 when Antonio and Walter Mastroberardino, heirs to an age-old wine tradition, parted company and set out on two different entrepreneurial pathways. The winery founded by Walter, and now run by his daughter and son Daniela and Paolo, has a very extensive range, with three lines: classics, vineyard selections and gran riservas. While we await the release of the new Taurasis, we were impressed by two of the whites. The focused Fiano di Avellino Terredora Di Paolo 2015 is immediate and expressive, fruit-rich with a good thrust of acidity, leading to a well-delineated, expansive finish. The resinous fragrance of the Greco di Tufo Loggia della Serra 2015 contrasts with its gutsy, fresh-tasting mouth; a lengthy finale with chamomile and hazelnut notes leaves its mark.

○ Fiano di Avellino Terredora Di Paolo '15	♟♟ 3
○ Greco di Tufo Loggia della Serra '15	♟♟ 3
● Irpinia Aglianico Il Principio '10	♟ 4
⊙ Irpinia Rosato Rosaenovae '15	♟ 3
● Taurasi Fatica Contadina '08	♟♟♟ 5
● Aglianico '11	♟♟ 2*
○ Falanghina '14	♟♟ 4
○ Fiano di Avellino Campore '12	♟♟ 5
○ Fiano di Avellino Campore '11	♟♟ 5
○ Greco di Tufo Loggia della Serra '13	♟♟ 3*
○ Irpinia Falanghina '14	♟♟ 4
○ Lacryma Christi del Vesuvio Bianco '14	♟♟ 4
○ Lacryma Christi del Vesuvio Rosso '13	♟♟ 3
● Taurasi Fatica Contadina '09	♟♟ 5
● Taurasi Pago dei Fusi '08	♟♟ 5

Torre a Oriente

LOC. MERCURI I, 19
82030 TORRECUSO [BN]
TEL. +39 0824874376
www.torreaoriente.eu

CELLAR SALES
PRE-BOOKED VISITS
ACCOMMODATION AND RESTAURANT SERVICE
ANNUAL PRODUCTION 40,000 bottles
HECTARES UNDER VINE 10.00
SUSTAINABLE WINERY

This Torrecuso estate is one of the region's emerging wineries, fruit of Patrizia Iannella and Giorgio Gentilcore's tireless work. They came together to make wine, preserves and olive oil, their mainstay being an excellent wine made from the ortice varietal. Ten organically-tended hectares of vines and a range dominated by no less than three versions of Falanghina. The flagship Biancuzita selection, with its strictly-controlled yields and generally late harvest, comes onto the market several years after harvest. Once again, Falanghina Biancuzita 2014, without doubt one of the best of its type, breezed its way to a Tre Bicchieri. A complete white of excellent structure, showing aromatic richness, acid verve and a mineral register. The full, fresh-tasting finale is reminiscent of green tea and basil. The Aglianico Janico 2011 and Falanghina Sannio Siriana 2015 are both pleasantly drinkable.

○ Falanghina del Sannio Biancuzita '14	♟♟♟ 3*
○ Falanghina del Sannio Taburno Siriana '15	♟ 2
○ Sannio Aglianico Janico '11	♟ 2
○ Falanghina del Sannio Biancuzita '12	♟♟♟ 3*
● Aglianico del Taburno U' Barone '08	♟♟ 3
○ Falanghina del Sannio Biancuzita '11	♟♟ 2*
○ Falanghina del Sannio Biancuzita '10	♟♟ 2*
○ Falanghina del Sannio Taburno Siriana '14	♟♟ 2*
● Janico '10	♟♟ 2*
● Sannio Aglianico Janico '10	♟♟ 2*

Traerte

C.DA VADIAPERTI
83030 MONTEFREDANE [AV]
TEL. +39 0825607270
info@traerte.it

CELLAR SALES
PRE-BOOKED VISITS
ANNUAL PRODUCTION 81,000 bottles
HECTARES UNDER VINE 6.00

Of the many genial, iconoclastic artists of
the Montefredane hills, few can match
Raffaele Troisi, who inherited his winery
from his father Antonio, one of the first
growers to set up his own vinification and
bottling business. After various financial
hiccoughs, the Traerte brand, epitomizing
all the best of Vadiaperti winemaking, was
created in 2011. Raffaele produces an
excellent Coda di Volpe, the Torama
selection is ever delightful, as are some of
the highly original Fiano di Avellinos and
Greco di Tufos. These wines open up
slowly in the glass, sculpted by salt and by
vibrant acid notes. The Fiano di Avellino
Aipierti 2015 is a worthy finalist, with an
attractively peaty profile, showing notes of
pollen and mountain herbs, encoring in the
lengthy rhythmic mouth, underpinned by a
slightly tannic finish providing grip and
texture. The intensely salty yet juicy and
spirited Coda di Volpe Torama 2015, the
region's best, shows splendid aromatic
development on the palate.

○ Fiano di Avellino Aipierti '15	🏆🏆 5
○ Irpinia Coda di Volpe Torama '15	🏆🏆 5
○ Greco di Tufo Tornante '15	🏆🏆 5
○ Irpinia Coda di Volpe '15	🏆🏆 2*
○ Fiano di Avellino '15	🏆 3
○ Fuori Limite Le Vecchie Vigne '15	🏆 5
○ Greco di Tufo '15	🏆 3
○ Fiano di Avellino Aipierti '14	🏆🏆 5
○ Fiano di Avellino Aipierti '13	🏆🏆 5
○ Fiano di Avellino Aipierti '12	🏆🏆 5
○ Greco di Tufo Tornante '14	🏆🏆 5
○ Greco di Tufo Tornante '13	🏆🏆 5
○ Greco di Tufo Tornante '12	🏆🏆 5
○ Irpinia Coda di Volpe Torama '14	🏆🏆 5
○ Irpinia Coda di Volpe Torama '13	🏆🏆 5

Antica Masseria Venditti

VIA SANNITICA, 120/122
82037 CASTELVENERE [BN]
TEL. +39 0824940306
www.venditti.it

CELLAR SALES
PRE-BOOKED VISITS
RESTAURANT SERVICE
ANNUAL PRODUCTION 61,000 bottles
HECTARES UNDER VINE 11.00
VITICULTURE METHOD Certified Organic
SUSTAINABLE WINERY

When we wrote the first edition of the
Guide back in 1988, one of the eight
Campania producer profiles we included
was Nicola Venditti's. He now has 11
hectares rather than seven, and still tends
his vines with the same passion and
respect for nature. The business was
founded in 1595, and today's range
includes finely-crafted wines, fruits of
environmentally-friendly viticultural
methods. The state-of-the-art winery
produces wines processed without
sulphites, focusing mainly on
Castelvenere's heirloom native grape, the
barbetta or barbera, not to be confused
with the Piedmontese variety of the same
name. A heady wild rose and blueberry
sweetness hallmark the Sannio Barbetta
Assenza 2015, with its intense juicy
aromatic swathe that is never excessive.
The Sannio Barbetta Barbera 2013 is
sounder, with notes of violet and
pomegranate. Smooth, penetrating tannins
for the Sannio Rosso Bosco Caldaia
Riserva 2011, a blend of aglianico,
montepulciano and piedirosso.

● Sannio Barbetta Assenza '15	🏆🏆 4
● Sannio Barbetta Barbera '13	🏆🏆 3
● Sannio Rosso Bosco Caldaia Ris. '11	🏆🏆 5
○ Falanghina del Sannio Assenza '15	🏆 4
○ Falanghina del Sannio Vàndari '15	🏆 3
● Sannio Rosso Sup. '14	🏆 2
○ Falanghina del Sannio Vàndari '13	🏆🏆 3
● Sannio Aglianico Marraioli '09	🏆🏆 4
● Sannio Aglianico Marraioli '08	🏆🏆 3
● Sannio Aglianico Marraioli '07	🏆🏆 3
● Sannio Barbera Barbetta '09	🏆🏆 3
● Sannio Rosso '10	🏆🏆 2*
● Solopaca Rosso Bosco Caldaia '07	🏆🏆 4

Vestini Campagnano

Via Costa dell'Aia, 9
81044 Conca della Campania [CE]
Tel. +39 0823679087
www.vestinicampagnano.it

CELLAR SALES
PRE-BOOKED VISITS
ANNUAL PRODUCTION 80,000 bottles
HECTARES UNDER VINE 7.00
VITICULTURE METHOD Certified Organic

In the 1990s, lawyer Alberto Barletta's winery led the revival of Caserta's native varietals, such as pallagrello bianco, pallagrello nero, or casavecchia. The winery, in Caiazzo, vaunts an extensive range that is showing significant growth across the board, especially for vintages, made with a polished and very focused touch. The new house style blends varietal stamping with drinkability, which bodes well for future harvests. The deliciously approachable Pallagrello Bianco 2015 shows succulent white-fleshed fruit, and is fragrant, creamy and mature, with a vibrant, well-sustained finish. The perfect vintage wine. We also enjoyed the Galluccio Rosso Concarosso 2015, with its extended, refined drinkability, fruity sensations and well-nuanced finish. The Kajanero 2015, a blend of casavecchia and pallagrello, topped up with aglianico, is fuller and riper with hints of green herbs. Asprinio 2015, Southern Italy's Vinho Verde shows good acid with hints of lime.

○ Pallagrello Bianco '15	♟♟♟ 3*
● Axilio '13	♟♟ 3
● Galluccio Rosso Concarosso '15	♟♟ 2*
● Kajanero '15	♟♟ 2*
○ Pallagrello Bianco Le Ortole '15	♟♟ 4
○ Asprinio '15	♟ 2
● Connubio '11	♟ 7
● Pallagrello Nero '13	♟ 5
☉ Vado Ceraso '15	♟ 3
● Casavecchia '11	♟♟ 5
● Connubio '08	♟♟ 7
○ Le Ortole '12	♟♟ 4
○ Pallagrello Bianco '13	♟♟ 3
● Pallagrello Nero '12	♟♟ 5

Villa Diamante

Via Toppole, 16
83030 Montefredane [AV]
Tel. +39 0825670014
villadiamante1996@gmail.com

CELLAR SALES
PRE-BOOKED VISITS
ANNUAL PRODUCTION 10,000 bottles
HECTARES UNDER VINE 4.50

With stubborn passion, Diamante Renna has taken over the helm from the outstanding vigneron Antoine Gaita, whose whole new vision for Fiano di Avellino had coaxed the best from the character of the Montefredane hills. She bottles two Fianos which defy the passage of time, occupying a special place in the hearts of aficionados. The Vigna della Congregazione stands on clay- and pebble-rich soils around Montefredane, while the Clos d'Haut expresses a plot near the top of Montefredane. Thicker sulphurous substrates make for an even more powerful and multifaceted, smoky sensation. Early release for both of oenologist Vincenzo Mercurio's Fianos. Once again unique, the Clos d'Haut 2015 shows an initial anarchic beeriness, making room for a crescendo of peaty, saline hints and a racy finale. A more measured, even elegant, canvas for the Vigna della Congregazione 2015, showing sun-drenched fruitiness and backbone, with a supple, layered finish of extraordinary length.

○ Fiano di Avellino V. della Congregazione '15	♟♟♟ 5
○ Fiano di Avellino Clos d'Haut '15	♟♟ 5
○ Fiano di Avellino Clos d'Haut '13	♟♟♟ 5
○ Fiano di Avellino V. della Congregazione '10	♟♟♟ 5
○ Fiano di Avellino V. della Congregazione '08	♟♟♟ 4
○ Fiano di Avellino Vigna della Congregazione '06	♟♟♟ 4
○ Fiano di Avellino Vigna della Congregazione '04	♟♟♟ 4
○ Fiano di Avellino V. della Congregazione '13	♟♟ 5
○ Fiano di Avellino V. della Congregazione '11	♟♟ 5

★Villa Matilde

S.S. DOMITIANA, 18
81030 CELLOLE [CE]
TEL. +39 0823932088
www.villamatilde.it

CELLAR SALES
PRE-BOOKED VISITS
ACCOMMODATION AND RESTAURANT SERVICE
ANNUAL PRODUCTION 700,000 bottles
HECTARES UNDER VINE 130.00
SUSTAINABLE WINERY

Production at Villa Matilde is driven by Francesco Avallone's innate curiosity for the history of winemaking, for the tales and anecdotes of Latin writers such as Pliny the Elder, Martial and Ovid. It is down to his tireless research, in conjunction with the Federico II University in Naples, that there is a space in every Guide for such an ancient designation as Falerno del Massico. Now run by his children Maria Ida and Salvatore, the estate has extended its holdings into Sannio, at Tenuta Rocca dei Leoni, and into Irpinia at Tenute di Altavilla, for a broad and comprehensive range. The creamy, caresssing Greco di Tufo 2015 white is true to type with hints of toasted almond and a juicy, well-paced, satisfying finish. Intriguingly baroque, the golden Falerno del Massico Bianco Vigna Caracci 2012 offers notes of dried fruit and wood resin, changing pace in the musky lip-smacking mouth, balancing full-bodied mouthfeel and good length.

○ Greco di Tufo Tenute di Altavilla '15	♥♥ 3*
● Aglianico Rocca dei Leoni '13	♥♥ 2*
○ Falerno del Massico Bianco V. Caracci '12	♥♥ 4
● Falerno del Massico Rosso '12	♥♥ 3
○ Falanghina Rocca dei Leoni '15	♥ 2
● Falerno del Massico Rosso V. Camarato Ris. '11	♥ 7
○ Fiano di Avellino Tenute di Altavilla '15	♥ 3
● Taurasi Tenute di Altavilla '15	♥ 5
⊙ Terre Cerase '15	♥ 2
○ Falerno del Massico Bianco V. Caracci '08	♥♥♥ 3
● Falerno del Massico Camarato '05	♥♥♥ 6
● Falerno del Massico Camarato '04	♥♥♥ 5

Villa Raiano

LOC. SAN MICHELE DI SERINO
VIA BOSCO SATRANO, 1
83020 SERINO [AV]
TEL. +39 0825595663
www.villaraiano.com

CELLAR SALES
PRE-BOOKED VISITS
ANNUAL PRODUCTION 300,000 bottles
HECTARES UNDER VINE 22.00
VITICULTURE METHOD Certified Organic

The Villa Raiano winemaking project is going full steam ahead. The estate affords panoramic views across the Sabato valley, covering 22 organically-tended hectares falling within three different Irpinia designations. From the slopes overlooking Montefredane, San Michele di Serino and Lapio come their fiano grapes, the greco from Montefusco, while the aglianico is from Castelfranci at an altitude of 600 m. Irpinia oenologist Fortunato Sebastiano is on hand for the production of two very distinct ranges, Linea Classica and Linea Vigne. These wines express excellent territorial faithfulness, remarkable stylistic focus and finesse. Without doubt one of this year's best Grecos in terms of compactness and stylistic precision, the Greco di Tufo Contrada Marotta 2014 is elegant and fine-grained, with fragrant notes of new-mown grass and flint. This deep, layered wine has a classy, lip-smacking, musky rhythm. The juicy Fiano di Avellino Alimata 2014, with its hazelnut, spice and black tea notes, also made it through to the final.

○ Fiano di Avellino Alimata '14	♥♥ 4
○ Greco di Tufo Contrada Marotta '14	♥♥ 4
○ Fiano di Avellino '15	♥♥ 3
○ Greco di Tufo '15	♥♥ 3
○ Falanghina '15	♥ 3
● Irpinia Campi Taurasini '12	♥ 3
○ Fiano di Avellino 22 '13	♥♥♥ 4*
○ Fiano di Avellino Alimata '10	♥♥♥ 4
● Taurasi Raiano '07	♥♥ 5
○ Fiano di Avellino '12	♥♥ 3
○ Fiano di Avellino 22 '12	♥♥ 4
○ Greco di Tufo '12	♥♥ 3
● Taurasi '10	♥♥ 5
● Taurasi '09	♥♥ 5
● Taurasi Raiano '08	♥♥ 5

Abbazia di Crapolla

LOC. AVIGLIANO
VIA SAN FILIPPO, 2
80069 VICO EQUENSE [NA]
TEL. +39 3383517280
www.abbaziadicrapolla.it

ANNUAL PRODUCTION 12,000 bottles
HECTARES UNDER VINE 2.00

○ Sireo Bianco '14	🍷🍷 5
● Noir '12	🍷🍷 5

Aia dei Colombi

C.DA SAPENZIE
82034 GUARDIA SANFRAMONDI [BN]
TEL. +39 0824817139
www.aiadeicolombi.it

CELLAR SALES
PRE-BOOKED VISITS
ANNUAL PRODUCTION 60,000 bottles
HECTARES UNDER VINE 10.00

○ Falanghina del Sannio Guardia Sanframondi '15	🍷🍷 2*
○ Falanghina del Sannio Guardia Sanframondi Vignasuprema '14	🍷🍷 2*

Albamarina

C.SO CARLO PISACANE, 28
84051 CENTOLA [SA]
TEL. +39 3495066001
www.fattorialbamarina.com

CELLAR SALES
PRE-BOOKED VISITS
ANNUAL PRODUCTION 20,000 bottles
HECTARES UNDER VINE 10.00

○ Primula '15	🍷🍷 3
○ Cilento Fiano Valmezzana '15	🍷 3

Amarano

C.DA TORRE, 32
83040 MONTEMARANO [AV]
TEL. +39 082763351
www.amarano.it

CELLAR SALES
PRE-BOOKED VISITS
ANNUAL PRODUCTION 20,000 bottles
HECTARES UNDER VINE 7.00

○ Fiano di Avellino Dulcinea '15	🍷🍷 3*
○ Irpinia Coda di Volpe Lucinda '15	🍷🍷 3
● Taurasi Principe Lagonessa '12	🍷🍷 5
● Irpinia Campi Taurasini Malambruno '12	🍷 3

Vitivinicola Anna Bosco

VIA SAN TOMMASO, 34
CASTELVENERE [BN]
TEL. +39 0824940483
vitivinicolaannabosco@gmail.com

ANNUAL PRODUCTION 10,000 bottles
HECTARES UNDER VINE 3.00

● Armonico '15	🍷🍷 2*
● Oro Rosso '15	🍷🍷 2*
○ Griecos's '15	🍷 2

Antico Castello

C.DA POPPANO, 11BIS
83050 SAN MANGO SUL CALORE [AV]
TEL. +39 3408062830
www.anticocastello.com

CELLAR SALES
PRE-BOOKED VISITS
ACCOMMODATION AND RESTAURANT SERVICE
ANNUAL PRODUCTION 50,000 bottles
HECTARES UNDER VINE 10.00
SUSTAINABLE WINERY

● Taurasi '12	🍷🍷 4
○ Irpinia Greco '15	🍷 2

Giuseppe Apicella

FRAZ. CAPITIGNANO
VIA CASTELLO SANTA MARIA, 1
84010 TRAMONTI [SA]
TEL. +39 089876075
www.giuseppeapicella.it

CELLAR SALES
PRE-BOOKED VISITS
ANNUAL PRODUCTION 60,000 bottles
HECTARES UNDER VINE 7.00
VITICULTURE METHOD Certified Organic

○ Costa d'Amalfi Tramonti Bianco '15	♥♥ 3
○ Costa d'Amalfi Tramonti Bianco Colle Santa Marina '15	♥♥ 2*
● Piedirosso '15	♥♥ 2*

Cantine Barone

VIA GIARDINO, 2
84070 RUTINO [SA]
TEL. +39 0974830463
www.cantinebarone.it

CELLAR SALES
PRE-BOOKED VISITS
ACCOMMODATION
ANNUAL PRODUCTION 100,000 bottles
HECTARES UNDER VINE 12.00
VITICULTURE METHOD Certified Organic

○ Marsia Bianco '15	♥♥ 1*
⊙ Primula Rosa '15	♥♥ 2*
○ Cilento Fiano Una Mattina '15	♥ 2
○ Cilento Fiano Vignolella '15	♥ 3

Bellaria

FRAZ. AREA PIP
LOC. CARRANI
83030 MONTEFALCIONE [AV]
TEL. +39 0825973467
www.agricolabellaria.it

CELLAR SALES
PRE-BOOKED VISITS
ANNUAL PRODUCTION 100,000 bottles
HECTARES UNDER VINE 15.00

● Aglianico '13	♥♥ 3
○ Fiano di Avellino '15	♥ 3
○ Greco di Tufo Oltre '15	♥ 4

Boccella

VIA SANT'EUSTACHIO
83040 CASTELFRANCI [AV]
TEL. +39 082772574
www.boccellavini.it

CELLAR SALES
PRE-BOOKED VISITS
ANNUAL PRODUCTION 10,000 bottles
HECTARES UNDER VINE 5.00
VITICULTURE METHOD Certified Organic

● Taurasi Sant'Eustachio '11	♥♥ 5
● Taurasi '11	♥♥ 5
○ Casefatte '15	♥ 2

Borgodangelo

C.DA BOSCO DELLA SELVA
S.DA PROV.LE 52 KM 10
83050 SANT'ANGELO ALL'ESCA [AV]
TEL. +39 082773027
www.borgodangelo.it

CELLAR SALES
PRE-BOOKED VISITS
RESTAURANT SERVICE
ANNUAL PRODUCTION 30,000 bottles
HECTARES UNDER VINE 8.50
SUSTAINABLE WINERY

⊙ Irpinia Rosato '15	♥♥ 2*
○ Fiano di Avellino '15	♥ 2
● Taurasi Ris. '10	♥ 4

Cantina dei Monaci

FRAZ. SANTA LUCIA, 206
83030 SANTA PAOLINA [AV]
TEL. +39 0825964350
www.cantinadeimonaci.it

CELLAR SALES
PRE-BOOKED VISITS
ANNUAL PRODUCTION 80,000 bottles
HECTARES UNDER VINE 9.50

○ Greco di Tufo Decimo Sesto '14	♥♥ 3
● Taurasi '08	♥♥ 5
○ Fiano di Avellino '15	♥ 3
○ Greco di Tufo '15	♥ 3

Cantina del Barone

VIA NOCELLETO, 21
83020 CESINALI [AV]
TEL. +39 0825666751
www.cantinadelbarone.it

CELLAR SALES
PRE-BOOKED VISITS
ANNUAL PRODUCTION 30,000 bottles
HECTARES UNDER VINE 2.50

○ Particella 928 '14	♟♟ 3*

Cantina Riccio

C.DA CAMPORE
83040 CHIUSANO DI SAN DOMENICO [AV]
TEL. +39 0825985631
www.cantinariccio.it

CELLAR SALES
PRE-BOOKED VISITS
ANNUAL PRODUCTION 50,000 bottles
HECTARES UNDER VINE 5.00

○ Fiano di Avellino I Vini di Janus '15	♟♟ 3
○ Greco di Tufo I Vini di Janus '15	♟ 2
● Irpinia Aglianico I Vini di Janus '15	♟ 2
● Taurasi Appia Antica '12	♟ 2

Cantine dell'Angelo

VIA SANTA LUCIA, 32
83010 TUFO [AV]
TEL. +39 3384512965
www.cantinedellangelo.com

CELLAR SALES
PRE-BOOKED VISITS
ANNUAL PRODUCTION 18,000 bottles
HECTARES UNDER VINE 5.00

○ Greco di Tufo '14	♟♟ 3
○ Greco di Tufo Torrefavale '14	♟♟ 3

Capolino Perlingieri

VIA MARRAIOLI, 58
82037 CASTELVENERE [BN]
TEL. +39 0824971541
www.capolinoperlingieri.com

CELLAR SALES
PRE-BOOKED VISITS
ANNUAL PRODUCTION 25,000 bottles
HECTARES UNDER VINE 13.00
VITICULTURE METHOD Certified Organic
SUSTAINABLE WINERY

○ Sannio Fiano Nembo '15	♟♟ 3
○ Falanghina del Sannio Preta '15	♟ 2
● Sannio Aglianico Talento '11	♟ 4
○ Sannio Greco Vento '15	♟ 3

Casebianche

C.DA CASE BIANCHE, 8
84076 TORCHIARA [SA]
TEL. +39 0974843244
www.casebianche.eu

CELLAR SALES
PRE-BOOKED VISITS
ANNUAL PRODUCTION 30,000 bottles
HECTARES UNDER VINE 5.50
VITICULTURE METHOD Certified Organic
SUSTAINABLE WINERY

○ La Matta Dosaggio Zero '15	♟♟ 3*
⊙ Il Fric '15	♟♟ 3
○ Cilento Fiano Cumalè '15	♟ 3

Tenute Casoli

VIA ROMA, 28
83040 CANDIDA [AV]
TEL. +39 3402958099
www.tenutecasoli.it

CELLAR SALES
PRE-BOOKED VISITS
ACCOMMODATION AND RESTAURANT SERVICE
ANNUAL PRODUCTION 100,000 bottles
HECTARES UNDER VINE 13.00

○ Fiano di Avellino Kryos '14	♟♟ 3
○ Greco di Tufo Cupavaticale '14	♟ 5
● Taurasi Armonia '11	♟ 6

Colle di San Domenico

S.DA ST.LE OFANTINA KM 7,500
83040 CHIUSANO DI SAN DOMENICO [AV]
TEL. +39 0825985423
www.cantinecolledisandomenico.it

CELLAR SALES
PRE-BOOKED VISITS
ANNUAL PRODUCTION 80,000 bottles
HECTARES UNDER VINE 10.00

○ Falanghina del Sannio '15	♟♟ 2*
○ Fiano di Avellino '15	♟ 3
○ Greco di Tufo '15	♟ 3
● Irpinia Campi Taurasini Principe '13	♟ 3

Colli di Castelfranci

C.DA BRAUDIANO
83040 CASTELFRANCI [AV]
TEL. +39 082772392
www.collidicastelfranci.com

CELLAR SALES
PRE-BOOKED VISITS
ACCOMMODATION AND RESTAURANT SERVICE
ANNUAL PRODUCTION 150,000 bottles
HECTARES UNDER VINE 25.00

○ Greco di Tufo Grotte '15	♟♟ 2*
● Taurasi Alta Valle Ris. '09	♟♟ 7
○ Fiano di Avellino Pendino '15	♟ 2
○ Irpinia Fiano Paladino '14	♟ 4

Contrada Salandra

FRAZ. COSTE DI CUMA
VIA TRE PICCIONI, 40
80078 POZZUOLI [NA]
TEL. +39 0815265258
www.dolciqualita.com

CELLAR SALES
PRE-BOOKED VISITS
ANNUAL PRODUCTION 15,000 bottles
HECTARES UNDER VINE 4.00

● Campi Flegrei Piedirosso '13	♟♟ 3*
○ Campi Flegrei Falanghina '14	♟♟ 2*

Cuomo
I Vini del Cavaliere

VIA FEUDO LA PILA, 16
84047 CAPACCIO [SA]
TEL. +39 0828725376
www.vinicuomo.com

CELLAR SALES
PRE-BOOKED VISITS
ANNUAL PRODUCTION 25,000 bottles
HECTARES UNDER VINE 4.00

○ Cilento Fiano Heraion '15	♟♟ 3
● Cilento Aglianico Granatum '14	♟ 3

D'Antiche Terre

C.DA LO PIANO
S.DA ST.LE 7BIS
83030 MANOCALZATI [AV]
TEL. +39 0825675358
www.danticheterre.it

CELLAR SALES
PRE-BOOKED VISITS
ACCOMMODATION AND RESTAURANT SERVICE
ANNUAL PRODUCTION 420,000 bottles
HECTARES UNDER VINE 40.00
SUSTAINABLE WINERY

● Coriliano '14	♟♟ 2*
○ Fiano di Avellino '15	♟ 3
○ Sannio Fiano '15	♟ 2
● Taurasi '09	♟ 5

Viticoltori De Conciliis

LOC. QUERCE, 1
84060 PRIGNANO CILENTO [SA]
TEL. +39 0974831090
www.viticoltorideconciliis.it

CELLAR SALES
PRE-BOOKED VISITS
ANNUAL PRODUCTION 200,000 bottles
HECTARES UNDER VINE 21.00
VITICULTURE METHOD Certified Organic
SUSTAINABLE WINERY

● Bacioilcielo Rosso '15	♟♟ 2*
● Aglianico Donnaluna '14	♟ 3
○ Bacioilcielo Bianco '15	♟ 2

Di Marzo

VIA GAETANO DI MARZO, 2
83010 TUFO [AV]
TEL. +39 0825998022
www.cantinedimarzo.it

CELLAR SALES
PRE-BOOKED VISITS
ANNUAL PRODUCTION 150,000 bottles
HECTARES UNDER VINE 23.00

○ Greco di Tufo '15	♟♟ 2*
○ Greco di Tufo Brut M. Cl. Anni Venti	♟♟ 4
○ Greco di Tufo Franciscus '15	♟ 3

Farro

LOC. FUSARO
VIA VIRGILIO, 16/24
80070 BACOLI [NA]
TEL. +39 0818545555
www.cantinefarro.it

CELLAR SALES
PRE-BOOKED VISITS
ANNUAL PRODUCTION 207,000 bottles
HECTARES UNDER VINE 20.00

○ Campi Flegrei Falanghina Le Cigliate '14	♟♟ 3
○ Campi Flegrei Falanghina '15	♟ 2
● Campi Flegrei Piedirosso '15	♟ 2

Cantine Federiciane Monteleone

FRAZ. SAN ROCCO
VIA ANTICA CONSOLARE CAMPANA, 34
80016 MARANO DI NAPOLI [NA]
TEL. +39 0815765294
www.federiciane.it

CELLAR SALES
PRE-BOOKED VISITS
ANNUAL PRODUCTION 200,000 bottles
HECTARES UNDER VINE 15.00

● Penisola Sorrentina Gragnano '15	♟♟ 2*
● Penisola Sorrentina Lettere '15	♟♟ 2*
● Campi Flegrei Piedirosso '15	♟ 2

Filadoro

C.DA CERRETO, 19
83030 LAPIO [AV]
TEL. +39 0825982536
www.filadoro.it

CELLAR SALES
PRE-BOOKED VISITS
ANNUAL PRODUCTION 40,000 bottles
HECTARES UNDER VINE 6.00

○ Fiano di Avellino '14	♟♟ 3
○ Frizzy '15	♟ 2

★Galardi

FRAZ. SAN CARLO
S.DA PROV.LE SESSA-MIGNANO
81037 SESSA AURUNCA [CE]
TEL. +39 08231440003
www.terradilavoro.com

CELLAR SALES
PRE-BOOKED VISITS
ANNUAL PRODUCTION 30,000 bottles
HECTARES UNDER VINE 10.00
VITICULTURE METHOD Certified Organic

● Terra di Lavoro '14	♟♟ 7

Raffaele Guastaferro

VIA GRAMSCI
83030 TAURASI [AV]
TEL. +39 082539244
www.guastaferro.it

CELLAR SALES
ANNUAL PRODUCTION 40,000 bottles
HECTARES UNDER VINE 10.00

● Taurasi Primum Ris. '07	♟♟ 4
● Irpinia Aglianico Memini '12	♟♟ 2*
○ Greco di Tufo Cardinale '15	♟ 3

Manimurci

S.DA ST.LE 164 KM 83,200
83052 PATERNOPOLI [AV]
TEL. +39 3938257033
www.peppebuiowinery.it

CELLAR SALES
PRE-BOOKED VISITS
ANNUAL PRODUCTION 300,000 bottles
HECTARES UNDER VINE 20.00

○ Falanghina del Sannio Falange '15	♥♥	2*
● Irpinia Campi Taurasini Rossocupo '14	♥♥	3
○ Greco di Tufo Zagreo '15	♥	2
● Taurasi Poema '11	♥	5

Salvatore Martusciello

VIA SPINELLI, 4
80010 QUARTO [NA]
TEL. +39 0818766123
www.salvatoremartusciello.it

ANNUAL PRODUCTION 87,000 bottles
HECTARES UNDER VINE 2.00

● Campi Flegrei Piedirosso Settevulcani '15	♥♥	3
● Penisola Sorrentina Lettere Ottouve '15	♥♥	3
○ Campi Flegrei Falanghina Settevulcani '15	♥	3
● Penisola Sorrentina Gragnano Ottouve '15	♥	3

Lorenzo Nifo Sarrapochiello

VIA PIANA, 62
82030 PONTE [BN]
TEL. +39 0824876450
www.nifo.eu

CELLAR SALES
PRE-BOOKED VISITS
ANNUAL PRODUCTION 70,000 bottles
HECTARES UNDER VINE 16.00
VITICULTURE METHOD Certified Organic

○ Sannio Fiano '15	♥♥	2*
○ Falanghina del Sannio Taburno '15	♥	2
○ Sannio Taburno Greco '15	♥	2

Raffaele Palma

LOC. SAN VITO
VIA ARSENALE, 8
84010 MAIORI [SA]
TEL. +39 3357601858
www.raffaelepalma.it

CELLAR SALES
ANNUAL PRODUCTION 20,000 bottles
HECTARES UNDER VINE 6.00
VITICULTURE METHOD Certified Organic
SUSTAINABLE WINERY

○ Costa d'Amalfi Bianco Puntacroce '15	♥♥	6
● Costa d'Amalfi Rosso Montecorvo '13	♥	6

Petilia

LOC. CAMPO FIORITO
C.DA PINCERA
83011 ALTAVILLA IRPINA [AV]
TEL. +39 0825991696
www.aziendaagricolapetilia.it

CELLAR SALES
PRE-BOOKED VISITS
ANNUAL PRODUCTION 80,000 bottles
HECTARES UNDER VINE 17.00
SUSTAINABLE WINERY

○ Fiano di Avellino '15	♥♥	3
○ Greco di Tufo 4 20 '15	♥♥	4
○ Irpinia Falanghina Hirpos '15	♥	3

Porto di Mola

VIA RISIERA
81050 GALLUCCIO [CE]
TEL. +39 0823925801
www.portodimola.it

CELLAR SALES
PRE-BOOKED VISITS
ANNUAL PRODUCTION 250,000 bottles
HECTARES UNDER VINE 50.00

○ Colle Lepre '15	♥♥	2*
○ Montecamino '15	♥	2
● Peppi '13	♥	2

Quadrigato

C.DA TAVERNA VECCHIA
82034 GUARDIA SANFRAMONDI [BN]
TEL. +39 0824864296
www.quadrigato.com

CELLAR SALES
PRE-BOOKED VISITS
ANNUAL PRODUCTION 70,000 bottles
HECTARES UNDER VINE 14.00

○ Falanghina del Sannio '15	🍷🍷 2*
○ Sannio Greco '15	🍷🍷 2*
○ Sannio Fiano '15	🍷 2

Regina Viarum

LOC. FALCIANO DEL MASSICO
VIA VELLARIA
81030 FALCIANO DEL MASSICO [CE]
TEL. +39 0823931299
www.reginaviarum.it

CELLAR SALES
PRE-BOOKED VISITS
ANNUAL PRODUCTION 19,000 bottles
HECTARES UNDER VINE 5.00
VITICULTURE METHOD Certified Organic
SUSTAINABLE WINERY

● Falerno del Massico Zero5 '13	🍷🍷 3
● Falerno del Massico Barone '11	🍷 5

Tenuta Scuotto

C.DA CAMPOMARINO, 2/3
83030 LAPIO [AV]
TEL. +39 08251851965
www.tenutascuotto.it

CELLAR SALES
PRE-BOOKED VISITS
ANNUAL PRODUCTION 40,000 bottles
HECTARES UNDER VINE 3.00

● Taurasi '12	🍷🍷 5
○ Greco di Tufo '15	🍷 3
○ Oi Ni '13	🍷 5

Andrea Reale

LOC. BORGO DI GETE
VIA CARDAMONE, 75
84010 TRAMONTI [SA]
TEL. +39 089856144
www.aziendaagricolareale.it

CELLAR SALES
PRE-BOOKED VISITS
ACCOMMODATION AND RESTAURANT SERVICE
ANNUAL PRODUCTION 12,500 bottles
HECTARES UNDER VINE 2.50
VITICULTURE METHOD Certified Organic

○ Costa d'Amalfi Tramonti Bianco Aliseo '15	🍷🍷 4
⊙ Costa d'Amalfi Tramonti Rosato Getis '15	🍷🍷 4
● Borgo di Gete '12	🍷 6

Sclavia

VIA CASE SPARSE
81040 LIBERI [CE]
TEL. +39 3356654770
www.sclavia.com

ANNUAL PRODUCTION 50,000 bottles
HECTARES UNDER VINE 13.00

○ Calù '15	🍷🍷 3*
● Granito '12	🍷🍷 3
● Liberi '12	🍷🍷 5
● Pallagrello Nero Montecardillo '13	🍷 3

Setaro

LOC. PARCO NAZIONALE DEL VESUVIO
VIA BOSCO DEL MONACO, 34
80040 TRECASE [NA]
TEL. +39 0818628956
www.casasetaro.it

ANNUAL PRODUCTION 50,000 bottles
HECTARES UNDER VINE 10.00

○ Caprettone Brut '12	🍷🍷 4
○ Falanghina Campanelle '15	🍷 2
○ Vesuvio Lacryma Christi Bianco Munazei '15	🍷 2

Sorrentino

VIA RIO, 26
80042 BOSCOTRECASE [NA]
TEL. +39 0818584963
www.sorrentinovini.com

CELLAR SALES
PRE-BOOKED VISITS
ACCOMMODATION AND RESTAURANT SERVICE
ANNUAL PRODUCTION 250,000 bottles
HECTARES UNDER VINE 30.00
VITICULTURE METHOD Certified Organic

⊙ Vesuvio Lacryma Christi Bianco V. Lapillo '15	🍷🍷 3
⊙ Vesuvio Lacryma Christi Rosato V. Lapillo '15	🍷🍷 3

Telaro

LOC. CALABRITTO
VIA CINQUE PIETRE, 2
81045 GALLUCCIO [CE]
TEL. +39 0823925841
www.vinitelaro.it

CELLAR SALES
PRE-BOOKED VISITS
ANNUAL PRODUCTION 550,000 bottles
HECTARES UNDER VINE 70.00
VITICULTURE METHOD Certified Organic

● Calivierno '13	🍷🍷 3
○ Galluccio Bianco Ripa Bianca '15	🍷🍷 2*
○ Fiano '15	🍷 2
● Galluccio Rosso Ara Mundi Ris. '13	🍷 3

Torre Varano

LOC. TORREVONO, 2
82030 TORRECUSO [BN]
TEL. +39 0824876372
www.torrevarano.it

CELLAR SALES
PRE-BOOKED VISITS
ANNUAL PRODUCTION 130,000 bottles
HECTARES UNDER VINE 12.00

● Aglianico del Taburno 36+6 '09	🍷🍷 5
● Aglianico '14	🍷 3
● Aglianico del Taburno '12	🍷 3
○ Falanghina del Sannio Taburno '15	🍷 2

Il Verro

LOC. ACQUAVALLE, LAUTONI
81040 FORMICOLA [CE]
TEL. +39 3456416200
www.ilverro.it

CELLAR SALES
ANNUAL PRODUCTION 20,000 bottles
HECTARES UNDER VINE 4.00

○ Pallagrello Bianco Verginiano '15	🍷🍷 2*
● Pallagrello Nero '15	🍷🍷 3
● Casavecchia Lautonis '15	🍷 2
○ Sheep '15	🍷 2

Vigne Guadagno

VIA TAGLIAMENTO, 237
83100 AVELLINO
TEL. +39 08251686379
www.vigneguadagno.it

CELLAR SALES
PRE-BOOKED VISITS
ANNUAL PRODUCTION 47,000 bottles
HECTARES UNDER VINE 10.00

○ Fiano di Avellino Contrada Sant'Aniello '13	🍷🍷 4
○ Greco di Tufo '15	🍷🍷 3
● Taurasi '10	🍷🍷 5

Vinosia

C.DA NOCELLETO
83052 PATERNOPOLI [AV]
TEL. +39 082771754
www.vinosia.com

CELLAR SALES
RESTAURANT SERVICE
ANNUAL PRODUCTION 800,000 bottles
HECTARES UNDER VINE 40.00
SUSTAINABLE WINERY

○ Fiano di Avellino Le Grade '15	🍷🍷 3
○ Greco di Tufo L'Ariella '15	🍷🍷 3
● Taurasi Marziacanale '09	🍷 5
● Taurasi Santandrea '12	🍷 4

BASILICATA

Basilicata is a precious source of wines and so far it has only been partially exploited. Most consumers are familiar with the region's foremost designation, Aglianico del Vulture, which was recently awarded DOCG status for its Superiore and Superiore Riserva versions. And it is precisely the Aglianico vinified on the spurs stretching from Vulture to Venosa that is found under Basilicata's most iconic labels. This year there are four award-winning wines, three of them (Terre degli Svevi, Cantine del Notaio and Titolo) are Tre Bicchieri old hands, while Grifalco di Lucania's superb Gricos 2014 is a debutant to the podium. The interesting fact that came to light during tastings was that 18 wines from Basilicata made our finals, all Aglianico del Vulture. The only exciting news came in the form of Terre dei Re's Vulcano 800, an elegant Pinot Nero from high altitude vineyards and offering an intuition of the potential of this unique terroir. Perhaps the epic adventures of Etna wines are now inspiring quiet Basilicata? Will we see new businesses opening and traditional names take their place on the international stage in years to come? We sincerely hope so, because the region has all the makings of a prosperous future. As we add the finishing touches to this edition of the Guide, news is coming in that a venerable brand like Paternoster has been taken over by leading Veneto group, Tommasi Viticoltori, coming hot on the heels of the recent acquisitions of Feudi di San Gregorio by Basilisco and Vigneti del Vulture by the Farnese group, not to mention the GIV buying a consolidated outfit like Terre degli Svevi. All proving our theory. The grapes, terroir and climate are some of the best in southern Italy for prestige wine production, and the success of the Paternoster brand, with two wines in our finals, is emblematic of this potential. But Basilicata viticulture is not just the Vulture area. There are names working hard to emerge, like Grottino di Roccanova, Terre dell'Alta Valdagri, and above all the Matera designation, all showing healthy vitals. The Matera DOC in particular, which comes in various types, including Moro and Primitivo, seems to show the most promise, and we are in no doubt that in the near future it will be up there with Vulture, revealing further aspects of the region's enormous winegrowing potential.

Basilisco

LOC. BARILE
VIA DELLE CANTINE, 20/22
85022 BARILE [PZ]
TEL. +39 0972771033
www.basiliscovini.it

CELLAR SALES
PRE-BOOKED VISITS
ACCOMMODATION
ANNUAL PRODUCTION 55,000 bottles
HECTARES UNDER VINE 27.00
VITICULTURE METHOD Certified Organic
SUSTAINABLE WINERY

When skilled, passionate Viviana Malafarina took over the helm of Feudi San Gregorio's Basilicata estate, a new phase began for Basilisco, one of the best-established names in the Vulture area. The new cellar in the centre of Barile and 27 hectares of vineyards scattered over classic local crus, like Macarico and Gelosia, provide the ingredients for a success story. There are plenty of heirloom vineyards too, even some ungrafted, which form the basis of special selections. The wines mature in the historic tuffstone Shesh caves, typical of Barile. Basilisco 2012 came close to our highest accolade this year. This well-structured, powerful, characterful, and fruity wine is both full-flavoured and austere, with attractive oaky hints, cherries and blackberries in the finish, and smooth, well-balanced tannins. The Aglianico del Vulture Storico Prefillosera 2012 selection is complex and rich in juicy fruit but suffers slightly from the wood used for maturation. Sophia is an interesting white made from fiano, malvasia bianca and traminer.

Cantine del Notaio

VIA ROMA, 159
85028 RIONERO IN VULTURE [PZ]
TEL. +39 0972723689
www.cantinedelnotaio.com

CELLAR SALES
PRE-BOOKED VISITS
RESTAURANT SERVICE
ANNUAL PRODUCTION 250,000 bottles
HECTARES UNDER VINE 30.00
VITICULTURE METHOD Certified Organic

With great passion Gerardo Giuratrabocchetti tends the 30 hectares of vineyards in the best growing areas of five municipalities in the Vulture DOC zone, where aglianico grapes play a leading role. The wines are fermented in the new Rionero cellar and aged in the 17th-century tuffstone caves built by Franciscan friars. The extensive house range covers all the different types and the wines, named in homage to Gerardo's notary father, are of a high overall standard. Alongside these, the Macarico line offers polished blends at reasonable prices. Il Repertorio, this year in the 2014 version, is again the star of our tastings. A stylish and expansive Aglianico del Vulture, it avoids wielding too much muscle in the structure and excessive extract, preferring grace and drinkability, with mouthfilling red and black berries, sweet tannins and nicely blended oaky sensations in the finish. The sumptuous 2013 La Firma is as richly extracted as ever. The Macarico line is polished and expansive.

● Aglianico del Vulture Basilisco '12	▼ 6
● Aglianico del Vulture Storico Prefillosera '12	▼▼ 5
○ Sophia '15	▼ 3
● Aglianico del Vulture Basilisco '09	▼▼▼ 5
● Aglianico del Vulture Basilisco '08	▼▼▼ 5
● Aglianico del Vulture Basilisco '07	▼▼▼ 5
● Aglianico del Vulture Basilisco '06	▼▼▼ 5
● Aglianico del Vulture Basilisco '04	▼▼▼ 5
● Aglianico del Vulture Basilisco '01	▼▼▼ 5
● Aglianico del Vulture Basilisco '11	▼▼ 6
● Aglianico del Vulture Teodosio '13	▼▼ 3*
● Aglianico del Vulture Teodosio '12	▼▼ 3

● Aglianico del Vulture Il Repertorio '14	▼▼▼ 4*
● Aglianico del Vulture La Firma '13	▼▼ 6
● Aglianico del Vulture Macari '14	▼▼ 2*
● Aglianico del Vulture Macarico '13	▼▼ 3
○ La Parcella '15	▼▼ 7
○ La Postilla	▼▼ 3
○ Il Preliminare '15	▼ 3
○ Macarico Xjnestra '15	▼ 2
● Aglianico del Vulture Il Repertorio '13	▼▼▼ 4*
● Aglianico del Vulture Il Repertorio '12	▼▼▼ 4*
● Aglianico del Vulture La Firma '10	▼▼▼ 6
● Aglianico del Vulture La Firma '00	▼▼▼ 5
● Aglianico del Vulture Il Sigillo '11	▼▼ 6
● Aglianico del Vulture La Firma '12	▼▼ 6

Casa Vinicola D'Angelo

VIA PADRE PIO, 8
85028 RIONERO IN VULTURE [PZ]
TEL. +39 0972721517
www.dangelowine.it

CELLAR SALES
PRE-BOOKED VISITS
ANNUAL PRODUCTION 300,000 bottles
HECTARES UNDER VINE 35.00

D'Angelo is a historic label in the classic
Aglianico del Vulture production zone
around Rionero, Barile and Rapolla. Now
run by his offspring Rocco and Erminia,
who inherited their father's passion for
wine, a stubborn character, and an interest
in producing wines true to the terroir. As
well as the 35-hectare estate, the
D'Angelos have two cellars, one for
vinification and the other for maturation in
barrels and barriques. From the estate's
extensive range this year we particularly
liked the two well-styled versions of
Aglianico 2014, D'Angelo and Tenuta del
Portale. The first is rich in fruit and
aromatic herbs, while the second is deeper,
smoky and intriguing. We were less
impressed with the two 2011 Riservas,
Caselle and Tenuta del Portale, and will
reserve our review for next year's edition.
The other wines are all sound.

Eubea

S.DA PROV.LE 8
85020 RIPACANDIDA [PZ]
TEL. +39 3284312789
www.agricolaeubea.com

CELLAR SALES
PRE-BOOKED VISITS
ANNUAL PRODUCTION 50,000 bottles
HECTARES UNDER VINE 16.00
VITICULTURE METHOD Certified Organic

Eugenia Sasso runs this lovely estate with
passionate enthusiasm: 16 hectares of
vineyards aged between 40 and 60 years,
scattered between Barile and Ripacandida
on some of the best-aspected hillside land
with well-drained tuffstone and volcanic
soil. Working alongside Eugenia is her
father, Professor Francesco Sasso, a
distinguished figure on the Basilicata wine
scene for over 50 years. The winery is
situated in an old, beautifully renovated
Ripacandida farmstead, which expresses all
the winegrowing history of this area.
Eugenia returns to the Guide with an
excellent performance. The Covo dei
Briganti 2013 stood out in our final tastings
for its generous, richly extracted, elegant
character with hints of blackberries and
blueberries, strongly present on nose and
palate, and the fresh balsamic hints slightly
held back by oaky notes that will surely
soften over time. Ròinos, from the same
vintage, has two aces up its sleeve: fruit
and attractive flavour.

● Aglianico del Vulture Tenuta del Portale '14	♟♟ 4
● Aglianico del Vulture '14	♟♟ 3
● Aglianico del Vulture Le Vigne a Capanno Tenuta del Portale '13	♟♟ 3
● Aglianico del Vulture Tecum '13	♟ 3
● Serra delle Querce '14	♟ 3
● Aglianico del Vulture V. Caselle Ris. '01	♟♟♟ 3*
● Aglianico del Vulture '13	♟♟ 3
● Aglianico del Vulture Le Vigne a Capanno Tenuta del Portale '12	♟♟ 3
● Aglianico del Vulture Tenuta del Portale Ris. '10	♟♟ 4
● Canneto '12	♟♟ 4
○ Villa dei Pini '14	♟♟ 2*

● Aglianico del Vulture Covo dei Briganti '13	♟♟ 3*
● Aglianico del Vulture Ròinos '13	♟♟ 5
⊙ La Vie en Rose M. Cl. '12	♟♟ 2*
● Le More '15	♟ 2
⊙ Le Rose '15	♟ 2
● Aglianico del Vulture Ròinos '01	♟♟♟ 8
● Aglianico del Vulture Covo dei Briganti '12	♟♟ 3
● Aglianico del Vulture Eubearosso '09	♟♟ 2*
● Aglianico del Vulture Covo dei Briganti '09	♟♟ 3
● Aglianico del Vulture Ròinos '12	♟♟ 5
● Aglianico del Vulture Roinos '09	♟♟ 5

★Elena Fucci

C.DA SOLAGNA DEL TITOLO
85022 BARILE [PZ]
TEL. +39 3204879945
www.elenafuccivini.com

CELLAR SALES
PRE-BOOKED VISITS
ANNUAL PRODUCTION 25,000 bottles
HECTARES UNDER VINE 6.70
SUSTAINABLE WINERY

Contrada Solagna del Titolo in Barile is the birthplace of Fucci's single great wine, Aglianico del Vulture Titolo. Since 2000 Salvatore Fucci and his daughter Elena, winemaker and owner, and the rest of the family, have worked their vineyards with passionate skill to make this noble, fresh and stylish wine. Now that the new zero-impact bioarchitecture cellar is completed, Elena and her husband Andrea continue to apply their sensitivity and techniques to expressing this terroir. The 2014 vintage offers another excellent Titolo: concentrated, generous and well-balanced, if lagging a little in development at the time of tasting. We enjoyed the stylish rich extract, mouthfilling fruit and smooth tannic texture, as well as its Mediterranean character and lingering aromas. It can only improve with time.

● Aglianico del Vulture Titolo '14	♥♥♥	6
● Aglianico del Vulture Titolo '13	♀♀♀	6
● Aglianico del Vulture Titolo '12	♀♀♀	5
● Aglianico del Vulture Titolo '11	♀♀♀	5
● Aglianico del Vulture Titolo '10	♀♀♀	5
● Aglianico del Vulture Titolo '09	♀♀♀	5
● Aglianico del Vulture Titolo '08	♀♀♀	6
● Aglianico del Vulture Titolo '07	♀♀♀	6
● Aglianico del Vulture Titolo '06	♀♀♀	5
● Aglianico del Vulture Titolo '05	♀♀♀	5
● Aglianico del Vulture Titolo '02	♀♀♀	5
● Aglianico del Vulture Titolo '04	♀♀	5
● Aglianico del Vulture Titolo '03	♀♀	5
● Aglianico del Vulture Titolo '01	♀♀	5
● Aglianico del Vulture Titolo '00	♀♀	4

Grifalco della Lucania

LOC. PIAN DI CAMERA
85029 VENOSA [PZ]
TEL. +39 097231002
grifalcodellalucania@email.it

CELLAR SALES
PRE-BOOKED VISITS
ANNUAL PRODUCTION 65,000 bottles
HECTARES UNDER VINE 15.00
VITICULTURE METHOD Certified Organic
SUSTAINABLE WINERY

Sangiovese and aglianico are the two grape varieties that embody the story of Fabrizio and Cecilia Piccin, who decided to move from their homeland of Tuscany to Venosa, and set up an estate dedicated to Aglianico del Vulture. Their winemaking experience gained in Montepulciano, helped the couple bring this winery to life in 2003, with the purchase of lovely vineyards in Ginestra, Maschito, Rapolla and Venosa. Today they follow certified organic farming methods and bottle wines of a remarkably high standard, offering several, always well-typed versions of Aglianico. The very appealing red Gricos 2014 certainly captivated our panel with rich extract and concentrated fruit, close-knit tannins, not without elegance and finesse, all supported by acidity lending fresh flavour and balance with a long, stylish finish on oaky, spicy notes and hints of aromatic herbs. A very well-deserved Tre Bicchieri.

● Aglianico del Vulture Gricos '14	♥♥♥	3*
● Aglianico del Vulture Damaschito '12	♀♀	4
● Aglianico del Vulture Grifalco '14	♀♀	4
⊙ Frà '15	♀	3
● Aglianico del Vulture Bosco Del Falco '07	♀♀	4
● Aglianico del Vulture Daginestra '11	♀♀	5
● Aglianico del Vulture Damaschito '08	♀♀	4
● Aglianico del Vulture Gricos '13	♀♀	3*
● Aglianico del Vulture Gricos '12	♀♀	2*
● Aglianico del Vulture Gricos '11	♀♀	2*
● Aglianico del Vulture Grifalco '13	♀♀	4
● Aglianico del Vulture Grifalco '12	♀♀	3*
● Aglianico del Vulture Grifalco '11	♀♀	3
● Aglianico del Vulture Grifalco '10	♀♀	3

Martino

via La Vista, 2a
85028 Rionero in Vulture [PZ]
Tel. +39 0972721422
www.martinovini.com

CELLAR SALES
PRE-BOOKED VISITS
ANNUAL PRODUCTION 250,000 bottles
HECTARES UNDER VINE 50.00

The Martino story started in the late 19th century at Rionero in Vulture, when they sold grapes, must and wine throughout Italy. The family began bottling wines under their own brand with Donato Martino, father of current owner, Armando, who now works alongside young Carolin, chairwoman of the Consorzio dell'Aglianico del Vulture. Today this estate is well established on the regional winegrowing scene and vaunts a modern, hi-tech cellar with plenty of underground space in the natural tuffstone caves, used for lengthy maturation of the wines. We really enjoyed the generous, fragrant qualities of the Aglianico del Vulture 2013. Lovely, dark ruby colour and stylish ripe red and black berry aromas, opening smooth and full-bodied onto the palate, supported by well-judged acidity that presents us with a lingering, ageable wine. The 2011 versions fell slightly short of our expectations, slightly too evolved overall for their age and compared to the excellent 2010.

● Aglianico del Vulture '13	❧❧	2*
● Aglianico del Vulture Bel Poggio '11	❧	2
● Aglianico del Vulture Oraziano '11	❧	5
● Aglianico del Vulture Pretoriano '11	❧	5
○ Greco I Sassi '15	❧	2
● Aglianico del Vulture '12	❧❧	2*
● Aglianico del Vulture '11	❧❧	2*
● Aglianico del Vulture Bel Poggio '10	❧❧	2*
● Aglianico del Vulture Bel Poggio '09	❧❧	2*
● Aglianico del Vulture Oraziano '10	❧❧	5
● Aglianico del Vulture Oraziano '09	❧❧	5
● Aglianico del Vulture Pretoriano '10	❧❧	5
● Aglianico del Vulture Pretoriano '09	❧❧	5

Paternoster

c.da Valle del Titolo
85022 Barile [PZ]
Tel. +39 0972770224
www.paternostervini.it

CELLAR SALES
PRE-BOOKED VISITS
ANNUAL PRODUCTION 150,000 bottles
HECTARES UNDER VINE 20.00
VITICULTURE METHOD Certified Organic

Established in 1925 by Anselmo Paternoster, this is one of Vulture's historic labels, and one of the first estates in southern Italy to bottles its own wines and create a brand. The estate has 20 hectares of vineyards as well as purchases in two main areas of Barile, Valle del Titolo and Macarico, and other prestigious crus like Gelosia, Pian di Carro, and Maschito. They have recently built a new, modern cellar. Today Vito Paternoster is at the helm of the family estate, assisted by his nephew, winemaker Fabio Mecca, who represents the fourth generation. The Aglianico del Vulture Don Anselmo 2012 is beautifully concentrated with rich aromas of ripe red and black berries alongside forward hints of spices and black pepper. The palate is expansive and harmonious with juicy fruit, but lacks length in the finish. In this phase, the Rotondo 2012 is more clenched and rugged, requiring longer in the bottle to achieve balance. The Giuv 2013 is taut and balsamic, while the Synthesi 2013 is excellent, as ever.

● Aglianico del Vulture Don Anselmo '12	❧❧	6
● Aglianico del Vulture Rotondo '12	❧❧	5
● Aglianico del Vulture Giuv '13	❧❧	2*
● Aglianico del Vulture Synthesi '13	❧❧	3
● Barigliòtt '15	❧	2
○ Biancorte '15	❧	3
● L'Antico Spumante	❧	3
⊙ Ros Retabli '15	❧	3
● Aglianico del Vulture Don Anselmo '09	❧❧❧	6
● Aglianico del Vulture Don Anselmo '94	❧❧❧	6
● Aglianico del Vulture Don Anselmo Ris. '05	❧❧❧	6
● Aglianico del Vulture Rotondo '11	❧❧❧	5

Re Manfredi
Cantina Terre degli Svevi

LOC. PIAN DI CAMERA
85029 VENOSA [PZ]
TEL. +39 097231263
www.cantineremanfredi.it

CELLAR SALES
PRE-BOOKED VISITS
RESTAURANT SERVICE
ANNUAL PRODUCTION 240,000 bottles
HECTARES UNDER VINE 120.00

This Venosa-based estate boasts 120 hectares of vineyards with the lion's share devoted to aglianico. Gruppo Italiano Vini bought Terre degli Svevi in 1988 and dedicated it to King Manfredi, the son of Frederick II, who once owned these lands. As well as aglianico, which is the basis for the Re Manfredi and other Aglianico del Vulture selections, the estate grows white grapes like traminer and müller thurgau used for its the Manfredi Bianco. Paolo Montrone and his team offer an excellent Aglianico del Vulture this year: the Re Manfredi 2013 in one of its best-ever versions. Beautiful dark ruby red colour and stylish complex aromas with fresh balsamic and spicy sensations alongside the fruit, closing on elegant nuances of new oak. The palate is generous, appealing and expansive, yet solid and deep, with medicinal herbs in the finish. The Serpara 2011 is smooth, richly extracted and fruity, while the pleasantly aromatic Manfredi Bianco is fresh and supple.

● Aglianico del Vulture Re Manfredi '13	▼▼▼ 6
● Aglianico del Vulture Serpara '11	▼▼ 5
○ Re Manfredi Bianco '15	▼▼ 4
● Aglianico del Vulture Re Manfredi '11	♀♀♀ 4*
● Aglianico del Vulture Re Manfredi '10	♀♀♀ 4*
● Aglianico del Vulture Re Manfredi '05	♀♀♀ 4
● Aglianico del Vulture Re Manfredi '99	♀♀♀ 4*
● Aglianico del Vulture Serpara '10	♀♀♀ 5
● Aglianico del Vulture Vign. Serpara '03	♀♀♀ 4*
● Aglianico del Vulture '09	♀♀ 3
● Aglianico del Vulture Re Manfredi '09	♀♀ 4
● Aglianico del Vulture Serpara '08	♀♀ 5
● Aglianico del Vulture Taglio del Tralcio '12	♀♀ 4
● Aglianico del Vulture Taglio del Tralcio '11	♀♀ 4

Taverna

C.DA TAVERNA, 15
75020 NOVA SIRI [MT]
TEL. +39 0835877083
www.aataverna.com

CELLAR SALES
PRE-BOOKED VISITS
ACCOMMODATION AND RESTAURANT SERVICE
ANNUAL PRODUCTION 50,000 bottles
HECTARES UNDER VINE 19.00

The history of the Taverna estate began in 1950 when Pasquale Lunati, who had bought a vineyard in the Nova Siri area, began a partnership with Conegliano's Istituto di Enologia to focus on making wine from native grape varieties. Today, current owner Pasquale, named after his grandfather, continues the Basilicata winemaking tradition with production of wines based on aglianico, greco and primitivo in the two provinces. A small part of the 280-hectare estate is under vine, on the most suitable terroir. Taverna is one of the best estates in the region, and upholds its reputation with an excellent version of Matera Moro, the 2014 I Sassi selection. This is a generous, fruity red, smooth and firm, in keeping with the style of the DOC. The Lagarino di Dionisio 2014 is a sturdy, fruity Bordeaux blend, while the Aglianico Il Lucano 2013 is a sound wine.

● Il Lagarino di Dioniso '14	▼▼ 4
● Il Lucano '13	▼▼ 4
● Matera Moro I Sassi '14	▼▼ 3
○ Greco San Basile '15	▼ 2
⊙ Primitivo Rosato Maddalena '15	▼ 2
● Aglianico del Vulture Loukania '12	♀♀ 4
● Aglianico del Vulture Loukania '10	♀♀ 4
○ Dry Muscat	♀♀ 2*
● Matera Moro I Sassi '13	♀♀ 3
● Matera Moro I Sassi '12	♀♀ 3
○ Matera San Basile '12	♀♀ 3
● Primitivo '12	♀♀ 3*
● Syrah '13	♀♀ 3
● Syrah '12	♀♀ 3

Terra dei Re

VIA MONTICCHIO KM 2,700
85028 RIONERO IN VULTURE [PZ]
TEL. +39 0972725116
www.terradeire.com

CELLAR SALES
PRE-BOOKED VISITS
ACCOMMODATION AND RESTAURANT SERVICE
ANNUAL PRODUCTION 70,000 bottles
HECTARES UNDER VINE 31.00
SUSTAINABLE WINERY

Terra dei Re was established a few years ago but inherited the Leone family's longstanding winegrowing tradition, now in partnership with the Rabasco family. The estate has a very modern, partly underground cellar, and 31 hectares of vines, on average more than 40 years old. These are in and around Barile, Rapolla, Melfi, and Rionero in Vulture in wine country for Aglianico del Vulture production: Piano di Carro, Colignelli, Calata delle Brecce and Querce di Annibale. Paride Leone is an enthusiastic experimenter, as demonstrated by the pinot nero vineyard he planted at 800 metres on Mount Vulture. From an area that has always grown aglianico, this year's outstanding wine is a Pinot Nero, Vulcano 800 2015. At such high altitudes this grape expresses graceful, varietal notes of red berries on the nose, moving on into Mediterranean herbs and a subtle hint of new oak. A stylish, fresh, invigorating palate foretells certain development over time. The two 2013 Aglianicos, Vultur and Nocte, are both of a good standard.

● Vulcano 800 '15	▼▼ 4
● Aglianico del Vulture Nocte '13	▼▼ 4
● Aglianico del Vulture Vultur '13	▼▼ 2*
○ Claris Bianco '15	▼ 2
● Claris Rosso '13	▼ 2
● Aglianico del Vulture Divinus '05	♀♀ 4
● Aglianico del Vulture Divinus '04	♀♀ 4
● Aglianico del Vulture Divinus '03	♀♀ 4
● Aglianico del Vulture Divinus '01	♀♀ 4
● Aglianico del Vulture Nocte '10	♀♀ 4
● Aglianico del Vulture Nocte '04	♀♀ 5
● Aglianico del Vulture Vultur '06	♀♀ 2*
● Aglianico del Vulture Vultur '01	♀♀ 2
● Pacus '06	♀♀ 3*
● Pacus '05	♀♀ 3*

Cantina di Venosa

LOC. VIGNALI
VIA APPIA
85029 VENOSA [PZ]
TEL. +39 097236702
www.cantinadivenosa.it

CELLAR SALES
PRE-BOOKED VISITS
ANNUAL PRODUCTION 800,000 bottles
HECTARES UNDER VINE 800.00
SUSTAINABLE WINERY

This is one of the most famous cooperative wineries in the south of Italy. Located in Venosa, it has 400 members and 800 hectares of vineyards in the municipalities of Venosa, Ripacandida, Ginestra and Maschito. Selection of the best aglianico grapes and attention to cellar techniques guarantee remarkable results for the production of excellent red wines like Carato Venusio, the winery's most typical product. However, all the wines, including the whites, are of a really high standard. Carato Venusio is this leading cooperative's flagship wine, and the 2012 vintage proves very polished and well-structured once again. This is one of the best Aglianico del Vultures tasted this year, thanks to complex aromas of ripe red and black berries, tempered by hints of Mediterranean scrubland and stylish hints of new oak. The palate is full-bodied and firm with generous hints of cherries, damsons and ripe blackberries, elegant tannins and a long, fruity finish. Although it falls just missed our highest accolade, the gap is closing.

● Aglianico del Vulture Carato Venusio '12	▼▼ 6
● Aglianico del Vulture Balì '13	▼▼ 2*
○ Terre di Orazio Dry Muscat '15	▼▼ 2*
● Aglianico del Vulture Balì'Aggio '13	▼ 2
⊙ Terre di Orazio Rosé '15	▼ 3
● Aglianico del Vulture Carato Venusio '11	♀♀ 6
● Aglianico del Vulture Gesualdo da Venosa '11	♀♀ 5
● Aglianico del Vulture Terre di Orazio '13	♀♀ 4
● Aglianico del Vulture Terre di Orazio '12	♀♀ 3*
● Aglianico del Vulture Vignali '13	♀♀ 2*
● Aglianico del Vulture Vignali '12	♀♀ 2*
○ D'Avalos di Gesualdo '12	♀♀ 3
○ Dry Muscat Terre di Orazio '13	♀♀ 2*
○ Dry Muscat Terre di Orazio '12	♀♀ 2*

Alovini

s.da prov.le 123 bis km 7,350
85013 Genzano di Lucania [PZ]
Tel. +39 0971776372
www.alovini.it

CELLAR SALES
PRE-BOOKED VISITS
ANNUAL PRODUCTION 170,000 bottles
HECTARES UNDER VINE 18.00

● Aglianico del Vulture Alvolo '12	♛♛	4
● Aglianico del Vulture Armand '12	♛♛	3
● Cabànico '12	♛	3
○ Greco Le Ralle '15	♛	2

Bisceglia

c.da Finocchiaro
85024 Lavello [PZ]
Tel. +39 0972877033
www.vinibisceglia.it

CELLAR SALES
PRE-BOOKED VISITS
RESTAURANT SERVICE
ANNUAL PRODUCTION 250,000 bottles
HECTARES UNDER VINE 45.00

● Aglianico del Vulture Gudarrà Ris. '08	♛♛	5
● Aglianico del Vulture Terra di Vulcano '14	♛♛	2*
○ Bosco delle Rose Chardonnay '15	♛	4
⊙ Bosco delle Rose Merlot Rosato '15	♛	3

Carbone

via Nitti, 48
85025 Melfi [PZ]
Tel. +39 3482338900
www.carbonevini.it

CELLAR SALES
PRE-BOOKED VISITS
ANNUAL PRODUCTION 30,000 bottles
HECTARES UNDER VINE 18.00
VITICULTURE METHOD Certified Organic

● Aglianico del Vulture Stupor Mundi '13	♛♛	5

Cantine Cerrolongo

c.da Cerrolongo, 1
75020 Nova Siri [MT]
Tel. +39 0835536174
www.cerrolongo.it

CELLAR SALES
PRE-BOOKED VISITS
ANNUAL PRODUCTION 25,000 bottles
HECTARES UNDER VINE 25.00
SUSTAINABLE WINERY

● Matera Primitivo Akratos '14	♛♛	2*
○ Matera Greco Le Paglie '15	♛	2
⊙ Matera Rosato Akratos '15	♛	2

Cifarelli

c.da San Vito
75010 Montescaglioso [MT]
Tel. +39 0835208436
www.cantinecifarelli.it

CELLAR SALES
PRE-BOOKED VISITS
ANNUAL PRODUCTION 25,000 bottles
HECTARES UNDER VINE 30.00

● La Regola '11	♛	4
● Matera Primitivo di San Vito '11	♛	3
● Rosso di San Vito '11	♛	2

Consorzio Viticoltori Associati del Vulture

s.s. 93
85022 Barile [PZ]
Tel. +39 0972770386
www.coviv.it

CELLAR SALES
PRE-BOOKED VISITS
ANNUAL PRODUCTION 130,000 bottles
HECTARES UNDER VINE 100.00

● Aglianico del Vulture Vetusto '09	♛♛	7
● Aglianico del Vulture '11	♛	3

Donato D'Angelo di Filomena Ruppi

VIA PADRE PIO, 10
85028 RIONERO IN VULTURE [PZ]
TEL. +39 0972724602
www.agrida.it

CELLAR SALES
PRE-BOOKED VISITS
ANNUAL PRODUCTION 80,000 bottles
HECTARES UNDER VINE 20.00

● Aglianico del Vulture
   Donato D'Angelo '13   ♟♟ 3*

Cantine Di Palma Strapellum

C.DA SCAVONE
85028 RIONERO IN VULTURE [PZ]
TEL. +39 3286629077
www.cantinedipalmasrl.com

CELLAR SALES
PRE-BOOKED VISITS
ANNUAL PRODUCTION 200,000 bottles
HECTARES UNDER VINE 27.70

● Aglianico del Vulture Il Nibbio Grigio '11   ♟♟ 4
⊙ Strapellum Kline Rosato '15   ♟ 1*
⊙ Strapellum Kline Rosato Vivace '15   ♟ 2

Eleano

FRAZ. PIAN DELL'ALTARE
S.DA PROV.LE 8
85028 RIPACANDIDA [PZ]
TEL. +39 0972722273
www.eleano.it

CELLAR SALES
PRE-BOOKED VISITS
ACCOMMODATION
ANNUAL PRODUCTION 53,000 bottles
HECTARES UNDER VINE 7.50

● Aglianico del Vulture Eleano '13   ♟♟ 5
● Aglianico del Vulture Dioniso '13   ♟♟ 3
⊙ Ambra Moscato V.T. '13   ♟♟ 4

Michele Laluce

VIA ROMA, 21
85020 GINESTRA [PZ]
TEL. +39 0972646145
www.vinilaluce.com

CELLAR SALES
PRE-BOOKED VISITS
ANNUAL PRODUCTION 40,000 bottles
HECTARES UNDER VINE 7.00
SUSTAINABLE WINERY

● Aglianico del Vulture Zimberno '12   ♟♟ 3
○ Morbino Bianco '15   ♟ 3

Tenuta Marino

C.DA PIANO DELLE ROSE
85035 NOEPOLI [PZ]
TEL. +39 0835815978
www.tenutamarino.it

CELLAR SALES
PRE-BOOKED VISITS
ANNUAL PRODUCTION 120,000 bottles
HECTARES UNDER VINE 26.00
VITICULTURE METHOD Certified Organic

● Terra Aspra '15   ♟♟ 3
● Matera Primitivo '09   ♟ 2

Vigne Mastrodomenico

VIA NAZIONALE PER RAPOLLA, 87
85022 BARILE [PZ]
TEL. +39 0972770108
www.vignemastrodomenico.com

CELLAR SALES
PRE-BOOKED VISITS
ANNUAL PRODUCTION 25,000 bottles
HECTARES UNDER VINE 8.00
VITICULTURE METHOD Certified Organic
SUSTAINABLE WINERY

● Aglianico del Vulture Likos '13   ♟♟ 3*

Musto Carmelitano

VIA PIETRO NENNI, 23
85020 MASCHITO [PZ]
TEL. +39 097233312
www.mustocarmelitano.it

CELLAR SALES
PRE-BOOKED VISITS
ACCOMMODATION AND RESTAURANT SERVICE
ANNUAL PRODUCTION 20,000 bottles
HECTARES UNDER VINE 14.00
VITICULTURE METHOD Certified Organic

● Aglianico del Vulture Maschitano Rosso '14	♟♟ 3
● Aglianico del Vulture Serra del Prete '13	♟♟ 4
⊙ Maschitano Rosato '15	♟ 3

Tenuta Parco dei Monaci

C.DA PARCO DEI MONACI
75100 MATERA
TEL. +39 0835259546
www.tenutaparcodeimonaci.it

PRE-BOOKED VISITS
ACCOMMODATION
ANNUAL PRODUCTION 20,000 bottles
HECTARES UNDER VINE 5.00

● Matera Moro Spaccasassi '13	♟♟ 6
● Matera Primitivo Monacello '14	♟♟ 5

Francesco Radino

VIA RIONE VETERA, 84
75100 MATERA
TEL. +39 3385882673
www.radino.it

CELLAR SALES
PRE-BOOKED VISITS
ANNUAL PRODUCTION 15,000 bottles
HECTARES UNDER VINE 4.00
VITICULTURE METHOD Certified Organic

● Aglianico del Vulture Colignelli '13	♟♟ 4
● Aglianico del Vulture Arcidiaconata '13	♟♟ 4
● Aglianico del Vulture Kataos '12	♟ 4

San Martino

C.DA SAN MARTINO
85023 FORENZA [PZ]
TEL. +39 097231002
lorenzo.sanmartino@email.it

CELLAR SALES
PRE-BOOKED VISITS
ANNUAL PRODUCTION 25,000 bottles
HECTARES UNDER VINE 4.00
VITICULTURE METHOD Certified Organic

● Aglianico del Volture Arberesko '14	♟♟ 4
● Aglianico del Volture Siir '14	♟♟ 3

I Talenti - Padri Trinitari

P.ZZA DON BOSCO, 3
85029 VENOSA [PZ]
TEL. +39 097234221
www.trinitarivenosa.it

CELLAR SALES
PRE-BOOKED VISITS
ANNUAL PRODUCTION 6,000 bottles
HECTARES UNDER VINE 5.00

○ Greco Muse '15	♟♟ 3
● Matera Moro Teorema '13	♟♟ 3

Vigneti del Vulture

C.DA PIPOLI
85011 ACERENZA [PZ]
TEL. +39 0971749363
www.vignetidelvulture.it

PRE-BOOKED VISITS
ANNUAL PRODUCTION 100,000 bottles
HECTARES UNDER VINE 56.00

● Aglianico del Vulture Pipoli Zero '14	♟♟ 2*
● Aglianico del Vulture Pipoli '13	♟♟ 2*
○ Pipoli Greco Fiano '15	♟ 2
⊙ Pipoli Rosato '15	♟ 2

PUGLIA

Puglia is such a large, complex region that it is difficult to read it as a single production area, but this year we feel it is important to concentrate more on the weather than on geographic variables. Over the last few years we have been able to state that the quality level is rising constantly in the region's wine industry, both with regard to flagships and to workaday products. This year, however, despite the best of intentions, wineries have had to throw in the towel because of climate trends during the last two seasons. For completely contrasting reasons these two years were particularly difficult and created a sort of "perfect storm" during our tastings. In actual fact, most of the young red wines we tasted this year were 2014s, and more or less anywhere in Puglia that meant low temperatures, rain and even hail. The result was almost inevitable, with wines that in most cases showed green notes, fragility and a rather uncharacteristic lack of structure for this region's products. There were very few exceptions considering that of the 36 wines to reach our finals, only a quarter were from the 2014 vintage. Almost all the white wines we tasted were from 2015 which, conversely, was a very hot summer, which impacted freshness and acidity virtually everywhere. These two aspects are already a habitual sore point for Puglia's whites, with the result that a series of wines may be fruit-rich, but not particularly pleasing, or are dragged down in the finale. The same goes for the rosés. None of this prevented us noting that quality continues to grow in wines from primitivo, particularly those from the Gioia del Colle or Manduria designations. In this respect, it must be said that the pure myth of primitivo-based wines that do not improve with time is being dispelled. Indeed, one of this year's Tre Bicchieri new entries is Coppi's 2010Il Senatore, a Gioia del Colle Primitivo. More Tre Bicchieri news includes other Primitivos, one from the same area, the 2013 Gioia del Colle Riserva by Tre Pini, and the other from Manduria, Paolo Leo's Primitivo di Manduria Passo del Cardinale 2014. For the rest, venerable wineries like Leone de Castris, Torrevento, Felline continue to confirm their expertise but are now being joined by cellars offering surefire quality with their wines, like Due Palme, Rubino, Polvanera, and Chiaromonte, whose 2014 Gioia del Colle Primitivo Muro Sant'Angelo Contrada Barbatto was our Red of the Year. We will also be keeping an eye on the up-and-coming wineries of passionate winegrowers like Vespa or Carvinea.

Cantina Albea

VIA DUE MACELLI, 8
70011 ALBEROBELLO [BA]
TEL. +39 0804323548
www.albeavini.com

CELLAR SALES
PRE-BOOKED VISITS
ANNUAL PRODUCTION 380,000 bottles
HECTARES UNDER VINE 40.00

Albea was founded in the early 20th
century, making it one of the oldest
wineries in the Alberobello area. The cellars
are entirely in stone, with vats for the wine
set in the rock, just like the rainwater tanks
for the trulli. There is also a wine museum.
The modern-style wines are produced
mainly from local varieties, especially nero
di Troia, primitivo, negroamaro,
susumaniello, verdeca and bianco
d'Alessano. The Primitivo Petranera 2014
displays intense aromas, with black berry
fruit to the fore, nuanced with spice and
chocolate, and a fruity, fresh-tasting,
pleasant palate. The Lui 2014 Nero di Troia
has a notch less brilliance, but is
well-made, with a nose of fresh red berries,
liquorice and caper, despite a stemmy,
clenched, over-oaked palate still rather
lacking some expression. The range also
offers a Negroamaro Raro 2014 and a
Locorotondo Il Selva 2015.

Cantele

S.DA PROV.LE SALICE SALENTINO-SAN DONACI KM 35,600
73010 GUAGNANO [LE]
TEL. +39 0832705010
www.cantele.it

CELLAR SALES
PRE-BOOKED VISITS
ANNUAL PRODUCTION 16,000,000 bottles
HECTARES UNDER VINE 200.00

Cousins Gianni, Paolo, Umberto, and Luisa
combine passion and expertise in their
running of Cantele, the family business
founded in 1979. Over the years it has
established itself as one of Puglia's most
interesting operations, with 50 hectares of
its own and a further 150 leased. The
winery grows local and international
varieties for quite a broad range of labels,
producing technically flawless, modern-
style wines that blend varietal stamping
with drinkability, and quantity with quality.
Cantele presented a fine array of wines.
First off was the Amativo 2014 blend of
60% primitivo and 40% negroamaro, a
fresh-tasting, nicely supple wine. The Fiano
Alticelli 2015 displays a good full body, with
appley scents, and shades of citrus and
aromatic herbs. The fruity Teresa Manara
Negroamaro 2014 has smoky and wood
resin notes; the Rohesia 2015 negroamaro
rosé is fresh and tangy; the Salice
Salentino Rosso Riserva 2013 is
well-defined but somewhat predictable.

● Lui '14	♟♟ 5
● Petranera '14	♟♟ 3
○ Locorotondo Il Selva '15	♟ 2
● Raro '14	♟ 3
● Lui '06	♟♟♟ 5
● Lui '05	♟♟♟ 5
● Lui '13	♟♟ 5
● Lui '12	♟♟ 5
● Lui '11	♟♟ 5
● Lui '10	♟♟ 5
● Petranera '13	♟♟ 3
● Raro '13	♟♟ 3
● Riservato '10	♟♟ 3*

● Amativo '14	♟♟ 4
○ Alticelli Fiano '15	♟♟ 2*
⊙ Rohesia '15	♟♟ 3
● Salice Salentino Rosso Ris. '13	♟♟ 2*
● Teresa Manara Negroamaro '14	♟♟ 3
⊙ Negroamaro Rosato '15	♟ 2
○ Teresa Manara Chardonnay '15	♟ 3
● Amativo '07	♟♟♟ 4*
● Amativo '03	♟♟♟ 3*
● Salice Salentino Rosso Ris. '09	♟♟♟ 2*
● Amativo '13	♟♟ 4
● Amativo '12	♟♟ 4
⊙ Negroamaro Rosato '14	♟♟ 2*
● Primitivo '13	♟♟ 2*
● Salice Salentino Rosso Ris. '12	♟♟ 2*

Cantine San Marzano

VIA REGINA MARGHERITA, 149
74020 SAN MARZANO DI SAN GIUSEPPE [TA]
TEL. +39 0999574181
www.cantinesanmarzano.com

PRE-BOOKED VISITS
ANNUAL PRODUCTION 8,500,000 bottles
HECTARES UNDER VINE 1,500.00
SUSTAINABLE WINERY

Founded by just 19 members back in 1962, numbers at this cooperative winery have now risen to around 1,200 vignerons, tending a total of 1,500 hectares under vine. Most of the vineyards are located around San Marzano, Sava and Francavilla Fontana, mainly on limestone soils dominated by terra rossa. They grow a wide range of varietals, from international grape types to traditional Salento cultivars, especially negroamaro and primitivo, with a number of bush-trained heirloom vines. As always, the Primitivo di Manduria Sessantanni is a compelling wine. The 2013 has overtones of black berry fruit and incense, and a long, fruity palate, showing distinctly sweet notes. In contrast, the supple Talò Malvasia Nera 2015 has good, rich flavour. Also of note is the Primitivo di Manduria 62 Anniversario Riserva 2013, with its shades of spice and Mediterranean scrub, and the fruit-rich F Negroamaro 2013 with more than a touch of sweetness.

Carvinea

LOC. PEZZA D'ARENA
VIA PER SERRANOVA
72012 CAROVIGNO [BR]
TEL. +39 0805862345
www.carvinea.com

CELLAR SALES
PRE-BOOKED VISITS
ACCOMMODATION AND RESTAURANT SERVICE
ANNUAL PRODUCTION 35,000 bottles
HECTARES UNDER VINE 12.00
VITICULTURE METHOD Certified Organic

Beppe di Maria's winery lies just a stone's throw from the famous Torre Guaceto nature reserve, in a 16th-century farmhouse known as Pezza d'Arena. The vineyards surrounding the winery are mainly planted with black varieties, including Montepulciano, aglianico, petit verdot, primitivo, negroamaro, and ottavianello, along with white fiano. Beppe produces a range of 11 wines, all by the book, and remarkably consistent in terms of quality. After concentrating mainly on non-native varietals, Beppe di Maria's new goal is to maximize the potential of native grapes, as we see in the TLC afforded to ottavianello. The spicy Otto 2014, a monovarietal ottavianello, shows aromas of garden vegetables, pleasing notes of black berry fruit and a lingering finish. Despite the difficult vintage, the Negroamaro 2014 and Primitivo 2014 are well-crafted and fruit-heavy with a savoury veneer.

● Malvasia Nera Talò '15	♀♀ 3*
● Primitivo di Manduria Sessantanni '13	♀♀ 5
● Collezione Cinquanta +1	♀♀ 5
● Negroamaro F '13	♀♀ 5
● Negroamaro Talò '15	♀♀ 3
● Primitivo di Manduria Anniversario 62 Ris. '13	♀♀ 5
● Primitivo di Manduria Talò '14	♀♀ 3
● Il Pumo Negroamaro '15	♀ 2
● Il Pumo Primitivo '15	♀ 2
● Primitivo di Manduria Talò '13	♀♀♀ 3*
● Collezione Cinquanta	♀♀ 5
● Il Pumo Primitivo '14	♀♀ 2*
● Primitivo di Manduria Anniversario 62 Ris. '12	♀♀ 5
● Salice Salentino Rosso Talò '12	♀♀ 3

● Negroamaro '14	♀♀♀ 5
● Otto '14	♀♀ 4
● Primitivo '14	♀♀ 5
⊙ Brut Rosé M. Cl. '11	♀ 5
○ Lucerna '15	♀ 2
⊙ Merula Rosa '15	♀ 2
● Frauma '08	♀♀♀ 4
● Merula '11	♀♀♀ 3*
● Negroamaro '13	♀♀♀ 5
● Negroamaro '11	♀♀♀ 3*
● Sierma '09	♀♀♀ 5
● Frauma '11	♀♀ 5
● Primitivo '13	♀♀ 5
● Sierma '12	♀♀ 5
● Sierma '11	♀♀ 5

Castello Monaci

VIA CASE SPARSE
73015 SALICE SALENTINO [LE]
TEL. +39 0831665700
www.castellomonaci.it

CELLAR SALES
PRE-BOOKED VISITS
RESTAURANT SERVICE
ANNUAL PRODUCTION 2,000,000 bottles
HECTARES UNDER VINE 150.00

Castello Monaci is an estate owned by the Gruppo Italiano Vini. The castle, settled by French monks in the early 16th century, and the wine cellar are surrounded by approximately 3,000 olive trees and 150 hectares under vine. The clayey topsoil is a metre or so in depth, with a thick underlying layer of tufa, which provides a water source during very dry spells, and is mainly planted to grape varieties native to Salento. The Salice Salentino Rosso Aiace Riserva 2013 is one of the best in the DOC zone. Its nose of black berry fruit and spices ushers in a very layered palate, sustained by a perky acidity which endows it with just the right freshness. Also well-crafted the pleasant, supple Negroamaro Maru 2015, with its hints of fresh dark berry fruit, and the Petraluce 2015, a monovarietal Verdeca, with aromas of yellow-fleshed fruit and garden vegetables, and a textured palate with good mouthfeel.

● Salice Salentino Aiace Ris. '13	♟♟♟ 3*
● Maru '15	♟♟ 2*
○ Petraluce '15	♟♟ 2*
○ Acante '15	♟ 2
○ Charà '15	♟ 3
● Pilùna '15	♟ 2
● Salice Salentino Rosso Liante '15	♟ 2
● Artas '07	♟♟♟ 4
● Artas '06	♟♟♟ 4
● Artas '05	♟♟♟ 4*
● Artas '04	♟♟♟ 3*
● Artas '13	♟♟ 5
● Maru '14	♟♟ 2*
● Pilùna '14	♟♟ 2*

Chiaromonte

VICO MURO SANT'ANGELO, 6
70021 ACQUAVIVA DELLE FONTI [BA]
TEL. +39 0803050432
www.tenutechiaromonte.com

CELLAR SALES
PRE-BOOKED VISITS
ANNUAL PRODUCTION 100,000 bottles
HECTARES UNDER VINE 27.00
VITICULTURE METHOD Certified Organic

The history of Tenute Chiaromonte dates back to 1826, but it was not until Nicola took over the family business in 1998 that this winery truly began to take off, gradually working its way up to the pinnacle of regional winemaking. Most of the estate vineyards are bush-trained, with vines ranging from 60 to over 100 years old, at an elevation of over 300 metres, on very mineral-rich limestone subsoils with thin topsoils of terra rossa and clay. The Gioia del Colle Primitivo Muro Sant'Angelo Contrada Barbatto 2013, Tre Bicchieri and Red Wine of the Year, remains a benchmark for anyone wishing to produce a Primitivo that is not just close-woven and fruity, but also elegant and drinkable. Here the nose notes of black berry fruit with spicy nuances usher in a palate whose sturdy alcohol is balanced by fresh acidity and rich flavour. The Riserva 2011 is more complex, but slightly less gutsy and spirited. Elè 2014 is pleasing and fruity.

● Gioia del Colle Primitivo Muro Sant'Angelo Contrada Barbatto '13	♟♟♟ 5
● Gioia del Colle Primitivo Ris. '11	♟♟ 8
● Elè '14	♟♟ 3
○ Kimìa '15	♟ 3
○ Kimìa Moscato '15	♟ 3
○ Kimìa Rosato '15	♟ 3
⊙ Gioia del Colle Primitivo Muro Sant'Angelo Contrada Barbatto '12	♟♟♟ 5
● Gioia del Colle Primitivo Muro Sant'Angelo Contrada Barbatto '11	♟♟♟ 5
● Gioia del Colle Primitivo Muro Sant'Angelo Contrada Barbatto '10	♟♟♟ 7
● Gioia del Colle Primitivo Muro Sant'Angelo Contrada Barbatto '09	♟♟♟ 5

Coppi

S.DA PROV.LE TURI - GIOIA DEL COLLE
70010 TURI [BA]
TEL. +39 0808915049
www.vinicoppi.it

CELLAR SALES
PRE-BOOKED VISITS
ANNUAL PRODUCTION 1,000,000 bottles
HECTARES UNDER VINE 100.00

The Coppi family estate was founded in 1976, when Antonio took over the 1882 wine cellar where he had been employed for around a decade. At the helm today are his children Lisia, Miriam and Doni, focusing on improving the quality of the estate's wines. On their 100 hectares under vine, half of which are bush-trained, they grow traditional varieties such as primitivo, negroamaro, malvasia nera, malvasia bianca and falanghina. Not long ago this estate's wines were cause for concern, and despite last year's considerable improvement, we hardly expected to award it a Tre Bicchieri so soon. The Gioia del Colle Primitivo Senatore 2010 thoroughly deserves the award for its intense, layered nose with nuances of forest fruits, leaf tobacco and chocolate; a palate of admirable structure is underpinned by fresh acidity and comes to a long, caressing finish. Other well-made wines include the Primitivo Don Antonio 2013, with its nose of Mediterranean scrub, and the freshly succulent Siniscalco 2014.

● Gioia del Colle Primitivo Senatore '10	▼▼▼ 3*
● Primitivo Don Antonio '13	▼▼ 3
● Primitivo Siniscalco '14	▼▼ 3
☉ Coré '15	▼ 3
● Gioia del Colle Primitivo Vanitoso Ris. '09	▼ 5
● Negroamaro Pellirosso '15	▼ 3
● Gioia del Colle Primitivo Senatore '08	▼▼ 3
● Gioia del Colle Primitivo Siniscalco '06	▼▼ 2*
○ Malvasia Bianca '08	▼▼ 1*
● Negroamaro Pellirosso '12	▼▼ 2*
● Primitivo '08	▼▼ 1*

★Cantine Due Palme

VIA SAN MARCO, 130
72020 CELLINO SAN MARCO [BR]
TEL. +39 0831617865
www.cantineduepalme.it

CELLAR SALES
PRE-BOOKED VISITS
ACCOMMODATION AND RESTAURANT SERVICE
ANNUAL PRODUCTION 10,000,000 bottles
HECTARES UNDER VINE 2,500.00
VITICULTURE METHOD Certified Organic
SUSTAINABLE WINERY

Launched in 1989 by Angelo Maci, Cantine Due Palme is a cooperative at the heart of Salento. In the meantime it has grown into one of Puglia's major wine producers with 1,000 members tending about 2,500 hectares under vine. Located in a triangle of land spanning the provinces of Brindisi, Taranto and Lecce, in all the outfit produces 25 different labels of modern, textbook wines that are fruit-rich and highly concentrated. The Salice Salentino Rosso Selvarossa Riserva is again among the best of its type, with the 2013 clocking up the tenth Tre Bicchieri in a row. The bouquet shows hints of leaf tobacco, black berry fruit and oriental spices, while the close-knit palate is fruity and textured, with a lengthy finish. Also appealing, the 1943 del Presidente 2013 lip-smacking, fruit-forward blend of primitivo and aglianico, still a tad heavy on the oak, and the fresh, well-balanced Susumaniello Serre 2015.

● Salice Salentino Rosso Selvarossa Ris. '13	▼▼▼ 4*
● 1943 del Presidente '13	▼▼ 6
● Serre '15	▼▼ 3
○ Anthea '15	▼ 2
○ Corerosa '15	▼ 3
○ Due Palme Brut M. Cl. '13	▼ 4
● Primitivo di Manduria Ettamiano Ris. '13	▼ 3
● Primitivo di Manduria San Gaetano '15	▼ 2
● Salice Salentino Rosso Selvarossa Ris. '12	▼▼▼ 4*
● Salice Salentino Rosso Selvarossa Ris. '11	▼▼▼ 4*
● Salice Salentino Rosso Selvarossa Ris. '10	▼▼▼ 4*

Tenute Eméra
di Claudio Quarta Vignaiolo

C.DA PORVICA
74123 LIZZANO [TA]
TEL. +39 0832704398
www.claudioquarta.it

CELLAR SALES
PRE-BOOKED VISITS
ACCOMMODATION
ANNUAL PRODUCTION 550,000 bottles
HECTARES UNDER VINE 50.00
SUSTAINABLE WINERY

Tenute Eméra is part of the Gruppo Magistravini, run by Claudio Quarta, along with his daughter Alessandra. Its vineyards include both native and international varietals, located mainly in a single area overlooking the Ionian coast, on permeable calcareous tufa soils, enhanced by a layer of debris and marl. In the last five years, the winery has also added a hectare in Guagnano, planted to negroamaro and malvasia nera, from which it makes Salice Salentino. Eméra's products gave a good overall performance, especially in the light of the taxing 2014 vintage. Alongside the Salice Salentino Rosso Moros Riserva 2013, with its spicy hints of leaf tobacco, and palate of black berry fruit, we enjoyed the pleasingly fresh, juicy Lizzano Superiore 2014, the Primitivo di Manduria Oro di Eméra 2014, with its fuller texture, and the Sud del Sud 2014, a close-knit Negroamaro with fruity and aromatic herb notes.

Felline

VIA SANTO STASI PRIMO, 42B
74024 MANDURIA [TA]
TEL. +39 0999711660
www.agricolafelline.it

CELLAR SALES
PRE-BOOKED VISITS
ANNUAL PRODUCTION 1,000,000 bottles
HECTARES UNDER VINE 120.00
VITICULTURE METHOD Certified Organic
SUSTAINABLE WINERY

Since 1994, Gregory Perrucci has been one of the leading lights in the renaissance of Salento winegrowing traditions, based around restoring and preserving native varieties and the area's bush-trained vines, as well as on producing modern, fruit-rich wines of great precision and aromatic focus. In the absence of his more ambitious labels, which Gregory chose not to produce in 2014, his Primitivo di Manduria 2015 took home a Tre Bicchieri, offering the finest expression of the qualities we expect from a vintage Primitivo di Manduria. The fruit-laden overtones show hints of violet, with an engaging, dynamic, focused palate and long finish. In short, a truly mouthwatering wine. Spicy with plenty of stuffing, though rather lacking in grip, the Primitivo di Manduria Cuvée Anniversario Riserva 2010, while the pleasing Alberello 2015, an equal blend of negroamaro and primitivo, is eminently drinkable.

● Lizzano Negroamaro Sup. '14	ΨΨ 2*
● Primitivo di Manduria Oro di Eméra '14	ΨΨ 5
● Salice Salentino Rosso Moros Ris. '13	ΨΨ 4
● Sud del Sud '14	ΨΨ 3
○ Amure '15	Ψ 2
○ Anima di Chardonnay '15	Ψ 2
● Primitivo di Manduria Anima di Primitivo '14	Ψ 3
⊙ Rose '15	Ψ 2
● Lizzano Negroamaro Sup. Anima di Negroamaro '13	ΨΨ 2*
● Lizzano Negroamaro Sup. Anima di Negroamaro '12	ΨΨ 2*
● Primitivo di Manduria Anima di Primitivo '12	ΨΨ 2*
● Salice Salentino Rosso '11	ΨΨ 2*
● Salice Salentino Rosso Moros Ris. '12	ΨΨ 4

● Primitivo di Manduria '15	ΨΨΨ 3*
● Primitivo di Manduria Cuvée Anniversario Ris. '10	ΨΨ 3*
● Alberello '15	ΨΨ 2*
● Nero di Troia '15	ΨΨ 2*
● Pietraluna Torre Guaceto '15	ΨΨ 2*
● Sum Torre Guaceto '15	ΨΨ 4
○ Verdeca '15	ΨΨ 2*
● Anarkos '15	Ψ 2
⊙ Cicala Rosé '15	Ψ 2
● Primitivo di Manduria Segnavento '15	Ψ 2
● Vigna del Feudo '97	ΨΨΨ 4*
● Alberello '11	ΨΨ 2*
● Primitivo di Manduria Archidamo '12	ΨΨ 2*
● Vigna del Feudo '09	ΨΨ 4

Gianfranco Fino

VIA PIAVE, 12
74028 SAVA [TA]
TEL. +39 0997773970
www.gianfrancofino.it

PRE-BOOKED VISITS
ANNUAL PRODUCTION 20,000 bottles
HECTARES UNDER VINE 20.00
SUSTAINABLE WINERY

Gianfranco and Simona Fino founded their winery in 2004, purchasing a vineyard of under 1.5 hectares in the Manduria area for production from venerable primitivo vines. Today there are 12 plots of head-trained vines, all between Manduria and Sava, on terra rossa and limestone, some of which have reached the ripe old age of 90. With time, the Primitivo di Manduria Es was gradually joined by another three labels: Jo, from the winery's one-hectare negroamaro vineyard, a sweet wine, and a Champagne-method sparkler. Once again, the only label presented for the tastings was the Primitivo di Manduria Es 2014. The nose is dominated by jammy hints of black berry fruit and dried fig while the palate, despite a good richness of flavour, is less stunning and firmly structured than in previous years. An Es deserving of praise for its authenticity and its expression of such a difficult vintage.

Vito Donato Giuliani

VIA GIOIA CANALE, 18
070010 TURI [BA]
TEL. +39 0808915335
www.vitivinicolagiuliani.com

ANNUAL PRODUCTION 100,000 bottles
HECTARES UNDER VINE 40.00

This year, the winery continues to perform well, earning itself another full-length profile. Founded in 1940, the Giuliani family estate has around 40 hectares under vine in the Murgia Barese, between Turi and Gioia del Colle, in a particularly fine primitivo-growing area. Indeed, primitivo is the most popular vine on the area's typical karst soils, made up of a thin terra rossa topsoil over a complex, mineral-rich, stony subsoil. Once again, the Giuliani estate's Gioia del Colle Primitivos are among the best around. The complex Gioia del Colle Primitivo Baronaggio Riserva 2013, a nose hinting at red berries and flint, with a mineral notes on the palate, has significant depth but is also fresh and gutsy. By contrast, the Gioia del Colle Primitivo Lavarossa 2013 shows spicy, earthy notes, is rich in fruit but less complex, with a full-flavoured finish lending support and length.

● Primitivo di Manduria Es '14	♟♟ 7
● Primitivo di Manduria Es '12	♟♟♟ 7
● Primitivo di Manduria Es '11	♟♟♟ 7
● Primitivo di Manduria Es '10	♟♟♟ 6
● Primitivo di Manduria Es '09	♟♟♟ 6
● Primitivo di Manduria Es '08	♟♟♟ 6
● Primitivo di Manduria Es '07	♟♟♟ 6
● Primitivo di Manduria Es '06	♟♟♟ 5
● Jo '08	♟♟ 6
● Jo '07	♟♟ 6
● Jo '06	♟♟ 5
● Primitivo di Manduria Dolce Naturale Es + Sole '12	♟♟ 7
● Primitivo di Manduria Es '13	♟♟ 7
● Primitivo di Manduria Es '05	♟♟ 5

● Gioia del Colle Baronaggio Ris. '13	♟♟ 5
● Gioia del Colle Primitivo Lavarossa '13	♟♟ 3
● Gioia del Colle Baronaggio Ris. '12	♟♟ 5
● Gioia del Colle Primitivo Lavarossa '12	♟♟ 3*

Cantine Paolo Leo

VIA TUTURANO, 21
72025 SAN DONACI [BR]
TEL. +39 0831635073
www.paololeo.it

CELLAR SALES
PRE-BOOKED VISITS
ACCOMMODATION
ANNUAL PRODUCTION 1,300,000 bottles
HECTARES UNDER VINE 35.00
VITICULTURE METHOD Certified Organic
SUSTAINABLE WINERY

Paolo Leo, the fourth generation of winegrowers here, radically modernized the estate, building a new cellar in 1989 and bottling wines that express the full potential of native Salento varietals of primitivo, negroamaro, malvasia nera and malvasia bianca. The winery's own vineyards lie mainly on limestone and tufa soils around San Dònaci, and are mostly planted to bush-trained vines over 40 years of age. Paolo Leo takes a Tre Bicchieri for his Primitivo di Manduria Passo del Cardinale 2014, with nose notes of Peruvian bark, plum and leaf tobacco nuanced with black olive tapenade, while the palate is austere, dense and close-knit. The Primitivo Fiore di Vigna 2014 is well-crafted, with floral nuances and hints of black berry fruit and sweet oak, while the compact palate is fresh, balanced and very pleasant. The Negroamaro Orfeo 2014 is a little subdued, unexciting and dragged down by unripe fruit notes.

● Primitivo di Manduria Passo del Cardinale '14	♟♟♟	3*
● Fiore di Vigna '14	♟♟	5
○ 350 Alture Minutolo '15	♟	3
○ Cala luna '15	♟	3
● Orfeo '14	♟	4
● Fiore di Vigna '13	♟♟	4
● Fiore di Vigna '12	♟♟	4
● Fiore di Vigna '10	♟♟	4
● Negramante '13	♟♟	3
● Orfeo '13	♟♟	4
● Orfeo '11	♟♟	4
● Taccorosso '13	♟♟	3*

★Leone de Castris

VIA SENATORE DE CASTRIS, 26
73015 SALICE SALENTINO [LE]
TEL. +39 0832731112
www.leonedecastris.com

PRE-BOOKED VISITS
ANNUAL PRODUCTION 2,500,000 bottles
HECTARES UNDER VINE 250.00
SUSTAINABLE WINERY

Founded in 1665 by the Conte di Lemos, Leone de Castris began bottling its wines back in 1925. Then, in 1943, it created Five Roses, Italy's first-ever bottled rosé, and in the early 1970s played a key role in the launch of the Salice Salentino designation. Today's winery offers a wide range of labels, from both native and international grapes, grown on various estates in Salice Salentino, Campi and Guagnano, creating wines with a modern, approachable style. The forthright Salice Salentino Rosso 50° Vendemmia 2014 is refreshing with dark, crunchy fruit, while the Salice Salentino Rosso Per Lui Riserva 2014 shows more mature notes, but is still balanced and full-flavoured with nice grip. Also well-crafted are the pleasingly fruity Per Lui Primitivo 2014, the floral Five Roses 72° Anniversario 2015 with its hints of wild strawberry, and the fresh-tasting fruity rosé Aleatico Aleikos, while the Salice Salentino Rosso Riserva 2014 displays good structure for the vintage.

● Salice Salentino Rosso 50° Vendemmia '14	♟♟♟	3*
⊙ Aleikos '15	♟♟	2*
⊙ Five Roses 72° Anniversario '15	♟♟	3
● Per Lui Primitivo '14	♟♟	6
● Salice Salentino Rosso Per Lui Ris. '14	♟♟	6
● Salice Salentino Rosso Ris. '14	♟♟	3
● Elo Veni '15	♟	2
⊙ Five Roses '15	♟	2
● Per Lui Susumaniello '14	♟	6
● Primitivo di Manduria Villa Santera '15	♟	3
⊙ Salice Salentino Brut Five Roses M. Cl. '13	♟	4
● Salice Salentino Rosso Per Lui Ris. '13	♟♟♟	6

Masseria Li Veli

S.DA PROV.LE CELLINO-CAMPI, KM 1
72020 CELLINO SAN MARCO [BR]
TEL. +39 0831618259
www.liveli.it

CELLAR SALES
PRE-BOOKED VISITS
ANNUAL PRODUCTION 350,000 bottles
HECTARES UNDER VINE 33.00
VITICULTURE METHOD Certified Organic

After 40 years in the Tuscan wine world, the Falvo family purchased Masseria Li Veli in 1999, moving to Puglia and renovating the premises. The estate's vineyards are planted mainly with native varieties. The black grapes are mostly grown around Cellino San Marco, with 85% of bush-trained vines planted in the ancient septunx pattern of a regular hexagon with six vertices, plus one vine in the middle. The white fruit comes from the Itria Valley. Good overall performance from this Falvo winery whose Salice Salentino Rosso Pezzo Morgana Riserva 2014 shows hints of black berry fruit and spice, with a well-defined palate and good length. The MLV 2013, a blend of 60% negroamaro and cabernet sauvignon, despite its generous fruit is held back by an injudicious use of wood. The Aleatico Passito 2009, with its notes of dried fig and chocolate, and the fresh, approachable Susumaniello 2015, are both well managed.

● Aleatico Passito '09	▼▼ 6
● MLV '13	▼▼ 5
● Salice Salentino Rosso Pezzo Morgana Ris. '14	▼▼ 4
● Susumaniello Askos '15	▼▼ 3
● Malvasia Nera Askos '15	▼ 3
⊙ Rosato '15	▼ 2
○ Verdeca Askos '15	▼ 3
● Masseria Li Veli '10	♀♀♀ 5
○ Fiano '14	♀♀ 2*
● MLV '12	♀♀ 5
● Susumaniello Askos '14	♀♀ 3

Morella

VIA PER UGGIANO, 147
74024 MANDURIA [TA]
TEL. +39 0999791482
www.morellavini.com

CELLAR SALES
PRE-BOOKED VISITS
ANNUAL PRODUCTION 26,000 bottles
HECTARES UNDER VINE 20.00
VITICULTURE METHOD Certified Biodynamic

Lisa Gilbee and Gaetano Morella's estate has been one of the leading lights in the Manduria area for some years now. Primitivo is undoubtedly king here, alongside negroamaro and fiano. Heirloom head-trained vines on terra rossa, up to a century in age, very low yields per plant, and non-intrusive cellarwork are the keys to understanding their wines. This year's entries left us rather baffled. The top-flight Primitivo Old Vines 2013 and La Signora 2013 both display a fair richness of fruit, with spicy notes of Mediterranean scrubland but considering the quality we have come to expect from this winery, there was a marked deterioration, with little thrust or focus. Though well-typed, both Mezzanotte 2015, a primitivo-led blend, and Fiano Mezzogiorno 2015, lack the lustre of previous vintages.

● Old Vines Primitivo '13	▼▼ 6
● Primitivo La Signora '13	▼▼ 6
● Mezzanotte '15	▼ 3
○ Mezzogiorno '15	▼ 3
● Primitivo La Signora '10	♀♀♀ 6
● Primitivo La Signora '07	♀♀♀ 5
● Primitivo Old Vines '09	♀♀♀ 5
● Primitivo Old Vines '08	♀♀♀ 5
● Primitivo Old Vines '07	♀♀♀ 5
● Negroamaro Primitivo Terre Rosse '12	♀♀ 4
● Primitivo La Signora '11	♀♀ 6
● Primitivo Malbek '11	♀♀ 4
● Primitivo Old Vines '11	♀♀ 6

Palamà

via A. Diaz, 6
73020 Cutrofiano [LE]
Tel. +39 0836542865
www.vinicolapalama.com

CELLAR SALES
PRE-BOOKED VISITS
ACCOMMODATION AND RESTAURANT SERVICE
ANNUAL PRODUCTION 200,000 bottles
HECTARES UNDER VINE 15.00

Now joined by the rest of his family, for the last quarter of a century Cosimo Palamà has been running the estate founded by his father Arcangelo in 1936. Their wines are made solely from native Puglia varietals like negroamaro, primitivo, malvasia nera, aleatico, malvasia bianca, and verdeca, grown around Cutrofiano and Matino, on moderately loose-packed, generally limestone soils. The estate's range is quite broad and offers traditional, textbook wines. The Palamà family's selection may not quite be up to previous versions, but it is still well-made. The outstanding label is the Metiusco Rosato 2015, an easy drinker which remains one of the best of its type, with a flowery, crisp tanginess and a veneer of red berries. The 75 Vendemmie 2015, a Negroamaro from heirloom bush vines, has a good structure, though slightly over-sweet, while the Metiusco Rosso 2015 and Metiusco Bianco 2015 are both pleasant and drinkable.

● 75 Vendemmie '15	🍷🍷 4
⊙ Metiusco Rosato '15	🍷🍷 2*
○ Metiusco Bianco '15	🍷 2
● Metiusco Rosso '15	🍷 2
● 75 Vendemmie '11	🍷🍷🍷 4*
● 75 Vendemmie '13	🍷🍷 4
● Albarossa Primitivo '13	🍷🍷 2*
● Mavro '13	🍷🍷 3*
● Mavro '12	🍷🍷 3*
● Mavro '11	🍷🍷 3
⊙ Metiusco Rosato '13	🍷🍷 2*
● Patrunale '12	🍷🍷 5
● Salice Salentino Rosso Albarossa '13	🍷🍷 1*

Plantamura

via V. Bodini, 9a
70023 Gioia del Colle [BA]
Tel. +39 3474711027
www.viniplantamura.it

CELLAR SALES
PRE-BOOKED VISITS
ANNUAL PRODUCTION 45,000 bottles
HECTARES UNDER VINE 8.00
VITICULTURE METHOD Certified Organic
SUSTAINABLE WINERY

Passion and expertise are the hallmarks of the small winery run by Mariangela Plantamura and her husband Vincenzo. They produce feisty, terroir-true wines typical of the Gioia del Colle Primitivo DOC zone. The estate vineyards are located in the municipality of Gioia del Colle, on marly terrain, about 350 metres above sea level, featuring both high-trained and heirloom bush-trained vines. Even though Plantamura wines failed to win the top award, they are excellent quality. Unlike previous years, the Gioia del Colle Primitivo Riserva impressed most. The nose on the 2013 shows hints of red berries and Mediterranean scrub while the palate is compact and fresh with plenty of thrust. Less gutsy are the Gioia del Colle Primitivo Etichetta Rossa Parco Largo 2015, with its good fruit, and the Gioia del Colle Primitivo Etichetta Nera Contrada San Pietro 2015, with its nuances of mulberry and aromatic herbs.

● Gioia del Colle Primitivo Ris. '13	🍷🍷 3*
● Gioia del Colle Primitivo Et. Nera Contrada San Pietro '15	🍷🍷 3
● Gioia del Colle Primitivo Et. Rossa Parco Largo '15	🍷🍷 3
● Gioia del Colle Primitivo Et. Nera Contrada San Pietro '13	🍷🍷🍷 3*
● Gioia del Colle Primitivo Et. Nera Contrada San Pietro '12	🍷🍷🍷 3*
● Gioia del Colle Primitivo Et. Rossa '11	🍷🍷🍷 4*
● Gioia del Colle Primitivo Et. Rossa Parco Largo '13	🍷🍷 3*
● Gioia del Colle Primitivo Ris. '12	🍷🍷 3
● Gioia del Colle Primitivo Ris. '10	🍷🍷 5

Polvanera

S.DA VICINALE LAMIE MARCHESANA, 601
70023 GIOIA DEL COLLE [BA]
TEL. +39 080758900
www.cantinepolvanera.it

CELLAR SALES
RESTAURANT SERVICE
ANNUAL PRODUCTION 300,000 bottles
HECTARES UNDER VINE 90.00
VITICULTURE METHOD Certified Organic

In just over a decade, Filippo Cassano's Polvanera winery has managed to turn the spotlight on the Gioia del Colle area and its primitivo. The estate vineyards are located between Acquaviva and Gioia del Colle, at an elevation of over 300 metres, on karst terrain, with a thin layer of soil on a base of solid rock. Vines aged 10–15 years are Guyot or cordon trained, while the heirloom bush-trained vineyards have reached the grand old age of 60. The 2013 vintage wins another Tre Bicchieri for the Gioia del Colle Primitivo 17, with a nose of black berry fruit, quinine and Mediterranean scrub, and a deep, juicy palate that is rich, full and big on structure. Also excellent is the spirited 2013 Gioia del Colle Primitivo 16 with its spicy notes, fruit-driven nuances, plenty of acid grip and lingering finish. The Gioia del Colle Primitivo 14 Vigneto Marchesana 2013 is agreeable and expansive.

● Gioia del Colle Primitivo 17 '13	♟♟♟ 5
● Gioia del Colle Primitivo 16 '13	♟♟ 5
● Gioia del Colle Primitivo 14 Vign. Marchesana '13	♟♟ 3
○ Minutolo '15	♟ 3
⊙ Rosato '15	♟ 2
● Gioia del Colle Primitivo 17 '10	♟♟♟ 5
● Gioia del Colle Primitivo 17 '09	♟♟♟ 5
● Gioia del Colle Primitivo 17 '08	♟♟♟ 4*
● Gioia del Colle Primitivo 17 Vign. Montevella '12	♟♟♟ 6
● Gioia del Colle Primitivo 17 Vign. Montevella '11	♟♟♟ 6

Rivera

C.DA RIVERA
S.DA PROV.LE 231 KM 60,500
76123 ANDRIA [BT]
TEL. +39 0883569510
www.rivera.it

CELLAR SALES
PRE-BOOKED VISITS
ANNUAL PRODUCTION 1,200,000 bottles
HECTARES UNDER VINE 75.00
SUSTAINABLE WINERY

Back in the 1940s, the De Corato della Rivera family founded this winery on the Castel del Monte estate bearing its name. Today, it vaunts a wide range of vineyards in the designation, on soils ranging from calcareous tufa to rocky limestone, as well as a series of trusted suppliers of wines from other areas. The extensive selection has now exceeded 20 labels, from Castel del Monte to Salento and Valle d'Itria wines. We were most impressed by the Castel del Monte Aglianico Cappellaccio Riserva 2010, a bouquet unfolding hints of red berries and pepper, with rooty shades, while the balanced palate is long and full-flavoured, with elegant, seamless tannins. The Castel del Monte Nero di Troia Violante 2014 has agreeable notes of red berries; the Castel del Monte Rosé 2015 is fresh-tasting and flowery; the Moscato di Trani Dolce Piani di Tufara 2015 offers candied orange peel and honeyed notes.

● Castel del Monte Aglianico Cappellaccio Ris. '10	♟♟ 2*
● Castel del Monte Nero di Troia Violante '14	♟♟ 2*
⊙ Castel del Monte Rosé '15	♟♟ 2*
○ Moscato di Trani Piani di Tufara '15	♟♟ 2*
○ Castel del Monte Chardonnay Preludio n° 1 '15	♟ 2
○ Castel del Monte Fedora '15	♟ 2
● Castel del Monte Nero di Troia Puer Apuliae '04	♟♟♟ 6
● Castel del Monte Nero di Troia Puer Apuliae '03	♟♟♟ 6
○ Moscato di Trani Piani di Tufara '14	♟♟ 2*
● Triusco '13	♟♟ 3

Tenute Rubino

VIA E. FERMI, 50
72100 BRINDISI
TEL. +39 0831571955
www.tenuterubino.com

CELLAR SALES
PRE-BOOKED VISITS
ANNUAL PRODUCTION 1,200,000 bottles
HECTARES UNDER VINE 200.00

Tenute Rubino is a project conceived in the mid-1980s by Tommaso. In just a few years, the family estate became one of Puglia's most successful and respected winemakers, with its four different holdings, from the Adriatic hills all the way down to the plains behind Brindisi: Jaddico, Marmorelle, Uggìo, and Punta Aquila. They produce a wide range of labels, with pride of place going to native varieties. The wines are characterized by wonderful technical rigour and a strong local identity. Way back when, the Rubinos were pioneers of the susumaniello grape, creating a vineyard entirely dedicated to this variety in the early 2000s. In the absence of the multi-award-winning Torre Testa, the Susumaniello Oltremé 2015 is the star performer, with its complex fruitiness of blackberry and black cherry, it is concentrated, lengthy and round. The fresh, spicy Brindisi Rosso Jaddico Riserva 2013 has good grip and length. The Chardonnay Marmorelle Bianco 2015 is pleasing.

Schola Sarmenti

VIA GENERALE CANTORE, 37
73048 NARDÒ [LE]
TEL. +39 0833567247
www.scholasarmenti.it

CELLAR SALES
PRE-BOOKED VISITS
ANNUAL PRODUCTION 240,000 bottles
HECTARES UNDER VINE 41.00
VITICULTURE METHOD Certified Organic

With around 85% of vines head-trained, some of which have reached the grand old age of 80, Luigi Carlo Marra and Benedetto Lorusso have made their winery into a benchmark for the tradition of Salento, and of the Nardò area in particular, which has lost huge swathes of its area under vine in recent decades. The vineyards are very much dominated by the native primitivo, negroamaro and malvasia nera. The wines offer a richness of fruit and excellent drinkability. The 2014 harvest greatly compromised Schola Sarmenti's wines. The Nardò Rosso Roccamora 2014 shows typical hints of black berry fruit, while the palate is a little husky but with well-textured mouthfeel. The Nauna 2014, a 60% negroamaro blend with primitivo has notes of quinine, printer's ink and mature plum, with an expansive, agreeable palate. We were less impressed by the Diciotto 2014, with its excess alcohol and notes of dried fruit, lacking balance.

● Oltremé Susumaniello '15	♟♟♟ 4*
● Brindisi Rosso Jaddico Ris. '13	♟♟ 6
○ Marmorelle Bianco '15	♟♟ 3
○ Giancòla '15	♟ 5
● Marmorelle Rosso '14	♟ 3
● Miraglio '14	♟ 4
● Punta Aquila '14	♟ 4
○ Saturnino '15	♟ 4
☉ Torre Testa Rosé '15	♟ 5
● Torre Testa '13	♟♟♟ 6
● Torre Testa '12	♟♟♟ 6
● Torre Testa '11	♟♟♟ 6
● Torre Testa '11	♟♟♟ 6
● Torre Testa '02	♟♟♟ 5
● Torre Testa '01	♟♟♟ 5
● Visellio '10	♟♟♟ 4*

● Nardò Rosso Roccamora '14	♟♟ 2*
● Nauna '14	♟♟ 5
● Cubardi '13	♟ 4
● Diciotto '14	♟ 8
○ Fiano '15	♟ 3
● Nardò Rosso Nerìo Ris. '13	♟ 3
● Cubardi '11	♟♟ 3
● Cubardi '10	♟♟ 3
● Diciotto '13	♟♟ 8
● Diciotto '12	♟♟ 7
● Nardò Nerìo Ris. '10	♟♟ 3
● Nardò Nerìo Ris. '09	♟♟ 3
● Nardò Rosso Roccamora '13	♟♟ 2*

Cantine Soloperto

S.DA ST.LE 7
74024 MANDURIA [TA]
TEL. +39 0999794286
www.soloperto.it

CELLAR SALES
PRE-BOOKED VISITS
ANNUAL PRODUCTION 1,500,000 bottles
HECTARES UNDER VINE 50.00

Established in 1967, the Soloperto family winery is a point of reference for the Primitivo di Manduria designation. Around half of its vines are gobelet-trained, growing in Salento's typical terrain, such as terra rossa and black soil, with older vines in the Bagnolo district up to a century old. The wide range of nicely-made wines goes from easy-drinkers to those of greater structure and complexity. In the absence of some major labels, we especially liked the vintage versions. The Vecchio Ceppo Primitivo 2015 interprets all of the qualities of its type: attractive, with hints of myrtle and red berries, a savoury, fresh and pleasurable palate with a long finish in which Mediterranean scrub is very much to the fore. Along the same lines, the supple Primitivo di Manduria 2015 shows fruity notes of mature plum on the palate.

● Vecchio Ceppo Primitivo '15	♟♟	2*
● Primitivo di Manduria '15	♟♟	1*
● Primitivo di Manduria Dolce Naturale Nektare '14	♟	3
● Primitivo di Manduria Rubinum Et. Blu '14	♟	2
● Primitivo di Manduria Centofuochi Tenuta Bagnolo '12	♟♟	4
● Primitivo di Manduria Mono '11	♟♟	3
● Primitivo di Manduria Patriarca '13	♟♟	4
● Primitivo di Manduria Rubinum 17 Et. Rossa '13	♟♟	2*
● Primitivo di Manduria Rubinum Et. Rossa '14	♟♟	2*
⊙ Rosato Salento '13	♟♟	2*

★Tormaresca

LOC. TOFANO
C.DA TORRE D'ISOLA
76013 MINERVINO MURGE [BT]
TEL. +39 0883692631
www.tormaresca.it

CELLAR SALES
PRE-BOOKED VISITS
ACCOMMODATION
ANNUAL PRODUCTION 3,000,000 bottles
HECTARES UNDER VINE 380.00
VITICULTURE METHOD Certified Organic
SUSTAINABLE WINERY

The Antinori family set up this winery in 1998, from two estates: Bocca di Lupo in Minervino Murge, in the Castel del Monte designation; and Masseria Maime in San Pietro Vernotico, in the Upper Salento. Tormaresca focuses mainly on local varietals including nero di Troia, aglianico, negroamaro, and primitivo, producing modern-styled wines of great balance and drinkability. The estate's wide range also includes international varieties such as chardonnay and cabernet sauvignon. The Negroamaro Masseria Maime 2013 has hints of fresh dark berries and spice on the nose, and a well-defined, fruit-rich, supple palate. Despite the difficult vintage and lack of structure, the Castel del Monte Chardonnay Pietrabianca 2014 is well-made, with attractive notes of white-fleshed fruit. Also worthy of note are a compact, balsamic Castel del Monte Rosso Trentangeli 2014, with its still rather edgy tannins, and a fruity, slightly predictable but highly drinkable Primitivo Torcicoda 2014.

● Masseria Maime '13	♟♟	5
○ Castel del Monte Chardonnay Pietrabianca '14	♟♟	4
● Castel del Monte Rosso Trentangeli '14	♟♟	3
● Torcicoda '14	♟♟	4
⊙ Calafuria '15	♟	3
● Fichimori '15	♟	2
○ Roycello '15	♟	3
● Castel del Monte Rosso Trentangeli '11	♟♟♟	3*
● Masseria Maime '12	♟♟♟	5
● Masseria Maime '08	♟♟♟	5
● Masseria Maime '07	♟♟♟	4
● Torcicoda '11	♟♟♟	4*
● Torcicoda '10	♟♟♟	3*
● Torcicoda '09	♟♟♟	3

★Torrevento

S.DA PROV.LE 234 KM 10,600
70033 CORATO [BA]
TEL. +39 0808980923
www.torrevento.it

CELLAR SALES
ACCOMMODATION AND RESTAURANT SERVICE
ANNUAL PRODUCTION 2,500,000 bottles
HECTARES UNDER VINE 450.00
SUSTAINABLE WINERY

Francesco Liantonio's winery has 450 hectares under vine within the Castel del Monte DOC zone, in the Parco Rurale della Murgia. Respect for the environment and sustainability have been two of the estate's underlying principles throughout. Torrevento's wide range of wines is made mainly from nero di Troia and other natives. The cellarwork is essentially non-invasive and respectful for wines that are refreshing, elegant and fruit-rich. Torrevento continues to be the flagship for the Castel del Monte DOC. The balanced Castel del Monte Nero di Troia Ottagono Riserva 2014 has spicy red berry fragrances, accompanied by hints of chocolate, good fruitiness and admirable length. On the nose, the Castel del Monte Vigna Pedale Riserva 2013 is focused more on black berry fruit with floral nuances, while the palate is balanced, rather fresh-tasting and drinkable.

Cantine Tre Pini

VIA VECCHIA PER ALTAMURA S.DA PROV.LE 79 KM 16
70020 CASSANO DELLE MURGE [BA]
TEL. +39 080764911
www.agriturismotrepini.com

CELLAR SALES
PRE-BOOKED VISITS
ACCOMMODATION AND RESTAURANT SERVICE
ANNUAL PRODUCTION 30,000 bottles
HECTARES UNDER VINE 7.00
VITICULTURE METHOD Certified Organic

Along the old road to Altamura, just outside Cassano Murge, within the confines of the Alta Murgia National Park, the Plantamura family's Tre Pini estate is made up of about 30 hectares of land, with seven under vine. They grow only two varietals in their vineyards, primitivo and malvasia bianca, with the former at an altitude of 450 metres and the latter at 400, on the typically Murge stony karst soils. We gave Tre Pini its first Tre Bicchieri for the Gioia del Colle Primitivo Riserva 2013, with its fruity fragrances preceding notes of autumn leaves, wood resin and cocoa powder, and showing a complex, dense palate with a leisurely finish that marches apace. Also well-made is the Gioia del Colle Primitivo Piscina delle Monache 2013, with berry fruit and aromatic herbs on the nose and a refined, balanced, flavoursome palate. The pleasing Primitivo Trullo di Carnevale 2014 is all about fresh-tasting fruit.

● Castel del Monte Nero di Troia Ottagono Ris. '14	♛♛♛ 5
● Castel del Monte Rosso V. Pedale Ris. '13	♛♛ 3*
⊙ Castel del Monte Rosato Primaronda '15	♛ 2*
● Infinitum '15	♛♛ 2*
● Passione Reale Appassimento '15	♛♛ 2*
○ Bacca Rara '15	♛ 3
● Castel del Monte Rosso Bolonero '14	♛ 2
● Torre del Falco '14	♛ 2
● Castel del Monte Rosso Bolonero '12	♛♛♛ 2*
● Castel del Monte Rosso V. Pedale Ris. '12	♛♛♛ 3*
● Castel del Monte Rosso V. Pedale Ris. '10	♛♛♛ 3*
● Castel del Monte Rosso V. Pedale Ris. '09	♛♛♛ 3*

● Gioia del Colle Primitivo Ris. '13	♛♛♛ 4*
● Gioia del Colle Primitivo Piscina delle Monache '13	♛♛ 3
● Trullo di Carnevale '14	♛♛ 2*
○ Pinus Brut M. Cl.	♛ 3
● Gioia del Colle Primitivo '11	♛♛ 4
● Gioia del Colle Primitivo Piscina delle Monache '12	♛♛ 3*
● Gioia del Colle Primitivo Ris. '12	♛♛ 4

Agricole Vallone

VIA XXV LUGLIO, 7
73100 LECCE
TEL. +39 0832308041
www.agricolevallone.it

PRE-BOOKED VISITS
ANNUAL PRODUCTION 424,000 bottles
HECTARES UNDER VINE 161.00
VITICULTURE METHOD Certified Organic
SUSTAINABLE WINERY

Changes on the horizon for the Vallone family estate. This venerable Puglia winemaker will now be in the hands of the next generation, namely Francesco, with new facilities being built north of Brindisi that add to an already outstanding viticultural heritage. The vineyards are divided into three estates: Flaminio, in the Brindisi designation; Iore, in the Salice Salentino district; and Castelserranova, just outside Carovigno, a stone's throw from the Adriatic. The time-honoured winery flagship Graticciaia Negroamaro, in the 2012 version, shows hints of ripe black berry fruit and dried flowers, accompanied by hints of quinine, while the sturdy alcohol on the expansive palate is offset by the rich fruit, with shades of dried fig on the finish. The Brindisi Rosso Vigna Flaminio Riserva 2012 has hints of plum and spices giving way to a consistent palate with nuances of orange peel and black mulberry. The Susumaniello 2015 is more predictable and approachable.

● Graticciaia '12	♟♟ 7
● Brindisi Rosso V. Flaminio Ris. '12	♟♟ 3
● Susumaniello '15	♟ 2
● Graticciaia '03	♟♟♟ 6
● Graticciaia '01	♟♟♟ 6
☉ Brindisi Rosato V. Flaminio '13	♟♟ 2*
☉ Brindisi Rosato V. Flaminio '11	♟♟ 2*
● Brindisi Rosso V. Flaminio '10	♟♟ 2*
● Brindisi Rosso V. Flaminio Ris. '09	♟♟ 3
● Brindisi Rosso V. Flaminio Ris. '06	♟♟ 2
● Graticciaia '10	♟♟ 7
○ Passo delle Viscarde '07	♟♟ 4
○ Salento Corte Valesio '12	♟♟ 2*
● Vigna Castello '11	♟♟ 5

Varvaglione

C.DA SANTA LUCIA
74020 LEPORANO [TA]
TEL. +39 0995315370
www.varvaglione.com

CELLAR SALES
PRE-BOOKED VISITS
ACCOMMODATION
ANNUAL PRODUCTION 3,000,000 bottles
HECTARES UNDER VINE 155.00
SUSTAINABLE WINERY

Four generations of Varvagliones have been involved in running the family estate since it opened in 1921, now that Cosimo and Maria Teresa have been joined by their son and daughter Angelo and Marzia. In addition to owning 20 hectares under vine, there are another 135 cultivated by trusted growers, with production focused mainly on natives, for textbook wines combining a classic feel with typical varietal characteristics. This estate's wines came up trumps, especially the current vintages from the 12 e mezzo range. The juicy, pleasing Primitivo 2015 offers a nose of black cherry and damson; the slightly sweet 2015 Negroamaro segues more towards spices and chocolate, true to type and with good length. The fresh Malvasia 2015 displays nuances of sage and peach. The Primitivo di Manduria Papale Linea Oro 2014 is less inspiring, indeed predictable, suffering from the difficult vintage.

○ 12 e mezzo Malvasia '15	♟♟ 2*
● 12 e mezzo Negroamaro '15	♟♟ 2*
● 12 e mezzo Primitivo '15	♟♟ 2*
● Primitivo di Manduria Papale Linea Oro '14	♟ 5
○ 12 e mezzo Malvasia '14	♟♟ 2*
● Passione '13	♟♟ 2*
● Primitivo di Manduria Gocce '12	♟♟ 2*
● Primitivo di Manduria Moi '12	♟♟ 2*
● Primitivo di Manduria Papale Linea Oro '13	♟♟ 5
● Primitivo di Manduria Papale Linea Oro '12	♟♟ 5
● Tatu '14	♟♟ 2*

Vecchia Torre

VIA MARCHE, 1
73045 LEVERANO [LE]
TEL. +39 0832925053
www.cantinavecchiatorre.it

CELLAR SALES
PRE-BOOKED VISITS
ANNUAL PRODUCTION 3,000,000 bottles
HECTARES UNDER VINE 1800.00

This cooperative winery remains a true benchmark for the whole Leverano area, with 1,300-plus members supplying grapes from a total area under vine of nearly 2,000 hectares, many of which are still Puglia bush-trained. The most common varieties are black natives like negroamaro, primitivo, and malvasia nera di Lecce, for a modern style of production that offers fantastic value for money. The well-textured Negroamaro 2014, with its earthy notes, and black berry fruit and cinchona on the nose, has a long, tangy finish. Also well-made is the 50° Anniversario 2013, an equal blend of negroamaro and syrah with a decidedly modern slant, and a bouquet expressing hints of chocolate, coffee and autumn leaves, while the soft, fruit-rich palate has good flesh. Finally, the pleasing Leverano Rosato 2015 hinges on fruitiness.

Vespa
Vignaioli per Passione

FRAZ. C.DA RENI
VIA MANDURIA - AVETRANA KM 3
74024 MANDURIA [TA]
TEL. +39 0637514609
www.vespavignaioli.it

ANNUAL PRODUCTION 150,000 bottles
HECTARES UNDER VINE 20.00
SUSTAINABLE WINERY

Together with his sons Alessandro and Federico, Italy's leading chat-show host Bruno Vespa has a share in a farmstead just outside Manduria, along with about 20 hectares under vine on clay and sandy loam, making his own wine with the help of oenologist Riccardo Cotarella. Naturally the estate is dominated by primitivo, but several other grape varieties are used, such as fiano, negroamaro, aleatico, and Montepulciano. The 2014 vintage affected the Primitivo di Manduria Raccontami very little, and it shows marked notes of alcohol, as well as nuances of jammy black berry fruit and sweet spice; the palate is rich and close-knit, with a nice supple finish. The Primitivo Il Rosso dei Vespa 2015 displays notes of fresh fruit and cocoa powder, while its palate is caressingly smooth.

● 50° Anniversario '13	♟♟ 3
☉ Leverano Rosato '15	♟♟ 2*
● Negroamaro '14	♟♟ 2*
● Arneide '13	♟ 3
● Leverano Rosso '14	♟ 2
● Leverano Rosso Ris. '11	♟ 2
☉ Negroamaro Rosato '15	♟ 2
● Salice Salentino Rosso '14	♟ 2
● 50° Anniversario '12	♟♟ 3*
● Arneide '11	♟♟ 3
☉ Leverano Rosato '14	♟♟ 2*
● Leverano Rosso '13	♟♟ 2*
● Primitivo '13	♟♟ 2*
● Salice Salentino Rosso '13	♟♟ 2*
○ Vermentino '14	♟♟ 2*

● Primitivo di Manduria Raccontami '14	♟♟♟ 5
● Il Rosso dei Vespa '15	♟♟ 3
☉ Brut Rosé M. Cl. Noi Tre '12	♟ 5
☉ Flarò Il Rosa dei Vespa '15	♟ 2
○ Il Bianco dei Vespa '15	♟ 2
● Il Bruno dei Vespa '15	♟ 2*
● Primitivo di Manduria Raccontami '13	♟♟♟ 5
☉ Brut Rosé M. Cl. Noi Tre '11	♟♟ 5
● Il Bruno dei Vespa '14	♟♟ 2*
● Il Bruno dei Vespa '13	♟♟ 2*
● Primitivo di Manduria Raccontami '12	♟♟ 5

Tenuta Viglione

S.DA PROV.LE 140 KM 4,100
70029 SANTERAMO IN COLLE [BA]
TEL. +39 0802123661
www.tenutaviglione.it

CELLAR SALES
PRE-BOOKED VISITS
ACCOMMODATION AND RESTAURANT SERVICE
ANNUAL PRODUCTION 400,000 bottles
HECTARES UNDER VINE 60.00
VITICULTURE METHOD Certified Organic

Straddling the provincial border between Bari and Taranto, along the ancient Appian Way, Giovanni Zullo's estate is one of the jewels of the Gioia del Colle designation. On the 40-hectare estate, as well as primitivo, they also grow aleatico, merlot, falanghina, trebbiano and malvasia, on mineral-rich karst soils, located about 450 metres above sea level in the Murgia Barese. The resulting wines are true expressions of the terroir. The 2012 version of the Gioia del Colle Primitivo Marpione Riserva is again one of the finest wines in this DOC. A nose of black berry fruit, coffee and Mediterranean scrub ushers in a textured, taut, gutsy palate, lacking only the touch of complexity that would have earned it our top accolade again, as in the previous two years. Also well-made is the Gioia del Colle Primitivo 2013, with its fruit notes segued by a bouquet of garden vegetables and a juicy, fresh-tasting and agreeable palate.

● Gioia del Colle Primitivo Marpione Ris. '12	🍷🍷 3*
● Gioia del Colle Primitivo '13	🍷🍷 2*
○ Fiano '15	🍷 2
● Nisia '15	🍷 2
● Gioia del Colle Primitivo Marpione Ris. '11	🍷🍷🍷 3*
● Gioia del Colle Primitivo Marpione Ris. '10	🍷🍷🍷 3*
● Gioia del Colle Primitivo '12	🍷🍷 2*
● Gioia del Colle Primitivo '10	🍷🍷 2*
● Johe '13	🍷🍷 2*
● Johe '12	🍷🍷 2*
● Nisia '14	🍷🍷 2*

★Conti Zecca

VIA CESAREA
73045 LEVERANO [LE]
TEL. +39 0832925613
www.contizecca.it

CELLAR SALES
PRE-BOOKED VISITS
ANNUAL PRODUCTION 2,800,000 bottles
HECTARES UNDER VINE 320.00
SUSTAINABLE WINERY

For five centuries, the Zecca noble family has lived on and tilled the land around Leverano, in the heart of Salento. They run four different estates, with Saracena, Donna Marzia and Santo Stefano located in Leverano, and Cantalupi in Salice Salentino. Each produces a wide range of labels, as well as flagship wines from the Selezioni range. The modern style and consistency are flanked by close attention to value for money. In the absence of its flagship wine, Nero, the spotlight turned to other Cantalupi wines, especially the beautifully-crafted, drinkable Salice Salentino Rosso Cantalupi Riserva 2013, with its tones of fresh red berries. Also well-made are the succulent, fruity Primitivo Cantalupi 2015, with its slightly spicy hints and the textured, fresh-tasting Primitivo Rodinò 2014, with shades of quinine and hints of black berry fruit.

● Salice Salentino Cantalupi Ris. '13	🍷🍷 3*
● Cantalupi Primitivo '15	🍷🍷 2*
● Rodinò '14	🍷🍷 7
○ Malvasia Bianca '15	🍷 3
● Negroamaro '13	🍷 3
○ Sole '15	🍷 2
○ Venus '15	🍷 3
● Nero '09	🍷🍷🍷 5
● Nero '08	🍷🍷🍷 5
● Nero '07	🍷🍷🍷 5
● Nero '06	🍷🍷🍷 5
● Nero '03	🍷🍷🍷 5
● Nero '02	🍷🍷🍷 5
● Nero '01	🍷🍷🍷 5

A Mano

VIA SAN GIOVANNI, 41
70015 NOCI [BA]
TEL. +39 0803434872
www.amanowine.it

CELLAR SALES
PRE-BOOKED VISITS
ANNUAL PRODUCTION 390,000 bottles
VITICULTURE METHOD Certified Organic

● Imprint '14	🍷🍷 2*
● Primitivo '15	🍷🍷 2*
○ A Mano Bianco '15	🍷 2
● Negroamaro '15	🍷 2

Masseria Altemura

S.DA PROV.LE 69 MESAGNE
72028 TORRE SANTA SUSANNA [BR]
TEL. +39 0831740485
www.masseriaaltemura.it

CELLAR SALES
PRE-BOOKED VISITS
ACCOMMODATION
ANNUAL PRODUCTION 400,000 bottles
HECTARES UNDER VINE 150.00

● Negroamaro '14	🍷🍷 3
● Sasseo '14	🍷🍷 4
● Pietravia '13	🍷 5
⊙ Rosato '15	🍷 3

Amastuola

VIA APPIA KM 632,200
74016 MASSAFRA [TA]
TEL. +39 0998805668
www.amastuola.it

CELLAR SALES
PRE-BOOKED VISITS
ACCOMMODATION AND RESTAURANT SERVICE
ANNUAL PRODUCTION 360,000 bottles
HECTARES UNDER VINE 101.00
VITICULTURE METHOD Certified Organic

● Aglianico '13	🍷🍷 3
● Centosassi '12	🍷 5
⊙ Ondarosa '15	🍷 2
● Primitivo '14	🍷 3

Apollonio

VIA SAN PIETRO IN LAMA, 7
73047 MONTERONI DI LECCE [LE]
TEL. +39 0832327182
www.apolloniovini.it

CELLAR SALES
PRE-BOOKED VISITS
ANNUAL PRODUCTION 1,500,000 bottles
HECTARES UNDER VINE 20.00

● Elfo Negroamaro '15	🍷🍷 2*
○ Elfo Bianco d'Alessano '15	🍷 2
● Elfo Susumaniello '15	🍷 2
● Terragnolo Negroamaro '11	🍷 5

Bonsegna

VIA A. VOLTA, 17
73048 NARDÒ [LE]
TEL. +39 0833561483
www.vinibonsegna.it

CELLAR SALES
PRE-BOOKED VISITS
ANNUAL PRODUCTION 100,000 bottles
HECTARES UNDER VINE 20.00

● Nardò Rosso Danze della Contessa '14	🍷🍷 2*
● Baia di Uluzzo Primitivo '13	🍷 2
● Nardò Rosso Barricato V. della Contessa '13	🍷 3

I Buongiorno

C.SO VITTORIO EMANUELE II, 71
72012 CAROVIGNO [BR]
TEL. +39 0831996286
www.giasottolarco.it

ANNUAL PRODUCTION 50,000 bottles
HECTARES UNDER VINE 10.00

● Negramaro '14	🍷🍷 2*
● Primitivo '14	🍷🍷 3
⊙ Rosalento '15	🍷 2

Francesco Cannito

C.DA PARCO BIZZARRO
70025 GRUMO APPULA [BA]
TEL. +39 080623529
www.agricolacannito.it

CELLAR SALES
PRE-BOOKED VISITS
ANNUAL PRODUCTION 60,000 bottles
HECTARES UNDER VINE 14.00
VITICULTURE METHOD Certified Organic
SUSTAINABLE WINERY

● Gioia del Colle Primitivo Drùmon '12	♟♟	5
● Gioia del Colle Primitivo Drùmon S '12	♟♟	6
☉ Gioia del Colle Rosato Drùmon Rosé '15	♟	5
● Gioia del Colle Rosso Cannito '12	♟	3

Cantolio Manduria

VIA PER LECCE KM 2,5
74024 MANDURIA [TA]
TEL. +39 0999796045
www.cantolio.it

CELLAR SALES
PRE-BOOKED VISITS
RESTAURANT SERVICE
ANNUAL PRODUCTION 500,000 bottles
HECTARES UNDER VINE 800.00
VITICULTURE METHOD Certified Organic

● Primitivo di Manduria 14,0 '13	♟♟	3
● Vero '15	♟♟	2*
☉ L'Opis '14	♟	2
● Primitivo di Manduria Urceus '15	♟	2

Cantine Cardone

LOC. LOCOROTONDO
VIA MARTIRI DELLA LIBERTÀ, 32
70010 LOCOROTONDO [BA]
TEL. +39 0804312561
www.cardonevini.com

CELLAR SALES
PRE-BOOKED VISITS
ANNUAL PRODUCTION 300,000 bottles
HECTARES UNDER VINE 9.00

● Carmerum '15	♟♟	3
● Dione '15	♟	2
● Primitivo di Manduria Primaio '15	♟	3
☉ Verdeca '15	♟	2

Giancarlo Ceci

C.DA SANT'AGOSTINO
76123 ANDRIA [BT]
TEL. +39 0883565220
www.agrinatura.net

ANNUAL PRODUCTION 520,000 bottles
HECTARES UNDER VINE 70.00
VITICULTURE METHOD Certified Biodynamic

○ Moscato di Trani Dolce Rosalia '15	♟♟	3
○ Castel del Monte Chardonnay Pozzo Sorgente '15	♟	2
● Castel del Monte Rosso Almagia '15	♟	2

Tenuta Coppadoro

S.DA PROV.LE 35 SAN SEVERO - LESINA KM 5,850
71016 SAN SEVERO [FG]
TEL. +39 0882223174
www.tenutacoppadoro.it

CELLAR SALES
PRE-BOOKED VISITS
ANNUAL PRODUCTION 360,000 bottles
HECTARES UNDER VINE 120.00

● Stibadium '13	♟♟	5
○ Diomede '15	♟	2
○ Fujente Brut	♟	3
○ Ratino '15	♟	2

D'Alfonso del Sordo

C.DA SANT'ANTONINO
71016 SAN SEVERO [FG]
TEL. +39 0882221444
www.dalfonsodelsordo.it

CELLAR SALES
PRE-BOOKED VISITS
ACCOMMODATION
ANNUAL PRODUCTION 250,000 bottles
HECTARES UNDER VINE 45.00

☉ Dammirose '15	♟♟	2*
● San Severo Rosso Posta Arignano '15	♟♟	2*
● Guado San Leo '13	♟	4
☉ San Severo Rosato Posta Arignano '15	♟	2

De Falco

VIA MILANO, 25
73051 NOVOLI [LE]
TEL. +39 0832711597
www.cantinedefalco.it

CELLAR SALES
PRE-BOOKED VISITS
ACCOMMODATION
ANNUAL PRODUCTION 300,000 bottles
HECTARES UNDER VINE 20.00

● Salice Salentino Rosso Falco Nero Ris. '13	♈♈ 3
● Squinzano Rosso Serre di Sant'Elia '14	♈♈ 2*
● Negroamaro '15	♈ 1*
⊙ Rosato '15	♈ 2

Feudi di Guagnano

VIA CELLINO, 3
73010 GUAGNANO [LE]
TEL. +39 0832705422
www.feudiguagnano.com

CELLAR SALES
PRE-BOOKED VISITS
ANNUAL PRODUCTION 200,000 bottles
HECTARES UNDER VINE 15.00

● Vegamaro '15	♈♈ 3
● Le Camarde '14	♈ 2
● Nero di Velluto '12	♈ 4
⊙ Rosarò '15	♈ 2

Feudi Salentini

FRAZ. LEPORANO
VIA AMENDOLA, 36
74020 TARANTO
TEL. +39 0995315370
www.feudisalentini.com

PRE-BOOKED VISITS
ANNUAL PRODUCTION 55,000 bottles
HECTARES UNDER VINE 25.00

● Primitivo di Manduria Gocce '14	♈♈ 5
● Primitivo di Manduria Sassirossi '15	♈♈ 3
● Uno/Due/Cinque Primitivo '15	♈♈ 2*
● Uno/Due/Cinque Negroamaro '15	♈ 2

Feudo di Santa Croce

C.DA CIVITELLA
74021 CAROSINO [TA]
TEL. +39 0995924445
www.tinazzi.it

CELLAR SALES
ANNUAL PRODUCTION 600,000 bottles
HECTARES UNDER VINE 66.00

● Primitivo di Manduria Byzantium '14	♈♈ 2*
● Primitivo di Manduria LXXIV '14	♈♈ 2*
● Malnera '14	♈ 2

Duca Carlo Guarini

L.GO FRISARI, 1
73020 SCORRANO [LE]
TEL. +39 0836460288
www.ducacarloguarini.it

CELLAR SALES
PRE-BOOKED VISITS
ACCOMMODATION AND RESTAURANT SERVICE
ANNUAL PRODUCTION 300,000 bottles
HECTARES UNDER VINE 70.00
VITICULTURE METHOD Certified Organic

● Boemondo '12	♈♈ 5
● Nativo '14	♈♈ 3
● Piutri '13	♈ 2
● Rarum '14	♈ 5

Cantine Imperatore

VIA MARCONI, 36
70010 ADELFIA [BA]
TEL. +39 0804594041
www.cantineimperatore.com

CELLAR SALES
PRE-BOOKED VISITS
ANNUAL PRODUCTION 20,000 bottles
HECTARES UNDER VINE 5.00

● Gioia del Colle Primitivo Il Sogno '14	♈♈ 5
● Gioia del Colle Primitivo Sonya '14	♈♈ 2*
⊙ Schietto '15	♈ 2
● VIII Decumano '14	♈ 5

Masca del Tacco

VIA TRIPOLI, 5/7
72020 ERCHIE [BR]
TEL. +39 0831759786
www.mascadeltacco.it

ANNUAL PRODUCTION 80,000 bottles
HECTARES UNDER VINE 50.00

● Primitivo di Manduria Li Filitti Ris. '12	♛♛ 4
○ L'Uetta '15	♛ 3
● Salice Salentino Lu Ceppu Ris. '11	♛ 4

Menhir

VIA SCARCIGLIA, 18
73027 MINERVINO DI LECCE [LE]
TEL. +39 0836818199
www.cantinemenhir.com

CELLAR SALES
PRE-BOOKED VISITS
RESTAURANT SERVICE
ANNUAL PRODUCTION 520,000 bottles
HECTARES UNDER VINE 18.00

● Fine '12	♛♛ 4
● Primitivo di Manduria '13	♛♛ 2*
○ Pass-O '15	♛ 3
● Quota 29 '13	♛ 2

Mottura Vini del Salento

P.ZZA MELICA, 4
73058 TUGLIE [LE]
TEL. +39 0833596601
www.motturavini.it

PRE-BOOKED VISITS
ANNUAL PRODUCTION 2,500,000 bottles
HECTARES UNDER VINE 200.00

● Negroamaro Villa Mottura '15	♛♛ 3
● Primitivo Le Pitre '14	♛♛ 6
● Negroamaro Le Pitre '14	♛ 5
● Primitivo di Manduria Villa Mottura '14	♛ 3

Tenuta Patruno Perniola

VIA VIC.LE MARAZAGAGLIA, 2603
70023 GIOIA DEL COLLE [BA]
TEL. +39 3383940830
www.tenutapatrunoperniola.it

CELLAR SALES
PRE-BOOKED VISITS
ACCOMMODATION AND RESTAURANT SERVICE
ANNUAL PRODUCTION 12,000 bottles
HECTARES UNDER VINE 3.00
VITICULTURE METHOD Certified Organic

● Gioia del Colle Primitivo 1821 Ris. '11	♛♛ 5
● Gioia del Colle Primitivo Marzagaglia '11	♛♛ 4

Giovanni Petrelli

VIA VILLA CONVENTO, 33
73041 CARMIANO [LE]
TEL. +39 0832603051
www.cantinapetrelli.com

CELLAR SALES
PRE-BOOKED VISITS
ANNUAL PRODUCTION 100,000 bottles
HECTARES UNDER VINE 15.00

● Don Pepè '13	♛♛ 4
⊙ Cavarletta '15	♛ 2
● Tenuta Scozzi 10000 '15	♛ 2

Pietraventosa

S.DA VIC.LE LATTA LATTA
70023 GIOIA DEL COLLE [BA]
TEL. +39 3355730274
www.pietraventosa.it

ANNUAL PRODUCTION 20,000 bottles
HECTARES UNDER VINE 5.40
VITICULTURE METHOD Certified Organic
SUSTAINABLE WINERY

● Gioia del Colle Primitivo Allegoria '13	♛♛ 3
⊙ EstRosa '15	♛ 3
● Ossimoro '12	♛ 3
● Volere Volare '13	♛ 2

Pietregiovani

C.DA RENZO
S.DA VIC.LE PRIMOCIELO
70010 ACQUAVIVA DELLE FONTI [BA]
TEL. +39 34926992453492699245
www.pietregiovani.com

ANNUAL PRODUCTION 15,000 bottles
HECTARES UNDER VINE 3.50
SUSTAINABLE WINERY

● Primitivo '13	🏆🏆 4
⊙ Negroamaro Rosato '15	🏆 3

Pirro Varone

VIA SENATORE LACAITA, 90
74024 MANDURIA [TA]
TEL. +39 3397429098
www.pirrovarone.eu

CELLAR SALES
PRE-BOOKED VISITS
ANNUAL PRODUCTION 90,000 bottles
HECTARES UNDER VINE 16.00
VITICULTURE METHOD Certified Organic

● Primitivo di Manduria '12	🏆🏆 3
● Primitivo di Manduria Naturale Tocy '12	🏆🏆 6
● Primitivo di Manduria Ris. '11	🏆🏆 4
● Primitivo di Manduria Casa Vecchia '13	🏆 4

Podere 29

C.SO NUNZIO RICCO, 61
76016 MARGHERITA DI SAVOIA [BT]
TEL. +39 3471917291
www.podere29.it

CELLAR SALES
ACCOMMODATION
ANNUAL PRODUCTION 60,000 bottles
HECTARES UNDER VINE 10.00

● Gelso d'Oro '14	🏆🏆 5
● Avia Pervia '15	🏆 2
● Gelso Nero '15	🏆 2
⊙ Gelso Rosa '15	🏆 2

Produttori Vini Manduria

VIA FABIO MASSIMO, 19
74024 MANDURIA [TA]
TEL. +39 0999735332
www.cpvini.com

CELLAR SALES
PRE-BOOKED VISITS
ANNUAL PRODUCTION 800,000 bottles
HECTARES UNDER VINE 900.00
SUSTAINABLE WINERY

● Amoroso '15	🏆🏆 2*
● Primitivo di Manduria Sonetto Ris. '12	🏆🏆 6
● Primitivo di Manduria Dolce Naturale Madrigale '13	🏆 3

Rasciatano

S.DA ST.LE 93, KM 13
76121 BARLETTA
TEL. +39 0883510999
www.rasciatano.com

CELLAR SALES
PRE-BOOKED VISITS
ANNUAL PRODUCTION 90,000 bottles
HECTARES UNDER VINE 18.00

● Tenute Nero di Troia '15	🏆🏆 3*
○ Rasciatano Malvasia Bianca '15	🏆 3

Risveglio Agricolo

C.DA TORRE MOZZA
72100 BRINDISI
TEL. +39 0831519948
www.cantinerisveglio.it

CELLAR SALES
PRE-BOOKED VISITS
ANNUAL PRODUCTION 100,000 bottles
HECTARES UNDER VINE 44.00

● 72100 Sel. Speciale '13	🏆🏆 3*
● 72100 '14	🏆🏆 2*

Rosa del Golfo

VIA GARIBALDI, 18
73011 ALEZIO [LE]
TEL. +39 0833281045
www.rosadelgolfo.com

CELLAR SALES
PRE-BOOKED VISITS
ANNUAL PRODUCTION 300,000 bottles
HECTARES UNDER VINE 40.00

○ Bolina '15	♟♟ 2*
○ Brut M. Cl. Bolina	♟ 4
● Portulano '13	♟ 2

Cantina Sociale Sampietrana

VIA MARE, 38
72027 SAN PIETRO VERNOTICO [BR]
TEL. +39 0831671120
www.cantinasampietrana.com

CELLAR SALES
PRE-BOOKED VISITS
ANNUAL PRODUCTION 1,500,000 bottles
HECTARES UNDER VINE 140.00

● Settebraccia '13	♟♟ 3
● Salice Salentino V. delle Monache Ris. '12	♟ 4
● Sessantenario '13	♟ 3

Cantina San Donaci

VIA MESAGNE, 62
72025 SAN DONACI [BR]
TEL. +39 0831681085
www.cantinasandonaci.eu

CELLAR SALES
PRE-BOOKED VISITS
ANNUAL PRODUCTION 350,000 bottles
HECTARES UNDER VINE 543.00

● Anticaia Negroamaro '14	♟♟ 2*
● Posta Vecchia '14	♟♟ 2*
⊙ Salice Salentino Rosato Anticaia '15	♟ 2
● Salice Salentino Rosso Anticaia Ris. '12	♟ 2

L'Antica Cantina di San Severo

V.LE SAN BERNARDINO, 94
71016 SAN SEVERO [FG]
TEL. +39 0882221125
www.anticacantina.it

CELLAR SALES
PRE-BOOKED VISITS
ANNUAL PRODUCTION 1,700,000 bottles
HECTARES UNDER VINE 1000.00
SUSTAINABLE WINERY

⊙ San Severo Castrum Rosato '15	♟♟ 2*
● San Severo Castrum Rosso '15	♟♟ 2*
● Capitolo Rosso '15	♟ 2
○ San Severo Castrum Bianco '15	♟ 2

Conte Spagnoletti Zeuli

C.DA SAN DOMENICO
S.DA PROV.LE 231 KM 60,000
70031 ANDRIA [BT]
TEL. +39 0883569511
www.contespagnolettizeuli.it

CELLAR SALES
PRE-BOOKED VISITS
ANNUAL PRODUCTION 400,000 bottles
HECTARES UNDER VINE 120.00

⊙ Castel del Monte Bombino Nero Colombaio '15	♟♟ 3
● Castel del Monte Rosso La Pozzacchera '15	♟♟ 3

Spelonga

VIA MENOLA
71047 STORNARA [FG]
TEL. +39 0885431048
www.cantinespelonga.com

CELLAR SALES
PRE-BOOKED VISITS
ANNUAL PRODUCTION 50,000 bottles
HECTARES UNDER VINE 17.00

⊙ Marilina Rosé '15	♟♟ 2*
● Samà Rosso '15	♟♟ 2*
● Nero di Troia '15	♟ 3
● Primitivo '14	♟ 3

Tagaro

C.DA MONTETESSA, 63
70010 LOCOROTONDO [BA]
TEL. +39 0802042313
www.tagaro.it

ANNUAL PRODUCTION 120,000 bottles
HECTARES UNDER VINE 15.00

● Cinquenoci '14	♈♈ 3
● Nero di Troia Pignataro '14	♈♈ 2*
● Primitivo Pignataro '15	♈ 2
○ Verdazzo '15	♈ 3

Cosimo Taurino

S.DA ST.LE 365 KM 1,400
73010 GUAGNANO [LE]
TEL. +39 0832706490
www.taurinovini.it

CELLAR SALES
PRE-BOOKED VISITS
ANNUAL PRODUCTION 900,000 bottles
HECTARES UNDER VINE 90.00

● Notarpanaro '11	♈♈ 3
⊙ Scaloti '15	♈ 2

Cantine Teanum

VIA CROCE SANTA, 48
71010 SAN SEVERO [FG]
TEL. +39 0882336332
www.teanum.it

CELLAR SALES
PRE-BOOKED VISITS
ANNUAL PRODUCTION 1,500,000 bottles
HECTARES UNDER VINE 170.00

● Gran Tiati Gold Vintage '12	♈♈ 5
● Ôtre Aglianico '13	♈♈ 3
● Ôtre Primitivo '14	♈♈ 3
○ Alta Falanghina '15	♈ 2

Torre Quarto

C.DA QUARTO, 5
71042 CERIGNOLA [FG]
TEL. +39 0885418453
www.torrequarto.it

CELLAR SALES
PRE-BOOKED VISITS
ACCOMMODATION AND RESTAURANT SERVICE
ANNUAL PRODUCTION 500,000 bottles
HECTARES UNDER VINE 70.00

● Sangue Blu '14	♈♈ 2*
○ Capriccio '15	♈ 2
● Primitivo di Manduria Regale '15	♈ 2
⊙ Tavoliere Rosato Intrigo '15	♈ 2

Vigneti Reale

VIA E. REALE, 55
73100 LECCE
TEL. +39 0832248433
www.vignetireale.it

PRE-BOOKED VISITS
ACCOMMODATION AND RESTAURANT SERVICE
ANNUAL PRODUCTION 100,000 bottles
HECTARES UNDER VINE 85.00
SUSTAINABLE WINERY

⊙ Malvasia Rosato '15	♈♈ 2*
● Salice Salentino Santa Croce Ris. '13	♈♈ 4
○ Blasi '15	♈ 2
● Rudiae '14	♈ 3

Vinicola Mediterranea

VIA MATERNITÀ E INFANZIA, 22
72027 SAN PIETRO VERNOTICO [BR]
TEL. +39 0831676323
www.vinicolamediterranea.it

CELLAR SALES
PRE-BOOKED VISITS
RESTAURANT SERVICE
ANNUAL PRODUCTION 500,000 bottles

● Don Vito Prestige '15	♈♈ 2*
● Salice Salentino Rosso Il Barone '14	♈♈ 2*
● Primonobile '14	♈ 3

CALABRIA

It is no mean feat to sum up a year of work in a region with such a complex and varied winemaking scenario as Calabria. Certainly, the quality is improving although the number of award-winning wines has not increased, as we saw in the overview offered by this year's tastings. The gap between the leaders and the other wineries is closing and quite quickly to boot. Indeed, Calabria has shifted from the doldrums of 20 years ago to a recent storm of exponential growth in the number of wineries operating here, forcing the long-standing operators to move with the times, reviewing production and sales strategies. Thus, in this last decade, many wineries have increased their vineyard estates, building modern new cellars, and have begun to research native grapes, working on the growing area, as well as cooperating with world-renowned oenologists. At the same time, attention to the environment and sustainability has increased, so organic or biodynamic growing is no longer an exception. And while the larger wineries, especially those of the Cirò district, are making wines of outstanding quality, the new wave of young winemakers favour an all-natural approach to vine and wine, and are already achieving very encouraging results for the future. Moreover, signs of change are being seen in the province of Reggio Calabria, where a couple of new cellars sent their wines in to our selections. Saracena is also revealing good producers and we were impressed by Cantine Diana's Moscato Passito 2014. Sadly, lack of space once again prevented the addition of several cellars worthy of a full profile: Chimento, Criserà, Malena, La Pizzuta del Principe, Le Moire, Masseria Falvo, Scala, and Zito.

Sergio Arcuri

VIA ROMA VICO PRIMO
88811 CIRÒ MARINA [KR]
TEL. +39 3280250255
www.sergioarcuri.it

CELLAR SALES
PRE-BOOKED VISITS
ANNUAL PRODUCTION 15,000 bottles
HECTARES UNDER VINE 3.68
VITICULTURE METHOD Certified Organic

The Arcuri family put down its roots in Cirò winemaking tradition in 1880, when great-grandfather Beppe founded the current winery. More than a century later, the baton passed to Sergio, entrusted with the task of continuing the family tradition. Our tastings suggest he went about it in the best possible way, banning synthetic chemical products in vineyard and cellar as soon as he took over, with no cultured yeasts used for fermentations, which are all spontaneous, and no controlled temperatures. The four hectares of bush-trained vineyards are divided into two production areas, La Piciara, planted in 1948 practically on the beach, and the other in Piana di Franze, a hilltop plateau that enjoys breezes from the nearby Ionian Sea. Tradition and terroir merge in the Cirò Riserva 2011, revealing a fine balance of tannins and fruit, acidity and structure, which point to a long future. The Cirò Aris 2013 is also austere and varietal.

● Cirò Rosso Cl. Sup. Aris '13	♟♟ 4
● Cirò Rosso Cl. Sup. Ris. '11	♟♟ 6
● Cirò Rosso Cl. Sup. Aris '12	♟♟ 4

Roberto Ceraudo

LOC. MARINA DI STRONGOLI
C.DA DATTILO
88815 CROTONE
TEL. +39 0962865613
www.dattilo.it

CELLAR SALES
PRE-BOOKED VISITS
ACCOMMODATION AND RESTAURANT SERVICE
ANNUAL PRODUCTION 70,000 bottles
HECTARES UNDER VINE 20.00
VITICULTURE METHOD Certified Organic

For Roberto Ceraudo, the striking Dattilo estate is a dream come true, after a lifetime devoted to growing with passion and competence. With a careful eye on biodiversity and the ecosystem, around 20 years ago he was one of the first to convert to organic farming, and a few years later to biodynamic. In recent times, thanks in part to the exceptional contribution of his children Giuseppe, Susy and Caterina, Dattilo has become a far more complex outfit, and now includes a thriving restaurant and pleasant farm accommodation. Dattilo wines are forthright and intriguing, at times even exciting, expressing grape varieties and territory in an exemplary manner. The Pecorello Grisara 2015 has an alluringly delicate nose of blossom and white-fleshed fruit, Mediterranean herbs and notes of iodine; the palate is harmonious and sensual, tangy and fruity. The intriguing gaglioppo and cabernet sauvignon Petraro 2012 is creamy with juicy fruit, close-woven, tannin-heavy and elegant.

○ Grisara '15	♟♟♟ 4*
● Petraro '12	♟♟ 5
● Dattilo '13	♟♟ 4
● Doro Bè '10	♟♟ 3
⊙ Grayasusi Et. Argento '15	♟♟ 5
⊙ Grayasusi Et. Rame '15	♟♟ 3
○ Imyr '15	♟♟ 5
○ Petelia '15	♟♟ 3
● Nanà '14	♟ 3
○ Grisara '14	♟♟♟ 3*
○ Grisara '13	♟♟♟ 3*
○ Grisara '12	♟♟♟ 3*
⊙ Grayasusi Et. Argento '14	♟♟ 4
⊙ Grayasusi Et. Rame '14	♟♟ 3
○ Petelia '14	♟♟ 3

iGreco

LOC. SALICE
C.DA GUARDAPIEDI
87062 CARIATI [CS]
TEL. +39 0983969441
www.igreco.it

CELLAR SALES
PRE-BOOKED VISITS
ACCOMMODATION AND RESTAURANT SERVICE
ANNUAL PRODUCTION 250,000 bottles
HECTARES UNDER VINE 80.00
SUSTAINABLE WINERY

With successful careers in other professional fields, the seven Greco siblings have also expanded the winery opened by their father Tommaso, in 1963. Indeed, their top-notch business now covers over 1,000 hectares, mostly planted to olive groves, in seven different municipalities around Crotone. The cellar and administrative headquarters of the winery have not moved from the original site, in Cariati. Its 80 hectares under vine, dotted across the Cirò district's finest soils, produce sparklers and other wines of great precision, versatility and drinkability. A Tre Bicchieri for the Calabrese Nero Masino 2014, with its aromas of ripe red berries, balsamic and flowery notes, plush on the palate with plenty of fruit underpinned by the tannins. Also good is the Gaglioppo Catà 2014 produced in the Cirò vineyards, showing a nose of primary shades of cherry and blackberry, with slightly smoky hints, paving the way for a fresh palate and a lingering finish.

● Masino '14	♟♟♟ 5
● Catà '14	♟♟ 3
○ Filù '15	♟ 3
⊙ Savù '15	♟ 3
● Masino '12	♟♟♟ 5
● Masino '11	♟♟♟ 5
● Masino '10	♟♟♟ 5
● Catà '13	♟♟ 3
● Catà '11	♟♟ 2*
○ Filù '13	♟♟ 2*
⊙ Gaglioppo Gran Cuvée Rosé '11	♟♟ 4
○ Greco Bianco Gran Cuvée '10	♟♟ 4
● Masino '13	♟♟ 5

Ippolito 1845

VIA TIRONE, 118
88811 CIRÒ MARINA [KR]
TEL. +39 096231106
www.ippolito1845.it

CELLAR SALES
PRE-BOOKED VISITS
ANNUAL PRODUCTION 1,000,000 bottles
HECTARES UNDER VINE 100.00

The Ippolito family has a long history of winemaking in Cirò Marina and the winery is located in town, as was once often the case. Gianluca and Vincenzo follow in the footsteps of several generations, whose credentials as winemakers are lost in the mists of time, dating back to well before 1845, when the Ippolito family officially established what is now one of southern Italy's oldest cellars. As also reflected in our tastings, the decision to focus on native varieties, such as gaglioppo, greco and pecorello, is paying handsome dividends. Another finalist was the Gaglioppo 160 Anni 2013, with part of the grapes left to dry on racks until November. The surprisingly fresh Cirò Riserva Ripe del Falco 2006 is also austere and layered. Another good performer was the Pecorello 2015, enjoyably grassy with a lip-smacking, fruit-driven palate.

● 160 Anni '13	♟♟ 5
○ Cirò Bianco Res Dei '15	♟♟ 2*
● Cirò Rosso Cl. Sup. Ripe del Falco Ris. '06	♟♟ 5
● I Mori '14	♟♟ 2*
○ Pecorello '15	♟♟ 2*
● Calabrise '15	♟ 2
⊙ Cirò Rosato Mabilia '15	♟ 2
● Cirò Rosso Cl. Sup. Colli del Mancuso Ris. '13	♟ 3
● Cirò Rosso Cl. Sup. Liber Pater '14	♟ 2
● 160 Anni '12	♟♟ 5
● Cirò Rosso Cl. Sup. Colli del Mancuso Ris. '12	♟♟ 3*

Cantine Lento

VIA DEL PROGRESSO, 1
88040 AMATO [CZ]
TEL. +39 096828028
www.cantinelento.it

CELLAR SALES
PRE-BOOKED VISITS
ANNUAL PRODUCTION 500,000 bottles
HECTARES UNDER VINE 70.00

The Lento family estate consists of three distinct production areas around Lamezia Terme. In the last decade, the original estates around Caracciolo, growing only native black grapes, and the Romeo plot dedicated to greco bianco, were joined by the huge Amato estate, approximately 80 hectares under vine, where a large, state-of-the-art cellar has been built. We are delighted to see that after taking a couple of years to settle in, and introducing a new oenologist, this long-established winery is once again producing labels at the levels we were used to. The Federico II 2012 was a star at our regional selections. This Cabernet Sauvignon has a dense, mature, fruit-rich nose and a fresh swathe of flavour, with edgy acidity that enlivens its luscious drinkability. Also well-made, the Magliocco 2012 is Mediterranean, with an elegant nose, and progression at once lively, fresh, juicy and lingering.

★Librandi

LOC. SAN GENNARO
S.S. JONICA 106
88811 CIRÒ MARINA [KR]
TEL. +39 096231518
www.librandi.it

CELLAR SALES
PRE-BOOKED VISITS
ANNUAL PRODUCTION 2,200,000 bottles
HECTARES UNDER VINE 232.00

This venerable cellar has 230 hectares under vine on three large estates: Duca San Felice, outside Cirò Marina; Critone, close to Strongoli; and Rosaneti, near Rocca di Neto. Since 1993, in conjunction with several Italian universities, the Librandi family has been working on a major study of native grapes. Originally concentrating on just arvino, magliocco, pecorello, and mantonico, this has now expanded to 25 of over 200 selections found in various parts of Calabria. To prevent them from being lost forever, in 2003 all the varieties recovered were planted in a vineyard at the centre of the Rosaneti estate, with an unusual spiral shape. A well-deserved Tre Bicchieri went to the elegant Gravello 2014, the best tasted so far of this cabernet and gaglioppo blend. Other finalists were the Cirò Duca Sanfelice 2014, with its authentic Mediterranean notes, and Efeso 2015, a Mantonico with mineral and peachy notes on the nose, ushering in a fresh, zesty palate and lingering finish.

● Federico II '12	♟♟ 4
○ Lamezia Greco '15	♟♟ 3
● Magliocco '12	♟♟ 5
○ Amatus Bianco '15	♟ 2
● Amatus Rosso '14	♟ 2
○ Contessa Emburga '15	♟ 3
○ Lamezia Bianco Dragone '15	♟ 2
● Lamezia Rosso Dragone '14	♟ 3
● Lamezia Rosso Salvatore Lento Ris. '12	♟ 4
● Federico II '11	♟♟ 4
● Federico II '10	♟♟ 4
● Federico II '09	♟♟ 5
○ Lamezia Greco '13	♟♟ 3
● Magliocco '11	♟♟ 5

● Gravello '14	♟♟♟ 5
● Cirò Rosso Cl. Duca Sanfelice '14	♟♟ 3*
○ Efeso '15	♟♟ 4
● Cirò Rosso Cl. '15	♟♟ 2*
○ Critone '15	♟♟ 2*
○ Le Passule '14	♟♟ 5
● Magno Megonio '14	♟♟ 4
⊙ Terre Lontane '15	♟♟ 2*
○ Cirò Bianco '15	♟ 2
⊙ Cirò Rosato '15	♟ 2
● Melissa Rosso Asylia '15	♟ 2
● Cirò Rosso Cl. Sup. Duca Sanfelice Ris. '11	♟♟♟ 3*
● Gravello '10	♟♟♟ 5
● Gravello '09	♟♟♟ 5
● Magno Megonio '13	♟♟♟ 4*
● Magno Megonio '12	♟♟♟ 4*

G.B. Odoardi

C.DA CAMPODORATO, 35
88047 NOCERA TERINESE [CZ]
TEL. +39 098429961
www.cantineodoardi.it

CELLAR SALES
ANNUAL PRODUCTION 120,000 bottles
HECTARES UNDER VINE 80.00

Commitment and expertise characterize
Barbara and Gregorio Odoardi's
management of their lovely 300-hectare
holding in Nocera Terinese, around 80
hectares of which are planted to vine, in
two separate production areas. The vines
are all densely planted, at around 11,000
per hectare, climbing from sea level all the
way up to above 600 metres, and enjoying
the breezes from the nearby Tyrrhenian
Sea. Their painstakingly meticulous work
in the vineyard and even more restrained
use of wood in the cellar have lent their
wines varietal definition and local identity,
without sacrificing any of their personality.
The GB Rosso 2013 mistakenly appeared
in last year's Guide but now sails into the
finals. This extractive wine is a variable
blend of gaglioppo, magliocco, nerello
cappuccino, and greco nero, depending on
the vintage, rich in polyphenols and nicely
elegant and balanced.

● GB Rosso '13	♟♟ 5
● Savuto '14	♟♟ 2*
○ Scavigna Bianco '15	♟ 2
⊙ Scavigna Rosato '15	♟ 2
● Scavigna V. Garrone '04	♟♟♟ 5
● Scavigna V. Garrone '03	♟♟♟ 5
● Scavigna V. Garrone '99	♟♟♟ 5
○ Odoardi GB '14	♟♟ 5
○ Odoardi GB '13	♟♟ 4
● Odoardi GB '11	♟♟ 6
● Savuto '13	♟♟ 2*
○ Terra Damia '14	♟♟ 2*
● Terra Damia '12	♟♟ 3

Fattoria San Francesco

LOC. QUATTROMANI
88813 CIRÒ [KR]
TEL. +39 096232228
www.fattoriasanfrancesco.it

CELLAR SALES
PRE-BOOKED VISITS
ANNUAL PRODUCTION 224,000 bottles
HECTARES UNDER VINE 40.00

A truly magnificent performance this year
from this ancient Cirò winery, founded in
the late 18th century by Benedetto Siciliani.
After a few years of transition and a change
of ownership, the excellent results we had
come to expect until a decade or so ago
are back with a vengeance. Fattoria San
Francesco, which now belongs to Cirò's
renowned luzzolini family of winemaking
entrepreneurs, farms around 40 hectares
under vine in the finest local production
areas, some of which reach altitudes of up
to 350 metres. Although they have yet to
come up with a winner, all the wines tasted
this year were outstanding for their
accuracy, with a modern style that does not
betray the strong local identity and sensory
profile of the grape type. Worth mentioning,
the focused and juicy Gaglioppo Ronco dei
Quattroventi 2013, with an elegant
aromatic profile.

○ Cirò Rosato '15	♟♟ 2*
● Cirò Rosso Cl. Sup. '14	♟♟ 2*
● Ronco dei Quattroventi '13	♟♟ 3
○ Cirò Bianco '15	♟ 2
⊙ Donna Rosa '15	♟ 3
○ Settemari '15	♟ 3
● Vignacorta '14	♟ 3
○ Cirò Bianco '14	♟♟ 2*
⊙ Cirò Rosato '13	♟♟ 2*
⊙ Cirò Rosato San Francesco '12	♟♟ 2*
● Cirò Rosso Cl. Ronco dei Quattroventi '08	♟♟ 5
● Cirò Rosso Cl. Sup. Duca dell'Argillone Ris. '10	♟♟ 4
● Donna Rosa '13	♟♟ 3

Santa Venere

LOC. TENUTA VOLTA GRANDE
S.DA PROV.LE 04 KM 10,00
88813 CIRÒ [KR]
TEL. +39 096238519
www.santavenere.com

CELLAR SALES
PRE-BOOKED VISITS
ANNUAL PRODUCTION 125,000 bottles
HECTARES UNDER VINE 25.00
VITICULTURE METHOD Certified Organic

Santa Venere is an all-round working farm that offers a traditional rural welcome. In addition it also produces olive oil and raises pedigree cattle. The farm is entirely organic, and a couple of years ago began to move towards a fully biodynamic approach, while also implementing a successful project to produce a Metodo Classico aged on the lees with no added sulphites. As well as making the most of Cirò's typical gaglioppo and greco vines, the Scala family has also revived production of wines using other local varieties such as guardavalle and marsigliana nera. The Cirò Rosso 2015, with its nose of intense fruit and spicy balsamic nuances, and fresh, invigorating, tannin-rich flavour on a juicy, compact fruitiness, is well-crafted. Elegant fragrances ranging from orange blossom through jasmine to damson and white peach characterize Guardavalle Vescovado 2015, with its palate of fresh acidity and soft fruitiness.

Serracavallo

C.DA SERRACAVALLO
87043 BISIGNANO [CS]
TEL. +39 098421144
www.viniserracavallo.it

CELLAR SALES
PRE-BOOKED VISITS
RESTAURANT SERVICE
ANNUAL PRODUCTION 80,000 bottles
HECTARES UNDER VINE 32.00
VITICULTURE METHOD Certified Organic

Demetrio Stancati tirelessly divides his time between his lovely Bisignano estate and running the newly-founded Terre di Cosenza Consortium. The cellar and part of the vineyards are found at an altitude of 600 metres, while other plots are planted on steep terraces rising up much higher slopes. In an area that was not known for outstanding grape varieties, Demetrio deserves credit for the courage he showed in concentrating on local varietals such as magliocco and mantonico, convincing other vignerons to follow suit. The winery's production philosophy has always been to go for quality over quantity. A place in the national finals goes to Magliocco Vigna Savuco 2012, thanks to a broad aromatic profile of fresh balsamic nuances, spices and red berries, and deep, rounded, fruit-rich flavours with a good tannic kick. Besidiae 2015, from pecorello, is a snappy early drinker, not without complexity and elegance.

○ Cirò Bianco '15	♟♟ 2*
⊙ Cirò Rosato '15	♟♟ 2*
● Cirò Rosso Cl. '15	♟♟ 2*
○ Vescovado '15	♟♟ 3
● Vurgadà '14	♟♟ 4
⊙ Scassabarile '15	♟ 3
● Speziale '15	♟ 3
● Cirò Cl. Sup. Federico Scala Ris. '12	♟♟ 5
● Cirò Rosso Cl. '13	♟♟ 2*
● Cirò Rosso Cl. Sup. Federico Scala Ris. '11	♟♟ 5
⊙ Rosé Brut SP 1 '11	♟♟ 4
● Speziale '14	♟♟ 3
● Speziale '13	♟♟ 3
⊙ Vescovado '14	♟♟ 3
● Vurgadà '12	♟♟ 3
● Vurgadà '11	♟♟ 3

● Vigna Savuco '12	♟♟ 6
○ Besidiae '15	♟♟ 2*
● Terre di Cosenza Sette Chiese '15	♟♟ 2*
⊙ Terre di Cosenza Don Filì '15	♟ 3
⊙ Terre di Cosenza Filì '15	♟ 2
● Terre di Cosenza Quattro Lustri '15	♟ 3
● Terre di Cosenza Terraccia '13	♟ 3
● Alta Quota '09	♟♟ 5
⊙ Filì '14	♟♟ 2*
● Terraccia '12	♟♟ 3
● Terraccia '11	♟♟ 3
● Vigna Savuco '11	♟♟ 6
● Vigna Savuco '10	♟♟ 6
● Vigna Savuco '09	♟♟ 6

Statti

c.da Lenti
88046 Lamezia Terme [CZ]
Tel. +39 0968456138
www.statti.com

CELLAR SALES
PRE-BOOKED VISITS
RESTAURANT SERVICE
ANNUAL PRODUCTION 300,000 bottles
HECTARES UNDER VINE 100.00

Over the last decade, Antonio and Alberto Statti's passion for wine has led them to turn their family estate on its head, investing heavily in the vineyards, which now cover almost 100 hectares, as well as in a state-of-the-art cellar vaunting all the space and technology needed to make Metodo Classico sparklers. Their extensive and reliable range of wines now also includes two elegant versions of the latter. With a close eye on the environment and on alternative energies, they have become energy-independent thanks to a modern biomass plant that uses winery waste to produce energy. The fine Gaglioppo Batasarro 2013 sailed into the finals with its focused morello cherry and blackcurrant fruitiness, echoed on the palate, against an elegant tannin-heavy background. We also took to the Arvino 2013, a blend of gaglioppo and cabernet, with its balsamic nose, and a mouth marked by sweet fruitiness.

● Batasarro '13	▼▼ 4
● Arvino '13	▼▼ 2*
● Gaglioppo '15	▼▼ 2*
● I Gelsi Rosso '15	▼▼ 2*
○ Mantonico '14	▼▼ 3
○ Greco '15	▼ 2
○ I Gelsi Bianco '15	▼ 2
◉ I Gelsi Rosato '15	▼ 2
● Arvino '12	♎♎ 2*
● Batasarro '12	♎♎ 4
● Gaglioppo '14	♎♎ 2*
○ Greco '14	♎♎ 2*
○ Greco '13	♎♎ 2*
● I Gelsi Rosso '13	♎♎ 1*
○ Mantonico '14	♎♎ 3

Luigi Viola

via Roma, 18
87010 Saracena [CS]
Tel. +39 0981349099
www.cantineviola.it

CELLAR SALES
PRE-BOOKED VISITS
ANNUAL PRODUCTION 15,000 bottles
HECTARES UNDER VINE 3.00
VITICULTURE METHOD Certified Organic

In retrospect, the battle Luigi Viola began almost 20 years ago could have turned into yet another tilt at windmills. At the time, this tenacious primary school teacher had decided to breathe new life into a wine which had gradually been forgotten: Moscato di Saracena, a passito made from moscatello, guarnacca and malvasia using a complex process. Nevertheless, not only did Luigi persuade the whole family to start vinifying this passito again, with excellent results, but he also managed to set in motion such a virtuous circle that today this tiny mountain village vaunts no less than ten producers of this noble wine. The Moscato's, close-knit, elegant nose of fresh aromatic herbs, candied tropical fruit, balsam and oriental spices ushers in a juicy, lingering palate with a long finale but a slightly lacklustre acidic vein.

○ Moscato Passito '15	▼▼ 6
○ Biancomargherita '14	▼ 3
● Rossoviola '13	▼ 3
○ Moscato Passito '14	♎♎♎ 6
○ Moscato Passito '13	♎♎♎ 6
○ Moscato Passito '12	♎♎♎ 6
○ Moscato Passito '11	♎♎♎ 6
○ Moscato Passito '10	♎♎♎ 6
○ Moscato Passito '09	♎♎♎ 6
○ Moscato Passito '08	♎♎♎ 6
○ Moscato Passito '07	♎♎♎ 6

Cataldo Calabretta

VIA MANDORLETO, 47
88811 CIRÒ MARINA [KR]
TEL. +39 3471866941
www.cataldocalabretta.it

CELLAR SALES
PRE-BOOKED VISITS
ANNUAL PRODUCTION 25,000 bottles
HECTARES UNDER VINE 13.50
VITICULTURE METHOD Certified Organic

○ Ansonica '15	♟♟ 3
○ Cirò Bianco '15	♟♟ 3
⊙ Cirò Rosato '15	♟ 3
● Cirò Rosso Cl. Sup. Ris. '13	♟ 2

Caparra & Siciliani

BIVIO S.S. 106
88811 CIRÒ MARINA [KR]
TEL. +39 0962373319
www.caparraesiciliani.com

CELLAR SALES
PRE-BOOKED VISITS
ANNUAL PRODUCTION 800,000 bottles
HECTARES UNDER VINE 180.00
VITICULTURE METHOD Certified Organic

● Cirò Rosso Cl. Sup. Volvito Ris. '13	♟♟ 2*
● Cirò Cl. Sup. Solagi '14	♟ 2
○ Curiale '15	♟ 2
⊙ Insidia '15	♟ 2

Capoano

C.DA CERAMIDIO
88072 CIRÒ MARINA [KR]
TEL. +39 096235801
www.capoano.it

CELLAR SALES
ANNUAL PRODUCTION 100,000 bottles
HECTARES UNDER VINE 20.00

● Cirò Rosso Cl. Sup. '14	♟♟ 2*
● Cirò Rosso Cl. Sup. Don Raffaele Ris. '13	♟♟ 5
○ Aeternum '13	♟ 4
⊙ Cirò Rosato '15	♟ 2

Wines Colacino

VIA COLLE MANCO
87054 ROGLIANO [CS]
TEL. +39 09841900252
www.colacino.it

CELLAR SALES
PRE-BOOKED VISITS
ANNUAL PRODUCTION 120,000 bottles
HECTARES UNDER VINE 21.00

● Savuto Si '15	♟♟ 2*
● Terre di Cosenza Magliocco '13	♟♟ 3
● Savuto Sup. Britto '13	♟ 4
● Savuto V. Colle Barabba '15	♟ 3

Tenuta del Conte

VIA TIRONE, 131
88811 CIRÒ MARINA [KR]
TEL. +39 096236239
www.tenutadelconte.it

PRE-BOOKED VISITS
ANNUAL PRODUCTION 90,000 bottles
HECTARES UNDER VINE 20.00

● Cirò Rosso Cl. Dagò '13	♟♟ 2*
○ Cirò Bianco '15	♟ 2
⊙ Cirò Rosato '15	♟ 2
● Cirò Rosso Cl. Dalla Terra Ris. '11	♟ 2

Cote di Franze

LOC. PIANA DI FRANZE
88811 CIRÒ MARINA [KR]
TEL. +39 3926911606
www.cotedifranze.it

CELLAR SALES
PRE-BOOKED VISITS
ANNUAL PRODUCTION 18,000 bottles
HECTARES UNDER VINE 9.00
VITICULTURE METHOD Certified Organic

⊙ Cirò Rosato '15	♟♟ 2*
● Cirò Rosso Cl. Sup. Ris. '12	♟♟ 3
○ Cirò Bianco '15	♟ 2

Cantina Enotria

LOC. SAN GENNARO
S.S. JONICA, 106
88811 CIRÒ MARINA [KR]
TEL. +39 0962371181
www.cantinaenotria.com

CELLAR SALES
PRE-BOOKED VISITS
ANNUAL PRODUCTION 1,000,000 bottles
HECTARES UNDER VINE 170.00

○ Cirò Bianco '15	♥♥ 2*
⊙ Cirò Rosato '15	♥ 2
● Cirò Rosso Cl. Sup. Piana delle Fate Ris. '13	♥ 5

Tenute Ferrocinto

C.DA FERROCINTO
87012 CASTROVILLARI [CS]
TEL. +39 0981415122
www.cantinecampoverde.it

CELLAR SALES
PRE-BOOKED VISITS
ANNUAL PRODUCTION 700,000 bottles
HECTARES UNDER VINE 45.00
VITICULTURE METHOD Certified Organic

● Terre di Cosenza Pollino Magliocco 24 Ris. '13	♥♥ 4
○ Terre di Cosenza Pollino Bianco '15	♥ 3
● Terre di Cosenza Pollino Rosso '14	♥ 3

Feudo dei Sanseverino

VIA VITTORIO EMANUELE, 108/110
87010 SARACENA [CS]
TEL. +39 098121461
www.feudodeisanseverino.it

CELLAR SALES
PRE-BOOKED VISITS
ANNUAL PRODUCTION 20,000 bottles
HECTARES UNDER VINE 6.00
VITICULTURE METHOD Certified Organic
SUSTAINABLE WINERY

○ Moscato Passito Mastro Terenzio '13	♥♥ 5
● Lacrima Nera Ris. '09	♥ 3

Tenuta Iuzzolini

LOC. FRASSÀ
88811 CIRÒ MARINA [KR]
TEL. +39 0962373893
www.tenutaiuzzolini.it

CELLAR SALES
PRE-BOOKED VISITS
ANNUAL PRODUCTION 1,000,000 bottles
HECTARES UNDER VINE 65.00

● Artino '14	♥♥ 3
⊙ Lumare '15	♥♥ 3
○ Prima Fila '15	♥♥ 3
● Principe Spinelli '15	♥ 3

Poderi Marini

LOC. SANT'AGATA
87069 SAN DEMETRIO CORONE [CS]
TEL. +39 0984947224
www.poderimarini.it

CELLAR SALES
ANNUAL PRODUCTION 42,000 bottles
HECTARES UNDER VINE 7.00
VITICULTURE METHOD Certified Organic

● Basileus '14	♥♥ 5
○ Collimarini Passito '15	♥♥ 4
● Elaphe '14	♥ 4
● Koronè Rosso '14	♥ 2

Nesci

VIA MARINA, 1
89038 PALIZZI [RC]
TEL. +39 3209785653
www.aziendanesci.it

ANNUAL PRODUCTION 28,000 bottles
HECTARES UNDER VINE 9.00

● Chapeaux '15	♥♥ 2*
● Esperanto '15	♥ 2
● Toto Corde '15	♥ 2

Tenute Pacelli

FRAZ. PAUCIURI
C.DA ROSE
87010 MALVITO [CS]
TEL. +39 0984501486
www.tenutepacelli.it

CELLAR SALES
PRE-BOOKED VISITS
ACCOMMODATION
ANNUAL PRODUCTION 15,000 bottles
HECTARES UNDER VINE 9.00
VITICULTURE METHOD Certified Organic
SUSTAINABLE WINERY

● Tèmeso '12	♟♟ 3
○ Barone Bianco '10	♟ 2
○ Zoe Brut	♟ 4

Senatore Vini

LOC. SAN LORENZO
88811 CIRÒ MARINA [KR]
TEL. +39 096232350
www.senatorevini.com

CELLAR SALES
PRE-BOOKED VISITS
ANNUAL PRODUCTION 280,000 bottles
HECTARES UNDER VINE 30.00

● Cirò Rosso Cl. Arcano Ris. '09	♟♟ 4
○ Alikia '15	♟ 3
○ Ciro Bianco Alalei '15	♟ 3
⊙ Cirò Rosato Puntalice '15	♟ 3

Spadafora Wines 1915

ZONA IND. PIANO LAGO, 18
87050 MANGONE [CS]
TEL. +39 0984969080
www.cantinespadafora.it

CELLAR SALES
PRE-BOOKED VISITS
ANNUAL PRODUCTION 600,000 bottles
HECTARES UNDER VINE 40.00

○ Terre di Cosenza Fiego Bianco '15	♟♟ 2*
● Terre di Cosenza Peperosso '15	♟♟ 2*
● Nerello '13	♟ 3
● Terre di Cosenza Telesio '13	♟ 4

Terre del Gufo - Muzzillo

C.DA ALBO SAN MARTINO, 22A
87100 COSENZA
TEL. +39 0984780364
www.terredelgufo.it

CELLAR SALES
PRE-BOOKED VISITS
ANNUAL PRODUCTION 25,500 bottles
HECTARES UNDER VINE 3.00

● Kaulos '15	♟♟ 3
● Terre di Cosenza Portapiana '14	♟♟ 4
● Timpamara '14	♟♟ 5
⊙ Terre di Cosenza Chiaroscuro '15	♟ 2

Tenuta Terre Nobili

LOC. CARIGLIALTO
87046 MONTALTO UFFUGO [CS]
TEL. +39 0984934005
www.tenutaterrenobili.it

CELLAR SALES
PRE-BOOKED VISITS
ACCOMMODATION
ANNUAL PRODUCTION 80,000 bottles
HECTARES UNDER VINE 15.00
VITICULTURE METHOD Certified Organic

● Alarico '14	♟♟ 3
● Cariglio '15	♟♟ 2*
● Ipazia '15	♟ 6
● Teodora '12	♟ 5

Tramontana

LOC. GALLICO MARINA
VIA CASA SAVOIA, 156
89139 REGGIO CALABRIA
TEL. +39 0965370067
www.vinitramontana.it

CELLAR SALES
PRE-BOOKED VISITS
ANNUAL PRODUCTION 200,000 bottles
HECTARES UNDER VINE 41.00

● Costa Viola '14	♟♟ 2*
● Palizzi '14	♟♟ 2*
○ 5 Generazioni '15	♟ 2
● Vorea '15	♟ 2

SICILY

Sicily took home an admirable 21 Tre Bicchieri awards, a record high that simply underscores how much the quality level continues to grow on this island. A very lively and dynamic regional setting, therefore, moving fast in some directions, underpinned by the growing areas, those macro districts with well-defined characteristics and landscapes. The most illuminating example is Etna, an area which continues to be on everyone's lips: a unique zone of amazing wine country, where new cellars are opening regularly, and we see new labels and new vineyard selections all the time. Etna garnered six Tre Bicchieri, of which two are first-timers: Cusumano's elegant Alta Mora 2014 and Tasca d'Almerita's refined Buonora 2015. Another name to look out for is Messina's Faro district, a small designation that was about to disappear, which not only confirmed last year's two Tre Bicchieri awards, but in the general and much augured expansion of base production, regaled us with Bonavita's excellent Faro 2014, just a whisker away from the top of the podium. The south east of the island, home to the vast Cerasuolo di Vittoria growing area, strengthens its already considerable heft by taking the number of award-winning wines to six, with two amazing Nero d'Avolas, both new entries this years: Nicosia's 2010 Sosta Tre Santi and Rudinì's traditional Saro. Western Sicily is also looking good with its seven Tre Bicchieri, including Baglio di Pianetto's elegant debut 2013 Shymer, from inland Palermo with its noteworthy quality growth, and Firriato's fascinating Favinia La Muciara 2015 , a perfect marriage of catarratto, grillo and zibibbo from the new Favignana estate on the stunning Egadi archipelago, where vines have finally returned after more than a century. Each example is part of the enchanting snapshot of viticultural Sicily, a region increasingly central to Italy's wine production scenario. Classic names confirm and consolidate rankings with ever-more focused wines, paring down concentration and improving elegance, and almost always obtained from countless local varieties. Nonetheless, in Sicily there is still, thankfully, plenty of room for a (re)-discovery of excellent terroirs and for new winemakers who know how to read all the nuances of this true vineyard country.

Abbazia Santa Anastasia

C.DA SANTA ANASTASIA
90013 CASTELBUONO [PA]
TEL. +39 0921671959
www.abbaziasantaanastasia.com

CELLAR SALES
PRE-BOOKED VISITS
ACCOMMODATION AND RESTAURANT SERVICE
ANNUAL PRODUCTION 250,000 bottles
HECTARES UNDER VINE 65.00
VITICULTURE METHOD Certified Biodynamic
SUSTAINABLE WINERY

This splendid estate on the slopes of the
Parco delle Madonie, buffeted by
impetuous winds from the nearby sea,
covers over 300 hectares of land, with 70
under vine. It revolves around a superbly
restored 12th-century abbey, inhabited
over the centuries by Theatine and
Benedictine monks, dedicated to study and
farming. In 1982, Franco Lena purchased
the property, and set about redeveloping it
with foresight and passion, engaging in
quality viticulture using certified organic
and biodynamic methods, with excellent
results. The monovarietal cabernet
sauvignon Litra 2012 made our finals,
confirming the qualities that made it
famous: inky ruby hue and a graceful nose
of cherry and damson, elegantly swathed in
sage, thyme and walnut skin, over a broad,
layered palate with impressive length. We
also loved the peerlessly complex, velvety
Montenero 2013, from nero d'Avola, merlot
and cabernet sauvignon.

● Litra '12	⚜⚜⚜ 6
● Montenero '13	⚜⚜⚜ 4
● Passomaggio '13	⚜⚜⚜ 3
○ Q 1000 M. Cl. '13	⚜⚜⚜ 5
○ Grillo '15	⚜ 2
● Nero d'Avola '15	⚜ 2
○ Sinestesia '15	⚜ 3
● Cannemasche '13	⚜⚜ 2*
● Litra '10	⚜⚜ 6
● Montenero '13	⚜⚜ 4
● Montenero '12	⚜⚜ 4
● Montenero '11	⚜⚜ 4
● Passomaggio '12	⚜⚜ 3
● Sens(i)nverso Cabernet Sauvignon '12	⚜⚜ 4
● Sens(i)nverso Nero d'Avola '12	⚜⚜ 4
● Sens(i)nverso Syrah '12	⚜⚜ 4

Alessandro di Camporeale

C.DA MANDRANOVA
90043 CAMPOREALE [PA]
TEL. +39 092437038
www.alessandrodicamporeale.it

CELLAR SALES
PRE-BOOKED VISITS
ANNUAL PRODUCTION 180,000 bottles
HECTARES UNDER VINE 35.00
VITICULTURE METHOD Certified Organic

The Alessandro family business has been
producing wine in Camporeale for four
generations, using artisanal methods which
are highly appreciated by consumers. The
operation is run by the brothers Natale,
Nino and Rosolino, and their children, all
busy with farming the 35 hectares of
organic vineyards, vinification, wine
tourism, and marketing in 15 countries.
Their passion for viticulture led them to
embark on a new adventure, with five
hectares of vineyards on Etna, at Piano
Filici near Castiglione di Sicilia, soon to
start producing. Carlo Ferrini has been the
winery consultant since 2015. The Syrah
Kaid 2014 made the finals, impressing us
with its balsamic, fruity depth and lingering
finesse. Just behind came the
concentrated, elegant Kaid Vendemmia
Tardiva 2015, with a harmoniously sweet,
leisurely palate, and the refreshing Kaid
Sauvignon 2015, offering focused tropical
notes. Equally good were the two Vigna di
Mandranova 2015 monovarietals,
respectively from grillo and catarratto.

● Sicilia Syrah Kaid '14	⚜⚜⚜ 3*
● Kaid V. T. '15	⚜⚜⚜ 5
○ Sicilia Catarratto Benedè '15	⚜⚜ 2*
○ Sicilia Catarratto V. di Mandranova '15	⚜⚜ 4
○ Sicilia Grillo V. di Mandranova '15	⚜⚜ 3
● Sicilia Nero d'Avola DonnaTà '15	⚜⚜ 2*
○ Sicilia Sauvignon Kaid '15	⚜⚜ 3
● DonnaTà '13	⚜⚜ 2*
● Kaid '13	⚜⚜ 3*
● Kaid Syrah '12	⚜⚜ 3*
● Kaid V. T. '14	⚜⚜ 5
● Sicilia DonnaTà '14	⚜⚜ 2*
○ Sicilia Grillo V. di Mandranova '14	⚜⚜ 3
○ Sicilia Kaid Sauvignon Blanc '14	⚜⚜ 3

Assuli

VIA ARCHI, 9
91100 TRAPANI
TEL. +39 0923546706
www.assuli.it

CELLAR SALES
ANNUAL PRODUCTION 100,000 bottles
HECTARES UNDER VINE 100.00

This was a year of changes: a new company structure saw the departure of Claudia Alliata di Villafranca, with Roberto Caruso taking her place at the helm. Consequently, the winery name changed from Alliata to Assuli, although the substance remains the same: the winery at Mazara and the same vineyards, around 100 hectares in four plots near Marsala, which have always been owned by the Caruso family. Quality has also remained a constant, both in the rows and the cellar, thanks in no small part to the technical expertise of Lorenzo Landi. The range of labels focuses increasingly on monovarietals from native grapes. Seamless, superb confirmation that garnered a Tre Bicchieri for the intensely deep Nero d'Avola Lorlando 2015, showing complexity and focused varietal notes over a generous palate with firmness and great length. It was joined in the finals by the Syrah Ruggiero 2015, with its fragrant, appley, balsamic fruit. The Grillo Fiordiligi 2015 showed a floral, herbaceous nose and deliciously fresh stuffing.

Baglio del Cristo di Campobello

C.DA FAVAROTTA
S.DA ST.LE 123 KM 19,200
92023 CAMPOBELLO DI LICATA [AG]
TEL. +39 0922 877709
www.cristodicampobello.it

CELLAR SALES
PRE-BOOKED VISITS
ANNUAL PRODUCTION 300,000 bottles
HECTARES UNDER VINE 30.00

Skilled, passionate farmers for generations, the Bonetta family have made their fine estate one of the benchmarks of modern Sicilian oenology. Their winning strategy has undoubtedly been to use local traditional viticultural methods, accompanied by a modern, farsighted vision of what the market demands. The lovely enclosed baglio farmstead is home to the cellar, and lies at the heart of a huge estate situated at an elevation of over 350 metres, caressed by the salty winds blowing in from the nearby coast. With its deep purple hue and exquisite hints of morello cherry, cloves, myrtle and juniper, the drinkable Adènzia Rosso 2014, from nero d'Avola and syrah, showed great character, and missed top honours by a whisker. Almost as good was the territorial Nero d'Avola Lu Patri 2014 and the fresh-tasting Lalùci 2015, a seductive Grillo with aromas of mint and white damson.

● Lorlando '15	♟♟♟ 2*
● Ruggiero '15	♟♟ 2*
○ Carinda '15	♟♟ 2*
● Fiordiligi '15	♟♟ 2*
● Besi '13	♟ 5
● Lorlando '14	♟♟♟ 2*
● Baltasàr '12	♟♟ 5
○ Grillo '13	♟♟ 2*
● Kaspàr '12	♟♟ 4
● Kaspàr '11	♟♟ 4
● Lorlando '13	♟♟ 2*
● Melkior '12	♟♟ 4
○ Mommo '13	♟♟ 3
● Ruggiero '14	♟♟ 2*
● Ruggiero '13	♟♟ 2*
○ Taya '14	♟♟ 4

● Sicilia Rosso Adènzia '14	♟♟ 3*
○ C'D'C' Cristo di Campobello Bianco '15	♟♟ 2*
○ C'D'C' Cristo di Campobello Rosato '15	♟♟ 2*
○ Sicilia Bianco Adènzia '15	♟♟ 3
○ Sicilia Grillo Lalùci '15	♟♟ 3
○ Sicilia Laudàri '14	♟♟ 4
● Sicilia Nero d'Avola Lu Patri '14	♟♟ 5
● Sicilia Syrah Lusira '14	♟♟ 5
● Lu Patri '09	♟♟♟ 5
○ Sicilia Chardonnay Laudàri '13	♟♟ 4
○ Sicilia Grillo Lalùci '14	♟♟ 3
● Sicilia Nero d'Avola Lu Patri '13	♟♟ 5
● Sicilia Syrah Lusirà '13	♟♟ 5

Baglio di Pianetto

LOC. PIANETTO
VIA FRANCIA
90030 SANTA CRISTINA GELA [PA]
TEL. +39 0918570002
www.bagliodipianetto.com

CELLAR SALES
PRE-BOOKED VISITS
ACCOMMODATION AND RESTAURANT SERVICE
ANNUAL PRODUCTION 550,000 bottles
HECTARES UNDER VINE 104.00
SUSTAINABLE WINERY

Paolo Marzotto's Sicilian dream come true is now 20 years old. He fell in love with the island in the 1950s, when he got to know its roads as a racing driver. The Pianetto and Baroni estates, with their respective cellars, are at the two extremes of the island: Santa Cristina Gela to the north, where the Conte has converted the ancient enclosed baglio farmstead into an elegant country house hotel; and Pachino, to the south, in Val di Noto, the heartland of nero d'Avola. In 2016, we saw the return of Renato De Bartoli, the winery's oenologist in the early years and now back as its managing director. A Tre Bicchieri went to the Shymer 2013, a blend of syrah from Noto and merlot from Santa Cristina Gela. An intense, focused nose with complex balsamic and spicy notes paves the way for a satisfyingly elegant palate and a long finish. The Moscato di Noto Ra'is 2012, in the more concentrated Essenza version, unleashes a nose of great finesse with autumn leaves and dried fruit, leading to a harmonious, refreshing palate.

● Shymer '13	♟♟♟	2*
● Carduni '12	♟♟	5
○ Moscato di Noto Ra'is Essenza '12	♟♟	5
● Salici '12	♟♟	4
● Sicilia Ramione '14	♟♟	4
● Agnus Ris. '11	♟	7
● Sicilia Cembali '13	♟	5
○ Sicilia Ficiligno '15	♟	3
○ Sicilia Ginolfo '13	♟	4
○ Sicilia Timeo '15	♟	3
● Ramione '04	♟♟♟	3*
● Sicilia Rosso Ramione '13	♟♟♟	3*
○ Sicilia Bianco Ficiligno '14	♟♟	4
● Sicilia Nero d'Avola Cembali '12	♟♟	6

Tenuta Bastonaca

C.DA BASTONACA
97019 VITTORIA [RG]
TEL. +39 0932686480
www.tenutabastonaca.it

CELLAR SALES
ACCOMMODATION
ANNUAL PRODUCTION 40,000 bottles
HECTARES UNDER VINE 10.00
SUSTAINABLE WINERY

Building on a family tradition in viticulture, a close young couple set up an operation covering around ten hectares, of which eight are currently under vine. At Contrada Bastonaca, in the heart of the Cerasuolo di Vittoria DOC zone, Giovanni Calcaterra and Silvana Raniolo focus on quality and respect for the environment, with conversion to organic farming methods is well underway. Their bush vines receive no irrigation so as to encourage the concentration of aromas and flavours. The winery is based in a nicely renovated 18th-century wine press. With its intense colour edged with violet, the superb, highly drinkable Cerasuolo di Vittoria 2014 impresses with its ripe nose of spice and black berry fruit swathed in delicate balsam, over an invigorating, elegant, leisurely palate. Equally good were the refreshing, fragrant Frappato, the fruity, intriguing Nero d'Avola and the zesty, sea-breezy Grillo, all from the 2015 growing year.

● Cerasuolo di Vittoria '14	♟♟	3
● Frappato '15	♟♟	3
○ Grillo '15	♟♟	3
● Nero d'Avola '15	♟♟	3

★Benanti

VIA G. GARIBALDI, 475
95029 VIAGRANDE [CT]
TEL. +39 0957893399
www.vinicolabenanti.it

CELLAR SALES
PRE-BOOKED VISITS
ANNUAL PRODUCTION 120,000 bottles
HECTARES UNDER VINE 45.00

If we had to make a documentary on the renaissance of Etna viticulture, it would be easy to choose a title: Giuseppe Benanti, the Cavaliere and the History. It would have been a fitting homage to the man who was the first grower, a solitary figure for many years, to try and establish a benchmark wine. He found what he was looking for in the tradition and history of the area around the volcano, in wines from native varieties that are a true expression of the terroir, without affectation. Today, his sons, Antonio and Salvino, also bring their enthusiasm to this prestigious operation. We saw an outstanding performance from the complex, concentrated Pietramarina 2012, boasting elegant nuances of quartz, flint, wisteria and fresh almond, followed by an extremely pleasurable, satisfying, leisurely palate. We liked all the other labels, from the fleshy, lively Serra della Contessa 2012, to the stylish, full-flavoured, juicy Nerello Cappuccio 2013.

○ Etna Bianco '14	♟♟	3
○ Etna Bianco Sup. Pietramarina '12	♟♟	5
● Etna Rosso '14	♟♟	4
● Etna Rosso Nerello Mascalese '13	♟♟	5
● Etna Rosso Rovittello '12	♟♟	5
● Etna Rosso Serra della Contessa '12	♟♟	7
● Nerello Cappuccio '13	♟♟	5
○ Etna Bianco Sup. Pietramarina '04	♟♟♟	6
○ Etna Bianco Sup. Pietramarina '02	♟♟♟	5
○ Etna Bianco Sup. Pietramarina '01	♟♟♟	5
○ Etna Bianco Sup. Pietramarina '00	♟♟♟	5
● Etna Rosso Serra della Contessa '04	♟♟♟	7
● Etna Rosso Serra della Contessa '03	♟♟♟	7
● Il Drappo '04	♟♟♟	5

Bonavita

LOC. FARO SUPERIORE
C.DA CORSO
98158 MESSINA
TEL. +39 3471754683
www.bonavitafaro.com

PRE-BOOKED VISITS
ANNUAL PRODUCTION 10,000 bottles
HECTARES UNDER VINE 2.50

When he was a boy, Giovanni Scarfone played near his grandfather in the small vineyard behind the house at Faro Superiore, where the family spent their summers. When the time came to decide what to do in life, Giovanni knew what he wanted: agricultural school, a degree in agronomics, and work experience around Italy before setting up on his own as a grower. His grandfather's vineyard is still there, with rootstock over 70 years in age, and joins another small plot at Curcuraci, for a total of two and a half hectares. Scarfone deals with the whole process himself, from digging the land to pruning and harvesting. The same holds true in the cellar, located in the garage of the ancestral home, large enough only for his slim build. His Faro 2014, a real vin de garage, seduced us with its hallmark aristocratic elegance, showing peach and pomegranate on the mineral nose, leading to a refreshing, dense, but supple palate and a captivating, concentrated finish of superb length.

● Faro '14	♟♟	5
⊙ Rosato '15	♟♟	2*
● Faro '13	♟♟	5
● Faro '12	♟♟	5
● Faro '11	♟♟	5
● Faro '10	♟♟	5
● Faro '09	♟♟	5
● Faro '08	♟♟	5
● Faro '07	♟♟	5
● Faro '06	♟♟	5
⊙ Rosato '14	♟♟	2*
⊙ Rosato '13	♟♟	2*
⊙ Rosato '12	♟♟	2*
⊙ Rosato '09	♟♟	2*

Le Casematte

LOC. FARO SUPERIORE
C.DA CORSO
98163 MESSINA
TEL. +39 0906409427
www.lecasematte.it

CELLAR SALES
ANNUAL PRODUCTION 30,000 bottles
HECTARES UNDER VINE 11.00
VITICULTURE METHOD Certified Organic
SUSTAINABLE WINERY

This unique winery lies in a magical setting, in the high hills overlooking the Straits of Messina, caressed by the sea breeze. It represents a dream come true for accountant Gianfranco Sabbatino and footballer Andrea Barzagli. They established the winery in 2008, naming it after three "casematte", pillboxes used during the two World Wars. The operation embodies the renaissance of the Faro DOC zone, with an artisanal approach much appreciated by demanding critics and wine enthusiasts. Top honours went to the stunning 2014 version of Faro, from nero d'Avola, nocera, nerello mascalese, and nerello cappuccio, which enchanted the panel with its charming black berry fruit, spice and Mediterranean herbs. This complex, extremely drinkable wine shows exceptional finesse, with glossy tannins, good length and grip. We were also won over by the elegant Rosato Rosematte Nerello Mascalese 2015.

● Faro '14	▼▼▼	5
○ Peloro Bianco '15	▼▼	3
● Peloro Rosso '14	▼▼	2*
⊙ Rosematte Nerello Mascalese '15	▼▼	3
● Faro '13	♀♀♀	5
● Faro Quattroenne '12	♀♀	5
● Faro Quattroenne '11	♀♀	5
● Figliodiennenne '11	♀♀	2*
● Figliodiennenne '10	♀♀	2*
○ Peloro Bianco '14	♀♀	3
● Peloro Rosso '13	♀♀	2*
⊙ Rosematte '14	♀♀	3
⊙ Rosematte '13	♀♀	3

Frank Cornelissen

FRAZ. SOLICCHIATA
VIA NAZIONALE, 297
95012 CASTIGLIONE DI SICILIA [CT]
TEL. +39 0942986315
www.frankcornelissen.it

CELLAR SALES
PRE-BOOKED VISITS
ANNUAL PRODUCTION 70,000 bottles
HECTARES UNDER VINE 18.00
VITICULTURE METHOD Certified Organic

Magma is the name of the first wine produced by Frank Cornelissen, determined to bottle the energy of the volcano and the complexity of nerello. For someone so madly in love with Etna's savage beauty, it was only natural to start producing wine from the old vineyards in the arid, metaphysical lunar landscapes sculpted by the lava flows. Frank's extremely intriguing wines are the result of a very personal and original interpretation of nerello, which in recent years have become cleaner-cut with greater varietal definition, without losing their initial spontaneity. The deeply concentrated, extremely drinkable Nerello Mascalese Magma 2014 made our finals with its rustic yet tantalizing aromas of smoked sea salt, ripe peach and aromatic herbs, over a dense, deep, fruit-driven palate, underpinned by fat tannins. Pomegranate, peach and apricot are the hallmarks of the complex, lingering, fruit-fuelled Munjebel Rosso Monte Colla 2014.

● Magma Dodicesima Edizione '14	▼▼	8
● Munjebel Rosso Le Vigne Alte '14	▼▼	7
● Munjebel Rosso Monte Colla '14	▼▼	7
● Munjebel Rosso PA - Vign. Porcaria '14	▼▼	7
● Contadino 10 '12	♀♀	4
○ Munjebel Bianco '14	♀♀	5
○ Munjebel Bianco '13	♀♀	5
● Munjebel Rosso '14	♀♀	6
● Munjebel Rosso '13	♀♀	6
● Munjebel Rosso Chiusa Spagnola '13	♀♀	7
● Munjebel Rosso Le Vigne Alte '13	♀♀	7
● Munjebel Rosso Monte Colla '13	♀♀	7
⊙ Susucaru '13	♀♀	4
● Vino del Contadino '14	♀♀	4

Cottanera

.oc. Iannazzo
s.da prov.le 89
95030 Castiglione di Sicilia [CT]
Tel. +39 0942963601
www.cottanera.it

CELLAR SALES
PRE-BOOKED VISITS
ANNUAL PRODUCTION 300,000 bottles
HECTARES UNDER VINE 65.00

Despite their youth, the Cambria brothers are keen to continue the work begun 20 years ago by their father Gugliemo, and with the same passion and dedication they obtain the same excellent results. The graceful wines are full of character, with a real sense of place, from vineyards covering over 60 hectares. The estate is unusually large for these parts and is tended with the loving care generally reserved for gardens. It is almost entirely planted to native varieties such as nerello mascalese, nerello cappuccio and carricante, in five different districts on the northern slopes of Etna, near Passopisciaro. The various Etnas were in fine fettle, starting with the Zottorinoto 2012, which romped off with a Tre Bicchieri thanks to a complex nose of red fruit, violets, autumn leaves and spice, backed up by a fresh, elegant palate, underpinned by close-knit, caressing tannins. Also on the podium was the appealing, harmonious Etna Diciassettesalme 2014, and the full-bodied Etna Bianco 2015, with a good acidic backbone.

● Etna Rosso Zottorinoto Ris. '12	♟♟♟ 8
○ Etna Bianco '15	♟♟ 3*
● Etna Rosso Diciassettesalme '14	♟♟ 3*
○ Etna Bianco Calderara '14	♟♟ 5
● Etna Rosso '13	♟♟ 5
● Etna Rosso Barbazzale '15	♟♟ 2*
● Sicilia L'Ardenza '12	♟♟ 4
● Sicilia Sole di Sesta '13	♟♟ 4
● Sicilia Fatagione '13	♟ 3
○ Etna Bianco '11	♟♟♟ 3*
● Etna Rosso '11	♟♟♟ 5
● Etna Rosso '07	♟♟♟ 5
● Etna Rosso '06	♟♟♟ 5
● Etna Rosso '05	♟♟♟ 5
● Etna Rosso Zottorinoto Ris. '11	♟♟♟ 8
● Sole di Sesta '00	♟♟♟ 5

★Cusumano

c.da San Carlo
s.da st. le 113 km 307
90047 Partinico [PA]
Tel. +39 0918908713
www.cusumano.it

CELLAR SALES
PRE-BOOKED VISITS
ANNUAL PRODUCTION 2,500,000 bottles
HECTARES UNDER VINE 520.00
SUSTAINABLE WINERY

Alberto and Diego Cusumano's winery, set up in the early 2000s, following in the footsteps of a family tradition, soon earned a reputation on all the main international markets, becoming a worldwide icon of Sicilian winemaking. This is the merit of the impeccable, modern, elegant wines, whose intriguing style expresses perfectly the traits of both native and international varieties, and of the various growing areas. The stylish cellar and headquarters at Partinico are the perfect example of the winery's philosophy. A Tre Bicchieri was never in doubt for the Alta Mora Bianco 2014, whose exceptional finesse is expressed in elegant nuances of blossom, citrus zest, white peach, and flint, echoed in the mouth, and sustained by a refreshing acidic vein of real class. Almost as good was the wonderfully subtle, mineral, spicy Alta Mora Rosso 2014, with delicate, lively tannins and good length. As always, Noà and Sàgana lived up to expectations.

○ Etna Bianco Alta Mora '14	♟♟♟ 3*
● Etna Rosso Alta Mora '14	♟♟ 4
● Sicilia Sàgana '14	♟♟ 4
○ Angimbé Tenuta Ficuzza '15	♟♟ 3
● Benuara Tenuta Presti e Pegni '15	♟♟ 3
○ Brut M. Cl. 700 '13	♟♟ 4
● Sicilia Noà '14	♟♟ 4
○ Sicilia Shamaris '15	♟♟ 3
○ Moscato dello Zucco '10	♟♟♟ 5
● Noà '10	♟♟♟ 4*
● Sàgana '12	♟♟♟ 4*
● Sàgana '11	♟♟♟ 4*
● Sàgana '09	♟♟♟ 4
● Sàgana '08	♟♟♟ 4
● Sàgana '07	♟♟♟ 4
● Sicilia Noà '13	♟♟♟ 4*

Di Giovanna

C.DA SAN GIACOMO
92017 SAMBUCA DI SICILIA [AG]
TEL. +39 09251955675
www.di-giovanna.com

CELLAR SALES
PRE-BOOKED VISITS
ANNUAL PRODUCTION 250,000 bottles
HECTARES UNDER VINE 50.00
VITICULTURE METHOD Certified Organic

This fine winery, dating back to the second half of the 19th century, whose most recent owners were Aurelio Di Giovanna and his German wife, Barbara. Now their sons Gunther and Klaus are at the helm of the company, combining Sicilian energy and Teutonic character perfectly. The estates are found around Sambuca di Sicilia and Contessa Entellina, at elevations of 400–800 metres, and benefit from excellent day-night temperature ranges. Their personal philosophy has led them to rely solely on organic farming methods. A fine range was presented this year, starting with the peerless, deliciously drinkable Grillo 2015, opening to a delicate greenish hue, and showing nuances of wisteria, green almond and white damson, exalted by salty, mineral notes. The refreshing, pleasurable Gerbino Rosato di Nerello Mascalese 2015 is an elegant, full-flavoured wine of great class, with notes of red berries.

⊙ Gerbino Rosato Nerello Mascalese '15	♥♥ 2*
● Gerbino Rosso '14	♥♥ 2*
○ Grillo '15	♥♥ 3
● Helios Rosso '14	♥♥ 5
● Nero d'Avola '14	♥♥ 3
○ Helios Bianco '15	♥ 3
○ Viognier '15	♥ 3
○ Grillo '14	♥♥ 2*
○ Grillo '12	♥♥ 2*
○ Helios '12	♥♥ 3*
○ Helios Bianco '14	♥♥ 3
○ Helios Bianco '13	♥♥ 3
● Helios Rosso '12	♥♥ 3

★Donnafugata

VIA SEBASTIANO LIPARI, 18
91025 MARSALA [TP]
TEL. +39 0923724200
www.donnafugata.it

CELLAR SALES
PRE-BOOKED VISITS
ANNUAL PRODUCTION 2,200,000 bottles
HECTARES UNDER VINE 338.00
SUSTAINABLE WINERY

Giacomo Rallo, who sadly passed away on 10 May, was a farsighted businessman with a forthright, generous nature, and a gentleman from a bygone age. His prestigious winery was set up in 1983, and later expanded to include cellars at Contessa Entellina and Pantelleria. The headquarters, in 19th-century premises in Marsala, are open to visitors and home to a magnificent underground barrique cellar of 2,000 square metres, completed in 2008. Giacomo's work is continued by his wife Gabriella and his sons José and Antonio, the latter recently elected national president of Unione Italiana Vino. The Ben Ryé 2014 took another memorable Tre Bicchieri, showing incomparable fullness and intensity in its elegant nose and a sumptuously cossetting yet dynamic palate of outstanding length. Giacomo's other two darlings also made our finals: the deep, full-bodied Milleunanotte 2011, balsamic with an elegant fruit encore on the palate; and the mature, characterful Tancredi 2012, showing concentration and length.

○ Passito di Pantelleria Ben Ryé '14	♥♥♥ 7
● Contessa Entellina Milleunanotte '11	♥♥ 7
● Tancredi '12	♥♥ 5
○ Contessa Entellina Chardonnay La Fuga '15	♥♥ 3
○ Contessa Entellina Chiarandà '13	♥♥ 5
● Sicilia Angheli '13	♥♥ 4
○ Sicilia Bianco V. di Gabri '14	♥♥ 3
○ Sicilia Brut Donnafugata '12	♥♥ 5
○ Sicilia Lighea '15	♥♥ 3
● Sicilia Sherazade '15	♥♥ 3
○ Sicilia Sursur '15	♥ 3
○ Passito di Pantelleria Ben Ryé '12	♥♥♥ 7
● Tancredi '11	♥♥♥ 5

Duca di Salaparuta

VIA NAZIONALE, S.DA ST.LE 113
90014 CASTELDACCIA [PA]
TEL. +39 091945201
www.duca.it

PRE-BOOKED VISITS
ANNUAL PRODUCTION 9,000,000 bottles
HECTARES UNDER VINE 155.00
SUSTAINABLE WINERY

Established in 1824 by Giuseppe Alliata di Villafranca, this cellar has played a key role in the evolution of Sicilian wine production for almost two centuries. Its pioneering start was followed by a long period of management by the regional government, until it was taken over by the ILLVA Saronno group in the early 2000s, together with another historic winery, Florio of Marsala. It boasts two famous brands: Corvo for the more approachable and innovative products, and Duca di Salaparuta for the iconic labels linked to the territory and to the winery's three estates at Vajasindi, Suor Marchesa and Risignolo. Good performance from the appealing, fresh Bianca di Valguarnera 2014, with oak to the fore as always. The delicately aromatic Irmàna Floris 2015, a blend of native varieties showing elegant notes of jasmine and white-fleshed fruit, over a fresh, crisp palate surprised us. And three interesting reds: the Vajasindi Làvico 2013 from nerello mascalese, and Vajasindi Pinot Nero Nawàri 2014, and the Calanìca Frappato Syrah 2014.

○ Bianca di Valguarnera '14	♥♥	6
● Calanìca Frappato Syrah '14	♥♥	3
○ Colomba Platino Risignolo '15	♥♥	4
● Duca Enrico '12	♥♥	8
○ Irmàna Floris Corvo '15	♥♥	3
● Làvico Vajasindi '13	♥♥	3
● Nawàri Vajasindi '14	♥♥	6
● Triskelè '13	♥♥	5
● Duca Enrico '03	♥♥♥	6
● Duca Enrico '01	♥♥♥	6
● Duca Enrico '92	♥♥♥	6
● Duca Enrico '90	♥♥♥	6
● Duca Enrico '88	♥♥♥	6
● Duca Enrico '86	♥♥♥	6
● Duca Enrico '85	♥♥♥	6
● Duca Enrico '84	♥♥♥	6

Tenuta di Fessina

C.DA ROVITTELLO
VIA NAZIONALE, 22 S.DA ST.LE 120
95012 CASTIGLIONE DI SICILIA [CT]
TEL. +39 0942395300
www.tenutadifessina.com

CELLAR SALES
PRE-BOOKED VISITS
ANNUAL PRODUCTION 70,000 bottles
HECTARES UNDER VINE 15.00
SUSTAINABLE WINERY

The love story between Tuscan grower Silvia Maestrelli and Etna started when she visited Sicily in the past and flourished in 2007 with the purchase of some small, very old vineyard plots around an 18th-century winepress. Seduced by the breathtaking beauty of the landscape and opportunities in the viticultural field, Silvia made rapid progress, and was soon producing wines of acknowledged elegance and character, to the point that her cellar became one of the best expressions of the Etna district's new wave. A' Puddara 2014, an extremely drinkable wine of great finesse, missed top honours by a whisker. This complex Carricante with forthright aromas of citron, apple, broom and white pepper, delighted us with its fresh, zesty palate with marked mineral notes. The subtly elegant, crystalline Erse Bianco 2015 showed tangy fruit, swathed in lavender, grapefruit, green almond, and curry plant.

○ Etna Bianco A' Puddara '14	♥♥	5
○ Etna Bianco Erse '15	♥♥	4
● Etna Rosso Erse '15	♥♥	4
● Laeneo Nerello Cappuccio '14	♥♥	3
⊙ Etna Rosato '15	♥	3
○ Etna Bianco A' Puddara '13	♥♥♥	5
○ Etna Bianco A' Puddara '12	♥♥♥	5
○ Etna Bianco A' Puddara '11	♥♥♥	5
○ Etna Bianco A' Puddara '10	♥♥♥	5
○ Etna Bianco A' Puddara '09	♥♥♥	5
● Etna Rosso Musmeci '07	♥♥♥	6
● Ero '13	♥♥	3
● Etna Rosso Musmeci Ris. '11	♥♥	6
● Laeneo '13	♥♥	3

Feudi del Pisciotto

C.DA PISCIOTTO
93015 NISCEMI [CL]
TEL. +39 09331930280
www.castellare.it

CELLAR SALES
PRE-BOOKED VISITS
ACCOMMODATION
ANNUAL PRODUCTION 200,000 bottles
HECTARES UNDER VINE 45.00

Just five years ago Paolo Panerai began his immense restoration project of the venerable Baglio del Pisciotto and its conversion into a wine resort. Only a restaurant was missing, which has just been opened. Alessandro Cellai tends the vineyard as if it were a garden, and carefully avoids the stress of excessive pruning or thinning. With passing time the vines have matured and only this can give the wines the desired depth. Feudo wines have benefited in terms of elegance and territorial character thanks also to work on extraction and oak ageing. A Tre Bicchieri for the austere Cerasuolo di Vittoria Giambattista Valli Paris 2012, with a fruity, balsamic nose, making way for an elegant, juicy myrtle and plum palate, its invigorating, caressing attack leads to a long, leisurely, spicy finish. The intense, complex Cabernet Sauvignon Missoni 2014 shows fruity stuffing, with a lively, racy palate and even-textured tannins.

● Cerasuolo di Vittoria Giambattista Valli Paris '12	▼▼▼	6
● Cabernet Sauvignon Missoni '14	▼▼	4
○ Passito Gianfranco Ferrè '14	▼▼	5
● Baglio del Sole Nero d'Avola '14	▼▼	2*
○ Chardonnay Alberta Ferretti '14	▼▼	4
● Frappato Carolina Marengo Kisa '14	▼▼	4
● L'Eterno '14	▼▼	7
● Nero d'Avola Versace '14	▼▼	4
○ Tirsat Gurra di Mare '14	▼▼	4
● Baglio del Sole Merlot Syrah '14	▼	2
● Cerasuolo di Vittoria Giambattista Valli Paris '11	♈♈♈	6
● Cerasuolo di Vittoria Giambattista Valli Paris '09	♈♈♈	6
● Frappato Carolina Marengo '11	♈♈♈	4*
● Nero d'Avola Versace '12	♈♈♈	4*

Feudo Arancio

C.DA PORTELLA MISILBESI
92017 SAMBUCA DI SICILIA [AG]
TEL. +39 0925579000
www.feudoarancio.it

CELLAR SALES
PRE-BOOKED VISITS
ANNUAL PRODUCTION 800,000 bottles
HECTARES UNDER VINE 690.00

This is one of the two Sicilian wineries owned by Mezzacorona, the Trentino-based international colossus established in 1904. The estate near Lake Arancio is set in a breathtaking landscape, and covers 240 hectares on windswept hillsides, while the Acate estate covers over 450, also in excellent wine country. A straightforward, modern approach to viticulture is based on a relationship with nature in which priority is given to safeguarding, respecting and keeping environmental impact to a minimum, as tradition dictates. The impressive Barone d'Albius 2014, an original blend of grillo, inzolia, zibibbo, chardonnay, and viognier, charms with delicate nuances of apricots, green almond, Mediterranean herbs, and tangerine, over an invigorating, pleasurably refreshing palate. We also liked its 2012 partner, a full, characterful red from nero d'Avola, syrah, cabernet sauvignon, pinot nero, and merlot.

○ Barone d'Albius '14	▼▼	5
● Barone d'Albius '12	▼▼	5
○ Dalila '14	▼▼	4
○ Hekate Passito '13	▼▼	5
○ Sicilia Grillo '15	▼▼	2*
● Cantodoro '13	▼	3
○ Inzolia '15	▼	3
● Sicilia Nero d'Avola '15	▼	3
● Sicilia Syrah '14	▼	4
● Barone d'Albius '11	♈♈	5
● Cantadoro '12	♈♈	4
○ Dalila '13	♈♈	4
○ Dalila '12	♈♈	3
○ Hekate Passito '12	♈♈	5
○ Sicilia Grillo '14	♈♈	2*

Feudo Maccari

C.DA MACCARI
S.DA PROV.LE PACHINO-NOTO KM 13,500
96017 NOTO [SR]
TEL. +39 0931596894
www.feudomaccari.it

CELLAR SALES
PRE-BOOKED VISITS
ANNUAL PRODUCTION 167,000 bottles
HECTARES UNDER VINE 50.00
SUSTAINABLE WINERY

In 2000, a passionate love for Sicily, the certainty of producing a great wine and a fair amount of tenacity pushed the Tuscan owner of Tenuta Sette Ponti, Antonio Moretti, to embark on the adventure of producing wine in the beautiful area between Noto and Pachino, near the Riserva di Vendicari. Antonio believes in respecting the territory, and being careful to protect traditions, especially when they go back centuries. This is why Feudo Maccari only has bush vines, almost entirely of nero d'Avola and grillo. A Tre Bicchieri went to the Nero d'Avola Saia 2014, whose elegant nose delights with focused, fragrant fruit, blackberries and cherries to the fore, accompanied by fresh notes of balsam and sea breeze, followed by an invigorating, vibrant palate with a satisfyingly long finish. We also liked the Mahâris 2014, a Syrah whose grassy Mediterranean notes, spice and balsam pave the way for firm structure and length in the mouth.

● Saia '14	♟♟♟ 4*
○ Family&Friends '15	♟♟ 5
● Sicilia Syrah Mahâris '14	♟♟ 5
○ Grillo '15	♟♟ 2*
● Nero d'Avola '15	♟♟ 2*
○ Sultana '13	♟ 5
● Saia '13	♟♟♟ 4*
● Saia '12	♟♟♟ 4*
● Saia '11	♟♟♟ 4*
● Saia '10	♟♟♟ 4*
● Saia '08	♟♟♟ 4*
● Saia '07	♟♟♟ 4*
● Saia '06	♟♟♟ 4
○ Grillo '14	♟♟ 2*
● Nero d'Avola '13	♟♟ 2*

Feudo Montoni

C.DA MONTONI VECCHI
90144 CAMMARATA [AG]
TEL. +39 091513106
www.feudomontoni.it

CELLAR SALES
PRE-BOOKED VISITS
ANNUAL PRODUCTION 205,000 bottles
HECTARES UNDER VINE 30.00
VITICULTURE METHOD Certified Organic
SUSTAINABLE WINERY

The winery, located in the green Cammarata hills at the heart of Sicily, dates back to 1469, when beautiful enclosed farmstead was built here. This is still today the pulsing heart of Fabio Sireci's fine operation, with 80 hectares planted to olive trees, wheat and vines, at elevations of between 500 and 700 metres. His family purchased it in the late 19th century, charmed by its unique setting and the day-night temperature range. Fabio has brought out its potential to the full, making it a benchmark for those who seek wines of character, focusing on natural, artisanal production methods. The peerless Nero d'Avola Vrucara 2012, with its beguiling deep ruby hue, displays focused notes of black damson, capers and juniper berries, swathed in attractive iodine notes. In the mouth, it shows an invigorating, stylish, lively character with impressive length. The highly drinkable Grillo Vigna della Timpa 2015 delights with citrus nuances, orange and tangerine to the fore.

● Nero d'Avola Vrucara '12	♟♟ 5
○ Sicilia Grillo V. della Timpa '15	♟♟ 3
○ Sicilia Inzolia dei Fornelli '15	♟♟ 3
● Sicilia Nero d'Avola V. Lagnusa '14	♟♟ 4
○ Sicilia Catarratto V. del Masso '15	♟ 2
○ Sicilia Nerello Mascalese Rose di Adele '15	♟ 2
○ Catarratto '11	♟♟ 2*
● Nero d'Avola Vrucara '10	♟♟ 5
● Nero d'Avola Vrucara '09	♟♟ 5
○ Sicilia Catarratto V. del Masso '13	♟♟ 3
○ Sicilia Grillo V. della Timpa '14	♟♟ 3
○ Sicilia Grillo V. della Timpa '13	♟♟ 3
● Sicilia Nero d'Avola V. Lagnusa '13	♟♟ 4
● Sicilia Perricone V. del Core '14	♟♟ 3

Feudo Principi di Butera

C.DA DELIELLA
93011 BUTERA [CL]
TEL. +39 0934347726
www.feudobutera.it

CELLAR SALES
PRE-BOOKED VISITS
ANNUAL PRODUCTION 900,000 bottles
HECTARES UNDER VINE 180.00
SUSTAINABLE WINERY

The Zonin group opened its Sicilian outfit 20 years ago, restoring this winery to its former splendour. The estate covers 350 hectares between the provinces of Caltanissetta and Agrigento, a few kilometres from the Gulf of Gela. In 2002, the large, modern cellar was opened near the renovated farmstead. The 180 hectares under vine require constant attention to ensure the vitality of the vine generated by the climate, limestone soils and coastal position. The results of this painstaking work in the rows are the raw materials for wines with a marked Mediterranean character. The Deliella 2014 was back in the finals and just missed the top honours. This monovarietal Nero d'Avola seduces with the intensity and depth of a richly nuanced nose, leading into a hefty, but not overpowering, dynamic palate with a long finish. Our finals were also graced by the balsamic, lingering Symposio 2014, an elegant, well-balanced blend of cabernet sauvignon, merlot and petit verdot.

● Sicilia Nero d'Avola Deliella '14	♟♟ 6
● Symposio '14	♟♟ 5
○ Sicilia Chardonnay '15	♟♟ 3
● Sicilia Merlot '14	♟♟ 3
● Sicilia Nero d'Avola '14	♟♟ 2*
● Sicilia Syrah '14	♟♟ 3
● Sicilia Cabernet Sauvignon '14	♟ 3
○ Sicilia Insolia Serò '15	♟ 3
● Cabernet Sauvignon '00	♟♟♟ 5
● Deliella '12	♟♟♟ 6
● Deliella '05	♟♟♟ 6
● Deliella '02	♟♟♟ 7
● Deliella '00	♟♟♟ 6
● Sicilia Deliella '13	♟♟♟ 6

★Firriato

VIA TRAPANI, 4
91027 PACECO [TP]
TEL. +39 0923882755
www.firriato.it

CELLAR SALES
PRE-BOOKED VISITS
ANNUAL PRODUCTION 6,000,000 bottles
HECTARES UNDER VINE 320.00
VITICULTURE METHOD Certified Organic

The Di Gaetano family can be defined custodians of the land. From Favignana to Etna, not to mention the countryside near Trapani, where everything began, Firriato has managed to draw out the individual qualities of its various production zones with great respect, reflected in the use of organic farming methods and environmental sustainability at every stage of the production process. Salvatore and Vinzia have been joined by their daughter Irene and son-in-law Federico Lombardo di Monte Iato. The winery also offers splendid hospitality at Baglio Soria, Cavanera and Calamoni. A Tre Bicchieri went to the Favinia La Muciara 2014, a charming blend of grillo, cattaratto and zibibbo, varieties imbued with intensity, minerality, elegance and deeply concentrated fruit thanks to the Favignana terroir and climate. The other finalists were the complex, firmly structured Nero d'Avola Harmonium 2014, and the stylish, lingering Etna Rosso Rovo delle Coturnie 2014.

○ Favinia La Muciara '14	♟♟♟ 5
● Etna Rosso Cavanera Rovo delle Coturnie '14	♟♟ 5
● Harmonium '14	♟♟ 5
○ Etna Bianco Cavanera Ripa di Scorciavacca '14	♟♟ 5
● Favinia Le Sciabiche '12	♟♟ 5
○ Favinia Passulè '12	♟♟ 6
○ L'Ecrù '14	♟♟ 5
○ Quater Bianco '15	♟♟ 4
● Quater Rosso '14	♟♟ 5
● Ribeca '14	♟♟ 5
● Santagostino Rosso Baglio Soria '14	♟♟ 4
● Harmonium '13	♟♟♟ 5
● Ribeca '10	♟♟♟ 5
● Santagostino Rosso Baglio Soria '12	♟♟♟ 4*

Cantine Florio

via Vincenzo Florio, 1
91025 Marsala [TP]
Tel. +39 0923781111
www.duca.it/cantineflorio

CELLAR SALES
PRE-BOOKED VISITS
ANNUAL PRODUCTION 3,500,000 bottles

The name of Florio has been linked to Marsala and the history of Sicily for 184 years, and evokes an age of splendour and prosperity that the winery still embodies as part of the ILLVA group, alongside Duca di Salaparuta. The venerable cellars, with their splendid ogival vaults, store reserves from centuries past and are parts of a superb visitor centre, with a terrace overlooking the sea. It is also a prestigious showcase for group products, in which Florio exudes Mediterranean sun, with its Marsalas and sweet and fortified wines from traditional growing areas. The Vergine Terre Arse 2004 made the finals with an intense, complex bouquet of great cleanness and finesse, leading to an impressive encore on the invigorating, long palate. The Targa 1840 Superiore Riserva Semisecco 2005 failed to match the previous vintage in terms of elegance, but showed the same personality and verve. The sweet, oak-aged Morsi di Luce 2013, from zibibbo, was as pleasurable as ever.

○ Marsala Vergine Terre Arse '04	🍷🍷 4
○ Ambar Moscato Liquoroso	🍷🍷 3
○ Marsala Sup. Semisecco Ambra Donna Franca Ris.	🍷🍷 6
○ Marsala Sup. Semisecco Targa 1840 Ris. '05	🍷🍷 4
○ Morsi di Luce '13	🍷🍷 5
○ Passito di Pantelleria '14	🍷🍷 6
○ Marsala Sup. Vecchio Florio Secco '12	🍷 3
○ Oxydia	🍷 3
○ Pantelleria Passito Liquoroso Zighidì '13	🍷 4
○ Marsala Sup. Semisecco Targa 1840 Ris. '04	🍷🍷🍷 4*
○ Marsala Sup. Vecchio Florio '11	🍷🍷 2*
○ Marsala Vergine Baglio Florio '02	🍷🍷 5
○ Morsi di Luce '12	🍷🍷 4
○ Passito di Pantelleria '12	🍷🍷 6

Graci

loc. Passopisciaro
c.da Feudo di Mezzo
95012 Castiglione di Sicilia [CT]
Tel. +39 3487016773
www.graci.eu

CELLAR SALES
PRE-BOOKED VISITS
ANNUAL PRODUCTION 65,000 bottles
HECTARES UNDER VINE 18.00
VITICULTURE METHOD Certified Organic

Despite his young age, Alberto Graci can consider himself one of the pioneers of Etna's new wave, to the point that in the space of only a few years he has become a benchmark for the entire area. His vineyards are now spread over six different districts, at elevations ranging from 650 to 1,000 metres. His wines express elegance and a sense of place, which are brought to the fore by organic farming methods, a light hand in the cellar, and ageing solely in concrete tanks and large oak. The impressively intense Etna Rosso Feudo di Mezzo 2014 boasts a focused mineral, balsamic character, but also rich red berries and rose tea, over an invigorating palate underpinned by silky tannins and a long, elegant finish. Also in the finals was the stylish, complex Etna Rosso Arcurìa 2014, offering attractive ripe fruit over mineral and balsam, for a deep, concentrated wine with firm structure.

● Etna Rosso Arcurìa '14	🍷🍷 6
● Etna Rosso Feudo di Mezzo '14	🍷🍷 6
○ Etna Bianco '15	🍷🍷 3
○ Etna Bianco Arcuria '14	🍷🍷 6
⊙ Etna Rosato '15	🍷🍷 3
● Etna Rosso '14	🍷🍷 3
○ Etna Bianco '10	🍷🍷🍷 4*
○ Etna Bianco Arcuria '11	🍷🍷🍷 5
○ Etna Bianco Quota 600 '10	🍷🍷🍷 5
● Etna Rosso Arcurìa '13	🍷🍷🍷 6
● Etna Rosso Arcurìa '12	🍷🍷🍷 6
○ Etna Bianco '14	🍷🍷 3*
○ Etna Bianco Arcuria '12	🍷🍷 6
⊙ Etna Rosato '14	🍷🍷 3

Gulfi

C.DA PATRIA
97012 CHIARAMONTE GULFI [RG]
TEL. +39 0932921654
www.gulfi.it

CELLAR SALES
PRE-BOOKED VISITS
ACCOMMODATION AND RESTAURANT SERVICE
ANNUAL PRODUCTION 280,000 bottles
HECTARES UNDER VINE 70.00
VITICULTURE METHOD Certified Organic

In 1996, Vito Catania's rediscovered love for his homeland and its traditions, left behind to seek his fortune in France and northern Italy, bore fruit in this prestigious operation. He decided to focus on native varieties and the infinite nuances provided by the various terroirs, from Pachino to Etna, on organic farming methods, and on bush vines. He also chose to forgo artificial irrigation and to harvest manually. The impressive results achieved and the strong personality of the wines have made this a cult winery. Among this year's entries we appreciated the Nero d'Avola Neromàccarj 2011 from the Pachino estate. Opening to a concentrated ruby hue, it charms with nuances of black cherry, violets, liquorice and quinine, over a chewy, balsamic palate, finishing harmonious and long. We also loved the firm, ripe Pinò 2012, from pinot nero grown on Etna.

Hauner

LOC. SANTA MARIA
VIA G.GRILLO, 61
98123 MESSINA
TEL. +39 0906413029
www.hauner.it

CELLAR SALES
PRE-BOOKED VISITS
ANNUAL PRODUCTION 80,000 bottles
HECTARES UNDER VINE 18.00

Salina, known in classical times as Didyme, is an island of harsh, intense beauty, whose twin volcanic cones are a challenge for viticulture. The results, however, can be delightful, such as the legendary Malvasia delle Lipari, a sweet wine that risked oblivion in the mid-19th century. Its survival has a great deal to do with the loving attentions of Carlo Hauner, a Brescia artist who visited the island in the early 1960s as a tourist, and soon became its adopted son, and a custodian and promoter of its traditional viticulture. His work continues through his son and heir, Carlo Junior. The Passito Riserva Carlo Hauner 2013 made the finals with its rich, complex nose of dried apricot, carob and candied citrus, over elegant hints of autumn leaves and bitter herbs. On the harmonious palate it shows concentrated, sweet and beautifully long. The Hierà 2014, a blend of calabrese, alicante and nocera, charms with elegant, ripe fruit. The attractive Salina Rosso 2014 also impressed.

● Neromàccarj '11	♛♛ 6
● Pinò '12	♛♛ 8
⊙ Rosà '15	♛♛ 3
● Nerobaronj '11	♛ 5
● Nerobufaleffj '11	♛ 6
● Nerosanlorè '11	♛ 6
● Nerobufaleffj '07	♛♛♛ 5
● Neromàccarj '08	♛♛♛ 6
● Neromàccarj '07	♛♛♛ 5
● Neromàccarj '04	♛♛♛ 5
● Nerosanlorè '05	♛♛♛ 5
● Nerobufaleffj '09	♛♛ 6
● Neromàccarj '10	♛♛ 6
○ Sicilia Carjcanti '12	♛♛ 5
○ Valcanzjria '13	♛♛ 3

○ Malvasia delle Lipari Passito Carlo Hauner Ris. '13	♛♛ 8
● Hierà '14	♛♛ 3
○ Malvasia delle Lipari Passito '14	♛♛ 5
● Salina Rosso '14	♛♛ 2*
○ Iancura '15	♛ 2
○ Malvasia delle Lipari '14	♛ 5
○ Salina Bianco '15	♛ 2
○ Salina Bianco Carlo Hauner '14	♛ 2
○ Malvasia delle Lipari Ris. '11	♛♛♛ 8
○ Malvasia delle Lipari Ris. '10	♛♛♛ 8
● Hierà '13	♛♛ 3
○ Malvasia delle Lipari Passito '13	♛♛ 6
○ Malvasia delle Lipari Passito Carlo Hauner '12	♛♛ 6

Morgante

C.DA RACALMARE
92020 GROTTE [AG]
TEL. +39 0922945579
www.morgantevini.it

CELLAR SALES
PRE-BOOKED VISITS
ANNUAL PRODUCTION 310,000 bottles
HECTARES UNDER VINE 52.00

In the beautiful area of Grotte, close to the sea and the Valle dei Templi, where there were once sulphur mines, we find a fine family-run winery with its roots in tradition. The star of the show here is nero d'Avola, and the Morgante family have brought out its greatness, capricious character, and extraordinary personality. Their love for the land and their pride as authentic growers have forged territorial wines of unforgettable focus, depth and elegance for the joy of fans of Sicily's most important black grape. The Nero d'Avola Don Antonio 2014 was in fine fettle this year, and made our finals thanks to its concentration, depth and character. On the nose, spice, topsoil, ripe plum, and myrtle pave the way for an elegant, plush palate, sustained by lively yet caressing tannins. The estate's second wine, the fresh, balsamic Nero d'Avola 2014, showed crisp, focused fruit and smooth tannins.

Cantine Nicosia

VIA LUIGI CAPUANA, 65
95039 TRECASTAGNI [CT]
TEL. +39 0957806767
www.cantinenicosia.it

CELLAR SALES
PRE-BOOKED VISITS
RESTAURANT SERVICE
ANNUAL PRODUCTION 1,800,000 bottles
HECTARES UNDER VINE 240.00
VITICULTURE METHOD Certified Organic
SUSTAINABLE WINERY

The Nicosia family have been producing wine on Etna for 119 years, and are based at Trecastagni, at the foot of Mount Gorna, on whose slopes terraced vineyards climb to elevations of up to 700 metres, alongside the cellar and an attractive wine tourism centre and agricultural museum. There are also vineyards further south, at Bonincontro, in the Cerasuolo di Vittoria DOC zone, and in total there are 240 hectares under vine. The vast range of labels includes not only organic wines, but also certified vegan labels. Top honours went to the Sosta Tre Santi 2010, from nero d'Avola topped up with 15% syrah from vineyards in Vittoria. An intense, complex and intriguing nose reveals superb body and finesse, and is echoed beautifully on the palate, which ends long, focused and satisfying. The new Contrada Monte Gorna 2012, a surprising Etna Bianco with a ripe citrus nose and a fresh, mineral palate, just missed the finals.

● Sicilia Nero d'Avola Don Antonio '14	❦❦ 6
○ Bianco di Morgante '15	❦❦ 3
● Sicilia Nero d'Avola '14	❦❦ 2*
● Don Antonio '07	❦❦❦ 4
● Don Antonio '06	❦❦❦ 4
● Don Antonio '03	❦❦❦ 4
● Don Antonio '02	❦❦❦ 4
● Don Antonio '01	❦❦❦ 4
● Don Antonio '00	❦❦❦ 5
● Don Antonio '99	❦❦❦ 5
● Don Antonio '98	❦❦❦ 5
○ Bianco di Morgante '14	♈♈ 2*
● Sicilia Nero d'Avola '13	♈♈ 2*
● Sicilia Nero d'Avola '12	♈♈ 2*
● Sicilia Nero d'Avola Don Antonio '13	♈♈ 5

● Nero d'Avola Sosta Tre Santi '10	❦❦❦ 5
○ Etna Bianco Contrada Monte Gorna '12	❦❦ 6
○ Etna Bianco Fondo Filara '15	❦❦ 4
● Etna Rosso Fondo Filara '13	❦❦ 4
● Sicilia Nerello Mascalese Fondo Filara '14	❦❦ 3
● Cerasuolo di Vittoria Cl. Fondo Filara '13	❦ 4
○ Etna Brut Sosta Tre Santi Collezione di Famiglia '13	❦ 5
● Sicilia Frappato Fondo Filara '15	❦ 3
● Cerasuolo di Vittoria Cl. Fondo Filara '12	♈♈ 4
● Etna Rosso Fondo Filara '12	♈♈ 4
● Nerello Mascalese Sosta Tre Santi '10	♈♈ 5
● Nero d'Avola Sosta Tre Santi '09	♈♈ 5
● Sicilia Frappato '14	♈♈ 3
● Sicilia Nerello Mascalese Fondo Filara '13	♈♈ 3

Occchipinti

S.DA PROV.LE 68 VITTORIA-PEDALINO KM 3,3
97019 VITTORIA [RG]
TEL. +39 09321865519
www.agricolaocchipinti.it

CELLAR SALES
PRE-BOOKED VISITS
ANNUAL PRODUCTION 130,000 bottles
HECTARES UNDER VINE 22.00
VITICULTURE METHOD Certified Organic
SUSTAINABLE WINERY

Now that the move to the newly-built winery has finally been completed, Arianna can put this period of transition behind her and get back to what she loves most, being a grower. In the modern, larger facility, it will be easier for her to pursue her ideal of wine, resulting from the combination of Vittoria's generous soils and the diverse characters of frappato and nero d'Avola, whose vines have always been separated by the dry stone walls typical of this part of Sicily. A Tre Bicchieri went to the SP 68 Rosso 2015, a blend of nero d'Avola and frappato, with exquisite aromas of red berry fruit and aromatic herbs, showing a fresh acidic vein on the elegant, most pleasing, leisurely palate. The racy Il Frappato 2014 also stood out, displaying sweet fruit and good length, with a nuanced nose of Mediterranean scrub, ripe red berries and spring flowers.

★Palari

LOC. SANTO STEFANO BRIGA
C.DA BARNA
98137 MESSINA
TEL. +39 090630194
www.palari.it

ANNUAL PRODUCTION 50,000 bottles
HECTARES UNDER VINE 7.00

The story of Salvatore Geraci: architect, restorer and gourmet, is well worth telling. In response to Gino Veronelli's appeal, he literally saved the life of Faro, the wine of his ancestors with a thousand-year history that risked extinction in the late 1980s. With his brother Giampiero, he took in hand seven hectares of old bush vines, planted on incredibly steep slopes, buffeted by the unpredictable winds of the Straits of Messina. In 1990 the winery, based in the family's 18th-century villa, presented the first vintage of Faro Palari, soon destined to enjoy international cult status. An extra year in the cellars clearly benefited the Faro 2012, which adds another Tre Bicchieri to a series with few equals. A seductively complex, tertiary nose offers notes of berry jam, peach, sweet spice, tobacco, leather and incense, over a velvety, dense palate of elegant solidity and outstanding length. The Rosso del Soprano 2014 plays on its ripeness, concentration and good texture.

● SP 68 Rosso '15	▼▼▼ 3*
● Il Frappato '14	▼▼ 6
● Siccagno '13	▼▼ 6
○ SP 68 Bianco '15	▼ 3
● Il Frappato '12	♀♀♀ 5
● Il Frappato '11	♀♀♀ 5
● Il Frappato '13	♀♀ 6
● Il Frappato '10	♀♀ 4
● Siccagno '12	♀♀ 6
● Siccagno '11	♀♀ 5
○ SP 68 Bianco '14	♀♀ 3
○ SP 68 Bianco '13	♀♀ 4
○ SP 68 Bianco '12	♀♀ 4
● SP 68 Rosso '14	♀♀ 3
● SP 68 Rosso '13	♀♀ 3
● SP 68 Rosso '12	♀♀ 3

● Faro Palari '12	▼▼▼ 6
● Rosso del Soprano '14	▼▼ 4
● Faro Palari '11	♀♀♀ 6
● Faro Palari '09	♀♀♀ 6
● Faro Palari '08	♀♀♀ 6
● Faro Palari '07	♀♀♀ 6
● Faro Palari '06	♀♀♀ 6
● Faro Palari '05	♀♀♀ 6*
● Faro Palari '04	♀♀♀ 7
● Faro Palari '03	♀♀♀ 6
● Faro Palari '02	♀♀♀ 6
● Faro Palari '01	♀♀♀ 6
● Rosso del Soprano '11	♀♀♀ 4*
● Rosso del Soprano '10	♀♀♀ 4*
● Rosso del Soprano '07	♀♀♀ 4

Carlo Pellegrino

VIA DEL FANTE, 39
91025 MARSALA [TP]
TEL. +39 0923719911
www.carlopellegrino.it

CELLAR SALES
PRE-BOOKED VISITS
ANNUAL PRODUCTION 6,900,000 bottles
HECTARES UNDER VINE 150.00
SUSTAINABLE WINERY

This prestigious winery is a fascinating part of Sicilian history, and was founded by Paolo Pellegrino in 1880. It has always enjoyed success on Italian and international markets, initially with Marsala and then increasingly with other types of wine, but always focusing on quality. Today, the cellar, managed expertly by Pietro Alagna and Benedetto Renda, respectively chairman and managing director, has implemented new ideas from the sixth generation of the owner families. A Tre Bicchieri went to the Tripudium Rosso 2013, a blend of Sicilian and international varieties, which won us over with its concentrated red berry fruit, black pepper, rose petals, and juniper. This attractively warm, deep wine shows great elegance, with even-textured, sumptuous tannins. We also loved the sweet, yet fresh and racy Passito Nes 2014, with subtle nuances of figs and dates.

Pietradolce

FRAZ. SOLICCHIATA
C.DA RAMPANTE
95012 CASTIGLIONE DI SICILIA [CT]
TEL. +39 3484037792
www.pietradolce.it

ANNUAL PRODUCTION 28,000 bottles
HECTARES UNDER VINE 13.00

The lovely underground cellar, with walls in lava stone and a roof covered by a metre of soil planted with Mediterranean herbs chosen meticulously from the Nebrodi mountains and Etna, is the latest project completed by Mario and Michele Faro. They drew inspiration from their grandparents, who farmed this land and introduced the two brothers to the wines of the mountain, the "muntagna", when they were boys. The cellar is an icon of contemporary Sicilian winemaking, beloved by enthusiasts all over the world for its artisanal style and elegant wines. A well-deserved Tre Bicchieri went to the Vigna Barbagalli 2013 from nerello mascalese. This superb, highly drinkable wine, with an elegant nose of violet, ripe berry fruit, spice, thyme and sage, confirms its character in the mouth with racy, silky tannins and great length. Hot on its heels was the concentrated Archineri 2014, a seductive, beautifully balanced wine of great depth.

● Tripudium Rosso Duca di Castelmonte '13	▼▼▼ 5
○ Passito di Pantelleria Nes Duca di Castelmonte '14	▼▼ 5
○ Gibelè Duca di Castelmonte '15	▼▼ 2*
○ Marsala Sup. Oro Dolce Ris.	▼▼ 3
○ Marsala Sup. Ambra Semisecco Ris. '85	♀♀♀ 4*
○ Marsala Vergine Ris. '81	♀♀♀ 6
○ Passito di Pantelleria Nes '09	♀♀♀ 5
● Tripudium Rosso Duca di Castelmonte '09	♀♀♀ 4*
○ Gibelè Duca di Castelmonte '14	♀♀ 2*
○ Marsala Vergine Ris. '00	♀♀ 6
○ Passito di Pantelleria Nes '12	♀♀ 5

● Etna Rosso V. Barbagalli '13	▼▼▼ 8
● Etna Rosso Archineri '14	▼▼ 6
○ Etna Bianco Archineri '15	▼▼ 6
○ Etna Bianco Pietradolce '15	▼▼ 4
● Etna Rosso Contrada Rampante '14	▼▼ 6
● Etna Rosso Pietradolce '15	▼▼ 4
● Etna Rosso Archineri '10	♀♀♀ 5
● Etna Rosso Archineri '08	♀♀♀ 3*
● Etna Rosso Archineri '07	♀♀♀ 3*
● Etna Rosso V. Barbagalli '12	♀♀♀ 8
● Etna Rosso V. Barbagalli '11	♀♀♀ 8
● Etna Rosso V. Barbagalli '10	♀♀♀ 8
○ Etna Bianco Pietradolce '14	♀♀ 4

★★Planeta

C.DA DISPENSA
92013 MENFI [AG]
TEL. +39 091327965
www.planeta.it

PRE-BOOKED VISITS
ACCOMMODATION AND RESTAURANT SERVICE
ANNUAL PRODUCTION 2,300,000 bottles
HECTARES UNDER VINE 390.00
SUSTAINABLE WINERY

In 1985 this family, who worked the land for centuries, planted its first vineyards around the Ulmo estate on the shores of Lake Arancio, and opened their winery here a decade later. This was followed by the acquisition of vineyards all over Sicily, but always in excellent wine country: Menfi, Vittoria, Noto, Etna and, most recently, Capo Milazzo. The individuality of each terroir is respected and brought to the fore, within a vision that embraces local culture and traditions, hospitality, art, communication, social commitment, and environmental sustainability. With the 2014 vintage, the Classico Dorilli takes home its third Tre Bicchieri in a row. This naturally eloquent wine offers irresistible fruit and grassy, mineral notes, over a dynamic, fresh, polished palate of impressive length. It was joined in the finals by the dense, harmonious Passito di Noto 2014, and the complex, mature and leisurely Cabernet Burdese 2011.

● Cerasuolo di Vittoria Cl. Dorilli '14	🍷🍷🍷 3*
● Burdese '11	🍷🍷 4
○ Passito di Noto '14	🍷🍷 5
● Cerasuolo di Vittoria '14	🍷🍷 3
○ Menfi Chardonnay '14	🍷🍷 5
○ Menfi Fiano Cometa '15	🍷🍷 5
○ Noto Moscato Bianco '15	🍷🍷 3
● Noto Santa Cecilia '13	🍷🍷 5
○ Sicilia Carricante Eruzione 1614 '15	🍷🍷 4
● Sicilia Merlot Sito dell'Ulmo '13	🍷🍷 5
● Sicilia Nerello Mascalese Eruzione 1614 '14	🍷🍷 4
● Vittoria Frappato '15	🍷🍷 3
● Cerasuolo di Vittoria Cl. Dorilli '13	🍷🍷🍷 3*
● Cerasuolo di Vittoria Cl. Dorilli '12	🍷🍷🍷 3*
● Noto Santa Cecilia '10	🍷🍷🍷 5

Poggio di Bortolone

FRAZ. ROCCAZZO
VIA BORTOLONE, 19
97010 CHIARAMONTE GULFI [RG]
TEL. +39 0932921161
www.poggiodibortolone.it

CELLAR SALES
PRE-BOOKED VISITS
ACCOMMODATION AND RESTAURANT SERVICE
ANNUAL PRODUCTION 80,000 bottles
HECTARES UNDER VINE 15.00
SUSTAINABLE WINERY

In the late 18th century the direct ancestors of the current owner, Pierluigi Cosenza, purchased the estate subsequently named Poggio di Bortolone, from the dialect name of the hill behind it. The modern farm operation is much more recent, and dates back to 1982, when Pierluigi's father, Ignazio, bottled the first Cerasuolo, a wine destined to become their flagship. From the outset, the estate's wines have showed remarkable consistency and a traditional style that perfectly expresses territory and varietal character. The austerely elegant Il Para Para 2012 charms with a balsamic, spicy nose with a potent fruit encore on the palate, barely reined in by a fine acidic backbone and close-knit, polished tannins. The Poggio di Bortolone 2013 reflects the growing year, and is warmer and riper than usual, without sacrificing finesse. Despite slightly jammy fruit, it remains fresh, invigorating, full-flavoured and long.

● Cerasuolo di Vittoria Cl. Poggio di Bortolone '13	🍷🍷 3*
● Cerasuolo di Vittoria Il Para Para '12	🍷🍷 4
● Addamanera '14	🍷🍷 2*
● Cerasuolo di Vittoria Cl. Contessa Costanza '13	🍷🍷 3
● Petit Verdò '14	🍷🍷 3
● Sicilia Rosso Pigi '14	🍷🍷 5
● Vittoria Frappato '15	🍷🍷 2*
⊙ Rosato '15	🍷 2
● Cerasuolo di Vittoria V. Para Para '05	🍷🍷🍷 4
● Cerasuolo di Vittoria V. Para Para '02	🍷🍷🍷 4*
● Addamanera '13	🍷🍷 2*
● Cerasuolo di Vittoria Cl. Para Para '11	🍷🍷 4
● Sicilia Rosso Pigi '13	🍷🍷 5
● Vittoria Frappato '14	🍷🍷 2*

Rallo

VIA VINCENZO FLORIO, 2
91025 MARSALA [TP]
TEL. +39 0923721633
www.cantinerallo.it

CELLAR SALES
PRE-BOOKED VISITS
ANNUAL PRODUCTION 420,000 bottles
HECTARES UNDER VINE 110.00
VITICULTURE METHOD Certified Organic

Andrea Vesco's enviable operation includes the 19th-century enclosed baglio farmstead, where Marsala was once produced, now converted into a state-of-the-art cellar, and three vineyards: nearby, at Piane Liquide, near Stagnone; at Patti Piccolo, in the Alcamo countryside; and on the Pantelleria estate, overlooking Lake Venere. Andrea, who has always been attentive to environmental issues, farms over 1,000 hectares of vineyards using certified organic methods. Elegant and well managed, his wines also offer great value for money. Our tastings showed a dynamic up-and-coming winery with an eye to the market and consumer demands. A well-deserved Tre Bicchieri went to the Catarratto Beleda 2015, showing complexity and finesse on a nose of citrus, jasmine and white-fleshed fruit, over a long zesty palate bursting with freshness. The exquisite Zibibbo Al Qasar 2015 also made the finals, impressing us with its delicate mint aromas.

○ Alcamo Beleda '15	♀♀♀ 4*
○ Al Qasar Zibibbo '15	♀♀ 3*
○ Passito di Pantelleria Bugeber '11	♀♀ 5
○ Sicilia Bianco Maggiore '15	♀♀ 3
○ Sicilia Evrò '15	♀♀ 3
● Sicilia Il Principe '15	♀♀ 2*
● Sicilia La Clarissa '12	♀♀ 2*
○ Sicilia Carta d'Oro '15	♀ 2
● Sicilia Lacuba '14	♀ 3
○ Alcamo Beleda '13	♀♀♀ 2*
○ Bianco Maggiore '12	♀♀♀ 3*
○ Sicilia Bianco Maggiore '14	♀♀♀ 3*
○ Al Qasar Zibibbo '14	♀♀ 3
○ Alcamo Beleda '14	♀♀ 2*
○ Bianco Maggiore '13	♀♀ 3*
● Siocilia Il Manto '13	♀♀ 3

Tenute Rapitalà

C.DA RAPITALÀ
90043 CAMPOREALE [PA]
TEL. +39 092437233
www.rapitala.it

CELLAR SALES
PRE-BOOKED VISITS
ANNUAL PRODUCTION 2,800,000 bottles
HECTARES UNDER VINE 175.00

The name Rapitalà derives from the Arabic Rabidh-Allah, or "river of Allah", and refers to the stream that still flows through this fine Sicilian estate owned by Gruppo Italiano Vini, run by Laurent Bernard de la Gatinais. The winery is situated between Camporeale and Alcamo and covers 175 hectares of vineyards on well-aspected hillside sites on a mixture of sand and clay soils. Today, almost 50 years after it was established, this leading company offers a wide range of well-made, reliable and, above all, highly drinkable wines. We saw an impressive performance from the wines of this historic estate. The Syrah Solinero 2013 opens to a nose of aromatic herbs, salted capers and dark berry fruit, leading to a firm, potent, yet elegant palate. The balanced, velvety Hugonis 2014 is a well-managed elegant blend of nero d'Avola and cabernet sauvignon, and the highly drinkable Grillo 2015 is brimming with blossom and Mediterranean herbs.

● Solinero '13	♀♀ 5
○ Conte Hugues Bernard de la Gatinais Grand Cru '14	♀♀ 4
● Hugonis '14	♀♀ 5
● Sicilia Alto Nero d'Avola '14	♀♀ 3
○ Sicilia Grillo '15	♀♀ 2*
○ Alcamo Bianco V. Casalj '15	♀ 3
○ Bouquet '15	♀ 3
● Sicilia Nuhar '14	♀ 3
○ Conte Hugues Bernard de la Gatinais Grand Cru '10	♀♀♀ 4*
● Hugonis '01	♀♀♀ 6
● Solinero '03	♀♀♀ 5
● Solinero '00	♀♀♀ 5

Riofavara

LOC. VAL DI NOTO
FRAZ. FAVARA
S.DA PROV.LE 49 ISPICA-PACHINO
97014 ISPICA [RG]
TEL. +39 0932705130
www.riofavara.it

CELLAR SALES
PRE-BOOKED VISITS
ACCOMMODATION
ANNUAL PRODUCTION 70,000 bottles
HECTARES UNDER VINE 16.00
VITICULTURE METHOD Certified Organic
SUSTAINABLE WINERY

Massimo and Marianta Padova are without doubt some of the best interpreters of the viticultural tradition of the Ispica area. The rows are tended according to strictly organic methods, with the utmost respect for biodiversity, and back at the cellar, vinification envisages minimum intervention and fermentation using ambient yeasts alone. Ever since the first bottling, the estate's red wines have been appreciated for their clear sense of place and the varietal traits typical of nero d'Avola. Our tastings highlighted the excellent quality of this estate's wines. Once again just missing top honours was the Sciavè 2013, a polished, well-balanced Nero d'Avola. We also liked the less complex but equally subtle and territorial Nero d'Avola Spaccaforno 2013. The fresh Moscato Mizzica 2015 performed well too, showing a rich, well-focused nose and mouth.

● Eloro Nero d'Avola Sciavè '13	🍷🍷 5
● Eloro Nero d'Avola Spaccaforno '13	🍷🍷 4
○ Marzaiolo '15	🍷🍷 3
○ Moscato di Noto Mizzica '15	🍷🍷 3
● San Basilio '14	🍷 3
● Eloro Nero d'Avola Sciavè '12	ΥΥ 5
● Eloro Nero d'Avola Spaccaforno '12	ΥΥ 3
○ Marzaiolo '14	ΥΥ 3
○ Marzaiolo '13	ΥΥ 2*
○ Marzaiolo '12	ΥΥ 2*
○ Moscato di Noto Notissimo '12	ΥΥ 3
● S. Basilio '13	ΥΥ 2*
● San Basilio '12	ΥΥ 3
● San Basilio '11	ΥΥ 3

Feudo Rudinì

C.DA CAMPOREALE
96018 PACHINO [SR]
TEL. +39 0931595333
www.vinirudini.it

PRE-BOOKED VISITS
ANNUAL PRODUCTION 300,000 bottles
HECTARES UNDER VINE 24.00

A long family tradition is behind this winery, run by Saro Di Pietro and his son Giuseppe, situated near Pachino at the southernmost tip of Sicily, with its white limestone soils. In the 19th century, here in the heartland of nero d'Avola, Barone Rudinì owned over 2,000 hectares of vineyards and exported 5,000,000 litres of wine obtained from the variety every year, using the nearby harbour at Marzamemi. The Di Pietro family dedicate particular care to traditional viticultural methods, above all by using bush vines, the original training system for nero d'Avola. Tre Bicchieri for the spectacular Eloro Pachino Saro 2013, a nero d'Avola selection from the winery's oldest vineyards. Intense, focused pomegranate and attractive notes of iodine and caper on the nose are followed by a fleshy, velvety palate and dense texture, with a leisurely, balsamic finish. The sweet, refreshing Moscato di Noto Baroque 2015 shows a subtle nose of melon and tropical fruit.

● Eloro Pachino Saro '13	🍷🍷🍷 3*
○ Moscato di Noto Baroque '15	🍷🍷 3
● Nero d'Avola Le Origini '15	🍷🍷 2*
○ Passito di Noto Scaramazzo '15	🍷🍷 4
● Eloro Pachino '05	ΥΥ 2
● Eloro Pachino Saro '06	ΥΥ 4

Girolamo Russo

LOC. PASSOPISCIARO
VIA REGINA MARGHERITA, 78
95012 CASTIGLIONE DI SICILIA [CT]
TEL. +39 3283840247
www.girolamorusso.it

CELLAR SALES
PRE-BOOKED VISITS
ANNUAL PRODUCTION 65,000 bottles
HECTARES UNDER VINE 15.00
VITICULTURE METHOD Certified Organic

Pianist and man of letters by education, grower by vocation and heritage, Giuseppe Russo farms the family vineyards on the slopes of Etna, between Passopisciaro and Randazzo: 12 hectares at San Lorenzo, six at Feudo and one at Feudo di Mezzo. He adopts the time-honoured traditional methods of local viticulture, with mainly bush vines up to a century old, farmed almost entirely without machinery and no use of synthetic chemicals. At the winery, his outstanding raw materials are vinified with the same loving care and respect. A Tre Bicchieri went to the vineyard selection San Lorenzo 2014, whose exceptional character bodes well for the future, showing an elegant nose over a leisurely palate with a captivating fruit encore. Our finals were also graced by the Feudo 2014, slightly more austere with its jammy fruit and spice, imposing character and hefty stuffing. We liked the polished fruit of the refreshing, fleshy Etna Rosato 2015.

● Etna Rosso San Lorenzo '14	♈♈♈ 6
● Etna Rosso Feudo '14	♈♈ 6
○ Etna Bianco Nerina '15	♈♈ 5
☉ Etna Rosato '15	♈♈ 4
● Etna Rosso 'A Rina '14	♈♈ 5
● Etna Rosso Feudo di Mezzo '14	♈♈ 6
● Etna Rosso 'A Rina '12	♈♈♈ 3*
● Etna Rosso Feudo '11	♈♈♈ 5
● Etna Rosso Feudo '10	♈♈♈ 5
● Etna Rosso Feudo '07	♈♈♈ 5
● Etna Rosso San Lorenzo '13	♈♈♈ 5
● Etna Rosso San Lorenzo '09	♈♈♈ 5
● Etna Rosso Feudo '13	♈♈ 5
● Etna Rosso Feudo '12	♈♈ 5

Emanuele Scammacca del Murgo

VIA ZAFFERANA, 13
95010 SANTA VENERINA [CT]
TEL. +39 095950520
www.murgo.it

CELLAR SALES
PRE-BOOKED VISITS
ACCOMMODATION AND RESTAURANT SERVICE
ANNUAL PRODUCTION 230,000 bottles
HECTARES UNDER VINE 35.00

The history of this winery is interwoven with that of a unique territory and a close-knit family who have been working the land here since 1860. The late Ambassdor Emanuele Scammacca del Murgo's amazing foresight persuaded him to give a new lease of life to the ancestral holdings, and in 1981 he converted them into a modern winemaking operation. The family's three estates produce wines that reflect and interpret perfectly the various terroirs and cultivars grown. These are mainly native, with some international varieties, a number grown on Etna since the 19th century. The outstanding Nerello Mascalese Tenuta San Michele 2014 presents an intriguing, inky violet hue, with elegant aromas of violet, flat peaches, red forest fruits, and a harmonious palate offset by delicate tannins. We also saw a fine performance from the Murgo Extra Brut 2009, a deep, floral, citrusy and attractively creamy Metodo Classico from nerello mascalese.

○ Etna Bianco '15	♈♈ 2*
● Etna Rosso Tenuta San Michele '14	♈♈ 2*
☉ Murgo Brut Rosé '12	♈♈ 4
○ Murgo Extra Brut '09	♈♈ 5
○ Murgo Brut '12	♈ 3
○ Arbiato '13	♈♈ 4
○ Etna Bianco '14	♈♈ 2*
○ Etna Bianco Tenuta San Michele '12	♈♈ 2*
☉ Etna Rosato '13	♈♈ 2*
● Etna Rosso '12	♈♈ 2*
● Etna Rosso Tenuta San Michele '12	♈♈ 2*
○ Murgo Brut '10	♈♈ 3
○ Murgo Extra Brut '07	♈♈ 5
○ Murgo Extra Brut '08	♈♈ 5
● Tenuta San Michele Pinot Nero '12	♈♈ 3

Cantine Settesoli

S.DA ST.LE 115
92013 MENFI [AG]
TEL. +39 092577111
www.cantinesettesoli.it

CELLAR SALES
PRE-BOOKED VISITS
ANNUAL PRODUCTION 20,000,000 bottles
HECTARES UNDER VINE 6000.00

Cantine Settesoli's vineyards are located at Menfi, on the southwestern coast of Sicily, in an unspoilt landscape of quality wine country with an ideal climate. The wines in the Mandrarossa line are based on selections from the best vineyards, after years of research into how the characteristics of the soil interact with the various cultivars. This major study has given excellent results, in the form of modern-styled, highly drinkable wines that faithfully express the territory and varieties used. The Nero d'Avola Mandrarossa Cartagho 2014 walked away with a Tre Bicchieri, thanks to its richly nuanced nose of violets, sea salt and black cherry, over a long palate boasting smooth tannins and juicy fruit. We were charmed by the Seligo Rosso 2015, a blend of nero d'Avola and syrah, with its delicate nose of spice, balsam and ripe peach over a fresh, lingering palate.

● Sicilia Mandrarossa Cartagho '14	🏆🏆🏆	3*
○ Sicilia Mandrarossa Urra di Mare '15	🏆🏆	2*
● Sicilia Seligo Rosso '15	🏆🏆	2*
● Mandrarossa Bonera '15	🏆🏆	3
● Mandrarossa Cavadiserpe '15	🏆🏆	3
● Mandrarossa Timperosse '15	🏆🏆	3
○ Mandrarossa Zibibbo '15	🏆🏆	2*
● Mandrarossa Frappato '15	🏆	2
● Cartagho Mandrarossa '09	🏆🏆🏆	3*
● Cartagho Mandrarossa '08	🏆🏆🏆	3*
● Cartagho Mandrarossa '06	🏆🏆🏆	3
● Timperosse Mandrarossa '14	🏆🏆🏆	3*
○ Santannella Mandrarossa '14	🏆🏆	3
○ Sicilia Urra di Mare Mandrarossa '14	🏆🏆	2*

★★Tasca d'Almerita

C.DA REGALEALI
90129 SCLAFANI BAGNI [PA]
TEL. +39 0916459711
www.tascadalmerita.it

CELLAR SALES
PRE-BOOKED VISITS
ACCOMMODATION AND RESTAURANT SERVICE
ANNUAL PRODUCTION 3,253,000 bottles
HECTARES UNDER VINE 388.00

Over the last two centuries this aristocratic family has played a fundamental role in the evolution of quality wine in Sicily. Conte Giuseppe gave the winery its modern structure, and his successors are son Lucio and grandsons Alberto and Giuseppe. Apart from Feudo di Regaleali, the original, stunning estate in the heart of Sicily, the Tasca family's pioneering spirit led them to experiment with other vineyards, including Capofaro on Salina, Tascante on Etna, the Whitaker estate on Mozia; and the Valle dello Jato estate run by their cousins, the Sallier de la Tour family. We saw a triumphant Etna white in the Tascante Buonora 2015, a Carricante with a magnificent nose of citrus blossom and jasmine, encoring with superb focus on the dense, fresh, lingering palate. The Rosso del Conte 2012 also made our finals, showing a gracefully complex nose of impressive intensity, over Mediterranean fruit and elegant hints of balsam in the mouth.

○ Sicilia Carricante Tascante Buonora '15	🏆🏆🏆	3*
● Contea di Sclafani Rosso del Conte '12	🏆🏆	6
● Contea di Sclafani Cabernet Sauvignon '13	🏆🏆	5
○ Malvasia Tenuta Capofaro '15	🏆🏆	5
○ Sicilia Grillo Whitaker '15	🏆🏆	3
● Sicilia Nero d'Avola Lamùri '14	🏆🏆	3
● Sicilia Perricone Guarnaccio '14	🏆🏆	3
● Sicilia Rosso Cygnus '13	🏆🏆	4
● Cabernet Sauvignon '08	🏆🏆🏆	5
● Contea di Sclafani Cabernet Sauvignon '10	🏆🏆🏆	5
● Contea di Sclafani Riserva del Conte '10	🏆🏆🏆	7
● Contea di Sclafani Rosso del Conte '10	🏆🏆🏆	6
● Contea di Sclafani Rosso del Conte '07	🏆🏆🏆	6
● Cygnus '10	🏆🏆🏆	4*

★Tenuta delle Terre Nere

C.DA CALDERARA
95036 RANDAZZO [CT]
TEL. +39 095924002
www.tenutaterrenere.com

CELLAR SALES
PRE-BOOKED VISITS
ANNUAL PRODUCTION 200,000 bottles
HECTARES UNDER VINE 30.00
VITICULTURE METHOD Certified Organic

As soon as he set foot on Etna, Marco de Grazia realized the great potential of this magic terroir, where the soils change according to the composition of the lava flows covering them over the centuries, even within the same vineyard. The microclimates also change, modified by the slope, elevation, and aspect. Consequently, right from the first harvest, Marco began to vinify and bottle vineyard by vineyard, while pursuing a successful campaign to change the Etna DOC production protocol, so that the cru of provenance is specified on the label. Elegance and a sense of place are the hallmark of Marco's range, but it is incredible how each wine offers different nose and palate nuances. A Tre Bicchieri went to his signature wine, the Prephilloxera La Vigna di Don Peppino 2014, as monumental as the heirloom vines from which it comes. This homage to elegance is a veritable explosion of crisp fruit, flavour and freshness. Hats off to Marco!

● Etna Rosso Prephylloxera La V. di Don Peppino '14	▼▼▼ 8
○ Etna Bianco Calderara Sottana Cuvée delle Vigne Niche '14	▼▼ 6
● Etna Rosso Guardiola '14	▼▼ 6
○ Etna Bianco '15	▼▼ 4
○ Etna Bianco Santo Spirito Cuvée delle Vigne Niche '14	▼▼ 6
⊙ Etna Rosato '15	▼▼ 4
● Etna Rosso '14	▼▼ 4
● Etna Rosso Calderara Sottana '14	▼▼ 6
● Etna Rosso Feudo di Mezzo Quadro delle Rose '14	▼▼ 6
● Etna Rosso Santo Spirito '14	▼▼ 6
● Etna Rosso Calderara Sottana '13	▼▼▼ 6
● Etna Rosso Santo Spirito '12	▼▼▼ 6
● Etna Rosso Santo Spirito '11	▼▼▼ 6

Terrazze dell'Etna

C.DA BOCCA D'ORZO
95036 RANDAZZO [CT]
TEL. +39 0916236343
www.terrazzedelletna.it

CELLAR SALES
PRE-BOOKED VISITS
ANNUAL PRODUCTION 120,000 bottles
HECTARES UNDER VINE 38.00

The fine estate run by engineer Nino Bevilacqua and his daughter Alessia covers 36 hectares of vineyards at Bocca d'Orzo, in the municipal district of Randazzo, within Etna National Park, in countryside of unspoilt beauty. Nearby, in Contrada Arena, we instead find an extremely modern, functional vinification and ageing facility. From the outset, the winery, celebrating its eighth harvest this year, has been characterized by the austere elegance of its wines and the extreme finesse and drinkability of its Metodo Classico sparklers. The top lines Cirneco and Cratere are staying in the cellars for a few more months, but the other labels are winners, starting with the Etna Rosso Carusu 2014, whose delicate nose of blossom and spice leads into a fresh, balanced, graceful palate. We liked the Ciuri 2015, from nerello mascalese fermented off the skins, with aromas of iodine, summer flowers and citrus over a fresh, zesty, supple palate.

○ Ciuri '15	▼▼ 3
○ Cuvée Brut '13	▼▼ 5
● Etna Rosso Carusu '14	▼▼ 4
⊙ Rosé Brut '13	▼▼ 5
● Etna Rosso Cirneco '09	▼▼▼ 6
● Etna Rosso Cirneco '08	▼▼▼ 5
○ Ciuri '14	▼▼ 3
● Cratere '11	▼▼ 4
○ Cuvée Brut '12	▼▼ 5
● Etna Rosso Carusu '12	▼▼ 4
● Etna Rosso Cirneco '12	▼▼ 6
● Etna Rosso Cirneco '11	▼▼ 6
⊙ Rosé Brut '12	▼▼ 5
⊙ Rosé Brut '11	▼▼ 5

Valle Dell'Acate

c.DA BIDINI
97011 ACATE [RG]
TEL. +39 0932874166
www.valledellacate.com

CELLAR SALES
PRE-BOOKED VISITS
ANNUAL PRODUCTION 400,000 bottles
HECTARES UNDER VINE 100.00
SUSTAINABLE WINERY

Dating back to the 19th century, this fine operation is owned by the Jacono and Ferreri families, whose great dedication and commitment turned it into a benchmark for quality in Sicilian winemaking. Today, they have been joined by the new generation, in the shape of Gaetana Jacono, the winery's brilliant image maker, and Francesco Ferreri, the authoritative president of Assovini. The splendid estate, in the immense valley below the town of Acate with the River Dirillo running through it, combines the area's winemaking history and tradition perfectly with a modern approach. The Frappato 2015 made our finals for its bright purplish hue and a gracefully nuanced nose of strawberry, raspberry and rose petals. These aromas encore perfectly on the elegant, racy palate, for an exceptionally drinkable, pleasurable wine. The well-structured, austere Nero d'Avola Il Moro 2013 offers ripe fruit and character.

Zisola

c.DA ZISOLA
96017 NOTO [SR]
TEL. +39 057773571
www.mazzei.it

CELLAR SALES
PRE-BOOKED VISITS
ANNUAL PRODUCTION 120,000 bottles
HECTARES UNDER VINE 21.00
SUSTAINABLE WINERY

Filippo Mazzei was one of the first to understand the great potential for winemaking of the part of Sicily falling within the Pachino, Noto and Vendicari Nature Reserve district. Naturally, as soon as he had a chance, he snapped up the Zisola estate, with its ancient enclosed baglio farmstead, which enjoys an stunning view over the Baroque town, just over a kilometre away. The decision to focus on nero d'Avola and use bush vines for the entire 21 hectares of the area under vine is also in keeping with local tradition. Our finals were graced by the highly drinkable Nero d'Avola Zisola 2014, an exceptional wine offering varietal aromas of iron filings, violet, salted capers and Mediterranean herbs, paving the way for a well-managed, crisp palate with unobtrusive tannins. The fruit-driven Doppiozeta 2013, also from selected nero d'Avola grapes, is still evolving. We liked all the other wines presented.

● Vittoria Frappato '15	▼▼ 3*
● Cerasuolo di Vittoria Cl. '13	▼▼ 4
● Sicilia Il Moro '13	▼▼ 3
● Sicilia Rusciano '13	▼▼ 4
○ Sicilia Bidis '14	▼ 4
○ Sicilia Zagra '15	▼ 3
● Cerasuolo di Vittoria Cl. '12	♀♀ 3*
● Cerasuolo di Vittoria Cl. '11	♀♀ 3
○ Sicilia Bidis '13	♀♀ 4
● Sicilia Il Moro '12	♀♀ 3
● Vittoria Il Frappato '14	♀♀ 3
● Vittoria Il Frappato '13	♀♀ 2*
○ Vittoria Inzolia '13	♀♀ 2*

● Noto Zisola '14	▼▼ 4
● Effe Emme '13	▼▼ 6
● Noto Zisola Doppiozeta '13	▼▼ 6
○ Sicilia Azisa '15	▼▼ 3
● Doppiozeta '10	♀♀ 6
● Doppiozeta '07	♀♀ 6
● Effe Emme '12	♀♀ 7
● Noto Doppiozeta '11	♀♀ 6
● Noto Zisola Doppiozeta '12	♀♀ 7
● Sicilia Zisola '13	♀♀ 4
○ Sicilia Zisola Azisa '14	♀♀ 4
● Zisola '12	♀♀ 5
● Zisola '10	♀♀ 5
● Zisola '08	♀♀ 4
● Zisola Nero d'Avola '11	♀♀ 5

Alagna

VIA SALEMI, 752
91025 MARSALA [TP]
TEL. +39 0923981022
www.alagnavini.com

CELLAR SALES
PRE-BOOKED VISITS
ACCOMMODATION
ANNUAL PRODUCTION 500,000 bottles
HECTARES UNDER VINE 50.00

○ Marsala Sup. Dolce Garibaldi	♟♟ 3
○ Marsala Sup. Secco S.O.M.	♟♟ 3
○ Marsala Vergine Baglio Baiata	♟ 5
○ Zibibbo Liquoroso	♟ 3

Ampelon

C.DA CALDERARA
95036 RANDAZZO [CT]
TEL. +39 3203298657
www.viniampelon.it

CELLAR SALES
ANNUAL PRODUCTION 50,000 bottles
HECTARES UNDER VINE 7.00
SUSTAINABLE WINERY

○ Etna Bianco Ampelon '14	♟♟ 3
● Etna Rosso Passo alle Sciare '12	♟♟ 3

Antichi Vinai 1877

LOC. PASSOPISCIARO
VIA CASTIGLIONE, 49
95030 CASTIGLIONE DI SICILIA [CT]
TEL. +39 0942983232
www.antichivinai.it

CELLAR SALES
PRE-BOOKED VISITS
ACCOMMODATION
ANNUAL PRODUCTION 300,000 bottles
HECTARES UNDER VINE 59.00

● d'A '13	♟♟ 4
● Etna Rosso Petralava '12	♟♟ 5
● Il Mascalese '15	♟♟ 4
○ Etna Bianco Petralava '15	♟ 5

Augustali

FRAZ. BOSCO FALCONERIA
S.DA ST.LE 113 ALCAMO-PARTINICO KM 318,700
90047 PARTINICO [PA]
TEL. +39 3396132334
www.augustali.com

ANNUAL PRODUCTION 25,000 bottles
HECTARES UNDER VINE 15.50

○ Terza Nota Bianco '15	♟♟ 3
● Terza Nota Rosso '15	♟♟ 3
○ Contrasto del Bianco Vermentino '13	♟ 5
● Contrasto del Rosso Nero d'Avola '12	♟ 5

Avide - Vigneti & Cantine

C.DA MASTRELLA, 346
97013 COMISO [RG]
TEL. +39 0932967456
www.avide.it

CELLAR SALES
PRE-BOOKED VISITS
ANNUAL PRODUCTION 250,000 bottles
HECTARES UNDER VINE 68.00

● Cerasuolo di Vittoria Cl. Barocco '11	♟♟ 6
○ Maria Stella Inzolia '15	♟♟ 4
○ Nutaru Brut M. Cl.	♟♟ 5
● Cerasuolo di Vittoria Cl. Etichetta Nera '14	♟ 3

Baglio Oro

C.DA PERINO, 235
91025 MARSALA [TP]
TEL. +39 0923967744
www.bagliooro.it

CELLAR SALES
PRE-BOOKED VISITS
ANNUAL PRODUCTION 80,000 bottles
HECTARES UNDER VINE 100.00

● Donsar '14	♟♟ 2*
○ Aralto '15	♟ 2
○ Kiggiari '15	♟ 2
○ Zafarà '15	♟ 2

Biscaris

VIA MARESCIALLO GIUDICE, 52
97011 ACATE [RG]
TEL. +39 0932990762
www.biscaris.it

CELLAR SALES
ANNUAL PRODUCTION 50,000 bottles
HECTARES UNDER VINE 10.00
VITICULTURE METHOD Certified Biodynamic

● Cerasuolo di Vittoria Pricipuzzu '15	♟♟ 3
● Nero d'Avola Cavalieri '15	♟♟ 2*
● Frappato Barunieddu '15	♟ 2
○ U' Duca '15	♟ 2

Calcagno

FRAZ. PASSOPISCIARO
VIA REGINA MARGHERITA,153
95012 CASTIGLIONE DI SICILIA [CT]
TEL. +39 3387772780
www.vinicalcagno.it

CELLAR SALES
PRE-BOOKED VISITS
ANNUAL PRODUCTION 13,000 bottles
HECTARES UNDER VINE 3.00

● Etna Rosso Arcuria '13	♟♟ 4
● Etna Rosso Feudo di Mezzo '13	♟♟ 4
⊘ Etna Rosato Arcuria '15	♟ 3
○ Ginestra '15	♟ 3

Paolo Calì

C.DA SALMÉ
VIA DEL FRAPPATO, 100
97019 VITTORIA [RG]
TEL. +39 0932510082
www.vinicali.it

CELLAR SALES
PRE-BOOKED VISITS
ANNUAL PRODUCTION 90,000 bottles
HECTARES UNDER VINE 15.00

⊙ Osa! Frappato Rosato '15	♟♟ 4
● Vittoria Frappato Mandragola '15	♟♟ 3
● Cerasuolo di Vittoria Cl. Manene '14	♟ 4
● Jazz '15	♟ 3

Cantina Viticoltori Associati Canicattì

C.DA AQUILATA
92024 CANICATTÌ [AG]
TEL. +39 0922829371
www.cvacanicatti.it

CELLAR SALES
PRE-BOOKED VISITS
ANNUAL PRODUCTION 900,000 bottles
HECTARES UNDER VINE 1000.00

○ Aquilae Catarratto '15	♟♟ 2*
● Diodoros '13	♟♟ 4
● Aquilae Nero d'Avola '14	♟ 2
● Sicilia Centouno '13	♟ 2

Caravaglio

LOC. MALFA SALINA
VIA NAZIONALE, 33
98050 MALFA [ME]
TEL. +39 3398115953
caravagliovini@virgilio.it

CELLAR SALES
PRE-BOOKED VISITS
ANNUAL PRODUCTION 40,000 bottles
HECTARES UNDER VINE 12.00
VITICULTURE METHOD Certified Organic
SUSTAINABLE WINERY

○ Infatata '15	♟♟ 3
○ Malvasia delle Lipari Passito '14	♟♟ 5
○ Occhio di Terra '15	♟♟ 3
● Nero du Munti '15	♟ 4

Caruso & Minini

VIA SALEMI, 3
91025 MARSALA [TP]
TEL. +39 0923982356
www.carusoeminini.it

CELLAR SALES
PRE-BOOKED VISITS
ANNUAL PRODUCTION 1,200,000 bottles
HECTARES UNDER VINE 120.00
VITICULTURE METHOD Certified Organic

● Delia Nivolelli Nero d'Avola Cutaja Ris. '13	♟♟ 3
● Sicilia Nero d'Avola Naturalmente Bio '15	♟♟ 3
● Delia Nivolelli Syrah Ris. '10	♟ 5
○ Sicilia Grillo Timpune '15	♟ 3

Centopassi

VIA PORTA PALERMO, 132
90048 SAN GIUSEPPE JATO [PA]
TEL. +39 0918577655
www.centopassisicilia.it

CELLAR SALES
PRE-BOOKED VISITS
ACCOMMODATION AND RESTAURANT SERVICE
ANNUAL PRODUCTION 500,000 bottles
HECTARES UNDER VINE 94.00
VITICULTURE METHOD Certified Organic
SUSTAINABLE WINERY

● Sicilia Rosso Centopassi '15	♟♟ 2*
● Syrah Marne di Saladino '14	♟♟ 4
○ Sicilia Bianco Centopassi '15	♟ 2
○ Tendoni di Trebbiano '14	♟ 4

Ceuso

C.DA VIVIGNATO
91013 CALATAFIMI [TP]
TEL. +39 092422836
www.ceuso.it

PRE-BOOKED VISITS
ANNUAL PRODUCTION 120,000 bottles
HECTARES UNDER VINE 50.00

● Ceuso '13	♟♟ 5
● Fastaia '14	♟♟ 3
○ Scurati Grillo '15	♟♟ 2*
● Scurati Nero d'Avola '15	♟ 2

Cantine Colosi

LOC. PACE DEL MELA
FRAZ. GIAMMORO
DIRAMAZIONE VIARIA C
98042 MESSINA
TEL. +39 0909385549
www.cantinecolosi.it

PRE-BOOKED VISITS
ANNUAL PRODUCTION 100,000 bottles
HECTARES UNDER VINE 10.00

⊙ Cariddi Rosato '15	♟♟ 2*
○ Passito '11	♟♟ 4
● Cariddi Rosso '14	♟ 3
○ Malvasia Delle Lipari Passito '10	♟ 5

Terra Costantino

VIA GARIBALDI, 417
95029 VIAGRANDE [CT]
TEL. +39 095434288
www.terracostantino.it

CELLAR SALES
PRE-BOOKED VISITS
ANNUAL PRODUCTION 40,000 bottles
HECTARES UNDER VINE 7.00

● Etna Rosso de Aetna '14	♟♟ 3
⊙ Etna Rosato de Aetna '15	♟ 3

Tenuta Coste Ghirlanda

LOC. PIANA DI GHIRLANDA
91017 PANTELLERIA [TP]
TEL. +39 3388244649
www.costeghirlanda.it

PRE-BOOKED VISITS
ANNUAL PRODUCTION 35,000 bottles
HECTARES UNDER VINE 7.00

○ Silenzio '14	♟♟ 6
○ Jardinu Zibibbo '14	♟♟ 6

Curatolo Arini

LOC. BAGLIO CURATOLO ARINI
VIA VITO CURATOLO ARINI, 5
91025 MARSALA [TP]
TEL. +39 0923989400
www.curatoloarini.com

ANNUAL PRODUCTION 2,000,000 bottles
HECTARES UNDER VINE 100.00

○ Coralto Grillo '14	♟♟ 3
● Paccamora Syrah '14	♟♟ 2*
○ Zibibbo '15	♟♟ 6
● Nero d'Avola '12	♟ 6

Curto

s.da st.le 115 Ispica-Rosolini km 358
97014 Ispica [RG]
Tel. +39 0932950161
www.curto.it

CELLAR SALES
PRE-BOOKED VISITS
ANNUAL PRODUCTION 70,000 bottles
HECTARES UNDER VINE 30.00

● Krio Syrah '12	🍷🍷4
○ Moscato Passito Dulce Netum '14	🍷🍷6
● Eloro Nero d'Avola Fontanelle '11	🍷4
○ Poiano Inzolia '15	🍷2

Di Legami

via Marzabotto, 7
91014 Castellammare del Golfo [TP]
Tel. +39 3381749679
www.cantinedilegami.it

ANNUAL PRODUCTION 30,000 bottles
HECTARES UNDER VINE 45.00

○ Zafaràna Inzolia '15	🍷🍷3
● Zafaràna Nero d'Avola '14	🍷🍷3
○ Berlinghieri Chardonnay '15	🍷2
○ Grillo Brut M. Cl. '13	🍷3

Gaspare Di Prima

loc. Sambuca di Sicilia
via G. Guasto, 27
92017 Sambuca di Sicilia [AG]
Tel. +39 0925941201
www.diprimavini.it

CELLAR SALES
PRE-BOOKED VISITS
ANNUAL PRODUCTION 50,000 bottles
HECTARES UNDER VINE 38.00
VITICULTURE METHOD Certified Organic

○ Sicilia Grillo del Lago '15	🍷🍷2*
● Sicilia Nero D'Avola Gibilmoro '13	🍷🍷3
● Villamaura Syrah '11	🍷🍷6
● Sicilia Pepita Rosso '14	🍷2

Feudo Disisa

fraz. Grisì
c.da Disisa
90046 Monreale [PA]
Tel. +39 0919127109
www.vinidisisa.it

CELLAR SALES
PRE-BOOKED VISITS
ANNUAL PRODUCTION 150,000 bottles
HECTARES UNDER VINE 150.00
VITICULTURE METHOD Certified Organic

● Adhara '14	🍷🍷2*
○ Sicilia Chardonnay Daliah '15	🍷🍷3
○ Sicilia Grillo '15	🍷🍷3
● Nero d'Avola '14	🍷2

Cantine Ermes

c.da Salinella
91029 Santa Ninfa [TP]
Tel. +39 092467153
www.cantineermes.it

CELLAR SALES
PRE-BOOKED VISITS
ANNUAL PRODUCTION 3,000,000 bottles
HECTARES UNDER VINE 4,642.00
VITICULTURE METHOD Certified Organic
SUSTAINABLE WINERY

● Marchese Montefusco Sangiovese '15	🍷🍷1*
● Vento di Mare Nero d'Avola Cabernet '15	🍷🍷2*
● Vento di Mare Nerello Mascalese '15	🍷2
● Vento di Mare Nero d'Avola '15	🍷2

Cantina Sociale Europa

loc. bivio Triglia Scaletta
s.da st.le 115, km 42,400
91020 Petrosino [TP]
Tel. +39 0923961866
info@cantinaeuropa.it

CELLAR SALES
PRE-BOOKED VISITS
ANNUAL PRODUCTION 2,000,000 bottles
HECTARES UNDER VINE 6,300.00

● Capofeto Nero d'Avola '15	🍷🍷1*
○ Eughenès Grillo Zibibbo '15	🍷🍷2*
○ Sicilia Grillo Eughenès '15	🍷🍷2*
○ Capofeto Grillo '15	🍷1*

Fazio Wines

FRAZ. FULGATORE
VIA CAPITAN RIZZO, 39
91010 ERICE [TP]
TEL. +39 0923811700
www.faziowines.com

ANNUAL PRODUCTION 750,000 bottles
HECTARES UNDER VINE 100.00
SUSTAINABLE WINERY

○ Erice Grillo Aegades '15	♥♥ 3
● Erice Nero d'Avola Torre dei Venti '14	♥♥ 4
● Erice Syrah Luce d' Oriente '14	♥♥ 3
● Sicilia Nero d'Avola Gàbal '14	♥ 4

Ferreri

C.DA SALINELLA
91029 SANTA NINFA [TP]
TEL. +39 092461871
www.ferrerivini.it

CELLAR SALES
PRE-BOOKED VISITS
ANNUAL PRODUCTION 70,000 bottles
HECTARES UNDER VINE 30.00

● Cabernet Sauvignon Karren '12	♥♥ 5
○ Zibibbo '15	♥♥ 3
○ Catarratto '15	♥ 3
○ Inzolia '15	♥ 3

Feudo di Santa Tresa

S.DA COM.LE MARANGIO, 35
97019 VITTORIA [RG]
TEL. +39 09321846555
www.santatresa.it

PRE-BOOKED VISITS
ANNUAL PRODUCTION 250,000 bottles
HECTARES UNDER VINE 38.00
VITICULTURE METHOD Certified Organic

● Avulisi '13	♥♥ 3
● Cerasuolo di Vittoria Cl. '13	♥♥ 2*
● Frappato '15	♥♥ 2*
○ Il Grillo di Santa Teresa Brut	♥ 4

Cantine Fina

C.DA BAUSA
91025 MARSALA [TP]
TEL. +39 0923733070
www.cantinefina.it

CELLAR SALES
PRE-BOOKED VISITS
ACCOMMODATION
ANNUAL PRODUCTION 250,000 bottles
HECTARES UNDER VINE 180.00
VITICULTURE METHOD Certified Organic

○ Kikè '15	♥♥ 3
● Perricone '15	♥♥ 3
○ Sauvignon Blanc '15	♥♥ 3
○ Kebrilla '15	♥ 2

Fischetti

C.DA MOSCAMENTO
FRAZ. ROVITTELLO
VIA NAZIONALE N. 2
95012 CASTIGLIONE DI SICILIA [CT]
TEL. +39 3341272527
www.fischettiwine.it

CELLAR SALES
PRE-BOOKED VISITS
ANNUAL PRODUCTION 8,000 bottles
HECTARES UNDER VINE 1.50

○ Etna Bianco Muscamento '15	♥♥ 4
● Etna Rosso Muscamento '13	♥♥ 4

Tenuta Gatti

C.DA CUPRANI
98064 LIBRIZZI [ME]
TEL. +39 0941368173
www.tenutagatti.com

CELLAR SALES
PRE-BOOKED VISITS
ANNUAL PRODUCTION 40,000 bottles
HECTARES UNDER VINE 15.00
VITICULTURE METHOD Certified Organic

● Mamertino Rosso Curpanè '12	♥♥ 3
● Nocera Sicè '14	♥♥ 4
● Franco '11	♥ 3

Geraci

VIA CORSICA, 18
90146 PALERMO
TEL. +39 0916154146
www.tarucco.com

CELLAR SALES
PRE-BOOKED VISITS
ANNUAL PRODUCTION 120,000 bottles
HECTARES UNDER VINE 15.00
VITICULTURE METHOD Certified Organic

○ Tarucco Chardonnay '15	♥♥ 3
○ Tarucco Grillo '15	♥♥ 2*
● Tarucco Merlot '14	♥ 3
● Tarucco Nero d'Avola '14	♥ 3

Tenuta Gorghi Tondi

C.DA SAN NICOLA
91026 MAZARA DEL VALLO [TP]
TEL. +39 0923719741
www.gorghitondi.com

CELLAR SALES
PRE-BOOKED VISITS
ACCOMMODATION AND RESTAURANT SERVICE
ANNUAL PRODUCTION 1,300,000 bottles
HECTARES UNDER VINE 130.00
VITICULTURE METHOD Certified Organic

○ Rajah '15	♥♥ 4
○ Sicilia Grillo Kheirè '15	♥♥ 4
● Sicilia Nero d'Avola Sorante '13	♥♥ 4
⊙ Palmarés Rosé Extra Dry	♥ 3

Hibiscus

C.DA TRAMONTANA
90010 USTICA [PA]
TEL. +39 0918449543
www.agriturismohibiscus.com

CELLAR SALES
PRE-BOOKED VISITS
ACCOMMODATION
ANNUAL PRODUCTION 10,000 bottles
HECTARES UNDER VINE 3.00

○ Grotta dell'Oro '15	♥♥ 2*
○ Zhabib Passito '15	♥♥ 4
○ L'Isola Bianco '15	♥ 2
● L'Isola Rosso '15	♥ 2

Judeka

C.DA SAN MAURO SOTTO
S.DA PROV.LE 39/11
95041 CALTAGIRONE [CT]
TEL. +39 09331895310
www.judeka.com

ANNUAL PRODUCTION 400,000 bottles
HECTARES UNDER VINE 33.00

○ Blandine '15	♥♥ 3
● Vittoria Frappato '14	♥♥ 2*
● Cerasuolo di Vittoria '14	♥ 3

Tenuta Enza La Fauci

C.DA MEZZANA-SPARTÀ
98163 MESSINA
TEL. +39 3476854318
www.tenutaenzalafauci.com

CELLAR SALES
ACCOMMODATION
ANNUAL PRODUCTION 14,000 bottles
HECTARES UNDER VINE 5.00

○ Case Bianche '15	♥♥ 4
● Faro Oblì '13	♥♥ 5

Tenuta La Favola

VIA PRINCIPE DI PIEMONTE, 39
96017 NOTO [SR]
TEL. +39 0931839216
www.tenutalafavola.it

CELLAR SALES
PRE-BOOKED VISITS
ANNUAL PRODUCTION 30,000 bottles
HECTARES UNDER VINE 10.00
VITICULTURE METHOD Certified Organic
SUSTAINABLE WINERY

● Fravolato '15	♥♥ 2*
● Synà '14	♥♥ 2*
● Eloro Pachino Nero d'Avola La Favola '14	♥ 3
○ Grillo Catarratto '15	♥ 2

Maggiovini

via Filippo Bonetti, 35
97019 Vittoria [RG]
Tel. +39 0932984771
www.maggiovini.it

CELLAR SALES
PRE-BOOKED VISITS
ACCOMMODATION
ANNUAL PRODUCTION 250,000 bottles
HECTARES UNDER VINE 45.00
VITICULTURE METHOD Certified Organic
SUSTAINABLE WINERY

● Sicilia Nero d'Avola V. di Pettineo '14	▼▼	3
● Vittoria Frappato V. di Pettineo '15	▼▼	3
○ Vittoria Grillo V. di Pettineo '15	▼▼	3

Marabino

c.da Buonivini
s.da prov.le Rosolini-Pachino km 8,5
97017 Noto [SR]
Tel. +39 3355284101
www.marabino.it

CELLAR SALES
PRE-BOOKED VISITS
ACCOMMODATION AND RESTAURANT SERVICE
ANNUAL PRODUCTION 100,000 bottles
HECTARES UNDER VINE 30.00
VITICULTURE METHOD Certified Organic

● Eloro Pachino Archimede Ris. '13	▼▼	5
○ Moscato di Noto Muscatedda '15	▼▼	3
● Noto Nero d'Avola '14	▼▼	2*
⊙ Eloro Nero d'Avola Rosato Rosa Nera '15	▼	3

Masseria del Feudo

c.da Grottarossa
93100 Caltanissetta
Tel. +39 0934569719
www.masseriadelfeudo.it

CELLAR SALES
PRE-BOOKED VISITS
ACCOMMODATION
ANNUAL PRODUCTION 100,000 bottles
HECTARES UNDER VINE 12.00
VITICULTURE METHOD Certified Organic

● Sicilia Il Giglio Syrah '15	▼▼	2*
● Sicilia Rosso delle Rose '14	▼▼	3
○ Sicilia Il Giglio Inzolia '15	▼	2
● Sicilia Il Giglio Nero d'Avola '15	▼	2

Miceli

c.da Piana Scunchipani, 190
92019 Sciacca [AG]
Tel. +39 092580188
www.miceli.uno

PRE-BOOKED VISITS
ANNUAL PRODUCTION 400,000 bottles
HECTARES UNDER VINE 60.00

○ Passito di Pantelleria Nun '13	▼▼	5
○ Baaria Grillo '15	▼	2
○ Pantelleria Bianco Yrnm '14	▼	4
○ Shahr Adonay '13	▼	4

Cantina Modica di San Giovanni

c.da Bufalefi
96017 Noto [SR]
Tel. +39 09311805181
www.vinidinoto.it

CELLAR SALES
PRE-BOOKED VISITS
RESTAURANT SERVICE
ANNUAL PRODUCTION 80,000 bottles
HECTARES UNDER VINE 40.00
SUSTAINABLE WINERY

● Dolcenero '12	▼▼	5
○ Moscato di Noto Dolcenoto '15	▼▼	3
○ Lupara '15	▼	2
⊙ Mamma Draja '15	▼	2

Cantine Mothia

via Giovanni Falcone, 22
91025 Marsala [TP]
Tel. +39 0923737295
www.cantine-mothia.com

CELLAR SALES
PRE-BOOKED VISITS
ANNUAL PRODUCTION 100,000 bottles
HECTARES UNDER VINE 25.00

● Mosaikon '15	▼▼	2*

Tenute Orestiadi

V.LE SANTA NINFA
91024 GIBELLINA [TP]
TEL. +39 092469124
www.tenuteorestiadi.it

CELLAR SALES
PRE-BOOKED VISITS
RESTAURANT SERVICE
ANNUAL PRODUCTION 1,000,000 bottles
HECTARES UNDER VINE 100.00
VITICULTURE METHOD Certified Organic
SUSTAINABLE WINERY

● Ludovico '11	♟♟ 5
● Molino a Vento Nero d'Avola '15	♟♟ 2*
● Perricone '14	♟♟ 3
● Molino a Vento Syrah '15	♟ 1*

Ottoventi

C.DA TORREBIANCA - FICO
91019 VALDERICE [TP]
TEL. +39 0923 1877151
www.cantinaottoventi.it

CELLAR SALES
PRE-BOOKED VISITS
ACCOMMODATION
ANNUAL PRODUCTION 300,000 bottles
HECTARES UNDER VINE 35.00

○ Grillo '15	♟♟ 4
○ Ottoventi Bianco '15	♟ 3
● Ottoventi Nero '14	♟ 3
○ Zibibbo '15	♟ 4

Tenute dei Paladini

VIA PALESTRO, 23
91025 MARSALA [TP]
TEL. +39 3463513366
www.tenutedeipaladini.com

ANNUAL PRODUCTION 40,000 bottles
HECTARES UNDER VINE 45.00

○ Grillo Palatium '15	♟♟ 3
● Nero d'Avola Palatium '15	♟♟ 3
○ Catarratto-Chardonnay Palatium '15	♟ 3
● San Giorgio '15	♟ 3

Cantine Paolini

C.DA GURGO, 168A
91025 MARSALA [TP]
TEL. +39 0923967042
www.cantinapaolini.com

ANNUAL PRODUCTION 4,000,000 bottles
HECTARES UNDER VINE 2739.00
VITICULTURE METHOD Certified Organic

● Lance Nero d'Avola '14	♟♟ 2*
● Nero d'Avola '15	♟♟ 2*
○ Zibibbo '15	♟♟ 2*
○ Sicilia Grillo Gurgò '15	♟ 2

Cantine Pepi

V.LE DEL LAVORO, 7
95040 MAZZARRONE [CT]
TEL. +39 093328001
wwww.cantinepepi.it

ANNUAL PRODUCTION 100,000 bottles
HECTARES UNDER VINE 35.00

● Agate Frappato '15	♟♟ 2*
● Tra Cielo e Terra Frappato Passito '15	♟♟ 5
● Cerasuolo di Vittoria Eore '14	♟ 3
● Ex Nero d'Avola '14	♟ 2

Pietracava

VIA LUIGI STURZO, 16
93011 BUTERA [CL]
TEL. +39 3392410117
www.pietracavawines.it

ANNUAL PRODUCTION 30,000 bottles
HECTARES UNDER VINE 30.00

○ Millelune Inzolia '15	♟♟ 2*
○ Pioggia di Luce '15	♟♟ 3
● Manaar '14	♟ 4
● Neofos '15	♟ 3

Quignones

VIA VITTORIO EMANUELE, 62
92027 LICATA [AG]
TEL. +39 0922773744
www.quignones.it

CELLAR SALES
PRE-BOOKED VISITS
ANNUAL PRODUCTION 90,000 bottles
HECTARES UNDER VINE 28.00

● Castel San Giacomo Rosso '13	♟♟ 2*
○ Castel San Giacomo Bianco '15	♟ 2
⊙ Fimmina Rosato di Nero d'Avola '15	♟ 2
● Lagasia Cabernet Sauvignon '10	♟ 2

Cantine Russo

LOC. CRASÀ
FRAZ. SOLICCHIATA
VIA CORVO
95014 CASTIGLIONE DI SICILIA [CT]
TEL. +39 0942986271
www.cantinerusso.eu

CELLAR SALES
PRE-BOOKED VISITS
ANNUAL PRODUCTION 190,000 bottles
HECTARES UNDER VINE 15.00

● Etna Luce di Lava '13	♟♟ 3
○ Etna Rampante Contrada Crasà '15	♟♟ 3
● Etna Rosso Rampante '10	♟ 4
⊙ Mon Pit Brut Rosé	♟ 6

Sallier de la Tour

C.DA PERNICE
90144 MONREALE [PA]
TEL. +39 0916459711
www.tascadalmerita.it

PRE-BOOKED VISITS
ANNUAL PRODUCTION 250,000 bottles
HECTARES UNDER VINE 41.00

● Monreale La Monaca '13	♟♟ 5
● Sicilia Nero d'Avola '14	♟♟ 2*
○ Sicilia Grillo '15	♟ 2
○ Sicilia Inzolia '15	♟ 2

Scilio

V.LE DELLE PROVINCIE, 52
95014 GIARRE [CT]
TEL. +39 095932822
www.scilio.com

CELLAR SALES
PRE-BOOKED VISITS
ACCOMMODATION AND RESTAURANT SERVICE
ANNUAL PRODUCTION 90,000 bottles
HECTARES UNDER VINE 22.00
VITICULTURE METHOD Certified Organic

○ Etna Bianco Valle Galfina '15	♟♟ 3
● Etna Rosso Valle Galfina '14	♟♟ 3

Solidea

C.DA KADDIUGGIA
91017 PANTELLERIA [TP]
TEL. +39 0923913016
www.solideavini.it

ANNUAL PRODUCTION 12,000 bottles
HECTARES UNDER VINE 1.80

○ Moscato di Pantelleria '15	♟♟ 4
○ Passito di Pantelleria '15	♟♟ 5
○ Ilios '15	♟ 3

Terre di Giurfo

VIA PALESTRO, 536
97019 VITTORIA [RG]
TEL. +39 0957221551
www.terredigiurfo.it

CELLAR SALES
PRE-BOOKED VISITS
ANNUAL PRODUCTION 100,000 bottles
HECTARES UNDER VINE 40.00

● Etna Rosso Nardalici '13	♟♟ 3
● Sicilia Nero d'Avola Kudyah '14	♟♟ 2*
● Vittoria Frappato Belsito '15	♟♟ 2*
● Sicilia Nero d'Avola Kuntàri '14	♟ 3

Todaro

C.DA FEOTTO
90048 SAN GIUSEPPE JATO [PA]
TEL. +39 3461056393
www.todarowinery.com

PRE-BOOKED VISITS
ANNUAL PRODUCTION 80,000 bottles
HECTARES UNDER VINE 25.00
VITICULTURE METHOD Certified Organic

● Shadir '14	♥♥ 2*
○ Lybra '15	♥ 2
○ Nihal '15	♥ 2
● Virgo '14	♥ 2

Girolamo Tola & C.

VIA GIACOMO MATEOTTI, 2
90047 PARTINICO [PA]
TEL. +39 0918781591
www.vinitola.it

ANNUAL PRODUCTION 180,000 bottles
HECTARES UNDER VINE 55.00

● Nero d'Avola '15	♥♥ 3
● Nero d'Avola Black Label '13	♥♥ 3
○ Chardonnay Insolia '15	♥ 2
○ Grillo '15	♥ 3

Cantine Trapani

LOC. BOVARELLA
VIA MONACI, 41
91018 SALEMI [TP]
TEL. +39 092469938
www.trapanivini.it

ANNUAL PRODUCTION 40,000 bottles
HECTARES UNDER VINE 40.00

● Goccia Nero d'Avola '15	♥♥ 2*
○ Vento del Sud Grillo '15	♥♥ 1*
● Vento del Sud Syrah '15	♥♥ 2*
○ Quiete Catarratto Grillo '15	♥ 2

Vaccaro

C.DA COMUNE
91020 SALAPARUTA [TP]
TEL. +39 092475151
www.vinivaccaro.it

CELLAR SALES
ANNUAL PRODUCTION 800,000 bottles
HECTARES UNDER VINE 40.00
VITICULTURE METHOD Certified Organic
SUSTAINABLE WINERY

○ Luna Grillo '15	♥♥ 1*
● Luna Nero d'Avola '15	♥♥ 4
● Salaparuta Rosso Zoe '14	♥♥ 4
⊙ Rosato di Nero d'Avola '15	♥ 2

Le Vigne di Eli

C.DA CALDERARA
95036 RANDAZZO [CT]
TEL. +39 095924002
www.tenutaterrenere.com

CELLAR SALES
PRE-BOOKED VISITS
ANNUAL PRODUCTION 200,000 bottles
HECTARES UNDER VINE 30.00
VITICULTURE METHOD Certified Organic

○ Etna Bianco Moganazzi Voltasciara '14	♥♥ 6
● Etna Rosso Moganazzi Voltasciara '14	♥♥ 6
● Etna Rosso Pignatuni '14	♥♥ 6
● Etna Rosso San Lorenzo '14	♥♥ 6

Vivera

C.DA MARTINELLA
S.DA PROV.LE 59 IV
95015 LINGUAGLOSSA [CT]
TEL. +39 095643837
www.vivera.it

PRE-BOOKED VISITS
ANNUAL PRODUCTION 120,000 bottles
HECTARES UNDER VINE 35.00
VITICULTURE METHOD Certified Organic

○ A'mami '13	♥♥ 3
○ Altrove '15	♥♥ 2*
● Etna Rosso Martinella '11	♥♥ 4
● Terra dei Sogni '13	♥ 2

SARDINIA

Casting an eye over the award-winning wines, but also over the multitude of labels that make the finals or pick up a Due Bicchieri, it is easy to come to the conclusion that the mission started several years ago is well underway. The mission, of course, involved the great traditional cultivars but grown only in areas where it is really worthwhile since the resulting wines are of a quality that will cut a swathe on global markets. So, even though the various regional designations do not make the most of smaller, confined growing areas, tastings this year point us in the direction of what is now proving to be real wine country. Add to all this the good 2015 growing year – even if hotter, less balanced and therefore not quite on a par with the previous vintage – able to offer some top-notch labels and lots of quaffable wines, although none particularly cellarable. Among the whites, we were pleased to see good performances not only from the renowned Gallura, but also from areas such as Campidano or the north west of the island. For the reds, the Cannonau di Sardegnas were predictably superb from the best terroirs like Ogliastra and Barbagia, as well as the south of the island. There were satisfactory results from Sulcis and its Carignanos, with some nice surprises from other natives, like nieddera or barbera sarda, sadly without a DOC zone. Among the prize winners, there were both old hands and newcomers. Some wines are sure-fire guarantees, year after year, like the Gabbas Cannonau di Sardegna Dule or the Capichera from the eponymous Arzachena cellar; Surrau's Vermentino di Gallura; Pala's lip-smacking Vermentino di Sardegna Stellato; the Carignano del Sulcis from Mesa and from Giba; and the D53, a great example of Cannonau from Ogliastra. Good results too for Contini's Barrile from nieddera, and for the Sella & Mosca Cuvée 161 from torbato grapes, both ambassadors for vine biodiversity. Then we meet three wines making their debut: the first vintage of Argiolas's Senes, a 2012 and typical Cannonau that charms with its typicity and elegance; the 2011 Falconaro from a blend of traditional grapes, which earned Cantina di Dolianova its first coveted Tre Bicchieri; lastly, the 2010 Latinia from Santadi, which demonstrated Sardinia's great potential for producing sweet wines from dried grapes.

★★Argiolas

VIA ROMA, 28/30
09040 SERDIANA [CA]
TEL. +39 070740606
www.argiolas.it

CELLAR SALES
PRE-BOOKED VISITS
ANNUAL PRODUCTION 2,200,000 bottles
HECTARES UNDER VINE 230.00
SUSTAINABLE WINERY

Ongoing research, extension and consolidation of the range, and consistent work towards exporting around the five continents. These are the main features of Argiolas, a venerable estate about which much has been said and written. Credit is due to a great wine-producing family headed by brothers Franco and Peppetto, still in the front line, although their children Valentina, Francesca and Antonio now manage all aspects of the estate. Annual production is over two million bottles, seemingly without dips in quality. Argiolas's new entry is Senes, a 2012 Riserva di Cannonau di Sardegna, whose name invokes the established longevity of Sardinian wines. This great Mediterranean red has roses and scrubland on the nose, and a fresh, balsamic flavour, with deep, plush tannins. A Tre Bicchieri for this surprise. The Turriga is sound as ever, although not its finest version. The rest of the range was at its usual high standard.

Capichera

S.S. ARZACHENA-SANT'ANTONIO, KM 4
07021 ARZACHENA [OT]
TEL. +39 078980612
www.capichera.it

CELLAR SALES
PRE-BOOKED VISITS
ANNUAL PRODUCTION 250,000 bottles
HECTARES UNDER VINE 50.00
SUSTAINABLE WINERY

Capichera is a well-known name in Italy and around the world, which should be no surprise considering that the Ragnedda brothers were among the first on the island to bottle and export great vermentino-based whites to other countries. This has certainly contributed to promoting Sardinia and the winegrowing area of Gallura, where they are based. Annual production is around 250,000 bottles, maintaining a very high standard across the range, not only for the whites. Capichera reds and whites are all elegant, characterful, terroir-true and above all, ageable. A very high standard once again from Capichera this year. The Vermentino di Gallura Vign'angena, youngest of their great Galluras, displays a fresh, pleasing yet very complex flavour. Capichera 2014 scales the absolute heights of quality: aromatic herbs, citrus and aniseed on the nose, and a fresh, tangy mouth with an almondy finish. The Vendemmia Tardiva is also a great wine.

● Cannonau di Sardegna Senes Ris. '12	♥♥♥ 5
● Turriga '12	♥♥ 8
○ Angialis '13	♥♥ 6
● Antonio Argiolas 100 '12	♥♥ 6
● Cannonau di Sardegna Costera '14	♥♥ 3
○ Cerdeña '12	♥♥ 7
○ Is Solinas '13	♥♥ 4
● Korem '13	♥♥ 5
● Monica di Sardegna Sup. Is Selis '14	♥♥ 3
● Monica di Sardegna Perdera '14	♥ 3
○ Nasco di Cagliari Is Selis '15	♥ 3
○ Nuragus di Cagliari S'Elegas '15	♥ 2
⊙ Serralori '15	♥ 2
○ Vermentino di Sardegna Costamolino '15	♥ 3
○ Vermentino di Sardegna Is Argiolas '15	♥ 3
○ Vermentino di Sardegna Merì '15	♥ 3

○ Capichera '14	♥♥♥ 6
○ Vermentino di Gallura Vign'angena '15	♥♥ 5
○ Capichera V.T. '14	♥♥ 8
● Lianti '14	♥ 4
⊙ Tambè '15	♥ 4
○ Capichera '13	♥♥♥ 6
○ Capichera '12	♥♥♥ 6
○ Capichera '11	♥♥♥ 6
○ Capichera '10	♥♥♥ 5
○ Capichera V.T. '00	♥♥♥ 6
○ Vermentino di Gallura Vign'angena '10	♥♥♥ 5
○ Vermentino di Gallura Vign'angena '09	♥♥♥ 5

Carpante

via Garibaldi, 151
07049 Usini [SS]
Tel. +39 079380614
www.carpante.it

CELLAR SALES
PRE-BOOKED VISITS
ANNUAL PRODUCTION 30,000 bottles
HECTARES UNDER VINE 8.00

Carpante is based in Usini, a small town in the north west of the island, considered the nerve centre for fine quality winegrowing. The estate's vineyards are situated at 250 metres above sea level, on loamy, limestone soil ideal for the production of vermentino-based whites, and cagnulari reds. A well-stocked range, despite the limited number of hectares and bottles, includes several incarnations of cagnulari and vermentino as well as some interesting cannonaus and carignanos. Carpante seems to be enjoying a particularly positive period, presenting an excellent range this year. The Lizzos 2012, a selection of cagnulari grapes, made the finals: spice and pipe tobacco on the nose, with ripe but clearly defined fruit and an austere palate with plush, polished tannins and an especially tangy, deep finish. Outstanding among the whites is the Vermentino di Sardegna Longhera 2015, which fully embodies its terroir of origin, Usini.

● Lizzos '12	🍷🍷 4
● Cagnulari '14	🍷🍷 3
● Carpante '12	🍷🍷 4
● Disizzu '14	🍷🍷 4
○ Vermentino di Sardegna Longhera '15	🍷🍷 2*
● Cannonau di Sardegna '14	🍷 3
○ Vermentino di Sardegna Frinas '15	🍷 4
● Carpante '11	🍷🍷 4
● Carpante '10	🍷🍷 4
● Carpante '09	🍷🍷 4
● Disizzu '12	🍷🍷 4
○ Vermentino di Sardegna Frinas '12	🍷🍷 4
○ Vermentino di Sardegna Frinas '10	🍷🍷 4
○ Vermentino di Sardegna Longhera '13	🍷🍷 2*

Giovanni Maria Cherchi

loc. Sa Pala e Sa Chessa
07049 Usini [SS]
Tel. +39 079380273
www.vinicolacherchi.it

CELLAR SALES
PRE-BOOKED VISITS
ANNUAL PRODUCTION 170,000 bottles
HECTARES UNDER VINE 30.00

The venerable Cherchi estate, based in Logudoro, was established by a great winegrowing family in the 1970s. Credit goes to them for promoting the Usini DOC zone, with authentic wines that offer a true interpretation of their land and microclimate of origin, and Vermentinos di Sardegna always among the best in their category with time-defying ageability. The reds are also excellent, led by the Cagnulari, made from the grape of the same name. Research goes on, and for a few years they have produced an increasingly delicate Metodo Classico, thanks to very lengthy maturation on the yeasts. Yet again a impressive range with the first-rate Vermentino di Sardegna Tuvaoes 2015 has hints of sage and citrus with a tangy palate. The Cannonau di Sardegna 2014 is fresh and juicy, as is the Cagnulari 2014, with truly enjoyable hints of spice, red berries and forest floor on the nose, and a compact, deep palate. Sound as ever, the Luzzana 2014 is a pleasing blend of cagnulari and cannonau.

● Cagnulari '14	🍷🍷 3
● Cagnulari Billia '15	🍷🍷 3
● Cannonau di Sardegna '14	🍷🍷 3
● Luzzana '14	🍷🍷 4
○ Vermentino di Sardegna Tuvaoes '15	🍷🍷 3
○ Tokaterra	🍷 3
○ Vermentino di Sardegna Billia '15	🍷 2
○ Vermentino di Sardegna Tuvaoes '88	🍷🍷🍷 4*
● Cagnulari '13	🍷🍷 3
● Cagnulari '12	🍷🍷 3
● Cagnulari Billia '12	🍷🍷 3
● Cannonau di Sardegna '13	🍷🍷 3
○ Vermentino di Sardegna Tuvaoes '14	🍷🍷 3

Chessa

VIA SAN GIORGIO
07049 USINI [SS]
TEL. +39 3283747069
www.cantinechessa.it

CELLAR SALES
PRE-BOOKED VISITS
ANNUAL PRODUCTION 43,000 bottles
HECTARES UNDER VINE 15.00

Giovanna owns the estate bearing her name, distinguishing itself in recent years as one of the island's most interesting wineries thanks to an accurate expression of the Usini terroir. The wines are authentic and characterful, starting with Cagnulari, which Giovanna has made more harmonious and elegant through meticulous vineyard procedures, despite the tricky nature of this grape variety. The other wines are all focused and cleanly made, from the Vermentino to the Moscato, the latter from super-ripe grapes. Cagnulari is always the most impressive wine in our tastings. The 2014 vintage brings us a stylish, subtle red with aromas of myrtle and sweet spice and minty, balsamic hints. A close-knit palate with spiky, but never drying, tannins and a tangy finish. The Mattariga is also excellent and the Vermentino di Sardegna 2015 is pleasant and fragrant.

● Cagnulari '14	♟♟ 3
○ Vermentino di Sardegna Mattariga '15	♟♟ 3
● Lugherra '13	♟ 5
● Cagnulari '13	♟♟ 3
● Cagnulari '12	♟♟ 3
● Cagnulari '11	♟♟ 3
● Cagnulari '10	♟♟ 3*
○ Kentàles	♟♟ 5
● Lugherra '12	♟♟ 5
● Lugherra '10	♟♟ 5
● Lugherra '09	♟♟ 5
○ Vermentino di Sardegna Mattariga '14	♟♟ 3
○ Vermentino di Sardegna Mattariga '13	♟♟ 3
○ Vermentino di Sardegna Mattariga '12	♟♟ 3
○ Vermentino di Sardegna Mattariga '10	♟♟ 3

Attilio Contini

VIA GENOVA, 48/50
09072 CABRAS [OR]
TEL. +39 0783290806
www.vinicontini.it

CELLAR SALES
PRE-BOOKED VISITS
ANNUAL PRODUCTION 800,000 bottles
HECTARES UNDER VINE 70.00
VITICULTURE METHOD Certified Organic
SUSTAINABLE WINERY

Contini is one of the biggest privately owned wine estates in Sardinia, both in number of bottles produced and in the standard of quality and prestige achieved. It has helped showcase the whole area, focusing on traditional grape varieties: the black nieddera grape and the white vernaccia di Oristano. A great deal of research has been carried out on the latter, and the cellar contains an amazing heritage of vintage reserves. The winery produces a very wide range from Vermentino and Cannonau di Sardegna to sparklers, also from nieddera and vernaccia. An excellent performance from this Oristano estate. The Barrile 2013 is a selection of nieddera, a native variety the winery has always believed in. The incredibly subtle and complex nose shows spice, ripe red berries, hints of flowers and scrubland; the close-knit palate is velvety, fresh and tangy. Tre Bicchieri. The latest version of the Vernaccia di Oristano is absolutely charming, a 1991 Riserva which even after 25 years continues to age without fear.

● Barrile '13	♟♟♟ 7
○ Vernaccia di Oristano Ris. '91	♟♟ 7
● Cannonau di Sardegna Sartiglia '10	♟♟ 3
● I Giganti Rosso '13	♟♟ 5
● Nieddera Rosso '15	♟♟ 3
○ Pontis	♟♟ 5
○ Vermentino di Gallura Elibaria '15	♟♟ 3
○ Vernaccia di Oristano Componidori '05	♟♟ 3
● Cannonau di Sardegna Tonaghe '15	♟ 2
○ I Giganti Bianco '13	♟ 5
○ Karmis '15	♟ 3
⊙ Nieddera Rosato '15	♟ 2
○ Vermentino di Sardegna Pariglia '15	♟ 2
○ Vermentino di Sardegna Tyrsos '15	♟ 2
○ Vernaccia di Oristano Flor '05	♟ 3
● Barrile '11	♟♟♟ 6

Ferruccio Deiana

LOC. SU LEUNAXI
VIA GIALETO, 7
09040 SETTIMO SAN PIETRO [CA]
TEL. +39 070749117
www.ferrucciodeiana.it

CELLAR SALES
PRE-BOOKED VISITS
ANNUAL PRODUCTION 520,000 bottles
HECTARES UNDER VINE 94.00

Skilled winegrower and winemaker
Ferruccio Deiana has succeeded in creating
a leading estate, both in number of bottles
produced and in estate under vine. There
are two main plots, Su Leunaxiu, one near
the winery, and the other at Sibiola in the
municipal area of Serdiana, which has
always been prime vineyard country. The
estate focuses on traditional grapes, in
many cases using separate vinifications,
with the exception of some leading wines
blended from different grapes. Into the Tre
Bicchieri finals for the Cannonau di
Sardegna Sileno Riserva 2013, successfully
combining complexity and drinkability, and
a very clean nose offering a good
expression of the island's native southern
varieties. The Ajana is a very nice blend of
traditional grapes while among the whites,
we recommend the Arvali 2015, a fresh,
supple Vermentino di Sardegna.

Cantine di Dolianova

LOC. SANT'ESU
S.S. 387 KM 17,150
09041 DOLIANOVA [CA]
TEL. +39 070744101
www.cantinedidolianova.it

CELLAR SALES
PRE-BOOKED VISITS
ANNUAL PRODUCTION 4,000,000 bottles
HECTARES UNDER VINE 1200.00

Dolianova is one of Sardinia's largest
cooperative wineries and a benchmark for
many growers in its local area of Parteolla.
In recent years the average quality has
improved considerably, from well-typed but
uninteresting wines to complex, authentic
products on a par with the island's greatest
labels. The very extensive range includes
still, sparkling and sweet wines, all showing
excellent value for money and obtained
exclusively from traditional grape varieties.
The enhanced quality from the Dolianova
cooperative in recent years is seen in the
range led by the Falconaro 2011:
complex aromas with hints of scrubland,
damson and aromatic resin, with a fresh,
long, tangy and balsamic flavour. This
blend of cannonau, Montepulciano and
carignano a very good example of a
full-bodied Mediterranean red, earns a
well-deserved Tre Bicchieri. The Blasio
and Terresicci are also excellent, the l
atter from barbera sarda.

● Cannonau di Sardegna Sileno Ris. '13	♟♟ 4
● Ajana '13	♟♟ 6
● Cannonau di Sardegna Sileno '14	♟♟ 3
○ Oirad '14	♟♟ 5
○ Vermentino di Sardegna Arvali '15	♟♟ 3
⊙ Bellarosa '15	♟ 2
● Monica di Sardegna Karel '14	♟ 2
○ Pluminus '14	♟ 6
○ Vermentino di Sardegna Donnikalia '15	♟ 2
● Ajana '02	♟♟♟ 6
● Cannonau di Sardegna Sileno Ris. '10	♟♟♟ 3*
● Ajana '12	♟♟ 6
● Cannonau di Sardegna Sileno '13	♟♟ 3
● Cannonau di Sardegna Sileno Ris. '12	♟♟ 4
○ Vermentino di Sardegna Arvali '14	♟♟ 3
○ Vermentino di Sardegna Donnikalia '14	♟♟ 2*

● Falconaro '11	♟♟♟ 3*
● Cannonau di Sardegna Blasio Ris. '11	♟♟ 3
● Terresicci '11	♟♟ 5
● Cannonau di Sardegna Anzenas San Pantaleo '14	♟ 2
○ Caralis Brut	♟ 2
○ Malvasia Scaleri Demi Sec	♟ 3
● Monica di Sardegna Arenada '14	♟ 2
○ Nuragus di Cagliari Perlas San Pantaleo '15	♟ 1*
⊙ Sibiola Rosé '15	♟ 2
○ Vermentino di Sardegna Naeli '15	♟ 2
○ Vermentino di Sardegna Prendas San Pantaleo '15	♟ 2
● Cannonau di Sardegna Blasio Ris. '10	♟♟ 3*
● Falconaro '10	♟♟ 3

Cantina Dorgali

via Piemonte, 11
08022 Dorgali [NU]
Tel. +39 078496143
www.cantinadorgali.com

CELLAR SALES
PRE-BOOKED VISITS
ANNUAL PRODUCTION 1,500,000 bottles
HECTARES UNDER VINE 600.00
SUSTAINABLE WINERY

Dorgali is the benchmark cooperative winery for the province of Nuoro, its vineyards rolling down towards the Tyrrhenian coast and encompassing the Ogliastra winegrowing zone. Here the cannonau grape reigns supreme, with many old bush-trained vineyards producing low yields but high quality. In recent years the winery has been able to exploit this rich heritage to the full, with a policy that begins in each grower's vineyards, which are the secret behind some of the island's best Cannonau di Sardegna. The main features of Dorgali wines are freshness, elegance and depth. The Cannonau di Sardegnas are the most impressive wines in the Dorgali range. The D53 2013 displays rose and blackberry aromas with a fresh, supple, stylish, deep palate. Tre Bicchieri. The Riserva 2013 Vinìola is also very good. The other wines are well made.

● Cannonau di Sardegna Cl. D53 '13	▼▼▼	4*
● Cannonau di Sardegna Vinìola Ris. '13	▼▼	4
● Norìolo '13	▼▼	4
⊙ Cannonau di Sardegna Rosato Filieri '15	▼	2
○ Vermentino di Sardegna Calaluna '15	▼	2
○ Vermentino di Sardegna Filine '15	▼	2
● Cannonau di Sardegna Cl. D53 '12	▽▽▽	4*
● Cannonau di Sardegna Vinìola Ris. '10	▽▽▽	4*
● Cannonau di Sardegna Vinìola Ris. '07	▽▽▽	3*
● Cannonau di Sardegna Vinìola Ris. '06	▽▽▽	3*
● Hortos '08	▽▽▽	6
● Cannonau di Sardegna Vinìola Ris. '12	▽▽	4
● Cannonau di Sardegna Vinìola Ris. '11	▽▽	4

Giuseppe Gabbas

via Trieste, 59
08100 Nuoro
Tel. +39 078433745
www.gabbas.it

CELLAR SALES
PRE-BOOKED VISITS
ANNUAL PRODUCTION 70,000 bottles
HECTARES UNDER VINE 20.00

Giuseppe Gabbas is a skilled and talented winegrower who has long since been taken as an example for his meticulous vineyard work and the character of his delicious wines. Here, a few kilometres from Oliena, the grapes grown on 20 or so hectares planted to cannonau produce four wines that differ according to the plot location and vinification method. A Vermentino di Sardegna Manzanile completes the range. All the wines stand out for their elegance, drinkability and sense of place. On top form this year, the Dule 2013 is a Cannonau di Sardegna Classico: an outstanding combination of complexity, elegance and great mouthfeel, with aromas of myrtle, medicinal herbs, spices and wild berries, and a fresh, flavoursome palate with gentle tannin and a long, clean finish. Tre Bicchieri. The Arbòre 2013 and the Lillové 2015 are both terrific.

● Cannonau di Sardegna Cl. Dule '13	▼▼▼	4*
● Cannonau di Sardegna Cl. Arbòre '13	▼▼	4
● Cannonau di Sardegna Lillové '15	▼▼	2*
○ Vermentino di Sardegna Manzanile '15	▼	3
● Cannonau di Sardegna Cl. Dule '12	▽▽▽	4*
● Cannonau di Sardegna Cl. Dule '11	▽▽▽	4*
● Cannonau di Sardegna Dule Ris. '10	▽▽▽	4*
● Cannonau di Sardegna Dule Ris. '09	▽▽▽	3*
● Cannonau di Sardegna Dule Ris. '08	▽▽▽	3*
● Cannonau di Sardegna Dule Ris. '07	▽▽▽	3*
● Cannonau di Sardegna Dule Ris. '06	▽▽▽	3*
● Cannonau di Sardegna Dule Ris. '05	▽▽▽	3*
● Cannonau di Sardegna Cl. Arbòre '12	▽▽	4
● Cannonau di Sardegna Cl. Arbòre '11	▽▽	4

Cantina Gallura

VIA VAL DI COSSU, 9
07029 TEMPIO PAUSANIA
TEL. +39 079631241
www.cantinagallura.com

CELLAR SALES
PRE-BOOKED VISITS
ANNUAL PRODUCTION 1,300,000 bottles
HECTARES UNDER VINE 350.00

The Gallura cooperative winery at Tempio, managed by skilled winemaker Dino Addis, is a benchmark for the whole of north-eastern Sardinia. Vermentino di Gallura takes the lion's share in a an extensive range of quality wines. Strict grape selection and vinification by individual vineyard allows the cooperative to produce excellent wines at excellent value for money, especially basic products which are far from commonplace. As well as Vermentino, also in sweet and sparkling versions, the winery offers a Moscato di Tempio Spumante and some interesting reds, always from traditional grape varieties. Another impressive range of wines this year, especially the Vermentinos, led by the Canayli Vendemma Tardiva. The 2015 shows peach and apricot aromas alongside aromatic herbs, broom flowers and orange blossom, with a supple, flavoursome palate. The Superiore del Canayli is also excellent, and the Piras delicious as ever. The other wines are all well-made.

○ Vermentino di Gallura Canayli V. T. '15	♥♥	4
○ Vermentino di Gallura Piras '15	♥♥	2*
○ Vermentino di Gallura Sup. Canayli '15	♥♥	2*
⊙ Campos '15	♥	2
● Cannonau di Sardegna Templum '14	♥	2
● Karana '15	♥	2
○ Moscato di Tempio Pausania	♥	2
○ Vermentino di Gallura Gemellae '15	♥	2
○ Vermentino di Gallura Mavriana '15	♥	2
○ Vermentino di Gallura Canayli V. T. '14	♥♥♥	4*
○ Vermentino di Gallura Sup. Genesi '10	♥♥♥	5
○ Vermentino di Gallura Sup. Genesi '08	♥♥♥	5
○ Vermentino di Gallura Piras '14	♥♥	2*
○ Vermentino di Gallura Sup. Canayli '14	♥♥	2*

Cantina Giba

VIA PRINCIPE DI PIEMONTE, 16
09010 GIBA [CI]
TEL. +39 0781689718
www.cantinagiba.it

CELLAR SALES
ANNUAL PRODUCTION 100,000 bottles
HECTARES UNDER VINE 15.00

Giba is a small town in the south-west of Sardinia, and lends its name to this winery specializing in Carignano del Sulcis obtained from old bush-trained vineyards. Previously known as 6Mura, which is now the name of the leading product line, this artisan winery offers authentic, seductive wines that are never predictable or commonplace, but true offspring of the Sulcis area. As well as two versions of Carignano and a new rosé, the winery produces two Vermentino di Sardegna from estate-grown grapes. The Carignano del Sulcis 6Mura 2011, from venerable ungrafted vineyards, won us over with its array of aromas from scrubland bushes to myrtle and red berries, and a creamy, soft palate, enlivened by well-focused tannin and textbook tanginess. The flavour is long and deep yet always fresh and lively. Tre Bicchieri. The Vermentino di Sardegna 6Mura 2015 has a salty tang of iodine.

● Carignano del Sulcis 6Mura '11	♥♥♥	5
⊙ Carignano del Sulcis Giba Rosato '15	♥♥	2*
○ Vermentino di Sardegna 6Mura '15	♥♥	4
○ Vermentino di Sardegna Giba '15	♥	2
● Carignano del Sulcis 6Mura '10	♥♥♥	5
● Carignano del Sulcis 6Mura '09	♥♥♥	5
● Carignano del Sulcis 6Mura '11	♥♥	5
● Carignano del Sulcis Giba '13	♥♥	2*
● Carignano del Sulcis Giba '12	♥♥	2*
● Carignano del Sulcis Giba '11	♥♥	2*
○ Vermentino di Sardegna '14	♥♥	4
○ Vermentino di Sardegna '12	♥♥	4
○ Vermentino di Sardegna Giba '13	♥♥	2*

Antichi Poderi Jerzu

VIA UMBERTO I, 1
08044 JERZU [OG]
TEL. +39 078270028
www.jerzuantichipoderi.it

CELLAR SALES
PRE-BOOKED VISITS
ANNUAL PRODUCTION 1,500,000 bottles
HECTARES UNDER VINE 750.00

Antichi Poderi di Jerzu is an Ogliastra cooperative specializing in Cannonau, which proudly represents the Jerzu subzone here. This is a very large estate with 750 hectares under vine, producing over 1.5 million bottles per year. The turning point in quality came a few years ago, following completion of zoning, when the estate began bottling its wines according to terrain, age and aspect of vineyards. The results have been encouraging and the Cannonau di Jerzu are increasingly well-typed, terroir-true and authentic. A few whites complete the range with a well-styled Monica di Sardegna. The Cannonau di Sardegna wines lead the pack unchallenged, starting with the Riservas, led by Josto Miglior 2013, with forest floor aromas and a fresh, balsamic palate. The Chierra 2013, not as compact, is equally good with softer tannin. Il Bantu 2015, a mouthwatering, moreish standard label Cannonau, is a dead cert. All the other wines are well made.

● Cannonau di Sardegna Bantu '15	♥♥ 2*
● Cannonau di Sardegna Chuerra Ris. '13	♥♥ 5
● Cannonau di Sardegna Josto Miglior Ris. '13	♥♥ 5
● Cannonau di Sardegna Marghìa '14	♥♥ 4
● Akratos '12	♥ 5
☉ Cannonau di Sardegna Isara '15	♥ 2
○ Vermentino di Sardegna Lucean Le Stelle '15	♥ 3
○ Vermentino di Sardegna Telavè '15	♥ 2
● Cannonau di Sardegna Josto Miglior Ris. '09	♥♥♥ 4*
● Cannonau di Sardegna Josto Miglior Ris. '05	♥♥♥ 4
● Radames '01	♥♥♥ 5
● Cannonau di Sardegna Josto Miglior Ris. '12	♥♥ 5

Alberto Loi

S.S. 125 KM 124,1
08040 CARDEDU [OG]
TEL. +39 070240866
www.albertoloi.it

CELLAR SALES
PRE-BOOKED VISITS
ACCOMMODATION
ANNUAL PRODUCTION 250,000 bottles
HECTARES UNDER VINE 53.00

Loi is a venerable wine-producing family based in Cardedu. Hats off for being the first to bottle fine Cannonau di Sardegna and the consequent promotion of this great Sardinian wine, produced here in the Jerzu subzone. Decades on, the estate is still rooted in artisan winegrowing traditions, as shown by the use of large, used oak barrels and selection of grapes from old bush-trained vineyards. The wide range of Cannonaus includes Riserva and Selezione versions, as well as a pinch of innovation with a cannonau-based white, and several blends of this variety with other traditional grapes. Once again this year, Loi wines prove to be authentic, unswayed by current trends, and excellent expressions of the Jerzu terroir. One prime example is the Alberto Loi Riserva, with the 2012 offering aromas of dried roses, gentle hints of resin and bark, closing on ripe red berries. The palate is warm with velvety tannins and a deep finish. The other versions of Cannonau di Sardegna are also reliably good.

● Cannonau di Sardegna Jerzu Alberto Loi Ris. '12	♥♥ 3
● Cannonau di Sardegna Jerzu Sa Mola '14	♥♥ 2*
● Tuvara '13	♥♥ 5
● Cannonau di Sardegna Jerzu Cardedo Ris. '13	♥ 3
● Monica di Sardegna Nibaru '15	♥ 2
○ Vermentino di Sardegna Theria '15	♥ 2
● Cannonau di Sardegna Jerzu Alberto Loi Ris. '11	♥♥ 3
● Cannonau di Sardegna Jerzu Cardedo Ris. '12	♥♥ 3
○ Leila '12	♥♥ 4
● Tuvara '11	♥♥ 5

Masone Mannu

LOC. SU CANALE
S.S. 199 KM 48
07020 MONTI [SS]
TEL. +39 078947140
www.masonemannu.com

CELLAR SALES
PRE-BOOKED VISITS
ANNUAL PRODUCTION 100,000 bottles
HECTARES UNDER VINE 19.00

Masone Mannu is one of Gallura's most attractive and important estates. Though still basically young, it has proved capable of showing the quality path it chose from the earliest vintages onwards, based on simple vineyard and vinification procedures, aiming to showcase the particular features of Gallura soil. The results are elegant, ageable wines with clean aromas, from the three versions of white Vermentino to the equally sound reds and rosés obtained from cannonau, syrah, carignano, and bovale. The Costarenas 2015, a Vermentino di Gallura Superiore, made the national finals thanks to complex leaf beet and citrus fruit aromas, and a tangy, fresh palate with excellent mouthfeel. The other Gallura, Petrizza 2015, is simpler but very well-focused. The Cannonau di Sardegna is a lovely surprise, graceful and alluring, while the Entu 2013, sound as always, is a mouthfilling red obtained from traditional grapes.

○ Vermentino di Gallura Sup. Costarenas '15	♥♥ 3*
● Cannonau di Sardegna Zòjosu '14	♥♥ 3
● Entu '13	♥♥ 5
○ Vermentino di Gallura Petrizza '15	♥♥ 3
○ Vermentino di Gallura Sup. Roccaìa '14	♥ 5
⊙ Zeluiu '15	♥ 3
● Cannonau di Sardegna Zòjosu '13	♀♀ 5
● Entu '12	♀♀ 5
● Mannu '11	♀♀ 8
○ Vermentino di Gallura Petrizza '14	♀♀ 3
○ Vermentino di Gallura Petrizza '13	♀♀ 3
○ Vermentino di Gallura Sup. Costarenas '14	♀♀ 3*
● Zùrria '14	♀♀ 3

Meloni Vini

VIA GALLUS, 79
09047 SELARGIUS [CA]
TEL. +39 070852822
www.melonivini.com

CELLAR SALES
PRE-BOOKED VISITS
ANNUAL PRODUCTION 1,000,000 bottles
HECTARES UNDER VINE 200.00
VITICULTURE METHOD Certified Organic
SUSTAINABLE WINERY

The Meloni family vaunts 200 hectares of vineyards in southern Sardinia, entirely organically farmed since way back when. After years of disappointing products, the cellar has made an excellent comeback with elegant, fresh-tasting wines with a beautifully satisfying flavour. The very well-stocked range focuses on traditional grapes and regional DOCs. Plenty of space is also reserved for aromatic varieties, above all Nasco and Girò di Cagliari, as well as Charmat-method sparklers, which have been available for several decades. Of the many wines tasted this year, the Donna Jolanda sweet wines had the biggest impact. The Girò di Cagliari 2012, made exclusively by this estate, is an aromatic red with hints of damson, chestnut flower honey and bottled cherries, and a sweet flavour with nicely contrasting freshness and a light streak of tannin. The Moscato di Sardegna 2012 is all about the sweetness, but never cloying, with a distinctive tangy finish.

● Cannonau di Sardegna Le Ghiaie Ris. '12	♥♥ 4
● Cannonau di Sardegna Le Sabbie '13	♥♥ 3
● Cannonau di Sardegna Terreforru '12	♥♥ 2*
● Girò di Cagliari Donna Jolanda '12	♥♥ 3
○ Moscato di Sardegna Donna Jolanda '12	♥♥ 2*
○ Vermentino di Sardegna Le Sabbie '15	♥♥ 3
○ Frius Brut	♥ 2
● Monica di Sardegna Jaccia '13	♥ 2
● Nue Bianco	♥ 2
● Nue Rosso	♥ 2
○ Vermentino di Sardegna Salike '15	♥ 2
● Cannonau di Sardegna Le Ghiaie Ris. '09	♀♀ 4
○ Malvasia di Cagliari Donna Jolanda '11	♀♀ 3
○ Moscato di Cagliari Donna Jolanda '09	♀♀ 3
○ Vermentino di Sardegna Le Sabbie '14	♀♀ 3

Mesa

LOC. SU BARONI
09010 SANT'ANNA ARRESI [CA]
TEL. +39 0781965057
www.cantinamesa.it

CELLAR SALES
PRE-BOOKED VISITS
ANNUAL PRODUCTION 750,000 bottles
HECTARES UNDER VINE 70.00

Mesa is one of the few privately owned
Sulcis estates, established several years
ago by advertising guru Gavino Sanna. After
the initial trial period, the estate settled on
very high levels of quality for the entire
range, from the basic everyday lines
upwards. The strongpoint is, of course,
Carignano del Sulcis, in various versions,
particularly an excellent version from dried
grapes, and several selections from old
ungrafted vines. The rest of the range is
outstanding, consisting of wines based on
traditional grapes purchased from the
island's best growing areas. Tre Bicchieri
again for the Buio Buio, a Riserva di
Carignano del Sulcis, this time the 2013,
from the estate's venerable vineyards. A
nose of scrubland, myrtle and damson, with
a close-knit palate with velvety tannin and
tangy finish. The Opale, a fresh, stylish
Vermentino di Sardegna with a hint of
iodine, is memorable. The other Carignanos
are well-typed, especially the mouthfilling
Riserva Gavino 2013.

Cantina di Mogoro Il Nuraghe

S.S. 131 KM 62
09095 MOGORO [OR]
TEL. +39 0783990285
www.cantinadimogoro.it

CELLAR SALES
PRE-BOOKED VISITS
ANNUAL PRODUCTION 850,000 bottles
HECTARES UNDER VINE 480.00

The Mogoro cooperative winery at
Campidano flies the quality flag for
Sardinian wine produced by cooperatives.
This is an extremely good area for
semidano, a native grape with the DOC
zone here at Mogoro, and for bovale sardo,
a tricky variety to grow but capable of
highly satisfactory results in some DOCs.
The range is headed up by Puisteris, a
Semidano di Mogoro which has proved
ageworthy and is therefore released after
three years' maturation with a fresh,
vibrant character. Puisteris was in fact the
most impressive wine in our tastings. The
2013 made the finals with complex
aromas of candied citrus peel, wild herbs
and apricots, while the palate is dry, lively
and full of energy. The excellent reds
include wines from bovale grapes,
particularly the Cavaliere Sardo, a 2013
Terralba Riserva. Lastly, a mention for the
Mora Bianca 2015, an unusual white
made from the rare monica bianca grape.

● Carignano del Sulcis Buio Buio Ris. '13	🍷🍷🍷	5
○ Vermentino di Sardegna Opale '14	🍷🍷	4
● Carignano del Sulcis Buio '15	🍷🍷	3
● Carignano del Sulcis Gavino Ris. '13	🍷🍷	5
⊙ Carignano del Sulcis Rosa Grande '15	🍷	3
● Malombra '12	🍷	6
○ Vermentino di Sardegna Giunco '15	🍷	3
● Buio Buio '10	🍷🍷🍷	4*
● Carignano del Sulcis Buio Buio Ris. '12	🍷🍷🍷	5
● Brace Cagnulari '14	🍷🍷	4
● Brama Syrah '14	🍷🍷	4
● Carignano del Sulcis Gavino Ris. '11	🍷🍷	5
○ Opale Dopo '12	🍷🍷	5
○ Orodoro '13	🍷🍷	5
○ Vermentino di Sardegna Giunco '13	🍷🍷	3

○ Semidano di Mogoro Sup. Puistèris '13	🍷🍷	4
○ Mora Bianca '15	🍷🍷	1*
● Sardegna Terralba '13	🍷🍷	3
● Sardegna Terralba Bovale Cavaliere Sardo Ris. '13	🍷🍷	3
● Sardegna Terralba Bovale Tiernu '14	🍷🍷	3
○ Anastasia Brut	🍷	3
⊙ Brut Rosato	🍷	2
● Cannonau di Sardegna Nero Sardo '14	🍷	2
● Monica di Sardegna San Bernardino '14	🍷	2
○ Moscato di Sardegna Capodolce '14	🍷	3
○ Moscato Spumante	🍷	2
○ Nuragus di Cagliari Ajò '15	🍷	2
○ Sardegna Semidano Mogoro Anastasia '15	🍷	2
○ Vermentino di Sardegna Don Giovanni '15	🍷	2

Giovanni Montisci

VIA ASIAGO, 7B
08024 MAMOIADA [NU]
TEL. +39 0784569021
www.barrosu.it

CELLAR SALES
PRE-BOOKED VISITS
ANNUAL PRODUCTION 6,000 bottles
HECTARES UNDER VINE 2.00

Giovanni Montisci is a true wine craftsman, passionate about vineyard work, and his small quantities of wine fully reflect the Mamoiada winegrowing tradition. These old bush-trained vineyards situated at high altitudes naturally have a low cluster yield per hectare. The wines are rich in extract with high alcohol content, but always display balsamic freshness to liven up the flavour, making them supple and vibrant. Two Cannonaus are produced, Barrosu and the Riserva Franzisca, from one 80-year-old vineyard. There is also a rosé, also from cannonau grapes, and a Moscato only in the best vintage years. Giovanni Montisci presents just one wine this year, his best selection of cannonau grapes named after the small old vineyard of origin. Cannonau di Sardegna Barrosu 2013 Riserva Franzisca is one of the best tasted in recent years: complex and close-knit, balanced by textbook freshness on the slender, supple palate. Only a few thousand bottles are produced of this exemplary Sardinian red.

● Cannonau di Sardegna Barrosu Franzisca Ris. '13	♟ 6
● Cannonau di Sardegna Barrosu Franzisca Ris. '11	♟♟♟ 6
● Cannonau di Sardegna Barrosu '09	♟♟ 6
● Cannonau di Sardegna Barrosu '08	♟♟ 5
● Cannonau di Sardegna Barrosu Ris. '11	♟♟ 6
● Cannonau di Sardegna Barrosu Ris. '10	♟♟ 6
● Cannonau di Sardegna Barrosu Ris. '09	♟♟ 6
● Cannonau di Sardegna Franzisca Ris. '12	♟♟ 6
● Cannonau di Sardegna Franzisca Ris. '10	♟♟ 6
● Cannonau di Sardegna Rosato '12	♟♟ 3

Mura

LOC. AZZANIDÒ, 1
07020 LOIRI PORTO SAN PAOLO [OT]
TEL. +39 078941070
www.vinimura.it

CELLAR SALES
PRE-BOOKED VISITS
RESTAURANT SERVICE
ANNUAL PRODUCTION 50,000 bottles
HECTARES UNDER VINE 12.00

This small 12-hectare estate is efficiently managed by brother and sister Salvatore and Marianna, who share the sales and wine production responsibilities. Here, in the heart of Gallura, the wines display an authentic quality linked to the terroir. Elegance, very drinkable flavour and clean aromas are the characteristic features of the range which includes Vermentino di Gallura and some well-made, nicely-typed reds. The whites show remarkable ageing potential. The Sienda 2015 is unquestionably the best in the range: aromas of chard, strawflowers and citrus fruit announce it as a great Vermentino di Gallura. Also delicious are the Cheremi 2015 and the Sienda II Decennio 2013, deliberately released three years after the harvest. The Cortes 2014 is a fragrant, tangy Cannonau di Sardegna with a moreish, succulent flavour.

○ Vermentino di Gallura Sienda '15	♟♟ 4
● Cannonau di Sardegna Cortes '14	♟♟ 3
○ Vermentino di Gallura Cheremi '15	♟♟ 3
○ Vermentino di Gallura Sup. Sienda II Decennio '13	♟♟ 3
● Baja '13	♟ 5
○ Vermentino di Sardegna Prisma '15	♟ 2
○ Vermentino di Gallura Sup. Sienda '13	♟♟♟ 3*
● Cannonau di Sardegna Cortes '14	♟♟ 3
○ Vermentino di Gallura Cheremi '14	♟♟ 3
○ Vermentino di Gallura Cheremi '13	♟♟ 3
○ Vermentino di Gallura Cheremi '12	♟♟ 3
○ Vermentino di Gallura Sup. Sienda '14	♟♟ 3*
○ Vermentino di Gallura Sup. Sienda '12	♟♟ 3*
○ Vermentino di Sardegna Prisma '13	♟♟ 2*

Pala

VIA VERDI, 7
09040 SERDIANA [CA]
TEL. +39 070740284
www.pala.it

CELLAR SALES
PRE-BOOKED VISITS
ANNUAL PRODUCTION 490,000 bottles
HECTARES UNDER VINE 98.00

Pala is a great wine-producing family led by Mario, who runs one of the most impressive wineries in Sardinia with his wife and three children. They are helped by longstanding and untiring sales director, Fabio Angius, who brings the Pala brand and its wines to the five continents. The basis is a vast acreage of old vineyards with particularly well-suited terrain, including ungrafted vineyards on sandy soil in the Oristano area, and masterly cellar work to achieve elegant, deep, ageable wines.. Once again the Vermentino di Sardegna Stellato proves itself as a great Sardinian white. This 2015 vintage shows spring flowers, aromatic herbs, and candied lemon peel followed by a tangy, fresh, supple and lively palate. Tre Bicchieri. The Cannonau di Sardegna Riserva and the Entemari, an IGT white from traditional grapes, are very good. The other wines are all well-made and very fairly priced.

○ Vermentino di Sardegna Stellato '15	♟♟♟ 4*
● Cannonau di Sardegna Ris. '14	♟♟ 3*
○ Entemari '14	♟♟ 5
● Cannonau di Sardegna I Fiori '15	♟♟ 3
● Siray '13	♟♟ 3
○ Stellato Nature '15	♟♟ 6
● Thesys '14	♟♟ 3
☉ Chiaro di Stelle '15	♟ 3
● Monica di Sardegna I Fiori '15	♟ 3
○ Nuragus di Cagliari I Fiori '15	♟ 2
○ Silenzi Bianco '15	♟ 2
☉ Silenzi Rosato '15	♟ 2
● Silenzi Rosso '15	♟ 2
○ Vermentino di Sardegna I Fiori '15	♟ 3
● Cannonau di Sardegna Ris. '12	♟♟♟ 3*
● Cannonau di Sardegna Ris. '11	♟♟♟ 3*
○ Vermentino di Sardegna Stellato '14	♟♟♟ 3*

Cantina Pedres

ZONA IND. SETTORE 7
07026 OLBIA
TEL. +39 0789595075
www.cantinapedres.it

CELLAR SALES
PRE-BOOKED VISITS
ANNUAL PRODUCTION 290,000 bottles
HECTARES UNDER VINE 40.00

The Pedres estate has 40 hectares under vine, producing around 300,000 bottles per year. Managed by Antonella Mancini, the young heir to a family who have produced wine in Gallura for centuries, working alongside her oenologist husband works for their product range. The feather in their cap is an elegant, subtle, vibrant, and very fresh version of Vermentino di Gallura. The other wines are good too, especially when they aim for supple drinkability, which is the only way to bring out all Gallura's granitic soul. Thilibas 2015, is a Vermentino di Gallura with a supple, lively palate enhanced by fresh acidity, lovely tangy flavour, and complex aromas with hints of almonds and citrus fruit. The Brino, another Vermentino, is also very good, simpler but not at all commonplace. Among the reds, the Sulità 2014 and Cerasio 2015 are two very good Cannonau di Sardinia versions: fragrant, mouthwatering, with wild berry aromas.

● Cannonau di Sardegna Cerasio '15	♟♟ 4
● Cannonau di Sardegna Sulità '14	♟♟ 3
○ Vermentino di Gallura Brino '15	♟♟ 3
○ Vermentino di Gallura Sup. Thilibas '15	♟♟ 4
○ Moscato di Sardegna Spumante	♟ 3
○ Vermentino di Gallura Sup. Thilibas '10	♟♟♟ 3*
○ Vermentino di Gallura Sup. Thilibas '09	♟♟♟ 3*
● Cannonau di Sardegna Cerasio '13	♟♟ 4
● Cannonau di Sardegna Sulità '13	♟♟ 3
● Cannonau di Sardegna Sulità '10	♟♟ 3
○ Moscato di Sardegna	♟♟ 3
○ Vermentino di Gallura Brino '13	♟♟ 3
○ Vermentino di Gallura Sup. Thilibas '14	♟♟ 4
○ Vermentino di Sardegna Colline '13	♟♟ 2*

Agricola Punica

VIA CAGLIARI, 78
09010 SANTADI [CI]
TEL. +39 0781941012
www.agripunica.it

PRE-BOOKED VISITS
ANNUAL PRODUCTION 300,000 bottles
HECTARES UNDER VINE 70.00

Agricola Punica is a lovely estate in Sulcis, established in the early 2000s by the Cantina di Santadi and its chairman Antonello Pilloni, Sebastiano Rosa of Tenuta San Guido, and late lamented winemaker Giacomo Tachis. The three wines produced, two reds and a white, are all blends of several grapes. The leading red is Barrua while the other originates from younger vineyards, and both consist of a pleasing blend of international varieties with carignano, the leading Sulcis grape. The white is a blend of sauvignon and vermentino. All the wines presented this year were very good. The Barrua is one to watch: the 2013 vintage offers ripe red berries, dried roses, and aromatic resin hints, with a fresh, soft, mouthfilling palate. Everything a southern red wine should be. The Montessu 2014 makes up for its less complex nature with a supple, slender palate, while the Samas 2015 is a fresh, tangy white with a hint of iodine.

● Barrua '13	♟♟ 6
● Montessu '14	♟♟ 4
○ Samas '15	♟ 3
● Barrua '12	♟♟♟ 6
● Barrua '10	♟♟♟ 6
● Barrua '07	♟♟♟ 6
● Barrua '05	♟♟♟ 5
● Barrua '11	♟♟ 6
● Barrua '09	♟♟ 6
● Barrua '08	♟♟ 6
● Montessu '13	♟♟ 4
● Montessu '12	♟♟ 4
● Montessu '11	♟♟ 4
● Montessu '10	♟♟ 4
● Montessu '09	♟♟ 4

Santa Maria La Palma

FRAZ. SANTA MARIA LA PALMA
07041 ALGHERO [SS]
TEL. +39 079999008
www.santamarialapalma.it

CELLAR SALES
PRE-BOOKED VISITS
ANNUAL PRODUCTION 4,000,000 bottles
HECTARES UNDER VINE 650.00

Santa Maria La Palma, in Alghero, is one of the larger Sardinian cooperative wineries, which have always worked well on the island, and in recent years the wines have followed their example by turning a significant corner in quality. Production is divided between native local grapes and international varieties, which have been present for many years in north-eastern Sardinia. The vast range includes all types, from Charmat-method sparklers and a Metodo Classico being researched, to still and sweet wines. Even the simplest wines display good quality and Aragosta is the proof: a delightful Vermentino di Sardinia, of which 1.5 million bottles are produced. An impressive range this year from the Alghero cooperative. The Alghero Sauvignon Estiu 2014 displays complex but never cloying aromas with hints of leaf beet, lemon zest and spring flowers, and a fresh, tangy palate. Iodine hints and ripe peaches and apricots for the Vermentino di Sardegna I Papiri 2015. The Cagnulari is up to its usual high standard. New sparkling additions, Palmì and Cantavigna, are both very enjoyable.

● Alghero Cagnulari '15	♟♟ 3
○ Alghero Chardonnay Triulas '14	♟♟ 3
● Alghero Rosso Cabirol '14	♟♟ 2*
○ Alghero Sauvignon Estiu '14	♟♟ 4
● Cannonau di Sardegna Ris. '14	♟♟ 3
○ Vermentino di Sardegna I Papiri '15	♟♟ 3
☉ Alghero Rosato Frizzante Cantavigna '15	♟ 2
● Cannonau di Sardegna Valmell '15	♟ 2
○ Vermentino di Sardegna Extra Dry Akenta '15	♟ 3
○ Vermentino di Sardegna Palmì '15	♟ 3
● Cannonau di Sardegna Le Bombarde '14	♟♟ 2*
● Cannonau di Sardegna Le Bombarde '13	♟♟ 2*
● Cannonau di Sardegna Valmell '14	♟♟ 2*
○ Vermentino di Sardegna Aragosta '14	♟♟ 2*
○ Vermentino di Sardegna I Papiri '14	♟♟ 3

★Cantina di Santadi

Via Cagliari, 78
09010 Santadi [CI]
Tel. +39 0781950127
www.cantinadisantadi.it

CELLAR SALES
PRE-BOOKED VISITS
ANNUAL PRODUCTION 1,740,000 bottles
HECTARES UNDER VINE 606.00

If any winery has given quality winegrowing a push in Sardinia, it is Santadi. This fact is even more impressive considering that the Sulcis-based winery is a cooperative. The prestigious acknowledgements and high quality achieved by Santadi are the fruit of a policy introduced in the mid-Seventies by Antonello Pilloni, chairman then and now. Selections of the best vineyards, some of which are very old, ungrafted and planted on sandy soil, specific guidelines given to growers, and ongoing research in the cellar have been the keys to Santadi's success. But work goes on, and so do the experiments, such as earthenware amphoras, which have confirmed recent policy. Santadi wines are always impressive. Latinia 2010 leads the pack this year, made from super-ripe grapes: a surprisingly complex nose with hints of ripe apricots, dried fruit, aromatic resins, and sweet spice. The palate is sweet but refreshed by a tangy streak adding lively mouthfeel. The Terre Brune 2012 is compact and austere.

○ Latinia '10	▼▼▼ 5
● Carignano del Sulcis Sup. Terre Brune '12	▼▼ 7
● Cannonau di Sardegna Noras '13	▼▼ 4
● Carignano del Sulcis Grotta Rossa '14	▼▼ 2*
● Carignano del Sulcis Rocca Rubia Ris. '13	▼▼ 4
○ Vermentino di Sardegna Villa Solais '15	▼▼ 2*
○ Brut Solais M. Cl.	▼ 5
⊙ Carignano del Sulcis Rosato Tre Torri '15	▼ 2
● Festa Noria	▼ 6
● Monica di Sardegna Antigua '15	▼ 2
○ Nuragus di Cagliari Pedraia '15	▼ 2
○ Vermentino di Sardegna Cala Silente '15	▼ 3
● Carignano del Sulcis Sup. Terre Brune '11	▼▼▼ 7

Sardus Pater

Via Rinascita, 46
09017 Sant'Antioco [CI]
Tel. +39 0781800274
www.cantinesarduspater.com

CELLAR SALES
PRE-BOOKED VISITS
ANNUAL PRODUCTION 600,000 bottles
HECTARES UNDER VINE 295.00

The island of Sant'Antiocco, joined to Sardinia by an isthmus of artificial land, has its own cooperative winery dating back to the 1950s, with an invaluable heritage of vineyards. Most of these are ungrafted and bush-trained, on sandy soil, and some as old as 90. The main wine produced is Carignano del Sulcis, in various versions: the fresher, basic version, a Riserva, a Superiore which uses only grapes from ungrafted vines, and Amentos, a dessert wine included in the DOC. Other wines in the range are all made from traditional grapes, including a Metodo Classico. The Carignano del Sulcis Is Arenas 2012 Riserva scales the heights with a nose of Mediterranean maquis and ripe red berries, and a soft, supple, balsamic palate with a tangy finish. The Arruga is compact, complex, and austere, though the oak still holds it back. The other wines are well-typed.

● Carignano del Sulcis Is Arenas Ris. '12	▼▼ 4
● Carignano del Sulcis Nur '14	▼▼ 3
● Carignano del Sulcis Sup. Arruga '10	▼▼ 6
● Carignano del Sulcis Is Solus '15	▼ 2
⊙ Carignano del Sulcis Rosato Horus '15	▼ 2
○ Vermentino di Sardegna Lugore '15	▼ 3
○ Vermentino di Sardegna Terre Fenicie '15	▼ 2
● Carignano del Sulcis Arenas Ris. '05	▼▼▼ 3*
● Carignano del Sulcis Is Arenas Ris. '09	▼▼▼ 4*
● Carignano del Sulcis Is Arenas Ris. '08	▼▼▼ 4*
● Carignano del Sulcis Is Arenas Ris. '07	▼▼▼ 3*
● Carignano del Sulcis Is Arenas Ris. '06	▼▼▼ 3*
● Carignano del Sulcis Sup. Arruga '09	▼▼▼ 6
● Carignano del Sulcis Sup. Arruga '07	▼▼▼ 5

Giuseppe Sedilesu

VIA VITTORIO EMANUELE II, 64
08024 MAMOIADA [NU]
TEL. +39 078456791
www.giuseppesedilesu.com

CELLAR SALES
PRE-BOOKED VISITS
ANNUAL PRODUCTION 120,000 bottles
HECTARES UNDER VINE 17.00

Sedilesu represents a great wine-producing family, now in its third generation. Credit goes to the family for the winegrowing renaissance in Mamoiada, a town and DOC zone where there is no lack of skilled and experienced vignerons. This is the realm of cannonau, the grape which succeeds in expressing its terroir of origin more than any other. These poor soils, high altitudes and old bush-trained vineyards yield well-structured, complex wines with a typical balsamic acidity that adds freshness and drinkability. In the absence of the Cannonaus, due to below par vintages and extended bottle ageing, the tastings were restricted to just a few wines this year. The Mamuthone 2014 is a mouthfilling Mediterranean red with well-ordered ripe fruit and floral hints of roses, while the alcohol warmth is nicely compensated by fresh tanginess on the silky, light palate.

● Cannonau di Sardegna Mamuthone '14	♟♟ 3*
○ Perda Pintà '14	♟♟ 5
● Cannonau di Sardegna Erèssia '15	♟ 3
○ Granazza '15	♟ 5
● Popassa	♟ 6
● Cannonau di Sardegna Mamuthone '12	♟♟♟ 3*
● Cannonau di Sardegna Mamuthone '11	♟♟♟ 3*
● Cannonau di Sardegna Mamuthone '08	♟♟♟ 3*
○ Perda Pintà '09	♟♟♟ 4
○ Perda Pintà '07	♟♟♟ 5
● Cannonau di Sardegna Giuseppe Sedilesu Ris. '10	♟♟ 3*
● Cannonau di Sardegna Gràssia Ris. '11	♟♟ 3
● Cannonau di Sardegna Sartiu '12	♟♟ 3
○ Perda Pintà '13	♟♟ 5

★★Tenute Sella & Mosca

LOC. I PIANI
07041 ALGHERO [SS]
TEL. +39 079997700
www.sellaemosca.com

CELLAR SALES
PRE-BOOKED VISITS
ANNUAL PRODUCTION 6,700,000 bottles
HECTARES UNDER VINE 541.00

Soundly based on production levels of almost seven million bottles per year and over 500 hectares under vine, the largest single vineyard in Europe, Sella & Mosca is one of Italy's leading historic estates. Owned by Campari for many years now, the winery has recently been overhauled by the group with policies to anchor it even more firmly to Sardinia's wine-producing economy. The very extensive range includes wines made from international grapes which have always been grown locally, as well as those from native varieties like torbato, of which Sella & Mosca are the sole producers. Three wines in the finals is already quite a result, but further gratification comes from the excellent Terre Bianche Cuvée 161. The Torbato selection is impressively subtle and stylish, with a complex nose and deep tangy flavour. Tre Bicchieri. The Marchese di Villamarina 2011 is still good, but falls short of its usual quality. The Vermentino di Gallura Monteoro 2015 is terroir-true.

○ Alghero Torbato Terre Bianche Cuvée 161 '15	♟♟♟ 4*
● Alghero Rosso Marchese di Villamarina '11	♟♟ 6
○ Vermentino di Gallura Sup. Monteoro '15	♟♟ 3*
● Alghero Anghelu Ruju Ris. '05	♟♟ 6
○ Alghero Bianco Le Arenarie '15	♟♟ 3
● Cannonau di Sardegna Dimonios Ris. '12	♟♟ 3
● Carignano del Sulcis Terre Rare Ris. '12	♟♟ 3
○ Alghero Bianco Parallelo 41 '15	♟ 4
⊙ Alghero Oleandro '15	♟ 3
○ Alghero Torbato Terre Bianche '15	♟ 3
● Monica di Sardegna Acino M '14	♟ 3
○ Vermentino di Sardegna Cala Reale '15	♟ 3
● Alghero Marchese di Villamarina '09	♟♟♟ 6
○ Vermentino di Gallura Sup. Monteoro '14	♟♟♟ 3*

Siddùra

Loc. Siddura
07020 Luogosanto [OT]
Tel. +39 0796513027
www.siddura.com

CELLAR SALES
PRE-BOOKED VISITS
ACCOMMODATION AND RESTAURANT SERVICE
ANNUAL PRODUCTION 250,000 bottles
HECTARES UNDER VINE 37.00
SUSTAINABLE WINERY

A young Luogosanto estate established
with significant investments matched by
equal ambitions for quality. The location is
in the heart of Gallura, a beautiful
landscape where vineyards alternate with
granite rock and Mediterranean scrubland.
Meticulous vineyard work and avant-garde
experimentation are the special features of
this estate, which focuses both on
typical Vermentino di Gallura and reds
obtained from grapes grown in other parts
of the island. The wines pursue finesse
and elegance with sheer drinkability, and
the complexity that reflects the Gallura
terroir. The wines presented this year
show an excellent standard. The
Vermentino di Gallura Spèra 2015 reveals
hints of medlar fruit alongside sage and
citrus, and a clear-cut, typical tang of
Gallura soil on the palate. The Cannonau
di Sardegna Fòla 2014 is also very good,
with airy mouthfeel and clean aromas. The
Bèru 2014, a Vermentino di Gallura
matured in oak, was less impressive.

● Cannonau di Sardegna Fòla '14	♟♟ 5
○ Vermentino di Gallura Spèra '15	♟♟ 3
○ Vermentino di Gallura Sup. Bèru '14	♟ 6
○ Vermentino di Gallura Maìa '14	♟♟♟ 4*
● Bàcco Cagnulari '14	♟♟ 5
● Bàcco Cagnulari '13	♟♟ 5
● Cannonau di Sardegna Fòla '13	♟♟ 5
● Cannonau di Sardegna Fòla '12	♟♟ 5
● Èrema '14	♟♟ 3
● Èrema '13	♟♟ 3
● Èrema '12	♟♟ 4
● Tiros '12	♟♟ 6
○ Vermentino di Gallura Spèra '12	♟♟ 3
○ Vermentino di Gallura Sup. Maìa '13	♟♟ 5
○ Vermentino di Gallura Sup. Maìa '12	♟♟ 5

Tenute Soletta

Loc. Signor'Anna
07040 Codrongianos [SS]
Tel. +39 079435067
www.tenutesoletta.it

CELLAR SALES
PRE-BOOKED VISITS
ANNUAL PRODUCTION 100,000 bottles
HECTARES UNDER VINE 15.00
VITICULTURE METHOD Certified Organic

Umberto Soletta is the passionate, skilled
director of this family estate in north-
western Sardinia, a part of the Logudoro
area especially suited to winegrowing. The
main distinguishing features of his wines
are weighty structure, complexity and rich
extract, especially in the case of the
Cannonaus, which aspire to ageability. The
whites are also impressive, mainly
vermentino-based with the addition of
international grapes in some cases. A
moscato dessert wine, one of the best in its
category, completes the range. The
best-typed wine is the Riserva 2011
Corona Majore, a Cannonau di Sardegna
with incense, myrtle and ripe damson
aromas, and a compact, tangy palate with
forward but velvety tannins. The IGT
Keramos 2010, mainly cannonau, is also
impressive. Among the whites we
recommend the Chimera, a flavoursome,
fresh and fruity Vermentino di Sardegna.

● Cannonau di Sardegna Corona Majore Ris. '11	♟♟ 3
● Keramos '10	♟♟ 5
○ Vermentino di Sardegna Chimera '15	♟♟ 4
○ Kianos '14	♟ 4
⊙ Prius '15	♟ 3
● Cannonau di Sardegna Keramos Ris. '07	♟♟♟ 5
● Cannonau di Sardegna Keramos Ris. '04	♟♟♟ 4
● Cannonau di Sardegna Corona Majore '12	♟♟ 4
● Cannonau di Sardegna Corona Majore '11	♟♟ 4
● Cannonau di Sardegna Keramos Ris. '11	♟♟ 5
○ Vermentino di Sardegna Chimera '14	♟♟ 4
○ Vermentino di Sardegna Chimera '13	♟♟ 4

Su Entu

S.DA PROV.LE KM 1,800
09025 SANLURI [CA]
TEL. +39 07093571200
www.cantinesuentu.com

CELLAR SALES
PRE-BOOKED VISITS
ANNUAL PRODUCTION 30,000 bottles
HECTARES UNDER VINE 32.00

Marmilla was once the cradle of wheat and vines, so it is nice to know that wineries like Su Entu have been established here with the purpose of restoring the former glory and prestige of this unique farming area. Salvatore Pilloni, a Sardinian entrepreneur involved in other fields but with a long-standing passion for vineyards and wine pursued his dream and a few years from the first harvest, the results are starting to come in. All thanks to the vines that are growing along with experience in the cellar, entrusted to skilled consultant Piero Cella. For now, focus is on vermentino and cannonau, as well as moscato and bovale, the latter traditionally grown in this DOC zone. The Mediterraneo 2014 aims to embody the renaissance of Marmilla reds: a blend of traditional grape varieties with hints of myrtle, red berries, aromatic resin and forest floor, and a very tangy, subtly fresh palate with velvety, mature tannins. The Bovale 2014 is also well-focused if slightly clenched by oaky, tannic sensations. The dry Aromatico 2015 from local aromatic grapes is fun and enjoyable.

● Mediterraneo '14	♥♥	3*
○ Aromatico '15	♥♥	3
● Bovale '14	♥♥	3
○ Passito '14	♥♥	5
● Cannonau di Sardegna '14	♥	3
○ Vermentino di Sardegna '15	♥	3
○ Vermentino di Sardegna + '13	♥	4
○ Aromatico '13	♀♀	3
● Bovale '13	♀♀	3*
● Cannonau di Sardegna '13	♀♀	3
● Cannonau di Sardegna '12	♀♀	3
● Cannonau di Sardegna '11	♀♀	3
○ Passito '13	♀♀	5
○ Vermentino di Sardegna '13	♀♀	3

Vigne Surrau

S.DA PROV.LE ARZACHENA - PORTO CERVO
07021 ARZACHENA [OT]
TEL. +39 078982933
www.vignesurrau.it

CELLAR SALES
PRE-BOOKED VISITS
ANNUAL PRODUCTION 300,000 bottles
HECTARES UNDER VINE 50.00
SUSTAINABLE WINERY

Surrau is one of the loveliest new estates to spring up in recent years and in a short space of time it has become a benchmark for Gallura wine production. It was established with the intention of growing great reds in this unusual granite-based terroir, but all the wines in the range are a guarantee of quality, from the fresh, stylish Vermentino di Gallura with its textbook tangy flavour as well as good ageing potential, to the reds, sweet wines and Metodo Classico sparklers, from vermentino and cannonau grapes processed in the estate cellar. Hospitality is offered in a beautiful building open all year round for exhibitions, conferences and cultural events. Sciala 2015 pursues the path that led it to excellence in recent years. This Vermentino di Gallura shows very typical hints of iodine, citrus and spring flowers on the nose. The structure is nicely balanced by a streak of acidity and tangy flavour, with a deep, clean, very fresh finish. Another well-deserved Tre Bicchieri this year. The Sincaru Riserva 2013 is also very good, proving that this granite-based terroir also produces sound reds.

○ Vermentino di Gallura Sup. Sciala '15	♥♥♥	5
● Cannonau di Sardegna Sincaru Ris. '13	♥♥	5
● Barriu '13	♥♥	5
● Cannonau di Sardegna Sincaru '14	♥♥	5
● Sole Ruju '14	♥♥	5
● Surrau '13	♥♥	4
○ Vermentino di Gallura Branu '15	♥♥	3
○ Vermentino di Gallura Spumante '12	♥♥	5
⊙ Brut Rosé '12	♥	5
○ Sole di Surrau '14	♥	5
● Surrau '09	♀♀♀	4*
○ Vermentino di Gallura Sup. Sciala '14	♀♀♀	5
○ Vermentino di Gallura Sup. Sciala '13	♀♀♀	5
○ Vermentino di Gallura Sup. Sciala '12	♀♀♀	5

Angelo Angioi

LOC. COLORAS
09079 TRESNURAGHES [OR]
TEL. +39 3409357227
saltodicoloras@gmail.com

CELLAR SALES
PRE-BOOKED VISITS
ANNUAL PRODUCTION 5,000 bottles
HECTARES UNDER VINE 2.80

○ Malvasia di Bosa Dolce Salto di Coloras Ris. '10	♔♔ 5
○ Malvasia di Bosa Dolce Salto di Coloras '14	♔♔ 4

Cantina Arvisionadu

VIA LODI, 4
07010 BENETUTTI [SS]
TEL. +39 079796947
www.cantina-arvisionadu.it

ANNUAL PRODUCTION 9,000 bottles
HECTARES UNDER VINE 2.00

○ G'Oceano Arvisionadu '15	♔♔ 3
● Burghera '14	♔ 3

Tenuta Asinara

LOC. MARRITZA
GOLFO DELL'ASINARA
07037 SORSO [SS]
TEL. +39 0793402017
www.tenutaasinara.com

CELLAR SALES
PRE-BOOKED VISITS
ANNUAL PRODUCTION 70,000 bottles
HECTARES UNDER VINE 19.00

● Cannonau di Sardegna Indolente '14	♔♔ 2*
● Hassan '13	♔♔ 3
● Herculis '13	♔ 4
○ Vermentino di Sardegna Indolente '15	♔ 2

Poderi Atha Ruja

LOC. PRADONOS
08022 DORGALI [NU]
TEL. +39 347 8693936
www.atharuja.com

CELLAR SALES
PRE-BOOKED VISITS
ACCOMMODATION
ANNUAL PRODUCTION 25,000 bottles
HECTARES UNDER VINE 5.00

● Cannonau di Sardegna V. Sorella '14	♔♔ 3
● Cannonau di Sardegna '12	♔ 3
● Muristellu '11	♔ 5
● Tuluj '10	♔ 5

Audarya

S.DA STATALE 466 KM 10,100
09040 SERDIANA [CA]
TEL. +39 070740437
www.audarya.it

CELLAR SALES
PRE-BOOKED VISITS
ANNUAL PRODUCTION 50,000 bottles
HECTARES UNDER VINE 35.00

○ Bisai '15	♔♔ 4
● Bovale Nuracada '14	♔♔ 4
○ Vermentino di Sardegna '15	♔♔ 2*
● Monica di Sardegna '15	♔ 2

Cantina di Calasetta

VIA ROMA, 134
09011 CALASETTA [CI]
TEL. +39 078188413
www.cantinadicalasetta.it

CELLAR SALES
PRE-BOOKED VISITS
ANNUAL PRODUCTION 100,000 bottles
HECTARES UNDER VINE 300.00

● Carignano del Sulcis Aina Ris. '13	♔♔ 4
● Carignano del Sulcis Piede Franco '14	♔♔ 2*
● Carignano del Sulcis Maccòri '14	♔ 2
○ Vermentino di Sardegna Cala di Seta '15	♔ 2

Cantina delle Vigne Piero Mancini

LOC. CALA SACCAIA
VIA MADAGASCAR, 17
07026 OLBIA
TEL. +39 078950717
www.pieromancini.it

CELLAR SALES
PRE-BOOKED VISITS
ANNUAL PRODUCTION 1,500,000 bottles
HECTARES UNDER VINE 100.00

○ Vermentino di Gallura Sup. Cucaione '15	🍷🍷 2*
○ Vermentino di Gallura Sup. Mancini Primo '15	🍷🍷 4

Cantina Castiadas

LOC. OLIA SPECIOSA
09040 CASTIADAS [CA]
TEL. +39 0709949004
www.cantinacastiadas.com

CELLAR SALES
PRE-BOOKED VISITS
ANNUAL PRODUCTION 120,000 bottles
HECTARES UNDER VINE 150.00

● Cannonau di Sardegna Capo Ferrato Rei '14	🍷🍷 2*
● Cannonau di Sardegna Capo Ferrato Ris. '12	🍷🍷 4

Consorzio San Michele

LOC. SAN MICHELE
07022 BERCHIDDA [OT]
TEL. +39 078923865
www.consorziosanmichele.com

CELLAR SALES
PRE-BOOKED VISITS
ANNUAL PRODUCTION 50,000 bottles
HECTARES UNDER VINE 10.00

○ Vermentino di Gallura Invidia Gallurese '15	🍷🍷 3
○ Vermentino di Gallura Sup. Superbia Gallurese '15	🍷🍷 4

Vigne Deriu

LOC. SIGNORANNA
07040 CODRONGIANOS [SS]
TEL. +39 079435101
www.vignederiu.it

CELLAR SALES
PRE-BOOKED VISITS
ANNUAL PRODUCTION 35,000 bottles
HECTARES UNDER VINE 6.00

● Cannonau di Sardegna '14	🍷🍷 3
○ Vermentino di Sardegna '15	🍷🍷 3
○ Moscato di Sardegna Passito Oroere '14	🍷 5
● Tiu Filippu '12	🍷 5

Fradiles

LOC. CRECCHERÌ
08030 ATZARA [NU]
TEL. +39 3331761683
www.fradiles.it

CELLAR SALES
PRE-BOOKED VISITS
ANNUAL PRODUCTION 20,000 bottles
HECTARES UNDER VINE 14.00
SUSTAINABLE WINERY

● Mandrolisai Azzarra '14	🍷🍷 2*
● Mandrolisai Fradiles '14	🍷🍷 3
● Mandrolisai Sup. Istentu '12	🍷🍷 8
● Mandrolisai Sup. Antiogu '12	🍷 5

Cantina Giogantinu

VIA MILANO, 30
07022 BERCHIDDA [OT]
TEL. +39 079704163
www.giogantinu.it

CELLAR SALES
PRE-BOOKED VISITS
ANNUAL PRODUCTION 1,500,000 bottles
HECTARES UNDER VINE 320.00

○ Vermentino di Gallura Sup. Aldia '15	🍷🍷 2*
○ Vermentino di Gallura Sup. Giogantinu '15	🍷🍷 2*
○ Vermentino di Gallura Sup. Vigne Storiche del Giogantinu '15	🍷🍷 4

Jankara

VIA REGINA ELENA, 55
07030 SANT'ANTONIO DI GALLURA [OT]
TEL. +39 399 4381296
www.vinijankara.com

ANNUAL PRODUCTION 14,000 bottles
HECTARES UNDER VINE 5.00

○ Vermentino di Gallura Sup. '15	♥♥	4
● Jankara '14	♥	2

Tenuta l'Ariosa

LOC. PREDDA NIEDDA SUD
S.DA 15
07100 SASSARI
TEL. +39 079261905
www.lariosa.it

ANNUAL PRODUCTION 40,000 bottles
HECTARES UNDER VINE 9.00

● Sass'Antico Cagnulari '15	♥♥	4
○ Vermentino di Sardegna Galatea '15	♥♥	3
● Cannonau di Sardegna Assolo '14	♥	3
○ Vermentino di Sardegna Arenu '15	♥	3

Andrea Ledda

VIA MUSIO, 13
07043 BONNANARO [SS]
TEL. +39 079845060
www.vitivinicolaledda.com

CELLAR SALES
PRE-BOOKED VISITS
ANNUAL PRODUCTION 25,000 bottles
HECTARES UNDER VINE 13.00

● Cannonau di Sardegna Mogano '13	♥♥	4
○ Vermentino di Sardegna Acero '15	♥♥	3

Li Duni

LOC. LI PARISI
07030 BADESI [OT]
TEL. +39 0799144480
www.cantinaliduni.com

CELLAR SALES
PRE-BOOKED VISITS
ANNUAL PRODUCTION 40,000 bottles
HECTARES UNDER VINE 25.00

● Nalboni '14	♥♥	2*
○ Vermentino di Gallura Sup. Renabianca '15	♥♥	3

Cantina Sociale del Mandrolisai

C.SO IV NOVEMBRE, 20
08038 SORGONO [NU]
TEL. +39 078460113
www.cantinadelmandrolisai.com

CELLAR SALES
PRE-BOOKED VISITS
ANNUAL PRODUCTION 200,000 bottles
HECTARES UNDER VINE 80.00

● Mandrolisai Kent'Annos '12	♥♥	4
● Mandrolisai Sup. V. V. '13	♥♥	2*
● Mandrolisai '14	♥	2
● Mandrolisai Sup. '13	♥	2

Tenute Massidda

LOC. GIUANNI PORCU
09040 DONORI [CA]
TEL. +39 3478088683
www.cantinemassidda.com

CELLAR SALES
PRE-BOOKED VISITS
ANNUAL PRODUCTION 200,000 bottles
HECTARES UNDER VINE 45.00

● Cannonau di Sardegna Arenargiu '13	♥♥	3
● Monica di Sardegna Bainosa '13	♥	3
○ Vermentino di Sardegna Cannisonis '15	♥	4

Abele Melis

VIA SANTA SUINA, 3
09098 TERRALBA [OR]
TEL. +39 0783851090
melis.vini@tiscali.it

CELLAR SALES
PRE-BOOKED VISITS
ANNUAL PRODUCTION 100,000 bottles
HECTARES UNDER VINE 35.00

● Terralba Bovale Dominariu '14	♥♥	3
● Cannonau di Sardegna Horreum '14	♥	3
○ Vermentino di Sardegna Iocalia '15	♥	2

Mora&Memo

VIA VERDI 9
09040 SERDIANA [CA]
TEL. +39 3311972266
www.moraememo.it

CELLAR SALES
PRE-BOOKED VISITS
ANNUAL PRODUCTION 35,000 bottles
HECTARES UNDER VINE 37.00
VITICULTURE METHOD Certified Organic

● Cannonau di Sardegna Nau '15	♥♥	4
○ Vermentino di Sardegna Tino '15	♥♥	4
● Nau&Co '15	♥	4
○ Tino Sur Lie '15	♥	4

Murales

LOC. PILIEZZU, 1
07026 OLBIA
TEL. +39 078953174
www.vinimurales.com

CELLAR SALES
PRE-BOOKED VISITS
ACCOMMODATION AND RESTAURANT SERVICE
ANNUAL PRODUCTION 80,000 bottles
HECTARES UNDER VINE 20.00

○ Vermentino di Gallura Miradas '15	♥♥	4
● Cannonau di Sardegna Arcanos '13	♥	3
● Nativo '14	♥	3
○ Vermentino di Sardegna Tuttiventi '15	♥	3

Olianas

LOC. PORRUDDU
08030 GERGEI [CA]
TEL. +39 0558300411
www.olianas.it

CELLAR SALES
PRE-BOOKED VISITS
ANNUAL PRODUCTION 120,000 bottles
HECTARES UNDER VINE 17.00
VITICULTURE METHOD Certified Organic
SUSTAINABLE WINERY

● Cannonau di Sardegna '15	♥♥	3
⊙ Cannonau di Sardegna Rosato '15	♥♥	3
○ Vermentino di Sardegna '15	♥	3

Cantina Cooperativa di Oliena

VIA NUORO, 112
08025 OLIENA [NU]
TEL. +39 0784287509
www.cantinasocialeoliena.it

ANNUAL PRODUCTION 300,000 bottles
HECTARES UNDER VINE 180.00

● Cannonau di Sardegna Nepente '14	♥♥	2*
● Lanaitto '14	♥♥	2*
● Cannonau di Sardegna Cl. '11	♥	2
● Cannonau di Sardegna Corrasi Ris. '10	♥	4

Cantine di Orgosolo

VIA ILOLE
08027 ORGOSOLO [NU]
TEL. +39 0784403096
www.cantinediorgosolo.it

CELLAR SALES
PRE-BOOKED VISITS
RESTAURANT SERVICE
ANNUAL PRODUCTION 17,000 bottles
HECTARES UNDER VINE 16.00
VITICULTURE METHOD Certified Organic

● Cannonau di Sardegna Neale '14	♥♥	3
● Cannonau di Sardegna Urùlu '14	♥♥	4
● Cannonau di Sardegna Luna Vona '15	♥	4

Orro

VIA G. VERDI
09070 TRAMATZA [OR]
TEL. +39 3477526617
www.famigliaorro.it

CELLAR SALES
PRE-BOOKED VISITS
ACCOMMODATION
ANNUAL PRODUCTION 15,000 bottles
HECTARES UNDER VINE 5.00

○ Crannatza '12	♥♥ 4
○ Passemtzia '13	♥♥ 5
○ Vernaccia di Oristano '09	♥♥ 5
⊙ Zenti Arrubia '15	♥ 2

Paulis
Cantina di Monserrato

VIA GIULIO CESARE, 2
09042 MONSERRATO [CA]
TEL. +39 070652641
enologo@cantinepaulis.it

ANNUAL PRODUCTION 1,200,000 bottles
HECTARES UNDER VINE 450.00

○ Nasco di Cagliari Ailis '14	♥♥ 4
○ Vermentino di Sardegna Evento '15	♥♥ 2*
● Cannonau di Sardegna Noah '13	♥ 3

Pusole

LOC. PERDA 'E CUBA
08040 LOTZORAI [OG]
TEL. +39 3334047219
roberto.pusole@gmail.com

CELLAR SALES
PRE-BOOKED VISITS
ACCOMMODATION
ANNUAL PRODUCTION 10,000 bottles
HECTARES UNDER VINE 7.50
SUSTAINABLE WINERY

● Cannonau di Sardegna '15	♥♥ 3*
⊙ Il Rosé di Pusole '15	♥ 3
○ Vermentino di Sardegna '15	♥ 5

Quartomoro di Sardegna

VIA DINO POLI, 33
09092 ARBOREA [OR]
TEL. +39 3467643522
www.quartomoro.it

CELLAR SALES
PRE-BOOKED VISITS
ANNUAL PRODUCTION 35,000 bottles
HECTARES UNDER VINE 2.50

○ Quartomoro Brut M. Cl.	♥♥ 4
○ Vermentino di Sardegna Memorie di Vite '13	♥ 4
○ Vermentino di Sardegna Orriu '15	♥ 3

Rigàtteri

LOC. SANTA MARIA LA PALMA
REG. FLUMELONGU, 56
07041 ALGHERO [SS]
TEL. +39 3408636375
www.rigatteri.com

CELLAR SALES
PRE-BOOKED VISITS
ANNUAL PRODUCTION 15,000 bottles
HECTARES UNDER VINE 10.00
SUSTAINABLE WINERY

● Cannonau di Sardegna Mirau '14	♥♥ 3
● Alghero Cagnulari '14	♥ 3
○ Vermentino di Sardegna Ardella '14	♥ 3
○ Vermentino di Sardegna Yiòs '15	♥ 2

Cantina Tani

LOC. CONCA SA RAIGHINA, 2
07020 MONTI [SS]
TEL. +39 3386432055
www.cantinatani.it

CELLAR SALES
PRE-BOOKED VISITS
ACCOMMODATION AND RESTAURANT SERVICE
ANNUAL PRODUCTION 65,000 bottles
HECTARES UNDER VINE 15.00

○ Vermentino di Gallura Sup. Taerra '15	♥♥ 3
○ Vermentino di Gallura Meoru '15	♥ 3

Cantina Trexenta

V.LE PIEMONTE, 40
09040 SENORBÌ [CA]
TEL. +39 0709808863
www.cantinatrexenta.it

CELLAR SALES
PRE-BOOKED VISITS
ANNUAL PRODUCTION 1,000,000 bottles
HECTARES UNDER VINE 350.00

● Cannonau di Sardegna Bingias '14	🍷🍷 2*
● Cannonau di Sardegna Corte Auda '14	🍷🍷 2*
● Cannonau di Sardegna Tanca su Conti Ris. '11	🍷🍷 4

U Tabarka Tanca Gioia

LOC. GIOIA
09014 CARLOFORTE [CI]
TEL. +39 3356359329
www.u-tabarka.com

CELLAR SALES
PRE-BOOKED VISITS
RESTAURANT SERVICE
ANNUAL PRODUCTION 30,000 bottles
HECTARES UNDER VINE 7.00

● Bovale Ciù Roussou '15	🍷🍷 3
● Carignano del Sulcis U-Tabarka Roussou '14	🍷🍷 3
☉ Flamingo	🍷 2

Cantina del Vermentino

VIA SAN PAOLO, 2
07020 MONTI [SS]
TEL. +39 078944012
www.vermentinomonti.it

CELLAR SALES
PRE-BOOKED VISITS
ANNUAL PRODUCTION 2,000,000 bottles
HECTARES UNDER VINE 500.00

○ Vermentino di Gallura Funtanaliras Oro '15	🍷🍷 3
○ Vermentino di Gallura S'Eleme Oro '15	🍷🍷 2*
● Cannonau di Sardegna Kiri '15	🍷 2

Cantina Sociale della Vernaccia

LOC. RIMEDIO
VIA ORISTANO, 6A
09170 ORISTANO
TEL. +39 078333383
www.vinovernaccia.com

CELLAR SALES
PRE-BOOKED VISITS
ANNUAL PRODUCTION 260,000 bottles
HECTARES UNDER VINE 120.00

● Nieddera Montiprama '13	🍷🍷 1*
○ Vernaccia di Oristano Jughissa '07	🍷🍷 3
● Cannonau di Sardegna Corash Ris. '13	🍷 3
○ Vermentino di Sardegna Benas '15	🍷 1*

Vigne Rada

REG. GUARDIA GRANDE, 12
07041 ALGHERO [SS]
TEL. +39 3274259136
wwww.vignerada.com

PRE-BOOKED VISITS
ANNUAL PRODUCTION 28,000 bottles
HECTARES UNDER VINE 6.00

● Alghero Cagnulari Arsenale '14	🍷🍷 6
● Cannonau di Sardegna Riviera '14	🍷🍷 5
○ Vermentino di Sardegna Stria '15	🍷 5

Vigneti Zanatta

VIA SPIRITO SANTO
07026 OLBIA
TEL. +39 3486679492
www.vignetizanatta.it

CELLAR SALES
PRE-BOOKED VISITS
ANNUAL PRODUCTION 300,000 bottles
HECTARES UNDER VINE 80.00

○ Vermentino di Gallura Renadoro '15	🍷🍷 3
● Cannonau di Sardegna Salana '14	🍷 2

INDEXES
wineries in alphabetical order
wineries by region

WINERIES IN ALPHABETICAL ORDER

Contadi Castaldi	230	Marisa Cuomo	810
Tenuta del Conte	882	Cuomo - I Vini del Cavaliere	836
Conte Guicciardini	580	Cupelli Spumanti	676
Tenuta Conte Romano	486	La Cura	583
Il Conte Villa Prandone	704	Curatolo Arini	911
Conte Vistarino	230	Curto	912
Diego Conterno	87	Custodi	758
Giacomo Conterno	87	Cantina di Custoza	409
Paolo Conterno	88	Cusumano	891
Conterno Fantino	88	Cuvage	184
Contesa	783	D'Alfonso del Sordo	869
Leone Conti	501	D'Ambra Vini d'Ischia	811
Conti degli Azzoni	730	Paolo e Noemia D'Amico	765
Conti di Buscareto	705	Casa Vinicola D'Angelo	843
Conti Ducco	260	Donato D'Angelo di Filomena Ruppi	849
Attilio Contini	922	D'Antiche Terre	836
Vignaioli Contrà Soarda	351	Cantina d'Isera	287
Michele Contrada	809	Angelo D'Uva	802
Contrada Salandra	836	Dacapo	184
Contrade di Taurasi	810	Giovanni Daglio	184
Contratto	183	Dal Cero - Tenuta di Corte Giacobbe	355
Contucci	580	Dal Cero - Tenuta Montecchiesi	676
Il Conventino	581	Dal Din	409
Dario Coos	431	Dal Maso	355
Tenuta Coppadoro	869	Dalle Nostre Mani	676
Coppi	855	Casale Daviddi	584
Vigne Marina Coppi	89	Tenuta De Angelis	706
Coppo	89	De Angelis Corvi	783
Cordeschi	773	Viticoltori De Conciliis	836
Giovanni Corino	90	De Falco	870
Renato Corino	90	Nicoletta De Fermo	784
Cantina Produttori Cormòns	431	De Stefani	356
Cornarea	91	De Toma	261
Frank Cornelissen	890	De Vescovi Ulzbach	275
Fattoria Coroncino	705	Decugnano dei Barbi	743
Matteo Correggia	91	Maria Caterina Dei	584
La Corsa	581	Ferruccio Deiana	923
Corte Adami	352	Delai	261
Corte Anna	261	Viticoltori Friulani La Delizia	486
Corte Aura	261	Deltetto	93
Corte dei Papi	773	Denavolo	502
Corte dei Venti	676	Derbusco Cives	232
Corte Figaretto	409	Vigne Deriu	937
Corte Gardoni	352	Fattoria Dezi	706
Corte Mainente	353	Di Barrò	28
Corte Moschina	353	Di Filippo	744
Corte Rugolin	354	Di Giovanna	892
Corte Sant'Alda	354	Di Legami	912
Giuseppe Cortese	92	di Lenardo	432
Villa Le Corti	582	Di Majo Norante	801
Fattoria Corzano e Paterno	582	Di Marzo	836
Clemente Cossetti	92	Di Meo	811
La Costa	231	Cantine Di Palma - Strapellum	849
Stefanino Costa	93	Gaspare Di Prima	912
Tenuta La Costa	261	Di Prisco	812
Costa Archi	501	Diadema	676
La Costaiola	261	Diana	262
Andrea Costanti	583	Dianella	676
Antonio Costantini	796	Emanuele Dianetti	707
Terra Costantino	911	Dievole	677
Costaripa	231	Fabrizio Dionisio	585
Coste del Faena	758	Dirupi	232
Coste di Brenta	796	Feudo Disisa	912
Tenuta Coste Ghirlanda	911	Divinalux	527
Cote di Franze	882	Gianni Doglia	94
Cottanera	891	Cantine di Dolianova	923
Paolo Cottini	409	Domodimonti	730
Crastin	432	Hartmann Donà	296
Les Crêtes	27	Tenuta Donà	323
La Crotta de Tanteun e Marietta	32	Marco Donati	287
La Crotta di Vegneron	27	Donelli	502

La Fortezza	815	Vito Donato Giuliani	857
Podere Fortuna	592	I Giusti & Zanza Vigneti	596
Fossa Mala	487	Giusti Wine	361
Le Fracce	235	Tenuta La Giustiniana	106
Fradiles	937	Glögglhof - Franz Gojer	300
Le Fraghe	359	Marchesi Gondi - Tenuta Bossi	679
La Fralluca	592	Tenuta Gorghi Tondi	914
Franca Contea	263	Gorgo	410
Paolo Francesconi	505	Gori	438
Frank & Serafico	593	Gotto d'Oro	774
Frascole	593	Tenuta di Gracciano della Seta	597
Frecciarossa	235	Graci	897
Cantina Frentana	797	Gradis'ciutta	438
Marchesi de' Frescobaldi	594	Bibi Graetz	597
Fattoria di Fubbiano	678	Elio Grasso	106
Elena Fucci	844	Silvio Grasso	107
Fuligni	594	Grattamacco	598
Marchesi Fumanelli	360	Gravner	439
La Fusina	185	Podere Grecchi	775
Giuseppe Gabbas	924	Gregoletto	361
Gabutti - Franco Boasso	99	Greppone Mazzi - Tenimenti Ruffino	679
Gaggino	100	Tenimenti Grieco	801
Gaierhof	288	Griesbauerhof - Georg Mumelter	300
Gaja	100	Grifalco della Lucania	844
Gajaudo - Cantina del Rossese	211	Fattoria di Grignano	679
Galardi	837	Grigoletti	278
Maria Galassi	505	Bruno Grigolli	288
Gallegati	506	Iole Grillo	439
Filippo Gallino	101	Bruna Grimaldi	107
Cantina Gallura	925	Giacomo Grimaldi	108
Gamba Gnirega	410	F.lli Grosjean	32
Garesio	185	Gruppo Cevico	506
Tenuta Garetto	101	Guado al Melo	598
Garlider - Christian Kerschbaumer	299	Tenuta Guado al Tasso	599
Gioacchino Garofoli	709	La Guardia	108
Cantine Garrone	185	La Guardiense	816
Gattavecchi	678	Duca Carlo Guarini	870
Enrico Gatti	236	Raffaele Guastaferro	837
Marco Gatti	710	Clemente Guasti	109
Tenuta Gatti	913	Albano Guerra	487
Gavioli	527	Luca Guerrieri	731
Generaj	102	Guerrieri Rizzardi	362
Gentile	786	Nicola Guglierame	211
Gentili	678	Tenute Guicciardini Strozzi	599
Geraci	914	Gulfi	898
La Gerla	679	Gummerhof - Malojer	301
Ettore Germano	102	Gumphof - Markus Prackwieser	301
I Gessi	236	Franz Haas	302
La Ghibellina	103	Haderburg	302
Tenuta di Ghizzano	595	Hauner	898
Alberto Giacobbe	774	Esther Hauser	731
Giacomelli	202	Hibiscus	914
Bruno Giacosa	103	Hilberg - Pasquero	109
Carlo Giacosa	104	Himmelreichhof	323
F.lli Giacosa	104	Humar	487
Donato Giangirolami	774	Icardi	110
Cantina Giba	925	iGreco	877
Gigante	437	Fattoria Il Lago	679
Giovanni Battista Gillardi	105	Tenuta L' Illuminata	185
La Ginestraia	202	Dino Illuminati	786
Gini	360	Cantine Imperatore	870
Marchesi Ginori Lisci	595	Inama	362
Giodo	596	Institut Agricole Régional	32
Cantina Giogantinu	937	Io Mazzucato	410
Giomi Zannoni	679	Ioppa	110
F.lli Giorgi	237	Ippolito 1845	877
La Giribaldina	185	Isimbarda	237
Cantina Girlan	299	Isola	527
Fattoria Giro di Vento	758	Isola Augusta	488
La Gironda	105	Isolabella della Croce	111
Giubertoni	263	Isole e Olena	600

WINERIES BY REGION